MATCH OF THE

FOOTBALL YEARBOOK

2007/2008

C000214774

Transfer talk: Torres, Forlan, Hargreaves and Bent

First published 2007

© Interact Publishing Limited

Photographs © Getty Images

Data collation by Warner Leach Ltd

ISBN 978095498198-3

Published by Interact Publishing Limited

www.footballyearbook.co.uk

Editor: Terry Pratt

Data interpretation: Tony Warner, Stephen Hall

Production: Stephen Hall, Jamie Stamper

Data management: Peter Watts, Tim Tyler. Sander Berends

Programming: Jonathan Proud

Additional writing: Jeff Fletcher, Jamie Stamper

European Data: Bas Abresch, Bob Boelens, Mike Boeschoten, Ivar Bos
Floris de Bruijn, Maarten Dekkers, Yvonne Drombakis, Glenn Duijzer,
Jeroen van den Kroonenberg, Patrick Leemans, Martijn Mooiweer, Jerd
de Laat, Nathalie Nuiten, Frederique van de Poll, Rudi Pronk, Daan
Schippers, Daniel Verwaijen, Leon Voskamp,Sander Zeldenrijk

Printed and bound by Butler & Tanner Limited.

By arrangement with the BBC

BBC logo © BBC 1996

Match of the Day logo © BBC 2007

THE OLD GUARD RETURN TO FORM

Inter, **United**, **Real Madrid**; some of the most famous names of European football showed a return to form in 2007. **Totti** was inspirational, **van Nistelrooy**, **Ronaldinho**, **Ronaldo** (the older version naturally) and **Pauleta** were firing goals; **Maldini**, **Vieira** and **Beckham** were leading teams to trophies.

And if it was business as usual for **Lyon** in France and **PSV** in Holland, Germany bucked the trend, picking up from the energy it generated from hosting the World Cup.

The **Bundesliga** provided the most thrilling end to the season in Europe and threw up a surprise champion.

VfB Stuttgart came through on a final day – which could also have seen **Werder Bremen** or **Schalke** finish champions – concluding a run of eight consecutive wins by coming from behind to beat **Cottbus**.

Traditional champions **Bayern Munich** were off the pace. The new stadia built for the World Cup contributed to the nearly 12m paying spectators; making it the best attended football division in the world.

Let me highlight a few noteworthy performances in this year's book:- Check out the Strike Rates on offer in **Serie A** where 14 players are averaging better than a goal every 200 minutes;

See the difference Argentinian keeper **Abbondanzieri** makes to **Getafe**;

The new guard coming through - **Cristiano Ronaldo**, breaking records and topping charts for United, **Messi** breaking into our Spanish charts, **Kaka's** extravagant talents lighting up the Champions League;

A wealth of transfer possibilities whose form you may want to look up: **Torres**, **Voronin**, **Hargreaves** and **Pizarro** to the Premiership? The hot strikers **Diego Milito**, **Forlan** and **Suazo** looking for more fashionable clubs on the continent?

Finally, see if you can track down the second worst disciplinary record on offer in Europe, a player desperate to show how much winning still means to him.

My usual thank you to all the people whose efforts pulled this book together after the Spanish Liga kicked their last ball: Steve Hall (who's wife Channy, gave birth to a little boy, Sachin, in the thick of the action!), Peter Watts, Jeff Fletcher, Jamie Stamper, Tony Warner and Jonathan Proud.

Terry Pratt

310
Totti takes on Inter
Record: Played 35, Goals 26; Assists 10; Shots 126. Totti turns into a one-man strike force in the Italian League

Totti scores the first goal in a 6-2 Coppa Italia thrashing of Inter

352
Dutch hot-shots
Huntelaar keeps up his phenomenal record, scoring 21 goals at a Strike Rate of one every 127 minutes – and he's still only fourth in Holland's Goalscoring chart

Still in striking form Klaas jan Huntelaar

390
Thrilling end to Bundesliga
Stuttgart supreme as Schalke stumble, Bremen are beaten off, Nuremberg clinch the cup and Bayern just aren't in it

Stuttgart fans anticipate clinching the Bundesliga Shield

428
Lyon invincible
OL move to their fourth manager (as Houllier steps down for Perrin) in six years, top players keep being snapped up, yet they remain the most dominant league team in Europe

Juninho; four different managers, six titles in a row

THE CLUBS

108
FA Cup

The return to Wembley appeared to have been blessed by the 'dream final' - instead it was almost comatose. All the games from the first round on…

Seven years of planning and construction leading to an FA Cup return

470
Champions League

Kaka uses the competition to display his talents and builds a persuasive case to be considered the World's best. Milan take on the cream of England and win

Kaka: AC Milan's champion

490
Uefa Cup

Seville confirm their class by retaining their hold on this trophy in a competition that shows the strength in depth in La Liga

Seville defend their Uefa Cup crown

494
Euro 2008

At the halfway stage several of Europe's big guns are struggling. Will Bosnia, Poland, Israel and Bulgaria be the surprise finalists in Switzerland and Austria next summer?

Bosnia & Herzegovina celebrate a win over Turkey to move into the final places

CHARTING PERFORMANCE

Goalkeepers
Newcastle's last line of defence

The reactions of Shay Given have come to the rescue of Newcastle's unsettled defence numerous times. When Given missed 22 games through injury last season, long-time reserve **Steve Harper** stepped in and fans would have been hard-pressed to notice the difference. In fact, on our stats, Harper came out top.

Goals Conceded in the League
The team conceded **18** goals in the **1445** minutes Harper played in league matches.

Goals Conceded in all competitions
Add in the five cup games he played in and he conceded **22** goals in total.

KEY GOALKEEPER	
Steve Harper	
Goals Conceded in the League Number of League goals conceded while the player was on the pitch	18
Goals Conceded in all competitions Total number of goals conceded while the player was on the pitch	22
League minutes played Number of minutes played in league matches	1445
Clean Sheets In games when player was on pitch for at least 70 minutesmins	6
Goals to Shots Ratio The average number of shots on target per each League goal conceded	6.67
Defensive Rating Ave mins between League goals conceded while on the pitch	80

Clean Sheets
In league games where Harper kept goal, he prevented the opposition from scoring in **6** games. We only measure games where he played for at least 70 minutes and the opposition finished goalless - a Counting Game.

Defensive Rating
This is the key statistic we use to compare keepers, how often a team scores against them in league games. Harper only let in a goal every **80** minutes on average.

Given's record for the season was every 69 minutes.

Goals to Shots Ratio
In the Premiership, we also record how many saves a keeper makes per goal conceded. We use the Shots on Target as the measure and by this measure Harper had the third best record in the Premiership, saving **6.67** shots on target for every goal he conceded. To put it in context, that ratio would have topped the Goals to Shots table in three of the last four seasons.

Given came seventh among the Premiership keepers with a 5.29 record. This was still better than he achieved in the 2005/06 season where he came ninth with 5.0.

Midfielders
Arca sparks Boro's midfield

Gareth Southgate surprised many pundits by plucking **Julio Arca** out of the ashes of Sunderland's record-breakingly bad 2005/06 Premiership season. After a first game injury Arca fought back to establish himself and our stats rate him the pick of the Boro midfield.

Goals in the League
Arca managed only **2** league goals in his 21 appearances.

Assists
He laid on just **2** goals for colleagues in the league, compared to the crossing of Stuart Downing, which delivered **13** goals for his forwards.

Defensive Rating
However, Arca's work rate and possession helped to keep opposition goals down. Boro only conceded a goal every **81** minutes when he was on the pitch. Only Jonathan Woodgate and ball-winning midfielder Lee Cattermole had higher Defensive Ratings at the club.

Contribution to Attacking Power
This is where Arca's value really shows through. Boro were a far more dangerous outfit when he was pulling the midfield strings. They scored a goal every **57** minutes when he was playing. Without him their average was a goal every 110 minutes. Only striker Mark Viduka had a better Attacking Power at the club.

KEY PLAYERS - MIDFIELDERS	
Julio Arca	
Goals in the League	2
Goals in all competitions	3
Assists League goals scored by a team mate where the player delivered the final pass	2
Defensive Rating Average number of mins between League goals conceded while on the pitch	81
Contribution to Attacking Power Average number of minutes between League team goals while on pitch	57
Scoring Difference Defensive Rating minus Contribution to Attacking Power	24

	PLAYER	GOALS LGE	GOALS ALL	ASSISTS	DEF RATE	POWER	SC
1	Julio Arca	2	3	2	81	57	24 m
2	Lee Cattermole	1	2	2	85	81	4 r
3	George Boateng	1	2	1	68	70	-2 r
4	Stewart Downing	2	2	13	64	70	-6 m

Scoring Difference
This measure is like a personal goal difference for a midfield player and we use it as a rough guide to compare top performers. It is found by taking away a player's Attacking Power from their Defensive Rating. With Arca it is **81** minus **57**, which makes his Scoring Difference **+24**. A positive figure means the team is more likely to score than concede when he is on the pitch. Negative results, like George Boateng's **-2**, show the team were more likely to let goals in than score when he was on the pitch.

Goalscorers
Spurs' three-pronged attack

Martin Jol rotates three top strikers, who would be regular starters in most other Premiership sides. **Jermain Defoe, Dimitar Berbatov** and **Robbie Keane** each bring something special to the side and all habitually find the net. It gives Spurs three of the top 16 Strike Rates in the division.

KEY PLAYERS - GOALSCORERS

Robbie Keane

Goals in the League	11
Goals in all competitions	22
Assists League goals scored by a team mate where the player delivered the final pass	6
Contribution to Attacking Power Average number of minutes between League team goals while on pitch	61
Player Strike Rate Average number of minutes between League goals scored by player	150
Club Strike Rate Average minutes between League goals scored by club	60

	PLAYER	GOALS LGE	GOALS ALL	ASSISTS	POWER	S RATE
1	Robbie Keane	11	22	6	61	150 mins
2	Jermain Defoe	10	18	3	62	193 mins
3	Dimitar Berbatov	12	23	13	52	226 mins
4	Jermaine Jenas	6	8	3	65	360 mins

Goals in the League
Berbatov shades this with **12** league goals, ahead of Keane with **11**, and the Bulgarian also scored the most in all competitions, **23** ahead of Keane on **22**.

Assists
Defoe creates goals for himself but not many for colleagues while Berbatov with **13** has the third highest Assists total in the division. Keane has **6** Assists.

Contribution to Attacking Power
This measures how potent Spurs' attack is when each player is on the pitch. When Berbatov plays they score every **52** minutes. With Keane it is a goal every **61** minutes.

Player Strike Rate
This is the main measure we use to rank Strikers. It shows how regularly they score. By this measure Keane is the pick of the trio. He scored a league goal every **150** minutes on average - the fifth best Strike Rate in the Premiership.

Club Strike Rate
This gives Spurs' Attacking Power as a club for the season. They scored 57 goals in the league (that's 3420 League minutes) or a goal every **60** minutes on average. When compared to a player's Attacking Power it shows whether the individual added to their team's potency.

Defenders
The costly loss of Gary Neville

Manchester United may have held on strongly in the league but their Defenders chart shows how badly they perhaps missed Gary Neville. The United captain was out injured for the last third of the season and it could have cost two cups.

Goals Conceded in the League
United conceded just **13** league goals while Neville was on the pitch.

Goals Conceded in all competitions
He conceded another 8 in cup appearances to make **21** in total.

Clean Sheets
We only measure Clean Sheets in league games where the player has influenced a game for at least 70 minutes. These we call Counting Games. There were **13** Clean Sheets in Neville's 21 Counting Games. You have to play at least 12 Counting Games in a season to qualify for the Key Defenders chart and 17+ Counting Games to get into the Divisional Round-up charts, so Neville is eligible for both.

Defensive Rating
This is the key measurement on which we sort Defenders. It shows how regularly a side concedes a goal when a particular defender is on the pitch. United conceded a goal every **152** minutes on average when Neville was playing. They conceded a goal every **103** minutes when he was absent.

KEY PLAYERS - DEFENDERS

Gary Neville

Goals Conceded in the League Number of League goals conceded while the player was on the pitch	13
Goals Conceded in all competitions Total number of goals conceded while the player was on the pitch	21
League minutes played Number of minutes played in league matches	1976
Clean Sheets In games when the player was on pitch for at least 70 minutes	11
Defensive Rating Average number of mins between League goals conceded while on the pitch	152
Club Defensive Rating Average number of mins between League goals conceded by the club this season	126

	PLAYER	CON LGE	CON ALL	MINS	C SHEETS	DEF RATE
1	Gary Neville	13	21	1976	11	152 mins
2	Patrice Evra	13	20	1852	10	142 mins
3	Nemanja Vidic	15	25	2139	11	142 mins
4	Rio Ferdinand	23	39	2925	14	127 mins

Club Defensive Rating
This provides a quick check on whether a Defender is tightening his club's defence. It shows how regularly the club concedes a league goal over the season. United let in a goal every **126** minutes on average, showing that they were stronger with Neville in the side.

Squad Appearances
Now with injuries and suspensions

This season we've started to keep track of injuries and suspensions to get a better view of a Premiership manager's selection policy. It helps show how a player has been used over a season.

Squares

A dark green square ■ shows the player was in the starting XI and finished the game. A light green square ▤ shows he was on the bench but didn't get subbed on. A blank square ☐ shows they didn't make it to the bench. A dark edged blank square ☐ means the player was *reported* injured.

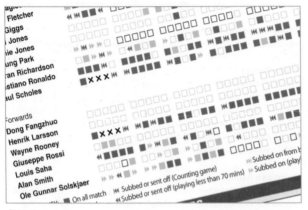

Arrows

A dark green arrow ◄◄ shows the player started the game but was subbed off or sent off. A light green arrow ►► shows they started on the bench but were subbed on. Still paler arrows show the player was subbed on but still didn't complete the 90 minutes.

Counting Games

A player registers a Counting Game when they play for 70 minutes or more in a particular game. Managers often take a view around the 70 minute mark and will rest key players. A dark green arrow with a small line before it ◄◄ means they were subbed off *after* 70 minutes and it counts as a Counting Game. A light green arrow with a small line after it means they were subbed on in the first 20 minutes and played a full 70 minutes after that – also a Counting Game.

Crosses

A black cross **x**, as in Rooney's second game above, shows a player was suspended for that game and not eligible for selection.

Competition Key

A quick guide to the Competition, Venue and Result is shown at the top of the Squad Appearances Chart. **H** or **A** in Venue refer to **H**ome and **A**way. The result is **W**, **L** or **D** and shown in the appropriate colour. The Competitions are: **L** = League; **F** = FA Cup; **C** = Champions League; **E** = Uefa Cup; **W** = the League Cup in the English or Scottish divisions; **O** = Other, e.g. a play-off match. Finally the numbers along the top refer to the game number and can be checked against the Results chart for more details. There's more information of how squads are used in the Premiership round up pages.

Team of the Season
Selecting the top performers

The club XI

Each club has a team of the season generated by our computers. The computer selects first from players who have played at least 12 Counting Games CG. We sometimes reset this to 11 to include a particularly strong performance but mark it with an asterisk.

Defence

If there is a choice of Keeper, it chooses the one with the best (highest) Defensive Rating **DR**. It then selects the best four Defensive Ratings among the club's Defenders. They will be the defenders who concede goals least often, regardless of whether they are central or full backs.

Midfield

The computer chooses its midfield based on the highest Scoring Differences **SD**. Positive figures mean the team has scored more often than it conceded when that individual played. **Arjan Robben** just qualifies for Chelsea's Team of the Season as he tallied **12** Counting Games in 2006-07, but he had the best Attacking Power at the club and a better Scoring Difference than Michael Ballack, who misses out.

Claude Makelele has the best defensive midfielder stats in the Premiership and tops the club's midfield charts.

Attack

In most divisions the computer selects the two best Strike Rates among he club forwards. In the Premiership, we give it more leeway. If a club plays with a withdrawn forward or advanced midfield player, we look at their Attacking Power. Chelsea usually played with two up. Andriy Shevchenko has a better Attacking Power than **Salomon Kalou** but a far worse Strike Rate so we've chosen Kalou on Strike Rate.

Occasionally we find a team that has chopped and changed so much we can't find a full 4-4-2 that has played sufficient Counting Games. Then the Computer selects on the next highest Counting Games or advances a utility player into the gap. We mark these with an asterisk.

Divisional Teams of the Season
The most effective players in each division are sorted into top 15-20 charts of Goalkeepers, Defenders, Midfielders or Goalscorers. For these we raise the Counting Games barrier to 17 or more games. The most effective 4-4-2 across a division is selected the same way with one difference – no team is allowed to have more then one of its players in any position. This means that **John Terry** gets into the Premiership team Defence therefore the unlucky **Wayne Bridge** misses out. The most any club can supply to the divisional team is therefore four players.

Goal Attempts
Pompey respond to home crowd

Shots For
We record Goal Attempts in Premiership League games. The Goal Attempts FOR chart details the featured side's attacking prowess. Shots On Target are split into Home and Away records and the overall Total is shown before being turned into an Average per league game. We do the same for Shots Off Target and note the total of all shots struck.

Portsmouth's Average of **12.4** shots a game is the fifth best in the division. They entertain far more at Home, hitting 62% of their Total

GOAL ATTEMPTS

FOR Goal attempts recorded in League games					AGAINST Goal attempts recorded in League games				
	HOME	AWAY	TOTAL	AVE		HOME	AWAY	TOTAL	AVE
shots on target	143	87	230	6.1	shots on target	89	145	234	6.2
shots off target	146	94	240	6.3	shots off target	91	130	221	5.8
TOTAL	289	181	470	12.4	TOTAL	180	275	455	12.0
Ratio of goals to shots Average number of shots on target per League goal scored			5.1		Ratio of goals to shots Average number of shots on target per League goal scored			5.6	
Accuracy rating Average percentage of total goal attempts which were on target			48.9		Accuracy rating Average percentage of total goal attempts which were on target			51.4	

Shots at Fratton Park. The Ratio of goals to shots shows Pompey needed **5.1** Shots On Target for each goal scored, which is average for the division. Under half of their Total Shots hit the target, giving them a **48.9%** Accuracy Rating. Europe rivals Reading were less Accurate at 47% but more deadly, needing only 3.3 Shots On Target per goal.

Shots Against
This is the defensive side of the shots coin, showing how often opponents shot at Pompey's goal. Again the defence performs far better at Home. Here the Ratio of goals to shots gives a feel for how the

goalkeeper is performing. **David James** saved **5.6** shots for every goal conceded. The Accuracy Rating reflects how much pressure opposition forwards were put under by the Pompey defence; **51.4%** is one of the poorer defensive results in the league.

Disciplinary Records
The league's bad boys

Red and Yellow cards are shown for all clubs. Blackburn have had one of the worst Disciplinary records in recent seasons. In 2006-07, the club totalled **76** yellows and **6** red cards in league games. **Lucas Neill** had the highest number of cards **8** yellows and **1** red before leaving for West Ham. However, we measure players by how often on average they receive a card and **Stephane Henchoz** received **5** cards in his **826** league minutes – an average of a card every **165** minutes.

BOOKINGS

Stephane Henchoz	
League Yellow	4
League Red	1
All competitions Yellow	4
All competitions Red	1

League Average 165 mins between cards

	PLAYER	LEAGUE		TOTAL		AVE
1	S. Henchoz	4Y	1R	4Y	1R	165
2	Lucas Neill	8	1	8	1	196
3	Robbie Savage	8	0	9	0	229
4	Jason Roberts	3	1	3	1	257
5	Z. Khizanishvili	6	0	8	0	261
6	Aaron Mokoena	6	0	11	1	281
7	David Dunn	2	0	4	0	295
8	Andy Todd	2	0	3	0	305
9	C. Samba	3	0	3	0	379
10	Benni McCarthy	8	0	11	0	381
	TOTAL	76	6	113	7	

Top Point Earners
The knack of turning draws into wins

Average points
Austrian **Paul Scharner** is a versatile player who can both shore up the defence and poach goals from midfield. He was Wigan's best points earner as they narrowly avoided relegation. In games when he played at least 70 minutes, they averaged **1.23** points.

TOP POINT EARNERS

Paul Scharner	
Counting Games League games when player was on pitch for at least 70 minutes	22
Average points Average League points taken in Counting games	1.23
Club Average points Average points taken in League games	1.00

	PLAYER	GAMES	PTS
1	Paul Scharner	22	1.23
2	Luis Antonio Valencia	12	1.17
3	Henri Camara	14	1.14
4	Emmerson Boyce	33	1.09
5	Lee McCulloch	23	1.09
6	Arjan De Zeeuw	19	1.05
7	Kevin Kilbane	24	1.04
8	Denny Landzaat	26	1.04
9	Leighton Baines	34	0.97
10	Chris Kirkland	25	0.96

Club Average Points
Overall Wigan gained 38 points, an average of **1.00** point per game. While Scharner was injured, suspended or making his way back from injury, they managed just 11 points from 16 games compared to 27 from the 22 Counting Games he played.

Most Missed Players
Amongst the masses of information in the Premiership Round-up, you can find the players who were most badly missed by their clubs. Had Scharner played in all the league games, enjoying the same average, Wigan would have finished comfortably in mid-table at 11th rather than just clinging onto their Premiership status.

THE PREMIERSHIP ROUND-UP

Cristiano Ronaldo was the pick of a free-scoring and versatile Manchester United attack that wrested back the league title from Chelsea. He broke **Frank Lampard's** recently set midfield Premiership goals record by hitting 17 and led the Assists and Attacking Power charts alongside **Ryan Giggs** – United scored every 39 minutes when they played. Lampard was second in midfield totals with 11 and **Gilberto Silva**, 10, and **Mikel Arteta** 9 next.

Didier Drogba led **Benni McCarthy** in the goals charts but Arsenal's injured duo **Thierry Henry** and **Robin van Persie** had better Strike Rates although neither played sufficient games to chart here.

Chelsea are the supreme defence, **Petr Cech** stopped 9.7 shots on target per goal conceded, while **Claude Makelele** still defends in midfield more effectively than anyone.

Daniel Agger is now a real force for Liverpool and his Defensive Rating is over 60 minutes better than his nearest colleague.

Reading were a model of attacking efficiency. Only **Watford** had less goal attempts but **Reading** needed just 3.3 shots on target to score. United hit more shots than we've ever recorded before.

CLUB STRIKE FORCE

1 Man Utd

Club Strike Rate (CSR) Average number of minutes between League goals scored by club				41

	CLUB	LGE	ALL	SoT	CSR
1	Man Utd	83	123	328	41
2	Chelsea	64	117	273	53
3	Arsenal	63	98	281	54
4	Liverpool	57	90	296	60
5	Tottenham	57	104	243	60
6	Reading	52	67	171	65
7	Everton	52	59	204	65
8	Blackburn	52	76	214	65
9	Bolton	47	56	186	72
10	Portsmouth	45	50	230	76
11	Middlesbrough	44	58	194	77
12	Aston Villa	43	49	216	79
13	Fulham	38	48	181	90
14	Newcastle	38	62	204	90
15	Wigan	37	38	207	92
16	West Ham	35	39	202	97
17	Charlton	34	39	169	100
18	Sheff Utd	32	35	204	106
19	Watford	29	41	174	117
20	Man City	29	39	197	117

Rooney and Ronaldo of Man Utd

Goals scored in the League	83

Goals scored in all competitions	123

Shots on target (SoT) Shots on target hit by the team recorded in League games	328

CLUB DEFENCES

1 Chelsea

Club Defensive Rate (CDR) Average number of minutes between League goals conceded by club				142

	CLUB	LGE	ALL	CS	SoT	CDR
1	Chelsea	24	43	22	129	142
2	Liverpool	27	52	20	134	126
3	Man Utd	27	51	16	175	126
4	Arsenal	35	53	12	164	97
5	Everton	36	42	14	252	95
6	Aston Villa	41	50	13	220	83
7	Portsmouth	42	49	12	234	81
8	Man City	44	52	14	193	77
9	Reading	47	62	13	261	72
10	Newcastle	47	64	7	263	72
11	Middlesbrough	49	64	9	240	69
12	Bolton	52	58	12	212	65
13	Blackburn	54	65	8	285	63
14	Tottenham	54	76	6	197	63
15	Sheff Utd	55	62	9	206	62
16	Watford	59	67	9	252	57
17	West Ham	59	66	9	247	57
18	Wigan	59	63	10	211	57
19	Charlton	60	66	11	271	57
20	Fulham	60	71	7	228	57

Chelsea's Portuguese defender Carvalho

Goals conceded in the League	24

Goals conceded in all competitions	43

Clean Sheets (CS) Number of league games where no goals were conceded	22

Shots on Target Against (SoT) Shots on Target conceded by team in League games	129

PLAYER NATIONALITIES

Overseas country with the most player appearances in the Premiership - France			
In the squad	746	Percentage of League action	6.53
Appearances in League games	671	Caps for France this season	0
Most appearances	Distin	Percentage of time on pitch	95.1

	COUNTRY	PLAYERS	IN SQUAD	LGE APP	% LGE ACT	CAPS	MOST APP	APP
	England	299	5172	4390	43.78	158	David James	100
1	France	42	746	671	6.53	40	Sylvain Distin	95.1
2	Rep of Ireland	27	557	479	4.78	78	Richard Dunne	100
3	Holland	17	391	340	3.21	50	George Boateng	89.1
4	Wales	17	347	317	3.16	48	Gary Speed	95.2
5	United States	13	324	302	3.11	26	Brad Friedel	98.7
6	Australia	14	303	241	2.66	19	Mark Schwarzer	94.7
7	Portugal	16	315	278	2.61	26	Cristiano Ronaldo	81.4
8	Nigeria	9	251	234	2.33	1	Joseph Yobo	100
9	Spain	15	272	224	2.31	27	Cesc Fabregas	93
10	Ivory Coast	7	196	194	2.06	18	Habib Kolo Toure	92.1
11	Senegal	7	191	184	1.89	0	El Hadji Diouf	78.7
12	Scotland	18	260	196	1.73	43	Lee McCulloch	67.9
13	Finland	6	133	114	1.29	17	Jussi Jaaskelainen	100
14	Denmark	9	160	128	1.24	38	Thomas Sorensen	74.4
15	Germany	6	147	128	1.24	15	Jens Lehmann	94.7
16	Iceland	5	140	122	1.16	0	Ivar Ingimarsson	100
17	N Ireland	6	148	112	1.05	29	Keith Gillespie	70.5
18	Norway	6	127	102	1.02	0	M Gamst Pedersen	90.8
19	Brazil	5	118	105	0.94	15	Gilberto Silva	88
20	Bulgaria	5	109	97	0.91	0	Dimitar Berbatov	79.4

CLUB MAKE-UP – HOME AND OVERSEAS PLAYERS

1 Arsenal

Overseas players in the squad	30	Home country players	8
Percent of overseas players	78.9	Percent of League action	99.02
Most appearances	Lehmann	Appearance percentage	94.7

	CLUB	OVERSEAS	HOME	% OVERSEAS	% LGE ACT	MOST APP	APP %
1	Arsenal	30	8	78.9	99.02	Jens Lehmann	94.7
2	Blackburn	23	10	69.7	81.04	Brad Friedel	98.7
3	Bolton	23	6	79.3	78.23	Jussi Jaaskelainen	100
4	Fulham	24	10	70.6	73.07	Brian McBride	84.7
5	Chelsea	22	10	68.8	71.07	Michael Essien	86.8
6	Liverpool	23	14	62.2	65.74	Jose Reina	92.1
7	Reading	19	13	59.4	65.28	Ivar Ingimarsson	100
8	Everton	19	11	63.3	64.31	Joseph Yobo	100
9	Wigan	21	14	60	62.29	P Chimbonda	85.6
10	Aston Villa	18	15	54.5	60.48	Olof Mellberg	98.7
11	Charlton	21	14	60	58.67	Talal El Karkouri	94.7
12	Man Utd	20	21	48.8	58.55	E van der Sar	84.2
13	Middlesbrough	13	19	40.6	54.74	Mark Schwarzer	94.7
14	Man City	15	17	46.9	53.47	Richard Dunne	100
15	Newcastle	21	13	61.8	52.2	Obafemi Martins	83.7
16	Tottenham	19	17	52.8	51.77	P Chimbonda	85.6
17	West Ham	15	19	44.1	51.1	Lucas Neill	79.7
18	Portsmouth	20	12	62.5	48.96	Nwankwo Kanu	79.2
19	Sheff Utd	11	27	28.9	34.65	Patrick Kenny	88.6
20	Watford	12	29	29.3	30.91	Jay DeMerit	83.3

CLUB STARTING FORMATIONS

1 Reading

Most used starting formation	4-4-2	How often the club used its most frequently used formation	**91.9%**
Number of different formations used	3		

	CLUB	Formation	Number	Used %
1	Reading	4-4-2	3	91.9
2	Tottenham	4-4-2	3	91.4
3	Wigan	4-4-2	4	89.2
4	Watford	4-4-2	5	86.5
5	West Ham	4-4-2	4	86.5
6	Blackburn	4-4-2	5	86.5
7	Portsmouth	4-4-2	5	81.1
8	Man Utd	4-4-2	4	78.9
9	Newcastle	4-4-2	3	78.4
10	Liverpool	4-4-2	5	77.1
11	Sheff Utd	4-4-2	6	73.7
12	Middlesbrough	4-4-2	5	69.4
13	Aston Villa	4-4-2	5	68.4
14	Fulham	4-4-2	5	63.2
15	Everton	4-4-2	3	60.5
16	Arsenal	4-4-2	4	59.5
17	Man City	4-4-2	7	57.9
18	Charlton	4-4-2	5	55.3
19	Chelsea	4-1-3-2	4	43.2
20	Bolton	4-3-3	7	28.9

We are recording the most commonly quoted formations for each Premier team at the start of each game.

The most commonly used formation in the Premiership is 4-4-2, which is used as the starting formation in 54% of matches.

It is followed by 4-5-1 and 4-1-4-1, both used in 11% of matches.

In all 17 different formations were recorded with Liverpool's Benitez using the most variations although Mourinho was the most flexible

Average number of different formations used by Premiership clubs	**5.35**

FINAL LEAGUE TABLE

		HOME					AWAY					TOTAL			
	P	W	D	L	F	A	W	D	L	F	A	F	A	DIF	PTS
Man Utd	38	15	2	2	46	12	13	3	3	37	15	83	27	56	89
Chelsea	38	12	7	0	37	11	12	4	3	27	13	64	24	40	83
Liverpool	38	14	4	1	39	7	6	4	9	18	20	57	27	30	68
Arsenal	38	12	6	1	43	16	7	5	7	20	19	63	35	28	68
Tottenham	38	12	3	4	34	22	5	6	8	23	32	57	54	3	60
Everton	38	11	4	4	33	17	4	9	6	19	19	52	36	16	58
Bolton	38	9	5	5	26	20	7	3	9	21	32	47	52	-5	56
Reading	38	11	2	6	29	20	5	5	9	23	27	52	47	5	55
Portsmouth	38	11	5	3	28	15	3	7	9	17	27	45	42	3	54
Blackburn	38	9	3	7	31	25	6	4	9	21	29	52	54	-2	52
Aston Villa	38	7	8	4	20	14	4	9	6	23	27	43	41	2	50
Middlesbrough	38	10	3	6	31	24	2	7	10	13	25	44	49	-5	46
Newcastle	38	7	7	5	23	20	4	3	12	15	27	38	47	-9	43
Man City	38	5	6	8	10	16	6	3	10	19	28	29	44	-15	42
West Ham	38	8	2	9	24	26	4	3	12	11	33	35	59	-24	41
Fulham	38	7	7	5	18	18	1	8	10	20	42	38	60	-22	39
Wigan	38	5	4	10	18	30	5	4	10	19	29	37	59	-22	38
Sheff Utd	38	7	6	6	24	21	3	2	14	8	34	32	55	-23	38
Charlton	38	7	5	7	19	20	1	5	13	15	40	34	60	-26	34
Watford	38	3	9	7	19	25	2	4	13	10	34	29	59	-30	28

CLUB GOAL ATTEMPTS FOR

United's goal poacher Ole Gunnar Solskjaer

1 Man Utd

Total shots					**633**	

	CLUB	SoT	Soff	Tot	SG	AR
1	Man Utd	328	305	633	4.0	51.8
2	Liverpool	296	313	609	5.2	48.6
3	Arsenal	281	290	571	4.5	49.2
4	Chelsea	273	280	553	4.3	49.4
5	Portsmouth	230	240	470	5.1	48.9
6	Blackburn	214	250	464	4.1	46.1
7	Tottenham	243	213	456	4.3	53.3
8	Wigan	207	229	436	5.6	47.5
9	Aston Villa	216	211	427	5.0	50.6
10	Sheff Utd	204	221	425	6.4	48.0
11	West Ham	202	217	419	5.8	48.2
12	Middlesbrough	194	222	416	4.4	46.6
13	Everton	204	211	415	3.9	49.2
14	Newcastle	204	206	410	5.4	49.8
15	Fulham	181	212	393	4.8	46.1
16	Man City	197	195	392	6.8	50.3
17	Bolton	186	182	368	4.0	50.5
18	Charlton	169	197	366	5.0	46.2
19	Reading	171	193	364	3.3	47.0
20	Watford	174	167	341	6.0	51.0

Shots on target	328
Shots off target	305
Ratio of shots on target to goals	4.0
Accuracy Rating	51.8

CLUB GOAL ATTEMPTS AGAINST

Charlton's impressive shot-stopper Carson

1 Charlton

Total shots against					**551**	

	CLUB	SoT	Soff	Tot	SG	AR
1	Charlton	271	280	551	4.5	49.2
2	Blackburn	285	234	519	5.3	54.9
3	Newcastle	263	256	519	5.6	50.7
4	Watford	252	264	516	4.3	48.8
5	Everton	252	264	516	7.0	48.8
6	Reading	261	253	514	5.6	50.8
7	West Ham	247	255	502	4.2	49.2
8	Middlesbrough	240	262	502	4.9	47.8
9	Fulham	228	261	489	3.8	46.6
10	Aston Villa	220	240	460	5.4	47.8
11	Portsmouth	234	221	455	5.6	51.4
12	Bolton	212	242	454	4.1	46.7
13	Sheff Utd	206	228	434	3.7	47.5
14	Man City	193	216	409	4.4	47.2
15	Tottenham	197	208	405	3.6	48.6
16	Wigan	211	186	397	3.6	53.1
17	Man Utd	175	187	362	6.5	48.3
18	Arsenal	164	175	339	4.7	48.4
19	Chelsea	129	180	309	5.4	41.7
20	Liverpool	134	142	276	5.0	48.6

Shots on target against	271
Shots off target against	280
Ratio of shots on target to goals	4.5
Accuracy Rating	49.2

STADIUM CAPACITY AND HOME CROWDS

	TEAM	CAPACITY		AVE	HIGH	LOW
1	Man Utd	76212		99.5	76098	75115
2	Arsenal	60432		99.3	60132	59912
3	Tottenham	36236		98.6	36170	34154
4	Reading	24200		98.5	24122	21954
5	Portsmouth	20288		98.0	20223	19105
6	Chelsea	42522		97.7	41953	38000
7	West Ham	35657		97.3	34977	33805
8	Newcastle	52387		96.8	52305	48145
9	Charlton	27111		96.6	27111	23423
10	Liverpool	45362		96.0	44403	41370
11	Sheff Utd	32609		93.6	32604	25011
12	Everton	40565		90.6	40004	32968
13	Fulham	24600		90.6	24554	17000
14	Watford	20800		90.2	19830	13760
15	Aston Villa	42573		85.1	42551	27450
16	Bolton	27879		84.7	27229	21140
17	Man City	47500		84.2	47244	35776
18	Middlesbrough	35120		79.0	32013	23638
19	Wigan	25000		72.7	24726	14636
20	Blackburn	31367		67.8	29342	16035

Key: Average. The percentage of each stadium filled in League games over the season (AVE), the stadium capacity and the highest and lowest crowds recorded.

AWAY ATTENDANCE

	TEAM		AVE	HIGH	LOW
1	Liverpool		97.4	75828	19746
2	Man Utd		96.8	60128	19453
3	Newcastle		93.6	75664	19225
4	Chelsea		93.5	75948	19398
5	Arsenal		93.4	75595	15311
6	Aston Villa		93.4	76078	18455
7	West Ham		92.7	75927	18344
8	Everton		92.6	75723	18149
9	Sheff Utd		92.5	75540	16322
10	Tottenham		92.2	75433	16506
11	Man City		91.1	75858	16235
12	Charlton		91.0	75883	16572
13	Middlesbrough		90.7	75967	17000
14	Wigan		90.5	76018	17859
15	Reading		90.0	75910	14636
16	Watford		89.6	76032	16035
17	Portsmouth		89.2	76004	15093
18	Fulham		89.2	75115	16001
19	Bolton		89.0	76058	18559
20	Blackburn		88.8	76098	13760

Key: Average. How close each club has come to filling grounds in its away league matches (AVE) and the highest and lowest crowds recorded.

PREMIERSHIP ROUND-UP

CHART-TOPPING MIDFIELDERS

1 Makelele - Chelsea	
Goals scored in the League	1
Assists in league games	0
Defensive Rating Av number of mins between League goals conceded while on the pitch	189
Contribution to Attacking Power Average number of minutes between League team goals while on pitch	55
Scoring Difference Defensive Rating minus Contribution to Attacking Power	134

	PLAYER	CLUB	GOALS	ASS	DEF R	POWER	SCORE DIFF
1	Claude Makelele	Chelsea	1	0	189	55	134 mins
2	Ryan Giggs	Man Utd	4	12	143	39	104 mins
3	Cristiano Ronaldo	Man Utd	17	15	139	39	100 mins
4	John Arne Riise	Liverpool	1	1	151	60	91 mins
5	Frank Lampard	Chelsea	11	12	141	52	89 mins
6	Paul Scholes	Man Utd	6	2	129	41	88 mins
7	Michael Carrick	Man Utd	3	4	119	40	79 mins
8	Michael Essien	Chelsea	2	3	129	52	77 mins
9	Michael Ballack	Chelsea	4	5	126	49	77 mins
10	Steven Gerrard	Liverpool	7	6	133	59	74 mins
11	Xabi Alonso	Liverpool	4	1	121	59	62 mins
12	Tomas Rosicky	Arsenal	3	2	107	52	55 mins
13	Cesc Fabregas	Arsenal	2	14	102	52	50 mins
14	Gilberto Silva	Arsenal	10	2	101	53	48 mins
15	Lee Carsley	Everton	1	4	102	66	36 mins
16	Alexander Hleb	Arsenal	2	4	87	52	35 mins
17	Mikel Arteta	Everton	9	9	101	66	35 mins
18	Leon Osman	Everton	3	4	100	66	34 mins
19	David Bentley	Blackburn	4	11	71	61	10 mins
20	Stephen Hunt	Reading	4	6	80	71	9 mins

The Divisional Round-up charts combine the records of chart-topping keepers, defenders, midfield players and forwards, from every club in the division.. The one above is for **the Chart-topping Midfielders**. The players are ranked by their Scoring Difference although other attributes are shown for you to compare.

CHART-TOPPING GOALSCORERS

1 Drogba - Chelsea	
Goals scored in the League (GL)	20
Goals scored in all competitions (ALL)	33
Contribution to Attacking Power Average number of minutes between League team goals while on pitch	52
Player Strike Rate (S Rate) Average number of minutes between League goals scored by player	147
Club Strike Rate (CSR) Average minutes between League goals scored by club	53

	PLAYER	CLUB	GOALS: LGE	ALL	POWER	CSR	S RATE
1	Didier Drogba	Chelsea	20	33	52	53	147 mins
2	Mark Viduka	Middlesbrough	14	19	54	77	148 mins
3	Cristiano Ronaldo	Man Utd	17	22	39	41	163 mins
4	Benni McCarthy	Blackburn	18	24	69	65	169 mins
5	Kevin Doyle	Reading	13	13	61	65	189 mins
6	Jermain Defoe	Tottenham	10	18	62	60	193 mins
7	Bobby Zamora	West Ham	11	11	79	97	195 mins
8	Wayne Rooney	Man Utd	14	23	40	41	209 mins
9	Dirk Kuyt	Liverpool	12	14	57	60	214 mins
10	Darren Bent	Charlton	13	15	95	100	220 mins
11	Dimitar Berbatov	Tottenham	12	23	52	60	226 mins
12	Andrew Johnson	Everton	11	12	66	65	246 mins
13	Emmanuel Adebayor	Arsenal	8	12	50	54	248 mins
14	Obafemi Martins	Newcastle	11	17	81	90	260 mins
15	Ayegbeni Yakubu	Middlesbrough	12	16	83	77	263 mins
16	Nwankwo Kanu	Portsmouth	10	12	73	76	270 mins
17	Craig Bellamy	Liverpool	7	9	68	60	272 mins
18	Nicolas Anelka	Bolton	11	12	71	72	273 mins
19	Salomon Kalou	Chelsea	7	9	48	53	277 mins
20	Emile Heskey	Wigan	10	10	99	92	278 mins

The Chart-topping Goalscorers measures the players by Strike Rate. They are most likely to be Forwards but Midfield players and even Defenders can come through the club tables. It is not a measure of the number of League goals scored - although that is also noted - but how often on average they have scored.

CHART-TOPPING DEFENDERS

1 Agger - Liverpool	
Goals Conceded in the League The number of League goals conceded while he was on the pitch	11
Goals Conceded in all competitions The number of goals conceded while he was on the pitch in all competitions	29
Clean Sheets In games when he played at least 70 mins	15
Defensive Rating Average number of minutes between League goals conceded while on the pitch	197
Club Defensive Rating Average mins between League goals conceded by the club this season	126

	PLAYER	CLUB	CON: LGE	ALL	CS	CDR	DEF RATE
1	Daniel Agger	Liverpool	11	29	15	126	197 mins
2	John Terry	Chelsea	14	27	16	142	172 mins
3	Gary Neville	Man Utd	13	21	11	126	152 mins
4	Nemanja Vidic	Man Utd	15	25	11	126	142 mins
5	Ricardo Carvalho	Chelsea	19	35	16	142	138 mins
6	Jamie Carragher	Liverpool	22	38	19	126	135 mins
7	Steve Finnan	Liverpool	22	34	18	126	131 mins
8	Rio Ferdinand	Man Utd	23	39	14	126	127 mins
9	Ashley Cole	Chelsea	15	29	9	142	123 mins
10	William Gallas	Arsenal	18	23	7	97	104 mins
11	Sami Hyypia	Liverpool	20	28	9	126	101 mins
12	Sol Campbell	Portsmouth	30	33	11	81	96 mins
13	Habib Kolo Toure	Arsenal	33	49	11	97	95 mins
14	Joseph Yobo	Everton	36	40	14	95	95 mins
15	Joleon Lescott	Everton	36	42	14	95	92 mins
16	Phil Neville	Everton	34	40	12	95	91 mins
17	Glen Johnson	Portsmouth	25	28	9	81	90 mins
18	Gael Clichy	Arsenal	27	35	7	97	87 mins
19	Alan Stubbs	Everton	23	23	7	95	86 mins
20	Olof Mellberg	Aston Villa	39	46	13	83	86 mins

The Chart-topping Defenders are resolved by their Defensive Rating, how often their team concedes a goal while they are playing. All these rightly favour players at the best performing clubs because good players win matches. However, good players in lower-table clubs will chart where they have lifted the team's performance.

CHART-TOPPING GOALKEEPERS

1 Cech - Chelsea	
Goals conceded in the League	9
Goals conceded in all comps (ALL)	21
Counting Games (CG) League games when he played at least 70 minutes	19
Clean Sheets (CS) In games when he played at least 70 mins	12
Goals to Shots Ratio (GSR) The average number of shots on target per each League goal conceded	9.67
Defensive Rating Average number of minutes between League goals conceded while on pitch	190

	PLAYER	CLUB	CG	CON: LGE	ALL	CS	GSR	DEF RATE
1	Petr Cech	Chelsea	19	9	21	12	9.67	190 mins
2	Jose Reina	Liverpool	35	23	36	19	5.26	136 mins
3	Edwin van der Sar	Man Utd	32	25	42	12	6.08	115 mins
4	Tim Howard	Everton	36	29	34	14	8.07	111 mins
5	Thomas Sorensen	Aston Villa	28	24	29	12	6.13	106 mins
6	Jens Lehmann	Arsenal	36	35	40	10	4.46	92 mins
7	David James	Portsmouth	38	42	48	12	5.57	81 mins
8	Nicky Weaver	Man City	23	28	36	9	4.71	76 mins
9	M Hahnemann	Reading	36	45	45	13	5.8	73 mins
10	Shay Given	Newcastle	20	27	40	3	5.63	69 mins
11	Mark Schwarzer	Middlesbrough	36	48	60	8	4.83	65 mins
12	Jussi Jaaskelainen	Bolton	38	52	56	12	4.08	65 mins
13	Patrick Kenny	Sheff Utd	33	46	46	8	3.91	65 mins
14	Paul Robinson	Tottenham	38	54	69	6	3.65	63 mins
15	Brad Friedel	Blackburn	37	54	65	8	5.28	62 mins
16	Antti Niemi	Fulham	30	45	45	6	3.89	61 mins
17	Robert Green	West Ham	26	39	41	9	4.59	60 mins
18	Scott Carson	Charlton	36	55	59	11	4.62	58 mins
19	Ben Foster	Watford	29	45	47	6	4.24	58 mins
20	Chris Kirkland	Wigan	26	43	43	7	3.42	55 mins

The Chart-topping Goalkeepers are positioned by their Defensive Rating. We also show Clean Sheets where the team has not conceded and the Keeper has played all or most (at least 70 minutes) of the game. Only the top keeper for each team is included in this chart.

GOALS

	PLAYER	TEAM	LGE	SR
1	Drogba	Chelsea	20	147
2	McCarthy	Blackburn	18	169
3	Ronaldo	Man Utd	17	163
4	Viduka	Middlesboro	14	148
5	Rooney	Man Utd	14	209
6	Doyle	Reading	13	189
7	Bent, D	Charlton	13	220
8	Kuyt	Liverpool	12	214
9	Berbatov	Tottenham	12	226
10	Yakubu	Middlesboro	12	263
11	van Persie	Arsenal	11	132
12	Keane	Tottenham	11	150
13	Zamora	West Ham	11	195
14	Johnson	Everton	11	246
15	Martins	Newcastle	11	260
16	Anelka	Bolton	11	273
17	Lampard	Chelsea	11	294
18	Henry	Arsenal	10	147
19	Defoe	Tottenham	10	193
20	Kanu	Portsmouth	10	270
21	Heskey	Wigan	10	278
22	Gilberto Silva	Arsenal	10	293
23	Crouch	Liverpool	9	167
24	McBride	Fulham	9	321
25	Arteta	Everton	9	348
26	Agbonlahor	Aston Villa	9	369

GOALS – MIDFIELDERS

	PLAYER	TEAM	LGE	SR
1	Ronaldo	Man Utd	17	163
2	Lampard	Chelsea	11	294
3	Gilberto Silva	Arsenal	10	293
4	Arteta	Everton	9	348
5	Taylor	Portsmouth	8	335
6	Barry	Aston Villa	8	389
7	Speed	Bolton	8	407
8	Gerrard	Liverpool	7	439
9	Jenas	Tottenham	6	360
10	Scholes	Man Utd	6	432
11	Barton	Man City	6	494
12	Pedersen	Blackburn	6	517
13	Park	Man Utd	5	154
14	Cahill	Everton	5	281
15	Dyer	Newcastle	5	336

GOALS – DEFENDERS

	PLAYER	TEAM	LGE	SR
1	Bocanegra	Fulham	5	466
2	O'Shea	Man Utd	4	434
3	Gallas	Arsenal	3	626
4	Vidic	Man Utd	3	713
5	Carvalho	Chelsea	3	879
6	Toure	Arsenal	3	1050
7	Baines	Wigan	3	1068
8	El Karkouri	Charlton	3	1080

ASSISTS

	PLAYER	TEAM	LGE	ALL
1	Ronaldo	Man Utd	13	15
2	Fabregas	Arsenal	13	14
3	Pedersen	Blackburn	12	13
4	Rooney	Man Utd	12	13
5	Lampard	Chelsea	12	12
6	Berbatov	Tottenham	10	13
7	Bentley	Blackburn	10	11
8	Arteta	Everton	9	9
9	Giggs	Man Utd	8	12
10	Lennon	Tottenham	8	12
11	Anelka	Bolton	8	8
12	Crouch	Liverpool	8	8
13	Downing	Middlesboro	7	13
14	Shevchenko	Chelsea	7	9
15	Diouf	Bolton	7	7
16	Sidwell	Reading	7	7
17	Davies	Bolton	6	7
18	Robben	Chelsea	6	7
19	Saha	Man Utd	6	7
20	Agbonlahor	Aston Villa	6	6
21	Johnson	Everton	6	6
22	Gerrard	Liverpool	6	6
23	Pennant	Liverpool	6	6
24	Milner	Newcastle	6	6
25	Hunt	Reading	6	6
26	Shorey	Reading	6	6
27	Kilbane	Wigan	6	6
28	Campo	Bolton	5	6

SHARE OF GOALS

	PLAYER	TEAM	% LGE GOALS
1	Bent, D	Charlton	38.24
2	McCarthy	Blackburn	34.62
3	Viduka	Middlesbrough	31.82
4	Zamora	West Ham	31.43
5	Drogba	Chelsea	31.25
6	Martins	Newcastle	28.95
7	Yakubu	Middlesbrough	27.27
8	Heskey	Wigan	26.32
9	Doyle	Reading	25.00
10	Hulse	Sheff Utd	25.00
11	McBride	Fulham	23.68
12	Anelka	Bolton	23.40
13	Kanu	Portsmouth	22.22
14	Johnson	Everton	21.15
15	Kuyt	Liverpool	21.05
16	Berbatov	Tottenham	21.05
17	Agbonlahor	Aston Villa	20.93
18	Barton	Man City	20.69
19	Ronaldo	Man Utd	20.48
20	Tevez	West Ham	20.00
21	Keane	Tottenham	19.30
22	Barry	Aston Villa	18.60
23	Taylor	Portsmouth	17.78
24	Defoe	Tottenham	17.54
25	van Persie	Arsenal	17.46

TEAM OF THE SEASON

CECH — CHELSEA — CG 19 DR 190

G.NEVILLE — MAN UTD — CG 21 DR 152
TERRY — CHELSEA — CG 27 DR 172
AGGER — LIVERPOOL — CG 23 DR 197
GALLAS — ARSENAL — CG 21 DR 104

ROSICKY — ARSENAL — CG 18 SD +55
MAKELELE — CHELSEA — CG 24 SD +134
GIGGS — MAN UTD — CG 22 SD +104
RIISE — LIVERPOOL — CG 27 SD +91

RONALDO — MAN UTD — CG 30 AP 39
DROGBA — CHELSEA — CG 30 SR 147

The Premiership Team of the Season shows a 4-4-2 of the best players in the Premiership based upon the selection criteria used for the chart-toppers. The players selected are taken from the lists for each club except that to get into a Divisional Team of the Season you must have played at least 17 Counting Games in the league (roughly half the league season) and not 12 as is the case in the club lists. The other restriction is that we are only allowing one player from each club in each position. So the maximum number of players one club can have in the divisional team is four.
- **The Divisional team's goalkeeper** is the player with the highest *Defensive Rating*
- **The Divisional team's defenders** are also tested by *Defensive Rating*, i.e. the average number of minutes between goals conceded while on the pitch.
- **The Divisional team's midfield** are selected on their *Scoring Difference*, i.e. their *Defensive Rating* minus their *Contribution to Attacking Power* (average number of minutes between league goals scored while on the pitch.
- **The Divisional team strikeforce** is made up of the striker with the highest *Strike Rate* (his average number of minutes between league goals scored while on the pitch) together with the striker with the highest *Contribution to Attacking Power*.

PREMIERSHIP CHART-TOPPING POINT EARNERS

1 Giggs - Man Utd

	PLAYER	TEAM	GAMES	POINTS	AVE
1	R Giggs	Man Utd	22	56	2.55
2	M Ballack	Chelsea	22	52	2.36
3	T Rosicky	Arsenal	18	38	2.11
4	D Agger	Liverpool	23	45	1.96
5	D Zokora	Tottenham	21	39	1.86
6	El H Diouf	Bolton	28	50	1.79
7	G Murty	Reading	21	36	1.71
8	W Bouma	Aston Villa	19	32	1.68
9	Sean Davis	Portsmouth	25	42	1.68
10	A Johnson	Everton	30	50	1.67
11	R Savage	Blackburn	20	31	1.55
12	Shay Given	Newcastle	20	31	1.55
13	Mark Viduka	Middlesboro	21	31	1.48
14	A Ferdinand	West Ham	28	37	1.32
15	Christanval	Fulham	18	23	1.28
16	N Weaver	Man City	23	29	1.26
17	Montgomery	Sheff Utd	19	24	1.26
18	P Scharner	Wigan	22	27	1.23
19	Matt Holland	Charlton	25	25	1.00
20	D Henderson	Watford	19	18	0.95

Counting Games Played at least 70mins.	22
Total Points Taken in Counting Games	56
Average Taken in Counting Games	2.55

For the Top Point Earners we have applied the same rule of only allowing one player per position for each club, the same as the Team of the Season. The most one club can have in the top 20 is four players, one keeper, one defender, one midfielder and a forward.

PREMIERSHIP MOST MISSED PLAYERS

	PLAYER	TEAM	AVERAGE	CLUB	DIFF
1	Shay Given	Newcastle	1.55	1.13	0.42
2	W Bouma	Aston Villa	1.68	1.32	0.36
3	T Rosicky	Arsenal	2.11	1.79	0.32
4	El H Diouf	Bolton	1.79	1.47	0.32
5	D Zokora	Tottenham	1.86	1.58	0.28
6	Mark Viduka	Middlesboro	1.48	1.21	0.27
7	Sean Davis	Portsmouth	1.68	1.42	0.26
10	G Murty	Reading	1.71	1.45	0.26
11	Montgomery	Sheff Utd	1.26	1.00	0.26
12	Christanval	Fulham	1.28	1.03	0.25
13	A Ferdinand	West Ham	1.32	1.08	0.24
14	P Scharner	Wigan	1.23	1.00	0.21
15	D Henderson	Watford	0.95	0.74	0.21
16	Ryan Giggs	Man Utd	2.55	2.34	0.21
17	M Ballack	Chelsea	2.36	2.18	0.18
18	R Savage	Blackburn	1.55	1.37	0.18
19	Daniel Agger	Liverpool	1.96	1.79	0.17
20	A Johnson	Everton	1.67	1.53	0.14

1 Given - Newcastle

Average points	1.55
Club average	1.13
Difference	0.42

The Most Missed Players we have applied the same rule of only allowing one player per position for each club, the same as the Team of the Season. The most one club can have in the top 20 is four players, one keeper, one defender, one midfielder and a forward.

MANAGERS - SUBSTITUTIONS USED

Club with the highest percentage of subs used - West Ham		Alan Curbishley	
Matches where no subs were used	0	Matches where one sub was used	0
Matches where two subs were used	5	Matches where three subs were used	33
Total subs used in season	109	Percentage of possible subs used	95.6

CLUB	MAIN MANAGER	0 SUBS	1 SUB	2 SUBS	3 SUBS	TOTAL	%
West Ham	Alan Curbishley	0	0	5	33	109	95.61
Chelsea	Jose Mourinho	0	1	6	31	106	92.98
Liverpool	Rafael Benitez	0	2	6	30	104	91.23
Charlton	Alan Pardew	0	3	9	26	99	86.84
Man City	Stuart Pearce	0	0	16	22	98	85.96
Portsmouth	Harry Redknapp	0	3	11	24	97	85.09
Reading	Steve Coppell	2	2	7	27	97	85.09
Middlesbrough	Gareth Southgate	0	3	12	23	96	84.21
Arsenal	Arsene Wenger	1	3	9	25	96	84.21
Sheff Utd	Neil Warnock	2	2	9	25	95	83.33
Man Utd	Sir Alex Ferguson	0	4	12	22	94	82.46
Fulham	Lawrie Sanchez	1	4	10	23	93	81.58
Bolton	Sam Allardyce	0	7	8	23	92	80.70
Wigan	Paul Jewell	0	5	12	21	92	80.70
Blackburn	Mark Hughes	1	3	14	20	91	79.82
Watford	Adrian Boothroyd	3	3	14	18	85	74.56
Newcastle	Glenn Roeder	1	7	13	17	84	73.68
Tottenham	Martin Jol	0	6	20	12	82	71.93
Everton	David Moyes	2	8	13	15	79	69.30
Aston Villa	Martin O'Neill	1	8	18	11	77	67.54

MANAGERS - SUBSTITUTION TIMES

Club with the highest percentage of subs used - West Ham		Alan Curbishley	
Substitutes made during first half	9	Substitutes made between 46 and 69 minutes (mainly tactical)	45
Substitutes made between 70-85 mins	49		
Substitutes made after 86 mins	6	Total subs used in season	109

CLUB	MANAGER	0-45 MINS	46-69	70-85	86+	TOTAL
West Ham	Alan Curbishley	9	45	49	6	109
Wigan	Paul Jewell	11	44	30	7	92
Chelsea	Jose Mourinho	5	42	44	15	106
Fulham	Lawrie Sanchez	4	42	40	7	93
Liverpool	Rafael Benitez	3	40	50	11	104
Man City	Stuart Pearce	8	40	39	11	98
Watford	Adrian Boothroyd	8	36	30	11	85
Portsmouth	Harry Redknapp	5	35	42	15	97
Man Utd	Sir Alex Ferguson	7	35	39	13	94
Sheff Utd	Neil Warnock	9	35	39	12	95
Arsenal	Arsene Wenger	4	34	45	13	96
Tottenham	Martin Jol	3	34	39	6	82
Charlton	Alan Pardew	10	33	45	11	99
Blackburn	Mark Hughes	5	33	44	9	91
Bolton	Sam Allardyce	9	32	31	20	92
Newcastle	Glenn Roeder	11	32	28	13	84
Middlesbrough	Gareth Southgate	4	31	44	17	96
Everton	David Moyes	5	24	36	14	79
Aston Villa	Martin O'Neill	5	23	41	8	77
Reading	Steve Coppell	10	22	51	14	97

LEAGUE PENALTY TAKERS

Arsenal's Gilberto Silva scores another pen

1 Gilberto - Arsenal; Barry - Aston Villa					
Penalties Taken Total number of penalties taken in the league					6

PLAYER	CLUB	TOTAL	Sc	Sa	Mi	%Scored
Gilberto Silva	Arsenal	6	5	1	0	83.33
Barry	Aston Villa	6	5	1	0	83.33
Speed	Bolton	5	5	0	0	100.00
Arteta	Everton	5	5	0	0	100.00
McCarthy	Blackburn	5	4	1	0	80.00
Yakubu	Middlesbrough	5	4	1	0	80.00
Defoe	Tottenham	4	3	1	0	75.00
Lampard	Chelsea	4	3	1	0	75.00
Ronaldo	Man Utd	4	3	1	0	75.00
Henry	Arsenal	3	3	0	0	100.00
Doyle	Reading	3	3	0	0	100.00
Fowler	Liverpool	3	3	0	0	100.00
Bent, D	Charlton	3	3	0	0	100.00
Solano	Newcastle	3	2	1	0	66.67
Jagielka	Sheff Utd	2	2	0	0	100.00
Beattie	Everton	2	2	0	0	100.00
Saha	Man Utd	2	2	0	0	100.00
Keane	Tottenham	2	2	0	0	100.00
Martins	Newcastle	2	1	0	1	50.00
Gerrard	Liverpool	2	1	0	1	50.00
Barton	Man City	2	1	0	1	50.00
Others (34)		34	19	11	4	44.12
TOTALS		111	86	19	6	77.48

Penalties scored - Gilberto Silva	5
Penalties saved	1
Penalties missed	0
League total	6
Percentage scored	83.3
% of all League penalties taken	5.4

CLUB - LEAGUE SQUAD USAGE

1 Bolton	
Players used Total number of players used by the club in the league	23

CLUB	Players used	% by 11	% by 16	Avge
Bolton	23	83.3	95.5	22.2
Reading	23	77.0	91.0	22.3
Arsenal	25	70.4	88.4	20.6
Fulham	25	70.9	89.3	20.4
Man Utd	25	66.2	87.2	20.5
Chelsea	26	68.6	87.2	20.2
Everton	26	79.7	92.5	19.1
Portsmouth	26	76.0	91.4	19.8
Tottenham	26	69.1	88.7	19.2
Middlesbrough	27	75.8	91.6	19.0
Blackburn	29	69.9	85.8	17.6
Liverpool	29	74.4	90.3	18.0
Man City	29	63.8	78.8	17.8
Newcastle	29	63.7	83.6	17.3
Aston Villa	30	69.2	83.7	16.5
Charlton	30	68.2	84.6	17.2
West Ham	30	63.2	81.5	17.6
Wigan	30	69.4	86.8	17.0
Sheff Utd	32	65.8	82.8	16.0
Watford	33	70.0	85.4	15.2
TOTAL	553			

Bolton players celebrate after scoring

% of games played by leading 11 players	83.3
% of games played by leading 16 players	95.5
Average number of appearances per player	22.2

LEADING APPEARANCES

DEFENDERS

	PLAYER	GAMES	TIME
1	Joseph Yobo	38	3420
2	Richard Dunne	38	3420
3	Ivar Ingimarsson	38	3420
4	Liam Rosenior	38	3397
5	Olof Mellberg	38	3375
6	Nicky Shorey	37	3330
7	Joleon Lescott	38	3318
8	Michael Dawson	37	3282
9	Sylvain Distin	37	3254
10	Talal El Karkouri	36	3240
11	Habib Kolo Toure	35	3150
12	Linvoy Primus	36	3142
13	Abdoulaye Meite	35	3127
14	Leighton Baines	35	3116
15	Phil Neville	35	3111
16	Emmerson Boyce	34	3020
17	Emanuel Pogatetz	35	3002
18	Jamie Carragher	35	2978

FORWARDS

	PLAYER	GAMES	TIME				
1	Gabriel Agbonlahor	38	3325	10	Dimitar Berbatov	33	2716
2	Ayegbeni Yakubu	37	3164	11	Andrew Johnson	33	2711
3	Benni McCarthy	36	3049	12	Nwankwo Kanu	36	2709
4	Nicolas Anelka	35	3010	13	Emile Heskey	34	2695
5	Didier Drogba	36	2944	14	El Hadji Diouf	33	2665
6	Wayne Rooney	35	2926	15	Dirk Kuyt	34	2577
7	Brian McBride	38	2897	16	Darius Vassell	32	2558
8	Darren Bent	32	2863	17	Kevin Davies	30	2521
9	Obafemi Martins	33	2863	18	Kevin Doyle	32	2469

MIDFIELDERS

	PLAYER	GAMES	TIME
1	Philip Jagielka	38	3420
2	Lee Carsley	38	3375
3	Gary Speed	38	3257
4	Frank Lampard	37	3243
5	James Harper	38	3199
6	Cesc Fabregas	38	3182
7	Mikel Arteta	35	3134
8	Gareth Barry	35	3119
9	Morten Gamst Pedersen	36	3104
10	Steven Sidwell	35	3092
11	Gary O'Neil	35	3088
12	Nigel Reo-Coker	35	3082
13	Steven Gerrard	36	3076
14	David Bentley	36	3069
15	Stewart Downing	34	3037
16	George Boateng	35	3017
17	Michael Essien	33	2970
18	Joey Barton	33	2966

FIRST SCORERS

SCORED FIRST

CLUB	MATCHES	WON	DRAWN	LOST
Chelsea	27	23	2	2
Man Utd	26	23	2	1
Blackburn	22	13	5	4
Everton	22	14	6	2
Bolton	20	12	6	2
Liverpool	20	19	0	1
Wigan	20	10	4	6
Tottenham	19	14	2	3
Portsmouth	17	12	3	2
Arsenal	16	14	2	0
Newcastle	16	9	4	3
Reading	16	12	2	2
Aston Villa	15	8	6	1
Fulham	15	7	6	2
Middlesbrough	15	10	3	2
Charlton	13	7	2	4
Sheff Utd	13	8	3	2
West Ham	13	10	1	2
Man City	12	11	1	0
Watford	9	4	4	1

CONCEDED FIRST

CLUB	MATCHES	WON	DRAWN	LOST
Chelsea	8	1	6	1
Man Utd	11	5	2	4
Liverpool	13	1	3	9
Everton	14	1	5	8
Blackburn	15	2	1	12
Portsmouth	15	2	3	10
Bolton	16	4	0	12
Wigan	16	0	2	14
Newcastle	17	2	1	14
Tottenham	17	3	5	9
Aston Villa	18	3	6	9
Middlesbrough	18	2	2	14
Fulham	19	1	5	13
Man City	19	0	1	18
Reading	19	4	2	13
Arsenal	20	5	7	8
Charlton	21	1	4	16
Sheff Utd	23	2	3	18
Watford	23	1	3	19
West Ham	24	2	3	19

CLUB DISCIPLINARY RECORDS

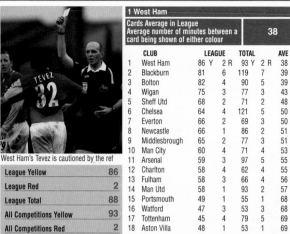

West Ham's Tevez is cautioned by the ref

1 West Ham

Cards Average in League		
Average number of minutes between a card being shown of either colour		38

	CLUB	LEAGUE		TOTAL		AVE
1	West Ham	86 Y	2 R	93 Y	2 R	38
2	Blackburn	81	6	119	7	39
3	Bolton	82	4	90	5	39
4	Wigan	75	3	77	3	43
5	Sheff Utd	68	2	71	2	48
6	Chelsea	64	4	121	5	50
7	Everton	66	2	69	3	50
8	Newcastle	66	1	86	2	51
9	Middlesbrough	65	2	77	3	51
10	Man City	60	4	71	4	53
11	Arsenal	59	3	97	5	55
12	Charlton	58	4	62	4	55
13	Fulham	58	3	66	4	56
14	Man Utd	58	1	93	2	57
15	Portsmouth	49	1	55	1	68
16	Watford	47	3	53	3	68
17	Tottenham	45	4	79	5	69
18	Aston Villa	48	1	53	1	69
19	Liverpool	43	0	71	0	79
20	Reading	40	3	51	3	79

League Yellow	86
League Red	2
League Total	88
All Competitions Yellow	93
All Competitions Red	2
TOTAL	95

PLAYER DISCIPLINARY RECORD

Everton's Anichebe in action for the Toffees

1 Anichebe - Everton

Cards Average in League		
Average number of minutes between a card being shown of either colour		104

	PLAYER		LEAGUE		TOTAL		AVE
1	Anichebe	Everton	6 Y	0 R	6 Y	0 R	104
2	Vaughan	Everton	5	0	5	0	130
3	Helguson	Fulham	10	1	10	1	133
4	Mikel	Chelsea	5	1	9	2	159
5	Senderos	Arsenal	3	2	7	2	161
6	Mido	Tottenham	4	0	4	0	163
7	Henchoz	Blackburn	4	1	4	1	165
8	Fernandes	Everton	4	0	4	0	179
9	van Persie	Arsenal	8	0	8	0	182
10	Diarra	Chelsea	3	0	10	0	185
11	Sankofa	Charlton	3	1	3	1	187
12	Thatcher	Man City	5	0	5	0	191
13	Richardson	Man Utd	4	0	6	0	195
14	Neill	Blackburn	8	1	8	1	196
15	Hamann	Man City	5	0	6	0	196
16	Cattermole	Middlesboro	10	0	12	0	196
17	Valencia	Wigan	6	1	6	1	196
18	Sheringh'm	West Ham	3	0	3	0	203
19	Dickov	Man City	4	0	5	0	204
20	Gardner	Bolton	6	0	6	0	205

(Playing a minimum of 500 minutes in the League)

League Yellow	6
League Red	0
League Total	6
All Competitions Yellow	6
All Competitions Red	0
TOTAL	6

REFEREES - PENALTIES

1 M. L. Dean

Penalties Average		
Average number of minutes between penalties awarded		180

	REF	Home	Away	Total	Avge
1	M. L. Dean	9	3	12	180
2	A. G. Wiley	7	6	13	200
3	H. M. Webb	4	7	11	229
4	C. J. Foy	5	4	9	230
5	U. D. Rennie	5	1	6	240
6	D. J. Gallagher	3	2	5	252
7	M. A. Riley	4	2	6	300
8	M. Clattenburg	3	4	7	308
9	R. Styles	3	5	8	315
10	M. Atkinson	4	2	6	345
11	P. Walton	4	0	4	360
12	L. Mason	2	1	3	360
13	G. Poll	3	4	7	372
14	M. R. Halsey	5	1	6	390
15	S. G. Bennett	3	0	3	810
16	P. Dowd	0	1	1	1440

Referee Mike Dean's decision is final

Games	25
Penalties awarded to home side	9
Penalties awarded to away side	3
Total	12

REFEREES - CARDS

1 M. L. Dean

Cards Average		
Average number of cards per match of either colour		4.24

	REF	Games	Y	Y/R	R	AVE
1	M. L. Dean	25	99	4	3	4.24
2	M. Clattenburg	27	112	0	0	4.15
3	H. M. Webb	28	110	3	1	4.07
4	U. D. Rennie	16	64	1	0	4.06
5	A. Marriner	6	23	1	0	4
6	M. A. Riley	22	78	2	4	3.82
7	G. Poll	31	105	3	1	3.52
8	S. G. Bennett	27	90	5	0	3.52
9	R. Styles	30	100	3	2	3.5
10	A. G. Wiley	30	96	1	2	3.3
11	M. Atkinson	24	74	2	2	3.25
12	P. Dowd	17	50	0	2	3.06
13	P. Walton	16	48	0	0	3
14	K. Stroud	1	3	0	0	3
15	L. Mason	12	28	0	1	2.42
16	M. R. Halsey	27	57	1	4	2.3
17	D. J. Gallagher	14	29	0	3	2.29
18	C. J. Foy	23	48	0	2	2.17
19	L. Probert	2	3	0	0	1.5
20	S. Tanner	3	2	0	0	0.67
	TOTALS	381	1219	26	27	3.34

Mark Clattenburg dishes out another card

Games	25
Yellow	99
Yellow/Red	4
Straight reds	3

CLUB - LEAGUE PENALTIES AWARDED

1 Arsenal

Penalties Awarded		
Total number of penalties awarded to the club in the league		10

CLUB	H	A	Total	Sc	Sa	M	%	No
Arsenal	7	3	10	8	2	0	9.5%	4
Blackburn	4	5	9	5	4	0	8.6%	4
Aston Villa	6	2	8	6	1	1	7.6%	2
Everton	5	2	7	7	0	0	6.7%	2
Newcastle	5	2	7	5	1	1	6.7%	4
Tottenham	3	3	6	6	0	0	5.7%	2
Bolton	2	4	6	5	1	0	5.7%	2
Liverpool	5	2	7	6	1	0	6.7%	3
Man Utd	3	3	6	5	1	0	5.7%	2
Middlesbrough	4	1	5	4	1	0	4.8%	1
Sheff Utd	4	1	5	2	3	0	4.8%	4
Charlton	1	3	4	4	0	0	3.8%	2
Chelsea	1	3	4	3	1	0	3.8%	1
Man City	4	0	4	2	0	2	3.8%	3
Wigan	0	4	4	2	1	1	3.8%	4
Reading	1	2	3	3	0	0	2.9%	1
Watford	2	1	3	3	0	0	2.9%	3
Portsmouth	3	0	3	2	1	0	2.9%	3
Fulham	2	0	2	2	0	0	1.9%	2
West Ham	1	1	2	1	1	0	1.9%	2
TOTALS	63	42	105	81	19	5		52

Arsenal's Hleb win a penalty for Arsenal

Awarded at home	7
Awarded away	3
Number scored	8
Number saved	2
Number missed	0
% of League penalties awarded	9.5
Number of takers	4

CLUB - LEAGUE PENALTIES CONCEDED

1 Blackburn

Penalties Conceded		
Total number of penalties conceded by the club in the league		11

CLUB	H	A	Total	Sc	Sa	M	%
Blackburn	6	5	11	6	5	0	10.5%
Sheff Utd	4	4	8	7	1	0	7.6%
Portsmouth	3	5	8	6	2	0	7.6%
Middlesbrough	3	4	7	7	0	0	6.7%
Tottenham	2	5	7	6	0	1	6.7%
Bolton	3	4	7	5	2	0	6.7%
Fulham	3	4	7	5	1	1	6.7%
Reading	2	4	6	6	0	0	5.7%
Watford	1	5	6	5	0	1	5.7%
Wigan	3	3	6	4	2	0	5.7%
Charlton	3	2	5	3	2	0	4.8%
West Ham	3	1	4	4	0	0	3.8%
Aston Villa	1	3	4	3	0	1	3.8%
Everton	1	3	4	2	1	1	3.8%
Man Utd	2	2	4	2	2	0	3.8%
Arsenal	1	2	3	3	0	0	2.9%
Chelsea	0	3	3	2	1	0	2.9%
Man City	1	1	2	2	0	0	1.9%
Newcastle	0	2	2	2	0	0	1.9%
Liverpool	0	1	1	1	0	0	1.0%
TOTALS	42	63	105	81	19	5	

Blackburn's Lucas Neill concedes a penalty

Conceded at home	6
Conceded away	5
League Total	11
Number scored	6
Number missed	5
% of League penalties conceded	10.5

PREMIERSHIP – AUGUST

LEAGUE PERFORMANCE FOR THE MONTH

	P	HOME					AWAY					TOTAL			
		W	D	L	F	A	W	D	L	F	A	F	A	DIF	PTS
Man Utd	3	1	0	0	5	1	2	0	0	5	1	10	2	8	9
Portsmouth	3	1	0	0	3	0	1	1	0	4	0	7	0	7	7
Aston Villa	3	2	0	0	4	1	0	1	0	1	1	5	2	3	7
Everton	3	1	0	0	2	1	1	1	0	3	1	5	2	3	7
Chelsea	3	1	0	0	3	0	1	0	1	3	2	6	2	4	6
West Ham	3	1	0	0	3	1	0	1	1	2	3	5	4	1	4
Liverpool	2	1	0	0	2	1	0	1	0	1	1	3	2	1	4
Bolton	3	1	0	0	2	0	0	1	1	1	3	3	3	0	4
Man City	3	1	1	0	1	0	0	0	1	0	3	1	3	-2	4
Fulham	3	1	1	0	2	1	0	0	1	1	5	3	6	-3	4
Wigan	2	1	0	0	1	0	0	0	1	1	2	2	2	0	3
Reading	3	1	0	0	3	2	0	0	2	1	3	4	5	-1	3
Newcastle	2	1	0	0	2	1	0	0	1	0	2	2	3	-1	3
Tottenham	3	1	0	1	2	2	0	0	1	0	2	2	4	-2	3
Charlton	3	1	0	1	2	3	0	0	1	1	3	3	6	-3	3
Middlesbrough	3	1	0	1	2	5	0	0	1	2	3	4	8	-4	3
Arsenal	2	0	1	0	1	1	0	0	1	0	1	1	2	-1	1
Watford	3	0	1	1	2	3	0	0	1	1	2	3	5	-2	1
Sheff Utd	3	0	1	0	1	1	0	0	2	0	3	1	4	-3	1
Blackburn	3	0	1	1	1	3	0	0	1	0	3	1	6	-5	1

GOAL OF THE MONTH

MATCH OF THE DAY

Daniel Agger
Liverpool v West Ham

Ivan Campo	*Bolton* v Tottenham
Wayne Rooney	*Man Utd* v Fulham
Didier Drogba	*Chelsea* v Manchester City
Marlon King	*Watford* v West Ham
Andrew Johnson	*Everton* v Tottenham

THE MONTH'S TOP GOALSCORERS

	GOALS IN THE MONTH		THE SEASON TO END OF MONTH	
Portsmouth	Kanu	4	Kanu	4 57.1%
West Ham	Zamora	4	Zamora	4 80.0%
Charlton	Bent, D	3	Bent, D	3 100.0%
Aston Villa	Angel	2	Angel	2 40.0%
Chelsea	Drogba, Lampard	2	Drogba, Lampard	2 33.3%
Everton	Johnson	2	Johnson	2 40.0%
Fulham	Bullard	2	Bullard	2 66.7%
Man Utd	Rooney, Saha	2	Rooney, Saha	2 20.0%
Watford	Francis	2	Francis	2 66.7%
Arsenal	Gilberto Silva	1	Gilberto Silva	1 100.0%
Blackburn	McCarthy	1	McCarthy	1 100.0%
Bolton	Campo, Davies, Diouf	1	Campo, Davies, Diouf	1 33.3%
Liverpool	Agger, Crouch, Fowler	1	Agger, Crouch, Fowler	1 33.3%
Man City	Barton	1	Barton	1 100.0%
Middlesboro	Downing, Pogatetz, Viduka, Yakubu	1	Downing, Pogatetz, Viduka, Yakubu	1 25.0%
Newcastle	Ameobi, Parker	1	Ameobi, Parker	1 50.0%
Reading	Doyle, Kitson, Lita, Sidwell	1	Doyle, Kitson, Lita, Sidwell	1 25.0%
Sheff Utd	Hulse	1	Hulse	1 100.0%
Tottenham	Berbatov, Jenas	1	Berbatov, Jenas	1 50.0%
Wigan	Heskey, McCulloch	1	Heskey, McCulloch	1 50.0%

BARCLAYS MANAGER OF THE MONTH

Sir Alex Ferguson - Manchester United

BARCLAYS PLAYER OF THE MONTH

Ryan Giggs - Manchester United

Sol Campbell signs two-year deal with Portsmouth after quitting Arsenal in July saying that he wanted a "fresh challenge and to make a major statement in a foreign league too"

Liverpool beat Chelsea 2-1 in the Millennium Stadium in Cardiff

Aston Villa name former Celtic and Leicester boss Martin O'Neill as their new manager

Aston Villa's board accept a £62.6m takeover bid of the club by American billionaire Randy Lerner. Long-standing chairman Doug Ellis is to stand down

Manchester United go to the top of the Premiership beating Charlton 3-0 at The Valley to make it two wins

Blackburn sign 32-year-old Dutch international Andre Ooijer from PSV Eindhoven

Premiership champions Chelsea open their league campaign with a 3-0 victory over Manchester City at Stamford Bridge

Aston Villa announce loss of £8.89m in the 12 months to 31 May

West Ham striker Dean Ashton suffers broken ankle while training with the England squad and faces lengthy spell out of action

New England boss Steve McClaren drops young Arsenal forward Theo Walcott to the Under-21 squad

Steve McClaren's reign as England manager starts brightly with a 4-0 win over Greece in international friendly at Old Trafford. Newly-appointed captain John Terry heads home the first goal

Manchester City ban their defender Ben Thatcher for six matches and fine him six weeks' wages for his brutal challenge on Pedro Mendes of Portsmouth

Chelsea skipper John Terry appointed England captain in succession to David Beckham. Liverpool's Steven Gerrard named vice-captain

Chelsea manager Jose Mourinho claims his midfielder Claude Makelele is being treated like "a slave" by the France national team

QUOTES FROM THE MONTH

"I hope to be the one who brings some success back to this club, but it is a long way off at the moment. I have to admit that I am petrified by the challenge, but this is an absolutely fantastic football club, and I'm raring to go."
- Martin O'Neill on his appointment as Aston Villa manager.

"The player's name, stature and history doesn't matter because the team always comes first. We could have Pele and Maradona but the best teams are always in front of the players. Nothing and nobody can change that."
- Chelsea boss Jose Mourinho on his team selection policy.

"I don't think there is much I can do. I play football the way I see it. I think referees are trying to grab the headlines too much instead of refereeing the game. In the Premier League the referees let it go a bit but the foreign refs slow it down and are quick with the cards."
- Manchester United striker Wayne Rooney after being sent off for the third time in 11 months in a friendly against Porto.

"I couldn't have wished for a better start. The most pleasing thing for me was that, in possession, we looked like a cohesive team. It bodes well."
- New England boss Steve McClaren after 4-0 win over Greece.

Chelsea claim they sold William Gallas to Arsenal because the French defender threatened to score an own goal if he was selected for their first game of the season

"We could have had ten," snarls Sir Alex Ferguson after Man Utd beat Celtic 3-2 in 'Battle of Britain' Champions League clash at Old Trafford. Hoops boss Gordon Strachan responds: "We should have scored six or seven"

Ashley Cole claims he snubbed a chance to join Real Madrid when he moved to Chelsea from Arsenal

Alan Pardew says he would quit as West Ham manager if he was forced to play new Argentinian signings Carlos Tevez or Javier Mascherano

Arsenal win 1-0 at Man Utd....Chelsea beat Liverpool 1-0 at Stamford Bridge in hyped-up 'grudge' Premiership matches

Xabi Alonso scores a stunning goal from his own half that has to be a contender for goal of the month in Liverpool's 2-0 win over Newcastle

Man Utd top the Premiership after beating Tottenham 1-0. Giggs scores the winner as Red Devils make it four wins out of four at the start of the season

Fulham's new midfielder Jimmy Bullard suffers sickening knee injury at Newcastle and is out for rest of season

Rio Ferdinand says he still dreams of becoming club captain at Man Utd despite losing out to Gary Neville last season

Brian Kidd, former Man Utd and England coach, joins backroom staff at Sheff United

Liverpool boss Rafael Benitez insists striker Craig Bellamy is a reformed character and finds him 'focused, mature and a very good example to the rest of the players.'

Man City defender Ben Thatcher given eight-game suspension by the FA for his assault on Portsmouth's Pedro Mendes at Eastlands in August

Football's European governing body, Uefa, advocates a life ban for anyone found guilty of taking an illegal payment from a transfer

The Premier League agrees £65.8m extension of its title sponsorship with Barclays – with new deal running from 2007 to 2010

PREMIERSHIP – SEPTEMBER

LEAGUE PERFORMANCE FOR THE MONTH

	P	HOME					AWAY					TOTAL			
		W	D	L	F	A	W	D	L	F	A	F	A	DIF	PTS
Arsenal	4	1	1	0	4	1	2	0	0	3	1	7	2	5	10
Chelsea	4	2	1	0	4	2	1	0	0	2	0	6	2	4	10
Bolton	4	2	1	0	3	0	1	0	0	1	0	4	0	4	10
Blackburn	3	1	0	0	4	2	1	1	0	1	0	5	2	3	7
Reading	3	1	1	0	2	1	1	0	0	2	1	4	2	2	7
Everton	4	1	2	0	6	3	0	1	0	1	1	7	4	3	6
Aston Villa	4	1	0	0	2	0	0	3	0	2	2	4	2	2	6
Portsmouth	3	1	0	1	1	1	1	0	0	1	0	2	1	1	6
Liverpool	5	2	0	0	5	0	0	0	3	0	6	5	6	-1	6
Man Utd	3	1	0	1	1	0	1	0	1	1	1	2	2	0	4
Man City	4	1	0	0	2	0	0	1	2	3	6	5	6	-1	4
Newcastle	4	0	1	1	2	3	1	0	1	2	2	4	5	-1	4
Fulham	3	0	0	1	0	2	1	1	0	2	1	2	3	-1	4
Sheff Utd	4	1	1	1	3	3	0	1	0	0	3	3	6	-3	4
Wigan	3	0	1	0	1	1	0	1	1	2	3	3	4	-1	2
Watford	3	0	1	0	0	0	0	1	1	1	2	1	2	-1	2
Middlesbrough	4	0	0	1	0	1	0	2	1	2	3	2	4	-2	2
West Ham	3	0	1	1	1	3	0	0	1	0	2	1	5	-4	1
Tottenham	3	0	1	0	0	0	0	0	2	0	4	0	4	-4	1
Charlton	4	0	0	2	1	3	0	0	2	1	4	2	7	-5	0

GOAL OF THE MONTH

Robin Van Persie
Charlton v *Arsenal*

The other contenders:

Didier Drogba	*Chelsea* v Liverpool
Xabi Alonso	*Liverpool* v Newcastle
Georgios Samaras	*Man City* v West Ham
Cristiano Ronaldo	Reading v *Man Utd*
Phil Jagielka	*Sheffield Utd* v Middlesbrough

THE MONTH'S TOP GOALSCORERS

	GOALS IN THE MONTH		THE SEASON TO END OF MONTH		
Everton	Johnson	4	Johnson	6	50.0%
Chelsea	Drogba	3	Drogba	5	41.7%
Reading	Doyle	2	Doyle	3	37.5%
Sheff Utd	Hulse	2	Hulse	3	75.0%
Arsenal	Henry, van Persie	2	Henry, van Persie	2	25.0%
Aston Villa	Agbonlahor	2	Agbonlahor, Angel, L Moore	2	22.2%
Bolton	Speed	2	Campo, Speed	2	28.6%
Liverpool	Kuyt	2	Kuyt	2	25.0%
Man City	Samaras	2	Barton, Samaras	2	33.3%
Wigan	Scharner	2	Scharner	2	40.0%
West Ham	Zamora	1	Zamora	5	83.3%
Charlton	D Bent, Hasselbaink	1	D Bent	4	80.0%
Portsmouth	LuaLua, Mwaruwari	1	Kanu	4	44.4%
Blackburn	Gallagher, McCarthy, Nonda, Pedersen	1	McCarthy	3	33.3%
Fulham	Bocanegra, McBride	1	Bullard	2	40.0%
Man Utd	Giggs, Ronaldo	1	Giggs, Ronaldo, Rooney, Saha	2	16.7%
Middlesboro	Morrison, Yakubu	1	Yakubu,	2	33.3%
Newcastle	Ameobi, Duff, Martins, Parker	1	Ameobi, Parker	2	33.3%
Watford	Bouazza	1	Francis	2	50.0%
Tottenham		0	Berbatov, Jenas	1	50.0%

QUOTES FROM THE MONTH

"I think Sven's time here will be looked upon as nearly, not quite. Three quarter-finals, a little bit of Groundhog Day about the last one, going out on penalties to Portugal"
- FA chief executive Brian Barwick on Sven-Goran Eriksson's spell as England head coach.

"It's not like buying a pair of shoes off a shelf, it's completely different. It's more like a game of poker - and don't forget, other clubs do not always want to sell their players."
- Newcastle chairman Freddy Shepherd on the business of signing new players.

"Berbatov may prove to be a good signing for Tottenham. We watched him quite a bit at Bayer Leverkusen and he's a really good player."
- Man Utd boss Sir Alex Ferguson on Spurs new striker Dimitar Berbatov.

England cruise to 5-0 win over Andorra in Euro 2008 qualifier at Old Trafford. "I've seen better pub teams"
- Chris Waddle, referring to the visiting team.

BARCLAYS MANAGER OF THE MONTH

Steve Coppell - Reading

BARCLAYS PLAYER OF THE MONTH

Andy Johnson - Everton

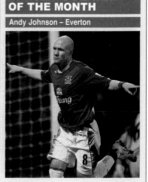

PREMIERSHIP – OCTOBER

LEAGUE PERFORMANCE FOR THE MONTH

		HOME					AWAY					TOTAL			
	P	W	D	L	F	A	W	D	L	F	A	F	A	DIF	PTS
Man Utd	4	2	0	0	4	0	2	0	0	7	1	11	1	10	12
Chelsea	3	1	0	0	2	1	2	0	0	3	0	5	1	4	9
Tottenham	4	2	0	0	3	1	0	2	0	1	1	4	2	2	8
Arsenal	3	1	1	0	4	1	1	0	0	4	0	8	1	7	7
Portsmouth	4	2	0	0	5	1	0	0	2	2	4	7	5	2	6
Wigan	4	1	0	1	5	3	1	0	1	2	2	7	5	2	6
Middlesbrough	4	2	0	0	3	1	0	0	1	0	1	3	2	1	6
Bolton	3	0	0	1	0	4	2	0	0	3	1	3	5	-2	6
Fulham	4	1	0	1	2	2	0	2	0	4	4	6	6	0	5
Everton	3	1	0	0	2	0	0	1	1	2	3	4	3	1	4
Liverpool	3	1	1	0	4	2	0	1	0	0	2	4	4	0	4
Blackburn	4	1	0	1	2	2	0	1	1	2	3	4	5	-1	4
Man City	3	1	1	0	1	0	0	0	1	0	4	1	4	-3	4
Watford	4	0	2	0	3	3	0	1	1	0	3	3	6	-3	3
West Ham	4	1	0	1	2	2	0	0	2	0	3	2	5	-3	3
Reading	4	0	0	2	0	5	1	0	1	2	3	2	8	-6	3
Charlton	3	0	1	0	0	0	0	1	1	1	2	1	2	-1	2
Aston Villa	3	0	2	0	2	2	0	0	1	1	3	3	5	-2	2
Newcastle	4	0	1	1	1	2	0	0	2	0	3	1	5	-4	1
Sheff Utd	3	0	0	1	0	2	0	1	1	0	2	0	4	-4	1

GOAL OF THE MONTH

Gareth Barry
Aston Villa v Tottenham

The other contenders:

Seol Ki-Hyeon	West Ham v *Reading*
Leighton Baines	*Wigan* v Man Utd
Emile Heskey	*Wigan* v Man City
Rio Ferdinand	*Man Utd* v Liverpool
Mido	*Spurs* v West Ham
Robin Van Persie	Reading v *Arsenal*
Wayne Rooney	Bolton v *Man Utd* (second goal)

THE MONTH'S TOP GOALSCORERS

	GOALS IN THE MONTH		THE SEASON TO END OF MONTH		
Portsmouth	Kanu	3	Kanu	7	43.8%
Arsenal	Henry	3	Henry	5	31.3%
Man Utd	Rooney, Solskjaer	3	Rooney	5	21.7%
Everton	Cahill	2	Johnson	6	37.5%
Chelsea	Ballack	2	Drogba, Lampard	5	29.4%
Blackburn	Bentley, McCarthy	2	McCarthy	4	40.0%
Middlesboro	Yakubu	2	Yakubu	4	44.4%
Aston Villa	Barry	2	Agbonlahor, Barry	3	25.0%
Bolton	Diouf	2	Campo, Diouf	3	30.0%
Fulham	McBride	2	McBride	3	27.3%
Wigan	Camara, Heskey	2	Camara, Heskey	3	25.0%
Watford	Young	2	Francis, Young	2	28.6%
Charlton	Bent, D	1	Bent, D	5	83.3%
West Ham	Mullina, Sheringham	1	Zamora	5	62.5%
Reading	Doyle, Seol	1	Doyle	4	40.0%
Liverpool	Bellamy, Crouch, Kuyt, Luis Garcia	1	Kuyt	3	25.0%
Newcastle	Ameobi	1	Ameobi	3	42.9%
Man City	Dunne	1	Barton, Samaras	3	28.6%
Tottenham	Defoe, Mido, Murphy	1	Berbatov, Defoe, Mido, Murphy	1	16.7%
Sheff Utd		0	Hulse	3	75.0%

BARCLAYS MANAGER OF THE MONTH

Sir Alex Ferguson - Manchester United

BARCLAYS PLAYER OF THE MONTH

Paul Scholes - Manchester United

Arsene Wenger celebrates 10 years as Arsenal manager with 2-1 win at Charlton and describes the second of Robin van Persie's strikes as one of the top five goals the Gunners have scored in his decade at the club

Paul Scholes plays his 500th match for Manchester United and scores the decisive first goal in 2-0 win over Liverpool at Old Trafford.

Liverpool boss Rafael Benitez defends his decision to play Steven Gerrard on the right side of midfield rather than in the centre of the park after rumours that the Reds skipper is unhappy with his role

Chelsea keeper Petr Cech suffers fractured skull and his replacement Carlo Cudicini is concussed in match at Reading. England skipper John Terry ends up in goal as Blues win 1-0 at the Madejski Stadium

Tottenham manager Martin Jol admits he may consider a bid for former England skipper David Beckham, who is unhappy with his lack of first-team action at Real Madrid

Manchester City midfielder Joey Barton celebrates Micah Richards' dramatic last-gasp equaliser by exposing his backside to the Goodison Park fans as he left the pitch and is charged with improper conduct by the FA

Manchester United striker Wayne Rooney ends personal goal drought by scoring his first Premiership hat-trick in 4-0 win at Bolton

Argentina coach Alfio Basile calls for Carlos Tevez and Javier Mascherano to leave West Ham for the sake of their careers

Steve McClaren's honeymoon period as England boss ends with dull goalless draw against Macedonia at Old Trafford

Television replays appear to show the England striker Jermain Defoe biting Javier Mascherano on the arm following a tackle from behind by West Ham's Argentine midfielder. Both players were booked and the FA takes no further action

Aston Villa training session is thrown open to free public access and nearly 4,000 fans turn up to watch the first-team squad practice at Villa Park

Four days later England lose 2-0 to Croatia in Zagreb and are booed by their own supporters, who call for the return of David Beckham

Blackburn miss two late penalties and Bolton skipper Kevin Nolan is red-carded in frantic final five minutes at Ewood Park. Bolton win the match 1-0

Public relations guru Max Clifford drops England boss Steve McClaren from his client list

Pressure mounts on West Ham boss Alan Pardew after the Hammers crash out of the Carling Cup after losing 2-1 at League One side Chesterfield

QUOTES FROM THE MONTH

"I stand by the reason why I made my decision over David. I'm looking to the future and the players coming through but the door is never closed to David Beckham."
- England head coach Steve McClaren on his decision to axe David Beckham from the national squad.

"Everyone has passion, but it's the way you express it. During 90 minutes I can show my passion for 10 minutes but Martin is 90 minutes. He shouts at everything and he complains about everything. Sometimes it is funny to look at him."
- Chelsea boss Jose Mourinho on Aston Villa manager martin O'Neill.

"I am not Abramovich's golden boy. I am just a player and he is my president, he takes care of all his players."
- Chelsea's £30 million striker Andrei Shevchenko on his relationship with club owner Roman Abramovich.

"I'm not Superman but what I need to do is to keep trying to score when my team needs it."
- Chelsea striker Didier Drogba after scoring the winner in 1-0 Champions League win over Barcelona.

Liverpool director Noel White resigns from the Anfield board after being quoted in a national newspaper questioning club manager Rafael Benitez's leadership and transfer dealings

Tottenham sporting director, Damien Comolli claims the club will endeavour to sign young British players in future and not copy Arsenal's policy of bringing in foreign stars

Manchester United manager Sir Alex Ferguson celebrates 20 years in charge at Old Trafford

Tottenham record first win over Chelsea in 16 years as goals from Michael Dawson and Aaron Lennon earn them a 2-1 victory at White Hart lane. Blues skipper John Terry is sent off

The FA launches investigation into claims by Chelsea players that referee Graham Poll targeted the champions in 2-1 defeat at Tottenham in order to "teaching them a lesson"

Premiership leaders Manchester United crash out of the Carling Cup after suffering shock 1-0 defeat at Southend. Self-confessed lifelong United fan Freddy Eastwood scores the winner

David Moyes's 200th match in charge of Everton ends in defeat with Arsenal securing a 1-0 Carling Cup victory at Goodison Park

Iain Dowie is sacked as Charlton Athletic manager after just six months - and 15 matches - in charge at The Valley. Les Reed is named as his successor

Manchester City defender Micah Richards senior England debut in 1-1 draw with Holland in Amsterdam. Wayne Rooney scores first goal for his country in more than a year

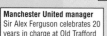

Consortium led by Icelandic businessman Eggert Magnusson completes his takeover of West Ham. Magnusson installs himself as chairman with Alan Pardew keeping his job as manager

Gareth Southgate is permitted to carry on as Middlesbrough manager after Premier League extends his dispensation to complete his coaching qualifications until the summer

The top of the table clash at Old Trafford between Manchester United and Chelsea ends in a 1-1 draw. French striker Louis Saha opens the scoring for United but then deflects Ricardo Carvalho's header past his own keeper Edwin van der Sar as the Blues grab a point

Fulham beat Arsenal 2-1 to record their first home win over the Gunners in 40 years. It was a stormy encounter at Craven Cottage with Arsenal defender Philippe Senderos sent-off and eight other players being shown yellow cards

Chelsea midfielder John Obi Mikel apologises to Blues manager Jose Mourinho after being criticized for his poor attitude in training and bad time-keeping

LEAGUE PERFORMANCE FOR THE MONTH

		HOME					AWAY					TOTAL		
	P	W	D	L	F	A	W	D	L	F	A	F	A	DIF	PTS
Man Utd	5	2	1	0	7	1	2	0	0	3	1	10	2	8	13
Chelsea	5	2	0	0	5	0	1	1	1	3	3	8	3	5	10
Reading	4	2	0	0	5	1	1	0	1	1	2	6	3	3	9
Aston Villa	5	1	1	1	4	4	1	1	0	1	0	5	4	1	8
Liverpool	5	2	1	0	3	0	0	1	1	0	3	3	3	0	8
Man City	5	1	1	0	3	1	1	0	2	3	3	6	4	2	7
Tottenham	4	2	0	0	5	2	0	1	1	2	4	7	6	1	7
Sheff Utd	5	0	1	1	3	4	2	0	1	2	1	5	5	0	7
Wigan	4	1	1	0	3	2	1	0	1	2	3	5	5	0	7
Fulham	5	2	0	1	3	2	0	1	1	2	4	5	6	-1	7
West Ham	4	2	0	0	2	0	0	0	2	0	2	2	2	0	6
Newcastle	4	1	0	1	1	1	0	2	0	1	1	2	2	0	5
Middlesbrough	4	1	1	0	1	0	0	1	1	1	3	2	3	-1	5
Portsmouth	5	1	0	1	3	2	0	1	2	0	4	3	6	-3	5
Arsenal	5	1	1	0	4	1	0	0	3	2	6	6	7	-1	4
Bolton	5	1	0	2	3	3	0	1	1	2	3	5	6	-1	4
Charlton	4	1	1	0	2	1	0	0	2	2	5	4	6	-2	4
Everton	5	1	0	1	1	1	0	1	2	1	5	2	6	-4	4
Watford	4	1	0	1	2	1	0	0	2	1	6	3	7	-4	3
Blackburn	3	0	1	1	1	2	0	0	1	0	2	1	4	-3	1

GOAL OF THE MONTH

MATCH OF THE DAY

Nicolas Anelka
Bolton v Arsenal

The other contenders:
Cristiano Ronaldo	*Man Utd v Portsmouth*
Claude Makelele	*Tottenham v Chelsea*
Colin Kazim-Richards	*Sheff Utd v Bolton*
Henri Camara	*Wigan v Charlton*
Mikel Arteta	*Everton v Bolton*
Tugay	*Blackburn v Tottenham*
Jermain Defoe	*Tottenham v Wigan*
Sylvain Distin	*Man City v Aston Villa*
Robin Van Persie	*Fulham v Arsenal*

THE MONTH'S TOP GOALSCORERS

	GOALS IN THE MONTH		THE SEASON TO END OF MONTH		
Chelsea	Drogba	3	Drogba	8	32.0%
Man Utd	Saha	3	Rooney	7	21.2%
Reading	Doyle	3	Doyle	7	43.8%
Aston Villa	Barry	2	Barry	5	29.4%
Liverpool	Kuyt	2	Kuyt	5	33.3%
Wigan	Camara, McCulloch	2	Camara	5	29.4%
Bolton	Anelka	2	Diouf	4	26.7%
Man City	Barton, Corradi	2	Barton	4	30.8%
Sheff Utd	Webber	2	Hulse	4	44.4%
Tottenham	Defoe, Lennon	2	Defoe	3	23.1%
Portsmouth	Cole, Kanu, LuaLua	1	Kanu	8	42.1%
Arsenal	Flamini, Gallas, Gilberto Silva, Henry, Toure, van Persie 1		Henry	6	27.3%
Charlton	Bent, D, Bent, M, Reid	1	Bent, D	6	60.0%
Everton	Arteta	1	Johnson	6	33.3%
West Ham	Harewood, Mullin	1	Zamora	5	50.0%
Blackburn	Tugay	1	McCarthy	4	36.4%
Fulham	Jensen, C, John, Knight, McBride, Radzinski 1		McBride	4	25.0%
Middlesboro	Christie, Maccarone	1	Yakubu	4	36.4%
Newcastle	Dyer, Sibierski	1	Ameobi	3	33.3%
Watford	DeMerit, Young	1	Young	3	30.0%

QUOTES FROM THE MONTH

"On Saturday I saw some fans leave early when we were looking for a goal. We were constantly attacking... I just wanted you to know that the players do notice it."
- Arsenal skipper Thierry Henry on supporters leaving the Emirates Stadium before the end of the game.

"I think it is scandalous that some people think I should retire - it is none of their bloody business."
- Sir Alex Ferguson on speculation about his future.

"I think it is a very minor incident. It was a little flurry and, quite honestly, it is a game played with great passion and people are passionate about it."
- Arsenal chairman Peter Hill-Wood on Gunners Boss Arsene Wenger's touchline bust-up with the West Ham manager.

"There are no suicides, no mass sackings, no need for counselling, but maybe a little bit of recrimination."
- Sir Alex Ferguson following Manchester United's 1-0 Carling Cup defeat at Southend.

BARCLAYS MANAGER OF THE MONTH

Steve Coppell - Reading

BARCLAYS PLAYER OF THE MONTH

Cristiano Ronaldo - Manchester United

PREMIERSHIP – DECEMBER

LEAGUE PERFORMANCE FOR THE MONTH

	P	HOME W	D	L	F	A	AWAY W	D	L	F	A	TOTAL F	A	DIF	PTS
Liverpool	6	2	0	0	6	0	3	0	1	8	1	14	1	13	15
Man Utd	6	3	0	0	9	4	2	0	1	5	2	14	6	8	15
Bolton	6	3	0	0	9	3	2	0	1	3	1	12	4	8	15
Arsenal	7	2	1	0	11	4	2	1	1	4	3	15	7	8	14
Chelsea	6	1	3	0	6	5	2	0	0	6	4	12	9	3	12
Newcastle	7	3	0	0	8	4	1	0	3	4	7	12	11	1	12
Tottenham	7	3	0	1	9	4	1	0	2	3	7	12	11	1	12
Blackburn	7	3	0	1	6	4	1	0	2	4	8	10	12	-2	12
Portsmouth	6	2	1	0	7	3	1	1	1	6	6	13	9	4	11
Everton	6	2	1	1	7	3	1	0	1	2	2	9	5	4	10
Sheff Utd	6	2	1	1	5	4	1	0	1	2	3	7	7	0	10
Man City	6	0	1	2	1	4	2	0	1	3	3	4	7	-3	7
Charlton	7	2	1	1	5	6	0	0	3	2	9	7	15	-8	7
Fulham	6	1	1	0	2	1	0	2	2	4	10	6	11	-5	6
Middlesbrough	7	1	1	1	4	3	0	1	3	3	6	7	9	-2	5
Reading	7	1	0	2	2	4	0	2	2	6	8	8	12	-4	5
Wigan	7	0	0	4	2	9	1	1	1	4	4	6	13	-7	4
West Ham	7	1	0	3	2	5	0	1	2	0	4	2	11	-9	4
Watford	5	0	1	1	1	2	0	1	2	1	4	2	6	-4	2
Aston Villa	6	0	0	2	0	4	0	2	2	6	8	6	12	-6	2

GOAL OF THE MONTH

MATCH OF THE DAY

Paul Scholes
Aston Villa v Man Utd

The other contenders:

Keith Gillespie	*Sheff Utd v Charlton*
Morten Gamst Pedersen	*Blackburn v Newcastle*
Matthew Taylor	*Portsmouth v Everton*
Michael Essien	*Chelsea v Arsenal*
David Bentley	Reading v *Blackburn*
Tom Huddlestone	Man City v *Tottenham*
Frank Lampard	Everton v *Chelsea*
Didier Drogba	Everton v *Chelsea*
Robin Van Persie	Watford v *Arsenal*

THE MONTH'S TOP GOALSCORERS

	GOALS IN THE MONTH		THE SEASON TO END OF MONTH		
Man Utd	Ronaldo	7	Ronaldo	12	25.5%
Newcastle	Martins	6	Martins	7	33.3%
Chelsea	Drogba	5	Drogba	13	35.1%
Portsmouth	Taylor	5	Kanu	9	28.1%
Arsenal	Gilberto Silva	5	van Persie	8	21.6%
Bolton	Anelka	5	Anelka	7	25.9%
Blackburn	McCarthy, Nonda	4	McCarthy	8	38.1%
Liverpool	Bellamy	4	Kuyt	6	20.7%
Aston Villa	Barry	3	Barry	8	34.8%
Reading	Harper	3	Doyle	8	33.3%
Middlesboro	Yakubu	3	Yakubu	7	38.9%
Tottenham	Berbatov, Defoe	3	Defoe	6	24.0%
Wigan	Heskey	3	Camara, Heskey	4	25.0%
Charlton	Bent, D	2	Bent, D	8	47.1%
Everton	Anichebe	2	Johnson	7	25.9%
Fulham	McBride	2	McBride	6	27.3%
Sheff Utd	Hulse	2	Hulse	6	37.5%
Man City	Barton, Beasley, Ireland, Trabelsi	1	Barton	5	29.4%
West Ham	Reo-Coker, Sheringham	1	Zamora	5	41.7%
Watford	Bouazza, Priskin, Smith, T	1	Young	3	23.1%

BARCLAYS MANAGER OF THE MONTH

Sam Allardyce - Bolton

BARCLAYS PLAYER OF THE MONTH

Cristiano Ronalo - Manchester United

Manchester United sign 35-year-old Swedish striker Henrik Larsson on a 10-week loan deal from Helsingborg

Middlesbrough boss Gareth Southgate calls winger Ronaldo a "diver" for his part in winning Manchester United a penalty against Boro

Arsenal skipper Thierry Henry storms out of training after being told he would be dropped for north London derby against Tottenham

Everton announce a £10m loss for the 2005-06 season

Arsenal, Celtic, Chelsea, Liverpool and Manchester United all qualify for the knockout round of the Champions' League

West Ham sack manager Alan Pardew after a series of disappointing results. First-team coach Kevin Keen takes temporary charge of team affairs

Michael Essien scores 84th minute equaliser with 35-yard piledriver to earn Chelsea a 1-1 draw with Arsenal and safeguard 51-game unbeaten run at Stamford Bridge in the Premiership under Jose Mourinho

Everton chairman Bill Kenwright says it is not an option for the club to remain at Goodison Park and reveals the club is investigating the possibility of building a new stadium in Kirkby

West Ham name Alan Curbishley as their new manager. The former Charlton boss has signed a three-and-a-half-year contract

Liverpool manager Rafael Benitez calls for top English clubs to be allowed to field second teams outside the Premiership in order to expose young players to more competitive football

Arsenal boss Arsene Wenger charged with "improper conduct" by the FA for "his words and behaviour towards the match officials" at half-time during match against Portsmouth

Sheffield United manager, Neil Warnock puts eight players up for sale or loan ahead of the January transfer window

Charlton appoint Alan Pardew as their new manager after sacking Les Reed who had been in charge at The Valley for just 41 days

Andy Johnson accepts an apology from Jose Mourinho following claims by the Chelsea manager that the Everton striker is a serial diver

Premiership leaders Manchester United end the year six points clear of Chelsea

QUOTES FROM THE MONTH

"If we ever play the way we did on Tuesday again, I'd probably give the money back to Sky. We were appalling, I nearly went home myself."
- Watford manager Adrian Boothroyd reflecting on the 1-0 home defeat by Sheffield United.

"If someone tripped you up in my day, most people would jump up and confront the guy who had done it. If you stayed down, the crowd would be shouting you were soft, or words to that effect."
- Blackburn manager Mark Hughes on the issue of "diving".

"Quite simply, it is true that I can be a pig! It is not a lie to say that. Sometimes, I feel that I am in the right even when I am wrong."
- Arsenal skipper Thierry Henry in an interview with French sports newspaper L'Equipe.

"They used to say that about us at Bayer Leverkusen, but we never won anything."
- German midfielder Michael Ballack when asked why Arsenal played much more attractive football than Chelsea.

Chelsea manager Jose Mourinho complains that several of his players are below form and and names Andrey Shevchenko, Salomon Kalou and Shaun Wright-Phillips as stars who have been "performing nothing for the team"

Watford sign 19-year-old Moses Ashikodi from Rangers for a nominal fee on a two-and-a-half-year contract

The Premier League confirms that it has sold its next set of overseas television rights for £625m, double the previous amount

West Ham suffer their heaviest Premiership defeat when they are trounced 6-0 at Reading

Robin van Persie and Thierry Henry hit two late goals as Arsenal come from behind to beat leaders Manchester United. However, celebrations for Gunners are tempered by news that van Persie broke the fifth metatarsal on his right foot in scoring his goal and faces a lengthy spell on sidelines

Aston Villa sign 6ft 4in striker John Carew from French champions Lyon in straight swap deal for Milan Baros. The Midlands club also complete the £9.65m signing of 21-year-old forward Ashley Young from Watford

Chelsea and England captain John Terry fined £10,000 by the FA for improper conduct. The Chelsea captain was charged in relation to comments made about referee Graham Poll after being sent off in the defeat against Tottenham on 5 November

Arsenal's Julio Baptista scores four goals and misses and penalty as Gunners thump Liverpool 6-3 in Carling Cup quarter-final

Former France midfielder Michel Platini is installed as the new president of Uefa

West Ham complete the £1.5m signing of Australian defender Lucas Neill from Blackburn.

David Beckham agrees agrees to move to Los Angeles Galaxy from Real Madrid in the summer on a five-year contract reported to be worth £128m

Fulham sign midfielder Simon Davies from Everton for initial fee of £2.5m

Chelsea keeper Petr Cech - who suffered a fractured skull at Reading in October - makes his comeback against Liverpool wearing a rugby style headguard. However, the Blues title hopes are dented by 2-0 defeat at Anfield

Manchester City manager Stuart Pearce is confirmed as the new part-time coach of the England Under-21 side

Newcastle concede five goals at home in the FA Cup for the first time since January 1914 after 5-1 defeat by Championship side Birmingham

Newcastle midfielder Emre Belozoglu becomes the first Premiership footballer to be charged by the FA with using racist language towards a fellow player after an incident during Newcastle's match at Goodison Park in December

Manchester United ban Cristiano Ronaldo from talking about media speculation linking the Portugal international with a possible move to Real Madrid

---

PREMIERSHIP – JANUARY

LEAGUE PERFORMANCE FOR THE MONTH

		HOME					AWAY					TOTAL		
	P	W	D	L	F	A	W	D	L	F	A	F	A	DIF	PTS
Liverpool	4	2	0	0	5	0	2	0	0	5	1	10	1	9	12
Reading	4	3	0	0	12	3	0	1	1	1	1	13	4	9	10
Middlesbrough	4	2	0	0	8	2	1	1	0	3	1	11	3	8	10
Arsenal	3	2	0	0	6	1	1	0	0	2	0	8	1	7	9
Newcastle	4	1	2	0	7	5	1	0	0	3	2	10	7	3	8
Man Utd	4	2	0	0	7	1	0	1	1	3	4	10	5	5	7
Chelsea	4	2	0	0	7	0	0	1	1	0	2	7	2	5	7
Blackburn	5	0	0	1	0	2	2	0	2	7	5	7	7	0	6
Everton	3	0	1	0	1	1	1	0	1	3	2	4	3	1	4
Sheff Utd	4	1	1	0	3	1	0	0	2	2	6	5	7	-2	4
Aston Villa	4	1	1	0	2	0	0	0	2	2	6	4	6	-2	4
Man City	3	1	0	1	2	4	0	1	0	0	0	2	4	-2	4
Charlton	4	0	0	1	1	3	1	1	1	2	5	3	8	-5	4
Watford	5	1	0	1	2	4	0	1	2	0	6	2	10	-8	4
Portsmouth	4	0	2	1	1	2	0	1	0	1	1	2	3	-1	3
Fulham	4	0	2	0	1	1	0	1	1	3	5	4	6	-2	3
Tottenham	3	0	0	1	2	3	0	2	0	2	2	4	5	-1	2
West Ham	4	0	1	1	4	5	0	1	1	2	8	6	13	-7	2
Bolton	4	0	2	0	1	1	0	0	2	1	8	2	9	-7	2
Wigan	4	0	0	2	0	5	0	0	2	2	7	2	12	-10	0

GOAL OF THE MONTH

MATCH OF THE DAY

Wayne Rooney
Man Utd v Portsmouth (F.A.)

The other contenders:

Peter Crouch	*Liverpool* v Bolton
James Milner	*Newcastle* v Man Utd
Tomas Rosicky	Liverpool v *Arsenal* (F.A.)
Yakubu	Charlton v *Middlesboro*
Thierry Henry	Blackburn v *Arsenal*
Obafemi Martins	Tottenham v *Newcastle*
Jermaine Pennant	*Liverpool* v Chelsea

THE MONTH'S TOP GOALSCORERS

	GOALS IN THE MONTH		THE SEASON TO END OF MONTH		
Liverpool	Crouch	4	Kuyt	9	23.1%
Arsenal	Henry, van Persie	3	van Persie	11	24.4%
Middlesboro	Viduka, Yakubu	3	Yakubu	10	34.5%
Newcastle	Milner	3	Martins	8	25.8%
Chelsea	Drogba, Lampard	2	Drogba	15	34.1%
Man Utd	Ronaldo, Rooney, Scholes	2	Ronaldo	14	24.6%
Blackburn	Derbyshire, McCarthy, Pedersen	2	McCarthy	10	35.7%
Reading	Doyle, Hunt, Lita, Long	2	Doyle	10	27.0%
Aston Villa	Agbonlahor	2	Barry	8	29.6%
Everton	Arteta	2	Johnson	8	25.8%
West Ham	Benayoun	2	Zamora	6	33.3%
Man City	Samaras	2	Barton	5	26.3%
Portsmouth	Mwaruwari, O'Neil	1	Kanu	9	26.5%
Bolton	Nolan, Pedersen	1	Anelka	7	24.1%
Fulham	Christanval, McBride, Montella, Radzinski	1	McBride	7	26.9%
Tottenham	Berbatov, Chimbonda, Defoe, Malbranque	1	Defoe	7	24.1%
Wigan	Heskey, Landzaat	1	Heskey	7	26.9%
Sheff Utd	Jagielka, Nade, Quinn, S, Stead, Tonge	1	Hulse	6	28.6%
Watford	DeMerit	1	Young	3	20.0%
Charlton	El Karkouri, Faye, Hasselbaink	1	El Karkouri, Hasselbaink, Reid	2	10.0%

QUOTES FROM THE MONTH

"Chelsea aren't getting their own way like they have done for the past couple of seasons and we are serious contenders now. I always said that if we got to January and we were top of the league I'd be happy with that and I am."
- Manchester United boss Sir Alex Ferguson on the race for the title

"My scouting department has done an excellent job but sometimes we go too slowly as a club to make the signings we need and when we do there is not a lot of money,"
- Liverpool boss Rafael Benitez on the Anfield transfer dealings

"It's not my club. I''m just the manager."
- Chelsea boss Jose Mourinho when asked to explain the lack of new signings at Stamford Bridge

"It would be disappointing for me [if he left], because I've enjoyed Jose's company the times we've met after games. He's got a good personality and I enjoy the competition against him," - Manchester United boss Sir Alex Ferguson on speculation that Jose Mourinho could quit as Chelsea manager at the end of the season.

BARCLAYS MANAGER OF THE MONTH

Rafa Benitez - Liverpool

BARCLAYS PLAYER OF THE MONTH

Francesc Fabregas - Arsenal

PREMIERSHIP – FEBRUARY

LEAGUE PERFORMANCE FOR THE MONTH

		HOME					AWAY					TOTAL		
	P	W	D	L	F	A	W	D	L	F	A	F	A	DIF	PTS
Man Utd	3	1	0	0	2	0	2	0	0	6	1	8	1	7	9
Everton	4	1	0	1	2	2	1	1	0	3	0	5	2	3	7
Wigan	4	2	0	0	2	0	0	1	1	2	3	4	3	1	7
Chelsea	2	1	0	0	3	0	1	0	0	1	0	4	0	4	6
Blackburn	3	2	0	0	5	1	0	0	1	0	1	5	2	3	6
Reading	3	1	0	0	2	0	1	0	1	3	2	5	2	3	6
Tottenham	4	1	0	1	4	5	1	0	1	3	3	7	8	-1	6
Bolton	3	1	0	0	2	1	1	0	1	2	4	4	5	-1	6
Liverpool	3	1	1	0	4	0	0	0	1	1	2	5	2	3	4
Arsenal	2	1	0	0	2	1	0	1	0	1	1	3	2	1	4
Middlesbrough	3	1	1	0	3	2	0	0	1	0	3	3	5	-2	4
Watford	4	0	1	2	1	5	1	0	0	1	0	2	5	-3	4
Charlton	3	1	0	1	4	1	0	0	1	0	2	4	3	1	3
Fulham	3	1	0	1	3	3	0	0	1	1	2	4	5	-1	3
Newcastle	3	1	0	0	2	1	0	0	2	1	3	3	4	-1	3
Aston Villa	2	1	0	0	1	0	0	0	1	0	2	1	2	-1	3
Portsmouth	3	1	0	0	2	1	0	0	2	0	4	2	5	-3	3
Sheff Utd	3	1	0	0	2	1	0	0	2	1	6	3	7	-4	3
Man City	2	0	0	1	0	2	0	0	1	1	2	1	4	-3	0
West Ham	3	0	0	1	0	1	0	0	2	0	5	0	6	-6	0

GOAL OF THE MONTH

MATCH OF THE DAY

Denny Landzaat
Arsenal v *Wigan*

The other contenders:
Steve Sidwell	*Reading* v Aston Villa
Pedro Mendes	*Portsmouth* v Man City
Freddie Ljungberg	Bolton v *Arsenal* (F.A.)
Michael Carrick	*Man Utd* v Reading (F.A.)
Stephen Ireland	Preston v *Man City* (F.A.)
Robbie Keane	Fulham v *Tottenham* (F.A.)
Cristiano Ronaldo	Fulham v *Man Utd*
Yakubu	*Middlesboro* v Reading
Benni McCarthy	*Blackburn* v Arsenal (F.A.)

THE MONTH'S TOP GOALSCORERS

GOALS IN THE MONTH

Tottenham	Jenas	3
Chelsea	Drogba	2
Man Utd	Giggs, Ronaldo	2
Middlesboro	Yakubu	2
Blackburn	Nonda, Pedersen	2
Everton	Johnson	2
Newcastle	Martins	2
Reading	Lita, Sidwell	2
Charlton	Thomas	2
Fulham	McBride	2
Liverpool	Fowler	2
Bolton	Speed	2
Watford	Henderson	2
Arsenal	Henry, Rosicky	1
Portsmouth	Kanu, Mendes	1
Aston Villa	Carew	1
Sheff Utd	Hulse, Jagielka, Stead	1
Wigan	Folan, Landzaat, McCulloch, Taylor	1
Man City	Corradi	1
West Ham		0

THE SEASON TO END OF MONTH

Berbatov, Defoe	7	19.4%
Drogba	17	35.4%
Ronaldo	16	24.6%
Yakubu	12	37.5%
McCarthy	10	30.3%
Johnson	10	27.8%
Martins	10	29.4%
Doyle	10	23.8%
Bent, D	9	37.5%
McBride	9	30.0%
Kuyt	9	20.5%
Anelka	8	24.2%
Bouazza, DeMerit, Francis, Henderson	2	11.8%
Henry	10	20.8%
Kanu	10	27.8%
Barry	8	28.6%
Hulse	7	29.2%
Heskey	7	23.3%
Barton	5	25.0%
Zamora	6	33.3%

BARCLAYS MANAGER OF THE MONTH

Sir Alex Ferguson - Manchester United

BARCLAYS PLAYER OF THE MONTH

Ryan Giggs - Manchester United

Tottenham captain Ledley King suffers setback in recovery from bruised foot and is ruled out for up to eight more weeks. He suffered injury against Aston Villa on Boxing Day

Manchester United keeper Edwin van der Sar suffers broken nose in 4-0 win at Tottenham and with all three substitutes on the field defender John O'Shea has to go in goal

American tycoons George Gillett Jr and Tom Hicks reach agreement to take over Liverpool

Real Madrid and Barcelona overtake Manchester United as biggest revenue-earning clubs in the world according to figures published in the Deloitte Money League table

Wigan boss Paul Jewell launches tirade against referee Phil Dowd after 2-1 defeat at Arsenal and says the match official "could cost us £50m" if club are relegated at the end of the season. The FA later charge Jewell with improper conduct

The FA charge Portsmouth manager Harry Redknapp with using abusive and/or insulting words towards a match official for apparent comments made to referee Mike Dean during 2-1 victory over Manchester City

Everton agree deal to sign on-loan keeper Tim Howard on the permanent basis from Manchester United at the end of the season

Howard, who has been on loan to Everton since losing his place at United to Edwin van der Sar, has agreed a five-year contract with the Toffees that will keep him at Goodison Park until 2012

England boss Steve McClaren has sends his team DVDs of their individual performances and statistical data with the promise that every player will be held "accountable"

Liverpool complete the signing of Javier Mascherano who had been playing for West Ham. The Argentina midfielder makes a gaffe, however, when he states: "I can consider myself a Red Devil"

Liverpool manager, Rafael Benitez promises an internal club investigation and potential disciplinary action following allegations that Craig Bellamy attacked team-mate John Arne Riise with a golf club at a training camp in Portugal

West Ham chairman Eggert Magnusson gives his "100 per cent backing" to manager Alan Curbishley despite only one win in 10 Premiership games since Curbishley replaced Alan Pardew

Chelsea beat Arsenal 2-1 in Carling Cup final but the match is marred by a head injury to Blues skipper John Terry and then a late mass brawl on the pitch which saw three players are red-carded

Craig Bellamy celebrates by miming a golf swing after scoring Liverpool's first goal in their 2-1 Champions League win at Barcelona

Manchester United captain Gary Neville calls for agents to be removed from football. "We've got the PFA - and they want to give, not take," says the England defender

Real Madrid coach Fabio Capello says Steve McClaren should follow his example and recall former skipper David Beckham to the England squad

Chelsea announce £80m losses in 12 months up to the end of June 2006, but the club's chief executive Peter Kenyon said that it was on track to break even by 2010

Lille players threaten to leave pitch after Ryan Giggs' goal from a quickly taken free-kick is allowed to stand as Manchester United claim 1-0 Champions League victory in France

QUOTES FROM THE MONTH

"One team wanted to win, the other wanted not to lose. They put nine men behind the ball and played narrow and compact. That's what small clubs do when they come here,"
- Liverpool boss Rafael Benitez after goalless goal against Everton at Anfield.

"As far as I am concerned there are no hard feelings. I think Joey is similar to myself. When he does interviews he is really honest and likes to say how he feels. I think every footballer has said things that they regret slightly and you learn from those things,"
- Liverpool captain Steven Gerrard on Manchester City midfielder Joey Barton's reported criticism of certain England players.

"We all know Henrik is a quality player. I have said before I think he is the best Scandinavian player since Michael Laudrup. His touch is something we can all learn from. You never stop learning as a player and Henrik has done a few tricks in training that have had us all looking and saying, 'We have not seen that before'."
- Manchester United stalwart Ole Gunnar Solskjaer on the club's on-loan striker Henrik Larsson.

"I think it's better you have an English guy. You savage them even quicker,"
- Arsenal boss Arsene Wenger on speculation that he might one day become England team manager.

The Premier League charge West Ham with breaching transfer regulations when they signed Argentine World Cup stars Carlos Tevez and Javier Mascherano in August

Liverpool concede first goal at home in the Premiership for 931 minutes as substitute John O'Shea scores the winner in Manchester United's 1-0 victory at Anfield

Tottenham board tells manager Martin Jol to pick the striker Dimitar Berbatov for FA Cup for the sixth-round game at Chelsea after he initially decided to rest the £10.9m Bulgarian star

Manchester United winger Ryan Giggs plays his 700th game in a Manchester United shirt

The FA confirm the 2007 Cup final will be played at the new national stadium at Wembley as scheduled on May 19

Tottenham keeper Paul Robinson scores a freakish goal from a 95-yard free-kick during 3-1 home victory over Watford.

England and Israel play out dull goalless Euro 2008 qualifier in Tel Aviv, while England Under-21 draw with Italy 3-3 in first international at new Wembley Stadium

Everton midfielder Tim Cahill suffers broken metatarsal at Sheffield United and will miss the rest of the season

Henrik Larsson scores Manchester United's winner in 1-0 Champions League second leg win against Lille in what is the Swedish striker last home game of is loan spell. United advance to the quarter-finals

Chelsea and Liverpool join Manchester United in the Champions League last eight draw, but Arsenal and Celtic are eliminated

England boss Steve McClaren storms out of post-match press conference after his team makes hard work of a 3-0 victory in Euro 2008 qualifier against Andorra

Arsenal announce that skipper Thierry Henry will not play again this season after suffering injuries to stomach and groin muscles

The FA charge Arsenal boss Arsene Wenger with improper conduct and/or bringing the game into disrepute following his comments after the Carling Cup final defeat by Chelsea

Chelsea midfielder Frank Lampard is attacked by a Tottenham fan as he celebrates the Blues' 2-1 win in bad-tempered FA Cup quarter-final replay at White Hart Lane

PREMIERSHIP – MARCH

LEAGUE PERFORMANCE FOR THE MONTH

		HOME					AWAY					TOTAL		
	P	W	D	L	F	A	W	D	L	F	A	F	A	DIF	PTS
Chelsea	4	1	0	0	3	0	3	0	0	4	0	7	0	7	12
Man Utd	3	2	0	0	8	2	1	0	0	1	0	9	2	7	9
Charlton	3	2	0	0	3	0	0	1	0	2	2	5	2	3	7
Tottenham	2	1	0	0	3	1	1	0	0	4	3	7	4	3	6
West Ham	3	1	0	1	5	4	1	0	0	2	1	7	5	2	6
Man City	4	0	0	2	0	2	2	0	0	3	0	3	2	1	6
Arsenal	4	1	0	0	2	1	1	0	2	2	5	4	6	-2	6
Liverpool	3	1	0	1	4	2	0	1	0	0	0	4	2	2	4
Everton	2	1	0	0	1	0	0	1	0	1	1	2	1	1	4
Wigan	3	0	1	0	0	0	1	0	1	1	1	1	1	0	4
Fulham	3	0	2	0	2	2	0	1	0	0	0	2	2	0	3
Blackburn	3	0	0	1	1	2	1	0	1	3	5	4	7	-3	3
Bolton	3	1	0	1	2	2	0	0	1	1	4	3	6	-3	3
Aston Villa	3	0	1	1	0	1	0	1	0	1	1	1	2	-1	2
Portsmouth	3	0	0	2	0	2	0	2	0	1	1	1	3	-2	2
Reading	2	0	1	0	0	0	0	0	1	1	2	1	2	-1	1
Watford	3	0	1	1	2	3	0	0	1	1	3	3	6	-3	1
Newcastle	3	0	1	1	0	1	0	0	1	0	2	0	3	-3	1
Sheff Utd	3	0	1	0	1	1	0	0	2	0	4	1	5	-4	1
Middlesbrough	3	0	0	1	0	2	0	1	1	0	2	0	4	-4	1

GOAL OF THE MONTH

Wayne Rooney
Man Utd v Bolton (first goal)

The other contenders:

Didier Drogba	Portsmouth v *Chelsea*
Hameur Bouazza	Plymouth Argyle v *Watford* (F.A.)
Paul Robinson	*Tottenham* v Watford
Andriy Shevchenko	Tottenham v *Chelsea* (F.A.)
Niko Krancjar	Fulham v *Portsmouth*
Peter Crouch	*Liverpool* v Arsenal (third goal)
Kevin Davies	*Bolton* v Sheff Utd
Paul Scholes	*Man Utd* v Blackburn

THE MONTH'S TOP GOALSCORERS

	GOALS IN THE MONTH		THE SEASON TO END OF MONTH		
Chelsea	Kalou	3	Drogba	18	32.7%
Man Utd	Park	3	Ronaldo	16	21.6%
Liverpool	Crouch	3	Crouch, Kuyt	9	18.8%
West Ham	Tevez, Zamora	3	Zamora	9	36.0%
Blackburn	McCarthy	2	McCarthy	12	32.4%
Man City	Mpenza	2	Barton	5	21.7%
Everton	Arteta, Johnson	1	Johnson	11	28.9%
Arsenal	Baptista, Diaby, Gallas, Gilberto Silva	1	Henry	10	19.2%
Charlton	Ambrose, Bent, D, Thomas, Young, Zheng, Z	1	Bent, D	10	34.5%
Portsmouth	Kranjcar	1	Kanu	10	27.0%
Bolton	Anelka, Davies, Speed	1	Anelka	9	25.0%
Fulham	Bocanegra, Pearce	1	McBride	9	28.1%
Aston Villa	Carew	1	Barry	8	27.6%
Sheff Utd	Hulse	1	Hulse	8	32.0%
Tottenham	Berbatov, Ghaly, Jenas, Robinson, Stalteri, Tainio	1	Berbatov, Defoe	8	18.6%
Wigan	Folan	1	Heskey	7	22.6%
Watford	Bouazza, Francis, Henderson	1	Bouazza, Francis, Henderson	3	15.0%
Middlesboro		0	Yakubu	12	37.5%
Newcastle		0	Martins	10	29.4%
Reading		0	Doyle	10	23.3%

QUOTES FROM THE MONTH

"I think Jose should button his lip now for good, for the rest of the season." - Manchester United manager Sir Alex Ferguson on complaints by Chelsea boss Jose Mourinho about United and their treatment from referees.

"If that happens I'll be a millionaire and I will get another club in a couple of months," - Jose Mourinho on the prospect of being sacked as Chelsea manager.

"If people boo me it's because I am dangerous and I am doing something good. For me it's not a problem - I keep my concentration and try to do good things to help my team," – Manchester United winger Cristiano Ronaldo on the hostility of opposition supporters.

"I was in the barbers when Steve McClaren rang with the news, but I didn't believe it was him, I thought it was someone messing me about, and I hung up on him. Thankfully, he rang straight back," - Manchester City defender Micah Richards on receiving the call from England manager Steve McClaren telling him he was in the squad for the friendly against Holland.

BARCLAYS MANAGER OF THE MONTH

Jose Mourinho - Chelsea

BARCLAYS PLAYER OF THE MONTH

Petr Cech - Chelsea

PREMIERSHIP ROUND-UP - MONTH BY MONTH

PREMIERSHIP – APRIL

LEAGUE PERFORMANCE FOR THE MONTH

	P	HOME					AWAY					TOTAL			
		W	D	L	F	A	W	D	L	F	A	F	A	DIF	PTS
Aston Villa	6	0	3	0	2	2	3	0	0	7	2	9	4	5	12
Arsenal	6	3	0	1	8	4	0	2	0	2	2	10	6	4	11
Liverpool	5	2	0	0	4	0	1	1	1	3	3	7	3	4	10
Reading	6	2	0	1	3	2	1	1	1	3	2	6	4	2	10
Portsmouth	5	3	0	0	6	3	0	1	1	2	4	8	7	1	10
West Ham	5	1	0	1	2	4	2	0	1	4	3	6	7	-1	9
Chelsea	4	1	1	0	3	2	1	1	0	4	1	7	3	4	8
Everton	6	2	0	1	8	6	0	2	1	2	3	10	9	1	8
Tottenham	5	1	1	0	3	2	1	1	1	6	6	9	8	1	8
Blackburn	4	2	0	1	8	4	0	1	0	1	1	9	5	4	7
Man Utd	4	1	1	0	3	1	1	0	1	5	4	8	5	3	7
Sheff Utd	5	2	0	1	5	2	0	1	1	1	3	6	5	1	7
Man City	6	0	2	1	0	2	1	1	1	5	5	5	7	-2	6
Bolton	5	0	1	1	2	4	1	1	1	6	5	8	9	-1	5
Newcastle	5	0	2	0	0	0	1	0	2	3	4	3	4	-1	5
Middlesbrough	5	1	0	2	7	7	0	1	1	1	3	8	10	-2	4
Watford	5	1	1	0	5	3	0	0	3	2	8	7	11	-4	4
Charlton	5	0	2	0	1	1	0	1	2	2	6	3	7	-4	4
Wigan	5	0	1	2	4	9	0	1	1	1	3	5	12	-7	2
Fulham	5	0	1	1	2	4	0	0	3	2	8	4	12	-8	1

GOAL OF THE MONTH

MATCH OF THE DAY

James McFadden
Everton v Charlton

The other contenders:

Gavin Mahon	*Watford* v Portsmouth
Michael Tonge	*Sheff Utd* v West Ham
Dimitar Berbatov	Wigan v *Tottenham*
Shaun Wright-Phillips	West Ham v *Chelsea*
Jonathan Stead	Charlton v *Sheff Utd*
Bobby Zamora	*West Ham* v Everton
Yossi Benayoun	Wigan v *West Ham*
Dimitar Berbatov	Middlesbro v *Tottenham*
Manuel Fernandes	*Everton* v Man Utd

THE MONTH'S TOP GOALSCORERS

	GOALS IN THE MONTH		THE SEASON TO END OF MONTH		
Tottenham	Keane	6	Berbatov, Keane	10	19.2%
Middlesbro	Viduka	4	Yakubu	12	30.0%
Blackburn	McCarthy, Roberts	3	McCarthy	15	32.6%
Liverpool	Kuyt	3	Kuyt	12	21.8%
Portsmouth	Taylor	3	Kanu	10	22.2%
Wigan	Heskey	3	Heskey	10	27.8%
Aston Villa	Agbonlahor	3	Agbonlahor, Barry	8	21.1%
Chelsea	Kalou, Wright-Phillips	2	Drogba	19	30.6%
Man Utd	O'Shea, Rooney	2	Ronaldo	16	19.5%
Charlton	Bent, D	2	Bent, D	12	37.5%
Reading	Doyle, Hunt	2	Doyle	12	24.5%
Bolton	Anelka, Davies, Teymourian	2	Anelka	11	25.0%
Everton	Lescott, Stubbs, Vaughan	2	Johnson	11	22.9%
West Ham	Zamora	2	Zamora	11	35.5%
Arsenal	Adebayor, Baptista, Fabregas, Rosicky	2	Gilberto Silva	9	14.5%
Fulham	Bocanegra	2	McBride	9	25.0%
Man City	Beasley, Vassell	2	Barton	6	21.4%
Watford	Bouazza, Priskin	2	Bouazza	5	18.5%
Sheff Utd	Stead	2	Jagielka, Stead	4	12.9%
Newcastle	Emre, Martins, Taylor	1	Martins	11	29.7%

BARCLAYS MANAGER OF THE MONTH

Martin O'Neill - Aston Villa

BARCLAYS PLAYER OF THE MONTH

Berbatov & Keane - Tottenham Hotspur

Middlesbrough captain, George Boateng is disciplined by his club after warning Manchester United winger Cristiano Ronaldo that his behaviour on the pitch could induce foul play

Table-toppers Manchester United lose 2-1 at Portsmouth and see their lead over second-placed Chelsea reduced to three points with six games to play after the Blues beat Tottenham 1-0

American billionaire Stan Kroenke completes the purchase of ITV's 9.99 per cent stake in Arsenal for £42m

Wayne Rooney hails his Manchester United team-mate Cristiano Ronaldo as the best player in the world

Fulham sack manager Chris Coleman and replaced him with Northern Ireland coach Lawrie Sanchez on a caretaker basis

Manchester United cruise into Champions League semi-finals after thrashing Roma 7-1 at Old Trafford

Liverpool beat PSV Eindhoven 4-0 on aggregate to set up Champions League semi-final clash with Chelsea, who overcame Valencia

Chelsea beat Blackburn 2-1 thanks to winner deep into extra-time to set up FA Cup final showdown with Manchester United, who beat Watford 4-1

Manchester United winger Ryan Giggs makes his 500th league appearance for the club in 2-0 win over Sheffield United

Watford are relegated after drawing 1-1 with Manchester City

David Dein leaves his position as Arsenal vice-chairman after a boardroom row about a proposed takeover of the club by the American billionaire Stan Kroenke

Chelsea chief executive Peter Kenyon insists the club have no plans to dismiss manager Jose Mourinho, saying: "We are not going to sack him he has the club's support. That's the situation and we are agreed on it."

West Ham escape a points deduction but are hit by a £5.5m fine over charges relating to the signings of Argentina World Cup stars Carlos Tevez and Javier Mascherano

Middlesbrough agree £7m deal to sign on-loan defender Jonathan Woodgate, 27, from Real Madrid on permanent four-year contract

England striker Michael Owen returns to action after more than 10 months on the sidelines with a serious knee injury in Newcastle's 1-0 defeat at Reading

Portsmouth announce plans to leave Fratton Park and build a new 36,000-seat stadium on a 13-acre site adjacent to the city's naval dockyards. The new ground should be ready in 2011

Manchester United winger Cristiano Ronaldo becomes the first man since Andy Gray in 1977 to win both the PFA Player and Young Player of the Year awards

England 1966 World Cup winner Alan Ball dies at the age of 61 of a heart attack

Sam Allardyce resigns as manager of Bolton with his assistant at the Reebok, Sammy Lee, named as his successor

QUOTES FROM THE MONTH

"He gets all the crosses, takes the penalties - I would score seven or eight goals over here with all the tap-ins. Fredi Kanoute was a terrific player. Especially at home."
- Tottenham boss Martin Jol on striker Fredi Kanoute who he sold to Seville in summer 2005.

"I said no to Real when they offered me more money than I get here, even though there maybe were greater expectations. Madrid may be my town but, although I have problems with my daughter's Scouse accent, we are really happy here."
- Liverpool manager Rafael Benitez on turning down the chance to rejoin Real Madrid.

"Next year will be a decisive year for us to fight for the championship. That is the main target and if it doesn't work then there will need to be much more money invested. I feel in the longer term it is always better to produce your own resources."
- Arsenal manager Arsene Wenger on the development of his young Gunners squad.

"We were good friends until we started beating them, but since then he has changed his mind. He has a good relationship with the managers of the teams Chelsea beat."
- Liverpool manager Rafael Benitez on Chelsea boss Jose Mourinho.

Manchester City suspend midfielder Joey Barton until the end of the season after a training ground incident involving team-mate Ousmane Dabo who required hospital treatment for cuts to his face

Bolton's new manager Sammy Lee names midfielder Gary Speed as his first-team player-coach

Liverpool beat Chelsea in a dramatic penalty shoot-out to reach Champions League final

AC Milan beat Manchester United 5-3 on aggregate to set up repeat of the 2005 Champions League final against Liverpool

Manchester United winger Cristiano Ronaldo voted Footballer of the Year by the Football Writers' Association - adding to his PFA Player and Young Player of the Year trophies

Manchester United declared Premiership champions after second-placed Chelsea draw 1-1 at Arsenal to leave United seven points clear with two games remaining

Charlton are relegated after losing 2-0 at home to Tottenham

Chelsea are held to a 1-1 draw by Everton but equal Liverpool's record of 63 home League games without defeat

Glenn Roeder resigns as Newcastle United manager after 15 months in charge including a spell as caretaker boss

Paul Jewell resigns as Wigan manager less than 24 hours after keeping the club in the top flight. Assistant boss Chris Hutchings named as Jewell's replacement

Sam Allardyce confirmed as new Newcastle manager on three-year contract

West Ham escape relegation on final day of the Premiership season after Carlos Tevez scores winning goal in 1-0 victory at champions Manchester United. Sheffield United are relegated after losing 2-1 at home to Wigan

Chelsea beat Manchester United 1-0 in the first FA Cup final to be played at the new Wembley stadium. The match is a disappointment with both sides cancelling each other out. Didier Drogba grabs a late winner for the Blues

Manchester City sack manager Stuart Pearce

Manager Neil Warnock leaves relegated Sheffield United by mutual consent

AC Milan beat Liverpool 2-1 in Champions League final to claim European Cup for the seventh time

PREMIERSHIP – MAY

LEAGUE PERFORMANCE FOR THE MONTH

	P	HOME					AWAY					TOTAL			
		W	D	L	F	A	W	D	L	F	A	F	A	DIF	PTS
Tottenham	3	1	1	0	3	2	1	0	0	2	0	5	2	3	7
Middlesbrough	2	1	0	0	3	1	1	0	0	1	0	4	1	3	6
West Ham	2	1	0	0	3	1	1	0	0	1	0	4	1	3	6
Blackburn	3	0	1	0	3	3	1	1	0	3	1	6	4	2	5
Aston Villa	2	1	0	0	3	0	0	1	0	2	2	5	2	3	4
Everton	2	1	0	0	3	0	0	1	0	1	1	4	1	3	4
Watford	2	0	1	0	1	1	1	0	0	2	0	3	1	2	4
Man Utd	3	0	1	1	1	1	1	1	0	1	0	1	1	0	4
Chelsea	3	0	2	0	1	1	0	1	0	1	1	2	2	0	3
Wigan	2	0	0	1	0	1	1	0	0	2	1	2	2	0	3
Fulham	2	1	0	0	1	0	0	0	1	1	3	2	3	-1	3
Arsenal	2	0	1	0	1	1	0	1	0	0	0	1	1	0	2
Liverpool	2	0	1	0	2	2	0	0	1	0	1	2	3	-1	1
Bolton	2	0	1	0	2	2	0	0	1	1	3	3	5	-2	1
Reading	2	0	0	1	0	2	0	1	0	3	3	3	5	-2	1
Charlton	2	0	1	0	0	2	0	1	0	2	2	2	4	-2	1
Newcastle	2	0	0	1	0	2	0	1	0	1	1	1	3	-2	1
Portsmouth	2	0	1	0	0	0	0	0	1	0	3	0	3	-3	1
Man City	2	0	0	1	0	1	0	0	1	1	2	1	3	-2	0
Sheff Utd	2	0	0	1	1	2	0	0	1	0	3	1	5	-4	0

GOAL OF THE SEASON

MATCH OF THE DAY

Wayne Rooney
Man Utd v Bolton (17th March)

Cristiano Ronaldo receives the ball on the edge of the United penalty area as Bolton attack. He breaks out, passing the ball 30 metres to Rooney via a nutmeg. Rooney wheels one way while one-touching the ball back into Ronaldo's path. Still deep in his own half, the Portuguese winger powers past the Bolton defenders through the centre of the pitch. He returns the ball to flying Rooney, having travelled to the final third. The United forward takes one touch into the Bolton area before nudging a chip over Jaskaalainen into the middle of the net. Nine touches and eight seconds from one end of the pitch to the other.

THE MONTH'S TOP GOALSCORERS

	GOALS IN THE MONTH		THE SEASON TO END OF MONTH		
Blackburn	McCarthy	3	McCarthy	18	34.6%
Middlesboro	Viduka	3	Viduka	14	31.8%
West Ham	Tevez	3	Zamora	11	31.4%
Tottenham	Berbatov, Defoe	2	Berbatov	12	21.1%
Bolton	Speed	2	Anelka	11	23.4%
Watford	King	2	King	4	13.3%
Chelsea	Drogba, Essien	1	Drogba	20	31.3%
Man Utd	Ronaldo	1	Ronaldo	17	20.5%
Charlton	Bent, D, Holland	1	Bent, D	13	38.2%
Reading	Doyle, Gunnarsson, Seol	1	Doyle	13	25.0%
Liverpool	Kewell, Xabi Alonso	1	Kuyt	12	21.1%
Newcastle	Dyer	1	Martins	11	28.9%
Arsenal	Gilberto Silva	1	Gilberto Silva	10	15.9%
Wigan	Scharner, Unsworth	1	Heskey	10	26.3%
Aston Villa	Agbonlahor, Berger, Gardner, Moore, L, Young	1	Agbonlahor	9	20.9%
Everton	Arteta, Naysmith, Vaughan, Yobo	1	Arteta	9	17.3%
Fulham	Davies, S, Dempsey	1	McBride	9	23.7%
Sheff Utd	Stead	1	Stead	5	15.6%
Man City	Mpenza	1	Samaras	4	13.8%
Portsmouth		0	Kanu	10	22.2%

QUOTES FROM THE MONTH

"It wouldn't be a problem getting into the Uefa Cup because I'd probably play the reserves. As far as I'm concerned we have a European Cup final every weekend in the Premiership. That's how much it means to everyone at this club."
- Reading boss Steve Coppell on the prospects of playing European club football next season.

"We feel we've given it a right good go since I came here. But the League table speaks for itself. There's no political involvements, no court case. This is where it's at. We've tried everything, smoke and mirrors, the whole shebang, to turn it around."
- Charlton manager Alan Pardew on his club's unsuccessful fight against relegation.

"I kept saying to people, 'Will somebody please shoot Drogba' because his performances were unbelievable. I thought he carried their team and he kept getting these incredible goals."
- Manchester United boss Sir Alex Ferguson on Chelsea striker Didier Drogba.

"When you see the quality of players Milan have, we have to think about improving. My first idea is to support my players who worked really hard and did their best tonight. Afterwards, you need to think about the future. We know we need to improve and we must."
- Liverpool boss Rafael Benitez speaking after losing to AC Milan in the Champions League final.

BARCLAYS MANAGER OF THE SEASON

Sir Alex Ferguson - Manchester United

BARCLAYS PLAYER OF THE SEASON

Cristiano Ronaldo - Manchester United

MANCHESTER UNITED

Cristiano Ronaldo beat Frank Lampard's midfield Premiership goals record and did it in his unique flamboyant style. His 17 goals came at a striker's rate of one every 163 minutes. **Louis Saha** and **Wayne Rooney** gave United three of the 12 best Strike Rates in the league. They hit more shots than we've ever recorded before.

Ronaldo topped the Premiership Assists table on 15 with Rooney, 13, and **Ryan Giggs**, 12, also in the top ten. On Scoring Difference Giggs led the way with the best Attacking Power in the division but five United players were prominent.

Captain **Gary Neville** was in flying form with a Defensive Rating of a goal conceded every 152 minutes, ten minutes better than last year's reported 'failures' (now regulars) Patrice Evra and Nemanja Vidic. The average Home gate was up 7,000 on last season.

NICKNAME: RED DEVILS   KEY: ■ Won □ Drawn ■ Lost

1	prem	Fulham	H W	5-1	Saha 7, Pearce 15 og, Rooney 16, 64, Ronaldo 19
2	prem	Charlton	A W	3-0	Fletcher 48, Saha 80, Solskjaer 90
3	prem	Watford	A W	2-1	Silvestre 12, Giggs 52
4	prem	Tottenham	H W	1-0	Giggs 9
5	ecgpf	Celtic	H W	3-2	Saha 30 pen, 40, Solskjaer 47
6	prem	Arsenal	H L	0-1	
7	prem	Reading	A D	1-1	Ronaldo 73
8	ecgpf	Benfica	A W	1-0	Saha 60
9	prem	Newcastle	H W	2-0	Solskjaer 40, 48
10	prem	Wigan	A W	3-1	Vidic 62, Saha 66, Solskjaer 90
11	ecgpf	Copenhagen	H W	3-0	Scholes 39, O'Shea 46, Richardson 83
12	prem	Liverpool	H W	2-0	Scholes 39, Ferdinand 66
13	ccr3	Crewe	A W	2-1	Solskjaer 26, Lee 119
14	prem	Bolton	A W	4-0	Rooney 10, 16, 89, Ronaldo 82
15	ecgpf	Copenhagen	A L	0-1	
16	prem	Portsmouth	H W	3-0	Saha 3 pen, Ronaldo 10, Vidic 66
17	ccr4	Southend	A L	0-1	
18	prem	Blackburn	A W	1-0	Saha 64
19	prem	Sheff Utd	A W	2-1	Rooney 30, 75
20	ecgpf	Celtic	A L	0-1	
21	prem	Chelsea	H D	1-1	Saha 29
22	prem	Everton	H W	3-0	Ronaldo 39, Evra 63, O'Shea 89
23	prem	Middlesbrough	A W	2-1	Saha 19 pen, Fletcher 68
24	ecgpf	Benfica	H W	3-1	Vidic 45, Giggs 61, Saha 75
25	prem	Man City	H W	3-1	Rooney 5, Saha 45, Ronaldo 84
26	prem	West Ham	A L	0-1	
27	prem	Aston Villa	A W	3-0	Ronaldo 58, 85, Scholes 64
28	prem	Wigan	H W	3-1	Ronaldo 47, 51, Solskjaer 59
29	prem	Reading	H W	3-2	Solskjaer 33, Ronaldo 59, 77
30	prem	Newcastle	A D	2-2	Scholes 40, 46
31	facr3	Aston Villa	H W	2-1	Larsson 55, Solskjaer 90
32	prem	Aston Villa	A W	3-1	Park 11, Carrick 13, Ronaldo 35
33	prem	Arsenal	A L	1-2	Rooney 53
34	facr4	Portsmouth	H W	2-1	Rooney 77, 83
35	prem	Watford	H W	4-0	Ronaldo 20 pen, Doyley 61 og, Larsson 70, Rooney 71
36	prem	Tottenham	A W	4-0	Ronaldo 45 pen, Vidic 48, Scholes 54, Giggs 77
37	prem	Charlton	H W	2-0	Park 24, Fletcher 82
38	facr5	Reading	H D	1-1	Carrick 45
39	eckl1	Lille	A W	1-0	Giggs 83
40	prem	Fulham	A W	2-1	Giggs 29, Ronaldo 88
41	facr5r	Reading	A W	3-2	Heinze 2, Saha 4, Solskjaer 6
42	prem	Liverpool	A W	1-0	O'Shea 90
43	eckl2	Lille	H W	1-0	Larsson 71
44	facqf	Middlesbrough	A D	2-2	Rooney 23, Ronaldo 68 pen
45	prem	Bolton	H W	4-1	Park 14, 25, Rooney 17, 74
46	facqfr	Middlesbrough	H W	1-0	Ronaldo 76 pen
47	prem	Blackburn	H W	4-1	Scholes 61, Carrick 73, Park 83, Solskjaer 90
48	ecqfl1	Roma	A L	1-2	Rooney 60
49	prem	Portsmouth	A L	1-2	O'Shea 90
50	ecqfl2	Roma	H W	7-1	Carrick 11, 60, Smith 17, Rooney 19, Ronaldo 44, 49, Evra 81
51	facsf	Watford	N W	4-1	Rooney 7, 66, Ronaldo 28, Richardson 82
52	prem	Sheff Utd	H W	2-0	Carrick 4, Rooney 50
53	prem	Middlesbrough	H D	1-1	Richardson 3
54	ecsfl1	AC Milan	H W	3-2	Ronaldo 5, Rooney 59, 90
55	prem	Everton	A W	4-2	O'Shea 61, P.Neville 67 og, Rooney 78, Eagles 90
56	ecsfl2	AC Milan	A L	0-3	
57	prem	Man City	A W	1-0	Ronaldo 33 pen
58	prem	Chelsea	A D	0-0	
59	prem	West Ham	H L	0-1	
60	facf	Chelsea	N L	0-1	

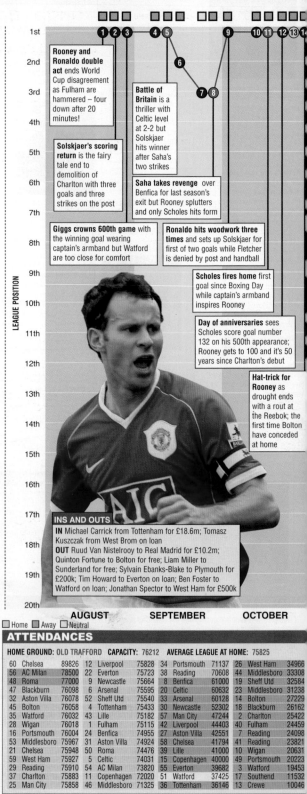

1st

□□□   □□□   □□ □   □ □□□□
① ② ③   ④ ⑤   ⑨   ⑩⑪ ⑫⑬ ⑭
              ⑥
           ⑦⑧

Rooney and Ronaldo double act ends World Cup disagreement as Fulham are hammered – four down after 20 minutes!

Battle of Britain is a thriller with Celtic level at 2-2 but Solskjaer hits winner after Saha's two strikes

Solskjaer's scoring return is the fairy tale end to demolition of Charlton with three goals and three strikes on the post

Saha takes revenge over Benfica for last season's exit but Rooney splutters and only Scholes hits form

Giggs crowns 600th game with the winning goal wearing captain's armband but Watford are too close for comfort

Ronaldo hits woodwork three times and sets up Solskjaer for first of two goals while Fletcher is denied by post and handball

Scholes fires home first goal since Boxing Day while captain's armband inspires Rooney

Day of anniversaries sees Scholes score goal number 132 on his 500th appearance; Rooney gets to 100 and it's 50 years since Charlton's debut

Hat-trick for Rooney as drought ends with a rout at the Reebok; the first time Bolton have conceded at home

2nd
3rd
4th
5th
6th
7th
8th
9th
10th
11th
12th
13th
14th
15th
16th
17th
18th
19th
20th

LEAGUE POSITION

INS AND OUTS
IN Michael Carrick from Tottenham for £18.6m; Tomasz Kuszczak from West Brom on loan
OUT Ruud Van Nistelrooy to Real Madrid for £10.2m; Quinton Fortune to Bolton for free; Liam Miller to Sunderland for free; Sylvain Ebanks-Blake to Plymouth for £200k; Tim Howard to Everton on loan; Ben Foster to Watford on loan; Jonathan Spector to West Ham for £500k

AUGUST   SEPTEMBER   OCTOBER

□ Home ■ Away □ Neutral

ATTENDANCES

HOME GROUND: OLD TRAFFORD   CAPACITY: 76212   AVERAGE LEAGUE AT HOME: 75825

60	Chelsea	89826	12	Liverpool	75828	34	Portsmouth	71137	26	West Ham	34966
56	AC Milan	78500	22	Everton	75723	38	Reading	70608	44	Middlesboro	33308
48	Roma	77000	9	Newcastle	75664	8	Benfica	61000	19	Sheff Utd	32584
47	Blackburn	76098	6	Arsenal	75595	20	Celtic	60632	23	Middlesboro	31541
32	Aston Villa	76078	52	Sheff Utd	75540	33	Arsenal	60128	14	Bolton	27229
45	Bolton	76058	4	Tottenham	75433	30	Newcastle	52302	18	Blackburn	27226
35	Watford	76032	43	Lille	75182	57	Man City	47244	2	Charlton	25422
28	Wigan	76018	1	Fulham	75115	42	Liverpool	44403	40	Fulham	24455
16	Portsmouth	76004	24	Benfica	74955	27	Aston Villa	42551	7	Reading	24098
53	Middlesboro	75967	31	Aston Villa	74924	58	Chelsea	41794	41	Reading	23821
21	Chelsea	75948	50	Roma	74476	39	Lille	41000	10	Wigan	20631
59	West Ham	75927	5	Celtic	74031	15	Copenhagen	40000	49	Portsmouth	20223
29	Reading	75910	54	AC Milan	73820	55	Everton	39682	3	Watford	19453
37	Charlton	75883	11	Copenhagen	72020	51	Watford	37425	17	Southend	11532
25	Man City	75858	46	Middlesboro	71325	36	Tottenham	36146	13	Crewe	10046

Ronaldo weaves a route to ninth title

Final Position: 1st

KEY: ● League ● Champions Lge ● UEFA Cup ● FA Cup ○ League Cup ● Other

16 17 18 19 20 21 22 23 24 25 26 27 28 29 30 31 32 · 33 34 35 36 · 37 38 39 40 41 42 43 44 45 46 · 47 48 49 50 51 52 53 54 55 56 57 58 59 60

Southend shocker as bottom Championship side snatch a Carling win against ten internationals

Trio of headers ensures group top spot after Benfica start with a thunderbolt

OAP Fergie celebrates going six points clear before his 65th birthday as Solskjaer and Ronaldo sink Reading

Outflanked in the last six minutes after Rooney claims lead with his first headed goal, Arsenal battle back to win

Giggs winner prompts uproar as quickly taken free kick surprises Lille who threaten to call their players off the pitch

Larsson's goodbye to Old Trafford is the header that ends Lille's carping and earns a first quarter-final berth since 2002

Final minute winner from man-of-the-match Rooney claims a narrow advantage but Kaka has two away goals for Milan

Over the line argues Giggs as best chance fails to break deadlock before Drogba's strike saves the 'tired' final from ending in penalties

End of run of seven wins as chances go begging in Denmark and Copenhagen spring a surprise

Saha's sweet strike earns lead against Champions but slack marking from corner gains Chelsea a deserved equaliser

King Henrik arrives to acclaim as he scores on debut, although it takes Solskjaer's late strike to break Villa

Van der Sar out for the count and so are Spurs as Ronaldo scores one and makes one with O'Shea keeping a clean sheet

Fergie's halftime talk sees turn-around as Scholes levels and Blackburn are destroyed in the last 30 minutes

Rooney rocks Everton and Chelsea, scoring the vital third after being 2-0 down on 60 minutes in a fighting win at Goodison to open up a five point gap

Ronaldo's 17th goal is a Premiership record for a midfield player as he defies City's roughhouse tactics

Outclassed by Kaka and Seedorf, whose clinical finishes from the edge of the box put the tie beyond a second half revival

Nine points clear as Rooney and Ronaldo romp through City's error-strewn defence and Giggs matches Bill Foulkes' 688 appearances

Scholes' brace gives him ten goals in ten games against Newcastle but his deflection gives Geordies a point

Ronaldo's run from his own half claims points that Fulham deserve but van der Sar denies them

Six minutes stun Reading who find themselves 3-0 down after United's best-ever start but it's tight at the end

Crowd trouble as supporters vent anger at Italian police's indiscriminate clubbings

MANCHESTER UNITED 7 AS ROMA 1

Roma blown away in best Champions League win with seven stunning goals including European firsts for Ronaldo and Carrick who both net a brace

MONTH BY MONTH POINTS TALLY

AUGUST	9	100%
SEPTEMBER	4	44%
OCTOBER	12	100%
NOVEMBER	13	87%
DECEMBER	15	83%
JANUARY	7	58%
FEBRUARY	9	100%
MARCH	9	100%
APRIL	7	58%
MAY	4	44%

INS AND OUTS

IN Henrik Larsson from Helsingborg on loan until 12th March 2007
OUT Phil Bardsley to Aston Villa on loan; Giuseppe Rossi to Parma on loan; David Jones to Derby for £1m; Jonny Evans and Danny Simpson to Sunderland on loan; Adam Eckersley to Barnsley on loan

Fifty years in Europe commemorated in charity game win over Lippi's XI

Champions for a ninth time with two games to go as Chelsea only draw at Arsenal

NOVEMBER · DECEMBER · JANUARY · FEBRUARY · MARCH · APRIL · MAY

GOAL ATTEMPTS

FOR
Goal attempts recorded in League games

	HOME	AWAY	TOTAL	AVE
shots on target	195	133	328	8.6
shots off target	177	128	305	8.0
TOTAL	372	261	633	16.7

Ratio of goals to shots
Average number of shots on target per League goal scored — **4.0**

Accuracy rating
Average percentage of total goal attempts which were on target — **51.8**

AGAINST
Goal attempts recorded in League games

	HOME	AWAY	TOTAL	AVE
shots on target	79	96	175	4.6
shots off target	90	97	187	4.9
TOTAL	169	193	362	9.5

Ratio of goals to shots
Average number of shots on target per League goal scored — **6.5**

Accuracy rating
Average percentage of total goal attempts which were on target — **48.3**

GOALS

Rooney

League	14
FA Cup	5
League Cup	0
Europe	4
Other	0
TOTAL	23

League Average 209 mins between goals

	PLAYER	LGE	FAC	LC	Euro	TOT	AVE
1	Rooney	14	5	0	4	23	209
2	Ronaldo	17	3	0	2	22	163
3	Saha	8	1	0	4	13	203
4	Solskjaer	7	2	1	1	11	132
5	Scholes	6	0	0	1	7	432
6	Giggs	4	0	0	2	6	575
7	Carrick	3	1	0	2	6	835
8	Park	5	0	0	0	5	154
9	O'Shea	4	0	0	1	5	434
10	Vidic	3	0	0	1	4	713
11	Larsson	1	1	0	1	3	459
12	Fletcher	3	0	0	0	3	476
13	Richardson	1	1	0	1	3	783
14	Evra	1	0	0	1	2	1852
15	Eagles	1	0	0	0	1	94
	Other	2	1	1	1	5	
	TOTAL	80	15	2	22	119	

SQUAD APPEARANCES

Match	1 2 3 4 5	6 7 8 9 10	11 12 13 14 15	16 17 18 19 20	21 22 23 24 25	26 27 28 29 30	31 32 33 34 35	36 37 38 39 40	41 42 43 44 45	46 47 48 49 50	51 52 53 54 55	56 57 58 59
Venue	H A A H H	H A A H A	H H A A A	H A A A A	H H A H H	A A H H A	H H A H H	A H H A A	A A H A H	H H A A H	N H H H A	A A A H
Competition	L L L L C	L L C L L	C L W L C	L W L L C	L L L C L	L L L L L	F L L F L	L L F C L	F L C F L	F L C L C	F L L C L	C L L L
Result	W W W W W	L D W W W	W W W W L	W L W W L	D W W W W	L W W W D	W W L W W	W W D W W	W W W D W	W W L L W	W W D W W	L W D L

Goalkeepers
Tom Heaton
Tomasz Kuszczak
Edwin van der Sar

Defenders
Wes Brown
Craig Cathcart
Patrice Evra
Rio Ferdinand
David Gray
Gabriel Ivan Heinze
Kieran Lee
Phil Marsh
Gary Neville
John O'Shea
Ryan Shawcross
Mikael Silvestre
Nemanja Vidic

Midfielders
Michael Barnes
Michael Carrick
Chris Eagles
Darren Fletcher
Ryan Giggs
David Jones
Ritchie Jones
Ji-Sung Park
Kirran Richardson
Cristiano Ronaldo
Paul Scholes

Forwards
Dong Fangzhuo
Henrik Larsson
Wayne Rooney
Giuseppe Rossi
Louis Saha
Alan Smith
Ole Gunnar Solskjaer

KEY: ■ On all match   ◄◄ Subbed or sent off (Counting game)   ▸▸▸ Subbed on from bench (Counting Game)   ▸▸ Subbed on and then subbed or sent off (Counting Game)   ☐ Not in 16   ☐ Injured
On bench   ◄ Subbed or sent off (playing less than 70 mins)   ▸▸ Subbed on (playing less than 70 mins)   ▸▸ Subbed on and then subbed or sent off (playing less than 70 min   ✕ Suspended

KEY PLAYERS - GOALSCORERS

Cristiano Ronaldo

Goals in the League	17
Goals in all competitions	22
Assists — League goals scored by a team mate where the player delivered the final pass	15
Contribution to Attacking Power — Average number of minutes between League team goals while on pitch	39
Player Strike Rate — Average number of minutes between League goals scored by player	163
Club Strike Rate — Average minutes between League goals scored by club	41

	PLAYER	GOALS LGE	GOALS ALL	ASSISTS	POWER	S RATE
1	Cristiano Ronaldo	17	22	15	39	163 mins
2	Louis Saha	8	13	7	45	203 mins
3	Wayne Rooney	14	23	13	40	209 mins
4	Paul Scholes	6	7	2	41	432 mins

KEY PLAYERS - MIDFIELDERS

Ryan Giggs

Goals in the League	4
Goals in all competitions	6
Assists — League goals scored by a team mate where the player delivered the final pass	12
Defensive Rating — Average number of mins between League goals conceded while on the pitch	143
Contribution to Attacking Power — Average number of minutes between League team goals while on pitch	39
Scoring Difference — Defensive Rating minus Contribution to Attacking Power	104

	PLAYER	GOALS LGE	GOALS ALL	ASSISTS	DEF RATE	POWER	SC DIF
1	Ryan Giggs	4	6	12	143	39	104 mins
2	Cristiano Ronaldo	17	22	15	139	39	100 mins
3	Darren Fletcher	3	3	2	158	59	99 mins
4	Paul Scholes	6	7	2	129	41	88 mins

PLAYER APPEARANCES

	AGE (on 01/07/07)	IN NAMED 16	APPEARANCES	COUNTING GAMES	MINUTES ON PITCH	APPEARANCES THIS SEASON	MINUTES ON PITCH THIS SEASON		HOME COUNTRY
Goalkeepers									
...m Heaton	21	4	0	0	0	0	0	-	England
...masz Kuszczak	25	37	6	6	540	13	1200	-	Poland
...win van der Sar	36	35	32	32	2880	47	4260	6	Holland
...fenders									
...es Brown	27	30	22	17	1604	37	3014	3	England
...aig Cathcart	18	1	0	0	0	0	0	-	England
...trice Evra	26	29	24	17	1852	36	2561	1	France
...o Ferdinand	28	34	33	32	2925	49	4299	7	England
...vid Gray	19	0	0	0	0	1	76	-	Scotland
...briel Ivan Heinze	29	24	22	15	1506	38	2907	2	Argentina
...ran Lee	19	2	1	1	90	3	150	-	England
...il Marsh	20	0	0	0	0	1	45	-	England
...ry Neville	32	24	24	21	1976	33	2786	4	England
...n O'Shea	26	36	32	16	1737	49	2705	8	Rep of Ireland
...an Shawcross	19	0	0	0	0	2	20	-	England
...kael Silvestre	29	19	14	5	612	21	1272	-	France
...manja Vidic	25	27	25	23	2139	38	3294	5	Serbia
...dfielders									
...chael Barnes	19	0	0	0	0	1	57	-	England
...chael Carrick	25	34	33	27	2505	52	4181	5	England
...ris Eagles	21	3	2	1	94	2	94	-	England
...rren Fletcher	23	28	24	14	1430	40	2428	6	Scotland
...an Giggs	33	31	30	22	2303	44	3451	8	Wales
...vid Jones	22	1	0	0	0	2	208	-	England
...chie Jones	20	0	0	0	0	1	120	-	England
...Sung Park	26	16	14	5	774	20	1137	3	South Korea
...ran Richardson	22	19	15	6	783	24	1202	4	England
...stiano Ronaldo	22	35	34	30	2783	53	4388	7	Portugal
...ul Scholes	32	32	30	28	2594	45	3736	-	England
...rwards									
...ng Fangzhuo	22	1	1	1	72	1	72	1	China
...nrik Larsson	35	7	7	4	459	13	896	-	Sweden
...yne Rooney	21	35	35	32	2926	55	4601	5	England
...seppe Rossi	20	2	0	0	0	0	0	-	Italy
...uis Saha	28	28	24	15	1628	34	2260	6	France
...n Smith	26	10	9	3	478	18	990	1	England
... Gunnar Solskjaer	34	24	19	7	925	32	1588	3	Norway

KEY: LEAGUE ALL COMPS CAPS (MAY FIFA RANKING)

TEAM OF THE SEASON

VAN DER SAR — CG 32 DR 115

G NEVILLE — CG 21 DR 152
FERDINAND — CG 32 DR 127
VIDIC — CG 23 DR 142
EVRA — CG 17 DR 142

RONALDO — CG 30 SD +100
FLETCHER — CG 14 SD +99
SCHOLES — CG 28 SD +88
GIGGS — CG 22 SD +104

ROONEY — CG 32 AP 40
SAHA — CG 15 SR 203

KEY: DR = Defensive Rate, SD = Scoring Difference AP = Attacking Power SR = Strike Rate, CG=Counting games − League games playing at least 70 minutes

TOP POINT EARNERS

Ryan Giggs

Counting Games League games when player was on pitch for at least 70 minutes		22
Average points Average League points taken in Counting games		2.55
Club Average points Average points taken in League games		2.34

	PLAYER	GAMES	PTS
1	Ryan Giggs	22	2.55
2	Patrice Evra	17	2.53
3	Nemanja Vidic	23	2.48
4	Louis Saha	15	2.47
5	Rio Ferdinand	32	2.44
6	Michael Carrick	27	2.44
7	Edwin van der Sar	32	2.38
8	Cristiano Ronaldo	30	2.33
9	Paul Scholes	28	2.29
10	Gary Neville	21	2.29

KEY PLAYERS - DEFENDERS

Gary Neville

Goals Conceded in the League Number of League goals conceded while the player was on the pitch	13
Goals Conceded in all competitions Total number of goals conceded while the player was on the pitch	21
League minutes played Number of minutes played in league matches	1976
Clean Sheets In games when the player was on pitch for at least 70 minutes	11
Defensive Rating Average number of mins between League goals conceded while on the pitch	152
Club Defensive Rating Average number of mins between League goals conceded by the club this season	126

	PLAYER	CON LGE	CON ALL	MINS	C SHEETS	DEF RATE
1	Gary Neville	13	21	1976	11	152 mins
2	Patrice Evra	13	20	1852	10	142 mins
3	Nemanja Vidic	15	25	2139	11	142 mins
4	Rio Ferdinand	23	39	2925	14	127 mins

KEY GOALKEEPER

Edwin van der Sar

Goals Conceded in the League Number of League goals conceded while the player was on the pitch	25
Goals Conceded in all competitions Total number of goals conceded while the player was on the pitch	42
League minutes played Number of minutes played in league matches	2880
Clean Sheets In games when the player was on pitch for at least 70 minutes	12
Goals to Shots Ratio The average number of shots on target per each League goal conceded	6.08
Defensive Rating Ave mins between League goals conceded while on the pitch	115

BOOKINGS

Keiran Richardson

League Yellow	4
League Red	0
All competitions Yellow	6
All competitions Red	0

League Average **195** mins between cards

	PLAYER	LEAGUE		TOTAL		AVE
1	Keiran Richardson	4 Y	0 R	6 Y	0 R	195
2	Paul Scholes	8	1	12	2	288
3	Gabriel I. Heinze	5	0	7	0	301
4	Nemanja Vidic	7	0	10	0	305
5	Henrik Larsson	1	0	2	0	459
6	Ryan Giggs	5	0	6	0	460
7	Patrice Evra	4	0	7	0	463
8	Alan Smith	1	0	4	0	478
9	Wes Brown	3	0	4	0	534
10	Wayne Rooney	5	0	9	0	585
11	John O'Shea	2	0	2	0	868
12	Ole G. Solskjaer	1	0	2	0	925
13	Gary Neville	2	0	2	0	988
14	Michael Carrick	2	0	4	0	1252
15	Cristiano Ronaldo	2	0	5	0	1391
	Other	4	0	7	0	
	TOTAL	56	1	89	2	

CHELSEA

Didier Drogba has won two Premiership titles without really hitting top form, now he's lost one while looking invincible. The Ivorian striker hit 33 goals with his 20 in the league coming at a Strike Rate of one every 147 minutes.

Frank Lampard is the inspiration in midfield, only missing one league game, scoring 11 times and equal seventh in the Assists chart with 12. **Claude Makelele** is the best ball-winning midfielder in the league with an astonishing Defensive Rating of a goal conceded every 189 minutes on average.

John Terry and **Petr Cech** were injured for key games but both top their respective club charts, in Cech's case only conceding a goal every 190 minutes and with the top Goals to Shots Ratio of 9.67 shots saved for every goal conceded.

NICKNAME: THE BLUES

KEY: ☐ Won ☐ Drawn ☐ Lost

#				Result	Scorers
1	facs	Liverpool	N L	1-2	Shevchenko 43
2	prem	Man City	H W	3-0	Terry 11, Lampard 26, Drogba 78
3	prem	Middlesbrough	A L	1-2	Shevchenko 15
4	prem	Blackburn	A W	2-0	Lampard 49 pen, Drogba 80
5	prem	Charlton	H W	2-1	Drogba 6, Carvalho 63
6	ecgpa	W Bremen	H W	2-0	Essien 24, Ballack 68 pen
7	prem	Liverpool	H W	1-0	Drogba 42
8	prem	Fulham	A W	2-0	Lampard 73 pen, 80
9	ecgpa	Levski Sofia	A W	3-1	Drogba 39, 52, 68
10	prem	Aston Villa	H D	1-1	Drogba 3
11	prem	Reading	A W	1-0	Ingimarsson 45 og
12	ecgpa	Barcelona	H W	1-0	Drogba 46
13	prem	Portsmouth	H W	2-1	Shevchenko 55, Ballack 57
14	ccr3	Blackburn	A W	2-0	J.Cole 53, Kalou 81
15	prem	Sheff Utd	A W	2-0	Lampard 43, Ballack 49
16	ecgpa	Barcelona	A D	2-2	Lampard 52, Drogba 90
17	prem	Tottenham	A L	1-2	Makelele 15
18	ccr4	Aston Villa	H W	4-0	Lampard 32, Shevchenko 65, Essien 82, Drogba 84
19	prem	Watford	H W	4-0	Drogba 27, 36, 69, Shevchenko 52
20	prem	West Ham	H W	1-0	Geremi 22
21	ecgpa	W Bremen	A L	0-1	
22	prem	Man Utd	A D	1-1	Carvalho 69
23	prem	Bolton	A W	1-0	Ballack 45
24	ecgpa	Levski Sofia	H W	2-0	Shevchenko 27, Wright-Phillips 83
25	prem	Arsenal	H D	1-1	Essien 84
26	prem	Newcastle	H W	1-0	Drogba 74
27	prem	Everton	A W	3-2	Howard 49 og, Lampard 81, Drogba 87
28	ccqf	Newcastle	A W	1-0	Drogba 78
29	prem	Wigan	A W	3-2	Lampard 13, Kalou 31, Robben 90
30	prem	Reading	H D	2-2	Drogba 38, 72
31	prem	Fulham	H D	2-2	Rosenior 35 og, Drogba 62
32	prem	Aston Villa	A D	0-0	
33	facr3	Macclesfield	H W	6-1	Lampard 16, 41, 51 pen, Wright-Phillips 68, Mikel 82, Carvalho 86
34	ccsfl1	Wycombe	A D	1-1	Bridge 36
35	prem	Wigan	H W	4-0	Lampard 13, Robben 63, Kirkland 70 og, Drogba 90
36	prem	Liverpool	A L	0-2	
37	ccsfl2	Wycombe	H W	4-0	Shevchenko 22, 43, Lampard 69, 90
38	facr4	Nottm Forest	H W	3-0	Shevchenko 9, Drogba 18, Mikel 45
39	prem	Blackburn	H W	3-0	Drogba 6, Lampard 67, Kalou 90
40	prem	Charlton	A W	1-0	Lampard 18
41	prem	Middlesbrough	H W	3-0	Drogba 45, 83, Xavier 66 og
42	facr5	Norwich	H W	4-0	Wright-Phillips 39, Drogba 51, Essien 90, Shevchenko 90
43	eckl1	Porto	A D	1-1	Shevchenko 15
44	cccf	Arsenal	N W	2-1	Drogba 20, 84
45	prem	Portsmouth	A W	2-0	Drogba 33, Kalou 82
46	eckl2	Porto	H W	2-1	Robben 48, Ballack 79
47	facqf	Tottenham	H D	3-3	Lampard 22, 71, Kalou 86
48	prem	Man City	A W	1-0	Lampard 28 pen
49	prem	Sheff Utd	H W	3-0	Shevchenko 4, Kalou 17, Ballack 58
50	facqfr	Tottenham	A W	2-1	Shevchenko 55, Wright-Phillips 61
51	prem	Watford	A W	1-0	Kalou 90
52	ecqfl1	Valencia	H D	1-1	Drogba 53
53	prem	Tottenham	H W	1-0	Carvalho 52
54	ecqfl2	Valencia	A W	2-1	Shevchenko 52, Essien 90
55	facsf	Blackburn	N W	2-1	Lampard 16, Ballack 109
56	prem	West Ham	A W	4-1	Wright-Phillips 31, 36, Kalou 52, Drogba 62
57	prem	Newcastle	A D	0-0	
58	ecsfl1	Liverpool	H W	1-0	J.Cole 29
59	prem	Bolton	H D	2-2	Kalou 22, Jaaskelainen 34 og
60	ecsfl2	Liverpool	A L	1-4*	(*on penalties)
61	prem	Arsenal	A D	1-1	Essien 70
62	prem	Man Utd	H D	0-0	
63	prem	Everton	H D	1-1	Drogba 57
64	facf	Man Utd	N W	1-0	Drogba 116

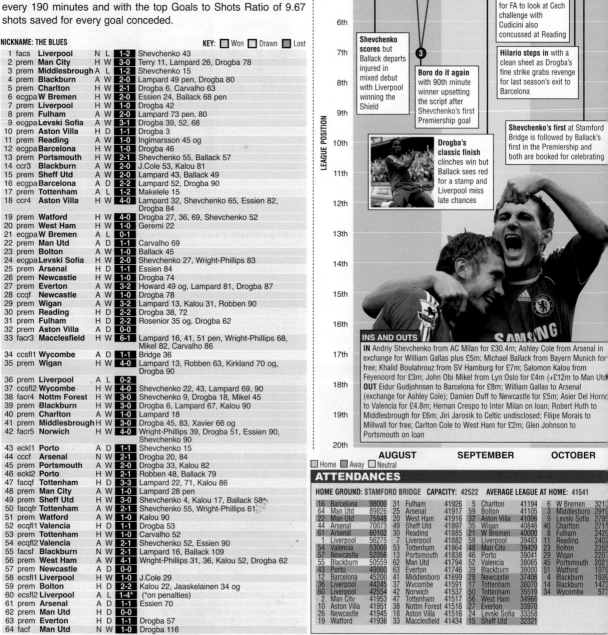

1st
2nd
3rd
4th
5th
6th
7th
8th
9th
10th
11th
12th
13th
14th
15th
16th
17th
18th
19th
20th

LEAGUE POSITION

Essien pounces on Bremen slip and Ballack takes over the penalty duties from Lampard to make it two

First hat-trick for Drogba takes season's tally to seven and dumps Bulgarians bottom of Group A

Two keepers down and Mourinho calls for FA to look at Cech challenge with Cudicini also concussed at Reading

Shevchenko scores but Ballack departs injured in mixed debut with Liverpool winning the Shield

Boro do it again with 90th minute winner upsetting the script after Shevchenko's first Premiership goal

Hilario steps in with a clean sheet as Drogba's fine strike grabs revenge for last season's exit to Barcelona

Drogba's classic finish clinches win but Ballack sees red for a stamp and Liverpool miss late chances

Shevchenko's first at Stamford Bridge is followed by Ballack's first in the Premiership and both are booked for celebrating

☐ Home ☐ Away ☐ Neutral

AUGUST · SEPTEMBER · OCTOBER

INS AND OUTS

IN Andriy Shevchenko from AC Milan for £30.4m; Ashley Cole from Arsenal in exchange for William Gallas plus £5m; Michael Ballack from Bayern Munich for free; Khalid Boulahrouz from SV Hamburg for £7m; Salomon Kalou from Feyenoord for £3m; John Obi Mikel from Lyn Oslo for £4m (+£12m to Man Utd)

OUT Eidur Gudjohnsen to Barcelona for £8m; William Gallas to Arsenal (exchange for Ashley Cole); Damien Duff to Newcastle for £5m; Asier Del Horno to Valencia for £4.8m; Hernan Crespo to Inter Milan on loan; Robert Huth to Middlesbrough for £6m; Jiri Jarosik to Celtic undisclosed; Filipe Morais to Millwall for free; Carlton Cole to West Ham for £2m; Glen Johnson to Portsmouth on loan

ATTENDANCES

HOME GROUND: STAMFORD BRIDGE   CAPACITY: 42522   AVERAGE LEAGUE AT HOME: 41541

16	Barcelona	98000	31	Fulham	41926	5	Charlton	41194	6	W Bremen	3213.
64	Man Utd	89826	25	Arsenal	41917	59	Bolton	41105	3	Middlesboro	2919.
22	Man Utd	75948	20	West Ham	41916	32	Aston Villa	41006	9	Levski Sofia	279.
44	Arsenal	70073	49	Sheff Utd	41897	35	Wigan	40846	40	Charlton	271.
61	Arsenal	60102	30	Reading	41885	21	W Bremen	40000	8	Fulham	242.
1	Liverpool	56275	7	Liverpool	41882	58	Liverpool	39483	11	Reading	240.
54	Valencia	53000	53	Tottenham	41864	48	Man City	39429	23	Bolton	235.
57	Newcastle	52056	13	Portsmouth	41838	46	Porto	39041	29	Wigan	202.
55	Blackburn	50559	62	Man Utd	41794	52	Valencia	38065	45	Portsmouth	202.
43	Porto	49000	63	Everton	41746	39	Blackburn	38000	51	Watford	192.
12	Barcelona	45200	41	Middlesboro	41699	28	Newcastle	37406	4	Blackburn	1939.
36	Liverpool	44245	37	Wycombe	41591	17	Tottenham	36070	14	Blackburn	1935.
60	Liverpool	42554	47	Norwich	41537	50	Tottenham	35519	34	Wycombe	193.
2	Man City	41953	47	Tottenham	41517	56	West Ham	34966			
10	Aston Villa	41951	38	Nottm Forest	41516	27	Everton	33970			
26	Newcastle	41945	18	Aston Villa	41516	24	Levski Sofia	33358			
19	Watford	41936	33	Macclesfield	41434	15	Sheff Utd	32321			

Two cups but injuries cost league title

Final Position: 2nd

KEY: ● League ● Champions Lge ● UEFA Cup ● FA Cup ○ League Cup ● Other

Merseyside misery as Agger's goal levels the aggregate score and Robben and Geremi both see penalties saved

17 18 19 20 21 22 23 24 25 26 27 28 29 30 31 32 33 34 35 36 37 38 39 40 41 42 43 44 45 46 47 48 49 50 51 52 53 54 55 56 57 58 59 60 61 62 63 64

"We can't defend" admits Mourinho as Terry is missed and it's eight goals conceded in five games

Terry's back against Boro and it's business as usual with Drogba scoring twice in a routine win

Two great strikes quash Spurs' spirit as Shevchenko and Wright-Phillips hit the net while Lampard is hit by a Spurs fan

"Almost lost" as United come back from 2-0 down at Everton and Bolton steal a point at the Bridge despite Kalou's brace

Poor night in Bremen as Drogba and Ballack are injured and Germans go joint top

Mourinho rings the changes but has to rely on old guard to snatch winner against Newcastle

Another Cole down as Ashley joins Joe on the injured list but Blackburn are rocked by Drogba and finished off by Lampard

Lampard's brace takes him to 19 for the season and Kalou finally levels Spurs' 3-1 first half lead to force a replay

Joe Cole flies in to get on the end of Drogba's powerful run and earn a first leg advantage in rivalry with Liverpool

Makelele scores first from open play but Spurs win for first time in 32 games and ref sends off Terry and disallows Drogba 'goal'

Essien scorcher answers Arsenal strike but woodwork thwarts Lampard and Ballack, leaving United eight points clear

Shevchenko goes second in the all-time list with 57th goal in European competition and Wright-Phillips scores first for club

Terry concussed in final thriller with Drogba ensuring victory over Arsenal's youngsters before Mikel sees red in 20-man free-for-all

Drogba's strike is first for a month and levels against Valencia whose Silva goal was a beauty

"Dream final", says scorer Ballack as his extra time goal builds on Cech's fine display to set up Wembley date with United

Cech's back in a protective helmet but gets no protection from Ferreira and Essien in Mourinho's first league defeat to Liverpool

Gap closes to three as Carvalho fires low bouncing winner past Robinson and Wright-Phillips looks sharp again

Essien snatches it in the 90th minute to come from behind and take a rare away win from Valencia's Mestalla stadium. Jose is ecstatic

Mourinho's shuffle earns point as Robben and Essien provide width and Carvalho levels against United

Ballack leads revival after Porto threaten with Quaresma's early strike and Mourinho's tinkering works in second half

Jose's collection is complete as the one moment of class sees Lampard one-two set up Drogba for goal to clinch FA Cup in extra time

NOVEMBER   DECEMBER   JANUARY   FEBRUARY   MARCH   APRIL   MAY

MONTH BY MONTH POINTS TALLY

Month	Points	%
AUGUST	6	67%
SEPTEMBER	10	83%
OCTOBER	9	100%
NOVEMBER	10	67%
DECEMBER	12	67%
JANUARY	7	58%
FEBRUARY	6	100%
MARCH	12	100%
APRIL	8	67%
MAY	3	33%

GOAL ATTEMPTS

FOR
Goal attempts recorded in League games

	HOME	AWAY	TOTAL	AVE
shots on target	147	126	273	7.2
shots off target	159	121	280	7.4
TOTAL	306	247	553	14.6

Ratio of goals to shots
Average number of shots on target per League goal scored: **4.3**

Accuracy rating
Average percentage of total goal attempts which were on target: **49.4**

AGAINST
Goal attempts recorded in League games

	HOME	AWAY	TOTAL	AVE
shots on target	54	75	129	3.4
shots off target	76	104	180	4.7
TOTAL	130	179	309	8.1

Ratio of goals to shots
Average number of shots on target per League goal scored: **5.4**

Accuracy rating
Average percentage of total goal attempts which were on target: **41.7**

GOALS

Drogba

League	20
FA Cup	3
League Cup	4
Europe	6
Other	0
TOTAL	33

League Average
147
mins between goals

	PLAYER	LGE	FAC	LC	Euro	TOT	AVE
1	Drogba	20	3	4	6	33	147
2	Lampard	11	6	3	1	21	294
3	Shevchenko	4	4	3	3	14	449
4	Kalou	7	1	1	0	9	277
5	Ballack	4	1	0	2	7	504
6	Wright-Phillips	2	3	0	1	6	635
7	Essien	2	1	1	2	6	1485
8	Carvalho	3	1	0	0	4	879
9	Robben	2	0	0	1	3	671
10	Mikel	0	2	0	0	2	
11	Cole, J	0	0	1	1	2	
12	Geremi	1	0	0	0	1	1156
13	Makelele	1	0	0	0	1	2268
14	Terry	1	0	0	0	1	2413
15	Bridge	0	0	1	0	1	
	Other	0	0	0	0	0	
	TOTAL	58	22	14	17	111	

PREMIERSHIP CLUBS – CHELSEA

SQUAD APPEARANCES

Match	1 2 3 4 5	6 7 8 9 10	11 12 13 14 15	16 17 18 19 20	21 22 23 24 25	26 27 28 29 30	31 32 33 34 35	36 37 38 39 40	41 42 43 44 45	46 47 48 49 50	51 52 53 54 55	56 57 58 59 60	61 62 6.
Venue	N H A A H	H H A A H	A H H A A	A A H H H	A A A H H	H A A A H	H A H A H	A H H H A	H H A N A	H H A H A	A H H A N	A A H H A	A H H
Competition	F L L L L	C L L C L	L C L W L	C L W L L	C L L C L	L L W L L	L L F W L	L W F L L	L F C W L	C F L L F	L C L C F	L L C L C	L L L
Result	L W L W W	W W W W D	W W W W W	D L W W W	L D W W D	W W W W W	D D W D W	L W W W W	W W D W W	W D W W W	W D W W W	W D W D L	D D D

Goalkeepers
Petr Cech
Carlo Cudicini
Magnus Hedman
Henrique Hilario
Y M Ma-Kalambay

Defenders
Khalid Boulahrouz
Wayne Bridge
Ricardo Carvalho
Ashley Cole
Paulo Ferreira
Geremi Nitjap
Michael Mancienne
Nuno Morais
John Terry

Midfielders
Michael Ballack
Joe Cole
Lassana Diarra
Michael Essien
Frank Lampard
Claude Makelele
John Obi Mikel
Arjen Robben
Michael Woods
S Wright-Phillips

Forwards
Didier Drogba
Salomon Kalou
Ben Sahar
Andriy Shevchenko
Scott Sinclair

KEY: ■ On all match ◄◄ Subbed or sent off (Counting game) ►► Subbed on from bench (Counting Game) ►► Subbed on and then subbed or sent off (Counting Game) □ Not in 16 ☐ Injured ■ On bench ◄◄ Subbed or sent off (playing less than 70 mins) ►► Subbed on (playing less than 70 mins) ►► Subbed on and then subbed or sent off (playing less than 70 min ✕ Suspended

KEY PLAYERS - GOALSCORERS

Didier Drogba

Goals in the League	20
Goals in all competitions	33
Assists — League goals scored by a team mate where the player delivered the final pass	9
Contribution to Attacking Power — Average number of minutes between League team goals while on pitch	52
Player Strike Rate — Average number of minutes between League goals scored by player	147
Club Strike Rate — Average minutes between League goals scored by club	53

	PLAYER	GOALS LGE	GOALS ALL	ASSISTS	POWER	S RATE
1	Didier Drogba	20	33	9	52	147 mins
2	Salomon Kalou	7	9	6	48	277 mins
3	Frank Lampard	11	21	12	52	294 mins
4	Andriy Shevchenko	4	14	9	46	449 mins

KEY PLAYERS - MIDFIELDERS

Claude Makelele

Goals in the League	1
Goals in all competitions	1
Assists — League goals scored by a team mate where the player delivered the final pass	0
Defensive Rating — Average number of mins between League goals conceded while on the pitch	189
Contribution to Attacking Power — Average number of minutes between League team goals while on pitch	55
Scoring Difference — Defensive Rating minus Contribution to Attacking Power	134

	PLAYER	GOALS LGE	GOALS ALL	ASSISTS	DEF RATE	POWER	SC DIF
1	Claude Makelele	1	1	0	189	55	134 mins
2	Frank Lampard	11	21	12	141	52	89 mins
3	Arjen Robben	2	3	7	134	47	87 mins
4	Michael Essien	2	6	3	129	52	77 mins

PLAYER APPEARANCES

	AGE (on 01/07/07)	IN NAMED 16	APPEARANCES	COUNTING GAMES	MINUTES ON PITCH	APPEARANCES	MINUTES ON PITCH THIS SEASON		HOME COUNTRY
Goalkeepers									
Petr Cech	27	20	20	19	1714	36	3244	8	Czech Republic
Carlo Cudicini	33	25	8	8	716	11	986	-	Italy
Magnus Hedman	34	8	0	0	0	0	0	-	Sweden
Henrique Hilario	31	21	11	11	990	18	1620	-	Portugal
M Ma-Kalambay	21	1	0	0	0	0	0	-	Belgium
Defenders									
Khalid Boulahrouz	25	25	13	8	812	23	1593	4	Holland
Wayne Bridge	26	25	22	16	1548	33	2491	2	England
Ricardo Carvalho	29	32	31	28	2638	51	4468	7	Portugal
Ashley Cole	26	23	23	18	1847	40	3291	7	England
Paulo Ferreira	28	27	24	17	1710	38	2688	6	Portugal
Geremi Njitap	28	23	19	8	1156	28	1842	4	Cameroon
Michael Mancienne	19	1	0	0	0	0	0	-	England
Nuno Morais	23	4	2	0	20	5	57	-	Portugal
John Terry	26	28	28	27	2413	45	3927	10	England
Midfielders									
Michael Ballack	30	26	26	21	2016	46	3647	7	Germany
Joe Cole	25	14	13	2	479	24	1095	3	England
Lassana Diarra	22	15	10	4	555	23	1418	-	France
Michael Essien	24	33	33	33	2970	55	4997	3	Ghana
Frank Lampard	29	37	37	35	3243	62	5356	10	England
Claude Makelele	34	31	29	24	2268	46	3615	8	France
John Obi Mikel	20	26	22	9	957	42	2343	1	Nigeria
Arjen Robben	23	21	21	12	1343	37	2225	6	Holland
Michael Woods	17	0	0	0	0	2	25	-	England
S Wright-Phillips	25	34	27	10	1270	44	1969	4	England
Forwards									
Didier Drogba	29	36	36	30	2944	60	4896	5	Ivory Coast
Salomon Kalou	21	33	33	18	1944	58	2838	1	Ivory Coast
Ben Sahar	17	4	3	0	67	5	112	3	Israel
Andriy Shevchenko	28	31	30	14	1797	51	3402	3	Ukraine
Scott Sinclair	18	2	2	0	64	3	65	-	England

KEY: LEAGUE   ALL COMPS   CAPS   (MAY FIFA RANKING)

TEAM OF THE SEASON

Player	CG		
CECH	19	DR	190
FERREIRA	17	DR	142
CARVALHO	28	DR	138
TERRY	27	DR	172
BRIDGE	16	DR	154
ESSIEN	33	SD	+77
LAMPARD	35	SD	+89
MAKELELE	24	SD	+134
ROBBEN*	12	SD	+87
KALOU	18	SR	277
DROGBA	30	SR	147

KEY: DR = Defensive Rate, SD = Scoring Difference AP = Attacking Power SR = Strike Rate, CG=Counting games – League games playing at least 70 minutes

TOP POINT EARNERS

Arjen Robben

Counting Games League games when player was on pitch for at least 70 minutes	12
Average points Average League points taken in Counting games	2.75
Club Average points Average points taken in League games	2.18

	PLAYER	GAMES	PTS
1	Arjen Robben	12	2.75
2	Andriy Shevchenko	14	2.50
3	Michael Ballack	22	2.36
4	Ricardo Carvalho	28	2.36
5	Petr Cech	19	2.32
6	Claude Makelele	24	2.29
7	Frank Lampard	35	2.23
8	John Terry	27	2.19
9	Didier Drogba	30	2.17
10	Michael Essien	33	2.12

KEY PLAYERS - DEFENDERS

John Terry

Goals Conceded in the League Number of League goals conceded while the player was on the pitch	14
Goals Conceded in all competitions Total number of goals conceded while the player was on the pitch	27
League minutes played Number of minutes played in league matches	2413
Clean Sheets In games when the player was on pitch for at least 70 minutes	16
Defensive Rating Average number of mins between League goals conceded while on the pitch	172
Club Defensive Rating Average number of mins between League goals conceded by the club this season	142

	PLAYER	CON LGE	CON ALL	MINS	C SHEETS	DEF RATE
1	John Terry	14	27	2413	16	172 mins
2	Wayne Bridge	10	15	1548	10	154 mins
3	Paulo Ferreira	12	20	1710	10	142 mins
4	Ricardo Carvalho	19	35	2638	16	138 mins

KEY GOALKEEPER

Petr Cech

Goals Conceded in the League Number of League goals conceded while the player was on the pitch	9
Goals Conceded in all competitions Total number of goals conceded while the player was on the pitch	21
League minutes played Number of minutes played in league matches	1714
Clean Sheets In games when the player was on pitch for at least 70 minutes	12
Goals to Shots Ratio The average number of shots on target per each League goal conceded	9.67
Defensive Rating Ave mins between League goals conceded while on the pitch	190

BOOKINGS

John Obi Mikel

League Yellow	5
League Red	1
All competitions Yellow	9
All competitions Red	2

League Average 159 mins between cards

	PLAYER	LEAGUE		TOTAL		AVE
1	John Obi Mikel	5Y	1R	9Y	2R	159
2	Joe Cole	3	0	6	0	159
3	Lassana Diarra	3	0	10	0	185
4	Michael Ballack	7	1	11	1	252
5	Khalid Boulahrouz	2	1	5	1	270
6	Didier Drogba	9	0	12	0	327
7	Paulo Ferreira	5	0	7	0	342
8	Ricardo Carvalho	6	0	8	0	439
9	Claude Makelele	5	0	8	0	453
10	Ashley Cole	4	0	10	0	461
11	Michael Essien	5	0	10	0	594
12	John Terry	2	1	5	1	804
13	Frank Lampard	3	0	8	0	1081
14	S. Wright-Phillips	1	0	1	0	1270
15	Arjen Robben	1	0	3	0	1343
	Other	3	0	8	0	
	TOTAL	64	4	121	5	

LIVERPOOL

Into American ownership but in other respects it seemed a typical Liverpool season, punching above their weight in Europe and disappointing at home. The use of top forward **Peter Crouch** summed it up; he played less than half a league season yet scored nine goals at a better Strike Rate than Benni McCarthy. Rafa Benitez saved Crouch's other nine goals for cups.

Jermaine Pennant justified his fee with six Assists and the Top Point Earners crown, averaging 2.13 points in his games.

However, defenders were Liverpool's stars with **Daniel Agger** boasting the best Defensive Rating in the league, while **Jamie Carragher**, and **Steve Finnan** also figured in the top ten. **Pepe Reina's** Defensive Rating of a goal conceded every 136 minutes was second only to Petr Cech.

NICKNAME: THE REDS   KEY: ☐ Won ☐ Drawn ☐ Lost

#	comp	Opponent			Score	Scorers
1	ecql1	Maccabi Haifa	H	W	2-1	Bellamy 33, M.Gonzalez 88
2	facs	Chelsea	N	W	2-1	Riise 9, Crouch 79
3	prem	Sheff Utd	A	D	1-1	Fowler 70 pen
4	ecql2	Maccabi Haifa	A	D	1-1	Crouch 54
5	prem	West Ham	H	W	2-1	Agger 42, Crouch 45
6	prem	Everton	A	L	0-3	
7	ecgpc	PSV Eindhoven	A	D	0-0	
8	prem	Chelsea	A	L	0-1	
9	prem	Newcastle	H	W	2-0	Kuyt 29, Xabi Alonso 79
10	prem	Tottenham	H	W	3-0	Gonzalez 63, Kuyt 73, Riise 89
11	ecgpc	Galatasaray	H	W	3-2	Crouch 8, 52, Luis Garcia 14
12	prem	Bolton	A	L	0-2	
13	prem	Blackburn	H	D	1-1	Bellamy 64
14	ecgpc	Bordeaux	A	W	1-0	Crouch 58
15	prem	Man Utd	A	L	0-2	
16	ccr3	Reading	H	W	4-3	Fowler 44, Riise 45, Paletta 50, Crouch 77
17	prem	Aston Villa	H	W	3-1	Kuyt 31, Crouch 38, Luis Garcia 44
18	ecgpc	Bordeaux	H	W	3-0	Luis Garcia 23, 76, Gerrard 71
19	prem	Reading	H	W	2-0	Kuyt 14, 73
20	ccr4	Birmingham	A	W	1-0	Agger 45
21	prem	Arsenal	A	L	0-3	
22	prem	Middlesbrough	A	D	0-0	
23	ecgpc	PSV Eindhoven	H	W	2-0	Gerrard 65, Crouch 88
24	prem	Man City	H	W	1-0	Gerrard 67
25	prem	Portsmouth	H	D	0-0	
26	prem	Wigan	A	W	4-0	Bellamy 9, 26, Kuyt 40, McCulloch 45 og
27	ecgpc	Galatasaray	A	L	2-3	Fowler 22, 90
28	prem	Fulham	H	W	4-0	Gerrard 54, Carragher 61, Luis Garcia 66, Gonzalez 90
29	prem	Charlton	A	W	3-0	Xabi Alonso 3 pen, Bellamy 82, Gerrard 88
30	prem	Watford	H	W	2-0	Bellamy 47, Xabi Alonso 88
31	prem	Blackburn	A	L	0-1	
32	prem	Tottenham	A	W	1-0	Luis Garcia 45
33	prem	Bolton	H	W	3-0	Crouch 61, Gerrard 63, Kuyt 83
34	facr3	Arsenal	H	L	1-3	Kuyt 71
35	ccqf	Arsenal	H	L	3-6	Fowler 32, Gerrard 68, Hyypia 80
36	prem	Watford	A	W	3-0	Bellamy 34, Crouch 39, 48
37	prem	Chelsea	H	W	2-0	Kuyt 4, Pennant 18
38	prem	West Ham	A	W	2-1	Kuyt 46, Crouch 53
39	prem	Everton	H	D	0-0	
40	prem	Newcastle	A	L	1-2	Bellamy 6
41	eckl1	Barcelona	A	W	2-1	Bellamy 43, Riise 74
42	prem	Sheff Utd	H	W	4-0	Fowler 20 pen, 25 pen, Hyypia 70, Gerrard 73
43	prem	Man Utd	H	L	0-1	
44	eckl2	Barcelona	H	L	0-1	
45	prem	Aston Villa	A	D	0-0	
46	prem	Arsenal	H	W	4-1	Crouch 4, 35, 81, Agger 60
47	ecqfl1	PSV Eindhoven	A	W	3-0	Gerrard 27, Riise 49, Crouch 63
48	prem	Reading	A	W	2-0	Arbeloa 15, Kuyt 86
49	ecqfl2	PSV Eindhoven	H	W	1-0	Crouch 68
50	prem	Man City	A	D	0-0	
51	prem	Middlesbrough	H	W	2-0	Gerrard 58, 65 pen
52	prem	Wigan	H	W	2-0	Kuyt 30, 68
53	ecsfl1	Chelsea	A	L	0-1	
54	prem	Portsmouth	A	L	1-2	Hyypia 59
55	ecsfl2	Chelsea	H	W	4-1*	Agger 22 (*on penalties)
56	prem	Fulham	A	L	0-1	
57	prem	Charlton	H	D	2-2	Xabi Alonso 62, Kewell 90 pen
58	ecfin	AC Milan	N	L	1-2	Kuyt 89

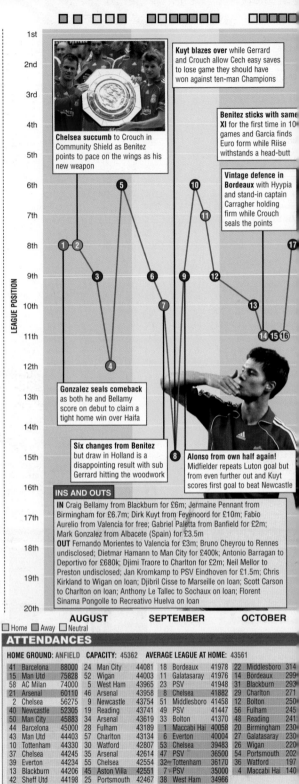

Kuyt blazes over while Gerrard and Crouch allow Cech easy saves to lose game they should have won against ten-man Champions

Benitez sticks with same XI for the first time in 100 games and Garcia finds Euro form while Riise withstands a head-butt

Chelsea succumb to Crouch in Community Shield as Benitez points to pace on the wings as his new weapon

Vintage defence in Bordeaux with Hyypia and stand-in captain Carragher holding firm while Crouch seals the points

Gonzalez seals comeback as both he and Bellamy score on debut to claim a tight home win over Haifa

Six changes from Benitez but draw in Holland is a disappointing result with sub Gerrard hitting the woodwork

Alonso from own half again! Midfielder repeats Luton goal from even further out and Kuyt scores first goal to beat Newcastle

LEAGUE POSITION: 1st, 2nd, 3rd, 4th, 5th, 6th, 7th, 8th, 9th, 10th, 11th, 12th, 13th, 14th, 15th, 16th, 17th, 18th, 19th, 20th

AUGUST   SEPTEMBER   OCTOBER

☐ Home ☐ Away ☐ Neutral

INS AND OUTS

IN Craig Bellamy from Blackburn for £6m; Jermaine Pennant from Birmingham for £6.7m; Dirk Kuyt from Feyenoord for £10m; Fabio Aurelio from Valencia for free; Gabriel Paletta from Banfield for £2m; Mark Gonzalez from Albacete (Spain) for £3.5m

OUT Fernando Morientes to Valencia for £3m; Bruno Cheyrou to Rennes undisclosed; Dietmar Hamann to Man City for £400k; Antonio Barragan to Deportivo for £680k; Djimi Traore to Charlton for £2m; Neil Mellor to Preston undisclosed; Jan Kromkamp to PSV Eindhoven for £1.5m; Chris Kirkland to Wigan on loan; Djibril Cisse to Marseille on loan; Scott Carson to Charlton on loan; Anthony Le Tallec to Sochaux on loan; Florent Sinama Pongolle to Recreativo Huelva on loan

ATTENDANCES

HOME GROUND: ANFIELD   CAPACITY: 45362   AVERAGE LEAGUE AT HOME: 43561

#	Opponent	Att		#	Opponent	Att		#	Opponent	Att		#	Opponent	Att
41	Barcelona	88000		24	Man City	44081		18	Bordeaux	41978		22	Middlesboro	314
15	Man Utd	75828		52	Wigan	44003		11	Galatasaray	41976		14	Bordeaux	299
58	AC Milan	74000		5	West Ham	43965		23	PSV	41948		31	Blackburn	293
21	Arsenal	60110		46	Arsenal	43958		8	Chelsea	41882		29	Charlton	271
2	Chelsea	56275		9	Newcastle	43754		51	Middlesboro	41458		12	Bolton	250
40	Newcastle	52305		19	Reading	43741		49	PSV	41447		56	Fulham	245
50	Man City	45883		34	Arsenal	43619		33	Bolton	41370		48	Reading	241
44	Barcelona	45000		28	Fulham	43189		1	Maccabi Hai	40058		20	Birmingham	230
43	Man Utd	44403		57	Charlton	43134		6	Everton	40004		27	Galatasaray	230
10	Tottenham	44330		30	Watford	42807		53	Chelsea	39483		26	Wigan	220
37	Chelsea	44245		35	Arsenal	42614		47	PSV	36500		54	Portsmouth	202
39	Everton	44234		55	Chelsea	42554		32	Tottenham	36170		36	Watford	197
13	Blackburn	44206		45	Aston Villa	42551		7	PSV	35000		4	Maccabi Hai	140
42	Sheff Utd	44198		25	Portsmouth	42467		38	West Ham	34966				
17	Aston Villa	44117		16	Reading	42445		3	Sheff Utd	31726				

New owners nearly see final repeat

Final Position: 3rd

Key: ● League ● Champions Lge ● UEFA Cup ● FA Cup ○ League Cup ● Other

Gap grows to 16 points as Portsmouth leave happy with a draw and Benitez worries over lack of attacking width

It's 11 from the last three games as Bellamy destroys Charlton but Kuyt misses a hat-trick of chances

Record defeat as Arsenal youngsters hit six at Anfield and Gonzalez and Garcia are stretchered off

Bellamy's stunning start against his old club is overturned as other chances go begging

Gerrard leads romp in Eindhoven to beat Rush's Champions League scoring record with first headed goal before Riise's blast and Crouch's header

Reina defies Lampard twice but can't prevent Joe Cole from giving Chelsea a first leg advantage

Kuyt double set up by Crouch's headers in first ever league meeting with Reading

Fortress Anfield crumbles to Gunners' counter attacks leaving Dudek exposed after eight games without conceding

Bellamy's clubbing ends with a goal celebration as he sets up Riise for an unlikely winner at the Nou Camp

Barcelona are second best despite a narrow win on the night as Riise and Sissoko hit the woodwork and Benitez triumphs over Rijkaard

Bring on Chelsea as Crouch takes his place at the top of the Champions League scorers' table

Reina supreme as his two penalty saves give Kuyt the winning penalty after Agger's superbly worked free kick to set up a repeat of 2005 final

Milan revenge Istanbul with a lucky Inzaghi deflection proving the pivotal moment despite Reds looking the better side but over-cautious

Run of 11 hours and 29 minutes without conceding ends as Blackburn grab a win while Crouch misfires and Friedel excels

Lucky United end 15 hours without conceding at Anfield as O'Shea snatches a late winner

Perfect hat-trick for Crouch's comeback with left foot, right foot and headed finishes in front of new American owners

Gerrard's 25 yard strike ends Boro's resistance and reclaims third spot in the table

Goalless for five successive away league defeats as linesman disallows two and Arsenal expose defensive frailty

Garcia bundles in vital goal for third away win but it's close as Spurs battle back

Nine men back as Everton come for a point and Benitez accuses them of having a 'small club' mentality

Group C won as Gerrard and Crouch despatch PSV but Alonso, Pennant and Gonzales are injured

Fowler's brace as he scores off his rump for first Euro goal for five years before adding a 90th minute consolation

Pennant's cracker is first goal for a year and ensures Benitez claims his league win over Mourinho at last

INS AND OUTS

IN Javier Mascherano from West Ham (and Media Sports Investments) for £1.5m; Alvaro Arbeloa from Deportivo La Coruna for £2.6m; Emiliano Insua from Boca Juniors on loan; Daniele Padelli from Sampdoria on loan
OUT Stephen Warnock to Blackburn for £1.5m; Salif Diao to Stoke on loan

MONTH BY MONTH POINTS TALLY

Month	Points	%
AUGUST	4	67%
SEPTEMBER	6	40%
OCTOBER	4	44%
NOVEMBER	8	53%
DECEMBER	15	83%
JANUARY	12	100%
FEBRUARY	4	44%
MARCH	4	44%
APRIL	10	67%
MAY	1	17%

NOVEMBER   DECEMBER   JANUARY   FEBRUARY   MARCH   APRIL   MAY

GOAL ATTEMPTS

FOR
Goal attempts recorded in League games

	HOME	AWAY	TOTAL	AVE
Shots on target	166	130	296	7.8
Shots off target	190	123	313	8.2
TOTAL	356	253	609	16.0

Ratio of goals to shots
Average number of shots on target per League goal scored: **5.2**

Accuracy rating
Average percentage of total goal attempts which were on target: **48.6**

AGAINST
Goal attempts recorded in League games

	HOME	AWAY	TOTAL	AVE
Shots on target	54	80	134	3.5
Shots off target	68	74	142	3.7
TOTAL	122	154	276	7.3

Ratio of goals to shots
Average number of shots on target per League goal scored: **5.0**

Accuracy rating
Average percentage of total goal attempts which were on target: **48.6**

GOALS

Crouch

League	9
FA Cup	1
League Cup	1
Europe	7
Other	0
TOTAL	18

League Average 167 mins between goals

	PLAYER	LGE	FAC	LC	Euro	TOT	AVE
1	Crouch	9	1	1	7	18	167
2	Kuyt	12	1	0	1	14	214
3	Gerrard	7	0	1	3	11	439
4	Bellamy	7	0	0	2	9	272
5	Fowler	3	0	2	2	7	203
6	Luis Garcia	3	0	0	3	6	333
7	Riise	1	1	1	2	5	2582
8	Xabi Alonso	4	0	0	0	4	665
9	Agger	2	0	1	1	4	1083
10	Gonzalez	2	0	0	1	3	607
11	Hyypia	2	0	1	0	3	1015
12	Kewell	1	0	0	0	1	48
13	Arbeloa	1	0	0	0	1	705
14	Pennant	1	0	0	0	1	1974
15	Carragher	1	0	0	0	1	2978
	Other	0	0	1	0	1	
	TOTAL	56	3	8	22	89	

PREMIERSHIP CLUBS – LIVERPOOL

SQUAD APPEARANCES

Match	1 2 3 4 5	6 7 8 9 10	11 12 13 14 15	16 17 18 19 20	21 22 23 24 25	26 27 28 29 30	31 32 33 34 35	36 37 38 39 40	41 42 43 44 45	46 47 48 49 50	51 52 53 54 55	56 57
Venue	H N A A H	A A A H H	H A H A A	H H H H A	A A H H H	A A H A H	A A H H H	A H A H A	A H H H A	H A A H A	H H A A H	A H
Competition	C F L C L	L C L L L	C L L C L	W L C L W	L L C L L	L C L L L	L L L F W	L L L L L	C L L C L	L C L C L	L L C L C	L L
Result	W W D D W	L D L W W	W L D W L	W W W W W	L D W W D	W L W W W	L W W L L	W W W D L	W W L L D	W W W W D	W W L L W	L D

Goalkeepers
Jerzy Dudek
David Martin
Daniele Padelli
Jose Reina

Defenders
Daniel Agger
Alvaro Arbeloa
Fabio Aurelio
Jamie Carragher
Steve Finnan
Jack Hobbs
Sami Hyypia
Emiliano Insua
Jan Kromkamp
Gabriel Paletta
Miguel Roque
James Smith
Stephen Warnock

Midfielders
Steven Gerrard
Mark Gonzalez
Danny Guthrie
Harry Kewell
Javier Mascherano
Lee Peltier
Jermaine Pennant
John Arne Riise
Momo Sissoko
Xabi Alonso
Boudewijn Zenden

Forwards
Craig Bellamy
Peter Crouch
Nabil El Zhar
Robbie Fowler
Dirk Kuyt
Javier Luis Garcia
F Sinama-Pongolle

KEY: ■ On all match ◄◄ Subbed or sent off (Counting game) ▸▸ Subbed on from bench (Counting Game) ▸ Subbed on and then subbed or sent off (Counting Game) ☐ Not in 16 ☐ Injured
■ On bench ◄ Subbed or sent off (playing less than 70 mins) ▸ Subbed on (playing less than 70 mins) ▸ Subbed on and then subbed or sent off (playing less than 70 min ✕ Suspended

---

KEY PLAYERS - GOALSCORERS

Peter Crouch

Goals in the League	9
Goals in all competitions	18
Assists — League goals scored by a team mate where the player delivered the final pass	8
Contribution to Attacking Power — Average number of minutes between League team goals while on pitch	48
Player Strike Rate — Average number of minutes between League goals scored by player	167
Club Strike Rate — Average minutes between League goals scored by club	60

	PLAYER	GOALS LGE	GOALS ALL	ASSISTS	POWER	S RATE
1	Peter Crouch	9	18	8	48	167 mins
2	Dirk Kuyt	12	14	5	57	214 mins
3	Craig Bellamy	7	9	4	68	272 mins
4	Steven Gerrard	7	11	6	59	439 mins

KEY PLAYERS - MIDFIELDERS

John Arne Riise

Goals in the League	1
Goals in all competitions	5
Assists — League goals scored by a team mate where the player delivered the final pass	1
Defensive Rating — Average number of mins between League goals conceded while on the pitch	151
Contribution to Attacking Power — Average number of minutes between League team goals while on pitch	60
Scoring Difference — Defensive Rating minus Contribution to Attacking Power	91

	PLAYER	GOALS LGE	GOALS ALL	ASSISTS	DEF RATE	POWER	SC DIFF
1	John Arne Riise	1	5	1	151	60	91 mins
2	Jermaine Pennant	1	1	6	151	63	88 mins
3	Steven Gerrard	7	11	6	133	59	74 mins
4	Xabi Alonso	4	4	1	121	59	62 mins

PLAYER APPEARANCES

	AGE (on 01/07/07)	IN NAMED 16	APPEARANCES	COUNTING GAMES	MINUTES ON PITCH	APPEARANCES THIS SEASON	MINUTES ON PITCH THIS SEASON	HOME COUNTRY
Goalkeepers								
Jerzy Dudek	34	33	2	2	180	6	540	1	Poland
David Martin	21	4	0	0	0	0	0	-	England
Daniele Padelli	21	4	1	1	90	1	90	-	Italy
Jose Reina	24	35	35	35	3150	51	4620	3	Spain
Defenders								
Daniel Agger	22	34	27	23	2167	43	3624	9	Denmark
Alvaro Arbeloa	24	9	9	7	705	14	1068	-	Spain
Fabio Aurelio	27	17	17	10	1016	25	1494	-	Brazil
Jamie Carragher	29	35	35	33	2978	51	4374	5	England
Steve Finnan	31	33	33	32	2889	47	4176	8	Rep of Ireland
Jack Hobbs	18	2	0	0	0	0	0	-	England
Sami Hyypia	33	36	23	22	2031	29	2571	8	Finland
Emiliano Insua	21	2	2	2	164	2	164	-	Argentina
Jan Kromkamp	26	2	1	1	90	1	90	-	Holland
Gabriel Paletta	21	9	3	2	210	8	583	-	Argentina
Miguel Roque	18	0	0	0	0	1	6	-	Spain
James Smith	21	0	0	0	0	1	17	-	England
Stephen Warnock	25	4	1	0	53	7	411	-	England
Midfielders								
Steven Gerrard	27	36	36	34	3076	51	4255	10	England
Mark Gonzalez	22	27	25	8	1214	36	1635	-	Chile
Danny Guthrie	20	4	3	0	35	7	222	-	England
Harry Kewell	27	2	2	0	48	3	80	-	Australia
Javier Mascherano	23	8	7	7	616	11	990	2	Argentina
Lee Peltier	20	0	0	0	0	4	343	-	England
Jermaine Pennant	24	35	34	16	1974	52	3136	-	England
John Arne Riise	26	33	33	27	2582	48	3880	3	Norway
Momo Sissoko	22	17	16	12	1222	28	2005	-	Mali
Xabi Alonso	25	32	32	29	2662	51	3983	8	Spain
Boudewijn Zenden	30	19	16	7	811	30	1779	-	Holland
Forwards								
Craig Bellamy	27	27	27	20	1908	42	2652	11	Wales
Peter Crouch	26	33	32	11	1511	49	2559	8	England
Nabil El Zhar	20	3	3	0	53	3	53	-	Morocco
Robbie Fowler	32	20	16	5	609	23	1041	-	England
Dirk Kuyt	26	35	34	26	2577	48	3626	9	Holland
Javier Luis Garcia	29	17	17	8	999	27	1681	7	Spain
Sinama-Pongolle	22	0	0	0	0	1	2	-	France

KEY: LEAGUE   ALL COMPS   CAPS   (MAY FIFA RANKING)

TEAM OF THE SEASON

REINA — CG 35   DR 136

 FINNAN — CG 32   DR 131

 CARRAGHER — CG 33   DR 135

 HYYPIA — CG 22   DR 101

 AGGER — CG 23   DR 197

 PENNANT — CG 16   SD +88

 GERRARD — CG 34   SD +74

 ALONSO — CG 29   SD +62

 RIISE — CG 27   SD +91

 KUYT — CG 26   AP 57

 CROUCH* — CG 11   SR 167

KEY: DR = Defensive Rate, SD = Scoring Difference AP = Attacking Power SR = Strike Rate, CG=Counting games – League games playing at least 70 minutes

TOP POINT EARNERS

Jermaine Pennant

Counting Games	
League games when player was on pitch for at least 70 minutes	16

Average points	
Average League points taken in Counting games	2.13

Club Average points	
Average points taken in League games	1.79

	PLAYER	GAMES	PTS
1	Jermaine Pennant	16	2.13
2	Daniel Agger	23	1.96
3	Dirk Kuyt	26	1.96
4	John Arne Riise	27	1.89
5	Jamie Carragher	33	1.85
6	Jose Reina	35	1.83
7	Steven Gerrard	34	1.82
8	Steve Finnan	32	1.81
9	Xabi Alonso	29	1.79
10	Sami Hyypia	22	1.77

KEY PLAYERS - DEFENDERS

Daniel Agger

Goals Conceded in the League	
Number of League goals conceded while the player was on the pitch	11

Goals Conceded in all competitions	
Total number of goals conceded while the player was on the pitch	29

League minutes played	
Number of minutes played in league matches	2167

Clean Sheets	
In games when the player was on pitch for at least 70 minutes	15

Defensive Rating	
Average number of mins between League goals conceded while on the pitch	197

Club Defensive Rating	
Average number of mins between League goals conceded by the club this season	126

	PLAYER	CON LGE	CON ALL	MINS	C SHEETS	DEF RATE
1	Daniel Agger	11	29	2167	15	197 mins
2	Jamie Carragher	22	38	2978	19	135 mins
3	Steve Finnan	22	34	2889	18	131 mins
4	Sami Hyypia	20	28	2031	9	101 mins

KEY GOALKEEPER

Jose Reina

Goals Conceded in the League	
Number of League goals conceded while the player was on the pitch	23

Goals Conceded in all competitions	
Total number of goals conceded while the player was on the pitch	36

League minutes played	
Number of minutes played in league matches	3150

Clean Sheets	
In games when the player was on pitch for at least 70 minutes	19

Goals to Shots Ratio	
The average number of shots on target per each League goal conceded	5.26

Defensive Rating	
Ave mins between League goals conceded while on the pitch	136

BOOKINGS

Momo Sissoko

League Yellow	5
League Red	0
All competitions Yellow	9
All competitions Red	0

League Average 244 mins between cards

	PLAYER	LEAGUE		TOTAL		AVE
1	Momo Sissoko	5 Y	0 R	9 Y	0 R	244
2	Xabi Alonso	9	0	13	0	295
3	Javier Luis Garcia	3	0	3	0	333
4	Jermaine Pennant	4	0	6	0	493
5	Robbie Fowler	1	0	1	0	609
6	Javier Mascherano	1	0	4	0	616
7	Sami Hyypia	3	0	4	0	677
8	Alvaro Arbeloa	1	0	2	0	705
9	Jamie Carragher	4	0	5	0	744
10	Peter Crouch	2	0	2	0	755
11	Craig Bellamy	2	0	3	0	954
12	Fabio Aurelio	1	0	1	0	1016
13	Steve Finnan	2	0	3	0	1444
14	Daniel Agger	1	0	3	0	2167
15	John Arne Riise	1	0	1	0	2582
	Other	1	0	7	0	
	TOTAL	**41**	**0**	**67**	**0**	

ARSENAL

Every manager is jealous of Arsenal's prodigious youngsters who went all the way to the Carling Cup final and made Chelsea's first XI work hard for a win. **Cesc Fabregas** is key to the future and his 14 Assists sums up the club's promise while his two league goals characterises its current problems – turning chances into goals!

Vital injuries to **Robin van Persie** and the departing **Thierry Henry** didn't help, as they had the two best Premiership Strike Rates with the Dutchman scoring a goal every 132 minutes on average. **Emmanuel Adebayor** also claimed a top 20 Strike Rate.

Tomas Rosicky and **Gilberto Silva** (with ten league goals) combined in a strong midfield but the defence was shaky with **Kolo Toure** and **William Gallas** both out of the top 15 defenders and **Jens Lehmann** poor in terms of shots saved per goals scored.

NICKNAME: THE GUNNERS

KEY: ■ Won ■ Drawn ■ Lost

#	Comp	Opponent	H/A	W/D/L	Score	Scorers
1	ecql1	Dinamo Zagreb	A	W	3-0	Fabregas 63, 79, van Persie 64
2	prem	Aston Villa	H	D	1-1	Gilberto Silva 84
3	ecql2	Dinamo Zagreb	H	W	2-1	Ljungberg 77, Flamini 90
4	prem	Man City	A	L	0-1	
5	prem	Middlesbrough	H	D	1-1	Henry 67 pen
6	ecgpg	Hamburg	A	W	2-1	Gilberto Silva 12 pen, Rosicky 53
7	prem	Man Utd	A	W	1-0	Adebayor 85
8	prem	Sheff Utd	H	W	3-0	Gallas 65, Jagielka 69 og, Henry 80
9	ecgpg	Porto	H	W	2-0	Henry 38, Hleb 48
10	prem	Charlton	A	W	2-1	van Persie 32, 49
11	prem	Watford	H	W	3-0	Stewart 33 og, Henry 43, Adebayor 67
12	ecgpg	CSKA Moscow	A	L	0-1	
13	prem	Reading	A	W	4-0	Henry 1, 70 pen, Hleb 39, van Persie 50
14	ccr3	West Brom	A	W	2-0	Aliadiere 33 pen, 49
15	prem	Everton	H	D	1-1	van Persie 71
16	ecgpg	CSKA Moscow	H	D	0-0	
17	prem	West Ham	A	L	0-1	
18	ccr4	Everton	A	W	1-0	Adebayor 85
19	prem	Liverpool	H	W	3-0	Flamini 41, Toure 56, Gallas 80
20	prem	Newcastle	H	D	1-1	Henry 70
21	ecgpg	Hamburg	H	W	3-1	van Persie 52, Eboue 83, Baptista 88
22	prem	Bolton	A	L	1-3	Gilberto Silva 45
23	prem	Fulham	A	L	1-2	van Persie 36
24	prem	Tottenham	H	W	3-0	Adebayor 20, Gilberto Silva 42 pen, 72 pen
25	ecgpg	Porto	A	D	0-0	
26	prem	Chelsea	A	D	1-1	Flamini 78
27	prem	Wigan	A	W	1-0	Adebayor 88
28	prem	Portsmouth	H	D	2-2	Adebayor 58, Gilberto Silva 60
29	prem	Blackburn	H	W	6-2	Gilberto Silva 10, Hleb 23, Adebayor 27 pen, van Persie 85, 88, Flamini 90
30	prem	Watford	A	W	2-1	Gilberto Silva 19, van Persie 83
31	prem	Sheff Utd	A	L	0-1	
32	prem	Charlton	H	W	4-0	Henry 30 pen, Hoyte 45, van Persie 75 pen, 90
33	facr3	Liverpool	A	W	3-1	Rosicky 37, 45, Henry 84
34	ccqf	Liverpool	A	W	6-3	Aliadiere 27, Baptista 40, 45, 60, 84, Song 45
35	prem	Blackburn	A	W	2-0	Toure 37, Henry 71
36	prem	Man Utd	H	W	2-1	van Persie 83, Henry 90
37	ccsfl1	Tottenham	A	D	2-2	Baptista 64, 77
38	facr4	Bolton	H	D	1-1	Toure 78
39	ccsfl2	Tottenham	H	W	3-1	Adebayor 77, Aliadiere 105, Chimbonda 113 og
40	prem	Middlesbrough	A	D	1-1	Henry 77
41	prem	Wigan	H	W	2-1	Hall 81 og, Rosicky 84
42	facr4r	Bolton	A	W	3-1	Adebayor 13, 120, Ljungberg 108
43	facr5	Blackburn	H	D	0-0	
44	eckl1	PSV Eindhoven	A	L	0-1	
45	cccf	Chelsea	A	L	1-2	Walcott 12
46	facr5r	Blackburn	A	L	0-1	
47	prem	Reading	H	W	2-1	Gilberto Silva 51 pen, Baptista 62
48	eckl2	PSV Eindhoven	H	D	1-1	Alex 58 og
49	prem	Aston Villa	A	W	1-0	Diaby 10
50	prem	Everton	A	L	0-1	
51	prem	Liverpool	A	L	1-4	Gallas 73
52	prem	West Ham	H	L	0-1	
53	prem	Newcastle	A	D	0-0	
54	prem	Bolton	H	W	2-1	Rosicky 31, Fabregas 46
55	prem	Man City	H	W	3-1	Rosicky 12, Fabregas 73, Baptista 80
56	prem	Tottenham	A	D	2-2	Toure 64, Adebayor 78
57	prem	Fulham	H	W	3-1	Baptista 4, Adebayor 84, Gilberto Silva 87 pen
58	prem	Chelsea	H	D	1-1	Gilberto Silva 43 pen
59	prem	Portsmouth	A	D	0-0	

LEAGUE POSITION (1st – 20th)

Betrayed claims Cole as he swaps places with Gallas and publishes his story

"It's inspirational" applauds Coppell on the end of a four-goal mauling instigated by Henry and Fabregas

Fabregas strikes twice and van Persie adds the third to give Dinamo a mountain to climb in second leg

Adebayor ends United's record with deserved winner as Gilberto misses a penalty and Rosicky pulls the strings in fluid midfield

Eboué's supreme cross connects with Henry's head for his 50th goal in Europe before Hleb makes sure to top group

First Emirates win comes courtesy of Walcott's 90th minute cross for Flamini to confirm Champions League qualification

Man City hang on despite Rosicky's energy and van Persie's dismal luck to record their first win

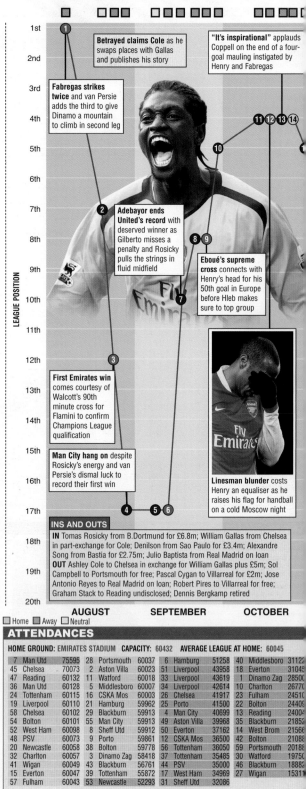

Linesman blunder costs Henry an equaliser as he raises his flag for handball on a cold Moscow night

INS AND OUTS

IN Tomas Rosicky from B.Dortmund for £6.8m; William Gallas from Chelsea in part-exchange for Cole; Denilson from Sao Paulo for £3.4m; Alexandre Song from Bastia for £2.75m; Julio Baptista from Real Madrid on loan
OUT Ashley Cole to Chelsea in exchange for William Gallas plus £5m; Sol Campbell to Portsmouth for free; Pascal Cygan to Villarreal for £2m; Jose Antonio Reyes to Real Madrid on loan; Robert Pires to Villarreal for free; Graham Stack to Reading undisclosed; Dennis Bergkamp retired

□ Home ■ Away □ Neutral

AUGUST SEPTEMBER OCTOBER

ATTENDANCES

HOME GROUND: EMIRATES STADIUM CAPACITY: 60432 AVERAGE LEAGUE AT HOME: 60045

#	Opponent	Att		#	Opponent	Att		#	Opponent	Att		#	Opponent	Att
7	Man Utd	75595		28	Portsmouth	60037		6	Hamburg	51258		40	Middlesboro	31122
45	Chelsea	70073		2	Aston Villa	60023		51	Liverpool	43958		18	Everton	31045
47	Reading	60132		11	Watford	60018		33	Liverpool	43619		1	Dinamo Zag	28500
36	Man Utd	60128		5	Middlesboro	60007		34	Liverpool	42614		10	Charlton	26770
24	Tottenham	60115		16	CSKA Mos	60003		26	Chelsea	41917		23	Fulham	24510
19	Liverpool	60110		21	Hamburg	59962		25	Porto	41500		22	Bolton	24409
58	Chelsea	60102		29	Blackburn	59913		4	Man City	40699		13	Reading	24004
54	Bolton	60101		55	Man City	59913		49	Aston Villa	39968		35	Blackburn	21852
52	West Ham	60098		8	Sheff Utd	59912		50	Everton	37162		14	West Brom	21566
48	PSV	60073		9	Porto	59861		12	CSKA Mos	36500		42	Bolton	21088
20	Newcastle	60058		38	Bolton	59778		56	Tottenham	36050		59	Portsmouth	20188
32	Charlton	60057		3	Dinamo Zag	58418		37	Tottenham	35485		30	Watford	19750
41	Wigan	60049		43	Blackburn	56761		44	PSV	35000		46	Blackburn	18882
15	Everton	60047		39	Tottenham	55872		17	West Ham	34969		27	Wigan	15311
57	Fulham	60043		53	Newcastle	52293		31	Sheff Utd	32086				

Fabregas leads the promise of youth

Final Position: 4th

● League ● Champions Lge ● UEFA Cup ● FA Cup ○ League Cup ● Other

ub Walcott turns game ying on goals for Eboué nd Baptista to overcome lamburg's early lead

Gilberto converts two from the spot following Adebayor's fine finish as Spurs are routed to nail Emirates 'myth'

Henry halts United with 93rd minute header after van Persie injures himself scoring the equaliser

Fabregas fluffs lines as he scuffs miss of the season at one end and flicks in an own goal at the other

First defeat of 2007 at the hands of PSV despite testing Gomes throughout

Crushed by Crouch as returning Liverpool striker scores a stunning hat-trick while returning Adebayor unlucky to hit woodwork twice

Second half rout with two goals and three strikes on the woodwork but Spurs level in the 95th minute

Adebayor silences Bolton in extra time after sub Ljungberg claims lead and Gilberto and Baptista miss penalties

Gilberto dooms Chelsea with penalty that makes United Champions despite Blues second half fightback

Anelka brace helps Bolton to a win despite three strikes against the woodwork and 68% possession

Blackburn succumb in the last five minutes of thrilling game as van Persie leads the way and Rovers are hit for six

Adebayor leads young guns to final with Spurs wilting and Aliadiere netting in extra time

Adebayor clinches win with a clinical finish after Fulham battle back from Baptista's early header

Toure's run and finish leaves Liverpool for dead before Gallas' second of the season adds a gloss

Rosicky rocks Reds with two sweetly hit goals before halftime, then Henry's individual effort ends holders' hopes

Smart Alex scores at both ends; first to give Wenger a lifeline and then knocking him out of a third cup in two weeks

Fabregas' first Premier goal of the season ends worst league run for 12 years with a win over fourth place rivals Bolton

Fireworks at Upton Park as Wenger and Pardew square up after Hleb penalty claim is dismissed and Hammers' manager 'celebrates over zealously'

Youngest ever back four thwarts Chelsea to claim a point after Flamini's strike is answered by Essien

Bizarre hat trick includes an own goal for Baptista plus two at the right end as youngsters hold Spurs

Walcott's first strike in an Arsenal shirt comes in final as wonder kids match Chelsea until Drogba's late header. A 20-man melee ends in red for Toure and Adebayor

Beaten at the Emirates by West Ham as Wenger admits his side 'should have scored ten' after 27 shots and two hits on the woodwork

Baptista blows them away, striking four and missing a penalty as young Guns hit a record six at Anfield

Boardroom break-up as David Dein loses bid to bring in US billionaire

MONTH BY MONTH POINTS TALLY

AUGUST	1	17%
SEPTEMBER	10	83%
OCTOBER	7	78%
NOVEMBER	4	27%
DECEMBER	14	67%
JANUARY	9	100%
FEBRUARY	4	67%
MARCH	6	50%
APRIL	11	61%
MAY	2	33%

NS AND OUTS

OUT Lauren to Portsmouth for £500k; Alexandre Song to Charlton on loan; Anthony Stokes to Sunderland for £2m; Niklas Bendtner to Birmingham on loan; Sebastian Larsson to Birmingham City for £1m; Joe O'Cearuill to Brighton on loan

NOVEMBER   DECEMBER   JANUARY   FEBRUARY   MARCH   APRIL   MAY

OAL ATTEMPTS

FOR
Goal attempts recorded in League games

	HOME	AWAY	TOTAL	AVE
ots on target	172	109	281	7.4
ots off target	147	143	290	7.6
TAL	319	252	571	15.0

Ratio of goals to shots verage number of shots on rget per League goal scored — **4.5**

ccuracy rating verage percentage of total goal empts which were on target — **49.2**

AGAINST
Goal attempts recorded in League games

	HOME	AWAY	TOTAL	AVE
shots on target	66	98	164	4.3
shots off target	63	112	175	4.6
TOTAL	129	210	339	8.9

Ratio of goals to shots Average number of shots on target per League goal scored — **4.7**

Accuracy rating Average percentage of total goal attempts which were on target — **48.4**

GOALS

van Persie

League	11
FA Cup	0
League Cup	0
Europe	2
Other	0
TOTAL	13

League Average **132** mins between goals

	PLAYER	LGE	FAC	LC	Euro	TOT	AVE
1	van Persie	11	0	0	2	13	132
2	Henry	10	1	0	1	12	147
3	Adebayor	8	2	2	0	12	248
4	Gilberto Silva	10	0	0	1	11	293
5	Baptista	3	0	6	1	10	379
6	Rosicky	3	2	0	1	6	609
7	Flamini	3	0	0	1	4	322
8	Toure	3	1	0	0	4	1050
9	Fabregas	2	0	0	2	4	1591
10	Aliadiere	0	0	4	0	4	
11	Gallas	3	0	0	0	3	626
12	Hleb	2	0	0	1	3	1177
13	Ljungberg	0	1	0	1	2	
14	Diaby	1	0	0	0	1	742
15	Hoyte	1	0	0	0	1	1503
	Other	0	0	2	1	3	
	TOTAL	60	7	14	12	93	

SQUAD APPEARANCES

Match	1 2 3 4 5	6 7 8 9 10	11 12 13 14 15	16 17 18 19 20	21 22 23 24 25	26 27 28 29 30	31 32 33 34 35	36 37 38 39 40	41 42 43 44 45	46 47 48 49 50	51 52 53 54 55	56 57 5
Venue	A H H A H	A A H H A	H A A A H	H A A H H	H A A H A	A A H H A	A H A A A	H A H H A	H A H A A	A H H A A	A H A H H	A H
Competition	C L C L L	C L L C L	L C L W L	C L W L L	C L L L C	L L L L L	L L F W L	L W F W L	L F F C W	F L C L L	L L L L L	L L
Result	W D W L D	W W W W W	W L W W D	D L W W D	W L L W D	D W D W W	L W W W W	W D D W D	W W D L L	L W D W L	L L D W W	D W

Goalkeepers
Manuel Almunia
Jens Lehmann
Mart Poom

Defenders
Gael Clichy
Matthew Connolly
Pascal Cygan
Johan Djourou
Emmanuel Eboue
William Gallas
Justin Hoyte
Etame Mayer Lauren
Philippe Senderos
Habib Kolo Toure
Armand Traore

Midfielders
Julio Baptista
Denilson
Vassiriki Diaby
Cesc Fabregas
Mathieu Flamini
Gilberto Silva
Alexander Hleb
Fredrik Ljungberg
Mark Randall
Jose Antonio Reyes
Tomas Rosicky
Alexandre Song
Theo Walcott

Forwards
Emmanuel Adebayor
Jeremie Aliadiere
Thierry Henry
Robin van Persie

KEY: ■ On all match ◀◀ Subbed or sent off (Counting game) ▶ Subbed on from bench (Counting Game) ◪ Subbed on and then subbed or sent off (Counting Game) ☐ Not in 16 ☐ Injured
■ On bench ◀◀ Subbed or sent off (playing less than 70 mins) ▶▶ Subbed on (playing less than 70 mins) ◪ Subbed on and then subbed or sent off (playing less than 70 min ✕ Suspended

KEY PLAYERS - GOALSCORERS

Robin van Persie

Goals in the League		11
Goals in all competitions		13
Assists — League goals scored by a team mate where the player delivered the final pass		5
Contribution to Attacking Power — Average number of minutes between League team goals while on pitch		40
Player Strike Rate — Average number of minutes between League goals scored by player		132
Club Strike Rate — Average minutes between League goals scored by club		54

	PLAYER	GOALS LGE	GOALS ALL	ASSISTS	POWER	S RATE
1	Robin van Persie	11	13	5	40	132 mins
2	Thierry Henry	10	12	4	47	147 mins
3	Emmanuel Adebayor	8	12	4	50	248 mins
4	Gilberto Silva	10	11	2	53	293 mins

KEY PLAYERS - MIDFIELDERS

Tomas Rosicky

Goals in the League		3
Goals in all competitions		6
Assists — League goals scored by a team mate where the player delivered the final pass		2
Defensive Rating — Average number of mins between League goals conceded while on pitch		107
Contribution to Attacking Power — Average number of minutes between League team goals while on pitch		52
Scoring Difference — Defensive Rating minus Contribution to Attacking Power		55

	PLAYER	GOALS LGE	GOALS ALL	ASSISTS	DEF RATE	POWER	SC DIF
1	Tomas Rosicky	3	6	2	107	52	55 min
2	Cesc Fabregas	2	4	14	102	52	50 min
3	Gilberto Silva	10	11	2	101	53	48 min
4	Fredrik Ljungberg	0	2	0	108	70	38 min

PLAYER APPEARANCES

	AGE (on 01/07/07)	IN NAMED 16	APPEARANCES	COUNTING GAMES	MINUTES ON PITCH	APPEARANCES	MINUTES ON PITCH THIS SEASON	HOME COUNTRY
Goalkeepers								
Manuel Almunia	30	36	1	1	90	14	1275	-	Spain
Jens Lehmann	37	36	36	36	3240	44	3960	8	Germany
Mart Poom	35	3	1	1	90	2	135	5	Estonia
Defenders								
Gael Clichy	21	28	27	26	2350	40	3312	-	France
Matthew Connolly	19	1	0	0	0	2	93	-	England
Pascal Cygan	33	2	0	0	0	0	0	-	France
Johan Djourou	20	27	21	15	1539	30	2334	5	Switzerland
Emmanuel Eboue	24	24	24	23	2059	35	2869	2	Ivory Coast
William Gallas	29	21	21	21	1880	29	2568	9	France
Justin Hoyte	22	28	22	15	1503	36	2618	-	England
Jerame Mayer Lauren	30	1	0	0	0	0	0	-	Cameroon
Philippe Senderos	22	27	14	7	809	25	1829	4	Switzerland
Habib Kolo Toure	26	35	35	35	3150	53	4763	3	Ivory Coast
Armand Traore	17	1	0	0	0	7	532	-	France
Midfielders								
Julio Baptista	25	27	24	8	1138	35	1771	3	Brazil
Denilson	19	14	10	3	388	19	1224	-	Brazil
Abou Diaby	21	12	12	6	742	18	1095	2	France
Cesc Fabregas	20	38	38	34	3182	54	4571	8	Spain
Mathieu Flamini	23	23	20	8	966	32	1730	-	France
Gilberto Silva	30	34	34	33	2933	47	4094	9	Brazil
Alexander Hleb	26	34	33	22	2355	48	3464	7	Belarus
Fredrik Ljungberg	30	18	18	13	1198	26	1745	5	Sweden
Mark Randall	17	1	0	0	0	2	34	-	England
Jose Antonio Reyes	23	0	0	0	0	0	0	1	Spain
Tomas Rosicky	26	26	26	18	1828	37	2698	8	Czech Republic
Alexandre Song	19	5	2	0	59	6	330	-	Cameroon
Theo Walcott	18	21	16	4	645	32	1395	-	England
Forwards								
Emmanuel Adebayor	23	31	29	20	1986	44	2998	1	Togo
Jeremie Aliadiere	24	12	11	3	427	23	1190	-	France
Thierry Henry	29	17	17	16	1474	27	2241	7	France
Robin van Persie	23	22	22	14	1457	31	2068	5	Holland

KEY: LEAGUE   ALL COMPS   CAPS   (MAY FIFA RANKING)

TEAM OF THE SEASON

LEHMANN — CG 36 | DR 92

HOYTE — CG 15 | DR 115

TOURE — CG 35 | DR 95

DJOUROU — CG 15 | DR 128

GALLAS — CG 21 | DR 104

ROSICKY — CG 18 | SD +55

GILBERTO — CG 33 | SD +48

FABREGAS — CG 34 | SD +50

LJUNGBERG — CG 13 | SD +50

VAN PERSIE — CG 14 | AP 40

HENRY — CG 16 | SR 147

KEY: DR = Defensive Rate, SD = Scoring Difference AP = Attacking Power SR = Strike Rate, CG=Counting games – League games playing at least 70 minutes

TOP POINT EARNERS

Johan Djourou

Counting Games	
League games when player was on pitch for at least 70 minutes	15

Average points	
Average League points taken in Counting games	2.13

Club Average points	
Average points taken in League games	1.79

	PLAYER	GAMES	PTS
1	Johan Djourou	15	2.13
2	Tomas Rosicky	18	2.11
3	Emmanuel Adebayor	20	1.95
4	Thierry Henry	16	1.94
5	Cesc Fabregas	34	1.88
6	William Gallas	21	1.86
7	Alexander Hleb	22	1.86
8	Gilberto Silva	34	1.85
9	Fredrik Ljungberg	13	1.85
10	Gael Clichy	26	1.81

KEY PLAYERS - DEFENDERS

Johan Djourou

Goals Conceded in the League	
Number of League goals conceded while the player was on the pitch	12

Goals Conceded in all competitions	
Total number of goals conceded while the player was on the pitch	19

League minutes played	
Number of minutes played in league matches	1539

Clean Sheets	
In games when the player was on pitch or at least 70 minutes	8

Defensive Rating	
Average number of mins between League goals conceded while on the pitch	128

Club Defensive Rating	
Average number of mins between League goals conceded by the club this season	97

	PLAYER	CON LGE	CON ALL	MINS	C SHEETS	DEF RATE
1	Johan Djourou	12	19	1539	8	128 mins
2	Justin Hoyte	13	26	1503	7	115 mins
3	William Gallas	18	23	1880	7	104 mins
4	Habib Kolo Toure	33	49	3150	11	95 mins

KEY GOALKEEPER

Jens Lehmann

Goals Conceded in the League	
Number of League goals conceded while the player was on the pitch	35

Goals Conceded in all competitions	
Total number of goals conceded while the player was on the pitch	40

League minutes played	
Number of minutes played in league matches	3240

Clean Sheets	
In games when the player was on pitch for at least 70 minutes	10

Goals to Shots Ratio	
The average number of shots on target per each League goal conceded	4.46

Defensive Rating	
Ave mins between League goals conceded while on the pitch	92

BOOKINGS

Philippe Senderos

League Yellow	3
League Red	2
All competitions Yellow	7
All competitions Red	2

League Average 161 mins between cards

	PLAYER	LEAGUE		TOTAL		AVE
1	Philippe Senderos	3Y	2R	7Y	2R	161
2	Robin van Persie	8	0	8	0	182
3	Mathieu Flamini	3	0	5	0	322
4	Jens Lehmann	8	0	8	0	405
5	Cesc Fabregas	7	0	9	0	454
6	William Gallas	4	0	4	0	470
7	Habib Kolo Toure	6	0	7	1	525
8	Fredrik Ljungberg	2	0	3	0	599
9	Tomas Rosicky	3	0	4	0	609
10	Vassiriki Diaby	2	0	2	0	742
11	Gilberto Silva	2	1	3	1	977
12	E. Adebayor	2	0	3	1	993
13	Emmanuel Eboue	2	0	4	0	1029
14	Gael Clichy	2	0	6	0	1175
15	Thierry Henry	1	0	4	0	1474
	Other	3	0	10	0	
	TOTAL	57	3	87	5	

TOTTENHAM HOTSPUR

Fuelled by three in-form strikers, Martin Jol made a late dash to reach fifth place for the second season. He wants to repeat a Uefa Cup run, only ended by eventual winners Seville. **Dimitar Berbatov** was a smart buy. He had twice struck 20 league goals for Bayer Leverkusen in previous seasons and top-scored for Jol with 12 league goals and 23 in total. **Robbie Keane** and **Jermain Defoe** both looked sharp and delivered sub-200 minute Strike Rates. Keane's goal every 150 minutes was the fifth best in the division.

Berbatov weighed in with 13 Assists and **Aaron Lennon** made 12 in a fluid midfield where seven players reached the 12 Counting Games mark - **Tom Huddlestone** had the top Scoring Difference.

The defence was overly generous with **Michael Dawson** starting 37 league games and **Paul Robinson** struggling in the keeping charts.

NICKNAME: SPURS   KEY: ☐ Won ☐ Drawn ■ Lost

#	comp	Opponent			Score	Scorers
1	prem	Bolton	A	L	0-2	
2	prem	Sheff Utd	H	W	2-0	Berbatov 8, Jenas 18
3	prem	Everton	H	L	0-2	
4	prem	Man Utd	A	L	0-1	
5	uc1rl1	Slavia Prague	A	W	1-0	Jenas 37
6	prem	Fulham	H	D	0-0	
7	prem	Liverpool	A	L	0-3	
8	uc1rl2	Slavia Prague	H	W	1-0	Keane 80
9	prem	Portsmouth	H	W	2-1	Murphy 1, Defoe 35 pen
10	prem	Aston Villa	A	D	1-1	Angel 76 og
11	ucgpb	Besiktas	A	W	2-0	Ghaly 31, Berbatov 63
12	prem	West Ham	H	W	1-0	Mido 45
13	ccr3	MK Dons	A	W	5-0	Mido 36, 59, Defoe 44, 51, Keane 90
14	prem	Watford	A	D	0-0	
15	ucgpb	Club Brugge	H	W	3-1	Berbatov 17, 73, Keane 63
16	prem	Chelsea	H	W	2-1	Dawson 25, Lennon 52
17	ccr4	Port Vale	H	W	3-1	Huddlestone 80, 99, Defoe 107
18	prem	Reading	A	L	1-3	Keane 23 pen
19	prem	Blackburn	A	D	1-1	Defoe 61 pen
20	ucgpb	B Leverkusen	A	W	1-0	Berbatov 36
21	prem	Wigan	H	W	3-1	Defoe 43, Berbatov 44, Lennon 90
22	prem	Arsenal	A	L	0-3	
23	prem	Middlesbrough	H	W	2-1	Berbatov 48, Keane 83
24	prem	Charlton	H	W	5-1	Berbatov 31, 66, Tainio 33, Malbranque 55, Defoe 63
25	ucgpb	D Bucharest	H	W	3-1	Berbatov 16, Defoe 39, 50
26	prem	Man City	A	W	2-1	Davenport 16, Huddlestone 24
27	ccqf	Southend	H	W	1-0	Defoe 115
28	prem	Newcastle	A	L	1-3	Murphy 15
29	prem	Aston Villa	H	W	2-1	Defoe 58, 77
30	prem	Liverpool	H	L	0-1	
31	prem	Portsmouth	A	D	1-1	Malbranque 50
32	facr3	Cardiff	A	D	0-0	
33	prem	Newcastle	H	L	2-3	Defoe 14, Berbatov 54
34	facr3r	Cardiff	H	W	4-0	Lennon 27, Keane 30, Malbranque 41, Defoe 81
35	prem	Fulham	A	D	1-1	Chimbonda 88
36	ccsfl1	Arsenal	H	D	2-2	Berbatov 12, Baptista 20 og
37	facr4	Southend	H	W	3-1	Keane 12, Jenas 50, Mido 76
38	ccsfl2	Arsenal	A	L	1-3	Mido 85
39	prem	Man Utd	H	L	0-4	
40	prem	Sheff Utd	A	L	1-2	Jenas 2
41	facr5	Fulham	A	W	4-0	Keane 6, 68, Berbatov 77, 90
42	prem	Everton	A	W	2-1	Berbatov 35, Jenas 88
43	prem	Bolton	H	W	4-1	Keane 11, 22, Jenas 19, Lennon 90
44	prem	West Ham	A	W	4-3	Defoe 50 pen, Tainio 63, Berbatov 89, Stalteri 90
45	uc3rl1	Braga	A	W	3-2	Keane 57, 90, Malbranque 72
46	facqf	Chelsea	A	D	3-3	Berbatov 5, Essien 28 og, Ghaly 36
47	uc4rl2	Braga	H	W	3-2	Berbatov 28, 42, Malbranque 76
48	prem	Watford	H	W	3-1	Jenas 41, Robinson 63, Ghaly 85
49	facqfr	Chelsea	H	L	1-2	Keane 79 pen
50	prem	Reading	H	W	1-0	Keane 36
51	ucqfl1	Seville	A	L	1-2	Keane 2
52	prem	Chelsea	A	L	0-1	
53	ucqfl2	Seville	H	D	2-2	Berbatov 65, Lennon 67
54	prem	Wigan	H	D	3-3	Berbatov 4, Keane 35 pen, 68
55	prem	Arsenal	H	D	2-2	Keane 30, Jenas 90
56	prem	Middlesbrough	A	W	3-2	Keane 12, 83, Defoe 47
57	prem	Charlton	H	W	2-0	Berbatov 7, Defoe 90
58	prem	Blackburn	H	D	1-1	Defoe 67
59	prem	Man City	H	W	2-1	Keane 10, Berbatov 32

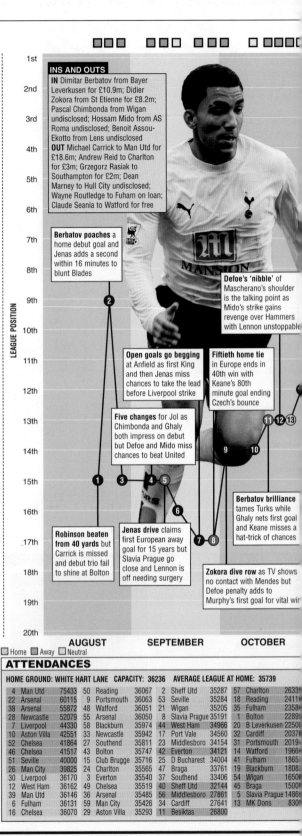

LEAGUE POSITION: 1st, 2nd, 3rd, 4th, 5th, 6th, 7th, 8th, 9th, 10th, 11th, 12th, 13th, 14th, 15th, 16th, 17th, 18th, 19th, 20th

☐☐☐   ☐☐☐   ☐☐☐   ☐ ☐☐☐☐

INS AND OUTS

IN Dimitar Berbatov from Bayer Leverkusen for £10.9m; Didier Zokora from St Etienne for £8.2m; Pascal Chimbonda from Wigan undisclosed; Hossam Mido from AS Roma undisclosed; Benoit Assou-Ekotto from Lens undisclosed

OUT Michael Carrick to Man Utd for £18.6m; Andrew Reid to Charlton for £3m; Grzegorz Rasiak to Southampton for £2m; Dean Marney to Hull City undisclosed; Wayne Routledge to Fuham on loan; Claude Seania to Watford for free

Berbatov poaches a home debut goal and Jenas adds a second within 16 minutes to blunt Blades

Defoe's 'nibble' of Mascherano's shoulder is the talking point as Mido's strike gains revenge over Hammers with Lennon unstoppable

Open goals go begging at Anfield as first King and then Jenas miss chances to take the lead before Liverpool strike

Fiftieth home tie in Europe ends in 40th win with Keane's 80th minute goal ending Czech's bounce

Five changes for Jol as Chimbonda and Ghaly both impress on debut but Defoe and Mido miss chances to beat United

Robinson beaten from 40 yards but Carrick is missed and debut trio fail to shine at Bolton

Jenas drive claims first European away goal for 15 years but Slavia Prague go close and Lennon is off needing surgery

Berbatov brilliance tames Turks while Ghaly nets first goal and Keane misses a hat-trick of chances

Zokora dive row as TV shows no contact with Mendes but Defoe penalty adds to Murphy's first goal for vital win

AUGUST	SEPTEMBER	OCTOBER

☐ Home ☐ Away ☐ Neutral

ATTENDANCES

HOME GROUND: WHITE HART LANE   CAPACITY: 36236   AVERAGE LEAGUE AT HOME: 35739

#	Opponent	Att		#	Opponent	Att		#	Opponent	Att
4	Man Utd	75433		50	Reading	36067		2	Sheff Utd	35287
22	Arsenal	60115		9	Portsmouth	36063		53	Seville	35284
38	Arsenal	55872		48	Watford	36051		21	Wigan	35205
28	Newcastle	52079		55	Arsenal	36050		8	Slavia Prague	35191
7	Liverpool	44330		58	Blackburn	35974		44	West Ham	34966
10	Aston Villa	42551		33	Newcastle	35942		17	Port Vale	34560
52	Chelsea	41864		27	Southend	35811		23	Middlesboro	34154
46	Chelsea	41517		43	Bolton	35747		42	Everton	34121
51	Seville	40000		15	Club Brugge	35716		25	D Bucharest	34004
26	Man City	39825		24	Charlton	35565		47	Braga	33761
30	Liverpool	36170		3	Everton	35540		37	Southend	33406
12	West Ham	36162		49	Chelsea	35519		40	Sheff Utd	32144
39	Man Utd	36146		36	Arsenal	35485		56	Middlesboro	27861
6	Fulham	36131		59	Man City	35426		34	Cardiff	27641
16	Chelsea	36070		29	Aston Villa	35293		11	Besiktas	26800
								57	Charlton	2633
								18	Reading	2411
								35	Fulham	2358
								1	Bolton	2289
								20	B Leverkusen	22500
								31	Portsmouth	2019
								14	Watford	1966
								19	Blackburn	1865
								54	Wigan	1650
								45	Braga	1650
								5	Slavia Prague	1486
								13	MK Dons	1486

Jol repeats 'best of the rest' finish

Final Position: 5th

KEY: ● League ○ Champions Lge ○ UEFA Cup ● FA Cup ○ League Cup ● Other

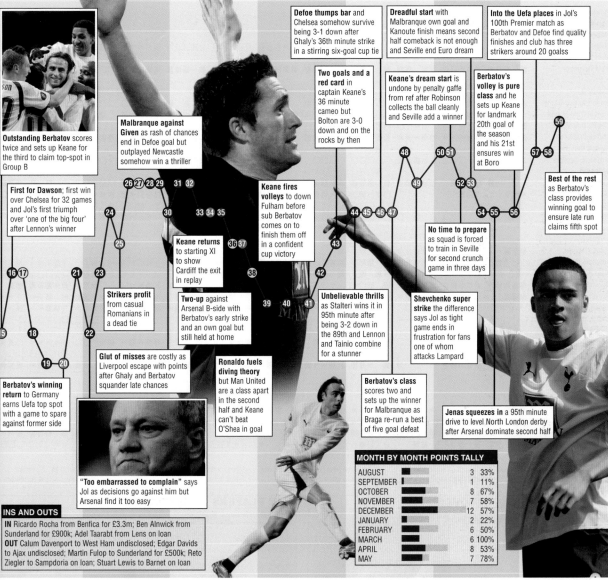

Defoe thumps bar and Chelsea somehow survive being 3-1 down after Ghaly's 36th minute strike in a stirring six-goal cup tie

Dreadful start with Malbranque own goal and Kanoute finish means second half comeback is not enough and Seville end Euro dream

Into the Uefa places in Jol's 100th Premier match as Berbatov and Defoe find quality finishes and club has three strikers around 20 goalss

Two goals and a red card in captain Keane's 36 minute cameo but Bolton are 3-0 down and on the rocks by then

Keane's dream start is undone by penalty gaffe from ref after Robinson collects the ball cleanly and Seville add a winner

Berbatov's volley is pure class and he sets up Keane for landmark 20th goal of the season and his 21st ensures win at Boro

Outstanding Berbatov scores twice and sets up Keane for the third to claim top-spot in Group B

Malbranque against Given as rash of chances end in Defoe goal but outplayed Newcastle somehow win a thriller

Keane fires volleys to down Fulham before sub Berbatov comes on to finish them off in a confident cup victory

Best of the rest as Berbatov's class provides winning goal to ensure late run claims fifth spot

First for Dawson; first win over Chelsea for 32 games and Jol's first triumph over 'one of the big four' after Lennon's winner

Keane returns to starting XI to show Cardiff the exit in replay

No time to prepare as squad is forced to train in Seville for second crunch game in three days

Strikers profit from casual Romanians in a dead tie

Two-up against Arsenal B-side with Berbatov's early strike and an own goal but still held at home

Unbelievable thrills as Stalteri wins it in 95th minute after being 3-2 down in the 89th and Lennon and Tainio combine for a stunner

Shevchenko super strike the difference says Jol as tight game ends in frustration for fans one of whom attacks Lampard

Berbatov's winning return to Germany earns Uefa top spot with a game to spare against former side

Glut of misses are costly as Liverpool escape with points after Ghaly and Berbatov squander late chances

Ronaldo fuels diving theory but Man United are a class apart in the second half and Keane can't beat O'Shea in goal

Berbatov's class scores two and sets up the winner for Malbranque as Braga re-run a best of five goal defeat

Jenas squeezes in a 95th minute drive to level North London derby after Arsenal dominate second half

"Too embarrassed to complain" says Jol as decisions go against him but Arsenal find it too easy

INS AND OUTS
IN Ricardo Rocha from Benfica for £3.3m; Ben Alnwick from Sunderland for £900k; Adel Taarabt from Lens on loan
OUT Calum Davenport to West Ham undisclosed; Edgar Davids to Ajax undisclosed; Martin Fulop to Sunderland for £500k; Reto Ziegler to Sampdoria on loan; Stuart Lewis to Barnet on loan

MONTH BY MONTH POINTS TALLY
Month	Points	%
AUGUST	3	33%
SEPTEMBER	1	11%
OCTOBER	8	67%
NOVEMBER	7	58%
DECEMBER	12	57%
JANUARY	2	22%
FEBRUARY	6	50%
MARCH	6	100%
APRIL	8	53%
MAY	7	78%

NOVEMBER   DECEMBER   JANUARY   FEBRUARY   MARCH   APRIL   MAY

GOAL ATTEMPTS

FOR				
Goal attempts recorded in League games				
	HOME	AWAY	TOTAL	AVE
shots on target	147	96	243	6.4
shots off target	121	92	213	5.6
TOTAL	**268**	**188**	**456**	**12.0**

Ratio of goals to shots
Average number of shots on target per League goal scored — **4.3**

Accuracy rating
Average percentage of total goal attempts which were on target — **53.3**

AGAINST				
Goal attempts recorded in League games				
	HOME	AWAY	TOTAL	AVE
shots on target	89	108	197	5.2
shots off target	96	112	208	5.5
TOTAL	**185**	**220**	**405**	**10.7**

Ratio of goals to shots
Average number of shots on target per League goal scored — **3.6**

Accuracy rating
Average percentage of total goal attempts which were on target — **48.6**

GOALS

Berbatov

League	12	
FA Cup	3	
League Cup	1	
Europe	7	
Other	0	
TOTAL	**23**	

League Average
226
mins between goals

	PLAYER	LGE	FAC	LC	Euro	TOT	AVE
1	Berbatov	12	3	1	7	23	226
2	Keane	11	5	1	5	22	150
3	Defoe	10	1	4	3	18	193
4	Jenas	6	1	0	1	8	360
5	Mido	1	1	3	0	5	653
6	Lennon	3	1	0	1	5	658
7	Malbranque	2	1	0	2	5	794
8	Ghaly	1	1	0	1	3	1394
9	Huddlestone	1	0	2	0	3	1510
10	Murphy	2	0	0	0	2	293
11	Tainio	2	0	0	0	2	745
12	Stalteri	1	0	0	0	1	185
13	Davenport	1	0	0	0	1	710
14	Chimbonda	1	0	0	0	1	2912
15	Dawson	1	0	0	0	1	3282
	Other	1	0	0	0	1	
	TOTAL	**56**	**14**	**11**	**20**	**101**	

PREMIERSHIP CLUBS – TOTTENHAM HOTSPUR

SQUAD APPEARANCES

Match	1 2 3 4 5	6 7 8 9 10	11 12 13 14 15	16 17 18 19 20	21 22 23 24 25	26 27 28 29 30	31 32 33 34 35	36 37 38 39 40	41 42 43 44 45	46 47 48 49 50	51 52 53 54 55	56 57 58
Venue	A H H A A	H A H H A	A H A A H	H H A A A	H A H H H	A H A H H	A A H H A	H H A H A	A A H A A	A H H H H	A A H A H	A A H
Competition	L L L L E	L L E L L	E L W L E	L W L L E	L L L L E	L W L L L	L F L F L	W F W L L	F L L L E	F E L F L	E L E L L	L L L
Result	L W L L W	D L W W D	W W W D W	W W L D W	W L W W W	W W L W L	D D L W D	D W L L L	W W W W W	D W W L W	L L D D D	W W D

Goalkeepers

| Ben Alnwick |
| Robert Burch |
| Radek Cerny |
| Marton Fulop |
| Paul Robinson |

Defenders

| Benoit Assou-Ekotto |
| Pascal Chimbonda |
| Calum Davenport |
| Michael Dawson |
| Dorian Dervite |
| Anthony Gardner |
| Philip Ifil |
| Ledley King |
| Young-Pyo Lee |
| Ricardo Rocha |
| Paul Stalteri |

Midfielders

| Edgar Davids |
| Hossam Ghaly |
| Tom Huddlestone |
| Jermaine Jenas |
| Aaron Lennon |
| Steed Malbranque |
| Danny Murphy |
| Jamie O'Hara |
| Teemu Tainio |
| Reto Ziegler |
| Didier Zokora |

Forwards

| Andy Barcham |
| Dimitar Berbatov |
| Jermain Defoe |
| Robbie Keane |
| Hossam Mido |
| Adel Taarabt |

KEY: ■ On all match ◄◄ Subbed or sent off (Counting game) ▶▶ Subbed on from bench (Counting Game) ▶▶ Subbed on and then subbed or sent off (Counting Game) ☐ Not in 16 ☐ Injured
■ On bench ◄◄ Subbed or sent off (playing less than 70 mins) ▶▶ Subbed on (playing less than 70 mins) ▶▶ Subbed on and then subbed or sent off (playing less than 70 min ✕ Suspended

KEY PLAYERS - GOALSCORERS

Robbie Keane

Goals in the League	11
Goals in all competitions	22
Assists — League goals scored by a team mate where the player delivered the final pass	6
Contribution to Attacking Power — Average number of minutes between League team goals while on pitch	61
Player Strike Rate — Average number of minutes between League goals scored by player	150
Club Strike Rate — Average minutes between League goals scored by club	60

	PLAYER	GOALS LGE	GOALS ALL	ASSISTS	POWER	S RATE
1	Robbie Keane	11	22	6	61	150 mins
2	Jermain Defoe	10	18	3	62	193 mins
3	Dimitar Berbatov	12	23	13	52	226 mins
4	Jermaine Jenas	6	8	3	65	360 mins

KEY PLAYERS - MIDFIELDERS

Tom Huddlestone

Goals in the League	1
Goals in all competitions	3
Assists — League goals scored by a team mate where the player delivered the final pass	5
Defensive Rating — Average number of mins between League goals conceded while on the pitch	65
Contribution to Attacking Power — Average number of minutes between League team goals while on pitch	52
Scoring Difference — Defensive Rating minus Contribution to Attacking Power	13

	PLAYER	GOALS LGE	GOALS ALL	ASSISTS	DEF RATE	POWER	SC DIFF
1	Tom Huddlestone	1	3	5	65	52	13 mins
2	Teemu Tainio	2	2	0	62	49	13 mins
3	Steed Malbranque	2	5	4	58	51	7 mins
4	Aaron Lennon	3	5	12	54	49	5 mins

PREMIERSHIP CLUBS – TOTTENHAM HOTSPUR

PLAYER APPEARANCES

	AGE (on 01/07/07)	IN NAMED 16	APPEARANCES	COUNTING GAMES	MINUTES ON PITCH	APPEARANCES THIS SEASON	MINUTES ON PITCH THIS SEASON		HOME COUNTRY
Goalkeepers									
Radek Cerny	33	38	0	0	0	5	480	-	Czech Republic
Paul Robinson	27	38	38	38	3420	54	4920	10	England
Defenders									
Benoit Assou-Ekotto	23	20	16	15	1395	25	2265	-	France
Pascal Chimbonda	28	33	33	32	2912	49	4367	-	France
Calum Davenport	24	11	10	8	710	15	1078	-	England
Michael Dawson	23	37	37	36	3282	58	5217	-	England
Dorian Dervite	18	0	0	0	0	1	120	-	France
Anthony Gardner	26	16	8	6	597	16	1132	-	England
Philip Ifil	20	5	1	1	90	2	210	-	England
Ledley King	26	21	21	21	1880	27	2397	3	England
Young-Pyo Lee	30	25	21	18	1764	31	2691	2	South Korea
Ricardo Rocha	28	11	9	8	765	13	1076	3	Portugal
Paul Stalteri	29	12	6	1	185	14	777	3	Canada
Midfielders									
Edgar Davids	34	12	9	4	516	13	811	-	Holland
Hossam Ghaly	25	24	21	12	1394	34	2099	3	Egypt
Tom Huddlestone	20	30	21	15	1510	35	2494	-	England
Jermaine Jenas	24	25	25	23	2160	34	3000	2	England
Aaron Lennon	20	26	26	21	1974	43	3201	5	England
Steed Malbranque	27	25	25	16	1589	41	2649	-	France
Danny Murphy	30	17	12	5	586	19	1046	-	England
Jamie O'Hara	21	3	0	0	0	0	0	-	England
Teemu Tainio	27	21	21	13	1491	32	2286	-	Finland
Reto Ziegler	21	6	1	0	34	4	196	-	Switzerland
Didier Zokora	26	32	31	21	2302	47	3730	4	Ivory Coast
Forwards									
Andy Barcham	20	0	0	0	0	1	65	-	England
Dimitar Berbatov	26	34	33	30	2716	49	3858	6	Bulgaria
Jermain Defoe	24	37	34	18	1933	49	2902	8	England
Robbie Keane	26	30	27	16	1655	44	2924	5	Rep of Ireland
Hossam Mido	24	15	12	6	653	23	1301	-	Egypt
Adel Taarabt	18	3	2	0	30	2	30	-	France

KEY: LEAGUE   ALL COMPS   CAPS   (MAY FIFA RANKING)

TEAM OF THE SEASON

ROBINSON — CG 38   DR 63

CHIMBONDA — CG 32   DR 63
DAWSON — CG 36   DR 63
KING — CG 21   DR 69
ASSOU-EKOTTO — CG 15   DR 69

LENNON — CG 21   SD +5
HUDDLESTONE — CG 15   SD +13
TAINIO — CG 13   SD +13
MALBRANQUE — CG 16   SD +7

BERBATOV — CG 30   AP 52
KEANE — CG 16   SR 150

KEY: DR = Defensive Rate, SD = Scoring Difference AP = Attacking Power SR = Strike Rate, CG = Counting games – League games playing at least 70 minutes

TOP POINT EARNERS

Didier Zokora

Counting Games — League games when player was on pitch for at least 70 minutes	21
Average points — Average League points taken in Counting games	1.86
Club Average points — Average points taken in League games	1.58

	PLAYER	GAMES	PTS
1	Didier Zokora	21	1.86
2	Teemu Tainio	13	1.85
3	Young-Pyo Lee	18	1.83
4	Ledley King	21	1.81
5	Aaron Lennon	21	1.76
6	Dimitar Berbatov	30	1.73
7	Jermain Defoe	18	1.72
8	Tom Huddlestone	15	1.67
9	Pascal Chimbonda	32	1.66
10	Jermaine Jenas	23	1.65

KEY PLAYERS - DEFENDERS

Benoit Assou-Ekotto

Goals Conceded in the League — Number of League goals conceded while the player was on the pitch	20
Goals Conceded in all competitions — Total number of goals conceded while the player was on the pitch	27
League minutes played — Number of minutes played in league matches	1395
Clean Sheets — In games when the player was on pitch for at least 70 minutes	4
Defensive Rating — Average number of mins between League goals conceded while on the pitch	69
Club Defensive Rating — Average number of mins between League goals conceded by the club this season	63

	PLAYER	CON LGE	CON ALL	MINS	C SHEETS	DEF RATE
1	Benoit Assou-Ekotto	20	27	1395	4	69 mins
2	Ledley King	27	30	1880	4	69 mins
3	Michael Dawson	52	74	3282	6	63 mins
4	Pascal Chimbonda	46	62	2912	5	63 mins

KEY GOALKEEPER

Paul Robinson

Goals Conceded in the League — Number of League goals conceded while the player was on the pitch	54
Goals Conceded in all competitions — Total number of goals conceded while the player was on the pitch	69
League minutes played — Number of minutes played in league matches	3420
Clean Sheets — In games when the player was on pitch for at least 70 minutes	6
Goals to Shots Ratio — The average number of shots on target per each League goal conceded	3.65
Defensive Rating — Ave mins between League goals conceded while on the pitch	63

BOOKINGS

Hossam Mido

League Yellow	4
League Red	0
All competitions Yellow	4
All competitions Red	0

League Average 163 mins between cards

	PLAYER	LEAGUE		TOTAL		AVE
1	Hossam Mido	4Y	0R	4Y	0R	163
2	Hossam Ghaly	4	1	8	1	278
3	Steed Malbranque	5	0	7	0	317
4	Calum Davenport	1	1	1	1	355
5	Ricardo Rocha	2	0	2	0	382
6	Edgar Davids	1	0	1	0	516
7	Jermaine Jenas	4	0	5	0	540
8	Michael Dawson	6	0	8	0	547
9	Robbie Keane	2	1	4	1	551
10	P. Chimbonda	5	0	8	0	582
11	Anthony Gardner	1	0	3	0	597
12	Didier Zokora	2	1	5	1	767
13	Jermain Defoe	2	0	5	0	966
14	B. Assou-Ekotto	1	0	2	0	1395
15	Teemu Tainio	1	0	3	1	1491
	Other	4	0	10	0	
	TOTAL	45	4	76	5	

EVERTON

Andrew Johnson added a cutting edge to the attack with 11 goals but a Strike Rate of one every 246 minutes shows room to improve. The new signing at the other end, **Tim Howard** was also key to reaching a Uefa Cup spot as he played all but the two Manchester United games. He had a top four Defensive Rating, only conceding a goal every 111 minutes on average. However, it's in the Goals to Shots Ratio that his worth really shows; second only to Petr Cech with over eight shots saved per goal conceded.

Between these two individual performances was a hard-working midfield with **Mikel Arteta** scoring nine plus nine Assists, while **Lee Carsley**, **Tim Cahill** and **Leon Osman** all boasted top 25 positions in the divisional midfield table on Scoring Difference.

Only 415 shots is a low total but better than one in four went in.

NICKNAME: THE TOFFEES

KEY: ■ Won □ Drawn ■ Lost

1	prem	**Watford**	H W	**2-1**	Johnson 15, Arteta 82 pen
2	prem	**Blackburn**	A D	**1-1**	Cahill 84
3	prem	**Tottenham**	A W	**2-0**	Davenport 53 og, Johnson 66
4	prem	**Liverpool**	H W	**3-0**	Cahill 24, Johnson 36, 90
5	prem	**Wigan**	H D	**2-2**	Johnson 49, Beattie 66 pen
6	ccr2	**Peterborough**	A W	**2-1**	Stirling 24 og, Cahill 87
7	prem	**Newcastle**	A D	**1-1**	Cahill 40
8	prem	**Man City**	H D	**1-1**	Johnson 44
9	prem	**Middlesbrough**	A L	**1-2**	Cahill 77
10	prem	**Sheff Utd**	H W	**2-0**	Arteta 13, Beattie 33 pen
11	ccr3	**Luton**	H W	**4-0**	Cahill 23, Keane 34 og, McFadden 53, Anichebe 83
12	prem	**Arsenal**	A D	**1-1**	Cahill 11
13	prem	**Fulham**	A L	**0-1**	
14	ccr4	**Arsenal**	H L	**0-1**	
15	prem	**Aston Villa**	H L	**0-1**	
16	prem	**Bolton**	H W	**1-0**	Arteta 60
17	prem	**Charlton**	A D	**1-1**	Hreidarsson 52 og
18	prem	**Man Utd**	A L	**0-3**	
19	prem	**West Ham**	H W	**2-0**	Osman 51, Vaughan 90
20	prem	**Portsmouth**	A L	**0-2**	
21	prem	**Chelsea**	H L	**2-3**	Arteta 38 pen, Yobo 64
22	prem	**Reading**	A W	**2-0**	Johnson 14, McFadden 47
23	prem	**Middlesbrough**	H D	**0-0**	
24	prem	**Newcastle**	H W	**3-0**	Anichebe 9, 58, P.Neville 62
25	prem	**Man City**	A L	**1-2**	Osman 84
26	facr3	**Blackburn**	H L	**1-4**	Johnson 68 pen
27	prem	**Reading**	H D	**1-1**	Johnson 81
28	prem	**Wigan**	A W	**2-0**	Arteta 65 pen, 90
29	prem	**Liverpool**	A D	**0-0**	
30	prem	**Blackburn**	H W	**1-0**	Johnson 10
31	prem	**Tottenham**	H L	**1-2**	Arteta 42
32	prem	**Watford**	A W	**3-0**	Fernandes 23, Johnson 25 pen, Osman 90
33	prem	**Sheff Utd**	A D	**1-1**	Arteta 75 pen
34	prem	**Arsenal**	H W	**1-0**	Johnson 90
35	prem	**Aston Villa**	A D	**1-1**	Lescott 14
36	prem	**Fulham**	H W	**4-1**	Carsley 25, Stubbs 34, Vaughan 45, Anichebe 80
37	prem	**Bolton**	A D	**1-1**	Vaughan 33
38	prem	**Charlton**	H W	**2-1**	Lescott 81, McFadden 90
39	prem	**West Ham**	A L	**0-1**	
40	prem	**Man Utd**	H L	**2-4**	Stubbs 12, Fernandes 50
41	prem	**Portsmouth**	H W	**3-0**	Arteta 59 pen, Yobo 62, Naysmith 90
42	prem	**Chelsea**	A D	**1-1**	Vaughan 50

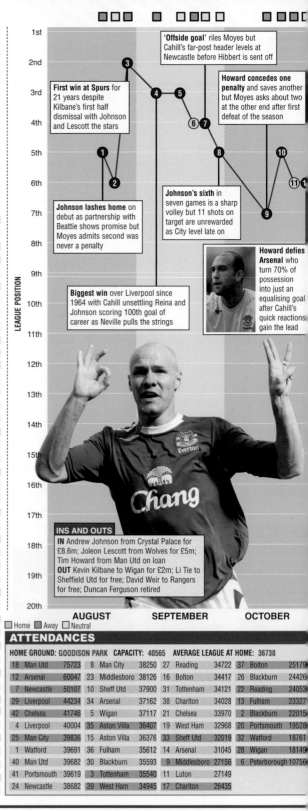

1st / 2nd / 3rd / 4th / 5th / 6th / 7th / 8th / 9th / 10th / 11th / 12th / 13th / 14th / 15th / 16th / 17th / 18th / 19th / 20th — LEAGUE POSITION

First win at Spurs for 21 years despite Kilbane's first half dismissal with Johnson and Lescott the stars

'Offside goal' riles Moyes but Cahill's far-post header levels at Newcastle before Hibbert is sent off

Howard concedes one penalty and saves another but Moyes asks about two at the other end after first defeat of the season

Johnson lashes home on debut as partnership with Beattie shows promise but Moyes admits second was never a penalty

Johnson's sixth in seven games is a sharp volley but 11 shots on target are unrewarded as City level late on

Biggest win over Liverpool since 1964 with Cahill unsettling Reina and Johnson scoring 100th goal of career as Neville pulls the strings

Howard defies Arsenal who turn 70% of possession into just an equalising goal after Cahill's quick reactions gain the lead

INS AND OUTS
IN Andrew Johnson from Crystal Palace for £8.6m; Joleon Lescott from Wolves for £5m; Tim Howard from Man Utd on loan
OUT Kevin Kilbane to Wigan for £2m; Li Tie to Sheffield Utd for free; David Weir to Rangers for free; Duncan Ferguson retired

AUGUST   SEPTEMBER   OCTOBER

□ Home ■ Away □ Neutral

ATTENDANCES

HOME GROUND: GOODISON PARK CAPACITY: **40565**   AVERAGE LEAGUE AT HOME: **36738**

18	Man Utd	75723	8	Man City	38250	27	Reading	34722	37	Bolton	25179
12	Arsenal	60047	23	Middlesboro	38126	16	Bolton	34417	26	Blackburn	24426
7	Newcastle	50107	10	Sheff Utd	37900	31	Tottenham	34121	22	Reading	24053
29	Liverpool	44234	34	Arsenal	37162	38	Charlton	34028	13	Fulham	23327
42	Chelsea	41746	5	Wigan	37117	21	Chelsea	33970	2	Blackburn	22015
4	Liverpool	40004	35	Aston Villa	36407	19	West Ham	32968	20	Portsmouth	19528
25	Man City	39836	15	Aston Villa	36376	33	Sheff Utd	32019	32	Watford	18761
1	Watford	39691	36	Fulham	35612	14	Arsenal	31045	28	Wigan	18149
40	Man Utd	39682	30	Blackburn	35593	9	Middlesboro	27156	6	Peterborough	10756
41	Portsmouth	39619	3	Tottenham	35540	11	Luton	27149			
24	Newcastle	38682	39	West Ham	34945	17	Charlton	26435			

New signings lead Moyes to Europe

Final Position: 6th

KEY: ● League ● Champions Lge ● UEFA Cup ■ FA Cup ○ League Cup ● Other

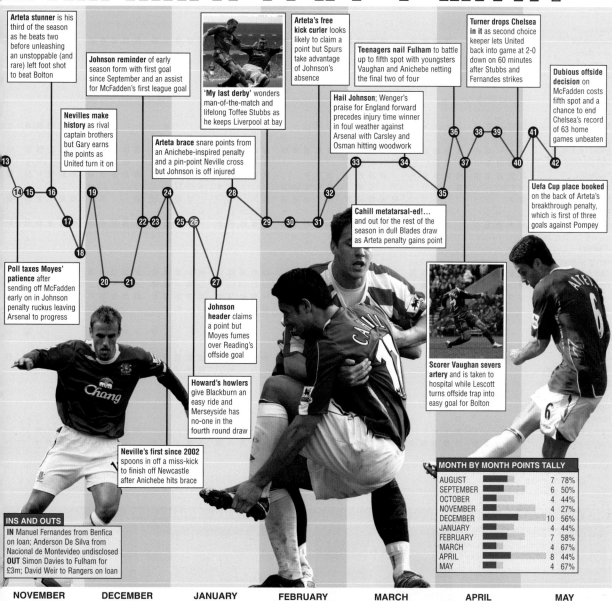

Arteta stunner is his third of the season as he beats two before unleashing an unstoppable (and rare) left foot shot to beat Bolton

Johnson reminder of early season form with first goal since September and an assist for McFadden's first league goal

Nevilles make history as rival captain brothers but Gary earns the points as United turn it on

Arteta brace snare points from an Anichebe-inspired penalty and a pin-point Neville cross but Johnson is off injured

'My last derby' wonders man-of-the-match and lifelong Toffee Stubbs as he keeps Liverpool at bay

Arteta's free kick curler looks likely to claim a point but Spurs take advantage of Johnson's absence

Teenagers nail Fulham to battle up to fifth spot with youngsters Vaughan and Anichebe netting the final two of four

Hail Johnson; Wenger's praise for England forward precedes injury time winner in foul weather against Arsenal with Carsley and Osman hitting woodwork

Turner drops Chelsea in it as second choice keeper lets United back into game at 2-0 down on 60 minutes after Stubbs and Fernandes strikes

Dubious offside decision on McFadden costs fifth spot and a chance to end Chelsea's record of 63 home games unbeaten

Uefa Cup place booked on the back of Arteta's breakthrough penalty, which is first of three goals against Pompey

Cahill metatarsal-ed!... and out for the rest of the season in dull Blades draw as Arteta penalty gains point

Poll taxes Moyes' patience after sending off McFadden early on in Johnson penalty ruckus leaving Arsenal to progress

Johnson header claims a point but Moyes fumes over Reading's offside goal

Scorer Vaughan severs artery and is taken to hospital while Lescott turns offside trap into easy goal for Bolton

Howard's howlers give Blackburn an easy ride and Merseyside has no-one in the fourth round draw

Neville's first since 2002 spoons in off a miss-kick to finish off Newcastle after Anichebe hits brace

INS AND OUTS
IN Manuel Fernandes from Benfica on loan; Anderson De Silva from Nacional de Montevideo undisclosed
OUT Simon Davies to Fulham for £3m; David Weir to Rangers on loan

MONTH BY MONTH POINTS TALLY		
AUGUST	7	78%
SEPTEMBER	6	50%
OCTOBER	4	44%
NOVEMBER	4	27%
DECEMBER	10	56%
JANUARY	4	44%
FEBRUARY	7	58%
MARCH	4	67%
APRIL	8	44%
MAY	4	67%

NOVEMBER   DECEMBER   JANUARY   FEBRUARY   MARCH   APRIL   MAY

GOAL ATTEMPTS

FOR
Goal attempts recorded in League games

	HOME	AWAY	TOTAL	AVE
shots on target	110	94	204	5.4
shots off target	114	97	211	5.6
TOTAL	224	191	415	10.9

Ratio of goals to shots	
Average number of shots on target per League goal scored	3.9

Accuracy rating	
Average percentage of total goal attempts which were on target	49.2

AGAINST
Goal attempts recorded in League games

	HOME	AWAY	TOTAL	AVE
shots on target	116	136	252	6.6
shots off target	121	143	264	6.9
TOTAL	237	279	516	13.6

Ratio of goals to shots	
Average number of shots on target per League goal scored	7.0

Accuracy rating	
Average percentage of total goal attempts which were on target	48.8

GOALS

Johnson

League	11
FA Cup	1
League Cup	0
Europe	0
Other	0
TOTAL	12

League Average	
246	mins between goals

	PLAYER	LGE	FAC	LC	Euro	TOT	AVE
1	Johnson	11	1	0	0	12	246
2	Arteta	9	0	0	0	9	348
3	Cahill	5	0	2	0	7	281
4	Vaughan	4	0	0	0	4	163
5	Anichebe	3	0	1	0	4	208
6	McFadden	2	0	1	0	3	397
7	Osman	3	0	0	0	3	936
8	Fernandes	2	0	0	0	2	358
9	Beattie	2	0	0	0	2	732
10	Stubbs	2	0	0	0	2	998
11	Lescott	2	0	0	0	2	1659
12	Yobo	2	0	0	0	2	1710
13	Naysmith	1	0	0	0	1	990
14	Neville	1	0	0	0	1	3111
15	Carsley	1	0	0	0	1	3375
	Other	0	0	0	0	0	
	TOTAL	50	1	4	0	55	

PREMIERSHIP CLUBS – EVERTON

SQUAD APPEARANCES

Match	1	2	3	4	5	6	7	8	9	10	11	12	13	14	15	16	17	18	19	20	21	22	23	24	25	26	27	28	29	30	31	32	33	34	35	36	37	38	39	40	41
Venue	H	A	A	H	H	A	A	H	A	H	H	A	A	H	H	H	A	A	H	A	H	A	H	H	A	H	H	A	A	H	H	A	A	H	A	H	A	H	A	H	H
Competition	L	L	L	L	L	W	L	L	L	L	W	L	L	L	W	L	L	L	L	L	L	L	L	L	L	F	L	L	L	L	L	L	L	L	L	L	L	L	L	L	L
Result	W	D	W	W	D	W	D	D	L	W	W	D	L	L	L	W	D	L	W	L	L	W	D	W	L	L	D	W	D	W	L	W	D	W	D	W	D	W	L	L	W

Goalkeepers
- Tim Howard
- John Ruddy
- Iain Turner
- Richard Wright

Defenders
- Patrick Boyle
- Tony Hibbert
- Mark Hughes
- Joleon Lescott
- Gary Naysmith
- Phil Neville
- Jorge Nuno Valente
- Alan Stubbs
- David Weir
- Joseph Yobo

Midfielders
- de Frenca Anderson
- Mikel Arteta
- Tim Cahill
- Lee Carsley
- Simon Davies
- Anderson De Silva
- Manuel Fernandes
- Kevin Kilbane
- Leon Osman
- Andy van der Meyde
- Bjarni Thor Vidarsson

Forwards
- Victor Anichebe
- James Beattie
- Andrew Johnson
- James McFadden
- James Vaughan

KEY: ■ On all match · ◄◄ Subbed or sent off (Counting game) · ►► Subbed on from bench (Counting Game) · Subbed on and then subbed or sent off (Counting Game) · □ Not in 16 · □ Injured
On bench · ◄◄ Subbed or sent off (playing less than 70 mins) · ►► Subbed on (playing less than 70 mins) · ►► Subbed on and then subbed or sent off (playing less than 70 min · ✕ Suspended

---

KEY PLAYERS - GOALSCORERS

Andrew Johnson

Goals in the League	11
Goals in all competitions	12
Assists — League goals scored by a team mate where the player delivered the final pass	6
Contribution to Attacking Power — Average number of minutes between League team goals while on pitch	66
Player Strike Rate — Average number of minutes between League goals scored by player	246
Club Strike Rate — Average minutes between League goals scored by club	65

	PLAYER	GOALS LGE	GOALS ALL	ASSISTS	POWER	S RATE
1	Andrew Johnson	11	12	6	66	246 mins
2	Tim Cahill	5	7	2	63	281 mins
3	Mikel Arteta	9	9	9	66	348 mins
4	James Beattie	2	2	3	86	732 mins

KEY PLAYERS - MIDFIELDERS

Tim Cahill

Goals in the League	5
Goals in all competitions	7
Assists — League goals scored by a team mate where the player delivered the final pass	2
Defensive Rating — Average number of mins between League goals conceded while on the pitch	140
Contribution to Attacking Power — Average number of minutes between League team goals while on pitch	63
Scoring Difference — Defensive Rating minus Contribution to Attacking Power	77

	PLAYER	GOALS LGE	GOALS ALL	ASSISTS	DEF RATE	POWER	SC DIFF
1	Tim Cahill	5	7	2	140	63	77 mins
2	Lee Carsley	1	1	4	102	66	36 mins
3	Mikel Arteta	9	9	9	101	66	35 mins
4	Leon Osman	3	3	4	100	66	34 mins

PLAYER APPEARANCES

	AGE (on 01/07/07)	IN NAMED 16	APPEARANCES	COUNTING GAMES	MINUTES ON PITCH	APPEARANCES THIS SEASON	MINUTES ON PITCH THIS SEASON		HOME COUNTRY
Goalkeepers									
Tim Howard	28	36	36	36	3240	38	3420	6	United States
John Ruddy	20	1	0	0	0	0	0	-	England
Iain Turner	23	7	1	1	90	2	180	-	Scotland
Richard Wright	29	32	1	1	90	2	180	-	England
Defenders									
Patrick Boyle	20	1	0	0	0	0	0	-	Scotland
Tony Hibbert	26	18	13	11	1014	13	1014	-	England
Mark Hughes	20	4	1	0	1	3	136	-	England
Joleon Lescott	24	38	38	36	3318	42	3678	-	England
Gary Naysmith	28	24	15	9	990	17	1100	6	Scotland
Phil Neville	30	35	35	34	3111	38	3381	4	England
Jorge Nuno Valente	32	17	14	8	898	17	1120	3	Portugal
Alan Stubbs	35	26	23	21	1997	24	2087	-	England
David Weir	37	18	5	1	152	6	197	8	Scotland
Joseph Yobo	26	38	38	38	3420	40	3587	4	Nigeria
Midfielders									
Mikel Arteta	25	35	35	35	3134	39	3432	-	Spain
Tim Cahill	27	18	18	14	1405	21	1613	3	Australia
Lee Carsley	33	38	38	37	3375	42	3734	5	Rep of Ireland
Simon Davies	27	18	15	12	1106	17	1265	11	Wales
Anderson De Silva	24	2	0	0	0	0	0	-	Brazil
Manuel Fernandes	21	10	9	8	716	9	716	-	Portugal
Kevin Kilbane	30	3	2	0	93	2	93	8	Rep of Ireland
Leon Osman	26	34	34	30	2808	37	3078	-	England
Andy van der Meyde	27	16	8	4	384	10	536	-	Holland
Bjarni T Vidarsson	19	1	0	0	0	0	0	-	Iceland
Forwards									
Victor Anichebe	19	23	19	4	626	23	828	-	Nigeria
James Beattie	29	38	33	10	1465	35	1578	-	England
Andrew Johnson	26	32	32	30	2711	35	2958	5	England
James McFadden	24	24	19	5	794	21	902	4	Scotland
James Vaughan	18	17	14	6	652	15	665	-	England

KEY: LEAGUE   ALL COMPS   CAPS   (MAY FIFA RANKING)

TEAM OF THE SEASON

HOWARD   CG 36   DR 111

 P NEVILLE   CG 34   DR 91

 YOBO   CG 38   DR 95

 STUBBS   CG 21   DR 66

 LESCOTT   CG 36   DR 92

 ARTETA   CG 35   SD +35

 CAHILL   CG 14   SD +77

 CARSLEY   CG 37   SD +36

 OSMAN   CG 30   SD +34

 BEATTIE*   CG 10   AP 86

 **JOHNSON**   CG 30   SR 246

KEY: DR = Defensive Rate, SD = Scoring Difference AP = Attacking Power SR = Strike Rate, CG=Counting games – League games playing at least 70 minutes

TOP POINT EARNERS

Tim Cahill

Counting Games League games when player was on pitch for at least 70 minutes		14
Average points Average League points taken in Counting games		1.71
Club Average points Average points taken in League games		1.53

	PLAYER	GAMES	PTS
1	Tim Cahill	14	1.71
2	Andrew Johnson	30	1.67
3	Tim Howard	36	1.61
4	Phil Neville	34	1.59
5	Mikel Arteta	35	1.54
6	Lee Carsley	37	1.54
7	Joseph Yobo	38	1.53
8	Leon Osman	30	1.50
9	Joleon Lescott	36	1.50
10	Alan Stubbs	21	1.38

KEY PLAYERS - DEFENDERS

Joseph Yobo

Goals Conceded in the League Number of League goals conceded while the player was on the pitch	36
Goals Conceded in all competitions Total number of goals conceded while the player was on the pitch	40
League minutes played Number of minutes played in league matches	3420
Clean Sheets In games when the player was on pitch for at least 70 minutes	14
Defensive Rating Average number of mins between League goals conceded while on the pitch	95
Club Defensive Rating Average number of mins between League goals conceded by the club this season	95

	PLAYER	CON LGE	CON ALL	MINS	C SHEETS	DEF RATE
1	Joseph Yobo	36	40	3420	14	95 mins
2	Joleon Lescott	36	42	3318	14	92 mins
3	Phil Neville	34	40	3111	12	91 mins
4	Alan Stubbs	23	23	1997	7	86 mins

KEY GOALKEEPER

Tim Howard

Goals Conceded in the League Number of League goals conceded while the player was on the pitch	29
Goals Conceded in all competitions Total number of goals conceded while the player was on the pitch	34
League minutes played Number of minutes played in league matches	3240
Clean Sheets In games when the player was on pitch for at least 70 minutes	14
Goals to Shots Ratio The average number of shots on target per each League goal conceded	8.07
Defensive Rating Ave mins between League goals conceded while on the pitch	111

BOOKINGS

Victor Anichebe

League Yellow	6
League Red	0
All competitions Yellow	6
All competitions Red	0

League Average   104 mins between cards

	PLAYER	LEAGUE		TOTAL		AVE
1	Victor Anichebe	6Y	0R	6Y	0R	104
2	James Vaughan	5	0	5	0	130
3	Manuel Fernandes	4	0	4	0	179
4	Tim Cahill	5	0	5	0	281
5	James Beattie	4	0	4	0	366
6	Mikel Arteta	8	0	8	0	391
7	Phil Neville	7	0	7	0	444
8	Tony Hibbert	1	1	1	1	507
9	Leon Osman	5	0	5	0	561
10	Alan Stubbs	3	0	3	0	665
11	Andrew Johnson	4	0	4	0	677
12	James McFadden	1	0	1	1	794
13	Nuno Valente	1	0	2	0	898
14	Simon Davies	1	0	1	0	1106
15	Lee Carsley	3	0	4	0	1125
	Other	6	0	7	0	
	TOTAL	**64**	**1**	**67**	**2**	

BOLTON WANDERERS

Holding onto a Uefa Cup spot was Sammy Lee's first success as a Premiership manager. Out of Sam Allardyce's shadow, Lee inherited a hard-working squad with a mercurial **Nicolas Anelka** as the only star name but a Strike Rate of 273 minutes per league goal only rated 25th in the Premiership. He did add eight Assists though.

Kevin Davies gave up the target man role but still struck eight in the league from deeper and there were goals through the midfield.

Captain **Kevin Nolan** claimed the only positive Scoring Difference in midfield as the team leaked goals.

Jussi Jaaskelainen was one of only three Premier keepers to play every minute of every league game and **Gary Speed** also made 38 appearances, scoring eight goals.

The club has one of the lowest shots averages in the division.

NICKNAME: THE TROTTERS   KEY: ☐ Won ☐ Drawn ■ Lost

1	prem	Tottenham	H	W	**2-0** Davies 9, Campo 13
2	prem	Fulham	A	D	**1-1** Diouf 74 pen
3	prem	Charlton	A	L	**0-2**
4	prem	Watford	H	W	**1-0** Speed 90 pen
5	prem	Middlesbrough	H	D	**0-0**
6	ccr2	Walsall	A	W	**3-1** Nolan 68, Campo 88, Anelka 90
7	prem	Portsmouth	A	W	**1-0** Nolan 22
8	prem	Liverpool	H	W	**2-0** Speed 30, Campo 51
9	prem	Newcastle	A	W	**2-1** Diouf 55, 56
10	prem	Blackburn	A	W	**1-0** Campo 62
11	ccr3	Charlton	A	L	**0-1**
12	prem	Man Utd	H	L	**0-4**
13	prem	Wigan	H	L	**0-1**
14	prem	Sheff Utd	A	D	**2-2** Diouf 34, Davies 59
15	prem	Everton	A	L	**0-1**
16	prem	Arsenal	H	W	**3-1** Faye 9, Anelka 45, 76
17	prem	Chelsea	H	L	**0-1**
18	prem	Reading	A	L	**0-1**
19	prem	West Ham	H	W	**4-0** Davies 17, 52, Diouf 77, Anelka 78
20	prem	Aston Villa	A	W	**1-0** Speed 75 pen
21	prem	Man City	A	W	**2-0** Anelka 8, 25
22	prem	Newcastle	H	W	**2-1** Ramage 32 og, Anelka 57
23	prem	Portsmouth	H	W	**3-2** Faye 30, Campo 40, Anelka 62
24	prem	Liverpool	A	L	**0-3**
25	facr3	Doncaster	A	W	**4-0** Davies 8, Teimourian 22, 49, Tal 33
26	prem	Man City	H	D	**0-0**
27	prem	Middlesbrough	A	L	**1-5** Nolan 25
28	facr4	Arsenal	A	D	**1-1** Nolan 50
29	prem	Charlton	H	D	**1-1** Pedersen 6
30	prem	Watford	A	W	**1-0** Anelka 63
31	prem	Fulham	H	W	**2-1** Speed 22 pen, Nolan 50
32	facr4r	Arsenal	H	L	**1-3** Meite 90
33	prem	Tottenham	A	L	**1-4** Speed 37 pen
34	prem	Blackburn	H	L	**1-2** Anelka 87
35	prem	Man Utd	A	L	**1-4** Speed 87 pen
36	prem	Sheff Utd	H	W	**1-0** Davies 80
37	prem	Wigan	A	W	**3-1** Anelka 44, Teimourian 68, 73
38	prem	Everton	H	D	**1-1** Davies 18
39	prem	Arsenal	A	L	**1-2** Anelka 11
40	prem	Reading	H	L	**1-3** Shorey 64 og
41	prem	Chelsea	A	D	**2-2** Michalik 19, Davies 54
42	prem	West Ham	A	L	**1-3** Speed 67
43	prem	Aston Villa	H	D	**2-2** Speed 32, Davies 58

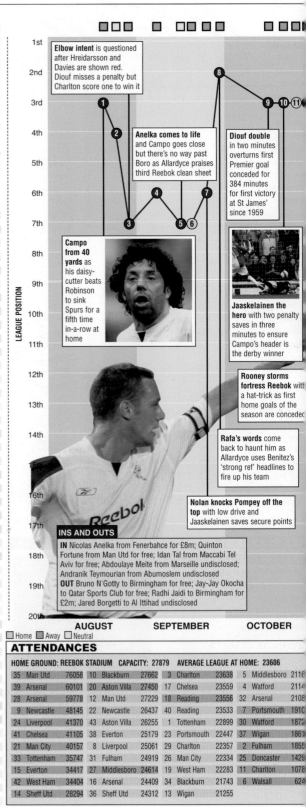

LEAGUE POSITION (1st–20th)

Elbow intent is questioned after Hreidarsson and Davies are shown red. Diouf misses a penalty but Charlton score one to win it

Anelka comes to life and Campo goes close but there's no way past Boro as Allardyce praises third Reebok clean sheet

Diouf double in two minutes overturns first Premier goal conceded for 384 minutes for first victory at St James' since 1959

Campo from 40 yards as his daisy-cutter beats Robinson to sink Spurs for a fifth time in-a-row at home

Jaaskelainen the hero with two penalty saves in three minutes to ensure Campo's header is the derby winner

Rooney storms fortress Reebok with a hat-trick as first home goals of the season are conceded

Rafa's words come back to haunt him as Allardyce uses Benitez's 'strong ref' headlines to fire up his team

Nolan knocks Pompey off the top with low drive and Jaaskelainen saves secure points

INS AND OUTS

IN Nicolas Anelka from Fenerbahce for £8m; Quinton Fortune from Man Utd for free; Idan Tal from Maccabi Tel Aviv for free; Abdoulaye Meite from Marseille undisclosed; Andranik Teymourian from Abumoslem undisclosed
OUT Bruno N'Gotty to Birmingham for free; Jay-Jay Okocha to Qatar Sports Club for free; Radhi Jaidi to Birmingham for £2m; Jared Borgetti to Al Ittihad undisclosed

AUGUST   SEPTEMBER   OCTOBER

☐ Home ■ Away ☐ Neutral

ATTENDANCES

HOME GROUND: REEBOK STADIUM   CAPACITY: 27879   AVERAGE LEAGUE AT HOME: 23606

35	Man Utd	76058	10	Blackburn	27662	3	Charlton	23638	5	Middlesboro	2116
39	Arsenal	60101	20	Aston Villa	27450	17	Chelsea	23559	4	Watford	2114
28	Arsenal	59778	12	Man Utd	27229	18	Reading	23556	32	Arsenal	2108
9	Newcastle	48145	22	Newcastle	26437	40	Reading	23533	7	Portsmouth	1910
24	Liverpool	41370	43	Aston Villa	26255	1	Tottenham	22899	30	Watford	1872
41	Chelsea	41105	38	Everton	25179	23	Portsmouth	22447	37	Wigan	186
21	Man City	40157	8	Liverpool	25061	29	Charlton	22357	2	Fulham	1855
33	Tottenham	35747	31	Fulham	24919	26	Man City	22334	25	Doncaster	1429
15	Everton	34417	27	Middlesboro	24614	19	West Ham	22283	11	Charlton	1078
42	West Ham	34404	16	Arsenal	24409	34	Blackburn	21743	6	Walsall	624
14	Sheff Utd	28294	36	Sheff Utd	24312	13	Wigan	21255			

Big Sam quits but Uefa spot secure

Final Position: 7th

KEY: ● League ● Champions Lge ● UEFA Cup ● FA Cup ● League Cup ● Other

■ □ ■ ■ ■ ■ ■ ■ ■ ■ ■ ■ ■ ■ ■ □ □ □ ■ ■ ■ ■ ■ ■ ■ ■ ■ ■ ■ ■ ■ ■ □

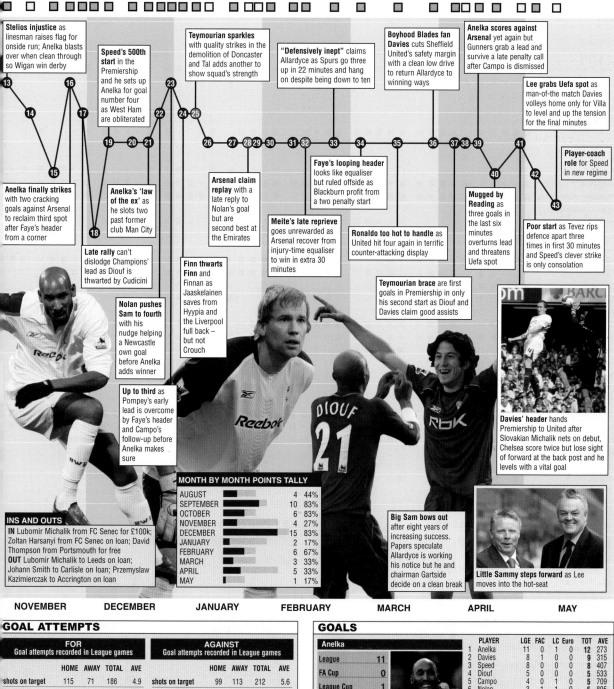

Stelios injustice as linesman raises flag for onside run; Anelka blasts over when clean through so Wigan win derby

Speed's 500th start in the Premiership and he sets up Anelka for goal number four as West Ham are obliterated

Teymourian sparkles with quality strikes in the demolition of Doncaster and Tal adds another to show squad's strength

"Defensively inept" claims Allardyce as Spurs go three up in 22 minutes and hang on despite being down to ten

Boyhood Blades fan Davies cuts Sheffield United's safety margin with a clean low drive to return Allardyce to winning ways

Anelka scores against Arsenal yet again but Gunners grab a lead and survive a late penalty call after Campo is dismissed

Lee grabs Uefa spot as man-of-the-match Davies volleys home only for Villa to level and up the tension for the final minutes

Player-coach role for Speed in new regime

Anelka finally strikes with two cracking goals against Arsenal to reclaim third spot after Faye's header from a corner

Anelka's 'law of the ex' as he slots two past former club Man City

Arsenal claim replay with a late reply to Nolan's goal but are second best at the Emirates

Faye's looping header looks like equaliser but ruled offside as Blackburn profit from a two penalty start

Mugged by Reading as three goals in the last six minutes overturns lead and threatens Uefa spot

Late rally can't dislodge Champions' lead as Diouf is thwarted by Cudicini

Meite's late reprieve goes unrewarded as Arsenal recover from injury-time equaliser to win in extra 30 minutes

Ronaldo too hot to handle as United hit four again in terrific counter-attacking display

Poor start as Tevez rips defence apart three times in first 30 minutes and Speed's clever strike is only consolation

Nolan pushes Sam to fourth with his nudge helping a Newcastle own goal before Anelka adds winner

Finn thwarts Finn and Finnan as Jaaskelainen saves from Hyypia and the Liverpool full back – but not Crouch

Teymourian brace are first goals in Premiership in only his second start as Diouf and Davies claim good assists

Davies' header hands Premiership to United after Slovakian Michalik nets on debut, Chelsea score twice but lose sight of forward at the back post and he levels with a vital goal

Up to third as Pompey's early lead is overcome by Faye's header and Campo's follow-up before Anelka makes sure

Big Sam bows out after eight years of increasing success. Papers speculate Allardyce is working his notice but he and chairman Gartside decide on a clean break

Little Sammy steps forward as Lee moves into the hot-seat

INS AND OUTS

IN Lubomir Michalik from FC Senec for £100k; Zoltan Harsanyi from FC Senec on loan; David Thompson from Portsmouth for free
OUT Lubomir Michalik to Leeds on loan; Johann Smith to Carlisle on loan; Przemyslaw Kazimierczak to Accrington on loan

MONTH BY MONTH POINTS TALLY

AUGUST	4	44%
SEPTEMBER	10	83%
OCTOBER	6	83%
NOVEMBER	4	27%
DECEMBER	15	83%
JANUARY	2	17%
FEBRUARY	6	67%
MARCH	3	33%
APRIL	5	33%
MAY	1	17%

NOVEMBER   DECEMBER   JANUARY   FEBRUARY   MARCH   APRIL   MAY

GOAL ATTEMPTS

FOR
Goal attempts recorded in League games

	HOME	AWAY	TOTAL	AVE
shots on target	115	71	186	4.9
shots off target	104	78	182	4.8
TOTAL	**219**	**149**	**368**	**9.7**

Ratio of goals to shots
Average number of shots on target per League goal scored — **4.0**

Accuracy rating
Average percentage of total goal attempts which were on target — **50.5**

AGAINST
Goal attempts recorded in League games

	HOME	AWAY	TOTAL	AVE
shots on target	99	113	212	5.6
shots off target	108	134	242	6.4
TOTAL	**207**	**247**	**454**	**11.9**

Ratio of goals to shots
Average number of shots on target per League goal scored — **4.1**

Accuracy rating
Average percentage of total goal attempts which were on target — **46.7**

GOALS

Anelka

League	11	
FA Cup	0	
League Cup	1	
Europe	0	
Other	0	
TOTAL	**12**	

League Average
273
mins between goals

	PLAYER	LGE	FAC	LC	Euro	TOT	AVE
1	Anelka	11	0	1	0	12	273
2	Davies	8	1	0	0	9	315
3	Speed	8	0	0	0	8	407
4	Diouf	5	0	0	0	5	533
5	Campo	4	0	1	0	5	709
6	Nolan	3	1	1	0	5	895
7	Teymourian	2	2	0	0	4	416
8	Faye	2	0	0	0	2	1260
9	Michalik	1	0	0	0	1	340
10	Pedersen	1	0	0	0	1	926
11	Tal	0	1	0	0	1	
12	Meite	0	1	0	0	1	
13	Al Habsi	0	0	0	0	0	
14	Cesar	0	0	0	0	0	
15	Augustyn	0	0	0	0	0	
	Other	0	0	0	0	0	
	TOTAL	**45**	**6**	**3**	**0**	**54**	

PREMIERSHIP CLUBS – BOLTON WANDERERS

SQUAD APPEARANCES

Match	1 2 3 4 5	6 7 8 9 10	11 12 13 14 15	16 17 18 19 20	21 22 23 24 25	26 27 28 29 30	31 32 33 34 35	36 37 38 39 40	41 42
Venue	H A A H H	A A H A A	A H H A A	H H A H A	A H H A A	H A A H A	H H A H A	H A H A H	A A
Competition	L L L L L	W L L L L	W L L L L	L L L L L	L L L L F	L L F L L	L F L L L	L L L L L	L L
Result	W D L W D	W W W W W	L L L D L	W L L W W	W W W L W	D L D D W	W L L L L	W W D L L	D L

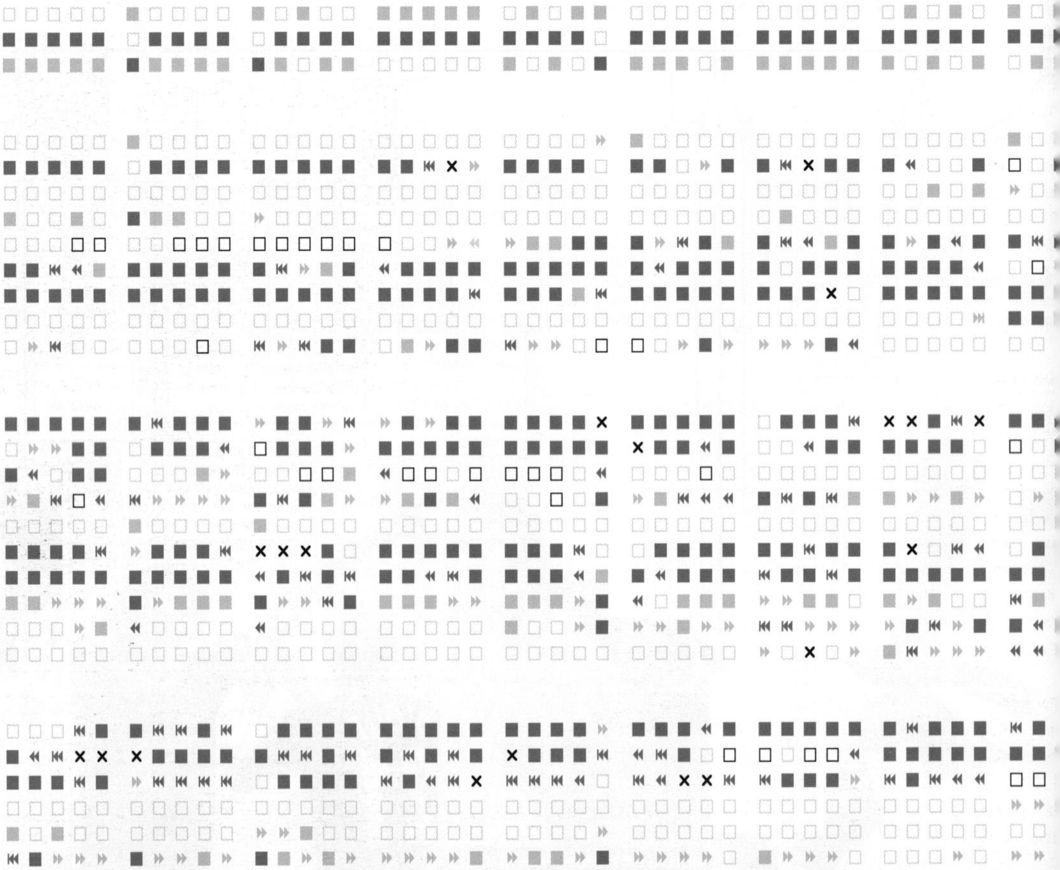

Goalkeepers

Ali Al Habsi
Jussi Jaaskelainen
Ian Walker

Defenders

Blazey Augustyn
Tal Ben Haim
Martin Cesar
Jaroslav Fojut
Ricardo Gardner
Nicky Hunt
Abdoulaye Meite
Lubomir Michalik
Henrik Pedersen

Midfielders

Ivan Campo
Abdoulaye Faye
Quinton Fortune
S Giannakopoulos
Scott Jamieson
Kevin Nolan
Gary Speed
Idan Tal
Andranik Teymourian
David Thompson

Forwards

Nicolas Anelka
Kevin Davies
El Hadji Diouf
James Sinclair
Johann Smith
Ricardo Vaz Te

KEY: ■ On all match ◄◄ Subbed or sent off (Counting game) ►►► Subbed on from bench (Counting Game) ▨ Subbed on and then subbed or sent off (Counting Game) ☐ Not in 16 ☐ Injured
☐ On bench ◄◄ Subbed or sent off (playing less than 70 mins) ►► Subbed on (playing less than 70 mins) ►► Subbed on and then subbed or sent off (playing less than 70 min ✗ Suspended

KEY PLAYERS - GOALSCORERS

Nicolas Anelka

Goals in the League	11
Goals in all competitions	12
Assists League goals scored by a team mate where the player delivered the final pass	8
Contribution to Attacking Power Average number of minutes between League team goals while on pitch	71
Player Strike Rate Average number of minutes between League goals scored by player	273
Club Strike Rate Average minutes between League goals scored by club	72

	PLAYER	GOALS LGE	GOALS ALL	ASSISTS	POWER	S RATE
1	Nicolas Anelka	11	12	8	71	273 mins
2	Kevin Davies	8	9	7	70	315 mins
3	Gary Speed	8	8	5	72	407 mins
4	El Hadji Diouf	5	5	7	70	533 mins

KEY PLAYERS - MIDFIELDERS

Kevin Nolan

Goals in the League	3
Goals in all competitions	5
Assists League goals scored by a team mate where the player delivered the final pass	1
Defensive Rating Average number of mins between League goals conceded while on the pitch	72
Contribution to Attacking Power Average number of minutes between League team goals while on pitch	67
Scoring Difference Defensive Rating minus Contribution to Attacking Power	5

	PLAYER	GOALS LGE	GOALS ALL	ASSISTS	DEF RATE	POWER	SC DIFF
1	Kevin Nolan	3	5	1	72	67	5 mins
2	Abdoulaye Faye	2	2	1	63	68	-5 mins
3	Gary Speed	8	8	5	66	72	-6 mins
4	Ivan Campo	4	5	6	64	78	-14 mins

PLAYER APPEARANCES

	AGE (on 01/07/07)	IN NAMED 16	APPEARANCES	COUNTING GAMES	MINUTES ON PITCH	APPEARANCES	MINUTES ON PITCH THIS SEASON		HOME COUNTRY
Goalkeepers									
Ali Al Habsi	25	12	0	0	0	0	0	-	Oman
Jussi Jaaskelainen	32	38	38	38	3420	40	3630	9	Finland
Ian Walker	35	25	0	0	0	3	270	-	England
Defenders									
Blazey Augustyn	19	2	0	0	0	1	8	-	Poland
Tal Ben Haim	25	32	32	29	2685	34	2891	6	Israel
Martin Cesar	30	3	1	0	1	1	1	-	Spain
Jaroslav Fojut	19	4	0	0	0	2	108	-	Poland
Ricardo Gardner	28	22	18	11	1234	21	1485	1	Jamaica
Nicky Hunt	23	35	33	28	2627	37	2987	-	England
Abdoulaye Meite	26	36	35	34	3127	40	3599	4	Ivory Coast
Lubomir Michalik	23	4	4	4	340	4	340	2	Slovakia
Henrik Pedersen	32	19	18	9	926	21	1047	-	Denmark
Midfielders									
Ivan Campo	33	34	34	31	2837	38	3165	-	Spain
Abdoulaye Faye	29	32	32	26	2520	34	2700	4	Senegal
Quinton Fortune	30	8	6	3	422	7	472	-	South Africa
S Giannakopoulos	32	31	23	6	934	28	1344	3	Greece
Scott Jamieson	18	0	0	0	0	0	0	-	Australia
Kevin Nolan	25	31	31	30	2687	34	2929	-	England
Gary Speed	37	38	38	33	3257	42	3619	-	Wales
Idan Tal	31	34	16	3	522	20	829	7	Israel
Andranik Teymourian	24	20	17	5	832	21	1118	4	Iran
David Thompson	29	9	8	1	287	8	287	-	England
Forwards									
Nicolas Anelka	28	35	35	33	3010	39	3328	7	France
Kevin Davies	30	30	30	27	2521	33	2773	-	England
El Hadji Diouf	26	33	33	27	2665	35	2801	3	Senegal
James Sinclair	19	3	2	0	46	2	46	-	England
Johann Smith	20	4	1	0	6	3	81	-	United States
Ricardo Vaz Te	20	32	25	2	659	30	983	-	Portugal

KEY: LEAGUE — ALL COMPS — CAPS — (MAY FIFA RANKING)

TEAM OF THE SEASON

JAASKELAINEN
CG 38 DR 65

HUNT CG 28 DR 75 | **BEN HAIM** CG 29 DR 68 | **MEITE** CG 34 DR 72 | **GARDNER*** CG 11 DR 47

NOLAN CG 30 SD +5 | **FAYE** CG 26 SD -5 | **CAMPO** CG 31 SD -14 | **SPEED** CG 33 SD -6

DAVIES CG 27 AP 70 | **ANELKA** CG 33 SR 273

KEY: DR = Defensive Rate, SD = Scoring Difference AP = Attacking Power SR = Strike Rate, CG=Counting games – League games playing at least 70 minutes

TOP POINT EARNERS

El Hadji Diouf	
Counting Games League games when player was on pitch for at least 70 minutes	**28**
Average points Average League points taken in Counting games	**1.79**
Club Average points Average points taken in League games	**1.47**

	PLAYER	GAMES	PTS
1	El Hadji Diouf	28	1.79
2	Kevin Nolan	30	1.67
3	Abdoulaye Faye	26	1.65
4	Nicky Hunt	28	1.64
5	Gary Speed	33	1.58
6	Abdoulaye Meite	34	1.56
7	Nicolas Anelka	33	1.52
8	Tal Ben Haim	29	1.52
9	Kevin Davies	27	1.48
10	Jussi Jaaskelainen	38	1.47

KEY PLAYERS - DEFENDERS

Nicky Hunt	
Goals Conceded in the League Number of League goals conceded while the player was on the pitch	**35**
Goals Conceded in all competitions Total number of goals conceded while the player was on the pitch	**38**
League minutes played Number of minutes played in league matches	**2627**
Clean Sheets In games when the player was on pitch for at least 70 minutes	**10**
Defensive Rating Average number of mins between League goals conceded while on the pitch	**75**
Club Defensive Rating Average number of mins between League goals conceded by the club this season	**65**

	PLAYER	CON LGE	CON ALL	MINS	C SHEETS	DEF RATE
1	Nicky Hunt	35	38	2627	10	75 mins
2	Abdoulaye Meite	43	49	3127	11	72 mins
3	Tal Ben Haim	39	42	2685	10	68 mins
4	Ricardo Gardner	26	28	1234	2	47 mins

KEY GOALKEEPER

Jussi Jaaskelainen	
Goals Conceded in the League Number of League goals conceded while the player was on the pitch	**52**
Goals Conceded in all competitions Total number of goals conceded while the player was on the pitch	**56**
League minutes played Number of minutes played in league matches	**3420**
Clean Sheets In games when the player was on pitch for at least 70 minutes	**12**
Goals to Shots Ratio The average number of shots on target per each League goal conceded	**4.08**
Defensive Rating Ave mins between League goals conceded while on the pitch	**65**

BOOKINGS

Ricardo Gardner	
League Yellow	**6**
League Red	**0**
All competitions Yellow	**6**
All competitions Red	**0**

League Average 205 mins between cards

	PLAYER	LEAGUE		TOTAL		AVE
1	Ricardo Gardner	6 Y	0 R	6 Y	0 R	205
2	Kevin Davies	10	1	10	1	229
3	Ivan Campo	11	1	12	1	236
4	Kevin Nolan	10	1	11	1	244
5	Abdoulaye Faye	9	0	10	0	280
6	El Hadji Diouf	7	1	7	1	333
7	Tal Ben Haim	7	0	9	1	383
8	Idan Tal	1	0	1	0	522
9	Gary Speed	4	0	4	0	814
10	Henrik Pedersen	1	0	1	0	926
11	S. Giannakopoulos	1	0	1	0	934
12	Abdoulaye Meite	3	0	4	0	1042
13	Jussi Jaaskelainen	3	0	3	0	1140
14	Nicky Hunt	2	0	3	0	1313
15	Nicolas Anelka	0	0	1	0	
	Other	0	0	0	0	
	TOTAL	**75**	**4**	**83**	**5**	

READING

The guile of Steve Coppell allied to the underrated talents of a squad, which was all in the Championship last year, surprised the pundits. **Kevin Doyle** hit 13 goals at the eighth highest Strike Rate in the league and **Leroy Lita** top-scored with seven in the cups.

There was plenty of variation out wide with **Glen Little** topping the midfield charts and maybe warranting more time on the pitch.

The side had the second lowest shots total in the league but easily the best Goals to Shots Ratio, needing 3.3 Shots on target to score.

Ivar Ingimarsson was one of only four outfield players in the league to play every minute of the season but finished behind skipper **Graeme Murty** in the defensive ratings. Murty was also Top Point Earner, averaging 1.71 a game. **Marcus Hahnemann** saved 5.8 shots for every goal he let in – the sixth best keeping record.

NICKNAME: THE ROYALS   KEY: ☐ Won ☐ Drawn ■ Lost

#	comp	Opponent	H/A	W/D/L	Score	Scorers
1	prem	Middlesbrough	H	W	3-2	Kitson 43, Sidwell 44, Lita 55
2	prem	Aston Villa	A	L	1-2	Doyle 4
3	prem	Wigan	A	L	0-1	
4	prem	Man City	H	W	1-0	Ingimarsson 22
5	prem	Sheff Utd	A	W	2-1	Doyle 1, Seol 25
6	ccr2	Darlington	H	W	4-2*	Lita 31, 35, Mate 86 (*on penalties)
7	prem	Man Utd	H	D	1-1	Doyle 48 pen
8	prem	West Ham	A	W	1-0	Seol 2
9	prem	Chelsea	H	L	0-1	
10	prem	Arsenal	H	L	0-4	
11	ccr3	Liverpool	A	L	3-4	Bikey 75, Lita 81, Long 85
12	prem	Portsmouth	A	L	1-3	Doyle 84
13	prem	Liverpool	A	L	0-2	
14	prem	Tottenham	H	W	3-1	Shorey 38, Sidwell 45, Doyle 79
15	prem	Charlton	H	W	2-0	Seol 18, Doyle 72
16	prem	Fulham	A	W	1-0	Doyle 17 pen
17	prem	Bolton	H	W	1-0	Doyle 33
18	prem	Newcastle	A	L	2-3	Harper 37, 42
19	prem	Watford	A	D	0-0	
20	prem	Blackburn	H	L	1-2	Harper 41
21	prem	Everton	H	L	0-2	
22	prem	Chelsea	A	D	2-2	Lita 67, Essien 85 og
23	prem	Man Utd	A	L	2-3	Sonko 38, Lita 90
24	prem	West Ham	H	W	6-0	Gunnarsson 12, Hunt 15, Ferdinand 30 og, Doyle 36, 78, Lita 53
25	facr3	Burnley	H	W	3-2	Lita 28, Long 37, Sodje 55
26	prem	Everton	A	D	1-1	Lescott 27 og
27	prem	Sheff Utd	H	W	3-1	Long 44, De La Cruz 50, Hunt 70
28	facr4	Birmingham	A	W	3-2	Kitson 3, Lita 41, 82
29	prem	Wigan	H	W	3-2	Ingimarsson 31, Long 51, Lita 88
30	prem	Man City	A	W	2-0	Lita 79, 89
31	prem	Aston Villa	H	W	2-0	Sidwell 16, 90
32	facr5	Man Utd	A	D	1-1	Gunnarsson 67
33	prem	Middlesbrough	A	L	1-2	Oster 87
34	facr5r	Man Utd	H	L	2-3	Kitson 23, Lita 84
35	prem	Arsenal	A	L	1-2	Fabregas 87 og
36	prem	Portsmouth	H	D	0-0	
37	prem	Tottenham	A	L	0-1	
38	prem	Liverpool	H	L	1-2	Gunnarsson 47
39	prem	Charlton	A	D	0-0	
40	prem	Fulham	H	W	1-0	Hunt 15
41	prem	Bolton	A	W	3-1	Doyle 84 pen, 89, Hunt 90
42	prem	Newcastle	H	W	1-0	Kitson 51
43	prem	Watford	H	L	0-2	
44	prem	Blackburn	A	D	3-3	Seol 36, Doyle 58, Gunnarsson 77

Doyle's charge nets in 16 seconds to blunt Blades and Seol adds a well-deserved second for first away win

Top billing on Match of the Day as comeback from two down fires Madejski Stadium with Seol in starring role

Sonko in a tangle and sees red to let Villa back in with a penalty to level Doyle's early strike

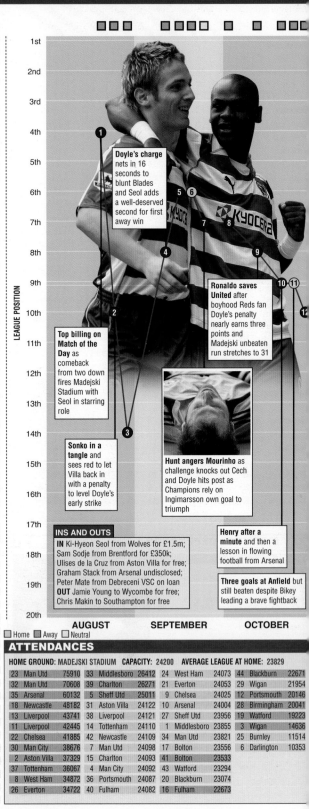

Ronaldo saves United after boyhood Reds fan Doyle's penalty nearly earns three points and Madejski unbeaten run stretches to 31

Hunt angers Mourinho as challenge knocks out Cech and Doyle hits post as Champions rely on Ingimarsson own goal to triumph

Henry after a minute and then a lesson in flowing football from Arsenal

Three goals at Anfield but still beaten despite Bikey leading a brave fightback

INS AND OUTS

IN Ki-Hyeon Seol from Wolves for £1.5m; Sam Sodje from Brentford for £350k; Ulises de la Cruz from Aston Villa for free; Graham Stack from Arsenal undisclosed; Peter Mate from Debreceni VSC on loan **OUT** Jamie Young to Wycombe for free; Chris Makin to Southampton for free

Chart axis: 1st, 2nd, 3rd, 4th, 5th, 6th, 7th, 8th, 9th, 10th, 11th, 12th, 13th, 14th, 15th, 16th, 17th, 18th, 19th, 20th — LEAGUE POSITION

AUGUST   SEPTEMBER   OCTOBER

☐ Home ■ Away ☐ Neutral

ATTENDANCES

HOME GROUND: MADEJSKI STADIUM   CAPACITY: 24200   AVERAGE LEAGUE AT HOME: 23829

23	Man Utd	75910	33	Middlesboro	26412	24	West Ham	24073	44	Blackburn	22671
32	Man Utd	70608	39	Charlton	26271	21	Everton	24053	29	Wigan	21954
35	Arsenal	60132	5	Sheff Utd	25011	9	Chelsea	24025	12	Portsmouth	20146
18	Newcastle	48182	31	Aston Villa	24122	10	Arsenal	24004	28	Birmingham	20041
13	Liverpool	43741	38	Liverpool	24121	27	Sheff Utd	23956	19	Watford	19223
11	Liverpool	42445	14	Tottenham	24110	1	Middlesboro	23855	3	Wigan	14636
22	Chelsea	41885	42	Newcastle	24109	34	Man Utd	23821	25	Burnley	11514
30	Man City	38676	7	Man Utd	24098	17	Bolton	23556	6	Darlington	10353
2	Aston Villa	37329	15	Charlton	24093	41	Bolton	23533			
37	Tottenham	36067	4	Man City	24092	43	Watford	23294			
8	West Ham	34872	36	Portsmouth	24087	20	Blackburn	23074			
26	Everton	34722	40	Fulham	24082	16	Fulham	22673			

Coppell's path doesn't reach to Europe

Final Position: 8th

KEY: ● League ○ Champions Lge ● UEFA Cup ● FA Cup ○ League Cup ● Other

Kitson returns and is on the score sheet after three minutes as Coppell's changes work at Birmingham

Lita proves point scoring first since August to start fight back against Chelsea who draw after own goal

Hammerered! Gunnarsson's first goal starts blitz of six as Doyle, Lita and Co. fire home Shorey's bullets in Coppell's dream start to 2007

Seven in eight games for Lita as Wigan's early lead is overturned in fourth straight home win

Nightmare start as United go three up in six minutes before Kitson and Lita make it tight and Gunnarsson hits the bar

Halford's horrible debut as ball bounces up awkwardly to be given as a Spurs' penalty in game of thrilling chances

Sidwell dropped from squad as he considers other options

Owen shown the way to goal as England forward makes his return but it's Kitson who scores – his first since August

Offside shout proves a clever Watford ploy as Duberry is held back for 'onside' Shittu to score and upset the script

Sidwell so close to claiming a point at the Emirates as his near-post shot brings best out of Lehmann

Doyle sets up Hunt for winner as Fulham prove tough opponents under new manager

Three times behind; three times level as end of season thriller is played out by two of the best sides not to reach Europe

Harper brace is overturned by Newcastle in a five goal thriller with a halftime melee in tunnel and a hotly disputed penalty

Sidwell strikes twice to sink Villa and take unbeaten run to eight matches with Hahnemann in top form

"We don't draw many", admits Coppell as Pompey claim a point in only second home draw

Uefa beckons as final six minutes turn a 1-0 deficit into a win with Doyle striking twice and Hunt adding a third

Federici brilliance keeps Larsson at bay and Gunnarsson header earns a return at the Madejski Stadium

Five at the back in first ever league meeting with Liverpool but Sodje, Sonko and the rest can't stop Kuyt

Three wins on the bounce puts Coppell within a point of top four as Doyle converts from the spot

Doyle's eighth of the season makes him a bargain buy at £80k and Bolton are overtaken in the league

INS AND OUTS

IN Michael Duberry from Stoke for £800k; Greg Halford from Colchester for £2.5m; Alan Bennett from Cork for an undisclosed fee; Mikkel Andersen from AB Copenhagen for £120k
OUT Jonathan Haynes to MK Dons on loan; Scott Golbourne to Wycombe on loan

MONTH BY MONTH POINTS TALLY

AUGUST	3	33%
SEPTEMBER	7	78%
OCTOBER	3	25%
NOVEMBER	9	75%
DECEMBER	5	24%
JANUARY	10	83%
FEBRUARY	6	67%
MARCH	1	17%
APRIL	10	56%
MAY	1	17%

NOVEMBER   DECEMBER   JANUARY   FEBRUARY   MARCH   APRIL   MAY

GOAL ATTEMPTS

FOR — Goal attempts recorded in League games

	HOME	AWAY	TOTAL	AVE
shots on target	107	64	171	4.5
shots off target	108	85	193	5.1
TOTAL	215	149	364	9.6

Ratio of goals to shots	
Average number of shots on target per League goal scored	3.3

Accuracy rating	
Average percentage of total goal attempts which were on target	47.0

AGAINST — Goal attempts recorded in League games

	HOME	AWAY	TOTAL	AVE
shots on target	117	144	261	6.9
shots off target	106	147	253	6.7
TOTAL	223	291	514	13.5

Ratio of goals to shots	
Average number of shots on target per League goal scored	5.6

Accuracy rating	
Average percentage of total goal attempts which were on target	50.8

GOALS

Lita

League	7
FA Cup	4
League Cup	3
Europe	0
Other	0
TOTAL	14

League Average	
286	mins between goals

	PLAYER	LGE	FAC	LC	Euro	TOT	AVE
1	Lita	7	4	3	0	14	286
2	Doyle	13	0	0	0	13	189
3	Gunnarsson	3	1	0	0	4	389
4	Kitson	2	2	0	0	4	402
5	Long	2	1	1	0	4	407
6	Seol	4	0	0	0	4	454
7	Hunt	4	0	0	0	4	606
8	Sidwell	4	0	0	0	4	773
9	Harper	3	0	0	0	3	1066
10	Ingimarsson	2	0	0	0	2	1710
11	De La Cruz	1	0	0	0	1	748
12	Oster	1	0	0	0	1	852
13	Sonko	1	0	0	0	1	1926
14	Shorey	1	0	0	0	1	3330
15	Sodje	0	1	0	0	1	
	Other	0	0	2	0	2	
	TOTAL	48	9	6	0	63	

SQUAD APPEARANCES

Match	1 2 3 4 5	6 7 8 9 10	11 12 13 14 15	16 17 18 19 20	21 22 23 24 25	26 27 28 29 30	31 32 33 34 35	36 37 38 39 40	41 42 43
Venue	H A A H A	H H A H H	A A A H H	A H A A H	H A A H H	A H A H A	H A A H A	H A H A H	A H H
Competition	L L L L L	W L L L L	W L L L L	L L L L L	L L L L F	L L F L L	L F L F L	L L L L L	L L L
Result	W L L W W	W D W L L	L L L W W	W W L D L	L D L W W	D W W W W	W D L L L	D L L D W	W W L

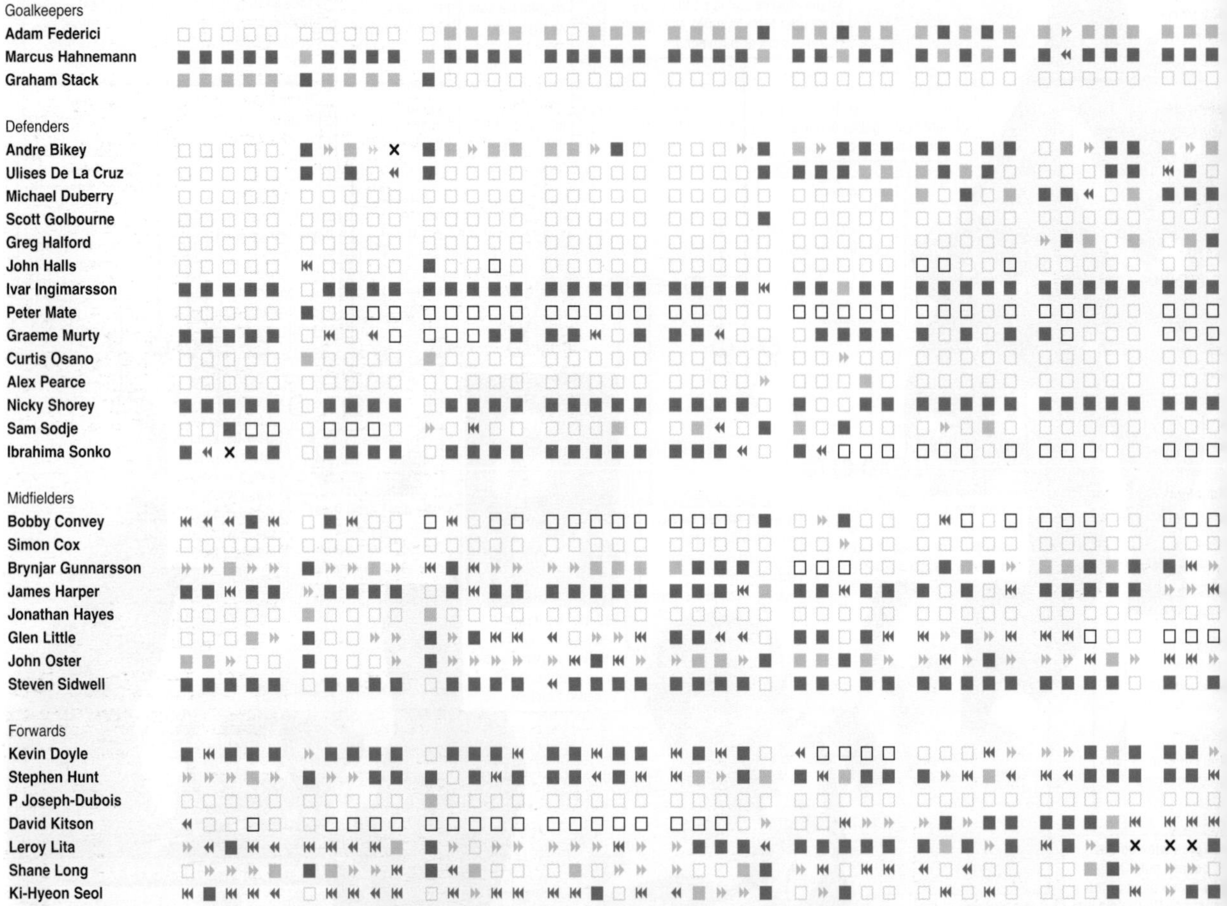

Goalkeepers

Adam Federici
Marcus Hahnemann
Graham Stack

Defenders

Andre Bikey
Ulises De La Cruz
Michael Duberry
Scott Golbourne
Greg Halford
John Halls
Ivar Ingimarsson
Peter Mate
Graeme Murty
Curtis Osano
Alex Pearce
Nicky Shorey
Sam Sodje
Ibrahima Sonko

Midfielders

Bobby Convey
Simon Cox
Brynjar Gunnarsson
James Harper
Jonathan Hayes
Glen Little
John Oster
Steven Sidwell

Forwards

Kevin Doyle
Stephen Hunt
P Joseph-Dubois
David Kitson
Leroy Lita
Shane Long
Ki-Hyeon Seol

KEY: ■ On all match ◄◄ Subbed or sent off (Counting game) ►► Subbed on from bench (Counting Game) ►►■ Subbed on and then subbed or sent off (Counting Game) ☐ Not in 16 ☐ Injured
■ On bench ◄◄ Subbed or sent off (playing less than 70 mins) ►► Subbed on (playing less than 70 mins) ►►■ Subbed on and then subbed or sent off (playing less than 70 min ✗ Suspended

KEY PLAYERS - GOALSCORERS

Kevin Doyle

Goals in the League	13
Goals in all competitions	13
Assists — League goals scored by a team mate where the player delivered the final pass	3
Contribution to Attacking Power — Average number of minutes between League team goals while on the pitch	61
Player Strike Rate — Average number of minutes between League goals scored by player	189
Club Strike Rate — Average minutes between League goals scored by club	65

	PLAYER	GOALS LGE	GOALS ALL	ASSISTS	POWER	S RATE
1	Kevin Doyle	13	13	3	61	189 mins
2	Leroy Lita	7	14	4	60	286 mins
3	Ki-Hyeon Seol	4	4	5	64	454 mins
4	Stephen Hunt	4	4	6	71	606 mins

KEY PLAYERS - MIDFIELDERS

Glen Little

Goals in the League	0
Goals in all competitions	0
Assists — League goals scored by a team mate where the player delivered the final pass	5
Defensive Rating — Average number of mins between League goals conceded while on the pitch	72
Contribution to Attacking Power — Average number of minutes between League team goals while on pitch	56
Scoring Difference — Defensive Rating minus Contribution to Attacking Power	16

	PLAYER	GOALS LGE	GOALS ALL	ASSISTS	DEF RATE	POWER	SC DIFF
1	Glen Little	0	0	5	72	56	16 mins
2	James Harper	3	3	3	71	65	6 mins
3	Steven Sidwell	4	4	7	70	65	5 mins
4	Brynjar Gunnarsson	3	4	0	58	55	3 mins

PLAYER APPEARANCES

	AGE (on 01/07/07)	IN NAMED 16	APPEARANCES	COUNTING GAMES	MINUTES ON PITCH	APPEARANCES	MINUTES ON PITCH	THIS SEASON	HOME COUNTRY
Goalkeepers									
Adam Federici	22	28	2	1	114	6	474	-	Australia
Marcus Hahnemann	35	38	38	36	3306	38	3306	-	United States
Graham Stack	25	9	0	0	0	2	210	-	England
Defenders									
Andre Bikey	22	26	15	7	832	21	1402	-	Cameroon
Ulises De La Cruz	33	13	9	8	748	15	1318	2	Ecuador
Michael Duberry	31	12	8	7	675	8	675	-	England
Scott Golbourne	19	0	0	0	0	1	90	-	England
Greg Halford	22	6	3	2	181	3	181	-	England
John Halls	25	0	0	0	0	2	191	-	England
Ivar Ingimarsson	29	38	38	38	3420	42	3763	7	Iceland
Peter Mate	22	0	0	0	0	1	120	-	Hungary
Graeme Murty	32	23	23	21	1981	24	2071	-	Scotland
Curtis Osano	20	0	0	0	0	1	1	-	England
Alex Pearce	18	1	0	0	0	1	17	-	England
Nicky Shorey	26	37	37	37	3330	39	3510	1	England
Sam Sodje	28	6	3	2	168	7	361	-	England
Ibrahima Sonko	26	23	23	20	1926	23	1926	-	Senegal
Midfielders									
Bobby Convey	24	9	9	6	613	12	863	1	United States
Simon Cox	20	0	0	0	0	1	13	-	England
Brynjar Gunnarsson	31	33	23	10	1167	27	1549	6	Iceland
James Harper	26	38	38	36	3199	40	3307	-	England
Jonathan Hayes	19	0	0	0	0	0	0	-	Rep of Ireland
Glen Little	31	25	24	15	1591	28	1825	-	England
John Oster	28	33	25	6	852	31	1417	-	Wales
Steven Sidwell	24	35	35	34	3092	37	3272	-	England
Forwards									
Kevin Doyle	23	33	32	27	2469	34	2591	1	Rep of Ireland
Stephen Hunt	25	37	35	25	2426	38	2656	4	Rep of Ireland
Joseph-Dubois	19	0	0	0	0	0	0	-	France
David Kitson	27	15	13	8	804	17	1092	-	England
Leroy Lita	22	34	33	19	2005	38	2332	-	England
Shane Long	20	27	21	5	814	24	1114	3	Rep of Ireland
Ki-Hyeon Seol	28	28	27	19	1818	31	2154	2	South Korea

KEY: LEAGUE   ALL COMPS   CAPS   (MAY FIFA RANKING)

TEAM OF THE SEASON

HAHNEMANN — CG 36 DR 73

 MURTY — CG 21 DR 79
 SONKO — CG 20 DR 68
 INGIMARSSON — CG 38 DR 71
 SHOREY — CG 37 DR 72

 LITTLE — CG 15 SD +16
 SIDWELL — CG 34 SD +5
 HARPER — CG 36 SD +6
 GUNNARSSON* — CG 10 SD +3

 **LITA** — CG 19 AP 60
 DOYLE — CG 27 SR 189

KEY: DR = Defensive Rate, SD = Scoring Difference AP = Attacking Power SR = Strike Rate, CG=Counting games – League games playing at least 70 minutes

TOP POINT EARNERS

Graeme Murty

Counting Games League games when player was on pitch for at least 70 minutes	21
Average points Average League points taken in Counting games	1.71
Club Average points Average points taken in League games	1.45

	PLAYER	GAMES	PTS
1	Graeme Murty	21	1.71
2	Stephen Hunt	25	1.64
3	Ki-Hyeon Seol	19	1.58
4	Marcus Hahnemann	36	1.50
5	Kevin Doyle	27	1.48
6	Ivar Ingimarsson	38	1.45
7	Nicky Shorey	37	1.41
8	Glen Little	15	1.40
9	James Harper	36	1.36
10	Ibrahima Sonko	21	1.33

KEY PLAYERS - DEFENDERS

Graeme Murty

Goals Conceded in the League Number of League goals conceded while the player was on the pitch	25
Goals Conceded in all competitions Total number of goals conceded while the player was on the pitch	27
League minutes played Number of minutes played in league matches	1981
Clean Sheets In games when the player was on pitch for at least 70 minutes	7
Defensive Rating Average number of mins between League goals conceded while on the pitch	79
Club Defensive Rating Average number of mins between League goals conceded by the club this season	72

	PLAYER	CON LGE	CON ALL	MINS	C SHEETS	DEF RATE
1	Graeme Murty	25	27	1981	7	79 mins
2	Ivar Ingimarsson	47	56	3420	13	72 mins
3	Nicky Shorey	46	50	3330	13	72 mins
4	Ibrahima Sonko	28	28	1926	6	68 mins

KEY GOALKEEPER

Marcus Hahnemann

Goals Conceded in the League Number of League goals conceded while the player was on the pitch	45
Goals Conceded in all competitions Total number of goals conceded while the player was on the pitch	45
League minutes played Number of minutes played in league matches	3306
Clean Sheets In games when the player was on pitch for at least 70 minutes	13
Goals to Shots Ratio The average number of shots on target per each League goal conceded	5.8
Defensive Rating Ave mins between League goals conceded while on the pitch	73

BOOKINGS

David Kitson

League Yellow	3
League Red	0
All competitions Yellow	4
All competitions Red	0

League Average   268 mins between cards

	PLAYER	LEAGUE		TOTAL		AVE
		3Y	0R	4Y	0R	
1	David Kitson	3Y	0R	4Y	0R	268
2	Andre Bikey	2	1	7	1	277
3	Shane Long	2	0	2	0	407
4	Ibrahima Sonko	3	1	3	1	481
5	Ki-Hyeon Seol	3	0	4	0	606
6	Stephen Hunt	4	0	4	0	606
7	Michael Duberry	1	0	1	0	675
8	John Oster	1	0	1	0	852
9	Ivar Ingimarsson	4	0	4	0	855
10	Graeme Murty	2	0	2	0	990
11	Steven Sidwell	3	0	3	0	1030
12	James Harper	3	0	4	0	1066
13	B. Gunnarsson	1	0	1	0	1167
14	Glen Little	1	0	2	0	1591
15	Nicky Shorey	2	0	2	0	1665
	Other	2	0	3	0	
	TOTAL	**37**	**2**	**47**	**2**	

PORTSMOUTH

The highest ever finish in the Premiership was the reward for Harry Redknapp's remodelled Pompey. **Nwankwo Kanu** hit six in his first eight games but tailed off to a 23rd in the division Strike Rate of one every 270 minutes. **Matthew Taylor** struck regularly from distance as the club recorded 470 shots – the fifth highest.

However, it was defensive solidity that kept Europe in sight. It was built around the signings of **Sol Campbell**, and **David James**, the form of **Linvoy Primus**, and the fitness of **Dejan Stefanovic**, who ended with the best defensive stats – conceding less than a goal a game on average. James set down a new all-time Premiership Clean Sheets record and played every minute of the league games.

Pedro Mendes was concussed at Man City but topped the club's midfield charts alongside Taylor.

NICKNAME: POMPEY

KEY: ☐ Won ☐ Drawn ☐ Lost

1	prem	**Blackburn**	H W	3-0	Todorov 26, Kanu 62, 84
2	prem	**Man City**	A D	0-0	
3	prem	**Middlesbrough**	A W	4-0	Kanu 7, 57, Mwaruwari 50, Todorov 90
4	prem	**Wigan**	H W	1-0	Mwaruwari 49
5	prem	**Charlton**	A W	1-0	LuaLua 74
6	ccr2	**Mansfield**	A W	2-1	Manuel Fernandes 5, Taylor 33
7	prem	**Bolton**	H L	0-1	
8	prem	**Tottenham**	A L	1-2	Kanu 40
9	prem	**West Ham**	H W	2-0	Kanu 24, Cole 82
10	prem	**Chelsea**	A L	1-2	Mwaruwari 69
11	ccr3	**Newcastle**	A L	0-3	
12	prem	**Reading**	H W	3-1	Gunnarsson 10 og, Kanu 52, Mendes 66
13	prem	**Man Utd**	A L	0-3	
14	prem	**Fulham**	H D	1-1	Cole 74
15	prem	**Watford**	H W	2-1	Kanu 44, LuaLua 89 pen
16	prem	**Newcastle**	A L	0-1	
17	prem	**Liverpool**	A D	0-0	
18	prem	**Aston Villa**	H D	2-2	Taylor 52, 80 pen
19	prem	**Everton**	H W	2-0	Taylor 14, Kanu 26
20	prem	**Arsenal**	A D	2-2	Pamarot 45, Taylor 47
21	prem	**Sheff Utd**	H W	3-1	Kozluk 48 og, Campbell 54, Pamarot 68
22	prem	**West Ham**	A W	2-1	Primus 16, 38
23	prem	**Bolton**	A L	2-3	Taylor 2, Cole 90
24	prem	**Tottenham**	H D	1-1	Mwaruwari 29
25	facr3	**Wigan**	H W	2-1	Cole 64, Kanu 90
26	prem	**Sheff Utd**	A D	1-1	O'Neil 81
27	prem	**Charlton**	H L	0-1	
28	facr4	**Man Utd**	A L	1-2	Kanu 87
29	prem	**Middlesbrough**	H D	0-0	
30	prem	**Wigan**	A L	0-1	
31	prem	**Man City**	H W	2-1	Mendes 5, Kanu 81
32	prem	**Blackburn**	A L	0-3	
33	prem	**Chelsea**	H L	0-2	
34	prem	**Reading**	A D	0-0	
35	prem	**Fulham**	A D	1-1	Kranjcar 4
36	prem	**Man Utd**	H W	2-1	Taylor 30, Ferdinand 89 og
37	prem	**Watford**	A L	2-4	Taylor 16, Mvuemba 81
38	prem	**Newcastle**	H W	2-1	Mwaruwari 7, Taylor 59
39	prem	**Aston Villa**	A D	0-0	
40	prem	**Liverpool**	H W	2-1	Mwaruwari 27, Kranjcar 32
41	prem	**Everton**	A L	0-3	
42	prem	**Arsenal**	H D	0-0	

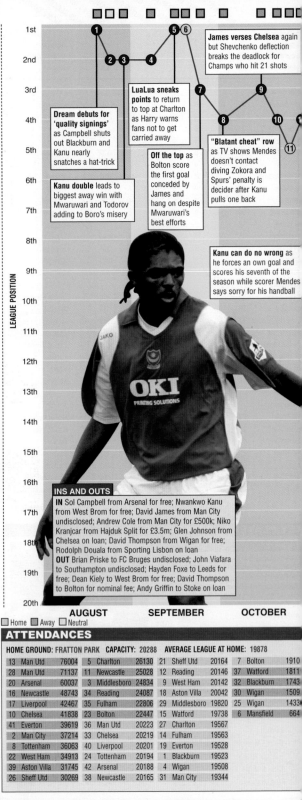

James verses Chelsea again but Shevchenko deflection breaks the deadlock for Champs who hit 21 shots

LuaLua sneaks points to return to top at Charlton as Harry warns fans not to get carried away

Dream debuts for 'quality signings' as Campbell shuts out Blackburn and Kanu nearly snatches a hat-trick

Off the top as Bolton score the first goal conceded by James and hang on despite Mwaruwari's best efforts

"Blatant cheat" row as TV shows Mendes doesn't contact diving Zokora and Spurs' penalty is decider after Kanu pulls one back

Kanu double leads to biggest away win with Mwaruwari and Todorov adding to Boro's misery

Kanu can do no wrong as he forces an own goal and scores his seventh of the season while scorer Mendes says sorry for his handball

LEAGUE POSITION

1st 2nd 3rd 4th 5th 6th 7th 8th 9th 10th 11th 12th 13th 14th 15th 16th 17th 18th 19th 20th

AUGUST **SEPTEMBER** **OCTOBER**

☐ Home ☐ Away ☐ Neutral

INS AND OUTS

IN Sol Campbell from Arsenal for free; Nwankwo Kanu from West Brom for free; David James from Man City undisclosed; Andrew Cole from Man City for £500k; Niko Kranjcar from Hajduk Split for £3.5m; Glen Johnson from Chelsea on loan; David Thompson from Wigan for free; Rodolph Douala from Sporting Lisbon on loan
OUT Brian Priske to FC Bruges undisclosed; John Viafara to Southampton undisclosed; Hayden Foxe to Leeds for free; Dean Kiely to West Brom for free; David Thompson to Bolton for nominal fee; Andy Griffin to Stoke on loan

ATTENDANCES

HOME GROUND: FRATTON PARK CAPACITY: 20288 AVERAGE LEAGUE AT HOME: 19878

13	Man Utd	76004	5	Charlton	26130	21	Sheff Utd	20164	7 Bolton 1910
28	Man Utd	71137	11	Newcastle	25028	12	Reading	20146	37 Watford 1811
20	Arsenal	60037	3	Middlesboro	24834	9	West Ham	20142	32 Blackburn 1743
16	Newcastle	48743	34	Reading	24087	18	Aston Villa	20042	30 Wigan 1509
17	Liverpool	42467	35	Fulham	22806	29	Middlesboro	19820	25 Wigan 1433
10	Chelsea	41838	23	Bolton	22447	15	Watford	19738	6 Mansfield 664
41	Everton	39619	36	Man Utd	20223	27	Charlton	19567	
2	Man City	37214	33	Chelsea	20219	14	Fulham	19563	
8	Tottenham	36063	40	Liverpool	20201	19	Everton	19523	
22	West Ham	34913	24	Tottenham	20194	1	Blackburn	19523	
39	Aston Villa	31745	42	Arsenal	20188	4	Wigan	19508	
26	Sheff Utd	30269	38	Newcastle	20165	31	Man City	19344	

James and Campbell closer to Europe

Final Position: 9th

KEY: ● League ○ Champions Lge ◐ UEFA Cup ● FA Cup ○ League Cup ● Other

"Jamo has been fantastic", Redknapp applauds keeper's performance but Newcastle still claim points

Pamarot's first goal unsettles Wenger and Taylor's sweet dink makes it 2-0 before Arsenal fight back at the Emirates

"As poor as we've been," admits Redknapp as Wigan end eight-game losing streak

Mwaruwari fires home but Spurs level despite Pamarot's high kick knocking out four of Ghaly's teeth

Mendes suffers again at City's hands after Barton stamp sees him stretchered off after scoring but Kanu supplies winner

Best season since the 50s thanks to home form

Liverpool kept at bay as defence snatches a rare point at Anfield

Cole close to levelling twice and Kanu also brings the best out of Cech but Champs claim points

James superb as United are repelled and beaten for the third time in four meetings at Fratton Park

Johnson's clumsy tackle lets in Everton to win the battle for Europe and highlights poor away run

Taylor-made: goal of the season thus far as he strikes a 42 metre volley and Kanu goes back to the top of the scoring charts

Cole strike gets Cup underway and sub Kanu clinches win after Wigan threaten replay

James beaten after 22 seconds at fault for second goal before saving penalty but Rovers defeat makes it one league win in eight

Taylor's missile into the corner is ninth goal of the season and another cracker in first win over Newcastle

Poll costs Uefa spot as ref interrupts Kranjcar's 'goal' celebration by wrongly calling offside while James makes a stunning penalty save

James' errors hand Bolton a three point gap in battle for Champions League spot despite good finishes from Taylor and Cole

Stefanovic return coincides with a James' 141st clean sheet to level Seaman's Premier record as defences rule at Reading

James claims record with his 142nd Premier clean sheet in a man-of-the-match performance against Villa

Kranjcar's curler flies into top corner for first goal of the season from Croatian international but James misses record after 92nd minute deflection

Campbell defies United for 77 minutes before Rooney settles it with Kanu deflecting in a consolation

Three defenders down and a dodgy penalty kick-starts Man United's comfortable win

Another notable scalp as James' long ball sets up Mwaruwari for first before Kranjcar's steers home a second against Liverpool

MONTH BY MONTH POINTS TALLY

Month	Points	%
AUGUST	7	78%
SEPTEMBER	6	67%
OCTOBER	6	50%
NOVEMBER	5	33%
DECEMBER	11	61%
JANUARY	3	25%
FEBRUARY	3	33%
MARCH	2	22%
APRIL	10	67%
MAY	1	17%

INS AND OUTS

IN Lauren from Arsenal for £500k; Djimi Traore from Charlton for £1m; Arnold Mvuemba from Rennes on loan
OUT Dean Kiely to West Brom for free; David Thompson to Bolton undisclosed; Andy Griffin to Stoke on loan; Richard Duffy to Swansea on loan

NOVEMBER   DECEMBER   JANUARY   FEBRUARY   MARCH   APRIL   MAY

GOAL ATTEMPTS

FOR
Goal attempts recorded in League games

	HOME	AWAY	TOTAL	AVE
shots on target	143	87	230	6.1
shots off target	146	94	240	6.3
TOTAL	289	181	470	12.4

Ratio of goals to shots Average number of shots on target per League goal scored	5.1
Accuracy rating Average percentage of total goal attempts which were on target	48.9

AGAINST
Goal attempts recorded in League games

	HOME	AWAY	TOTAL	AVE
shots on target	89	145	234	6.2
shots off target	91	130	221	5.8
TOTAL	180	275	455	12.0

Ratio of goals to shots Average number of shots on target per League goal scored	5.6
Accuracy rating Average percentage of total goal attempts which were on target	51.4

GOALS

Kanu

League	10
FA Cup	2
League Cup	0
Europe	0
Other	0
TOTAL	12

| League Average | 270 | mins between goals |

	PLAYER	LGE	FAC	LC	Euro	TOT	AVE
1	Kanu	10	2	0	0	12	270
2	Taylor	8	0	1	0	9	335
3	Mwaruwari	6	0	0	0	6	338
4	Cole	3	1	0	0	4	227
5	Todorov	2	0	0	0	2	51
6	LuaLua	2	0	0	0	2	478
7	Kranjcar	2	0	0	0	2	644
8	Pamarot	2	0	0	0	2	903
9	Mendes	2	0	0	0	2	1037
10	Primus	2	0	0	0	2	1571
11	Mvuemba	1	0	0	0	1	226
12	Campbell	1	0	0	0	1	2880
13	O'Neil	1	0	0	0	1	3088
14	Fernandes	0	0	1	0	1	
15	Lauren	0	0	0	0	0	
	Other	0	0	0	0	0	
	TOTAL	42	3	2	0	47	

SQUAD APPEARANCES

Match	1	2	3	4	5	6	7	8	9	10	11	12	13	14	15	16	17	18	19	20	21	22	23	24	25	26	27	28	29	30	31	32	33	34	35	36	37	38	39	40	41
Venue	H	A	A	H	A		A	H	A	H	A		A	H	A	H	H		A	A	H	H	H	A		A	H	A	H	A		H	A	H	A	A		H	A	H	A	H	A
Competition	L	L	L	L	L		W	L	L	L	L		W	L	L	L	L		L	L	L	L	L	L		L	L	F	L	L		L	L	F	L	L		L	L	L	L	L	L	L
Result	W	D	W	W	W		W	L	L	W	L		L	W	L	D	W		L	D	D	W	D			W	W	L	D	W		D	L	L	D	L		W	L	L	D	D		W	L	W	D	W		L

Goalkeepers
Jamie Ashdown
David James
Dean Kiely

Defenders
Sol Campbell
Richard Duffy
Andrew Griffin
Glen Johnson
Etame Mayer Lauren
Andy O'Brien
Noe Pamarot
Linvoy Primus
Dejan Stefanovic
Djimi Traore

Midfielders
Sean Davis
Richard Hughes
Ognijen Koroman
Niko Kranjcar
Manuel Fernandes
Pedro Mendes
Arnold Mvuemba
Gary O'Neil
Franck Songo'o
Matthew Taylor
David Thompson

Forwards
Andy Cole
Rudolph Mbela Douala
Nwankwo Kanu
Lomana LuaLua
Benjani Mwaruwari
Svetoslav Todorov

KEY: ■ On all match ◄◄ Subbed or sent off (Counting game) ►► Subbed on from bench (Counting Game) ►◄ Subbed on and then subbed or sent off (Counting Game) □ Not in 16 ▢ Injured
□ On bench ◄◄ Subbed or sent off (playing less than 70 mins) ►► Subbed on (playing less than 70 mins) ►◄ Subbed on and then subbed or sent off (playing less than 70 min) ✕ Suspended

KEY PLAYERS - GOALSCORERS

Nwankwo Kanu

Goals in the League	10
Goals in all competitions	12
Assists — League goals scored by a team mate where the player delivered the final pass	3
Contribution to Attacking Power — Average number of minutes between League team goals while on pitch	73
Player Strike Rate — Average number of minutes between League goals scored by player	270
Club Strike Rate — Average minutes between League goals scored by club	76

	PLAYER	GOALS LGE	GOALS ALL	ASSISTS	POWER	S RATE
1	Nwankwo Kanu	10	12	3	73	270 mins
2	Matthew Taylor	8	9	5	72	335 mins
3	Benjani Mwaruwari	6	6	3	70	338 mins
4	Niko Kranjcar	2	2	2	92	644 mins

KEY PLAYERS - MIDFIELDERS

Pedro Mendes

Goals in the League	2
Goals in all competitions	2
Assists — League goals scored by a team mate where the player delivered the final pass	5
Defensive Rating — Average number of mins between League goals conceded while on the pitch	83
Contribution to Attacking Power — Average number of minutes between League team goals while on pitch	76
Scoring Difference — Defensive Rating minus Contribution to Attacking Power	7

	PLAYER	GOALS LGE	GOALS ALL	ASSISTS	DEF RATE	POWER	SC DIFF
1	Pedro Mendes	2	2	5	83	76	7 mins
2	Matthew Taylor	8	9	5	79	72	7 mins
3	Gary O'Neil	1	1	5	79	73	6 mins
4	Sean Davis	0	0	4	69	67	2 mins

PLAYER APPEARANCES

	AGE (on 01/07/07)	IN NAMED 16	APPEARANCES	COUNTING GAMES	MINUTES ON PITCH	APPEARANCES	MINUTES ON PITCH THIS SEASON	MINUTES ON PITCH THIS SEASON	HOME COUNTRY
Goalkeepers									
Jamie Ashdown	26	25	0	0	0	0	0	-	England
David James	36	38	38	38	3420	41	3690	-	England
Dean Kiely	36	10	0	0	0	1	90	-	Rep of Ireland
Defenders									
Sol Campbell	32	32	32	32	2880	34	3060	-	England
Richard Duffy	21	0	0	0	0	1	90	6	Wales
Andrew Griffin	28	1	0	0	0	0	0	-	England
Glen Johnson	22	26	26	25	2258	28	2438	-	England
Dame Mayer Lauren	30	10	10	8	797	11	887	-	Cameroon
Andy O'Brien	28	16	3	1	107	5	287	4	Rep of Ireland
Noe Pamarot	28	32	23	19	1807	25	1987	-	France
Linvoy Primus	33	36	36	34	3142	39	3412	-	England
Dejan Stefanovic	32	20	20	17	1703	20	1703	-	Serbia
Djimi Traore	27	12	10	8	804	10	804	-	France
Midfielders									
Sean Davis	27	33	31	25	2491	33	2653	-	England
Richard Hughes	28	21	18	11	1055	21	1244	-	Scotland
Gagnijen Koroman	28	5	1	0	18	3	139	8	Serbia
Niko Kranjcar	22	27	24	12	1289	28	1569	9	Croatia
Manuel Fernandes	21	12	10	5	594	9	658	-	Portugal
Pedro Mendes	28	26	26	22	2075	28	2255	-	Portugal
Arnold Mvuemba	22	10	7	1	226	7	226	-	France
Gary O'Neil	24	35	35	34	3088	37	3268	-	England
Franck Songo'o	20	0	0	0	0	0	0	-	France
Matthew Taylor	25	35	35	27	2687	39	3047	-	England
David Thompson	29	17	12	4	445	15	531	-	England
Forwards									
Andy Cole	35	19	18	5	681	22	1012	-	England
Mbela Douala	28	9	7	1	249	10	300	-	Cameroon
Nwankwo Kanu	30	37	36	30	2709	38	2783	3	Nigeria
Lomana LuaLua	26	24	22	6	957	24	1119	2	Congo DR
Benjani Mwaruwari	28	31	31	17	2030	34	2104	2	Zimbabwe
Svetoslav Todorov	28	5	4	0	103	4	103	-	Bulgaria

KEY: LEAGUE   ALL COMPS   CAPS   (MAY FIFA RANKING)

TEAM OF THE SEASON

JAMES CG 38 DR 81			
JOHNSON CG 25 DR 90	**PRIMUS** CG 34 DR 84	**CAMPBELL** CG 32 DR 96	**STEFANOVIC** CG 17 DR 100
O'NEIL CG 34 SD +6	**DAVIS** CG 25 SD +2	**MENDES** CG 22 SD +7	**TAYLOR** CG 27 SD +7
MWARUWARI CG 17 AP 70	**KANU** CG 30 SR 270		

KEY: DR = Defensive Rate, SD = Scoring Difference AP = Attacking Power SR = Strike Rate, CG=Counting games − League games playing at least 70 minutes

TOP POINT EARNERS

Dejan Stefanovic			PLAYER	GAMES	PTS
Counting Games League games when player was on pitch for at least 70 minutes		17	1 Dejan Stefanovic	17	1.88
			2 Benjani Mwaruwari	17	1.71
			3 Sean Davis	25	1.68
Average points Average League points taken in Counting games		1.88	4 Matthew Taylor	27	1.63
			5 Glen Johnson	25	1.52
			6 Gary O'Neil	34	1.50
Club Average points Average points taken in League games		1.42	7 Sol Campbell	32	1.47
			8 Nwankwo Kanu	30	1.47
			9 David James	38	1.42
			10 Pedro Mendes	22	1.41

KEY PLAYERS - DEFENDERS

Dejan Stefanovic	
Goals Conceded in the League Number of League goals conceded while the player was on the pitch	17
Goals Conceded in all competitions Total number of goals conceded while the player was on the pitch	17
League minutes played Number of minutes played in league matches	1703
Clean Sheets In games when the player was on pitch for at least 70 minutes	7
Defensive Rating Average number of mins between League goals conceded while on the pitch	100
Club Defensive Rating Average number of mins between League goals conceded by the club this season	81

	PLAYER	CON LGE	CON ALL	MINS	C SHEETS	DEF RATE
1	Dejan Stefanovic	17	17	1703	7	100 mins
2	Sol Campbell	30	33	2880	11	96 mins
3	Glen Johnson	25	28	2258	9	90 mins
4	Linvoy Primus	37	43	3142	12	84 mins

KEY GOALKEEPER

David James	
Goals Conceded in the League Number of League goals conceded while the player was on the pitch	42
Goals Conceded in all competitions Total number of goals conceded while the player was on the pitch	48
League minutes played Number of minutes played in league matches	3420
Clean Sheets In games when the player was on pitch for at least 70 minutes	12
Goals to Shots Ratio The average number of shots on target per each League goal conceded	5.57
Defensive Rating Ave mins between League goals conceded while on the pitch	81

BOOKINGS

Richard Hughes	
League Yellow	4
League Red	0
All competitions Yellow	5
All competitions Red	0

League Average 263 mins between cards

	PLAYER	LEAGUE		TOTAL		AVE
1	Richard Hughes	4Y	0R	5Y	0R	263
2	Gary O'Neil	8	0	8	0	386
3	Dejan Stefanovic	4	0	4	0	425
4	Sean Davis	5	0	6	0	498
5	Pedro Mendes	3	1	3	1	518
6	Glen Johnson	4	0	4	0	564
7	Noe Pamarot	3	0	4	0	602
8	Matthew Taylor	4	0	4	0	671
9	Andy Cole	1	0	1	0	681
10	Lauren	1	0	1	0	797
11	Nwankwo Kanu	3	0	3	0	903
12	David James	2	0	2	0	1710
13	Sol Campbell	1	0	1	0	2880
14	Linvoy Primus	1	0	1	0	3142
15	Manuel Fernandes	0	0	1	0	
	Other	1	0	1	0	
	TOTAL	**44**	**1**	**49**	**1**	

BLACKBURN ROVERS

Benni McCarthy was the revelation as Mark Hughes rebuilt his strike force and finished the season looking full of goals with 26 in the last 13 games. McCarthy struck 24 and his 18 in the league was second only to Didier Drogba. **Matt Derbyshire** hit nine with his league goals coming at a Strike Rate of one every 156 minutes. **Shabani Nonda** performed well and **Jason Roberts** finished strongly after a long lay-off.

Both wings were potent with 15 goals coming between **Morten Gamst Pedersen** and **David Bentley**. The duo also set up colleagues for 24 goals– and both are in the top ten Assists table.

Injuries disrupted the defence but **Ryan Nelsen's** return from injury and the signings of **Stephen Warnock** and **Christopher Samba** saw it remodelled successfully without **Lucas Neill**.

NICKNAME: ROVERS

KEY: ☐ Won ☐ Drawn ☐ Lost

#	comp	Opponent			Score	Scorers
1	prem	**Portsmouth**	A	L	0-3	
2	prem	**Everton**	H	D	1-1	McCarthy 50
3	prem	**Chelsea**	H	L	0-2	
4	prem	**Sheff Utd**	A	D	0-0	
5	ucr1l1	**Salzburg**	A	D	2-2	Savage 32, McCarthy 39
6	prem	**Man City**	H	W	4-2	Sinclair 16 og, Pedersen 43, McCarthy 66, Gallagher 88
7	prem	**Middlesbrough**	A	W	1-0	Nonda 27
8	ucr1l2	**Salzburg**	H	W	2-0	McCarthy 32, Bentley 56
9	prem	**Wigan**	H	W	2-1	Bentley 45, McCarthy 81
10	prem	**Liverpool**	A	D	1-1	McCarthy 17
11	ucgpe	**Wisla Krakow**	A	W	2-1	Savage 56, Bentley 89
12	prem	**Bolton**	H	L	0-1	
13	ccr3	**Chelsea**	H	L	0-2	
14	prem	**West Ham**	A	L	1-2	Bentley 90
15	ucgpe	**Basel**	H	W	3-0	Tugay 75, Jeffers 89 pen, McCarthy 90
16	ucgpe	**Aston Villa**	A	L	0-2	
17	prem	**Man Utd**	H	L	0-1	
18	prem	**Tottenham**	H	D	1-1	Tugay 22
19	ucgpe	**Feyenoord**	A	D	0-0	
20	prem	**Fulham**	H	W	2-0	Nonda 6, McCarthy 24
21	prem	**Charlton**	A	L	0-1	
22	prem	**Newcastle**	H	L	1-3	Pedersen 47
23	ucgpe	**Nancy**	H	W	1-0	Neill 90
24	prem	**Reading**	A	W	2-1	McCarthy 64, Bentley 84
25	prem	**Arsenal**	A	L	2-6	Nonda 3 pen, 69
26	prem	**Liverpool**	H	W	1-0	McCarthy 49
27	prem	**Middlesbrough**	H	W	2-1	Nonda 9, McCarthy 74
28	prem	**Wigan**	A	W	3-0	Heskey 37 og, Derbyshire 58, McCarthy 76 pen
29	facr3	**Everton**	A	W	4-1	Derbyshire 5, Pedersen 21, Gallagher 38, McCarthy 90
30	prem	**Arsenal**	H	L	0-2	
31	prem	**Man City**	A	W	3-0	Pedersen 44, 62, Derbyshire 90
32	prem	**Watford**	A	L	1-2	McCarthy 45
33	facr4	**Luton**	A	W	4-0	Derbyshire 10, 56, McCarthy 36, Pedersen 74
34	prem	**Chelsea**	A	L	0-3	
35	prem	**Sheff Utd**	H	W	2-1	Pedersen 22, 90
36	prem	**Everton**	A	L	0-1	
37	ucr2l1	**B Leverkusen**	A	L	2-3	Bentley 39, Nonda 86
38	facr5	**Arsenal**	A	D	0-0	
39	ucr2l2	**B Leverkusen**	H	D	0-0	
40	prem	**Portsmouth**	H	W	3-0	Nonda 1, 25, Warnock 50
41	facr5r	**Arsenal**	H	W	1-0	McCarthy 87
42	prem	**Bolton**	A	W	2-1	McCarthy 58 pen, 68 pen
43	facqf	**Man City**	H	W	2-0	Mokoena 28, Derbyshire 90
44	prem	**West Ham**	H	L	1-2	Samba 47
45	prem	**Man Utd**	A	L	1-4	Derbyshire 29
46	prem	**Aston Villa**	H	L	1-2	McCarthy 24 pen
47	facsf	**Chelsea**	N	L	1-2	Roberts 64
48	prem	**Watford**	H	W	3-1	Samba 7, Roberts 10, McCarthy 32
49	prem	**Fulham**	A	D	1-1	McCarthy 61
50	prem	**Charlton**	H	W	4-1	Roberts 60, 80, Hreidarsson 77 og, Derbyshire 83
51	prem	**Newcastle**	A	W	2-0	McCarthy 14, Roberts 73
52	prem	**Tottenham**	A	D	1-1	McCarthy 33
53	prem	**Reading**	H	D	3-3	McCarthy 21, Bentley 56, Derbyshire 67

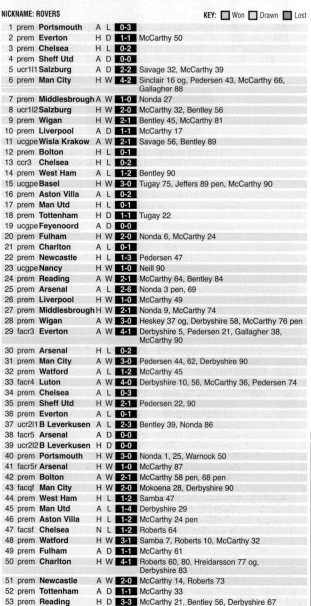

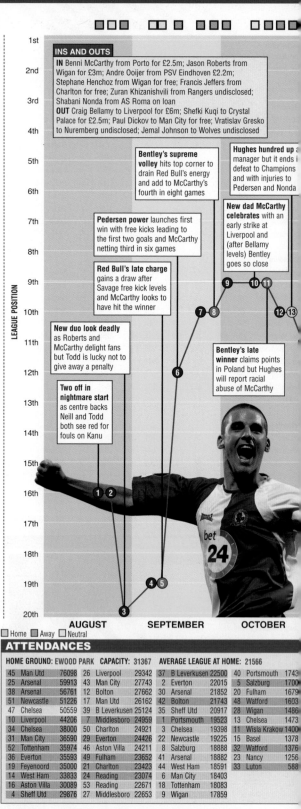

LEAGUE POSITION

1st 2nd 3rd 4th 5th 6th 7th 8th 9th 10th 11th 12th 13th 14th 15th 16th 17th 18th 19th 20th

☐ Home ☐ Away ☐ Neutral

AUGUST SEPTEMBER OCTOBER

INS AND OUTS

IN Benni McCarthy from Porto for £2.5m; Jason Roberts from Wigan for £3m; Andre Ooijer from PSV Eindhoven £2.2m; Stephane Henchoz from Wigan for free; Francis Jeffers from Charlton for free; Zuran Khizanishvili from Rangers undisclosed; Shabani Nonda from AS Roma on loan

OUT Craig Bellamy to Liverpool for £6m; Shefki Kuqi to Crystal Palace for £2.5m; Paul Dickov to Man City for free; Vratislav Gresko to Nuremberg undisclosed; Jemal Johnson to Wolves undisclosed

Bentley's supreme volley hits top corner to drain Red Bull's energy and add to McCarthy's fourth in eight games

Hughes hundred up a manager but it ends i defeat to Champions and with injuries to Pedersen and Nonda

Pedersen power launches first win with free kicks leading to the first two goals and McCarthy netting third in six games

New dad McCarthy celebrates with an early strike at Liverpool and (after Bellamy levels) Bentley goes so close

Red Bull's late charge gains a draw after Savage free kick levels and McCarthy looks to have hit the winner

New duo look deadly as Roberts and McCarthy delight fans but Todd is lucky not to give away a penalty

Bentley's late winner claims points in Poland but Hughes will report racial abuse of McCarthy

Two off in nightmare start as centre backs Neill and Todd both see red for fouls on Kanu

ATTENDANCES

HOME GROUND: EWOOD PARK **CAPACITY:** 31367 **AVERAGE LEAGUE AT HOME:** 21566

45	Man Utd	76098	26	Liverpool	29342	37	B Leverkusen	22500	40	Portsmouth	1743
25	Arsenal	59913	43	Man City	27743	2	Everton	22015	5	Salzburg	1700
38	Arsenal	56761	12	Bolton	27662	30	Arsenal	21852	20	Fulham	1679
51	Newcastle	51226	17	Man Utd	26162	42	Bolton	21743	48	Watford	1603
47	Chelsea	50559	39	B Leverkusen	25124	35	Sheff Utd	20917	28	Wigan	1486
10	Liverpool	44206	7	Middlesboro	24959	1	Portsmouth	19523	13	Chelsea	1473
34	Chelsea	38000	50	Charlton	24921	3	Chelsea	19398	11	Wisla Krakow	1400
31	Man City	36590	29	Everton	24426	22	Newcastle	19225	15	Basel	1378
52	Tottenham	35974	46	Aston Villa	24211	8	Salzburg	18888	32	Watford	1376
36	Everton	35593	49	Fulham	23652	41	Arsenal	18882	23	Nancy	1256
19	Feyenoord	35000	21	Charlton	23423	44	West Ham	18591	33	Luton	588
14	West Ham	33833	24	Reading	23074	6	Man City	18403			
16	Aston Villa	30089	53	Reading	22671	18	Tottenham	18083			
4	Sheff Utd	29876	27	Middlesboro	22653	9	Wigan	17859			

McCarthy pick of the new strike force

Final Position: 10th

KEY: ● League ○ Champions Lge ○ UEFA Cup ● FA Cup ○ League Cup ○ Other

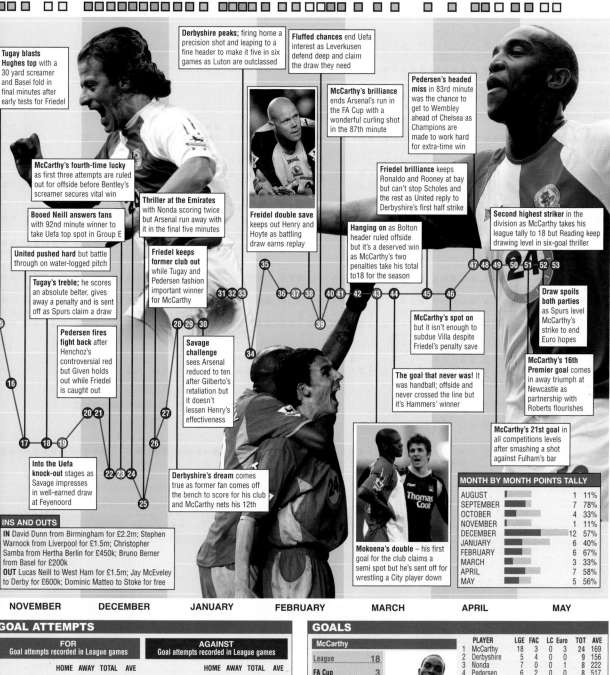

Tugay blasts Hughes top with a 30 yard screamer and Basel fold in final minutes after early tests for Friedel

Derbyshire peaks; firing home a precision shot and leaping to a fine header to make it five in six games as Luton are outclassed

Fluffed chances end Uefa interest as Leverkusen defend deep and claim the draw they need

Pedersen's headed miss in 83rd minute was the chance to get to Wembley ahead of Chelsea as Champions are made to work hard for extra-time win

McCarthy's fourth-time lucky as first three attempts are ruled out for offside before Bentley's screamer secures vital win

McCarthy's brilliance ends Arsenal's run in the FA Cup with a wonderful curling shot in the 87th minute

Booed Neill answers fans with 92nd minute winner to take Uefa top spot in Group E

Friedel brilliance keeps Ronaldo and Rooney at bay but can't stop Scholes and the rest as United reply to Derbyshire's first half strike

Thriller at the Emirates with Nonda scoring twice but Arsenal run away with it in the final five minutes

Freidel double save keeps out Henry and Hoyte as battling draw earns replay

Second highest striker in the division as McCarthy takes his league tally to 18 but Reading keep drawing level in six-goal thriller

United pushed hard but battle through on water-logged pitch

Friedel keeps former club out while Tugay and Pedersen fashion important winner for McCarthy

Hanging on as Bolton header ruled offside but it's a deserved win as McCarthy's two penalties take his total to18 for the season

Tugay's treble; he scores an absolute belter, gives away a penalty and is sent off as Spurs claim a draw

Draw spoils both parties as Spurs level McCarthy's strike to end Euro hopes

Pedersen fires fight back after Henchoz's controversial red but Given holds out while Friedel is caught out

Savage challenge sees Arsenal reduced to ten after Gilberto's retaliation but it doesn't lessen Henry's effectiveness

McCarthy's spot on but it isn't enough to subdue Villa despite Friedel's penalty save

McCarthy's 16th Premier goal comes in away triumph at Newcastle as partnership with Roberts flourishes

The goal that never was! It was handball; offside and never crossed the line but it's Hammers' winner

McCarthy's 21st goal in all competitions levels after smashing a shot against Fulham's bar

Into the Uefa knock-out stages as Savage impresses in well-earned draw at Feyenoord

Derbyshire's dream comes true as former fan comes off the bench to score for his club and McCarthy nets his 12th

Mokoena's double – his first goal for the club claims a semi spot but he's sent off for wrestling a City player down

INS AND OUTS

IN David Dunn from Birmingham for £2.2m; Stephen Warnock from Liverpool for £1.5m; Christopher Samba from Hertha Berlin for £450k; Bruno Berner from Basel for £200k
OUT Lucas Neill to West Ham for £1.5m; Jay McEveley to Derby for £600k; Dominic Matteo to Stoke for free

MONTH BY MONTH POINTS TALLY		
AUGUST	1	11%
SEPTEMBER	7	78%
OCTOBER	4	33%
NOVEMBER	1	11%
DECEMBER	12	57%
JANUARY	6	40%
FEBRUARY	6	67%
MARCH	3	33%
APRIL	7	58%
MAY	5	56%

NOVEMBER DECEMBER JANUARY FEBRUARY MARCH APRIL MAY

GOAL ATTEMPTS

FOR
Goal attempts recorded in League games

	HOME	AWAY	TOTAL	AVE
shots on target	121	93	214	5.6
shots off target	130	120	250	6.6
TOTAL	251	213	464	12.2

Ratio of goals to shots
Average number of shots on target per League goal scored — **4.1**

Accuracy rating
Average percentage of total goal attempts which were on target — **46.1**

AGAINST
Goal attempts recorded in League games

	HOME	AWAY	TOTAL	AVE
shots on target	115	170	285	7.5
shots off target	103	131	234	6.2
TOTAL	218	301	519	13.7

Ratio of goals to shots
Average number of shots on target per League goal scored — **5.3**

Accuracy rating
Average percentage of total goal attempts which were on target — **54.9**

GOALS

McCarthy

League	18
FA Cup	3
League Cup	0
Europe	3
Other	0
TOTAL	24

League Average
169
mins between goals

	PLAYER	LGE	FAC	LC	Euro	TOT	AVE
1	McCarthy	18	3	0	3	24	169
2	Derbyshire	5	4	0	0	9	156
3	Nonda	7	0	0	1	8	222
4	Pedersen	6	2	0	0	8	517
5	Bentley	4	0	0	3	7	767
6	Roberts	4	1	0	0	5	257
7	Gallagher	1	1	0	0	2	340
8	Samba	2	0	0	0	2	568
9	Tugay	1	0	0	1	2	2202
10	Savage	0	0	0	2	2	
11	Warnock	1	0	0	0	1	1167
12	Jeffers	0	0	0	1	1	
13	Mokoena	0	1	0	0	1	
14	Neill	0	0	0	1	1	
15	Nelsen	0	0	0	0	1	
	Other	0	0	0	0	0	
	TOTAL	49	12	0	12	73	

PREMIERSHIP CLUBS – BLACKBURN

SQUAD APPEARANCES

Match	1 2 3 4 5	6 7 8 9 10	11 12 13 14 15	16 17 18 19 20	21 22 23 24 25	26 27 28 29 30	31 32 33 34 35	36 37 38 39 40	41 42 43 44 45	46 47 48 49 50	51 52
Venue	A H H A A	H A H H A	A H H A H	A H H A H	A H H A A	H H A A H	A A A A H	A A A H H	H A H H A	H N H A H	A A
Competition	L L L L E	L L E L L	E L W L E	L L L E L	L L E L L	L L L F L	L L F L L	L E F E L	F L F L L	L F L L L	L L
Result	L D L D D	W W W W D	W L L L W	L L D D W	L L W W L	W W W W L	W L W L W	L L D D W	W W W L L	L L W D W	W D

Goalkeepers

Jason Brown
Peter Enckelman
Brad Friedel

Defenders

Bruno Berner
Michael Gray
Stephane Henchoz
Zurab Khizanishvili
Dominic Matteo
James McEveley
Lucas Neill
Ryan Nelsen
Eddie Nolan
Andre Ooijer
Christopher Samba
Andy Todd
Stephen Warnock

Midfielders

David Bentley
David Dunn
Brett Emerton
Aaron Mokoena
M Gamst Pedersen
Sergio Peter
Steven Reid
Robbie Savage
Kerimoglu Tugay

Forwards

Matthew Derbyshire
Paul Gallagher
Francis Jeffers
Shefki Kuqi
Benni McCarthy
Shabani Nonda
Jason Roberts

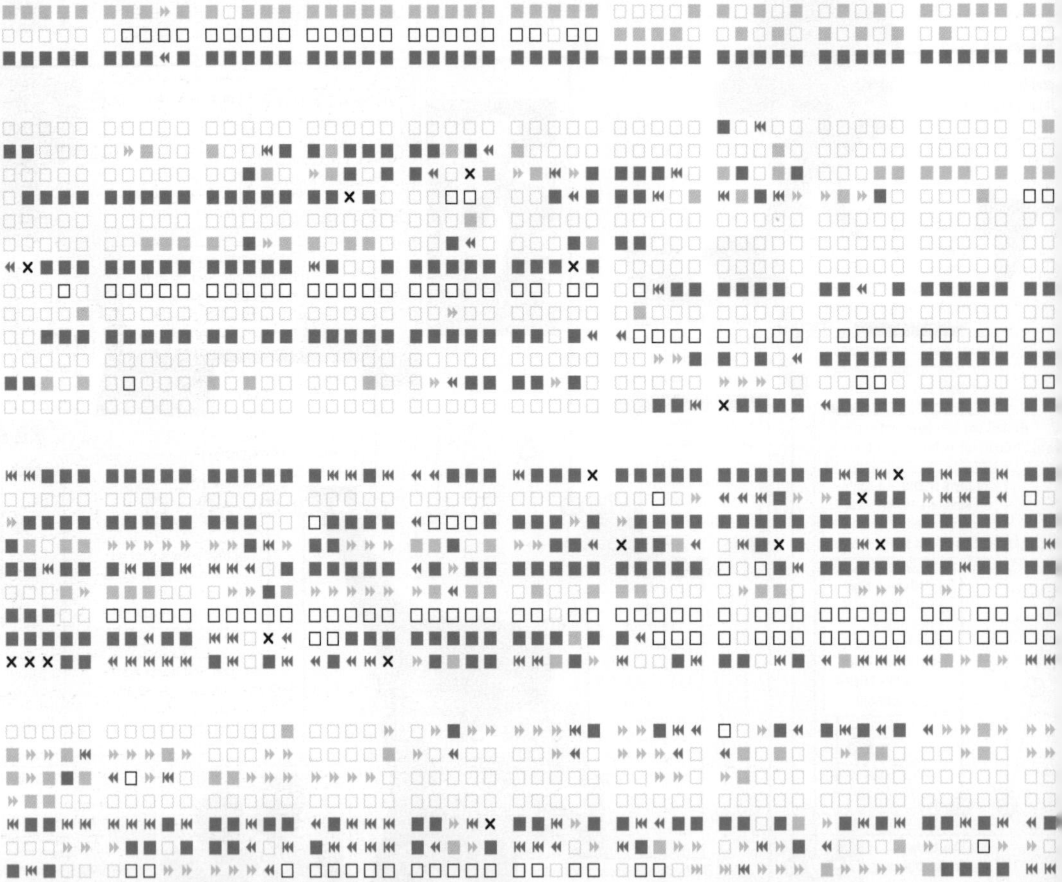

KEY: ■ On all match ◄◄ Subbed or sent off (Counting game) ►► Subbed on from bench (Counting Game) ►► Subbed on and then subbed or sent off (Counting Game) ☐ Not in 16 ☐ Injured
■ On bench ◄◄ Subbed or sent off (playing less than 70 mins) ►► Subbed on (playing less than 70 mins) ►► Subbed on and then subbed or sent off (playing less than 70 min ✗ Suspended

KEY PLAYERS - GOALSCORERS

Benni McCarthy

Goals in the League	18
Goals in all competitions	24
Assists League goals scored by a team mate where the player delivered the final pass	2
Contribution to Attacking Power Average number of minutes between League team goals while on pitch	69
Player Strike Rate Average number of minutes between League goals scored by player	169
Club Strike Rate Average minutes between League goals scored by club	65

	PLAYER	GOALS LGE	GOALS ALL	ASSISTS	POWER	S RATE
1	Benni McCarthy	18	24	2	69	169 mins
2	Shabani Nonda	7	8	1	64	222 mins
3	Morten Gamst Pedersen	6	8	13	60	517 mins
4	David Bentley	4	7	11	61	767 mins

KEY PLAYERS - MIDFIELDERS

Aaron Mokoena

Goals in the League	0
Goals in all competitions	1
Assists League goals scored by a team mate where the player delivered the final pass	0
Defensive Rating Average number of mins between League goals conceded while on the pitch	67
Contribution to Attacking Power Average number of mins between League team goals while on pitch	56
Scoring Difference Defensive Rating minus Contribution to Attacking Power	11

	PLAYER	GOALS LGE	GOALS ALL	ASSISTS	DEF RATE	POWER	SC DIFF
1	Aaron Mokoena	0	1	0	67	56	11 mins
2	David Bentley	4	7	11	71	61	10 mins
3	Brett Emerton	0	0	4	68	61	7 mins
4	Morten Gamst Pedersen	6	8	13	63	60	3 mins

PLAYER APPEARANCES

	AGE (on 01/07/07)	IN NAMED 16	APPEARANCES	COUNTING GAMES	MINUTES ON PITCH	APPEARANCES	MINUTES ON PITCH THIS SEASON		HOME COUNTRY
Goalkeepers									
...son Brown	25	33	1	0	45	1	45	1	Wales
...ter Enckelman	30	4	0	0	0	0	0	-	Finland
...ad Friedel	36	38	38	37	3375	53	4755	-	United States
Defenders									
...uno Berner	29	2	1	1	90	2	157	-	Switzerland
...ichael Gray	32	13	11	9	864	13	1044	-	England
...ephane Henchoz	32	25	12	9	826	16	1149	-	Switzerland
...urab Khizanishvili	25	21	18	17	1567	30	2484	4	Georgia
...ominic Matteo	33	1	0	0	0	0	0	-	Scotland
...mes McEveley	22	9	4	2	235	7	505	-	England
...cas Neill	36	20	20	19	1768	26	2308	3	Australia
...an Nelsen	29	12	12	12	1080	19	1674	1	New Zealand
...die Nolan	18	1	0	0	0	1	63	-	Rep of Ireland
...dre Ooijer	32	20	20	18	1712	27	2342	6	Holland
...ristopher Samba	23	14	14	12	1137	19	1548	2	Congo
...dy Todd	32	10	9	6	611	13	730	-	England
...ephen Warnock	25	13	13	13	1167	20	1782	-	England
Midfielders									
...vid Bentley	22	36	36	34	3069	51	4443	-	England
...vid Dunn	27	11	11	5	591	16	967	-	England
...ett Emerton	32	34	34	31	2929	47	4067	4	Australia
...ron Mokoena	26	33	27	16	1686	40	2600	3	South Africa
... Gamst Pedersen	25	36	36	35	3104	49	4179	4	Norway
...rgio Peter	20	19	9	1	216	16	386	-	Germany
...even Reid	26	3	3	3	270	3	270	2	Rep of Ireland
...bbie Savage	32	21	21	20	1839	27	2292	-	Wales
...rimoglu Tugay	36	33	30	21	2202	40	3019	-	Turkey
Forwards									
...atthew Derbyshire	21	23	22	4	784	30	1332	-	England
...ul Gallagher	22	22	16	0	340	22	578	-	England
...ancis Jeffers	26	13	10	2	356	15	422	-	England
...efki Kuqi	30	3	1	0	9	1	9	4	Finland
...nni McCarthy	29	37	36	34	3049	50	4094	-	South Africa
...abani Nonda	30	27	26	13	1555	36	2131	2	DR Congo
...son Roberts	29	19	18	10	1031	25	1290	-	Grenada

KEY: LEAGUE   ALL COMPS   CAPS (MAY FIFA RANKING)

TEAM OF THE SEASON

FRIEDEL — CG 37, DR 62

NEILL	KHIZANISHVILI	OOIJER	SAMBA*
CG 19, DR 63	CG 17, DR 78	CG 18, DR 65	CG 12, DR 59

EMERTON	MOKOENA	BENTLEY	PEDERSEN
CG 31, SD +7	CG 16, SD +11	CG 34, SD +10	CG 35, SD +3

NONDA — CG 13, AP 64

McCARTHY — CG 34, SR 169

KEY: DR = Defensive Rate, SD = Scoring Difference AP = Attacking Power SR = Strike Rate, CG=Counting games – League games playing at least 70 minutes

TOP POINT EARNERS

Stephen Warnock

Counting Games League games when player was on pitch for at least 70 minutes	**13**
Average points Average League points taken in Counting games	**1.62**
Club Average points Average points taken in League games	**1.37**

	PLAYER	GAMES	PTS
1	Stephen Warnock	13	1.62
2	Robbie Savage	20	1.55
3	David Bentley	34	1.53
4	Ryan Nelsen	12	1.50
5	Christopher Samba	12	1.50
6	Morten Gamst Pedersen	35	1.49
7	Brett Emerton	31	1.48
8	Shabani Nonda	13	1.46
9	Benni McCarthy	34	1.35
10	Andre Ooijer	18	1.33

KEY PLAYERS - DEFENDERS

Zurab Khizanishvili

Goals Conceded in the League Number of League goals conceded while the player was on the pitch	**20**
Goals Conceded in all competitions Total number of goals conceded while the player was on the pitch	**25**
League minutes played Number of minutes played in league matches	**1567**
Clean Sheets In games when the player was on pitch for at least 70 minutes	**4**
Defensive Rating Average number of mins between League goals conceded while on the pitch	**78**
Club Defensive Rating Average number of mins between League goals conceded by the club this season	**63**

	PLAYER	CON LGE	CON ALL	MINS	C SHEETS	DEF RATE
1	Zurab Khizanishvili	20	25	1567	4	78 mins
2	Andre Ooijer	26	30	1712	4	65 mins
3	Lucas Neill	28	33	1768	5	63 mins
4	Christopher Samba	19	21	1137	1	59 mins

KEY GOALKEEPER

Brad Friedel

Goals Conceded in the League Number of League goals conceded while the player was on the pitch	**54**
Goals Conceded in all competitions Total number of goals conceded while the player was on the pitch	**65**
League minutes played Number of minutes played in league matches	**3375**
Clean Sheets In games when the player was on pitch for at least 70 minutes	**8**
Goals to Shots Ratio The average number of shots on target per each League goal conceded	**5.28**
Defensive Rating Ave mins between League goals conceded while on the pitch	**62**

BOOKINGS

Stephane Henchoz

League Yellow	4
League Red	1
All competitions Yellow	4
All competitions Red	1

League Average 165 mins between cards

	PLAYER	LEAGUE		TOTAL		AVE
		4Y	1R	4Y	1R	
1	S. Henchoz	4Y	1R	4Y	1R	165
2	Lucas Neill	8	1	8	1	196
3	Robbie Savage	8	0	9	0	229
4	Jason Roberts	3	1	3	1	257
5	Z. Khizanishvili	6	0	8	0	261
6	Aaron Mokoena	6	0	11	1	281
7	David Dunn	2	0	4	0	295
8	Andy Todd	2	0	3	0	305
9	C. Samba	3	0	3	0	379
10	Benni McCarthy	8	0	10	0	381
11	Stephen Warnock	2	1	4	1	389
12	David Bentley	6	1	11	1	438
13	Kerimoglu Tugay	3	1	5	1	550
14	Andre Ooijer	3	0	6	0	570
15	Brett Emerton	5	0	7	0	585
	Other	7	0	16	0	
	TOTAL	**76**	**6**	**113**	**7**	

ASTON VILLA

Gabriel Agbonlahor went from converted winger to fully fledged striker under Martin O'Neill's guidance. A Strike Rate of a goal every 369 minutes is well below what's needed in a top ten Premiership side but the youngster started and ended strongly, mirroring his club's season. **Luke Moore** hit four goals at an average of one every 160 minutes and could form a strong partnership with **John Carew**. New skipper **Gareth Barry** weighed in with eight goals including five penalties converted from six.

Thomas Sorensen had a top five Defensive Rating of a goal conceded every 106 minutes and his record of saving 6.13 Shots On Target per goal let in was the fourth best. **Phil Bardsley** contributed to a nine-match unbeaten run at the end of the season to top the Defensive Rankings. Home attendance rose 2,000.

NICKNAME: THE VILLANS

KEY: ☐ Won ☐ Drawn ☐ Lost

1	prem	Arsenal	A	D	1-1	Mellberg 53
2	prem	Reading	H	W	2-1	Angel 33 pen, Barry 62
3	prem	Newcastle	H	W	2-0	L.Moore 5, Angel 38
4	prem	West Ham	A	D	1-1	Ridgewell 4
5	prem	Watford	A	D	0-0	
6	ccr2	Scunthorpe	A	W	2-1	Angel 42, 64
7	prem	Charlton	H	W	2-0	Agbonlahor 35, L.Moore 62
8	prem	Chelsea	A	D	1-1	Agbonlahor 45
9	prem	Tottenham	H	D	1-1	Barry 81
10	prem	Fulham	H	D	1-1	Barry 26 pen
11	ccr3	Leicester	A	W	3-2	Angel 5, Barry 45 pen, Agbonlahor 119
12	prem	Liverpool	A	L	1-3	Agbonlahor 56
13	prem	Blackburn	H	W	2-0	Barry 39 pen, Angel 50
14	ccr4	Chelsea	A	L	0-4	
15	prem	Everton	A	W	1-0	Sutton 42
16	prem	Wigan	A	D	0-0	
17	prem	Middlesbrough	H	D	1-1	Barry 45 pen
18	prem	Man City	H	L	1-3	McCann 66
19	prem	Portsmouth	A	D	2-2	Barry 37 pen, Angel 82
20	prem	Sheff Utd	A	D	2-2	Petrov 2, Baros 65
21	prem	Bolton	H	L	0-1	
22	prem	Man Utd	H	L	0-3	
23	prem	Tottenham	A	L	1-2	Barry 81
24	prem	Charlton	A	L	1-2	Barry 39 pen
25	prem	Chelsea	H	D	0-0	
26	facr3	Man Utd	A	L	1-2	Baros 74
27	prem	Man Utd	A	L	1-3	Agbonlahor 52
28	prem	Watford	H	W	2-0	Mahon 86 og, Agbonlahor 90
29	prem	Newcastle	A	L	1-3	Young 25
30	prem	West Ham	H	W	1-0	Carew 36
31	prem	Reading	A	L	0-2	
32	prem	Fulham	A	D	1-1	Carew 21
33	prem	Arsenal	H	L	0-1	
34	prem	Liverpool	H	D	0-0	
35	prem	Everton	H	D	1-1	Agbonlahor 83
36	prem	Blackburn	A	W	2-1	Berger 34, Agbonlahor 73
37	prem	Wigan	H	D	1-1	Agbonlahor 50
38	prem	Middlesbrough	A	W	3-1	Gardner 45, L.Moore 70, Petrov 77
39	prem	Portsmouth	H	D	0-0	
40	prem	Man City	A	W	2-0	Carew 24, Maloney 75
41	prem	Sheff Utd	H	W	3-0	Agbonlahor 25, Young 42, Berger 59
42	prem	Bolton	A	D	2-2	Gardner 37, L.Moore 81

O'Neill works his magic as a Mellberg header leaves Arsenal chasing the game to claim a point

Angel thrives on width as Lerner sees his new team hit form with Agbonlahor and Moore flying at Newcastle

Petrov sparkles on his debut and goes so-close to a winner after Hammers level Ridgewell's opener

LEAGUE POSITION: 1st, 2nd, 3rd, 4th, 5th, 6th, 7th, 8th, 9th, 10th, 11th, 12th, 13th, 14th, 15th, 16th, 17th, 18th, 19th, 20th

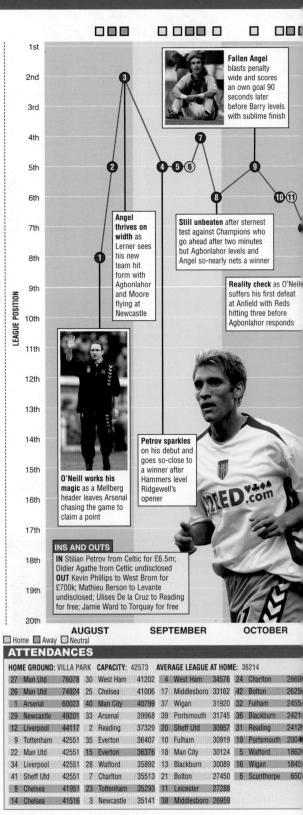

Fallen Angel blasts penalty wide and scores an own goal 90 seconds later before Barry levels with sublime finish

Still unbeaten after sternest test against Champions who go ahead after two minutes but Agbonlahor levels and Angel so-nearly nets a winner

Reality check as O'Neill suffers his first defeat at Anfield with Reds hitting three before Agbonlahor responds

☐ Home ☐ Away ☐ Neutral

AUGUST SEPTEMBER OCTOBER

INS AND OUTS
IN Stilian Petrov from Celtic for £6.5m; Didier Agathe from Celtic undisclosed **OUT** Kevin Phillips to West Brom for £700k; Mathieu Berson to Levante undisclosed; Ulises De la Cruz to Reading for free; Jamie Ward to Torquay for free

ATTENDANCES

HOME GROUND: VILLA PARK **CAPACITY:** 42573 **AVERAGE LEAGUE AT HOME:** 36214

27	Man Utd	76078	30	West Ham	41202	4	West Ham	34576	24	Charlton	2669
26	Man Utd	74924	25	Chelsea	41006	17	Middlesboro	33162	42	Bolton	2625
1	Arsenal	60023	40	Man City	40799	37	Wigan	31920	32	Fulham	2455
29	Newcastle	49201	33	Arsenal	39968	39	Portsmouth	31745	36	Blackburn	2421
12	Liverpool	44117	2	Reading	37329	20	Sheff Utd	30957	31	Reading	2412
9	Tottenham	42551	35	Everton	36407	10	Fulham	30919	19	Portsmouth	2004
22	Man Utd	42551	15	Everton	36376	18	Man City	30124	5	Watford	1862
34	Liverpool	42551	28	Watford	35892	13	Blackburn	30089	16	Wigan	1845
41	Sheff Utd	42551	7	Charlton	35513	21	Bolton	27450	6	Scunthorpe	650
8	Chelsea	41951	23	Tottenham	35293	11	Leicester	27288			
14	Chelsea	41516	3	Newcastle	35141	38	Middlesboro	26959			

O'Neill unleashes Agbonlahor's talent

Final Position: 11th

KEY: ● League ○ Champions Lge ○ UEFA Cup ● FA Cup ○ League Cup ○ Other

Barry's fifth penalty flies in before his handball gives Pompey a spot-kick lead, only for sub Angel to level

Cruel for Kiraly as United strike in injury time with a shot that squirms under his body

Lucky Osbourne sees wayward header hit his own post as Sorensen keeps out Wigan

Barry's back injury leaves door open and Chelsea steam through to hit four without reply

Sutton starts against his old side and earns a dubious penalty for Barry to score before Angel nets his sixth of the season

Ron Saunders invited back after 22 years to witness United's flowing win

Champions held again as five man midfield 'stops the rot' and gains a point

New signings click on home debut with Young setting up Carew and Barry celebrates England call-up with fine game

Agbonlahor's cool finish averts the boos, which came at halftime, by levelling against Everton

Berger dances through Blades' defence for one of the best worked goals of the season to delight O'Neill

Careless Sorensen gifts Boro the lead but Gardner levels with first ever goal and Moore scores on his return before Petrov seals it

Nine games unbeaten is a strong end to the season as youngsters Gardner and Moore level to take a point from Bolton

Lucky deflection earns Arsenal the points as Sorenson sees a poor shot career in off Diaby's heel

Unlucky at Reading as chances go begging with Hahnemann saving from Carew and debutant Maloney

Eight without a win as Barry takes the battle to Spurs who hang on

"Excellent" Carew scores one and comes closest to winning it but Premiership draw specialists end up level

Debutants deserve better as Young scores and Carew heads into the net but sees it wrongly disallowed as Newcastle claim win

Double penalty! Two Liverpool defenders foul Petrov in the six yard box but ref waves play on

James draws record-breaking blank as Gardner and Carew are frustrated by the Pompey keeper's clean sheet

Berger beefs up attack with goal and assist to gain a well-deserved win at Blackburn despite Barry's penalty miss

INS AND OUTS

IN Ashley Young from Watford for £9.65m; John Carew from Lyon in swap for Milan Baros; Shaun Maloney from Celtic for £1m; Phil Bardsley from Man Utd on loan
OUT Milan Baros to Lyon in swap for Carew; Eric Djemba-Djemba to Burnley on loan; Lee Hendrie to Stoke on loan; Peter Whittingham to Cardiff for £350k

MONTH BY MONTH POINTS TALLY

AUGUST	7	78%
SEPTEMBER	6	50%
OCTOBER	2	22%
NOVEMBER	8	53%
DECEMBER	2	11%
JANUARY	4	33%
FEBRUARY	3	50%
MARCH	2	22%
APRIL	12	67%
MAY	4	67%

NOVEMBER   DECEMBER   JANUARY   FEBRUARY   MARCH   APRIL   MAY

GOAL ATTEMPTS

FOR — Goal attempts recorded in League games

	HOME	AWAY	TOTAL	AVE
shots on target	111	105	216	5.7
shots off target	125	86	211	5.6
TOTAL	236	191	427	11.2

Ratio of goals to shots — Average number of shots on target per League goal scored	5.0
Accuracy rating — Average percentage of total goal attempts which were on target	50.6

AGAINST — Goal attempts recorded in League games

	HOME	AWAY	TOTAL	AVE
shots on target	87	133	220	5.8
shots off target	91	149	240	6.3
TOTAL	178	282	460	12.1

Ratio of goals to shots — Average number of shots on target per League goal scored	5.4
Accuracy rating — Average percentage of total goal attempts which were on target	47.8

GOALS

Agbonlahor

League	9
FA Cup	0
League Cup	1
Europe	0
Other	0
TOTAL	10

League Average	369 mins between goals

	PLAYER	LGE	FAC	LC	Euro	TOT	AVE
1	Agbonlahor	9	0	1	0	10	369
2	Barry	8	0	1	0	9	389
3	Angel	4	0	3	0	7	373
4	Moore	4	0	0	0	4	160
5	Carew	3	0	0	0	3	300
6	Berger	2	0	0	0	2	280
7	Gardner	2	0	0	0	2	485
8	Young	2	0	0	0	2	489
9	Baros	1	1	0	0	2	875
10	Petrov	2	0	0	0	2	1317
11	Maloney	1	0	0	0	1	450
12	Sutton	1	0	0	0	1	591
13	Ridgewell	1	0	0	0	1	1766
14	McCann	1	0	0	0	1	2421
15	Mellberg	1	0	0	0	1	3375
	Other	0	0	0	0	0	
	TOTAL	42	1	5	0	48	

SQUAD APPEARANCES

Match	1	2	3	4	5	6	7	8	9	10	11	12	13	14	15	16	17	18	19	20	21	22	23	24	25	26	27	28	29	30	31	32	33	34	35	36	37	38	39	40	41
Venue	A	H	H	A	A	A	H	A	H	H	A	A	H	A	A	A	H	H	A	A	H	H	A	A	H	A	A	H	A	H	A	A	H	H	H	A	H	A	H	A	H
Competition	L	L	L	L	L	W	L	L	L	L	W	L	L	L	W	L	L	L	L	L	L	L	L	L	L	F	L	L	L	L	L	L	L	L	L	L	L	L	L	L	L
Result	D	W	W	D	D	W	W	D	D	D	W	L	W	L	W	D	D	L	D	D	L	L	L	L	D	L	L	W	L	W	L	D	L	D	D	W	D	W	D	W	W

Goalkeepers
Gabor Kiraly
Robert Olejnik
Thomas Sorensen
Stuart Taylor

Defenders
Didier Agathe
Phillip Bardsley
Wilfred Bouma
Gary Cahill
Mark Delaney
Aaron Hughes
Martin Laursen
Olof Mellberg
Liam Ridgewell
Jlloyd Samuel

Midfielders
Gareth Barry
Patrik Berger
Steven Davis
Eric Djemba-Djemba
Craig Gardner
Lee Hendrie
Gavin McCann
Isaiah Osbourne
Stilian Petrov
Peter Whittingham

Forwards
Gabriel Agbonlahor
Juan Pablo Angel
Milan Baros
John Alieu Carew
Shaun Maloney
Luke Moore
Kevin Phillips
Chris Sutton
Ashley Young

KEY: ■ On all match ◀◀ Subbed or sent off (Counting game) ▶▶ Subbed on from bench (Counting Game) ▶▶ Subbed on and then subbed or sent off (Counting Game) □ Not in 16 □ Injured
■ On bench ◀◀ Subbed or sent off (playing less than 70 mins) ▶▶ Subbed on (playing less than 70 mins) ▶▶ Subbed on and then subbed or sent off (playing less than 70 min ✕ Suspended

KEY PLAYERS - GOALSCORERS

John Alieu Carew

Goals in the League	3
Goals in all competitions	3
Assists — League goals scored by a team mate where the player delivered the final pass	3
Contribution to Attacking Power — Average number of minutes between League team goals while on pitch	90
Player Strike Rate — Average number of minutes between League goals scored by player	300
Club Strike Rate — Average minutes between League goals scored by club	79

	PLAYER	GOALS LGE	GOALS ALL	ASSISTS	POWER	S RATE
1	John Alieu Carew	3	3	3	90	300 mins
2	Gabriel Agbonlahor	9	10	6	79	369 mins
3	Juan Pablo Angel	4	7	1	82	373 mins
4	Gareth Barry	8	9	4	77	389 mins

KEY PLAYERS - MIDFIELDERS

Steven Davis

Goals in the League	0
Goals in all competitions	0
Assists — League goals scored by a team mate where the player delivered the final pass	1
Defensive Rating — Average number of mins between League goals conceded while on the pitch	86
Contribution to Attacking Power — Average number of minutes between League team goals while on pitch	78
Scoring Difference — Defensive Rating minus Contribution to Attacking Power	8

	PLAYER	GOALS LGE	GOALS ALL	ASSISTS	DEF RATE	POWER	SC DIFF
1	Steven Davis	0	0	1	86	78	8 mins
2	Gareth Barry	8	9	4	82	77	5 mins
3	Stilian Petrov	2	2	3	84	90	-6 mins
4	Gavin McCann	1	1	2	80	89	-9 mins

PLAYER APPEARANCES

	AGE (on 01/07/07)	IN NAMED 16	APPEARANCES	COUNTING GAMES	MINUTES ON PITCH	APPEARANCES	MINUTES ON PITCH THIS SEASON		HOME COUNTRY
Goalkeepers									
Gabor Kiraly	31	5	5	5	450	6	540	4	Hungary
Robert Olejnik	20	9	0	0	0	0	0	-	Austria
Thomas Sorensen	31	29	29	28	2544	31	2724	9	Denmark
Stuart Taylor	26	33	6	4	426	7	546	-	England
Defenders									
Didier Agathe	31	5	5	0	171	6	201	-	France
Phillip Bardsley	22	13	13	13	1145	13	1145	-	England
Wilfred Bouma	29	30	25	19	1973	28	2167	4	Holland
Gary Cahill	21	25	20	19	1745	21	1835	-	England
Mark Delaney	31	1	0	0	0	0	0	2	Wales
Aaron Hughes	27	29	19	13	1292	23	1682	8	N Ireland
Martin Laursen	29	20	14	11	1054	15	1099	1	Denmark
Olof Mellberg	29	38	38	37	3375	41	3675	5	Sweden
Liam Ridgewell	22	26	21	19	1766	25	2111	-	England
Lloyd Samuel	26	5	4	1	205	5	230	-	England
Midfielders									
Gareth Barry	26	35	35	34	3119	39	3464	1	England
Patrik Berger	33	20	13	5	561	14	606	-	Czech Republic
Steven Davis	22	35	28	17	1652	31	1902	7	N Ireland
Eric Djemba-Djemba	26	3	1	0	2	1	2	-	Cameroon
Craig Gardner	20	17	13	10	971	13	971	-	England
Lee Hendrie	30	4	1	0	8	1	8	-	England
Gavin McCann	29	31	30	26	2421	33	2643	-	England
Isaiah Osbourne	19	12	11	5	647	13	843	-	England
Stilian Petrov	27	30	30	29	2634	34	2999	5	Bulgaria
Peter Whittingham	22	9	3	1	172	4	220	-	England
Forwards									
Gabriel Agbonlahor	20	38	38	37	3325	42	3715	-	Englandi
Juan Pablo Angel	31	26	23	14	1493	27	1845	-	Colombia
Milan Baros	25	21	17	7	875	21	1020	7	Czech Republic
John Alieu Carew	27	11	11	11	902	11	902	4	Norway
Shaun Maloney	24	10	8	3	450	8	450	4	Scotland
Luke Moore	21	15	13	6	642	14	710	-	England
Kevin Phillips	33	1	0	0	0	0	0	-	England
Chris Sutton	34	8	8	6	591	9	646	-	England
Ashley Young	21	13	13	10	978	13	978	-	England

KEY: LEAGUE ... ALL COMPS ... CAPS ... (MAY FIFA RANKING)

TEAM OF THE SEASON

SORENSEN — CG 28 | DR 106

BARDSLEY — CG 13 | DR 104

MELLBERG — CG 37 | DR 86

LAURSEN* — CG 11 | DR 131

BOUMA — CG 19 | DR 82

DAVIS — CG 17 | SD +8

McCANN — CG 26 | SD -9

BARRY — CG 34 | SD +5

PETROV — CG 29 | SD -6

AGBONLAHOR — CG 37 | AP 79

CAREW* — CG 11 | SR 300

KEY: DR = Defensive Rate, SD = Scoring Difference AP = Attacking Power SR = Strike Rate, CG=Counting games – League games playing at least 70 minutes

TOP POINT EARNERS

Juan Pablo Angel

Counting Games — League games when player was on pitch for at least 70 minutes	14
Average points — Average League points taken in Counting games	1.79
Club Average points — Average points taken in League games	1.32

	PLAYER	GAMES	PTS
1	Juan Pablo Angel	14	1.79
2	Wilfred Bouma	19	1.68
3	Thomas Sorensen	28	1.61
4	Phillip Bardsley	13	1.54
5	Aaron Hughes	13	1.54
6	Olof Mellberg	37	1.35
7	Gabriel Agbonlahor	37	1.32
8	Gareth Barry	35	1.29
9	Steven Davis	17	1.24
10	Gavin McCann	26	1.23

KEY PLAYERS - DEFENDERS

Martin Laursen

Goals Conceded in the League — Number of League goals conceded while the player was on the pitch	8
Goals Conceded in all competitions — Total number of goals conceded while the player was on the pitch	9
League minutes played — Number of minutes played in league matches	1054
Clean Sheets — In games when the player was on pitch for at least 70 minutes	5
Defensive Rating — Average number of mins between League goals conceded while on the pitch	131
Club Defensive Rating — Average number of mins between League goals conceded by the club this season	83

	PLAYER	CON LGE	CON ALL	MINS	C SHEETS	DEF RATE
1	Martin Laursen	8	9	1054	5	131 mins
2	Phillip Bardsley	11	11	1145	5	104 mins
3	Olof Mellberg	39	46	3375	13	86 mins
4	Wilfred Bouma	24	30	1973	10	82 mins

KEY GOALKEEPER

Thomas Sorensen

Goals Conceded in the League — Number of League goals conceded while the player was on the pitch	24
Goals Conceded in all competitions — Total number of goals conceded while the player was on the pitch	29
League minutes played — Number of minutes played in league matches	2544
Clean Sheets — In games when the player was on pitch for at least 70 minutes	12
Goals to Shots Ratio — The average number of shots on target per each League goal conceded	6.13
Defensive Rating — Ave mins between League goals conceded while on the pitch	106

BOOKINGS

Gavin McCann

League Yellow	9
League Red	0
All competitions Yellow	10
All competitions Red	0

League Average 269 mins between cards

	PLAYER	LEAGUE		TOTAL		AVE
1	Gavin McCann	9Y	0R	10Y	0R	269
2	Chris Sutton	2	0	2	0	295
3	Gareth Barry	7	1	8	1	389
4	Olof Mellberg	8	0	9	0	421
5	John Alieu Carew	2	0	2	0	451
6	Gary Cahill	3	0	4	0	581
7	Isaiah Osbourne	1	0	1	0	647
8	Stilian Petrov	4	0	4	0	658
9	Juan Pablo Angel	2	0	2	0	746
10	Milan Baros	1	0	1	0	875
11	Craig Gardner	1	0	1	0	971
12	Ashley Young	1	0	1	0	978
13	Phillip Bardsley	1	0	1	0	1145
14	Steven Davis	1	0	1	0	1652
15	G. Agbonlahor	2	0	2	0	1662
	Other	1	0	2	0	
	TOTAL	**46**	**1**	**51**	**1**	

MIDDLESBROUGH

Gareth Southgate inherited **Mark Viduka** in his debut management season and the Aussie struck 14 goals at the fourth best Strike Rate in the division to lift Boro to mid-table respectability. **Ayegbeni Yakubu** powered in another 12 but made harder work of it.

In midfield **Stuart Downing** laid on 13 Assists, the third highest total, while **Julio Arca** looked a smart acquisition by Southgate, helping to prompt the attack and having both the club's best Scoring Difference and the best points average, 1.87 – Champions League form! **Lee Cattermole** picked up ten bookings.

Jonathan Woodgate was another important buy and always seems to deliver the best Defensive Rating at his clubs. A mention too for **Emanuel Pogatetz**, switched to centre back and making 35 appearances there.

NICKNAME: BORO   KEY: ☐ Won ☐ Drawn ■ Lost

#	comp	Opponent	H/A	Result	Scorers
1	prem	Reading	A L	2-3	Downing 11, Yakubu 21
2	prem	Chelsea	H W	2-1	Pogatetz 80, Viduka 90
3	prem	Portsmouth	H L	0-4	
4	prem	Arsenal	A D	1-1	Morrison 22
5	prem	Bolton	A D	0-0	
6	ccr2	Notts County	H L	0-1	
7	prem	Blackburn	H L	0-1	
8	prem	Sheff Utd	A L	1-2	Yakubu 49
9	prem	Everton	H W	2-1	Yakubu 27 pen, Viduka 71
10	prem	Newcastle	H W	1-0	Yakubu 84
11	prem	Man City	A L	0-1	
12	prem	Watford	A L	0-2	
13	prem	West Ham	H W	1-0	Maccarone 74
14	prem	Liverpool	H D	0-0	
15	prem	Aston Villa	A D	1-1	Christie 43
16	prem	Man Utd	H L	1-2	Morrison 66
17	prem	Tottenham	A L	1-2	Huth 79
18	prem	Wigan	H D	1-1	Yakubu 67
19	prem	Fulham	A L	1-2	Viduka 74
20	prem	Charlton	H W	2-0	Yakubu 29, Arca 52
21	prem	Everton	A D	0-0	
22	prem	Blackburn	A L	1-2	Yakubu 61 pen
23	prem	Sheff Utd	H W	3-1	Viduka 36, Yakubu 69, 76 pen
24	facr3	Hull City	A D	1-1	Viduka 73
25	prem	Charlton	A W	3-1	Cattermole 45, Arca 63, Yakubu 68
26	facr3r	Hull City	H W	4-3	Hines 32, Viduka 49, 64, Yakubu 57 pen
27	prem	Bolton	H W	5-1	Speed 6 og, Xavier 10, Viduka 23, 84, Downing 43
28	facr4	Bristol City	A D	2-2	Yakubu 4, Christie 23
29	prem	Portsmouth	A D	0-0	
30	prem	Arsenal	H D	1-1	Yakubu 63 pen
31	prem	Chelsea	A L	0-3	
32	facr4r	Bristol City	H W	5-4*	Viduka 69, Yakubu 102 (*on penalties)
33	facr5	West Brom	H D	2-2	Arca 29, Yakubu 43 pen
34	prem	Reading	H W	2-1	Viduka 7, Yakubu 69
35	facr5r	West Brom	A W	5-4*	Viduka 63 (*on penalties)
36	prem	Newcastle	A D	0-0	
37	facqf	Man Utd	H D	2-2	Cattermole 45, Boateng 47
38	prem	Man City	H L	0-2	
39	facqfr	Man Utd	A L	0-1	
40	prem	West Ham	A L	0-2	
41	prem	Watford	H W	4-1	Viduka 5, 75, Boateng 27, Rochemback 79
42	prem	Aston Villa	H L	1-3	Rochemback 13
43	prem	Liverpool	A L	0-2	
44	prem	Man Utd	A D	1-1	Viduka 45
45	prem	Tottenham	H L	2-3	Viduka 66, Pogatetz 89
46	prem	Wigan	A W	1-0	Viduka 29
47	prem	Fulham	H W	3-1	Viduka 34, 47, Wheater 45

Viduka claims Champions' scalp with last minute strike to complete a win begun by Pogatetz's headed equaliser in re-run of last season's shock

Woodgate's great debut erases spectre of 7-0 defeat by Arsenal last season as Morrison goal earns a draw

Powerful header from Yakubu earns North East bragging rights but Newcastle rue missed chances

Woodgate profligate with short-range volley and Yakubu fires open goal chance against the post before Blades cut through late on

Two-goal start evaporates before halftime as Southgate sees management debut sunk by Reading's fight back

Yakubu squanders chance to beat Bolton in the last minute as Euell puts him clear and he fires wide

Yakubu on the spot with initial penalty but sees second saved before Viduka makes sure of Everton's first defeat

LEAGUE POSITION: 1st, 2nd, 3rd, 4th, 5th, 6th, 7th, 8th, 9th, 10th, 11th, 12th, 13th, 14th, 15th, 16th, 17th, 18th, 19th, 20th

AUGUST   SEPTEMBER   OCTOBER

☐ Home ■ Away ☐ Neutral

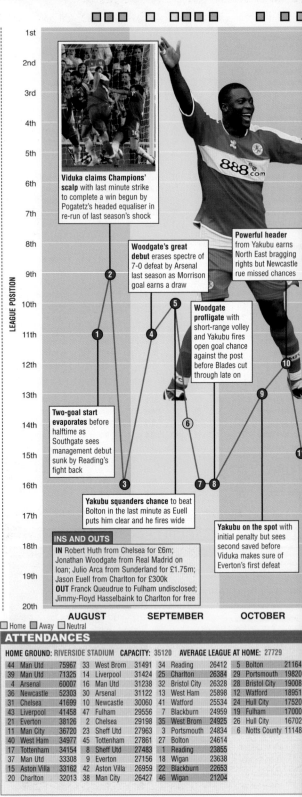

INS AND OUTS

IN Robert Huth from Chelsea for £6m; Jonathan Woodgate from Real Madrid on loan; Julio Arca from Sunderland for £1.75m; Jason Euell from Charlton for £300k
OUT Franck Queudrue to Fulham undisclosed; Jimmy-Floyd Hasselbaink to Charlton for free

ATTENDANCES

HOME GROUND: RIVERSIDE STADIUM   CAPACITY: 35120   AVERAGE LEAGUE AT HOME: 27729

#	Opponent	Att	#	Opponent	Att	#	Opponent	Att	#	Opponent	Att
44	Man Utd	75967	33	West Brom	31491	34	Reading	26412	5	Bolton	21164
39	Man Utd	71325	14	Liverpool	31424	25	Charlton	26384	29	Portsmouth	19820
4	Arsenal	60007	16	Man Utd	31238	32	Bristol City	26328	28	Bristol City	19008
36	Newcastle	52303	30	Arsenal	31122	18	West Ham	25898	12	Watford	18951
31	Chelsea	41699	10	Newcastle	30060	41	Watford	25534	24	Hull City	17520
43	Liverpool	41458	47	Fulham	29556	7	Blackburn	24959	19	Fulham	17000
21	Everton	38126	2	Chelsea	29198	35	West Brom	24925	26	Hull City	16702
11	Man City	36720	23	Sheff Utd	27963	3	Portsmouth	24834	6	Notts County	11148
40	West Ham	34977	45	Tottenham	27861	27	Bolton	24614			
17	Tottenham	34154	8	Sheff Utd	27483	1	Reading	23855			
37	Man Utd	33308	9	Everton	27156	18	Wigan	23638			
15	Aston Villa	33162	42	Aston Villa	26959	22	Blackburn	22653			
20	Charlton	32013	38	Man City	26427	46	Wigan	21204			

iduka salvages Southgate's debut

Final Position: 12th

● League ● Champions Lge ● UEFA Cup ● FA Cup ○ League Cup ● Other

Super-sub Maccarone changes the game within five minutes of joining the action with a winner from a tight angle

Downing on fire; setting up the first three goals and scoring the fourth as Bolton get a thumping

Woodgate in his pomp at Portsmouth as goalless draw shows defensive backbone

Yakubu kicks air instead of connecting to score a simple rebound from Euell's header in goalless draw with Liverpool

Southgate angry with players' attitude after Villa storm back from soft Rochemback goal

"I was offside" admits Christie as returning forward scores first of the season but Villa level from the spot

Deflections gift two goals to Hammers but Southgate says he didn't see poor performance coming and Downing is booed for England association

Downing loses his feet and wins a game as miss-kick fools Wigan defence and falls to Viduka to guarantee safety

Penalties needed again as FA Cup run stretches to ten hours of playing time before Boateng converts pressure kick

"We switched off again" moans Southgate as Huth levels only for Spurs to regain the lead moments later and Boateng sees red

Viduka brace take him to 14 league goals for the season and into new contract talks

Morrison frustration with show-boating Ronaldo leads to red after United winger earns penalty winner to end cup run

Schwarzer non-plussed as Ronaldo wins penalty without contact, then Morrison's sweet strike is trumped by United

So cool Yakubu sends Lehmann the wrong way after winning penalty but Henry levels for ten men

Newcastle's regret that they didn't secure Woodgate's services is brought home with classy display at St James' Park

Johnson's jinks bring the best out of Viduka as Watford are slammed with Aussie striker picking up two goals and an assist

Viduka's headed flick breathes life into pursuit of Spurs but Robinson's saves and breakaway third goal claim points

Hines scoring debut with first goal of seven in replay thriller but Viduka brace finally breaches Hull resistance

Southgate anger at Drogba challenges but Viduka leads list of missed chances as Champs take revenge

Ref deaf to Dong-Gook penalty claim but Pogatetz's defensive heroics dent United's title hopes

IN AND OUTS

IN Lee Dong-Gook from Pohang Steelers for free

OUT Ugo Ehiogu to Rangers for free; Ray Parlour released (joined Hull in February); Massimo Maccarone to Siena for free

MONTH BY MONTH POINTS TALLY

Month	Points	%
AUGUST	3	33%
SEPTEMBER	2	17%
OCTOBER	6	67%
NOVEMBER	5	42%
DECEMBER	5	24%
JANUARY	10	83%
FEBRUARY	4	44%
MARCH	1	11%
APRIL	4	27%
MAY	6	100%

NOVEMBER   DECEMBER   JANUARY   FEBRUARY   MARCH   APRIL   MAY

GOAL ATTEMPTS

FOR
Goal attempts recorded in League games

	HOME	AWAY	TOTAL	AVE
ots on target	124	70	194	5.1
ots off target	140	82	222	5.8
TAL	264	152	416	10.9

Ratio of goals to shots
Average number of shots on target per League goal scored: **4.4**

Accuracy rating
Average percentage of total goal attempts which were on target: **46.6**

AGAINST
Goal attempts recorded in League games

	HOME	AWAY	TOTAL	AVE
shots on target	109	131	240	6.3
shots off target	92	170	262	6.9
TOTAL	201	301	502	13.2

Ratio of goals to shots
Average number of shots on target per League goal scored: **4.9**

Accuracy rating
Average percentage of total goal attempts which were on target: **47.8**

GOALS

Viduka

League	14
FA Cup	5
League Cup	0
Europe	0
Other	0
TOTAL	19

League Average 148 mins between goals

	PLAYER	LGE	FAC	LC	Euro	TOT	AVE
1	Viduka	14	5	0	0	19	148
2	Yakubu	12	4	0	0	16	263
3	Arca	2	1	0	0	3	769
4	Christie	1	1	0	0	2	371
5	Morrison	2	0	0	0	2	761
6	Rochemback	2	0	0	0	2	768
7	Pogatetz	2	0	0	0	2	1501
8	Downing	2	0	0	0	2	1518
9	Cattermole	1	1	0	0	2	1960
10	Boateng	1	1	0	0	2	3017
11	Wheater	1	0	0	0	1	93
12	Maccarone	1	0	0	0	1	180
13	Huth	1	0	0	0	1	794
14	Xavier	1	0	0	0	1	1257
15	Hines	0	1	0	0	1	
	Other	0	0	0	0	0	
	TOTAL	43	14	0	0	57	

PREMIERSHIP CLUBS – MIDDLESBROUGH

SQUAD APPEARANCES

Match	1 2 3 4 5	6 7 8 9 10	11 12 13 14 15	16 17 18 19 20	21 22 23 24 25	26 27 28 29 30	31 32 33 34 35	36 37 38 39 40	41 42 43 44 45
Venue	A H H A A	H H A H H	A A H H A	H A H A H	A A H A A	H H A A H	A H H H A	A H H A A	H H A A H
Competition	L L L L L	W L L L L	L L L L L	L L L L L	L L L F L	F L F L L	L F F L F	L F L F L	L L L L L
Result	L W L D D	L L L W W	L L W D D	L L D L W	D L W D W	W W D D D	L W D W W	D D L L L	W L L D L

Goalkeepers
Brad Jones
Mark Schwarzer
Ross Turnbull

Defenders
Matthew Bates
Andrew Davies
Ugo Ehiogu
Seb Hines
Robert Huth
Anthony McMahon
Stuart Parnaby
Emanuel Pogatetz
Chris Riggott
Andrew Taylor
David Wheater
Jonathan Woodgate
Abel Xavier

Midfielders
Julio Arca
George Boateng
Lee Cattermole
Stewart Downing
Adam Johnson
Gaizka Mendieta
James Morrison
Fabio Rochemback

Forwards
Malcolm Christie
Jason Euell
Danny Graham
Lee Dong-Gook
Massimo Maccarone
Mark Viduka
Ayegbeni Yakubu

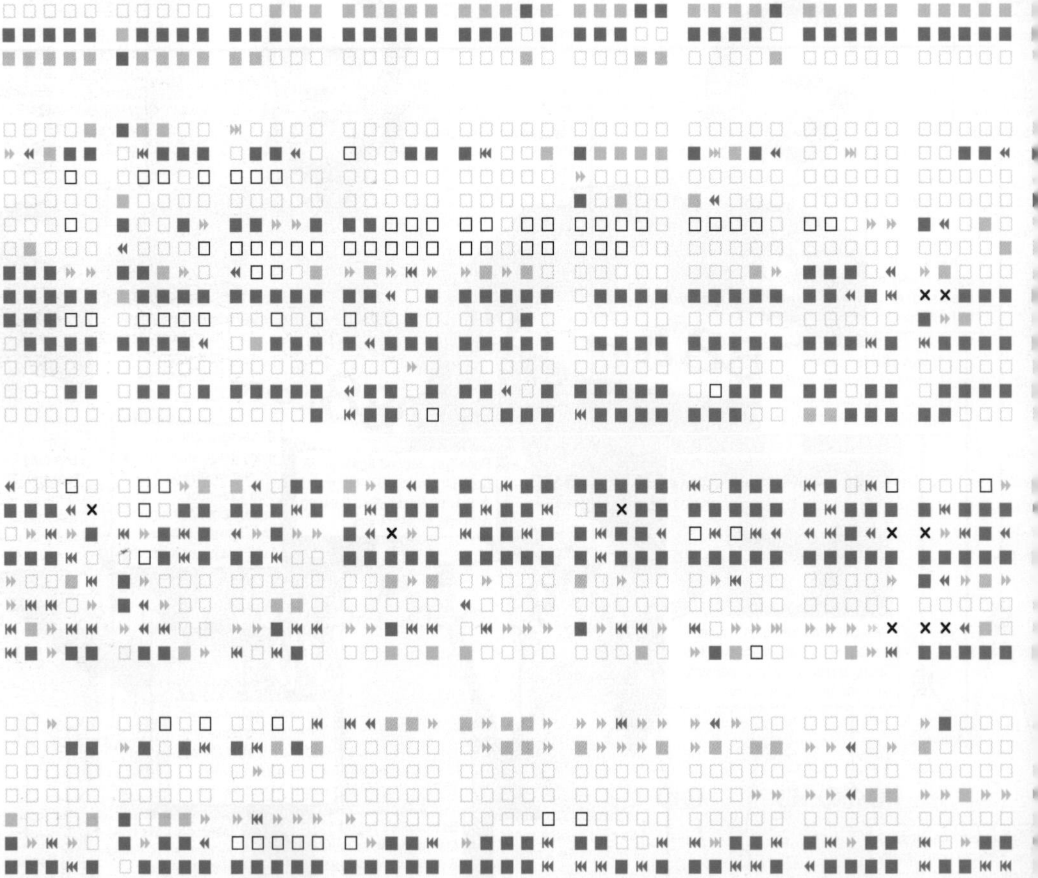

KEY: ■ On all match ◄◄ Subbed or sent off (Counting game) ▶▶ Subbed on from bench (Counting Game) ▷▷ Subbed on and then subbed or sent off (Counting Game) ☐ Not in 16 ☐ Injured
On bench ◄◄ Subbed or sent off (playing less than 70 mins) ▶▶ Subbed on (playing less than 70 mins) ▷▷ Subbed on and then subbed or sent off (playing less than 70 min ✕ Suspended

KEY PLAYERS - GOALSCORERS

Mark Viduka

Goals in the League	14
Goals in all competitions	19
Assists — League goals scored by a team mate where the player delivered the final pass	5
Contribution to Attacking Power — Average number of minutes between League team goals while on pitch	54
Player Strike Rate — Average number of minutes between League goals scored by player	148
Club Strike Rate — Average minutes between League goals scored by club	77

	PLAYER	GOALS LGE	GOALS ALL	ASSISTS	POWER	S RATE
1	Mark Viduka	14	19	5	54	148 mins
2	Ayegbeni Yakubu	12	16	4	83	263 mins
3	James Morrison	2	2	4	117	761 mins
4	Fabio Rochemback	2	2	4	80	768 mins

KEY PLAYERS - MIDFIELDERS

Julio Arca

Goals in the League	2
Goals in all competitions	3
Assists — League goals scored by a team mate where the player delivered the final pass	2
Defensive Rating — Average number of mins between League goals conceded while on the pitch	81
Contribution to Attacking Power — Average number of minutes between League team goals while on pitch	57
Scoring Difference — Defensive Rating minus Contribution to Attacking Power	24

	PLAYER	GOALS LGE	GOALS ALL	ASSISTS	DEF RATE	POWER	SC D
1	Julio Arca	2	3	2	81	57	24 mi
2	Lee Cattermole	1	2	2	85	81	4 m
3	George Boateng	1	2	1	68	70	-2 m
4	Stewart Downing	2	2	13	64	70	-6 m

PLAYER APPEARANCES

	AGE (on 01/07/07)	IN NAMED 16	APPEARANCES	COUNTING GAMES	MINUTES ON PITCH	APPEARANCES	MINUTES ON PITCH THIS SEASON		HOME COUNTRY
Goalkeepers									
Brad Jones	25	27	2	2	180	4	390	1	Australia
Mark Schwarzer	34	36	36	36	3240	42	3810	3	Australia
Ross Turnbull	22	13	0	0	0	1	90	-	England
Defenders									
Matthew Bates	20	4	1	1	69	2	159	-	England
Andrew Davies	22	28	23	19	1900	26	2120	-	England
Ugo Ehiogu	34	0	0	0	0	1	20	-	England
Seb Hines	19	1	0	0	0	2	135	-	England
Robert Huth	22	13	12	7	794	14	887	-	Germany
Anthony McMahon	21	2	0	0	0	1	60	-	England
Stuart Parnaby	24	24	18	7	860	21	1105	-	England
Emanuel Pogatetz	24	35	35	33	3002	42	3692	-	Austria
Chris Riggott	26	8	6	5	488	7	578	-	England
Andrew Taylor	20	35	34	32	2966	42	3743	-	England
David Wheater	20	2	2	1	93	2	93	-	England
Jonathan Woodgate	27	30	30	28	2597	36	3167	1	England
Abel Xavier	34	15	14	14	1257	20	1807	-	Portugal
Midfielders									
Julio Arca	26	24	21	15	1539	28	2177	-	Argentina
George Boateng	31	35	35	33	3017	41	3615	-	Holland
Lee Cattermole	19	31	31	17	1960	39	2530	-	England
Stewart Downing	22	34	34	34	3037	42	3817	9	England
Adam Johnson	19	16	12	2	353	16	570	-	England
Gaizka Mendieta	33	9	7	2	291	8	381	-	Spain
James Morrison	21	30	28	13	1523	36	1885	-	England
Fabio Rochemback	25	26	20	16	1536	22	1678	-	Brazil
Forwards									
Malcolm Christie	28	17	13	3	371	17	503	-	England
Jason Euell	30	24	17	7	798	20	836	-	England
Danny Graham	21	1	1	0	11	1	11	-	England
Lee Dong-Gook	28	11	9	1	282	11	319	-	South Korea
Massimo Maccarone	27	11	7	1	180	8	270	-	Italy
Mark Viduka	31	29	29	21	2081	37	2779	1	Australia
Aiyegbeni Yakubu	24	37	37	35	3164	45	3931	1	Nigeria

KEY: LEAGUE   ALL COMPS   CAPS   (MAY FIFA RANKING)

TEAM OF THE SEASON

SCHWARZER — CG 36 DR 67

DAVIES — CG 19 DR 76
WOODGATE — CG 28 DR 86
POGATETZ — CG 33 DR 73
TAYLOR — CG 32 DR 74

CATTERMOLE — CG 17 SD +4
BOATENG — CG 33 SD -2
ARCA — CG 15 SD +24
DOWNING — CG 34 SD -6

YAKUBU — CG 35 AP 83
VIDUKA — CG 21 SR 148

KEY: DR = Defensive Rate, SD = Scoring Difference AP = Attacking Power SR = Strike Rate, CG=Counting games — League games playing at least 70 minutes

TOP POINT EARNERS

Julio Arca

Counting Games League games when player was on pitch for at least 70 minutes	15
Average points Average League points taken in Counting games	1.87
Club Average points Average points taken in League games	1.21

	PLAYER	GAMES	PTS
1	Julio Arca	15	1.87
2	Mark Viduka	21	1.48
3	Lee Cattermole	17	1.47
4	Andrew Davies	19	1.32
5	Emanuel Pogatetz	33	1.27
6	Stewart Downing	34	1.26
7	Andrew Taylor	32	1.25
8	George Boateng	34	1.24
9	Mark Schwarzer	36	1.22
10	Jonathan Woodgate	28	1.21

KEY PLAYERS - DEFENDERS

Jonathan Woodgate

Goals Conceded in the League Number of League goals conceded while the player was on the pitch	30
Goals Conceded in all competitions Total number of goals conceded while the player was on the pitch	41
League minutes played Number of minutes played in league matches	2597
Clean Sheets In games when the player was on pitch for at least 70 minutes	9
Defensive Rating Average number of mins between League goals conceded while on the pitch	86
Club Defensive Rating Average number of mins between League goals conceded by the club this season	69

	PLAYER	CON LGE	CON ALL	MINS	C SHEETS	DEF RATE
1	Jonathan Woodgate	30	41	2597	9	86 mins
2	Andrew Davies	25	30	1900	6	76 mins
3	Andrew Taylor	40	52	2966	8	74 mins
4	Emanuel Pogatetz	41	52	3002	9	73 mins

KEY GOALKEEPER

Mark Schwarzer

Goals Conceded in the League Number of League goals conceded while the player was on the pitch	48
Goals Conceded in all competitions Total number of goals conceded while the player was on the pitch	60
League minutes played Number of minutes played in league matches	3240
Clean Sheets In games when the player was on pitch for at least 70 minutes	8
Goals to Shots Ratio The average number of shots on target per each League goal conceded	4.83
Defensive Rating Ave mins between League goals conceded while on the pitch	67

BOOKINGS

Lee Cattermole

League Yellow	10
League Red	0
All competitions Yellow	12
All competitions Red	0

League Average 196 mins between cards

	PLAYER	LEAGUE		TOTAL		AVE
1	Lee Cattermole	10Y	0R	12Y	0R	196
2	Robert Huth	3	0	3	0	264
3	E. Pogatetz	10	0	12	0	300
4	F. Rochemback	5	0	6	0	307
5	George Boateng	6	2	8	2	377
6	Jason Euell	2	0	3	0	399
7	Stuart Parnaby	2	0	2	0	430
8	Chris Riggott	1	0	1	0	488
9	Julio Arca	3	0	3	0	513
10	Andrew Davies	3	0	3	0	633
11	Stewart Downing	3	0	4	0	759
12	J. Woodgate	3	0	5	0	865
13	Andrew Taylor	3	0	3	0	988
14	Mark Viduka	2	0	2	0	1040
15	Abel Xavier	1	0	3	0	1257
	Other	3	0	3	1	
	TOTAL	**61**	**2**	**73**	**3**	

NEWCASTLE UNITED

Glenn Roeder lifted Newcastle to Europe last year but failed to build on that and was sacked. He struggled with a dreadful run of injuries, notably to **Michael Owen** and new signing **Damien Duff** leaving **Obafemi Martins** to carry the goal threat with 11 league goals and 17 in total. His Strike Rate of a goal every 260 minutes on average was not enough without support.

Kieron Dyer returned in the second half of the season to reap the only positive Scoring Difference in midfield and hit seven goals.

Injuries meant defensive turmoil with Roeder barely picking the same four twice running and **Titus Bramble** led the ratings. **Steve Harper** deputised for **Shay Given** and out-performed him with a Defensive Rating of 80 and the third best Goals to Shots Ratio in the league – 6.67 shots saved per goal conceded.

NICKNAME: THE MAGPIES

KEY: ☐ Won ☐ Drawn ■ Lost

1	ucql1	**FK Ventspils**	A	W	1-0	Bramble 70
2	prem	**Wigan**	H	W	2-1	Parker 38, Ameobi 62
3	ucql2	**FK Ventspils**	H	D	0-0	
4	prem	**Aston Villa**	A	L	0-2	
5	prem	**Fulham**	H	L	1-2	Parker 54
6	uc1rl1	**Levadia Tallinn**	A	W	1-0	Sibierski 10
7	prem	**West Ham**	A	W	2-0	Duff 49, Martins 74
8	prem	**Liverpool**	A	L	0-2	
9	prem	**Everton**	H	D	1-1	Ameobi 14
10	uc1rl2	**Levadia Tallinn**	H	W	2-1	Martins 47, 50
11	prem	**Man Utd**	A	L	0-2	
12	prem	**Bolton**	H	L	1-2	Ameobi 17 pen
13	ucgph	**Fenerbahce**	H	W	1-0	Sibierski 79
14	prem	**Middlesbrough**	A	L	0-1	
15	ccr3	**Portsmouth**	H	W	3-0	Rossi 48, Solano 53, 90
16	prem	**Charlton**	H	D	0-0	
17	ucgph	**Palermo**	A	W	1-0	Luque 37
18	prem	**Sheff Utd**	H	L	0-1	
19	ccr4	**Watford**	A	W	5-4*	Sibierski 3, Parker 116 (*on penalties)
20	prem	**Man City**	A	D	0-0	
21	prem	**Arsenal**	A	D	1-1	Dyer 30
22	ucgph	**Celta Vigo**	H	W	2-1	Sibierski 37, Taylor 86
23	prem	**Portsmouth**	H	W	1-0	Sibierski 69
24	ucgph	**Eintr Frankfurt**	A	D	0-0	
25	prem	**Reading**	H	W	3-2	Sibierski 23, Martins 57 pen, Emre Belozoglu 84
26	prem	**Blackburn**	A	W	3-1	Martins 31, 90, Taylor 35
27	prem	**Chelsea**	A	L	0-1	
28	prem	**Watford**	H	W	2-1	Martins 49, 85
29	ccqf	**Chelsea**	H	L	0-1	
30	prem	**Tottenham**	H	W	3-1	Dyer 3, Martins 7, Parker 34
31	prem	**Bolton**	A	L	1-2	Dyer 8
32	prem	**Everton**	A	L	0-3	
33	prem	**Man Utd**	H	D	2-2	Milner 33, Edgar 73
34	facr3	**Birmingham**	A	D	2-2	Taylor 40, Dyer 54
35	prem	**Tottenham**	A	W	3-2	Huntington 16, Martins 72, Butt 74
36	facr3r	**Birmingham**	H	L	1-5	Milner 56
37	prem	**West Ham**	H	D	2-2	Milner 45, Solano 53 pen
38	prem	**Aston Villa**	H	W	3-1	Milner 5, Dyer 7, Sibierski 90
39	prem	**Fulham**	A	L	1-2	Martins 90
40	prem	**Liverpool**	H	W	2-1	Martins 26, Solano 70 pen
41	uc2rl1	**Zulte-Waregem**	A	W	3-1	Dindeleux 47 og, Martins 59 pen, Sibierski 76
42	uc2rl2	**Zulte-Waregem**	H	W	1-0	Martins 68
43	prem	**Wigan**	A	L	0-1	
44	prem	**Middlesbrough**	H	D	0-0	
45	uc3rl1	**AZ Alkmaar**	H	W	4-2	Steinsson 7 og, Dyer 22, Martins 23, 37
46	uc3rl2	**AZ Alkmaar**	A	L	0-2	
47	prem	**Charlton**	A	L	0-1	
48	prem	**Man City**	H	L	0-1	
49	prem	**Sheff Utd**	A	W	2-1	Martins 17, Taylor 80
50	prem	**Arsenal**	H	D	0-0	
51	prem	**Portsmouth**	A	L	1-2	Emre Belozoglu 69 pen
52	prem	**Chelsea**	H	D	0-0	
53	prem	**Reading**	A	L	0-1	
54	prem	**Blackburn**	H	L	0-2	
55	prem	**Watford**	A	D	1-1	Dyer 29

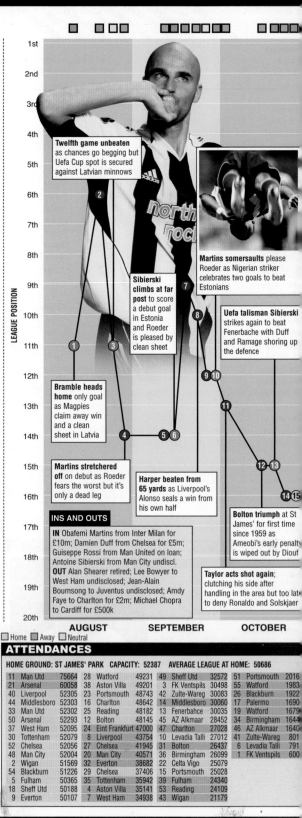

Twelfth game unbeaten as chances go begging but Uefa Cup spot is secured against Latvian minnows

Martins somersaults please Roeder as Nigerian striker celebrates two goals to beat Estonians

Sibierski climbs at far post to score a debut goal in Estonia and Roeder is pleased by clean sheet

Uefa talisman Sibierski strikes again to beat Fenerbache with Duff and Ramage shoring up the defence

Bramble heads home only goal as Magpies claim away win and a clean sheet in Latvia

Martins stretchered off on debut as Roeder fears the worst but it's only a dead leg

Harper beaten from 65 yards as Liverpool's Alonso seals a win from his own half

Bolton triumph at St James' for first time since 1959 as Ameobi's early penalty is wiped out by Diouf

Taylor acts shot again; clutching his side after handling in the area but too late to deny Ronaldo and Solskjaer

INS AND OUTS

IN Obafemi Martins from Inter Milan for £10m; Damien Duff from Chelsea for £5m; Guiseppe Rossi from Man United on loan; Antoine Sibierski from Man City undiscl. **OUT** Alan Shearer retired; Lee Bowyer to West Ham undisclosed; Jean-Alain Boumsong to Juventus undisclosed; Amdy Faye to Charlton for £2m; Michael Chopra to Cardiff for £500k

☐ Home ☐ Away ☐ Neutral

1st				
2nd				
3rd				
4th				
5th				
6th				
7th				
8th				
9th				
10th				
11th				
12th				
13th				
14th				
15th				
16th				
17th				
18th				
19th				
20th				

LEAGUE POSITION

AUGUST SEPTEMBER OCTOBER

ATTENDANCES

HOME GROUND: ST JAMES' PARK   CAPACITY: 52387   AVERAGE LEAGUE AT HOME: 50686

11	Man Utd	75664	28	Watford	49231	49	Sheff Utd	32572	51	Portsmouth	2016
21	Arsenal	60058	38	Aston Villa	49201	3	FK Ventspils	30498	55	Watford	1983
40	Liverpool	52305	23	Portsmouth	48743	42	Zulte-Wareg	30083	26	Blackburn	1922
44	Middlesboro	52303	16	Charlton	48642	14	Middlesboro	30060	17	Palermo	1690
33	Man Utd	52302	25	Reading	48182	13	Fenerbache	30035	19	Watford	1679
50	Arsenal	52293	12	Bolton	48145	45	AZ Alkmaar	28452	34	Birmingham	1644
37	West Ham	52095	24	Eint Frankfurt	47000	47	Charlton	27028	46	AZ Alkmaar	1642
30	Tottenham	52079	8	Liverpool	43754	10	Levadia Talli	27012	41	Zulte-Wareg	801
52	Chelsea	52056	27	Chelsea	41945	31	Bolton	26437	6	Levadia Talli	791
48	Man City	52004	20	Man City	40571	36	Birmingham	26099	1	FK Ventspils	600
2	Wigan	51569	32	Everton	38682	22	Celta Vigo	25079			
54	Blackburn	51226	29	Chelsea	37406	15	Portsmouth	25028			
5	Fulham	50365	35	Tottenham	35942	39	Fulham	24340			
18	Sheff Utd	50188	4	Aston Villa	35141	53	Reading	24109			
9	Everton	50107	7	West Ham	34938	43	Wigan	21179			

Roeder makes way for Big Sam

Final Position: 13th

KEY: ● League ○ Champions Lge ● UEFA Cup ● FA Cup ○ League Cup ● Other

INS AND OUTS
IN Oguchi Onyewu from Standard Liege on loan until end of the season

AZ win on away goals as the lapses in defence at St James' Park in the first leg cost Roeder's side a place in the Quarter finals

Solano's double block on the line keeps Arsenal goalless while Milner hits bar at the other end and Given is injured

Martins lashes home at 84mph before setting up Butt for a thrilling winner in a game where Given excels

Dyer claims big scalp as his early goal unsettles Spurs and Martins and Parker wrap up win

Parker unlucky with tight offside decision and Taylor, Butt and Carr all go close before City escape with the points

Owen's back with the ball in the net but offside at Reading who claim a tight win

Ramage push is the key moment as Bolton nudge him into an own goal past third choice Srnicek

Luque delivers an unlikely win in Sicily thanks to debut keeper Krul performing heroics and Carroll, 17, becoming the youngest Euro player

Fifth game without a home goal is worst run since 1951 as Owen 's first start at St James' ends in defeat

Taylor's headed winner ensures Uefa progress with a game to spare against quality side from Spain

Sixth match unbeaten and no injuries as Frankfurt's shooting is dreadful

Belgians blasted as Sibierski secures two goal lead for second leg despite a first half of missed chances

Roeder has words at halftime as team is 'carrying four players' but Emre penalty can't prevent Pompey's win

Bramble returns to acclaim as he and Taylor keep the Champions goalless at St James' Park

Owen injury by his own player is major talking point with Pearson stepping in as caretaker for an end of season draw

Given supreme to claim a point at Arsenal as only Henry's pin-point free kick answers Dyer's breakaway goal

Was it in? Martins' shot comes down from the bar and no-one can tell but Chelsea are given benefit and go on to win

Martins' 12th goal levels Bellamy strike before Solano's penalty earns a comeback win over Liverpool

Martins on fire in first half demolition of Alkmaar but late reply leaves work to do in Holland

Owen scores on his first friendly run-out after injury

Roeder pays the price and resigns after season of injuries with Allardyce now free and favourite

Unlucky at the Bridge as Champions have to call on Drogba to find a route past Given

Fight back from two down with Milner goal given despite Parker being offside but Given and Ramage are injured

Edgar's dream goal takes point off leaders while Milner thunderbolt is his first and Given works wonders behind young back four

Allardyce drops in by helicoptor to press conference with mandate to challenge the big four

MONTH BY MONTH POINTS TALLY

Month	Points	%
AUGUST	3	50%
SEPTEMBER	4	33%
OCTOBER	1	8%
NOVEMBER	5	42%
DECEMBER	12	57%
JANUARY	8	67%
FEBRUARY	3	33%
MARCH	1	11%
APRIL	5	33%
MAY	1	17%

NOVEMBER   DECEMBER   JANUARY   FEBRUARY   MARCH   APRIL   MAY

GOAL ATTEMPTS

FOR — Goal attempts recorded in League games

	HOME	AWAY	TOTAL	AVE
shots on target	122	82	204	5.4
shots off target	119	87	206	5.4
TOTAL	241	169	410	10.8

Ratio of goals to shots — Average number of shots on target per League goal scored	5.4
Accuracy rating — Average percentage of total goal attempts which are on target	49.8

AGAINST — Goal attempts recorded in League games

	HOME	AWAY	TOTAL	AVE
shots on target	112	151	263	6.9
shots off target	109	147	256	6.7
TOTAL	221	298	519	13.7

Ratio of goals to shots — Average number of shots on target per League goal scored	5.6
Accuracy rating — Average percentage of total goal attempts which are on target	50.7

GOALS

Martins

League	11
FA Cup	0
League Cup	0
Europe	6
Other	0
TOTAL	17

League Average 260 mins between goals

	PLAYER	LGE	FAC	LC	Euro	TOT	AVE
1	Martins	11	0	0	6	17	260
2	Sibierski	3	0	1	4	8	484
3	Dyer	5	1	0	1	7	336
4	Parker	3	0	1	0	4	806
5	Milner	3	1	0	0	4	893
6	Solano	2	0	2	0	4	1071
7	Taylor	2	1	0	1	4	1192
8	Ameobi	3	0	0	0	3	252
9	Emre Belozoglu	2	0	0	0	2	909
10	Edgar	1	0	0	0	1	241
11	Huntington	1	0	0	0	1	901
12	Duff	1	0	0	0	1	1725
13	Butt	1	0	0	0	1	2290
14	Bramble	0	0	0	1	1	
15	Luque	0	0	1	0	1	
	Other	1	0	1	0	1	
	TOTAL	38	3	5	14	60	

SQUAD APPEARANCES

Match	1 2 3 4 5	6 7 8 9 10	11 12 13 14 15	16 17 18 19 20	21 22 23 24 25	26 27 28 29 30	31 32 33 34 35	36 37 38 39 40	41 42 43 44 45	46 47 48 49 50	51 52 53 54
Venue	A H H A H	A A A H H	A H H A H	H A H A A	A H H A H	A A H H H	A A H A A	H H H A H	A H A H H	A A H A H	A H A H
Competition	E L E L L	E L L L E	L L E L W	L E L W L	L E L E L	L L L W L	L L L F L	F L L L L	E E L L E	E L L L L	L L L L
Result	W W D L L	W W L D W	L L W L W	D W L W D	D W W D W	W L W L W	L L D D W	L D W L W	W W L D W	L L L W D	L D L L

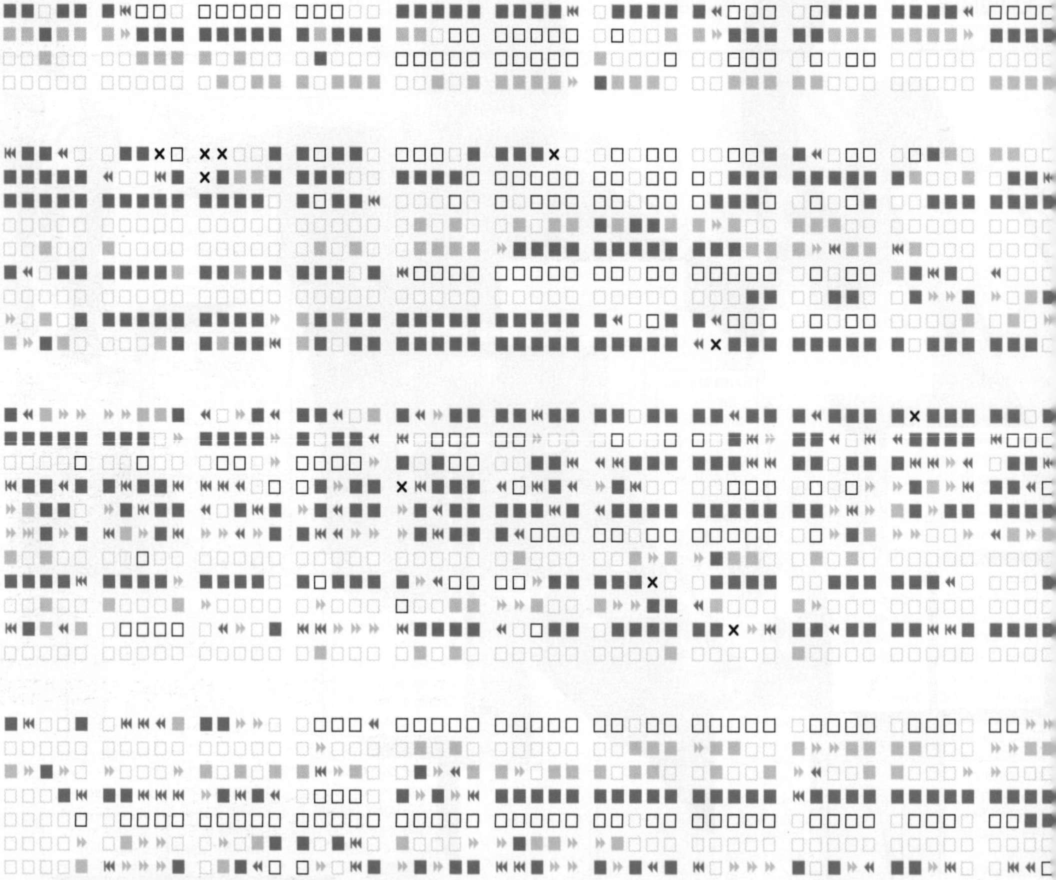

Goalkeepers
Shay Given
Steve Harper
Tim Krul
Pavel Srnicek

Defenders
Celestine Babayaro
Titus Bramble
Stephen Carr
David Edgar
Paul Huntington
Craig Moore
Oguchi Onyewu
Peter Ramage
Steven Taylor

Midfielders
Nicky Butt
Damien Duff
Kieron Dyer
Emre Belozoglu
James Milner
Charles N'Zogbia
Alan O'Brien
Scott Parker
Matty Pattison
Nolberto Solano
James Troisi

Forwards
Shola Ameobi
Andrew Carroll
Alberto Luque
Obafemi Martins
Michael Owen
Giuseppe Rossi
Antoine Sibierski

KEY: ■ On all match   ◄◄ Subbed or sent off (Counting game)   ►► Subbed on from bench (Counting Game)   ►► Subbed on and then subbed or sent off (Counting Game)   Not in 16   ☐ Injured
■ On bench   ◄◄ Subbed or sent off (playing less than 70 mins)   ►► Subbed on (playing less than 70 mins)   ►► Subbed on and then subbed or sent off (playing less than 70 min   ✗ Suspended

---

KEY PLAYERS - GOALSCORERS

Obafemi Martins

Goals in the League	11
Goals in all competitions	17
Assists League goals scored by a team mate where the player delivered the final pass	5
Contribution to Attacking Power Average number of minutes between League team goals while on pitch	81
Player Strike Rate Average number of minutes between League goals scored by player	260
Club Strike Rate Average minutes between League goals scored by club	90

	PLAYER	GOALS LGE	GOALS ALL	ASSISTS	POWER	S RATE
1	Obafemi Martins	11	17	5	81	260 mins
2	Kieron Dyer	5	7	3	76	336 mins
3	Antoine Sibierski	3	8	5	80	484 mins
4	Scott Parker	3	4	1	100	806 mins

KEY PLAYERS - MIDFIELDERS

Kieron Dyer

Goals in the League	5
Goals in all competitions	7
Assists League goals scored by a team mate where the player delivered the final pass	3
Defensive Rating Average number of mins between League goals conceded while on pitch	80
Contribution to Attacking Power Average number of minutes between League team goals while on pitch	76
Scoring Difference Defensive Rating minus Contribution to Attacking Power	4

	PLAYER	GOALS LGE	GOALS ALL	ASSISTS	DEF RATE	POWER	SC DIFF
1	Kieron Dyer	5	7	3	80	76	4 mins
2	Nolberto Solano	2	4	5	69	79	-10 mins
3	James Milner	3	4	6	72	83	-11 mins
4	Nicky Butt	1	1	1	69	84	-15 mins

PLAYER APPEARANCES

	AGE (on 01/07/07)	IN NAMED 16	APPEARANCES	COUNTING GAMES	MINUTES ON PITCH	APPEARANCES	MINUTES ON PITCH THIS SEASON		HOME COUNTRY
Goalkeepers									
ay Given	31	22	22	20	1880	31	2690	4	Rep of Ireland
eve Harper	32	29	18	15	1445	25	2105	-	England
n Krul	19	4	0	0	0	1	90	-	Holland
vel Srnicek	39	21	2	1	95	2	95	-	Czech Republic
Defenders									
lestine Babayaro	28	15	12	11	1035	18	1555	-	Nigeria
us Bramble	25	20	17	17	1493	29	2518	-	England
phen Carr	30	23	23	23	2055	30	2715	2	Rep of Ireland
vid Edgar	20	9	3	2	241	4	331	-	Canada
ul Huntington	19	18	11	10	901	16	1301	-	England
aig Moore	31	17	17	15	1404	21	1764	1	Australia
uchi Onyewu	25	12	11	7	749	11	749	4	United States
ter Ramage	23	25	21	18	1706	32	2552	-	England
even Taylor	21	31	27	26	2385	42	3731	-	England
Midfielders									
cky Butt	32	34	31	22	2290	46	3432	-	England
mien Duff	28	22	22	17	1725	33	2585	7	Rep of Ireland
ron Dyer	28	22	22	18	1683	30	2344	4	England
re Belozoglu	26	25	24	16	1819	36	2716	1	Turkey
mes Milner	21	36	35	27	2680	51	3964	-	England
arles N'Zogbia	21	25	22	8	1130	33	1785	-	France
an O'Brien	22	8	2	1	114	4	193	-	England
ott Parker	26	29	29	26	2420	39	3206	1	England
atty Pattison	20	11	7	2	302	11	488	4	South Africa
lberto Solano	32	29	28	21	2142	42	3261	-	Peru
mes Troisi	18	1	0	0	0	0	0	-	Australia
Forwards									
ola Ameobi	25	12	12	6	757	14	863	-	England
drew Carroll	18	12	4	0	91	7	129	-	England
erto Luque	29	16	7	0	112	15	527	-	Spain
afemi Martins	22	33	33	32	2863	46	3818	-	Nigeria
chael Owen	27	3	3	2	246	3	246	2	England
useppe Rossi	20	16	11	3	388	13	577	-	Italy
toine Sibierski	32	28	26	12	1453	39	2401	-	France

KEY: LEAGUE   ALL COMPS   CAPS   (MAY FIFA RANKING)

TEAM OF THE SEASON

HARPER — CG 15 DR 80

CARR — CG 23 DR 76
BRAMBLE — CG 17 DR 87
MOORE — CG 15 DR 78
BABAYARO* — CG 11 DR 79

SOLANO — CG 21 SD -10
BUTT — CG 22 SD -15
DYER — CG 18 SD +4
MILNER — CG 27 SD -11

SIBIERSKI — CG 12 AP 80

MARTINS — CG 32 SR 260

KEY: DR = Defensive Rate, SD = Scoring Difference AP = Attacking Power SR = Strike Rate, CG=Counting games – League games playing at least 70 minutes

TOP POINT EARNERS

Shay Given

Counting Games - League games when player was on pitch for at least 70 minutes	20
Average points - Average League points taken in Counting games	1.55
Club Average points - Average points taken in League games	1.13

	PLAYER	GAMES	PTS
1	Shay Given	20	1.55
2	Antoine Sibierski	12	1.50
3	Peter Ramage	18	1.39
4	Nolberto Solano	21	1.38
5	Kieron Dyer	18	1.33
6	Steven Taylor	26	1.31
7	James Milner	27	1.30
8	Nicky Butt	22	1.23
9	Obafemi Martins	32	1.16
10	Emre Belozoglu	16	1.06

KEY PLAYERS - DEFENDERS

Titus Bramble

Goals Conceded in the League — Number of League goals conceded while the player was on the pitch	17
Goals Conceded in all competitions — Total number of goals conceded while the player was on the pitch	24
League minutes played — Number of minutes played in league matches	1493
Clean Sheets — In games when the player was on pitch for at least 70 minutes	4
Defensive Rating — Average number of mins between League goals conceded while on the pitch	87
Club Defensive Rating — Average number of mins between League goals conceded by the club this season	72

	PLAYER	CON LGE	CON ALL	MINS	C SHEETS	DEF RATE
1	Titus Bramble	17	24	1493	4	87 mins
2	Celestine Babayaro	13	16	1035	2	79 mins
3	Craig Moore	18	18	1404	4	78 mins
4	Stephen Carr	27	32	2055	5	76 mins

KEY GOALKEEPER

Steve Harper

Goals Conceded in the League — Number of League goals conceded while the player was on the pitch	18
Goals Conceded in all competitions — Total number of goals conceded while the player was on the pitch	22
League minutes played — Number of minutes played in league matches	1445
Clean Sheets — In games when the player was on pitch for at least 70 minutes	3
Goals to Shots Ratio — The average number of shots on target per each League goal conceded	6.67
Defensive Rating — Ave mins between League goals conceded while on the pitch	80

BOOKINGS

Celestine Babayaro

League Yellow	5
League Red	0
All competitions Yellow	6
All competitions Red	0

League Average 207 mins between cards

	PLAYER	LEAGUE		TOTAL		AVE
1	C. Babayaro	5Y	0R	6Y	0R	207
2	Paul Huntington	4	0	4	0	225
3	Titus Bramble	5	1	6	1	248
4	Scott Parker	9	0	9	0	268
5	Emre Belozoglu	6	0	8	0	303
6	Craig Moore	4	0	6	0	351
7	Nolberto Solano	3	0	5	0	357
8	Nicky Butt	6	0	10	0	381
9	Charles N'Zogbia	2	0	3	0	565
10	Steven Taylor	4	0	6	1	596
11	Shola Ameobi	1	0	1	0	757
12	Peter Ramage	2	0	2	0	853
13	James Milner	3	0	5	0	893
14	Stephen Carr	2	0	2	0	1027
15	Kieron Dyer	1	0	1	0	1683
	Other	3	0	6	0	
	TOTAL	63	1	83	2	

MANCHESTER CITY

The lowest home goals total in the Premiership was the record that led to the demise of Stuart Pearce. **Joey Barton** showed his talent to earn an England call up before confirming his reputation as hot-headed and was suspended by the club. With **Ben Thatcher's** dreadful assault on Pedro Mendes, it made it a season to forget.

Only the defence held up for Pearce. **Nicky Weaver** kept out **Andreas Isaksson** for most of the season with a Defensive Rating of a goal conceded every 76 minutes. Isaksson's rating was 73.

Nedium Onuoha's 18 appearances earned a top 20 Defensive Rating of a goal conceded every 101 minutes. He also led the Top Point Earners table, averaging 1.36 points per game. Thatcher left with five yellows, an eight game suspension and a sub 200-minute Disciplinary record. The average home gate dropped by 2,000.

NICKNAME: BLUES/CITIZENS

KEY: ☐ Won ☐ Drawn ☐ Lost

#	comp	Opponent			Score	Scorers
1	prem	Chelsea	A	L	0-3	
2	prem	Portsmouth	H	D	0-0	
3	prem	Arsenal	H	W	1-0	Barton 41 pen
4	prem	Reading	A	L	0-1	
5	prem	Blackburn	A	L	2-4	Barton 39, Ooijer 44 og
6	ccr2	Chesterfield	A	L	1-2	Samaras 40
7	prem	West Ham	H	W	2-0	Samaras 50, 63
8	prem	Everton	A	D	1-1	Richards 90
9	prem	Sheff Utd	H	D	0-0	
10	prem	Wigan	A	L	0-4	
11	prem	Middlesbrough	H	W	1-0	Dunne 23
12	prem	Charlton	A	L	0-1	
13	prem	Newcastle	H	D	0-0	
14	prem	Fulham	H	W	3-1	Corradi 12, 32, Barton 45
15	prem	Liverpool	A	L	0-1	
16	prem	Aston Villa	A	W	3-1	Vassell 18, Barton 32, Distin 75
17	prem	Watford	H	D	0-0	
18	prem	Man Utd	A	L	1-3	Trabelsi 72
19	prem	Tottenham	H	L	1-2	Barton 64
20	prem	Bolton	H	L	0-2	
21	prem	Sheff Utd	A	W	1-0	Ireland 78
22	prem	West Ham	A	W	1-0	Beasley 83
23	prem	Everton	H	W	2-1	Samaras 50, 72 pen
24	facr3	Sheff Wed	A	D	1-1	Samaras 78 pen
25	prem	Bolton	A	D	0-0	
26	facr3r	Sheff Wed	H	W	2-1	Ireland 44, Vassell 56
27	prem	Blackburn	H	L	0-3	
28	facr4	Southampton	H	W	3-1	Vassell 26, Barton 45, Beasley 70
29	prem	Reading	H	L	0-2	
30	prem	Portsmouth	A	L	1-2	Corradi 62
31	facr5	Preston	A	W	3-1	Ball 35, Hill 84 og, Ireland 90
32	prem	Wigan	H	L	0-1	
33	facqf	Blackburn	A	L	0-2	
34	prem	Chelsea	H	L	0-1	
35	prem	Middlesbrough	A	W	2-0	Distin 61, Mpenza 74
36	prem	Newcastle	A	W	1-0	Mpenza 80
37	prem	Charlton	H	D	0-0	
38	prem	Fulham	A	W	3-1	Barton 21, Beasley 36, Vassell 59
39	prem	Liverpool	H	D	0-0	
40	prem	Arsenal	A	L	1-3	Beasley 41
41	prem	Watford	A	D	1-1	Vassell 53
42	prem	Aston Villa	H	L	0-2	
43	prem	Man Utd	H	L	0-1	
44	prem	Tottenham	A	L	1-2	Mpenza 40

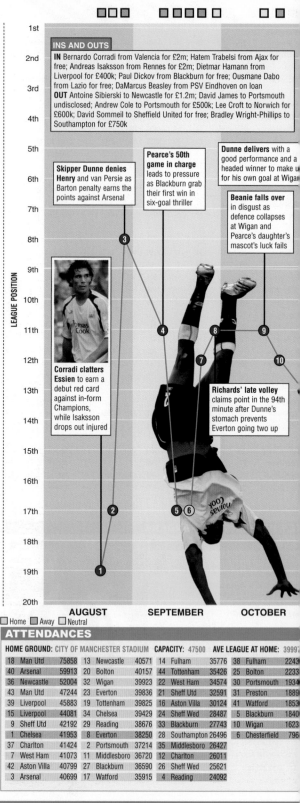

INS AND OUTS

IN Bernardo Corradi from Valencia for £2m; Hatem Trabelsi from Ajax for free; Andreas Isaksson from Rennes for £2m; Dietmar Hamann from Liverpool for £400k; Paul Dickov from Blackburn for free; Ousmane Dabo from Lazio for free; DaMarcus Beasley from PSV Eindhoven on loan **OUT** Antoine Sibierski to Newcastle for £1.2m; David James to Portsmouth undisclosed; Andrew Cole to Portsmouth for £500k; Lee Croft to Norwich for £600k; David Sommeil to Sheffield United for free; Bradley Wright-Phillips to Southampton for £750k

Skipper Dunne denies Henry and van Persie as Barton penalty earns the points against Arsenal

Pearce's 50th game in charge leads to pressure as Blackburn grab their first win in six-goal thriller

Dunne delivers with a good performance and a headed winner to make up for his own goal at Wigan

Beanie falls over in disgust as defence collapses at Wigan and Pearce's daughter's mascot's luck fails

Corradi clatters Essien to earn a debut red card against in-form Champions, while Isaksson drops out injured

Richards' late volley claims point in the 94th minute after Dunne's stomach prevents Everton going two up

League Position axis: 1st–20th

☐ Home ☐ Away ☐ Neutral

AUGUST · **SEPTEMBER** · **OCTOBER**

ATTENDANCES

HOME GROUND: CITY OF MANCHESTER STADIUM · **CAPACITY:** 47500 · **AVE LEAGUE AT HOME:** 39997

18	Man Utd	75858	13	Newcastle	40571	14	Fulham	35776	38	Fulham	2243
40	Arsenal	59913	20	Bolton	40157	44	Tottenham	35426	25	Bolton	2233
36	Newcastle	52004	32	Wigan	39923	22	West Ham	34574	30	Portsmouth	1934
43	Man Utd	47244	23	Everton	39836	21	Sheff Utd	32591	31	Preston	1889
39	Liverpool	45883	19	Tottenham	39825	16	Aston Villa	30124	41	Watford	1853
15	Liverpool	44081	34	Chelsea	39429	24	Sheff Wed	28487	5	Blackburn	1840
9	Sheff Utd	42192	29	Reading	38676	33	Blackburn	27743	10	Wigan	1623
1	Chelsea	41953	8	Everton	38250	28	Southampton	26496	6	Chesterfield	796
37	Charlton	41424	2	Portsmouth	37214	35	Middlesboro	26427			
7	West Ham	41073	11	Middlesboro	36720	12	Charlton	26011			
42	Aston Villa	40799	27	Blackburn	36590	26	Sheff Wed	25621			
3	Arsenal	40699	17	Watford	35915	4	Reading	24092			

Pearce is discarded as goals dry up

Final Position: 14th

KEY: ● League ● Champions Lge ● UEFA Cup ● FA Cup ● League Cup ● Other

MONTH BY MONTH POINTS TALLY		
AUGUST	4	44%
SEPTEMBER	4	33%
OCTOBER	4	44%
NOVEMBER	7	47%
DECEMBER	7	39%
JANUARY	4	44%
FEBRUARY	0	0%
MARCH	6	50%
APRIL	6	33%
MAY	0	0%

City slackers! Dunne derides signings for lack of effort

FA to investigate Ball stamp while Pearce contemplates Barton fall out and new Premiership record low with only ten home goals scored

Corradi 'knights' Barton with the corner flag in goal celebration after Italian striker breaks his duck with two well-taken strikes to over-run Fulham

Double miss as first Corradi, then Barton fail to tap in Vassell's cross as City fans boycott Bolton

Poor pass spoils good defensive display as Barton lets in Gerrard for only goal of the game at Anfield

Was it over? Dickov claims it was, ref and technology say 'not over the line' as Barton sees red and Anelka claims goals

Redknapp anger over Barton's 'stamp' on Mendes which ends Pompey scorer's match

Mpenza clinches second away win and Pearce praises 'stout' defence as Newcastle go close at the end

"I wouldn't pay to watch us" says Barton, before missing a vital penalty kick in Villa defeat

Barton suspended by club for the rest of the season for training ground assault on Dabo

Barton can't celebrate England call-up as two chances go begging and Reading pounce in the last 11 minutes

Vital win comes courtesy of Distin's second goal of the season before loan-star Mpenza makes sure

Beasley rocks bar as his late drive nearly claims a win over Liverpool but Barton tackle on Gerrard looks reckless

"I was only ever a caretaker"; Pearce is sacrificed to allow new owners to choose their man

"It's lack of goals" says Pearce as Spurs drive home the point with their surplus of strikers

Ball's first goal levels at Preston before Samaras shot deflects in and Ireland's volley secures quarter final spot

Sub Samaras strikes first goals since September to defeat Everton and make it three wins on the spin

Samaras heads in but Poll disallows crucial goal in game of good chances – especially for Barton and Corradi

Trabelsi alarms United but it turns into consolation after Corradi is sent off for blatant dive

Home record ends with first defeat by Spurs who withstand Barton's fight-back as crowd jeer

Three match ban for Ball after apology

Ten points from 12 as Barton dooms Fulham with opening goal and an assist for Beasley before halftime

Saints succumb after early lead with Vassell and Barton converting before Beasley adds a third

Richards gifts Lampard a penalty that beats Isaksson and claims the points but it's a better performance

Vassell pounces on keeper's error to relegate Watford who level and earn Pearce's praise

Ball breaker; full back stamps on Ronaldo, trips him for a penalty and falls to earn another, which Vassell misses, at the other end

INS AND OUTS

IN Emile Mpenza as a free agent; Michael Ball from PSV Eindhoven for £200k; Djamel Abdoun from Ajaccio on loan **OUT** Ben Thatcher to Charlton for £500k; Claudio Reyna to New York Red Bulls for free; Marc Laird to Northampton on loan; Matthew Mills to Colchester on loan; Kasper Schmeichel to Falkirk on loan; Joe Hart to Tranmere on loan

NOVEMBER DECEMBER JANUARY FEBRUARY MARCH APRIL MAY

GOAL ATTEMPTS

FOR Goal attempts recorded in League games	HOME	AWAY	TOTAL	AVE
shots on target	96	101	197	5.2
shots off target	106	89	195	5.1
TOTAL	202	190	392	10.3

Ratio of goals to shots Average number of shots on target per League goal scored	6.8
Accuracy rating Average percentage of total goal attempts which were on target	50.3

AGAINST Goal attempts recorded in League games	HOME	AWAY	TOTAL	AVE
shots on target	63	130	193	5.1
shots off target	98	118	216	5.7
TOTAL	161	248	409	10.8

Ratio of goals to shots Average number of shots on target per League goal scored	4.4
Accuracy rating Average percentage of total goal attempts which were on target	47.2

GOALS

Barton

League	6
FA Cup	1
League Cup	0
Europe	0
Other	0
TOTAL	7

League Average	494
mins between goals	

	PLAYER	LGE	FAC	LC	Euro	TOT	AVE
1	Barton	6	1	0	0	7	494
2	Samaras	4	1	1	0	6	426
3	Vassell	3	2	0	0	5	852
4	Beasley	3	1	0	0	4	342
5	Mpenza	3	0	0	0	3	275
6	Corradi	3	0	0	0	3	527
7	Ireland	1	2	0	0	3	1338
8	Distin	2	0	0	0	2	1627
9	Trabelsi	1	0	0	0	1	1367
10	Richards	1	0	0	0	1	2342
11	Dunne	1	0	0	0	1	3420
12	Ball	0	1	0	0	1	
13	Abdoun	0	0	0	0	0	
14	Onuoha	0	0	0	0	0	
15	Reyna	0	0	0	0	0	
	Other	0	0	0	0	0	
	TOTAL	28	8	1	0	37	

SQUAD APPEARANCES

Match	1 2 3 4 5	6 7 8 9 10	11 12 13 14 15	16 17 18 19 20	21 22 23 24 25	26 27 28 29 30	31 32 33 34 35	36 37 38 39 40	41 42 43 4
Venue	A H H A A	A H A H A	H A H A H A	A H A H H	A A H A A	H H H H A	A H A H A	A H A H A	A H H A
Competition	L L L L L	W L L L L	L L L L L	L L L L L	L L L F L	F L F L L	F L F L L	L L L L L	L L L L
Result	L D W L L	L W D D L	W L D W L	W D L L L	W W W D D	W L W L L	W L L L W	W D W D L	D L L L

Goalkeepers
Joe Hart
Andreas Isaksson
Kasper Schmeichel
Nicky Weaver

Defenders
Michael Ball
Sylvain Distin
Richard Dunne
Stephen Jordan
Danny Mills
Matthew Mills
Nedum Onuoha
Micah Richards
Sun Jihai
Ben Thatcher

Midfielders
Joey Barton
DaMarcus Beasley
Ousmane Dabo
Dietmar Hamann
Stephen Ireland
Michael Johnson
Marc Laird
Ishmael Miller
Claudio Reyna
Trevor Sinclair
Hatem Trabelsi

Forwards
Djamel Abdoun
Bernardo Corradi
Paul Dickov
Emile Mpenza
Georgios Samaras
Daniel Sturridge
Darius Vassell

KEY: ■ On all match ◄◄ Subbed or sent off (Counting game) ►► Subbed on from bench (Counting Game) ►► Subbed on and then subbed or sent off (Counting Game) □ Not in 16 □ Injured
■ On bench ◄◄ Subbed or sent off (playing less than 70 mins) ►► Subbed on (playing less than 70 mins) ►► Subbed on and then subbed or sent off (playing less than 70 min ✗ Suspended

KEY PLAYERS - GOALSCORERS

Georgios Samaras

Goals in the League	4
Goals in all competitions	6
Assists — League goals scored by a team mate where the player delivered the final pass	5
Contribution to Attacking Power — Average number of minutes between League team goals while on pitch	94
Player Strike Rate — Average number of minutes between League goals scored by player	426
Club Strike Rate — Average minutes between League goals scored by club	117

	PLAYER	GOALS LGE	GOALS ALL	ASSISTS	POWER	S RATE
1	Georgios Samaras	4	6	5	94	426 mins
2	Joey Barton	6	7	5	118	494 mins
3	Bernardo Corradi	3	3	5	113	527 mins
4	Darius Vassell	3	5	2	111	852 mins

KEY PLAYERS - MIDFIELDERS

Hatem Trabelsi

Goals in the League	1
Goals in all competitions	1
Assists — League goals scored by a team mate where the player delivered the final pass	1
Defensive Rating — Average number of mins between League goals conceded while on the pitch	80
Contribution to Attacking Power — Average number of minutes between League team goals while on pitch	113
Scoring Difference — Defensive Rating minus Contribution to Attacking Power	-33

	PLAYER	GOALS LGE	GOALS ALL	ASSISTS	DEF RATE	POWER	SC DIFF
1	Hatem Trabelsi	1	1	1	80	113	-33
2	Joey Barton	6	7	5	80	118	-38
3	Trevor Sinclair	0	0	1	81	185	-104
4	Stephen Ireland	1	3	2	70	334	-264

PLAYER APPEARANCES

	AGE (on 01/07/07)	IN NAMED 16	APPEARANCES	COUNTING GAMES	MINUTES ON PITCH	APPEARANCES	MINUTES ON PITCH	THIS SEASON	HOME COUNTRY
Goalkeepers									
Joe Hart	20	17	1	1	90	1	90	-	England
Andreas Isaksson	25	23	14	12	1181	14	1181	3	Sweden
Kasper Schmeichel	20	1	0	0	0	0	0	-	Denmark
Nicky Weaver	28	35	25	23	2149	31	2689	-	England
Defenders									
Michael Ball	27	12	12	12	1075	14	1255	-	England
Sylvain Distin	29	37	37	36	3254	43	3794	-	France
Richard Dunne	27	38	38	38	3420	44	3960	6	Rep of Ireland
Stephen Jordan	25	14	13	11	1041	16	1304	-	England
Danny Mills	30	3	1	0	11	1	11	-	England
Matthew Mills	20	3	1	0	59	1	59	-	England
Nedum Onuoha	20	22	18	14	1324	19	1414	-	England
Micah Richards	19	28	28	25	2342	34	2882	4	England
Sun Jihai	29	14	13	9	998	14	1054	-	China PR
Ben Thatcher	31	12	11	10	955	11	955	3	Wales
Midfielders									
Joey Barton	24	33	33	33	2966	38	3411	1	England
DaMarcus Beasley	25	23	18	8	1027	22	1231	5	United States
Ousmane Dabo	30	18	13	8	882	17	1238	-	France
Dietmar Hamann	33	21	16	7	981	19	1138	-	Germany
Stephen Ireland	20	27	24	11	1338	29	1711	4	Rep of Ireland
Michael Johnson	19	13	10	10	900	10	900	-	England
Marc Laird	21	2	0	0	0	0	0	-	England
Ishmael Miller	20	20	16	2	454	19	500	-	England
Claudio Reyna	33	16	15	9	956	16	1026	-	United States
Trevor Sinclair	34	18	18	13	1296	21	1522	-	England
Hatem Trabelsi	30	24	20	14	1367	23	1591	-	Tunisia
Forwards									
Djamel Abdoun	21	0	0	0	0	1	2	-	France
Bernardo Corradi	31	29	25	15	1582	29	1917	-	Italy
Paul Dickov	34	23	16	4	816	18	827	-	England
Emile Mpenza	28	10	10	8	826	11	836	5	Belgium
Georgios Samaras	22	38	36	11	1706	42	2081	4	Greece
Daniel Sturridge	17	2	2	0	22	2	22	-	England
Darius Vassell	27	32	32	28	2558	36	2915	-	England

KEY: LEAGUE   ALL COMPS   CAPS   (MAY FIFA RANKING)

TEAM OF THE SEASON

WEAVER — CG 23 — DR 76

 ONUOHA — CG 14 — DR 101

 DUNNE — CG 38 — DR 77

 DISTIN — CG 36 — DR 85

 BALL — CG 12 — DR 89

 TRABELSI — CG 14 — SD -33

 IRELAND* — CG 11 — SD -264

 BARTON — CG 33 — SD -38

 SINCLAIR — CG 13 — SD -104

 **CORRADI** — CG 15 — AP 113

 SAMARAS* — CG 11 — SR 426

KEY: DR = Defensive Rate, SD = Scoring Difference AP = Attacking Power SR = Strike Rate,
CG=Counting games – League games playing at least 70 minutes

TOP POINT EARNERS

Nedum Onuoha

Counting Games League games when player was on pitch for at least 70 minutes		14
Average points Average League points taken in Counting games		1.36
Club Average points Average points taken in League games		1.11

	PLAYER	GAMES	PTS
1	Nedum Onuoha	14	1.36
2	Hatem Trabelsi	14	1.29
3	Nicky Weaver	23	1.26
4	Darius Vassell	28	1.21
5	Micah Richards	25	1.20
6	Sylvain Distin	36	1.17
7	Bernardo Corradi	16	1.13
8	Richard Dunne	38	1.11
9	Joey Barton	33	1.09
10	Trevor Sinclair	13	1.08

KEY PLAYERS - DEFENDERS

Nedum Onuoha

Goals Conceded in the League Number of League goals conceded while the player was on the pitch		13
Goals Conceded in all competitions Total number of goals conceded while the player was on the pitch		14
League minutes played Number of minutes played in league matches		1324
Clean Sheets In games when the player was on pitch for at least 70 minutes		6
Defensive Rating Average number of mins between League goals conceded while on the pitch		101
Club Defensive Rating Average number of mins between League goals conceded by the club this season		77

	PLAYER	CON LGE	CON ALL	MINS	C SHEETS	DEF RATE
1	Nedum Onuoha	13	14	1324	6	101 mins
2	Michael Ball	12	15	1075	4	89 mins
3	Sylvain Distin	38	46	3254	14	85 mins
4	Richard Dunne	44	52	3420	14	77 mins

KEY GOALKEEPER

Nicky Weaver

Goals Conceded in the League Number of League goals conceded while the player was on the pitch		28
Goals Conceded in all competitions Total number of goals conceded while the player was on the pitch		36
League minutes played Number of minutes played in league matches		2149
Clean Sheets In games when the player was on pitch for at least 70 minutes		9
Goals to Shots Ratio The average number of shots on target per each League goal conceded		4.71
Defensive Rating Ave mins between League goals conceded while on the pitch		76

BOOKINGS

Ben Thatcher

League Yellow	5
League Red	0
All competitions Yellow	5
All competitions Red	0

League Average 191 mins between cards

	PLAYER	LEAGUE		TOTAL		AVE
		5Y	0R	5Y	0R	
1	Ben Thatcher	5Y	0R	5Y	0R	191
2	Dietmar Hamann	5	0	6	0	196
3	Paul Dickov	4	0	5	0	204
4	Ousmane Dabo	3	1	3	1	220
5	Bernardo Corradi	2	2	4	2	263
6	Joey Barton	10	1	11	1	269
7	Trevor Sinclair	4	0	5	0	324
8	Darius Vassell	6	0	7	0	426
9	Ishmael Miller	1	0	1	0	454
10	Claudio Reyna	2	0	2	0	478
11	Stephen Jordan	2	0	2	0	520
12	Hatem Trabelsi	2	0	3	0	683
13	Emile Mpenza	1	0	1	0	826
14	Richard Dunne	1	0	6	0	855
15	Michael Johnson	1	0	1	0	900
	Other	6	0	9	0	
	TOTAL	60	4	71	4	

WEST HAM UNITED

Eggert Magnusson arrived from Iceland and was almost undone by the buy none get two free deal done between his predecessors and Kia Joorabchian, 'owner' of **Carlos Tevez** and **Javier Mascherano**. The duo's star status unsettled Alan Pardew's squad and East London unsettled them. Mascherano escaped to Liverpool, and Tevez didn't score for 17 games. Then he hit seven in ten to help new manager Alan Curbishley avoid relegation.

Bobby Zamora struck 11 times for a sub-200 minute Strike Rate and **Teddy Sheringham** became the Premiership's oldest outfield player. **James Collins** had the club's best Defensive Rating and also led the Top Point Earners chart; the club earned 1.67 points on average when he played. **Lee Bowyer** also had a good points' average and led some poor midfield stats.

NICKNAME: THE HAMMERS   KEY: ☐ Won ☐ Drawn ■ Lost

1	prem	**Charlton**	H	W	3-1	Zamora 52, 66, C.Cole 90
2	prem	**Watford**	A	D	1-1	Zamora 65
3	prem	**Liverpool**	A	L	1-2	Zamora 12
4	prem	**Aston Villa**	H	D	1-1	Zamora 51
5	uc1rl1	**Palermo**	H	L	0-1	
6	prem	**Newcastle**	H	L	0-2	
7	prem	**Man City**	A	L	0-2	
8	uc1rl2	**Palermo**	A	L	0-3	
9	prem	**Reading**	H	L	0-1	
10	prem	**Portsmouth**	A	L	0-2	
11	prem	**Tottenham**	A	L	0-1	
12	ccr3	**Chesterfield**	A	L	1-2	Harewood 4
13	prem	**Blackburn**	H	W	2-1	Sheringham 21, Mullins 80
14	prem	**Arsenal**	H	W	1-0	Harewood 89
15	prem	**Middlesbrough**	A	L	0-1	
16	prem	**Chelsea**	A	L	0-1	
17	prem	**Sheff Utd**	H	W	1-0	Mullins 36
18	prem	**Everton**	A	L	0-2	
19	prem	**Wigan**	H	L	0-2	
20	prem	**Bolton**	A	L	0-4	
21	prem	**Man Utd**	H	W	1-0	Reo-Coker 75
22	prem	**Fulham**	A	D	0-0	
23	prem	**Portsmouth**	H	L	1-2	Sheringham 81
24	prem	**Man City**	H	L	0-1	
25	prem	**Reading**	A	L	0-6	
26	facr3	**Brighton**	H	W	3-0	Noble 49, Cole 58, Mullins 90
27	prem	**Fulham**	H	D	3-3	Zamora 28, Benayoun 46, 64
28	prem	**Newcastle**	A	D	2-2	Cole 18, Harewood 22
29	facr4	**Watford**	H	L	0-1	
30	prem	**Liverpool**	H	L	1-2	Blanco 77
31	prem	**Aston Villa**	A	L	0-1	
32	prem	**Watford**	H	L	0-1	
33	prem	**Charlton**	A	L	0-4	
34	prem	**Tottenham**	H	L	3-4	Noble 16, Tevez 40, Zamora 84
35	prem	**Blackburn**	A	W	2-1	Tevez 71 pen, Zamora 75
36	prem	**Middlesbrough**	H	W	2-0	Zamora 2, Tevez 45
37	prem	**Arsenal**	A	W	1-0	Zamora 45
38	prem	**Sheff Utd**	A	L	0-3	
39	prem	**Chelsea**	H	L	1-4	Tevez 35
40	prem	**Everton**	H	W	1-0	Zamora 13
41	prem	**Wigan**	A	W	3-0	Boa Morte 30, Benayoun 57, Harewood 83
42	prem	**Bolton**	H	W	3-1	Tevez 10, 21, Noble 29
43	prem	**Man Utd**	A	W	1-0	Tevez 45

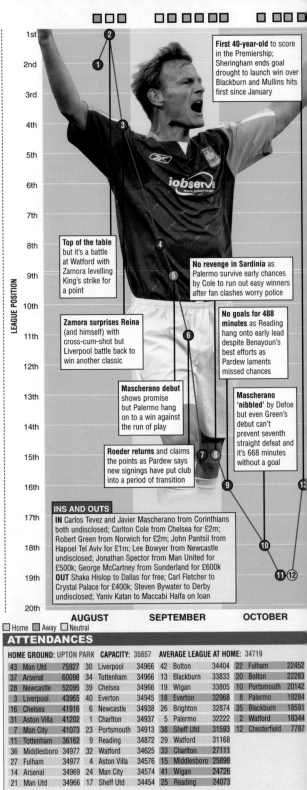

LEAGUE POSITION (1st – 20th, AUGUST SEPTEMBER OCTOBER)

☐ Home ■ Away ☐ Neutral

First 40-year-old to score in the Premiership; Sheringham ends goal drought to launch win over Blackburn and Mullins first since January

Top of the table but it's a battle at Watford with Zamora levelling King's strike for a point

No revenge in Sardinia as Palermo survive early chances by Cole to run out easy winners after fan clashes worry police

Zamora surprises Reina (and himself) with cross-cum-shot but Liverpool battle back to win another classic

No goals for 488 minutes as Reading hang onto early lead despite Benayoun's best efforts as Pardew laments missed chances

Mascherano debut shows promise but Palermo hang on to a win against the run of play

Mascherano 'nibbled' by Defoe but even Green's debut can't prevent seventh straight defeat and it's 668 minutes without a goal

Roeder returns and claims the points as Pardew says new signings have put club into a period of transition

INS AND OUTS

IN Carlos Tevez and Javier Mascherano from Corinthians both undisclosed; Carlton Cole from Chelsea for £2m; Robert Green from Norwich for £2m; John Pantsil from Hapoel Tel Aviv for £1m; Lee Bowyer from Newcastle undisclosed; Jonathan Spector from Man United for £500k; George McCartney from Sunderland for £600k **OUT** Shaka Hislop to Dallas for free; Carl Fletcher to Crystal Palace for £400k; Steven Bywater to Derby undisclosed; Yaniv Katan to Maccabi Haifa on loan

ATTENDANCES

HOME GROUND: UPTON PARK   CAPACITY: 35657   AVERAGE LEAGUE AT HOME: 34719

43	Man Utd	75927	30	Liverpool	34966	42	Bolton	34404	22	Fulham	22452
37	Arsenal	60098	34	Tottenham	34966	13	Blackburn	33833	20	Bolton	22283
28	Newcastle	52095	39	Chelsea	34966	19	Wigan	33805	10	Portsmouth	20142
3	Liverpool	43965	40	Everton	34945	18	Everton	32968	8	Palermo	19284
16	Chelsea	41916	6	Newcastle	34938	26	Brighton	32874	35	Blackburn	18591
1	Aston Villa	41202	1	Charlton	34937	5	Palermo	32222	2	Watford	18344
7	Man City	41073	23	Portsmouth	34913	38	Sheff Utd	31593	12	Chesterfield	7787
11	Tottenham	36162	9	Reading	34872	29	Watford	31168			
36	Middlesboro	34977	32	Watford	34625	33	Charlton	27111			
27	Fulham	34977	4	Aston Villa	34576	15	Middlesboro	25898			
14	Arsenal	34969	24	Man City	34574	41	Wigan	24726			
21	Man Utd	34966	17	Sheff Utd	34454	25	Reading	24073			

Icelandic invasion saved by Tevez

Final Position: 15th

KEY: ● League ● Champions Lge ● UEFA Cup ● FA Cup ○ League Cup ● Other

INS AND OUTS

IN Luis Boa Morte from Fulham for £5m; Matthew Upson from Birmingham for £6m; Lucas Neill from Blackburn for £1.5m; Nigel Quashie from West Brom for £1.5m; Calum Davenport from Tottenham undisclosed; Kepa Blanco from Seville on loan **OUT** Javier Mascherano to Liverpool on loan (ultimately sale, following registration by the FA); Tyrone Mears to Derby on loan

MONTH BY MONTH POINTS TALLY

AUGUST	4	44%
SEPTEMBER	1	11%
OCTOBER	3	25%
NOVEMBER	6	50%
DECEMBER	4	19%
JANUARY	2	17%
FEBRUARY	0	0%
MARCH	6	67%
APRIL	9	60%
MAY	6	100%

No points deducted but £5.5m fine for playing Tevez as an ineligible player

Legal threat fades away with evidence of Tevez contract with Kia Joorabchian being ended

Legal challenge from other clubs to FA decision to allow Tevez to keep playing

Wenger won't shake hands after Pardew celebrates a late Harewood winner to a thrilling game but thrown coin hits van Persie

Reo-Coker proves a point with winner against leaders and Green denies Ronaldo as Curbishley makes instant impact

Sheringham nets against his former club but Redknapp and Pompey inflict first Curbishley defeat

FA to press charges for misleading Premiership over registrations of the two Argentinians

Zamora smashes winner – his fifth goal in seven games – to beat Everton after Tevez picks up player of the season award

Tevez ensures Premier status with a clever breakaway goal to beat the new Champions and doom Sheffield United

Green can't get close to 'perfect free kick' at Chelsea but Champions are pushed all the way although starter Tevez doesn't impress

Rennie gives Curbishley indigestion as ref allows Newcastle comeback goal despite interference in front of Carroll but Davenport impresses on debut

Blades cut lifeline as comprehensive defeat in six-pointer rocks confidence and Tevez is booked for a dive

Level with Wigan as Boa Morte's bravery claims first and his unselfishness adds third for a confident win in six-pointer

Winning start for new regime but Tevez heads down tunnel and keeps going after being subbed

Heartbreak for Tevez who has a hand in three goals and still ends up losing to Spurs 95th minute breakaway in best of seven thriller

Green light for relegation hopes as keeper defies Arsenal to inflict Gunners' first loss at the Emirates despite a tally of 27 shots against

Horror show at Reading as defence goes to sleep and are hit for six with chairman Magnusson looking daggers from the stand

"You're not fit to wear the shirt" sing fans as Pardew inspires Charlton to devastating victory in six pointer

Zamora pounces on deflected cross for his ninth goal and Tevez makes sure of win, which gives Curbishley hope

Pardew pays the price for dreadful performance as Magnusson acts two weeks after promising manager his support

Harewood horror as missed penalty leads to an unthinkable defeat against relegation rivals Watford

Tevez clears on the line for Blackburn but the linesman flags for a goal and it's a vital ray of hope for Curbishley

Out of the zone with a game to go as Tevez destroys Bolton with two goals and an assist to make it six wins in eight

"A tough day" admits Pardew as Gabbidon is missed and new owner winces at Bolton's avalanche

Loan sub Blanco nets on his debut but it's too little too late to prevent Liverpool leaving with the points

NOVEMBER DECEMBER JANUARY FEBRUARY MARCH APRIL MAY

GOAL ATTEMPTS

FOR
Goal attempts recorded in League games

	HOME	AWAY	TOTAL	AVE
shots on target	123	79	202	5.3
shots off target	129	88	217	5.7
TOTAL	252	167	419	11.0

Ratio of goals to shots Average number of shots on target per League goal scored — **5.8**

Accuracy rating Average percentage of total goal attempts which were on target — **48.2**

AGAINST
Goal attempts recorded in League games

	HOME	AWAY	TOTAL	AVE
shots on target	104	143	247	6.5
shots off target	111	144	255	6.7
TOTAL	215	287	502	13.2

Ratio of goals to shots Average number of shots on target per League goal scored — **4.2**

Accuracy rating Average percentage of total goal attempts which were on target — **49.2**

GOALS

Zamora

League	11
FA Cup	0
League Cup	0
Europe	0
Other	0
TOTAL	11
League Average	195
mins between goals	

	PLAYER	LGE	FAC	LC	Euro	TOT	AVE
1	Zamora	11	0	0	0	11	195
2	Tevez	7	0	0	0	7	242
3	Harewood	3	0	1	0	4	585
4	Cole	2	1	0	0	3	270
5	Noble	2	1	0	0	3	418
6	Benayoun	3	0	0	0	3	756
7	Mullins	2	1	0	0	3	1037
8	Sheringham	2	0	0	0	2	305
9	Blanco	1	0	0	0	1	175
10	Boa Morte	1	0	0	0	1	774
11	Reo-Coker	1	0	0	0	1	3082
12	Upson	0	0	0	0	0	
13	Walker	0	0	0	0	0	
14	Spector	0	0	0	0	0	
15	Neill	0	0	0	0	0	
	Other	0	0	0	0	0	
	TOTAL	35	3	1	0	39	

PREMIERSHIP CLUBS – WEST HAM UNITED

SQUAD APPEARANCES

Match	1 2 3 4 5	6 7 8 9 10	11 12 13 14 15	16 17 18 19 20	21 22 23 24 25	26 27 28 29 30	31 32 33 34 35	36 37 38 39 40	41 42 4
Venue	H A A H H	H A A H A	A A H H A	A H A H A	H A H H A	H H A H H	A H A H A	H A A H H	A H
Competition	L L L L E	L L E L L	L W L L L	L L L L L	L L L L L	F L L F L	L L L L L	L L L L L	L L
Result	W D L D L	L L L L L	L L W W L	L W L L L	W D L L L	W D D L L	L L L L W	W W L L W	W W W

Goalkeepers
Roy Carroll
Robert Green
Gabor Kiraly
James Walker

Defenders
James Collins
Christian Dailly
Calum Davenport
Anton Ferdinand
Daniel Gabbidon
Paul Konchesky
George McCartney
Tyrone Mears
Lucas Neill
John Paintsil
Jonathan Spector
Matthew Upson

Midfielders
Yossi Benayoun
Luis Boa Morte
Lee Bowyer
Matthew Etherington
Javier Mascherano
Hayden Mullins
Shaun Newton
Mark Noble
Nigel Quashie
Kyel Reid
Nigel Reo-Coker

Forwards
Kepa Blanco
Carlton Cole
Hogan Ephraim
Marlon Harewood
Teddy Sheringham
Carlos Tevez
Bobby Zamora

KEY: ■ On all match ◀ Subbed or sent off (Counting game) ▶ Subbed on from bench (Counting Game) ▶ Subbed on and then subbed or sent off (Counting Game) □ Not in 16 □ Injured
■ On bench ◀ Subbed or sent off (playing less than 70 mins) ▶ Subbed on (playing less than 70 mins) ▶ Subbed on and then subbed or sent off (playing less than 70 min) ✕ Suspended

KEY PLAYERS – GOALSCORERS

Bobby Zamora

Goals in the League	11
Goals in all competitions	11
Assists League goals scored by a team mate where the player delivered the final pass	3
Contribution to Attacking Power Average number of minutes between League team goals while on pitch	79
Player Strike Rate Average number of minutes between League goals scored by player	195
Club Strike Rate Average minutes between League goals scored by club	97

	PLAYER	GOALS LGE	GOALS ALL	ASSISTS	POWER	S RATE
1	Bobby Zamora	11	11	3	79	195 mins
2	Carlos Tevez	7	7	3	94	242 mins
3	Marlon Harewood	3	4	1	125	585 mins
4	Yossi Benayoun	3	3	3	94	756 mins

KEY PLAYERS – MIDFIELDERS

Lee Bowyer

Goals in the League	0
Goals in all competitions	0
Assists League goals scored by a team mate where the player delivered the final pass	3
Defensive Rating Average number of mins between League goals conceded while on the pitch	75
Contribution to Attacking Power Average number of minutes between League team goals while on pitch	84
Scoring Difference Defensive Rating minus Contribution to Attacking Power	-9

	PLAYER	GOALS LGE	GOALS ALL	ASSISTS	DEF RATE	POWER	SC DIFF
1	Lee Bowyer	0	0	3	75	84	-9 mins
2	Nigel Reo-Coker	1	1	1	61	96	-35 mins
3	Yossi Benayoun	3	3	3	58	94	-36 mins
4	Matthew Etherington	0	0	1	72	155	-83 mins

PREMIERSHIP CLUBS – WEST HAM UNITED

PLAYER APPEARANCES

	AGE (on 01/07/07)	IN NAMED 16	APPEARANCES	COUNTING GAMES	MINUTES ON PITCH	APPEARANCES	MINUTES ON PITCH	THIS SEASON	HOME COUNTRY
Goalkeepers									
Roy Carroll	29	27	12	12	1080	16	1440	2	N Ireland
Robert Green	27	35	26	26	2340	27	2430	-	England
Gabor Kiraly	31	3	0	0	0	0	0	4	Hungary
James Walker	33	8	0	0	0	0	0	-	England
Defenders									
James Collins	23	18	16	15	1360	17	1450	7	Wales
Christian Dailly	33	18	14	10	993	17	1263	4	Scotland
Calum Davenport	24	11	6	6	530	6	530	-	England
Anton Ferdinand	22	31	31	28	2647	34	2871	-	England
Daniel Gabbidon	27	18	18	16	1553	22	1913	7	Wales
Paul Konchesky	26	22	22	22	1964	25	2166	-	England
George McCartney	26	25	22	14	1456	25	1704	-	N Ireland
Tyrone Mears	24	5	5	1	216	6	306	-	England
Lucas Neill	36	11	11	10	932	12	979	3	Australia
John Paintsil	26	7	5	3	345	7	478	-	Ghana
Jonathan Spector	21	29	25	17	1787	28	2013	5	United States
Matthew Upson	28	2	2	0	39	2	39	-	England
Midfielders									
Yossi Benayoun	27	31	29	24	2268	32	2471	7	Israel
Luis Boa Morte	29	14	14	7	774	16	922	-	Portugal
Lee Bowyer	30	21	20	14	1431	22	1579	-	England
Matthew Etherington	25	27	27	20	2018	30	2098	-	England
Javier Mascherano	23	9	5	1	235	7	392	2	Argentina
Hayden Mullins	28	35	30	22	2075	32	2255	-	England
Shaun Newton	31	3	3	1	101	5	183	-	England
Mark Noble	20	11	10	9	837	11	927	-	England
Nigel Quashie	28	7	7	7	608	8	698	2	Scotland
Kyel Reid	19	0	0	0	0	1	56	-	England
Nigel Reo-Coker	23	35	35	34	3082	39	3442	-	England
Forwards									
Kepa Blanco	23	8	8	0	175	8	175	-	Spain
Carlton Cole	23	20	17	4	540	21	770	-	England
Hogan Ephraim	19	0	0	0	0	0	0	-	England
Marlon Harewood	27	32	32	12	1757	35	1887	-	England
Teddy Sheringham	41	20	17	3	611	20	700	-	England
Carlos Tevez	23	30	26	15	1696	29	1953	2	Argentina
Bobby Zamora	26	34	32	18	2149	37	2459	-	England

KEY: LEAGUE   ALL COMPS   CAPS   (MAY FIFA RANKING)

TEAM OF THE SEASON

GREEN

| CG | 26 | DR | 60 |

SPECTOR	**FERDINAND**	**COLLINS**	**McCARTNEY**
CG 17 DR 68	CG 28 DR 64	CG 15 DR 71	CG 14 DR 66

BENAYOUN	**BOWYER**	**REO-COKER**	**ETHERINGTON**
CG 24 SD -36	CG 14 SD -9	CG 34 SD -35	CG 20 SD -83

 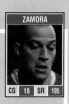

TEVEZ	**ZAMORA**
CG 15 AP 94	CG 18 SR 195

KEY: DR = Defensive Rate, SD = Scoring Difference AP = Attacking Power SR = Strike Rate, CG=Counting games – League games playing at least 70 minutes

TOP POINT EARNERS

James Collins

Counting Games	
League games when player was on pitch for at least 70 minutes	15
Average points	
Average League points taken in Counting games	1.67
Club Average points	
Average points taken in League games	1.08

	PLAYER	GAMES	PTS
1	James Collins	15	1.67
2	Lee Bowyer	14	1.43
3	George McCartney	14	1.43
4	Carlos Tevez	15	1.40
5	Anton Ferdinand	28	1.32
6	Robert Green	26	1.31
7	Matthew Etherington	20	1.25
8	Nigel Reo-Coker	34	1.12
9	Yossi Benayoun	24	1.00
10	Bobby Zamora	19	0.84

KEY PLAYERS - DEFENDERS

James Collins

Goals Conceded in the League Number of League goals conceded while the player was on the pitch	19
Goals Conceded in all competitions Total number of goals conceded while the player was on the pitch	22
League minutes played Number of minutes played in league matches	1360
Clean Sheets In games when the player was on pitch for at least 70 minutes	6
Defensive Rating Average number of mins between League goals conceded while on the pitch	71
Club Defensive Rating Average number of mins between League goals conceded by the club this season	57

	PLAYER	CON LGE	CON ALL	MINS	C SHEETS	DEF RATE
1	James Collins	19	22	1360	6	71 mins
2	Jonathan Spector	26	30	1787	4	68 mins
3	George McCartney	22	24	1456	4	66 mins
4	Anton Ferdinand	41	44	2647	8	64 mins

KEY GOALKEEPER

Robert Green

Goals Conceded in the League Number of League goals conceded while the player was on the pitch	39
Goals Conceded in all competitions Total number of goals conceded while the player was on the pitch	41
League minutes played Number of minutes played in league matches	2340
Clean Sheets In games when the player was on pitch for at least 70 minutes	9
Goals to Shots Ratio The average number of shots on target per each League goal conceded	4.59
Defensive Rating Ave mins between League goals conceded while on the pitch	60

BOOKINGS

Teddy Sheringham

League Yellow	3
League Red	0
All competitions Yellow	3
All competitions Red	0

League Average 203 mins between cards

	PLAYER	LEAGUE		TOTAL		AVE
		3Y	0R	3Y	0R	
1	T Sheringham	3Y	0R	3Y	0R	203
2	Nigel Reo-Coker	13	0	14	0	237
3	Paul Konchesky	7	1	7	1	245
4	Carlton Cole	2	0	4	0	270
5	Lee Bowyer	5	0	5	0	286
6	Nigel Quashie	2	0	3	0	304
7	James Collins	4	0	4	0	340
8	Marlon Harewood	5	0	5	0	351
9	Jonathan Spector	5	0	5	0	357
10	George McCartney	4	0	4	0	364
11	Mark Noble	2	0	2	0	418
12	Carlos Tevez	4	0	4	0	424
13	Bobby Zamora	4	1	4	1	429
14	Lucas Neill	2	0	3	0	466
15	Hayden Mullins	4	0	4	0	518
	Other	17	0	19	0	
	TOTAL	**83**	**2**	**89**	**2**	

FULHAM

As the draws mounted Chris Coleman found himself drifting too close to the relegation zone and paid the price. He can count himself unlucky in a season-long injury to his star signing **Jimmy Bullard** but a dreadful defensive record was the real reason.

The usually reliable **Antti Niemi** suffered with injuries but conceded 45 goals and was in the bottom four in his Goals to Shots Ratio. In front of him the central pair chopped and changed while **Leroy Rosenior** played in all 38 league games, so reflected the club's poor Defensive Rating.

Brian McBride missed only one game all season and scored 12 times but a Strike Rate of a goal every 321 minutes barely rates a top 30 place. **Heider Helguson** saw ten yellows and a red - a card every 133 minutes – one of the worst disciplinary records around.

NICKNAME: THE COTTAGERS

KEY: ☐ Won ☐ Drawn ■ Lost

1	prem	**Man Utd**	A	L	1-5 Ferdinand 40 og
2	prem	**Bolton**	H	D	1-1 Bullard 90 pen
3	prem	**Sheff Utd**	H	W	1-0 Bullard 40
4	prem	**Newcastle**	A	W	2-1 McBride 82, Bocanegra 89
5	prem	**Tottenham**	A	D	0-0
6	ccr2	**Wycombe**	H	L	1-2 Helguson 47
7	prem	**Chelsea**	H	L	0-2
8	prem	**Watford**	A	D	3-3 McBride 71, Helguson 83, Francis 87 og
9	prem	**Charlton**	H	W	2-1 McBride 65, C.Jensen 68
10	prem	**Aston Villa**	A	D	1-1 Volz 45
11	prem	**Wigan**	H	L	0-1
12	prem	**Everton**	H	W	1-0 C.Jensen 66
13	prem	**Portsmouth**	A	D	1-1 Knight 57
14	prem	**Man City**	A	L	1-3 John 62
15	prem	**Reading**	H	L	0-1
16	prem	**Arsenal**	H	W	2-1 McBride 6, Radzinski 19
17	prem	**Blackburn**	A	L	0-2
18	prem	**Liverpool**	A	L	0-4
19	prem	**Middlesbrough**	H	W	2-1 Helguson 12 pen, McBride 35
20	prem	**West Ham**	H	D	0-0
21	prem	**Charlton**	A	D	2-2 McBride 13, Queudrue 90
22	prem	**Chelsea**	A	D	2-2 Volz 16, Bocanegra 84
23	prem	**Watford**	H	D	0-0
24	facr3	**Leicester**	A	D	2-2 McBride 69, Volz 83
25	prem	**West Ham**	A	D	3-3 Radzinski 16, McBride 59, Christanval 90
26	facr3r	**Leicester**	H	W	4-3 McBride 35, Montella 51, 60, Routledge 90
27	prem	**Tottenham**	H	D	1-1 Montella 84 pen
28	facr4	**Stoke**	H	W	3-0 Montella 11, McBride 38, Radzinski 54
29	prem	**Sheff Utd**	A	L	0-2
30	prem	**Newcastle**	H	W	2-1 Helguson 49, McBride 73
31	prem	**Bolton**	A	L	1-2 Knight 66
32	facr5	**Tottenham**	H	L	0-4
33	prem	**Man Utd**	H	L	1-2 McBride 17
34	prem	**Aston Villa**	H	D	1-1 Bocanegra 23
35	prem	**Wigan**	A	D	0-0
36	prem	**Portsmouth**	H	D	1-1 Pearce 90
37	prem	**Everton**	A	L	1-4 Bocanegra 22
38	prem	**Man City**	H	L	1-3 Bocanegra 76
39	prem	**Reading**	A	L	0-1
40	prem	**Blackburn**	H	D	1-1 Montella 10
41	prem	**Arsenal**	A	L	1-3 S.Davies 78
42	prem	**Liverpool**	H	W	1-0 Dempsey 69
43	prem	**Middlesbrough**	A	L	1-3 S.Davies 42

☐☐☐ ☐ ☐☐☐ ☐ ☐☐ ☐

INS AND OUTS

IN Jimmy Bullard from Wigan for £2.5m; Clint Dempsey from New England Revolution for £1.5m; Franck Queudrue from Middlesbrough undisclosed; Simon Davies from Everton undisclosed; Alexei Smertin from Dynamo Moscow for free; Wayne Routledge from Tottenham on loan; Jan Lastuvka from Shakhtar Donetsk on loan
OUT Steed Malbranque tp Tottenham for £2.5m; Sylvain Legwinski to Ipswich undisclosed; Wayne Bridge to Chelsea loan return; Dean Leacock to Derby for £375k

Boa Morte fractures cheekbone to add to list of injuries but reshuffled team earns a point at Spurs

Coleman anger at Halsey; claiming ref favours the big teams as two penalty decisions go Chelsea's way

Claus Jensen sinks former club with an assist and a goal after coming on as sub against Charlton

Six goal thriller sees Helguson level against his old club to battle back from two down before points are shared at Watford

Routed by Rooney as Man United run rampant scoring four in the first 20 minutes

McBride masters Magpies with crisp volley and header against the bar that Bocanegra turns home after Bullard's horrific injury

Deadly from distance; Bullard strikes from a free kick and judders the bar after Radzinski wastes chance

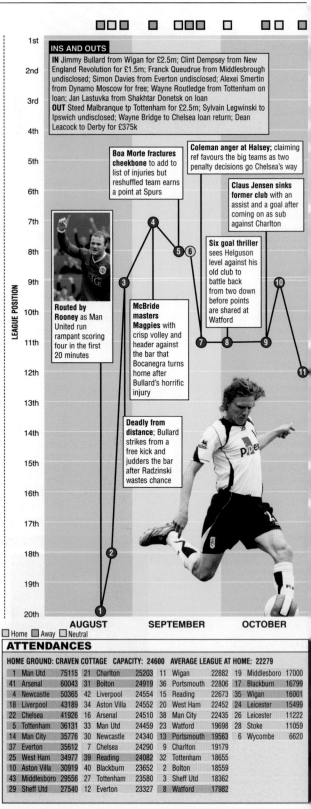

LEAGUE POSITION

1st 2nd 3rd 4th 5th 6th 7th 8th 9th 10th 11th 12th 13th 14th 15th 16th 17th 18th 19th 20th

AUGUST **SEPTEMBER** **OCTOBER**

☐ Home ☐ Away ☐ Neutral

ATTENDANCES

HOME GROUND: CRAVEN COTTAGE   CAPACITY: 24600   AVERAGE LEAGUE AT HOME: 22279

1	Man Utd	75115	21	Charlton	25203	11	Wigan	22882	19	Middlesboro	17000
41	Arsenal	60043	31	Bolton	24919	36	Portsmouth	22806	17	Blackburn	16799
4	Newcastle	50365	42	Liverpool	24554	15	Reading	22673	35	Wigan	16001
18	Liverpool	43189	34	Aston Villa	24552	20	West Ham	22452	24	Leicester	15499
22	Chelsea	41926	16	Arsenal	24510	38	Man City	22435	26	Leicester	11222
5	Tottenham	36131	33	Man Utd	24459	23	Watford	19698	28	Stoke	11059
14	Man City	35776	30	Newcastle	24340	13	Portsmouth	19563	6	Wycombe	6620
37	Everton	35612	7	Chelsea	24290	9	Charlton	19179			
25	West Ham	34977	39	Reading	24082	32	Tottenham	18655			
10	Aston Villa	30919	40	Blackburn	23652	2	Bolton	18559			
43	Middlesboro	29556	27	Tottenham	23580	3	Sheff Utd	18362			
29	Sheff Utd	27540	12	Everton	23327	8	Watford	17982			

Coleman the loser in relegation scrap

Final Position: 16th

KEY: ● League ● Champions Lge ● UEFA Cup ● FA Cup ○ League Cup ● Other

□ □ □ □□□ □□ □ □□□□□□□□□□ □ □ □ □   □   □□□ □ □ □ □□ □

MONTH BY MONTH POINTS TALLY

AUGUST	4	44%
SEPTEMBER	4	44%
OCTOBER	5	42%
NOVEMBER	7	47%
DECEMBER	6	33%
JANUARY	3	25%
FEBRUARY	3	33%
MARCH	3	33%
APRIL	1	7%
MAY	3	50%

'No alternative' claims club as Coleman is sacked after ten years service and Northern Ireland boss Lawrie Sanchez takes over

Best performance yet claims Coleman as Arsenal succumb to McBride and Radzinski, who is injured on the hoardings after scoring

Mourinho shocked by 15,000th – Volz scores a landmark Premiership goal and Bocanegra adds another to draw at Chelsea

Welcome to the Premiership as Niemi injury gives Czech Lastuvka his debut but he's a goal down in six minutes at Blackburn

Christanval snatches point against Hammers with his first strike in the 93rd minute of a six-goal thriller

Man-of-the-match Davies brings the best out of van der Sar before Ronaldo claims United a late and ill-deserved win

Knight-mare as defender lets Spurs fire four to end FA Cup dream

Dragged into the dogfight after Bocanegra's early goal is swamped by Everton come-back

Boos ring out before halftime as Man City defeat makes it just one win in last 15 although Bocanegra strikes third goal in five

Radzinski so close to earning an unlikely point at Bolton after Knight header starts fight back

Brave Pearce stays on to score deflected equaliser and snatch a point despite being injured and reduced to hobbling around the pitch

Montella's flick wafts Diop's header past Friedel but Blackburn level despite Niemi's heroics

Simon Davies's 42nd minute equaliser isn't enough to take any points from the Riverside as Boro prove too strong

Hat-trick of sorts for John as he hits the Man City net three times - but two are ruled offside

Coppell pleads Pearce's case that penalty foul does not warrant a red card but it's all over after spot kick is converted on 17 minutes

"Bitterly disappointed" says Coleman after Liverpool's four goal second half blitz

"Worthy point" claims Coleman but it's dull fare in survival scrap at Wigan

Naivety as Davies' lobbed equaliser lifts hope of a win only for Arsenal to win it with a breakaway

All but safe after Dempsey's first goal is winner over Liverpool but Brown's butt on Alonso is the talking point

Loan star Montella hits a brace to battle back from 3-1 down before Routledge clinches win in 93rd minute

Diop's by-line run sets up McBride for a snap-shot winner after Helguson's fine finish sets the tone against Newcastle

Bocanegra's dive heads home third of the season but returning Niemi makes a crucial late save for point

Reed appointed to coach as former Charlton boss gets back into football

INS AND OUTS

IN Simon Davies from Everton for £3m; Clint Dempsey from New England Revolution for £2m; Vincenzo Montella from Roma on loan **OUT** Luis Boa Morte to West Ham for £5m; Niclas Jensen to FC Copenhagen for free; Bjorn Runstorm to Luton on loan

Helguson's double yellow leaves ten men to battle to a fine draw against Spurs

NOVEMBER	DECEMBER	JANUARY	FEBRUARY	MARCH	APRIL	MAY

GOAL ATTEMPTS

FOR
Goal attempts recorded in League games

	HOME	AWAY	TOTAL	AVE
shots on target	102	79	181	4.8
shots off target	120	92	212	5.6
TOTAL	222	171	393	10.3

Ratio of goals to shots Average number of shots on target per League goal scored — **4.8**

Accuracy rating Average percentage of total goal attempts which were on target — **46.1**

AGAINST
Goal attempts recorded in League games

	HOME	AWAY	TOTAL	AVE
shots on target	89	139	228	6.0
shots off target	124	137	261	6.9
TOTAL	213	276	489	12.9

Ratio of goals to shots Average number of shots on target per League goal scored — **3.8**

Accuracy rating Average percentage of total goal attempts which were on target — **46.6**

GOALS

McBride

League	9
FA Cup	3
League Cup	0
Europe	0
Other	0
TOTAL	12

League Average — **321** mins between goals

	PLAYER	LGE	FAC	LC	Euro	TOT	AVE
1	McBride	9	3	0	0	12	321
2	Montella	2	3	0	0	5	158
3	Bocanegra	5	0	0	0	5	466
4	Helguson	3	0	1	0	4	488
5	Volz	2	1	0	0	3	1010
6	Radzinski	2	1	0	0	3	1118
7	Bullard	2	0	0	0	2	152
8	Jensen, C	2	0	0	0	2	456
9	Davies, S	2	0	0	0	2	618
10	Knight	2	0	0	0	2	1016
11	Dempsey	1	0	0	0	1	261
12	John	1	0	0	0	1	916
13	Christanval	1	0	0	0	1	1696
14	Pearce	1	0	0	0	1	1838
15	Queudrue	1	0	0	0	1	2515
	Other	0	1	0	0	1	
	TOTAL	**36**	**9**	**1**	**0**	**46**	

SQUAD APPEARANCES

Match	1 2 3 4 5	6 7 8 9 10	11 12 13 14 15	16 17 18 19 20	21 22 23 24 25	26 27 28 29 30	31 32 33 34 35	36 37 38 39 40	41 42
Venue	A H H A A	H H A H A	H H A A H	H A A H H	A A H A A	H H H A H	A H H H A	H A H A H	A H
Competition	L L L L L	W L L L L	L L L L L	L L L L L	L L L F L	F L F L L	L F L L L	L L L L L	L L
Result	L D W W D	L L D W D	L W D L L	W L L W D	D D D D D	W D W L W	L L L D D	D L L L D	L W

Goalkeepers
Ricardo Batista
Mark Crossley
Jaroslav Drobny
Jan Lastuvka
Antti Niemi
Tony Warner

Defenders
Carlos Bocanegra
Matthew Briggs
Philippe Christanval
Niclas Jensen
Zatyiah Knight
Elliot Omozusi
Ian Pearce
Franck Queudrue
Liam Rosenior
Moritz Volz
Gabriel Zakuani

Midfielders
Luis Boa Morte
Michael Brown
Jimmy Bullard
Matthew Collins
Simon Davies
Papa Bouba Diop
Claus Jensen
Wayne Routledge
Alexei Smertin
Michael Timlin

Forwards
Clint Dempsey
Heidar Helguson
Collins John
Brian McBride
Vincenzo Montella
Tomasz Radzinski
Bjorn Runstrom

KEY: ■ On all match ◄◄ Subbed or sent off (Counting game) ▶▶ Subbed on from bench (Counting Game) ▷▷ Subbed on and then subbed or sent off (Counting Game) ☐ Not in 16 ☐ Injured
■ On bench ◄◄ Subbed or sent off (playing less than 70 mins) ▶▶ Subbed on (playing less than 70 mins) ▷▷ Subbed on and then subbed or sent off (playing less than 70 min ✕ Suspended

---

KEY PLAYERS - GOALSCORERS

Brian McBride

Goals in the League	9
Goals in all competitions	12
Assists — League goals scored by a team mate where the player delivered the final pass	2
Contribution to Attacking Power — Average number of minutes between League team goals while on pitch	85
Player Strike Rate — Average number of minutes between League goals scored by player	321
Club Strike Rate — Average minutes between League goals scored by club	90

	PLAYER	GOALS LGE	GOALS ALL	ASSISTS	POWER	S RATE
1	Brian McBride	9	12	2	85	321 mins
2	Simon Davies	2	2	4	103	618 mins
3	Tomasz Radzinski	2	3	5	74	1118 mins
4	Wayne Routledge	0	1	1	67	0 mins

KEY PLAYERS - MIDFIELDERS

Wayne Routledge

Goals in the League	0
Goals in all competitions	1
Assists — League goals scored by a team mate where the player delivered the final pass	1
Defensive Rating — Average number of mins between League goals conceded while on the pitch	64
Contribution to Attacking Power — Average number of minutes between League team goals while on pitch	67
Scoring Difference — Defensive Rating minus Contribution to Attacking Power	-3

	PLAYER	GOALS LGE	GOALS ALL	ASSISTS	DEF RATE	POWER	SC DIF
1	Wayne Routledge	0	1	1	64	67	-3 mins
2	Papa Bouba Diop	0	0	2	56	89	-33 mins
3	Michael Brown	0	0	1	57	91	-34 mins
4	Luis Boa Morte	0	0	1	55	100	-45 mins

PLAYER APPEARANCES

	AGE (on 01/07/07)	IN NAMED 16	APPEARANCES	COUNTING GAMES	MINUTES ON PITCH	APPEARANCES ON PITCH	MINUTES ON PITCH THIS SEASON		HOME COUNTRY
oalkeepers									
...ardo Batista	20	3	0	0	0	0	0	-	Portugal
...rk Crossley	38	1	0	0	0	0	0	-	Wales
...roslav Drobny	27	2	0	0	0	0	0	-	Czech Republic
...n Lastuvka	24	34	8	7	660	12	1020	-	Czech Republic
...tti Niemi	35	31	31	30	2760	31	2760	-	Finland
...ny Warner	33	4	0	0	0	1	90	-	England
fenders									
...rlos Bocanegra	28	33	30	24	2332	34	2659	5	United States
...tthew Briggs	16	1	1	0	14	1	14	-	England
...ilippe Christanval	28	22	20	18	1696	23	1966	-	France
...las Jensen	32	2	0	0	0	1	64	7	Denmark
...yiah Knight	27	26	23	22	2033	24	2123	-	England
...ot Omozusi	18	5	0	0	0	2	123	-	England
...Pearce	33	23	22	20	1838	23	1903	-	England
...nck Queudrue	28	29	29	27	2515	32	2785	-	France
...m Rosenior	22	38	38	37	3397	42	3667	-	England
...ritz Volz	24	32	29	20	2020	34	2470	-	Germany
...briel Zakuani	21	8	0	0	0	2	115	-	Zaire
dfielders									
...s Boa Morte	29	15	15	11	1103	15	1103	-	Portugal
...chael Brown	30	34	34	31	2930	37	3200	-	England
...mmy Bullard	28	4	4	3	304	4	304	-	England
...tthew Collins	21	0	0	0	0	0	0	-	Wales
...non Davies	27	14	14	13	1237	16	1353	11	Wales
...pa Bouba Diop	29	23	23	17	1704	24	1794	5	Senegal
...us Jensen	30	16	12	9	912	14	1016	5	Denmark
...yne Routledge	22	31	24	12	1419	28	1779	-	England
...xei Smertin	32	7	7	5	533	8	623	1	Russia
...chael Timlin	22	0	0	0	0	1	90	-	England
rwards									
...nt Dempsey	24	13	10	1	261	12	315	6	United States
...dar Helguson	29	37	30	9	1466	34	1777	1	Iceland
...lins John	21	26	23	5	916	25	958	-	Holland
...an McBride	35	38	38	29	2897	42	3169	-	United States
...cenzo Montella	33	11	10	1	316	14	469	-	Italy
...masz Radzinski	33	38	35	22	2236	40	2662	1	Canada
...rn Runstrom	23	7	1	0	7	2	84	-	Sweden

KEY: LEAGUE   ALL COMPS   CAPS   (MAY FIFA RANKING)

TEAM OF THE SEASON

NIEMI — CG 30 DR 61
ROSENIOR — CG 37 DR 58
I PEARCE — CG 20 DR 61
BOCANEGRA — CG 24 DR 61
QUEUDRUE — CG 27 DR 67
ROUTLEDGE — CG 12 SD -3
DIOP — CG 17 SD -33
BROWN — CG 31 SD -34
BOA MORTE* — CG 11 SD -45
RADZINSKI — CG 22 AP 74
McBRIDE — CG 29 SR 321

KEY: DR = Defensive Rate, SD = Scoring Difference AP = Attacking Power SR = Strike Rate, CG=Counting games − League games playing at least 70 minutes

TOP POINT EARNERS

Wayne Routledge

Counting Games — League games when player was on pitch for at least 70 minutes	**12**
Average points — Average League points taken in Counting games	**1.33**
Club Average points — Average points taken in League games	**1.03**

	PLAYER	GAMES	PTS
1	Wayne Routledge	12	1.33
2	Philippe Christanval	18	1.28
3	Brian McBride	29	1.21
4	Franck Queudrue	27	1.19
5	Papa Bouba Diop	17	1.12
6	Antti Niemi	30	1.10
7	Zatyiah Knight	22	1.05
8	Tomasz Radzinski	22	1.05
9	Liam Rosenior	37	1.05
10	Michael Brown	31	1.03

KEY PLAYERS - DEFENDERS

Franck Queudrue

Goals Conceded in the League — number of League goals conceded while the player was on the pitch	**37**
Goals Conceded in all competitions — total number of goals conceded while the player was on the pitch	**44**
League minutes played — number of minutes played in league matches	**2515**
Clean Sheets — in games when the player was on pitch for at least 70 minutes	**6**
Defensive Rating — average number of mins between League goals conceded while on the pitch	**67**
Club Defensive Rating — average number of mins between League goals conceded by the club this season	**57**

	PLAYER	CON LGE	CON ALL	MINS	C SHEETS	DEF RATE
1	Franck Queudrue	37	44	2515	6	67 mins
2	Carlos Bocanegra	38	45	2332	6	61 mins
3	Ian Pearce	30	30	1838	4	61 mins
4	Liam Rosenior	58	63	3397	7	58 mins

KEY GOALKEEPER

Antti Niemi

Goals Conceded in the League — Number of League goals conceded while the player was on the pitch	**45**
Goals Conceded in all competitions — Total number of goals conceded while the player was on the pitch	**45**
League minutes played — Number of minutes played in league matches	**2760**
Clean Sheets — In games when the player was on pitch for at least 70 minutes	**6**
Goals to Shots Ratio — The average number of shots on target per each League goal conceded	**3.89**
Defensive Rating — Ave mins between League goals conceded while on the pitch	**61**

BOOKINGS

Heidar Helguson

League Yellow	**10**
League Red	**1**
All competitions Yellow	**10**
All competitions Red	**1**

League Average 133 mins between cards

	PLAYER	LEAGUE		TOTAL		AVE
1	Heidar Helguson	10 Y	1 R	10 Y	1 R	133
2	Michael Brown	10	0	10	0	293
3	Franck Queudrue	8	0	9	0	314
4	Papa Bouba Diop	4	1	5	1	340
5	Ian Pearce	3	1	3	1	459
6	Carlos Bocanegra	5	0	7	0	466
7	Luis Boa Morte	2	0	2	0	551
8	Moritz Volz	3	0	4	0	673
9	Zatyiah Knight	3	0	3	0	677
10	Tomasz Radzinski	3	0	3	0	745
11	Simon Davies	1	0	1	0	1237
12	Wayne Routledge	1	0	1	0	1419
13	P Christanval	1	0	1	0	1696
14	Liam Rosenior	2	0	3	0	1698
15	Antti Niemi	1	0	1	0	2760
	Other	0	0	0	0	
	TOTAL	**57**	**3**	**63**	**3**	

WIGAN ATHLETIC

It was too much for Paul Jewell and must have tested the pulse rate of every fan, but Premiership survival was achieved by the width of a goal post. Why so close? The Squad Appearances table shows overlapping injuries to **Arjan De Zeeuw**, **Henri Camara**, **Antonio Valencia** and **Paul Scharner** during a run of nine defeats.

Emile Heskey won plaudits for his work rate but a good Strike Rate has always eluded him. Camara tops that table without ever looking as dangerous as the previous year. Valencia heads the midfield quartet while De Zeeuw has a Defensive Rating ten minutes better than his colleagues. Scharner has the best points average.

The Goal Attempts tell a story; Wigan hit plenty but had one of the lower 'on target' averages and only converted one in every 5.6 of those, while opponents only needed 3.6 shots on target to score.

NICKNAME: THE LATICS

KEY: ☐ Won ☐ Drawn ☐ Lost

1	prem	**Newcastle**	A L	**1-2**	McCulloch 59
2	prem	**Reading**	H W	**1-0**	Heskey 38
3	prem	**Portsmouth**	A L	**0-1**	
4	prem	**Everton**	A D	**2-2**	Scharner 62, 68
5	ccr2	**Crewe**	A L	**0-2**	
6	prem	**Watford**	H D	**1-1**	Camara 29
7	prem	**Blackburn**	A L	**1-2**	Heskey 2
8	prem	**Man Utd**	H L	**1-3**	Baines 4
9	prem	**Man City**	H W	**4-0**	Heskey 2, Dunne 4 og, Camara 65, Valencia 67
10	prem	**Fulham**	A W	**1-0**	Camara 83
11	prem	**Bolton**	A W	**1-0**	McCulloch 79
12	prem	**Charlton**	H W	**3-2**	McCulloch 13, Camara 41, Jackson 78
13	prem	**Aston Villa**	H D	**0-0**	
14	prem	**Tottenham**	A L	**1-3**	Camara 25
15	prem	**Liverpool**	H L	**0-4**	
16	prem	**West Ham**	A W	**2-0**	Cotterill 51, Spector 58 og
17	prem	**Middlesbrough**	A D	**1-1**	Camara 24 pen
18	prem	**Arsenal**	H L	**0-1**	
19	prem	**Sheff Utd**	H L	**0-1**	
20	prem	**Chelsea**	H L	**2-3**	Heskey 45, 75
21	prem	**Man Utd**	A L	**1-3**	Baines 90 pen
22	prem	**Blackburn**	H L	**0-3**	
23	facr3	**Portsmouth**	A L	**1-2**	McCulloch 83
24	prem	**Chelsea**	A L	**0-4**	
25	prem	**Everton**	H L	**0-2**	
26	prem	**Reading**	A L	**2-3**	Heskey 3, Landzaat 90
27	prem	**Portsmouth**	H W	**1-0**	McCulloch 68
28	prem	**Arsenal**	A L	**1-2**	Landzaat 35
29	prem	**Watford**	A D	**1-1**	Folan 40
30	prem	**Newcastle**	H W	**1-0**	Taylor 40
31	prem	**Man City**	A W	**1-0**	Folan 18
32	prem	**Fulham**	H D	**0-0**	
33	prem	**Charlton**	A L	**0-1**	
34	prem	**Bolton**	H L	**1-3**	Heskey 32
35	prem	**Aston Villa**	A D	**1-1**	Heskey 21
36	prem	**Tottenham**	H D	**3-3**	Heskey 1, Baines 30, Kilbane 60
37	prem	**Liverpool**	A L	**0-2**	
38	prem	**West Ham**	H L	**0-3**	
39	prem	**Middlesbrough**	H L	**0-1**	
40	prem	**Sheff Utd**	A W	**2-1**	Scharner 14, Unsworth 45 pen

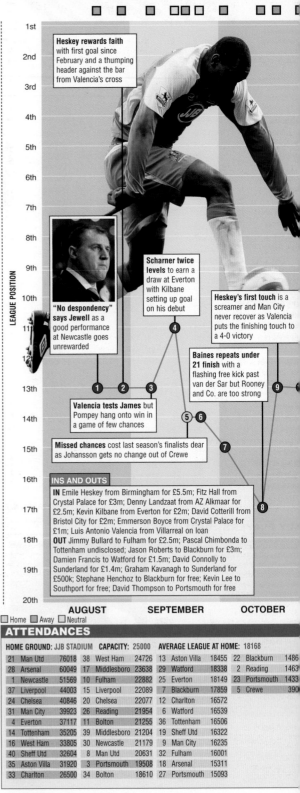

Heskey rewards faith with first goal since February and a thumping header against the bar from Valencia's cross

"No despondency" says Jewell as a good performance at Newcastle goes unrewarded

Scharner twice levels to earn a draw at Everton with Kilbane setting up goal on his debut

Heskey's first touch is a screamer and Man City never recover as Valencia puts the finishing touch to a 4-0 victory

Baines repeats under 21 finish with a flashing free kick past van der Sar but Rooney and Co. are too strong

Valencia tests James but Pompey hang onto win in a game of few chances

Missed chances cost last season's finalists dear as Johansson gets no change out of Crewe

LEAGUE POSITION (vertical axis: 1st–20th)

☐ Home ☐ Away ☐ Neutral

AUGUST   SEPTEMBER   OCTOBER

INS AND OUTS

IN Emile Heskey from Birmingham for £5.5m; Fitz Hall from Crystal Palace for £3m; Denny Landzaat from AZ Alkmaar for £2.5m; Kevin Kilbane from Everton for £2m; David Cotterill from Bristol City for £2m; Emmerson Boyce from Crystal Palace for £1m; Luis Antonio Valencia from Villarreal on loan

OUT Jimmy Bullard to Fulham for £2.5m; Pascal Chimbonda to Tottenham undisclosed; Jason Roberts to Blackburn for £3m; Damien Francis to Watford for £1.5m; David Connolly to Sunderland for £1.4m; Graham Kavanagh to Sunderland for £500k; Stephane Henchoz to Blackburn for free; Kevin Lee to Southport for free; David Thompson to Portsmouth for free

ATTENDANCES

HOME GROUND: JJB STADIUM   CAPACITY: 25000   AVERAGE LEAGUE AT HOME: 18168

21	Man Utd	76018	38	West Ham	24726	13	Aston Villa	18455	22	Blackburn	1486
28	Arsenal	60049	17	Middlesboro	23638	29	Watford	18338	2	Reading	1463
1	Newcastle	51569	10	Fulham	22882	25	Everton	18149	23	Portsmouth	1433
37	Liverpool	44003	15	Liverpool	22089	7	Blackburn	17859	5	Crewe	390
24	Chelsea	40846	20	Chelsea	22077	12	Charlton	16572			
31	Man City	39923	26	Reading	21954	6	Watford	16539			
4	Everton	37117	11	Bolton	21255	36	Tottenham	16506			
14	Tottenham	35205	39	Middlesboro	21204	19	Sheff Utd	16322			
16	West Ham	33805	30	Newcastle	21179	9	Man City	16173			
40	Sheff Utd	32604	8	Man Utd	20631	32	Fulham	16001			
35	Aston Villa	31920	3	Portsmouth	19508	18	Arsenal	15311			
33	Charlton	26500	34	Bolton	18610	27	Portsmouth	15093			

ewell quits after nail-biting finale

KEY: ● League ● Champions Lge ● UEFA Cup ● FA Cup ● League Cup ● Other

MONTH BY MONTH POINTS TALLY

AUGUST	3	50%
SEPTEMBER	2	22%
OCTOBER	6	50%
NOVEMBER	7	58%
DECEMBER	4	19%
JANUARY	0	0%
FEBRUARY	7	58%
MARCH	4	44%
APRIL	2	13%
MAY	3	50%

Filan's flying saves keep Villa down to one 'offside' goal for a point after Heskey's early lead and Valencia's red card

Whelan weighs in on decision to let Tevez keep playing despite eligibility questions

McCulloch's stunning finish is worth third successive win as sub scores the only goal at Bolton to go tenth

'Exhausted' Jewell calls a halt after the battle to stay in the Premiership and Chris Hutchins steps into the role

"Catalogue of mistakes", Jewell rages at ref Dowd's performance as Heskey penalty is denied and Arsenal level from offside position

Jewell seethes over penalty decision that gives Charlton win in six-pointer, which his side had dominated

In awe of top teams concludes Jewell as Arsenal hold on and pinch a late winner

Heskey a handful as Champions go 2-0 up and then are taken to the wire for the second season in a row

Jackson clinches win with third goal against Charlton. It's the club captain's first in the Premiership for 13 years!

McCulloch levels at Fratton Park with seven minutes to go but still Pompey inflict sixth straight defeat

Taylor's 30-yard free kick lifts relegation gap to six points with Filan's penalty save crucial in keeping Newcastle blank

Three times ahead with Camara back and dangerous, but pulled back each time by Spurs leaves Jewell's pulling his hair out

Camara's fifth of the season claims deserved lead but Spurs battle back and make most of De Zeeuw's absence

Haestad horror show as Champions are gifted three goals including a dreadful pass back by Norwegian debutant

"It wasn't pretty" but both sides take solace in a point and a clean sheet

Into the bottom three as 'two touch' free kick catches defence sleeping for Boro's goal while McCulloch header hits bar

McCulloch misses a sitter at one end and scores an own goal at the other as Liverpool are rampant in first half

Ninth successive defeat comes at Reading despite Heskey's early goal boost and Landzaat's first goal

Striking duo a handful as six pointer against Man City is decided by Folan's header and some stout defending

"A poor poor performance", admits Jewell as Hammers run away with it and draw level on points

Unsworth put on the spot he scores the penalty that keeps his current side safe at the expense of his former one

INS AND OUTS

IN Julius Agahowa from Shakhtar Donetsk £2.1m; Caleb Folan from Chesterfield for £500k; David Unsworth from Sheff Utd for free; Kristofer Haestad from IK Start on loan; Andreas Garnqvist from Helsingborg on loan **OUT** Gary Teale to Derby for £600k; Mike Pollitt to Burnley on loan; Andy Webster to Rangers on loan; David Wright to Ipswich undisclosed

Baines adds penalty to free kick for home and away goals against Man United but it's only consolation

Out of the fog comes the result Jewell's been working for as McCulloch's low drive sinks Pompey and ends freefall

Heskey strike goes unrewarded as Bolton battle back with three goals to re-awaken relegation fears

NOVEMBER	DECEMBER	JANUARY	FEBRUARY	MARCH	APRIL	MAY

GOAL ATTEMPTS

FOR
Goal attempts recorded in League games

	HOME	AWAY	TOTAL	AVE
shots on target	112	95	207	5.4
shots off target	132	97	229	6.0
TOTAL	244	192	436	11.5

Ratio of goals to shots
Average number of shots on target per League goal scored — **5.6**

Accuracy rating
Average percentage of total goal attempts which were on target — **47.5**

AGAINST
Goal attempts recorded in League games

	HOME	AWAY	TOTAL	AVE
shots on target	91	120	211	5.6
shots off target	74	112	186	4.9
TOTAL	165	232	397	10.4

Ratio of goals to shots
Average number of shots on target per League goal scored — **3.6**

Accuracy rating
Average percentage of total goal attempts which were on target — **53.1**

GOALS

Heskey

League	10
FA Cup	0
League Cup	0
Europe	0
Other	0
TOTAL	10

League Average
278
mins between goals

	PLAYER	LGE	FAC	LC	Euro	TOT	AVE
1	Heskey	10	0	0	0	10	278
2	Camara	6	0	0	0	6	269
3	McCulloch	4	1	0	0	5	576
4	Scharner	3	0	0	0	3	684
5	Baines	3	0	0	0	3	1068
6	Folan	2	0	0	0	2	346
7	Landzaat	2	0	0	0	2	1304
8	Unsworth	1	0	0	0	1	637
9	Cotterill	1	0	0	0	1	722
10	Taylor	1	0	0	0	1	1110
11	Valencia	1	0	0	0	1	1375
12	Jackson	1	0	0	0	1	1531
13	Kilbane	1	0	0	0	1	2447
14	Kirkland	0	0	0	0	0	
15	Aghahowa	0	0	0	0	0	
	Other	0	0	0	0	0	
	TOTAL	36	1	0	0	37	

SQUAD APPEARANCES

Match	1	2	3	4	5	6	7	8	9	10	11	12	13	14	15	16	17	18	19	20	21	22	23	24	25	26	27	28	29	30	31	32	33	34	35	36	37	38	39
Venue	A	H	A	A	A	H	A	H	H	A	A	H	H	A	H	A	A	H	H	H	A	H	A	A	H	A	H	A	A	H	A	H	A	H	A	H	A	H	H
Competition	L	L	L	L	W	L	L	L	L	L	L	L	L	L	L	L	L	L	F	L	L	L	F	L	L	L	L	L	L	L	L	L	L	L	L	L	L	L	L
Result	L	W	L	D	L	D	L	L	W	W	W	W	D	L	L	W	D	L	L	L	L	L	L	L	L	L	W	L	D	W	W	D	L	L	D	D	L	L	L

Goalkeepers
- John Filan
- Chris Kirkland
- Carlo Nash
- Mike Pollitt

Defenders
- Leighton Baines
- Emmerson Boyce
- Pascal Chimbonda
- Arjan De Zeeuw
- Andreas Granqvist
- Fitz Hall
- Matt Jackson
- Ryan Taylor
- David Unsworth
- Andy Webster
- David Wright

Midfielders
- Tomasz Cywka
- Kristofer Haestad
- Andreas Johansson
- Graham Kavanagh
- Kevin Kilbane
- Denny Landzaat
- Lee McCulloch
- Lewis Montrose
- Paul Scharner
- Josip Skoko
- Gary Teale
- L Antonio Valencia

Forwards
- Julius Aghahowa
- Henri Camara
- David Connolly
- David Cotterill
- Caleb Folan
- Emile Heskey
- Svetoslav Todorov

KEY: ■ On all match |◄◄ Subbed or sent off (Counting game) ►►| Subbed on from bench (Counting Game) ►►► Subbed on and then subbed or sent off (Counting Game) ☐ Not in 16 ☐ Injured
☐ On bench ◄◄ Subbed or sent off (playing less than 70 mins) ►► Subbed on (playing less than 70 mins) ►► Subbed on and then subbed or sent off (playing less than 70 min ✗ Suspended

KEY PLAYERS - GOALSCORERS

Henri Camara

Goals in the League	6
Goals in all competitions	6
Assists — League goals scored by a team mate where the player delivered the final pass	0
Contribution to Attacking Power — Average number of minutes between League team goals while on pitch	89
Player Strike Rate — Average number of minutes between League goals scored by player	269
Club Strike Rate — Average minutes between League goals scored by club	92

	PLAYER	GOALS LGE	GOALS ALL	ASSISTS	POWER	S RATE
1	Henri Camara	6	6	0	89	269 mins
2	Emile Heskey	10	10	2	99	278 mins
3	Lee McCulloch	4	5	5	100	576 mins
4	Paul Scharner	3	3	1	76	684 mins

KEY PLAYERS - MIDFIELDERS

Luis Antonio Valencia

Goals in the League	1
Goals in all competitions	1
Assists — League goals scored by a team mate where the player delivered the final pass	1
Defensive Rating — Average number of mins between League goals conceded while on the pitch	76
Contribution to Attacking Power — Average number of mins between League team goals while on pitch	80
Scoring Difference — Defensive Rating minus Contribution to Attacking Power	-4

	PLAYER	GOALS LGE	GOALS ALL	ASSISTS	DEF RATE	POWER	SC DIFF
1	Luis Antonio Valencia	1	1	1	76	80	-4
2	Paul Scharner	3	3	1	58	76	-18
3	Kevin Kilbane	1	1	6	58	81	-23
4	Denny Landzaat	2	2	1	66	93	-27

PLAYER APPEARANCES

	AGE (on 01/07/07)	IN NAMED 16	APPEARANCES	COUNTING GAMES	MINUTES ON PITCH	APPEARANCES	MINUTES ON PITCH THIS SEASON		HOME COUNTRY
Goalkeepers									
...n Filan	37	19	10	10	900	10	900	-	Australia
...ris Kirkland	26	26	26	25	2295	26	2295	1	England
...lo Nash	33	7	0	0	0	0	0	-	England
...ke Pollitt	35	23	3	2	225	5	405	-	England
...fenders									
...ghton Baines	22	35	35	34	3116	37	3296	-	England
...mmerson Boyce	27	34	34	33	3020	35	3110	-	England
...scal Chimbonda	28	1	1	0	15	1	15	-	France
...an De Zeeuw	37	21	21	19	1763	22	1801	-	Holland
...dreas Granqvist	22	2	0	0	0	1	79	-	Sweden
... Hall	26	24	24	17	1822	26	1964	-	England
...t Jackson	35	30	20	16	1531	22	1632	-	England
...an Taylor	22	17	16	10	1110	16	1110	-	England
...vid Unsworth	33	15	10	5	637	10	637	-	England
...dy Webster	25	7	4	2	273	4	273	-	Scotland
...vid Wright	27	13	12	5	679	13	769	-	England
...dfielders									
...masz Cywka	19	3	0	0	0	1	62	-	Poland
...stofer Haestad	23	4	2	1	73	3	98	-	Norway
...dreas Johansson	28	20	12	4	452	14	612	1	Sweden
...ham Kavanagh	33	2	2	0	17	2	17	1	Rep of Ireland
...in Kilbane	30	35	31	24	2357	33	2516	-	Rep of Ireland
...nny Landzaat	31	37	33	26	2519	35	2674	10	Holland
... McCulloch	29	30	29	23	2306	30	2396	4	Scotland
...vis Montrose	18	0	0	0	0	1	28	-	England
...l Scharner	27	25	25	22	2053	26	2143	-	Austria
...ip Skoko	31	29	28	22	2159	28	2159	2	Australia
...y Teale	28	13	12	4	533	14	644	5	Scotland
...ntonio Valencia	21	23	22	11	1375	22	1375	-	Ecuador
...wards									
...us Aghahowa	25	9	6	2	311	6	311	-	Nigeria
...ri Camara	30	25	23	14	1617	23	1617	-	Senegal
...vid Connolly	30	2	2	1	72	2	72	-	Rep of Ireland
...vid Cotterill	19	22	15	2	632	16	722	5	Wales
...eb Folan	24	13	13	5	692	13	692	-	England
...le Heskey	29	34	34	25	2695	36	2805	-	England
...toslav Todorov	28	7	5	2	227	5	227	-	Bulgaria

KEY: LEAGUE   ALL COMPS   CAPS   (MAY FIFA RANKING)

TEAM OF THE SEASON

KIRKLAND — CG 25   DR 55

 JACKSON — CG 16   DR 51

 BOYCE — CG 33   DR 56

 DE ZEEUW — CG 19   DR 68

 BAINES — CG 34   DR 53

 SCHARNER — CG 22   SD -18

 LANDZAAT — CG 26   SD -27

 VALENCIA* — CG 11   SD -4

 KILBANE — CG 24   SD -23

 HESKEY — CG 25   AP 99

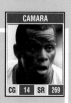 CAMARA — CG 14   SR 269

KEY: DR = Defensive Rate, SD = Scoring Difference AP = Attacking Power SR = Strike Rate, CG=Counting games – League games playing at least 70 minutes

TOP POINT EARNERS

Paul Scharner

Counting Games League games when player was on pitch for at least 70 minutes	22
Average points Average League points taken in Counting games	1.23
Club Average points Average points taken in League games	1.00

	PLAYER	GAMES	PTS
1	Paul Scharner	22	1.23
2	Luis Antonio Valencia	12	1.17
3	Henri Camara	14	1.14
4	Emmerson Boyce	33	1.09
5	Lee McCulloch	23	1.09
6	Arjan De Zeeuw	19	1.05
7	Kevin Kilbane	24	1.04
8	Denny Landzaat	26	1.04
9	Leighton Baines	34	0.97
10	Chris Kirkland	25	0.96

KEY PLAYERS - DEFENDERS

Arjan De Zeeuw

Goals Conceded in the League Number of League goals conceded while the player was on the pitch	27
Goals Conceded in all competitions Total number of goals conceded while the player was on the pitch	28
League minutes played Number of minutes played in league matches	1853
Clean Sheets Games when the player was on pitch for at least 70 minutes	6
Defensive Rating Average number of mins between League goals conceded while on the pitch	68
Club Defensive Rating Average number of mins between League goals conceded by the club this season	58

	PLAYER	CON LGE	CON ALL	MINS	C SHEETS	DEF RATE
1	Arjan De Zeeuw	27	28	1853	6	68 mins
2	Emmerson Boyce	55	57	3110	9	56 mins
3	Leighton Baines	60	64	3206	7	53 mins
4	Matt Jackson	30	33	1531	5	51 mins

KEY GOALKEEPER

Chris Kirkland

Goals Conceded in the League Number of League goals conceded while the player was on the pitch	43
Goals Conceded in all competitions Total number of goals conceded while the player was on the pitch	43
League minutes played Number of minutes played in league matches	2385
Clean Sheets In games when the player was on pitch for at least 70 minutes	7
Goals to Shots Ratio The average number of shots on target per each League goal conceded	3.42
Defensive Rating Ave mins between League goals conceded while on the pitch	55

BOOKINGS

Luis Antonio Valencia

League Yellow	6
League Red	1
All competitions Yellow	6
All competitions Red	1
League Average	196 mins between cards

	PLAYER	LEAGUE		TOTAL		AVE
1	Luis A. Valencia	6Y	1R	6Y	1R	196
2	Ryan Taylor	5	0	5	0	222
3	Paul Scharner	9	0	9	0	228
4	David Cotterill	3	0	3	0	240
5	John Filan	3	0	3	0	300
6	Lee McCulloch	6	1	6	1	329
7	Caleb Folan	2	0	2	0	346
8	Arjan De Zeeuw	5	0	6	0	370
9	Emile Heskey	7	0	7	0	397
10	Leighton Baines	8	0	8	0	400
11	Fitz Hall	3	1	4	1	455
12	Henri Camara	3	0	3	0	539
13	David Unsworth	1	0	1	0	637
14	Josip Skoko	3	0	3	0	749
15	David Wright	1	0	1	0	769
	Other	8	0	8	0	
	TOTAL	**73**	**3**	**75**	**3**	

SHEFFIELD UNITED

A sense of disbelief, as much as injustice, accompanied the slip into the bottom three as Hammers completed an unlikely escape at Old Trafford. Ten-man Wigan hung on as the Blades pounded them with everything. That summed up the season – it lacked cutting edge. The Blades had the second worst Ratio of goals to shots after Man City; they needed 6.4 shots on target to score once.

Rob Hulse's injury added to the problem but only Jonathan Stead had even a half-decent Strike Rate and he played less than a third of the season.

Neil Warnock mixed, matched and patched but **Phil Jagielka's** stats suffered from swapping between midfield and defence. **Paddy Kenny** had one of the poorest Goals to Shots Ratios in the division, saving only 3.9 shots for each goal conceded.

NICKNAME: THE BLADES

KEY: □ Won □ Drawn □ Lost

#		Opponent	H/A	Result	Score	Scorers
1	prem	Liverpool	H	D	1-1	Hulse 46
2	prem	Tottenham	A	L	0-2	
3	prem	Fulham	A	L	0-1	
4	prem	Blackburn	H	D	0-0	
5	prem	Reading	H	L	1-2	Hulse 61
6	ccr2	Bury	H	W	1-0	Nade 16
7	prem	Arsenal	A	L	0-3	
8	prem	Middlesbrough	H	W	2-1	Hulse 35, Jagielka 90
9	prem	Man City	A	D	0-0	
10	prem	Everton	A	L	0-2	
11	ccr3	Birmingham	H	L	2-4	Akinbiyi 21, Montgomery 85
12	prem	Chelsea	H	L	0-2	
13	prem	Newcastle	A	W	1-0	Webber 68
14	prem	Bolton	H	D	2-2	Hulse 70, Kazim-Richards 73
15	prem	Man Utd	H	L	1-2	Gillespie 13
16	prem	West Ham	A	L	0-1	
17	prem	Watford	A	W	1-0	Webber 88
18	prem	Charlton	H	W	2-1	Morgan 64, Gillespie 88
19	prem	Aston Villa	H	D	2-2	S.Quinn 50, Webber 64
20	prem	Wigan	A	W	1-0	Hulse 45
21	prem	Portsmouth	A	L	1-3	Hulse 4
22	prem	Man City	H	L	0-1	
23	prem	Arsenal	H	W	1-0	Nade 41
24	prem	Middlesbrough	A	L	1-3	Jagielka 45 pen
25	facr3	Swansea	H	L	0-3	
26	prem	Portsmouth	H	D	1-1	S.Quinn 22
27	prem	Reading	A	L	1-3	Nade 77
28	prem	Fulham	H	W	2-0	Stead 23, Tonge 28
29	prem	Blackburn	A	L	1-2	Stead 25
30	prem	Tottenham	H	W	2-1	Hulse 27, Jagielka 62 pen
31	prem	Liverpool	A	L	0-4	
32	prem	Everton	H	D	1-1	Hulse 52
33	prem	Chelsea	A	L	0-3	
34	prem	Bolton	A	L	0-1	
35	prem	Newcastle	H	L	1-2	Nade 74
36	prem	West Ham	H	W	3-0	Tonge 39, Jagielka 68, Stead 78
37	prem	Man Utd	A	L	0-2	
38	prem	Charlton	A	D	1-1	Stead 69
39	prem	Watford	H	W	1-0	Powell 44 og
40	prem	Aston Villa	A	L	0-3	
41	prem	Wigan	H	L	1-2	Stead 38

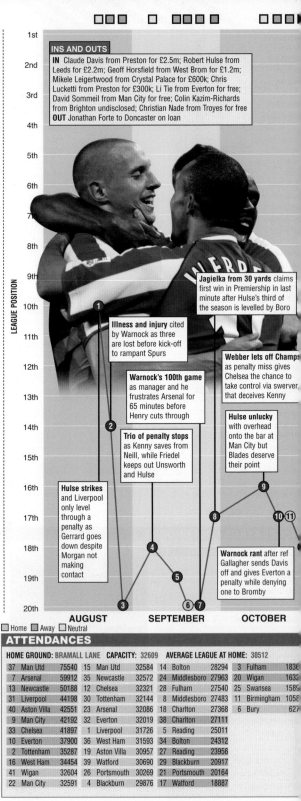

LEAGUE POSITION: 1st, 2nd, 3rd, 4th, 5th, 6th, 7th, 8th, 9th, 10th, 11th, 12th, 13th, 14th, 15th, 16th, 17th, 18th, 19th, 20th

Jagielka from 30 yards claims first win in Premiership in last minute after Hulse's third of the season is levelled by Boro

Illness and injury cited by Warnock as three are lost before kick-off to rampant Spurs

Webber lets off Champs as penalty miss gives Chelsea the chance to take control via swerver that deceives Kenny

Warnock's 100th game as manager and he frustrates Arsenal for 65 minutes before Henry cuts through

Hulse unlucky with overhead onto the bar at Man City but Blades deserve their point

Trio of penalty stops as Kenny saves from Neill, while Friedel keeps out Unsworth and Hulse

Hulse strikes and Liverpool only level through a penalty as Gerrard goes down despite Morgan not making contact

Warnock rant after ref Gallagher sends Davis off and gives Everton a penalty while denying one to Bromby

AUGUST   SEPTEMBER   OCTOBER

□ Home □ Away □ Neutral

ATTENDANCES

HOME GROUND: BRAMALL LANE   **CAPACITY:** 32609   **AVERAGE LEAGUE AT HOME:** 30512

#			#			#			#		
37	Man Utd	75540	15	Man Utd	32584	14	Bolton	28294	3	Fulham	1838?
7	Arsenal	59912	35	Newcastle	32572	24	Middlesboro	27963	20	Wigan	1632?
13	Newcastle	50188	12	Chelsea	32321	28	Fulham	27540	25	Swansea	1589?
31	Liverpool	44198	30	Tottenham	32144	8	Middlesboro	27483	11	Birmingham	1058?
40	Aston Villa	42551	23	Arsenal	32086	18	Charlton	27368	6	Bury	627?
9	Man City	42192	32	Everton	32019	38	Charlton	27111			
33	Chelsea	41897	1	Liverpool	31726	5	Reading	25011			
10	Everton	37900	36	West Ham	31593	34	Bolton	24312			
2	Tottenham	35287	19	Aston Villa	30957	27	Reading	23956			
16	West Ham	34454	39	Watford	30690	29	Blackburn	20917			
41	Wigan	32604	26	Portsmouth	30269	21	Portsmouth	20164			
22	Man City	32591	4	Blackburn	29876	17	Watford	18887			

op flight slips away on final day

Y: ● League ○ Champions Lge ● UEFA Cup ● FA Cup ○ League Cup ● Other

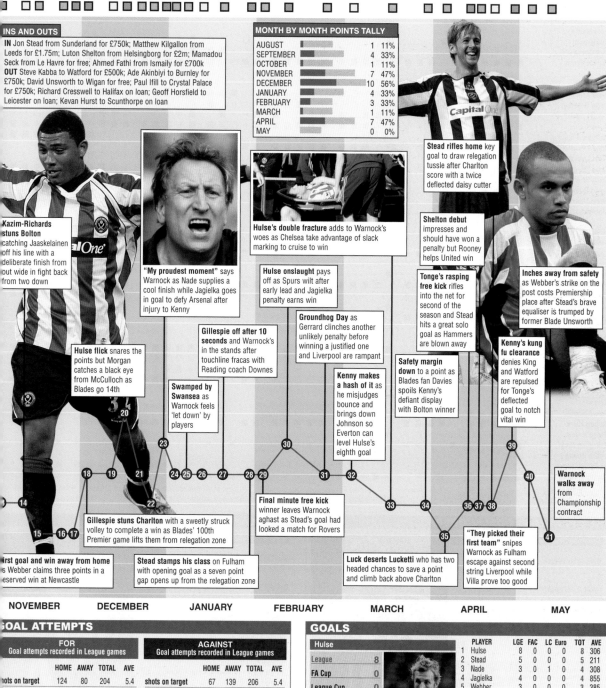

INS AND OUTS

IN Jon Stead from Sunderland for £750k; Matthew Kilgallon from Leeds for £1.75m; Luton Shelton from Helsingborg for £2m; Mamadou Seck from Le Havre for free; Ahmed Fathi from Ismaily for £700k
OUT Steve Kabba to Watford for £500k; Ade Akinbiyi to Burnley for £750k; David Unsworth to Wigan for free; Paul Ifill to Crystal Palace for £750k; Richard Cresswell to Halifax on loan; Geoff Horsfield to Leicester on loan; Kevan Hurst to Scunthorpe on loan

MONTH BY MONTH POINTS TALLY

AUGUST	1	11%
SEPTEMBER	4	33%
OCTOBER	1	11%
NOVEMBER	7	47%
DECEMBER	10	56%
JANUARY	4	33%
FEBRUARY	3	33%
MARCH	1	11%
APRIL	7	47%
MAY	0	0%

Stead rifles home key goal to draw relegation tussle after Charlton score with a twice deflected daisy cutter

Shelton debut impresses and should have won a penalty but Rooney helps United win

Inches away from safety as Webber's strike on the post costs Premiership place after Stead's brave equaliser is trumped by former Blade Unsworth

Kazim-Richards stuns Bolton catching Jaaskelainen off his line with a deliberate finish from out wide in fight back from two down

Hulse's double fracture adds to Warnock's woes as Chelsea take advantage of slack marking to cruise to win

"My proudest moment" says Warnock as Nade supplies a cool finish while Jagielka goes in goal to defy Arsenal after injury to Kenny

Hulse onslaught pays off as Spurs wilt after early lead and Jagielka penalty earns win

Tonge's rasping free kick rifles into the net for second of the season and Stead hits a great solo goal as Hammers are blown away

Kenny's kung fu clearance denies King and Watford are repulsed for Tonge's deflected goal to notch vital win

Hulse flick snares the points but Morgan catches a black eye from McCulloch as Blades go 14th

Gillespie off after 10 seconds and Warnock's in the stands after touchline fracas with Reading coach Downes

Groundhog Day as Gerrard clinches another unlikely penalty before winning a justified one and Liverpool are rampant

Safety margin down to a point as Blades fan Davies spoils Kenny's defiant display with Bolton winner

Kenny makes a hash of it as he misjudges bounce and brings down Johnson so Everton can level Hulse's eighth goal

Swamped by Swansea as Warnock feels 'let down' by players

Warnock walks away from Championship contract

Gillespie stuns Charlton with a sweetly struck volley to complete a win as Blades' 100th Premier game lifts them from relegation zone

Final minute free kick winner leaves Warnock aghast as Stead's goal had looked a match for Rovers

"They picked their first team" snipes Warnock as Fulham escape against second string Liverpool while Villa prove too good

irst goal and win away from home s Webber claims three points in a eserved win at Newcastle

Stead stamps his class on Fulham with opening goal as a seven point gap opens up from the relegation zone

Luck deserts Lucketti who has two headed chances to save a point and climb back above Charlton

14 15 16 17 18 19 21 22 23 24 25 26 27 28 29 30 31 32 33 34 35 36 37 38 39 40 41

NOVEMBER	DECEMBER	JANUARY	FEBRUARY	MARCH	APRIL	MAY

GOAL ATTEMPTS

FOR
Goal attempts recorded in League games

	HOME	AWAY	TOTAL	AVE
hots on target	124	80	204	5.4
hots off target	110	111	221	5.8
OTAL	234	191	425	11.2

atio of goals to shots
verage number of shots on rget per League goal scored — **6.4**

ccuracy rating
verage percentage of total goal tempts which were on target — **48.0**

AGAINST
Goal attempts recorded in League games

	HOME	AWAY	TOTAL	AVE
shots on target	67	139	206	5.4
shots off target	104	124	228	6.0
TOTAL	171	263	434	11.4

Ratio of goals to shots
Average number of shots on target per League goal scored — **3.7**

Accuracy rating
Average percentage of total goal attempts which were on target — **47.5**

GOALS

Hulse

League	8
FA Cup	0
League Cup	0
Europe	0
Other	0
TOTAL	8

League Average
306
mins between goals

	PLAYER	LGE	FAC	LC	Euro	TOT	AVE
1	Hulse	8	0	0	0	8	306
2	Stead	5	0	0	0	5	211
3	Nade	3	0	1	0	4	308
4	Jagielka	4	0	0	0	4	855
5	Webber	3	0	0	0	3	385
6	Quinn, S	2	0	0	0	2	600
7	Tonge	2	0	0	0	2	1006
8	Gillespie	2	0	0	0	2	1188
9	Kazim-Richards	1	0	0	0	1	1506
10	Morgan	1	0	0	0	1	2033
11	Akinbiyi	0	0	1	0	1	
12	Montgomery	0	0	1	0	1	
	Other	0	0	0	0	0	
	TOTAL	31	0	3	0	34	

PREMIERSHIP CLUBS – SHEFFIELD UNITED

SQUAD APPEARANCES

Match	1	2	3	4	5	6	7	8	9	10	11	12	13	14	15	16	17	18	19	20	21	22	23	24	25	26	27	28	29	30	31	32	33	34	35	36	37	38	39	40
Venue	H	A	A	H	H	H	A	H	A	A	H	H	A	H	H	A	A	H	H	A	A	H	H	A	H	H	A	H	A	H	A	H	A	A	H	H	A	A	H	A
Competition	L	L	L	L	L	W	L	L	L	L	W	L	L	L	L	L	L	L	L	L	L	L	L	L	F	L	L	L	L	L	L	L	L	L	L	L	L	L	L	L
Result	D	L	L	D	L	W	L	W	D	L	L	L	W	D	L	L	W	W	D	W	L	L	W	L	L	D	L	W	L	W	L	D	L	L	L	W	L	D	W	L

Goalkeepers
Ian Bennett
Paul Gerrard
Patrick Kenny

Defenders
Chris Armstrong
Leigh Bromby
Claude Davis
Derek Geary
Matthew Kilgallon
Robert Kozluk
Chris Lucketti
Chris Morgan
Craig Short
David Sommeil
David Unsworth
Alan Wright

Midfielders
Ahmed Fathi
Keith Gillespie
Kevan Hurst
Paul Ifill
Philip Jagielka
C Kazim-Richards
Nicholas Law
Mikele Leigertwood
Li Tie
Colin Marrison
Nick Montgomery
Alan Quinn
Stephen Quinn
Michael Tonge

Forwards
Ade Akinbiyi
Robert Hulse
Steve Kabba
Christian Nade
Luton Shelton
Jonathan Stead
Danny Webber

KEY: ■ On all match ■ On bench ⏮ Subbed or sent off (Counting game) ⏪ Subbed or sent off (playing less than 70 mins) ⏭ Subbed on from bench (Counting Game) ⏩ Subbed on (playing less than 70 mins) ⏭ Subbed on and then subbed or sent off (Counting Game) ⏩ Subbed on and then subbed or sent off (playing less than 70 min □ Not in 16 □ Injured ✕ Suspended

KEY PLAYERS - GOALSCORERS

Jonathan Stead

Goals in the League	5
Goals in all competitions	5
Assists League goals scored by a team mate where the player delivered the final pass	0
Contribution to Attacking Power Average number of minutes between League team goals while on pitch	75
Player Strike Rate Average number of minutes between League goals scored by player	211
Club Strike Rate Average minutes between League goals scored by club	106

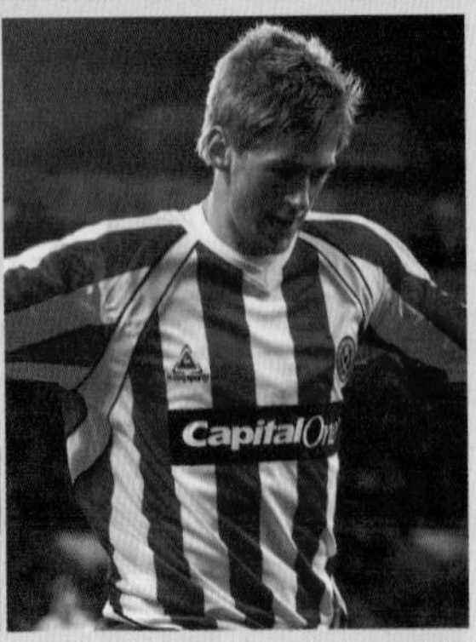

	PLAYER	GOALS LGE	GOALS ALL	ASSISTS	POWER	S RATE
1	Jonathan Stead	5	5	0	75	211 mins
2	Robert Hulse	8	8	2	102	306 mins
3	Stephen Quinn	2	2	3	80	600 mins
4	Philip Jagielka	4	4	0	106	855 mins

KEY PLAYERS - MIDFIELDERS

Colin Kazim-Richards

Goals in the League	1
Goals in all competitions	1
Assists League goals scored by a team mate where the player delivered the final pass	3
Defensive Rating Average number of mins between League goals conceded while on the pitch	60
Contribution to Attacking Power Average number of minutes between League team goals while on pitch	88
Scoring Difference Defensive Rating minus Contribution to Attacking Power	-28

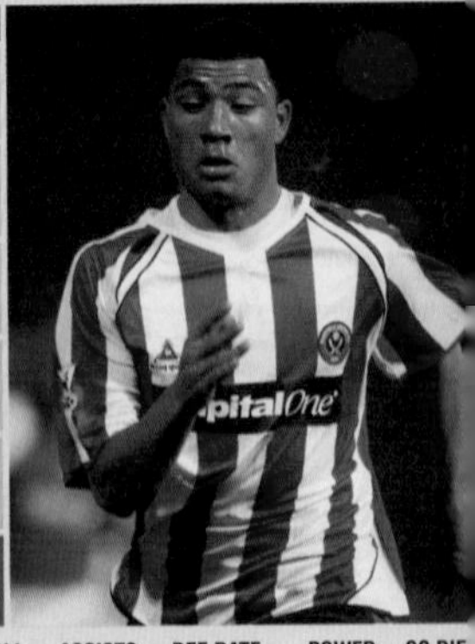

	PLAYER	GOALS LGE	GOALS ALL	ASSISTS	DEF RATE	POWER	SC DIF
1	Colin Kazim-Richards	1	1	3	60	88	-28 min
2	Stephen Quinn	2	2	3	52	80	-28 min
3	Nick Montgomery	0	1	4	60	99	-39 min
4	Philip Jagielka	4	4	0	62	106	-44 min

PLAYER APPEARANCES

	AGE (on 01/07/07)	IN NAMED 16	APPEARANCES	COUNTING GAMES	MINUTES ON PITCH	APPEARANCES	MINUTES ON PITCH THIS SEASON		HOME COUNTRY
Goalkeepers									
...o Bennett	35	5	2	2	180	4	360	-	England
...ul Gerrard	34	4	2	2	180	3	270	-	England
...trick Kenny	29	34	34	33	3031	34	3031	2	Rep of Ireland
Defenders									
...ris Armstrong	24	30	27	23	2214	28	2304	-	England
...igh Bromby	27	25	17	11	1139	18	1229	-	England
...aude Davis	28	24	21	13	1494	22	1584	-	Jamaica
...rek Geary	27	29	26	24	2217	28	2324	-	Rep of Ireland
...atthew Kilgallon	23	6	6	6	540	6	540	-	England
...bert Kozluk	29	27	19	16	1489	20	1579	-	England
...ris Lucketti	36	9	8	7	661	9	706	-	England
...ris Morgan	29	31	24	21	2033	25	2123	-	England
...aig Short	39	2	0	0	0	2	135	-	England
...vid Sommeil	32	9	5	3	327	7	507	-	France
...vid Unsworth	33	5	5	3	375	6	465	-	England
...n Wright	35	1	1	1	90	2	135	-	England
Midfielders									
...med Fathi	22	6	3	2	199	3	199	2	Egypt
...th Gillespie	32	32	31	24	2376	31	2376	7	N Ireland
...van Hurst	21	0	0	0	0	1	61	-	England
...ul Ifill	27	4	3	0	166	4	256	-	England
...ilip Jagielka	24	38	38	38	3420	38	3420	-	England
...Kazim-Richards	20	33	27	14	1506	29	1686	-	England
...cholas Law	19	7	4	2	212	7	421	-	England
...kele Leigertwood	24	21	19	14	1410	19	1410	-	England
...Tie	29	0	0	0	0	1	90	-	China PR
...in Marrison	21	0	0	0	0	1	16	-	England
...k Montgomery	25	29	26	19	1988	28	2168	-	England
...n Quinn	28	29	19	7	970	21	1150	2	Rep of Ireland
...phen Quinn	21	15	15	12	1200	17	1274	-	Rep of Ireland
...chael Tonge	24	27	27	22	2012	28	2017	-	England
Forwards									
...e Akinbiyi	32	6	3	2	185	5	325	-	England
...bert Hulse	27	29	29	27	2450	29	2450	-	England
...ve Kabba	26	8	7	0	120	8	210	-	England
...istian Nade	22	33	25	5	926	28	1101	4	France
...on Shelton	21	7	4	1	200	4	200	2	Jamaica
...nathan Stead	24	15	14	11	1059	14	1059	-	England
...nny Webber	25	28	22	10	1156	24	1314	-	England

KEY: LEAGUE   ALL COMPS   CAPS   (MAY FIFA RANKING)

TEAM OF THE SEASON

KENNY — CG 33 | DR 65

KOZLUK — CG 16 | DR 59
MORGAN — CG 21 | DR 63
DAVIS — CG 13 | DR 64
GEARY — CG 24 | DR 61

KAZIM-RICHARDS — CG 14 | SD -28
JAGIELKA — CG 38 | SD -44
MONTGOMERY — CG 19 | SD -39
S. QUINN — CG 12 | SD -28

HULSE — CG 27 | AP 102

STEAD* — CG 11 | SR 211

KEY: DR = Defensive Rate, SD = Scoring Difference AP = Attacking Power SR = Strike Rate, CG=Counting games — League games playing at least 70 minutes

TOP POINT EARNERS

Nick Montgomery

Counting Games League games when player was on pitch for at least 70 minutes	19
Average points Average League points taken in Counting games	1.26
Club Average points Average points taken in League games	1.00

	PLAYER	GAMES	PTS
1	Nick Montgomery	19	1.26
2	Stephen Quinn	12	1.25
3	Derek Geary	24	1.25
4	Colin Kazim-Richards	14	1.21
5	Keith Gillespie	24	1.17
6	Robert Kozluk	16	1.13
7	Robert Hulse	27	1.04
8	Patrick Kenny	33	1.03
9	Chris Armstrong	23	1.00
10	Philip Jagielka	38	1.00

KEY PLAYERS - DEFENDERS

Claude Davis

Goals Conceded in the League Number of League goals conceded while the player was on the pitch	23
Goals Conceded in all competitions Total number of goals conceded while the player was on the pitch	23
League minutes played Number of minutes played in league matches	1494
Clean Sheets Games when the player was on pitch for at least 70 minutes	3
Defensive Rating Average number of mins between League goals conceded while on the pitch	64
Club Defensive Rating Average number of mins between League goals conceded by the club this season	62

	PLAYER	CON LGE	CON ALL	MINS	C SHEETS	DEF RATE
1	Claude Davis	23	23	1494	3	64 mins
2	Chris Morgan	32	36	2033	5	63 mins
3	Derek Geary	36	41	2217	6	61 mins
4	Robert Kozluk	25	25	1489	4	59 mins

KEY GOALKEEPER

Patrick Kenny

Goals Conceded in the League Number of League goals conceded while the player was on the pitch	46
Goals Conceded in all competitions Total number of goals conceded while the player was on the pitch	46
League minutes played Number of minutes played in league matches	3031
Clean Sheets In games when the player was on pitch for at least 70 minutes	8
Goals to Shots Ratio The average number of shots on target per each League goal conceded	3.91
Defensive Rating Ave mins between League goals conceded while on the pitch	65

BOOKINGS

Leigh Bromby

League Yellow	5
League Red	0
All competitions Yellow	5
All competitions Red	0

League Average **227** mins between cards

	PLAYER	LEAGUE		TOTAL		AVE
1	Leigh Bromby	5Y 0R		5Y 0R		227
2	Nick Montgomery	7	0	7	0	284
3	Michael Tonge	6	0	6	0	335
4	Chris Morgan	6	0	6	0	338
5	Robert Kozluk	4	0	4	0	372
6	Claude Davis	3	1	3	1	373
7	Robert Hulse	6	0	6	0	408
8	Christian Nade	2	0	2	0	463
9	M. Leigertwood	3	0	3	0	470
10	Jonathan Stead	2	0	2	0	529
11	Derek Geary	4	0	5	0	554
12	Keith Gillespie	3	1	3	1	594
13	Chris Lucketti	1	0	1	0	661
14	C Kazim-Richards	2	0	3	0	753
15	Patrick Kenny	4	0	4	0	757
	Other	7	0	7	0	
	TOTAL	65	2	67	2	

CHARLTON ATHLETIC

The goals of **Darren Bent** were not enough to salvage the club from a sequence of management uncertainty. The striker confirmed his Premiership class with 13 league goals and a fair Strike Rate, for a relegated team player, of one every 220 minutes – the 14th best in the division.

However, he had little striking support and the injury hit **Jerome Thomas** had the next best Strike Rate despite only playing for 1360 minutes. Thomas was the pick of the midfield, somehow conjuring a positive Scoring Difference of +29 and was way ahead of the rest in the Top Point Earners chart with the side averaging 1.62 points a game when he played.

Scott Carson only missed the two Liverpool league games but 11 Clean Sheets was a good return.

NICKNAME: THE ADDICKS   KEY: ☐ Won ☐ Drawn ■ Lost

1	prem	**West Ham**	A	L	**1-3** D.Bent 15 pen
2	prem	**Man Utd**	H	L	**0-3**
3	prem	**Bolton**	H	W	**2-0** D.Bent 65 pen, 85
4	prem	**Chelsea**	A	L	**1-2** Hasselbaink 54
5	prem	**Portsmouth**	H	L	**0-1**
6	ccr2	**Carlisle**	H	W	**1-0** D.Bent 57
7	prem	**Aston Villa**	A	L	**0-2**
8	prem	**Arsenal**	H	L	**1-2** D.Bent 21
9	prem	**Fulham**	A	L	**1-2** D.Bent 78
10	prem	**Watford**	H	D	**0-0**
11	ccr3	**Bolton**	H	W	**1-0** M.Bent 17
12	prem	**Newcastle**	A	D	**0-0**
13	prem	**Man City**	H	W	**1-0** D.Bent 28
14	ccr4	**Chesterfield**	A	W	**4-3*** Hasselbaink 40, 93, D.Bent 73 (*on penalties)
15	prem	**Wigan**	A	L	**2-3** De Zeeuw 52 og, M.Bent 90
16	prem	**Reading**	A	L	**0-2**
17	prem	**Everton**	H	D	**1-1** Reid 68
18	prem	**Sheff Utd**	A	L	**1-2** Reid 17
19	prem	**Blackburn**	H	W	**1-0** El Karkouri 90
20	prem	**Tottenham**	A	L	**1-5** Dawson 43 og
21	prem	**Liverpool**	H	L	**0-3**
22	ccqf	**Wycombe**	H	L	**0-1**
23	prem	**Middlesbrough**	A	L	**0-2**
24	prem	**Fulham**	H	D	**2-2** Ambrose 19, D.Bent 45
25	prem	**Aston Villa**	H	W	**2-1** D.Bent 57, Hughes 90
26	prem	**Arsenal**	A	L	**0-4**
27	facr3	**Nottm Forest**	A	L	**0-2**
28	prem	**Middlesbrough**	H	L	**1-3** Hasselbaink 27
29	prem	**Portsmouth**	A	W	**1-0** Faye 79
30	prem	**Bolton**	A	D	**1-1** El Karkouri 12
31	prem	**Chelsea**	H	L	**0-1**
32	prem	**Man Utd**	A	L	**0-2**
33	prem	**West Ham**	H	W	**4-0** Ambrose 24, Thomas 34, 80, D.Bent 41
34	prem	**Watford**	A	D	**2-2** Young 67, Ambrose 89
35	prem	**Newcastle**	H	W	**2-0** Z.Zheng 53, Thomas 88 pen
36	prem	**Wigan**	H	W	**1-0** D.Bent 86 pen
37	prem	**Man City**	A	D	**0-0**
38	prem	**Reading**	H	D	**0-0**
39	prem	**Everton**	A	L	**1-2** D.Bent 89
40	prem	**Sheff Utd**	H	D	**1-1** El Karkouri 59
41	prem	**Blackburn**	A	L	**1-4** D.Bent 71
42	prem	**Tottenham**	H	L	**0-2**
43	prem	**Liverpool**	A	D	**2-2** Holland 2, D.Bent 72

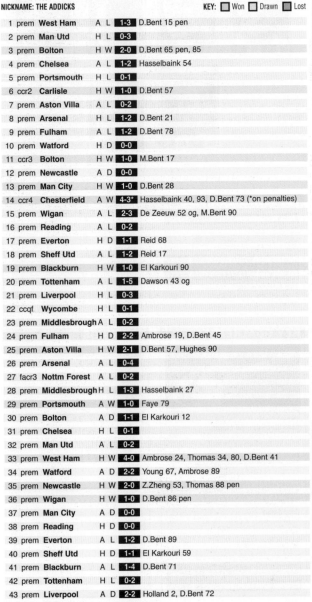

☐☐☐ ☐ ☐☐☐☐ ☐☐☐

LEAGUE POSITION: 1st, 2nd, 3rd, 4th, 5th, 6th, 7th, 8th, 9th, 10th, 11th, 12th, 13th, 14th, 15th, 16th, 17th, 18th, 19th, 20th

AUGUST   SEPTEMBER   OCTOBER

☐ Home ■ Away ☐ Neutral

Carson overwhelmed as United notch up chances before settling on three goal win to leave Dowie bottom

Traore's moment of madness undermines Darren Bent's good start to the season as Hammers take ten men apart

Wonder volley wins it for Arsenal after Darren Bent gives an early lead and Hasselbaink misses header for a point

Hasselbaink apologetic as he scores against Chelsea but Blues still win despite Carson's penalty save

El Karkhouri impresses to gain away point at Newcastle and Darren Bent misses late chance

Five defeats in-a-row leave Dowie cursing poor finishing from Rommedahl's pacy wing play

ATTENDANCES

HOME GROUND: THE VALLEY   CAPACITY: 27111   AVERAGE LEAGUE AT HOME: 26195

32	Man Utd	75883	18	Sheff Utd	27368	28	Middlesboro	26384
26	Arsenal	60057	21	Liverpool	27111	42	Tottenham	26339
12	Newcastle	48642	33	West Ham	27111	38	Reading	26271
43	Liverpool	43134	31	Chelsea	27111	5	Portsmouth	26130
37	Man City	41424	40	Sheff Utd	27111	13	Man City	26011
4	Chelsea	41194	35	Newcastle	27028	2	Man Utd	25422
20	Tottenham	35565	10	Watford	27011	24	Fulham	25203
7	Aston Villa	35513	8	Arsenal	26770	41	Blackburn	24921
1	West Ham	34937	25	Aston Villa	26699	16	Reading	24093
39	Everton	34028	36	Wigan	26500	3	Bolton	23638
23	Middlesboro	32013	17	Everton	26435	19	Blackburn	23423
30	Bolton		223?					
34	Watford		197?					
29	Portsmouth		195?					
9	Fulham		191?					
27	Nottm Forest		190?					
22	Wycombe		189?					
15	Wigan		165?					
11	Bolton		107?					
6	Carlisle		81?					
14	Chesterfield		70?					

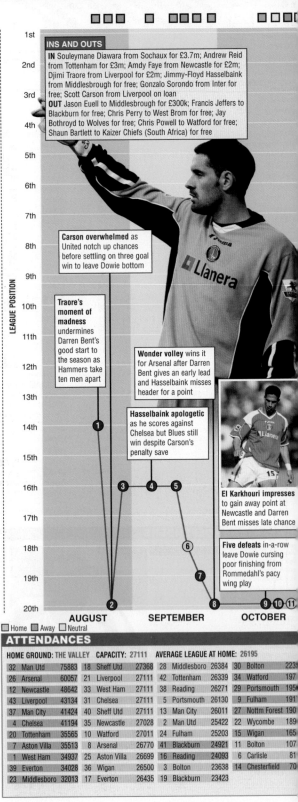

Managerial muddle leads to the drop

Final Position: 19th

Key: ● League ○ Champions Lge ○ UEFA Cup ● FA Cup ○ League Cup ● Other

INS AND OUTS

IN Alexandre Song Billong from Arsenal on loan; Madjid Bougherra from Sheff Wed for £2.5m; Ben Thatcher from Man City for £500k; Zheng Zhi from Shandong Luneng (China) on loan
OUT Djimi Traore to Portsmouth for £1m; Stephan Andersen to Brondby undisclosed; Jonathan Fortune to Stoke on loan; Stephan Andersen to Brondby (Denmark) for a nominal fee

Fans get Pardew for Xmas as patience with Reed runs out after 41 days

MONTH BY MONTH POINTS TALLY

AUGUST	3	33%
SEPTEMBER	0	0%
OCTOBER	2	22%
NOVEMBER	4	33%
DECEMBER	7	33%
JANUARY	4	33%
FEBRUARY	3	33%
MARCH	7	78%
APRIL	3	20%
MAY	1	17%

Dowie is first manager out this Premier season as board decide they have to act

Captain Darren Bent scores eighth goal but sub Hughes snatches win in 91st minute over ten-man Villa

Wycombe, we saw we conquered; League Two strugglers pile on the misery for Reed and fans bay their disapproval

Traore's high kicking gives his old side a penalty start and then it's one-way traffic

Rolled over at Tottenham with only an own goal to show for and five against

Giant-killers halted by Hreidarsson's decisive penalty after Hasselbaink hits two against Chesterfield

Defence crumbles despite Darren Bent forcing an own goal and Marcus Bent pulls back a late consolation

Reid strikes for Reed's first point after a slow start with the first signs of returning confidence

Hasselbaink nets against his old side to earn lead but it's too easy as Boro blast back

Faye's double first; his first goal in English football and first away win of the season comes at Pompey

Class keepers make it tight at the Valley but Carson is beaten while Cech keeps Faye at bay

Twenty points needed says Pardew as remaining games dwindle to 11 after United defeat

Thomas twists knife in Curbishley's hopes as Hammers are swamped by four goals plus two strikes against the woodwork

Song Billong's in Premiership as his passes set up comeback goals against Watford with Ambrose levelling in 89th minute

Pardew salutes Chinese captain as Zheng scores first goal and earns penalty for second in win that makes it seven point from nine

Points gap cut to just one from safety as Marcus Bent is tripped and Darren slots away penalty for third home win on the spin

Injuries disrupt against Reading as Hreidarsson and Marcus Bent take knocks but El Karkouri thumps bar

Heartbreak after Darren Bent levels in 89 minute only for Everton's McFadden to hit a peach of a winner

Relegated after seven years in the top flight as Song goes closest but Spurs show their quality

Bowing out with a draw at Anfield as Darren Bent takes Premier tally to 13 and Liverpool only level with a last-minute penalty

Out of the bottom three for the first time in seven months as Pardew claims a point at Man City

NOVEMBER — DECEMBER — JANUARY — FEBRUARY — MARCH — APRIL — MAY

GOAL ATTEMPTS

FOR — Goal attempts recorded in League games

	HOME	AWAY	TOTAL	AVE
shots on target	107	62	169	4.4
shots off target	117	80	197	5.2
TOTAL	224	142	366	9.6

Ratio of goals to shots — Average number of shots on target per League goal scored	5.0
Accuracy rating — Average percentage of total goal attempts which were on target	46.2

AGAINST — Goal attempts recorded in League games

	HOME	AWAY	TOTAL	AVE
shots on target	126	145	271	7.1
shots off target	127	153	280	7.4
TOTAL	253	298	551	14.5

Ratio of goals to shots — Average number of shots on target per League goal scored	4.5
Accuracy rating — Average percentage of total goal attempts which were on target	49.2

GOALS

Bent, D

League	13
FA Cup	0
League Cup	2
Europe	0
Other	0
TOTAL	15

League Average — 220 mins between goals

	PLAYER	LGE	FAC	LC	Euro	TOT	AVE
1	Bent, D	13	0	2	0	15	220
2	Hasselbaink	2	0	2	0	4	557
3	Thomas	3	0	0	0	3	453
4	Ambrose	3	0	0	0	3	582
5	El Karkouri	3	0	0	0	3	1080
6	Reid	2	0	0	0	2	600
7	Bent, M	1	0	1	0	2	1484
8	Zheng	1	0	0	0	1	842
9	Hughes	1	0	0	0	1	1480
10	Faye	1	0	0	0	1	2081
11	Holland	1	0	0	0	1	2443
12	Young	1	0	0	0	1	2587
13	Traore	0	0	0	0	0	
14	Walker	0	0	0	0	0	
15	Rommedahl	0	0	0	0	0	
	Other	0	0	0	0	0	
	TOTAL	32	0	5	0	37	

SQUAD APPEARANCES

Match	1	2	3	4	5	6	7	8	9	10	11	12	13	14	15	16	17	18	19	20	21	22	23	24	25	26	27	28	29	30	31	32	33	34	35	36	37	38	39	40	41	42
Venue	A	H	H	A	H		H	A	H	A	H		H	A	H	A	A		A	H	A	H	A		H	H	A	H	H		A	A	H	A	A		H	A	H	A	H		A	H
Competition	L	L	L	L	L		W	L	L	L	L		W	L	L	W	L		L	L	L	L	L		L	L	W	L	L		L	F	L	L	L		L	L	L	L	L		L	L
Result	L	L	W	L	L		W	L	L	L	D		W	D	W	W	L		L	D	L	W	L		L	L	L	D	W		L	L	W	D	W		W	D	D	L	D		L	L

Goalkeepers
Stephan Andersen
Scott Carson
Robert Elliot
Thomas Myhre
Darren Randolph

Defenders
Nathan Ashton
Madjid Bougherra
Souleymane Diawara
Talal El Karkouri
Jonathan Fortune
Hermann Hreidarsson
Radostin Kishishev
Osei Sankofa
Ben Thatcher
Djimi Traore
Luke Young

Midfielders
Darren Ambrose
Amdy Faye
Matt Holland
Bryan Hughes
Alistair John
Omar Pouso
Andrew Reid
Dennis Rommedahl
Lloyd Sam
Alexandre Song
Gonzalo Sorondo
Jerome Thomas
Zhi Zheng

Forwards
Darren Bent
Marcus Bent
J-Floyd Hasselbaink
Kevin Lisbie
James Walker

KEY: ■ On all match ◄◄ Subbed or sent off (Counting game) ▶▶ Subbed on from bench (Counting Game) ▷▷ Subbed on and then subbed or sent off (Counting Game) ☐ Not in 16 ☐ Injured
■ On bench ◄ Subbed or sent off (playing less than 70 mins) ▶ Subbed on (playing less than 70 mins) ▷ Subbed on and then subbed or sent off (playing less than 70 min ✕ Suspended

---

KEY PLAYERS - GOALSCORERS

Darren Bent

Goals in the League	13
Goals in all competitions	15
Assists — League goals scored by a team mate where the player delivered the final pass	2
Contribution to Attacking Power — Average number of minutes between League team goals while on pitch	95
Player Strike Rate — Average number of minutes between League goals scored by player	220
Club Strike Rate — Average minutes between League goals scored by club	100

	PLAYER	GOALS LGE	GOALS ALL	ASSISTS	POWER	S RATE
1	Darren Bent	13	15	2	95	220 mins
2	Jerome Thomas	3	3	2	75	453 mins
3	Darren Ambrose	3	3	2	87	582 mins
4	Marcus Bent	1	2	3	106	1484 mins

KEY PLAYERS - MIDFIELDERS

Jerome Thomas

Goals in the League	3
Goals in all competitions	3
Assists — League goals scored by a team mate where the player delivered the final pass	2
Defensive Rating — Average number of mins between League goals conceded while on the pitch	104
Contribution to Attacking Power — Average number of minutes between League team goals while on pitch	75
Scoring Difference — Defensive Rating minus Contribution to Attacking Power	29

	PLAYER	GOALS LGE	GOALS ALL	ASSISTS	DEF RATE	POWER	SC DIF
1	Jerome Thomas	3	3	2	104	75	29 min
2	Alexandre Song	0	0	1	70	81	-11 min
3	Darren Ambrose	3	3	2	56	87	-31 min
4	Andrew Reid	2	2	1	52	100	-48 min

PLAYER APPEARANCES

	AGE (on 01/07/07)	IN NAMED 16	APPEARANCES	COUNTING GAMES	MINUTES ON PITCH	APPEARANCES	MINUTES ON PITCH THIS SEASON		HOME COUNTRY
Goalkeepers									
Stephan Andersen	25	5	0	0	0	0	0	-	Denmark
Scott Carson	21	36	36	36	3240	38	3450	-	England
Thomas Myhre	33	19	1	1	90	4	360	1	Norway
Darren Randolph	20	15	1	1	90	1	90	-	Rep of Ireland
Defenders									
Nathan Ashton	20	3	0	0	0	1	90	-	England
Madjid Bougherra	24	9	5	2	221	5	221	-	Algeria
Souleymane Diawara	28	25	23	17	1649	26	1923	-	Senegal
Talal El Karkouri	30	36	36	36	3240	39	3501	5	Morocco
Jonathan Fortune	26	15	8	6	643	13	1123	-	England
Hreidarsson	32	31	31	28	2590	33	2800	5	Iceland
Radostin Kishishev	32	19	14	4	653	18	977	4	Bulgaria
Osei Sankofa	22	11	9	8	748	12	839	-	England
Ben Thatcher	31	11	11	9	912	11	912	3	Wales
Djimi Traore	27	11	11	7	794	13	974	-	France
Luke Young	27	29	29	28	2587	32	2887	-	England
Midfielders									
Darren Ambrose	23	30	26	16	1746	30	2037	-	England
Amdy Faye	30	30	27	20	2081	31	2312	4	Senegal
Matt Holland	33	37	33	25	2443	36	2644	-	Rep of Ireland
Bryan Hughes	31	26	24	14	1480	27	1720	-	Wales
Alistair John	19	0	0	0	0	0	0	-	England
Omar Pouso	27	1	1	0	57	1	57	-	Uruguay
Andrew Reid	24	16	16	12	1201	17	1321	2	Rep of Ireland
Dennis Rommedahl	28	34	28	15	1749	32	1998	7	Denmark
Lloyd Sam	22	6	5	2	190	7	219	-	England
Alexandre Song	19	12	12	11	981	12	981	-	Cameroon
Gonzalo Sorondo	27	1	1	0	62	1	62	-	Uruguay
Jerome Thomas	24	20	20	13	1360	24	1612	-	England
Zhi Zheng	26	12	12	8	842	12	842	3	China PR
Forwards									
Darren Bent	23	32	32	32	2863	35	3103	1	England
Marcus Bent	29	33	30	12	1484	35	1903	-	England
J-Floyd Hasselbaink	35	29	25	7	1114	29	1431	-	Holland
Kevin Lisbie	28	10	8	1	192	9	193	-	Jamaica
James Walker	19	0	0	0	0	0	0	-	England

KEY: LEAGUE ■■■■ ALL COMPS ■■■■ CAPS (MAY FIFA RANKING)

TEAM OF THE SEASON

CARSON
CG 36 DR 58

YOUNG — CG 28 DR 61

DIAWARA — CG 17 DR 61

EL KARKOURI — CG 36 DR 57

HREIDARSSON — CG 28 DR 56

AMBROSE — CG 16 SD -31

SONG* — CG 11 SD -11

REID — CG 12 SD -48

THOMAS — CG 13 SD +29

M BENT* — CG 12 AP 106

D BENT — CG 32 SR 220

KEY: DR = Defensive Rate, SD = Scoring Difference AP = Attacking Power SR = Strike Rate, CG=Counting games − League games playing at least 70 minutes

TOP POINT EARNERS

Jerome Thomas	
Counting Games League games when player was on pitch for at least 70 minutes	13
Average points Average League points taken in Counting games	1.62
Club Average points Average points taken in League games	0.89

	PLAYER	GAMES	PTS
1	Jerome Thomas	13	1.62
2	Andrew Reid	12	1.00
3	Souleymane Diawara	17	1.00
4	Matt Holland	25	1.00
5	Hermann Hreidarsson	29	0.97
6	Darren Bent	32	0.94
7	Luke Young	28	0.93
8	Scott Carson	36	0.92
9	Talal El Karkouri	36	0.92
10	Amdy Faye	20	0.85

KEY PLAYERS - DEFENDERS

Luke Young

Goals Conceded in the League Number of League goals conceded while the player was on the pitch	42
Goals Conceded in all competitions Total number of goals conceded while the player was on the pitch	45
League minutes played Number of minutes played in league matches	2587
Clean Sheets In games when the player was on pitch for at least 70 minutes	10
Defensive Rating Average number of mins between League goals conceded while on the pitch	61
Club Defensive Rating Average number of mins between League goals conceded by the club this season	57

	PLAYER	CON LGE	CON ALL	MINS	C SHEETS	DEF RATE
1	Luke Young	42	45	2587	10	61 mins
2	Souleymane Diawara	27	33	1649	8	61 mins
3	Talal El Karkouri	56	58	3240	11	57 mins
4	Hermann Hreidarsson	46	49	2590	8	56 mins

KEY GOALKEEPER

Scott Carson

Goals Conceded in the League Number of League goals conceded while the player was on the pitch	55
Goals Conceded in all competitions Total number of goals conceded while the player was on the pitch	59
League minutes played Number of minutes played in league matches	3240
Clean Sheets In games when the player was on pitch for at least 70 minutes	11
Goals to Shots Ratio The average number of shots on target per each League goal conceded	4.62
Defensive Rating Ave mins between League goals conceded while on the pitch	58

BOOKINGS

Osei Sankofa	
League Yellow	3
League Red	1
All competitions Yellow	3
All competitions Red	1

League Average 187 mins between cards

	PLAYER	LEAGUE 3Y 1R	TOTAL 3Y 1R	AVE
1	Osei Sankofa	3Y 1R	3Y 1R	187
2	Jonathan Fortune	3 0	4 0	214
3	Djimi Traore	2 1	2 1	264
4	Ben Thatcher	2 1	2 1	304
5	Alexandre Song	3 0	3 0	327
6	S. Diawara	5 0	6 0	329
7	Amdy Faye	6 0	7 0	346
8	J-F. Hasselbaink	3 0	3 0	371
9	Talal El Karkouri	8 0	8 0	405
10	H. Hreidarsson	5 1	5 1	431
11	Andrew Reid	2 0	2 0	600
12	R. Kishishev	1 0	1 0	653
13	Bryan Hughes	2 0	3 0	740
14	Zhi Zheng	1 0	1 0	842
15	Luke Young	3 0	3 0	862
	Other	6 0	6 0	
	TOTAL	**55 4**	**59 4**	

WATFORD

Deprived of the inspiration and goals of **Marlon King**, Aidy Boothroyd was left with copious amounts of hard work, energy and spirit – it wasn't enough. King's 12 performances yielded four goals at a rate of one every 280 minutes. **Ashley Young** looked the next biggest threat but departed in the January transfer window.

In defence **Ben Foster** received his England call up on the back of several eye-catching performances and also surprisingly won the battle of the three England hopefuls. His Goals to Shots Ratio of 4.24 Shots on Target saved for every goal conceded was better than both current keeper, Paul Robinson, 3.65, and Wigan's Chris Kirkland, 3.42.

Darius Henderson had a miserable season with just three goals in 37 appearances but he led the club's Top Point Earners table

NICKNAME: THE HORNETS

KEY: ■ Won □ Drawn ■ Lost

#	comp	Opponent	H/A	Result	Result	Scorers
1	prem	Everton	A	L	1-2	Francis 90
2	prem	West Ham	H	D	1-1	King 63
3	prem	Man Utd	H	L	1-2	Francis 34
4	prem	Bolton	A	L	0-1	
5	prem	Aston Villa	H	D	0-0	
6	ccr2	Accrington	H	W	6-5*	(*on penalties)
7	prem	Wigan	A	D	1-1	Bouazza 63
8	prem	Fulham	H	D	3-3	King 23, Young 46, 89
9	prem	Arsenal	A	L	0-3	
10	prem	Charlton	A	D	0-0	
11	ccr3	Hull City	H	W	2-1	Young 2, Priskin 54
12	prem	Tottenham	H	D	0-0	
13	prem	Middlesbrough	H	W	2-0	Woodgate 6 og, Young 60
14	ccr4	Newcastle	H	L	4-5*	Francis 69, Shittu 108 (*on penalties)
15	prem	Chelsea	A	L	0-4	
16	prem	Portsmouth	A	L	1-2	DeMerit 32
17	prem	Sheff Utd	H	L	0-1	
18	prem	Man City	A	D	0-0	
19	prem	Reading	H	D	0-0	
20	prem	Newcastle	A	L	1-2	Bouazza 57
21	prem	Liverpool	A	L	0-2	
22	prem	Arsenal	H	L	1-2	T.Smith 23
23	prem	Fulham	A	D	0-0	
24	facr3	Stockport	H	W	4-1	Mackay 30, 76, T.Smith 48, Ashikodi 82
25	prem	Liverpool	H	L	0-3	
26	prem	Aston Villa	A	L	0-2	
27	prem	Blackburn	H	W	2-1	Emerton 12 og, DeMerit 70
28	facr4	West Ham	A	W	1-0	McNamee 42
29	prem	Man Utd	A	L	0-4	
30	prem	Bolton	H	L	0-1	
31	prem	West Ham	A	W	1-0	Henderson 12 pen
32	facr5	Ipswich	H	W	1-0	Francis 88
33	prem	Wigan	H	D	1-1	Henderson 24
34	prem	Everton	H	L	0-3	
35	prem	Charlton	H	D	2-2	Bouazza 15, Francis 21
36	facqf	Plymouth	A	W	1-0	Bouazza 21
37	prem	Tottenham	A	L	1-3	Henderson 89
38	prem	Chelsea	H	L	0-1	
39	prem	Middlesbrough	A	L	1-4	Francis 23
40	prem	Portsmouth	H	W	4-2	Bouazza 28 pen, 72, Mahon 45, Priskin 51
41	facsf	Man Utd	N	L	1-4	Bouazza 26
42	prem	Blackburn	A	L	1-3	Rinaldi 21
43	prem	Man City	H	D	1-1	Priskin 75
44	prem	Sheff Utd	A	L	0-1	
45	prem	Reading	A	W	2-0	Shittu 60, King 85
46	prem	Newcastle	H	D	1-1	King 52 pen

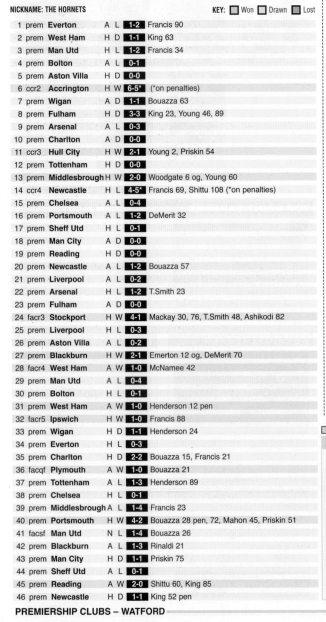

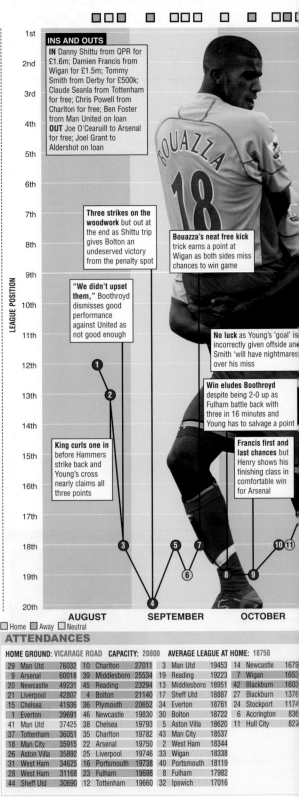

INS AND OUTS

IN Danny Shittu from QPR for £1.6m; Damien Francis from Wigan for £1.5m; Tommy Smith from Derby for £500k; Claude Seanla from Tottenham for free; Chris Powell from Charlton for free; Ben Foster from Man United on loan
OUT Joe O'Cearuill to Arsenal for free; Joel Grant to Aldershot on loan

Three strikes on the woodwork but out at the end as Shittu trip gives Bolton an undeserved victory from the penalty spot

Bouazza's neat free kick trick earns a point at Wigan as both sides miss chances to win game

"We didn't upset them," Boothroyd dismisses good performance against United as not good enough

No luck as Young's 'goal' is incorrectly given offside and Smith 'will have nightmares over his miss

Win eludes Boothroyd despite being 2-0 up as Fulham battle back with three in 16 minutes and Young has to salvage a point

King curls one in before Hammers strike back and Young's cross nearly claims all three points

Francis first and last chances but Henry shows his finishing class in comfortable win for Arsenal

LEAGUE POSITION: 1st, 2nd, 3rd, 4th, 5th, 6th, 7th, 8th, 9th, 10th, 11th, 12th, 13th, 14th, 15th, 16th, 17th, 18th, 19th, 20th

AUGUST SEPTEMBER OCTOBER

□ Home □ Away □ Neutral

ATTENDANCES

HOME GROUND: VICARAGE ROAD **CAPACITY:** 20800 **AVERAGE LEAGUE AT HOME:** 18750

#	Opponent	Att		#	Opponent	Att		#	Opponent	Att		#	Opponent	Att
29	Man Utd	76032		10	Charlton	27011		3	Man Utd	19453		14	Newcastle	16791
9	Arsenal	60018		39	Middlesboro	25534		19	Reading	19223		7	Wigan	16531
20	Newcastle	49231		45	Reading	23294		13	Middlesboro	18951		42	Blackburn	16033
21	Liverpool	42807		4	Bolton	21140		17	Sheff Utd	18887		27	Blackburn	13762
15	Chelsea	41936		36	Plymouth	20652		34	Everton	18761		24	Stockport	11742
1	Everton	39691		46	Newcastle	19830		30	Bolton	18722		6	Accrington	8366
41	Man Utd	37425		38	Chelsea	19793		5	Aston Villa	18620		11	Hull City	8221
37	Tottenham	36051		35	Charlton	19782		43	Man City	18537				
18	Man City	35915		22	Arsenal	19750		2	West Ham	18344				
26	Aston Villa	35892		25	Liverpool	19746		33	Wigan	18338				
31	West Ham	34625		16	Portsmouth	19738		40	Portsmouth	18119				
28	West Ham	31168		23	Fulham	19698		8	Fulham	17982				
44	Sheff Utd	30690		12	Tottenham	19660		32	Ipswich	17016				

King injury makes it mission impossible

Final Position: 20th

Key: ● League ● Champions Lge ● UEFA Cup ● FA Cup ○ League Cup ● Other

INS AND OUTS

IN Steve Kabba from Sheff Utd for £500k; Moses Ashikodi from Rangers for nominal fee; Cedic Avinel from Creteil for free; Johan Cavalli from Istres for free
OUT Ashley Young to Aston Villa for £9.65m; Matthew Spring to Luton for £200k

MONTH BY MONTH POINTS TALLY

Month	Points	%
AUGUST	1	11%
SEPTEMBER	2	22%
OCTOBER	3	25%
NOVEMBER	3	25%
DECEMBER	2	13%
JANUARY	4	27%
FEBRUARY	4	33%
MARCH	1	11%
APRIL	4	27%
MAY	4	67%

Carlisle returns from cruciate ligament injury for first Premier appearance

Foster deceived by bounce as England rival Robinson's free kick flies over his head for a rare keeper score

"No regrets" says Boothroyd as draw confirms relegation after Foster gifts Man City their opener

Nine points from safety as Bouazza run and cross brings equaliser but Arsenal breakaway wins it

Francis fires home for a quarter final place but Boothroyd admits that ten-man Ipswich were the better side

First win at last as Bouazza's shot flies in off Woodgate and Young's clinical finish makes sure of the points against Boro

Foster returns to a lot of action at Anfield but Bangura misses best chance and Liverpool secure win

Henderson at last! Striker nets first goal from the spot to win six pointer with Hammers squandering their own penalty chance

Bouazza's sharp finish keeps it tight until United run away with it in the last quarter as chances go begging

Down but not out of spirit as Shittu foils Reading's offside trap and King converts Smith's deflected cross for second away win

Shittu so close to quarters with extra time goal but Newcastle level and go through on penalties

Ten points from safety as Bolton snatch win from Foster's poor punch

Skipper scorcher is first of the season for Mahon as Bouazza takes tally to seven and Pompey are hit for four in confidence-building display

Overrun by Chelsea, whose stars turn it on to reinforce Boothroyd's point about budget differences

Quality tells after DeMerit's tug and Doyley's own goal help set United on the scoring trail

Bouazza fizzing strike powers into the roof of the net to claim a semi final spot and end Plymouth's dreams

Kabba stretches champions with overhead kick and lets them off with miss-kick before Chelsea snatch a 92nd minute winner

"They will never give up"; Boothroyd praises his team as they take game to Newcastle and end up unlucky losers

McNamee improvises his first goal since November 2005 to ensure belief continues for second game

"We choked," says Boothroyd after poor performance against Reds leaves him ten points from safety

Off the bottom but it feels like a loss as Charlton are on the ropes at 2-0 down but battle back to almost steal it

King claims point with final goal from the spot, while Foster earns a standing ovation in his last game

NOVEMBER | DECEMBER | JANUARY | FEBRUARY | MARCH | APRIL | MAY

GOAL ATTEMPTS

FOR — Goal attempts recorded in League games

	HOME	AWAY	TOTAL	AVE
shots on target	95	79	174	4.6
shots off target	95	72	167	4.4
TOTAL	190	151	341	9.0

Ratio of goals to shots — Average number of shots on target per League goal scored: **6.0**

Accuracy rating — Average percentage of total goal attempts which were on target: **51.0**

AGAINST — Goal attempts recorded in League games

	HOME	AWAY	TOTAL	AVE
shots on target	109	143	252	6.6
shots off target	113	151	264	6.9
TOTAL	222	294	516	13.6

Ratio of goals to shots — Average number of shots on target per League goal scored: **4.3**

Accuracy rating — Average percentage of total goal attempts which were on target: **48.8**

GOALS

Bouazza

League	5
FA Cup	2
League Cup	0
Europe	0
Other	0
TOTAL	7

League Average **469** mins between goals

	PLAYER	LGE	FAC	LC	Euro	TOT	AVE
1	Bouazza	5	2	0	0	7	469
2	Francis	4	1	1	0	6	620
3	King	4	0	0	0	4	280
4	Priskin	3	0	1	0	4	281
5	Young	3	0	1	0	4	630
6	Henderson	3	0	0	0	3	732
7	DeMerit	2	0	0	0	2	1424
8	Shittu	1	0	1	0	2	2433
9	Smith, T	1	1	0	0	2	2687
10	Mackay	0	2	0	0	2	
11	Rinaldi	1	0	0	0	1	434
12	Mahon	1	0	0	0	1	3027
13	McNamee	0	1	0	0	1	
14	Ashikodi	0	1	0	0	1	
15	Avinel	0	1	0	0	1	
	Other	0	0	0	0	0	
	TOTAL	28	8	4	0	40	

SQUAD APPEARANCES

Match	1 2 3 4 5	6 7 8 9 10	11 12 13 14 15	16 17 18 19 20	21 22 23 24 25	26 27 28 29 30	31 32 33 34 35	36 37 38 39 40	41 42 43 44 45
Venue	A H H A H	H A H A A	H H H H A	A H A H A	A H A H H	A H A A H	A H H H H	A A H A H	N A H A A
Competition	L L L L L	W L L L L	W L L L W L	L L L L L	L L L F L	L L F L L	L F L L L	F L L L L	F L L L L
Result	L D L L D	W D D L D	W D W L L	L L L D D L	L L D W L	L W W L L	W W D L D	W L L L W	L L D L W

Goalkeepers
Alec Chamberlain
Ben Foster
Richard Lee
Scott Loach

Defenders
Clarke Carlisle
James Chambers
Jay DeMerit
Lloyd Doyley
Sheku Kamara
Malcolm Mackay
Adrian Mariappa
Jordan Parkes
Chris Powell
Danny Shittu
Jordan Stewart

Midfielders
Cedric Avinel
Alhassan Bangura
Dominic Blizzard
Johan Cavalli
Toumani Diagouraga
Damian Francis
Albert Jarrett
Gavin Mahon
Anthony McNamee
Douglas Rinaldi
Tommy Smith
Matthew Spring
Gareth Williams
Lee Williamson

Forwards
Moses Ashikodi
Hameur Bouazza
Darius Henderson
William Hoskins
Steve Kabba
Marlon King
Tamas Priskin
Theo Robinson
Claude Seanla
Ashley Young

KEY: ■ On all match　◄◄ Subbed or sent off (Counting game)　▸▸ Subbed on from bench (Counting Game)　▸▸ Subbed on and then subbed or sent off (Counting Game)　☐ Not in 16　☐ Injured
■ On bench　◄ Subbed or sent off (playing less than 70 mins)　▸ Subbed on (playing less than 70 mins)　▸ Subbed on and then subbed or sent off (playing less than 70 min　✗ Suspended

KEY PLAYERS - GOALSCORERS

Marlon King

Goals in the League	4
Goals in all competitions	4
Assists League goals scored by a team mate where the player delivered the final pass	1
Contribution to Attacking Power Average number of minutes between League team goals while on pitch	102
Player Strike Rate Average number of minutes between League goals scored by player	280
Club Strike Rate Average minutes between League goals scored by club	117

	PLAYER	GOALS LGE	GOALS ALL	ASSISTS	POWER	S RATE
1	Marlon King	4	4	1	102	280 mins
2	Hameur Bouazza	5	7	4	106	469 mins
3	Damian Francis	4	6	1	124	620 mins
4	Ashley Young	3	4	3	145	630 mins

KEY PLAYERS - MIDFIELDERS

Tommy Smith

Goals in the League	1
Goals in all competitions	2
Assists League goals scored by a team mate where the player delivered the final pass	6
Defensive Rating Average number of mins between League goals conceded while on the pitch	58
Contribution to Attacking Power Average number of minutes between League team goals while on pitch	107
Scoring Difference Defensive Rating minus Contribution to Attacking Power	-49

	PLAYER	GOALS LGE	GOALS ALL	ASSISTS	DEF RATE	POWER	SC DIF
1	Tommy Smith	1	2	6	58	107	-49 min
2	Alhassan Bangura	0	0	0	73	130	-57 min
3	Gavin Mahon	1	1	0	59	116	-57 min
4	Damian Francis	4	6	1	55	124	-69 min

PLAYER APPEARANCES

	AGE (on 01/07/07)	IN NAMED 16	APPEARANCES	COUNTING GAMES	MINUTES ON PITCH	APPEARANCES	MINUTES ON PITCH THIS SEASON		HOME COUNTRY
Goalkeepers									
c Chamberlain	43	8	1	0	1	1	1	-	England
n Foster	24	29	29	28	2564	33	2924	1	England
hard Lee	24	33	10	9	855	14	1275	-	England
ott Loach	19	2	0	0	0	0	0	-	England
Defenders									
rke Carlisle	27	5	4	3	302	5	392	-	England
nes Chambers	26	13	12	6	684	15	905	-	England
DeMerit	27	34	32	29	2758	39	3418	3	United States
yd Doyley	24	31	21	16	1621	25	1841	-	England
eku Kamara	19	0	0	0	0	1	63	-	England
lcolm Mackay	35	21	14	12	1182	17	1361	-	Scotland
rian Mariappa	20	22	19	16	1558	25	2125	-	England
dan Parkes	17	0	0	0	0	1	120	-	England
ris Powell	37	18	15	8	864	18	1063	-	England
nny Shittu	26	32	30	25	2343	34	2727	-	Nigeria
dan Stewart	25	33	31	29	2681	36	3161	-	England
Midfielders									
dric Avinel	20	2	1	0	45	1	45	-	France
assan Bangura	19	24	16	11	1087	20	1418	-	Sierra Leone
minic Blizzard	23	0	0	0	0	1	57	-	England
an Cavalli	25	3	2	1	119	3	184	-	France
mani Diagouraga	20	0	0	0	0	2	149	-	France
mian Francis	28	33	32	27	2481	39	3112	-	England
ert Jarrett	22	2	1	0	20	2	140	-	England
vin Mahon	30	34	34	32	2937	38	3297	-	England
thony McNamee	22	12	7	7	348	10	629	-	England
uglas Rinaldi	23	7	7	4	434	7	434	-	Brazil
mmy Smith	27	32	32	29	2597	37	3047	-	England
tthew Spring	27	13	6	1	262	9	503	-	England
eth Williams	25	6	3	1	196	3	196	-	Scotland
Williamson	25	6	5	3	332	5	332	-	England
Forwards									
ses Ashikodi	20	3	2	0	25	3	115	-	England
meur Bouazza	22	32	32	22	2348	38	2853	2	Algeria
rius Henderson	25	35	35	19	2196	41	2671	-	England
liam Hoskins	20	10	9	3	423	9	423	-	England
ve Kabba	26	12	11	5	617	14	784	-	England
rlon King	27	13	13	12	1122	14	1135	-	England
mas Priskin	20	27	16	4	755	22	1188	3	Hungary
o Robinson	18	1	1	0	4	1	4	-	England
ude Seanla	19	0	0	0	0	1	16	-	Ivory Coast
ley Young	21	20	20	20	1800	23	2033	-	England

KEY: LEAGUE ALL COMPS CAPS (MAY FIFA RANKING)

TEAM OF THE SEASON

FOSTER — CG 28 DR 58

DOYLEY	SHITTU	MACKAY	STEWART
CG 16 DR 55	CG 25 DR 62	CG 12 DR 65	CG 29 DR 58

SMITH	BANGURA*	MAHON	FRANCIS
CG 29 SD -49	CG 11 SD -57	CG 32 SD -57	CG 27 SD -69

BOUAZZA — CG 22 AP 106

KING* — CG 12 SR 280

KEY: DR = Defensive Rate, SD = Scoring Difference AP = Attacking Power SR = Strike Rate, CG=Counting games — League games playing at least 70 minutes

TOP POINT EARNERS

Darius Henderson	
Counting Games League games when player was on pitch for at least 70 minutes	19
Average points Average League points taken in Counting games	0.95
Club Average points Average points taken in League games	0.74

	PLAYER	GAMES	PTS
1	Darius Henderson	19	0.95
2	Tommy Smith	29	0.86
3	Malcolm Mackay	12	0.83
4	Hameur Bouazza	22	0.82
5	Damian Francis	27	0.81
6	Adrian Mariappa	16	0.81
7	Ben Foster	28	0.79
8	Jordan Stewart	29	0.76
9	Marlon King	12	0.75
10	Gavin Mahon	32	0.69

KEY PLAYERS - DEFENDERS

Malcolm Mackay

Goals Conceded in the League Number of League goals conceded while the player was on the pitch	18
Goals Conceded in all competitions Total number of goals conceded while the player was on the pitch	19
League minutes played Number of minutes played in league matches	1182
Clean Sheets In games when the player was on pitch for at least 70 minutes	2
Defensive Rating Average number of mins between League goals conceded while on the pitch	65
Club Defensive Rating Average number of mins between League goals conceded by the club this season	58

	PLAYER	CON LGE	CON ALL	MINS	C SHEETS	DEF RATE
1	Malcolm Mackay	18	19	1182	2	65 mins
2	Danny Shittu	39	42	2433	7	62 mins
3	Jordan Stewart	47	55	2771	8	58 mins
4	Lloyd Doyley	29	32	1621	4	55 mins

KEY GOALKEEPER

Ben Foster

Goals Conceded in the League Number of League goals conceded while the player was on the pitch	45
Goals Conceded in all competitions Total number of goals conceded while the player was on the pitch	47
League minutes played Number of minutes played in league matches	2654
Clean Sheets In games when the player was on pitch for at least 70 minutes	6
Goals to Shots Ratio The average number of shots on target per each League goal conceded	4.24
Defensive Rating Ave mins between League goals conceded while on the pitch	58

BOOKINGS

Tamas Priskin

League Yellow	2
League Red	1
All competitions Yellow	2
All competitions Red	1
League Average	281 mins between cards

	PLAYER	LEAGUE		TOTAL		AVE
1	Tamas Priskin	2Y	1R	2Y	1R	281
2	Malcolm Mackay	3	0	3	0	394
3	Gavin Mahon	7	0	7	0	432
4	Chris Powell	1	1	1	1	432
5	Damian Francis	5	0	5	0	496
6	Alhassan Bangura	2	0	2	0	588
7	James Chambers	1	0	2	0	684
8	Jay DeMerit	4	0	5	0	712
9	Darius Henderson	3	0	3	0	732
10	Hameur Bouazza	3	0	3	0	782
11	Adrian Mariappa	2	0	2	0	824
12	Ashley Young	2	0	2	0	945
13	Tommy Smith	2	0	2	0	1343
14	Jordan Stewart	2	0	2	0	1385
15	Lloyd Doyley	1	0	2	0	1621
	Other	1	0	3	0	
	TOTAL	41	2	46	2	

THE AXA FA CUP

1ST ROUND

Cheltenham 0 **Scunthorpe** 0
2,721

Barrow 2 **Bristol Rovers** 3
Pope 69, Rogan 77   R.Walker 35, Disley 62
   Anthony 67
   2,939

Bishops S 3 **Kings Lynn** 5
Essandoh 36,   Smith 27, 45
Morgan 40, Martin 81   Frew 55, 61
   O'Halloran 71
   1,750

Bournemouth 4 **Boston** 0
Fletcher 5, 42,
Hayter 59, Hollands 90   4,263

Bradford 4 **Crewe** 0
Bridge-Wilkinson 3
Schumacher 61,
Windass 70, Kempson 77   3,483

Brentford 0 **Doncaster** 1
   Guy 32
   3,607

Brighton 8 **Northwich** 0
Cox 8, 90
Robinson 18, 55, 78
Revell 64, Gatting 82
Rents 89   4,487

Burton 1 **Tamworth** 2
Clare 49   Poole o.g. 59
   Stevenson 90
   4,150

Chelmsford City 1 **Aldershot** 1
Minton 51 pen   Chenery o.g. 59 2,838

Chesterfield 0 **Basingstoke** 1
   Warner 25 3,539

Clevedon 1 **Chester** 4
Pitcher 90   Wilson 7, Hand 49
   Walters 60, Blundell 74
   2,261

Exeter 1 **Stockport** 2
Phillips 45   Bramble 21, Proudlock 82
   4,454

Gainsborough 1 **Barnet** 3
Ellis 75   Sinclair 14, Kandol 78, 90 pen
   1,914

Gillingham 4 **Bromley** 1
Bentley 31, 59   McDonnell 70
Ndumbu-Nsungu 84, 90   5,547

Huddersfield 0 **Blackpool** 1
   Hoolahan 70 pen 6,597

Kettering 3 **Oldham** 4
McIlwain 52,   Gregan 43, Warne 56
Abbey 62, Solkhon 84   Trotman 60 C.Hall 90
   3,481

Lewes 1 **Darlington** 4
Farrell 79   Smith 38, 90 Collins 62
   Ngoma 82 1,500

Leyton Orient 2 **Notts County** 1
Corden 12, Miller 58   Dudfield 90 3,011

Mansfield 1 **Accrington** 0
Barker 44 pen   3,909

Morecambe 2 **Kidderminster** 1
Curtis 44 pen, Twiss 73   Hurren 89 1,673

Newport 1 **Swansea** 3
Hillier 48   Trundle 7, Iriekpen 31
   Britton 45 4,660

Northampton 0 **Grimsby** 0
   4,092

Nottm Forest 5 **Yeading** 0
Commons 19, 32, 45,
Agogo 54 pen, 63   7,704

Peterborough 3 **Rotherham** 0
Butcher 29, McLean 59
Crow 73   4,281

Port Vale 2 **Lincoln** 1
Whitaker 29,   Frecklington 84
A.Sodje 38
   3,884

Rochdale 1 **Hartlepool** 1
Doolan 62   Brown 41
   2,098

Rushden & D 3 **Yeovil** 1
Hope 28   Cohen 62
Rankine 54, 75
   2,530

Salisbury 3 **Fleetwood** 0
Tubbs 12, Holmes 60,
Bartlett 69   2,684

Shrewsbury 0 **Hereford** 0
   5,574

Stafford 1 **Maidenhead** 1
Daniel 13   Lee 52
   1,526

Swindon 3 **Carlisle** 1
Lumsdon 9 og,   Gray 43
Roberts 70, 90
   4,938

Torquay 2 **Leatherhead** 1
Ward 57, McPhee 72   Hendry 2
   2,218

Tranmere 4 **Woking** 2
Taylor 19, 48   Jackson 63
Greenacre 37, 83   McAllister 69
   4,591

Wrexham 1 **Stevenage** 0
D.Williams 40   2,863

Wycombe 2 **Oxford** 1
Antwi 58, Oakes 86   G.Johnson 85
   6,279

York 0 **Bristol City** 1
   McCombe 53
   3,525

Farsley 0 **MK Dons** 0
   2,200

Weymouth 2 **Bury** 2
Weatherstone 50   Pugh 26, Bishop 75
Logan 55
   2,503

Havant & W 1 **Millwall** 2
Baptiste 57   May 6, Dunne 71
   5,753

Macclesfield 0 **Walsall** 0
   2,018

FA 1st Round replay

Hartlepool 0 **Rochdale** 0
Hartlepool win 4-2 on penalties 2,788

Aldershot 2 **Chelmsford City** 0
Barnard 53 pen, Grant 80   2,731

Bury 4 **Weymouth** 3
Mattis 10, 67,   Downer 16, Purser 20
Bishop 23, 74   Tully 30 2,231

Grimsby 0 **Northampton** 1
   Whittle 18 og, Burnell 45
   2,657

Hereford 2 **Shrewsbury** 0
Connell 85, Webb 88   4,224

Maidenhead 0 **Stafford** 2
Murray 9, 78   1,934

MK Dons 2 **Farsley** 0
McLeod 63, 76 pen   2,676

Scunthorpe 2 **Cheltenham** 0
Baraclough 26, B.Sharp 74   3,074

Walsall 0 **Macclesfield** 1
3,114   McNulty 83

2ND ROUND

Bradford 0 **Millwall** 0
   4,346

Kings Lynn 0 **Oldham** 2
   Porter 10, C.Hall 82
   5,444

Stockport 2 **Wycombe** 1
Proudlock 43 pen, 75   Easter 34 3,821

Aldershot 1 **Basingstoke** 1
Grant 77   Bruce 45 4,525

Barnet 4 **Northampton** 1
Birchall 49, Sinclair 53   McGleish 45
Hendon 67 pen, Vieira 87   2,786

Brighton 3 **Stafford** 0
Hammond 18, Revell 66
Robinson 90   5,741

Bristol Rovers 1 **Bournemouth** 1
R.Walker 45 pen   Hayter 73 6,252

Bury 2 **Chester** 2
Bishop 66, Baker 69   Steele 63, 73 3,428

Darlington 1 **Swansea** 3
Smith 2   Britton 15, Robinson 52
   Akinfenwa 79 4,183

Hereford 4 **Port Vale** 0
Webb 41,
Purdie 49 pen, 51, Ferrell 83   4,076

Macclesfield 2 **Hartlepool** 1
McIntyre 45 pen,   Regan 8 og
Murphy 52   1,992

Mansfield 1 **Doncaster** 1
Barker 23 pen   Stock 90 4,837

MK Dons 0 **Blackpool** 2
   Parker 31, Morrell 48
   3,837

Rushden & D 1 **Tamworth** 2
Shaw 85   Burton 42, McGrath 77
   2,815

Scunthorpe 0 **Wrexham** 2
   Mark Jones 49, Smith 66
   5,054

Swindon 1 **Morecambe** 0
Roberts 89 pen   5,942

Torquay 1 **Leyton Orient** 1
Ward 60 pen   Corden 76 2,392

Tranmere 1 **Peterborough** 2
Sherriff 30   Crow 45, 70 6,308

Bristol City 4 **Gillingham** 3
Jevons 21, 44, 45,   Mulligan 49
Showunmi 64   Flynn 66, 90 pen 5,663

Salisbury 1 **Nottm Forest** 1
Tubbs 61   Tyson 27 3,100

FA 2nd Round replay

Basingstoke 1 **Aldershot** 3
Roach 4   Soares 14, 30, Barnard 51
   3,300

Bournemouth 0 **Bristol Rovers** 1
   R.Walker 64   4,153

Chester 1 **Bury** 3
Wilson 3   Bishop 36, Hurst 48
   Mattis 54 2,810

Doncaster 2 **Mansfield** 0
McCammon 23, Heffernan 50   5,338

Leyton Orient 1 **Torquay** 2
J.Walker 58   Robertson 52, 81
   2,384

Millwall 1 **Bradford** 0
Doyle 114 og   3,220

Nottm Forest 2 **Salisbury** 0
Tyson 53, Southall 81   6,177

3RD ROUND

Bristol Rovers 1 **Hereford**
R.Walker 22 pen   8,9

Stoke 2 **Millwall**
Elliott 82 og, Fuller 87   8,0

Birmingham 2 **Newcastle**
Campbell 15, Larsson 86   Taylor 40, Dyer
   16,

Blackpool 4 **Aldershot**
Vernon 4, Morrell 7, 73,   John.Grant
Burgess 80 pen   Pritchard
   6,

Bristol City 3 **Coventry**
Brooker 14,   Cameron 13, McKenzie
Showunmi 18,   John
Jevons 21   13,3

England midfielder Lampard scores a hat-trick as a depleted Chelsea side hammer ten-man Macclesfield, who have keeper Lee red-carded. Town defender Morley takes over in goal but it's one-way traffic

Chelsea 6 **Macclesfield**
Lampard 16, 41, 51 pen   Murphy
Wright-Phillips 68,
Mikel 82, Carvalho 86   41,4

Chester 0 **Ipswich**
   4,3

Crystal Palace 2 **Swindon**
Kuqi 8, McAnuff 70   Ifi
   10,

Derby 3 **Wrexham**
Lupoli 32, 56, 85   McEvilly
   15,

Doncaster 0 **Bolton**
   Davie
   Teimourian 22, 49, Ta
   14,

Hull City 1 **Middlesbrough**
Forster 79   Viduka
   17,

Leicester 2 **Fulham**
Kisnorbo 80   McBride 69, Volz
Cadamarteri 90   15,4

Liverpool 1 **Arsenal**
Kuijt 71   Rosicky 37, 45, Henry
   9,

Nottm Forest 2 **Charlton**
Agogo 28, Grant.Holt 32   19,

Peterborough 1 **Plymouth**
McLean 78   Aljofree 74
   6,

Portsmouth 2 **Wigan**
Cole 64, Kanu 90   McCulloch

reston 1 Sunderland 0
rmerod 31 10,318

PR 2 Luton 2
ackstock 32 Vine 45
aidoo 76 Feeney 46 10,064

heff Utd 0 Swansea 3
Butler 53, 59
Britton 67 pen 15,896

outhend 1 Barnsley 1
ower 58 Coulson 90 5,485

amworth 1 Norwich 4
orer 68 Dublin 40, 62
Huckerby 42, 51
3,165

orquay 0 Southampton 3
Rasiak 43, 72
5,396

New signing Ashikodi scores on his debut for Watford who hit four against Stockport at Vicarage Road.

atford 4 Stockport 1
ackay 30, 76, Poole 23
Smith 48, Ashikodi 82 11,745

est Brom 3 Leeds 1
McShane 7, Hartson 15 Robinson 90 og
hillips 82 16,957

est Ham 3 Brighton 0
oble 49, Cole 58
ullins 90 32,874

olverhampton 2 Oldham 2
ofinjana 35 Warne 19, C.Hall 78
avies 42 14,524

ardiff 0 Tottenham 0
20,376

verton 1 Blackburn 4
ohnson 68 pen Derbyshire 5, Pedersen 21
, Gallagher 38, McCarthy 90
24,426

an Utd 2 Aston Villa 2
arsson 55 Baros 74
olskjaer 90 74,924

heff Wed 1 Man City 1
acLean 79 Samaras 78 pen
28,487

uncheon is the hero for League Two Barnet as he scores ten minutes from ime to defeat Championship favourites Colchester

arnet 2 Colchester 1
akubu 61 Cureton 35
uncheon 80 3,075

Reading 3 Burnley 2
Lita 28, Long 37, Akinbiyi 69
Sodje 55 G.O'Connor 90
11,514

FA 3rd Round replay

Barnsley 0 Southend 2
Maher 22, Bradbury 58
4,944

Coventry 0 Bristol City 2
Murray 39, Showunmi 54
13,055

Ipswich 1 Chester 0
Richards 84 11,732

Man City 2 Sheff Wed 1
Ireland 44, Vassell 56 Bullen 51
25,621

Yakubu's 64th-min penalty gives rampant Middlesbrough a 3-0 lead but they have to survive a remarkable fightback by Hull before securing a fourth round place

Middlesbrough 4 Hull City 3
Hines 32, Viduka 49, 64, Dawson 59, 69
Yakubu 57 pen Parkin 63 pen
16,702

Oldham 0 Wolverhampton 2
Potter 56, C.Davies 75
9,628

Plymouth 2 Peterborough 1
Hayles 18, Norris 27 McLean 13
9,973

Fulham 4 Leicester 3
McBride 35 Fryatt 13, McAuley 45
Montella 51, 60 Wesolowski 47
Routledge 90 11,222

DJ Campbell puts the final gloss on Birmingham's humiliation of Newcastle at St James' Park. McSheffrey starts the game with a typically clinical finish and a Solano own goal on halftime leaves the home side with too much to do

Newcastle 1 Birmingham 5
Milner 56 McSheffrey 5
Solano 45 og, N'Gotty 59,
Larsson 83, Campbell 89
26,099

Tottenham 4 Cardiff 0
Lennon 27, Keane 30,
Malbranque 41, Defoe 81 27,641

Luton 1 QPR 0
Rehman 80 og 7,494

4TH ROUND

Barnet 0 Plymouth 2
Aljofree 67 pen, Sinclair 83
5,204

Birmingham 2 Reading 3
Martin.Taylor 47, Kitson 3, Lita 41, 82
Larsson 90 20,041

Blackpool 1 Norwich 1
Evatt 52 Huckerby 45 9,491

Bristol City 2 Middlesbrough 2
Keogh 53, Murray 59 Yakubu 4, Christie 23
19,008

Crystal Palace 0 Preston 2
Nugent 46, Wilson 83
8,422

Derby 1 Bristol Rovers 0
Peschisolido 82 25,033

Fulham 3 Stoke 0
Montella 11, McBride 38,
Radzinski 54 11,059

Ipswich 1 Swansea 0
Lee 64 pen 16,635

Derbyshire's brace of goals help Blackburn to an emphatic victory over Luton and earns a congratulatory pat from Bentley and Pedersen

Luton 0 Blackburn 4
Derbyshire 10, 56
McCarthy 36,
Pedersen 74
5,887

Man Utd 2 Portsmouth 1
Rooney 77, 83 Kanu 87 71,137

Tottenham 3 Southend 1
Keane 12, Jenas 50 Eastwood 69 pen
Mido 76 33,406

West Ham 0 Watford 1
McNamee 42 31,168

Flamini tussles with Meite at the Emirates Stadium where Toure's diving header 12 mins from time earns Arsenal a replay after Nolan gives Bolton the lead

Arsenal 1 Bolton 1
Toure 78 Nolan 50 59,778

Chelsea 3 Nottm Forest 0
Shevchenko 9, 41,516
Drogba 18, Mikel 45

Man City 3 Southampton 1
Vassell 26, Barton 45 Jones 23
Beasley 70 26,496

Wolverhampton 0 West Brom 3
Kamara 44, Phillips 48
Gera 78 28,107

FA 4th Round replay

Middlesbrough keeper Mark Schwarzer is mobbed by team-mates after his saves from Jevons and Woodman see Gareth Southgate's side win a penalty shoot-out against Bristol City

Middlesbrough 2 Bristol City 2
Viduka 69, Noble 23
Yakubu 102 , McCombe 117
Boro win 5-4 on penalties 26,328

Teenage striker Martin scores his first goal for Norwich City with an extra-time winner against Blackpool at Carrow Road. Huckerby hits two as Canaries fight back after conceding an early goal to Jackson

Norwich 3 Blackpool 2
Huckerby 78, 95 Jackson 37
Martin 112 Barker 108
19,120

Bolton 1 Arsenal 3
Meite 90 Adebayor 13, 120
Ljungberg 108
21,088

5TH ROUND

Arsenal	0	Blackburn	0
			56,761

Chelsea	4	Norwich	0
Wright-Phillips 39			
Drogba 51, Essien 90			
Shevchenko 90			41,537

Reading boss Coppell salutes the crowd after watching his side come from behind to earn a deserved draw at Old Trafford thanks to Gunnarsson's second-half headed equaliser

Man Utd	1	Reading	1
Carrick 45		Gunnarsson 67	
			70,608

Middlesbrough	2	West Brom	2
Arca 29,		Kamara 41, Phillips 58	
Yakubu 43 pen			31,491

Plymouth	2	Derby	0
Gallen 14 pen			
Sinclair 84			18,026

Watford	1	Ipswich	0
Francis 88			17,016

Sub Berbatov grabs two goals for Spurs to add to two from Keane

Fulham	0	Tottenham	4
		Keane 6, 68	
		Berbatov 77, 90	
			18,655

Preston	1	Man City	3
Nugent 8		Ball 35, Hill 84 og	
		Ireland 90	
			18,890

FA Cp 5th Round replay

Reading	2	Man Utd	3
Kitson 23, Lita 84		Heinze 2, Saha 4	
		Solskjaer 6	
			23,821

West Brom	1	Middlesbrough	1
Carter 26		Viduka 63	
Bro win 5-4 on penalties			24,925

McCarthy comes off the Blackburn bench to lash home a late winner in a tie dominated by the defences

Blackburn	1	Arsenal	0
McCarthy 87			18,882

QUARTER-FINALS

Middlesbrough	2	Man Utd	2
Cattermole 45,		Rooney 23	
Boateng 47		Ronaldo 68 pen	
			33,308

Boateng wheels away after heading home Downing's corner to give Middlesbrough the lead early on the second half. But referee Rob Styles then awards United a penalty for handball against the Boro skipper and Ronaldo makes no mistake from the spot to earn a replay

Man Utd	1	Middlesbrough	0
Ronaldo 76 pen			71,325

Manchester United's penalty king does it again - sending Schwarzer the wrong way to break Middlesbrough's resistance

Blackburn	2	Man City	0
Mokoena 28,			
Derbyshire 90			27,743

Derbyshire seals victory in stoppage time for Blackburn after Mokoena scores his first goal for Rovers in two and a half years at Ewood Park

Chelsea	3	Tottenham	3
Lampard 22, 71		Berbatov 5	
Kalou 86		Essien 28 og, Ghaly 36	
			41,517

Spurs produce a stunning first-half attacking display to lead Chelsea 3-1 at the break with Lennon superb in midfield. In the second half Mourinho waves his magic wand and the Blues stage a great fightback to earn a replay

Tottenham	1	Chelsea	2
Keane 79 pen		Shevchenko 55	
		Wright-Phillips 61	
			35,519

Wright-Phillips scores Chelsea's second goal with a magnificent volley. Keane's late penalty is just consolation for Spurs

Plymouth	0	Watford	1
		Bouazza 21	
			20,652

Premiership strugglers Watford put their relegation battle to one side as Bouazza's drive from the edge of the area puts and end to the FA Cup dreams of Plymouth supporters at Home Park

SEMI-FINALS

Watford	1	Man Utd	4
Bouazza 26		Rooney 7, 66	
		Ronaldo 28	
		Richardson 82	
			37,425

Rooney shows his England class with two goals against Adrian Boothroyd's battling Watford. United overcome loss of Ferdinand with a groin injury to book their place in the final but the scoreline flatters them

Blackburn	1	Chelsea	2
Roberts 64		Lampard 16	
		Ballack 109	
			50,559

Samba celebrates Blackburn's equalising goal as Roberts flicks home Pedersen's low free-kick. Both sides squander clear goal-scoring chances before Chelsea midfielder Ballack scores the winner in extra-time to set up a final showdown against Manchester United

FINAL

Chelsea	1	Man Utd	0
Drogba 116			
			89,826

Chelsea celebrate their hard-earned victory in the first FA Cup final at the new Wembley Stadium. Both sides look weary after a long season and cancel each other out in what proves to be a tactical, low-key match.
Ronaldo is given little space by the Chelsea defence and precious few chances are created by the top two Premiership sides. The match is in extra-time and heading for a penalty shoot-out when Drogba plays a neat one-two with Lampard before knocking home his 33rd goal of the season. Giggs has the best chance of the game and appeals that the ball has crossed the line

THE CARLING FOOTBALL LEAGUE CUP

1ST ROUND

Accrington 1 **Nottm Forest** 0
Mullin 61
2,146

Birmingham 1 **Shrewsbury** 0
Larsson 83
12,428

Blackpool 2 **Barnsley** 2
Vernon 71, 120 Williams 53 pen
Devaney 117
Barnsley win 4-2 on penalties 3,938

Bournemouth 1 **Southend** 3
Fletcher 47 Gower 33
Eastwood 56 pen, 67
3,764

Bristol Rovers (3) 1 **Luton** (5) 1
Walker 61 Boyd 3
Luton win 5-3 on penalties 2,882

Burnley 0 **Hartlepool** 1
Porter 72 pen 3,853

Bury 2 **Sunderland** 0
Fitzgerald 82, Bishop 88
2,930

Cardiff 0 **Barnet** 2
Kandol 33, 54 3,305

Carlisle 1 **Bradford** 1
Holmes 31 E.Johnson 81
Carlisle win 4-3 on penalties 4,757

Cheltenham 2 **Bristol City** 1
Guinan 24, Wilson 33 Cotterill 40
3,713

Crystal Palace 1 **Notts County** 2
Hughes 17 Dudfield 23, Martin 84
4,481

Doncaster 3 **Rochdale** 2
McCammon 55, 67 Rundle 45, Doolan 79
Coppinger 56 3,690

Grimsby 0 **Crewe** 3
Maynard 39, O'Connor 73
Lowe 89 pen
1,635

Hereford 3 **Coventry** 1
Fleetwood 1, 57, 64 Adebola 59
3,404

Huddersfield 0 **Mansfield** 2
Boulding 45, Barker 47
5,111

Hull City 2 **Tranmere** 1
Burgess 56, Duffy 110 Sherriff 31
6,075

Leeds 1 **Chester** 0
Bakke 57
10,013

Leicester 2 **Macclesfield** 0
O'Grady 24, McCarthy 89
6,298

Millwall 2 **Gillingham** 1
Braniff 39, Hubertz 86 Mulligan 81
5,040

MK Dons 1 **Colchester** 0
McLeod 94
2,747

Peterborough 2 **Ipswich** 2
Benjamin 45 pen, De Vos 90
Branston 96 Clarke 105
Peterborough win 4-2 on penalties 4,792

Plymouth 0 **Walsall** 1
Dann 85 6,407

QPR 3 **Northampton** 2
Cook 18, Gallen 50 Watt 55, Kirk 78
R.Jones 87 4,569

Rotherham 3 **Oldham** 1
Sharps 48, Hoskins 54 Rocastle 41
Partridge 88 3,065

Scunthorpe 4 **Lincoln** 3
Torpey 7, Mulligan 58, Stallard 69
Paul 105, Frecklington 80
Baraclough 106 Beevers 93
3,455

Stockport 0 **Derby** 1
M.Johnson 45
3,394

Stoke 1 **Darlington** 2
Pericard 29 Logan 45, Joachim 54
3,573

Swansea 2 **Wycombe** 3
Williamson 72 og Easter 50, Oakes 64
Pratley 81 Williamson 114
5,892

Swindon 2 **Brentford** 2
Nicholas 38, O'Connor 9
P.Evans 72 Kuffour 25
Brentford win 4-3 on penalties 5,582

Brighton 1 **Boston** 0
Reid 73
2,533

Chesterfield 0 **Wolverhampton** 0
Chesterfield win 6-5 on penalties 4,136

Port Vale 2 **Preston** 1
A.Sodje 52 Whaley 72
Constantine 82 3,522

Sheff Wed 1 **Wrexham** 4
Whelan 79 N.Roberts 33
Llewellyn 39
Done 64, Ma.Jones 84
8,047

Southampton 5 **Yeovil** 2
Cohen 25 og, Skacel 32, Gray 30
Wright-Phillips 37, 8 Harrold 40
Dyer 69, Jones 7 20,653

Torquay 0 **Norwich** 2
McKenzie 48, Etuhu 64 3,100

Leyton Orient 0 **West Brom** 3
3,058 Nicholson 41
Carter 71, Greening 76

2ND ROUND

Barnsley 1 **MK Dons** 2
McIndoe 66 Wilbraham 28, 90
4,411

Birmingham 4 **Wrexham** 1
Jerome 41, 7 Llewellyn 29
McSheffrey 102, 113
Bendtner 11 10,491

Brentford 0 **Luton** 3
Morgan 10, Feeney 53
, Vine 90
3,005

Charlton 1 **Carlisle** 0
D.Bent 57 8,190

Crewe 2 **Wigan** 2
Jack 42, Maynard 90 3,907

Hereford 1 **Leicester** 3
Purdie 56 pen Hammond 27
Stearman 66,
Hume 76 pen
4,073

Hull City 0 **Hartlepool** 0
Hull City win 3-2 on penalties 6,392

Leeds 3 **Barnet** 1
Blake 7, Moore 55, 74 Vieira 78
7,220

Mansfield 1 **Portsmouth** 2
Reet 81 Manuel Fernandes 5
Taylor 33 6,646

Millwall 0 **Southampton** 4
Belmadi 20
Wright-Phillips 43, 9
McGoldrick 9
5,492

Peterborough 1 **Everton** 2
Benjamin 56 Stirling 24 og, Cahill 87
10,756

Port Vale 3 **QPR** 2
J.Smith 19, Whitaker 28 Nygaard 9
Walker 61 Stewart 78
3,550

Reading 3 **Darlington** 3
Lita 31, 35, Mate 86 Johnson 19 pen
Joachim 34, 52
Reading win 4-2 on penalties 10,353

Rotherham 2 **Norwich** 4
Keane 24, Thorne 6
Williamson 49 pen Ryan.Jarvis 53, 90
Fleming 54
3,958

Sheff Utd 1 **Bury** 0
Nade 16
6,273

Southend 3 **Brighton** 2
Paynter 87, Hunt 88, Cox 71, El-Abd 90
Eastwood 90
4,819

Walsall 1 **Bolton** 3
Butler 74 Nolan 68, Campo 88
Anelka 90
6,243

Watford 0 **Accrington** 0
Watford win 6-5 on penalties 8,368

West Brom 3 **Cheltenham** 1
Wallwork 48 Odejayi 45
Ellington 60 pen
Nicholson 68 pen 10,974

Chesterfield 2 **Man City** 1
Folan 51, Niven 67 Samaras 40 7,960

Doncaster 3 **Derby** 3
Forte 6, 57, Stock 29 Howard 74, Moore 78
Lupoli 90
Doncaster win 8-7 on penalties 5,598

Fulham 1 **Wycombe** 2
Helguson 47 Easter 8
Mooney 41 pen
6,620

Middlesbrough 0 **Notts County** 1
N'Toya 26 11,148

Scunthorpe 1 **Aston Villa** 2
B.Sharp 73 Angel 42, 64 6,502

3RD ROUND

Chesterfield 2 **West Ham** 1
Larkin 54, Folan 87 Harewood 4
7,787

Everton 4 **Luton** 0
Cahill 23, Keane 34 og
McFadden 53
Anichebe 83 27,149

Leeds 1 **Southend** 3
Moore 44 Hammell 34 pen
Hooper 36, 64
10,449

Agbonlahor scores a last-gasp winner to give Villa boss O'Neill a victory on his return to his former club Leicester

Leicester 2 **Aston Villa** 3
Stearman 42 Angel 5, Barry 45 pen
Kisnorbo 85 Agbonlahor 119
27,288

Notts County 2 **Southampton** 0
Edwards 13, J.Lee 44 6,731

Port Vale 0 **Norwich** 0
Port Vale win 3-2 on penalties 4,518

Sheff Utd 2 **Birmingham** 4
Akinbiyi 21 Campbell 41, Bendtner 70
Montgomery 85 Jerome 79, Larsson 90
10,584

Watford 2 **Hull City** 1
Young 2, Priskin 54 Barmby 71 8,274

West Brom 0 **Arsenal** 2
Aliadiere 33 pen, 45
21,566

Wycombe 2 **Doncaster** 2
Oakes 71, Easter 116 Forte 65, Lee 97
Wycombe win 3-2 on penalties 3,308

Blackburn 0 **Chelsea** 2
J.Cole 53, Kalou 81
14,732

Charlton 1 **Bolton** 0
M.Bent 17 10,788

Crewe 1 **Man Utd** 2
Varney 73 Solskjaer 26, Lee 119
10,046

Liverpool 4 **Reading** 3
Fowler 44, Riise 45 Bikey 75, Lita 81
Paletta 50, Crouch 77 Long 85 42,445

MK Dons 0 **Tottenham** 5
Mido 36, 59, Defoe 44, 51
Keane 90 8,306

Newcastle 3 **Portsmouth** 0
Rossi 48,
Solano 53, 90 25,028

4TH ROUND

Chesterfield 3 **Charlton** 3
Larkin 3, Folan 47, Hasselbaink 40, 93
Allison 119 D.Bent 73
7,000

Notts County 0 **Wycombe** 1
Easter 50
7,395

Life-long Manchester United supporter Eastwood hits the winner for Southend and sends the holders crashing out of the competition

Southend 1 **Man Utd** 0
Eastwood 27 11,532

Watford 2 **Newcastle** 2
Francis 69, Shittu 108 Sibierski 3, Parker 116
Newcastle win 5-4 on penalties 16,791

Birmingham 0 **Liverpool** 1
Agger 45
23,061

Chelsea 4 **Aston Villa** 0
Lampard 32,
Shevchenko 65,
Essien 82, Drogba 84
41,516

Everton 0 **Arsenal** 1
Adebayor 85
31,045

Tottenham 3 **Port Vale** 1
Huddlestone 80, 99, Constantine 64
Defoe 107 34,560

QUARTER-FINALS

Charlton	0	Wycombe	1
		Easter 35	
		18,940	

Charlton are booed off the pitch after Easter's 25-yard piledriver earns Wycombe a 1-0 win at The Valley

Newcastle	0	Chelsea	1
		Drogba 78	
		37,406	

Drogba comes off the bench to fire home the winner from 20 yards after a clever short free-kick move with Ballack. Both sides rattle the woodwork but it's Chelsea who grab a deserved place in last four

Tottenham	1	Southend	0
Defoe 115			
		35,811	

Defoe finally breaks the deadlock for Spurs with five minutes of extra-time remaining when he slides in to convert a cross from Mido

Liverpool	3	Arsenal	6
Fowler 32, Gerrard 68		Aliadiere 27	
Hyypia 80		Baptista 40, 45, 60, 84	
		Song 45	
		42,614	

Liverpool are humiliated in front of a bemused Kop. Bapista scores four and misses a penalty as a Gunners side - with six teenagers in their line-up - see Liverpool concede six goals at home for first time since 1930

SEMI-FINALS

Wycombe	1	Chelsea	1
Easter 77		Bridge 36	
		5,771	

Chelsea	(1) 4	Wycombe	(1) 0
Shevchenko 22, 43,			
Lampard 69, 90			41,591

The superstars of Chelsea are made to work hard over the two legs by a battling Wycombe side. Two goals apiece from Shevchenko and Lampard in the second match at Stamford Bridge warrant a place in the final but the 5-1 aggregate is harsh on the lower league club

Tottenham	2	Arsenal	2
Berbatov 12		Baptista 64, 77	
Baptista 20 og			35,485

Arsenal	(2) 3	Tottenham	(2) 1
Adebayor 77		Mido 85	
Aliadiere 105			
Chimbonda 113 og			55,872

Arsenal win the battle of North London but they certainly leave it late. It takes two goals in extra-time at the end of a topsy-turvy second leg at the Emirates Stadium to secure the Gunners a trip to Cardiff

FINAL

Chelsea	2	Arsenal	1
Drogba 20, 84		Walcott 12	
		70,073	

Chelsea come from behind to collect the trophy courtesy of two goals from Drogba after an impressive young Gunners side dominate the first hour. A magnificent occasion is marred, however, by a mass brawl on the pitch towards the end of the match that results in Arsenal's Toure and Adebayor plus Chelsea substitute Mikel being red-carded.
Both clubs are later fined £100,000 each for failing to control their players, while Gunners boss Wenger also falls foul of the FA for comments made about an assistant linesman

CHAMPIONSHIP LEAGUE ROUND-UP

FINAL LEAGUE TABLE

	P	HOME					AWAY					TOTAL			
		W	D	L	F	A	W	D	L	F	A	F	A	DIF	PTS
Sunderland	46	15	4	4	38	18	12	3	8	38	29	76	47	29	88
Birmingham	46	15	5	3	37	18	11	3	9	30	24	67	42	25	86
Derby	46	13	6	4	33	19	12	3	8	29	27	62	46	16	84
West Brom	46	14	4	5	51	24	8	6	9	30	31	81	55	26	76
Wolves	46	12	5	6	33	28	10	5	8	26	28	59	56	3	76
Southampton	46	13	6	4	36	20	8	6	9	41	33	77	53	24	75
Preston	46	15	4	4	38	17	7	4	12	26	36	64	53	11	74
Stoke	46	12	8	3	35	16	7	8	8	27	25	62	41	21	73
Sheff Wed	46	10	6	7	38	36	10	5	8	32	30	70	66	4	71
Colchester	46	15	4	4	46	19	5	5	13	24	37	70	56	14	69
Plymouth	46	10	8	5	36	26	7	8	8	27	36	63	62	1	67
Crystal Palace	46	12	3	8	33	22	6	8	9	26	29	59	51	8	65
Cardiff	46	11	7	5	33	18	6	6	11	24	35	57	53	4	64
Ipswich	46	13	2	8	40	29	5	6	12	24	30	64	59	5	62
Burnley	46	10	6	7	35	23	5	6	12	17	26	52	49	3	57
Norwich	46	10	5	8	29	25	6	4	13	27	46	56	71	-15	57
Coventry	46	11	4	8	30	25	5	4	14	17	37	47	62	-15	56
QPR	46	9	6	8	31	29	5	5	13	23	39	54	68	-14	53
Leicester	46	6	8	9	26	31	7	6	10	23	33	49	64	-15	53
Barnsley	46	9	4	10	27	29	6	1	16	26	56	53	85	-32	50
Hull	46	8	3	12	33	33	5	7	11	18	35	51	67	-16	49
Southend	46	6	6	11	29	38	4	6	13	18	42	47	80	-33	42
Luton	46	7	5	11	33	40	3	5	15	20	41	53	81	-28	40
Leeds*	46	10	4	9	27	30	3	3	17	19	42	46	72	-26	36

CLUB STRIKE FORCE

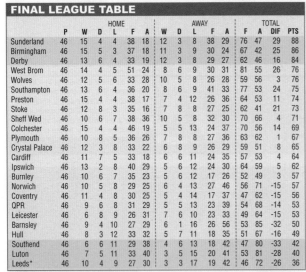

West Brom's Kamara & Phillips celebrate

	CLUB	GOALS	CSR
1	West Brom	81	51
2	Southampton	77	53
3	Sunderland	76	54
4	Sheff Wed	70	59
5	Colchester	70	59
6	Birmingham	67	61
7	Ipswich	64	64
8	Preston	64	64
9	Plymouth	63	65
10	Stoke	62	66
11	Derby	62	66
12	Crystal Palace	59	70
13	Wolverhampton	59	70
14	Cardiff	57	72
15	Norwich	56	73
16	QPR	54	76
17	Luton	53	78
18	Barnsley	53	78
19	Burnley	52	79
20	Hull City	51	81
21	Leicester	49	84
22	Coventry	47	88
23	Southend	47	88
24	Leeds	46	90

1 West Brom

Goals scored in the League	81
Club Strike Rate (CSR) Average number of minutes between League goals scored by club	51

CLUB DISCIPLINARY RECORDS

Leeds's Robert Bayly is sent off

	CLUB	Y	R	TOTAL	AVE
1	Leeds	97	6	103	40
2	QPR	101	2	103	40
3	West Brom	91	9	100	41
4	Ipswich	94	6	100	41
5	Derby	95	2	97	42
6	Burnley	87	6	93	44
7	Hull City	84	3	87	47
8	Stoke	83	4	87	47
9	Coventry	83	2	85	48
10	Sheff Wed	80	6	86	48
11	Plymouth	79	4	83	49
12	Barnsley	79	5	84	49
13	Leicester	79	3	82	50
14	Preston	75	4	79	52
15	Birmingham	68	8	76	54
16	Luton	70	5	75	55
17	Wolverhampton	68	6	74	55
18	Southend	69	4	73	56
19	Norwich	64	3	67	61
20	Sunderland	63	2	65	63
21	Cardiff	55	9	64	64
22	Southampton	54	1	55	75
23	Colchester	51	2	53	78
24	Crystal Palace	50	1	51	81

1 Leeds

League Yellow	97
League Red	6
League Total	103
Cards Average in League Average number of minutes between a card being shown of either colour	40

CLUB DEFENCES

	CLUB	LGE	CS	CDR
1	Stoke	41	16	100
2	Birmingham	42	18	98
3	Derby	46	15	90
4	Sunderland	47	17	88
5	Burnley	49	16	84
6	Crystal Palace	51	15	81
7	Cardiff	53	15	78
8	Preston	53	15	78
9	Southampton	53	16	78
10	West Brom	55	13	75
11	Wolverhampton	56	17	73
12	Colchester	56	13	73
13	Ipswich	59	7	70
14	Plymouth	62	10	66
15	Coventry	62	11	66
16	Leicester	64	10	64
17	Sheff Wed	66	8	62
18	Hull City	67	11	61
19	QPR	68	9	60
20	Norwich	71	10	58
21	Leeds	72	8	57
22	Luton	81	8	51
23	Southend	80	10	51
24	Barnsley	85	10	48

Stoke's Carl Hoefkens wins the ball

1 Stoke

Goals conceded in the League	41
Clean Sheets (CS) Number of league games where no goals were conceded	16
Club Defensive Rate (CDR) Average number of minutes between League goals conceded by club	100

STADIUM CAPACITY AND HOME CROWDS

TEAM	CAPACITY	AVE	HIGH	LOW
1 Norwich	26034	94.3	25476	23311
2 Colchester	6143	88.9	6065	4249
3 Luton	10155	84.2	10260	7441
4 Southend	12343	81.2	11415	7901
5 Derby	33597	77.2	31920	21295
6 Birmingham	29949	74.4	29431	15854
7 Ipswich	30311	74.3	28355	19337
8 Hull City	25404	73.8	25512	14895
9 West Brom	28000	73.1	26606	17417
10 Southampton	32689	72.1	32008	18736
11 Wolverhampton	29277	71.6	28016	16772
12 Leicester	32500	71.4	30457	18677
13 Cardiff	21432	71.0	20109	11549
14 Preston	20600	70.1	19603	11601
15 QPR	19148	67.6	16741	10811
16 Crystal Palace	26257	66.8	21523	15985
17 Sunderland	49000	64.3	44448	24242
18 Coventry	32000	63.6	27212	16178
19 Plymouth	20922	60.1	17088	1655
20 Sheff Wed	39814	59.4	29103	18752
21 Stoke	28218	55.8	23017	11626
22 Leeds	40232	52.8	31269	16268
23 Burnley	22516	51.4	15061	1039
24 Barnsley	25000	50.9	21253	9479

Key: Average. The percentage of each stadium filled in League games over the season (AVE), the stadium capacity and the highest and lowest crowds recorded.

AWAY ATTENDANCE

TEAM	AVE	HIGH	LOW
1 Leeds	77.7	40116	5916
2 Sunderland	76.3	29103	6042
3 Sheff Wed	74.5	36764	5097
4 QPR	72.0	39206	5246
5 Derby	71.4	36049	4574
6 Wolverhampton	71.1	31920	5893
7 Birmingham	70.0	27212	5918
8 West Brom	69.2	28016	4934
9 Burnley	68.0	44448	4934
10 Hull City	67.2	38448	5373
11 Coventry	67.2	33591	5453
12 Ipswich	66.6	31269	6065
13 Southend	66.6	33576	5954
14 Barnsley	66.5	30457	4249
15 Leicester	66.1	35104	5915
16 Norwich	65.8	28287	5851
17 Southampton	65.4	25667	5893
18 Crystal Palace	65.4	30548	5857
19 Luton	64.8	30445	5427
20 Cardiff	64.5	28223	1655
21 Plymouth	64.5	25775	4627
22 Preston	64.3	30460	5245
23 Stoke	63.5	31358	5245
24 Colchester	63	28355	1039

Key: Average. How close each club has come to filling grounds in its away league matches (AVE) and the highest and lowest crowds recorded.

CHART-TOPPING MIDFIELDERS

1 Diao - Stoke

Goals scored in the League	0
Defensive Rating Av number of mins between League goals conceded while on the pitch	137
Contribution to Attacking Power Average number of minutes between League team goals while on pitch	64
Scoring Difference Defensive Rating minus Contribution to Attacking Power	73

	PLAYER	CLUB	GOALS	DEF RATE	POWER	S DIFF
1	Salif Diao	Stoke	0	137	64	73
2	Stephen Clemence	Birmingham	4	129	63	66
3	Liam Miller	Sunderland	2	119	53	66
4	Lee Hendrie	Stoke	3	120	63	57
5	Sebastian Larsson	Birmingham	4	103	56	47
6	Rudolf Skacel	Southampton	3	85	45	40
7	Fabrice Muamba	Birmingham	0	115	80	35
8	Darel Russell	Stoke	7	98	66	32
9	Dean Whitehead	Sunderland	4	86	54	32
10	Damien Johnson	Birmingham	1	103	72	31
11	Matthew Oakley	Derby	6	94	63	31
12	Liam Lawrence	Stoke	5	94	63	31
13	David Jones	Derby	6	105	77	28
14	Grant Leadbitter	Sunderland	7	83	57	26
15	Wade Elliott	Burnley	4	102	77	25

CHART-TOPPING GOALSCORERS

1 Earnshaw - Norwich

Goals scored in the League	19
Contribution to Attacking Power (AP) Average number of minutes between League team goals while on pitch	66
Club Strike Rate (CSR) Average minutes between League goals scored by club	77
Player Strike Rate Average number of minutes between League goals scored by player	133

	PLAYER	CLUB	GOALS: LGE	POWER	CSR	S RATE
1	Robert Earnshaw	Norwich	19	66	77	133
2	Diomansy Kamara	West Brom	20	50	51	143
3	Kenwyne Jones	Southampton	14	57	53	148
4	Grzegorz Rasiak	Southampton	18	54	53	155
5	Jamie Cureton	Colchester	23	57	59	162
6	Kevin Phillips	West Brom	16	48	51	163
7	Michael Chopra	Cardiff	22	65	72	167
8	Rowan Vine	Luton	12	67	79	186
9	Chris Iwelumo	Colchester	18	57	59	195
10	David Connolly	Sunderland	13	56	54	205
11	Martin Rowlands	QPR	10	80	76	216
12	Andy Gray	Burnley	14	63	83	218
13	Alan Lee	Ipswich	15	64	64	218
14	Clinton Morrison	Crystal Palace	12	83	70	222
15	Ricardo Fuller	Stoke	10	65	68	224

CHART-TOPPING DEFENDERS

1 Loovens - Cardiff

Goals Conceded in the League The number of League goals conceded while he was on the pitch	21
Clean Sheets In games when he played at least 70 mins	12
Club Defensive Rating Average mins between League goals conceded by the club this season	78
Defensive Rating Average number of minutes between League goals conceded while on pitch	120

	PLAYER	CLUB	CON: LGE	CS	CDR	DEF RATE
1	Glenn Loovens	Cardiff	21	12	78	120
2	Stephen Kelly	Birmingham	28	15	102	113
3	Andrew Griffin	Stoke	25	13	103	113
4	Darren Moore	Derby	23	10	90	111
5	Matthew Sadler	Birmingham	30	16	102	107
6	Carl Hoefkens	Stoke	36	16	103	105
7	Michael Duberry	Stoke	25	13	103	104
8	Danny Higginbotham	Stoke	38	15	103	102
9	Danny Butterfield	Crystal Palace	22	9	81	99
10	Bruno N'Gotty	Birmingham	22	9	102	97
11	Radhi Jaidi	Birmingham	34	13	102	97
12	Nayron Nosworthy	Sunderland	25	11	88	97
13	Martin Taylor	Birmingham	27	12	102	96
14	Mohammed Camara	Derby	18	8	90	95
15	Marc Edworthy	Derby	35	13	90	94

CHART-TOPPING GOALKEEPERS

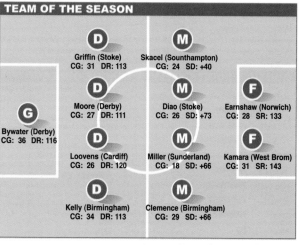

1 Bywater - Derby

Counting Games Games in which he played at least 70 minutes	36
Goals Conceded in the League The number of League goals conceded while he was on the pitch	28
Clean Sheets In games when he played at least 70 mins	14
Defensive Rating Average number of minutes between League goals conceded while on pitch	116

	PLAYER	CLUB	CG	CONC	CS	DEF RATE
1	Stephen Bywater	Derby	36	28	14	116
2	Colin Doyle	Birmingham	19	15	7	114
3	Darren Ward	Sunderland	30	27	11	100
4	Steve Simonsen	Stoke	46	41	16	100
5	Carlo Nash	Preston	28	27	11	93
6	Maik Taylor	Birmingham	27	27	11	90
7	Brian Jensen	Burnley	31	31	14	89
8	Neil Alexander	Cardiff	39	42	15	83
9	Gabor Kiraly	Crystal Palace	29	32	8	81
10	Dean Gerken	Colchester	27	32	8	75
11	Matt Murray	Wolverhampton	43	52	17	74
12	Kelvin Davis	Southampton	38	46	12	74
13	Andy Marshall	Coventry	41	50	10	73
14	Aidan Davison	Colchester	19	24	5	71
15	Paul Henderson	Leicester	28	36	7	70

PLAYER DISCIPLINARY RECORD

Simon Walton is shown the red card

	PLAYER		LY	LR	TOT	AVE
1	Foxe	Leeds	9	1	10	116
2	Walton	Ipswich	7	1	8	148
3	Kyle	Coventry	11	0	11	163
4	Tiatto	Leicester	11	0	11	164
5	McNamee	Coventry	6	1	7	174
6	Bolder	QPR	8	0	8	174
7	Carter	West Brom	10	1	11	174
8	McCormack	Southend	10	0	10	176
9	Dichio	Preston	6	1	7	194
10	McCarthy	Leicester	8	1	9	198
11	Fuller	Stoke	9	2	11	203
12	Whing	Coventry	6	0	6	205
13	Timoska	QPR	4	1	5	206
14	Noble	Ipswich	5	0	5	209
15	Nicholls	Leeds	4	1	5	214

1. Hayden Foxe

Cards Average mins between cards	116
League Yellow	9
League Red	1
TOTAL	10

TEAM OF THE SEASON

D Griffin (Stoke) CG: 31 DR: 113

M Skacel (Sounthampton) CG: 24 SD: +40

D Moore (Derby) CG: 27 DR: 111

M Diao (Stoke) CG: 26 SD: +73

F Earnshaw (Norwich) CG: 28 SR: 133

G Bywater (Derby) CG: 36 DR: 116

D Loovens (Cardiff) CG: 26 DR: 120

M Miller (Sunderland) CG: 18 SD: +66

F Kamara (West Brom) CG: 31 SR: 143

D Kelly (Birmingham) CG: 34 DR: 113

M Clemence (Birmingham) CG: 29 SD: +66

SUNDERLAND

Final Position: **1st**

NICKNAME: MACKEMS/BLACKCATS   KEY: ☐ Won ☐ Drawn ☐ Lost   Attendance

				Result	Scorers	Attendance
1	div1	Coventry	A L	1-2	D.Murphy 52	22,366
2	div1	Birmingham	H L	0-1		26,668
3	div1	Plymouth	H L	2-3	Murphy 1, S.Elliott 67	24,377
4	div1	Southend	A L	1-1	Stead 90	9,848
5	ccr1	Bury	A L	0-2		2,930
6	div1	West Brom	H W	2-0	Whitehead 33, N.Collins 47	24,242
7	div1	Derby	A W	2-1	Brown 62, Wallace 64	26,502
8	div1	Leeds	A W	3-0	L.Miller 28, Kavanagh 45, S.Elliott 48	23,037
9	div1	Leicester	H D	1-1	Hysen 66	35,104
10	div1	Ipswich	A L	1-3	De Vos 29 og	23,311
11	div1	Sheff Wed	H W	1-0	Leadbitter 58	36,764
12	div1	Preston	A L	1-4	Varga 56	19,603
13	div1	Stoke	A L	1-2	Yorke 28	14,482
14	div1	Barnsley	H W	2-0	Whitehead 82, Brown 88	27,918
15	div1	Hull City	A W	1-0	Wallace 90	25,512
16	div1	Cardiff	H L	1-2	Brown 10	26,528
17	div1	Norwich	A L	0-1		24,652
18	div1	Southampton	H D	1-1	Wallace 62	25,667
19	div1	Colchester	H W	3-1	S.Elliott 45, 53, Connolly 90	25,197
20	div1	Wolverhampton	A D	1-1	S.Elliott 80	27,203
21	div1	QPR	A W	2-1	Murphy 17, Leadbitter 45	13,108
22	div1	Norwich	H W	1-0	Murphy 76	27,934
23	div1	Luton	H W	2-1	Murphy 9, Connolly 53	30,445
24	div1	Burnley	A D	2-2	Leadbitter 80, Connolly 90	14,798
25	div1	Crystal Palace	A L	0-1		17,439
26	div1	Leeds	H W	2-0	Connolly 65, Leadbitter 81	40,116
27	div1	Preston	H L	0-1		30,460
28	div1	Leicester	A W	2-0	Hysen 79, Connolly 83	21,975
29	facr3	Preston	A L	0-1		10,318
30	div1	Ipswich	H W	1-0	Connolly 13	27,604
31	div1	Sheff Wed	A W	4-2	Yorke 21, Hartley 45, Connolly 58, Edwards 89	29,103
32	div1	Crystal Palace	H D	0-0		26,958
33	div1	Coventry	H W	2-0	Yorke 19, Edwards 84	33,591
34	div1	Plymouth	A W	2-0	Stokes 69, Connolly 71	15,247
35	div1	Southend	H W	4-0	Connolly 4, Hysen 13, John 77, 78	33,576
36	div1	Birmingham	A D	1-1	Edwards 27	20,941
37	div1	Derby	H W	2-1	Connolly 27 pen, L.Miller 90	36,049
38	div1	West Brom	A W	2-1	Yorke 23, John 49	23,252
39	div1	Barnsley	A W	2-0	Leadbitter 66, Connolly 90	18,207
40	div1	Stoke	H D	2-2	Whitehead 24, Murphy 90	31,358
41	div1	Hull City	H W	2-0	Evans 3, John 90	38,448
42	div1	Cardiff	A W	1-0	Wallace 72	19,353
43	div1	Wolverhampton	H W	2-1	Murphy 15, Wallace 63	40,748
44	div1	Southampton	A W	2-1	Edwards 77, Leadbitter 87	25,766
45	div1	QPR	H W	2-1	Whitehead 7, Leadbitter 76	39,206
46	div1	Colchester	A L	1-3	Yorke 55	6,042
47	div1	Burnley	H W	3-2	Murphy 14, Connolly 54 pen, Edwards 80	44,448
48	div1	Luton	A W	5-0	Stokes 4, Murphy 6, 46, Wallace 77, Connolly 86	10,260

LEAGUE APPEARANCES, BOOKINGS AND CAPS

	AGE (on 01/07/07)	IN NAMED 16	APPEARANCES	COUNTING GAMES	MINUTES ON PITCH	LEAGUE GOALS	▯	▮
Goalkeepers								
Ben Alnwick	20	16	11	11	990	0	0	0
Marton Fulop	24	25	5	5	450	0	0	0
Darren Ward	33	43	30	30	2700	0	0	0
Defenders								
Stephen Caldwell	26	14	11	9	853	0	2	0
Danny Collins	26	43	38	36	3298	0	4	0
Neill Collins	23	10	7	5	464	1	0	0
Kenny Cunningham	36	13	11	10	945	0	1	0
Robbie Elliott	33	12	7	6	585	0	1	0
Jonny Evans	19	18	18	17	1575	1	3	0
Nayron Nosworthy	26	31	29	27	2446	0	4	0
Lewin Nyatanga	18	14	11	9	897	0	0	0
Danny Simpson	20	14	13	11	1043	0	1	0
Stanislav Varga	34	23	20	20	1800	1	7	0
Stephen Wright	27	6	3	3	251	0	1	0
Midfielders								
Rory Delap	30	6	6	6	519	0	1	0
Carlos Edwards	28	15	15	13	1259	5	1	0
Tobias Hysen	25	29	26	10	1381	3	0	0
Graham Kavanagh	33	15	14	10	956	1	3	0
Liam Lawrence	25	14	12	8	834	0	1	0
Grant Leadbitter	21	46	44	21	2429	7	1	0
Liam Miller	26	35	30	18	2029	2	7	1
Ross Wallace	22	33	32	15	1894	6	5	2
Dean Whitehead	25	45	45	41	3822	4	7	0
Forwards								
Chris Brown	22	17	16	8	911	3	4	0
David Connolly	30	37	36	29	2670	13	1	0
Stephen Elliott	23	25	24	13	1403	5	0	0
Stern John	30	15	15	4	785	4	0	0
Tommy Miller	28	3	3	2	242	0	0	0
Daryl Murphy	24	39	38	22	2390	10	1	0
Anthony Stokes	18	15	15	7	834	2	1	0
Dwight Yorke	35	35	32	23	2414	5	6	0

TEAM OF THE SEASON

D Jonny Evans — CG: 17 DR: 112
M Liam Miller — CG: 18 SD: 66
D Nayron Nosworthy — CG: 27 DR: 97
M Carlos Edwards — CG: 13 SD: 63
F David Connolly — CG: 29 SR: 205
G Darren Ward — CG: 30 DR: 100
D Danny Collins — CG: 36 DR: 86
M Ross Wallace — CG: 15 SD: 39
F Daryl Murphy — CG: 22 SR: 239
D Stanislav Varga — CG: 20 DR: 85
M Dean Whitehead — CG: 41 SD: 32

MONTHLY POINTS TALLY

Month	Points	%
AUGUST		3 20%
SEPTEMBER		10 67%
OCTOBER		6 40%
NOVEMBER		8 53%
DECEMBER		10 56%
JANUARY		10 83%
FEBRUARY		13 87%
MARCH		13 87%
APRIL		12 80%
MAY		3 100%

LEAGUE GOALS

	PLAYER	MINS	GOALS	S RATE
1	Connolly	2670	13	205
2	Murphy	2390	10	239
3	Leadbitter	2429	7	347
4	Wallace	1894	6	315
5	Edwards	1259	5	251
6	Elliott, S	1403	5	280
7	Yorke	2414	5	482
8	John	785	4	196
9	Whitehead	3822	4	955
10	Brown	911	3	303
11	Hysen	1381	3	460
12	Stokes	834	2	417
13	Miller, L	2029	2	1014
	Other		5	
	TOTAL		**74**	

TOP POINT EARNERS

	PLAYER	GAMES	AV PTS
1	Carlos Edwards	13	2.62
2	Jonny Evans	17	2.59
3	Ross Wallace	14	2.36
4	Liam Miller	18	2.22
5	Nayron Nosworthy	27	2.15
6	Darren Ward	30	2.07
7	David Connolly	29	1.97
8	Dwight Yorke	22	1.95
9	Danny Collins	36	1.92
10	Dean Whitehead	40	1.90
	CLUB AVERAGE:		**1.91**

DISCIPLINARY RECORDS

	PLAYER	YELLOW	RED	AVE
1	Chris Brown	4	0	227
2	Ross Wallace	5	2	270
3	Stanislav Varga	7	0	300
4	Graham Kavanagh	3	0	318
5	Liam Miller	7	1	338
6	Dwight Yorke	6	0	402
7	Stephen Caldwell	2	0	426
8	Rory Delap	1	0	519
9	Jonny Evans	3	0	525
10	Dean Whitehead	7	0	546
11	Robbie Elliott	1	0	585
12	Nayron Nosworthy	4	0	611
13	Grant Leadbitter	3	0	809
	Other	11	0	
	TOTAL	**64**	**3**	

KEY GOALKEEPER

Darren Ward

Goals Conceded in the League	27	Counting Games League games when player was on pitch for at least 70 minutes		30
Defensive Rating Ave number of mins between League goals conceded while on the pitch	100	Clean Sheets In League games when player was on pitch for at least 70 minutes		11

KEY PLAYERS - DEFENDERS

Jonny Evans

Goals Conceded Number of League goals conceded while the player was on the pitch	14	Clean Sheets In League games when player was on pitch for at least 70 minutes		8
Defensive Rating Ave number of mins between League goals conceded while on the pitch	112	Club Defensive Rating Average number of mins between League goals conceded by the club this season		88

	PLAYER	CON LGE	CLEAN SHEETS	DEF RATE
1	Jonny Evans	14	8	112 mins
2	Nayron Nosworthy	25	11	97 mins
3	Danny Collins	38	12	86 mins
4	Stanislav Varga	21	7	85 mins

KEY PLAYERS - MIDFIELDERS

Liam Miller

Goals in the League	2	Contribution to Attacking Power Average number of minutes between League team goals while on pitch		53
Defensive Rating Average number of mins between League goals conceded while on the pitch	119	Scoring Difference Defensive Rating minus Contribution to Attacking Power		66

	PLAYER	LGE GOALS	DEF RATE	POWER	SCORE DIFF
1	Liam Miller	2	119	53	66 mins
2	Carlos Edwards	5	104	41	63 mins
3	Ross Wallace	6	90	51	39 mins
4	Dean Whitehead	4	86	54	32 mins

KEY PLAYERS - GOALSCORERS

David Connolly

Goals in the League	13	Player Strike Rate Average number of minutes between League goals scored by player		205
Contribution to Attacking Power Average number of minutes between League team goals while on pitch	56	Club Strike Rate Average number of minutes between League goals scored by club		54

	PLAYER	LGE GOALS	POWER	STRIKE RATE
1	David Connolly	13	56	205 mins
2	Daryl Murphy	10	59	239 mins
3	Carlos Edwards	5	41	251 mins
4	Stephen Elliott	5	56	280 mins

David Connolly

SQUAD APPEARANCES

Match	1 2 3 4 5	6 7 8 9 10	11 12 13 14 15	16 17 18 19 20	21 22 23 24 25	26 27 28 29 30	31 32 33 34 35	36 37 38 39 40	41 42 43 44 45	46 47 48
Venue	A H H A A	H A A H A	H A A H A	H A H H A	A H H A A	H H A H H	A H H A H	A H A A H	H A H A H	A H A
Competition	L L L L W	L L L L L	L L L L L	L L L L L	L L L L L	L L L F L	L L L L L	L L L L L	L L L L L	L L L
Result	L L L L L	W W W D L	W L L W W	L L D W D	W W W D L	W L W L W	W D W W W	D W W W D	L L L L L	L W W

Goalkeepers
Ben Alnwick
Trevor Carson
Marton Fulop
Darren Ward

Defenders
Stephen Caldwell
Clive Clarke
Danny Collins
Neill Collins
Kenny Cunningham
Robbie Elliott
Jonny Evans
Peter Hartley
Nayron Nosworthy
Lewin Nyatanga
Danny Simpson
Daniel Smith
Stanislav Varga
Stephen Wright

Midfielders
Rory Delap
Carlos Edwards
Tobias Hysen
Graham Kavanagh
Liam Lawrence
Grant Leadbitter
Liam Miller
Tommy Miller
Arnau Riera
Ross Wallace
Andrew Welsh
Dean Whitehead

Forwards
Chris Brown
David Connolly
Stephen Elliott
Stern John
Kevin Kyle
Tommy Miller
Daryl Murphy
Kevin Smith
Jonathan Stead
Anthony Stokes
Dwight Yorke

KEY: ■ On all match   ◄◄ Subbed or sent off (Counting game)   ►► Subbed on from bench (Counting Game)   ►► Subbed on and then subbed or sent off (Counting Game)   ☐ Not in 16
   ■ On bench   ◄◄ Subbed or sent off (playing less than 70 minutes)   ►► Subbed on (playing less than 70 minutes)   ►► Subbed on and then subbed or sent off (playing less than 70 minutes)

CHAMPIONSHIP - SUNDERLAND

BIRMINGHAM

Final Position: 2nd

NICKNAME: THE BLUES   KEY: ☐ Won ☐ Drawn ☐ Lost

						Attendance
1	div1	Colchester	H W	2-1	Campbell 30, Bendtner 79	24,238
2	div1	Sunderland	A W	1-0	Forssell 40 pen	26,668
3	div1	Stoke	A D	0-0		12,347
4	div1	Crystal Palace	H W	2-1	Bendtner 23, Larsson 90	20,223
5	ccr1	Shrewsbury	H W	1-0	Larsson 83	12,428
6	div1	Cardiff	A L	0-2		20,109
7	div1	Hull City	H W	2-1	Campbell 16, Bendtner 53	19,228
8	div1	QPR	A W	2-0	N'Gotty 23, Jerome 90	10,936
9	div1	Ipswich	H D	2-2	Campbell 74, Dunn 86	20,841
10	ccr2	Wrexham	H W	4-1	Jerome 41, McSheffrey 102, 113, Bendtner 117	10,491
11	div1	Leeds	A L	2-3	Warner 13 og, Bendtner 74	18,898
12	div1	Leicester	H D	1-1	McSheffrey 58	18,002
13	div1	Luton	A L	2-3	Campbell 14, Danns 66	9,275
14	div1	Norwich	H L	0-1		20,537
15	div1	Derby	A W	1-0	Clemence 84	25,673
16	ccr3	Sheff Utd	A W	4-2	Campbell 41, Bendtner 70, Jerome 79, Larsson 90	10,584
17	div1	West Brom	H W	2-0	McSheffrey 18, 90	21,009
18	div1	Coventry	A W	1-0	Bendtner 26	27,212
19	div1	Plymouth	A W	1-0	Jaidi 75	17,008
20	ccr4	Liverpool	H L	0-1		23,061
21	div1	Barnsley	H W	2-0	McSheffrey 35, Danns 90	19,344
22	div1	Wolverhampton	H D	1-1	McSheffrey 30	22,256
23	div1	Burnley	A W	2-1	Bendtner 15, Campbell 83	12,889
24	div1	Southampton	A L	3-4	Jerome 68, Bendtner 72, Jaidi 90	21,889
25	div1	Plymouth	H W	3-0	Bendtner 21, Upson 30, McSheffrey 41	22,592
26	div1	Preston	H W	3-1	McSheffrey 32, 40, 89 pen	23,159
27	div1	Sheff Wed	A W	3-0	Clemence 42, McSheffrey 65, Jerome 90	26,083
28	div1	Southend	A W	4-0	Campbell 8, Clemence 38, McSheffrey 54, Jaidi 84	9,781
29	div1	QPR	H W	2-1	Upson 22, Jerome 62	29,431
30	div1	Luton	H D	2-2	McSheffrey 31, Danns 90	24,642
31	div1	Ipswich	A L	0-1		22,436
32	facr3	Newcastle	H D	2-2	Campbell 15, Larsson 86	16,444
33	facr3r	Newcastle	A W	5-1	McSheffrey 5, Solano 45 og, N'Gotty 59, Larsson 83, Campbell 89	26,099
34	facr4	Reading	H L	2-3	Martin.Taylor 47, Larsson 90	20,041
35	div1	Southend	H L	1-3	Clarke 9 og	19,177
36	div1	Colchester	A D	1-1	Clemence 66	5,918
37	div1	Stoke	H W	1-0	McSheffrey 71	15,854
38	div1	Crystal Palace	A W	1-0	Jerome 34	17,233
39	div1	Sunderland	H D	1-1	Campbell 90	20,941
40	div1	Hull City	A L	0-2		18,811
41	div1	Leeds	H W	1-0	Bendtner 15	18,363
42	div1	Cardiff	H W	1-0	Larsson 56	28,223
43	div1	Derby	H W	1-0	Vine 45	20,962
44	div1	Norwich	A L	0-1		23,504
45	div1	West Brom	A D	1-1	Johnson 86	21,434
46	div1	Coventry	H W	3-0	Jaidi 13, Campbell 65, 78	25,424
47	div1	Burnley	H L	0-1		28,777
48	div1	Barnsley	A L	0-1		15,857
49	div1	Southampton	H W	2-1	Jaidi 32, Bendtner 79	19,754
50	div1	Leicester	A W	2-1	Jaidi 16, Larsson 19	24,290
51	div1	Wolverhampton	A W	3-2	Cole 53, Bendtner 77, Jerome 88	22,754
52	div1	Sheff Wed	H W	2-0	Jerome 74, Larsson 84	29,317
53	div1	Preston	A L	0-1		16,837

LEAGUE APPEARANCES, BOOKINGS AND CAPS

	AGE (on 01/07/07)	IN NAMED 16	APPEARANCES	COUNTING GAMES	MINUTES ON PITCH	LEAGUE GOALS		
Goalkeepers								
Colin Doyle	22	46	19	19	1710	0	0	0
Maik Taylor	35	45	27	27	2430	0	0	0
Defenders								
Radhi Jaidi	31	38	38	36	3316	6	5	2
Stephen Kelly	23	37	36	34	3169	0	5	0
Bruno N'Gotty	36	25	25	23	2135	1	2	1
Marcos Painter	20	1	1	1	90	0	1	0
Matthew Sadler	22	36	36	36	3234	0	3	0
Martin Taylor	27	39	31	28	2603	0	1	0
Olivier Tebily	31	9	6	5	490	0	1	0
Matthew Upson	28	10	9	8	719	2	2	0
Midfielders								
Stephen Clemence	29	34	34	29	2715	4	6	0
Neil Danns	24	35	29	8	1095	3	2	0
David Dunn	27	11	11	7	766	1	3	0
Julian Gray	27	9	7	1	245	0	2	0
Damien Johnson	28	27	27	24	2174	1	2	0
Neil Kilkenny	21	13	8	0	164	0	1	0
Sebastian Larsson	22	43	43	25	2583	4	9	0
Fabrice Muamba	19	38	34	25	2421	0	9	1
Mehdi Nafti	28	39	32	15	1596	0	7	0
Forwards								
Nicklas Bendtner	19	42	42	36	3383	11	5	0
Dudley Campbell	25	42	32	10	1303	9	1	0
Andy Cole	35	5	5	3	368	1	0	0
Mikael Forssell	26	13	8	1	322	1	0	0
Cameron Jerome	20	39	37	11	1865	7	3	1
Gary McSheffrey	24	40	40	39	3521	13	4	0
Rowan Vine	24	19	17	7	914	1	0	0

TEAM OF THE SEASON

G Colin Doyle — CG: 19 DR: 114

D Stephen Kelly — CG: 34 DR: 113
D Matthew Sadler — CG: 36 DR: 107
D Bruno N'Gotty — CG: 23 DR: 97
D Radhi Jaidi — CG: 36 DR: 97

M Stephen Clemence — CG: 29 SD: 66
M Sebastian Larsson — CG: 25 SD: 47
M Mehdi Nafti — CG: 15 SD: 40
M Fabrice Muamba — CG: 25 SD: 35

F Gary McSheffrey — CG: 39 SR: 270
F Nicklas Bendtner — CG: 36 SR: 307

MONTHLY POINTS TALLY

AUGUST		10	67%
SEPTEMBER		8	53%
OCTOBER		9	60%
NOVEMBER		10	67%
DECEMBER		16	89%
JANUARY		0	0%
FEBRUARY		11	61%
MARCH		7	58%
APRIL		15	71%
MAY		0	0%

LEAGUE GOALS

	PLAYER	MINS	GOALS	S RATE
1	McSheffrey	3521	13	270
2	Bendtner	3383	11	307
3	Campbell	1303	9	144
4	Jerome	1865	7	266
5	Jaidi	3316	6	552
6	Larsson	2583	4	645
7	Clemence	2715	4	678
8	Danns	1095	3	365
9	Upson	719	2	359
10	Forssell	322	1	322
11	Cole	368	1	368
12	Dunn	766	1	766
13	Vine	914	1	914
	Other		2	
	TOTAL		**65**	

TOP POINT EARNERS

	PLAYER	GAMES	AV PTS
1	Fabrice Muamba	25	2.28
2	Stephen Clemence	29	2.21
3	Nicklas Bendtner	37	2.11
4	Stephen Kelly	34	2.09
5	Sebastian Larsson	25	2.00
6	Bruno N'Gotty	23	2.00
7	Maik Taylor	27	1.96
8	Martin Taylor	28	1.86
9	Matthew Sadler	36	1.86
10	Radhi Jaidi	37	1.86
	CLUB AVERAGE:		**1.87**

DISCIPLINARY RECORDS

	PLAYER	YELLOW	RED	AVE
1	Fabrice Muamba	9	1	242
2	David Dunn	3	0	255
3	Mehdi Nafti	7	0	266
4	Sebastian Larsson	9	0	322
5	Stephen Clemence	6	0	452
6	Cameron Jerome	3	1	466
7	Olivier Tebily	1	0	490
8	Gary McSheffrey	6	1	503
9	Nicklas Bendtner	5	1	563
10	Stephen Kelly	5	0	633
11	Bruno N'Gotty	2	1	711
12	Matthew Upson	2	0	719
13	Damien Johnson	2	1	724
	Other	12	2	
	TOTAL	**72**	**8**	

KEY GOALKEEPER

Colin Doyle

Goals Conceded in the League	15	Counting Games League games when player was on pitch for at least 70 minutes	19
Defensive Rating Ave number of mins between League goals conceded while on the pitch	114	Clean Sheets In games when player was on pitch for at least 70 minutes	7

KEY PLAYERS - DEFENDERS

Stephen Kelly

Goals Conceded Number of League goals conceded while the player was on the pitch	28	Clean Sheets In League games when player was on pitch for at least 70 minutes	15
Defensive Rating Ave number of mins between League goals conceded while on the pitch	113	Club Defensive Rating Average number of mins between League goals conceded by the club this season	102

	PLAYER	CON LGE	CLEAN SHEETS	DEF RATE
1	Stephen Kelly	28	15	113 mins
2	Matthew Sadler	30	16	107 mins
3	Bruno N'Gotty	22	9	97 mins
4	Radhi Jaidi	34	13	97 mins

KEY PLAYERS - MIDFIELDERS

Stephen Clemence

Goals in the League	4	Contribution to Attacking Power Average number of minutes between League team goals while on pitch	63
Defensive Rating Average number of mins between League goals conceded while on the pitch	129	Scoring Difference Defensive Rating minus Contribution to Attacking Power	66

	PLAYER	LGE GOALS	DEF RATE	POWER	SCORE DIFF
1	Stephen Clemence	4	129	63	66 mins
2	Sebastian Larsson	4	103	56	47 mins
3	Mehdi Nafti	0	88	48	40 mins
4	Fabrice Muamba	0	115	80	35 mins

KEY PLAYERS - GOALSCORERS

Gary McSheffrey

Goals in the League	13	Player Strike Rate Average number of minutes between League goals scored by player	270
Contribution to Attacking Power Average number of minutes between League team goals while on pitch	64	Club Strike Rate Average number of minutes between League goals scored by club	64

	PLAYER	LGE GOALS	POWER	STRIKE RATE
1	Gary McSheffrey	13	64	270 mins
2	Nicklas Bendtner	11	62	307 mins
3	Sebastian Larsson	4	56	645 mins
4	Stephen Clemence	4	63	678 mins

Damien Johnson and Stephen Clemence

SQUAD APPEARANCES

Match	1 2 3 4 5	6 7 8 9 10	11 12 13 14 15	16 17 18 19 20	21 22 23 24 25	26 27 28 29 30	31 32 33 34 35	36 37 38 39 40	41 42 43 44 45	46 47 48 49 50	51 52 53
Venue	H A A H H	A H A H H	A H A H A	A H A A H	H H A A H	H A A H H	A H A H H	A H A H A	H H H A A	H H A H A	A H A
Competition	L L L L W	L L L L W	L L L L L	W L L L W	L L L L L	L L L L L	L F F F L	L L L L L	L L L L L	L L L L L	L L L
Result	W W D W W	L W W D W	L D L L W	W W W W L	W D W L W	W W W W D	L D W L L	D W W D L	W W W L D	W L L W W	W W L

KEY: On all match · Subbed or sent off (Counting game) · Subbed on from bench (Counting Game) · Subbed on and then subbed or sent off (Counting Game) · Not in 16 · On bench · Subbed or sent off (playing less than 70 minutes) · Subbed on (playing less than 70 minutes) · Subbed on and then subbed or sent off (playing less than 70 minutes)

CHAMPIONSHIP - BIRMINGHAM

DERBY COUNTY

PROMOTED VIA THE PLAY-OFFS Final Position: **3rd**

NICKNAME: THE RAMS KEY: ☐ Won ☐ Drawn ☐ Lost Attendance

#	Comp	Opponent			Score	Scorers	Attendance
1	div1	Southampton	H	D	2-2	Se.Johnson 35, Peschisolido 90	21,939
2	div1	Stoke	A	L	0-2		20,013
3	div1	Hull City	A	W	2-1	Oakley 7, T.Smith 74 pen	15,621
4	div1	Norwich	H	D	0-0		22,196
5	ccr1	Stockport	A	W	1-0	M.Johnson 45	3,394
6	div1	Colchester	A	L	3-4	Lupoli 42, 80, Peschisolido 89	4,574
7	div1	Sunderland	H	L	1-2	Oakley 45	26,502
8	div1	Wolverhampton	A	W	1-0	Howard 34	21,546
9	div1	Preston	H	D	1-1	Howard 44 pen	22,220
10	ccr2	Doncaster	A	L	7-8*	Howard 74, Moore 78, Lupoli 90 (*on penalties)	5,598
11	div1	Sheff Wed	A	W	2-1	Peschisolido 79, Howard 90	23,659
12	div1	Southend	H	W	3-0	Lupoli 40, 63, M.Johnson 48	22,395
13	div1	Plymouth	A	L	1-3	Lupoli 45	13,622
14	div1	QPR	H	W	2-1	Bisgaard 4, Howard 33	10,882
15	div1	Birmingham	H	L	0-1		25,673
16	div1	Cardiff	A	D	2-2	Howard 66, Barnes 90	17,371
17	div1	Barnsley	H	W	2-1	Barnes 72, 76	21,295
18	div1	West Brom	H	W	2-1	Oakley 69, Barnes 72	25,342
19	div1	Coventry	A	W	2-1	Stead 11, Howard 76	19,701
20	div1	Luton	A	W	2-0	Stead 72, Howard 75	9,708
21	div1	Leicester	H	W	1-0	Stead 53	28,315
22	div1	Ipswich	A	W	2-1	Howard 54, Lupoli 90	22,606
23	div1	West Brom	A	L	0-1		20,494
24	div1	Leeds	A	W	1-0	Barnes 9	20,087
25	div1	Crystal Palace	H	W	1-0	D.Jones 22	23,875
26	div1	Burnley	A	D	0-0		12,825
27	div1	Wolverhampton	H	L	0-2		31,920
28	div1	Plymouth	H	W	1-0	Bisgaard 81	25,775
29	div1	Preston	A	W	2-1	Howard 48, 51 pen	19,204
30	facr3	Wrexham	H	W	3-1	Lupoli 32, 56, 85	15,609
31	div1	Sheff Wed	H	W	1-0	D.Jones 90	28,936
32	div1	Southend	A	W	1-0	Howard 33	10,745
33	facr4	Bristol Rovers	H	W	1-0	Peschisolido 82	25,033
34	div1	Burnley	H	W	1-0	Howard 4	23,122
35	div1	Southampton	A	W	1-0	Howard 83	27,656
36	div1	Hull City	H	D	2-2	Teale 29, Moore 45	28,140
37	facr5	Plymouth	A	L	0-2		18,026
38	div1	Stoke	H	L	0-2		24,897
39	div1	Sunderland	A	L	1-2	Barnes 59	36,049
40	div1	Colchester	H	W	5-1	D.Jones 2, Lupoli 20, Barnes 30, Howard 62 pen, Barker 69 og	26,704
41	div1	Norwich	A	W	2-1	D.Jones 62, 72	23,462
42	div1	Birmingham	A	L	0-1		20,962
43	div1	QPR	H	D	1-1	Moore 87	27,567
44	div1	Cardiff	H	W	3-1	Howard 28 pen, 60, Barnes 49	27,689
45	div1	Barnsley	A	W	2-1	D.Jones 11, Oakley 48	17,059
46	div1	Leicester	A	D	1-1	Fagan 23	24,704
47	div1	Coventry	H	D	1-1	Oakley 79	29,940
48	div1	Ipswich	A	L	1-2	Oakley 9	24,319
49	div1	Luton	H	W	1-0	Nyatanga 37	28,499
50	div1	Crystal Palace	A	L	0-2		19,545
51	div1	Leeds	H	W	2-0	Currie 45, Mears 86	31,183
52	d1po1	Southampton	A	W	2-1	Howard 36, 58 pen	30,602
53	d1po2	Southampton	H	W	4-3*	Moore 3, Best 66 og (*on penalties)	31,569
54	d1pof	West Brom	H	W	1-0	Pearson 61	74,993

LEAGUE APPEARANCES, BOOKINGS AND CAPS

	AGE (on 01/07/07)	IN NAMED 16	APPEARANCES	COUNTING GAMES	MINUTES ON PITCH	LEAGUE GOALS		
Goalkeepers								
Stephen Bywater	26	40	37	36	3267	0	2	1
Lee Camp	22	3	3	3	270	0	0	0
Lee Grant	24	28	7	6	602	0	1	0
Defenders								
Paul Boertien	28	14	11	9	835	0	1	0
Mohammed Camara	32	24	19	19	1710	0	6	0
Marc Edworthy	34	42	38	35	3298	0	10	0
Richard Jackson	27	13	5	4	327	0	0	0
Michael Johnson	33	34	29	18	1856	1	7	0
Dean Leacock	23	38	38	35	3212	0	9	0
Robert Malcolm	26	16	9	3	463	0	2	0
James McEveley	22	15	15	15	1340	0	4	0
Tyrone Mears	24	16	13	9	932	1	3	0
Darren Moore	33	37	35	27	2557	2	8	1
Lewin Nyatanga	18	11	7	5	508	1	1	0
Midfielders								
Giles Barnes	18	40	39	29	2913	8	2	1
Morten Bisgaard	33	35	32	12	1674	2	3	0
Adam Bolder	26	18	13	8	810	2	2	0
Darren Currie	32	7	7	1	348	1	0	0
Inigo Idiakez	33	5	5	3	307	0	0	0
Seth Johnson	28	33	27	15	1673	1	5	0
David Jones	22	28	28	26	2329	6	5	0
Matthew Oakley	29	38	37	35	3125	6	12	0
Stephen Pearson	24	11	9	6	599	0	2	0
Ryan Smith	20	19	15	2	590	0	2	0
Gary Teale	28	17	16	7	962	1	0	0
Forwards								
Craig Fagan	24	17	17	9	1011	2	2	0
Steven Howard	31	43	43	42	3846	16	12	0
Arturo Lupoli	20	38	35	16	1761	7	4	1
Jonathan Macken	29	9	8	1	328	0	1	0
Paul Peschisolido	36	22	14	1	320	3	4	0
Tommy Smith	27	5	5	4	405	1	0	0
Jonathan Stead	24	17	17	12	1281	3	2	0

TEAM OF THE SEASON

- **G** Stephen Bywater CG: 36 DR: 116
- **D** Darren Moore CG: 27 DR: 111
- **D** Mohammed Camara CG: 19 DR: 95
- **D** Marc Edworthy CG: 35 DR: 94
- **D** Dean Leacock CG: 35 DR: 94
- **M** Matthew Oakley CG: 35 SD: 31
- **M** David Jones CG: 26 SD: 28
- **M** Morten Bisgaard CG: 12 SD: 26
- **M** Giles Barnes CG: 29 SD: 20
- **F** Steven Howard CG: 42 SR: 240
- **F** Arturo Lupoli CG: 16 SR: 251

MONTHLY POINTS TALLY

Month		Pts	%
AUGUST		5	33%
SEPTEMBER		10	67%
OCTOBER		4	33%
NOVEMBER		18	100%
DECEMBER		10	56%
JANUARY		12	100%
FEBRUARY		4	33%
MARCH		13	72%
APRIL		5	33%
MAY		3	100%

LEAGUE GOALS

	PLAYER	MINS	GOALS	S RATE
1	Howard	3846	16	240
2	Barnes	2913	8	364
3	Lupoli	1761	7	251
4	Jones, D	2329	6	388
5	Oakley	3125	6	520
6	Peschisolido	320	3	106
7	Stead	1281	3	427
8	Bisgaard	1674	2	837
9	Moore	2557	2	1278
10	Currie	348	1	348
11	Smith, T	405	1	405
12	Nyatanga	508	1	508
13	Mears	932	1	932
	Other		4	
	TOTAL		**61**	

TOP POINT EARNERS

	PLAYER	GAMES	AV PTS
1	Seth Johnson	14	2.14
2	Dean Leacock	35	2.06
3	Mohammed Camara	19	2.05
4	Stephen Bywater	37	2.00
5	Jonathan Stead	13	2.00
6	Darren Moore	27	1.89
7	Marc Edworthy	35	1.89
8	David Jones	26	1.88
9	Matthew Oakley	34	1.88
10	Giles Barnes	29	1.79
	CLUB AVERAGE:		**1.83**

DISCIPLINARY RECORDS

	PLAYER	YELLOW	RED	AVE
1	Mohammed Camara	6	0	285
2	Michael Johnson	7	0	309
3	Matthew Oakley	12	0	312
4	Steven Howard	12	0	320
5	Marc Edworthy	10	0	329
6	James McEveley	4	0	335
7	Adam Bolder	2	0	405
8	Darren Moore	8	1	426
9	Dean Leacock	9	0	458
10	Robert Malcolm	1	0	463
11	Tyrone Mears	3	0	466
12	Craig Fagan	2	0	505
13	Lewin Nyatanga	1	0	508
	Other	29	3	
	TOTAL	**106**	**4**	

KEY GOALKEEPER

Stephen Bywater

Goals Conceded in the League	28	Counting Games League games when player was on pitch for at least 70 minutes	36
Defensive Rating Ave number of mins between League goals conceded while on the pitch	116	Clean Sheets In League games when player was on pitch for at least 70 minutes	15

KEY PLAYERS - DEFENDERS

Darren Moore

Goals Conceded Number of League goals conceded while the player was on the pitch	23	Clean Sheets In League games when player was on pitch for at least 70 minutes	10
Defensive Rating Ave number of mins between League goals conceded while on the pitch	111	Club Defensive Rating Average number of mins between League goals conceded by the club this season	90

	PLAYER	CON LGE	CLEAN SHEETS	DEF RATE
1	Darren Moore	23	10	111 mins
2	Mohammed Camara	18	8	95 mins
3	Marc Edworthy	35	13	94 mins
4	Dean Leacock	34	13	94 mins

KEY PLAYERS - MIDFIELDERS

Matthew Oakley

Goals in the League	6	Contribution to Attacking Power Average number of minutes between League team goals while on pitch	63
Defensive Rating Average number of mins between League goals conceded while on the pitch	94	Scoring Difference Defensive Rating minus Contribution to Attacking Power	31

	PLAYER	LGE GOALS	DEF RATE	POWER	SCORE DIFF
1	Matthew Oakley	6	94	63	31 mins
2	David Jones	6	105	77	28 mins
3	Morten Bisgaard	2	88	62	26 mins
4	Giles Barnes	8	83	63	20 mins

KEY PLAYERS - GOALSCORERS

Steven Howard

Goals in the League	16	Player Strike Rate Average number of minutes between League goals scored by player	240
Contribution to Attacking Power Average number of minutes between League team goals while on pitch	67	Club Strike Rate Average number of minutes between League goals scored by club	66

	PLAYER	LGE GOALS	POWER	STRIKE RATE
1	Steven Howard	16	67	240 mins
2	Arturo Lupoli	7	58	251 mins
3	Giles Barnes	8	63	364 mins
4	David Jones	6	77	388 mins

Steven Howard

SQUAD APPEARANCES

Match	1 2 3 4 5	6 7 8 9 10	11 12 13 14 15	16 17 18 19 20	21 22 23 24 25	26 27 28 29 30	31 32 33 34 35	36 37 38 39 40	41 42 43 44 45	46 47 48 49 50	51 52 53 54
Venue	H A A H A	A H A H A	A H A A H	A H H A A	H H A A H	A H H A H	H A H H A	H A H A H	A A H H A	A H A H A	H A H H
Competition	L L L L W	L L L L W	L L L L L	L L L L L	L L L L L	L L L L F	L L F L L	L F L L L	L L L L L	L L L L L	L O O O
Result	D L W D W	L L W D L	W W L W L	D W W W W	W W L W W	D L W W W	W W W W W	D L L L W	W L D W W	D D L W L	W W W W

Goalkeepers
Stephen Bywater
Lee Camp
Lee Grant

Defenders
Paul Boertien
Mohammed Camara
Marc Edworthy
Richard Jackson
Michael Johnson
Dean Leacock
Robert Malcolm
James McEveley
Tyrone Mears
Darren Moore
Lewin Nyatanga

Midfielders
Giles Barnes
Morten Bisgaard
Adam Bolder
Darren Currie
Inigo Idiakez
Seth Johnson
David Jones
Matthew Oakley
Stephen Pearson
Ryan Smith
Gary Teale

Forwards
Craig Fagan
Steven Howard
Arturo Lupoli
Jonathan Macken
Paul Peschisolido
Tommy Smith
Jonathan Stead

KEY: ■ On all match   ◄◄ Subbed or sent off (Counting game)   ►► Subbed on from bench (Counting Game)   ►► Subbed on and then subbed or sent off (Counting Game)   □ Not in 16
  ■ On bench   ◄◄ Subbed or sent off (playing less than 70 minutes)   ►► Subbed on (playing less than 70 minutes)   ►► Subbed on and then subbed or sent off (playing less than 70 minutes)

CHAMPIONSHIP - DERBY COUNTY

WEST BROMWICH ALBION

Final Position: 4th

NICKNAME: BAGGIES

KEY: ☐ Won ☐ Drawn ☐ Lost

					Attendance
1	div1	**Hull City**	H W	**2-0** Hartson 57, 90	20,682
2	div1	**Cardiff**	A D	**1-1** Gera 4	18,506
3	div1	**Southampton**	A D	**0-0**	24,233
4	div1	**Colchester**	H W	**2-1** Ellington 11 pen, Wallwork 41	17,509
5	ccr1	**Leyton Orient**	A W	**3-0** Nicholson 41, Carter 71, Greening 76	3,058
6	div1	**Sunderland**	A L	**0-2**	24,242
7	div1	**Leicester**	H W	**2-0** Kenton 83 og, Phillips 86 pen	19,322
8	div1	**Preston**	A L	**0-1**	12,119
9	div1	**Southend**	H D	**1-1** Ellington 61	19,576
10	ccr2	**Cheltenham**	H W	**3-1** Wallwork 48, Ellington 60 pen, Nicholson 68 pen	10,974
11	div1	**Luton**	A D	**2-2** Carter 34, Gera 61	9,332
12	div1	**Leeds**	H W	**4-2** Albrechtsen 40, Kamara 65, 90, Phillips 79	21,435
13	div1	**Ipswich**	A W	**5-1** Kamara 29, 56, Phillips 40, 54, 90	22,581
14	div1	**Crystal Palace**	A W	**2-0** Gera 45, Kamara 48	16,105
15	div1	**Wolverhampton**	H W	**3-0** Greening 11, Kamara 27, Hartson 85 pen	26,606
16	ccr3	**Arsenal**	H L	**0-2**	21,566
17	div1	**Birmingham**	H L	**0-2**	21,009
18	div1	**QPR**	H D	**3-3** Ellington 8, Kamara 40, 54	17,417
19	div1	**Derby**	A L	**1-2** Chaplow 26	25,342
20	div1	**Norwich**	H L	**0-1**	18,718
21	div1	**Burnley**	H W	**3-0** Koumas 5, Ellington 7, Carter 45	18,707
22	div1	**Stoke**	A L	**0-1**	18,282
23	div1	**Sheff Wed**	A L	**1-3** Koumas 89	21,695
24	div1	**Derby**	H W	**1-0** Hartson 89	20,494
25	div1	**Barnsley**	A D	**1-1** Koumas 30	9,512
26	div1	**Coventry**	H W	**5-0** Kamara 1, 22 pen, Koumas 39, Phillips 57, Robinson 83	20,370
27	div1	**Plymouth**	A D	**2-2** Phillips 45, 45	15,172
28	div1	**Preston**	H W	**4-2** Koumas 6, Kamara 25, Ellington 75, 87	22,905
29	div1	**Ipswich**	H W	**2-0** Kamara 53, Koumas 67	20,328
30	div1	**Southend**	A L	**1-3** Hartson 63	9,907
31	facr3	**Leeds**	H W	**3-1** McShane 7, Hartson 15, Phillips 82	16,957
32	div1	**Luton**	H W	**3-2** Koumas 45, Phillips 88, 90	19,927
33	div1	**Leeds**	A W	**3-2** Greening 7, Kamara 19, 45	20,019
34	facr4	**Wolverhampton**	A W	**3-0** Kamara 44, Phillips 48, Gera 78	28,107
35	div1	**Plymouth**	H W	**2-1** Kamara 41 pen, 50	19,894
36	div1	**Hull City**	A W	**1-0** Kamara 59	18,005
37	div1	**Southampton**	H D	**1-1** Phillips 45	21,138
38	div1	**Colchester**	A W	**2-1** McShane 51, Kamara 52	5,611
39	facr5	**Middlesbrough**	A D	**2-2** Kamara 41, Phillips 58	31,491
40	div1	**Cardiff**	H W	**1-0** Ellington 66	18,802
41	div1	**Leicester**	A D	**1-1** Carter 27 pen	25,581
42	facr5r	**Middlesbrough**	H L	**4-5*** Carter 26 (*on penalties)	24,925
43	div1	**Sunderland**	H L	**1-2** Carter 72	23,252
44	div1	**Wolverhampton**	A L	**0-1**	28,016
45	div1	**Crystal Palace**	H L	**2-3** Clement 26, Phillips 76	17,960
46	div1	**Birmingham**	H D	**1-1** McShane 64	21,434
47	div1	**QPR**	A W	**2-1** Phillips 48, Gera 84	14,784
48	div1	**Stoke**	H L	**1-3** Koumas 74	20,386
49	div1	**Norwich**	A W	**2-1** Sodje 73, Kamara 90	25,422
50	div1	**Sheff Wed**	H L	**0-1**	20,415
51	div1	**Burnley**	A L	**2-3** Koumas 6, Ellington 8	12,500
52	div1	**Coventry**	A W	**1-0** Robinson 37	26,343
53	div1	**Barnsley**	H W	**7-0** Phillips 21, 53, 71, Ellington 25 pen, 36, Koren 40, Gera 75	23,568
54	d1po1	**Wolverhampton**	A W	**3-2** Phillips 25, 54, Kamara 73	27,750
55	d1po2	**Wolverhampton**	H W	**1-0** Phillips 65	27,415
56	d1pof	**Derby**	A L	**0-1**	74,993

LEAGUE APPEARANCES, BOOKINGS AND CAPS

	AGE (on 01/07/07)	IN NAMED 16	APPEARANCES	COUNTING GAMES	MINUTES ON PITCH	LEAGUE GOALS	
Goalkeepers							
Russell Hoult	34	22	14	14	1260	0	0	0
Dean Kiely	36	17	17	17	1530	0	1	0
Pascal Zuberbuhler	36	23	15	15	1350	0	1	0
Defenders							
Martin Albrechtsen	27	40	31	22	2214	1	2	1
Neil Clement	28	20	20	14	1417	1	3	2
Curtis Davies	22	32	32	30	2755	0	3	1
Jared Hodgkiss	20	15	5	1	171	0	0	0
Paul McShane	21	39	32	27	2643	2	11	2
Chris Perry	34	24	23	22	2025	0	6	0
Paul Robinson	28	42	42	42	3771	2	11	2
Sam Sodje	28	7	7	4	517	1	2	0
Midfielders							
Darren Carter	23	38	33	18	1920	3	12	1
Richard Chaplow	22	37	28	12	1500	1	2	0
Zoltan Gera	28	43	40	24	2666	5	6	0
Jonathan Greening	28	43	42	36	3481	2	10	0
Junichi Inamoto	27	4	3	0	34	0	1	0
Robert Koren	26	19	18	14	1367	1	1	0
Jason Koumas	27	40	39	30	2953	9	5	0
Nigel Quashie	28	21	20	16	1542	0	5	0
Ronnie Wallwork	29	14	10	9	790	1	4	0
Steve Watson	33	18	12	8	811	0	1	0
Forwards							
Nathan Ellington	25	37	34	11	1717	10	0	1
John Hartson	32	26	21	11	1209	5	5	0
Diomansy Kamara	26	35	34	31	2874	20	12	1
Sherjili MacDonald	22	10	9	0	227	0	0	0
Kevin Phillips	33	37	36	23	2611	16	6	0

TEAM OF THE SEASON

G Pascal Zuberbuhler CG: 15 DR: 84

D Neil Clement CG: 14 DR: 88
D Chris Perry CG: 22 DR: 81
D Curtis Davies CG: 30 DR: 78
D Paul Robinson CG: 42 DR: 78

M Nigel Quashie CG: 16 SD: 43
M Robert Koren CG: 14 SD: 24
M Jason Koumas CG: 30 SD: 23
M Darren Carter CG: 18 SD: 22

F Diomansy Kamara CG: 31 SR: 143
F Kevin Phillips CG: 23 SR: 163

MONTHLY POINTS TALLY

AUGUST	8	53%
SEPTEMBER	8	53%
OCTOBER	10	67%
NOVEMBER	3	20%
DECEMBER	14	78%
JANUARY	9	75%
FEBRUARY	11	73%
MARCH	4	27%
APRIL	6	40%
MAY	3	100%

LEAGUE GOALS

	PLAYER	MINS	GOALS	S RATE
1	Kamara	2874	20	143
2	Phillips	2611	16	163
3	Ellington	1717	10	171
4	Koumas	2953	9	328
5	Hartson	1209	5	241
6	Gera	2666	5	533
7	Carter	1920	3	640
8	McShane	2643	2	1321
9	Greening	3481	2	1740
10	Robinson	3771	2	1885
11	Sodje	517	1	517
12	Wallwork	790	1	790
13	Koren	1367	1	1367
	Other		3	
	TOTAL		**80**	

TOP POINT EARNERS

	PLAYER	GAMES	AV PTS
1	Kevin Phillips	23	2.00
2	Robert Koren	14	1.93
3	Neil Clement	14	1.93
4	Richard Chaplow	12	1.92
5	Jonathan Greening	35	1.83
6	Martin Albrechtsen	22	1.73
7	Pascal Zuberbuhler	15	1.73
8	Paul Robinson	42	1.71
9	Paul McShane	29	1.66
10	Russell Hoult	14	1.64
	CLUB AVERAGE:		**1.65**

DISCIPLINARY RECORDS

	PLAYER	YELLOW	RED	AVE
1	Darren Carter	12	1	174
2	Ronnie Wallwork	4	0	197
3	Paul McShane	11	2	264
4	Diomansy Kamara	12	1	287
5	John Hartson	5	0	302
6	Nigel Quashie	5	0	308
7	Paul Robinson	11	2	342
8	Jonathan Greening	10	0	348
9	Neil Clement	3	2	354
10	Chris Perry	6	0	405
11	Kevin Phillips	6	0	435
12	Zoltan Gera	6	0	444
13	Jason Koumas	5	0	590
	Other	13	3	
	TOTAL	**109**	**11**	

KEY GOALKEEPER

Pascal Zuberbuhler

Goals Conceded in the League	16	Counting Games League games when player was on pitch for at least 70 minutes	15
Defensive Rating Ave number of mins between League goals conceded while on the pitch	84	Clean Sheets In League games when player was on pitch for at least 70 minutes	5

KEY PLAYERS - DEFENDERS

Neil Clement

Goals Conceded Number of League goals conceded while the player was on the pitch	16	Clean Sheets In League games when player was on pitch for at least 70 minutes	3
Defensive Rating Ave number of mins between League goals conceded while on the pitch	88	Club Defensive Rating Average number of mins between League goals conceded by the club this season	75

	PLAYER	CON LGE	CLEAN SHEETS	DEF RATE
1	Neil Clement	16	3	88 mins
2	Chris Perry	25	8	81 mins
3	Curtis Davies	35	9	78 mins
4	Paul Robinson	48	12	78 mins

KEY PLAYERS - MIDFIELDERS

Nigel Quashie

Goals in the League	0	Contribution to Attacking Power Average number of minutes between League team goals while on pitch	59
Defensive Rating Average number of mins between League goals conceded while on the pitch	102	Scoring Difference Defensive Rating minus Contribution to Attacking Power	43

	PLAYER	LGE GOALS	DEF RATE	POWER	SCORE DIFF
1	Nigel Quashie	0	102	59	43 mins
2	Robert Koren	1	71	47	24 mins
3	Jason Koumas	9	68	45	23 mins
4	Darren Carter	3	83	61	22 mins

KEY PLAYERS - GOALSCORERS

Diomansy Mehdi Kamara

Goals in the League	20	Player Strike Rate Average number of minutes between League goals scored by player	143
Contribution to Attacking Power Average number of minutes between League team goals while on pitch	50	Club Strike Rate Average number of minutes between League goals scored by club	51

	PLAYER	LGE GOALS	POWER	STRIKE RATE
1	Diomansy Mehdi Kamara	20	50	143 mins
2	Kevin Phillips	16	48	163 mins
3	Jason Koumas	9	45	328 mins
4	Zoltan Gera	5	56	533 mins

Diomansy Mehdi Kamara

SQUAD APPEARANCES

Match	1 2 3 4 5	6 7 8 9 10	11 12 13 14 15	16 17 18 19 20	21 22 23 24 25	26 27 28 29 30	31 32 33 34 35	36 37 38 39 40	41 42 43 44 45	46 47 48 49 50	51 52 53 54 55	56
Venue	H A A H A	A H A H H	A H A A H	H A H A H	H A A H A	H A H H A	H H A A H	A H A A H	A H H A H	H A H A H	A A H A H	A
Competition	L L L L W	L L L L W	L L L L L	W L L L L	L L L L W	L L L L L	F L L F L	L L L F L	L F L L L	L L L L L	L L L O O	O
Result	W D D W W	L W L D W	D W W W W	L L D L L	W L L W D	W D W W L	W W W W W	W D W D W	D L L L L	D W L W L	L W W W W	L

Goalkeepers
Luke Daniels
Russell Hoult
Dean Kiely
Tomasz Kuszczak
Luke Steele
Pascal Zuberbuhler

Defenders
Martin Albrechtsen
Neil Clement
Curtis Davies
Jeff Forsyth
Jared Hodgkiss
Paul McShane
Chris Perry
Paul Robinson
Sam Sodje

Midfielders
Darren Carter
Richard Chaplow
Rob Davies
Zoltan Gera
Jonathan Greening
Junichi Inamoto
Robert Koren
Jason Koumas
Nigel Quashie
Ronnie Wallwork
Steve Watson

Forwards
Nathan Ellington
John Hartson
Diomansy Mehdi Kamara
Sherjili MacDonald
Stuart Nicholson
Kevin Phillips

KEY: ■ On all match ◄◄ Subbed or sent off (Counting game)　►► Subbed on from bench (Counting Game)　►► Subbed on and then subbed or sent off (Counting Game)　□ Not in 16
■ On bench　◄◄ Subbed or sent off (playing less than 70 minutes)　►► Subbed on (playing less than 70 minutes)　►► Subbed on and then subbed or sent off (playing less than 70 minutes)

CHAMPIONSHIP - WEST BROMWICH ALBION

WOLVERHAMPTON WANDERERS

Final Position: 5th

NICKNAME: WOLVES **KEY:** ☐ Won ☐ Drawn ☐ Lost Attendance

#	Comp	Opponent			Score	Scorers	Attendance
1	div1	Plymouth	A	D	1-1	Doumbe 47 og	15,964
2	div1	Ipswich	H	W	1-0	Bothroyd 27	19,199
3	div1	Preston	H	L	1-3	Bothroyd 14	17,410
4	div1	Burnley	A	W	1-0	Johnson 19	12,245
5	ccr1	Chesterfield	A	L	5-6*	(*on penalties)	4,136
6	div1	Luton	H	W	1-0	Johnson 47	19,378
7	div1	Leeds	A	W	1-0	Bothroyd 90	16,268
8	div1	Derby	H	L	0-1		21,546
9	div1	Barnsley	A	L	0-1		11,350
10	div1	Stoke	H	W	2-0	Clarke 21, Olofinjana 68	19,489
11	div1	Cardiff	A	L	0-4		19,915
12	div1	Colchester	H	W	1-0	Bothroyd 51	19,318
13	div1	Coventry	H	W	1-0	Ward 20 og	19,823
14	div1	West Brom	A	L	0-3		26,606
15	div1	Sheff Wed	H	D	2-2	Clarke 30, 73	20,637
16	div1	Southampton	A	L	0-2		18,979
17	div1	Southend	H	W	3-1	Clarke 10, 22, Craddock 12	17,904
18	div1	Hull City	A	L	0-2		16,962
19	div1	Birmingham	A	D	1-1	Craddock 89	22,256
20	div1	Sunderland	H	D	1-1	Johnson 43	27,203
21	div1	Crystal Palace	H	D	1-1	Gobern 63	17,806
22	div1	Southend	A	W	1-0	Craddock 61	9,411
23	div1	Leicester	H	L	1-2	Gobern 81	18,600
24	div1	QPR	A	W	1-0	Kightly 49	12,323
25	div1	Norwich	H	D	2-2	Henry 36, Craddock 90	22,910
26	div1	Derby	A	W	2-0	Olofinjana 66, Kightly 90	31,920
27	div1	Colchester	A	L	1-2	N.Collins 90	5,893
28	div1	Barnsley	H	W	2-0	Henry 52, Olofinjana 78	20,064
29	facr3	Oldham	H	D	2-2	Olofinjana 35, Davies 42	14,524
30	div1	Stoke	A	D	1-1	N.Collins 63	15,882
31	facr3r	Oldham	A	W	2-0	Potter 56, C.Davies 75	9,628
32	div1	Cardiff	H	L	1-2	Olofinjana 58	16,772
33	facr4	West Brom	H	L	0-3		28,107
34	div1	Norwich	A	W	1-0	Kightly 53	23,311
35	div1	Plymouth	H	D	2-2	Ward 33, Olofinjana 69	19,082
36	div1	Preston	A	W	1-0	Olofinjana 8	15,748
37	div1	Burnley	H	W	2-1	Kightly 5, Ward 40	19,521
38	div1	Ipswich	A	W	1-0	Ward 33	20,602
39	div1	Leeds	H	W	1-0	Kightly 76	24,314
40	div1	Luton	A	W	3-2	Breen 10, Keogh 53, Henry 66	10,002
41	div1	West Brom	H	W	1-0	Bothroyd 83	28,016
42	div1	Coventry	A	L	1-2	Kightly 45	22,099
43	div1	Sheff Wed	A	D	2-2	McIndoe 35, Keogh 90	24,181
44	div1	Southampton	H	L	0-6		24,804
45	div1	Sunderland	A	L	1-2	Keogh 65	40,748
46	div1	Hull City	H	W	3-1	Bothroyd 18, 47, Olofinjana 39	20,772
47	div1	Crystal Palace	A	D	2-2	Bothroyd 13, 22	17,981
48	div1	Birmingham	H	L	2-3	McIndoe 66, 71	22,754
49	div1	QPR	H	W	2-0	Keogh 57, Kightly 64	24,931
50	div1	Leicester	A	W	4-1	Olofinjana 24, Kightly 33, McAuley 53 og, Keogh 84 pen	30,282
51	d1po1	West Brom	H	L	2-3	Craddock 44, Olofinjana 52	27,750
52	d1po2	West Brom	A	L	0-1		27,415

LEAGUE APPEARANCES, BOOKINGS AND CAPS

	AGE (on 01/07/07)	IN NAMED 16	APPEARANCES	COUNTING GAMES	MINUTES ON PITCH	LEAGUE GOALS	
Goalkeepers							
Jan Budtz	28	14	4	2	244	0	0
Carl Ikeme	21	17	1	0	4	0	0
Matt Murray	26	44	44	43	3892	0	0
Defenders							
Gary Breen	33	40	40	35	3396	1	7
Jamie Clapham	31	32	26	20	2046	0	2
Leon Clarke	22	23	21	5	916	5	2
Mark Clyde	24	3	3	1	194	0	0
Neill Collins	23	23	21	19	1790	2	3
Jody Craddock	31	37	34	26	2581	4	4
Rob Edwards	24	37	33	23	2325	0	6
Craig Fleming	35	1	1	1	90	0	0
Daniel Jones	20	11	8	6	611	0	1
Mark Little	18	31	26	17	1780	0	4
Jackie McNamara	33	21	19	15	1539	0	5
Charles Mulgrew	24	8	6	2	315	0	1
Lee Naylor	27	3	3	2	228	0	0
David Wheater	20	3	1	1	90	0	0
Midfielders							
Mark Davies	19	38	25	2	577	0	0
Lewis Gobern	22	13	12	5	634	2	1
Karl Henry	24	35	34	34	3047	3	6
Michael Kightly	21	24	24	21	2029	8	4
Michael McIndoe	27	27	27	22	2136	3	1
Kevin O'Connor	21	3	3	3	270	0	1
Seyi Olofinjana	27	44	44	40	3768	8	7
Darren Potter	22	42	38	32	3067	0	8
Rohan Ricketts	24	22	19	11	1253	0	2
Forwards							
Jay Bothroyd	25	35	34	11	1711	9	4
Carl Cort	29	10	10	6	672	0	0
Craig Davies	21	6	5	3	282	0	0
Jemal Johnson	22	23	20	10	1167	3	2
Andrew Keogh	21	17	17	17	1510	5	2
Stephen Ward	21	18	18	10	1004	3	1

TEAM OF THE SEASON

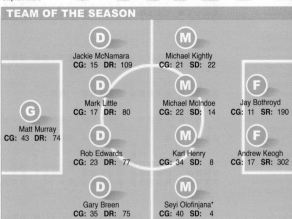

- **Matt Murray** CG: 43 DR: 74
- **Jackie McNamara** CG: 15 DR: 109
- **Mark Little** CG: 17 DR: 80
- **Rob Edwards** CG: 23 DR: 77
- **Gary Breen** CG: 35 DR: 75
- **Michael Kightly** CG: 21 SD: 22
- **Michael McIndoe** CG: 22 SD: 14
- **Karl Henry** CG: 34 SD: 8
- **Seyi Olofinjana*** CG: 40 SD: 4
- **Jay Bothroyd** CG: 11 SR: 190
- **Andrew Keogh** CG: 17 SR: 302

MONTHLY POINTS TALLY

Month		Pts	%
AUGUST		10	67%
SEPTEMBER		6	40%
OCTOBER		7	58%
NOVEMBER		6	33%
DECEMBER		10	56%
JANUARY		7	58%
FEBRUARY		13	87%
MARCH		7	47%
APRIL		7	47%
MAY		3	100%

LEAGUE GOALS

	PLAYER	MINS	GOALS	S RATE
1	Bothroyd	1711	9	190
2	Kightly	2029	8	253
3	Olofinjana	3768	8	471
4	Clarke	916	5	183
5	Keogh	1510	5	302
6	Craddock	2581	4	645
7	Ward	1004	3	334
8	Johnson	1167	3	389
9	McIndoe	2136	3	712
10	Henry	3047	3	1015
11	Gobern	634	2	317
12	Collins, N	1790	2	895
13	Breen	3396	1	3396
	Other		0	
	TOTAL		56	

TOP POINT EARNERS

	PLAYER	GAMES	AV PTS
1	Jackie McNamara	16	2.19
2	Michael Kightly	21	2.10
3	Andrew Keogh	17	1.94
4	Rob Edwards	23	1.83
5	Seyi Olofinjana	40	1.78
6	Michael McIndoe	22	1.77
7	Karl Henry	34	1.74
8	Neill Collins	19	1.74
9	Darren Potter	32	1.66
10	Matt Murray	43	1.65
	CLUB AVERAGE:		1.65

DISCIPLINARY RECORDS

	PLAYER	YELLOW	RED	AVE
1	Jackie McNamara	5	2	219
2	Gary Breen	7	2	377
3	Jay Bothroyd	4	0	427
4	Mark Little	4	1	445
5	Leon Clarke	2	0	458
6	Rob Edwards	6	0	484
7	Karl Henry	6	0	507
8	Michael Kightly	4	0	507
9	Darren Potter	8	0	511
10	Jemal Johnson	2	0	583
11	Neill Collins	3	0	596
12	Daniel Jones	1	0	611
13	Rohan Ricketts	2	0	626
	Other	18	1	
	TOTAL	72	6	

KEY GOALKEEPER

Matt Murray

Goals Conceded in the League	52	Counting Games League games when player was on pitch for at least 70 minutes	43
Defensive Rating Ave number of mins between League goals conceded while on the pitch	74	Clean Sheets In League games when player was on pitch for at least 70 minutes	17

KEY PLAYERS - DEFENDERS

Jackie McNamara

Goals Conceded Number of League goals conceded while the player was on the pitch	14	Clean Sheets In League games when player was on pitch for at least 70 minutes	9
Defensive Rating Ave number of mins between League goals conceded while on the pitch	109	Club Defensive Rating Average number of mins between League goals conceded by the club this season	73

	PLAYER	CON LGE	CLEAN SHEETS	DEF RATE
1	Jackie McNamara	14	9	109 mins
2	Mark Little	22	5	80 mins
3	Rob Edwards	30	10	77 mins
4	Gary Breen	45	12	75 mins

KEY PLAYERS - MIDFIELDERS

Michael Kightly

Goals in the League	8	Contribution to Attacking Power Average number of minutes between League team goals while on pitch	53
Defensive Rating Average number of mins between League goals conceded while on the pitch	75	Scoring Difference Defensive Rating minus Contribution to Attacking Power	22

	PLAYER	LGE GOALS	DEF RATE	POWER	SCORE DIFF
1	Michael Kightly	8	75	53	22 mins
2	Michael McIndoe	3	68	54	14 mins
3	Karl Henry	3	84	76	8 mins
4	Seyi Olofinjana	8	75	71	4 mins

KEY PLAYERS - GOALSCORERS

Jay Bothroyd

Goals in the League	9	Player Strike Rate Average number of minutes between League goals scored by player	190
Contribution to Attacking Power Average number of minutes between League team goals while on pitch	61	Club Strike Rate Average number of minutes between League goals scored by club	70

	PLAYER	LGE GOALS	POWER	STRIKE RATE
1	Jay Bothroyd	9	61	190 mins
2	Michael Kightly	8	53	253 mins
3	Andrew Keogh	5	52	302 mins
4	Seyi Olofinjana	8	71	471 mins

Darren Potter

SQUAD APPEARANCES

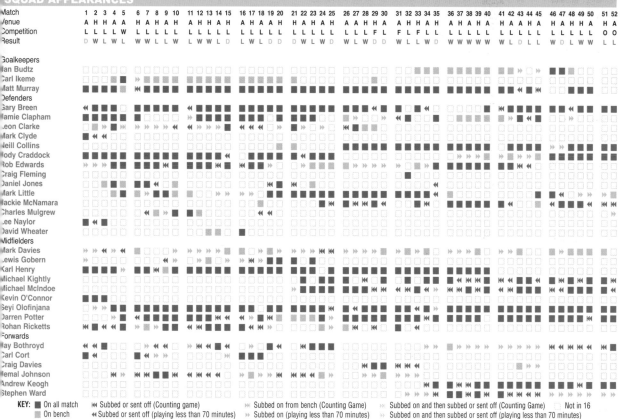

Match	1	2	3	4	5		6	7	8	9	10		11	12	13	14	15		16	17	18	19	20		21	22	23	24	25		26	27	28	29	30		31	32	33	34	35		36	37	38	39	40		41	42	43	44	45		46	47	48	49	50		51	52
Venue	A	H	H	A	A		H	A	H	A	H		A	H	H	A	H		A	H	A	A	H		H	A	H	A	H		A	A	H	H	A		A	H	H	A	H		A	H	A	H	A		H	A	A	H	A		H	A	H	H	A		H	A
Competition	L	L	L	L	W		L	L	L	L	L		L	L	L	L	L		L	L	L	L	L		L	L	L	L	L		L	L	L	F	L		F	L	F	L	L		L	L	L	L	L		L	L	L	L	L		L	L	L	L	L		O	O
Result	D	W	L	W	L		W	W	L	L	W		L	W	W	L	D		L	W	L	D	D		D	W	L	W	D		W	L	W	D	D		W	L	L	W	D		W	W	W	W	W		W	L	D	L	L		W	D	L	W	W		L	L

Goalkeepers
Ian Budtz
Carl Ikeme
Matt Murray

Defenders
Gary Breen
Jamie Clapham
Leon Clarke
Mark Clyde
Neill Collins
Jody Craddock
Rob Edwards
Craig Fleming
Daniel Jones
Mark Little
Jackie McNamara
Charles Mulgrew
Lee Naylor
David Wheater

Midfielders
Mark Davies
Lewis Gobern
Karl Henry
Michael Kightly
Michael McIndoe
Kevin O'Connor
Seyi Olofinjana
Darren Potter
Rohan Ricketts

Forwards
Jay Bothroyd
Carl Cort
Craig Davies
Jemal Johnson
Andrew Keogh
Stephen Ward

KEY: ■ On all match ◀◀ Subbed or sent off (Counting game) ▶▶ Subbed on from bench (Counting Game) ▶▶ Subbed on and then subbed or sent off (Counting Game) ☐ Not in 16

■ On bench ◀◀ Subbed or sent off (playing less than 70 minutes) ▶▶ Subbed on (playing less than 70 minutes) ▶▶ Subbed on and then subbed or sent off (playing less than 70 minutes)

CHAMPIONSHIP - WOLVERHAMPTON WANDERERS

SOUTHAMPTON

Final Position: **6th**

NICKNAME: THE SAINTS   **KEY:** ☐ Won ☐ Drawn ☐ Lost   Attendance

1	div1	Derby	A	D	2-2	Bale 62, B.Wright-Phillips 68	21,939
2	div1	Coventry	H	W	2-0	Bale 61, Rasiak 86 pen	21,088
3	div1	West Brom	H	D	0-0		24,233
4	div1	Barnsley	A	D	2-2	Rasiak 47, 74 pen	11,306
5	ccr1	Yeovil	H	W	5-2	Cohen 25 og, Skacel 32, Wright-Phillips 37, Dyer 69, Jones 78	20,653
6	div1	Preston	H	D	1-1	Rasiak 43	20,712
7	div1	Ipswich	A	L	1-2	Jones 3	21,422
8	div1	Crystal Palace	A	W	2-0	Jones 2, Rasiak 49	17,084
9	div1	Plymouth	H	W	1-0	Rasiak 52	22,514
10	ccr2	Millwall	A	W	4-0	Belmadi 20, Wright-Phillips 43, 90, McGoldrick 90	5,492
11	div1	Burnley	A	W	3-2	Rasiak 18, 73, Skacel 54	13,051
12	div1	QPR	H	L	1-2	Wright 3	25,185
13	div1	Leicester	A	L	2-3	Viafara 45, Idiakez 64	21,347
14	div1	Cardiff	A	L	0-1		19,345
15	div1	Stoke	H	W	1-0	Licka 54	20,531
16	ccr3	Notts County	A	L	0-2		6,731
17	div1	Colchester	A	L	0-2		5,893
18	div1	Wolverhampton	H	W	2-0	Wright-Phillips 39, Jones 70	18,979
19	div1	Hull City	H	D	0-0		20,560
20	div1	Sunderland	A	D	1-1	Bale 90	25,667
21	div1	Leeds	A	W	3-0	Rasiak 29, 75, Skacel 69	19,467
22	div1	Luton	H	W	2-1	Baird 15, Rasiak 38 pen	20,482
23	div1	Birmingham	H	W	4-3	Jones 14, 17, Skacel 19, Wright-Phillips 78	21,889
24	div1	Hull City	A	W	4-2	Rasiak 19, 75, Bale 25, Wright-Phillips 82	15,697
25	div1	Southend	A	L	1-2	Rasiak 87	10,867
26	div1	Norwich	H	W	2-1	Bale 41, Jones 65	25,919
27	div1	Sheff Wed	A	D	3-3	Rasiak 14, Jones 26, Wright-Phillips 50	23,739
28	div1	Crystal Palace	H	D	1-1	Baird 47	30,548
29	div1	Leicester	H	W	2-0	Pele 9, Prutton 53	24,447
30	div1	Plymouth	A	D	1-1	Rasiak 5	15,377
31	facr3	Torquay	A	W	2-0	Rasiak 43, 72	5,396
32	div1	Burnley	H	D	0-0		20,486
33	div1	QPR	A	W	2-0	Rasiak 81, Wright-Phillips 90	14,686
34	facr4	Man City	A	L	1-3	Jones 23	26,496
35	div1	Sheff Wed	H	W	2-1	Jones 7, 58	20,230
36	div1	Derby	H	L	0-1		27,656
37	div1	West Brom	A	D	1-1	Jones 18	21,138
38	div1	Barnsley	H	W	5-2	Surman 11, 80, 90 pen, Jones 48, 73 pen	22,460
39	div1	Coventry	A	L	1-2	Saganowski 14	17,194
40	div1	Ipswich	H	W	1-0	Saganowski 1	27,974
41	div1	Preston	A	L	1-3	Rasiak 57	13,065
42	div1	Stoke	A	L	1-2	Saganowski 17	13,404
43	div1	Cardiff	H	D	2-2	Baird 30, Wright-Phillips 44	20,383
44	div1	Colchester	H	L	1-2	Saganowski 26	18,736
45	div1	Wolverhampton	A	W	6-0	Saganowski 24, 36, 83, Breen 27 og, Best 55, Surman 79	24,804
46	div1	Luton	A	W	2-0	Saganowski 45, Viafara 45	9,171
47	div1	Sunderland	H	L	1-2	Saganowski 67	25,766
48	div1	Birmingham	A	L	1-2	Saganowski 85	19,754
49	div1	Leeds	H	W	1-0	Wright-Phillips 84	29,012
50	div1	Norwich	A	W	1-0	Best 30	25,437
51	div1	Southend	H	W	4-1	Jones 29, 81, Best 48, 80	32,008
52	d1po1	Derby	H	L	1-2	Surman 7	30,602
53	d1po2	Derby	A	L	3-4*	Viafara 4, 54, Rasiak 89 (*on penalties)	31,569

LEAGUE APPEARANCES, BOOKINGS AND CAPS

	AGE (on 01/07/07)	IN NAMED 16	APPEARANCES	COUNTING GAMES	MINUTES ON PITCH	LEAGUE GOALS		
Goalkeepers								
Bartosz Bialkowski	19	29	8	8	720	0	0	0
Kelvin Davis	30	43	38	38	3420	0	1	0
Defenders								
Chris Baird	25	44	44	43	3915	3	5	0
Gareth Bale	17	40	38	37	3374	5	4	0
Claus Lundekvam	34	33	33	30	2794	0	6	0
Chris Makin	34	25	22	18	1796	0	1	0
Alexander Ostlund	28	31	20	18	1700	0	4	0
Pedro Pele	29	44	37	34	3103	1	6	0
Darren Powell	31	8	8	6	641	0	3	0
Midfielders								
Djamel Belmadi	31	15	14	8	862	1	2	0
Danny Guthrie	20	10	10	8	764	0	0	0
Inigo Idiakez	33	17	14	9	1056	1	5	0
Mario Licka	25	18	15	6	748	1	3	0
David Prutton	25	3	3	0	133	1	0	0
Rudolf Skacel	27	38	37	24	2651	3	3	0
Andrew Surman	20	40	37	23	2390	4	3	0
John Eduis Viafara	28	41	36	27	2697	2	7	0
Jermaine Wright	31	42	42	39	3589	1	0	0
Forwards								
Leon Best	20	10	9	4	470	4	1	0
Nathan Dyer	19	25	18	6	810	0	1	0
Ricardo Fuller	27	2	1	0	54	0	0	0
Kenwyne Jones	22	34	34	19	2080	14	2	1
Adam Lallana	19	5	1	0	45	0	0	0
David McGoldrick	19	12	9	1	183	0	0	0
Grzegorz Rasiak	28	42	39	29	2797	18	0	0
Marek Saganowski	28	13	13	9	911	10	0	0
Bradl Wright-Phillips	22	45	39	13	1773	8	2	0

TEAM OF THE SEASON

D Chris Makin CG: 18 DR: 81
M Rudolf Skacel CG: 24 SD: 40
D Gareth Bale CG: 37 DR: 78
M Jermaine Wright CG: 39 SD: 22
F Kenwyne Jones CG: 19 SR: 148
G Kelvin Davis CG: 38 DR: 74
D Claus Lundekvam CG: 30 DR: 77
M Andrew Surman CG: 23 SD: 20
F Grzegorz Rasiak CG: 29 SR: 155
D Pedro Pele CG: 34 DR: 77
M John Eduis Viafara CG: 27 SD: 12

MONTHLY POINTS TALLY

AUGUST		7	47%
SEPTEMBER		9	60%
OCTOBER		3	25%
NOVEMBER		14	78%
DECEMBER		11	61%
JANUARY		8	67%
FEBRUARY		7	47%
MARCH		4	27%
APRIL		9	60%
MAY		3	100%

LEAGUE GOALS

	PLAYER	MINS	GOALS	S RATE
1	Rasiak	2797	18	155
2	Jones	2080	14	148
3	Saganowski	911	10	91
4	Wright-Phillips	1773	8	221
5	Bale	3374	5	674
6	Best	470	4	117
7	Surman	2390	4	597
8	Skacel	2651	3	883
9	Baird	3915	3	1305
10	Viafara	2697	2	1348
11	Prutton	133	1	133
12	Licka	748	1	748
13	Idiakez	1056	1	1056
	Other		2	
	TOTAL		**76**	

TOP POINT EARNERS

	PLAYER	GAMES	AV PTS
1	Rudolf Skacel	24	2.13
2	Kenwyne Jones	19	1.89
3	Pedro Pele	34	1.85
4	Alexander Ostlund	18	1.83
5	Andrew Surman	23	1.83
6	Chris Makin	18	1.72
7	Grzegorz Rasiak	29	1.68
8	Jermaine Wright	39	1.64
9	Claus Lundekvam	30	1.63
10	Chris Baird	43	1.60
	CLUB AVERAGE:		**1.63**

DISCIPLINARY RECORDS

	PLAYER	YELLOW	RED	AVE
1	Mario Licka	3	0	249
2	Inigo Idiakez	5	0	264
3	Darren Powell	3	0	320
4	John Eduis Viafara	7	0	385
5	Djamel Belmadi	2	0	431
6	Claus Lundekvam	6	0	465
7	Leon Best	1	0	470
8	Alexander Ostlund	4	0	566
9	Pedro Pele	6	0	620
10	Chris Baird	5	0	783
11	Nathan Dyer	1	0	810
12	Gareth Bale	4	0	843
13	Rudolf Skacel	3	0	883
	Other	10	1	
	TOTAL	**60**	**1**	

KEY GOALKEEPER

Kelvin Davis

Goals Conceded in the League	46	Counting Games League games when player was on pitch for at least 70 minutes	38
Defensive Rating Ave number of mins between League goals conceded while on the pitch	74	Clean Sheets In League games when player was on pitch for at least 70 minutes	12

KEY PLAYERS - DEFENDERS

Chris Makin

Goals Conceded Number of League goals conceded while the player was on the pitch	22	Clean Sheets In League games when player was on pitch for at least 70 minutes	8
Defensive Rating Ave number of mins between League goals conceded while on the pitch	81	Club Defensive Rating Average number of mins between League goals conceded by the club this season	78

	PLAYER	CON LGE	CLEAN SHEETS	DEF RATE
1	Chris Makin	22	8	81 mins
2	Gareth Bale	43	12	78 mins
3	Claus Lundekvam	36	10	77 mins
4	Pedro Pele	40	12	77 mins

KEY PLAYERS - MIDFIELDERS

Rudolf Skacel

Goals in the League	3	Contribution to Attacking Power Average number of minutes between League team goals while on pitch	45
Defensive Rating Average number of mins between League goals conceded while on the pitch	85	Scoring Difference Defensive Rating minus Contribution to Attacking Power	40

	PLAYER	LGE GOALS	DEF RATE	POWER	SCORE DIFF
1	Rudolf Skacel	3	85	45	40 mins
2	Jermaine Wright	1	76	54	22 mins
3	Andrew Surman	4	66	46	20 mins
4	John Eduis Viafara	2	70	58	12 mins

KEY PLAYERS - GOALSCORERS

Kenwyne Jones

Goals in the League	14	Player Strike Rate Average number of minutes between League goals scored by player	148
Contribution to Attacking Power Average number of minutes between League team goals while on pitch	57	Club Strike Rate Average number of minutes between League goals scored by club	53

	PLAYER	LGE GOALS	POWER	STRIKE RATE
1	Kenwyne Jones	14	57	148 mins
2	Grzegorz Rasiak	18	54	155 mins
3	Bradley Wright-Phillips	8	53	221 mins
4	Andrew Surman	4	46	597 mins

Grzegorz Rasiak

SQUAD APPEARANCES

Match	1 2 3 4 5	6 7 8 9 10	11 12 13 14 15	16 17 18 19 20	21 22 23 24 25	26 27 28 29 30	31 32 33 34 35	36 37 38 39 40	41 42 43 44 45	46 47 48 49 50	51 52 53
Venue	A H H A H	H A A H A	A H A A H	A A H H A	A H H A A	H A H H A	A H A A H	H A H A H	A A H H A	A H A H A	H H A
Competition	L L L L W	L L L L W	L L L L L	W L L L L	L L L L L	L L L L L	F L L F L	L L L L L	L L L L L	L L L L L	L O O
Result	D W D D W	D L W W W	W L L L W	L L W D D	W W W W L	W D D W D	W D W L W	L D W L W	L L D L W	W L L W W	W L L

Goalkeepers
- Bartosz Bialkowski
- Kelvin Davis
- Kevin Miller
- Michael Poke

Defenders
- Chris Baird
- Gareth Bale
- Martin Cranie
- Claus Lundekvam
- Chris Makin
- Alexander Ostlund
- Pedro Pele
- Darren Powell

Midfielders
- Djamel Belmadi
- Danny Guthrie
- Inigo Idiakez
- Mario Licka
- David Prutton
- Marcelo Sarmiento
- Rudolf Skacel
- Andrew Surman
- John Eduis Viafara
- Jermaine Wright

Forwards
- Leon Best
- Nathan Dyer
- Ricardo Fuller
- Kenwyne Jones
- Adam Lallana
- David McGoldrick
- Grzegorz Rasiak
- Marek Saganowski
- Bradley Wright-Phillips

KEY: ■ On all match   ◄◄ Subbed or sent off (Counting game)   ►► Subbed on from bench (Counting Game)   ◄► Subbed on and then subbed or sent off (Counting Game)   ☐ Not in 16
    ■ On bench   ◄ Subbed or sent off (playing less than 70 minutes)   ►► Subbed on (playing less than 70 minutes)   ►► Subbed on and then subbed off (playing less than 70 minutes)

CHAMPIONSHIP - SOUTHAMPTON

PRESTON NORTH END

Final Position: 7th

NICKNAME: THE LILYWHITES

KEY: ☐ Won ☐ Drawn ☐ Lost

Attendance

1	div1	Sheff Wed	H	D	0-0		15,650
2	div1	Norwich	A	L	0-2		24,676
3	div1	Wolverhampton	A	W	3-1	Nugent 22, 65, Whaley 90	17,410
4	div1	QPR	H	D	1-1	McKenna 86	11,879
5	ccr1	Port Vale	A	L	1-2	Whaley 72	3,522
6	div1	Southampton	A	D	1-1	Whaley 50	20,712
7	div1	Cardiff	H	W	2-1	Agyemang 47, Pugh 65	12,435
8	div1	West Brom	H	W	1-0	Agyemang 78	12,119
9	div1	Derby	A	D	1-1	Pugh 45	22,220
10	div1	Barnsley	H	W	1-0	Agyemang 30	11,728
11	div1	Stoke	A	D	1-1	Agyemang 63	14,342
12	div1	Sunderland	H	W	4-1	Dichio 18, Alexander 31 pen, Whitehead 35 og, Whaley 55	19,603
13	div1	Ipswich	A	W	3-2	Nugent 53, Chilvers 56, Whaley 65	19,337
14	div1	Hull City	H	W	2-1	Dichio 1, 37	13,728
15	div1	Burnley	A	L	2-3	Whaley 77, Ormerod 80	14,871
16	div1	Leeds	H	W	4-1	Dichio 19, Pugh 22, Nugent 47, L.Neal 84	16,168
17	div1	Luton	H	W	3-0	Alexander 51 pen, Agyemang 60, Ormerod 87	13,094
18	div1	Southend	A	D	0-0		9,263
19	div1	Leicester	A	W	1-0	Agyemang 15	22,721
20	div1	Crystal Palace	H	D	0-0		14,202
21	div1	Coventry	H	D	1-1	Nugent 35	13,104
22	div1	Luton	A	L	0-2		7,665
23	div1	Birmingham	A	L	1-3	Ormerod 45	23,159
24	div1	Plymouth	H	W	3-0	Pugh 12, Ormerod 41, Alexander 56 pen	13,171
25	div1	Colchester	H	W	1-0	Nugent 33	14,225
26	div1	West Brom	A	L	2-4	Alexander 35 pen, Nugent 67	22,905
27	div1	Sunderland	A	W	1-0	Nugent 36	30,460
28	div1	Derby	H	L	1-2	Nugent 79	19,204
29	facr3	Sunderland	H	W	1-0	Ormerod 31	10,318
30	div1	Barnsley	A	W	1-0	Chilvers 55	10,810
31	div1	Stoke	H	W	3-2	McKenna 65, Nugent 74, Wilson 89	15,151
32	facr4	Crystal Palace	A	W	2-0	Nugent 46, Wilson 83	8,422
33	div1	Colchester	A	L	0-1		5,085
34	div1	Sheff Wed	A	W	3-1	Ormerod 6, Nugent 45, 55	22,441
35	div1	Wolverhampton	H	L	0-1		15,748
36	facr5	Man City	H	L	1-3	Nugent 8	18,890
37	div1	Norwich	H	W	2-1	Pergl 28, Dichio 43	11,601
38	div1	Cardiff	A	L	1-4	Alexander 53 pen	12,889
39	div1	Southampton	H	W	3-2	Mellor 45, Nugent 75, Baird 81 og	13,065
40	div1	Hull City	A	L	0-2		17,118
41	div1	Ipswich	H	W	1-0	Ricketts 6	13,100
42	div1	Burnley	H	W	2-0	Nugent 33, Agyemang 75	17,666
43	div1	Leeds	A	L	1-2	Ormerod 5	18,433
44	div1	QPR	A	L	0-1		11,910
45	div1	Crystal Palace	A	L	0-3		15,985
46	div1	Southend	H	L	2-3	St Ledger 51, Alexander 79 pen	13,684
47	div1	Coventry	A	W	4-0	Sedgwick 8, Nugent 17, Ormerod 49, 56	21,117
48	div1	Leicester	H	L	0-1		14,725
49	div1	Plymouth	A	L	0-2		13,813
50	div1	Birmingham	H	W	1-0	Whaley 85	16,837

LEAGUE APPEARANCES, BOOKINGS AND CAPS

	AGE (on 01/07/07)	IN NAMED 16	APPEARANCES	COUNTING GAMES	MINUTES ON PITCH	LEAGUE GOALS	
Goalkeepers							
Wayne Henderson	23	16	4	4	360	0	0
Andrew Lonergan	23	41	13	13	1170	0	0
Carlo Nash	33	29	28	28	2520	0	1
Chris Neal	21	6	2	1	157	0	0
Defenders							
Graham Alexander	35	42	42	42	3779	6	7
Liam Chilvers	25	45	45	44	4005	2	4
Matthew Hill	26	39	38	35	3195	0	5
Seyfo Soley	27	11	6	6	519	0	2
Sean St Ledger	22	45	41	39	3517	1	5
Kelvin Wilson	21	42	21	12	1269	1	2
Midfielders							
Joe Anyinsah	22	4	3	0	23	0	0
Callum Davidson	31	18	15	10	1022	0	4
Jason Jarrett	27	8	5	4	349	0	1
Alan McCormack	23	7	3	0	64	0	0
Paul McKenna	29	33	33	31	2880	2	4
Tommy Miller	28	8	7	3	363	0	0
Lewis Neal	25	28	23	2	501	1	0
Pavel Pergl	29	7	6	5	509	1	1
Danny Pugh	24	45	45	45	3976	4	10
Chris Sedgwick	27	46	43	39	3581	1	6
Franck Songo'o	20	6	6	2	328	0	2
Brian Stock	25	4	2	0	82	0	0
Simon Whaley	22	40	40	30	2785	0	0
Forwards							
Patrick Agyemang	26	32	30	5	1186	7	1
Danny Dichio	32	33	30	9	1364	5	6
Neil Mellor	24	6	5	1	215	1	0
David Nugent	22	44	44	39	3587	15	11
Brett Ormerod	30	30	29	13	1448	8	2
Michael Ricketts	28	16	14	6	670	1	2

TEAM OF THE SEASON

G Carlo Nash CG: 28 DR: 93

D Matthew Hill CG: 35 DR: 86
D Liam Chilvers CG: 44 DR: 80
D Graham Alexander CG: 42 DR: 78
D Sean St Ledger CG: 39 DR: 76

M Paul McKenna CG: 31 SD: 24
M Chris Sedgwick CG: 39 SD: 20
M Danny Pugh CG: 45 SD: 17
M Simon Whaley CG: 30 SD: 15

F Brett Ormerod CG: 13 SR: 181
F David Nugent CG: 39 SR: 239

MONTHLY POINTS TALLY

AUGUST		6	40%
SEPTEMBER		11	73%
OCTOBER		12	80%
NOVEMBER		9	60%
DECEMBER		9	50%
JANUARY		6	50%
FEBRUARY		6	50%
MARCH		9	60%
APRIL		3	17%
MAY		3	100%

LEAGUE GOALS

	PLAYER	MINS	GOALS	S RATE
1	Nugent	3587	15	239
2	Ormerod	1448	8	181
3	Agyemang	1186	7	169
4	Whaley	2785	6	464
5	Alexander	3779	6	629
6	Dichio	1364	5	272
7	Pugh	3976	4	994
8	McKenna	2880	2	1440
9	Chilvers	4005	2	2002
10	Mellor	215	1	215
11	Neal, L	501	1	501
12	Pergl	509	1	509
13	Ricketts	670	1	670
	Other		3	
	TOTAL		**62**	

TOP POINT EARNERS

	PLAYER	GAMES	AV PTS
1	Carlo Nash	28	1.89
2	Matthew Hill	35	1.83
3	Paul McKenna	31	1.81
4	Simon Whaley	30	1.72
5	Chris Sedgwick	39	1.64
6	David Nugent	39	1.64
7	Brett Ormerod	13	1.62
8	Liam Chilvers	44	1.61
9	Graham Alexander	42	1.60
10	Danny Pugh	45	1.58
	CLUB AVERAGE:		**1.61**

DISCIPLINARY RECORDS

	PLAYER	YELLOW	RED	AVE
1	Danny Dichio	6	1	194
2	Callum Davidson	4	0	255
3	Seyfo Soley	2	0	259
4	David Nugent	11	1	298
5	Michael Ricketts	2	0	335
6	Kelvin Wilson	2	1	423
7	Graham Alexander	7	1	472
8	Danny Pugh	10	0	497
9	Pavel Pergl	1	0	509
10	Chris Sedgwick	6	0	596
11	Sean St Ledger	5	0	703
12	Paul McKenna	4	0	720
13	Brett Ormerod	2	0	720
	Other	13	0	
	TOTAL	**75**	**4**	

KEY GOALKEEPER

Carlo Nash

Goals Conceded in the League	27	Counting Games League games when player was on pitch for at least 70 minutes	28
Defensive Rating Ave number of mins between League goals conceded while on the pitch	93	Clean Sheets In League games when player was on pitch for at least 70 minutes	11

KEY PLAYERS - DEFENDERS

Matthew Hill

Goals Conceded Number of League goals conceded while the player was on the pitch	37	Clean Sheets In League games when player was on pitch for at least 70 minutes	15
Defensive Rating Ave number of mins between League goals conceded while on the pitch	86	Club Defensive Rating Average number of mins between League goals conceded by the club this season	78

	PLAYER	CON LGE	CLEAN SHEETS	DEF RATE
1	Matthew Hill	37	15	86 mins
2	Liam Chilvers	50	14	80 mins
3	Graham Alexander	48	15	78 mins
4	Sean St Ledger	46	14	76 mins

KEY PLAYERS - MIDFIELDERS

Paul McKenna

Goals in the League	2	Contribution to Attacking Power Average number of mins between League team goals while on pitch	60
Defensive Rating Average number of mins between League goals conceded while on the pitch	84	Scoring Difference Defensive Rating minus Contribution to Attacking Power	24

	PLAYER	LGE GOALS	DEF RATE	POWER	SCORE DIFF
1	Paul McKenna	2	84	60	24 mins
2	Chris Sedgwick	1	87	67	20 mins
3	Danny Pugh	4	81	64	17 mins
4	Simon Whaley	6	75	60	15 mins

KEY PLAYERS - GOALSCORERS

Brett Ormerod

Goals in the League	8	Player Strike Rate Average number of minutes between League goals scored by player	181
Contribution to Attacking Power Average number of minutes between League team goals while on pitch	62	Club Strike Rate Average number of minutes between League goals scored by club	64

	PLAYER	LGE GOALS	POWER	STRIKE RATE
1	Brett Ormerod	8	62	181 mins
2	David Nugent	15	64	239 mins
3	Simon Whaley	6	60	464 mins
4	Danny Pugh	4	64	994 mins

David Nugent

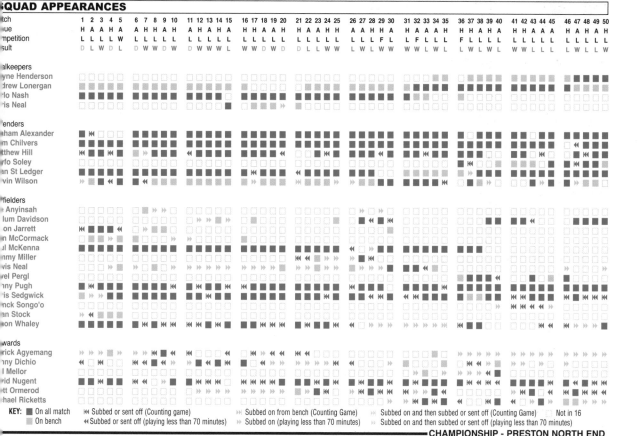

SQUAD APPEARANCES

Match: 1 2 3 4 5 6 7 8 9 10 11 12 13 14 15 16 17 18 19 20 21 22 23 24 25 26 27 28 29 30 31 32 33 34 35 36 37 38 39 40 41 42 43 44 45 46 47 48 49 50

Venue: H A A H A A H H A H A H A H A H H A A H H A A H H A A H H A H A A A H H H A H A H H A A A H A H A H

Competition: L L L L W L L L L L L L L L L L L L L L L L L L L L L L L L L F L L L F L L L L L L L L L L L L L L

Result: D L W D L D W W D W D W W W L W W D W D D L L W W L W L W W W W L W L L W L W L W W L L L L W L L W

Goalkeepers
Wayne Henderson
Andrew Lonergan
Carlo Nash
Chris Neal

Defenders
Graham Alexander
Liam Chilvers
Matthew Hill
Youl Soley
Sean St Ledger
Kevin Wilson

Midfielders
Paul Anyinsah
Callum Davidson
Jason Jarrett
Alan McCormack
Paul McKenna
Jimmy Miller
Lewis Neal
Pavel Pergl
Danny Pugh
Chris Sedgwick
Franck Songo'o
Brian Stock
Simon Whaley

Forwards
Patrick Agyemang
Danny Dichio
Neil Mellor
David Nugent
Brett Ormerod
Michael Ricketts

KEY: ■ On all match ◄◄ Subbed or sent off (Counting game) ►◄ Subbed on from bench (Counting Game) ►► Subbed on and then subbed or sent off (Counting Game) ☐ Not in 16
On bench ◄ Subbed or sent off (playing less than 70 minutes) ►► Subbed on (playing less than 70 minutes) ►► Subbed on and then subbed or sent off (playing less than 70 minutes)

CHAMPIONSHIP - PRESTON NORTH END

STOKE CITY

Final Position: **8th**

NICKNAME: THE POTTERS   KEY: ☐ Won ☐ Drawn ☐ Lost   Attendance

1	div1	Southend	A	L	0-1	8,971
2	div1	Derby	H	W	2-0	Pericard 18, Russell 58	20,013
3	div1	Birmingham	H	D	0-0	12,347
4	div1	Luton	A	D	2-2	Sweeney 10, Chadwick 70	7,727
5	ccr1	Darlington	H	L	1-2	Pericard 29	3,573
6	div1	Plymouth	H	D	1-1	Sidibe 39	11,626
7	div1	Barnsley	A	D	2-2	Hill 3, Chadwick 23	10,464
8	div1	Sheff Wed	A	D	1-1	Paterson 34	19,966
9	div1	Burnley	H	L	0-1	12,247
10	div1	Wolverhampton	A	L	0-2	19,489
11	div1	Preston	H	D	1-1	Fuller 41	14,342
12	div1	Leeds	A	W	4-0	Hendrie 7, Griffin 58, Higginbotham 62, Fuller 88	18,173
13	div1	Sunderland	H	W	2-1	Hendrie 50, Pericard 54	14,482
14	div1	Southampton	A	L	0-1	20,531
15	div1	Norwich	H	W	5-0	Hendrie 22, Fuller 38, Higginbotham 74 pen, Chadwick 79, Russell 90	13,444
16	div1	Leicester	A	L	1-2	Fuller 42	21,107
17	div1	Coventry	H	W	1-0	Griffin 60	19,055
18	div1	Crystal Palace	A	W	1-0	Russell 38	18,868
19	div1	Hull City	A	W	2-0	Higginbotham 2, Russell 80	16,940
20	div1	West Brom	H	W	1-0	Higginbotham 40 pen	18,282
21	div1	Cardiff	H	W	3-0	Fuller 60, Lawrence 63, Sidibe 65	15,039
22	div1	Coventry	A	D	0-0	19,073
23	div1	QPR	H	W	1-0	Higginbotham 17 pen	16,487
24	div1	Colchester	A	L	0-3	5,245
25	div1	Ipswich	A	W	1-0	Lawrence 71	20,369
26	div1	Sheff Wed	H	L	1-2	Sidibe 60	23,003
27	div1	Leeds	H	W	3-1	Sidibe 12, Ehiogu 54 og, Fuller 77	18,128
28	facr3	Millwall	H	W	2-0	Elliott 82 og, Fuller 87	8,024
29	div1	Wolverhampton	H	D	1-1	Hill 85	15,882
30	div1	Preston	A	L	2-3	Lawrence 2, Sidibe 7	15,151
31	div1	Burnley	A	W	1-0	Sidibe 24	12,109
32	facr4	Fulham	A	L	0-3	11,059
33	div1	Ipswich	H	D	0-0	11,812
34	div1	Southend	H	D	1-1	Fuller 31	23,017
35	div1	Birmingham	A	L	0-1	15,854
36	div1	Luton	H	D	0-0	12,375
37	div1	Derby	A	W	2-0	Higginbotham 15 pen, Matteo 26	24,897
38	div1	Barnsley	H	L	0-1	13,114
39	div1	Plymouth	A	D	1-1	Russell 55	12,539
40	div1	Southampton	H	W	2-1	Fortune 34, Martin 72	13,404
41	div1	Sunderland	A	D	2-2	Russell 22, Hoefkens 47	31,358
42	div1	Norwich	A	L	0-1	24,293
43	div1	Leicester	H	W	4-2	Parkin 18, Fuller 29 pen, Sidibe 79, Lawrence 90	13,303
44	div1	West Brom	A	W	3-1	Fuller 14, Greening 21 og, Parkin 22	20,386
45	div1	Crystal Palace	H	W	2-1	Parkin 20, Fuller 27	13,616
46	div1	Cardiff	A	D	1-1	Hoefkens 30	11,664
47	div1	Hull City	H	D	1-1	Lawrence 45	17,109
48	div1	Colchester	H	W	3-1	Russell 53, Sidibe 57, Higginbotham 62	20,108
49	div1	QPR	A	D	1-1	Sidibe 84	16,741

LEAGUE APPEARANCES, BOOKINGS AND CAPS

	AGE (on 01/07/07)	IN NAMED 16	APPEARANCES	COUNTING GAMES	MINUTES ON PITCH	LEAGUE GOALS
Goalkeepers						
Steve Simonsen	28	46	46	46	4140	0	3
Defenders						
Carl Dickinson	20	21	12	5	610	0	1
Michael Duberry	31	29	29	29	2610	0	7
Jonathan Fortune	26	14	14	14	1241	1	2
Andrew Griffin	28	33	33	31	2839	2	9
Danny Higginbotham	28	44	44	43	3893	7	3
Clinton Hill	28	22	18	15	1367	2	4
Carl Hoefkens	30	46	45	41	3814	2	3
Dominic Matteo	33	9	9	7	709	1	1
Andy Wilkinson	22	12	4	2	230	0	1
Gabriel Zakuani	21	14	9	7	724	0	1
Midfielders						
Patrik Berger	33	8	6	1	211	0	0
David Brammer	32	27	22	10	1084	0	5
Luke Chadwick	26	15	15	9	1004	3	1
Rory Delap	30	2	2	1	101	0	0
Salif Diao	30	27	27	26	2339	0	10
John Eustace	27	24	15	7	806	0	1
Kevin Harper	31	5	3	0	36	0	0
Lee Hendrie	30	28	28	23	2169	3	7
Liam Lawrence	25	27	27	26	2365	5	3
Lee Martin	20	17	13	5	498	1	2
Darel Russell	26	43	43	38	3545	7	6
Peter Sweeney	22	22	13	7	829	1	1
Jeff Whitley	32	5	3	0	60	0	1
Forwards						
Sambegou Bangoura	25	11	4	0	94	0	1
Ricardo Fuller	27	30	30	23	2241	10	10
Jonathan Parkin	25	6	6	1	370	3	1
Martin Paterson	20	14	9	1	245	1	0
Vincent Pericard	24	34	28	11	1392	2	1
Adam Rooney	19	14	10	0	140	0	0
Mamady Sidibe	27	43	43	39	3633	9	2
Hannes Sigurdsson	24	5	2	0	36	0	0

TEAM OF THE SEASON

D Andrew Griffin CG: 31 DR: 113
M Salif Diao CG: 26 SD: 73
D Carl Hoefkens CG: 41 DR: 105
M Lee Hendrie CG: 23 SD: 57
F Ricardo Fuller CG: 23 SR: 224
G Steve Simonsen CG: 46 DR: 100
D Michael Duberry CG: 29 DR: 104
M Darel Russell CG: 38 SD: 32
F Mamady Sidibe CG: 39 SR: 403
D Danny Higginbotham CG: 43 DR: 102
M Liam Lawrence CG: 26 SD: 31

MONTHLY POINTS TALLY

AUGUST	6	40%
SEPTEMBER	3	20%
OCTOBER	9	60%
NOVEMBER	15	100%
DECEMBER	10	56%
JANUARY	5	42%
FEBRUARY	5	33%
MARCH	8	53%
APRIL	11	73%
MAY	1	33%

LEAGUE GOALS

	PLAYER	MINS	GOALS	S RATE
1	Fuller	2241	10	224
2	Sidibe	3633	9	403
3	Russell	3545	7	506
4	Higginbotham	3893	7	556
5	Lawrence	2365	5	473
6	Parkin	370	3	123
7	Chadwick	1004	3	334
8	Hendrie	2169	3	723
9	Hill	1367	2	683
10	Pericard	1392	2	696
11	Griffin	2839	2	1419
12	Hoefkens	3814	2	1907
13	Paterson	245	1	245
	Other		4	
	TOTAL		60	

TOP POINT EARNERS

	PLAYER	GAMES	AV PTS
1	Salif Diao	26	1.92
2	Lee Hendrie	23	1.91
3	Carl Hoefkens	41	1.71
4	Liam Lawrence	26	1.69
5	Danny Higginbotham	43	1.62
6	Darel Russell	38	1.61
7	Steve Simonsen	46	1.59
8	Andrew Griffin	31	1.58
9	Ricardo Fuller	25	1.56
10	Michael Duberry	29	1.55
	CLUB AVERAGE:		1.59

DISCIPLINARY RECORDS

	PLAYER	YELLOW	RED	AV
1	Ricardo Fuller	10	2	20
2	David Brammer	5	0	21
3	Salif Diao	10	0	23
4	Lee Martin	2	0	24
5	Clinton Hill	4	1	27
6	Andrew Griffin	9	1	28
7	Lee Hendrie	7	0	30
8	Michael Duberry	7	0	37
9	Darel Russell	6	0	59
10	Jonathan Fortune	2	0	62
11	Dominic Matteo	1	0	70
12	Gabriel Zakuani	1	0	72
13	Liam Lawrence	3	0	78
	Other	15	0	
	TOTAL	82	4	

KEY GOALKEEPER

Steve Simonsen

Goals Conceded in the League	41	Counting Games League games when player was on pitch for at least 70 minutes	46
Defensive Rating Ave number of mins between League goals conceded while on the pitch	100	Clean Sheets In League games when player was on pitch for at least 70 minutes	16

KEY PLAYERS - DEFENDERS

Andrew Griffin

Goals Conceded Number of League goals conceded while the player was on the pitch	25	Clean Sheets In League games when player was on pitch for at least 70 minutes	13
Defensive Rating Ave number of mins between League goals conceded while on the pitch	113	Club Defensive Rating Average number of mins between League goals conceded by the club this season	103

	PLAYER	CON LGE	CLEAN SHEETS	DEF RATE
1	Andrew Griffin	25	13	113 mins
2	Carl Hoefkens	36	16	105 mins
3	Michael Duberry	25	13	104 mins
4	Danny Higginbotham	38	15	102 mins

KEY PLAYERS - MIDFIELDERS

Salif Diao

Goals in the League	0	Contribution to Attacking Power Average number of minutes between League team goals while on pitch	64
Defensive Rating Average number of mins between League goals conceded while on the pitch	137	Scoring Difference Defensive Rating minus Contribution to Attacking Power	73

	PLAYER	LGE GOALS	DEF RATE	POWER	SCORE DIFF
1	Salif Diao	0	137	64	73 mins
2	Lee Hendrie	3	120	63	57 mins
3	Darel Russell	7	98	66	32 mins
4	Liam Lawrence	5	94	63	31 mins

KEY PLAYERS - GOALSCORERS

Ricardo Fuller

Goals in the League	10	Player Strike Rate Average number of minutes between League goals scored by player	224
Contribution to Attacking Power Average number of minutes between League team goals while on pitch	65	Club Strike Rate Average number of minutes between League goals scored by club	68

	PLAYER	LGE GOALS	POWER	STRIKE RATE
1	Ricardo Fuller	10	65	224 mins
2	Mamady Sidibe	9	66	403 mins
3	Liam Lawrence	5	63	473 mins
4	Darel Russell	7	66	506 mins

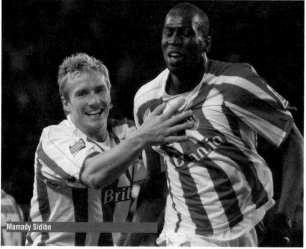

Mamady Sidibe

SQUAD APPEARANCES

KEY: ■ On all match · ◄◄ Subbed or sent off (Counting game) · ►► Subbed on from bench (Counting Game) · ►► Subbed on and then subbed or sent off (Counting Game) · Not in 16 · On bench · ◄◄ Subbed or sent off (playing less than 70 minutes) · ►► Subbed on (playing less than 70 minutes) · ►► Subbed on and then subbed or sent off (playing less than 70 minutes)

CHAMPIONSHIP - STOKE CITY

SHEFFIELD WEDNESDAY
Final Position: **9th**

NICKNAME: THE OWLS   KEY: ☐ Won ☐ Drawn ☐ Lost   Attendance

#		Opponent			Score	Scorers	Attendance
1	div1	Preston	A	D	0-0		15,650
2	div1	Luton	H	L	0-1		22,613
3	div1	Burnley	H	D	1-1	MacLean 67 pen	22,425
4	div1	Plymouth	A	W	2-1	McAllister 52, O'Brien 83	14,507
5	ccr1	Wrexham	H	L	1-4	Whelan 79	8,047
6	div1	Leeds	H	L	0-1		23,792
7	div1	Southend	A	D	0-0		9,639
8	div1	Stoke	H	D	1-1	Brunt 40 pen	19,966
9	div1	Hull City	A	L	1-2	Burton 4 pen	17,685
10	div1	Derby	H	L	1-2	Brunt 62	23,659
11	div1	Sunderland	A	L	0-1		36,764
12	div1	Barnsley	H	W	2-1	Whelan 4, Brunt 90	28,687
13	div1	Colchester	A	L	0-4		5,097
14	div1	QPR	H	W	3-2	Tudgay 13, 45, MacLean 70 pen	23,813
15	div1	Wolverhampton	A	D	2-2	Small 36, Brunt 53	20,637
16	div1	Crystal Palace	H	W	3-2	Tudgay 45, Coughlan 73, MacLean 90	19,034
17	div1	Leicester	H	W	2-1	Tudgay 34, 55	22,451
18	div1	Ipswich	A	W	2-0	Tudgay 11, Bougherra 82	21,830
19	div1	Coventry	A	L	1-3	Brunt 22	19,489
20	div1	Cardiff	H	D	0-0		23,935
21	div1	West Brom	H	W	3-1	Whelan 11, Bougherra 15, MacLean 90 pen	21,695
22	div1	Leicester	A	W	4-1	Brunt 43 pen, 53, Whelan 70, Tudgay 72	22,378
23	div1	Norwich	A	W	2-1	Camp 80 og, Burton 83	24,816
24	div1	Birmingham	H	L	0-3		26,083
25	div1	Southampton	H	D	3-3	Whelan 28, 69, Crossley 90	23,739
26	div1	Stoke	A	W	2-1	MacLean 35, Burton 79	23,003
27	div1	Barnsley	A	W	3-0	Andrews 11, Brunt 60, MacLean 68	21,253
28	div1	Hull City	H	L	1-2	Burton 53	28,600
29	facr3	Man City	H	D	1-1	MacLean 79	28,487
30	div1	Derby	A	L	0-1		28,936
31	facr3r	Man City	A	L	1-2	Bullen 51	25,621
32	div1	Sunderland	H	L	2-4	Brunt 82, Small 87	29,103
33	div1	Southampton	A	L	1-2	MacLean 52	20,230
34	div1	Preston	H	L	1-3	Burton 4	22,441
35	div1	Burnley	A	D	1-1	Burton 58	12,745
36	div1	Luton	A	L	2-3	Burton 25, Whelan 60	8,011
37	div1	Southend	H	W	3-2	Tudgay 16, Prior 29 og, MacLean 90 pen	24,116
38	div1	Leeds	A	W	3-2	Tudgay 7, Brunt 37, J.Johnson 54	25,297
39	div1	Plymouth	H	D	1-1	MacLean 21	19,449
40	div1	QPR	A	D	1-1	Brunt 56	15,188
41	div1	Colchester	H	W	2-0	Simek 27, M.Mills 35 og	18,752
42	div1	Wolverhampton	H	D	2-2	Burton 22, MacLean 47	24,181
43	div1	Crystal Palace	A	W	2-1	Burton 57, Tudgay 85	21,523
44	div1	Cardiff	A	W	2-1	Clarke 39, Burton 67	13,621
45	div1	Ipswich	H	W	2-0	Whelan 47, MacLean 59	23,232
46	div1	West Brom	A	W	1-0	Burton 59	20,415
47	div1	Coventry	H	W	2-1	Tudgay 17, MacLean 70	23,632
48	div1	Birmingham	A	L	0-2		29,317
49	div1	Norwich	H	W	3-2	J.Johnson 26, Burton 45, Etuhu 50 og	28,287

LEAGUE APPEARANCES, BOOKINGS AND CAPS

	AGE (on 01/07/07)	IN NAMED 16	APPEARANCES	COUNTING GAMES	MINUTES ON PITCH	LEAGUE GOALS
Goalkeepers						
Chris Adamson	28	45	4	3	293	0	0
Mark Crossley	38	17	17	17	1530	1	1
Brad Jones	25	15	15	14	1324	0	1
Iain Turner	23	11	11	11	990	0	0
Defenders						
Mark Beevers	17	3	2	2	180	0	0
Madjid Bougherra	24	28	28	28	2502	2	5
Lee Bullen	36	43	38	31	2983	0	4
Leon Clarke	22	11	10	1	348	1	3
Graham Coughlan	32	27	18	13	1257	1	3
Peter Gilbert	23	11	6	5	453	0	0
John Hills	29	18	16	13	1265	0	4
Frankie Simek	22	41	41	40	3635	1	7
Tommy Spurr	19	41	36	31	2846	0	7
Richard Wood	21	12	12	12	1080	0	3
Midfielders						
Steve Adams	26	3	3	0	119	0	1
Chris Brunt	22	44	44	41	3695	11	6
Yoann Folly	22	35	29	19	1855	0	0
Jermaine Johnson	27	8	7	4	449	2	0
Kenny Lunt	27	42	37	26	2685	0	8
Sean McAllister	19	12	6	1	155	1	0
Burton O'Brien	26	26	21	12	1267	1	0
Lloyd Sam	22	4	4	3	290	0	2
Wade Small	23	20	20	10	1052	2	2
Steve Watson	33	11	11	10	926	0	1
Glenn Whelan	23	41	38	34	3124	7	9
Forwards						
Wayne Andrews	29	9	9	4	572	1	2
Deon Burton	30	42	41	28	2918	12	9
David Graham	28	9	1	0	41	0	0
Steven MacLean	24	41	41	17	2095	12	3
Drew Talbot	20	9	8	1	220	0	0
Marcus Tudgay	24	40	40	32	3135	11	4

TEAM OF THE SEASON

- **D** Richard Wood — CG: 12 DR: 83
- **M** Glenn Whelan — CG: 34 SD: 11
- **D** John Hills — CG: 13 DR: 66
- **M** Chris Brunt — CG: 41 SD: 9
- **F** Steven MacLean — CG: 17 SR: 174
- **G** Brad Jones — CG: 14 DR: 69
- **D** Graham Coughlan — CG: 13 DR: 66
- **M** Kenny Lunt — CG: 26 SD: 8
- **F** Deon Burton — CG: 28 SR: 265
- **D** Madjid Bougherra — CG: 28 DR: 65
- **M** Yoann Folly — CG: 19 SD: -10

MONTHLY POINTS TALLY

Month	Points	%
AUGUST	5	33%
SEPTEMBER	2	13%
OCTOBER	10	67%
NOVEMBER	10	67%
DECEMBER	13	72%
JANUARY	0	0%
FEBRUARY	4	33%
MARCH	12	67%
APRIL	12	80%
MAY	3	100%

LEAGUE GOALS

	PLAYER	MINS	GOALS	S RATE
1	MacLean	2095	12	174
2	Burton	2918	12	265
3	Tudgay	3135	11	285
4	Brunt	3695	11	335
5	Whelan	3124	7	446
6	Johnson, J	449	2	224
7	Small	1052	2	526
8	Bougherra	2502	2	1251
9	McAllister	155	1	155
10	Clarke	348	1	348
11	Andrews	572	1	572
12	Coughlan	1257	1	1257
13	O'Brien	1267	1	1267
	Other		2	
	TOTAL		**65**	

TOP POINT EARNERS

	PLAYER	GAMES	AV PTS
1	Richard Wood	12	2.25
2	Kenny Lunt	26	1.92
3	Marcus Tudgay	33	1.76
4	Lee Bullen	32	1.72
5	John Hills	13	1.69
6	Chris Brunt	41	1.68
7	Deon Burton	28	1.64
8	Glenn Whelan	34	1.56
9	Steven MacLean	17	1.50
10	Frankie Simek	40	1.48
	CLUB AVERAGE:		**1.54**

DISCIPLINARY RECORDS

	PLAYER	YELLOW	RED	AV
1	Wayne Andrews	2	0	28
2	John Hills	4	0	31
3	Wade Small	2	1	35
4	Richard Wood	3	0	36
5	Kenny Lunt	8	0	38
6	Glenn Whelan	9	0	39
7	Tommy Spurr	7	0	40
8	Deon Burton	8	0	40
9	Frankie Simek	7	1	44
10	Madjid Bougherra	5	0	50
11	Chris Brunt	6	1	62
12	Marcus Tudgay	4	1	62
13	Graham Coughlan	3	0	62
	Other	10	2	
	TOTAL	**78**	**6**	

KEY GOALKEEPER

Brad Jones

Goals Conceded in the League	19	Counting Games League games when player was on pitch for at least 70 minutes	14
Defensive Rating Ave number of mins between League goals conceded while on the pitch	69	Clean Sheets In League games when player was on pitch for at least 70 minutes	3

KEY PLAYERS - DEFENDERS

Richard Wood

Goals Conceded Number of League goals conceded while the player was on the pitch	13	Clean Sheets In League games when player was on pitch for at least 70 minutes	3
Defensive Rating Ave number of mins between League goals conceded while on the pitch	83	Club Defensive Rating Average number of mins between League goals conceded by the club this season	62

	PLAYER	CON LGE	CLEAN SHEETS	DEF RATE
1	Richard Wood	13	3	83 mins
2	John Hills	19	3	66 mins
3	Graham Coughlan	19	2	66 mins
4	Madjid Bougherra	38	5	65 mins

KEY PLAYERS - MIDFIELDERS

Glenn Whelan

Goals in the League	7	Contribution to Attacking Power Average number of minutes between League team goals while on pitch	55
Defensive Rating Average number of mins between League goals conceded while on the pitch	66	Scoring Difference Defensive Rating minus Contribution to Attacking Power	11

	PLAYER	LGE GOALS	DEF RATE	POWER	SCORE DIFF
1	Glenn Whelan	7	66	55	11 mins
2	Chris Brunt	11	64	55	9 mins
3	Kenny Lunt	0	62	54	8 mins
4	Yoann Folly	0	53	63	-10 mins

KEY PLAYERS - GOALSCORERS

Steven MacLean

Goals in the League	12	Player Strike Rate Average number of minutes between League goals scored by player	174
Contribution to Attacking Power Average number of minutes between League team goals while on pitch	61	Club Strike Rate Average number of minutes between League goals scored by club	59

	PLAYER	LGE GOALS	POWER	STRIKE RATE
1	Steven MacLean	12	61	174 mins
2	Deon Burton	11	58	265 mins
3	Marcus Tudgay	11	53	285 mins
4	Chris Brunt	11	55	335 mins

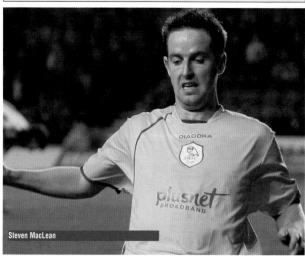

Steven MacLean

SQUAD APPEARANCES

Match	1 2 3 4 5	6 7 8 9 10	11 12 13 14 15	16 17 18 19 20	21 22 23 24 25	26 27 28 29 30	31 32 33 34 35	36 37 38 39 40	41 42 43 44 45	46 47 48 49
Venue	A H H A H	H A H A H	A H A H A	H H A A H	H A A H H	A A H H A	A H A H A	A H A H A	H H A A H	A H A H
Competition	L L L L W	L L L L L	L L L L L	L L L L L	L L L L L	L L L F L	F L L L L	L L L L L	L L L L L	L L L L
Result	D L D W L	L D D L L	L W L W D	W W W L D	W W W L D	W W L D L	L L L L D	L W W D D	W D W W W	W W L W

KEY: ■ On all match ◄◄ Subbed or sent off (Counting game) ►► Subbed on from bench (Counting Game) ►► Subbed on and then subbed or sent off (Counting Game) □ Not in 16
◻ On bench ◄◄ Subbed or sent off (playing less than 70 minutes) ►► Subbed on (playing less than 70 minutes) ►► Subbed on and then subbed or sent off (playing less than 70 minutes)

CHAMPIONSHIP - SHEFFIELD WEDNESDAY

COLCHESTER UNITED

Final Position: **10th**

NICKNAME: THE U'S   KEY: ☐ Won ☐ Drawn ☐ Lost

#		Opponent		Result	Scorers	Attendance
1	div1	Birmingham	A L	1-2	Garcia 51	24,238
2	div1	Plymouth	H L	0-1		4,627
3	div1	Barnsley	H L	1-2	Halford 42	4,249
4	div1	West Brom	A L	1-2	Guy 83	17,509
5	ccr1	MK Dons	A L	0-1		2,747
6	div1	Derby	H W	4-3	Cureton 28, 30, 67, Iwelumo 49 pen	4,574
7	div1	Burnley	A W	2-1	Watson 26, Iwelumo 54 pen	1,039
8	div1	Luton	A D	1-1	Cureton 40	7,609
9	div1	QPR	H W	2-1	Iwelumo 9, Garcia 18	5,246
10	div1	Leicester	A D	0-0		22,449
11	div1	Ipswich	H W	1-0	Duguid 9	6,065
12	div1	Wolverhampton	A L	0-1		19,318
13	div1	Sheff Wed	H W	4-0	Cureton 28, Halford 56, Iwelumo 61, Duguid 83	5,097
14	div1	Coventry	A L	1-2	Guy 85	16,178
15	div1	Southampton	H W	2-0	McLeod 3, Cureton 90	5,893
16	div1	Norwich	A D	1-1	Cureton 53	25,065
17	div1	Cardiff	H W	3-1	McLeod 49, Guy 84, Cureton 90 pen	5,393
18	div1	Leeds	A L	0-3		17,678
19	div1	Sunderland	A L	1-3	Iwelumo 79	25,197
20	div1	Southend	H W	3-0	Halford 68, Baldwin 74, Cureton 85	5,954
21	div1	Hull City	H W	5-1	Iwelumo 19, 53 pen, 66, 79, Cureton 57	5,373
22	div1	Cardiff	A D	0-0		13,512
23	div1	Crystal Palace	A W	3-1	Duguid 63, Garcia 70, Iwelumo 90 pen	16,762
24	div1	Stoke	H W	3-0	Cureton 2, 17, Garcia 63	5,245
25	div1	Preston	A L	0-1		14,225
26	div1	Luton	H W	4-1	McLeod 23, Iwelumo 41, 65, Garcia 59	5,427
27	div1	Wolverhampton	H W	2-1	Cureton 4, Iwelumo 45	5,893
28	div1	QPR	A L	0-1		11,319
29	facr3	Barnet	A L	1-2	Cureton 35	3,075
30	div1	Leicester	H D	1-1	Iwelumo 48 pen	5,915
31	div1	Ipswich	A L	2-3	Duguid 15, Iwelumo 90 pen	28,355
32	div1	Preston	H W	1-0	Richards 67	5,085
33	div1	Birmingham	H D	1-1	Izzet 55	5,918
34	div1	Barnsley	A W	3-0	Duguid 3, Cureton 10, Ephraim 83	11,192
35	div1	West Brom	H L	1-2	Jackson 55	5,611
36	div1	Plymouth	A L	0-3		12,895
37	div1	Burnley	H D	0-0		4,934
38	div1	Derby	A L	1-5	Jackson 56	26,704
39	div1	Coventry	H D	0-0		5,453
40	div1	Sheff Wed	A L	0-2		18,752
41	div1	Southampton	A W	2-1	Cureton 4, 27	18,736
42	div1	Norwich	H W	3-0	Cureton 52, Garcia 64, Iwelumo 73	5,851
43	div1	Southend	A W	3-0	Cureton 1, 63, 79	10,552
44	div1	Leeds	H W	2-1	Iwelumo 82, Cureton 90	5,916
45	div1	Hull City	A D	1-1	Cureton 63	20,887
46	div1	Sunderland	H W	3-1	Brown 45, Garcia 82, Cureton 89 pen	6,042
47	div1	Stoke	A L	1-3	Iwelumo 38 pen	20,108
48	div1	Crystal Palace	H L	0-2		5,857

LEAGUE APPEARANCES, BOOKINGS AND CAPS

	AGE (on 01/07/07)	IN NAMED 16	APPEARANCES	COUNTING GAMES	MINUTES ON PITCH	LEAGUE GOALS	
Goalkeepers							
Aidan Davison	39	41	19	19	1710	0	0
Dean Gerken	21	45	27	27	2430	0	0
Defenders							
Pat Baldwin	24	43	38	33	3136	1	3
Chris Barker	27	39	38	38	3382	0	5
Wayne Brown	29	46	46	46	4140	1	4
George Elokobi	21	20	11	7	726	0	1
Greg Halford	22	28	28	28	2517	3	3
Matthew Mills	20	10	9	7	706	0	2
Garry Richards	21	16	5	3	321	1	0
John White	20	37	16	5	727	0	0
Midfielders							
Karl Duguid	29	44	44	41	3759	5	5
Hogan Ephraim	19	25	21	3	725	1	4
Kemal Izzet	26	45	45	43	3846	1	6
Johnnie Jackson	24	40	32	22	2300	2	2
Ritchie Jones	20	6	6	0	136	0	1
Kevin McLeod	26	34	24	6	1129	3	3
Kevin Watson	33	40	40	35	3308	1	2
Forwards							
Jamie Cureton	31	44	44	42	3736	23	3
Richard Garcia	25	35	35	28	2769	7	5
Jamie Guy	19	43	31	1	490	3	1
Chris Iwelumo	28	46	46	36	3521	18	2

TEAM OF THE SEASON

G Dean Gerken CG: 27 DR: 75

D Pat Baldwin CG: 33 DR: 89
D Greg Halford CG: 28 DR: 81
D Chris Barker CG: 38 DR: 75
D Wayne Brown CG: 46 DR: 73

M Kemal Izzet CG: 43 SD: 18
M Kevin Watson CG: 35 SD: 15
M Johnnie Jackson CG: 22 SD: 12
M Karl Duguid CG: 41 SD: 10

F Jamie Cureton CG: 42 SR: 162
F Chris Iwelumo CG: 36 SR: 195

MONTHLY POINTS TALLY

AUGUST		3	20%
SEPTEMBER		11	73%
OCTOBER		7	47%
NOVEMBER		9	60%
DECEMBER		13	72%
JANUARY		4	33%
FEBRUARY		5	33%
MARCH		7	47%
APRIL		10	67%
MAY		0	0%

LEAGUE GOALS

	PLAYER	MINS	GOALS	S RATE
1	Cureton	3736	23	162
2	Iwelumo	3521	18	195
3	Garcia	2769	7	395
4	Duguid	3759	5	751
5	Guy	490	3	163
6	McLeod	1129	3	376
7	Halford	2517	3	839
8	Jackson	2300	2	1150
9	Richards	321	1	321
10	Ephraim	725	1	725
11	Baldwin	3136	1	3136
12	Watson	3308	1	3308
13	Izzet	3846	1	3846
	Other		1	
	TOTAL		**70**	

TOP POINT EARNERS

	PLAYER	GAMES	AV PTS
1	Pat Baldwin	33	1.85
2	Chris Iwelumo	36	1.77
3	Jamie Cureton	42	1.66
4	Chris Barker	38	1.63
5	Greg Halford	28	1.57
6	Dean Gerken	27	1.56
7	Johnnie Jackson	22	1.55
8	Kemal Izzet	43	1.53
9	Wayne Brown	46	1.50
10	Kevin Watson	35	1.49
	CLUB AVERAGE:		**1.50**

DISCIPLINARY RECORDS

	PLAYER	YELLOW	RED	AVE
1	Hogan Ephraim	4	0	181
2	Matthew Mills	2	0	353
3	Kevin McLeod	3	0	376
4	Chris Barker	5	2	483
5	Jamie Guy	1	0	490
6	Richard Garcia	5	0	553
7	Kemal Izzet	6	0	641
8	George Elokobi	1	0	726
9	Karl Duguid	5	0	751
10	Wayne Brown	4	0	1035
11	Pat Baldwin	3	0	1045
12	Johnnie Jackson	2	0	1150
13	Jamie Cureton	3	0	1245
	Other	7	0	
	TOTAL	**51**	**2**	

KEY GOALKEEPER

Dean Gerken

Goals Conceded in the League	32	Counting Games League games when player was on pitch for at least 70 minutes	27
Defensive Rating Ave number of mins between League goals conceded while on the pitch	75	Clean Sheets In League games when player was on pitch for at least 70 minutes	8

KEY PLAYERS - DEFENDERS

Pat Baldwin

Goals Conceded Number of League goals conceded while the player was on the pitch	35	Clean Sheets In League games when player was on pitch for at least 70 minutes	10
Defensive Rating Ave number of mins between League goals conceded while on the pitch	89	Club Defensive Rating Average number of mins between League goals conceded by the club this season	73

	PLAYER	CON LGE	CLEAN SHEETS	DEF RATE
1	Pat Baldwin	35	10	89 mins
2	Greg Halford	31	7	81 mins
3	Chris Barker	45	12	75 mins
4	Wayne Brown	56	13	73 mins

KEY PLAYERS - MIDFIELDERS

Kemal Izzet

Goals in the League	1	Contribution to Attacking Power Average number of minutes between League team goals while on pitch	58
Defensive Rating Average number of mins between League goals conceded while on the pitch	76	Scoring Difference Defensive Rating minus Contribution to Attacking Power	18

	PLAYER	LGE GOALS	DEF RATE	POWER	SCORE DIFF
1	Kemal Izzet	1	76	58	18 mins
2	Kevin Watson	1	75	60	15 mins
3	Johnnie Jackson	2	74	62	12 mins
4	Karl Duguid	5	70	60	10 mins

KEY PLAYERS - GOALSCORERS

Jamie Cureton

Goals in the League	23	Player Strike Rate Average number of minutes between League goals scored by player	162
Contribution to Attacking Power Average number of minutes between League team goals while on pitch	57	Club Strike Rate Average number of minutes between League goals scored by club	59

	PLAYER	LGE GOALS	POWER	STRIKE RATE
1	Jamie Cureton	23	57	162 mins
2	Chris Iwelumo	18	57	195 mins
3	Richard Garcia	7	60	395 mins
4	Karl Duguid	5	60	751 mins

Jamie Cureton

SQUAD APPEARANCES

Match	1 2 3 4 5	6 7 8 9 10	11 12 13 14 15	16 17 18 19 20	21 22 23 24 25	26 27 28 29 30	31 32 33 34 35	36 37 38 39 40	41 42 43 44 45	46 47 48
Venue	A H H A A	H A A H A	H A H A H	A H A A H	H A A H A	H H A A H	A H H A H	A H A H A	A H A H A	H A H
Competition	L L L L W	L L L L L	L L L L L	L L L L L	L L L L L	L L L L L	L L L F L	L L L L L	L L L L L	L L L
Result	L L L L L	W W D W D	W L W L W	D W L L W	W D W W L	W W L L D	L W D W L	L D L D L	W W W W D	W L L

PLYMOUTH ARGYLE

Final Position: **11th**

NICKNAME: THE PILGRIMS KEY: ☐ Won ☐ Drawn ☐ Lost Attendance

						Attendance
1	div1	Wolverhampton	H	D	1-1 Hayles 35	15,964
2	div1	Colchester	A	W	1-0 Summerfield 30	4,627
3	div1	Sunderland	A	W	3-2 Norris 8, Hayles 39, Chadwick 82	24,377
4	div1	Sheff Wed	H	L	1-2 Wotton 43 pen	14,507
5	ccr1	Walsall	H	L	0-1	6,407
6	div1	Stoke	A	D	1-1 Hayles 78	11,626
7	div1	QPR	H	D	1-1 Ebanks-Blake 31	12,138
8	div1	Cardiff	H	D	3-3 McNaughton 69 og, Hayles 74, Purse 88 og	1,655
9	div1	Southampton	A	L	0-1	22,514
10	div1	Norwich	H	W	3-1 Doherty 14 og, Seip 47, Norris 74	11,813
11	div1	Coventry	A	W	1-0 Samba 82	19,545
12	div1	Derby	H	W	3-1 Wotton 44 pen, 63 pen, Seip 79	13,622
13	div1	Barnsley	A	D	2-2 Ebanks-Blake 29, Hayles 34	9,479
14	div1	Burnley	H	D	0-0	12,817
15	div1	Crystal Palace	A	W	1-0 Chadwick 39	17,084
16	div1	Ipswich	H	D	1-1 Wotton 22	12,210
17	div1	Birmingham	H	L	0-1	17,008
18	div1	Leicester	A	D	2-2 Nalis 31, Hayles 90	21,703
19	div1	Southend	A	D	1-1 Djordjic 5	9,469
20	div1	Leeds	H	L	1-2 Djordjic 40	17,088
21	div1	Luton	H	W	1-0 Djordjic 61	9,965
22	div1	Birmingham	A	L	0-3	22,592
23	div1	Hull City	H	W	1-0 Ebanks-Blake 71	12,101
24	div1	Preston	A	L	0-3	13,171
25	div1	West Brom	H	D	2-2 Hayles 23, Nalis 40	15,172
26	div1	Cardiff	A	D	2-2 Norris 34, 59	17,299
27	div1	Derby	A	L	0-1	25,775
28	div1	Southampton	H	D	1-1 Hayles 66	15,377
29	facr3	Peterborough	A	D	1-1 Aljofree 74 pen	6,255
30	div1	Norwich	A	W	3-1 Hayles 59, Buzsaky 63, 75	23,513
31	facr3r	Peterborough	H	W	2-1 Hayles 18, Norris 27	9,973
32	div1	Coventry	H	W	3-2 Gallen 18, Buzsaky 32, Hayles 48	9,841
33	facr4	Barnet	A	W	2-0 Aljofree 67 pen, Sinclair 83	5,204
34	div1	West Brom	A	L	1-2 Fallon 70	19,894
35	div1	Wolverhampton	A	D	2-2 Sinclair 27, Timar 36	19,082
36	div1	Sunderland	H	L	0-2	15,247
37	facr5	Derby	H	W	2-0 Gallen 14 pen, Sinclair 84	18,026
38	div1	Colchester	H	W	3-0 Norris 12, Ebanks-Blake 59 pen, Gosling 67	12,895
39	div1	QPR	A	D	1-1 Nalis 32	13,757
40	div1	Stoke	H	D	1-1 Ebanks-Blake 40 pen	12,539
41	div1	Sheff Wed	A	D	1-1 Gosling 56	19,449
42	facqf	Watford	H	L	0-1	20,652
43	div1	Barnsley	H	L	2-4 Nalis 15, Ebanks-Blake 41	10,265
44	div1	Crystal Palace	H	W	1-0 Sinclair 48	11,239
45	div1	Ipswich	A	L	0-3	21,078
46	div1	Burnley	A	L	0-4	9,793
47	div1	Leeds	A	L	1-2 Halmosi 36	-
48	div1	Leicester	H	W	3-0 Halmosi 15, Ebanks-Blake 46, Hayles 62	10,900
49	div1	Luton	A	W	2-1 Norris 4, Halmosi 40	7,601
50	div1	Southend	H	W	2-1 Ebanks-Blake 6, Hayles 90	11,097
51	div1	Preston	H	W	2-0 Ebanks-Blake 77 pen, Hayles 85	13,813
52	div1	Hull City	A	W	2-1 Halmosi 45, Ebanks-Blake 59	20,661

LEAGUE APPEARANCES, BOOKINGS AND CAPS

	AGE (on 01/07/07)	IN NAMED 16	APPEARANCES	COUNTING GAMES	MINUTES ON PITCH	LEAGUE GOALS
Goalkeepers						
Romain Larrieu	30	21	6	6	540	0	0
Luke McCormick	23	46	40	40	3600	0	1
Defenders						
Hasney Aljofree	28	28	25	21	2000	0	10
Anthony Barness	35	4	1	0	55	0	0
Paul Connolly	23	38	38	36	3362	0	8
Mathias Doumbe	27	34	29	26	2423	0	5
Gary Sawyer	21	38	22	18	1739	0	5
Marcel Seip	25	38	37	36	3285	2	7
Krisztian Timar	27	15	9	8	721	1	2
Paul Wotton	29	22	22	18	1802	4	3
Midfielders						
Akos Buzsaky	25	38	36	22	2373	3	4
Anthony Capaldi	25	34	31	29	2646	0	8
Bojan Djordjic	25	30	17	5	653	3	0
Dan Gosling	17	18	12	7	720	2	1
Peter Halmosi	27	17	16	12	1205	4	0
Lee Hodges	33	19	15	9	945	0	0
Lilian Nalis	35	42	41	39	3469	4	4
David Norris	26	41	41	41	3690	6	9
Reuben Reid	18	13	6	1	160	0	0
Luke Summerfield	28	37	23	9	1081	1	1
Forwards						
Nick Chadwick	24	17	16	4	717	2	3
Sylvain Ebanks-Blake	21	41	41	25	2583	10	7
Rory Fallon	25	18	15	4	552	1	1
Kevin Gallen	31	15	13	4	572	1	0
Barry Hayles	35	39	39	36	3267	13	12
Chemo Samba	22	13	13	2	375	1	1
Scott Sinclair	18	15	15	7	844	2	1

TEAM OF THE SEASON

D Gary Sawyer CG: 18 DR: 79
M David Norris CG: 41 SD: 8
D Mathias Doumbe CG: 26 DR: 75
M Lilian Nalis CG: 39 SD: 7
F Barry Hayles CG: 36 SR: 251
G Luke McCormick CG: 40 DR: 65
D Paul Wotton CG: 18 DR: 72
M Akos Buzsaky CG: 22 SD: 6
F S Ebanks-Blake CG: 25 SR: 258
D Paul Connolly CG: 36 DR: 70
M Peter Halmosi CG: 12 SD: 6

MONTHLY POINTS TALLY

AUGUST		8	53%
SEPTEMBER		8	53%
OCTOBER		9	60%
NOVEMBER		5	33%
DECEMBER		5	28%
JANUARY		7	58%
FEBRUARY		5	42%
MARCH		5	33%
APRIL		12	67%
MAY		3	100%

LEAGUE GOALS

	PLAYER	MINS	GOALS	S RATE
1	Hayles	3267	13	251
2	Ebanks-Blake	2583	10	258
3	Norris	3690	6	615
4	Halmosi	1205	4	301
5	Wotton	1802	4	450
6	Nalis	3469	4	867
7	Djordjic	653	3	217
8	Buzsaky	2373	3	791
9	Chadwick	717	2	358
10	Gosling	720	2	360
11	Sinclair	844	2	422
12	Seip	3285	2	1642
13	Samba	375	1	375
	Other		4	
	TOTAL		**60**	

TOP POINT EARNERS

	PLAYER	GAMES	AV PTS
1	Gary Sawyer	18	2.06
2	Peter Halmosi	12	1.92
3	Mathias Doumbe	28	1.68
4	Akos Buzsaky	22	1.62
5	Paul Wotton	18	1.61
6	Marcel Seip	36	1.56
7	Sylvain Ebanks-Blake	25	1.56
8	David Norris	41	1.51
9	Paul Connolly	36	1.50
10	Luke McCormick	40	1.45
	CLUB AVERAGE:		1.46

DISCIPLINARY RECORDS

	PLAYER	YELLOW	RED	AV
1	Barry Hayles	12	1	25
2	Hasney Aljofree	10	0	28
3	Mathias Doumbe	5	2	34
4	Nick Chadwick	3	0	35
5	Krisztian Timar	2	0	36
6	David Norris	9	0	41
7	S Ebanks-Blake	7	0	43
8	Anthony Capaldi	8	0	44
9	Rory Fallon	1	0	55
10	Paul Connolly	8	0	56
11	Gary Sawyer	5	0	57
12	Akos Buzsaky	4	0	59
13	Paul Wotton	3	0	60
	Other	15	1	
	TOTAL	**92**	**5**	

KEY GOALKEEPER

Luke McCormick

Goals Conceded in the League	55	Counting Games League games when player was on pitch for at least 70 minutes		40
Defensive Rating Ave number of mins between League goals conceded while on the pitch	65	Clean Sheets In League games when player was on pitch for at least 70 minutes		9

KEY PLAYERS - DEFENDERS

Gary Sawyer

Goals Conceded Number of League goals conceded while the player was on the pitch	22	Clean Sheets In League games when player was on pitch for at least 70 minutes		6
Defensive Rating Ave number of mins between League goals conceded while on the pitch	79	Club Defensive Rating Average number of mins between League goals conceded by the club this season		66

	PLAYER	CON LGE	CLEAN SHEETS	DEF RATE
1	Gary Sawyer	22	6	79 mins
2	Mathias Doumbe	32	7	75 mins
3	Paul Wotton	25	5	72 mins
4	Paul Connolly	48	8	70 mins

KEY PLAYERS - MIDFIELDERS

David Norris

Goals in the League	6	Contribution to Attacking Power Average number of minutes between League team goals while on pitch		62
Defensive Rating Average number of mins between League goals conceded while on the pitch	70	Scoring Difference Defensive Rating minus Contribution to Attacking Power		8

	PLAYER	LGE GOALS	DEF RATE	POWER	SCORE DIFF
1	David Norris	6	70	62	8 mins
2	Lilian Nalis	4	68	61	7 mins
3	Akos Buzsaky	3	71	65	6 mins
4	Peter Halmosi	4	63	57	6 mins

KEY PLAYERS - GOALSCORERS

Barry Hayles

Goals in the League	13	Player Strike Rate Average number of minutes between League goals scored by player		251
Contribution to Attacking Power Average number of minutes between League team goals while on pitch	64	Club Strike Rate Average number of minutes between League goals scored by club		65

	PLAYER	LGE GOALS	POWER	STRIKE RATE
1	Barry Hayles	13	64	251 mins
2	Sylvain Ebanks-Blake	10	63	258 mins
3	Peter Halmosi	4	57	301 mins
4	David Norris	6	62	615 mins

Sylvain Ebanks-Blake

SQUAD APPEARANCES

Match	1	2	3	4	5		6	7	8	9	10		11	12	13	14	15		16	17	18	19	20		21	22	23	24	25		26	27	28	29	30		31	32	33	34	35		36	37	38	39	40		41	42	43	44	45		46	47	48	49	50		51	52
Venue	H	A	A	H	H		A	H	H	A	H		A	H	A	H	A		H	H	A	A	H		H	A	H	A	H		A	A	H	A	A		H	H	A	A	A		H	H	H	A	H		A	H	H	A	A		A	A	H	A	H		H	A
Competition	L	L	L	L	W		L	L	L	L	L		L	L	L	L	L		L	L	L	L	L		L	L	L	L	L		L	L	L	F	L		F	L	F	L	L		L	F	L	L	L		L	F	L	L	L		L	L	L	L	L		L	L
Result	D	W	W	L	L		D	D	D	L	W		W	W	D	D	W		D	L	D	D	L		W	L	W	L	D		D	L	D	D	W		W	W	W	L	D		L	W	W	D	D		D	L	L	W	L		L	L	W	W	W		W	W

Goalkeepers

Romain Larrieu
Luke McCormick

Defenders

Rasney Aljofree
Anthony Barness
Paul Connolly
Mathias Doumbe
Gary Sawyer
Marcel Seip
Krisztian Timar
Paul Wotton

Midfielders

Akos Buzsaky
Anthony Capaldi
Bojan Djordjic
Dan Gosling
Peter Halmosi
Lee Hodges
Lilian Nalis
David Norris
Reuben Reid
Luke Summerfield

Forwards

Nick Chadwick
Sylvain Ebanks-Blake
Rory Fallon
Kevin Gallen
Barry Hayles
Nemo Samba
Scott Sinclair

KEY: ■ On all match ◄◄ Subbed or sent off (Counting game) ►►► Subbed on from bench (Counting Game) ►► Subbed on and then subbed or sent off (Counting Game) ☐ Not in 16
 ■ On bench ◄◄ Subbed or sent off (playing less than 70 minutes) ►► Subbed on (playing less than 70 minutes) ►► Subbed on and then subbed or sent off (playing less than 70 minutes)

CHAMPIONSHIP - PLYMOUTH ARGYLE

CRYSTAL PALACE

Final Position: **12th**

NICKNAME: THE EAGLES KEY: ☐ Won ☐ Drawn ☐ Lost Attendance

#	Comp	Opp	H/A	Result		Scorers	Attendance
1	div1	Ipswich	A	W	2-1	McAnuff 58, Scowcroft 61	25,413
2	div1	Southend	H	W	3-1	Cort 52, Freedman 55, Hudson 61	18,072
3	div1	Leeds	H	W	1-0	Morrison 90	17,218
4	div1	Birmingham	A	L	1-2	McAnuff 11	20,223
5	ccr1	Notts County	H	L	1-2	Hughes 17	4,481
6	div1	Burnley	H	D	2-2	Cort 48, Scowcroft 74	16,396
7	div1	Luton	A	L	1-2	Scowcroft 90	9,187
8	div1	Southampton	H	L	0-2		17,084
9	div1	Norwich	A	W	1-0	Kuqi 90	24,618
10	div1	Coventry	H	W	1-0	Morrison 55	16,093
11	div1	Hull City	A	D	1-1	Cort 57	18,099
12	div1	Cardiff	H	L	1-2	Green 40	18,876
13	div1	West Brom	H	L	0-2		16,105
14	div1	Leicester	A	D	1-1	Soares 16	28,762
15	div1	Plymouth	H	L	0-1		17,084
16	div1	Sheff Wed	A	L	2-3	Kuqi 21, Soares 64	19,034
17	div1	QPR	A	L	2-4	Soares 30, Morrison 43	13,989
18	div1	Stoke	H	L	0-1		18,868
19	div1	Barnsley	H	W	2-0	Scowcroft 16, Morrison 32	20,159
20	div1	Preston	A	D	0-0		14,202
21	div1	Wolverhampton	A	D	1-1	Freedman 84	17,806
22	div1	QPR	H	W	3-0	Freedman 13, Kuqi 32, Morrison 86	17,017
23	div1	Colchester	H	L	1-3	Morrison 87	16,762
24	div1	Derby	A	L	0-1		23,875
25	div1	Sunderland	H	W	1-0	Hudson 41	17,439
26	div1	Southampton	A	D	1-1	McAnuff 54	30,548
27	div1	Cardiff	A	D	0-0		13,704
28	div1	Norwich	H	W	3-1	Hudson 26, Kuqi 29, Green 45	16,765
29	facr3	Swindon	H	W	2-1	Kuqi 8, McAnuff 70	10,238
30	div1	Coventry	A	W	4-2	Fletcher 19, Kuqi 27, Cort 28, McAnuff 39	16,582
31	div1	Hull City	H	D	1-1	Fletcher 51	17,012
32	facr4	Preston	H	L	0-2		8,422
33	div1	Sunderland	A	D	0-0		26,958
34	div1	Ipswich	H	W	2-0	Cort 33, Ifill 51	17,090
35	div1	Leeds	A	L	1-2	Cort 83	19,220
36	div1	Birmingham	H	L	0-1		17,233
37	div1	Southend	A	W	1-0	Ifill 65	10,419
38	div1	Luton	H	W	2-1	Morrison 45, 68	16,177
39	div1	Burnley	A	D	1-1	Morrison 15	10,659
40	div1	Leicester	H	W	2-0	Fletcher 14, Watson 90 pen	16,969
41	div1	West Brom	A	W	3-2	Morrison 35, Watson 42 pen, Grabban 90	17,960
42	div1	Plymouth	A	L	0-1		11,239
43	div1	Sheff Wed	H	L	1-2	Morrison 80	21,523
44	div1	Preston	H	W	3-0	Kuqi 16, 21, Cort 68	15,985
45	div1	Stoke	A	L	1-2	Zakuani 30 og	13,616
46	div1	Wolverhampton	H	D	2-2	Hudson 12, McAnuff 37	17,981
47	div1	Barnsley	A	L	0-2		10,277
48	div1	Derby	H	W	2-0	Morrison 29, Kennedy 67	19,545
49	div1	Colchester	A	W	2-0	Scowcroft 11, Watson 69	5,857

LEAGUE APPEARANCES, BOOKINGS AND CAPS

	AGE (on 01/07/07)	IN NAMED 16	APPEARANCES	COUNTING GAMES	MINUTES ON PITCH	LEAGUE GOALS
Goalkeepers						
Scott Flinders	21	22	8	7	697	0	1
Gabor Kiraly	31	34	29	29	2610	0	1
Julian Speroni	28	27	5	5	450	0	0
Iain Turner	23	5	5	4	383	0	0
Defenders						
Gary Borrowdale	21	28	25	24	2150	0	3
Danny Butterfield	27	38	28	22	2183	0	3
Leon Cort	27	38	37	37	3330	7	0
Danny Granville	32	17	15	15	1350	0	1
Mark Hudson	25	42	39	37	3420	4	3
Matt Lawrence	33	43	33	29	2741	0	5
Darren Ward	28	27	20	20	1782	0	1
Midfielders						
Carl Fletcher	27	40	37	27	2800	3	5
Stuart Green	26	16	14	4	591	2	0
Michael Hughes	35	17	16	10	1067	0	1
Paul Ifill	27	13	13	4	651	2	0
Mark Kennedy	31	42	38	32	2975	1	2
David Martin	22	7	4	0	68	0	0
Jobi McAnuff	25	34	34	28	2763	5	2
Marco Reich	29	9	6	1	255	0	0
Tom Soares	20	37	37	28	2811	3	4
Lewis Spence	19	2	2	0	86	0	0
Ben Watson	21	26	25	15	1608	3	4
Forwards						
Dougie Freedman	33	38	34	9	1436	3	0
Lewis Grabban	19	9	8	0	120	1	0
Shefki Kuqi	30	36	35	20	2131	7	2
Jonathan Macken	29	2	1	0	45	0	0
Clinton Morrison	28	46	41	27	2673	12	4
James Scowcroft	33	37	35	25	2348	5	8

TEAM OF THE SEASON

D Danny Butterfield CG: 22 DR: 99
M Ben Watson CG: 15 SD: 21
D Mark Hudson CG: 37 DR: 87
M Carl Fletcher CG: 27 SD: 15
F Clinton Morrison CG: 27 SR: 222
G Gabor Kiraly CG: 29 DR: 81
D Darren Ward CG: 20 DR: 84
M Jobi McAnuff CG: 28 SD: 14
F Shefki Kuqi CG: 20 SR: 304
D Gary Borrowdale CG: 24 DR: 82
M Mark Kennedy CG: 32 SD: 2

MONTHLY POINTS TALLY

Month	Points	%
AUGUST	10	67%
SEPTEMBER	7	47%
OCTOBER	1	7%
NOVEMBER	5	33%
DECEMBER	8	44%
JANUARY	8	67%
FEBRUARY	9	60%
MARCH	7	47%
APRIL	7	47%
MAY	3	100%

LEAGUE GOALS

	PLAYER	MINS	GOALS	S RATE
1	Morrison	2673	12	222
2	Kuqi	2131	7	304
3	Cort	3330	7	475
4	Scowcroft	2348	5	469
5	McAnuff	2763	5	552
6	Hudson	3420	4	855
7	Freedman	1436	3	478
8	Watson	1608	3	536
9	Fletcher	2800	3	933
10	Soares	2811	3	937
11	Green	591	2	295
12	Ifill	651	2	325
13	Grabban	120	1	120
	Other		1	
	TOTAL		**58**	

TOP POINT EARNERS

	PLAYER	GAMES	AV PTS
1	James Scowcroft	22	1.73
2	Danny Butterfield	22	1.70
3	Carl Fletcher	27	1.67
4	Jobi McAnuff	28	1.61
5	Ben Watson	15	1.60
6	Mark Hudson	37	1.54
7	Mark Kennedy	32	1.41
8	Leon Cort	37	1.41
9	Darren Ward	20	1.40
10	Tom Soares	28	1.39
	CLUB AVERAGE:		**1.41**

DISCIPLINARY RECORDS

	PLAYER	YELLOW	RED	AVE
1	James Scowcroft	8	0	293
2	Ben Watson	4	0	402
3	Matt Lawrence	5	0	548
4	Carl Fletcher	5	0	560
5	Tom Soares	4	1	562
6	Clinton Morrison	4	0	668
7	Scott Flinders	1	0	697
8	Gary Borrowdale	3	0	716
9	Danny Butterfield	3	0	727
10	Shefki Kuqi	2	0	1065
11	Michael Hughes	1	0	1067
12	Mark Hudson	3	0	1140
13	Danny Granville	1	0	1350
	Other	5	0	
	TOTAL	**49**	**1**	

KEY GOALKEEPER

Gabor Kiraly

Goals Conceded in the League	32	Counting Games League games when player was on pitch for at least 70 minutes	29
Defensive Rating Ave number of mins between League goals conceded while on the pitch	81	Clean Sheets In League games when player was on pitch for at least 70 minutes	8

KEY PLAYERS - DEFENDERS

Danny Butterfield

Goals Conceded Number of League goals conceded while the player was on the pitch	22	Clean Sheets In League games when player was on pitch for at least 70 minutes	9
Defensive Rating Ave number of mins between League goals conceded while on the pitch	99	Club Defensive Rating Average number of mins between League goals conceded by the club this season	81

	PLAYER	CON LGE	CLEAN SHEETS	DEF RATE
1	Danny Butterfield	22	9	99 mins
2	Mark Hudson	39	13	87 mins
3	Darren Ward	21	7	84 mins
4	Gary Borrowdale	26	8	82 mins

KEY PLAYERS - MIDFIELDERS

Ben Watson

Goals in the League	3	Contribution to Attacking Power Average number of minutes between League team goals while on pitch	73
Defensive Rating Average number of mins between League goals conceded while on the pitch	94	Scoring Difference Defensive Rating minus Contribution to Attacking Power	21

	PLAYER	LGE GOALS	DEF RATE	POWER	SCORE DIFF
1	Ben Watson	3	94	73	21 mins
2	Carl Fletcher	3	80	65	15 mins
3	Jobi McAnuff	5	83	69	14 mins
4	Mark Kennedy	1	80	78	2 mins

KEY PLAYERS - GOALSCORERS

Clinton Morrison

Goals in the League	12	Player Strike Rate Average number of minutes between League goals scored by player	222
Contribution to Attacking Power Average number of minutes between League team goals while on pitch	83	Club Strike Rate Average number of minutes between League goals scored by club	70

	PLAYER	LGE GOALS	POWER	STRIKE RATE
1	Clinton Morrison	12	83	222 mins
2	Shefki Kuqi	7	62	304 mins
3	James Scowcroft	5	83	469 mins
4	Ben Watson	3	73	536 mins

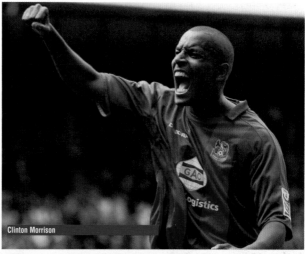

Clinton Morrison

SQUAD APPEARANCES

Match	1 2 3 4 5	6 7 8 9 10	11 12 13 14 15	16 17 18 19 20	21 22 23 24 25	26 27 28 29 30	31 32 33 34 35	36 37 38 39 40	41 42 43 44 45	46 47 48 49
Venue	A H H A H	H A H A H	A H H A H	A A H H A	A H H A H	A A H H A	H H A H A	H A H A H	A A H H A	H A H A
Competition	L L L L L	L L L L L	L L L L L	L L L L W	L L L L L	L L L L W	L L L F L	L F L L L	L L L L L	L L L L
Result	W W W L L	D L L W W	D L L D L	L L L W D	D W L L W	D D W W W	D L D W L	L W W D W	W L L W L	D L W W

Goalkeepers
Scott Flinders
Gabor Kiraly
Julian Speroni
Len Turner

Defenders
Gary Borrowdale
Danny Butterfield
Leon Cort
Danny Granville
Mark Hudson
Matt Lawrence
Darren Ward

Midfielders
Carl Fletcher
Stuart Green
Michael Hughes
Paul Ifill
Mark Kennedy
David Martin
Jobi McAnuff
Marco Reich
Tom Soares
Lewis Spence
Ben Watson

Forwards
Dougie Freedman
Lewis Grabban
Shefki Kuqi
Jonathan Macken
Clinton Morrison
James Scowcroft

KEY: ■ On all match ◄◄ Subbed or sent off (Counting game) ►► Subbed on from bench (Counting Game) ►►► Subbed on and then subbed or sent off (Counting Game) ☐ Not in 16
☐ On bench ◄◄ Subbed or sent off (playing less than 70 minutes) ►► Subbed on (playing less than 70 minutes) ►► Subbed on and then subbed or sent off (playing less than 70 minutes)

CHAMPIONSHIP - CRYSTAL PALACE

CARDIFF CITY

Final Position: **13th**

NICKNAME: THE BLUEBIRDS   KEY: ☐ Won ☐ Drawn ☐ Lost   Attendance

1	div1	Barnsley	A W	**2-1**	Ledley 19, Thompson 22	12,082
2	div1	West Brom	H D	**1-1**	Scimeca 33	18,506
3	div1	Coventry	H W	**1-0**	Chopra 79	13,965
4	div1	Leeds	A W	**1-0**	Flood 83	18,246
5	ccr1	Barnet	H L	**0-2**		3,305
6	div1	Birmingham	H W	**2-0**	Ledley 12, Parry 75	20,109
7	div1	Preston	A L	**1-2**	Chopra 51	12,435
8	div1	Plymouth	A D	**3-3**	Thompson 8, Chopra 29, 49	1,655
9	div1	Luton	H W	**4-1**	Purse 10 pen, Parry 30, Chopra 58, 77	14,108
10	div1	Southend	A W	**3-0**	Purse 10, Scimeca 45, Ledley 65	7,901
11	div1	Wolverhampton	H W	**4-0**	Scimeca 40, Craddock 50 og, Kamara 70, Parry 78	19,915
12	div1	Crystal Palace	A W	**2-1**	Chopra 2, Scimeca 84	18,876
13	div1	Southampton	H W	**1-0**	Thompson 84	19,345
14	div1	Norwich	A L	**0-1**		25,014
15	div1	Derby	H D	**2-2**	Loovens 52, Chopra 74	17,371
16	div1	Sunderland	A W	**2-1**	Chopra 4, 37	26,528
17	div1	Colchester	A L	**1-3**	Chopra 66	5,393
18	div1	Burnley	H W	**1-0**	Scimeca 23	15,744
19	div1	QPR	H L	**0-1**		13,250
20	div1	Sheff Wed	A D	**0-0**		23,935
21	div1	Stoke	A L	**0-3**		15,039
22	div1	Colchester	H D	**0-0**		13,512
23	div1	Ipswich	H D	**2-2**	Purse 3, 66 pen	16,015
24	div1	Hull City	A L	**1-4**	Chopra 55	23,089
25	div1	Leicester	A D	**0-0**		22,274
26	div1	Plymouth	H D	**2-2**	Thompson 47, 52	17,299
27	div1	Crystal Palace	H D	**0-0**		13,704
28	div1	Luton	A D	**0-0**		8,004
29	facr3	Tottenham	H D	**0-0**		20,376
30	div1	Southend	H L	**0-1**		13,822
31	facr3r	Tottenham	A L	**0-4**		27,641
32	div1	Wolverhampton	A W	**2-1**	Chopra 27, Byrne 82	16,772
33	div1	Leicester	H W	**3-2**	Chopra 21, 57, 69	12,057
34	div1	Barnsley	H W	**2-0**	Whittingham 11, Chopra 44	11,549
35	div1	Coventry	A D	**2-2**	Chopra 45 pen, Whittingham 58	17,107
36	div1	Leeds	H W	**1-0**	Chopra 45	16,644
37	div1	West Brom	A L	**0-1**		18,802
38	div1	Preston	H W	**4-1**	Whittingham 44, Chopra 51 pen, 67, Johnson 54	12,889
39	div1	Birmingham	A L	**0-1**		28,223
40	div1	Norwich	H W	**1-0**	Parry 3	13,276
41	div1	Southampton	A D	**2-2**	Thompson 61, Whittingham 85	20,383
42	div1	Derby	A L	**1-3**	Parry 32	27,689
43	div1	Sunderland	H L	**0-1**		19,353
44	div1	Sheff Wed	H L	**1-2**	Johnson 45	13,621
45	div1	Burnley	A L	**0-2**		11,347
46	div1	Stoke	H D	**1-1**	Chopra 90	11,664
47	div1	QPR	A L	**0-1**		12,710
48	div1	Hull City	H L	**0-1**		12,421
49	div1	Ipswich	A L	**1-3**	Parry 37	26,488

LEAGUE APPEARANCES, BOOKINGS AND CAPS

	AGE (on 01/07/07)	IN NAMED 16	APPEARANCES	COUNTING GAMES	MINUTES ON PITCH	LEAGUE GOALS	
Goalkeepers							
Neil Alexander	29	45	39	39	3510	0	0
David Forde	27	19	7	7	630	0	0
Defenders							
James Chambers	26	7	7	7	630	0	2
Kerrea Gilbert	20	25	24	17	1726	0	5
Chris Gunter	17	23	15	9	945	0	1
Roger Johnson	24	46	32	26	2465	2	2
Glenn Loovens	23	32	30	26	2525	1	5
Kevin McNaughton	24	42	42	37	3440	0	3
Darren Purse	30	32	31	30	2717	4	3
Alan Wright	35	9	7	4	519	0	1
Midfielders							
Darcy Blake	18	16	10	3	368	0	1
Kevin Cooper	32	5	4	0	48	0	0
Willo Flood	22	35	25	4	776	1	4
Malvin Kamara	23	20	15	2	490	1	0
Joe Ledley	20	46	46	43	3999	3	3
Stephen McPhail	27	43	43	42	3826	0	4
Paul Parry	26	42	42	38	3472	6	2
Riccardo Scimeca	32	35	35	33	3049	5	1
Simon Walton	19	9	6	5	487	0	2
Peter Whittingham	22	19	19	15	1497	4	3
Forwards							
Jason Byrne	29	11	10	1	229	1	0
Kevin Campbell	37	31	19	2	465	0	0
Michael Chopra	23	42	42	40	3678	22	10
Warren Feeney	26	7	6	3	335	0	0
Andrea Ferretti	20	1	1	0	65	0	0
Luigi Glombard	22	18	6	0	87	0	0
Matthew Green	20	10	6	0	89	0	0
Iwan Redan	26	4	2	0	38	0	0
Steven Thompson	28	43	43	35	3287	6	6

TEAM OF THE SEASON

D Glenn Loovens CG: 26 DR: 120
M Riccardo Scimeca CG: 33 SD: 21
D Kerrea Gilbert CG: 17 DR: 107
M Stephen McPhail CG: 42 SD: 16
F Michael Chopra CG: 40 SR: 167
G Neil Alexander CG: 39 DR: 83
D Darren Purse CG: 30 DR: 77
M Paul Parry CG: 38 SD: 11
F Steven Thompson CG: 35 SR: 547
D Kevin McNaughton CG: 37 DR: 68
M Joe Ledley CG: 43 SD: 4

MONTHLY POINTS TALLY

AUGUST	13	87%
SEPTEMBER	10	67%
OCTOBER	10	67%
NOVEMBER	4	27%
DECEMBER	5	28%
JANUARY	7	58%
FEBRUARY	10	67%
MARCH	4	27%
APRIL	1	7%
MAY	0	0%

LEAGUE GOALS

	PLAYER	MINS	GOALS	S RATE
1	Chopra	3678	22	167
2	Thompson	3287	6	547
3	Parry	3472	6	578
4	Scimeca	3049	5	609
5	Whittingham	1497	4	374
6	Purse	2717	4	679
7	Ledley	3999	3	1333
8	Johnson	2465	2	1232
9	Byrne	229	1	229
10	Kamara	490	1	490
11	Flood	776	1	776
12	Loovens	2525	1	2525
13	McKoy	0	0	
	Other		0	
	TOTAL		**56**	

TOP POINT EARNERS

	PLAYER	GAMES	AV PTS
1	Glenn Loovens	28	1.89
2	Kerrea Gilbert	17	1.88
3	Riccardo Scimeca	33	1.58
4	Michael Chopra	41	1.56
5	Neil Alexander	39	1.54
6	Paul Parry	38	1.50
7	Stephen McPhail	42	1.48
8	Steven Thompson	35	1.40
9	Joe Ledley	43	1.38
10	Peter Whittingham	15	1.33
	CLUB AVERAGE:		**1.39**

DISCIPLINARY RECORDS

	PLAYER	YELLOW	RED	AVE
1	Simon Walton	2	2	121
2	Willo Flood	4	0	258
3	Kerrea Gilbert	5	1	287
4	James Chambers	2	0	315
5	Michael Chopra	10	1	334
6	Glenn Loovens	5	2	360
7	Peter Whittingham	3	0	499
8	Alan Wright	1	0	519
9	Stephen McPhail	4	2	637
10	Steven Thompson	6	0	657
11	Darren Purse	3	1	679
12	Chris Gunter	1	0	945
13	Kevin McNaughton	3	0	1146
	Other	8	0	
	TOTAL	**57**	**9**	

KEY GOALKEEPER

Neil Alexander

Goals Conceded in the League	42	Counting Games League games when player was on pitch for at least 70 minutes	39
Defensive Rating Average number of mins between League goals conceded while on the pitch	83	Clean Sheets In League games when player was on pitch for at least 70 minutes	15

KEY PLAYERS - DEFENDERS

Glenn Loovens

Goals Conceded Number of League goals conceded while the player was on the pitch	21	Clean Sheets In League games when player was on pitch for at least 70 minutes	12
Defensive Rating Average number of mins between League goals conceded while on the pitch	120	Club Defensive Rating Average number of mins between League goals conceded by the club this season	78

	PLAYER	CON LGE	CLEAN SHEETS	DEF RATE
1	Glenn Loovens	21	12	120 mins
2	Kerrea Gilbert	16	7	107 mins
3	Darren Purse	35	11	77 mins
4	Kevin McNaughton	50	11	68 mins

KEY PLAYERS - MIDFIELDERS

Riccardo Scimeca

Goals in the League	5	Contribution to Attacking Power Average number of minutes between League team goals while on pitch	66
Defensive Rating Average number of mins between League goals conceded while on the pitch	87	Scoring Difference Defensive Rating minus Contribution to Attacking Power	21

	PLAYER	LGE GOALS	DEF RATE	POWER	SCORE DIFF
1	Riccardo Scimeca	5	87	66	21 mins
2	Stephen McPhail	0	86	70	16 mins
3	Paul Parry	6	75	64	11 mins
4	Joe Ledley	3	78	74	4 mins

KEY PLAYERS - GOALSCORERS

Michael Chopra

Goals in the League	22	Player Strike Rate Average number of minutes between League goals scored by player	167
Contribution to Attacking Power Average number of minutes between League team goals while on pitch	65	Club Strike Rate Average number of minutes between League goals scored by club	72

	PLAYER	LGE GOALS	POWER	STRIKE RATE
1	Michael Chopra	22	65	167 mins
2	Peter Whittingham	4	74	374 mins
3	Steven Thompson	6	68	547 mins
4	Paul Parry	6	64	578 mins

Michael Chopra

SQUAD APPEARANCES

Match	1	2	3	4	5	6	7	8	9	10	11	12	13	14	15	16	17	18	19	20	21	22	23	24	25	26	27	28	29	30	31	32	33	34	35	36	37	38	39	40	41	42	43	44	45	46	47	48	49
Venue	A	H	H	A	H	H	A	A	H	A	H	A	H	A	H	A	A	H	H	A	A	H	H	A	A	H	H	H	H	A	H	H	H	A	H	A	A	H	H	A	A	H	H	H	A	H	A	H	A
Competition	L	L	L	W	L	L	L	L	L	L	L	L	L	L	L	L	L	L	L	L	L	L	L	L	L	L	L	L	L	F	L	L	L	F	L	F	L	L	L	L	L	L	L	L	L	L	L	L	L
Result	W	D	W	W	L	W	L	D	W	W	W	W	W	L	D	W	L	W	L	D	L	D	D	L	D	D	D	D	D	L	L	W	W	W	D	W	L	W	L	W	D	L	L	L	L	D	L	L	L

Goalkeepers

Neil Alexander
David Forde
Mark Howard

Defenders

James Chambers
Kerrea Gilbert
Chris Gunter
Joe Jacobson
Roger Johnson
Glenn Loovens
Kevin McNaughton
Darren Purse
Rhys Weston
Ian Wright

Midfielders

Darcy Blake
Kevin Cooper
Michael Corcoran
Willo Flood
Malvin Kamara
Joe Ledley
Mark McKoy
Stephen McPhail
Paul Parry
Aaron Ramsey
Riccardo Scimeca
Simon Walton
Jeff Whitley
Peter Whittingham

Forwards

Jason Byrne
Kevin Campbell
Michael Chopra
Warren Feeney
Andrea Ferretti
Luigi Glombard
Matthew Green
Ian Redan
Steven Thompson

KEY: ■ On all match ◄◄ Subbed or sent off (Counting game) ►► Subbed on from bench (Counting Game) ►► Subbed on and then subbed or sent off (Counting Game) ☐ Not in 16
■ On bench ◄◄ Subbed or sent off (playing less than 70 minutes) ►► Subbed on (playing less than 70 minutes) ►► Subbed on and then subbed or sent off (playing less than 70 minutes)

IPSWICH TOWN

Final Position: **14th**

NICKNAME: TRACTOR BOYS KEY: ☐ Won ☐ Drawn ☐ Lost Attendance

							Attendance
1	div1	Crystal Palace	H	L	1-2	Forster 30	25,413
2	div1	Wolverhampton	A	L	0-1		19,199
3	div1	Leicester	A	L	1-3	Richards 85	18,820
4	div1	Hull City	H	D	0-0		19,790
5	ccr1	Peterborough	A	L	2-4*	De Vos 90, Clarke 105 (*on penalties)	4,792
6	div1	QPR	A	W	3-1	Walton 61 pen, De Vos 67, Bowditch 86	10,918
7	div1	Southampton	H	W	2-1	Walton 67 pen, Clarke 78	21,422
8	div1	Coventry	H	W	2-1	Noble 51, Clarke 85	19,465
9	div1	Birmingham	A	D	2-2	Krause 48, Walton 78	20,841
10	div1	Sunderland	H	W	3-1	Currie 32, Lee 63, 66	23,311
11	div1	Colchester	A	L	0-1		6,065
12	div1	West Brom	H	L	1-5	Perry 36 og	22,581
13	div1	Preston	H	L	2-3	Macken 10 pen, Lee 37	19,337
14	div1	Southend	A	W	3-0	Clarke 30, Legwinski 47, Lee 50	11,415
15	div1	Luton	H	W	5-0	Legwinski 19, Peters 54, Lee 65, 75, 89 pen	20,975
16	div1	Plymouth	A	D	1-1	Legwinski 1	12,210
17	div1	Burnley	A	L	0-1		11,709
18	div1	Sheff Wed	H	L	0-2		21,830
19	div1	Norwich	H	W	3-1	Legwinski 40, Haynes 77, 90	27,276
20	div1	Barnsley	A	L	0-1		10,556
21	div1	Derby	A	L	1-2	Roberts 39	22,606
22	div1	Burnley	H	D	1-1	Lee 90 pen	20,254
23	div1	Cardiff	A	D	2-2	Macken 48, 73 pen	16,015
24	div1	Leeds	H	W	1-0	Williams 45	23,661
25	div1	Stoke	H	L	0-1		20,369
26	div1	Coventry	A	W	2-1	Macken 62, Lee 85	22,154
27	div1	West Brom	A	L	0-2		20,328
28	div1	Birmingham	H	W	1-0	Williams 90	22,436
29	facr3	Chester	A	D	0-0		4,330
30	div1	Sunderland	A	L	0-1		27,604
31	facr3r	Chester	H	W	1-0	Richards 84	11,732
32	div1	Colchester	H	W	3-2	Lee 30 pen, Legwinski 56, Haynes 82	28,355
33	facr4	Swansea	H	W	1-0	Lee 64 pen	16,635
34	div1	Stoke	A	D	0-0		11,812
35	div1	Crystal Palace	A	L	0-2		17,090
36	div1	Leicester	H	L	0-2		21,221
37	facr5	Watford	A	L	0-1		17,016
38	div1	Wolverhampton	H	L	0-1		20,602
39	div1	Southampton	A	L	0-1		27,974
40	div1	QPR	H	W	2-1	Lee 26, Walters 54	21,412
41	div1	Hull City	A	W	5-2	Jeffers 23, Peters 41, Lee 49, De Vos 62, Haynes 81	18,056
42	div1	Southend	H	L	0-2		24,051
43	div1	Preston	A	L	0-1		13,100
44	div1	Luton	A	W	2-0	Lee 39, Richards 62	8,880
45	div1	Plymouth	H	W	3-0	Garvan 9, Lee 15, Haynes 90	21,078
46	div1	Barnsley	H	W	5-1	Roberts 2, O'Callaghan 43, Haynes 82, Jeffers 86, Walters 90	20,585
47	div1	Sheff Wed	A	L	0-2		23,232
48	div1	Derby	H	W	2-1	Jeffers 69, Haynes 88 pen	24,319
49	div1	Norwich	A	D	1-1	Wright 61	25,476
50	div1	Leeds	A	D	1-1	Lee 88	31,269
51	div1	Cardiff	H	W	3-1	Jeffers 4, Walters 68, 79	26,488

LEAGUE APPEARANCES, BOOKINGS AND CAPS

	AGE (on 01/07/07)	IN NAMED 16	APPEARANCES	COUNTING GAMES	MINUTES ON PITCH	LEAGUE GOALS	
Goalkeepers							
Lewis Price	22	41	34	33	2977	0	0
Shane Supple	20	45	12	12	1073	0	0
Defenders							
Matthew Bates	20	2	2	1	155	0	0
Alex Bruce	22	43	41	37	3507	0	12
Jason De Vos	33	39	39	39	3489	2	3
Dan Harding	23	42	42	38	3578	0	11
Richard Naylor	30	28	25	21	1952	0	5
Luis Castro Sito	27	13	7	5	497	0	3
Fabian Wilnis	36	26	22	18	1734	0	2
David Wright	27	19	19	19	1709	1	1
Midfielders							
Darren Currie	32	18	13	5	635	1	2
Owen Garvan	19	28	27	23	2135	1	6
Danny Haynes	19	35	31	2	817	7	3
Sylvain Legwinski	33	32	32	28	2706	5	6
Mark Noble	20	13	13	11	1045	1	5
George O'Callaghan	27	16	11	3	419	1	2
Jamie Peters	20	29	23	17	1672	2	0
Matthew Richards	22	35	28	14	1761	2	0
Gary Roberts	20	34	33	25	2509	2	7
Simon Walton	19	21	19	12	1184	3	7
Gavin Williams	26	30	29	20	2194	2	9
Forwards							
Dean Bowditch	21	10	9	1	271	1	0
Billy Clarke	19	31	27	6	1036	3	5
Nick Forster	33	4	4	3	315	1	0
Francis Jeffers	26	9	9	4	552	4	1
Alan Lee	28	42	41	33	3271	15	11
Jonathan Macken	29	19	14	9	1000	4	1
Jonathan Walters	23	16	16	10	1045	4	0

TEAM OF THE SEASON

D David Wright CG: 19 DR: 81
M Gavin Williams CG: 20 SD: 19
D Fabian Wilnis CG: 18 DR: 78
M Jamie Peters CG: 17 SD: 13
F Alan Lee CG: 33 SR: 218
G Shane Supple CG: 12 DR: 71
D Jason De Vos CG: 39 DR: 69
M Simon Walton CG: 12 SD: 13
F Jonathan Walters* CG: 10 SR: 261
D Alex Bruce CG: 37 DR: 68
M Matthew Richards CG: 14 SD: 7

MONTHLY POINTS TALLY

AUGUST	4	27%
SEPTEMBER	10	67%
OCTOBER	7	47%
NOVEMBER	3	20%
DECEMBER	8	44%
JANUARY	7	58%
FEBRUARY	0	0%
MARCH	12	67%
APRIL	8	53%
MAY	3	100%

LEAGUE GOALS

	PLAYER	MINS	GOALS	S RATE
1	Lee	3271	15	218
2	Haynes	817	7	116
3	Legwinski	2706	5	541
4	Jeffers	552	4	138
5	Macken	1000	4	250
6	Walters	1045	4	261
7	Clarke	1036	3	345
8	Walton	1184	3	394
9	Peters	1672	2	836
10	Richards	1761	2	880
11	Williams	2194	2	1097
12	Roberts, G	2509	2	1254
13	De Vos	3489	2	1744
	Other		7	
	TOTAL		**62**	

TOP POINT EARNERS

	PLAYER	GAMES	AV PTS
1	Gavin Williams	20	1.70
2	Fabian Wilnis	18	1.61
3	Alan Lee	33	1.52
4	Alex Bruce	38	1.50
5	Jamie Peters	17	1.47
6	Gary Roberts	24	1.46
7	Matthew Richards	14	1.43
8	David Wright	19	1.42
9	Owen Garvan	23	1.39
10	Simon Walton	13	1.38
	CLUB AVERAGE:		**1.35**

DISCIPLINARY RECORDS

	PLAYER	YELLOW	RED	AV
1	Simon Walton	7	1	14
2	Mark Noble	5	0	20
3	Gavin Williams	9	0	243
4	Billy Clarke	5	0	25
5	Alan Lee	11	1	29
6	Owen Garvan	6	1	30
7	Darren Currie	2	0	31
8	Alex Bruce	12	1	31
9	Dan Harding	11	0	35
10	Danny Haynes	3	0	40
11	Gary Roberts	7	0	41
12	Sylvain Legwinski	5	0	45
13	Richard Naylor	5	0	48
	Other	10	2	
	TOTAL	**99**	**6**	

KEY GOALKEEPER

Shane Supple

Goals Conceded in the League	15	Counting Games League games when player was on pitch for at least 70 minutes	12
Defensive Rating Ave number of mins between League goals conceded while on the pitch	71	Clean Sheets In League games when player was on pitch for at least 70 minutes	1

KEY PLAYERS - DEFENDERS

David Wright

Goals Conceded Number of League goals conceded while the player was on the pitch	21	Clean Sheets In League games when player was on pitch for at least 70 minutes	3
Defensive Rating Ave number of mins between League goals conceded while on the pitch	81	Club Defensive Rating Average number of mins between League goals conceded by the club this season	70

	PLAYER	CON LGE	CLEAN SHEETS	DEF RATE
1	David Wright	21	3	81 mins
2	Fabian Wilnis	22	4	78 mins
3	Jason De Vos	50	6	69 mins
4	Alex Bruce	51	6	68 mins

KEY PLAYERS - MIDFIELDERS

Gavin Williams

Goals in the League	2	Contribution to Attacking Power Average number of minutes between League team goals while on pitch	68
Defensive Rating Average number of mins between League goals conceded while on the pitch	87	Scoring Difference Defensive Rating minus Contribution to Attacking Power	19

	PLAYER	LGE GOALS	DEF RATE	POWER	SCORE DIFF
1	Gavin Williams	2	87	68	19 mins
2	Jamie Peters	2	66	53	13 mins
3	Simon Walton	3	69	56	13 mins
4	Matthew Richards	2	65	58	7 mins

KEY PLAYERS - GOALSCORERS

Alan Lee

Goals in the League	15	Player Strike Rate Average number of minutes between League goals scored by player	218
Contribution to Attacking Power Average number of minutes between League team goals while on pitch	64	Club Strike Rate Average number of minutes between League goals scored by club	64

	PLAYER	LGE GOALS	POWER	STRIKE RATE
1	Alan Lee	15	64	218 mins
2	Simon Walton	3	56	394 mins
3	Sylvain Legwinski	5	71	541 mins
4	Jamie Peters	2	53	836 mins

Jason De Vos

SQUAD APPEARANCES

CHAMPIONSHIP - IPSWICH TOWN

BURNLEY

Final Position: **15th**

NICKNAME: THE CLARETS   KEY: ☐ Won ☐ Drawn ☐ Lost   Attendance

#		Opponent			Score	Scorers	Attendance
1	div1	QPR	H	W	2-0	Jones 59, 69	12,190
2	div1	Leicester	A	W	1-0	Gray 45	19,035
3	div1	Sheff Wed	A	D	1-1	J.O'Connor 82	22,425
4	div1	Wolverhampton	H	L	0-1		12,245
5	ccr1	Hartlepool	H	L	0-1		3,853
6	div1	Crystal Palace	A	D	2-2	Mahon 23, Lafferty 52	16,396
7	div1	Colchester	H	L	1-2	Gray 88	1,039
8	div1	Barnsley	H	W	4-2	Harley 42, Noel-Williams 57, 83, 90	10,304
9	div1	Stoke	A	W	1-0	Gray 1	12,247
10	div1	Southampton	H	L	2-3	Jones 4, Gray 33	13,051
11	div1	Norwich	A	W	4-1	J.O'Connor 32, Gray 45, 64, Mahon 89	24,717
12	div1	Hull City	H	W	2-0	Duff 10, Noel-Williams 13	11,530
13	div1	Southend	H	D	0-0		10,461
14	div1	Plymouth	A	D	0-0		12,817
15	div1	Preston	H	W	3-2	J.O'Connor 44, St Ledger 81 og, Gray 89	14,871
16	div1	Luton	A	W	2-0	Gray 31, 36	7,664
17	div1	Ipswich	H	W	1-0	McCann 90	11,709
18	div1	Cardiff	A	L	0-1		15,744
19	div1	West Brom	A	L	0-3		18,707
20	div1	Birmingham	H	L	1-2	McCann 4	12,889
21	div1	Leeds	H	W	2-1	Noel-Williams 67, Gray 69	15,061
22	div1	Ipswich	A	D	1-1	Lafferty 86	20,254
23	div1	Coventry	A	L	0-1		18,362
24	div1	Sunderland	H	D	2-2	Lafferty 9, 52	14,798
25	div1	Derby	H	D	0-0		12,825
26	div1	Barnsley	A	L	0-1		12,842
27	div1	Hull City	A	L	0-2		17,731
28	facr3	Reading	A	L	2-3	Akinbiyi 69, G.O'Connor 90	11,514
29	div1	Southampton	A	D	0-0		20,486
30	div1	Stoke	H	L	0-1		12,109
31	div1	Derby	A	L	0-1		23,122
32	div1	QPR	H	L	1-3	McCann 18	10,811
33	div1	Sheff Wed	H	D	1-1	Elliott 55	12,745
34	div1	Wolverhampton	A	L	1-2	McCann 53	19,521
35	div1	Leicester	H	L	0-1		10,274
36	div1	Colchester	A	D	0-0		4,934
37	div1	Crystal Palace	H	D	1-1	Akinbiyi 38	10,659
38	div1	Southend	A	L	0-1		8,855
39	div1	Preston	A	L	0-2		17,666
40	div1	Luton	H	D	0-0		11,088
41	div1	Plymouth	H	W	4-0	Duff 13, McVeigh 20, Jones 38, Elliott 61	9,793
42	div1	Birmingham	A	W	1-0	Spicer 80	28,777
43	div1	Cardiff	H	W	2-0	Jones 4, 48	11,347
44	div1	Leeds	A	L	0-1		23,528
45	div1	Norwich	H	W	3-0	Akinbiyi 30, Gray 86, Elliott 89	9,681
46	div1	West Brom	H	W	3-2	Gray 15, 48, McCann 87	12,500
47	div1	Sunderland	A	L	2-3	Gray 38 pen, Elliott 50	44,448
48	div1	Coventry	H	L	1-2	McVeigh 62	12,830

LEAGUE APPEARANCES, BOOKINGS AND CAPS

	AGE (on 01/07/07)	IN NAMED 16	APPEARANCES	COUNTING GAMES	MINUTES ON PITCH	LEAGUE GOALS
Goalkeepers						
Danny Coyne	33	29	12	11	1007	0	0
Brian Jensen	32	34	31	31	2773	0	0
Mike Pollitt	35	4	4	4	360	0	0
Defenders						
Stephen Caldwell	26	17	17	15	1421	0	5
Graham Coughlan	32	9	2	1	93	0	0
Mike Duff	28	46	44	42	3864	2	9
Stephen Foster	26	33	17	5	749	0	2
Jon Harley	27	45	45	43	3901	1	11
John McGreal	35	26	22	18	1775	0	3
Frank Sinclair	35	22	19	15	1464	0	5
Wayne Thomas	28	36	33	30	2787	0	4
Midfielders						
Graham Branch	35	11	5	0	97	0	1
Eric Djemba-Djemba	26	19	15	12	1179	0	3
Wade Elliott	28	45	42	34	3176	4	8
Johannes Gudjonsson	27	12	11	6	744	0	5
Micah Hyde	32	24	23	17	1728	0	7
Alan Mahon	29	28	25	6	980	2	1
Christopher McCann	19	44	38	21	2206	5	3
Paul McVeigh	29	8	8	5	562	2	0
Gareth O'Connor	28	21	8	0	74	0	0
James O'Connor	27	43	43	36	3395	3	10
John Spicer	23	20	11	0	153	1	0
Forwards						
Ade Akinbiyi	32	20	20	13	1315	2	0
Andy Gray	29	35	35	34	3055	14	5
Steve Jones	30	43	41	34	3180	6	1
Kyle Lafferty	19	38	35	13	1678	4	4
Gifton Noel-Williams	27	24	23	17	1714	5	1

TEAM OF THE SEASON

G Brian Jensen   CG: 31   DR: 89

D Stephen Caldwell   CG: 15   DR: 88
D Frank Sinclair   CG: 15   DR: 86
D Mike Duff   CG: 42   DR: 84
D Wayne Thomas   CG: 30   DR: 84

M Wade Elliott   CG: 34   SD: 25
M Eric Djemba-Djemba   CG: 12   SD: 25
M Micah Hyde   CG: 17   SD: 21
M James O'Connor   CG: 36   SD: 6

F Andy Gray   CG: 34   SR: 218
F G Noel-Williams   CG: 17   SR: 342

MONTHLY POINTS TALLY

Month		Points	%
AUGUST		8	53%
SEPTEMBER		6	50%
OCTOBER		14	78%
NOVEMBER		6	40%
DECEMBER		3	17%
JANUARY		1	11%
FEBRUARY		2	13%
MARCH		2	17%
APRIL		15	71%
MAY		0	0%

LEAGUE GOALS

	PLAYER	MINS	GOALS	S RATE
1	Gray	3055	14	218
2	Jones	3180	6	530
3	Noel-Williams	1714	5	342
4	McCann	2206	5	441
5	Lafferty	1678	4	419
6	Elliott	3176	4	794
7	O'Connor, J	3395	3	1131
8	McVeigh	562	2	281
9	Mahon	980	2	490
10	Akinbiyi	1315	2	657
11	Duff	3864	2	1932
12	Spicer	153	1	153
13	Harley	3901	1	3901
	Other		0	
	TOTAL		**51**	

TOP POINT EARNERS

	PLAYER	GAMES	AV PTS
1	Micah Hyde	17	1.71
2	Frank Sinclair	15	1.67
3	Steve Jones	32	1.66
4	Wade Elliott	34	1.61
5	Andy Gray	34	1.56
6	Brian Jensen	31	1.55
7	Eric Djemba-Djemba	12	1.42
8	Mike Duff	42	1.31
9	Jon Harley	42	1.31
10	Gifton Noel-Williams	17	1.29
	CLUB AVERAGE:		**1.24**

DISCIPLINARY RECORDS

	PLAYER	YELLOW	RED	AV
1	J Gudjonsson	5	0	14
2	Micah Hyde	7	1	21
3	Frank Sinclair	5	1	24
4	Stephen Foster	2	1	24
5	Stephen Caldwell	5	0	28
6	E Djemba-Djemba	3	1	29
7	James O'Connor	10	0	33
8	Jon Harley	11	0	35
9	Wade Elliott	8	0	39
10	Kyle Lafferty	4	0	41
11	Mike Duff	9	0	42
12	Andy Gray	5	1	50
13	Wayne Thomas	4	2	55
	Other	9	0	
	TOTAL	**87**	**7**	

KEY GOALKEEPER

Brian Jensen

Goals Conceded in the League	31	Counting Games League games when player was on pitch for at least 70 minutes		31
Defensive Rating Ave number of mins between League goals conceded while on the pitch	89	Clean Sheets In League games when player was on pitch for at least 70 minutes		14

KEY PLAYERS - DEFENDERS

Stephen Caldwell

Goals Conceded Number of League goals conceded while the player was on the pitch	16	Clean Sheets In League games when player was on pitch for at least 70 minutes	6
Defensive Rating Ave number of mins between League goals conceded while on the pitch	88	Club Defensive Rating Average number of mins between League goals conceded by the club this season	88

	PLAYER	CON LGE	CLEAN SHEETS	DEF RATE
1	Stephen Caldwell	16	6	88 mins
2	Frank Sinclair	17	7	86 mins
3	Mike Duff	46	14	84 mins
4	Wayne Thomas	33	10	84 mins

KEY PLAYERS - MIDFIELDERS

Wade Elliott

Goals in the League	4	Contribution to Attacking Power Average number of minutes between League team goals while on pitch	77
Defensive Rating Average number of mins between League goals conceded while on the pitch	102	Scoring Difference Defensive Rating minus Contribution to Attacking Power	25

	PLAYER	LGE GOALS	DEF RATE	POWER	SCORE DIFF
1	Wade Elliott	4	102	77	25 mins
2	Eric Djemba-Djemba	0	98	73	25 mins
3	Micah Hyde	0	82	61	21 mins
4	James O'Connor	3	84	78	6 mins

KEY PLAYERS - GOALSCORERS

Andy Gray

Goals in the League	14	Player Strike Rate Average number of minutes between League goals scored by player	218
Contribution to Attacking Power Average number of minutes between League team goals while on pitch	63	Club Strike Rate Average number of minutes between League goals scored by club	83

	PLAYER	LGE GOALS	POWER	STRIKE RATE
1	Andy Gray	14	63	218 mins
2	Gifton Noel-Williams	5	85	342 mins
3	Kyle Lafferty	4	98	419 mins
4	Christopher McCann	5	110	441 mins

Andy Gray

SQUAD APPEARANCES

Match	1 2 3 4 5	6 7 8 9 10	11 12 13 14 15	16 17 18 19 20	21 22 23 24 25	26 27 28 29 30	31 32 33 34 35	36 37 38 39 40	41 42 43 44 45	46 47 48
Venue	H A A H H	A H H A H	A H H A H	A H A A H	H A A H H	A A A A H	A A H A H	A H A A H	H A H A H	H A H
Competition	L L L L W	L L L L L	L L L L L	L L L L L	L L L L L	L L F L L	L L L L L	L L L L L	L L L L L	L L L
Result	W W D L L	D L W W L	W W D D W	W W L L L	W D L D D	L L L D L	L L D L L	D D L L D	W W W L W	W L L

Goalkeepers
Danny Coyne
Brian Jensen
Mike Pollitt

Defenders
Stephen Caldwell
Graham Coughlan
Mike Duff
Stephen Foster
Jon Harley
John McGreal
Frank Sinclair
Wayne Thomas

Midfielders
Graham Branch
Eric Djemba-Djemba
Wade Elliott
Johannes Gudjonsson
Micah Hyde
Alan Mahon
Christopher McCann
Paul McVeigh
Gareth O'Connor
James O'Connor
John Spicer

Forwards
Ade Akinbiyi
Andy Gray
Steve Jones
Kyle Lafferty
Gifton Noel-Williams

KEY: ■ On all match ◄◄ Subbed or sent off (Counting game) ▸▸ Subbed on from bench (Counting Game) ▸ Subbed on and then subbed or sent off (Counting Game) ▫ Not in 16
■ On bench ◄ Subbed or sent off (playing less than 70 minutes) ▸ Subbed on (playing less than 70 minutes) ▸ Subbed on and then subbed or sent off (playing less than 70 minutes)

CHAMPIONSHIP - BURNLEY

NORWICH

Final Position: **16th**

NICKNAME: THE CANARIES   KEY: ☐ Won ☐ Drawn ☐ Lost

#	Comp	Opponent		Result	Scorers	Attendance
1	div1	Leeds	A L	0-1		22,417
2	div1	Preston	H W	2-0	St Ledger 56 og, Earnshaw 82	24,676
3	div1	Luton	H W	3-2	Huckerby 57, Croft 67, Earnshaw 71	23,863
4	div1	Derby	A D	0-0		22,196
5	ccr1	Torquay	A W	2-0	McKenzie 48, Etuhu 64	3,100
6	div1	Barnsley	H W	5-1	Earnshaw 13 pen, 69, Robinson 27, Croft 57, Huckerby 64	24,876
7	div1	Coventry	A L	0-3		20,006
8	div1	Southend	A D	3-3	Earnshaw 34, 39, Etuhu 47	11,072
9	div1	Crystal Palace	H L	0-1		24,618
10	ccr2	Rotherham	A W	4-2	Thorne 6, Ryan.Jarvis 53, 90, Fleming 54	3,958
11	div1	Plymouth	A L	1-3	Earnshaw 90	11,813
12	div1	Burnley	H L	1-4	Earnshaw 82	24,717
13	div1	QPR	A D	3-3	Huckerby 4, Dublin 72, Earnshaw 84	14,793
14	div1	Birmingham	A W	1-0	Shackell 66	20,537
15	div1	Cardiff	H W	1-0	Etuhu 7	25,014
16	ccr3	Port Vale	A L	2-3*	(*on penalties)	4,518
17	div1	Stoke	A L	0-5		13,444
18	div1	Colchester	H D	1-1	Etuhu 72	25,065
19	div1	Sunderland	H W	1-0	Earnshaw 51	24,652
20	div1	West Brom	H W	1-0	Earnshaw 57	18,718
21	div1	Ipswich	A L	1-3	Chadwick 26	27,276
22	div1	Hull City	H D	1-1	Earnshaw 72	24,129
23	div1	Leicester	H W	3-1	Robinson 45, Earnshaw 59, McAuley 90 og	23,896
24	div1	Sunderland	A L	0-1		27,934
25	div1	Sheff Wed	H L	1-2	Dublin 85	24,816
26	div1	Southampton	A L	1-2	Earnshaw 21	25,919
27	div1	Wolverhampton	A D	2-2	Earnshaw 10, 77	22,910
28	div1	Southend	H D	0-0		25,433
29	div1	QPR	H W	1-0	Dublin 69	25,113
30	div1	Crystal Palace	A L	1-3	Earnshaw 45 pen	16,765
31	facr3	Tamworth	A W	4-1	Dublin 40, 62, Huckerby 42, 51	3,165
32	div1	Plymouth	H L	1-3	Safri 45	23,513
33	facr4	Blackpool	A D	1-1	Huckerby 45	9,491
34	div1	Wolverhampton	H L	0-1		23,311
35	div1	Leeds	H W	2-1	Dublin 59, Huckerby 78	25,018
36	facr4r	Blackpool	H W	3-2	Huckerby 78, 95, Martin 112	19,120
37	facr5	Chelsea	A L	0-4		41,537
38	div1	Preston	A L	1-2	Shackell 62	11,601
39	div1	Coventry	H D	1-1	Martin 81	24,220
40	div1	Luton	A W	3-2	Martin 26, Shackell 73, Lappin 90 fk	8,868
41	div1	Barnsley	A W	3-1	Huckerby 7, Croft 26, Martin 41	11,010
42	div1	Derby	H L	1-2	Martin 52	23,462
43	div1	Cardiff	A L	0-1		13,276
44	div1	Birmingham	H W	1-0	Huckerby 47	23,504
45	div1	Stoke	H W	1-0	Huckerby 31	24,293
46	div1	Colchester	A L	0-3		5,851
47	div1	Hull City	A W	2-0	Huckerby 39, Etuhu 55	19,053
48	div1	West Brom	H L	1-2	Etuhu 58	25,422
49	div1	Leicester	A W	2-1	Earnshaw 74 pen, Maybury 78 og	21,483
50	div1	Burnley	A L	0-3		9,681
51	div1	Ipswich	H D	1-1	Etuhu 72	25,476
52	div1	Southampton	H L	0-1		25,437
53	div1	Sheff Wed	A L	2-3	Earnshaw 56, Dublin 75	28,287

LEAGUE APPEARANCES, BOOKINGS AND CAPS

	AGE (on 01/07/07)	IN NAMED 16	APPEARANCES	COUNTING GAMES	MINUTES ON PITCH	LEAGUE GOALS		
Goalkeepers								
Jamie Ashdown	26	5	2	2	161	0	0	1
Lee Camp	22	11	3	3	270	0	0	0
Paul Gallacher	27	41	27	26	2358	0	1	0
David Marshall	22	2	2	2	180	0	1	0
Tony Warner	33	13	13	13	1170	0	1	0
Defenders								
Patrick Boyle	20	3	3	2	225	0	0	0
Jurgen Colin	26	39	33	28	2657	0	5	0
Gary Doherty	27	34	34	32	2983	0	3	1
Adam Drury	28	39	39	34	3192	0	7	0
Craig Fleming	35	18	10	3	444	1	1	0
Jason Shackell	23	43	43	41	3759	3	7	0
Midfielders								
Lee Croft	22	36	36	27	2688	3	6	0
Robert Eagle	20	19	10	2	358	0	1	0
Dickson Etuhu	25	43	43	40	3729	6	8	0
Mark Fotheringham	23	15	14	10	942	0	4	0
Andrew Hughes	29	41	36	25	2534	0	5	0
Simon Lappin	24	14	14	14	1240	1	1	0
Paul McVeigh	29	35	20	5	709	0	0	1
Carl Robinson	30	27	27	23	2173	2	6	0
Youssef Safri	30	37	35	29	2729	1	7	0
Michael Spillane	18	10	5	3	334	0	0	0
Forwards								
Chris Brown	22	4	4	2	233	0	1	1
Dion Dublin	38	34	33	20	2154	5	3	0
Robert Earnshaw	26	30	30	28	2542	19	1	0
Darren Huckerby	31	41	41	39	3605	8	10	0
Chris Martin	18	19	18	12	1209	4	1	0
Leon McKenzie	29	4	4	0	55	1	1	0
Peter Thorne	34	22	15	3	551	1	0	0

TEAM OF THE SEASON

D Jason Shackell CG: 41 DR: 60
M Youssef Safri CG: 29 SD: -1
D Adam Drury CG: 34 DR: 58
M Simon Lappin CG: 14 SD: -6
F Robert Earnshaw CG: 28 SR: 133
G Tony Warner CG: 13 DR: 61
D Gary Doherty CG: 32 DR: 58
M Lee Croft CG: 27 SD: -8
F Chris Martin CG: 12 SR: 302
D Jurgen Colin CG: 28 DR: 57
M Dickson Etuhu CG: 40 SD: -14

MONTHLY POINTS TALLY

AUGUST	10	67%
SEPTEMBER	1	8%
OCTOBER	8	44%
NOVEMBER	10	67%
DECEMBER	5	28%
JANUARY	0	0%
FEBRUARY	7	58%
MARCH	9	50%
APRIL	7	39%
MAY	0	0%

LEAGUE GOALS

	PLAYER	MINS	GOALS	S RATE
1	Earnshaw	2542	19	133
2	Huckerby	3605	8	450
3	Etuhu	3729	6	621
4	Dublin	2154	5	430
5	Martin	1209	4	302
6	Croft	2688	3	896
7	Shackell	3759	3	1253
8	Robinson	2173	2	1086
9	Chadwick	129	1	129
10	Lappin	1240	1	1240
11	Safri	2729	1	2729
12	Lewis	0	0	
13	Marshall	180	0	
	Other		0	
	TOTAL		**53**	

TOP POINT EARNERS

	PLAYER	GAMES	AV PTS
1	Youssef Safri	29	1.68
2	Lee Croft	27	1.54
3	Darren Huckerby	39	1.36
4	Simon Lappin	14	1.36
5	Chris Martin	12	1.33
6	Jason Shackell	41	1.32
7	Jurgen Colin	28	1.29
8	Dickson Etuhu	40	1.28
9	Dion Dublin	20	1.25
10	Robert Earnshaw	28	1.25
	CLUB AVERAGE:		**1.24**

DISCIPLINARY RECORDS

	PLAYER	YELLOW	RED	AVE
1	Mark Fotheringham	4	0	314
2	Lee Croft	6	0	448
3	Darren Huckerby	10	0	450
4	Youssef Safri	7	0	454
5	Adam Drury	7	0	456
6	Jason Shackell	7	0	537
7	Carl Robinson	6	0	543
8	Dickson Etuhu	6	0	621
9	Andrew Hughes	5	0	633
10	Paul McVeigh	0	1	709
11	Dion Dublin	3	0	718
12	Gary Doherty	3	1	994
13	Tony Warner	1	0	1170
	Other	9	0	
	TOTAL	**76**	**2**	

KEY GOALKEEPER

Tony Warner

Goals Conceded in the League	19	Counting Games League games when player was on pitch for at least 70 minutes	13
Defensive Rating Ave number of mins between League goals conceded while on the pitch	61	Clean Sheets In League games when player was on pitch for at least 70 minutes	2

KEY PLAYERS - DEFENDERS

Jason Shackell

Goals Conceded Number of League goals conceded while the player was on the pitch	62	Clean Sheets In League games when player was on pitch for at least 70 minutes	10
Defensive Rating Ave number of mins between League goals conceded while on the pitch	60	Club Defensive Rating Average number of mins between League goals conceded by the club this season	60

	PLAYER	CON LGE	CLEAN SHEETS	DEF RATE
1	Jason Shackell	62	10	60 mins
2	Adam Drury	55	7	58 mins
3	Gary Doherty	51	8	58 mins
4	Jurgen Colin	46	8	57 mins

KEY PLAYERS - MIDFIELDERS

Youssef Safri

Goals in the League	1	Contribution to Attacking Power Average number of minutes between League team goals while on pitch	69
Defensive Rating Average number of mins between League goals conceded while on the pitch	68	Scoring Difference Defensive Rating minus Contribution to Attacking Power	-1

	PLAYER	LGE GOALS	DEF RATE	POWER	SCORE DIFF
1	Youssef Safri	1	68	69	-1 mins
2	Simon Lappin	1	62	68	-6 mins
3	Lee Croft	3	62	70	-8 mins
4	Dickson Etuhu	6	62	76	-14 mins

KEY PLAYERS - GOALSCORERS

Robert Earnshaw

Goals in the League	19	Player Strike Rate Average number of minutes between League goals scored by player	133
Contribution to Attacking Power Average number of minutes between League team goals while on pitch	66	Club Strike Rate Average number of minutes between League goals scored by club	77

	PLAYER	LGE GOALS	POWER	STRIKE RATE
1	Robert Earnshaw	19	66	133 mins
2	Chris Martin	4	71	302 mins
3	Dion Dublin	5	82	430 mins
4	Darren Huckerby	8	72	450 mins

Robert Earnshaw

SQUAD APPEARANCES

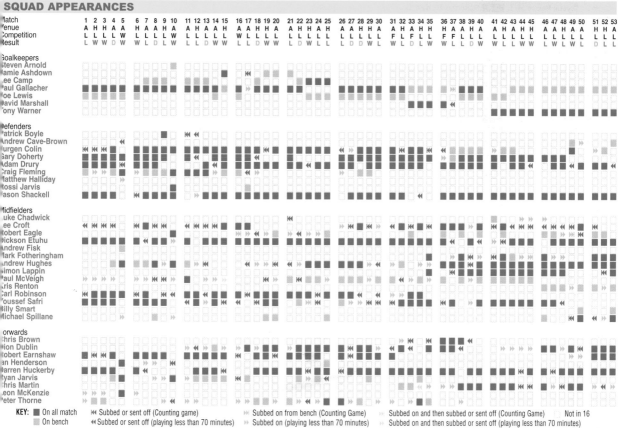

KEY: ■ On all match   ◄◄ Subbed or sent off (Counting game)   ►► Subbed on from bench (Counting Game)   ►► Subbed on and then subbed or sent off (Counting Game)   ☐ Not in 16
  ☐ On bench   ◄◄ Subbed or sent off (playing less than 70 minutes)   ►► Subbed on (playing less than 70 minutes)   ►► Subbed on and then subbed or sent off (playing less than 70 minutes)

COVENTRY CITY

Final Position: **17th**

NICKNAME: THE SKY BLUES KEY: ☐ Won ☐ Drawn ☐ Lost Attendance

#	comp	Opponent			Score	Scorers	Attendance
1	div1	Sunderland	H	W	2-1	John 72, McSheffrey 78	22,366
2	div1	Southampton	A	L	0-2		21,088
3	div1	Cardiff	A	L	0-1		13,965
4	div1	Leicester	H	D	0-0		20,261
5	ccr1	Hereford	A	L	1-3	Adebola 59	3,404
6	div1	Hull City	A	W	1-0	Thornton 85	16,145
7	div1	Norwich	H	W	3-0	Birchall 12, Kyle 63, John 67	20,006
8	div1	Ipswich	A	L	1-2	Ward 72	19,465
9	div1	Leeds	H	W	1-0	John 26	22,146
10	div1	Crystal Palace	A	L	0-1		16,093
11	div1	Plymouth	H	L	0-1		19,545
12	div1	Southend	A	W	3-2	Hughes 42, Cameron 47 pen, Adebola 80	9,821
13	div1	Wolverhampton	A	L	0-1		19,823
14	div1	Colchester	H	W	2-1	John 45, Doyle 69	16,178
15	div1	Barnsley	A	W	1-0	Andrews 84	10,470
16	div1	Birmingham	H	L	0-1		27,212
17	div1	Stoke	A	L	0-1		19,055
18	div1	Derby	H	L	1-2	John 22	19,701
19	div1	Sheff Wed	H	W	3-1	Bougherra 25 og, McKenzie 51, 55	19,489
20	div1	QPR	A	W	1-0	Adebola 48	12,840
21	div1	Preston	A	D	1-1	Adebola 80	13,104
22	div1	Stoke	H	D	0-0		19,073
23	div1	Burnley	H	W	1-0	Cameron 31 pen	18,362
24	div1	West Brom	A	L	0-5		20,370
25	div1	Luton	A	L	1-3	Brkovic 59 og	8,299
26	div1	Ipswich	H	L	1-2	Doyle 90	22,154
27	div1	Southend	H	D	1-1	Ward 12	16,623
28	div1	Leeds	A	L	1-2	Virgo 43	18,158
29	facr3	Bristol City	A	D	3-3	Cameron 13, McKenzie 33, John 81	13,336
30	div1	Crystal Palace	H	L	2-4	McKenzie 45, Kyle 57	16,582
31	facr3r	Bristol City	H	L	0-2		13,055
32	div1	Plymouth	A	L	2-3	Birchall 22, Mifsud 70	9,841
33	div1	Luton	H	W	1-0	McKenzie 76	18,781
34	div1	Sunderland	A	L	0-2		33,591
35	div1	Cardiff	H	D	2-2	McKenzie 8, Adebola 71	17,107
36	div1	Leicester	A	L	0-3		25,816
37	div1	Southampton	H	W	2-1	Adebola 5, Kyle 30	17,194
38	div1	Norwich	A	D	1-1	Tabb 42	24,220
39	div1	Hull City	H	W	2-0	Doyle 21 pen, McKenzie 34	21,079
40	div1	Colchester	A	D	0-0		5,453
41	div1	Wolverhampton	H	W	2-1	Adebola 26, Ward 71	22,099
42	div1	Barnsley	H	W	4-1	Tabb 27, Mifsud 32, Adebola 38, 50	21,609
43	div1	Birmingham	A	L	0-3		25,424
44	div1	QPR	H	L	0-1		22,850
45	div1	Derby	A	D	1-1	McKenzie 73	29,940
46	div1	Preston	H	L	0-4		21,117
47	div1	Sheff Wed	A	L	1-2	Mifsud 37	23,632
48	div1	West Brom	H	L	0-1		26,343
49	div1	Burnley	A	W	2-1	Mifsud 40, Tabb 55	12,830

LEAGUE APPEARANCES, BOOKINGS AND CAPS

	AGE (on 01/07/07)	IN NAMED 16	APPEARANCES	COUNTING GAMES	MINUTES ON PITCH	LEAGUE GOALS		
Goalkeepers								
Andy Marshall	32	41	41	41	3690	0	0	0
Luke Steele	22	21	5	5	450	0	0	0
Defenders								
Mikkel Bischoff	25	8	3	2	210	0	0	0
Clive Clarke	27	13	12	10	974	0	1	0
Richard Duffy	21	13	13	13	1157	0	4	0
Marcus Hall	31	41	40	37	3439	0	5	0
Colin Hawkins	29	13	13	12	1142	0	1	0
Matt Heath	26	13	7	7	618	0	0	0
David McNamee	26	16	16	13	1219	0	6	1
Robert Page	32	34	29	28	2548	0	10	0
Adam Virgo	24	25	15	9	962	1	3	0
Elliott Ward	22	39	39	38	3480	3	5	0
Andrew Whing	22	17	16	12	1233	0	7	0
Midfielders								
Christopher Birchall	23	38	28	11	1470	2	0	0
Colin Cameron	34	31	24	12	1453	2	1	0
Darren Currie	32	8	8	5	536	0	2	0
Michael Doyle	25	41	40	38	3492	3	10	0
Mustapha El Idrissi	29	1	1	0	37	0	0	0
Khalilou Fadiga	32	7	5	1	146	0	1	0
Stephen Hughes	30	39	37	34	3118	1	4	0
Don Hutchison	36	17	14	1	317	0	1	0
Isaac Osbourne	21	23	19	14	1407	0	3	0
Jay Tabb	23	36	31	19	2037	3	5	0
Kevin Thornton	20	17	11	3	468	1	3	0
Ben Turner	19	4	1	0	44	0	1	0
Forwards								
Dele Adebola	32	45	40	24	2624	8	2	0
Wayne Andrews	29	5	3	0	40	1	0	0
Liam Davis	20	3	3	1	139	0	0	0
Stern John	30	24	23	18	1713	5	1	0
Kevin Kyle	26	34	31	16	1795	3	12	0
Leon McKenzie	29	32	31	21	2162	7	5	0
Gary McSheffrey	24	3	3	3	247	1	0	0
Michael Mifsud	26	19	19	10	1075	4	0	0

TEAM OF THE SEASON

G — Andy Marshall CG: 41 DR: 73

D — Elliott Ward CG: 38 DR: 75
D — Colin Hawkins CG: 12 DR: 71
D — Marcus Hall CG: 37 DR: 68
D — Richard Duffy CG: 13 DR: 68

M — Jay Tabb CG: 19 SD: -7
M — Michael Doyle CG: 38 SD: -9
M — Isaac Osbourne CG: 14 SD: -21
M — Stephen Hughes CG: 34 SD: -25

F — Leon McKenzie CG: 21 SR: 308
F — Dele Adebola CG: 24 SR: 328

MONTHLY POINTS TALLY

AUGUST	7	47%
SEPTEMBER	6	40%
OCTOBER	9	60%
NOVEMBER	7	47%
DECEMBER	5	28%
JANUARY	3	25%
FEBRUARY	5	33%
MARCH	10	83%
APRIL	1	6%
MAY	3	100%

LEAGUE GOALS

	PLAYER	MINS	GOALS	S RATE
1	Adebola	2624	8	328
2	McKenzie	2162	7	308
3	John	1713	5	342
4	Mifsud	1075	4	268
5	Kyle	1795	3	598
6	Tabb	2037	3	679
7	Ward	3480	3	1160
8	Doyle	3492	3	1164
9	Cameron	1453	2	726
10	Birchall	1470	2	735
11	Andrews	40	1	40
12	McSheffrey	247	1	247
13	Thornton	468	1	468
	Other		2	
	TOTAL		45	

TOP POINT EARNERS

	PLAYER	GAMES	AV PTS
1	Colin Hawkins	12	1.75
2	Michael Doyle	38	1.44
3	Kevin Kyle	15	1.40
4	Dele Adebola	24	1.33
5	Colin Cameron	12	1.33
6	Jay Tabb	19	1.32
7	Richard Duffy	13	1.31
8	Andy Marshall	41	1.29
9	Elliott Ward	38	1.29
10	Leon McKenzie	21	1.25
	CLUB AVERAGE:		1.22

DISCIPLINARY RECORDS

	PLAYER	YELLOW	RED	AVE
1	Kevin Thornton	3	0	156
2	Kevin Kyle	12	0	163
3	David McNamee	6	1	174
4	Andrew Whing	7	0	205
5	Robert Page	10	0	254
6	Richard Duffy	4	0	289
7	Jay Tabb	5	0	407
8	Leon McKenzie	5	0	432
9	Michael Doyle	10	0	469
10	Isaac Osbourne	3	0	469
11	Adam Virgo	3	0	481
12	Marcus Hall	5	0	688
13	Elliott Ward	5	0	696
	Other	10	0	
	TOTAL	88	1	

KEY GOALKEEPER

Andy Marshall

Goals Conceded in the League	50	Counting Games League games when player was on pitch for at least 70 minutes	41
Defensive Rating Ave number of mins between League goals conceded while on the pitch	73	Clean Sheets In League games when player was on pitch for at least 70 minutes	10

KEY PLAYERS - DEFENDERS

Elliott Ward

Goals Conceded Number of League goals conceded while the player was on the pitch	46	Clean Sheets In League games when player was on pitch for at least 70 minutes	10
Defensive Rating Ave number of mins between League goals conceded while on the pitch	75	Club Defensive Rating Average number of mins between League goals conceded by the club this season	66

	PLAYER	CON LGE	CLEAN SHEETS	DEF RATE
1	Elliott Ward	46	10	75 mins
2	Colin Hawkins	16	3	71 mins
3	Marcus Hall	50	9	68 mins
4	Richard Duffy	17	4	68 mins

KEY PLAYERS - MIDFIELDERS

Jay Tabb

Goals in the League	3	Contribution to Attacking Power Average number of minutes between League team goals while on pitch	72
Defensive Rating Average number of mins between League goals conceded while on the pitch	65	Scoring Difference Defensive Rating minus Contribution to Attacking Power	-7

	PLAYER	LGE GOALS	DEF RATE	POWER	SCORE DIFF
1	Jay Tabb	3	65	72	-7 mins
2	Michael Doyle	3	74	83	-9 mins
3	Isaac Osbourne	0	61	82	-21 mins
4	Stephen Hughes	1	64	89	-25 mins

KEY PLAYERS - GOALSCORERS

Leon McKenzie

Goals in the League	7	Player Strike Rate Average number of minutes between League goals scored by player	308
Contribution to Attacking Power Average number of minutes between League team goals while on pitch	94	Club Strike Rate Average number of minutes between League goals scored by club	88

	PLAYER	LGE GOALS	POWER	STRIKE RATE
1	Leon McKenzie	7	94	308 mins
2	Dele Adebola	8	93	328 mins
3	Stern John	5	95	342 mins
4	Kevin Kyle	3	81	598 mins

Elliott Ward

SQUAD APPEARANCES

Match	1 2 3 4 5	6 7 8 9 10	11 12 13 14 15	16 17 18 19 20	21 22 23 24 25	26 27 28 29 30	31 32 33 34 35	36 37 38 39 40	41 42 43 44 45	46 47 48 49
Venue	H A A H A	A H A H A	H A A H A	H A H H A	A H H A A	H H A A H	H A H A H	A H A H A	H H A H A	H A H A
Competition	L L L L W	L L L L L	L L L L L	L L L L L	L L L L L	L L L L F	F L L L L	L L L L L	L L L L L	L L L L
Result	W L L D L	W W L W L	L W L W W	L L L W W	D D W L L	L D L D L	L L W L D	L W D W D	W W L L D	L L L W

KEY: On all match · On bench · Subbed or sent off (Counting game) · Subbed or sent off (playing less than 70 minutes) · Subbed on from bench (Counting Game) · Subbed on (playing less than 70 minutes) · Subbed on and then subbed or sent off (Counting Game) · Subbed on and then subbed or sent off (playing less than 70 minutes) · Not in 16

QUEENS PARK RANGERS

Final Position: 18th

NICKNAME: RANGERS   KEY: ☐ Won ☐ Drawn ☐ Lost   Attendance

					Attendance
1 div1	Burnley	A L	0-2		12,190
2 div1	Leeds	H D	2-2	Rowlands 81 pen, Baidoo 90	13,996
3 div1	Southend	H W	2-0	Rowlands 31, Ward 41	12,368
4 div1	Preston	A D	1-1	Ainsworth 5	11,879
5 ccr1	Northampton	H W	3-2	Cook 18, Gallen 50, R.Jones 87	4,569
6 div1	Ipswich	H L	1-3	Gallen 58	10,918
7 div1	Plymouth	A D	1-1	Blackstock 17	12,138
8 div1	Birmingham	H L	0-2		10,936
9 div1	Colchester	A L	1-2	Brown 76 og	5,246
10 ccr2	Port Vale	A L	1-2	Nygaard 9, Stewart 78	3,550
11 div1	Hull City	H W	2-0	R.Jones 60, Blackstock 80	11,381
12 div1	Southampton	A W	2-1	Blackstock 34, R.Jones 40	25,185
13 div1	Norwich	H D	3-3	Smith 24, Rowlands 45, 90	14,793
14 div1	Derby	H L	1-2	Smith 7	10,882
15 div1	Sheff Wed	A L	2-3	Blackstock 50, 54	23,813
16 div1	Leicester	H D	1-1	Rowlands 68 pen	12,430
17 div1	West Brom	A L	2-4	Stewart 45, Gallen 48, Nygaard 83	17,417
18 div1	Crystal Palace	H W	4-2	Smith 34, 69, Lomas 59, Gallen 66 pen	13,989
19 div1	Luton	A W	3-2	Smith 33, Heikkinen 51 og, Blackstock 54	9,007
20 div1	Cardiff	A W	1-0	R.Jones 87	13,250
21 div1	Coventry	H L	0-1		12,840
22 div1	Sunderland	H L	1-2	R.Jones 73	13,108
23 div1	Crystal Palace	A L	0-3		17,017
24 div1	Stoke	A L	0-1		16,487
25 div1	Wolverhampton	H L	0-1		12,323
26 div1	Barnsley	H W	1-0	Rowlands 15	11,307
27 div1	Birmingham	A L	1-2	Cook 31	29,431
28 div1	Norwich	A L	0-1		25,113
29 div1	Colchester	H W	1-0	R.Jones 36	11,319
30 facr3	Luton	H D	2-2	Blackstock 32, Baidoo 76	10,064
31 div1	Hull City	A L	1-2	Blackstock 45	19,791
32 div1	Southampton	H L	0-2		14,686
33 facr3r	Luton	A L	0-1		7,494
34 div1	Barnsley	A L	0-2		9,890
35 div1	Burnley	H W	3-1	Cook 13, Blackstock 55, Lomas 72	10,811
36 div1	Southend	A L	0-5		10,217
37 div1	Leeds	A D	0-0		29,593
38 div1	Plymouth	H D	1-1	Cook 59	13,757
39 div1	Ipswich	A L	1-2	Furlong 71	21,412
40 div1	Sheff Wed	H D	1-1	Rowlands 72 pen	15,188
41 div1	Derby	A D	1-1	Rowlands 14	27,567
42 div1	Leicester	A W	3-1	Idiakez 47, Nygaard 51 pen, 68	24,558
43 div1	West Brom	H L	1-2	Blackstock 63	14,784
44 div1	Preston	H W	1-0	Blackstock 51	11,910
45 div1	Coventry	A W	1-0	Smith 53	22,850
46 div1	Luton	H W	3-2	Blackstock 41, 81 pen, Furlong 90	14,360
47 div1	Sunderland	A L	1-2	Rowlands 23 pen	39,206
48 div1	Cardiff	H W	1-0	Blackstock 23	12,710
49 div1	Wolverhampton	A L	0-2		24,931
50 div1	Stoke	H D	1-1	Rowlands 6	16,741

LEAGUE APPEARANCES, BOOKINGS AND CAPS

	AGE (on 01/07/07)	IN NAMED 16	APPEARANCES	COUNTING GAMES	MINUTES ON PITCH	LEAGUE GOALS		
Goalkeepers								
Lee Camp	22	11	11	11	990	0	2	0
Jake Cole	21	33	3	3	270	0	1	0
Paul Jones	40	18	12	12	1080	0	2	0
Simon Royce	35	26	20	20	1800	0	0	0
Defenders								
Marcus Bignot	32	34	33	31	2835	0	6	0
Danny Cullip	30	13	13	12	1108	0	5	0
Patrick Kanyuka	19	29	11	5	708	0	1	0
Michael Mancienne	19	29	28	26	2408	0	2	0
Mauro Milanese	35	21	14	13	1207	0	2	0
Zeshan Rehman	23	27	25	23	2093	0	5	0
Matthew Rose	31	14	11	8	787	0	1	0
Damion Stewart	26	45	45	45	4050	2	4	0
Sampsa Timoska	28	14	14	9	1031	0	0	0
Midfielders								
Gareth Ainsworth	34	22	22	15	1554	1	4	0
Stefan Bailey	19	18	10	5	656	0	3	1
Marc Bircham	29	18	17	5	879	0	3	0
Adam Bolder	26	16	16	16	1399	0	8	0
Lee Cook	24	38	37	35	3236	3	7	1
Inigo Idiakez	33	5	5	1	240	1	1	0
Steve Lomas	33	34	34	27	2560	2	6	0
Egutu Oliseh	26	3	2	2	180	0	0	0
Martin Rowlands	28	30	29	22	2163	10	4	0
Jimmy Smith	20	34	29	23	2097	6	7	0
Nick Ward	22	24	19	11	1158	1	2	0
Forwards								
Shabazz Baidoo	19	16	9	2	276	1	0	0
Dextor Blackstock	21	39	39	32	3092	13	6	0
Adam Czerkas	22	3	3	1	169	0	0	0
Paul Furlong	38	25	22	7	942	2	4	0
Kevin Gallen	31	19	18	9	926	3	1	0
Ray Jones	18	34	31	16	1700	5	7	0
Stefan Moore	23	6	3	3	248	0	1	0
Marc Nygaard	30	27	23	13	1504	3	3	0

TEAM OF THE SEASON

G Paul Jones CG: 12 DR: 54

D Danny Cullip CG: 12 DR: 79
D Marcus Bignot CG: 31 DR: 65
D Mauro Milanese CG: 13 DR: 63
D Michael Mancienne CG: 26 DR: 61

M Gareth Ainsworth CG: 15 SD: 5
M Lee Cook CG: 35 SD: -9
M Adam Bolder CG: 16 SD: -11
M Martin Rowlands CG: 22 SD: -19

F Dextor Blackstock CG: 32 SR: 237
F Ray Jones CG: 16 SR: 340

MONTHLY POINTS TALLY

AUGUST	5	33%
SEPTEMBER	7	47%
OCTOBER	3	20%
NOVEMBER	9	60%
DECEMBER	3	17%
JANUARY	3	25%
FEBRUARY	5	42%
MARCH	5	33%
APRIL	12	67%
MAY	1	33%

LEAGUE GOALS

	PLAYER	MINS	GOALS	S RATE
1	Blackstock	3092	13	237
2	Rowlands	2163	10	216
3	Smith	2097	6	349
4	Jones, R	1700	5	340
5	Gallen	926	3	308
6	Nygaard	1504	3	501
7	Cook	3236	3	1078
8	Furlong	942	2	471
9	Lomas	2560	2	1280
10	Idiakez	240	1	240
11	Baidoo	276	1	276
12	Ward	1158	1	1158
13	Ainsworth	1554	1	1554
	Other		1	
	TOTAL		**52**	

TOP POINT EARNERS

	PLAYER	GAMES	AV PTS
1	Gareth Ainsworth	15	1.73
2	Danny Cullip	12	1.58
3	Dextor Blackstock	32	1.39
4	Adam Bolder	16	1.38
5	Marc Nygaard	13	1.38
6	Marcus Bignot	31	1.29
7	Lee Cook	35	1.23
8	Damion Stewart	45	1.18
9	Paul Jones	12	1.08
10	Steve Lomas	27	1.07
	CLUB AVERAGE:		**1.15**

DISCIPLINARY RECORDS

	PLAYER	YELLOW	RED	AVE
1	Adam Bolder	8	0	174
2	Sampsa Timoska	4	1	206
3	Danny Cullip	5	0	221
4	Paul Furlong	4	0	235
5	Ray Jones	7	0	242
6	Marc Bircham	3	0	293
7	Jimmy Smith	7	0	299
8	Stefan Bailey	3	1	328
9	Gareth Ainsworth	4	0	388
10	Lee Cook	7	1	404
11	Zeshan Rehman	5	0	418
12	Steve Lomas	6	0	426
13	Marcus Bignot	6	0	472
	Other	30	0	
	TOTAL	**99**	**3**	

KEY GOALKEEPER

Paul Jones

Goals Conceded in the League	20	Counting Games League games when player was on pitch for at least 70 minutes	12
Defensive Rating Ave number of mins between League goals conceded while on the pitch	54	Clean Sheets In League games when player was on pitch for at least 70 minutes	2

KEY PLAYERS - DEFENDERS

Danny Cullip

Goals Conceded Number of League goals conceded while the player was on the pitch	14	Clean Sheets In League games when player was on pitch for at least 70 minutes	3
Defensive Rating Ave number of mins between League goals conceded while on the pitch	79	Club Defensive Rating Average number of mins between League goals conceded by the club this season	60

	PLAYER	CON LGE	CLEAN SHEETS	DEF RATE
1	Danny Cullip	14	3	79 mins
2	Marcus Bignot	43	6	65 mins
3	Mauro Milanese	19	1	63 mins
4	Michael Mancienne	39	5	61 mins

KEY PLAYERS - MIDFIELDERS

Gareth Ainsworth

Goals in the League	1	Contribution to Attacking Power Average number of minutes between League team goals while on pitch	59
Defensive Rating Average number of mins between League goals conceded while on the pitch	64	Scoring Difference Defensive Rating minus Contribution to Attacking Power	5

	PLAYER	LGE GOALS	DEF RATE	POWER	SCORE DIFF
1	Gareth Ainsworth	1	64	59	5 mins
2	Lee Cook	3	61	70	-9 mins
3	Adam Bolder	0	66	77	-11 mins
4	Martin Rowlands	10	61	80	-19 mins

KEY PLAYERS - GOALSCORERS

Martin Rowlands

Goals in the League	10	Player Strike Rate Average number of minutes between League goals scored by player	216
Contribution to Attacking Power Average number of minutes between League team goals while on pitch	80	Club Strike Rate Average number of minutes between League goals scored by club	76

	PLAYER	LGE GOALS	POWER	STRIKE RATE
1	Martin Rowlands	10	80	216 mins
2	Dextor Blackstock	13	71	237 mins
3	Ray Jones	5	80	340 mins
4	Jimmy Smith	6	74	349 mins

Martin Rowlands

SQUAD APPEARANCES

Match	1 2 3 4 5	6 7 8 9 10	11 12 13 14 15	16 17 18 19 20	21 22 23 24 25	26 27 28 29 30	31 32 33 34 35	36 37 38 39 40	41 42 43 44 45	46 47 48 49 50
Venue	A H H A H	H A H A A	H A H A A	H A H A A	H H A A H	H A A H H	A H A A H	A A H A H	A A H H A	H A H A H
Competition	L L L L W	L L L L W	L L L L L	L L L L L	L L L L L	L L L L L	L L F L L	L L L L L	L L L L L	L L L L L
Result	L D W D W	L D L L L	W W D L L	D D W W W	L L L L L	L W L L W	L L L L W	L D D L D	D W L W W	W L W L D

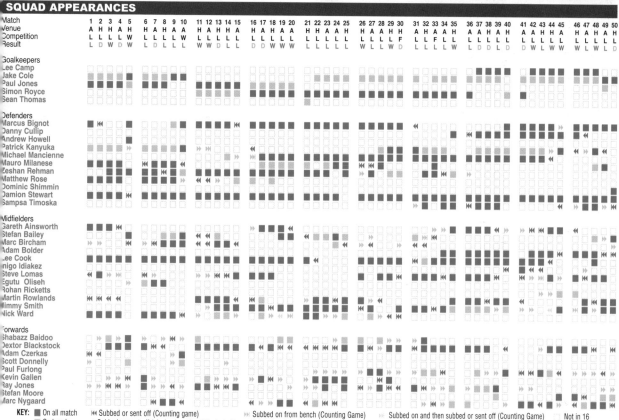

Goalkeepers
Lee Camp
Jake Cole
Paul Jones
Simon Royce
Sean Thomas

Defenders
Marcus Bignot
Danny Cullip
Andrew Howell
Patrick Kanyuka
Michael Mancienne
Mauro Milanese
Zeshan Rehman
Matthew Rose
Dominic Shimmin
Damion Stewart
Sampsa Timoska

Midfielders
Gareth Ainsworth
Stefan Bailey
Marc Bircham
Adam Bolder
Lee Cook
Inigo Idiakez
Steve Lomas
Egutu Oliseh
Rohan Ricketts
Martin Rowlands
Jimmy Smith
Nick Ward

Forwards
Shabazz Baidoo
Dextor Blackstock
Adam Czerkas
Scott Donnelly
Paul Furlong
Kevin Gallen
Ray Jones
Stefan Moore
Marc Nygaard

KEY: ■ On all match   ◄◄ Subbed or sent off (Counting game)   ►► Subbed on from bench (Counting Game)   ►► Subbed on and then subbed or sent off (Counting Game)   □ Not in 16
■ On bench   ◄◄ Subbed or sent off (playing less than 70 minutes)   ►► Subbed on (playing less than 70 minutes)   ►► Subbed on and then subbed or sent off (playing less than 70 minutes)

CHAMPIONSHIP - QUEENS PARK RANGERS

LEICESTER CITY

Final Position: 19th

NICKNAME: THE FOXES   **KEY:** ☐ Won ☐ Drawn ☐ Lost   Attendance

#					Result	Scorers	Attendance
1	div1	Luton	A	L	0-2		8,131
2	div1	Burnley	H	L	0-1		19,035
3	div1	Ipswich	H	W	3-1	Kisnorbo 8, Hughes 50, Hume 90	18,820
4	div1	Coventry	A	D	0-0		20,261
5	ccr1	Macclesfield	H	W	2-0	O'Grady 24, McCarthy 89	6,298
6	div1	Southend	H	W	1-0	Kisnorbo 40	19,427
7	div1	West Brom	A	L	0-2		19,322
8	div1	Hull City	H	L	0-1		18,677
9	div1	Sunderland	A	D	1-1	Fryatt 48	35,104
10	ccr2	Hereford	A	W	3-1	Hammond 27, Stearman 66, Hume 76 pen	4,073
11	div1	Colchester	H	D	0-0		22,449
12	div1	Birmingham	A	D	1-1	Hammond 86	18,002
13	div1	Southampton	H	W	3-2	Hume 35, 62, Stearman 65	21,347
14	div1	Leeds	A	W	2-1	Tiatto 29, Hume 82	16,477
15	div1	Crystal Palace	H	D	1-1	Hume 37 pen	28,762
16	ccr3	Aston Villa	H	L	2-3	Stearman 42, Kisnorbo 85	27,288
17	div1	QPR	A	D	1-1	Kisnorbo 7	12,430
18	div1	Stoke	H	W	2-1	Hume 45, Hughes 64	21,107
19	div1	Sheff Wed	A	L	1-2	Fryatt 72	22,451
20	div1	Plymouth	H	D	2-2	Hume 29, Porter 75	21,703
21	div1	Preston	H	L	0-1		22,721
22	div1	Derby	A	L	0-1		28,315
23	div1	Norwich	A	L	1-3	McCarthy 23	23,896
24	div1	Sheff Wed	H	W	1-4	Hughes 57	22,378
25	div1	Wolverhampton	A	W	2-1	Hammond 38, Porter 90	18,600
26	div1	Barnsley	H	W	2-0	Hammond 45, Porter 52	30,457
27	div1	Cardiff	H	D	0-0		22,274
28	div1	Hull City	A	W	2-1	Kisnorbo 55, Williams 68	18,523
29	div1	Southampton	A	L	0-2		24,447
30	div1	Sunderland	H	L	0-2		21,975
31	facr3	Fulham	H	D	2-2	Kisnorbo 80, Cadamarteri 90	15,499
32	div1	Colchester	A	D	1-1	Hume 19	5,915
33	facr3r	Fulham	A	L	3-4	Fryatt 13, McAuley 45, Wesolowski 47	11,222
34	div1	Cardiff	A	L	2-3	Kisnorbo 71, Hammond 89	12,057
35	div1	Luton	H	D	1-1	Yeates 6	20,410
36	div1	Ipswich	A	W	2-0	McAuley 28, 56	21,221
37	div1	Coventry	H	W	3-0	Horsfield 11, 26, Johnson 18	25,816
38	div1	Burnley	A	W	1-0	McGreal 67 og	10,274
39	div1	West Brom	H	D	1-1	McAuley 35	25,581
40	div1	Southend	A	D	2-2	Hume 9, 81	10,528
41	div1	Crystal Palace	A	L	0-2		16,969
42	div1	Leeds	H	D	1-1	Hume 45	25,165
43	div1	QPR	H	L	1-3	Hume 90 pen	24,558
44	div1	Stoke	A	L	2-4	Kenton 16, Hammond 58	13,303
45	div1	Derby	H	D	1-1	Fryatt 68	24,704
46	div1	Plymouth	A	L	0-3		10,900
47	div1	Norwich	H	L	1-2	Kenton 1	21,483
48	div1	Birmingham	H	L	1-2	Newton 82	24,290
49	div1	Preston	A	W	1-0	Johansson 90	14,725
50	div1	Barnsley	A	W	1-0	Austin 49 og	20,012
51	div1	Wolverhampton	H	L	1-2	Hume 3	30,282

LEAGUE APPEARANCES, BOOKINGS AND CAPS

	AGE (on 01/07/07)	IN NAMED 16	APPEARANCES	COUNTING GAMES	MINUTES ON PITCH	LEAGUE GOALS	☐	☐
Goalkeepers								
Paul Henderson	31	46	28	28	2520	0	1	0
Conrad Logan	21	46	18	18	1620	0	3	0
Defenders								
Nils-Eric Johansson	27	41	36	35	3209	1	5	0
Darren Kenton	28	28	23	16	1672	2	2	0
Patrick Kisnorbo	26	40	40	39	3571	5	7	2
Alan Maybury	28	35	27	24	2210	0	4	0
Gareth McAuley	27	34	30	25	2435	3	4	1
Patrick McCarthy	24	25	22	19	1784	1	8	1
Richard Stearman	19	44	35	21	2279	1	7	0
Midfielders								
Stephen Hughes	24	41	41	31	3161	3	4	0
Jason Jarrett	27	12	12	11	1035	0	3	0
Andy Johnson	33	24	23	21	1931	1	3	0
Joshua Low	28	19	16	8	973	0	1	0
Joe Mattock	17	4	4	3	283	0	0	0
Shaun Newton	31	9	9	8	776	1	3	0
Levi Porter	20	36	33	24	2389	3	2	0
Mohammed Sylla	30	7	6	3	306	0	1	0
Danny Tiatto	27	30	25	16	1807	1	11	0
Andrew Welsh	23	10	7	3	438	0	1	0
James Wesolowski	19	25	18	8	987	0	0	0
Gareth Williams	25	15	14	10	1032	1	1	0
Forwards								
Danny Cadamarteri	27	10	8	0	139	0	0	0
Matty Fryatt	21	33	32	12	1852	3	3	0
Elvis Hammond	26	36	31	12	1695	5	1	1
Geoff Horsfield	33	16	13	5	806	2	1	0
Iain Hume	23	46	45	36	3492	13	9	0
Chris O'Grady	21	12	10	3	501	0	0	0
Mark Yeates	22	10	9	4	446	1	0	0

TEAM OF THE SEASON

G — Paul Henderson — CG: 28 DR: 70

D — Nils-Eric Johansson — CG: 35 DR: 78
D — Gareth McAuley — CG: 25 DR: 76
D — Patrick McCarthy — CG: 19 DR: 68
D — Patrick Kisnorbo — CG: 39 DR: 64

M — Andy Johnson — CG: 21 SD: 3
M — Danny Tiatto — CG: 16 SD: -12
M — Levi Porter — CG: 24 SD: -17
M — Stephen Hughes — CG: 31 SD: -29

F — Iain Hume — CG: 36 SR: 268
F — Matty Fryatt — CG: 12 SR: 617

MONTHLY POINTS TALLY

Month	Points	%
AUGUST	7	47%
SEPTEMBER	3	20%
OCTOBER	11	73%
NOVEMBER	1	7%
DECEMBER	10	56%
JANUARY	1	11%
FEBRUARY	11	73%
MARCH	2	13%
APRIL	7	39%
MAY	0	0%

LEAGUE GOALS

	PLAYER	MINS	GOALS	S RATE
1	Hume	3492	13	268
2	Hammond	1695	5	339
3	Kisnorbo	3571	5	714
4	Fryatt	1852	3	617
5	Porter	2389	3	796
6	McAuley	2435	3	811
7	Hughes	3161	3	1053
8	Horsfield	806	2	403
9	Kenton	1672	2	836
10	Yeates	446	1	446
11	Newton	776	1	776
12	Williams	1032	1	1032
13	McCarthy	1784	1	1784
	Other		4	
	TOTAL		**47**	

TOP POINT EARNERS

	PLAYER	GAMES	AV PTS
1	Andy Johnson	20	1.45
2	Gareth McAuley	26	1.42
3	Nils-Eric Johansson	35	1.34
4	Danny Tiatto	16	1.33
5	Paul Henderson	28	1.18
6	Levi Porter	23	1.17
7	Stephen Hughes	31	1.16
8	Patrick Kisnorbo	40	1.13
9	Conrad Logan	18	1.11
10	Richard Stearman	21	1.10
	CLUB AVERAGE:		**1.15**

DISCIPLINARY RECORDS

	PLAYER	YELLOW	RED	AVE
1	Danny Tiatto	11	0	164
2	Patrick McCarthy	8	1	198
3	Shaun Newton	3	0	258
4	Jason Jarrett	3	0	345
5	Richard Stearman	7	0	379
6	Iain Hume	9	0	388
7	Patrick Kisnorbo	7	2	608
8	Gareth McAuley	4	1	608
9	Matty Fryatt	3	0	617
10	Nils-Eric Johansson	5	0	641
11	Andy Johnson	3	0	643
12	Alan Maybury	4	0	736
13	Stephen Hughes	4	0	790
	Other	12	1	
	TOTAL	**83**	**5**	

KEY GOALKEEPER

Paul Henderson

Goals Conceded in the League	36	Counting Games League games when player was on pitch for at least 70 minutes	28
Defensive Rating Ave number of mins between League goals conceded while on the pitch	70	Clean Sheets In League games when player was on pitch for at least 70 minutes	7

KEY PLAYERS - DEFENDERS

Nils-Eric Johansson

Goals Conceded Number of League goals conceded while the player was on the pitch	41	Clean Sheets In League games when player was on pitch for at least 70 minutes	10
Defensive Rating Ave number of mins between League goals conceded while on the pitch	78	Club Defensive Rating Average number of mins between League goals conceded by the club this season	66

	PLAYER	CON LGE	CLEAN SHEETS	DEF RATE
1	Nils-Eric Johansson	41	10	78 mins
2	Gareth McAuley	32	7	76 mins
3	Patrick McCarthy	26	3	68 mins
4	Patrick Kisnorbo	55	9	64 mins

KEY PLAYERS - MIDFIELDERS

Andy Johnson

Goals in the League	1	Contribution to Attacking Power Average number of minutes between League team goals while on pitch	77
Defensive Rating Average number of mins between League goals conceded while on the pitch	80	Scoring Difference Defensive Rating minus Contribution to Attacking Power	3

	PLAYER	LGE GOALS	DEF RATE	POWER	SCORE DIFF
1	Andy Johnson	1	80	77	3 mins
2	Danny Tiatto	1	66	78	-12 mins
3	Levi Porter	3	68	85	-17 mins
4	Stephen Hughes	3	61	90	-29 mins

KEY PLAYERS - GOALSCORERS

Iain Hume

Goals in the League	13	Player Strike Rate Average number of minutes between League goals scored by player	268
Contribution to Attacking Power Average number of minutes between League team goals while on pitch	81	Club Strike Rate Average number of minutes between League goals scored by club	86

	PLAYER	LGE GOALS	POWER	STRIKE RATE
1	Iain Hume	13	81	268 mins
2	Matty Fryatt	3	123	617 mins
3	Levi Porter	3	85	796 mins
4	Stephen Hughes	3	90	1053 mins

Geoff Horsfield

SQUAD APPEARANCES

Match	1 2 3 4 5	6 7 8 9 10	11 12 13 14 15	16 17 18 19 20	21 22 23 24 25	26 27 28 29 30	31 32 33 34 35	36 37 38 39 40	41 42 43 44 45	46 47 48 49 50	51
Venue	A H H A H	H A H A A	H A H A H	H A H A H	H A A H A	H H A A H	H A A A H	A H A H A	A H H A H	A H H A A	H
Competition	L L L L W	L L L L W	L L L L L	W L L L L	L L L L L	L L L L L	F L F L L	L L L L L	L L L L L	L L L L L	L
Result	L L W D W	W L L D W	D D W W D	L D W L D	L L L L W	W D W L L	D D L L D	W W W D D	L D L L D	L L L W W	L

Goalkeepers
Paul Henderson
Conrad Logan

Defenders
Nils-Eric Johansson
Darren Kenton
Patrick Kisnorbo
Alan Maybury
Gareth McAuley
Patrick McCarthy
Richard Stearman

Midfielders
Stephen Hughes
Jason Jarrett
Andy Johnson
Joshua Low
Joe Mattock
Shaun Newton
Levi Porter
Mohammed Sylla
Danny Tiatto
Andrew Welsh
James Wesolowski
Gareth Williams

Forwards
Danny Cadamarteri
Matty Fryatt
Elvis Hammond
Geoff Horsfield
Iain Hume
Chris O'Grady
Mark Yeates

KEY: ■ On all match ◄◄ Subbed or sent off (Counting game) ►► Subbed on from bench (Counting Game) ►► Subbed on and then subbed or sent off (Counting Game) □ Not in 16
   ■ On bench ◄◄ Subbed or sent off (playing less than 70 minutes) ►► Subbed on (playing less than 70 minutes) ►► Subbed on and then subbed or sent off (playing less than 70 minutes)

BARNSLEY

Final Position: 20th

NICKNAME: THE TYKES | KEY: ☐ Won ☐ Drawn ☐ Lost | Attendance

1	div1	Cardiff	H L	1-2	Howard 31	12,082
2	div1	Hull City	A W	3-2	McIndoe 45, Richards 49, Hayes 73	18,207
3	div1	Colchester	A W	2-1	Richards 57, Howard 78	4,249
4	div1	Southampton	H D	2-2	Richards 45, Hayes 71 pen	11,306
5	ccr1	Blackpool	A W	4-2*	Williams 53 pen, Devaney 117 (*on penalties)	3,938
6	div1	Norwich	A L	1-5	Hayes 38	24,876
7	div1	Stoke	H D	2-2	Wright 73, Hayes 76	10,464
8	div1	Burnley	A L	2-4	McIndoe 21, 32	10,304
9	div1	Wolverhampton	H W	1-0	Richards 10	11,350
10	ccr2	MK Dons	H L	1-2	McIndoe 66	4,411
11	div1	Preston	A L	0-1		11,728
12	div1	Luton	H L	1-2	Howard 48	10,175
13	div1	Sheff Wed	A L	1-2	Howard 56	28,687
14	div1	Plymouth	H D	2-2	Kay 2, Richards 50	9,479
15	div1	Sunderland	A L	0-2		27,918
16	div1	Coventry	H L	0-1		10,470
17	div1	Derby	A L	1-2	Hassell 13	21,295
18	div1	Leeds	H W	3-2	Devaney 30, McIndoe 62, Howard 76	16,943
19	div1	Birmingham	A L	0-2		19,344
20	div1	Crystal Palace	A L	0-2		20,159
21	div1	Ipswich	H W	1-0	McCann 90	10,556
22	div1	Southend	H W	2-0	Howard 24, K.Reid 87	9,588
23	div1	Leeds	A D	2-2	Nardiello 3, 36	21,378
24	div1	West Brom	H D	1-1	Hayes 35	9,512
25	div1	Leicester	A L	0-2		30,457
26	div1	QPR	A L	0-1		11,307
27	div1	Burnley	H W	1-0	Devaney 30	12,842
28	div1	Sheff Wed	H L	0-3		21,253
29	div1	Wolverhampton	A L	0-2		20,064
30	facr3	Southend	A D	1-1	Coulson 90	5,485
31	div1	Preston	H L	0-1		10,810
32	facr3r	Southend	H L	0-2		4,944
33	div1	Luton	A W	2-0	Howard 7, Devaney 90	7,441
34	div1	QPR	H W	2-0	Richards 45, Howard 90	9,890
35	div1	Cardiff	A L	0-2		11,549
36	div1	Colchester	H L	0-3		11,192
37	div1	Southampton	A L	2-5	Nardiello 2, Ferenczi 68	22,460
38	div1	Hull City	H W	3-0	Ferenczi 16, 76, Rajczi 46	12,526
39	div1	Stoke	A W	1-0	Ferenczi 43	13,114
40	div1	Norwich	H L	1-3	Ferenczi 45	11,010
41	div1	Sunderland	H L	0-2		18,207
42	div1	Plymouth	A W	4-2	Nyatanga 20, Devaney 31, 61, Ferenczi 90	10,265
43	div1	Coventry	A L	1-4	Hassell 79	21,609
44	div1	Derby	H L	1-2	Togwell 90	17,059
45	div1	Ipswich	A L	1-5	Nardiello 79	-
46	div1	Birmingham	H W	1-0	Nardiello 52	15,857
47	div1	Southend	A W	3-1	Nardiello 15, 51, K.Reid 29	10,089
48	div1	Crystal Palace	H W	2-0	Nardiello 15, 68 pen	10,277
49	div1	Leicester	H L	0-1		20,012
50	div1	West Brom	A L	0-7		23,568

LEAGUE APPEARANCES, BOOKINGS AND CAPS

	AGE (on 01/07/07)	IN NAMED 16	APPEARANCES	COUNTING GAMES	MINUTES ON PITCH	LEAGUE GOALS		
Goalkeepers								
Nick Colgan	33	45	44	41	3778	0	2	1
David Lucas	29	18	3	1	189	0	0	0
Vito Mannone	19	9	2	2	172	0	0	0
Defenders								
Robert Atkinson	20	14	6	6	540	0	1	0
Neil Austin	24	33	23	18	1814	0	4	0
Adam Eckersley	21	9	6	5	474	0	0	0
Bobby Hassell	27	40	39	36	3301	2	8	0
Paul Heckingbottom	29	39	32	28	2636	0	4	1
Antony Kay	24	34	32	30	2756	1	8	1
Lewin Nyatanga	18	10	10	10	900	1	1	0
Paul Reid	25	37	37	35	3196	0	4	0
Robbie Williams	23	22	14	6	683	0	5	0
Midfielders								
Martin Devaney	27	42	41	34	3108	5	7	0
Colin Healy	27	14	8	0	117	0	1	0
Brian Howard	24	43	42	39	3602	8	5	0
Ritchie Jones	20	10	4	1	135	0	1	0
Dwayne Mattis	25	6	3	1	210	0	0	0
Grant McCann	27	26	22	16	1584	1	2	0
Michael McIndoe	27	18	18	18	1615	4	2	0
Luke Potter	17	1	1	1	90	0	0	0
Kyel Reid	19	27	26	10	1275	2	2	1
Sam Togwell	22	45	44	43	3854	1	8	0
Dale Tonge	22	7	6	2	223	0	0	0
Ronnie Wallwork	29	2	2	2	180	0	1	0
Forwards								
Michael Coulson	20	3	2	0	36	0	1	0
Istvan Ferenczi	29	16	16	13	1247	6	3	0
Paul Hayes	23	30	30	21	2123	5	2	0
Leon Knight	24	9	9	5	513	0	0	0
Daniel Nardiello	24	32	31	16	1790	9	6	1
Peter Rajczi	26	15	15	8	803	1	4	0
Marc Richards	24	34	31	16	1743	6	4	0
Tommy Wright	22	18	17	3	544	1	3	0

TEAM OF THE SEASON

G Nick Colgan CG: 41 DR: 51

D Antony Kay CG: 30 DR: 62
D Paul Heckingbottom CG: 28 DR: 57
D Paul Reid CG: 35 DR: 47
D Bobby Hassell CG: 36 DR: 47

M Sam Togwell CG: 43 SD: -24
M Brian Howard CG: 39 SD: -26
M Michael McIndoe CG: 18 SD: -29
M Grant McCann CG: 16 SD: -32

F Daniel Nardiello CG: 16 SR: 198
F Istvan Ferenczi CG: 13 SR: 207

MONTHLY POINTS TALLY

AUGUST	7	47%
SEPTEMBER	4	27%
OCTOBER	1	8%
NOVEMBER	9	50%
DECEMBER	5	28%
JANUARY	6	50%
FEBRUARY	6	40%
MARCH	3	20%
APRIL	9	60%
MAY	0	0%

LEAGUE GOALS

	PLAYER	MINS	GOALS	S RATE
1	Nardiello	1790	9	198
2	Howard	3602	8	450
3	Ferenczi	1247	6	207
4	Richards	1743	6	290
5	Hayes	2123	5	424
6	Devaney	3108	5	621
7	McIndoe	1615	4	403
8	Reid, K	1275	2	637
9	Hassell	3301	2	1650
10	Wright, T	544	1	544
11	Rajczi	803	1	803
12	Nyatanga	900	1	900
13	McCann	1584	1	1584
	Other		2	
	TOTAL		53	

TOP POINT EARNERS

	PLAYER	GAMES	AV PTS
1	Istvan Ferenczi	13	1.38
2	Grant McCann	16	1.38
3	Martin Devaney	31	1.26
4	Paul Heckingbottom	29	1.24
5	Antony Kay	31	1.23
6	Sam Togwell	43	1.16
7	Marc Richards	14	1.14
8	Nick Colgan	42	1.12
9	Daniel Nardiello	16	1.06
10	Paul Reid	35	1.06
	CLUB AVERAGE:		1.09

DISCIPLINARY RECORDS

	PLAYER	YELLOW	RED	AVE
1	Peter Rajczi	4	0	200
2	Tommy Wright	3	0	272
3	Daniel Nardiello	6	1	298
4	Antony Kay	8	1	306
5	Bobby Hassell	8	0	412
6	Istvan Ferenczi	3	0	415
7	Kyel Reid	2	1	425
8	Marc Richards	4	0	435
9	Martin Devaney	7	0	444
10	Paul Heckingbottom	4	1	527
11	Robert Atkinson	1	0	540
12	Sam Togwell	8	0	550
13	Neil Austin	4	0	604
	Other	19	1	
	TOTAL	81	5	

KEY GOALKEEPER

Nick Colgan

Goals Conceded in the League	73	Counting Games League games when player was on pitch for at least 70 minutes		41
Defensive Rating Ave number of mins between League goals conceded while on the pitch	51	Clean Sheets In League games when player was on pitch for at least 70 minutes		12

KEY PLAYERS - GOALSCORERS

Daniel Nardiello

Goals in the League	9	Player Strike Rate Average number of minutes between League goals scored by player		198
Contribution to Attacking Power Average number of minutes between League team goals while on pitch	89	Club Strike Rate Average number of minutes between League goals scored by club		78

	PLAYER	LGE GOALS	POWER	STRIKE RATE
1	Daniel Nardiello	9	89	198 mins
2	Istvan Ferenczi	6	62	207 mins
3	Marc Richards	6	83	290 mins
4	Michael McIndoe	4	73	403 mins

KEY PLAYERS - DEFENDERS

Antony Kay

Goals Conceded Number of League goals conceded while the player was on the pitch	44	Clean Sheets In League games when player was on pitch for at least 70 minutes		8
Defensive Rating Ave number of mins between League goals conceded while on the pitch	62	Club Defensive Rating Average number of mins between League goals conceded by the club this season		48

	PLAYER	CON LGE	CLEAN SHEETS	DEF RATE
1	Antony Kay	44	8	62 mins
2	Paul Heckingbottom	46	6	57 mins
3	Paul Reid	67	6	47 mins
4	Bobby Hassell	70	8	47 mins

KEY PLAYERS - MIDFIELDERS

Sam Togwell

Goals in the League	1	Contribution to Attacking Power Average number of minutes between League team goals while on pitch		74
Defensive Rating Average number of mins between League goals conceded while on the pitch	50	Scoring Difference Defensive Rating minus Contribution to Attacking Power		-24

	PLAYER	LGE GOALS	DEF RATE	POWER	SCORE DIFF
1	Sam Togwell	1	50	74	-24 mins
2	Brian Howard	8	47	73	-26 mins
3	Michael McIndoe	4	44	73	-29 mins
4	Grant McCann	1	56	88	-32 mins

Istvan Ferenczi and Peter Rajczi

SQUAD APPEARANCES

Match	1	2	3	4	5	6	7	8	9	10	11	12	13	14	15	16	17	18	19	20	21	22	23	24	25	26	27	28	29	30	31	32	33	34	35	36	37	38	39	40	41	42	43	44	45	46	47	48	49	50
Venue	H	A	A	H	A	A	H	A	H	H	A	H	A	H	A	H	A	H	A	A	H	H	A	H	A	A	H	A	H	A	H	H	A	H	A	H	A	H	H	A	H	A	A	H	A	H	A	H	H	A
Competition	L	L	L	L	W	L	L	L	L	W	L	L	L	L	L	L	L	L	L	L	L	L	L	L	L	A	L	L	L	F	L	F	L	L	L	L	L	L	L	L	L	L	L	L	L	L	L	L	L	L
Result	L	W	W	D	W	L	D	L	W	L	L	L	L	D	L	L	L	W	L	L	W	W	D	D	L	L	W	L	L	D	L	L	W	W	L	L	L	W	W	L	L	W	L	L	L	W	W	W	L	L

Goalkeepers
Nick Colgan
Kyle Letheren
David Lucas
Tito Mannone

Defenders
Robert Atkinson
Neil Austin
Adam Eckersley
Bobby Hassell
Paul Heckingbottom
Antony Kay
Lewin Nyatanga
Paul Reid
Robbie Williams

Midfielders
Colin Healy
Simon Heslop
Brian Howard
Ritchie Jones
Dwayne Mattis
Grant McCann
Michael McIndoe
Anthony McParland
Luke Potter
Kyel Reid
Sam Togwell
Dale Tonge
Ronnie Wallwork
Nicky Wroe

Forwards
Michael Coulson
Martin Devaney
Istvan Ferenczi
Paul Hayes
Nathan Jarman
Leon Knight
Daniel Nardiello
Peter Rajczi
Marc Richards
Tommy Wright

KEY: ■ On all match ◄◄ Subbed or sent off (Counting game) ►►› Subbed on from bench (Counting Game) ›› Subbed on and then subbed or sent off (Counting Game) □ Not in 16
■ On bench ◄◄ Subbed or sent off (playing less than 70 minutes) ›› Subbed on (playing less than 70 minutes) ›› Subbed on and then subbed or sent off (playing less than 70 minutes)

CHAMPIONSHIP - BARNSLEY

HULL CITY

Final Position: **21st**

NICKNAME: THE TIGERS KEY: ☐ Won ☐ Drawn ☐ Lost   Attendance

1	div1	**West Brom**	A L	0-2		20,682
2	div1	**Barnsley**	H L	2-3	Parkin 6, 9	18,207
3	div1	**Derby**	H L	1-2	Parkin 45 pen	15,621
4	div1	**Ipswich**	A D	0-0		19,790
5	ccr1	**Tranmere**	H W	2-1	Burgess 56, Duffy 110	6,075
6	div1	**Coventry**	H L	0-1		16,145
7	div1	**Birmingham**	A L	1-2	Livermore 67	19,228
8	div1	**Leicester**	A W	1-0	Bridges 58	18,677
9	div1	**Sheff Wed**	H L	2-1	Parkin 11, 17	17,685
10	ccr2	**Hartlepool**	H W	3-2*	(*on penalties)	6,392
11	div1	**QPR**	A L	0-2		11,381
12	div1	**Crystal Palace**	H D	1-1	Turner 90	18,099
13	div1	**Burnley**	A L	0-2		11,530
14	div1	**Luton**	H D	0-0		14,895
15	div1	**Preston**	A L	1-1	Welsh 58	13,728
16	ccr3	**Watford**	A L	1-2	Barmby 71	8,274
17	div1	**Sunderland**	H L	0-1		25,512
18	div1	**Southend**	A W	3-2	Parkin 35, Elliott 56, Fagan 65	10,234
19	div1	**Southampton**	A D	0-0		20,560
20	div1	**Wolverhampton**	H W	2-0	Fagan 13, Elliott 75	16,962
21	div1	**Stoke**	H L	0-2		16,940
22	div1	**Norwich**	A D	1-1	Turner 90	24,129
23	div1	**Colchester**	A L	1-5	Forster 16	5,373
24	div1	**Southampton**	H L	2-4	Barmby 44, Fagan 45	15,697
25	div1	**Plymouth**	A L	0-1		12,101
26	div1	**Cardiff**	H W	4-1	Delaney 6, Marney 9, Fagan 36,	
					Bridges 71	23,089
27	div1	**Leeds**	A D	0-0		22,578
28	div1	**Leicester**	H L	1-2	Fagan 45	18,523
29	div1	**Burnley**	H W	2-0	Marney 6, Fagan 23 pen	17,731
30	div1	**Sheff Wed**	A W	2-1	Barmby 9, 65	28,600
31	facr3	**Middlesbrough**	H D	1-1	Forster 79	17,520
32	div1	**QPR**	H W	2-1	Elliott 85, 90	19,791
33	facr3r	**Middlesbrough**	A L	3-4	Dawson 59, 69, Parkin 63 pen	16,702
34	div1	**Crystal Palace**	A D	1-1	Ashbee 72	17,012
35	div1	**Leeds**	H L	1-2	Forster 45	24,311
36	div1	**West Brom**	H L	0-1		18,005
37	div1	**Derby**	A D	2-2	Dawson 33, Livermore 88	28,140
38	div1	**Barnsley**	A L	0-3		12,526
39	div1	**Birmingham**	H W	2-0	Windass 10, 57 pen	18,811
40	div1	**Coventry**	A L	0-2		21,079
41	div1	**Ipswich**	H L	2-5	Windass 22, 83 pen	18,056
42	div1	**Preston**	H W	2-0	Forster 29, Livermore 70	17,118
43	div1	**Luton**	A W	2-1	Livermore 22, Turner 62	7,777
44	div1	**Sunderland**	A L	0-2		38,448
45	div1	**Southend**	H W	4-0	Windass 43, 73, 79, Ricketts 81	19,629
46	div1	**Norwich**	H L	1-2	Dawson 88	19,053
47	div1	**Wolverhampton**	A L	1-3	Forster 61	20,772
48	div1	**Colchester**	H D	1-1	Forster 24	20,887
49	div1	**Stoke**	A D	1-1	Barmby 90	17,109
50	div1	**Cardiff**	A W	1-0	Windass 52	12,421
51	div1	**Plymouth**	H L	1-2	Elliott 61	20,661

LEAGUE APPEARANCES, BOOKINGS AND CAPS

	AGE (on 01/07/07)	IN NAMED 16	APPEARANCES	COUNTING GAMES	MINUTES ON PITCH	LEAGUE	GOALS	
Goalkeepers								
Boaz Myhill	24	46	46	45	4108	0	1	0
Defenders								
Danny Coles	25	33	21	16	1498	0	3	1
Sam Collins	30	7	6	6	540	0	2	0
Andrew Dawson	28	40	38	36	3313	2	6	0
Damien Delaney	25	37	37	36	3241	1	9	0
Nathan Doyle	20	3	1	1	90	0	1	0
Danny Mills	30	9	9	9	810	0	5	0
Samuel Ricketts	25	41	40	40	3585	1	2	0
Alton Thelwell	26	9	2	1	115	0	0	0
Michael Turner	23	46	43	42	3805	3	2	0
Midfielders								
Ian Ashbee	30	35	35	34	3096	1	8	1
Ryan France	26	26	24	11	1403	0	1	0
Jason Jarrett	27	3	3	3	270	0	1	0
David Livermore	27	26	25	22	2069	4	8	0
Dean Marney	23	39	37	24	2439	2	4	0
Ray Parlour	34	15	15	11	1109	0	2	0
Lee Peltier	20	7	7	3	371	0	0	0
John Welsh	23	21	18	6	735	1	3	0
Forwards								
Nick Barmby	33	25	20	5	823	5	5	0
Michael Bridges	28	20	15	5	732	2	5	0
Darryl Duffy	23	11	9	2	398	0	2	0
Stuart Elliott	28	36	32	16	1806	5	5	0
Craig Fagan	24	27	27	27	2404	6	8	0
Nick Forster	33	38	35	22	2390	5	3	0
Stephen McPhee	26	15	12	2	533	0	1	0
Jonathan Parkin	25	31	29	15	1774	6	6	1
Ricardo Vaz Te	20	6	6	1	196	0	1	0
Dean Windass	38	18	18	14	1397	8	1	0
Mark Yeates	22	9	5	2	250	0	0	0

TEAM OF THE SEASON

Ⓓ Andrew Dawson **CG:** 36 **DR:** 66

Ⓜ Ian Ashbee **CG:** 34 **SD:** -12

Ⓓ Michael Turner **CG:** 42 **DR:** 64

Ⓜ Dean Marney **CG:** 24 **SD:** -15

Ⓕ Dean Windass **CG:** 14 **SR:** 174

Ⓖ Boaz Myhill **CG:** 45 **DR:** 61

Ⓓ Samuel Ricketts **CG:** 40 **DR:** 60

Ⓜ David Livermore **CG:** 22 **SD:** -15

Ⓕ Jonathan Parkin **CG:** 15 **SR:** 295

Ⓓ Damien Delaney **CG:** 36 **DR:** 57

Ⓜ Ray Parlour **CG:** 11 **SD:** -15

MONTHLY POINTS TALLY

AUGUST		1	7%
SEPTEMBER		7	47%
OCTOBER		4	27%
NOVEMBER		5	33%
DECEMBER		7	39%
JANUARY		7	58%
FEBRUARY		4	33%
MARCH		9	50%
APRIL		5	33%
MAY		0	0%

LEAGUE GOALS

	PLAYER	MINS	GOALS	S RATE
1	Windass	1397	8	174
2	Parkin	1774	6	295
3	Fagan	2404	6	400
4	Elliott	1806	5	361
5	Forster	2390	5	478
6	Barmby	823	4	205
7	Livermore	2069	4	517
8	Turner	3805	3	1268
9	Bridges	732	2	366
10	Marney	2439	2	1219
11	Dawson	3313	2	1656
12	Welsh	735	1	735
13	Ashbee	3096	1	3096
	Other		2	
	TOTAL		51	

TOP POINT EARNERS

	PLAYER	GAMES	AV PTS
1	Jonathan Parkin	15	1.43
2	Stuart Elliott	16	1.38
3	David Livermore	22	1.36
4	Dean Windass	14	1.21
5	Ian Ashbee	35	1.20
6	Andrew Dawson	36	1.14
7	Damien Delaney	36	1.11
8	Michael Turner	42	1.10
9	Samuel Ricketts	40	1.05
10	Dean Marney	24	1.04
	CLUB AVERAGE:		1.07

DISCIPLINARY RECORDS

	PLAYER	YELLOW	RED	AVE
1	Danny Mills	5	0	162
2	Nick Barmby	5	0	205
3	Jonathan Parkin	6	1	253
4	David Livermore	8	0	258
5	Sam Collins	2	0	270
6	Craig Fagan	8	0	300
7	Ian Ashbee	8	1	344
8	Damien Delaney	9	0	360
9	John Welsh	3	0	367
10	Danny Coles	3	1	374
11	Stephen McPhee	1	0	533
12	Andrew Dawson	6	0	552
13	Ray Parlour	2	0	555
	Other	17	0	
	TOTAL	83	3	

KEY GOALKEEPER

Boaz Myhill

Goals Conceded in the League	67	Counting Games League games when player was on pitch for at least 70 minutes	45
Defensive Rating Ave number of mins between League goals conceded while on the pitch	61	Clean Sheets In League games when player was on pitch for at least 70 minutes	11

KEY PLAYERS - DEFENDERS

Andrew Dawson

Goals Conceded Number of League goals conceded while the player was on the pitch	50	Clean Sheets In League games when player was on pitch for at least 70 minutes	8
Defensive Rating Ave number of mins between League goals conceded while on the pitch	66	Club Defensive Rating Average number of minutes between League goals conceded by the club this season	61

	PLAYER	CON LGE	CLEAN SHEETS	DEF RATE
1	Andrew Dawson	50	8	66 mins
2	Michael Turner	59	11	64 mins
3	Samuel Ricketts	59	10	60 mins
4	Damien Delaney	56	8	57 mins

KEY PLAYERS - MIDFIELDERS

Ian Ashbee

Goals in the League	1	Contribution to Attacking Power Average number of minutes between League team goals while on pitch	73
Defensive Rating Average number of mins between League goals conceded while on the pitch	61	Scoring Difference Defensive Rating minus Contribution to Attacking Power	-12

	PLAYER	LGE GOALS	DEF RATE	POWER	SCORE DIFF
1	Ian Ashbee	1	61	73	-12 mins
2	Ray Parlour	0	58	73	-15 mins
3	Dean Marney	2	58	73	-15 mins
4	David Livermore	4	64	79	-15 mins

KEY PLAYERS - GOALSCORERS

Dean Windass

Goals in the League	8	Player Strike Rate Average number of minutes between League goals scored by player	174
Contribution to Attacking Power Average number of minutes between League team goals while on pitch	66	Club Strike Rate Average number of minutes between League goals scored by club	81

	PLAYER	LGE GOALS	POWER	STRIKE RATE
1	Dean Windass	8	66	174 mins
2	Jonathan Parkin	6	93	295 mins
3	Stuart Elliott	5	66	361 mins
4	Craig Fagan	6	89	400 mins

Dean Windass

SQUAD APPEARANCES

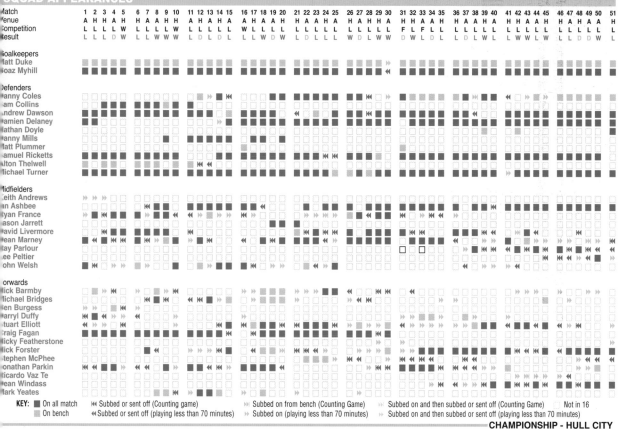

Match	1 2 3 4 5	6 7 8 9 10	11 12 13 14 15	16 17 18 19 20	21 22 23 24 25	26 27 28 29 30	31 32 33 34 35	36 37 38 39 40	41 42 43 44 45	46 47 48 49 50	51
Venue	A H H A H	H A H A H	A H A H A	A H A H A	H A A H A	H A H H A	H H A A H	H A A H A	H H A A H	H A H A A	H
Competition	L L L L W	L L L L W	L L L L L	W L L L L	L L L L L	L L L L L	F L F L L	L L L L L	L L L L L	L L L L L	L
Result	L L L D W	L L W W W	L D L D L	L L W D W	L D L L L	W D L W W	D W L D L	L D L W L	L W W L W	L L D D W	L

Key: ■ On all match |◄◄ Subbed or sent off (Counting game)   ▶▶| Subbed on from bench (Counting Game)   ▶▶ Subbed on and then subbed or sent off (Counting Game)   □ Not in 16
    ■ On bench   ◄◄ Subbed or sent off (playing less than 70 minutes)   ▶▶ Subbed on (playing less than 70 minutes)   ▶▶ Subbed on and then subbed or sent off (playing less than 70 minutes)

SOUTHEND UNITED

Final Position: 22nd

NICKNAME: THE SHRIMPERS   KEY: ☐ Won ☐ Drawn ☐ Lost   Attendance

						Attendance
1	div1	Stoke	H W	1-0	Eastwood 14 pen	8,971
2	div1	Crystal Palace	A L	1-3	Eastwood 42	18,072
3	div1	QPR	A L	0-2		12,368
4	div1	Sunderland	H W	3-1	Barrett 45, 68, Bradbury 89	9,848
5	ccr1	Bournemouth	A W	3-1	Gower 33, Eastwood 56 pen, 67	3,764
6	div1	Leicester	A L	0-1		19,427
7	div1	Sheff Wed	H D	0-0		9,639
8	div1	Norwich	H D	3-3	Eastwood 9, Hammell 68, Gower 90	11,072
9	div1	West Brom	A D	1-1	Harrold 82	19,576
10	ccr2	Brighton	H W	3-2	Paynter 87, Hunt 88, Eastwood 90	4,819
11	div1	Cardiff	H L	0-3		7,901
12	div1	Derby	A L	0-3		22,395
13	div1	Coventry	H L	2-3	Eastwood 29 pen, 73	9,821
14	div1	Burnley	A D	0-0		10,461
15	div1	Ipswich	H L	1-3	Francis 65	11,415
16	ccr3	Leeds	A W	3-1	Hammell 34 pen, Hooper 36, 64	10,449
17	div1	Leeds	A L	0-2		19,528
18	div1	Hull City	H L	2-3	Harrold 28, Eastwood 51	10,234
19	div1	Wolverhampton	A L	1-3	Harrold 57	17,904
20	ccr4	Man Utd	H W	1-0	Eastwood 27	11,532
21	div1	Preston	H D	0-0		9,263
22	div1	Plymouth	H D	1-1	Gower 59	9,469
23	div1	Colchester	A L	0-3		5,954
24	div1	Barnsley	A L	0-2		9,588
25	div1	Wolverhampton	H L	0-1		9,411
26	div1	Southampton	H W	2-1	Eastwood 22, McCormack 64	10,867
27	div1	Luton	A D	0-0		7,468
28	ccqf	Tottenham	A L	0-1		35,811
29	div1	Birmingham	H L	0-4		9,781
30	div1	Norwich	A D	0-0		25,433
31	div1	Coventry	A D	1-1	Gower 54	16,623
32	div1	West Brom	H W	3-1	Campbell-Ryce 11, 28, Hunt 42	9,907
33	facr3	Barnsley	H D	1-1	Gower 58	5,485
34	div1	Cardiff	A W	1-0	Bradbury 23	13,822
35	facr3r	Barnsley	A W	2-0	Maher 22, Bradbury 58	4,944
36	div1	Derby	H L	0-1		10,745
37	facr4	Tottenham	A L	1-3	Eastwood 69 pen	33,406
38	div1	Birmingham	A W	3-1	Maher 22, Eastwood 48, Gower 84	19,177
39	div1	Stoke	A D	1-1	Eastwood 86	23,017
40	div1	QPR	H W	5-0	Bradbury 8, Gower 70, E.Sodje 79, Maher 90, 90	10,217
41	div1	Sunderland	A L	0-4		33,576
42	div1	Crystal Palace	H L	0-1		10,419
43	div1	Sheff Wed	A L	2-3	Hunt 15, Eastwood 61	24,116
44	div1	Leicester	H D	2-2	Eastwood 53, McCormack 90	10,528
45	div1	Ipswich	A W	2-0	Gower 35, Clarke 42	24,051
46	div1	Burnley	H W	1-0	Foran 90	8,855
47	div1	Leeds	H D	1-1	Gower 24	11,274
48	div1	Hull City	A L	0-4		19,629
49	div1	Colchester	H L	0-3		10,552
50	div1	Preston	A W	3-2	Maher 41, 90, McCormack 88	13,684
51	div1	Barnsley	H L	1-3	Gower 69	10,089
52	div1	Plymouth	A L	1-2	Clarke 25	11,097
53	div1	Luton	H L	1-3	Bradbury 66	10,276
54	div1	Southampton	A L	1-4	Barrett 13	32,008

LEAGUE APPEARANCES, BOOKINGS AND CAPS

	AGE (on 01/07/07)	IN NAMED 16	APPEARANCES	COUNTING GAMES	MINUTES ON PITCH	LEAGUE GOALS	
Goalkeepers							
Stephen Collis	26	30	1	0	47	0	0
Darryl Flahavan	28	46	46	45	4093	0	2	0
Defenders							
Adam Barrett	27	30	28	26	2384	3	6	0
Peter Clarke	25	45	38	34	3153	2	8	0
Simon Francis	22	44	40	31	2946	1	8	0
Steven Hammell	25	42	39	37	3344	1	6	0
Lewis Hunt	24	43	35	30	2814	2	3	0
Franck Moussa	17	15	4	2	204	0	0	0
Spencer Prior	36	24	17	13	1209	0	1	0
Efetobore Sodje	34	33	24	22	2056	1	4	1
Che Wilson	28	4	2	1	123	0	0	0
Midfielders							
Jamal Campbell-Ryce	24	44	43	33	3216	2	5	0
Mitchell Cole	21	10	4	1	162	0	0	0
Mark Gower	28	43	43	38	3567	8	2	1
Luke Guttridge	25	19	17	14	1311	0	2	0
Gary Hooper	19	28	19	1	463	0	2	0
Kevin Maher	30	41	41	39	3590	5	8	1
Alan McCormack	23	22	22	18	1765	3	12	0
Arnau Riera	25	4	2	0	70	0	0	0
Forwards							
Lee Bradbury	31	32	31	28	2448	4	6	0
Freddy Eastwood	23	42	42	38	3521	11	2	0
Ritchie Foran	27	15	15	9	973	1	2	1
Matt Harrold	22	38	36	10	1360	3	1	0
William Paynter	22	13	9	4	485	0	1	0
Michael Ricketts	28	2	2	0	46	0	0	0

TEAM OF THE SEASON

- **G** Darryl Flahavan CG: 45 DR: 51
- **D** Spencer Prior CG: 13 DR: 54
- **D** Lewis Hunt CG: 30 DR: 52
- **D** Efetobore Sodje CG: 22 DR: 52
- **D** Adam Barrett CG: 26 DR: 51
- **M** Alan McCormack CG: 18 SD: -17
- **M** Kevin Maher CG: 39 SD: -30
- **M** Jamal Campbell-Ryce CG: 33 SD: -32
- **M** Mark Gower CG: 38 SD: -34
- **F** Freddy Eastwood CG: 38 SR: 320
- **F** Lee Bradbury CG: 28 SR: 612

MONTHLY POINTS TALLY

AUGUST	6	40%
SEPTEMBER	3	20%
OCTOBER	1	7%
NOVEMBER	2	13%
DECEMBER	6	33%
JANUARY	9	75%
FEBRUARY	4	27%
MARCH	8	53%
APRIL	3	20%
MAY	0	0%

LEAGUE GOALS

	PLAYER	MINS	GOALS	S RATE
1	Eastwood	3521	11	320
2	Gower	3567	8	445
3	Maher	3590	5	718
4	Bradbury	2448	4	612
5	Harrold	1360	3	453
6	McCormack	1765	3	588
7	Barrett	2384	3	794
8	Hunt	2814	2	1407
9	Clarke	3153	2	1576
10	Campbell-Ryce	3216	2	1608
11	Foran	973	1	973
12	Sodje, E	2056	1	2056
13	Francis	2946	1	2946
	Other		1	
	TOTAL		**47**	

TOP POINT EARNERS

	PLAYER	GAMES	AV PTS
1	Alan McCormack	18	1.28
2	Lee Bradbury	28	1.15
3	Mark Gower	39	1.08
4	Jamal Campbell-Ryce	33	1.03
5	Adam Barrett	26	1.00
6	Freddy Eastwood	38	0.97
7	Kevin Maher	40	0.95
8	Darryl Flahavan	45	0.93
9	Lewis Hunt	30	0.93
10	Luke Guttridge	14	0.93
	CLUB AVERAGE:		**0.91**

DISCIPLINARY RECORDS

	PLAYER	YELLOW	RED	AVE
1	Alan McCormack	12	0	176
2	Gary Hooper	2	0	231
3	Ritchie Foran	2	1	324
4	Peter Clarke	8	0	394
5	Lee Bradbury	6	0	408
6	Kevin Maher	8	0	448
7	Adam Barrett	6	0	476
8	Simon Francis	8	0	491
9	Efetobore Sodje	4	1	514
10	J Campbell-Ryce	5	0	643
11	Luke Guttridge	2	0	655
12	Lewis Hunt	3	0	938
13	Steven Hammell	6	0	1114
	Other	9	1	
	TOTAL	**81**	**4**	

KEY GOALKEEPER

Darryl Flahavan

Goals Conceded in the League	80	Counting Games League games when player was on pitch for at least 70 minutes	45
Defensive Rating Ave number of mins between League goals conceded while on the pitch	51	Clean Sheets In League games when player was on pitch for at least 70 minutes	10

KEY PLAYERS - DEFENDERS

Spencer Prior

Goals Conceded Number of League goals conceded while the player was on the pitch	22	Clean Sheets In League games when player was on pitch for at least 70 minutes	3
Defensive Rating Ave number of mins between League goals conceded while on the pitch	54	Club Defensive Rating Average number of mins between League goals conceded by the club this season	51

	PLAYER	CON LGE	CLEAN SHEETS	DEF RATE
1	Spencer Prior	22	3	54 mins
2	Lewis Hunt	54	7	52 mins
3	Efetobore Sodje	39	5	52 mins
4	Adam Barrett	46	5	51 mins

KEY PLAYERS - MIDFIELDERS

Alan McCormack

Goals in the League	3	Contribution to Attacking Power Average number of minutes between League team goals while on pitch	70
Defensive Rating Average number of mins between League goals conceded while on the pitch	53	Scoring Difference Defensive Rating minus Contribution to Attacking Power	-17

	PLAYER	LGE GOALS	DEF RATE	POWER	SCORE DIFF
1	Alan McCormack	3	53	70	-17 mins
2	Kevin Maher	5	53	83	-30 mins
3	Jamal Campbell-Ryce	2	59	91	-32 mins
4	Mark Gower	8	55	89	-34 mins

KEY PLAYERS - GOALSCORERS

Freddy Eastwood

Goals in the League	11	Player Strike Rate Average number of minutes between League goals scored by player	320
Contribution to Attacking Power Average number of minutes between League team goals while on pitch	97	Club Strike Rate Average number of minutes between League goals scored by club	88

	PLAYER	LGE GOALS	POWER	STRIKE RATE
1	Freddy Eastwood	11	97	320 mins
2	Mark Gower	8	89	445 mins
3	Alan McCormack	3	70	588 mins
4	Lee Bradbury	4	81	612 mins

Freddy Eastwood

SQUAD APPEARANCES

Match	1 2 3 4	6 7 8 9 10	11 12 13 14 15	16 17 18 19 20	21 22 23 24 25	26 27 28 29 30	31 32 33 34 35	36 37 38 39 40	41 42 43 44 45	46 47 48 49 50	51 52 53 54
Venue	H A A H A	A H H A H	H A H A H	A A H A H	H H A A H	H A A H A	A H H A A	H A A A H	A H A H A	H H A H A	H A H A
Competition	L L L L W	L L L L W	L L L L L	W L L L W	L L L L L	L L W L L	L L F L F	L F L L L	L L L L L	L L L L L	L L L L
Result	W L L W W	L D D D W	L L L D L	W L L L W	D D L L L	W D L L D	D W D W W	L L W D W	L L L D W	W D L L W	L L L L

Goalkeepers

Stephen Collis

Darryl Flahavan

Defenders

Adam Barrett

Peter Clarke

Simon Francis

Steven Hammell

Lewis Hunt

Franck Moussa

Spencer Prior

Efetobore Sodje

Che Wilson

Midfielders

Jamal Campbell-Ryce

Mitchell Cole

Mark Gower

Luke Guttridge

Gary Hooper

Kevin Maher

Alan McCormack

Arnau Riera

Forwards

Lee Bradbury

Freddy Eastwood

Ritchie Foran

Matt Harrold

William Paynter

Michael Ricketts

KEY: ■ On all match   ◄◄ Subbed or sent off (Counting game)   ►► Subbed on from bench (Counting Game)   ◄► Subbed on and then subbed or sent off (Counting Game)   ☐ Not in 16

☐ On bench   ◄◄ Subbed or sent off (playing less than 70 minutes)   ►► Subbed on (playing less than 70 minutes)   ►► Subbed on and then subbed or sent off (playing less than 70 minutes)

LUTON TOWN

Final Position: 23rd

NICKNAME: THE HATTERS   KEY: ☐ Won ☐ Drawn ☐ Lost

#		Opponent			Score	Scorers	Attendance
1	div1	Leicester	H	W	2-0	Barnett 8, Edwards 79	8,131
2	div1	Sheff Wed	A	W	1-0	Emanuel 45	22,613
3	div1	Norwich	A	L	2-3	Vine 15, Morgan 52	23,863
4	div1	Stoke	H	D	2-2	Barnett 54, Langley 60 pen	7,727
5	ccr1	Bristol Rovers	A	D	1-1	Boyd 3	2,882
6	div1	Wolverhampton	A	L	0-1		19,378
7	div1	Crystal Palace	H	W	2-1	Edwards 2, Vine 61	9,187
8	div1	Colchester	H	D	1-1	Parkin 32	7,609
9	div1	Cardiff	A	L	1-4	Vine 45	147,108
10	ccr2	Brentford	A	W	3-0	Morgan 10, Feeney 53, Vine 90	3,005
11	div1	West Brom	H	D	2-2	Vine 27, 36	9,332
12	div1	Barnsley	A	W	2-1	Edwards 47, Brkovic 90	10,175
13	div1	Birmingham	H	W	3-2	Vine 28 pen, 29, Bell 81	9,275
14	div1	Hull City	A	D	0-0		14,895
15	div1	Leeds	H	W	5-1	Edwards 12, 90, Vine 55, Bell 56, Heikkinen 73	10,260
16	ccr3	Everton	A	L	0-4		27,149
17	div1	Ipswich	A	L	0-5		20,975
18	div1	Burnley	H	L	0-2		7,664
19	div1	Preston	A	L	0-3		13,094
20	div1	QPR	H	L	2-3	Boyd 45, Brkovic 45	9,007
21	div1	Derby	H	L	0-2		9,708
22	div1	Southampton	H	L	1-2	Perrett 67	20,482
23	div1	Plymouth	A	L	0-1		9,965
24	div1	Preston	H	W	2-0	Vine 2, Edwards 19	7,665
25	div1	Sunderland	A	L	1-2	Morgan 5	30,445
26	div1	Southend	H	D	0-0		7,468
27	div1	Coventry	H	W	3-1	Brkovic 45, Vine 66, Morgan 68	8,299
28	div1	Colchester	A	L	1-4	Vine 85 pen	5,427
29	div1	Birmingham	A	D	2-2	Vine 44, Feeney 77	24,642
30	div1	Cardiff	H	D	0-0		8,004
31	facr3	QPR	A	D	2-2	Vine 45, Feeney 46	10,064
32	div1	West Brom	A	L	2-3	Keane 60, Feeney 70	19,927
33	div1	Barnsley	H	L	0-2		7,441
34	facr3r	QPR	H	W	1-0	Rehman 80 og	7,494
35	facr4	Blackburn	H	L	0-4		5,887
36	div1	Coventry	A	L	0-1		18,781
37	div1	Leicester	A	D	1-1	Morgan 33	20,410
38	div1	Stoke	A	D	0-0		12,375
39	div1	Sheff Wed	H	W	3-2	Runstrom 33, Spurr 54 og, Talbot 63	8,011
40	div1	Crystal Palace	A	L	1-2	Hudson 55 og	16,177
41	div1	Norwich	H	L	2-3	Runstrom 11, Talbot 48	8,868
42	div1	Wolverhampton	H	L	2-3	Emanuel 22, Barnett 45	10,002
43	div1	Leeds	A	L	0-1		27,138
44	div1	Hull City	H	L	1-2	Talbot 70	7,777
45	div1	Ipswich	H	L	0-2		8,880
46	div1	Burnley	A	D	0-0		11,088
47	div1	Southampton	H	L	0-2		-
48	div1	QPR	A	L	2-3	Coyne 45, Bell 51 pen	14,360
49	div1	Plymouth	H	L	1-2	O'Leary 51	7,601
50	div1	Derby	A	L	0-1		28,499
51	div1	Southend	A	W	3-1	Andrew 20, Spring 39, Idrizaj 87	10,276
52	div1	Sunderland	H	L	0-5		10,260

LEAGUE APPEARANCES, BOOKINGS AND CAPS

	AGE (on 01/07/07)	IN NAMED 16	APPEARANCES	COUNTING GAMES	MINUTES ON PITCH	LEAGUE GOALS		
Goalkeepers								
Marlon Beresford	37	39	26	24	2242	0	0	1
Dean Brill	20	34	11	9	907	0	0	0
Dean Kiely	36	11	11	11	990	0	0	0
Defenders								
Leon Barnett	21	40	39	37	3405	3	9	1
Clarke Carlisle	27	5	5	4	380	0	1	0
Chris Coyne	28	20	18	12	1249	1	2	0
Sol Davis	27	25	24	17	1710	0	2	1
Kevin Foley	22	40	39	35	3331	0	0	0
Markus Heikkinen	28	37	37	35	3250	1	7	0
Russell Perrett	34	22	10	7	725	1	2	0
Midfielders								
David Bell	23	35	34	27	2579	3	3	1
Ahmet Brkovic	32	27	20	12	1306	3	3	0
Carlos Edwards	28	26	26	24	2273	6	1	0
Lewis Emanuel	23	40	40	27	3056	2	5	1
Peter Holmes	26	11	5	3	313	0	2	0
Keith Keane	20	29	19	17	1582	1	3	0
Richard Langley	27	36	29	13	1670	1	4	0
Dean Morgan	23	40	36	15	2076	4	4	0
Stephen O'Leary	22	18	7	4	430	1	1	0
Steve Robinson	32	38	38	36	3308	0	5	0
Matthew Spring	27	16	14	13	1195	1	2	0
Forwards								
Calvin Andrew	20	7	7	5	503	1	3	0
Adam Boyd	25	30	19	4	630	1	0	0
Warren Feeney	26	34	29	10	1374	2	2	0
Sam Parkin	26	8	8	6	600	1	1	0
Bjorn Runstrom	23	9	8	7	614	2	2	0
Drew Talbot	20	16	15	11	1062	3	1	0
Rowan Vine	24	26	26	25	2234	12	9	0

TEAM OF THE SEASON

G Marlon Beresford — CG: 24 DR: 53

D Sol Davis — CG: 17 DR: 74
D Markus Heikkinen — CG: 35 DR: 55
D Kevin Foley — CG: 35 DR: 51
D Leon Barnett — CG: 37 DR: 50

M Carlos Edwards — CG: 24 SD: -14
M Dean Morgan — CG: 15 SD: -20
M David Bell — CG: 27 SD: -23
M Lewis Emanuel — CG: 27 SD: -25

F Rowan Vine — CG: 25 SR: 186
F Drew Talbot* — CG: 11 SR: 354

MONTHLY POINTS TALLY

Month	Pts	%
AUGUST	7	47%
SEPTEMBER	8	53%
OCTOBER	7	47%
NOVEMBER	0	0%
DECEMBER	8	44%
JANUARY	1	8%
FEBRUARY	5	33%
MARCH	1	7%
APRIL	3	20%
MAY	0	0%

LEAGUE GOALS

	PLAYER	MINS	GOALS	S RATE
1	Vine	2234	12	186
2	Edwards	2273	6	378
3	Morgan	2076	4	519
4	Talbot	1062	3	354
5	Brkovic	1306	3	435
6	Bell	2579	3	859
7	Barnett	3405	3	1135
8	Runstrom	614	2	307
9	Feeney	1374	2	687
10	Emanuel	3056	2	1528
11	Idrizaj	317	1	317
12	O'Leary	430	1	430
13	Andrew	503	1	503
	Other		8	
	TOTAL		**51**	

TOP POINT EARNERS

	PLAYER	GAMES	AV PTS
1	Carlos Edwards	24	1.25
2	Sol Davis	17	1.24
3	Rowan Vine	25	1.12
4	Kevin Foley	35	1.09
5	Marlon Beresford	25	1.08
6	Markus Heikkinen	35	1.03
7	Richard Langley	14	1.00
8	Leon Barnett	37	0.92
9	Lewis Emanuel	28	0.89
10	Dean Morgan	15	0.86
	CLUB AVERAGE:		**0.87**

DISCIPLINARY RECORDS

	PLAYER	YELLOW	RED	AVE
1	Calvin Andrew	3	0	167
2	Rowan Vine	9	0	248
3	Bjorn Runstrom	2	0	307
4	Russell Perrett	2	0	362
5	Richard Langley	4	1	417
6	Leon Barnett	9	1	435
7	Ahmet Brkovic	3	0	435
8	Markus Heikkinen	7	0	464
9	Lewis Emanuel	5	1	509
10	Sol Davis	2	1	570
11	Matthew Spring	2	0	597
12	Sam Parkin	1	0	600
13	David Bell	3	1	644
	Other	18	1	
	TOTAL	**70**	**6**	

KEY GOALKEEPER

Marlon Beresford

Goals Conceded in the League	42	Counting Games League games when player was on pitch for at least 70 minutes	24
Defensive Rating Ave number of mins between League goals conceded while on the pitch	53	Clean Sheets In League games when player was on pitch for at least 70 minutes	5

KEY PLAYERS - DEFENDERS

Sol Davis

Goals Conceded Number of League goals conceded while the player was on the pitch	23	Clean Sheets In League games when player was on pitch for at least 70 minutes	5
Defensive Rating Ave number of mins between League goals conceded while on the pitch	74	Club Defensive Rating Average number of minutes between League goals conceded by the club this season	52

	PLAYER	CON LGE	CLEAN SHEETS	DEF RATE
1	Sol Davis	23	5	74 mins
2	Markus Heikkinen	59	7	55 mins
3	Kevin Foley	65	6	51 mins
4	Leon Barnett	68	6	50 mins

KEY PLAYERS - MIDFIELDERS

Carlos Edwards

Goals in the League	6	Contribution to Attacking Power Average number of minutes between League team goals while on pitch	68
Defensive Rating Average number of mins between League goals conceded while on the pitch	54	Scoring Difference Defensive Rating minus Contribution to Attacking Power	-14

	PLAYER	LGE GOALS	DEF RATE	POWER	SCORE DIFF
1	Carlos Edwards	6	54	68	-14 mins
2	Dean Morgan	4	51	71	-20 mins
3	David Bell	3	52	75	-23 mins
4	Lewis Emanuel	2	51	76	-25 mins

KEY PLAYERS - GOALSCORERS

Rowan Vine

Goals in the League	12	Player Strike Rate Average number of minutes between League goals scored by player	186
Contribution to Attacking Power Average number of minutes between League team goals while on pitch	67	Club Strike Rate Average number of minutes between League goals scored by club	79

	PLAYER	LGE GOALS	POWER	STRIKE RATE
1	Rowan Vine	12	67	186 mins
2	Drew Talbot	3	75	354 mins
3	Carlos Edwards	6	68	378 mins
4	Ahmet Brkovic	3	108	435 mins

Dean Morgan

SQUAD APPEARANCES

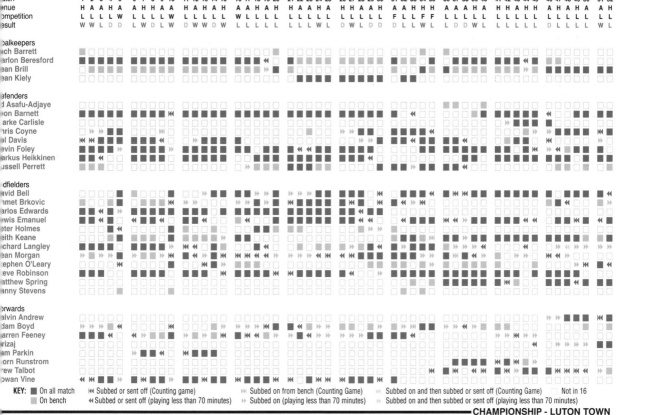

KEY: ■ On all match |◄◄ Subbed or sent off (Counting game)   ►► Subbed on from bench (Counting Game)   ►► Subbed on and then subbed or sent off (Counting Game)   □ Not in 16
□ On bench   ◄◄ Subbed or sent off (playing less than 70 minutes)   ►► Subbed on (playing less than 70 minutes)   ►► Subbed on and then subbed or sent off (playing less than 70 minutes)

LEEDS UNITED

Final Position: **24th**

NICKNAME: UNITED   KEY: ☐ Won ☐ Drawn ☐ Lost   Attendance

1	div1	Norwich	H	W	1-0	Healy 41 pen	22,417
2	div1	QPR	A	D	2-2	Lewis 65, Horsfield 82	13,996
3	div1	Crystal Palace	A	L	0-1		17,218
4	div1	Cardiff	H	L	0-1		18,246
5	ccr1	Chester	H	W	1-0	Bakke 57	10,013
6	div1	Sheff Wed	A	W	1-0	Healy 66 pen	23,792
7	div1	Wolverhampton	H	L	0-1		16,268
8	div1	Sunderland	H	L	0-3		23,037
9	div1	Coventry	A	L	0-1		22,146
10	ccr2	Barnet	H	W	3-1	Blake 7, Moore 55, 74	7,220
11	div1	Birmingham	H	W	3-2	Healy 6, 15 pen, Tebily 85 og	18,898
12	div1	West Brom	A	L	2-4	Horsfield 82, Stone 88	21,435
13	div1	Stoke	H	L	0-4		18,173
14	div1	Leicester	H	L	1-2	Butler 87	16,477
15	div1	Luton	A	L	1-5	Foxe 17	10,260
16	ccr3	Southend	H	L	1-3	Moore 44	10,449
17	div1	Southend	H	W	2-0	Moore 40, Blake 88	19,528
18	div1	Preston	A	L	1-4	Healy 80	16,168
19	div1	Barnsley	A	L	2-3	Derry 44, Blake 45	16,943
20	div1	Colchester	H	W	3-0	Blake 36, 53 pen, Cresswell 48	17,678
21	div1	Southampton	H	L	0-3		19,467
22	div1	Plymouth	A	W	2-1	Blake 3, Lewis 61	17,088
23	div1	Burnley	A	L	1-2	Healy 87	15,061
24	div1	Barnsley	H	D	2-2	Kandol 8, Ehiogu 45	21,378
25	div1	Derby	H	L	0-1		20,087
26	div1	Ipswich	A	L	0-1		23,661
27	div1	Hull City	H	D	0-0		22,578
28	div1	Sunderland	A	L	0-2		40,116
29	div1	Stoke	A	L	1-3	Moore 41	18,128
30	div1	Coventry	H	W	2-1	Healy 15, Douglas 53	18,158
31	facr3	West Brom	A	L	1-3	Robinson 90 og	16,957
32	div1	West Brom	H	L	2-3	Flo 3, Thompson 66	20,019
33	div1	Hull City	A	W	2-1	Heath 21, Thompson 50	24,311
34	div1	Norwich	A	L	1-2	Howson 20	25,018
35	div1	Crystal Palace	H	W	2-1	Heath 27, Blake 72	19,220
36	div1	Cardiff	A	L	0-1		16,644
37	div1	QPR	H	D	0-0		29,593
38	div1	Wolverhampton	A	L	0-1		24,314
39	div1	Birmingham	A	L	0-1		18,363
40	div1	Sheff Wed	H	L	2-3	Bullen 88 og, Cresswell 89	25,297
41	div1	Luton	H	W	1-0	Cresswell 50	27,138
42	div1	Leicester	A	D	1-1	Blake 45	25,165
43	div1	Southend	A	D	1-1	Healy 88	11,274
44	div1	Preston	H	W	2-1	Blake 51, Healy 90	18,433
45	div1	Plymouth	H	W	2-1	Healy 45, Michalik 87	30,034
46	div1	Colchester	A	L	1-2	Lewis 53	5,916
47	div1	Burnley	H	W	1-0	Heath 21	23,528
48	div1	Southampton	A	L	0-1		29,012
49	div1	Ipswich	H	D	1-1	Cresswell 12	31,269
50	div1	Derby	A	L	0-2		31,183

LEAGUE APPEARANCES, BOOKINGS AND CAPS

	AGE (on 01/07/07)	IN NAMED 16	APPEARANCES	COUNTING GAMES	MINUTES ON PITCH	LEAGUE GOALS
Goalkeepers						
Casper Ankergren	27	16	14	14	1260	0	1
Graham Stack	25	24	12	12	1080	0	1
Neil Sullivan	37	15	7	7	630	0	0
Tony Warner	33	27	13	13	1170	0	1
Defenders						
Paul Butler	34	16	16	16	1440	1	4
Stephen Crainey	26	20	19	18	1624	0	4
Ugo Ehiogu	34	6	6	6	521	1	4
Robbie Elliott	33	10	8	4	441	0	4
Hayden Foxe	30	28	18	10	1162	1	10
Michael Gray	32	6	6	6	526	0	1
Matt Heath	26	27	26	26	2340	3	1
Gary Kelly	32	16	16	15	1395	0	1
Matthew Kilgallon	23	21	19	17	1603	0	3
Radostin Kishishev	32	10	10	10	892	0	1
Rui Manuel Marques	29	18	16	13	1236	0	2
Lubomir Michalik	23	7	7	7	630	1	3
Miguel Armando Sa	31	11	11	6	610	0	1
Midfielders						
Eirik Bakke	29	3	3	1	184	0	1
Sebastien Carole	24	24	16	5	640	0	0
Shaun Derry	29	23	23	21	1985	1	8
Jonathan Douglas	25	35	35	34	3101	1	15
Adam Johnson	19	7	5	3	324	0	0
Eddie Lewis	33	42	41	37	3365	3	3
Kevin Nicholls	28	13	13	11	1071	0	4
Frazer Richardson	24	28	22	17	1702	0	0
Steve Stone	35	10	10	3	470	1	0
Alan Thompson	33	11	11	7	770	2	3
Ian Westlake	23	29	27	16	1743	0	6
Forwards						
Jermaine Beckford	23	8	5	1	129	0	1
Robbie Blake	31	41	36	17	2176	8	3
Richard Cresswell	29	22	22	18	1737	4	5
Tore Andre Flo	34	1	1	1	90	1	1
David Healy	27	42	41	25	2760	10	7
Geoff Horsfield	33	15	14	6	796	2	0
Jonathan Howson	19	15	9	4	577	1	1
Jemal Johnson	22	10	5	2	260	0	1
Tresor Kandol	25	20	18	10	1097	1	5
Ian Moore	30	42	32	12	1459	2	2

TEAM OF THE SEASON

D Matt Heath CG: 26 DR: 73

M Frazer Richardson CG: 17 SD: -20

D Rui Manuel Marques CG: 13 DR: 65

M Jonathan Douglas CG: 34 SD: -28

F Robbie Blake CG: 17 SR: 272

G Casper Ankergren CG: 14 DR: 96

D Stephen Crainey CG: 18 DR: 52

M Eddie Lewis CG: 37 SD: -29

F David Healy CG: 25 SR: 276

D Matthew Kilgallon CG: 17 DR: 50

M Shaun Derry CG: 21 SD: -35

MONTHLY POINTS TALLY

AUGUST		7	47%
SEPTEMBER		3	20%
OCTOBER		3	20%
NOVEMBER		6	40%
DECEMBER		2	11%
JANUARY		6	67%
FEBRUARY		4	22%
MARCH		8	53%
APRIL		7	47%
MAY		0	0%

LEAGUE GOALS

	PLAYER	MINS	GOALS	S RATE
1	Healy	2760	10	276
2	Blake	2176	8	272
3	Cresswell	1737	4	434
4	Heath	2340	3	780
5	Lewis	3365	3	1121
6	Thompson	770	2	385
7	Horsfield	796	2	398
8	Moore	1459	2	729
9	Flo	90	1	90
10	Stone	470	1	470
11	Ehiogu	521	1	521
12	Howson	577	1	577
13	Michalik	630	1	630
	Other		5	
	TOTAL		44	

TOP POINT EARNERS

	PLAYER	GAMES	AV PTS
1	Robbie Blake	17	1.41
2	Casper Ankergren	14	1.36
3	Richard Cresswell	18	1.22
4	David Healy	24	1.13
5	Matt Heath	26	1.12
6	Eddie Lewis	37	1.12
7	Frazer Richardson	17	1.12
8	Ian Moore	12	1.08
9	Matthew Kilgallon	18	1.06
10	Jonathan Douglas	34	1.03
	CLUB AVERAGE:		0.78

DISCIPLINARY RECORDS

	PLAYER	YELLOW	RED	AVE
1	Hayden Foxe	10	1	116
2	Alan Thompson	3	1	192
3	Lubomir Michalik	3	0	210
4	Kevin Nicholls	4	1	214
5	Tresor Kandol	5	0	219
6	Jonathan Douglas	15	0	238
7	Shaun Derry	8	0	248
8	Ian Westlake	6	0	290
9	Richard Cresswell	5	0	347
10	Paul Butler	4	0	360
11	David Healy	7	0	394
12	Matthew Kilgallon	3	1	400
13	Michael Gray	1	0	526
	Other	21	1	
	TOTAL	95	5	

KEY GOALKEEPER

Casper Ankergren

Goals Conceded in the League	13	Counting Games League games when player was on pitch for at least 70 minutes	14
Defensive Rating Ave number of mins between League goals conceded while on the pitch	96	Clean Sheets In League games when player was on pitch for at least 70 minutes	3

KEY PLAYERS - DEFENDERS

Matt Heath

Goals Conceded Number of League goals conceded while the player was on the pitch	32	Clean Sheets In League games when player was on pitch for at least 70 minutes	5
Defensive Rating Ave number of mins between League goals conceded while on the pitch	73	Club Defensive Rating Average number of mins between League goals conceded by the club this season	58

	PLAYER	CON LGE	CLEAN SHEETS	DEF RATE
1	Matt Heath	32	5	73 mins
2	Rui Manuel Marques	19	1	65 mins
3	Stephen Crainey	31	3	52 mins
4	Matthew Kilgallon	32	4	50 mins

KEY PLAYERS - MIDFIELDERS

Frazer Richardson

Goals in the League	0	Contribution to Attacking Power Average number of minutes between League team goals while on pitch	94
Defensive Rating Average number of mins between League goals conceded while on the pitch	74	Scoring Difference Defensive Rating minus Contribution to Attacking Power	-20

	PLAYER	LGE GOALS	DEF RATE	POWER	SCORE DIFF
1	Frazer Richardson	0	74	94	-20 mins
2	Jonathan Douglas	1	55	83	-28 mins
3	Eddie Lewis	3	64	93	-29 mins
4	Shaun Derry	1	47	82	-35 mins

KEY PLAYERS - GOALSCORERS

Robbie Blake

Goals in the League	8	Player Strike Rate Average number of minutes between League goals scored by player	272
Contribution to Attacking Power Average number of minutes between League team goals while on pitch	77	Club Strike Rate Average number of minutes between League goals scored by club	91

	PLAYER	LGE GOALS	POWER	STRIKE RATE
1	Robbie Blake	8	77	272 mins
2	David Healy	10	92	276 mins
3	Richard Cresswell	4	91	434 mins
4	Ian Moore	2	72	729 mins

David Healy

SQUAD APPEARANCES

LEAGUE ONE ROUND-UP

FINAL LEAGUE TABLE

	P	HOME					AWAY					TOTAL			
		W	D	L	F	A	W	D	L	F	A	F	A	DIF	PTS
Scunthorpe	46	15	6	2	40	17	11	7	5	33	18	73	35	38	91
Bristol City	46	15	5	3	35	20	10	5	8	28	19	63	39	24	85
Blackpool	46	12	6	5	40	25	12	5	6	36	24	76	49	27	83
Nottm Forest	46	14	5	4	37	17	9	8	6	28	24	65	41	24	82
Yeovil	46	14	3	6	22	12	9	7	7	33	27	55	39	16	79
Oldham	46	13	4	6	36	18	8	8	7	33	29	69	47	22	75
Swansea	46	12	6	5	36	20	8	6	9	33	33	69	53	16	72
Carlisle	46	12	5	6	35	24	7	6	10	19	31	54	55	-1	68
Tranmere	46	13	5	5	33	22	5	8	10	25	31	58	53	5	67
Millwall	46	11	8	4	33	19	8	1	14	26	43	59	62	-3	66
Doncaster	46	8	10	5	30	23	8	5	10	22	24	52	47	5	63
Port Vale	46	12	3	8	35	26	6	3	14	29	39	64	65	-1	60
Crewe	46	11	4	8	39	38	6	5	12	27	34	66	72	-6	60
Northampton	46	8	5	10	27	28	7	9	7	21	23	48	51	-3	59
Huddersfield	46	9	8	6	37	33	5	9	9	23	36	60	69	-9	59
Gillingham	46	14	2	7	29	24	3	6	14	27	53	56	77	-21	59
Cheltenham	46	8	6	9	25	27	7	3	13	24	34	49	61	-12	54
Brighton	46	5	7	11	23	34	9	4	10	26	24	49	58	-9	53
Bournemouth	46	10	5	8	28	27	3	8	12	22	37	50	64	-14	52
Leyton Orient	46	6	10	7	30	32	6	5	12	31	45	61	77	-16	51
Chesterfield	46	9	5	9	29	22	3	6	14	16	31	45	53	-8	47
Bradford	46	5	9	9	27	31	6	5	12	20	34	47	65	-18	47
Rotherham*	46	8	4	11	37	39	5	5	13	21	36	58	75	-17	38
Brentford	46	5	8	10	24	41	3	5	15	16	38	40	79	-39	37

CLUB STRIKE FORCE

Blackpool striker Andy Morrell

	CLUB	GOALS	CSR
1	Blackpool	76	54
2	Scunthorpe	73	56
3	Swansea	69	60
4	Oldham	69	60
5	Crewe	66	62
6	Nottm Forest	65	63
7	Port Vale	64	64
8	Bristol City	63	65
9	Leyton Orient	61	67
10	Huddersfield	60	69
11	Millwall	59	70
12	Rotherham	58	71
13	Tranmere	58	71
14	Gillingham	56	73
15	Carlisle	55	75
16	Yeovil	55	75
17	Doncaster	52	79
18	Bournemouth	50	82
19	Cheltenham	49	84
20	Brighton	49	84
21	Northampton	48	86
22	Bradford	47	88
23	Chesterfield	45	92
24	Brentford	40	103

1 Blackpool

Goals scored in the League	76
Club Strike Rate (CSR) Average number of minutes between League goals scored by club	54

CLUB DISCIPLINARY RECORDS

Millwall's Chris Zebroski: 8 cards

	CLUB	Y	R	TOTAL	AVE
1	Millwall	91	3	94	44
2	Huddersfield	84	8	92	45
3	Swansea	79	8	87	47
4	Bradford	79	7	86	48
5	Tranmere	78	4	82	50
6	Brighton	73	7	80	51
7	Brentford	73	6	79	52
8	Leyton Orient	73	6	79	52
9	Scunthorpe	73	5	78	53
10	Nottm Forest	71	3	74	55
11	Bristol City	71	2	73	56
12	Oldham	67	6	73	56
13	Carlisle	67	3	70	59
14	Cheltenham	64	3	67	61
15	Bournemouth	63	3	66	62
16	Northampton	64	1	65	63
17	Blackpool	58	4	62	66
18	Chesterfield	60	2	62	66
19	Port Vale	56	4	60	69
20	Rotherham	54	4	58	71
21	Gillingham	53	5	58	71
22	Yeovil	53	2	55	75
23	Doncaster	50	2	52	79
24	Crewe	32	1	33	125

1 Millwall

League Yellow	91
League Red	3
League Total	94
Cards Average in League Average number of minutes between a card being shown of either colour	44

CLUB DEFENCES

	CLUB	LGE	CS	CDR
1	Scunthorpe	35	23	118
2	Yeovil	39	18	106
3	Bristol City	39	18	106
4	Nottm Forest	42	18	98
5	Oldham	47	17	88
6	Doncaster	47	19	88
7	Blackpool	49	10	84
8	Northampton	51	14	81
9	Swansea	53	17	78
10	Tranmere	53	14	78
11	Chesterfield	53	12	78
12	Carlisle	55	18	75
13	Brighton	58	11	71
14	Cheltenham	61	10	67
15	Millwall	62	14	66
16	Bournemouth	64	14	64
17	Bradford	65	9	63
18	Port Vale	65	13	63
19	Huddersfield	69	8	60
20	Crewe	72	8	57
21	Rotherham	75	6	55
22	Leyton Orient	77	11	53
23	Gillingham	77	7	53
24	Brentford	79	6	52

Scunthorpe defender Foster gets stuck in

1 Scunthorpe

Goals conceded in the League	35
Clean Sheets (CS) Number of league games where no goals were conceded	23
Club Defensive Rate (CDR) Average number of minutes between League goals conceded by club	118

STADIUM CAPACITY AND HOME CROWDS

TEAM		CAPACITY	AVE	HIGH	LOW
1	Brighton	6973	86.7	7749	5146
2	Doncaster	10593	73.1	14470	5190
3	Northampton	7653	72.8	7172	4184
4	Blackpool	9491	72.5	9482	4600
5	Nottm Forest	30602	67.4	27875	16785
6	Scunthorpe	9088	62.4	8906	3473
7	Swansea	20500	62.1	18903	9675
8	Leyton Orient	7804	61.9	7206	3529
9	Yeovil	9634	59.9	9009	4709
10	Cheltenham	7289	59.8	6554	3036
11	Bristol City	21479	59.6	19517	9726
12	Bournemouth	10770	56.3	8001	4538
13	Gillingham	11400	55.1	8216	5103
14	Crewe	10046	54.4	7632	4062
15	Chesterfield	8502	49.8	6641	3341
16	Rotherham	9624	49.5	7809	3223
17	Carlisle	16291	48.7	12031	6087
18	Oldham	13624	46.5	10207	4652
19	Millwall	20146	45.9	12547	6251
20	Brentford	12763	43.8	7023	4296
21	Huddersfield	24500	43.2	14772	8723
22	Tranmere	16789	41.3	11444	5528
23	Bradford	25136	34.6	14925	7134
24	Port Vale	19892	23.8	7388	3077

Key: Average. The percentage of each stadium filled in League games over the season (AVE), the stadium capacity and the highest and lowest crowds recorded.

AWAY ATTENDANCE

TEAM		AVE	HIGH	LOW
1	Nottm Forest	68.3	19249	6554
2	Bristol City	57.5	23466	3471
3	Rotherham	55.9	27875	3525
4	Huddersfield	55.7	19070	3720
5	Yeovil	54.9	19002	4184
6	Bradford	53.5	19665	3529
7	Millwall	53.5	19410	3973
8	Carlisle	53.5	19535	3831
9	Scunthorpe	53.3	22640	3036
10	Port Vale	53.1	22999	3473
11	Oldham	52.8	17446	4054
12	Leyton Orient	52.2	23109	3665
13	Blackpool	52.1	18903	4025
14	Doncaster	51.9	16785	3868
15	Bournemouth	51.8	19898	3657
16	Brighton	51.7	18686	3984
17	Tranmere	50.8	19729	3697
18	Northampton	50.8	24567	3224
19	Swansea	50.6	19034	3697
20	Crewe	50.5	27472	3154
21	Brentford	49.2	18003	3697
22	Cheltenham	49.1	22640	3340
23	Chesterfield	49.0	19480	3697
24	Gillingham	46.6	17950	3077

Key: Average. How close each club has come to filling grounds in its away league matches (AVE) and the highest and lowest crowds recorded.

CHART-TOPPING MIDFIELDERS

1 Goodwin - Scunthorpe	
Goals scored in the League	1
Defensive Rating Av number of mins between League goals conceded while on the pitch	131
Contribution to Attacking Power Average number of minutes between League team goals while on pitch	57
Scoring Difference Defensive Rating minus Contribution to Attacking Power	74

	PLAYER	CLUB	GOALS	DEF RATE	POWER	S DIFF
1	James Goodwin	Scunthorpe	1	131	57	74
2	Cleveland Taylor	Scunthorpe	3	122	54	68
3	Matthew Sparrow	Scunthorpe	4	113	54	59
4	Sammy Clingan	Nottm Forest	0	119	63	56
5	Scott Murray	Bristol City	7	118	69	49
6	Ian Baraclough	Scunthorpe	1	101	53	48
7	Aaron Davies	Yeovil	6	122	75	47
8	J-P Kamudimba Kalala	Yeovil	1	114	68	46
9	David Fox	Blackpool	4	94	53	41
10	Andy Liddell	Oldham	10	97	57	40
11	Gary Holt	Nottm Forest	2	101	62	39
12	Chris Taylor	Oldham	4	92	54	38
13	Lee Johnson	Bristol City	5	102	67	35
14	Kristian Commons	Nottm Forest	9	91	56	35
15	Gary McDonald	Oldham	7	90	57	33

CHART-TOPPING GOALSCORERS

1 Hoskins - Rotherham	
Goals scored in the League	15
Contribution to Attacking Power (AP) Average number of minutes between League team goals while on pitch	52
Club Strike Rate (CSR) Average minutes between League goals scored by club	74
Player Strike Rate Average number of minutes between League goals scored by player	132

	PLAYER	CLUB	GOALS: LGE	POWER	CSR	S RATE
1	William Hoskins	Rotherham	15	52	74	132
2	Billy Sharp	Scunthorpe	30	57	59	134
3	Chris Porter	Oldham	21	54	61	138
4	Nicky Maynard	Crewe	16	61	66	142
5	Lee Trundle	Swansea	19	57	61	148
6	Darren Byfield	Millwall	16	60	70	159
7	Luke Varney	Crewe	17	61	66	167
8	Leon Constantine	Port Vale	22	59	67	168
9	Scott McGleish	Northampton	12	96	91	176
10	Andy Morrell	Blackpool	16	46	56	181
11	Keigan Parker	Blackpool	13	41	56	187
12	Dean Windass	Bradford	11	72	90	192
13	Luke Beckett	Huddersfield	15	67	69	194
14	Chris Greenacre	Tranmere	17	76	75	212
15	Paul Heffernan	Doncaster	9	61	81	217

CHART-TOPPING DEFENDERS

1 Keogh - Bristol City	
Goals Conceded in the League The number of League goals conceded while he was on the pitch	13
Clean Sheets In games when he played at least 70 mins	11
Club Defensive Rating Average mins between League goals conceded by the club this season	106
Defensive Rating Average number of minutes between League goals conceded while on pitch	155

	PLAYER	CLUB	CON: LGE	CS	CDR	DEF RATE
1	Richard Keogh	Bristol City	13	11	106	155
2	Marcus Williams	Scunthorpe	19	16	123	141
3	Clifford Byrne	Scunthorpe	13	12	123	133
4	Julian Bennett	Nottm Forest	18	11	103	122
5	Richard Hinds	Scunthorpe	27	17	123	121
6	Stephen Foster	Scunthorpe	31	19	123	119
7	James Perch	Nottm Forest	33	20	103	116
8	Jamie McCombe	Bristol City	30	14	106	115
9	Louis Carey	Bristol City	29	14	106	112
10	Nathan Jones	Yeovil	33	18	108	112
11	James McAllister	Bristol City	23	9	106	109
12	Terry Skiverton	Yeovil	30	13	108	109
13	Gareth Roberts	Doncaster	23	13	90	108
14	Andrew Crosby	Scunthorpe	30	14	123	108
15	Dave Mulligan	Scunthorpe	17	8	123	106

CHART-TOPPING GOALKEEPERS

1 Murphy - Scunthorpe	
Counting Games Games in which he played at least 70 minutes	45
Goals Conceded in the League The number of League goals conceded while he was on the pitch	35
Clean Sheets In games when he played at least 70 mins	22
Defensive Rating Average number of minutes between League goals conceded while on pitch	115

	PLAYER	CLUB	CG	CONC	CS	DEF RATE
1	Joe Murphy	Scunthorpe	45	35	22	115
2	Steve Mildenhall	Yeovil	46	39	18	106
3	Paul Smith	Nottm Forest	45	38	19	106
4	Adriano Basso	Bristol City	44	38	18	105
5	Leslie Pogliacomi	Oldham	38	37	15	93
6	Rhys Evans	Blackpool	32	36	5	80
7	Mark Bunn	Northampton	43	49	12	78
8	Willy Gueret	Swansea	42	48	16	78
9	Gavin Ward	Tranmere	35	43	12	77
10	Barry Roche	Chesterfield	40	47	11	77
11	Kieren Westwood	Carlisle	46	55	18	75
12	Lenny Pidgeley	Millwall	42	56	14	68
13	Mark Goodlad	Port Vale	24	32	7	67
14	Neil Moss	Bournemouth	27	36	10	67
15	Shane Higgs	Cheltenham	35	48	6	66

PLAYER DISCIPLINARY RECORD

	PLAYER		LY	LR	TOT	AVE
1	Leary	Brentford	10	0	10	145
2	Bentham	Bradford	6	0	6	179
3	Prutton	Nottm Forest	5	0	5	206
4	Lester	Nottm Forest	10	0	10	209
5	Williams	Millwall	8	0	8	210
6	Garner	Carlisle	6	1	7	211
7	Best	Bournemouth	5	0	5	217
8	Zebroski	Millwall	5	0	5	219
9	Guttridge	Leyton Orient	5	1	6	220
10	Bennett	Nottm Forest	10	0	10	221
11	Goodwin	Scunthorpe	10	0	10	224
12	Chambers	Leyton Orient	13	1	14	233
13	Worthington	Huddersfield	9	0	9	251
14	Brandon	Huddersfield	6	0	6	255
15	Hughes	Northampton	6	0	6	255

Tough tackler Leary in action for Brentford

1. Michael Leary - Brentford	
Cards Average mins between cards	145
League Yellow	10
League Red	0
TOTAL	10

TEAM OF THE SEASON

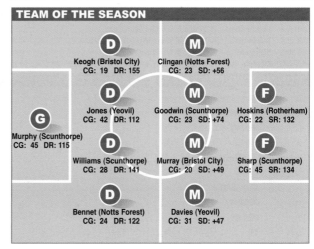

D Keogh (Bristol City) CG: 19 DR: 155
M Clingan (Notts Forest) CG: 23 SD: +56
D Jones (Yeovil) CG: 42 DR: 112
M Goodwin (Scunthorpe) CG: 23 SD: +74
F Hoskins (Rotherham) CG: 22 SR: 132
G Murphy (Scunthorpe) CG: 45 DR: 115
D Williams (Scunthorpe) CG: 28 DR: 141
M Murray (Bristol City) CG: 20 SD: +49
F Sharp (Scunthorpe) CG: 45 SR: 134
D Bennet (Notts Forest) CG: 24 DR: 122
M Davies (Yeovil) CG: 31 SD: +47

SCUNTHORPE UNITED

Final Position: **1st**

NICKNAME: THE IRON KEY: ☐ Won ☐ Drawn ☐ Lost Attendance

#	Comp	Opponent	H/A	Result	Scorers	Attendance
1	div2	Bristol City	A	L	0-1		13,268
2	div2	Swansea	H	D	2-2	Crosby 49 pen, B.Sharp 67	4,187
3	div2	Crewe	H	D	2-2	B.Sharp 39, Crosby 66 pen	4,329
4	div2	Rotherham	A	L	1-2	B.Sharp 6	4,708
5	ccr1	Lincoln	H	W	4-3	Torpey 7, Mulligan 58, Paul 105, Baraclough 106	3,455
6	div2	Brentford	H	D	1-1	Mousinho 70 og	3,942
7	div2	Gillingham	A	W	2-0	Hinds 40, Sparrow 45	5,749
8	div2	Oldham	A	L	0-1		4,812
9	div2	Port Vale	H	W	3-0	B.Sharp 9, 45, Morris 65	3,473
10	div2	Cheltenham	H	W	1-0	Keogh 90	4,288
11	ccr2	Aston Villa	H	L	1-2	B.Sharp 73	6,502
12	div2	Bournemouth	A	D	1-1	MacKenzie 19	5,256
13	div2	Chesterfield	A	W	1-0	B.Sharp 13	4,849
14	div2	Doncaster	H	W	2-0	B.Sharp 54, Keogh 68	6,441
15	div2	Nottm Forest	A	W	4-0	Taylor 28, Keogh 36, Morris 66, B.Sharp 90	22,640
16	div2	Brighton	H	L	1-2	B.Sharp 43	5,607
17	div2	Bradford	A	W	1-0	B.Sharp 79	8,723
18	div2	Leyton Orient	H	W	3-1	B.Sharp 6, 57, Sparrow 38	4,795
19	div2	Huddersfield	A	D	1-1	Sparrow 55	10,456
20	facr1	Cheltenham	A	D	0-0		2,721
21	div2	Northampton	H	W	1-0	Crosby 86 pen	4,758
22	facr1r	Cheltenham	H	W	2-0	Baraclough 26, B.Sharp 74	3,074
23	div2	Yeovil	A	W	2-0	B.Sharp 7, 62	5,921
24	facr2	Wrexham	H	L	0-2		5,054
25	div2	Tranmere	H	D	1-1	Keogh 42	4,572
26	div2	Carlisle	A	W	2-0	B.Sharp 52, Keogh 90	6,954
27	div2	Blackpool	H	L	1-3	Baraclough 90	4,527
28	div2	Millwall	A	W	1-0	Torpey 74	7,192
29	div2	Chesterfield	H	W	1-0	B.Sharp 49	6,123
30	div2	Bournemouth	H	W	3-2	Crosby 8, Keogh 29, B.Sharp 44	4,794
31	div2	Port Vale	A	D	0-0		4,869
32	div2	Oldham	H	D	1-1	Gregan 54 og	7,685
33	div2	Cheltenham	A	D	1-1	B.Sharp 79	-
34	div2	Doncaster	A	D	2-2	Keogh 15, Talbot 23	12,414
35	div2	Millwall	H	W	3-0	Goodwin 50, Crosby 53 pen, Beckford 79	5,001
36	div2	Bristol City	H	W	1-0	B.Sharp 40	5,108
37	div2	Rotherham	H	W	1-0	Beckford 17	5,978
38	div2	Swansea	A	W	2-0	B.Sharp 3, Beckford 71	10,746
39	div2	Gillingham	H	W	3-1	Hinds 24, Mulligan 65, Morris 90	5,312
40	div2	Crewe	A	W	3-1	B.Sharp 29, 62, Beckford 40	4,842
41	div2	Brentford	A	W	2-0	Beckford 40, Taylor 89	5,645
42	div2	Nottm Forest	H	D	1-1	B.Sharp 46	8,906
43	div2	Brighton	A	D	1-1	Beckford 64	6,276
44	div2	Leyton Orient	A	D	2-2	MacKenzie 51, B.Sharp 90	5,869
45	div2	Bradford	H	W	2-0	B.Sharp 56, Beckford 76	6,437
46	div2	Yeovil	H	W	1-0	Jones 39 og	7,883
47	div2	Northampton	A	L	1-2	B.Sharp 57	6,361
48	div2	Huddersfield	H	W	2-0	B.Sharp 68, 84 pen	7,518
49	div2	Tranmere	A	W	2-0	Ward 55 og, B.Sharp 70	6,721
50	div2	Blackpool	A	L	1-3	B.Sharp 41	9,482
51	div2	Carlisle	H	W	3-0	Taylor 41, Sparrow 47, Beckford 64	8,720

LEAGUE APPEARANCES, BOOKINGS AND CAPS

	AGE (on 01/07/07)	IN NAMED 16	APPEARANCES	COUNTING GAMES	MINUTES ON PITCH	LEAGUE GOALS	
Goalkeepers							
Josh Lillis	20	45	1	1	90	0	0
Joe Murphy	26	45	45	45	4050	0	6
Defenders							
Andy Butler	23	23	10	4	449	0	1
Clifford Byrne	25	33	24	18	1732	0	3
Andrew Crosby	34	41	39	34	3262	5	9
Stephen Foster	32	44	44	40	3715	0	4
Richard Hinds	26	46	44	35	3286	1	4
Dave Mulligan	25	31	24	20	1812	1	4
Lee Ridley	24	22	18	14	1393	0	3
Marcus Williams	21	39	34	28	2680	0	5
Midfielders							
Ian Baraclough	36	37	32	22	2127	1	4
Robbie Foy	21	12	5	0	107	0	0
James Goodwin	25	33	30	23	2241	1	10
Kevan Hurst	21	14	13	6	805	0	1
Neil MacKenzie	31	34	23	8	1015	2	1
Ian Morris	20	31	28	13	1646	3	1
Matthew Sparrow	23	29	29	26	2385	4	6
Cleveland Taylor	23	45	45	37	3672	3	2
Forwards							
Jermaine Beckford	23	18	18	17	1545	8	2
Andrea Ferretti	20	5	4	0	78	0	0
Andrew Keogh	21	28	28	24	2259	7	4
Daniel McBreen	30	11	6	1	126	0	0
Billy Sharp	21	45	45	45	4023	30	10
Drew Talbot	20	3	3	2	197	1	1
Steve Torpey	36	16	14	3	523	1	1

TEAM OF THE SEASON

D Marcus Williams CG: 28 DR: 141
M James Goodwin CG: 23 SD: 74
D Clifford Byrne CG: 18 DR: 133
M Ian Morris CG: 13 SD: 70
F Billy Sharp CG: 45 SR: 134
G Joe Murphy CG: 45 DR: 115
D Richard Hinds CG: 35 DR: 121
M Cleveland Taylor CG: 37 SD: 68
F Jermaine Beckford CG: 17 SR: 193
D Stephen Foster CG: 40 DR: 119
M Matthew Sparrow CG: 26 SD: 59

MONTHLY POINTS TALLY

Month		Pts	%
AUGUST		3	20%
SEPTEMBER		16	76%
OCTOBER		9	75%
NOVEMBER		7	78%
DECEMBER		13	72%
JANUARY		7	47%
FEBRUARY		15	100%
MARCH		9	60%
APRIL		9	60%
MAY		3	100%

LEAGUE GOALS

	PLAYER	MINS	GOALS	S RATE
1	Sharp, B	4023	30	134
2	Beckford	1545	8	193
3	Keogh	2259	7	322
4	Crosby	3262	5	652
5	Sparrow	2385	4	596
6	Morris	1646	3	548
7	Taylor	3672	3	1224
8	MacKenzie	1015	2	507
9	Hinds	3286	2	1643
10	Talbot	197	1	197
11	Torpey	523	1	523
12	Mulligan	1812	1	1812
13	Baraclough	2127	1	2127
	Other		1	
	TOTAL		69	

TOP POINT EARNERS

	PLAYER	GAMES	AV PTS
1	Cleveland Taylor	38	2.26
2	Ian Morris	13	2.25
3	James Goodwin	23	2.22
4	Jermaine Beckford	17	2.18
5	Clifford Byrne	18	2.17
6	Marcus Williams	28	2.04
7	Billy Sharp	45	2.00
8	Joe Murphy	45	1.96
9	Ian Baraclough	22	1.91
10	Richard Hinds	35	1.91
	CLUB AVERAGE:		1.98

DISCIPLINARY RECORDS

	PLAYER	YELLOW	RED	AVE
1	James Goodwin	10	0	224
2	Steve Torpey	1	1	261
3	Matthew Sparrow	6	1	397
4	Billy Sharp	10	0	402
5	Clifford Byrne	3	1	433
6	Dave Mulligan	4	0	453
7	Lee Ridley	3	0	464
8	Andrew Crosby	9	0	466
9	Ian Baraclough	4	0	531
10	Marcus Williams	5	0	670
11	Stephen Foster	4	1	743
12	Jermaine Beckford	2	0	772
13	Kevan Hurst	1	0	805
	Other	18	1	
	TOTAL	80	5	

KEY GOALKEEPER

Joe Murphy

Goals Conceded in the League	35	Counting Games League games when player was on pitch for at least 70 minutes	45
Defensive Rating Ave number of mins between League goals conceded while on the pitch	115	Clean Sheets In games when player was on pitch for at least 70 minutes	22

KEY PLAYERS - DEFENDERS

Marcus Williams

Goals Conceded Number of League goals conceded while the player was on the pitch	19	Clean Sheets In League games when player was on pitch for at least 70 minutes	16
Defensive Rating Ave number of mins between League goals conceded while on the pitch	141	Club Defensive Rating Average number of mins between League goals conceded by the club this season	123

	PLAYER	CON LGE	CLEAN SHEETS	DEF RATE
1	Marcus Williams	19	16	141 mins
2	Clifford Byrne	13	12	133 mins
3	Richard Hinds	27	17	121 mins
4	Stephen Foster	31	19	119 mins

KEY PLAYERS - MIDFIELDERS

James Goodwin

Goals in the League	1	Contribution to Attacking Power Average number of minutes between League team goals while on pitch	57
Defensive Rating Average number of mins between League goals conceded while on the pitch	131	Scoring Difference Defensive Rating minus Contribution to Attacking Power	74

	PLAYER	LGE GOALS	DEF RATE	POWER	SCORE DIFF
1	James Goodwin	1	131	57	74 mins
2	Ian Morris	3	126	56	70 mins
3	Cleveland Taylor	3	122	54	68 mins
4	Matthew Sparrow	4	113	54	59 mins

KEY PLAYERS - GOALSCORERS

Billy Sharp

Goals in the League	30	Player Strike Rate Average number of minutes between League goals scored by player	134
Contribution to Attacking Power Average number of minutes between League team goals while on pitch	57	Club Strike Rate Average number of minutes between League goals scored by club	59

	PLAYER	LGE GOALS	POWER	STRIKE RATE
1	Billy Sharp	30	57	134 mins
2	Jermaine Beckford	8	49	193 mins
3	Andrew Keogh	7	61	322 mins
4	Ian Morris	3	56	548 mins

Billy Sharp

SQUAD APPEARANCES

Match	1	2	3	4	5	6	7	8	9	10	11	12	13	14	15	16	17	18	19	20	21	22	23	24	25	26	27	28	29	30	31	32	33	34	35	36	37	38	39	40	41	42	43	44	45	46	47	48	49	50	51
Venue	A	H	H	A	H	H	A	A	H	H	H	A	A	H	A	H	A	H	A	A	H	H	A	H	H	A	H	A	H	H	A	H	A	A	H	H	H	A	H	A	A	H	A	A	H	H	A	H	A	A	H
Competition	L	L	L	L	W	L	L	L	L	L	W	L	L	L	L	L	L	L	L	F	L	F	L	F	L	L	L	L	L	L	L	L	L	L	L	L	L	L	L	L	L	L	L	L	L	L	L	L	L	L	L
Result	L	D	D	L	W	D	W	L	W	W	L	D	W	W	W	L	W	W	D	D	W	W	W	L	D	W	L	W	W	W	D	D	D	D	W	W	W	W	W	W	W	D	D	D	W	W	L	W	W	L	W

Goalkeepers

Josh Lillis

Joe Murphy

Defenders

Andy Butler

Clifford Byrne

Andrew Crosby

Stephen Foster

Richard Hinds

Dave Mulligan

Joe Ridley

Marcus Williams

Midfielders

Ian Baraclough

Robbie Foy

James Goodwin

Ivan Hurst

Gil MacKenzie

Ian Morris

Matthew Sparrow

Cleveland Taylor

Forwards

Jermaine Beckford

Andrea Ferretti

Andrew Keogh

Daniel McBreen

Billy Sharp

Drew Talbot

Steve Torpey

KEY: ■ On all match ◄◄ Subbed or sent off (Counting game) ►► Subbed on from bench (Counting Game) ►► Subbed on and then subbed or sent off (Counting Game) □ Not in 16
◻ On bench ◄◄ Subbed or sent off (playing less than 70 minutes) ►► Subbed on (playing less than 70 minutes) ►► Subbed on and then subbed or sent off (playing less than 70 minutes)

BRISTOL CITY

Final Position: **2nd**

NICKNAME: THE ROBINS KEY: ☐ Won ☐ Drawn ☐ Lost   Attendance

#	Comp	Opponent		Result	Scorers	Attendance
1	div2	Scunthorpe	H W	1-0	Showunmi 69	13,268
2	div2	Bradford	A L	1-2	Murray 2	7,356
3	div2	Huddersfield	A L	1-2	Jevons 49	10,492
4	div2	Blackpool	H L	2-4	Showunmi 43, 64 pen	10,630
5	ccr1	Cheltenham	A L	1-2	Cotterill 40	3,713
6	div2	Northampton	A W	3-1	Jevons 32 pen, Brooker 71, Cotterill 90 pen	4,919
7	div2	Brighton	H W	1-0	Brown 21	10,552
8	div2	Tranmere	A L	0-1		8,111
9	div2	Leyton Orient	H W	2-1	Jevons 18, Showunmi 44	9,726
10	div2	Chesterfield	H W	3-1	Carey 3, Brown 40, Myrie-Williams 51	10,398
11	div2	Port Vale	A W	2-0	Brown 45, Jevons 76	5,295
12	div2	Bournemouth	A W	1-0	Jevons 70	6,484
13	div2	Oldham	H D	0-0		11,656
14	div2	Brentford	A D	1-1	McCombe 41	6,740
15	div2	Crewe	H W	2-1	Murray 26, Brown 32	11,899
16	div2	Nottm Forest	A L	0-1		23,466
17	div2	Doncaster	H W	1-0	Carey 37	11,909
18	div2	Yeovil	A L	1-2	Jevons 90 pen	9,009
19	facr1	York	A W	1-0	McCombe 53	3,525
20	div2	Gillingham	H W	3-1	Keogh 29, Showunmi 77, Murray 90	11,823
21	div2	Swansea	A D	0-0		15,531
22	facr2	Gillingham	H W	4-3	Jevons 21, 44, 45, Showunmi 64	5,663
23	div2	Carlisle	H W	1-0	Showunmi 85	10,792
24	div2	Rotherham	A D	1-1	Murray 72	4,862
25	div2	Millwall	H W	1-0	Murray 1	12,067
26	div2	Cheltenham	A D	2-2	Orr 53, McCombe 90	5,863
27	div2	Bournemouth	H D	2-2	Murray 74, Johnson 80	13,848
28	div2	Port Vale	H W	2-1	Brooker 69, Murray 76	12,776
29	div2	Leyton Orient	A D	1-1	Johnson 68	4,814
30	facr3	Coventry	H D	3-3	Brooker 14, Showunmi 18, Jevons 23	13,336
31	div2	Tranmere	H W	3-2	Showunmi 48, Jevons 59, Myrie-Williams 68	10,822
32	facr3r	Coventry	A W	2-0	Murray 39, Showunmi 54	13,055
33	div2	Oldham	A W	3-0	Showunmi 9, McAllister 37, Andrews 65	6,924
34	facr4	Middlesbrough	H D	2-2	Keogh 53, Murray 59	19,008
35	div2	Cheltenham	H L	0-1		12,227
36	div2	Scunthorpe	A L	0-1		5,108
37	div2	Huddersfield	H D	1-1	Johnson 88	11,636
38	facr4r	Middlesbrough	A L	4-5*	Noble 23, McCombe 117 (*on penalties)	26,328
39	div2	Blackpool	A W	1-0	Andrews 53	6,696
40	div2	Brighton	A W	2-0	Jevons 43, 84 pen	6,280
41	div2	Northampton	H W	1-0	Betsy 19	11,965
42	div2	Chesterfield	A W	3-1	Keogh 8, Johnson 36, Noble 45	3,471
43	div2	Brentford	H W	1-0	Jevons 5 pen	11,826
44	div2	Bradford	H L	2-3	Jevons 13, Russell 90	13,021
45	div2	Crewe	A W	1-0	Showunmi 85	5,731
46	div2	Doncaster	A W	1-0	McCombe 88	7,945
47	div2	Nottm Forest	H D	1-1	Orr 38	19,249
48	div2	Swansea	H D	0-0		14,025
49	div2	Gillingham	A L	0-1		6,292
50	div2	Yeovil	H W	2-0	Johnson 43, Orr 71 pen	19,002
51	div2	Carlisle	A W	3-1	McCombe 45, Showunmi 65, Orr 84	10,232
52	div2	Millwall	A L	0-1		12,547
53	div2	Rotherham	H W	3-1	Noble 8, 44, Russell 55	19,517

LEAGUE APPEARANCES, BOOKINGS AND CAPS

	AGE (on 01/07/07)	IN NAMED 16	APPEARANCES	COUNTING GAMES	MINUTES ON PITCH	LEAGUE GOALS	
Goalkeepers							
Adriano Basso	32	45	45	44	4024	0	0
John Ruddy	20	1	1	1	90	0	0
Chris Weale	25	18	1	0	26	0	0
Defenders							
Louis Carey	30	38	38	35	3271	2	11
Liam Fontaine	21	34	30	20	2041	0	3
Richard Keogh	20	37	31	19	2019	2	8
James McAllister	29	33	31	27	2524	1	11
Jamie McCombe	24	43	41	37	3454	4	6
James Wilson	18	19	19	17	1523	0	2
Craig Woodman	24	18	11	5	515	0	1
Midfielders							
Kevin Betsy	29	17	17	16	1469	1	2
Scott Brown	22	17	15	9	942	4	0
Lee Johnson	26	43	42	39	3487	5	5
Scott Murray	33	29	28	20	2006	7	5
David Noble	25	34	26	12	1545	3	4
Bradley Orr	24	39	35	24	2522	4	5
Alex Russell	34	42	29	17	1826	2	4
Cole Skuse	21	43	42	27	2807	0	2
Nick Wright	19	4	4	1	172	0	1
Forwards							
Wayne Andrews	29	7	7	1	301	2	0
Stephen Brooker	26	23	23	13	1404	2	0
Barry Corr	22	3	3	1	109	0	0
David Cotterill	19	5	5	2	275	1	1
Phil Jevons	27	43	41	26	2781	11	4
Jennison Myrie-Williams	19	27	25	12	1466	2	3
Enoch Showunmi	24	33	33	26	2505	10	5
Andrew Smith	26	13	9	5	364	0	1

TEAM OF THE SEASON

Richard Keogh D — CG: 19 DR: 155	**Alex Russell** M — CG: 17 SD: 87
James Wilson D — CG: 17 DR: 152	**Kevin Betsy** M — CG: 16 SD: 77
Adriano Basso G — CG: 44 DR: 105	**Enoch Showunmi** F — CG: 26 SR: 250
Jamie McCombe D — CG: 37 DR: 115	**Scott Murray** M — CG: 20 SD: 49
Louis Carey D — CG: 35 DR: 112	**Phil Jevons** F — CG: 26 SR: 252
	Lee Johnson M — CG: 39 SD: 35

MONTHLY POINTS TALLY

Month	Points	%
AUGUST	6	40%
SEPTEMBER	16	76%
OCTOBER	7	58%
NOVEMBER	4	44%
DECEMBER	12	67%
JANUARY	7	58%
FEBRUARY	7	58%
MARCH	16	76%
APRIL	7	47%
MAY	3	100%

LEAGUE GOALS

	PLAYER	MINS	GOALS	S RATE
1	Jevons	2781	11	252
2	Showunmi	2505	10	250
3	Murray	2006	7	286
4	Johnson	3487	5	697
5	Brown, S	942	4	235
6	Orr	2522	4	630
7	McCombe	3454	4	863
8	Noble	1545	3	515
9	Andrews	301	2	150
10	Brooker	1404	2	702
11	Myrie-Williams	1466	2	733
12	Russell	1826	2	913
13	Keogh	2019	2	1009
	Other		5	
	TOTAL		**63**	

TOP POINT EARNERS

	PLAYER	GAMES	AV PTS
1	Richard Keogh	19	2.26
2	Alex Russell	17	2.25
3	Liam Fontaine	20	1.95
4	Louis Carey	35	1.94
5	James McAllister	27	1.93
6	Jamie McCombe	37	1.89
7	Kevin Betsy	16	1.88
8	James Wilson	17	1.88
9	Stephen Brooker	13	1.85
10	Adriano Basso	45	1.82
	CLUB AVERAGE:		**1.85**

DISCIPLINARY RECORDS

	PLAYER	YELLOW	RED	AV
1	James McAllister	11	0	28
2	Richard Keogh	8	0	28
3	Louis Carey	11	0	32
4	David Noble	4	0	38
5	J Myrie-Williams	3	0	48
6	Scott Murray	5	0	50
7	Bradley Orr	5	1	50
8	Craig Woodman	1	0	51
9	Jamie McCombe	6	0	57
10	Alex Russell	4	0	60
11	Kevin Betsy	2	0	73
12	James Wilson	2	0	76
13	Enoch Showunmi	5	0	83
	Other	14	1	
	TOTAL	**81**	**2**	

KEY GOALKEEPER

Adriano Basso

Goals Conceded in the League	38	**Counting Games** League games when player was on pitch for at least 70 minutes	44
Defensive Rating Ave number of mins between League goals conceded while on the pitch	105	**Clean Sheets** In League games when player was on pitch for at least 70 minutes	18

KEY PLAYERS - DEFENDERS

Richard Keogh

Goals Conceded Number of League goals conceded while the player was on the pitch	13	**Clean Sheets** In League games when player was on pitch for at least 70 minutes	11
Defensive Rating Ave number of mins between League goals conceded while on the pitch	155	**Club Defensive Rating** Average number of mins between League goals conceded by the club this season	106

	PLAYER	CON LGE	CLEAN SHEETS	DEF RATE
1	Richard Keogh	13	11	155 mins
2	James Wilson	10	9	152 mins
3	Jamie McCombe	30	14	115 mins
4	Louis Carey	29	14	112 mins

KEY PLAYERS - MIDFIELDERS

Alex Russell

Goals in the League	2	**Contribution to Attacking Power** Average number of minutes between League team goals while on pitch	65
Defensive Rating Average number of mins between League goals conceded while on pitch	152	**Scoring Difference** Defensive Rating minus Contribution to Attacking Power	87

	PLAYER	LGE GOALS	DEF RATE	POWER	SCORE DIFF
1	Alex Russell	2	152	65	87 mins
2	Kevin Betsy	1	146	69	77 mins
3	Scott Murray	7	118	69	49 mins
4	Lee Johnson	5	102	67	35 mins

KEY PLAYERS - GOALSCORERS

Enoch Showunmi

Goals in the League	10	**Player Strike Rate** Average number of minutes between League goals scored by player	250
Contribution to Attacking Power Average number of minutes between League team goals while on pitch	69	**Club Strike Rate** Average number of minutes between League goals scored by club	65

	PLAYER	LGE GOALS	POWER	STRIKE RATE
1	Enoch Showunmi	10	69	250 mins
2	Phil Jevons	11	69	252 mins
3	Scott Murray	7	69	286 mins
4	David Noble	3	55	515 mins

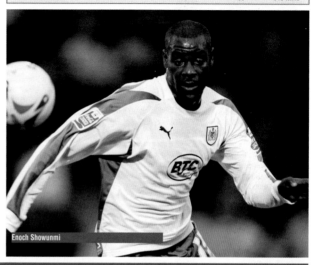

Enoch Showunmi

SQUAD APPEARANCES

Match	1 2 3 4 5	6 7 8 9 10	11 12 13 14 15	16 17 18 19 20	21 22 23 24 25	26 27 28 29 30	31 32 33 34 35	36 37 38 39 40	41 42 43 44 45	46 47 48 49 50	51 52 53
Venue	H A A H A	A H A H H	A A H A H	A H A A H	A H H A H	A H H A H	H A A H H	A H A A A	H A H H A	A H H A H	A A H
Competition	L L L L W	L L L L L	L L L L L	L L L F L	L F L L L	L L L L F	L F L F L	L L F L L	L L L L L	L L L L L	L L L
Result	W L L L L	W W L W W	W W D D W	L W L W W	D W W D W	D D W D D	W W W D L	L D L W W	W W W L W	W D D L W	W L W

Goalkeepers
Adriano Basso
John Ruddy
Chris Weale

Defenders
Louis Carey
Liam Fontaine
Richard Keogh
James McAllister
Jamie McCombe
James Wilson
Craig Woodman

Midfielders
Kevin Betsy
Scott Brown
Lee Johnson
Scott Murray
David Noble
Bradley Orr
Alex Russell
Cole Skuse
Nick Wright

Forwards
Wayne Andrews
Stephen Brooker
Barry Corr
David Cotterill
Phil Jevons
Jennison Myrie-Williams
Enoch Showunmi
Andrew Smith

KEY: ■ On all match ◄◄ Subbed or sent off (Counting game) ►► Subbed on from bench (Counting Game) ►► Subbed on and then subbed or sent off (Counting Game) □ Not in 16
■ On bench ◄◄ Subbed or sent off (playing less than 70 minutes) ►► Subbed on (playing less than 70 minutes) ►► Subbed on and then subbed or sent off (playing less than 70 minutes)

LEAGUE 1 - BRISTOL CITY

BLACKPOOL

PROMOTED VIA THE PLAY-OFFS Final Position: **3rd**

NICKNAME: THE SEASIDERS   KEY: ☐ Won ☐ Drawn ☐ Lost   Attendance

#					Result	Scorers	Attendance
1	div2	Brentford	A	L	0-1		6,048
2	div2	Nottm Forest	H	L	0-1		7,635
3	div2	Rotherham	H	L	0-1		5,677
4	div2	Bristol City	A	W	4-2	Vernon 27, Jackson 50, Parker 77, Graham 89	10,630
5	ccr1	Barnsley	H	L	2-4*	Vernon 71, 120 (*on penalties)	3,938
6	div2	Gillingham	H	D	1-1	Vernon 34	5,056
7	div2	Millwall	A	D	0-0		7,692
8	div2	Port Vale	A	L	1-2	Southern 90	5,171
9	div2	Chesterfield	H	D	1-1	Gillett 32	4,600
10	div2	Oldham	H	D	2-2	Vernon 41, Morrell 90	6,794
11	div2	Doncaster	A	D	0-0		5,424
12	div2	Carlisle	A	L	0-1		8,401
13	div2	Leyton Orient	H	W	3-0	Morrell 21, Hoolahan 82 pen, Parker 86	5,298
14	div2	Brighton	A	W	3-0	Southern 17, Vernon 61, 87	5,146
15	div2	Yeovil	H	D	1-1	Vernon 57	6,812
16	div2	Crewe	A	W	2-1	Morrell 3, Barker 90	5,765
17	div2	Bradford	H	W	4-1	Fox 39, Hoolahan 45 pen, Parker 64, 70	7,937
18	div2	Northampton	A	D	1-1	Morrell 20	5,762
19	facr1	Huddersfield	A	W	1-0	Hoolahan 70 pen	6,597
20	div2	Huddersfield	H	W	3-1	Parker 26, Southern 30, Morrell 60	7,414
21	div2	Tranmere	A	L	0-2		8,247
22	facr2	MK Dons	A	W	2-0	Parker 31, Morrell 48	3,837
23	div2	Cheltenham	H	W	2-1	Morrell 29, Hoolahan 80	4,851
24	div2	Swansea	H	D	1-1	Vernon 83	6,216
25	div2	Scunthorpe	A	W	3-1	Morrell 27, Hoolahan 58 pen, Parker 88	4,527
26	div2	Bournemouth	A	W	3-1	Parker 47, 52, Fox 88	5,758
27	div2	Carlisle	H	W	2-1	Murphy 5 og, Parker 29	9,473
28	div2	Doncaster	H	W	3-1	Vernon 77, 83, Barker 81	7,952
29	div2	Chesterfield	A	L	0-2		4,351
30	facr3	Aldershot	H	W	4-2	Vernon 4, Morrell 7, 73, Burgess 80 pen	6,355
31	div2	Port Vale	H	W	2-1	Morrell 72, Fox 76	6,661
32	div2	Leyton Orient	A	W	1-0	Southern 85	5,217
33	facr4	Norwich	H	D	1-1	Evatt 52	9,491
34	div2	Brentford	H	L	1-3	Vernon 90	6,086
35	facr4r	Norwich	A	L	1-2	Jackson 37, Barker 108	19,120
36	div2	Bristol City	H	L	0-1		6,696
37	div2	Nottm Forest	A	D	1-1	Hoolahan 90 pen	16,849
38	div2	Millwall	H	L	0-1		6,547
39	div2	Oldham	A	W	1-0	Morrell 67	6,956
40	div2	Gillingham	A	D	2-2	Burgess 12, Fox 64	5,949
41	div2	Bournemouth	H	W	2-0	Forbes 36, Burgess 54	6,184
42	div2	Brighton	H	D	0-0		8,164
43	div2	Yeovil	A	W	1-0	Morrell 57	6,012
44	div2	Bradford	A	W	3-1	Williams 6, Morrell 77, Vernon 90	8,984
45	div2	Rotherham	A	L	0-1		4,025
46	div2	Crewe	H	W	2-1	Hoolahan 15, Williams 57	7,203
47	div2	Tranmere	H	W	3-2	Parker 9, Hoolahan 36, Morrell 73	8,091
48	div2	Huddersfield	A	W	2-0	Jorgensen 29, Williams 59	11,432
49	div2	Northampton	H	W	4-1	Brandon 49, 62, Hoolahan 55 pen, Dyche 84 og	7,334
50	div2	Cheltenham	A	W	2-1	Williams 39, Southern 85	5,093
51	div2	Scunthorpe	H	W	3-1	Jorgensen 8, Parker 26, Barker 56	9,482
52	div2	Swansea	A	W	6-3	Morrell 25, 57, 61, 78, Parker 32, 89	18,903
53	d2po1	Oldham	A	W	2-1	Barker 52, Hoolahan 87	12,154
54	d2po2	Oldham	H	W	3-1	Southern 28, Morrell 75, Parker 90	9,453
55	d2pof	Yeovil	A	W	2-0	Williams 43, Parker 52	59,313

LEAGUE APPEARANCES, BOOKINGS AND CAPS

	AGE (on 01/07/07)	IN NAMED 16	APPEARANCES	COUNTING GAMES	MINUTES ON PITCH	LEAGUE GOALS	
Goalkeepers							
Lewis Edge	20	7	1	1	90	0	0	0
Rhys Evans	25	37	32	32	2880	0	1	0
Joe Hart	20	5	5	5	450	0	0	0
Paul Rachubka	26	12	8	8	720	0	0	0
Defenders							
Shaun Barker	24	45	45	44	4018	3	4	1
Danny Coid	25	25	18	14	1360	0	1	0
Carl Dickinson	20	7	7	7	630	0	1	0
Ian Evatt	25	45	44	42	3808	0	1	0
Vincent Fernandez	20	5	1	0	40	0	1	0
Kaspar Gorkss	25	16	9	7	627	0	0	0
Michael Jackson	33	44	44	37	3659	1	5	0
Marc Joseph	30	22	8	3	442	0	1	0
Paul Tierney	24	14	10	6	614	0	1	0
Andy Wilkinson	22	8	7	4	415	0	0	0
Midfielders							
Marcus Bean	22	16	6	2	243	0	1	0
Chris Brandon	31	5	5	3	325	2	1	1
Adrian Forbes	28	36	34	19	2125	1	4	0
David Fox	23	40	37	31	2848	4	5	0
Simon Gillett	21	32	31	19	1846	1	5	1
Wesley Hoolahan	25	44	43	36	3360	8	8	1
Claus Jorgensen	31	34	31	18	1874	2	3	0
Rory Prendergast	29	7	5	2	247	0	1	0
Keith Southern	23	39	39	37	3321	5	7	0
Robbie Williams	22	9	9	9	805	4	3	0
Forwards							
Ben Burgess	25	29	27	11	1354	2	0	0
Danny Graham	21	5	4	1	132	1	0	0
Andy Morrell	32	41	39	29	2905	16	6	0
Keigan Parker	25	45	44	22	2442	13	9	0
Scott Vernon	23	43	38	15	1843	11	0	0

TEAM OF THE SEASON

D Danny Coid CG: 14 DR: 123	**M** David Fox CG: 31 SD: 41	
D Ian Evatt CG: 42 DR: 84	**M** Adrian Forbes CG: 19 SD: 31	**F** Scott Vernon CG: 15 SR: 167
G Rhys Evans CG: 32 DR: 80		
D Shaun Barker CG: 44 DR: 83	**M** Claus Jorgensen CG: 18 SD: 28	**F** Andy Morrell CG: 29 SR: 181
D Michael Jackson CG: 37 DR: 79	**M** Wesley Hoolahan CG: 36 SD: 26	

MONTHLY POINTS TALLY

AUGUST		4	27%
SEPTEMBER		7	33%
OCTOBER		10	83%
NOVEMBER		4	44%
DECEMBER		16	89%
JANUARY		6	67%
FEBRUARY		4	27%
MARCH		14	67%
APRIL		15	100%
MAY		3	100%

LEAGUE GOALS

	PLAYER	MINS	GOALS	S RATE
1	Morrell	2905	16	181
2	Parker	2442	13	187
3	Vernon	1843	11	167
4	Hoolahan	3360	8	420
5	Southern	3321	5	664
6	Williams	805	4	201
7	Fox	2848	4	712
8	Barker	4018	3	1339
9	Brandon	325	2	162
10	Burgess	1354	2	677
11	Jorgensen	1874	2	937
12	Graham	132	1	132
13	Gillett	1846	1	1846
	Other		2	
	TOTAL		74	

TOP POINT EARNERS

	PLAYER	GAMES	AV PTS
1	Andy Morrell	28	2.39
2	Claus Jorgensen	17	2.35
3	Keigan Parker	21	2.14
4	David Fox	31	2.00
5	Adrian Forbes	19	1.94
6	Michael Jackson	37	1.92
7	Ian Evatt	42	1.90
8	Wesley Hoolahan	36	1.83
9	Shaun Barker	45	1.78
10	Keith Southern	36	1.78
	CLUB AVERAGE:		1.80

DISCIPLINARY RECORDS

	PLAYER	YELLOW	RED	AVE
1	Simon Gillett	5	1	307
2	Wesley Hoolahan	10	1	336
3	Keigan Parker	9	0	348
4	Robbie Williams	3	0	402
5	Andy Morrell	6	0	484
6	David Fox	5	0	569
7	Carl Dickinson	1	0	630
8	Adrian Forbes	4	0	708
9	Michael Jackson	5	0	914
10	Claus Jorgensen	3	0	937
11	Ian Evatt	4	0	952
12	Shaun Barker	3	1	1339
13	Danny Coid	1	0	1360
	Other	9	0	
	TOTAL	68	3	

KEY GOALKEEPER

Rhys Evans

Goals Conceded in the League	36	Counting Games	League games when player was on pitch for at least 70 minutes	32
Defensive Rating	Average number of mins between League goals conceded while on the pitch	80	Clean Sheets	In League games when player was on pitch for at least 70 minutes	5

KEY PLAYERS - DEFENDERS

Danny Coid

Goals Conceded	Number of League goals conceded while the player was on the pitch	11	Clean Sheets	In League games when player was on pitch for at least 70 minutes	7
Defensive Rating	Average number of mins between League goals conceded while on the pitch	123	Club Defensive Rating	Average number of mins between League goals conceded by the club this season	88

	PLAYER	CON LGE	CLEAN SHEETS	DEF RATE
1	Danny Coid	11	7	123 mins
2	Ian Evatt	45	10	84 mins
3	Shaun Barker	48	9	83 mins
4	Michael Jackson	46	6	79 mins

KEY PLAYERS - MIDFIELDERS

David Fox

Goals in the League	4	Contribution to Attacking Power	Average number of minutes between League team goals while on pitch	53
Defensive Rating	Average number of mins between League goals conceded while on the pitch	94	Scoring Difference	Defensive Rating minus Contribution to Attacking Power	41

	PLAYER	LGE GOALS	DEF RATE	POWER	SCORE DIFF
1	David Fox	4	94	53	41 mins
2	Adrian Forbes	1	88	57	31 mins
3	Claus Jorgensen	2	74	46	28 mins
4	Wesley Hoolahan	8	81	55	26 mins

KEY PLAYERS - GOALSCORERS

Scott Vernon

Goals in the League	11	Player Strike Rate	Average number of minutes between League goals scored by player	167
Contribution to Attacking Power	Average number of minutes between League team goals while on pitch	83	Club Strike Rate	Average number of minutes between League goals scored by club	56

	PLAYER	LGE GOALS	POWER	STRIKE RATE
1	Scott Vernon	11	83	167 mins
2	Andy Morrell	16	46	181 mins
3	Keigan Parker	13	41	187 mins
4	Wesley Hoolahan	8	55	420 mins

Andy Morrell

SQUAD APPEARANCES

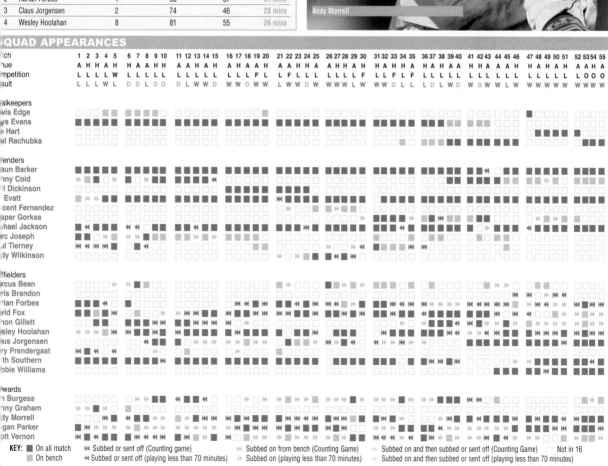

Match	1 2 3 4 5	6 7 8 9 10	11 12 13 14 15	16 17 18 19 20	21 22 23 24 25	26 27 28 29 30	31 32 33 34 35	36 37 38 39 40	41 42 43 44 45 46	47 48 49 50 51	52 53 54 55
Venue	A H H A H	H A A H H	A A H A H	A H A A H	A A H H A	A H H A H	H A H H A	H A H A A	H H A A A H	H A H A H	A A H A
Competition	L L L L W	L L L L L	L L L L L	L L L F L	L F L L L	L L L L F	L L F L F	L L L L L	L L L L L L	L L L L L	L O O O
Result	L L L W L	D D L D D	D L W W D	W W D W W	L W W D W	W W W L W	W W D L L	L D L W D	W D W L W	W W W W W	W W W W

Goalkeepers
- Lewis Edge
- Rhys Evans
- Joe Hart
- Paul Rachubka

Defenders
- Shaun Barker
- Danny Coid
- Liam Dickinson
- Ian Evatt
- Vincent Fernandez
- Kaspar Gorkss
- Michael Jackson
- Marc Joseph
- Paul Tierney
- Andy Wilkinson

Midfielders
- Marcus Bean
- Chris Brandon
- Adrian Forbes
- David Fox
- Simon Gillett
- Wesley Hoolahan
- Claus Jorgensen
- Gary Prendergast
- Keith Southern
- Robbie Williams

Forwards
- Ben Burgess
- Danny Graham
- Andy Morrell
- Keigan Parker
- Scott Vernon

KEY: ■ On all match   ◄◄ Subbed or sent off (Counting game)   ►► Subbed on from bench (Counting Game)   ►► Subbed on and then subbed or sent off (Counting Game)   ☐ Not in 16
   ■ On bench   ◄◄ Subbed or sent off (playing less than 70 minutes)   ►► Subbed on (playing less than 70 minutes)   ►► Subbed on and then subbed or sent off (playing less than 70 minutes)

LEAGUE 1 - BLACKPOOL

NOTTINGHAM FOREST

Final Position: 4th

NICKNAME: THE REDS   KEY: ☐ Won ☐ Drawn ☐ Lost   Attendance

#	Comp	Opponent	H/A	Result		Scorers	Attendance
1	div2	Bradford	H W	1-0		Bennett 10	19,665
2	div2	Blackpool	A W	2-0		Lester 45, Grant.Holt 73	7,635
3	div2	Northampton	A W	1-0		Doig 46 og	7,172
4	div2	Brighton	H W	2-1		Grant.Holt 63 pen, 78	18,686
5	ccr1	Accrington	A L	0-1			2,146
6	div2	Huddersfield	A D	1-1		Grant.Holt 34	11,720
7	div2	Chesterfield	H W	4-0		Lester 35, Harris 45, Grant.Holt 50 pen, Southall 70	19,480
8	div2	Yeovil	A W	1-0		Gary.Holt 88	6,925
9	div2	Oldham	H L	0-2			17,446
10	div2	Carlisle	H L	0-1			19,535
11	div2	Tranmere	A D	0-0			11,444
12	div2	Port Vale	A D	1-1		Breckin 33	7,388
13	div2	Swansea	H W	3-1		Perch 54, Commons 56, Agogo 67	19,034
14	div2	Scunthorpe	H L	0-4			22,640
15	div2	Gillingham	A W	1-0		Southall 57	7,800
16	div2	Bristol City	H W	1-0		Southall 9	23,466
17	div2	Cheltenham	A W	2-0		Southall 32, 36	6,554
18	div2	Brentford	H W	2-0		Commons 10, 37	18,003
19	facr1	Yeading	H W	5-0		Commons 19, 32, 45, Agogo 54 pen, 63	7,704
20	div2	Rotherham	A D	1-1		Tyson 88	7,809
21	div2	Millwall	H W	3-1		Agogo 65, Perch 67, Breckin 82	19,410
22	facr2	Salisbury	A D	1-1		Tyson 27	3,100
23	div2	Bournemouth	A L	0-2			7,067
24	div2	Crewe	A W	4-1		Grant.Holt 31, Tyson 37, 43, 45	7,253
25	facr2r	Salisbury	H W	2-0		Tyson 53, Southall 81	6,177
26	div2	Leyton Orient	H L	1-3		Breckin 58	23,109
27	div2	Doncaster	A L	0-1			8,923
28	div2	Port Vale	H W	3-0		Tyson 13, Grant.Holt 65, 90	22,999
29	div2	Tranmere	H D	1-1		Perch 72	19,729
30	div2	Oldham	A L	0-5			9,768
31	facr3	Charlton	H W	2-0		Agogo 28, Grant.Holt 32	19,017
32	div2	Yeovil	H W	1-0		Grant.Holt 48	17,885
33	div2	Swansea	A D	0-0			16,849
34	facr4	Chelsea	A L	0-3			41,516
35	div2	Carlisle	A L	0-1			9,022
36	div2	Bradford	A D	2-2		Tyson 10, Lester 18	10,160
37	div2	Northampton	H W	1-0		Bennett 66	24,567
38	div2	Brighton	A L	1-2		Lester 55	7,749
39	div2	Blackpool	H D	1-1		Agogo 16	16,849
40	div2	Chesterfield	A W	2-1		Agogo 56, 62 pen	6,641
41	div2	Huddersfield	H W	5-1		Agogo 6, 60, McGugan 17, Grant.Holt 19, Perch 33	19,070
42	div2	Doncaster	H L	0-1			16,785
43	div2	Scunthorpe	A D	1-1		Commons 18	8,906
44	div2	Gillingham	H W	1-0		McGugan 85	17,950
45	div2	Cheltenham	H W	3-0		Gary.Holt 33, Perch 57, Tyson 90 pen	22,640
46	div2	Bristol City	A D	1-1		Grant.Holt 5	19,249
47	div2	Millwall	A L	0-1			12,035
48	div2	Rotherham	H D	1-1		Grant.Holt 21 pen	27,875
49	div2	Brentford	A W	4-2		Prutton 52, Commons 68, 90, Grant.Holt 74 pen	6,637
50	div2	Bournemouth	H W	3-0		Commons 23, 54, Prutton 66	19,898
51	div2	Leyton Orient	A W	3-1		Lester 18, 58, Commons 29	7,206
52	div2	Crewe	H D	0-0			27,472
53	d2po1	Yeovil	A W	2-0		Commons 23 pen, Perch 90 pen	8,935
54	d2po2	Yeovil	H L	2-5		Dobie 47, Gary.Holt 93	27,819

LEAGUE APPEARANCES, BOOKINGS AND CAPS

	AGE (on 01/07/07)	IN NAMED 16	APPEARANCES	COUNTING GAMES	MINUTES ON PITCH	LEAGUE GOALS
Goalkeepers						
Rune Pedersen	27	40	1	1	90	0	0
Paul Smith	27	45	45	45	4050	0	0
Defenders						
Julian Bennett	22	35	29	24	2211	2	11
Ian Breckin	31	46	46	46	4121	3	7
Luke Chambers	21	16	14	10	973	0	1
Danny Cullip	30	20	20	16	1575	0	2
John Curtis	28	44	41	35	3320	0	5
Wes Morgan	23	40	38	31	2921	0	2
James Perch	21	46	46	43	3856	6	8
John Thompson	26	23	14	5	573	0	1
Alan Wright	35	9	9	8	756	0	0
Midfielders						
Sammy Clingan	23	30	28	23	2146	0	4
Kristian Commons	23	32	32	25	2373	9	5
Gary Holt	34	42	38	28	2730	2	4
Robert Hughes	20	7	2	0	25	0	0
Lewis McGugan	18	16	12	9	878	2	1
David Prutton	25	12	12	11	1032	2	6
Nicky Southall	35	27	27	25	2290	5	5
Forwards						
Junior Agogo	27	30	29	16	1848	7	0
Scott Dobie	28	24	19	1	359	0	1
Neil Harris	29	20	18	9	982	1	1
Grant Holt	26	45	43	28	2853	13	7
Jack Lester	31	39	35	18	2097	6	12
Nathan Tyson	25	24	24	7	1067	7	3

TEAM OF THE SEASON

Paul Smith CG: 45 DR: 106 (G)

Julian Bennett CG: 23 DR: 122 (D)
James Perch CG: 43 DR: 116 (D)
Danny Cullip CG: 16 DR: 105 (D)
Ian Breckin CG: 46 DR: 103 (D)

Sammy Clingan CG: 23 SD: 56 (M)
David Prutton* CG: 11 SD: 46 (M)
Gary Holt CG: 28 SD: 39 (M)
Kristian Commons CG: 25 SD: 35 (M)

Grant Holt CG: 26 SR: 219 (F)
Junior Agogo CG: 15 SR: 264 (F)

MONTHLY POINTS TALLY

Month	Points	%
AUGUST	13	87%
SEPTEMBER	11	52%
OCTOBER	9	75%
NOVEMBER	7	78%
DECEMBER	7	39%
JANUARY	4	33%
FEBRUARY	8	53%
MARCH	11	61%
APRIL	10	67%
MAY	1	33%

LEAGUE GOALS

	PLAYER	MINS	GOALS	S RATE
1	Holt, Grant	2853	13	219
2	Commons	2373	9	263
3	Tyson	1067	7	152
4	Agogo	1848	7	264
5	Lester	2097	6	349
6	Southall	2290	5	458
7	Perch	3856	5	771
8	Breckin	4121	3	1373
9	McGugan	878	2	439
10	Prutton	1032	2	516
11	Bennett	2211	2	1105
12	Holt, Gary	2730	2	1365
13	Harris	982	1	982
	Other		0	
	TOTAL		**64**	

TOP POINT EARNERS

	PLAYER	GAMES	AV PTS
1	Danny Cullip	17	1.94
2	Junior Agogo	15	1.93
3	Jack Lester	17	1.88
4	Nicky Southall	25	1.84
5	James Perch	43	1.81
6	Paul Smith	45	1.80
7	Kristian Commons	25	1.80
8	John Curtis	35	1.77
9	Ian Breckin	46	1.76
10	Sammy Clingan	24	1.75
	CLUB AVERAGE:		**1.78**

DISCIPLINARY RECORDS

	PLAYER	YELLOW	RED	AV
1	David Prutton	6	1	20
2	Jack Lester	12	0	20
3	Julian Bennett	11	0	22
4	Nathan Tyson	3	1	26
5	Grant Holt	7	0	40
6	James Perch	8	0	48
7	Sammy Clingan	4	1	51
8	John Thompson	1	0	57
9	Ian Breckin	7	0	68
10	Nicky Southall	5	0	76
11	Danny Cullip	2	1	78
12	Kristian Commons	5	0	83
13	John Curtis	5	0	83
	Other	9	0	
	TOTAL	**85**	**4**	

KEY GOALKEEPER

Paul Smith

Goals Conceded in the League	38	Counting Games League games when player was on pitch for at least 70 minutes	45
Defensive Rating Ave number of mins between League goals conceded while on the pitch	106	Clean Sheets In League games when player was on pitch for at least 70 minutes	19

KEY PLAYERS - DEFENDERS

Julian Bennett

Goals Conceded Number of League goals conceded while the player was on the pitch	18	Clean Sheets In League games when player was on pitch for at least 70 minutes	11
Defensive Rating Ave number of mins between League goals conceded while on the pitch	122	Club Defensive Rating Average number of mins between League goals conceded by the club this season	103

	PLAYER	CON LGE	CLEAN SHEETS	DEF RATE
1	Julian Bennett	18	11	122 mins
2	James Perch	33	20	116 mins
3	Danny Cullip	15	8	105 mins
4	Ian Breckin	40	19	103 mins

KEY PLAYERS - MIDFIELDERS

Sammy Clingan

Goals in the League	0	Contribution to Attacking Power Average number of minutes between League team goals while on pitch	63
Defensive Rating Average number of mins between League goals conceded while on the pitch	119	Scoring Difference Defensive Rating minus Contribution to Attacking Power	56

	PLAYER	LGE GOALS	DEF RATE	POWER	SCORE DIFF
1	Sammy Clingan	0	119	63	56 mins
2	David Prutton	2	103	57	46 mins
3	Gary Holt	2	101	62	39 mins
4	Kristian Commons	9	91	56	35 mins

KEY PLAYERS - GOALSCORERS

Grant Holt

Goals in the League	13	Player Strike Rate Average number of minutes between League goals scored by player	219
Contribution to Attacking Power Average number of minutes between League team goals while on pitch	55	Club Strike Rate Average number of minutes between League goals scored by club	63

	PLAYER	LGE GOALS	POWER	STRIKE RATE
1	Grant Holt	13	55	219 mins
2	Kristian Commons	9	56	263 mins
3	Junior Agogo	7	61	264 mins
4	Jack Lester	6	61	349 mins

Grant Holt

SQUAD APPEARANCES

Match	1 2 3 4 5	6 7 8 9 10	11 12 13 14 15	16 17 18 19 20	21 22 23 24 25	26 27 28 29 30	31 32 33 34 35	36 37 38 39 40	41 42 43 44 45	46 47 48 49 50	51 52 53 54
Venue	H A A H A	A H A H H	A A H H A	H A H H A	H A A A H	H A H H A	H H A A A	A H A H A	H H A H H	A A H A H	A H A H
Competition	L L L L W	L L L L L	L L L L L	L L L W L	L F L L L	F L L F L	L L L L L	F L L F L	L L L L L	L L L L L	L L O O
Result	W W W W L	D W W L L	D D W L W	W W W W D	W D L W W	L L W D L	W W D L L	D W L D W	W L D W W	D L D W W	W D W L

Goalkeepers

| Rune Pedersen | ■ ■ ■ ■ ■ | ■ ■ ■ ■ ■ | ■ ■ ■ ■ ■ | ■ ■ ■ ■ ■ | ■ ■ ■ ■ ■ | □ □ ■ ■ ■ | ■ ■ ■ ■ ■ | ■ ■ ■ ■ ■ | ■ ■ ■ ■ ■ | ■ ■ ■ ■ ■ | ■ ■ ■ ■ |
| Paul Smith | ■ ■ ■ ■ ■ | ■ ■ ■ ■ ■ | ■ ■ ■ ■ ■ | ■ ■ ■ ■ ■ | ■ ■ ■ ■ ■ | □ □ ■ ■ ■ | ■ ■ ■ ■ ■ | ■ ■ ■ ■ ■ | ■ ■ ■ ■ ■ | ■ ■ ■ ■ ■ | ■ ■ ■ ■ |

Defenders

Julian Bennett	■ ◀◀ ◀◀ ■ □	■ ■ ■ ◀◀ ■	■ ■ ■ ■ □	■ ■ ■ ■ ■	□ □ □ ■ ■	■ ■ ■ ■ ■	■ ■ ■ ■ ■	■ ■ ■ ■ ■	■ ■ ■ ■ ■	■ ■▶ ▶▶ ■ ■	□ ▶▶ ■ ■
Ian Breckin	■ ■ ■ ■ ■	■ ■ ■ ■ ■	■ ■ ■ ■ ■	■ ■ ■ ■ ■	■ ■ ■ ■ ■	■ ■ ■ ■ ■	■ ■ ■ ■ ■	■ ■ ■ ■ ■	■ ■ ■ ◀◀ ■	■ ■ ■ ■ ■	■ ■ ■ ■
Luke Chambers	□ ■ ◀◀ □ □	□ □ □ □ □	□ □ □ □ □	□ □ □ □ □	□ □ □ □ □	□ □ □ □ □	□ □ □ □ □	▶▶ □ ■ ▶▶ □	■ ▶▶ ■ ■ ■	■ ■ ■ ■ ■	■ ■ ■ ■
Danny Cullip	◀◀ ■ ■ ■ ■	■ ■ ◀◀ ■ ■	□ □ □ □ ■	■ ■ ■ ■ ■	□ □ □ □ ◀◀	■ ■ ■ ■ ■	■ ◀◀ □ □ □	□ □ □ □ □	□ □ □ □ □	■ ■ ■ ■ ■	■ ■ ■ ■
John Curtis	▶▶ ■ ▶▶ ■ ▶▶	■ ◀◀ ◀◀ □ □	■ ■ ■ ■ ■	□ □ □ □ □	◀◀ ■ ■ ■ ■	■ ■ ■ ■ ■	□ □ ◀◀ □ □	□ □ □ □ □	◀◀ ■ ◀◀ □ □	□ □ □ □ □	□ ■ ■ ■
Wes Morgan	■ ■ ■ ■ ◀◀	■ ▶▶ ▶▶ ◀◀ ■	■ ■ ■ ■ ■	■ ■ ■ ■ ■	■ ■ ■ ■ ■	■ ■ ■ ■ ■	■ ■ ■ ■ ■	■ ■ ■ ■ ■	□ ■ ■ ▶▶ ■	■ ■ ■ ■ ■	■ ■ ■ ■
James Perch	■ ■ ◀◀ ■ ■	■ ■ ■ ■ ■	■ ■ ■ ■ ■	■ ◀◀ ▶▶ ■ ■	■ ■ ■ ■ ■	▶▶ □ □ ■ ■	■ ■ ■ ■ ■	■ ■ ■ ■ ■	■ ■ ■ ■ ■	◀◀ ■ ■ ■ ■	■ ■ ■ ■
John Thompson	■▶ ■ ■ ▶▶ ▶▶	■▶ ■▶ ■ ▶▶ ■	▶▶ □ □ □ □	□ ◀◀ □ □ □	□ □ □ □ □	□ □ ■ ■ ■	□ ◀◀ ■ ■ ■	■ ■ ■ ■ ■	□ □ □ □ □	□ □ □ □ □	□ □ □ □
Ian Wright	□ □ □ □ □	□ □ □ □ □	□ □ □ □ □	□ □ □ □ □	□ □ □ □ □	□ □ □ □ □	□ □ □ □ □	□ □ □ □ □	□ □ □ □ □	□ □ ■ ■ ◀◀	◀◀ ◀◀ ■ ■

Midfielders

Sammy Clingan	■ ■ ■ ◀◀ □	◀◀ □ ■▶ ▶▶ □	■ ■ ▶▶ ■ ■	■ □ □ ▶▶ ■	◀◀ □ ■ ■ ■	◀◀ ■ ■ ◀◀ □	■ ■ ◀◀ □ □	□ ◀◀ ■ ■ ◀◀	◀◀ ■ ◀◀ ■ ■	■ ■ ◀◀ ◀◀ ■	■ ■ ◀◀ ◀◀
Kristian Commons	□ □ □ □ □	□ ■ ◀◀ ◀◀ ■	◀◀ ◀◀ ■ ■ ■	■ ◀◀ ■ ■ ■	■ ◀◀ ▶▶ ◀◀ ■	▶▶ ■ ■ ▶▶ ■	■ ■ ■ ■ □	◀◀ ■ ◀◀ ■ ◀◀	■ ■ ■ ■ ■	■ ■ ■ ■ ■	■ ■ ▶▶ ▶▶
Gary Holt	■ ■ ■ ◀◀ □	■ ■ ■ ■ ◀◀	□ □ ◀◀ □ □	■ ◀◀ □ ◀◀ ■	▶▶ ■ ■ ▶▶ ■	■ ▶▶ ■ ■ ▶▶	□ ▶▶ ■ ■ ■	■ ■ ■ ■ ■	■ ■ ■ ◀◀ ■	■ ■ ■ ■ ■	▶▶ ■ ▶▶ ■
Robert Hughes	□ □ □ □ □	□ □ □ □ □	□ □ ▶▶ □ □	□ □ □ □ □	□ □ □ □ □	□ □ □ □ □	□ □ □ □ □	□ □ □ □ □	◀◀ ■ ■ ▶▶ □	□ □ □ □ □	□ □ □ □
Lewis McGugan	□ □ □ □ □	□ □ □ □ □	□ □ □ □ □	□ □ □ □ □	□ □ □ □ □	□ □ □ □ □	□ □ □ □ □	□ □ □ □ □	□ □ □ ◀◀ ◀◀	■ ◀◀ ■ ▶▶ ▶▶	◀◀ ◀◀ ■ ■
David Prutton	□ □ □ □ □	□ □ □ □ □	□ □ □ □ □	□ □ □ □ □	□ □ □ □ □	□ □ □ □ □	□ □ □ □ □	□ □ □ □ □	□ □ □ □ □	▶▶ □ ■ ■ ■	■ ■ ■ ■
Nicky Southall	■ ■ ■ ■ ▶▶	◀◀ ■ ■ ■ ■	◀◀ ■ ▶▶ ■ ■	■ ■ ■ ■ ■	■ ■ ◀◀ ▶▶ □	□ □ □ □ □	□ □ □ □ □	□ □ □ □ □	□ □ □ □ □	□ □ □ □ □	□ □ □ □

Forwards

Junior Agogo	□ □ □ □ □	□ ▶▶ ▶▶ ■ ◀◀	◀◀ ◀◀ ◀◀ □ □	◀◀ ◀◀ ◀◀ ■ ■	◀◀ □ □ □ ◀◀	◀◀ ▶▶ ▶▶ ◀◀ ■	■ ▶▶ ▶▶ ◀◀ ■	□ ◀◀ ■ ■ ■	□ □ □ □ □	□ □ □ □ □	□ □ □ □
Scott Dobie	□ □ □ □ □	□ □ □ □ □	□ □ □ □ □	□ □ □ □ □	□ □ ▶▶ ▶▶ ■	◀◀ □ ▶▶ ▶▶ ▶▶	▶▶ □ ◀◀ ◀◀ □	□ □ □ □ □	□ □ □ □ □	□ □ □ □ □	□ □ □ □
Neil Harris	▶▶ ▶▶ ▶▶ ■ ◀◀	▶▶ ■ ■ ◀◀ ◀◀	◀◀ ▶▶ □ ▶▶ ◀◀	◀◀ ◀◀ ◀◀ ◀◀ ◀◀	▶▶ □ ◀◀ ▶▶ □	□ ■ ◀◀ ◀◀ ■	□ □ □ □ □	□ □ □ □ □	□ □ □ □ □	□ □ □ □ □	□ □ □ □
Grant Holt	□ □ □ □ □	□ □ □ □ □	□ □ □ □ ■	■ ◀◀ ■ ■ ■	■ ■ ■ ■ ■	■ ■ ■ ■ ■	■ ■ ■ ■ ■	■ ■ ■ ■ ■	■ ■ ■ ■ ◀◀	◀◀ ■ ■ ■ ■	■ ■ ◀◀ ■
Jack Lester	◀◀ ◀◀ ◀◀ ◀◀ □	◀◀ ◀◀ ◀◀ ◀◀ ■	▶▶ ▶▶ ◀◀ ■ □	◀◀ □ □ □ □	□ □ □ □ ■	■ ■ ■ ■ ■	■ ■ ■ ■ ■	◀◀ ◀◀ ■ ■ ◀◀	■ ■ ■ ◀◀ ◀◀	◀◀ ◀◀ ■ ■ ■	◀◀ ◀◀ □ □
Nathan Tyson	◀◀ □ □ □ □	□ □ □ □ □	□ □ □ □ □	□ □ □ □ □	▶▶ ◀◀ ◀◀ ◀◀ ◀◀	◀◀ ◀◀ ◀◀ ◀◀ □	◀◀ ◀◀ ◀◀ ◀◀ ■	■ ◀◀ ◀◀ ◀◀ ◀◀	◀◀ ◀◀ ◀◀ ◀◀ ◀◀	◀◀ ◀◀ ◀◀ ◀◀ ◀◀	◀◀ ◀◀ ◀◀ ◀◀

KEY: ■ On all match   ◀◀ Subbed or sent off (Counting game)   ▶▶ Subbed on from bench (Counting Game)   ■▶ Subbed on and then subbed or sent off (Counting Game)   □ Not in 16
   ■ On bench   ◀◀ Subbed or sent off (playing less than 70 minutes)   ▶▶ Subbed on (playing less than 70 minutes)   ▶▶ Subbed on and then subbed or sent off (playing less than 70 minutes)

LEAGUE 1 - NOTTINGHAM FOREST

YEOVIL

Final Position: 5th

NICKNAME: THE GLOVERS   KEY: ☐ Won ☐ Drawn ☐ Lost   Attendance

#		Opponent			Score	Scorers	Attendance
1	div2	Millwall	A	D	1-1	Gray 35	10,012
2	div2	Bournemouth	H	D	0-0		6,451
3	div2	Carlisle	H	W	2-1	Cohen 16, Welsh 42	4,709
4	div2	Tranmere	A	L	1-2	Cohen 44	6,023
5	ccr1	Southampton	A	L	2-5	Gray 30, Harrold 90	20,653
6	div2	Port Vale	H	W	1-0	Terry 4	4,827
7	div2	Swansea	A	D	1-1	Stewart 53	14,513
8	div2	Nottm Forest	H	L	0-1		6,925
9	div2	Northampton	A	D	1-1	Stewart 68	4,184
10	div2	Huddersfield	A	W	3-2	Morris 13, Davies 51, Cohen 77	9,573
11	div2	Crewe	H	W	2-0	B.Williams 45 og, Terry 71	5,333
12	div2	Brighton	H	W	2-0	Stewart 6, Gray 82	5,243
13	div2	Brentford	A	W	2-1	Skiverton 57, Cohen 88	5,770
14	div2	Cheltenham	H	L	0-1		6,220
15	div2	Blackpool	A	D	1-1	Stewart 86	6,812
16	div2	Oldham	H	W	1-0	Skiverton 45	5,741
17	div2	Chesterfield	A	D	1-1	Stewart 89	5,413
18	div2	Bristol City	H	W	2-1	Davies 78, Gray 90	9,009
19	facr1	Rushden & D	A	L	1-3	Cohen 62	2,530
20	div2	Leyton Orient	A	D	0-0		4,842
21	div2	Scunthorpe	H	L	0-2		5,921
22	div2	Rotherham	A	L	2-3	Best 25, Morris 31	4,823
23	div2	Gillingham	H	W	2-0	Best 17, Cohen 59	4,933
24	div2	Bradford	H	D	0-0		6,208
25	div2	Brighton	A	W	3-1	Best 38, Morris 47, Davies 59	6,554
26	div2	Crewe	A	W	3-2	Best 5, 8, Morris 70	5,450
27	div2	Northampton	H	D	0-0		5,361
28	div2	Huddersfield	H	W	3-1	Morris 4, Best 23, Hardy 36 og	5,554
29	div2	Nottm Forest	A	L	0-1		17,885
30	div2	Brentford	H	W	1-0	Best 56	5,373
31	div2	Bradford	A	W	2-0	Davies 5, 67	7,474
32	div2	Millwall	H	L	0-1		5,810
33	div2	Carlisle	A	W	4-1	Gray 49, Best 72, 90, Cohen 90	7,112
34	div2	Tranmere	H	L	0-2		5,168
35	div2	Bournemouth	A	W	2-0	Gray 30, Best 77	7,285
36	div2	Swansea	H	W	1-0	Stewart 56	5,984
37	div2	Doncaster	A	D	0-0		8,046
38	div2	Port Vale	A	L	2-4	Gray 37, Stewart 38	4,202
39	div2	Cheltenham	A	W	2-1	Gray 20, 63	5,314
40	div2	Blackpool	H	L	0-1		6,012
41	div2	Chesterfield	H	W	1-0	Jones 90	4,735
42	div2	Oldham	A	L	0-1		6,035
43	div2	Scunthorpe	A	L	0-1		7,883
44	div2	Leyton Orient	H	W	2-1	Gray 77 pen, Davies 83	5,206
45	div2	Bristol City	A	L	0-2		19,002
46	div2	Rotherham	H	W	1-0	Stewart 45	5,878
47	div2	Doncaster	H	W	1-0	Gray 72	6,253
48	div2	Gillingham	A	W	2-0	Kalala 63, Gray 68	7,484
49	d2po1	Nottm Forest	H	L	0-2		8,935
50	d2po2	Nottm Forest	A	W	5-2	Davies 22, 109, Wright 82 og, Stewart 87, Morris 92	27,819
51	d2pof	Blackpool	H	L	0-2		59,313

LEAGUE 1 - YEOVIL

LEAGUE APPEARANCES, BOOKINGS AND CAPS

	AGE (on 01/07/07)	IN NAMED 16	APPEARANCES	COUNTING GAMES	MINUTES ON PITCH	LEAGUE GOALS	
Goalkeepers							
Steve Mildenhall	29	46	46	46	4140	0	0
Defenders							
Craig Alcock	19	2	1	0	17	0	0
Chris Cohen	20	44	44	44	3960	6	9
Martin Cranie	20	12	12	11	992	0	2
Terrell Forbes	25	46	46	45	4095	0	2
Scott Guyett	31	41	16	8	1013	0	2
Nathan Jones	34	42	42	42	3728	1	11
Mark Lynch	25	17	17	17	1530	0	0
Matthew Rose	31	11	9	6	636	0	0
Terry Skiverton	32	39	39	35	3290	2	2
Anthony Tonkin	27	21	5	1	196	0	2
Midfielders							
Anthony Barry	21	40	24	9	1200	0	4
Martin Brittain	22	21	15	11	1042	0	0
Kevin Cooper	32	5	4	4	301	0	2
Aaron Davies	23	43	38	31	2939	6	3
J-P Kamudimba Kalala	25	43	38	32	3102	1	7
Nicholas Law	19	8	6	5	447	0	0
Andrew Lindegaard	26	14	14	11	1107	0	2
David Poole	22	4	4	1	159	0	0
Peter Sweeney	22	13	8	5	464	0	0
Paul Terry	28	20	20	16	1664	2	1
Ishmael Welsh	19	28	18	4	554	1	1
Forwards							
Leon Best	20	15	15	14	1301	10	2
Tom Clarke	18	1	1	0	56	0	0
Wayne Gray	26	46	46	23	2498	11	3
Matt Harrold	22	5	5	1	183	0	0
Kevin James	27	6	6	1	239	0	0
Darryl Knights	19	6	4	0	86	0	0
Lee Morris	27	36	33	15	1748	5	6
Adam Rooney	19	8	3	0	112	0	0
Marcus Stewart	34	32	31	28	2598	8	2
Daniel Webb	23	9	4	0	68	0	0

TEAM OF THE SEASON

D Nathan Jones — CG: 42 DR: 112
M Andrew Lindegaard* — CG: 11 SD: 59
D Terry Skiverton — CG: 35 DR: 109
M Aaron Davies — CG: 31 SD: 47
F Leon Best — CG: 14 SR: 130
G Steve Mildenhall — CG: 46 DR: 106
D Terrell Forbes — CG: 45 DR: 105
M J-P Kamudimba Kalala — CG: 32 SD: 46
F Wayne Gray — CG: 23 SR: 227
D Chris Cohen — CG: 44 DR: 104
M Paul Terry — CG: 16 SD: 13

MONTHLY POINTS TALLY

Month	Points	%
AUGUST		8 53%
SEPTEMBER		14 67%
OCTOBER		5 42%
NOVEMBER		4 44%
DECEMBER		10 67%
JANUARY		10 67%
FEBRUARY		10 56%
MARCH		6 40%
APRIL		9 60%
MAY		3 100%

LEAGUE GOALS

	PLAYER	MINS	GOALS	S RATE
1	Gray	2498	11	227
2	Best	1301	10	130
3	Stewart	2598	8	324
4	Davies	2939	6	489
5	Cohen	3960	6	660
6	Morris	1748	5	349
7	Terry	1664	2	832
8	Skiverton	3290	2	1645
9	Welsh	554	1	554
10	Kalala	3102	1	3102
11	Jones	3728	1	3728
12	Knights	86	0	
13	Law	447	0	
	Other		0	
	TOTAL		53	

TOP POINT EARNERS

	PLAYER	GAMES	AV PTS
1	Aaron Davies	31	1.97
2	J-P Kamudimba Kalala	32	1.94
3	Leon Best	14	1.86
4	Nathan Jones	42	1.74
5	Chris Cohen	44	1.73
6	Steve Mildenhall	46	1.72
7	Mark Lynch	17	1.71
8	Terrell Forbes	45	1.69
9	Terry Skiverton	35	1.69
10	Paul Terry	16	1.63
	CLUB AVERAGE:		1.72

DISCIPLINARY RECORDS

	PLAYER	YELLOW	RED	AVE
1	Nathan Jones	11	0	372
2	Anthony Barry	4	0	400
3	Lee Morris	6	0	437
4	Chris Cohen	9	0	495
5	Martin Cranie	2	0	496
6	Scott Guyett	0	2	506
7	J-P Kamud Kalala	7	0	517
8	Ishmael Welsh	1	0	554
9	Leon Best	2	0	650
10	Wayne Gray	3	0	832
11	Andrew Lindegaard	2	0	1107
12	Marcus Stewart	2	0	1299
13	Aaron Davies	3	0	1469
	Other	5	0	
	TOTAL	57	2	

KEY GOALKEEPER

Steve Mildenhall

Goals Conceded in the League	39	Counting Games League games when player was on pitch for at least 70 minutes	46
Defensive Rating Ave number of mins between League goals conceded while on the pitch	106	Clean Sheets In League games when player was on pitch for at least 70 minutes	18

KEY PLAYERS - DEFENDERS

Nathan Jones

Goals Conceded Number of League goals conceded while the player was on the pitch	33	Clean Sheets In League games when player was on pitch for at least 70 minutes	18
Defensive Rating Ave number of mins between League goals conceded while on the pitch	112	Club Defensive Rating Average number of mins between League goals conceded by the club this season	108

	PLAYER	CON LGE	CLEAN SHEETS	DEF RATE
1	Nathan Jones	33	18	112 mins
2	Terry Skiverton	30	13	109 mins
3	Terrell Forbes	39	18	105 mins
4	Chris Cohen	38	17	104 mins

KEY PLAYERS - MIDFIELDERS

Andrew Lindegaard

Goals in the League	0	Contribution to Attacking Power Average number of minutes between League team goals while on pitch	79
Defensive Rating Average number of mins between League goals conceded while on the pitch	138	Scoring Difference Defensive Rating minus Contribution to Attacking Power	59

	PLAYER	LGE GOALS	DEF RATE	POWER	SCORE DIFF
1	Andrew Lindegaard	0	138	79	59 mins
2	Aaron Davies	6	122	75	47 mins
3	Jean-Paul Kamudimba Kalala	1	114	68	46 mins
4	Paul Terry	2	92	79	13 mins

KEY PLAYERS - GOALSCORERS

Leon Best

Goals in the League	10	Player Strike Rate Average number of minutes between League goals scored by player	130
Contribution to Attacking Power Average number of minutes between League team goals while on pitch	59	Club Strike Rate Average number of minutes between League goals scored by club	76

	PLAYER	LGE GOALS	POWER	STRIKE RATE
1	Leon Best	10	59	130 mins
2	Wayne Gray	11	75	227 mins
3	Marcus Stewart	8	96	324 mins
4	Lee Morris	5	76	349 mins

Marcus Stewart

SQUAD APPEARANCES

Match	1 2 3 4 5	6 7 8 9 10	11 12 13 14 15	16 17 18 19 20	21 22 23 24 25	26 27 28 29 30	31 32 33 34 35	36 37 38 39 40	41 42 43 44 45	46 47 48 49 50	51
Venue	A H H A A	H A H A A	H H A H A	H A H A A	H A H H A	A H H A H	A H A H A	H A A A H	H A A H A	H H A H A	H
Competition	L L L L W	L L L L L	L L L L L	L L L F L	L L L L L	L L L L L	L L L L L	L L L L L	L L L L L	L L L O O	O
Result	D D W L L	W D L D W	W W W L D	W D W L D	L L W D W	W D W L W	W L W L W	W D L W L	W L L W L	W W W L W	L

Goalkeepers

Steve Mildenhall

Defenders

Craig Alcock

Chris Cohen

Martin Cranie

Terrell Forbes

Scott Guyett

Nathan Jones

Mark Lynch

Matthew Rose

Terry Skiverton

Anthony Tonkin

Midfielders

Anthony Barry

Martin Brittain

Kevin Cooper

Aaron Davies

J-P Kamudimba Kalala

Nicholas Law

Andrew Lindegaard

David Poole

Peter Sweeney

Paul Terry

Ishmael Welsh

Forwards

Leon Best

Tom Clarke

Wayne Gray

Matt Harrold

Kevin James

Darryl Knights

Lee Morris

Adam Rooney

Marcus Stewart

Daniel Webb

KEY: ■ On all match   ◄◄ Subbed or sent off (Counting game)   ►► Subbed on from bench (Counting Game)   ►► Subbed on and then subbed or sent off (Counting Game)   ☐ Not in 16

◻ On bench   ◄◄ Subbed or sent off (playing less than 70 minutes)   ►► Subbed on (playing less than 70 minutes)   ►► Subbed on and then subbed or sent off (playing less than 70 minutes)

OLDHAM ATHLETIC

Final Position: 6th

NICKNAME: THE LATICS   KEY: ☐ Won ☐ Drawn ☐ Lost   Attendance

#	Comp	Opponent			Score	Scorers	Attendance
1	div2	Tranmere	A	L	0-1		8,586
2	div2	Port Vale	H	L	0-1		4,975
3	div2	Swansea	H	W	1-0	Molango 67	4,708
4	div2	Millwall	A	L	0-1		7,455
5	ccr1	Rotherham	A	L	1-3	Rocastle 41	3,065
6	div2	Carlisle	H	D	0-0		6,080
7	div2	Bournemouth	A	L	2-3	Liddell 47 pen, 79	4,838
8	div2	Scunthorpe	H	W	1-0	McDonald 34	4,812
9	div2	Nottm Forest	A	W	2-0	Porter 28, 45	17,446
10	div2	Blackpool	A	D	2-2	Wellens 63, Porter 72	6,794
11	div2	Gillingham	H	W	4-1	Haining 4, Porter 23, 90, Charlton 46	4,652
12	div2	Rotherham	H	W	2-0	Stam 51, Warne 76	4,880
13	div2	Bristol City	A	D	0-0		11,656
14	div2	Doncaster	A	D	1-1	Porter 45	6,241
15	div2	Leyton Orient	H	D	3-3	Porter 78, 83, Liddell 90 pen	5,014
16	div2	Yeovil	A	L	0-1		5,741
17	div2	Brentford	H	W	3-0	Warne 15, McDonald 47, Wellens 90	4,708
18	div2	Cheltenham	A	W	2-1	Warne 23, McDonald 41	4,054
19	facr1	Kettering	A	W	4-3	Gregan 43, Warne 56, Trotman 60, C.Hall 90	3,481
20	div2	Bradford	H	W	2-0	Porter 79, 82	6,001
21	div2	Huddersfield	A	W	3-0	McDonald 16, Porter 59, Warne 67	13,280
22	facr2	Kings Lynn	A	W	2-0	Porter 10, C.Hall 82	5,444
23	div2	Crewe	H	W	1-0	Porter 45	4,798
24	div2	Chesterfield	A	L	1-2	Eardley 45	4,059
25	div2	Brighton	H	D	1-1	Warne 18	9,321
26	div2	Northampton	H	W	3-0	McDonald 22, Porter 37, Liddell 61	10,207
27	div2	Rotherham	A	W	3-2	Porter 29, 67, Haining 42	6,512
28	div2	Gillingham	A	W	3-0	Porter 26, Liddell 36 pen, Eardley 54	6,790
29	div2	Nottm Forest	H	W	5-0	Warne 30, Porter 39, Liddell 43 pen, 68 pen, Rocastle 90	9,768
30	facr3	Wolverhampton	A	D	2-2	Warne 19, C.Hall 78	14,524
31	div2	Scunthorpe	A	D	1-1	McDonald 90	7,685
32	facr3r	Wolverhampton	H	L	0-2		9,628
33	div2	Bristol City	H	L	0-3		6,924
34	div2	Northampton	A	W	3-2	Wellens 2, Warne 44, Porter 58	5,662
35	div2	Tranmere	H	W	1-0	C.Hall 90	6,944
36	div2	Swansea	A	W	1-0	Warne 32	9,880
37	div2	Millwall	H	L	1-2	Warne 55	6,181
38	div2	Port Vale	A	L	0-3		4,061
39	div2	Bournemouth	H	L	1-2	Liddell 45 pen	5,429
40	div2	Blackpool	H	L	0-1		6,956
41	div2	Carlisle	A	D	1-1	C.Taylor 13	7,951
42	div2	Doncaster	H	W	4-0	Clarke 8, Rocastle 74, C.Taylor 76, 90	6,619
43	div2	Leyton Orient	A	D	2-2	C.Taylor 73, Liddell 81 pen	5,443
44	div2	Brentford	A	D	2-2	Clarke 86, 90 pen	4,720
45	div2	Yeovil	H	W	1-0	McDonald 37	6,035
46	div2	Huddersfield	H	D	1-1	Porter 23	7,096
47	div2	Bradford	A	D	1-1	Glombard 87	9,940
48	div2	Cheltenham	H	L	0-2		5,426
49	div2	Crewe	A	L	1-2	Wellens 85	6,304
50	div2	Brighton	A	W	2-1	Porter 18, Liddell 40	7,588
51	div2	Chesterfield	H	W	1-0	Porter 58	8,148
52	d2po1	Blackpool	H	L	1-2	Liddell 75 pen	12,154
53	d2po2	Blackpool	A	L	1-3	Wolfenden 83	9,453

LEAGUE APPEARANCES, BOOKINGS AND CAPS

	AGE (on 01/07/07)	IN NAMED 16	APPEARANCES	COUNTING GAMES	MINUTES ON PITCH	LEAGUE GOALS		
Goalkeepers								
Alan Blayney	25	14	3	2	225	0	0	0
Chris Howarth	22	4	3	3	261	0	0	0
David Knight	20	3	2	1	128	0	0	1
Leslie Pogliacomi	31	42	40	38	3460	0	2	1
Defenders								
Hasney Aljofree	28	5	5	5	428	0	2	0
Simon Charlton	35	34	34	32	2942	1	5	0
Leon Clarke	22	5	5	5	445	3	1	0
Neil Eardley	19	36	36	32	3105	2	5	1
Sean Gregan	33	27	27	27	2409	0	6	0
Will Haining	24	44	44	42	3848	2	7	0
Kelvin Lomax	20	16	9	4	530	0	0	0
Miguel Roque	18	7	4	1	118	0	0	0
Stefan Stam	30	28	22	17	1664	1	2	0
Chris Swailes	36	4	4	4	354	0	0	0
Marc Tierney	21	5	5	1	200	0	1	0
Ben Turner	19	2	1	1	89	0	0	1
Midfielders								
Paul Edwards	27	30	25	10	1189	0	4	0
Andy Liddell	34	46	46	40	3816	10	3	0
Gary McDonald	25	45	43	37	3349	7	7	0
Craig Rocastle	25	44	34	12	1538	2	7	0
Chris Taylor	20	46	44	37	3430	4	4	1
Richard Wellens	27	42	42	42	3757	4	10	1
Forwards								
Luigi Glombard	22	8	8	3	331	1	0	0
Lewis Grabban	19	10	9	1	168	0	0	0
Christopher Hall	20	26	19	1	447	1	2	0
Maheta Molango	24	6	5	1	259	1	0	0
Chris Porter	23	35	35	32	2910	21	2	0
Paul Warne	34	46	46	39	3669	9	5	0
Neil Wood	24	13	5	2	214	0	0	0

TEAM OF THE SEASON

G Leslie Pogliacomi — CG: 38 DR: 93

D Stefan Stam — CG: 17 DR: 97
D Sean Gregan — CG: 27 DR: 92
D Neil Eardley — CG: 32 DR: 91
D Simon Charlton — CG: 32 DR: 91

M Andy Liddell — CG: 40 SD: 40
M Chris Taylor — CG: 37 SD: 38
M Gary McDonald — CG: 37 SD: 33
M Richard Wellens — CG: 42 SD: 32

F Chris Porter — CG: 32 SR: 138
F Paul Warne — CG: 39 SR: 407

MONTHLY POINTS TALLY

Month		Pts	%
AUGUST		4	27%
SEPTEMBER		14	67%
OCTOBER		5	42%
NOVEMBER		9	100%
DECEMBER		13	72%
JANUARY		7	58%
FEBRUARY		6	33%
MARCH		9	60%
APRIL		5	33%
MAY		3	100%

LEAGUE GOALS

	PLAYER	MINS	GOALS	S RATE
1	Porter	2910	21	138
2	Liddell	3816	10	381
3	Warne	3669	9	407
4	McDonald	3349	7	478
5	Taylor, C	3430	4	857
6	Wellens	3757	4	939
7	Clarke	445	3	148
8	Rocastle	1538	2	769
9	Eardley	3105	2	1552
10	Haining	3848	2	1924
11	Molango	259	1	259
12	Glombard	331	1	331
13	Hall, C	447	1	447
	Other		2	
	TOTAL		**69**	

TOP POINT EARNERS

	PLAYER	GAMES	AV PTS
1	Chris Porter	32	1.91
2	Leslie Pogliacomi	38	1.87
3	Andy Liddell	40	1.83
4	Sean Gregan	27	1.77
5	Paul Warne	39	1.77
6	Simon Charlton	32	1.75
7	Neil Eardley	32	1.72
8	Will Haining	42	1.71
9	Gary McDonald	37	1.69
10	Richard Wellens	42	1.69
	CLUB AVERAGE:		**1.63**

DISCIPLINARY RECORDS

	PLAYER	YELLOW	RED	AVE
1	Craig Rocastle	6	0	256
2	Paul Edwards	4	0	396
3	Richard Wellens	10	1	417
4	Sean Gregan	6	0	481
5	Will Haining	7	0	549
6	Simon Charlton	5	0	588
7	Gary McDonald	7	0	669
8	Chris Taylor	4	1	686
9	Paul Warne	5	0	733
10	Neil Eardley	5	1	776
11	Stefan Stam	2	0	832
12	Leslie Pogliacomi	2	1	1153
13	Andy Liddell	3	0	1272
	Other	2	0	
	TOTAL	**68**	**4**	

KEY GOALKEEPER

Leslie Pogliacomi

Goals Conceded in the League	37	Counting Games League games when player was on pitch for at least 70 minutes	38
Defensive Rating Ave number of mins between League goals conceded while on the pitch	93	Clean Sheets In League games when player was on pitch for at least 70 minutes	16

KEY PLAYERS - GOALSCORERS

Chris Porter

Goals in the League	21	Player Strike Rate Average number of minutes between League goals scored by player	138
Contribution to Attacking Power Average number of minutes between League team goals while on pitch	54	Club Strike Rate Average number of minutes between League goals scored by club	61

	PLAYER	LGE GOALS	POWER	STRIKE RATE
1	Chris Porter	21	54	138 mins
2	Andy Liddell	10	57	381 mins
3	Paul Warne	9	56	407 mins
4	Gary McDonald	7	57	478 mins

KEY PLAYERS - DEFENDERS

Stefan Stam

Goals Conceded Number of League goals conceded while the player was on the pitch	17	Clean Sheets In League games when player was on pitch for at least 70 minutes	7
Defensive Rating Ave number of mins between League goals conceded while on the pitch	97	Club Defensive Rating Average number of mins between League goals conceded by the club this season	90

	PLAYER	CON LGE	CLEAN SHEETS	DEF RATE
1	Stefan Stam	17	7	97 mins
2	Sean Gregan	26	11	92 mins
3	Neil Eardley	34	13	91 mins
4	Simon Charlton	32	14	91 mins

KEY PLAYERS - MIDFIELDERS

Andy Liddell

Goals in the League	10	Contribution to Attacking Power Average number of minutes between League team goals while on pitch	57
Defensive Rating Average number of mins between League goals conceded while on the pitch	97	Scoring Difference Defensive Rating minus Contribution to Attacking Power	40

	PLAYER	LGE GOALS	DEF RATE	POWER	SCORE DIFF
1	Andy Liddell	10	97	57	40 mins
2	Chris Taylor	4	92	54	38 mins
3	Gary McDonald	7	90	57	33 mins
4	Richard Wellens	4	91	59	32 mins

Chris Porter

SQUAD APPEARANCES

Match	1 2 3 4 5	6 7 8 9 10	11 12 13 14 15	16 17 18 19 20	21 22 23 24 25	26 27 28 29 30	31 32 33 34 35	36 37 38 39 40	41 42 43 44 45	46 47 48 49 50	51 52 53
Venue	A H H A A	H A H A A	H H A A H	A H A A H	A A H A H	H A A H A	A H H A H	A H A H H	A H A A H	H A H A A	H H A
Competition	L L L L W	L L L L L	L L L L L	L L L L L	L F L L L	L L L L F	L F L L L	L L L L L	L L L L L	L L L L L	L O O
Result	L L W L L	D L W W D	W W D D D	L W L W W	W W W L D	W W W W D	D L L W W	W L L L L	D W D D W	D D L L W	W L L

Goalkeepers
Alan Blayney
Chris Howarth
David Knight
Leslie Pogliacomi

Defenders
Hasney Aljofree
Simon Charlton
Leon Clarke
Neil Eardley
Sean Gregan
Will Haining
Kelvin Lomax
Miguel Roque
Stefan Stam
Chris Swailes
Marc Tierney
Ben Turner

Midfielders
Paul Edwards
Andy Liddell
Gary McDonald
Craig Rocastle
Chris Taylor
Richard Wellens

Forwards
Luigi Glombard
Lewis Grabban
Christopher Hall
Maheta Molango
Chris Porter
Paul Warne
Neil Wood

KEY: ■ On all match　◄◄ Subbed or sent off (Counting game)　►► Subbed on from bench (Counting Game)　►► Subbed on and then subbed or sent off (Counting Game)　☐ Not in 16
■ On bench　◄◄ Subbed or sent off (playing less than 70 minutes)　►► Subbed on (playing less than 70 minutes)　►► Subbed on and then subbed or sent off (playing less than 70 minutes)

LEAGUE 1 - OLDHAM ATHLETIC

SWANSEA

Final Position: 7th

NICKNAME: THE SWANS   KEY: ☐ Won ☐ Drawn ☐ Lost   Attendance

#	Comp	Opponent	H/A	Result	Score	Scorers	Attendance
1	div2	Cheltenham	H	L	1-2	Knight 77	15,199
2	div2	Scunthorpe	A	D	2-2	Robinson 45, Fallon 78	4,187
3	div2	Oldham	A	L	0-1		4,708
4	div2	Doncaster	H	W	2-0	Trundle 83, 90	12,218
5	ccr1	Wycombe	H	L	2-3	Williamson 72 og, Pratley 81	5,892
6	div2	Leyton Orient	A	W	1-0	Knight 54	4,162
7	div2	Yeovil	H	D	1-1	Trundle 64 pen	14,513
8	div2	Bradford	H	W	1-0	Robinson 73	11,481
9	div2	Brentford	A	W	2-0	Knight 36, 55	5,392
10	div2	Gillingham	A	L	1-3	Knight 85	5,500
11	div2	Huddersfield	H	L	1-2	Knight 81	12,202
12	div2	Crewe	H	W	2-1	Fallon 24, Knight 53	10,031
13	div2	Nottm Forest	A	L	1-3	Fallon 42	19,034
14	div2	Tranmere	H	D	0-0		12,347
15	div2	Chesterfield	A	W	3-2	Britton 4, Trundle 35, 67 pen	3,915
16	div2	Millwall	H	W	2-0	Lawrence 17, Britton 51	13,975
17	div2	Northampton	A	L	0-1		5,444
18	div2	Bournemouth	H	W	4-2	Iriekpen 4, Fallon 58, 60, Trundle 90	11,795
19	facr1	Newport	A	W	3-1	Trundle 7, Iriekpen 31, Britton 45	4,660
20	div2	Port Vale	A	W	2-0	Butler 90, Trundle 90	4,615
21	div2	Bristol City	H	D	0-0		15,531
22	facr2	Darlington	A	W	3-1	Britton 15, Robinson 52, Akinfenwa 79	4,183
23	div2	Brighton	A	L	2-3	Lawrence 59, Fallon 90	5,209
24	div2	Blackpool	A	D	1-1	Dickinson 21 og	6,216
25	div2	Carlisle	H	W	5-0	Lawrence 8, Fallon 15, 62, Robinson 27, Pratley 59	12,550
26	div2	Rotherham	H	D	1-1	Akinfenwa 90	12,327
27	div2	Crewe	A	W	3-1	Trundle 3, 23, Lawrence 47	6,083
28	div2	Huddersfield	A	L	2-3	Trundle 9 pen, 43	9,399
29	div2	Brentford	H	W	2-0	Akinfenwa 29, Osborne 41 og	12,554
30	facr3	Sheff Utd	A	W	3-0	Butler 53, 59, Britton 67 pen	15,896
31	div2	Bradford	A	D	2-2	O'Leary 33, Akinfenwa 52	7,347
32	div2	Nottm Forest	H	D	0-0		16,849
33	div2	Gillingham	H	W	2-0	Akinfenwa 6, Robinson 72	9,675
34	facr4	Ipswich	A	L	0-1		16,635
35	div2	Cheltenham	A	L	1-2	Trundle 17	5,221
36	div2	Oldham	H	L	0-1		9,880
37	div2	Doncaster	A	D	2-2	Akinfenwa 20, Trundle 45 pen	7,900
38	div2	Scunthorpe	H	L	0-2		10,746
39	div2	Yeovil	A	L	0-1		5,984
40	div2	Rotherham	A	W	2-1	Abbott 20, Trundle 61	3,697
41	div2	Leyton Orient	H	D	0-0		12,901
42	div2	Tranmere	A	W	2-0	Robinson 6, Trundle 52	7,467
43	div2	Chesterfield	H	W	2-0	Robinson 74 pen, Iriekpen 78	11,384
44	div2	Northampton	H	W	2-1	Lawrence 45, Robinson 46	11,071
45	div2	Millwall	A	L	0-2		9,249
46	div2	Bristol City	A	D	0-0		14,025
47	div2	Port Vale	H	W	3-0	Trundle 19, D.Duffy 26, 59	12,465
48	div2	Bournemouth	A	D	2-2	Tate 83, Trundle 88	6,786
49	div2	Brighton	H	W	2-1	D.Duffy 21, 41	11,972
50	div2	Carlisle	A	W	2-1	Trundle 1, D.Duffy 90	10,578
51	div2	Blackpool	H	L	3-6	Iriekpen 14, 55, Trundle 47	18,903

LEAGUE APPEARANCES, BOOKINGS AND CAPS

	AGE (on 01/07/07)	IN NAMED 16	APPEARANCES	COUNTING GAMES	MINUTES ON PITCH	LEAGUE GOALS		
Goalkeepers								
Willy Gueret	33	45	42	42	3780	0	4	0
Andy Oakes	30	42	5	4	379	0	1	0
Defenders								
Kevin Amankwaah	25	35	29	18	2012	0	7	0
Kevin Austin	34	35	30	23	2275	0	6	0
Richard Duffy	21	14	12	7	796	0	2	0
Ezomo Iriekpen	25	39	32	30	2771	4	2	0
Dennis Lawrence	33	39	39	36	3329	5	3	0
Gary Monk	28	3	2	1	118	0	1	0
Marcos Painter	20	23	23	21	1963	0	3	0
Alan Tate	24	38	38	32	3100	1	8	2
Tommy Williams	26	34	29	16	2658	0	4	0
Midfielders								
Leon Britton	24	41	41	35	3371	2	7	1
Thomas Butler	26	36	29	11	568	1	3	0
Ian Craney	24	27	27	22	2167	0	4	0
Shaun MacDonald	19	12	8	2	319	0	1	0
Kevin McLeod	26	4	4	1	194	0	0	0
Kristian O'Leary	29	25	23	14	1581	1	4	1
Darren Pratley	22	28	28	23	2240	1	6	1
Andy Robinson	23	39	39	29	2889	7	10	0
Owain Tudur-Jones	22	6	3	2	231	0	0	0
Darren Way	27	10	9	4	447	0	0	0
Forwards								
Pawel Abbott	25	18	18	6	831	1	3	0
Adebayo Akinfenwa	25	30	25	10	1238	5	2	0
Darryl Duffy	23	7	7	5	490	5	1	0
Rory Fallon	25	27	24	18	1837	8	2	0
Leon Knight	24	12	11	7	788	7	4	1
Lee Trundle	30	34	34	29	2823	19	4	2

TEAM OF THE SEASON

D Tommy Williams CG: 16 DR: 106
M Ian Craney CG: 22 SD: 26
D Marcos Painter CG: 21 DR: 93
M Leon Britton CG: 35 SD: 26
F Lee Trundle CG: 29 SR: 148
G Willy Gueret CG: 42 DR: 78
D Alan Tate CG: 32 DR: 91
M Darren Pratley CG: 23 SD: 19
F Rory Fallon CG: 18 SR: 229
D Kevin Amankwaah CG: 18 DR: 83
M Andy Robinson CG: 29 SD: 7

MONTHLY POINTS TALLY

Month	Points	%
AUGUST	7	47%
SEPTEMBER	10	48%
OCTOBER	7	58%
NOVEMBER	7	78%
DECEMBER	8	44%
JANUARY	8	67%
FEBRUARY	4	22%
MARCH	10	67%
APRIL	11	73%
MAY	0	0%

LEAGUE GOALS

	PLAYER	MINS	GOALS	S RATE
1	Trundle	2823	19	148
2	Fallon	1837	8	229
3	Knight	788	7	112
4	Robinson	2889	7	412
5	Duffy, D	490	5	98
6	Akinfenwa	1238	5	247
7	Lawrence	3329	5	665
8	Iriekpen	2771	4	692
9	Britton	3371	2	1685
10	Butler	568	1	568
11	Abbott	831	1	831
12	O'Leary	1581	1	1581
13	Pratley	2240	1	2240
	Other		1	
	TOTAL		**67**	

TOP POINT EARNERS

	PLAYER	GAMES	AV PTS
1	Rory Fallon	18	1.94
2	Kevin Austin	23	1.83
3	Alan Tate	34	1.74
4	Leon Britton	35	1.68
5	Ian Craney	22	1.68
6	Marcos Painter	21	1.62
7	Dennis Lawrence	36	1.61
8	Lee Trundle	30	1.60
9	Willy Gueret	42	1.57
10	Ezomo Iriekpen	30	1.57
	CLUB AVERAGE:		**1.53**

DISCIPLINARY RECORDS

	PLAYER	YELLOW	RED	AVE
1	Leon Knight	4	1	157
2	Thomas Butler	3	0	189
3	Pawel Abbott	3	0	277
4	Kristian O'Leary	4	1	316
5	Alan Tate	8	2	344
6	Andy Robinson	10	0	361
7	Kevin Austin	6	0	379
8	Kevin Amankwaah	7	0	402
9	Darren Pratley	6	1	448
10	Lee Trundle	4	2	470
11	Leon Britton	7	1	481
12	Darryl Duffy	1	0	490
13	Ian Craney	4	0	541
	Other	22	0	
	TOTAL	**89**	**8**	

KEY GOALKEEPER

Willy Gueret

Goals Conceded in the League	48	Counting Games League games when player was on pitch for at least 70 minutes	42
Defensive Rating Ave number of mins between League goals conceded while on the pitch	78	Clean Sheets In League games when player was on pitch for at least 70 minutes	16

KEY PLAYERS - DEFENDERS

Tommy Williams

Goals Conceded Number of League goals conceded while the player was on the pitch	25	Clean Sheets In League games when player was on pitch for at least 70 minutes	7
Defensive Rating Ave number of mins between League goals conceded while on the pitch	106	Club Defensive Rating Average number of mins between League goals conceded by the club this season	79

	PLAYER	CON LGE	CLEAN SHEETS	DEF RATE
1	Tommy Williams	25	7	106 mins
2	Marcos Painter	21	9	93 mins
3	Alan Tate	34	14	91 mins
4	Kevin Amankwaah	24	8	83 mins

KEY PLAYERS - MIDFIELDERS

Ian Craney

Goals in the League	0	Contribution to Attacking Power Average number of minutes between League team goals while on pitch	54
Defensive Rating Average number of mins between League goals conceded while on the pitch	80	Scoring Difference Defensive Rating minus Contribution to Attacking Power	26

	PLAYER	LGE GOALS	DEF RATE	POWER	SCORE DIFF
1	Ian Craney	0	80	54	26 mins
2	Leon Britton	2	84	58	26 mins
3	Darren Pratley	1	77	58	19 mins
4	Andy Robinson	7	67	60	7 mins

KEY PLAYERS - GOALSCORERS

Lee Trundle

Goals in the League	19	Player Strike Rate Average number of minutes between League goals scored by player	148
Contribution to Attacking Power Average number of minutes between League team goals while on pitch	57	Club Strike Rate Average number of minutes between League goals scored by club	61

	PLAYER	LGE GOALS	POWER	STRIKE RATE
1	Lee Trundle	19	57	148 mins
2	Rory Fallon	8	52	229 mins
3	Andy Robinson	7	60	412 mins
4	Kristian O'Leary	1	83	1581 mins

Lee Trundle

SQUAD APPEARANCES

Match	1 2 3 4 5	6 7 8 9 10	11 12 13 14 15	16 17 18 19 20	21 22 23 24 25	26 27 28 29 30	31 32 33 34 35	36 37 38 39 40	41 42 43 44 45	46 47 48 49 50	51
Venue	H A A H H	A H H A A	H H A H A	H A H A A	H A A A H	H A A H A	A H H A A	H A H A A	H A H H A	A H A H A	H
Competition	L L L L W	L L L L L	L L L L L	L L L F L	L F L L L	L L L L F	L L L F L	L L L L L	L L L L L	L L L L L	L
Result	L D L W L	W D W W L	L W L D W	W L W W W	D W L D W	D W L W W	D D W L L	L D L L W	D W W W L	D W D W W	L

Goalkeepers
Willy Gueret
Andy Oakes

Defenders
Kevin Amankwaah
Kevin Austin
Richard Duffy
Ezomo Iriekpen
Dennis Lawrence
Gary Monk
Marcos Painter
Alan Tate
Tommy Williams

Midfielders
Leon Britton
Thomas Butler
Ian Craney
Shaun MacDonald
Kevin McLeod
Kristian O'Leary
Darren Pratley
Andy Robinson
Owain Tudur-Jones
Darren Way

Forwards
Pawel Abbott
Adebayo Akinfenwa
Darryl Duffy
Rory Fallon
Leon Knight
Lee Trundle

KEY: ■ On all match ◄◄ Subbed or sent off (Counting game) ►► Subbed on from bench (Counting Game) ►► Subbed on and then subbed or sent off (Counting Game) □ Not in 16
■ On bench ◄◄ Subbed or sent off (playing less than 70 minutes) ►► Subbed on (playing less than 70 minutes) ►► Subbed on and then subbed or sent off (playing less than 70 minutes)

LEAGUE 1 - SWANSEA

CARLISLE

Final Position: **8th**

NICKNAME: THE FOXES KEY: ☐ Won ☐ Drawn ☐ Lost   Attendance

#	Comp	Opponent		Result	Scorers	Attendance
1	div2	Doncaster	H W	1-0	P.Murray 4	12,031
2	div2	Chesterfield	A D	0-0		4,525
3	div2	Yeovil	A L	1-2	Gall 23	4,709
4	div2	Leyton Orient	H W	3-1	Gall 24, 59, Hawley 49	7,160
5	ccr1	Bradford	H W	4-3*	Holmes 31 (*on penalties)	4,757
6	div2	Oldham	A D	0-0		6,080
7	div2	Cheltenham	H W	2-0	Gall 27, Hawley 45	7,248
8	div2	Northampton	H D	1-1	Hawley 56	7,602
9	div2	Bradford	A D	1-1	Lumsden 50	7,966
10	div2	Nottm Forest	A L	0-1		19,535
11	ccr2	Charlton	A L	0-1		8,190
12	div2	Brighton	H W	3-1	Hawley 6, Gray 31, Hackney 81	7,704
13	div2	Blackpool	H W	2-0	Lumsden 18, Hawley 88	8,401
14	div2	Crewe	A L	1-5	Hawley 24	5,989
15	div2	Millwall	H L	1-2	Beckford 33	8,413
16	div2	Huddersfield	A L	1-2	Hackney 43	10,830
17	div2	Tranmere	H W	1-0	Gall 35	7,328
18	div2	Gillingham	A L	0-2		5,973
19	div2	Rotherham	H D	1-1	Gray 64	7,247
20	facr1	Swindon	A L	1-3	Gray 43	4,938
21	div2	Bournemouth	A W	1-0	Hawley 5 pen	5,682
22	div2	Port Vale	H W	3-2	Holmes 66, Hawley 77, Murphy 81	7,543
23	div2	Bristol City	A L	0-1		10,792
24	div2	Scunthorpe	H L	0-2		6,954
25	div2	Swansea	A L	0-5		12,550
26	div2	Brentford	H W	2-0	Holmes 69, McDermott 74	6,805
27	div2	Blackpool	A L	1-2	Hawley 73	9,473
28	div2	Brighton	A W	2-1	Aranalde 56, McDermott 82	5,436
29	div2	Bradford	H W	1-0	Hawley 26	7,548
30	div2	Northampton	A L	2-3	Graham 82, Gall 86	5,549
31	div2	Crewe	H L	0-2		7,075
32	div2	Brentford	A D	0-0		5,381
33	div2	Nottm Forest	H W	1-0	Hawley 45	9,022
34	div2	Doncaster	A W	2-1	J.Smith 56, Hawley 78	9,036
35	div2	Yeovil	H L	1-4	Garner 43	7,112
36	div2	Leyton Orient	A D	1-1	Garner 15	4,449
37	div2	Chesterfield	H D	0-0		6,196
38	div2	Cheltenham	A W	1-0	Garner 15	3,831
39	div2	Oldham	H D	1-1	Holmes 87	7,951
40	div2	Millwall	A L	0-2		10,415
41	div2	Huddersfield	H W	1-0	Garner 45	6,629
42	div2	Gillingham	H W	5-0	P.Murray 14, Joyce 81, Gall 83, Graham 88 pen, 90	6,087
43	div2	Tranmere	A W	2-0	Graham 10, Gall 67	7,289
44	div2	Port Vale	A W	2-0	Graham 27, Garner 90	4,882
45	div2	Bournemouth	H W	3-1	Graham 3 pen, Livesey 29, McDermott 85	8,989
46	div2	Rotherham	A W	1-0	Gray 68	4,428
47	div2	Bristol City	H L	1-3	Graham 5	10,232
48	div2	Swansea	H L	1-2	Johann.Smith 49	10,578
49	div2	Scunthorpe	A L	0-3		8,720

LEAGUE APPEARANCES, BOOKINGS AND CAPS

	AGE (on 01/07/07)	IN NAMED 16	APPEARANCES	COUNTING GAMES	MINUTES ON PITCH	LEAGUE GOALS	🟨	🟥
Goalkeepers								
Kieren Westwood	22	46	46	46	4140	0	1	0
Defenders								
Zigor Aranalde	34	43	43	42	3825	1	12	0
Paul Arnison	29	23	11	6	716	0	3	0
Simon Grand	23	12	4	1	139	0	2	0
Kevin Gray	35	42	31	26	2437	3	3	0
James Krause	20	8	3	3	240	0	0	0
Danny Livesey	22	40	31	28	2590	1	1	0
Peter Murphy	26	34	33	32	2925	0	5	0
David Raven	22	35	35	34	3098	0	9	0
Midfielders								
Chris Billy	34	24	20	11	1360	0	1	0
Simon Hackney	23	21	18	13	1302	2	1	0
Kevin Harper	31	7	7	7	566	0	0	0
Luke Joyce	19	23	16	8	823	1	3	1
Chris Lumsden	27	39	39	33	3070	2	4	0
Neale McDermott	22	25	15	7	708	3	2	0
Paul Murray	30	21	21	21	1783	1	0	0
Jeff Smith	27	17	17	17	1529	1	1	0
Paul Thirlwell	28	30	30	28	2582	0	8	1
Shaun Vipond	18	6	4	0	79	0	0	0
Forwards								
Jermaine Beckford	23	5	4	3	306	1	1	0
Michael Bridges	28	5	5	5	438	0	2	0
Kevin Gall	25	45	45	40	3841	8	3	0
Joe Garner	19	18	18	15	1481	5	6	1
Danny Graham	21	11	11	10	918	7	0	0
Karl Hawley	25	33	32	29	2668	12	1	0
Stephen Hindmarch	17	13	7	0	78	0	0	0
Derek Holmes	28	43	36	6	1074	3	1	0
Johann Smith	20	16	13	6	758	1	1	0

TEAM OF THE SEASON

- **G** Kieren Westwood — CG: 46 DR: 75
- **D** Peter Murphy — CG: 32 DR: 88
- **D** David Raven — CG: 34 DR: 86
- **D** Zigor Aranalde — CG: 42 DR: 79
- **D** Kevin Gray — CG: 26 DR: 78
- **M** Jeff Smith — CG: 17 SD: 15
- **M** Paul Murray — CG: 21 SD: 15
- **M** Chris Lumsden — CG: 33 SD: -9
- **M** Paul Thirlwell — CG: 28 SD: -12
- **F** Karl Hawley — CG: 29 SR: 222
- **F** Joe Garner — CG: 15 SR: 296

MONTHLY POINTS TALLY

AUGUST	8	53%
SEPTEMBER	14	67%
OCTOBER	3	25%
NOVEMBER	7	78%
DECEMBER	6	33%
JANUARY	7	47%
FEBRUARY	8	53%
MARCH	8	53%
APRIL	9	60%
MAY	0	0%

LEAGUE GOALS

	PLAYER	MINS	GOALS	S RATE
1	Hawley	2668	12	222
2	Gall	3841	8	480
3	Graham	918	7	131
4	Garner	1481	5	296
5	McDermott	708	3	236
6	Holmes	1074	3	358
7	Gray	2437	3	812
8	Hackney	1302	2	651
9	Lumsden	3070	2	1535
10	Beckford	306	1	306
11	Smith, Johann	758	1	758
12	Joyce	823	1	823
13	Smith, Jeff	1529	1	1529
	Other		3	
	TOTAL		**52**	

TOP POINT EARNERS

	PLAYER	GAMES	AV PTS
1	Kevin Gall	40	1.70
2	Paul Murray	21	1.65
3	Jeff Smith	17	1.65
4	Karl Hawley	29	1.59
5	Peter Murphy	32	1.56
6	Kevin Gray	26	1.54
7	David Raven	34	1.53
8	Kieren Westwood	46	1.52
9	Zigor Aranalde	42	1.52
10	Joe Garner	15	1.47
	CLUB AVERAGE:		**1.48**

DISCIPLINARY RECORDS

	PLAYER	YELLOW	RED	AVE
1	Luke Joyce	3	1	205
2	Joe Garner	6	1	211
3	Paul Arnison	3	0	238
4	Paul Thirlwell	8	1	322
5	David Raven	9	0	344
6	Zigor Aranalde	12	0	347
7	Neale McDermott	2	0	354
8	Peter Murphy	5	0	585
9	Johann Smith	1	0	758
10	Kevin Gray	3	0	812
11	Chris Lumsden	4	0	1023
12	Derek Holmes	1	0	1074
13	Kevin Gall	3	0	1280
	Other	6	0	
	TOTAL	**66**	**3**	

KEY GOALKEEPER

Kieren Westwood

Goals Conceded in the League	55	Counting Games League games when player was on pitch for at least 70 minutes	46
Defensive Rating Ave number of mins between League goals conceded while on the pitch	75	Clean Sheets In League games when player was on pitch for at least 70 minutes	18

KEY PLAYERS - DEFENDERS

Peter Murphy

Goals Conceded Number of League goals conceded while the player was on the pitch	33	Clean Sheets In League games when player was on pitch for at least 70 minutes	15
Defensive Rating Ave number of mins between League goals conceded while on the pitch	88	Club Defensive Rating Average number of mins between League goals conceded by the club this season	75

	PLAYER	CON LGE	CLEAN SHEETS	DEF RATE
1	Peter Murphy	33	15	88 mins
2	David Raven	36	14	86 mins
3	Zigor Aranalde	48	17	79 mins
4	Kevin Gray	31	10	78 mins

KEY PLAYERS - MIDFIELDERS

Jeff Smith

Goals in the League	1	Contribution to Attacking Power Average number of minutes between League team goals while on pitch	69
Defensive Rating Average number of mins between League goals conceded while on the pitch	84	Scoring Difference Defensive Rating minus Contribution to Attacking Power	15

	PLAYER	LGE GOALS	DEF RATE	POWER	SCORE DIFF
1	Jeff Smith	1	84	69	15 mins
2	Paul Murray	1	99	84	15 mins
3	Chris Lumsdon	2	69	78	-9 mins
4	Paul Thirlwell	0	71	83	-12 mins

KEY PLAYERS - GOALSCORERS

Karl Hawley

Goals in the League	12	Player Strike Rate Average number of minutes between League goals scored by player	222
Contribution to Attacking Power Average number of minutes between League team goals while on pitch	80	Club Strike Rate Average number of minutes between League goals scored by club	76

	PLAYER	LGE GOALS	POWER	STRIKE RATE
1	Karl Hawley	12	80	222 mins
2	Joe Garner	5	87	296 mins
3	Kevin Gall	8	73	480 mins
4	Simon Hackney	2	81	651 mins

Karl Hawley

SQUAD APPEARANCES

Match	1 2 3 4 5	6 7 8 9 10	11 12 13 14 15	16 17 18 19 20	21 22 23 24 25	26 27 28 29 30	31 32 33 34 35	36 37 38 39 40	41 42 43 44 45	46 47 48 49
Venue	H A A H H	A H H A A	A H H A H	A H A H A	A H A H A	H A A H A	H A H A H	A H A H A	H H A A H	A H H A
Competition	L L L L W	L L L L L	W L L L L	L L L L F	L L L L L	L L L L L	L L L L L	L L L L L	L L L L L	L L L L
Result	W D L W W	D W D D W	L W W L L	L W L D L	W W L L L	W L W W W	L D W W L	D D W D L	D W W W W	W L L L

Goalkeepers
Kieren Westwood

Defenders
Zigor Aranalde
Paul Arnison
Simon Grand
Kevin Gray
James Krause
Danny Livesey
Peter Murphy
David Raven

Midfielders
Chris Billy
Simon Hackney
Kevin Harper
Luke Joyce
Chris Lumsdon
Neale McDermott
Paul Murray
Jeff Smith
Paul Thirlwell
Shaun Vipond

Forwards
Jermaine Beckford
Michael Bridges
Kevin Gall
Joe Garner
Danny Graham
Karl Hawley
Stephen Hindmarch
Derek Holmes
Johann Smith

KEY: ■ On all match   ⊩ Subbed or sent off (Counting game)   ⊪ Subbed on from bench (Counting Game)   ⊯ Subbed on and then subbed or sent off (Counting Game)   □ Not in 16

   ▨ On bench   ◀ Subbed or sent off (playing less than 70 minutes)   ⊳ Subbed on (playing less than 70 minutes)   ⊳⊳ Subbed on and then subbed or sent off (playing less than 70 minutes)

LEAGUE 1 - CARLISLE

TRANMERE ROVERS

Final Position: 9th

NICKNAME: ROVERS   KEY: ☐ Won ☐ Drawn ☐ Lost   Attendance

#	Comp	Opponent	H/A	Result	Scorers	Att
1	div2	Oldham	H	W	1-0 Greenacre 24	8,586
2	div2	Cheltenham	A	L	0-1	3,875
3	div2	Doncaster	A	D	0-0	6,014
4	div2	Yeovil	H	W	2-1 Ellison 35, Mullin 54	6,023
5	ccr1	Hull City	A	L	1-2 Sherriff 31	6,075
6	div2	Chesterfield	A	W	2-0 Downes 45 og, Taylor 68	4,163
7	div2	Leyton Orient	H	W	3-0 Ward 9, Greenacre 12, 80	6,446
8	div2	Bristol City	H	W	1-0 Mullin 85	8,111
9	div2	Rotherham	A	L	1-2 Ellison 28	3,732
10	div2	Northampton	A	W	3-1 Zola 14, Taylor 35, Mullin 57 pen	5,334
11	div2	Nottm Forest	H	D	0-0	11,444
12	div2	Huddersfield	H	D	2-2 Zola 11, Greenacre 38	6,702
13	div2	Bradford	A	L	0-2	8,877
14	div2	Swansea	A	D	0-0	12,347
15	div2	Port Vale	H	L	1-2 Greenacre 57	7,866
16	div2	Carlisle	A	L	0-1	7,328
17	div2	Bournemouth	H	W	1-0 Ellison 41	6,076
18	div2	Millwall	H	W	3-1 Taylor 19, McCready 22, Shuker 89	7,114
19	facr1	Woking	H	W	4-2 Taylor 19, 48, Greenacre 37, 83	4,591
20	div2	Brighton	A	W	1-0 Greenacre 20	6,069
21	div2	Blackpool	H	W	2-0 Greenacre 2, Davies 67	8,247
22	facr2	Peterborough	H	L	1-2 Sherriff 30	6,308
23	div2	Scunthorpe	A	D	1-1 Sherriff 53	4,572
24	div2	Brentford	A	D	1-1 Shuker 45	4,878
25	div2	Gillingham	H	L	2-3 Greenacre 2, Shuker 5	6,407
26	div2	Huddersfield	A	D	2-2 Greenacre 39, 51	10,228
27	div2	Nottm Forest	A	D	1-1 Taylor 49	19,729
28	div2	Rotherham	H	W	2-1 Sherriff 28, Taylor 43	6,675
29	div2	Northampton	H	D	1-1 Mullin 87	6,089
30	div2	Bristol City	A	L	2-3 McCombe 25 og, McLaren 44	10,822
31	div2	Crewe	H	W	1-0 Taylor 19	5,708
32	div2	Bradford	H	D	1-1 Taylor 9	6,567
33	div2	Gillingham	A	L	0-2	5,378
34	div2	Oldham	A	L	0-1	6,944
35	div2	Doncaster	H	W	1-0 Greenacre 6	5,965
36	div2	Yeovil	A	W	2-0 Shuker 53, 83	5,168
37	div2	Cheltenham	H	D	2-2 Shuker 49, Greenacre 90	5,576
38	div2	Leyton Orient	A	L	1-3 Greenacre 34	4,832
39	div2	Chesterfield	H	W	2-0 Mullin 21, Greenacre 73	6,254
40	div2	Swansea	H	L	0-2	7,467
41	div2	Port Vale	A	W	3-2 Greenacre 3, 35 pen, Ellison 83	4,809
42	div2	Bournemouth	A	L	0-2	5,640
43	div2	Carlisle	H	L	0-2	7,289
44	div2	Blackpool	A	L	2-3 Zola 29, 46	8,091
45	div2	Brighton	H	W	2-1 Curran 76, Greenacre 90 pen	5,528
46	div2	Millwall	A	D	2-2 Sherriff 9, Zola 69	10,036
47	div2	Scunthorpe	H	L	0-2	6,721
48	div2	Crewe	A	D	1-1 Harrison 49	5,777
49	div2	Brentford	H	W	3-1 Curran 5, 7, 36	6,529

LEAGUE APPEARANCES, BOOKINGS AND CAPS

	AGE (on 01/07/07)	IN NAMED 16	APPEARANCES	COUNTING GAMES	MINUTES ON PITCH	LEAGUE GOALS	🟨	🟥
Goalkeepers								
John Achterberg	35	27	4	1	160	0	0	0
Joe Hart	20	6	6	6	540	0	0	0
Ben Hinchcliffe	18	12	2	2	160	0	0	0
Gavin Ward	37	45	38	35	3311	1	2	1
Defenders								
Ian Goodison	34	41	40	40	3608	0	6	1
Chris McCready	25	44	42	40	3730	1	5	0
Shane Sherriff	24	43	41	37	3594	3	8	0
Robbie Stockdale	27	41	36	33	3089	0	8	0
John Thompson	26	13	12	12	1080	0	5	0
Carl Tremarco	21	38	24	14	1422	0	5	0
Midfielders								
Kevin Ellison	28	41	34	20	2091	4	3	0
Danny Harrison	24	33	11	7	758	1	2	0
Stephen Jennings	22	10	2	1	74	0	0	0
Jason McAteer	36	26	18	7	994	0	2	1
Paul McLaren	30	42	42	40	3680	1	7	0
John Mullin	31	40	40	37	3375	5	9	1
Chris Shuker	25	45	45	42	3813	6	7	0
Forwards								
Craig Curran	17	10	4	2	195	4	0	0
Steve Davies	19	43	28	16	1684	1	4	0
Chris Greenacre	29	44	44	38	3617	17	4	0
Gareth Taylor	34	39	37	35	3197	6	4	0
Calvin Zola	22	37	29	12	1440	5	2	0

TEAM OF THE SEASON

G Gavin Ward — CG: 35 DR: 77

D John Thompson — CG: 12 DR: 108
D Chris McCready — CG: 40 DR: 88
D Ian Goodison — CG: 40 DR: 80
D Robbie Stockdale — CG: 33 DR: 79

M Paul McLaren — CG: 40 SD: 17
M Kevin Ellison — CG: 20 SD: 7
M Chris Shuker — CG: 42 SD: 6
M John Mullin — CG: 37 SD: 5

F Chris Greenacre — CG: 38 SR: 212
F Calvin Zola — CG: 12 SR: 288

MONTHLY POINTS TALLY

Month	Points	%
AUGUST	10	67%
SEPTEMBER	11	52%
OCTOBER	4	33%
NOVEMBER	9	100%
DECEMBER	4	27%
JANUARY	8	44%
FEBRUARY	7	47%
MARCH	6	40%
APRIL	5	33%
MAY	3	100%

LEAGUE GOALS

	PLAYER	MINS	GOALS	S RATE
1	Greenacre	3617	17	212
2	Taylor	3197	6	532
3	Shuker	3813	6	635
4	Zola	1440	5	288
5	Mullin	3375	5	675
6	Curran	195	4	48
7	Ellison	2091	4	522
8	Sherriff	3594	3	1198
9	Harrison	758	1	758
10	Davies	1684	1	1684
11	Ward	3311	1	3311
12	McLaren	3680	1	3680
13	McCready	3730	1	3730
	Other		0	
	TOTAL		**55**	

TOP POINT EARNERS

	PLAYER	GAMES	AV PTS
1	John Thompson	12	2.00
2	Gareth Taylor	35	1.63
3	Ian Goodison	40	1.58
4	Steve Davies	16	1.56
5	Chris McCready	40	1.55
6	Shane Sherriff	37	1.54
7	Paul McLaren	40	1.53
8	Chris Shuker	42	1.50
9	Chris Greenacre	38	1.47
10	Gavin Ward	36	1.42
	CLUB AVERAGE:		**1.46**

DISCIPLINARY RECORDS

	PLAYER	YELLOW	RED	AVE
1	Carl Tremarco	5	0	284
2	Jason McAteer	2	1	331
3	John Mullin	9	1	337
4	Robbie Stockdale	8	0	386
5	Steve Davies	4	0	421
6	Shane Sherriff	7	0	513
7	Ian Goodison	6	1	515
8	Paul McLaren	7	0	525
9	Chris Shuker	7	0	544
10	Kevin Ellison	3	0	697
11	Calvin Zola	2	0	720
12	Chris McCready	5	0	746
13	Danny Harrison	1	0	758
	Other	10	1	
	TOTAL	**76**	**4**	

KEY GOALKEEPER

Gavin Ward

Goals Conceded in the League	43	Counting Games — League games when player was on pitch for at least 70 minutes	35
Defensive Rating — Ave number of mins between League goals conceded while on the pitch	77	Clean Sheets — In League games when player was on pitch for at least 70 minutes	13

KEY PLAYERS - GOALSCORERS

Chris Greenacre

Goals in the League	17	Player Strike Rate — Average number of minutes between League goals scored by player	212
Contribution to Attacking Power — Average number of minutes between League team goals while on pitch	76	Club Strike Rate — Average number of minutes between League goals scored by club	75

	PLAYER	LGE GOALS	POWER	STRIKE RATE
1	Chris Greenacre	17	76	212 mins
2	Calvin Zola	5	65	288 mins
3	Kevin Ellison	4	83	522 mins
4	Gareth Taylor	6	66	532 mins

KEY PLAYERS - DEFENDERS

John Thompson

Goals Conceded — Number of League goals conceded while the player was on the pitch	10	Clean Sheets — In League games when player was on pitch for at least 70 minutes	4
Defensive Rating — Ave number of mins between League goals conceded while on the pitch	108	Club Defensive Rating — Average number of mins between League goals conceded by the club this season	82

	PLAYER	CON LGE	CLEAN SHEETS	DEF RATE
1	John Thompson	10	4	108 mins
2	Chris McCready	42	14	88 mins
3	Ian Goodison	45	12	80 mins
4	Robbie Stockdale	39	10	79 mins

KEY PLAYERS - MIDFIELDERS

Paul McLaren

Goals in the League	1	Contribution to Attacking Power — Average number of minutes between League team goals while on pitch	70
Defensive Rating — Average number of mins between League goals conceded while on the pitch	87	Scoring Difference — Defensive Rating minus Contribution to Attacking Power	17

	PLAYER	LGE GOALS	DEF RATE	POWER	SCORE DIFF
1	Paul McLaren	1	87	70	17 mins
2	Kevin Ellison	4	90	83	7 mins
3	Chris Shuker	6	77	71	6 mins
4	John Mullin	5	78	73	5 mins

Ian Goodison

SQUAD APPEARANCES

Match	1 2 3 4 5	6 7 8 9 10	11 12 13 14 15	16 17 18 19 20	21 22 23 24 25	26 27 28 29 30	31 32 33 34 35	36 37 38 39 40	41 42 43 44 45	46 47 48 49
Venue	H A A H A	A H H A A	H H A A H	A H H H A	H H A A H	A A H H A	H H A A H	A H A H H	A A H A H	A H A H
Competition	L L L L W	L L L L L	L L L L L	L L L F L	L F L L L	L L L L L	L L L L L	L L L L L	L L L L L	L L L L
Result	W L D W L	W W W L W	D D L D L	L W W W W	W L D D L	D D W D L	W D L L W	W D L W L	W L L L W	D L D W

KEY: ■ On all match · ■ On bench · ◀◀ Subbed or sent off (Counting game) · ◀◀ Subbed or sent off (playing less than 70 minutes) · ▶▶ Subbed on from bench (Counting Game) · ▶▶ Subbed on (playing less than 70 minutes) · ▶▶ Subbed on and then subbed or sent off (Counting Game) · ▶▶ Subbed on and then subbed or sent off (playing less than 70 minutes) · □ Not in 16

LEAGUE 1 - TRANMERE ROVERS

MILLWALL

Final Position: 10th

NICKNAME: THE LIONS KEY: ☐ Won ☐ Drawn ☐ Lost Attendance

#	Comp	Opponent	H/A	Result	Scorers	Attendance
1	div2	Yeovil	H	D	1-1 Byfield 82	10,012
2	div2	Leyton Orient	A	L	0-2	6,142
3	div2	Chesterfield	A	L	1-5 Braniff 72	4,136
4	div2	Oldham	H	W	1-0 Hubertz 79	7,455
5	ccr1	Gillingham	H	W	2-1 Braniff 39, Hubertz 86	5,040
6	div2	Cheltenham	A	L	2-3 McInnes 24, Williams 45	4,386
7	div2	Blackpool	H	D	0-0	7,692
8	div2	Brighton	H	L	0-1	9,372
9	div2	Gillingham	A	L	1-2 Hubertz 88	7,934
10	div2	Crewe	A	L	0-1	4,875
11	ccr2	Southampton	H	L	0-4	5,492
12	div2	Northampton	H	L	0-1	7,432
13	div2	Brentford	H	D	1-1 Dunne 27	7,618
14	div2	Rotherham	A	W	3-2 Haynes 45 pen, 86, Dunne 90	4,977
15	div2	Carlisle	A	W	2-1 Dunne 27, Hubertz 39	8,413
16	div2	Bournemouth	H	W	1-0 Hackett 45	9,838
17	div2	Swansea	A	L	0-2	13,975
18	div2	Port Vale	H	D	1-1 Zebroski 20	10,819
19	div2	Tranmere	A	L	1-3 Hackett 41	7,114
20	facr1	Havant & W	A	W	2-1 May 6, Dunne 71	5,753
21	div2	Doncaster	H	D	2-2 Byfield 40, Hackett 59	8,670
22	div2	Nottm Forest	A	L	1-3 May 4	19,410
23	facr2	Bradford	A	D	0-0	4,346
24	div2	Huddersfield	H	D	0-0	6,251
25	div2	Bradford	H	W	2-0 Morais 6, Byfield 33 pen	7,588
26	facr2r	Bradford	H	W	1-0 Doyle 114 og	3,220
27	div2	Bristol City	A	L	0-1	12,067
28	div2	Scunthorpe	H	L	0-1	7,192
29	div2	Brentford	A	W	4-1 Hubertz 1, 57, P.Robinson 62, Byfield 83 pen	6,925
30	div2	Gillingham	H	W	4-1 Zebroski 38, Byfield 50 pen, 79, 85	10,055
31	facr3	Stoke	A	L	0-2	8,024
32	div2	Brighton	A	W	1-0 Byfield 22	6,226
33	div2	Rotherham	H	W	4-0 Harris 16, Zebroski 26, Byfield 39, 90	9,534
34	div2	Northampton	A	L	0-3	5,834
35	div2	Scunthorpe	A	L	0-3	5,001
36	div2	Yeovil	A	W	1-0 May 12	5,810
37	div2	Chesterfield	H	W	2-1 Byfield 10, Hubertz 85	9,711
38	div2	Oldham	A	W	2-1 Williams 61, Byfield 82 pen	6,181
39	div2	Leyton Orient	H	L	2-5 Alexander 66 og, Hubertz 69	10,356
40	div2	Blackpool	A	W	1-0 Brammer 29	6,547
41	div2	Cheltenham	H	W	2-0 Byfield 33, Brighton 42	10,261
42	div2	Carlisle	H	W	2-0 Harris 52, 82	10,415
43	div2	Crewe	H	D	2-2 Byfield 44, Hubertz 90	8,867
44	div2	Bournemouth	A	L	0-1	7,194
45	div2	Port Vale	A	L	0-2	3,973
46	div2	Swansea	H	W	2-0 Harris 31, 70 pen	9,249
47	div2	Nottm Forest	H	W	1-0 Harris 53	12,035
48	div2	Doncaster	A	W	2-1 Williams 38, Hubertz 83	7,870
49	div2	Tranmere	H	D	2-2 Dunne 49, 67	10,036
50	div2	Huddersfield	A	L	2-4 Byfield 9, Dunne 90	9,406
51	div2	Bristol City	H	W	1-0 P.Robinson 78	12,547
52	div2	Bradford	A	D	2-2 Byfield 46, Craig 71	7,134

LEAGUE APPEARANCES, BOOKINGS AND CAPS

	AGE (on 01/07/07)	IN NAMED 16	APPEARANCES	COUNTING GAMES	MINUTES ON PITCH	LEAGUE GOALS		
Goalkeepers								
Chris Day	31	46	5	4	413	0	0	0
Lenny Pidgeley	22	45	42	41	3725	0	4	1
Defenders								
Zoumana Bakayogo	20	7	4	1	160	0	0	0
Tony Craig	22	31	30	26	2460	1	2	1
Mark Phillips	24	17	12	8	820	0	3	0
Paul Robinson	25	41	38	37	3369	2	6	0
Maurice Ross	26	16	15	12	1177	0	2	0
Danny Senda	26	37	36	32	3036	0	2	0
Richard Shaw	38	41	41	41	3690	0	7	0
Zak Whitbread	23	14	14	11	1136	0	5	0
Midfielders								
Neal Ardley	34	27	20	9	1219	0	0	0
David Brammer	32	17	17	17	1520	1	3	0
Alan Dunne	24	34	32	28	2593	6	9	1
Marvin Elliott	22	42	42	39	3578	0	3	0
Ali Fuseini	18	12	7	3	412	0	2	0
Chris Hackett	24	37	33	14	1841	3	6	0
Danny Haynes	19	5	5	4	415	2	2	0
Charlie Lee	20	7	5	4	338	0	1	0
Samy Mawene	22	6	4	3	292	0	1	0
Derek McInnes	35	16	13	6	752	1	3	0
Filipe Morais	21	15	12	5	672	1	3	0
Ryan Smith	20	7	6	5	443	0	1	0
Liam Trotter	18	5	2	1	108	0	0	0
Forwards								
Kevin Braniff	24	7	7	3	409	1	2	0
Tom Brighton	23	16	16	9	1068	1	1	0
Darren Byfield	30	31	31	26	2454	16	9	0
Gavin Grant	26	7	4	1	165	0	0	0
Neil Harris	29	21	21	19	1777	6	5	0
Poul Hubertz	30	44	33	14	1790	10	7	0
Ben May	23	14	13	5	788	2	3	0
Marvin Williams	19	30	29	11	1595	3	8	0
Chris Zebroski	20	28	25	7	1098	3	8	0

TEAM OF THE SEASON

G — Lenny Pidgeley CG: 42 DR: 68

D — Paul Robinson CG: 37 DR: 78
D — Danny Senda CG: 32 DR: 76
D — Maurice Ross CG: 12 DR: 73
D — Richard Shaw CG: 41 DR: 70

M — Alan Dunne CG: 28 SD: 19
M — David Brammer CG: 17 SD: 14
M — Chris Hackett CG: 14 SD: 2
M — Marvin Elliott CG: 39 SD: -9

F — Darren Byfield CG: 27 SR: 159
F — Poul Hubertz CG: 15 SR: 188

MONTHLY POINTS TALLY

Month	Points	%
AUGUST	4	27%
SEPTEMBER	5	24%
OCTOBER	7	58%
NOVEMBER	1	11%
DECEMBER	7	47%
JANUARY	9	60%
FEBRUARY	12	80%
MARCH	10	56%
APRIL	10	67%
MAY	1	33%

LEAGUE GOALS

	PLAYER	MINS	GOALS	S RATE
1	Byfield	2544	16	159
2	Hubertz	1880	10	188
3	Harris	1777	6	296
4	Dunne	2683	6	447
5	Zebroski	1098	3	366
6	Williams	1685	3	561
7	Hackett	1931	3	643
8	Haynes	415	2	207
9	May	788	2	394
10	Robinson, P	3459	2	1729
11	Braniff	409	1	409
12	Morais	672	1	672
13	McInnes	752	1	752
	Other		3	
	TOTAL		59	

TOP POINT EARNERS

	PLAYER	GAMES	AV PTS
1	David Brammer	17	1.94
2	Neil Harris	19	1.89
3	Tony Craig	27	1.85
4	Poul Hubertz	14	1.71
5	Darren Byfield	26	1.58
6	Lenny Pidgeley	42	1.55
7	Danny Senda	32	1.53
8	Alan Dunne	28	1.50
9	Paul Robinson	37	1.49
10	Richard Shaw	41	1.44
	CLUB AVERAGE:		1.43

DISCIPLINARY RECORDS

	PLAYER	YELLOW	RED	AVE
1	Marvin Williams	8	0	210
2	Chris Zebroski	8	0	219
3	Derek McInnes	3	0	250
4	Darren Byfield	9	0	282
5	Zak Whitbread	5	0	284
6	Poul Hubertz	7	0	313
7	Alan Dunne	9	1	335
8	Filipe Morais	3	0	336
9	Neil Harris	5	0	355
10	Chris Hackett	6	0	386
11	Ben May	3	0	394
12	David Brammer	3	0	506
13	Richard Shaw	7	0	540
	Other	20	2	
	TOTAL	96	3	

KEY GOALKEEPER

Lenny Pidgeley

Goals Conceded in the League	56	Counting Games League games when player was on pitch for at least 70 minutes	42
Defensive Rating Ave number of mins between League goals conceded while on the pitch	68	Clean Sheets In League games when player was on pitch for at least 70 minutes	14

KEY PLAYERS - DEFENDERS

Paul Robinson

Goals Conceded Number of League goals conceded while the player was on the pitch	44	Clean Sheets In League games when player was on pitch for at least 70 minutes	15
Defensive Rating Ave number of mins between League goals conceded while on the pitch	78	Club Defensive Rating Average number of mins between League goals conceded by the club this season	69

	PLAYER	CON LGE	CLEAN SHEETS	DEF RATE
1	Paul Robinson	44	15	78 mins
2	Danny Senda	41	14	76 mins
3	Maurice Ross	16	3	73 mins
4	Richard Shaw	54	15	70 mins

KEY PLAYERS - MIDFIELDERS

Alan Dunne

Goals in the League	6	Contribution to Attacking Power Average number of minutes between League team goals while on pitch	62
Defensive Rating Average number of mins between League goals conceded while on the pitch	81	Scoring Difference Defensive Rating minus Contribution to Attacking Power	19

	PLAYER	LGE GOALS	DEF RATE	POWER	SCORE DIFF
1	Alan Dunne	6	81	62	19 mins
2	David Brammer	1	72	58	14 mins
3	Chris Hackett	3	66	64	2 mins
4	Marvin Elliott	0	65	74	-9 mins

KEY PLAYERS - GOALSCORERS

Darren Byfield

Goals in the League	16	Player Strike Rate Average number of minutes between League goals scored by player	159
Contribution to Attacking Power Average number of minutes between League team goals while on pitch	60	Club Strike Rate Average number of minutes between League goals scored by club	70

	PLAYER	LGE GOALS	POWER	STRIKE RATE
1	Darren Byfield	16	60	159 mins
2	Poul Hubertz	10	58	188 mins
3	Neil Harris	6	68	296 mins
4	Alan Dunne	6	62	447 mins

Poul Hubertz

SQUAD APPEARANCES

Match	1 2 3 4 5	6 7 8 9 10	11 12 13 14 15	16 17 18 19 20	21 22 23 24 25	26 27 28 29 30	31 32 33 34 35	36 37 38 39 40	41 42 43 44 45	46 47 48 49 50	51 52
Venue	H A A H H	A H H A A	H H H A A	H A H A A	H A A H H	H A H A H	A A H A A	A H A H A	H H H A A	H H A H A	H A
Competition	L L L L W	L L L L L	W L L L L	L L L L F	L L F L L	F L L L L	F L L L L	L L L L L	L L L L L	L L L L L	L L
Result	D L L W W	L D L L L	L L D W W	W L D L W	D L D D W	W L L W W	L W W L L	W W W L W	W W D L L	W W W D L	W D

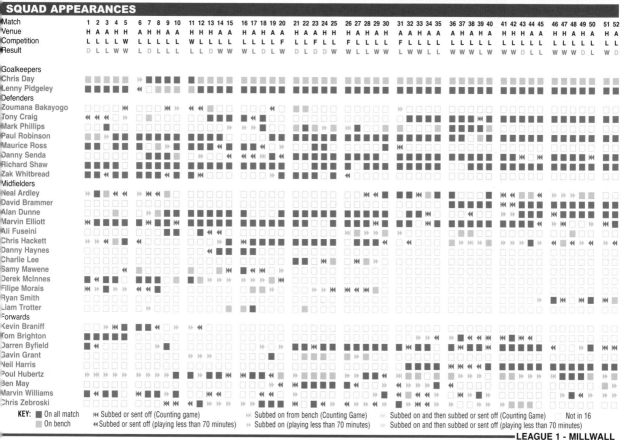

KEY: ■ On all match ◄◄ Subbed or sent off (Counting game) ►► Subbed on from bench (Counting Game) ►► Subbed on and then subbed or sent off (Counting Game) ☐ Not in 16
■ On bench ◄◄ Subbed or sent off (playing less than 70 minutes) ►► Subbed on (playing less than 70 minutes) ►► Subbed on and then subbed or sent off (playing less than 70 minutes)

DONCASTER ROVERS

Final Position: 11th

NICKNAME: ROVERS   KEY: ☐ Won ☐ Drawn ☐ Lost   Attendance

#	comp	Opponent	H/A	Result	Scorers	Attendance
1	div2	Carlisle	A	L 0-1		12,031
2	div2	Crewe	H	W 3-1	Dyer 19, Horlock 63, Coppinger 71	6,081
3	div2	Tranmere	H	D 0-0		6,014
4	div2	Swansea	A	L 0-2		12,218
5	ccr1	Rochdale	H	W 3-2	McCammon 55, 67, Coppinger 56	3,690
6	div2	Bournemouth	H	D 1-1	Guy 60	5,190
7	div2	Port Vale	A	W 2-1	Heffernan 88 pen, 90	4,862
8	div2	Gillingham	H	L 1-2	Clohessy 78 og	5,772
9	div2	Huddersfield	A	D 0-0		10,151
10	div2	Rotherham	A	D 0-0		6,348
11	ccr2	Derby	H	W 8-7*	Forte 6, 57, Stock 29 (*on penalties)	5,598
12	div2	Blackpool	H	D 0-0		5,424
13	div2	Bradford	H	D 3-3	Green 43, 52, Coppinger 54	6,304
14	div2	Scunthorpe	A	L 0-2		6,441
15	div2	Oldham	H	D 1-1	Lee 23	6,241
16	div2	Cheltenham	A	W 2-0	Guy 45, Forte 82	3,872
17	div2	Chesterfield	H	W 1-0	Forte 24	6,280
18	ccr3	Wycombe	A	L 2-3*	Forte 65, Lee 97 (*on penalties)	3,308
19	div2	Bristol City	A	L 0-1		11,909
20	div2	Leyton Orient	H	D 0-0		5,447
21	facr1	Brentford	A	W 1-0	Guy 32	3,607
22	div2	Millwall	A	D 2-2	Forte 16, Price 53	8,670
23	div2	Brighton	H	W 1-0	McCammon 25	5,804
24	facr2	Mansfield	A	D 1-1	Stock 90	4,837
25	div2	Brentford	A	W 4-0	Price 25, Forte 53, J.O'Connor 64, Heffernan 73	4,296
26	div2	Northampton	A	W 2-0	Heffernan 75, Guy 86	5,131
27	facr2r	Mansfield	H	W 2-0	McCammon 23, Heffernan 50	5,338
28	div2	Nottm Forest	H	W 1-0	Streete 60	8,923
29	div2	Bradford	A	W 1-0	Heffernan 14	10,069
30	div2	Blackpool	A	L 1-3	Heffernan 90	7,952
31	div2	Huddersfield	H	W 3-0	McCammon 9, Heffernan 47, Forte 51	14,470
32	facr3	Bolton	H	L 0-4		14,297
33	div2	Gillingham	A	W 2-0	Price 81, Stock 88	6,202
34	div2	Scunthorpe	H	D 2-2	Lee 57, Price 59	12,414
35	div2	Rotherham	H	W 3-2	Heffernan 12, 59, Lee 47	12,126
36	div2	Carlisle	H	L 1-2	Coppinger 3	9,036
37	div2	Tranmere	A	L 0-1		5,965
38	div2	Swansea	H	D 2-2	Price 32, Heffernan 59	7,900
39	div2	Crewe	A	L 1-2	Heffernan 58 pen	4,483
40	div2	Port Vale	H	W 1-0	Price 49	7,848
41	div2	Yeovil	H	D 0-0		8,046
42	div2	Bournemouth	A	L 0-2		6,166
43	div2	Nottm Forest	A	W 1-0	Stock 44	16,785
44	div2	Oldham	A	L 0-4		6,619
45	div2	Cheltenham	H	L 0-2		6,777
46	div2	Chesterfield	A	D 1-1	Stock 25	3,868
47	div2	Bristol City	H	L 0-1		7,945
48	div2	Brighton	A	W 2-0	Lee 28, Cadamarteri 47	6,267
49	div2	Millwall	H	L 1-2	Coppinger 13	7,870
50	div2	Leyton Orient	A	D 1-1	Lockwood 54	4,697
51	div2	Brentford	H	W 3-0	Lockwood 45, Wilson 67, Guy 76 pen	8,713
52	div2	Yeovil	A	L 0-1		6,253
53	div2	Northampton	H	D 2-2	Nelthorpe 13, G.Roberts 59	7,534

LEAGUE APPEARANCES, BOOKINGS AND CAPS

	AGE (on 01/07/07)	IN NAMED 16	APPEARANCES	COUNTING GAMES	MINUTES ON PITCH	LEAGUE GOALS	🟨	🟥
Goalkeepers								
Alan Blayney	25	8	8	7	674	0	0	0
Jan Budtz	28	12	7	6	586	0	0	0
John Filan	37	3	3	3	270	0	0	0
Benjamin Smith	20	24	13	13	1170	0	1	0
Neil Sullivan	37	16	16	16	1440	0	0	0
Defenders								
Peter Gilbert	23	4	4	4	358	0	0	0
Sam Hird	19	12	5	0	119	0	0	0
Graeme Lee	29	41	39	35	3239	4	8	1
Adam Lockwood	25	45	44	41	3728	2	4	0
Sean McDaid	21	23	20	15	1419	0	2	0
James O'Connor	22	41	40	39	3555	1	3	0
Gareth Roberts	29	32	30	28	2496	1	2	1
Stephen Roberts	27	23	21	13	1304	0	3	0
Theo Streete	19	11	6	1	193	1	1	0
Harry Worley	18	11	10	8	807	0	2	0
Alan Wright	35	3	3	3	270	0	0	0
Midfielders								
James Coppinger	26	39	39	33	3042	4	4	0
Paul Green	24	44	41	32	3125	2	1	0
Anthony Griffith	20	5	2	2	167	0	1	0
Kevin Horlock	34	3	2	2	180	1	1	0
Craig Nelthorpe	20	7	6	2	206	1	0	0
Jason Price	30	33	29	14	1712	6	3	0
Brian Stock	25	36	36	35	3162	3	4	0
Sean Thornton	24	38	30	13	1444	0	3	0
Mark Wilson	28	25	22	15	1468	1	3	0
Forwards								
Danny Cadamarteri	27	6	6	6	534	1	0	0
Michele di Piedi	26	3	3	1	117	0	0	0
Bruce Dyer	32	23	15	7	797	1	2	0
Jonathan Forte	20	45	41	27	2814	5	2	0
Lewis Guy	21	39	35	17	1727	4	3	0
Paul Heffernan	25	33	28	20	1957	10	4	0
Mark McCammon	28	27	22	14	1396	2	5	0

TEAM OF THE SEASON

G Neil Sullivan — CG: 16 DR: 96

D Gareth Roberts — CG: 28 DR: 108
D Graeme Lee — CG: 35 DR: 95
D James O'Connor — CG: 39 DR: 88
D Adam Lockwood — CG: 41 DR: 86

M Paul Green — CG: 32 SD: 15
M Jason Price — CG: 14 SD: 10
M Brian Stock — CG: 35 SD: 9
M James Coppinger — CG: 33 SD: 4

F Paul Heffernan — CG: 20 SR: 217
F Lewis Guy — CG: 17 SR: 431

MONTHLY POINTS TALLY

Month	Points	%
AUGUST	5	33%
SEPTEMBER	7	33%
OCTOBER	7	58%
NOVEMBER	5	56%
DECEMBER	12	80%
JANUARY	10	83%
FEBRUARY	5	28%
MARCH	4	22%
APRIL	7	47%
MAY	1	33%

LEAGUE GOALS

	PLAYER	MINS	GOALS	S RATE
1	Heffernan	1957	9	217
2	Price	1712	6	285
3	Forte	2814	5	562
4	Guy	1727	4	431
5	Coppinger	3042	4	760
6	Lee	3239	4	809
7	Stock	3162	3	1054
8	McCammon	1396	2	698
9	Green, P	3125	2	1562
10	Lockwood	3728	2	1864
11	Horlock	180	1	180
12	Streete	193	1	193
13	Nelthorpe	206	1	206
	Other		5	
	TOTAL		**49**	

TOP POINT EARNERS

	PLAYER	GAMES	AV PTS
1	Mark McCammon	14	1.86
2	Jonathan Forte	27	1.70
3	Paul Green	32	1.53
4	Neil Sullivan	16	1.50
5	Graeme Lee	35	1.49
6	Mark Wilson	15	1.47
7	Benjamin Smith	13	1.46
8	Gareth Roberts	28	1.46
9	Jason Price	14	1.43
10	James Coppinger	33	1.42
	CLUB AVERAGE:		**1.37**

DISCIPLINARY RECORDS

	PLAYER	YELLOW	RED	AVE
1	Graeme Lee	8	1	359
2	Bruce Dyer	2	0	398
3	Mark McCammon	3	0	465
4	Sean Thornton	3	0	481
5	Paul Heffernan	4	0	489
6	Mark Wilson	3	0	489
7	James Coppinger	4	0	760
8	Brian Stock	4	0	790
9	Gareth Roberts	2	1	832
10	Jason Price	2	0	856
11	Lewis Guy	3	0	863
12	James O'Connor	3	0	1185
13	Adam Lockwood	4	0	1242
	Other	7	0	
	TOTAL	**52**	**2**	

KEY GOALKEEPER

Neil Sullivan

Goals Conceded in the League	15	Counting Games League games when player was on pitch for at least 70 minutes	16
Defensive Rating Ave number of mins between League goals conceded while on the pitch	96	Clean Sheets In League games when player was on pitch for at least 70 minutes	8

KEY PLAYERS - DEFENDERS

Gareth Roberts

Goals Conceded Number of League goals conceded while the player was on the pitch	23	Clean Sheets In League games when player was on pitch for at least 70 minutes	13
Defensive Rating Ave number of mins between League goals conceded while on the pitch	108	Club Defensive Rating Average number of mins between League goals conceded by the club this season	90

	PLAYER	CON LGE	CLEAN SHEETS	DEF RATE
1	Gareth Roberts	23	13	108 mins
2	Graeme Lee	34	16	95 mins
3	James O'Connor	40	16	88 mins
4	Adam Lockwood	43	16	86 mins

KEY PLAYERS - MIDFIELDERS

Paul Green

Goals in the League	2	Contribution to Attacking Power Average number of minutes between League team goals while on pitch	82
Defensive Rating Average number of mins between League goals conceded while on the pitch	97	Scoring Difference Defensive Rating minus Contribution to Attacking Power	15

	PLAYER	LGE GOALS	DEF RATE	POWER	SCORE DIFF
1	Paul Green	2	97	82	15 mins
2	Jason Price	6	95	85	10 mins
3	Brian Stock	3	90	81	9 mins
4	James Coppinger	4	76	72	4 mins

KEY PLAYERS - GOALSCORERS

Paul Heffernan

Goals in the League	9	Player Strike Rate Average number of minutes between League goals scored by player	217
Contribution to Attacking Power Average number of minutes between League team goals while on pitch	61	Club Strike Rate Average number of minutes between League goals scored by club	81

	PLAYER	LGE GOALS	POWER	STRIKE RATE
1	Paul Heffernan	9	61	217 mins
2	Jason Price	6	85	285 mins
3	Lewis Guy	4	86	431 mins
4	Jonathan Forte	5	80	562 mins

Paul Heffernan

SQUAD APPEARANCES

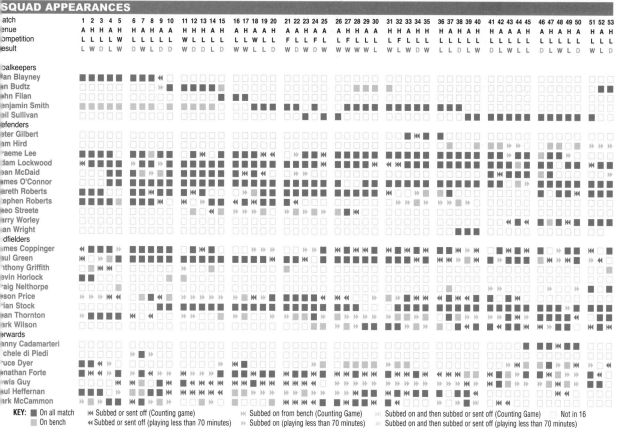

Match	1 2 3 4 5	6 7 8 9 10	11 12 13 14 15	16 17 18 19 20	21 22 23 24 25	26 27 28 29 30	31 32 33 34 35	36 37 38 39 40	41 42 43 44 45	46 47 48 49 50	51 52 53
Venue	A H H A H	H A H A A	H H H A H	A H A A H	A A H A A	A H H A A	H H A H H	H A H A H	H A A A H	A H A H A	H A H
Competition	L L L L W	L L L L L	W L L L L	L L W L L	F L L L F	L F L L L	L F L L L	L L L L L	L L L L L	L L L L L	L L L
Result	L W D L W	D W L D D	W D D L D	W W L L D	W D W D W	W W W W L	W L W D W	L L D L W	D L W L L	D L W L D	W L D

Goalkeepers
Alan Blayney
Jan Budtz
John Filan
Benjamin Smith
Neil Sullivan

Defenders
Peter Gilbert
Sam Hird
Graeme Lee
Adam Lockwood
Sean McDaid
James O'Connor
Gareth Roberts
Stephen Roberts
Theo Streete
Barry Worley
Ian Wright

Midfielders
James Coppinger
Paul Green
Anthony Griffith
Kevin Horlock
Craig Nelthorpe
Jason Price
Brian Stock
Sean Thornton
Mark Wilson

Forwards
Danny Cadamarteri
Michele di Piedi
Bruce Dyer
Jonathan Forte
Lewis Guy
Paul Heffernan
Mark McCammon

KEY: ■ On all match ◄◄ Subbed or sent off (Counting game) ►► Subbed on from bench (Counting Game) ►◄ Subbed on and then subbed or sent off (Counting game) □ Not in 16
■ On bench ◄ Subbed or sent off (playing less than 70 minutes) ►► Subbed on (playing less than 70 minutes) ►► Subbed on and then subbed or sent off (playing less than 70 minutes)

PORT VALE

Final Position: **12th**

NICKNAME: THE VALIANTS   KEY: ☐ Won ☐ Drawn ☐ Lost   Attendance

#	Comp	Opponent		Result	Scorers	Attendance
1	div2	Leyton Orient	H W	3-0	Constantine 43, 72, Sodje 78	5,631
2	div2	Oldham	A W	1-0	A.Sodje 66	4,975
3	div2	Cheltenham	A W	1-0	Constantine 55	4,309
4	div2	Chesterfield	H W	3-2	Constantine 44, 87, Pilkington 77	5,622
5	ccr1	Preston	H W	2-1	A.Sodje 52, Constantine 82	3,522
6	div2	Yeovil	A L	0-1		4,827
7	div2	Doncaster	H L	1-2	Whitaker 43	4,862
8	div2	Blackpool	H W	2-1	Constantine 44, A.Sodje 68	5,171
9	div2	Scunthorpe	A L	0-3		3,473
10	div2	Bradford	A L	0-2		7,829
11	ccr2	QPR	H W	3-2	J.Smith 19, Whitaker 28, Walker 61	3,550
12	div2	Bristol City	H L	0-2		5,295
13	div2	Nottm Forest	H D	1-1	Husbands 1	7,388
14	div2	Northampton	A W	2-0	Pilkington 12, S.Moore 32	5,316
15	div2	Rotherham	H L	1-3	Constantine 74 pen	4,810
16	div2	Tranmere	A W	2-1	J.Smith 31, Constantine 45	7,866
17	div2	Huddersfield	H L	1-2	Constantine 33	5,225
18	ccr3	Norwich	H W	3-2*	(*on penalties)	4,518
19	div2	Millwall	A D	1-1	A.Sodje 72	10,819
20	div2	Crewe	A L	1-2	Abbey 36	7,632
21	ccr4	Tottenham	A L	1-3	Constantine 64	34,560
22	facr1	Lincoln	H W	2-1	Whitaker 29, A.Sodje 38	3,884
23	div2	Swansea	H L	0-2		4,615
24	div2	Carlisle	A L	2-3	Harsley 26, J.Smith 40	7,543
25	facr2	Hereford	A L	0-4		4,076
26	div2	Gillingham	H W	2-0	Gardner 8, Constantine 75	3,077
27	div2	Bournemouth	A W	4-0	Constantine 3, 68, Pilkington 13, A.Sodje 80	4,538
28	div2	Brentford	H W	1-0	Pilkington 87	4,166
29	div2	Brighton	H W	2-1	Constantine 13, 23 pen	4,349
30	div2	Nottm Forest	A L	0-3		22,999
31	div2	Bristol City	A L	1-2	J.Smith 68	12,776
32	div2	Scunthorpe	H D	0-0		4,869
33	div2	Bradford	H L	0-1		4,146
34	div2	Blackpool	A L	1-2	A.Sodje 90 pen	6,661
35	div2	Brighton	A D	0-0		5,177
36	div2	Leyton Orient	A L	1-2	Gardner 12	4,295
37	div2	Northampton	H W	1-0	Whitaker 47	3,353
38	div2	Chesterfield	A L	0-3		3,752
39	div2	Oldham	H W	3-0	Whitaker 18, Pilkington 49, Constantine 79 pen	4,061
40	div2	Doncaster	A L	0-1		7,848
41	div2	Yeovil	H W	4-2	Constantine 15, 80, Whitaker 17, Rose 49 og	4,202
42	div2	Cheltenham	H D	1-1	Kamara 41	3,340
43	div2	Rotherham	A W	5-1	A.Sodje 11, 25, 29, 78, Pilkington 44	3,854
44	div2	Tranmere	H L	2-3	Sonner 36, Constantine 73	4,809
45	div2	Millwall	H W	2-0	Whitaker 18, A.Sodje 53	3,973
46	div2	Huddersfield	A D	2-2	A.Sodje 35, 68	10,313
47	div2	Carlisle	H L	0-2		4,882
48	div2	Swansea	A L	0-3		12,465
49	div2	Crewe	H W	3-0	Hulbert 36, Constantine 59, Rodgers 63	5,740
50	div2	Gillingham	A L	2-3	Whitaker 78, Constantine 90 pen	5,928
51	div2	Brentford	A L	3-4	Rodgers 55, Constantine 59, 83	5,125
52	div2	Bournemouth	H W	2-1	A.Sodje 51, Rodgers 57	5,080

LEAGUE APPEARANCES, BOOKINGS AND CAPS

	AGE (on 01/07/07)	IN NAMED 16	APPEARANCES	COUNTING GAMES	MINUTES ON PITCH	LEAGUE GOALS	CAPS
Goalkeepers							
Joe Anyon	20	46	22	22	1976	0	0	0
Mark Goodlad	27	25	25	24	2164	0	2	0
Defenders							
George Abbey	28	28	24	17	1745	1	3	0
Clayton Fortune	24	14	13	9	1001	0	0	0
Mark McGregor	30	39	32	26	2539	0	6	0
Colin Miles	28	34	28	16	1733	0	4	1
George Pilkington	25	46	46	46	4140	6	3	0
Jason Talbot	21	23	22	18	1682	0	2	2
Richard Walker	26	28	14	11	1102	0	2	0
Michael Walsh	29	23	18	13	1341	0	4	0
Rhys Weston	26	15	15	15	1281	0	5	0
Midfielders							
Joe Cardle	20	20	6	0	194	0	0	0
Ross Gardner	21	22	16	7	885	2	2	0
Paul Harsley	29	33	32	25	2538	1	4	0
Robin Hulbert	27	22	19	15	1425	1	5	0
Richie Humphreys	29	7	7	5	491	0	0	1
Malvin Kamara	23	18	18	12	1197	1	1	0
Christian Smith	19	3	1	0	15	0	0	0
Jeff Smith	27	27	27	22	2097	3	4	0
Danny Sonner	35	33	33	31	2823	1	5	0
Danny Whitaker	26	45	45	43	3951	6	0	0
Forwards							
Leon Constantine	29	42	42	41	3707	22	3	0
Michael Husbands	23	31	23	3	603	1	3	0
Nathan Lowndes	30	21	12	1	270	0	0	0
Stefan Moore	23	13	12	4	646	1	1	0
Luke Rodgers	34	9	8	5	500	3	1	0
Akpo Sodje	27	43	43	36	3393	14	1	0

TEAM OF THE SEASON

Position	Player	CG	DR/SD/SR
G	Mark Goodlad	24	DR: 67
D	Jason Talbot	17	DR: 76
D	Colin Miles	16	DR: 75
D	Michael Walsh	13	DR: 67
D	Mark McGregor	26	DR: 66
M	Danny Sonner	31	SD: 12
M	Malvin Kamara	12	SD: 11
M	Robin Hulbert	15	SD: 7
M	Jeff Smith	22	SD: 5
F	Leon Constantine	41	SR: 168
F	Akpo Sodje	36	SR: 242

MONTHLY POINTS TALLY

Month	Points	%
AUGUST	12	80%
SEPTEMBER	7	33%
OCTOBER	4	33%
NOVEMBER	0	0%
DECEMBER	12	67%
JANUARY	2	17%
FEBRUARY	6	40%
MARCH	11	61%
APRIL	3	20%
MAY	3	100%

LEAGUE GOALS

	PLAYER	MINS	GOALS	S RATE
1	Constantine	3707	22	168
2	Sodje, A	3393	14	242
3	Whitaker	3951	6	658
4	Pilkington	4140	6	690
5	Rodgers	500	3	166
6	Smith, Jeff	2097	3	699
7	Gardner	885	2	442
8	Husbands	603	1	603
9	Moore, S	646	1	646
10	Kamara	1197	1	1197
11	Hulbert	1425	1	1425
12	Abbey	1745	1	1745
13	Harsley	2538	1	2538
	Other		1	
	TOTAL		**63**	

TOP POINT EARNERS

	PLAYER	GAMES	AV PTS
1	Colin Miles	17	1.65
2	Danny Sonner	31	1.62
3	Mark McGregor	26	1.54
4	George Abbey	17	1.47
5	Mark Goodlad	24	1.46
6	Jeff Smith	22	1.45
7	Leon Constantine	41	1.44
8	Danny Whitaker	42	1.38
9	George Pilkington	46	1.30
10	Akpo Sodje	36	1.28
	CLUB AVERAGE:		**1.30**

DISCIPLINARY RECORDS

	PLAYER	YELLOW	RED	AVE
1	Michael Husbands	3	0	201
2	Rhys Weston	5	0	256
3	Robin Hulbert	5	0	285
4	Michael Walsh	4	0	335
5	Jason Talbot	2	2	420
6	Mark McGregor	6	0	423
7	Ross Gardner	2	0	442
8	Richie Humphreys	0	1	491
9	Luke Rodgers	1	0	500
10	Jeff Smith	4	0	524
11	Richard Walker	2	0	551
12	Danny Sonner	5	0	564
13	Colin Miles	4	1	577
	Other	18	0	
	TOTAL	**61**	**4**	

KEY GOALKEEPER

Mark Goodlad

Goals Conceded in the League	32	Counting Games League games when player was on pitch for at least 70 minutes	24
Defensive Rating Ave number of mins between League goals conceded while on the pitch	67	Clean Sheets In League games when player was on pitch for at least 70 minutes	8

KEY PLAYERS - DEFENDERS

Jason Talbot

Goals Conceded Number of League goals conceded while the player was on the pitch	22	Clean Sheets In League games when player was on pitch for at least 70 minutes	5
Defensive Rating Ave number of mins between League goals conceded while on the pitch	76	Club Defensive Rating Average number of mins between League goals conceded by the club this season	66

	PLAYER	CON LGE	CLEAN SHEETS	DEF RATE
1	Jason Talbot	22	5	76 mins
2	Colin Miles	23	7	75 mins
3	Michael Walsh	20	5	67 mins
4	Mark McGregor	38	7	66 mins

KEY PLAYERS - MIDFIELDERS

Danny Sonner

Goals in the League	1	Contribution to Attacking Power Average number of minutes between League team goals while on pitch	60
Defensive Rating Average number of mins between League goals conceded while on the pitch	72	Scoring Difference Defensive Rating minus Contribution to Attacking Power	12

	PLAYER	LGE GOALS	DEF RATE	POWER	SCORE DIFF
1	Danny Sonner	1	72	60	12 mins
2	Malvin Kamara	1	63	52	11 mins
3	Robin Hulbert	1	61	54	7 mins
4	Jeff Smith	3	74	69	5 mins

KEY PLAYERS - GOALSCORERS

Leon Constantine

Goals in the League	22	Player Strike Rate Average number of minutes between League goals scored by player	168
Contribution to Attacking Power Average number of minutes between League team goals while on pitch	59	Club Strike Rate Average number of minutes between League goals scored by club	67

	PLAYER	LGE GOALS	POWER	STRIKE RATE
1	Leon Constantine	22	59	168 mins
2	Akpo Sodje	14	65	242 mins
3	Danny Whitaker	6	61	658 mins
4	Jeff Smith	3	69	699 mins

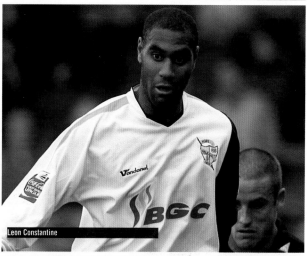

Leon Constantine

SQUAD APPEARANCES

Match	1	2	3	4	5	6	7	8	9	10	11	12	13	14	15	16	17	18	19	20	21	22	23	24	25	26	27	28	29	30	31	32	33	34	35	36	37	38	39	40	41	42	43	44	45	46	47	48	49	50	51	52
Venue	H	A	A	H	H		A	H	H	A	A		H	H	H	A	H		A	H	H	A	A		A	H	H	A	A		H	A	H	H		A	H	H	A	A		A	H	A	H	A		H	H	A	H	H		A	H	A	H	A		A	H
Competition	L	L	L	L	W		L	L	L	L	L		W	L	L	L	L		L	L	W	L	L		W	F	L	L	F		L	L	L	L		L	L	L	L		L	L	L	L	L		L	L	L	L	L		L	L
Result	W	W	W	W	W		L	L	W	L	L		W	L	D	W	L		W	L	W	D	L		L	W	L	L	L		W	W	W	W		L	D	L	L	D		L	W	L	W	L		W	D	W	L	W		D	L	L	W	L		L	W

Goalkeepers
Joe Anyon
Mark Goodlad

Defenders
George Abbey
Clayton Fortune
Mark McGregor
Colin Miles
George Pilkington
Jason Talbot
Richard Walker
Michael Walsh
Rhys Weston

Midfielders
Joe Cardle
Ross Gardner
Paul Harsley
Robin Hulbert
Richie Humphreys
Malvin Kamara
Christian Smith
Jeff Smith
Danny Sonner
Danny Whitaker

Forwards
Leon Constantine
Michael Husbands
Nathan Lowndes
Stefan Moore
Luke Rodgers
Akpo Sodje

KEY: ■ On all match   ◄◄ Subbed or sent off (Counting game)   ►► Subbed on from bench (Counting Game)   ►► Subbed on and then subbed or sent off (Counting game)   ☐ Not in 16
☐ On bench   ◄◄ Subbed or sent off (playing less than 70 minutes)   ►► Subbed on (playing less than 70 minutes)   ►► Subbed on and then subbed or sent off (playing less than 70 minutes)

CREWE ALEXANDRA

Final Position: **13th**

NICKNAME: THE RAILWAYMEN KEY: ☐ Won ☐ Drawn ☐ Lost Attendance

				Result	Scorers	Att
1	div2	Northampton	H D	2-2	Lowe 7, Vaughan 19	5,553
2	div2	Doncaster	A L	1-3	Maynard 11	6,081
3	div2	Scunthorpe	A D	2-2	Rodgers 30 pen, Vaughan 49	4,329
4	div2	Bradford	H L	0-3		5,274
5	ccr1	Grimsby	A W	3-0	Maynard 39, O'Connor 73, Lowe 89 pen	1,635
6	div2	Brighton	A W	4-1	B.Jones 44, Lowe 45 pen, Maynard 56, 84	5,848
7	div2	Huddersfield	H W	2-0	Maynard 41, 53	4,868
8	div2	Bournemouth	A L	0-1		5,627
9	div2	Cheltenham	H W	3-1	Maynard 21, Cox 70, Varney 81	4,062
10	div2	Millwall	H W	1-0	Varney 65	4,875
11	ccr2	Wigan	H W	2-0	Jack 42, Maynard 90	3,907
12	div2	Yeovil	A L	0-2		5,333
13	div2	Swansea	A L	1-2	Roberts 32 pen	10,031
14	div2	Carlisle	H W	5-1	Varney 42, 73, Lowe 45, 63, 90	5,989
15	div2	Gillingham	H W	4-3	Maynard 36, Jack 69, O'Donnell 88, Varney 90	5,022
16	div2	Bristol City	A L	1-2	Varney 60	11,899
17	div2	Blackpool	H L	1-2	Maynard 67	5,765
18	ccr3	Man Utd	H L	1-2	Varney 73	10,046
19	div2	Rotherham	A L	1-5	Varney 10	5,407
20	div2	Port Vale	H W	2-1	Maynard 32, Rodgers 90 pen	7,632
21	facr1	Bradford	A L	0-4		3,483
22	div2	Brentford	A W	4-0	Varney 5, 63, Rix 58, Vaughan 67	4,771
23	div2	Chesterfield	H D	2-2	Varney 64, Rodgers 89	5,078
24	div2	Oldham	A L	0-1		4,798
25	div2	Nottm Forest	H L	1-4	Roberts 36 pen	7,253
26	div2	Leyton Orient	A D	1-1	Maynard 30	4,371
27	div2	Swansea	H L	1-3	Varney 59	6,083
28	div2	Yeovil	H L	2-3	Maynard 77, Roberts 80	5,450
29	div2	Cheltenham	A D	1-1	Varney 15	3,154
30	div2	Bournemouth	H W	2-0	Varney 9, Maynard 62	4,739
31	div2	Tranmere	A L	0-1		5,708
32	div2	Carlisle	A W	2-0	Baudet 53, Maynard 90	7,075
33	div2	Leyton Orient	H L	0-4		5,280
34	div2	Northampton	A W	2-1	Varney 26, 57	5,262
35	div2	Bradford	A W	1-0	Lowe 89	7,778
36	div2	Doncaster	H W	2-1	Rix 50, Higdon 90	4,483
37	div2	Huddersfield	A W	2-1	Higdon 45, Lowe 69	10,052
38	div2	Scunthorpe	H L	1-3	Varney 26	4,842
39	div2	Brighton	H D	1-1	Varney 18	5,202
40	div2	Gillingham	A L	0-1		6,373
41	div2	Millwall	A D	2-2	Higdon 30, Moss 84	8,867
42	div2	Bristol City	H L	0-1		5,731
43	div2	Rotherham	H W	1-0	Moss 16	5,675
44	div2	Blackpool	A L	1-2	Miller 90	7,203
45	div2	Chesterfield	A L	1-2	Miller 8	3,698
46	div2	Brentford	H W	3-1	Vaughan 18, Lowe 23, Maynard 70	4,667
47	div2	Port Vale	A L	0-3		5,740
48	div2	Oldham	H W	2-1	Maynard 25, 71	6,304
49	div2	Tranmere	H D	1-1	Miller 90	5,777
50	div2	Nottm Forest	A D	0-0		27,472

LEAGUE APPEARANCES, BOOKINGS AND CAPS

	AGE (on 01/07/07)	IN NAMED 16	APPEARANCES	COUNTING GAMES	MINUTES ON PITCH	LEAGUE GOALS	CAPS
Goalkeepers							
Stuart Tomlinson	23	27	7	7	630	0	0
Ben Williams	24	44	38	38	3420	0	1
Owain fon Williams	20	8	1	1	90	0	0
Defenders							
Julien Baudet	28	42	42	40	3671	1	3
Paul Bignot	21	19	11	9	861	0	2
Neil Cox	35	31	31	28	2596	1	2
Billy Jones	20	41	41	37	3485	1	2
Darren Kempson	22	14	7	5	512	0	1
Darren Moss	26	30	22	19	1789	2	2
Daniel O'Donnell	21	41	25	19	1955	1	0
Jon Otsemobor	24	28	27	26	2325	0	2
Andy Taylor	21	4	4	4	360	0	0
Dan Woodards	28	11	11	7	786	0	1
Midfielders							
Mark Carrington	20	9	3	0	49	0	0
Christopher Flynn	19	2	1	1	74	0	0
Tony Grant	32	6	4	3	264	0	0
Michael Higdon	23	33	25	12	1262	3	1
Ryan Lowe	28	41	37	27	2710	8	2
Anthony McNamee	22	6	5	3	381	0	0
Michael O'Connor	19	30	29	23	2149	0	3
Isaac Osbourne	21	2	2	2	180	0	0
Ben Rix	23	37	31	23	2170	2	1
Gary Roberts	20	43	43	40	3667	3	3
David Vaughan	24	29	29	24	2327	4	1
Forwards							
Rodney Jack	34	34	29	16	1648	1	2
Lee Matthews	28	11	10	0	173	0	0
Nicky Maynard	20	31	31	23	2287	16	2
Shaun Miller	19	9	7	2	280	3	0
Tom Pope	21	13	4	0	64	0	0
Luke Rodgers	34	13	12	4	468	3	1
Luke Varney	24	36	34	31	2842	17	2

TEAM OF THE SEASON

- **D** Darren Moss — CG: 19 DR: 66
- **D** Neil Cox — CG: 28 DR: 63
- **G** Ben Williams — CG: 38 DR: 57
- **D** Billy Jones — CG: 37 DR: 61
- **D** Daniel O'Donnell — CG: 19 DR: 59
- **M** Ben Rix — CG: 23 SD: 2
- **M** Michael O'Connor — CG: 23 SD: 0
- **M** David Vaughan — CG: 24 SD: 0
- **M** Gary Roberts — CG: 40 SD: -3
- **F** Nicky Maynard — CG: 23 SR: 142
- **F** Luke Varney — CG: 31 SR: 167

MONTHLY POINTS TALLY

AUGUST	5	33%
SEPTEMBER	12	57%
OCTOBER	3	25%
NOVEMBER	7	78%
DECEMBER	1	7%
JANUARY	7	47%
FEBRUARY	12	80%
MARCH	5	28%
APRIL	7	47%
MAY	1	33%

LEAGUE GOALS

	PLAYER	MINS	GOALS	S RATE
1	Varney	2842	17	167
2	Maynard	2287	16	142
3	Lowe	2710	8	338
4	Vaughan	2327	4	581
5	Miller	280	3	93
6	Rodgers	468	3	156
7	Higdon	1262	3	420
8	Roberts	3487	3	1162
9	Moss	1789	2	894
10	Rix	2170	2	1085
11	Jack	1648	1	1648
12	O'Donnell	1955	1	1955
13	Cox	2596	1	2596
	Other		2	
	TOTAL		**66**	

TOP POINT EARNERS

	PLAYER	GAMES	AV PTS
1	Rodney Jack	16	1.63
2	Michael O'Connor	23	1.52
3	Daniel O'Donnell	19	1.47
4	Ben Rix	23	1.45
5	Darren Moss	19	1.44
6	Gary Roberts	40	1.38
7	Luke Varney	31	1.35
8	Jon Otsemobor	26	1.35
9	Nicky Maynard	23	1.35
10	Neil Cox	28	1.32
	CLUB AVERAGE:		**1.30**

DISCIPLINARY RECORDS

	PLAYER	YELLOW	RED	AVE
1	Luke Rodgers	1	0	468
2	Darren Kempson	1	0	512
3	Michael O'Connor	3	0	716
4	Dan Woodards	1	0	786
5	Rodney Jack	2	0	824
6	Paul Bignot	2	0	861
7	Gary Roberts	3	1	871
8	Darren Moss	2	0	894
9	Nicky Maynard	2	0	1143
10	Jon Otsemobor	2	0	1162
11	Michael Higdon	2	0	1262
12	Neil Cox	2	0	1298
13	Ryan Lowe	2	0	1355
	Other	10	0	
	TOTAL	**34**	**1**	

KEY GOALKEEPER

Ben Williams

Goals Conceded in the League	60	Counting Games League games when player was on pitch for at least 70 minutes	38
Defensive Rating Ave number of mins between League goals conceded while on the pitch	57	Clean Sheets In League games when player was on pitch for at least 70 minutes	6

KEY PLAYERS - DEFENDERS

Darren Moss

Goals Conceded Number of League goals conceded while the player was on the pitch	27	Clean Sheets In League games when player was on pitch for at least 70 minutes	4
Defensive Rating Ave number of mins between League goals conceded while on the pitch	66	Club Defensive Rating Average number of mins between League goals conceded by the club this season	61

	PLAYER	CON LGE	CLEAN SHEETS	DEF RATE
1	Darren Moss	27	4	66 mins
2	Neil Cox	41	5	63 mins
3	Billy Jones	57	7	61 mins
4	Daniel O'Donnell	33	4	59 mins

KEY PLAYERS - MIDFIELDERS

Ben Rix

Goals in the League	2	Contribution to Attacking Power Average number of minutes between League team goals while on pitch	60
Defensive Rating Average number of mins between League goals conceded while on the pitch	62	Scoring Difference Defensive Rating minus Contribution to Attacking Power	2

	PLAYER	LGE GOALS	DEF RATE	POWER	SCORE DIFF
1	Ben Rix	2	62	60	2 mins
2	Michael O'Connor	0	58	58	0 mins
3	David Vaughan	4	59	59	0 mins
4	Gary Roberts	3	60	63	-3 mins

KEY PLAYERS - GOALSCORERS

Nicky Maynard

Goals in the League	16	Player Strike Rate Average number of minutes between League goals scored by player	142
Contribution to Attacking Power Average number of minutes between League team goals while on pitch	61	Club Strike Rate Average number of minutes between League goals scored by club	66

	PLAYER	LGE GOALS	POWER	STRIKE RATE
1	Nicky Maynard	16	61	142 mins
2	Luke Varney	17	61	167 mins
3	Ryan Lowe	8	69	338 mins
4	Michael Higdon	3	74	420 mins

Luke Varney

SQUAD APPEARANCES

Match	1 2 3 4 5	6 7 8 9 10	11 12 13 14 15	16 17 18 19 20	21 22 23 24 25	26 27 28 29 30	31 32 33 34 35	36 37 38 39 40	41 42 43 44 45	46 47 48 49 50
Venue	H A A H A	A H A H H	H A A H H	A H H A H	A A H A H	A H H A H	A A H A A	H A H H A	A H H A A	H A H H A
Competition	L L L L L	L L L L L	W L L L L	L L W L L	F L L L L	L L L L L	L L L L L	L L L L L	L L L L L	L L L L L
Result	D L D L W	W W L W W	W L L W W	L L L L W	L W D L L	D L L D W	L W L W W	W W L D L	D L W L L	W L W D D

KEY: ■ On all match ◄◄ Subbed or sent off (Counting game) ►► Subbed on from bench (Counting Game) ►► Subbed on and then subbed or sent off (Counting Game) Not in 16
☐ On bench ◄◄ Subbed or sent off (playing less than 70 minutes) ►► Subbed on (playing less than 70 minutes) ►► Subbed on and then subbed or sent off (playing less than 70 minutes)

LEAGUE 1 - CREWE ALEXANDRA

NORTHAMPTON TOWN

Final Position: 14th

NICKNAME: THE COBBLERS   KEY: ☐ Won ☐ Drawn ☐ Lost   Attendance

1	div2	Crewe	A D	2-2	McGleish 12, Kirk 42	5,553
2	div2	Brentford	H L	0-1		5,707
3	div2	Nottm Forest	H L	0-1		7,172
4	div2	Gillingham	A W	1-0	Kirk 23	5,654
5	ccr1	QPR	A L	2-3	Watt 55, Kirk 78	4,569
6	div2	Bristol City	H L	1-3	Kirk 18	4,919
7	div2	Rotherham	A W	2-1	McGleish 74, 83	4,971
8	div2	Carlisle	A D	1-1	McGleish 47	7,602
9	div2	Yeovil	H D	1-1	Crowe 31	4,184
10	div2	Tranmere	H L	1-3	McGleish 74	5,334
11	div2	Millwall	A W	1-0	Cole 42	7,432
12	div2	Cheltenham	A W	2-0	Kirk 66, McGleish 83 pen	3,224
13	div2	Port Vale	H L	0-2		5,316
14	div2	Bournemouth	A D	0-0		5,746
15	div2	Bradford	A D	0-0		5,625
16	div2	Brighton	A D	1-1	Quinn 84	5,862
17	div2	Swansea	H W	1-0	Chambers 55	5,444
18	div2	Blackpool	H D	1-1	Jess 62	5,762
19	facr1	Grimsby	H D	0-0		4,092
20	div2	Scunthorpe	A L	0-1		4,758
21	facr1r	Grimsby	A W	2-0	Whittle 18 og, Burnell 45	2,657
22	facr2	Barnet	A L	1-4	McGleish 45	2,786
23	div2	Chesterfield	A D	0-0		3,341
24	div2	Doncaster	H L	0-2		5,131
25	div2	Huddersfield	A D	1-1	Burnell 19	8,723
26	div2	Leyton Orient	H L	0-1		4,728
27	div2	Oldham	A L	0-3		10,207
28	div2	Cheltenham	H W	2-0	McGleish 45, 74 pen	5,239
29	div2	Yeovil	A D	0-0		5,361
30	div2	Tranmere	A L	1-6	McGleish 11	6,089
31	div2	Carlisle	H W	3-2	Kirk 45, McGleish 47, 71	5,549
32	div2	Millwall	H W	3-0	McGleish 46, Holt 71, Bradley.Johnson 90	5,834
33	div2	Oldham	H L	2-3	Kirk 24, Robertson 88	5,662
34	div2	Crewe	H L	1-2	Bradley.Johnson 55	5,262
35	div2	Port Vale	A L	0-1		3,353
36	div2	Nottm Forest	A L	0-1		24,567
37	div2	Gillingham	H D	1-1	Robertson 86	5,618
38	div2	Brentford	A W	1-0	Crowe 31	5,164
39	div2	Rotherham	H W	3-0	Deuchar 15, Hughes 21, Taylor 45	4,564
40	div2	Bristol City	A L	0-1		11,965
41	div2	Bournemouth	H W	3-1	Robertson 17, Deuchar 77, Kirk 85	5,921
42	div2	Bradford	A W	2-1	Bradley.Johnson 64, Deuchar 87	8,190
43	div2	Swansea	A L	1-2	Bradley.Johnson 6	11,071
44	div2	Brighton	H L	0-2		6,613
45	div2	Leyton Orient	A W	2-0	Cox 12, Palmer 40 og	5,459
46	div2	Scunthorpe	H W	2-1	Pearce 16, Bradley.Johnson 90	6,361
47	div2	Blackpool	A L	1-4	Cox 42	7,334
48	div2	Chesterfield	H W	1-0	Cox 78	5,730
49	div2	Huddersfield	H D	1-1	Holt 63	5,842
50	div2	Doncaster	A D	2-2	Crowe 45, Hughes 64	7,534

LEAGUE APPEARANCES, BOOKINGS AND CAPS

	AGE (on 01/07/07)	IN NAMED 16	APPEARANCES	COUNTING GAMES	MINUTES ON PITCH	LEAGUE GOALS
Goalkeepers						
Mark Bunn	22	44	42	42	3780	0	4
Lee Harper	35	14	4	4	360	0	0
Defenders						
Pedj Bojic	23	27	26	13	1649	0	3
Luke Chambers	21	29	29	28	2552	1	3
Jason Crowe	28	43	43	41	3807	3	9
Chris Doig	26	39	39	37	3373	0	5
Sean Dyche	36	34	21	18	1792	0	2
Andy Holt	29	35	35	31	2895	2	2
Mark Hughes	20	17	17	17	1530	2	6
Brett Johnson	21	6	3	1	197	0	0
Danny May	18	5	3	1	153	0	0
Alex Pearce	18	15	15	14	1322	1	0
Midfielders						
Sam Aiston	30	28	21	10	1192	0	3
Joe Burnell	26	25	24	22	1948	1	2
Mitchell Cole	21	8	8	3	420	1	1
Simon Cox	20	8	8	6	573	3	4
Liam Dolman	19	2	1	1	82	0	0
Ryan Gilligan	20	32	24	13	1484	0	5
David Hunt	24	36	29	20	1992	0	5
Eoin Jess	36	33	26	17	1820	1	1
Bradley Johnson	20	29	28	21	2003	5	4
Marc Laird	21	7	6	1	240	0	1
Ian Taylor	39	37	32	23	2348	1	5
Jerome Watt	22	13	10	0	337	0	0
Nick Wright	19	4	4	1	187	0	0
Forwards						
Kenny Deuchar	26	17	17	13	1301	3	1
Andy Kirk	28	46	44	27	2728	7	0
Scott McGleish	33	25	25	22	2112	12	1
James Quinn	32	26	18	1	528	1	0
Jordan Robertson	19	17	17	6	806	3	1

TEAM OF THE SEASON

G Mark Bunn CG: 43 DR: 78

D Chris Doig CG: 37 DR: 93
D Luke Chambers CG: 28 DR: 88
D Pedj Bojic CG: 13 DR: 82
D Andy Holt CG: 31 DR: 80

M Bradley Johnson CG: 21 SD: 8
M David Hunt CG: 20 SD: -4
M Eoin Jess CG: 17 SD: -20
M Ian Taylor CG: 23 SD: -20

F Scott McGleish CG: 22 SR: 176
F Andy Kirk CG: 27 SR: 402

MONTHLY POINTS TALLY

AUGUST	4	27%
SEPTEMBER	11	52%
OCTOBER	6	50%
NOVEMBER	1	17%
DECEMBER	5	28%
JANUARY	8	53%
FEBRUARY	7	39%
MARCH	6	40%
APRIL	10	67%
MAY	1	33%

LEAGUE GOALS

	PLAYER	MINS	GOALS	S RATE
1	McGleish	2112	12	176
2	Kirk	2818	7	402
3	Johnson, B	2003	5	400
4	Cox	573	3	191
5	Robertson	806	3	268
6	Deuchar	1301	3	433
7	Crowe	3897	3	1299
8	Hughes	1530	2	765
9	Holt	2985	2	1492
10	Cole	420	1	420
11	Quinn	528	1	528
12	Pearce	1322	1	1322
13	Jess	1910	1	1910
	Other		3	
	TOTAL		47	

TOP POINT EARNERS

	PLAYER	GAMES	AV PTS
1	Eoin Jess	17	1.69
2	Alex Pearce	14	1.64
3	Bradley Johnson	21	1.48
4	David Hunt	20	1.45
5	Mark Hughes	17	1.41
6	Sean Dyche	18	1.39
7	Ryan Gilligan	13	1.38
8	Pedj Bojic	13	1.38
9	Mark Bunn	42	1.33
10	Jason Crowe	41	1.32
	CLUB AVERAGE:		1.28

DISCIPLINARY RECORDS

	PLAYER	YELLOW	RED	AVE
1	Mark Hughes	6	0	255
2	Ryan Gilligan	5	0	314
3	Sam Aiston	3	0	397
4	David Hunt	5	0	398
5	Jason Crowe	9	0	433
6	Bradley Johnson	4	0	500
7	Simon Cox	1	0	573
8	Pedj Bojic	3	0	579
9	Ian Taylor	5	0	609
10	Chris Doig	5	0	692
11	Jordan Robertson	1	0	806
12	Luke Chambers	3	0	880
13	Mark Bunn	4	0	967
	Other	9	1	
	TOTAL	63	1	

KEY GOALKEEPER

Mark Bunn

Goals Conceded in the League	49	Counting Games — League games when player was on pitch for at least 70 minutes	43
Defensive Rating — Ave number of mins between League goals conceded while on the pitch	78	Clean Sheets — In League games when player was on pitch for at least 70 minutes	12

KEY PLAYERS - DEFENDERS

Chris Doig

Goals Conceded — Number of League goals conceded while the player was on the pitch	37	Clean Sheets — In League games when player was on pitch for at least 70 minutes	13
Defensive Rating — Ave number of mins between League goals conceded while on the pitch	93	Club Defensive Rating — Average number of mins between League goals conceded by the club this season	84

	PLAYER	CON LGE	CLEAN SHEETS	DEF RATE
1	Chris Doig	37	13	93 mins
2	Luke Chambers	30	10	88 mins
3	Pedj Bojic	21	7	82 mins
4	Andy Holt	37	8	80 mins

KEY PLAYERS - MIDFIELDERS

Bradley Johnson

Goals in the League	5	Contribution to Attacking Power — Average number of minutes between League team goals while on pitch	69
Defensive Rating — Average number of mins between League goals conceded while on the pitch	77	Scoring Difference — Defensive Rating minus Contribution to Attacking Power	8

	PLAYER	LGE GOALS	DEF RATE	POWER	SCORE DIFF
1	Bradley Johnson	5	77	69	8 mins
2	David Hunt	0	90	94	-4 mins
3	Eoin Jess	1	86	106	-20 mins
4	Ian Taylor	1	90	110	-20 mins

KEY PLAYERS - GOALSCORERS

Scott McGleish

Goals in the League	12	Player Strike Rate — Average number of minutes between League goals scored by player	176
Contribution to Attacking Power — Average number of minutes between League team goals while on pitch	96	Club Strike Rate — Average number of minutes between League goals scored by club	91

	PLAYER	LGE GOALS	POWER	STRIKE RATE
1	Scott McGleish	12	96	176 mins
2	Bradley Johnson	5	69	400 mins
3	Andy Kirk	7	97	402 mins
4	Kenny Deuchar	3	81	433 mins

Scott McGleish

SQUAD APPEARANCES

Match	1 2 3 4 5	6 7 8 9 10	11 12 13 14 15	16 17 18 19 20	21 22 23 24 25	26 27 28 29 30	31 32 33 34 35	36 37 38 39 40	41 42 43 44 45	46 47 48 49 50
Venue	A H H A A	H A A H H	A A H A H	A H H H A	A A A H A	H A H A A	H H H H A	A H A H A	H A A H A	H A H H A
Competition	L L L L W	L L L L L	L L L L L	L L L F L	F F L L L	L L L L L	L L L L L	L L L L L	L L L L L	L L L L L
Result	D L L W L	L W D D L	W W L D D	D W D D L	W L D L D	L L W D D	W W L L L	L D W W L	W W L L W	W L W D D

Goalkeepers
Mark Bunn
Lee Harper

Defenders
Pedj Bojic
Luke Chambers
Jason Crowe
Chris Doig
Sean Dyche
Andy Holt
Mark Hughes
Brett Johnson
Danny May
Alex Pearce

Midfielders
Sam Aiston
Joe Burnell
Mitchell Cole
Simon Cox
Liam Dolman
Ryan Gilligan
David Hunt
Eoin Jess
Bradley Johnson
Marc Laird
Ian Taylor
Jerome Watt
Nick Wright

Forwards
Kenny Deuchar
Andy Kirk
Scott McGleish
James Quinn
Jordan Robertson

KEY: ■ On all match — ◄◄ Subbed or sent off (Counting game) — ►► Subbed on from bench (Counting Game) — ►► Subbed on and then subbed or sent off (Counting Game) — □ Not in 16
□ On bench — ◄◄ Subbed or sent off (playing less than 70 minutes) — ►► Subbed on (playing less than 70 minutes) — ►► Subbed on and then subbed or sent off (playing less than 70 minutes)

LEAGUE 1 - NORTHAMPTON TOWN

HUDDERSFIELD TOWN

Final Position: 15th

NICKNAME: THE TERRIERS   KEY: ☐ Won ☐ Drawn ☐ Lost   Attendance

#		Opponent		Result	Scorers	Attendance
1	div2	Gillingham	A L	1-2	Taylor-Fletcher 81	6,075
2	div2	Rotherham	H W	3-0	Beckett 36 pen, Abbott 45, Taylor-Fletcher 79	10,161
3	div2	Bristol City	H W	2-1	Beckett 64, Abbott 90	10,492
4	div2	Brentford	A D	2-2	Schofield 72, Beckett 90	5,709
5	ccr1	Mansfield	H L	0-2		5,111
6	div2	Nottm Forest	H D	1-1	Taylor-Fletcher 72	11,720
7	div2	Crewe	A L	0-2		4,868
8	div2	Cheltenham	A L	1-2	Abbott 86	3,720
9	div2	Doncaster	H D	0-0		10,151
10	div2	Yeovil	H L	2-3	Hudson 26, Taylor-Fletcher 63	9,573
11	div2	Swansea	A W	2-1	Taylor-Fletcher 50, 60	12,202
12	div2	Tranmere	A D	2-2	Booth 56, Taylor-Fletcher 78	6,702
13	div2	Bournemouth	H D	2-2	Taylor-Fletcher 27, Beckett 69	11,350
14	div2	Bradford	A W	1-0	Hudson 25	14,925
15	div2	Carlisle	H W	2-1	Beckett 21, 32 pen	10,830
16	div2	Port Vale	A W	2-1	Booth 77, Collins 79	5,225
17	div2	Brighton	H L	0-3		10,616
18	div2	Scunthorpe	H D	1-1	Booth 86	10,456
19	facr1	Blackpool	H L	0-1		6,597
20	div2	Blackpool	A L	1-3	Taylor-Fletcher 45	7,414
21	div2	Oldham	H L	0-3		13,280
22	div2	Millwall	A D	0-0		6,251
23	div2	Leyton Orient	A L	0-1		4,300
24	div2	Northampton	H D	1-1	Schofield 65	8,723
25	div2	Chesterfield	A D	0-0		4,472
26	div2	Tranmere	H D	2-2	Booth 9, Schofield 60 pen	10,228
27	div2	Swansea	H W	3-2	Worthington 67, Abbott 75, 90 pen	9,399
28	div2	Doncaster	A L	0-3		14,470
29	div2	Yeovil	A L	1-3	Taylor-Fletcher 50	5,554
30	div2	Cheltenham	H W	2-0	Beckett 31, Booth 43	9,813
31	div2	Bournemouth	A W	2-1	Worthington 12, Schofield 85	5,263
32	div2	Chesterfield	H D	1-1	Young 53	9,872
33	div2	Gillingham	H W	3-1	Beckett 3, Booth 8, 83	9,167
34	div2	Bristol City	A D	1-1	Taylor-Fletcher 52	11,636
35	div2	Brentford	H L	0-2		10,520
36	div2	Rotherham	A W	3-2	Beckett 3, 46, Collins 59	4,448
37	div2	Crewe	H L	1-2	Brandon 22	10,052
38	div2	Nottm Forest	A L	1-5	Young 82	19,070
39	div2	Bradford	H W	2-0	Hayes 3, Schofield 75	14,772
40	div2	Carlisle	A D	1-1	Beckett 26	6,629
41	div2	Brighton	A D	0-0		5,974
42	div2	Port Vale	H D	2-2	Beckett 4, McAliskey 46	10,313
43	div2	Oldham	A D	1-1	Beckett 78	7,096
44	div2	Blackpool	H L	0-2		11,432
45	div2	Scunthorpe	A L	0-2		7,518
46	div2	Millwall	H W	4-2	Collins 20, Hudson 59, Beckett 73 pen, 79	9,406
47	div2	Northampton	A D	1-1	Mirfin 75	5,842
48	div2	Leyton Orient	H W	3-1	Collins 11, Holdsworth 26, 45	10,842

LEAGUE APPEARANCES, BOOKINGS AND CAPS

	AGE (on 01/07/07)	IN NAMED 16	APPEARANCES	COUNTING GAMES	MINUTES ON PITCH	LEAGUE GOALS	
Goalkeepers							
Mathew Glennon	28	46	46	46	4140	0	1	0
Paul Rachubka	26	22	0	0	0	0	0	0
Defenders							
Daniel Adams	31	23	23	22	2017	0	5	2
Nathan Clarke	23	18	16	15	1371	0	3	0
Tom Clarke	19	13	8	4	482	0	0	0
Aaron Hardy	21	12	9	6	574	0	2	0
John McCombe	22	31	7	4	432	0	1	0
Martin McIntosh	36	29	26	22	2145	0	5	1
David Mirfin	22	40	38	38	3420	1	4	0
Frank Sinclair	35	13	13	12	1144	0	2	1
Joe Skarz	17	20	17	14	1340	0	1	0
Andy Taylor	21	8	8	7	653	0	3	0
Midfielders							
Adnan Ahmed	23	17	9	5	458	0	2	1
Lucas Akins	18	2	2	0	24	0	0	0
James Berrett	18	3	2	0	67	0	0	0
Chris Brandon	31	24	23	14	1534	1	6	0
Michael Collins	21	43	42	37	3446	4	8	0
James Hand	20	6	1	0	45	0	0	0
Andy Holdsworth	23	36	35	31	2951	2	9	1
Mark Hudson	26	34	32	27	2632	3	3	0
Danny Racchi	19	5	3	0	44	0	0	0
Danny Schofield	27	35	34	19	2122	5	5	0
John Worthington	24	28	28	23	2263	2	10	0
Matthew Young	21	33	29	12	1585	2	3	0
Forwards							
Pawel Abbott	25	21	17	6	894	5	2	1
Luke Beckett	30	46	40	31	2917	15	1	0
Andy Booth	33	34	34	26	2582	7	4	0
Paul Hayes	23	4	4	4	338	1	1	0
John McAliskey	22	28	8	3	270	1	0	0
Gary Taylor-Fletcher	26	39	38	36	3170	11	7	0

TEAM OF THE SEASON

G Mathew Glennon — CG: 46 DR: 60

D Martin McIntosh — CG: 22 DR: 67
D Joe Skarz — CG: 14 DR: 67
D Nathan Clarke — CG: 15 DR: 62
D David Mirfin — CG: 38 DR: 61

M John Worthington — CG: 23 SD: 7
M Andy Holdsworth — CG: 31 SD: 3
M Chris Brandon — CG: 14 SD: -5
M Danny Schofield — CG: 19 SD: -8

F Luke Beckett — CG: 31 SR: 194
F Gary Taylor-Fletcher — CG: 36 SR: 288

MONTHLY POINTS TALLY

Month		Pts	%
AUGUST		8	53%
SEPTEMBER		6	29%
OCTOBER		9	75%
NOVEMBER		1	11%
DECEMBER		7	39%
JANUARY		7	47%
FEBRUARY		7	47%
MARCH		6	40%
APRIL		5	33%
MAY		3	100%

LEAGUE GOALS

	PLAYER	MINS	GOALS	S RATE
1	Beckett	2917	15	194
2	Taylor-Fletcher	3170	11	288
3	Booth	2582	7	368
4	Abbott	894	5	178
5	Schofield	2122	5	424
6	Collins	3446	4	861
7	Hudson	2632	3	877
8	Young	1585	2	792
9	Worthington	2263	2	1131
10	Holdsworth	2951	2	1475
11	McAliskey	270	1	270
12	Hayes	338	1	338
13	Brandon	1534	1	1534
	Other		1	
	TOTAL		**60**	

TOP POINT EARNERS

	PLAYER	GAMES	AV PTS
1	John Worthington	23	1.70
2	Chris Brandon	14	1.62
3	Martin McIntosh	23	1.61
4	Andy Holdsworth	32	1.53
5	Matthew Young	12	1.50
6	Joe Skarz	14	1.43
7	Danny Schofield	19	1.42
8	Luke Beckett	31	1.39
9	Nathan Clarke	15	1.33
10	Mathew Glennon	46	1.28
	CLUB AVERAGE:		**1.28**

DISCIPLINARY RECORDS

	PLAYER	YELLOW	RED	AVE
1	Adnan Ahmed	2	1	152
2	Andy Taylor	3	0	217
3	John Worthington	10	0	251
4	Chris Brandon	6	0	255
5	Aaron Hardy	2	0	287
6	Daniel Adams	5	2	288
7	Pawel Abbott	2	1	298
8	Martin McIntosh	5	1	357
9	Andy Holdsworth	9	1	368
10	Frank Sinclair	2	1	381
11	Danny Schofield	5	0	424
12	Michael Collins	8	1	430
13	Gary Taylor-Fletcher	7	0	452
	Other	20	0	
	TOTAL	**86**	**8**	

KEY GOALKEEPER

Mathew Glennon

Goals Conceded in the League	69	Counting Games League games when player was on pitch for at least 70 minutes	46
Defensive Rating Ave number of mins between League goals conceded while on the pitch	60	Clean Sheets In League games when player was on pitch for at least 70 minutes	8

KEY PLAYERS - DEFENDERS

Martin McIntosh

Goals Conceded Number of League goals conceded while the player was on the pitch	32	Clean Sheets In League games when player was on pitch for at least 70 minutes	4
Defensive Rating Ave number of mins between League goals conceded while on the pitch	67	Club Defensive Rating Average number of mins between League goals conceded by the club this season	60

	PLAYER	CON LGE	CLEAN SHEETS	DEF RATE
1	Martin McIntosh	32	4	67 mins
2	Joe Skarz	20	2	67 mins
3	Nathan Clarke	22	3	62 mins
4	David Mirfin	56	7	61 mins

KEY PLAYERS - MIDFIELDERS

John Worthington

Goals in the League	2	Contribution to Attacking Power Average number of minutes between League team goals while on pitch	61
Defensive Rating Average number of mins between League goals conceded while on the pitch	68	Scoring Difference Defensive Rating minus Contribution to Attacking Power	7

	PLAYER	LGE GOALS	DEF RATE	POWER	SCORE DIFF
1	John Worthington	2	68	61	7 mins
2	Andy Holdsworth	2	68	65	3 mins
3	Chris Brandon	1	56	61	-5 mins
4	Danny Schofield	5	58	66	-8 mins

KEY PLAYERS - GOALSCORERS

Luke Beckett

Goals in the League	15	Player Strike Rate Average number of minutes between League goals scored by player	194
Contribution to Attacking Power Average number of minutes between League team goals while on pitch	67	Club Strike Rate Average number of minutes between League goals scored by club	69

	PLAYER	LGE GOALS	POWER	STRIKE RATE
1	Luke Beckett	15	67	194 mins
2	Gary Taylor-Fletcher	11	64	288 mins
3	Andy Booth	7	89	368 mins
4	Danny Schofield	5	66	424 mins

Andy Booth

SQUAD APPEARANCES

Match	1 2 3 4 5	6 7 8 9 10	11 12 13 14 15	16 17 18 19 20	21 22 23 24 25	26 27 28 29 30	31 32 33 34 35	36 37 38 39 40	41 42 43 44 45	46 47 48
Venue	A H H A H	H A A H H	A A H A H	A H H H A	H A A H A	H H A A H	A H H A H	A H A H A	A H A H A	H A H
Competition	L L L L W	L L L L L	L L L L L	L L L F L	L L L L L	L L L L L	L L L L L	L L L L L	L L L L L	L L L
Result	L W W D L	D L L D L	W D D W W	W L D L L	L D L D D	D W L L W	W D W D L	W L L W D	D D D L L	W D W

Goalkeepers
Mathew Glennon
Paul Rachubka

Defenders
Daniel Adams
Nathan Clarke
Tom Clarke
Aaron Hardy
John McCombe
Martin McIntosh
David Mirfin
Frank Sinclair
Joe Skarz
Andy Taylor

Midfielders
Adnan Ahmed
Lucas Akins
James Berrett
Chris Brandon
Michael Collins
James Hand
Andy Holdsworth
Mark Hudson
Danny Racchi
Danny Schofield
John Worthington
Matthew Young

Forwards
Pawel Abbott
Luke Beckett
Andy Booth
Paul Hayes
John McAliskey
Gary Taylor-Fletcher

KEY: ■ On all match ◄◄ Subbed or sent off (Counting game) ►►► Subbed on from bench (Counting Game) ►►► Subbed on and then subbed or sent off (Counting Game) ☐ Not in 16
On bench ◄◄ Subbed or sent off (playing less than 70 minutes) ►► Subbed on (playing less than 70 minutes) ►► Subbed on and then subbed or sent off (playing less than 70 minutes)

LEAGUE 1 - HUDDERSFIELD TOWN

GILLINGHAM

Final Position: 16th

NICKNAME: THE GILLS   KEY: ☐ Won ☐ Drawn ☐ Lost   Attendance

1	div2	Huddersfield	H W	2-1	Jarvis 57, McDonald 67	6,075
2	div2	Brighton	A L	0-1		6,643
3	div2	Bradford	A L	2-4	Bentley 6, Flynn 14	7,807
4	div2	Northampton	H L	0-1		5,654
5	ccr1	Millwall	A L	1-2	Mulligan 81	5,040
6	div2	Blackpool	A D	1-1	Ndumbu-Nsungu 3	5,056
7	div2	Scunthorpe	H L	0-2		5,749
8	div2	Doncaster	A W	2-1	Crofts 9, Flynn 38 pen	5,772
9	div2	Millwall	H W	2-1	Easton 13, Jarvis 64	7,934
10	div2	Swansea	H W	3-1	Cox 13, 79, Jarvis 26	5,500
11	div2	Oldham	A L	1-4	Flynn 51 pen	4,652
12	div2	Leyton Orient	A D	3-3	Bentley 43, Ndumbu-Nsungu 45, Jarvis 57	3,978
13	div2	Cheltenham	H W	2-1	Jarvis 13, Bentley 45	5,688
14	div2	Crewe	A L	3-4	Pouton 21, Flynn 28, McDonald 45	5,022
15	div2	Nottm Forest	H L	0-1		7,800
16	div2	Brentford	A D	2-2	Flynn 26 pen, 74	5,759
17	div2	Carlisle	H W	2-0	Bentley 8, Mulligan 89	5,973
18	div2	Chesterfield	H W	2-1	McDonald 90, Mulligan 90	5,856
19	facr1	Bromley	H W	4-1	Bentley 31, 59, Ndumbu-Nsungu 84, 90	5,547
20	div2	Bristol City	A L	1-3	Flynn 15	11,823
21	div2	Rotherham	H W	1-0	Mulligan 23	5,103
22	facr2	Bristol City	A L	3-4	Mulligan 49, Flynn 66, 90 pen	5,663
23	div2	Port Vale	A L	0-2		3,077
24	div2	Yeovil	A L	0-2		4,933
25	div2	Bournemouth	H D	1-1	Crofts 90	6,296
26	div2	Tranmere	A W	3-2	Mulligan 11, 19, Chorley 42	6,407
27	div2	Leyton Orient	H W	2-1	Saah 81 og, Ndumbu-Nsungu 88 pen	8,216
28	div2	Oldham	H L	0-3		6,790
29	div2	Millwall	A L	1-4	Mulligan 10	10,055
30	div2	Doncaster	H L	0-2		6,202
31	div2	Cheltenham	A D	1-1	Savage 6	3,598
32	div2	Swansea	A L	0-2		9,675
33	div2	Tranmere	H W	2-0	McCready 22 og, Crofts 29	5,378
34	div2	Huddersfield	A L	1-3	Mulligan 70	9,167
35	div2	Bradford	H W	1-0	L.Johnson 45	5,513
36	div2	Northampton	A D	1-1	McDonald 61	5,618
37	div2	Brighton	H L	0-1		6,609
38	div2	Scunthorpe	A L	1-3	Jarvis 54	5,312
39	div2	Blackpool	H D	2-2	McDonald 9, Crofts 34	5,949
40	div2	Crewe	H W	1-0	Flynn 71	6,373
41	div2	Nottm Forest	A L	0-1		17,950
42	div2	Carlisle	A L	0-5		6,087
43	div2	Brentford	H W	2-1	Crofts 29, Jackman 88	6,113
44	div2	Rotherham	A L	2-3	Bastians 21, Crofts 24	3,223
45	div2	Bristol City	H W	1-0	McDonald 55	6,292
46	div2	Chesterfield	A W	1-0	Crofts 90	3,867
47	div2	Port Vale	H W	3-2	Cox 37, Flynn 49, 53	5,928
48	div2	Bournemouth	A D	1-1	Crofts 24	8,001
49	div2	Yeovil	H L	0-2		7,484

LEAGUE APPEARANCES, BOOKINGS AND CAPS

	AGE (on 01/07/07)	IN NAMED 16	APPEARANCES	COUNTING GAMES	MINUTES ON PITCH	LEAGUE GOALS	
Goalkeepers							
Dean Brill	20	8	8	8	720	0	0
Scott Flinders	21	9	9	9	810	0	3
Kelvin Jack	31	10	9	9	810	0	1
Romain Larrieu	30	14	14	14	1260	0	1
Darren Randolph	20	3	3	3	270	0	0
Simon Royce	35	3	3	3	270	0	0
Defenders							
Ben Chorley	24	30	27	22	2142	1	2
Sean Clohessy	20	14	6	3	373	0	0
Ian Cox	36	42	33	31	2862	3	1
Danny Jackman	24	44	31	29	2665	1	4
Duncan Jupp	32	29	27	26	2326	0	4
Brent Sancho	30	30	26	18	1763	0	2
Midfielders							
Felix Bastians	19	5	5	3	397	1	0
Mark Bentley	29	41	41	40	3593	4	7
Andrew Crofts	23	43	43	41	3736	8	4
Clint Easton	29	40	32	22	2323	1	6
Michael Flynn	26	45	45	40	3798	10	4
Leon Johnson	26	40	24	23	2102	1	2
Alan Pouton	30	23	8	3	362	1	1
Nicky Southall	35	15	15	15	1350	0	2
Daniel Spiller	26	35	25	10	1182	0	0
Craig Stone	18	6	3	2	209	0	1
Dale Tonge	22	6	3	3	262	0	0
Forwards							
Francis Collin	20	21	3	0	27	0	1
Matthew Jarvis	21	35	35	34	3059	6	1
Dean McDonald	21	36	26	10	1461	6	2
Gary Mulligan	22	39	38	32	3069	7	1
Guylain Ndumbu-Nsungu	24	40	32	10	1382	3	5
Andy Pugh	18	6	3	0	74	0	0
Basir Savage	25	18	14	6	666	0	1

TEAM OF THE SEASON

D Ben Chorley CG: 22 DR: 57
M Leon Johnson CG: 23 SD: -10
D Danny Jackman CG: 29 DR: 56
M Mark Bentley CG: 40 SD: -13
F Gary Mulligan CG: 32 SR: 438
G Romain Larrieu CG: 14 DR: 66
D Ian Cox CG: 31 DR: 56
M Clint Easton CG: 22 SD: -16
F Matthew Jarvis CG: 34 SR: 509
D Duncan Jupp CG: 26 DR: 50
M Andrew Crofts CG: 41 SD: -17

MONTHLY POINTS TALLY

AUGUST	4	27%
SEPTEMBER	13	62%
OCTOBER	4	33%
NOVEMBER	6	67%
DECEMBER	7	39%
JANUARY	4	27%
FEBRUARY	4	27%
MARCH	7	47%
APRIL	10	67%
MAY	0	0%

LEAGUE GOALS

	PLAYER	MINS	GOALS	S RATE
1	Flynn	3798	10	379
2	Crofts	3736	8	467
3	Mulligan	3069	7	438
4	McDonald	1461	6	243
5	Jarvis	3059	6	509
6	Bentley	3593	4	898
7	N-Nsungu	1382	3	460
8	Cox	2862	3	954
9	Pouton	362	1	362
10	Bastians	397	1	397
11	Savage	666	1	666
12	Johnson, L	2102	1	2102
13	Chorley	2142	1	2142
	Other		2	
	TOTAL		**54**	

TOP POINT EARNERS

	PLAYER	GAMES	AV PTS
1	Ian Cox	33	1.45
2	Romain Larrieu	14	1.43
3	Nicky Southall	15	1.40
4	Leon Johnson	23	1.39
5	Andrew Crofts	41	1.37
6	Mark Bentley	40	1.35
7	Michael Flynn	40	1.33
8	Danny Jackman	30	1.33
9	Duncan Jupp	26	1.31
10	Ben Chorley	23	1.30
	CLUB AVERAGE:		**1.28**

DISCIPLINARY RECORDS

	PLAYER	YELLOW	RED	AVE
1	Scott Flinders	3	0	270
2	G Ndumbu-Nsungu	5	0	276
3	Clint Easton	6	0	464
4	Mark Bentley	7	1	513
5	Danny Jackman	4	1	533
6	Basir Savage	1	0	666
7	Nicky Southall	2	0	675
8	Ben Chorley	2	1	714
9	Dean McDonald	2	0	730
10	Duncan Jupp	4	0	775
11	Kelvin Jack	1	0	810
12	Brent Sancho	2	0	881
13	Andrew Crofts	4	0	934
	Other	10	2	
	TOTAL	**53**	**5**	

KEY GOALKEEPER

Romain Larrieu

Goals Conceded in the League	19	Counting Games League games when player was on pitch for at least 70 minutes	14
Defensive Rating Ave number of mins between League goals conceded while on the pitch	66	Clean Sheets In League games when player was on pitch for at least 70 minutes	5

KEY PLAYERS - DEFENDERS

Ben Chorley

Goals Conceded Number of League goals conceded while the player was on the pitch	37	Clean Sheets In League games when player was on pitch for at least 70 minutes	5
Defensive Rating Ave number of mins between League goals conceded while on the pitch	57	Club Defensive Rating Average number of mins between League goals conceded by the club this season	53

	PLAYER	CON LGE	CLEAN SHEETS	DEF RATE
1	Ben Chorley	37	5	57 mins
2	Danny Jackman	47	5	56 mins
3	Ian Cox	51	4	56 mins
4	Duncan Jupp	46	2	50 mins

KEY PLAYERS - MIDFIELDERS

Leon Johnson

Goals in the League	1	Contribution to Attacking Power Average number of minutes between League team goals while on pitch	65
Defensive Rating Average number of mins between League goals conceded while on the pitch	55	Scoring Difference Defensive Rating minus Contribution to Attacking Power	-10

	PLAYER	LGE GOALS	DEF RATE	POWER	SCORE DIFF
1	Leon Johnson	1	55	65	-10 mins
2	Mark Bentley	4	58	71	-13 mins
3	Clint Easton	1	48	64	-16 mins
4	Andrew Crofts	8	59	76	-17 mins

KEY PLAYERS - GOALSCORERS

Michael Flynn

Goals in the League	10	Player Strike Rate Average number of minutes between League goals scored by player	379
Contribution to Attacking Power Average number of minutes between League team goals while on pitch	75	Club Strike Rate Average number of minutes between League goals scored by club	73

	PLAYER	LGE GOALS	POWER	STRIKE RATE
1	Michael Flynn	10	75	379 mins
2	Gary Mulligan	7	78	438 mins
3	Andrew Crofts	8	76	467 mins
4	Matthew Jarvis	6	74	509 mins

Andrew Crofts

SQUAD APPEARANCES

Match	1 2 3 4 5	6 7 8 9 10	11 12 13 14 15	16 17 18 19 20	21 22 23 24 25	26 27 28 29 30	31 32 33 34 35	36 37 38 39 40	41 42 43 44 45	46 47 48 49
Venue	H A A H A	A H A H H	A A H A H	A H H H A	H A A A H	A H H A H	A A H A H	A H A H H	A A H A H	A H A H
Competition	L L L L W	L L L L L	L L L L L	L L L F L	L F L L L	L L L L L	L L L L L	L L L L L	L L L L L	L L L L
Result	W L L L L	D L W W W	L D W L L	D W W W L	W L L L D	W W L L L	D L W L W	D L L D W	L L W L W	W W D L

Goalkeepers
Dean Brill
Scott Flinders
Kelvin Jack
Romain Larrieu
Darren Randolph
Simon Royce

Defenders
Ben Chorley
Sean Clohessy
Ian Cox
Danny Jackman
Duncan Jupp
Brent Sancho

Midfielders
Felix Bastians
Mark Bentley
Andrew Crofts
Clint Easton
Michael Flynn
Leon Johnson
Alan Pouton
Nicky Southall
Daniel Spiller
Craig Stone
Dale Tonge

Forwards
Francis Collin
Matthew Jarvis
Dean McDonald
Gary Mulligan
Guylain Ndumbu-Nsungu
Andy Pugh
Yasir Savage

KEY: ■ On all match ◄◄ Subbed or sent off (Counting game) ►►► Subbed on from bench (Counting Game) ►◄ Subbed on and then subbed or sent off (Counting Game) □ Not in 16
  ▨ On bench ◄◄ Subbed or sent off (playing less than 70 minutes) ►► Subbed on (playing less than 70 minutes) ►► Subbed on and then subbed or sent off (playing less than 70 minutes)

LEAGUE 1 - GILLINGHAM

CHELTENHAM

Final Position: **17th**

NICKNAME: THE ROBINS

KEY: ☐ Won ☐ Drawn ☐ Lost Attendance

#		Opponent		Result	Scorers	Attendance
1	div2	**Swansea**	A W	2-1	Odejayi 48, McCann 54	15,199
2	div2	**Tranmere**	H W	1-0	Odejayi 8	3,875
3	div2	**Port Vale**	H L	0-1		4,309
4	div2	**Bournemouth**	A L	1-2	McCann 15	5,378
5	ccr1	**Bristol City**	H W	2-1	Guinan 24, Wilson 33	3,713
6	div2	**Millwall**	H W	3-2	McCann 13 pen, Odejayi 67, Melligan 82	4,386
7	div2	**Carlisle**	A L	0-2		7,248
8	div2	**Huddersfield**	H W	2-1	McCann 10, Melligan 71	3,720
9	div2	**Crewe**	A L	1-3	Wilson 38	4,062
10	div2	**Scunthorpe**	A L	0-1		4,288
11	ccr2	**West Brom**	A L	1-3	Odejayi 45	10,974
12	div2	**Bradford**	H L	1-2	Odejayi 41	3,830
13	div2	**Northampton**	H L	0-2		3,224
14	div2	**Gillingham**	A L	1-2	McCann 28	5,688
15	div2	**Yeovil**	A W	1-0	Melligan 88	6,220
16	div2	**Doncaster**	H L	0-2		3,872
17	div2	**Leyton Orient**	A L	0-2		4,500
18	div2	**Nottm Forest**	H L	0-2		6,554
19	div2	**Oldham**	H L	1-2	Odejayi 90	4,054
20	facr1	**Scunthorpe**	H D	0-0		2,721
21	div2	**Chesterfield**	A L	0-1		3,488
22	facr1r	**Scunthorpe**	A L	0-2		3,074
23	div2	**Brentford**	H W	2-0	Odejayi 5, 75	3,646
24	div2	**Blackpool**	A L	1-2	Spencer 14	4,851
25	div2	**Brighton**	A L	1-2	Victory 74	5,386
26	div2	**Rotherham**	H W	2-0	Wilson 65, Bird 90	3,525
27	div2	**Bristol City**	H D	2-2	O'Leary 36, Bird 38	5,863
28	div2	**Northampton**	A L	0-2		5,239
29	div2	**Bradford**	A D	2-2	Finnigan 57 pen, Odejayi 60	7,264
30	div2	**Crewe**	H D	1-1	Finnigan 31	3,154
31	div2	**Huddersfield**	A L	0-2		9,813
32	div2	**Scunthorpe**	H D	1-1	Gillespie 17	-
33	div2	**Gillingham**	H D	1-1	Melligan 17	3,598
34	div2	**Bristol City**	A W	1-0	Spencer 44	12,227
35	div2	**Swansea**	H W	2-1	Odejayi 40, Connor 67	5,221
36	div2	**Bournemouth**	H W	1-0	Spencer 90	4,530
37	div2	**Tranmere**	A D	2-2	Lowe 18, Odejayi 26	5,576
38	div2	**Carlisle**	H L	0-1		3,831
39	div2	**Millwall**	A L	0-1		10,261
40	div2	**Port Vale**	A D	1-1	Townsend 70	3,340
41	div2	**Yeovil**	H L	1-2	Finnigan 90	5,314
42	div2	**Doncaster**	A W	2-0	Gillespie 34, Odejayi 71	6,777
43	div2	**Nottm Forest**	A L	0-3		22,640
44	div2	**Leyton Orient**	H W	2-1	Finnigan 13, Melligan 61	4,300
45	div2	**Brentford**	A W	2-0	Gillespie 8, Melligan 47	4,831
46	div2	**Chesterfield**	H D	0-0		5,089
47	div2	**Oldham**	A W	2-0	Odejayi 21, Finnigan 31	5,426
48	div2	**Blackpool**	H L	1-2	Finnigan 51 pen	5,093
49	div2	**Rotherham**	A W	4-2	Odejayi 44, Gillespie 46, 56, Melligan 88	3,876
50	div2	**Brighton**	H D	1-1	Finnigan 87 pen	6,232

LEAGUE APPEARANCES, BOOKINGS AND CAPS

	AGE (on 01/07/07)	IN NAMED 16	APPEARANCES	COUNTING GAMES	MINUTES ON PITCH	LEAGUE GOALS	
Goalkeepers							
Scott Brown	22	46	11	10	946	0	1
Shane Higgs	30	36	36	35	3194	0	0
Defenders							
Mick Bell	35	10	6	2	353	0	0
Gavin Caines	23	46	39	26	2535	0	3
Shane Duff	25	34	34	31	2932	0	6
Jeremy Gill	36	40	39	35	3294	0	8
Keith Lowe	21	26	16	12	1226	1	0
Michael Townsend	21	33	30	27	2458	1	4
Jamie Victory	31	12	10	7	721	1	0
Michael Wylde	20	22	7	4	403	0	0
Midfielders							
Craig Armstrong	32	42	42	41	3705	0	6
David Bird	22	33	32	26	2474	2	1
Scott Brown	22	4	4	3	279	0	0
Adam Connolly	21	14	7	4	420	0	0
John Finnigan	31	41	40	36	3447	7	6
Grant McCann	27	15	15	14	1327	5	6
John Melligan	26	43	43	35	3267	7	8
Kristian O'Leary	29	5	5	5	450	1	2
Denes Rosa	30	5	4	1	225	0	0
Ashley Vincent	22	5	5	0	107	0	1
Brian Wilson	24	25	25	21	2023	2	1
Sosthene Yao	19	24	15	2	422	0	2
Forwards							
Paul Connor	28	19	15	4	763	1	1
Robert Elvins	20	6	5	0	60	0	0
Stephen Gillespie	23	26	23	12	1299	5	4
Stephen Guinan	31	22	19	13	1321	0	0
Kayode Odejayi	25	45	45	37	3456	13	6
Craig Reid	18	12	6	0	79	0	0
Andrew Smith	26	2	2	1	152	0	1
Damian Spencer	25	28	27	22	2103	3	5

TEAM OF THE SEASON

G Shane Higgs CG: 35 DR: 66

D Michael Townsend CG: 27 DR: 72
D Shane Duff CG: 31 DR: 69
D Jeremy Gill CG: 35 DR: 65
D Gavin Caines CG: 26 DR: 60

M John Melligan CG: 35 SD: -5
M Craig Armstrong CG: 41 SD: -11
M John Finnigan CG: 36 SD: -14
M David Bird CG: 26 SD: -23

F Stephen Gillespie CG: 13 SR: 259
F Kayode Odejayi CG: 37 SR: 265

MONTHLY POINTS TALLY

AUGUST		9	60%
SEPTEMBER		3	14%
OCTOBER		3	25%
NOVEMBER		3	33%
DECEMBER		5	28%
JANUARY		6	40%
FEBRUARY		7	58%
MARCH		7	39%
APRIL		10	67%
MAY		1	33%

LEAGUE GOALS

	PLAYER	MINS	GOALS	S RATE
1	Odejayi	3456	13	265
2	Melligan	3267	7	466
3	Finnigan	3447	7	492
4	Gillespie	1299	5	259
5	McCann	1327	5	265
6	Spencer	2103	3	701
7	Wilson	2023	2	1011
8	Bird	2474	2	1237
9	O'Leary	450	1	450
10	Victory	721	1	721
11	Connor	763	1	763
12	Lowe	1226	1	1226
13	Townsend	2458	1	2458
	Other		0	
	TOTAL		49	

TOP POINT EARNERS

	PLAYER	GAMES	AV PTS
1	Stephen Gillespie	13	1.62
2	John Melligan	35	1.43
3	Michael Townsend	27	1.33
4	John Finnigan	36	1.28
5	Jeremy Gill	35	1.23
6	Stephen Guinan	13	1.23
7	Damian Spencer	22	1.23
8	Craig Armstrong	41	1.22
9	Kayode Odejayi	37	1.19
10	Shane Duff	31	1.16
	CLUB AVERAGE:		1.17

DISCIPLINARY RECORDS

	PLAYER	YELLOW	RED	AVE
1	Stephen Gillespie	4	1	259
2	Grant McCann	6	0	331
3	Damian Spencer	5	1	350
4	John Melligan	8	0	466
5	Jeremy Gill	8	0	470
6	Shane Duff	6	0	488
7	John Finnigan	6	1	492
8	Michael Townsend	4	0	614
9	Kayode Odejayi	6	0	691
10	Craig Armstrong	6	0	741
11	Paul Connor	1	0	763
12	Gavin Caines	3	0	845
13	Scott Brown	1	0	946
	Other	2	1	
	TOTAL	66	4	

KEY GOALKEEPER

Shane Higgs

Goals Conceded in the League	48	Counting Games League games when player was on pitch for at least 70 minutes	35
Defensive Rating Ave number of mins between League goals conceded while on the pitch	66	Clean Sheets In League games when player was on pitch for at least 70 minutes	7

KEY PLAYERS - DEFENDERS

Michael Townsend

Goals Conceded Number of League goals conceded while the player was on the pitch	34	Clean Sheets In League games when player was on pitch for at least 70 minutes	7
Defensive Rating Ave number of mins between League goals conceded while on the pitch	72	Club Defensive Rating Average number of mins between League goals conceded by the club this season	70

	PLAYER	CON LGE	CLEAN SHEETS	DEF RATE
1	Michael Townsend	34	7	72 mins
2	Shane Duff	42	7	69 mins
3	Jeremy Gill	50	8	65 mins
4	Gavin Caines	42	4	60 mins

KEY PLAYERS - MIDFIELDERS

John Melligan

Goals in the League	7	Contribution to Attacking Power Average number of minutes between League team goals while on pitch	79
Defensive Rating Average number of mins between League goals conceded while on the pitch	74	Scoring Difference Defensive Rating minus Contribution to Attacking Power	-5

	PLAYER	LGE GOALS	DEF RATE	POWER	SCORE DIFF
1	John Melligan	7	74	79	-5 mins
2	Craig Armstrong	0	71	82	-11 mins
3	John Finnigan	7	68	82	-14 mins
4	David Bird	2	65	88	-23 mins

KEY PLAYERS - GOALSCORERS

Stephen Gillespie

Goals in the League	5	Player Strike Rate Average number of minutes between League goals scored by player	259
Contribution to Attacking Power Average number of minutes between League team goals while on pitch	64	Club Strike Rate Average number of minutes between League goals scored by club	88

	PLAYER	LGE GOALS	POWER	STRIKE RATE
1	Stephen Gillespie	5	64	259 mins
2	Grant McCann	5	102	265 mins
3	Kayode Odejayi	13	80	265 mins
4	John Melligan	7	79	466 mins

Craig Armstrong

SQUAD APPEARANCES

Match	1 2 3 4 5	6 7 8 9 10	11 12 13 14 15	16 17 18 19 20	21 22 23 24 25	26 27 28 29 30	31 32 33 34 35	36 37 38 39 40	41 42 43 44 45	46 47 48 49 50
Venue	A H H A H	H A H A A	A H H A A	H A H H H	A A H A A	H H A A H	A H H A H	H A H A A	H A A H A	H A H A H
Competition	L L L L W	L L L L L	W L L L L	L L L L F	L F L L L	L L L L L	L L L L L	L L L L L	L L L L L	L L L L L
Result	W W L L W	W L W L L	L L L L W	L L L L D	L L W L L	W D L D D	L D D W W	W D L L L	L W L W W	D W L W D

Goalkeepers
Scott Brown
Shane Higgs
Defenders
Mick Bell
Gavin Caines
Shane Duff
Jeremy Gill
Keith Lowe
Michael Townsend
Jamie Victory
Michael Wylde
Midfielders
Craig Armstrong
David Bird
Scott Brown
Adam Connolly
John Finnigan
Grant McCann
John Melligan
Kristian O'Leary
Denes Rosa
Ashley Vincent
Brian Wilson
Sosthene Yao
Forwards
Paul Connor
Robert Elvins
Stephen Gillespie
Stephen Guinan
Kayode Odejayi
Craig Reid
Andrew Smith
Damian Spencer

KEY:
- ■ On all match
- ■ On bench
- ◄◄ Subbed or sent off (Counting game)
- ◄◄ Subbed or sent off (playing less than 70 minutes)
- ▶▶ Subbed on from bench (Counting Game)
- ▶▶ Subbed on (playing less than 70 minutes)
- ■▶ Subbed on and then subbed or sent off (Counting Game)
- ▶▶ Subbed on and then subbed or sent off (playing less than 70 minutes)
- ☐ Not in 16

LEAGUE 1 - CHELTENHAM

BRIGHTON & HOVE ALBION

Final Position: **18th**

NICKNAME: THE SEAGULLS **KEY:** ☐ Won ☐ Drawn ☐ Lost Attendance

1	div2	Rotherham	A W	1-0	Revell 43	4,998
2	div2	Gillingham	H W	1-0	Robinson 67	6,643
3	div2	Brentford	H D	2-2	Hammond 10 pen, Hart 13	6,745
4	div2	Nottm Forest	A L	1-2	Robinson 39	18,686
5	ccr1	Boston	H W	1-0	Reid 73	2,533
6	div2	Crewe	H L	1-4	Cox 39	5,848
7	div2	Bristol City	A L	0-1		10,552
8	div2	Millwall	A W	1-0		9,372
9	div2	Bournemouth	H D	2-2	Hammond 53, Revell 60	5,958
10	div2	Leyton Orient	H W	4-1	Reid 15, El-Abd 30, Cox 45, Loft 90	6,003
11	ccr2	Southend	A L	2-3	Cox 71, El-Abd 90	4,819
12	div2	Carlisle	A L	1-3	Revell 87	7,704
13	div2	Yeovil	A L	0-2		5,243
14	div2	Chesterfield	H L	1-2	Williams 54	5,499
15	div2	Blackpool	H L	0-3		5,146
16	div2	Scunthorpe	A W	2-1	Cox 23, Hart 52	5,607
17	div2	Northampton	H D	1-1	Robinson 39	5,862
18	div2	Huddersfield	A W	3-0	Robinson 23, 30, 50	10,616
19	div2	Bradford	A W	3-0	Revell 13, Hammond 48 pen, Bowditch 89	7,610
20	facr1	Northwich	H W	8-0	Cox 8, 90, Robinson 18, 55, 78, Revell 64, Gatting 82, Rents 89	4,487
21	div2	Tranmere	H L	0-1		6,069
22	div2	Doncaster	A L	0-1		5,804
23	facr2	Stafford	H W	3-0	Hammond 18, Revell 66, Robinson 90	5,741
24	div2	Swansea	H W	3-2	Cox 13, Revell 66, 81	5,209
25	div2	Cheltenham	H W	2-1	Hammond 56, 89 pen	5,386
26	div2	Oldham	A D	1-1	Hammond 61	9,321
27	div2	Port Vale	A L	1-2	Fraser 84	4,349
28	div2	Yeovil	H L	1-3	Gatting 72	6,554
29	div2	Carlisle	H L	1-2	Gatting 37	5,436
30	div2	Bournemouth	A L	0-1		6,686
31	facr3	West Ham	A L	0-3		32,874
32	div2	Millwall	H L	0-1		6,226
33	div2	Chesterfield	A W	1-0	Gatting 50	3,984
34	div2	Port Vale	H D	0-0		5,177
35	div2	Rotherham	H D	0-0		5,444
36	div2	Brentford	A L	0-1		7,023
37	div2	Leyton Orient	A W	4-1	Hammond 39, Savage 57, Gatting 67, Cox 89	4,670
38	div2	Nottm Forest	H W	2-1	Hammond 72, Ward 73	7,749
39	div2	Gillingham	A W	1-0	Savage 18	6,609
40	div2	Bristol City	H L	0-2		6,280
41	div2	Crewe	A D	1-1	Savage 31	5,202
42	div2	Blackpool	A D	0-0		8,164
43	div2	Scunthorpe	H D	1-1	Savage 72	6,276
44	div2	Huddersfield	H D	0-0		5,974
45	div2	Northampton	A W	2-0	Savage 60, 66	6,613
46	div2	Doncaster	H L	0-2		6,267
47	div2	Tranmere	A L	1-2	Goodison 11 og	5,528
48	div2	Bradford	H L	0-1		5,757
49	div2	Swansea	A L	1-2	Revell 14	11,972
50	div2	Oldham	H L	1-2	Cox 85	7,588
51	div2	Cheltenham	A D	1-1	Elder 23	6,232

LEAGUE APPEARANCES, BOOKINGS AND CAPS

	AGE (on 01/07/07)	IN NAMED 16	APPEARANCES	COUNTING GAMES	MINUTES ON PITCH	LEAGUE GOALS	
Goalkeepers							
Scott Flinders	21	12	12	12	1080	0	0
Wayne Henderson	23	24	20	20	1800	0	1
Michel Kuipers	33	43	14	14	1260	0	1
Defenders							
Guy Butters	37	34	31	31	2752	0	3
Adam El-Abd	22	42	41	37	3447	1	10
Adam Hinshelwood	23	12	12	9	926	0	0
Joel Lynch	19	40	37	30	2970	0	2
Kerry Mayo	29	33	30	25	2447	0	7
Joe O'Cearuill	20	10	8	6	578	0	3
Zeshan Rehman	23	8	8	8	720	0	2
Paul Reid	27	10	10	8	809	1	0
Sam Rents	20	28	25	18	1735	0	2
Georges Santos	36	12	11	6	595	0	2
Andrew Whing	22	12	12	12	1080	0	3
Midfielders							
Alexis Bertin	27	16	16	15	1347	0	4
Richard Carpenter	34	16	15	11	1107	0	2
Dean Cox	19	43	42	39	3568	6	10
Tommy Elphick	19	19	3	2	200	0	0
Tommy Fraser	19	32	27	12	1548	1	2
Alexandre Frutos	25	18	9	3	439	0	1
Dean Hammond	24	37	37	35	3279	8	6
Gary Hart	30	26	25	18	1646	2	5
Alistair John	19	6	4	1	151	0	1
Douglas Loft	20	13	11	4	439	1	1
Tony Stokes	20	6	6	4	404	0	0
Nick Ward	22	10	8	3	477	1	1
Forwards							
Dean Bowditch	21	3	3	0	113	1	0
Nathan Elder	19	18	13	1	268	1	1
Joe Gatting	19	33	23	7	885	4	0
Maheta Molango	24	1	1	0	45	0	0
Alex Revell	23	38	38	32	3095	7	3
Jake Robinson	20	41	37	28	2729	6	2
Basir Savage	25	15	15	12	1164	6	1
Sam Williams	20	3	3	2	212	1	0

TEAM OF THE SEASON

Scott Flinders G — CG: 12 DR: 83

Guy Butters D — CG: 31 DR: 88
Adam El-Abd D — CG: 37 DR: 76
Joel Lynch D — CG: 30 DR: 74
Kerry Mayo D — CG: 25 DR: 67

Dean Hammond M — CG: 35 SD: -1
Alexis Bertin M — CG: 14 SD: -7
Dean Cox M — CG: 39 SD: -13
Gary Hart M — CG: 18 SD: -14

Basir Savage F — CG: 12 SR: 194
Alex Revell F — CG: 32 SR: 442

MONTHLY POINTS TALLY

AUGUST	7	47%
SEPTEMBER	7	33%
OCTOBER	7	58%
NOVEMBER	3	33%
DECEMBER	7	39%
JANUARY	4	33%
FEBRUARY	10	56%
MARCH	7	47%
APRIL	0	0%
MAY	1	33%

LEAGUE GOALS

	PLAYER	MINS	GOALS	S RATE
1	Hammond	3279	8	409
2	Revell	3095	7	442
3	Savage	1164	6	194
4	Robinson	2729	6	454
5	Cox	3568	6	594
6	Gatting	885	4	221
7	Hart	1646	2	823
8	Bowditch	113	1	113
9	Williams, S	212	1	212
10	Elder	268	1	268
11	Loft	439	1	439
12	Ward	477	1	477
13	Reid	809	1	809
	Other		2	
	TOTAL		**47**	

TOP POINT EARNERS

	PLAYER	GAMES	AV PTS
1	Michel Kuipers	14	1.57
2	Andrew Whing	12	1.42
3	Dean Hammond	35	1.37
4	Basir Savage	12	1.33
5	Joel Lynch	30	1.27
6	Alexis Bertin	14	1.21
7	Dean Cox	40	1.20
8	Kerry Mayo	27	1.19
9	Gary Hart	18	1.17
10	Adam El-Abd	37	1.14
	CLUB AVERAGE:		**1.15**

DISCIPLINARY RECORDS

	PLAYER	YELLOW	RED	AVE
1	Joe O'Cearuill	3	0	192
2	Georges Santos	2	0	297
3	Kerry Mayo	7	2	305
4	Dean Cox	10	1	324
5	Alexis Bertin	4	0	336
6	Adam El-Abd	10	1	344
7	Andrew Whing	3	0	360
8	Zeshan Rehman	2	0	360
9	Richard Carpenter	2	1	369
10	Gary Hart	5	0	411
11	Nick Ward	1	0	477
12	Tommy Fraser	2	1	516
13	Dean Hammond	6	0	546
	Other	16	0	
	TOTAL	**73**	**6**	

KEY GOALKEEPER

Scott Flinders

Goals Conceded in the League	13	Counting Games League games when player was on pitch for at least 70 minutes	12
Defensive Rating Ave number of mins between League goals conceded while on the pitch	83	Clean Sheets In League games when player was on pitch for at least 70 minutes	4

KEY PLAYERS - DEFENDERS

Guy Butters

Goals Conceded Number of League goals conceded while the player was on the pitch	31	Clean Sheets In League games when player was on pitch for at least 70 minutes	8
Defensive Rating Ave number of mins between League goals conceded while on the pitch	88	Club Defensive Rating Average number of mins between League goals conceded by the club this season	71

	PLAYER	CON LGE	CLEAN SHEETS	DEF RATE
1	Guy Butters	31	8	88 mins
2	Adam El-Abd	45	11	76 mins
3	Joel Lynch	40	9	74 mins
4	Kerry Mayo	36	7	67 mins

KEY PLAYERS - MIDFIELDERS

Dean Hammond

Goals in the League	8	Contribution to Attacking Power Average number of minutes between League team goals while on pitch	79
Defensive Rating Average number of mins between League goals conceded while on the pitch	78	Scoring Difference Defensive Rating minus Contribution to Attacking Power	-1

	PLAYER	LGE GOALS	DEF RATE	POWER	SCORE DIFF
1	Dean Hammond	8	78	79	-1 mins
2	Alexis Bertin	0	89	96	-7 mins
3	Dean Cox	6	71	84	-13 mins
4	Gary Hart	2	68	82	-14 mins

KEY PLAYERS - GOALSCORERS

Basir Savage

Goals in the League	6	Player Strike Rate Average number of minutes between League goals scored by player	194
Contribution to Attacking Power Average number of minutes between League team goals while on pitch	89	Club Strike Rate Average number of minutes between League goals scored by club	86

	PLAYER	LGE GOALS	POWER	STRIKE RATE
1	Basir Savage	6	89	194 mins
2	Dean Hammond	8	79	409 mins
3	Alex Revell	7	77	442 mins
4	Jake Robinson	6	94	454 mins

Dean Cox

SQUAD APPEARANCES

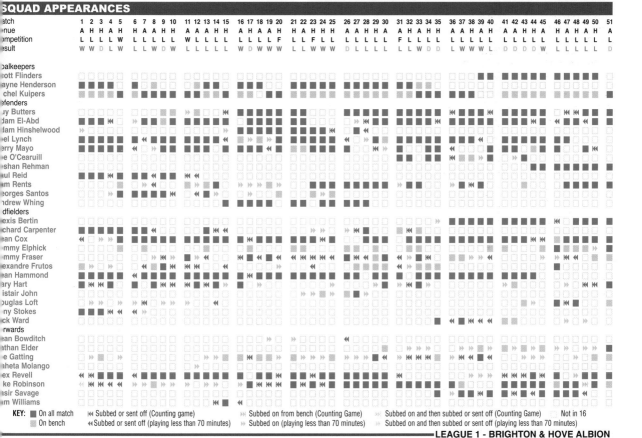

KEY: ■ On all match ◄◄ Subbed or sent off (Counting game) ►► Subbed on from bench (Counting Game) ►► Subbed on and then subbed or sent off (Counting Game) ☐ Not in 16
☐ On bench ◄◄ Subbed or sent off (playing less than 70 minutes) ►► Subbed on (playing less than 70 minutes) ►► Subbed on and then subbed or sent off (playing less than 70 minutes)

LEAGUE 1 - BRIGHTON & HOVE ALBION

BOURNEMOUTH

Final Position: **19th**

NICKNAME: THE CHERRIES KEY: ☐ Won ☐ Drawn ☐ Lost

					Attendance
1	div2	Chesterfield	H L	0-3	5,499
2	div2	Yeovil	A D	0-0	6,451
3	div2	Leyton Orient	A L	2-3	Hayter 57, Cooke 62	4,474
4	div2	Cheltenham	H W	2-1	Fletcher 2, Best 55	5,378
5	ccr1	Southend	H L	1-3	Fletcher 47	3,764
6	div2	Doncaster	A D	1-1	Hayter 90 pen	5,190
7	div2	Oldham	H W	3-2	Hayter 29, 43, Browning 90	4,838
8	div2	Crewe	H W	1-0	Best 23	5,627
9	div2	Brighton	A D	2-2	Foley 34, Howe 74	5,958
10	div2	Brentford	A D	0-0		6,272
11	div2	Scunthorpe	H D	1-1	Anderton 22	5,256
12	div2	Bristol City	H L	0-1		6,484
13	div2	Huddersfield	A D	2-2	Hayter 10, Best 48	11,350
14	div2	Northampton	H D	0-0		5,746
15	div2	Millwall	A L	0-1		9,838
16	div2	Rotherham	H L	1-3	Gowling 31	5,544
17	div2	Tranmere	A L	0-1		6,076
18	div2	Swansea	A L	2-4	Hollands 79, Pitman 85	11,795
19	facr1	Boston	H W	4-0	Fletcher 5, 42, Hayter 59, Hollands 90	4,263
20	div2	Carlisle	H L	0-1		5,682
21	div2	Bradford	A D	0-0		10,347
22	facr2	Bristol Rovers	A D	1-1	Hayter 73	6,252
23	div2	Nottm Forest	H W	2-0	Connolly 51, Pitman 89 pen	7,067
24	div2	Port Vale	H L	0-4		4,538
25	facr2r	Bristol Rovers	H L	0-1		4,153
26	div2	Gillingham	A D	1-1	Vokes 38	6,296
27	div2	Blackpool	H L	1-3	Gillett 82	5,758
28	div2	Bristol City	A D	2-2	Pitman 16, Browning 47	13,848
29	div2	Scunthorpe	A L	2-3	Vokes 46, 74	4,794
30	div2	Brighton	H W	1-0	Pitman 90	6,686
31	div2	Brentford	H W	1-0	Anderton 42	5,782
32	div2	Crewe	A L	0-2		4,739
33	div2	Huddersfield	H L	1-2	Purches 43	5,263
34	div2	Chesterfield	A W	1-0	Hayter 52	3,854
35	div2	Leyton Orient	H W	5-0	Wilson 10, Anderton 16, 47, 53, Hayter 68	5,985
36	div2	Cheltenham	A L	0-1		4,530
37	div2	Yeovil	H L	0-2		7,285
38	div2	Oldham	A W	2-1	McGoldrick 29, Vidarsson 31	5,429
39	div2	Doncaster	H W	2-0	Pitman 45, McGoldrick 47	6,166
40	div2	Blackpool	A L	0-2		6,184
41	div2	Northampton	A L	1-3	Wilson 55	5,921
42	div2	Millwall	H W	1-0	Anderton 19	7,194
43	div2	Tranmere	H W	2-0	McGoldrick 13, Hayter 57 pen	5,640
44	div2	Rotherham	A W	2-0	McGoldrick 12, Hayter 28	3,657
45	div2	Bradford	H D	1-1	McGoldrick 61	6,440
46	div2	Carlisle	A L	1-3	Vokes 62	8,989
47	div2	Swansea	H D	2-2	Wilson 22, McGoldrick 60	6,786
48	div2	Nottm Forest	A L	0-3		19,898
49	div2	Gillingham	H D	1-1	Hayter 45	8,001
50	div2	Port Vale	A L	1-2	Summerfield 80	5,080

LEAGUE APPEARANCES, BOOKINGS AND CAPS

	AGE (on 01/07/07)	IN NAMED 16	APPEARANCES	COUNTING GAMES	MINUTES ON PITCH	LEAGUE GOALS
Goalkeepers						
Neil Moss	32	43	27	27	2430	0	1
Gareth Stewart	27	46	19	19	1710	0	0
Defenders						
Ryan Bertrand	17	6	6	6	540	0	0
Karl Broadhurst	27	33	26	23	2165	0	4
Matthew Connolly	19	6	5	3	286	1	1
Warren Cummings	26	32	31	26	2412	0	4
Josh Gowling	23	40	34	24	2331	1	2
Callum Hart	21	17	8	7	662	0	0
Eddie Howe	29	16	15	14	1265	1	3
Shaun Maher	29	10	7	5	469	0	3
Stephen Purches	27	43	43	37	3569	1	2
Marc Wilson	19	20	19	17	1647	3	5
Neil Young	33	35	34	30	2879	0	6
Midfielders						
Lionel Ainsworth	19	8	7	1	189	0	0
Darren Anderton	35	28	28	22	2222	6	6
Marcus Browning	36	22	21	13	1352	2	3
Stephen Cooke	24	16	10	6	645	1	0
Shaun Cooper	23	34	33	23	2495	0	2
Jack Cork	18	7	7	6	559	0	1
Steve Foley	21	20	18	14	1343	1	0
Simon Gillett	21	7	7	7	619	1	1
Danny Hollands	21	42	33	14	1585	1	3
Franck Songo'o	20	4	4	1	227	0	1
Luke Summerfield	28	8	3	2	409	1	0
Bjarni Thor Vidarsson	19	6	6	2	329	1	0
Josh Walker	25	6	6	4	449	0	1
Forwards						
Leon Best	20	15	15	10	1088	3	5
Steve Claridge	41	1	1	0	57	0	0
Steve Fletcher	35	44	41	26	2772	1	3
James Hayter	28	42	42	41	3691	10	3
James Lawson	19	4	4	1	184	0	3
David McGoldrick	19	13	12	12	1036	6	3
Brett Pitman	19	33	29	6	1070	5	3
Sam Vokes	17	19	13	3	701	4	0

TEAM OF THE SEASON

G Neil Moss CG: 27 DR: 67

D Warren Cummings CG: 26 DR: 67
D Eddie Howe CG: 15 DR: 74
D Marc Wilson CG: 17 DR: 74
D Stephen Purches CG: 37 DR: 66

M Darren Anderton CG: 22 SD: -9
M Marcus Browning CG: 13 SD: 29
M Shaun Cooper CG: 23 SD: 6
M Steve Foley CG: 14 SD: -34

F David McGoldrick CG: 12 SR: 172
F James Hayter CG: 41 SR: 369

MONTHLY POINTS TALLY

AUGUST		5	33%
SEPTEMBER		10	48%
OCTOBER		1	8%
NOVEMBER		1	11%
DECEMBER		5	28%
JANUARY		6	50%
FEBRUARY		9	60%
MARCH		12	67%
APRIL		3	20%
MAY		0	0%

LEAGUE GOALS

	PLAYER	MINS	GOALS	S RATE
1	Hayter	3691	10	369
2	McGoldrick	1036	6	172
3	Anderton	2222	6	370
4	Pitman	1070	5	214
5	Vokes	701	4	175
6	Best	1088	3	362
7	Wilson	1647	3	549
8	Browning	1352	2	676
9	Connolly	286	1	286
10	Vidarsson	329	1	329
11	Summerfield	409	1	409
12	Gillett	619	1	619
13	Cooke	645	1	645
	Other		6	
	TOTAL		50	

TOP POINT EARNERS

	PLAYER	GAMES	AV PTS
1	Marcus Browning	14	1.71
2	Eddie Howe	14	1.57
3	Shaun Cooper	23	1.52
4	David McGoldrick	12	1.42
5	Marc Wilson	17	1.41
6	Neil Moss	27	1.30
7	Karl Broadhurst	23	1.22
8	Warren Cummings	26	1.12
9	Steve Fletcher	24	1.08
10	Steve Foley	14	1.08
	CLUB AVERAGE:		1.13

DISCIPLINARY RECORDS

	PLAYER	YELLOW	RED	AVE
1	Shaun Maher	3	0	156
2	Leon Best	5	0	217
3	Marc Wilson	5	0	329
4	Marcus Browning	3	1	338
5	David McGoldrick	3	0	345
6	Brett Pitman	3	0	356
7	Darren Anderton	6	1	370
8	Neil Young	6	1	411
9	Eddie Howe	3	0	421
10	Danny Hollands	3	0	528
11	Karl Broadhurst	4	0	541
12	Jack Cork	1	0	559
13	Warren Cummings	4	0	603
	Other	13	0	
	TOTAL	62	3	

KEY GOALKEEPER

Neil Moss

Goals Conceded in the League	36	Counting Games League games when player was on pitch for at least 70 minutes	27
Defensive Rating Ave number of mins between League goals conceded while on the pitch	67	Clean Sheets In League games when player was on pitch for at least 70 minutes	10

KEY PLAYERS - DEFENDERS

Eddie Howe

Goals Conceded Number of League goals conceded while the player was on the pitch	17	Clean Sheets In League games when player was on pitch for at least 70 minutes	6
Defensive Rating Ave number of mins between League goals conceded while on the pitch	74	Club Defensive Rating Average number of mins between League goals conceded by the club this season	64

	PLAYER	CON LGE	CLEAN SHEETS	DEF RATE
1	Eddie Howe	17	6	74 mins
2	Marc Wilson	22	6	74 mins
3	Warren Cummings	36	7	67 mins
4	Stephen Purches	54	11	66 mins

KEY PLAYERS - MIDFIELDERS

Marcus Browning

Goals in the League	2	Contribution to Attacking Power Average number of minutes between League team goals while on pitch	61
Defensive Rating Average number of mins between League goals conceded while on the pitch	90	Scoring Difference Defensive Rating minus Contribution to Attacking Power	29

	PLAYER	LGE GOALS	DEF RATE	POWER	SCORE DIFF
1	Marcus Browning	2	90	61	29 mins
2	Shaun Cooper	0	73	67	6 mins
3	Darren Anderton	6	67	76	-9 mins
4	Steve Foley	1	55	89	-34 mins

KEY PLAYERS - GOALSCORERS

David McGoldrick

Goals in the League	6	Player Strike Rate Average number of minutes between League goals scored by player	172
Contribution to Attacking Power Average number of minutes between League team goals while on pitch	74	Club Strike Rate Average number of minutes between League goals scored by club	82

	PLAYER	LGE GOALS	POWER	STRIKE RATE
1	David McGoldrick	6	74	172 mins
2	James Hayter	10	85	369 mins
3	Darren Anderton	6	76	370 mins
4	Marcus Browning	2	61	676 mins

Darren Anderton

SQUAD APPEARANCES

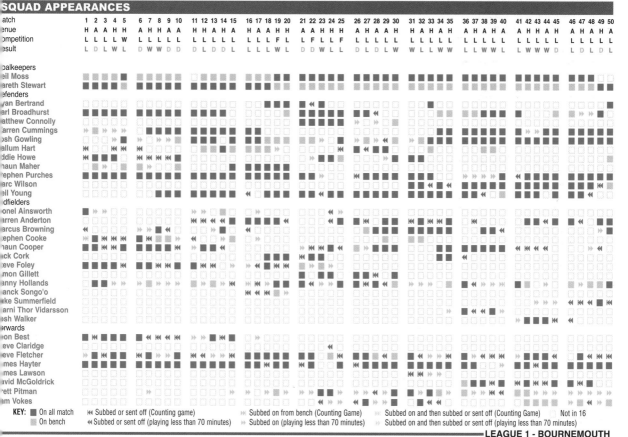

Match	1 2 3 4 5	6 7 8 9 10	11 12 13 14 15	16 17 18 19 20	21 22 23 24 25	26 27 28 29 30	31 32 33 34 35	36 37 38 39 40	41 42 43 44 45	46 47 48 49 50
Venue	H A A H H	A H H A A	H H A H A	H A A H H	A A H H H	A H A A H	H A H A H	A H A H A	A H H A H	A H A H A
Competition	L L L L W	D L L L L	L L L L L	L L L W L	D D W L L	D L D L W	W L L W W	L L W W L	L W W W D	L D L D L
Result	L D L W L	D W W D D	D L D D L	L L L W L	D D W L L	D L D L W	W L L W W	L L W W L	L W W W D	L D L D L

Goalkeepers
Neil Moss
Gareth Stewart

Defenders
Ryan Bertrand
Carl Broadhurst
Matthew Connolly
Warren Cummings
Josh Gowling
Callum Hart
Eddie Howe
Shaun Maher
Stephen Purches
Marc Wilson
Neil Young

Midfielders
Lionel Ainsworth
Darren Anderton
Marcus Browning
Stephen Cooke
Shaun Cooper
Jack Cork
Steve Foley
Simon Gillett
Danny Hollands
Franck Songo'o
Luke Summerfield
Marni Thor Vidarsson
Josh Walker

Forwards
Leon Best
Steve Claridge
Steve Fletcher
James Hayter
James Lawson
David McGoldrick
Brett Pitman
Sam Vokes

KEY: ■ On all match ◄◄ Subbed or sent off (Counting game) ►► Subbed on from bench (Counting Game) ►◄ Subbed on and then subbed or sent off (Counting Game) □ Not in 16
■ On bench ◄◄ Subbed or sent off (playing less than 70 minutes) ►► Subbed on (playing less than 70 minutes) ►► Subbed on and then subbed or sent off (playing less than 70 minutes)

LEYTON ORIENT

Final Position: **20th**

NICKNAME: THE O'S   KEY: ☐ Won ☐ Drawn ☐ Lost   Attendance

				Result	Scorers	Attendance
1	div2	Port Vale	A L	0-3		5,631
2	div2	Millwall	H W	2-0	Steele 45, Alexander 78	6,142
3	div2	Bournemouth	H W	3-2	Alexander 28, Steele 67, 90	4,474
4	div2	Carlisle	A L	1-3	Steele 68	7,160
5	ccr1	West Brom	H L	0-3		3,058
6	div2	Swansea	H L	0-1		4,162
7	div2	Tranmere	A L	0-3		6,446
8	div2	Brentford	H D	1-1	Simpson 15	5,420
9	div2	Bristol City	A L	1-2	Lockwood 63 pen	9,726
10	div2	Brighton	A L	1-4	Lockwood 82 pen	6,003
11	div2	Rotherham	H L	2-3	A.Chambers 20, Miller 68	4,063
12	div2	Gillingham	H D	3-3	Lockwood 77 pen, 85, 88	3,978
13	div2	Blackpool	A L	0-3		5,298
14	div2	Chesterfield	H D	0-0		4,309
15	div2	Oldham	A D	3-3	Ibehre 9, Alexander 60, 86	5,014
16	div2	Cheltenham	H W	2-0	Alexander 6, Lockwood 66 pen	4,500
17	div2	Scunthorpe	A L	1-3	Easton 10	4,795
18	div2	Doncaster	A D	0-0		5,447
19	facr1	Notts County	H W	2-1	Corden 12, Miller 58	3,011
20	div2	Yeovil	H D	0-0		4,842
21	facr2	Torquay	A D	1-1	Corden 76	2,392
22	div2	Bradford	H L	1-2	Thelwell 29	3,529
23	div2	Huddersfield	H W	1-0	Alexander 28	4,300
24	facr2r	Torquay	H L	1-2	J.Walker 58	2,384
25	div2	Nottm Forest	A W	3-1	Guttridge 25, A.Chambers 45, Corden 69	23,109
26	div2	Northampton	A W	1-0	Connor 79	4,728
27	div2	Crewe	H D	1-1	Lockwood 47 pen	4,371
28	div2	Gillingham	A L	1-2	J.Walker 35	8,216
29	div2	Rotherham	A D	2-2	A.Chambers 15, Alexander 52	4,715
30	div2	Bristol City	H D	1-1	Lockwood 62 pen	4,814
31	div2	Brentford	A D	2-2	Ibehre 26, Connor 84	6,765
32	div2	Blackpool	H L	0-1		5,217
33	div2	Crewe	A W	4-0	A.Chambers 45, Corden 51, Ibehre 67, Tudor 83	5,280
34	div2	Port Vale	H W	2-1	Lockwood 68, Ibehre 86	4,295
35	div2	Bournemouth	A L	0-5		5,985
36	div2	Brighton	H L	1-4	Demetriou 87	4,670
37	div2	Carlisle	H D	1-1	Lockwood 47	4,449
38	div2	Millwall	A W	5-2	Alexander 5, Ryan.Jarvis 7, 12, 76, J.Walker 90	10,356
39	div2	Tranmere	H W	3-1	Miller 18, Ryan.Jarvis 29, 39	4,832
40	div2	Swansea	A D	0-0		12,901
41	div2	Chesterfield	A W	1-0	Tudor 53	3,665
42	div2	Oldham	H D	2-2	Alexander 13, Hooper 70	5,443
43	div2	Scunthorpe	H D	2-2	Corden 41, Hooper 87	5,869
44	div2	Cheltenham	A L	1-2	Alexander 63	4,300
45	div2	Northampton	H L	0-2		5,459
46	div2	Yeovil	A L	1-2	Ryan.Jarvis 31	5,206
47	div2	Doncaster	H D	1-1	Alexander 36	4,697
48	div2	Bradford	A W	2-0	Alexander 62, Tann 65	10,665
49	div2	Nottm Forest	H L	1-3	Lockwood 9	7,206
50	div2	Huddersfield	A L	1-3	Demetriou 59	10,842

LEAGUE APPEARANCES, BOOKINGS AND CAPS

	AGE (on 01/07/07)	IN NAMED 16	APPEARANCES	COUNTING GAMES	MINUTES ON PITCH	LEAGUE GOALS
Goalkeepers						
Glyn Garner	30	44	43	43	3870	0	3
Glenn Morris	23	46	3	3	270	0
Defenders						
Donny Barnard	23	31	18	7	855	0	2
Jason Demetriou	19	24	15	2	428	2	2
Clayton Fortune	24	10	9	7	733	0	2
Matthew Lockwood	30	41	41	40	3619	11	6
John Mackie	30	35	35	27	2691	0	6
Justin Miller	26	33	31	26	2455	2	2
Aiden Palmer	20	10	6	4	444	0
David Partridge	28	2	1	1	90	0	1
Adam Tann	25	25	21	11	1288	1	3
Alton Thelwell	26	23	22	19	1793	1
Midfielders						
Adam Chambers	26	38	37	36	3270	4	13
Wayne Corden	31	46	42	31	3084	3	3
Derek Duncan	20	7	3	0	48	0
Craig Easton	28	30	30	28	2578	1	8
Luke Guttridge	25	17	17	14	1321	1	5
Gary Hooper	19	4	4	2	251	2
Joe Keith	28	17	11	7	735	0
Daryl McMahon	24	11	8	3	370	0	1
Phillip Mulryne	29	4	2	0	65	0
Brian Saah	20	37	32	31	2783	0	5
Michael Simpson	33	15	15	15	1321	1
Peter Till	21	4	4	4	349	0
Shane Tudor	25	33	33	24	2358	2	2
Forwards						
Gary Alexander	27	44	44	38	3619	12	8
Paul Connor	28	24	18	2	523	2
Efe Echanomi	20	3	3	0	68	0
Jabo Ibehre	24	33	29	11	1320	4	2
Ryan Jarvis	20	14	14	11	1116	6	1
Lee Steele	33	12	11	6	719	4	1
James Walker	19	16	14	9	821	2

TEAM OF THE SEASON

D Justin Miller — CG: 26 DR: 66	**M** Luke Guttridge — CG: 14 SD: 7
G Glyn Garner — CG: 43 DR: 57	**D** John Mackie — CG: 27 DR: 57	**M** Craig Easton — CG: 28 SD: 5	**F** Ryan Jarvis* — CG: 11 SR: 186
D Matthew Lockwood — CG: 40 DR: 54	**M** Wayne Corden — CG: 31 SD: -9	**F** Gary Alexander — CG: 38 SR: 301
D Alton Thelwell — CG: 19 DR: 54	**M** Brian Saah — CG: 31 SD: -11

MONTHLY POINTS TALLY

AUGUST		6	40%
SEPTEMBER		2	10%
OCTOBER		5	42%
NOVEMBER		2	33%
DECEMBER		11	52%
JANUARY		5	42%
FEBRUARY		10	56%
MARCH		6	40%
APRIL		4	27%
MAY		0	0%

LEAGUE GOALS

	PLAYER	MINS	GOALS	S RATE
1	Alexander	3619	12	301
2	Lockwood	3619	11	329
3	Jarvis, Ryan	1116	6	186
4	Steele	719	4	179
5	Ibehre	1320	4	330
6	Chambers, A	3270	4	817
7	Corden	3084	3	1028
8	Hooper	251	2	125
9	Demetriou	428	2	214
10	Connor	523	2	261
11	Walker, J	821	2	410
12	Tudor	2358	2	1179
13	Miller	2455	2	1227
	Other		5	
	TOTAL		**61**	

TOP POINT EARNERS

	PLAYER	GAMES	AV PTS
1	Craig Easton	28	1.39
2	Luke Guttridge	14	1.36
3	Justin Miller	27	1.33
4	John Mackie	29	1.31
5	Shane Tudor	24	1.25
6	Matthew Lockwood	40	1.20
7	Glyn Garner	43	1.19
8	Gary Alexander	38	1.18
9	Wayne Corden	31	1.16
10	Adam Chambers	36	1.11
	CLUB AVERAGE:		**1.11**

DISCIPLINARY RECORDS

	PLAYER	YELLOW	RED	AVE
1	Luke Guttridge	5	1	220
2	Adam Chambers	13	1	233
3	Craig Easton	8	0	322
4	Clayton Fortune	2	0	366
5	Gary Alexander	8	1	402
6	Adam Tann	3	0	429
7	John Mackie	6	2	448
8	Matthew Lockwood	6	0	603
9	Jabo Ibehre	2	0	660
10	Brian Saah	5	0	695
11	Lee Steele	1	0	719
12	Justin Miller	2	1	818
13	Donny Barnard	1	0	855
	Other	9	0	
	TOTAL	**71**	**6**	

KEY GOALKEEPER

Glyn Garner

Goals Conceded in the League	67	Counting Games League games when player was on pitch for at least 70 minutes	43
Defensive Rating Ave number of mins between League goals conceded while on the pitch	57	Clean Sheets In League games when player was on pitch for at least 70 minutes	11

KEY PLAYERS - DEFENDERS

Justin Miller

Goals Conceded Number of League goals conceded while the player was on the pitch	37	Clean Sheets In League games when player was on pitch for at least 70 minutes	7
Defensive Rating Ave number of mins between League goals conceded while on the pitch	66	Club Defensive Rating Average number of mins between League goals conceded by the club this season	54

	PLAYER	CON LGE	CLEAN SHEETS	DEF RATE
1	Justin Miller	37	7	66 mins
2	John Mackie	47	9	57 mins
3	Alton Thelwell	33	6	54 mins
4	Matthew Lockwood	66	11	54 mins

KEY PLAYERS - MIDFIELDERS

Luke Guttridge

Goals in the League	1	Contribution to Attacking Power Average number of minutes between League team goals while on pitch	66
Defensive Rating Average number of mins between League goals conceded while on the pitch	73	Scoring Difference Defensive Rating minus Contribution to Attacking Power	7

	PLAYER	LGE GOALS	DEF RATE	POWER	SCORE DIFF
1	Luke Guttridge	1	73	66	7 mins
2	Craig Easton	1	66	61	5 mins
3	Wayne Corden	3	61	70	-9 mins
4	Brian Saah	0	53	64	-11 mins

KEY PLAYERS - GOALSCORERS

Ryan Jarvis

Goals in the League	6	Player Strike Rate Average number of minutes between League goals scored by player	186
Contribution to Attacking Power Average number of minutes between League team goals while on pitch	62	Club Strike Rate Average number of minutes between League goals scored by club	69

	PLAYER	LGE GOALS	POWER	STRIKE RATE
1	Ryan Jarvis	6	62	186 mins
2	Gary Alexander	12	72	301 mins
3	Jabo Ibehre	4	57	330 mins
4	Adam Chambers	4	66	817 mins

Gary Alexander

SQUAD APPEARANCES

Match	1	2	3	4	5		6	7	8	9	10		11	12	13	14	15		16	17	18	19	20		21	22	23	24	25		26	27	28	29	30		31	32	33	34	35		36	37	38	39	40		41	42	43	44	45		46	47	48	49	50
Venue	A	H	H	A	H		H	A	H	A	A		H	H	A	H	A		H	A	A	H	H		A	H	H	H	A		A	H	A	A	H		A	H	A	H	A		H	H	A	H	A		A	H	H	A	H		A	H	A	H	A
Competition	L	L	L	L	W		L	L	L	L	L		L	L	L	L	L		L	L	L	F	L		F	L	L	F	L		L	L	L	L	L		L	L	L	L	L		L	L	L	L	L		L	L	L	L	L		L	L	L	L	L
Result	L	W	W	L	L		L	L	D	L	L		L	D	L	D	D		W	L	D	W	D		D	L	W	L	W		W	D	L	D	D		D	L	W	W	L		L	D	W	W	D		W	D	D	L	L		L	D	W	L	L

Goalkeepers
Glyn Garner
Glenn Morris

Defenders
Lenny Barnard
Jason Demetriou
Clayton Fortune
Matthew Lockwood
John Mackie
Justin Miller
Aiden Palmer
David Partridge
Adam Tann
Alton Thelwell

Midfielders
Adam Chambers
Wayne Corden
Derek Duncan
Craig Easton
Luke Guttridge
Gary Hooper
Joe Keith
Daryl McMahon
Phillip Mulryne
Brian Saah
Michael Simpson
Peter Till
Shane Tudor

Forwards
Gary Alexander
Paul Connor
Joe Echanomi
Jabo Ibehre
Ryan Jarvis
Joe Steele
James Walker

KEY: ■ On all match   ◄◄ Subbed or sent off (Counting game)   ►► Subbed on from bench (Counting Game)   ►◄ Subbed on and then subbed or sent off (Counting Game)   ☐ Not in 16
   ▨ On bench   ◄◄ Subbed or sent off (playing less than 70 minutes)   ►► Subbed on (playing less than 70 minutes)   ►► Subbed on and then subbed or sent off (playing less than 70 minutes)

LEAGUE 1 - LEYTON ORIENT

CHESTERFIELD

Final Position: **21st**

NICKNAME: THE SPIREITES   KEY: ☐ Won ☐ Drawn ☐ Lost   Attendance

#	Comp	Opponent	H/A	Res	Score	Scorers	Attendance
1	div2	Bournemouth	A	W	3-0	Niven 47, Larkin 62, Shaw 90	5,499
2	div2	Carlisle	H	D	0-0		4,525
3	div2	Millwall	H	W	5-1	Hall 13, 51, Allison 24, 65, Folan 32	4,136
4	div2	Port Vale	A	L	2-3	Downes 23, Folan 85	5,622
5	ccr1	Wolverhampton	H	W	6-5*	(*on penalties)	4,136
6	div2	Tranmere	H	L	0-2		4,163
7	div2	Nottm Forest	A	L	0-4		19,480
8	div2	Rotherham	H	W	2-1	Folan 9, Shaw 28	4,803
9	div2	Blackpool	A	D	1-1	Hurst 60	4,600
10	div2	Bristol City	A	L	1-3	Larkin 20	10,398
11	ccr2	Man City	H	W	2-1	Folan 51, Niven 67	7,960
12	div2	Brentford	H	W	3-1	Folan 30, 40, Shaw 37	3,877
13	div2	Scunthorpe	H	L	0-1		4,849
14	div2	Brighton	A	W	2-0	Folan 20, Niven 74	5,499
15	div2	Leyton Orient	A	D	0-0		4,309
16	div2	Swansea	H	L	2-3	Hall 47, Hazell 77	3,915
17	div2	Doncaster	A	L	0-1		6,280
18	ccr3	West Ham	H	W	2-1	Larkin 54, Folan 87	7,787
19	div2	Yeovil	H	D	1-1	O'Hare 50	5,413
20	div2	Gillingham	A	L	1-2	Hughes 39	5,856
21	ccr4	Charlton	H	L	3-4*	Larkin 3, Folan 47, Allison 119 (*on penalties)	7,000
22	facr1	Basingstoke	H	L	0-1		-
23	div2	Cheltenham	H	W	1-0	O'Hare 48	3,488
24	div2	Crewe	A	D	2-2	Niven 85, Hurst 90	5,078
25	div2	Northampton	H	D	0-0		3,341
26	div2	Oldham	H	W	2-1	Larkin 14, 33	4,059
27	div2	Bradford	A	L	0-1		7,228
28	div2	Huddersfield	H	D	0-0		4,472
29	div2	Scunthorpe	A	L	0-1		6,123
30	div2	Brentford	A	L	1-2	Hazell 79	4,540
31	div2	Blackpool	H	W	2-0	Hurst 13, Folan 42	4,351
32	div2	Rotherham	A	W	1-0	Folan 33	5,188
33	div2	Brighton	H	L	0-1		3,984
34	div2	Huddersfield	A	D	1-1	Holmes 23	9,872
35	div2	Bournemouth	H	L	0-1		3,854
36	div2	Millwall	A	L	1-2	Hall 58	9,711
37	div2	Port Vale	H	W	3-0	Picken 38, Ward 79, Allison 90	3,752
38	div2	Carlisle	A	D	0-0		6,196
39	div2	Nottm Forest	H	L	1-2	Downes 67	6,641
40	div2	Tranmere	A	L	0-2		6,254
41	div2	Bristol City	H	L	1-3	Allison 59	3,471
42	div2	Leyton Orient	H	L	0-1		3,665
43	div2	Swansea	A	L	0-2		11,384
44	div2	Doncaster	H	D	1-1	Hall 41 pen	3,868
45	div2	Yeovil	A	L	0-1		4,735
46	div2	Crewe	H	W	2-1	Downes 29, Shaw 67	3,698
47	div2	Cheltenham	A	D	0-0		5,089
48	div2	Gillingham	H	L	0-1		3,867
49	div2	Northampton	A	L	0-1		5,730
50	div2	Bradford	H	W	3-0	Ward 15, 28, Bower 60 og	5,207
51	div2	Oldham	A	L	0-1		8,148

LEAGUE APPEARANCES, BOOKINGS AND CAPS

	AGE (on 01/07/07)	IN NAMED 16	APPEARANCES	COUNTING GAMES	MINUTES ON PITCH	LEAGUE GOALS	
Goalkeepers							
Michael Jordan	21	37	6	6	540	0	0
Barry Roche	25	45	40	40	3630	0	2
Defenders							
Alex Bailey	23	35	30	23	2316	0	4
Paul Boertien	28	4	4	3	337	0	0
Kyle Critchell	20	13	10	5	537	0	1
Kevin Dawson	26	2	2	2	180	0	0
Aaron Downes	22	43	42	42	3810	2	4
Sebastien Grimaldi	27	12	8	7	708	0	2
Reuben Hazell	28	44	39	39	3510	2	8
Janos Kovacs	21	29	6	4	429	0	0
James Lowry	20	13	8	6	605	0	0
Shane Nicholson	37	6	2	0	47	0	0
Alan O'Hare	24	19	17	14	1393	2	3
Phil Picken	21	42	39	38	3428	1	9
Midfielders							
Mark Allott	29	39	39	38	3487	0	10
Charlie Daniels	20	2	2	1	127	0	0
Gareth Davies	24	23	15	6	747	0	2
Paul Hall	34	46	46	39	3688	5	1
Peter Holmes	26	10	10	9	814	1	1
Mark Hughes	23	3	2	1	152	1	0
Kevan Hurst	21	25	25	22	2110	3	1
James Meredith	19	1	1	1	120	0	0
Derek Niven	23	45	45	45	4032	3	7
Nicky Rizzo	28	5	4	1	148	0	0
Jamie Ward	21	9	9	8	712	3	1
Forwards							
Wayne Allison	38	42	36	12	1544	4	0
Caleb Folan	24	23	23	17	1666	8	5
Jamie Jackson	20	20	14	1	398	0	1
Colin Larkin	25	44	39	18	2286	4	1
Paul Shaw	33	36	29	16	1843	4	2
Adam Smith	21	17	13	3	524	0	0

TEAM OF THE SEASON

G Barry Roche — CG: 40 DR: 77

D Aaron Downes — CG: 42 DR: 82
D Reuben Hazell — CG: 39 DR: 79
D Alex Bailey — CG: 23 DR: 77
D Phil Picken — CG: 38 DR: 76

M Kevan Hurst — CG: 22 SD: -3
M Mark Allott — CG: 38 SD: -6
M Derek Niven — CG: 45 SD: -10
M Paul Hall — CG: 39 SD: -16

F Caleb Folan — CG: 17 SR: 208
F Paul Shaw — CG: 16 SR: 460

MONTHLY POINTS TALLY

Month	Points	%
AUGUST	7	47%
SEPTEMBER	10	48%
OCTOBER	2	17%
NOVEMBER	4	44%
DECEMBER	5	28%
JANUARY	7	58%
FEBRUARY	4	27%
MARCH	1	6%
APRIL	7	47%
MAY	0	0%

LEAGUE GOALS

	PLAYER	MINS	GOALS	S RATE
1	Folan	1666	8	208
2	Hall	3688	5	737
3	Allison	1544	4	386
4	Shaw	1843	4	460
5	Larkin	2286	4	571
6	Ward	712	3	237
7	Hurst	2110	3	703
8	Niven	4032	3	1344
9	O'Hare	1393	2	696
10	Hazell	3510	2	1755
11	Downes	3810	2	1905
12	Hughes	152	1	152
13	Holmes	814	1	814
	Other		1	
	TOTAL		**43**	

TOP POINT EARNERS

	PLAYER	GAMES	AV PTS
1	Kevan Hurst	22	1.27
2	Caleb Folan	17	1.24
3	Paul Shaw	16	1.19
4	Alan O'Hare	14	1.14
5	Mark Allott	38	1.13
6	Aaron Downes	42	1.12
7	Reuben Hazell	39	1.10
8	Alex Bailey	23	1.09
9	Barry Roche	40	1.08
10	Paul Hall	39	1.05
	CLUB AVERAGE:		**1.02**

DISCIPLINARY RECORDS

	PLAYER	YELLOW	RED	AVE
1	Mark Allott	10	1	317
2	Sebastien Grimaldi	2	0	354
3	Gareth Davies	2	0	373
4	Caleb Folan	5	1	416
5	Phil Picken	9	0	428
6	Alan O'Hare	3	0	464
7	Reuben Hazell	8	0	501
8	Kyle Critchell	1	0	537
9	Alex Bailey	4	0	579
10	Derek Niven	7	0	672
11	Jamie Ward	1	0	712
12	Peter Holmes	1	0	814
13	Paul Shaw	2	0	921
	Other	9	0	
	TOTAL	**64**	**2**	

KEY GOALKEEPER

Barry Roche

Goals Conceded in the League	47	Counting Games League games when player was on pitch for at least 70 minutes	40
Defensive Rating Ave number of mins between League goals conceded while on the pitch	77	Clean Sheets In League games when player was on pitch for at least 70 minutes	11

KEY PLAYERS - DEFENDERS

Aaron Downes

Goals Conceded Number of League goals conceded while the player was on the pitch	46	Clean Sheets In League games when player was on pitch for at least 70 minutes	12
Defensive Rating Ave number of mins between League goals conceded while on the pitch	82	Club Defensive Rating Average number of mins between League goals conceded by the club this season	78

	PLAYER	CON LGE	CLEAN SHEETS	DEF RATE
1	Aaron Downes	46	12	82 mins
2	Reuben Hazell	44	10	79 mins
3	Alex Bailey	30	7	77 mins
4	Phil Picken	45	10	76 mins

KEY PLAYERS - MIDFIELDERS

Kevan Hurst

Goals in the League	3	Contribution to Attacking Power Average number of minutes between League team goals while on pitch	75
Defensive Rating Average number of mins between League goals conceded while on the pitch	72	Scoring Difference Defensive Rating minus Contribution to Attacking Power	-3

	PLAYER	LGE GOALS	DEF RATE	POWER	SCORE DIFF
1	Kevan Hurst	3	72	75	-3 mins
2	Mark Allott	0	77	83	-6 mins
3	Derek Niven	3	79	89	-10 mins
4	Paul Hall	5	73	89	-16 mins

KEY PLAYERS - GOALSCORERS

Caleb Folan

Goals in the League	8	Player Strike Rate Average number of minutes between League goals scored by player	208
Contribution to Attacking Power Average number of minutes between League team goals while on pitch	72	Club Strike Rate Average number of minutes between League goals scored by club	92

	PLAYER	LGE GOALS	POWER	STRIKE RATE
1	Caleb Folan	8	72	208 mins
2	Paul Shaw	4	115	460 mins
3	Colin Larkin	4	163	571 mins
4	Kevan Hurst	3	75	703 mins

Derek Niven

SQUAD APPEARANCES

Match	1 2 3 4 5	6 7 8 9 10	11 12 13 14 15	16 17 18 19 20	21 22 23 24 25	26 27 28 29 30	31 32 33 34 35	36 37 38 39 40	41 42 43 44 45	46 47 48 49 50	51
Venue	A H H A H	H A H A A	H H H A A	H A H H A	H H H A H	H A H A A	H A H A H	A H A H A	H H A H A	H A H A H	A
Competition	L L L L W	L L L L L	W L L L L	L L W L L	W F L L L	L L L L L	L L L L L	L L L L L	L L L L L	L L L L L	L
Result	W D W L W	L L W D L	W W L W D	L L W D L	L L W D D	W L D L L	W W L D L	L W D L L	L L L D L	W D L L W	L

Goalkeepers
Michael Jordan
Barry Roche

Defenders
Alex Bailey
Paul Boertien
Kyle Critchell
Kevin Dawson
Aaron Downes
Sebastien Grimaldi
Reuben Hazell
Janos Kovacs
James Lowry
Shane Nicholson
Alan O'Hare
Phil Picken

Midfielders
Mark Allott
Charlie Daniels
Gareth Davies
Paul Hall
Peter Holmes
Mark Hughes
Kevan Hurst
James Meredith
Derek Niven
Nicky Rizzo
Jamie Ward

Forwards
Wayne Allison
Caleb Folan
Jamie Jackson
Colin Larkin
Paul Shaw
Adam Smith

KEY: ■ On all match ◄◄ Subbed or sent off (Counting game) ▶▷ Subbed on from bench (Counting Game) ▷▷ Subbed on and then subbed or sent off (Counting Game) ☐ Not in 16
■ On bench ◄ Subbed or sent off (playing less than 70 minutes) ▷ Subbed on (playing less than 70 minutes) ▷▷ Subbed on and then subbed or sent off (playing less than 70 minutes)

LEAGUE 1 - CHESTERFIELD

BRADFORD CITY

Final Position: **22nd**

NICKNAME: THE BANTAMS   KEY: ☐ Won ☐ Drawn ☐ Lost   Attendance

#	Comp	Opponent			Score	Scorers	Attendance
1	div2	Nottm Forest	A	L	0-1		19,665
2	div2	Bristol City	H	W	2-1	Graham 42, Windass 42	7,356
3	div2	Gillingham	H	W	4-2	Bower 43, Windass 61, 82, J.Johnson 90	7,807
4	div2	Crewe	A	W	3-0	E.Johnson 44, 57, Bridge-Wilkinson 55	5,274
5	ccr1	Carlisle	A	L	3-4*	E.Johnson 81 (*on penalties)	4,757
6	div2	Rotherham	H	D	1-1	Windass 76	8,669
7	div2	Brentford	A	L	1-2	Bower 14	5,471
8	div2	Swansea	A	L	0-1		11,481
9	div2	Carlisle	H	D	1-1	Windass 21	7,966
10	div2	Port Vale	H	W	2-0	Bridge-Wilkinson 62, Graham 64	7,829
11	div2	Cheltenham	A	W	2-1	Graham 52, J.Johnson 69	3,830
12	div2	Doncaster	A	D	3-3	Windass 1, 23, Bridge-Wilkinson 83	6,304
13	div2	Tranmere	H	W	2-0	Bower 54, Schumacher 71	8,877
14	div2	Huddersfield	H	L	0-1		14,925
15	div2	Northampton	A	D	0-0		5,625
16	div2	Scunthorpe	H	L	0-1		8,723
17	div2	Blackpool	A	L	1-4	J.Johnson 84	7,937
18	div2	Brighton	H	L	2-3	Windass 56 pen, Schumacher 80	7,610
19	facr1	Crewe	H	W	4-0	Bridge-Wilkinson 3, Schumacher 61, Windass 70, Kempson 77	3,483
20	div2	Oldham	A	L	0-2		6,001
21	div2	Bournemouth	H	D	0-0		10,347
22	facr2	Millwall	H	D	0-0		4,346
23	div2	Leyton Orient	A	W	2-1	E.Johnson 4, Bridge-Wilkinson 34	3,529
24	div2	Millwall	A	L	0-2		7,588
25	facr2r	Millwall	A	L	0-1		3,220
26	div2	Chesterfield	H	W	1-0	Windass 57	7,228
27	div2	Yeovil	A	D	0-0		6,208
28	div2	Doncaster	H	L	0-1		10,069
29	div2	Cheltenham	H	D	2-2	Wetherall 15, J.Johnson 65	7,264
30	div2	Carlisle	A	L	0-1		7,548
31	div2	Port Vale	A	W	1-0	Schumacher 54	4,146
32	div2	Swansea	H	D	2-2	Windass 23, 88 pen	7,347
33	div2	Tranmere	A	D	1-1	Schumacher 34	6,567
34	div2	Yeovil	H	L	0-2		7,474
35	div2	Nottm Forest	H	D	2-2	Dyer 8	10,160
36	div2	Gillingham	A	L	0-1		5,513
37	div2	Crewe	H	L	0-1		7,778
38	div2	Brentford	H	D	1-1	Schumacher 88 pen	7,627
39	div2	Rotherham	A	L	1-4	Daley 54	4,568
40	div2	Huddersfield	A	L	0-2		14,772
41	div2	Bristol City	A	W	3-2	Paynter 44, Ashikodi 49, Schumacher 55	13,021
42	div2	Northampton	H	L	1-2	Paynter 62	8,190
43	div2	Blackpool	H	L	1-3	Daley 61	8,984
44	div2	Scunthorpe	A	L	0-2		6,437
45	div2	Bournemouth	A	D	1-1	Weir-Daley 90	6,440
46	div2	Oldham	H	D	1-1	Ashikodi 65	9,940
47	div2	Brighton	A	W	1-0	Paynter 35	5,757
48	div2	Leyton Orient	H	L	0-2		10,665
49	div2	Chesterfield	A	L	0-3		5,207
50	div2	Millwall	H	D	2-2	Barrau 45, 67	7,134

LEAGUE APPEARANCES, BOOKINGS AND CAPS

	AGE (on 01/07/07)	IN NAMED 16	APPEARANCES	COUNTING GAMES	MINUTES ON PITCH	LEAGUE GOALS	
Goalkeepers							
Donovan Ricketts	30	46	46	46	4140	0	2
Defenders							
Simon Ainge	19	15	9	5	521	0	1
Craig Bentham	22	27	17	11	1076	0	6
Mark Bower	27	46	46	46	4140	3	5
Matthew Clarke	26	28	8	5	549	0	5
Nathan Doyle	20	28	28	25	2330	0	5
Richard Edghill	32	35	24	18	1786	0	5
Ben Parker	19	41	38	30	2956	0	6
Alan Rogers	30	11	7	3	360	0	2
David Wetherall	36	43	41	38	3559	1	4
Kelly Youga	21	12	11	9	892	0	2
Midfielders							
Xavier Barrau	24	5	3	1	102	2	1
Thomas Black	30	5	4	2	246	0	0
Marc Bridge-Wilkinson	28	39	39	37	3359	4	3
Joe Brown	19	12	6	1	181	0	1
Joe Colbeck	20	34	31	13	1557	0	4
Omar Daley	26	17	14	12	1121	2	3
Colin Healy	27	3	2	2	180	0	1
Lee Holmes	20	16	16	15	1333	0	4
Jermaine Johnson	27	27	27	24	2222	4	4
Carlos Logan	21	4	3	1	179	0	0
Ben Muirhead	24	7	4	0	136	0	0
Thomas Penford	22	9	3	1	103	0	0
Steve Schumacher	23	44	44	44	3939	6	8
Forwards							
Moses Ashikodi	20	8	8	7	650	2	5
Bruce Dyer	32	5	5	2	239	1	0
David Graham	28	24	23	14	1534	3	0
Dave Hibbert	21	9	8	4	398	0	1
Eddie Johnson	22	37	31	13	1666	3	4
William Paynter	22	15	15	13	1258	3	2
Spencer Weir-Daley	21	5	5	2	231	1	2
Dean Windass	38	25	25	23	2116	11	1

TEAM OF THE SEASON

Nathan Doyle CG: 25 DR: 80	**Lee Holmes** CG: 15 SD: 3
David Wetherall CG: 38 DR: 67	**Jermaine Johnson** CG: 24 SD: -10 **Dean Windass** CG: 23 SR: 192
G — **Donovan Ricketts** CG: 46 DR: 63	
Mark Bower CG: 46 DR: 63	**Joe Colbeck** CG: 13 SD: -17 **William Paynter** CG: 13 SR: 419
Ben Parker CG: 30 DR: 59	**Marc Bridge-Wilkinson** CG: 37 SD: -20

MONTHLY POINTS TALLY

Month		Pts	%
AUGUST		10	67%
SEPTEMBER		11	52%
OCTOBER		1	8%
NOVEMBER		1	11%
DECEMBER		8	44%
JANUARY		5	33%
FEBRUARY		2	17%
MARCH		3	17%
APRIL		5	33%
MAY		1	33%

LEAGUE GOALS

	PLAYER	MINS	GOALS	S RATE
1	Windass	2116	11	192
2	Schumacher	3939	6	656
3	Johnson, J	2222	4	555
4	Br.-Wilkinson	3359	4	839
5	Paynter	1258	3	419
6	Graham	1534	3	511
7	Johnson, E	1666	3	555
8	Bower	4140	3	1380
9	Barrau	102	2	51
10	Ashikodi	650	2	325
11	Daley	1121	2	560
12	Weir-Daley	231	1	231
13	Dyer	239	1	239
	Other		1	
	TOTAL		46	

TOP POINT EARNERS

	PLAYER	GAMES	AV PTS
1	Lee Holmes	15	1.50
2	David Graham	12	1.42
3	Jermaine Johnson	24	1.25
4	Dean Windass	24	1.21
5	Marc Bridge-Wilkinson	37	1.11
6	Ben Parker	30	1.10
7	Joe Colbeck	13	1.08
8	Nathan Doyle	25	1.08
9	Mark Bower	46	1.02
10	Donovan Ricketts	46	1.02
	CLUB AVERAGE:		1.02

DISCIPLINARY RECORDS

	PLAYER	YELLOW	RED	AVE
1	Moses Ashikodi	5	0	130
2	Craig Bentham	6	0	179
3	Kelly Youga	2	1	297
4	Joe Colbeck	4	0	311
5	Dean Windass	5	1	352
6	Richard Edghill	5	0	357
7	Omar Daley	3	0	373
8	Eddie Johnson	4	0	416
9	Jermaine Johnson	4	1	444
10	Nathan Doyle	5	0	466
11	Steve Schumacher	8	1	492
12	Ben Parker	5	0	492
13	Simon Ainge	1	0	521
	Other	17	1	
	TOTAL	75	6	

KEY GOALKEEPER

Donovan Ricketts

Goals Conceded in the League	65	Counting Games League games when player was on pitch for at least 70 minutes	46
Defensive Rating Ave number of mins between League goals conceded while on the pitch	63	Clean Sheets In League games when player was on pitch for at least 70 minutes	9

KEY PLAYERS - DEFENDERS

Nathan Doyle

Goals Conceded Number of League goals conceded while the player was on the pitch	29	Clean Sheets In League games when player was on pitch for at least 70 minutes	8
Defensive Rating Ave number of mins between League goals conceded while on the pitch	80	Club Defensive Rating Average number of mins between League goals conceded by the club this season	63

	PLAYER	CON LGE	CLEAN SHEETS	DEF RATE
1	Nathan Doyle	29	8	80 mins
2	David Wetherall	53	9	67 mins
3	Mark Bower	65	9	63 mins
4	Ben Parker	50	6	59 mins

KEY PLAYERS - MIDFIELDERS

Lee Holmes

Goals in the League	0	Contribution to Attacking Power Average number of minutes between League team goals while on pitch	63
Defensive Rating Average number of mins between League goals conceded while on the pitch	66	Scoring Difference Defensive Rating minus Contribution to Attacking Power	3

	PLAYER	LGE GOALS	DEF RATE	POWER	SCORE DIFF
1	Lee Holmes	0	66	63	3 mins
2	Jermaine Johnson	4	69	79	-10 mins
3	Joe Colbeck	0	57	74	-17 mins
4	Marc Bridge-Wilkinson	4	68	88	-20 mins

KEY PLAYERS - GOALSCORERS

Dean Windass

Goals in the League	11	Player Strike Rate Average number of minutes between League goals scored by player	192
Contribution to Attacking Power Average number of minutes between League team goals while on pitch	72	Club Strike Rate Average number of minutes between League goals scored by club	90

	PLAYER	LGE GOALS	POWER	STRIKE RATE
1	Dean Windass	11	72	192 mins
2	William Paynter	3	114	419 mins
3	David Graham	3	85	511 mins
4	Jermaine Johnson	4	79	555 mins

Steve Schumacher

SQUAD APPEARANCES

Match	1 2 3 4 5	6 7 8 9 10	11 12 13 14 15	16 17 18 19 20	21 22 23 24 25	26 27 28 29 30	31 32 33 34 35	36 37 38 39 40	41 42 43 44 45	46 47 48 49 50
Venue	A H H A A	H A A H H	A A H H A	H A H H A	H H A A A	H A H H A	A H A H H	A H H A A	A H H A A	H A H A H
Competition	L L L L W	L L L L L	L L L L L	L L L F L	L F L L F	L L L L L	L L L L L	L L L L L	L L L L L	L L L L L
Result	L W W W L	D L L D W	W D W L D	L L L W L	D D W L L	W D L D L	W D D L D	L L D L L	W L L L D	D W L L D

Goalkeepers

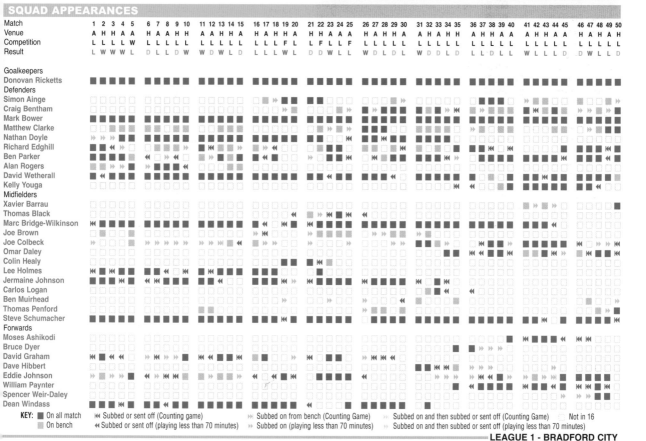

Defenders
Simon Ainge
Craig Bentham
Mark Bower
Matthew Clarke
Nathan Doyle
Richard Edghill
Ben Parker
Alan Rogers
David Wetherall
Kelly Youga

Midfielders
Xavier Barrau
Thomas Black
Marc Bridge-Wilkinson
Joe Brown
Joe Colbeck
Omar Daley
Colin Healy
Lee Holmes
Jermaine Johnson
Carlos Logan
Ben Muirhead
Thomas Penford
Steve Schumacher

Forwards
Moses Ashikodi
Bruce Dyer
David Graham
Dave Hibbert
Eddie Johnson
William Paynter
Spencer Weir-Daley
Dean Windass

KEY: ■ On all match   ◄◄ Subbed or sent off (Counting game)   ►► Subbed on from bench (Counting Game)   ►► Subbed on and then subbed or sent off (Counting Game)   □ Not in 16
■ On bench   ◄◄ Subbed or sent off (playing less than 70 minutes)   ►► Subbed on (playing less than 70 minutes)   ►► Subbed on and then subbed or sent off (playing less than 70 minutes)

LEAGUE 1 - BRADFORD CITY

ROTHERHAM UNITED

Final Position: 23rd

NICKNAME: THE MERRY MILLERS   KEY: ☐ Won ☐ Drawn ☐ Lost   Attendance

#					Score	Scorers	Attendance
1	div2	Brighton	H	L	0-1		4,998
2	div2	Huddersfield	A	L	0-3		10,161
3	div2	Blackpool	A	W	1-0	Hoskins 78	5,677
4	div2	Scunthorpe	H	W	2-1	Bopp 7, Mills 45	4,708
5	ccr1	Oldham	H	W	3-1	Sharps 48, Hoskins 54, Partridge 88	3,065
6	div2	Bradford	A	D	1-1	Hoskins 31	8,669
7	div2	Northampton	H	L	1-2	Hibbert 8	4,971
8	div2	Chesterfield	A	L	1-2	Hoskins 11	4,803
9	div2	Tranmere	H	W	2-1	Williamson 18, Hoskins 38	3,732
10	div2	Doncaster	H	D	0-0		6,348
11	ccr2	Norwich	H	L	2-4	Keane 24, Williamson 49 pen	3,958
12	div2	Leyton Orient	A	W	3-2	Sharps 20, Hoskins 45, Wiseman 82	4,063
13	div2	Oldham	A	L	1-2	Hoskins 68	4,880
14	div2	Millwall	H	L	2-3	Hoskins 30, Sharps 40	4,977
15	div2	Port Vale	A	W	3-1	Cochrane 47, Hibbert 53, Hoskins 85	4,810
16	div2	Brentford	H	W	2-0	Williamson 50, 61 pen	4,722
17	div2	Bournemouth	A	W	3-1	Bopp 18, Hoskins 33, Williamson 36	5,544
18	div2	Crewe	H	W	5-1	Bopp 32, Partridge 41, 74, Williamson 45 pen, Hoskins 65	5,407
19	div2	Carlisle	A	D	1-1	Facey 21	7,247
20	facr1	Peterborough	A	L	0-3		4,281
21	div2	Nottm Forest	H	D	1-1	Hoskins 59	7,809
22	div2	Gillingham	A	L	0-1		5,103
23	div2	Yeovil	H	W	3-2	Facey 11, Skiverton 13 og, Hoskins 45 pen	4,823
24	div2	Bristol City	H	D	1-1	Facey 53	4,862
25	div2	Cheltenham	A	L	0-2		3,525
26	div2	Swansea	A	D	1-1	Bopp 56	12,327
27	div2	Oldham	H	L	2-3	Bopp 54, Hoskins 81 pen	6,512
28	div2	Leyton Orient	H	D	2-2	Hoskins 69, 81	4,715
29	div2	Tranmere	A	L	1-2	Facey 82	6,675
30	div2	Chesterfield	H	L	0-1		5,188
31	div2	Millwall	A	L	0-4		9,534
32	div2	Doncaster	A	L	2-3	Partridge 10, Woods 71	12,126
33	div2	Brighton	A	D	0-0		5,444
34	div2	Scunthorpe	A	L	0-1		5,978
35	div2	Huddersfield	H	L	2-3	O'Grady 31 pen, Facey 71	4,448
36	div2	Northampton	A	L	0-3		4,564
37	div2	Swansea	H	L	1-2	Woods 90	3,697
38	div2	Bradford	H	W	4-1	Facey 4, 72, Woods 66, 88	4,568
39	div2	Port Vale	H	L	1-5	Facey 67	3,854
40	div2	Brentford	A	W	1-0	Facey 13	4,937
41	div2	Crewe	A	L	0-1		5,675
42	div2	Blackpool	H	W	1-0	O'Grady 60	4,025
43	div2	Bournemouth	H	L	0-2		3,657
44	div2	Gillingham	H	W	3-2	Facey 7, O'Grady 75, Newsham 86	3,223
45	div2	Nottm Forest	A	D	1-1	O'Grady 10	27,875
46	div2	Carlisle	H	L	0-1		4,428
47	div2	Yeovil	A	L	0-1		5,878
48	div2	Cheltenham	H	L	2-4	Newsham 14, Henderson 22	3,876
49	div2	Bristol City	A	L	1-3	Newsham 58	19,517

LEAGUE APPEARANCES, BOOKINGS AND CAPS

	AGE (on 01/07/07)	IN NAMED 16	APPEARANCES	COUNTING GAMES	MINUTES ON PITCH	LEAGUE GOALS		
Goalkeepers								
Neil Cutler	30	43	41	40	3643	0	3	0
Gary Montgomery	24	46	6	5	497	0	0	0
Defenders								
Stephen Brogan	19	28	23	19	1784	0	4	0
Craig Fleming	35	17	17	16	1485	0	1	0
Paul Hurst	32	15	12	10	953	0	2	0
Rossi Jarvis	19	10	10	10	884	0	1	0
Liam King	19	13	6	3	384	0	2	0
Pablo Mills	23	36	30	26	2500	1	4	0
Colin Murdock	31	6	4	3	273	0	1	0
Gregor Robertson	23	21	18	15	1486	0	2	0
Ian Sharps	26	39	38	36	3309	3	7	0
Theo Streete	19	7	4	3	316	0	1	0
Che Wilson	28	8	6	4	439	0	0	0
Scott Wiseman	21	27	18	10	988	1	1	0
David Worrell	29	43	41	37	3461	0	3	0
Midfielders								
Eugen Bopp	23	29	29	22	2182	5	2	1
Justin Cochrane	25	34	31	24	2433	1	5	1
Toumani Diagouraga	20	7	7	4	378	0	1	0
Michael Keane	24	23	22	13	1394	0	3	0
Natt Kerr	19	3	3	1	127	0	0	0
Ritchie Partridge	26	36	33	23	2408	3	1	0
Lee Williamson	25	19	19	17	1588	5	3	0
Martin Woods	21	41	36	29	2879	4	4	0
Forwards								
Delroy Facey	27	40	40	33	3167	10	1	0
Ian Henderson	22	18	18	17	1561	2	1	1
Dave Hibbert	21	24	21	10	1066	2	0	0
William Hoskins	20	24	24	22	1982	15	2	1
Marc Newsham	20	32	15	1	516	3	1	0
Chris O'Grady	21	18	13	10	1009	4	0	0
Ryan Taylor	19	15	10	1	232	0	1	0
Jamie Yates	18	8	3	1	155	0	1	0

TEAM OF THE SEASON

G Neil Cutler — CG: 40 DR: 60

D Gregor Robertson — CG: 15 DR: 64
D David Worrell — CG: 37 DR: 64
D Pablo Mills — CG: 26 DR: 62
D Ian Sharps — CG: 36 DR: 55

M Lee Williamson — CG: 17 SD: 24
M Michael Keane — CG: 13 SD: 5
M Eugen Bopp — CG: 22 SD: -18
M Ritchie Partridge — CG: 23 SD: -19

F William Hoskins — CG: 22 SR: 132
F Delroy Facey — CG: 33 SR: 316

MONTHLY POINTS TALLY

Month	Points	%
AUGUST	7	47%
SEPTEMBER	7	33%
OCTOBER	12	100%
NOVEMBER	2	22%
DECEMBER	6	33%
JANUARY	0	0%
FEBRUARY	1	7%
MARCH	9	50%
APRIL	4	27%
MAY	0	0%

LEAGUE GOALS

	PLAYER	MINS	GOALS	S RATE
1	Hoskins	1982	15	132
2	Facey	3167	10	316
3	Williamson	1588	5	317
4	Bopp	2182	5	436
5	O'Grady	1009	4	252
6	Woods	2879	4	719
7	Newsham	516	3	172
8	Partridge	2408	3	802
9	Hibbert	1066	2	533
10	Sharps	3309	2	1654
11	Wiseman	988	1	988
12	Henderson	1561	1	1561
13	Cochrane	2433	1	2433
	Other		1	
	TOTAL		**57**	

TOP POINT EARNERS

	PLAYER	GAMES	AV PTS
1	Lee Williamson	17	1.59
2	Michael Keane	13	1.54
3	William Hoskins	22	1.41
4	Pablo Mills	26	1.35
5	Gregor Robertson	15	1.27
6	David Worrell	37	1.14
7	Neil Cutler	40	1.13
8	Eugen Bopp	22	1.09
9	Justin Cochrane	24	1.08
10	Delroy Facey	33	1.03
	CLUB AVERAGE:		**0.83**

DISCIPLINARY RECORDS

	PLAYER	YELLOW	RED	AVE
1	Justin Cochrane	5	1	405
2	Stephen Brogan	4	0	446
3	Paul Hurst	2	0	476
4	Marc Newsham	1	0	516
5	Ian Henderson	2	1	520
6	Lee Williamson	3	0	529
7	Ian Sharps	7	0	551
8	William Hoskins	2	1	660
9	Michael Keane	3	0	697
10	Eugen Bopp	2	1	727
11	Gregor Robertson	2	0	743
12	Pablo Mills	4	0	833
13	Rossi Jarvis	1	0	884
	Other	14	0	
	TOTAL	**52**	**4**	

KEY GOALKEEPER

Neil Cutler

Goals Conceded in the League	60	Counting Games League games when player was on pitch for at least 70 minutes	40
Defensive Rating Ave number of mins between League goals conceded while on the pitch	60	Clean Sheets In League games when player was on pitch for at least 70 minutes	6

KEY PLAYERS - DEFENDERS

Gregor Robertson

Goals Conceded Number of League goals conceded while the player was on the pitch	23	Clean Sheets In League games when player was on pitch for at least 70 minutes	2
Defensive Rating Ave number of mins between League goals conceded while on the pitch	64	Club Defensive Rating Average number of mins between League goals conceded by the club this season	57

	PLAYER	CON LGE	CLEAN SHEETS	DEF RATE
1	Gregor Robertson	23	2	64 mins
2	David Worrell	54	6	64 mins
3	Pablo Mills	40	3	62 mins
4	Ian Sharps	60	6	55 mins

KEY PLAYERS - MIDFIELDERS

Lee Williamson

Goals in the League	5	Contribution to Attacking Power Average number of minutes between League team goals while on pitch	51
Defensive Rating Average number of mins between League goals conceded while on the pitch	75	Scoring Difference Defensive Rating minus Contribution to Attacking Power	24

	PLAYER	LGE GOALS	DEF RATE	POWER	SCORE DIFF
1	Lee Williamson	5	75	51	24 mins
2	Michael Keane	0	63	58	5 mins
3	Eugen Bopp	5	54	72	-18 mins
4	Ritchie Partridge	3	56	75	-19 mins

KEY PLAYERS - GOALSCORERS

William Hoskins

Goals in the League	15	Player Strike Rate Average number of minutes between League goals scored by player	132
Contribution to Attacking Power Average number of minutes between League team goals while on pitch	52	Club Strike Rate Average number of minutes between League goals scored by club	74

	PLAYER	LGE GOALS	POWER	STRIKE RATE
1	William Hoskins	15	52	132 mins
2	Delroy Facey	10	77	316 mins
3	Lee Williamson	5	51	317 mins
4	Eugen Bopp	5	72	436 mins

Delroy Facey

SQUAD APPEARANCES

Match	1 2 3 4 5	6 7 8 9 10	11 12 13 14 15	16 17 18 19 20	21 22 23 24 25	26 27 28 29 30	31 32 33 34 35	36 37 38 39 40	41 42 43 44 45	46 47 48 49
Venue	H A A H H	A H A H H	H A A H A	H A H A A	H A H H A	A H H A H	A A A A H	A H H H A	A H H H A	H A H A
Competition	L L L L W	L L L L L	W L L L L	L L L L F	L L L L L	L L L L L	L L L L L	L L L L L	L L L L L	L L L L
Result	L L W W W	D L L W D	L W L L W	W W W D L	D L W D L	D L D L L	L L D L L	L L W L W	L W L W D	L L L L

LEAGUE 1 - ROTHERHAM UNITED

BRENTFORD

Final Position: **24th**

NICKNAME: THE BEES   KEY: ☐ Won ☐ Drawn ☐ Lost   Attendance

#	Comp	Opponent	H/A	Result	Score	Scorers	Attendance
1	div2	Blackpool	H	W	1-0	Skulason 74	6,048
2	div2	Northampton	A	W	1-0	Moore 71	5,707
3	div2	Brighton	A	D	2-2	O'Connor 38, Moore 90	6,745
4	div2	Huddersfield	H	D	2-2	Kuffour 70, 89	5,709
5	ccr1	Swindon	A	W	4-3*	O'Connor 9, Kuffour 25 (*on penalties)	5,582
6	div2	Scunthorpe	A	D	1-1	Kuffour 39	3,942
7	div2	Bradford	H	W	2-1	O'Connor 74, Kuffour 81	5,471
8	div2	Leyton Orient	A	D	1-1	Tillen 88	5,420
9	div2	Swansea	H	L	0-2		5,392
10	div2	Bournemouth	H	D	0-0		6,272
11	ccr2	Luton	H	L	0-3		3,005
12	div2	Chesterfield	A	L	1-3	Griffiths 45	3,877
13	div2	Millwall	A	D	1-1	Willock 13	7,618
14	div2	Yeovil	H	L	1-2	Kuffour 80	5,770
15	div2	Bristol City	H	D	1-1	O'Connor 58 pen	6,740
16	div2	Rotherham	A	L	0-2		4,722
17	div2	Gillingham	H	D	2-2	Heywood 36, Willock 45	5,759
18	div2	Oldham	A	L	0-3		4,708
19	div2	Nottm Forest	A	L	0-2		18,003
20	facr1	Doncaster	H	L	0-1		3,607
21	div2	Crewe	H	L	0-4		4,771
22	div2	Cheltenham	H	L	0-2		3,646
23	div2	Doncaster	H	L	0-4		4,296
24	div2	Tranmere	H	D	1-1	Ide 38	4,878
25	div2	Port Vale	A	L	0-1		4,166
26	div2	Carlisle	A	L	0-2		6,805
27	div2	Millwall	H	L	1-4	O'Connor 78 pen	6,925
28	div2	Chesterfield	H	W	2-1	Kuffour 2, 67	4,540
29	div2	Swansea	A	L	0-2		12,554
30	div2	Bournemouth	A	L	0-2		5,782
31	div2	Leyton Orient	H	D	2-2	Ide 66, 90	6,765
32	div2	Yeovil	A	L	0-1		5,373
33	div2	Carlisle	H	D	0-0		5,381
34	div2	Blackpool	A	W	3-1	Frampton 13, Kuffour 29, 30	6,086
35	div2	Brighton	H	W	1-0	Kuffour 31	7,023
36	div2	Huddersfield	A	W	2-0	Ide 49, Kuffour 58	10,520
37	div2	Northampton	H	L	0-1		5,164
38	div2	Bradford	A	D	1-1	O'Connor 48 pen	7,627
39	div2	Scunthorpe	H	L	0-1		5,645
40	div2	Bristol City	A	L	0-1		11,826
41	div2	Rotherham	H	L	0-1		4,937
42	div2	Oldham	H	D	2-2	Richards 59, J.Keith 85	4,720
43	div2	Gillingham	A	L	1-2	Kuffour 7	6,113
44	div2	Cheltenham	H	L	0-2		4,831
45	div2	Crewe	A	L	1-3	O'Connor 69 pen	4,667
46	div2	Nottm Forest	H	L	2-4	Pinault 16, Ide 47	6,637
47	div2	Doncaster	A	L	0-3		8,713
48	div2	Port Vale	H	W	4-3	Ide 2, 39, J.Keith 68 pen, Charles 89	5,125
49	div2	Tranmere	A	L	1-3	Willock 35	6,529

LEAGUE APPEARANCES, BOOKINGS AND CAPS

	AGE (on 01/07/07)	IN NAMED 16	APPEARANCES	COUNTING GAMES	MINUTES ON PITCH	LEAGUE GOALS		
Goalkeepers								
Nathan Abbey	28	20	16	16	1440	0	1	0
Clark Masters	20	30	11	10	922	0	0	1
Stuart Nelson	25	25	19	19	1710	0	1	0
Defenders								
Andrew Frampton	27	32	32	32	2880	1	4	0
Adam Griffiths	27	40	37	30	2857	1	11	0
Matthew Heywood	27	29	28	26	2325	1	4	0
John Mousinho	21	39	34	28	2633	0	5	0
Kevin O'Connor	25	39	39	37	3416	7	2	0
Karleigh Osborne	19	29	21	13	1556	0	7	1
David Partridge	28	3	3	2	185	0	1	1
Garry Richards	21	10	10	9	875	1	2	0
Sam Tillen	22	37	33	20	2201	1	1	0
Che Wilson	28	3	3	3	269	0	1	1
Midfielders								
Paul Brooker	31	39	33	20	2249	0	4	0
Karle Carder-Andrews	18	11	5	1	141	0	1	0
Darius Charles	19	25	18	8	962	1	2	0
Simon Cox	20	13	13	10	951	0	4	0
Lewis Dark	18	3	3	2	172	0	0	0
Charlie Ide	19	30	26	20	1918	7	3	1
Joe Keith	28	18	18	16	1471	2	0	0
Michael Leary	24	17	17	15	1458	0	10	0
Thomas Pinault	25	40	26	23	2138	1	7	0
Olafur Ingi Skulason	24	13	10	8	843	1	2	0
Forwards								
Jonathan Osei Kuffour	25	39	39	36	3324	13	3	1
Ross Montague	18	4	4	0	65	0	1	0
Chris Moore	27	17	16	7	832	2	4	1
Folawiyo Onibuje	22	2	2	0	61	0	0	0
Lloyd Owusu	30	7	7	4	425	0	1	0
Ryan Peters	19	16	13	0	236	0	1	0
Alex Rhodes	25	15	14	4	672	0	1	0
Neil Shipperley	32	11	11	10	929	0	1	0
Scott Taylor	31	6	6	2	283	0	1	0
Gavin Tomlin	23	12	12	5	651	0	0	0
Clyde Wijnhard	33	10	9	5	604	0	0	0
Callum Willock	25	34	28	15	1598	3	1	0

TEAM OF THE SEASON

D Karleigh Osborne — CG: 13 DR: 55
M Joe Keith — CG: 16 SD: -23
D Andrew Frampton — CG: 32 DR: 53
M Paul Brooker — CG: 20 SD: -41
F Jonathan O Kuffour — CG: 36 SR: 277
G Nathan Abbey — CG: 16 DR: 72
D Sam Tillen — CG: 20 DR: 53
M Charlie Ide — CG: 20 SD: -42
F Callum Willock — CG: 15 SR: 532
D Matthew Heywood — CG: 26 DR: 52
M Thomas Pinault — CG: 23 SD: -46

MONTHLY POINTS TALLY

Month	Points	%
AUGUST		9 60%
SEPTEMBER		6 29%
OCTOBER		2 17%
NOVEMBER		0 0%
DECEMBER		4 22%
JANUARY		2 13%
FEBRUARY		10 67%
MARCH		1 7%
APRIL		3 20%
MAY		0 0%

LEAGUE GOALS

	PLAYER	MINS	GOALS	S RATE
1	Kuffour	3324	12	277
2	Ide	1918	7	274
3	O'Connor	3416	6	569
4	Willock	1598	3	532
5	Moore	832	2	416
6	Keith, J	1471	2	735
7	Skulason	843	1	843
8	Richards	875	1	875
9	Charles	962	1	962
10	Pinault	2138	1	2138
11	Tillen	2201	1	2201
12	Heywood	2325	1	2325
13	Griffiths	2857	1	2857
	Other		1	
	TOTAL		**40**	

TOP POINT EARNERS

	PLAYER	GAMES	AV PTS
1	Sam Tillen	20	1.15
2	Nathan Abbey	16	1.13
3	Joe Keith	16	1.00
4	Karleigh Osborne	14	1.00
5	Thomas Pinault	23	0.91
6	Jonathan Osei Kuffour	36	0.89
7	Matthew Heywood	26	0.81
8	Charlie Ide	20	0.80
9	Callum Willock	15	0.79
10	Andrew Frampton	32	0.78
	CLUB AVERAGE:		**0.80**

DISCIPLINARY RECORDS

	PLAYER	YELLOW	RED	AVE
1	Michael Leary	10	0	145
2	Karleigh Osborne	7	1	259
3	Chris Moore	4	1	277
4	Adam Griffiths	11	0	317
5	Simon Cox	4	0	317
6	Thomas Pinault	7	0	356
7	Olafur Ingi Skulason	2	0	421
8	Garry Richards	2	0	437
9	Darius Charles	2	0	481
10	Matthew Heywood	4	0	581
11	Charlie Ide	3	1	639
12	John Mousinho	5	0	658
13	Andrew Frampton	4	0	720
	Other	14	2	
	TOTAL	**79**	**5**	

KEY GOALKEEPER

Nathan Abbey

Goals Conceded in the League	20	Counting Games League games when player was on pitch for at least 70 minutes	16
Defensive Rating Ave number of mins between League goals conceded while on the pitch	72	Clean Sheets In League games when player was on pitch for at least 70 minutes	3

KEY PLAYERS - DEFENDERS

Karleigh Osborne

Goals Conceded Number of League goals conceded while the player was on the pitch	28	Clean Sheets In League games when player was on pitch for at least 70 minutes	2
Defensive Rating Ave number of mins between League goals conceded while on the pitch	55	Club Defensive Rating Average number of mins between League goals conceded by the club this season	52

	PLAYER	CON LGE	CLEAN SHEETS	DEF RATE
1	Karleigh Osborne	28	2	55 mins
2	Andrew Frampton	54	5	53 mins
3	Sam Tillen	41	4	53 mins
4	Matthew Heywood	44	3	52 mins

KEY PLAYERS - MIDFIELDERS

Joe Keith

Goals in the League	2	Contribution to Attacking Power Average number of minutes between League team goals while on pitch	81
Defensive Rating Average number of mins between League goals conceded while on the pitch	58	Scoring Difference Defensive Rating minus Contribution to Attacking Power	-23

	PLAYER	LGE GOALS	DEF RATE	POWER	SCORE DIFF
1	Joe Keith	2	58	81	-23 mins
2	Paul Brooker	0	48	89	-41 mins
3	Charlie Ide	7	58	100	-42 mins
4	Thomas Pinault	1	46	92	-46 mins

KEY PLAYERS - GOALSCORERS

Charlie Ide

Goals in the League	7	Player Strike Rate Average number of minutes between League goals scored by player	274
Contribution to Attacking Power Average number of minutes between League team goals while on pitch	100	Club Strike Rate Average number of minutes between League goals scored by club	103

	PLAYER	LGE GOALS	POWER	STRIKE RATE
1	Charlie Ide	7	100	274 mins
2	Jonathan Osei Kuffour	12	107	277 mins
3	Callum Willock	3	94	532 mins
4	Joe Keith	2	81	735 mins

Jonathan Osei Kuffour

SQUAD APPEARANCES

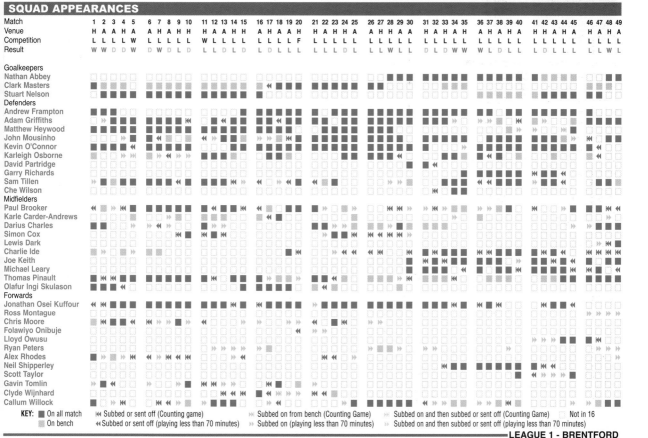

Match	1 2 3 4 5	6 7 8 9 10	11 12 13 14 15	16 17 18 19 20	21 22 23 24 25	26 27 28 29 30	31 32 33 34 35	36 37 38 39 40	41 42 43 44 45	46 47 48 49
Venue	H A A H A	A H A H H	H A A H H	A H A A H	A H A A	A H H A A	H A H A H	A H A H A	H H A H A	H A H A
Competition	L L L L W	L L L L L	W L L L L	L L L L F	L L L L L	L L L L L	L L L L L	L L L L L	L L L L L	L L L L
Result	W W D D W	D W D L D	L L D L D	L D L L L	L L L D L	L L W L L	D L D W W	W L D L L	L D L L L	L L W L

Goalkeepers
Nathan Abbey
Clark Masters
Stuart Nelson

Defenders
Andrew Frampton
Adam Griffiths
Matthew Heywood
John Mousinho
Kevin O'Connor
Karleigh Osborne
David Partridge
Garry Richards
Sam Tillen
Che Wilson

Midfielders
Paul Brooker
Karle Carder-Andrews
Darius Charles
Simon Cox
Lewis Dark
Charlie Ide
Joe Keith
Michael Leary
Thomas Pinault
Olafur Ingi Skulason

Forwards
Jonathan Osei Kuffour
Ross Montague
Chris Moore
Folawiyo Onibuje
Lloyd Owusu
Ryan Peters
Alex Rhodes
Neil Shipperley
Scott Taylor
Gavin Tomlin
Clyde Wijnhard
Callum Willock

KEY: ■ On all match ◄◄ Subbed or sent off (Counting game) ►► Subbed on from bench (Counting Game) ►► Subbed on and then subbed or sent off (Counting Game) □ Not in 16
■ On bench ◄◄ Subbed or sent off (playing less than 70 minutes) ►► Subbed on (playing less than 70 minutes) ►► Subbed on and then subbed or sent off (playing less than 70 minutes)

LEAGUE 1 - BRENTFORD

LEAGUE TWO ROUND-UP

FINAL LEAGUE TABLE

	P	HOME W	D	L	F	A	AWAY W	D	L	F	A	TOTAL F	A	DIF	PTS
Walsall	46	16	4	3	39	13	9	10	4	27	21	66	34	32	89
Hartlepool	46	14	5	4	34	17	12	5	6	31	23	65	40	25	88
Swindon	46	15	4	4	34	17	10	6	7	24	21	58	38	20	85
M K Dons	46	14	4	5	41	26	11	5	7	35	32	76	58	18	84
Lincoln City	46	12	4	7	36	28	9	7	7	34	31	70	59	11	74
Bristol Rovers	46	13	5	5	27	14	7	7	9	22	28	49	42	7	72
Shrewsbury	46	11	7	5	38	23	7	10	6	30	23	68	46	22	71
Stockport	46	14	4	5	41	25	7	4	12	24	29	65	54	11	71
Rochdale	46	9	6	8	33	24	9	6	8	37	30	70	50	20	66
Peterborough	46	10	6	7	48	36	8	5	10	22	25	70	61	9	65
Darlington	46	10	6	7	28	30	7	8	8	24	26	52	56	-4	65
Wycombe	46	8	11	4	23	14	8	3	12	29	33	52	47	5	62
Notts County	46	8	6	9	29	25	8	8	7	26	28	55	53	2	62
Barnet	46	12	5	6	35	30	4	6	13	20	40	55	70	-15	59
Grimsby	46	11	4	8	33	32	6	4	13	24	41	57	73	-16	59
Hereford	46	9	7	7	23	17	5	6	12	22	36	45	53	-8	55
Mansfield	46	10	4	9	38	31	4	8	11	20	32	58	63	-5	54
Chester	46	7	9	7	23	23	6	5	12	17	25	40	48	-8	53
Wrexham	46	8	8	7	23	21	5	4	14	20	44	43	65	-22	51
Acc Stanley	46	10	6	7	42	33	3	5	15	28	48	70	81	-11	50
Bury	46	4	7	12	22	35	9	4	10	24	26	46	61	-15	50
Macclesfield	46	8	7	8	36	34	4	5	14	19	43	55	77	-22	48
Boston Utd*	46	9	5	9	29	32	3	5	15	22	48	51	80	-29	36
Torquay	46	5	8	10	19	22	2	6	15	17	41	36	63	-27	35

CLUB STRIKE FORCE

Izale McLeod scores for MK Dons

	CLUB	GOALS	CSR
1	MK Dons	76	54
2	Lincoln	70	59
3	Peterborough	70	59
4	Rochdale	70	59
5	Accrington	70	59
6	Shrewsbury	68	60
7	Walsall	66	62
8	Stockport	65	63
9	Hartlepool	65	63
10	Swindon	58	71
11	Mansfield	58	71
12	Grimsby	57	72
13	Barnet	55	75
14	Macclesfield	55	75
15	Notts County	55	75
16	Darlington	52	79
17	Wycombe	52	79
18	Boston	51	81
19	Bristol Rovers	49	84
20	Bury	46	90
21	Hereford	45	92
22	Wrexham	43	96
23	Chester	40	103
24	Torquay	36	115

1 MK Dons

Goals scored in the League	76

Club Strike Rate (CSR) Average number of minutes between League goals scored by club	54

CLUB DISCIPLINARY RECORDS

Accrington's Robbie Williams: 10 cards

	CLUB	Y	R	TOTAL	AVE
1	Accrington	101	9	110	37
2	Chester	92	7	99	41
3	Swindon	89	3	92	45
4	Macclesfield	86	6	92	45
5	Boston	83	8	91	45
6	MK Dons	85	5	90	46
7	Wycombe	81	7	88	47
8	Barnet	81	7	88	47
9	Wrexham	80	7	87	47
10	Notts County	80	4	84	49
11	Torquay	71	4	75	55
12	Darlington	61	6	67	61
13	Shrewsbury	63	1	64	64
14	Rochdale	61	2	63	65
15	Bury	56	5	61	67
16	Stockport	57	4	61	67
17	Grimsby	56	5	61	67
18	Peterborough	50	4	54	76
19	Walsall	52	2	54	76
20	Hartlepool	48	5	53	78
21	Bury	50	2	52	79
22	Mansfield	49	2	51	81
23	Bristol Rovers	43	5	48	86
24	Hereford	33	4	37	111

1 Accrington

League Yellow	101

League Red	9

League Total	110

Cards Average in League Average number of minutes between a card being shown of either colour	37

CLUB DEFENCES

	CLUB	LGE	CS	CDR
1	Walsall	34	21	121
2	Swindon	38	15	108
3	Hartlepool	40	22	103
4	Bristol Rovers	42	22	98
5	Shrewsbury	46	14	90
6	Wycombe	47	19	88
7	Chester	48	13	86
8	Rochdale	50	18	82
9	Notts County	53	14	78
10	Hereford	53	16	78
11	Stockport	54	19	76
12	Darlington	56	14	73
13	MK Dons	58	13	71
14	Lincoln	59	14	70
15	Peterborough	61	16	67
16	Bury	61	10	67
17	Mansfield	63	7	65
18	Torquay	63	9	65
19	Wrexham	65	12	63
20	Barnet	70	9	59
21	Grimsby	73	10	56
22	Macclesfield	77	9	53
23	Boston	80	6	51
24	Accrington	81	4	51

Walsall defender Scott Dann in action

1 Walsall

Goals conceded in the League	34

Clean Sheets (CS) Number of league games where no goals were conceded	21

Club Defensive Rate (CDR) Average number of minutes between League goals conceded by club	121

STADIUM CAPACITY AND HOME CROWDS

	TEAM	CAPACITY		AVE	HIGH	LOW
1	MK Dons	8630		69.9	8102	4564
2	Hartlepool	7629		66.6	7629	3659
3	Shrewsbury	8000		59.1	7782	3369
4	Lincoln	10127		51.1	6820	3913
5	Stockport	10817		51.1	7860	4089
6	Swindon	14540		51.0	14731	5462
7	Walsall	11200		50.4	8345	4070
8	Wycombe	10000		49.8	7150	3885
9	Bristol Rovers	11626		47.1	9902	4327
10	Accrington	5057		44.6	4004	1234
11	Grimsby	10033		43.5	6137	3012
12	Torquay	6104		43.1	4047	1588
13	Barnet	5560		40.9	2958	1461
14	Chester	6000		39.9	3779	1527
15	Macclesfield	6208		39.1	4451	1472
16	Wrexham	15500		32.4	12374	3401
17	Boston	6643		32.3	4327	1571
18	Mansfield	9954		31.9	6182	2023
19	Peterborough	15460		30.1	8405	3193
20	Rochdale	10249		28.2	5846	1982
21	Notts County	20300		24.5	10034	3010
22	Hereford	13777		24.1	5201	2176
23	Bury	11699		22.1	5075	1775
24	Darlington	25000		15.2	9987	2321

Key: Average. The percentage of each stadium filled in League games over the season (AVE), the stadium capacity and the highest and lowest crowds recorded.

AWAY ATTENDANCE

	TEAM		AVE	HIGH	LOW
1	Walsall		44.3	14731	2007
2	Lincoln		43.4	8405	1930
3	Swindon		42.9	9902	2101
4	Mansfield		40.9	10472	1234
5	Notts County		39.8	6805	1702
6	Hartlepool		39.4	9987	1787
7	Bury		39.3	7246	1642
8	Stockport		38.5	6868	1796
9	Bristol Rovers		38.4	10010	1302
10	Wrexham		38.0	7057	1588
11	Accrington		38	8102	1564
12	Peterborough		37.5	7329	1808
13	Torquay		37.3	7389	1836
14	MK Dons		37.3	8304	1384
15	Grimsby		36.8	7782	1588
16	Darlington		36.7	7458	1870
17	Rochdale		36.6	6771	1472
18	Boston		36.6	12374	1461
19	Shrewsbury		36.5	8405	1571
20	Chester		36.3	6801	1752
21	Wycombe		35.8	8878	1574
22	Macclesfield		35.8	6575	1816
23	Hereford		35.5	6910	1731
24	Barnet		31.4	7475	1591

Key: Average. How close each club has come to filling grounds in its away league matches (AVE) and the highest and lowest crowds recorded.

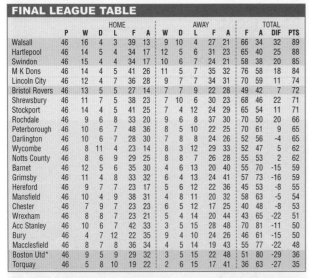

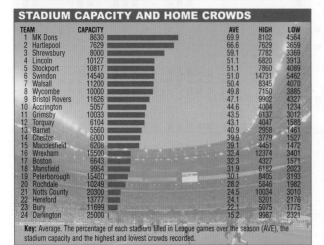

CHART-TOPPING MIDFIELDERS

1 Monkhouse - Hartlepool	
Goals scored in the League	7
Defensive Rating Av number of mins between League goals conceded while on the pitch	150
Contribution to Attacking Power Average number of minutes between League team goals while on pitch	57
Scoring Difference Defensive Rating minus Contribution to Attacking Power	93

	PLAYER	CLUB	GOALS	DEF RATE	POWER	S DIFF
1	Andy Monkhouse	Hartlepool	7	150	57	93
2	Dean Keates	Walsall	12	139	61	78
3	Mark Wright	Walsall	2	129	55	74
4	Craig Pead	Walsall	0	118	55	63
5	Willie Boland	Hartlepool	0	131	74	57
6	Richie Humphreys	Hartlepool	3	122	70	52
7	Michael Pook	Swindon	2	122	71	51
8	Kris Taylor	Walsall	1	108	59	49
9	Gary Liddle	Hartlepool	3	103	59	44
10	David Poole	Stockport	4	100	59	41
11	Rickie Lambert	Bristol Rovers	8	116	79	37
12	Antony Sweeney	Hartlepool	4	96	60	36
13	Gareth Edds	MK Dons	2	87	54	33
14	John Doolan	Rochdale	3	89	57	32
15	Curtis Weston	Swindon	0	94	62	32

CHART-TOPPING GOALSCORERS

1 McLeod - MK Dons	
Goals scored in the League	21
Contribution to Attacking Power (AP) Average number of minutes between League team goals while on pitch	47
Club Strike Rate (CSR) Average minutes between League goals scored by club	55
Player Strike Rate Average number of minutes between League goals scored by player	130

	PLAYER	CLUB	GOALS: LGE	POWER	CSR	S RATE
1	Izale McLeod	MK Dons	21	47	55	130
2	Jermaine Easter	Wycombe	17	79	79	150
3	Glenn Murray	Rochdale	16	48	61	158
4	Anthony Elding	Stockport	11	58	65	159
5	Chris Dagnall	Rochdale	17	63	61	164
6	Richard Barker	Hartlepool	9	53	63	178
7	Richard Barker	Mansfield	12	73	73	184
8	Clive Platt	MK Dons	18	58	55	187
9	Jamie Forrester	Lincoln	18	55	59	189
10	Jamie Ward	Torquay	9	105	115	199
11	Jason Lee	Notts County	15	66	75	217
12	Glynn Hurst	Bury	11	72	93	231
13	Mark Stallard	Lincoln	15	60	59	237
14	Jonathan Walters	Chester	9	77	108	241
15	Andrew Bishop	Bury	15	86	93	248

CHART-TOPPING DEFENDERS

1 Anthony - Bristol Rovers	
Goals Conceded in the League The number of League goals conceded while he was on the pitch	11
Clean Sheets In games when he played at least 70 mins	12
Club Defensive Rating Average mins between League goals conceded by the club this season	100
Defensive Rating Average number of minutes between League goals conceded while on pitch	166

	PLAYER	CLUB	CON: LGE	CS	CDR	DEF RATE
1	Byron Anthony	Bristol Rovers	11	12	100	166
2	Michael Barron	Hartlepool	16	14	103	140
3	Anthony Gerrard	Walsall	20	14	121	136
4	Sofiane Zaaboub	Swindon	15	8	111	129
5	Ian Roper	Walsall	17	13	121	127
6	Andrew Nicholas	Swindon	22	11	111	121
7	Michael Dobson	Walsall	29	18	121	119
8	Ben Clark	Hartlepool	30	20	103	118
9	Rory McArdle	Rochdale	19	12	86	118
10	Daniel Fox	Walsall	33	20	121	118
11	Robert Clare	Stockport	21	16	78	116
12	Scott Dann	Walsall	20	9	121	114
13	Jamie Vincent	Swindon	27	12	111	112
14	Mike Williamson	Wycombe	26	16	88	112
15	Ryan Green	Bristol Rovers	23	15	100	111

CHART-TOPPING GOALKEEPERS

1 Ince - Walsall	
Counting Games Games in which he played at least 70 minutes	45
Goals Conceded in the League The number of League goals conceded while he was on the pitch	34
Clean Sheets In games when he played at least 70 mins	20
Defensive Rating Average number of minutes between League goals conceded while on pitch	119

	PLAYER	CLUB	CG	CONC	CS	DEF RATE
1	Clayton Ince	Walsall	45	34	20	119
2	Phil Smith	Swindon	31	26	10	107
3	D Konstantopoulos	Hartlepool	46	40	22	103
4	Steve Phillips	Bristol Rovers	44	41	21	96
5	Chris MacKenzie	Shrewsbury	20	19	8	94
6	Ricardo Batista	Wycombe	27	27	10	92
7	Wayne Brown	Hereford	39	39	16	89
8	John Danby	Chester	46	48	13	86
9	Scott Shearer	Shrewsbury	20	21	5	85
10	Mathew Gilks	Rochdale	46	50	18	82
11	Jamie Young	Wycombe	18	20	8	81
12	Kevin Pilkington	Notts County	39	44	12	79
13	Sam Russell	Darlington	31	38	11	73
14	Lee Harper	MK Dons	22	27	7	73
15	Alan Marriott	Lincoln	46	59	14	70

PLAYER DISCIPLINARY RECORD

Wycombe's Tommy Doherty in action

	PLAYER		LY	LR	TOT	AVE
1	Doherty	Wycombe	10	2	12	147
2	Welch	Accrington	13	1	14	176
3	Broughton	Boston	10	2	12	186
4	Harris	Accrington	11	1	12	189
5	Hadfield	Macclesfield	14	1	15	190
6	Lee	Notts County	17	0	17	192
7	Grant	Wycombe	14	2	16	192
8	Daly	Hartlepool	5	1	6	195
9	Dickinson	Stockport	5	1	6	195
10	Albrighton	Boston	5	0	5	203
11	Valentine	Wrexham	12	1	13	213
12	Timlin	Swindon	7	1	8	214
13	Hatch	Barnet	7	1	8	215
14	Hessenthaler	Barnet	8	0	8	217
15	Ravenhill	Grimsby	6	0	6	220

1. Tommy Doherty - Wycombe	
Cards Average mins between cards	147
League Yellow	10
League Red	2
TOTAL	12

TEAM OF THE SEASON

D Zaaboub (Swindon) CG: 27 DR: 129

M Monkhouse (Hartlepool) CG: 26 SD: +93

G Ince (Walsall) CG: 45 DR: 119

D Gerrard (Walsall) CG: 35 DR: 136

M Pook (Swindon) CG: 38 SD: +51

F McLeod (MK Dons) CG: 34 SR: 130

D Barron (Hartlepool) CG: 29 DR: 140

M Poole (Stockport) CG: 31 SD: +41

F Easter (Wycombe) CG: 38 SR: 150

D Anthony (Bristol Rovers) CG: 23 DR: 166

M Keates (Walsall) CG: 39 SD: +78

WALSALL

Final Position: **1st**

NICKNAME: THE SADDLERS KEY: ☐Won ☐Drawn ☐Lost Attendance

						Attendance
1	div3	Rochdale	A W	1-0	Butler 48	3,218
2	div3	Stockport	H W	2-0	Butler 16, Roper 48	4,877
3	div3	Hartlepool	H W	2-0	Keates 18, 29	5,637
4	div3	Lincoln	A D	2-2	K.Taylor 79, Fangueiro 90	4,565
5	ccr1	Plymouth	A W	1-0	Dann 85	6,407
6	div3	Darlington	H W	1-0	Butler 45	4,651
7	div3	Barnet	A D	1-1	Keates 60	2,356
8	div3	Grimsby	A L	1-2	Butler 10	3,669
9	div3	Peterborough	H W	5-0	Fox 7, Dobson 16, 26, Butler 75, 79	4,070
10	div3	Macclesfield	H W	2-0	Sam 37, Dann 88	4,657
11	ccr2	Bolton	H L	1-3	Butler 74	6,243
12	div3	Bristol Rovers	A W	2-1	Dann 8, Fox 28 pen	5,260
13	div3	Shrewsbury	A D	1-1	Bedeau 5	6,593
14	div3	Mansfield	H W	4-0	Wright 51, Keates 62, 76, Gerrard 90	5,429
15	div3	Chester	A D	0-0		3,241
16	div3	Wycombe	H W	2-0	Sam 33, Kinsella 60	6,745
17	div3	Accrington	A W	2-1	Sam 40, Wright 85	3,142
18	div3	MK Dons	H D	0-0		6,275
19	div3	Torquay	H W	1-0	Roper 53	5,806
20	facr1	Macclesfield	A D	0-0		2,018
21	div3	Hereford	A W	1-0	Westwood 63	4,462
22	facr1r	Macclesfield	H L	0-1		3,114
23	div3	Notts County	H W	2-1	Wright 27, Keates 45	5,402
24	div3	Bury	A W	2-1	Roper 75, Sam 85	2,148
25	div3	Swindon	H L	0-2		6,812
26	div3	Wrexham	A D	1-1	Sam 27	4,270
27	div3	Boston	A D	1-1	T.Wright 72	2,083
28	div3	Shrewsbury	H W	1-0	Westwood 50	8,345
29	div3	Bristol Rovers	H D	2-2	Sam 46, Dann 88	5,941
30	div3	Peterborough	A W	2-0	Fox 14, Westwood 23	4,405
31	div3	Grimsby	H W	2-0	Butler 28, 79	4,889
32	div3	Mansfield	A L	1-2	Roper 9	3,737
33	div3	Boston	H D	1-1	Butler 19	5,058
34	div3	Macclesfield	A W	2-0	Keates 2 pen, 90	2,007
35	div3	Rochdale	H D	1-1	Dann 90	5,046
36	div3	Hartlepool	A L	1-3	Butler 3	5,847
37	div3	Lincoln	H L	1-2	Sam 16	4,885
38	div3	Stockport	A L	0-1		6,005
39	div3	Barnet	H W	4-1	Hendon 33 og, Dobson 54, Harper 65, 77	4,635
40	div3	Darlington	A D	0-0		3,745
41	div3	Chester	H W	1-0	Keates 67 pen	5,282
42	div3	Wycombe	A D	0-0		5,625
43	div3	MK Dons	A D	1-1	Wrack 77	8,044
44	div3	Accrington	H W	3-2	Harper 21, Keates 75 pen, Butler 85	6,062
45	div3	Torquay	A W	2-1	Benjamin 10, Keates 16 pen	4,047
46	div3	Hereford	H W	1-0		5,658
47	div3	Notts County	A W	2-1	Harper 17, Benjamin 84	7,080
48	div3	Bury	H L	0-1		6,568
49	div3	Wrexham	H W	1-0	Demontagnac 61	7,057
50	div3	Swindon	A D	1-1	Keates 90	14,731

KEY PLAYER APPEARANCES

	PLAYER	POS	AGE	APP	MINS ON	GOALS	CARDS(Y/R)	
1	Clayton Ince	GK	34	45	4050	0	0	0
2	Daniel Fox	DEF	21	44	3898	3	10	0
3	Martin Butler	ATT	32	44	3863	11	6	0
4	Michael Dobson	DEF	26	39	3452	3	0	0
5	Chris Westwood	DEF	30	40	3352	3	3	0
6	Dean Keates	MID	29	39	3200	12	4	0
7	Craig Pead	MID	25	41	2847	0	3	1
8	Anthony Gerrard	DEF	20	35	2733	1	5	1
9	Mark Wright	MID	25	37	2590	2	1	0
10	Kris Taylor	MID	23	35	2506	1	2	0
11	Scott Dann	DEF	20	30	2293	4	3	0
12	Hector Sam	ATT	29	42	2288	7	2	0
13	Ian Roper	DEF	30	27	2160	4	4	0
14	Kevin Harper	MID	31	10	832	4	0	0
15	Darren Wrack	MID	31	18	733	1	1	0
16	Mark Kinsella	MID	34	11	706	1	1	0
17	Anthony Bedeau	MID	28	18	675	1	3	0
18	Trevor Benjamin	ATT	28	8	608	2	0	0

KEY PLAYERS - GOALSCORERS

Dean Keates			Player Strike Rate		
Goals in the League	12		Average number of minutes between League goals scored by player		266
Contribution to Attacking Power			Club Strike Rate		
Average number of minutes between League team goals while on pitch	61		Average number of minutes between League goals scored by club		63

	PLAYER	GOALS LGE	POWER	STRIKE RATE
1	Dean Keates	12	61	266 mins
2	Hector Sam	7	61	326 mins
3	Martin Butler	11	63	351 mins
4	Mark Wright	2	55	1295 mins

KEY PLAYERS - MIDFIELDERS

Dean Keates			Contribution to Attacking Power		
Goals in the League	12		Average number of minutes between League team goals while on pitch		61
Defensive Rating			Scoring Difference		
Average number of mins between League goals conceded while on the pitch	139		Defensive Rating minus Contribution to Attacking Power		78

	PLAYER	GOALS LGE	DEF RATE	POWER	SCORE DIFF
1	Dean Keates	12	139	61	78 mins
2	Mark Wright	2	129	55	74 mins
3	Craig Pead	0	118	55	63 mins
4	Kris Taylor	1	108	59	49 mins

KEY PLAYERS - DEFENDERS

Anthony Gerrard			Clean Sheets		
Goals Conceded when he was on pitch	20		In games when he played at least 70 minutes		14
Defensive Rating			Club Defensive Rating		
Ave number of mins between League goals conceded while on the pitch	136		Average number of mins between League goals conceded by the club this season.		121

	PLAYER	CON LGE	CLEAN SHEETS	DEF RATE
1	Anthony Gerrard	20	14	136 mins
2	Ian Roper	17	13	127 mins
3	Michael Dobson	29	18	119 mins
4	Daniel Fox	33	20	118 mins

TEAM OF THE SEASON

D Anthony Gerrard CG: 29 DR: 136
M Dean Keates CG: 35 SD: 78
D Ian Roper CG: 23 DR: 127
M Mark Wright CG: 23 SD: 74
F Hector Sam CG: 12 SR: 326
G Clayton Ince CG: 45 DR: 119
D Michael Dobson CG: 38 DR: 119
M Craig Pead CG: 26 SD: 63
F Martin Butler CG: 43 SR: 351
D Daniel Fox CG: 43 DR: 118
M Kris Taylor CG: 22 SD: 49

KEY GOALKEEPER

Clayton Ince	
Goals Conceded in the League	34
Defensive Rating Ave number of mins between League goals conceded while on the pitch.	119
Counting Games Games when he played at least 70 mins	45
Clean Sheets In games when he played at least 70 mins	20

TOP POINT EARNERS

	PLAYER	GAMES	AV PTS
1	Mark Wright	23	2.17
2	Kris Taylor	22	2.05
3	Ian Roper	23	2.04
4	Dean Keates	35	2.00
5	Clayton Ince	45	1.96
6	Michael Dobson	38	1.95
7	Anthony Gerrard	29	1.93
8	Craig Pead	26	1.92
9	Daniel Fox	43	1.91
10	Martin Butler	43	1.91
	CLUB AVERAGE:		1.93

HARTLEPOOL

Final Position: **2nd**

CKNAME: THE POOL   KEY: ☐ Won ☐ Drawn ☐ Lost   Attendance

#					Score		Attendance
1	div3	Swindon	H	L	0-1		4,690
2	div3	Macclesfield	A	D	0-0		1,843
3	div3	Walsall	A	L	0-2		5,637
4	div3	Torquay	H	D	1-1	Bullock 81	3,688
5	ccr1	Burnley	A	W	1-0	Porter 72 pen	3,853
6	div3	Hereford	A	L	1-3	Brown 53	3,156
7	div3	Boston	H	W	2-1	Sweeney 30, Daly 72	4,054
8	div3	MK Dons	A	D	0-0		5,630
9	div3	Mansfield	H	W	2-0	Porter 77, 90	3,899
10	div3	Shrewsbury	H	L	0-3		4,291
1	ccr2	Hull City	A	L	2-3*	(*on penalties)	6,392
2	div3	Peterborough	A	W	5-3	Liddle 30, 53, Daly 32 pen, 45, Robson 84	3,916
3	div3	Grimsby	A	W	4-1	Daly 45 pen, 85, Liddle 52, Porter 90	3,486
4	div3	Wrexham	H	W	3-0	Daly 20, 22, 68	4,452
5	div3	Lincoln	A	L	0-2		5,332
6	div3	Stockport	H	D	1-1	Robson 43	4,372
7	div3	Chester	A	L	1-2	Porter 9	2,580
8	div3	Darlington	H	D	0-0		7,458
9	div3	Barnet	H	L	0-1		3,778
0	facr1	Rochdale	A	D	1-1	Brown 41	2,098
1	div3	Accrington	A	W	2-1	E.Williams 75, Humphreys 90	1,787
2	facr1r	Rochdale	H	W	4-2*	(*on penalties)	2,788
3	div3	Wycombe	H	W	2-0	Duffy 24, 49	3,711
4	facr2	Macclesfield	A	L	1-2	Regan 8 og	1,992
5	div3	Notts County	A	W	1-0	Monkhouse 8	3,546
6	div3	Bristol Rovers	A	W	2-0	Clark 79, Duffy 90	4,906
7	div3	Rochdale	H	W	1-0	Duffy 17	3,659
8	div3	Bury	A	W	1-0	Sweeney 46	2,839
9	div3	Grimsby	H	W	2-0	Daly 52, Monkhouse 82	5,290
0	div3	Peterborough	H	W	1-0	Duffy 90	4,654
1	div3	Mansfield	A	W	1-0	Monkhouse 77	3,531
2	div3	Shrewsbury	A	D	1-1	Brown 35	4,334
3	div3	MK Dons	H	W	1-0	Sweeney 55	4,851
4	div3	Wrexham	A	D	1-1	Barker 9	3,828
5	div3	Bury	H	W	2-0	Brown 33, Sweeney 57	4,901
6	div3	Swindon	A	W	1-0	Monkhouse 49	6,841
7	div3	Walsall	H	W	3-1	Nelson 52, Humphreys 88, Barker 90	5,847
8	div3	Torquay	A	W	1-0	E.Williams 7	2,194
9	div3	Macclesfield	H	W	3-2	Brown 26, Barker 60, Morley 88 og	5,242
0	div3	Boston	A	W	1-0	Humphreys 64	2,120
1	div3	Hereford	H	W	3-2	Clark 32, Brown 54, E.Williams 68	5,535
2	div3	Lincoln	H	D	1-1	Barker 90 pen	6,903
3	div3	Stockport	A	D	3-3	Monkhouse 38, Barker 47 pen, 65	7,860
4	div3	Darlington	A	W	3-0	E.Williams 39, 51, Monkhouse 80	9,987
5	div3	Chester	H	W	3-0	Barker 3, Monkhouse 26, Clark 71	6,059
6	div3	Barnet	A	L	1-2	E.Williams 77	2,906
7	div3	Accrington	H	W	1-0	Barker 65 pen	5,867
8	div3	Wycombe	A	W	1-0	Barker 81	5,540
9	div3	Notts County	H	D	1-1	Brown 3	6,174
0	div3	Rochdale	A	L	0-2		5,846
1	div3	Bristol Rovers	H	L	1-2	Porter 32	7,629

KEY PLAYER APPEARANCES

	PLAYER	POS	AGE	APP	MINS ON	GOALS	CARDS(Y/R)	
1	D Konstantopoulos	GK	28	46	4140	0	0	0
2	Gary Liddle	MID	21	42	3719	3	8	0
3	Michael Nelson	DEF	25	42	3662	1	4	0
4	Ben Clark	DEF	24	40	3541	3	5	1
5	Richie Humphreys	MID	29	38	3306	3	3	0
6	Antony Sweeney	MID	23	35	2701	4	0	1
7	James Brown	ATT	20	36	2519	6	3	0
8	Eifion Williams	ATT	31	40	2514	6	1	0
9	Andy Monkhouse	MID	26	26	2258	7	1	1
10	Michael Barron	DEF	32	29	2253	0	6	0
11	Willie Boland	MID	31	27	2239	0	5	0
12	Darren Williams	DEF	30	26	1741	0	3	0
13	Richard Barker	ATT	32	18	1604	9	2	1
14	Matty Robson	DEF	22	20	1550	2	1	0
15	Joel Porter	ATT	28	22	1234	5	2	0
16	Jon Daly	ATT	24	19	1173	9	6	1
17	Lee Bullock	MID	26	25	1101	1	1	0
18	Alistair Gibb	MID	31	25	1093	0	1	0

KEY PLAYERS - GOALSCORERS

Richard Barker

Goals in the League	9		Player Strike Rate Average number of minutes between League goals scored by player	178

Contribution to Attacking Power Average number of minutes between League team goals while on pitch	53		Club Strike Rate Average number of minutes between League goals scored by club	63

	PLAYER	GOALS LGE	POWER	STRIKE RATE
1	Richard Barker	9	53	178 mins
2	Andy Monkhouse	7	57	322 mins
3	James Brown	6	64	419 mins
4	Eifion Williams	6	64	419 mins

KEY PLAYERS - MIDFIELDERS

Andy Monkhouse

Goals in the League	7		Contribution to Attacking Power Average number of minutes between League team goals while on pitch	57

Defensive Rating Average number of mins between League goals conceded while on the pitch	150		Scoring Difference Defensive Rating minus Contribution to Attacking Power	93

	PLAYER	GOALS LGE	DEF RATE	POWER	SCORE DIFF
1	Andy Monkhouse	7	150	57	93 mins
2	Willie Boland	0	131	74	57 mins
3	Richie Humphreys	3	122	70	52 mins
4	Gary Liddle	3	103	59	44 mins

KEY PLAYERS - DEFENDERS

Michael Barron

Goals Conceded when he was on pitch	16		Clean Sheets In games when he played at least 70 minutes	14

Defensive Rating Ave number of mins between League goals conceded while on the pitch	140		Club Defensive Rating Average number of mins between League goals conceded by the club this season.	103

	PLAYER	CON LGE	CLEAN SHEETS	DEF RATE
1	Michael Barron	16	14	140 mins
2	Ben Clark	30	20	118 mins
3	Michael Nelson	36	19	101 mins
4	Darren Williams	23	6	75 mins

KEY GOALKEEPER

Demitrios Konstantopoulos

Goals Conceded in the League	40
Defensive Rating Ave number of mins between League goals conceded while on the pitch.	103
Counting Games Games when he played at least 70 mins	46
Clean Sheets In games when he played at least 70 mins	22

TOP POINT EARNERS

	PLAYER	GAMES	AV PTS
1	Andy Monkhouse	26	2.46
2	Michael Barron	22	2.36
3	Antony Sweeney	27	2.22
4	James Brown	24	2.13
5	Richard Barker	18	2.11
6	Ben Clark	39	2.03
7	Gary Liddle	41	2.02
8	Willie Boland	22	2.00
9	Richie Humphreys	36	1.97
10	Michael Nelson	40	1.95
	CLUB AVERAGE:		1.91

TEAM OF THE SEASON

D Michael Barron CG: 22 DR: 140
M Andy Monkhouse CG: 26 SD: 93
G D Konstantopoulos CG: 46 DR: 103
D Ben Clark CG: 39 DR: 118
M Willie Boland CG: 22 SD: 57
F Richard Barker CG: 18 SR: 178
D Michael Nelson CG: 40 DR: 101
M Richie Humphreys CG: 36 SD: 52
F James Brown CG: 24 SR: 419
D Darren Williams CG: 17 DR: 75
M Gary Liddle CG: 41 SD: 44

SWINDON TOWN

Final Position: 3rd

NICKNAME: THE ROBINS   KEY: ☐ Won ☐ Drawn ☐ Lost   Attendance

#				Result	Scorers	Attendance
1	div3	Hartlepool	A W	1-0	Peacock 11	4,690
2	div3	Barnet	H W	2-1	Shakes 54, Brownlie 90	7,475
3	div3	Rochdale	H W	1-0	Goodall 44 og	6,771
4	div3	Darlington	A W	2-1	P.Evans 6, Roberts 21	4,571
5	ccr1	Brentford	H L	3-4*	Nicholas 38, P.Evans 72 (*on penalties)	5,582
6	div3	Stockport	H W	2-0	Brown 33, Roberts 63	6,868
7	div3	Chester	A W	2-0	Peacock 48, 74	3,382
8	div3	Wrexham	A L	1-2	P.Evans 29	5,257
9	div3	MK Dons	H W	2-1	J.Smith 45 pen, P.Evans 56 pen	8,304
10	div3	Peterborough	H L	0-1		7,329
11	div3	Notts County	A D	1-1	Onibuje 47	6,079
12	div3	Wycombe	A D	1-1	Brownlie 52	6,090
13	div3	Boston	H D	1-1	Monkhouse 25	6,074
14	div3	Accrington	A D	1-1	Peacock 68	3,083
15	div3	Grimsby	H W	3-0	Pook 33, Monkhouse 44, Peacock 88	5,719
16	div3	Shrewsbury	A W	2-0	Onibuje 12, Brown 81	5,218
17	div3	Lincoln	H L	0-1		7,685
18	div3	Hereford	H L	1-2	Roberts 32	6,910
19	facr1	Carlisle	H W	3-1	Lumsdon 9 og, Roberts 70, 90	4,938
20	div3	Torquay	A W	1-0	Roberts 62 pen	4,029
21	div3	Bury	H W	2-1	Roberts 34, Fitzgerald 90 og	5,628
22	facr2	Morecambe	H W	1-0	Roberts 89 pen	5,942
23	div3	Mansfield	A L	0-2		2,274
24	div3	Walsall	A W	2-0	Jutkiewicz 23, Roberts 69 pen	6,812
25	div3	Bristol Rovers	H W	2-1	Jutkiewicz 15, Brown 17	10,010
26	div3	Macclesfield	A L	1-2	Peacock 64	2,377
27	div3	Wycombe	H W	2-1	Jutkiewicz 45, Peacock 53	8,878
28	div3	Notts County	H D	1-1	Timlin 77	6,805
29	div3	MK Dons	A W	1-0	Peacock 31	6,797
30	facr3	Crystal Palace	A L	1-2	Ifil 85	10,238
31	div3	Wrexham	H W	2-0	Zaaboub 9, Roberts 71 pen	6,130
32	div3	Boston	A W	3-1	Roberts 10, Pook 59, Sturrock 88	2,101
33	div3	Macclesfield	H W	2-0	Shakes 45, Peacock 52	6,062
34	div3	Peterborough	A D	1-1	Sturrock 88	3,516
35	div3	Hartlepool	H L	0-1		6,841
36	div3	Darlington	H D	1-1	Nicholas 9	5,570
37	div3	Barnet	A L	0-1		2,639
38	div3	Chester	H W	1-0	J.Smith 9 pen	5,462
39	div3	Stockport	A L	0-3		6,594
40	div3	Accrington	H W	2-0	J.Smith 45 pen, Nicholas 48	6,197
41	div3	Grimsby	A L	0-1		4,595
42	div3	Lincoln	A W	3-2	Roberts 17, Corr 34, Peacock 49	5,741
43	div3	Shrewsbury	H W	2-1	Corr 67, Roberts 73	7,335
44	div3	Rochdale	A D	0-0		2,544
45	div3	Hereford	A D	0-0		4,740
46	div3	Torquay	H W	2-1	Sturrock 2, Jutkiewicz 83	7,389
47	div3	Bury	A W	1-0	Jutkiewicz 85	2,401
48	div3	Mansfield	H W	2-0	Corr 4, Hjelde 38 og	10,472
49	div3	Bristol Rovers	A L	0-1		9,902
50	div3	Walsall	H D	1-1	Ifil 52	14,731

KEY PLAYER APPEARANCES

	PLAYER	POS	AGE	APP	MINS ON	GOALS	CARDS(Y/R)	
1	Jerel Ifil	DEF	25	40	3563	1	11	2
2	Lee Peacock	ATT	30	42	3498	10	5	0
3	Jack Smith	DEF	23	40	3454	3	10	0
4	Christian Roberts	ATT	27	42	3345	10	9	0
5	Jamie Vincent	DEF	32	34	3026	0	5	0
6	Michael Pook	MID	21	38	2951	2	7	0
7	Phil Smith	GK	27	31	2790	0	0	0
8	Andrew Nicholas	DEF	23	35	2679	2	4	0
9	Adrian Williams	DEF	35	27	2430	0	2	0
10	Ricky Shakes	ATT	22	32	2190	2	2	0
11	Sofiane Zaaboub	DEF	24	27	1936	1	7	0
12	Curtis Weston	MID	20	27	1882	0	8	0
13	Michael Timlin	MID	22	24	1715	1	7	1
14	Lucas Jutkiewicz	ATT	18	33	1416	5	0	0
15	Aaron Brown	MID	27	30	1377	3	5	0
16	Peter Brezovan	GK	27	14	1247	0	1	0
17	Paul Evans	MID	32	15	1030	3	3	0
18	Ashley Westwood	DEF	30	9	792	0	2	0

KEY PLAYERS - GOALSCORERS

Lucas Jutkiewicz

Goals in the League	5	Player Strike Rate Average number of minutes between League goals scored by player	283
Contribution to Attacking Power Average number of minutes between League team goals while on pitch	78	Club Strike Rate Average number of minutes between League goals scored by club	72

	PLAYER	GOALS LGE	POWER	STRIKE RATE
1	Lucas Jutkiewicz	5	78	283 mins
2	Christian Roberts	10	72	334 mins
3	Lee Peacock	10	71	349 mins
4	Aaron Brown	3	65	459 mins

KEY PLAYERS - MIDFIELDERS

Michael Pook

Goals in the League	2	Contribution to Attacking Power Average number of minutes between League team goals while on pitch	71
Defensive Rating Average number of mins between League goals conceded while on the pitch	122	Scoring Difference Defensive Rating minus Contribution to Attacking Power	51

	PLAYER	GOALS LGE	DEF RATE	POWER	SCORE DIFF
1	Michael Pook	2	122	71	51 mins
2	Curtis Weston	0	94	62	32 mins
3	Aaron Brown	3	86	65	21 mins
4	Michael Timlin	1	100	81	19 mins

KEY PLAYERS - DEFENDERS

Sofiane Zaaboub

Goals Conceded when he was on pitch	15	Clean Sheets In games when he played at least 70 minutes	8
Defensive Rating Ave number of mins between League goals conceded while on the pitch	129	Club Defensive Rating Average number of mins between League goals conceded by the club this season.	111

	PLAYER	CON LGE	CLEAN SHEETS	DEF RATE
1	Sofiane Zaaboub	15	8	129 mins
2	Andrew Nicholas	22	11	121 mins
3	Jamie Vincent	27	12	112 mins
4	Jerel Ifil	32	13	111 mins

KEY GOALKEEPER

Peter Brezovan

Goals Conceded in the League	10
Defensive Rating Ave number of mins between League goals conceded while on the pitch.	124
Counting Games Games when he played at least 70 mins	14
Clean Sheets In games when he played at least 70 mins	5

TOP POINT EARNERS

	PLAYER	GAMES	AV PTS
1	Sofiane Zaaboub	21	2.19
2	Ricky Shakes	21	2.05
3	Peter Brezovan	14	2.00
4	Christian Roberts	39	1.97
5	Jerel Ifil	40	1.95
6	Jack Smith	37	1.95
7	Michael Pook	32	1.91
8	Curtis Weston	20	1.90
9	Adrian Williams	27	1.89
10	Andrew Nicholas	28	1.86
	CLUB AVERAGE:		1.85

TEAM OF THE SEASON

D Sofiane Zaaboub   CG: 21   DR: 129
M Michael Pook   CG: 32   SD: 51
D Andrew Nicholas   CG: 28   DR: 121
M Curtis Weston   CG: 20   SD: 32
F Lucas Jutkiewicz   CG: 12   SR: 283
G Peter Brezovan   CG: 14   DR: 124
D Jamie Vincent   CG: 34   DR: 112
M Aaron Brown   CG: 12   SD: 21
F Christian Roberts   CG: 39   SR: 334
D Jerel Ifil   CG: 40   DR: 111
M Michael Timlin   CG: 18   SD: 19

MK DONS

Final Position: **4th**

ICKNAME: THE DONS/WOMBLES   KEY: ☐ Won ☐ Drawn ☐ Lost   Attendance

1	div3	Bury	H	W	2-1	McLeod 59 pen, 83	5,329
2	div3	Mansfield	A	L	1-2	Wilbraham 10	4,033
3	div3	Macclesfield	A	W	2-1	Platt 35, Swailes 80 og	1,711
4	div3	Bristol Rovers	H	W	2-0	Dyer 30, Platt 64	5,125
5	ccr1	Colchester	H	W	1-0	McLeod 94	2,747
6	div3	Boston	A	W	1-0	Platt 50	2,032
7	div3	Notts County	H	W	3-2	Dyer 45, 53, Taylor 73	6,323
8	div3	Hartlepool	H	D	0-0		5,630
9	div3	Swindon	A	L	1-2	McGovern 16	8,304
10	div3	Lincoln	A	W	3-2	McLeod 4 pen, Wilbraham 25, Platt 53	5,310
11	ccr2	Barnsley	A	W	2-1	Wilbraham 28, 90	4,411
12	div3	Chester	H	L	1-2	Platt 35	5,476
13	div3	Torquay	H	W	3-2	McLeod 50 pen, 59, Wilbraham 84	5,378
14	div3	Barnet	A	D	3-3	O'Hanlon 43, Chorley 69 pen, Dyer 90	2,819
15	div3	Peterborough	H	L	0-2		6,647
16	div3	Wrexham	A	W	2-0	McLeod 46, O'Hanlon 77	3,828
17	div3	Hereford	H	L	1-3	McLeod 59	5,609
18	ccr3	Tottenham	H	L	0-5		8,306
19	div3	Walsall	A	D	0-0		6,275
20	div3	Grimsby	A	W	3-1	McLeod 53, Wilbraham 60, 79	3,268
21	facr1	Farsley	A	D	0-0		2,200
22	div3	Shrewsbury	H	W	2-0	Edds 28, Platt 58	5,830
23	facr1r	Farsley	H	W	2-0	McLeod 63, 76 pen	2,676
24	div3	Darlington	A	L	0-1		4,017
25	facr2	Blackpool	H	L	0-2		3,837
26	div3	Stockport	H	W	2-0	McLeod 61, 75	4,564
27	div3	Accrington	A	W	4-3	McLeod 16, Wilbraham 54, 58, O'Hanlon 81	1,384
28	div3	Wycombe	H	W	3-1	Andrews 17, McLeod 25 pen, 87	5,977
29	div3	Rochdale	H	W	2-1	McLeod 80, Stanton 88 og	5,459
30	div3	Torquay	A	W	2-0	Platt 27, McLeod 39 pen	2,715
31	div3	Chester	A	W	3-0	Platt 60, McLeod 65, McGovern 76	2,271
32	div3	Swindon	H	L	0-1		6,797
33	div3	Lincoln	H	D	2-2	McLeod 6, Edds 90	7,140
34	div3	Hartlepool	A	L	0-1		4,851
35	div3	Barnet	H	W	3-1	Platt 12, 67, 72	6,447
36	div3	Rochdale	A	L	0-5		2,493
37	div3	Bury	A	W	2-0	Knight 32, Andrews 50	2,325
38	div3	Bristol Rovers	A	D	1-1	McGovern 55	5,489
39	div3	Mansfield	H	D	1-1	Taylor 50	5,070
40	div3	Notts County	A	D	2-2	Dyer 26, Lewington 32	4,031
41	div3	Boston	H	W	3-2	Platt 3, 84, McLeod 75	6,605
42	div3	Peterborough	A	L	0-4		5,880
43	div3	Macclesfield	H	W	3-0	McLeod 2, Platt 45, Lee 79 og	5,681
44	div3	Wrexham	H	W	2-0	Andrews 38 pen, Platt 85	5,712
45	div3	Walsall	H	D	1-1	McLeod 52	8,044
46	div3	Hereford	A	D	0-0		2,715
47	div3	Grimsby	H	L	1-2	Andrews 71	6,101
48	div3	Shrewsbury	A	L	1-2	Platt 9	5,238
49	div3	Darlington	H	W	1-0	Platt 57	5,730
50	div3	Stockport	A	W	2-1	Platt 24, Andrews 55	5,681
51	div3	Wycombe	A	W	2-0	G.Smith 88, McLeod 90	7,150
52	div3	Accrington	H	W	3-1	Andrews 55 pen, Mitchell 69, Stirling 83	8,102
53	d3po1	Shrewsbury	A	D	0-0		7,126
54	d3po2	Shrewsbury	H	L	1-2	Andrews 74	8,212

TEAM OF THE SEASON

D Drissa Diallo **CG:** 38 **DR:** 85
M Gareth Edds **CG:** 23 **SD:** 33
D Dean Lewington **CG:** 42 **DR:** 77
M Keith Andrews **CG:** 33 **SD:** 23
F Izale McLeod **CG:** 28 **SR:** 130
G Lee Harper **CG:** 22 **DR:** 73
D Sean O'Hanlon **CG:** 30 **DR:** 69
M John-Paul McGovern **CG:** 36 **SD:** 20
F Clive Platt **CG:** 32 **SR:** 187
D Paul Butler **CG:** 17 **DR:** 63
M Lloyd Dyer **CG:** 32 **SD:** 14

KEY PLAYER APPEARANCES

	PLAYER	POS	AGE	APP	MINS ON	GOALS	CARDS(Y/R)	
1	Dean Lewington	DEF	23	45	3896	1	6	0
2	Drissa Diallo	DEF	34	40	3495	0	9	0
3	John-Paul McGovern	MID	26	44	3452	3	6	0
4	Clive Platt	ATT	29	42	3366	18	5	0
5	Lloyd Dyer	MID	24	41	3230	5	4	0
6	Keith Andrews	MID	26	34	3012	6	7	0
7	Sean O'Hanlon	DEF	24	36	2903	3	9	0
8	Izale McLeod	ATT	22	34	2732	21	8	3
9	Aaron Wilbraham	ATT	27	32	2607	7	8	0
10	Gareth Edds	MID	26	35	2363	2	6	0
11	Lee Harper	GK	35	22	1980	0	0	0
12	Adolfo Baines	GK	35	19	1656	0	2	1
13	Paul Butler	DEF	34	17	1530	0	3	0
14	Jamie Smith	DEF	32	17	1195	0	3	0
15	Gary Smith	MID	23	22	1144	1	3	0
16	Ben Chorley	DEF	24	13	1053	1	2	0
17	Paul Mitchell	DEF	25	20	958	0	1	0
18	Scott Taylor	ATT	31	27	817	2	3	0

KEY PLAYERS - GOALSCORERS

Izale McLeod

Goals in the League	21	Player Strike Rate Average number of minutes between League goals scored by player	130
Contribution to Attacking Power Average number of minutes between League team goals while on pitch	47	Club Strike Rate Average number of minutes between League goals scored by club	55

	PLAYER	GOALS LGE	POWER	STRIKE RATE
1	Izale McLeod	21	47	130 mins
2	Clive Platt	18	58	187 mins
3	Aaron Wilbraham	7	51	372 mins
4	Keith Andrews	6	54	502 mins

KEY PLAYERS - MIDFIELDERS

Gareth Edds

Goals in the League	2	Contribution to Attacking Power Average number of minutes between League team goals while on pitch	54
Defensive Rating Average number of mins between League goals conceded while on the pitch	87	Scoring Difference Defensive Rating minus Contribution to Attacking Power	33

	PLAYER	GOALS LGE	DEF RATE	POWER	SCORE DIFF
1	Gareth Edds	2	87	54	33 mins
2	Keith Andrews	6	77	54	23 mins
3	John-Paul McGovern	3	73	53	20 mins
4	Lloyd Dyer	5	67	53	14 mins

KEY PLAYERS - DEFENDERS

Drissa Diallo

Goals Conceded when he was on pitch	41	Clean Sheets In games when he played at least 70 minutes	13
Defensive Rating Ave number of mins between League goals conceded while on the pitch	85	Club Defensive Rating Average number of mins between League goals conceded by the club this season.	72

	PLAYER	CON LGE	CLEAN SHEETS	DEF RATE
1	Drissa Diallo	41	13	85 mins
2	Dean Lewington	50	13	77 mins
3	Sean O'Hanlon	42	9	69 mins
4	Paul Butler	24	4	63 mins

KEY GOALKEEPER

Lee Harper

Goals Conceded in the League	27
Defensive Rating Ave number of mins between League goals conceded while on the pitch.	73
Counting Games Games when he played at least 70 mins	22
Clean Sheets In games when he played at least 70 mins	7

TOP POINT EARNERS

	PLAYER	GAMES	AV PTS
1	Lloyd Dyer	32	2.00
2	John-Paul McGovern	36	1.97
3	Gareth Edds	23	1.96
4	Sean O'Hanlon	30	1.93
5	Izale McLeod	28	1.89
6	Clive Platt	32	1.88
7	Drissa Diallo	38	1.87
8	Dean Lewington	42	1.86
9	Adolfo Baines	19	1.84
10	Paul Butler	17	1.76
	CLUB AVERAGE:		1.83

LINCOLN CITY

Final Position: **5th**

NICKNAME: THE RED IMPS KEY: ☐ Won ☐ Drawn ☐ Lost Attendance

#	Comp	Opponent	H/A	Result	Scorers	Attendance
1	div3	Notts County	H	D 1-1	Moses 10	6,046
2	div3	Hereford	A	W 2-1	Stallard 11, 29	4,405
3	div3	Torquay	A	W 2-1	Gritton 90, Morgan 90	3,192
4	div3	Walsall	H	D 2-2	Kerr 12, Frecklington 22	4,565
5	ccr1	Scunthorpe	A	L 3-4	Stallard 69, Frecklington 80, Beevers 93	3,455
6	div3	Mansfield	A	W 4-2	Forrester 14 pen, 23, 29, 49 pen	4,596
7	div3	Accrington	H	W 3-1	Gritton 7, Stallard 40, 69	4,999
8	div3	Shrewsbury	A	W 1-0	Frecklington 29	4,083
9	div3	Macclesfield	H	W 2-1	Kerr 13, Beevers 40	4,184
10	div3	MK Dons	H	L 2-3	Frecklington 44, Beevers 58	5,310
11	div3	Wycombe	A	W 3-1	Frecklington 45, Stallard 64, 73	5,247
12	div3	Boston	A	L 0-1		4,327
13	div3	Bury	H	L 0-2		4,748
14	div3	Hartlepool	H	W 2-0	Forrester 40, Hughes 60	5,332
15	div3	Barnet	A	W 5-0	Forrester 26, 33 pen, 54 pen, Beevers 38, Mettam 90	2,409
16	div3	Rochdale	H	W 7-1	Forrester 11, 44, 49, Stallard 16, 65, Hughes 56, 77	5,194
17	div3	Swindon	A	W 1-0	Forrester 63	7,685
18	div3	Stockport	A	L 0-2		5,497
19	facr1	Port Vale	A	L 1-2	Frecklington 84	3,884
20	div3	Darlington	H	L 1-3	Mayo 82	5,292
21	div3	Wrexham	A	L 1-1	Stallard 64	3,619
22	div3	Bristol Rovers	H	W 1-0	Forrester 45 pen	3,913
23	div3	Chester	A	L 1-4	Brown 64	2,142
24	div3	Grimsby	H	W 2-0	Forrester 43, Frecklington 73	5,919
25	div3	Peterborough	A	W 2-1	Amoo 22, 72	8,405
26	div3	Boston	H	W 2-1	Stallard 16, Hughes 60	6,820
27	div3	Wycombe	H	W 1-0	Hughes 72	5,465
28	div3	Macclesfield	A	L 1-2	Hughes 15	2,869
29	div3	MK Dons	A	D 2-2	Forrester 51 pen, Weir-Daley 84	7,140
30	div3	Shrewsbury	H	D 1-1	Frecklington 17	4,811
31	div3	Bury	A	D 2-2	Forrester 37, Frecklington 76	2,476
32	div3	Peterborough	H	W 1-0	Stallard 71	6,606
33	div3	Notts County	A	L 1-3	Weir-Daley 89	7,019
34	div3	Torquay	H	W 1-0	Stallard 25	4,881
35	div3	Walsall	A	W 2-1	Weir-Daley 15, 42	4,885
36	div3	Hereford	H	L 1-4	Weir-Daley 56	4,695
37	div3	Accrington	A	D 2-2	Beevers 15, Kerr 56	1,930
38	div3	Mansfield	H	L 1-2	Forrester 74	5,316
39	div3	Hartlepool	A	D 1-1	Green 7	6,903
40	div3	Barnet	H	W 1-0	Frecklington 51	4,339
41	div3	Swindon	H	L 2-3	Stallard 13, 77	5,741
42	div3	Rochdale	A	L 0-2		2,911
43	div3	Stockport	H	D 0-0		5,320
44	div3	Darlington	A	D 1-1	Beevers 77	3,878
45	div3	Wrexham	H	L 0-3		4,279
46	div3	Bristol Rovers	A	D 0-0		6,828
47	div3	Grimsby	A	D 0-0		6,137
48	div3	Chester	H	W 2-0	Stallard 64, Forrester 90 pen	5,267
49	d3po1	Bristol Rovers	A	L 1-2	Hughes 31	10,654
50	d3po2	Bristol Rovers	H	L 3-5	Hughes 25, 90, Stallard 43	7,694

TEAM OF THE SEASON

D Jeff Hughes CG: 36 DR: 84
M Scott Kerr CG: 41 SD: 20
D Nicky Eaden CG: 30 DR: 76
M Lee Frecklington CG: 38 SD: 13
F Jamie Forrester CG: 38 SR: 189
G Alan Marriott CG: 46 DR: 70
D Lee Beevers CG: 41 DR: 75
M Ryan Amoo CG: 33 SD: 11
F Mark Stallard CG: 40 SR: 237
D Nathaniel Brown CG: 27 DR: 67
M Paul Green* CG: 11 SD: -59

KEY PLAYER APPEARANCES

	PLAYER	POS	AGE	APP	MINS ON	GOALS	CARDS(Y/R)	
1	Alan Marriott	GK	28	46	4140	0	0	0
2	Scott Kerr	MID	25	43	3752	3	4	0
3	Lee Beevers	DEF	23	44	3675	5	7	1
4	Mark Stallard	ATT	32	41	3563	15	8	0
5	Lee Frecklington	MID	21	42	3467	8	6	0
6	Jamie Forrester	ATT	32	41	3408	18	1	1
7	Jeff Hughes	DEF	22	41	3365	7	3	0
8	Ryan Amoo	MID	23	43	3172	2	5	0
9	Nicky Eaden	DEF	35	33	2825	0	2	0
10	Paul Morgan	DEF	28	33	2516	1	2	1
11	Paul Mayo	DEF	25	34	2491	1	3	0
12	Nathaniel Brown	DEF	26	28	2372	1	3	0
13	Adrian Moses	DEF	32	32	2266	1	3	0
14	Paul Green	MID	20	14	993	1	2	0
15	Martin Gritton	ATT	29	17	546	2	3	0
16	Shane Nicholson	DEF	37	8	543	0	0	0
17	Spencer Weir-Daley	ATT	21	11	460	5	2	0
18	Dany N'Guessan	MID	19	9	381	0	2	0

KEY PLAYERS - GOALSCORERS

Jamie Forrester

Goals in the League	18

Player Strike Rate — Average number of minutes between League goals scored by player	189

Contribution to Attacking Power — Average number of minutes between League team goals while on pitch	55

Club Strike Rate — Average number of minutes between League goals scored by club	59

	PLAYER	GOALS LGE	POWER	STRIKE RATE
1	Jamie Forrester	18	55	189 mins
2	Mark Stallard	15	60	237 mins
3	Lee Frecklington	8	56	433 mins
4	Paul Green	1	141	993 mins

KEY PLAYERS - MIDFIELDERS

Scott Kerr

Goals in the League	3

Contribution to Attacking Power — Average number of minutes between League team goals while on pitch	58

Defensive Rating — Average number of mins between League goals conceded while on the pitch	78

Scoring Difference — Defensive Rating minus Contribution to Attacking Power	20

	PLAYER	GOALS LGE	DEF RATE	POWER	SCORE DIFF
1	Scott Kerr	3	78	58	20 mins
2	Lee Frecklington	8	69	56	13 mins
3	Ryan Amoo	2	66	55	11 mins
4	Paul Green	1	82	141	-59 mins

KEY PLAYERS - DEFENDERS

Jeff Hughes

Goals Conceded when he was on pitch	40

Clean Sheets — In games when he played at least 70 minutes	13

Defensive Rating — Ave number of mins between League goals conceded while on the pitch	84

Club Defensive Rating — Average number of mins between League goals conceded by the club this season.	70

	PLAYER	CON LGE	CLEAN SHEETS	DEF RATE
1	Jeff Hughes	40	13	84 mins
2	Nicky Eaden	37	12	76 mins
3	Lee Beevers	49	13	75 mins
4	Nathaniel Brown	35	9	67 mins

KEY GOALKEEPER

Alan Marriott

Goals Conceded in the League	59

Defensive Rating — Ave number of mins between League goals conceded while on the pitch.	70

Counting Games — Games when he played at least 70 mins	46

Clean Sheets — In games when he played at least 70 mins	14

TOP POINT EARNERS

	PLAYER	GAMES	AV PTS
1	Nicky Eaden	30	1.80
2	Paul Morgan	27	1.78
3	Scott Kerr	41	1.76
4	Lee Frecklington	38	1.71
5	Lee Beevers	41	1.71
6	Ryan Amoo	33	1.70
7	Nathaniel Brown	27	1.67
8	Paul Mayo	26	1.65
9	Adrian Moses	23	1.65
10	Mark Stallard	40	1.65
	CLUB AVERAGE:		1.61

BRISTOL ROVERS

PROMOTED VIA THE PLAY-OFFS Final Position: **6th**

CKNAME: THE PIRATES   KEY: ☐ Won ☐ Drawn ☐ Lost   Attendance

#	Comp	Opponent	H/A	Result	Scorers	Attendance
1	div3	Peterborough	A	L 1-4	Igoe 52	4,890
2	div3	Wycombe	H	L 1-2	Hunt 72	5,349
3	div3	Grimsby	H	W 1-0	Sandell 50	4,596
4	div3	MK Dons	A	L 0-2		5,125
5	ccr1	Luton	H	L 1-1	Walker 61 (Luton won 5-3 on penalties)	2,882
6	div3	Shrewsbury	H	W 1-0	Haldane 21	4,774
7	div3	Stockport	A	L 1-2	Walker 83	4,846
8	div3	Rochdale	H	D 0-0		4,689
9	div3	Torquay	A	D 0-0		3,145
10	div3	Darlington	A	D 1-1	Haldane 54	3,654
11	div3	Walsall	H	L 1-2	Sandell 90	5,260
12	div3	Hereford	H	W 2-1	J.Walker 67, 68	4,975
13	div3	Chester	A	L 0-2		2,151
14	div3	Boston	H	W 1-0	Walker 52	4,327
15	div3	Notts County	A	W 2-1	R.Walker 54, Haldane 67	5,797
16	div3	Macclesfield	H	D 0-0		5,130
17	div3	Wrexham	A	L 0-2		3,803
18	div3	Mansfield	H	W 1-0	Disley 87	5,044
19	facr1	Barrow	A	W 3-2	R.Walker 35, Disley 62, Anthony 67	2,939
20	div3	Bury	A	W 2-0	Haldane 74, R.Walker 86	2,635
21	div3	Barnet	H	W 2-0	Nicholson 60, Lambert 90	5,351
22	facr2	Bournemouth	H	D 1-1	R.Walker 45 pen	6,252
23	div3	Lincoln	A	L 0-1		3,913
24	div3	Hartlepool	H	L 0-2		4,906
25	facr2r	Bournemouth	A	W 1-0	R.Walker 64	4,153
26	div3	Swindon	A	L 1-2	R.Walker 12	10,010
27	div3	Accrington	H	W 4-0	R.Walker 6, 26 pen, Elliott 22, Nicholson 88	5,205
28	div3	Hereford	A	D 0-0		5,201
29	div3	Walsall	A	D 2-2	Elliott 65, 90	5,941
30	div3	Torquay	H	W 1-0	Sandell 84	6,475
31	facr3	Hereford	H	W 1-0	R.Walker 22 pen	8,978
32	div3	Rochdale	A	W 1-0	Lambert 54	2,547
33	div3	Chester	H	D 0-0		5,694
34	facr4	Derby	A	L 0-1		25,033
35	div3	Peterborough	H	W 3-2	Lambert 14, R.Walker 52, Campbell 90	5,700
36	div3	Darlington	H	L 1-2	Disley 89	5,511
37	div3	Grimsby	A	L 3-4	Disley 14, 90, Haldane 20	5,883
38	div3	MK Dons	H	D 1-1	Nicholson 80	5,489
39	div3	Shrewsbury	A	D 0-0		4,227
40	div3	Accrington	A	D 1-1	R.Walker 58	1,302
41	div3	Boston	A	L 1-2	Haldane 68	1,697
42	div3	Notts County	H	W 2-0	Nicholson 53, 72	4,642
43	div3	Stockport	H	W 2-1	Lambert 15 pen, Nicholson 61	4,725
44	div3	Wrexham	H	L 0-1		5,209
45	div3	Wycombe	A	W 1-0	Elliott 16	4,299
46	div3	Mansfield	A	W 1-0	Elliott 35	2,392
47	div3	Bury	H	W 2-0	Lambert 30, 61	6,266
48	div3	Barnet	A	D 1-1	R.Walker 12	2,541
49	div3	Lincoln	H	D 0-0		6,828
50	div3	Macclesfield	A	W 1-0	Rigg 76	1,940
51	div3	Swindon	H	W 1-0	Lambert 27	9,902
52	div3	Hartlepool	A	W 2-1	R.Walker 54 pen, Lambert 86	7,629
53	d3po1	Lincoln	H	W 2-1	Disley 10, R.Walker 54	10,654
54	d3po2	Lincoln	A	W 5-3	Campbell 3, Lambert 11, R.Walker 36, Igoe 82, Rigg 90	7,694
55	d3pof	Shrewsbury	H	W 3-1	R.Walker 22, 36, Igoe 90	61,589

KEY PLAYER APPEARANCES

	PLAYER	POS	AGE	APP	MINS ON	GOALS	CARDS(Y/R)
1	Steve Phillips	GK	29	44	3960	0	0 0
2	Craig Disley	MID	25	45	3583	5	0 0
3	Steve Elliott	DEF	28	39	3510	5	3 0
4	Richard Walker	ATT	29	45	3330	11	4 0
5	Stuart Campbell	MID	29	41	3170	1	5 1
6	Sam Igoe	MID	31	39	3050	1	5 1
7	Chris Carruthers	DEF	23	38	2981	0	4 0
8	Aaron Lescott	MID	28	34	2791	0	5 2
9	Lewis Haldane	ATT	22	45	2788	6	7 0
10	Ryan Green	DEF	26	33	2561	0	1 0
11	Craig Hinton	DEF	29	30	2521	0	4 1
12	Rickie Lambert	MID	25	36	2456	8	0 0
13	Andy Sandell	MID	23	36	1888	3	2 0
14	Byron Anthony	DEF	22	23	1835	0	4 0
15	Stuart Nicholson	ATT	20	22	1159	6	3 0
16	James Hunt	MID	30	14	1094	1	1 1
17	Joe Jacobson	DEF	20	11	742	0	1 0
18	Samuel Oji	DEF	21	5	450	0	1 0

KEY PLAYERS - GOALSCORERS

Richard Walker

Goals in the League	11

Player Strike Rate Average number of minutes between League goals scored by player	302

Contribution to Attacking Power Average number of minutes between League team goals while on pitch	83

Club Strike Rate Average number of minutes between League goals scored by club	86

	PLAYER	GOALS LGE	POWER	STRIKE RATE
1	Richard Walker	11	83	302 mins
2	Rickie Lambert	8	79	307 mins
3	Lewis Haldane	6	99	464 mins
4	Andy Sandell	3	78	629 mins

KEY PLAYERS - MIDFIELDERS

Andy Sandell

Goals in the League	3

Contribution to Attacking Power Average number of minutes between League team goals while on pitch	78

Defensive Rating Average number of mins between League goals conceded while on the pitch	125

Scoring Difference Defensive Rating minus Contribution to Attacking Power	47

	PLAYER	GOALS LGE	DEF RATE	POWER	SCORE DIFF
1	Andy Sandell	3	125	78	47 mins
2	Rickie Lambert	8	116	79	37 mins
3	Stuart Campbell	1	102	79	23 mins
4	Craig Disley	4	96	85	11 mins

KEY PLAYERS - DEFENDERS

Byron Anthony

Goals Conceded when he was on pitch	11

Clean Sheets In games when he played at least 70 minutes	12

Defensive Rating Ave number of mins between League goals conceded while on the pitch	166

Club Defensive Rating Average number of mins between League goals conceded by the club this season.	100

	PLAYER	CON LGE	CLEAN SHEETS	DEF RATE
1	Byron Anthony	11	12	166 mins
2	Ryan Green	23	15	111 mins
3	Chris Carruthers	30	16	99 mins
4	Steve Elliott	36	19	97 mins

KEY GOALKEEPER

Steve Phillips

Goals Conceded in the League	41
Defensive Rating Ave number of mins between League goals conceded while on the pitch.	96
Counting Games Games when he played at least 70 mins	44
Clean Sheets In games when he played at least 70 mins	21

TOP POINT EARNERS

	PLAYER	GAMES	AV PTS
1	Byron Anthony	19	1.89
2	Stuart Campbell	32	1.78
3	Craig Disley	37	1.70
4	Rickie Lambert	23	1.70
5	Richard Walker	34	1.68
6	Chris Carruthers	32	1.66
7	Ryan Green	28	1.64
8	Andy Sandell	15	1.60
9	Steve Phillips	44	1.55
10	Lewis Haldane	24	1.54
	CLUB AVERAGE:		1.57

TEAM OF THE SEASON

D Byron Anthony CG: 19 DR: 166
M Andy Sandell CG: 15 SD: 47
D Ryan Green CG: 28 DR: 111
M Rickie Lambert CG: 23 SD: 37
F Richard Walker CG: 34 SR: 302
G Steve Phillips CG: 44 DR: 96
D Chris Carruthers CG: 32 DR: 99
M Stuart Campbell CG: 32 SD: 23
F Lewis Haldane CG: 24 SR: 464
D Steve Elliott CG: 39 DR: 97
M Craig Disley CG: 37 SD: 11

SHREWSBURY TOWN

Final Position: 7th

NICKNAME: THE SHREWS   KEY: ☐ Won ☐ Drawn ☐ Lost   Attendance

#		Opponent			Score	Scorers	Attendance
1	div3	Mansfield	H	D	2-2	Drummond 22, Edwards 31	5,066
2	div3	Notts County	A	D	1-1	Davies 46	4,386
3	div3	Bury	A	W	2-1	Langmead 67, Davies 78 pen	2,329
4	div3	Boston	H	W	5-0	Davies 27 pen, Asamoah 42, 67, Symes 83, Edwards 90	3,502
5	ccr1	Birmingham	A	L	0-1		12,428
6	div3	Bristol Rovers	A	L	0-1		4,774
7	div3	Lincoln	H	L	0-1		4,083
8	div3	Stockport	A	W	3-0	Cooke 43, 57, 78	4,089
9	div3	Hartlepool	A	W	3-0	Daly 10 og, Drummond 76, Symes 80	4,291
10	div3	Darlington	H	D	2-2	Symes 64, Davies 85 pen	3,931
11	div3	Walsall	H	D	1-1	Sorvel 28	6,593
12	div3	Rochdale	A	D	1-1	Cooke 62	2,942
13	div3	Macclesfield	H	W	2-1	Herd 1, Langmead 90	4,816
14	div3	Peterborough	A	L	1-2	Davies 84 pen	4,171
15	div3	Swindon	H	L	1-2	Davies 68	5,218
16	div3	Torquay	A	D	0-0		2,262
17	div3	Wycombe	H	D	0-0		4,116
18	facr1	Hereford	H	D	0-0		5,574
19	div3	MK Dons	A	L	0-2		5,830
20	facr1r	Hereford	A	L	0-2		4,224
21	div3	Chester	H	W	2-1	Davies 50, Symes 90 pen	4,464
22	div3	Accrington	A	D	3-3	Asamoah 4 pen, Fortune-West 40, Symes 84	1,602
23	div3	Grimsby	A	L	1-2	Symes 53	4,076
24	div3	Hereford	H	W	3-0	Cooke 35, 66, Edwards 78	4,177
25	div3	Barnet	H	L	0-1		3,620
26	div3	Walsall	A	L	0-1		8,345
27	div3	Darlington	A	W	2-1	Symes 45, Edwards 87	2,825
28	div3	Stockport	H	W	4-2	Davies 4, Cooke 21, 48, 90	4,569
29	div3	Hartlepool	H	D	1-1	Symes 78	4,334
30	div3	Lincoln	A	D	1-1	M.Jones 63	4,811
31	div3	Mansfield	A	D	1-1	Asamoah 13	3,250
32	div3	Boston	A	W	3-0	Burton 6, Cooke 45, Davies 66	1,571
33	div3	Notts County	H	W	2-0	Asamoah 32, Fortune-West 45	3,369
34	div3	Wrexham	A	W	3-1	Fortune-West 8, 51, Asamoah 38	5,605
35	div3	Bristol Rovers	H	D	0-0		4,227
36	div3	Macclesfield	A	D	2-2	Swailes 63 og, Fortune-West 73	2,928
37	div3	Peterborough	H	W	2-1	Davies 61, Asamoah 81	4,027
38	div3	Barnet	A	D	0-0		1,672
39	div3	Torquay	H	W	1-0	Asamoah 77	4,678
40	div3	Rochdale	H	W	3-0	Fortune-West 48, Edwards 65, Drummond 78	4,363
41	div3	Swindon	A	L	1-2	Fortune-West 40	7,335
42	div3	Bury	H	L	1-3	Asamoah 45	4,419
43	div3	Wycombe	A	D	1-1	Symes 37	5,299
44	div3	MK Dons	H	W	2-1	Asamoah 53, Ashton 75	5,238
45	div3	Chester	A	D	0-0		3,266
46	div3	Accrington	H	W	2-1	Ashton 33, Davies 62	5,438
47	div3	Wrexham	H	L	0-1		6,749
48	div3	Hereford	A	W	1-0	Drummond 45	4,359
49	div3	Grimsby	H	D	2-2	Davies 63 pen, Langmead 74	7,782
50	d3po1	MK Dons	H	D	0-0		7,126
51	d3po2	MK Dons	A	W	2-1	Cooke 58, 76	8,212
52	d3pof	Bristol Rovers	A	L	1-3	Drummond 3	61,589

KEY PLAYER APPEARANCES

	PLAYER	POS	AGE	APP	MINS ON	GOALS	CARDS(Y/R)	
1	Kelvin Langmead	ATT	22	45	3961	3	3	0
2	Ben Davies	MID	26	43	3869	12	8	0
3	Stuart Drummond	MID	31	44	3841	5	5	0
4	Neil Ashton	DEF	22	43	3703	2	9	0
5	David Edwards	MID	21	45	3581	5	3	0
6	Derek Asamoah	ATT	26	39	2992	10	2	0
7	Richard Hope	DEF	29	32	2692	0	4	0
8	Ben Herd	DEF	22	32	2611	1	3	0
9	Sagi Burton	DEF	29	28	2208	1	7	0
10	Daniel Hall	DEF	23	27	1984	0	6	0
11	Andrew Cooke	ATT	33	34	1902	10	9	0
12	Michael Symes	ATT	23	33	1894	9	1	1
13	Chris MacKenzie	GK	29	20	1800	0	0	0
14	Scott Shearer	GK	26	20	1800	0	0	0
15	Marc Tierney	DEF	21	18	1575	0	4	1
16	Neil Sorvel	MID	34	18	1390	1	0	0
17	Leo Fortune-West	ATT	36	18	847	7	4	0
18	Ryan Esson	GK	27	6	540	0	0	0

KEY PLAYERS - GOALSCORERS

Andrew Cooke			**Player Strike Rate** Average number of minutes between League goals scored by player	**190**
Goals in the League	10			
Contribution to Attacking Power Average number of minutes between League team goals while on pitch	79		**Club Strike Rate** Average number of minutes between League goals scored by club	**66**

	PLAYER	GOALS LGE	POWER	STRIKE RATE
1	Andrew Cooke	10	79	190 mins
2	Michael Symes	9	61	210 mins
3	Derek Asamoah	10	62	299 mins
4	Ben Davies	12	61	322 mins

KEY PLAYERS - MIDFIELDERS

Ben Davies		**Contribution to Attacking Power** Average number of minutes between League team goals while on pitch	**61**
Goals in the League	12		
Defensive Rating Average number of mins between League goals conceded while on the pitch	92	**Scoring Difference** Defensive Rating minus Contribution to Attacking Power	**31**

	PLAYER	GOALS LGE	DEF RATE	POWER	SCORE DIFF
1	Ben Davies	12	92	61	31 mins
2	David Edwards	5	89	58	31 mins
3	Stuart Drummond	4	87	62	25 mins
4	Neil Sorvel	1	81	63	18 mins

KEY PLAYERS - DEFENDERS

Marc Tierney		**Clean Sheets** In games when he played at least 70 minutes	**8**
Goals Conceded when he was on pitch	14		
Defensive Rating Ave number of mins between League goals conceded while on the pitch	112	**Club Defensive Rating** Average number of mins between League goals conceded by the club this season.	**97**

	PLAYER	CON LGE	CLEAN SHEETS	DEF RATE
1	Marc Tierney	14	8	112 mins
2	Neil Ashton	41	12	90 mins
3	Richard Hope	30	9	89 mins
4	Ben Herd	30	8	87 mins

KEY GOALKEEPER

Scott Shearer	
Goals Conceded in the League	21
Defensive Rating Ave number of mins between League goals conceded while on the pitch.	85
Counting Games Games when he played at least 70 mins	20
Clean Sheets In games when he played at least 70 mins	5

TOP POINT EARNERS

	PLAYER	GAMES	AV PTS
1	Marc Tierney	17	1.76
2	Ben Herd	29	1.72
3	Chris MacKenzie	20	1.70
4	Andrew Cooke	16	1.69
5	Daniel Hall	20	1.65
6	Derek Asamoah	32	1.63
7	Kelvin Langmead	43	1.58
8	Sagi Burton	23	1.57
9	David Edwards	38	1.55
10	Richard Hope	28	1.54
	CLUB AVERAGE:		1.54

TEAM OF THE SEASON

D Marc Tierney CG: 17 DR: 112
M Ben Davies CG: 43 SD: 31
D Neil Ashton CG: 40 DR: 90
M David Edwards CG: 38 SD: 31
F Andrew Cooke CG: 16 SR: 190
G Scott Shearer CG: 20 DR: 85
D Richard Hope CG: 28 DR: 89
M Stuart Drummond CG: 42 SD: 25
F Michael Symes CG: 16 SR: 210
D Ben Herd CG: 29 DR: 87
M Neil Sorvel CG: 14 SD: 18

STOCKPORT COUNTY

Final Position: 8th

NICKNAME: COUNTY   KEY: ☐ Won ☐ Drawn ☐ Lost   Attendance

							Attendance
1	div3	Hereford	H	L	0-2		5,297
2	div3	Walsall	A	L	0-2		4,877
3	div3	Mansfield	A	D	1-1	Briggs 24	3,856
4	div3	Accrington	H	D	1-1	G.Murray 12	5,291
5	ccr1	Derby	H	L	0-1		3,394
6	div3	Swindon	A	L	0-2		6,868
7	div3	Bristol Rovers	H	W	2-1	G.Murray 39, 53	4,846
8	div3	Boston	A	L	1-2	J.Taylor 28	1,796
9	div3	Shrewsbury	H	L	0-3		4,089
10	div3	Wrexham	H	W	5-2	Le Fondre 23, 54, 84, 86, Robinson 23 pen	4,884
11	div3	Grimsby	A	W	1-0	Briggs 37	4,708
12	div3	Notts County	A	L	0-1		4,021
13	div3	Peterborough	H	L	0-1		4,775
14	div3	Barnet	H	W	2-0	Poole 31, Le Fondre 52	4,133
15	div3	Hartlepool	A	D	1-1	Griffin 30	4,372
16	div3	Torquay	H	W	1-0	Le Fondre 38	4,663
17	div3	Rochdale	A	W	3-1	A.Williams 19, Robinson 45 pen, Bramble 80	3,709
18	div3	Lincoln	H	W	2-0	Rose 56, Malcolm 90	5,497
19	facr1	Exeter	A	W	2-1	Bramble 21, Proudlock 82	4,454
20	div3	Chester	A	D	1-1	Poole 27	3,624
21	div3	Macclesfield	H	D	1-1	Proudlock 75	6,575
22	facr2	Wycombe	H	W	2-1	Proudlock 43 pen, 75	3,821
23	div3	MK Dons	A	L	0-2		4,564
24	div3	Darlington	H	W	5-2	Bramble 18, 36, Proudlock 24, Dinning 32, Gleeson 62	4,564
25	div3	Bury	A	L	0-2		4,466
26	div3	Wycombe	A	L	0-2		4,559
27	div3	Notts County	H	W	2-0	Pilkington 47, Dickinson 90	5,823
28	div3	Grimsby	H	W	3-0	Barnes 8 og, Dickinson 29, Malcolm 78	5,032
29	div3	Shrewsbury	A	L	2-4	Pilkington 49, 69	4,569
30	facr3	Watford	A	L	1-4	Poole 23	11,745
31	div3	Boston	H	W	2-0	Proudlock 25, Bramble 79	4,568
32	div3	Peterborough	A	W	3-0	Elding 20, Rose 31, Griffin 90	4,330
33	div3	Wycombe	H	W	2-0	Elding 21, Gleeson 47	5,353
34	div3	Wrexham	A	W	1-0	Dickinson 90	4,060
35	div3	Hereford	H	W	2-0	Bramble 33, Elding 38	3,310
36	div3	Mansfield	H	W	1-0	Elding 17	5,656
37	div3	Accrington	A	W	1-0	Griffin 45	3,004
38	div3	Walsall	H	W	1-0	Elding 52	6,005
39	div3	Swindon	H	W	3-0	Elding 16, 50, Dickinson 84	6,594
40	div3	Barnet	A	L	1-3	Bramble 33	2,647
41	div3	Hartlepool	H	D	3-3	Le Fondre 24 pen, Elding 28, Dickinson 36	7,860
42	div3	Bristol Rovers	A	L	1-2	Rose 68	4,725
43	div3	Rochdale	H	L	2-7	Elding 32, Dickinson 35	6,679
44	div3	Torquay	A	L	0-1		3,005
45	div3	Lincoln	A	D	0-0		5,320
46	div3	Chester	H	W	2-0	Pilkington 22, Dinning 47	5,719
47	div3	Macclesfield	A	L	0-1		4,451
48	div3	MK Dons	H	L	1-2	Pilkington 80	5,681
49	div3	Bury	H	D	0-0		7,246
50	div3	Darlington	A	W	5-0	Elding 35 pen, 80, Poole 49, 68, Dickinson 61	5,184

TEAM OF THE SEASON

Player	CG	DR/SD/SR
Wayne Hennessey (G)	15	DR: 84
Robert Clare (D)	26	DR: 116
Gareth Owen (D)	38	DR: 80
Ashley Williams (D)	45	DR: 79
Michael Rose (D)	18	DR: 79
David Poole (M)	24	SD: 41
Stephen Gleeson (M)	14	SD: 37
Adam Griffin (M)	28	SD: 23
Jason Taylor (M)	43	SD: 10
Anthony Elding (F)	20	SR: 159
Adam Le Fondre (F)	12	SR: 181

KEY PLAYER APPEARANCES

	PLAYER	POS	AGE	APP	MINS ON	GOALS	CARDS(Y/R)
1	Ashley Williams	DEF	22	46	4116	1	2	2
2	Jason Taylor	MID	20	45	3937	1	7	0
3	Gareth Owen	DEF	24	39	3480	0	5	0
4	Adam Griffin	MID	22	42	2934	3	4	0
5	Robert Clare	DEF	24	30	2451	0	3	1
6	Tony Dinning	MID	32	33	2444	2	8	0
7	David Poole	MID	22	31	2421	4	1	0
8	Michael Rose	DEF	24	25	1917	3	1	0
9	Tesfaye Bramble	ATT	26	31	1771	6	4	0
10	Anthony Elding	ATT	25	20	1758	11	2	0
11	Anthony Pilkington	ATT	19	24	1644	5	2	0
12	James Spencer	GK	22	15	1350	0	0	0
13	Wayne Hennessey	GK	20	15	1350	0	0	0
14	Keith Briggs	DEF	25	20	1325	2	0	0
15	Adam Le Fondre	ATT	20	21	1273	7	2	0
16	Stephen Gleeson	MID	0	14	1244	2	3	0
17	Adam Proudlock	ATT	26	23	1176	3	5	0
18	Liam Dickinson	ATT	21	32	1170	7	5	1

KEY PLAYERS - GOALSCORERS

Anthony Elding

Goals in the League	11

Player Strike Rate Average number of minutes between League goals scored by player: **159**

Contribution to Attacking Power Average number of minutes between League team goals while on pitch: **58**

Club Strike Rate Average number of minutes between League goals scored by club: **65**

	PLAYER	GOALS LGE	POWER	STRIKE RATE
1	Anthony Elding	11	58	159 mins
2	Adam Le Fondre	7	67	181 mins
3	Tesfaye Bramble	6	53	295 mins
4	Anthony Pilkington	5	63	328 mins

KEY PLAYERS - MIDFIELDERS

David Poole

Goals in the League	4

Contribution to Attacking Power Average number of minutes between League team goals while on pitch: **59**

Defensive Rating Average number of mins between League goals conceded while on the pitch: **100**

Scoring Difference Defensive Rating minus Contribution to Attacking Power: **41**

	PLAYER	GOALS LGE	DEF RATE	POWER	SCORE DIFF
1	David Poole	4	100	59	41 mins
2	Stephen Gleeson	2	88	51	37 mins
3	Adam Griffin	3	88	65	23 mins
4	Jason Taylor	1	74	64	10 mins

KEY PLAYERS - DEFENDERS

Robert Clare

Goals Conceded when he was on pitch	21

Clean Sheets In games when he played at least 70 minutes: **16**

Defensive Rating Ave number of mins between League goals conceded while on the pitch: **116**

Club Defensive Rating Average number of mins between League goals conceded by the club this season: **78**

	PLAYER	CON LGE	CLEAN SHEETS	DEF RATE
1	Robert Clare	21	16	116 mins
2	Gareth Owen	43	18	80 mins
3	Ashley Williams	52	19	79 mins
4	Michael Rose	24	11	79 mins

KEY GOALKEEPER

Wayne Hennessey

Goals Conceded in the League	16
Defensive Rating Ave number of mins between League goals conceded while on the pitch.	84
Counting Games Games when he played at least 70 mins	15
Clean Sheets In games when he played at least 70 mins	10

TOP POINT EARNERS

	PLAYER	GAMES	AV PTS
1	Michael Rose	18	2.11
2	Robert Clare	26	2.00
3	Wayne Hennessey	15	1.93
4	Stephen Gleeson	14	1.86
5	Anthony Elding	20	1.80
6	Tesfaye Bramble	14	1.79
7	David Poole	24	1.75
8	Anthony Pilkington	17	1.71
9	Adam Griffin	28	1.64
10	Gareth Owen	38	1.58
	CLUB AVERAGE:		1.54

ROCHDALE

Final Position: **9th**

NICKNAME: THE DALE   KEY: ☐ Won ☐ Drawn ☐ Lost   Attendance

#	Comp	Opponent	H/A	W/D/L	Score	Scorers	Attendance
1	div3	Walsall	H	L	0-1		3,218
2	div3	Torquay	A	L	0-1		3,039
3	div3	Swindon	A	L	0-1		6,771
4	div3	Notts County	H	L	0-1		2,321
5	ccr1	Doncaster	A	L	2-3	Rundle 45, Doolan 79	3,690
6	div3	Accrington	A	D	1-1	Dagnall 20	3,045
7	div3	Hereford	H	D	1-1	Jones 90 pen	2,146
8	div3	Bristol Rovers	A	D	0-0		4,689
9	div3	Grimsby	H	W	1-0	Sako 57	1,997
10	div3	Wycombe	H	L	0-2		2,313
11	div3	Boston	A	W	3-0	Dagnall 7, 33, Doolan 90	1,709
12	div3	Wrexham	A	W	2-1	Dagnall 48, 77	3,577
13	div3	Shrewsbury	H	D	1-1	J.Sharp 7	2,942
14	div3	Darlington	A	W	5-0	Sako 7, 35, Goodall 20, Dagnall 45, Moyo-Modise 82	3,752
15	div3	Chester	H	D	0-0		3,149
16	div3	Lincoln	A	L	1-7	Goodall 23	5,194
17	div3	Stockport	H	L	1-3	Jones 53	3,709
18	div3	Bury	H	L	1-3	Dagnall 11	4,499
19	facr1	Hartlepool	H	D	1-1	Doolan 62	2,098
20	div3	Barnet	A	L	2-3	Clarke 22, G.Murray 59	1,972
21	facr1r	Hartlepool	A	L	2-4*	(*on penalties)	2,788
22	div3	Mansfield	H	W	2-0	Dagnall 24, Doolan 41	2,378
23	div3	Macclesfield	A	L	0-1		1,472
24	div3	Peterborough	H	L	0-1		1,982
25	div3	Hartlepool	A	L	0-1		3,659
26	div3	MK Dons	A	L	1-2	Harper 58 og	5,459
27	div3	Wrexham	H	D	2-2	G.Murray 63, Doolan 78	2,837
28	div3	Boston	H	W	4-0	Jones 44, Dagnall 62, Mocquet 65, G.Murray 70	2,159
29	div3	Grimsby	A	W	4-0	Ramsden 13, 72, G.Murray 45, Rundle 66	4,302
30	div3	Wycombe	A	D	1-1	Etuhu 80	4,067
31	div3	Bristol Rovers	H	L	0-1		2,547
32	div3	MK Dons	H	W	5-0	Le Fondre 5, 62, Ramsden 10, Prendergast 16, Etuhu 84	2,493
33	div3	Walsall	A	D	1-1	Ince 5 og	5,046
34	div3	Notts County	A	W	2-1	G.Murray 80, Muirhead 83	4,493
35	div3	Torquay	H	W	2-0	G.Murray 19, Le Fondre 90 pen	2,456
36	div3	Hereford	A	D	0-0		3,090
37	div3	Accrington	H	W	4-2	Rundle 14, G.Murray 25, 32, Le Fondre 82 pen	3,433
38	div3	Darlington	H	D	0-0		3,256
39	div3	Chester	A	W	1-0	Dodds 5	2,197
40	div3	Stockport	A	W	7-2	G.Murray 4, 53, Goodall 11, Rundle 15 pen, Muirhead 17, 46, Dagnall 89	6,679
41	div3	Shrewsbury	A	L	0-3		4,363
42	div3	Lincoln	H	W	2-0	Dagnall 89, Rundle 90	2,911
43	div3	Swindon	H	D	0-0		2,544
44	div3	Bury	A	W	1-0	G.Murray 74	5,075
45	div3	Barnet	H	L	0-2		2,525
46	div3	Mansfield	A	W	2-1	G.Murray 9, Dodds 90	2,023
47	div3	Macclesfield	H	W	5-0	Dagnall 20, 41, 45, G.Murray 47, 59	2,989
48	div3	Hartlepool	H	W	2-0	G.Murray 2, Dagnall 76 pen	5,846
49	div3	Peterborough	A	D	3-3	G.Murray 11, Dagnall 63, 69	6,011

TEAM OF THE SEASON

D Rory McArdle   CG: 25 DR: 118
M David Perkins   CG: 14 SD: 51
D Lee Crooks   CG: 18 DR: 84
M Ben Muirhead*   CG: 11 SD: 44
F Glenn Murray   CG: 26 SR: 158
G Mathew Gilks   CG: 46 DR: 82
D Alan Goodall   CG: 45 DR: 81
M John Doolan   CG: 38 SD: 32
F Chris Dagnall   CG: 29 SR: 164
D Gary Brown   CG: 13 DR: 80
M Gary Jones   CG: 25 SD: 16

KEY PLAYER APPEARANCES

	PLAYER	POS	AGE	APP	MINS ON	GOALS	CARDS(Y/R)	
1	Mathew Gilks	GK	25	46	4140	0	2	0
2	Alan Goodall	DEF	25	45	4050	3	8	0
3	John Doolan	MID	33	40	3496	3	7	1
4	Nathan Stanton	DEF	26	35	3015	0	10	0
5	Simon Ramsden	DEF	25	34	2795	3	2	0
6	Chris Dagnall	ATT	22	37	2793	17	3	0
7	Glenn Murray	ATT	23	31	2528	16	2	0
8	Gary Jones	MID	30	27	2317	3	2	0
9	Rory McArdle	DEF	20	25	2250	0	2	0
10	Lee Crooks	DEF	29	31	2186	0	4	0
11	Adam Rundle	ATT	22	29	1779	4	0	0
12	David Perkins	MID	25	18	1377	0	3	0
13	Gary Brown	DEF	21	21	1287	0	0	0
14	Morike Sako	ATT	25	17	1202	3	4	0
15	Ernie Cooksey	MID	27	19	1061	0	3	0
16	James Sharp	DEF	31	12	1041	1	2	0
17	Ben Muirhead	MID	24	12	981	3	1	0
18	Mark Jackson	DEF	29	12	908	0	2	0

KEY PLAYERS - GOALSCORERS

Glenn Murray

Goals in the League	16

Player Strike Rate — Average number of minutes between League goals scored by player	158

Contribution to Attacking Power — Average number of minutes between League team goals while on pitch	48

Club Strike Rate — Average number of minutes between League goals scored by club	61

	PLAYER	GOALS LGE	POWER	STRIKE RATE
1	Glenn Murray	16	48	158 mins
2	Chris Dagnall	17	63	164 mins
3	Ben Muirhead	3	54	327 mins
4	Morike Sako	3	75	400 mins

KEY PLAYERS - MIDFIELDERS

David Perkins

Goals in the League	0

Contribution to Attacking Power — Average number of minutes between League team goals while on pitch	47

Defensive Rating — Average number of mins between League goals conceded while on the pitch	98

Scoring Difference — Defensive Rating minus Contribution to Attacking Power	51

	PLAYER	GOALS LGE	DEF RATE	POWER	SCORE DIFF
1	David Perkins	0	98	47	51 mins
2	Ben Muirhead	3	98	54	44 mins
3	John Doolan	3	89	57	32 mins
4	Gary Jones	3	72	56	16 mins

KEY PLAYERS - DEFENDERS

Rory McArdle

Goals Conceded when he was on pitch	19

Clean Sheets — In games when he played at least 70 minutes	12

Defensive Rating — Ave number of mins between League goals conceded while on the pitch	118

Club Defensive Rating — Average number of mins between League goals conceded by the club this season.	86

	PLAYER	CON LGE	CLEAN SHEETS	DEF RATE
1	Rory McArdle	19	12	118 mins
2	Lee Crooks	26	7	84 mins
3	Alan Goodall	50	17	81 mins
4	Gary Brown	16	4	80 mins

KEY GOALKEEPER

Mathew Gilks

Goals Conceded in the League	50

Defensive Rating — Ave number of mins between League goals conceded while on the pitch.	82

Counting Games — Games when he played at least 70 mins	46

Clean Sheets — In games when he played at least 70 mins	18

TOP POINT EARNERS

	PLAYER	GAMES	AV PTS
1	David Perkins	14	2.00
2	Rory McArdle	25	1.80
3	Adam Rundle	16	1.75
4	Lee Crooks	18	1.67
5	Glenn Murray	26	1.62
6	John Doolan	38	1.55
7	Mathew Gilks	46	1.43
8	Alan Goodall	45	1.40
9	Simon Ramsden	30	1.40
10	Gary Brown	13	1.38
	CLUB AVERAGE:		1.43

PETERBOROUGH UNITED

Final Position: **10th**

NICKNAME: THE POSH **KEY:** ☐ Won ☐ Drawn ☐ Lost Attendance

#		Opponent			Score	Scorers	Attendance
1	div3	Bristol Rovers	H	W	4-1	Day 10, Butcher 32, Yeo 35, Opara 77	4,890
2	div3	Boston	A	W	1-0	Yeo 86	3,528
3	div3	Wrexham	A	D	0-0		4,706
4	div3	Macclesfield	H	W	3-1	Benjamin 46, 48, Teague 62 og	4,136
5	ccr1	Ipswich	H	W	4-2*	Benjamin 45 pen, Branston 96 (*on penalties)	4,792
6	div3	Notts County	A	D	0-0		6,353
7	div3	Bury	H	L	0-1		5,561
8	div3	Darlington	H	L	1-3	Crow 81	3,848
9	div3	Walsall	A	L	0-5		4,070
10	div3	Swindon	A	W	1-0	Benjamin 45	7,329
11	ccr2	Everton	H	L	1-2	Benjamin 56	10,756
12	div3	Hartlepool	H	L	3-5	Butcher 59, Gain 61, Holden 70	3,916
13	div3	Barnet	H	D	1-1	Gain 36	3,193
14	div3	Stockport	A	W	1-0	Benjamin 46	4,775
15	div3	MK Dons	A	W	2-0	Arber 70, Richards 81	6,647
16	div3	Shrewsbury	H	W	2-1	Benjamin 42, Crow 65	4,171
17	div3	Wycombe	A	L	0-2		4,924
18	div3	Grimsby	H	D	2-2	Futcher 61, Benjamin 79	4,203
19	div3	Accrington	H	W	4-2	Benjamin 57 pen, Crow 58, 88, McLean 60	3,990
20	facr1	Rotherham	H	W	3-0	Butcher 29, McLean 59, Crow 73	4,281
21	div3	Mansfield	A	W	2-0	McLean 39, Crow 67	3,550
22	div3	Torquay	H	W	5-2	Huke 12, Thorpe 26 og, Futcher 36, McLean 59, Butcher 60	4,452
23	facr2	Tranmere	A	W	2-1	Crow 45, 70	6,308
24	div3	Hereford	A	D	0-0		2,309
25	div3	Rochdale	A	W	1-0	McLean 73	1,982
26	div3	Chester	H	L	0-2		4,491
27	div3	Lincoln	H	L	1-2	Gain 42	8,405
28	div3	Barnet	A	L	0-1		2,958
29	div3	Hartlepool	A	L	0-1		4,654
30	div3	Walsall	H	L	0-2		4,405
31	facr3	Plymouth	H	D	1-1	McLean 78	6,255
32	div3	Darlington	A	L	1-3	Smith 23	2,321
33	facr3r	Plymouth	A	L	1-2	McLean 13	9,973
34	div3	Stockport	H	L	0-3		4,330
35	div3	Lincoln	A	L	0-1		6,606
36	div3	Swindon	H	D	1-1	Gain 71	3,516
37	div3	Bristol Rovers	A	L	2-3	Crow 65, McLean 74	5,700
38	div3	Wrexham	H	W	3-0	McLean 23, Boyd 53, S.Evans 82 og	3,839
39	div3	Macclesfield	A	L	1-2	McLean 50	2,274
40	div3	Boston	H	D	1-1	Boyd 75	4,882
41	div3	Bury	A	W	3-0	Mackail-Smith 53, Futcher 57, Strachan 64	2,085
42	div3	Notts County	H	W	2-0	Boyd 51, Morgan 55	5,014
43	div3	MK Dons	H	W	4-0	Gain 25, Strachan 39, Mackail-Smith 79, Butcher 85	5,880
44	div3	Shrewsbury	A	L	1-2	Gain 22	4,027
45	div3	Grimsby	A	W	2-0	Boyd 46, White 73	5,164
46	div3	Wycombe	H	D	3-3	Mackail-Smith 8, 75, Newton 59	6,062
47	div3	Accrington	A	L	2-3	Mackail-Smith 43, Low 54	1,808
48	div3	Mansfield	H	W	2-0	Mackail-Smith 87, White 89	4,276
49	div3	Torquay	A	D	1-1	Mackail-Smith 77 pen	2,106
50	div3	Hereford	H	W	3-0	Mackail-Smith 1, White 13, Strachan 50	3,759
51	div3	Chester	A	D	1-1	Artell 71 og	1,905
52	div3	Rochdale	H	D	3-3	Boyd 22, 26, Blanchett 54	6,011

KEY PLAYER APPEARANCES

	PLAYER	POS	AGE	APP	MINS ON	GOALS	CARDS(Y/R)	
1	Adam Newton	DEF	26	43	3759	1	6	0
2	Mark Tyler	GK	30	41	3690	0	0	0
3	Richard Butcher	MID	26	43	3116	4	1	0
4	Mark Arber	DEF	29	34	2723	1	5	0
5	Peter Gain	MID	30	34	2477	6	5	0
6	Danny Crow	ATT	21	35	2196	6	1	0
7	Guy Branston	DEF	28	24	2002	0	7	1
8	Craig Morgan	DEF	22	23	1995	1	2	0
9	Ben Futcher	DEF	26	25	1963	3	6	0
10	Dean Holden	DEF	27	21	1800	1	3	0
11	Micah Hyde	MID	32	18	1614	0	1	0
12	George Boyd	MID	21	20	1612	6	3	0
13	Joshua Low	MID	28	19	1551	1	1	0
14	Trevor Benjamin	ATT	28	27	1485	7	2	0
15	Jamie Day	MID	21	24	1425	1	1	0
16	Aaron McLean	ATT	24	16	1357	7	4	0
17	Jude Stirling	DEF	24	22	1286	0	2	0
18	Craig Mackail-Smith	ATT	23	15	1174	8	2	0

KEY PLAYERS - GOALSCORERS

Craig Mackail-Smith

Goals in the League	8	Player Strike Rate Average number of minutes between League goals scored by player	146
Contribution to Attacking Power Average number of minutes between League team goals while on pitch	40	Club Strike Rate Average number of minutes between League goals scored by club	59

	PLAYER	GOALS LGE	POWER	STRIKE RATE
1	Craig Mackail-Smith	8	40	146 mins
2	Aaron McLean	7	71	193 mins
3	Trevor Benjamin	7	70	212 mins
4	George Boyd	6	52	268 mins

KEY PLAYERS - MIDFIELDERS

Shane Blackett

Goals in the League	0	Contribution to Attacking Power Average number of minutes between League team goals while on pitch	42
Defensive Rating Average number of mins between League goals conceded while on the pitch	91	Scoring Difference Defensive Rating minus Contribution to Attacking Power	49

	PLAYER	GOALS LGE	DEF RATE	POWER	SCORE DIFF
1	Shane Blackett	0	91	42	49 mins
2	Jamie Day	1	79	50	29 mins
3	George Boyd	6	70	52	18 mins
4	Micah Hyde	0	62	48	14 mins

KEY PLAYERS - DEFENDERS

Guy Branston

Goals Conceded when he was on pitch	27	Clean Sheets In games when he played at least 70 minutes	8
Defensive Rating Ave number of mins between League goals conceded while on the pitch	74	Club Defensive Rating Average number of mins between League goals conceded by the club this season.	67

	PLAYER	CON LGE	CLEAN SHEETS	DEF RATE
1	Guy Branston	27	8	74 mins
2	Adam Newton	55	14	68 mins
3	Ben Futcher	29	8	67 mins
4	Craig Morgan	31	6	64 mins

KEY GOALKEEPER

Mark Tyler

Goals Conceded in the League	52
Defensive Rating Ave number of mins between League goals conceded while on the pitch.	70
Counting Games Games when he played at least 70 mins	41
Clean Sheets In games when he played at least 70 mins	16

TOP POINT EARNERS

	PLAYER	GAMES	AV PTS
1	Jamie Day	12	2.08
2	Shane Blackett	12	1.83
3	Trevor Benjamin	14	1.79
4	Craig Mackail-Smith	13	1.77
5	Mark Tyler	41	1.56
6	Ben Futcher	20	1.55
7	George Boyd	17	1.53
8	Peter Gain	24	1.46
9	Dean Holden	20	1.45
10	Guy Branston	22	1.45
	CLUB AVERAGE:		1.41

TEAM OF THE SEASON

D Guy Branston **CG:** 22 **DR:** 74
M Shane Blackett **CG:** 12 **SD:** 49
D Adam Newton **CG:** 41 **DR:** 68
M Jamie Day **CG:** 12 **SD:** 29
F Craig Mackail-Smith **CG:** 13 **SR:** 146
G Mark Tyler **CG:** 41 **DR:** 70
D Ben Futcher **CG:** 20 **DR:** 67
M George Boyd **CG:** 17 **SD:** 18
F Aaron McLean **CG:** 15 **SR:** 193
D Craig Morgan **CG:** 22 **DR:** 64
M Micah Hyde **CG:** 18 **SD:** 14

DARLINGTON

Final Position: **11th**

NICKNAME: THE QUAKERS

KEY: ☐ Won ☐ Drawn ☐ Lost

Attendance

1	div3	Macclesfield	H W	**4-0**	Giallanza 12, Conlon 32, 41, 73	4,095
2	div3	Accrington	A W	**2-0**	Cummins 33, Smith 43	2,667
3	div3	Boston	A L	**1-4**	Conlon 30	1,934
4	div3	Swindon	H L	**1-2**	Giallanza 45	4,571
5	ccr1	Stoke	A W	**2-1**	Logan 45, Joachim 54	3,573
6	div3	Walsall	A L	**0-1**		4,651
7	div3	Torquay	H D	**1-1**	Ngoma 45	4,007
8	div3	Peterborough	A W	**3-1**	Conlon 3 pen, Joachim 22, 25	3,848
9	div3	Bury	H W	**1-0**	Conlon 67 pen	3,335
10	div3	Bristol Rovers	H D	**1-1**	Stamp 90	3,654
11	ccr2	Reading	A L	**2-4***	Johnson 19 pen, Joachim 34, 52 (*on penalties)	10,353
12	div3	Shrewsbury	A D	**2-2**	Giallanza 29, Wainwright 70	3,931
13	div3	Mansfield	A L	**0-1**		2,794
14	div3	Grimsby	H D	**2-2**	Armstrong 8, Smith 25	3,636
15	div3	Rochdale	H L	**0-5**		3,752
16	div3	Hereford	A D	**1-1**	Armstrong 37	2,838
17	div3	Barnet	H W	**2-0**	Johnson 75, Devera 78 og	3,268
18	div3	Hartlepool	A D	**0-0**		7,458
19	div3	Chester	H W	**1-0**	Cummins 18	3,630
20	facr1	Lewes	A W	**4-1**	Smith 38, 90, Collins 62, Ngoma 82	1,500
21	div3	Lincoln	A W	**3-1**	Holloway 43, Cummins 55, Johnson 73	5,292
22	div3	MK Dons	H W	**1-0**	Wainwright 38	4,017
23	facr2	Swansea	H L	**1-3**	Smith 2	4,183
24	div3	Wycombe	A L	**0-1**		3,885
25	div3	Stockport	A L	**2-5**	Smith 7, Keltie 40 pen	4,564
26	div3	Notts County	H L	**0-1**		3,253
27	div3	Wrexham	A L	**0-1**		3,401
28	div3	Mansfield	H L	**0-2**		3,808
29	div3	Shrewsbury	H L	**1-2**	Joachim 48	2,825
30	div3	Peterborough	H W	**3-1**	Wheater 41, Joachim 51, 61	2,321
31	div3	Bury	A D	**1-1**	J.Wright 87	1,870
32	div3	Grimsby	A W	**1-0**	T.Ryan 83	3,282
33	div3	Wrexham	H D	**1-1**	T.Wright 45 pen	3,301
34	div3	Macclesfield	A D	**1-1**	Ravenhill 34	2,173
35	div3	Bristol Rovers	A W	**2-1**	Blundell 7, Cummins 70	5,511
36	div3	Boston	H W	**2-0**	Miller 59, Wainwright 64	2,764
37	div3	Swindon	A D	**1-1**	Smith 71	5,570
38	div3	Accrington	H W	**2-1**	T.Wright 21, Blundell 29	2,790
39	div3	Torquay	A W	**1-0**	Joachim 87	2,109
40	div3	Walsall	H D	**0-0**		3,745
41	div3	Rochdale	A D	**0-0**		3,256
42	div3	Hereford	H W	**1-0**	T.Wright 67	3,165
43	div3	Hartlepool	H L	**0-3**		9,987
44	div3	Barnet	A L	**1-2**	Wheater 22	2,364
45	div3	Chester	A D	**1-1**	Blundell 89 pen	1,942
46	div3	Lincoln	H D	**1-1**	Joachim 39	3,878
47	div3	MK Dons	A L	**0-1**		5,730
48	div3	Wycombe	H W	**3-2**	Wainwright 26, 47, Rowson 70	2,727
49	div3	Notts County	A W	**1-0**	Rowson 82	5,264
50	div3	Stockport	H L	**0-5**		5,184

KEY PLAYER APPEARANCES

	PLAYER	POS	AGE	APP	MINS ON	GOALS	CARDS(Y/R)
1	Michael Cummins	MID	29	39	3347	4	4	0
2	Sam Russell	GK	24	31	2790	0	2	0
3	Neil Wainwright	MID	29	41	2691	5	3	0
4	Patrick Collins	DEF	22	31	2566	0	5	0
5	Martin Smith	MID	32	34	2487	4	3	0
6	Julian Joachim	ATT	32	36	2386	7	0	0
7	Brian Close	DEF	25	27	2351	0	4	0
8	Clark Keltie	MID	23	27	2199	1	6	1
9	Craig James	DEF	24	23	1877	0	4	2
10	David Rowson	DEF	30	24	1783	2	2	0
11	Evan Horwood	DEF	21	20	1647	0	2	2
12	Alun Armstrong	ATT	32	28	1385	2	2	0
13	David Wheater	DEF	20	15	1350	2	2	0
14	Greg Blundell	ATT	31	15	1292	3	2	0
15	Joey Hutchinson	MID	25	13	1170	0	0	0
16	Darren Holloway	DEF	29	21	1159	1	2	1
17	Kaluswivikako Ngoma	DEF	29	17	1157	1	2	0
18	Richard Ravenhill	MID	26	15	1121	1	4	0

KEY PLAYERS - GOALSCORERS

Julian Joachim

Goals in the League	7	Player Strike Rate Average number of minutes between League goals scored by player	340
Contribution to Attacking Power Average number of minutes between League team goals while on pitch	79	Club Strike Rate Average number of minutes between League goals scored by club	81

	PLAYER	GOALS LGE	POWER	STRIKE RATE
1	Julian Joachim	7	79	340 mins
2	Greg Blundell	3	99	430 mins
3	Neil Wainwright	5	86	538 mins
4	Martin Smith	4	82	621 mins

KEY PLAYERS - MIDFIELDERS

Clark Keltie

Goals in the League	1	Contribution to Attacking Power Average number of minutes between League team goals while on pitch	70
Defensive Rating Average number of mins between League goals conceded while on the pitch	87	Scoring Difference Defensive Rating minus Contribution to Attacking Power	17

	PLAYER	GOALS LGE	DEF RATE	POWER	SCORE DIFF
1	Clark Keltie	1	87	70	17 mins
2	Joey Hutchinson	0	73	68	5 mins
3	Michael Cummins	4	79	76	3 mins
4	Martin Smith	4	75	82	-7 mins

KEY PLAYERS - DEFENDERS

David Wheater

Goals Conceded when he was on Pitch	12	Clean Sheets In games when he played at least 70 minutes	6
Defensive Rating Ave number of mins between League goals conceded while on the pitch	112	Club Defensive Rating Average number of mins between League goals conceded by the club this season.	75

	PLAYER	CON LGE	CLEAN SHEETS	DEF RATE
1	David Wheater	12	6	112 mins
2	Evan Horwood	16	6	102 mins
3	Brian Close	25	7	94 mins
4	David Rowson	27	4	66 mins

TEAM OF THE SEASON

D David Wheater CG: 15 DR: 112

M Clark Keltie CG: 25 SD: 17

D Evan Horwood CG: 18 DR: 102

M Joey Hutchinson CG: 13 SD: 5

F Julian Joachim CG: 22 SR: 340

G Sam Russell CG: 31 DR: 73

D Brian Close CG: 26 DR: 94

M Michael Cummins CG: 36 SD: 3

F Greg Blundell CG: 14 SR: 430

D David Rowson CG: 17 DR: 66

M Martin Smith CG: 24 SD: -7

KEY GOALKEEPER

Sam Russell

Goals Conceded in the League	38
Defensive Rating Ave number of mins between League goals conceded while on the pitch.	73
Counting Games Games when he played at least 70 mins	31
Clean Sheets In games when he played at least 70 mins	11

TOP POINT EARNERS

	PLAYER	GAMES	AV PTS
1	David Wheater	15	1.80
2	Evan Horwood	18	1.72
3	Neil Wainwright	25	1.64
4	Clark Keltie	25	1.60
5	Brian Close	26	1.58
6	Martin Smith	24	1.54
7	David Rowson	17	1.53
8	Greg Blundell	14	1.50
9	Joey Hutchinson	13	1.46
10	Sam Russell	31	1.42
	CLUB AVERAGE:		1.41

WYCOMBE WANDERERS

Final Position: 12th

KNAME: THE CHAIRBOYS **KEY:** ☐ Won ☐ Drawn ☐ Lost   Attendance

div3	Wrexham	H	D	1-1	Mooney 6	4,763
div3	Bristol Rovers	A	W	2-1	Betsy 50, Mooney 59	5,349
div3	Notts County	A	L	0-1		4,053
div3	Bury	H	W	3-0	Easter 60, 72, 85	4,184
ccr1	Swansea	A	W	3-2	Easter 50, Oakes 64, Williamson 114	5,892
div3	Macclesfield	A	W	2-0	Easter 16, Mooney 35	1,574
div3	Mansfield	H	W	1-0	Easter 59	4,754
div3	Chester	H	W	1-0	Betsy 28	4,277
div3	Hereford	A	W	2-1	Easter 32, 74	2,585
div3	Rochdale	A	W	2-0	Mooney 15, Dixon 90	2,313
ccr2	Fulham	A	W	2-1	Easter 8, Mooney 41 pen	6,620
div3	Lincoln	H	L	1-3	Mooney 1	5,247
div3	Swindon	H	D	1-1	Mooney 90	6,090
div3	Accrington	A	L	1-2	Antwi 55	2,243
div3	Torquay	H	W	2-0	Mooney 5, Martin 80	4,769
div3	Walsall	A	L	0-2		6,745
div3	Peterborough	H	W	2-0	Betsy 64, Easter 84	4,924
ccr3	Doncaster	H	W	3-2*	Oakes 71, Easter 116 (*on penalties)	3,308
div3	Boston	A	W	1-0	Bloomfield 90	1,762
div3	Shrewsbury	A	D	0-0		4,116
ccr4	Notts County	A	W	1-0	Easter 50	7,395
facr1	Oxford	H	W	2-1	Antwi 58, Oakes 86	6,279
div3	Grimsby	H	D	1-1	Golbourne 77	5,037
div3	Hartlepool	A	L	0-2		3,711
facr2	Stockport	A	L	1-2	Easter 34	3,821
div3	Darlington	H	W	1-0	Easter 3	3,885
div3	Barnet	H	D	1-1	Mooney 80	4,711
div3	MK Dons	A	L	1-3	Mooney 31	5,977
ccqf	Charlton	A	W	1-0	Easter 35	18,940
div3	Stockport	H	W	2-0	Betsy 2, Easter 63	4,559
div3	Swindon	A	L	1-2	Easter 81	8,878
div3	Lincoln	A	L	0-1		5,465
div3	Hereford	H	D	0-0		4,851
div3	Rochdale	H	D	1-1	Easter 51	4,067
ccsfl1	Chelsea	H	D	1-1	Easter 77	5,771
div3	Chester	A	W	1-0	Easter 88	2,336
div3	Accrington	H	D	1-1	Betsy 59	5,884
ccsfl2	Chelsea	A	L	0-4		41,591
div3	Stockport	A	L	0-2		5,353
div3	Wrexham	A	W	2-0	Williamson 23, Easter 52	3,607
div3	Notts County	H	D	0-0		4,836
div3	Bury	A	W	4-0	Doherty 38, McGleish 43, Mooney 65, Easter 90	1,988
div3	Mansfield	A	L	2-3	McGleish 27, 37	2,711
div3	Macclesfield	H	W	3-0	Doherty 40, Martin 54, Bloomfield 65	5,450
div3	Torquay	A	L	0-3		3,060
div3	Walsall	H	D	0-0		5,625
div3	Boston	H	D	0-0		4,417
div3	Bristol Rovers	H	L	0-1		4,299
div3	Peterborough	A	D	3-3	Bloomfield 23, Stockley 28, Mooney 86 pen	6,062
div3	Shrewsbury	H	D	1-1	Mooney 32	5,299
div3	Grimsby	A	D	2-2	McGleish 22, Easter 25	4,271
div3	Hartlepool	H	L	0-1		5,540
div3	Darlington	A	L	2-3	Bloomfield 11, Easter 50	2,727
div3	MK Dons	H	L	0-2		7,150
div3	Barnet	A	L	1-2	McGleish 32	2,707

KEY PLAYER APPEARANCES

	PLAYER	POS	AGE	APP	MINS ON	GOALS	CARDS(Y/R)	
1	Tommy Mooney	ATT	35	42	3549	12	6	0
2	Matt Bloomfield	MID	23	41	3380	4	5	0
3	Anthony Grant	MID	20	40	3072	0	17	2
4	Russell Martin	MID	21	42	3052	2	10	0
5	Sam Stockley	DEF	29	34	2955	1	5	0
6	Mike Williamson	DEF	23	33	2921	2	7	0
7	Scott Golbourne	DEF	19	34	2920	1	4	0
8	Stefan Oakes	MID	28	35	2606	3	4	1
9	Kevin Betsy	MID	29	29	2592	5	3	0
10	Jermaine Easter	ATT	25	38	2551	17	8	1
11	Ricardo Batista	GK	20	29	2504	0	5	1
12	Will Antwi	DEF	24	25	2167	2	6	1
13	Chris Palmer	MID	23	32	2028	0	2	0
14	Tommy Doherty	MID	28	26	1770	2	11	2
15	Jamie Young	GK	22	19	1636	0	1	0
16	Scott McGleish	ATT	33	14	965	5	2	0
17	Sergio Torres	MID	23	19	903	0	0	0
18	Leon Crooks	DEF	21	10	900	0	0	0

KEY PLAYERS - GOALSCORERS

Jermaine Easter

Goals in the League	17	Player Strike Rate Average number of minutes between League goals scored by player	150
Contribution to Attacking Power Average number of minutes between League team goals while on pitch	79	Club Strike Rate Average number of minutes between League goals scored by club	79

	PLAYER	GOALS LGE	POWER	STRIKE RATE
1	Jermaine Easter	17	79	150 mins
2	Tommy Mooney	12	84	295 mins
3	Kevin Betsy	5	81	518 mins
4	Matt Bloomfield	4	82	845 mins

KEY PLAYERS - MIDFIELDERS

Kevin Betsy

Goals in the League	5	Contribution to Attacking Power Average number of minutes between League team goals while on pitch	81
Defensive Rating Average number of mins between League goals conceded while on the pitch	108	Scoring Difference Defensive Rating minus Contribution to Attacking Power	27

	PLAYER	GOALS LGE	DEF RATE	POWER	SCORE DIFF
1	Kevin Betsy	5	108	81	27 mins
2	Stefan Oakes	0	100	81	19 mins
3	Tommy Doherty	2	98	80	18 mins
4	Chris Palmer	0	78	67	11 mins

KEY PLAYERS - DEFENDERS

Mike Williamson

Goals Conceded when he was on pitch	26	Clean Sheets In games when he played at least 70 minutes	16
Defensive Rating Ave number of mins between League goals conceded while on the pitch	112	Club Defensive Rating Average number of mins between League goals conceded by the club this season.	88

	PLAYER	CON LGE	CLEAN SHEETS	DEF RATE
1	Mike Williamson	26	16	112 mins
2	Will Antwi	21	10	103 mins
3	Sam Stockley	32	14	92 mins
4	Scott Golbourne	32	15	91 mins

KEY GOALKEEPER

Ricardo Batista

Goals Conceded in the League	27
Defensive Rating Ave number of mins between League goals conceded while on the pitch.	92
Counting Games Games when he played at least 70 mins	27
Clean Sheets In games when he played at least 70 mins	12

TOP POINT EARNERS

	PLAYER	GAMES	AV PTS
1	Will Antwi	24	1.71
2	Mike Williamson	32	1.66
3	Kevin Betsy	29	1.62
4	Tommy Doherty	16	1.56
5	Stefan Oakes	25	1.48
6	Chris Palmer	17	1.47
7	Sam Stockley	33	1.45
8	Scott Golbourne	32	1.44
9	Ricardo Batista	28	1.43
10	Jermaine Easter	25	1.32
	CLUB AVERAGE:		1.35

TEAM OF THE SEASON

D Mike Williamson **CG:** 32 **DR:** 112
M Kevin Betsy **CG:** 29 **SD:** 27
D Will Antwi **CG:** 24 **DR:** 103
M Stefan Oakes **CG:** 25 **SD:** 19
F Jermaine Easter **CG:** 25 **SR:** 150
G Ricardo Batista **R:** 27 **DR:** 92
D Sam Stockley **CG:** 33 **DR:** 92
M Tommy Doherty **CG:** 16 **SD:** 18
F Tommy Mooney **CG:** 38 **SR:** 295
D Scott Golbourne **CG:** 32 **DR:** 91
M Chris Palmer **CG:** 17 **SD:** 11

NOTTS COUNTY

Final Position: 13th

NICKNAME: THE MAGPIES

KEY: ☐ Won ☐ Drawn ☐ Lost

				Result		Attendance
1	div3	Lincoln	A D	1-1	Hughes 55 og	6,046
2	div3	Shrewsbury	H D	1-1	Edwards 53	4,386
3	div3	Wycombe	H W	1-0	Junior Mendes 17	4,053
4	div3	Rochdale	A W	1-0	White 51	2,321
5	ccr1	Crystal Palace	A W	2-1	Dudfield 23, Martin 84	4,481
6	div3	Peterborough	H D	0-0		6,353
7	div3	MK Dons	A L	2-3	J.Lee 78, Martin 83	6,323
8	div3	Accrington	H W	3-2	Edwards 11, Martin 29, 35	4,677
9	div3	Chester	A D	0-0		1,818
10	div3	Barnet	A W	3-2	White 31, Parkinson 36, J.Lee 54	2,317
11	ccr2	Middlesbrough	A W	1-0	N'Toya 26	11,148
12	div3	Swindon	H D	1-1	White 67	6,079
13	div3	Stockport	H W	1-0	Junior Mendes 40	4,021
14	div3	Torquay	A W	1-0	Dudfield 90	2,815
15	div3	Mansfield	A D	2-2	Edwards 71, Dudfield 86	6,182
16	div3	Bristol Rovers	H L	1-2	Mendes 66	5,797
17	div3	Grimsby	A W	2-0	Mendes 60, J.Lee 83	4,029
18	ccr3	Southampton	H W	2-0	Edwards 13, J.Lee 44	6,731
19	div3	Bury	H L	0-1		4,770
20	div3	Boston	A D	3-3	J.Lee 28, 48, White 47	2,539
21	ccr4	Wycombe	H L	0-1		7,395
22	facr1	Leyton Orient	A L	1-2	Dudfield 90	3,011
23	div3	Wrexham	H W	2-1	Parkinson 37, J.Lee 60	4,416
24	div3	Walsall	A L	1-2	Ross 72	5,402
25	div3	Hartlepool	H L	0-1		3,546
26	div3	Macclesfield	H L	1-2	Martin 90	4,036
27	div3	Darlington	A W	1-0	White 84	3,253
28	div3	Hereford	H L	0-1		4,106
29	div3	Stockport	A L	0-2		5,823
30	div3	Swindon	A D	1-1	Dudfield 35	6,805
31	div3	Chester	H L	1-2	J.Lee 45	4,019
32	div3	Accrington	A W	2-1	Dudfield 9, J.Lee 20	1,702
33	div3	Torquay	H W	5-2	Mendes 23, Smith 39, Parkinson 40, J.Lee 83, 90	4,311
34	div3	Hereford	A L	2-3	J.Lee 7, 64	3,280
35	div3	Barnet	H D	1-1	Dudfield 17 pen	3,010
36	div3	Lincoln	H W	3-1	Smith 2, J.Lee 45, Dudfield 61	7,019
37	div3	Wycombe	A D	0-0		4,836
38	div3	Rochdale	H L	1-2	J.Lee 53	4,493
39	div3	Shrewsbury	A L	0-2		3,369
40	div3	MK Dons	H D	2-2	Smith 40 pen, Hunt 90	4,031
41	div3	Peterborough	A L	0-2		5,014
42	div3	Mansfield	H D	0-0		10,034
43	div3	Bristol Rovers	A L	0-2		4,642
44	div3	Bury	A W	1-0	N'Toya 40	2,310
45	div3	Grimsby	H W	2-0	Newey 52 og, Smith 86	4,724
46	div3	Boston	H W	2-0	J.Lee 11, Somner 70	4,170
47	div3	Wrexham	A W	1-0	Spender 88 og	4,557
48	div3	Walsall	H L	1-2	Dudfield 41	7,080
49	div3	Hartlepool	A D	1-1	Parkinson 45	6,174
50	div3	Darlington	H L	0-1		5,264
51	div3	Macclesfield	A D	1-1	Parkinson 38	4,114

KEY PLAYER APPEARANCES

	PLAYER	POS	AGE	APP	MINS ON	GOALS	CARDS(Y/R)	
1	Michael Edwards	DEF	27	45	3928	4	4	0
2	Austin McCann	DEF	27	43	3870	0	5	0
3	Kevin Pilkington	GK	33	39	3510	0	1	0
4	Andy Parkinson	ATT	28	45	3491	5	2	0
5	David Pipe	MID	23	39	3349	0	6	1
6	Jason Lee	ATT	36	38	3269	15	18	0
7	Matt Somner	MID	24	38	2939	1	7	1
8	Alan White	DEF	31	35	2921	5	8	1
9	Lawrie Dudfield	ATT	27	41	2618	7	5	0
10	Stephen Hunt	DEF	22	32	2293	1	3	1
11	Ian Ross	MID	21	35	2267	1	5	0
12	Jay Smith	MID	25	27	2238	4	5	0
13	Gary Silk	DEF	22	29	2106	0	5	0
14	Dan Gleeson	DEF	22	17	1368	0	5	0
15	Junior Mendes	ATT	30	23	1930	5	1	0
16	Daniel Martin	DEF	20	29	1243	5	4	0
17	Saul Deeney	GK	24	7	630	0	0	0

KEY PLAYERS - GOALSCORERS

Jason Lee

Goals in the League	15
Player Strike Rate Average number of minutes between League goals scored by player	**217**
Contribution to Attacking Power Average number of minutes between League team goals while on pitch	66
Club Strike Rate Average number of minutes between League goals scored by club	**75**

	PLAYER	GOALS LGE	POWER	STRIKE RAT
1	Jason Lee	15	66	217 mins
2	Lawrie Dudfield	7	74	374 mins
3	Junior Mendes	5	89	384 mins
4	Jay Smith	4	79	559 mins

KEY PLAYERS - MIDFIELDERS

Matt Somner

Goals in the League	1
Contribution to Attacking Power Average number of minutes between League team goals while on pitch	73
Defensive Rating Average number of mins between League goals conceded while on the pitch	97
Scoring Difference Defensive Rating minus Contribution to Attacking Power	24

	PLAYER	GOALS LGE	DEF RATE	POWER	SCORE DIF
1	Matt Somner	1	97	73	24 mins
2	Ian Ross	1	90	70	20 mins
3	David Pipe	0	83	88	-5 mins
4	Jay Smith	4	69	79	-10 mins

KEY PLAYERS - DEFENDERS

Dan Gleeson

Goals Conceded when he was on pitch	16
Clean Sheets In games when he played at least 70 minutes	7
Defensive Rating Ave number of mins between League goals conceded while on the pitch	85
Club Defensive Rating Average number of mins between League goals conceded by the club this season.	78

	PLAYER	CON LGE	CLEAN SHEETS	DEF RAT
1	Dan Gleeson	16	7	85 min
2	Austin McCann	47	14	82 min
3	Stephen Hunt	29	7	79 min
4	Michael Edwards	50	14	78 min

TEAM OF THE SEASON

Dan Gleeson CG: 14 DR: 85 (D)
Matt Somner CG: 30 SD: 24 (M)
Austin McCann CG: 43 DR: 82 (D)
Ian Ross CG: 21 SD: 20 (M)
Jason Lee CG: 36 SR: 217 (F)
Kevin Pilkington CG: 39 DR: 79 (G)
Stephen Hunt CG: 23 DR: 79 (D)
David Pipe CG: 38 SD: -5 (M)
Lawrie Dudfield CG: 25 SR: 374 (F)
Michael Edwards CG: 43 DR: 78 (D)
Jay Smith CG: 24 SD: -10 (M)

KEY GOALKEEPER

Kevin Pilkington

Goals Conceded in the League	44
Defensive Rating Ave number of mins between League goals conceded while on the pitch.	79
Counting Games Games when he played at least 70 mins	39
Clean Sheets In games when he played at least 70 mins	12

TOP POINT EARNERS

	PLAYER	GAMES	AV PT
1	Dan Gleeson	14	1.71
2	Matt Somner	30	1.57
3	Kevin Pilkington	39	1.46
4	Michael Edwards	43	1.42
5	Stephen Hunt	23	1.39
6	Jason Lee	36	1.36
7	David Pipe	38	1.34
8	Ian Ross	21	1.33
9	Austin McCann	43	1.30
10	Andy Parkinson	34	1.29
	CLUB AVERAGE:		**1.35**

BARNET

Final Position: **14th**

CKNAME: THE BEES   KEY: ☐ Won ☐ Drawn ☐ Lost   Attendance

1	div3	Torquay	H	L	0-1		2,827
2	div3	Swindon	A	L	1-2	Bailey 18	7,475
3	div3	Accrington	A	L	1-2	King 89	1,639
4	div3	Hereford	H	W	3-0	Grazioli 28, Bailey 62, Puncheon 90	1,945
5	ccr1	Cardiff	A	W	2-0	Kandol 33, 54	3,305
6	div3	Wrexham	A	D	1-1	Kandol 62	4,304
7	div3	Walsall	H	D	1-1	Sinclair 15	2,356
8	div3	Macclesfield	A	W	3-2	Hendon 59 pen, Cogan 64, Bailey 74	1,770
9	div3	Boston	H	D	3-3	Vieira 28, 62, Grazioli 90	1,461
10	div3	Notts County	H	L	2-3	Hendon 24 pen, Puncheon 29	2,317
11	ccr2	Leeds	A	L	1-3	Vieira 78	7,220
12	div3	Bury	A	D	2-2	Kandol 21, Hendon 81 pen	1,901
13	div3	Peterborough	A	D	1-1	Hessenthaler 46	3,193
14	div3	MK Dons	H	D	3-3	Hendon 38 pen, Kandol 52, Graham 57	2,819
15	div3	Stockport	A	L	0-2		4,133
16	div3	Lincoln	H	L	0-5		2,409
17	div3	Darlington	A	L	0-2		3,268
18	div3	Chester	H	W	1-0	Sinclair 29 pen	2,301
19	div3	Hartlepool	A	W	1-0	Cogan 83	3,778
20	facr1	Gainsborough	A	W	3-1	Sinclair 14, Kandol 78, 90 pen	1,914
21	div3	Rochdale	H	W	3-2	Kandol 39, 49, 90	1,972
22	div3	Bristol Rovers	A	L	0-2		5,351
23	facr2	Northampton	H	W	4-1	Birchall 49, Sinclair 53, Hendon 67 pen, Vieira 87	2,786
24	div3	Grimsby	H	L	0-1		1,588
25	div3	Wycombe	A	D	1-1	Hatch 60	4,711
26	div3	Mansfield	H	W	2-1	Yakubu 45, Gross 54	1,790
27	div3	Shrewsbury	A	W	1-0	Puncheon 82	3,620
28	div3	Peterborough	H	W	1-0	Birchall 13	2,958
29	div3	Bury	H	W	2-1	Bailey 7, Birchall 18	1,959
30	div3	Boston	A	L	1-2	Graham 12	1,780
31	facr3	Colchester	H	W	2-1	Yakubu 61, Puncheon 80	3,075
32	div3	Macclesfield	H	W	1-0	Birchall 40	2,018
33	div3	MK Dons	A	L	1-3	King 27	6,447
34	facr4	Plymouth	H	L	0-2		5,204
35	div3	Notts County	A	D	1-1	Bailey 74	3,010
36	div3	Torquay	A	D	1-1	Nicolau 89	1,942
37	div3	Accrington	H	L	1-2	Birchall 45	2,041
38	div3	Hereford	A	L	0-2		2,608
39	div3	Swindon	H	W	1-0	Allen 6	2,639
40	div3	Walsall	A	L	1-4	Allen 22	4,635
41	div3	Wrexham	H	L	1-2	Allen 27	2,180
42	div3	Stockport	H	W	3-1	Allen 44, Sinclair 47, Hatch 82	2,647
43	div3	Lincoln	A	L	0-1		4,339
44	div3	Shrewsbury	H	D	0-0		1,672
45	div3	Chester	A	L	0-2		1,591
46	div3	Darlington	H	W	2-1	Sinclair 4, Hatch 52	2,364
47	div3	Hartlepool	H	W	2-1	Birchall 4, Puncheon 81	2,906
48	div3	Rochdale	A	W	2-0	Cogan 24, Sinclair 33	2,525
49	div3	Bristol Rovers	H	D	1-1	Puncheon 45	2,541
50	div3	Grimsby	A	L	0-5		3,675
51	div3	Mansfield	A	L	1-2	Birchall 68	2,446
52	div3	Wycombe	H	W	2-1	Sinclair 53, Vieira 89	2,707

TEAM OF THE SEASON

Ishmail Yakubu CG: 27 DR: 77
Jason Puncheon CG: 32 SD: -9
Joe Devera CG: 23 DR: 76
Dean Sinclair CG: 42 SD: -13
Tresor Kandol CG: 14 SR: 215
Ross Flitney G: 12 DR: 61
Simon King CG: 41 DR: 62
Nick Bailey CG: 43 SD: -18
Adam Birchall CG: 21 SR: 321
Adam Gross CG: 24 DR: 58
Barry Cogan CG: 29 SD: -20

KEY PLAYER APPEARANCES

	PLAYER	POS	AGE	APP	MINS ON	GOALS	CARDS(Y/R)
1	Nick Bailey	MID	23	44	3872	5	8	0
2	Simon King	DEF	24	43	3796	2	4	0
3	Dean Sinclair	MID	22	42	3711	6	6	2
4	Jason Puncheon	MID	21	37	3005	5	6	1
5	Barry Cogan	MID	22	39	2823	3	3	1
6	Ishmail Yakubu	DEF	22	29	2473	1	1	0
7	Lee Harrison	GK	35	28	2427	0	1	0
8	Adam Gross	DEF	21	27	2235	1	9	1
9	Joe Devera	DEF	20	26	2128	0	5	0
10	Ian Hendon	DEF	35	26	2120	4	8	1
11	Richard Graham	MID	27	34	1931	2	0	0
12	Adam Birchall	ATT	22	23	1927	6	2	0
13	Andy Hessenthaler	MID	41	24	1740	1	8	0
14	Liam Hatch	ATT	25	31	1727	3	8	1
15	Nicky Nicolau	MID	23	22	1652	1	3	0
16	Tresor Kandol	ATT	25	16	1291	6	5	0
17	Anthony Charles	DEF	26	17	1274	0	4	0
18	Ross Flitney	GK	23	15	1173	0	3	0

KEY PLAYERS - GOALSCORERS

Tresor Kandol

Goals in the League	6	Player Strike Rate Average number of minutes between League goals scored by player	215
Contribution to Attacking Power Average number of minutes between League team goals while on pitch	53	Club Strike Rate Average number of minutes between League goals scored by club	75

	PLAYER	GOALS LGE	POWER	STRIKE RATE
1	Tresor Kandol	6	53	215 mins
2	Adam Birchall	6	87	321 mins
3	Liam Hatch	3	90	575 mins
4	Jason Puncheon	5	71	601 mins

KEY PLAYERS - MIDFIELDERS

Jason Puncheon

Goals in the League	5	Contribution to Attacking Power Average number of minutes between League team goals while on pitch	71
Defensive Rating Average number of mins between League goals conceded while on the pitch	62	Scoring Difference Defensive Rating minus Contribution to Attacking Power	-9

	PLAYER	GOALS LGE	DEF RATE	POWER	SCORE DIFF
1	Jason Puncheon	5	62	71	-9 mins
2	Dean Sinclair	6	59	72	-13 mins
3	Nick Bailey	5	57	75	-18 mins
4	Barry Cogan	3	56	76	-20 mins

KEY PLAYERS - DEFENDERS

Ishmail Yakubu

Goals Conceded when he was on pitch	32	Clean Sheets In games when he played at least 70 minutes	7
Defensive Rating Ave number of mins between League goals conceded while on the pitch	77	Club Defensive Rating Average number of mins between League goals conceded by the club this season.	59

	PLAYER	CON LGE	CLEAN SHEETS	DEF RATE
1	Ishmail Yakubu	32	7	77 mins
2	Joe Devera	28	6	76 mins
3	Simon King	61	9	62 mins
4	Adam Gross	38	3	58 mins

KEY GOALKEEPER

Ross Flitney

Goals Conceded in the League	19
Defensive Rating Ave number of mins between League goals conceded while on the pitch.	61
Counting Games Games when he played at least 70 mins	12
Clean Sheets In games when he played at least 70 mins	5

TOP POINT EARNERS

	PLAYER	GAMES	AV PTS
1	Barry Cogan	29	1.55
2	Lee Harrison	26	1.54
3	Joe Devera	23	1.52
4	Jason Puncheon	33	1.52
5	Ishmail Yakubu	27	1.52
6	Adam Birchall	21	1.38
7	Simon King	41	1.37
8	Dean Sinclair	42	1.36
9	Nicky Nicolau	17	1.35
10	Tresor Kandol	14	1.29
	CLUB AVERAGE:		1.28

GRIMSBY TOWN

Final Position: **15th**

NICKNAME: THE MARINERS | KEY: ☐ Won ☐ Drawn ☐ Lost | Attendance

#	Comp	Opponent	H/A	Result	Scorers	Attendance
1	div3	Boston	H W	3-2	Bore 68, 79, Rankin 73	5,012
2	div3	Wrexham	A L	0-3		5,180
3	div3	Bristol Rovers	A L	0-1		4,596
4	div3	Mansfield	H D	1-1	Bore 73	4,604
5	ccr1	Crewe	H L	0-3		1,635
6	div3	Bury	A L	0-3		2,118
7	div3	Macclesfield	H D	1-1	Toner 18 pen	3,638
8	div3	Walsall	H W	2-1	Bolland 38, Bore 73	3,669
9	div3	Rochdale	A L	0-1		1,997
10	div3	Chester	A W	2-0	Jones 90, Taylor 90	1,957
11	div3	Stockport	H L	0-1		4,708
12	div3	Hartlepool	H L	1-4	Fenton 16	3,486
13	div3	Darlington	A D	2-2	Toner 66 pen, Ravenhill 82	3,636
14	div3	Hereford	H W	2-1	Jones 9, 61	4,147
15	div3	Swindon	A L	0-3		5,719
16	div3	Notts County	H L	0-2		4,029
17	div3	Peterborough	A D	2-2	Toner 52, Bore 73 pen	4,203
18	div3	MK Dons	H L	1-3	Ravenhill 90	3,268
19	facr1	Northampton	A D	0-0		4,092
20	div3	Wycombe	A D	1-1	Jones 71	5,037
21	facr1r	Northampton	H L	0-2		2,657
22	div3	Accrington	H W	2-0	Paterson 12, Jones 56	4,511
23	div3	Barnet	A W	1-0	Paterson 28	1,588
24	div3	Shrewsbury	H W	2-1	Paterson 38, 72	4,076
25	div3	Lincoln	A L	0-2		5,919
26	div3	Torquay	H W	2-0	Rankin 18, Fenton 78	4,666
27	div3	Hartlepool	A L	0-2		5,290
28	div3	Stockport	A L	0-3		5,032
29	div3	Rochdale	H L	0-4		4,302
30	div3	Chester	H L	0-2		3,012
31	div3	Walsall	A L	0-2		4,889
32	div3	Darlington	H L	0-1		3,282
33	div3	Torquay	A L	1-4	Paterson 88	2,095
34	div3	Boston	A W	6-0	Bore 4, 42, 78, Hunt 7, Toner 20, Paterson 63	2,915
35	div3	Bristol Rovers	H W	4-3	North 33, Whittle 48, Boshell 53, Toner 66	5,883
36	div3	Mansfield	A W	2-0	Bolland 42, North 83	4,033
37	div3	Wrexham	H W	2-1	Bolland 45, Toner 90	5,850
38	div3	Macclesfield	A L	1-2	Jones 78	2,598
39	div3	Bury	H W	2-0	North 10, Toner 24	4,733
40	div3	Hereford	A W	1-0	Bolland 76	2,914
41	div3	Swindon	H W	1-0	Toner 73	4,595
42	div3	Peterborough	H L	0-2		5,164
43	div3	Notts County	A L	0-2		4,724
44	div3	MK Dons	A W	2-1	Boshell 32, Hunt 53	6,101
45	div3	Wycombe	H D	2-2	Jones 71, Bolland 83	4,271
46	div3	Accrington	A L	1-4	Newey 41	1,818
47	div3	Barnet	H W	5-0	Jones 26, North 39, 72, 90 pen, Fenton 80	3,675
48	div3	Lincoln	H D	0-0		6,137
49	div3	Shrewsbury	A D	2-2	Taylor 29, Fenton 90	7,782

KEY PLAYER APPEARANCES

	PLAYER	POS	AGE	APP	MINS ON	GOALS	CARDS(Y/R)	
1	Philip Barnes	GK	28	46	4140	0	1	0
2	Tom Newey	MID	24	42	3700	1	5	1
3	Paul Bolland	MID	27	39	3312	5	4	0
4	Nicky Fenton	DEF	27	38	3222	4	6	1
5	Justin Whittle	DEF	36	37	2975	1	3	0
6	Gary Jones	ATT	32	39	2885	8	2	2
7	Ciaran Toner	MID	26	33	2801	8	1	0
8	Gary Croft	DEF	33	28	2206	0	4	1
9	Danny Boshell	MID	26	29	2045	2	5	0
10	Peter Bore	MID	19	32	2039	8	0	0
11	John McDermott	DEF	38	23	1745	0	1	0
12	Peter Till	MID	21	22	1438	0	1	0
13	Richard Ravenhill	MID	26	17	1323	2	6	0
14	Martin Paterson	ATT	20	15	1307	6	2	0
15	Isaiah Rankin	ATT	29	20	1289	2	3	0
16	James Hunt	MID	30	15	1213	2	3	0
17	Danny North	ATT	19	20	1118	6	2	0
18	Gary Harkins	MID	22	17	1033	0	1	0

KEY PLAYERS - GOALSCORERS

Martin Paterson		Player Strike Rate	
		Average number of minutes between	217
Goals in the League	6	League goals scored by player	
Contribution to Attacking Power		Club Strike Rate	
Average number of minutes between	76	Average number of minutes between	72
League team goals while on pitch		League goals scored by club	

	PLAYER	GOALS LGE	POWER	STRIKE RATE
1	Martin Paterson	6	76	217 mins
2	Peter Bore	8	55	254 mins
3	Ciaran Toner	8	70	350 mins
4	Gary Jones	8	73	360 mins

KEY PLAYERS - MIDFIELDERS

Danny Boshell		Contribution to Attacking Power	
		Average number of minutes between	58
Goals in the League	2	League team goals while on pitch	
Defensive Rating		Scoring Difference	
Average number of mins between League	61	Defensive Rating minus Contribution to	3
goals conceded while on the pitch		Attacking Power	

	PLAYER	GOALS LGE	DEF RATE	POWER	SCORE DIFF
1	Danny Boshell	2	61	58	3 mins
2	Peter Bore	8	53	55	-2 mins
3	Paul Bolland	5	56	67	-11 mins
4	Tom Newey	1	61	72	-11 mins

KEY PLAYERS - DEFENDERS

Nicky Fenton		Clean Sheets	
		In games when he played at least 70	9
Goals Conceded when he was on pitch	54	minutes	
Defensive Rating		Club Defensive Rating	
Ave number of mins between League	59	Average number of mins between League	56
goals conceded while on the pitch		goals conceded by the club this season.	

	PLAYER	CON LGE	CLEAN SHEETS	DEF RATE
1	Nicky Fenton	54	9	59 mins
2	Justin Whittle	50	7	59 mins
3	John McDermott	31	4	56 mins
4	Gary Croft	42	4	52 mins

TEAM OF THE SEASON

D Nicky Fenton CG: 35 DR: 59
M Danny Boshell CG: 18 SD: 3
D Justin Whittle CG: 32 DR: 59
M Peter Bore CG: 18 SD: -2
F Martin Paterson CG: 15 SR: 217
G Philip Barnes CG: 46 DR: 56
D John McDermott CG: 18 DR: 56
M Paul Bolland CG: 34 SD: -11
F Gary Jones CG: 26 SR: 360
D Gary Croft CG: 23 DR: 52
M Tom Newey CG: 41 SD: -11

KEY GOALKEEPER

Philip Barnes	
Goals Conceded in the League	73
Defensive Rating	
Ave number of mins between League	56
goals conceded while on the pitch.	
Counting Games	
Games when he played at least 70 mins	46
Clean Sheets	
In games when he played at least 70 mins	10

TOP POINT EARNERS

	PLAYER	GAMES	AV PTS
1	Danny Boshell	18	1.78
2	Peter Bore	18	1.50
3	Nicky Fenton	35	1.49
4	Martin Paterson	15	1.40
5	James Hunt	13	1.38
6	Tom Newey	41	1.34
7	Justin Whittle	32	1.34
8	John McDermott	18	1.33
9	Paul Bolland	34	1.32
10	Philip Barnes	46	1.28
	CLUB AVERAGE:		1.28

HEREFORD UNITED

Final Position: **16th**

NICKNAME: THE BULLS KEY: ☐ Won ☐ Drawn ☐ Lost   Attendance

1	div3	Stockport	A W	2-0	Fleetwood 36, Mkandawire 59	5,297
2	div3	Lincoln	H L	1-2	Purdie 77 pen	4,405
3	div3	Chester	H W	2-0	Fleetwood 71, Rose 73	3,834
4	div3	Barnet	A L	0-3		1,945
5	ccr1	Coventry	H W	3-1	Fleetwood 1, 57, 64	3,404
6	div3	Hartlepool	H W	3-1	T.Sills 33, Purdie 51 pen, Williams 73	3,156
7	div3	Rochdale	A D	1-1	Purdie 90 pen	2,146
8	div3	Mansfield	A L	1-4	Connell 69	3,242
9	div3	Wycombe	H L	1-2	Williams 51	2,585
10	div3	Bury	H W	1-0	Williams 80	2,885
11	ccr2	Leicester	H L	1-3	Purdie 56 pen	4,073
12	div3	Wrexham	A L	0-1		4,705
13	div3	Bristol Rovers	A L	1-2	Purdie 18 pen	4,975
14	div3	Macclesfield	H W	1-0	Connell 80	2,705
15	div3	Grimsby	A L	1-2	Purdie 26 pen	4,147
16	div3	Darlington	H D	1-1	Mkandawire 71	2,838
17	div3	MK Dons	A W	3-1	Connell 8, Purdie 22 pen, Fleetwood 90	5,609
18	div3	Accrington	H W	1-0	Connell 85	3,391
19	div3	Swindon	A W	2-1	Williams 36, 81	6,910
20	facr1	Shrewsbury	A D	0-0		5,574
21	div3	Walsall	H L	0-1		4,462
22	facr1r	Shrewsbury	H W	2-1	Connell 85, Webb 88	4,224
23	div3	Boston	A D	1-1	Williams 68	1,731
24	facr2	Port Vale	H W	4-0	Webb 41, Purdie 49 pen, 51, Ferrell 68	4,076
25	div3	Peterborough	H D	0-0		2,309
26	div3	Torquay	H D	1-1	Jeannin 33	3,078
27	div3	Shrewsbury	A L	0-3		4,177
28	div3	Notts County	A W	1-0	T.Sills 81	4,106
29	div3	Bristol Rovers	H D	0-0		5,201
30	div3	Wrexham	H W	2-0	Connell 37, 88	3,444
31	div3	Wycombe	A D	0-0		4,851
32	facr3	Bristol Rovers	A L	0-1		8,978
33	div3	Mansfield	H L	1-3	Sheldon 90	3,048
34	div3	Macclesfield	A L	0-3		2,494
35	div3	Notts County	H W	3-2	McClenahan 9, Guinan 27, 68	3,280
36	div3	Bury	A D	2-2	Adams 63 og, Williams 78	1,775
37	div3	Stockport	H L	0-2		3,310
38	div3	Barnet	H W	2-0	B.Smith 48, Thomas 90	2,608
39	div3	Lincoln	A W	4-1	Connell 3, Guinan 36, 46, 54	4,695
40	div3	Rochdale	H D	0-0		3,090
41	div3	Chester	A D	1-1	Connell 82	1,842
42	div3	Hartlepool	A L	2-3	Thomas 46, Guinan 56	5,535
43	div3	Grimsby	H L	0-1		2,914
44	div3	Darlington	A L	0-1		3,165
45	div3	Accrington	A L	0-2		1,848
46	div3	MK Dons	H D	0-0		2,715
47	div3	Swindon	H D	0-0		4,740
48	div3	Walsall	A L	0-1		5,658
49	div3	Boston	H W	3-0	Guinan 56, Williams 71, Connell 90	2,176
50	div3	Peterborough	A L	0-3		3,759
51	div3	Shrewsbury	H L	0-1		4,359
52	div3	Torquay	A D	0-0		2,942

KEY PLAYER APPEARANCES

	PLAYER	POS	AGE	APP	MINS ON	GOALS	CARDS(Y/R)
1	Rob Purdie	MID	24	44	3812	6	1 0
2	Wayne Brown	GK	30	39	3490	0	1 0
3	Tamika Mkandawire	DEF	24	39	3439	2	5 0
4	Simon Travis	DEF	30	36	3039	0	2 0
5	Andrew Williams	ATT	20	41	2971	8	3 0
6	Alan Connell	ATT	24	44	2881	9	3 0
7	Dean Beckwith	DEF	23	32	2763	0	3 2
8	Richard Rose	DEF	24	33	2636	1	1 0
9	Phil Gulliver	DEF	24	26	2225	0	1 0
10	Trent McClenahan	DEF	22	26	2105	1	2 1
11	Tim Sills	ATT	27	36	2014	2	3 1
12	Stuart Fleetwood	ATT	21	26	1835	3	2 0
13	Ben Smith	MID	28	18	1602	1	0 0
14	Stephen Guinan	ATT	31	16	1416	7	2 0
15	Andy Ferrell	MID	23	21	1411	0	2 1
16	Danny Thomas	DEF	26	15	1286	2	1 0
17	Luke Webb	MID	20	21	1254	0	0 0
18	Alexandre Jeannin	DEF	29	12	1016	1	2 0

KEY PLAYERS - GOALSCORERS

Stephen Guinan

Goals in the League	7

Player Strike Rate — Average number of minutes between League goals scored by player	202

Contribution to Attacking Power — Average number of minutes between League team goals while on pitch	88

Club Strike Rate — Average number of minutes between League goals scored by club	94

	PLAYER	GOALS LGE	POWER	STRIKE RATE
1	Stephen Guinan	7	88	202 mins
2	Alan Connell	9	84	320 mins
3	Andrew Williams	8	90	371 mins
4	Stuart Fleetwood	3	76	611 mins

KEY PLAYERS - MIDFIELDERS

Andy Ferrell

Goals in the League	0

Contribution to Attacking Power — Average number of minutes between League team goals while on pitch	78

Defensive Rating — Average number of mins between League goals conceded while on the pitch	74

Scoring Difference — Defensive Rating minus Contribution to Attacking Power	-4

	PLAYER	GOALS LGE	DEF RATE	POWER	SCORE DIFF
1	Andy Ferrell	0	74	78	-4 mins
2	Ben Smith	1	84	94	-10 mins
3	Rob Purdie	6	79	103	-24 mins
4	Luke Webb	0	125	313	-188 mins

KEY PLAYERS - DEFENDERS

Danny Thomas

Goals Conceded when he was on pitch	12

Clean Sheets — In games when he played at least 70 minutes	7

Defensive Rating — Ave number of mins between League goals conceded while on the pitch	107

Club Defensive Rating — Average number of mins between League goals conceded by the club this season.	81

	PLAYER	CON LGE	CLEAN SHEETS	DEF RATE
1	Danny Thomas	12	7	107 mins
2	Dean Beckwith	31	11	89 mins
3	Trent McClenahan	24	11	87 mins
4	Tamika Mkandawire	42	13	81 mins

KEY GOALKEEPER

Wayne Brown

Goals Conceded in the League	39

Defensive Rating — Ave number of mins between League goals conceded while on the pitch.	89

Counting Games — Games when he played at least 70 mins	39

Clean Sheets — In games when he played at least 70 mins	16

TOP POINT EARNERS

	PLAYER	GAMES	AV PTS
1	Trent McClenahan	23	1.48
2	Stuart Fleetwood	17	1.47
3	Richard Rose	29	1.34
4	Phil Gulliver	23	1.30
5	Wayne Brown	39	1.23
6	Alan Connell	31	1.23
7	Rob Purdie	42	1.21
8	Andy Ferrell	15	1.20
9	Dean Beckwith	31	1.19
10	Andrew Williams	30	1.17
	CLUB AVERAGE:		1.20

TEAM OF THE SEASON

D Danny Thomas CG: 14 DR: 107
M Andy Ferrell CG: 15 SD: -4
D Dean Beckwith CG: 31 DR: 89
M Ben Smith CG: 18 SD: -10
F Stephen Guinan CG: 16 SR: 202
G Wayne Brown CG: 39 DR: 89
D Trent McClenahan CG: 23 DR: 87
M Rob Purdie CG: 42 SD: -24
F Alan Connell CG: 31 SR: 320
D Tamika Mkandawire CG: 38 DR: 81
M Luke Webb CG: 13 SD: -188

MANSFIELD TOWN

Final Position: **17th**

NICKNAME: THE STAGS

KEY: ☐ Won ☐ Drawn ☐ Lost

#			Result	Scorers	Attendance
1	div3	Shrewsbury	A D 2-2	Hamshaw 17, Brown 43	5,066
2	div3	MK Dons	H W 2-1	Barker 29, Boulding 37	4,033
3	div3	Stockport	H D 1-1	Hamshaw 84	3,856
4	div3	Grimsby	A D 1-1	Hamshaw 51	4,604
5	ccr1	Huddersfield	A W 2-0	Boulding 45, Barker 47	5,111
6	div3	Lincoln	H L 2-4	Reet 66, Barker 90 pen	4,596
7	div3	Wycombe	A L 0-1		4,754
8	div3	Hereford	H W 4-1	Mkandawire 20 og, Barker 38, 72 pen, Reet 49	3,242
9	div3	Hartlepool	A L 0-2		3,899
10	div3	Torquay	A L 0-1		2,660
11	ccr2	Portsmouth	H L 1-2	Reet 81	6,646
12	div3	Accrington	H D 2-2	Hamshaw 58, Boulding 81	3,088
13	div3	Darlington	H W 1-0	Reet 60	2,794
14	div3	Walsall	A L 0-4		5,429
15	div3	Notts County	H D 2-2	Reet 10, 19	6,182
16	div3	Boston	A D 1-1	Barker 72 pen	2,314
17	div3	Wrexham	H W 3-0	Barker 21, 36, Reet 69	2,971
18	div3	Macclesfield	A W 3-2	Coke 65, Barker 83, 90 pen	2,599
19	div3	Bristol Rovers	A L 0-1		5,044
20	facr1	Accrington	H W 1-0	Barker 44 pen	3,909
21	div3	Peterborough	H L 0-2		3,550
22	div3	Rochdale	A L 0-2		2,378
23	facr2	Doncaster	H D 1-1	Barker 23 pen	4,837
24	div3	Swindon	H W 2-0	Barker 3, Brown 38	2,274
25	div3	Bury	H L 0-2		2,197
26	facr2r	Doncaster	A L 0-2		5,338
27	div3	Barnet	A L 1-2	Barker 84	1,790
28	div3	Darlington	A W 2-0	Barker 5, Arnold 62	3,808
29	div3	Hartlepool	H L 0-1		3,531
30	div3	Hereford	A W 3-1	Conlon 10, M.Boulding 79, Gritton 90	3,048
31	div3	Accrington	A L 2-3	Conlon 32, Dawson 43	1,234
32	div3	Walsall	H W 2-1	Conlon 14, Gritton 57	3,737
33	div3	Chester	A D 1-1	Buxton 32	2,129
34	div3	Torquay	H W 5-0	M.Boulding 14, Gritton 39, 59, 77 pen, Baptiste 64	2,573
35	div3	Shrewsbury	H D 1-1	Brown 60	3,250
36	div3	Stockport	A L 0-1		5,656
37	div3	Grimsby	H L 1-2	M.Boulding 30	4,033
38	div3	MK Dons	A D 1-1	Arnold 90	5,070
39	div3	Wycombe	H W 3-2	Mullins 21, Gritton 36, D'Laryea 87	2,711
40	div3	Lincoln	A W 2-1	Conlon 15 pen, Arnold 51	5,316
41	div3	Chester	H W 2-1	Brown 27, Baptiste 82	2,366
42	div3	Notts County	A D 0-0		10,034
43	div3	Boston	H L 1-2	Conlon 30	2,790
44	div3	Macclesfield	H L 1-2	Mullins 68	2,414
45	div3	Wrexham	A D 0-0		7,752
46	div3	Bristol Rovers	H L 0-1		2,392
47	div3	Peterborough	A L 0-2		4,276
48	div3	Rochdale	H L 1-2	Hjelde 45	2,023
49	div3	Swindon	A L 0-2		10,472
50	div3	Barnet	H W 2-1	Conlon 45, Brown 66	2,446
51	div3	Bury	A D 1-1	Baptiste 25	3,532

TEAM OF THE SEASON

Jon-Olav Hjelde D — CG: 23 DR: 68
Stephen Dawson M — CG: 28 SD: 15
Gareth Jelleyman D — CG: 38 DR: 67
Simon Brown M — CG: 25 SD: 7
Richard Barker F — CG: 23 SR: 184
Jason White G — CG: 31 DR: 69
John Mullins D — CG: 38 DR: 66
Jonathan D'Laryea M — CG: 35 SD: 1
Martin Gritton F — CG: 12 SR: 201
Jake Buxton D — CG: 27 DR: 64
Matthew Hamshaw M — CG: 34 SD: -9

KEY PLAYER APPEARANCES

	PLAYER	POS	AGE	APP	MINS ON	GOALS	CARDS(Y/R)	
1	Alex Baptiste	DEF	21	46	4061	3	3	0
2	Gareth Jelleyman	DEF	26	40	3485	0	5	0
3	John Mullins	DEF	21	43	3477	2	5	0
4	Jonathan D'Laryea	MID	21	37	3248	1	0	0
5	Matthew Hamshaw	MID	25	40	3235	4	2	1
6	Stephen Dawson	MID	21	34	2746	1	8	0
7	Jason White	GK	21	31	2745	0	1	0
8	Simon Brown	MID	23	34	2554	5	7	0
9	Jake Buxton	DEF	22	30	2491	1	7	0
10	Michael Boulding	ATT	31	39	2295	6	0	0
11	Jon-Olav Hjelde	DEF	34	28	2179	1	3	0
12	Richard Barker	ATT	32	24	2126	12	2	0
13	Carl Muggleton	GK	38	16	1395	0	0	0
14	Barry Conlon	ATT	28	17	1338	6	2	1
15	Giles Coke	MID	21	21	1257	1	4	0
16	Martin Gritton	ATT	29	19	1207	6	1	0
17	Danny Reet	ATT	20	21	896	6	4	0
18	Nathan Arnold	MID	19	22	830	3	0	0

KEY PLAYERS - GOALSCORERS

Richard Barker

Goals in the League	12

Player Strike Rate Average number of minutes between League goals scored by player	184

Contribution to Attacking Power Average number of minutes between League team goals while on pitch	73

Club Strike Rate Average number of minutes between League goals scored by club	73

	PLAYER	GOALS LGE	POWER	STRIKE RATE
1	Richard Barker	12	73	184 mins
2	Martin Gritton	6	63	201 mins
3	Barry Conlon	6	66	223 mins
4	Michael Boulding	6	68	397 mins

KEY PLAYERS - MIDFIELDERS

Stephen Dawson

Goals in the League	1

Contribution to Attacking Power Average number of minutes between League team goals while on pitch	59

Defensive Rating Average number of mins between League goals conceded while on the pitch	74

Scoring Difference Defensive Rating minus Contribution to Attacking Power	15

	PLAYER	GOALS LGE	DEF RATE	POWER	SCORE DIFF
1	Stephen Dawson	1	74	59	15 mins
2	Simon Brown	5	73	66	7 mins
3	Jonathan D'Laryea	1	65	64	1 mins
4	Matthew Hamshaw	4	64	73	-9 mins

KEY PLAYERS - DEFENDERS

Jon-Olav Hjelde

Goals Conceded when he was on pitch	32

Clean Sheets In games when he played at least 70 minutes	4

Defensive Rating Ave number of mins between League goals conceded while on the pitch	68

Club Defensive Rating Average number of mins between League goals conceded by the club this season.	67

	PLAYER	CON LGE	CLEAN SHEETS	DEF RATE
1	Jon-Olav Hjelde	32	4	68 mins
2	Gareth Jelleyman	53	7	67 mins
3	John Mullins	54	4	66 mins
4	Jake Buxton	40	5	64 mins

KEY GOALKEEPER

Jason White

Goals Conceded in the League	41

Defensive Rating Ave number of mins between League goals conceded while on the pitch.	69

Counting Games Games when he played at least 70 mins	31

Clean Sheets In games when he played at least 70 mins	6

TOP POINT EARNERS

	PLAYER	GAMES	AV PTS
1	Simon Brown	25	1.40
2	Jonathan D'Laryea	35	1.40
3	Martin Gritton	12	1.33
4	Stephen Dawson	28	1.32
5	Jon-Olav Hjelde	23	1.30
6	Jake Buxton	27	1.26
7	Jason White	30	1.23
8	Barry Conlon	15	1.20
9	Richard Barker	23	1.17
10	Gareth Jelleyman	38	1.16
	CLUB AVERAGE:		1.17

CHESTER CITY

Final Position: 18th

NICKNAME: THE BLUES   KEY: ☐ Won ☐ Drawn ☐ Lost

							Attendance
1	div3	Accrington	H	W	2-0	Broughton 15, Blundell 86 pen	3,779
2	div3	Bury	A	W	3-1	Woodthorpe 36 og, Walters 49, 90	2,719
3	div3	Hereford	A	L	0-2		3,834
4	div3	Wrexham	H	L	1-2	Hand 81	4,206
5	ccr1	Leeds	A	L	0-1		10,013
6	div3	Torquay	A	D	2-2	Broughton 55, Martinez 90	2,541
7	div3	Swindon	H	L	0-2		3,382
8	div3	Wycombe	A	L	0-1		4,277
9	div3	Notts County	H	D	0-0		1,818
10	div3	Grimsby	H	L	0-2		1,957
1	div3	MK Dons	A	W	2-1	Westwood 57, Walters 88	5,476
2	div3	Macclesfield	A	D	1-1	Sandwith 61	2,022
3	div3	Bristol Rovers	H	W	2-0	Sandwith 18, Martinez 37	2,151
4	div3	Walsall	H	D	0-0		3,241
5	div3	Rochdale	A	D	0-0		3,149
6	div3	Hartlepool	H	W	2-1	Westwood 45, Walters 53	2,580
7	div3	Barnet	A	L	0-1		2,301
8	div3	Darlington	A	L	0-1		3,630
9	facr1	Clevedon	A	W	4-1	Wilson 7, Hand 49, Walters 60, Blundell 74	2,261
10	div3	Stockport	H	D	1-1	Walters 59	3,624
1	div3	Shrewsbury	A	L	1-2	Blundell 8	4,464
2	facr2	Bury	A	D	2-2	Steele 63, 73	3,428
3	div3	Boston	H	W	3-1	Blundell 50, 65 pen, Walters 72	1,527
4	div3	Lincoln	H	W	4-1	Martinez 20, Walters 54, Blundell 76, Wilson 82	2,142
5	facr2r	Bury	H	L	1-3	Wilson 3	2,810
6	div3	Peterborough	A	W	2-0	Walters 9, Arber 40 og	4,491
7	div3	Macclesfield	H	L	0-3		3,365
8	div3	MK Dons	H	L	0-3		2,271
9	div3	Notts County	A	W	2-1	Walters 34, Westwood 79	4,019
10	facr3	Ipswich	H	D	0-0		4,330
1	div3	Grimsby	A	W	2-0	Artell 53, Blundell 72	3,012
2	div3	Wycombe	H	L	0-1		2,336
3	facr3r	Ipswich	A	L	0-1		11,732
4	div3	Bristol Rovers	A	D	0-0		5,694
5	div3	Mansfield	H	D	1-1	Steele 62	2,129
6	div3	Accrington	A	W	1-0	Linwood 23	1,900
7	div3	Wrexham	A	D	0-0		6,801
8	div3	Bury	H	W	1-0	Yeo 90 pen	1,642
9	div3	Swindon	A	L	0-1		5,462
10	div3	Hereford	H	D	1-1	Yeo 71	1,842
1	div3	Torquay	H	D	1-1	Bennett 53	1,996
2	div3	Mansfield	A	L	1-2	Maylett 9	2,366
3	div3	Walsall	A	L	0-1		5,282
4	div3	Rochdale	H	L	0-1		2,197
5	div3	Barnet	H	W	2-0	Bolland 45, Hand 58	1,591
6	div3	Hartlepool	A	L	0-3		6,059
7	div3	Darlington	H	D	1-1	Yeo 51	1,942
8	div3	Stockport	A	L	0-2		5,719
9	div3	Shrewsbury	H	D	0-0		3,266
10	div3	Boston	A	L	0-2		1,752
1	div3	Peterborough	H	D	1-1	Yeo 13	1,905
2	div3	Lincoln	A	L	0-2		5,267

KEY PLAYER APPEARANCES

	PLAYER	POS	AGE	APP	MINS ON	GOALS	CARDS(Y/R)	
1	John Danby	GK	23	46	4140	0	2	0
2	Jamie Hand	MID	23	43	3870	1	13	0
3	David Artell	DEF	26	43	3634	1	8	0
4	Lawrence Wilson	DEF	20	41	3148	2	5	1
5	Paul Linwood	DEF	23	37	3085	1	11	1
6	Roberto Martinez	MID	33	31	2739	3	10	1
7	Kevin Sandwith	MID	29	32	2423	2	3	1
8	Dean Bennett	MID	29	32	2196	1	5	0
9	Jonathan Walters	ATT	23	26	2176	9	3	0
10	Simon Marples	DEF	31	30	2157	0	2	0
11	Philip Bolland	DEF	30	26	2119	1	8	1
12	Sean Hessey	DEF	28	26	1961	0	6	0
13	Greg Blundell	ATT	31	27	1880	6	5	0
14	Ashley Westwood	DEF	30	21	1672	3	6	1
15	Stephen Vaughan	DEF	22	19	1554	0	4	0
16	Simon Yeo	ATT	33	15	1190	4	3	0
17	Lee Steele	ATT	33	20	949	2	2	1
18	Chris Holroyd	ATT	20	22	855	0	2	0

KEY PLAYERS - GOALSCORERS

Jonathan Walters		Player Strike Rate	
Goals in the League	9	Average number of minutes between League goals scored by player	241
Contribution to Attacking Power		Club Strike Rate	
Average number of minutes between League team goals while on pitch	77	Average number of minutes between League goals scored by club	108

	PLAYER	GOALS LGE	POWER	STRIKE RATE
1	Jonathan Walters	9	77	241 mins
2	Simon Yeo	4	170	297 mins
3	Greg Blundell	6	78	313 mins
4	Roberto Martinez	3	91	913 mins

KEY PLAYERS - MIDFIELDERS

Roberto Martinez		Contribution to Attacking Power	
Goals in the League	3	Average number of minutes between League team goals while on pitch	91
Defensive Rating		Scoring Difference	
Average number of mins between League goals conceded while on the pitch	94	Defensive Rating minus Contribution to Attacking Power	3

	PLAYER	GOALS LGE	DEF RATE	POWER	SCORE DIFF
1	Roberto Martinez	3	94	91	3 mins
2	Kevin Sandwith	2	93	110	-17 mins
3	Jamie Hand	2	82	99	-17 mins
4	Dean Bennett	1	95	146	-51 mins

KEY PLAYERS - DEFENDERS

Simon Marples		Clean Sheets	
Goals Conceded when he was on pitch	20	In games when he played at least 70 minutes	7
Defensive Rating		Club Defensive Rating	
Ave number of mins between League goals conceded while on the pitch	107	Average number of mins between League goals conceded by the club this season.	90

	PLAYER	CON LGE	CLEAN SHEETS	DEF RATE
1	Simon Marples	20	7	107 mins
2	Philip Bolland	24	6	88 mins
3	David Artell	41	12	88 mins
4	Ashley Westwood	19	5	88 mins

KEY GOALKEEPER

John Danby	
Goals Conceded in the League	48
Defensive Rating Ave number of mins between League goals conceded while on the pitch.	86
Counting Games Games when he played at least 70 mins	46
Clean Sheets In games when he played at least 70 mins	13

TOP POINT EARNERS

	PLAYER	GAMES	AV PTS
1	Greg Blundell	18	1.50
2	Ashley Westwood	18	1.50
3	Stephen Vaughan	17	1.47
4	Roberto Martinez	30	1.40
5	Jonathan Walters	24	1.33
6	Simon Marples	22	1.27
7	Lawrence Wilson	34	1.24
8	David Artell	39	1.23
9	Kevin Sandwith	26	1.19
10	John Danby	46	1.15
	CLUB AVERAGE:		1.15

TEAM OF THE SEASON

D Simon Marples CG: 22 DR: 107

M Roberto Martinez CG: 30 SD: 3

D Philip Bolland CG: 23 DR: 88

M Kevin Sandwith CG: 26 SD: -17

F Jonathan Walters CG: 24 SR: 241

G John Danby CG: 46 DR: 86

D David Artell CG: 39 DR: 88

M Jamie Hand CG: 43 SD: -17

F Simon Yeo CG: 13 SR: 297

D Ashley Westwood CG: 18 DR: 88

M Dean Bennett CG: 21 SD: -51

WREXHAM

Final Position: **19th**

NICKNAME: THE ROBINS   KEY: ☐ Won ☐ Drawn ☐ Lost   Attendance

1	div3	Wycombe	A	D	1-1	Ma.Jones 32	4,763
2	div3	Grimsby	H	W	3-0	Evans 16, Llewellyn 34, Done 68	5,180
3	div3	Peterborough	H	D	0-0		4,706
4	div3	Chester	A	W	2-1	N.Roberts 42 pen, Ma.Jones 52	4,206
5	ccr1	Sheff Wed	A	W	4-1	N.Roberts 33, Llewellyn 39, Done 64, Ma.Jones 84	8,047
6	div3	Barnet	H	D	1-1	Ma.Jones 15	4,304
7	div3	Swindon	H	W	2-1	Valentine 68 pen, Ma.Jones 70	5,257
8	div3	Accrington	A	L	0-5		2,689
9	div3	Stockport	A	L	2-5	D.Williams 42, 60	4,884
10	ccr2	Birmingham	A	L	1-4	Llewellyn 29	10,491
11	div3	Hereford	H	W	1-0	S.Evans 28	4,705
12	div3	Rochdale	H	L	1-2	Llewellyn 12	3,577
13	div3	Hartlepool	A	L	0-3		4,452
14	div3	MK Dons	H	L	1-2	N.Roberts 20	3,828
15	div3	Mansfield	A	L	0-3		2,971
16	div3	Bristol Rovers	H	W	2-0	Llewellyn 22, Craddock 90	3,803
17	div3	Macclesfield	H	D	0-0		3,568
18	div3	Bury	A	L	0-1		2,506
19	facr1	Stevenage	H	W	1-0	D.Williams 40	2,863
20	div3	Notts County	A	L	1-2	Llewellyn 65	4,416
21	div3	Lincoln	H	W	2-1	Ma.Jones 24, Llewellyn 44	3,619
22	facr2	Scunthorpe	A	W	2-0	Ma.Jones 49, Smith 66	5,054
23	div3	Torquay	A	D	1-1	Smith 7	1,588
24	div3	Boston	A	L	0-4		1,706
25	div3	Walsall	H	D	1-1	Llewellyn 68	4,270
26	div3	Darlington	H	W	1-0	Holloway 19 og	3,401
27	div3	Rochdale	A	D	2-2	McEvilly 48, Llewellyn 55	2,837
28	div3	Hereford	A	L	0-2		3,444
29	div3	Accrington	H	L	1-3	Johnson 45	3,805
30	facr3	Derby	A	L	1-3	McEvilly 61	15,609
31	div3	Swindon	A	L	1-2	Marc.Williams 8	6,130
32	div3	Hartlepool	H	D	1-1	Llewellyn 64	3,828
33	div3	Darlington	A	D	1-1	Spender 31	3,301
34	div3	Stockport	H	L	0-1		4,060
35	div3	Wycombe	H	L	0-2		3,607
36	div3	Peterborough	A	L	0-3		3,839
37	div3	Chester	H	D	0-0		6,801
38	div3	Grimsby	A	L	1-2	McEvilly 28	5,850
39	div3	Shrewsbury	H	L	1-3	D.Williams 55	5,605
40	div3	Barnet	A	W	2-1	McEvilly 57, 60	2,180
41	div3	Bury	H	D	1-1	McEvilly 33	7,030
42	div3	MK Dons	A	L	1-2	McEvilly 12	5,712
43	div3	Bristol Rovers	A	W	1-0	Whitley 87	5,209
44	div3	Mansfield	H	D	0-0		7,752
45	div3	Macclesfield	A	L	0-2		4,142
46	div3	Notts County	H	L	0-1		4,557
47	div3	Lincoln	A	W	3-0	Spender 18, Kerr 29 og, McEvilly 52	4,279
48	div3	Torquay	H	W	1-0	N.Roberts 79	6,057
49	div3	Shrewsbury	A	W	1-0	Proctor 79	6,749
50	div3	Walsall	A	L	0-1		7,057
51	div3	Boston	H	W	3-1	Valentine 56 pen, Llewellyn 87, Proctor 90	12,374

TEAM OF THE SEASON

(D) Ryan Valentine CG: 30 DR: 71
(M) Matt Done CG: 23 SD: 6
(D) Simon Spender CG: 17 DR: 70
(M) Mark Jones CG: 25 SD: -24
(F) Lee McEvilly CG: 17 SR: 266
(G) Michael Ingham CG: 31 DR: 60
(D) Shaun Pejic CG: 32 DR: 69
(M) Darren Ferguson CG: 19 SD: -24
(F) Chris Llewellyn CG: 39 SR: 381
(D) Stephen Evans CG: 32 DR: 64
(M) Danny Williams CG: 38 SD: -26

KEY PLAYER APPEARANCES

	PLAYER	POS	AGE	APP	MINS ON	GOALS	CARDS(Y/R)
1	Danny Williams	MID	27	40	3465	3	11	0
2	Chris Llewellyn	ATT	27	39	3437	9	7	2
3	Shaun Pejic	DEF	24	33	2922	0	2	0
4	Michael Ingham	GK	26	31	2790	0	1	0
5	Stephen Evans	DEF	28	34	2783	2	3	3
6	Ryan Valentine	DEF	24	34	2777	2	13	1
7	Matt Done	MID	18	34	2442	1	2	0
8	Mark Jones	MID	23	30	2425	5	6	0
9	Lee Roche	DEF	26	28	2260	0	9	1
10	Mike Williams	DEF	20	31	2085	0	2	0
11	Simon Spender	DEF	21	25	1895	2	1	0
12	Lee McEvilly	ATT	25	28	1868	7	6	0
13	Darren Ferguson	MID	35	20	1690	0	2	0
14	Neil Roberts	ATT	29	19	1341	3	2	0
15	Jeff Whitley	MID	32	11	990	1	0	0
16	Gareth Evans	DEF	20	13	980	0	3	0
17	Matt Crowell	MID	22	15	974	0	2	0
18	Josh Johnson	ATT	26	22	961	1	1	0

KEY PLAYERS - GOALSCORERS

Lee McEvilly		Player Strike Rate Average number of minutes between League goals scored by player	266
Goals in the League	7		
Contribution to Attacking Power Average number of minutes between League team goals while on pitch	93	Club Strike Rate Average number of minutes between League goals scored by club	100

	PLAYER	GOALS LGE	POWER	STRIKE RATE
1	Lee McEvilly	7	93	266 mins
2	Chris Llewellyn	9	85	381 mins
3	Neil Roberts	3	78	447 mins
4	Mark Jones	5	83	485 mins

KEY PLAYERS - MIDFIELDERS

Matt Done		Contribution to Attacking Power Average number of minutes between League team goals while on pitch	87
Goals in the League	1		
Defensive Rating Average number of mins between League goals conceded while on the pitch	93	Scoring Difference Defensive Rating minus Contribution to Attacking Power	6

	PLAYER	GOALS LGE	DEF RATE	POWER	SCORE DIFF
1	Matt Done	1	93	87	6 mins
2	Mark Jones	5	59	83	-24 mins
3	Darren Ferguson	0	52	76	-24 mins
4	Danny Williams	3	65	91	-26 mins

KEY PLAYERS - DEFENDERS

Ryan Valentine		Clean Sheets In games when he played at least 70 minutes	9
Goals Conceded when he was on pitch	39		
Defensive Rating Ave number of mins between League goals conceded while on the pitch	71	Club Defensive Rating Average number of mins between League goals conceded by the club this season.	66

	PLAYER	CON LGE	CLEAN SHEETS	DEF RATE
1	Ryan Valentine	39	9	71 mins
2	Simon Spender	27	8	70 mins
3	Shaun Pejic	42	7	69 mins
4	Stephen Evans	43	10	64 mins

KEY GOALKEEPER

Michael Ingham	
Goals Conceded in the League	46
Defensive Rating Ave number of mins between League goals conceded while on the pitch.	60
Counting Games Games when he played at least 70 mins	31
Clean Sheets In games when he played at least 70 mins	6

TOP POINT EARNERS

	PLAYER	GAMES	AV PTS
1	Neil Roberts	13	1.69
2	Simon Spender	17	1.47
3	Matt Done	23	1.35
4	Ryan Valentine	30	1.30
5	Shaun Pejic	32	1.22
6	Darren Ferguson	19	1.21
7	Danny Williams	38	1.21
8	Chris Llewellyn	39	1.18
9	Lee McEvilly	17	1.18
10	Stephen Evans	32	1.13
	CLUB AVERAGE:		1.11

ACCRINGTON STANLEY

Final Position: **20th**

NICKNAME: THE STANS   KEY: ☐ Won ☐ Drawn ☐ Lost   Attendance

#					Result	Scorers	Attendance
1	div3	Chester	A	L	0-2		3,779
2	div3	Darlington	H	L	0-2		2,667
3	div3	Barnet	H	W	2-1	Boco 35, 53	1,639
4	div3	Stockport	A	D	1-1	Welch 78	5,291
5	ccr1	Nottm Forest	H	W	1-0	Mullin 61	2,146
6	div3	Rochdale	H	D	1-1	G.Roberts 76 pen	3,045
7	div3	Lincoln	A	L	1-3	G.Roberts 84	4,999
8	div3	Notts County	A	L	2-3	Mullin 90, G.Roberts 90 pen	4,677
9	div3	Wrexham	H	W	5-0	Mullin 40, Craney 48, G.Roberts 52, 66, Cavanagh 54	2,689
10	div3	Boston	H	W	2-1	G.Roberts 10, Todd 90	1,916
11	ccr2	Watford	A	L	5-6*	(*on penalties)	8,368
12	div3	Mansfield	A	D	2-2	Mullin 16, 85	3,088
13	div3	Bury	A	D	2-2	G.Roberts 12, Boco 37	2,912
14	div3	Wycombe	H	W	2-1	Craney 27, Mangan 90	2,243
15	div3	Swindon	H	D	1-1	Todd 33	3,083
16	div3	Torquay	A	W	2-0	Welch 47, G.Roberts 73	2,743
17	div3	Walsall	H	L	1-2	Craney 78	3,142
18	div3	Hereford	A	L	0-1		3,391
19	div3	Peterborough	A	L	2-4	Craney 23, 79	3,990
20	facr1	Mansfield	A	L	0-1		3,909
21	div3	Hartlepool	H	L	1-2	Todd 38	1,787
22	div3	Grimsby	A	L	0-2		4,511
23	div3	Shrewsbury	H	D	3-3	Todd 19 pen, Edwards 55, Wiliams 89	1,602
24	div3	MK Dons	H	L	3-4	Todd 39, Mullin 43, Mangan 83	1,384
25	div3	Macclesfield	A	D	3-3	McGivern 27, Jacobson 75, Mangan 90	2,242
26	div3	Bristol Rovers	A	L	0-4		5,205
27	div3	Bury	H	D	1-1	Todd 5 pen	3,225
28	div3	Wrexham	A	W	3-1	Mullin 17, D.Brown 83, 86	3,805
29	div3	Boston	A	L	0-1		1,664
30	div3	Notts County	H	L	1-2	D.Brown 14	1,702
31	div3	Mansfield	H	W	3-2	Mullin 1, Welch 60, Whalley 83	1,234
32	div3	Wycombe	A	D	1-1	Harris 63	5,884
33	div3	Chester	H	L	0-1		1,900
34	div3	Barnet	A	W	2-1	Todd 40 pen, Proctor 84	2,041
35	div3	Stockport	H	L	0-1		3,004
36	div3	Darlington	A	L	1-2	Mullin 50	2,790
37	div3	Lincoln	H	D	2-2	Todd 23, Mullin 73	1,930
38	div3	Rochdale	A	L	2-4	Mullin 70, Mangan 90	3,433
39	div3	Bristol Rovers	H	D	1-1	Whalley 90	1,302
40	div3	Swindon	A	L	0-2		6,197
41	div3	Torquay	H	W	1-0	Cavanagh 90	4,004
42	div3	Hereford	H	W	2-0	D.Brown 26, Cavanagh 54	1,848
43	div3	Walsall	A	L	2-3	Mullin 25, Wiliams 65	6,062
44	div3	Peterborough	H	W	3-2	Todd 2, 90, Harris 45	1,808
45	div3	Hartlepool	A	L	0-1		5,867
46	div3	Grimsby	H	W	4-1	Mullin 32, Todd 44 pen, Doherty 55, Cavanagh 88	1,818
47	div3	Shrewsbury	A	L	1-2	Mullin 10	5,438
48	div3	Macclesfield	H	W	3-2	Wiliams 11, Proctor 45, 48	3,012
49	div3	MK Dons	A	L	1-3	D.Brown 14	8,102

KEY PLAYER APPEARANCES

	PLAYER	POS	AGE	APP	MINS ON	GOALS	CARDS(Y/R)	
1	Paul Mullin	ATT	33	46	4081	13	0	0
2	Andy Todd	MID	28	45	3885	11	4	0
3	Robbie Wiliams	DEF	28	43	3681	3	9	1
4	Andrew Proctor	MID	24	42	3287	3	4	1
5	Leam Richardson	DEF	27	38	3092	0	8	0
6	Phil Edwards	DEF	21	33	2662	1	12	0
7	Romauld Boco	MID	21	32	2446	3	3	0
8	Michael Welch	DEF	25	30	2378	3	13	1
9	Peter Cavanagh	DEF	25	26	2264	4	9	1
10	Jay Harris	MID	20	31	2179	2	11	1
11	Ian Dunbavin	GK	27	23	1996	0	4	0
12	Ian Craney	MID	24	18	1610	5	3	0
13	Shaun Whalley	ATT	19	20	1357	2	6	0
14	Andrew Mangan	ATT	20	33	1248	4	2	2
15	Gary Roberts	MID	20	13	1170	8	1	0
16	Sean Doherty	MID	22	18	884	1	1	0
17	David Martin	GK	21	10	798	0	0	0
18	Godwin Antwi	DEF	19	9	774	0	2	0

KEY PLAYERS - GOALSCORERS

Gary Roberts

Goals in the League	8

Player Strike Rate	
Average number of minutes between League goals scored by player	146

Contribution to Attacking Power	
Average number of minutes between League team goals while on pitch	50

Club Strike Rate	
Average number of minutes between League goals scored by club	59

	PLAYER	GOALS LGE	POWER	STRIKE RATE
1	Gary Roberts	8	50	146 mins
2	Paul Mullin	13	58	320 mins
3	Ian Craney	5	61	322 mins
4	Andy Todd	11	57	353 mins

KEY PLAYERS - MIDFIELDERS

Gary Roberts

Goals in the League	8

Contribution to Attacking Power	
Average number of minutes between League team goals while on pitch	50

Defensive Rating	
Average number of mins between League goals conceded while on the pitch	58

Scoring Difference	
Defensive Rating minus Contribution to Attacking Power	8

	PLAYER	GOALS LGE	DEF RATE	POWER	SCORE DIFF
1	Gary Roberts	8	58	50	8 mins
2	Ian Craney	5	55	61	-6 mins
3	Andrew Proctor	3	49	56	-7 mins
4	Andy Todd	12	49	57	-8 mins

KEY PLAYERS - DEFENDERS

Peter Cavanagh

Goals Conceded when he was on pitch	39

Clean Sheets	
In games when he played at least 70 minutes	4

Defensive Rating	
Ave number of mins between League goals conceded while on the pitch	58

Club Defensive Rating	
Average number of mins between League goals conceded by the club this season.	51

	PLAYER	CON LGE	CLEAN SHEETS	DEF RATE
1	Peter Cavanagh	39	4	58 mins
2	Robbie Wiliams	66	4	57 mins
3	Leam Richardson	60	4	53 mins
4	Michael Welch	48	1	51 mins

KEY GOALKEEPER

Ian Dunbavin

Goals Conceded in the League	41

Defensive Rating	
Ave number of mins between League goals conceded while on the pitch.	50

Counting Games	
Games when he played at least 70 mins	23

Clean Sheets	
In games when he played at least 70 mins	2

TOP POINT EARNERS

	PLAYER	GAMES	AV PTS
1	Peter Cavanagh	25	1.40
2	Romauld Boco	23	1.39
3	Gary Roberts	13	1.31
4	Jay Harris	21	1.19
5	Robbie Wiliams	40	1.15
6	Leam Richardson	34	1.12
7	Paul Mullin	46	1.11
8	Ian Craney	18	1.11
9	Shaun Whalley	14	1.08
10	Andy Todd	44	1.07
	CLUB AVERAGE:		1.09

TEAM OF THE SEASON

D Peter Cavanagh — CG: 25 DR: 58

M Gary Roberts — CG: 13 SD: 8

D Robbie Wiliams — CG: 40 DR: 57

M Ian Craney — CG: 18 SD: -6

F Paul Mullin — CG: 46 SR: 320

G Ian Dunbavin — CG: 23 DR: 50

D Leam Richardson — CG: 34 DR: 53

M Andrew Proctor — CG: 35 SD: -7

F Shaun Whalley — CG: 14 SR: 723

D Michael Welch — CG: 25 DR: 51

M Andy Todd — CG: 44 SD: -8

BURY

Final Position: 21st

NICKNAME: THE SHAKERS   KEY: ☐ Won ☐ Drawn ☐ Lost   Attendance

#	Comp	Opponent	H/A	Result	Scorers	Att
1	div3	MK Dons	A	L	1-2	Bishop 81 pen	5,329
2	div3	Chester	H	L	1-3	Pittman 45	2,719
3	div3	Shrewsbury	H	L	1-2	Fitzgerald 34	2,329
4	div3	Wycombe	A	L	0-3		4,184
5	ccr1	Sunderland	H	W	2-0	Fitzgerald 82, Bishop 88	2,930
6	div3	Grimsby	H	W	3-0	Youngs 6, 20, Adams 45	2,118
7	div3	Peterborough	A	W	1-0	Bishop 90 pen	5,561
8	div3	Torquay	H	L	0-1		2,317
9	div3	Darlington	A	L	0-1		3,335
10	div3	Hereford	A	L	0-1		2,885
11	ccr2	Sheff Utd	A	L	0-1		6,273
12	div3	Barnet	H	D	2-2	Hurst 15, 74	1,901
13	div3	Accrington	H	D	2-2	Bishop 7, 36	2,912
14	div3	Lincoln	A	W	2-0	Baker 43, Hurst 54	4,748
15	div3	Macclesfield	A	W	3-0	Baker 32, 49, Hurst 60	2,512
16	div3	Boston	H	W	2-1	Hurst 70, Pugh 73	2,246
17	div3	Notts County	A	W	1-0	Bishop 31	4,770
18	div3	Rochdale	A	W	3-1	Fitzgerald 15, Bishop 29 pen, 90 pen	4,499
19	div3	Wrexham	H	W	1-0	Mattis 7	2,506
20	facr1	Weymouth	A	D	2-2	Pugh 26, Bishop 75	2,503
21	div3	Bristol Rovers	H	L	0-2		2,635
22	facr1r	Weymouth	H	W	4-3	Mattis 10, 67, Bishop 23, 74	2,231
23	div3	Swindon	A	L	1-2	Scott 21	5,628
24	facr2	Chester	H	D	2-2	Bishop 66, Baker 69	3,428
25	div3	Walsall	H	L	1-2	Scott 52	2,148
26	div3	Mansfield	A	W	2-0	Pugh 18, Hurst 51	2,197
27	facr2r	Chester	A	W	3-1*	Bishop 36, Hurst 48, Mattis 54	2,810
28	div3	Stockport	H	W	2-0	Hurst 2, Bishop 66	4,466
29	div3	Hartlepool	H	L	0-1		2,839
30	div3	Accrington	A	D	1-1	Bishop 77	3,225
31	div3	Barnet	A	L	1-2	Baker 3 pen	1,959
32	div3	Torquay	A	D	2-2	Pugh 79, Bishop 90 pen	2,063
33	div3	Darlington	H	D	1-1	Bishop 42 pen	1,870
34	div3	Lincoln	H	D	2-2	Bishop 5, Fitzgerald 79	2,476
35	div3	Hartlepool	A	L	0-2		4,901
36	div3	Hereford	H	D	2-2	Baker 29, Hurst 58	1,775
37	div3	MK Dons	H	L	0-2		2,325
38	div3	Wycombe	H	L	0-4		1,988
39	div3	Chester	A	L	0-1		1,642
40	div3	Peterborough	H	L	0-3		2,085
41	div3	Grimsby	A	L	0-2		4,733
42	div3	Wrexham	A	D	1-1	Hurst 90	7,030
43	div3	Macclesfield	H	D	1-1	Hurst 75	2,561
44	div3	Notts County	H	L	0-1		2,310
45	div3	Boston	A	W	1-0	Bishop 86	1,946
46	div3	Shrewsbury	A	W	3-1	Bishop 1, 51, Hurst 65	4,419
47	div3	Rochdale	H	L	0-1		5,075
48	div3	Bristol Rovers	A	L	0-2		6,266
49	div3	Swindon	H	L	0-1		2,401
50	div3	Walsall	A	W	1-0	Youngs 42	6,568
51	div3	Stockport	A	D	0-0		7,246
52	div3	Mansfield	H	D	1-1	Youngs 50	3,532

* Bury lose FA Cup tie for fielding an ineligible player and Chester go through

TEAM OF THE SEASON

D Darren Kempson — CG: 12 DR: 89
M Dwayne Mattis — CG: 21 SD: 5
D Paul Scott — CG: 44 DR: 68
M Marc Pugh — CG: 26 SD: -9
F Glynn Hurst — CG: 26 SR: 231
G Kasper Schmeichel — CG: 14 DR: 96
D David Challinor — CG: 43 DR: 67
M David Buchanan — CG: 30 SD: -15
F Andrew Bishop — CG: 40 SR: 248
D Chris Brass — CG: 19 DR: 67
M Richie Baker — CG: 32 SD: -18

KEY PLAYER APPEARANCES

	PLAYER	POS	AGE	APP	MINS ON	GOALS	CARDS(Y/R)
1	Paul Scott	DEF	27	46	4044	2	6	0
2	David Challinor	DEF	31	43	3870	0	4	0
3	Andrew Bishop	ATT	24	43	3726	15	1	0
4	Thomas Kennedy	DEF	22	37	3122	0	1	0
5	David Buchanan	MID	21	41	3063	0	3	0
6	Richie Baker	MID	19	39	3050	5	7	0
7	Glynn Hurst	ATT	31	35	2550	11	1	0
8	Marc Pugh	MID	20	35	2513	3	2	0
9	Dwayne Mattis	MID	25	22	1941	2	5	0
10	Andy Warrington	GK	31	20	1795	0	0	0
11	John Fitzgerald	DEF	23	23	1773	1	1	1
12	Chris Brass	DEF	31	22	1755	0	4	0
13	Kasper Schmeichel	GK	20	14	1260	0	0	0
14	Colin Woodthorpe	DEF	38	15	1117	0	2	0
15	Jason Kennedy	MID	20	12	1080	0	1	0
16	Darren Kempson	DEF	22	12	1074	0	2	1
17	Nicky Adams	MID	20	19	1058	1	2	0
18	Tom Youngs	ATT	27	19	821	4	1	0

KEY PLAYERS - GOALSCORERS

Glynn Hurst

Goals in the League	11	Player Strike Rate — Average number of minutes between League goals scored by player	231
Contribution to Attacking Power — Average number of minutes between League team goals while on pitch	72	Club Strike Rate — Average number of minutes between League goals scored by club	93

	PLAYER	GOALS LGE	POWER	STRIKE RATE
1	Glynn Hurst	11	72	231 mins
2	Andrew Bishop	15	86	248 mins
3	Richie Baker	5	82	610 mins
4	Marc Pugh	3	76	837 mins

KEY PLAYERS - MIDFIELDERS

Dwayne Mattis

Goals in the League	1	Contribution to Attacking Power — Average number of minutes between League team goals while on pitch	66
Defensive Rating — Average number of mins between League goals conceded while on the pitch	71	Scoring Difference — Defensive Rating minus Contribution to Attacking Power	5

	PLAYER	GOALS LGE	DEF RATE	POWER	SCORE DIFF
1	Dwayne Mattis	1	71	66	5 mins
2	Marc Pugh	3	67	76	-9 mins
3	David Buchanan	0	80	95	-15 mins
4	Richie Baker	5	64	82	-18 mins

KEY PLAYERS - DEFENDERS

Darren Kempson

Goals Conceded when he was on pitch	12	Clean Sheets — In games when he played at least 70 minutes	3
Defensive Rating — Ave number of mins between League goals conceded while on the pitch	89	Club Defensive Rating — Average number of mins between League goals conceded by the club this season.	70

	PLAYER	CON LGE	CLEAN SHEETS	DEF RATE
1	Darren Kempson	12	3	89 mins
2	Paul Scott	59	10	68 mins
3	David Challinor	57	9	67 mins
4	Chris Brass	26	5	67 mins

KEY GOALKEEPER

Kasper Schmeichel

Goals Conceded in the League	13
Defensive Rating — Ave number of mins between League goals conceded while on the pitch.	96
Counting Games — Games when he played at least 70 mins	14
Clean Sheets — In games when he played at least 70 mins	5

TOP POINT EARNERS

	PLAYER	GAMES	AV PTS
1	Kasper Schmeichel	14	1.64
2	Glynn Hurst	26	1.46
3	David Buchanan	30	1.43
4	Dwayne Mattis	21	1.43
5	Marc Pugh	26	1.23
6	Chris Brass	19	1.21
7	Andrew Bishop	40	1.20
8	Thomas Kennedy	34	1.15
9	Paul Scott	44	1.11
10	John Fitzgerald	19	1.11
	CLUB AVERAGE:		1.09

MACCLESFIELD

Final Position: **22nd**

NICKNAME: THE SILKMEN   KEY: ☐ Won ☐ Drawn ☐ Lost   Attendance

#		Opponent	H/A	W/D/L	Score	Scorers	Attendance
1	div3	Darlington	A	L	0-4		4,095
2	div3	Hartlepool	H	D	0-0		1,843
3	div3	MK Dons	H	L	1-2	McIntyre 58 pen	1,711
4	div3	Peterborough	A	L	1-3	Swailes 90	4,136
5	ccr1	Leicester	A	L	0-2		6,298
6	div3	Wycombe	H	L	0-2		1,574
7	div3	Grimsby	A	D	1-1	Teague 49	3,638
8	div3	Barnet	H	L	2-3	McNeil 52, Tipton 67	1,770
9	div3	Lincoln	A	L	1-2	Scott 45	4,184
10	div3	Walsall	A	L	0-2		4,657
11	div3	Torquay	H	D	3-3	Morley 43, Bullock 48, Swailes 90	1,836
12	div3	Chester	H	D	1-1	Bullock 10	2,022
13	div3	Hereford	A	L	0-1		2,705
14	div3	Shrewsbury	A	L	1-2	Weir-Daley 56	4,816
15	div3	Bury	H	L	2-3	Scott 28, Weir-Daley 77	2,512
16	div3	Bristol Rovers	A	D	0-0		5,130
17	div3	Mansfield	H	L	2-2	Heath 49, Morley 81	2,599
18	div3	Wrexham	A	D	0-0		3,568
19	facr1	Walsall	H	D	0-0		2,018
20	div3	Boston	H	L	2-3	Heath 17 pen, Regan 90	1,895
21	facr1r	Walsall	A	W	1-0	McNulty 83	3,114
22	div3	Stockport	A	D	1-1	McIntyre 42 pen	6,575
23	facr2	Hartlepool	H	W	2-1	McIntyre 45 pen, Murphy 52	1,992
24	div3	Rochdale	H	W	1-0	McNeil 52	1,472
25	div3	Notts County	A	W	2-1	Heath 25, McIntyre 33 pen	4,036
26	div3	Accrington	H	D	3-3	Tolley 48, Bullock 73, Murphy 89	2,242
27	div3	Swindon	H	W	2-1	Murphy 27, Swailes 52	2,377
28	div3	Chester	A	W	3-0	Tipton 10, McIntyre 70, Murphy 78	3,365
29	div3	Torquay	A	W	1-0	Morley 90	2,169
30	div3	Lincoln	H	W	2-1	McIntyre 6 pen, 65 pen	2,869
31	facr3	Chelsea	A	L	1-6	Murphy 40	41,434
32	div3	Barnet	A	L	0-1		2,018
33	div3	Hereford	H	W	3-0	McIntyre 17 pen, Murphy 61, 83	2,494
34	div3	Swindon	A	L	0-2		6,062
35	div3	Walsall	H	L	0-2		2,007
36	div3	Darlington	H	D	1-1	Navarro 86	2,173
37	div3	Peterborough	H	W	2-1	Bullock 45, Navarro 53	2,274
38	div3	Hartlepool	A	L	2-3	Hadfield 65, Tipton 70	5,242
39	div3	Grimsby	H	W	2-1	McIntyre 5 pen, Heath 20	2,598
40	div3	Wycombe	A	L	0-3		5,450
41	div3	Shrewsbury	H	D	2-2	Tipton 29, 52	2,928
42	div3	MK Dons	A	L	0-3		5,681
43	div3	Bury	A	D	1-1	McIntyre 90 pen	2,561
44	div3	Mansfield	A	W	2-1	Miles 54, McNeil 66	2,414
45	div3	Wrexham	H	W	2-0	McNeil 34, Murphy 62	4,142
46	div3	Boston	A	L	1-4	Holgate 77	1,816
47	div3	Stockport	H	W	2-0	Murphy 19, Miles 69	4,451
48	div3	Rochdale	A	L	0-5		2,989
49	div3	Bristol Rovers	H	L	0-1		1,940
50	div3	Accrington	A	L	2-3	Miles 30, 36	3,012
51	div3	Notts County	H	D	1-1	Miles 6	4,114

KEY PLAYER APPEARANCES

	PLAYER	POS	AGE	APP	MINS ON	GOALS	CARDS(Y/R)	
1	Kevin McIntyre	MID	29	44	3880	9	6	1
2	Danny Swailes	DEF	28	38	3403	3	7	1
3	Carl Regan	DEF	26	38	3325	1	9	0
4	Martin Bullock	MID	32	42	3264	4	4	1
5	David Morley	DEF	29	35	3090	3	5	0
6	Tommy Lee	GK	21	34	3060	0	0	1
7	Jordan Hadfield	MID	20	37	2855	1	15	1
8	Matty McNeil	ATT	30	35	2518	4	6	0
9	Alan Navarro	MID	26	31	2347	2	9	1
10	John Murphy	ATT	30	29	2261	7	2	0
11	Rob Scott	DEF	33	25	1909	2	8	0
12	John Miles	ATT	25	29	1867	5	3	0
13	Jamie Tolley	MID	24	23	1784	1	5	1
14	Matthew Tipton	ATT	27	33	1634	5	3	0
15	Jim McNulty	DEF	22	15	1288	0	0	0
16	Colin Heath	ATT	23	25	1225	4	3	0
17	Andrew Teague	DEF	21	13	920	1	0	0
18	Jonathan Brain	GK	24	9	741	0	1	0

KEY PLAYERS - GOALSCORERS

John Murphy

		Player Strike Rate	
Goals in the League	7	Average number of minutes between League goals scored by player	323

Contribution to Attacking Power		Club Strike Rate	
Average number of minutes between League team goals while on pitch	68	Average number of minutes between League goals scored by club	76

	PLAYER	GOALS LGE	POWER	STRIKE RATE
1	John Murphy	7	68	323 mins
2	Matthew Tipton	5	74	326 mins
3	John Miles	5	62	373 mins
4	Kevin McIntyre	9	73	431 mins

KEY PLAYERS - MIDFIELDERS

Jordan Hadfield

		Contribution to Attacking Power	
Goals in the League	1	Average number of minutes between League team goals while on pitch	67

Defensive Rating		Scoring Difference	
Average number of mins between League goals conceded while on the pitch	52	Defensive Rating minus Contribution to Attacking Power	-15

	PLAYER	GOALS LGE	DEF RATE	POWER	SCORE DIFF
1	Jordan Hadfield	1	52	67	-15 mins
2	Alan Navarro	2	58	78	-20 mins
3	Kevin McIntyre	9	53	73	-20 mins
4	Jamie Tolley	1	46	68	-22 mins

KEY PLAYERS - DEFENDERS

Carl Regan

		Clean Sheets	
Goals Conceded when he was on pitch	55	In games when he played at least 70 minutes	9

Defensive Rating		Club Defensive Rating	
Ave number of mins between League goals conceded while on the pitch	60	Average number of mins between League goals conceded by the club this season.	54

	PLAYER	CON LGE	CLEAN SHEETS	DEF RATE
1	Carl Regan	55	9	60 mins
2	Danny Swailes	61	7	55 mins
3	David Morley	57	8	54 mins
4	Rob Scott	42	4	45 mins

TEAM OF THE SEASON

D Carl Regan CG: 36 DR: 60
M Jordan Hadfield CG: 30 SD: -15
D Danny Swailes CG: 38 DR: 55
M Alan Navarro CG: 24 SD: -20
F John Murphy CG: 22 SR: 323
G Tommy Lee CG: 34 DR: 51
D David Morley CG: 34 DR: 54
M Kevin McIntyre CG: 43 SD: -20
F Matthew Tipton CG: 12 SR: 326
D Rob Scott CG: 19 DR: 45
M Jamie Tolley CG: 18 SD: -22

KEY GOALKEEPER

Tommy Lee

Goals Conceded in the League	59
Defensive Rating — Ave number of mins between League goals conceded while on the pitch.	51
Counting Games — Games when he played at least 70 mins	34
Clean Sheets — In games when he played at least 70 mins	6

TOP POINT EARNERS

	PLAYER	GAMES	AV PTS
1	John Murphy	22	1.45
2	John Miles	17	1.29
3	Matty McNeil	25	1.28
4	Jordan Hadfield	30	1.23
5	Carl Regan	36	1.19
6	Tommy Lee	34	1.12
7	Danny Swailes	38	1.11
8	Kevin McIntyre	43	1.09
9	Alan Navarro	24	1.08
10	David Morley	34	1.03
	CLUB AVERAGE:		1.04

BOSTON UNITED

Final Position: **23rd**

NICKNAME: THE PILGRIMS KEY: ☐ Won ☐ Drawn ☐ Lost Attendance

1	div3	**Grimsby**	A L	2-3	Green 16, Joachim 54	5,012
2	div3	**Peterborough**	H L	0-1		3,528
3	div3	**Darlington**	H W	4-1	Tait 13, T.Ryan 68 pen, Joachim 76, 90	1,934
4	div3	**Shrewsbury**	A L	0-5		3,502
5	ccr1	**Brighton**	A L	2-3		2,533
6	div3	**MK Dons**	H L	0-1		2,032
7	div3	**Hartlepool**	A L	1-2	N'Guessan 83	4,054
8	div3	**Stockport**	H W	2-1	T.Ryan 25 pen, Elding 39	1,796
9	div3	**Barnet**	A D	3-3	Galbraith 23, T.Ryan 43 pen, 84 pen	1,461
10	div3	**Accrington**	A L	1-2	Farrell 48	1,916
11	div3	**Rochdale**	H L	0-3		1,709
12	div3	**Lincoln**	H W	1-0	Green 59	4,327
13	div3	**Swindon**	A D	1-1	N'Guessan 88	6,074
14	div3	**Bristol Rovers**	A L	0-1		4,327
15	div3	**Mansfield**	H D	1-1	N'Guessan 25	2,314
16	div3	**Bury**	A L	1-2	Tait 78	2,246
17	div3	**Wycombe**	H L	0-1		1,762
18	div3	**Notts County**	H D	3-3	Stevens 24, Elding 75, Green 86	2,539
19	facr1	**Bournemouth**	A L	0-4		4,263
20	div3	**Macclesfield**	A W	3-2	Ellender 3, Broughton 18, Greaves 40	1,895
21	div3	**Hereford**	H D	1-1	Clarke 74	1,731
22	div3	**Chester**	A L	1-3	N'Guessan 88	1,527
23	div3	**Wrexham**	H W	4-0	Elding 22, 83, Broughton 48, 69	1,706
24	div3	**Torquay**	A W	1-0	Elding 41	2,107
25	div3	**Walsall**	H D	1-1	N'Guessan 55	2,083
26	div3	**Lincoln**	A L	1-2	Kennedy 38	6,820
27	div3	**Rochdale**	A L	0-4		2,159
28	div3	**Barnet**	H W	2-1	Greaves 8, Yakubu 46 og	1,780
29	div3	**Accrington**	H W	1-0	Broughton 72	1,664
30	div3	**Stockport**	A L	0-1		4,568
31	div3	**Swindon**	H L	1-3	Thomas 17	2,101
32	div3	**Walsall**	A D	1-1	Dann 25 og	5,058
33	div3	**Grimsby**	H L	0-6		2,915
34	div3	**Darlington**	A L	0-2		2,764
35	div3	**Shrewsbury**	H L	0-1		1,571
36	div3	**Peterborough**	A D	1-1	Joynes 61	4,882
37	div3	**Hartlepool**	H L	0-1		2,120
38	div3	**MK Dons**	A L	2-3	Thomas 20, Broughton 32	6,605
39	div3	**Bristol Rovers**	H W	2-1	Jarrett 3 pen, 9	1,697
40	div3	**Mansfield**	A W	2-1	Talbot 18, Broughton 40	2,790
41	div3	**Wycombe**	A D	0-0		4,417
42	div3	**Bury**	H L	0-1		1,946
43	div3	**Notts County**	A L	0-2		4,170
44	div3	**Macclesfield**	H W	4-1	Galbraith 22, Broughton 44, Greaves 65, Clarke 80 pen	1,816
45	div3	**Hereford**	A L	0-3		2,176
46	div3	**Chester**	H W	1-0	Stevens 83	1,752
47	div3	**Torquay**	H D	1-1	Broughton 83	2,664
48	div3	**Wrexham**	A L	1-3	Green 39	12,374

KEY PLAYER APPEARANCES

	PLAYER	POS	AGE	APP	MINS ON	GOALS	CARDS(Y/R)
1	Andy Marriott	GK	36	46	4140	0	1 0
2	Paul Ellender	DEF	32	42	3496	1	10 1
3	Mark Greaves	DEF	32	39	3381	3	8 0
4	Francis Green	ATT	27	38	2995	4	4 1
5	Jamie Clarke	MID	24	35	2700	2	5 0
6	Dave Farrell	MID	35	39	2321	1	4 0
7	Drewe Broughton	ATT	28	26	2236	8	10 2
8	Tim Ryan	DEF	32	23	2069	4	5 1
9	David Galbraith	MID	23	30	1941	2	4 1
10	Anthony Elding	ATT	25	19	1519	5	0 0
11	Stewart Talbot	MID	34	18	1384	1	4 0
12	Colin Cryan	DEF	26	15	1350	0	0 0
13	Lee Canoville	MID	26	16	1268	0	3 0
14	Dany N'Guessan	MID	19	23	1263	5	2 0
15	Jason Kennedy	MID	20	13	1116	1	1 0
16	Chris Holland	MID	31	15	1062	0	1 0
17	Ernie Cooksey	MID	27	16	1042	0	3 0
18	Jamie Stevens	DEF	18	12	1033	2	2 0

KEY PLAYERS - GOALSCORERS

Drewe Broughton

Goals in the League	8

Player Strike Rate – Average number of minutes between League goals scored by player	279

Contribution to Attacking Power – Average number of minutes between League team goals while on pitch	79

Club Strike Rate – Average number of minutes between League goals scored by club	81

	PLAYER	GOALS LGE	POWER	STRIKE RATE
1	Drewe Broughton	8	79	279 mins
2	Anthony Elding	5	66	303 mins
3	Francis Green	4	74	748 mins
4	David Galbraith	2	92	970 mins

KEY PLAYERS - MIDFIELDERS

Jason Kennedy

Goals in the League	1

Contribution to Attacking Power – Average number of minutes between League team goals while on pitch	62

Defensive Rating – Average number of mins between League goals conceded while on the pitch	62

Scoring Difference – Defensive Rating minus Contribution to Attacking Power	0

	PLAYER	GOALS LGE	DEF RATE	POWER	SCORE DIFF
1	Jason Kennedy	1	62	62	0 mins
2	Stewart Talbot	1	69	76	-7 mins
3	Lee Canoville	0	50	70	-20 mins
4	Jamie Clarke	2	45	72	-27 mins

KEY PLAYERS - DEFENDERS

Colin Cryan

Goals Conceded when he was on pitch	23

Clean Sheets – In games when he played at least 70 minutes	2

Defensive Rating – Ave number of mins between League goals conceded while on the pitch	58

Club Defensive Rating – Average number of mins between League goals conceded by the club this season.	51

	PLAYER	CON LGE	CLEAN SHEETS	DEF RATE
1	Colin Cryan	23	2	58 mins
2	Tim Ryan	39	3	53 mins
3	Mark Greaves	66	5	51 mins
4	Paul Ellender	69	5	50 mins

TEAM OF THE SEASON

D Colin Cryan CG: 15 DR: 58
M Jason Kennedy CG: 12 SD: 0
D Tim Ryan CG: 23 DR: 53
M Stewart Talbot CG: 14 SD: -7
F Drewe Broughton CG: 25 SR: 279
G Andy Marriott CG: 46 DR: 51
D Mark Greaves CG: 37 DR: 51
M Lee Canoville CG: 13 SD: -20
F Anthony Elding CG: 16 SR: 303
D Paul Ellender CG: 38 DR: 50
M Jamie Clarke CG: 27 SD: -27

KEY GOALKEEPER

Andy Marriott

Goals Conceded in the League	80

Defensive Rating – Ave number of mins between League goals conceded while on the pitch.	51

Counting Games – Games when he played at least 70 mins	46

Clean Sheets – In games when he played at least 70 mins	6

TOP POINT EARNERS

	PLAYER	GAMES	AV PTS
1	Jason Kennedy	12	1.33
2	Anthony Elding	16	1.25
3	David Galbraith	16	1.25
4	Francis Green	33	1.21
5	Drewe Broughton	25	1.16
6	Jamie Clarke	27	1.15
7	Colin Cryan	15	1.00
8	Lee Canoville	13	1.00
9	Mark Greaves	37	1.00
10	Paul Ellender	38	1.00
	CLUB AVERAGE:		0.78

TORQUAY

Final Position: 24th

NICKNAME: THE GULLS KEY: ☐ Won ☐ Drawn ☐ Lost Attendance

				Result	Scorers	Attendance
1	div3	Barnet	A W	1-0	Thorpe 90	2,827
2	div3	Rochdale	H W	1-0	Mansell 87	3,039
3	div3	Lincoln	H L	1-2	Garner 52	3,192
4	div3	Hartlepool	A D	1-1	Phillips 5	3,688
5	ccr1	Norwich	H L	0-2		3,100
6	div3	Chester	H D	2-2	Ward 43, 74	2,541
7	div3	Darlington	A D	1-1	Thorpe 33 pen	4,007
8	div3	Bury	A W	1-0	Evans 33	2,317
9	div3	Bristol Rovers	H D	0-0		3,145
10	div3	Mansfield	H W	1-0	Ward 36	2,660
11	div3	Macclesfield	A D	3-3	Mansell 33, Thorpe 67, Ward 85	1,836
12	div3	MK Dons	A L	2-3	Ward 8, 45	5,378
13	div3	Notts County	H L	0-1		2,815
14	div3	Wycombe	A L	0-2		4,769
15	div3	Accrington	H L	0-2		2,743
16	div3	Stockport	A L	0-1		4,663
17	div3	Shrewsbury	H D	0-0		2,262
18	div3	Walsall	A L	0-1		5,806
19	facr1	Leatherhead	H W	2-1	Ward 57, McPhee 72	2,218
20	div3	Swindon	H L	0-1		4,029
21	div3	Peterborough	A L	2-5	Mansell 7, Robertson 90	4,452
22	facr2	Leyton Orient	H D	1-1	Ward 60 pen	2,392
23	div3	Wrexham	H D	1-1	Robertson 51	1,588
24	div3	Hereford	A D	1-1	Angus 2	3,078
25	facr2r	Leyton Orient	A W	2-1	Robertson 52, 81	2,384
26	div3	Boston	H L	0-1		2,107
27	div3	Grimsby	A L	0-2		4,666
28	div3	MK Dons	H L	0-2		2,715
29	div3	Macclesfield	H L	0-1		2,169
30	div3	Bristol Rovers	A L	0-1		6,475
31	facr3	Southampton	H L	0-2		5,396
32	div3	Bury	H D	2-2	Ward 32 pen, 49 pen	2,063
33	div3	Notts County	A L	2-5	Cooke 25, Dickson 35	4,311
34	div3	Grimsby	H W	4-1	Ward 3, Thorpe 44, 59, 83 pen	2,095
35	div3	Mansfield	A L	0-5		2,573
36	div3	Barnet	H D	1-1	Taylor 45	1,942
37	div3	Lincoln	A L	0-1		4,881
38	div3	Hartlepool	H L	0-1		2,194
39	div3	Rochdale	A L	0-1		2,456
40	div3	Darlington	H L	0-1		2,109
41	div3	Chester	A D	1-1	Thorpe 90 pen	1,996
42	div3	Wycombe	H W	3-0	Kerry 20, Williams 40, Robertson 76	3,060
43	div3	Accrington	A L	0-1		4,004
44	div3	Shrewsbury	A L	0-1		4,678
45	div3	Stockport	H W	1-0	Reid 90	3,005
46	div3	Walsall	H L	1-2	Reid 58	4,047
47	div3	Swindon	A L	1-2	Thorpe 82 pen	7,389
48	div3	Peterborough	H D	1-1	Hill 45	2,106
49	div3	Wrexham	A L	0-1		6,057
50	div3	Boston	A D	1-1	Mansell 49	2,664
51	div3	Hereford	H D	0-0		2,942

TEAM OF THE SEASON

D Mark Robinson CG: 18 DR: 76
M Jamie Ward CG: 18 SD: -43
D Matt Hockley CG: 22 DR: 71
M Kevin Hill CG: 21 SD: -43
F Lee Thorpe CG: 38 SR: 429
G Nathan Abbey CG: 24 DR: 67
D Lee Andrews CG: 45 DR: 67
M Lee Mansell CG: 42 SD: -46
F Micky Evans CG: 12 SR: 1153
D Stephen Woods CG: 32 DR: 63
M Adam Murray CG: 18 SD: -132

KEY PLAYER APPEARANCES

	PLAYER	POS	AGE	APP	MINS ON	GOALS	CARDS(Y/R)	
1	Lee Andrews	DEF	24	46	4093	0	4	0
2	Lee Mansell	MID	24	45	3844	4	6	1
3	Lee Thorpe	ATT	31	41	3438	8	6	2
4	Stephen Woods	DEF	30	32	2874	0	5	0
5	Stevland Angus	DEF	26	36	2758	1	3	1
6	Matt Hockley	DEF	25	37	2303	0	8	0
7	Kevin Hill	MID	31	36	2228	1	8	0
8	Nathan Abbey	GK	28	24	2152	0	0	0
9	Jamie Ward	MID	21	25	1799	9	7	0
10	Adam Murray	MID	25	21	1785	0	5	0
11	Mark Robinson	DEF	25	18	1613	0	3	0
12	Chris McPhee	ATT	24	37	1395	0	1	0
13	Micky Evans	ATT	34	14	1153	1	2	0
14	Craig Taylor	DEF	33	13	1050	1	1	0
15	Steven Reed	DEF	22	15	960	0	2	0
16	Simon Rayner	GK	23	10	900	0	0	0
17	Chris Robertson	DEF	20	9	810	0	1	0
18	Martin Phillips	MID	31	14	765	1	0	0

KEY PLAYERS - GOALSCORERS

Jamie Ward

Goals in the League	9

Player Strike Rate — Average number of minutes between League goals scored by player	199

Contribution to Attacking Power — Average number of minutes between League team goals while on pitch	105

Club Strike Rate — Average number of minutes between League goals scored by club	115

	PLAYER	GOALS LGE	POWER	STRIKE RATE
1	Jamie Ward	9	105	199 mins
2	Lee Thorpe	8	107	429 mins
3	Lee Mansell	4	113	961 mins
4	Micky Evans	1	104	1153 mins

KEY PLAYERS - MIDFIELDERS

Jamie Ward

Goals in the League	9

Contribution to Attacking Power — Average number of minutes between League team goals while on pitch	105

Defensive Rating — Average number of mins between League goals conceded while on the pitch	62

Scoring Difference — Defensive Rating minus Contribution to Attacking Power	-43

	PLAYER	GOALS LGE	DEF RATE	POWER	SCORE DIFF
1	Jamie Ward	9	62	105	-43 mins
2	Kevin Hill	1	63	106	-43 mins
3	Lee Mansell	4	67	113	-46 mins
4	Adam Murray	0	66	198	-132 mins

KEY PLAYERS - DEFENDERS

Mark Robinson

Goals Conceded when he was on pitch	21

Clean Sheets — In games when he played at least 70 minutes	4

Defensive Rating — Ave number of mins between League goals conceded while on the pitch	76

Club Defensive Rating — Average number of mins between League goals conceded by the club this season.	65

	PLAYER	CON LGE	CLEAN SHEETS	DEF RATE
1	Mark Robinson	21	4	76 mins
2	Matt Hockley	32	5	71 mins
3	Lee Andrews	61	9	67 mins
4	Stephen Woods	45	5	63 mins

KEY GOALKEEPER

Nathan Abbey

Goals Conceded in the League	32

Defensive Rating — Ave number of mins between League goals conceded while on the pitch.	67

Counting Games — Games when he played at least 70 mins	24

Clean Sheets — In games when he played at least 70 mins	6

TOP POINT EARNERS

	PLAYER	GAMES	AV PTS
1	Micky Evans	12	1.42
2	Kevin Hill	21	0.90
3	Nathan Abbey	24	0.83
4	Lee Thorpe	38	0.82
5	Lee Mansell	42	0.79
6	Lee Andrews	45	0.78
7	Mark Robinson	18	0.78
8	Matt Hockley	22	0.77
9	Stevland Angus	29	0.72
10	Stephen Woods	32	0.66
	CLUB AVERAGE:		0.76

SCOTTISH PREMIERSHIP ROUND-UP

FINAL LEAGUE TABLE

	P	HOME					AWAY					TOTAL			
	P	W	D	L	F	A	W	D	L	F	A	F	A	DIF	PTS
Celtic	38	16	1	2	36	13	10	5	4	29	21	65	34	31	84
Rangers	38	11	6	2	35	10	10	3	6	26	22	61	32	29	72
Aberdeen	38	11	3	5	33	21	8	5	6	22	17	55	38	17	65
Hearts	38	9	4	6	26	19	8	6	5	21	16	47	35	12	61
Kilmarnock	38	7	5	6	24	22	9	2	9	23	32	47	54	-7	55
Hibernian	38	9	6	4	32	20	4	4	11	24	26	56	46	10	49
Falkirk	38	10	2	8	24	19	5	3	10	25	28	49	47	2	50
Inverness CT	38	8	6	5	25	20	3	7	9	17	28	42	48	-6	46
Dundee Utd	38	5	8	6	17	24	5	4	10	23	35	40	59	-19	42
Motherwell	38	5	3	11	25	34	5	5	9	16	27	41	61	-20	38
St Mirren	38	3	6	10	13	23	5	6	8	18	28	31	51	-20	36
Dunfermline	38	6	4	9	17	28	2	4	13	9	27	26	55	-29	32

CLUB STRIKE FORCE

Celtic's Hesselink and McManus celebrate

	CLUB	GOALS	CSR
1	Celtic	65	52
2	Rangers	61	56
3	Hibernian	56	61
4	Aberdeen	55	62
5	Falkirk	49	69
6	Hearts	47	72
7	Kilmarnock	47	72
8	Inverness CT	42	81
9	Motherwell	41	83
10	Dundee Utd	40	85
11	St Mirren	31	110
12	Dunfermline	26	131

1 Celtic

Goals scored in the League	65
Club Strike Rate (CSR) Average number of minutes between League goals scored by club	52

CLUB DISCIPLINARY RECORDS

Dunfermline's Gary Mason gets stuck in

	CLUB	Y	R	TOTAL	AVE
1	Dunfermline	95	6	101	33
2	Hearts	86	7	93	36
3	Hibernian	82	10	92	37
4	Falkirk	74	8	82	41
5	Dundee Utd	69	8	77	44
6	Inverness CT	67	5	72	47
7	Kilmarnock	61	4	65	52
8	Aberdeen	62	2	64	53
9	Rangers	61	2	63	54
10	Motherwell	57	6	63	54
11	Celtic	52	3	55	62
12	St Mirren	55	0	55	62

1 Dunfermline

League Yellow	95
League Red	6
League Total	101
Cards Average in League Average number of minutes between a card being shown of either colour	33

CLUB DEFENCES

	CLUB	LGE	CS	CDR
1	Rangers	32	16	106
2	Celtic	34	11	100
3	Hearts	35	14	97
4	Aberdeen	38	13	90
5	Hibernian	46	10	74
6	Falkirk	47	11	72
7	Inverness CT	48	10	71
8	St Mirren	51	10	67
9	Kilmarnock	54	12	63
10	Dunfermline	55	8	62
11	Dundee Utd	59	10	57
12	Motherwell	61	9	56

Ranger's Alan Hutton battles for the ball

1 Rangers

Goals conceded in the League	32
Clean Sheets (CS) Number of league games where no goals were conceded	16
Club Defensive Rate (CDR) Average number of minutes between League goals conceded by club	106

STADIUM CAPACITY AND HOME CROWDS

TEAM	CAPACITY	AVE	HIGH	LOW
1 Rangers	50444	99.03	50488	48218
2 Celtic	60355	95.98	59659	54620
3 Hearts	17700	95.69	17369	15912
4 Inverness CT	5580	87.43	7522	3517
5 Hibernian	17458	83.55	16747	10674
6 Falkirk	8000	67.33	7245	3129
7 Aberdeen	21474	58.09	20045	9379
8 St Mirren	10752	52.16	10251	3576
9 Dunfermline	11998	50.89	8561	4200
10 Dundee Utd	14223	50.25	12329	5036
11 Motherwell	13757	42.72	11745	3640
12 Kilmarnock	18128	41.72	13623	4732

Key: Average. The percentage of each stadium filled in League games over the season (AVE), the stadium capacity and the highest and lowest crowds recorded.

AWAY ATTENDANCE

TEAM	AVE	HIGH	LOW
1 Rangers	89.02	59425	7245
2 Celtic	86.61	50418	6438
3 Aberdeen	83.35	59510	4530
4 Hearts	83.12	59510	4389
5 St Mirren	77.29	58382	4246
6 Kilmarnock	75.98	57236	3728
7 Falkirk	74.67	55000	3640
8 Dunfermline	74.25	59131	3517
9 Hibernian	74.07	59659	4031
10 Dundee Utd	73.87	57343	3586
11 Motherwell	73.65	58654	3576
12 Inverness CT	69.35	56637	3129

Key: Average. How close each club has come to filling grounds in its away league matches (AVE) and the highest and lowest crowds recorded.

CHART-TOPPING MIDFIELDERS

1 Nakamura - Celtic	
Goals scored in the League	9
Defensive Rating Av number of mins between League goals conceded while on the pitch	114
Contribution to Attacking Power Average number of minutes between League team goals while on pitch	51
Scoring Difference Defensive Rating minus Contribution to Attacking Power	63

	PLAYER	CLUB	GOALS	DEF RATE	POWER	S DIFF
1	Shunsuke Nakamura	Celtic	9	114	51	63
2	Jeremy Clement	Rangers	0	106	48	58
3	Barry Ferguson	Rangers	4	109	57	52
4	Barry Nicholson	Aberdeen	6	111	62	49
5	Neil Lennon	Celtic	0	107	58	49
6	Charlie Adam	Rangers	11	104	60	44
7	Bruno Aguiar	Hearts	2	122	83	39
8	Michael Stewart	Hibernian	1	95	62	33
9	Christopher Clark	Aberdeen	1	88	63	25
10	Scott Severin	Aberdeen	4	85	61	24
11	Richard Foster	Aberdeen	3	85	65	20
12	Aiden McGeady	Celtic	5	85	65	20
13	Paul Hartley	Hearts	3	91	71	20
14	Steven Whittaker	Hibernian	1	73	59	14
15	Jack Ross	Falkirk	0	76	67	9

CHART-TOPPING GOALSCORERS

1 Boyd - Rangers	
Goals scored in the League	20
Contribution to Attacking Power (AP) Average number of minutes between League team goals while on pitch	46
Club Strike Rate (CSR) Average minutes between League goals scored by club	56
Player Strike Rate Average number of minutes between League goals scored by player	114

	PLAYER	CLUB	GOALS: LGE	POWER	CSR	S RATE
1	Kris Boyd	Rangers	20	46	56	114
2	Scott McDonald	Motherwell	15	75	87	182
3	Noel Hunt	Dundee Utd	10	84	85	210
4	Craig Dargo	Inverness CT	10	78	81	212
5	Steven Naismith	Kilmarnock	15	69	72	212
6	Darren Mackie	Aberdeen	13	58	63	220
7	John Sutton	St Mirren	12	101	113	220
8	Barry Robson	Dundee Utd	11	76	85	235
9	Andrius Velicka	Hearts	8	94	72	236
10	Charlie Adam	Rangers	11	60	56	247
11	Ritchie Foran	Motherwell	7	76	87	271
12	Shunsuke Nakamura	Celtic	9	51	52	357
13	Steven Fletcher	Hibernian	6	74	61	361
14	Stevie Crawford	Dunfermline	5	161	131	387
15	Aiden McGeady	Celtic	5	65	52	429

CHART-TOPPING DEFENDERS

1 Svensson - Rangers	
Goals Conceded in the League The number of League goals conceded while he was on the pitch	15
Clean Sheets In games when he played at least 70 mins	9
Club Defensive Rating Average mins between League goals conceded by the club this season	106
Defensive Rating Average number of minutes between League goals conceded while on pitch	119

	PLAYER	CLUB	CON: LGE	CS	CDR	DEF RATE
1	Karl Svensson	Rangers	15	9	106	119
2	Ibrahim Hemdani	Rangers	27	16	106	117
3	Marius Zaliukas	Hearts	20	9	97	113
4	Gary Caldwell	Celtic	16	6	100	109
5	Lee Naylor	Celtic	27	10	100	106
6	Alan Hutton	Rangers	27	13	106	106
7	Paul Telfer	Celtic	17	7	100	105
8	Russell Anderson	Aberdeen	30	14	92	101
9	Stephen McManus	Celtic	28	9	100	96
10	Christophe Berra	Hearts	32	13	97	93
11	Michael Hart	Aberdeen	34	10	92	87
12	Kenny Milne	Falkirk	36	11	72	80
13	David Murphy	Hibernian	36	8	74	80
14	Andrew Considine	Aberdeen	27	9	92	77
15	Christian Kalvenes	Dundee Utd	32	9	57	77

CHART-TOPPING GOALKEEPERS

2 Boruc - Celtic	
Counting Games Games in which he played at least 70 minutes	35
Goals Conceded in the League The number of League goals conceded while he was on the pitch	30
Clean Sheets In games when he played at least 70 mins	11
Defensive Rating Average number of minutes between League goals conceded while on pitch	106

	PLAYER	CLUB	GG	CONC	CS	DEF RATE
1	Allan McGregor	Rangers	31	24	15	116
2	Artur Boruc	Celtic	35	30	11	106
3	James Langfield	Aberdeen	38	38	13	90
4	Craig Gordon	Hearts	34	35	10	87
5	Chris Smith	St Mirren	21	26	6	72
6	Mark Brown	Inverness CT	23	29	6	71
7	Zibigniew Malkowski	Hibernian	19	25	4	68
8	Dorus de Vries	Dunfermline	26	37	7	64
9	Derek Stillie	Dundee Utd	37	54	10	61
10	Graeme Smith	Motherwell	22	34	5	60
11	Graeme Smith	Kilmarnock	27	43	6	56

PLAYER DISCIPLINARY RECORD

Dunfermline's McGuire fouls another player

1. Stephen O'Donnell - Falkirk	
Cards Average mins between cards	139
League Yellow	11
League Red	1
TOTAL	12

	PLAYER		LY	LR	TOT	AVE
1	O'Donnell	Falkirk	11	1	12	139
2	Black	Inverness CT	12	1	13	142
3	McGuire	Dunfermline	13	0	13	148
4	Wilkie	Dundee Utd	6	1	7	173
5	Young	Dunfermline	10	0	10	177
6	Hamilton	Dunfermline	8	1	9	181
7	Neilson	Hearts	5	1	6	194
8	Brellier	Hearts	7	0	7	196
9	Sproule	Hibernian	7	2	9	200
10	Killen	Hibernian	4	2	6	207
11	Lasley	Motherwell	6	0	6	207
12	Nish	Kilmarnock	9	1	10	212
13	Brown	Hibernian	11	1	12	221
14	Novo	Rangers	9	0	9	221
15	Stewart	Hibernian	8	0	8	249

TEAM OF THE SEASON

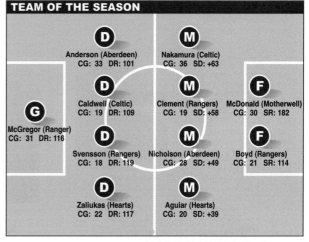

D Anderson (Aberdeen) CG: 33 DR: 101
M Nakamura (Celtic) CG: 36 SD: +63
D Caldwell (Celtic) CG: 19 DR: 109
M Clement (Rangers) CG: 19 SD: +58
F McDonald (Motherwell) CG: 30 SR: 182
G McGregor (Ranger) CG: 31 DR: 116
D Svensson (Rangers) CG: 18 DR: 119
M Nicholson (Aberdeen) CG: 28 SD: +49
F Boyd (Rangers) CG: 21 SR: 114
D Zaliukas (Hearts) CG: 22 DR: 117
M Aguiar (Hearts) CG: 20 SD: +39

EACH MONTH IN THE SCOTTISH PREMIER LEAGUE

AUGUST

The 2006/7 season kicks off at the end of July with a new Mitre golden football - the new official ball of the Scottish Premier League

Champions Celtic start their campaign with an emphatic 4-1 win over Kilmarnock at Parkhead, while Paul Le Guen gets his reign as Rangers manager off to winning start with a 2-1 victory over Motherwell at Fir Park

Newly-promoted St Mirren are the shock early leaders of the SPL after two successive victories

Rangers go top of the table after beating Hearts 2-0 at Ibrox Park...Kris Boyd scores both goals

Celtic sign 6ft 3in tall Dutch striker Jan Vennegoor of Hesselink from PSV Eindhoven and Danish midfielder Thomas Gravesen from Real Madrid

Celtic take over as SPL leaders with a 2-1 victory against Hibs. Jan Vennegoor of Hesselink scores the winner on his debut. Kris Boyd scores two more goals for Rangers but the Gers are held 2-2 by Kilmarnock

Rangers sign Bosnia defender Sasa Papac from Austria Vienna on transfer deadline day

AUGUST

SEPTEMBER

Tony Mowbray signs new 12-month rolling contract with Hibs. Assistant boss Mark Venus also commits his future to the club

Rangers rename their Main Stand at Ibrox Park in honour of legendary former manager Bill Struth, who was in charge of the club for 34 years until 1954

Jimmy Calderwood plus his assistants Jimmy Nicholl and Sandy Clark sign new contracts with Aberdeen to keep them at Pittodrie until summer 2008

OLD FIRM

Celtic win first Old Firm derby of the season with 2-0 win over Rangers at Parkhead. Thomas Gravesen scores his first goal for the Bhoys with Kenny Miller netting the second

Rangers goalkeeper Allan McGregor named Bank of Scotland Premier League Player of the Month for September

SEPTEMBER

OCTOBER

Celtic go six points clear at the top of the table after winning 4-1 at Dundee United. Shunsuke Nakamura scores a hat-trick

Scottish Premier League announce new sponsorship deal with Clydesdale Bank to start July 2007 and will be worth up to £8 million

Inverness shock Rangers with 1-0 win at Ibrox

Tony Mowbray leaves Easter Road to become manager at West Bromwich Albion

Jim Leishman steps down as Dunfermline manager to take up previous role as director of football at East End Park

Bottom club Dundee United name Craig Levein as their new manager as replacement for Craig Brewster, who left the club by mutual agreement

Hibernian appoint former player John Collins as their new manager

Hearts captain Steven Pressley says at a press conference flanked by team-mates Craig Gordon and Paul Hartley that there is "significant unrest in the Hearts dressing room"

OCTOBER

NOVEMBER

Celtic go 13 points clear after coming from behind to beat Hearts 2-1

New Dundee United boss Craig Levein makes winning start as the Tangerines recover from a goal down to beat Rangers 2-1 at Tannadice

Falkirk striker Anthony Stokes scores second sucessive SPL hat-trick in 3-0 victory at Dunfermline

Dunfermline confirm former Derry City boss Stephen Kenny as their new manager

Danish midfielder Thomas Gravesen scores a hat-trick as Celtic win 3-1 at St Mirren to go 15 points clear

Motherwell's Scott McDonald claims the honour of scoring the 5000th Scottish Premier League goal in the 4-2 victory over Falkirk at Fir Park

Hibernian captain Kevin Thomson dismisses speculation about his future by insisting he wants to sign a new contract at Easter Road

New Dundee United boss Craig Levein named Bank of Scotland Premier League Manager of the Month for November

NOVEMBER

DECEMBER

Motherwell midfielder Keith Lasley suffers suspected knee ligament damage against Inverness and could be sidelined for two months

Falkirk beat Rangers 1-0 to record their first league victory over the Light Blues since the 1970/71 season. Mark Twaddle scores the first-half winner

Rangers striker Kris Boyd suffers ankle injury in the defeat by the Bairns and is ruled out until New Year

Rangers end Hibernian's unbeaten run under John Collins with 3-0 win at Ibrox

Lee Robinson signs new Rangers club contract that keeps the Sunderland-born 'keeper at Ibrox until 2009

Defender Stephen Craigan signs new contract that will keep him at Fir Park Motherwell until 2010

Steven Pressley parts company with Hearts and the defender signs for Celtic as a free agent

Aberdeen sign 40-year-old former Dundee United and Hibernian striker Craig Brewster until the end of the season. Brewster left his post as player-manager at Tannadice in October

OLD FIRM

Old Firm derby ends in a 1-1 draw as the season reaches the halfway stage with the Hoops 14 points clear at the top

DECEMBER

Celtic complete domestic double

2006 – 07

JANUARY

Barry Ferguson is stripped of the Rangers captaincy of Rangers and reports say he will not play for the club again under Paul Le Guen. Gavin Rae is appointed as the new Light Blues skipper

Rangers part company with Paul Le Guen by mutual consent

Walter Smith is confirmed as Rangers manager having resigned as Scotland national team boss. Former Ibrox favourite Ally McCoist is appointed assistant boss

Barry Ferguson is reinstated as Rangers captain

Hibernian striker Chris Killen ruled out for rest of season after suffering Achilles injury during 2-2 Scottish Cup match with Aberdeen

Rangers sign defender David Weir from Everton until the end of the season; defender 34-year-old Ugo Ehiogu on 18-month contract on free transfer from Middlesbrough; midfielder Kevin Thomson from Hibernian for reported fee of £2m

Celtic sign goalkeeper Mark Brown from Inverness on a three-and-a-half year contract; defender Jean-Joel Perrier-Doumbe from Rennes on loan with view to permanent transfer; midfielder Paul Hartley from Hearts

Celtic stretch lead to 19 points after 2-1 win at Inverness. Jan Vennegoor of Hesselink scores the last-minute winner but was then sent-off after rushing into the crowd in celebration

FEBRUARY

Falkirk midfielder Alan Gow signs pre-contract agreement with Rangers and will move to Ibrox in the close season

Bottom club Dunfermline beat Hearts 1-0 to knock the holders out of the Scottish Cup

Hibernian sign striker Thomas Sowunmi on short-term contract until end of season

Stevie Crawford ends Dunfermline's nine-match goal drought when he converts a penalty in 1-1 draw with Hearts

Motherwell forward Steven McGarry signs two-year extension to his current contract

Celtic's 18-year-old striker Cillian Sheridan handed new three-year contract just days after making first-team debut for the Hoops

Celtic maintain 19-point lead at the top of the SPL with 2-1 win over Dunfermline at Parkhead

Rangers stay second after 2-0 win at Hibernian. Charlie Adam scored both goals from free-kicks

Motherwell boss Maurice Malpas named Bank of Scotland Premier League Manager of the Month for February

MARCH

St Mirren defender Kirk Broadfoot signs pre-contract agreement with Rangers and will move to Ibrox in close season

OLD FIRM

Celtic's 27-match unbeaten run in the SPL comes to an end as Rangers win 1-0 at Parkhead. Gers defender Ugo Ehiogu is unlikely match winner with superb overhead kick

Celtic defender Darren O'Shea signs new contract that will keep him at Parkhead until 2010

Leaders Celtic suffer another defeat as Steven Thomson scores only goal of the match to give Falkirk a famous victory

Kris Boyd scores a first-half hat-trick in 3-0 defeat of Aberdeen

Manager John Collins leads Hibernian to their first trophy in 16 years with 5-1 victory over Kilmarnock in CIS Cup Final

Hearts head coach Valdas Ivanauskas leaves the club by mutual consent. Sporting director Anatoly Korobochka remains temporarily in charge of team matters at Easter Road assisted by first-team coach Stevie Frail

APRIL

Rangers defender David Weir signs new contract that keeps him at Ibrox until end of 2008/09 season

Celtic crowned SPL champions for second successive season after 2-1 win at Kilmarnock. Shunsuke Nakamura scores the winner in stoppage time with trademark free-kick to secure title for the Hoops with four games to spare

Celtic star Shunsuke Nakamura wins SPFA Player of the Year award

Celtic's John Kennedy makes first-team comeback at Kilmarnock after being sidelined since March 2004 with serious knee injury and then signs new three-year contract with the Hoops

Gretna win promotion to the SPL as First Division champions after beating Ross County 3-2 at Victoria Park

MAY

Celtic boss Gordon Strachan is named Scottish Football Writers' Association Manager of the Year; Celtic playmaker Shunsuke Nakamura wins Player of the Year award and Hibernian's Scott Brown is Young Player of the Year

OLD FIRM

Rangers secure runners-up spot in the SPL and a place in the Champions League qualifiers after beating Celtic 2-0 in the final Old Firm derby of season

Dunfermline are relegated from the SPL after 2-1 defeat at Inverness

Andy Millen becomes the oldest ever SPL player at 41 years 10 months 26 days after starting for St Mirren at Dundee United

Kilmarnock's 1-0 victory at Rangers sees Walter Smith lose his first league match since returning as Rangers manager

The final weekend of the season sees Aberdeen secure place in UEFA cup beating Rangers 2-0 at Pittodrie

A much-changed Celtic side loses 2-1 at Hearts but the champions still finish 12 points ahead of runners-up Rangers

A total of 146,846 attend the six SPL matches on Saturday 12 and Sunday 13 to set new record for single round of fixtures

Celtic win the Scottish Cup for the 34th time when they beat Dunfermline 1-0 in the final at Hampden. Defender Jean-Joel Perrier-Doumbe scores the late winner to seal another league and cup double for the Hoops

SCOTTISH PREMIER LEAGUE ROUND-UP

CELTIC

Final Position: **1st**

NICKNAME: THE BHOYS   KEY: ☐ Won ☐ Drawn ☐ Lost   Attendance

#		Opponent		Result	Scorers	Attendance
1	spl	Kilmarnock	H W	4-1	Zurawski 25, 90, Jarosik 38, Nakamura 75	54,620
2	spl	Hearts	A L	1-2	Petrov 65	16,822
3	spl	St Mirren	H W	2-0	McManus 28, Petrov 65	56,579
4	spl	Inverness CT	A D	1-1	Pearson 26	7,332
5	spl	Hibernian	H W	2-1	Zurawski 62, Vennegoor 66	58,078
6	spl	Aberdeen	A W	1-0	Vennegoor 79	15,304
7	ecgpf	Man Utd	A L	2-3	Vennegoor 21, Nakamura 43	74,031
8	spl	Dunfermline	H W	1-0	McManus 31	55,894
9	sccc3	St Mirren	H W	2-0	Beattie 76, Zurawski 87	32,587
10	spl	Rangers	H W	2-0	Gravesen 35, Miller 74	59,341
11	ecgpf	Copenhagen	H W	1-0	Miller 36 pen	57,598
12	spl	Falkirk	A W	1-0	McGeady 84	7,139
13	spl	Dundee Utd	A W	4-1	Nakamura 44, 48, 58, Vennegoor 52	10,504
14	ecgpf	Benfica	H W	3-0	Miller 56, 66, Pearson 90	58,313
15	spl	Motherwell	A W	2-1	Craigan 16 og, Zurawski 66	57,742
16	spl	Kilmarnock	A W	2-1	Nakamura 55, Miller 75	10,083
17	ecgpf	Benfica	A L	0-3		49,000
18	spl	Hearts	H W	2-1	Jarosik 86, Gordon 90 og	58,971
19	sccqf	Falkirk	H L	4-5*	Zurawski 99 (*on penalties)	18,684
20	spl	St Mirren	A W	3-1	Gravesen 2, 21, 68	8,445
21	spl	Inverness CT	H W	3-0	Dods 43 og, Vennegoor 72, Jarosik 85	56,637
22	ecgpf	Man Utd	H W	1-0	Nakamura 81 fk	60,632
23	spl	Hibernian	A D	2-2	Sno 70, McGeady 73	16,747
24	spl	Aberdeen	H W	1-0	Zurawski 72	58,911
25	ecgpf	Copenhagen	A L	1-3	Jarosik 75	41,500
26	spl	Dunfermline	A W	2-1	McGeady 49, Zurawski 68	7,080
27	spl	Rangers	A D	1-1	Gravesen 38	50,418
28	spl	Falkirk	H W	1-0	Gravesen 24	55,000
29	spl	Dundee Utd	H D	2-2	O'Dea 78, Nakamura 80	57,343
30	spl	Motherwell	A D	1-1	Riordan 36	9,769
31	spl	Kilmarnock	H W	2-0	O'Dea 39, McGeady 90	57,236
32	scr3	Dumbarton	H W	4-0	Zurawski 4, 9, Vennegoor 43, Riordan 69	18,685
33	spl	Hearts	A W	2-1	Vennegoor 59, Jarosik 82	17,129
34	spl	St Mirren	H W	5-1	Vennegoor 16, 61 pen, 75, McGeady 69, Miller 82	58,382
35	spl	Inverness CT	A W	2-1	Riordan 37, Vennegoor 90	7,484
36	scr4	Livingston	A W	4-1	O'Dea 30, Riordan 45, 59, Vennegoor 61	7,281
37	spl	Hibernian	H W	1-0	Beattie 54	59,659
38	spl	Aberdeen	A W	2-1	Beattie 9, Nakamura 20	16,711
39	eckl1	AC Milan	H D	0-0		58,785
40	scpqf	Inverness CT	A W	2-1	Pressley 89, Miller 90	7,119
41	spl	Dunfermline	H W	2-1	Miller 4, Vennegoor 76	59,131
42	eckl2	AC Milan	A L	0-1		65,000
43	spl	Rangers	H L	0-1		59,425
44	spl	Falkirk	A L	0-1		6,438
45	spl	Dundee Utd	A D	1-1	Nakamura 48	11,363
46	spl	Motherwell	H W	1-0	Riordan 52	58,654
47	scsf	St Johnstone	A W	2-1	Vennegoor 13 pen, 54	28,339
48	spl	Kilmarnock	A W	2-1	Vennegoor 24, Nakamura 90	13,623
49	spl	Hearts	H L	1-3	Pressley 63	59,510
50	spl	Rangers	A L	0-2		50,384
51	spl	Aberdeen	H W	2-1	Vennegoor 33, 49	59,510
52	spl	Hibernian	A L	1-2	Riordan 56	13,885
53	scfin	Dunfermline	H W	1-0	Perrier-Doumbe 85	49,600

LEAGUE APPEARANCES, BOOKINGS AND CAPS

	AGE (on 01/07/07)	IN NAMED 18	APPEARANCES	COUNTING GAMES	MINUTES ON PITCH	YELLOW CARDS	RED CARDS	CAPS THIS SEASON	NATIONAL SIDE
Goalkeepers									
Artur Boruc	27	36	36	35	3195	2	0	5	Poland
Mark Brown	26	14	1	1	90	0	0	-	Scotland
David Marshall	22	22	2	1	135	0	0	-	Scotland
Defenders									
Dianbobo Balde	31	13	6	5	488	2	0	-	France
Gary Caldwell	26	24	21	19	1752	3	0	4	Scotland
Mohammed Camara	32	1	1	1	90	0	0	-	Guinea
John Kennedy	23	4	3	3	270	1	0	-	Scotland
Stephen McManus	24	31	31	29	2714	4	1	5	Scotland
Lee Naylor	27	32	32	32	2880	7	0	-	England
Darren O'Dea	20	32	14	9	980	2	0	-	Rep of Ireland
J-J Perrier-Doumbe	28	9	4	3	291	0	0	-	Cameroon
Steven Pressley	33	14	14	13	1195	3	0	4	Scotland
Paul Telfer	35	26	21	20	1801	3	0	-	Scotland
Mark Wilson	23	15	12	12	1065	1	0	-	Scotland
Midfielders									
Theodor Bjarnson	20	5	1	1	90	0	0	1	Iceland
Thomas Gravesen	31	27	22	14	1491	2	0	2	Denmark
Paul Hartley	30	10	10	10	896	3	0	8	Scotland
Jiri Jarosik	29	32	25	13	1506	3	0	-	Czech Republic
Neil Lennon	36	32	31	30	2693	6	1	-	N Ireland
Aiden McGeady	21	37	34	20	2147	3	0	6	Rep of Ireland
Shunsuke Nakamura	29	37	37	36	3219	1	0	1	Japan
Stephen Pearson	24	17	12	3	387	2	0	-	Scotland
Stilian Petrov	27	3	3	3	270	0	0	-	Bulgaria
Evander Sno	20	30	18	7	800	1	0	-	Holland
Ross Wallace	22	4	2	1	145	0	0	-	Scotland
Forwards									
Craig Beattie	23	21	16	5	780	1	0	-	Scotland
Shaun Maloney	24	10	9	3	539	0	0	4	Scotland
Kenny Miller	27	35	31	16	1827	2	0	5	Scotland
Derek Riordan	24	28	17	5	681	1	0	-	Scotland
Jan V of Hesselink	28	21	21	15	1583	3	1	4	Holland
Maciej Zurawski	30	27	26	13	1562	0	0	10	Poland

TEAM OF THE SEASON

Gary Caldwell — D — CG: 18 DR: 109

Mark Wilson — D — CG: 12 DR: 106

Lee Naylor — D — CG: 32 DR: 106

Paul Telfer — D — CG: 20 DR: 105

Artur Boruc — G — CG: 35 DR: 106

Shunsuke Nakamura — M — CG: 36 SD: 63

Neil Lennon — M — CG: 30 SD: 49

Thomas Gravesen — M — CG: 13 SD: 59

Jiri Jarosik — M — CG: 13 SD: 52

Jan Vennegoor — F — CG: 15 SR: 121

Maciej Zurawski — F — CG: 12 SR: 260

MONTHLY POINTS TALLY

AUGUST	7	58%
SEPTEMBER	9	100%
OCTOBER	12	100%
NOVEMBER	10	83%
DECEMBER	12	67%
JANUARY	12	100%
FEBRUARY	6	100%
MARCH	4	33%
APRIL	6	67%
MAY	3	33%

LEAGUE GOALS

	PLAYER	MINS	GOALS	S RATE
1	Vennegoor	1583	13	121
2	Nakamura	3219	9	357
3	Gravesen	1491	6	248
4	Zurawski	1562	6	260
5	McGeady	2147	5	429
6	Riordan	681	4	170
7	Jarosik	1506	4	376
8	Miller	1827	4	456
9	Petrov	270	2	135
10	Beattie	780	2	390
11	O'Dea	980	2	490
12	McManus	2714	2	1357
13	Pearson	387	1	387
	Other		2	
	TOTAL		**62**	

TOP POINT EARNERS

	PLAYER	GAMES	AV PTS
1	Kenny Miller	16	2.56
2	Paul Telfer	20	2.55
3	Thomas Gravesen	13	2.54
4	Gary Caldwell	18	2.44
5	Maciej Zurawski	12	2.42
6	Lee Naylor	32	2.31
7	Artur Boruc	35	2.29
8	Neil Lennon	30	2.27
9	Jan Vennegoor	15	2.27
10	Shunsuke Nakamura	36	2.25
	CLUB AVERAGE:		**2.21**

DISCIPLINARY RECORDS

	PLAYER	YELLOW	RED	AVE
1	Dianbobo Balde	2	0	244
2	Paul Hartley	3	0	298
3	Neil Lennon	9	1	384
4	Jan Vennegoor	3	1	395
5	Steven Pressley	4	0	398
6	Lee Naylor	8	0	411
7	Jiri Jarosik	5	0	502
8	Stephen McManus	8	1	542
9	Gary Caldwell	3	0	584
10	Derek Riordan	1	0	681
11	Aiden McGeady	5	0	715
12	Thomas Gravesen	3	0	745
13	Craig Beattie	1	0	780
	Other	15	0	
	TOTAL	**70**	**3**	

KEY GOALKEEPER

Artur Boruc

Goals Conceded in the League	30	Counting Games League games when player was on pitch for at least 70 minutes	35
Defensive Rating Ave number of mins between League goals conceded while on the pitch	106	Clean Sheets In games when player was on pitch for at least 70 minutes	12

KEY PLAYERS - DEFENDERS

Gary Caldwell

Goals Conceded Number of League goals conceded while the player was on the pitch	16	Clean Sheets In League games when player was on pitch for at least 70 minutes	6
Defensive Rating Ave number of mins between League goals conceded while on the pitch	109	Club Defensive Rating Average number of mins between League goals conceded by the club this season	100

	PLAYER	CON LGE	CLEAN SHEETS	DEF RATE
1	Gary Caldwell	16	6	109 mins
2	Lee Naylor	27	10	106 mins
3	Mark Wilson	10	3	106 mins
4	Paul Telfer	17	7	105 mins

KEY PLAYERS - MIDFIELDERS

Shunsuke Nakamura

Goals in the League	9	Contribution to Attacking Power Average number of minutes between League team goals while on pitch	51
Defensive Rating Average number of mins between League goals conceded while on the pitch	114	Scoring Difference Defensive Rating minus Contribution to Attacking Power	63

	PLAYER	LGE GOALS	DEF RATE	POWER	SCORE DIFF
1	Shunsuke Nakamura	9	114	51	63 mins
2	Thomas Gravesen	6	114	55	59 mins
3	Jiri Jarosik	4	100	48	52 mins
4	Neil Lennon	0	107	58	49 mins

KEY PLAYERS - GOALSCORERS

Jan Vennegoor of Hesselink

Goals in the League	13	Player Strike Rate Average number of minutes between League goals scored by player	121
Contribution to Attacking Power Average number of minutes between League team goals while on pitch	42	Club Strike Rate Average number of minutes between League goals scored by club	52

	PLAYER	LGE GOALS	POWER	STRIKE RATE
1	Jan Vennegoor of Hesselink	13	42	121 mins
2	Thomas Gravesen	6	55	248 mins
3	Maciej Zurawski	6	60	260 mins
4	Shunsuke Nakamura	9	51	357 mins

Kenny Miller

SQUAD APPEARANCES

Match	1 2 3 4 5	6 7 8 9 10	11 12 13 14 15	16 17 18 19 20	21 22 23 24 25	26 27 28 29 30	31 32 33 34 35	36 37 38 39 40	41 42 43 44 45	46 47 48 49 50	51 52 53
Venue	H A H A H	A A H H H	H A A H H	A A H H A	H H A H A	A A H H A	H H A H A	A H A H A	H A H A A	H A A H A	H A N
Competition	L L L L L	L C L W L	C L L C L	L C L W L	L C L L C	L L L L L	L F L L L	F L L C F	L C L L L	L F L L L	L L F
Result	W L W D W	W L W W W	W W W W W	W L W L W	W W D W L	W D W D D	W W W W W	W W W D W	W L L L D	W W W L L	W L W

Goalkeepers

Artur Boruc
Mark Brown
David Marshall

Defenders

Dianbobo Balde
Gary Caldwell
Mohammed Camara
John Kennedy
Stephen McManus
Lee Naylor
Darren O'Dea
J-J Perrier-Doumbe
Steven Pressley
Paul Telfer
Mark Wilson

Midfielders

Theodor Bjarnson
Thomas Gravesen
Paul Hartley
Jiri Jarosik
Neil Lennon
Aiden McGeady
Shunsuke Nakamura
Stephen Pearson
Stilian Petrov
Evander Sno
Ross Wallace

Forwards

Craig Beattie
Shaun Maloney
Kenny Miller
Derek Riordan
Jan V of Hesselink
Maciej Zurawski

KEY: ■ On all match ◄◄ Subbed or sent off (Counting game) ►► Subbed on from bench (Counting Game) ►► Subbed on and then subbed or sent off (Counting Game) □ Not in 16
On bench ◄◄ Subbed or sent off (playing less than 70 minutes) ►► Subbed on (playing less than 70 minutes) ►► Subbed on and then subbed or sent off (playing less than 70 minutes)

SCOTTISH PREMIERSHIP - CELTIC

RANGERS

Final Position: **2nd**

NICKNAME: THE GERS   KEY: ☐ Won ☐ Drawn ☐ Lost   Attendance

				Result	Scorers	Attendance
1	spl	Motherwell	A W	2-1	Sionko 8, Prso 65	11,745
2	spl	Dundee Utd	H D	2-2	Burke 57, Robb 79 og	50,394
3	spl	Dunfermline	A D	1-1	Buffel 63	8,561
4	spl	Hearts	H W	2-0	Boyd 47 pen, 49	50,239
5	spl	Kilmarnock	A D	2-2	Boyd 43, 85	13,506
6	spl	Falkirk	H W	4-0	Bardsley 17, Prso 28, Boyd 68 pen, Buffel 78	50,196
7	ucrl1	Molde	A D	0-0		6,569
8	spl	Hibernian	A L	1-2	Sebo 65	16,450
9	sccc3	Dunfermline	A W	2-0	Bamba 65 og, Boyd 73	5,702
10	spl	Celtic	A L	0-2		59,341
11	ucrl2	Molde	H W	2-0	Buffel 12, Ferguson 45	48,024
12	spl	Aberdeen	H W	1-0	Sebo 88	50,488
13	spl	Inverness CT	H L	0-1		49,494
14	ucgpa	Livorno	A W	3-2	Adam 27, Boyd 29 pen, Novo 35	13,200
15	spl	St Mirren	A W	3-2	Adam 18, Buffel 26, Novo 85	8,384
16	spl	Motherwell	H D	1-1	Boyd 36	49,785
17	ucgpa	Maccabi Haifa	H W	2-0	Novo 5, Adam 89 pen	43,062
18	spl	Dundee Utd	A L	1-2	Adam 50	10,392
19	sccqf	St Johnstone	H L	0-2		31,074
20	spl	Dunfermline	H W	2-0	Boyd 61, S.Smith 77	48,218
21	spl	Hearts	A W	1-0	Novo 78	17,040
22	ucgpa	Auxerre	A D	2-2	Novo 61, Boyd 84	8,305
23	spl	Kilmarnock	H W	3-0	Adam 23, Boyd 28, Prso 58	48,289
24	spl	Falkirk	A L	0-1		7,245
25	spl	Hibernian	H W	3-0	Prso 16, Sionko 32, Ferguson 36	49,702
26	ucgpa	Partizan	H W	1-0	Hutton 55	45,129
27	spl	Celtic	H D	1-1	Hemdani 88	50,418
28	spl	Aberdeen	A L	1-2	Novo 22, Sionko 24	20,045
29	spl	Inverness CT	A L	1-2	Novo 22 pen	7,522
30	spl	St Mirren	H D	1-1	Boyd 19	50,273
31	spl	Motherwell	A W	1-0	Boyd 70 pen	10,338
32	scr3	Dunfermline	A L	2-3	Boyd 54, 68	7,231
33	spl	Dundee Utd	H W	5-0	Adam 23, Burke 36, Boyd 59, 68, Ferguson 88	50,276
34	spl	Dunfermline	A W	1-0	Adam 9	7,868
35	spl	Hearts	H D	0-0		50,321
36	spl	Kilmarnock	A W	3-1	Boyd 8 pen, 30, 60 pen	11,894
37	uc2rl1	H Tel-Aviv	A L	1-2	Novo 53	13,000
38	spl	Falkirk	H W	2-0	Boyd 34, Ferguson 73	49,850
39	uc2rl2	H Tel-Aviv	H W	4-0	Ferguson 24, 73, Boyd 35, Adam 90	46,213
40	spl	Hibernian	A W	2-0	Adam 4, 60	16,265
41	uc3rl1	Osasuna	H D	1-1	Hemdani 90	50,290
42	spl	Celtic	A W	1-0	Ehiogu 50	59,425
43	uc4rl2	Osasuna	A L	0-1		35,000
44	spl	Aberdeen	H W	3-0	Boyd 8, 25, 31	50,354
45	spl	Inverness CT	H D	1-1	Adam 15	50,278
46	spl	St Mirren	A W	1-0	Novo 4	7,308
47	spl	Hearts	H W	2-1	G.Rae 52, Ferguson 79	50,099
48	spl	Hibernian	A D	3-3	Adam 24, 78, Hutton 54	16,747
49	spl	Celtic	H W	2-0	Boyd 34, Adam 55	50,384
50	spl	Kilmarnock	H L	0-1		50,085
51	spl	Aberdeen	A L	0-2		20,010

LEAGUE APPEARANCES, BOOKINGS AND CAPS

	AGE (on 01/07/07)	IN NAMED 18	APPEARANCES	COUNTING GAMES	MINUTES ON PITCH	YELLOW CARDS	RED CARDS	CAPS THIS SEASON	NATIONAL SIDE
Goalkeepers									
Stefan Klos	35	20	1	1	90	0	0	-	Germany
Lionel Letizi	34	7	7	7	630	0	0	-	France
Allan McGregor	25	37	31	31	2790	1	1	1	Scotland
Defenders									
Phillip Bardsley	22	7	5	4	424	2	1	-	England
Ugo Ehiogu	34	10	9	8	745	1	0	-	England
Ibrahim Hemdani	29	37	36	35	3175	1	0	-	France
Alan Hutton	22	36	33	31	2875	11	0	-	Scotland
Sasa Papac	27	29	21	17	1718	2	0	-	Bosnia
Julien Rodriguez	29	17	13	12	1063	2	0	-	France
Steven Smith	21	18	17	16	1480	6	0	-	Scotland
Karl Svensson	23	33	21	18	1786	1	0	2	Sweden
David Weir	37	14	14	14	1260	2	0	8	Scotland
Midfielders									
Charlie Adam	21	36	32	30	2719	7	0	-	Scotland
Thomas Buffel	26	21	17	8	908	1	0	1	Belgium
Chris Burke	23	22	22	7	1111	3	0	-	Scotland
Jeremy Clement	22	20	19	19	1710	5	0	-	France
Barry Ferguson	29	32	32	31	2836	8	0	6	Scotland
Steven Lennon	19	11	3	0	61	0	0	-	Scotland
Lee Martin	20	8	7	3	349	1	0	-	England
Ian Murray	26	16	13	12	1121	2	0	-	Scotland
Makhtar N'Diaye	25	6	1	0	1	0	0	-	Senegal
Gavin Rae	29	34	9	3	309	1	0	-	Scotland
Andrew Shinnie	17	8	2	0	18	0	0	-	Scotland
Libor Sionko	30	24	18	9	1041	0	0	5	Czech Republic
Kevin Thomson	22	10	9	7	664	1	0	-	Scotland
Forwards									
Kris Boyd	23	33	32	21	2285	6	0	7	Scotland
Nacho Novo	28	30	28	17	1995	11	0	-	Spain
Dado Prso	32	28	28	17	1846	6	1	-	Croatia
Filip Sebo	23	29	24	4	681	2	0	-	Slovakia

TEAM OF THE SEASON

G Allan McGregor CG: 31 DR: 116

D David Weir CG: 14 DR: 126
D Karl Svensson CG: 18 DR: 119
D Alan Hutton CG: 31 DR: 106
D Ibrahim Hemdani CG: 35 DR: 117

M Ian Murray CG: 12 SD: 133
M Charlie Adam CG: 30 SD: 44
M Jeremy Clement CG: 19 SD: 58
M Barry Ferguson CG: 31 SD: 52

F Kris Boyd CG: 21 SR: 114
F Nacho Novo CG: 17 SR: 399

MONTHLY POINTS TALLY

AUGUST	6	50%
SEPTEMBER	3	33%
OCTOBER	7	58%
NOVEMBER	9	75%
DECEMBER	8	44%
JANUARY	10	83%
FEBRUARY	6	100%
MARCH	10	83%
APRIL	7	78%
MAY	3	33%

LEAGUE GOALS

	PLAYER	MINS	GOALS	S RATE
1	Boyd	2285	20	114
2	Adam	2719	11	247
3	Novo	1995	5	399
4	Prso	1846	4	461
5	Ferguson	2836	4	709
6	Buffel	908	3	302
7	Sionko	1041	3	347
8	Sebo	681	2	340
9	Burke	1111	2	555
10	Rae, G	309	1	309
11	Bardsley	424	1	424
12	Ehiogu	745	1	745
13	Smith, S	1480	1	1480
	Other		2	
	TOTAL		**60**	

TOP POINT EARNERS

	PLAYER	GAMES	AV PTS
1	Kris Boyd	21	2.24
2	Ian Murray	12	2.17
3	David Weir	14	2.14
4	Karl Svensson	18	2.06
5	Dado Prso	16	2.06
6	Ibrahim Hemdani	35	2.06
7	Alan Hutton	31	2.03
8	Allan McGregor	31	1.94
9	Charlie Adam	29	1.93
10	Nacho Novo	17	1.88
	CLUB AVERAGE:		**1.89**

DISCIPLINARY RECORDS

	PLAYER	YELLOW	RED	AVE
1	Nacho Novo	11	0	221
2	Filip Sebo	2	0	340
3	Jeremy Clement	5	0	342
4	Dado Prso	6	1	369
5	Alan Hutton	11	0	410
6	Charlie Adam	7	0	453
7	Kris Boyd	6	0	457
8	Steven Smith	6	0	493
9	Julien Rodriguez	2	0	531
10	Chris Burke	3	0	555
11	Barry Ferguson	8	0	567
12	David Weir	2	0	630
13	Kevin Thomson	1	0	664
	Other	9	1	
	TOTAL	**79**	**2**	

KEY GOALKEEPER

Allan McGregor

Goals Conceded in the League	24	Counting Games League games when player was on pitch for at least 70 minutes	31
Defensive Rating Ave number of mins between League goals conceded while on the pitch	116	Clean Sheets In League games when player was on pitch for at least 70 minutes	15

KEY PLAYERS - DEFENDERS

David Weir

Goals Conceded Number of League goals conceded while the player was on the pitch	10	Clean Sheets In League games when player was on pitch for at least 70 minutes	7
Defensive Rating Ave number of mins between League goals conceded while on the pitch	126	Club Defensive Rating Average number of mins between League goals conceded by the club this season	106

	PLAYER	CON LGE	CLEAN SHEETS	DEF RATE
1	David Weir	10	7	126 mins
2	Karl Svensson	15	9	119 mins
3	Ibrahim Hemdani	27	16	117 mins
4	Alan Hutton	27	13	106 mins

KEY PLAYERS - MIDFIELDERS

Ian Murray

Goals in the League	0	Contribution to Attacking Power Average number of minutes between League team goals while on pitch	53
Defensive Rating Average number of mins between League goals conceded while on the pitch	186	Scoring Difference Defensive Rating minus Contribution to Attacking Power	133

	PLAYER	LGE GOALS	DEF RATE	POWER	SCORE DIFF
1	Ian Murray	0	186	53	133 mins
2	Jeremy Clement	0	106	48	58 mins
3	Barry Ferguson	4	109	57	52 mins
4	Charlie Adam	11	104	60	44 mins

KEY PLAYERS - GOALSCORERS

Kris Boyd

Goals in the League	20	Player Strike Rate Average number of minutes between League goals scored by player	114
Contribution to Attacking Power Average number of minutes between League team goals while on pitch	46	Club Strike Rate Average number of minutes between League goals scored by club	56

	PLAYER	LGE GOALS	POWER	STRIKE RATE
1	Kris Boyd	20	46	114 mins
2	Charlie Adam	11	60	247 mins
3	Nacho Novo	5	55	399 mins
4	Dado Prso	4	54	461 mins

Kris Boyd

SQUAD APPEARANCES

Match	1 2 3 4 5	6 7 8 9 10	11 12 13 14 15	16 17 18 19 20	21 22 23 24 25	26 27 28 29 30	31 32 33 34 35	36 37 38 39 40	41 42 43 44 45	46 47 48 49 50	51
Venue	A H A H A	H A A A A	H H H A A	H H A H H	A A H A H	H H A A H	A A H A H	A A H H A	H A A H H	A H A H H	A
Competition	L L L L L	L E L W L	E L L E L	L E L W L	L E L L L	E L L L L	L F L L L	L E L E L	E L E L L	L L L L L	L
Result	W D D W D	W D L W L	W W L W W	D W L L W	W D W L W	W D W L D	W L W W D	W L W W W	D W L W D	W W D W L	L

Goalkeepers
- Stefan Klos
- Lionel Letizi
- Allan McGregor

Defenders
- Phillip Bardsley
- Ugo Ehiogu
- Ibrahim Hemdani
- Alan Hutton
- Sasa Papac
- Julien Rodriguez
- Steven Smith
- Karl Svensson
- David Weir

Midfielders
- Charlie Adam
- Thomas Buffel
- Chris Burke
- Jeremy Clement
- Barry Ferguson
- Steven Lennon
- Lee Martin
- Ian Murray
- Makhtar N'Diaye
- Gavin Rae
- Andrew Shinnie
- Libor Sionko
- Kevin Thomson

Forwards
- Kris Boyd
- Nacho Novo
- Dado Prso
- Filip Sebo

KEY: ■ On all match   ◄◄ Subbed or sent off (Counting game)   ►► Subbed on from bench (Counting Game)   ►► Subbed on and then subbed or sent off (Counting Game)   ☐ Not in 16
  ☐ On bench   ◄◄ Subbed or sent off (playing less than 70 minutes)   ►► Subbed on (playing less than 70 minutes)   ►► Subbed on and then subbed or sent off (playing less than 70 minutes)

ABERDEEN

Final Position: 3rd

NICKNAME: THE DONS **KEY:** ☐ Won ☐ Drawn ☐ Lost   Attendance

1 spl	Hibernian	A D	1-1	Crawford 19	15,046
2 spl	Inverness CT	H D	1-1	Crawford 29	11,955
3 spl	Motherwell	A W	2-0	Mackie 33, 61	5,186
4 spl	St Mirren	A D	1-1	Crawford 33	5,344
5 sccc2	Queens Park	A L	3-5*	(*on penalties)	1,588
6 spl	Dunfermline	H W	1-0	Severin 68	9,889
7 spl	Celtic	H L	0-1		15,304
8 spl	Falkirk	A W	2-0	Dempsey 51, Daal 81	5,812
9 spl	Hearts	H L	1-3	Daal 82	11,160
10 spl	Rangers	A L	0-1		50,488
11 spl	Kilmarnock	A L	0-1		5,744
12 spl	Dundee Utd	H W	3-1	Mackie 39, Nicholson 47, 71	10,747
13 spl	Hibernian	H W	2-1	Miller 56, Severin 90	11,179
14 spl	Inverness CT	A D	1-1	Lovell 90	5,744
15 spl	Motherwell	H W	2-1	J.Smith 56, Miller 86	10,527
16 spl	St Mirren	H W	2-0	Mackie 77, 85	11,426
17 spl	Dunfermline	A W	3-0	Miller 54, Mackie 83, 85	6,501
18 spl	Celtic	A L	0-1		58,911
19 spl	Falkirk	H W	2-1	Mackie 17, Clark 44	10,594
20 spl	Hearts	A W	1-0	Lovell 87	17,274
21 spl	Rangers	H L	1-2	Lovell 84	20,045
22 spl	Kilmarnock	H W	3-1	Maguire 6, Nicholson 9, Lovell 87	11,887
23 spl	Dundee Utd	A L	1-3	Severin 56	12,329
24 spl	Hibernian	A D	0-0		16,278
25 scr3	Hibernian	H D	2-2	Brewster 58, Nicholson 89	7,905
26 spl	Inverness CT	H D	1-1	Lovell 90	10,300
27 scr3r	Hibernian	A L	1-4	Nicholson 10	11,375
28 spl	St Mirren	A W	2-0	Considine 8, 36	4,921
29 spl	Dunfermline	H W	3-0	Mackie 33, Nicholson 58 pen, Lovell 83	9,379
30 spl	Celtic	H L	1-2	Mackie 90	16,711
31 spl	Falkirk	A W	2-1	Dempsey 16, Foster 61	5,825
32 spl	Hearts	H W	1-0	Lovell 7	13,964
33 spl	Motherwell	A W	2-0	Fitzpatrick 31 og, Foster 90	4,530
34 spl	Rangers	A L	0-3		50,354
35 spl	Kilmarnock	A W	2-1	Fowler 59 og, Anderson 69	7,236
36 spl	Dundee Utd	H L	2-4	Lovell 8, Mackie 10 pen	12,148
37 spl	Hibernian	H D	2-2	Anderson 25, Foster 80	9,753
38 spl	Kilmarnock	H W	3-0	Nicholson 7 pen, Miller 49, Mackie 62	10,046
39 spl	Hearts	A D	1-1	Nicholson 90	17,208
40 spl	Celtic	A L	1-2	Mackie 41	59,510
41 spl	Rangers	H W	2-0	Severin 21, Lovell 32	20,010

LEAGUE APPEARANCES, BOOKINGS AND CAPS

	AGE (on 01/07/07)	IN NAMED 18	APPEARANCES	COUNTING GAMES	MINUTES ON PITCH	YELLOW CARDS	RED CARDS	CAPS THIS SEASON	NATIONAL SIDE
Goalkeepers									
James Langfield	27	38	38	38	3420	0	0	-	Scotland
Derek Soutar	28	35	0	0	0	0	0	-	Scotland
Defenders									
Russell Anderson	28	35	35	33	3054	6	0	-	Scotland
Richie Byrne	25	5	5	4	369	1	0	-	Rep of Ireland
Andrew Considine	20	37	33	20	2105	6	0	-	Scotland
Alexander Diamond	22	29	21	12	1421	5	0	-	Scotland
David Donald	19	18	0	0	0	0	0	-	Scotland
Michael Hart	27	34	34	32	2988	7	1	-	Scotland
Kyle Macauley	-	9	0	0	0	0	0	-	Scotland
Daniel Smith	20	31	6	2	245	0	0	-	Scotland
Karim Touzani	26	26	11	4	519	0	0	-	Holland
Midfielders									
Christopher Clark	26	37	37	34	3189	6	0	-	Scotland
Gary Dempsey	26	32	26	16	1743	0	0	-	Rep of Ireland
Richard Foster	21	37	37	35	3155	6	0	-	Scotland
Barry Nicholson	28	31	31	28	2677	4	1	-	Scotland
Scott Severin	28	35	35	34	3064	6	0	-	Scotland
Jamie Smith	26	22	21	17	1686	3	0	-	Scotland
Forwards									
Craig Brewster	40	13	12	4	569	3	0	-	Scotland
Stevie Crawford	33	4	4	3	298	0	0	-	Scotland
Dyron Daal	23	10	7	1	183	1	0	-	Holland
Steve Lovell	26	27	27	10	1363	5	0	-	England
Darren Mackie	25	37	36	30	2867	2	0	-	Scotland
Christopher Maguire	18	33	19	1	439	3	0	-	Scotland
Lee Miller	24	33	32	22	2141	2	0	-	Scotland
Michael Paton	18	3	0	0	0	0	0	-	Scotland
John Stewart	21	5	4	0	99	0	0	-	Scotland
Jamie Winter	21	20	0	0	0	0	0	-	Scotland

TEAM OF THE SEASON

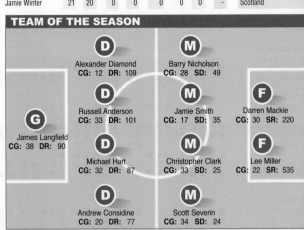

D Alexander Diamond CG: 12 DR: 109
M Barry Nicholson CG: 28 SD: 49
D Russell Anderson CG: 33 DR: 101
M Jamie Smith CG: 17 SD: 35
F Darren Mackie CG: 30 SR: 220
G James Langfield CG: 38 DR: 90
D Michael Hart CG: 32 DR: 87
M Christopher Clark CG: 33 SD: 25
F Lee Miller CG: 22 SR: 535
D Andrew Considine CG: 20 DR: 77
M Scott Severin CG: 34 SD: 24

MONTHLY POINTS TALLY

AUGUST	8	67%
SEPTEMBER	3	33%
OCTOBER	6	50%
NOVEMBER	10	83%
DECEMBER	9	50%
JANUARY	5	56%
FEBRUARY	3	50%
MARCH	12	80%
APRIL	4	44%
MAY	4	44%

LEAGUE GOALS

	PLAYER	MINS	GOALS	S RATE
1	Mackie	2867	13	220
2	Lovell	1363	9	151
3	Nicholson	2677	6	446
4	Miller	2141	4	535
5	Severin	3064	4	766
6	Crawford	298	3	99
7	Foster	3155	3	1051
8	Daal	183	2	91
9	Dempsey	1743	2	871
10	Considine	2105	2	1052
11	Anderson	3054	2	1527
12	Maguire	439	1	439
13	Smith, J	1686	1	1686
	Other		1	
	TOTAL		53	

TOP POINT EARNERS

	PLAYER	GAMES	AV PTS
1	Russell Anderson	33	1.94
2	Jamie Smith	17	1.94
3	Barry Nicholson	28	1.82
4	Christopher Clark	33	1.82
5	Andrew Considine	20	1.75
6	Scott Severin	34	1.74
7	James Langfield	38	1.71
8	Darren Mackie	30	1.70
9	Gary Dempsey	16	1.69
10	Richard Foster	35	1.66
	CLUB AVERAGE:		1.71

DISCIPLINARY RECORDS

	PLAYER	YELLOW	RED	AVE
1	Craig Brewster	3	0	189
2	Steve Lovell	5	0	272
3	Alexander Diamond	5	0	284
4	Andrew Considine	6	0	421
5	Michael Hart	7	1	426
6	Russell Anderson	6	0	509
7	Richard Foster	6	0	525
8	Christopher Clark	6	0	531
9	Barry Nicholson	4	1	535
10	Jamie Smith	3	0	562
11	Scott Severin	6	0	612
12	Darren Mackie	2	0	1433
13	Lee Miller	2	0	2141
	Other	0	0	
	TOTAL	61	2	

KEY GOALKEEPER

James Langfield

Goals Conceded in the League	38	Counting Games League games when player was on pitch for at least 70 minutes	38
Defensive Rating Ave number of mins between League goals conceded while on the pitch	90	Clean Sheets In League games when player was on pitch for at least 70 minutes	13

KEY PLAYERS - DEFENDERS

Alexander Diamond

Goals Conceded Number of League goals conceded while the player was on the pitch	13	Clean Sheets In League games when player was on pitch for at least 70 minutes	5
Defensive Rating Ave number of mins between League goals conceded while on the pitch	109	Club Defensive Rating Average number of mins between League goals conceded by the club this season	92

	PLAYER	CON LGE	CLEAN SHEETS	DEF RATE
1	Alexander Diamond	13	5	109 mins
2	Russell Anderson	30	14	101 mins
3	Michael Hart	34	10	87 mins
4	Andrew Considine	27	9	77 mins

KEY PLAYERS - MIDFIELDERS

Barry Nicholson

Goals in the League	6	Contribution to Attacking Power Average number of minutes between League team goals while on pitch	62
Defensive Rating Average number of mins between League goals conceded while on the pitch	111	Scoring Difference Defensive Rating minus Contribution to Attacking Power	49

	PLAYER	LGE GOALS	DEF RATE	POWER	SCORE DIFF
1	Barry Nicholson	6	111	62	49 mins
2	Jamie Smith	1	93	58	35 mins
3	Christopher Clark	1	88	63	25 mins
4	Scott Severin	4	85	61	24 mins

KEY PLAYERS - GOALSCORERS

Darren Mackie

Goals in the League	13	Player Strike Rate Average number of minutes between League goals scored by player	220
Contribution to Attacking Power Average number of minutes between League team goals while on pitch	58	Club Strike Rate Average number of minutes between League goals scored by club	63

	PLAYER	LGE GOALS	POWER	STRIKE RATE
1	Darren Mackie	13	58	220 mins
2	Barry Nicholson	6	62	446 mins
3	Lee Miller	4	66	535 mins
4	Scott Severin	4	61	766 mins

Darren Mackie

SQUAD APPEARANCES

Match	1	2	3	4	5	6	7	8	9	10	11	12	13	14	15	16	17	18	19	20	21	22	23	24	25	26	27	28	29	30	31	32	33	34	35	36	37	38	39	40	41
Venue	A	H	A	A	A	H	H	A	H	A	A	H	H	A	H	H	A	A	H	A	H	H	A	A	H	H	A	H	H	A	A	H	A	A	A	H	H	H	A	A	H
Competition	L	L	L	W	L	L	L	L	L	L	L	L	L	L	L	L	L	L	L	L	L	L	L	L	F	L	F	L	L	L	L	L	L	L	L	L	L	L	L	L	L
Result	D	D	W	D	L	W	L	W	L	L	L	W	W	D	W	W	W	L	W	W	L	W	L	D	D	D	L	W	W	L	W	W	W	L	W	L	D	W	D	L	W

Goalkeepers
James Langfield
Derek Soutar

Defenders
Russell Anderson
Richie Byrne
Andrew Considine
Alexander Diamond
David Donald
Michael Hart
Kyle Macauley
Daniel Smith
Karim Touzani

Midfielders
Christopher Clark
Gary Dempsey
Richard Foster
Barry Nicholson
Scott Severin
Jamie Smith

Forwards
Craig Brewster
Stevie Crawford
Dyron Daal
Steve Lovell
Darren Mackie
Christopher Maguire
Lee Miller
Michael Paton
John Stewart
Jamie Winter

KEY: ■ On all match   ◄◄ Subbed or sent off (Counting game)   ►► Subbed on from bench (Counting Game)   ►► Subbed on and then subbed or sent off (Counting Game)   ☐ Not in 16
■ On bench   ◄◄ Subbed or sent off (playing less than 70 minutes)   ►► Subbed on (playing less than 70 minutes)   ►► Subbed on and then subbed or sent off (playing less than 70 minutes)

SCOTTISH PREMIERSHIP - ABERDEEN

HEART OF MIDLOTHIAN

Final Position: **4th**

NICKNAME: THE JAM TARTS — KEY: ☐ Won ☐ Drawn ☐ Lost — Attendance

#	Comp	Opponent	H/A	Result		Scorers	Attendance
1	spl	Dunfermline	A	W	2-1	Bednar 15, Pospisil 78	7,936
2	ecql2	Siroki Brijeg	A	D	0-0		6,000
3	spl	Celtic	H	W	2-1	Bednar 49, 87	16,822
4	ecql1	AEK Athens	H	L	1-2	Mikoliunas 62	32,459
5	spl	Falkirk	H	D	0-0		16,127
6	spl	Rangers	A	L	0-2		50,239
7	ecql2	AEK Athens	A	L	0-3		31,500
8	spl	Inverness CT	H	W	4-1	Pinilla 20, Mole 42, Driver 80, Aguiar 90	15,912
9	spl	St Mirren	H	L	0-1		16,823
10	uc1rl1	Sparta Prague	H	L	0-2		27,255
11	spl	Motherwell	A	W	1-0	Mole 69	5,931
12	sccc3	Alloa	A	W	4-0	Makela 34, 46, 82, Aguiar 88	2,551
13	spl	Aberdeen	A	W	3-1	Berra 63, Pinilla 76, Mikoliunas 81	11,160
14	uc1rl2	Sparta Prague	A	D	0-0		16,505
15	spl	Dundee Utd	H	W	4-0	Archibald 30 og, Makela 39, Hartley 88 pen, Mole 89	16,849
16	spl	Hibernian	A	D	2-2	Velicka 28, 72	16,623
17	spl	Kilmarnock	H	L	0-2		16,849
18	spl	Dunfermline	H	D	1-1	Velicka 12	17,031
19	spl	Celtic	A	L	1-2	Velicka 74	58,971
20	sccqf	Hibernian	A	L	0-1		15,825
21	spl	Falkirk	A	D	1-1	Velicka 65	6,289
22	spl	Rangers	H	L	0-1		17,040
23	spl	Inverness CT	A	D	0-0		5,603
24	spl	St Mirren	A	D	2-2	Mikoliunas 1, Zaliukas 51	5,728
25	spl	Motherwell	H	W	4-1	Fyssas 9, P.Quinn 55 og, Velicka 58, Aguiar 64	16,753
26	spl	Aberdeen	H	L	0-1		17,274
27	spl	Dundee Utd	A	W	1-0	Hartley 55 pen	7,789
28	spl	Hibernian	H	W	3-2	Hartley 2, Jankauskas 49, Mikoliunas 70	17,369
29	spl	Kilmarnock	A	D	0-0		7,302
30	spl	Dunfermline	A	W	1-0	Pospisil 16	7,004
31	scr3	Stranraer	A	W	4-0	Velicka 17, 43, 90, Bednar 79	-
32	spl	Celtic	H	L	1-2	Mikoliunas 28	17,129
33	spl	Falkirk	H	W	1-0	Bednar 74	17,247
34	spl	Rangers	A	D	0-0		50,321
35	scr4	Dunfermline	A	L	0-1		9,597
36	spl	Inverness CT	H	W	1-0	Pospisil 82	16,631
37	spl	St Mirren	H	D	1-1	L.Kingston 71	17,195
38	spl	Motherwell	A	W	2-0	Tall 37, Craigan 66 og	4,389
39	spl	Aberdeen	A	L	0-1		13,964
40	spl	Dundee Utd	H	L	0-4		17,172
41	spl	Hibernian	A	W	1-0	Zaliukas 82	15,953
42	spl	Kilmarnock	H	W	1-0	Pospisil 78	17,019
43	spl	Rangers	A	L	1-2	Velicka 16	50,099
44	spl	Celtic	A	W	3-1	Ivaskevicius 57, Driver 61, Pospisil 71 pen	59,510
45	spl	Aberdeen	H	D	1-1	Velicka 15	17,208
46	spl	Hibernian	H	W	2-0	Pospisil 1, Driver 23	17,349
47	spl	Kilmarnock	A	L	0-1		11,030

LEAGUE APPEARANCES, BOOKINGS AND CAPS

	AGE (on 01/07/07)	IN NAMED 18	APPEARANCES	COUNTING GAMES	MINUTES ON PITCH	YELLOW CARDS	RED CARDS	CAPS THIS SEASON	NATIONAL SIDE
Goalkeepers									
Steve Banks	35	35	4	4	360	0	0	-	England
Craig Gordon	24	35	34	34	3060	3	0	8	Scotland
Defenders									
Nerijus Barasa	29	12	10	6	675	4	0	-	Lithuania
Christophe Berra	22	35	35	33	2994	7	0	-	Scotland
Panagiotis Fyssas	34	28	21	15	1611	3	0	-	Greece
Jose Goncalves	21	13	11	7	755	0	1	-	Portugal
Tomas Kancelskis	31	7	5	1	255	2	0	-	Lithuania
Christos Karipidis	24	24	12	10	975	4	0	-	Greece
Robbie Neilson	27	22	14	12	1168	6	1	1	Scotland
Steven Pressley	33	14	13	13	1170	3	0	4	Scotland
Lee Wallace	19	31	17	11	1224	1	0	-	Scotland
Marius Zaliukas	23	32	27	22	2277	6	0	-	Lithuania
Midfielders									
Bruno Aguiar	26	27	25	20	1833	8	1	-	Portugal
Mirsad Beslija	27	7	5	1	213	0	0	-	Bosnia
Julien Brellier	25	25	22	13	1376	9	1	-	France
Deividas Cesnauskis	26	9	9	3	424	0	0	-	Lithuania
Andrew Driver	19	23	20	16	1535	9	0	-	Scotland
Paul Hartley	30	21	21	18	1642	4	1	8	Scotland
Kestutis Ivaskevicius	22	12	9	8	773	5	0	-	Lithuania
Laryea Kingston	26	10	10	9	850	2	1	-	Ghana
Neil McCann	32	28	21	13	1324	4	1	-	Scotland
Ibrahim Tall	31	27	23	16	1578	2	1	-	Senegal
Forwards									
Roman Bednar	24	22	18	11	1212	2	0	1	Czech Republic
Calum Elliot	20	13	10	4	527	1	0	-	Scotland
Edgaras Jankauskas	32	17	13	4	686	2	0	-	Lithuania
Saulius Mikoliunas	23	32	31	23	2382	8	1	-	Lithuania
Jamie Mole	19	17	10	3	517	0	0	-	England
Linas Pilibaitis	22	7	5	3	338	2	0	-	Lithuania
Mauricio Pinilla	23	3	3	2	201	1	1	-	Chile
Michel Pospisil	28	26	24	9	1232	4	0	-	Czech Republic
Andrius Velicka	28	27	27	18	1895	4	0	-	Lithuania

TEAM OF THE SEASON

- **D** Panagiotis Fyssas — CG: 15 DR: 115
- **M** Andrew Driver — CG: 16 SD: 59
- **G** Craig Gordon — CG: 34 DR: 87
- **D** Marius Zaliukas — CG: 22 DR: 113
- **M** Neil McCann — CG: 12 SD: 51
- **F** Andrius Velicka — CG: 18 SR: 236
- **D** Steven Pressley — CG: 13 DR: 97
- **M** Bruno Aguiar — CG: 20 SD: 39
- **F** Paul Hartley — CG: 18 SR: 547
- **D** Robbie Neilson — CG: 12 DR: 97
- **M** Ibrahim Tall — CG: 15 SD: 22

MONTHLY POINTS TALLY

Month	Points	%
AUGUST	7	58%
SEPTEMBER	6	67%
OCTOBER	5	42%
NOVEMBER	2	17%
DECEMBER	11	61%
JANUARY	7	58%
FEBRUARY	4	67%
MARCH	3	33%
APRIL	9	75%
MAY	4	44%

LEAGUE GOALS

	PLAYER	MINS	GOALS	S RATE
1	Velicka	1895	8	236
2	Pospisil	1232	6	205
3	Bednar	1212	4	303
4	Mikoliunas	2382	4	595
5	Mole	517	3	172
6	Driver	1535	3	511
7	Hartley	1642	3	547
8	Pinilla	201	2	100
9	Aguiar	1833	2	916
10	Zaliukas	2277	2	1138
11	Makela	133	1	133
12	Jankauskas	686	1	686
13	Ivaskevicius	773	1	773
	Other		4	
	TOTAL		**44**	

TOP POINT EARNERS

	PLAYER	GAMES	AV PTS
1	Marius Zaliukas	22	1.82
2	Julien Brellier	13	1.77
3	Andrew Driver	16	1.75
4	Steven Pressley	13	1.69
5	Bruno Aguiar	20	1.65
6	Paul Hartley	18	1.61
7	Neil McCann	12	1.58
8	Christophe Berra	33	1.55
9	Panagiotis Fyssas	15	1.53
10	Saulius Mikoliunas	23	1.52
	CLUB AVERAGE:		**1.61**

DISCIPLINARY RECORDS

	PLAYER	YELLOW	RED	AVE
1	Nerijus Barasa	4	0	168
2	K Ivaskevicius	5	0	193
3	Robbie Neilson	6	1	194
4	Julien Brellier	9	1	196
5	Laryea Kingston	2	1	283
6	Saulius Mikoliunas	8	1	305
7	Bruno Aguiar	8	1	305
8	Michel Pospisil	4	0	308
9	Christos Karipidis	4	0	325
10	Paul Hartley	4	1	328
11	Edgaras Jankauskas	2	0	343
12	Andrew Driver	9	0	390
13	Steven Pressley	3	0	390
	Other	33	3	
	TOTAL	**97**	**9**	

KEY GOALKEEPER

Craig Gordon

Goals Conceded in the League	35	Counting Games League games when player was on pitch for at least 70 minutes	34
Defensive Rating Ave number of mins between League goals conceded while on the pitch	87	Clean Sheets In League games when player was on pitch for at least 70 minutes	10

KEY PLAYERS - DEFENDERS

Panagiotis Fyssas

Goals Conceded Number of League goals conceded while the player was on the pitch	14	Clean Sheets In League games when player was on pitch for at least 70 minutes	7
Defensive Rating Ave number of mins between League goals conceded while on the pitch	115	Club Defensive Rating Average number of mins between League goals conceded by the club this season	97

	PLAYER	CON LGE	CLEAN SHEETS	DEF RATE
1	Panagiotis Fyssas	14	7	115 mins
2	Marius Zaliukas	20	9	113 mins
3	Steven Pressley	12	4	97 mins
4	Robbie Neilson	12	5	97 mins

KEY PLAYERS - MIDFIELDERS

Andrew Driver

Goals in the League	3	Contribution to Attacking Power Average number of minutes between League team goals while on pitch	80
Defensive Rating Average number of mins between League goals conceded while on the pitch	139	Scoring Difference Defensive Rating minus Contribution to Attacking Power	59

	PLAYER	LGE GOALS	DEF RATE	POWER	SCORE DIFF
1	Andrew Driver	3	139	80	59 mins
2	Neil McCann	0	120	69	51 mins
3	Bruno Aguiar	2	122	83	39 mins
4	Ibrahim Tall	1	87	65	22 mins

KEY PLAYERS - GOALSCORERS

Andrius Velicka

Goals in the League	8	Player Strike Rate Average number of minutes between League goals scored by player	236
Contribution to Attacking Power Average number of minutes between League team goals while on pitch	94	Club Strike Rate Average number of minutes between League goals scored by club	72

	PLAYER	LGE GOALS	POWER	STRIKE RATE
1	Andrius Velicka	8	94	236 mins
2	Andrew Driver	3	80	511 mins
3	Paul Hartley	3	71	547 mins
4	Saulius Mikoliunas	4	68	595 mins

Craig Gordon

SQUAD APPEARANCES

Match	1 2 3 4 5	6 7 8 9 10	11 12 13 14 15	16 17 18 19 20	21 22 23 24 25	26 27 28 29 30	31 32 33 34 35	36 37 38 39 40	41 42 43 44 45	46 47
Venue	A A H H H	A A H H H	A A A A H	A H H A A	A H A A H	H A H A A	A H H A A	H H A A H	A H A A H	H A
Competition	L C L C L	L C L L E	L W L E L	L L L L W	L L L L L	L L L L L	F L L L F	L L L L L	L L L L L	W L
Result	W D W L D	L L W L L	W W W D W	D L D L L	D L D D W	L W W D W	W L W D L	W D W L L	W W L W D	W L

Goalkeepers
Steve Banks
Craig Gordon
Defenders
Nerijus Barasa
Christophe Berra
Panagiotis Fyssas
Jose Goncalves
Tomas Kancelskis
Christos Karipidis
Robbie Neilson
Steven Pressley
Lee Wallace
Marius Zaliukas
Midfielders
Bruno Aguiar
Mirsad Beslija
Julien Brellier
Deividas Cesnauskis
Andrew Driver
Paul Hartley
Kestutis Ivaskevicius
Laryea Kingston
Neil McCann
Ibrahim Tall
Forwards
Roman Bednar
Calum Elliot
Edgaras Jankauskas
Saulius Mikoliunas
Jamie Mole
Linas Pilibaitis
Mauricio Pinilla
Michel Pospisil
Andrius Velicka

KEY: ■ On all match ◄◄ Subbed or sent off (Counting game) ►► Subbed on from bench (Counting Game) ►► Subbed on and then subbed or sent off (Counting Game) □ Not in 16
■ On bench ◄◄ Subbed or sent off (playing less than 70 minutes) ►► Subbed on (playing less than 70 minutes) ►► Subbed on and then subbed or sent off (playing less than 70 minutes)

SCOTTISH PREMIERSHIP - HEART OF MIDLOTHIAN

KILMARNOCK

Final Position: **5th**

NICKNAME: KILLIE   KEY: ☐ Won ☐ Drawn ☐ Lost   Attendance

#	Comp	Opponent		Result	Scorers	Attendance
1	spl	Celtic	A L	1-4	Naismith 87	54,620
2	spl	Hibernian	H W	2-1	Nish 48, Naismith 72	6,299
3	spl	Dundee Utd	H D	0-0		5,328
4	spl	Falkirk	A W	2-1	Wales 45, Di Giacomo 87	5,022
5	sccc2	Queen of South	A W	2-1		2,452
6	spl	Rangers	H D	2-2	Wright 63, Naismith 90 pen	13,506
7	spl	Dunfermline	A L	2-3	Invincibile 9, Wales 52	4,510
8	spl	St Mirren	A W	1-0	Broadfoot 70 og	5,277
9	sccc3	Livingston	H W	2-1	Wales 57, Wright 115	3,573
10	spl	Inverness CT	H D	1-1	Nish 7	4,809
11	spl	Motherwell	A L	0-5		4,765
12	spl	Aberdeen	H W	1-0	Wales 69	5,744
13	spl	Hearts	A W	2-0	Invincibile 28, Wales 35	16,849
14	spl	Celtic	H L	1-2	Nish 49	10,083
15	spl	Hibernian	A D	2-2	Martis 49 og, Naismith 65	13,510
16	sccqf	Motherwell	H W	3-2	Wright 6, 45, Invincibile 71	5,601
17	spl	Dundee Utd	A L	0-1		5,815
18	spl	Falkirk	H W	2-1	Hay 59, O'Donnell 70 og	5,666
19	spl	Rangers	A L	0-3		48,289
20	spl	Dunfermline	H W	5-1	Greer 7, Di Giacomo 19, 25, Nish 27, 72	4,750
21	spl	St Mirren	H D	1-1	Di Giacomo 54	5,978
22	spl	Inverness CT	A W	4-3	Naismith 29, 68 pen, Nish 35, 50	3,728
23	spl	Motherwell	H L	1-2	Naismith 38	5,576
24	spl	Aberdeen	A L	1-3	Naismith 89	11,887
25	spl	Hearts	H D	0-0		7,302
26	spl	Celtic	A L	0-2		57,236
27	scr3	G Morton	A L	1-3	Nish 47	6,649
28	spl	Hibernian	H L	0-2		4,963
29	spl	Dundee Utd	H W	1-0	Leven 61	4,732
30	spl	Falkirk	A W	2-0	Nish 22, Naismith 28	4,696
31	sfcqf	Falkirk	H W	3-0	Naismith 30, 71, 78 pen	10,722
32	spl	Rangers	H L	1-3	Naismith 73	11,894
33	spl	Dunfermline	A D	1-1	Naismith 10	4,500
34	spl	St Mirren	A W	2-0	Nish 59, 79	4,778
35	spl	Inverness CT	H W	3-2	Di Giacomo 17, 27, Naismith 40	7,630
36	scccf	Hibernian	N L	1-5	Greer 78	52,000
37	spl	Aberdeen	H L	1-2	Naismith 86 pen	7,236
38	spl	Motherwell	A W	1-0	Nish 90	3,784
39	spl	Hearts	A L	0-1		17,019
40	spl	Celtic	H L	1-2	Nish 50	13,623
41	spl	Aberdeen	A L	0-3		10,046
42	spl	Hibernian	A W	1-0	Nish 49	10,674
43	spl	Rangers	A W	1-0	Naismith 53	50,085
44	spl	Hearts	H W	1-0	Naismith 82 pen	11,030

LEAGUE APPEARANCES, BOOKINGS AND CAPS

	AGE (on 01/07/07)	IN NAMED 18	APPEARANCES	COUNTING GAMES	MINUTES ON PITCH	YELLOW CARDS	RED CARDS	CAPS THIS SEASON	NATIONAL SIDE
Goalkeepers									
Alan Combe	33	22	11	11	990	1	0	-	Scotland
Graeme Smith	24	35	27	27	2430	0	0	-	Scotland
Defenders									
Simon Ford	25	21	16	8	990	0	1	-	England
James Fowler	26	38	38	38	3420	5	0	-	Scotland
Gordon Greer	26	33	33	32	2925	6	0	-	Scotland
Jamie Hamill	20	12	4	2	181	0	0	-	Scotland
Garry Hay	29	30	29	26	2460	3	1	-	Scotland
David Lilley	29	10	7	6	551	1	0	-	Scotland
Grant Murray	31	33	30	29	2613	7	0	-	Scotland
Ryan O'Leary	19	24	7	5	535	1	0	-	Scotland
Fraser Wright	27	35	35	34	3086	9	0	-	Scotland
Midfielders									
Rhian Dodds	27	23	9	3	303	1	0	-	Canada
William Gibson	22	9	7	0	194	1	0	-	Scotland
Danny Invincibile	28	25	25	23	2051	0	0	-	Australia
Allan Johnston	33	29	28	24	2241	6	0	-	Scotland
Peter Leven	23	34	27	19	1808	3	0	-	Scotland
Gary Locke	32	13	12	3	545	3	0	-	Scotland
Stephen Murray	24	21	9	0	171	0	0	-	Scotland
Rocco Quinn	20	12	6	3	385	0	0	-	Scotland
Mohammed Sylla	30	11	11	8	860	3	0	-	Guinea
Forwards									
Andrew Barrowman	22	4	3	0	52	0	0	-	Scotland
Paul Di Giacomo	25	31	22	6	755	2	0	-	Scotland
David Fernandez	31	8	8	6	596	1	0	-	Spain
Aime Koudou	30	10	5	0	163	0	0	-	Ivory Coast
Steven Naismith	20	37	37	35	3193	3	0	-	Scotland
Colin Nish	26	33	33	17	2125	9	1	-	Scotland
Gary Wales	28	30	28	18	1929	4	1	-	Scotland

TEAM OF THE SEASON

G Graeme Smith   CG: 27   DR: 56

D Fraser Wright   CG: 34   DR: 64
D Garry Hay   CG: 26   DR: 64
D Gordon Greer   CG: 32   DR: 63
D Grant Murray   CG: 29   DR: 59

M James Fowler   CG: 38   SD: -9
M Danny Invincibile   CG: 23   SD: -18
M Peter Leven   CG: 19   SD: -30
M Mohammed Sylla   CG: 8   SD: 36

F Colin Nish   CG: 17   SR: 163
F Steven Naismith   CG: 35   SR: 212

MONTHLY POINTS TALLY

Month		Points	%
AUGUST		8	67%
SEPTEMBER		4	33%
OCTOBER		6	67%
NOVEMBER		4	33%
DECEMBER		8	44%
JANUARY		6	50%
FEBRUARY		1	17%
MARCH		6	67%
APRIL		3	25%
MAY		9	100%

LEAGUE GOALS

	PLAYER	MINS	GOALS	S RATE
1	Naismith	3193	15	212
2	Nish	2125	13	163
3	Di Giacomo	755	6	125
4	Wales	1929	4	482
5	Invincible	2051	2	1025
6	Leven	1808	1	1808
7	Hay	2460	1	2460
8	Greer	2925	1	2925
9	Wright	3086	1	3086
10	O'Leary	535	0	
11	Quinn	385	0	
12	Skora	0	0	
13	Smith	2430	0	
	Other		0	
	TOTAL		**44**	

TOP POINT EARNERS

	PLAYER	GAMES	AV PTS
1	Colin Nish	17	1.82
2	Allan Johnston	24	1.63
3	Fraser Wright	34	1.59
4	Steven Naismith	35	1.54
5	Garry Hay	26	1.46
6	James Fowler	38	1.45
7	Gordon Greer	32	1.41
8	Grant Murray	29	1.34
9	Graeme Smith	27	1.33
10	Danny Invincibile	23	1.30
	CLUB AVERAGE:		**1.45**

DISCIPLINARY RECORDS

	PLAYER	YELLOW	RED	AVE
1	Colin Nish	9	1	212
2	Gary Locke	3	0	272
3	Mohammed Sylla	3	0	286
4	Fraser Wright	9	0	385
5	Gary Wales	4	1	385
6	Grant Murray	7	0	435
7	Allan Johnston	6	0	448
8	Ryan O'Leary	1	0	535
9	David Lilley	1	0	551
10	Gordon Greer	6	0	585
11	Peter Leven	3	0	602
12	James Fowler	5	0	684
13	Paul Di Giacomo	2	0	755
	Other	8	2	
	TOTAL	**67**	**4**	

KEY GOALKEEPER

Graeme Smith

Goals Conceded in the League	43	Counting Games League games when player was on pitch for at least 70 minutes	27
Defensive Rating Ave number of mins between League goals conceded while on the pitch	56	Clean Sheets In League games when player was on pitch for at least 70 minutes	6

KEY PLAYERS - DEFENDERS

Fraser Wright

Goals Conceded Number of League goals conceded while the player was on the pitch	48	Clean Sheets In League games when player was on pitch for at least 70 minutes	11
Defensive Rating Ave number of mins between League goals conceded while on the pitch	64	Club Defensive Rating Average number of mins between League goals conceded by the club this season	63

	PLAYER	CON LGE	CLEAN SHEETS	DEF RATE
1	Fraser Wright	48	11	64 mins
2	Garry Hay	38	7	64 mins
3	Gordon Greer	46	9	63 mins
4	James Fowler	54	12	63 mins

KEY PLAYERS - MIDFIELDERS

Mohammed Sylla

Goals in the League	0	Contribution to Attacking Power Average number of minutes between League team goals while on pitch	107
Defensive Rating Average number of mins between League goals conceded while on the pitch	143	Scoring Difference Defensive Rating minus Contribution to Attacking Power	36

	PLAYER	LGE GOALS	DEF RATE	POWER	SCORE DIFF
1	Mohammed Sylla	0	143	107	36 mins
2	James Fowler	0	63	72	-9 mins
3	Danny Invincibile	2	52	70	-18 mins
4	Peter Leven	1	56	86	-30 mins

KEY PLAYERS - GOALSCORERS

Colin Nish

Goals in the League	13	Player Strike Rate Average number of minutes between League goals scored by player	163
Contribution to Attacking Power Average number of minutes between League team goals while on pitch	62	Club Strike Rate Average number of minutes between League goals scored by club	72

	PLAYER	LGE GOALS	POWER	STRIKE RATE
1	Colin Nish	13	62	163 mins
2	Steven Naismith	15	69	212 mins
3	Gary Wales	4	101	482 mins
4	Danny Invincibile	2	70	1025 mins

Steven Naismith

SQUAD APPEARANCES

Match	1 2 3 4 5	6 7 8 9 10	11 12 13 14 15	16 17 18 19 20	21 22 23 24 25	26 27 28 29 30	31 32 33 34 35	36 37 38 39 40	41 42 43 44
Venue	A H H A A	H A A H H	A H A H A	H A H A H	H A H A H	A A H H A	H H A A H	N H A A H	A A A H
Competition	L L L L W	L L L W L	L L L L L	W L L L L	L L L L L	L F L L L	F L L L L	F L L L L	L L L L
Result	L W D W W	D L W W D	L W W L D	W L W L W	D W L L D	L L L W W	W L D W W	L L W L L	L W W W

Goalkeepers
Alan Combe
Graeme Smith

Defenders
Simon Ford
James Fowler
Gordon Greer
Jamie Hamill
Garry Hay
David Lilley
Grant Murray
Ryan O'Leary
Fraser Wright

Midfielders
Rhian Dodds
William Gibson
Danny Invincibile
Allan Johnston
Peter Leven
Gary Locke
Stephen Murray
Rocco Quinn
Mohammed Sylla

Forwards
Andrew Barrowman
Paul Di Giacomo
David Fernandez
Aime Koudou
Steven Naismith
Colin Nish
Gary Wales

KEY: ■ On all match ◄◄ Subbed or sent off (Counting game) ▸▸ Subbed on from bench (Counting Game) ▸▸ Subbed on and then subbed or sent off (Counting Game) □ Not in 16
⬜ On bench ◄◄ Subbed or sent off (playing less than 70 minutes) ▸▸ Subbed on (playing less than 70 minutes) ▸▸ Subbed on and then subbed or sent off (playing less than 70 minutes)

SCOTTISH PREMIERSHIP - KILMARNOCK

HIBERNIAN

Final Position: **6th**

NICKNAME: THE HIBEES   KEY: ☐ Won ☐ Drawn ☐ Lost   Attendance

						Result	Scorers	Attendance
1	spl	Aberdeen	H	D	1-1		D.Shiels 31	15,046
2	spl	Kilmarnock	A	L	1-2		D.Shiels 31	6,299
3	spl	Inverness CT	A	D	0-0			4,623
4	spl	Motherwell	H	W	3-1		Benjelloun 30, Scott.Brown 65, R.Jones 82	13,274
5	sccc2	Peterhead	H	W	4-0		Good 7 og, Benjelloun 32, Brown 52, McCluskey 66 pen	7,834
6	spl	Celtic	A	L	1-2		Scott.Brown 8	58,078
7	spl	Dundee Utd	A	W	3-0		Killen 52, D.Shiels 81, Sproule 89	6,387
8	spl	Rangers	H	W	2-1		Killen 8, 82	16,450
9	sccc3	Gretna	H	W	6-0		Fletcher 11, Scott.Brown 18, R.Jones 20, D.Shiels 24, 63, Benjelloun 72	10,700
10	spl	Falkirk	H	L	0-1			14,828
11	spl	St Mirren	A	L	0-1			6,008
12	spl	Hearts	H	D	2-2		Zemmama 5, Killen 16	16,623
13	spl	Dunfermline	A	W	4-0		Sproule 44, Killen 62, 90, Benjelloun 89	6,057
14	spl	Aberdeen	A	L	1-2		Killen 47	11,179
15	spl	Kilmarnock	H	D	2-2		Stewart 53, Fletcher 57	13,510
16	scccqf	Hearts	H	W	1-0		R.Jones 32	15,825
17	spl	Inverness CT	H	W	2-0		Fletcher 65, Killen 83 pen	12,868
18	spl	Motherwell	A	W	6-1		Scott.Brown 10, Killen 25, Sproule 29, 40, R.Jones 73, D.Shiels 90	6,190
19	spl	Celtic	H	D	2-2		Sproule 12, Thomson 63	16,747
20	spl	Dundee Utd	H	W	2-1		R.Jones 45, Fletcher 73	14,032
21	spl	Rangers	A	L	0-3			49,702
22	spl	Falkirk	A	L	1-2		Fletcher 56	6,142
23	spl	St Mirren	H	W	5-1		Beuzelin 21, Killen 32, D.Shiels 58, Zemmama 65, Benjelloun 74	13,053
24	spl	Hearts	A	L	2-3		Killen 55, D.Shiels 61 pen	17,369
25	spl	Dunfermline	H	W	2-0		Killen 63, 72 pen	14,061
26	spl	Aberdeen	H	D	0-0			16,278
27	scr3	Aberdeen	A	D	2-2		Sproule 43, Killen 73	7,905
28	spl	Kilmarnock	A	W	2-0		Sproule 51, Fletcher 87	4,963
29	scr3r	Aberdeen	H	W	4-1		Fletcher 13, Stewart 45, Benjelloun 47, 56	11,375
30	spl	Inverness CT	A	L	0-3			4,577
31	spl	Motherwell	H	W	2-0		Scott.Brown 66, Benjelloun 90	14,280
32	slc5	St Johnstone	A	W	3-1		Fletcher 3, Murphy 92, Benjelloun 120	16,112
33	scr4	Gretna	H	W	3-1		R.Jones 28, Sleming 54 og, Benjelloun 59	14,075
34	spl	Celtic	A	L	0-1			59,659
35	spl	Dundee Utd	A	D	0-0			6,453
36	scpqf	Queen of South	A	W	2-1		Murphy 45, Sowunmi 51	6,400
37	spl	Rangers	H	L	0-2			16,265
38	spl	Falkirk	H	W	2-0		Benjelloun 52, 74	12,572
39	scccf	Kilmarnock	A	W	5-1		R.Jones 27, Benjelloun 59, 85, Fletcher 66, 87	52,000
40	spl	Hearts	H	L	0-1			15,953
41	spl	St Mirren	A	D	1-1		R.Jones 20	4,031
42	spl	Dunfermline	A	L	0-1			6,001
43	scsf	Dunfermline	H	D	0-0			25,336
44	spl	Aberdeen	A	D	2-2		Gray 19, D.Shiels 44	9,753
45	scsfr	Dunfermline	A	L	0-1			8,536
46	spl	Rangers	H	D	3-3		Fletcher 20, McCann 45, Whittaker 62	16,747
47	spl	Kilmarnock	H	L	0-1			10,674
48	spl	Hearts	A	L	0-2			17,349
49	spl	Celtic	H	W	2-1		Scott.Brown 60, Sproule 90	13,885

LEAGUE APPEARANCES, BOOKINGS AND CAPS

	AGE (on 01/07/07)	IN NAMED 18	APPEARANCES	COUNTING GAMES	MINUTES ON PITCH	YELLOW CARDS	RED CARDS	CAPS THIS SEASON	NATIONAL SIDE
Goalkeepers									
Simon Brown	30	19	4	4	360	0	0	-	England
Zibigniew Malkowski	29	20	19	19	1710	0	0	-	Poland
Andrew McNeil	20	33	15	15	1350	1	0	-	Scotland
Defenders									
Chris Hogg	22	30	15	15	1350	2	0	-	England
Robert Jones	27	34	34	33	2981	8	0	-	England
Oumar Konde	27	9	2	2	169	1	0	-	Switzerland
Shelton Martis	24	35	27	26	2384	4	0	-	Holland
Dermot McCaffrey	-	2	1	1	88	1	1	-	N Ireland
Kevin McCann	19	18	8	6	624	3	0	-	Scotland
David Murphy	23	33	33	31	2881	4	0	-	England
Lewis Stevenson	19	22	16	11	1147	4	0	-	Scotland
Midfielders									
Guillaume Beuzelin	28	26	25	13	1684	4	0	-	France
Ross Chisholm	-	10	6	4	406	2	0	-	Scotland
Steven Fletcher	20	34	31	22	2166	5	0	-	Scotland
Stephen Glass	31	22	10	2	379	0	0	-	Scotland
Jamie McCluskey	19	13	5	0	106	0	0	-	Scotland
Jay Shields	22	16	4	2	189	0	0	-	Scotland
Ivan Sproule	26	32	32	13	1807	7	0	3	N Ireland
Michael Stewart	26	30	29	18	1996	9	0	-	Scotland
Kevin Thomson	22	23	23	16	1753	6	1	-	Scotland
Steven Whittaker	23	37	35	34	3085	7	0	-	Scotland
Merouane Zemmama	23	24	23	11	1441	2	0	-	Morocco
Forwards									
A Benjelloun	22	36	33	13	1850	7	0	-	Morocco
Scott Brown	22	30	30	30	2660	13	1	2	Scotland
Ross Campbell	19	12	3	0	99	0	0	-	Scotland
Paul Dalglish	30	2	2	0	82	0	0	-	Scotland
Damon Gray	-	5	3	0	106	0	0	-	England
Christopher Killen	25	19	18	9	1244	6	2	-	New Zealand
Amadou Konte	26	4	2	1	109	0	0	-	Mali
Sean Lynch	20	7	3	0	124	1	1	-	Scotland
Dean Shiels	22	30	23	3	986	2	1	1	N Ireland
Thomas Sowunmi	28	6	5	0	121	0	0	-	Hungary

TEAM OF THE SEASON

G Andrew McNeil CG: 15 DR: 84

D David Murphy CG: 30 DR: 80
D Robert Jones CG: 33 DR: 76
D Shelton Martis CG: 26 DR: 70
D Chris Hogg CG: 15 DR: 67

M Michael Stewart CG: 17 SD: 33
M Kevin Thomson CG: 16 SD: 14
M Steven Whittaker CG: 34 SD: 14
M Ivan Sproule CG: 12 SD: 9

F A Benjelloun CG: 13 SR: 308
F Scott Brown CG: 30 SR: 532

MONTHLY POINTS TALLY

Month	Pts	%
AUGUST	4	33%
SEPTEMBER	6	50%
OCTOBER	4	44%
NOVEMBER	8	67%
DECEMBER	9	50%
JANUARY	7	58%
FEBRUARY	1	17%
MARCH	3	50%
APRIL	3	20%
MAY	3	33%

LEAGUE GOALS

	PLAYER	MINS	GOALS	S RATE
1	Killen	1244	13	95
2	Shiels, D	986	7	140
3	Sproule	1807	7	258
4	Benjelloun	1850	6	308
5	Fletcher	2166	6	361
6	Brown, Scott	2660	5	532
7	Jones, R	2981	4	745
8	Zemmama	1441	2	720
9	Gray	106	1	106
10	McCann	624	1	624
11	Beuzelin	1684	1	1684
12	Thomson	1753	1	1753
13	Stewart	1996	1	1996
	Other		1	
	TOTAL		**56**	

TOP POINT EARNERS

	PLAYER	GAMES	AV PTS
1	Ivan Sproule	13	1.54
2	Zibigniew Malkowski	19	1.47
3	Shelton Martis	26	1.46
4	Scott Brown	30	1.43
5	Robert Jones	33	1.42
6	Kevin Thomson	17	1.41
7	David Murphy	30	1.40
8	Steven Whittaker	34	1.29
9	Michael Stewart	17	1.29
10	Andrew McNeil	15	1.27
	CLUB AVERAGE:		**1.29**

DISCIPLINARY RECORDS

	PLAYER	YELLOW	RED	AVE
1	Ivan Sproule	7	2	200
2	Christopher Killen	6	2	207
3	Kevin McCann	3	0	208
4	Scott Brown	13	1	221
5	Michael Stewart	9	0	249
6	Kevin Thomson	6	1	292
7	A Benjelloun	7	0	370
8	Robert Jones	8	0	372
9	Lewis Stevenson	4	0	382
10	Guillaume Beuzelin	4	1	421
11	Dean Shiels	2	1	493
12	Steven Whittaker	7	0	514
13	Chris Hogg	2	0	675
	Other	16	0	
	TOTAL	**94**	**8**	

KEY GOALKEEPER

Andrew McNeil

Goals Conceded in the League	16	Counting Games League games when player was on pitch for at least 70 minutes	15
Defensive Rating Ave number of mins between League goals conceded while on the pitch	84	Clean Sheets In League games when player was on pitch for at least 70 minutes	5

KEY PLAYERS - DEFENDERS

David Murphy

Goals Conceded Number of League goals conceded while the player was on the pitch	36	Clean Sheets In League games when player was on pitch for at least 70 minutes	8
Defensive Rating Ave number of mins between League goals conceded while on the pitch	80	Club Defensive Rating Average number of mins between League goals conceded by the club this season	74

	PLAYER	CON LGE	CLEAN SHEETS	DEF RATE
1	David Murphy	36	8	80 mins
2	Robert Jones	39	10	76 mins
3	Shelton Martis	34	7	70 mins
4	Chris Hogg	20	3	67 mins

KEY PLAYERS - MIDFIELDERS

Michael Stewart

Goals in the League	1	Contribution to Attacking Power Average number of minutes between League team goals while on pitch	62
Defensive Rating Average number of mins between League goals conceded while on the pitch	95	Scoring Difference Defensive Rating minus Contribution to Attacking Power	33

	PLAYER	LGE GOALS	DEF RATE	POWER	SCORE DIFF
1	Michael Stewart	1	95	62	33 mins
2	Kevin Thomson	1	67	53	14 mins
3	Steven Whittaker	1	73	59	14 mins
4	Ivan Sproule	7	69	60	9 mins

KEY PLAYERS - GOALSCORERS

Ivan Sproule

Goals in the League	7	Player Strike Rate Average number of minutes between League goals scored by player	258
Contribution to Attacking Power Average number of minutes between League team goals while on pitch	60	Club Strike Rate Average number of minutes between League goals scored by club	61

	PLAYER	LGE GOALS	POWER	STRIKE RATE
1	Ivan Sproule	7	60	258 mins
2	Abdessalam Benjelloun	6	63	308 mins
3	Steven Fletcher	6	74	361 mins
4	Scott Brown	5	64	532 mins

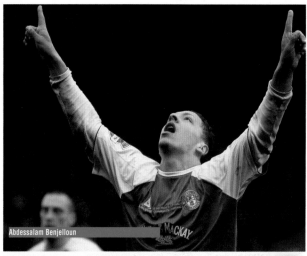

Abdessalam Benjelloun

SQUAD APPEARANCES

Match	1 2 3 4 5	6 7 8 9 10	11 12 13 14 15	16 17 18 19 20	21 22 23 24 25	26 27 28 29 30	31 32 33 34 35	36 37 38 39 40	41 42 43 44 45	46 47 48 49
Venue	H A A H H	A A H H H	A H A A H	H H A H H	A A H A H	H A A H A	H A H A A	A H H N H	A A H A A	H H A H
Competition	L L L L W	L W W W L	L L L L L	W L L L L	L L L L L	L F L F L	L W F L L	F L L W L	L L F L F	L L L W
Result	D L D W W	L W W W L	L D W L D	W W W D W	L L W L W	D D W L W	W W W L D	W L W W L	D L D D L	D L L W

Goalkeepers
Simon Brown
Zbigniew Malkowski
Andrew McNeil

Defenders
Chris Hogg
Robert Jones
Oumar Konde
Shelton Martis
Dermot McCaffrey
Kevin McCann
David Murphy
Lewis Stevenson

Midfielders
Guillaume Beuzelin
Ross Chisholm
Steven Fletcher
Stephen Glass
Jamie McCluskey
Jay Shields
Ian Sproule
Michael Stewart
Kevin Thomson
Steven Whittaker
Merouane Zemmama

Forwards
Benjelloun
Scott Brown
Ross Campbell
Paul Dalglish
Eamon Gray
Christopher Killen
Amadou Konte
Sean Lynch
Dean Shiels
Thomas Sowunmi

KEY: ■ On all match | ◄◄ Subbed or sent off (Counting game) | ►► Subbed on from bench (Counting Game) | ►► Subbed on and then subbed or sent off (Counting Game) | ☐ Not in 16
■ On bench | ◄◄ Subbed or sent off (playing less than 70 minutes) | ►► Subbed on (playing less than 70 minutes) | ►► Subbed on and then subbed or sent off (playing less than 70 minutes)

FALKIRK

Final Position: **7th**

NICKNAME: THE BAIRNS | KEY: ☐ Won ☐ Drawn ☐ Lost | Attendance

#					Result	Scorers	Attendance
1	spl	Dundee Utd	A	W	2-1	Latapy 23, Craig 59	6,616
2	spl	Dunfermline	H	W	1-0	Barr 11	5,542
3	spl	Hearts	A	D	0-0		16,127
4	spl	Kilmarnock	H	L	1-2	Latapy 44	5,022
5	sccc2	Cowdenbeath	A	W	5-0	Craig 35, Moutinho 50, 81, Twaddle 74, Stewart 84	1,530
6	spl	Motherwell	H	L	0-1		4,594
7	spl	Rangers	A	L	0-4		50,196
8	spl	Aberdeen	H	L	0-2		5,812
9	sccc3	Inverness CT	A	W	1-0	Stokes 60	1,198
10	spl	Hibernian	A	W	1-0	Milne 9	14,828
11	spl	Celtic	H	L	0-1		7,139
12	spl	St Mirren	H	D	1-1	Stokes 81	4,961
13	spl	Inverness CT	A	L	2-3	Stokes 41, 51	3,749
14	spl	Dundee Utd	H	W	5-1	Latapy 2, Stokes 39, 48, 89 pen, Twaddle 75	5,386
15	spl	Dunfermline	A	W	3-0	Stokes 1, 59, 80	6,504
16	sccqf	Celtic	A	W	5-4*	Stokes 100 (*on penalties)	18,684
17	spl	Hearts	H	D	1-1	Latapy 84	6,289
18	spl	Kilmarnock	A	L	1-2	Stokes 42	5,666
19	spl	Motherwell	A	L	2-4	Stokes 36, Latapy 71	4,970
20	spl	Rangers	H	W	1-0	Twaddle 26	7,245
21	spl	Aberdeen	A	L	1-2	Gow 69	10,594
22	spl	Hibernian	H	W	2-1	Martis 14 og, Craig 21	6,142
23	spl	Celtic	A	L	0-1		55,000
24	spl	St Mirren	A	L	0-1		5,212
25	spl	Inverness CT	H	W	3-1	Stokes 33, 37, 45	4,516
26	spl	Dundee Utd	A	W	5-1	Cregg 17 pen, O'Donnell 45, Gow 63, 76, 89	6,261
27	scr3	Berwick	A	W	2-0	Gow 9, Craig 51	1,910
28	spl	Dunfermline	H	W	1-0	Gow 90	6,051
29	spl	Hearts	A	L	0-1		17,247
30	spl	Kilmarnock	H	L	0-2		4,696
31	slc5	Kilmarnock	A	L	0-3		10,722
32	scr4	St Johnstone	H	L	0-3		3,908
33	spl	Motherwell	H	L	1-2	Cregg 47	4,478
34	spl	Rangers	A	L	1-2	Finnigan 64	49,850
35	spl	Aberdeen	H	L	1-2	Holden 66	5,825
36	spl	Hibernian	A	L	0-2		12,572
37	spl	Celtic	H	W	1-0	S.Thomson 16	6,438
38	spl	St Mirren	H	W	2-0	Moutinho 20, O'Donnell 40	5,863
39	spl	Inverness CT	A	D	1-1	Finnigan 80	4,435
40	spl	St Mirren	H	L	0-2		4,441
41	spl	Motherwell	A	D	3-3	Scobbie 48, Craigan 49 og, Cregg 55	3,640
42	spl	Inverness CT	H	W	1-0	Finnigan 78	3,129
43	spl	Dundee Utd	H	W	2-0	Latapy 5, Gow 51	4,161
44	spl	Dunfermline	A	W	3-0	S.Thomson 49, Gow 57, Moutinho 90	5,087

LEAGUE APPEARANCES, BOOKINGS AND CAPS

	AGE (on 01/07/07)	IN NAMED 18	APPEARANCES	COUNTING GAMES	MINUTES ON PITCH	YELLOW CARDS	RED CARDS	CAPS THIS SEASON	NATIONAL SIDE
Goalkeepers									
Scott Higgins	31	23	15	14	1325	1	0	-	Australia
Jeroen Lambers	26	37	9	8	745	0	0	-	Holland
Kasper Schmeichel	20	15	15	15	1350	1	0	-	Denmark
Defenders									
Brian Allison	19	7	3	1	105	0	0	-	Scotland
Darren Barr	22	36	36	36	3240	8	0	-	Scotland
Karl Dodd	26	26	17	12	1227	3	1	-	Australia
Dean Holden	27	11	9	5	653	3	1	-	England
Kenny Milne	27	34	34	31	2909	11	0	-	Scotland
Thomas Scobbie	19	35	21	13	1466	3	1	-	Scotland
Mark Twaddle	20	25	16	10	1072	3	0	-	Scotland
Cedric Uras	29	22	9	8	712	2	0	-	France
Midfielders									
Liam Craig	20	37	28	16	1708	3	1	-	Scotland
Patrick Cregg	21	32	32	32	2858	10	0	-	Rep of Ireland
Russell Latapy	38	38	37	33	3037	0	0	-	Trinidad & Tobago
Vitor Santos Lima	27	38	22	16	1535	4	0	-	Portugal
Stephen O'Donnell	21	29	25	16	1678	13	1	-	Rep of Ireland
Dayne Robertson	19	6	2	0	7	0	0	-	Scotland
Jack Ross	31	38	36	35	3121	5	0	-	Scotland
Steven Thomson	29	28	22	16	1549	3	1	-	Scotland
Forwards									
Carl Finnigan	20	12	12	8	857	2	1	-	England
Alan Gow	24	36	36	34	3038	2	0	-	Scotland
Tom McManus	26	16	5	0	72	0	0	-	Scotland
Ryan McStay	21	23	5	0	70	1	0	-	Scotland
Pedro Moutinho	27	24	21	11	1259	1	0	-	Portugal
John Stewart	21	14	10	3	307	0	0	-	Scotland
Mark Stewart	19	11	8	1	166	2	0	-	England
Anthony Stokes	18	16	16	16	1389	2	1	2	Rep of Ireland

TEAM OF THE SEASON

G Kasper Schmeichel — CG: 15 DR: 79

D Karl Dodd — CG: 12 DR: 81
D Kenny Milne — CG: 31 DR: 80
D Darren Barr — CG: 36 DR: 75
D Thomas Scobbie — CG: 13 DR: 69

M Vitor Santos Lima — CG: 16 SD: 19
M Liam Craig — CG: 16 SD: 14
M Jack Ross — CG: 35 SD: 9
M Russell Latapy — CG: 33 SD: 8

F Anthony Stokes — CG: 16 SR: 99
F Alan Gow — CG: 33 SR: 434

MONTHLY POINTS TALLY

AUGUST	4	33%
SEPTEMBER	3	33%
OCTOBER	4	33%
NOVEMBER	4	33%
DECEMBER	9	50%
JANUARY	6	50%
FEBRUARY	0	0%
MARCH	6	50%
APRIL	2	22%
MAY	9	100%

LEAGUE GOALS

	PLAYER	MINS	GOALS	S RATE
1	Stokes	1389	14	99
2	Gow	3038	7	434
3	Latapy	3037	6	506
4	Finnigan	857	3	285
5	Cregg	2858	3	952
6	Twaddle	1072	2	536
7	Moutinho	1259	2	629
8	Thomson, S	1549	2	774
9	O'Donnell	1678	2	839
10	Craig	1687	2	843
11	Holden	653	1	653
12	Scobbie	1466	1	1466
13	Milne	2909	1	2909
	Other		1	
	TOTAL		**47**	

TOP POINT EARNERS

	PLAYER	GAMES	AV PTS
1	Vitor Santos Lima	16	1.88
2	Liam Craig	16	1.63
3	Kenny Milne	31	1.52
4	Russell Latapy	33	1.52
5	Alan Gow	33	1.42
6	Jack Ross	35	1.40
7	Darren Barr	36	1.39
8	Kasper Schmeichel	15	1.33
9	Steven Thomson	16	1.31
10	Karl Dodd	13	1.31
	CLUB AVERAGE:		**1.32**

DISCIPLINARY RECORDS

	PLAYER	YELLOW	RED	AVE
1	Stephen O'Donnell	13	1	139
2	Dean Holden	3	1	163
3	Kenny Milne	11	0	290
4	Karl Dodd	3	1	306
5	Cedric Uras	2	0	356
6	Mark Twaddle	3	0	357
7	Thomas Scobbie	3	1	366
8	Vitor Santos Lima	4	0	383
9	Steven Thomson	3	1	387
10	Darren Barr	8	0	405
11	Carl Finnigan	2	1	428
12	Anthony Stokes	2	1	463
13	Patrick Cregg	10	0	476
	Other	12	0	
	TOTAL	**79**	**7**	

KEY GOALKEEPER

Kasper Schmeichel

Goals Conceded in the League	17	Counting Games League games when player was on pitch for at least 70 minutes	15
Defensive Rating Ave number of mins between League goals conceded while on the pitch	79	Clean Sheets In League games when player was on pitch for at least 70 minutes	6

KEY PLAYERS - DEFENDERS

Karl Dodd

Goals Conceded Number of League goals conceded while the player was on the pitch	15	Clean Sheets In League games when player was on pitch for at least 70 minutes	3
Defensive Rating Ave number of mins between League goals conceded while on the pitch	81	Club Defensive Rating Average number of mins between League goals conceded by the club this season	72

	PLAYER	CON LGE	CLEAN SHEETS	DEF RATE
1	Karl Dodd	15	3	81 mins
2	Kenny Milne	36	11	80 mins
3	Darren Barr	43	11	75 mins
4	Thomas Scobbie	21	4	69 mins

KEY PLAYERS - MIDFIELDERS

Vitor Santos Lima

Goals in the League	0	Contribution to Attacking Power Average number of minutes between League team goals while on pitch	61
Defensive Rating Average number of mins between League goals conceded while on the pitch	80	Scoring Difference Defensive Rating minus Contribution to Attacking Power	19

	PLAYER	LGE GOALS	DEF RATE	POWER	SCORE DIFF
1	Vitor Santos Lima	0	80	61	19 mins
2	Liam Craig	2	84	70	14 mins
3	Jack Ross	0	76	67	9 mins
4	Russell Latapy	6	77	69	8 mins

KEY PLAYERS - GOALSCORERS

Anthony Stokes

Goals in the League	14	Player Strike Rate Average number of minutes between League goals scored by player	99
Contribution to Attacking Power Average number of minutes between League team goals while on pitch	63	Club Strike Rate Average number of minutes between League goals scored by club	69

	PLAYER	LGE GOALS	POWER	STRIKE RATE
1	Anthony Stokes	14	63	99 mins
2	Alan Gow	7	72	434 mins
3	Russell Latapy	6	69	506 mins
4	Steven Thomson	2	64	774 mins

Jack Ross

SQUAD APPEARANCES

Match	1	2	3	4	5	6	7	8	9	10	11	12	13	14	15	16	17	18	19	20	21	22	23	24	25	26	27	28	29	30	31	32	33	34	35	36	37	38	39	40	41	42	43	44
Venue	A	H	A	H	A	H	A	H	A	A	H	H	A	H	A	A	H	A	A	H	A	H	A	A	H	A	A	H	A	H	A	H	H	A	H	A	H	H	A	H	A	H	H	A
Competition	L	L	L	L	W	L	L	L	W	L	L	L	L	L	L	W	L	L	L	W	L	L	L	L	L	L	F	L	L	L	W	F	L	L	L	L	L	L	L	L	L	L	L	L
Result	W	W	D	L	W	L	L	L	W	W	L	D	L	W	W	W	D	L	L	W	L	W	L	L	W	W	W	W	L	L	L	L	L	L	L	L	W	W	D	L	D	W	W	W

Goalkeepers
Scott Higgins
Jeroen Lambers
Kasper Schmeichel

Defenders
Brian Allison
Darren Barr
Karl Dodd
Sean Holden
Kenny Milne
Thomas Scobbie
Mark Twaddle
Cedric Uras

Midfielders
Liam Craig
Patrick Cregg
Russell Latapy
Vitor Santos Lima
Stephen O'Donnell
Wayne Robertson
Jack Ross
Steven Thomson

Forwards
Carl Finnigan
Alan Gow
Tom McManus
Ryan McStay
Pedro Moutinho
John Stewart
Mark Stewart
Anthony Stokes

KEY: ■ On all match ◄◄ Subbed or sent off (Counting game) ►► Subbed on from bench (Counting Game) ►► Subbed on and then subbed or sent off (Counting Game) ☐ Not in 16
☐ On bench ◄◄ Subbed or sent off (playing less than 70 minutes) ►► Subbed on (playing less than 70 minutes) ►► Subbed on and then subbed or sent off (playing less than 70 minutes)

INVERNESS CALEDONIAN THISTLE

Final Position: 8th

NICKNAME: CALEY THISTLE   KEY: ☐ Won ☐ Drawn ☐ Lost   Attendance

1	spl	St Mirren	H L	1-2	Dargo 48	4,267
2	spl	Aberdeen	A D	1-1	Wilson 89	11,955
3	spl	Hibernian	H D	0-0		4,623
4	spl	Celtic	H D	1-1	Munro 79	7,332
5	sccc2	Dumbarton	H W	3-1		1,085
6	spl	Hearts	A L	1-4	Bayne 31	15,912
7	spl	Motherwell	A W	4-1	Tokely 25, Dargo 48, Munro 79, McAllister 87	4,091
8	spl	Dundee Utd	H D	0-0		3,586
9	sccc3	Falkirk	H L	0-1		1,198
10	spl	Kilmarnock	A D	1-1	Dargo 19	4,809
11	spl	Dunfermline	H W	1-0	Tokely 90	3,517
12	spl	Rangers	A W	1-0	Bayne 74	49,494
13	spl	Falkirk	H W	3-2	Dargo 70, Rankin 82, 86	3,749
14	spl	St Mirren	A D	1-1	Dargo 34	4,432
15	spl	Aberdeen	H D	1-1	Bayne 78	5,744
16	spl	Hibernian	A L	0-2		12,868
17	spl	Celtic	A L	0-3		56,637
18	spl	Hearts	H D	0-0		5,603
19	spl	Motherwell	H L	0-1		3,668
20	spl	Dundee Utd	A L	1-3	Wilson 15	5,294
21	spl	Kilmarnock	H L	3-4	Dods 6, 39, Dargo 45 pen	3,728
22	spl	Dunfermline	A D	0-0		4,216
23	spl	Rangers	H W	2-1	Dods 40, Rankin 90	7,522
24	spl	Falkirk	A L	1-3	Rankin 90	4,516
25	spl	St Mirren	H W	2-1	Bayne 5, Wyness 22	4,246
26	scr3	Stirling	A W	6-1	Dargo 8, 41, Wyness 13, McBain 22, Wilson 47, Morgan 69	1,521
27	spl	Aberdeen	A D	1-1	Rankin 86	10,300
28	spl	Hibernian	H W	3-0	Dargo 20, McBain 30, Wilson 42	4,577
29	spl	Celtic	H L	1-2	Bayne 57	7,484
30	scr4	Dundee Utd	H W	1-0	Duncan 16	3,402
31	spl	Hearts	A L	0-1		16,631
32	spl	Motherwell	A L	0-1		4,258
33	scpqf	Celtic	H L	1-2	Bayne 19	7,119
34	spl	Dundee Utd	H W	1-0	Wilson 90	3,901
35	spl	Kilmarnock	A L	2-3	Ma.Paatelainen 10, Dods 48	7,630
36	spl	Dunfermline	H L	1-3	Ma.Paatelainen 23	4,447
37	spl	Rangers	A D	1-1	Dargo 82	50,278
38	spl	Falkirk	H D	1-1	Rankin 86	4,435
39	spl	Motherwell	H W	2-0	Dargo 14, 45	3,804
40	spl	Dundee Utd	A D	1-1	Bayne 58	5,273
41	spl	Falkirk	A L	0-1		3,129
42	spl	Dunfermline	H W	2-1	Hastings 77, McAllister 89	6,464
43	spl	St Mirren	A W	1-0	McCaffrey 74	4,834

LEAGUE APPEARANCES, BOOKINGS AND CAPS

	AGE (on 01/07/07)	IN NAMED 18	APPEARANCES	COUNTING GAMES	MINUTES ON PITCH	YELLOW CARDS	RED CARDS	CAPS THIS SEASON	NATIONAL SIDE
Goalkeepers									
Mark Brown	26	23	23	23	2060	0	1	-	Scotland
Mike Fraser	23	38	16	15	1359	0	0	-	Scotland
Defenders									
Darren Dods	42	36	35	34	3069	3	2	-	Scotland
Stuart Golabek	32	1	1	1	77	0	0	-	Scotland
Richard Hastings	30	37	37	35	3251	4	0	-	Canada
Stuart McCaffrey	28	38	13	10	921	2	0	-	Scotland
Alan Morgan	23	17	6	1	138	0	0	-	Scotland
Grant Munro	26	36	36	36	3223	6	1	-	Scotland
Ross Tokely	28	35	34	34	3034	9	0	-	Scotland
Midfielders									
Ian Black	22	32	26	20	1858	13	1	-	Scotland
Russell Duncan	26	37	28	19	1893	3	0	-	Scotland
Richard Hart	29	19	16	8	846	2	0	-	Scotland
Roy McBain	32	32	32	29	2654	6	0	-	Scotland
Markus Paatelainen	24	14	11	4	502	0	0	-	Finland
John Rankin	24	38	34	30	2802	5	0	-	Scotland
Alexander Sutherland	19	33	5	1	168	1	0	-	Scotland
Barry Wilson	35	35	34	28	2584	7	0	-	Scotland
Forwards									
Graham Bayne	27	38	38	29	2763	4	0	-	Scotland
Craig Dargo	29	28	27	24	2122	7	0	-	Scotland
Liam Keogh	25	9	8	1	185	0	0	-	Scotland
Rory McAllister	20	35	19	5	636	2	0	-	Scotland
Gary McSwegan	36	14	9	1	225	0	0	-	Scotland
Dennis Wyness	30	23	20	10	1113	1	0	-	Scotland

TEAM OF THE SEASON

G Mike Fraser — CG: 15 DR: 71

D Grant Munro — CG: 36 DR: 76
D Richard Hastings — CG: 35 DR: 73
D Darren Dods — CG: 34 DR: 73
D Ross Tokely — CG: 34 DR: 70

M Barry Wilson — CG: 26 SD: 2
M John Rankin — CG: 30 SD: -11
M Russell Duncan — CG: 18 SD: -12
M Ian Black — CG: 20 SD: -16

F Craig Dargo — CG: 21 SR: 212
F Graham Bayne — CG: 29 SR: 460

MONTHLY POINTS TALLY

AUGUST	3	25%
SEPTEMBER	8	67%
OCTOBER	7	78%
NOVEMBER	2	17%
DECEMBER	4	22%
JANUARY	7	58%
FEBRUARY	0	0%
MARCH	4	33%
APRIL	5	56%
MAY	6	67%

LEAGUE GOALS

	PLAYER	MINS	GOALS	S RATE
1	Dargo	2122	10	212
2	Bayne	2763	6	460
3	Rankin	2802	6	467
4	Wilson	2584	4	646
5	Dods	3069	4	767
6	Paatelainen	502	2	251
7	McAllister	636	2	318
8	Tokely	3034	2	1517
9	Munro	3223	2	1611
10	McCaffrey	921	1	921
11	Wyness	1113	1	1113
12	McBain	2654	1	2654
13	Hastings	3251	1	3251
	Other		0	
	TOTAL		**42**	

TOP POINT EARNERS

	PLAYER	GAMES	AV PTS
1	John Rankin	30	1.30
2	Ian Black	21	1.29
3	Grant Munro	36	1.28
4	Ross Tokely	34	1.24
5	Barry Wilson	26	1.23
6	Richard Hastings	35	1.23
7	Russell Duncan	18	1.22
8	Mark Brown	23	1.22
9	Graham Bayne	29	1.21
10	Darren Dods	35	1.20
	CLUB AVERAGE:		**1.21**

DISCIPLINARY RECORDS

	PLAYER	YELLOW	RED	AVE
1	Ian Black	13	1	142
2	Craig Dargo	7	0	303
3	Rory McAllister	2	0	318
4	Ross Tokely	9	0	379
5	Barry Wilson	7	0	430
6	Roy McBain	6	0	442
7	Stuart McCaffrey	2	0	460
8	Grant Munro	6	1	537
9	John Rankin	5	0	560
10	Russell Duncan	3	0	631
11	Darren Dods	3	2	767
12	Richard Hart	1	0	846
13	Graham Bayne	4	0	921
	Other	5	1	
	TOTAL	**73**	**5**	

KEY GOALKEEPER

Mike Fraser

Goals Conceded in the League	19	Counting Games League games when player was on pitch for at least 70 minutes	15
Defensive Rating Ave number of mins between League goals conceded while on the pitch	71	Clean Sheets In League games when player was on pitch for at least 70 minutes	4

KEY PLAYERS - DEFENDERS

Grant Munro

Goals Conceded Number of League goals conceded while the player was on the pitch	42	Clean Sheets In League games when player was on pitch for at least 70 minutes	10
Defensive Rating Ave number of mins between League goals conceded while on the pitch	76	Club Defensive Rating Average number of mins between League goals conceded by the club this season	71

	PLAYER	CON LGE	CLEAN SHEETS	DEF RATE
1	Grant Munro	42	10	76 mins
2	Richard Hastings	44	10	73 mins
3	Darren Dods	42	10	73 mins
4	Ross Tokely	43	9	70 mins

KEY PLAYERS - MIDFIELDERS

Barry Wilson

Goals in the League	4	Contribution to Attacking Power Average number of minutes between League team goals while on pitch	76
Defensive Rating Average number of mins between League goals conceded while on the pitch	78	Scoring Difference Defensive Rating minus Contribution to Attacking Power	2

	PLAYER	LGE GOALS	DEF RATE	POWER	SCORE DIFF
1	Barry Wilson	4	78	76	2 mins
2	John Rankin	6	71	82	-11 mins
3	Russell Duncan	0	82	94	-12 mins
4	Ian Black	0	58	74	-16 mins

KEY PLAYERS - GOALSCORERS

Craig Dargo

Goals in the League	10	Player Strike Rate Average number of minutes between League goals scored by player	212
Contribution to Attacking Power Average number of minutes between League team goals while on pitch	78	Club Strike Rate Average number of minutes between League goals scored by club	81

	PLAYER	LGE GOALS	POWER	STRIKE RATE
1	Craig Dargo	10	78	212 mins
2	Graham Bayne	6	81	460 mins
3	John Rankin	6	82	467 mins
4	Barry Wilson	4	76	646 mins

Craig Dargo

SQUAD APPEARANCES

Match	1 2 3 4 5	6 7 8 9 10	11 12 13 14 15	16 17 18 19 20	21 22 23 24 25	26 27 28 29 30	31 32 33 34 35	36 37 38 39 40	41 42 43
Venue	H A H H H	A A H H A	H A H A H	A A H H A	H A H A H	A A H H H	A A H H A	H A H H A	A H A
Competition	L L L L W	L L L W L	L L L L L	L L L L L	L L L L L	F L L L F	L L F L L	L L L L L	L L L
Result	L D D D W	L W D L D	W W W D D	L L D L L	L D W L W	W D W L W	L L L W L	L D D W D	L W W

Goalkeepers: Mark Brown, Mike Fraser

Defenders: Darren Dods, Stuart Golabek, Richard Hastings, Stuart McCaffrey, Ian Morgan, Grant Munro, Ross Tokely

Midfielders: Ian Black, Russell Duncan, Richard Hart, Roy McBain, Markus Paatelainen, John Rankin, Alexander Sutherland, Barry Wilson

Forwards: Graham Bayne, Craig Dargo, Liam Keogh, Barry McAllister, Barry McSwegan, Dennis Wyness

KEY: ■ On all match ◄◄ Subbed or sent off (Counting game) ►► Subbed on from bench (Counting Game) ►► Subbed on and then subbed or sent off (Counting Game) Not in 16
□ On bench ◄◄ Subbed or sent off (playing less than 70 minutes) ►► Subbed on (playing less than 70 minutes) ►► Subbed on and then subbed or sent off (playing less than 70 minutes)

SCOTTISH PREMIERSHIP - INVERNESS CALEDONIAN THISTLE

DUNDEE UNITED

Final Position: **9th**

NICKNAME: THE TERRORS/ ARABS　　　KEY: ☐ Won ☐ Drawn ☐ Lost　　　Attendance

1 spl	Falkirk	H L	1-2	Robson 17		6,616
2 spl	Rangers	A D	2-2	Hunt 15, Kalvenes 56		50,394
3 spl	Kilmarnock	A D	0-0			5,328
4 spl	Dunfermline	H D	0-0			6,171
5 sccc2	Airdrie	H W	1-0			2,851
6 spl	St Mirren	A W	3-1	Robson 12, 53, Duff 34		4,902
7 spl	Hibernian	H L	0-3			6,387
8 spl	Inverness CT	A D	0-0			3,586
9 sccc3	St Johnstone	A L	0-3			4,653
10 spl	Motherwell	H D	1-1	Hunt 64		5,036
11 spl	Hearts	A L	0-4			16,849
12 spl	Celtic	H L	1-4	Hunt 5		10,504
13 spl	Aberdeen	A L	1-3	Robson 70 pen		10,747
14 spl	Falkirk	A L	1-5	Samuel 69		5,386
15 spl	Rangers	H W	2-1	Kenneth 77, Mair 82		10,392
16 spl	Kilmarnock	H W	1-0	Hunt 71		5,815
17 spl	Dunfermline	A L	1-2	Robson 52		6,129
18 spl	St Mirren	H W	1-0	Hunt 64		5,681
19 spl	Hibernian	A L	1-2	Martis 24 og		14,032
20 spl	Inverness CT	H W	3-1	Hunt 22, 65, Robertson 78		5,294
21 spl	Motherwell	A W	3-2	Samuel 29, McCracken 45, Hunt 79		4,420
22 spl	Hearts	H L	0-1			7,789
23 spl	Celtic	A D	2-2	Robertson 17, Samuel 57		57,343
24 spl	Aberdeen	H W	3-1	Samuel 62, 90, Robson 81 pen		12,329
25 spl	Falkirk	H L	1-5	Robson 41		6,261
26 spl	Rangers	A L	0-5			50,276
27 scr3	St Mirren	H W	3-2	Robson 31, Kenneth 46, Robertson 90		6,875
28 spl	Kilmarnock	A L	0-1			4,732
29 spl	Dunfermline	H D	0-0			6,295
30 scr4	Inverness CT	A L	0-1			3,402
31 spl	St Mirren	A W	1-0	Robson 78		3,849
32 spl	Hibernian	H D	0-0			6,453
33 spl	Inverness CT	A L	0-1			3,901
34 spl	Motherwell	H D	1-1	Robb 29		5,183
35 spl	Hearts	A W	4-0	Robson 51, 59, 78, Hunt 70		17,172
36 spl	Celtic	H D	1-1	Daly 90		11,363
37 spl	Aberdeen	A W	4-2	Daly 1 pen, Hunt 14, Cameron 17, 51		12,148
38 spl	Dunfermline	A L	0-1			5,131
39 spl	Inverness CT	H D	1-1	Robertson 41		5,273
40 spl	St Mirren	H L	0-2			6,875
41 spl	Falkirk	A L	0-2			4,161
42 spl	Motherwell	H D	0-0			6,070

LEAGUE APPEARANCES, BOOKINGS AND CAPS

	AGE (on 01/07/07)	IN NAMED 18	APPEARANCES	COUNTING GAMES	MINUTES ON PITCH	YELLOW CARDS	RED CARDS	CAPS THIS SEASON	NATIONAL SIDE
Goalkeepers									
Ewan McLean	21	37	1	1	90	0	0	-	Scotland
Derek Stillie	33	38	37	37	3330	0	0	-	Scotland
Defenders									
Alan Archibald	29	25	16	14	1328	2	0	-	Scotland
Sean Dillon	23	15	15	15	1350	1	0	-	Rep of Ireland
William Easton	20	21	7	0	123	0	0	-	Scotland
Christian Kalvenes	30	29	29	27	2490	6	1	-	Norway
Gary Kenneth	20	25	11	9	922	2	0	-	Scotland
Lee Mair	26	32	18	17	1532	6	0	-	Scotland
David McCracken	25	35	33	32	2937	4	0	-	Scotland
David Proctor	23	14	12	8	805	2	0	-	Scotland
Keith Watson	17	12	1	0	1	0	0	-	Scotland
Lee Wilkie	27	16	14	13	1213	7	1	-	Scotland
Midfielders									
Gregg Burnett	20	6	1	0	45	0	0	-	Scotland
Greg Cameron	19	31	25	20	1798	3	0	-	Scotland
Craig Conway	22	32	30	16	1908	0	0	-	Scotland
Stuart Duff	25	35	28	21	2026	3	0	-	Scotland
Morgaro Gomis	21	15	12	5	713	2	0	-	France
Mark Kerr	25	36	36	32	3067	8	0	-	Scotland
Stephen Robb	25	18	15	5	705	1	0	-	Scotland
David Robertson	20	32	26	9	1848	5	1	-	Scotland
Barry Robson	28	30	29	29	2595	8	2	-	Scotland
William Russell	18	2	2	0	19	0	0	-	Scotland
Grant Smith	27	14	6	3	340	1	0	-	Scotland
Forwards									
Craig Brewster	40	5	3	1	122	1	0	-	Scotland
Jon Daly	24	12	11	10	885	4	0	-	Rep of Ireland
David Goodwillie	18	29	16	1	531	0	0	-	Scotland
Noel Hunt	24	29	28	19	2108	6	2	-	Rep of Ireland
Lee Miller	24	4	3	0	99	2	1	-	Scotland
Collin Samuel	25	37	37	22	2397	2	0	-	Trinidad & Tobago

TEAM OF THE SEASON

G Derek Stillie CG: 37 DR: 61

D Sean Dillon CG: 15 DR: 79
D Christian Kalvenes CG: 27 DR: 77
D Lee Wilkie CG: 13 DR: 75
D Lee Mair CG: 17 DR: 54

M Barry Robson CG: 29 SD: -16
M Mark Kerr CG: 32 SD: -22
M Craig Conway CG: 16 SD: -25
M Greg Cameron CG: 20 SD: -31

F Noel Hunt CG: 19 SR: 210
F Collin Samuel CG: 22 SR: 479

MONTHLY POINTS TALLY

AUGUST	6	50%
SEPTEMBER	2	22%
OCTOBER	0	0%
NOVEMBER	9	75%
DECEMBER	10	56%
JANUARY	1	8%
FEBRUARY	4	67%
MARCH	5	42%
APRIL	4	44%
MAY	1	11%

LEAGUE GOALS

	PLAYER	MINS	GOALS	S RATE
1	Robson	2595	11	235
2	Hunt	2108	10	210
3	Samuel	2397	5	479
4	Robertson	1848	3	616
5	Daly	885	2	442
6	Cameron	1798	2	899
7	Robb	705	1	705
8	Kenneth	922	1	922
9	Mair	1532	1	1532
10	Duff	2026	1	2026
11	Kalvenes	2490	1	2490
12	McCracken	2937	1	2937
13	McLean	90	0	
	Other		0	
	TOTAL		39	

TOP POINT EARNERS

	PLAYER	GAMES	AV PTS
1	David Robertson	19	1.47
2	Craig Conway	16	1.38
3	Noel Hunt	21	1.33
4	Christian Kalvenes	28	1.29
5	Lee Mair	17	1.29
6	Mark Kerr	32	1.25
7	Barry Robson	29	1.24
8	Derek Stillie	37	1.14
9	David McCracken	32	1.09
10	Lee Wilkie	13	1.08
	CLUB AVERAGE:		1.11

DISCIPLINARY RECORDS

	PLAYER	YELLOW	RED	AVE
1	Lee Wilkie	7	1	173
2	Lee Mair	6	0	255
3	Noel Hunt	6	2	263
4	Jon Daly	4	0	295
5	David Robertson	5	1	308
6	Barry Robson	8	2	324
7	Christian Kalvenes	6	1	355
8	Morgaro Gomis	2	0	356
9	Mark Kerr	8	0	383
10	David Proctor	2	0	402
11	Gary Kenneth	2	0	461
12	Alan Archibald	2	0	664
13	Stephen Robb	1	0	705
	Other	11	0	
	TOTAL	70	7	

KEY GOALKEEPER

Derek Stillie

Goals Conceded in the League	54	Counting Games League games when player was on pitch for at least 70 minutes	37
Defensive Rating Ave number of mins between League goals conceded while on the pitch	61	Clean Sheets In League games when player was on pitch for at least 70 minutes	10

KEY PLAYERS - DEFENDERS

Sean Dillon

Goals Conceded Number of League goals conceded while the player was on the pitch	17	Clean Sheets In League games when player was on pitch for at least 70 minutes	5
Defensive Rating Ave number of mins between League goals conceded while on the pitch	79	Club Defensive Rating Average number of mins between League goals conceded by the club this season	57

	PLAYER	CON LGE	CLEAN SHEETS	DEF RATE
1	Sean Dillon	17	5	79 mins
2	Christian Kalvenes	32	9	77 mins
3	Lee Wilkie	16	4	75 mins
4	Lee Mair	28	4	54 mins

KEY PLAYERS - MIDFIELDERS

Barry Robson

Goals in the League	11	Contribution to Attacking Power Average number of minutes between League team goals while on pitch	76
Defensive Rating Average number of mins between League goals conceded while on the pitch	60	Scoring Difference Defensive Rating minus Contribution to Attacking Power	-16

	PLAYER	LGE GOALS	DEF RATE	POWER	SCORE DIFF
1	Barry Robson	11	60	76	-16 mins
2	Mark Kerr	0	58	80	-22 mins
3	Craig Conway	0	54	79	-25 mins
4	Greg Cameron	2	54	85	-31 mins

KEY PLAYERS - GOALSCORERS

Noel Hunt

Goals in the League	10	Player Strike Rate Average number of minutes between League goals scored by player	210
Contribution to Attacking Power Average number of minutes between League team goals while on pitch	84	Club Strike Rate Average number of minutes between League goals scored by club	85

	PLAYER	LGE GOALS	POWER	STRIKE RATE
1	Noel Hunt	10	84	210 mins
2	Barry Robson	11	76	235 mins
3	Collin Samuel	5	95	479 mins
4	David Robertson	3	97	616 mins

Barry Robson

SQUAD APPEARANCES

Match	1	2	3	4	5	6	7	8	9	10	11	12	13	14	15	16	17	18	19	20	21	22	23	24	25	26	27	28	29	30	31	32	33	34	35	36	37	38	39	40	41	42
Venue	H	A	A	H	H	A	H	A	A	H	A	H	A	A	H	H	A	H	A	H	A	H	A	H	H	A	H	A	H	A	A	H	A	H	A	H	A	A	H	H	A	H
Competition	L	L	L	L	W	L	L	L	L	W	L	L	L	L	W	L	L	L	L	L	L	L	L	L	L	L	F	L	L	F	L	L	L	L	L	L	L	L	L	L	L	L
Result	L	D	D	D	W	W	L	D	L	D	L	L	L	L	W	W	L	W	L	W	W	L	D	W	L	L	W	L	D	L	W	D	L	D	W	D	W	L	D	L	L	D

Goalkeepers
Ewan McLean
Derek Stillie

Defenders
Alan Archibald
Sean Dillon
William Easton
Christian Kalvenes
Gary Kenneth
Lee Mair
David McCracken
David Proctor
Keith Watson
Lee Wilkie

Midfielders
Gregg Burnett
Greg Cameron
Craig Conway
Stuart Duff
Morgaro Gomis
Mark Kerr
Stephen Robb
David Robertson
Barry Robson
William Russell
Grant Smith

Forwards
Craig Brewster
Jon Daly
David Goodwillie
Noel Hunt
Lee Miller
Collin Samuel

KEY: ■ On all match   ◄◄ Subbed or sent off (Counting game)   ►► Subbed on from bench (Counting Game)   ►► Subbed on and then subbed or sent off (Counting Game)   □ Not in 16
    ▨ On bench   ◄◄ Subbed or sent off (playing less than 70 minutes)   ►► Subbed on (playing less than 70 minutes)   ►► Subbed on and then subbed or sent off (playing less than 70 minutes)

SCOTTISH PREMIERSHIP - DUNDEE UNITED

MOTHERWELL

Final Position: **10th**

NICKNAME: THE WELL   KEY: ☐ Won ☐ Drawn ☐ Lost   Attendance

				Result	Scorers	Attendance
1	spl	Rangers	H L	1-2	O'Donnell 52	11,745
2	spl	St Mirren	A L	0-2		5,036
3	spl	Aberdeen	H L	0-2		5,186
4	spl	Hibernian	A L	1-3	Scott.McDonald 90	13,274
5	sccc2	Partick	H W	3-2		3,752
6	spl	Falkirk	A W	1-0	Scott.McDonald 58	4,594
7	spl	Inverness CT	H L	1-4	Scott.McDonald 72	4,091
8	spl	Hearts	H L	0-1		5,931
9	sccc3	Queens Park	A W	3-0	Foran 24, 47, 54 pen	2,408
10	spl	Dundee Utd	A D	1-1	Elliot 61	5,036
11	spl	Kilmarnock	H W	5-0	Foran 15, Reynolds 20, Kerr 23, Scott.McDonald 82, 86	4,765
12	spl	Dunfermline	H W	2-1	Scott.McDonald 61, Clarkson 84	4,527
13	spl	Celtic	A L	1-2	Scott.McDonald 77	57,742
14	spl	Rangers	A D	1-1	Kerr 51	49,785
15	spl	St Mirren	H D	0-0		5,337
16	sccqf	Kilmarnock	A L	2-3	Foran 25 pen, Clarkson 59	5,601
17	spl	Aberdeen	A L	1-2	Hart 61 og	10,527
18	spl	Hibernian	H L	1-6	McGarry 83	6,190
19	spl	Falkirk	H W	4-2	Foran 45 pen, 49 pen, Scott.McDonald 75, Elliot 83	4,970
20	spl	Inverness CT	A W	1-0	Foran 90 pen	3,668
21	spl	Hearts	A L	1-4	Foran 20	16,753
22	spl	Dundee Utd	H L	2-3	Foran 62 pen, Reynolds 68	4,420
23	spl	Kilmarnock	A W	2-1	Foran 15, Paterson 20	5,576
24	spl	Dunfermline	A W	2-0	Fitzpatrick 26, Scott.McDonald 79	4,200
25	spl	Celtic	H D	1-1	DL.Smith 90	9,769
26	spl	Rangers	H L	0-1		10,338
27	scr3	Airdrie Utd	A W	1-0	Foran 31	5,924
28	spl	Hibernian	A L	0-2		14,280
29	scr4	G Morton	H W	2-0	Kerr 10, Scott.McDonald 34	9,394
30	spl	Falkirk	A W	2-1	Scott.McDonald 66, DL.Smith 67	4,478
31	spl	Inverness CT	H W	1-0	Scott.McDonald 45	4,258
32	spl	St Mirren	A D	0-0		3,576
33	scpqf	St Johnstone	H L	1-2	R.McCormack 85	5,788
34	spl	Hearts	H L	0-2		4,389
35	spl	Dundee Utd	A D	1-1	Murphy 37	5,183
36	spl	Aberdeen	H L	0-2		4,530
37	spl	Dunfermline	H W	2-0	Scott.McDonald 51 pen, 62	4,511
38	spl	Kilmarnock	H L	0-1		3,784
39	spl	Celtic	A L	0-1		58,654
40	spl	Inverness CT	A L	0-2		3,804
41	spl	Falkirk	H D	3-3	DL.Smith 18, Scott.McDonald 37, Clarkson 58	3,640
42	spl	Dunfermline	A L	1-4	Scott.McDonald 87 pen	6,662
43	spl	St Mirren	H L	2-3	R.McCormack 38, 49 pen	9,277
44	spl	Dundee Utd	A D	0-0		6,070

LEAGUE APPEARANCES, BOOKINGS AND CAPS

	AGE (on 01/07/07)	IN NAMED 18	APPEARANCES	COUNTING GAMES	MINUTES ON PITCH	YELLOW CARDS	RED CARDS	CAPS THIS SEASON	NATIONAL SIDE
Goalkeepers									
Colin Meldrum	31	35	16	14	1355	0	0	-	Scotland
Graeme Smith	24	38	24	22	2065	0	0	-	Scotland
Defenders									
Martyn Corrigan	29	22	22	18	1689	4	0	-	Scotland
Stephen Craigan	30	35	34	33	3024	6	0	8	N Ireland
Marc Fitzpatrick	21	38	24	12	1415	1	1	-	Scotland
William Kinniburgh	22	21	6	4	396	1	0	-	Scotland
Brian McLean	22	5	4	1	137	0	0	-	N Ireland
Danny Murphy	24	13	13	9	969	2	0	-	England
Paul Quinn	22	36	26	23	2195	7	1	-	Scotland
Mark Reynolds	20	36	35	34	3127	0	1	-	Scotland
Midfielders									
Kenneth Connolly	20	28	2	1	100	0	0	-	Scotland
Robert Donnelly	20	6	2	2	180	1	0	-	Scotland
Brian Kerr	25	36	35	34	3105	4	0	-	Scotland
Keith Lasley	27	14	14	14	1243	6	0	-	Scotland
Kevin McBride	26	30	17	8	956	0	0	-	Scotland
Steven McGarry	27	38	29	19	1999	3	0	-	Scotland
Philip O'Donnell	35	3	3	3	270	0	0	-	Scotland
Jamie Paterson	27	34	34	30	2785	6	1	-	Scotland
Krisztian Vadocz	22	14	11	11	990	0	0	-	Hungary
Forwards									
David Clarkson	21	32	29	15	1653	5	1	-	Scotland
Adam Coakley	19	13	2	0	41	0	0	-	England
Calum Elliot	20	15	15	7	848	2	0	-	Scotland
Ritchie Foran	27	24	23	20	1902	6	0	-	Rep of Ireland
Jim Hamilton	31	3	3	2	192	0	0	-	Scotland
Paul Keegan	34	14	8	3	357	0	0	-	Rep of Ireland
Ross McCormack	20	21	12	4	553	1	0	-	Scotland
Scott McDonald	23	32	32	30	2734	8	1	-	Australia
Trevor Molloy	30	12	6	0	139	0	0	-	Rep of Ireland
Jamie Murphy	17	3	2	1	101	0	0	-	Scotland
Darren Lee Smith	19	20	17	9	1010	1	0	-	Scotland

TEAM OF THE SEASON

D Stephen Craigan CG: 33 DR: 59

M Keith Lasley CG: 14 SD: -11

D Martyn Corrigan CG: 18 DR: 56

M Jamie Paterson CG: 29 SD: -23

F Scott McDonald CG: 30 SR: 182

G Colin Meldrum CG: 14 DR: 50

M Brian Kerr CG: 34 SD: -26

F Ritchie Foran CG: 20 SR: 271

D Mark Fitzpatrick CG: 12 DR: 88

D Mark Reynolds CG: 34 DR: 59

M Steven McGarry CG: 19 SD: -32

MONTHLY POINTS TALLY

AUGUST	3	25%
SEPTEMBER	4	33%
OCTOBER	4	44%
NOVEMBER	4	33%
DECEMBER	10	56%
JANUARY	0	0%
FEBRUARY	7	78%
MARCH	4	33%
APRIL	1	8%
MAY	1	11%

LEAGUE GOALS

	PLAYER	MINS	GOALS	S RATE
1	McDonald, S	2734	15	182
2	Foran	1902	7	271
3	Smith, DL	1010	3	336
4	McCormack, R	553	2	276
5	Elliot	848	2	424
6	Clarkson	1653	2	826
7	Kerr	3105	2	1552
8	Reynolds	3127	2	1563
9	O'Donnell	270	1	270
10	Murphy, D	969	1	969
11	Fitzpatrick	1415	1	1415
12	McGarry	1999	1	1999
13	Paterson	2785	1	2785
	Other		0	
	TOTAL		40	

TOP POINT EARNERS

	PLAYER	GAMES	AV PTS
1	Mark Fitzpatrick	12	**1.33**
2	Keith Lasley	14	**1.29**
3	Scott McDonald	30	**1.20**
4	Ritchie Foran	20	**1.20**
5	Mark Reynolds	35	**1.09**
6	Colin Meldrum	14	**1.07**
7	Brian Kerr	34	**1.06**
8	Jamie Paterson	30	**1.03**
9	David Clarkson	15	**1.00**
10	Martyn Corrigan	18	**1.00**
	CLUB AVERAGE:		**1.00**

DISCIPLINARY RECORDS

	PLAYER	YELLOW	RED	AVE
1	Keith Lasley	6	0	207
2	Paul Quinn	7	1	274
3	Ritchie Foran	6	0	317
4	David Clarkson	5	1	330
5	Scott McDonald	8	1	341
6	Jamie Paterson	6	1	397
7	Martyn Corrigan	4	0	422
8	Ross McCormack	1	0	553
9	Stephen Craigan	6	0	604
10	Steven McGarry	3	0	666
11	Mark Fitzpatrick	1	1	707
12	Brian Kerr	4	0	776
13	Calum Elliot	2	0	848
	Other	3	1	
	TOTAL	62	6	

KEY GOALKEEPER

Colin Meldrum

Goals Conceded in the League	27	**Counting Games** League games when player was on pitch for at least 70 minutes	14
Defensive Rating Ave number of mins between League goals conceded while on the pitch	50	**Clean Sheets** In League games when player was on pitch for at least 70 minutes	4

KEY PLAYERS - DEFENDERS

Marc Fitzpatrick

Goals Conceded Number of League goals conceded while the player was on the pitch	16	**Clean Sheets** In League games when player was on pitch for at least 70 minutes	4
Defensive Rating Ave number of mins between League goals conceded while on the pitch	88	**Club Defensive Rating** Average number of mins between League goals conceded by the club this season	59

	PLAYER	CON LGE	CLEAN SHEETS	DEF RATE
1	Marc Fitzpatrick	16	4	88 mins
2	Mark Reynolds	53	9	59 mins
3	Stephen Craigan	51	8	59 mins
4	Martyn Corrigan	30	4	56 mins

KEY PLAYERS - MIDFIELDERS

Keith Lasley

Goals in the League	0	**Contribution to Attacking Power** Average number of minutes between League team goals while on pitch	65
Defensive Rating Average number of mins between League goals conceded while on the pitch	54	**Scoring Difference** Defensive Rating minus Contribution to Attacking Power	-11

	PLAYER	LGE GOALS	DEF RATE	POWER	SCORE DIFF
1	Keith Lasley	0	54	65	-11 mins
2	Jamie Paterson	1	58	81	-23 mins
3	Brian Kerr	2	55	81	-26 mins
4	Steven McGarry	1	51	83	-32 mins

KEY PLAYERS - GOALSCORERS

Scott McDonald

Goals in the League	15	**Player Strike Rate** Average number of minutes between League goals scored by player	182
Contribution to Attacking Power Average number of minutes between League team goals while on pitch	75	**Club Strike Rate** Average number of minutes between League goals scored by club	87

	PLAYER	LGE GOALS	POWER	STRIKE RATE
1	Scott McDonald	15	75	182 mins
2	Ritchie Foran	7	76	271 mins
3	David Clarkson	2	127	826 mins
4	Mark Fitzpatrick	1	78	1415 mins

Scott McDonald

SQUAD APPEARANCES

Match	1 2 3 4 5	6 7 8 9 10	11 12 13 14 15	16 17 18 19 20	21 22 23 24 25	26 27 28 29 30	31 32 33 34 35	36 37 38 39 40	41 42 43 44
Venue	H A H A H	A H H A A	H H A A H	A A H H A	A H A A H	H A A H A	H A H H A	H H A A	H A H A
Competition	L L L L W	L L L W L	L L L L L	W L L L L	L L L L L	L F L F L	L L F L L	L L L L L	L L L L
Result	L L L L W	W L L W D	W W L D D	L L L W W	L L W W D	L W L W W	W D L L D	L W L L L	D L L D

Goalkeepers
Colin Meldrum
Graeme Smith

Defenders
Martyn Corrigan
Stephen Craigan
Marc Fitzpatrick
William Kinniburgh
Ryan McLean
Danny Murphy
Paul Quinn
Mark Reynolds

Midfielders
Kenneth Connolly
Robert Donnelly
Brian Kerr
Keith Lasley
Kevin McBride
Steven McGarry
Phillip O'Donnell
Jamie Paterson
Krisztian Vadocz

Forwards
David Clarkson
Liam Coakley
Callum Elliot
Ritchie Foran
Jim Hamilton
Paul Keegan
Ross McCormack
Scott McDonald
Ivor Molloy
Jamie Murphy
Darren Lee Smith

KEY: ■ On all match   ◄◄ Subbed or sent off (Counting game)   ►► Subbed on from bench (Counting Game)   ►► Subbed on and then subbed or sent off (Counting Game)   ☐ Not in 16

■ On bench   ◄◄ Subbed or sent off (playing less than 70 minutes)   ►► Subbed on (playing less than 70 minutes)   ►► Subbed on and then subbed or sent off (playing less than 70 minutes)

ST MIRREN

Final Position: **11th**

NICKNAME: BUDDIES/SAINTS KEY: ☐ Won ☐ Drawn ☐ Lost Attendance

#	comp	Opponent	H/A	Result	Scorers	Attendance
1	spl	Inverness CT	A	W 2-1	Sutton 55, 75	4,267
2	spl	Motherwell	H	W 2-0	Sutton 17, Quinn 51 og	5,036
3	spl	Celtic	A	L 0-2		56,579
4	spl	Aberdeen	H	D 1-1	Broadfoot 87	5,344
5	sccc2	Stenhousemuir	H	W 3-1		1,707
6	spl	Dundee Utd	H	L 1-3	Brady 48	4,902
7	spl	Hearts	A	W 1-0	Kean 82	16,823
8	spl	Kilmarnock	H	L 0-1		5,277
9	sccc3	Celtic	A	L 0-2		32,587
10	spl	Dunfermline	A	L 1-2	Sutton 10	4,914
11	spl	Hibernian	H	W 1-0	van Zanten 39	6,008
12	spl	Falkirk	A	D 1-1	Mehmet 69	4,961
13	spl	Rangers	H	L 2-3	Sutton 5, 78 pen	8,384
14	spl	Inverness CT	H	D 1-1	Sutton 65	4,432
15	spl	Motherwell	A	D 0-0		5,337
16	spl	Celtic	H	L 1-3	Sutton 56	8,445
17	spl	Aberdeen	A	L 0-2		11,426
18	spl	Dundee Utd	A	L 0-1		5,681
19	spl	Hearts	H	D 2-2	Kean 19, 21	5,728
20	spl	Kilmarnock	A	D 1-1	Corcoran 75	5,978
21	spl	Dunfermline	H	D 0-0		4,246
22	spl	Hibernian	A	L 1-5	Sutton 41	13,053
23	spl	Falkirk	H	W 1-0	Lappin 67	5,212
24	spl	Rangers	A	D 1-1	Brittain 14	50,273
25	spl	Inverness CT	A	L 1-2	Broadfoot 77	4,246
26	scr3	Dundee Utd	A	L 2-3	Brittain 76 pen, Sutton 81	6,875
27	spl	Celtic	A	L 1-5	McGinn 47	58,382
28	spl	Aberdeen	H	L 0-2		4,921
29	spl	Dundee Utd	H	L 0-1		3,849
30	spl	Hearts	A	D 1-1	O'Donnell 14	17,195
31	spl	Motherwell	H	D 0-0		3,576
32	spl	Kilmarnock	H	L 0-2		4,778
33	spl	Dunfermline	A	D 0-0		7,149
34	spl	Falkirk	A	L 0-2		5,863
35	spl	Hibernian	H	D 1-1	Sutton 89	4,031
36	spl	Rangers	H	L 0-1		7,308
37	spl	Falkirk	A	W 2-0	Kean 37 pen, Brady 57	4,441
38	spl	Dunfermline	H	L 0-1		10,251
39	spl	Dundee Utd	A	W 2-0	Murray 23, Broadfoot 88	6,875
40	spl	Motherwell	A	W 3-2	Sutton 56, 84, Mehmet 59	9,277
41	spl	Inverness CT	H	L 0-1		4,834

LEAGUE APPEARANCES, BOOKINGS AND CAPS

	AGE (on 01/07/07)	IN NAMED 18	APPEARANCES	COUNTING GAMES	MINUTES ON PITCH	YELLOW CARDS	RED CARDS	CAPS THIS SEASON	NATIONAL SIDE
Goalkeepers									
Tony Bullock	35	22	17	17	1530	0	0	-	England
Chris Smith	21	38	21	21	1890	0	0	-	Scotland
Defenders									
Kirk Broadfoot	22	37	37	37	3330	9	0	-	Scotland
Ian Maxwell	32	24	16	14	1317	1	0	-	Scotland
Kevin McGowne	37	20	19	18	1586	2	0	-	Scotland
Andy Millen	42	33	23	19	1916	1	0	-	Scotland
John-Paul Potter	27	29	26	24	2245	6	0	-	Scotland
David van Zanten	25	37	37	37	3330	8	0	-	Rep of Ireland
Midfielders									
Garry Brady	30	35	29	21	2155	1	0	-	Scotland
Richard Brittain	23	33	31	24	2343	7	0	-	Scotland
Simon Lappin	24	24	24	23	2109	2	0	-	Scotland
Paul Lawson	23	9	4	3	281	1	0	-	Scotland
Brian Mackay	19	20	2	0	71	0	0	-	Scotland
Edward Malone	22	11	6	3	329	1	0	-	Scotland
Ryan McCay	21	11	2	0	29	0	0	-	Scotland
Stephen McGinn	18	10	4	1	174	0	0	-	Scotland
Craig Molloy	21	19	12	5	587	2	0	-	Scotland
Hugh Murray	28	31	31	30	2718	10	0	-	Scotland
Stephen O'Donnell	23	6	5	4	399	1	0	-	Scotland
Alan Reid	26	31	22	17	1751	0	0	-	Scotland
Forwards									
Alex Burke	29	16	13	1	429	0	0	-	Scotland
Mark Corcoran	26	31	27	10	1260	1	0	-	Scotland
Scott Gemmill	20	12	5	1	107	0	0	-	Scotland
Stewart Kean	24	31	31	18	1846	0	0	-	Scotland
David McKenna	20	32	10	0	157	0	0	-	Scotland
Billy Mehmet	23	26	25	9	1178	3	0	-	Rep of Ireland
John Sutton	23	36	33	29	2641	1	0	-	England

TEAM OF THE SEASON

D Ian Maxwell CG: 14 DR: 73

M Hugh Murray CG: 29 SD: -24

D John-Paul Potter CG: 24 DR: 72

M Simon Lappin CG: 23 SD: -47

F John Sutton CG: 29 SR: 220

G Chris Smith CG: 21 DR: 72

D Kirk Broadfoot CG: 37 DR: 67

M Garry Brady CG: 20 SD: -49

F Stewart Kean CG: 17 SR: 461

D David van Zanten CG: 37 DR: 67

M Richard Brittain CG: 23 SD: -65

MONTHLY POINTS TALLY

Month		Points	%
AUGUST		4	33%
SEPTEMBER		6	50%
OCTOBER		2	22%
NOVEMBER		1	8%
DECEMBER		7	39%
JANUARY		0	0%
FEBRUARY		2	22%
MARCH		1	11%
APRIL		4	33%
MAY		6	67%

LEAGUE GOALS

	PLAYER	MINS	GOALS	S RATE
1	Sutton	2641	12	220
2	Kean	1846	4	461
3	Broadfoot	3330	3	1110
4	Mehmet	1178	2	589
5	Brady	2155	2	1077
6	McGinn	174	1	174
7	O'Donnell	399	1	399
8	Corcoran	1260	1	1260
9	Lappin	2109	1	2109
10	Brittain	2343	1	2343
11	Murray	2718	1	2718
12	van Zanten	3330	1	3330
13	Millen	1916	0	
	Other		0	
	TOTAL		**30**	

TOP POINT EARNERS

	PLAYER	GAMES	AV PTS
1	Stewart Kean	17	1.35
2	Kevin McGowne	16	1.19
3	Hugh Murray	29	1.14
4	Chris Smith	21	1.10
5	Simon Lappin	23	1.00
6	Ian Maxwell	14	1.00
7	Kirk Broadfoot	37	0.97
8	David van Zanten	37	0.97
9	John-Paul Potter	24	0.96
10	Andy Millen	19	0.89
	CLUB AVERAGE:		**0.95**

DISCIPLINARY RECORDS

	PLAYER	YELLOW	RED	AV
1	Hugh Murray	10	0	27
2	Craig Molloy	2	0	29
3	Richard Brittain	7	0	33
4	John-Paul Potter	6	0	37
5	Billy Mehmet	3	0	39
6	Kirk Broadfoot	8	0	41
7	David van Zanten	8	0	41
8	Kevin McGowne	2	0	79
9	Simon Lappin	2	0	105
10	Mark Corcoran	1	0	126
11	Ian Maxwell	1	0	131
12	Garry Brady	1	0	215
13	John Sutton	1	0	264
	Other	1	0	
	TOTAL	**53**	**0**	

KEY GOALKEEPER

Chris Smith

Goals Conceded in the League	26	Counting Games League games when player was on pitch for at least 70 minutes	21
Defensive Rating Ave number of mins between League goals conceded while on the pitch	72	Clean Sheets In League games when player was on pitch for at least 70 minutes	6

KEY PLAYERS - DEFENDERS

Ian Maxwell

Goals Conceded Number of League goals conceded while the player was on the pitch	18	Clean Sheets In League games when player was on pitch for at least 70 minutes	4
Defensive Rating Ave number of mins between League goals conceded while on the pitch	73	Club Defensive Rating Average number of mins between League goals conceded by the club this season	68

	PLAYER	CON LGE	CLEAN SHEETS	DEF RATE
1	Ian Maxwell	18	4	73 mins
2	John-Paul Potter	31	6	72 mins
3	Kirk Broadfoot	49	10	67 mins
4	David van Zanten	49	10	67 mins

KEY PLAYERS - MIDFIELDERS

Hugh Murray

Goals in the League	1	Contribution to Attacking Power Average number of minutes between League team goals while on pitch	97
Defensive Rating Average number of mins between League goals conceded while on the pitch	73	Scoring Difference Defensive Rating minus Contribution to Attacking Power	-24

	PLAYER	LGE GOALS	DEF RATE	POWER	SCORE DIFF
1	Hugh Murray	1	73	97	-24 mins
2	Simon Lappin	1	58	105	-47 mins
3	Garry Brady	2	58	107	-49 mins
4	Richard Brittain	1	65	130	-65 mins

KEY PLAYERS - GOALSCORERS

John Sutton

Goals in the League	12	Player Strike Rate Average number of minutes between League goals scored by player	220
Contribution to Attacking Power Average number of minutes between League team goals while on pitch	101	Club Strike Rate Average number of minutes between League goals scored by club	113

	PLAYER	LGE GOALS	POWER	STRIKE RATE
1	John Sutton	12	101	220 mins
2	Stewart Kean	4	97	461 mins
3	Garry Brady	2	107	1077 mins
4	Simon Lappin	1	105	2109 mins

John Sutton

SQUAD APPEARANCES

Match	1	2	3	4	5	6	7	8	9	10	11	12	13	14	15	16	17	18	19	20	21	22	23	24	25	26	27	28	29	30	31	32	33	34	35	36	37	38	39	40	41
Venue	A	H	A	H	H	H	A	H	A	A	H	A	H	H	A	H	A	A	H	A	H	A	H	A	A	A	A	H	H	A	H	H	A	A	H	H	A	H	A	A	H
Competition	L	L	L	L	W	L	L	L	W	L	L	L	L	L	L	L	L	L	L	L	L	L	L	L	L	F	L	L	L	L	L	L	L	L	L	L	L	L	L	L	L
Result	W	W	L	D	W	L	W	L	L	L	W	D	L	D	D	L	L	L	D	D	D	L	W	D	L	L	L	L	L	D	D	L	D	L	D	L	W	L	W	W	L

Goalkeepers
Tony Bullock
Chris Smith

Defenders
Kirk Broadfoot
Ian Maxwell
Kevin McGowne
Andy Millen
John-Paul Potter
David van Zanten

Midfielders
Garry Brady
Richard Brittain
Simon Lappin
Paul Lawson
Ian Mackay
Edward Malone
Ian McCay
Stephen McGinn
Craig Molloy
Hugh Murray
Stephen O'Donnell
Ian Reid

Forwards
Alex Burke
Mark Corcoran
Scott Gemmill
Stewart Kean
David McKenna
Billy Mehmet
John Sutton

KEY: ■ On all match ◄◄ Subbed or sent off (Counting game) ►► Subbed on from bench (Counting Game) ►► Subbed on and then subbed or sent off (Counting Game) □ Not in 16
■ On bench ◄ Subbed or sent off (playing less than 70 minutes) ►► Subbed on (playing less than 70 minutes) ►► Subbed on and then subbed or sent off (playing less than 70 minutes)

SCOTTISH PREMIERSHIP - ST MIRREN

DUNFERMLINE

Final Position: 12th

NICKNAME: THE PARS KEY: ☐ Won ☐ Drawn ☐ Lost   Attendance

1 spl	Hearts	H L	1-2	Simmons 62	7,936
2 spl	Falkirk	A L	0-1		5,542
3 spl	Rangers	H D	1-1	O.Morrison 69	8,561
4 spl	Dundee Utd	A D	0-0		6,171
5 sccc2	Ayr	A W	7-6*	(*on penalties)	1,507
6 spl	Aberdeen	A L	0-1		9,889
7 spl	Kilmarnock	H W	3-2	Darren.Young 42, Mason 73, Crawford 84	4,510
8 spl	Celtic	A L	0-1		55,894
9 sccc3	Rangers	H L	0-2		5,702
10 spl	St Mirren	H W	2-1	Darren.Young 46, Crawford 73	4,914
11 spl	Inverness CT	A L	0-1		3,517
12 spl	Motherwell	A L	1-2	Crawford 69	4,527
13 spl	Hibernian	H L	0-4		6,057
14 spl	Hearts	A D	1-1	Hamilton 48	17,031
15 spl	Falkirk	H L	0-3		6,504
16 spl	Rangers	A L	0-2		48,218
17 spl	Dundee Utd	H W	2-1	Shields 76, Mason 89	6,129
18 spl	Aberdeen	H L	0-3		6,501
19 spl	Kilmarnock	A L	1-5	Crawford 11	4,750
20 spl	Celtic	H L	1-2	Simmons 90	7,080
21 spl	St Mirren	A D	0-0		4,246
22 spl	Inverness CT	H D	0-0		4,216
23 spl	Motherwell	H L	0-2		4,200
24 spl	Hibernian	A L	0-2		14,061
25 spl	Hearts	H L	0-1		7,004
26 scr3	Rangers	H W	3-2	Hamilton 17, Simmons 29, McGuire 46	7,231
27 spl	Falkirk	A L	0-1		6,051
28 spl	Rangers	H L	0-1		7,868
29 spl	Dundee Utd	A D	0-0		6,295
30 scr4	Hearts	H W	1-0	S.Wilson 90	9,597
31 spl	Aberdeen	A L	0-3		9,379
32 spl	Kilmarnock	H D	1-1	Crawford 45 pen	4,500
33 scpqf	Partick	H W	2-0	Simmons 4, 86	7,090
34 spl	Celtic	A L	1-2	Hamill 87	59,131
35 spl	St Mirren	H D	0-0		7,149
36 spl	Inverness CT	A W	3-1	Glass 48, 79 pen, McIntyre 61	4,447
37 spl	Motherwell	A L	0-2		4,511
38 spl	Hibernian	H W	1-0	McGuire 84	6,001
39 scsf	Hibernian	A D	0-0		25,336
40 spl	Dundee Utd	H W	1-0	McManus 34	5,131
41 scsfr	Hibernian	H W	1-0	McIntyre 88 pen	8,536
42 spl	St Mirren	A W	1-0	McManus 58	10,251
43 spl	Motherwell	H W	4-1	O'Brien 6, S.Wilson 11, Glass 58 pen, Hamilton 90	6,662
44 spl	Inverness CT	A L	1-2	McIntyre 37	6,464
45 spl	Falkirk	H L	0-3		5,087
46 scfin	Celtic	N L	0-1		49,600

LEAGUE APPEARANCES, BOOKINGS AND CAPS

	AGE (on 01/07/07)	IN NAMED 18	APPEARANCES	COUNTING GAMES	MINUTES ON PITCH	YELLOW CARDS	RED CARDS	CAPS THIS SEASON	NATIONAL SIDE
Goalkeepers									
Dorus de Vries	26	32	27	26	2404	3	0	-	Holland
Roddy McKenzie	31	36	12	11	1016	0	0	-	Scotland
Defenders									
Souleymane Bamba	22	32	23	20	1895	7	1	-	France
Iain Campbell	22	3	1	0	24	1	0	-	Scotland
Aaron Labonte	23	15	13	11	1058	1	0	-	England
Philip McGuire	27	25	24	21	1927	14	0	-	Scotland
Scott Morrison	22	18	12	12	1049	4	0	-	Scotland
Greg Ross	20	33	26	14	1577	5	0	-	Scotland
Greg Shields	30	29	29	27	2489	5	0	-	Scotland
Andy Tod	35	16	10	6	560	2	1	-	Scotland
Scott Wilson	30	31	31	27	2635	10	1	-	Scotland
Callum Woods	20	27	12	8	783	3	0	-	Scotland
Midfielders									
Stephen Glass	31	11	11	11	980	1	0	-	Scotland
Adam Hamill	19	13	13	8	916	2	0	-	England
Gary Mason	27	36	36	34	3120	12	0	-	Scotland
Jamie McCunnie	24	24	14	8	834	1	0	-	Scotland
Owen Morrison	25	27	24	6	1102	1	0	-	N Ireland
Scott Muirhead	22	29	26	12	1607	1	0	-	Scotland
Stephen Simmons	25	25	23	17	1745	7	0	-	Scotland
Calum Smith	19	5	1	0	16	0	0	-	Scotland
Iain Williamson	19	21	4	0	41	0	0	-	Scotland
Darren Young	28	23	21	19	1773	11	0	-	Scotland
Forwards									
Mark Burchill	26	22	20	9	1088	3	0	-	Scotland
Stevie Crawford	33	26	25	20	1939	4	1	-	Scotland
Frederic Daquin	28	23	20	5	805	1	0	-	France
Jim Hamilton	31	28	25	16	1633	8	1	-	Scotland
James McIntyre	35	11	10	7	637	1	0	-	Scotland
Tom McManus	26	8	8	6	559	1	1	-	Scotland
James O'Brien	19	14	13	13	1127	3	0	-	Scotland
Bobby Ryan	28	7	5	1	172	0	0	-	Rep of Ireland
Craig Wilson	21	8	3	0	17	0	0	-	Scotland

TEAM OF THE SEASON

G Dorus de Vries CG: 26 DR: 64

D Scott Wilson CG: 27 DR: 73
D Philip McGuire CG: 21 DR: 71
D Souleymane Bamba CG: 20 DR: 67
D Greg Ross CG: 14 DR: 63

M Gary Mason CG: 34 SD: -58
M Darren Young CG: 19 SD: -120
M Scott Muirhead CG: 12 SD: -60
M Stephen Glass CG: 11 SD: +8

F Stevie Crawford CG: 19 SR: 387
F Jim Hamilton CG: 15 SR: 816

MONTHLY POINTS TALLY

AUGUST	2	17%
SEPTEMBER	6	50%
OCTOBER	1	11%
NOVEMBER	3	25%
DECEMBER	2	11%
JANUARY	1	8%
FEBRUARY	1	17%
MARCH	4	33%
APRIL	9	100%
MAY	3	33%

LEAGUE GOALS

	PLAYER	MINS	GOALS	S RATE
1	Crawford	1939	5	387
2	Glass	980	3	326
3	McManus	559	2	279
4	McIntyre	637	2	318
5	Hamilton	1633	2	816
6	Simmons	1745	2	872
7	Young, Darren	1773	2	886
8	Mason	3120	2	1560
9	Hamill	916	1	916
10	Morrison, O	1102	1	1102
11	O'Brien	1127	1	1127
12	McGuire	1927	1	1927
13	Shields	2489	1	2489
	Other		1	
	TOTAL		**26**	

TOP POINT EARNERS

	PLAYER	GAMES	AV PTS
1	James O'Brien	13	1.38
2	Dorus de Vries	26	1.12
3	Gary Mason	34	0.94
4	Scott Wilson	27	0.93
5	Souleymane Bamba	20	0.90
6	Jim Hamilton	15	0.87
7	Greg Shields	27	0.81
8	Scott Morrison	12	0.75
9	Philip McGuire	21	0.71
10	Greg Ross	14	0.71
	CLUB AVERAGE:		**0.84**

DISCIPLINARY RECORDS

	PLAYER	YELLOW	RED	AVE
1	Philip McGuire	14	0	148
2	Darren Young	11	0	177
3	Jim Hamilton	8	1	181
4	Andy Tod	2	1	186
5	Scott Morrison	4	0	262
6	Souleymane Bamba	6	1	270
7	Tom McManus	1	1	279
8	Gary Mason	12	0	312
9	Greg Ross	5	0	315
10	Scott Wilson	10	1	329
11	Stephen Simmons	7	0	349
12	Stevie Crawford	4	1	387
13	Callum Woods	2	0	391
	Other	21	0	
	TOTAL	**107**	**6**	

KEY GOALKEEPER

Dorus de Vries

Goals Conceded in the League	37	Counting Games League games when player was on pitch for at least 70 minutes	26
Defensive Rating Ave number of mins between League goals conceded while on the pitch	64	Clean Sheets In League games when player was on pitch for at least 70 minutes	7

KEY PLAYERS - DEFENDERS

Scott Wilson

Goals Conceded Number of League goals conceded while the player was on the pitch	36	Clean Sheets In League games when player was on pitch for at least 70 minutes	8
Defensive Rating Ave number of mins between League goals conceded while on the pitch	73	Club Defensive Rating Average number of mins between League goals conceded by the club this season	62

	PLAYER	CON LGE	CLEAN SHEETS	DEF RATE
1	Scott Wilson	36	8	73 mins
2	Philip McGuire	27	5	71 mins
3	Souleymane Bamba	28	5	67 mins
4	Greg Ross	25	4	63 mins

KEY PLAYERS - MIDFIELDERS

Stephen Glass

Goals in the League	3	Contribution to Attacking Power Average number of minutes between League team goals while on pitch	81
Defensive Rating Average number of mins between League goals conceded while on the pitch	89	Scoring Difference Defensive Rating minus Contribution to Attacking Power	8

	PLAYER	LGE GOALS	DEF RATE	POWER	SCORE DIFF
1	Stephen Glass	3	89	81	8 mins
2	Gary Mason	2	62	120	-58 mins
3	Scott Muirhead	0	73	133	-60 mins
4	Darren Young	2	57	177	-120 mins

KEY PLAYERS - GOALSCORERS

Stevie Crawford

Goals in the League	5	Player Strike Rate Average number of minutes between League goals scored by player	387
Contribution to Attacking Power Average number of minutes between League team goals while on pitch	161	Club Strike Rate Average number of mins between League goals scored by club	131

	PLAYER	LGE GOALS	POWER	STRIKE RATE
1	Stevie Crawford	5	161	387 mins
2	Jim Hamilton	2	163	816 mins
3	Stephen Simmons	2	218	872 mins
4	Darren Young	2	177	886 mins

Stevie Crawford

SQUAD APPEARANCES

Match	1 2 3 4 5	6 7 8 9 10	11 12 13 14 15	16 17 18 19 20	21 22 23 24 25	26 27 28 29 30	31 32 33 34 35	36 37 38 39 40	41 42 43 44 45	46
Venue	H A H A A	A H A H H	A A H A H	A H H A H	A H H A H	H A H A H	A H H A H	A A H A H	H A H A H	N
Competition	L L L L W	L W L L W	L L L L L	L L L L L	L L L L L	L L L L L	F L L L F	L L F L L	F L L L L	F
Result	L L D D W	L W L L W	L L L D L	L W L L L	D D L L L	W L L D W	L D W L D	W L W D W	W W W L L	L

Goalkeepers
Dorus de Vries
Roddy McKenzie
Defenders
Souleymane Bamba
Iain Campbell
Aaron Labonte
Philip McGuire
Scott Morrison
Greg Ross
Greg Shields
Andy Tod
Scott Wilson
Callum Woods
Midfielders
Stephen Glass
Adam Hamill
Gary Mason
Jamie McCunnie
Owen Morrison
Scott Muirhead
Stephen Simmons
Calum Smith
Iain Williamson
Darren Young
Forwards
Mark Burchill
Stevie Crawford
Frederic Daquin
Jim Hamilton
James McIntyre
Tom McManus
James O'Brien
Bobby Ryan
Craig Wilson

KEY: ■ On all match ◄◄ Subbed or sent off (Counting game) ►► Subbed on from bench (Counting Game) ►► Subbed on and then subbed or sent off (Counting Game) □ Not in 16
■ On bench ◄◄ Subbed or sent off (playing less than 70 minutes) ►► Subbed on (playing less than 70 minutes) ►► Subbed on and then subbed or sent off (playing less than 70 minutes)

SCOTTISH PREMIERSHIP - DUNFERMLINE

SPANISH LEAGUE ROUND-UP

FINAL LEAGUE TABLE

	P	W	D	L	F	A	W	D	L	F	A	F	A	DIF	PTS
			HOME					AWAY					TOTAL		
Real Madrid	38	12	4	3	32	18	11	3	5	34	22	66	40	26	76
Barcelona	38	14	5	0	41	12	8	5	6	37	21	78	33	45	76
Seville	38	15	2	2	41	13	6	6	7	23	22	64	35	29	71
Valencia	38	14	2	3	40	16	6	4	9	17	26	57	42	15	66
Villarreal	38	10	4	5	23	18	8	4	7	25	26	48	44	4	62
Real Zaragoza	38	12	5	2	33	16	4	7	8	22	27	55	43	12	60
Atletico Madrid	38	8	6	5	20	20	9	3	7	26	19	46	39	7	60
Recreativo	38	9	4	6	27	23	6	5	8	27	29	54	52	2	54
Getafe	38	9	7	3	21	11	5	3	11	18	22	39	33	6	52
R Santander	38	9	4	6	25	25	3	10	6	17	23	42	48	-6	50
Espanyol	38	7	6	6	26	27	5	7	7	20	26	46	53	-7	49
Mallorca	38	8	5	6	22	19	6	2	11	19	28	41	47	-6	49
Deportivo	38	9	4	6	19	16	3	7	9	13	29	32	45	-13	47
Osasuna	38	6	6	7	26	24	7	1	11	25	25	51	49	2	46
Levante	38	6	7	6	22	25	4	5	10	15	28	37	53	-16	42
Real Betis	38	4	9	6	17	22	4	7	8	19	27	36	49	-13	40
Athletic Bilbao	38	6	4	9	19	28	4	6	9	25	34	44	62	-18	40
Celta Vigo	38	4	5	10	21	31	6	3	10	19	28	40	59	-19	39
Real Sociedad	38	6	4	9	20	24	2	7	10	12	23	32	47	-15	35
Gimnastic	38	4	4	11	23	36	3	3	13	11	33	34	69	-35	28

CLUB STRIKE FORCE

Barcelona's Puyol and his team celebrate

1 Barcelona

Goals scored in the League	78
Club Strike Rate (CSR) Average number of minutes between League goals scored by club	43

	CLUB	GOALS	CSR
1	Barcelona	78	43
2	Real Madrid	66	51
3	Seville	64	53
4	Valencia	57	60
5	Real Zaragoza	55	62
6	Recreativo Huelva	54	63
7	Osasuna	51	67
8	Villarreal	48	71
9	Atl Madrid	46	74
10	Espanyol	46	74
11	Athl Bilbao	44	77
12	R Santander	42	81
13	Mallorca	41	83
14	Celta Vigo	40	85
15	Getafe	39	87
16	Levante	37	92
17	Real Betis	36	95
18	Gimnastic	34	100
19	Deportivo	32	106
20	Real Sociedad	32	106

CLUB DISCIPLINARY RECORDS

Madrid's Ramos disagrees with the referee

1 Real Madrid

League Yellow	117
League Red	11
League Total	128
Cards Average in League Average number of minutes between a card being shown of either colour	26

	CLUB	Y	R	TOTAL	AVE
1	Real Madrid	117	11	128	26
2	Deportivo	115	11	126	27
3	Atl Madrid	114	10	124	27
4	R Santander	114	9	123	27
5	Levante	112	13	125	27
6	Osasuna	112	6	118	28
7	Real Zaragoza	110	8	118	28
8	Espanyol	104	9	113	30
9	Celta Vigo	101	11	112	30
10	Seville	96	11	107	31
11	Valencia	101	9	110	31
12	Real Betis	95	11	106	32
13	Villarreal	95	5	100	34
14	Getafe	92	6	98	34
15	Mallorca	90	7	97	35
16	Athl Bilbao	89	8	97	35
17	Real Sociedad	90	5	95	36
18	Gimnastic	88	7	95	36
19	Barcelona	80	7	87	39
20	Recreativo Huelva	61	3	64	53

CLUB DEFENCES

Barcelona's French defender Lilian Thuram

1 Barcelona

Goals conceded in the League	33
Clean Sheets (CS) Number of league games where no goals were conceded	15
Club Defensive Rate (CDR) Average number of minutes between League goals conceded by club	103

	CLUB	LGE	CS	CDR
1	Barcelona	33	15	103
2	Getafe	33	15	103
3	Seville	35	14	97
4	Atl Madrid	39	13	87
5	Real Madrid	40	11	85
6	Valencia	42	14	81
7	Real Zaragoza	43	13	79
8	Villarreal	44	13	77
9	Deportivo	45	16	76
10	Real Sociedad	47	9	72
11	Mallorca	47	12	72
12	R Santander	48	13	71
13	Real Betis	49	10	69
14	Osasuna	49	9	69
15	Recreativo Huelva	52	11	65
16	Espanyol	53	9	64
17	Levante	53	11	64
18	Celta Vigo	59	5	57
19	Athl Bilbao	62	11	55
20	Gimnastic	69	8	49

PLAYER NATIONALITIES

Overseas country with the most player appearances in the Spanish League - Argentina

746 league appearances by Argentinian players

	COUNTRY	PLAYERS	IN SQUAD	LGE APP	% LGE ACT	CAPS	MOST APP	APP
1	Spain	292	7652	5799	55.53	117	Cesar Sanchez	100.0
2	Argentina	33	923	746	7.45	30	Gabriel Milito	96.2
3	Brazil	33	783	671	6.49	23	Daniel Alves	88.2
4	France	17	412	328	3.09	12	Peter Luccin	77.9
5	Portugal	14	342	263	2.46	27	J C Araujo Nunes	91.4
6	Uruguay	11	290	229	2.1	4	Diego Forlan	88.1
7	Italy	9	208	170	1.59	16	Fabio Cannavaro	82.4
8	Serbia	4	110	96	0.89	5	Darko Kovacevic	71.3
9	Cameroon	4	98	91	0.82	0	Carlos Kameni	94.7
10	Mali	2	68	65	0.7	0	Mahamadou Diarra	77.8
11	Holland	3	83	63	0.66	7	Ruud van Nistelrooy	93
12	Switzerland	3	69	61	0.62	4	Fabio Celestini	88.9
13	Greece	2	68	60	0.59	0	Giorgios Seitaridis	74.2
14	Israel	1	38	38	0.45	0	Dudu Aouate	100
15	Denmark	3	56	49	0.44	16	Christian Poulsen	72.1
16	Venezuela	1	37	37	0.39	0	Juan Arango	85.1
17	Chile	1	32	30	0.34	0	P A Fica Contreras	74.8
18	Ghana	1	34	33	0.33	0	R Mustapha Riga	72.1
19	Ivory Coast	1	35	34	0.3	0	Felix Dja Ettien	66.4
20	Colombia	1	33	25	0.27	1	Luis Perea	58.9

CLUB MAKE-UP – HOME AND OVERSEAS PLAYERS

1 Villarreal

76.7% of appearances by overseas players

	CLUB	OVERSEAS	HOME	% OVERSEAS	% LGE ACT	MOST APP	APP
1	Villarreal	23	7	76.7	69.84	Diego Forlan	88.1
2	Celta Vigo	25	11	69.4	67.03	Diego Placente	87.8
3	Atl Madrid	25	8	75.8	65.26	Leonardo Franco	82.9
4	Barcelona	17	7	70.8	63.97	Ronaldinho	81.4
5	Levante	21	9	70	61.75	Olivier Kapo	73.1
6	Gimnastic	20	12	62.5	58	Anibal Matellan	64.6
7	Real Madrid	19	14	57.6	56.3	Ruud v Nistelrooy	93
8	Seville	17	13	56.7	55.33	Daniel Alves	88.2
9	Recreativo Huelva	17	13	56.7	52.43	Jésus Vásquez	90.6
10	Mallorca	13	12	52	50.42	J C Araujo Nunes	91.4
11	Real Zaragoza	17	13	56.7	46.56	Gabriel Milito	96.2
12	Deportivo	18	15	54.5	45.61	Dudu Aouate	100
13	Real Betis	16	18	47.1	38.08	L E Schmidt Edu	66.3
14	Valencia	19	18	51.4	33.16	Roberto Ayala	76.3
15	Getafe	9	16	36	31.98	R Abbondanzieri	94
16	R Santander	12	21	36.4	28.64	Nicola Zigic	81.8
17	Real Sociedad	11	20	35.5	26.63	Claudio Bravo	90.6
18	Osasuna	16	18	47.1	26.25	Valmiro Valdo	55.1
19	Espanyol	13	23	36.1	22.41	Carlos Kameni	94.7
20	Athl Bilbao	4	24	14.3	10.47	Josu Sarriegi	94.6

CHART-TOPPING MIDFIELDERS

1 Edmilson - Barcelona	
Goals scored in the League	0
Defensive Rating Av number of mins between League goals conceded while on the pitch	120
Contribution to Attacking Power Average number of minutes between League team goals while on pitch	47
Scoring Difference Defensive Rating minus Contribution to Attacking Power	73

	PLAYER	CLUB	GOALS	DEF RATE	POWER	S DIFF
1	Moraes Edmilson	Barcelona	0	120	47	73
2	Deco	Barcelona	1	112	44	68
3	Xavi Hernandez	Barcelona	3	106	44	62
4	Antonio Puerta	Seville	2	107	49	58
5	Mahamadou Diarra	Real Madrid	3	95	43	52
6	Lionel Messi	Barcelona	14	95	45	50
7	Christian Poulsen	Seville	1	94	48	46
8	Jesus Navas	Seville	1	99	54	45
9	Andres Iniesta	Barcelona	6	89	46	43
10	Francisco Casquero	Getafe	5	111	79	32
11	Dirnei Renato	Seville	5	88	56	32
12	David Silva	Valencia	4	91	60	31
13	Emerson F da Rosa	Real Madrid	1	85	55	30
14	David Albelda	Valencia	0	80	50	30
15	Maniche	Atl Madrid	4	88	61	27

CHART-TOPPING GOALSCORERS

1 Kanoute - Seville	
Goals scored in the League	22
Contribution to Attacking Power (AP) Average number of minutes between League team goals while on pitch	48
Club Strike Rate (CSR) Average minutes between League goals scored by club	53
Player Strike Rate Average number of minutes between League goals scored by player	117

	PLAYER	CLUB	GOALS: LGE	POWER	CSR	S RATE
1	Frederic Kanoute	Seville	22	48	53	117
2	Ruud van Nistelrooy	Real Madrid	25	52	51	127
3	Ronaldinho	Barcelona	21	40	43	130
4	Diego Milito	Real Zaragoza	23	62	62	136
5	Lionel Messi	Barcelona	14	45	43	142
6	Diego Forlan	Villarreal	19	68	71	158
7	Raul Tamudo	Espanyol	15	70	74	159
8	Roberto Soldado	Osasuna	11	59	67	161
9	Daniel Gonzalez Guiza	Getafe	11	70	87	173
10	David Villa	Valencia	15	55	60	195
11	Fernando Baiano	Celta Vigo	15	78	85	199
12	Fernando Torres	Atl Madrid	15	79	74	205
13	Javier Portillo	Gimnastic	11	99	100	244
14	Luis Garcia	Espanyol	10	73	74	265
15	Aritz Aduriz	Athl Bilbao	9	85	77	266

CHART-TOPPING DEFENDERS

1 Alexis - Getafe	
Goals Conceded in the League The number of League goals conceded while he was on the pitch	13
Clean Sheets In games when he played at least 70 mins	13
Club Defensive Rating Average mins between League goals conceded by the club this season	103
Defensive Rating Average number of minutes between League goals conceded while on pitch	162

	PLAYER	CLUB	CON: LGE	CS	CDR	DEF RATE
1	Ruano Alexis	Getafe	13	13	103	162
2	Lilian Thuram	Barcelona	15	12	103	130
3	Gio Van Bronckhorst	Barcelona	17	6	103	104
4	David Belenguer	Getafe	29	15	103	103
5	Gianluca Zambrotta	Barcelona	23	11	103	101
6	Carlos Puyol	Barcelona	30	12	103	101
7	Javier Arango Paredes	Getafe	31	13	103	98
8	Jose S Dias Enrique	Villarreal	21	9	77	98
9	Luis Perea	Atl Madrid	21	6	87	95
10	I Gorostola Ansotegi	Real Sociedad	18	7	72	95
11	Julien Escude	Seville	27	11	97	95
12	Daniel Alves	Seville	32	12	97	94
13	Ivan Helguera	Real Madrid	21	6	85	93
14	Javi Navarro	Seville	23	7	97	93
15	Pablo Ibanez	Atl Madrid	23	8	87	91

CHART-TOPPING GOALKEEPERS

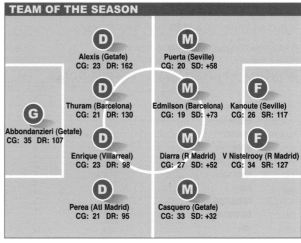

1 Abbondanzieri - Getafe	
Counting Games Games in which he played at least 70 minutes	35
Goals Conceded in the League The number of League goals conceded while he was on the pitch	30
Clean Sheets In games when he played at least 70 mins	14
Defensive Rating Average number of minutes between League goals conceded while on pitch	107

	PLAYER	CLUB	CG	CONC	CS	DEF RATE
1	Roberto Abbondanzieri	Getafe	35	30	14	107
2	Victor Valdes	Barcelona	38	33	15	103
3	Leonardo Franco	Atl Madrid	31	28	11	101
4	Sebastian Viera	Villarreal	27	25	11	99
5	Andres Palop	Seville	33	32	11	94
6	Claudio Bravo	Real Sociedad	28	27	8	93
7	Antonio Doblas	Real Betis	22	23	7	86
8	Iker Casillas	Real Madrid	38	40	11	85
9	Santiago Canizares	Valencia	31	33	12	84
10	Cesar Sanchez	Real Zaragoza	38	43	13	79
11	Francisco Molina	Levante	32	37	10	77
12	Dudu Aouate	Deportivo	38	45	16	76
13	Javier Lopez Vallejo	Recreativo Huelva	30	36	11	76
14	A Rodriguez Tono	R Santander	32	39	11	74
15	Lopez Ricardo	Osasuna	35	45	8	70

PLAYER DISCIPLINARY RECORD

Celta Vigo's Garcia gets stuck in

1. Pablo Garcia - Celta Vigo	
Cards Average mins between cards	89
League Yellow	9
League Red	2
TOTAL	11

	PLAYER		LY	LR	TOT	AVE
1	Garcia	Celta Vigo	9	2	11	89
2	Beckham	Real Madrid	12	1	13	108
3	Tacchinardi	Villarreal	10	0	10	110
4	Salgado	Real Madrid	9	0	9	137
5	Marti	Seville	10	1	11	143
6	Luccin	Atl Madrid	15	3	18	145
7	Diogo	Real Zaragoza	16	2	18	147
8	Murillo	Athl Bilbao	16	1	17	162
9	Pernia	Atl Madrid	9	0	9	162
10	Melo	R Santander	5	1	6	162
11	Pinilla	Gimnastic	10	0	10	164
12	Deco	Barcelona	14	1	15	165
13	Gago	Real Madrid	6	0	6	166
14	Tamas	Celta Vigo	11	2	13	167
15	Contra	Getafe	9	1	10	167

TEAM OF THE SEASON

D — Alexis (Getafe) CG: 23 DR: 162

M — Puerta (Seville) CG: 20 SD: +58

D — Thuram (Barcelona) CG: 21 DR: 130

M — Edmilson (Barcelona) CG: 19 SD: +73

F — Kanoute (Seville) CG: 26 SR: 117

G — Abbondanzieri (Getafe) CG: 35 DR: 107

D — Enrique (Villarreal) CG: 23 DR: 98

M — Diarra (R Madrid) CG: 27 SD: +52

F — V Nistelrooy (R Madrid) CG: 34 SR: 127

D — Perea (Atl Madrid) CG: 21 DR: 95

M — Casquero (Getafe) CG: 33 SD: +32

REAL MADRID

Final Position: 1st

NICKNAME: LOS BLANCOS KEY: ☐ Won ☐ Drawn ☐ Lost Attendance

				Score	Scorers	Attendance
1	sppr1	Villarreal	H D	0-0		65,000
2	sppr1	Levante	A W	4-1	van Nistelrooy 16, 56, 90, Cassano 26	18,677
3	ecgpe	Lyon	A L	0-2		40,013
4	sppr1	Real Sociedad	H W	2-0	Reyes 70, Beckham 90	71,500
5	sppr1	Real Betis	A W	1-0	Diarra 6	45,000
6	ecgpe	Dinamo Kiev	H W	5-1	van Nistelrooy 19, 70 pen, Raul 27, 61, Reyes 45	70,000
7	sppr1	Atl Madrid	H D	1-1	Raul 37	75,000
8	sppr1	Getafe	A L	0-1		17,000
9	ecgpe	St Bucharest	A W	4-1	Sergio Ramos 9, Raul 34, Robinho 56, van Nistelrooy 76	20,000
10	sppr1	Barcelona	H W	2-0	Raul 3, van Nistelrooy 51	75,000
11	sppr1	Gimnastic	A W	3-1	Roberto Carlos 44, Helguera 50, Robinho 85	14,000
12	ecgpe	St Bucharest	H W	1-0	Nicolita 70 og	69,000
13	sppr1	Celta Vigo	H L	1-2	Emerson 43	77,088
14	sppr1	Osasuna	A W	4-1	van Nistelrooy 12, 27, 45, 84	19,000
15	sppr1	R Santander	H W	3-1	Sergio Ramos 5, Reyes 58, Diarra 71	75,000
16	ecgpe	Lyon	H D	2-2	Diarra 39, van Nistelrooy 83	78,677
17	sppr1	Valencia	A W	1-0	Raul 52	50,000
18	sppr1	Athl Bilbao	H W	2-1	Ronaldo 65, Roberto Carlos 82	78,000
19	ecgpe	Dinamo Kiev	A D	2-2	Ronaldo 86, 88 pen	33,000
20	sppr1	Seville	A L	1-2	Beckham 13	45,000
21	sppr1	Espanyol	A W	1-0	van Nistelrooy 50	25,000
22	sppr1	Recreativo H	H L	0-3		50,000
23	sppr1	Deportivo	A L	0-2		32,000
24	sppr1	Real Zaragoza	H W	1-0	van Nistelrooy 41	69,000
25	sppr1	Mallorca	A W	1-0	Reyes 78	25,000
26	sppr1	Villarreal	A L	0-1		20,000
27	sppr1	Levante	H L	0-1		65,000
28	sppr1	Real Sociedad	A W	2-1	Beckham 37 , van Nistelrooy 49	23,000
29	sppr1	Real Betis	H D	0-0		70,000
30	eckl1	Bayern Munich	H W	3-2	Raul 10, 28, van Nistelrooy 34	80,000
31	sppr1	Atl Madrid	A D	1-1	Higuain 62	56,000
32	sppr1	Getafe	H D	1-1	van Nistelrooy 45 pen	65,000
33	eckl2	Bayern Munich	A L	1-2	van Nistelrooy 83 pen	66,000
34	sppr1	Barcelona	A D	3-3	van Nistelrooy 5, 13 pen, Sergio Ramos 73	90,000
35	sppr1	Gimnastic	H W	2-0	Robinho 55, David Garcia 80 og	70,000
36	sppr1	Celta Vigo	A W	2-1	van Nistelrooy 27 pen, Robinho 83	22,000
37	sppr1	Osasuna	H W	2-0	Raul 24, Robinho 80	72,270
38	sppr1	R Santander	A L	1-2	Raul 33	19,000
39	sppr1	Valencia	H W	2-1	van Nistelrooy 18, Sergio Ramos 73	75,000
40	sppr1	Athl Bilbao	A W	4-1	Sergio Ramos 13, van Nistelrooy 34, 50, Guti 84	39,000
41	sppr1	Seville	H W	3-2	van Nistelrooy 63, 85, Robinho 78	80,300
42	sppr1	Espanyol	H W	4-3	van Nistelrooy 30, Raul 49, Reyes 57, Higuain 88	75,000
43	sppr1	Recreativo H	A W	3-2	Robinho 9, van Nistelrooy 54 pen, Roberto Carlos 90	20,092
44	sppr1	Deportivo	H W	3-1	Sergio Ramos 28, Raul 57, van Nistelrooy 75	75,000
45	sppr1	Real Zaragoza	A D	2-2	van Nistelrooy 57, 88	34,500
46	sppr1	Mallorca	H W	3-1	Reyes 68, 83, Diarra 80	80,000

LEAGUE APPEARANCES, BOOKINGS AND CAPS

	AGE (on 01/07/07)	IN NAMED 18	APPEARANCES	COUNTING GAMES	MINUTES ON PITCH	YELLOW CARDS	RED CARDS	CAPS THIS SEASON	NATIONAL SIDE
Goalkeepers									
Iker Casillas	26	38	38	38	3420	1	0	8	Spain
Diego Lopez	25	37	0	0	0	0	0	-	Spain
Defenders									
Fabio Cannavaro	33	33	32	30	2775	13	2	8	Italy
Cicinho	27	18	7	3	363	0	0	3	Brazil
Ivan Helguera	32	28	23	21	1963	6	1	-	Spain
V da Silva J Marcelo	19	11	6	1	176	0	0	1	Brazil
Alvaro Mejia	25	29	9	3	429	2	1	-	Spain
Raul Bravo	26	18	8	3	439	0	0	-	Spain
Roberto Carlos	34	25	23	21	1955	5	0	-	Brazil
Michel Salgado	31	24	16	12	1240	9	0	2	Spain
Sergio Ramos	26	33	33	31	2893	15	2	10	Spain
Miguel Torres	21	18	18	15	1476	3	0	-	-
Midfielders									
Julio Baptista	25	1	0	0	0	0	0	3	Brazil
David Beckham	32	23	22	12	1410	12	1	2	England
Ruben De la Red	22	10	7	0	144	1	0	-	Spain
Mahamadou Diarra	26	33	33	27	2661	12	0	-	Mali
Emerson F da Rosa	31	33	28	21	2210	3	0	-	Brazil
Fernando Gago	21	18	13	9	999	6	0	2	Argentina
Jose Maria Guti	30	31	30	19	1896	9	2	-	Spain
Jose Antonio Reyes	23	32	30	5	1269	3	0	1	Spain
Forwards									
Antonio Cassano	24	20	7	1	349	3	0	2	Italy
Gonzalo Higuain	19	20	19	12	1261	1	0	-	Argentina
Miguel Nieto	21	4	2	0	29	0	0	-	Spain
Gonzalez Raul	30	35	35	26	2709	2	0	3	Spain
R de Souza Robinho	23	36	32	16	1959	3	1	9	Brazil
Ronaldo	30	9	6	1	321	1	1	-	Brazil
Ruud van Nistelrooy	31	37	37	34	3179	5	0	-	Holland

TEAM OF THE SEASON

Position	Player	Stats
G	Iker Casillas	CG: 38 DR: 85
D	Miguel Torres	CG: 15 DR: 98
D	Ivan Helguera	CG: 21 DR: 93
D	Fabio Cannavaro	CG: 30 DR: 89
D	Roberto Carlos	CG: 21 DR: 81
M	Mahamadou Diarra	CG: 27 SD: 52
M	Emerson F da Rosa	CG: 21 SD: 30
M	Jose Maria Guti	CG: 19 SD: 22
M	David Beckham	CG: 12 SD: 18
F	Ruud van Nistelrooy	CG: 34 SR: 127
F	R de S Robinho	CG: 16 SR: 326

MONTHLY POINTS TALLY

Month	Points	%
AUGUST	1	33%
SEPTEMBER	9	100%
OCTOBER	7	58%
NOVEMBER	9	75%
DECEMBER	6	50%
JANUARY	6	50%
FEBRUARY	5	42%
MARCH	5	56%
APRIL	12	80%
MAY	12	100%
JUNE	4	67%

LEAGUE GOALS

	PLAYER	MINS	GOALS	S RATE
1	van Nistelrooy	3179	25	127
2	Raul	2709	7	387
3	Reyes	1269	6	211
4	Robinho	1959	6	326
5	Sergio Ramos	2623	5	524
6	Roberto Carlos	1955	3	651
7	Diarra	2661	3	887
8	Higuain	1261	2	630
9	Beckham	1410	2	705
10	Ronaldo	321	1	321
11	Cassano	349	1	349
12	Guti	1896	1	1896
13	Helguera	1963	1	1963
	Other		1	
	TOTAL		**64**	

TOP POINT EARNERS

	PLAYER	GAMES	AV PTS
1	R de Souza Robinho	16	2.50
2	Mahamadou Diarra	27	2.37
3	Michel Salgado	12	2.25
4	Sergio Ramos	29	2.10
5	Fabio Cannavaro	31	2.10
6	Gonzalez Raul	26	2.08
7	Miguel Torres	15	2.07
8	Roberto Carlos	21	2.05
9	Ruud van Nistelrooy	34	2.03
10	Iker Casillas	38	2.00
	CLUB AVERAGE:		**2.00**

DISCIPLINARY RECORDS

	PLAYER	YELLOW	RED	AVE
1	David Beckham	12	1	108
2	Michel Salgado	9	0	137
3	Fernando Gago	6	0	166
4	Jose Maria Guti	10	2	172
5	Sergio Ramos	16	2	174
6	Fabio Cannavaro	15	2	185
7	Maham Diarra	14	1	221
8	Ivan Helguera	6	1	280
9	Roberto Carlos	7	0	391
10	J Antonio Reyes	3	0	423
11	R de S Robinho	3	1	489
12	Miguel Torres	3	0	492
13	Ruud v Nistelrooy	5	0	635
	Other	8	0	
	TOTAL	**117**	**10**	

KEY GOALKEEPER

Iker Casillas

Goals Conceded in the League	40	Counting Games League games when player was on pitch for at least 70 minutes	38
Defensive Rating Ave number of mins between League goals conceded while on the pitch	85	Clean Sheets In League games when player was on pitch for at least 70 minutes	11

KEY PLAYERS - DEFENDERS

Miguel Torres

Goals Conceded Number of League goals conceded while the player was on the pitch	15	Clean Sheets In League games when player was on pitch for at least 70 minutes	4
Defensive Rating Ave number of mins between League goals conceded while on the pitch	98	Club Defensive Rating Average number of mins between League goals conceded by the club this season	85

	PLAYER	CON LGE	CLEAN SHEETS	DEF RATE
1	Miguel Torres	15	4	98 mins
2	Ivan Helguera	21	6	93 mins
3	Fabio Cannavaro	31	10	89 mins
4	Roberto Carlos	24	5	81 mins

KEY PLAYERS - MIDFIELDERS

Mahamadou Diarra

Goals in the League	3	Contribution to Attacking Power Average number of minutes between League team goals while on pitch	43
Defensive Rating Average number of mins between League goals conceded while on the pitch	95	Scoring Difference Defensive Rating minus Contribution to Attacking Power	52

	PLAYER	LGE GOALS	DEF RATE	POWER	SCORE DIFF
1	Mahamadou Diarra	3	95	43	52 mins
2	Emerson Ferreira da Rosa	1	85	55	30 mins
3	Jose Maria Guti	1	70	48	22 mins
4	David Beckham	2	70	52	18 mins

KEY PLAYERS - GOALSCORERS

Ruud van Nistelrooy

Goals in the League	25	Player Strike Rate Average number of minutes between League goals scored by player	127
Contribution to Attacking Power Average number of minutes between League team goals while on pitch	52	Club Strike Rate Average number of minutes between League goals scored by club	51

	PLAYER	LGE GOALS	POWER	STRIKE RATE
1	Ruud van Nistelrooy	25	52	127 mins
2	Robson de Souza Robinho	6	44	326 mins
3	Gonzalez Raul	7	52	387 mins
4	Gonzalo Higuain	2	50	630 mins

Ruud van Nistelrooy

SQUAD APPEARANCES

Match	1 2 3 4 5	6 7 8 9 10	11 12 13 14 15	16 17 18 19 20	21 22 23 24 25	26 27 28 29 30	31 32 33 34 35	36 37 38 39 40	41 42 43 44 45	46
Venue	H A A H A	H H A A H	A H H A H	H A H A A	A H A H A	A H A H H	A H A A H	A H A A H	H H A H A	H
Competition	L L C L L	C L L C L	L C L L L	C L L C L	L L L L L	L L L L C	L L C L L	L L L L L	L L L L L	L
Result	D W L W W	W D L W W	W W L W W	D W W W D L	W L L W W	L L W D W	D D L D W	W W L W W	W W W W D	W

Goalkeepers
Iker Casillas
Diego Lopez

Defenders
Fabio Cannavaro
Cicinho
Ivan Helguera
da Silva J Marcelo
Alvaro Mejia
Raul Bravo
Roberto Carlos
Michel Salgado
Sergio Ramos
Miguel Torres

Midfielders
Julio Baptista
David Beckham
Ruben De la Red
Mahamadou Diarra
Emerson F da Rosa
Fernando Gago
Jose Maria Guti
Jose Antonio Reyes

Forwards
Antonio Cassano
Gonzalo Higuain
Miguel Nieto
Gonzalez Raul
de Souza Robinho
Ronaldo
Ruud van Nistelrooy

KEY: ■ On all match | ▐◀ Subbed or sent off (Counting game) | ▶▷ Subbed on from bench (Counting Game) | ◢ Subbed on and then subbed or sent off (Counting Game) | □ Not in 16
■ On bench | ◀◀ Subbed or sent off (playing less than 70 minutes) | ▶▶ Subbed on (playing less than 70 minutes) | ▷▷ Subbed on and then subbed or sent off (playing less than 70 minutes)

SPAIN - REAL MADRID

BARCELONA

Final Position: 2nd

NICKNAME: BARCA KEY: ☐ Won ☐ Drawn ☐ Lost Attendance

#	Comp	Opponent	H/A	Result	Scorers	Attendance
1	escup	Seville	H L	0-3		18,000
2	sppr1	Celta Vigo	A W	3-2	Eto'o 55, Messi 60, Gudjohnsen 88	25,000
3	sppr1	Osasuna	H W	3-0	Eto'o 1, 27, Messi 37	63,720
4	ecgpa	Levski Sofia	H W	5-0	Iniesta 7, Giuly 39, Puyol 49, Eto'o 58, Ronaldinho 90	91,326
5	sppr1	R Santander	A W	3-0	Eto'o 18, Giuly 83, Ronaldinho 90 pen	19,241
6	sppr1	Valencia	H D	1-1	Iniesta 49	75,000
7	ecgpa	W Bremen	A D	1-1	Messi 89	41,256
8	sppr1	Athl Bilbao	A W	3-1	Ustaritz 45, Gudjohnsen 61, Saviola 77	39,000
9	sppr1	Seville	H W	3-1	Ronaldinho 28, 39, Messi 80	91,220
10	ecgpa	Chelsea	A L	0-1		45,999
11	sppr1	Real Madrid	A L	0-2		75,000
12	sppr1	Recreativo H	H W	3-0	Ronaldinho 28 pen, 57, Xavi 60	65,000
13	ecgpa	Chelsea	H D	2-2	Deco 3, Gudjohnsen 58	98,000
14	sppr1	Deportivo	A D	1-1	Ronaldinho 40 pen	34,000
15	sppr1	Real Zaragoza	H W	3-1	Ronaldinho 31, 86, Saviola 90	80,000
16	sppr1	Mallorca	A W	4-1	Gudjohnsen 43, 57, Iniesta 86, Ezquerro 90	20,000
17	ecgpa	Levski Sofia	A W	2-0	Giuly 5, Iniesta 65	43,340
18	sppr1	Villarreal	H W	4-0	Ronaldinho 35 pen, 88, Gudjohnsen 56, Iniesta 70	75,000
19	sppr1	Levante	A D	1-1	Deco 41	18,000
20	ecgpa	W Bremen	H W	2-0	Ronaldinho 13, Gudjohnsen 18	98,787
21	sppr1	Real Sociedad	H W	1-0	Ronaldinho 61	75,000
22	sppr1	Atl Madrid	H D	1-1	Ronaldinho 41	53,685
23	sppr1	Getafe	A D	1-1	Xavi 69	17,000
24	sppr1	Espanyol	A L	1-3	Saviola 60	31,450
25	sppr1	Gimnastic	H W	3-0	Saviola 18, Giuly 68, Iniesta 81	60,000
26	sppr1	Real Betis	A D	1-1	Marquez 61	40,000
27	sppr1	Celta Vigo	H W	3-1	Saviola 34, Ronaldinho 78 pen, Giuly 86	65,000
28	sppr1	Osasuna	A D	0-0		18,000
29	sppr1	R Santander	H W	2-0	Ronaldinho 51, 67	70,000
30	sppr1	Valencia	A L	1-2	Ronaldinho 90	50,000
31	eckl1	Liverpool	H L	1-2	Deco 14	88,000
32	sppr1	Athl Bilbao	H W	3-0	Amorebieta 23 og, Xavi 30, Eto'o 41	68,000
33	sppr1	Seville	A L	1-2	Ronaldinho 14	45,500
34	eckl2	Liverpool	A W	1-0	Gudjohnsen 75	45,000
35	sppr1	Real Madrid	H D	3-3	Messi 11, 28, 90	90,000
36	sppr1	Recreativo H	A W	4-0	Eto'o 3, 41, Zambrotta 38, Messi 86	20,000
37	sppr1	Deportivo	H W	2-1	Messi 45, Eto'o 51	70,000
38	sppr1	Real Zaragoza	A L	0-1		34,100
39	sppr1	Mallorca	H W	1-0	Navarro 89 og	70,441
40	sppr1	Villarreal	A L	0-2		23,000
41	sppr1	Levante	H W	1-0	Eto'o 28	70,000
42	sppr1	Real Sociedad	A W	2-0	Iniesta 47, Eto'o 88	29,777
43	sppr1	Real Betis	H D	1-1	Ronaldinho 5 pen	77,747
44	sppr1	Atl Madrid	A W	6-0	Messi 39, 80, Zambrotta 43, Eto'o 45, Ronaldinho 58, Iniesta 90	55,000
45	sppr1	Getafe	H W	1-0	Ronaldinho 2	90,000
46	sppr1	Espanyol	H D	2-2	Messi 43, 57	90,695
47	sppr1	Gimnastic	A W	5-1	Puyol 20, Messi 35, 51, Ronaldinho 38, Zambrotta 90	14,000

LEAGUE APPEARANCES, BOOKINGS AND CAPS

	AGE (on 01/07/07)	IN NAMED 18	APPEARANCES	COUNTING GAMES	MINUTES ON PITCH	YELLOW CARDS	RED CARDS	CAPS THIS SEASON	NATIONAL SIDE
Goalkeepers									
Albert Jorquera	28	36	0	0	0	0	0	-	Spain
Victor Valdes	25	38	38	38	3420	2	0	-	Spain
Defenders									
Juliano Belletti	31	26	13	7	798	2	0	-	Brazil
Rafael Marquez	28	24	21	19	1724	9	0	2	Mexico
Presas Oleguer	27	33	25	10	1228	3	1	-	Spain
Jesus Olmo	22	2	1	0	2	0	0	-	Spain
Carlos Puyol	29	36	35	32	3030	3	0	6	Spain
Sylvinho	33	25	13	11	977	1	1	-	Brazil
Lilian Thuram	35	29	23	21	1959	2	0	9	France
Gio Van Bronckhorst	32	34	23	18	1776	3	0	7	Holland
Gianluca Zambrotta	30	31	29	24	2323	9	1	6	Italy
Midfielders									
Deco	29	32	31	22	2479	14	1	7	Portugal
J G Moraes Edmilson	30	33	26	19	1813	5	0	6	Brazil
Ludovic Giuly	30	36	27	10	1468	0	1	-	France
Andres Iniesta	23	38	37	27	2696	3	0	9	Spain
Lionel Messi	20	26	26	21	1999	2	0	3	Argentina
Thiago Motta	24	26	14	4	546	3	1	-	Brazil
Xavi Hernandez	27	37	35	31	2864	3	0	7	Spain
Forwards									
Samuel Eto'o	26	20	19	15	1477	5	0	2	Cameroon
Santiago Ezquerro	30	23	9	1	269	0	0	-	Spain
Eidur Gudjohnsen	28	35	25	9	1173	1	0	6	Iceland
Ronaldinho	27	32	32	30	2733	8	1	7	Brazil
Javier Saviola	25	26	18	1	671	2	0	3	Argentina

TEAM OF THE SEASON

- **D** Lilian Thuram CG: 21 DR: 130
- **M** Deco CG: 22 SD: 68
- **D** Carlos Puyol CG: 32 DR: 101
- **M** Xavi Hernandez CG: 31 SD: 62
- **F** Ronaldinho CG: 30 SR: 130
- **G** Victor Valdes CG: 38 DR: 103
- **D** Gianluca Zambrotta CG: 24 DR: 101
- **M** Lionel Messi CG: 21 SD: 50
- **F** Samuel Eto'o CG: 15 SR: 134
- **D** Gio Van Bronckhorst CG: 18 DR: 104
- **M** J G Moraes Edmilson CG: 19 SD: 73

MONTHLY POINTS TALLY

Month	Points	%
AUGUST	3	100%
SEPTEMBER	10	83%
OCTOBER	6	67%
NOVEMBER	10	83%
DECEMBER	5	56%
JANUARY	8	53%
FEBRUARY	7	58%
MARCH	7	58%
APRIL	6	50%
MAY	10	83%
JUNE	4	67%

LEAGUE GOALS

	PLAYER	MINS	GOALS	S RATE
1	Ronaldinho	2733	21	130
2	Messi	1999	14	142
3	Eto'o	1477	11	134
4	Iniesta	2696	6	449
5	Saviola	671	5	134
6	Gudjohnsen	1173	5	234
7	Giuly	1468	3	489
8	Zambrotta	2323	3	774
9	Xavi	2864	3	954
10	Ezquerro	269	1	269
11	Marquez	1724	1	1724
12	Deco	2479	1	2479
13	Puyol	3030	1	3030
	Other		0	
	TOTAL		75	

TOP POINT EARNERS

	PLAYER	GAMES	AV PTS
1	Samuel Eto'o	15	2.40
2	J Gomes M Edmilson	19	2.26
3	Gio Van Bronckhorst	18	2.22
4	Gianluca Zambrotta	24	2.17
5	Ronaldinho	31	2.10
6	Lilian Thuram	21	2.10
7	Victor Valdes	38	2.00
8	Lionel Messi	21	1.95
9	Xavi Hernandez	31	1.90
10	Rafael Marquez	19	1.89
	CLUB AVERAGE:		2.00

DISCIPLINARY RECORDS

	PLAYER	YELLOW	RED	AVE
1	Thiago Motta	5	1	136
2	Deco	15	1	165
3	Rafael Marquez	9	0	191
4	Gia Zambrotta	10	1	232
5	Samuel Eto'o	5	0	295
6	Ronaldinho	8	1	303
7	Presas Oleguer	3	1	307
8	Javier Saviola	2	0	335
9	J G M Edmilson	6	0	362
10	Juliano Belletti	3	0	399
11	Sylvinho	2	1	488
12	Gio V Bronckhorst	4	0	592
13	Andres Iniesta	3	0	898
	Other	18	1	
	TOTAL	93	7	

KEY GOALKEEPER

Victor Valdes

Goals Conceded in the League	33	Counting Games League games when player was on pitch for at least 70 minutes	38
Defensive Rating Ave number of mins between League goals conceded while on the pitch	103	Clean Sheets In games when player was on pitch for at least 70 minutes	15

KEY PLAYERS - DEFENDERS

Lilian Thuram

Goals Conceded Number of League goals conceded while the player was on the pitch	15	Clean Sheets In League games when player was on pitch for at least 70 minutes	12
Defensive Rating Ave number of mins between League goals conceded while on the pitch	130	Club Defensive Rating Average number of mins between League goals conceded by the club this season	103

	PLAYER	CON LGE	CLEAN SHEETS	DEF RATE
1	Lilian Thuram	15	12	130 mins
2	Giovanni Van Bronckhorst	17	6	104 mins
3	Gianluca Zambrotta	23	11	101 mins
4	Carlos Puyol	30	12	101 mins

KEY PLAYERS - MIDFIELDERS

Jose Gomes Moraes Edmilson

Goals in the League	0	Contribution to Attacking Power Average number of minutes between League team goals while on pitch	47
Defensive Rating Average number of minutes between League goals conceded while on the pitch	120	Scoring Difference Defensive Rating minus Contribution to Attacking Power	73

	PLAYER	LGE GOALS	DEF RATE	POWER	SCORE DIFF
1	Jose Gomes Moraes Edmilson	0	120	47	73 mins
2	Deco	1	112	44	68 mins
3	Xavi Hernandez	3	106	44	62 mins
4	Lionel Messi	14	95	45	50 mins

KEY PLAYERS - GOALSCORERS

Ronaldinho

Goals in the League	21	Player Strike Rate Average number of minutes between League goals scored by player	130
Contribution to Attacking Power Average number of minutes between League team goals while on pitch	40	Club Strike Rate Average number of minutes between League goals scored by club	43

	PLAYER	LGE GOALS	POWER	STRIKE RATE
1	Ronaldinho	21	40	130 mins
2	Samuel Eto'o	11	38	134 mins
3	Lionel Messi	14	45	142 mins
4	Andres Iniesta	6	46	449 mins

Rafael Marquez, Ronaldinho and Carlos Puyol

SQUAD APPEARANCES

Match	1 2 3 4 5	6 7 8 9 10	11 12 13 14 15	16 17 18 19 20	21 22 23 24 25	26 27 28 29 30	31 32 33 34 35	36 37 38 39 40	41 42 43 44 45	46 47
Venue	H A H H A	H A A H A	A H H A H	A A H A H	H H A A H	A H A H A	H H A A H	A H A H A	H A H A H	H A
Competition	O L L C L	L C L L C	L L C L L	L C L L C	L L L L L	L L L L L	C L L C L	L L L L L	L L L L L	L L
Result	L W W W W	D D W W L	L W D D W	W W W D W	W D D L W	D W D W L	L W L W D	W W L W L	W W D W W	D W

Goalkeepers

Albert Jorquera
Victor Valdes

Defenders

Juliano Belletti
Rafael Marquez
Presas Oleguer
Jesus Olmo
Carlos Puyol
Sylvinho
Lilian Thuram
Gio Van Bronckhorst
Gianluca Zambrotta

Midfielders

Deco
J G Moraes Edmilson
Ludovic Giuly
Andres Iniesta
Lionel Messi
Thiago Motta
Xavi Hernandez

Forwards

Samuel Eto'o
Santiago Ezquerro
Eidur Gudjohnsen
Ronaldinho
Javier Saviola

KEY: ■ On all match ◄◄ Subbed or sent off (Counting game) ►◄ Subbed on from bench (Counting Game) ►► Subbed on and then subbed or sent off (Counting Game) □ Not in 16
■ On bench ◄◄ Subbed or sent off (playing less than 70 minutes) ►► Subbed on (playing less than 70 minutes) ►► Subbed on and then subbed or sent off (playing less than 70 minutes)

SPAIN - BARCELONA

FC SEVILLE

Final Position: **3rd**

NICKNAME: SEVILLISTAS   KEY: ☐ Won ☐ Drawn ☐ Lost   Attendance

#	Comp	Opponent		Result	Scorers	Attendance
1	escup	Barcelona	A W	3-0	Renato 7, Kanoute 45, Maresca 90 pen	18,000
2	sppr1	Levante	H W	4-0	Kanoute 8, Kepa 28, 51, 87	45,000
3	sppr1	Real Sociedad	A W	3-1	Renato 8, Kanoute 75, 89	20,983
4	ucrl1	Atromitos	A W	2-1	Kepa 15, Duda 42	2,500
5	sppr1	Real Betis	H W	3-2	Kanoute 26, 58, Renato 85	45,500
6	sppr1	Atl Madrid	A L	1-2	Renato 40	40,000
7	ucrl2	Atromitos	H W	4-0	Rocha 1 og, Ioannou 10 og, Fabiano 29, Blanco-Gonzalez 86	35,000
8	sppr1	Getafe	H W	1-0	Renato 31	45,000
9	sppr1	Barcelona	A L	1-3	Kanoute 37	91,220
10	ucgpc	Slovan Liberec	A D	0-0		8,000
11	sppr1	Gimnastic	H W	2-1	Kanoute 21, 26	45,000
12	sppr1	Celta Vigo	A W	2-1	Poulsen 31, Adriano Correia 61	20,000
13	sppr1	Osasuna	H W	2-0	Kanoute 50 pen, Adriano Correia 88	45,500
14	sppr1	R Santander	A D	0-0		17,000
15	sppr1	Valencia	H W	3-0	Escude 19, Fabiano 55, Kanoute 71	45,000
16	ucgpc	Braga	H W	2-0	Fabiano 40, Chevanton 76	40,000
17	sppr1	Athl Bilbao	A W	3-1	Fabiano 5, 90, Marti 10	38,000
18	ucgpc	Grasshoppers	A W	4-0	Daniel Alves 12, 53, Chevanton 62, Kepa 84	7,300
19	sppr1	Espanyol	A L	1-2	Kanoute 26 pen	18,000
20	sppr1	Real Madrid	H W	2-1	Kanoute 17, Chevanton 77	45,000
21	ucgpc	AZ Alkmaar	H L	1-2	Chevanton 52 pen	20,000
22	sppr1	Recreativo H	A W	3-1	Fabiano 11, Kanoute 35, J.Navas 53	18,000
23	sppr1	Deportivo	H W	4-0	Kanoute 29, 64 pen, Fabiano 67, Daniel Alves 73	45,000
24	sppr1	Real Zaragoza	A L	1-2	Fabiano 70	25,000
25	sppr1	Mallorca	H L	1-2	Kanoute 22 pen	45,000
26	sppr1	Villarreal	A D	0-0		18,000
27	sppr1	Levante	A W	4-2	Kanoute 35, Kerzhakov 55, Tommasi 66 og, Alfaro 76	21,000
28	sppr1	Real Sociedad	H D	0-0		45,000
29	sppr1	Real Betis	A D	0-0		45,000
30	ucrl1	St Bucharest	A W	2-0	Poulsen 41, Kanoute 76 pen	28,000
31	sppr1	Atl Madrid	H W	3-1	Kanoute 15, 73, Daniel Alves 22	45,000
32	ucrl2	St Bucharest	H W	1-0	Kerzhakov 45	25,000
33	sppr1	Getafe	A D	0-0		14,000
34	sppr1	Barcelona	H W	2-1	Kerzhakov 39, Daniel Alves 61	45,500
35	ucrl1	Shakhtar Don	H D	2-2	Marti 8 pen, Maresca 88 pen	35,000
36	sppr1	Gimnastic	A L	0-1		14,000
37	ucrl2	Shakhtar Don	A W	3-2	Maresca 53, Palop 90, Chevanton 106	30,000
38	sppr1	Celta Vigo	H W	2-0	Kanoute 52 pen, Kerzhakov 90	40,000
39	sppr1	Osasuna	A D	0-0		18,000
40	ucqfl1	Tottenham	H W	2-1	Kanoute 19 pen, Kerzhakov 36	40,000
41	sppr1	R Santander	H D	0-0		41,405
42	ucqfl2	Tottenham	A D	2-2	Malbranque 3 og, Kanoute 8	35,284
43	sppr1	Valencia	A L	0-2		50,000
44	sppr1	Athl Bilbao	H W	4-1	Kerzhakov 49, Puerta 55, Chevanton 69, Fabiano 83	45,500
45	ucsfl1	Osasuna	A L	0-1		19,500
46	sppr1	Espanyol	H W	3-1	Puerta 51, Chevanton 53, Marti 74	42,000
47	ucsfl2	Osasuna	H W	2-0	Fabiano 37, Renato 53	45,000
48	sppr1	Real Madrid	A L	2-3	Maresca 41, Chevanton 90	80,300
49	sppr1	Recreativo H	H W	2-1	Maresca 14, Fabiano 81 pen	42,000
50	ucfin	Espanyol	A W	3-1*	Adriano Correia 18, Kanoute 105 (*on penalties)	50,000
51	sppr1	Deportivo	A W	2-1	Renato 76, Kanoute 83	12,000
52	sppr1	Real Zaragoza	H W	3-1	Fabiano 27, Kerzhakov 82, Kanoute 90	45,500
53	sppr1	Mallorca	A D	0-0		45,000
54	sppr1	Villarreal	H L	0-1		45,000

LEAGUE APPEARANCES, BOOKINGS AND CAPS

	AGE (on 01/07/07)	IN NAMED 18	APPEARANCES	COUNTING GAMES	MINUTES ON PITCH	YELLOW CARDS	RED CARDS	CAPS THIS SEASON	NATIONAL SIDE
Goalkeepers									
David Cobeno	25	36	5	4	405	0	0	-	Spain
Andres Palop	33	34	34	33	3015	3	0	-	Spain
Defenders									
Aitor Ocio	30	24	16	12	1195	2	3	-	Spain
Daniel Alves	24	34	34	33	3015	16	0	2	Brazil
Castedo David	33	25	18	16	1515	2	0	-	Spain
Ivica Dragutinovic	31	34	25	21	1921	4	1	5	Serbia
Julien Escude	27	35	30	28	2575	7	1	3	France
Andreas Hinkel	25	30	13	2	607	1	1	-	Germany
Javi Navarro	33	27	26	22	2149	10	1	4	Spain
Midfielders									
Claro Adriano Correia	22	28	27	17	1926	2	0	1	Brazil
Alejandro Alfaro	20	15	9	1	301	1	0	-	Spain
Bruno	22	3	1	0	29	0	0	-	Spain
Diego Capel	19	1	0	0	0	0	0	-	Spain
Sergio Duda	27	25	11	1	333	2	1	2	Portugal
Jesuli	29	2	1	0	3	0	0	-	Spain
Enzo Maresca	27	32	25	8	1321	2	0	-	Italy
Jose Luis Marti	32	35	30	12	1578	10	1	-	Spain
Jesus Navas	21	31	29	24	2380	1	0	-	Spain
Christian Poulsen	27	34	33	24	2467	9	0	9	Denmark
Antonio Puerta	22	34	30	20	2033	4	0	1	Spain
Dirnei Renato	28	33	33	24	2393	1	0	-	Brazil
Forwards									
Kepa Blanco	23	15	9	2	429	0	0	-	Spain
Ernesto Chevanton	26	24	17	2	657	5	0	-	Uruguay
Luis Fabiano	26	30	27	15	1799	9	2	-	Brazil
Frederic Kanoute	29	35	32	26	2576	2	0	2	Mali
Alexander Kerzhakov	24	49	15	5	789	2	0	5	Russia
Fernando Sales	29	4	0	0	0	0	0	-	Spain

TEAM OF THE SEASON

- **D** Aitor Ocio — CG: 12 DR: 108
- **D** Castedo David — CG: 16 DR: 108
- **G** Andres Palop — CG: 33 DR: 94
- **D** Julien Escude — CG: 28 DR: 95
- **D** Daniel Alves — CG: 33 DR: 94
- **M** Antonio Puerta — CG: 20 SD: 58
- **M** Claro Adriano Correia — CG: 17 SD: 47
- **M** Christian Poulsen — CG: 24 SD: 46
- **M** Jesus Navas — CG: 24 SD: 45
- **F** Frederic Kanoute — CG: 26 SR: 117
- **F** Luis Fabiano — CG: 14 SR: 191

MONTHLY POINTS TALLY

Month	Points	%
AUGUST	3	100%
SEPTEMBER	6	67%
OCTOBER	9	75%
NOVEMBER	10	83%
DECEMBER	9	75%
JANUARY	4	33%
FEBRUARY	6	50%
MARCH	6	67%
APRIL	8	53%
MAY	9	75%
JUNE	1	17%

LEAGUE GOALS

	PLAYER	MINS	GOALS	S RATE
1	Kanoute	2576	22	117
2	Fabiano	1726	9	191
3	Kerzhakov	789	5	157
4	Renato	2393	5	478
5	Chevanton	657	4	164
6	Blanco	429	3	143
7	Daniel Alves	3015	3	1005
8	Maresca	1321	2	660
9	Marti	1578	2	789
10	Puerta	1763	2	881
11	Adriano Correia	1926	2	963
12	Alfaro	301	1	301
13	Navas, J	2380	1	2380
	Other		2	
	TOTAL		63	

TOP POINT EARNERS

	PLAYER	GAMES	AV PTS
1	Aitor Ocio	14	2.50
2	Castedo David	16	2.25
3	Jesus Navas	24	2.17
4	Luis Fabiano	14	2.00
5	Christian Poulsen	24	1.96
6	Andres Palop	33	1.91
7	Daniel Alves	33	1.91
8	Julien Escude	29	1.86
9	Frederic Kanoute	26	1.85
10	Antonio Puerta	17	1.82
	CLUB AVERAGE:		1.87

DISCIPLINARY RECORDS

	PLAYER	YELLOW	RED	AVE
1	Ernesto Chevanton	5	0	131
2	Jose Luis Marti	12	1	143
3	Luis Fabiano	14	1	172
4	Daniel Alves	17	0	188
5	Javi Navarro	12	1	195
6	Aitor Ocio	3	3	239
7	Christian Poulsen	11	0	274
8	Andreas Hinkel	1	1	303
9	Julien Escude	10	1	321
10	Ivica Dragutinovic	6	1	384
11	Alex Kerzhakov	3	0	394
12	Antonio Puerta	5	0	587
13	Enzo Maresca	3	0	660
	Other	22	0	
	TOTAL	124	9	

KEY GOALKEEPER

Andres Palop

Goals Conceded in the League	32	Counting Games League games when player was on pitch for at least 70 minutes	33
Defensive Rating Ave number of mins between League goals conceded while on the pitch	94	Clean Sheets In League games when player was on pitch for at least 70 minutes	12

KEY PLAYERS - DEFENDERS

Aitor Ocio

Goals Conceded Number of League goals conceded while the player was on the pitch	11	Clean Sheets In League games when player was on pitch for at least 70 minutes	6
Defensive Rating Ave number of mins between League goals conceded while on the pitch	108	Club Defensive Rating Average number of mins between League goals conceded by the club this season	97

	PLAYER	CON LGE	CLEAN SHEETS	DEF RATE
1	Aitor Ocio	11	6	108 mins
2	Castedo David	14	7	108 mins
3	Julien Escude	27	11	95 mins
4	Daniel Alves	32	12	94 mins

KEY PLAYERS - MIDFIELDERS

Antonio Puerta

Goals in the League	2	Contribution to Attacking Power Average number of minutes between League team goals while on pitch	49
Defensive Rating Average number of mins between League goals conceded while on the pitch	107	Scoring Difference Defensive Rating minus Contribution to Attacking Power	58

	PLAYER	LGE GOALS	DEF RATE	POWER	SCORE DIFF
1	Antonio Puerta	2	107	49	58 mins
2	Claro Adriano Correia	2	107	60	47 mins
3	Christian Poulsen	1	94	48	46 mins
4	Jesus Navas	1	99	54	45 mins

KEY PLAYERS - GOALSCORERS

Frederic Kanoute

Goals in the League	22	Player Strike Rate Average number of minutes between League goals scored by player	117
Contribution to Attacking Power Average number of minutes between League team goals while on pitch	48	Club Strike Rate Average number of minutes between League goals scored by club	53

	PLAYER	LGE GOALS	POWER	STRIKE RATE
1	Frederic Kanoute	22	48	117 mins
2	Luis Fabiano	9	52	191 mins
3	Dirnei Renato	5	56	478 mins
4	Jose Luis Marti	2	56	789 mins

Frederic Kanoute

SQUAD APPEARANCES

Match	1 2 3 4 5	6 7 8 9 10	11 12 13 14 15	16 17 18 19 20	21 22 23 24 25	26 27 28 29 30	31 32 33 34 35	36 37 38 39 40	41 42 43 44 45	46 47 48 49 50	51 52 53 54
Venue	A H A A H	A H H A A	H A H A H	H A A A H	H A H A H	A A H A A	H H A H H	A A H A H	H A A H A	H H A H A	A H A H
Competition	O L L E L	L E L L E	L L L L L	E L E L L	E L L L L	L L L L E	L E L L E	L E L L E	L E L L E	L E L L E	L L L L
Result	W W W W W	L W W L D	W W W W D	W W W L W	L W W L L	D W D D W	W W D W D	L W W D W	D D L W L	W W L W W	W W D L

Goalkeepers
David Cobeno
Andres Palop

Defenders
Aitor Ocio
Daniel Alves
Castedo David
Ivica Dragutinovic
Julien Escude
Andreas Hinkel
Javi Navarro

Midfielders
Claro Adriano Correia
Alejandro Alfaro
Bruno
Diego Capel
Sergio Duda
Jesuli
Enzo Maresca
Jose Luis Marti
Jesus Navas
Christian Poulsen
Antonio Puerta
Dirnei Renato

Forwards
Kepa Blanco
Ernesto Chevanton
Luis Fabiano
Frederic Kanoute
Alexander Kerzhakov
Fernando Sales

KEY: ■ On all match   ◄◄ Subbed or sent off (Counting game)   ►► Subbed on from bench (Counting Game)   ►► Subbed on and then subbed or sent off (Counting Game)   □ Not in 16
  ■ On bench   ◄◄ Subbed or sent off (playing less than 70 minutes)   ►► Subbed on (playing less than 70 minutes)   ►► Subbed on and then subbed or sent off (playing less than 70 minutes)

SPAIN - FC SEVILLE

VALENCIA

Final Position: 4th

NICKNAME: THE BATS **KEY:** ☐ Won ☐ Drawn ☐ Lost Attendance

#	Comp	Opponent	H/A	Result		Scorers	Attendance
1	ecql2	Salzburg	H	W	3-0	Morientes 13, Villa 33, Silva 90	52,000
2	sppr1	Real Betis	H	W	2-1	Morientes 33, Raul Albiol 61	35,000
3	sppr1	Atl Madrid	A	W	1-0	Villa 7	50,000
4	ecgpd	Olympiakos	A	W	4-2	Morientes 34, 39, 89, Albiol 86	34,500
5	sppr1	Getafe	H	W	2-0	Morientes 45, Vicente 67	44,000
6	sppr1	Barcelona	A	D	1-1	Villa 17	75,000
7	ecgpd	Roma	H	W	2-1	Angulo 13, Villa 29	48,000
8	sppr1	Gimnastic	H	W	4-0	Morientes 14, Villa 54, 79, Angulo 84	40,000
9	sppr1	Celta Vigo	A	L	2-3	Navarro 40, Morientes 63	24,000
10	ecgpd	Shakhtar Don	H	W	2-0	Villa 31, 45	40,000
11	sppr1	Osasuna	H	W	1-0	Villa 16	45,000
12	sppr1	R Santander	A	L	0-1		15,000
13	ecgpd	Shakhtar Don	A	D	2-2	Morientes 18, Ayala 68	25,000
14	sppr1	Espanyol	A	D	1-1	David Silva 43	23,000
15	sppr1	Athl Bilbao	H	D	1-1	Morientes 44	49,000
16	sppr1	Seville	A	L	0-3		45,000
17	ecgpd	Olympiakos	H	W	2-0	Angulo 45, Morientes 46	35,000
18	sppr1	Real Madrid	H	L	0-1		50,000
19	ecgpd	Roma	A	L	0-2		45,000
20	ecgpd	Roma	A	L	0-2		45,000
21	sppr1	Deportivo	H	W	4-0	Angulo 10, Villa 39 pen, 75, Vicente 90	45,000
22	sppr1	Real Zaragoza	A	W	1-0	Angulo 42	29,000
23	sppr1	Mallorca	H	W	3-1	Vicente 39, Villa 57, Morientes 82	40,000
24	sppr1	Villarreal	A	W	1-0	Angulo 75	23,000
25	sppr1	Levante	H	W	3-0	Viana 52, Morientes 56, Ayala 80	45,000
26	sppr1	Real Sociedad	A	W	1-0	Villa 29	22,000
27	sppr1	Real Betis	A	L	1-2	Villa 10	40,000
28	sppr1	Atl Madrid	H	W	3-1	Ayala 15, Morientes 53, 68	42,000
29	sppr1	Getafe	A	L	0-3		12,000
30	sppr1	Barcelona	H	W	2-1	Angulo 52, Silva 56	50,000
31	eckl1	Inter Milan	A	D	2-2	Villa 64 , Silva 89	65,000
32	sppr1	Gimnastic	A	D	1-1	Joaquin 63	13,000
33	sppr1	Celta Vigo	H	W	1-0	Morientes 67	44,000
34	eckl2	Inter Milan	H	D	0-0		53,000
35	sppr1	Osasuna	A	D	1-1	Morientes 90	17,000
36	sppr1	R Santander	H	L	0-2		40,000
37	sppr1	Espanyol	H	W	3-2	Villa 12, Vicente 26, Angulo 58	45,000
38	ecqfl1	Chelsea	A	D	1-1	Silva 30	38,065
39	sppr1	Athl Bilbao	A	L	0-1		39,000
40	ecqfl2	Chelsea	H	L	1-2	Morientes 32	53,000
41	sppr1	Seville	H	W	2-0	Villa 27, 50 pen	50,000
42	sppr1	Real Madrid	A	L	1-2	Morientes 52	75,000
43	sppr1	Recreativo H	H	W	2-0	Joaquin 59, 62	40,000
44	sppr1	Deportivo	A	W	2-1	Viana 39, Silva 74	20,000
45	sppr1	Real Zaragoza	H	W	2-0	Moretti 21, Silva 44	48,000
46	sppr1	Mallorca	A	W	1-0	Joaquin 90	18,000
47	sppr1	Villarreal	H	L	2-3	Villa 20 pen, Moretti 90	45,000
48	sppr1	Levante	A	L	2-4	Joaquin 16, Baraja 88	24,052
49	sppr1	Real Sociedad	H	D	3-3	Villa 6, Lopez 19 og, Estrada 82 og	40,000

LEAGUE APPEARANCES, BOOKINGS AND CAPS

	AGE (on 01/07/07)	IN NAMED 18	APPEARANCES	COUNTING GAMES	MINUTES ON PITCH	YELLOW CARDS	RED CARDS	CAPS THIS SEASON	NATIONAL SIDE
Goalkeepers									
Ludovic Butelle	24	36	8	7	637	2	0	-	France
Santiago Canizares	37	35	32	31	2781	5	1	-	Spain
Defenders									
Roberto Ayala	34	34	29	28	2572	15	1	3	Argentina
David Cerra	23	8	5	4	352	4	0	-	Spain
David Corcoles	22	1	1	1	90	0	0	-	Spain
Asier Del Horno	26	14	6	6	532	2	0	-	Spain
Carlos Marchena	27	23	22	16	1584	8	1	4	Spain
Luis Garcia Miguel	27	33	30	27	2483	5	0	7	Portugal
Emiliano Moretti	26	26	23	22	2040	6	1	-	Italy
David Navarro	27	21	13	10	1006	6	0	-	Spain
Curro Torres	30	35	18	16	1468	4	0	-	Spain
Midfielders									
David Albelda	29	27	25	18	2013	13	1	9	Spain
Raul Albiol	21	36	36	36	3185	6	0	-	Spain
Ruben Baraja	31	18	14	7	805	5	0	-	Spain
Edu	29	10	10	9	819	3	0	-	Brazil
Jaime Gavilan	22	13	10	2	384	2	1	-	Spain
Nacho Insa	21	3	1	0	6	0	0	-	Spain
Sanchez Joaquin	26	36	35	18	2132	5	0	3	Spain
Jorge Lopez	28	30	14	1	298	2	0	-	Spain
Miguel Pallardo	20	20	10	2	390	2	0	-	Spain
Mario Regueiro	28	12	6	2	228	1	1	-	Uruguay
David Silva	21	36	36	25	2654	7	1	5	Spain
Hugo Viana	24	31	25	7	989	4	0	3	Portugal
Forwards									
Miguel Angulo	30	1	1	0	13	0	0	-	Spain
Miguel Angel Angulo	30	34	34	16	2124	3	1	-	Spain
Javi Guerra	24	6	2	0	14	0	0	-	Spain
Fernando Morientes	31	31	25	14	1611	0	0	4	Spain
Francesco Tavano	28	5	3	0	45	0	0	-	Italy
Rodriguez Vicente	25	18	16	12	1135	2	0	-	Spain
David Villa	25	36	36	31	2934	8	0	11	Spain

TEAM OF THE SEASON

G Santiago Canizares CG: 31 DR: 84

D Luis Garcia Miguel CG: 27 DR: 91
D Curro Torres CG: 16 DR: 86
D Roberto Ayala CG: 28 DR: 85
D Carlos Marchena CG: 16 DR: 83

M David Silva CG: 25 SD: 31
M David Albelda CG: 18 SD: 30
M Raul Albiol CG: 36 SD: 25
M Sanchez Joaquin CG: 18 SD: 22

F Fernando Morientes CG: 14 SR: 134
F David Villa CG: 31 SR: 195

MONTHLY POINTS TALLY

AUGUST	3	100%
SEPTEMBER	7	78%
OCTOBER	6	50%
NOVEMBER	2	17%
DECEMBER	9	75%
JANUARY	9	75%
FEBRUARY	7	58%
MARCH	7	58%
APRIL	6	50%
MAY	9	75%
JUNE	1	17%

LEAGUE GOALS

	PLAYER	MINS	GOALS	S RATE
1	Villa	2934	15	195
2	Morientes	1611	12	134
3	Angulo	2124	6	354
4	Joaquin	2132	5	426
5	Vicente	1135	4	283
6	Silva	2654	4	663
7	Viana	989	2	494
8	Moretti	2040	2	1020
9	Ayala	2572	2	1286
10	Baraja	805	1	805
11	Navarro	1006	1	1006
12	Albiol	3185	1	3185
13	Angulo	13	0	
	Other		0	
	TOTAL		**55**	

TOP POINT EARNERS

	PLAYER	GAMES	AV PTS
1	Rodriguez Vicente	12	2.08
2	David Albelda	19	1.95
3	Carlos Marchena	17	1.88
4	Curro Torres	16	1.88
5	Luis Garcia Miguel	27	1.85
6	David Villa	31	1.84
7	Raul Albiol	36	1.81
8	Miguel Angel Angulo	16	1.81
9	Fernando Morientes	14	1.79
10	Emiliano Moretti	23	1.78
	CLUB AVERAGE:		**1.74**

DISCIPLINARY RECORDS

	PLAYER	YELLOW	RED	AVE
1	Ruben Baraja	5	0	161
2	David Navarro	6	0	167
3	Carlos Marchena	8	1	198
4	David Albelda	13	1	223
5	Roberto Ayala	15	1	233
6	Hugo Viana	4	0	247
7	Ludovic Butelle	2	0	318
8	Emiliano Moretti	6	1	340
9	Curro Torres	4	0	367
10	David Silva	7	1	379
11	Edu	3	0	409
12	David Villa	8	0	419
13	Sanchez Joaquin	5	0	426
	Other	23	2	
	TOTAL	**109**	**7**	

KEY GOALKEEPER

Santiago Canizares				
Goals Conceded in the League	33	Counting Games League games when player was on pitch for at least 70 minutes	31
Defensive Rating Ave number of mins between League goals conceded while on the pitch	84	Clean Sheets In League games when player was on pitch for at least 70 minutes	12

KEY PLAYERS - DEFENDERS

Luis Garcia Miguel				
Goals Conceded Number of League goals conceded while the player was on the pitch	27	Clean Sheets In League games when player was on pitch for at least 70 minutes	12
Defensive Rating Ave number of mins between League goals conceded while on the pitch	91	Club Defensive Rating Average number of mins between League goals conceded by the club this season	81

	PLAYER	CON LGE	CLEAN SHEETS	DEF RATE
1	Luis Garcia Miguel	27	12	91 mins
2	Curro Torres	17	6	86 mins
3	Roberto Ayala	30	11	85 mins
4	Carlos Marchena	19	6	83 mins

KEY PLAYERS - MIDFIELDERS

David Silva				
Goals in the League	4	Contribution to Attacking Power Average number of minutes between League team goals while on pitch	60
Defensive Rating Average number of mins between League goals conceded while on the pitch	91	Scoring Difference Defensive Rating minus Contribution to Attacking Power	31

	PLAYER	LGE GOALS	DEF RATE	POWER	SCORE DIFF
1	David Silva	4	91	60	31 mins
2	David Albelda	0	80	50	30 mins
3	Raul Albiol	1	83	58	25 mins
4	Sanchez Joaquin	5	82	60	22 mins

KEY PLAYERS - GOALSCORERS

Fernando Morientes				
Goals in the League	12	Player Strike Rate Average number of minutes between League goals scored by player	134
Contribution to Attacking Power Average number of minutes between League team goals while on pitch	64	Club Strike Rate Average number of minutes between League goals scored by club	60

	PLAYER	LGE GOALS	POWER	STRIKE RATE
1	Fernando Morientes	12	64	134 mins
2	David Villa	15	55	195 mins
3	Rodriguez Vicente	4	54	283 mins
4	Miguel Angel Angulo	6	68	354 mins

David Villa

SQUAD APPEARANCES

Match	1 2 3 4 5	6 7 8 9 10	11 12 13 14 15	16 17 18 19 20	21 22 23 24 25	26 27 28 29 30	31 32 33 34 35	36 37 38 39 40	41 42 43 44 45	46 47 48 49
Venue	H H A A H	A H H A H	H A A A H	A H H A A	H A H A H	A A H A H	A A H H A	H H A A H	H A H A H	A H A H
Competition	C L L C L	L C L L C	L L L C L L	L C L L C	L L L L L	L L L L L	C L L C L	L L C L C	L L L L L	L L L L
Result	W W W W W	D W W L W	W L D D D	L W L L L	W W W W W	W L W L W	D D W D D	L W D L L	W L W W W	W L L D

Goalkeepers

Ludovic Butelle

Santiago Canizares

Defenders

Roberto Ayala

David Cerra

David Corcoles

Asier Del Horno

Carlos Marchena

Luis Garcia Miguel

Emiliano Moretti

David Navarro

Curro Torres

Midfielders

David Albelda

Raul Albiol

Ruben Baraja

Edu

Jaime Gavilan

Nacho Insa

Sanchez Joaquin

Jorge Lopez

Miguel Pallardo

Mario Regueiro

David Silva

Hugo Viana

Forwards

Miguel Angulo

Miguel Angel Angulo

Javi Guerra

Fernando Morientes

Francesco Tavano

Rodriguez Vicente

David Villa

KEY: ■ On all match ◄◄ Subbed or sent off (Counting game) ►► Subbed on from bench (Counting Game) ►► Subbed on and then subbed or sent off (Counting Game) □ Not in 16
■ On bench ◄◄ Subbed or sent off (playing less than 70 minutes) ►► Subbed on (playing less than 70 minutes) ►► Subbed on and then subbed or sent off (playing less than 70 minutes)

SPAIN - VALENCIA

VILLARREAL

Final Position: **5th**

NICKNAME: YELLOW SUBMARINES   KEY: ☐ Won ☐ Drawn ☐ Lost   Attendance

1	sppr1	Real Madrid	A D	0-0	65,000
2	sppr1	Recreativo H	H L	0-1	18,000
3	sppr1	Deportivo	A L	0-2	22,000
4	sppr1	Real Zaragoza	H W	3-2	Cani 49, Forlan 60, Riquelme 80 pen	18,000
5	sppr1	Mallorca	A W	2-1	Forlan 21, 25	15,000
6	sppr1	Espanyol	H D	0-0	22,000
7	sppr1	Levante	H D	1-1	Jonathan 66	17,000
8	sppr1	Real Sociedad	A W	1-0	Arruabarrena 82	19,000
9	sppr1	Real Betis	H W	3-2	Forlan 21, Cygan 57, Cani 60	16,000
10	sppr1	Atl Madrid	A L	1-3	Fuentes 14	40,000
11	sppr1	Getafe	H W	1-0	Abbondanzieri 50 og	15,000
12	sppr1	Barcelona	A L	0-4	75,000
13	sppr1	Gimnastic	H W	2-0	Fuentes 24, Franco 29	17,000
14	sppr1	Celta Vigo	A D	1-1	Forlan 64	12,000
15	sppr1	Osasuna	H L	1-4	Cani 61	19,000
16	sppr1	R Santander	A L	1-2	Marcos 87	13,414
17	sppr1	Valencia	H L	0-1	23,000
18	sppr1	Athl Bilbao	A W	1-0	Forlan 70	38,000
19	sppr1	Seville	H D	0-0	18,000
20	sppr1	Real Madrid	H W	1-0	Marcos 68	20,000
21	sppr1	Recreativo H	A L	1-2	Tomasson 78	17,000
22	sppr1	Deportivo	H L	0-2	18,000
23	sppr1	Real Zaragoza	A L	0-1	28,000
24	sppr1	Mallorca	H W	2-1	Tomasson 38, Fuentes 90	18,000
25	sppr1	Espanyol	A D	1-1	Forlan 54	28,000
26	sppr1	Levante	A W	2-0	Forlan 8, Tomasson 72	18,000
27	sppr1	Real Sociedad	H D	1-1	Josico 58	20,000
28	sppr1	Real Betis	A D	3-3	Forlan 1, 47, Pires 78	35,000
29	sppr1	Atl Madrid	H L	0-1	20,000
30	sppr1	Getafe	A L	0-3	12,000
31	sppr1	Barcelona	H W	2-0	Pires 56, Marcos 85	23,000
32	sppr1	Gimnastic	A W	3-0	Forlan 18, 79, Fernandez 90	13,000
33	sppr1	Celta Vigo	H W	1-0	Franco 68	20,000
34	sppr1	Osasuna	A W	4-1	Pires 6, Forlan 64, 87, 90	18,545
35	sppr1	R Santander	H W	2-1	Tacchinardi 39, Cani 59	15,000
36	sppr1	Valencia	A W	3-2	Forlan 34, 86, Tomasson 78	45,000
37	sppr1	Athl Bilbao	H W	3-1	Forlan 37 pen, 38, Ustaritz 51 og	22,000
38	sppr1	Seville	A W	1-0	Fuentes 51	45,000

LEAGUE APPEARANCES, BOOKINGS AND CAPS

	AGE (on 01/07/07)	IN NAMED 18	APPEARANCES	COUNTING GAMES	MINUTES ON PITCH	YELLOW CARDS	RED CARDS	CAPS THIS SEASON	NATIONAL SIDE
Goalkeepers									
Mariano D Barbosa	22	37	11	10	945	1	0	-	Argentina
Sebastian Viera	23	36	28	27	2475	3	0	-	Uruguay
Defenders									
Quique Alvarez	31	29	15	13	1207	6	0	-	Spain
Rodolfo Arruabarrena	31	33	22	15	1428	3	1	1	Argentina
Pascal Cygan	33	24	21	18	1749	4	0	-	France
Jose S Dias Enrique	21	30	23	23	2059	6	0	-	Spain
Fabricio Fuentes	30	35	33	31	2913	7	0	-	Argentina
Javi Venta	31	25	20	18	1669	5	0	-	Spain
Miguel Josemi	27	35	22	19	1790	8	0	-	Spain
Juan Manuel Pena	34	11	6	4	431	1	0	-	Bolivia
Gonzalo Rodriguez	23	11	6	6	540	1	0	-	Argentina
Midfielders									
Bruno Soriano	23	11	2	0	26	1	0	-	Spain
Ruben Cani	25	35	35	22	2423	4	1	-	Spain
Matias Fernandez	21	20	20	13	1248	2	0	-	Chile
Josico	32	27	26	13	1606	6	0	-	Spain
Garcia Marcos	20	34	29	16	1831	1	0	-	Spain
Robert Pires	33	11	11	6	662	0	1	-	France
Juan R. Riquelme	29	13	13	13	1163	1	0	1	Argentina
Marcos Senna	30	34	33	30	2817	10	0	1	Spain
Leandro Somoza	26	31	24	8	1120	4	0	2	Argentina
Alessio Tacchinardi	31	25	22	7	1104	10	0	-	Italy
Forwards									
Diego Forlan	28	36	36	32	3013	2	0	2	Uruguay
Guillermo Franco	30	28	27	12	1411	5	1	-	Mexico
Pereira R Jonathan	20	16	4	0	78	2	0	-	Spain
Jose Mari	28	21	18	6	790	3	1	-	Spain
Kahveci Nihat	27	11	9	3	521	2	0	3	Turkey
Jon Dahl Tomasson	30	16	11	5	654	0	0	7	Denmark

TEAM OF THE SEASON

J Sanchez Dias Enrique — CG: 23 DR: 98
Matias Fernandez — CG: 13 SD: 20
Quique Alvarez — CG: 13 DR: 86
Ruben Cani — CG: 22 SD: 20
Diego Forlan — CG: 32 SR: 158
Sebastian Viera — CG: 27 DR: 99
Javi Venta — CG: 18 DR: 83
Josico — CG: 13 SD: 8
Guillermo Franco — CG: 12 SR: 705
Fabricio Fuentes — CG: 31 DR: 76
Garcia Marcos — CG: 16 SD: 4

MONTHLY POINTS TALLY

AUGUST	1	33%
SEPTEMBER	3	33%
OCTOBER	8	67%
NOVEMBER	6	50%
DECEMBER	4	33%
JANUARY	7	58%
FEBRUARY	3	25%
MARCH	6	50%
APRIL	6	50%
MAY	12	100%
JUNE	6	100%

LEAGUE GOALS

	PLAYER	MINS	GOALS	S RATE
1	Forlan	3013	19	158
2	Tomasson	654	4	163
3	Cani	2423	4	605
4	Fuentes	2913	4	728
5	Pires	662	3	220
6	Marcos	1831	3	610
7	Franco	1411	2	705
8	Jonathan	78	1	78
9	Tacchinardi	1104	1	1104
10	Riquelme	1163	1	1163
11	Fernandez	1248	1	1248
12	Arruabarrena	1341	1	1341
13	Josico	1606	1	1606
	Other		1	
	TOTAL		**46**	

TOP POINT EARNERS

	PLAYER	GAMES	AV PTS
1	Javi Venta	18	2.06
2	Ruben Cani	22	2.05
3	Sebastian Viera	27	1.93
4	J Sanchez D Enrique	23	1.83
5	Fabricio Fuentes	31	1.81
6	Diego Forlan	32	1.75
7	Josico	13	1.69
8	Garcia Marcos	16	1.63
9	Marcos Senna	30	1.57
10	Pascal Cygan	18	1.56
	CLUB AVERAGE:		**1.63**

DISCIPLINARY RECORDS

	PLAYER	YELLOW	RED	AVE
1	A Tacchinardi	10	0	110
2	Jose Mari	3	1	197
3	Quique Alvarez	6	0	201
4	Miguel Josemi	8	0	223
5	Guillermo Franco	5	1	235
6	Kahveci Nihat	2	0	260
7	Josico	6	0	267
8	Leandro Somoza	4	0	280
9	Marcos Senna	10	0	281
10	Javi Venta	5	0	333
11	Fabricio Fuentes	7	0	416
12	Pascal Cygan	4	0	437
13	R Arruabarrena	3	0	447
	Other	18	2	
	TOTAL	**91**	**4**	

KEY GOALKEEPER

Sebastian Viera

Goals Conceded in the League	25	Counting Games League games when player was on pitch for at least 70 minutes	27
Defensive Rating Ave number of mins between League goals conceded while on the pitch	99	Clean Sheets In League games when player was on pitch for at least 70 minutes	12

KEY PLAYERS - DEFENDERS

Jose Sanchez Dias Enrique

Goals Conceded Number of League goals conceded while the player was on the pitch	21	Clean Sheets In League games when player was on pitch for at least 70 minutes	9
Defensive Rating Ave number of mins between League goals conceded while on the pitch	98	Club Defensive Rating Average number of mins between League goals conceded by the club this season	77

	PLAYER	CON LGE	CLEAN SHEETS	DEF RATE
1	Jose Sanchez Dias Enrique	21	9	98 mins
2	Quique Alvarez	14	5	86 mins
3	Javi Venta	20	7	83 mins
4	Fabricio Fuentes	38	10	76 mins

KEY PLAYERS - MIDFIELDERS

Matias Fernandez

Goals in the League	1	Contribution to Attacking Power Average number of minutes between League team goals while on pitch	69
Defensive Rating Average number of mins between League goals conceded while on the pitch	89	Scoring Difference Defensive Rating minus Contribution to Attacking Power	20

	PLAYER	LGE GOALS	DEF RATE	POWER	SCORE DIFF
1	Matias Fernandez	1	89	69	20 mins
2	Ruben Cani	4	89	69	20 mins
3	Josico	1	84	76	8 mins
4	Garcia Marcos	3	87	83	4 mins

KEY PLAYERS - GOALSCORERS

Diego Forlan

Goals in the League	19	Player Strike Rate Average number of minutes between League goals scored by player	158
Contribution to Attacking Power Average number of minutes between League team goals while on pitch	68	Club Strike Rate Average number of minutes between League goals scored by club	71

	PLAYER	LGE GOALS	POWER	STRIKE RATE
1	Diego Forlan	19	68	158 mins
2	Ruben Cani	4	69	605 mins
3	Garcia Marcos	3	83	610 mins
4	Guillermo Franco	2	64	705 mins

Diego Forlan

SQUAD APPEARANCES

Match	1	2	3	4	5	6	7	8	9	10	11	12	13	14	15	16	17	18	19	20	21	22	23	24	25	26	27	28	29	30	31	32	33	34	35	36	37	38
Venue	A	H	A	H	A	H	H	A	H	A	H	A	H	A	H	A	H	A	H	H	A	H	A	H	A	A	H	A	H	A	H	A	H	A	H	A	H	A
Competition	L	L	L	L	L	L	L	L	L	L	L	L	L	L	L	L	L	L	L	L	L	L	L	L	L	L	L	L	L	L	L	L	L	L	L	L	L	L
Result	D	L	L	W	W	D	D	W	W	L	W	L	W	D	L	L	L	W	D	W	L	L	L	W	D	W	D	D	L	L	W	W	W	W	W	W	W	W

Goalkeepers
Mariano D Barbosa
Sebastian Viera

Defenders
Quique Alvarez
Rodolfo Arruabarrena
Pascal Cygan
Jose S Dias Enrique
Fabricio Fuentes
Javi Venta
Miguel Josemi
Juan Manuel Pena
Gonzalo Rodriguez

Midfielders
Bruno Soriano
Ruben Cani
Matias Fernandez
Josico
Garcia Marcos
Robert Pires
Juan Roman Riquelme
Marcos Senna
Leandro Somoza
Alessio Tacchinardi

Forwards
Diego Forlan
Guillermo Franco
Pereira R Jonathan
Jose Mari
Kahveci Nihat
Jon Dahl Tomasson

KEY: ■ On all match ◄◄ Subbed or sent off (Counting game) ►► Subbed on from bench (Counting Game) ►► Subbed on and then subbed or sent off (Counting Game) ☐ Not in 16
■ On bench ◄ Subbed or sent off (playing less than 70 minutes) ►► Subbed on (playing less than 70 minutes) ►► Subbed on and then subbed or sent off (playing less than 70 minutes)

SPAIN - VILLARREAL

REAL ZARAGOZA

Final Position: 6th

NICKNAME: BLANQUILLOS KEY: ☐ Won ☐ Drawn ☐ Lost Attendance

#			Result	Scorers	Attendance
1	sppr1 Deportivo	A L	2-3	D.Milito 9, Ewerthon 80	16,000
2	sppr1 Espanyol	H W	3-0	Aimar 37, D.Milito 81, Oscar 83	28,000
3	sppr1 Mallorca	H W	2-0	Ewerthon 58, Sergio Garcia 79	26,700
4	sppr1 Villarreal	A L	2-3	Aimar 22, Pique 90	18,000
5	sppr1 Levante	H D	2-2	Celades 60, D.Milito 79	28,000
6	sppr1 Real Sociedad	A W	3-1	D.Milito 34 pen, 59, Diogo 55	23,000
7	sppr1 Real Betis	H W	2-1	D.Milito 13, 30	28,000
8	sppr1 Atl Madrid	A W	1-0	Oscar 88	50,000
9	sppr1 Getafe	H W	3-1	Diogo 39, D.Milito 74, Ewerthon 90	27,000
10	sppr1 Barcelona	A L	1-3	G.Milito 17	80,000
11	sppr1 Gimnastic	H W	3-0	Aimar 51, Oscar 55, Pique 70	25,000
12	sppr1 Celta Vigo	A D	1-1	D.Milito 7	15,000
13	sppr1 Osasuna	H L	1-2	D.Milito 19	28,000
14	sppr1 R Santander	A W	2-0	D.Milito 60, Lafita 80	16,000
15	sppr1 Valencia	H L	0-1		29,000
16	sppr1 Athl Bilbao	A D	0-0		40,000
17	sppr1 Seville	H W	2-1	Diogo 14, D.Milito 51	25,000
18	sppr1 Real Madrid	A L	0-1		69,000
19	sppr1 Recreativo H	H D	0-0		20,000
20	sppr1 Deportivo	H D	1-1	D.Milito 79 pen	27,000
21	sppr1 Espanyol	A W	2-1	Sergio Garcia 55, 87	23,500
22	sppr1 Mallorca	A L	1-2	D.Milito 55	15,000
23	sppr1 Villarreal	H W	1-0	D.Milito 32	28,000
24	sppr1 Levante	A D	0-0		13,000
25	sppr1 Real Sociedad	H W	3-2	Aimar 53, D.Milito 75 pen, Ewerthon 81	25,000
26	sppr1 Real Betis	A D	1-1	D.Milito 23	40,000
27	sppr1 Atl Madrid	H W	1-0	D.Milito 21	25,000
28	sppr1 Getafe	A D	2-2	Sergio Garcia 22, D'Alessandro 36	12,000
29	sppr1 Barcelona	H W	1-0	D.Milito 57	34,100
30	sppr1 Gimnastic	A L	0-1		12,000
31	sppr1 Celta Vigo	H W	2-0	Ewerthon 72, 76	27,000
32	sppr1 Osasuna	A D	2-2	Aimar 12, Sergio Garcia 90	16,000
33	sppr1 R Santander	H D	0-0		29,000
34	sppr1 Valencia	A L	0-2		48,000
35	sppr1 Athl Bilbao	H W	4-3	D.Milito 16, Diogo 19, Sergio Garcia 37, Murillo 45 og	30,000
36	sppr1 Seville	A L	1-3	D'Alessandro 74	45,500
37	sppr1 Real Madrid	H D	2-2	D.Milito 32 pen, 64	34,500
38	sppr1 Recreativo H	A D	1-1	D.Milito 75	15,000

LEAGUE APPEARANCES, BOOKINGS AND CAPS

	AGE (on 01/07/07)	IN NAMED 18	APPEARANCES	COUNTING GAMES	MINUTES ON PITCH	YELLOW CARDS	RED CARDS	CAPS THIS SEASON	NATIONAL SIDE
Goalkeepers									
Cesar Sanchez	35	38	38	38	3420	5	0	-	Spain
Miguel Martinez	25	19	0	0	0	0	0	-	Spain
Defenders									
Agustin Aranzabal	34	12	1	0	12	0	0	-	Spain
Carlos Cuartero	32	1	1	1	90	0	0	-	Spain
Carlos Diogo	23	30	30	29	2658	16	2	-	Uruguay
Chus Herrero	23	28	10	8	721	6	0	-	Spain
Juanfran	30	33	33	32	2921	7	1	-	Spain
Gabriel Milito	26	36	36	35	3172	11	2	4	Argentina
Gustavo Nery	29	7	4	0	55	1	0	-	Brazil
Gerard Pique	20	32	22	15	1562	8	1	-	Spain
Sergio Fernandez	30	32	29	28	2565	11	0	-	Spain
Midfielders									
Pablo Aimar	27	31	31	25	2516	7	0	2	Argentina
Albert Celades	31	29	22	10	1288	3	0	-	Spain
Andres D'Alessandro	26	36	36	30	2845	10	0	-	Argentina
Angel Lafita	22	35	28	3	672	0	0	-	Spain
Antonio Longes	22	30	9	0	224	0	0	-	Spain
Jose Movilla	32	37	22	11	1352	4	0	-	Spain
Oscar G Marcos	24	37	30	5	1039	4	0	-	Spain
Leonardo Ponzio	25	15	11	6	684	2	1	1	Argentina
Sergio Garcia	24	35	32	17	1988	2	0	-	Spain
Alberto Zapater	22	36	36	35	3158	7	1	-	Spain
Forwards									
Ewerthon	26	34	28	7	1325	1	0	-	Brazil
Diego Milito	28	37	37	34	3136	2	0	2	Argentina

TEAM OF THE SEASON

G Cesar Sanchez CG: 38 DR: 79
D Juanfran CG: 32 DR: 88
D Carlos Diogo CG: 29 DR: 83
D Gabriel Milito CG: 35 DR: 79
D Sergio Fernandez CG: 28 DR: 73
M Sergio Garcia CG: 17 SD: 68
M Albert Celades CG: 10 SD: 46
M Andres D'Alessandro CG: 30 SD: 22
M Alberto Zapater CG: 35 SD: 20
F Diego Milito CG: 34 SR: 136
F Ewerthon* CG: 7 SR: 220

MONTHLY POINTS TALLY

AUGUST	0	0%
SEPTEMBER	6	67%
OCTOBER	10	83%
NOVEMBER	7	58%
DECEMBER	4	33%
JANUARY	5	42%
FEBRUARY	7	58%
MARCH	7	78%
APRIL	8	53%
MAY	4	33%
JUNE	2	33%

LEAGUE GOALS

	PLAYER	MINS	GOALS	S RATE
1	Milito, D	3136	23	136
2	Ewerthon	1325	6	220
3	Sergio Garcia	1988	6	331
4	Aimar	2516	5	503
5	Diogo	2658	4	664
6	Oscar Gonzalez	1039	3	346
7	Pique	1562	2	781
8	D'Alessandro	2845	2	1422
9	Lafita	672	1	672
10	Celades	1288	1	1288
11	Milito, G	3172	1	3172
12	Movilla	1352	0	
13	Nery	55	0	
	Other		0	
	TOTAL		54	

TOP POINT EARNERS

	PLAYER	GAMES	AV PTS
1	Carlos Diogo	29	1.79
2	Sergio Garcia	17	1.76
3	Juanfran	32	1.69
4	Andres D'Alessandro	30	1.67
5	Alberto Zapater	36	1.64
6	Gerard Pique	16	1.63
7	Cesar Sanchez	38	1.58
8	Sergio Fernandez	28	1.57
9	Diego Milito	34	1.56
10	Gabriel Milito	35	1.51
	CLUB AVERAGE:		1.58

DISCIPLINARY RECORDS

	PLAYER	YELLOW	RED	AVE
1	Chus Herrero	6	0	120
2	Carlos Diogo	16	2	147
3	Gerard Pique	8	1	173
4	Angel Lafita	3	0	224
5	Leonardo Ponzio	2	1	228
6	Sergio Fernandez	11	0	233
7	Gabriel Milito	11	2	244
8	Oscar G Marcos	4	0	259
9	A D'Alessandro	10	0	284
10	Jose Movilla	4	0	338
11	Pablo Aimar	7	0	359
12	Juanfran	7	1	365
13	Alberto Zapater	7	1	394
	Other	13	0	
	TOTAL	109	8	

KEY GOALKEEPER

Cesar Sanchez

Goals Conceded in the League	43	Counting Games League games when player was on pitch for at least 70 minutes	38
Defensive Rating Ave number of mins between League goals conceded while on the pitch	79	Clean Sheets In League games when player was on pitch for at least 70 minutes	13

KEY PLAYERS - DEFENDERS

Juanfran

Goals Conceded Number of League goals conceded while the player was on the pitch	33	Clean Sheets In League games when player was on pitch for at least 70 minutes	12
Defensive Rating Ave number of mins between League goals conceded while on the pitch	88	Club Defensive Rating Average number of mins between League goals conceded by the club this season	79

	PLAYER	CON LGE	CLEAN SHEETS	DEF RATE
1	Juanfran	33	12	88 mins
2	Carlos Diogo	32	11	83 mins
3	Gabriel Milito	40	10	79 mins
4	Sergio Fernandez	35	9	73 mins

KEY PLAYERS - MIDFIELDERS

Sergio Garcia

Goals in the League	6	Contribution to Attacking Power Average number of minutes between League team goals while on pitch	56
Defensive Rating Average number of mins between League goals conceded while on the pitch	124	Scoring Difference Defensive Rating minus Contribution to Attacking Power	68

	PLAYER	LGE GOALS	DEF RATE	POWER	SCORE DIFF
1	Sergio Garcia	6	124	56	68 mins
2	Albert Celades	1	107	61	46 mins
3	Andres D'Alessandro	2	88	66	22 mins
4	Alberto Zapater	0	78	58	20 mins

KEY PLAYERS - GOALSCORERS

Diego Milito

Goals in the League	23	Player Strike Rate Average number of minutes between League goals scored by player	136
Contribution to Attacking Power Average number of minutes between League team goals while on pitch	62	Club Strike Rate Average number of minutes between League goals scored by club	62

	PLAYER	LGE GOALS	POWER	STRIKE RATE
1	Diego Milito	23	62	136 mins
2	Ewerthon	6	57	220 mins
3	Sergio Garcia	6	56	331 mins
4	Pablo Aimar	5	62	503 mins

Diego Milito

SQUAD APPEARANCES

Match	1	2	3	4	5	6	7	8	9	10	11	12	13	14	15	16	17	18	19	20	21	22	23	24	25	26	27	28	29	30	31	32	33	34	35	36	37	38
Venue	A	H	H	A	H	A	H	A	H	A	H	A	H	A	H	A	H	A	H	H	A	A	H	A	H	A	H	A	H	A	H	A	H	A	H	A	H	A
Competition	L	L	L	L	L	L	L	L	L	L	L	L	L	L	L	L	L	L	L	L	L	L	L	L	L	L	L	L	L	L	L	L	L	L	L	L	L	L
Result	L	W	W	L	D	W	W	W	W	L	W	D	L	W	L	D	W	L	D	D	W	L	W	D	W	D	W	D	W	L	W	D	D	L	W	L	D	D

Goalkeepers

Cesar Sanchez
Miguel Martinez

Defenders

Agustin Aranzabal
Carlos Cuartero
Carlos Diogo
Chus Herrero
Juanfran
Gabriel Milito
Gustavo Nery
Gerard Pique
Adrian Ripa
Sergio Fernandez

Midfielders

Pablo Aimar
Albert Celades
Andres D'Alessandro
Angel Lafita
Antonio Longes
Jose Movilla
Oscar G Marcos
Leonardo Ponzio
Sergio Garcia
Alberto Zapater

Forwards

Ewerthon
Diego Milito

KEY: ■ On all match ◀◀ Subbed or sent off (Counting game) ▶▶ Subbed on from bench (Counting Game) ▶▶ Subbed on and then subbed or sent off (Counting Game) □ Not in 16
■ On bench ◀◀ Subbed or sent off (playing less than 70 minutes) ▶▶ Subbed on (playing less than 70 minutes) ▶▶ Subbed on and then subbed or sent off (playing less than 70 minutes)

SPAIN - REAL ZARAGOZA

ATLETICO MADRID

Final Position: **7th**

NICKNAME: LOS INDIOS   KEY: ☐ Won ☐ Drawn ☐ Lost   Attendance

#		Opponent		Result		Scorers	Attendance
1	sppr1	R Santander	A	W	1-0	Torres 12	17,897
2	sppr1	Valencia	H	L	0-1		50,000
3	sppr1	Athl Bilbao	A	W	4-1	Rodriguez 18, Petrov 37, Aguero 64, Galletti 90	38,800
4	sppr1	Seville	H	W	2-1	Rodriguez 85, Torres 89	40,000
5	sppr1	Real Madrid	A	D	1-1	Mista Ferrer 6	75,000
6	sppr1	Recreativo H	H	W	2-1	Torres 71 pen, Aguero 77	48,000
7	sppr1	Deportivo	A	L	0-1		20,000
8	sppr1	Real Zaragoza	H	L	0-1		50,000
9	sppr1	Mallorca	A	D	0-0		17,000
10	sppr1	Villarreal	H	W	3-1	Ze Castro 37, Torres 45 pen, Aguero 64	40,000
11	sppr1	Levante	A	W	3-0	Torres 33 pen, Maniche 68, 75	15,000
12	sppr1	Real Sociedad	H	D	1-1	Mikel.Gonzalez 77 og	40,000
13	sppr1	Real Betis	A	W	1-0	Galletti 33	38,000
14	sppr1	Espanyol	H	L	1-2	Torres 56	40,000
15	sppr1	Getafe	H	W	1-0	Maniche 24	30,000
16	sppr1	Barcelona	A	D	1-1	Aguero 60	53,685
17	sppr1	Gimnastic	H	D	0-0		40,000
18	sppr1	Celta Vigo	A	W	3-1	Torres 13, 21, Aguero 54	12,000
19	sppr1	Osasuna	H	W	1-0	Ze Castro 83	40,000
20	sppr1	R Santander	H	D	1-1	Pablo Ibanez 75	12,000
21	sppr1	Valencia	A	L	1-3	Mista 56	42,000
22	sppr1	Athl Bilbao	H	W	1-0	Aguero 64	40,000
23	sppr1	Seville	A	L	1-3	Pablo Ibanez 82	45,000
24	sppr1	Real Madrid	H	D	1-1	Torres 11	56,000
25	sppr1	Recreativo H	A	L	0-1		17,000
26	sppr1	Deportivo	H	W	2-0	Galletti 1, Mista 85	40,000
27	sppr1	Real Zaragoza	A	L	0-1		25,000
28	sppr1	Mallorca	H	D	1-1	Torres 16	40,000
29	sppr1	Villarreal	A	W	1-0	Eller 32	20,000
30	sppr1	Levante	H	W	1-0	Torres 60	40,000
31	sppr1	Real Sociedad	A	L	0-2		27,426
32	sppr1	Real Betis	H	D	0-0		45,000
33	sppr1	Espanyol	A	L	1-2	Petrov 90	20,450
34	sppr1	Getafe	A	W	4-1	Torres 2, 64, Maniche 17, Galletti 88 pen	13,680
35	sppr1	Barcelona	H	L	0-6		55,000
36	sppr1	Gimnastic	A	W	2-0	Torres 11, 54 pen	12,000
37	sppr1	Celta Vigo	H	L	2-3	Rodriguez 28, 70	45,000
38	sppr1	Osasuna	A	W	2-1	Rodriguez 38, Monreal 53 og	18,000

LEAGUE APPEARANCES, BOOKINGS AND CAPS

	AGE (on 01/07/07)	IN NAMED 18	APPEARANCES	COUNTING GAMES	MINUTES ON PITCH	YELLOW CARDS	RED CARDS	CAPS THIS SEASON	NATIONAL SIDE
Goalkeepers									
Ivan Cuellar Pichu	23	35	7	6	585	1	0	-	Spain
Leonardo Franco	30	33	32	31	2835	3	0	-	Argentina
Defenders									
Azcarate	23	5	1	1	90	0	0	-	Argentina
Fabiano Eller	29	12	12	12	1033	3	2	-	Brazil
Antonio Lopez	25	36	33	29	2723	7	0	5	Spain
Pablo Ibanez	25	29	24	23	2096	5	0	5	Spain
Luis Perea	28	33	25	21	2015	8	0	1	Colombia
Mariano Pernia	30	35	22	13	1460	9	0	2	Spain
Giorgios Seitaridis	26	34	31	26	2485	9	2	6	Greece
Jose Ze Castro	24	37	22	20	1838	2	0	-	Portugal
Midfielders									
Victor Bravo	23	9	2	2	142	0	0	-	Spain
Francisco Costinha	33	33	24	10	1240	6	1	2	Portugal
Fernandez Gabi	23	29	20	6	885	8	1	-	Spain
Luciano Galletti	27	36	35	23	2394	10	0	-	Argentina
Jacobo	23	7	1	0	1	0	0	-	Spain
Jose Jurado	21	35	33	16	1988	2	0	-	Spain
Peter Luccin	28	33	31	28	2617	15	3	-	France
Maniche	29	28	28	22	2200	6	0	2	Portugal
Adrian Pollo	24	2	1	0	1	0	0	-	Spain
Maxi Rodriguez	26	10	10	6	626	2	0	2	Argentina
Juan Valera	22	24	8	5	465	2	0	-	Spain
Forwards									
Sergio Aguero	19	38	38	20	2482	4	0	3	Argentina
J Fernando Marques	22	6	3	0	56	0	0	-	Spain
Mista	28	34	29	5	1224	4	0	-	Spain
Martin Petrov	28	13	13	9	906	3	0	5	Bulgaria
Fernando Torres	23	36	36	33	3086	5	1	8	Spain

TEAM OF THE SEASON

G Leonardo Franco — CG: 31 DR: 101

D Mariano Pernia — CG: 13 DR: 112
D Luis Perea — CG: 21 DR: 95
D Pablo Ibanez — CG: 23 DR: 91
D Antonio Lopez — CG: 29 DR: 87

M Maniche — CG: 22 SD: 27
M Luciano Galletti — CG: 23 SD: 21
M Peter Luccin — CG: 28 SD: 12
M Jose Jurado — CG: 16 SD: 0

F Fernando Torres — CG: 33 SR: 205
F Sergio Aguero — CG: 20 SR: 413

MONTHLY POINTS TALLY

AUGUST	3	100%
SEPTEMBER	6	67%
OCTOBER	4	33%
NOVEMBER	8	67%
DECEMBER	7	58%
JANUARY	8	67%
FEBRUARY	4	33%
MARCH	3	33%
APRIL	8	53%
MAY	6	50%
JUNE	3	50%

LEAGUE GOALS

	PLAYER	MINS	GOALS	S RATE
1	Torres	3086	15	205
2	Aguero	2482	6	413
3	Rodriguez	626	5	125
4	Maniche	2200	4	550
5	Mista	1224	3	408
6	Galletti	2394	3	798
7	Petrov	906	2	453
8	Ze Castro	1838	2	919
9	Pablo Ibanez	2096	2	1048
10	Eller	1033	1	1033
11	Falcon	0	0	
12	Franco	2835	0	
13	Gabi	885	0	
	Other		0	
	TOTAL		43	

TOP POINT EARNERS

	PLAYER	GAMES	AV PTS
1	Giorgios Seitaridis	27	1.78
2	Mariano Pernia	13	1.77
3	Antonio Lopez	29	1.69
4	Maniche	22	1.68
5	Luis Perea	21	1.67
6	Jose Ze Castro	20	1.65
7	Peter Luccin	29	1.59
8	Fabiano Eller	12	1.58
9	Leonardo Franco	31	1.58
10	Luciano Galletti	23	1.57
	CLUB AVERAGE:		1.58

DISCIPLINARY RECORDS

	PLAYER	YELLOW	RED	AVE
1	Fernandez Gabi	8	1	98
2	Peter Luccin	15	3	145
3	Mariano Pernia	9	0	162
4	Francisco Costinha	6	1	177
5	Fabiano Eller	3	2	206
6	Giorgios Seitaridis	9	2	225
7	Juan Valera	2	0	232
8	Luciano Galletti	10	0	239
9	Luis Perea	7	0	287
10	Martin Petrov	3	0	302
11	Mista	4	0	306
12	Maxi Rodriguez	2	0	313
13	Maniche	6	0	366
	Other	29	1	
	TOTAL	113	10	

KEY GOALKEEPER

Leonardo Franco

Goals Conceded in the League	28	Counting Games League games when player was on pitch for at least 70 minutes	31
Defensive Rating Ave number of mins between League goals conceded while on the pitch	101	Clean Sheets In League games when player was on pitch for at least 70 minutes	12

KEY PLAYERS - DEFENDERS

Mariano Pernia

Goals Conceded Number of League goals conceded while the player was on the pitch	13	Clean Sheets In League games when player was on pitch for at least 70 minutes	7
Defensive Rating Ave number of mins between League goals conceded while on the pitch	112	Club Defensive Rating Average number of mins between League goals conceded by the club this season	87

	PLAYER	CON LGE	CLEAN SHEETS	DEF RATE
1	Mariano Pernia	13	7	112 mins
2	Luis Perea	21	6	95 mins
3	Pablo Ibanez	23	8	91 mins
4	Antonio Lopez	31	9	87 mins

KEY PLAYERS - MIDFIELDERS

Maniche

Goals in the League	4	Contribution to Attacking Power Average number of minutes between League team goals while on pitch	61
Defensive Rating Average number of mins between League goals conceded while on the pitch	88	Scoring Difference Defensive Rating minus Contribution to Attacking Power	27

	PLAYER	LGE GOALS	DEF RATE	POWER	SCORE DIFF
1	Maniche	4	88	61	27 mins
2	Luciano Galletti	3	95	74	21 mins
3	Peter Luccin	0	84	72	12 mins
4	Jose Jurado	0	79	79	0 mins

KEY PLAYERS - GOALSCORERS

Fernando Torres

Goals in the League	15	Player Strike Rate Average number of minutes between League goals scored by player	205
Contribution to Attacking Power Average number of minutes between League team goals while on pitch	79	Club Strike Rate Average number of minutes between League goals scored by club	74

	PLAYER	LGE GOALS	POWER	STRIKE RATE
1	Fernando Torres	15	79	205 mins
2	Sergio Aguero	6	73	413 mins
3	Maniche	4	61	550 mins
4	Luciano Galletti	3	74	798 mins

Fernando Torres

SQUAD APPEARANCES

Match	1	2	3	4	5	6	7	8	9	10	11	12	13	14	15	16	17	18	19	20	21	22	23	24	25	26	27	28	29	30	31	32	33	34	35	36	37	38
Venue	A	H	A	H	A	H	A	H	A	H	A	H	A	H	H	A	H	A	H	H	A	H	A	H	A	H	A	H	A	H	A	H	A	A	H	A	H	A
Competition	L	L	L	L	L	L	L	L	L	L	L	L	L	L	L	L	L	L	L	L	L	L	L	L	L	L	L	L	L	L	L	L	L	L	L	L	L	L
Result	W	L	W	W	D	W	L	L	L	W	W	D	W	L	W	D	D	W	W	D	L	W	L	D	L	W	L	D	W	W	L	D	L	W	L	W	L	W

Goalkeepers

Ivan Cuellar Pichu

Leonardo Franco

Defenders

Azcarate

Fabiano Eller

Antonio Lopez

Pablo Ibanez

Luis Perea

Mariano Pernia

Giorgios Seitaridis

Jose Ze Castro

Midfielders

Victor Bravo

Francisco Costinha

Fernandez Gabi

Luciano Galletti

Jacobo

Jose Jurado

Peter Luccin

Maniche

Adrian Pollo

Maxi Rodriguez

Juan Valera

Forwards

Sergio Aguero

J Fernando Marques

Mista

Martin Petrov

Fernando Torres

KEY: ■ On all match   ◄◄ Subbed or sent off (Counting game)   ►► Subbed on from bench (Counting Game)   ►► Subbed on and then subbed or sent off (Counting Game)   ▫ Not in 16

□ On bench   ◄◄ Subbed or sent off (playing less than 70 minutes)   ►► Subbed on (playing less than 70 minutes)   ►► Subbed on and then subbed or sent off (playing less than 70 minutes)

SPAIN - ATLETICO MADRID

RECREATIVO HUELVA

Final Position: **8th**

NICKNAME: RECRE   KEY: ☐ Won ☐ Drawn ☐ Lost   Attendance

#		Opponent			Score	Scorers	Attendance
1	sppr1	Mallorca	H	D	1-1	Cazorla 90	18,500
2	sppr1	Villarreal	A	W	1-0	Cazorla 82	18,000
3	sppr1	Levante	H	L	0-1		18,100
4	sppr1	Real Sociedad	A	W	3-2	Calle 39, 49, Sinama-Pongolle 90	20,000
5	sppr1	Real Betis	H	W	2-0	Sinama-Pongolle 84, Guerrero 88	18,000
6	sppr1	Atl Madrid	A	L	1-2	Guerrero 62 pen	48,000
7	sppr1	Getafe	H	L	1-2	Sinama-Pongolle 54	18,000
8	sppr1	Barcelona	A	L	0-3		65,000
9	sppr1	Gimnastic	H	W	2-1	Guerrero 31, Mario 90	17,000
10	sppr1	Celta Vigo	A	W	2-1	Sinama-Pongolle 48, Uche 57	12,000
11	sppr1	Osasuna	H	W	2-0	Guerrero 45, Uche 76	18,000
12	sppr1	R Santander	A	L	3-4	Oriol 29 og, Uche 61, Vasquez 90	16,000
13	sppr1	Valencia	H	W	2-0	Aitor 1, Sinama-Pongolle 82	18,000
14	sppr1	Athl Bilbao	A	L	2-4	Uche 55, Sarriegui 88 og	38,000
15	sppr1	Seville	H	L	1-3	Vasquez 19	18,000
16	sppr1	Real Madrid	A	W	3-0	Sinama-Pongolle 35, Uche 52, Viqueira 90	50,000
17	sppr1	Espanyol	A	W	1-0	Vasquez 56	25,000
18	sppr1	Deportivo	H	D	1-1	Guerrero 11	18,000
19	sppr1	Real Zaragoza	A	D	0-0		20,000
20	sppr1	Mallorca	A	L	1-2	Juanma 49	12,000
21	sppr1	Villarreal	H	W	2-1	Juanma 13, Sinama-Pongolle 46	17,000
22	sppr1	Levante	A	L	1-2	Sinama-Pongolle 55 pen	13,000
23	sppr1	Real Sociedad	H	W	1-0	Beto 49	16,000
24	sppr1	Real Betis	A	D	0-0		35,000
25	sppr1	Atl Madrid	H	W	1-0	Sinama-Pongolle 10 pen	17,000
26	sppr1	Getafe	A	D	1-1	Uche 4	12,000
27	sppr1	Barcelona	H	L	0-4		20,000
28	sppr1	Gimnastic	A	D	1-1	Sinama-Pongolle 11	13,000
29	sppr1	Celta Vigo	H	W	4-2	Vasquez 37 pen, Rosu 85, 87, Gonzalez 90	17,820
30	sppr1	Osasuna	A	D	1-1	Sinama-Pongolle 51	16,000
31	sppr1	R Santander	H	W	4-2	Uche 2, Pablo Amo 32, Cazorla 39, Rosu 65	18,000
32	sppr1	Valencia	A	L	0-2		40,000
33	sppr1	Athl Bilbao	H	D	0-0		18,500
34	sppr1	Seville	A	L	1-2	Vasquez 89	42,000
35	sppr1	Real Madrid	H	L	2-3	Vasquez 74 pen, Uche 86	20,092
36	sppr1	Espanyol	H	L	0-1		15,048
37	sppr1	Deportivo	A	W	5-2	Gonzalez 16, Guerrero 18, Cazorla 58, 69, Sinama-Pongolle 75	15,000
38	sppr1	Real Zaragoza	H	D	1-1	Guerrero 3	15,000

LEAGUE APPEARANCES, BOOKINGS AND CAPS

	AGE (on 01/07/07)	IN NAMED 18	APPEARANCES	COUNTING GAMES	MINUTES ON PITCH	YELLOW CARDS	RED CARDS	CAPS THIS SEASON	NATIONAL SIDE
Goalkeepers									
Javier Lopez Vallejo	31	35	31	30	2745	3	0	-	Spain
Bertrand Laquait	30	35	8	7	675	1	0	-	France
Defenders									
Cesar Amposta Arzo	21	33	24	17	1687	8	0	-	Spain
Dani Bautista	26	33	23	19	1809	4	1	-	Spain
Roberto Severo Beto	31	29	25	18	1979	2	1	-	Portugal
Iago Amoedo Bouzon	24	23	6	2	289	0	0	-	Spain
Castillo Edu Moya	26	23	15	14	1292	4	0	-	Spain
Juanma	30	2	1	0	8	0	0	-	Spain
P A Abrante Mario	25	29	24	22	2020	4	0	-	Spain
Juan Merino	36	28	23	21	1970	3	1	-	Spain
Pablo Amo	29	18	14	11	1046	1	0	-	Spain
Fernandez Poli	30	25	18	17	1533	4	0	-	Spain
Midfielders									
Tornavaca Aitor	31	38	37	24	2579	4	0	-	Spain
Rafael Barber	26	28	21	14	1426	5	0	-	Spain
Santiago Cazorla	22	34	34	30	2816	1	0	-	Spain
J M Gonzalez Cheli	28	15	11	1	270	0	0	-	Spain
Gomes Juanma	26	29	27	9	1407	1	0	-	Spain
Jesus Vasquez	26	37	37	32	3100	7	0	-	Spain
Emilio Jose Viqueira	32	25	24	18	1842	2	0	-	Spain
Forwards									
Pablo Bernal	20	6	5	0	173	0	0	-	Spain
Antonio Calle	28	16	7	2	460	0	0	-	Spain
J Garcia Guerrero	30	29	23	7	1209	0	0	-	Spain
D Laurentiu Rosu	31	34	26	4	1059	1	0	9	Romania
F Sinama-Pongolle	22	35	34	13	2007	3	0	-	France
Ikechukwu Uche	23	31	31	18	2163	1	0	-	Nigeria

TEAM OF THE SEASON

	Fernandez Poli CG: 17 DR: 90		Emilio Jose Viqueira CG: 18 SD: 9	
	Cesar Amposta Arzo CG: 17 DR: 88		Santiago Cazorla CG: 30 SD: 5	F Sinama-Pongolle CG: 13 SR: 167
Javier Lopez Vallejo CG: 30 DR: 76	Juan Merino CG: 21 DR: 70		Jesus Vasquez CG: 32 SD: 0	Ikechukwu Uche CG: 18 SR: 270
	P Alvarez Abrante Mario CG: 22 DR: 69		Tornavaca Aitor CG: 24 SD: -5	

MONTHLY POINTS TALLY

Month			%
AUGUST		1	33%
SEPTEMBER		6	67%
OCTOBER		3	25%
NOVEMBER		9	75%
DECEMBER		6	50%
JANUARY		5	42%
FEBRUARY		7	58%
MARCH		4	44%
APRIL		8	53%
MAY		1	8%
JUNE		4	67%

LEAGUE GOALS

	PLAYER	MINS	GOALS	S RATE
1	S-Pongolle	2007	12	167
2	Uche	2163	8	270
3	Guerrero	1209	7	172
4	Vasquez	3100	6	516
5	Cazorla	2816	5	563
6	Rosu	1059	3	353
7	Calle	460	2	230
8	Juanma	1407	2	703
9	Gonzalez	270	1	270
10	Pablo Amo	1046	1	1046
11	Viqueira	1842	1	1842
12	Beto	1979	1	1979
13	Mario	2020	1	2020
	Other		1	
	TOTAL		**51**	

TOP POINT EARNERS

	PLAYER	GAMES	AV PTS
1	Emilio Jose Viqueira	18	1.61
2	Dani Bautista	19	1.58
3	Santiago Cazorla	30	1.57
4	Castillo Edu Moya	14	1.57
5	Javier Lopez Vallejo	30	1.57
6	Cesar Amposta Arzo	17	1.53
7	Jesus Vasquez	32	1.50
8	Tornavaca Aitor	24	1.46
9	Pedro A Abrante Mario	22	1.45
10	Ikechukwu Uche	18	1.44
	CLUB AVERAGE:		**1.42**

DISCIPLINARY RECORDS

	PLAYER	YELLOW	RED	AVE
1	C Amposta Arzo	8	0	210
2	Rafael Barber	5	0	285
3	Castillo Edu Moya	4	0	323
4	Dani Bautista	4	1	361
5	Fernandez Poli	4	0	383
6	Jesus Vasquez	7	0	442
7	Juan Merino	3	1	492
8	Pedro A A Mario	4	0	505
9	Tornavaca Aitor	4	0	644
10	Roberto S Beto	2	1	659
11	F Sinama-Pongolle	3	0	669
12	Bertrand Laquait	1	0	675
13	Javier L Vallejo	3	0	915
	Other	8	0	
	TOTAL	**60**	**3**	

KEY GOALKEEPER

Javier Lopez Vallejo

Goals Conceded in the League	36	Counting Games League games when player was on pitch for at least 70 minutes	30
Defensive Rating Ave number of mins between League goals conceded while on the pitch	76	Clean Sheets In League games when player was on pitch for at least 70 minutes	12

KEY PLAYERS - DEFENDERS

Fernandez Poli

Goals Conceded Number of League goals conceded while the player was on the pitch	17	Clean Sheets In League games when player was on pitch for at least 70 minutes	7
Defensive Rating Ave number of mins between League goals conceded while on the pitch	90	Club Defensive Rating Average number of mins between League goals conceded by the club this season	65

	PLAYER	CON LGE	CLEAN SHEETS	DEF RATE
1	Fernandez Poli	17	7	90 mins
2	Cesar Amposta Arzo	19	7	88 mins
3	Juan Merino	28	8	70 mins
4	Pedro Alvarez Abrante Mario	29	7	69 mins

KEY PLAYERS - MIDFIELDERS

Emilio Jose Viqueira

Goals in the League	1	Contribution to Attacking Power Average number of minutes between League team goals while on pitch	59
Defensive Rating Average number of mins between League goals conceded while on the pitch	68	Scoring Difference Defensive Rating minus Contribution to Attacking Power	9

	PLAYER	LGE GOALS	DEF RATE	POWER	SCORE DIFF
1	Emilio Jose Viqueira	1	68	59	9 mins
2	Santiago Cazorla	5	67	62	5 mins
3	Jesus Vasquez	6	59	59	0 mins
4	Tornavaca Aitor	1	59	64	-5 mins

KEY PLAYERS - GOALSCORERS

Florent Sinama-Pongolle

Goals in the League	12	Player Strike Rate Average number of minutes between League goals scored by player	167
Contribution to Attacking Power Average number of minutes between League team goals while on pitch	60	Club Strike Rate Average number of minutes between League goals scored by club	63

	PLAYER	LGE GOALS	POWER	STRIKE RATE
1	Florent Sinama-Pongolle	12	60	167 mins
2	Ikechukwu Uche	8	55	270 mins
3	Jesus Vasquez	6	59	516 mins
4	Santiago Cazorla	5	62	563 mins

Florent Sinama-Pongolle

SQUAD APPEARANCES

Match	1 2 3 4 5	6 7 8 9 10	11 12 13 14 15	16 17 18 19 20	21 22 23 24 25	26 27 28 29 30	31 32 33 34 35	36 37 38
Venue	H A H A H	A H A H A	H A H A H	A A H A A	H A H A H	A H A H A	H A H A H	H A H
Competition	L L L L L	L L L L L	L L L L L	L L L L L	L L L L L	L L L L L	L L L L L	L L L
Result	D W L W W	L L L W W	W L W L L	W W D D L	W L W D W	D L D W D	W L D L L	L W D

Goalkeepers

Javier Lopez Vallejo
Bertrand Laquait

Defenders

Cesar Amposta Arzo
Dani Bautista
Roberto Severo Beto
Iago Amoedo Bouzon
Castillo Edu Moya
Juanma
P A Abrante Mario
Juan Merino
Pablo Amo
Fernandez Poli

Midfielders

Tornavaca Aitor
Rafael Barber
Santiago Cazorla
J M Gonzalez Cheli
Gomes Juanma
Jesus Vasquez
Emilio Jose Viqueira

Forwards

Pablo Bernal
Antonio Calle
J Garcia Guerrero
D Laurentiu Rosu
F Sinama-Pongolle
Ikechukwu Uche

KEY: ■ On all match ◄◄ Subbed or sent off (Counting game) ►► Subbed on from bench (Counting Game) ►► Subbed on and then subbed or sent off (Counting Game) ☐ Not in 16
■ On bench ◄◄ Subbed or sent off (playing less than 70 minutes) ►► Subbed on (playing less than 70 minutes) ►► Subbed on and then subbed or sent off (playing less than 70 minutes)

SPAIN - RECREATIVO HUELVA

GETAFE

Final Position: 9th

NICKNAME: LOS AZULONES KEY: ☐ Won ☐ Drawn ☐ Lost Attendance

#		Opponent			Score	Scorers	Attendance
1	sppr1	Osasuna	A	W	2-0	Celestini 53, Nacho 75	15,506
2	sppr1	R Santander	H	W	1-0	Guiza 60	8,000
3	sppr1	Valencia	A	L	0-2		44,000
4	sppr1	Athl Bilbao	H	D	0-0		10,000
5	sppr1	Seville	A	L	0-1		45,000
6	sppr1	Real Madrid	H	W	1-0	Alexis 60	17,000
7	sppr1	Recreativo H	A	W	2-1	Pachon 42, Del Moral 72	18,000
8	sppr1	Deportivo	H	W	2-0	Del Moral 11, Nacho 68	9,000
9	sppr1	Real Zaragoza	A	L	1-3	Del Moral 68	27,000
10	sppr1	Mallorca	H	W	1-0	Nacho 60	9,000
11	sppr1	Villarreal	A	L	0-1		15,000
12	sppr1	Levante	H	D	0-0		12,000
13	sppr1	Real Sociedad	A	D	0-0		19,000
14	sppr1	Real Betis	H	D	1-1	Guiza 50	10,000
15	sppr1	Atl Madrid	A	L	0-1		30,000
16	sppr1	Espanyol	H	L	0-1		6,000
17	sppr1	Barcelona	H	D	1-1	Guiza 54	17,000
18	sppr1	Gimnastic	A	W	3-1	Vivar Dorado 12, Guiza 42, Casquero 75	12,000
19	sppr1	Celta Vigo	H	W	1-0	Del Moral 1	7,000
20	sppr1	Osasuna	H	W	2-0	Guiza 28, 45	12,000
21	sppr1	R Santander	A	L	0-1		14,000
22	sppr1	Valencia	H	W	3-0	Mario Cotelo 46, Guiza 58, Nacho 79	12,000
23	sppr1	Athl Bilbao	A	L	0-2		36,000
24	sppr1	Seville	H	D	0-0		14,000
25	sppr1	Real Madrid	A	D	1-1	Guiza 38	65,000
26	sppr1	Recreativo H	H	D	1-1	Guiza 24	12,000
27	sppr1	Deportivo	A	L	0-1		12,000
28	sppr1	Real Zaragoza	H	D	2-2	Del Moral 43, Casquero 61	12,000
29	sppr1	Mallorca	A	L	0-2		14,553
30	sppr1	Villarreal	H	W	3-0	Casquero 31, Maris 64, Pachon 84	12,000
31	sppr1	Levante	A	D	1-1	Belenguer 57	22,192
32	sppr1	Real Sociedad	H	W	1-0	Alexis 71	12,000
33	sppr1	Real Betis	A	W	2-0	Guiza 16, Casquero 35	45,000
34	sppr1	Atl Madrid	H	L	1-4	Del Moral 60	13,680
35	sppr1	Espanyol	A	W	5-1	Casquero 8, Del Moral 42, 71, Pulido 55, Guiza 65	20,200
36	sppr1	Barcelona	A	L	0-1		90,000
37	sppr1	Gimnastic	H	L	0-1		12,000
38	sppr1	Celta Vigo	A	L	1-2	Redondo 26	20,000

LEAGUE APPEARANCES, BOOKINGS AND CAPS

	AGE (on 01/07/07)	IN NAMED 18	APPEARANCES	COUNTING GAMES	MINUTES ON PITCH	YELLOW CARDS	RED CARDS	CAPS THIS SEASON	NATIONAL SIDE
Goalkeepers									
R Abbondanzieri	34	36	36	35	3216	3	0	5	Argentina
Luis Garcia	28	36	3	2	204	0	0	-	Spain
Defenders									
Ruano Alexis	21	26	24	23	2114	4	1	-	Spain
David Belenguer	34	35	34	33	3011	7	1	-	Spain
David Cortes	27	26	21	17	1670	1	0	-	Spain
Lucas Mathias Licht	26	19	7	2	334	1	0	-	Argentina
J Arango Paredes	24	34	34	34	3060	11	0	-	Spain
Martin Pulido	28	27	16	11	1078	2	1	-	Spain
Manuel Tena	30	21	10	8	741	2	0	-	Spain
Midfielders									
Aguilar Leiva Alberto	22	31	14	4	532	1	0	-	Spain
Juan Angel Albin	20	17	13	1	381	1	0	-	Uruguay
Francisco Casquero	30	36	36	33	3015	11	1	-	Spain
Fabio Celestini	31	34	34	33	2984	10	1	-	Switzerland
Cosmin Contra	31	29	20	17	1670	9	1	7	Romania
Gutierrez M Cotelo	32	33	31	26	2470	6	0	-	Spain
Nacho	27	35	33	19	2113	6	0	-	Spain
Pablo Redondo	25	31	22	10	1224	2	0	-	Spain
Francisco David Sousa	27	27	15	6	662	1	0	-	Spain
Angel Vivar Dorado	30	18	14	5	756	1	0	-	Spain
Forwards									
Manu Del Moral	23	31	30	25	2211	1	0	-	Spain
Daniel Gonzalez Guiza	26	29	29	22	1911	4	0	-	Spain
Valentin Pachon	30	28	24	6	916	0	0	-	Spain
Veljko Paunovic	29	16	14	6	655	2	0	-	Serbia
Maris Verpakovskis	27	18	13	2	483	0	0	6	Latvia

TEAM OF THE SEASON

G R Abbondanzieri **CG:** 35 **DR:** 107

D Ruano Alexis **CG:** 23 **DR:** 162
D David Belenguer **CG:** 33 **DR:** 103
D Javier Arango Paredes **CG:** 34 **DR:** 98
D David Cortes **CG:** 17 **DR:** 98

M Francisco Casquero **CG:** 33 **SD:** 32
M Gutierrez Mario Cotelo **CG:** 26 **SD:** 25
M Cosmin Contra **CG:** 17 **SD:** 25
M Nacho **CG:** 19 **SD:** 24

F D Gonzalez Guiza **CG:** 22 **SR:** 173
F Manu Del Moral **CG:** 25 **SR:** 276

MONTHLY POINTS TALLY

Month		Points	%
AUGUST		3	100%
SEPTEMBER		4	44%
OCTOBER		9	75%
NOVEMBER		4	33%
DECEMBER		2	17%
JANUARY		10	83%
FEBRUARY		4	33%
MARCH		2	22%
APRIL		8	53%
MAY		6	50%
JUNE		0	0%

LEAGUE GOALS

	PLAYER	MINS	GOALS	S RATE
1	Guiza	1911	11	173
2	Del Moral	2211	8	276
3	Casquero	3015	5	603
4	Nacho	2113	4	528
5	Pachon	916	2	458
6	Alexis	2114	2	1057
7	Vivar Dorado	756	1	756
8	Pulido	1078	1	1078
9	Redondo	1224	1	1224
10	Mario Cotelo	2470	1	2470
11	Celestini	2984	1	2984
12	Belenguer	3011	1	3011
13	Licht	334	0	
	Other		0	
	TOTAL		38	

TOP POINT EARNERS

	PLAYER	GAMES	AV PTS
1	Daniel Gonzalez Guiza	22	1.59
2	Gutierrez Mario Cotelo	26	1.58
3	Francisco Casquero	34	1.50
4	Ruano Alexis	23	1.48
5	Roberto Abbondanzieri	35	1.46
6	Cosmin Contra	18	1.44
7	Manu Del Moral	25	1.40
8	Nacho	19	1.37
9	David Belenguer	33	1.36
10	Fabio Celestini	34	1.32
	CLUB AVERAGE:		1.37

DISCIPLINARY RECORDS

	PLAYER	YELLOW	RED	AVE
1	Cosmin Contra	9	1	167
2	Franc Casquero	11	1	251
3	J Arango Paredes	11	0	278
4	Fabio Celestini	9	1	298
5	Veljko Paunovic	2	0	327
6	Nacho	6	0	352
7	Martin Pulido	2	1	359
8	Manuel Tena	2	0	370
9	David Belenguer	7	1	376
10	G Mario Cotelo	6	0	411
11	Ruano Alexis	4	1	422
12	D Gonzalez Guiza	4	0	477
13	Aguilar L Alberto	1	0	532
	Other	9	0	
	TOTAL	83	6	

KEY GOALKEEPER

Roberto Abbondanzieri

Goals Conceded in the League	30	Counting Games League games when player was on pitch for at least 70 minutes	35
Defensive Rating Ave number of mins between League goals conceded while on the pitch	107	Clean Sheets In League games when player was on pitch for at least 70 minutes	15

KEY PLAYERS - DEFENDERS

Ruano Alexis

Goals Conceded Number of League goals conceded while the player was on the pitch	13	Clean Sheets In League games when player was on pitch for at least 70 minutes	13
Defensive Rating Ave number of mins between League goals conceded while on the pitch	162	Club Defensive Rating Average number of mins between League goals conceded by the club this season	103

	PLAYER	CON LGE	CLEAN SHEETS	DEF RATE
1	Ruano Alexis	13	13	162 mins
2	David Belenguer	29	15	103 mins
3	Javier Arango Paredes	31	13	98 mins
4	David Cortes	17	7	98 mins

KEY PLAYERS - MIDFIELDERS

Francisco Casquero

Goals in the League	5	Contribution to Attacking Power Average number of minutes between League team goals while on pitch	79
Defensive Rating Average number of mins between League goals conceded while on the pitch	111	Scoring Difference Defensive Rating minus Contribution to Attacking Power	32

	PLAYER	LGE GOALS	DEF RATE	POWER	SCORE DIFF
1	Francisco Casquero	5	111	79	32 mins
2	Gutierrez Mario Cotelo	1	107	82	25 mins
3	Cosmin Contra	0	104	79	25 mins
4	Nacho	4	105	81	24 mins

KEY PLAYERS - GOALSCORERS

Daniel Gonzalez Guiza

Goals in the League	11	Player Strike Rate Average number of minutes between League goals scored by player	173
Contribution to Attacking Power Average number of minutes between League team goals while on pitch	70	Club Strike Rate Average number of minutes between League goals scored by club	87

	PLAYER	LGE GOALS	POWER	STRIKE RATE
1	Daniel Gonzalez Guiza	11	70	173 mins
2	Manu Del Moral	8	76	276 mins
3	Nacho	4	81	528 mins
4	Francisco Casquero	5	79	603 mins

Daniel Gonzalez Guiza

SQUAD APPEARANCES

Match	1	2	3	4	5	6	7	8	9	10	11	12	13	14	15	16	17	18	19	20	21	22	23	24	25	26	27	28	29	30	31	32	33	34	35	36	37	38
Venue	A	H	A	H	A	H	A	H	A	H	A	H	A	H	A	H	H	A	H	H	A	H	A	H	A	H	A	H	A	H	A	H	A	H	A	A	H	A
Competition	L	L	L	L	L	L	L	L	L	L	L	L	L	L	L	L	L	L	L	L	L	L	L	L	L	L	L	L	L	L	L	L	L	L	L	L	L	L
Result	W	W	L	D	L	W	W	W	L	W	L	D	D	D	L	L	D	W	W	W	L	W	L	D	D	D	L	D	L	W	D	W	W	L	W	L	L	L

Goalkeepers

Roberto Abbondanzieri

Luis Garcia

Defenders

Ruano Alexis

David Belenguer

David Cortes

Lucas Mathias Licht

Arango Paredes

Martin Pulido

Manuel Tena

Midfielders

Aguilar Leiva Alberto

Juan Angel Albin

Francisco Casquero

Fabio Celestini

Cosmin Contra

Gutierrez M Cotelo

Nacho

Pablo Redondo

Francisco David Sousa

Angel Vivar Dorado

Forwards

Manu Del Moral

Daniel Gonzalez Guiza

Valentin Pachon

Zeljko Paunovic

Maris Verpakovskis

KEY: ■ On all match   ◀◀ Subbed or sent off (Counting game)   ▶▶ Subbed on from bench (Counting Game)   ▶ Subbed on and then subbed or sent off (Counting Game)   Not in 16

□ On bench   ◀◀ Subbed or sent off (playing less than 70 minutes)   ▶▶ Subbed on (playing less than 70 minutes)   ▶▶ Subbed on and then subbed or sent off (playing less than 70 minutes)

SPAIN - GETAFE

RACING SANTANDER

Final Position: **10th**

NICKNAME: RACING

KEY: ☐ Won ☐ Drawn ☐ Lost

#		Opponent			Score	Scorers	Attendance
1	sppr1	Atl Madrid	H	L	0-1		17,897
2	sppr1	Getafe	A	L	0-1		8,000
3	sppr1	Barcelona	H	L	0-3		19,241
4	sppr1	Gimnastic	A	D	2-2	Zigic 48, 90	12,000
5	sppr1	Celta Vigo	H	D	1-1	Zigic 25	20,000
6	sppr1	Osasuna	A	W	1-0	Melo 53 pen	19,000
7	sppr1	Espanyol	A	D	2-2	Munitis 25, Chica 87 og	17,450
8	sppr1	Valencia	H	W	1-0	Munitis 57	15,000
9	sppr1	Athl Bilbao	A	D	0-0		38,000
10	sppr1	Seville	H	D	0-0		17,000
11	sppr1	Real Madrid	A	L	1-3	Garay 76	75,000
12	sppr1	Recreativo H	H	W	4-3	Zigic 14, 65, Garay 34, Colsa 42	16,000
13	sppr1	Deportivo	A	D	0-0		16,000
14	sppr1	Real Zaragoza	H	L	0-2		16,000
15	sppr1	Mallorca	A	W	2-1	Ruben 64, Balboa Osa 88	17,000
16	sppr1	Villarreal	H	W	2-1	Ruben 48, Colsa 64	13,414
17	sppr1	Levante	A	L	0-2		19,000
18	sppr1	Real Sociedad	H	W	1-0	Garay 90 pen	14,000
19	sppr1	Real Betis	A	D	1-1	Garay 85 pen	35,000
20	sppr1	Atl Madrid	A	D	1-1	Zigic 73	12,000
21	sppr1	Getafe	H	W	1-0	Garay 7	14,000
22	sppr1	Barcelona	A	L	0-2		70,000
23	sppr1	Gimnastic	H	W	4-1	Scaloni 60, Matellan 68 og, Colsa 75, Munitis 83	15,000
24	sppr1	Celta Vigo	A	D	2-2	Munitis 55, Cristian Alvarez 79 pen	12,000
25	sppr1	Osasuna	H	W	1-0	Juanjo 79	15,000
26	sppr1	Espanyol	H	D	1-1	Garay 10 pen	15,000
27	sppr1	Valencia	A	W	2-0	Munitis 19, Oriol 62	40,000
28	sppr1	Athl Bilbao	H	W	5-4	Christian 59, Garay 66 pen, Zigic 70, 89, Murillo 78 og	15,000
29	sppr1	Seville	A	D	0-0		41,405
30	sppr1	Real Madrid	H	W	2-1	Garay 73 pen, 89 pen	19,000
31	sppr1	Recreativo H	A	L	2-4	Garay 8, Zigic 66	18,000
32	sppr1	Deportivo	H	D	0-0		18,000
33	sppr1	Real Zaragoza	A	D	0-0		29,000
34	sppr1	Mallorca	H	L	0-2		15,845
35	sppr1	Villarreal	A	L	1-2	Melo 65	15,000
36	sppr1	Levante	H	L	2-3	Zigic 32, Melo 78	12,667
37	sppr1	Real Sociedad	A	D	0-0		23,348
38	sppr1	Real Betis	H	L	0-2		15,000

LEAGUE APPEARANCES, BOOKINGS AND CAPS

	AGE (on 01/07/07)	IN NAMED 18	APPEARANCES	COUNTING GAMES	MINUTES ON PITCH	YELLOW CARDS	RED CARDS	CAPS THIS SEASON	NATIONAL SIDE
Goalkeepers									
Juan Calatayud	28	36	6	5	509	0	0	-	Spain
A Rodriguez Tono	27	38	33	32	2910	2	1	-	Spain
Defenders									
Pablo Alfaro	38	16	5	4	386	2	0	-	Spain
F Sales Christian	21	16	10	8	802	5	0	-	Spain
Cristian Alvarez	29	31	22	5	858	3	0	-	Argentina
Luis Fernandez	34	21	16	15	1381	4	0	-	Spain
Ezequiel Garay	20	32	31	30	2723	3	0	-	Spain
Jose Moraton	27	3	1	0	27	0	0	-	Spain
Lozano Oriol	26	31	20	17	1639	3	1	-	Spain
Pablo Pinillos	32	35	35	33	3057	12	1	-	Spain
Ruben Gonzalez	25	34	34	31	2951	9	1	-	Spain
Midfielders									
Javier Balboa	22	36	30	6	1087	1	0	-	Spain
Gonzalo Colsa	28	38	37	32	3020	8	0	-	Spain
Juan Jose Juanjo	21	36	24	5	727	3	0	-	Spain
Sergio Matabuena	28	16	4	1	137	1	0	-	Spain
Felipe Melo	23	15	15	10	977	5	1	-	Brazil
J Figueroa Momo	24	26	13	1	319	0	0	-	Spain
Lionel Scaloni	29	30	30	29	2567	9	0	-	Argentina
Antonio Tomas	22	32	20	5	796	7	0	-	Spain
Vitolo	23	33	32	23	2352	10	1	-	Spain
Forwards									
David Aganzo	26	11	6	0	142	0	0	-	Spain
Pedro Munitis	32	34	34	32	2947	8	2	-	Spain
Portilla	18	1	1	0	25	0	0	-	Spain
Ruben Castro	26	1	1	0	24	0	0	-	Spain
Oscar Serrano	25	33	31	23	2306	6	0	-	Spain
Nicola Zigic	26	32	32	31	2784	12	1	6	Serbia

TEAM OF THE SEASON

G A Rodriguez Tono CG: 32 DR: 74

D Ezequiel Garay CG: 30 DR: 77
D Luis Fernandez CG: 15 DR: 72
D Pablo Pinillos CG: 33 DR: 71
D Ruben Gonzalez CG: 31 DR: 67

M Lionel Scaloni CG: 29 SD: -3
M Vitolo CG: 23 SD: -8
M Gonzalo Colsa CG: 32 SD: -18
M Felipe Melo CG: 10 SD: -19

F Nicola Zigic CG: 31 SR: 278
F Pedro Munitis CG: 32 SR: 589

MONTHLY POINTS TALLY

Month			
AUGUST		0	0%
SEPTEMBER		1	11%
OCTOBER		8	67%
NOVEMBER		5	42%
DECEMBER		7	58%
JANUARY		5	42%
FEBRUARY		7	58%
MARCH		7	78%
APRIL		8	53%
MAY		1	8%
JUNE		1	17%

LEAGUE GOALS

	PLAYER	MINS	GOALS	S RATE
1	Garay	2723	10	272
2	Zigic	2784	10	278
3	Munitis	2947	5	589
4	Melo	977	3	325
5	Colsa	3020	3	1006
6	R Gonzalez	2951	2	1475
7	Juanjo	727	1	727
8	Christian	802	1	802
9	Cristian Alvarez	858	1	858
10	Balboa	1087	1	1087
11	Oriol	1639	1	1639
12	Scaloni	2567	1	2567
13	Serrano	2306	0	
	Other		0	
	TOTAL		**39**	

TOP POINT EARNERS

	PLAYER	GAMES	AV PTS
1	Oscar Serrano	23	1.65
2	Nicola Zigic	31	1.58
3	Ezequiel Garay	30	1.57
4	Lionel Scaloni	29	1.48
5	Pedro Munitis	34	1.47
6	Gonzalo Colsa	32	1.44
7	Pablo Pinillos	33	1.39
8	Ruben Gonzalez	31	1.39
9	A Rodriguez Tono	32	1.31
10	Vitolo	23	1.26
	CLUB AVERAGE:		**1.32**

DISCIPLINARY RECORDS

	PLAYER	YELLOW	RED	AVE
1	Antonio Tomas	7	0	113
2	F Sales Christian	5	0	160
3	Felipe Melo	5	1	162
4	Vitolo	10	1	213
5	Nicola Zigic	12	1	214
6	Pablo Pinillos	12	1	235
7	Juan Jose Juanjo	3	0	242
8	Lionel Scaloni	9	0	285
9	Cristian Alvarez	3	0	286
10	Pedro Munitis	8	2	294
11	Ruben Gonzalez	9	1	295
12	Luis Fernandez	4	0	345
13	Gonzalo Colsa	8	0	377
	Other	14	2	
	TOTAL	**109**	**9**	

KEY GOALKEEPER

Antonio Rodriguez Tono

Goals Conceded in the League	39	Counting Games League games when player was on pitch for at least 70 minutes	32
Defensive Rating Ave number of mins between League goals conceded while on the pitch	74	Clean Sheets In League games when player was on pitch for at least 70 minutes	11

KEY PLAYERS - DEFENDERS

Ezequiel Garay

Goals Conceded Number of League goals conceded while the player was on the pitch	35	Clean Sheets In League games when player was on pitch for at least 70 minutes	12
Defensive Rating Ave number of mins between League goals conceded while on the pitch	77	Club Defensive Rating Average number of mins between League goals conceded by the club this season	71

	PLAYER	CON LGE	CLEAN SHEETS	DEF RATE
1	Ezequiel Garay	35	12	77 mins
2	Luis Fernandez	19	5	72 mins
3	Pablo Pinillos	43	12	71 mins
4	Ruben Gonzalez	44	10	67 mins

KEY PLAYERS - MIDFIELDERS

Lionel Scaloni

Goals in the League	1	Contribution to Attacking Power Average number of minutes between League team goals while on pitch	80
Defensive Rating Average number of mins between League goals conceded while on the pitch	77	Scoring Difference Defensive Rating minus Contribution to Attacking Power	-3

	PLAYER	LGE GOALS	DEF RATE	POWER	SCORE DIFF
1	Lionel Scaloni	1	77	80	-3 mins
2	Vitolo	0	67	75	-8 mins
3	Gonzalo Colsa	3	73	91	-18 mins
4	Felipe Melo	3	69	88	-19 mins

KEY PLAYERS - GOALSCORERS

Nicola Zigic

Goals in the League	10	Player Strike Rate Average number of minutes between League goals scored by player	278
Contribution to Attacking Power Average number of minutes between League team goals while on pitch	67	Club Strike Rate Average number of minutes between League goals scored by club	81

	PLAYER	LGE GOALS	POWER	STRIKE RATE
1	Nicola Zigic	10	67	278 mins
2	Felipe Melo	3	88	325 mins
3	Pedro Munitis	5	75	589 mins
4	Gonzalo Colsa	3	91	1006 mins

Gonzalo Colsa

SQUAD APPEARANCES

Match	1	2	3	4	5	6	7	8	9	10	11	12	13	14	15	16	17	18	19	20	21	22	23	24	25	26	27	28	29	30	31	32	33	34	35	36	37	38
Venue	H	A	H	A	H	A	A	H	A	H	A	H	L	L	A	H	A	H	A	H	L	H	L	H	A	H	A	H	A	H	A	H	A	H	A	H	A	H
Competition	L	L	L	L	L	L	L	L	L	L	L	L	L	L	L	L	L	L	L	L	L	L	L	L	L	L	L	L	L	L	L	L	L	L	L	L	L	L
Result	L	L	L	D	D	W	D	W	D	D	L	W	D	L	W	W	L	W	D	D	W	L	W	D	W	D	W	W	D	W	L	D	D	L	L	L	D	L

Goalkeepers
Juan Calatayud
A Rodriguez Tono

Defenders
Pablo Alfaro
F Sales Christian
Cristian Alvarez
De Abreu
Luis Fernandez
Ezequiel Garay
Marcano
Jose Moraton
Lozano Oriol
Pablo Pinillos
Ruben Gonzalez

Midfielders
Javier Balboa
Gonzalo Colsa
Juan Jose Juanjo
Sergio Matabuena
Felipe Melo
J Figueroa Momo
Lionel Scaloni
Antonio Tomas
Vitolo

Forwards
David Aganzo
Pedro Munitis
Platero
Portilla
Ruben Castro
Oscar Serrano
Nicola Zigic

KEY: ■ On all match   ◄◄ Subbed or sent off (Counting game)   ►► Subbed on from bench (Counting Game)   ►► Subbed on and then subbed or sent off (Counting Game)   ☐ Not in 16
■ On bench   ◄◄ Subbed or sent off (playing less than 70 minutes)   ►► Subbed on (playing less than 70 minutes)   ►► Subbed on and then subbed or sent off (playing less than 70 minutes)

SPAIN - RACING SANTANDER

ESPANYOL

Final Position: 11th

NICKNAME: PARAKEETS

KEY: ☐ Won ☐ Drawn ☐ Lost

#		Opponent		Result	Scorers	Attendance
1	sppr1	Gimnastic	H L	0-1		24,198
2	sppr1	Real Zaragoza	A L	0-3		28,000
3	ucrl1	Art Bratislava	A D	2-2	Riera 31, Pandiani 53	3,480
4	sppr1	Celta Vigo	H W	2-1	Moises Hurtado 49, Jonatas 55	49,000
5	sppr1	Mallorca	A L	0-1		15,000
6	ucrl2	Art Bratislava	H W	3-1	Pandiani 19, 80, Corominas 66	8,100
7	sppr1	Osasuna	H D	0-0		18,000
8	sppr1	Villarreal	A D	0-0		22,000
9	ucgpf	Sparta Prague	A W	2-0	Luis Garcia 17 pen, Riera 85	11,020
10	sppr1	R Santander	H D	2-2	Tamudo 45, 90 pen	17,450
11	sppr1	Levante	A D	0-0		15,000
12	sppr1	Valencia	H D	1-1	Riera 23	23,000
13	sppr1	Real Sociedad	A D	1-1	Luis Garcia 54	19,000
14	sppr1	Athl Bilbao	H W	3-2	Tamudo 54, 61, Pandiani 90	17,000
15	ucgpf	Zulte-Waregem	H W	6-2	Corominas 9, Pandiani 14, 83, Luis Garcia 19, 27 pen, 73	10,000
16	sppr1	Real Betis	A D	1-1	Pandiani 90	35,000
17	ucgpf	Ajax	A W	2-0	Pandiani 36, Corominas 77	41,248
18	sppr1	Seville	H W	2-0	Tamudo 68, Luis Garcia 80	18,000
19	sppr1	Atl Madrid	A W	2-1	Tamudo 8, Luis Garcia 62	40,000
20	ucgpf	Austria Vienna	H W	1-0	Pandiani 57	5,580
21	sppr1	Real Madrid	H L	0-1		25,000
22	sppr1	Getafe	A W	1-0	Tamudo 74	6,000
23	sppr1	Recreativo H	H L	0-1		25,000
24	sppr1	Barcelona	H W	3-1	Luis Garcia 31, Tamudo 65, Rufete 90	31,450
25	sppr1	Deportivo	A D	0-0		15,000
26	sppr1	Gimnastic	A L	0-4		10,000
27	sppr1	Real Zaragoza	H L	1-2	Luis Garcia 85	23,500
28	sppr1	Celta Vigo	A W	2-0	Luis Garcia 23, Pandiani 57	13,000
29	ucrl1	Livorno	A W	2-1	Pandiani 28 pen, Moha 59	18,000
30	sppr1	Mallorca	H W	3-1	Luis Garcia 29 , 79, Costa 90	18,550
31	ucrl2	Livorno	H W	2-0	Lacruz Gomez 16, Corominas 49	10,000
32	sppr1	Osasuna	A W	2-0	Corominas 13, Tamudo 66	16,000
33	sppr1	Villarreal	H D	1-1	Tamudo 29	28,000
34	ucrl1	Maccabi Haifa	A D	0-0		15,000
35	sppr1	R Santander	A D	1-1	Riera 6	15,000
36	ucrl2	Maccabi Haifa	H W	4-0	De La Pena 53, Tamudo 59, Luis Garcia 61, Pandiani 90	16,000
37	sppr1	Levante	H D	1-1	Luis Garcia 19	19,000
38	sppr1	Valencia	A L	2-3	Riera 14, Luis Garcia 63	45,000
39	ucqfl1	Benfica	H W	3-2	Tamudo 15, Nelson 33 og, Pandiani 58	20,000
40	sppr1	Real Sociedad	H W	1-0	Corominas 58	40,320
41	ucqfl2	Benfica	A D	0-0		40,000
42	sppr1	Athl Bilbao	A L	1-2	Jonatas 4	35,000
43	sppr1	Real Betis	H D	2-2	Riera 9, Tamudo 90 pen	20,150
44	ucsfl1	W Bremen	H W	3-0	Moises Hurtado 20, Pandiani 50, Corominas 88	35,000
45	sppr1	Seville	A L	1-3	Corominas 60	42,000
46	ucsfl2	W Bremen	A W	2-0	Corominas 50, Lacruz Gomez 61	37,000
47	sppr1	Atl Madrid	H W	2-1	Moha 10, Pandiani 75	20,450
48	sppr1	Real Madrid	A L	3-4	Pandiani 15, 26, 34	75,000
49	ucfin	Seville	H L	1-3*	Riera 28, Jonatas 115 (*on penalties)	50,000
50	sppr1	Getafe	H L	1-5	Corominas 4	20,200
51	sppr1	Recreativo H	A W	1-0	Tamudo 82	15,048
52	sppr1	Barcelona	A D	2-2	Tamudo 29, 90	90,695
53	sppr1	Deportivo	H L	1-3	Tamudo 48 pen	20,000

LEAGUE APPEARANCES, BOOKINGS AND CAPS

	AGE (on 01/07/07)	IN NAMED 18	APPEARANCES	COUNTING GAMES	MINUTES ON PITCH	YELLOW CARDS	RED CARDS	CAPS THIS SEASON	NATIONAL SIDE
Goalkeepers									
Gorka Iraizoz	26	35	2	2	180	0	0	-	Spain
Carlos Kameni	23	36	36	36	3240	3	0	1	Cameroon
Defenders									
Francisco Chica	22	30	27	27	2428	12	1	-	Spain
David Garcia	26	12	11	5	609	2	0	-	Spain
Daniel Jarque	24	36	36	33	3035	7	1	-	Spain
Jesus Lacruz Gomez	29	34	20	19	1758	2	0	-	Spain
Moises Hurtado	26	34	28	24	2364	15	1	-	Spain
Sergio Sanchez	21	4	2	0	110	4	0	-	Spain
Alberto Serran	22	3	2	1	95	0	0	-	Spain
Marc Torrejon Moya	21	37	29	26	2402	3	0	-	Spain
Juan Velasco	30	30	20	14	1435	5	0	-	Spain
Midfielders									
Angel Martinez	21	8	7	3	384	2	0	-	Spain
Ferran Corominas	24	37	30	13	1563	2	0	-	Spain
Eduardo Costa	24	19	16	8	890	5	1	-	Brazil
Ivan De La Pena	31	27	26	19	1948	9	0	-	Spain
Julian De Lerma	20	11	7	0	236	1	0	-	Spain
Fredson	26	7	2	1	151	0	0	-	Brazil
Ito	32	33	29	9	410	3	1	-	Spain
Domingos Jonatas	24	22	20	9	1199	6	0	-	Brazil
El Yaagoubi Moha	29	30	19	13	1187	6	0	-	Spain
Albert Riera	25	30	28	19	1951	6	3	-	Spain
Francisco Rufete	30	33	29	17	2111	10	0	-	Spain
Pablo Javier Zabaleta	22	25	20	16	1520	11	0	2	Argentina
Forwards									
Luis Garcia	26	36	35	29	2656	9	1	-	Spain
Miguel Palanca	19	1	1	0	23	0	0	-	Spain
Walter Pandiani	31	35	34	7	1243	7	1	-	Uruguay
Raul Tamudo	29	32	31	25	2389	6	0	-	Spain

TEAM OF THE SEASON

D Moises Hurtado CG: 24 DR: 73
M El Yaagoubi Moha CG: 13 SD: 4
D Marc Torrejon Moya CG: 26 DR: 70
M Ivan De La Pena CG: 20 SD: -4
F Raul Tamudo CG: 25 SR: 159
G Carlos Kameni CG: 36 DR: 64
D Francisco Chica CG: 27 DR: 62
M Albert Riera CG: 19 SD: -8
F Luis Garcia CG: 29 SR: 265
D Daniel Jarque CG: 33 DR: 61
M Pablo Javier Zabaleta CG: 16 SD: -11

MONTHLY POINTS TALLY

Month		Points	%
AUGUST		0	0%
SEPTEMBER		3	33%
OCTOBER		4	33%
NOVEMBER		6	50%
DECEMBER		9	75%
JANUARY		4	33%
FEBRUARY		9	75%
MARCH		3	25%
APRIL		4	33%
MAY		6	50%
JUNE		1	17%

LEAGUE GOALS

	PLAYER	MINS	GOALS	S RATE
1	Tamudo	2389	15	159
2	Luis Garcia	2656	10	265
3	Pandiani	1243	7	177
4	Corominas	1563	4	390
5	Riera	1951	4	487
6	Jonatas	1199	2	599
7	Costa	890	1	890
8	Moha	1187	1	1187
9	Rufete	2111	1	2111
10	M Hurtado	2364	1	2364
11	Palanca	23	0	
12	Pedraza	0	0	
13	Sergio Sanchez	110	0	
	Other		0	
	TOTAL		46	

TOP POINT EARNERS

	PLAYER	GAMES	AV PTS
1	Moises Hurtado	24	1.75
2	El Yaagoubi Moha	13	1.69
3	Marc Torrejon Moya	26	1.50
4	Francisco Chica	27	1.48
5	Raul Tamudo	25	1.40
6	Pablo Javier Zabaleta	16	1.38
7	Luis Garcia	29	1.38
8	Ivan De La Pena	20	1.35
9	Albert Riera	20	1.35
10	Francisco Rufete	17	1.29
	CLUB AVERAGE:		1.29

DISCIPLINARY RECORDS

	PLAYER	YELLOW	RED	AVE
1	Moises Hurtado	15	1	197
2	El Yaagoubi Moha	6	0	197
3	Domingos Jonatas	6	0	199
4	P Javier Zabaleta	11	0	217
5	Eduardo Costa	5	1	222
6	Francisco Chica	12	1	242
7	Walter Pandiani	7	1	248
8	Francisco Rufete	10	0	263
9	Ivan De La Pena	9	0	278
10	Albert Riera	6	3	278
11	David Garcia	2	0	304
12	Juan Velasco	5	0	358
13	Raul Tamudo	6	0	398
	Other	26	2	
	TOTAL	126	9	

KEY GOALKEEPER

Carlos Kameni

Goals Conceded in the League	50	Counting Games League games when player was on pitch for at least 70 minutes	36
Defensive Rating Ave number of mins between League goals conceded while on the pitch	64	Clean Sheets In League games when player was on pitch for at least 70 minutes	8

KEY PLAYERS - DEFENDERS

Moises Hurtado

Goals Conceded Number of League goals conceded while the player was on the pitch	32	Clean Sheets In League games when player was on pitch for at least 70 minutes	7
Defensive Rating Ave number of mins between League goals conceded while on the pitch	73	Club Defensive Rating Average number of mins between League goals conceded by the club this season	64

	PLAYER	CON LGE	CLEAN SHEETS	DEF RATE
1	Moises Hurtado	32	7	73 mins
2	Marc Torrejon Moya	34	7	70 mins
3	Francisco Chica	39	7	62 mins
4	Daniel Jarque	49	7	61 mins

KEY PLAYERS - MIDFIELDERS

El Yaagoubi Moha

Goals in the League	1	Contribution to Attacking Power Average number of minutes between League team goals while on pitch	65
Defensive Rating Average number of mins between League goals conceded while on the pitch	69	Scoring Difference Defensive Rating minus Contribution to Attacking Power	4

	PLAYER	LGE GOALS	DEF RATE	POWER	SCORE DIFF
1	El Yaagoubi Moha	1	69	65	4 mins
2	Ivan De La Pena	0	77	81	-4 mins
3	Albert Riera	4	67	75	-8 mins
4	Pablo Javier Zabaleta	0	84	95	-11 mins

KEY PLAYERS - GOALSCORERS

Raul Tamudo

Goals in the League	15	Player Strike Rate Average number of minutes between League goals scored by player	159
Contribution to Attacking Power Average number of minutes between League team goals while on pitch	70	Club Strike Rate Average number of minutes between League goals scored by club	74

	PLAYER	LGE GOALS	POWER	STRIKE RATE
1	Raul Tamudo	15	70	159 mins
2	Luis Garcia	10	73	265 mins
3	Ferran Corominas	4	86	390 mins
4	Albert Riera	4	75	487 mins

Luis Garcia and David Garcia

SQUAD APPEARANCES

Match	1 2 3 4	6 7 8 9 10	11 12 13 14 15	16 17 18 19 20	21 22 23 24 25	26 27 28 29 30	31 32 33 34 35	36 37 38 39 40	41 42 43 44 45	46 47 48 49 50	51 52 53
Venue	H A A H A	H H A A H	A H A H H	A A H A H	H A H H A	A H A A H	H A H A A	H H A H H	A A H H A	A H A H H	A A H
Competition	L L E L L	E L L E L	L L L L E	L E L L E	L L L L L	L L L E L	E L L E L	E L L E L	E L L E L	E L L E L	L L L
Result	L L D W L	W D D W D	D D D W W	D W W W W	L W L W D	L L W W W	W W D D D	W D L W W	D L D W L	W W L L L	W D L

Goalkeepers
Iorka Iraizoz
Carlos Kameni

Defenders
Francisco Chica
David Garcia
Daniel Jarque
Jesus Lacruz Gomez
Moises Hurtado
Sergio Sanchez
Alberto Serran
Marc Torrejon Moya
Juan Velasco

Midfielders
Angel Martinez
Ferran Corominas
Eduardo Costa
Ivan De La Pena
Julian Lopez De Lerma
Fredson
Io
Domingos Jonatas
El Yaagoubi Moha
Albert Riera
Francisco Rufete
Pablo Javier Zabaleta

Forwards
Luis Garcia
Miguel Palanca
Walter Pandiani
Raul Tamudo

KEY: ■ On all match   ◄◄ Subbed or sent off (Counting game)   ►► Subbed on from bench (Counting Game)   ◄►► Subbed on and then subbed or sent off (Counting Game)   □ Not in 16
■ On bench   ◄◄ Subbed or sent off (playing less than 70 minutes)   ►► Subbed on (playing less than 70 minutes)   ►► Subbed on and then subbed or sent off (playing less than 70 minutes)

SPAIN - ESPANYOL

MALLORCA

Final Position: **12th**

NICKNAME: BARRALETS   KEY: ☐ Won ☐ Drawn ☐ Lost   Attendance

				Result	Scorers	Attendance
1	sppr1	Recreativo H	A D	1-1	Arango 86	18,500
2	sppr1	Deportivo	H D	0-0		16,000
3	sppr1	Real Zaragoza	A L	0-2		26,700
4	sppr1	Espanyol	H W	1-0	Lopez 77	15,000
5	sppr1	Villarreal	H L	1-2	Jankovic 58	15,000
6	sppr1	Levante	A W	1-0	Arango 22	18,000
7	sppr1	Real Sociedad	H D	0-0		16,000
8	sppr1	Real Betis	A W	1-0	Jankovic 77	35,000
9	sppr1	Atl Madrid	H D	0-0		17,000
10	sppr1	Getafe	A L	0-1		9,000
11	sppr1	Barcelona	H L	1-4	Victor 70	20,000
12	sppr1	Gimnastic	A W	3-2	Jankovic 56, Victor 63, Arango 88	13,000
13	sppr1	Celta Vigo	H D	2-2	Jonas 6, Jankovic 52	17,000
14	sppr1	Osasuna	A L	0-3		17,000
15	sppr1	R Santander	H L	1-2	Jankovic 17	17,000
16	sppr1	Valencia	A L	1-3	Jonas 87 pen	40,000
17	sppr1	Athl Bilbao	H L	1-3	Exposito 82	18,000
18	sppr1	Seville	A W	2-1	Nunes 48, Lopez 62	45,000
19	sppr1	Real Madrid	H L	0-1		25,000
20	sppr1	Recreativo H	H W	2-1	Ballesteros 39, Nunes 45	12,000
21	sppr1	Deportivo	A L	0-1		18,000
22	sppr1	Real Zaragoza	H W	2-1	Nunes 57, Jankovic 83	15,000
23	sppr1	Espanyol	A L	1-3	Jankovic 44	18,550
24	sppr1	Villarreal	A L	1-2	Pereyra 26	18,000
25	sppr1	Levante	H W	3-1	Jankovic 48, Victor Casadesus 51, Arango 90	15,000
26	sppr1	Real Sociedad	A L	1-3	Ibagaza 40	20,000
27	sppr1	Real Betis	H W	2-0	Pereyra 1, Arango 2	18,000
28	sppr1	Atl Madrid	A D	1-1	Arango 53	40,000
29	sppr1	Getafe	H W	2-0	Nunes 64, Oscar Trejo 90	14,553
30	sppr1	Barcelona	A L	0-1		70,441
31	sppr1	Gimnastic	H W	1-0	Victor Casadesus 20	17,000
32	sppr1	Celta Vigo	A W	3-0	Arango 10, Varela 22, Lopez 80	23,000
33	sppr1	Osasuna	H W	3-1	Varela 37, Jonas 66, Jankovic 80	17,000
34	sppr1	R Santander	A W	2-0	Navarro 53, Arango 60	15,845
35	sppr1	Valencia	H L	0-1		18,000
36	sppr1	Athl Bilbao	A L	0-1		38,800
37	sppr1	Seville	H D	0-0		18,000
38	sppr1	Real Madrid	A L	1-3	Varela 17	80,000

LEAGUE APPEARANCES, BOOKINGS AND CAPS

	AGE (on 01/07/07)	IN NAMED 18	APPEARANCES	COUNTING GAMES	MINUTES ON PITCH	YELLOW CARDS	RED CARDS	CAPS THIS SEASON	NATIONAL SIDE
Goalkeepers									
Miguel Moya	23	35	17	17	1530	2	0	-	Spain
Antonio Prats	35	37	21	21	1890	3	0	-	Spain
Defenders									
Sergio Ballesteros	31	35	35	35	3139	9	1	-	Spain
Del Pino B Hector	32	29	21	20	1845	4	0	-	Spain
Javier Dorado	29	25	2	1	113	1	0	-	Spain
Fernando Navarro	25	37	37	37	3330	9	0	-	Spain
Jose C Araujo Nunes	30	36	36	33	3098	7	1	-	Portugal
Ivan Ramis	22	27	7	5	565	2	0	-	Spain
Fernando Varela	27	34	31	24	2277	6	2	-	Spain
Midfielders									
Juan Arango	27	37	37	32	2911	3	0	-	Venezuela
Angelos Basinas	31	34	29	16	1902	3	0	4	Greece
J Manuel Gutierrez	23	37	36	32	3011	2	1	1	Argentina
Ariel Ibagaza	30	29	29	25	2303	9	0	-	Argentina
Bosko Jankovic	23	33	28	14	1633	5	0	6	Serbia
Lopez Felpeto Jordi	26	30	24	11	1374	3	0	-	Spain
Daniel Kome	27	10	5	0	125	1	0	-	Cameroon
Guillermo Pereyra	27	33	28	21	2189	5	0	-	Argentina
Forwards									
Maxi Lopez	23	37	29	10	1410	5	1	-	Argentina
Guido Oscar Trejo	19	10	8	0	91	0	0	-	Argentina
L Nicolas Pisculichi	23	8	4	1	266	1	0	-	Argentina
Diego Tristan	31	17	13	4	527	1	0	-	Spain
Antoni Tuni	25	24	11	1	273	2	0	-	Spain
C Victor Casadesus	22	38	38	11	1714	5	0	-	Spain

TEAM OF THE SEASON

Del Pino B Hector
CG: 20 DR: 83

Ariel Ibagaza
CG: 25 SD: 18

Jose Carlos A Nunes
CG: 33 DR: 81

Jonas M Gutierrez
CG: 32 SD: -7

C Victor Casadesus
CG: 11 SR: 428

Antonio Prats
CG: 21 DR: 63

Fernando Varela
CG: 24 DR: 78

Juan Arango
CG: 32 SD: -10

Maxi Lopez
CG: 10 SR: 470

Fernando Navarro
CG: 37 DR: 75

Guillermo Pereyra
CG: 21 SD: -14

MONTHLY POINTS TALLY

AUGUST	1	33%
SEPTEMBER	4	44%
OCTOBER	7	58%
NOVEMBER	4	33%
DECEMBER	1	8%
JANUARY	6	50%
FEBRUARY	3	25%
MARCH	6	67%
APRIL	10	67%
MAY	6	50%
JUNE	1	17%

LEAGUE GOALS

	PLAYER	MINS	GOALS	S RATE
1	Jankovic	1633	9	181
2	Arango	2911	8	363
3	V Casadesus	1714	4	428
4	Nunes	3098	4	774
5	Lopez	1410	3	470
6	Varela	2277	3	759
7	Gutierrez	3011	3	1003
8	Pereyra	2189	2	1094
9	Oscar Trejo	91	1	91
10	Ibagaza	2303	1	2303
11	Ballesteros	3139	1	3139
12	Navarro	3330	1	3330
13	Basinas	1902	0	
	Other		0	
	TOTAL		40	

TOP POINT EARNERS

	PLAYER	GAMES	AV PTS
1	Miguel Moya	17	1.53
2	Ariel Ibagaza	25	1.52
3	Del Pino B Hector	20	1.45
4	Jonas Manuel Gutierrez	32	1.41
5	Sergio Ballesteros	35	1.40
6	Fernando Navarro	37	1.32
7	Jose C Araujo Nunes	34	1.32
8	Juan Arango	32	1.31
9	Guillermo Pereyra	21	1.14
10	Antonio Prats	21	1.10
	CLUB AVERAGE:		1.29

DISCIPLINARY RECORDS

	PLAYER	YELLOW	RED	AVE
1	Maxi Lopez	5	1	235
2	Ariel Ibagaza	9	0	255
3	Ivan Ramis	2	0	282
4	Fernando Varela	6	2	284
5	Sergio Ballesteros	9	1	313
6	Bosko Jankovic	5	0	326
7	C Victor Casadesus	5	0	342
8	Fernando Navarro	9	0	370
9	J C Araujo Nunes	7	1	387
10	Guillermo Pereyra	5	0	437
11	Lopez Felpeto Jordi	3	0	458
12	Del Pino B Hector	4	0	461
13	Diego Tristan	1	0	527
	Other	13	1	
	TOTAL	83	6	

KEY GOALKEEPER

Antonio Prats

Goals Conceded in the League	30	Counting Games League games when player was on pitch for at least 70 minutes	21
Defensive Rating Ave number of mins between League goals conceded while on the pitch	63	Clean Sheets In League games when player was on pitch for at least 70 minutes	6

KEY PLAYERS - DEFENDERS

Del Pino Berenguel Hector

Goals Conceded Number of League goals conceded while the player was on the pitch	22	Clean Sheets In League games when player was on pitch for at least 70 minutes	6
Defensive Rating Ave number of mins between League goals conceded while on the pitch	83	Club Defensive Rating Average number of mins between League goals conceded by the club this season	72

	PLAYER	CON LGE	CLEAN SHEETS	DEF RATE
1	Del Pino Berenguel Hector	22	6	83 mins
2	Jose Carlos Araujo Nunes	38	12	81 mins
3	Fernando Varela	29	9	78 mins
4	Fernando Navarro	44	12	75 mins

KEY PLAYERS - MIDFIELDERS

Ariel Ibagaza

Goals in the League	1	Contribution to Attacking Power Average number of minutes between League team goals while on pitch	74
Defensive Rating Average number of mins between League goals conceded while on the pitch	92	Scoring Difference Defensive Rating minus Contribution to Attacking Power	18

	PLAYER	LGE GOALS	DEF RATE	POWER	SCORE DIFF
1	Ariel Ibagaza	1	92	74	18 mins
2	Jonas Manuel Gutierrez	3	79	86	-7 mins
3	Juan Arango	8	78	88	-10 mins
4	Guillermo Pereyra	2	64	78	-14 mins

KEY PLAYERS - GOALSCORERS

Bosko Jankovic

Goals in the League	9	Player Strike Rate Average number of minutes between League goals scored by player	181
Contribution to Attacking Power Average number of minutes between League team goals while on pitch	71	Club Strike Rate Average number of minutes between League goals scored by club	83

	PLAYER	LGE GOALS	POWER	STRIKE RATE
1	Bosko Jankovic	9	71	181 mins
2	Juan Arango	8	88	363 mins
3	Castano Victor Casadesus	4	63	428 mins
4	Maxi Lopez	3	100	470 mins

Fernando Navarro

SQUAD APPEARANCES

Match	1	2	3	4	5	6	7	8	9	10	11	12	13	14	15	16	17	18	19	20	21	22	23	24	25	26	27	28	29	30	31	32	33	34	35	36	37	38
Venue	A	H	A	H	H	A	H	A	H	A	H	A	H	A	H	A	H	A	H	H	A	H	A	A	H	A	H	A	H	A	H	A	H	A	H	A	H	A
Competition	L	L	L	L	L	L	L	L	L	L	L	L	L	L	L	L	L	L	L	L	L	L	L	L	L	L	L	L	L	L	L	L	L	L	L	L	L	L
Result	D	D	L	W	L	W	D	W	D	L	L	W	D	L	L	L	L	W	L	W	L	W	L	L	W	L	W	D	W	L	W	W	W	W	L	L	D	L

Goalkeepers

Miguel Moya

Antonio Prats

Defenders

Sergio Ballesteros

Del Pino B Hector

Javier Dorado

Fernando Navarro

Jose C Araujo Nunes

Ivan Ramis

Fernando Varela

Midfielders

Juan Arango

Angelos Basinas

Jonas Manuel Gutierrez

Ariel Ibagaza

Bosko Jankovic

Lopez Felpeto Jordi

Daniel Kome

Guillermo Pereyra

Forwards

Maxi Lopez

Guido Oscar Trejo

Nicolas Pisculichi

Diego Tristan

Antoni Tuni

Victor Casadesus

KEY: ■ On all match ◄◄ Subbed or sent off (Counting game) ►► Subbed on from bench (Counting Game) ►► Subbed on and then subbed or sent off (Counting Game) ☐ Not in 16
■ On bench ◄◄ Subbed or sent off (playing less than 70 minutes) ►► Subbed on (playing less than 70 minutes) ►► Subbed on and then subbed or sent off (playing less than 70 minutes)

SPAIN - MALLORCA

DEPORTIVO LA CORUNA

Final Position: **13th**

NICKNAME: DEPOR   KEY: ☐ Won ☐ Drawn ☐ Lost   Attendance

#		Opponent	H/A	Result	Scorers	Result	Attendance
1	sppr1	Real Zaragoza	H	W	**3-2**	Juan Rodriguez 17, Sergio 38, Arizmendi 75	16,000
2	sppr1	Mallorca	A	D	**0-0**		16,000
3	sppr1	Villarreal	H	W	**2-0**	Capdevila 4, 67	22,000
4	sppr1	Levante	A	L	**0-2**		15,000
5	sppr1	Real Sociedad	H	W	**2-0**	Barragan 83, Riki 88	20,000
6	sppr1	Real Betis	A	D	**1-1**	Arizmendi 48	32,000
7	sppr1	Atl Madrid	H	W	**1-0**	Arizmendi 66	20,000
8	sppr1	Getafe	A	L	**0-2**		9,000
9	sppr1	Barcelona	H	D	**1-1**	Juan Rodriguez 73	34,000
10	sppr1	Gimnastic	A	D	**0-0**		14,000
11	sppr1	Celta Vigo	H	L	**0-1**		16,000
12	sppr1	Osasuna	A	L	**1-4**	Juan Rodriguez 30	15,000
13	sppr1	R Santander	H	D	**0-0**		16,000
14	sppr1	Valencia	A	L	**0-4**		45,000
15	sppr1	Athl Bilbao	H	L	**0-2**		20,000
16	sppr1	Seville	A	L	**0-4**		45,000
17	sppr1	Real Madrid	H	W	**2-0**	Capdevila 10, Cristian 56	32,000
18	sppr1	Recreativo H	A	D	**1-1**	Arizmendi 20	18,000
19	sppr1	Espanyol	H	D	**0-0**		15,000
20	sppr1	Real Zaragoza	A	D	**1-1**	Taborda 21	27,000
21	sppr1	Mallorca	H	W	**1-0**	Estoyanoff 45 pen	18,000
22	sppr1	Villarreal	A	W	**2-0**	Senna 19 og, Verdu 79	18,000
23	sppr1	Levante	H	D	**0-0**		15,000
24	sppr1	Real Sociedad	A	W	**1-0**	Arizmendi 29	24,424
25	sppr1	Real Betis	H	L	**0-1**		23,000
26	sppr1	Atl Madrid	A	L	**0-2**		40,000
27	sppr1	Getafe	H	W	**1-0**	Barragan 80	12,000
28	sppr1	Barcelona	A	L	**1-2**	Adrian 68	70,000
29	sppr1	Gimnastic	H	W	**1-0**	Iago 58	23,182
30	sppr1	Celta Vigo	A	L	**0-1**		24,000
31	sppr1	Osasuna	H	W	**1-0**	Lopo 90	14,000
32	sppr1	R Santander	A	D	**0-0**		18,000
33	sppr1	Valencia	H	L	**1-2**	Taborda 69	20,000
34	sppr1	Athl Bilbao	A	D	**1-1**	Riki 63	35,012
35	sppr1	Seville	H	L	**1-2**	Bodipo 72	12,000
36	sppr1	Real Madrid	A	L	**1-3**	Capdevila 54	75,000
37	sppr1	Recreativo H	H	L	**2-5**	Bodipo 71, Juan Rodriguez 79 pen	15,000
38	sppr1	Espanyol	A	W	**3-1**	Iago 61, Sergio 63, Riki 84	20,000

LEAGUE APPEARANCES, BOOKINGS AND CAPS

	AGE (on 01/07/07)	IN NAMED 18	APPEARANCES	COUNTING GAMES	MINUTES ON PITCH	YELLOW CARDS	RED CARDS	CAPS THIS SEASON	NATIONAL SIDE
Goalkeepers									
Dudu Aouate	29	38	38	38	3420	3	0	-	Israel
Gustavo Munua	29	30	0	0	0	0	0	-	Uruguay
Defenders									
Jorge Andrade	29	22	22	21	1903	7	1	6	Portugal
Alvaro Arbeloa	24	20	20	20	1763	5	0	-	Spain
Antonio Barragan	19	30	16	8	910	4	0	-	Spain
Joan Capdevila	29	5	5	5	450	2	0	-	Spain
Fabricio Coloccini	25	29	26	22	2201	8	0	1	Argentina
Luis Filipe	28	27	18	8	977	2	1	-	Portugal
Juanma	30	19	7	6	569	5	2	-	Spain
Alberto Lopo	28	33	31	29	2695	10	1	-	Spain
Manuel Pablo	31	31	15	12	1184	2	0	-	Spain
Sergio Rodri	22	6	1	0	1	0	0	-	Spain
Midfielders									
Pablo Alvarez	27	10	7	3	343	2	0	-	Spain
Juan Capdevila	29	29	29	29	2585	7	1	-	Spain
Julian De Guzman	26	25	20	14	1445	6	1	-	Canada
Aldo Duscher	28	17	15	7	938	5	0	-	Argentina
Fabian Estoyanoff	24	29	28	11	1629	8	1	2	Uruguay
Iago	23	18	9	1	260	0	0	-	Spain
Juan Rodriguez	25	36	31	21	2196	6	0	-	Spain
Gonzalez Sergio	30	35	28	16	1962	8	0	-	Spain
Juan Carlos Valeron	32	2	1	0	1	0	0	-	Spain
Joan Verdu	24	30	27	10	1367	3	0	-	Spain
Forwards									
Adrian	19	21	15	4	752	2	0	-	Spain
Javier Arizmendi	23	33	33	28	2726	4	1	1	Spain
Rodolfo Diaz Bodipo	29	7	7	0	267	0	0	-	Spain
Hidalgo Cristian	23	30	29	20	2032	7	1	-	Spain
Ivan Riki	26	34	33	20	2218	4	0	-	Spain
Ruben Rivera Corral	22	1	1	0	56	0	0	-	Spain
Sebastian Taborda	26	22	16	1	510	2	1	-	Uruguay

TEAM OF THE SEASON

Dudu Aouate (G) CG: 38 DR: 76

Alberto Lopo (D) CG: 29 DR: 84
Jorge Andrade (D) CG: 21 DR: 82
Alvaro Arbeloa (D) CG: 20 DR: 76
Fabricio Coloccini (D) CG: 22 DR: 71

Julian De Guzman (M) CG: 14 SD: 15
Fabian Estoyanoff (M) CG: 11 SD: -9
Juan Rodriguez (M) CG: 21 SD: -45
Gonzalez Sergio (M) CG: 16 SD: -58

Javier Arizmendi (F) CG: 28 SR: 545
Ivan Riki (F) CG: 20 SR: 739

MONTHLY POINTS TALLY

Month		Points	%
AUGUST		3	100%
SEPTEMBER		4	44%
OCTOBER		7	58%
NOVEMBER		2	17%
DECEMBER		1	8%
JANUARY		6	50%
FEBRUARY		10	83%
MARCH		3	25%
APRIL		7	58%
MAY		1	8%
JUNE		3	50%

LEAGUE GOALS

	PLAYER	MINS	GOALS	S RATE
1	Arizmendi, J	2726	5	545
2	J Rodriguez	2196	4	549
3	Riki	2218	3	739
4	Iago	260	2	130
5	Bodipo	267	2	133
6	Capdevila	450	2	225
7	Taborda	510	2	255
8	Barragan	910	2	455
9	Sergio	1962	2	981
10	Capdevila	2585	2	1292
11	Adrian	752	1	752
12	Verdu	1367	1	1367
13	Estoyanoff	1629	1	1629
	Other		2	
	TOTAL		**31**	

TOP POINT EARNERS

	PLAYER	GAMES	AV PTS
1	Julian De Guzman	14	1.43
2	Hidalgo Cristian	20	1.40
3	Ivan Riki	20	1.40
4	Javier Arizmendi	29	1.38
5	Jorge Andrade	22	1.36
6	Alberto Lopo	29	1.31
7	Fabricio Coloccini	22	1.27
8	Dudu Aouate	38	1.24
9	Alvaro Arbeloa	20	1.15
10	Manuel Pablo	12	1.08
	CLUB AVERAGE:		**1.24**

DISCIPLINARY RECORDS

	PLAYER	YELLOW	RED	AVE
1	Juanma	5	2	81
2	Sebastian Taborda	2	1	170
3	Fabian Estoyanoff	8	1	181
4	Aldo Duscher	5	0	187
5	Julian De Guzman	6	1	206
6	Antonio Barragan	4	0	227
7	Jorge Andrade	7	1	237
8	Alberto Lopo	10	1	245
9	Gonzalez Sergio	8	0	245
10	Hidalgo Cristian	7	1	254
11	Fabricio Coloccini	8	0	275
12	Juan Capdevila	7	1	323
13	Luis Filipe	2	1	325
	Other	29	1	
	TOTAL	**108**	**11**	

KEY GOALKEEPER

Dudu Aouate

Goals Conceded in the League	45	Counting Games League games when player was on pitch for at least 70 minutes	38
Defensive Rating Ave number of mins between League goals conceded while on the pitch	76	Clean Sheets In League games when player was on pitch for at least 70 minutes	16

KEY PLAYERS - DEFENDERS

Alberto Lopo

Goals Conceded Number of League goals conceded while the player was on the pitch	32	Clean Sheets In League games when player was on pitch for at least 70 minutes	13
Defensive Rating Ave number of mins between League goals conceded while on the pitch	84	Club Defensive Rating Average number of mins between League goals conceded by the club this season	76

	PLAYER	CON LGE	CLEAN SHEETS	DEF RATE
1	Alberto Lopo	32	13	84 mins
2	Jorge Andrade	23	10	82 mins
3	Alvaro Arbeloa	23	8	76 mins
4	Fabricio Coloccini	31	8	71 mins

KEY PLAYERS - MIDFIELDERS

Julian De Guzman

Goals in the League	0	Contribution to Attacking Power Average number of minutes between League team goals while on pitch	96
Defensive Rating Average number of mins between League goals conceded while on the pitch	111	Scoring Difference Defensive Rating minus Contribution to Attacking Power	15

	PLAYER	LGE GOALS	DEF RATE	POWER	SCORE DIFF
1	Julian De Guzman	0	111	96	15 mins
2	Fabian Estoyanoff	1	116	125	-9 mins
3	Juan Rodriguez	4	54	99	-45 mins
4	Gonzalez Sergio	2	72	130	-58 mins

KEY PLAYERS - GOALSCORERS

Javier Arizmendi

Goals in the League	5	Player Strike Rate Average number of minutes between League goals scored by player	545
Contribution to Attacking Power Average number of minutes between League team goals while on pitch	109	Club Strike Rate Average number of minutes between League goals scored by club	106

	PLAYER	LGE GOALS	POWER	STRIKE RATE
1	Javier Arizmendi	5	109	545 mins
2	Juan Rodriguez	4	99	549 mins
3	Ivan Riki	3	130	739 mins
4	Gonzalez Sergio	2	130	981 mins

Javier Arizmendi

SQUAD APPEARANCES

Match	1	2	3	4	5	6	7	8	9	10	11	12	13	14	15	16	17	18	19	20	21	22	23	24	25	26	27	28	29	30	31	32	33	34	35	36	37	38
Venue	H	A	H	A	H		A	H	A	H		H	A	H	A	H		A	H	A	H	A		H	A	H	A	H		A	H	A	H	A	H		A	H	A
Competition	L	L	L	L	L		L	L	L	L		L	L	L	L	L		L	L	L	L		L	L	L	L		L	L	L	L	L		L	L	L	L		L	L	L
Result	W	D	W	L	W		D	W	L	D	D		L	L	D	L	L		L	W	D	D	D		W	W	D	W	L		L	W	L	W	L		W	D	L	D	L		L	L	W

Goalkeepers
Dudu Aouate
Gustavo Munua

Defenders
Jorge Andrade
Alvaro Arbeloa
Antonio Barragan
Joan Capdevila
Fabricio Coloccini
Luis Filipe
Juanma
Alberto Lopo
Manuel Pablo
Sergio Rodri

Midfielders
Pablo Alvarez
Juan Capdevila
Julian De Guzman
Aldo Duscher
Fabian Estoyanoff
Ngo
Juan Rodriguez
Gonzalez Sergio
Juan Carlos Valeron
Joan Verdu

Forwards
Adrian
Javier Arizmendi
Rodolfo Diaz Bodipo
Hidalgo Cristian
Ivan Riki
Ruben Rivera Corral
Sebastian Taborda

KEY: ■ On all match ◄◄ Subbed or sent off (Counting game) ►►I Subbed on from bench (Counting Game) ◄I Subbed on and then subbed or sent off (Counting Game) □ Not in 16
■ On bench ◄◄ Subbed or sent off (playing less than 70 minutes) ►► Subbed on (playing less than 70 minutes) ►► Subbed on and then subbed or sent off (playing less than 70 minutes)

SPAIN - DEPORTIVO LA CORUNA

OSASUNA

Final Position: **14th**

NICKNAME: LOS ROJILLOS   KEY: ☐ Won ☐ Drawn ☐ Lost   Attendance

#	Comp	Opponent	H/A	Result	Result	Scorers	Attendance
1	ecql1	Hamburg	A	D	0-0		47,458
2	ecql2	Hamburg	H	D	1-1	Cuellar 6	18,766
3	sppr1	Getafe	H	L	0-2		15,506
4	sppr1	Barcelona	A	L	0-3		63,720
5	ucrl1	Trabzonspor	A	D	2-2	Valdo 21, Juanlu 52	49,991
6	sppr1	Gimnastic	H	W	2-0	Webo 1, Milosevic 90	18,900
7	sppr1	Celta Vigo	A	W	2-0	Valdo 35, Juanfran 90	17,000
8	ucrl2	Trabzonspor	H	D	0-0		15,000
9	sppr1	Espanyol	A	D	0-0		18,000
10	sppr1	R Santander	H	L	0-1		19,000
11	ucgpd	Heerenveen	H	D	0-0		20,000
12	sppr1	Valencia	A	L	0-1		45,000
13	sppr1	Athl Bilbao	H	D	1-1	Soldado 54	18,210
14	ucgpd	Lens	A	L	1-3	Valdo 46	26,000
15	sppr1	Seville	A	L	0-2		45,500
16	sppr1	Real Madrid	H	L	1-4	Valdo 63	19,000
17	sppr1	Recreativo H	A	L	0-2		18,000
18	sppr1	Deportivo	H	W	4-1	Soldado 5, 60, Valdo 22, Milosevic 90	15,000
19	ucgpd	Odense	H	W	3-1	Punal 29, 67, Romeo 87	13,000
20	sppr1	Real Zaragoza	A	W	2-1	R.Garcia 82, Ponzio 90 og	28,000
21	sppr1	Mallorca	H	W	3-0	Milosevic 60, J.Flano 68, Punal 80 pen	17,000
22	ucgpd	Parma	A	W	3-0	David Lopez 33, 44, Juanfran 82	3,109
23	sppr1	Villarreal	A	W	4-1	Webo 13, Nekounam 42, Lopez 56 pen, Juanfran 70	19,000
24	sppr1	Levante	H	W	2-1	Cruchaga 57, Soldado 69	14,943
25	sppr1	Real Sociedad	A	L	1-2	R.Garcia 55	20,000
26	sppr1	Real Betis	H	W	5-1	Soldado 16, 58, Punal 29, Lopez 57, Webo 72	15,000
27	sppr1	Atl Madrid	A	L	0-1		40,000
28	sppr1	Getafe	A	L	0-2		12,000
29	sppr1	Barcelona	H	D	0-0		18,000
30	sppr1	Gimnastic	A	W	3-2	Cuellar 13, Soldado 71, 75	11,000
31	ucrl1	Bordeaux	A	D	0-0		20,000
32	sppr1	Celta Vigo	H	L	0-1		15,647
33	ucrl2	Bordeaux	H	W	1-0	Nekounam 120	14,000
34	sppr1	Espanyol	H	L	0-2		16,000
35	sppr1	R Santander	A	L	0-1		15,000
36	ucrl1	Rangers	A	D	1-1	Raul Garcia 17	50,290
37	sppr1	Valencia	H	D	1-1	Punal 35 pen	17,000
38	ucrl2	Rangers	H	W	1-0	Webo 71	35,000
39	sppr1	Athl Bilbao	A	W	3-0	Munoz 30 pen, David Lopez 47, Izquierdo 72	38,000
40	sppr1	Seville	H	D	0-0		18,000
41	ucqfl1	B Leverkusen	A	W	3-0	Cuellar 1, David Lopez 72, Webo 73	22,500
42	sppr1	Real Madrid	A	L	0-2		72,270
43	ucqfl2	B Leverkusen	H	W	1-0	Juanlu 62	19,800
44	sppr1	Recreativo H	H	D	1-1	Cruchaga 54	16,000
45	sppr1	Deportivo	A	L	0-1		14,000
46	ucsfl1	Seville	H	W	1-0	Soldado 55	19,500
47	sppr1	Real Zaragoza	H	D	2-2	Juanlu 5, Valdo 55	16,000
48	ucsfl2	Seville	A	L	0-2		45,000
49	sppr1	Mallorca	A	L	1-3	Raul Garcia 60	17,000
50	sppr1	Villarreal	H	L	1-4	Valdo 17	18,545
51	sppr1	Levante	A	W	4-1	Soldado 18, 32, 64, Raul Garcia 45	21,294
52	sppr1	Real Sociedad	H	W	2-0	David Lopez 26, Nekounam 33	18,274
53	sppr1	Real Betis	A	W	5-0	M.Flano 32, Webo 62, Valdo 72, Echaide 76, 88	35,000
54	sppr1	Atl Madrid	H	L	1-2	Milosevic 47	18,000

LEAGUE APPEARANCES, BOOKINGS AND CAPS

	AGE (on 01/07/07)	IN NAMED 18	APPEARANCES	COUNTING GAMES	MINUTES ON PITCH	YELLOW CARDS	RED CARDS	CAPS THIS SEASON	NATIONAL SIDE
Goalkeepers									
Juan Elia	37	38	3	2	239	0	0	-	Spain
Lopez Ricardo	35	37	36	35	3180	5	1	-	Spain
Defenders									
Enrique Corrales	25	28	28	28	2505	16	0	-	Spain
Cesar Cruchaga	33	33	18	17	1538	4	0	-	Spain
Carlos Cuellar	35	31	23	22	2018	11	1	-	Spain
Javier Flano	22	35	27	26	2349	11	0	-	Spain
Miguel Flano	22	30	17	17	1530	3	0	-	Spain
Jose Izquierdo	26	21	11	10	965	4	1	-	Spain
Jose Romero Josetxo	32	31	19	19	1692	11	1	-	Spain
Nacho Monreal	21	13	10	10	900	4	0	-	Spain
Midfielders									
Cesar Azpilicueta	17	1	1	0	25	0	0	-	Spain
David Lopez	24	32	30	24	2258	4	0	-	Spain
Ludovic Delporte	27	9	8	6	560	6	0	-	Spain
Ion Echaide	19	1	1	0	21	0	0	-	Spain
Ion Erice	21	6	5	4	368	0	0	-	Spain
Romero Hector Font	23	26	16	5	672	5	0	-	Spain
Juanfran	22	30	28	13	1581	6	0	-	Spain
Javad Nekounam	26	30	24	20	1866	5	0	-	Iran
Francisco Punal	31	34	32	24	2441	10	0	-	Spain
Raul Garcia	20	35	33	24	2512	15	1	-	Spain
Luis Sota	25	2	1	0	19	1	0	-	Spain
Valmiro Valdo	26	27	26	19	1886	9	0	-	Brazil
Forwards									
Juanlu	27	24	18	1	715	2	0	-	Spain
Savo Milosevic	33	26	24	14	1634	3	0	-	Serbia
Inaki Munoz	28	28	21	5	742	5	0	-	Spain
Bernardo Romeo	29	14	8	1	293	1	0	-	Argentina
Roberto Soldado	22	30	29	18	1779	9	1	2	Spain
Pierre Webo	25	32	31	8	1294	4	0	5	Cameroon

TEAM OF THE SEASON

D   Miguel Flano   CG: 17 DR: 102
M   David Lopez   CG: 24 SD: 16

D   Cesar Cruchaga   CG: 17 DR: 76
M   Javad Nekounam   CG: 20 SD: 10
F   Roberto Soldado   CG: 18 SR: 161

G   Lopez Ricardo   CG: 35 DR: 70

D   Enrique Corrales   CG: 28 DR: 73
M   Juanfran   CG: 13 SD: 10
F   Savo Milosevic   CG: 14 SR: 408

D   Carlos Cuellar   CG: 22 DR: 67
M   Raul Garcia   CG: 24 SD: 2

MONTHLY POINTS TALLY

Month		Points	%
AUGUST		0	0%
SEPTEMBER		6	67%
OCTOBER		2	17%
NOVEMBER		3	25%
DECEMBER		12	100%
JANUARY		3	25%
FEBRUARY		4	33%
MARCH		4	44%
APRIL		3	20%
MAY		6	50%
JUNE		3	50%

LEAGUE GOALS

	PLAYER	MINS	GOALS	S RATE
1	Soldado	1779	11	161
2	Valdo	1886	6	314
3	Webo	1294	4	323
4	Milosevic	1634	4	408
5	Raul Garcia	2512	4	628
6	David Lopez	2258	3	752
7	Punal	2441	3	813
8	Echaide	21	2	10
9	Cruchaga	1538	2	769
10	Juanfran	1581	2	790
11	Nekounam	1866	2	933
12	Juanlu	715	1	715
13	Munoz	742	1	742
	Other		4	
	TOTAL		49	

TOP POINT EARNERS

	PLAYER	GAMES	AV PTS
1	Miguel Flano	17	1.59
2	Javad Nekounam	20	1.50
3	Valmiro Valdo	19	1.42
4	Roberto Soldado	18	1.39
5	Enrique Corrales	28	1.39
6	Cesar Cruchaga	17	1.29
7	David Lopez	24	1.29
8	Javier Flano	26	1.23
9	Lopez Ricardo	35	1.23
10	Francisco Punal	24	1.21
	CLUB AVERAGE:		1.21

DISCIPLINARY RECORDS

	PLAYER	YELLOW	RED	AVE
1	R Hector Font	5	0	134
2	Ludovic Delporte	6	0	140
3	Jose R Josetxo	11	1	188
4	Carlos Cuellar	11	1	201
5	Raul Garcia	15	1	209
6	Enrique Corrales	16	0	227
7	Inaki Munoz	5	0	247
8	Roberto Soldado	9	1	254
9	Javier Flano	11	0	261
10	Valmiro Valdo	9	0	269
11	Nacho Monreal	4	0	300
12	Juanfran	6	0	316
13	Francisco Punal	10	0	406
	Other	34	2	
	TOTAL	152	6	

KEY GOALKEEPER

Lopez Ricardo

Goals Conceded in the League	45	**Counting Games** League games when player was on pitch for at least 70 minutes	35
Defensive Rating Ave number of mins between League goals conceded while on the pitch	70	**Clean Sheets** In League games when player was on pitch for at least 70 minutes	9

KEY PLAYERS - DEFENDERS

Miguel Flano

Goals Conceded Number of League goals conceded while the player was on the pitch	15	**Clean Sheets** In League games when player was on pitch for at least 70 minutes	9
Defensive Rating Ave number of mins between League goals conceded while on the pitch	102	**Club Defensive Rating** Average number of mins between League goals conceded by the club this season	69

	PLAYER	CON LGE	CLEAN SHEETS	DEF RATE
1	Miguel Flano	15	9	102 mins
2	Cesar Cruchaga	20	3	76 mins
3	Enrique Corrales	34	7	73 mins
4	Carlos Cuellar	30	6	67 mins

KEY PLAYERS - MIDFIELDERS

David Lopez

Goals in the League	3	**Contribution to Attacking Power** Average number of minutes between League team goals while on pitch	61
Defensive Rating Average number of mins between League goals conceded while on the pitch	77	**Scoring Difference** Defensive Rating minus Contribution to Attacking Power	16

	PLAYER	LGE GOALS	DEF RATE	POWER	SCORE DIFF
1	David Lopez	3	77	61	16 mins
2	Javad Nekounam	2	66	56	10 mins
3	Juanfran	2	68	58	10 mins
4	Raul Garcia	4	69	67	2 mins

KEY PLAYERS - GOALSCORERS

Roberto Soldado

Goals in the League	11	**Player Strike Rate** Average number of minutes between League goals scored by player	161
Contribution to Attacking Power Average number of minutes between League team goals while on pitch	59	**Club Strike Rate** Average number of minutes between League goals scored by club	67

	PLAYER	LGE GOALS	POWER	STRIKE RATE
1	Roberto Soldado	11	59	161 mins
2	Valmiro Valdo	6	65	314 mins
3	Savo Milosevic	4	74	408 mins
4	Raul Garcia	4	67	628 mins

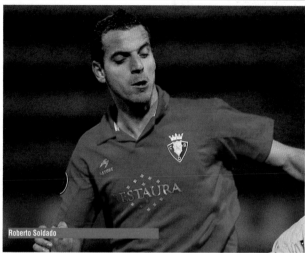

Roberto Soldado

SQUAD APPEARANCES

Match	1 2 3 4	6 7 8 9 10	11 12 13 14 15	16 17 18 19 20	21 22 23 24 25	26 27 28 29 30	31 32 33 34 35	36 37 38 39 40	41 42 43 44 45	46 47 48 49 50	51 52 53 54
Venue	A H H A A	H A H A H	H A H A A	H A H H A	H A A H A	H A A H A	A H H H A	A H H A A	A A H H A	H H A A H	A H A H
Competition	C C L L E	L L E L L	E L E L E	L L L E L	L E L L L	L L L L L	E L E L L	E L E L L	E L E L L	E L E L L	L L L L
Result	D D L L D	W W D D L	D L D L L	L L W W W	W W W W L	W L L D W	D L W L L	D D W W D	W L W D L	W D L L L	W W W

Goalkeepers
Juan Elia
Lopez Ricardo

Defenders
Enrique Corrales
Cesar Cruchaga
Carlos Cuellar
Javier Flano
Miguel Flano
Jose Izquierdo
Jose Romero Josetxo
Nacho Monreal

Midfielders
Cesar Azpilicueta
David Lopez
Ludovic Delporte
Jon Echaide
Jon Erice
Romero Hector Font
Juanfran
Javad Nekounam
Francisco Punal
Raul Garcia
Luis Sota
Valmiro Valdo

Forwards
Juanlu
Savo Milosevic
Iaki Munoz
Bernardo Romeo
Roberto Soldado
Pierre Webo

KEY: ■ On all match ◄◄ Subbed or sent off (Counting game) ►► Subbed on from bench (Counting Game) ►► Subbed on and then subbed or sent off (Counting Game) □ Not in 16
■ On bench ◄◄ Subbed or sent off (playing less than 70 minutes) ►► Subbed on (playing less than 70 minutes) ►► Subbed on and then subbed or sent off (playing less than 70 minutes)

SPAIN - OSASUNA

LEVANTE

Final Position: **15th**

NICKNAME: FROGS   KEY: ☐ Won ☐ Drawn ☐ Lost   Attendance

#		Opponent		Result	Scorers	Attendance
1	sppr1	Seville	A L	0-4		45,000
2	sppr1	Real Madrid	H L	1-4	Ettien 36	18,677
3	sppr1	Recreativo H	A W	1-0	Alexis 85	18,100
4	sppr1	Deportivo	H W	2-0	Kapo 17, 76	15,000
5	sppr1	Real Zaragoza	A D	2-2	Camacho 22, Kapo 44	28,000
6	sppr1	Mallorca	H L	0-1		18,000
7	sppr1	Villarreal	A D	1-1	Camacho 48	17,000
8	sppr1	Espanyol	H D	0-0		15,000
9	sppr1	Real Sociedad	H W	2-0	Meyong Ze 40, Courtois 87	6,500
10	sppr1	Real Betis	A L	1-2	Riga 63	30,000
11	sppr1	Atl Madrid	H L	0-3		15,000
12	sppr1	Getafe	A D	0-0		12,000
13	sppr1	Barcelona	H D	1-1	Alvaro 77	18,000
14	sppr1	Gimnastic	A L	1-2	Riga 28	12,000
15	sppr1	Celta Vigo	H D	1-1	Alvaro 51	20,000
16	sppr1	Osasuna	A L	1-2	Nino 90	14,943
17	sppr1	R Santander	H W	2-0	Camacho 61, Kapo 76	19,000
18	sppr1	Valencia	A L	0-3		45,000
19	sppr1	Athl Bilbao	H D	0-0		12,000
20	sppr1	Seville	H L	2-4	Dehu 68, Reggi 73	21,000
21	sppr1	Real Madrid	A W	1-0	Salva 10 pen	65,000
22	sppr1	Recreativo H	H W	2-1	Salva 16, 42	13,000
23	sppr1	Deportivo	A D	0-0		15,000
24	sppr1	Real Zaragoza	H D	0-0		13,000
25	sppr1	Mallorca	A L	1-3	Kapo 74	15,000
26	sppr1	Villarreal	H L	0-2		18,000
27	sppr1	Espanyol	A D	1-1	Reggi 14	19,000
28	sppr1	Real Sociedad	A L	0-1		18,000
29	sppr1	Real Betis	H D	1-1	Descarga 34	20,400
30	sppr1	Atl Madrid	A L	0-1		40,000
31	sppr1	Getafe	H D	1-1	Mustapha Riga 4	22,192
32	sppr1	Barcelona	A L	0-1		70,000
33	sppr1	Gimnastic	H W	2-0	Cesar Navas 29 og, Mustapha Riga 40	18,000
34	sppr1	Celta Vigo	A W	2-1	Reggi 41 pen, Mustapha Riga 49	18,000
35	sppr1	Osasuna	H L	1-4	Descarga 44	21,294
36	sppr1	R Santander	A W	3-2	Ettien 11, Mustapha Riga 38, 73	12,667
37	sppr1	Valencia	H W	4-2	Mustapha Riga 3, 49, Salva 11, Courtois 75	24,052
38	sppr1	Athl Bilbao	A L	0-2		40,000

LEAGUE APPEARANCES, BOOKINGS AND CAPS

	AGE (on 01/07/07)	IN NAMED 18	APPEARANCES	COUNTING GAMES	MINUTES ON PITCH	YELLOW CARDS	RED CARDS	CAPS THIS SEASON	NATIONAL SIDE
Goalkeepers									
Pablo Cavallero	33	35	7	7	624	1	1	-	Argentina
Francisco Molina	36	35	33	32	2885	4	1	-	Spain
Defenders									
Suarez Alexis	33	36	34	33	2980	15	0	-	Spain
Maior Alvaro	30	25	23	22	2031	6	1	-	Brazil
Martin Cesar	30	13	4	1	195	1	1	-	Spain
Frederic Dehu	34	24	12	8	802	2	2	-	France
Inaki Descarga	30	35	21	20	1769	4	1	-	Spain
Ian Harte	29	6	6	3	329	0	0	1	Rep of Ireland
Gaspar Haro Manolo	26	18	13	11	1013	5	0	-	Spain
Luis Rubiales	29	30	29	24	2415	6	0	-	Spain
Jose Serrano	26	10	8	8	720	2	0	-	Spain
Ze Maria	33	26	15	9	961	0	0	-	Brazil
Midfielders									
Mathieu Berson	27	32	27	20	2025	8	1	-	France
Diego Camacho	30	35	33	27	2612	10	0	-	Spain
Gonzalez J Carmelo	23	8	6	2	259	1	0	-	Spain
Laurent Courtois	28	32	29	20	2053	6	0	-	France
Felix Dja Ettien	27	35	34	21	2272	5	0	-	Ivory Coast
Olivier Kapo	26	30	30	26	2444	6	2	-	France
R Mustapha Riga	25	34	33	24	2429	5	1	-	Ghana
Sylvain N'Diaye	31	26	17	4	730	1	0	-	Senegal
Damiano Tommasi	33	35	29	17	1914	9	0	-	Italy
Forwards									
Peguy Luyindula	28	12	10	0	247	1	0	-	France
Albert Meyong Ze	26	17	11	1	358	3	0	-	Cameroon
F Martines Nino	27	28	19	7	925	0	0	-	Spain
G Enrique Reggi	34	20	18	3	575	4	0	-	Argentina
Laurent Robert	32	20	13	1	596	2	1	-	France
Ballesta Salva	32	14	14	12	1121	5	0	-	Spain

TEAM OF THE SEASON

G — Francisco Molina — CG: 32 DR: 77

D — Luis Rubiales — CG: 24 DR: 69
D — Suarez Alexis — CG: 33 DR: 78
D — Maior Alvaro — CG: 22 DR: 75
D — Inaki Descarga — CG: 20 DR: 73

M — Felix Dja Ettien — CG: 21 SD: -13
M — Mathieu Berson — CG: 20 SD: -17
M — Olivier Kapo — CG: 26 SD: -27
M — R Mustapha Riga — CG: 24 SD: -28

F — Ballesta Salva — CG: 12 SR: 280
F — F Martines Nino* — CG: 7 SR: 925

MONTHLY POINTS TALLY

Month		Pts	%
AUGUST		0	0%
SEPTEMBER		6	67%
OCTOBER		3	25%
NOVEMBER		4	33%
DECEMBER		2	17%
JANUARY		4	33%
FEBRUARY		8	67%
MARCH		1	8%
APRIL		2	17%
MAY		9	75%
JUNE		3	50%

LEAGUE GOALS

	PLAYER	MINS	GOALS	S RATE
1	Mustapha Riga	2429	9	269
2	Kapo	2444	5	488
3	Salva	1121	4	280
4	Reggi	575	3	191
5	Camacho	2612	3	870
6	Descarga	1769	2	884
7	Alvaro	2031	2	1015
8	Courtois	2053	2	1026
9	Ettien	2272	2	1136
10	Meyong Ze	358	1	358
11	Dehu	802	1	802
12	Nino	925	1	925
13	Alexis	2980	1	2980
	Other		0	
	TOTAL		**36**	

TOP POINT EARNERS

	PLAYER	GAMES	AV PTS
1	Luis Rubiales	24	1.42
2	Maior Alvaro	22	1.27
3	Ballesta Salva	12	1.25
4	Damiano Tommasi	17	1.24
5	Mathieu Berson	21	1.24
6	Inaki Descarga	20	1.20
7	R Mustapha Riga	25	1.20
8	Felix Dja Ettien	21	1.19
9	Suarez Alexis	33	1.18
10	Olivier Kapo	27	1.11
	CLUB AVERAGE:		**1.11**

DISCIPLINARY RECORDS

	PLAYER	YELLOW	RED	AVE
1	G Enrique Reggi	4	0	143
2	Suarez Alexis	15	0	198
3	Laurent Robert	2	1	198
4	Frederic Dehu	2	2	202
5	Gaspar Manolo	5	0	202
6	Damiano Tommasi	9	0	212
7	Ballesta Salva	5	0	224
8	Mathieu Berson	8	1	225
9	Diego Camacho	10	1	237
10	Maior Alvaro	6	1	239
11	Olivier Kapo	6	2	305
12	Laurent Courtois	6	0	342
13	Inaki Descarga	4	1	353
	Other	23	2	
	TOTAL	**105**	**11**	

KEY GOALKEEPER

Francisco Molina

Goals Conceded in the League	37	Counting Games League games when player was on pitch for at least 70 minutes	32
Defensive Rating Ave number of mins between League goals conceded while on the pitch	77	Clean Sheets In League games when player was on pitch for at least 70 minutes	11

KEY PLAYERS - DEFENDERS

Suarez Alexis

Goals Conceded Number of League goals conceded while the player was on the pitch	38	Clean Sheets In League games when player was on pitch for at least 70 minutes	11
Defensive Rating Ave number of mins between League goals conceded while on the pitch	78	Club Defensive Rating Average number of mins between League goals conceded by the club this season	64

	PLAYER	CON LGE	CLEAN SHEETS	DEF RATE
1	Suarez Alexis	38	11	78 mins
2	Maior Alvaro	27	6	75 mins
3	Inaki Descarga	24	6	73 mins
4	Luis Rubiales	35	7	69 mins

KEY PLAYERS - MIDFIELDERS

Felix Dja Ettien

Goals in the League	2	Contribution to Attacking Power Average number of minutes between League team goals while on pitch	84
Defensive Rating Average number of mins between League goals conceded while on the pitch	71	Scoring Difference Defensive Rating minus Contribution to Attacking Power	-13

	PLAYER	LGE GOALS	DEF RATE	POWER	SCORE DIFF
1	Felix Dja Ettien	2	71	84	-13 mins
2	Mathieu Berson	0	75	92	-17 mins
3	Olivier Kapo	5	74	101	-27 mins
4	Rahamat Mustapha Riga	9	65	93	-28 mins

KEY PLAYERS - GOALSCORERS

Rahamat Mustapha Riga

Goals in the League	9	Player Strike Rate Average number of minutes between League goals scored by player	269
Contribution to Attacking Power Average number of minutes between League team goals while on pitch	93	Club Strike Rate Average number of minutes between League goals scored by club	92

	PLAYER	LGE GOALS	POWER	STRIKE RATE
1	Rahamat Mustapha Riga	9	93	269 mins
2	Ballesta Salva	4	86	280 mins
3	Olivier Kapo	5	101	488 mins
4	Diego Camacho	3	100	870 mins

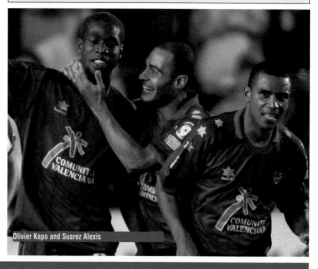

Olivier Kapo and Suarez Alexis

SQUAD APPEARANCES

Match	1 2 3 4 5	6 7 8 9 10	11 12 13 14 15	16 17 18 19 20	21 22 23 24 25	26 27 28 29 30	31 32 33 34 35	36 37 38
Venue	A H A H A	H A H H A	H A H A H	A H A H H	A H A H A	H A A H A	H A H A H	A H A
Competition	L L L L L	L L L L L	L L L L L	L L L L L	L L L L L	L L L L L	L L L L L	L L L
Result	L L W W D	L D D W L	L D D L D	L W L D L	W W D D L	L D L D L	D L W W L	W W L

Goalkeepers
Pablo Cavallero
Francisco Molina

Defenders
Suarez Alexis
Maior Alvaro
Martin Cesar
Frederic Dehu
Inaki Descarga
Ian Harte
Gaspar Haro Manolo
Luis Rubiales
Jose Serrano
De Maria

Midfielders
Mathieu Berson
Diego Camacho
Gonzalez J Carmelo
Laurent Courtois
Felix Dja Ettien
Olivier Kapo
Mustapha Riga
Sylvain N'Diaye
Damiano Tommasi

Forwards
Neguy Luyindula
Albert Meyong Ze
Martines Nino
Enrique Reggi
Laurent Robert
Ballesta Salva

KEY: ■ On all match ◄◄ Subbed or sent off (Counting game) ►► Subbed on from bench (Counting Game) ►► Subbed on and then subbed or sent off (Counting Game) □ Not in 16
■ On bench ◄◄ Subbed or sent off (playing less than 70 minutes) ►► Subbed on (playing less than 70 minutes) ►► Subbed on and then subbed or sent off (playing less than 70 minutes)

REAL BETIS

Final Position: **16th**

NICKNAME: BETICOS   KEY: ☐ Won ☐ Drawn ☐ Lost   Attendance

1	sppr1 Valencia	A L	1-2	Xisco 53	50,000
2	sppr1 Athl Bilbao	H W	3-0	Juanito 19, Edu 39, Capi 83	30,000
3	sppr1 Seville	A L	2-3	Sobis 40, 55	45,500
4	sppr1 Real Madrid	H L	0-1		45,000
5	sppr1 Recreativo H	A L	0-2		18,000
6	sppr1 Deportivo	H D	1-1	Robert 90 pen	32,000
7	sppr1 Real Zaragoza	A L	1-2	Robert 52	28,000
8	sppr1 Mallorca	H L	0-1		35,000
9	sppr1 Villarreal	A L	2-3	Edu 4, Rivera 48	16,000
10	sppr1 Levante	H W	2-1	Edu 5, Capi 90	30,000
11	sppr1 Real Sociedad	A D	0-0		19,000
12	sppr1 Espanyol	H D	1-1	Robert 32 pen	35,000
13	sppr1 Atl Madrid	H L	0-1		38,000
14	sppr1 Getafe	A D	1-1	Juanito 86	10,000
15	sppr1 Gimnastic	A W	1-0	Assuncao 65 pen	10,000
16	sppr1 Celta Vigo	H W	1-0	Sobis 60	36,000
17	sppr1 Osasuna	A L	1-5	Arzu 45	15,000
18	sppr1 R Santander	H D	1-1	Xisco 87	35,000
19	sppr1 Barcelona	H D	1-1	Robert 37	40,000
20	sppr1 Valencia	H W	2-1	Robert 14, 68 pen	40,000
21	sppr1 Athl Bilbao	A W	2-1	Robert 18, Pancrate 77	38,000
22	sppr1 Seville	H D	0-0		45,000
23	sppr1 Real Madrid	A D	0-0		70,000
24	sppr1 Recreativo H	H D	0-0		35,000
25	sppr1 Deportivo	A W	1-0	Fernando 80	23,000
26	sppr1 Real Zaragoza	H D	1-1	Assuncao 45 pen	40,000
27	sppr1 Mallorca	A L	0-2		18,000
28	sppr1 Villarreal	H D	3-3	Fernando 10, Edu 72, Juanito 90	35,000
29	sppr1 Levante	A D	1-1	Robert 80	20,400
30	sppr1 Real Sociedad	H L	0-1		45,000
31	sppr1 Espanyol	A D	2-2	Edu 45, 77	20,150
32	sppr1 Atl Madrid	A D	0-0		45,000
33	sppr1 Getafe	H L	0-2		45,000
34	sppr1 Barcelona	A D	1-1	Sobis 89	77,747
35	sppr1 Gimnastic	H D	1-1	Xisco 90	45,000
36	sppr1 Celta Vigo	A L	1-2	Robert 31	12,803
37	sppr1 Osasuna	H L	0-5		35,000
38	sppr1 R Santander	A W	2-0	Edu 80, 90	15,000

LEAGUE APPEARANCES, BOOKINGS AND CAPS

	AGE (on 01/07/07)	IN NAMED 18	APPEARANCES	COUNTING GAMES	MINUTES ON PITCH	YELLOW CARDS	RED CARDS	CAPS THIS SEASON	NATIONAL SIDE
Goalkeepers									
Pedro Contreras	35	36	16	16	1439	1	1	-	Spain
Antonio Doblas	27	32	22	22	1980	4	0	-	Spain
Defenders									
Branko Ilic	24	17	13	12	1121	4	0	-	Slovenia
Gomez Isidoro	20	9	8	7	635	4	0	-	Spain
J Gutierrez Juanito	30	34	34	34	3053	4	0	3	Spain
Daniel Lembo	29	8	2	1	124	0	1	-	Uruguay
Juan Alberto Melli	23	35	27	25	2323	9	0	-	Spain
Victoriano Nano	26	25	21	19	1811	3	2	-	Spain
H Oscar Lopez	27	1	1	1	90	1	0	-	Spain
David Rivas	28	16	11	10	943	2	0	-	Spain
Enrique Romero	36	18	18	17	1567	3	0	-	Spain
Fernando Vega	22	28	16	13	1226	4	0	-	Spain
Midfielders									
Arturo Arzu	26	20	16	11	1139	3	0	-	Spain
Marcos Assuncao	30	29	27	20	1985	8	1	-	Brazil
Juan Pablo Caffa	22	14	7	0	299	0	0	-	Argentina
Jesus Capitan Capi	30	31	29	12	1706	6	1	-	Spain
Luis E Schmidt Edu	28	29	29	23	2218	4	2	-	Brazil
Fernandez Fernando	33	35	24	10	1309	1	0	-	Spain
Juan de Dios Juande	21	9	7	5	542	3	0	-	Spain
Miguel Angel	28	31	23	14	1486	7	1	-	Spain
Alberto Rivera	29	32	27	15	1907	4	0	-	Spain
Johann Vogel	30	20	17	12	1257	4	1	4	Switzerland
Roger Jorge Wagner	25	15	10	1	395	1	0	-	Switzerland
Forwards									
Daniel Martin Dani	25	21	14	1	473	3	0	-	Spain
F Jose Maldonado	26	21	15	4	636	2	0	-	Spain
David Odonkor	23	15	13	4	674	2	0	5	Germany
Fabrice Pancrate	27	7	7	3	402	0	0	-	France
Robert	26	31	29	13	1792	3	0	-	Brazil
Rafael Sobis	22	33	31	21	2176	2	1	5	Brazil
Francisco Xisco	26	26	15	2	746	3	0	-	Spain

TEAM OF THE SEASON

G Antonio Doblas
CG: 22 DR: 86

D Fernando Vega
CG: 13 DR: 122

D Branko Ilic
CG: 12 DR: 101

D Victoriano Nano
CG: 19 DR: 72

D Juan Alberto Melli
CG: 25 DR: 70

M Johann Vogel
CG: 12 SD: -11

M Jesus Capitan Capi
CG: 12 SD: -21

M Alberto Rivera
CG: 15 SD: -22

M Luis E Schmidt Edu
CG: 23 SD: -27

F Robert
CG: 13 SR: 199

F Rafael Sobis
CG: 21 SR: 544

MONTHLY POINTS TALLY

AUGUST		0	0%
SEPTEMBER		3	33%
OCTOBER		1	8%
NOVEMBER		5	42%
DECEMBER		4	44%
JANUARY		8	53%
FEBRUARY		6	50%
MARCH		5	42%
APRIL		3	25%
MAY		2	17%
JUNE		3	50%

LEAGUE GOALS

	PLAYER	MINS	GOALS	S RATE
1	Robert	1792	9	199
2	Edu	2218	8	277
3	Sobis	2176	4	544
4	Xisco	746	3	248
5	Juanito	3053	3	1017
6	Fernando	1309	2	654
7	Capi	1706	2	853
8	Assuncao	1985	2	992
9	Pancrate	402	1	402
10	Arzu	1139	1	1139
11	Rivera	1907	1	1907
12	Romero	1567	0	
13	Rivas	943	0	
	Other		0	
	TOTAL		**36**	

TOP POINT EARNERS

	PLAYER	GAMES	AV PTS
1	Fernando Vega	13	1.62
2	Johann Vogel	12	1.33
3	Branko Ilic	12	1.33
4	Rafael Sobis	21	1.29
5	Antonio Doblas	22	1.14
6	Marcos Assuncao	20	1.10
7	Robert	13	1.08
8	Jesus Capitan Capi	13	1.00
9	Luis E Schmidt Edu	24	1.00
10	Juan Gutierrez Juanito	34	1.00
	CLUB AVERAGE:		**1.05**

DISCIPLINARY RECORDS

	PLAYER	YELLOW	RED	AVE
1	Daniel Martin Dani	3	0	157
2	Gomez Isidoro	4	0	158
3	J de Dios Juande	3	0	180
4	Miguel Angel	7	1	185
5	Marcos Assuncao	8	1	220
6	Jesus Capitan Capi	6	1	243
7	Johann Vogel	4	1	251
8	Juan Alberto Melli	9	0	258
9	Branko Ilic	4	0	280
10	Fernando Vega	4	0	306
11	F Jose Maldonado	2	0	318
12	David Odonkor	2	0	337
13	Victoriano Nano	3	2	362
	Other	33	4	
	TOTAL	**92**	**10**	

KEY GOALKEEPER

Antonio Doblas

Goals Conceded in the League	23	Counting Games League games when player was on pitch for at least 70 minutes	22
Defensive Rating Ave number of mins between League goals conceded while on the pitch	86	Clean Sheets In League games when player was on pitch for at least 70 minutes	7

KEY PLAYERS - DEFENDERS

Fernando Vega

Goals Conceded Number of League goals conceded while the player was on the pitch	10	Clean Sheets In League games when player was on pitch for at least 70 minutes	6
Defensive Rating Ave number of mins between League goals conceded while on the pitch	122	Club Defensive Rating Average number of mins between League goals conceded by the club this season	69

	PLAYER	CON LGE	CLEAN SHEETS	DEF RATE
1	Fernando Vega	10	6	122 mins
2	Branko Ilic	11	5	101 mins
3	Victoriano Nano	25	6	72 mins
4	Juan Alberto Melli	33	7	70 mins

KEY PLAYERS - MIDFIELDERS

Johann Vogel

Goals in the League	0	Contribution to Attacking Power Average number of minutes between League team goals while on pitch	89
Defensive Rating Average number of mins between League goals conceded while on the pitch	78	Scoring Difference Defensive Rating minus Contribution to Attacking Power	-11

	PLAYER	LGE GOALS	DEF RATE	POWER	SCORE DIFF
1	Johann Vogel	0	78	89	-11 mins
2	Jesus Capitan Capi	2	68	89	-21 mins
3	Alberto Rivera	1	73	95	-22 mins
4	Luis Eduardo Schmidt Edu	8	65	92	-27 mins

KEY PLAYERS - GOALSCORERS

Robert

Goals in the League	9	Player Strike Rate Average number of minutes between League goals scored by player	199
Contribution to Attacking Power Average number of minutes between League team goals while on pitch	94	Club Strike Rate Average number of minutes between League goals scored by club	95

	PLAYER	LGE GOALS	POWER	STRIKE RATE
1	Robert	9	94	199 mins
2	Luis Eduardo Schmidt Edu	8	92	277 mins
3	Rafael Sobis	4	120	544 mins
4	Jesus Capitan Capi	2	89	853 mins

Robert

SQUAD APPEARANCES

Match	1 2 3 4 5	6 7 8 9 10	11 12 13 14 15	16 17 18 19 20	21 22 23 24 25	26 27 28 29 30	31 32 33 34 35	36 37 38
Venue	A H A H A	H A H A H	A H H A A	H A H H H	A H A H A	H A H A H	A A H A H	A H A
Competition	L L L L L	L L L L L	L L L L L	L L L L L	L L L L L	L L L L L	L L L L L	L L L
Result	L W L L L	D L L L W	D D L D W	W L D D W	W D D D W	D L D D L	D D L D D	L L W

Goalkeepers

Pedro Contreras
Antonio Doblas

Defenders

Branko Ilic
Gomez Isidoro
J Gutierrez Juanito
Daniel Lembo
Juan Alberto Melli
Victoriano Nano
H Oscar Lopez
David Rivas
Enrique Romero
Fernando Vega

Midfielders

Arturo Arzu
Marcos Assuncao
Juan Pablo Caffa
Jesus Capitan Capi
Luis E Schmidt Edu
Fernandez Fernando
Juan de Dios Juande
Miguel Angel
Alberto Rivera
Johann Vogel
Roger Jorge Wagner

Forwards

Daniel Martin Dani
F Jose Maldonado
David Odonkor
Fabrice Pancrate
Robert
Rafael Sobis
Francisco Xisco

KEY: ■ On all match ◄◄ Subbed or sent off (Counting game) ►► Subbed on from bench (Counting Game) ►► Subbed on and then subbed or sent off (Counting Game) ☐ Not in 16
■ On bench ◄◄ Subbed or sent off (playing less than 70 minutes) ►► Subbed on (playing less than 70 minutes) ►► Subbed on and then subbed or sent off (playing less than 70 minutes)

SPAIN - REAL BETIS

ATHLETIC BILBAO

Final Position: **17th**

NICKNAME: LIONS   KEY: ☐ Won ☐ Drawn ☐ Lost   Attendance

#		Match	H/A	Result	Score	Scorers	Attendance
1	sppr1	Real Sociedad	H	D	1-1	Aduriz 38	40,000
2	sppr1	Real Betis	A	L	0-3		30,000
3	sppr1	Atl Madrid	H	L	1-4	Martinez 86	38,800
4	sppr1	Getafe	A	D	0-0		10,000
5	sppr1	Barcelona	H	L	1-3	Yeste 11	39,000
6	sppr1	Gimnastic	A	W	3-2	Yeste 11 pen, 50, Iraola 29	13,000
7	sppr1	Celta Vigo	H	L	0-1		38,000
8	sppr1	Osasuna	A	D	1-1	Gabilondo 29	18,210
9	sppr1	R Santander	H	D	0-0		38,000
10	sppr1	Valencia	A	D	1-1	Llorente 90	49,000
11	sppr1	Espanyol	A	L	2-3	Yeste 48 pen, Aduriz 67	17,000
12	sppr1	Seville	H	L	1-3	Aduriz 69	38,000
13	sppr1	Real Madrid	A	L	1-2	Prieto 35	78,000
14	sppr1	Recreativo H	H	W	4-2	Bautista 6 og, Urzaiz 27, 41, Garmendia 60	38,000
15	sppr1	Deportivo	A	W	2-0	Martinez 9, 90	20,000
16	sppr1	Real Zaragoza	H	D	0-0		40,000
17	sppr1	Mallorca	A	W	3-1	Urzaiz 30, 53, Etxeberria 84	18,000
18	sppr1	Villarreal	H	L	0-1		38,000
19	sppr1	Levante	A	D	0-0		12,000
20	sppr1	Real Sociedad	A	W	2-0	Iraola 13, 69	22,000
21	sppr1	Real Betis	H	L	1-2	Urzaiz 90	38,000
22	sppr1	Atl Madrid	A	L	0-1		40,000
23	sppr1	Getafe	H	W	2-0	Aduriz 30, 50	36,000
24	sppr1	Barcelona	A	L	0-3		68,000
25	sppr1	Gimnastic	H	L	0-2		35,000
26	sppr1	Celta Vigo	A	D	1-1	Aduriz 71	13,000
27	sppr1	Osasuna	H	L	0-3		38,000
28	sppr1	R Santander	A	L	4-5	Prieto 7, Etxeberria 63, 80, Iraola 83	15,000
29	sppr1	Valencia	H	W	1-0	Gabilondo 27	39,000
30	sppr1	Espanyol	H	W	2-1	Urzaiz 62, 78	35,000
31	sppr1	Seville	A	L	1-4	Yeste 78	45,500
32	sppr1	Real Madrid	H	L	1-4	Llorente 81	39,000
33	sppr1	Recreativo H	A	D	0-0		18,500
34	sppr1	Deportivo	H	D	1-1	Murillo 57	35,012
35	sppr1	Real Zaragoza	A	L	3-4	Aduriz 35, 74 pen, 78	30,000
36	sppr1	Mallorca	H	W	1-0	Urzaiz 64 pen	38,800
37	sppr1	Villarreal	A	L	1-3	Iraola 21	22,000
38	sppr1	Levante	H	W	2-0	Serrano 61 og, Gabilondo 77	40,000

LEAGUE APPEARANCES, BOOKINGS AND CAPS

	AGE (on 01/07/07)	IN NAMED 18	APPEARANCES	COUNTING GAMES	MINUTES ON PITCH	YELLOW CARDS	RED CARDS	CAPS THIS SEASON	NATIONAL SIDE
Goalkeepers									
Daniel Aranzubia	27	34	29	28	2548	2	0	-	Spain
Inaki Lafuente	31	27	10	9	872	0	0	-	Spain
Defenders									
Fernando Amorebieta	22	34	27	16	1788	8	1	-	Venezuela
Javier Casas	25	28	20	15	1485	3	1	-	Spain
Unai Exposito	27	36	30	30	2629	6	0	-	Spain
Andoni Iraola	25	35	35	35	3093	5	0	-	Spain
Ander Murillo	23	36	33	29	2760	16	1	-	Spain
Luis Prieto	28	24	19	17	1579	4	0	-	Spain
Josu Sarriegi	28	37	36	36	3235	9	1	-	Spain
Ald Ustaritz	24	19	13	11	1037	3	0	-	Spain
Iban Zubiaurre	24	12	1	0	32	0	0	-	Spain
Midfielders									
Benat	20	3	1	0	6	0	0	-	Spain
Markel Bergara	21	6	1	0	13	1	0	-	Spain
Igor Gabilondo	28	37	33	17	2159	2	1	-	Spain
Joseba Garmendia	21	21	16	3	617	0	0	-	Spain
Javier Iturriaga	23	22	4	0	104	1	0	-	Mexico
Javi Gonzalez	33	15	13	9	939	1	0	-	Spain
Javi Martinez	18	33	33	26	2605	7	0	-	Spain
Pablo Orbaiz	28	9	9	6	673	3	0	-	Spain
Roberto Tiko	30	5	5	1	154	2	0	-	Spain
Francisco Yeste	27	38	38	27	2734	5	0	-	Spain
Forwards									
Aritz Aduriz	26	35	34	24	2395	4	3	-	Spain
Mikel Danobeitia	21	23	4	0	85	0	0	-	Spain
Joseba Etxeberria	29	31	28	10	1578	1	0	-	Spain
Fernando Llorente	22	34	23	0	442	0	0	-	Spain
Ismael Urzaiz	35	37	33	12	1838	5	0	-	Spain

TEAM OF THE SEASON

Inaki Lafuente (G) CG: 9 DR: 43

Javier Casas (D) CG: 15 DR: 82
Unai Exposito (D) CG: 30 DR: 57
Josu Sarriegi (D) CG: 36 DR: 59
Andoni Iraola (D) CG: 35 DR: 57

Francisco Yeste (M) CG: 27 SD: -21
Javi Gonzalez* (M) CG: 9 SD: -28
Javi Martinez (M) CG: 26 SD: -29
Igor Gabilondo (M) CG: 17 SD: -32

Ismael Urzaiz (F) CG: 12 SR: 229
Aritz Aduriz (F) CG: 24 SR: 266

MONTHLY POINTS TALLY

Month		Pts	%
AUGUST		1	33%
SEPTEMBER		1	8%
OCTOBER		4	44%
NOVEMBER		2	17%
DECEMBER		7	58%
JANUARY		7	58%
FEBRUARY		3	25%
MARCH		1	11%
APRIL		6	40%
MAY		5	42%
JUNE		3	50%

LEAGUE GOALS

	PLAYER	MINS	GOALS	S RATE
1	Aduriz	2395	9	266
2	Urzaiz	1838	8	229
3	Yeste	2734	5	546
4	Iraola	3093	5	618
5	Etxeberria	1578	3	526
6	Gabilondo	2159	3	719
7	Martinez	2605	3	868
8	Llorente	442	2	221
9	Prieto	1579	2	789
10	Garmendia	617	1	617
11	Murillo	2760	1	2760
12	Orbaiz	673	0	
13	Sarriegi	3235	0	
	Other		0	
	TOTAL		**42**	

TOP POINT EARNERS

	PLAYER	GAMES	AV PTS
1	Ismael Urzaiz	12	1.33
2	Javier Casas	16	1.31
3	Luis Prieto	17	1.29
4	Daniel Aranzubia	28	1.21
5	Josu Sarriegi	36	1.11
6	Andoni Iraola	35	1.11
7	Unai Exposito	30	1.07
8	Javi Martinez	26	1.04
9	Ander Murillo	29	1.00
10	Igor Gabilondo	18	1.00
	CLUB AVERAGE:		**1.05**

DISCIPLINARY RECORDS

	PLAYER	YELLOW	RED	AVE
1	Ander Murillo	16	1	162
2	F Amorebieta	8	1	198
3	Pablo Orbaiz	3	0	224
4	Josu Sarriegi	9	1	323
5	Aritz Aduriz	4	3	342
6	A Ustaritz	3	0	345
7	Ismael Urzaiz	5	0	367
8	Javier Casas	3	1	371
9	Javi Martinez	7	0	372
10	Luis Prieto	4	0	394
11	Unai Exposito	5	0	525
12	Francisco Yeste	5	0	546
13	Andoni Iraola	5	0	618
	Other	6	1	
	TOTAL	**83**	**8**	

KEY GOALKEEPER

Inaki Lafuente

Goals Conceded in the League	20	Counting Games League games when player was on pitch for at least 70 minutes	9
Defensive Rating Ave number of mins between League goals conceded while on the pitch	43	Clean Sheets In League games when player was on pitch for at least 70 minutes	1

KEY PLAYERS - DEFENDERS

Javier Casas

Goals Conceded Number of League goals conceded while the player was on the pitch	18	Clean Sheets In League games when player was on pitch for at least 70 minutes	6
Defensive Rating Ave number of mins between League goals conceded while on the pitch	82	Club Defensive Rating Average number of mins between League goals conceded by the club this season	55

	PLAYER	CON LGE	CLEAN SHEETS	DEF RATE
1	Javier Casas	18	6	82 mins
2	Josu Sarriegi	54	11	59 mins
3	Andoni Iraola	54	11	57 mins
4	Unai Exposito	46	9	57 mins

KEY PLAYERS - MIDFIELDERS

Francisco Yeste

Goals in the League	5	Contribution to Attacking Power Average number of minutes between League team goals while on pitch	75
Defensive Rating Average number of mins between League goals conceded while on the pitch	54	Scoring Difference Defensive Rating minus Contribution to Attacking Power	-21

	PLAYER	LGE GOALS	DEF RATE	POWER	SCORE DIFF
1	Francisco Yeste	5	54	75	-21 mins
2	Javi Gonzalez	0	44	72	-28 mins
3	Javi Martinez	3	57	86	-29 mins
4	Igor Gabilondo	3	51	83	-32 mins

KEY PLAYERS - GOALSCORERS

Ismael Urzaiz

Goals in the League	8	Player Strike Rate Average number of minutes between League goals scored by player	229
Contribution to Attacking Power Average number of minutes between League team goals while on pitch	76	Club Strike Rate Average number of minutes between League goals scored by club	77

	PLAYER	LGE GOALS	POWER	STRIKE RATE
1	Ismael Urzaiz	8	76	229 mins
2	Aritz Aduriz	9	85	266 mins
3	Joseba Etxeberria	3	58	526 mins
4	Francisco Yeste	5	75	546 mins

Francisco Yeste

SQUAD APPEARANCES

Match	1	2	3	4	5	6	7	8	9	10	11	12	13	14	15	16	17	18	19	20	21	22	23	24	25	26	27	28	29	30	31	32	33	34	35	36	37	38
Venue	H	A	H	A	H	A	H	A	H	A	A	H	A	H	A	H	A	H	A	A	H	A	H	A	H	A	H	A	H	H	A	H	A	H	A	H	A	H
Competition	L	L	L	L	L	L	L	L	L	L	L	L	L	L	L	L	L	L	L	L	L	L	L	L	L	L	L	L	L	L	L	L	L	L	L	L	L	L
Result	D	L	L	D	L	W	L	D	D	D	L	L	L	W	W	D	W	L	D	W	L	L	W	L	L	D	L	L	W	W	L	L	D	D	L	W	L	W

Goalkeepers
Daniel Aranzubia
Inaki Lafuente

Defenders
Fernando Amorebieta
Javier Casas
Unai Exposito
Andoni Iraola
Ander Murillo
Luis Prieto
Josu Sarriegi
David Ustaritz
Aitor Zubiaurre

Midfielders
Gurpegi
Markel Bergara
Igor Gabilondo
Joseba Garmendia
Javier Iturriaga
Javi Gonzalez
Javi Martinez
Pablo Orbaiz
Roberto Tiko
Francisco Yeste

Forwards
Aritz Aduriz
Mikel Danobeitia
Joseba Etxeberria
Fernando Llorente
Ismael Urzaiz

KEY: ■ On all match ◄◄ Subbed or sent off (Counting game) ►► Subbed on from bench (Counting Game) ›› Subbed on and then subbed or sent off (Counting Game) ☐ Not in 16
□ On bench ◄ Subbed or sent off (playing less than 70 minutes) ›› Subbed on (playing less than 70 minutes) ›› Subbed on and then subbed or sent off (playing less than 70 minutes)

SPAIN - ATHLETIC BILBAO

CELTA VIGO

Final Position: **18th**

NICKNAME: LITTLE CELTS   KEY: ☐Won ☐Drawn ☐Lost   Attendance

#		Opponent			Result	Scorers	Attendance
1	sppr1	Barcelona	H	L	2-3	Baiano 42, Gustavo Lopez 65	25,000
2	sppr1	Gimnastic	A	W	2-1	Baiano 49, Nene 74	13,000
3	ucrl1	Standard Liege	A	W	1-0	Gustavo Lopez 37	11,500
4	sppr1	Espanyol	A	L	1-2	Canobbio 52	49,000
5	sppr1	Osasuna	H	L	0-2		17,000
6	ucrl2	Standard Liege	H	W	3-0	Baiano 21, 83, Canobbio 69	8,000
7	sppr1	R Santander	A	D	1-1	Nene 56	20,000
8	sppr1	Valencia	H	W	3-2	Baiano 45, Iriney 52, Canobbio 56	24,000
9	sppr1	Athl Bilbao	A	W	1-0	Baiano 6	38,000
10	sppr1	Seville	H	L	1-2	Nene 8	20,000
11	ucgph	Eintr Frankfurt	H	D	1-1	Perera 11	10,000
12	sppr1	Real Madrid	A	W	2-1	Nene 36, Jorge 82	77,088
13	sppr1	Recreativo H	H	L	1-2	Guayre 82	12,000
14	sppr1	Deportivo	A	W	1-0	Nene 74	16,000
15	ucgph	Newcastle	A	L	1-2	Canobbio 9	25,079
16	sppr1	Real Zaragoza	H	D	1-1	Baiano 52	15,000
17	ucgph	Fenerbahce	H	W	1-0	Canobbio 77	10,000
18	sppr1	Mallorca	A	D	2-2	Baiano 57, Perera 85	17,000
19	sppr1	Villarreal	H	D	1-1	Baiano 17	12,000
20	ucgph	Palermo	A	D	1-1	Baiano 59	10,222
21	sppr1	Levante	A	D	1-1	Baiano 1	20,000
22	sppr1	Real Sociedad	H	D	0-0		8,000
23	sppr1	Real Betis	A	L	0-1		36,000
24	sppr1	Atl Madrid	H	L	1-3	Nene 70	12,000
25	sppr1	Getafe	A	L	0-1		7,000
26	sppr1	Barcelona	A	L	1-3	Nene 67 pen	65,000
27	sppr1	Gimnastic	H	D	1-1	Oubina 50	12,000
28	sppr1	Espanyol	H	L	0-2		13,000
29	ucrl1	Spart Moscow	A	D	1-1	Nunez 41	30,000
30	sppr1	Osasuna	A	W	1-0	Baiano 2	15,647
31	ucrl2	Spart Moscow	H	W	2-1	Nene 19, Jonathan 78	7,000
32	sppr1	R Santander	H	D	2-2	Baiano 25 pen, Bamogo 33	12,000
33	sppr1	Valencia	A	L	0-1		44,000
34	ucrl1	W Bremen	H	L	0-1		20,000
35	sppr1	Athl Bilbao	H	D	1-1	Angel 36	13,000
36	ucrl2	W Bremen	A	L	0-2		28,000
37	sppr1	Seville	A	L	0-2		40,000
38	sppr1	Real Madrid	H	L	1-2	Angel 44	22,000
39	sppr1	Recreativo H	A	L	2-4	Nene 74 pen, 90	17,820
40	sppr1	Deportivo	H	W	1-0	Baiano 61	24,000
41	sppr1	Real Zaragoza	A	L	0-2		27,000
42	sppr1	Mallorca	H	L	0-3		23,000
43	sppr1	Villarreal	A	L	0-1		20,000
44	sppr1	Levante	H	L	1-2	Baiano 62	18,000
45	sppr1	Real Sociedad	A	L	1-3	Gustavo Lopez 20	27,015
46	sppr1	Real Betis	H	W	2-1	Gustavo Lopez 42, Baiano 90 pen	12,803
47	sppr1	Atl Madrid	A	W	3-2	Baiano 31 pen, 67, Yago 48	45,000
48	sppr1	Getafe	H	W	2-1	Bamogo 36, Lequi 66	20,000

LEAGUE APPEARANCES, BOOKINGS AND CAPS

	AGE (on 01/07/07)	IN NAMED 18	APPEARANCES	COUNTING GAMES	MINUTES ON PITCH	YELLOW CARDS	RED CARDS	CAPS THIS SEASON	NATIONAL SIDE
Goalkeepers									
Andres Esteban	32	36	4	4	360	0	0	-	Spain
J M Pinto Colorado	31	37	34	34	3060	5	0	-	Spain
Defenders									
Lopez Ruano Angel	26	35	35	35	3133	8	1	3	Spain
M Alexandre Areias	30	10	1	1	90	0	0	-	Portugal
P A Fica Contreras	28	32	30	28	2556	12	1	-	Chile
A Juncal Jonathan	25	28	21	7	945	4	0	-	Spain
Matias Emanuel Lequi	26	29	26	22	2061	9	1	-	Argentina
George Lucas	23	2	2	1	147	0	0	-	Brazil
Diego Placente	30	37	35	33	3003	13	0	-	Argentina
Gabriel Tamas	23	33	29	24	2180	14	2	8	Romania
Alonso-Fueyo Yago	27	17	4	3	326	0	0	-	Spain
Midfielders									
Dani Abalo	19	4	1	0	12	0	0	-	Spain
Fabian Canobbio	27	34	34	26	2565	6	2	-	Uruguay
Daniel de Ridder	23	12	3	0	36	0	0	-	Holland
Pablo Garcia	30	16	14	9	989	11	2	-	Uruguay
Pablo Gustavo Lopez	34	32	31	23	2205	7	1	-	Argentina
Santos da Silva Iriney	26	27	26	18	2029	9	1	-	Brazil
Larena Jorge	25	30	16	2	503	1	0	-	Spain
Anderson Nene	25	38	38	30	2999	4	0	-	Brazil
Antonio Nunez	28	33	24	7	989	3	0	-	Spain
B Melendez Oubina	25	32	30	30	2685	5	0	2	Spain
Jonathan Vila	24	16	6	0	97	1	0	-	Spain
Forwards									
Fernando Baiano	28	35	35	33	2993	6	0	-	Brazil
Habib Bamogo	25	16	15	5	644	0	0	-	France
Antonio Guayre	27	16	10	2	320	2	0	-	Spain
Iago	19	5	2	1	121	0	0	-	Spain
Jose Jesus Perera	27	30	17	1	392	2	0	-	Spain

TEAM OF THE SEASON

D P A Fica Contreras CG: 28 DR: 60
D Lopez Ruano Angel CG: 35 DR: 60
D Diego Placente CG: 33 DR: 60
D Gabriel Tamas CG: 24 DR: 55
G J M Pinto Colorado CG: 34 DR: 62
M Pablo Gustavo Lopez CG: 23 SD: -15
M Borja Melendez Oubina CG: 30 SD: -22
M Fabian Canobbio CG: 26 SD: -24
M Anderson Nene CG: 30 SD: -24
F Fernando Baiano CG: 33 SR: 199
F Habib Bamogo* CG: 5 SR: 322

MONTHLY POINTS TALLY

AUGUST	0	0%
SEPTEMBER	3	33%
OCTOBER	7	58%
NOVEMBER	7	58%
DECEMBER	4	33%
JANUARY	0	0%
FEBRUARY	5	42%
MARCH	1	11%
APRIL	3	20%
MAY	3	25%
JUNE	6	100%

LEAGUE GOALS

	PLAYER	MINS	GOALS	S RATE
1	Baiano	2993	15	199
2	Nene	2999	9	333
3	Gustavo Lopez	2205	3	735
4	Bamogo	644	2	322
5	Canobbio	2565	2	1282
6	Angel	3133	2	1566
7	Guayre	320	1	320
8	Yago	326	1	326
9	Perera	392	1	392
10	Jorge	503	1	503
11	Iriney	2029	1	2029
12	Lequi	2061	1	2061
13	Oubina	2685	1	2685
	Other		0	
	TOTAL		**40**	

TOP POINT EARNERS

	PLAYER	GAMES	AV PTS
1	Fabian Canobbio	27	1.22
2	Santos da Silva Iriney	18	1.17
3	Jose M Pinto Colorado	34	1.15
4	Pablo A Fica Contreras	28	1.11
5	Borja Melendez Oubina	30	1.10
6	Matias Emanuel Lequi	22	1.09
7	Diego Placente	33	1.06
8	Lopez Ruano Angel	35	1.06
9	Fernando Baiano	33	1.00
10	Anderson Nene	30	0.93
	CLUB AVERAGE:		**1.03**

DISCIPLINARY RECORDS

	PLAYER	YELLOW	RED	AV
1	Pablo Garcia	11	2	8
2	Gabriel Tamas	14	2	16
3	P A Fica Contreras	12	1	23
4	S da Silva Iriney	9	1	25
5	M Emanuel Lequi	9	1	25
6	P Gustavo Lopez	7	1	31
7	Antonio Nunez	3	0	32
8	Diego Placente	13	0	33
9	Lopez Ruano Angel	8	1	39
10	Fabian Canobbio	6	2	42
11	Aspas J Jonathan	4	0	49
12	Fernando Baiano	6	0	49
13	Larena Jorge	1	0	50
	Other	14	0	
	TOTAL	**116**	**11**	

KEY GOALKEEPER

Jose Manuel Pinto Colorado

Goals Conceded in the League	49	Counting Games: League games when player was on pitch for at least 70 minutes	34
Defensive Rating: Ave number of mins between League goals conceded while on the pitch	62	Clean Sheets: In League games when player was on pitch for at least 70 minutes	5

KEY PLAYERS - DEFENDERS

Pablo Andres Fica Contreras

Goals Conceded: Number of League goals conceded while the player was on the pitch	42	Clean Sheets: In League games when player was on pitch for at least 70 minutes	4
Defensive Rating: Ave number of mins between League goals conceded while on the pitch	60	Club Defensive Rating: Average number of mins between League goals conceded by the club this season	57

	PLAYER	CON LGE	CLEAN SHEETS	DEF RATE
1	Pablo Andres Fica Contreras	42	4	60 mins
2	Lopez Ruano Angel	52	5	60 mins
3	Diego Placente	50	5	60 mins
4	Gabriel Tamas	39	2	55 mins

KEY PLAYERS - MIDFIELDERS

Pablo Gustavo Lopez –

Goals in the League	3	Contribution to Attacking Power: Average number of minutes between League team goals while on pitch	78
Defensive Rating: Average number of mins between League goals conceded while on the pitch	63	Scoring Difference: Defensive Rating minus Contribution to Attacking Power	-15

	PLAYER	LGE GOALS	DEF RATE	POWER	SCORE DIFF
1	Pablo Gustavo Lopez	3	63	78	-15 mins
2	Borja Melendez Oubina	1	52	74	-22 mins
3	Fabian Canobbio	2	61	85	-24 mins
4	Anderson Nene	9	57	81	-24 mins

KEY PLAYERS - GOALSCORERS

Fernando Baiano

Goals in the League	15	Player Strike Rate: Average number of minutes between League goals scored by player	199
Contribution to Attacking Power: Average number of minutes between League team goals while on pitch	78	Club Strike Rate: Average number of minutes between League goals scored by club	85

	PLAYER	LGE GOALS	POWER	STRIKE RATE
1	Fernando Baiano	15	78	199 mins
2	Habib Bamogo	2	80	322 mins
3	Anderson Nene	9	81	333 mins
4	Pablo Gustavo Lopez	3	78	735 mins

Fernando Baiano

SQUAD APPEARANCES

Match	1 2 3 4	5 6 7 8 9 10	11 12 13 14 15	16 17 18 19 20	21 22 23 24 25	26 27 28 29 30	31 32 33 34 35	36 37 38 39 40	41 42 43 44 45	46 47 48
Venue	H A A A H	H A H A A	H A H A A	H H A H A	A H A H A	A H H A A	H H A H H	A A H A H	A H A H A	H A H
Competition	L L E L L	E L L L L	E L L L E	L E L E L	L L L L L	L L L E L	E L E L	E L E L	L L L L L	L L L
Result	L W W L L	W D W W L	D W L W L	D W D D D	D D L L L	L D L D W	W D L L D	L L L L W	L L L L L	W W W

Goalkeepers
Andres Esteban
J M Pinto Colorado

Defenders
Lopez Ruano Angel
M Alexandre Areias
P A Fica Contreras
A Juncal Jonathan
Matias Emanuel Lequi
George Lucas
Diego Placente
Gabriel Tamas
Alonso-Fueyo Yago

Midfielders
Dani Abalo
Fabian Canobbio
Daniel de Ridder
Pablo Garcia
Pablo Gustavo Lopez
Santos da Silva Iriney
Larena Jorge
Anderson Nene
Antonio Nunez
B Melendez Oubina
Jonathan Vila

Forwards
Fernando Baiano
Habib Bamogo
Antonio Guayre
Iago
Jose Jesus Perera

KEY: ■ On all match ◄◄ Subbed or sent off (Counting game) ►► Subbed on from bench (Counting Game) ►►► Subbed on and then subbed or sent off (Counting Game) ☐ Not in 16
■ On bench ◄ Subbed or sent off (playing less than 70 minutes) ►► Subbed on (playing less than 70 minutes) ►► Subbed on and then subbed or sent off (playing less than 70 minutes)

SPAIN - CELTA VIGO

REAL SOCIEDAD

Final Position: 19th

NICKNAME: TXURI-URDIN   KEY: ☐ Won ☐ Drawn ☐ Lost   Attendance

#		Opponent			Score	Scorers	Attendance
1	sppr1	Athl Bilbao	A	D	1-1	Aramburu 87	40,000
2	sppr1	Seville	H	L	1-3	de Cerio 90	20,983
3	sppr1	Real Madrid	A	L	0-2		71,500
4	sppr1	Recreativo H	H	L	2-3	Uranga 65, Novo 76 pen	20,000
5	sppr1	Deportivo	A	L	0-2		20,000
6	sppr1	Real Zaragoza	H	L	1-3	Prieto 29	23,000
7	sppr1	Mallorca	A	D	0-0		16,000
8	sppr1	Villarreal	H	L	0-1		19,000
9	sppr1	Levante	A	L	0-2		6,500
10	sppr1	Espanyol	H	D	1-1	de Cerio 31	19,000
11	sppr1	Real Betis	H	D	0-0		19,000
12	sppr1	Atl Madrid	A	D	1-1	Uranga 24	40,000
13	sppr1	Getafe	H	D	0-0		19,000
14	sppr1	Barcelona	A	L	0-1		75,000
15	sppr1	Gimnastic	H	W	3-2	Mingo 48 og, Juanito 54, Diego Rivas 60	19,000
16	sppr1	Celta Vigo	A	D	0-0		8,000
17	sppr1	Osasuna	H	W	2-1	Prieto 19 pen, Aranburu 88	20,000
18	sppr1	R Santander	A	L	0-1		14,000
19	sppr1	Valencia	H	L	0-1		22,000
20	sppr1	Athl Bilbao	H	L	0-2		22,000
21	sppr1	Seville	A	D	0-0		45,000
22	sppr1	Real Madrid	H	L	1-2	Aranburu 8	23,000
23	sppr1	Recreativo H	A	L	0-1		16,000
24	sppr1	Deportivo	H	L	0-1		24,424
25	sppr1	Real Zaragoza	A	L	2-3	Herrera 17, de Cerio 90	25,000
26	sppr1	Mallorca	H	W	3-1	Savio 27, Kovacevic 45, Prieto 90	20,000
27	sppr1	Villarreal	A	D	1-1	Savio 40	20,000
28	sppr1	Levante	H	W	1-0	Ansotegi 38	18,000
29	sppr1	Espanyol	A	L	0-1		40,320
30	sppr1	Real Betis	A	W	1-0	Garrido 33	45,000
31	sppr1	Atl Madrid	H	W	2-0	Kovacevic 7, Savio 84	27,426
32	sppr1	Getafe	A	L	0-1		12,000
33	sppr1	Barcelona	H	L	0-2		29,777
34	sppr1	Gimnastic	A	W	3-1	Garitano 12, Savio 24, Ansotegi 72	9,000
35	sppr1	Celta Vigo	H	W	3-1	Kovacevic 46, Savio 51, Lopez Rekarte 77	27,015
36	sppr1	Osasuna	A	L	0-2		18,274
37	sppr1	R Santander	H	D	0-0		23,348
38	sppr1	Valencia	A	D	3-3	Garitano 3, de Cerio 36, Moretti 90 og	40,000

LEAGUE APPEARANCES, BOOKINGS AND CAPS

	AGE (on 01/07/07)	IN NAMED 18	APPEARANCES	COUNTING GAMES	MINUTES ON PITCH	YELLOW CARDS	RED CARDS	CAPS THIS SEASON	NATIONAL SIDE
Goalkeepers									
Claudio Bravo	24	35	28	28	2520	3	0	-	Chile
Asier Riesgo	23	38	10	10	900	0	0	-	Spain
Defenders									
Ion G Ansotegi	24	29	20	19	1726	2	0	-	Spain
Daniel A Cifuentes	26	5	1	0	55	1	0	-	Spain
Javier Garrido	22	34	27	24	2217	5	0	-	Spain
Garcia Gerardo	32	34	30	25	2430	9	2	-	Spain
Mikel Gonzalez	21	25	19	18	1610	6	1	-	Spain
Juanito	27	36	28	21	2186	6	0	-	Spain
Mikel Labaka	26	25	11	11	990	2	0	-	Spain
Victor Lopez	28	17	17	17	1508	5	0	-	Argentina
Lopez Rekarte	31	34	27	23	2180	6	0	-	Spain
Adriano Rossato	29	4	2	0	59	0	0	-	Brazil
Midfielders									
Mikel Alonso	27	24	18	3	765	0	0	-	Spain
Mikel Aranburu	28	36	29	17	1904	1	1	-	Spain
G Elustondo Urkola	20	11	6	4	427	0	0	-	Spain
Daniel Estrada	20	8	8	5	473	1	0	-	Spain
Fabio Felicio	25	11	10	2	381	3	0	-	Portugal
Gaizka Garitano	31	33	30	20	2078	9	0	-	Spain
Jesuli	29	11	11	8	764	1	0	-	Spain
Alvaro Novo	29	29	12	3	456	3	0	-	Spain
Xabier Prieto	23	34	33	29	2717	3	0	-	Spain
Diego Rivas	27	29	22	14	1589	4	1	-	Spain
Bortolini Savio	33	19	19	18	1619	2	0	-	Brazil
Dalibor Stevanovic	22	5	1	0	53	0	0	-	Slovenia
Forwards									
Imanol Agirretxe	20	8	6	0	75	0	0	-	Spain
Diaz de Cerio	23	28	27	6	1076	4	0	-	Spain
G Gustavo Herrera	23	21	19	3	796	3	0	-	Argentina
Darko Kovacevic	33	34	33	23	2438	6	0	-	Serbia
Morten Skoubo	27	6	5	0	171	0	0	-	Denmark
Garikoitz Uranga	27	20	20	15	1449	5	0	-	Spain

TEAM OF THE SEASON

- **Claudio Bravo** (G) — CG: 28 DR: 93
- **Ion Gorostola Ansotegi** (D) — CG: 19 DR: 95
- **Lopez Rekarte** (D) — CG: 23 DR: 80
- **Victor Lopez** (D) — CG: 17 DR: 79
- **Mikel Gonzalez** (D) — CG: 18 DR: 76
- **Gaizka Garitano** (M) — CG: 20 SD: -8
- **Bortolini Savio** (M) — CG: 18 SD: -10
- **Xabier Prieto** (M) — CG: 29 SD: -40
- **Mikel Aranburu** (M) — CG: 17 SD: -42
- **Garikoitz Uranga** (F) — CG: 15 SR: 724
- **Darko Kovacevic** (F) — CG: 23 SR: 812

MONTHLY POINTS TALLY

Month	Points	%
AUGUST	1	33%
SEPTEMBER	0	0%
OCTOBER	1	8%
NOVEMBER	3	25%
DECEMBER	5	42%
JANUARY	3	25%
FEBRUARY	1	8%
MARCH	7	58%
APRIL	6	50%
MAY	6	50%
JUNE	2	33%

LEAGUE GOALS

	PLAYER	MINS	GOALS	S RATE
1	Savio	1619	5	323
2	de Cerio	1076	4	269
3	Aranburu	1904	3	634
4	Kovacevic	2438	3	812
5	Prieto	2717	3	905
6	Uranga	1449	2	724
7	Ansotegi	1726	2	863
8	Garitano	2078	2	1039
9	Novo	456	1	456
10	Herrera	796	1	796
11	Rivas	1589	1	1589
12	Lopez Rekarte	2180	1	2180
13	Juanito	2186	1	2186
	Other		1	
	TOTAL		30	

TOP POINT EARNERS

	PLAYER	GAMES	AV PTS
1	Gaizka Garitano	20	1.30
2	Darko Kovacevic	23	1.26
3	Victor Lopez	17	1.24
4	Bortolini Savio	18	1.22
5	Ion Gorostola Ansotegi	19	1.21
6	Claudio Bravo	28	1.11
7	Garcia Gerardo	24	1.04
8	Juanito	21	0.95
9	Xabier Prieto	29	0.90
10	Javier Garrido	24	0.83
	CLUB AVERAGE:		0.92

DISCIPLINARY RECORDS

	PLAYER	YELLOW	RED	AVE
1	Alvaro Novo	3	0	152
2	Gaizka Garitano	9	0	230
3	Mikel Gonzalez	6	1	230
4	Garcia Gerardo	8	1	260
5	G Gustavo Herrera	3	0	265
6	Diaz de Cerio	4	0	269
7	Garikoitz Uranga	5	0	289
8	Victor Lopez	5	0	301
9	Diego Rivas	4	1	317
10	Lopez Rekarte	6	0	363
11	Juanito	6	0	364
12	Darko Kovacevic	6	0	406
13	Javier Garrido	5	0	443
	Other	15	1	
	TOTAL	85	4	

KEY GOALKEEPER

Claudio Bravo

Goals Conceded in the League	27	Counting Games League games when player was on pitch for at least 70 minutes	28
Defensive Rating Ave number of mins between League goals conceded while on the pitch	93	Clean Sheets In League games when player was on pitch for at least 70 minutes	8

KEY PLAYERS - DEFENDERS

Ion Gorostola Ansotegi

Goals Conceded Number of League goals conceded while the player was on the pitch	18	Clean Sheets In League games when player was on pitch for at least 70 minutes	7
Defensive Rating Ave number of mins between League goals conceded while on the pitch	95	Club Defensive Rating Average number of mins between League goals conceded by the club this season	72

	PLAYER	CON LGE	CLEAN SHEETS	DEF RATE
1	Ion Gorostola Ansotegi	18	7	95 mins
2	Lopez Rekarte	27	4	80 mins
3	Victor Lopez	19	4	79 mins
4	Mikel Gonzalez	21	4	76 mins

KEY PLAYERS - MIDFIELDERS

Gaizka Garitano

Goals in the League	2	Contribution to Attacking Power Average number of minutes between League team goals while on pitch	94
Defensive Rating Average number of mins between League goals conceded while on the pitch	86	Scoring Difference Defensive Rating minus Contribution to Attacking Power	-8

	PLAYER	LGE GOALS	DEF RATE	POWER	SCORE DIFF
1	Gaizka Garitano	2	86	94	-8 mins
2	Bortolini Savio	5	85	95	-10 mins
3	Xabier Prieto	3	73	113	-40 mins
4	Mikel Aranburu	3	70	112	-42 mins

KEY PLAYERS - GOALSCORERS

Bortolini Savio

Goals in the League	5	Player Strike Rate Average number of minutes between League goals scored by player	323
Contribution to Attacking Power Average number of minutes between League team goals while on pitch	95	Club Strike Rate Average number of minutes between League goals scored by club	106

	PLAYER	LGE GOALS	POWER	STRIKE RATE
1	Bortolini Savio	5	95	323 mins
2	Mikel Aranburu	3	112	634 mins
3	Garikoitz Uranga	2	161	724 mins
4	Darko Kovacevic	3	90	812 mins

Darko Kovacevic

SQUAD APPEARANCES

Match	1	2	3	4	5		6	7	8	9	10		11	12	13	14	15		16	17	18	19	20		21	22	23	24	25		26	27	28	29	30		31	32	33	34	35		36	37	38
Venue	A	H	A	H	A		H	A	H	A	H		H	A	H	A	H		A	H	A	H	H		A	H	A	H	A		H	A	H	A	A		H	A	H	A	H		A	H	A
Competition	L	L	L	L	L		L	L	L	L	L		L	L	L	L	L		L	L	L	L	L		L	L	L	L	L		L	L	L	L	L		L	L	L	L	L		L	L	L
Result	D	L	L	L	L		L	D	L	L	D		D	D	D	L	W		D	W	L	L	L		D	L	L	L	L		W	D	W	L	W		W	L	L	W	W		L	D	D

Goalkeepers
Claudio Bravo
Asier Riesgo

Defenders
Ion G Ansotegi
Daniel A Cifuentes
Javier Garrido
Garcia Gerardo
Mikel Gonzalez
Juanito
Mikel Labaka
Victor Lopez
Lopez Rekarte
Adriano Rossato

Midfielders
Mikel Alonso
Mikel Aranburu
G Elustondo Urkola
Daniel Estrada
Fabio Felicio
Gaizka Garitano
Jesuli
Alvaro Novo
Xabier Prieto
Diego Rivas
Bortolini Savio
Dalibor Stevanovic

Forwards
Imanol Agirretxe
Diaz de Cerio
G Gustavo Herrera
Darko Kovacevic
Morten Skoubo

KEY: ■ On all match ◄◄ Subbed or sent off (Counting game) ►► Subbed on from bench (Counting Game) ►► Subbed on and then subbed or sent off (Counting Game) ☐ Not in 16
■ On bench ◄◄ Subbed or sent off (playing less than 70 minutes) ►► Subbed on (playing less than 70 minutes) ►► Subbed on and then subbed or sent off (playing less than 70 minutes)

SPAIN - REAL SOCIEDAD

GIMNASTIC

Final Position: 20th

NICKNAME: NASTIC KEY: ☐ Won ☐ Drawn ☐ Lost Attendance

					Scorers	Att
1	sppr1	Espanyol	A	W	1-0	Campano 51	24,198
2	sppr1	Celta Vigo	H	L	1-2	Portillo 67 pen	13,000
3	sppr1	Osasuna	A	L	0-2		18,900
4	sppr1	R Santander	H	D	2-2	Cuellar 37, Portillo 66	12,000
5	sppr1	Valencia	A	L	0-4		40,000
6	sppr1	Athl Bilbao	H	L	2-3	Sarriegui 55 og, Makukula 71	13,000
7	sppr1	Seville	A	L	1-2	Cuellar 68	45,000
8	sppr1	Real Madrid	H	L	1-3	Buades 30 pen	14,000
9	sppr1	Recreativo H	A	L	1-2	Irurzun 7	17,000
10	sppr1	Deportivo	H	D	0-0		14,000
11	sppr1	Real Zaragoza	A	L	0-3		25,000
12	sppr1	Mallorca	H	L	2-3	Campano 40, Lopez 73	13,000
13	sppr1	Villarreal	A	L	0-2		17,000
14	sppr1	Levante	H	W	2-1	Garcia 41, 76	12,000
15	sppr1	Real Sociedad	A	L	2-3	Llera 18, Castro 50	19,000
16	sppr1	Real Betis	H	L	0-1		10,000
17	sppr1	Atl Madrid	A	D	0-0		40,000
18	sppr1	Getafe	H	L	1-3	Llera 61	12,000
19	sppr1	Barcelona	A	L	0-3		60,000
20	sppr1	Espanyol	H	W	4-0	Portillo 8, Campano 19, Pinilla 26, Cesar Navas 43	10,000
21	sppr1	Celta Vigo	A	D	1-1	Portillo 77	12,000
22	sppr1	Osasuna	H	L	2-3	Portillo 34, Cesar Navas 59	11,000
23	sppr1	R Santander	A	L	1-4	Grahn 59	15,000
24	sppr1	Valencia	H	D	1-1	Ruben Castro 90	13,000
25	sppr1	Athl Bilbao	A	W	2-0	Portillo 37, Pinilla 72	35,000
26	sppr1	Seville	H	W	1-0	Portillo 76	14,000
27	sppr1	Real Madrid	A	L	0-2		70,000
28	sppr1	Recreativo H	H	D	1-1	Portillo 15	13,000
29	sppr1	Deportivo	A	L	0-1		23,182
30	sppr1	Real Zaragoza	H	W	1-0	Portillo 81	12,000
31	sppr1	Mallorca	A	L	0-1		17,000
32	sppr1	Villarreal	H	L	0-3		13,000
33	sppr1	Levante	A	L	0-2		18,000
34	sppr1	Real Sociedad	H	L	1-3	Portillo 31	9,000
35	sppr1	Real Betis	A	D	1-1	Portillo 90 pen	45,000
36	sppr1	Atl Madrid	H	L	0-2		12,000
37	sppr1	Getafe	A	W	1-0	Irurzun 79	12,000
38	sppr1	Barcelona	H	L	1-5	Grahn 83	14,000

LEAGUE APPEARANCES, BOOKINGS AND CAPS

	AGE (on 01/07/07)	IN NAMED 18	APPEARANCES	COUNTING GAMES	MINUTES ON PITCH	YELLOW CARDS	RED CARDS	CAPS THIS SEASON	NATIONAL SIDE
Goalkeepers									
A Benjamin Bizzarri	29	37	22	22	1980	3	0	-	Argentina
Ruben Perez	26	22	16	16	1440	1	0	-	-
Defenders									
Julio Cesar Caceres	27	14	11	11	990	1	0	-	Paraguay
Jose Maria Calvo	25	19	19	19	1695	5	0	-	Argentina
Cesar Navas	27	20	19	18	1624	4	1	-	Spain
Haro David Garcia	27	26	16	14	1367	5	0	-	Spain
Miguel Angel Llera	27	19	12	12	1071	5	1	-	Spain
Martinez Lara Manolo	27	6	3	0	109	1	0	-	Spain
Antonio Marco Ortega	30	20	14	14	1260	3	0	-	Spain
Anibal Matellan	30	32	26	24	2208	6	0	-	Argentina
Carles Mingo	29	19	16	14	1357	7	1	-	Spain
Hernandez O Lopez	27	2	2	2	180	0	0	-	Spain
Manuel Ruz	21	26	17	14	1353	6	2	-	Spain
Midfielders									
Abel Buades	29	20	18	15	1450	1	0	-	Spain
Alejandro Campano	28	35	29	13	1768	0	1	-	Spain
Sebastien Chabaud	30	18	16	13	1287	3	0	-	France
David Cuellar Tainta	27	33	28	16	1926	0	0	-	Spain
David Generelo	24	32	26	11	1626	2	0	-	Spain
Dias Prendes Juan	30	36	30	15	1837	6	0	-	Spain
Antonio Lopez	25	1	1	0	31	1	0	-	Spain
Carlos Merino	27	21	17	3	713	2	0	-	Spain
Angel Morales	31	32	24	16	1686	6	0	-	Spain
Jesus Maria Serrano	34	7	2	1	119	1	0	-	Spain
Forwards									
G R Goncalves Gil	26	25	19	6	1027	3	0	-	Brazil
Tobias Grahn	27	11	9	0	222	0	0	-	Sweden
Ismael Irurzun	32	26	21	5	959	2	0	-	Spain
Ariza Makukula	26	18	12	4	550	0	1	-	Portugal
Antonio Pinilla	36	30	28	15	1649	10	0	-	Spain
Javier Portillo	25	35	34	26	2687	2	0	-	Spain
Ruben Castro	26	24	19	9	1132	1	0	-	Spain

TEAM OF THE SEASON

- **Jose Maria Calvo** (D) CG: 19 DR: 56
- **Angel Morales** (M) CG: 16 SD: -30
- **Haro David Garcia** (D) CG: 14 DR: 56
- **Alejandro Campano** (M) CG: 13 SD: -36
- **Javier Portillo** (F) CG: 26 SR: 244
- **Ruben Perez** (G) CG: 16 DR: 46
- **Cesar Navas** (D) CG: 18 DR: 54
- **David Cuellar Tainta** (M) CG: 16 SD: -59
- **Antonio Pinilla** (F) CG: 15 SR: 824
- **Antonio Marco Ortega** (D) CG: 14 DR: 54
- **David Generelo*** (M) CG: 11 SD: -64

MONTHLY POINTS TALLY

AUGUST	3	100%
SEPTEMBER	1	11%
OCTOBER	0	0%
NOVEMBER	1	8%
DECEMBER	3	25%
JANUARY	4	33%
FEBRUARY	2	17%
MARCH	6	67%
APRIL	4	27%
MAY	1	8%
JUNE	3	50%

LEAGUE GOALS

	PLAYER	MINS	GOALS	S RATE
1	Portillo	2687	11	244
2	Campano	1768	3	589
3	Grahn	222	2	111
4	Irurzun	959	2	479
5	Llera	1071	2	535
6	Ruben Castro	1132	2	566
7	David Garcia	1367	2	683
8	Cesar Navas	1624	2	812
9	Pinilla	1649	2	824
10	Cuellar	1926	2	963
11	Lopez	211	1	211
12	Makukula	550	1	550
13	Buades	1450	1	1450
	Other		0	
	TOTAL		**33**	

TOP POINT EARNERS

	PLAYER	GAMES	AV PTS
1	Antonio Pinilla	15	1.07
2	Antonio Marco Ortega	14	1.00
3	Jose Maria Calvo	19	1.00
4	Haro David Garcia	14	1.00
5	Cesar Navas	19	0.95
6	Angel Morales	16	0.94
7	Javier Portillo	26	0.88
8	A Benjamin Bizzarri	22	0.86
9	Sebastien Chabaud	13	0.85
10	Alejandro Campano	14	0.79
	CLUB AVERAGE:		**0.74**

DISCIPLINARY RECORDS

	PLAYER	YELLOW	RED	AVE
1	Antonio Pinilla	10	0	164
2	Carles Mingo	7	1	169
3	Manuel Ruz	6	2	169
4	Miguel Angel Llera	5	1	178
5	Haro David Garcia	5	0	273
6	Angel Morales	6	0	281
7	Dias Prendes Juan	6	0	306
8	Cesar Navas	4	1	324
9	Jose Maria Calvo	5	0	339
10	G R Goncalves Gil	3	0	342
11	Carlos Merino	2	0	356
12	Anibal Matellan	6	0	368
13	A Marco Ortega	3	0	420
	Other	16	2	
	TOTAL	**84**	**7**	

KEY GOALKEEPER

Ruben Perez

Goals Conceded in the League	31	**Counting Games** League games when player was on pitch for at least 70 minutes	16
Defensive Rating Ave number of mins between League goals conceded while on the pitch	46	**Clean Sheets** In League games when player was on pitch for at least 70 minutes	3

KEY PLAYERS - DEFENDERS

Jose Maria Calvo

Goals Conceded Number of League goals conceded while the player was on the pitch	30	**Clean Sheets** In League games when player was on pitch for at least 70 minutes	5
Defensive Rating Ave number of mins between League goals conceded while on the pitch	56	**Club Defensive Rating** Average number of mins between League goals conceded by the club this season	49

	PLAYER	CON LGE	CLEAN SHEETS	DEF RATE
1	Jose Maria Calvo	30	5	56 mins
2	Haro David Garcia	24	4	56 mins
3	Cesar Navas	30	5	54 mins
4	Antonio Marco Ortega	23	4	54 mins

KEY PLAYERS - MIDFIELDERS

Angel Morales

Goals in the League	0	**Contribution to Attacking Power** Average number of minutes between League team goals while on pitch	88
Defensive Rating Average number of mins between League goals conceded while on the pitch	58	**Scoring Difference** Defensive Rating minus Contribution to Attacking Power	-30

	PLAYER	LGE GOALS	DEF RATE	POWER	SCORE DIFF
1	Angel Morales	0	58	88	-30 mins
2	Alejandro Campano	3	52	88	-36 mins
3	David Cuellar Tainta	2	42	101	-59 mins
4	David Generelo	0	52	116	-64 mins

KEY PLAYERS - GOALSCORERS

Javier Portillo

Goals in the League	11	**Player Strike Rate** Average number of minutes between League goals scored by player	244
Contribution to Attacking Power Average number of minutes between League team goals while on pitch	99	**Club Strike Rate** Average number of minutes between League goals scored by club	100

	PLAYER	LGE GOALS	POWER	STRIKE RATE
1	Javier Portillo	11	99	244 mins
2	Alejandro Campano	3	88	589 mins
3	Antonio Pinilla	2	109	824 mins
4	David Cuellar Tainta	2	101	963 mins

Javier Portillo

SQUAD APPEARANCES

Match	1	2	3	4	5	6	7	8	9	10	11	12	13	14	15	16	17	18	19	20	21	22	23	24	25	26	27	28	29	30	31	32	33	34	35	36	37	38
Venue	A	H	A	H	A	H	A	H	A	H	A	H	A	H	A	H	A	H	A	H	A	H	A	H	A	H	A	H	A	H	A	H	A	H	A	H	A	H
Competition	L	L	L	L	L	L	L	L	L	L	L	L	L	L	L	L	L	L	L	L	L	L	L	L	L	L	L	L	L	L	L	L	L	L	L	L	L	L
Result	W	L	L	D	L	L	L	L	L	D	L	L	L	W	L	L	D	L	L	W	L	D	L	D	W	W	L	D	L	W	L	L	L	L	D	L	W	L

Goalkeepers
Benjamin Bizzarri
Ruben Perez

Defenders
Julio Cesar Caceres
Jose Maria Calvo
Cesar Navas
Haro David Garcia
Miguel Angel Llera
Martinez Lara Manolo
Antonio Marco Ortega
Anibal Matellan
Carles Mingo
Hernandez O Lopez
Manuel Ruz

Midfielders
Abel Buades
Alejandro Campano
Sebastien Chabaud
David Cuellar Tainta
David Generelo
Mias Prendes Juan
Antonio Lopez
Carlos Merino
Angel Morales
Jesus Maria Serrano

Forwards
R Goncalves Gil
Tobias Grahn
Ismael Irurzun
Ariza Makukula
Antonio Pinilla
Javier Portillo
Ruben Castro

KEY: ■ On all match ⁞◄ Subbed or sent off (Counting game) ▸▸ Subbed on from bench (Counting Game) ▸▸ Subbed on and then subbed or sent off (Counting Game) ☐ Not in 16
■ On bench ◀◀ Subbed or sent off (playing less than 70 minutes) ▸▸ Subbed on (playing less than 70 minutes) ▸▸ Subbed on and then subbed or sent off (playing less than 70 minutes)

SPAIN - GIMNASTIC

ITALIAN LEAGUE ROUND-UP

FINAL LEAGUE TABLE

	P	W	D	L	F	A	W	D	L	F	A	F	A	DIF	PTS
			HOME					AWAY					TOTAL		
Inter Milan	38	15	3	1	42	19	15	4	0	38	15	80	34	46	97
Roma	38	13	4	2	43	12	9	5	5	31	22	74	34	40	75
Lazio*	38	10	6	3	25	9	8	5	6	34	24	59	33	26	62
AC Milan*	38	12	3	4	30	17	7	9	3	27	19	57	36	21	61
Palermo	38	9	3	7	37	28	7	7	5	21	23	58	51	7	58
Fiorentina*	38	15	2	2	44	12	6	8	5	18	19	62	31	31	58
Empoli	38	10	7	2	29	16	4	5	10	13	27	42	43	-1	54
Atalanta	38	8	9	2	34	22	4	5	10	22	32	56	54	2	50
Sampdoria	38	9	7	3	30	19	4	3	12	14	29	44	48	-4	49
Udinese	38	8	4	7	26	21	4	6	9	23	34	49	55	-6	46
Livorno	38	8	3	8	24	15	2	5	12	17	39	41	54	-13	43
Parma	38	9	4	6	25	24	1	8	10	16	32	41	56	-15	42
Catania	38	7	6	6	29	29	3	5	11	17	39	46	68	-22	41
Reggina*	38	7	8	4	26	19	5	7	7	26	31	52	50	2	40
Siena*	38	5	8	6	23	24	4	6	9	12	21	35	45	-10	40
Cagliari	38	7	7	5	19	19	2	6	11	16	27	35	46	-11	40
Torino	38	6	6	9	15	22	4	6	9	12	25	27	47	-20	40
Chievo	38	7	6	6	21	18	2	6	11	17	30	38	48	-10	39
Ascoli	38	3	8	8	24	32	2	4	13	12	35	36	67	-31	27
Messina	38	5	7	7	20	26	0	4	15	17	43	37	69	-32	26

CLUB STRIKE FORCE

Inter's Argentinean striker Hernan Crespo

1 Inter Milan		
Goals scored in the League		**80**
Club Strike Rate (CSR) Average number of minutes between League goals scored by club		**42**

	CLUB	GOALS	CSR
1	Inter Milan	80	42
2	Roma	74	46
3	Fiorentina	62	55
4	Lazio	59	57
5	Palermo	58	58
6	AC Milan	57	60
7	Atalanta	56	61
8	Reggina	52	65
9	Udinese	49	69
10	Catania	46	74
11	Sampdoria	44	77
12	Empoli	42	81
13	Livorno	41	83
14	Parma	41	83
15	Chievo	38	90
16	Ascoli	36	95
17	Messina	36	95
18	Siena	35	97
19	Cagliari	35	97
20	Torino	27	126

CLUB DISCIPLINARY RECORDS

Messina's Zoro argues with the referee

1 Messina		
League Yellow		**107**
League Red		**13**
League Total		**120**
Cards Average in League Average number of minutes between a card being shown of either colour		**28**

	CLUB	Y	R	TOTAL	AVE
1	Messina	107	13	120	28
2	Ascoli	107	8	115	29
3	Reggina	104	5	109	31
4	Parma	99	6	105	32
5	Catania	95	11	106	32
6	Siena	92	12	104	32
7	Atalanta	94	7	101	33
8	Lazio	90	9	99	34
9	Udinese	88	12	100	34
10	Palermo	85	8	93	36
11	Torino	86	8	94	36
12	Inter Milan	83	5	88	38
13	Chievo	81	9	90	38
14	Sampdoria	82	7	89	38
15	Fiorentina	80	4	84	40
16	Livorno	77	6	83	41
17	Roma	79	2	81	42
18	Empoli	68	4	72	47
19	AC Milan	65	3	68	50
20	Cagliari	60	6	66	51

CLUB DEFENCES

Ujfalusi of Fiorentina battles for the ball

1 Fiorentina		
Goals conceded in the League		**31**
Clean Sheets (CS) Number of league games where no goals were conceded		**19**
Club Defensive Rate (CDR) Average number of minutes between League goals conceded by club		**110**

	CLUB	LGE	CS	CDR
1	Fiorentina	31	19	110
2	Lazio	33	18	103
3	Roma	34	14	100
4	Inter Milan	34	15	100
5	AC Milan	36	17	95
6	Empoli	43	16	79
7	Siena	45	9	76
8	Cagliari	46	12	74
9	Chievo	47	9	72
10	Torino	47	14	72
11	Sampdoria	48	12	71
12	Reggina	50	8	68
13	Palermo	51	11	67
14	Livorno	54	12	63
15	Atalanta	54	6	63
16	Udinese	55	9	62
17	Parma	56	9	61
18	Ascoli	67	5	51
19	Catania	68	7	50
20	Messina	69	5	49

PLAYER NATIONALITIES

Overseas country with the most player appearances in the Italian League - Brazil

644 league appearances by Brazilian players

	COUNTRY	PLAYERS	IN SQUAD	LGE APP	% LGE ACT	CAPS	MOST APP	APP
1	Italy	415	10231	7985	77.4	100	Armando Pantanelli	100
2	Brazil	35	812	644	6.1	28	F Enrico Simplicio	84.8
3	Argentina	18	450	338	3	11	Javier Zanetti	91.6
4	France	12	306	250	2.4	8	Sebastian Frey	100
5	Chile	4	134	120	1.3	0	D Marcelo Pizarro	79.3
6	Serbia	7	194	154	1.3	14	Dejan Stankovic	79.6
7	Romania	5	133	110	1.2	27	Adrian Mutu	82.3
8	Ghana	4	118	103	1.1	5	Mark Edusei	78.7
9	Croatia	4	112	94	0.9	6	Igor Budan	80.2
10	Czech Republic	4	92	86	0.8	22	Tomas Ujfalusi	78.9
11	Honduras	3	88	83	0.8	0	David Suazo	93.8
12	Colombia	4	97	75	0.7	2	C Eduardo Zapata	92.2
13	Australia	3	96	69	0.7	9	Mark Bresciano	73.8
14	Portugal	5	127	90	0.6	0	Luis Figo	60.3
15	Nigeria	5	99	84	0.6	0	Christian Obodo	74.4
16	Albania	4	108	88	0.6	0	Erjon Bogdani	60.1
17	Uruguay	7	126	77	0.5	0	Diego Luis Lopez	86.7
18	Ivory Coast	4	97	71	0.5	0	Marc Andre Zoro	46.8
19	Denmark	4	98	68	0.5	9	Martin Jorgensen	65.7
20	Austria	1	38	38	0.4	0	Alex Manninger	100

CLUB MAKE-UP – HOME AND OVERSEAS PLAYERS

1 Inter Milan	95.5% of appearances by overseas players

	CLUB	OVERSEAS	HOME	% OVERSEAS	% LGE ACT	MOST APP	APP
1	Inter Milan	27	7	79.4	95.5	Javier Zanetti	91.6
2	AC Milan	17	19	47.2	51.0	Ricardo Kaka	77.6
3	Roma	15	14	51.7	44.5	Alexander Doni	84.2
4	Udinese	23	16	59	41.5	C Eduardo Zapata	92.2
5	Fiorentina	16	15	51.6	38.2	Sebastian Frey	100
6	Siena	10	22	31.3	36.3	Alex Manninger	100
7	Lazio	10	19	34.5	33.0	C Daniel Ledesma	85.9
8	Parma	14	20	41.2	30.5	Igor Budan	80.2
9	Messina	12	28	30	26.6	Vincent Candela	66.9
10	Ascoli	10	28	26.3	26.4	Viktor Boudianski	78
11	Livorno	15	16	48.4	25.5	Marc Pfertzel	56.4
12	Palermo	15	19	44.1	21.1	F Enrico Simplicio	84.8
13	Atalanta	12	20	37.5	19.6	A Ferreira Pinto	64.8
14	Chievo	8	27	22.9	18.9	Erjon Bogdani	60.1
15	Catania	8	22	26.7	18.7	Mark Edusei	78.7
16	Cagliari	8	23	25.8	18.4	David Suazo	93.8
17	Empoli	5	24	17.2	7.4	Sergio Almiron	52.1
18	Torino	7	27	20.6	6.1	Nikola Lazetic	52.1
19	Reggina	8	23	25.8	5.1	Julio Cesar Leon	36.5
20	Sampdoria	12	26	31.6	4.0	R Ariel Olivera	20.5

CHART-TOPPING MIDFIELDERS

1 Vieira - Inter Milan

Goals scored in the League	1
Defensive Rating Av number of mins between League goals conceded while on the pitch	120
Contribution to Attacking Power Average number of minutes between League team goals while on pitch	40
Scoring Difference Defensive Rating minus Contribution to Attacking Power	80

	PLAYER	CLUB	GOALS	DEF RATE	POWER	S DIFF
1	Patrick Vieira	Inter Milan	1	120	40	80
2	David Marcelo Pizarro	Roma	1	123	46	77
3	Stefano Mauri	Lazio	6	128	54	74
4	Riccardo Montolivo	Fiorentina	2	119	50	69
5	Massimo Mutarelli	Lazio	2	121	53	68
6	Daniele De Rossi	Roma	2	105	43	62
7	Dejan Stankovic	Inter Milan	6	100	40	60
8	Fabio Liverani	Fiorentina	1	113	55	58
9	Luis Figo	Inter Milan	2	103	45	58
10	Cristian D Ledesma	Lazio	2	112	56	56
11	Rodrigo Taddei	Roma	5	96	45	51
12	Simone Perrotta	Roma	8	98	49	49
13	Luciano Zauri	Lazio	0	101	54	47
14	Gaby Mudingayi	Lazio	0	103	57	46
15	Max Tonetto	Roma	0	94	50	44

CHART-TOPPING GOALSCORERS

1 Rigano - Messina

Goals scored in the League	19
Contribution to Attacking Power Average number of minutes between League team goals while on pitch	86
Club Strike Rate (CSR) Average minutes between League goals scored by club	97
Player Strike Rate Average number of minutes between League goals scored by player	118

	PLAYER	CLUB	GOALS: LGE	POWER	CSR	S RATE
1	Christian Rigano	Messina	19	86	97	118
2	Francesco Totti	Roma	25	44	47	120
3	Cristiano Lucarelli	Livorno	20	86	85	133
4	Luca Toni	Fiorentina	16	55	56	144
5	Zlatan Ibrahimovic	Inter Milan	15	41	43	144
6	Nicola Amoruso	Reggina	17	58	67	151
7	Gianatha Spinesi	Catania	17	74	76	157
8	Cristiano Doni	Atalanta	13	55	62	158
9	Rolando Bianchi	Reggina	18	63	67	173
10	Alberto Gilardino	AC Milan	12	56	61	174
11	Adrian Mutu	Fiorentina	16	56	56	175
12	Vincenzo Iaquinta	Udinese	14	80	71	183
13	Luca Saudati	Empoli	14	75	85	187
14	Tommaso Rocchi	Lazio	16	58	59	188
15	Fabio Quagliarella	Sampdoria	13	81	79	213

CHART-TOPPING DEFENDERS

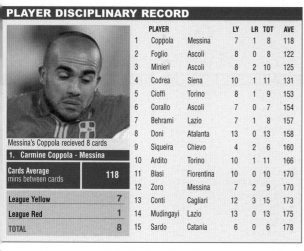

1 Lucchini - Empoli

Goals Conceded in the League The number of League goals conceded while he was on the pitch	15
Clean Sheets In games when he played at least 70 mins	11
Club Defensive Rating Average mins between League goals conceded by the club this season	83
Defensive Rating Average number of minutes between League goals conceded while on pitch	136

	PLAYER	CLUB	CON: LGE	CS	CDR	DEF RATE
1	Stefano Lucchini	Empoli	15	11	83	136
2	E Sanchez Cribari	Lazio	15	13	106	135
3	Matteo Ferrari	Roma	16	11	103	133
4	Alessandro Gamberini	Fiorentina	19	14	113	127
5	Tomas Ujfalusi	Fiorentina	24	15	113	112
6	Marco Materazzi	Inter Milan	21	10	103	112
7	Sebastiano Siviglia	Lazio	24	15	106	112
8	Alessandro Mancini	Roma	19	9	103	109
9	Manuel Pasqual	Fiorentina	28	17	113	108
10	Guglielmo Stendardo	Lazio	16	7	106	106
11	Nicolas Burdisso	Inter Milan	18	10	103	104
12	Daniele Bonera	AC Milan	20	10	97	101
13	Javier Zanetti	Inter Milan	31	14	103	101
14	Marco Cassetti	Roma	17	6	103	101
15	Christian Panucci	Roma	27	11	103	100

CHART-TOPPING GOALKEEPERS

1 Dida - AC Milan

Counting Games Games in which he played at least 70 minutes	25
Goals Conceded in the League The number of League goals conceded while he was on the pitch	19
Clean Sheets In games when he played at least 70 mins	13
Defensive Rating Average number of minutes between League goals conceded while on pitch	118

	PLAYER	CLUB	CG	CONC	CS	DEF RATE
1	Nelson Dida	AC Milan	25	19	13	118
2	Alexander Doni	Roma	32	25	13	115
3	Sebastian Frey	Fiorentina	38	31	19	110
4	Angelo Peruzzi	Lazio	26	24	11	99
5	Julio Cesar	Inter Milan	32	30	12	96
6	Daniele Balli	Empoli	32	31	15	92
7	Lorenzo Squizzi	Chievo	21	24	5	78
8	Luca Bucci	Parma	25	30	8	77
9	Christian Abbiati	Torino	36	42	14	76
10	Alex Manninger	Siena	38	45	9	76
11	Antonio Chimenti	Cagliari	20	25	7	74
12	Luca Castellazzi	Sampdoria	27	34	8	71
13	Alberto Fontana	Palermo	29	38	9	69
14	Ivan Pelizzoli	Reggina	21	28	5	67
15	Alex Calderoni	Atalanta	37	50	6	66

PLAYER DISCIPLINARY RECORD

Messina's Coppola received 8 cards

1. Carmine Coppola - Messina

Cards Average	118
mins between cards	
League Yellow	7
League Red	1
TOTAL	8

	PLAYER		LY	LR	TOT	AVE
1	Coppola	Messina	7	1	8	118
2	Foglio	Ascoli	8	0	8	122
3	Minieri	Ascoli	8	2	10	125
4	Codrea	Siena	10	1	11	131
5	Cioffi	Torino	8	1	9	153
6	Corallo	Ascoli	7	0	7	154
7	Behrami	Lazio	7	1	8	157
8	Doni	Atalanta	13	0	13	158
9	Siqueira	Chievo	4	2	6	160
10	Ardito	Torino	10	1	11	166
11	Blasi	Fiorentina	10	0	10	170
12	Zoro	Messina	7	2	9	170
13	Conti	Cagliari	12	3	15	173
14	Mudingayi	Lazio	13	0	13	175
15	Sardo	Catania	6	0	6	178

TEAM OF THE SEASON

G Dida (AC Milan) CG: 25 DR: 118

D Gamberini (Fiorentina) CG: 27 DR: 127

D Lucchini (Empoli) CG: 19 DR: 136

D Ferrari (Roma) CG: 22 DR: 133

D Cribari (Lazio) CG: 23 DR: 135

M Mauri (Lazio) CG: 27 SD: +74

M Vieira (Inter) CG: 19 SD: +80

M Pizzaro (Roma) CG: 29 SD: +77

M Montolivo (Fiorentina) CG: 25 SD: +69

F Riggano (Messina) CG: 27 SR: 118

F Totti (Roma) CG: 34 SR: 120

ITALIAN LEAGUE ROUND-UP

INTER MILAN

Final Position: 1st

NICKNAME: INTER   KEY: ☐ Won ☐ Drawn ☐ Lost   Attendance

#		Opponent		Result	Scorers	Attendance
1	itpr1	**Fiorentina**	A W	3-2	Cambiasso 11, 41, Ibrahimovic 61	41,334
2	ecgpb	**Sp Lisbon**	A L	0-1		30,000
3	itpr1	**Sampdoria**	H D	1-1	Bonanni 79	45,194
4	itpr1	**Roma**	A W	1-0	Crespo 44	56,476
5	itpr1	**Chievo**	H W	4-3	Crespo 11, 70, Samuel 58, D.Stankovic 64	41,357
6	ecgpb	**Bayern Munich**	H L	0-2		79,000
7	itpr1	**Cagliari**	A D	1-1	Grosso 38	18,000
8	itpr1	**Catania**	H W	2-1	D.Stankovic 29, 75	47,505
9	ecgpb	**Spar Moscow**	H W	2-1	Cruz 2, 9	40,000
10	itpr1	**Udinese**	A D	0-0		20,000
11	itpr1	**Livorno**	H W	4-1	Pfertzel 2, Materazzi 13, Ibrahimovic 71, Cruz 78	39,057
12	itpr1	**AC Milan**	A W	4-3	Crespo 17, D.Stankovic 22, Ibrahimovic 47, Materazzi 68	79,000
13	ecgpb	**Spar Moscow**	A W	1-0	Cruz 2	60,000
14	itpr1	**Ascoli**	H W	2-0	J.Zanetti 41, Cudini 53 og	35,000
15	itpr1	**Parma**	A W	2-0	Ibrahimovic 15, Cruz 90	18,000
16	itpr1	**Reggina**	H W	1-0	Crespo 4	45,000
17	ecgpb	**Sp Lisbon**	H W	1-0	Crespo 36	40,000
18	itpr1	**Palermo**	A W	2-1	Ibrahimovic 7, Vieira 61	35,000
19	itpr1	**Siena**	H W	2-0	Burdisso 11, Crespo 55	42,299
20	ecgpb	**Bayern Munich**	A D	1-1	Vieira 90	66,000
21	itpr1	**Empoli**	A W	3-0	Crespo 60, Ibrahimovic 78, Samuel 87	11,000
22	itpr1	**Messina**	H W	2-0	Materazzi 49, Ibrahimovic 59	45,000
23	itpr1	**Lazio**	A W	2-0	Cambiasso 39, Materazzi 85	50,000
24	itpr1	**Atalanta**	H W	2-1	Adriano 65, Loria 74 og	43,000
25	itpr1	**Torino**	A W	3-1	Adriano 24, Ibrahimovic 60, Materazzi 85 pen	23,000
26	itpr1	**Fiorentina**	H W	3-1	D.Stankovic 19, Adriano 24, Ibrahimovic 71	50,000
27	itpr1	**Sampdoria**	A W	2-0	Ibrahimovic 38, Maicon 75	25,000
28	itpr1	**Chievo**	A W	2-0	Adriano 1, Crespo 51	0
29	itpr1	**Cagliari**	H W	1-0	Burdisso 11	30,000
30	eckl1	**Valencia**	H D	2-2	Cambiasso 28, Maicon 76	65,000
31	eckl2	**Catania**	A W	5-2	Samuel 45, Solari 49, Grosso 57, Ibrahimovic 67, Cruz 78	0
32	itpr1	**Udinese**	H D	1-1	Crespo 67	35,000
33	itpr1	**Livorno**	A W	2-1	Cruz 35, Ibrahimovic 66	5,641
34	eckl2	**Valencia**	A D	0-0		53,000
35	itpr1	**AC Milan**	H W	2-1	Cruz 55, Ibrahimovic 75	63,681
36	itpr1	**Ascoli**	A W	2-1	Ibrahimovic 65, 73	4,787
37	itpr1	**Parma**	H W	2-0	Maxwell 56, Crespo 70	48,888
38	itpr1	**Reggina**	A D	0-0		18,506
39	itpr1	**Palermo**	H D	2-2	Cruz 67, Adriano 74	46,611
40	itpr1	**Roma**	H L	1-3	Materazzi 52 pen	60,000
41	itpr1	**Siena**	A W	2-1	Materazzi 18, 60 pen	14,027
42	itpr1	**Empoli**	H W	3-1	Cruz 27, Recoba 59, D.Stankovic 60	61,839
43	itpr1	**Messina**	A W	1-0	Crespo 72	13,410
44	itpr1	**Lazio**	H W	4-3	Crespo 20, 35, 81, Materazzi 85	45,429
45	itpr1	**Atalanta**	A D	1-1	Figo 58 pen	22,899
46	itpr1	**Torino**	H W	3-0	Materazzi 12 pen, Maicon 60, Figo 67 pen	64,758

LEAGUE APPEARANCES, BOOKINGS AND CAPS

	AGE (on 01/07/07)	IN NAMED 18	APPEARANCES	COUNTING GAMES	MINUTES ON PITCH	YELLOW CARDS	RED CARDS	CAPS THIS SEASON	NATIONAL SIDE
Goalkeepers									
Julio Cesar	27	34	32	32	2880	1	0	2	Brazil
Francesco Toldo	35	36	6	6	540	1	0	-	Italy
Defenders									
Marco Andreolli	21	12	4	3	334	0	0	-	Italy
Nicolas Burdisso	26	32	24	20	1888	8	0	1	Argentina
Ivan Cordoba	30	31	29	24	2272	10	0	1	Colombia
Fabio Grosso	29	32	23	13	1620	1	1	-	Italy
D Sisenando Maicon	25	34	32	27	2597	8	1	8	Brazil
Marco Materazzi	33	33	28	26	2372	13	1	6	Italy
Walter Samuel	29	23	18	10	1068	6	0	1	Argentina
Javier Zanetti	33	38	37	34	3133	3	0	2	Argentina
Midfielders									
Esteban Cambiasso	26	24	20	16	1586	0	0	2	Argentina
Olivier Dacourt	32	29	24	12	1481	7	0	-	France
Luis Figo	34	36	32	18	2063	5	0	-	Portugal
Mariano Gonzalez	26	24	13	3	454	1	0	-	Argentina
Scherer Maxwell	25	27	20	11	1223	2	0	-	Brazil
Santiago H Solari	30	35	21	5	922	1	0	-	Argentina
Dejan Stankovic	28	34	34	30	2721	10	0	8	Serbia
Patrick Vieira	31	20	20	19	1690	7	2	7	France
Forwards									
Leite Adriano	25	25	23	11	1415	1	0	2	Brazil
Lambros Choutos	27	4	1	0	12	0	0	-	Greece
Hernan Crespo	31	33	29	17	1902	3	0	2	Argentina
Julio Cruz	32	21	15	4	778	2	0	-	Argentina
Zlatan Ibrahimovic	25	29	27	22	2167	8	3	3	Sweden
Ibrahim Maaroufi	18	2	1	0	9	0	0	-	Belgium
Alvaro Recoba	31	18	13	1	416	0	0	-	Uruguay

TEAM OF THE SEASON

D Marco Materazzi CG: 26 DR: 112

M Esteban Cambiasso CG: 16 SD: 102

D Nicolas Burdisso CG: 20 DR: 104

M Patrick Vieira CG: 19 SD: 80

F Hernan Crespo CG: 17 SR: 135

G Julio Cesar CG: 32 DR: 96

D Javier Zanetti CG: 34 DR: 101

M Dejan Stankovic CG: 30 SD: 60

F Zlatan Ibrahimovic CG: 22 SR: 144

D D Sisenando Maicon CG: 27 DR: 99

M Luis Figo CG: 18 SD: 58

MONTHLY POINTS TALLY

Month	Points	%
SEPTEMBER	10	83%
OCTOBER	11	73%
NOVEMBER	12	100%
DECEMBER	15	100%
JANUARY	9	100%
FEBRUARY	10	83%
MARCH	9	100%
APRIL	11	61%
MAY	10	83%

LEAGUE GOALS

	PLAYER	MINS	GOALS	S RATE
1	Ibrahimovic	2167	15	144
2	Crespo	1902	14	135
3	Materazzi	2372	10	237
4	Cruz	778	7	111
5	Stankovic, D	2721	6	453
6	Adriano	1415	5	283
7	Samuel	1068	3	356
8	Cambiasso	1586	3	528
9	Grosso	1620	2	810
10	Burdisso	1888	2	944
11	Figo	2063	2	1031
12	Maicon	2597	2	1298
13	Recoba	416	1	416
	Other		4	
	TOTAL		**76**	

TOP POINT EARNERS

	PLAYER	GAMES	AV PTS
1	Patrick Vieira	19	2.79
2	Hernan Crespo	17	2.76
3	Dejan Stankovic	30	2.63
4	Nicolas Burdisso	20	2.60
5	Javier Zanetti	34	2.56
6	Julio Cesar	32	2.53
7	D Sisenando Maicon	27	2.52
8	Marco Materazzi	26	2.50
9	Olivier Dacourt	12	2.50
10	Zlatan Ibrahimovic	22	2.50
	CLUB AVERAGE:		**2.55**

DISCIPLINARY RECORDS

	PLAYER	YELLOW	RED	AVE
1	Marco Materazzi	13	1	197
2	Olivier Dacourt	7	0	211
3	Walter Samuel	6	0	213
4	Patrick Vieira	7	2	241
5	Nicolas Burdisso	8	0	269
6	Zlatan Ibrahimovic	8	3	270
7	Ivan Cordoba	10	0	284
8	Dejan Stankovic	10	0	302
9	D Sisenando Maicon	8	1	371
10	Julio Cruz	2	0	389
11	Mariano Gonzalez	1	0	454
12	Luis Figo	5	0	515
13	Scherer Maxwell	2	0	611
	Other	11	1	
	TOTAL	**98**	**8**	

KEY GOALKEEPER

Julio Cesar

Goals Conceded in the League	30	Counting Games League games when player was on pitch for at least 70 minutes	32
Defensive Rating Ave number of mins between League goals conceded while on the pitch	96	Clean Sheets In games when player was on pitch for at least 70 minutes	12

KEY PLAYERS - DEFENDERS

Marco Materazzi

Goals Conceded Number of League goals conceded while the player was on the pitch	21	Clean Sheets In League games when player was on pitch for at least 70 minutes	10
Defensive Rating Ave number of mins between League goals conceded while on the pitch	112	Club Defensive Rating Average number of mins between League goals conceded by the club this season	103

	PLAYER	CON LGE	CLEAN SHEETS	DEF RATE
1	Marco Materazzi	21	10	112 mins
2	Nicolas Burdisso	18	10	104 mins
3	Javier Zanetti	31	14	101 mins
4	Douglas Sisenando Maicon	26	10	99 mins

KEY PLAYERS - MIDFIELDERS

Esteban Cambiasso

Goals in the League	3	Contribution to Attacking Power Average number of minutes between League team goals while on pitch	42
Defensive Rating Average number of mins between League goals conceded while on the pitch	144	Scoring Difference Defensive Rating minus Contribution to Attacking Power	102

	PLAYER	LGE GOALS	DEF RATE	POWER	SCORE DIFF
1	Esteban Cambiasso	3	144	42	102 mins
2	Patrick Vieira	1	120	40	80 mins
3	Dejan Stankovic	6	100	40	60 mins
4	Luis Figo	2	103	45	58 mins

KEY PLAYERS - GOALSCORERS

Hernan Crespo

Goals in the League	14	Player Strike Rate Average number of minutes between League goals scored by player	135
Contribution to Attacking Power Average number of minutes between League team goals while on pitch	46	Club Strike Rate Average number of minutes between League goals scored by club	43

	PLAYER	LGE GOALS	POWER	STRIKE RATE
1	Hernan Crespo	14	46	135 mins
2	Zlatan Ibrahimovic	15	41	144 mins
3	Dejan Stankovic	6	40	453 mins
4	Esteban Cambiasso	3	42	528 mins

Zlatan Ibrahimovic and Luis Figo

SQUAD APPEARANCES

Match	1 2 3 4	6 7 8 9 10	11 12 13 14 15	16 17 18 19 20	21 22 23 24 25	26 27 28 29 30	31 32 33 34 35	36 37 38 39 40	41 42 43 44 45	46
Venue	A A H A H	H A H H A	H A A H A	H H A H A	A H A H A	H A A H H	A H A A H	A H A H H	A H A H A	H
Competition	L C L L L	C L L L C L	L L C L L	L C L L C	L L L L L	L L L L C	L L L C L	L L L L L	L L L L L	L
Result	W L D W W	L D W W D	W W W W W	W W W W D	W W W W W	W W W W D	W D W D W	W W D D L	W W W W D	W

Goalkeepers

Julio Cesar

Francesco Toldo

Defenders

Marco Andreolli

Nicolas Burdisso

Ivan Cordoba

Fabio Grosso

D Sisenando Maicon

Marco Materazzi

Walter Samuel

Javier Zanetti

Midfielders

Esteban Cambiasso

Olivier Dacourt

Luis Figo

Mariano Gonzalez

Scherer Maxwell

Santiago H Solari

Dejan Stankovic

Patrick Vieira

Forwards

Leite Adriano

Lambros Choutos

Hernan Crespo

Julio Cruz

Zlatan Ibrahimovic

Ibrahim Maaroufi

Alvaro Recoba

KEY: ■ On all match ⋈ Subbed or sent off (Counting game) ▸▸ Subbed on from bench (Counting Game) ⋙ Subbed on and then subbed or sent off (Counting Game) ☐ Not in 16
■ On bench ◂◂ Subbed or sent off (playing less than 70 minutes) ▸ Subbed on (playing less than 70 minutes) ⋙ Subbed on and then subbed or sent off (playing less than 70 minutes)

ITALY - INTER MILAN

ROMA

Final Position: **2nd**

NICKNAME: GIALLOROSSI KEY: ☐Won ☐Drawn ☐Lost Attendance

1	itpr1	Livorno	H	W	2-0	De Rossi 45, Mancini 54	38,529
2	ecgpd	Shakh Donetsk	H	W	4-0	Taddei 67, Totti 76, De Rossi 79, Pizarro 89	75,000
3	itpr1	Siena	A	W	3-1	Taddei 47, Pizarro 70, Okaka 90	11,136
4	itpr1	Inter Milan	H	L	0-1		56,476
5	itpr1	Parma	A	W	4-0	Montella 5, Perrotta 45, Rosi 54, Aquilani 90	15,495
6	ecgpd	Valencia	A	L	1-2	Totti 18 pen	48,000
7	itpr1	Empoli	H	W	1-0	Montella 23	35,000
8	itpr1	Reggina	A	L	0-1		11,719
9	ecgpd	Olympiakos	A	W	1-0	Perrotta 76	33,000
10	itpr1	Chievo	H	D	1-1	Totti 66	35,000
11	itpr1	Ascoli	H	D	2-2	Totti 50, Mexes 90	33,000
12	itpr1	Udinese	A	W	1-0	Ferrari 66	19,000
13	ecgpd	Olympiakos	H	D	1-1	Totti 66	40,000
14	itpr1	Fiorentina	H	W	3-1	De Rossi 38, Taddei 49, 66	37,000
15	itpr1	AC Milan	A	W	2-1	Totti 7, 83	75,000
16	itpr1	Catania	H	W	7-0	Panucci 12, 48, Mancini 19, Perrotta 24, 40, Montella 59, Totti 70	32,000
17	ecgpd	Shakh Donetsk	A	L	0-1		25,000
18	itpr1	Sampdoria	A	W	4-2	Totti 12, 74, Perrotta 32, Panucci 44	19,000
19	itpr1	Atalanta	H	W	2-1	Totti 50 pen, 63 pen	33,745
20	ecgpd	Valencia	H	W	1-0	Panucci 13	45,000
21	itpr1	Lazio	A	L	0-3		70,000
22	itpr1	Palermo	H	W	4-0	Mancini 45, 83, Totti 56 pen, Biava 90 og	40,000
23	itpr1	Torino	A	W	2-1	Totti 37, Mancini 80	25,000
24	itpr1	Cagliari	H	W	2-0	Taddei 5, Mancini 56	35,000
25	itpr1	Messina	A	D	1-1	Mancini 39	20,000
26	itpr1	Livorno	A	D	1-1	Totti 74	9,000
27	itpr1	Siena	H	W	1-0	Vucinic 62	38,000
28	itpr1	Parma	H	W	3-0	Totti 50, Perrotta 66, Taddei 90	28,216
29	itpr1	Empoli	A	L	0-1		0
30	eckL1	Lyon	H	D	0-0		55,000
31	itpr1	Reggina	H	W	3-0	Tavano 55, Mexes 65, Panucci 90	43,000
32	itpr1	Chievo	A	D	2-2	Totti 34, 49	4,000
33	itpr1	Ascoli	A	D	1-1	Wilhelmsson 85	5,000
34	eckL2	Lyon	A	W	2-0	Totti 22, Mancini 44	41,000
35	itpr1	Udinese	H	W	3-1	Totti 33 pen, 60, Perrotta 39	30,817
36	itpr1	Fiorentina	A	D	0-0		23,900
37	itpr1	AC Milan	H	D	1-1	Mexes 4	43,830
38	ecqfl1	Man Utd	H	W	2-1	Taddei 43, Vucinic 66	77,000
39	itpr1	Catania	A	W	2-0	Tavano 37, Vucinic 83	0
40	ecqfl2	Man Utd	A	L	1-7	De Rossi 69	74,476
41	itpr1	Sampdoria	H	W	4-0	Totti 21, 66, Ferrari 71, Panucci 86	31,875
42	itpr1	Inter Milan	A	W	3-1	Perrotta 44, Totti 89, Cassetti 90	60,000
43	itpr1	Atalanta	A	L	1-2	Perrotta 64	12,258
44	itpr1	Lazio	H	D	0-0		61,292
45	itpr1	Palermo	A	W	2-1	Totti 17, Cassetti 36	24,680
46	itpr1	Torino	H	L	0-1		32,242
47	itpr1	Cagliari	A	L	2-3	Totti 29, 85	20,000
48	itpr1	Messina	H	W	4-3	Totti 10, 73, Mancini 19, Rosi 84	28,191

LEAGUE APPEARANCES, BOOKINGS AND CAPS

	AGE (on 01/07/07)	IN NAMED 18	APPEARANCES	COUNTING GAMES	MINUTES ON PITCH	YELLOW CARDS	RED CARDS	CAPS THIS SEASON	NATIONAL SIDE
Goalkeepers									
Gianluca Curci	21	36	6	6	540	0	0	-	Italy
Alexander Doni	27	35	32	32	2880	2	0	1	Brazil
Defenders									
Marco Cassetti	30	32	28	18	1725	9	0	-	Italy
Christian Chivu	26	29	26	26	2303	6	0	6	Romania
Ricardo Faty	20	27	11	2	313	1	0	-	France
Matteo Ferrari	27	30	27	22	2133	6	1	-	Italy
Alessandro Mancini	26	29	29	21	2075	6	0	-	Brazil
Philippe Mexes	25	31	27	27	2411	12	0	1	France
Christian Panucci	34	35	34	29	2706	6	0	-	Italy
Midfielders									
Alberto Aquilani	22	17	13	6	710	4	0	1	Italy
Daniele De Rossi	22	36	36	31	2944	9	0	7	Italy
Simone Perrotta	29	34	34	29	2747	9	0	5	Italy
David Marcelo Pizarro	27	32	32	29	2711	13	0	-	Chile
Aleandro Rosi	20	37	19	4	668	3	0	-	Italy
Rodrigo Taddei	27	29	29	24	2309	2	0	-	Brazil
Max Tonetto	32	30	30	24	2358	3	0	1	Italy
Chris Wilhelmsson	27	20	19	7	1010	2	0	8	Sweden
Forwards									
Vincenzo Montella	33	17	12	3	546	2	0	-	Italy
Okaka Chuka Stefano	17	17	5	0	33	0	0	-	Nigeria
Francesco Tavano	28	18	14	4	661	0	0	-	Italy
Francesco Totti	30	35	35	34	3010	4	1	-	Italy
Valerio Virga	21	13	4	0	115	0	0	-	Italy
Mirko Vucinic	23	28	25	4	710	2	0	1	Montenegro

TEAM OF THE SEASON

D Matteo Ferrari **CG:** 22 **DR:** 133
M David Marcelo Pizarro **CG:** 29 **SD:** 77
D Alessandro Mancini **CG:** 21 **DR:** 109
M Daniele De Rossi **CG:** 31 **SD:** 62
F Simone Perrotta* **CG:** 29 **SR:** 343
G Alexander Doni **CG:** 32 **DR:** 115
D Marco Cassetti **CG:** 18 **DR:** 101
M Rodrigo Taddei **CG:** 24 **SD:** 51
F Francesco Totti **CG:** 34 **SR:** 120
D Christian Panucci **CG:** 29 **DR:** 100
M Max Tonetto **CG:** 24 **SD:** 44

MONTHLY POINTS TALLY

SEPTEMBER	9	75%
OCTOBER	8	53%
NOVEMBER	12	100%
DECEMBER	12	80%
JANUARY	5	56%
FEBRUARY	7	58%
MARCH	6	50%
APRIL	10	67%
MAY	6	50%

LEAGUE GOALS

	PLAYER	MINS	GOALS	S RATE
1	Totti	3010	25	120
2	Mancini	2075	8	259
3	Perrotta	2747	8	343
4	Taddei	2309	5	461
5	Panucci	2706	5	541
6	Montella	546	3	182
7	Mexes	2411	3	803
8	Tavano	661	2	330
9	Rosi	668	2	334
10	Vucinic	710	2	355
11	Cassetti	1725	2	862
12	Ferrari	2133	2	1066
13	De Rossi	2944	2	1472
	Other		4	
	TOTAL		**73**	

TOP POINT EARNERS

	PLAYER	GAMES	AV PTS
1	Alessandro Mancini	21	2.38
2	Philippe Mexes	27	2.22
3	Daniele De Rossi	31	2.13
4	David Marcelo Pizarro	29	2.10
5	Marco Cassetti	18	2.06
6	Francesco Totti	34	2.03
7	Rodrigo Taddei	24	2.00
8	Doni	22	2.00
9	Matteo Ferrari	22	2.00
10	Christian Panucci	28	2.00
	CLUB AVERAGE:		1.97

DISCIPLINARY RECORDS

	PLAYER	YELLOW	RED	AVE
1	Aleandro Rosi	3	0	222
2	Alberto Aquilani	4	0	236
3	Philippe Mexes	12	0	241
4	Marco Cassetti	9	0	246
5	Vincenzo Montella	2	0	273
6	D Marcelo Pizarro	13	0	338
7	Matteo Ferrari	6	1	355
8	Mirko Vucinic	2	0	355
9	Christian Chivu	6	0	383
10	Alessandro Mancini	6	0	415
11	Daniele De Rossi	9	0	420
12	C Wilhelmsson	2	0	505
13	Christian Panucci	6	0	541
	Other	20	1	
	TOTAL	100	2	

KEY GOALKEEPER

Alexander Doni

Goals Conceded in the League	25	**Counting Games** League games when player was on pitch for at least 70 minutes	32
Defensive Rating Ave number of mins between League goals conceded while on the pitch	115	**Clean Sheets** In League games when player was on pitch for at least 70 minutes	13

KEY PLAYERS - DEFENDERS

Matteo Ferrari

Goals Conceded Number of League goals conceded while the player was on the pitch	16	**Clean Sheets** In League games when player was on pitch for at least 70 minutes	11
Defensive Rating Ave number of mins between League goals conceded while on the pitch	133	**Club Defensive Rating** Average number of mins between League goals conceded by the club this season	103

	PLAYER	CON LGE	CLEAN SHEETS	DEF RATE
1	Matteo Ferrari	16	11	133 mins
2	Alessandro Mancini	19	9	109 mins
3	Marco Cassetti	17	6	101 mins
4	Christian Panucci	27	11	100 mins

KEY PLAYERS - MIDFIELDERS

David Marcelo Pizarro

Goals in the League	1	**Contribution to Attacking Power** Average number of minutes between League team goals while on pitch	46
Defensive Rating Average number of mins between League goals conceded while on the pitch	123	**Scoring Difference** Defensive Rating minus Contribution to Attacking Power	77

	PLAYER	LGE GOALS	DEF RATE	POWER	SCORE DIFF
1	David Marcelo Pizarro	1	123	46	77 mins
2	Daniele De Rossi	2	105	43	62 mins
3	Rodrigo Taddei	5	96	45	51 mins
4	Max Tonetto	0	94	50	44 mins

KEY PLAYERS - GOALSCORERS

Francesco Totti

Goals in the League	25	**Player Strike Rate** Average number of minutes between League goals scored by player	120
Contribution to Attacking Power Average number of minutes between League team goals while on pitch	44	**Club Strike Rate** Average number of minutes between League goals scored by club	47

	PLAYER	LGE GOALS	POWER	STRIKE RATE
1	Francesco Totti	25	44	120 mins
2	Simone Perrotta	8	49	343 mins
3	Rodrigo Taddei	5	45	461 mins
4	Daniele De Rossi	2	43	1472 mins

Francesco Totti

SQUAD APPEARANCES

Match	1 2 3 4	6 7 8 9 10	11 12 13 14 15	16 17 18 19 20	21 22 23 24 25	26 27 28 29 30	31 32 33 34 35	36 37 38 39 40	41 42 43 44 45	46 47 48
Venue	H H A H	A H A A H	H A H H A	H A A H H	A H A H A	A H H A H	H A A A H	A H H A A	H A A H A	H A H
Competition	L C L L	C L L C L	L L C L L	L C L L C	L L L L L	L L L L L	L L L C L	L L C L C	L L L L L	L L L
Result	W W W L W	L W L W D	D W D W W	W L W W W	L W W W D	D W W L D	W D D W W	D D W W L	W W L D W	L L W

Goalkeepers

Gianluca Curci										
Alexander Doni										

Defenders

Marco Cassetti
Christian Chivu
Ricardo Faty
Matteo Ferrari
Alessandro Mancini
Philippe Mexes
Christian Panucci

Midfielders

Alberto Aquilani
Daniele De Rossi
Simone Perrotta
David Marcelo Pizarro
Aleandro Rosi
Rodrigo Taddei
Max Tonetto
Chris Wilhelmsson

Forwards

Vincenzo Montella
Okaka Chuka Stefano
Francesco Tavano
Francesco Totti
Valerio Virga
Mirko Vucinic

KEY: ■ On all match ◄◄ Subbed or sent off (Counting game) ▸▸ Subbed on from bench (Counting Game) ▸▸ Subbed on and then subbed or sent off (Counting Game) □ Not in 16
■ On bench ◄◄ Subbed or sent off (playing less than 70 minutes) ▸▸ Subbed on (playing less than 70 minutes) ▸▸ Subbed on and then subbed or sent off (playing less than 70 minutes)

ITALY - ROMA

LAZIO

Final Position: **3rd**

NICKNAME: BIANCOCELESTI　　**KEY:** ☐ Won ☐ Drawn ☐ Lost　　Attendance

1	itpr1	**AC Milan**	A	L	1-2	Makinwa 73	44,770
2	itpr1	**Palermo**	H	L	1-2	Rocchi 73	20,395
3	itpr1	**Chievo**	A	W	1-0	Oddo 63 pen	5,232
4	itpr1	**Atalanta**	H	W	1-0	Siviglia 69	19,339
5	itpr1	**Torino**	A	W	4-0	Rocchi 49, Oddo 55 pen, 68, Mauri 71	18,000
6	itpr1	**Cagliari**	H	D	0-0		19,402
7	itpr1	**Catania**	A	L	1-3	Rocchi 56	0
8	itpr1	**Sampdoria**	A	L	0-2		20,000
9	itpr1	**Reggina**	H	D	0-0		13,000
10	itpr1	**Empoli**	A	D	1-1	Pandev 17	4,500
11	itpr1	**Udinese**	H	W	5-0	Rocchi 33, 82, Mauri 41, 74, Oddo 78	19,000
12	itpr1	**Messina**	A	W	4-1	Mauri 10, 82, Pandev 59, Makinwa 84	20,000
13	itpr1	**Ascoli**	H	W	3-1	Belleri 8, Pandev 25, Foggia 84	19,000
14	itpr1	**Fiorentina**	A	L	0-1		30,000
15	itpr1	**Roma**	H	W	3-0	Ledesma 44, Oddo 50 pen, Mutarelli 72	70,000
16	itpr1	**Livorno**	A	D	1-1	Pandev 25	9,000
17	itpr1	**Inter Milan**	H	L	0-2		50,000
18	itpr1	**Parma**	A	W	3-1	Stendardo 30, Pandev 34, Rocchi 43	15,000
19	itpr1	**Siena**	H	D	1-1	Rocchi 61	38,000
20	itpr1	**AC Milan**	H	D	0-0		35,000
21	itpr1	**Palermo**	A	W	3-0	Rocchi 45, 78 pen, Siviglia 52	22,000
22	itpr1	**Atalanta**	A	D	0-0		0
23	itpr1	**Torino**	H	W	2-0	Pandev 11, 60	10,000
24	itpr1	**Cagliari**	A	W	2-0	Cribari 21, Rocchi 34	10,000
25	itpr1	**Catania**	H	W	3-1	Pandev 60, Siviglia 88, Rocchi 90	20,000
26	itpr1	**Sampdoria**	H	W	1-0	Rocchi 23	16,000
27	itpr1	**Reggina**	A	W	3-2	Manfredini 45, Pandev 45, Makinwa 79	10,236
28	itpr1	**Empoli**	H	W	3-1	Pandev 8, Rocchi 27, Manfredini 74	25,527
29	itpr1	**Udinese**	A	W	4-2	Stendardo 18, Mauri 50, Behrami 51, Rocchi 59 pen	13,652
30	itpr1	**Messina**	H	W	1-0	Stendardo 45	24,106
31	itpr1	**Ascoli**	A	D	2-2	Rocchi 73, Jimenez 84	11,380
32	itpr1	**Chievo**	H	D	0-0		25,000
33	itpr1	**Fiorentina**	H	L	0-1		25,723
34	itpr1	**Roma**	A	D	0-0		61,292
35	itpr1	**Livorno**	H	W	1-0	Jimenez 27	14,809
36	itpr1	**Inter Milan**	A	L	3-4	Pandev 3, Mutarelli 4, Ledesma 41	45,429
37	itpr1	**Parma**	H	D	0-0		37,914
38	itpr1	**Siena**	A	L	1-2	Rocchi 73 pen	10,803

LEAGUE APPEARANCES, BOOKINGS AND CAPS

	AGE (on 01/07/07)	IN NAMED 18	APPEARANCES	COUNTING GAMES	MINUTES ON PITCH	YELLOW CARDS	RED CARDS	CAPS THIS SEASON	NATIONAL SIDE
Goalkeepers									
Marco Ballotta	43	37	11	9	866	0	0	-	Italy
Tommaso Berni	24	10	2	2	174	0	0	-	Italy
Angelo Peruzzi	37	28	28	26	2380	0	0	-	Italy
Defenders									
Manuel Belleri	29	35	22	9	1036	3	0	-	Italy
Riccardo Bonetto	28	28	9	4	438	1	0	-	Italy
E Sanchez Cribari	27	30	23	23	2032	4	1	-	Brazil
Lorenzo De Silvestri	19	2	2	1	103	0	0	-	Italy
Mobido Diakite	20	7	3	2	182	1	0	-	France
Massimo Oddo	31	16	15	14	1304	5	1	7	Italy
Sebastiano Siviglia	34	32	32	29	2707	2	2	-	Italy
Guglielmo Stendardo	26	31	21	18	1701	4	1	-	Italy
Midfielders									
Roberto Baronio	29	23	10	4	497	2	0	-	Italy
Valon Behrami	22	21	17	12	1260	7	1	2	Switzerland
Fabio Firmani	29	26	11	4	414	1	0	-	Italy
A Luis Jimenez	23	17	16	6	816	1	0	-	Italy
C Daniel Ledesma	28	34	33	33	2937	10	1	-	Argentina
Christian Manfredini	32	30	25	12	1420	2	0	-	Italy
Stefano Mauri	27	29	29	27	2440	8	0	1	Italy
Gaby Mudingayi	25	28	28	25	2280	13	0	5	Belgium
Massimo Mutarelli	29	27	24	23	2073	11	0	-	Italy
Alberto Quadri	24	4	1	0	59	0	0	-	-
Luciano Zauri	29	36	36	36	3239	4	1	-	Italy
Forwards									
Pasquale Foggia	24	17	11	2	371	2	0	-	Italy
Simone Inzaghi	31	10	5	0	66	1	0	-	Italy
S Ayodele Makinwa	23	28	25	5	812	1	0	-	Nigeria
Goran Pandev	23	37	36	23	2512	3	0	6	Macedonia
Tommaso Rocchi	29	36	36	32	3019	3	1	3	Italy
Igli Tare	33	27	13	1	283	1	0	3	Albania

TEAM OF THE SEASON

G Angelo Peruzzi CG: 26 DR: 99

D E Sanchez Cribari CG: 23 DR: 135
D Massimo Oddo CG: 14 DR: 118
D Sebastiano Siviglia CG: 29 DR: 112
D Guglielmo Stendardo CG: 18 DR: 106

M Stefano Mauri CG: 27 SD: 74
M Massimo Mutarelli CG: 23 SD: 68
M C Daniel Ledesma CG: 33 SD: 56
M Valon Behrami* CG: 12 SD: 51

F Tommaso Rocchi CG: 32 SR: 188
F Goran Pandev CG: 23 SR: 228

MONTHLY POINTS TALLY

SEPTEMBER	9	60%
OCTOBER	2	17%
NOVEMBER	10	83%
DECEMBER	7	47%
JANUARY	5	56%
FEBRUARY	10	83%
MARCH	9	100%
APRIL	9	50%
MAY	4	33%

LEAGUE GOALS

	PLAYER	MINS	GOALS	S RATE
1	Rocchi	3019	16	188
2	Pandev	2512	11	228
3	Mauri	2440	6	406
4	Oddo	1304	5	260
5	Makinwa	812	3	270
6	Stendardo	1701	3	567
7	Siviglia	2707	3	902
8	Jimenez	816	2	408
9	Manfredini	1420	2	710
10	Mutarelli	2073	2	1036
11	Ledesma	2937	2	1468
12	Foggia	371	1	371
13	Belleri	1036	1	1036
	Other		2	
	TOTAL		59	

TOP POINT EARNERS

	PLAYER	GAMES	AV PTS
1	Goran Pandev	21	2.24
2	Valon Behrami	13	2.15
3	Christian Manfredini	12	2.00
4	Stefano Mauri	27	1.96
5	Guglielmo Stendardo	18	1.83
6	Luciano Zauri	36	1.78
7	Cristian Daniel Ledesma	32	1.78
8	Sebastiano Siviglia	30	1.77
9	Tommaso Rocchi	33	1.76
10	Massimo Mutarelli	23	1.74
	CLUB AVERAGE:		1.63

DISCIPLINARY RECORDS

	PLAYER	YELLOW	RED	AVE
1	Valon Behrami	7	1	157
2	Gaby Mudingayi	13	0	175
3	Massimo Mutarelli	11	0	188
4	Massimo Oddo	5	1	217
5	Roberto Baronio	2	0	248
6	C Daniel Ledesma	10	1	267
7	Stefano Mauri	8	0	305
8	Guglielmo Stendardo	4	1	340
9	Manuel Belleri	3	0	345
10	E Sanchez Cribari	4	1	406
11	Luciano Zauri	4	1	647
12	Sebastiano Siviglia	2	2	676
13	Christian Manfredini	2	0	710
	Other	8	1	
	TOTAL	83	9	

KEY GOALKEEPER

Angelo Peruzzi

Goals Conceded in the League	24	Counting Games League games when player was on pitch for at least 70 minutes	26
Defensive Rating Ave number of mins between League goals conceded while on the pitch	99	Clean Sheets In League games when player was on pitch for at least 70 minutes	11

KEY PLAYERS - DEFENDERS

Emilson Sanchez Cribari

Goals Conceded Number of League goals conceded while the player was on the pitch	15	Clean Sheets In League games when player was on pitch for at least 70 minutes	13
Defensive Rating Ave number of mins between League goals conceded while on the pitch	135	Club Defensive Rating Average number of mins between League goals conceded by the club this season	106

	PLAYER	CON LGE	CLEAN SHEETS	DEF RATE
1	Emilson Sanchez Cribari	15	13	135 mins
2	Massimo Oddo	11	7	118 mins
3	Sebastiano Siviglia	24	15	112 mins
4	Guglielmo Stendardo	16	7	106 mins

KEY PLAYERS - MIDFIELDERS

Stefano Mauri

Goals in the League	6	Contribution to Attacking Power Average number of minutes between League team goals while on pitch	54
Defensive Rating Average number of mins between League goals conceded while on the pitch	128	Scoring Difference Defensive Rating minus Contribution to Attacking Power	74

	PLAYER	LGE GOALS	DEF RATE	POWER	SCORE DIFF
1	Stefano Mauri	6	128	54	74 mins
2	Massimo Mutarelli	2	121	53	68 mins
3	Cristian Daniel Ledesma	2	112	56	56 mins
4	Valon Behrami	1	96	45	51 mins

KEY PLAYERS - GOALSCORERS

Tommaso Rocchi

Goals in the League	16	Player Strike Rate Average number of minutes between League goals scored by player	188
Contribution to Attacking Power Average number of minutes between League team goals while on pitch	58	Club Strike Rate Average number of minutes between League goals scored by club	59

	PLAYER	LGE GOALS	POWER	STRIKE RATE
1	Tommaso Rocchi	16	58	188 mins
2	Goran Pandev	11	55	228 mins
3	Stefano Mauri	6	54	406 mins
4	Christian Manfredini	2	74	710 mins

Tommaso Rocchi

SQUAD APPEARANCES

Match	1	2	3	4	5	6	7	8	9	10	11	12	13	14	15	16	17	18	19	20	21	22	23	24	25	26	27	28	29	30	31	32	33	34	35	36	37	38
Venue	A	H	A	H	A	H	A	A	H	A	H	A	H	A	H	A	H	A	H	H	A	A	H	A	H	H	A	H	A	H	A	H	H	A	H	A	H	A
Competition	L	L	L	L	L	L	L	L	L	L	L	L	L	L	L	L	L	L	L	L	L	L	L	L	L	L	L	L	L	L	L	L	L	L	L	L	L	L
Result	L	L	W	W	W	D	L	L	D	D	W	W	W	L	W	D	L	W	D	D	W	D	W	W	W	W	W	W	W	W	D	D	L	D	W	L	D	L

Goalkeepers
Marco Ballotta
Tommaso Berni
Angelo Peruzzi

Defenders
Manuel Belleri
Riccardo Bonetto
E Sanchez Cribari
Lorenzo De Silvestri
Mobido Diakite
Massimo Oddo
Sebastiano Siviglia
Guglielmo Stendardo

Midfielders
Roberto Baronio
Valon Behrami
Fabio Firmani
A Luis Jimenez
C Daniel Ledesma
Christian Manfredini
Stefano Mauri
Gaby Mudingayi
Massimo Mutarelli
Alberto Quadri
Luciano Zauri

Forwards
Pasquale Foggia
Simone Inzaghi
S Ayodele Makinwa
Goran Pandev
Tommaso Rocchi
gli Tare

KEY: ■ On all match　◄◄ Subbed or sent off (Counting game)　►► Subbed on from bench (Counting Game)　►► Subbed on and then subbed or sent off (Counting Game)　□ Not in 16
　　　■ On bench　◄◄ Subbed or sent off (playing less than 70 minutes)　►► Subbed on (playing less than 70 minutes)　►► Subbed on and then subbed or sent off (playing less than 70 minutes)

ITALY - LAZIO

AC MILAN

Final Position: 4th

NICKNAME: LA ROSSONERI KEY: ☐ Won ☐ Drawn ☐ Lost Attendance

#	Comp	Opponent	H/A	Result	Scorers	Attendance
1	ecql1	**Crvena Zvezda**	H W	1-0	Inzaghi 22	55,000
2	ecql2	**Crvena Zvezda**	A W	2-1	Inzaghi 29, Seedorf 79	55,000
3	itpr1	**Lazio**	H W	2-1	Inzaghi 27, Oliveira 70	44,770
4	ecgph	**AEK Athens**	H W	3-0	Inzaghi 17, Gourcuff 41, Kaka 76 pen	45,000
5	itpr1	**Parma**	A W	2-0	Seedorf 25, Kaka 86 pen	18,617
6	itpr1	**Ascoli**	H W	1-0	Jankulovski 68	43,085
7	itpr1	**Livorno**	A D	0-0		17,000
8	ecgph	**Lille**	A D	0-0		35,000
9	itpr1	**Siena**	H D	0-0		44,650
10	itpr1	**Sampdoria**	A D	1-1	Kaladze 84	25,324
11	ecgph	**Anderlecht**	A W	1-0	Kaka 58	20,129
12	itpr1	**Palermo**	H L	0-2		50,028
13	itpr1	**Chievo**	A W	1-0	Jankulovski 31	17,000
14	itpr1	**Inter Milan**	H L	3-4	Seedorf 50, Gilardino 76, Kaka 90	79,000
15	ecgph	**Anderlecht**	H W	4-1	Kaka 6 pen, 22, 56, Gilardino 88	42,300
16	itpr1	**Atalanta**	A L	0-2		25,000
17	itpr1	**Roma**	H L	1-2	Brocchi 56	75,000
18	itpr1	**Empoli**	A D	0-0		7,327
19	ecgph	**AEK Athens**	A L	0-1		70,000
20	itpr1	**Messina**	H W	1-0	Maldini 13	45,000
21	itpr1	**Cagliari**	A D	2-2	Gilardino 48, Borriello 70	20,000
22	ecgph	**Lille**	H L	0-2		27,067
23	itpr1	**Torino**	H D	0-0		50,000
24	itpr1	**Fiorentina**	A D	2-2	Gilardino 4, 89	47,000
25	itpr1	**Catania**	H W	3-0	Kaka 5, 88, Gilardino 82	55,000
26	itpr1	**Udinese**	A W	3-0	Kaka 28 pen, Gilardino 35, Oliveira 76	20,000
27	itpr1	**Reggina**	H W	3-1	Pirlo 6, Seedorf 35, Gilardino 77	43,996
28	itpr1	**Lazio**	A D	0-0		35,000
29	itpr1	**Parma**	H W	1-0	Inzaghi 76	44,000
30	itpr1	**Livorno**	H W	2-1	Gattuso 29, Jankulovski 68	21,694
31	itpr1	**Siena**	A W	4-3	Ronaldo 15, 82, Oliveira 29, Ambrosini 90	10,000
32	eckl1	**Celtic**	A D	0-0		58,785
33	itpr1	**Sampdoria**	H W	1-0	Ambrosini 90	21,000
34	itpr1	**Palermo**	A D	0-0		28,000
35	itpr1	**Chievo**	H W	3-1	Gilardino 33, Oddo 55, Seedorf 90	40,000
36	eckl2	**Celtic**	H W	1-0	Kaka 93	65,000
37	itpr1	**Inter Milan**	A L	1-2	Ronaldo 40	63,681
38	itpr1	**Atalanta**	H W	1-0	Ambrosini 40	45,491
39	itpr1	**Roma**	A D	1-1	Gilardino 62	43,830
40	ecqfl1	**Bayern Munich**	H D	2-2	Pirlo 40, Kaka 84 pen	60,000
41	itpr1	**Empoli**	H W	3-1	Ronaldo 12, Gilardino 44, Favalli 78	45,566
42	ecqfl2	**Bayern Munich**	A W	2-0	Seedorf 27, Inzaghi 31	66,000
43	itpr1	**Messina**	A W	3-1	Kaka 14, Favalli 30, Ronaldo 86	17,521
44	itpr1	**Ascoli**	A W	5-2	Gilardino 3, 26, Kaka 25 pen, 35, Seedorf 75	5,000
45	itpr1	**Cagliari**	H W	3-1	Ronaldo 14, 69, Pirlo 80	43,728
46	ecsfl1	**Man Utd**	A L	2-3	Kaka 22, 37	73,820
47	itpr1	**Torino**	A W	1-0	Seedorf 25	22,539
48	ecsfl2	**Man Utd**	H W	3-0	Kaka 11, Seedorf 30, Gilardino 78	78,500
49	itpr1	**Fiorentina**	H D	0-0		55,078
50	itpr1	**Catania**	A D	1-1	Seedorf 6	4,000
51	itpr1	**Udinese**	H L	2-3	Gourcuff 36, Costacurta 57 pen	51,124
52	ecfin	**Liverpool**	N W	2-1	Inzaghi 45, 82	74,000
53	itpr1	**Reggina**	A L	0-2		20,835

LEAGUE APPEARANCES, BOOKINGS AND CAPS

	AGE (on 01/07/07)	IN NAMED 18	APPEARANCES	COUNTING GAMES	MINUTES ON PITCH	YELLOW CARDS	RED CARDS	CAPS THIS SEASON	NATIONAL SIDE
Goalkeepers									
Nelson Dida	33	25	25	25	2250	1	0	-	Brazil
Zeljko Kalac	34	34	10	10	900	0	0	1	Australia
Marco Storari	30	8	3	3	270	0	0	-	Italy
Defenders									
Daniele Bonera	26	34	25	22	2025	11	1	-	Italy
Cafu	37	31	24	22	1949	3	0	-	Brazil
A Costacurta	41	11	3	1	165	1	0	-	Italy
Giuseppe Favalli	35	20	15	10	1075	2	0	-	Italy
Leandro Grimi	22	5	3	1	108	0	0	-	Argentina
Kakha Kaladze	29	20	18	15	1365	2	1	3	Georgia
Paolo Maldini	39	20	18	14	1399	4	0	-	Italy
Alessandro Nesta	31	16	14	12	1131	1	0	-	Italy
Massimo Oddo	31	10	6	6	656	0	1	7	Italy
Dario Simic	31	31	22	16	1592	3	0	6	Croatia
Midfielders									
Massimo Ambrosini	30	22	19	8	949	4	0	2	Italy
Christian Brocchi	31	34	29	22	2159	4	0	1	Italy
Gennaro Gattuso	29	30	30	23	2173	12	0	6	Italy
Yoann Gourcuff	20	33	21	7	972	4	0	-	France
Alex Guerci	22	2	1	0	15	0	0	-	Italy
Marek Jankulovski	30	33	33	24	2423	5	0	9	Czech Republic
Ricardo Kaka	25	32	31	28	2653	3	0	9	Brazil
Andrea Pirlo	28	34	34	30	2778	5	1	7	Italy
Clarence Seedorf	31	32	32	23	2269	3	0	4	Holland
Serginho	36	6	6	2	258	1	0	-	Brazil
Forwards									
Marco Borriello	25	17	9	3	403	0	0	-	Italy
Davide Di Gennaro	19	2	1	0	33	0	0	-	Italy
Alberto Gilardino	24	35	30	20	2093	6	0	3	Italy
Filippo Inzaghi	33	29	20	8	1060	0	0	5	Italy
Ricardo Oliveira	27	34	26	9	1309	5	0	2	Brazil
Ronaldo	30	14	14	12	1059	1	0	-	Brazil

TEAM OF THE SEASON

D Dario Simic — CG: 16 DR: 122
M Gennaro Gattuso — CG: 23 SD: 40
D Daniele Bonera — CG: 22 DR: 101
M Andrea Pirlo — CG: 30 SD: 39
F Ronaldo* — CG: 12 SR: 151
G Nelson Dida — CG: 25 DR: 118
D Cafu — CG: 22 DR: 92
M Clarence Seedorf — CG: 23 SD: 39
F Alberto Gilardino — CG: 20 SR: 174
D Paolo Maldini — CG: 14 DR: 87
M Marek Jankulovski — CG: 24 SD: 38

MONTHLY POINTS TALLY

Month	Points	%
SEPTEMBER	10	83%
OCTOBER	5	33%
NOVEMBER	4	33%
DECEMBER	9	60%
JANUARY	7	78%
FEBRUARY	10	83%
MARCH	7	58%
APRIL	15	100%
MAY	2	17%

LEAGUE GOALS

	PLAYER	MINS	GOALS	S RATE
1	Gilardino	2093	12	174
2	Kaka	2653	8	331
3	Ronaldo	1059	7	151
4	Seedorf	2269	7	324
5	Ambrosini	949	3	316
6	Oliveira	1309	3	436
7	Jankulovski	2423	3	807
8	Inzaghi	1060	2	530
9	Favalli	1075	2	537
10	Pirlo	2778	2	1389
11	Costacurta	165	1	165
12	Borriello	403	1	403
13	Oddo	656	1	656
	Other		5	
	TOTAL		57	

TOP POINT EARNERS

	PLAYER	GAMES	AV PTS
1	Daniele Bonera	20	2.15
2	Alberto Gilardino	20	2.10
3	Marek Jankulovski	24	2.04
4	Dario Simic	16	1.94
5	Andrea Pirlo	29	1.93
6	Christian Brocchi	22	1.86
7	Cafu	22	1.86
8	Gennaro Gattuso	22	1.82
9	Kakha Kaladze	13	1.77
10	Ricardo Kaka	28	1.75
	CLUB AVERAGE:		1.61

DISCIPLINARY RECORDS

	PLAYER	YELLOW	RED	AVE
1	Daniele Bonera	11	1	225
2	Gennaro Gattuso	12	0	241
3	Yoann Gourcuff	4	0	243
4	Ricardo Oliveira	5	0	327
5	Filippo Inzaghi	3	0	353
6	Andrea Pirlo	5	1	463
7	Massimo Ambrosini	4	0	474
8	Dario Simic	3	0	530
9	Giuseppe Favalli	2	0	537
10	Christian Brocchi	4	0	539
11	Cafu	3	0	649
12	Massimo Oddo	0	1	656
13	Kakha Kaladze	2	1	682
	Other	24	0	
	TOTAL	82	4	

KEY GOALKEEPER

Nelson Dida

Goals Conceded in the League	19	Counting Games League games when player was on pitch for at least 70 minutes	25
Defensive Rating Ave number of mins between League goals conceded while on the pitch	118	Clean Sheets In League games when player was on pitch for at least 70 minutes	13

KEY PLAYERS - DEFENDERS

Dario Simic

Goals Conceded Number of League goals conceded while the player was on the pitch	13	Clean Sheets In League games when player was on pitch for at least 70 minutes	9
Defensive Rating Ave number of mins between League goals conceded while on the pitch	122	Club Defensive Rating Average number of mins between League goals conceded by the club this season	97

	PLAYER	CON LGE	CLEAN SHEETS	DEF RATE
1	Dario Simic	13	9	122 mins
2	Daniele Bonera	20	10	101 mins
3	Cafu	21	10	92 mins
4	Paolo Maldini	16	6	87 mins

KEY PLAYERS - MIDFIELDERS

Gennaro Gattuso

Goals in the League	1	Contribution to Attacking Power Average number of minutes between League team goals while on pitch	63
Defensive Rating Average number of mins between League goals conceded while on the pitch	103	Scoring Difference Defensive Rating minus Contribution to Attacking Power	40

	PLAYER	LGE GOALS	DEF RATE	POWER	SCORE DIFF
1	Gennaro Gattuso	1	103	63	40 mins
2	Andrea Pirlo	2	95	56	39 mins
3	Clarence Seedorf	7	103	64	39 mins
4	Marek Jankulovski	3	100	62	38 mins

KEY PLAYERS - GOALSCORERS

Ronaldo

Goals in the League	7	Player Strike Rate Average number of minutes between League goals scored by player	151
Contribution to Attacking Power Average number of minutes between League team goals while on pitch	44	Club Strike Rate Average number of minutes between League goals scored by club	61

	PLAYER	LGE GOALS	POWER	STRIKE RATE
1	Ronaldo	7	44	151 mins
2	Alberto Gilardino	12	56	174 mins
3	Clarence Seedorf	7	64	324 mins
4	Ricardo Kaka	8	63	331 mins

Ricardo Kaka and Alberto Gilardino

SQUAD APPEARANCES

Match	1 2 3 4 5	6 7 8 9 10	11 12 13 14 15	16 17 18 19 20	21 22 23 24 25	26 27 28 29 30	31 32 33 34 35	36 37 38 39 40	41 42 43 44 45	46 47 48 49 50	51 52 53
Venue	H A H H A	H A A H A	A H A H H	A H A A H	A H H A H	A H A H H	A A H A H	H A H A H	H A A A H	A A H H A	H N A
Competition	C C L C L	L L C L L	C L L L C	L L L C L	L C L L L	L L L L L	L C L L L	C L L L C	L C L L L	C L C L L	L C L
Result	W W W W	W D D D D	W L W L W	L L D L W	D L D D W	W W D W W	W D W D W	W L W D D	W W W W W	L W W D D	L W L

Goalkeepers
Nelson Dida
Valerio Fiori
Zeljko Kalac
Marco Storari

Defenders
Daniele Bonera
Cafu
A Costacurta
Giuseppe Favalli
Leandro Grimi
Lakha Kaladze
Paolo Maldini
Alessandro Nesta
Massimo Oddo
Dario Simic

Midfielders
Massimo Ambrosini
Christian Brocchi
Gennaro Gattuso
Yoann Gourcuff
Alex Guerci
Marek Jankulovski
Ricardo Kaka
Matteo Lunati
Andrea Pirlo
Clarence Seedorf
Serginho

Forwards
Marco Borriello
Davide Di Gennaro
Alberto Gilardino
Filippo Inzaghi
Ricardo Oliveira
Ronaldo

KEY: ■ On all match ◄◄ Subbed or sent off (Counting game) ▸▸ Subbed on from bench (Counting Game) ▣ Subbed on and then subbed or sent off (Counting Game) □ Not in 16
■ On bench ◄◄ Subbed or sent off (playing less than 70 minutes) ▸▸ Subbed on (playing less than 70 minutes) ▸▸ Subbed on and then subbed or sent off (playing less than 70 minutes)

ITALY - AC MILAN

PALERMO

Final Position: 5th

NICKNAME: ROSANERO   KEY: ☐ Won ☐ Drawn ☐ Lost   Attendance

1 itpr1	Reggina	H W	4-3	Bresciano 11, Biava 17, Corini 27 pen, Amauri 67	24,500
2 ucrl1	West Ham	A W	1-0	Caracciolo 45	32,222
3 itpr1	Lazio	A W	2-1	Di Michele 11, 38	20,395
4 itpr1	Catania	H W	5-3	Tedesco 27, Simplicio 47, Corini 68, Amauri 74, Barzagli 80	34,261
5 itpr1	Empoli	A L	0-2		4,672
6 ucrl2	West Ham	H W	3-0	Simplicio 35, 62, Di Michele 68	19,284
7 itpr1	Chievo	A W	1-0	Corini 30	3,500
8 itpr1	Atalanta	H L	2-3	Bresciano 18, Corini 45	21,716
9 ucgph	Eintr Frankfurt	A W	2-1	Brienza 49, Zaccardo 87	45,000
10 itpr1	AC Milan	A W	2-0	Bresciano 48, Amauri 74	50,028
11 itpr1	Messina	H W	2-1	Zaccardo 25, Di Michele 41 pen	28,547
12 itpr1	Fiorentina	A W	2-1	Di Michele 9, Amauri 80, 90	34,000
13 ucgph	Newcastle	H L	0-1		16,904
14 itpr1	Sampdoria	H W	2-0	Corini 35, Zaccardo 70	22,244
15 itpr1	Torino	H W	3-0	Corini 43, Di Michele 69, Amauri 79	24,000
16 itpr1	Cagliari	A L	0-1		21,655
17 ucgph	Fenerbahce	A L	0-3		45,000
18 itpr1	Inter Milan	H L	1-2	Amauri 45	35,000
19 itpr1	Parma	A D	0-0		15,000
20 itpr1	Livorno	H W	3-0	Simplicio 2, 78, Amauri 36	20,000
21 ucgph	Celta Vigo	H D	1-1	Tedesco 70	10,222
22 itpr1	Roma	A L	0-4		40,000
23 itpr1	Ascoli	H W	4-0	Bresciano 15, Corini 53, Tedesco 84, Capuano 90	20,000
24 itpr1	Siena	A D	1-1	Simplicio 41	7,000
25 itpr1	Udinese	H W	2-0	Caracciolo 32, Zaccardo 75	20,913
26 itpr1	Reggina	A D	0-0		13,000
27 itpr1	Lazio	H L	0-3		22,000
28 itpr1	Catania	A W	2-1	Caracciolo 50, Di Michele 83	15,000
29 itpr1	Empoli	H L	0-1		19,144
30 itpr1	Chievo	H D	1-1	Di Michele 23	25,000
31 itpr1	Atalanta	A D	1-1	Diana 58	8,800
32 itpr1	AC Milan	H D	0-0		28,000
33 itpr1	Messina	A L	0-2		15,000
34 itpr1	Fiorentina	H D	1-1	Cavani 71	22,476
35 itpr1	Sampdoria	A D	1-1	Cavani 53	17,000
36 itpr1	Torino	A D	0-0		20,932
37 itpr1	Cagliari	H L	1-3	Bresciano 3	21,655
38 itpr1	Inter Milan	A D	2-2	Caracciolo 3, Zaccardo 45	46,611
39 itpr1	Parma	H L	3-4	Bresciano 36, Di Michele 45 pen, Zaccardo 90	21,472
40 itpr1	Livorno	A W	2-1	Corini 48, Di Michele 75	7,750
41 itpr1	Roma	H L	1-2	Tedesco 86	24,680
42 itpr1	Ascoli	A L	2-3	Simplicio 10, Matusiak 31	4,352
43 itpr1	Siena	H W	2-1	Corini 26, Caracciolo 45	20,043
44 itpr1	Udinese	A W	2-1	Caracciolo 14, Corini 71	5,000

LEAGUE APPEARANCES, BOOKINGS AND CAPS

	AGE (on 01/07/07)	IN NAMED 18	APPEARANCES	COUNTING GAMES	MINUTES ON PITCH	YELLOW CARDS	RED CARDS	CAPS THIS SEASON	NATIONAL SIDE
Goalkeepers									
Federico Agliardi	24	30	10	8	765	0	0	-	Italy
Alberto Fontana	40	38	30	29	2655	2	0	-	Italy
Defenders									
Andrea Barzagli	26	36	36	36	3229	2	0	4	Italy
Giuseppe Biava	30	28	24	19	1846	9	1	-	Italy
Cesare Bovo	24	3	1	0	13	0	0	-	Italy
Ciro Capuano	25	14	7	0	204	1	0	-	Italy
Mattia Cassani	23	32	29	21	2056	7	0	-	Italy
H Paolo Dellafiore	22	26	7	5	493	1	0	-	Argentina
Marco Pisano	25	34	33	29	2761	8	1	-	Italy
Cristian Zaccardo	25	36	36	35	3171	7	0	1	Italy
Midfielders									
Mark Bresciano	27	35	33	22	2524	3	0	4	Australia
Franco Brienza	28	36	22	4	880	4	0	-	Italy
Maurizio Ciaramitaro	25	8	6	1	254	2	0	-	Italy
Eugenio Corini	36	30	27	25	2261	9	0	-	Italy
Stefano Aimo Diana	29	27	26	18	1850	4	0	1	Italy
Guillermo Giacomazzi	29	16	7	0	72	1	0	-	Uruguay
Roberto Guana	26	33	33	27	2642	12	1	-	Italy
Francesco Parravicini	25	19	8	0	193	2	0	-	Italy
Fabio E Simplicio	27	33	33	32	2843	7	4	-	Brazil
Giovanni Tedesco	35	36	26	6	893	1	0	-	Italy
Forwards									
C De O Amauri	27	17	17	15	1397	4	0	-	Brazil
Andrea Caracciolo	25	34	27	16	1645	4	1	1	Italy
Edison Cavani	20	7	7	4	456	3	0	-	Uruguay
David Di Michele	31	35	29	24	2243	7	0	-	Italy
Radoslav Matusiak	25	7	3	0	93	0	0	-	Poland

TEAM OF THE SEASON

Position	Player	Stats
G	Alberto Fontana	CG: 29 DR: 69
D	Cristian Zaccardo	CG: 35 DR: 70
D	Mattia Cassani	CG: 21 DR: 68
D	Andrea Barzagli	CG: 36 DR: 65
D	Marco Pisano	CG: 29 DR: 64
M	Eugenio Corini	CG: 25 SD: 22
M	Fabio Enrico Simplicio	CG: 32 SD: 14
M	Roberto Guana	CG: 27 SD: 8
M	Mark Bresciano	CG: 22 SD: 6
F	C De Ol Amauri	CG: 15 SR: 174
F	David Di Michele	CG: 24 SR: 249

MONTHLY POINTS TALLY

SEPTEMBER	9	75%
OCTOBER	12	80%
NOVEMBER	6	50%
DECEMBER	8	53%
JANUARY	4	44%
FEBRUARY	6	40%
MARCH	2	22%
APRIL	5	33%
MAY	6	50%

LEAGUE GOALS

	PLAYER	MINS	GOALS	S RATE
1	Corini	2261	10	226
2	Di Michele	2243	9	249
3	Amauri	1397	8	174
4	Bresciano	2524	6	420
5	Caracciolo	1645	5	329
6	Simplicio	2843	5	568
7	Zaccardo	3171	5	634
8	Tedesco	893	3	297
9	Cavani	456	2	228
10	Matusiak	93	1	93
11	Capuano	204	1	204
12	Biava	1846	1	1846
13	Diana	1850	1	1850
	Other		1	
	TOTAL		**58**	

TOP POINT EARNERS

	PLAYER	GAMES	AV PTS
1	C De Oliveira Amauri	15	2.07
2	Eugenio Corini	25	1.84
3	Mark Bresciano	21	1.67
4	Fabio Enrico Simplicio	32	1.63
5	Cristian Zaccardo	35	1.63
6	Guiseppe Biava	19	1.58
7	Andrea Barzagli	36	1.56
8	Stefano Aimo Diana	18	1.56
9	Andrea Caracciolo	15	1.53
10	David Di Michele	23	1.52
	CLUB AVERAGE:		**1.53**

DISCIPLINARY RECORDS

	PLAYER	YELLOW	RED	AVE
1	Edison Cavani	3	0	152
2	Guiseppe Biava	9	1	184
3	Franco Brienza	4	0	220
4	Roberto Guana	12	1	264
5	Eugenio Corini	9	0	282
6	Fabio Enrico Simplicio	7	4	284
7	C De Oliveira Amauri	4	0	349
8	David Di Michele	7	0	373
9	Marco Pisano	8	1	394
10	Mattia Cassani	7	0	411
11	Stefano Aimo Diana	4	0	462
12	Cristian Zaccardo	7	0	528
13	Andrea Caracciolo	4	1	548
	Other	9	0	
	TOTAL	**94**	**8**	

KEY GOALKEEPER

Alberto Fontana

Goals Conceded in the League	38	Counting Games League games when player was on pitch for at least 70 minutes	29
Defensive Rating Ave number of mins between League goals conceded while on the pitch	69	Clean Sheets In League games when player was on pitch for at least 70 minutes	9

KEY PLAYERS - DEFENDERS

Cristian Zaccardo

Goals Conceded Number of League goals conceded while the player was on the pitch	45	Clean Sheets In League games when player was on pitch for at least 70 minutes	11
Defensive Rating Ave number of mins between League goals conceded while on the pitch	70	Club Defensive Rating Average number of mins between League goals conceded by the club this season	67

	PLAYER	CON LGE	CLEAN SHEETS	DEF RATE
1	Cristian Zaccardo	45	11	70 mins
2	Mattia Cassani	30	7	68 mins
3	Andrea Barzagli	49	11	65 mins
4	Marco Pisano	43	8	64 mins

KEY PLAYERS - MIDFIELDERS

Eugenio Corini

Goals in the League	10	Contribution to Attacking Power Average number of minutes between League team goals while on pitch	50
Defensive Rating Average number of mins between League goals conceded while on the pitch	72	Scoring Difference Defensive Rating minus Contribution to Attacking Power	22

	PLAYER	LGE GOALS	DEF RATE	POWER	SCORE DIFF
1	Eugenio Corini	10	72	50	22 mins
2	Fabio Enrico Simplicio	5	72	58	14 mins
3	Roberto Guana	0	69	61	8 mins
4	Mark Bresciano	6	64	58	6 mins

KEY PLAYERS - GOALSCORERS

Carvalho De Oliveira Amauri

Goals in the League	8	Player Strike Rate Average number of minutes between League goals scored by player	174
Contribution to Attacking Power Average number of minutes between League team goals while on pitch	45	Club Strike Rate Average number of minutes between League goals scored by club	58

	PLAYER	LGE GOALS	POWER	STRIKE RATE
1	Carvalho De Oliveira Amauri	8	45	174 mins
2	Eugenio Corini	10	50	226 mins
3	David Di Michele	9	60	249 mins
4	Andrea Caracciolo	5	82	329 mins

Carvalho De Oliveira Amauri

SQUAD APPEARANCES

Match	1 2 3 4 5	6 7 8 9 10	11 12 13 14 15	16 17 18 19 20	21 22 23 24 25	26 27 28 29 30	31 32 33 34 35	36 37 38 39 40	41 42 43 44
Venue	H A A H A	H A H A A	H A H H H	A A H A H	H A H A H	A H A H H	A H A H A	A H A H A	H A H A
Competition	L E L L L	E L L E L	L L E L L	L E L L L	E L L L L	L L L L L	L L L L L	L L L L L	L L L L
Result	W W W W L	W W L W W	W W L W W	L L L D W	D L W D W	D L W L D	D D L D D	D L D L W	L L W W

Goalkeepers
Federico Agliardi
Alberto Fontana

Defenders
Andrea Barzagli
Giuseppe Biava
Cesare Bovo
Ciro Capuano
Mattia Cassani
Paolo Dellafiore
Marco Pisano
Cristian Zaccardo

Midfielders
Mark Bresciano
Franco Brienza
Maurizio Ciaramitaro
Eugenio Corini
Stefano Aimo Diana
Guillermo Giacomazzi
Roberto Guana
Francesco Parravicini
Fabio E Simplicio
Giovanni Tedesco

Forwards
De O Amauri
Andrea Caracciolo
Edison Cavani
David Di Michele
Radoslav Matusiak

KEY: ■ On all match   ◄◄ Subbed or sent off (Counting game)   ►► Subbed on from bench (Counting Game)   ►► Subbed on and then subbed or sent off (Counting Game)   □ Not in 16
   ■ On bench   ◄◄ Subbed or sent off (playing less than 70 minutes)   ►► Subbed on (playing less than 70 minutes)   ►► Subbed on and then subbed or sent off (playing less than 70 minutes)

ITALY - PALERMO

FIORENTINA

Final Position: **6th**

NICKNAME: VIOLA   **KEY:** ☐ Won ☐ Drawn ☐ Lost   Attendance

#		Opponent		Result	Scorers	Attendance
1	itpr1	Inter Milan	H L	2-3	Toni 68, 79	41,334
2	itpr1	Livorno	A L	0-1		10,964
3	itpr1	Parma	H W	1-0	Mutu 17	28,445
4	itpr1	Udinese	A L	0-1		15,273
5	itpr1	Catania	H W	3-0	Jorgensen 54, Toni 79, Dainelli 83	30,000
6	itpr1	Empoli	A W	2-1	Mutu 67, Toni 77	11,783
7	itpr1	Reggina	H W	3-0	Mutu 30, Santana 43, Blasi 55	28,960
8	itpr1	Torino	A W	1-0	Jorgensen 13	19,000
9	itpr1	Palermo	H L	2-3	Barzagli 32 og, Mutu 88	34,000
10	itpr1	Roma	A L	1-3	Ujfalusi 15	37,000
11	itpr1	Atalanta	H W	3-1	Mutu 26, Pazzini 90, 90	29,000
12	itpr1	Ascoli	A D	1-1	Toni 45	7,000
13	itpr1	Siena	A D	1-1	Mutu 38	11,000
14	itpr1	Lazio	H W	1-0	Toni 15	30,000
15	itpr1	Chievo	A W	1-0	Mutu 80	13,000
16	itpr1	AC Milan	H D	2-2	Mutu 20 pen, 76	47,000
17	itpr1	Cagliari	A W	2-0	Toni 32, 75	15,000
18	itpr1	Messina	H W	4-0	Toni 17, Potenza 22, Liverani 45, Mutu 51	30,000
19	itpr1	Sampdoria	A D	0-0		22,000
20	itpr1	Inter Milan	A L	1-3	Toni 5	50,000
21	itpr1	Livorno	H W	2-1	Toni 68, Jorgensen 82	30,000
22	itpr1	Udinese	H W	2-0	Reginaldo 16, Pazzini 44	0
23	itpr1	Catania	A W	1-0	Toni 87	0
24	itpr1	Empoli	H W	2-0	Mutu 27, Toni 75	24,000
25	itpr1	Reggina	A D	1-1	Mutu 87 pen	9,000
26	itpr1	Torino	H W	5-1	Toni 31, 34, Franceschini 52 og, Gamberini 74, 83	23,900
27	itpr1	Palermo	A D	1-1	Mutu 33	22,476
28	itpr1	Roma	H D	0-0		23,900
29	itpr1	Atalanta	A D	2-2	Reginaldo 27, Pazzini 32	13,035
30	itpr1	Ascoli	H W	4-0	Reginaldo 4, Montolivo 45, Toni 56, Kroldrup 70	29,123
31	itpr1	Siena	H W	1-0	Mutu 43	33,467
32	itpr1	Parma	A L	0-2		13,000
33	itpr1	Lazio	A W	1-0	Mutu 71	25,723
34	itpr1	Chievo	H W	1-0	Reginaldo 64	30,724
35	itpr1	AC Milan	A D	0-0		55,078
36	itpr1	Cagliari	H W	1-0	Pazzini 7	19,312
37	itpr1	Messina	A D	2-2	Pazzini 25 pen, Gamberini 58	10,648
38	itpr1	Sampdoria	H W	5-1	Mutu 5, Montolivo 36, Pazzini 49, Reginaldo 72, 90	29,312

LEAGUE APPEARANCES, BOOKINGS AND CAPS

	AGE (on 01/07/07)	IN NAMED 18	APPEARANCES	COUNTING GAMES	MINUTES ON PITCH	YELLOW CARDS	RED CARDS	CAPS THIS SEASON	NATIONAL SIDE
Goalkeepers									
Sebastian Frey	27	38	38	38	3420	0	0	-	France
Bogdan Lonut Lobont	29	12	0	0	0	0	0	7	Romania
Cristiano Lupatelli	29	26	0	0	0	0	0	-	Italy
Defenders									
Davide Brivio	18	13	1	0	24	0	0	-	Italy
Dario Dainelli	28	35	31	27	2531	6	1	-	Italy
Samuele Di Carmine	18	6	2	0	23	0	0	-	Italy
Alessandro Gamberini	25	34	28	27	2421	2	1	-	Italy
Per Kroldrup	27	34	21	16	1559	3	0	1	Denmark
Manuel Pasqual	25	34	34	34	3044	3	0	1	Italy
Alessandro Potenza	23	31	19	9	1074	1	0	-	Italy
Tomas Ujfalusi	29	33	31	30	2699	7	0	10	Czech Republic
Midfielders									
Manuele Blasi	26	34	31	11	1705	10	0	-	Italy
Marco Donadel	24	19	19	18	1665	4	0	-	Italy
Massimo Gobbi	26	26	16	6	753	0	0	-	Italy
Martin Jorgensen	31	37	35	17	2247	3	0	8	Denmark
Zdravko Kuzmanovic	19	17	4	0	124	0	0	1	Serbia
Fabio Liverani	31	37	36	24	2611	6	0	1	Italy
Riccardo Montolivo	22	37	36	25	2628	7	0	-	Italy
Michele Pazienza	24	30	21	12	1296	4	0	-	Italy
Mario Santana	25	9	8	3	333	1	0	-	Argentina
Forwards									
Adrian Mutu	28	33	33	30	2813	13	0	8	Romania
Giampaolo Pazzini	22	29	24	7	1083	3	1	-	Italy
Reginaldo F Da Silva	33	35	27	6	1159	3	0	-	Brazil
Luca Toni	30	29	29	25	2311	3	1	3	Italy

TEAM OF THE SEASON

Position	Player		
G	Sebastian Frey	CG: 38	DR: 110
D	Alessandro Gamberini	CG: 27	DR: 127
D	Tomas Ujfalusi	CG: 30	DR: 112
D	Manuel Pasqual	CG: 34	DR: 108
D	Dario Dainelli	CG: 27	DR: 97
M	Michele Pazienza*	CG: 12	SD: 201
M	Riccardo Montolivo	CG: 25	SD: 69
M	Martin Jorgensen	CG: 17	SD: 65
M	Fabio Liverani	CG: 24	SD: 58
F	Luca Toni	CG: 25	SR: 144
F	Adrian Mutu	CG: 30	SR: 175

MONTHLY POINTS TALLY

Month	Points	%
SEPTEMBER	3	25%
OCTOBER	12	80%
NOVEMBER	5	42%
DECEMBER	13	87%
JANUARY	4	44%
FEBRUARY	10	83%
MARCH	5	56%
APRIL	13	72%
MAY	8	67%

LEAGUE GOALS

	PLAYER	MINS	GOALS	S RATE
1	Toni	2311	16	144
2	Mutu	2813	16	175
3	Pazzini	1083	7	154
4	Reginaldo	1159	6	193
5	Jorgensen	2247	3	749
6	Gamberini	2421	3	807
7	Montolivo	2628	2	1314
8	Santana	333	1	333
9	Potenza	1074	1	1074
10	Kroldrup	1559	1	1559
11	Blasi	1705	1	1705
12	Dainelli	2531	1	2531
13	Liverani	2611	1	2611
	Other		1	
	TOTAL		**60**	

TOP POINT EARNERS

	PLAYER	GAMES	AV PTS
1	Michele Pazienza	12	2.33
2	Fabio Liverani	23	2.22
3	Alessandro Gamberini	27	2.07
4	Tomas Ujfalusi	30	2.03
5	Manuel Pasqual	34	1.94
6	Sebastian Frey	38	1.92
7	Riccardo Montolivo	25	1.92
8	Martin Jorgensen	17	1.88
9	Dario Dainelli	27	1.85
10	Adrian Mutu	29	1.83
	CLUB AVERAGE:		**1.53**

DISCIPLINARY RECORDS

	PLAYER	YELLOW	RED	AVE
1	Manuele Blasi	10	0	170
2	Adrian Mutu	13	0	216
3	Giampaolo Pazzini	3	1	270
4	Michele Pazienza	4	0	324
5	Dario Dainelli	6	1	361
6	Riccardo Montolivo	7	0	375
7	Tomas Ujfalusi	7	0	385
8	R Ferreira Da Silva	3	0	386
9	Marco Donadel	4	0	416
10	Fabio Liverani	6	0	435
11	Per Kroldrup	3	0	519
12	Luca Toni	3	1	577
13	Martin Jorgensen	3	0	749
	Other	6	1	
	TOTAL	**78**	**4**	

KEY GOALKEEPER

Sebastian Frey

Goals Conceded in the League	31	Counting Games League games when player was on pitch for at least 70 minutes	38
Defensive Rating Ave number of mins between League goals conceded while on the pitch	110	Clean Sheets In League games when player was on pitch for at least 70 minutes	19

KEY PLAYERS - DEFENDERS

Alessandro Gamberini

Goals Conceded Number of League goals conceded while the player was on the pitch	19	Clean Sheets In League games when player was on pitch for at least 70 minutes	14
Defensive Rating Ave number of mins between League goals conceded while on the pitch	127	Club Defensive Rating Average number of mins between League goals conceded by the club this season	113

	PLAYER	CON LGE	CLEAN SHEETS	DEF RATE
1	Alessandro Gamberini	19	14	127 mins
2	Tomas Ujfalusi	24	15	112 mins
3	Manuel Pasqual	28	17	108 mins
4	Dario Dainelli	26	11	97 mins

KEY PLAYERS - MIDFIELDERS

Michele Pazienza

Goals in the League	0	Contribution to Attacking Power Average number of minutes between League team goals while on pitch	58
Defensive Rating Average number of mins between League goals conceded while on the pitch	259	Scoring Difference Defensive Rating minus Contribution to Attacking Power	201

	PLAYER	LGE GOALS	DEF RATE	POWER	SCORE DIFF
1	Michele Pazienza	0	259	58	201 mins
2	Riccardo Montolivo	2	119	50	69 mins
3	Martin Jorgensen	3	124	59	65 mins
4	Fabio Liverani	1	113	55	58 mins

KEY PLAYERS - GOALSCORERS

Luca Toni

Goals in the League	16	Player Strike Rate Average number of minutes between League goals scored by player	144
Contribution to Attacking Power Average number of minutes between League team goals while on pitch	55	Club Strike Rate Average number of minutes between League goals scored by club	56

	PLAYER	LGE GOALS	POWER	STRIKE RATE
1	Luca Toni	16	55	144 mins
2	Adrian Mutu	16	56	175 mins
3	Martin Jorgensen	3	59	749 mins
4	Riccardo Montolivo	2	50	1314 mins

Luca Toni

SQUAD APPEARANCES

Match	1	2	3	4	5	6	7	8	9	10	11	12	13	14	15	16	17	18	19	20	21	22	23	24	25	26	27	28	29	30	31	32	33	34	35	36	37	38
Venue	H	A	H	A	H	A	H	A	H	A	H	A	A	H	A	H	A	H	A	A	H	H	A	H	A	H	A	H	A	H	H	A	A	H	A	H	A	H
Competition	L	L	L	L	L	L	L	L	L	L	L	L	L	L	L	L	L	L	L	L	L	L	L	L	L	L	L	L	L	L	L	L	L	L	L	L	L	L
Result	L	L	W	L	W	W	W	W	L	L	W	D	D	W	W	D	W	W	D	L	W	W	W	W	D	W	D	D	D	W	W	L	W	W	D	W	D	W

Goalkeepers

Sebastian Frey
Bogdan Lonut Lobont
Cristiano Lupatelli

Defenders

Davide Brivio
Dario Dainelli
Samuele Di Carmine
Alessandro Gamberini
Per Kroldrup
Manuel Pasqual
Alessandro Potenza
Tomas Ujfalusi

Midfielders

Manuele Blasi
Marco Donadel
Massimo Gobbi
Martin Jorgensen
Zdravko Kuzmanovic
Fabio Liverani
Riccardo Montolivo
Michele Pazienza
Mario Santana

Forwards

Adrian Mutu
Giampaolo Pazzini
Reginaldo F Da Silva
Luca Toni

KEY: ■ On all match ◄◄ Subbed or sent off (Counting game) ►► Subbed on from bench (Counting Game) ⋈ Subbed on and then subbed or sent off (Counting Game) ☐ Not in 16
■ On bench ◄◄ Subbed or sent off (playing less than 70 minutes) ►► Subbed on (playing less than 70 minutes) ►► Subbed on and then subbed or sent off (playing less than 70 minutes)

ITALY - FIORENTINA

EMPOLI

Final Position: 7th

NICKNAME: AZZURRI

KEY: ☐ Won ☐ Drawn ☐ Lost   Attendance

1 itpr1	Sampdoria	A W	2-1	Busce 26, Saudati 51 pen	19,000
2 itpr1	Chievo	H D	1-1	Vannucchi 61	3,504
3 itpr1	Atalanta	A D	0-0		11,069
4 itpr1	Palermo	H W	2-0	Saudati 28, Almiron 54	4,672
5 itpr1	Roma	A L	0-1		35,000
6 itpr1	Fiorentina	H L	1-2	Matteini 28	11,783
7 itpr1	Messina	A D	2-2	Saudati 32, Busce 64	16,000
8 itpr1	Udinese	H D	1-1	Matteini 60	5,000
9 itpr1	Livorno	A D	0-0		8,379
10 itpr1	Lazio	H D	1-1	Vannucchi 87	4,500
11 itpr1	Ascoli	A W	1-0	Busce 7	7,000
12 itpr1	AC Milan	H D	0-0		7,327
13 itpr1	Cagliari	H W	1-0	Vannucchi 9	4,000
14 itpr1	Torino	A L	0-1		20,000
15 itpr1	Inter Milan	H L	0-3		11,000
16 itpr1	Siena	H W	1-0	Marianini 47	5,000
17 itpr1	Reggina	A L	1-4	Saudati 65 pen	9,000
18 itpr1	Parma	H W	2-0	Raggi 26, Matteini 77	5,000
19 itpr1	Sampdoria	H W	2-0	Saudati 56 pen, Matteini 87	5,000
20 itpr1	Catania	A L	1-2	Busce 54	15,000
21 itpr1	Chievo	A D	0-0		6,000
22 itpr1	Palermo	A W	1-0	Almiron 46	19,144
23 itpr1	Roma	H W	1-0	Pozzi 4	0
24 itpr1	Fiorentina	A L	0-2		24,000
25 itpr1	Messina	H W	3-1	Saudati 14, 62, Marzoratti 35	1,000
26 itpr1	Udinese	A W	1-0	Pozzi 18	10,000
27 itpr1	Livorno	H D	2-2	Pratali 28, Almiron 45	4,925
28 itpr1	Lazio	A L	1-3	Almiron 90	25,527
29 itpr1	Ascoli	H W	4-1	Pozzi 44, 74, Saudati 53 pen, 71	4,151
30 itpr1	AC Milan	A L	1-3	Saudati 43	45,566
31 itpr1	Cagliari	A D	0-0		8,000
32 itpr1	Atalanta	H W	2-0	Saudati 35, Almiron 54	4,000
33 itpr1	Torino	H D	0-0		5,201
34 itpr1	Inter Milan	A L	1-3	Saudati 57	61,839
35 itpr1	Catania	H W	2-1	Pozzi 23, Almiron 26	4,345
36 itpr1	Siena	A L	0-2		6,216
37 itpr1	Reggina	H D	3-3	Vannucchi 9, Moro 22, Saudati 23	4,893
38 itpr1	Parma	A L	1-3	Saudati 29	16,449

LEAGUE APPEARANCES, BOOKINGS AND CAPS

	AGE (on 01/07/07)	IN NAMED 18	APPEARANCES	COUNTING GAMES	MINUTES ON PITCH	YELLOW CARDS	RED CARDS	CAPS THIS SEASON	NATIONAL SIDE
Goalkeepers									
Daniele Balli	39	38	31	31	2790	1	0	-	Italy
Davide Bassi	22	37	7	7	630	0	0	-	Italy
Defenders									
Daniele Adani	32	19	15	7	883	1	0	-	Italy
Nicola Ascoli	27	25	13	6	754	5	0	-	Italy
Ivano Baldanzeddu	21	5	2	0	49	0	0	-	Italy
Stefano Lucchini	26	28	27	19	2044	6	0	-	Italy
Lino Marzoratti	20	36	25	12	1486	2	0	-	Italy
Davide Moro	25	37	36	35	3144	10	0	-	Italy
Francesco Pratali	28	28	27	24	2290	6	0	-	Italy
Andrea Raggi	23	35	35	32	3029	5	0	-	Italy
Vittorio Tosto	33	22	20	14	1466	4	1	-	Italy
Richard Vanigli	36	31	23	11	1341	5	1	-	Italy
Midfielders									
Sergio Almiron	26	31	30	26	2396	4	0	-	Argentina
Antonio Busce	31	35	35	34	3069	1	0	-	Italy
Daniele Buzzegoli	24	8	2	0	16	0	0	-	Italy
Fabrizio Ficini	33	36	10	3	445	2	1	-	Italy
Simone Iacoponi	20	5	1	0	25	0	0	-	Italy
Francesco Marianini	28	38	32	18	1926	3	0	-	Italy
Ighli Vannucchi	29	38	38	33	3159	3	0	-	Italy
Forwards									
Salvatore Caturano	16	1	1	0	11	0	0	-	Italy
Claudio Coralli	24	9	3	0	48	0	0	-	Italy
Citadin Martins Eder	20	15	5	2	284	0	0	-	Brazil
Mirco Gasparetto	27	18	8	2	269	0	1	-	Italy
Davide Matteini	25	34	32	13	1822	4	0	-	Italy
Nicola Pozzi	21	31	30	10	1626	5	0	-	Italy
Luca Saudati	29	35	34	23	2535	5	0	-	Italy

TEAM OF THE SEASON

Stefano Lucchini CG: 19 DR: 136

Sergio Almiron CG: 27 SD: 8

Davide Moro CG: 36 DR: 87

Ighli Vannucchi CG: 34 SD: -2

Luca Saudati CG: 24 SR: 187

Daniele Balli CG: 32 DR: 92

Lino Marzoratti CG: 13 DR: 82

Antonio Busce CG: 35 SD: -4

Davide Matteini CG: 13 SR: 455

Francesco Pratali CG: 25 DR: 79

Francesco Marianini CG: 19 SD: -22

MONTHLY POINTS TALLY

SEPTEMBER	8	67%
OCTOBER	3	20%
NOVEMBER	8	67%
DECEMBER	3	25%
JANUARY	7	58%
FEBRUARY	9	75%
MARCH	4	44%
APRIL	8	44%
MAY	4	33%

LEAGUE GOALS

	PLAYER	MINS	GOALS	S RATE
1	Saudati	2625	14	187
2	Almiron	2486	6	414
3	Pozzi	1626	5	325
4	Matteini	1822	4	455
5	Busce	3159	4	789
6	Vannucchi	3249	4	812
7	Marianini	2016	1	2016
8	Pratali	2380	1	2380
9	Raggi	3029	1	3029
10	Moro	3234	1	3234
11	Nicoletti	0	0	
12	Marzoratti	1576	0	
13	Ascoli	754	0	
	Other		0	
	TOTAL		**41**	

TOP POINT EARNERS

	PLAYER	GAMES	AV PTS
1	Stefano Lucchini	19	1.74
2	Vittorio Tosto	14	1.57
3	Sergio Almiron	26	1.54
4	Francesco Marianini	18	1.50
5	Daniele Balli	31	1.48
6	Davide Moro	35	1.46
7	Ighli Vannucchi	33	1.45
8	Richard Vanigli	12	1.42
9	Davide Matteini	13	1.38
10	Francesco Pratali	24	1.38
	CLUB AVERAGE:		**1.42**

DISCIPLINARY RECORDS

	PLAYER	YELLOW	RED	AVE
1	Richard Vanigli	5	1	223
2	Vittorio Tosto	4	1	311
3	Davide Moro	10	0	323
4	Nicola Pozzi	5	0	325
5	Stefano Lucchini	6	0	340
6	Francesco Pratali	6	0	396
7	Davide Matteini	4	0	455
8	Luca Saudati	5	0	525
9	Andrea Raggi	5	0	605
10	Sergio Almiron	4	0	621
11	Francesco Marianini	3	0	672
12	Nicola Ascoli	1	0	754
13	Lino Marzoratti	2	0	788
	Other	6	0	
	TOTAL	**66**	**2**	

KEY GOALKEEPER

Daniele Balli				
Goals Conceded in the League	31	Counting Games League games when player was on pitch for at least 70 minutes	32
Defensive Rating Ave number of mins between League goals conceded while on the pitch	92	Clean Sheets In League games when player was on pitch for at least 70 minutes	15

KEY PLAYERS - GOALSCORERS

Luca Saudati				
Goals in the League	14	Player Strike Rate Average number of minutes between League goals scored by player	187
Contribution to Attacking Power Average number of minutes between League team goals while on pitch	75	Club Strike Rate Average number of minutes between League goals scored by club	85

	PLAYER	LGE GOALS	POWER	STRIKE RATE
1	Luca Saudati	14	75	187 mins
2	Sergio Almiron	6	80	414 mins
3	Davide Matteini	4	86	455 mins
4	Antonio Busce	4	85	789 mins

KEY PLAYERS - DEFENDERS

Stefano Lucchini				
Goals Conceded Number of League goals conceded while the player was on the pitch	15	Clean Sheets In League games when player was on pitch for at least 70 minutes	11
Defensive Rating Ave number of mins between League goals conceded while on the pitch	136	Club Defensive Rating Average number of mins between League goals conceded by the club this season	83

	PLAYER	CON LGE	CLEAN SHEETS	DEF RATE
1	Stefano Lucchini	15	11	136 mins
2	Davide Moro	37	18	87 mins
3	Lino Marzoratti	19	7	82 mins
4	Francesco Pratali	30	9	79 mins

Luca Saudati

KEY PLAYERS - MIDFIELDERS

Sergio Almiron				
Goals in the League	6	Contribution to Attacking Power Average number of minutes between League team goals while on pitch	80
Defensive Rating Average number of mins between League goals conceded while on the pitch	88	Scoring Difference Defensive Rating minus Contribution to Attacking Power	8

	PLAYER	LGE GOALS	DEF RATE	POWER	SCORE DIFF
1	Sergio Almiron	6	88	80	8 mins
2	Ighli Vannucchi	4	77	79	-2 mins
3	Antonio Busce	4	81	85	-4 mins
4	Francesco Marianini	1	69	91	-22 mins

SQUAD APPEARANCES

Match	1	2	3	4	5	6	7	8	9	10	11	12	13	14	15	16	17	18	19	20	21	22	23	24	25	26	27	28	29	30	31	32	33	34	35	36	37	38
Venue	A	H	A	H	A	H	A	H	A	H	A	H	H	A	H	H	A	H	H	A	A	A	H	A	H	A	H	A	H	A	H	H	H	A	H	A	H	A
Competition	L	L	L	L	L	L	L	L	L	L	L	L	L	L	L	L	L	L	L	L	L	L	L	L	L	L	L	L	L	L	L	L	L	L	L	L	L	L
Result	W	D	D	W	L	L	D	D	D	D	W	D	W	L	L	W	L	W	W	L	D	W	W	L	W	W	D	L	W	L	D	W	D	L	W	L	D	L

Goalkeepers

Daniele Balli

Davide Bassi

Defenders

Daniele Adani

Nicola Ascoli

Ivano Baldanzeddu

Stefano Lucchini

Lino Marzoratti

Davide Moro

Francesco Pratali

Andrea Raggi

Vittorio Tosto

Richard Vanigli

Midfielders

Sergio Almiron

Antonio Busce

Daniele Buzzegoli

Fabrizio Ficini

Simone Iacoponi

Francesco Marianini

Ighli Vannucchi

Forwards

Salvatore Caturano

Claudio Coralli

Citadin Martins Eder

Mirco Gasparetto

Davide Matteini

Nicola Pozzi

Luca Saudati

KEY:
- ■ On all match
- ■ On bench
- ◄◄ Subbed or sent off (Counting game)
- ◄◄ Subbed or sent off (playing less than 70 minutes)
- ►► Subbed on from bench (Counting Game)
- ►► Subbed on (playing less than 70 minutes)
- ►► Subbed on and then subbed or sent off (Counting Game)
- ►► Subbed on and then subbed or sent off (playing less than 70 minutes)
- □ Not in 16

ITALY - EMPOLI

ATALANTA

Final Position: 8th

NICKNAME: NERAZZURRI　　　KEY: ☐ Won ☐ Drawn ☐ Lost　　　Attendance

1 itpr1	Ascoli	H W	**3-1**	Zampagna 32, Ventola 38, 44	11,000
2 itpr1	Catania	A D	**0-0**		18,400
3 itpr1	Empoli	H D	**0-0**		11,069
4 itpr1	Lazio	A L	**0-1**		19,339
5 itpr1	Reggina	H D	**1-1**	Loria 2	13,000
6 itpr1	Palermo	A W	**3-2**	Doni 14, Rivalta 31, Tissone 56	21,716
7 itpr1	Sampdoria	H W	**3-2**	Doni 38 pen, 85 pen, Zampagna 89	12,000
8 itpr1	Cagliari	H D	**3-3**	Loria 4, Ventola 58, Doni 69	13,000
9 itpr1	Parma	A L	**1-3**	Doni 58	14,637
10 itpr1	AC Milan	H W	**2-0**	Ventola 50, Soncin 90	25,000
11 itpr1	Fiorentina	A L	**1-3**	Migliaccio 25	29,000
12 itpr1	Chievo	A D	**2-2**	Zampagna 72, Loria 74	6,000
13 itpr1	Torino	H L	**1-2**	Loria 90	12,000
14 itpr1	Roma	A L	**1-2**	Zampagna 19	33,745
15 itpr1	Messina	H W	**3-2**	Bombardini 28, Ferreira Pinto 57, Doni 67	13,000
16 itpr1	Siena	A D	**1-1**	Migliaccio 36	6,500
17 itpr1	Udinese	H L	**1-2**	Tissone 46	15,000
18 itpr1	Inter Milan	A L	**1-2**	Doni 16	43,000
19 itpr1	Livorno	H W	**5-1**	Doni 38, 45, Donati 57, Ariatti 66, Ventola 90	13,000
20 itpr1	Ascoli	A W	**3-1**	Zampagna 51, Adriano 84, Doni 86	8,000
21 itpr1	Catania	H D	**1-1**	Zampagna 30	12,000
22 itpr1	Lazio	H D	**0-0**		0
23 itpr1	Reggina	A D	**1-1**	Talamonti 74	7,000
24 itpr1	Palermo	H D	**1-1**	Zampagna 13	8,800
25 itpr1	Sampdoria	A L	**1-2**	Ventola 8	20,000
26 itpr1	Cagliari	A L	**0-2**		10,000
27 itpr1	Parma	H D	**1-1**	Defendi 52	8,092
28 itpr1	AC Milan	A L	**0-1**		45,491
29 itpr1	Fiorentina	H D	**2-2**	Loria 39, Doni 65	13,035
30 itpr1	Chievo	H W	**1-0**	Doni 54	11,845
31 itpr1	Torino	A W	**2-1**	Bellini 1, Zampagna 8	19,845
32 itpr1	Empoli	A L	**0-2**		4,000
33 itpr1	Roma	H W	**2-1**	Doni 37, Zampagna 44	12,258
34 itpr1	Messina	A D	**0-0**		10,752
35 itpr1	Siena	H W	**3-1**	Ariatti 11, Vieri 65, Carrozzieri 90	11,388
36 itpr1	Udinese	A W	**3-2**	Zampagna 45 pen, Tissone 74, Vieri 86	13,652
37 itpr1	Inter Milan	H D	**1-1**	Ferreira Pinto 10	22,899
38 itpr1	Livorno	A L	**2-4**	Zampagna 51, Bombardini 65	8,587

LEAGUE APPEARANCES, BOOKINGS AND CAPS

	AGE (on 01/07/07)	IN NAMED 18	APPEARANCES	COUNTING GAMES	MINUTES ON PITCH	YELLOW CARDS	RED CARDS	CAPS THIS SEASON	NATIONAL SIDE
Goalkeepers									
Alex Calderoni	31	37	37	37	3330	0	0	-	Italy
Andrea Ivan	34	33	1	1	90	0	0	-	Italy
Defenders									
P da Silva Adriano	25	32	25	13	1649	7	2	-	Brazil
Giampaolo Bellini	27	32	32	27	2655	4	1	-	Italy
Morris Carrozzieri	26	26	19	16	1496	8	0	-	Italy
Kewullay Conteh	29	7	1	0	3	0	0	-	Sierra Leone
Simone Loria	30	30	28	26	2378	8	2	-	Italy
Claudio Rivalta	29	34	32	28	2710	5	0	-	Italy
Leonardo Talamonti	25	30	20	18	1722	5	0	-	Argentina
Midfielders									
Nelson Abeijon	33	19	5	0	120	2	0	-	Uruguay
Luca Ariatti	28	36	36	34	3029	9	0	-	Italy
Antonio Bernardini	33	35	24	16	1575	4	0	-	Italy
Davide Bombardini	33	35	22	2	875	4	0	-	Italy
Massimo Donati	26	34	32	25	2342	7	1	-	Italy
Cristiano Doni	34	26	26	23	2062	13	0	-	Italy
Giulio Migliaccio	26	34	33	31	2864	3	1	-	Italy
F Damian Tissone	20	37	33	13	1529	0	0	-	Argentina
Forwards									
Karamoko Cisse	18	4	3	0	74	0	0	-	Guinea
Mario Defendi	21	24	17	9	885	2	0	-	Italy
Adriano Ferreira Pinto	27	37	32	21	2215	2	0	-	Brazil
Andrea Soncin	28	11	6	1	186	0	0	-	Italy
Nicola Ventola	29	30	29	13	1537	2	0	-	Italy
Christian Vieri	33	7	7	0	237	0	0	-	Italy
Riccardo Zampagna	32	30	28	17	1891	6	0	-	Italy

TEAM OF THE SEASON

G Alex Calderoni CG: 37 DR: 66

D Morris Carrozzieri CG: 16 DR: 78
D Leonardo Talamonti CG: 18 DR: 71
D Giampaolo Bellini CG: 27 DR: 66
D Claudio Rivalta CG: 28 DR: 61

M Cristiano Doni CG: 23 SD: 11
M Giulio Migliaccio CG: 31 SD: 10
M F Damian Tissone CG: 13 SD: 7
M Massimo Donati CG: 25 SD: 5

F Riccardo Zampagna CG: 17 SR: 171
F Nicola Ventola CG: 13 SR: 256

MONTHLY POINTS TALLY

SEPTEMBER	6	40%
OCTOBER	7	58%
NOVEMBER	4	33%
DECEMBER	4	27%
JANUARY	7	78%
FEBRUARY	3	25%
MARCH	1	11%
APRIL	11	61%
MAY	7	58%

LEAGUE GOALS

	PLAYER	MINS	GOALS	S RATE
1	Doni	2062	13	158
2	Zampagna	1891	11	171
3	Ventola	1537	6	256
4	Loria	2378	5	475
5	Tissone	1529	3	509
6	Vieri	237	2	118
7	Bombardini	875	2	437
8	Ferreira Pinto	2215	2	1107
9	Migliaccio	2864	2	1432
10	Ariatti	3029	2	1514
11	Soncin	186	1	186
12	Defendi	885	1	885
13	Carrozzieri	1496	1	1496
	Other		5	
	TOTAL		**56**	

TOP POINT EARNERS

	PLAYER	GAMES	AV PTS
1	Pereira da Silva Adriano	15	1.80
2	Adriano Ferreira Pinto	20	1.60
3	Leonardo Talamonti	18	1.56
4	Morris Carrozzieri	16	1.50
5	Giulio Migliaccio	31	1.48
6	Cristiano Doni	22	1.45
7	Riccardo Zampagna	16	1.44
8	Luca Ariatti	33	1.39
9	Alex Calderoni	37	1.35
10	Giampaolo Bellini	28	1.32
	CLUB AVERAGE:		**1.32**

DISCIPLINARY RECORDS

	PLAYER	YELLOW	RED	AVE
1	Cristiano Doni	13	0	158
2	P da Silva Adriano	7	2	183
3	Morris Carrozzieri	8	0	187
4	Davide Bombardini	4	0	218
5	Simone Loria	8	2	237
6	Massimo Donati	7	1	292
7	Riccardo Zampagna	6	0	315
8	Luca Ariatti	9	0	336
9	Leonardo Talamonti	5	0	344
10	Antonio Bernardini	4	0	393
11	Mario Defendi	2	0	442
12	Giampaolo Bellini	4	1	531
13	Claudio Rivalta	5	0	542
	Other	7	1	
	TOTAL	**89**	**7**	

KEY GOALKEEPER

Alex Calderoni

Goals Conceded in the League	50	Counting Games League games when player was on pitch for at least 70 minutes	37
Defensive Rating Ave number of mins between League goals conceded while on the pitch	66	Clean Sheets In League games when player was on pitch for at least 70 minutes	6

KEY PLAYERS - DEFENDERS

Morris Carrozzieri

Goals Conceded Number of League goals conceded while the player was on the pitch	19	Clean Sheets In League games when player was on pitch for at least 70 minutes	3
Defensive Rating Ave number of mins between League goals conceded while on the pitch	78	Club Defensive Rating Average number of mins between League goals conceded by the club this season	65

	PLAYER	CON LGE	CLEAN SHEETS	DEF RATE
1	Morris Carrozzieri	19	3	78 mins
2	Leonardo Talamonti	24	4	71 mins
3	Giampaolo Bellini	40	4	66 mins
4	Claudio Rivalta	44	5	61 mins

KEY PLAYERS - MIDFIELDERS

Cristiano Doni

Goals in the League	13	Contribution to Attacking Power Average number of minutes between League team goals while on pitch	55
Defensive Rating Average number of minutes between League goals conceded while on the pitch	66	Scoring Difference Defensive Rating minus Contribution to Attacking Power	11

	PLAYER	LGE GOALS	DEF RATE	POWER	SCORE DIFF
1	Cristiano Doni	13	66	55	11 mins
2	Giulio Migliaccio	2	69	59	10 mins
3	Fernando Damian Tissone	3	63	56	7 mins
4	Massimo Donati	1	66	61	5 mins

KEY PLAYERS - GOALSCORERS

Cristiano Doni

Goals in the League	13	Player Strike Rate Average number of minutes between League goals scored by player	158
Contribution to Attacking Power Average number of minutes between League team goals while on pitch	55	Club Strike Rate Average number of minutes between League goals scored by club	62

	PLAYER	LGE GOALS	POWER	STRIKE RATE
1	Cristiano Doni	13	55	158 mins
2	Riccardo Zampagna	11	55	171 mins
3	Nicola Ventola	6	66	256 mins
4	Fernando Damian Tissone	3	56	509 mins

Cristiano Doni

SQUAD APPEARANCES

Match	1	2	3	4	5	6	7	8	9	10	11	12	13	14	15	16	17	18	19	20	21	22	23	24	25	26	27	28	29	30	31	32	33	34	35	36	37	38
Venue	H	A	H	A	H	A	H	H	A	H	A	A	H	A	H	A	H	A	H	A	H	H	A	H	A	A	H	A	H	H	A	A	H	A	H	A	H	A
Competition	L	L	L	L	L	L	L	L	L	L	L	L	L	L	L	L	L	L	L	L	L	L	L	L	L	L	L	L	L	L	L	L	L	L	L	L	L	L
Result	W	D	D	L	D	W	W	D	L	W	L	D	L	L	W	D	L	L	W	W	D	D	D	D	L	L	D	L	D	W	W	L	W	D	W	W	D	L

Goalkeepers
Alex Calderoni
Andrea Ivan

Defenders
da Silva Adriano
Giampaolo Bellini
Morris Carrozzieri
Kewullay Conteh
Simone Loria
Claudio Rivalta
Leonardo Talamonti

Midfielders
Nelson Abeijon
Luca Ariatti
Antonio Bernardini
Davide Bombardini
Massimo Donati
Cristiano Doni
Giulio Migliaccio
F Damian Tissone

Forwards
Karamoko Cisse
Mario Defendi
Adriano Ferreira Pinto
Andrea Soncin
Nicola Ventola
Christian Vieri
Riccardo Zampagna

KEY: ■ On all match ■ On bench ◄◄ Subbed or sent off (Counting game) ◄◄ Subbed or sent off (playing less than 70 minutes) ►► Subbed on from bench (Counting Game) ►► Subbed on (playing less than 70 minutes) ►► Subbed on and then subbed or sent off (Counting Game) ►► Subbed on and then subbed or sent off (playing less than 70 minutes) □ Not in 16

ITALY - ATALANTA

SAMPDORIA

Final Position: **9th**

NICKNAME: BLUCERCHIATI   KEY: ☐ Won ☐ Drawn ☐ Lost   Attendance

#				Result	Scorers	Attendance
1	itpr1	Empoli	H L	1-2	Bonazzoli 9	19,000
2	itpr1	Inter Milan	A D	1-1	Flachi 48 pen	45,194
3	itpr1	Udinese	H D	3-3	Delvecchio 44, Volpi 68, Flachi 77	18,100
4	itpr1	Ascoli	A D	1-1	Delvecchio 65	7,809
5	itpr1	Parma	H W	3-2	Franceschini 23, Delvecchio 53, Bonazzoli 64	19,000
6	itpr1	AC Milan	H D	1-1	Bonazzoli 69	25,324
7	itpr1	Atalanta	A L	2-3	Quagliarella 4, 11	12,000
8	itpr1	Lazio	H W	2-0	Quagliarella 53, Volpi 75	20,000
9	itpr1	Cagliari	A L	0-1		10,000
10	itpr1	Palermo	A L	0-2		22,244
11	itpr1	Chievo	H W	3-0	Bonazzoli 19, Quagliarella 28, 36	18,000
12	itpr1	Torino	A L	0-1		20,000
13	itpr1	Roma	H L	2-4	Volpi 13, Flachi 45 pen	19,000
14	itpr1	Messina	A W	2-0	Franceschini 20, Quagliarella 90	20,000
15	itpr1	Siena	H D	0-0		20,000
16	itpr1	Reggina	A W	1-0	Quagliarella 68	10,000
17	itpr1	Livorno	H W	4-1	Franceschini 25, Flachi 30, Quagliarella 47, 57	25,000
18	itpr1	Catania	A L	2-4	Palombo 22, Franceschini 40	17,000
19	itpr1	Fiorentina	H D	0-0		22,000
20	itpr1	Empoli	A L	0-2		5,000
21	itpr1	Inter Milan	H L	0-2		25,000
22	itpr1	Ascoli	H W	2-0	Maggio 48, Franceschini 75	17,000
23	itpr1	Parma	A W	1-0	Quagliarella 57	14,501
24	itpr1	AC Milan	A L	0-1		21,000
25	itpr1	Atalanta	H W	2-1	Bazzani 71, Volpi 83 pen	20,000
26	itpr1	Lazio	A L	0-1		16,000
27	itpr1	Cagliari	H D	1-1	Palombo 40	17,259
28	itpr1	Palermo	H D	1-1	Quagliarella 56	17,000
29	itpr1	Chievo	A D	1-1	Quagliarella 27	5,765
30	itpr1	Torino	H W	1-0	Bonazzoli 17	18,648
31	itpr1	Roma	A L	0-4		31,875
32	itpr1	Udinese	A L	0-1		13,500
33	itpr1	Messina	H W	3-1	Ziegler 13, Franceschini 83, Delvecchio 89	16,673
34	itpr1	Siena	A W	2-0	Maggio 39, Delvecchio 89	5,277
35	itpr1	Reggina	H D	0-0		17,264
36	itpr1	Livorno	A L	0-1		13,209
37	itpr1	Catania	H W	1-0	Zenoni 66	17,303
38	itpr1	Fiorentina	A L	1-5	Quagliarella 40	29,312

LEAGUE APPEARANCES, BOOKINGS AND CAPS

	AGE (on 01/07/07)	IN NAMED 18	APPEARANCES	COUNTING GAMES	MINUTES ON PITCH	YELLOW CARDS	RED CARDS	CAPS THIS SEASON	NATIONAL SIDE
Goalkeepers									
Gianluca Berti	40	25	10	10	900	2	0	-	Italy
Luca Castellazzi	31	37	27	27	2430	2	0	-	Italy
Carlo Zotti	24	9	1	1	90	0	0	-	Italy
Defenders									
Pietro Accardi	24	35	27	25	2323	8	0	-	Italy
Alessandro Bastrini	20	15	6	3	338	0	0	-	Italy
Guilio Falcone	33	32	32	24	2533	6	3	1	Italy
Cristian Maggio	25	33	31	28	2698	2	0	-	Italy
Mirko Pieri	28	34	24	14	1445	2	0	-	Italy
Alessandro Romeo	20	4	4	0	131	1	0	-	Italy
Luigi Sala	33	36	24	18	1812	9	0	-	Italy
Christian Terlizzi	27	8	4	4	356	1	1	1	Italy
Cristian Zenoni	30	36	35	31	2958	8	0	-	Italy
Midfielders									
Massimo Bonanni	25	15	7	2	351	1	0	-	Italy
F Bruno Da Mota	19	5	1	0	11	0	0	-	Italy
Gennaro Delvecchio	29	31	30	12	1747	7	1	-	Italy
Daniele Franceschini	31	37	36	20	2358	1	0	-	Italy
Vladimir Koman	18	5	4	1	183	0	0	-	Hungary
Ruben Ariel Olivera	24	28	20	1	649	4	1	-	Uruguay
Angelo Palombo	25	36	36	33	3043	0	0	2	Italy
Andrea Parola	28	27	21	8	1101	4	0	-	Italy
Danilo Soddimo	19	6	2	0	80	0	0	-	Italy
Sergio Volpi	33	30	30	28	2560	8	0	-	Italy
Reto Ziegler	21	16	15	1	606	1	0	-	Switzerland
Forwards									
Pietro Arnulfo	18	1	1	0	2	0	0	-	Italy
Fabio Bazzani	30	27	21	8	1042	2	0	-	Italy
Emiliano Bonazzoli	28	27	27	16	1817	4	0	1	Italy
Marco Delvecchio	34	1	1	0	34	1	1	-	Italy
Francesco Flachi	32	13	13	10	975	0	0	-	Italy
Fabio Quagliarella	33	35	35	30	2772	8	0	3	Italy

TEAM OF THE SEASON

D Pietro Accardi CG: 25 DR: 89
M Daniele Franceschini CG: 20 SD: 8
D Mirko Pieri CG: 14 DR: 85
M Gennaro Delvecchio* CG: 12 SD: 3
F Fabio Quagliarella CG: 30 SR: 213
G Luca Castellazzi CG: 27 DR: 71
D Guilio Falcone CG: 24 DR: 79
M Sergio Volpi CG: 28 SD: 0
F Emiliano Bonazzoli CG: 16 SR: 363
D Cristian Maggio CG: 28 DR: 71
M Angelo Palombo CG: 33 SD: -10

MONTHLY POINTS TALLY

SEPTEMBER	3	25%
OCTOBER	7	47%
NOVEMBER	3	25%
DECEMBER	10	67%
JANUARY	1	11%
FEBRUARY	9	75%
MARCH	2	22%
APRIL	10	56%
MAY	4	33%

LEAGUE GOALS

	PLAYER	MINS	GOALS	S RATE
1	Quagliarella	2772	13	213
2	Franceschini	2358	6	393
3	Delvecchio	1747	5	349
4	Bonazzoli	1817	5	363
5	Flachi	975	4	243
6	Volpi	2560	4	640
7	Maggio	2698	2	1349
8	Palombo	3043	2	1521
9	Ziegler	606	1	606
10	Bazzani	1042	1	1042
11	Zenoni	2958	1	2958
12	Parola	1101	0	
13	Pieri	1445	0	
	Other		0	
	TOTAL		**44**	

TOP POINT EARNERS

	PLAYER	GAMES	AV PTS
1	Gennaro Delvecchio	13	1.62
2	Pietro Accardi	25	1.44
3	Sergio Volpi	28	1.43
4	Daniele Franceschini	20	1.40
5	Luca Castellazzi	27	1.37
6	Cristian Maggio	28	1.36
7	Guilio Falcone	27	1.33
8	Fabio Quagliarella	30	1.33
9	Angelo Palombo	33	1.27
10	Cristian Zenoni	31	1.23
	CLUB AVERAGE:		**1.29**

DISCIPLINARY RECORDS

	PLAYER	YELLOW	RED	AVE
1	Ruben Ariel Olivera	4	1	129
2	Luigi Sala	9	0	201
3	Gennaro Delvecchio	7	1	218
4	Andrea Parola	4	0	275
5	Guilio Falcone	6	3	281
6	Pietro Accardi	8	0	290
7	Sergio Volpi	8	0	320
8	Fabio Quagliarella	8	0	346
9	Cristian Zenoni	8	0	369
10	Emiliano Bonazzoli	4	0	454
11	Fabio Bazzani	2	0	521
12	Reto Ziegler	1	0	606
13	Mirko Pieri	2	0	722
	Other	6	0	
	TOTAL	**77**	**5**	

KEY GOALKEEPER

Luca Castellazzi

Goals Conceded in the League	34	Counting Games League games when player was on pitch for at least 70 minutes	27
Defensive Rating Ave number of mins between League goals conceded while on the pitch	71	Clean Sheets In League games when player was on pitch for at least 70 minutes	8

KEY PLAYERS - GOALSCORERS

Fabio Quagliarella

Goals in the League	13	Player Strike Rate Average number of minutes between League goals scored by player	213
Contribution to Attacking Power Average number of minutes between League team goals while on pitch	81	Club Strike Rate Average number of minutes between League goals scored by club	79

	PLAYER	LGE GOALS	POWER	STRIKE RATE
1	Fabio Quagliarella	13	81	213 mins
2	Gennaro Delvecchio	5	64	349 mins
3	Emiliano Bonazzoli	5	58	363 mins
4	Daniele Franceschini	6	73	393 mins

KEY PLAYERS - DEFENDERS

Pietro Accardi

Goals Conceded Number of League goals conceded while the player was on the pitch	26	Clean Sheets In League games when player was on pitch for at least 70 minutes	11
Defensive Rating Ave number of mins between League goals conceded while on the pitch	89	Club Defensive Rating Average number of mins between League goals conceded by the club this season	73

	PLAYER	CON LGE	CLEAN SHEETS	DEF RATE
1	Pietro Accardi	26	11	89 mins
2	Mirko Pieri	17	4	85 mins
3	Guilio Falcone	32	9	79 mins
4	Cristian Maggio	38	8	71 mins

KEY PLAYERS - MIDFIELDERS

Daniele Franceschini

Goals in the League	6	Contribution to Attacking Power Average number of minutes between League team goals while on pitch	73
Defensive Rating Average number of mins between League goals conceded while on the pitch	81	Scoring Difference Defensive Rating minus Contribution to Attacking Power	8

	PLAYER	LGE GOALS	DEF RATE	POWER	SCORE DIFF
1	Daniele Franceschini	6	81	73	8 mins
2	Gennaro Delvecchio	5	67	64	3 mins
3	Sergio Volpi	4	71	71	0 mins
4	Angelo Palombo	2	64	74	-10 mins

Fabio Quagliarella

SQUAD APPEARANCES

Match	1	2	3	4	5	6	7	8	9	10	11	12	13	14	15	16	17	18	19	20	21	22	23	24	25	26	27	28	29	30	31	32	33	34	35	36	37	38
Venue	H	A	H	A	H	H	A	H	A	A	H	A	H	A	H	A	H	A	H	A	H	H	A	A	H	A	H	H	A	H	A	A	H	A	H	A	H	A
Competition	L	L	L	L	L	L	L	L	L	L	L	L	L	L	L	L	L	L	L	L	L	L	L	L	L	L	L	L	L	L	L	L	L	L	L	L	L	L
Result	L	D	D	D	W	D	L	W	L	L	W	L	L	W	D	W	W	L	D	L	L	W	W	L	W	L	D	D	D	W	L	L	W	W	D	L	W	L

Goalkeepers
Gianluca Berti
Luca Castellazzi
Carlo Zotti

Defenders
Pietro Accardi
Alessandro Bastrini
Guilio Falcone
Cristian Maggio
Mirko Pieri
Alessandro Romeo
Luigi Sala
Christian Terlizzi
Cristian Zenoni

Midfielders
Massimo Bonanni
F Bruno Da Mota
Gennaro Delvecchio
Daniele Franceschini
Vladimir Koman
Ruben Ariel Olivera
Angelo Palombo
Andrea Parola
Danilo Soddimo
Sergio Volpi
Reto Ziegler

Forwards
Pietro Arnulfo
Fabio Bazzani
Emiliano Bonazzoli
Marco Delvecchio
Francesco Flachi
Fabio Quagliarella

KEY: ■ On all match   ◄◄ Subbed or sent off (Counting game)   ►►► Subbed on from bench (Counting Game)   ►► Subbed on and then subbed or sent off (Counting Game)   Not in 16
■ On bench   ◄◄ Subbed or sent off (playing less than 70 minutes)   ►► Subbed on (playing less than 70 minutes)   ►► Subbed on and then subbed or sent off (playing less than 70 minutes)

ITALY - SAMPDORIA

UDINESE

Final Position: 10th

NICKNAME: ZEBRETTE

KEY: ☐ Won ☐ Drawn ☐ Lost

Attendance

#				Result	Scorers	Attendance
1	itpr1	Messina	A L	0-1		12,000
2	itpr1	Torino	H W	2-0	Di Natale 25, Felipe Dal Belo 65	14,555
3	itpr1	Sampdoria	A D	3-3	Di Natale 4, Iaquinta 16, Asamoah 43	18,100
4	itpr1	Fiorentina	H W	1-0	Iaquinta 40	15,273
5	itpr1	Ascoli	H D	0-0		14,000
6	itpr1	Parma	A W	3-0	Muntari 9, Iaquinta 12 pen, 66	12,250
7	itpr1	Inter Milan	H D	0-0		20,000
8	itpr1	Empoli	A D	1-1	Obodo 57	5,000
9	itpr1	Roma	H L	0-1		19,000
10	itpr1	Livorno	A L	0-1		7,500
11	itpr1	Lazio	A L	0-5		19,000
12	itpr1	Siena	H W	3-0	Asamoah 19, Iaquinta 44, 79	15,000
13	itpr1	Chievo	A L	0-2		6,000
14	itpr1	Reggina	H D	1-1	Iaquinta 69	13,000
15	itpr1	Catania	A L	0-1		19,000
16	itpr1	Cagliari	H W	3-1	Pinzi 17, Iaquinta 27, Obodo 52	14,000
17	itpr1	Atalanta	A W	2-1	De Martino 51, Di Natale 90	15,000
18	itpr1	AC Milan	H L	0-3		20,000
19	itpr1	Palermo	A L	0-2		20,913
20	itpr1	Messina	H W	1-0	Iaquinta 76	15,000
21	itpr1	Torino	A W	3-2	Obodo 18, Barreto De Souza 32, Asamoah 61	22,000
22	itpr1	Fiorentina	A L	0-2		0
23	itpr1	Ascoli	A D	2-2	Iaquinta 36, Barreto De Souza 42	400
24	itpr1	Parma	H D	3-3	Di Natale 41, 68 pen, Obodo 84	13,652
25	itpr1	Inter Milan	A D	1-1	Obodo 48	35,000
26	itpr1	Empoli	H L	0-1		10,000
27	itpr1	Roma	A L	1-3	Asamoah 69	30,817
28	itpr1	Livorno	H W	4-0	Di Natale 34, 69, Asamoah 37, Barreto De Souza 83 pen	13,652
29	itpr1	Lazio	H L	2-4	Di Natale 58 pen, Iaquinta 90	13,652
30	itpr1	Siena	A D	2-2	Di Natale 42, Iaquinta 60	6,463
31	itpr1	Chievo	H W	2-1	Iaquinta 34, Di Natale 74	21,804
32	itpr1	Sampdoria	H W	1-0	Iaquinta 53 pen	13,500
33	itpr1	Reggina	A D	1-1	Muntari 26	10,622
34	itpr1	Catania	H L	0-1		13,652
35	itpr1	Cagliari	A L	1-2	Muntari 44	7,000
36	itpr1	Atalanta	H L	2-3	Asamoah 28, 68	13,652
37	itpr1	AC Milan	A W	3-2	Asamoah 10, Di Natale 53, Barreto De Souza 61	51,124
38	itpr1	Palermo	H L	1-2	Sivok 21	5,000

LEAGUE APPEARANCES, BOOKINGS AND CAPS

	AGE (on 01/07/07)	IN NAMED 18	APPEARANCES	COUNTING GAMES	MINUTES ON PITCH	YELLOW CARDS	RED CARDS	CAPS THIS SEASON	NATIONAL SIDE
Goalkeepers									
Fabrizio Casazza	36	16	1	0	45	0	0	-	Italy
Morgan De Sanctis	30	36	36	35	3195	2	0	-	Italy
Gabriele Paoletti	29	18	2	2	180	0	0	-	Italy
Defenders									
Andrea Coda	22	35	22	22	1954	5	1	-	Italy
Andrea Dossena	25	26	19	18	1842	3	1	-	Italy
Felipe Dal Belo	22	14	13	11	994	3	1	-	Brazil
Massimo Gotti	21	7	2	0	41	0	0	-	Italy
Aleksandar Lukovic	24	14	5	2	185	1	0	2	Serbia
Marco Motta	21	23	16	13	1235	0	1	-	Italy
Cesare Natali	28	33	32	31	2799	10	0	-	Italy
C Eduardo Zapata	20	36	36	35	3154	8	0	-	Colombia
Tomas Zapotocny	26	14	11	8	780	3	0	3	Czech Republic
Midfielders									
Gaetano D'Agostino	25	29	23	13	1412	3	1	-	Italy
Raffaele De Martino	21	32	18	3	648	5	1	-	Italy
Roman Eremenko	20	12	6	1	214	1	0	1	Finland
Jose Montiel	19	12	8	0	153	0	0	-	Olimpia Asuncion
Sulley Ali Muntari	22	28	28	26	2343	9	3	5	Ghana
Christian Obodo	23	30	30	27	2545	4	0	2	Nigeria
Giampiero Pinzi	26	32	32	31	2801	14	0	-	Italy
Guilherme Siqueira	21	26	16	1	490	0	0	-	Brazil
Tomas Sivok	23	12	11	4	512	1	0	-	Czech Republic
Damiano Zenoni	30	20	20	20	1800	4	0	1	Italy
Forwards									
Gyan Asamoah	21	28	25	13	1544	3	0	-	Ghana
P Vitor B De Souza	21	27	25	10	1356	3	0	-	Brazil
Antonio Di Natale	29	31	31	27	2552	4	2	4	Italy
Federico Gerardi	19	11	1	0	9	0	0	-	Italy
Vincenzo Iaquinta	27	30	30	27	2564	2	1	2	Italy
T M S Schumacher	20	1	1	0	7	0	0	-	Brazil
Christian Tiboni	19	8	2	0	24	0	0	-	Italy
Jani Virtanen	19	1	1	0	1	0	0	-	Finland

TEAM OF THE SEASON

G Morgan De Sanctis CG: 35 DR: 63

D Cesare Natali CG: 31 DR: 71
D Andrea Dossena CG: 19 DR: 65
D Cristian Eduardo Zapata CG: 35 DR: 61
D Marco Motta CG: 13 DR: 58

M Sulley Ali Muntari CG: 26 SD: 18
M Giampiero Pinzi CG: 31 SD: -1
M Christian Obodo CG: 27 SD: -2
M Damiano Zenoni CG: 20 SD: -3

F Vincenzo Iaquinta CG: 27 SR: 183
F Gyan Asamoah CG: 13 SR: 193

MONTHLY POINTS TALLY

Month	Points	%
SEPTEMBER	7	58%
OCTOBER	6	40%
NOVEMBER	3	25%
DECEMBER	7	47%
JANUARY	6	67%
FEBRUARY	3	25%
MARCH	3	33%
APRIL	8	44%
MAY	3	25%

LEAGUE GOALS

	PLAYER	MINS	GOALS	S RATE
1	Iaquinta	2564	14	183
2	Di Natale	2552	11	232
3	Asamoah	1544	8	193
4	Obodo	2545	5	509
5	B De Souza	1356	4	339
6	Muntari	2343	3	781
7	Sivok	512	1	512
8	De Martino	648	1	648
9	Felipe Dal Belo	994	1	994
10	Pinzi	2801	1	2801
11	Rinaldi	0	0	
12	Schumacher	7	0	
13	Sciarrone	0	0	
	Other		0	
	TOTAL		**49**	

TOP POINT EARNERS

	PLAYER	GAMES	AV PTS
1	Sulley Ali Muntari	27	1.52
2	Damiano Zenoni	20	1.45
3	Andrea Dossena	19	1.42
4	Antonio Di Natale	27	1.33
5	Morgan De Sanctis	35	1.31
6	Gyan Asamoah	13	1.31
7	Giampiero Pinzi	31	1.29
8	Andrea Coda	22	1.27
9	Christian Obodo	27	1.22
10	Vincenzo Iaquinta	27	1.19
	CLUB AVERAGE:		**1.21**

DISCIPLINARY RECORDS

	PLAYER	YELLOW	RED	AVE
1	Raffaele De Martino	5	1	108
2	Sulley Ali Muntari	9	3	195
3	Giampiero Pinzi	14	0	200
4	Felipe Dal Belo	3	1	248
5	Tomas Zapotocny	3	0	260
6	Cesare Natali	10	0	279
7	Andrea Coda	5	1	325
8	Gaetano D'Agostino	3	1	353
9	C Eduardo Zapata	8	0	394
10	Antonio Di Natale	4	2	425
11	Damiano Zenoni	4	0	450
12	P V B De Souza	3	0	452
13	Andrea Dossena	3	1	460
	Other	12	2	
	TOTAL	**86**	**12**	

KEY GOALKEEPER

Morgan De Sanctis

Goals Conceded in the League	50	Counting Games League games when player was on pitch for at least 70 minutes	35
Defensive Rating Ave number of mins between League goals conceded while on the pitch	63	Clean Sheets In League games when player was on pitch for at least 70 minutes	9

KEY PLAYERS - DEFENDERS

Cesare Natali

Goals Conceded Number of League goals conceded while the player was on the pitch	39	Clean Sheets In League games when player was on pitch for at least 70 minutes	7
Defensive Rating Ave number of mins between League goals conceded while on the pitch	71	Club Defensive Rating Average number of mins between League goals conceded by the club this season	63

	PLAYER	CON LGE	CLEAN SHEETS	DEF RATE
1	Cesare Natali	39	7	71 mins
2	Andrea Dossena	28	5	65 mins
3	Cristian Eduardo Zapata	51	8	61 mins
4	Marco Motta	21	2	58 mins

KEY PLAYERS - MIDFIELDERS

Sulley Ali Muntari

Goals in the League	3	Contribution to Attacking Power Average number of minutes between League team goals while on pitch	53
Defensive Rating Average number of mins between League goals conceded while on the pitch	71	Scoring Difference Defensive Rating minus Contribution to Attacking Power	18

	PLAYER	LGE GOALS	DEF RATE	POWER	SCORE DIFF
1	Sulley Ali Muntari	3	71	53	18 mins
2	Giampiero Pinzi	1	70	71	-1 mins
3	Christian Obodo	5	72	74	-2 mins
4	Damiano Zenoni	0	75	78	-3 mins

KEY PLAYERS - GOALSCORERS

Vincenzo Iaquinta

Goals in the League	14	Player Strike Rate Average number of minutes between League goals scored by player	183
Contribution to Attacking Power Average number of minutes between League team goals while on pitch	80	Club Strike Rate Average number of minutes between League goals scored by club	71

	PLAYER	LGE GOALS	POWER	STRIKE RATE
1	Vincenzo Iaquinta	14	80	183 mins
2	Gyan Asamoah	8	59	193 mins
3	Antonio Di Natale	11	63	232 mins
4	Christian Obodo	5	74	509 mins

Vincenzo Iaquinta

SQUAD APPEARANCES

Match	1	2	3	4	5	6	7	8	9	10	11	12	13	14	15	16	17	18	19	20	21	22	23	24	25	26	27	28	29	30	31	32	33	34	35	36	37	38
Venue	A	H	A	H	H	A	H	A	H	A	A	H	A	H	A	H	A	H	A	H	A	A	A	H	A	H	A	H	H	A	H	H	A	H	A	H	A	H
Competition	L	L	L	L	L	L	L	L	L	L	L	L	L	L	L	L	L	L	L	L	L	L	L	L	L	L	L	L	L	L	L	L	L	L	L	L	L	L
Result	L	W	D	W	D	W	D	D	L	L	L	W	L	D	L	W	W	L	L	W	W	L	D	D	D	L	L	W	L	D	W	W	D	L	L	L	W	L

Goalkeepers
Fabrizio Casazza
Morgan De Sanctis
Gabriele Paoletti

Defenders
Andrea Coda
Andrea Dossena
Felipe Dal Belo
Massimo Gotti
Aleksandar Lukovic
Marco Motta
Cesare Natali
C Eduardo Zapata
Tomas Zapotocny

Midfielders
Gaetano D'Agostino
Raffaele De Martino
Roman Eremenko
Jose Montiel
Sulley Ali Muntari
Christian Obodo
Giampiero Pinzi
Guilherme Siqueira
Tomas Sivok
Damiano Zenoni

Forwards
Gyan Asamoah
Vitor B De Souza
Antonio Di Natale
Federico Gerardi
Vincenzo Iaquinta
M S Schumacher
Christian Tiboni
Claudio David Vargas
Jani Virtanen

KEY:
- ■ On all match
- ◄◄ Subbed or sent off (Counting game)
- ►► Subbed on from bench (Counting Game)
- ►► Subbed on and then subbed or sent off (Counting Game)
- ☐ Not in 16
- ■ On bench
- ◄◄ Subbed or sent off (playing less than 70 minutes)
- ►► Subbed on (playing less than 70 minutes)
- ►► Subbed on and then subbed or sent off (playing less than 70 minutes)

ITALY - UDINESE

LIVORNO

Final Position: **11th**

NICKNAME: AMARANTO   KEY: ☐ Won ☐ Drawn ☐ Lost   Attendance

#		Opponent			Result	Scorers	Attendance
1	itpr1	Roma	A	L	0-2		38,529
2	ucrl1	Pasching	H	W	2-0	Danilevicus 42, C.Lucarelli 48	7,600
3	itpr1	Fiorentina	H	W	1-0	C.Lucarelli 56	10,964
4	itpr1	Cagliari	A	D	2-2	Bakayoko 8, Danilevicus 61 pen	10,000
5	itpr1	AC Milan	H	D	0-0		17,000
6	ucrl2	Pasching	A	W	1-0	Bakayoko 55	4,100
7	itpr1	Messina	A	W	1-0	Danilevicus 76	18,000
8	itpr1	Ascoli	A	W	2-0	Danilevicus 24, A.Filippini 63	7,078
9	ucgpa	Rangers	H	L	2-3	C.Lucarelli 33 pen, 89	13,200
10	itpr1	Siena	H	D	0-0		8,646
11	itpr1	Inter Milan	A	L	1-4	C.Lucarelli 70	39,057
12	itpr1	Empoli	H	D	0-0		8,379
13	ucgpa	Partizan	A	D	1-1	Amelia 88	12,170
14	itpr1	Udinese	H	W	1-0	Bakayoko 73	7,500
15	itpr1	Catania	A	L	2-3	Bakayoko 45, Pantanelli 60	19,000
16	itpr1	Parma	H	W	3-0	Pfertzel 26, Ferronetti 71 og, C.Lucarelli	827,445
17	itpr1	Reggina	A	D	2-2	Galante 23, C.Lucarelli 27	10,000
18	ucgpa	Maccabi Haifa	H	D	1-1	C.Lucarelli 20	7,874
19	itpr1	Chievo	H	L	0-2		7,500
20	itpr1	Palermo	A	L	0-3		20,000
21	ucgpa	Auxerre	A	W	1-0	C.Lucarelli 59	8,000
22	itpr1	Lazio	H	D	1-1	C.Lucarelli 65	9,000
23	itpr1	Sampdoria	A	L	1-4	Vigiani 12	25,000
24	itpr1	Torino	H	D	1-1	C.Lucarelli 61	8,000
25	itpr1	Atalanta	A	L	1-5	Pfertzel 52	13,000
26	itpr1	Roma	H	D	1-1	C.Lucarelli 22 pen	9,000
27	itpr1	Fiorentina	A	L	1-2	C.Lucarelli 27	30,000
28	itpr1	AC Milan	A	L	1-2	C.Lucarelli 31	21,694
29	ucrl1	Espanyol	H	L	1-2	Galante 82	18,200
30	itpr1	Messina	H	W	2-1	Fiore 26, C.Lucarelli 69	0
31	ucrl2	Espanyol	A	L	0-2		10,000
32	itpr1	Ascoli	H	D	0-0		5,641
33	itpr1	Siena	A	D	0-0		7,000
34	itpr1	Inter Milan	H	L	1-2	C.Lucarelli 27	5,641
35	itpr1	Empoli	A	D	2-2	Rezaei 58, C.Lucarelli 90	4,925
36	itpr1	Udinese	A	L	0-4		13,652
37	itpr1	Catania	H	W	4-1	C.Lucarelli 20, 83 pen, 90, Fiore 45	5,641
38	itpr1	Parma	A	L	0-1		13,080
39	itpr1	Reggina	H	D	1-1	C.Lucarelli 28	8,643
40	itpr1	Cagliari	H	W	2-1	C.Lucarelli 5, Knezevic 67	5,500
41	itpr1	Chievo	A	L	1-2	C.Lucarelli 18	5,433
42	itpr1	Palermo	H	L	1-2	AR.Cesar 57 pen	7,750
43	itpr1	Lazio	A	L	0-1		14,809
44	itpr1	Sampdoria	H	W	1-0	A.Filippini 72	13,209
45	itpr1	Torino	A	D	0-0		22,036
46	itpr1	Atalanta	H	W	4-2	C.Lucarelli 45, 57, Morrone 47, Paulinho Betanin 83	8,587

LEAGUE APPEARANCES, BOOKINGS AND CAPS

	AGE (on 01/07/07)	IN NAMED 18	APPEARANCES	COUNTING GAMES	MINUTES ON PITCH	YELLOW CARDS	RED CARDS	CAPS THIS SEASON	NATIONAL SIDE
Goalkeepers									
Marco Amelia	25	31	30	30	2700	3	0	2	Italy
Emanuele Manitta	30	35	8	8	720	0	0	-	Italy
Defenders									
Stefano Argilli	34	8	2	0	81	0	0	-	Italy
David Balleri	38	33	25	11	1322	6	0	-	Italy
Cesar Luis Prates	32	9	4	1	168	1	0	-	Brazil
A Rodrigues Cesar	32	15	9	3	457	2	2	-	Brazil
Fabio Galante	33	35	32	28	2669	5	0	-	Italy
Alessandro Grandoni	29	37	34	33	3020	6	0	-	Italy
Dario Knezevic	25	20	11	7	742	0	0	-	Croatia
Samuel Osei Kuffour	30	27	18	16	1548	7	0	-	Ghana
Giovanni Pasquale	25	34	31	27	2498	10	3	-	Italy
Simone Pavan	33	19	13	11	1071	3	0	-	Italy
Marc Pfertzel	26	34	30	17	1929	4	0	-	France
Midfielders									
Martin Bergvold	23	8	5	0	127	0	0	-	Denmark
Carmine Coppola	28	16	11	2	506	3	1	-	Italy
Antonio Filippini	33	36	35	34	3062	10	0	-	Italy
Stefano Fiore	32	17	17	13	1324	0	0	-	Italy
Stefano Morrone	28	37	37	33	3044	8	0	-	Italy
Dario Passoni	33	32	32	29	2734	11	1	-	Italy
Rahman Rezaei	32	24	16	12	1185	3	0	2	Iran
Jose Luis Vidigal	34	32	18	4	587	5	0	-	Portugal
Luca Vigiani	30	19	14	9	937	0	0	-	Italy
Forwards									
Ibrahim Bakayoko	30	18	16	8	904	1	0	-	Ivory Coast
Tomas Danilevicus	28	17	13	3	520	1	0	-	Lithuania
Cristiano Lucarelli	31	35	34	27	2671	5	0	2	Italy
P Sergio P Betanin	21	34	19	6	967	2	0	-	Brazil

TEAM OF THE SEASON

D Fabio Galante CG: 28 DR: 72
M Stefano Fiore CG: 13 SD: 0
D Giovanni Pasquale CG: 27 DR: 67
M Dario Passoni CG: 29 SD: -10
F Cristiano Lucarelli CG: 27 SR: 133
G Marco Amelia CG: 30 DR: 58
D Alessandro Grandoni CG: 33 DR: 65
M Antonio Filippini CG: 34 SD: -20
F Ibrahim Bakayoko* CG: 8 SR: 301
D Marc Pfertzel CG: 17 DR: 58
M Stefano Morrone CG: 33 SD: -23

MONTHLY POINTS TALLY

Month	Points	%
SEPTEMBER	5	42%
OCTOBER	8	53%
NOVEMBER	7	58%
DECEMBER	2	13%
JANUARY	1	11%
FEBRUARY	5	42%
MARCH	1	11%
APRIL	7	39%
MAY	7	58%

LEAGUE GOALS

	PLAYER	MINS	GOALS	S RATE
1	Lucarelli, C	2671	20	133
2	Danilevicus	520	3	173
3	Bakayoko	904	3	301
4	Fiore	1324	2	662
5	Pfertzel	1929	2	964
6	Filippini, A	3062	2	1531
7	Cesar, AR	457	1	457
8	Knezevic	742	1	742
9	Vigiani	937	1	937
10	Paulinho Betanin	967	1	967
11	Rezaei	1185	1	1185
12	Galante	2669	1	2669
13	Morrone	3044	1	3044
	Other		0	
	TOTAL		**39**	

TOP POINT EARNERS

	PLAYER	GAMES	AV PTS
1	Stefano Fiore	12	1.33
2	Fabio Galante	28	1.29
3	Antonio Filippini	34	1.21
4	Giovanni Pasquale	25	1.20
5	Dario Passoni	29	1.17
6	Rahman Rezaei	12	1.17
7	Marco Amelia	30	1.17
8	Stefano Morrone	33	1.12
9	Alessandro Grandoni	33	1.12
10	Cristiano Lucarelli	27	1.04
	CLUB AVERAGE:		**1.13**

DISCIPLINARY RECORDS

	PLAYER	YELLOW	RED	AVE
1	Carmine Coppola	3	1	126
2	Giovanni Pasquale	10	3	208
3	David Balleri	6	0	220
4	A Rodrigues Cesar	2	2	228
5	Dario Passoni	11	1	248
6	Jose Luis Vidigal	5	0	293
7	Samuel Osei Kuffour	7	0	309
8	Simone Pavan	3	0	357
9	Antonio Filippini	10	0	382
10	P S Paulinho Betanin	2	0	483
11	Stefano Morrone	8	0	507
12	Tomas Danilevicus	1	0	520
13	Rahman Rezaei	3	0	592
	Other	24	0	
	TOTAL	**95**	**7**	

KEY GOALKEEPER

Marco Amelia

Goals Conceded in the League	46	Counting Games League games when player was on pitch for at least 70 minutes	30
Defensive Rating Ave number of mins between League goals conceded while on the pitch	58	Clean Sheets In League games when player was on pitch for at least 70 minutes	10

KEY PLAYERS - DEFENDERS

Fabio Galante

Goals Conceded Number of League goals conceded while the player was on the pitch	37	Clean Sheets In League games when player was on pitch for at least 70 minutes	11
Defensive Rating Ave number of mins between League goals conceded while on the pitch	72	Club Defensive Rating Average number of mins between League goals conceded by the club this season	65

	PLAYER	CON LGE	CLEAN SHEETS	DEF RATE
1	Fabio Galante	37	11	72 mins
2	Giovanni Pasquale	37	8	67 mins
3	Alessandro Grandoni	46	12	65 mins
4	Marc Pfertzel	33	6	58 mins

KEY PLAYERS - MIDFIELDERS

Stefano Fiore

Goals in the League	2	Contribution to Attacking Power Average number of minutes between League team goals while on pitch	73
Defensive Rating Average number of mins between League goals conceded while on the pitch	73	Scoring Difference Defensive Rating minus Contribution to Attacking Power	0

	PLAYER	LGE GOALS	DEF RATE	POWER	SCORE DIFF
1	Stefano Fiore	2	73	73	0 mins
2	Dario Passoni	0	70	80	-10 mins
3	Antonio Filippini	2	65	85	-20 mins
4	Stefano Morrone	1	59	82	-23 mins

KEY PLAYERS - GOALSCORERS

Cristiano Lucarelli

Goals in the League	20	Player Strike Rate Average number of minutes between League goals scored by player	133
Contribution to Attacking Power Average number of minutes between League team goals while on pitch	86	Club Strike Rate Average number of minutes between League goals scored by club	85

	PLAYER	LGE GOALS	POWER	STRIKE RATE
1	Cristiano Lucarelli	20	86	133 mins
2	Ibrahim Bakayoko	3	64	301 mins
3	Stefano Fiore	2	73	662 mins
4	Luca Vigiani	1	104	937 mins

Cristiano Lucarelli

SQUAD APPEARANCES

Match	1	2	3	4	5	6	7	8	9	10	11	12	13	14	15	16	17	18	19	20	21	22	23	24	25	26	27	28	29	30	31	32	33	34	35	36	37	38	39	40	41	42	43	44	45	46
Venue	A	H	H	A	H	A	A	A	H	H	A	H	A	H	A	H	A	H	H	H	A	H	A	H	A	H	A	A	H	H	A	H	A	H	A	A	H	A	H	H	A	H	A	H	A	H
Competition	L	E	L	L	L	E	L	L	E	L	L	L	E	L	L	L	L	E	L	L	E	L	L	L	L	L	L	L	E	L	E	L	L	L	L	L	L	L	L	L	L	L	L	L	L	L
Result	L	W	W	D	D	W	W	W	L	D	L	D	D	W	L	W	D	D	L	L	W	D	L	D	L	D	L	L	L	W	L	D	D	L	D	L	W	L	D	W	L	L	L	W	D	W

Goalkeepers
Marco Amelia
Emanuele Manitta

Defenders
Stefano Argilli
David Balleri
Cesar Luis Prates
A Rodrigues Cesar
Fabio Galante
Alessandro Grandoni
Dario Knezevic
Samuel Osei Kuffour
Giovanni Pasquale
Simone Pavan
Marc Pfertzel

Midfielders
Martin Bergvold
Carmine Coppola
Antonio Filippini
Stefano Fiore
Stefano Morrone
Dario Passoni
Rahman Rezaei
Jose Luis Vidigal
Luca Vigiani

Forwards
Ibrahim Bakayoko
Tomas Danilevicus
Cristiano Lucarelli
Sergio P Betanin

KEY: On all match — Subbed or sent off (Counting game) — Subbed on from bench (Counting Game) — Subbed on and then subbed or sent off (Counting Game) — Not in 16
On bench — Subbed or sent off (playing less than 70 minutes) — Subbed on (playing less than 70 minutes) — Subbed on and then subbed or sent off (playing less than 70 minutes)

PARMA

Final Position: **12th**

NICKNAME: CROCIATI   KEY: ☐ Won ☐ Drawn ☐ Lost   Attendance

#		Opponent		Result	Scorers	Attendance
1	itpr1	Torino	A D	1-1	Budan 55	23,000
2	ucrl1	Rubin Kazan	A W	1-0	Dessena 79	10,000
3	itpr1	AC Milan	H L	0-2		18,617
4	itpr1	Fiorentina	A L	0-1		28,445
5	itpr1	Roma	H L	0-4		15,495
6	ucrl2	Rubin Kazan	H W	1-0	Paponi 49	2,501
7	itpr1	Sampdoria	A L	2-3	Dessena 4, Contini 78 pen	19,000
8	itpr1	Udinese	H L	0-3		12,250
9	ucgpd	Odense	A W	2-1	Dessena 40, Budan 50	12,559
10	itpr1	Ascoli	H W	1-0	Budan 10	12,814
11	itpr1	Reggina	A L	2-3	Budan 39, Gasbarroni 84	15,000
12	itpr1	Atalanta	H W	3-1	Budan 1, Grella 70 pen, Muslimovic 87	14,637
13	itpr1	Siena	A D	2-2	Morfeo 35, Bucci 70	8,000
14	itpr1	Inter Milan	H L	1-2	Budan 26	18,000
15	itpr1	Livorno	A L	0-1		7,445
16	ucgpd	Heerenveen	H W	2-1	Budan 24, 73	3,632
17	itpr1	Catania	A L	0-2		18,000
18	ucgpd	Lens	A W	2-1	Dedic 77, Paponi 90	32,341
19	itpr1	Palermo	H D	0-0		15,000
20	itpr1	Cagliari	A D	0-0		10,000
21	ucgpd	Osasuna	H L	0-3		3,109
22	itpr1	Chievo	H D	2-2	Budan 25, Dessena 57	15,000
23	itpr1	Messina	A D	1-1	Paponi 77	15,000
24	itpr1	Lazio	H L	1-3	Budan 19	15,000
25	itpr1	Empoli	A L	0-1		5,000
26	itpr1	Torino	H W	1-0	Rossi 74	13,000
27	itpr1	AC Milan	A L	0-1		44,000
28	itpr1	Roma	A L	0-3		28,216
29	ucrl1	Braga	A L	0-1		6,127
30	itpr1	Sampdoria	H L	0-1		14,501
31	ucrl2	Braga	H L	0-1		3,861
32	itpr1	Udinese	A D	3-3	Budan 8, Parravicini 78, Rossi 86 pen	13,652
33	itpr1	Ascoli	A D	0-0		4,800
34	itpr1	Reggina	H D	2-2	Budan 22, G.Rossi 90	13,500
35	itpr1	Atalanta	A D	1-1	Coly 87	8,092
36	itpr1	Siena	H W	1-0	Gasbarroni 17	12,777
37	itpr1	Inter Milan	A L	0-2		48,888
38	itpr1	Livorno	H W	1-0	G.Rossi 90	13,080
39	itpr1	Catania	H D	1-1	Couto 32	13,427
40	itpr1	Fiorentina	H W	2-0	G.Rossi 26, 89 pen	13,000
41	itpr1	Palermo	A W	4-3	Budan 25, Couto 47, Gasbarroni 72, G.Rossi 81	21,472
42	itpr1	Cagliari	H W	2-1	Budan 28, Gasbarroni 77 pen	14,225
43	itpr1	Chievo	A L	0-1		11,934
44	itpr1	Messina	H W	4-1	G.Rossi 23, 31, Muslimovic 29, Gasbarroni 34	13,833
45	itpr1	Lazio	A D	0-0		37,914
46	itpr1	Empoli	H W	3-1	Muslimovic 9, Budan 16, Gasbarroni 88	16,449

LEAGUE APPEARANCES, BOOKINGS AND CAPS

	AGE (on 01/07/07)	IN NAMED 18	APPEARANCES	COUNTING GAMES	MINUTES ON PITCH	YELLOW CARDS	RED CARDS	CAPS THIS SEASON	NATIONAL SIDE
Goalkeepers									
Luca Bucci	38	30	26	25	2317	3	0	-	Italy
Alfonso De Lucia	23	36	13	12	1103	3	0	-	Italy
Defenders									
Antonio Bocchetti	27	29	17	6	846	3	0	-	Italy
Giuseppe Cardone	33	8	5	2	236	1	0	-	Italy
Paoli Castellini	28	38	33	28	2725	3	0	-	Italy
Ferdinand Coly	33	34	27	23	2210	8	1	-	Senegal
Matteo Contini	27	30	28	27	2430	11	1	-	Italy
Fernando Couto	37	23	23	20	1908	11	1	-	Portugal
Damiano Ferronetti	22	28	16	11	1190	4	0	-	Italy
Massimo Paci	29	30	24	22	1993	4	0	-	Italy
Armando Perna	26	11	6	6	519	2	0	-	Italy
Marco Rossi	19	11	4	3	307	3	0	-	Italy
Midfielders									
Jorge Bolano	30	28	10	4	486	2	0	-	Colombia
Maurizio Ciaramitaro	25	18	17	12	1272	4	0	-	Italy
Luca Cigarini	21	36	21	13	1371	5	0	-	Italy
Daniele Dessena	20	36	34	23	2308	12	0	-	Italy
Andrea Gasbarroni	25	32	28	14	1652	4	0	-	Italy
Vincenzo Grella	27	27	26	20	1949	8	1	4	Australia
Domenico Morfeo	31	25	23	12	1355	3	1	-	Italy
Francesco Parravicini	25	16	16	14	1327	2	0	-	Italy
Forwards									
Igor Budan	27	35	35	23	2704	5	1	-	Croatia
Zlatko Dedic	23	6	6	0	107	2	0	-	Bosnia
Vitaly Kutuzov	27	12	9	0	316	1	0	4	Belarus
Zlatan Muslimovic	26	30	28	14	1648	0	0	6	Bosnia
Daniele Paponi	19	18	11	0	331	1	0	-	Italy
Andrea Pisanu	25	22	20	12	1336	6	0	-	Italy
Giuseppe Rossi	20	19	19	14	1520	3	0	-	Italy

TEAM OF THE SEASON

Alfonso De Lucia G — CG: 12 DR: 42

Fernando Couto D — CG: 20 DR: 76
Massimo Paci D — CG: 22 DR: 68
Ferdinand Coly D — CG: 23 DR: 63
Paoli Castellini D — CG: 28 DR: 63

Francesco Parravicini M — CG: 14 SD: 16
Domenico Morfeo M — CG: 12 SD: -8
Vincenzo Grella M — CG: 20 SD: -14
Daniele Dessena M — CG: 23 SD: -16

Giuseppe Rossi F — CG: 14 SR: 168
Igor Budan F — CG: 23 SR: 225

MONTHLY POINTS TALLY

Month		Points	%
SEPTEMBER		1	8%
OCTOBER		6	40%
NOVEMBER		1	8%
DECEMBER		4	27%
JANUARY		3	33%
FEBRUARY		2	17%
MARCH		5	56%
APRIL		13	72%
MAY		7	58%

LEAGUE GOALS

	PLAYER	MINS	GOALS	S RATE
1	Budan	2704	12	225
2	Rossi, G.	1520	9	168
3	Gasbarroni	1652	6	275
4	Muslimovic	1648	3	549
5	Couto	1908	2	954
6	Dessena	2308	2	1154
7	Paponi	331	1	331
8	Parravicini	1327	1	1327
9	Morfeo	1355	1	1355
10	Grella	1949	1	1949
11	Coly	2210	1	2210
12	Contini	2430	1	2430
13	Bocchetti	846	0	
	Other		0	
	TOTAL		**40**	

TOP POINT EARNERS

	PLAYER	GAMES	AV PTS
1	Francesco Parravicini	13	1.62
2	Luca Cigarini	13	1.54
3	Luca Bucci	25	1.36
4	Giuseppe Rossi, G.	14	1.36
5	Ferdinand Coly	24	1.33
6	Fernando Couto	20	1.30
7	Daniele Dessena	22	1.23
8	Paoli Castellini	28	1.21
9	Massimo Paci	22	1.14
10	Andrea Gasbarroni	12	1.08
	CLUB AVERAGE:		**1.11**

DISCIPLINARY RECORDS

	PLAYER	YELLOW	RED	AVE
1	Fernando Couto	11	1	190
2	Daniele Dessena	12	0	209
3	Vincenzo Grella	8	1	216
4	Matteo Contini	11	1	220
5	Jorge Bolano	2	0	243
6	Ferdinand Coly	8	1	245
7	Armando Perna	2	0	259
8	Andrea Pisanu	6	0	267
9	Antonio Bocchetti	3	0	282
10	Maurizio Ciaramitaro	4	0	318
11	Domenico Morfeo	3	1	338
12	Luca Cigarini	5	0	342
13	Alfonso De Lucia	3	0	367
	Other	28	1	
	TOTAL	**106**	**6**	

KEY GOALKEEPER

Alfonso De Lucia

Goals Conceded in the League	26	Counting Games League games when player was on pitch for at least 70 minutes	12
Defensive Rating Ave number of mins between League goals conceded while on the pitch	42	Clean Sheets In League games when player was on pitch for at least 70 minutes	1

KEY PLAYERS - DEFENDERS

Fernando Couto

Goals Conceded Number of League goals conceded while the player was on the pitch	25	Clean Sheets In League games when player was on pitch for at least 70 minutes	8
Defensive Rating Ave number of mins between League goals conceded while on the pitch	76	Club Defensive Rating Average number of minutes between League goals conceded by the club this season	62

	PLAYER	CON LGE	CLEAN SHEETS	DEF RATE
1	Fernando Couto	25	8	76 mins
2	Massimo Paci	29	5	68 mins
3	Ferdinand Coly	35	6	63 mins
4	Paoli Castellini	43	7	63 mins

KEY PLAYERS - MIDFIELDERS

Francesco Parravicini

Goals in the League	1	Contribution to Attacking Power Average number of minutes between League team goals while on pitch	66
Defensive Rating Average number of mins between League goals conceded while on the pitch	82	Scoring Difference Defensive Rating minus Contribution to Attacking Power	16

	PLAYER	LGE GOALS	DEF RATE	POWER	SCORE DIFF
1	Francesco Parravicini	1	82	66	16 mins
2	Domenico Morfeo	1	67	75	-8 mins
3	Vincenzo Grella	1	67	81	-14 mins
4	Daniele Dessena	2	60	76	-16 mins

KEY PLAYERS - GOALSCORERS

Giuseppe Rossi

Goals in the League	9	Player Strike Rate Average number of minutes between League goals scored by player	168
Contribution to Attacking Power Average number of minutes between League team goals while on pitch	69	Club Strike Rate Average number of minutes between League goals scored by club	85

	PLAYER	LGE GOALS	POWER	STRIKE RATE
1	Giuseppe Rossi	9	69	168 mins
2	Igor Budan	12	75	225 mins
3	Andrea Gasbarroni	6	82	275 mins
4	Zlatan Muslimovic	3	74	549 mins

Zlatko Dedic and Igor Budan

SQUAD APPEARANCES

Match	1 2 3 4 5	6 7 8 9 10	11 12 13 14 15	16 17 18 19 20	21 22 23 24 25	26 27 28 29 30	31 32 33 34 35	36 37 38 39 40	41 42 43 44 45	46
Venue	A A H A H	H A H A H	A H A H A	H A A H A	H H A H A	H A A A H	H A A H A	H A H H H	A H A H A	H
Competition	L E L L L	E L L E L	L L L L L	E L E L L	E L L L L	L L L E L	E L L L L	L L L L L	L L L L L	L
Result	D W L L L	W L L W W	L W D L L	W L W D D	L D D L L	W L L L L	L D D D D	W L W D W	W W L W D	W

Goalkeepers

Luca Bucci
Alfonso De Lucia

Defenders

Antonio Bocchetti
Giuseppe Cardone
Paoli Castellini
Ferdinand Coly
Matteo Contini
Fernando Couto
Damiano Ferronetti
Massimo Paci
Armando Perna
Marco Rossi

Midfielders

Jorge Bolano
Maurizio Ciaramitaro
Luca Cigarini
Daniele Dessena
Andrea Gasbarroni
Vincenzo Grella
Domenico Morfeo
Francesco Parravicini

Forwards

Igor Budan
Zlatko Dedic
Vitaly Kutuzov
Zlatan Muslimovic
Daniele Paponi
Andrea Pisanu
Giuseppe Rossi

KEY: ■ On all match   ⊷ Subbed or sent off (Counting game)   ⊷ Subbed on from bench (Counting Game)   ⊷ Subbed on and then subbed or sent off (Counting Game)   ☐ Not in 16
    ☐ On bench   ⊷ Subbed or sent off (playing less than 70 minutes)   ⊷ Subbed on (playing less than 70 minutes)   ⊷ Subbed on and then subbed or sent off (playing less than 70 minutes)

ITALY - PARMA

CATANIA

Final Position: 13th

NICKNAME: ROSSAZZURRI

KEY: ☐ Won ☐ Drawn ☐ Lost   Attendance

#		Opponent			Result	Scorers	Attendance
1	itpr1	Cagliari	A	W	1-0	Corona 55	15,000
2	itpr1	Atalanta	H	D	0-0		18,400
3	itpr1	Palermo	A	L	3-5	Corona 26, Mascara 64, Spinesi 90	34,261
4	itpr1	Messina	H	D	2-2	Mascara 58, Spinesi 61	19,029
5	itpr1	Fiorentina	A	L	0-3		30,000
6	itpr1	Inter Milan	A	L	1-2	Mascara 16	47,505
7	itpr1	Lazio	H	W	3-1	Colucci 36, 53, Spinesi 45	0
8	itpr1	Siena	A	D	1-1	Corona 90	6,500
9	itpr1	Torino	H	D	1-1	Spinesi 20	0
10	itpr1	Reggina	A	W	1-0	Corona 69	10,000
11	itpr1	Livorno	H	W	3-2	Spinesi 35, Caserta 61, Corona 90	19,000
12	itpr1	Roma	A	L	0-7		32,000
13	itpr1	Parma	H	W	2-0	Spinesi 67 pen, Caserta 84	18,000
14	itpr1	Ascoli	A	D	2-2	Stovini 53, Spinesi 90	7,000
15	itpr1	Udinese	H	W	1-0	Spinesi 68	19,000
16	itpr1	AC Milan	A	L	0-3		55,000
17	itpr1	Sampdoria	H	W	4-2	Spinesi 7, 45 pen, 88, Caserta 37	17,000
18	itpr1	Chievo	A	L	1-2	Stovini 37	6,409
19	itpr1	Cagliari	H	L	0-1		18,000
20	itpr1	Empoli	H	W	2-1	Caserta 52, Mascara 61	15,000
21	itpr1	Atalanta	A	D	1-1	Morimoto 88	12,000
22	itpr1	Palermo	H	L	1-2	Caserta 59	15,000
23	itpr1	Messina	A	D	1-1	Mascara 60	0
24	itpr1	Fiorentina	H	L	0-1		0
25	itpr1	Inter Milan	H	L	2-5	Spinesi 65, Corona 74	0
26	itpr1	Lazio	A	L	1-3	Colucci 17	20,000
27	itpr1	Siena	H	D	1-1	Corona 56	0
28	itpr1	Torino	A	L	0-1		19,777
29	itpr1	Reggina	H	L	1-4	Rossini 90	0
30	itpr1	Livorno	A	L	1-4	Sottil 14	5,641
31	itpr1	Roma	H	L	0-2		0
32	itpr1	Parma	A	D	1-1	Spinesi 20	13,427
33	itpr1	Udinese	A	W	1-0	Spinesi 52 pen	13,652
34	itpr1	Ascoli	H	D	3-3	Mascara 21, Caserta 69, Spinesi 76 pen	0
35	itpr1	Empoli	A	L	1-2	Spinesi 28	4,345
36	itpr1	AC Milan	H	D	1-1	Spinesi 61	4,000
37	itpr1	Sampdoria	A	L	0-1		17,303
38	itpr1	Chievo	H	W	2-0	Rossini 66, Minelli 80	18,207

LEAGUE APPEARANCES, BOOKINGS AND CAPS

	AGE (on 01/07/07)	IN NAMED 18	APPEARANCES	COUNTING GAMES	MINUTES ON PITCH	YELLOW CARDS	RED CARDS	CAPS THIS SEASON	NATIONAL SIDE
Goalkeepers									
Armando Pantanelli	36	37	37	37	3330	3	0	-	Italy
Ciro Polito	28	18	1	1	90	0	0	-	Italy
Defenders									
Vi C de Luca Cesar	28	17	8	6	615	3	0	-	Brazil
Gianluca Falsini	31	8	5	4	390	1	0	-	Italy
Giorgio Lucenti	31	28	24	14	1480	4	0	-	Italy
Mauro Minelli	26	32	10	5	550	1	1	-	Italy
Gennaro Sardo	28	33	17	10	1073	6	0	-	Italy
Cristian Silvestri	32	32	25	20	1894	3	1	-	Italy
Andrea Sottil	33	33	29	29	2610	8	0	-	Italy
Lorenzo Stovini	30	35	35	35	3140	7	1	-	Italy
Midfielders									
Davide Baiocco	32	33	33	32	2943	9	2	-	Italy
Marco Biagianti	23	3	2	0	57	0	0	-	Italy
Mattia Biso	30	21	15	4	653	5	1	-	Italy
Fabio Caserta	28	35	35	34	3035	9	0	-	Italy
Giuseppe Colucci	26	27	24	18	1771	6	0	-	Italy
Mark Edusei	30	33	31	29	2602	8	0	-	Ghana
Mariano Julio Izco	24	32	18	10	1020	2	0	-	Argentina
Francesco Millesi	26	28	9	1	274	0	0	-	Italy
Jorge Vargas	31	35	33	28	2639	6	0	-	Chile
Forwards									
Giorgio Corona	33	36	31	15	1692	3	0	-	Italy
Umberto Del Core	27	14	11	2	253	0	0	-	Italy
Guiseppe Mascara	27	28	28	23	2265	5	3	-	Italy
Takayuki Morimoto	19	10	5	0	58	0	0	-	Japan
Fausto Rossini	29	19	15	1	325	2	0	-	Italy
Gianatha Spinesi	29	33	32	26	2582	4	1	-	Italy

TEAM OF THE SEASON

Position	Player	CG	DR/SD/SR
D	Cristian Silvestri	CG: 21	DR: 55
M	Giuseppe Colucci	CG: 19	SD: -15
G	Armando Pantanelli	CG: 38	DR: 50
D	Giorgio Lucenti	CG: 15	DR: 54
M	Davide Baiocco	CG: 33	SD: -24
F	Gianatha Spinesi	CG: 27	SR: 157
D	Lorenzo Stovini	CG: 36	DR: 50
M	Fabio Caserta	CG: 35	SD: -28
F	Giorgio Corona	CG: 15	SR: 241
D	Andrea Sottil	CG: 30	DR: 47
M	Jorge Vargas	CG: 28	SD: -29

MONTHLY POINTS TALLY

Month	Points	%
SEPTEMBER	5	42%
OCTOBER	5	33%
NOVEMBER	9	75%
DECEMBER	7	58%
JANUARY	4	33%
FEBRUARY	1	7%
MARCH	1	11%
APRIL	4	33%
MAY	5	33%

LEAGUE GOALS

	PLAYER	MINS	GOALS	S RATE
1	Spinesi	2672	17	157
2	Corona	1692	7	241
3	Mascara	2355	6	392
4	Caserta	3125	6	520
5	Colucci	1861	3	620
6	Rossini	325	2	162
7	Stovini	3230	2	1615
8	Morimoto	58	1	58
9	Minelli	550	1	550
10	Sottil	2700	1	2700
11	Spadavecchia	0	0	
12	Sardo	1073	0	
13	Silvestri	1984	0	
	Other		0	
	TOTAL		**46**	

TOP POINT EARNERS

	PLAYER	GAMES	AV PTS
1	Giorgio Corona	14	1.36
2	Giuseppe Colucci	18	1.28
3	Cristian Silvestri	20	1.20
4	Lorenzo Stovini	35	1.09
5	Gianatha Spinesi	26	1.08
6	Fabio Caserta	33	1.06
7	Jorge Vargas	28	1.04
8	Andrea Sottil	29	1.03
9	Davide Baiocco	33	1.03
10	Armando Pantanelli	37	1.03
	CLUB AVERAGE:		**1.08**

DISCIPLINARY RECORDS

	PLAYER	YELLOW	RED	AVE
1	Mattia Biso	5	1	108
2	Gennaro Sardo	6	0	178
3	V C de Luca Cesar	3	0	205
4	Davide Baiocco	9	2	275
5	Mauro Minelli	1	1	275
6	Guiseppe Mascara	5	3	294
7	Giuseppe Colucci	6	0	310
8	Mark Edusei	8	0	336
9	Andrea Sottil	8	0	337
10	Fabio Caserta	9	0	347
11	Giorgio Lucenti	4	0	392
12	Lorenzo Stovini	7	1	403
13	Jorge Vargas	6	0	439
	Other	15	2	
	TOTAL	**92**	**10**	

KEY GOALKEEPER

Armando Pantanelli

Goals Conceded in the League	68	Counting Games League games when player was on pitch for at least 70 minutes	38
Defensive Rating Ave number of mins between League goals conceded while on the pitch	50	Clean Sheets In League games when player was on pitch for at least 70 minutes	7

KEY PLAYERS - DEFENDERS

Cristian Silvestri

Goals Conceded Number of League goals conceded while the player was on the pitch	36	Clean Sheets In League games when player was on pitch for at least 70 minutes	5
Defensive Rating Ave number of mins between League goals conceded while on the pitch	55	Club Defensive Rating Average number of mins between League goals conceded by the club this season	51

	PLAYER	CON LGE	CLEAN SHEETS	DEF RATE
1	Cristian Silvestri	36	5	55 mins
2	Giorgio Lucenti	29	4	54 mins
3	Lorenzo Stovini	64	7	50 mins
4	Andrea Sottil	57	7	47 mins

KEY PLAYERS - MIDFIELDERS

Giuseppe Colucci

Goals in the League	3	Contribution to Attacking Power Average number of minutes between League team goals while on pitch	71
Defensive Rating Average number of mins between League goals conceded while on the pitch	56	Scoring Difference Defensive Rating minus Contribution to Attacking Power	-15

	PLAYER	LGE GOALS	DEF RATE	POWER	SCORE DIFF
1	Giuseppe Colucci	3	56	71	-15 mins
2	Davide Baiocco	0	48	72	-24 mins
3	Fabio Caserta	6	48	76	-28 mins
4	Jorge Vargas	0	46	75	-29 mins

KEY PLAYERS - GOALSCORERS

Gianatha Spinesi

Goals in the League	17	Player Strike Rate Average number of minutes between League goals scored by player	157
Contribution to Attacking Power Average number of minutes between League team goals while on pitch	74	Club Strike Rate Average number of minutes between League goals scored by club	76

	PLAYER	LGE GOALS	POWER	STRIKE RATE
1	Gianatha Spinesi	17	74	157 mins
2	Giorgio Corona	7	76	241 mins
3	Guiseppe Mascara	6	81	392 mins
4	Fabio Caserta	6	76	520 mins

Gianatha Spinesi

SQUAD APPEARANCES

Match	1	2	3	4	5	6	7	8	9	10	11	12	13	14	15	16	17	18	19	20	21	22	23	24	25	26	27	28	29	30	31	32	33	34	35	36	37	38
Venue	A	H	A	H	A	A	H	A	H	A	H	A	H	A	H	A	H	A	H	H	A	H	A	H	H	A	H	A	H	A	H	A	A	H	A	H	A	H
Competition	L	L	L	L	L	L	L	L	L	L	L	L	L	L	L	L	L	L	L	L	L	L	L	L	L	L	L	L	L	L	L	L	L	L	L	L	L	L
Result	W	D	L	D	L	L	W	D	D	W	W	L	W	D	W	L	W	L	L	W	D	L	D	L	L	L	D	L	L	L	L	D	W	D	L	D	L	W

Goalkeepers

Armando Pantanelli

Ciro Polito

Defenders

Vi C de Luca Cesar

Gianluca Falsini

Giorgio Lucenti

Mauro Minelli

Gennaro Sardo

Cristian Silvestri

Andrea Sottil

Lorenzo Stovini

Midfielders

Davide Baiocco

Marco Biagianti

Mattia Biso

Fabio Caserta

Giuseppe Colucci

Mark Edusei

Mariano Julio Izco

Francesco Millesi

Jorge Vargas

Forwards

Giorgio Corona

Umberto Del Core

Guiseppe Mascara

Takayuki Morimoto

Fausto Rossini

Gianatha Spinesi

KEY: ■ On all match ｜◄ Subbed or sent off (Counting game) ｜▸ Subbed on from bench (Counting Game) ｜▸ Subbed on and then subbed or sent off (Counting Game) ☐ Not in 16
☐ On bench ◄◄ Subbed or sent off (playing less than 70 minutes) ▸▸ Subbed on (playing less than 70 minutes) ▸▸ Subbed on and then subbed or sent off (playing less than 70 minutes)

ITALY - CATANIA

REGGINA

Final Position: **14th**

NICKNAME: AMARANTO   KEY: ☐ Won ☐ Drawn ☐ Lost   Attendance

1	itpr1	Palermo	A L	3-4 Bianchi 42, 55, 79 pen	24,500
2	itpr1	Cagliari	H W	2-1 A.Lucarelli 52, Bianchi 90	9,634
3	itpr1	Messina	A L	0-2	19,625
4	itpr1	Torino	H D	1-1 Modesto 56	9,559
5	itpr1	Atalanta	A D	1-1 Tedesco 6	13,000
6	itpr1	Roma	H W	1-0 Amoruso 49	11,719
7	itpr1	Fiorentina	A L	0-3	28,960
8	itpr1	Parma	H W	3-2 Amoruso 33, 77, Bianchi 76	15,000
9	itpr1	Lazio	A D	0-0	13,000
10	itpr1	Catania	H L	0-1	10,000
11	itpr1	Siena	A W	1-0 Bianchi 70 pen	7,000
12	itpr1	Inter Milan	A L	0-1	45,000
13	itpr1	Livorno	H D	2-2 Bianchi 63, Leon 77	10,000
14	itpr1	Udinese	A D	1-1 Bianchi 35	13,000
15	itpr1	Ascoli	H W	2-1 A.Lucarelli 29, Amoruso 78	9,000
16	itpr1	Sampdoria	H L	0-1	10,000
17	itpr1	Chievo	A L	2-3 Amoruso 17, Modesto 78	6,000
18	itpr1	Empoli	H W	4-1 Leon 4, Amoruso 8, 28, Bianchi 44	9,000
19	itpr1	AC Milan	A L	1-3 Bianchi 66	43,996
20	itpr1	Palermo	H D	0-0	13,000
21	itpr1	Cagliari	A W	2-0 Vigiani 46, Modesto 58	8,000
22	itpr1	Torino	A W	2-1 Bianchi 48, 58	18,000
23	itpr1	Atalanta	H D	1-1 Amoruso 63	7,000
24	itpr1	Roma	A L	0-3	43,000
25	itpr1	Fiorentina	H D	1-1 Foggia 57	9,000
26	itpr1	Parma	A D	2-2 Bianchi 13, 39	13,500
27	itpr1	Lazio	H L	2-3 Tedesco 26, Foggia 65	10,236
28	itpr1	Catania	A W	4-1 Amoruso 58, Foggia 62, Bianchi 85, Esteves 88	0
29	itpr1	Siena	H L	0-1	17,234
30	itpr1	Inter Milan	H D	0-0	18,506
31	itpr1	Livorno	A D	1-1 Bianchi 31	8,643
32	itpr1	Messina	H W	3-1 Bianchi 13, Amoruso 54, 72 pen	11,000
33	itpr1	Udinese	H D	1-1 Amoruso 85 pen	10,622
34	itpr1	Ascoli	A W	3-2 Amoruso 24, 32, Foggia 52	5,896
35	itpr1	Sampdoria	A D	0-0	17,264
36	itpr1	Chievo	H D	1-1 Bianchi 53	13,164
37	itpr1	Empoli	A D	3-3 Vigiani 52, Amoruso 56, 84 pen	4,893
38	itpr1	AC Milan	H W	2-0 Amoruso 8, Amerini 68	20,835

LEAGUE APPEARANCES, BOOKINGS AND CAPS

	AGE (on 01/07/07)	IN NAMED 18	APPEARANCES	COUNTING GAMES	MINUTES ON PITCH	YELLOW CARDS	RED CARDS	CAPS THIS SEASON	NATIONAL SIDE
Goalkeepers									
Andrea Campagnolo	29	30	15	14	1309	0	0	-	Italy
Ivan Pelizzoli	26	21	21	21	1890	0	0	-	Italy
Christian Puggioni	26	16	3	2	221	0	0	-	Italy
Defenders									
Salvatore Aronica	29	35	35	34	3121	10	1	-	Italy
Palmiro Di Dio	21	25	6	5	430	1	0	-	Italy
Antonio Giosa	23	25	15	6	864	3	0	-	Italy
Maurizio Lanzaro	25	32	32	29	2719	10	1	-	Italy
Alessandro Lucarelli	29	34	34	31	2935	11	1	-	Italy
Francesco Modesto	25	35	35	33	3013	6	0	-	Italy
Midfielders									
Daniele Amerini	32	36	36	21	2385	7	0	-	Italy
Antonino Barilla	19	19	4	0	51	0	0	-	Italy
Filippo Carobbio	27	17	11	1	231	3	0	-	Italy
Ricardo Esteves	27	29	14	3	477	2	0	-	Portugal
Alessandro Gazzi	24	11	9	1	319	2	0	-	Italy
Julio Cesar Leon	27	16	16	12	1250	4	0	3	Honduras
Giandomenico Mesto	25	33	33	29	2751	6	0	-	Italy
Riccardo Nardini	24	18	12	2	301	0	0	-	Italy
Nicki Billie Nielsen	19	19	7	0	73	0	0	-	Denmark
Giacomo Tedesco	31	35	35	34	3116	11	1	-	Italy
Luca Vigiani	30	15	15	10	1069	3	0	-	Italy
Forwards									
Nicola Amoruso	32	34	34	25	2578	5	0	-	Italy
Rolando Bianchi	24	37	37	32	3114	6	0	-	Italy
Pasquale Foggia	24	15	15	10	1034	3	0	-	Italy
Simone Missiroli	21	32	22	1	551	6	0	-	Italy
Leonel Rios	24	10	5	0	123	1	0	-	Argentina
Luca Tognozzi	29	33	24	16	1560	4	0	-	Italy

TEAM OF THE SEASON

Ivan Pelizzoli CG: 21 DR: 67 (G)

Maurizio Lanzaro CG: 29 DR: 75 (D)
Salvatore Aronica CG: 34 DR: 70 (D)
Francesco Modesto CG: 33 DR: 65 (D)
Alessandro Lucarelli CG: 31 DR: 63 (D)

Giacomo Tedesco CG: 34 SD: 0 (M)
Julio Cesar Leon CG: 12 SD: -4 (M)
Daniele Amerini CG: 21 SD: -10 (M)
Giandomenico Mesto CG: 29 SD: -11 (M)

Nicola Amoruso CG: 25 SR: 151 (F)
Rolando Bianchi CG: 32 SR: 173 (F)

MONTHLY POINTS TALLY

SEPTEMBER		5	33%
OCTOBER		7	58%
NOVEMBER		4	33%
DECEMBER		7	47%
JANUARY		4	44%
FEBRUARY		5	42%
MARCH		4	33%
APRIL		9	60%
MAY		6	50%

LEAGUE GOALS

	PLAYER	MINS	GOALS	S RATE
1	Bianchi	3114	18	173
2	Amoruso	2578	17	151
3	Foggia	1034	4	258
4	Modesto	3013	3	1004
5	Vigiani	1069	2	534
6	Leon	1250	2	625
7	Lucarelli, A	2935	2	1467
8	Tedesco	3116	2	1558
9	Esteves	477	1	477
10	Amerini	2385	1	2385
11	Aronica	3121	0	
12	Barilla	51	0	
13	Campagnolo	1309	0	
	Other		0	
	TOTAL		**52**	

TOP POINT EARNERS

	PLAYER	GAMES	AV PTS
1	Andrea Campagnolo	14	1.43
2	Francesco Modesto	32	1.41
3	Giacomo Tedesco	34	1.38
4	Nicola Amoruso	25	1.36
5	Rolando Bianchi	31	1.35
6	Salvatore Aronica	35	1.34
7	Alessandro Lucarelli	32	1.34
8	Giandomenico Mesto	29	1.34
9	Julio Cesar Leon	12	1.33
10	Maurizio Lanzaro	30	1.30
	CLUB AVERAGE:		**1.05**

DISCIPLINARY RECORDS

	PLAYER	YELLOW	RED	AVE
1	Simone Missiroli	6	0	91
2	Ricardo Esteves	2	0	238
3	Alessandro Lucarelli	11	1	244
4	Maurizio Lanzaro	10	1	247
5	Giacomo Tedesco	11	1	259
6	Salvatore Aronica	10	1	283
7	Antonio Giosa	3	0	288
8	Julio Cesar Leon	4	0	312
9	Daniele Amerini	7	0	340
10	Pasquale Foggia	3	0	344
11	Luca Vigiani	3	0	356
12	Luca Tognozzi	4	0	390
13	Giandomenico Mesto	6	0	458
	Other	17	0	
	TOTAL	**97**	**4**	

KEY GOALKEEPER

Ivan Pelizzoli

Goals Conceded in the League	28	Counting Games League games when player was on pitch for at least 70 minutes	21
Defensive Rating Ave number of mins between League goals conceded while on the pitch	67	Clean Sheets In League games when player was on pitch for at least 70 minutes	5

KEY PLAYERS - DEFENDERS

Maurizio Lanzaro

Goals Conceded Number of League goals conceded while the player was on the pitch	36	Clean Sheets In League games when player was on pitch for at least 70 minutes	7
Defensive Rating Ave number of mins between League goals conceded while on the pitch	75	Club Defensive Rating Average of mins between League goals conceded by the club this season	70

	PLAYER	CON LGE	CLEAN SHEETS	DEF RATE
1	Maurizio Lanzaro	36	7	75 mins
2	Salvatore Aronica	44	8	70 mins
3	Francesco Modesto	46	7	65 mins
4	Alessandro Lucarelli	46	5	63 mins

KEY PLAYERS - MIDFIELDERS

Giacomo Tedesco

Goals in the League	2	Contribution to Attacking Power Average number of minutes between League team goals while on pitch	64
Defensive Rating Average of mins between League goals conceded while on the pitch	64	Scoring Difference Defensive Rating minus Contribution to Attacking Power	0

	PLAYER	LGE GOALS	DEF RATE	POWER	SCORE DIFF
1	Giacomo Tedesco	2	64	64	0 mins
2	Julio Cesar Leon	2	65	69	-4 mins
3	Daniele Amerini	1	64	74	-10 mins
4	Giandomenico Mesto	0	63	74	-11 mins

KEY PLAYERS - GOALSCORERS

Nicola Amoruso

Goals in the League	17	Player Strike Rate Average number of minutes between League goals scored by player	151
Contribution to Attacking Power Average number of minutes between League team goals while on pitch	58	Club Strike Rate Average number of minutes between League goals scored by club	67

	PLAYER	LGE GOALS	POWER	STRIKE RATE
1	Nicola Amoruso	17	58	151 mins
2	Rolando Bianchi	18	63	173 mins
3	Julio Cesar Leon	2	69	625 mins
4	Giacomo Tedesco	2	64	1558 mins

Rolando Bianchi

SQUAD APPEARANCES

Match	1	2	3	4	5		6	7	8	9	10		11	12	13	14	15		16	17	18	19	20		21	22	23	24	25		26	27	28	29	30		31	32	33	34	35		36	37	38
Venue	A	H	A	H	A		H	A	H	A	H		A	A	H	A	H		H	A	H	A	H		A	A	H	A	H		A	H	A	H	H		A	H	H	A	A		H	A	H
Competition	L	L	L	L	L		L	L	L	L	L		L	L	L	L	L		L	L	L	L	L		L	L	L	L	L		L	L	L	L	L		L	L	L	L	L		L	L	L
Result	L	W	L	D	D		W	L	W	D	L		W	L	D	D	W		L	L	W	D	L		W	W	D	L	D		D	L	W	L	D		D	W	D	W	D		D	D	W

Goalkeepers
Andrea Campagnolo
Ivan Pelizzoli
Christian Puggioni

Defenders
Salvatore Aronica
Palmiro Di Dio
Antonio Giosa
Maurizio Lanzaro
Alessandro Lucarelli
Francesco Modesto

Midfielders
Daniele Amerini
Antonino Barilla
Filippo Carobbio
Ricardo Esteves
Alessandro Gazzi
Julio Cesar Leon
Giandomenico Mesto
Riccardo Nardini
Nicki Billie Nielsen
Giacomo Tedesco
Luca Vigiani

Forwards
Nicola Amoruso
Rolando Bianchi
Pasquale Foggia
Simone Missiroli
Leonel Rios
Luca Tognozzi

KEY: ■ On all match ◄◄ Subbed or sent off (Counting game) ►► Subbed on from bench (Counting Game) ►► Subbed on and then subbed or sent off (Counting Game) Not in 16
■ On bench ◄◄ Subbed or sent off (playing less than 70 minutes) ►► Subbed on (playing less than 70 minutes) ►► Subbed on and then subbed or sent off (playing less than 70 minutes)

ITALY - REGGINA

SIENA

Final Position: 15th

NICKNAME: BIANCONERI KEY: ☐ Won ☐ Drawn ☐ Lost Attendance

				Result	Scorers	Attendance
1	itpr1	Chievo	A W	2-1	Brevi 74, Chiesa 89	5,253
2	itpr1	Roma	H L	1-3	Frick 87	11,136
3	itpr1	Torino	A W	2-1	Frick 4, 35	21,396
4	itpr1	Cagliari	H D	0-0		6,592
5	itpr1	AC Milan	A D	0-0		44,650
6	itpr1	Messina	H W	3-1	Konko 45, Cozza 90, Frick 90	11,231
7	itpr1	Livorno	A D	0-0		8,646
8	itpr1	Catania	H D	1-1	Frick 47	6,500
9	itpr1	Ascoli	A W	1-0	Codrea 86	12,000
10	itpr1	Parma	H D	2-2	Bogdani 77, 90	8,000
11	itpr1	Reggina	H L	0-1		7,000
12	itpr1	Udinese	A L	0-3		15,000
13	itpr1	Fiorentina	H D	1-1	Antonini 18	11,000
14	itpr1	Inter Milan	A L	0-2		42,299
15	itpr1	Sampdoria	A D	0-0		20,000
16	itpr1	Atalanta	H D	1-1	Frick 85	6,500
17	itpr1	Empoli	A L	0-1		5,000
18	itpr1	Palermo	H D	1-1	Rinaudo 42	7,000
19	itpr1	Lazio	A D	1-1	Cozza 85	38,000
20	itpr1	Chievo	H W	2-1	Antonini 62, Portanova 67	6,000
21	itpr1	Roma	A L	0-1		38,000
22	itpr1	Cagliari	A D	2-2	Corvia 29, Codrea 82	8,000
23	itpr1	AC Milan	H L	3-4	Vergassola 19, Maccarone 30, 90	10,000
24	itpr1	Messina	A L	0-1		10,000
25	itpr1	Livorno	H D	0-0		7,000
26	itpr1	Catania	A D	1-1	Cozza 74	0
27	itpr1	Ascoli	H L	0-1		10,792
28	itpr1	Parma	A L	0-1		12,777
29	itpr1	Reggina	A W	1-0	Bertotto 45	17,234
30	itpr1	Udinese	H D	2-2	Maccarone 76, Negro 81	6,463
31	itpr1	Fiorentina	A L	0-1		33,467
32	itpr1	Torino	H W	1-0	Antonini 65	7,000
33	itpr1	Inter Milan	H L	1-2	Negro 21	14,027
34	itpr1	Sampdoria	H L	0-2		5,277
35	itpr1	Atalanta	A L	1-3	Vergassola 58 pen	11,388
36	itpr1	Empoli	H W	2-0	Portanova 12, Maccarone 90	6,216
37	itpr1	Palermo	A L	1-2	Maccarone 90	20,043
38	itpr1	Lazio	H W	2-1	Maccarone 23 pen, Negro 85	10,803

LEAGUE APPEARANCES, BOOKINGS AND CAPS

	AGE (on 01/07/07)	IN NAMED 18	APPEARANCES	COUNTING GAMES	MINUTES ON PITCH	YELLOW CARDS	RED CARDS	CAPS THIS SEASON	NATIONAL SIDE
Goalkeepers									
Francesco Benussi	25	18	0	0	0	0	0	-	Italy
Alex Manninger	30	38	38	38	3420	3	0	-	Austria
Nicola Pavarini	33	14	0	0	0	0	0	-	Italy
Defenders									
Valerio Bertotto	34	30	27	24	2320	3	1	-	Italy
Daniele Gastaldello	24	31	20	16	1589	5	0	-	Italy
Christian Molinaro	23	37	36	35	3194	4	0	-	Italy
Paolo Negro	35	33	19	14	1354	4	0	-	Italy
Daniele Portanova	28	29	28	27	2492	7	2	-	Italy
Leandro Rinaudo	24	33	28	26	2402	7	0	-	Italy
Andrea Rossi	20	11	4	3	266	2	0	-	Italy
Midfielders									
Do Carmo Neto A	32	23	16	4	753	2	1	-	Brazil
Luca Antonini	25	33	32	23	2386	8	0	-	Italy
Ezio Brevi	37	33	22	9	1104	4	1	-	Italy
Paul Codrea	26	27	22	13	1449	10	1	6	Romania
Francesco Cozza	33	20	18	5	875	2	0	-	Italy
Roberto D'aversa	31	15	11	6	699	1	0	-	Italy
Roman Eremenko	20	15	10	2	376	1	0	1	Finland
Tomas Locatelli	31	25	23	7	1200	3	1	-	Italy
Simone Vergassola	31	36	35	34	3093	8	0	-	Italy
Forwards									
Erjon Bogdani	30	17	15	6	854	2	0	5	Albania
Vincent Candela	33	17	14	7	889	1	1	-	France
Enrico Chiesa	36	32	23	5	1069	2	0	-	Italy
Daniele Corvia	22	25	20	8	1179	4	2	-	Italy
Mario Frick	32	36	33	17	2162	3	0	6	Liechtenstein
Daniele Galloppa	22	11	10	6	626	2	0	-	Italy
Abdulay Konko	23	16	14	7	901	2	1	-	France
Massimo Maccarone	27	11	11	8	828	2	0	-	Italy
Federico Melchiorri	20	1	1	0	1	0	0	-	Italy

TEAM OF THE SEASON

G Alex Manninger CG: 38 DR: 76

D Leandro Rinaudo CG: 26 DR: 88
D Valerio Bertotto CG: 24 DR: 77
D Christian Molinaro CG: 35 DR: 77
D Daniele Portanova CG: 27 DR: 73

M Simone Vergassola CG: 34 SD: -22
M Paul Codrea CG: 13 SD: -27
M Luca Antonini CG: 23 SD: -45
M Ezio Brevi* CG: 9 SD: -69

F M Maccarone* CG: 8 SR: 138
F Mario Frick CG: 17 SR: 360

MONTHLY POINTS TALLY

SEPTEMBER	7	58%
OCTOBER	9	60%
NOVEMBER	2	17%
DECEMBER	3	20%
JANUARY	4	44%
FEBRUARY	2	17%
MARCH	4	33%
APRIL	4	27%
MAY	6	50%

LEAGUE GOALS

	PLAYER	MINS	GOALS	S RATE
1	Maccarone	828	6	138
2	Frick	2162	6	360
3	Cozza	875	3	291
4	Negro	1354	3	451
5	Antonini	2386	3	795
6	Bogdani	854	2	427
7	Codrea	1449	2	724
8	Portanova	2492	2	1246
9	Vergassola	3093	2	1546
10	Konko	901	1	901
11	Chiesa	1069	1	1069
12	Brevi	1104	1	1104
13	Corvia	1179	1	1179
	Other		2	
	TOTAL		**35**	

TOP POINT EARNERS

	PLAYER	GAMES	AV PTS
1	Valerio Bertotto	24	1.38
2	Mario Frick	17	1.18
3	Christian Molinaro	35	1.14
4	Leandro Rinaudo	26	1.12
5	Daniele Portanova	28	1.11
6	Alex Manninger	38	1.08
7	Simone Vergassola	34	1.06
8	Daniele Gastaldello	16	1.00
9	Paul Codrea	13	0.77
10	Luca Antonini	23	0.74
	CLUB AVERAGE:		**1.08**

DISCIPLINARY RECORDS

	PLAYER	YELLOW	RED	AVE
1	Paul Codrea	10	1	131
2	Daniele Corvia	4	2	196
3	Ezio Brevi	4	1	220
4	Do C Neto Alberto	2	1	251
5	Daniele Portanova	7	2	276
6	Luca Antonini	8	0	298
7	Tomas Locatelli	3	1	300
8	Abdulay Konko	2	1	300
9	Daniele Galloppa	2	0	313
10	Daniele Gastaldello	5	0	317
11	Leandro Rinaudo	7	0	343
12	Simone Vergassola	8	0	386
13	Massimo Maccarone	2	0	414
	Other	24	2	
	TOTAL	**88**	**11**	

KEY GOALKEEPER

Alex Manninger

Goals Conceded in the League	45	Counting Games League games when player was on pitch for at least 70 minutes	38
Defensive Rating Ave number of mins between League goals conceded while on the pitch	76	Clean Sheets In League games when player was on pitch for at least 70 minutes	9

KEY PLAYERS - DEFENDERS

Leandro Rinaudo

Goals Conceded Number of League goals conceded while the player was on the pitch	27	Clean Sheets In League games when player was on pitch for at least 70 minutes	7
Defensive Rating Ave number of mins between League goals conceded while on the pitch	88	Club Defensive Rating Average number of mins between League goals conceded by the club this season	78

	PLAYER	CON LGE	CLEAN SHEETS	DEF RATE
1	Leandro Rinaudo	27	7	88 mins
2	Valerio Bertotto	30	6	77 mins
3	Christian Molinaro	41	9	77 mins
4	Daniele Portanova	34	5	73 mins

KEY PLAYERS - MIDFIELDERS

Simone Vergassola

Goals in the League	2	Contribution to Attacking Power Average number of minutes between League team goals while on pitch	99
Defensive Rating Average number of mins between League goals conceded while on the pitch	77	Scoring Difference Defensive Rating minus Contribution to Attacking Power	-22

	PLAYER	LGE GOALS	DEF RATE	POWER	SCORE DIFF
1	Simone Vergassola	2	77	99	-22 mins
2	Paul Codrea	2	69	96	-27 mins
3	Luca Antonini	3	74	119	-45 mins
4	Ezio Brevi	1	69	138	-69 mins

KEY PLAYERS - GOALSCORERS

Massimo Maccarone

Goals in the League	6	Player Strike Rate Average number of minutes between League goals scored by player	138
Contribution to Attacking Power Average number of minutes between League team goals while on pitch	75	Club Strike Rate Average number of minutes between League goals scored by club	100

	PLAYER	LGE GOALS	POWER	STRIKE RATE
1	Massimo Maccarone	6	75	138 mins
2	Mario Frick	6	102	360 mins
3	Paul Codrea	2	96	724 mins
4	Luca Antonini	3	119	795 mins

Mario Frick

SQUAD APPEARANCES

Match	1	2	3	4	5	6	7	8	9	10	11	12	13	14	15	16	17	18	19	20	21	22	23	24	25	26	27	28	29	30	31	32	33	34	35	36	37	38
Venue	A	H	A	H	A	H	A	H	A	H	H	A	H	A	A	H	A	H	A	H	A	A	H	A	H	A	H	A	A	H	A	H	H	H	A	H	A	H
Competition	L	L	L	L	L	L	L	L	L	L	L	L	L	L	L	L	L	L	L	L	L	L	L	L	L	L	L	L	L	L	L	L	L	L	L	L	L	L
Result	W	L	W	D	D	W	D	D	W	D	L	L	D	L	D	D	L	D	D	W	L	D	L	L	D	D	L	L	W	D	L	W	L	L	L	W	L	W

Goalkeepers
Francesco Benussi
Alex Manninger
Nicola Pavarini

Defenders
Valerio Bertotto
Daniele Gastaldello
Christian Molinaro
Paolo Negro
Daniele Portanova
Leandro Rinaudo
Andrea Rossi

Midfielders
Do Carmo Neto A
Luca Antonini
Ezio Brevi
Paul Codrea
Francesco Cozza
Roberto D'aversa
Roman Eremenko
Tomas Locatelli
Simone Vergassola

Forwards
Erjon Bogdani
Vincent Candela
Enrico Chiesa
Daniele Corvia
Mario Frick
Daniele Galloppa
Abdulay Konko
Massimo Maccarone
Federico Melchiorri

KEY: ■ On all match ◄◄ Subbed or sent off (Counting game) ▸▸ Subbed on from bench (Counting Game) ▸◂ Subbed on and then subbed or sent off (Counting Game) ☐ Not in 16
■ On bench ◄ Subbed or sent off (playing less than 70 minutes) ▹ Subbed on (playing less than 70 minutes) ▹▹ Subbed on and then subbed or sent off (playing less than 70 minutes)

CAGLIARI

Final Position: **16th**

NICKNAME: ISOLANI   KEY: ☐ Won ☐ Drawn ☐ Lost   Attendance

#				Result	Scorers	Attendance
1	itpr1	Catania	H L	0-1		15,000
2	itpr1	Reggina	A L	1-2	Suazo 62 pen	9,634
3	itpr1	Livorno	H D	2-2	Ferri 12, Suazo 57	10,000
4	itpr1	Siena	A D	0-0		6,592
5	itpr1	Inter Milan	H D	1-1	Colucci 17	18,000
6	itpr1	Lazio	A D	0-0		19,402
7	itpr1	Torino	H D	0-0		10,000
8	itpr1	Atalanta	A D	3-3	Bianco 6, D'Agostino 30, Suazo 54	13,000
9	itpr1	Sampdoria	H W	1-0	Conti 45	10,000
10	itpr1	Chievo	A D	0-0		5,426
11	itpr1	Messina	A D	2-2	Esposito 53, Conti 90	12,000
12	itpr1	Palermo	H W	1-0	Pepe 90	18,000
13	itpr1	Empoli	A L	0-1		4,000
14	itpr1	AC Milan	H D	2-2	Suazo 53 pen, Capone 65	20,000
15	itpr1	Parma	H D	0-0		10,000
16	itpr1	Udinese	A L	1-3	Cocco 82	14,000
17	itpr1	Fiorentina	H L	0-2		15,000
18	itpr1	Roma	A L	0-2		35,000
19	itpr1	Ascoli	H W	1-0	Suazo 15 pen	10,000
20	itpr1	Catania	A W	1-0	Suazo 8 pen	18,000
21	itpr1	Reggina	H L	0-2		8,000
22	itpr1	Siena	H D	2-2	Capone 38, Suazo 66	8,000
23	itpr1	Inter Milan	A L	0-1		30,000
24	itpr1	Lazio	H L	0-2		10,000
25	itpr1	Torino	A L	0-1		13,000
26	itpr1	Atalanta	H W	2-0	Suazo 4, Pepe 71	10,000
27	itpr1	Sampdoria	A D	1-1	Suazo 63	17,259
28	itpr1	Chievo	H L	0-2		8,000
29	itpr1	Messina	H W	2-0	Biondini 12, Budel 24	7,000
30	itpr1	Palermo	A W	3-1	Suazo 37 pen, 86, Pepe 83	21,655
31	itpr1	Empoli	H D	0-0		8,000
32	itpr1	Livorno	A L	1-2	Suazo 61 pen	5,500
33	itpr1	AC Milan	A L	1-3	Suazo 74 pen	43,728
34	itpr1	Parma	A L	1-2	Conti 67	14,225
35	itpr1	Udinese	H W	2-1	Marchini 66, Capone 85	7,000
36	itpr1	Fiorentina	A L	0-1		19,312
37	itpr1	Roma	H W	3-2	Suazo 13, Marchini 40, 68	20,000
38	itpr1	Ascoli	A L	1-2	Mancosu 13	5,427

LEAGUE APPEARANCES, BOOKINGS AND CAPS

	AGE (on 01/07/07)	IN NAMED 18	APPEARANCES	COUNTING GAMES	MINUTES ON PITCH	YELLOW CARDS	RED CARDS	CAPS THIS SEASON	NATIONAL SIDE
Goalkeepers									
Simone Aresti	21	14	1	0	45	0	0	-	Italy
Antonio Chimenti	37	24	22	20	1862	0	0	-	Italy
Marco Fortin	32	36	17	17	1513	0	0	-	Italy
Defenders									
Alessandro Agostini	27	34	27	19	1872	0	0	-	Italy
Paulo Bianco	29	35	35	35	3150	4	0	-	Italy
Joe Bizera	27	29	10	4	566	0	1	-	Uruguay
Michele Canini	22	12	4	3	269	1	0	-	Italy
Cristiano Del Grosso	24	29	22	17	1639	1	0	-	Italy
Michele Ferri	26	29	23	19	1849	4	0	-	Italy
Diego Luis Lopez	32	35	35	32	2964	3	0	-	Uruguay
Francesco Pisano	21	30	23	15	1477	2	0	-	Italy
Jose Vitor Semedo	22	7	3	1	107	1	1	-	Portugal
Midfielders									
Davide Biondini	24	34	31	26	2468	6	0	-	Italy
Alessandro Budel	26	37	30	15	1781	4	0	-	Italy
Salvatore Burrai	20	3	1	0	9	0	0	-	-
Leonardo Colucci	34	31	26	20	2022	3	0	-	Italy
Daniele Conti	28	30	30	28	2595	12	3	-	Italy
Alessandro Conticchio	33	16	5	0	113	2	0	-	Italy
Antonino D'Agostino	28	28	27	11	1554	1	0	-	Italy
Mauro Esposito	28	18	18	15	1489	2	0	1	Italy
Davide Marchini	26	18	17	9	984	3	0	-	Italy
Gabriel Penalba	22	4	3	0	61	0	0	-	Argentina
Forwards									
Andrea Capone	26	31	25	7	1191	2	0	-	Italy
Andrea Cocco	21	7	3	0	32	0	0	-	Italy
Antonio Langella	30	21	16	3	701	4	1	-	Italy
Marco Mancosu	19	1	1	0	57	0	0	-	Italy
Simone Pepe	23	37	35	15	1992	3	0	-	Italy
Roberto Puddu	20	3	2	0	38	0	0	-	Italy
David Suazo	27	36	36	36	3209	2	0	-	Honduras

TEAM OF THE SEASON

D Diego Luis Lopez
CG: 32 DR: 84

M Leonardo Colucci
CG: 20 SD: -12

D Paulo Bianco
CG: 35 DR: 78

M Daniele Conti
CG: 28 SD: -14

F David Suazo
CG: 36 SR: 229

G Marco Fortin
CG: 17 DR: 75

D Alessandro Agostini
CG: 19 DR: 78

M Mauro Esposito
CG: 15 SD: -27

F Simone Pepe
CG: 15 SR: 664

D Michele Ferri
CG: 19 DR: 77

M Davide Biondini
CG: 26 SD: -39

MONTHLY POINTS TALLY

SEPTEMBER	2	17%
OCTOBER	7	47%
NOVEMBER	5	42%
DECEMBER	2	13%
JANUARY	6	67%
FEBRUARY	1	8%
MARCH	4	44%
APRIL	7	39%
MAY	6	50%

LEAGUE GOALS

	PLAYER	MINS	GOALS	S RATE
1	Suazo	3209	14	229
2	Marchini	984	3	328
3	Capone	1191	3	397
4	Pepe	1992	3	664
5	Conti	2595	3	865
6	Cocco	32	1	32
7	Mancosu	57	1	57
8	Esposito	1489	1	1489
9	D'Agostino	1554	1	1554
10	Budel	1781	1	1781
11	Ferri	1849	1	1849
12	Colucci	2022	1	2022
13	Biondini	2468	1	2468
	Other		1	
	TOTAL		35	

TOP POINT EARNERS

	PLAYER	GAMES	AV PTS
1	Leonardo Colucci	19	1.37
2	Daniele Conti	28	1.21
3	Antonio Chimenti	20	1.20
4	Diego Luis Lopez	32	1.19
5	Davide Biondini	25	1.16
6	Paulo Bianco	35	1.14
7	Francesco Pisano	15	1.13
8	Michele Ferri	19	1.11
9	David Suazo	36	1.08
10	Simone Pepe	15	1.00
	CLUB AVERAGE:		1.05

DISCIPLINARY RECORDS

	PLAYER	YELLOW	RED	AVE
1	Antonio Langella	4	1	140
2	Daniele Conti	12	3	173
3	Davide Marchini	3	0	328
4	Davide Biondini	6	0	411
5	Alessandro Budel	4	0	445
6	Michele Ferri	4	0	462
7	Joe Bizera	0	1	566
8	Andrea Capone	2	0	595
9	Simone Pepe	3	0	664
10	Leonardo Colucci	3	0	674
11	Francesco Pisano	2	0	738
12	Mauro Esposito	2	0	744
13	Paulo Bianco	4	0	787
	Other	7		
	TOTAL	56	5	

KEY GOALKEEPER

Marco Fortin

Goals Conceded in the League	20	Counting Games League games when player was on pitch for at least 70 minutes	17
Defensive Rating Ave number of mins between League goals conceded while on the pitch	75	Clean Sheets In League games when player was on pitch for at least 70 minutes	6

KEY PLAYERS - DEFENDERS

Diego Luis Lopez

Goals Conceded Number of League goals conceded while the player was on the pitch	35	Clean Sheets In League games when player was on pitch for at least 70 minutes	12
Defensive Rating Ave number of mins between League goals conceded while on the pitch	84	Club Defensive Rating Average number of mins between League goals conceded by the club this season	76

	PLAYER	CON LGE	CLEAN SHEETS	DEF RATE
1	Diego Luis Lopez	35	12	84 mins
2	Paulo Bianco	40	12	78 mins
3	Alessandro Agostini	24	7	78 mins
4	Michele Ferri	24	5	77 mins

KEY PLAYERS - MIDFIELDERS

Leonardo Colucci

Goals in the League	1	Contribution to Attacking Power Average number of minutes between League team goals while on pitch	96
Defensive Rating Average number of mins between League goals conceded while on the pitch	84	Scoring Difference Defensive Rating minus Contribution to Attacking Power	-12

	PLAYER	LGE GOALS	DEF RATE	POWER	SCORE DIFF
1	Leonardo Colucci	1	84	96	-12 mins
2	Daniele Conti	3	78	92	-14 mins
3	Mauro Esposito	1	87	114	-27 mins
4	Davide Biondini	1	68	107	-39 mins

KEY PLAYERS - GOALSCORERS

David Suazo

Goals in the League	14	Player Strike Rate Average number of minutes between League goals scored by player	229
Contribution to Attacking Power Average number of minutes between League team goals while on pitch	100	Club Strike Rate Average number of minutes between League goals scored by club	100

	PLAYER	LGE GOALS	POWER	STRIKE RATE
1	David Suazo	14	100	229 mins
2	Simone Pepe	3	86	664 mins
3	Daniele Conti	3	92	865 mins
4	Mauro Esposito	1	114	1489 mins

David Suazo

SQUAD APPEARANCES

Match	1	2	3	4	5	6	7	8	9	10	11	12	13	14	15	16	17	18	19	20	21	22	23	24	25	26	27	28	29	30	31	32	33	34	35	36	37	38
Venue	H	A	H	A	H		A	H	A	H	A		A	H	A	H	H		A	H	A	H	A		H	H	A	H	A		H	A	H	H	A		A	H	A
Competition	L	L	L	L	L		L	L	L	L	L		L	L	L	L	L		L	L	L	L	L		W	W		L	D		L	L	L	L	L		L	L	L
Result	L	L	D	D	D		D	D	D	W	D		D	W	L	D	D		L	L	L	W	W		L	D	L	L	L		W	D	L	W	W		D	L	L	L	L	W		L	W	L

KEY:
- ■ On all match
- ◄◄ Subbed or sent off (Counting game)
- ►► Subbed on from bench (Counting Game)
- ►► Subbed on and then subbed or sent off (Counting Game)
- ☐ Not in 16
- ■ On bench
- ◄◄ Subbed or sent off (playing less than 70 minutes)
- ►► Subbed on (playing less than 70 minutes)
- ►► Subbed on and then subbed or sent off (playing less than 70 minutes)

TORINO

Final Position: **17th**

NICKNAME: GRANATA

KEY: ☐ Won ☐ Drawn ☐ Lost — Attendance

1	itpr1	Parma	H D	1-1	Stellone 90	23,000
2	itpr1	Udinese	A L	0-2		14,555
3	itpr1	Siena	H L	1-2	Muzzi 40	21,396
4	itpr1	Reggina	A D	1-1	Comotto 66	9,559
5	itpr1	Lazio	H L	0-4		18,000
6	itpr1	Chievo	H W	1-0	Stellone 48	18,945
7	itpr1	Cagliari	A D	0-0		10,000
8	itpr1	Fiorentina	H L	0-1		19,000
9	itpr1	Catania	A D	1-1	Franceschini 85	0
10	itpr1	Messina	H D	1-1	Stellone 61	18,000
11	itpr1	Palermo	A L	0-3		24,000
12	itpr1	Sampdoria	H W	1-0	Rosina 80 pen	20,000
13	itpr1	Atalanta	A W	2-1	Lazetic 78, Rosina 88	12,000
14	itpr1	Empoli	H W	1-0	Comotto 88	20,000
15	itpr1	AC Milan	A D	0-0		50,000
16	itpr1	Ascoli	A W	2-0	Rosina 59 pen, 90	8,000
17	itpr1	Roma	H L	1-2	Rosina 89	25,000
18	itpr1	Livorno	A D	1-1	Cioffi 23	8,000
19	itpr1	Inter Milan	H L	1-3	Materazzi 59 og	23,000
20	itpr1	Parma	A L	0-1		13,000
21	itpr1	Udinese	H L	2-3	Abbruscato 77, 90	22,000
22	itpr1	Reggina	H L	1-2	Comotto 50	18,000
23	itpr1	Lazio	A L	0-2		10,000
24	itpr1	Chievo	A L	0-3		5,000
25	itpr1	Cagliari	H W	1-0	Bovo 23	13,000
26	itpr1	Fiorentina	A L	1-5	Rosina 15	23,900
27	itpr1	Catania	H W	1-0	Rosina 77	19,777
28	itpr1	Messina	A W	3-0	Muzzi 26, Rosina 77 pen, Stellone 85	11,915
29	itpr1	Palermo	H D	0-0		20,932
30	itpr1	Sampdoria	A L	0-1		18,648
31	itpr1	Atalanta	H L	1-2	Abbruscato 70	19,845
32	itpr1	Siena	A L	0-1		7,000
33	itpr1	Empoli	A D	0-0		5,201
34	itpr1	AC Milan	H L	0-1		22,539
35	itpr1	Ascoli	H W	1-0	Rosina 17	20,048
36	itpr1	Roma	A W	1-0	Muzzi 14	32,242
37	itpr1	Livorno	H D	0-0		22,036
38	itpr1	Inter Milan	A L	0-3		64,758

LEAGUE APPEARANCES, BOOKINGS AND CAPS

	AGE (on 01/07/07)	IN NAMED 18	APPEARANCES	COUNTING GAMES	MINUTES ON PITCH	YELLOW CARDS	RED CARDS	CAPS THIS SEASON	NATIONAL SIDE
Goalkeepers									
Christian Abbiati	29	36	36	36	3232	0	1	-	Italy
Antonio Fontana	32	1	1	0	22	0	0	-	Italy
Massimo Taibi	37	37	3	2	165	1	0	-	Italy
Defenders									
Cesare Bovo	24	8	7	6	602	3	0	-	Italy
Oscar Brevi	29	30	22	21	1835	5	1	-	Italy
Gabriele Cioffi	32	31	18	15	1385	8	1	-	Italy
Gianluca Comotto	28	35	35	35	3143	6	0	-	Italy
Marco Di Loreto	32	31	23	21	1979	5	1	-	Italy
Diaw Doudou	31	3	2	1	106	0	0	-	Guinea
Ivan Franceschini	30	34	30	28	2594	8	1	-	Italy
Luigi Martinelli	36	8	4	0	113	0	0	-	Italy
A Obinze Ogbona	19	9	4	1	185	1	0	-	Italy
Giuseppe Pancaro	35	20	10	9	863	2	0	-	Italy
Midfielders									
Andrea Ardito	30	27	26	18	1826	10	1	-	Italy
Jacopo Balestri	32	37	31	30	2723	5	0	-	Italy
Simone Barone	29	34	33	27	2513	8	1	1	Italy
Francesco Coco	30	6	3	0	120	1	0	-	Italy
Diego De Ascentis	30	33	30	21	2152	5	0	-	Italy
Claudio Ferrarese	28	1	1	0	17	0	0	-	Italy
Stefano Fiore	32	21	19	10	1041	1	0	-	Italy
Fabio Gallo	36	29	23	10	1192	4	0	-	Italy
Nikola Lazetic	29	32	27	17	1781	3	0	-	Serbia
Vedin Music	34	4	1	0	13	0	0	4	Bosnia
Alessandro Rosina	22	36	35	29	2773	2	0	-	Italy
Forwards									
Elvis Abbruscato	26	34	29	11	1442	1	0	-	Italy
H Axel Cedric Konan	24	14	5	0	136	0	0	-	Ivory Coast
Roberto Muzzi	35	32	28	5	1313	3	1	-	Italy
Mashasi Oguro	27	17	7	1	250	0	0	-	Japan
Roberto Stellone	29	33	32	18	1986	5	0	-	Italy

TEAM OF THE SEASON

G Christian Abbiati — CG: 36 DR: 76

D Gianluca Comotto — CG: 35 DR: 80
D Gabriele Cioffi — CG: 15 DR: 76
D Oscar Brevi — CG: 21 DR: 73
D Ivan Franceschini — CG: 28 DR: 68

M Andrea Ardito — CG: 18 SD: -25
M Nikola Lazetic — CG: 17 SD: -48
M Jacopo Balestri — CG: 30 SD: -54
M Alessandro Rosina — CG: 29 SD: -57

F Elvis Abbruscato* — CG: 11 SR: 480
F Roberto Stellone — CG: 18 SR: 496

MONTHLY POINTS TALLY

SEPTEMBER		2	13%
OCTOBER		5	42%
NOVEMBER		7	58%
DECEMBER		8	53%
JANUARY		0	0%
FEBRUARY		3	25%
MARCH		6	67%
APRIL		2	11%
MAY		7	58%

LEAGUE GOALS

	PLAYER	MINS	GOALS	S RATE
1	Rosina	2773	9	308
2	Stellone	1986	4	496
3	Muzzi	1313	3	437
4	Abbruscato	1442	3	480
5	Comotto	3143	3	1047
6	Bovo	602	1	602
7	Cioffi	1385	1	1385
8	Lazetic	1781	1	1781
9	Franceschini	2594	1	2594
10	Gallo	1192	0	
11	Konan	136	0	
12	Schiattarella	0	0	
13	Taibi	165	0	
	Other		0	
	TOTAL		**26**	

TOP POINT EARNERS

	PLAYER	GAMES	AV PTS
1	Nikola Lazetic	17	1.53
2	Andrea Ardito	18	1.33
3	Marco Di Loreto	21	1.29
4	Gabriele Cioffi	15	1.27
5	Alessandro Rosina	28	1.18
6	Roberto Stellone	17	1.18
7	Gianluca Comotto	35	1.14
8	Christian Abbiati	36	1.11
9	Jacopo Balestri	30	1.10
10	Ivan Franceschini	29	0.90
	CLUB AVERAGE:		**1.05**

DISCIPLINARY RECORDS

	PLAYER	YELLOW	RED	AVE
1	Gabriele Cioffi	8	1	153
2	Andrea Ardito	10	1	166
3	Cesare Bovo	3	0	200
4	Simone Barone	8	1	279
5	Ivan Franceschini	8	1	288
6	Fabio Gallo	4	0	298
7	Oscar Brevi	5	1	305
8	Roberto Muzzi	3	1	328
9	Marco Di Loreto	5	1	329
10	Roberto Stellone	5	0	397
11	Diego De Ascentis	5	0	430
12	Giuseppe Pancaro	2	0	431
13	Gianluca Comotto	6	0	523
	Other	11	1	
	TOTAL	**83**	**8**	

KEY GOALKEEPER

Christian Abbiati			
Goals Conceded in the League	42	Counting Games League games when player was on pitch for at least 70 minutes	36
Defensive Rating Ave number of mins between League goals conceded while on the pitch	76	Clean Sheets In League games when player was on pitch for at least 70 minutes	14

KEY PLAYERS - DEFENDERS

Gianluca Comotto			
Goals Conceded Number of League goals conceded while the player was on the pitch	39	Clean Sheets In League games when player was on pitch for at least 70 minutes	14
Defensive Rating Ave number of mins between League goals conceded while on the pitch	80	Club Defensive Rating Average number of mins between League goals conceded by the club this season	74

	PLAYER	CON LGE	CLEAN SHEETS	DEF RATE
1	Gianluca Comotto	39	14	80 mins
2	Gabriele Cioffi	18	5	76 mins
3	Oscar Brevi	25	9	73 mins
4	Ivan Franceschini	38	9	68 mins

KEY PLAYERS - MIDFIELDERS

Andrea Ardito			
Goals in the League	0	Contribution to Attacking Power Average number of minutes between League team goals while on pitch	121
Defensive Rating Average number of mins between League goals conceded while on the pitch	96	Scoring Difference Defensive Rating minus Contribution to Attacking Power	-25

	PLAYER	LGE GOALS	DEF RATE	POWER	SCORE DIFF
1	Andrea Ardito	0	96	121	-25 mins
2	Nikola Lazetic	1	89	137	-48 mins
3	Jacopo Balestri	0	69	123	-54 mins
4	Alessandro Rosina	9	81	138	-57 mins

KEY PLAYERS - GOALSCORERS

Alessandro Rosina			
Goals in the League	9	Player Strike Rate Average number of minutes between League goals scored by player	308
Contribution to Attacking Power Average number of minutes between League team goals while on pitch	138	Club Strike Rate Average number of minutes between League goals scored by club	130

	PLAYER	LGE GOALS	POWER	STRIKE RATE
1	Alessandro Rosina	9	138	308 mins
2	Elvis Abbruscato	3	96	480 mins
3	Roberto Stellone	4	141	496 mins
4	Nikola Lazetic	1	137	1781 mins

Alessandro Rosina

SQUAD APPEARANCES

Match	1	2	3	4	5		6	7	8	9	10		11	12	13	14	15		16	17	18	19	20		21	22	23	24	25		26	27	28	29	30		31	32	33	34	35		36	37	38
Venue	H	A	H	A	H		H	A	H	A	H		A	H	A	H	A		A	H	A	H	A		H	H	A	A	H		A	H	A	H	A		H	A	A	H	H		A	H	A
Competition	L	L	L	L	L		L	L	L	L	L		L	L	L	L	L		L	L	L	L	L		L	L	L	L	L		L	L	L	L	L		L	L	L	L	L		L	L	L
Result	D	L	L	D	L		W	D	L	D	D		L	W	W	W	D		W	L	D	L	L		L	L	L	L	W		L	W	W	D	L		L	L	D	L	W		W	D	L

Goalkeepers
Christian Abbiati
Antonio Fontana
Massimo Taibi

Defenders
Cesare Bovo
Oscar Brevi
Gabriele Cioffi
Gianluca Comotto
Marco Di Loreto
Diaw Doudou
Ivan Franceschini
Luigi Martinelli
A Obinze Ogbona
Guiseppe Pancaro

Midfielders
Andrea Ardito
Jacopo Balestri
Simone Barone
Francesco Coco
Diego De Ascentis
Claudio Ferrarese
Stefano Fiore
Fabio Gallo
Nikola Lazetic
Vedin Music
Alessandro Rosina

Forwards
Elvis Abbruscato
H Axel Cedric Konan
Roberto Muzzi
Mashasi Oguro
Roberto Stellone

KEY: ■ On all match ◄◄ Subbed or sent off (Counting game) ►►| Subbed on from bench (Counting Game) ►► Subbed on and then subbed or sent off (Counting Game) ☐ Not in 16
■ On bench ◄◄ Subbed or sent off (playing less than 70 minutes) ►► Subbed on (playing less than 70 minutes) ►► Subbed on and then subbed or sent off (playing less than 70 minutes)

CHIEVO VERONA

Final Position: 18th

NICKNAME: MUSSI VOLANTI

KEY: ☐ Won ☐ Drawn ☐ Lost

#		Opponent			Result	Scorers	Attendance
1	ecql1	Levski Sofia	A	L	0-2		26,000
2	ecql2	Levski Sofia	H	D	2-2	Amauri 48, 81	44,000
3	itpr1	Siena	H	L	1-2	Pellissier 31	5,253
4	ucrl1	Braga	A	L	0-2		20,000
5	itpr1	Empoli	A	D	1-1	Mandelli 15	3,504
6	itpr1	Lazio	H	L	0-1		5,232
7	itpr1	Inter Milan	A	L	3-4	Pellissier 77 pen, Tiribocchi 86, Brighi 88	41,357
8	ucrl2	Braga	H	W	2-1	Tiribocchi 37, Godeas 67	4,624
9	itpr1	Palermo	H	L	0-1		3,500
10	itpr1	Torino	A	L	0-1		18,945
11	itpr1	Roma	A	D	1-1	Pellissier 40	35,000
12	itpr1	AC Milan	H	L	0-1		17,000
13	itpr1	Messina	A	D	1-1	Tiribocchi 32	15,000
14	itpr1	Cagliari	H	D	0-0		5,426
15	itpr1	Sampdoria	A	L	0-2		18,000
16	itpr1	Atalanta	H	D	2-2	Zanchetta 25, Pellissier 57	6,000
17	itpr1	Udinese	H	W	2-0	Obinna 31, 72	6,000
18	itpr1	Livorno	A	W	2-0	Obinna 72, 78	7,500
19	itpr1	Fiorentina	H	L	0-1		13,000
20	itpr1	Parma	A	D	2-2	Zanchetta 23 pen, D'Anna 67	15,000
21	itpr1	Reggina	H	W	3-2	Sammarco 26, Cossato 44, Tiribocchi 88	6,000
22	itpr1	Ascoli	A	L	0-3		7,000
23	itpr1	Catania	H	W	2-1	Semioli 58, Pellissier 64 pen	6,409
24	itpr1	Siena	A	L	1-2	Brighi 25	6,000
25	itpr1	Empoli	H	D	0-0		6,000
26	itpr1	Inter Milan	H	L	0-2		0
27	itpr1	Palermo	A	D	1-1	Obinna 45	25,000
28	itpr1	Torino	H	W	3-0	Bogdani 2, 45, Brighi 47	5,000
29	itpr1	Roma	H	D	2-2	Bogdani 17, Semioli 33	4,000
30	itpr1	AC Milan	A	L	1-3	Pellissier 17	40,000
31	itpr1	Messina	H	D	1-1	Sammarco 73	4,221
32	itpr1	Cagliari	A	W	2-0	Brighi 50, Bogdani 55	8,000
33	itpr1	Sampdoria	H	D	1-1	Brighi 32	5,765
34	itpr1	Atalanta	A	L	0-1		11,845
35	itpr1	Udinese	A	L	1-2	Pellissier 9	21,804
36	itpr1	Lazio	A	D	0-0		25,000
37	itpr1	Livorno	H	W	2-1	Pellissier 55, Bogdani 76	5,433
38	itpr1	Fiorentina	A	L	0-1		30,724
39	itpr1	Parma	H	W	1-0	Pellissier 5	11,934
40	itpr1	Reggina	A	D	1-1	Brighi 51	13,164
41	itpr1	Ascoli	H	W	1-0	Marcolini 43	12,706
42	itpr1	Catania	A	L	0-2		18,207

LEAGUE APPEARANCES, BOOKINGS AND CAPS

	AGE (on 01/07/07)	IN NAMED 18	APPEARANCES	COUNTING GAMES	MINUTES ON PITCH	YELLOW CARDS	RED CARDS	CAPS THIS SEASON	NATIONAL SIDE
Goalkeepers									
Vincenzo Sicignano	32	23	17	17	1530	1	0	-	Italy
Lorenzo Squizzi	33	36	21	21	1890	2	0	-	Italy
Defenders									
Lorenzo D'Anna	35	21	21	19	1811	4	1	-	Italy
Salvatore Lanna	30	33	31	31	2763	4	2	-	Italy
Marco Malago	28	29	21	18	1728	6	0	-	Italy
Davide Mandelli	30	36	36	36	3240	8	0	-	Italy
Andrea Mantovani	23	33	18	13	1291	4	1	-	Italy
Giovanni Marchese	22	24	9	7	614	3	1	-	Italy
Fabio Moro	31	20	19	16	1558	6	1	-	Italy
C Rickler Del Mare	20	14	5	2	228	1	0	-	Italy
Giuseppe Scurto	22	5	5	4	383	2	0	-	Italy
Midfielders									
Matteo Brighi	26	29	28	20	2163	2	1	-	Italy
Federico Giunti	35	11	8	6	571	1	0	-	Italy
Vincenzo Italiano	29	19	17	12	1220	2	0	-	Italy
Kamil Kosowski	29	34	23	1	908	1	0	-	Poland
Luciano Siqueira	31	17	14	8	962	4	2	-	Brazil
Mattia Marchesetti	23	8	5	0	162	2	0	-	Italy
Michele Marcolini	31	33	25	13	1526	6	0	-	Italy
Paolo Sammarco	24	37	32	27	2658	9	2	-	Italy
Franco Semioli	27	32	32	24	2520	3	0	2	Italy
Michele Troiano	22	6	3	0	106	0	0	-	Italy
Andrea Zanchetta	32	13	11	9	834	4	1	-	Italy
Forwards									
C De Oliveira Amauri	27	2	2	2	180	0	0	-	Brazil
Erjon Bogdani	30	19	19	7	1203	4	0	5	Albania
Salvatore Bruno	27	9	4	0	148	0	0	-	Italy
Federico Cossato	34	18	17	1	498	2	1	-	Italy
Giuseppe Cozzolino	21	7	5	0	120	0	0	-	Italy
Denis Godeas	31	9	5	3	309	0	0	-	Italy
Victor Obinna	20	24	24	11	1448	4	1	-	Nigeria
Sergio Pellissier	28	36	36	20	2371	3	0	-	Italy
Simone Tiribocchi	29	17	15	2	541	2	0	-	Italy

TEAM OF THE SEASON

G Lorenzo Squizzi
CG: 21 DR: 78

D Andrea Mantovani
CG: 13 DR: 92

D Salvatore Lanna
CG: 31 DR: 78

D Fabio Moro
CG: 16 DR: 74

D Davide Mandelli
CG: 36 DR: 73

M Vincenzo Italiano
CG: 12 SD: -6

M Michele Marcolini
CG: 13 SD: -8

M Franco Semioli
CG: 24 SD: -14

M Paolo Sammarco
CG: 27 SD: -16

F Sergio Pellissier
CG: 20 SR: 263

F Victor Obinna*
CG: 11 SR: 289

MONTHLY POINTS TALLY

SEPTEMBER	1	8%
OCTOBER	2	13%
NOVEMBER	5	42%
DECEMBER	7	47%
JANUARY	4	44%
FEBRUARY	5	42%
MARCH	4	44%
APRIL	5	28%
MAY	7	58%

LEAGUE GOALS

	PLAYER	MINS	GOALS	S RATE
1	Pellissier	2371	9	263
2	Brighi	2163	6	360
3	Bogdani	1203	5	240
4	Obinna	1448	5	289
5	Tiribocchi	541	3	180
6	Zanchetta	834	2	417
7	Semioli	2520	2	1260
8	Sammarco	2658	2	1329
9	Cossato	498	1	498
10	Marcolini	1526	1	1526
11	D'Anna	1811	1	1811
12	Mandelli	3240	1	3240
13	Mantovani	1291	0	
	Other		0	
	TOTAL		**38**	

TOP POINT EARNERS

	PLAYER	GAMES	AV PTS
1	Victor Obinna	12	1.33
2	Matteo Brighi	20	1.30
3	Marco Malago	18	1.28
4	Michele Marcolini	13	1.23
5	Paolo Sammarco	28	1.21
6	Franco Semioli	24	1.21
7	Sergio Pellissier	18	1.17
8	Andrea Mantovani	13	1.15
9	Lorenzo D'Anna	20	1.15
10	Vincenzo Italiano	12	1.08
	CLUB AVERAGE:		**1.03**

DISCIPLINARY RECORDS

	PLAYER	YELLOW	RED	AVE
1	Luciano Siqueira	4	2	160
2	Federico Cossato	2	1	166
3	Fabio Moro	6	1	259
4	Simone Tiribocchi	2	0	270
5	Marco Malago	6	0	288
6	Victor Obinna	4	1	289
7	Erjon Bogdani	4	0	300
8	Michele Marcolini	6	0	305
9	Giovanni Marchese	3	1	307
10	Andrea Mantovani	4	1	322
11	Paolo Sammarco	9	2	332
12	Lorenzo D'Anna	4	1	362
13	Andrea Zanchetta	4	1	417
	Other	27	3	
	TOTAL	**85**	**14**	

KEY GOALKEEPER

Lorenzo Squizzi

Goals Conceded in the League	24	**Counting Games** League games when player was on pitch for at least 70 minutes	21
Defensive Rating Ave number of mins between League goals conceded while on the pitch	78	**Clean Sheets** In League games when player was on pitch for at least 70 minutes	5

KEY PLAYERS - DEFENDERS

Andrea Mantovani

Goals Conceded Number of League goals conceded while the player was on the pitch	14	**Clean Sheets** In League games when player was on pitch for at least 70 minutes	5
Defensive Rating Ave number of mins between League goals conceded while on the pitch	92	**Club Defensive Rating** Average number of mins between League goals conceded by the club this season	74

	PLAYER	CON LGE	CLEAN SHEETS	DEF RATE
1	Andrea Mantovani	14	5	92 mins
2	Salvatore Lanna	35	8	78 mins
3	Fabio Moro	21	3	74 mins
4	Davide Mandelli	44	9	73 mins

KEY PLAYERS - MIDFIELDERS

Vincenzo Italiano

Goals in the League	0	**Contribution to Attacking Power** Average number of minutes between League team goals while on pitch	87
Defensive Rating Average number of mins between League goals conceded while on the pitch	81	**Scoring Difference** Defensive Rating minus Contribution to Attacking Power	-6

	PLAYER	LGE GOALS	DEF RATE	POWER	SCORE DIFF
1	Vincenzo Italiano	0	81	87	-6 mins
2	Michele Marcolini	1	72	80	-8 mins
3	Franco Semioli	2	76	90	-14 mins
4	Paolo Sammarco	2	69	85	-16 mins

KEY PLAYERS - GOALSCORERS

Sergio Pellissier

Goals in the League	9	**Player Strike Rate** Average number of minutes between League goals scored by player	263
Contribution to Attacking Power Average number of minutes between League team goals while on pitch	87	**Club Strike Rate** Average number of minutes between League goals scored by club	92

	PLAYER	LGE GOALS	POWER	STRIKE RATE
1	Sergio Pellissier	9	87	263 mins
2	Victor Obinna	5	96	289 mins
3	Matteo Brighi	6	86	360 mins
4	Franco Semioli	2	90	1260 mins

Franco Semioli and Erjon Bogdani

SQUAD APPEARANCES

Match	1 2 3 4 5	6 7 8 9 10	11 12 13 14 15	16 17 18 19 20	21 22 23 24 25	26 27 28 29 30	31 32 33 34 35	36 37 38 39 40	41 42
Venue	A H H A A	H A H H A	A H A H A	H H A H A	H A H A H	H A H H A	H A H A A	A H A H A	H A
Competition	C C L E L	L L E L L	L L L L L	L L L L L	L L L L L	L L L L L	L L L L L	L L L L L	L L
Result	L D L L D	L L W L L	D L D D L	D W W L D	W L W L D	L D W D L	D W D L L	D W L W D	W L

Goalkeepers
Vincenzo Sicignano
Lorenzo Squizzi

Defenders
Lorenzo D'Anna
Salvatore Lanna
Marco Malago
Davide Mandelli
Andrea Mantovani
Giovanni Marchese
Fabio Moro
C Rickler Del Mare
Giuseppe Scurto

Midfielders
Matteo Brighi
Federico Giunti
Vincenzo Italiano
Kamil Kosowski
Luciano Siqueira
Mattia Marchesetti
Michele Marcolini
Paolo Sammarco
Franco Semioli
Michele Troiano
Andrea Zanchetta

Forwards
C De Oliveira Amauri
Erjon Bogdani
Salvatore Bruno
Federico Cossato
Giuseppe Cozzolino
Denis Godeas
Victor Obinna
Sergio Pellissier
Simone Tiribocchi

KEY: ■ On all match ◄◄ Subbed or sent off (Counting game) ►► Subbed on from bench (Counting Game) ►► Subbed on and then subbed or sent off (Counting Game) ☐ Not in 16
■ On bench ◄◄ Subbed or sent off (playing less than 70 minutes) ►► Subbed on (playing less than 70 minutes) ►► Subbed on and then subbed or sent off (playing less than 70 minutes)

ITALY - CHIEVO VERONA

ASCOLI

Final Position: **19th**

NICKNAME: PICCHIO   KEY: ☐ Won ☐ Drawn ☐ Lost   Attendance

#				Result	Scorers	Attendance
1	itpr1	Atalanta	A L	1-3	Bjelanovic 59	11,000
2	itpr1	Messina	H D	1-1	Perrulli 87	7,000
3	itpr1	AC Milan	A L	0-1		43,085
4	itpr1	Sampdoria	H D	1-1	Delvecchio 15	7,809
5	itpr1	Udinese	A D	0-0		14,000
6	itpr1	Livorno	H L	0-2		7,078
7	itpr1	Parma	A L	0-1		12,814
8	itpr1	Roma	A D	2-2	Delvecchio 22, Bjelanovic 64	33,000
9	itpr1	Siena	H L	0-1		12,000
10	itpr1	Inter Milan	A L	0-2		35,000
11	itpr1	Empoli	H L	0-1		7,000
12	itpr1	Fiorentina	H D	1-1	Bjelanovic 84	7,000
13	itpr1	Lazio	A L	1-3	Mauri 15	19,000
14	itpr1	Catania	H D	2-2	Bjelanovic 12, 39	7,000
15	itpr1	Reggina	A L	1-2	Pecorari 84	9,000
16	itpr1	Torino	H L	0-2		8,000
17	itpr1	Palermo	A L	0-4		20,000
18	itpr1	Chievo	H W	3-0	Paolucci 8, Bjelanovic 14, 37	7,000
19	itpr1	Cagliari	A L	0-1		10,000
20	itpr1	Atalanta	H L	1-3	Paolucci 73	8,000
21	itpr1	Messina	A W	2-1	Paolucci 89, 90	13,000
22	itpr1	Sampdoria	A L	0-2		17,000
23	itpr1	Udinese	H D	2-2	Soncin 58, 69	400
24	itpr1	Livorno	A D	0-0		5,641
25	itpr1	Parma	H D	0-0		4,800
26	itpr1	Roma	H D	1-1	Soncin 31	5,000
27	itpr1	Siena	A W	1-0	Bjelanovic 22	10,792
28	itpr1	Inter Milan	H L	1-2	Bonanni 90 pen	4,787
29	itpr1	Empoli	A L	1-4	Soncin 50	4,151
30	itpr1	Fiorentina	A L	0-4		29,123
31	itpr1	Lazio	H D	2-2	Soncin 70, Di Biagio 76 pen	11,380
32	itpr1	AC Milan	H L	2-5	Di Biagio 33 pen, Guberti 41	5,000
33	itpr1	Reggina	H L	2-3	Fini 15, Bonanni 78	5,896
34	itpr1	Catania	A D	3-3	Boudianski 36, Perrulli 49, Zanetti 52	0
35	itpr1	Torino	A L	0-1		20,048
36	itpr1	Palermo	H W	3-2	Boudianski 25, 61, Paolucci 47	4,352
37	itpr1	Chievo	A L	0-1		12,706
38	itpr1	Cagliari	H W	2-1	Soncin 17, Paolucci 78	5,427

LEAGUE APPEARANCES, BOOKINGS AND CAPS

	AGE (on 01/07/07)	IN NAMED 18	APPEARANCES	COUNTING GAMES	MINUTES ON PITCH	YELLOW CARDS	RED CARDS	CAPS THIS SEASON	NATIONAL SIDE
Goalkeepers									
D Eleftheropoulos	30	30	14	13	1219	1	0	-	Greece
Gianluca Pagliuca	40	23	23	23	2070	2	0	-	Italy
Defenders									
Guiseppe Bellusci	17	4	3	1	111	0	0	-	Italy
Ricardo Corallo	27	17	12	12	1080	7	0	-	Italy
Mirko Cudini	33	19	18	18	1590	1	0	-	Italy
Paolo Foglio	31	12	11	11	979	8	0	-	Italy
Aleksandar Lukovic	24	10	10	9	841	3	0	2	Serbia
Matteo Melara	27	18	16	15	1338	4	1	-	Italy
Michelangelo Minieri	26	27	19	10	1258	8	2	-	Italy
Vasile Nastase	32	32	29	26	2457	9	0	-	Romania
Marco Pecorari	29	18	15	13	1247	3	0	-	Italy
Gaetano Vastola	29	24	17	10	1110	3	0	-	Italy
Midfielders									
Massimo Bonanni	25	17	14	3	733	4	1	-	Italy
Viktor Boudianski	23	33	31	28	2669	8	0	-	Ukraine
Luigi Di Biagio	36	9	7	5	496	2	1	-	Italy
Michele Fini	33	32	32	26	2529	5	0	-	Italy
Gaetano Fontana	37	18	10	7	714	4	0	-	Italy
Domenico Giampa	30	19	11	2	510	1	0	-	Italy
Stefano Guberti	22	30	22	9	1242	0	0	-	Italy
Stefano Lombardi	30	10	10	8	780	5	1	-	Italy
Fabio Pecchia	33	14	7	2	318	0	0	-	Italy
Giampietro Perrulli	22	33	26	5	977	2	0	-	Italy
Simone Pesce	24	31	28	18	1775	3	1	-	Italy
Ervin Skela	30	9	7	1	298	1	0	4	Albania
Paolo Zanetti	24	32	30	26	2490	6	0	-	Italy
Forwards									
Sasa Bjelanovic	28	26	26	20	1999	4	0	-	Croatia
Marco Delvecchio	34	10	10	2	422	3	1	-	Italy
Daniele Galloppa	22	15	13	6	797	1	0	-	Italy
Thomas Herve Job	22	10	4	1	185	1	0	-	Cameroon
Michele Paolucci	21	36	32	16	1838	3	0	-	Italy
Andrea Soncin	28	16	16	10	1064	3	0	-	Italy

TEAM OF THE SEASON

D Mirko Cudini CG: 18 DR: 54
M Simone Pesce CG: 18 SD: -18
D Marco Pecorari CG: 13 DR: 54
M Viktor Boudianski CG: 28 SD: -32
F Sasa Bjelanovic CG: 20 SR: 249
G Gianluca Pagliuca CG: 23 DR: 54
D Vasile Nastase CG: 26 DR: 53
M Paolo Zanetti CG: 26 SD: -45
F Michele Paolucci CG: 16 SR: 306
D Matteo Melara CG: 15 DR: 49
M Michele Fini CG: 26 SD: -69

MONTHLY POINTS TALLY

SEPTEMBER	2	17%
OCTOBER	2	13%
NOVEMBER	1	8%
DECEMBER	4	27%
JANUARY	3	33%
FEBRUARY	3	25%
MARCH	4	44%
APRIL	1	7%
MAY	7	47%

LEAGUE GOALS

	PLAYER	MINS	GOALS	S RATE
1	Bjelanovic	1999	8	249
2	Soncin	1064	6	177
3	Paolucci	1838	6	306
4	Boudianski	2669	3	889
5	Delvecchio	422	2	211
6	Di Biagio	496	2	248
7	Bonanni	733	2	366
8	Perrulli	977	2	488
9	Guberti	1242	1	1242
10	Pecorari	1247	1	1247
11	Zanetti	2490	1	2490
12	Fini	2529	1	2529
13	Foglio	979	0	
	Other		0	
	TOTAL		**35**	

TOP POINT EARNERS

	PLAYER	GAMES	AV PTS
1	Michele Paolucci	15	1.20
2	Matteo Melara	14	1.14
3	Simone Pesce	18	1.06
4	Viktor Boudianski	27	0.89
5	D Eleftheropoulos	13	0.85
6	Ricardo Corallo	12	0.75
7	Paolo Zanetti	25	0.72
8	Michele Fini	24	0.63
9	Gianluca Pagliuca	23	0.57
10	Vasile Nastase	26	0.54
	CLUB AVERAGE:		**0.71**

DISCIPLINARY RECORDS

	PLAYER	YELLOW	RED	AVE
1	Paolo Foglio	8	0	122
2	Michelangelo Minieri	8	2	125
3	Stefano Lombardi	5	1	130
4	Massimo Bonanni	4	1	146
5	Ricardo Corallo	7	0	154
6	Luigi Di Biagio	2	1	165
7	Gaetano Fontana	4	0	178
8	Matteo Melara	4	1	267
9	Vasile Nastase	9	0	273
10	Aleksandar Lukovic	3	0	280
11	Viktor Boudianski	8	0	333
12	Andrea Soncin	3	0	354
13	Gaetano Vastola	3	0	370
	Other	32	1	
	TOTAL	**100**	**7**	

KEY GOALKEEPER

Gianluca Pagliuca

Goals Conceded in the League	38	Counting Games League games when player was on pitch for at least 70 minutes	23
Defensive Rating ...ve number of mins between League ...goals conceded while on the pitch	54	Clean Sheets In League games when player was on pitch for at least 70 minutes	2

KEY PLAYERS - DEFENDERS

Mirko Cudini

Goals Conceded Number of League goals conceded while the player was on the pitch	29	Clean Sheets In League games when player was on pitch for at least 70 minutes	1
Defensive Rating ...ve number of mins between League ...goals conceded while on the pitch	54	Club Defensive Rating Average number of mins between League goals conceded by the club this season	52

	PLAYER	CON LGE	CLEAN SHEETS	DEF RATE
1	Mirko Cudini	29	1	54 mins
2	Marco Pecorari	23	0	54 mins
3	Vasile Nastase	46	4	53 mins
4	Matteo Melara	27	3	49 mins

KEY PLAYERS - MIDFIELDERS

Simone Pesce

Goals in the League	0	Contribution to Attacking Power Average number of minutes between League team goals while on pitch	71
Defensive Rating Average number of mins between League goals conceded while on the pitch	53	Scoring Difference Defensive Rating minus Contribution to Attacking Power	-18

	PLAYER	LGE GOALS	DEF RATE	POWER	SCORE DIFF
1	Simone Pesce	0	53	71	-18 mins
2	Viktor Boudianski	3	51	83	-32 mins
3	Paolo Zanetti	1	54	99	-45 mins
4	Michele Fini	1	51	120	-69 mins

KEY PLAYERS - GOALSCORERS

Sasa Bjelanovic

Goals in the League	8	Player Strike Rate Average number of minutes between League goals scored by player	249
Contribution to Attacking Power Average number of minutes between League team goals while on pitch	105	Club Strike Rate Average number of minutes between League goals scored by club	97

	PLAYER	LGE GOALS	POWER	STRIKE RATE
1	Sasa Bjelanovic	8	105	249 mins
2	Michele Paolucci	6	79	306 mins
3	Viktor Boudianski	3	83	889 mins
4	Paolo Zanetti	1	99	2490 mins

Michele Paolucci

SQUAD APPEARANCES

	1	2	3	4	5		6	7	8	9	10		11	12	13	14	15		16	17	18	19	20		21	22	23	24	25		26	27	28	29	30		31	32	33	34	35		36	37	38
...ue	A	H	A	H	A		H	A	A	H	A		H	H	H	A	H		A	H	A	H	A		A	A	H	A	H		H	A	H	A	A		H	H	H	A	A		H	A	H
...mpetition	L	L	L	L	L		L	L	L	L	L		L	L	L	L	L		L	L	L	L	L		L	L	L	L	L		L	L	L	L	L		L	L	L	L	L		L	L	L
...sult	L	D	L	D	D		L	L	D	L	L		L	D	L	D	L		L	L	W	L	L		W	L	D	D	D		D	W	L	L	L		D	L	L	D	L		W	L	W

Goalkeepers
- ...leftheropoulos
- ...nluca Pagliuca

Defenders
- ...seppe Bellusci
- ...ardo Corallo
- ...ko Cudini
- ...olo Foglio
- ...ksandar Lukovic
- ...tteo Melara
- ...helangelo Minieri
- ...ile Nastase
- ...rco Pecorari
- ...etano Vastola

Midfielders
- ...ssimo Bonanni
- ...tor Boudianski
- ...gi Di Biagio
- ...hele Fini
- ...etano Fontana
- ...menico Giampa
- ...fano Guberti
- ...fano Lombardi
- ...io Pecchia
- ...mpietro Perrulli
- ...one Pesce
- ...in Skela
- ...olo Zanetti

Forwards
- ...a Bjelanovic
- ...rco Delvecchio
- ...iele Galloppa
- ...ars Gauracs
- ...hele Paolucci
- ...drea Soncin

KEY: ■ On all match ◄◄ Subbed or sent off (Counting game) ►►◄ Subbed on from bench (Counting Game) ►► Subbed on and then subbed or sent off (Counting Game) □ Not in 16
□ On bench ◄ Subbed or sent off (playing less than 70 minutes) ►► Subbed on (playing less than 70 minutes) ►► Subbed on and then subbed or sent off (playing less than 70 minutes)

MESSINA

Final Position: **20th**

NICKNAME: BIANCOSCUDATI   KEY: ☐ Won ☐ Drawn ☐ Lost   Attendance

#				Score	Scorers	Attendance
1	itpr1	Udinese	H W	1-0	Zanchi 73	12,000
2	itpr1	Ascoli	A D	1-1	Rigano 63	7,000
3	itpr1	Reggina	H W	2-0	Rigano 24, 85	19,625
4	itpr1	Catania	A D	2-2	Floccari 32, Cordova 64	19,029
5	itpr1	Livorno	H L	0-1		18,000
6	itpr1	Siena	A L	1-3	Rigano 20	11,231
7	itpr1	Empoli	H D	2-2	Rigano 9, Ogasawara 50	16,000
8	itpr1	Palermo	A L	1-2	Rigano 7	28,547
9	itpr1	Chievo	H D	1-1	Rigano 45	15,000
10	itpr1	Torino	A D	1-1	Cordova 36	18,000
11	itpr1	Cagliari	H D	2-2	Cordova 35, Rigano 64	12,000
12	itpr1	Lazio	H L	1-4	Rigano 57 pen	20,000
13	itpr1	AC Milan	A L	0-1		45,000
14	itpr1	Sampdoria	H L	0-2		20,000
15	itpr1	Atalanta	A L	2-3	Cordova 76, Di Napoli 85	13,000
16	itpr1	Inter Milan	A L	0-2		45,000
17	itpr1	Parma	H D	1-1	Di Napoli 73	15,000
18	itpr1	Fiorentina	A L	0-4		30,000
19	itpr1	Roma	H D	1-1	Parisi 90 pen	20,000
20	itpr1	Udinese	A L	0-1		15,000
21	itpr1	Ascoli	H L	1-2	Parisi 75 pen	13,000
22	itpr1	Catania	H D	1-1	Zanchi 35	0
23	itpr1	Livorno	A L	1-2	Zoro 78	0
24	itpr1	Siena	H W	1-0	Alvarez 90	10,000
25	itpr1	Empoli	A L	1-3	Alvarez 89	1,000
26	itpr1	Palermo	H W	2-0	Rigano 45, 65	15,000
27	itpr1	Chievo	A D	1-1	Rigano 87 pen	4,221
28	itpr1	Torino	H L	0-3		11,915
29	itpr1	Cagliari	A L	0-2		7,000
30	itpr1	Lazio	A L	0-1		24,106
31	itpr1	AC Milan	H L	1-3	Masiello 90	17,521
32	itpr1	Reggina	A L	1-3	Rigano 27 pen	11,000
33	itpr1	Sampdoria	A L	1-3	Rigano 54	16,673
34	itpr1	Atalanta	H D	0-0		10,752
35	itpr1	Inter Milan	H L	0-1		13,410
36	itpr1	Parma	A L	1-4	Rigano 87	13,833
37	itpr1	Fiorentina	H D	2-2	Rigano 80, 88 pen	10,648
38	itpr1	Roma	A L	3-4	Rigano 10, 58, Cordova 75	28,191

LEAGUE APPEARANCES, BOOKINGS AND CAPS

	AGE (on 01/07/07)	IN NAMED 18	APPEARANCES	COUNTING GAMES	MINUTES ON PITCH	YELLOW CARDS	RED CARDS	CAPS THIS SEASON	NATIONAL SIDE
Goalkeepers									
Nicholas Caglioni	24	27	7	7	630	0	0	-	Italy
Alessandro Cesaretti	38	6	1	1	90	0	0	-	Italy
Gabriele Paoletti	29	19	11	11	990	1	0	-	Italy
Marco Storari	30	19	19	19	1710	2	0	-	Italy
Defenders									
Gaetano Cala	18	3	2	1	135	0	0	-	Italy
Andrea Giallombardo	26	18	15	8	975	2	0	-	Italy
Mark Iuliano	33	22	21	18	1679	8	1	-	Italy
Enrico Morello	30	24	17	6	860	2	1	-	Italy
Alessandro Parisi	30	31	30	23	2272	9	2	-	Italy
Angelo Rea	25	28	23	16	1673	8	1	-	Italy
Marco Zanchi	30	32	32	30	2758	9	2	-	Italy
Midfielders									
Edgar A R Alvarez	27	36	31	18	1956	1	0	3	Honduras
Carmine Coppola	28	13	13	9	951	7	1	-	Italy
N Andrea Cordova	28	35	23	13	1513	3	1	-	Chile
Roberto D'aversa	31	16	12	9	964	2	0	-	Italy
Daniele De Vezze	27	29	27	19	1873	8	1	-	Italy
Luigi Lavecchia	25	35	31	24	2334	7	0	-	Italy
Salvatore Masiello	25	37	36	32	2991	7	0	-	Italy
Massimo Minetti	29	11	2	0	35	0	0	-	Italy
Mitsuo Ogasawara	28	20	6	2	311	1	0	-	Japan
Manolo Pestrin	28	17	16	9	1204	4	0	-	Italy
Salvatore Sullo	35	16	4	2	187	1	0	-	Italy
Marc Andre Zoro	23	23	22	15	1538	7	2	-	Ivory Coast
Forwards									
Ibrahim Bakayoko	30	12	6	3	398	0	0	-	Ivory Coast
Vincent Candela	33	16	16	14	1360	4	1	-	France
Arturo Di Napoli	33	30	22	10	1132	3	0	-	Italy
Sergio Floccari	25	30	27	13	1517	1	0	-	Italy
Ivica Iliev	27	31	21	7	969	1	0	-	Serbia
Antonio Montella	21	2	2	0	32	0	0	-	Italy
Christian Rigano	33	27	27	24	2242	8	0	-	Italy

TEAM OF THE SEASON

D Angelo Rea — CG: 16 DR: 55
M N Andrea Cordova — CG: 13 SD: -29
G Marco Storari — CG: 19 DR: 51
D Alessandro Parisi — CG: 23 DR: 55
M Edgar A Reyes Alvarez — CG: 18 SD: -31
F Christian Rigano — CG: 24 SR: 118
D Marco Zanchi — CG: 30 DR: 53
M Luigi Lavecchia — CG: 24 SD: -39
F Sergio Floccari — CG: 13 SR: 1517
D Mark Iuliano — CG: 18 DR: 46
M Salvatore Masiello — CG: 32 SD: -49

MONTHLY POINTS TALLY

SEPTEMBER	8	67%
OCTOBER	2	13%
NOVEMBER	2	17%
DECEMBER	1	7%
JANUARY	1	11%
FEBRUARY	4	33%
MARCH	4	44%
APRIL	1	6%
MAY	1	8%

LEAGUE GOALS

	PLAYER	MINS	GOALS	S RATE
1	Rigano	2242	19	118
2	Cordova	1513	5	302
3	Di Napoli	1132	2	566
4	Alvarez	1956	2	978
5	Parisi	2272	2	1136
6	Zanchi	2758	2	1379
7	Ogasawara	311	1	311
8	Floccari	1517	1	1517
9	Zoro	1538	1	1538
10	Masiello	2991	1	2991
11	Minetti	35	0	
12	Montalto	0	0	
13	Montella	32	0	
	Other		0	
	TOTAL		36	

TOP POINT EARNERS

	PLAYER	GAMES	AV PTS
1	Luigi Lavecchia	23	0.87
2	Alessandro Parisi	22	0.82
3	Angelo Rea	17	0.76
4	Marco Storari	19	0.74
5	E Antonio Reyes Alvarez	17	0.71
6	Marco Zanchi	30	0.70
7	Salvatore Masiello	30	0.67
8	Sergio Floccari	13	0.62
9	Christian Rigano	23	0.61
10	Nicolas Andrea Cordova	14	0.57
	CLUB AVERAGE:		0.68

DISCIPLINARY RECORDS

	PLAYER	YELLOW	RED	AV
1	Carmine Coppola	7	1	11
2	Marc Andre Zoro	7	2	17
3	Angelo Rea	8	1	18
4	Mark Iuliano	8	1	18
5	Alessandro Parisi	9	2	20
6	Daniele De Vezze	8	1	20
7	Marco Zanchi	9	2	25
8	Vincent Candela	4	1	27
9	Christian Rigano	8	0	28
10	Enrico Morello	2	1	28
11	Manolo Pestrin	4	0	30
12	Luigi Lavecchia	7	0	33
13	Arturo Di Napoli	3	0	37
	Other	19	1	
	TOTAL	103	13	

KEY GOALKEEPER

Marco Storari

Goals Conceded in the League	33	Counting Games League games when player was on pitch for at least 70 minutes	19
Defensive Rating Ave number of mins between League goals conceded while on the pitch	51	Clean Sheets In League games when player was on pitch for at least 70 minutes	2

KEY PLAYERS - DEFENDERS

Angelo Rea

Goals Conceded Number of League goals conceded while the player was on the pitch	30	Clean Sheets In League games when player was on pitch for at least 70 minutes	3
Defensive Rating Ave number of mins between League goals conceded while on the pitch	55	Club Defensive Rating Average number of mins between League goals conceded by the club this season	50

	PLAYER	CON LGE	CLEAN SHEETS	DEF RATE
1	Angelo Rea	30	3	55 mins
2	Alessandro Parisi	41	5	55 mins
3	Marco Zanchi	52	4	53 mins
4	Mark Iuliano	36	2	46 mins

KEY PLAYERS - MIDFIELDERS

Nicolas Andrea Cordova

Goals in the League	5	Contribution to Attacking Power Average number of minutes between League team goals while on pitch	79
Defensive Rating Average number of minutes between League goals conceded while on the pitch	50	Scoring Difference Defensive Rating minus Contribution to Attacking Power	-29

	PLAYER	LGE GOALS	DEF RATE	POWER	SCORE DIFF
1	Nicolas Andrea Cordova	5	50	79	-29 mins
2	Edgar Antonio Reyes Alvarez	2	47	78	-31 mins
3	Luigi Lavecchia	0	47	86	-39 mins
4	Salvatore Masiello	1	50	99	-49 mins

KEY PLAYERS - GOALSCORERS

Christian Rigano

Goals in the League	19	Player Strike Rate Average number of minutes between League goals scored by player	118
Contribution to Attacking Power Average number of minutes between League team goals while on pitch	86	Club Strike Rate Average number of minutes between League goals scored by club	97

	PLAYER	LGE GOALS	POWER	STRIKE RATE
1	Christian Rigano	19	86	118 mins
2	Nicolas Andrea Cordova	5	79	302 mins
3	Edgar Antonio Reyes Alvarez	2	78	978 mins
4	Sergio Floccari	1	108	1517 mins

Marco Zanchi

SQUAD APPEARANCES

Match	1 2 3 4 5	6 7 8 9 10	11 12 13 14 15	16 17 18 19 20	21 22 23 24 25	26 27 28 29 30	31 32 33 34 35	36 37 38
Venue	H A H A H	A H A H A	H H A H A	A H A H A	H H A H A	H A H A A	H A H H	A H A
Competition	L L L L L	L L L L L	L L L L L	L L L L L	L L L L L	L L L L L	L L L L L	L L L
Result	W D W D L	L D L D D	D L L L L	L D L D L	L D L W L	W D L L L	L L L D L	L D L

KEY: ■ On all match   ◄◄ Subbed or sent off (Counting game)   ►► Subbed on from bench (Counting Game)   ►► Subbed on and then subbed or sent off (Counting Game)   □ Not in 16
  ■ On bench   ◄◄ Subbed or sent off (playing less than 70 minutes)   ►► Subbed on (playing less than 70 minutes)   ►► Subbed on and then subbed or sent off (playing less than 70 minutes)

Goalkeepers
Nicholas Caglioni
Alessandro Cesaretti
Gabriele Paoletti
Marco Storari
Defenders
Gaetano Cala
Andrea Giallombardo
Mark Iuliano
Enrico Morello
Alessandro Parisi
Angelo Rea
Marco Zanchi
Midfielders
Edgar A R Alvarez
Carmine Coppola
N Andrea Cordova
Roberto D'aversa
Daniele De Vezze
Luigi Lavecchia
Salvatore Masiello
Massimo Minetti
Mitsuo Ogasawara
Manolo Pestrin
Salvatore Sullo
Marc Andre Zoro
Forwards
Ibrahim Bakayoko
Vincent Candela
Arturo Di Napoli
Sergio Floccari
Ivica Iliev
Antonio Montella
Christian Rigano

DUTCH LEAGUE ROUND-UP

FINAL LEAGUE TABLE

			HOME				AWAY					TOTAL		
	P	W	D	L	F	A	W	D	L	F	A	F	A	DIF	PTS
PSV	34	15	0	2	53	14	8	6	3	22	11	75	25	50	75
Ajax	34	12	3	2	44	12	11	3	3	40	23	84	35	49	75
AZ	34	10	6	1	44	13	11	3	3	39	18	83	31	52	72
FC Twente	34	13	3	1	47	15	6	6	5	20	22	67	37	30	66
Heerenveen	34	10	4	3	35	14	6	3	8	25	29	60	43	17	55
Roda JC	34	11	2	4	29	14	4	7	6	18	22	47	36	11	54
Feyenoord	34	10	5	2	29	24	5	3	9	27	42	56	66	-10	53
FC Groningen	34	8	4	5	32	26	7	2	8	22	28	54	54	0	51
FC Utrecht	34	11	4	2	30	11	2	5	10	11	33	41	44	-3	48
NEC	34	8	3	6	22	20	4	5	8	14	24	36	44	-8	44
NAC	34	6	7	4	22	21	6	0	11	21	33	43	54	-11	43
Vitesse	34	7	4	6	30	23	3	4	10	20	32	50	55	-5	38
Sparta	34	6	5	6	20	24	4	2	11	20	42	40	66	-26	37
Heracles	34	7	6	4	27	19	6	5	12	5	45	32	64	-32	32
Willem II	34	7	2	8	21	27	1	5	11	10	37	31	64	-33	31
Excelsior	34	6	3	8	27	28	2	3	12	16	37	43	65	-22	30
RKC	34	5	5	7	19	24	1	4	12	14	36	33	60	-27	27
ADO Den Haag	34	2	4	11	19	36	1	4	12	21	36	40	72	-32	17

CLUB STRIKE FORCE

Ajax's Jaap Stam & Klaas Jan Huntelaar

1 Ajax

Goals scored in the League 84

Club Strike Rate (CSR) Average number of minutes between League goals scored by club — 36

	CLUB	GOALS	CSR
1	Ajax	84	36
2	AZ Alkmaar	83	36
3	PSV Eindhoven	75	40
4	Twente	67	45
5	Heerenveen	60	51
6	Feyenoord	56	54
7	Groningen	54	56
8	Vitesse Arnhem	50	61
9	Roda JC Kerk	47	65
10	NAC Breda	43	71
11	Excelsior	43	71
12	Utrecht	41	74
13	S Rotterdam	40	76
14	Den Haag	40	76
15	NEC Nijmegen	36	85
16	RKC Waalwijk	33	92
17	Heracles	32	95
18	Willem II Tilb	31	98

CLUB DISCIPLINARY RECORDS

Den Haag's aggressive midfielder Bakkati

1 Den Haag

League Yellow 82

League Red 8

League Total 90

Cards Average in League Average number of minutes between a card being shown of either colour — 34

	CLUB	Y	R	TOTAL	AVE
1	Den Haag	82	8	90	34
2	RKC Waalwijk	66	4	70	43
3	NAC Breda	67	3	70	43
4	Vitesse Arnhem	64	6	70	43
5	Feyenoord	63	4	67	45
6	Utrecht	64	4	68	45
7	Roda JC Kerk	60	5	65	47
8	Ajax	59	4	63	48
9	Heracles	57	6	63	48
10	Willem II Tilb	57	3	60	51
11	NEC Nijmegen	55	2	57	53
12	Twente	49	5	54	56
13	Groningen	52	1	53	57
14	S Rotterdam	47	2	49	62
15	AZ Alkmaar	47	1	48	63
16	Heerenveen	45	3	48	63
17	Excelsior	41	6	47	65
18	PSV Eindhoven	32	1	33	92

CLUB DEFENCES

PSV's Carlos Salcido gets stuck in

1 PSV Eindhoven

Goals conceded in the League 25

Clean Sheets (CS) Number of league games where no goals were conceded — 17

Club Defensive Rate (CDR) Average number of minutes between League goals conceded by club — 122

	CLUB	LGE	CS	CDR
1	PSV Eindhoven	25	17	122
2	AZ Alkmaar	31	16	98
3	Ajax	35	13	87
4	Roda JC Kerk	36	15	85
5	Twente	37	11	82
6	Heerenveen	43	14	71
7	Utrecht	44	16	69
8	NEC Nijmegen	44	11	69
9	NAC Breda	54	9	56
10	Groningen	54	8	56
11	Vitesse Arnhem	55	7	55
12	RKC Waalwijk	60	3	51
13	Willem II Tilb	64	8	47
14	Heracles	64	9	47
15	Excelsior	65	2	47
16	Feyenoord	66	6	46
17	S Rotterdam	66	7	46
18	Den Haag	72	1	42

PLAYER NATIONALITIES

Overseas country with the most player appearances in the Dutch League - Belgium

806 league appearances by Belgian players

	COUNTRY	PLAYERS	IN SQUAD	LGE APP	% LGE ACT	CAPS	MOST APP	APP
1	Holland	346	6810	5113	61.8	96	Peter Wisgerhof	100
2	Belgium	47	1042	806	9.2	27	Brian Vandenbussche	100
3	Brazil	11	267	250	3.2	9	Heurelho Gomes	94.1
4	Sweden	8	227	213	2.8	19	Kennedy Bakircioglu	97.1
5	Ghana	10	247	211	2.6	4	Emmanuel Boakye	88.2
6	Denmark	12	243	187	2.0	6	Thomas Baelum	90.8
7	Morocco	11	235	169	1.7	0	Adil Ramzi	90.2
8	Australia	5	145	117	1.4	5	Brett Holman	87.2
9	Serbia	6	141	112	1.4	9	Goran Bunjevcevic	65.1
10	Canada	6	145	114	1.2	0	Jonathan de Guzman	86.6
11	Norway	3	89	82	1.1	0	Pa-Modou Kah	82.3
12	France	5	115	80	1.1	0	Sebastien Sansoni	81.2
13	Spain	4	98	78	0.9	0	G Garcia de la Torre	82.3
14	Greece	4	99	80	0.9	0	Angelos Charisteas	76.5
15	Hungary	5	118	81	0.9	0	Gabor Babos	100
16	Sierra Leone	2	65	62	0.9	0	Ibrahim Kargbo	92.9
17	Germany	5	81	67	0.8	0	Martin Pieckenhagen	97.1
18	Czech Republic	3	85	71	0.8	5	Zdenek Grygera	58.6
19	Uruguay	3	72	66	0.8	0	Luis Suarez	75.5
20	Estonia	2	65	64	0.7	0	Andres Oper	79.7

CLUB MAKE-UP – HOME AND OVERSEAS PLAYERS

1 PSV Eindhoven

63.9% of appearances by overseas players

	CLUB	OVERSEAS	HOME	% OVERSEAS	% LGE ACT	MOST APP	APP
1	PSV Eindhoven	23	13	63.9	74.7	Timmy Simons	100
2	Heerenveen	18	16	52.9	67.8	B Vandenbussche	100
3	Roda JC Kerk	15	9	62.5	65.8	Davy De Fauw	96.5
4	Groningen	10	24	29.4	62.1	Gibril Sankoh	87.5
5	Heracles	14	14	50	62.0	M Pieckenhagen	97.1
6	Ajax	15	17	46.9	55.5	G G de la Torre	82.3
7	Willem II Tilb	15	17	46.9	47.2	Ibrahim Kargbo	92.9
8	Feyenoord	16	18	47.1	47.2	J de Guzman	86.6
9	Utrecht	11	22	33.3	44.7	Tom Caluwe	90.1
10	Vitesse Arnhem	13	20	39.4	40.8	Danko Lazovic	92.1
11	Twente	13	18	41.9	39.9	K Bakircioglu	97.1
12	NEC Nijmegen	9	22	29	38.7	Gabor Babos	100
13	Den Haag	12	23	34.3	37.9	Laurent Delorge	74.5
14	RKC Waalwijk	13	23	36.1	37.8	Anthony Obodai	85.2
15	AZ Alkmaar	10	20	33.3	34.7	Maarten Martens	72.9
16	S Rotterdam	9	23	28.1	27.1	Sepp De Roover	99.5
17	NAC Breda	7	23	23.3	21.1	Glen Salmon	67.9
18	Excelsior	4	24	14.3	13.0	Jarda Simr	55

353

CHART-TOPPING MIDFIELDERS

1 de Zeeuw - AZ Alkmaar

Goals scored in the League	5
Defensive Rating Av number of mins between League goals conceded while on the pitch	119
Contribution to Attacking Power Average number of minutes between League team goals while on pitch	37
Scoring Difference Defensive Rating minus Contribution to Attacking Power	82

	PLAYER	CLUB	GOALS	DEF RATE	POWER	S DIFF
1	Demy de Zeeuw	AZ Alkmaar	5	119	37	82
2	Timmy Simons	PSV Eindhoven	5	122	40	82
3	Edison Mendez	PSV Eindhoven	5	111	38	73
4	Phillip Cocu	PSV Eindhoven	7	112	41	71
5	Wesley Sneijder	Ajax	18	92	38	54
6	Maarten Martens	AZ Alkmaar	10	89	37	52
7	Orlando Engelaar	Twente	4	89	43	46
8	G Garcia de la Torre	Ajax	5	83	38	45
9	Karim El Ahmadi	Twente	2	87	49	38
10	Kemy Agustien	Roda JC Kerk	2	97	67	30
11	Marcel Meeuwis	Roda JC Kerk	2	90	65	25
12	Danijel Pranjic	Heerenveen	2	73	53	20
13	Paul Bosvelt	Heerenveen	1	63	51	12
14	Andre Hanssen	Heerenveen	0	55	44	11
15	Adil Ramzi	Roda JC Kerk	8	76	67	9

CHART-TOPPING GOALSCORERS

1 Alves - Heerenveen

Goals scored in the League	34
Contribution to Attacking Power (AP) Average number of minutes between League team goals while on pitch	48
Club Strike Rate (CSR) Average minutes between League goals scored by club	51
Player Strike Rate Average number of minutes between League goals scored by player	79

	PLAYER	CLUB	GOALS: LGE	POWER	CSR	S RATE
1	Afonso Alves	Heerenveen	34	48	51	79
2	Danny Koevermans	AZ Alkmaar	22	34	36	100
3	Jefferson Farfan	PSV Eindhoven	21	38	40	121
4	Klaas-Jan Huntelaar	Ajax	21	38	36	127
5	Blaise N'Kufo	Twente	22	46	45	134
6	Wesley Sneijder	Ajax	18	38	36	138
7	Danko Lazovic	Vitesse Arnhem	19	56	61	146
8	Shota Arveladze	AZ Alkmaar	14	37	36	154
9	Santi Kolk	Den Haag	12	69	76	190
10	Erik Nevland	Groningen	13	54	56	192
11	Kennedy Bakircioglu	Twente	15	45	45	198
12	Andwele Slory	Excelsior	12	72	71	212
13	Andres Oper	Roda JC Kerk	11	59	65	220
14	Maarten Martens	AZ Alkmaar	10	37	36	223
15	Luis Suarez	Groningen	10	56	56	231

CHART-TOPPING DEFENDERS

1 Alex - PSV Eindhoven

Goals Conceded in the League The number of League goals conceded while he was on the pitch	15
Clean Sheets In games when he played at least 70 mins	15
Club Defensive Rating Average mins between League goals conceded by the club this season	122
Defensive Rating Average number of minutes between League goals conceded while on pitch	167

	PLAYER	CLUB	CON: LGE	CS	CDR	DEF RATE
1	Alex	PSV Eindhoven	15	15	122	167
2	Jan Kromkamp	PSV Eindhoven	18	11	122	130
3	Carlos Salcido	PSV Eindhoven	25	16	122	118
4	Gretar Rafn Steinsson	AZ Alkmaar	18	9	98	107
5	Kew Jaliens	AZ Alkmaar	26	13	98	95
6	Patrick Mtiliga	NAC Breda	20	10	56	95
7	Tim de Cler	AZ Alkmaar	31	13	98	91
8	Jaap Stam	Ajax	22	6	87	90
9	John Heitinga	Ajax	31	11	87	90
10	Gianni Zuiverloon	Heerenveen	26	10	71	88
11	Davy De Fauw	Roda JC Kerk	34	14	85	86
12	Zdenek Grygera	Ajax	21	8	87	85
13	Urby Emanuelson	Ajax	31	13	87	85
14	David Mendes Da Silva	AZ Alkmaar	23	10	98	84
15	Pa-Modou Kah	Roda JC Kerk	30	12	85	83

CHART-TOPPING GOALKEEPERS

1 Gomes - PSV Eindhoven

Counting Games Games in which he played at least 70 minutes	32
Goals Conceded in the League The number of League goals conceded while he was on the pitch	24
Clean Sheets In games when he played at least 70 mins	16
Defensive Rating Average number of minutes between League goals conceded while on pitch	120

	PLAYER	CLUB	CG	CONC	CS	DEF RATE
1	Heurelho Gomes	PSV Eindhoven	32	24	16	120
2	Vladan Kujovic	Roda JC Kerk	20	18	10	103
3	Maarten Stekelenburg	Ajax	32	33	12	87
4	Sander Boschker	Twente	33	37	11	81
5	Brian Vandenbussche	Heerenveen	34	43	12	71
6	Michel Vorm	Utrecht	33	42	16	70
7	Gabor Babos	NEC Nijmegen	34	44	11	69
8	Edwin Zoetebier	NAC Breda	32	49	9	58
9	Harald Wapenaar	Vitesse Arnhem	19	31	4	55
10	Martin Pieckenhagen	Heracles	33	57	6	52
11	Bas Roorda	Groningen	29	50	6	51
12	Henk Timmer	Feyenoord	31	58	6	48
13	Theo Zwarthoed	Excelsior	26	52	0	45
14	Rob van Dijk	RKC Waalwijk	19	38	1	45
15	Bjorn Sengier	Willem II Tilb	23	48	4	43

PLAYER DISCIPLINARY RECORD

AZ's Simon Cziommer: 6 cards

1. Virgilio Teixeira - RKC Waalwijk

Cards Average mins between cards	156
League Yellow	7
League Red	1
TOTAL	8

	PLAYER		LY	LR	TOT	AVE
1	Teixeira	RKC Waalwijk	7	1	8	156
2	Bosschaart	Den Haag	10	1	11	172
3	Bakens	RKC Waalwijk	7	0	7	173
4	Gudde	S Rotterdam	5	1	6	178
5	Cziommer	AZ Alkmaar	6	0	6	179
6	Pieters	Utrecht	7	1	8	180
7	Niedzielan	NEC Nijmegen	6	0	6	199
8	Leonardo	NAC Breda	5	1	6	213
9	Knol	Vitesse Arnhem	7	1	8	213
10	Vreven	Den Haag	7	1	8	220
11	Nelisse	Utrecht	5	0	5	224
12	Prager	Heerenveen	6	1	7	229
13	Davids	Ajax	3	1	4	235
14	den Bergh	RKC Waalwijk	6	0	6	235
15	Snoyl	NEC Nijmegen	8	0	8	238

TEAM OF THE SEASON

Alex (PSV) — CG: 27 DR: 167
de Zeeuw (AZ Alk) — CG: 25 SD: + 82
Stam (Ajax) — CG: 19 DR: 90
Simons (PSV) — CG: 34 SD: +82
Alves (Heerenveen) — CG: 30 SR: 79
Gomes (PSV) — CG: 32 DR: 120
Mtiliga (NAC Breda) — CG: 21 DR: 95
Sneijder (Ajax) — CG: 28 SD: +54
Koevermans (AZ Alk) — CG: 20 SR: 100
Steinsson (AZ Alk) — CG: 20 DR: 107
Engelaar (Twente) — CG: 28 SD: +46

PSV EINDHOVEN

Final Position: **1st**

NICKNAME: BOEREN　　　KEY: ☐ Won ☐ Drawn ☐ Lost　　　Attendance

#		Opponent			Score	Scorers	Attendance
1	jcs	Ajax	A	L	1-3	Cocu 49	35,000
2	hopr1	NEC Nijmegen	H	W	3-1	Cocu 44, Alex 45, Vennegoor 57	33,400
3	hopr1	Twente	A	L	0-1		13,000
4	hopr1	Willem II Tilb	A	W	3-1	Mendez 14, 21, Farfan 45 pen	14,000
5	ecgpc	Liverpool	H	D	0-0		35,000
6	hopr1	Feyenoord	H	W	2-1	Farfan 7, Alex 42	35,000
7	hocr2	Kozakken Boys	A	W	2-0	Kone 74, Simons 83 pen	5,000
8	hopr1	Den Haag	A	W	2-0	Tardelli 57, Mendez 85	7,133
9	ecgpc	Bordeaux	A	W	1-0	Vayrynen 65	26,000
10	hopr1	Heerenveen	A	D	0-0		25,400
11	hopr1	Roda JC Kerk	H	W	4-1	Farfan 75, Alex 77, Aissati 90, Beerens 90	34,500
12	ecgpc	Galatasaray	A	W	2-1	Kromkamp 59, Kone 72	45,000
13	hopr1	AZ Alkmaar	A	W	3-1	da Costa 12, Kone 45, Mendez 45	17,000
14	hopr1	S Rotterdam	H	W	7-0	Kone 5, 39, Farfan 21 pen, 28, 81, Reiziger 78, Simons 90 pen	33,800
15	hopr1	RKC Waalwijk	A	W	3-0	Afellay 52, Kone 59, 90	7,000
16	ecgpc	Galatasaray	H	W	2-0	Simons 59, Kone 84	35,000
17	hopr1	NAC Breda	H	W	3-0	Farfan 27, 85, Cocu 42	34,000
18	hocr3	Vitesse Arnhem	A	W	4-0	Kone 19, Culina 25, Farfan 79, Simons 84 pen	9,600
19	hopr1	Ajax	A	W	1-0	Simons 63	50,496
20	hopr1	Excelsior	H	W	4-0	Kone 29, Alex 44, Farfan 80, Salcido 85	33,000
21	ecgpc	Liverpool	A	L	0-2		41,948
22	hopr1	Utrecht	H	W	5-0	Nelisse 8 og, Afellay 28, Farfan 39, 76, Kone 54	33,114
23	hopr1	Vitesse Arnhem	A	W	1-0	Mendez 23	19,000
24	ecgpc	Bordeaux	H	L	1-3	Alex 87	26,000
25	hopr1	Groningen	A	W	2-0	Afellay 62, Kone 87	19,000
26	hopr1	Heracles	H	W	3-0	Simons 25 pen, Cocu 51, Kluivert 64	33,500
27	hopr1	Willem II Tilb	H	W	4-0	Afellay 4, Kone 16, Simons 22, Tardelli 71	33,000
28	hopr1	Feyenoord	A	D	1-1	Cocu 24	40,000
29	hopr1	Den Haag	H	W	2-0	Kluivert 33, Farfan 48	32,800
30	hopr1	Heerenveen	H	W	3-1	Simons 14 pen, Kone 22, Farfan 35 pen	33,212
31	hocr4	G A Eagles	H	W	3-2	Simons 58 pen, Farfan 74, Kone 79	25,000
32	hopr1	Roda JC Kerk	A	L	0-2		18,000
33	hopr1	AZ Alkmaar	H	L	2-3	Farfan 20, Cocu 65	33,300
34	hopr1	S Rotterdam	A	D	1-1	Culina 46	10,350
35	hopr1	Heracles	A	W	2-0	Farfan 74, Tardelli 90	8,500
36	eckl1	Arsenal	H	W	1-0	Mendez 61	35,000
37	hopr1	Groningen	H	W	1-0	Alex 85	33,400
38	hocqf	NAC Breda	A	L	0-3		16,000
39	hopr1	RKC Waalwijk	A	W	2-0	Farfan 3, Alcides 19	33,300
40	eckl2	Arsenal	A	D	1-1	Alex 83	60,073
41	hopr1	Excelsior	A	D	0-0		2,900
42	hopr1	Ajax	H	L	1-5	Kluivert 67	35,100
43	hopr1	NAC Breda	A	D	1-1	Farfan 74	16,580
44	ecqfl1	Liverpool	H	L	0-3		36,500
45	hopr1	NEC Nijmegen	A	L	1-2	Cocu 61	12,500
46	ecqfl2	Liverpool	A	L	0-1		41,447
47	hopr1	Twente	H	W	2-0	Farfan 19, 20	33,600
48	hopr1	Utrecht	A	D	1-1	Afellay 11	23,500
49	hopr1	Vitesse Arnhem	H	W	5-1	Alex 8, Farfan 9, 65, Afellay 58, Cocu 76	34,000

LEAGUE APPEARANCES, BOOKINGS AND CAPS

	AGE (on 01/07/07)	IN NAMED 18	APPEARANCES	COUNTING GAMES	MINUTES ON PITCH	YELLOW CARDS	RED CARDS	CAPS THIS SEASON	NATIONAL SIDE
Goalkeepers									
Heurelho Gomes	26	32	32	32	2880	0	0	4	Brazil
Oscar Moens	34	33	2	2	180	0	0	-	Holland
Defenders									
Eric Addo	28	31	14	5	663	1	0	-	Ghana
Eduardo Alcides	22	10	9	5	564	0	0	-	Brazil
Alex	25	29	29	27	2515	3	0	3	Brazil
Manuel da Costa	21	25	15	9	1059	4	0	-	Portugal
Jan Kromkamp	26	28	28	25	2342	3	0	-	Holland
Michael Lamey	27	12	7	5	526	2	1	-	Holland
Michael Reiziger	34	21	11	7	839	3	0	-	Holland
Carlos Salcido	27	33	33	33	2970	4	0	-	Mexico
Xiang Sun	25	8	5	2	294	1	0	-	China PR
Midfielders									
Ibrahim Afellay	21	27	27	17	1951	3	0	1	Holland
Ismael Aissati	18	17	10	0	259	0	0	-	Morocco
Phillip Cocu	36	32	32	27	2706	4	0	-	Holland
Jason Culina	26	30	28	7	1268	0	0	3	Australia
Csaba Feher	31	22	3	2	187	2	0	-	Hungary
Edison Mendez	28	28	26	22	2120	5	1	-	Ecuador
Timmy Simons	30	34	34	34	3060	2	0	8	Belgium
Mika Vayrynen	25	24	17	3	604	5	0	6	Finland
Forwards									
Roy Beerens	19	12	7	2	296	0	0	-	Holland
Jefferson Farfan	22	32	30	29	2560	3	0	1	Peru
Patrick Kluivert	31	19	16	1	541	1	0	-	Holland
Arouna Kone	23	31	31	30	2689	0	0	3	Ivory Coast
Diego Tardelli	22	22	13	2	422	1	0	-	Brazil
Jan V of Hesselink	28	1	1	1	73	0	0	4	Holland
Genero Zeefuik	17	5	5	0	72	0	0	-	Holland

TEAM OF THE SEASON

G Heurelho Gomes — CG: 32 DR: 120

D Alex — CG: 27 DR: 167
D Jan Kromkamp — CG: 25 DR: 130
D Carlos Salcido — CG: 33 DR: 118
D Manuel Da Costa* — CG: 9 DR: 117

M Ibrahim Afellay — CG: 17 SD: 119
M Timmy Simons — CG: 34 SD: 82
M Edison Mendez — CG: 22 SD: 73
M Phillip Cocu — CG: 27 SD: 71

F Jefferson Farfan — CG: 29 SR: 121
F Arouna Kone — CG: 30 SR: 268

MONTHLY POINTS TALLY

Month	Points	%
AUGUST	3	50%
SEPTEMBER	9	100%
OCTOBER	13	87%
NOVEMBER	12	100%
DECEMBER	16	89%
JANUARY	3	50%
FEBRUARY	7	58%
MARCH	5	42%
APRIL	7	58%

LEAGUE GOALS

	PLAYER	MINS	GOALS	S RATE
1	Farfan	2560	21	121
2	Kone	2689	10	268
3	Cocu	2706	7	386
4	Afellay	1951	6	325
5	Alex	2515	6	419
6	Mendez	2120	5	424
7	Simons	3060	5	612
8	Tardelli	422	3	140
9	Kluivert	541	3	180
10	Vennegoor	73	1	73
11	Aissati	259	1	259
12	Beerens	296	1	296
13	Alcides	564	1	564
	Other		4	
	TOTAL		74	

TOP POINT EARNERS

	PLAYER	GAMES	AV PTS
1	Alex	27	2.37
2	Arouna Kone	30	2.33
3	Edison Mendez	22	2.32
4	Jan Kromkamp	25	2.24
5	Heurelho Gomes	32	2.22
6	Timmy Simons	34	2.21
7	Carlos Salcido	33	2.18
8	Jefferson Farfan	29	2.14
9	Phillip Cocu	27	2.07
10	Ibrahim Afellay	17	2.06
	CLUB AVERAGE:		2.21

DISCIPLINARY RECORDS

	PLAYER	YELLOW	RED	AVE
1	Mika Vayrynen	5	0	201
2	Michael Lamey	2	1	263
3	Michael Reiziger	3	0	419
4	Edison Mendez	5	1	424
5	Manuel da Costa	4	0	529
6	Ibrahim Afellay	3	0	650
7	Eric Addo	1	0	663
8	Alex	3	0	838
9	Jefferson Farfan	3	0	853
10	Phillip Cocu	4	0	902
11	Jan Kromkamp	3	0	1171
12	Carlos Salcido	4	0	2970
13	Timmy Simons	2	0	3060
	Other	1	0	
	TOTAL	43	2	

KEY GOALKEEPER

Heurelho Gomes

Goals Conceded in the League	24	**Counting Games** League games when player was on pitch for at least 70 minutes	32
Defensive Rating Ave number of mins between League goals conceded while on the pitch	120	**Clean Sheets** In League games when player was on pitch for at least 70 minutes	16

KEY PLAYERS - DEFENDERS

Alex

Goals Conceded Number of League goals conceded while the player was on the pitch	15	**Clean Sheets** In League games when player was on pitch for at least 70 minutes	15
Defensive Rating Ave number of mins between League goals conceded while on the pitch	167	**Club Defensive Rating** Average number of mins between League goals conceded by the club this season	122

	PLAYER	CON LGE	CLEAN SHEETS	DEF RATE
1	Alex	15	15	167 mins
2	Jan Kromkamp	18	11	130 mins
3	Carlos Salcido	25	16	118 mins
4	Manuel da Costa	9	5	117 mins

KEY PLAYERS - MIDFIELDERS

Ibrahim Afellay

Goals in the League	6	**Contribution to Attacking Power** Average number of minutes between League team goals while on pitch	43
Defensive Rating Average number of mins between League goals conceded while on the pitch	162	**Scoring Difference** Defensive Rating minus Contribution to Attacking Power	119

	PLAYER	LGE GOALS	DEF RATE	POWER	SCORE DIFF
1	Ibrahim Afellay	6	162	43	119 mins
2	Timmy Simons	5	122	40	82 mins
3	Edison Mendez	5	111	38	73 mins
4	Phillip Cocu	7	112	41	71 mins

KEY PLAYERS - GOALSCORERS

Jefferson Farfan

Goals in the League	21	**Player Strike Rate** Average number of minutes between League goals scored by player	121
Contribution to Attacking Power Average number of minutes between League team goals while on pitch	38	**Club Strike Rate** Average number of minutes between League goals scored by club	40

	PLAYER	LGE GOALS	POWER	STRIKE RATE
1	Jefferson Farfan	21	38	121 mins
2	Arouna Kone	10	37	268 mins
3	Ibrahim Afellay	6	43	325 mins
4	Phillip Cocu	7	41	386 mins

Arouna Kone and Phillip Cocu

SQUAD APPEARANCES

Match	1 2 3 4	6 7 8 9 10	11 12 13 14 15 16 17	18 19 20 21	22 23	24 25 26 27	28 29 30 31 32 33 34	35 36 37 38 39	40 41 42 43 44	45 46 47 48 49
Venue	A H A A H	H A A A A	H A A H A H H	A A H A	H A	H A H H	A H H H H A	A H H A	A A H A H	A A H A H
Competition	O L L L C	L O L C L	L C L L L L C L	O L L C	L L	C L L L	L L L O L L L	L C L O L	C L L L C	L C L L L
Result	L W L W D	W W W W D	W W W W W W W	W W W L	W W	L W W W	D W W W L L D	W W W L W	D D L D L	L L W D W

Goalkeepers

Player										
Heurelho Gomes										
Oscar Moens										

Defenders

Player
Eric Addo
Eduardo Alcides
Alex
Manuel da Costa
Jan Kromkamp
Michael Lamey
Michael Reiziger
Carlos Salcido
Xiang Sun

Midfielders

Player
Ibrahim Afellay
Ismael Aissati
Phillip Cocu
Jason Culina
Csaba Feher
Edison Mendez
Timmy Simons
Mika Vayrynen

Forwards

Player
Roy Beerens
Jefferson Farfan
Patrick Kluivert
Arouna Kone
Diego Tardelli
Jan V of Hesselink
Genero Zeefuik

KEY: ■ On all match — ▶◀ Subbed or sent off (Counting game) — ▶▶ Subbed on from bench (Counting Game) — ▶▶ Subbed on and then subbed or sent off (Counting Game) — ☐ Not in 16
■ On bench — ◀◀ Subbed or sent off (playing less than 70 minutes) — ▶▶ Subbed on (playing less than 70 minutes) — ▶▶ Subbed on and then subbed or sent off (playing less than 70 minutes)

HOLLAND - PSV EINDHOVEN

AJAX

Final Position: **2nd**

NICKNAME: GODENZONEN   KEY: ☐ Won ☐ Drawn ☐ Lost   Attendance

#	Comp	Opponent		Result	Scorers	Attendance
1	ecql1	Copenhagen	A W	2-1	Huntelaar 38, 84	40,014
2	jcs	PSV Eindhoven	H W	3-1	Rosales 7, Perez 69, Sneijder 82	35,000
3	hopr1	RKC Waalwijk	H W	5-0	Babel 33, Sneijder 44, 69, Heitinga 53, Rosales 89	48,000
4	ecql2	Copenhagen	H L	0-2		35,617
5	hopr1	NAC Breda	A W	2-1	Sneijder 73, 83	15,432
6	hopr1	Vitesse Arnhem	H W	3-0	Huntelaar 32, 55, Roger 45	46,001
7	ucrl1	IK Start	A W	5-2	Huntelaar 17, 87, Rosenberg 43, Sneijder 63, Roger 67	1,840
8	hopr1	Roda JC Kerk	A L	0-2		15,000
9	hocr2	RKC Waalwijk	A W	5-2	Rosenberg 22, 85, Maduro 29, Perez 48, Huntelaar 57	7,000
10	hopr1	NEC Nijmegen	H W	2-0	Perez 58, 82	46,081
11	ucrl2	IK Start	H W	4-0	Rosenberg 6, 25, Grygera 41, Babel 68	26,467
12	hopr1	Utrecht	A W	3-2	Gabri 7, Heitinga 45, Perez 87	24,000
13	hopr1	Groningen	H W	3-2	Babel 51, 74, Emanuelson 80	49,782
14	hopr1	Feyenoord	A W	4-0	Huntelaar 11, 37, Perez 49 pen, 61	41,000
15	hopr1	Den Haag	H W	2-0	Gabri 30, Sneijder 32	45,757
16	hopr1	Heerenveen	A W	2-0	de Mul 17, Sneijder 75	26,000
17	ucgpf	Austria Vienna	H W	3-0	Huntelaar 35, 68, Manucharyan 65	30,000
18	hopr1	Heracles	A W	3-0	Perez 39, 82 pen, Sneijder 87	8,500
19	hocr3	Den Haag	H W	2-0	Stam 8, Huntelaar 65	7,909
20	hopr1	PSV Eindhoven	H L	0-1		50,496
21	hopr1	Twente	H D	1-1	Sneijder 48	49,364
22	ucgpf	Sparta Prague	A D	0-0		12,230
23	hopr1	S Rotterdam	A L	0-3		10,500
24	ucgpf	Espanyol	H L	0-2		41,248
25	hopr1	Willem II Tilb	H W	6-0	Grygera 4, Emanuelson 10, Mitea 19, Huntelaar 23, 45, de Mul 78	46,695
26	hopr1	AZ Alkmaar	H D	2-2	Heitinga 35, Huntelaar 75	50,649
27	ucgpf	Zulte-Waregem	A W	3-0	Huntelaar 3, 57, Heitinga 83	12,000
28	hopr1	Excelsior	A W	3-1	Huntelaar 24, 48, 74	3,500
29	hopr1	Vitesse Arnhem	A L	2-4	Grygera 4, de Mul 35	24,450
30	hopr1	Roda JC Kerk	H W	2-0	Sneijder 15, Grygera 41	50,334
31	hopr1	NEC Nijmegen	A D	2-2	Perez 62, Gabri 80	12,500
32	hopr1	Utrecht	H W	2-0	Heitinga 11, Sneijder 21	44,740
33	hocr4	Haarlem	H W	4-0	Frankel 7 og, Leonardo 33, Perez 40, 90	23,100
34	hopr1	Groningen	A W	3-2	Stam 53, Heitinga 82, Leonardo 90	19,000
35	hopr1	Feyenoord	H W	4-1	Sneijder 20, 32, 87, de Mul 34	50,490
36	hopr1	Den Haag	A W	2-1	Heitinga 58, Huntelaar 70	8,276
37	ucrl1	W Bremen	A L	0-3		38,150
38	hopr1	Excelsior	H D	2-2	Davids 19, Huntelaar 38	47,905
39	ucrl2	W Bremen	H W	3-1	Leonardo 3, Huntelaar 60, Babel 74	35,227
40	hopr1	AZ Alkmaar	A D	1-1	Perez 65	16,458
41	hocqf	Willem II Tilb	A W	2-0	Huntelaar 14, Heitinga 80	12,000
42	hopr1	Heerenveen	H L	0-1		50,174
43	hopr1	Twente	A W	4-1	Huntelaar 21, 30, 74, Babel 44	13,250
44	hopr1	PSV Eindhoven	A W	5-1	Huntelaar 17, 72, Sneijder 44, Gabri 72, Perez 89	35,100
45	hopr1	Heracles	H W	3-0	Sneijder 11, Huntelaar 50, 52	50,109
46	hopr1	RKC Waalwijk	A D	2-2	Gabri 9, Sneijder 21	7,500
47	hopr1	NAC Breda	H W	2-0	Perez 18 pen, Babel 64	49,737
48	hocsf	RKC Waalwijk	H W	3-1	Sneijder 12, Gabri 66, Mitea 88	34,600
49	hopr1	S Rotterdam	H W	5-2	Sneijder 9, 17, Huntelaar 21, Perez 76 pen, Mitea 82	50,364
50	hopr1	Willem II Tilb	A W	2-0	Emanuelson 18, Huntelaar 69	14,000
51	hocf	AZ Alkmaar	A W	8-7*	Huntelaar 51 (*on penalties)	35,000
52	erepo	Heerenveen	A L	0-1		23,500
53	erepo	Heerenveen	H W	4-0	Huntelaar 21, 61 pen, Babel 23, Perez 85	30,000
54	erepo	AZ Alkmaar	A L	1-2	Sneijder 13	17,000
55	erepo	AZ Alkmaar	H W	3-0	Heitinga 56, Donk 58 og, Gabri 90	51,000

LEAGUE APPEARANCES, BOOKINGS AND CAPS

	AGE (on 01/07/07)	IN NAMED 18	APPEARANCES	COUNTING GAMES	MINUTES ON PITCH	YELLOW CARDS	RED CARDS	CAPS THIS SEASON	NATIONAL SIDE
Goalkeepers									
Dennis Gentenaar	31	24	2	2	180	0	0	-	Holland
Maarten Stekelenburg	24	32	32	32	2880	0	0	4	Holland
Defenders									
Vurnon Anita	18	1	1	1	90	0	0	-	Holland
Urby Emanuelson	21	31	31	29	2649	4	0	6	Holland
Zdenek Grygera	27	24	22	19	1794	4	0	5	Czech Republic
John Heitinga	23	32	32	31	2803	7	1	6	Holland
George Ogararu	27	33	28	17	1916	5	0	-	Romania
Jaap Stam	34	25	25	19	2001	6	0	-	Holland
Gregory Van der Wiel	19	8	4	3	280	0	0	-	Holland
Thomas Vermaelen	21	23	23	14	1587	5	0	7	Belgium
Midfielders									
Edgar Davids	34	11	11	10	943	3	1	-	Holland
G Garcia de la Torre	28	31	31	24	2497	8	1	-	Spain
Olaf Lindenbergh	33	30	12	3	532	1	0	-	Holland
Hedwiges Maduro	22	26	15	7	840	4	0	1	Holland
Roger Garcia Junyent	30	26	11	3	520	1	0	-	Spain
Wesley Sneijder	23	30	30	28	2488	5	1	8	Holland
Jan Vertonghen	20	7	3	1	148	0	0	1	Belgium
Forwards									
Ryan Babel	20	27	27	23	2102	1	0	7	Holland
Angelos Charisteas	27	1	1	0	18	0	0	4	Greece
Tom de Mul	21	29	28	15	1750	1	0	-	Belgium
Klaas-Jan Huntelaar	23	33	32	29	2685	4	0	7	Holland
Michael Krohn-Dehli	24	4	3	0	100	0	0	1	Denmark
Leonardo	24	7	7	4	425	0	0	-	Brazil
Edgar Manucharyan	20	14	5	0	70	0	0	-	Armenia
Nicolae Mitea	22	16	8	1	279	0	0	-	Romania
Kenneth Perez	32	29	27	6	1148	0	0	-	Denmark
M Damian Rosales	26	21	12	5	612	0	0	-	Argentina
Markus Rosenberg	24	17	9	0	138	0	0	6	Sweden

TEAM OF THE SEASON

G Maarten Stekelenburg CG: 32 DR: 87

D George Ogararu CG: 17 DR: 112
D Jaap Stam CG: 19 DR: 90
D John Heitinga CG: 31 DR: 90
D Thomas Vermaelen CG: 12 DR: 90

M Wesley Sneijder CG: 28 SD: 54
M G Garcia de la Torre CG: 24 SD: 45
M Edgar Davids CG: 10 SD: 64
M Hedwiges Maduro CG: 7 SD: 36

F K-Jan Huntelaar CG: 29 SR: 127
F Ryan Babel CG: 23 SR: 420

MONTHLY POINTS TALLY

Month		Points	%
AUGUST		6	100%
SEPTEMBER		6	67%
OCTOBER		15	100%
NOVEMBER		4	33%
DECEMBER		11	61%
JANUARY		6	100%
FEBRUARY		8	67%
MARCH		6	67%
APRIL		13	87%

LEAGUE GOALS

	PLAYER	MINS	GOALS	S RATE
1	Huntelaar	2685	21	127
2	Sneijder	2488	18	138
3	Perez	1148	12	95
4	Heitinga	2803	6	467
5	Babel	2102	5	420
6	Gabri	2497	5	499
7	de Mul	1750	4	437
8	Grygera	1794	3	598
9	Emanuelson	2649	3	883
10	Mitea	279	2	139
11	Leonardo	425	1	425
12	Roger	520	1	520
13	Rosales	612	1	612
	Other		2	
	TOTAL		84	

TOP POINT EARNERS

	PLAYER	GAMES	AV PTS
1	George Ogararu	17	2.47
2	Edgar Davids	11	2.45
3	Thomas Vermaelen	12	2.33
4	Ryan Babel	23	2.26
5	John Heitinga	32	2.25
6	Maarten Stekelenburg	32	2.22
7	Wesley Sneijder	29	2.21
8	Urby Emanuelson	29	2.21
9	Jaap Stam	19	2.16
10	Klaas-Jan Huntelaar	29	2.14
	CLUB AVERAGE:		2.21

DISCIPLINARY RECORDS

	PLAYER	YELLOW	RED	AVE
1	Hedwiges Maduro	7	0	210
2	Edgar Davids	5	1	235
3	Thomas Vermaelen	6	0	272
4	G G de la Torre	12	2	277
5	Jaap Stam	9	0	333
6	John Heitinga	9	1	350
7	George Ogararu	9	1	383
8	Wesley Sneijder	13	1	414
9	Zdenek Grygera	5	0	448
10	Roger G Junyent	2	0	520
11	Olaf Lindenbergh	1	0	532
12	Urby Emanuelson	7	1	662
13	Klaas-Jan Huntelaar	9	1	671
	Other	7	0	
	TOTAL	102	7	

KEY GOALKEEPER

Maarten Stekelenburg

Goals Conceded in the League	33	Counting Games League games when player was on pitch for at least 70 minutes	32
Defensive Rating Ave number of mins between League goals conceded while on the pitch	87	Clean Sheets In League games when player was on pitch for at least 70 minutes	12

KEY PLAYERS - DEFENDERS

George Ogararu

Goals Conceded Number of League goals conceded while the player was on the pitch	17	Clean Sheets In League games when player was on pitch for at least 70 minutes	7
Defensive Rating Ave number of mins between League goals conceded while on the pitch	112	Club Defensive Rating Average number of mins between League goals conceded by the club this season	87

	PLAYER	CON LGE	CLEAN SHEETS	DEF RATE
1	George Ogararu	17	7	112 mins
2	Jaap Stam	22	6	90 mins
3	John Heitinga	31	11	90 mins
4	Thomas Vermaelen	15	5	90 mins

KEY PLAYERS - MIDFIELDERS

Edgar Davids

Goals in the League	1	Contribution to Attacking Power Average number of minutes between League team goals while on pitch	30
Defensive Rating Average number of mins between League goals conceded while on the pitch	94	Scoring Difference Defensive Rating minus Contribution to Attacking Power	64

	PLAYER	LGE GOALS	DEF RATE	POWER	SCORE DIFF
1	Edgar Davids	1	94	30	64 mins
2	Wesley Sneijder	18	92	38	54 mins
3	Gabriel Garcia de la Torre	5	83	38	45 mins
4	Hedwiges Maduro	0	64	28	36 mins

KEY PLAYERS - GOALSCORERS

Klaas-Jan Huntelaar

Goals in the League	21	Player Strike Rate Average number of minutes between League goals scored by player	127
Contribution to Attacking Power Average number of minutes between League team goals while on pitch	38	Club Strike Rate Average number of minutes between League goals scored by club	36

	PLAYER	LGE GOALS	POWER	STRIKE RATE
1	Klaas-Jan Huntelaar	21	38	127 mins
2	Wesley Sneijder	18	38	138 mins
3	Ryan Babel	5	34	420 mins
4	Tom de Mul	4	37	437 mins

Klaas-Jan Huntelaar

SQUAD APPEARANCES

Match	1 2 3 4 5	6 7 8 9 10	11 12 13 14 15 16 17	18 19 20 21 22 23 24 25 26 27 28	29 30 31 32 33	34 35 36 37 38 39 40 41 42	43 44 45 46 47 48 49 50	51 52 53 54 55
Venue	A H H H A	H A A A H	H A H A H A H	A H H H A A	A H A H H	A H A A H H A A H	A A H A H H H A	A A H A H
Competition	C O L C L	L E L O L	E L L L L L E L	O L L E L E L L L E L	L L L L O	L L L E L E L O L	L L L L L O L L	O O O O O
Result	W W W L W	W W L W W	W W W W W W W W	W W L D D L L W D W	L W D W W	W W W L D W D W L	W W W D W W W W	W L W L W

Goalkeepers
Dennis Gentenaar
Maarten Stekelenburg

Defenders
Vurnon Anita
Urby Emanuelson
Zdenek Grygera
John Heitinga
George Ogararu
Jaap Stam
Gregory Van der Wiel
Thomas Vermaelen

Midfielders
Edgar Davids
G Garcia de la Torre
Olaf Lindenbergh
Hedwiges Maduro
Roger Garcia Junyent
Wesley Sneijder
Jan Vertonghen

Forwards
Ryan Babel
Angelos Charisteas
Tom de Mul
Klaas-Jan Huntelaar
Michael Krohn-Dehli
Leonardo
Edgar Manucharyan
Nicolae Mitea
Kenneth Perez
M Damian Rosales
Markus Rosenberg

KEY: ■ On all match   ◄◄ Subbed or sent off (Counting game)   ►► Subbed on from bench (Counting Game)   ►► Subbed on and then subbed or sent off (Counting Game)   □ Not in 16
  ▨ On bench   ◄◄ Subbed or sent off (playing less than 70 minutes)   ►► Subbed on (playing less than 70 minutes)   ►► Subbed on and then subbed or sent off (playing less than 70 minutes)

AZ ALKMAAR

Final Position: 3rd

NICKNAME: AZ   KEY: ☐ Won ☐ Drawn ☐ Lost   Attendance

#					Score	Scorers	Attendance
1	hopr1	NAC Breda	H	W	8-1	Koevermans 32, 71, Cziommer 40, 56, 80, J.Mathijsen 54, Schaars 57, de Cler 63	17,023
2	hopr1	Vitesse Arnhem	A	W	3-1	Koevermans 20, Schaars 57, de Zeeuw 90	20,000
3	hopr1	NEC Nijmegen	A	W	2-0	Arveladze 31, Schaars 80	11,800
4	ucrl1	Kayserispor	H	W	3-2	Koevermans 7 pen, Molhoek 33, Arveladze 64	12,621
5	hopr1	Twente	H	D	2-2	Arveladze 57, Dembele 88	17,000
6	hocr2	Bennekom	A	W	10-0	de Zeeuw 17, Martens 30, 65, Cziommer 33, 50, 55, Dembele 37, 41, Mendes Da Silva 45, Schaars 64	2,500
7	hopr1	Roda JC Kerk	A	W	2-0	Arveladze 69, Dembele 78	13,000
8	ucrl2	Kayserispor	A	D	1-1	Cora 55 og	17,000
9	hopr1	Den Haag	H	D	2-2	Koevermans 10, Jaliens 69	15,478
10	hopr1	S Rotterdam	A	W	2-0	Steinsson 69, Koevermans 79	10,500
11	ucgpc	Braga	H	W	3-0	Arveladze 36, Koevermans 74, Schaars 79	13,534
12	hopr1	PSV Eindhoven	H	L	1-3	de Zeeuw 71	17,000
13	hopr1	Willem II Tilb	A	W	4-0	de Zeeuw 13, Martens 53, Dembele 63, Koevermans 84	12,200
14	hopr1	Utrecht	H	W	5-1	Schaars 23, Arveladze 49, Mendes Da Silva 53, 73, Martens 88	15,297
15	ucgpc	Grasshoppers	A	W	5-2	Arveladze 49, de Zeeuw 56, Dembele 78, 90, Martens 90	5,000
16	hopr1	RKC Waalwijk	A	W	2-0	Dembele 6, Koevermans 31	7,000
17	hocr3	Meersen	H	W	10-1	Martens 10, 89, Schaars 15, 65, de Cler 32, Cziommer 41, Jenner 78, Koevermans 82 pen, 85, de Zeeuw 89	5,421
18	hopr1	Heracles	H	W	5-0	Schaars 2, de Zeeuw 23, Arveladze 81, 88, Koevermans 90	15,485
19	hopr1	Feyenoord	A	L	2-3	de Zeeuw 32, Koevermans 73	45,000
20	hopr1	Heerenveen	A	W	3-1	Arveladze 81, Martens 85	26,000
21	ucgpc	Slovan Liberec	H	D	2-2	Steinsson 69, Jenner 89	15,745
22	hopr1	Excelsior	H	W	5-0	Arveladze 10, 56, Koevermans 27, 43, Gyan 77 og	15,000
23	hopr1	Ajax	A	D	2-2	Arveladze 51, Mendes Da Silva 57	50,649
24	ucgpc	Seville	A	W	2-1	Arveladze 62, 90	20,000
25	hopr1	Groningen	H	W	2-0	Luirink 26, Koevermans 40 pen	15,000
26	hopr1	NEC Nijmegen	H	D	0-0		16,000
27	hopr1	Twente	A	L	0-3		13,000
28	hopr1	Roda JC Kerk	H	D	2-2	Opdam 65, Koevermans 84	15,240
29	hopr1	Den Haag	A	W	3-1	Mendes Da Silva 45 pen, Koevermans 57, Martens 84	6,405
30	hocr4	MVV Maastricht	H	W	5-0	Mendes Da Silva 21, 43 pen, 60, Dembele 23, Cziommer 45	5,796
31	hopr1	S Rotterdam	H	W	3-0	Arveladze 22, Olfers 47, Martens 52	15,000
32	hopr1	PSV Eindhoven	A	W	3-2	Dembele 50, Jenner 62, Koevermans 88	33,300
33	hopr1	Willem II Tilb	H	W	2-0	Koevermans 15, Martens 71	15,978
34	ucrl1	Fenerbahce	A	D	3-3	de Zeeuw 15, Boukhari 62, Jenner 63	38,000
35	hopr1	Groningen	A	D	1-1	Koevermans 26	19,186
36	ucrl2	Fenerbahce	H	D	2-2	Martens 64, Opdam 86	16,191
37	hopr1	Ajax	H	D	1-1	Martens 79	16,458
38	hocqf	Utrecht	A	W	2-1	Boukhari 28, 33	19,000
39	hopr1	Utrecht	A	W	4-0	Martens 18, Arveladze 22, Dembele 68, Koevermans 84	20,200
40	ucrl1	Newcastle	A	L	2-4	Arveladze 31, Koevermans 73	28,452
41	hopr1	Feyenoord	H	D	0-0		16,529
42	ucrl2	Newcastle	H	W	2-0	Arveladze 14, Koevermans 56	16,401
43	hopr1	Heracles	A	D	0-0		8,419
44	hopr1	RKC Waalwijk	H	W	2-0	Arveladze 24, Jenner 77	16,181
45	ucqfl1	W Bremen	H	D	0-0		16,000
46	hopr1	NAC Breda	A	W	4-1	Koevermans 27, 79, Penders 54 og, Martens 69	14,780
47	ucqfl2	W Bremen	A	L	1-4	Dembele 32	35,000
48	hopr1	Vitesse Arnhem	H	W	1-0	Arveladze 23 pen	16,088
49	hocsf	NAC Breda	H	W	6-0	Cziommer 41, 58, Arveladze 51 pen, Martens 60, 63, Steinsson 82	14,198
50	hopr1	Heerenveen	H	W	3-1	Cziommer 14, 88, Martens 38	16,272
51	hopr1	Excelsior	A	L	2-3	Cziommer 24, Koevermans 70	3,000
52	hocf	Ajax	H	L	7-8*	Dembele 4 (*on penalties)	35,000
53	erepo	Twente	A	D	1-1	Cziommer 13	13,000
54	erepo	Twente	H	W	2-0	de Cler 71, Lens 89	14,000
55	erepo	Ajax	H	W	2-1	Cziommer 2, Arveladze 89	17,000
56	erepo	Ajax	A	L	0-3		51,000

LEAGUE APPEARANCES, BOOKINGS AND CAPS

	AGE (on 01/07/07)	IN NAMED 18	APPEARANCES	COUNTING GAMES	MINUTES ON PITCH	YELLOW CARDS	RED CARDS	CAPS THIS SEASON	NATIONAL SIDE
Goalkeepers									
Job Bulters	21	19	3	2	197	0	0	-	Holland
Joseph Didulica	29	7	7	7	630	1	0	-	Croatia
Khalid Sinouh	32	23	11	10	909	0	0	-	Morocco
Boy Waterman	23	12	11	9	872	0	1	-	Holland
Ronald Waterreus	36	5	5	5	450	0	0	-	Holland
Defenders									
Tim de Cler	28	33	32	31	2835	6	0	-	Holland
Ryan Donk	21	29	18	11	1224	5	0	-	Holland
Kew Jaliens	28	29	28	27	2484	5	0	5	Holland
Gijs Luirink	23	23	16	10	1063	5	0	-	Holland
Joris Mathijsen	27	1	1	1	90	0	0	11	Holland
D Mendes Da Silva	24	24	24	20	1939	3	0	1	Holland
Barry Opdam	31	27	24	17	1855	10	0	-	Holland
Gretar Rafn Steinsson	25	28	25	20	1930	8	0	7	Iceland
Ruud Vormer	19	13	3	0	42	1	0	-	Holland
Midfielders									
Simon Cziommer	26	22	18	9	1077	8	0	-	Germany
Demy de Zeeuw	24	34	32	25	2504	6	0	3	Holland
Johannes Gudjonsson	27	13	5	1	166	1	0	4	Iceland
Maarten Martens	22	33	31	22	2231	1	0	-	Belgium
Rogier Molhoek	25	26	10	5	590	5	0	-	Holland
Stijn Schaars	23	22	18	11	1346	2	0	6	Holland
Forwards									
Shota Arveladze	34	30	29	18	2163	6	0	4	Georgia
Nourdine Boukhari	27	12	10	4	597	1	0	-	Morocco
Moussa Dembele	19	33	33	18	1992	4	0	5	Belgium
Julian Jenner	23	32	25	12	1509	1	0	-	Holland
Danny Koevermans	28	31	31	20	2219	3	0	1	Holland
Jeremain Lens	19	23	14	1	342	0	0	-	Holland
Martijn Meerdink	30	13	6	3	331	2	0	-	Holland

TEAM OF THE SEASON

Gretar Rafn Steinsson — **CG: 20 DR: 107** (D)
Demy de Zeeuw — **CG: 25 SD: 82** (M)
Tim De Cler — **CG: 31 DR: 91** (D)
Simon Cziommer — **CG: 9 SD: 60** (M)
Danny Koevermans — **CG: 20 SR: 100** (F)
Boy Waterman — **CG: 9 DR: 218** (G)
Barry Opdam — **CG: 17 DR: 103** (D)
Stijn Schaars — **CG: 11 SD: 52** (M)
Shota Arveladze — **CG: 18 SR: 154** (F)
Kew Jaliens — **CG: 27 DR: 95** (D)
Maarten Martens — **CG: 22 SD: 52** (M)

MONTHLY POINTS TALLY

AUGUST	6	100%
SEPTEMBER	7	78%
OCTOBER	10	67%
NOVEMBER	9	75%
DECEMBER	9	50%
JANUARY	6	100%
FEBRUARY	8	67%
MARCH	8	67%
APRIL	9	75%

LEAGUE GOALS

	PLAYER	MINS	GOALS	S RATE
1	Koevermans	2219	22	100
2	Arveladze	2163	14	154
3	Martens	2231	10	223
4	Cziommer	1077	6	179
5	Dembele	1992	6	332
6	Schaars	1346	5	269
7	de Zeeuw	2504	5	500
8	M Da Silva	1939	4	484
9	Jenner	1509	2	754
10	Mathijsen, J	90	1	90
11	Luirink	1063	1	1063
12	Opdam	1855	1	1855
13	Steinsson	1930	1	1930
	Other		2	
	TOTAL		80	

TOP POINT EARNERS

	PLAYER	GAMES	AV PTS
1	Stijn Schaars	11	2.64
2	Danny Koevermans	20	2.45
3	Demy de Zeeuw	25	2.28
4	David Mendes Da Silva	20	2.20
5	Julian Jenner	12	2.17
6	Maarten Martens	22	2.14
7	Kew Jaliens	27	2.11
8	Tim de Cler	31	2.10
9	Gretar Rafn Steinsson	20	2.10
10	Barry Opdam	17	2.06
	CLUB AVERAGE:		2.12

DISCIPLINARY RECORDS

	PLAYER	YELLOW	RED	AVE
1	Simon Cziommer	8	0	179
2	Gijs Luirink	5	0	354
3	Barry Opdam	10	0	371
4	G Rafn Steinsson	8	0	386
5	Ryan Donk	5	0	408
6	Rogier Molhoek	5	0	590
7	Demy de Zeeuw	6	0	626
8	Tim de Cler	6	0	708
9	Shota Arveladze	6	0	721
10	Kew Jaliens	5	0	828
11	Boy Waterman	0	1	872
12	Moussa Dembele	4	0	996
13	Danny Koevermans	3	0	1109
	Other	9	0	
	TOTAL	80	0	

KEY GOALKEEPER

Boy Waterman

Goals Conceded in the League	4	Counting Games League games when player was on pitch for at least 70 minutes		9
Defensive Rating Ave number of mins between League goals conceded while on the pitch	218	Clean Sheets In games when player was on pitch for at least 70 minutes		7

KEY PLAYERS - GOALSCORERS

Danny Koevermans

Goals in the League	22	Player Strike Rate Average number of minutes between League goals scored by player		100
Contribution to Attacking Power Average number of minutes between League team goals while on pitch	34	Club Strike Rate Average number of minutes between League goals scored by club		36

	PLAYER	LGE GOALS	POWER	STRIKE RATE
1	Danny Koevermans	22	34	100 mins
2	Shota Arveladze	14	37	154 mins
3	Simon Cziommer	6	37	179 mins
4	Maarten Martens	10	37	223 mins

KEY PLAYERS - DEFENDERS

Gretar Rafn Steinsson

Goals Conceded (GC) Number of League goals conceded while the player was on the pitch	18	Clean Sheets In League games when player was on pitch for at least 70 minutes		9
Defensive Rating Ave number of mins between League goals conceded while on the pitch	107	Club Defensive Rating Average number of mins between League goals conceded by the club this season		98

	PLAYER	CON LGE	CLEAN SHEETS	DEF RATE
1	Gretar Rafn Steinsson	18	9	107 mins
2	Barry Opdam	18	8	103 mins
3	Kew Jaliens	26	13	95 mins
4	Tim de Cler	31	13	91 mins

Shota Arveladze and Danny Koevermans

KEY PLAYERS - MIDFIELDERS

Demy de Zeeuw

Goals in the League	5	Contribution to Attacking Power Average number of minutes between League team goals while on pitch		37
Defensive Rating Average number of mins between League goals conceded while on the pitch	119	Scoring Difference Defensive Rating minus Contribution to Attacking Power		82

	PLAYER	LGE GOALS	DEF RATE	POWER	SCORE DIFF
1	Demy de Zeeuw	5	119	37	82 mins
2	Simon Cziommer	6	97	37	60 mins
3	Stijn Schaars	5	84	32	52 mins
4	Maarten Martens	10	89	37	52 mins

SQUAD APPEARANCES

Match	1 2 3 4	5 6 7 8 9 10	11 12 13 14 15 16 17 18 19 20 21 22	23 24 25	26 27 28 29 30 31	32 33 34 35	36 37 38 39 40	41 42 43 44 45	46 47 48 49 50 51 52 53 54 55 56
Venue	H A A H H	A A A H A	H H A H A A H H A A H H	A A H	H A H A H H	A H A A	H H A A A	H H A H H	A A H H H A H A H H A
Competition	L L L E L	O L E L L	E L L L E L O L L L E L	L E L	L E L L L L O	L L E L	E L O L E	L E L L E	L E L O L L O O O O O
Result	W W W D	W W D D W	L W W W W W W L W	D W	D W W D	L D W W W	W D D	D D W W L	D W D W D	W L W W W L L D W W L

Goalkeepers
Job Bulters	
Joseph Didulica	
Khalid Sinouh	
Boy Waterman	
Ronald Waterreus	

Defenders
Tim de Cler	
Ryan Donk	
Kew Jaliens	
Gijs Luirink	
Joris Mathijsen	
D Mendes Da Silva	
Barry Opdam	
Gretar Rafn Steinsson	
Ruud Vormer	

Midfielders
Simon Cziommer	
Demy de Zeeuw	
Johannes Gudjonsson	
Maarten Martens	
Rogier Molhoek	
Stijn Schaars	

Forwards
Shota Arveladze	
Nourdine Boukhari	
Moussa Dembele	
Julian Jenner	
Danny Koevermans	
Jeremain Lens	
Martijn Meerdink	

KEY: ■ On all match ◄◄ Subbed or sent off (Counting game) ▸▸ Subbed on from bench (Counting Game) ▸▸ Subbed on and then subbed or sent off (Counting Game) □ Not in 16
▨ On bench ◄◄ Subbed or sent off (playing less than 70 minutes) ▸▸ Subbed on (playing less than 70 minutes) ▸▸ Subbed on and then subbed or sent off (playing less than 70 minutes)

HOLLAND - AZ ALKMAAR

TWENTE ENSCHEDE

Final Position: 4th

NICKNAME: THE TUKKERS   KEY: ☐ Won ☐ Drawn ☐ Lost   Attendance

						Attendance
1	ucql1	Levadia Tallinn	H	D	1-1 Heubach 55	8,100
2	hopr1	Heracles	A	L	0-3	8,500
3	ucql2	Levadia Tallinn	A	L	0-1	4,500
4	hopr1	PSV Eindhoven	H	W	1-0 N'Kufo 71	13,000
5	hopr1	Roda JC Kerk	H	D	2-2 Wielaert 24, Bakircioglu 49	12,000
6	hopr1	AZ Alkmaar	A	D	2-2 N'Kufo 14 pen, Touma 81	17,000
7	hocr2	DOTO	A	W	7-1 N'Kufo 6, Touma 35, 38, 69, Bakircioglu 45, 85, Gerk 66	1,700
8	hopr1	S Rotterdam	H	W	2-0 van Bueren 19 og, N'Kufo 49	13,000
9	hopr1	RKC Waalwijk	H	W	4-3 Engelaar 45, Touma 70, N'Kufo 73, Bakircioglu 88	13,100
10	hopr1	Den Haag	A	W	2-1 N'Kufo 58 pen, Bakircioglu 74	6,453
11	hopr1	Excelsior	H	W	4-1 Touma 22, Bakkal 29, Engelaar 56, N'Kufo 64	13,125
12	hopr1	Feyenoord	A	L	1-2 Touma 30	38,000
13	hopr1	NEC Nijmegen	H	W	4-0 Wielaert 10, Bakkal 12, 16, N'Kufo 89	13,225
14	hopr1	Utrecht	A	D	0-0	19,700
15	hocr3	NEC Nijmegen	H	W	3-1 Bakkal 6, Engelaar 45, Bakircioglu 79	8,300
16	hopr1	Groningen	H	W	7-1 N'Kufo 16 pen, 71, Bakircioglu 45, 52, Wilkshire 85, Zijler 89, 90	13,000
17	hopr1	Ajax	A	D	1-1 Engelaar 8	49,364
18	hopr1	Vitesse Arnhem	H	W	2-0 Bakircioglu 34, N'Kufo 89	13,250
19	hopr1	NAC Breda	A	D	0-0	15,000
20	hopr1	Willem II Tilb	A	W	3-1 N'Kufo 31, 42, 67	12,067
21	hopr1	Heerenveen	H	W	5-1 N'Kufo 7, 72, Touma 41, Heubach 57, Bakircioglu 80	13,250
22	hopr1	Roda JC Kerk	A	L	0-2	13,000
23	hopr1	AZ Alkmaar	H	W	3-0 N'Kufo 30, Bakircioglu 42, Wilkshire 59	13,000
24	hopr1	S Rotterdam	A	L	0-3	10,000
25	hopr1	RKC Waalwijk	A	W	2-1 Bakircioglu 13, Engelaar 85	5,400
26	hocr4	NAC Breda	H	L	1-2 Touma 75 pen	12,500
27	hopr1	Den Haag	H	W	3-1 Heubach 15, Touma 59, Aissati 89	13,000
28	hopr1	Excelsior	A	W	2-1 El Ahmadi 33, N'Kufo 45	2,968
29	hopr1	Feyenoord	H	W	3-0 Heubach 25, Bakircioglu 58, 88	13,250
30	hopr1	Heerenveen	A	W	2-1 N'Kufo 14, Bakircioglu 33	25,000
31	hopr1	Willem II Tilb	H	D	0-0	13,000
32	hopr1	NEC Nijmegen	A	W	3-0 Bakircioglu 49, Touma 54, 69	12,000
33	hopr1	Ajax	H	L	1-4 N'Kufo 7	13,250
34	hopr1	Groningen	A	D	1-1 Touma 27	19,764
35	hopr1	Utrecht	H	W	3-0 Zomer 10, N'Kufo 25, Bakircioglu 90	13,250
36	hopr1	Heracles	H	D	1-1 El Ahmadi 22	13,250
37	hopr1	PSV Eindhoven	A	L	0-2	33,600
38	hopr1	Vitesse Arnhem	A	D	1-1 N'Kufo 87	24,250
39	hopr1	NAC Breda	H	W	2-1 Bakircioglu 12, N'Kufo 77	13,250
40	erepo	AZ Alkmaar	H	D	1-1 Bakircioglu 48	13,000
41	erepo	AZ Alkmaar	A	L	0-2	14,000

LEAGUE APPEARANCES, BOOKINGS AND CAPS

	AGE (on 01/07/07)	IN NAMED 18	APPEARANCES	COUNTING GAMES	MINUTES ON PITCH	YELLOW CARDS	RED CARDS	CAPS THIS SEASON	NATIONAL SIDE
Goalkeepers									
Sander Boschker	36	34	34	33	3006	3	0	-	Holland
Cees Paauwe	29	34	1	0	54	0	0	-	Holland
Defenders									
Edson Braafheid	24	12	11	5	604	1	0	-	Holland
Jeroen Heubach	32	31	31	28	2612	9	1	-	Holland
Peter Niemeyer	23	15	15	10	1096	3	0	-	Germany
Resit Schuurman	28	10	2	1	97	1	0	-	Holland
Rob Wielaert	28	34	34	34	3060	6	0	-	Holland
Luke Wilkshire	25	28	28	25	2253	4	1	2	Australia
Ramon Zomer	24	32	31	25	2523	7	1	-	Holland
Midfielders									
Ismael Aissati	18	14	14	10	1006	2	0	-	Morocco
Wout Brama	20	31	18	6	788	3	0	-	Holland
Karim El Ahmadi	22	23	22	21	1916	7	0	-	Holland
Orlando Engelaar	27	30	30	28	2583	5	0	2	Holland
Anatoli Gerk	22	19	8	0	75	0	0	-	Russia
Niels Oude Kamphuis	29	8	6	2	294	0	0	-	Holland
Rahim Ouedraogo	26	4	1	0	14	0	0	-	Burkina Faso
Bas Sibum	24	20	12	2	421	1	0	-	Holland
Arnar Vidarsson	29	29	2	0	24	0	0	3	Iceland
Niels Wellenberg	24	26	11	3	414	1	0	-	Holland
Forwards									
Guilherme Afonso	21	3	1	0	19	0	0	-	Switzerland
Marko Arnautovic	18	5	2	0	26	0	0	-	Austria
Kennedy Bakircioglu	26	34	34	33	2972	1	0	3	Sweden
Otman Bakkal	22	32	31	12	1649	1	1	-	Holland
Georgi Gakhokidze	31	3	2	0	48	0	0	-	Georgia
Patrick Gerritsen	20	5	3	0	77	0	0	-	Holland
Marcel Kleizen	21	1	1	0	18	0	0	-	Holland
Blaise N'Kufo	32	34	34	33	2958	1	0	-	Switzerland
Sharbel Touma	28	32	32	28	2564	1	1	-	Sweden
Sergio Zijler	19	24	12	1	290	0	0	-	Holland

TEAM OF THE SEASON

D Luke Wilkshire CG: 25 DR: 83	**M** Ismael Aissati* CG: 10 SD: 59
D Rob Wielaert CG: 34 DR: 82	**M** Wout Brama * CG: 6 SD: 48 · **F** Blaise N'Kufo CG: 33 SR: 134
G Sander Boschker CG: 33 DR: 81	
D Ramon Zomer CG: 25 DR: 81	**M** Orlando Engelaar CG: 28 SD: 46 · **F** K Bakircioglu CG: 33 SR: 198
D Jeroen Heubach CG: 28 DR: 81	**M** Karim El Ahmadi CG: 21 SD: 38

MONTHLY POINTS TALLY

AUGUST	3	50%
SEPTEMBER	8	67%
OCTOBER	9	75%
NOVEMBER	8	67%
DECEMBER	10	56%
JANUARY	6	100%
FEBRUARY	10	83%
MARCH	4	44%
APRIL	8	53%

LEAGUE GOALS

	PLAYER	MINS	GOALS	S RATE
1	N'Kufo	2958	22	134
2	Bakircioglu	2972	15	198
3	Touma	2564	9	284
4	Engelaar	2583	4	645
5	Bakkal	1649	3	549
6	Heubach	2612	3	870
7	Zijler	290	2	145
8	El Ahmadi	1916	2	958
9	Wilkshire	2253	2	1126
10	Wielaert	3060	2	1530
11	Aissati	1006	1	1006
12	Zomer	2523	1	2523
13	Kleizen	18	0	
	Other		0	
	TOTAL		66	

TOP POINT EARNERS

	PLAYER	GAMES	AV PTS
1	Ramon Zomer	26	2.23
2	Orlando Engelaar	28	2.04
3	Jeroen Heubach	28	2.04
4	Blaise N'Kufo	33	1.97
5	Rob Wielaert	34	1.94
6	Kennedy Bakircioglu	33	1.91
7	Sander Boschker	33	1.91
8	Sharbel Touma	29	1.90
9	Luke Wilkshire	26	1.88
10	Karim El Ahmadi	21	1.86
	CLUB AVERAGE:		1.94

DISCIPLINARY RECORDS

	PLAYER	YELLOW	RED	AVE
1	Jeroen Heubach	9	1	261
2	Karim El Ahmadi	7	0	319
3	Ramon Zomer	7	1	360
4	Wout Brama	3	0	394
5	Luke Wilkshire	4	1	450
6	Peter Niemeyer	3	0	548
7	Edson Braafheid	1	0	604
8	Rob Wielaert	6	0	612
9	Orlando Engelaar	5	0	645
10	Otman Bakkal	1	1	824
11	Sander Boschker	3	0	1002
12	Ismael Aissati	2	0	1006
13	Sharbel Touma	1	1	1282
	Other	2	0	
	TOTAL	54	5	

KEY GOALKEEPER

Sander Boschker

Goals Conceded in the League	37	Counting Games League games when player was on pitch for at least 70 minutes	33
Defensive Rating Ave number of mins between League goals conceded while on the pitch	81	Clean Sheets In League games when player was on pitch for at least 70 minutes	11

KEY PLAYERS - DEFENDERS

Luke Wilkshire

Goals Conceded Number of League goals conceded while the player was on the pitch	27	Clean Sheets In League games when player was on pitch for at least 70 minutes	8
Defensive Rating Ave number of mins between League goals conceded while on the pitch	83	Club Defensive Rating Average number of mins between League goals conceded by the club this season	82

	PLAYER	CON LGE	CLEAN SHEETS	DEF RATE
1	Luke Wilkshire	27	8	83 mins
2	Rob Wielaert	37	11	82 mins
3	Ramon Zomer	31	9	81 mins
4	Jeroen Heubach	32	10	81 mins

KEY PLAYERS - MIDFIELDERS

Ismael Aissati

Goals in the League	1	Contribution to Attacking Power Average number of minutes between League team goals while on pitch	52
Defensive Rating Average number of mins between League goals conceded while on the pitch	111	Scoring Difference Defensive Rating minus Contribution to Attacking Power	59

	PLAYER	LGE GOALS	DEF RATE	POWER	SCORE DIFF
1	Ismael Aissati	1	111	52	59 mins
2	Wout Brama	0	87	39	48 mins
3	Orlando Engelaar	4	89	43	46 mins
4	Karim El Ahmadi	2	87	49	38 mins

KEY PLAYERS - GOALSCORERS

Blaise N'Kufo

Goals in the League	22	Player Strike Rate Average number of minutes between League goals scored by player	134
Contribution to Attacking Power Average number of minutes between League team goals while on pitch	46	Club Strike Rate Average number of minutes between League goals scored by club	45

	PLAYER	LGE GOALS	POWER	STRIKE RATE
1	Blaise N'Kufo	22	46	134 mins
2	Kennedy Bakircioglu	15	45	198 mins
3	Sharbel Touma	9	49	284 mins
4	Otman Bakkal	3	38	549 mins

Bas Sibum

SQUAD APPEARANCES

Match	1	2	3	4	5	6	7	8	9	10	11	12	13	14	15	16	17	18	19	20	21	22	23	24	25	26	27	28	29	30	31	32	33	34	35	36	37	38	39	40	41
Venue	H	A	A	H	H		L	O	L	L		H	A	H	A	H		H	A	H	A	A	A	H	A	H	H		A	H	A	H	A		H	A	H	H	A	A	H	A
Competition	E	L	E	L	L		L	O	L	L		L	L	L	L	O		L	L	L	L	L	L	L	L	O	L		A	L	L	L	L		H	L	L	H	A	A	H	A
Result	D	L	L	W	D		D	W	W	W		W	L	W	D	W		W	D	W	W	L	W	L	W	L	W		W	W	W	D	W		L	D	W	D	L	D	W	L

Goalkeepers
Sander Boschker
Kees Paauwe

Defenders
Edson Braafheid
Jeroen Heubach
Peter Niemeyer
Wesit Schuurman
Rob Wielaert
Luke Wilkshire
Ramon Zomer

Midfielders
Ismael Aissati
Wout Brama
Karim El Ahmadi
Orlando Engelaar
Anatoli Gerk
Niels Oude Kamphuis
Rahim Ouedraogo
Bas Sibum
Arnar Vidarsson
Niels Wellenberg

Forwards
Guilherme Afonso
Marko Arnautovic
Kennedy Bakircioglu
Otman Bakkal
Georgi Gakhokidze
Patrick Gerritsen
Marcel Kleizen
Blaise N'Kufo
Sharbel Touma
Sergio Zijler

KEY:
- ■ On all match
- ■ On bench
- ◄◄ Subbed or sent off (Counting game)
- ◄ Subbed or sent off (playing less than 70 minutes)
- ►► Subbed on from bench (Counting Game)
- ►► Subbed on (playing less than 70 minutes)
- ►► Subbed on and then subbed or sent off (Counting Game)
- ►► Subbed on and then subbed or sent off (playing less than 70 minutes)
- □ Not in 16

HOLLAND - TWENTE ENSCHEDE

HEERENVEEN

Final Position: **5th**

NICKNAME: TROT VAN HET NOORDEN   KEY: ☐ Won ☐ Drawn ☐ Lost   Attendance

#		Opponent		Result	Scorers	Attendance
1	hopr1	**Den Haag**	A W	3-2	Bosvelt 42, Yildirim 82, Alves 93	6,900
2	hopr1	**Willem II Tilb**	H W	5-0	Zuiverloon 2, Alves 11, 42, Nilsson 23, Friend 46	25,000
3	hopr1	**Excelsior**	A L	1-3	Hansson 4	3,000
4	ucrl1	**Setubal**	A W	3-0	Alves 59, 65, Nilsson 90	3,027
5	hopr1	**NEC Nijmegen**	H W	3-0	Alves 29, Nilsson 64, Pranjic 77	25,000
6	hocr2	**Roda JC Kerk**	H L	0-2		10,300
7	hopr1	**Utrecht**	A L	0-1		19,000
8	ucrl2	**Setubal**	H D	0-0		16,800
9	hopr1	**PSV Eindhoven**	H D	0-0		25,400
10	hopr1	**Heracles**	A L	0-1		8,500
11	ucgpd	**Osasuna**	A D	0-0		20,000
12	hopr1	**Groningen**	H W	4-2	Alves 14, 74, 79, Friend 68	26,000
13	hopr1	**Ajax**	H L	0-2		26,000
14	ucgpd	**Odense**	H L	0-2		17,500
15	hopr1	**S Rotterdam**	H W	2-0	Nilsson 29, Alves 54	25,800
16	hopr1	**NAC Breda**	A D	1-1	Alves 5	14,045
17	hopr1	**RKC Waalwijk**	A W	2-0	Nilsson 13, Alves 22	5,500
18	ucgpd	**Parma**	A L	1-2	Pranjic 21	3,632
19	hopr1	**AZ Alkmaar**	H L	1-3	Alves 20	26,000
20	hopr1	**Vitesse Arnhem**	A W	3-1	Alves 56, 60, 77 pen	17,600
21	hopr1	**Feyenoord**	A L	3-4	Alves 24, Friend 74, 78	40,000
22	hopr1	**Roda JC Kerk**	H W	1-0	Tarvajarvi 87	25,200
23	ucgpd	**Lens**	H W	1-0	Alves 90	17,000
24	hopr1	**Twente**	A L	1-5	Alves 24	13,250
25	hopr1	**Excelsior**	H W	2-0	Alves 24, Nilsson 42	25,000
26	hopr1	**NEC Nijmegen**	A W	2-0	Alves 15, Johnson 82	12,250
27	hopr1	**Utrecht**	H D	0-0		26,000
28	hopr1	**PSV Eindhoven**	A L	1-3	Alves 21	33,212
29	hopr1	**Heracles**	H W	5-1	Nilsson 2, Alves 39, 43, Pranjic 63, Friend 75	25,200
30	hopr1	**Groningen**	A D	1-1	Alves 70	19,846
31	hopr1	**Vitesse Arnhem**	H D	0-0		25,000
32	hopr1	**Twente**	H L	1-2	Hansson 67	25,000
33	hopr1	**Roda JC Kerk**	A L	0-1		13,000
34	hopr1	**Ajax**	A W	1-0	Nilsson 18	50,174
35	hopr1	**RKC Waalwijk**	H W	1-0	Hansson 30	25,500
36	hopr1	**NAC Breda**	H W	4-2	Alves 9, 39, 68, Nilsson 64	25,300
37	hopr1	**S Rotterdam**	A D	2-2	Hansson 11, Garcia-Garcia 22	10,800
38	hopr1	**Den Haag**	H D	1-1	Alves 24	25,000
39	hopr1	**Willem II Tilb**	A W	3-1	Alves 49, 52, 69	13,600
40	hopr1	**AZ Alkmaar**	A L	1-3	Alves 72	16,272
41	hopr1	**Feyenoord**	H W	5-1	Alves 32, 64, 65, 75 pen, Nilsson 79	26,000
42	erepo	**Ajax**	H W	1-0	Nilsson 18	23,500
43	erepo	**Ajax**	A L	0-4		30,000

LEAGUE APPEARANCES, BOOKINGS AND CAPS

	AGE (on 01/07/07)	IN NAMED 18	APPEARANCES	COUNTING GAMES	MINUTES ON PITCH	YELLOW CARDS	RED CARDS	CAPS THIS SEASON	NATIONAL SIDE
Goalkeepers									
Brian Vandenbussche	25	34	34	34	3090	3	1	-	Belgium
Boy Waterman	23	19	0	0	0	0	0	-	Holland
Defenders									
Michel Breuer	27	32	31	28	2664	6	0	-	Holland
Michael Dingsdag	24	34	34	33	3029	6	0	-	Holland
Jeroen Drost	20	16	9	5	646	1	0	-	Holland
Petter Hansson	30	29	29	28	2529	4	1	9	Sweden
Timmi Johansen	20	9	3	0	99	2	0	-	Denmark
Calvin Jong-a-Pin	20	17	9	6	597	1	1	-	Holland
Gianni Zuiverloon	20	31	30	21	2309	9	0	-	Holland
Midfielders									
Paul Bosvelt	37	31	28	19	2148	4	0	-	Holland
Michael Bradley	19	34	21	4	838	4	0	7	United States
Andre Hanssen	26	27	21	18	1777	3	0	-	Norway
Abdelkarim Kissi	27	11	5	1	152	0	0	-	Morocco
Jakob Poulsen	23	32	20	9	1133	0	0	-	Denmark
Thomas Prager	21	24	21	17	1607	6	1	-	Austria
Danijel Pranjic	25	34	34	33	3009	1	0	-	Croatia
Forwards									
Afonso Alves	26	31	31	30	2707	2	0	-	Brazil
Age Hains Boersma	25	3	1	0	10	0	0	-	Holland
Rob Friend	26	22	19	8	936	3	0	-	Canada
Gonzalo Garcia-Garcia	23	9	8	4	543	1	0	-	Uruguay
Reza Ghoochannejhad	19	1	0	0	0	0	0	-	Holland
Will Johnson	20	17	14	0	217	0	0	-	Canada
Lasse Nilsson	25	34	34	30	2668	2	1	1	Sweden
Bo Storm	20	14	3	0	26	0	0	-	Denmark
Niklas Tarvajarvi	24	20	13	1	286	0	0	-	Finland
Ugur Yildirim	25	21	18	3	753	0	0	-	Holland

TEAM OF THE SEASON

D Gianni Zuiverloon CG: 21 DR: 88

M Thomas Prager CG: 17 SD: 34

G Brian Vandenbussche CG: 34 DR: 71

D Michael Dingsdag CG: 33 DR: 79

M Danijel Pranjic CG: 33 SD: 20

F Afonso Alves CG: 30 SR: 79

D Michel Breuer CG: 28 DR: 70

M Paul Bosvelt CG: 19 SD: 12

F Lasse Nilsson CG: 30 SR: 296

D Petter Hansson CG: 28 DR: 68

M Andre Hanssen CG: 18 SD: 11

MONTHLY POINTS TALLY

AUGUST	6	100%
SEPTEMBER	3	33%
OCTOBER	4	33%
NOVEMBER	10	67%
DECEMBER	10	56%
JANUARY	3	50%
FEBRUARY	2	17%
MARCH	9	100%
APRIL	8	53%

LEAGUE GOALS

	PLAYER	MINS	GOALS	S RATE
1	Alves	2707	34	79
2	Nilsson	2668	9	296
3	Friend	936	5	187
4	Hansson	2529	4	632
5	Pranjic	3009	2	1504
6	Johnson	217	1	217
7	Tarvajarvi	286	1	286
8	Garcia-Garcia	543	1	543
9	Yildirim	753	1	753
10	Bosvelt	2148	1	2148
11	Zuiverloon	2309	1	2309
12	Storm	26	0	
13	Sulejmani	0	0	
	Other		0	
	TOTAL		**60**	

TOP POINT EARNERS

	PLAYER	GAMES	AV PTS
1	Gianni Zuiverloon	21	2.10
2	Paul Bosvelt	19	1.84
3	Lasse Nilsson	30	1.83
4	Afonso Alves	30	1.70
5	Michel Breuer	28	1.68
6	Michael Dingsdag	33	1.67
7	Andre Hanssen	18	1.67
8	Brian Vandenbussche	34	1.62
9	Danijel Pranjic	33	1.58
10	Petter Hansson	29	1.55
	CLUB AVERAGE:		**1.62**

DISCIPLINARY RECORDS

	PLAYER	YELLOW	RED	AVE
1	Thomas Prager	6	1	229
2	Michael Bradley	4	0	279
3	Gianni Zuiverloon	9	0	288
4	Calvin Jong-a-Pin	1	1	298
5	Michel Breuer	6	0	444
6	Petter Hansson	4	1	505
7	G Garcia-Garcia	1	0	543
8	Jeroen Drost	1	0	646
9	Michael Dingsdag	6	0	757
10	Rob Friend	3	0	936
11	B Vandenbussche	3	1	1030
12	Paul Bosvelt	4	0	1074
13	Andre Hanssen	3	0	1777
	Other	5	1	
	TOTAL	**56**	**5**	

KEY GOALKEEPER

Brian Vandenbussche

Goals Conceded in the League	43	Counting Games League games when player was on pitch for at least 70 minutes	34
Defensive Rating Ave number of mins between League goals conceded while on the pitch	71	Clean Sheets In League games when player was on pitch for at least 70 minutes	12

KEY PLAYERS - DEFENDERS

Gianni Zuiverloon

Goals Conceded Number of League goals conceded while the player was on the pitch	26	Clean Sheets In League games when player was on pitch for at least 70 minutes	10
Defensive Rating Ave number of mins between League goals conceded while on the pitch	88	Club Defensive Rating Average number of mins between League goals conceded by the club this season	71

	PLAYER	CON LGE	CLEAN SHEETS	DEF RATE
1	Gianni Zuiverloon	26	10	88 mins
2	Michael Dingsdag	38	12	79 mins
3	Michel Breuer	38	9	70 mins
4	Petter Hansson	37	8	68 mins

KEY PLAYERS - MIDFIELDERS

Thomas Prager

Goals in the League	0	Contribution to Attacking Power Average number of minutes between League team goals while on pitch	73
Defensive Rating Average number of mins between League goals conceded while on the pitch	107	Scoring Difference Defensive Rating minus Contribution to Attacking Power	34

	PLAYER	LGE GOALS	DEF RATE	POWER	SCORE DIFF
1	Thomas Prager	0	107	73	34 mins
2	Danijel Pranjic	2	73	53	20 mins
3	Paul Bosvelt	1	63	51	12 mins
4	Andre Hanssen	0	55	44	11 mins

KEY PLAYERS - GOALSCORERS

Afonso Alves

Goals in the League	34	Player Strike Rate Average number of minutes between League goals scored by player	79
Contribution to Attacking Power Average number of minutes between League team goals while on pitch	48	Club Strike Rate Average number of minutes between League goals scored by club	51

	PLAYER	LGE GOALS	POWER	STRIKE RATE
1	Afonso Alves	34	48	79 mins
2	Lasse Nilsson	9	50	296 mins
3	Danijel Pranjic	2	53	1504 mins
4	Paul Bosvelt	1	51	2148 mins

Afonso Alves

SQUAD APPEARANCES

Match	1	2	3	4	5	6	7	8	9	10	11	12	13	14	15	16	17	18	19	20	21	22	23	24	25	26	27	28	29	30	31	32	33	34	35	36	37	38	39	40	41	42	43
Venue	A	H	A	A	H	H	A	H	H	A	A	H	H	H	H	A	A	A	H	A	A	H	H	A	H	A	H	A	H	A	H	H	A	A	H	H	A	H	A	A	H	H	A
Competition	L	L	L	E	L	O	L	E	L	L	E	L	E	L	L	L	L	E	L	L	L	L	E	L	L	W	D	L	W	D	L	L	L	L	L	L	L	L	L	L	L	O	O
Result	W	W	L	W	W	L	L	D	D	L	D	W	L	L	W	D	W	L	L	W	L	W	W	L	W	W	D	L	W	D	D	L	L	W	W	W	D	D	W	L	W	W	L

Goalkeepers
Brian Vandenbussche
Roy Waterman

Defenders
Michel Breuer
Michael Dingsdag
Jeroen Drost
Petter Hansson
Kimmi Johansen
Calvin Jong-a-Pin
Gianni Zuiverloon

Midfielders
Paul Bosvelt
Michael Bradley
Andre Hanssen
Abdelkarim Kissi
Jakob Poulsen
Thomas Prager
Danijel Pranjic

Forwards
Afonso Alves
Ge Hains Boersma
Rob Friend
Gonzalo Garcia-Garcia
Geza Ghoochannejhad
Will Johnson
Lasse Nilsson
Bo Storm
Niklas Tarvajarvi
Ugur Yildirim

KEY: ■ On all match   ◄◄ Subbed or sent off (Counting game)   ►► Subbed on from bench (Counting Game)   ►► Subbed on and then subbed or sent off (Counting Game)   ☐ Not in 16
☐ On bench   ◄◄ Subbed or sent off (playing less than 70 minutes)   ►► Subbed on (playing less than 70 minutes)   ►► Subbed on and then subbed or sent off (playing less than 70 minutes)

RODA JC KERK

Final Position: 6th

NICKNAME: KOEMPELS **KEY:** ☐ Won ☐ Drawn ☐ Lost   Attendance

				Score	Scorers	Attendance
1	hopr1	**Excelsior**	A W	1-0	Gyan 10 og	2,825
2	hopr1	**Den Haag**	H W	1-0	Vandamme 78	11,000
3	hopr1	**Twente**	A D	2-2	Ramzi 11, 27	12,000
4	hopr1	**Ajax**	H W	2-0	De Fauw 8, Oper 66	15,000
5	hocr2	**Heerenveen**	A W	2-0	Ramzi 69, Vandamme 90	10,300
6	hopr1	**AZ Alkmaar**	H L	0-2		13,000
7	hopr1	**Willem II Tilb**	A W	1-0	Ramzi 63	8,900
8	hopr1	**PSV Eindhoven** A L		1-4	De Fauw 4	34,500
9	hopr1	**S Rotterdam**	H W	2-1	Meeuwis 59 pen, Van Tornhout 90	15,000
10	hopr1	**NEC Nijmegen**	A D	0-0		11,750
11	hopr1	**Feyenoord**	H L	1-2	Ramzi 20	16,000
12	hopr1	**Groningen**	A L	1-2	De Fauw 59	19,000
13	hocr3	**ASWH**	H W	5-0	Bouchiba 2, Vandamme 8, De Fauw 27, Agustien 41, Cisse 54	7,000
14	hopr1	**RKC Waalwijk**	H D	1-1	Ramzi 19	15,000
15	hopr1	**Utrecht**	A L	0-2		19,000
16	hopr1	**NAC Breda**	H W	3-2	Oper 53, De Fauw 63, Ramzi 81	14,000
17	hopr1	**Heracles**	A D	1-1	Saeijs 29	8,500
18	hopr1	**Heerenveen**	A L	0-1		25,200
19	hopr1	**Vitesse Arnhem** H L		2-4	Cisse 25, Oper 29	12,000
20	hopr1	**Twente**	H W	2-0	Van Tornhout 2, 31	13,000
21	hopr1	**Ajax**	A L	0-2		50,334
22	hopr1	**AZ Alkmaar**	A D	2-2	Oper 23, 67	15,240
23	hopr1	**Willem II Tilb**	H W	2-1	Cisse 26, Agustien 55	13,300
24	hocr4	**AZ Alkmaar**	H W	2-1	Ramzi 58, Van Tornhout 62	3,500
25	hopr1	**PSV Eindhoven** H W		2-0	Saeijs 21, Oper 87	18,000
26	hopr1	**S Rotterdam**	A D	2-2	Bodor 5, Oper 78	9,750
27	hopr1	**NEC Nijmegen**	H W	1-0	Sibum 32	13,000
28	hopr1	**Vitesse Arnhem** A D		0-0		19,500
29	hopr1	**Heerenveen**	H W	1-0	Oper 43	13,000
30	hocqf	**RKC Waalwijk**	A L	0-1		5,000
31	hopr1	**Feyenoord**	A D	1-1	Cisse 57	42,000
32	hopr1	**Utrecht**	H D	0-0		13,800
33	hopr1	**RKC Waalwijk**	A L	2-3	Ramzi 31, Vandamme 61	6,000
34	hopr1	**Groningen**	H L	0-1		14,200
35	hopr1	**Excelsior**	H W	2-0	Kah 48, Oper 90	15,184
36	hopr1	**Den Haag**	A W	2-0	De Fauw 48, Meeuwis 60 pen	8,477
37	hopr1	**NAC Breda**	A W	2-0	Kah 35, Ramzi 73	14,120
38	hopr1	**Heracles**	H W	7-0	Oper 13, 86, Cisse 41, Bosnar 45 og, Agustien 53, Vandamme 56, Bodor 62	14,000
39	erepo	**Utrecht**	A D	0-0		13,000
40	erepo	**Utrecht**	H D	1-1	Oper 14	15,000

LEAGUE APPEARANCES, BOOKINGS AND CAPS

	AGE (on 01/07/07)	IN NAMED 18	APPEARANCES	COUNTING GAMES	MINUTES ON PITCH	YELLOW CARDS	RED CARDS	CAPS THIS SEASON	NATIONAL SIDE
Goalkeepers									
Bram Castro	24	33	14	13	1192	1	0	-	Belgium
Vladan Kujovic	28	33	21	20	1866	2	1	-	Serbia
Kay Van Eijk	19	2	0	0	0	0	0	-	Holland
Defenders									
Roy Bejas	20	10	0	0	0	0	0	-	Holland
Davy De Fauw	25	33	33	32	2929	6	1	-	Belgium
Marcel de Jong	20	32	27	20	1978	6	0	-	Holland
Pa-Modou Kah	26	31	30	27	2519	7	0	-	Norway
Vincent Lachambre	26	30	25	17	1739	3	0	-	Belgium
Kevin Leemans	24	27	5	2	182	1	0	-	Belgium
Humphrey Rudge	29	4	0	0	0	0	0	-	Holland
Jan-Paul Saeijs	29	32	30	26	2407	6	1	-	Holland
Ger Senden	35	32	14	6	819	3	0	-	Holland
Midfielders									
Kemy Agustien	20	33	31	26	2436	3	0	-	Holland
Boldiszar Bodor	25	33	29	17	1883	4	0	2	Hungary
Elbekay Bouchiba	28	33	15	1	229	3	0	-	Morocco
Marcel Meeuwis	26	33	33	30	2799	5	0	-	Holland
Adil Ramzi	29	31	31	31	2760	3	1	-	Morocco
Bas Sibum	24	13	13	11	1054	4	0	-	Holland
Alexander Voigt	29	9	0	0	0	0	0	-	Germany
Forwards									
Sekou Cisse	22	27	26	12	1549	4	0	-	Ivory Coast
Andres Oper	29	32	32	24	2427	4	1	3	Estonia
Edrissa Sonko	27	8	5	0	99	0	0	-	Gambia
Dieter Van Tornhout	22	29	25	10	1284	4	0	-	Belgium
Jamaique Vandamme	21	31	28	12	1438	0	0	-	Belgium

TEAM OF THE SEASON

D Vincent Lachambre **CG:** 17 **DR:** 102

M Boldiszar Bodor **CG:** 17 **SD:** 32

D Davy De Fauw **CG:** 32 **DR:** 86

M Kemy Agustien **CG:** 26 **SD:** 30

F Andres Oper **CG:** 24 **SR:** 220

G Vladan Kujovic **CG:** 20 **DR:** 103

D Jan-Paul Saeijs **CG:** 26 **DR:** 83

M Marcel Meeuwis **CG:** 30 **SD:** 25

F Sekou Cisse **CG:** 12 **SR:** 387

D Pa-Modou Kah **CG:** 27 **DR:** 83

M Adil Ramzi **CG:** 31 **SD:** 9

MONTHLY POINTS TALLY

AUGUST	6	100%
SEPTEMBER	7	58%
OCTOBER	4	33%
NOVEMBER	4	33%
DECEMBER	5	28%
JANUARY	6	100%
FEBRUARY	8	67%
MARCH	2	17%
APRIL	12	100%

LEAGUE GOALS

	PLAYER	MINS	GOALS	S RATE
1	Oper	2427	11	220
2	Ramzi	2760	8	345
3	De Fauw	2929	5	585
4	Cisse	1549	4	387
5	Van Tornhout	1284	3	428
6	Vandamme	1438	3	479
7	Bodor	1883	2	941
8	Saeijs	2407	2	1203
9	Agustien	2436	2	1218
10	Kah	2519	2	1259
11	Meeuwis	2799	2	1399
12	Sibum	1054	1	1054
13	Sonko	99	0	
	Other		0	
	TOTAL		**45**	

TOP POINT EARNERS

	PLAYER	GAMES	AV PTS
1	Bas Sibum	11	2.09
2	Kemy Agustien	26	1.77
3	Boldiszar Bodor	17	1.76
4	Vincent Lachambre	17	1.76
5	Bram Castro	13	1.69
6	Marcel Meeuwis	30	1.67
7	Andres Oper	24	1.67
8	Jan-Paul Saeijs	26	1.62
9	Davy De Fauw	33	1.55
10	Vladan Kujovic	21	1.52
	CLUB AVERAGE:		**1.59**

DISCIPLINARY RECORDS

	PLAYER	YELLOW	RED	AVE
1	Ger Senden	3	0	273
2	Dieter Van Tornhout	4	0	321
3	Jan-Paul Saeijs	6	1	343
4	Bas Sibum	4	0	351
5	Sekou Cisse	4	0	387
6	Marcel de Jong	6	0	395
7	Pa-Modou Kah	7	0	419
8	Boldiszar Bodor	4	0	470
9	Davy De Fauw	6	1	488
10	Vincent Lachambre	3	0	579
11	Vladan Kujovic	2	1	622
12	Adil Ramzi	3	1	690
13	Marcel Meeuwis	5	0	699
	Other	8	1	
	TOTAL	**65**	**5**	

KEY GOALKEEPER

Vladan Kujovic

Goals Conceded in the League	18	**Counting Games** League games when player was on pitch for at least 70 minutes	20
Defensive Rating Ave number of mins between League goals conceded while on the pitch	103	**Clean Sheets** In League games when player was on pitch for at least 70 minutes	10

KEY PLAYERS - DEFENDERS

Vincent Lachambre

Goals Conceded Number of League goals conceded while the player was on the pitch	17	**Clean Sheets** In League games when player was on pitch for at least 70 minutes	10
Defensive Rating Ave number of mins between League goals conceded while on the pitch	102	**Club Defensive Rating** Average number of mins between League goals conceded by the club this season	85

	PLAYER	CON LGE	CLEAN SHEETS	DEF RATE
1	Vincent Lachambre	17	10	102 mins
2	Davy De Fauw	34	14	86 mins
3	Jan-Paul Saeijs	29	12	83 mins
4	Pa-Modou Kah	30	12	83 mins

KEY PLAYERS - MIDFIELDERS

Boldiszar Bodor

Goals in the League	2	**Contribution to Attacking Power** Average number of minutes between League team goals while on pitch	62
Defensive Rating Average number of mins between League goals conceded while on the pitch	94	**Scoring Difference** Defensive Rating minus Contribution to Attacking Power	32

	PLAYER	LGE GOALS	DEF RATE	POWER	SCORE DIFF
1	Boldiszar Bodor	2	94	62	32 mins
2	Kemy Agustien	2	97	67	30 mins
3	Marcel Meeuwis	2	90	65	25 mins
4	Adil Ramzi	8	76	67	9 mins

KEY PLAYERS - GOALSCORERS

Andres Oper

Goals in the League	11	**Player Strike Rate** Average number of minutes between League goals scored by player	220
Contribution to Attacking Power Average number of minutes between League team goals while on pitch	59	**Club Strike Rate** Average number of minutes between League goals scored by club	65

	PLAYER	LGE GOALS	POWER	STRIKE RATE
1	Andres Oper	11	59	220 mins
2	Adil Ramzi	8	67	345 mins
3	Sekou Cisse	4	67	387 mins
4	Jamaique Vandamme	3	62	479 mins

Andres Oper and Jamaique Vandamme

SQUAD APPEARANCES

Match	1	2	3	4	5	6	7	8	9	10	11	12	13	14	15	16	17	18	19	20	21	22	23	24	25	26	27	28	29	30	31	32	33	34	35	36	37	38	39	40
Venue	A	H	A	H	A	H	A	A	H	A	H	A	H	A	H	A	H	A	H	A	H	A	A	H	H	A	H	A	H	A	A	H	A	H	H	A	H	A	H	H
Competition	L	L	L	O	L	L	L	L	L	L	L	L	O	L	L	L	L	L	L	L	L	L	L	O	L	L	L	L	L	O	L	L	L	L	L	L	L	L	O	O
Result	W	W	D	W	W	L	W	L	W	D	L	L	W	D	L	W	D	L	L	W	D	W	L	D	W	D	W	D	W	L	D	D	L	L	W	W	W	W	D	D

Goalkeepers

Bram Castro

Vladan Kujovic

Clay Van Eijk

Defenders

Roy Bejas

Davy De Fauw

Marcel de Jong

Pa-Modou Kah

Vincent Lachambre

Kevin Leemans

Humphrey Rudge

Jan-Paul Saeijs

Peter Senden

Midfielders

Kemy Agustien

Boldiszar Bodor

Ibekay Bouchiba

Marcel Meeuwis

Adil Ramzi

Jonas Sibum

Alexander Voigt

Forwards

Sekou Cisse

Andres Oper

Idrissa Sonko

Pieter Van Tornhout

Jamaique Vandamme

KEY: ■ On all match ◀◀ Subbed or sent off (Counting game) ▶▶ Subbed on from bench (Counting Game) ◀▶ Subbed on and then subbed or sent off (Counting Game) ☐ Not in 16
☐ On bench ◀ Subbed or sent off (playing less than 70 minutes) ▶ Subbed on (playing less than 70 minutes) ▶ Subbed on and then subbed off (playing less than 70 minutes)

HOLLAND - RODA JC KERK

FEYENOORD

Final Position: **7th**

NICKNAME: DE CLUB VAN ZUID   KEY: ☐ Won ☐ Drawn ☐ Lost   Attendance

#				Result	Scorers	Attendance
1	hopr1	Groningen	A L	0-3		19,814
2	hopr1	Heracles	H D	0-0		40,000
3	hopr1	S Rotterdam	A W	4-1	Hofs 10, 14, Lucius 85 pen, Boussaboun 88	11,000
4	ucrl1	Loko Sofia	A D	2-2	Lucius 45 pen, Greene 59	8,000
5	hopr1	PSV Eindhoven	A L	1-2	de Guzman 45	35,000
6	hocr2	Veendam	A W	3-2	Lucius 26, Bahia 67, Boussaboun 90	5,600
7	hopr1	Excelsior	H W	1-0	de Guzman 8	39,000
8	ucrl2	Loko Sofia	H D	0-0		22,000
9	hopr1	NAC Breda	H W	3-2	Buijs 33, Hofs 45, van Hooijdonk 63	38,000
10	hopr1	RKC Waalwijk	A D	2-2	Boussaboun 38, Lucius 45 pen	7,500
11	ucgpe	Basel	A D	1-1	Huysegems 76	16,000
12	hopr1	Ajax	H L	0-4		41,000
13	hopr1	Twente	H W	2-1	Huysegems 47, de Guzman 85	38,000
14	hopr1	Roda JC Kerk	A W	2-1	Charisteas 39, Huysegems 66	16,000
15	hopr1	Vitesse Arnhem	H W	2-1	Bahia 22, Lucius 71	40,000
16	hocr3	RKC Waalwijk	A L	2-3	Lucius 83, Keller 101 og	3,250
17	hopr1	Willem II Tilb	A W	5-3	Huysegems 10, Buijs 33, 74, Kolkka 55, 61	12,750
18	hopr1	AZ Alkmaar	H W	3-2	Hofs 29, 81, Derijck 57	45,000
19	ucgpe	Blackburn	H D	0-0		35,000
20	hopr1	NEC Nijmegen	A L	1-4	Pothuizen 90 og	12,000
21	ucgpe	Nancy	A L	0-3		19,840
22	hopr1	Heerenveen	H W	4-3	Huysegems 45, 51, Lucius 65 pen, de Guzman 84	40,000
23	hopr1	Den Haag	H W	3-1	Hofs 55, de Guzman 59, Charisteas 85 pen	36,000
24	ucgpe	Wisla Krakow	H W	3-1	Hofs 16, de Guzman 41, Charisteas 67	24,000
25	hopr1	Utrecht	A L	1-2	Vlaar 89	21,750
26	hopr1	S Rotterdam	H W	3-2	Charisteas 17, Lucius 29 pen, Vincken 76	44,000
27	hopr1	PSV Eindhoven	H D	1-1	Charisteas 38	40,000
28	hopr1	Excelsior	A W	3-1	Buijs 31, Hofs 40, Huysegems 50	3,527
29	hopr1	NAC Breda	A L	1-4	van Hooijdonk 86 pen	16,480
30	hopr1	RKC Waalwijk	H W	3-1	de Guzman 27, Bahia 34, Charisteas 85	40,500
31	hopr1	Ajax	A L	1-4	Charisteas 42	50,490
32	hopr1	Twente	A L	0-3		13,250
33	hopr1	Utrecht	H W	2-0	de Guzman 7, Charisteas 19	38,000
34	hopr1	Den Haag	A D	3-3	Kolkka 19, Charisteas 55, 73	8,814
35	hopr1	Roda JC Kerk	H D	1-1	van Hooijdonk 84	42,000
36	hopr1	AZ Alkmaar	A D	0-0		16,529
37	hopr1	Willem II Tilb	H D	0-0		41,000
38	hopr1	Vitesse Arnhem	A W	1-0	van Hooijdonk 79	22,900
39	hopr1	Groningen	H L	0-4		46,000
40	hopr1	Heracles	A L	1-4	van Hooijdonk 50	8,500
41	hopr1	NEC Nijmegen	H D	1-1	Castelen 53	45,500
42	hopr1	Heerenveen	A L	1-5	Buijs 55	26,000
43	erepo	Groningen	A L	1-2	Castelen 14	19,300
44	erepo	Groningen	H D	1-1	van Hooijdonk 8	18,000

LEAGUE APPEARANCES, BOOKINGS AND CAPS

	AGE (on 01/07/07)	IN NAMED 18	APPEARANCES	COUNTING GAMES	MINUTES ON PITCH	YELLOW CARDS	RED CARDS	CAPS THIS SEASON	NATIONAL SIDE
Goalkeepers									
Sherif Ekramy	24	16	3	2	234	0	0	-	Egypt
Henk Timmer	35	32	32	31	2826	0	0	2	Holland
Defenders									
Andre Bahia	23	32	29	26	2428	5	0	-	Brazil
Pieter Collen	27	13	2	0	88	0	0	1	Belgium
Timothy Derijck	20	28	18	6	876	2	0	-	Belgium
Royston Drenthe	25	31	26	23	2245	12	1	-	Holland
Serginho Greene	25	24	22	21	1874	7	0	-	Holland
Philippe Leonard	33	14	2	0	73	1	0	2	Belgium
Karim Saidi	23	15	12	7	752	3	0	-	Tunisia
Dwight Tiendalli	21	18	13	11	1024	3	1	-	Surinam
Ron Vlaar	22	20	20	18	1699	4	0	-	Holland
Midfielders									
Pascal Bosschaart	27	2	1	1	90	0	0	-	Holland
Danny Buijs	25	27	27	25	2376	8	1	-	Holland
Jonathan de Guzman	19	32	32	27	2651	3	1	3	Canada
Nick Hofs	24	19	19	16	1513	6	0	-	Holland
Jacob Lensky	18	5	1	0	45	0	0	-	Canada
Theo Lucius	30	27	27	25	2335	8	0	-	Holland
Sebastien Pardo	25	16	10	4	498	3	1	-	Chile
Alfred Schreuder	34	16	10	7	668	1	0	-	Holland
Georginio Wijnaldum	16	4	3	2	224	0	0	-	Holland
Forwards									
Ali Boussaboun	28	18	11	3	452	2	0	-	Morocco
Romeo Castelen	24	12	12	10	935	1	0	2	Holland
Angelos Charisteas	27	29	28	26	2324	4	0	4	Greece
Benjamin De Ceulaer	23	2	2	0	81	0	0	-	Belgium
Stijn Huysegems	25	34	25	14	1572	0	0	2	Belgium
Joonas Kolkka	32	33	22	13	1507	2	0	6	Finland
Pierre van Hooijdonk	37	32	26	15	1496	4	1	-	Holland
Tim Vincken	20	28	23	3	726	3	0	-	Holland

TEAM OF THE SEASON

Position	Player	Stats
D	Serginho Greene	CG: 21 DR: 50
M	Nick Hofs	CG: 16 SD: 8
D	Royston Drenthe	CG: 23 DR: 48
M	Theo Lucius	CG: 25 SD: -3
F	Angelos Charisteas	CG: 26 SR: 258
G	Henk Timmer	CG: 31 DR: 48
D	Andre Bahia	CG: 26 DR: 47
M	Danny Buijs	CG: 25 SD: -5
F	Stein Huysegems	CG: 14 SR: 262
D	Ron Vlaar	CG: 18 DR: 45
M	Jonathan de Guzman	CG: 27 SD: -10

MONTHLY POINTS TALLY

Month		Points	%
AUGUST		1	17%
SEPTEMBER		6	67%
OCTOBER		10	67%
NOVEMBER		9	75%
DECEMBER		13	72%
JANUARY		3	50%
FEBRUARY		4	33%
MARCH		3	33%
APRIL		4	27%

LEAGUE GOALS

	PLAYER	MINS	GOALS	S RATE
1	Charisteas	2324	9	258
2	Hofs	1513	7	216
3	de Guzman	2651	7	378
4	Huysegems	1572	6	262
5	van Hooijdonk	1496	5	299
6	Lucius	2335	5	467
7	Buijs	2376	5	475
8	Kolkka	1507	3	502
9	Boussaboun	452	2	226
10	Bahia	2428	2	1214
11	Vincken	726	1	726
12	Derijck	876	1	876
13	Castelen	935	1	935
	Other		1	
	TOTAL		55	

TOP POINT EARNERS

	PLAYER	GAMES	AV PTS
1	Stein Huysegems	14	2.21
2	Nick Hofs	16	2.06
3	Dwight Tiendalli	11	1.82
4	Serginho Greene	21	1.81
5	Theo Lucius	25	1.72
6	Joonas Kolkka	13	1.69
7	Henk Timmer	31	1.68
8	Royston Drenthe	23	1.65
9	Danny Buijs	25	1.64
10	Andre Bahia	26	1.62
	CLUB AVERAGE:		1.56

DISCIPLINARY RECORDS

	PLAYER	YELLOW	RED	AVE
1	Sebastien Pardo	3	1	124
2	Tim Vincken	3	0	242
3	Royston Drenthe	12	1	249
4	Dwight Tiendalli	3	1	256
5	Nick Hofs	6	0	302
6	Danny Buijs	8	1	339
7	Serginho Greene	7	0	374
8	P van Hooijdonk	4	1	374
9	Ron Vlaar	4	0	424
10	Timothy Derijck	2	0	438
11	Ali Boussaboun	2	0	452
12	Theo Lucius	8	0	467
13	Angelos Charisteas	4	0	581
	Other	15	1	
	TOTAL	81	6	

KEY GOALKEEPER

Henk Timmer

Goals Conceded in the League	58	Counting Games League games when player was on pitch for at least 70 minutes	31
Defensive Rating Ave number of mins between League goals conceded while on the pitch	48	Clean Sheets In League games when player was on pitch for at least 70 minutes	6

KEY PLAYERS - DEFENDERS

Serginho Greene

Goals Conceded Number of League goals conceded while the player was on the pitch	37	Clean Sheets In League games when player was on pitch for at least 70 minutes	4
Defensive Rating Ave number of mins between League goals conceded while on the pitch	50	Club Defensive Rating Average number of mins between League goals conceded by the club this season	46

	PLAYER	CON LGE	CLEAN SHEETS	DEF RATE
1	Serginho Greene	37	4	50 mins
2	Royston Drenthe	46	5	48 mins
3	Andre Bahia	51	5	47 mins
4	Ron Vlaar	37	4	45 mins

KEY PLAYERS - MIDFIELDERS

Nick Hofs

Goals in the League	7	Contribution to Attacking Power Average number of minutes between League team goals while on pitch	40
Defensive Rating Average number of mins between League goals conceded while on the pitch	48	Scoring Difference Defensive Rating minus Contribution to Attacking Power	8

	PLAYER	LGE GOALS	DEF RATE	POWER	SCORE DIFF
1	Nick Hofs	7	48	40	8 mins
2	Theo Lucius	5	44	47	-3 mins
3	Danny Buijs	5	49	54	-5 mins
4	Jonathan de Guzman	7	47	57	-10 mins

KEY PLAYERS - GOALSCORERS

Nick Hofs

Goals in the League	7	Player Strike Rate Average number of minutes between League goals scored by player	216
Contribution to Attacking Power Average number of minutes between League team goals while on pitch	40	Club Strike Rate Average number of minutes between League goals scored by club	54

	PLAYER	LGE GOALS	POWER	STRIKE RATE
1	Nick Hofs	7	40	216 mins
2	Angelos Charisteas	9	52	258 mins
3	Stein Huysegems	6	46	262 mins
4	Pierre van Hooijdonk	5	68	299 mins

Royston Drenthe

SQUAD APPEARANCES

Match	1	2	3	4	5	6	7	8	9	10	11	12	13	14	15	16	17	18	19	20	21	22	23	24	25	26	27	28	29	30	31	32	33	34	35	36	37	38	39	40	41	42	43	44
Venue	A	H	A	A	A	A	H	H	H	A	A	H	H	A	H	A	A	H	H	A	A	H	H	H	A	H	H	A	A	H	A	A	H	A	H	A	A	H	A	H	A	H	A	H
Competition	L	L	L	E	L	O	L	E	L	L	E	L	L	L	L	O	L	L	E	L	E	L	L	E	L	L	L	L	L	L	L	L	L	L	L	L	L	L	L	L	L	L	O	O
Result	L	D	W	D	L	W	W	D	W	D	D	L	W	W	W	L	W	W	D	L	L	W	W	W	L	W	D	W	L	W	L	L	W	D	D	D	D	W	L	L	D	L	L	D

Goalkeepers

Sherif Ekramy

Henk Timmer

Defenders

Andre Bahia

Pieter Collen

Timothy Derijck

Royston Drenthe

Serginho Greene

Philippe Leonard

Karim Saidi

Dwight Tiendalli

Ron Vlaar

Midfielders

Pascal Bosschaart

Danny Buijs

Jonathan de Guzman

Nick Hofs

Jacob Lensky

Theo Lucius

Sebastien Pardo

Alfred Schreuder

Georginio Wijnaldum

Forwards

Ali Boussaboun

Romeo Castelen

Angelos Charisteas

Benjamin De Ceulaer

Stijn Huysegems

Joonas Kolkka

Pierre van Hooijdonk

Tim Vincken

KEY: ■ On all match ◄◄ Subbed or sent off (Counting game) ►► Subbed on from bench (Counting Game) ►► Subbed on and then subbed or sent off (Counting Game) ☐ Not in 16
■ On bench ◄ Subbed or sent off (playing less than 70 minutes) ►► Subbed on (playing less than 70 minutes) ►► Subbed on and then subbed or sent off (playing less than 70 minutes)

FC GRONINGEN
Final Position: 8th

NICKNAME: PRIDE OF THE NORTH KEY: ☐ Won ☐ Drawn ☐ Lost   Attendance

#	Comp	Opponent	H/A	Result	Score	Scorers	Attendance
1	hopr1	Feyenoord	H	W	3-0	Nevland 54, van de Laak 60, Salmon 67	19,814
2	hopr1	NEC Nijmegen	A	D	1-1	Salmon 34	11,800
3	hopr1	Heracles	H	W	2-1	van de Laak 62, Levchenko 69 pen	19,000
4	ucrl1	Partizan	A	L	2-4	Fledderus 58, Suarez 90	11,500
5	hopr1	S Rotterdam	A	W	1-0	Seedorf 88	7,000
6	hocr2	TOP Oss	H	W	2-1	Lindgren 28, Suarez 51	4,600
7	hopr1	RKC Waalwijk	H	D	1-1	Nevland 10	19,000
8	ucrl2	Partizan	H	W	1-0	van de Laak 60 pen	20,000
9	hopr1	Vitesse Arnhem	H	W	4-3	Levchenko 37, van de Laak 82 pen, Suarez 89, 90	18,754
10	hopr1	Ajax	A	L	2-3	Levchenko 56 pen, Suarez 60	49,782
11	hopr1	Heerenveen	A	L	2-4	Levchenko 81 pen, 83	26,000
12	hopr1	Excelsior	H	W	2-1	Nevland 23, 68	18,000
13	hopr1	NAC Breda	A	D	0-0		14,985
14	hopr1	Roda JC Kerk	H	W	2-1	Nevland 71, Suarez 90	19,000
15	hocr3	NAC Breda	H	L	1-3	Levchenko 24 pen	16,000
16	hopr1	Twente	A	L	1-7	Lovre 22	13,000
17	hopr1	Willem II Tilb	H	W	4-1	Nevland 38, 56, Levchenko 85 pen, Salmon 90	19,000
18	hopr1	Den Haag	H	L	2-5	Lovre 13, Nevland 28	18,747
19	hopr1	Utrecht	A	L	0-3		19,000
20	hopr1	PSV Eindhoven	H	L	0-2		19,000
21	hopr1	AZ Alkmaar	A	L	0-2		15,000
22	hopr1	Heracles	A	W	1-0	Lovre 62	8,221
23	hopr1	S Rotterdam	H	L	0-1		19,000
24	hopr1	RKC Waalwijk	A	W	2-0	van de Laak 25 pen, Nevland 48	5,000
25	hopr1	Vitesse Arnhem	A	L	2-3	Suarez 31, 63	18,650
26	hopr1	Ajax	H	L	2-3	Levchenko 19 pen, Suarez 39	19,000
27	hopr1	Heerenveen	H	D	1-1	van der Linden 62	19,846
28	hopr1	Excelsior	A	W	2-0	Lovre 23, Suarez 49	3,000
29	hopr1	AZ Alkmaar	H	D	1-1	Nevland 56	19,186
30	hopr1	PSV Eindhoven	A	L	0-1		33,400
31	hopr1	NAC Breda	H	W	3-1	Fledderus 6, Nevland 67, van de Laak 79 pen	18,443
32	hopr1	Willem II Tilb	A	L	0-3		12,500
33	hopr1	Twente	H	D	1-1	Suarez 70	19,764
34	hopr1	Roda JC Kerk	A	W	1-0	Lovre 37	14,200
35	hopr1	Feyenoord	A	W	4-0	Lovre 50, 64, van de Laak 59, 70	46,000
36	hopr1	NEC Nijmegen	H	W	4-1	Levchenko 33 pen, 90, Svejdik 40, Suarez 64	19,159
37	hopr1	Den Haag	A	W	3-1	Nevland 11, 45, Lovre 25	7,800
38	hopr1	Utrecht	H	L	0-2		19,000
39	erepo	Feyenoord	H	W	2-1	Nevland 45, Sankoh 72	19,300
40	erepo	Feyenoord	A	D	1-1	Lovre 73	18,000
41	erepo	Utrecht	A	W	2-0	Suarez 54, 76	15,500
42	erepo	Utrecht	H	W	2-1	Suarez 4, Levchenko 14 pen	19,500

LEAGUE APPEARANCES, BOOKINGS AND CAPS

	Age (on 01/07/07)	In named 18	Appearances	Counting games	Minutes on pitch	Yellow cards	Red cards	Caps this season	National side
Goalkeepers									
Bas Roorda	34	34	29	29	2593	0	0	-	Holland
Brian van Loo	32	33	6	5	467	1	0	-	Holland
Defenders									
Mathias Floren	30	19	13	6	725	2	0	-	Sweden
Ewald Koster	22	5	1	0	14	0	0	-	Holland
Arnold Kruiswijk	22	26	25	24	2169	3	0	-	Holland
Gibril Sankoh	24	33	30	30	2676	7	0	-	Sierra Leone
Bruno R Silva Barone	27	31	29	24	2250	2	0	-	Uruguay
Donovan Slijngard	19	9	2	0	19	0	0	-	Holland
Ondrej Svejdik	24	34	22	16	1629	3	0	-	Czech Republic
A van der Linden	31	29	28	26	2442	3	0	-	Holland
Midfielders									
Danny Buijs	25	2	2	2	180	0	0	-	Holland
Mark-Jan Fledderus	22	21	18	13	1352	7	0	2	Belgium
Danny Holla	19	24	6	6	494	2	0	-	Holland
Yevgeniy Levchenko	29	30	29	24	2388	8	0	-	Ukraine
Rasmus Lindgren	22	30	30	27	2562	5	1	-	Sweden
Goran Lovre	25	33	30	14	1760	2	0	-	Serbia
Paul Matthijs	30	15	11	4	572	2	0	-	Holland
Marcel Pannekoek	21	3	1	0	16	0	0	-	Holland
Stefano Seedorf	25	21	12	3	456	0	0	-	Holland
Forwards									
Yuri Cornelisse	32	27	22	8	1005	0	0	-	Holland
Robbin Kieft	20	2	1	0	1	0	0	-	Holland
Marnix Kolder	26	14	7	1	130	0	0	-	Holland
Martijn Meerdink	30	11	10	3	448	5	0	-	Holland
Erik Nevland	29	31	31	25	2505	2	0	1	Norway
Glen Salmon	29	17	17	6	746	2	0	-	South Africa
Luis Suarez	20	32	29	24	2310	8	0	-	Uruguay
Koen van de Laak	24	25	25	16	1740	7	0	-	Holland

TEAM OF THE SEASON

G Bas Roorda CG: 29 DR: 51

D Ondrej Svejdik CG: 16 DR: 58
D Arnold Kruiswijk CG: 24 DR: 58
D Antoine van der Linden CG: 26 DR: 56
D Gibril Sankoh CG: 30 DR: 56

M Mark-Jan Fledderus CG: 13 SD: 23
M Goran Lovre CG: 14 SD: 16
M Rasmus Lindgren CG: 27 SD: -1
M Yevgeniy Levchenko CG: 24 SD: -10

F Erik Nevland CG: 25 SR: 192
F Luis Suarez CG: 24 SR: 231

MONTHLY POINTS TALLY

Month	Points	%
AUGUST	4	67%
SEPTEMBER	7	78%
OCTOBER	7	47%
NOVEMBER	6	50%
DECEMBER	6	33%
JANUARY	0	0%
FEBRUARY	5	42%
MARCH	7	58%
APRIL	9	75%

LEAGUE GOALS

	PLAYER	MINS	GOALS	S RATE
1	Nevland	2505	13	192
2	Suarez	2310	10	231
3	Levchenko	2388	9	265
4	Lovre	1760	8	220
5	van de Laak	1740	7	248
6	Salmon	746	3	248
7	Seedorf	456	1	456
8	Fledderus	1352	1	1352
9	Svejdik	1629	1	1629
10	van der Linden	2442	1	2442
11	van Loo	467	0	
12	Velten	0	0	
13	Van der Laan	0	0	
	Other		0	
	TOTAL		54	

TOP POINT EARNERS

	PLAYER	GAMES	AV PTS
1	Mark-Jan Fledderus	13	1.85
2	Goran Lovre	14	1.79
3	Arnold Kruiswijk	24	1.63
4	Ondrej Svejdik	16	1.63
5	Gibril Sankoh	30	1.57
6	Erik Nevland	25	1.56
7	Koen van de Laak	16	1.50
8	Antoine van der Linden	26	1.50
9	Rasmus Lindgren	27	1.44
10	Bas Roorda	29	1.34
	CLUB AVERAGE:		1.50

DISCIPLINARY RECORDS

	PLAYER	YELLOW	RED	AVE
1	Mark-Jan Fledderus	7	0	270
2	Mathias Floren	2	0	362
3	Glen Salmon	2	0	373
4	Luis Suarez	8	0	385
5	Yevgeniy Levchenko	8	0	398
6	Brian van Loo	1	0	467
7	Danny Holla	2	0	494
8	Rasmus Lindgren	5	1	512
9	Gibril Sankoh	7	0	535
10	Ondrej Svejdik	3	0	543
11	Paul Matthijs	2	0	572
12	Koen van de Laak	7	0	580
13	Goran Lovre	2	0	880
	Other	10	0	
	TOTAL	66	1	

KEY GOALKEEPER

Bas Roorda

Goals Conceded in the League	50	Counting Games League games when player was on pitch for at least 70 minutes	29
Defensive Rating Ave number of mins between League goals conceded while on the pitch	51	Clean Sheets In League games when player was on pitch for at least 70 minutes	6

KEY PLAYERS - DEFENDERS

Ondrej Svejdik

Goals Conceded Number of League goals conceded while the player was on the pitch	28	Clean Sheets In League games when player was on pitch for at least 70 minutes	6
Defensive Rating Ave number of mins between League goals conceded while on the pitch	58	Club Defensive Rating Average number of mins between League goals conceded by the club this season	56

	PLAYER	CON LGE	CLEAN SHEETS	DEF RATE
1	Ondrej Svejdik	28	6	58 mins
2	Arnold Kruiswijk	37	5	58 mins
3	Antoine van der Linden	43	5	56 mins
4	Gibril Sankoh	47	7	56 mins

KEY PLAYERS - MIDFIELDERS

Mark-Jan Fledderus

Goals in the League	1	Contribution to Attacking Power Average number of minutes between League team goals while on pitch	67
Defensive Rating Average number of mins between League goals conceded while on the pitch	90	Scoring Difference Defensive Rating minus Contribution to Attacking Power	23

	PLAYER	LGE GOALS	DEF RATE	POWER	SCORE DIFF
1	Mark-Jan Fledderus	1	90	67	23 mins
2	Goran Lovre	8	58	42	16 mins
3	Rasmus Lindgren	0	55	56	-1 mins
4	Yevgeniy Levchenko	9	51	61	-10 mins

KEY PLAYERS - GOALSCORERS

Erik Nevland

Goals in the League	13	Player Strike Rate Average number of minutes between League goals scored by player	192
Contribution to Attacking Power Average number of minutes between League team goals while on pitch	54	Club Strike Rate Average number of minutes between League goals scored by club	56

	PLAYER	LGE GOALS	POWER	STRIKE RATE
1	Erik Nevland	13	54	192 mins
2	Goran Lovre	8	42	220 mins
3	Luis Suarez	10	56	231 mins
4	Koen van de Laak	7	52	248 mins

Goran Lovre

SQUAD APPEARANCES

Match	1 2 3 4 5	6 7 8 9 10 11	12 13 14 15	16 17 18 19 20 21 22	23 24 25 26 27	28 29 30 31 32	33 34 35 36 37	38 39 40 41 42
Venue	H A H A A	H H H H A A	H A H H	A H H A H A A	H A A H H	A H A H A	H A A H A	H H A A H
Competition	L L L E L	O L E L L L	L L L O	L L L L L L L	L L L L L	L L L L L	L L L L L	L O O O O
Result	W D W L W	W D W W L L	W D W L	L W L L L L W	L W L L D	W D L W L	D W W W W	L W D W W

HOLLAND - FC GRONINGEN

UTRECHT

Final Position: **9th**

NICKNAME: UTREG

KEY: ☐ Won ☐ Drawn ☐ Lost   Attendance

#						Attendance
1	hopr1	Willem II Tilb	A	L	**1-2** Fortune 2	10,700
2	hopr1	S Rotterdam	H	D	**2-2** Caluwe 25, 45	19,000
3	hopr1	RKC Waalwijk	H	W	**5-0** Fortune 15, Kopteff 20, 41, Cornelisse 29, 43	20,000
4	hopr1	Heracles	A	L	**0-3**	8,000
5	hocr2	AGOVV	H	W	**3-1** Fortune 14, Caluwe 43, Dickoh 71	2,500
6	hopr1	Heerenveen	H	W	**1-0** van Dijk 90 pen	19,000
7	hopr1	Ajax	H	L	**2-3** van Dijk 80 pen, Fortune 85	24,000
8	hopr1	Excelsior	A	W	**1-0** van der Gun 45	2,835
9	hopr1	Den Haag	H	W	**2-0** Kruys 24, van der Gun 37	19,000
10	hopr1	NAC Breda	A	L	**1-2** Fortune 50	14,834
11	hopr1	AZ Alkmaar	A	L	**1-5** Fortune 90 pen	15,297
12	hopr1	Twente	H	D	**0-0**	19,700
13	hocr3	Rijnsb Boys	H	W	**5-0** van Dijk 37, Kruys 71, Nelisse 73, 79, Fortune 75	5,000
14	hopr1	Vitesse Arnhem	A	L	**2-4** Kopteff 71, Nelisse 77	19,000
15	hopr1	Roda JC Kerk	H	W	**2-0** Kruys 26, van Dijk 70 pen	19,000
16	hopr1	PSV Eindhoven	A	L	**0-5**	33,114
17	hopr1	Groningen	H	W	**3-0** Keller 4, van der Gun 35, 52	19,000
18	hopr1	NEC Nijmegen	A	L	**0-2**	12,000
19	hopr1	Feyenoord	H	W	**2-1** van Dijk 9 pen, Nelisse 17	21,750
20	hopr1	RKC Waalwijk	A	D	**1-1** Caluwe 25	2,500
21	hopr1	Heracles	H	D	**0-0**	20,000
22	hopr1	Heerenveen	A	D	**0-0**	26,000
23	hopr1	Ajax	A	L	**0-2**	44,740
24	hocr4	Roosendaal	H	W	**1-0** Kruys 68	7,100
25	hopr1	Excelsior	H	W	**1-0** Somers 41	19,000
26	hopr1	Den Haag	A	D	**1-1** Caluwe 17	7,160
27	hopr1	NAC Breda	H	W	**1-0** Kopteff 76	18,750
28	hopr1	Feyenoord	A	L	**0-2**	38,000
29	hopr1	NEC Nijmegen	H	W	**3-0** Somers 45, Rossini 48, Caluwe 63	19,000
30	hocqf	AZ Alkmaar	H	L	**1-2** Loval 54	19,000
31	hopr1	AZ Alkmaar	H	L	**0-4**	20,200
32	hopr1	Roda JC Kerk	A	D	**0-0**	13,800
33	hopr1	Vitesse Arnhem	H	W	**2-0** Dickoh 20, Caluwe 51	21,400
34	hopr1	Twente	A	L	**0-3**	13,250
35	hopr1	Willem II Tilb	H	W	**3-0** Caluwe 14, Somers 29, Cornelisse 66	21,230
36	hopr1	S Rotterdam	A	D	**1-1** George 68	10,500
37	hopr1	PSV Eindhoven	H	D	**1-1** Schut 86	23,500
38	hopr1	Groningen	A	W	**2-0** Loval 6, Keller 34	19,000
39	erepo	Roda JC Kerk	H	D	**0-0**	13,000
40	erepo	Roda JC Kerk	A	D	**1-1** Cornelisse 38	15,000
41	erepo	Groningen	H	L	**0-2**	15,500
42	erepo	Groningen	A	L	**1-2** van Dijk 79 pen	19,500
43	erepo	Vitesse Arnhem	A	D	**2-2** Rossini 64, Loval 67	8,750
44	erepo	Vitesse Arnhem	H	D	**0-0**	15,000

LEAGUE APPEARANCES, BOOKINGS AND CAPS

	AGE (on 01/07/07)	IN NAMED 18	APPEARANCES	COUNTING GAMES	MINUTES ON PITCH	YELLOW CARDS	RED CARDS	CAPS THIS SEASON	NATIONAL SIDE
Goalkeepers									
Franck Grandel	29	34	1	1	90	0	0	-	France
Michel Vorm	23	33	33	33	2970	2	0	-	Holland
Defenders									
Edson Braafheid	24	13	13	12	1137	3	0	-	Holland
Tim Cornelisse	29	29	29	29	2610	7	0	-	Holland
Francis Dickoh	24	29	29	29	2610	6	0	4	Ghana
Sander Keller	27	15	8	6	596	4	0	-	Holland
Erik Pieters	18	31	29	15	1446	8	1	-	Holland
Alje Schut	26	13	7	2	271	2	0	-	Holland
Etienne Shew-Atjon	27	11	7	4	473	3	0	-	Holland
Dwight Tiendalli	21	1	1	1	90	0	0	-	Surinam
Jahri Valentijn	22	3	1	0	29	0	0	-	Holland
Kees van Buuren	20	16	9	3	481	1	0	-	Holland
Leen van Steensel	23	3	1	0	37	0	0	-	Holland
Midfielders									
Jasper Bolland	21	4	1	0	17	0	0	-	Holland
Joost Broerse	28	34	28	21	2183	6	0	-	Holland
Tom Caluwe	32	33	33	30	2758	4	0	-	Belgium
Jean-Paul de Jong	36	33	21	6	695	2	0	-	Holland
Ricky Kruys	21	32	27	17	1767	7	0	-	Holland
Lucian Sanmartean	27	1	1	0	45	0	0	-	Romania
Hans Somers	29	33	31	17	1905	4	0	-	Belgium
Gregoor van Dijk	25	28	28	27	2467	6	1	-	Holland
Forwards									
Ali Boussaboun	28	9	9	7	670	1	1	-	Morocco
Darl Douglas	27	18	11	1	257	0	0	-	Holland
Marc-Antoine Fortune	25	22	22	22	1980	0	0	-	France
Leroy George	20	4	3	0	92	0	0	-	Holland
Peter Kopteff	28	33	30	18	1966	3	0	-	Finland
Loic Loval	25	12	12	8	772	1	0	-	France
Nassir Maachi	21	8	2	0	67	0	0	-	Holland
Robin Nelisse	29	27	18	10	1121	5	0	-	Holland
Guiseppe Rossini	20	29	17	5	583	0	1	-	Italy
Cedric van der Gun	28	18	18	13	1360	3	0	-	Holland

TEAM OF THE SEASON

G Michel Vorm — CG: 33 DR: 70

D Erik Pieters — CG: 15 DR: 76
D Francis Dickoh — CG: 29 DR: 68
D Tim Cornelisse — CG: 29 DR: 68
D Edson Braafheid — CG: 12 DR: 49

M Ricky Kruys — CG: 17 SD: 8
M Tom Caluwe — CG: 30 SD: -2
M Gregoor van Dijk — CG: 27 SD: -2
M Hans Somers — CG: 17 SD: -16

F C van der Gun — CG: 13 SR: 340
F Marc-A Fortune — CG: 22 SR: 396

MONTHLY POINTS TALLY

AUGUST	1	17%
SEPTEMBER	6	67%
OCTOBER	6	40%
NOVEMBER	4	33%
DECEMBER	9	50%
JANUARY	3	50%
FEBRUARY	7	58%
MARCH	4	44%
APRIL	8	53%

LEAGUE GOALS

	PLAYER	MINS	GOALS	S RATE
1	Caluwe	2758	7	394
2	Fortune	1980	5	396
3	van der Gun	1360	4	340
4	Kopteff	1966	4	491
5	van Dijk	2467	4	616
6	Somers	1905	3	635
7	Cornelisse	2610	3	870
8	Keller	596	2	298
9	Nelisse	1121	2	560
10	Kruys	1767	2	883
11	George	92	1	92
12	Schut	271	1	271
13	Rossini	583	1	583
	Other		2	
	TOTAL		**41**	

TOP POINT EARNERS

	PLAYER	GAMES	AV PTS
1	Ricky Kruys	17	1.65
2	Joost Broerse	21	1.57
3	Cedric van der Gun	13	1.54
4	Francis Dickoh	29	1.52
5	Tom Caluwe	30	1.50
6	Michel Vorm	33	1.45
7	Tim Cornelisse	29	1.41
8	Gregoor van Dijk	27	1.37
9	Hans Somers	17	1.35
10	Peter Kopteff	18	1.33
	CLUB AVERAGE:		**1.41**

DISCIPLINARY RECORDS

	PLAYER	YELLOW	RED	AVE
1	Etienne Shew-Atjon	3	0	157
2	Erik Pieters	8	1	180
3	Robin Nelisse	5	0	224
4	Ricky Kruys	7	0	252
5	Sander Keller	4	0	298
6	Ali Boussaboun	1	1	335
7	Jean-Paul de Jong	2	0	347
8	Edson Braafheid	3	0	379
9	Cedric van der Gun	3	0	453
10	Hans Somers	4	0	476
11	Kees van Buuren	1	0	481
12	Gregoor van Dijk	6	1	493
13	Francis Dickoh	6	0	522
	Other	23	1	
	TOTAL	**76**	**4**	

KEY GOALKEEPER

Michel Vorm

Goals Conceded in the League	42	Counting Games League games when player was on pitch for at least 70 minutes	33
Defensive Rating Ave number of mins between League goals conceded while on the pitch	70	Clean Sheets In League games when player was on pitch for at least 70 minutes	16

KEY PLAYERS - DEFENDERS

Erik Pieters

Goals Conceded Number of League goals conceded while the player was on the pitch	19	Clean Sheets In League games when player was on pitch for at least 70 minutes	7
Defensive Rating Ave number of mins between League goals conceded while on the pitch	76	Club Defensive Rating Average number of mins between League goals conceded by the club this season	69

	PLAYER	CON LGE	CLEAN SHEETS	DEF RATE
1	Erik Pieters	19	7	76 mins
2	Francis Dickoh	38	14	68 mins
3	Tim Cornelisse	38	14	68 mins
4	Edson Braafheid	23	5	49 mins

KEY PLAYERS - MIDFIELDERS

Ricky Kruys

Goals in the League	2	Contribution to Attacking Power Average number of minutes between League team goals while on pitch	65
Defensive Rating Average number of mins between League goals conceded while on the pitch	73	Scoring Difference Defensive Rating minus Contribution to Attacking Power	8

	PLAYER	LGE GOALS	DEF RATE	POWER	SCORE DIFF
1	Ricky Kruys	2	73	65	8 mins
2	Tom Caluwe	7	72	74	-2 mins
3	Gregoor van Dijk	4	70	72	-2 mins
4	Hans Somers	3	63	79	-16 mins

KEY PLAYERS - GOALSCORERS

Cedric van der Gun

Goals in the League	4	Player Strike Rate Average number of minutes between League goals scored by player	340
Contribution to Attacking Power Average number of minutes between League team goals while on pitch	64	Club Strike Rate Average number of minutes between League goals scored by club	74

	PLAYER	LGE GOALS	POWER	STRIKE RATE
1	Cedric van der Gun	4	64	340 mins
2	Tom Caluwe	7	74	394 mins
3	Marc-Antoine Fortune	5	73	396 mins
4	Peter Kopteff	4	67	491 mins

Ali Boussaboun

SQUAD APPEARANCES

Match	1	2	3	4	5	6	7	8	9	10	11	12	13	14	15	16	17	18	19	20	21	22	23	24	25	26	27	28	29	30	31	32	33	34	35	36	37	38	39	40	41	42	43	44
Venue	A	H	H	A	H	H	H	A	H	A	A	H	H	A	H	A	H	A	H	A	A	H	H	A	H	H	A	H	H	A	H	A	H	A	H	A	H	A	H	A	H	A	A	H
Competition	L	L	L	L	O	L	L	L	L	L	L	L	O	L	L	L	L	L	L	L	L	L	L	O	L	L	L	L	L	O	L	L	L	L	L	L	L	L	L	O	O	O	O	O
Result	L	D	W	L	W	W	L	W	W	W	L	L	D	W	L	W	L	W	L	W	D	D	D	L	W	W	D	W	L	W	L	L	D	W	L	W	D	D	W	D	D	L	L	D

Goalkeepers
Franck Grandel
Michel Vorm
Defenders
Edson Braafheid
Tim Cornelisse
Francis Dickoh
Sander Keller
Erik Pieters
Alje Schut
Etienne Shew-Atjon
Dwight Tiendalli
Jahri Valentijn
Kees van Buuren
Leen van Steensel
Midfielders
Jasper Bolland
Joost Broerse
Tom Caluwe
Jean-Paul de Jong
Ricky Kruys
Lucian Sanmartean
Hans Somers
Gregoor van Dijk
Forwards
Ali Boussaboun
Darl Douglas
Marc-Antoine Fortune
Leroy George
Peter Kopteff
Loic Loval
Nassir Maachi
Robin Nelisse
Guiseppe Rossini
Cedric van der Gun

KEY: ■ On all match ◄◄ Subbed or sent off (Counting game) ►► Subbed on from bench (Counting Game) ►►◄ Subbed on and then subbed or sent off (Counting Game) □ Not in 16
□ On bench ◄◄ Subbed or sent off (playing less than 70 minutes) ►► Subbed on (playing less than 70 minutes) ►►◄ Subbed on and then subbed or sent off (playing less than 70 minutes)

NEC NIJMEGEN

Final Position: 10th

NICKNAME: N.E.C. KEY: ☐ Won ☐ Drawn ☐ Lost Attendance

1	hopr1	PSV Eindhoven	A L	1-3	Worm 89	33,400
2	hopr1	Groningen	H D	1-1	Denneboom 8	11,800
3	hopr1	AZ Alkmaar	H L	0-2		11,800
4	hopr1	Heerenveen	A L	0-3		25,000
5	hocr2	EVV	A W	2-0	Eagles 68, Denneboom 88	1,700
6	hopr1	Ajax	A L	0-2		46,081
7	hopr1	Heracles	H W	2-0	Boutahar 11, 74	11,800
8	hopr1	NAC Breda	A W	2-0	Denneboom 17, 21	15,000
9	hopr1	Vitesse Arnhem	H W	1-0	El-Akchaoui 93 pen	12,500
10	hopr1	Roda JC Kerk	H D	0-0		11,750
11	hopr1	Twente	A L	0-4		13,225
12	hopr1	Willem II Tilb	H L	1-2	Holman 30	12,000
13	hocr3	Twente	A L	1-3	Holman 42	8,300
14	hopr1	Excelsior	A D	1-1	Snoyl 90	2,915
15	hopr1	S Rotterdam	H L	1-2	Denneboom 77	12,000
16	hopr1	Feyenoord	H W	4-1	Holman 54, Eagles 80, Kivuvu 83, Niedzielan 87	12,000
17	hopr1	Den Haag	A W	2-0	Niedzielan 45, Snoyl 67	6,738
18	hopr1	Utrecht	H W	2-0	Olsson 6, Wisgerhof 47	12,000
19	hopr1	RKC Waalwijk	A W	1-0	Denneboom 37	7,000
20	hopr1	AZ Alkmaar	A D	0-0		16,000
21	hopr1	Heerenveen	H L	0-2		12,250
22	hopr1	Ajax	H D	2-2	Denneboom 77, Wisgerhof 78	12,500
23	hopr1	Heracles	A D	0-0		8,412
24	hopr1	NAC Breda	H W	2-1	Holman 22, Denneboom 35	12,000
25	hopr1	Vitesse Arnhem	A L	1-1	Beerens 53	21,200
26	hopr1	Roda JC Kerk	A L	0-1		13,000
27	hopr1	RKC Waalwijk	H W	1-0	Barreto 60 fk	11,750
28	hopr1	Utrecht	A L	0-3		19,000
29	hopr1	Twente	H L	0-3		12,000
30	hopr1	S Rotterdam	A W	4-0	Barreto 10, Beerens 45, Olsson 54, Holman 64	10,115
31	hopr1	Excelsior	H L	0-1		12,000
32	hopr1	Willem II Tilb	A L	0-1		13,300
33	hopr1	PSV Eindhoven	H W	2-1	Holman 22, 24	12,500
34	hopr1	Groningen	A L	1-4	Holman 22	19,159
35	hopr1	Feyenoord	A D	1-1	Denneboom 57	45,500
36	hopr1	Den Haag	H W	3-2	Denneboom 38 pen, Delorge 69 og, Jans 74	12,000
37	erepo	S Rotterdam	A D	1-1	Jans 13	9,156
38	erepo	S Rotterdam	H W	2-1	Wisgerhof 36, Pothuizen 60	4,000
39	erepo	Vitesse Arnhem	A L	0-1		11,425
40	erepo	Vitesse Arnhem	H L	0-2		8,000

LEAGUE APPEARANCES, BOOKINGS AND CAPS

	AGE (on 01/07/07)	IN NAMED 18	APPEARANCES	COUNTING GAMES	MINUTES ON PITCH	YELLOW CARDS	RED CARDS	CAPS THIS SEASON	NATIONAL SIDE
Goalkeepers									
Gabor Babos	32	34	34	34	3060	2	0	-	Hungary
R van Emmerik	27	31	0	0	0	0	0	-	Holland
Defenders									
Youssef El-Akchaoui	26	27	23	20	1901	3	0	-	Holland
Muslu Nalbantoglu	23	34	32	28	2698	3	0	-	Holland
Jonas Olsson	24	32	32	32	2863	10	1	-	Sweden
Mark Otten	21	32	27	23	2193	4	0	-	Holland
Patrick Pothuizen	35	29	18	8	1121	4	1	-	Holland
Ferne Snoyl	22	27	25	19	1907	9	0	-	Holland
G Vanaudenaerde	23	28	9	1	205	1	0	-	Belgium
Bob Verweij	20	0	0	0	0	0	0	-	Holland
Peter Wisgerhof	27	34	34	34	3060	3	0	-	Holland
Midfielders									
Edgar Barreto	22	30	29	21	2170	5	0	1	Paraguay
Said Boutahar	24	20	12	6	777	0	0	-	Morocco
Lorenzo Davids	20	12	9	5	546	2	0	-	Holland
Chris Eagles	21	17	15	6	719	2	0	-	England
Dominique Kivuvu	19	33	23	18	1775	1	0	-	Holland
Dominique Scholten	19	5	0	0	0	0	0	-	Holland
Bart Van Brakel	20	1	0	0	0	0	0	-	Holland
Forwards									
Roy Beerens	19	14	14	10	963	0	0	-	Holland
Romano Denneboom	26	33	33	30	2782	5	0	-	Holland
Karim Fachtali	19	1	1	0	10	0	0	-	Holland
Guillano Grot	24	2	1	1	72	0	0	-	Holland
Brett Holman	23	32	32	29	2669	2	0	5	Australia
Paul Jans	25	26	8	0	155	2	0	-	Holland
Andrzej Niedzielan	28	22	22	9	1199	6	0	-	Poland
Saidi Ntibazonkiza	20	11	7	0	145	1	0	-	Burundi
Rutger Worm	21	34	21	2	630	1	0	-	Holland

TEAM OF THE SEASON

Peter Wisgerhof CG: 34 DR: 69

Dominique Kivuvu CG: 18 SD: 4

Mark Otten CG: 23 DR: 75

Chris Eagles CG: 6 SD: 0

R Denneboom CG: 30 SR: 309

Gabor Babos CG: 34 DR: 69

Jonas Olsson CG: 32 DR: 73

Edgar Barreto CG: 21 SD: -15

Brett Holman CG: 29 SR: 381

Muslu Nalbantoglu CG: 28 DR: 72

Said Boutahar CG: 6 SD: -60

MONTHLY POINTS TALLY

AUGUST	1	17%
SEPTEMBER	3	25%
OCTOBER	7	58%
NOVEMBER	4	33%
DECEMBER	11	61%
JANUARY	4	67%
FEBRUARY	4	33%
MARCH	3	25%
APRIL	7	58%

LEAGUE GOALS

	PLAYER	MINS	GOALS	S RATE
1	Denneboom	2782	9	309
2	Holman	2669	7	381
3	Boutahar	777	2	388
4	Beerens	963	2	481
5	Niedzielan	1199	2	599
6	Snoyl	1907	2	953
7	Barreto	2170	2	1085
8	Olsson	2863	2	1431
9	Wisgerhof	3060	2	1530
10	Jans	155	1	155
11	Worm	630	1	630
12	Eagles	719	1	719
13	Kivuvu	1775	1	1775
	Other		1	
	TOTAL		**35**	

TOP POINT EARNERS

	PLAYER	GAMES	AV PTS
1	Dominique Kivuvu	18	1.61
2	Mark Otten	23	1.39
3	Romano Denneboom	30	1.37
4	Gabor Babos	34	1.29
5	Muslu Nalbantoglu	28	1.29
6	Peter Wisgerhof	34	1.29
7	Brett Holman	29	1.28
8	Jonas Olsson	32	1.28
9	Ferne Snoyl	19	1.26
10	Edgar Barreto	21	1.24
	CLUB AVERAGE:		**1.29**

DISCIPLINARY RECORDS

	PLAYER	YELLOW	RED	AVE
1	Andrzej Niedzielan	6	0	199
2	Ferne Snoyl	9	0	238
3	Lorenzo Davids	2	0	273
4	Jonas Olsson	10	1	357
5	Chris Eagles	2	0	359
6	Patrick Pothuizen	4	1	373
7	Edgar Barreto	5	0	434
8	Mark Otten	4	0	548
9	Rutger Worm	1	0	630
10	R Denneboom	5	0	695
11	Yous El-Akchaoui	3	0	950
12	Peter Wisgerhof	3	0	1020
13	Brett Holman	2	0	1334
	Other	6	0	
	TOTAL	**62**	**2**	

KEY GOALKEEPER

Gabor Babos

Goals Conceded in the League	44	Counting Games League games when player was on pitch for at least 70 minutes	34
Defensive Rating Ave number of mins between League goals conceded while on the pitch	69	Clean Sheets In League games when player was on pitch for at least 70 minutes	11

KEY PLAYERS - DEFENDERS

Mark Otten

Goals Conceded Number of League goals conceded while the player was on the pitch	29	Clean Sheets In League games when player was on pitch for at least 70 minutes	9
Defensive Rating Ave number of mins between League goals conceded while on the pitch	75	Club Defensive Rating Average number of mins between League goals conceded by the club this season	69

	PLAYER	CON LGE	CLEAN SHEETS	DEF RATE
1	Mark Otten	29	9	75 mins
2	Jonas Olsson	39	11	73 mins
3	Muslu Nalbantoglu	37	11	72 mins
4	Peter Wisgerhof	44	11	69 mins

KEY PLAYERS - MIDFIELDERS

Dominique Kivuvu

Goals in the League	1	Contribution to Attacking Power Average number of minutes between League team goals while on pitch	73
Defensive Rating Average number of mins between League goals conceded while on the pitch	77	Scoring Difference Defensive Rating minus Contribution to Attacking Power	4

	PLAYER	LGE GOALS	DEF RATE	POWER	SCORE DIFF
1	Dominique Kivuvu	1	77	73	4 mins
2	Chris Eagles	1	79	79	0 mins
3	Edgar Barreto	2	65	80	-15 mins
4	Said Boutahar	2	51	111	-60 mins

KEY PLAYERS - GOALSCORERS

Romano Denneboom

Goals in the League	9	Player Strike Rate Average number of minutes between League goals scored by player	309
Contribution to Attacking Power Average number of minutes between League team goals while on pitch	89	Club Strike Rate Average number of minutes between League goals scored by club	85

	PLAYER	LGE GOALS	POWER	STRIKE RATE
1	Romano Denneboom	9	89	309 mins
2	Brett Holman	7	102	381 mins
3	Said Boutahar	2	111	388 mins
4	Roy Beerens	2	68	481 mins

Romano Denneboom

SQUAD APPEARANCES

Match	1 2 3 4 5 6 7 8 9 10 11	12 13 14 15 16	17 18 19 20 21	22 23 24 25 26	27 28 29 30 31	32 33 34 35 36 37 38 39 40
Venue	A H H A A H A H H A	H A A H H	A H A A H	H A H A A	H A H A H	A H A A H A H A H
Competition	L L L L O L L L L L	L O L L L	L L L L L	L L L L L	L L L L L	L L L L L O O O O
Result	L D L L W L W W W D L	L L D L W	W W W D L	D D W D L	W L L W L	L W L D W D W L L

Goalkeepers
Gabor Babos
R van Emmerik

Defenders
Youssef El-Akchaoui
Muslu Nalbantoglu
Jonas Olsson
Mark Otten
Patrick Pothuizen
Ferne Snoyl
G Vanaudenaerde
Bob Verweij
Peter Wisgerhof

Midfielders
Edgar Barreto
Said Boutahar
Lorenzo Davids
Chris Eagles
Dominique Kivuvu
Dominique Scholten
Bart Van Brakel

Forwards
Roy Beerens
Romano Denneboom
Karim Fachtali
Guillano Grot
Brett Holman
Paul Jans
Andrzej Niedzielan
Saidi Ntibazonkiza
Rutger Worm

KEY: ■ On all match ◄◄ Subbed or sent off (Counting game) ►► Subbed on from bench (Counting Game) ►► Subbed on and then subbed or sent off (Counting Game) □ Not in 16
□ On bench ◄◄ Subbed or sent off (playing less than 70 minutes) ►► Subbed on (playing less than 70 minutes) ►► Subbed on and then subbed or sent off (playing less than 70 minutes)

HOLLAND - NEC NIJMEGEN

NAC BREDA

Final Position: **11th**

NICKNAME: PEARL OF THE SOUTH   KEY: □ Won □ Drawn □ Lost   Attendance

1	hopr1	**AZ Alkmaar**	A L	**1-8** Stam 46	17,023
2	hopr1	**Ajax**	H L	**1-2** de Graaf 64	15,432
3	hopr1	**Den Haag**	A W	**2-0** Leonardo 1, de Graaf 79 pen	6,600
4	hopr1	**Vitesse Arnhem**	A W	**1-0** Zonneveld 90	19,251
5	hocr2	**Ijsselmeervo**	A W	**4-2** Peto 23, Leonardo 31, 44, Rigters 35	2,500
6	hopr1	**Willem II Tilb**	H D	**0-0**	15,000
7	hopr1	**Feyenoord**	A L	**2-3** Rigters 13, Zonneveld 36	38,000
8	hopr1	**NEC Nijmegen**	H L	**0-2**	15,000
9	hopr1	**RKC Waalwijk**	A W	**1-0** Mulder 66 og	6,000
10	hopr1	**Utrecht**	H W	**2-1** Zwaanswijk 9, Slot 90	14,834
11	hopr1	**Groningen**	H D	**0-0**	14,985
12	hopr1	**PSV Eindhoven**	A L	**0-3**	34,000
13	hocr3	**Groningen**	A W	**3-1** de Graaf 9, Zonneveld 45, Leonardo 54	16,000
14	hopr1	**Heerenveen**	H D	**1-1** de Graaf 81	14,045
15	hopr1	**Heracles**	A L	**0-2**	8,000
16	hopr1	**Roda JC Kerk**	A L	**2-3** de Graaf 40, Zonneveld 86	14,000
17	hopr1	**Twente**	H D	**0-0**	15,000
18	hopr1	**Excelsior**	H W	**2-1** Stam 36, Zonneveld 66	15,121
19	hopr1	**S Rotterdam**	A W	**3-0** Pinas 9, Mtliga 28, Rigters 45	10,000
20	hopr1	**Den Haag**	H D	**2-2** Slot 32, Leonardo 81	14,628
21	hopr1	**Vitesse Arnhem**	H W	**2-1** Slot 33, Sikora 89	13,520
22	hopr1	**Willem II Tilb**	A W	**2-0** Salmon 84, Zonneveld 90	14,000
23	hopr1	**Feyenoord**	H W	**4-1** van Gessel 12, Zonneveld 21, Salmon 60, 81	16,480
24	hocr4	**Twente**	A W	**2-1** Salmon 31, Zonneveld 89	12,500
25	hopr1	**NEC Nijmegen**	A L	**1-2** van Gessel 59	12,000
26	hopr1	**RKC Waalwijk**	H W	**2-1** Salmon 27, 73	14,760
27	hopr1	**Utrecht**	A L	**0-1**	18,750
28	hopr1	**S Rotterdam**	H W	**3-1** Salmon 32, de Graaf 54, Rigters 78	14,375
29	hopr1	**Excelsior**	A W	**2-0** Mtliga 51, Diba 73	3,312
30	hocqf	**PSV Eindhoven**	H W	**3-0** de Graaf 47, Diba 67, Salmon 70	16,000
31	hopr1	**Groningen**	A L	**1-3** de Graaf 50	18,443
32	hopr1	**Heracles**	H D	**1-1** Slot 33	14,812
33	hopr1	**Heerenveen**	A L	**2-4** Salmon 29, 82	25,300
34	hopr1	**PSV Eindhoven**	H D	**1-1** Slot 62	16,580
35	hopr1	**AZ Alkmaar**	H L	**1-4** Penders 45	14,780
36	hopr1	**Ajax**	A L	**0-2**	49,737
37	hocsf	**AZ Alkmaar**	A L	**0-6**	14,198
38	hopr1	**Roda JC Kerk**	H L	**0-2**	14,120
39	hopr1	**Twente**	A L	**1-2** Slot 79 pen	13,250
40	erepo	**Vitesse Arnhem**	A L	**2-3** Zonneveld 66 pen, 69	11,450
41	erepo	**Vitesse Arnhem**	H L	**0-1**	5,520

LEAGUE APPEARANCES, BOOKINGS AND CAPS

	AGE (on 01/07/07)	IN NAMED 18	APPEARANCES	COUNTING GAMES	MINUTES ON PITCH	YELLOW CARDS	RED CARDS	CAPS THIS SEASON	NATIONAL SIDE
Goalkeepers									
Arno van Zwam	37	34	2	2	180	0	0	-	Holland
Edwin Zoetebier	37	32	32	32	2880	0	0	-	Holland
Defenders									
Aykut Demir	18	25	1	1	90	0	0	-	Turkey
Kurt Elshot	29	22	14	10	976	5	0	-	Surinam
Wilmer Kousemaker	21	13	2	0	48	0	0	-	Holland
Patrick Mtliga	26	23	22	21	1903	7	0	-	Denmark
Rob Penders	31	27	25	23	2126	2	0	-	Holland
Patrick Zwaanswijk	32	32	32	31	2791	9	0	-	Holland
Midfielders									
Edwin de Graaf	27	32	32	31	2736	5	0	-	Holland
Fouad Idabdelhay	19	1	0	0	0	0	0	-	Holland
Danny Mathijssen	24	29	23	17	1611	4	0	-	Holland
Tamas Peto	33	18	8	2	262	3	0	-	Hungary
Brian Pinas	28	25	23	7	1049	4	0	-	Holland
Arne Slot	28	32	29	20	2083	4	0	-	Holland
Ronnie Stam	23	31	27	25	2329	7	0	-	Holland
Sander van Gessel	30	31	29	21	2060	6	0	-	Holland
Mike Zonneveld	26	31	31	28	2529	9	1	-	Holland
Forwards									
Anouar Diba	24	29	29	24	2257	4	0	-	Holland
Andro Franca	19	8	0	0	0	0	0	-	Holland
Leonardo	24	17	17	14	1283	5	0	-	Brazil
Maceo Rigters	23	34	32	22	2343	2	0	-	Holland
Glen Salmon	29	15	15	15	1332	1	0	-	South Africa
Victor Sikora	29	18	9	1	217	3	1	-	Holland
Gertjan Tamerus	26	10	1	1	172	1	0	-	Holland
Rogier Veenstra	19	23	8	1	259	1	0	-	Holland

TEAM OF THE SEASON

D Patrick Mtliga — CG: 21 DR: 95
M Danny Mathijssen — CG: 17 SD: 4
G Edwin Zoetebier — CG: 32 DR: 58
D Patrick Zwaanswijk — CG: 31 DR: 63
M Edwin de Graaf — CG: 31 SD: -16
F Glen Salmon — CG: 15 SR: 166
D Rob Penders — CG: 23 DR: 62
M Ronnie Stam — CG: 25 SD: -18
F Leonardo — CG: 14 SR: 641
D Kurt Elshot — CG: 10 DR: 46
M Sander van Gessel — CG: 21 SD: -22

MONTHLY POINTS TALLY

AUGUST	0	0%
SEPTEMBER	7	78%
OCTOBER	7	47%
NOVEMBER	1	8%
DECEMBER	11	73%
JANUARY	6	67%
FEBRUARY	9	75%
MARCH	2	17%
APRIL	0	0%

LEAGUE GOALS

	PLAYER	MINS	GOALS	S RATE
1	Salmon	1332	8	166
2	Slot	2083	6	347
3	Zonneveld	2529	6	421
4	de Graaf	2736	6	456
5	Rigters	2343	3	781
6	Leonardo	1283	2	641
7	Mtliga	1903	2	951
8	van Gessel	2060	2	1030
9	Stam	2329	2	1164
10	Sikora	217	1	217
11	Pinas	1049	1	1049
12	Penders	2126	1	2126
13	Diba	2257	1	2257
	Other		1	
	TOTAL		**42**	

TOP POINT EARNERS

	PLAYER	GAMES	AV PTS
1	Patrick Mtliga	21	**1.90**
2	Maceo Rigters	22	**1.55**
3	Danny Mathijssen	17	**1.53**
4	Leonardo	15	**1.47**
5	Edwin Zoetebier	32	**1.34**
6	Ronnie Stam	25	**1.32**
7	Patrick Zwaanswijk	31	**1.29**
8	Edwin de Graaf	31	**1.29**
9	Anouar Diba	24	**1.25**
10	Glen Salmon	15	**1.13**
	CLUB AVERAGE:		**1.26**

DISCIPLINARY RECORDS

	PLAYER	YELLOW	RED	AVE
1	Leonardo	5	1	213
2	Kurt Elshot	5	0	244
3	Mike Zonneveld	9	1	281
4	Patrick Mtliga	7	0	317
5	Brian Pinas	4	0	349
6	Ronnie Stam	7	0	388
7	Patrick Zwaanswijk	9	0	398
8	Sander van Gessel	6	0	515
9	Arne Slot	4	0	520
10	Danny Mathijssen	4	0	537
11	Edwin de Graaf	5	0	547
12	Anouar Diba	4	0	752
13	Rob Penders	2	0	1063
	Other	3	0	
	TOTAL	**74**	**2**	

KEY GOALKEEPER

Edwin Zoetebier

Goals Conceded in the League	49	Counting Games League games when player was on pitch for at least 70 minutes	32
Defensive Rating Ave number of mins between League goals conceded while on the pitch	58	Clean Sheets In League games when player was on pitch for at least 70 minutes	9

KEY PLAYERS - DEFENDERS

Patrick Mtiliga

Goals Conceded Number of League goals conceded while the player was on the pitch	20	Clean Sheets In League games when player was on pitch for at least 70 minutes	10
Defensive Rating Ave number of mins between League goals conceded while on the pitch	95	Club Defensive Rating Average number of mins between League goals conceded by the club this season	56

	PLAYER	CON LGE	CLEAN SHEETS	DEF RATE
1	Patrick Mtiliga	20	10	95 mins
2	Patrick Zwaanswijk	44	9	63 mins
3	Rob Penders	34	7	62 mins
4	Kurt Elshot	21	4	46 mins

KEY PLAYERS - MIDFIELDERS

Danny Mathijssen

Goals in the League	0	Contribution to Attacking Power Average number of minutes between League team goals while on pitch	76
Defensive Rating Average number of mins between League goals conceded while on the pitch	80	Scoring Difference Defensive Rating minus Contribution to Attacking Power	4

	PLAYER	LGE GOALS	DEF RATE	POWER	SCORE DIFF
1	Danny Mathijssen	0	80	76	4 mins
2	Edwin de Graaf	6	54	70	-16 mins
3	Ronnie Stam	2	50	68	-18 mins
4	Sander van Gessel	2	49	71	-22 mins

KEY PLAYERS - GOALSCORERS

Glen Salmon

Goals in the League	8	Player Strike Rate Average number of minutes between League goals scored by player	166
Contribution to Attacking Power Average number of minutes between League team goals while on pitch	63	Club Strike Rate Average number of minutes between League goals scored by club	71

	PLAYER	LGE GOALS	POWER	STRIKE RATE
1	Glen Salmon	8	63	166 mins
2	Arne Slot	6	74	347 mins
3	Mike Zonneveld	6	76	421 mins
4	Edwin de Graaf	6	70	456 mins

Ronnie Stam

SQUAD APPEARANCES

Match	1	2	3	4	5	6	7	8	9	10	11	12	13	14	15	16	17	18	19	20	21	22	23	24	25	26	27	28	29	30	31	32	33	34	35	36	37	38	39	40	41
Venue	A	H	A	A	H	A	H	A	H	H	A	A	H	A	A	H	H	A	H	H	A	H	A	A	H	A	H	A	H	A	H	A	H	A	H	A	A	H	A	A	H
Competition	L	L	L	L	O	L	L	L	L	L	L	O	L	L	L	L	L	L	L	L	L	L	L	L	O	L	L	L	L	O	L	L	L	L	L	L	O	L	L	O	O
Result	L	L	W	W	W	D	L	L	W	W	D	L	W	D	L	L	D	W	W	D	W	W	W	L	W	L	W	W	W	L	D	L	D	L		L	L	L	L	L	L

Goalkeepers
Arno van Zwam
Edwin Zoetebier

Defenders
Aykut Demir
Kurt Elshot
Wilmer Kousemaker
Patrick Mtiliga
Rob Penders
Patrick Zwaanswijk

Midfielders
Edwin de Graaf
Fouad Idabdelhay
Danny Mathijssen
Tamas Peto
Brian Pinas
Arne Slot
Ronnie Stam
Sander van Gessel
Mike Zonneveld

Forwards
Anouar Diba
Andro Franca
Leonardo
Maceo Rigters
Glen Salmon
Victor Sikora
Gertjan Tamerus
Rogier Veenstra

KEY: ■ On all match ◄◄ Subbed or sent off (Counting game) ►► Subbed on from bench (Counting Game) ►► Subbed on and then subbed or sent off (Counting Game) □ Not in 16
■ On bench ◄◄ Subbed or sent off (playing less than 70 minutes) ►► Subbed on (playing less than 70 minutes) ►► Subbed on and then subbed or sent off (playing less than 70 minutes)

HOLLAND - NAC BREDA

VITESSE ARNHEM

Final Position: **12th**

NICKNAME: GEEL EN ZWART

KEY: ☐ Won ☐ Drawn ☐ Lost   Attendance

#		Match			Result	Scorers	Attendance
1	hopr1	S Rotterdam	A	W	2-1	Lazovic 2, Knol 32 pen	7,689
2	hopr1	AZ Alkmaar	H	L	1-3	Lazovic 89	20,000
3	hopr1	Ajax	A	L	0-3		46,001
4	hopr1	NAC Breda	H	L	0-1		19,251
5	hocr2	Argon	A	W	3-1	Esajas 8, 24, Lazovic 58	3,000
6	hopr1	Heracles	H	W	4-0	Lazovic 37, 57, 75, Pryor 66	19,650
7	hopr1	Groningen	A	L	3-4	Pryor 2, Hersi 53, 79	18,754
8	hopr1	Willem II Tilb	H	W	1-0	Kaya 45	19,284
9	hopr1	NEC Nijmegen	A	L	0-1		12,500
10	hopr1	Excelsior	A	D	2-2	Pryor 27, Lazovic 35	3,000
11	hopr1	Feyenoord	A	L	1-2	Lazovic 59	40,000
12	hocr3	PSV Eindhoven	H	L	0-4		9,600
13	hopr1	Utrecht	H	W	4-2	Esajas 7, Kaya 25, Sansoni 50, Lazovic 89 pen	19,000
14	hopr1	Den Haag	A	W	3-0	Lazovic 21 pen, Pryor 47, Bunjevcevic 66 og	7,483
15	hopr1	Twente	A	L	0-2		13,250
16	hopr1	Heerenveen	H	L	1-3	Benson 24	17,600
17	hopr1	PSV Eindhoven	H	L	0-1		19,000
18	hopr1	RKC Waalwijk	H	W	3-1	Lazovic 22, Junker 24, Hersi 68	20,750
19	hopr1	Roda JC Kerk	A	W	4-2	Lazovic 38, 74, Pryor 49, Benson 90	12,000
20	hopr1	Ajax	H	W	4-2	Lazovic 49, Junker 51, Benson 89, Hersi 90	24,450
21	hopr1	NAC Breda	A	L	1-2	Verhaegh 10	13,520
22	hopr1	Heracles	A	D	2-2	Lazovic 7, Benson 70	8,183
23	hopr1	Groningen	H	W	3-2	Kaya 8, Lazovic 49 pen, Benson 51	18,650
24	hopr1	Willem II Tilb	A	D	0-0		12,000
25	hopr1	NEC Nijmegen	H	D	1-1	Junker 74	21,200
26	hopr1	Heerenveen	A	D	0-0		25,000
27	hopr1	Roda JC Kerk	H	D	0-0		19,500
28	hopr1	RKC Waalwijk	A	L	1-3	Lazovic 19 pen	6,014
29	hopr1	Excelsior	H	L	2-3	Lazovic 15, Knol 72	19,450
30	hopr1	Den Haag	H	D	2-2	Junker 15, Benson 90	18,285
31	hopr1	Utrecht	A	L	0-2		21,400
32	hopr1	Feyenoord	H	L	0-1		22,900
33	hopr1	S Rotterdam	H	W	3-0	Lazovic 4 pen, 83, Verhaegh 20	21,200
34	hopr1	AZ Alkmaar	A	L	0-1		16,088
35	hopr1	Twente	H	D	1-1	Knol 57 pen	24,250
36	hopr1	PSV Eindhoven	A	L	1-5	Janssen 13	34,000
37	erepo	NAC Breda	H	W	3-2	Benson 9, 36, Junker 26	11,450
38	erepo	NAC Breda	A	W	1-0	Pryor 51	5,520
39	erepo	NEC Nijmegen	H	W	1-0	Lazovic 45	11,425
40	erepo	NEC Nijmegen	A	W	2-0	Pryor 29, Lazovic 78	8,000
41	erepo	Utrecht	H	D	2-2	Janssen 42, Knol 82 pen	8,750
42	erepo	Utrecht	A	D	0-0		15,000

LEAGUE APPEARANCES, BOOKINGS AND CAPS

	AGE (on 01/07/07)	IN NAMED 18	APPEARANCES	COUNTING GAMES	MINUTES ON PITCH	YELLOW CARDS	RED CARDS	CAPS THIS SEASON	NATIONAL SIDE
Goalkeepers									
Vladimir Stojkovic	23	11	8	7	675	0	0	9	Serbia
Piet Velthuizen	20	27	8	7	675	0	0	-	Holland
Harald Wapenaar	37	19	19	19	1710	1	0	-	Holland
Defenders									
Siebe Blondelle	21	28	12	4	623	4	1	-	Belgium
Geovanny Espinoza	30	10	10	8	759	0	1	-	Ecuador
Purrel Frankel	30	30	28	19	1990	8	0	-	Surinam
Michael Jansen	23	2	2	2	180	0	0	-	Holland
Ruud Knol	26	26	23	18	1709	7	1	-	Holland
Sebastien Sansoni	29	28	28	28	2484	6	0	-	France
Civard Sprockel	24	33	31	28	2659	4	0	-	Holland
Gill Swerts	24	3	2	0	17	0	0	-	Belgium
Kevin van Diermen	17	1	1	0	22	0	0	-	Holland
Paul Verhaegh	23	32	32	31	2819	9	0	-	Holland
Midfielders									
Jaime Bruinier	20	7	2	1	106	0	0	-	Holland
Tim de Meersman	22	3	1	0	29	0	0	-	Belgium
Anders Due	25	31	18	11	1191	3	0	-	Denmark
Youssouf Hersi	24	29	27	14	1714	6	0	-	Holland
Theo Janssen	25	20	20	17	1652	4	1	2	Holland
Onur Kaya	21	32	29	18	2137	8	0	-	Belgium
Remco v. der Schaaf	28	15	14	10	1037	4	0	-	Holland
Colin van Mourik	21	9	1	0	61	0	0	4	Ghana
Abubakari Yakubu	25	8	4	0	112	2	0	-	Ghana
Forwards									
Fred Benson	23	32	26	7	1012	2	0	-	Holland
Etienne Esajas	22	32	21	9	1158	1	0	-	Holland
Mads Junker	26	33	27	16	1750	2	1	1	Denmark
Danko Lazovic	24	32	32	31	2780	6	2	9	Serbia
Rihairo Meulens	19	23	8	0	78	2	0	-	Holland
Anduelle Pryor	22	33	30	22	2215	2	1	-	Holland
Eldridge Rojer	23	3	1	0	45	0	0	-	Holland
Yu Hai	20	6	2	0	42	0	0	-	China PR

TEAM OF THE SEASON

D Civard Sprockel — CG: 28 DR: 66
M Theo Janssen — CG: 17 SD: 0
D Sebastien Sansoni — CG: 28 DR: 56
M Youssouf Hersi — CG: 14 SD: -2
F Danko Lazovic — CG: 31 SR: 146
G Harald Wapenaar — CG: 19 DR: 55
D Paul Verhaegh — CG: 31 DR: 54
M Remco v d Schaff* — CG: 10 SD: 2
F Mads Junker — CG: 16 SR: 437
D Ruud Knol — CG: 18 DR: 51
M Andres Due — CG: 11 SD: -8

MONTHLY POINTS TALLY

Month		%
AUGUST	3	50%
SEPTEMBER	3	33%
OCTOBER	4	33%
NOVEMBER	6	40%
DECEMBER	10	56%
JANUARY	4	67%
FEBRUARY	3	25%
MARCH	1	11%
APRIL	4	27%

LEAGUE GOALS

	PLAYER	MINS	GOALS	S RATE
1	Lazovic	2780	19	146
2	Benson	1012	6	168
3	Pryor	2215	5	443
4	Hersi	1714	4	428
5	Junker	1750	4	437
6	Knol	1709	3	569
7	Kaya	2137	3	712
8	Verhaegh	2819	2	1409
9	Esajas	1158	1	1158
10	Janssen	1652	1	1652
11	Sansoni	2484	1	2484
12	Snijders	0	0	
13	Sprockel	2659	0	
	Other		0	
	TOTAL		**49**	

TOP POINT EARNERS

	PLAYER	GAMES	AV PTS
1	Theo Janssen	17	1.35
2	Harald Wapenaar	19	1.32
3	Mads Junker	16	1.31
4	Youssouf Hersi	14	1.29
5	Sebastien Sansoni	28	1.25
6	Civard Sprockel	28	1.25
7	Anduelle Pryor	23	1.22
8	Purrel Frankel	19	1.21
9	Onur Kaya	18	1.17
10	Paul Verhaegh	31	1.16
	CLUB AVERAGE:		**1.12**

DISCIPLINARY RECORDS

	PLAYER	YELLOW	RED	AVE
1	Siebe Blondelle	4	1	124
2	Ruud Knol	7	1	213
3	R van der Schaaf	4	0	259
4	Youssouf Hersi	6	0	285
5	Purrel Frankel	8	0	331
6	Onur Kaya	7	0	356
7	Anders Due	3	0	397
8	Paul Verhaegh	9	0	402
9	Sebastien Sansoni	6	0	496
10	Fred Benson	2	0	506
11	Theo Janssen	4	1	550
12	Danko Lazovic	6	2	695
13	Anduelle Pryor	2	1	738
	Other	4	2	
	TOTAL	**72**	**8**	

KEY GOALKEEPER

Harald Wapenaar

Goals Conceded in the League	31	Counting Games League games when player was on pitch for at least 70 minutes	19
Defensive Rating Ave number of mins between League goals conceded while on the pitch	55	Clean Sheets In League games when player was on pitch for at least 70 minutes	4

KEY PLAYERS - DEFENDERS

Civard Sprockel

Goals Conceded Number of League goals conceded while the player was on the pitch	40	Clean Sheets In League games when player was on pitch for at least 70 minutes	8
Defensive Rating Ave average of mins between League goals conceded while on the pitch	66	Club Defensive Rating Average number of mins between League goals conceded by the club this season	55

	PLAYER	CON LGE	CLEAN SHEETS	DEF RATE
1	Civard Sprockel	40	8	66 mins
2	Sebastien Sansoni	44	6	56 mins
3	Paul Verhaegh	52	7	54 mins
4	Ruud Knol	33	6	51 mins

KEY PLAYERS - MIDFIELDERS

Remco van der Schaaf

Goals in the League	0	Contribution to Attacking Power Average number of minutes between League team goals while on pitch	49
Defensive Rating Average number of mins between League goals conceded while on the pitch	51	Scoring Difference Defensive Rating minus Contribution to Attacking Power	2

	PLAYER	LGE GOALS	DEF RATE	POWER	SCORE DIFF
1	Remco van der Schaaf	0	51	49	2 mins
2	Theo Janssen	1	63	63	0 mins
3	Youssouf Hersi	4	59	61	-2 mins
4	Anders Due	0	62	70	-8 mins

KEY PLAYERS - GOALSCORERS

Danko Lazovic

Goals in the League	19	Player Strike Rate Average number of minutes between League goals scored by player	146
Contribution to Attacking Power Average number of minutes between League team goals while on pitch	56	Club Strike Rate Average number of minutes between League goals scored by club	61

	PLAYER	LGE GOALS	POWER	STRIKE RATE
1	Danko Lazovic	19	56	146 mins
2	Youssouf Hersi	4	61	428 mins
3	Mads Junker	4	67	437 mins
4	Anduelle Pryor	5	51	443 mins

Remco van der Schaaf

SQUAD APPEARANCES

Match	1	2	3	4	5	6	7	8	9	10	11	12	13	14	15	16	17	18	19	20	21	22	23	24	25	26	27	28	29	30	31	32	33	34	35	36	37	38	39	40	41	42
Venue	A	H	A	H	A	H	A	H	A	A	A	H	H	A	H	A	A	H	H	H	A	H	A	A	H	A	H	A	H	H	A	H	H	A	H	A	H	A	H	A	H	A
Competition	L	L	L	L	O	L	L	L	L	L	L	O	L	L	L	L	L	L	L	L	L	L	L	L	L	L	L	L	L	L	L	L	L	L	L	L	O	O	O	O	O	O
Result	W	L	L	L	W	W	L	W	L	D	L	L	W	W	L	L	W	W	W	L	D	W	D	D	D	D	L	L	D	L	L	L	W	L	D	L	W	W	W	W	D	D

Goalkeepers
Vladimir Stojkovic
Piet Velthuizen
Harald Wapenaar
Defenders
Siebe Blondelle
Geovanny Espinoza
Purrel Frankel
Michael Jansen
Ruud Knol
Sebastien Sansoni
Civard Sprockel
Gill Swerts
Kevin van Diermen
Paul Verhaegh
Midfielders
Jaime Bruinier
Tim de Meersman
Anders Due
Youssouf Hersi
Theo Janssen
Onur Kaya
Remco van der Schaaf
Colin van Mourik
Abubakari Yakubu
Forwards
Fred Benson
Etienne Esajas
Mads Junker
Danko Lazovic
Rihairo Meulens
Anduelle Pryor
Eldridge Rojer
Yu Hai

KEY: ■ On all match   ◄◄ Subbed or sent off (Counting game)   ►► Subbed on from bench (Counting Game)   ►► Subbed on and then subbed or sent off (Counting Game)   □ Not in 16
  ■ On bench   ◄◄ Subbed or sent off (playing less than 70 minutes)   ►► Subbed on (playing less than 70 minutes)   ►► Subbed on and then subbed or sent off (playing less than 70 minutes)

HOLLAND - VITESSE ARNHEM

SPARTA ROTTERDAM

Final Position: **13th**

NICKNAME: SPARTA KEY: ☐ Won ☐ Drawn ☐ Lost Attendance

1	hopr1	Vitesse Arnhem	H	L	1-2	Schenkel 74	7,689
2	hopr1	Utrecht	A	D	2-2	Rose 37, Olfers 84	19,000
3	hopr1	Feyenoord	H	L	1-4	Anastasiou 17 pen	11,000
4	hopr1	Groningen	H	L	0-1		7,000
5	hocr2	De Treffers	A	W	6-2	Oost 9, Gudde 13, Rose 21, Medunjanin 33 pen,	4,500
						Rumathe 69 og, van Dijk 75	
6	hopr1	Twente	A	L	0-2		13,000
7	hopr1	Excelsior	A	L	1-3	Medunjanin 85	3,531
8	hopr1	AZ Alkmaar	H	L	0-2		10,500
9	hopr1	Roda JC Kerk	A	L	1-2	van Dijk 74	15,000
10	hopr1	PSV Eindhoven	A	L	0-7		33,800
11	hopr1	Willem II Tilb	H	W	1-0	Cvetkov 70	10,134
12	hopr1	Heerenveen	A	L	0-2		25,800
13	hocr3	Achilles	A	W	4-0	Rose 48, 71, 84, Cvetkov 73	650
14	hopr1	Den Haag	H	W	2-1	Rose 40, Schenkel 90	9,072
15	hopr1	NEC Nijmegen	A	W	2-1	Vlug 34, Rose 58	12,000
16	hopr1	Ajax	H	W	3-0	Rose 35, Polak 60 pen, Medunjanin 84	10,500
17	hopr1	RKC Waalwijk	A	L	1-2	Vlug 38	6,200
18	hopr1	Heracles	A	W	3-2	Medunjanin 33, 45, Vlug 57	8,500
19	hopr1	NAC Breda	H	L	0-3		10,000
20	hopr1	Feyenoord	A	L	2-3	Cvetkov 16, Moreno Freire 46	44,000
21	hopr1	Groningen	A	W	1-0	van Bueren 64	19,000
22	hopr1	Twente	H	W	3-0	Polak 24 pen, Bouaouzan 31, Cvetkov 88	10,000
23	hopr1	Excelsior	H	W	2-1	Schenkel 19, Medunjanin 39	10,025
24	hocr4	RKC Waalwijk	H	L	2-3	Moreno Freire 9, Rose 58	3,500
25	hopr1	AZ Alkmaar	A	L	0-3		15,000
26	hopr1	Roda JC Kerk	H	D	2-2	Polak 52 pen, Lopes 59	9,750
27	hopr1	PSV Eindhoven	H	D	1-1	Medunjanin 76	10,350
28	hopr1	NAC Breda	A	L	1-3	Polak 81 pen	14,375
29	hopr1	Heracles	H	D	0-0		10,150
30	hopr1	Willem II Tilb	A	D	0-0		12,200
31	hopr1	NEC Nijmegen	H	L	0-4		10,115
32	hopr1	Den Haag	A	W	4-2	Polak 36 pen, 43, Lopes 56,	7,500
						Krohn-Dehli 77	
33	hopr1	Heerenveen	H	D	2-2	Roberts 48, Polak 74 pen	10,800
34	hopr1	Vitesse Arnhem	A	L	0-3		21,200
35	hopr1	Utrecht	H	D	1-1	Roberts 25	10,500
36	hopr1	Ajax	A	L	2-5	Bouaouzan 37, Moreno Freire 47	50,364
37	hopr1	RKC Waalwijk	H	W	1-0	Medunjanin 61	10,000
38	erepo	NEC Nijmegen	H	D	1-1	Adeleye 21	9,156
39	erepo	NEC Nijmegen	A	L	1-2	Schenkel 26	4,000

LEAGUE APPEARANCES, BOOKINGS AND CAPS

	AGE (on 01/07/07)	IN NAMED 18	APPEARANCES	COUNTING GAMES	MINUTES ON PITCH	YELLOW CARDS	RED CARDS	CAPS THIS SEASON	NATIONAL SIDE
Goalkeepers									
Rene Ponk	35	18	7	6	585	1	0	-	Holland
Joost Terol	27	32	15	14	1305	1	0	-	Holland
Harald Wapenaar	37	13	13	13	1170	2	0	-	Holland
Defenders									
Ayodele Adeleye	18	12	5	3	336	2	0	-	Nigeria
Sepp De Roover	22	34	34	34	3045	2	0	-	Belgium
Wouter Gudde	22	32	18	8	1069	6	1	-	Holland
Steve Olfers	25	33	32	27	2593	2	0	-	Holland
Sjaak Polak	31	28	27	23	2215	4	0	-	Holland
Danny Schenkel	29	29	26	23	2156	4	1	-	Holland
Midfielders									
Sani Kaita	21	22	4	2	222	1	0	-	Nigeria
Haris Medunjanin	22	34	32	22	2277	2	0	-	Holland
Iderlindo M Freire	22	28	14	8	970	3	0	-	Holland
Anthony Obodai	24	19	19	17	1616	2	0	-	Ghana
Nathan Rutjes	23	7	1	0	19	0	0	-	Holland
Edwin van Bueren	27	29	27	25	2355	6	0	-	Holland
Dominique van Dijk	27	21	15	4	690	0	0	-	Holland
Forwards									
Yannis Anastasiou	34	33	16	5	635	1	0	-	Greece
Rachid Bouaouzan	23	28	28	20	2173	3	0	-	Holland
Ivan Cvetkov	27	14	14	9	942	1	0	-	Bulgaria
Marvin Emnes	19	21	16	4	603	0	0	-	Holland
Michael Krohn-Dehli	24	12	12	8	892	0	0	1	Denmark
Cecilio Lopes	28	8	8	5	584	1	0	-	Holland
Jason Oost	24	30	28	13	1540	0	0	-	Holland
Darryl Roberts	23	5	5	3	335	0	0	-	Trinidad & Tobago
Yuri Rose	28	27	26	22	2070	3	0	-	Holland
Jeffrey Vlug	21	29	22	10	1230	2	0	-	Holland

TEAM OF THE SEASON

G Harald Wapenaar CG: 13 DR: 43

D Danny Schenkel CG: 23 DR: 51
D Sjaak Polak CG: 23 DR: 48
D Steve Olfers CG: 27 DR: 47
D Sepp De Roover CG: 34 DR: 46

M Edwin van Bueren CG: 25 SD: -26
M Haris Medunjanin CG: 22 SD: -31
M Anthony Obodai CG: 17 SD: -39
M Iderlindo Moreno Freire CG: 8 SD: -32

F Yuri Rose CG: 22 SR: 517
F Rachid Bouaouzan CG: 20 SR: 1086

MONTHLY POINTS TALLY

AUGUST		1	17%
SEPTEMBER		0	0%
OCTOBER		3	25%
NOVEMBER		9	75%
DECEMBER		9	50%
JANUARY		3	50%
FEBRUARY		3	25%
MARCH		4	44%
APRIL		5	33%

LEAGUE GOALS

	PLAYER	MINS	GOALS	S RATE
1	Polak	2215	7	316
2	Medunjanin	2277	7	325
3	Rose	2070	4	517
4	Cvetkov	942	3	314
5	Vlug	1230	3	410
6	Schenkel	2156	3	718
7	Roberts	335	2	167
8	Lopes	584	2	292
9	Moreno Freire	970	2	485
10	Bouaouzan	2173	2	1086
11	Anastasiou	635	1	635
12	van Dijk	690	1	690
13	Krohn-Dehli	892	1	892
	Other		2	
	TOTAL		**40**	

TOP POINT EARNERS

	PLAYER	GAMES	AV PTS
1	Joost Terol	14	1.50
2	Sjaak Polak	23	1.30
3	Danny Schenkel	23	1.26
4	Edwin van Bueren	25	1.16
5	Steve Olfers	27	1.15
6	Haris Medunjanin	22	1.14
7	Sepp De Roover	34	1.09
8	Rachid Bouaouzan	20	1.05
9	Yuri Rose	22	1.05
10	Anthony Obodai	17	0.94
	CLUB AVERAGE:		**1.09**

DISCIPLINARY RECORDS

	PLAYER	YELLOW	RED	AVE
1	Wouter Gudde	6	1	178
2	I Moreno Freire	3	0	323
3	Edwin van Bueren	6	0	392
4	Danny Schenkel	4	1	431
5	Cecilio Lopes	1	0	584
6	Harald Wapenaar	2	0	585
7	Rene Ponk	1	0	585
8	Jeffrey Vlug	2	0	615
9	Yannis Anastasiou	1	0	635
10	Yuri Rose	3	0	690
11	Rachid Bouaouzan	3	0	724
12	Sjaak Polak	4	0	738
13	Anthony Obodai	2	0	808
	Other	8	0	
	TOTAL	**46**	**2**	

KEY GOALKEEPER

Harald Wapenaar

Goals Conceded in the League	27	Counting Games League games when player was on pitch for at least 70 minutes	13
Defensive Rating Ave number of mins between League goals conceded while on the pitch	43	Clean Sheets In League games when player was on pitch for at least 70 minutes	2

KEY PLAYERS - DEFENDERS

Danny Schenkel

Goals Conceded Number of League goals conceded while the player was on the pitch	42	Clean Sheets In League games when player was on pitch for at least 70 minutes	5
Defensive Rating Ave number of mins between League goals conceded while on the pitch	51	Club Defensive Rating Average number of mins between League goals conceded by the club this season	46

	PLAYER	CON LGE	CLEAN SHEETS	DEF RATE
1	Danny Schenkel	42	5	51 mins
2	Sjaak Polak	46	5	48 mins
3	Steve Olfers	55	7	47 mins
4	Sepp De Roover	65	7	46 mins

KEY PLAYERS - MIDFIELDERS

Edwin van Bueren

Goals in the League	1	Contribution to Attacking Power Average number of minutes between League team goals while on pitch	75
Defensive Rating Average number of mins between League goals conceded while on the pitch	49	Scoring Difference Defensive Rating minus Contribution to Attacking Power	-26

	PLAYER	LGE GOALS	DEF RATE	POWER	SCORE DIFF
1	Edwin van Bueren	1	49	75	-26 mins
2	Haris Medunjanin	7	42	73	-31 mins
3	Iderlindo Moreno Freire	2	48	80	-32 mins
4	Anthony Obodai	0	41	80	-39 mins

KEY PLAYERS - GOALSCORERS

Haris Medunjanin

Goals in the League	7	Player Strike Rate Average number of minutes between League goals scored by player	325
Contribution to Attacking Power Average number of minutes between League team goals while on pitch	73	Club Strike Rate Average number of minutes between League goals scored by club	76

	PLAYER	LGE GOALS	POWER	STRIKE RATE
1	Haris Medunjanin	7	73	325 mins
2	Yuri Rose	4	86	517 mins
3	Rachid Bouaouzan	2	83	1086 mins
4	Edwin van Bueren	1	75	2355 mins

Sjaak Polak

SQUAD APPEARANCES

Match	1	2	3	4	5	6	7	8	9	10	11	12	13	14	15	16	17	18	19	20	21	22	23	24	25	26	27	28	29	30	31	32	33	34	35	36	37	38	39
Venue	H	A	H	H	A	A	A	H	A	A	H	A	A	H	A	H	A	A	H	A	A	H	H	A	H	H	A	H	A	H	A	H	A	H	A	H	A	H	A
Competition	L	L	L	L	O	L	L	L	L	L	L	L	O	L	L	L	L	L	L	L	L	L	L	O	L	L	L	L	L	L	L	L	L	L	L	L	L	O	O
Result	L	D	L	L	W	L	L	L	L	L	W	L	W	W	W	W	L	W	L	L	W	W	W	L	L	D	D	L	D	D	L	W	D	L	D	L	W	D	L

Goalkeepers
Rene Ponk
Joost Terol
Harald Wapenaar

Defenders
Ayodele Adeleye
Sepp De Roover
Wouter Gudde
Steve Olfers
Sjaak Polak
Danny Schenkel

Midfielders
Sani Kaita
Haris Medunjanin
Iderlindo M Freire
Anthony Obodai
Nathan Rutjes
Edwin van Bueren
Dominique van Dijk

Forwards
Yannis Anastasiou
Rachid Bouaouzan
Ivan Cvetkov
Marvin Emnes
Michael Krohn-Dehli
Cecilio Lopes
Jason Oost
Darryl Roberts
Yuri Rose
Jeffrey Vlug

KEY:
■ On all match
■ On bench
◄◄ Subbed or sent off (Counting game)
◄◄ Subbed or sent off (playing less than 70 minutes)
►► Subbed on from bench (Counting Game)
►► Subbed on (playing less than 70 minutes)
►► Subbed on and then subbed or sent off (Counting Game)
►► Subbed on and then subbed or sent off (playing less than 70 minutes)
☐ Not in 16

HOLLAND - SPARTA ROTTERDAM

SC HERACLES

Final Position: **14th**

NICKNAME: HERACLIEDEN   KEY: ☐ Won ☐ Drawn ☐ Lost   Attendance

#				Score	Scorers	Attendance
1	hopr1	Twente	H W	3-0	Quansah 37, Tanghe 80, Biseswar 90	8,500
2	hopr1	Feyenoord	A D	0-0		40,000
3	hopr1	Groningen	A L	1-2	Kruiswijk 1 og	19,000
4	hopr1	Utrecht	H W	3-0	Quansah 5, Everton 26, 82	8,000
5	hocr2	FC Eindhoven	A L	2-3	Schilder 94	4,300
6	hopr1	Vitesse Arnhem	A L	0-4		19,650
7	hopr1	NEC Nijmegen	A L	0-2		11,800
8	hopr1	Heerenveen	H W	1-0	Everton 25	8,500
9	hopr1	Willem II Tilb	A L	0-2		11,500
10	hopr1	RKC Waalwijk	H D	1-1	Schilder 22	8,500
11	hopr1	Den Haag	A L	0-2		7,630
12	hopr1	Ajax	H L	0-3		8,500
13	hopr1	AZ Alkmaar	A L	0-5		15,485
14	hopr1	NAC Breda	H W	2-0	Everton 14, Tanghe 89	8,000
15	hopr1	Excelsior	A L	1-6	Everton 15	3,328
16	hopr1	Roda JC Kerk	H D	1-1	Everton 70	8,500
17	hopr1	S Rotterdam	H L	2-3	Biseswar 72, Quansah 90	8,500
18	hopr1	PSV Eindhoven	A L	0-3		33,500
19	hopr1	Groningen	H L	0-1		8,221
20	hopr1	Utrecht	A D	0-0		20,000
21	hopr1	Vitesse Arnhem	H D	2-2	Klavan 37, Everton 41	8,183
22	hopr1	NEC Nijmegen	H D	0-0		8,412
23	hopr1	Heerenveen	A L	1-5	Quansah 51	25,200
24	hopr1	Willem II Tilb	H D	2-2	Tanghe 80, Everton 90	8,500
25	hopr1	RKC Waalwijk	A L	0-2		5,460
26	hopr1	PSV Eindhoven	H L	0-2		8,500
27	hopr1	S Rotterdam	A D	0-0		10,150
28	hopr1	Den Haag	H W	3-1	Maas 36 pen, Gluscevic 77, Bridji 83	8,361
29	hopr1	NAC Breda	A D	1-1	Gluscevic 53	14,812
30	hopr1	AZ Alkmaar	H D	0-0		8,419
31	hopr1	Ajax	A L	0-3		50,109
32	hopr1	Twente	A D	1-1	Gluscevic 8	13,250
33	hopr1	Feyenoord	H W	4-1	Friend 20, 88, Gluscevic 66, Smit 86	8,500
34	hopr1	Excelsior	H W	3-2	Bridji 58, Friend 79, Everton 80	8,500
35	hopr1	Roda JC Kerk	A L	0-7		14,000

LEAGUE APPEARANCES, BOOKINGS AND CAPS

	AGE (on 01/07/07)	IN NAMED 18	APPEARANCES	COUNTING GAMES	MINUTES ON PITCH	YELLOW CARDS	RED CARDS	CAPS THIS SEASON	NATIONAL SIDE
Goalkeepers									
Remko Pasveer	23	33	1	1	90	0	0	-	Holland
Martin Pieckenhagen	35	34	33	33	2970	0	0	-	Germany
Defenders									
Emmanuel Boakye	22	31	30	29	2618	6	1	-	Ghana
Eddy Bosnar	27	33	28	23	2273	1	1	-	Australia
Bjorn Daelemans	29	19	11	6	657	1	0	-	Belgium
Ragnar Klavan	21	33	32	24	2301	4	0	-	Estonia
Mark Looms	26	32	22	20	1815	4	0	-	Holland
Peter Reekers	26	18	7	3	382	2	1	-	Holland
Marnix Smit	31	33	21	14	1384	1	0	-	Holland
Jan Wuytens	22	25	6	3	428	1	1	-	Belgium
Midfielders									
Karim Bridji	25	27	19	6	910	0	0	-	Holland
Remon de Vries	27	27	23	18	1738	6	1	-	Holland
Rob Maas	37	31	31	30	2712	5	0	-	Holland
Kai Michalke	31	1	1	0	14	0	0	-	Germany
Robbert Schilder	21	32	31	25	2387	6	0	-	Holland
Stefaan Tanghe	35	30	30	26	2499	5	0	-	Belgium
Forwards									
Diego Biseswar	19	28	26	14	1517	6	0	-	Holland
R da Silva Everton	24	25	24	13	1588	1	1	-	Brazil
Rob Friend	26	12	12	11	1056	3	0	-	Canada
Igor Gluscevic	33	13	12	8	770	0	0	-	Serbia
Sota Hirayama	22	2	1	0	64	0	0	-	Japan
Marc Hocher	22	21	11	1	316	0	0	-	Holland
Bernard Hofstede	26	14	11	3	449	0	0	-	Holland
Kwame Quansah	24	33	32	24	2438	5	0	-	Ghana

TEAM OF THE SEASON

D Eddy Bosnar — CG: 23 DR: 55
M Remon de Vries — CG: 18 SD: -43
D Marnix Smit — CG: 14 DR: 53
M Robbert Schilder — CG: 25 SD: -46
F R da Silva Everton — CG: 13 SR: 176
G Martin Pieckenhagen — CG: 33 DR: 52
D Ragnar Klavan — CG: 24 DR: 50
M Stefaan Tanghe — CG: 26 SD: -47
F Kwame Quansah — CG: 24 SR: 609
D Emmanuel Boakye — CG: 29 DR: 50
M Rob Maas — CG: 30 SD: -57

MONTHLY POINTS TALLY

Month			
AUGUST		4	67%
SEPTEMBER		3	25%
OCTOBER		4	33%
NOVEMBER		3	25%
DECEMBER		3	17%
JANUARY		1	17%
FEBRUARY		2	17%
MARCH		5	56%
APRIL		7	47%

LEAGUE GOALS

	PLAYER	MINS	GOALS	S RATE
1	Everton	1588	9	176
2	Gluscevic	770	4	192
3	Quansah	2438	4	609
4	Friend	1056	3	352
5	Tanghe	2499	3	833
6	Bridji	910	2	455
7	Biseswar	1517	2	758
8	Smit	1384	1	1384
9	Klavan	2301	1	2301
10	Schilder	2387	1	2387
11	Maas	2712	1	2712
12	Michalke	14	0	
13	Pasveer	90	0	
	Other		0	
	TOTAL		**31**	

TOP POINT EARNERS

	PLAYER	GAMES	AV PTS
1	Rob Friend	11	1.27
2	Robbert Schilder	25	1.08
3	Diego Biseswar	14	1.00
4	Remon de Vries	18	1.00
5	Emmanuel Boakye	30	0.97
6	Martin Pieckenhagen	33	0.97
7	Ramos da Silva Everton	14	0.93
8	Ragnar Klavan	24	0.92
9	Eddy Bosnar	24	0.88
10	Mark Looms	20	0.85
	CLUB AVERAGE:		**0.94**

DISCIPLINARY RECORDS

	PLAYER	YELLOW	RED	AVE
1	Remon de Vries	6	1	248
2	Diego Biseswar	6	0	252
3	Rob Friend	3	0	352
4	Emmanuel Boakye	6	1	374
5	Robbert Schilder	6	0	397
6	Mark Looms	4	0	453
7	Kwame Quansah	5	0	487
8	Stefaan Tanghe	5	0	499
9	Rob Maas	5	0	542
10	Ragnar Klavan	4	0	575
11	Bjorn Daelemans	1	0	657
12	R da Silva Everton	1	1	794
13	Eddy Bosnar	1	1	1136
	Other	1	0	
	TOTAL	**54**	**4**	

KEY GOALKEEPER

Martin Pieckenhagen

Goals Conceded in the League	57	Counting Games League games when player was on pitch for at least 70 minutes	33
Defensive Rating Ave number of mins between League goals conceded while on the pitch	52	Clean Sheets In League games when player was on pitch for at least 70 minutes	9

KEY PLAYERS - DEFENDERS

Eddy Bosnar

Goals Conceded Number of League goals conceded while the player was on the pitch	41	Clean Sheets In League games when player was on pitch for at least 70 minutes	7
Defensive Rating Ave number of mins between League goals conceded while on the pitch	55	Club Defensive Rating Average number of mins between League goals conceded by the club this season	47

	PLAYER	CON LGE	CLEAN SHEETS	DEF RATE
1	Eddy Bosnar	41	7	55 mins
2	Marnix Smit	26	3	53 mins
3	Ragnar Klavan	46	6	50 mins
4	Emmanuel Boakye	52	9	50 mins

KEY PLAYERS - MIDFIELDERS

Remon de Vries

Goals in the League	0	Contribution to Attacking Power Average number of minutes between League team goals while on pitch	86
Defensive Rating Average number of mins between League goals conceded while on the pitch	43	Scoring Difference Defensive Rating minus Contribution to Attacking Power	-43

	PLAYER	LGE GOALS	DEF RATE	POWER	SCORE DIFF
1	Remon de Vries	0	43	86	-43 mins
2	Robbert Schilder	1	45	91	-46 mins
3	Stefaan Tanghe	3	49	96	-47 mins
4	Rob Maas	1	51	108	-57 mins

KEY PLAYERS - GOALSCORERS

Ramos da Silva Everton

Goals in the League	9	Player Strike Rate Average number of minutes between League goals scored by player	176
Contribution to Attacking Power Average number of minutes between League team goals while on pitch	83	Club Strike Rate Average number of minutes between League goals scored by club	95

	PLAYER	LGE GOALS	POWER	STRIKE RATE
1	Ramos da Silva Everton	9	83	176 mins
2	Kwame Quansah	4	116	609 mins
3	Diego Biseswar	2	94	758 mins
4	Stefaan Tanghe	3	96	833 mins

Ramos da Silva Everton

SQUAD APPEARANCES

Match	1	2	3	4	5	6	7	8	9	10	11	12	13	14	15	16	17	18	19	20	21	22	23	24	25	26	27	28	29	30	31	32	33	34	35
Venue	H	A	A	H	A	A	A	H	A	H	A	H	A	H	A	H	H	A	H	A	H	H	A	H	A	H	A	H	A	H	A	A	H	H	A
Competition	L	L	L	L	O	L	L	L	L	L	L	L	L	L	L	L	L	L	L	L	L	L	L	L	L	L	L	L	L	L	L	L	L	L	L
Result	W	D	L	W	L	L	L	W	L	D	L	L	L	W	L	D	L	L	L	D	D	D	L	D	L	L	D	W	D	D	L	D	W	W	L

KEY: ■ On all match ◀◀ Subbed or sent off (Counting game) ▶▶ Subbed on from bench (Counting Game) ▶▶ Subbed on and then subbed or sent off (Counting Game) □ Not in 16
■ On bench ◀◀ Subbed or sent off (playing less than 70 minutes) ▶▶ Subbed on (playing less than 70 minutes) ▶▶ Subbed on and then subbed or sent off (playing less than 70 minutes)

HOLLAND - SC HERACLES

WILLEM II TILBURG

Final Position: **15th**

NICKNAME: KING'S ARMY

KEY: ☐ Won ☐ Drawn ☐ Lost   Attendance

1	hopr1	**Utrecht**	H W	2-1	El Hamdaoui 23 pen, Redan 82	10,700
2	hopr1	**Heerenveen**	A L	0-5		25,000
3	hopr1	**PSV Eindhoven**	H L	1-3	Messoudi 7	14,000
4	hopr1	**Excelsior**	A L	2-3	El Hamdaoui 45, 83	3,295
5	hocr2	**Flevo Boys**	A W	2-0	Imschoot 69, Bobson 81	2,000
6	hopr1	**NAC Breda**	A D	0-0		15,000
7	hopr1	**Roda JC Kerk**	H L	0-1		8,900
8	hopr1	**Vitesse Arnhem**	A L	0-1		19,284
9	hopr1	**Heracles**	H W	2-0	Kerekes 57 pen, den Ouden 87	11,500
10	hopr1	**AZ Alkmaar**	H L	0-4		12,200
11	hopr1	**S Rotterdam**	A L	0-1		10,134
12	hopr1	**NEC Nijmegen**	A W	2-1	Bobson 35, Assou-Ekotto 77	12,000
13	hocr3	**Be Quick**	A W	5-2	Redan 22, Hadouir 31, 56, van der Struijk 49, Messoudi 70	3,210
14	hopr1	**Feyenoord**	H L	3-5	Baelum 56, Redan 60, Hadouir 78 pen	12,750
15	hopr1	**Groningen**	A L	1-4	Hadouir 67	19,000
16	hopr1	**RKC Waalwijk**	H W	3-1	Bobson 5, 29, van der Struijk 90	13,100
17	hopr1	**Ajax**	A L	0-6		46,695
18	hopr1	**Twente**	H L	1-3	Bobson 45	12,067
19	hopr1	**Den Haag**	A L	1-2	Kargbo 53	6,600
20	hopr1	**PSV Eindhoven**	A L	0-4		33,000
21	hopr1	**Excelsior**	H W	2-1	Imschoot 82, 85	11,750
22	hopr1	**NAC Breda**	H L	0-2		14,000
23	hopr1	**Roda JC Kerk**	A L	1-2	Bobson 39	13,300
24	hocr4	**De Graafschap**	H W	4-2	Hadouir 9, 66, Boutahar 11, 14	6,500
25	hopr1	**Vitesse Arnhem**	H D	0-0		12,000
26	hopr1	**Heracles**	A D	2-2	Boutahar 30, Imschoot 90 pen	8,500
27	hopr1	**AZ Alkmaar**	A L	0-2		15,978
28	hopr1	**Den Haag**	H W	2-1	Cristiano 32, 62	12,500
29	hopr1	**Twente**	A D	0-0		13,000
30	hocqf	**Ajax**	H L	0-2		12,000
31	hopr1	**S Rotterdam**	H D	0-0		12,200
32	hopr1	**Groningen**	H W	3-0	Cristiano 1, Hadouir 32, 70	12,500
33	hopr1	**Feyenoord**	A D	0-0		41,000
34	hopr1	**NEC Nijmegen**	H W	1-0	Hadouir 23	13,300
35	hopr1	**Utrecht**	A L	0-3		21,230
36	hopr1	**Heerenveen**	H L	1-3	Cristiano 51	13,600
37	hopr1	**RKC Waalwijk**	A D	1-1	Cristiano 7	7,000
38	hopr1	**Ajax**	H L	0-2		14,000

LEAGUE APPEARANCES, BOOKINGS AND CAPS

	AGE (on 01/07/07)	IN NAMED 18	APPEARANCES	COUNTING GAMES	MINUTES ON PITCH	YELLOW CARDS	RED CARDS	CAPS THIS SEASON	NATIONAL SIDE
Goalkeepers									
Maikel Aerts	30	7	7	7	630	0	0	-	Holland
Tristan Peersman	27	4	3	3	270	0	0	-	Belgium
Bjorn Sengier	27	32	23	23	2070	0	0	-	Belgium
Peter Zois	29	22	1	1	90	0	0	-	Australia
Defenders									
Thomas Baelum	29	32	32	30	2778	6	1	-	Denmark
Edwin Hermans	33	22	10	9	815	1	0	-	Holland
Delano Hill	32	14	14	14	1260	4	0	-	Holland
Jens Janse	21	25	16	14	1302	3	0	-	Holland
Arjan Swinkels	22	17	9	2	230	0	0	-	Holland
Jose Valencia	25	19	18	17	1515	3	1	-	Ecuador
Frank van der Struijk	22	34	33	28	2640	3	0	-	Holland
Nuelson Wau	26	29	26	20	1912	7	0	-	Holland
Midfielders									
Mathieu Assou-Ekotto	29	19	17	16	1481	3	0	-	France
Said Boutahar	24	15	15	13	1243	2	0	-	Morocco
Kristof Imschoot	26	33	29	9	1365	3	0	-	Belgium
Ibrahim Kargbo	25	32	32	31	2798	6	1	-	Sierra Leone
Joe Keenan	24	28	4	0	163	1	0	-	England
Mohamed Messoudi	23	32	26	10	1357	2	0	-	Belgium
Steef Nieuwendaal	21	31	17	4	571	3	0	-	Holland
Forwards									
Kevin Bobson	26	32	32	30	2753	5	0	-	Holland
Cristiano	26	12	12	11	987	2	0	-	Brazil
Geert den Ouden	30	30	17	4	532	1	0	-	Holland
Mounir El Hamdaoui	24	4	4	4	360	1	0	-	Holland
Anouar Hadouir	24	25	24	17	1725	3	0	-	Holland
Zsombor Kerekes	33	11	7	3	333	0	0	-	Hungary
Rydell Poepon	19	8	8	5	476	2	0	-	Holland
Iwan Redan	26	15	15	13	1245	1	1	-	Holland
Ronnie Reniers	19	1	1	0	16	0	0	-	Holland
Jonathan Wilmet	21	22	15	5	627	1	0	-	Belgium

TEAM OF THE SEASON

G Bjorn Sengier CG: 23 DR: 43

D Delano Hill CG: 14 DR: 78
D Jens Janse CG: 14 DR: 76
D Frank van der Struijk CG: 28 DR: 57
D Thomas Baelum CG: 30 DR: 47

M Ibrahim Kargbo CG: 31 SD: -50
M Mathieu Assou-Ekotto CG: 16 SD: -51
M Said Boutahar CG: 13 SD: -56
M Mohamed Messoudi CG: 10 SD: -46

F Anouar Hadouir CG: 17 SR: 345
F Kevin Bobson CG: 30 SR: 550

MONTHLY POINTS TALLY

AUGUST	3	50%
SEPTEMBER	1	8%
OCTOBER	3	25%
NOVEMBER	6	50%
DECEMBER	3	20%
JANUARY	1	11%
FEBRUARY	5	42%
MARCH	8	67%
APRIL	1	8%

LEAGUE GOALS

	PLAYER	MINS	GOALS	S RATE
1	Cristiano	987	5	197
2	Hadouir	1725	5	345
3	Bobson	2753	5	550
4	El Hamdaoui	360	3	120
5	Imschoot	1365	3	455
6	Redan	1245	2	622
7	Kerekes	333	1	333
8	den Ouden	532	1	532
9	Boutahar	1243	1	1243
10	Messoudi	1357	1	1357
11	Assou-Ekotto	1481	1	1481
12	van der Struijk	2640	1	2640
13	Baelum	2778	1	2778
	Other		1	
	TOTAL		31	

TOP POINT EARNERS

	PLAYER	GAMES	AV PTS
1	Cristiano	11	1.18
2	Delano Hill	14	1.07
3	Anouar Hadouir	17	1.06
4	Kevin Bobson	30	1.03
5	Thomas Baelum	30	1.00
6	Ibrahim Kargbo	32	0.97
7	Said Boutahar	13	0.92
8	Nuelson Wau	20	0.90
9	Frank van der Struijk	28	0.89
10	Iwan Redan	14	0.86
	CLUB AVERAGE:		**0.91**

DISCIPLINARY RECORDS

	PLAYER	YELLOW	RED	AVE
1	Steef Nieuwendaal	3	0	190
2	Rydell Poepon	2	0	238
3	Nuelson Wau	7	0	273
4	Delano Hill	4	0	315
5	Jose Valencia	3	1	378
6	Jens Janse	3	0	434
7	Ibrahim Kargbo	6	1	466
8	M Assou-Ekotto	3	0	493
9	Cristiano	2	0	493
10	Geert den Ouden	1	0	532
11	Kevin Bobson	5	0	550
12	Anouar Hadouir	3	0	575
13	Said Boutahar	2	0	621
	Other	17	2	
	TOTAL	61	4	

KEY GOALKEEPER

Bjorn Sengier

Goals Conceded in the League	48	Counting Games League games when player was on pitch for at least 70 minutes	23
Defensive Rating Ave number of mins between League goals conceded while on the pitch	43	Clean Sheets In League games when player was on pitch for at least 70 minutes	4

KEY PLAYERS - DEFENDERS

Delano Hill

Goals Conceded Number of League goals conceded while the player was on the pitch	16	Clean Sheets In League games when player was on pitch for at least 70 minutes	6
Defensive Rating Ave number of mins between League goals conceded while on the pitch	78	Club Defensive Rating Average number of mins between League goals conceded by the club this season	47

	PLAYER	CON LGE	CLEAN SHEETS	DEF RATE
1	Delano Hill	16	6	78 mins
2	Jens Janse	17	6	76 mins
3	Frank van der Struijk	46	9	57 mins
4	Thomas Baelum	58	7	47 mins

KEY PLAYERS - MIDFIELDERS

Mohamed Messoudi

Goals in the League	1	Contribution to Attacking Power Average number of minutes between League team goals while on pitch	84
Defensive Rating Average number of mins between League goals conceded while on the pitch	38	Scoring Difference Defensive Rating minus Contribution to Attacking Power	-46

	PLAYER	LGE GOALS	DEF RATE	POWER	SCORE DIFF
1	Mohamed Messoudi	1	38	84	-46 mins
2	Ibrahim Kargbo	1	49	99	-50 mins
3	Mathieu Assou-Ekotto	1	36	87	-51 mins
4	Said Boutahar	1	82	138	-56 mins

KEY PLAYERS - GOALSCORERS

Anouar Hadouir

Goals in the League	5	Player Strike Rate Average number of minutes between League goals scored by player	345
Contribution to Attacking Power Average number of minutes between League team goals while on pitch	82	Club Strike Rate Average number of minutes between League goals scored by club	98

	PLAYER	LGE GOALS	POWER	STRIKE RATE
1	Anouar Hadouir	5	82	345 mins
2	Kevin Bobson	5	94	550 mins
3	Iwan Redan	2	69	622 mins
4	Said Boutahar	1	138	1243 mins

Nuelson Wau

SQUAD APPEARANCES

Match	1	2	3	4	5	6	7	8	9	10	11	12	13	14	15	16	17	18	19	20	21	22	23	24	25	26	27	28	29	30	31	32	33	34	35	36	37	38
Venue	H	A	H	A	A		A	H	A	H	H		A	A	H	A	H	A	A	H	H	A		A	H	A	H	A	H	A	A	H	H	H	A	H	A	H
Competition	L	L	L	L	O		L	L	L	L		L	L	O	L	L	L	L	L	L	L	L		L	O	L	L	L	L	L	O	L	L	L	L	L	L	L
Result	W	L	L	L	W		D	L	L	W	L		L	W	W	L	L	W	L	L	L	W		L	W	D	D	L	W	D	L	D	W	D	W	L	L	D	L

Goalkeepers: Maikel Aerts, Tristan Peersman, Bjorn Sengier, Peter Zois

Defenders: Thomas Baelum, Edwin Hermans, Delano Hill, Jens Janse, Arjan Swinkels, Jose Valencia, Frank van der Struijk, Nuelson Wau

Midfielders: Mathieu Assou-Ekotto, Said Boutahar, Kristof Imschoot, Ibrahim Kargbo, Joe Keenan, Mohamed Messoudi, Steef Nieuwendaal

Forwards: Kevin Bobson, Cristiano, Geert den Ouden, Mounir El Hamdaoui, Anouar Hadouir, Zsombor Kerekes, Rydell Poepon, Iwan Redan, Ronnie Reniers, Jonathan Wilmet

KEY:
- ■ On all match
- ■ On bench
- ◄◄ Subbed or sent off (Counting game)
- ◄◄ Subbed or sent off (playing less than 70 minutes)
- ►►► Subbed on from bench (Counting Game)
- ►► Subbed on (playing less than 70 minutes)
- ►► Subbed on and then subbed or sent off (Counting Game)
- ►► Subbed on and then subbed or sent off (playing less than 70 minutes)
- ☐ Not in 16

EXCELSIOR

Final Position: 16th

NICKNAME: THE KRALINGERS

KEY: ☐ Won ☐ Drawn ☐ Lost

#			H/A	W/D/L	Result	Scorers	Attendance
1	hopr1	Roda JC Kerk	H	L	0-1		2,825
2	hopr1	RKC Waalwijk	A	D	1-1	Slory 53	5,000
3	hopr1	Heerenveen	H	W	3-1	Bruins 11 pen, 72, Slory 83	3,000
4	hopr1	Willem II Tilb	H	W	3-2	Steur 35, 38, Slory 41	3,295
5	hocr2	Schijndel	A	W	1-0	Slory 107	900
6	hopr1	Feyenoord	A	L	0-1		39,000
7	hopr1	S Rotterdam	H	W	3-1	Simr 36, Steur 75, Guijo-Velasco 81	3,531
8	hopr1	Utrecht	H	L	0-1		2,835
9	hopr1	Twente	A	L	1-4	Simr 88	13,125
10	hopr1	Groningen	A	L	1-2	Grot 45	18,000
11	hopr1	Vitesse Arnhem	H	D	2-2	Bruins 61 pen, Voskamp 90	3,000
12	hopr1	Den Haag	A	D	2-2	Slory 41, 60	7,514
13	hocr3	G A Eagles	A	L	0-2		2,100
14	hopr1	NEC Nijmegen	H	D	1-1	Dijkhuizen 90 pen	2,915
15	hopr1	PSV Eindhoven	A	L	0-4		33,000
16	hopr1	Heracles	H	W	6-1	Slory 31, van Nieuwstadt 45, Bruins 54 pen, 69, Steur 58, Grot 78	3,328
17	hopr1	AZ Alkmaar	A	L	0-5		15,000
18	hopr1	NAC Breda	A	L	1-2	Slory 24	15,121
19	hopr1	Ajax	H	L	1-3	Pique 90	3,500
20	hopr1	Heerenveen	A	L	0-2		25,000
21	hopr1	Willem II Tilb	A	L	1-2	Slory 11	11,750
22	hopr1	Feyenoord	H	L	1-3	Voskamp 81	3,527
23	hopr1	S Rotterdam	A	L	1-2	Rojer 17	10,025
24	hopr1	Utrecht	A	L	0-1		19,000
25	hopr1	Twente	H	L	1-2	Voskamp 34	2,968
26	hopr1	Groningen	H	L	0-2		3,000
27	hopr1	Ajax	A	D	2-2	Slory 25, Rojer 30	47,905
28	hopr1	NAC Breda	H	L	0-2		3,312
29	hopr1	Vitesse Arnhem	A	W	3-2	Voskamp 64, Rojer 84, Slory 86	19,450
30	hopr1	PSV Eindhoven	H	D	0-0		2,900
31	hopr1	NEC Nijmegen	A	W	1-0	Slory 39	12,000
32	hopr1	Den Haag	H	W	3-1	Simr 10, Rojer 30, Guijo-Velasco 61	2,825
33	hopr1	Roda JC Kerk	A	L	0-2		15,184
34	hopr1	RKC Waalwijk	H	L	0-3		3,624
35	hopr1	Heracles	A	L	2-3	Braber 32, Slory 90	8,500
36	hopr1	AZ Alkmaar	H	W	3-2	Bruins 21 pen, Drost 60, Voskamp 90	3,000
37	honac	Veendam	A	W	1-0	Voskamp 84	3,521
38	honac	Veendam	H	W	3-0	Zijm 45, Slory 48, 69	2,130
39	honac	Roosendaal	A	D	1-1	Bruins 6	3,200
40	honac	Roosendaal	H	W	1-0	Slory 77	3,000

LEAGUE APPEARANCES, BOOKINGS AND CAPS

	AGE (on 01/07/07)	IN NAMED 18	APPEARANCES	COUNTING GAMES	MINUTES ON PITCH	YELLOW CARDS	RED CARDS	CAPS THIS SEASON	NATIONAL SIDE
Goalkeepers									
Ronald Graafland	28	34	8	8	720	1	0	-	Holland
J. v. Nieuwenhuizen	28	2	1	1	90	0	0	-	Holland
Theo Zwarthoed	24	33	26	26	2370	0	0	-	Holland
Defenders									
Sigourney Bandjar	23	31	27	24	2254	6	0	-	Holland
Henrico Drost	20	30	30	28	2579	1	1	-	Holland
Christian Gyan	28	22	16	11	1069	0	0	-	Ghana
Rudy Jansen	28	28	14	10	1024	1	0	-	Holland
Mitchell Pique	28	34	27	16	1753	3	0	-	Holland
Jos van Nieuwstadt	27	32	32	31	2855	3	1	-	Holland
Sieme Zijm	29	32	26	19	1855	5	2	-	Holland
Midfielders									
Luigi Bruins	20	30	30	28	2516	3	0	-	Holland
Daniel Guijo-Velasco	23	32	24	14	1610	2	0	-	Belgium
Damien Hertog	32	0	0	0	0	0	0	-	Holland
Kees Luijckx	21	14	12	6	700	0	0	-	Holland
Jarda Simr	28	27	27	17	1684	2	0	-	Czech Republic
Rene van Dieren	26	32	32	31	2801	9	1	-	Holland
Forwards									
Robert Braber	24	14	8	5	510	1	0	-	Holland
Marinus Dijkhuizen	35	17	11	1	318	0	0	-	Holland
Guillano Grot	24	24	21	7	931	1	0	-	Holland
Robin Hofman	21	2	0	0	0	0	0	-	Holland
Eldridge Rojer	23	11	11	8	866	0	0	-	Holland
Gert Jan Rothman	23	22	6	0	152	0	0	-	Holland
Andwele Slory	24	29	29	28	2551	6	0	2	Holland
Sebastiaan Steur	23	26	25	13	1563	4	1	-	Holland
Johan Voskamp	22	31	21	10	1082	1	0	-	Holland

TEAM OF THE SEASON

D Jos van Nieuwstadt CG: 31 DR: 50

M Daniel Guijo-Velasco CG: 14 SD: -17

D Sigourney Bandjar CG: 24 DR: 49

M Jarda Simr CG: 17 SD: -21

F Andwele Slory CG: 28 SR: 212

G Theo Zwarthoed CG: 26 DR: 45

D Henrico Drost CG: 28 DR: 45

M Rene van Dieren CG: 31 SD: -23

F Sebastiaan Steur CG: 13 SR: 390

D Sieme Zijm CG: 19 DR: 44

M Luigi Bruins CG: 28 SD: -23

MONTHLY POINTS TALLY

Month	Points	%
AUGUST	1	17%
SEPTEMBER	9	75%
OCTOBER	1	8%
NOVEMBER	5	42%
DECEMBER	0	0%
JANUARY	0	0%
FEBRUARY	1	8%
MARCH	7	78%
APRIL	6	40%

LEAGUE GOALS

	PLAYER	MINS	GOALS	S RATE
1	Slory	2551	12	212
2	Bruins	2516	6	419
3	Voskamp	1082	5	216
4	Rojer	866	4	216
5	Steur	1563	4	390
6	Simr	1684	3	561
7	Grot	931	2	465
8	Guijo-Velasco	1610	2	805
9	Dijkhuizen	318	1	318
10	Braber	510	1	510
11	Pique	1753	1	1753
12	Drost	2579	1	2579
13	van Nieuwstadt	2855	1	2855
	Other		0	
	TOTAL		**43**	

TOP POINT EARNERS

	PLAYER	GAMES	AV PTS
1	Daniel Guijo-Velasco	14	1.29
2	Sebastiaan Steur	13	1.15
3	Henrico Drost	28	1.00
4	Rene van Dieren	31	0.97
5	Jos van Nieuwstadt	32	0.94
6	Jarda Simr	17	0.94
7	Andwele Slory	28	0.93
8	Sieme Zijm	20	0.90
9	Mitchell Pique	16	0.88
10	Sigourney Bandjar	24	0.83
	CLUB AVERAGE:		**0.88**

DISCIPLINARY RECORDS

	PLAYER	YELLOW	RED	AVE
1	Sieme Zijm	5	2	309
2	Sebastiaan Steur	4	1	312
3	Rene van Dieren	9	1	350
4	Sigourney Bandjar	6	0	450
5	Andwele Slory	6	0	510
6	Robert Braber	1	0	510
7	Jos van Nieuwstadt	3	1	713
8	Ronald Graafland	1	0	720
9	Jarda Simr	2	0	842
10	Mitchell Pique	3	0	876
11	Guillano Grot	1	0	931
12	Rudy Jansen	1	0	1024
13	Johan Voskamp	1	0	1082
	Other	6	1	
	TOTAL	**49**	**6**	

KEY GOALKEEPER

Theo Zwarthoed

Goals Conceded in the League	52	Counting Games League games when player was on pitch for at least 70 minutes	26
Defensive Rating Ave number of mins between League goals conceded while on the pitch	45	Clean Sheets In League games when player was on pitch for at least 70 minutes	0

KEY PLAYERS - DEFENDERS

Jos van Nieuwstadt

Goals Conceded Number of League goals conceded while the player was on the pitch	57	Clean Sheets In League games when player was on pitch for at least 70 minutes	2
Defensive Rating Ave number of mins between League goals conceded while on the pitch	50	Club Defensive Rating Average number of mins between League goals conceded by the club this season	47

	PLAYER	CON LGE	CLEAN SHEETS	DEF RATE
1	Jos van Nieuwstadt	57	2	50 mins
2	Sigourney Bandjar	46	2	49 mins
3	Henrico Drost	57	2	45 mins
4	Sieme Zijm	42	0	44 mins

KEY PLAYERS - MIDFIELDERS

Daniel Guijo-Velasco

Goals in the League	2	Contribution to Attacking Power Average number of minutes between League team goals while on pitch	67
Defensive Rating Average number of mins between League goals conceded while on the pitch	50	Scoring Difference Defensive Rating minus Contribution to Attacking Power	-17

	PLAYER	LGE GOALS	DEF RATE	POWER	SCORE DIFF
1	Daniel Guijo-Velasco	2	50	67	-17 mins
2	Jarda Simr	3	52	73	-21 mins
3	Rene van Dieren	0	48	71	-23 mins
4	Luigi Bruins	6	48	71	-23 mins

KEY PLAYERS - GOALSCORERS

Andwele Slory

Goals in the League	12	Player Strike Rate Average number of minutes between League goals scored by player	212
Contribution to Attacking Power Average number of minutes between League team goals while on pitch	72	Club Strike Rate Average number of minutes between League goals scored by club	71

	PLAYER	LGE GOALS	POWER	STRIKE RATE
1	Andwele Slory	12	72	212 mins
2	Sebastiaan Steur	4	78	390 mins
3	Luigi Bruins	6	71	419 mins
4	Jarda Simr	3	73	561 mins

Henrico Drost

SQUAD APPEARANCES

Match	1 2 3 4 5	6 7 8 9 10	11 12 13 14 15	16 17 18 19 20	21 22 23 24 25	26 27 28 29 30 31 32 33 34 35 36 37 38 39 40
Venue	H A H H A	A H H A A	H A A H A	H A A H A	A H A A H	H A H A H A H A H A H A H A H
Competition	L L L L O	L L L L L	L L O L L	L L L L L	L L L L L	L L L L L L L L L L L O O O O
Result	L D W W W	L W L L L	D D L D L	W L L L L	L L L L L	L D L W D W W L L W W W D W

Goalkeepers

Ronald Graafland
Jorg van Nieuwenhuijzen
Theo Zwarthoed

Defenders

Sigourney Bandjar
Henrico Drost
Christian Gyan
Rudy Jansen
Mitchell Pique
Jos van Nieuwstadt
Sieme Zijm

Midfielders

Luigi Bruins
Daniel Guijo-Velasco
Damien Hertog
Kees Luijckx
Jarda Simr
Rene van Dieren

Forwards

Robert Braber
Marinus Dijkhuizen
Guillano Grot
Robin Hofman
Eldridge Rojer
Gert Jan Rothman
Andwele Slory
Sebastiaan Steur
Johan Voskamp

KEY: ■ On all match ◄◄ Subbed or sent off (Counting game) ▸▸ Subbed on from bench (Counting Game) ▸▸ Subbed on and then subbed or sent off (Counting Game) ☐ Not in 16
■ On bench ◄◄ Subbed or sent off (playing less than 70 minutes) ▸▸ Subbed on (playing less than 70 minutes) ▸▸ Subbed on and then subbed or sent off (playing less than 70 minutes)

HOLLAND - EXCELSIOR

RKC WAALWIJK

Final Position: 17th

NICKNAME: RKC   KEY: ☐ Won ☐ Drawn ☐ Lost   Attendance

#				Score	Scorers	Attendance
1	hopr1	Ajax	A L	0-5		48,000
2	hopr1	Excelsior	H D	1-1	Teixeira 3	5,000
3	hopr1	Utrecht	A L	0-5		20,000
4	hopr1	Den Haag	H W	1-0	Janssen 86	6,000
5	hocr2	Dordrecht	H W	3-2	Reuser 68, Janssen 72, Ikedia 87	400
6	hopr1	Groningen	A D	1-1	Janssen 58	19,000
7	hopr1	Twente	A L	3-4	Janssen 17, 63, Ikedia 24	13,100
8	hopr1	Feyenoord	H D	2-2	van Diemen 21, Reuser 28	7,500
9	hopr1	NAC Breda	H L	0-1		6,000
10	hopr1	Heracles	A D	1-1	Berger 9	8,500
11	hopr1	PSV Eindhoven	H L	0-3		7,000
12	hopr1	AZ Alkmaar	H L	0-2		7,000
13	hocr3	Feyenoord	H W	3-2	van Diemen 58, Fuchs 96, Keller 108	3,250
14	hopr1	Roda JC Kerk	A D	1-1	van den Bergh 58	15,000
15	hopr1	Heerenveen	H L	0-2		5,500
16	hopr1	Willem II Tilb	A L	1-3	van de Haar 68	13,100
17	hopr1	S Rotterdam	H W	2-1	Ikedia 26, D..Mulder 86	6,200
18	hopr1	Vitesse Arnhem	A L	1-3	Remacle 18	20,750
19	hopr1	NEC Nijmegen	H L	0-1		7,000
20	hopr1	Utrecht	H D	1-1	Fuchs 7	2,500
21	hopr1	Den Haag	A D	1-1	Janssen 45	8,360
22	hopr1	Groningen	H L	0-2		5,000
23	hopr1	Twente	H L	1-2	van den Bergh 26 pen	5,400
24	hocr4	S Rotterdam	A W	3-2	Olfers 17 og, van de Haar 39, Garcia 96	3,500
25	hopr1	Feyenoord	A L	1-3	van den Bergh 53 pen	40,500
26	hopr1	NAC Breda	H L	1-2	Berger 30	14,760
27	hopr1	Heracles	H W	2-0	Vertonghen 35, van den Bergh 85	5,460
28	hopr1	NEC Nijmegen	A L	0-1		11,750
29	hopr1	Vitesse Arnhem	H W	3-1	Vertonghen 36, van de Haar 74, Janssen 84	6,014
30	hocqf	Roda JC Kerk	H W	1-0	van den Bergh 6	5,000
31	hopr1	PSV Eindhoven	A L	0-2		33,300
32	hopr1	Heerenveen	A L	0-1		25,500
33	hopr1	Roda JC Kerk	H W	3-2	De Fauw 16 og, Berger 34, van den Bergh 71	6,000
34	hopr1	AZ Alkmaar	A L	0-2		16,181
35	hopr1	Ajax	H D	2-2	Vertonghen 10, Berger 71	7,500
36	hopr1	Excelsior	A W	3-0	Janssen 54, 58, 90	3,624
37	hocsf	Ajax	A L	1-3	Heitinga 32 og	34,600
38	hopr1	Willem II Tilb	H D	1-1	Janssen 61	7,000
39	hopr1	S Rotterdam	A L	0-1		10,000
40	honac	Dordrecht	A L	0-2		3,210
41	honac	Dordrecht	H W	2-0	van den Bergh 37 pen, De Ceulaer 82	5,531
42	honac	Dordrecht	A W	3-0	De Ceulaer 19, Sektioui 70, 76	4,200
43	honac	VVV	A L	0-2		5,946
44	honac	VVV	H W	1-0	Janssen 4	6,100
45	honac	VVV	A L	0-3		6,000

LEAGUE APPEARANCES, BOOKINGS AND CAPS

	AGE (on 01/07/07)	IN NAMED 18	APPEARANCES	COUNTING GAMES	MINUTES ON PITCH	YELLOW CARDS	RED CARDS	CAPS THIS SEASON	NATIONAL SIDE
Goalkeepers									
Erwin Lemmens	31	11	10	10	888	0	0	-	Belgium
Rob van Dijk	38	22	19	19	1710	0	0	-	Holland
Jurgen Wevers	28	31	6	5	462	0	0	-	Holland
Defenders									
Tim Bakens	24	22	16	12	1211	7	0	-	Holland
Ryan Donk	21	2	2	2	180	0	0	-	Holland
Cerezo Fung A Wing	23	16	14	13	1136	1	0	-	Holland
Stephan Keller	28	25	16	14	1270	5	0	-	Switzerland
Milano Koenders	19	32	30	29	2642	5	0	-	Holland
Virgilio Teixeira	33	28	17	13	1251	7	1	-	Portugal
Patrick van Diemen	35	26	26	25	2265	6	0	-	Holland
Ramon van Haaren	34	27	17	13	1323	5	0	-	Holland
Frank van Mosselveld	23	5	5	4	389	2	0	-	Holland
Midfielders									
Ruud Berger	27	27	25	18	1826	5	0	-	Holland
Robert Fuchs	32	19	13	7	901	5	0	-	Holland
Dustley Mulder	22	33	25	18	1892	4	0	-	Holland
Hans Mulder	20	9	7	3	414	0	2	-	Holland
Anthony Obodai	24	11	11	11	990	2	0	-	Ghana
Jordan Remacle	20	22	19	2	498	2	0	-	Belgium
Jan Vertonghen	20	12	12	12	1080	6	0	1	Belgium
Ivan Vicelich	30	22	19	13	1363	2	0	-	New Zealand
Forwards									
Benjamin De Ceulaer	23	10	7	2	385	3	0	-	Belgium
Luwamo Garcia	22	24	14	7	824	2	0	-	Angola
Pius Ikedia	26	24	24	17	1639	1	0	-	Nigeria
Jochen Janssen	31	1	1	0	45	0	0	-	Holland
Tim Janssen	21	30	27	14	1563	3	0	-	Holland
Eddy Putter	25	9	5	2	249	0	0	-	Holland
Martijn Reuser	32	28	20	11	1247	2	0	-	Holland
Tarik Sektioui	30	9	9	6	606	4	1	-	Morocco
Hans van de Haar	32	29	26	14	1696	4	0	-	Holland
Ricky van den Bergh	26	24	23	12	1414	8	0	-	Holland
Nick van der Velden	25	6	4	1	176	0	0	-	Holland

TEAM OF THE SEASON

G Rob van Dijk   CG: 19   DR: 45

D Milano Koenders   CG: 29   DR: 55
D Cerezo Fung A Wing   CG: 13   DR: 54
D Stephan Keller   CG: 14   DR: 52
D Patrick van Diemen   CG: 25   DR: 49

M Jan Vertonghen   CG: 12   SD: 0
M Ruud Berger   CG: 18   SD: -8
M Dustley Mulder   CG: 18   SD: -53
M Ivan Vicelich   CG: 13   SD: -72

F Tim Janssen   CG: 14   SR: 156
F R van den Bergh   CG: 12   SR: 282

MONTHLY POINTS TALLY

Month		
AUGUST	1	17%
SEPTEMBER	4	33%
OCTOBER	2	17%
NOVEMBER	1	8%
DECEMBER	5	28%
JANUARY	0	0%
FEBRUARY	6	50%
MARCH	3	25%
APRIL	5	42%

LEAGUE GOALS

	PLAYER	MINS	GOALS	S RATE
1	Janssen	1563	10	156
2	van den Bergh	1414	5	282
3	Berger	1826	4	456
4	Vertonghen	1080	3	360
5	Ikedia	1639	2	819
6	van de Haar	1696	2	848
7	Remacle	498	1	498
8	Fuchs	901	1	901
9	Reuser	1247	1	1247
10	Teixeira	1251	1	1251
11	Mulder, D.	1892	1	1892
12	van Diemen	2265	1	2265
13	van Dijk, R	1710	0	
	Other		0	
	TOTAL		**32**	

TOP POINT EARNERS

	PLAYER	GAMES	AV PTS
1	Anthony Obodai	11	1.27
2	Jan Vertonghen	12	1.17
3	Stephan Keller	14	1.14
4	Ruud Berger	18	1.11
5	Pius Ikedia	17	1.06
6	Hans van de Haar	14	0.93
7	Cerezo Fung A Wing	13	0.92
8	Tim Janssen	14	0.86
9	Tim Bakens	12	0.83
10	Martijn Reuser	11	0.82
	CLUB AVERAGE:		**0.79**

DISCIPLINARY RECORDS

	PLAYER	YELLOW	RED	AVE
1	Virgilio Teixeira	7	1	156
2	Tim Bakens	7	0	173
3	Tarik Sektioui	4	1	202
4	R van den Bergh	8	0	235
5	Stephan Keller	5	0	254
6	Jan Vertonghen	6	0	270
7	Robert Fuchs	5	0	300
8	Ramon van Haaren	5	0	330
9	Patrick van Diemen	6	0	453
10	Ruud Berger	5	0	456
11	Dustley Mulder	4	0	473
12	Anthony Obodai	2	0	495
13	Hans van de Haar	4	0	565
	Other	18	0	
	TOTAL	**86**	**2**	

KEY GOALKEEPER

Rob van Dijk

Goals Conceded in the League	38	Counting Games League games when player was on pitch for at least 70 minutes	19
Defensive Rating Ave number of mins between League goals conceded while on the pitch	45	Clean Sheets In League games when player was on pitch for at least 70 minutes	1

KEY PLAYERS - DEFENDERS

Milano Koenders

Goals Conceded Number of League goals conceded while the player was on the pitch	48	Clean Sheets In League games when player was on pitch for at least 70 minutes	2
Defensive Rating Ave number of mins between League goals conceded while on the pitch	55	Club Defensive Rating Average number of mins between League goals conceded by the club this season	51

	PLAYER	CON LGE	CLEAN SHEETS	DEF RATE
1	Milano Koenders	48	2	55 mins
2	Cerezo Fung A Wing	21	0	54 mins
3	Stephan Keller	24	2	52 mins
4	Patrick van Diemen	46	2	49 mins

KEY PLAYERS - MIDFIELDERS

Jan Vertonghen

Goals in the League	3	Contribution to Attacking Power Average number of minutes between League team goals while on pitch	72
Defensive Rating Average number of mins between League goals conceded while on the pitch	72	Scoring Difference Defensive Rating minus Contribution to Attacking Power	0

	PLAYER	LGE GOALS	DEF RATE	POWER	SCORE DIFF
1	Jan Vertonghen	3	72	72	0 mins
2	Ruud Berger	4	65	73	-8 mins
3	Dustley Mulder	1	52	105	-53 mins
4	Ivan Vicelich	0	41	113	-72 mins

KEY PLAYERS - GOALSCORERS

Tim Janssen

Goals in the League	10	Player Strike Rate Average number of minutes between League goals scored by player	156
Contribution to Attacking Power Average number of minutes between League team goals while on pitch	67	Club Strike Rate Average number of minutes between League goals scored by club	92

	PLAYER	LGE GOALS	POWER	STRIKE RATE
1	Tim Janssen	10	67	156 mins
2	Ricky van den Bergh	5	108	282 mins
3	Jan Vertonghen	3	72	360 mins
4	Ruud Berger	4	73	456 mins

Anthony Obodai

SQUAD APPEARANCES

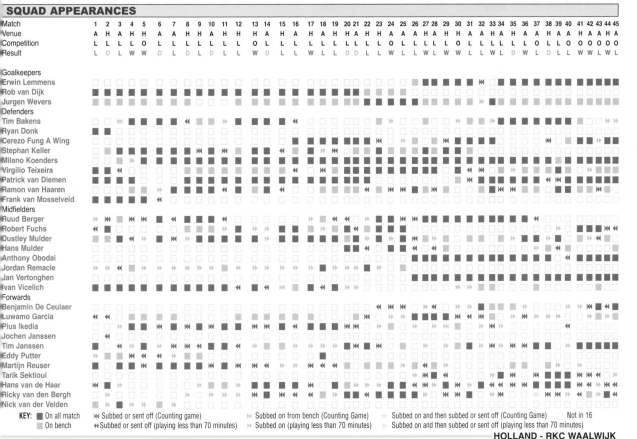

Match	1 2 3 4 5 6 7 8 9 10 11 12 13 14 15 16 17 18 19 20 21 22 23 24 25 26 27 28 29 30 31 32 33 34 35 36 37 38 39 40 41 42 43 44 45
Venue	A H A H H A A H H A H H H A H A H A H A H H A H H H A A A H A H H A A H A H A A H A A H A
Competition	L L L L O L L L L L L L O L L L L L L L L L L L O L L L L L L O L L L L L L O L L O O O O O
Result	L D L W W D L D L D L L W D L L W L L D D L L W L L L W L W W L L W L D W L D L L W W L W L

Goalkeepers
Erwin Lemmens
Rob van Dijk
Jurgen Wevers

Defenders
Tim Bakens
Ryan Donk
Cerezo Fung A Wing
Stephan Keller
Milano Koenders
Virgilio Teixeira
Patrick van Diemen
Ramon van Haaren
Frank van Mosselveld

Midfielders
Ruud Berger
Robert Fuchs
Dustley Mulder
Hans Mulder
Anthony Obodai
Jordan Remacle
Jan Vertonghen
Ivan Vicelich

Forwards
Benjamin De Ceulaer
Luwamo Garcia
Pius Ikedia
Jochen Janssen
Tim Janssen
Eddy Putter
Martijn Reuser
Tarik Sektioui
Hans van de Haar
Ricky van den Bergh
Nick van der Velden

KEY: ■ On all match ◄◄ Subbed or sent off (Counting game) ►► Subbed on from bench (Counting Game) ►◄ Subbed on and then subbed or sent off (Counting Game) ☐ Not in 16
■ On bench ◄◄ Subbed or sent off (playing less than 70 minutes) ►► Subbed on (playing less than 70 minutes) ►► Subbed on and then subbed or sent off (playing less than 70 minutes)

HOLLAND - RKC WAALWIJK

ADO DEN HAAG

Final Position: **18th**

NICKNAME: DEN HAAG KEY: ☐Won ☐Drawn ☐Lost Attendance

#		Opponent			Score	Scorers	Attendance
1	hopr1	Heerenveen	H	L	2-3	Rankovic 40, Tininho 58 pen	6,900
2	hopr1	Roda JC Kerk	A	L	0-1		11,000
3	hopr1	NAC Breda	H	L	0-2		6,600
4	hopr1	RKC Waalwijk	A	L	0-1		6,000
5	hocr2	Turkiyemspor	A	W	6-1	Elia 4, 6, 38, 51, Verschraagen 66 og, Kolk 87	400
6	hopr1	PSV Eindhoven	H	L	0-2		7,133
7	hopr1	AZ Alkmaar	A	D	2-2	Knopper 5, Mols 34	15,478
8	hopr1	Twente	H	L	1-2	Mols 38	6,453
9	hopr1	Utrecht	A	L	0-2		19,000
10	hopr1	Ajax	A	L	0-2		45,757
11	hopr1	Heracles	H	W	2-0	Kolk 57, Elia 89	7,630
12	hopr1	Excelsior	H	D	2-2	Mols 43, Tininho 84 pen	7,514
13	hocr3	Ajax	A	L	0-2		7,909
14	hopr1	S Rotterdam	A	L	1-2	Delorge 79	9,072
15	hopr1	Vitesse Arnhem	H	L	0-3		7,483
16	hopr1	Groningen	A	W	5-2	Bunjevcevic 2, Knopper 26, Delorge 50, Kolk 70, 85	18,747
17	hopr1	NEC Nijmegen	H	L	0-2		6,738
18	hopr1	Feyenoord	A	L	1-3	Kolk 90	36,000
19	hopr1	Willem II Tilb	H	W	2-1	Elia 8, Kolk 20	6,600
20	hopr1	NAC Breda	A	D	2-2	Elia 17, Mols 45	14,628
21	hopr1	RKC Waalwijk	H	D	1-1	Kolk 87	8,360
22	hopr1	PSV Eindhoven	A	L	1-2	Verhoek 78	32,800
23	hopr1	AZ Alkmaar	H	L	1-3	Rankovic 72	6,405
24	hopr1	Twente	A	L	1-3	Delorge 33	13,000
25	hopr1	Utrecht	H	D	1-1	Hoogendorp 33	7,160
26	hopr1	Ajax	H	L	1-2	Kolk 20	8,276
27	hopr1	Willem II Tilb	A	L	1-2	Kolk 16	12,500
28	hopr1	Feyenoord	H	D	3-3	Hoogendorp 40, 62 pen, Delorge 66	8,814
29	hopr1	Heracles	A	L	1-3	Mols 68	8,361
30	hopr1	Vitesse Arnhem	A	D	2-2	Kolk 11, 38 pen	18,285
31	hopr1	S Rotterdam	H	L	2-4	Rankovic 60, de Vries 80	0
32	hopr1	Excelsior	A	L	1-3	Kolk 67	2,825
33	hopr1	Heerenveen	A	D	1-1	Kolk 42	25,000
34	hopr1	Roda JC Kerk	H	L	0-2		8,477
35	hopr1	Groningen	H	L	1-3	Delorge 85	8,000
36	hopr1	NEC Nijmegen	A	L	2-3	Bodde 49 pen, de Vries 81	12,000

LEAGUE APPEARANCES, BOOKINGS AND CAPS

	AGE (on 01/07/07)	IN NAMED 18	APPEARANCES	COUNTING GAMES	MINUTES ON PITCH	YELLOW CARDS	RED CARDS	CAPS THIS SEASON	NATIONAL SIDE
Goalkeepers									
Stefan Postma	30	5	5	4	418	0	0	-	Holland
Sergio Sanchez	30	9	9	9	810	0	0	-	Spain
R van Nieuwkoop	20	11	3	3	253	0	0	-	Holland
Josh Wagenaar	22	23	5	2	274	0	0	-	Canada
Robert Zwinkels	22	19	15	14	1305	1	0	-	Holland
Defenders									
Said Bakkati	25	32	19	16	1587	4	0	-	Holland
Goran Bunjevcevic	34	24	24	22	1993	7	0	-	Serbia
Samir El-Moussaoui	20	9	5	3	330	1	1	-	Holland
Christiaan Kum	21	19	12	7	795	4	0	-	Holland
K Loumpoutis	28	6	6	3	367	2	0	-	Greece
Angelo Martha	25	10	4	2	288	1	0	-	Holland
Daniel Rijaard	30	19	7	6	604	1	0	-	Holland
Alberto Saavedra	25	32	27	19	1962	7	1	-	Spain
Stijn Vreven	33	24	20	19	1766	7	1	-	Belgium
Midfielders									
Ferrie Bodde	25	27	27	24	2292	8	1	-	Holland
Pascal Bosschaart	27	23	23	20	1895	10	1	-	Holland
Laurent Delorge	27	29	28	25	2280	4	0	-	Belgium
Jesper Hakansson	26	8	5	2	213	1	0	-	Denmark
Richard Knopper	29	18	15	9	957	1	0	-	Holland
Aleksandar Rankovic	28	27	17	8	1082	2	1	-	Serbia
Levi Schwiebbe	20	27	21	13	1467	3	0	-	Holland
Tininho	29	26	23	20	1932	5	0	-	Brazil
Forwards									
Nick Coster	21	13	4	2	243	0	0	-	Holland
Mark de Vries	31	32	27	2	730	3	1	-	Holland
Eljero Elia	20	29	25	12	1422	4	1	-	Holland
Rick Hoogendorp	32	10	8	7	629	1	0	-	Holland
Santi Kolk	25	33	29	23	2290	3	0	-	Holland
Michael Mols	36	33	31	26	2407	2	0	-	Holland
Paulus Roiha	26	3	1	0	16	0	0	-	Finland
Wesley Verhoek	20	23	20	5	806	2	0	-	Holland

TEAM OF THE SEASON

- **D** Stijn Vreven — CG: 19 DR: 46
- **M** Tininho — CG: 20 SD: -23
- **G** Robert Zwinkels — CG: 14 DR: 48
- **D** Said Bakkati — CG: 16 DR: 46
- **M** Levi Schwiebbe — CG: 13 SD: -25
- **F** Santi Kolk — CG: 23 SR: 190
- **D** Goran Bunjevcevic — CG: 22 DR: 42
- **M** Laurent Delorge — CG: 25 SD: -29
- **F** Eljero Elia — CG: 12 SR: 474
- **D** Alberto Saavedra — CG: 19 DR: 40
- **M** Pascal Bosschaart — CG: 20 SD: -38

MONTHLY POINTS TALLY

Month		Points	%
AUGUST		0	0%
SEPTEMBER		0	0%
OCTOBER		4	27%
NOVEMBER		4	33%
DECEMBER		5	28%
JANUARY		0	0%
FEBRUARY		2	17%
MARCH		1	11%
APRIL		1	7%

LEAGUE GOALS

	PLAYER	MINS	GOALS	S RATE
1	Kolk	2290	12	190
2	Delorge	2280	5	456
3	Mols	2407	5	481
4	Hoogendorp	629	3	209
5	Rankovic	1082	3	360
6	Elia	1422	3	474
7	de Vries	730	2	365
8	Knopper	957	2	478
9	Tininho	1932	2	966
10	Verhoek	806	1	806
11	Bunjevcevic	1993	1	1993
12	Bodde	2292	1	2292
13	Bosschaart	1895	0	
	Other		0	
	TOTAL		40	

TOP POINT EARNERS

	PLAYER	GAMES	AV PTS
1	Robert Zwinkels	14	0.86
2	Eljero Elia	12	0.83
3	Santi Kolk	23	0.70
4	Tininho	20	0.70
5	Levi Schwiebbe	13	0.69
6	Stijn Vreven	20	0.60
7	Alberto Saavedra	19	0.58
8	Michael Mols	26	0.54
9	Ferrie Bodde	25	0.52
10	Goran Bunjevcevic	22	0.50
	CLUB AVERAGE:		0.50

DISCIPLINARY RECORDS

	PLAYER	YELLOW	RED	AVE
1	Pascal Bosschaart	10	1	172
2	Mark de Vries	3	1	182
3	Stijn Vreven	7	1	220
4	Alberto Saavedra	7	1	245
5	Ferrie Bodde	8	1	254
6	Christiaan Kum	4	0	265
7	Goran Bunjevcevic	7	0	284
8	Eljero Elia	4	1	284
9	Tininho	5	0	386
10	Said Bakkati	4	0	396
11	Wesley Verhoek	2	0	403
12	Levi Schwiebbe	3	0	489
13	Aleks Rankovic	2	1	541
	Other	13	0	
	TOTAL	79	7	

KEY GOALKEEPER

Robert Zwinkels

Goals Conceded in the League	27	Counting Games League games when player was on pitch for at least 70 minutes	14
Defensive Rating Ave number of mins between League goals conceded while on the pitch	48	Clean Sheets In League games when player was on pitch for at least 70 minutes	1

KEY PLAYERS - DEFENDERS

Stijn Vreven

Goals Conceded Number of League goals conceded while the player was on the pitch	38	Clean Sheets In League games when player was on pitch for at least 70 minutes	1
Defensive Rating Ave number of mins between League goals conceded while on the pitch	46	Club Defensive Rating Average number of mins between League goals conceded by the club this season	42

	PLAYER	CON LGE	CLEAN SHEETS	DEF RATE
1	Stijn Vreven	38	1	46 mins
2	Said Bakkati	34	0	46 mins
3	Goran Bunjevcevic	47	1	42 mins
4	Alberto Saavedra	48	0	40 mins

KEY PLAYERS - MIDFIELDERS

Tininho

Goals in the League	2	Contribution to Attacking Power Average number of minutes between League team goals while on pitch	71
Defensive Rating Average number of mins between League goals conceded while on the pitch	48	Scoring Difference Defensive Rating minus Contribution to Attacking Power	-23

	PLAYER	LGE GOALS	DEF RATE	POWER	SCORE DIFF
1	Tininho	2	48	71	-23 mins
2	Levi Schwiebbe	0	44	69	-25 mins
3	Laurent Delorge	5	40	69	-29 mins
4	Pascal Bosschaart	0	40	78	-38 mins

KEY PLAYERS - GOALSCORERS

Santi Kolk

Goals in the League	12	Player Strike Rate Average number of minutes between League goals scored by player	190
Contribution to Attacking Power Average number of minutes between League team goals while on pitch	69	Club Strike Rate Average number of minutes between League goals scored by club	76

	PLAYER	LGE GOALS	POWER	STRIKE RATE
1	Santi Kolk	12	69	190 mins
2	Laurent Delorge	5	69	456 mins
3	Eljero Elia	3	83	474 mins
4	Michael Mols	5	75	481 mins

Jesper Hakansson

SQUAD APPEARANCES

Match	1 2 3 4 5	6 7 8 9 10	11 12 13 14 15	16 17 18 19 20	21 22 23 24 25	26 27 28 29 30	31 32 33 34 35 36
Venue	H A H A A	H A H A A	H H A A H	A H A H A	H A H A H	H A H A A	A H A A H A
Competition	L L L L O	L L L L L	L L O L L	L L L L L	L L L L L	L L L L L	L L L L L L
Result	L L L L W	L D L L L	W D L L L	W L L W D	D L L L D	L L D L D	L L L D L L

Goalkeepers
Stefan Postma
Sergio Sanchez
R van Nieuwkoop
Josh Wagenaar
Robert Zwinkels

Defenders
Said Bakkati
Goran Bunjevcevic
Samir El-Moussaoui
Christiaan Kum
K Loumpoutis
Angelo Martha
Daniel Rijaard
Alberto Saavedra
Stijn Vreven

Midfielders
Ferrie Bodde
Pascal Bosschaart
Laurent Delorge
Jesper Hakansson
Richard Knopper
Aleksandar Rankovic
Levi Schwiebbe
Tininho

Forwards
Nick Coster
Mark de Vries
Eljero Elia
Rick Hoogendorp
Santi Kolk
Michael Mols
Paulus Roiha
Wesley Verhoek

KEY: ■ On all match ◄◄ Subbed or sent off (Counting game) ►► Subbed on from bench (Counting Game) ►► Subbed on and then subbed or sent off (Counting Game) □ Not in 16
■ On bench ◄◄ Subbed or sent off (playing less than 70 minutes) ►► Subbed on (playing less than 70 minutes) ►► Subbed on and then subbed or sent off (playing less than 70 minutes)

HOLLAND - ADO DEN HAAG

GERMAN LEAGUE ROUND-UP

FINAL LEAGUE TABLE

	P	W	D	L	F	A	W	D	L	F	A	F	A	DIF	PTS
			HOME					AWAY					TOTAL		
VfB Stuttgart	34	12	3	2	30	13	9	4	4	31	24	61	37	24	70
Schalke 04	34	13	2	2	30	11	8	3	6	23	21	53	32	21	68
Werder Bremen	34	11	1	5	33	18	9	5	3	43	22	76	40	36	66
Bayern Munich	34	11	4	2	29	14	7	2	8	26	26	55	40	15	60
B Leverkusen	34	8	3	6	28	23	7	3	7	26	26	54	49	5	51
Nuremberg	34	8	7	2	26	16	3	8	6	17	16	43	32	11	48
Hamburg	34	4	9	4	22	19	6	6	5	21	18	43	37	6	45
VFL Bochum	34	7	1	9	23	30	6	5	6	26	20	49	50	-1	45
B Dortmund	34	6	6	5	19	17	6	2	9	22	26	41	43	-2	44
Hertha Berlin	34	8	3	6	29	25	4	5	8	21	30	50	55	-5	44
Hannover 96	34	6	6	5	23	24	7	2	8	18	26	41	50	-9	44
Arminia B	34	8	4	5	29	24	3	5	9	18	25	47	49	-2	42
Cottbus	34	6	5	6	21	22	5	3	9	17	27	38	49	-11	41
E Frankfurt	34	5	5	7	21	30	4	8	5	25	28	46	58	-12	40
Wolfsburg	34	6	6	5	22	22	2	7	8	15	23	37	45	-8	37
Mainz	34	6	4	7	20	28	2	6	9	14	29	34	57	-23	34
Alemania A	34	5	4	8	28	37	4	3	10	18	33	46	70	-24	34
B M'gladbach	34	5	6	6	15	16	1	2	14	8	28	23	44	-21	26

CLUB STRIKE FORCE

Werder Bremen's Brazilian forward Diego

1 Werder Bremen

Goals scored in the League	78
Club Strike Rate (CSR) Average number of minutes between League goals scored by club	40

	CLUB	GOALS	CSR
1	W Bremen	76	40
2	Stuttgart	61	50
3	Bayern Munich	55	55
4	B Leverkusen	54	56
5	Schalke	53	57
6	Hertha Berlin	50	61
7	Bochum	49	62
8	Arminia B	47	65
9	Eintr Frankfurt	46	66
10	Alem Aachen	46	66
11	Nuremberg	43	71
12	Hamburg	43	71
13	Hannover 96	41	74
14	B Dortmund	41	74
15	Cottbus	38	80
16	Wolfsburg	37	82
17	Mainz	34	90
18	B M'gladbach	23	133

CLUB DISCIPLINARY RECORDS

Cottbus's Timo Rost; 10 cards

1 Cottbus

League Yellow	86
League Red	3
League Total	89
Cards Average in League Average number of minutes between a card being shown of either colour	34

	CLUB	Y	R	TOTAL	AVE
1	Cottbus	86	3	89	34
2	B Leverkusen	77	8	85	36
3	Hertha Berlin	76	7	83	36
4	Alem Aachen	77	5	82	37
5	Hamburg	65	7	72	42
6	Nuremberg	67	2	69	44
7	Schalke	64	2	66	46
8	B Dortmund	64	2	66	46
9	B M'gladbach	63	3	66	46
10	Wolfsburg	64	1	65	47
11	W Bremen	62	0	62	49
12	Bochum	59	3	62	49
13	Mainz	59	2	61	50
14	Stuttgart	54	6	60	51
15	Bayern Munich	58	0	58	52
16	Hannover 96	54	3	57	53
17	Eintr Frankfurt	46	7	53	57
18	Arminia B	50	2	52	58

CLUB DEFENCES

Nuremberg's Brazilian defender Glauber

1 Nuremberg

Goals conceded in the League	32
Clean Sheets (CS) Number of league games where no goals were conceded	12
Club Defensive Rate (CDR) Average number of minutes between League goals conceded by club	95

	CLUB	LGE	CS	CDR
1	Nuremberg	32	12	95
2	Schalke	32	14	95
3	Stuttgart	37	14	82
4	Hamburg	37	12	82
5	W Bremen	40	11	76
6	Bayern Munich	40	8	76
7	B Dortmund	43	9	71
8	B M'gladbach	44	6	69
9	Wolfsburg	45	9	68
10	B Leverkusen	49	7	62
11	Arminia B	49	5	62
12	Cottbus	49	8	62
13	Bochum	50	9	61
14	Hannover 96	50	10	61
15	Hertha Berlin	55	6	55
16	Mainz	57	7	53
17	Eintr Frankfurt	58	7	52
18	Alem Aachen	70	6	43

PLAYER NATIONALITIES

Overseas country with the most player appearances in the German League - Brazil		543 league appearances by Brazilian players	

	COUNTRY	PLAYERS	IN SQUAD	LGE APP	% LGE ACT	CAPS	MOST APP	APP
1	Germany	275	5301	3783	45.17	144	Roman Weidenfeller	100
2	Brazil	25	619	543	7.13	42	R da C Santos Diego	95.9
3	Holland	15	381	336	4.34	24	Jeffrey Leiwakabessy	99
4	Czech Republic	14	327	267	3.01	15	Tomas Galasek	89.4
5	Switzerland	11	302	254	2.84	32	Alexander Frei	85.1
6	Poland	9	244	216	2.79	7	Mariusz Kukielka	93.6
7	Argentina	9	243	225	2.77	0	Javier Horacio Pinola	88.6
8	Denmark	18	335	237	2.52	29	Kasper Bogelund	58.7
9	Bosnia	6	192	176	2.27	1	Tomislav Piplica	100
10	Croatia	14	282	193	1.76	23	Josip Simunic	73.5
11	Serbia	6	142	132	1.47	9	Marko Pantelic	83.2
12	Romania	4	110	105	1.34	0	Sergiu Marian Radu	95.7
13	Hungary	4	112	101	1.3	0	Szabolcs Huszti	82.9
14	Portugal	5	132	111	1.28	5	José Ze Antonio	88.2
15	Cameroon	5	99	96	1.27	0	Pierre Nlend Wome	76.4
16	Macedonia	4	89	84	1.23	0	Nikolce Noveski	91.2
17	Greece	3	86	86	1.15	0	Theofanis Gekas	90.8
18	Turkey	7	129	110	1.07	3	Halil Altintop	70.4
19	Belgium	8	118	89	1.03	12	Daniel Van Buyten	89.1
20	United States	6	97	82	1.03	13	Steve Cherundolo	94.2

CLUB MAKE-UP – HOME AND OVERSEAS PLAYERS

1 Cottbus		60.7% of appearances by overseas players	

	CLUB	OVERSEAS	HOME	% OVERSEAS	% LGE ACT	MOST APP	APP
1	Cottbus	17	11	60.7	77.57	Tomislav Piplica	100
2	Hamburg	18	17	51.4	70.1	Joris Mathijsen	92.6
3	Wolfsburg	17	12	58.6	66.77	Tom van der Leegte	91.8
4	B M'gladbach	20	15	57.1	66.76	José Ze Antonio	88.2
5	Schalke	13	17	43.3	66.05	Rafinha	87.5
6	Nuremberg	17	8	68	63.95	Tomas Galasek	89.4
7	Bayern Munich	16	13	55.2	61.59	Daniel Van Buyten	89.1
8	Hannover 96	14	16	46.7	59.69	Steve Cherundolo	94.2
9	Bochum	15	15	50	58.84	Tomasz Zdebel	91.9
10	Hertha Berlin	15	14	51.7	57.49	Gilberto	84.8
11	Stuttgart	12	17	41.4	55.56	Pavel Pardo	97.1
12	B Dortmund	11	17	39.3	51.48	Tinga	88.1
13	W Bremen	13	16	44.8	50.66	R da Santos Diego	95.9
14	B Leverkusen	16	13	55.2	49.56	Sergei Barbarez	86
15	Eintr Frankfurt	10	20	33.3	42.44	Christoph Spycher	83.4
16	Mainz	17	15	53.1	41.99	Nikolce Noveski	91.2
17	Arminia B	11	18	37.9	33.81	Artur Wichniarek	79.4
18	Alem Aachen	10	21	32.3	31.16	Jeffrey Leiwakabessy	99

CHART-TOPPING MIDFIELDERS

1 Mnari - Nuremberg	
Goals scored in the League	3
Defensive Rating Av number of mins between League goals conceded while on the pitch	120
Contribution to Attacking Power Average number of minutes between League team goals while on pitch	64
Scoring Difference Defensive Rating minus Contribution to Attacking Power	56

	PLAYER	CLUB	GOALS	DEF RATE	POWER	S DIFF
1	Jawhar Mnari	Nuremberg	3	120	64	56
2	Thomas Hitzlsperger	Stuttgart	7	96	51	45
3	Clemens Fritz	W Bremen	1	82	40	42
4	Levan Kobiashvili	Schalke	3	97	56	41
5	Ludovic Magnin	Stuttgart	1	86	46	40
6	Andreas Ottl	Bayern Munich	1	87	48	39
7	Torsten Frings	W Bremen	1	78	39	39
8	Fabian Ernst	Schalke	0	105	67	38
9	Lincoln	Schalke	3	92	59	33
10	R da C Santos Diego	W Bremen	13	73	40	33
11	Pavel Pardo	Stuttgart	1	80	48	32
12	Hasan Salihamidzic	Bayern Munich	4	88	57	31
13	Rafael Van der Vaart	Hamburg	8	99	70	29
14	Tomas Galasek	Nuremberg	2	97	68	29
15	Roberto Hilbert	Stuttgart	7	77	49	28

CHART-TOPPING GOALSCORERS

1 Gekas - Bochum	
Goals scored in the League	21
Contribution to Attacking Power Average number of minutes between League team goals while on pitch	59
Club Strike Rate (CSR) Average minutes between League goals scored by club	62
Player Strike Rate Average number of minutes between League goals scored by player	132

	PLAYER	CLUB	GOALS: LGE	POWER	CSR	S RATE
1	Theofanis Gekas	Bochum	21	59	62	132
2	Mario Gomez	Stuttgart	13	49	50	152
3	Alexander Frei	B Dortmund	16	83	74	162
4	Roy Makaay	Bayern Munich	16	53	55	162
5	Christian Gimenez	Hertha Berlin	12	61	61	179
6	Kevin Kuranyi	Schalke	15	56	57	192
7	Marko Pantelic	Hertha Berlin	13	60	61	195
8	Jeronimo Cacau	Stuttgart	13	51	50	201
9	Andriy Voronin	B Leverkusen	10	51	56	206
10	Miroslav Klose	W Bremen	13	39	40	207
11	Naohiro Takahara	Eintr Frankfurt	11	61	66	212
12	Sergiu Marian Radu	Cottbus	13	79	80	225
13	R da Cunha S Diego	W Bremen	13	40	40	225
14	Vlad Munteanu	Cottbus	12	79	80	226
15	Ioannis Amanatidis	Eintr Frankfurt	8	64	66	234

CHART-TOPPING DEFENDERS

1 Atouba - Hamburg	
Goals Conceded in the League The number of League goals conceded while he was on the pitch	15
Clean Sheets In games when he played at least 70 mins	10
Club Defensive Rating Average mins between League goals conceded by the club this season	82
Defensive Rating Average number of minutes between League goals conceded while on pitch	118

	PLAYER	CLUB	CON: LGE	CS	CDR	DEF RATE
1	Timothee Atouba	Hamburg	15	10	82	118
2	Andreas Wolf	Nuremberg	27	12	95	105
3	Javier Horacio Pinola	Nuremberg	27	10	95	100
4	Rafinha	Schalke	27	12	95	99
5	Ricardo Osorio	Stuttgart	22	10	82	96
6	Dominik Reinhardt	Nuremberg	27	11	95	95
7	Per Mertesacker	W Bremen	23	10	76	94
8	Bastian Reinhardt	Hamburg	23	10	82	93
9	Jose Marcelo Bordon	Schalke	27	12	95	91
10	Mladen Krstajic	Schalke	26	9	95	90
11	Dario Rodriguez	Schalke	24	7	95	86
12	Joris Mathijsen	Hamburg	33	12	82	85
13	Mathieu Delpierre	Stuttgart	35	14	82	83
14	Serdar Tasci	Stuttgart	24	10	82	83
15	Christian Worns	B Dortmund	26	7	71	82

CHART-TOPPING GOALKEEPERS

1 Neuer - Schalke	
Counting Games Games in which he played at least 70 minutes	27
Goals Conceded in the League The number of League goals conceded while he was on the pitch	21
Clean Sheets In games when he played at least 70 mins	13
Defensive Rating Average number of minutes between League goals conceded while on pitch	115

	PLAYER	CLUB	CG	CONC	CS	DEF RATE
1	Manuel Neuer	Schalke	27	21	13	115
2	Raphael Schafer	Nuremberg	33	32	12	93
3	Timo Hildebrand	Stuttgart	33	37	13	80
4	Tim Wiese	W Bremen	31	35	10	79
5	Oliver Kahn	Bayern Munich	32	37	8	77
6	Kasey Keller	B M'gladbach	27	34	6	72
7	Roman Weidenfeller	B Dortmund	34	43	9	71
8	Simon Jentzsch	Wolfsburg	34	45	9	68
9	Tomislav Piplica	Cottbus	34	49	8	62
10	Robert Enke	Hannover 96	34	50	10	61
11	Hans-Jorg Butt	B Leverkusen	21	32	3	59
12	Mathias Hain	Arminia B	30	46	4	59
13	Christian Fiedler	Hertha Berlin	32	49	6	58
14	Dimo Wache	Mainz	26	41	5	57
15	Oka Nikolov	Eintr Frankfurt	19	34	5	50

PLAYER DISCIPLINARY RECORD

Sascha Dum of Aachen battles for the ball

	PLAYER		LY	LR	TOT	AVE
1	Dum	Alem Aachen	7	1	8	144
2	Ramelow	B Leverkusen	5	2	7	145
3	Gohouri	B M'gladbach	6	2	8	156
4	Andreasen	Mainz	7	1	8	164
5	Jarolim	Hamburg	14	1	15	169
6	Haggui	B Leverkusen	11	0	11	173
7	Ziebig	Cottbus	8	1	9	184
8	Pinto	Alem Aachen	10	0	10	192
9	Silva	Cottbus	9	0	9	200
10	Boateng	Hertha Berlin	7	0	7	207
11	Zdebel	Bochum	13	0	13	216
12	de Jong	Hamburg	6	0	6	216
13	Wolf	Nuremberg	13	0	13	219
14	Hofland	Wolfsburg	12	0	12	222
15	Leegte	Wolfsburg	12	0	12	234

1. Sascha Dum - Alem Aachen	
Cards Average mins between cards	144
League Yellow	7
League Red	1
TOTAL	8

TEAM OF THE SEASON

D Atouba (Hamburg) CG: 19 DR: 118

M Fritz (W Bremen) CG: 31 SD: +42

D Wolf (Nuremburg) CG: 32 DR: 105

M Hitzelsperger (Stuttgart) CG: 22 SD: +45

F Gekas (Bochum) CG: 31 SR: 132

G Neuer (Schalke) CG: 27 DR: 115

D Osorio (Stuttgart) CG: 20 DR: 96

M Kobiashvili (Schalke) CG: 22 SD: +41

F Gomez (Stuttgart) CG: 20 SR: 152

D Rafina (Schalke) CG: 29 DR: 99

M Mnari (Nuremburg) CG: 18 SD: +56

VfB STUTTGART

Final Position: **1st**

NICKNAME: DIE SCHWABEN   KEY: ☐ Won ☐ Drawn ☐ Lost   Attendance

#		Match		Score	Scorers	Attendance
1	grpr1	Nurnberg	H L	0-3		40,000
2	grpr1	Arminia B	A W	3-2	Meira 39, Cacau 73, 82	22,095
3	grpr1	B Dortmund	H L	1-3	Tasci 30	38,000
4	grpr1	W Bremen	A W	3-2	Hilbert 37, Pardo 57, Gomez 86	40,000
5	grpr1	Eintr Frankfurt	H D	1-1	Gomez 73	40,000
6	grpr1	Hertha Berlin	A D	2-2	Gomez 4, Cacau 57	48,637
7	grpr1	B Leverkusen	H W	3-0	Gomez 22, Boka 47, Hitzlsperger 76	35,000
8	grpr1	Wolfsburg	A D	1-1	Gomez 30	21,927
9	grpr1	Schalke	H W	3-0	Khedira 32, 46, Tasci 75	50,000
10	grpr1	Alem Aachen	A W	4-2	Gomez 23, Hitzlsperger 26, Streller 46, 63	21,000
11	grpr1	Hamburg	H W	2-0	Gomez 80, Hitzlsperger 85	45,000
12	grpr1	Hannover 96	A W	2-1	Hitzlsperger 49, Cacau 54	28,847
13	grpr1	Bayern Munich	A L	1-2	Gomez 7	69,000
14	grpr1	B M'gladbach	H W	1-0	Cacau 6	46,000
15	grpr1	Mainz	A D	0-0		20,300
16	grpr1	Bochum	H W	1-0	Streller 87	45,000
17	grpr1	Cottbus	A D	0-0		12,000
18	grpr1	Nurnberg	A L	1-4	Cacau 33	35,082
19	grpr1	Arminia B	H W	3-2	Gomez 9, 59, Cacau 52	28,000
20	grpr1	B Dortmund	A W	1-0	Gomez 59	63,600
21	grpr1	W Bremen	H W	4-1	Hilbert 3, Gomez 15, Magnin 33, Streller 86	58,000
22	grpr1	Eintr Frankfurt	A W	4-0	Hilbert 2, Gomez 16, Osorio 44, Hitzlsperger 78	46,000
23	grpr1	Hertha Berlin	H D	0-0		41,000
24	grpr1	B Leverkusen	A L	1-3	Cacau 73	22,500
25	grpr1	Wolfsburg	H D	0-0		48,000
26	grpr1	Schalke	A L	0-1		61,482
27	grpr1	Alem Aachen	H W	3-1	Streller 29, Lauth 75, Cacau 84	43,000
28	grpr1	Hamburg	A W	4-2	Cacau 10, Khedira 13, Hilbert 27, Meira 51	57,000
29	grpr1	Hannover 96	H W	2-1	Hilbert 2, Zuraw 76	53,000
30	grpr1	Bayern Munich	H W	2-0	Cacau 23, 25	57,400
31	grpr1	B M'gladbach	A W	1-0	Hilbert 53	48,014
32	grpr1	Mainz	H W	2-0	Meira 26, Hilbert 64	56,000
33	grpr1	Bochum	A W	3-2	Hitzlsperger 24, Gomez 62, Cacau 73	31,328
34	grpr1	Cottbus	H W	2-1	Hitzlsperger 27, Khedira 63	56,000

LEAGUE APPEARANCES, BOOKINGS AND CAPS

	AGE (on 01/07/07)	IN NAMED 18	APPEARANCES	COUNTING GAMES	MINUTES ON PITCH	YELLOW CARDS	RED CARDS	CAPS THIS SEASON	NATIONAL SIDE
Goalkeepers									
Timo Hildebrand	28	33	33	33	2970	0	0	2	Germany
Michael Langer	22	31	1	1	90	0	0	-	Austria
Defenders									
Markus Babbel	34	15	2	1	98	0	0	-	Germany
Andreas Beck	20	15	3	0	22	0	0	-	Germany
Arthur Boka	24	25	19	15	1435	5	1	4	Ivory Coast
Mathieu Delpierre	26	33	33	32	2922	4	0	-	France
Tobias Feisthammel	19	3	0	0	0	0	0	-	Germany
Fernando Meira	29	20	20	17	1653	5	0	4	Portugal
Ricardo Osorio	27	30	27	20	2127	1	1	-	Mexico
Serdar Tasci	20	28	26	21	2007	4	1	-	Germany
Midfielders									
Daniel Bierofka	28	24	12	2	497	2	0	-	Germany
Antonio da Silva	29	30	28	15	1817	3	1	-	Brazil
Alexander Farnerud	23	16	10	1	351	1	0	-	Sweden
Christian Gentner	21	24	15	1	501	0	0	-	Germany
Heiko Gerber	34	3	0	0	0	0	0	-	Germany
Roberto Hilbert	22	34	34	31	2794	2	0	2	Germany
Thomas Hitzlsperger	25	31	30	22	2224	5	2	9	Germany
Sami Khedira	20	22	22	11	1355	1	0	-	Germany
Ludovic Magnin	28	32	22	19	1736	6	0	7	Switzerland
Silvio Meissner	34	6	1	0	5	0	0	-	Germany
Pavel Pardo	30	33	33	33	2970	6	0	-	Mexico
Forwards									
Jeronimo Cacau	26	34	32	30	2618	3	0	-	Brazil
Mario Gomez	21	26	25	20	1980	2	0	3	Germany
Benjamin Lauth	25	16	11	1	409	1	0	-	Germany
Bernd Nehrig	20	1	1	0	12	0	0	-	Germany
Marco Streller	26	33	27	5	755	3	0	2	Switzerland
Jon Dahl Tomasson	30	7	4	1	186	0	0	7	Denmark

TEAM OF THE SEASON

G Timo Hildebrand CG: 33 DR: 80

D Ricardo Osorio CG: 20 DR: 96
D Arthur Boka CG: 15 DR: 95
D Serdar Tasci CG: 21 DR: 83
D Mathieu Delpierre CG: 32 DR: 83

M Antonio da Silva CG: 15 SD: 48
M Sami Khedira CG: 11 SD: 48
M Thomas Hitzlsperger CG: 22 SD: 45
M Ludovic Magnin CG: 19 SD: 40

F Mario Gomez CG: 20 SR: 152
F Jeronimo Cacau CG: 30 SR: 201

MONTHLY POINTS TALLY

Month		Points	%
AUGUST		3	33%
SEPTEMBER		4	67%
OCTOBER		8	67%
NOVEMBER		12	80%
DECEMBER		5	56%
JANUARY		3	50%
FEBRUARY		10	83%
MARCH		4	33%
APRIL		12	100%
MAY		9	100%

LEAGUE GOALS

	PLAYER	MINS	GOALS	S RATE
1	Gomez	1980	13	152
2	Cacau	2618	13	201
3	Hitzlsperger	2224	7	317
4	Hilbert	2794	7	399
5	Streller	755	5	151
6	Khedira	1355	4	338
7	Meira	1653	3	551
8	Tasci	2007	2	1003
9	Lauth	409	1	409
10	Boka	1435	1	1435
11	Magnin	1736	1	1736
12	Osorio	2127	1	2127
13	Pardo	2970	1	2970
	Other		0	
	TOTAL		59	

TOP POINT EARNERS

	PLAYER	GAMES	AV PTS
1	Arthur Boka	15	2.20
2	Ricardo Osorio	21	2.14
3	Roberto Hilbert	31	2.13
4	Ludovic Magnin	19	2.11
5	Mario Gomez	20	2.10
6	Pavel Pardo	33	2.09
7	Timo Hildebrand	33	2.09
8	Antonio da Silva	15	2.07
9	Fernando Meira	17	2.06
10	Thomas Hitzlsperger	23	2.04
	CLUB AVERAGE:		2.06

DISCIPLINARY RECORDS

	PLAYER	YELLOW	RED	AVE
1	Arthur Boka	5	1	239
2	Daniel Bierofka	2	0	248
3	Marco Streller	3	0	251
4	Ludovic Magnin	6	0	289
5	Thom Hitzlsperger	5	2	317
6	Fernando Meira	5	0	330
7	Serdar Tasci	4	1	401
8	Antonio da Silva	3	1	454
9	Pavel Pardo	6	0	495
10	Mathieu Delpierre	4	0	730
11	Jeronimo Cacau	3	0	872
12	Mario Gomez	2	0	990
13	Ricardo Osorio	1	1	1063
	Other	3	0	
	TOTAL	52	6	

KEY GOALKEEPER

Timo Hildebrand

Goals Conceded in the League	37	Counting Games League games when player was on pitch for at least 70 minutes	33
Defensive Rating Ave number of mins between League goals conceded while on the pitch	80	Clean Sheets In League games when player was on pitch for at least 70 minutes	13

KEY PLAYERS - DEFENDERS

Ricardo Osorio

Goals Conceded Number of League goals conceded while the player was on the pitch	22	Clean Sheets In League games when player was on pitch for at least 70 minutes	10
Defensive Rating Ave number of mins between League goals conceded while on the pitch	96	Club Defensive Rating Average number of mins between League goals conceded by the club this season	82

	PLAYER	CON LGE	CLEAN SHEETS	DEF RATE
1	Ricardo Osorio	22	10	96 mins
2	Arthur Boka	15	6	95 mins
3	Serdar Tasci	24	10	83 mins
4	Mathieu Delpierre	35	14	83 mins

KEY PLAYERS - MIDFIELDERS

Antonio da Silva

Goals in the League	0	Contribution to Attacking Power Average number of mins between League team goals while on pitch	42
Defensive Rating Average number of mins between League goals conceded while on the pitch	90	Scoring Difference Defensive Rating minus Contribution to Attacking Power	48

	PLAYER	LGE GOALS	DEF RATE	POWER	SCORE DIFF
1	Antonio da Silva	0	90	42	48 mins
2	Sami Khedira	4	96	48	48 mins
3	Thomas Hitzlsperger	7	96	51	45 mins
4	Ludovic Magnin	1	86	46	40 mins

KEY PLAYERS - GOALSCORERS

Mario Gomez

Goals in the League	13	Player Strike Rate Average number of minutes between League goals scored by player	152
Contribution to Attacking Power Average number of minutes between League team goals while on pitch	49	Club Strike Rate Average number of minutes between League goals scored by club	50

	PLAYER	LGE GOALS	POWER	STRIKE RATE
1	Mario Gomez	13	49	152 mins
2	Jeronimo Cacau	13	51	201 mins
3	Thomas Hitzlsperger	7	51	317 mins
4	Sami Khedira	4	48	338 mins

Marco Streller, Mario Gomez, Antonio da Silva

SQUAD APPEARANCES

Match	1	2	3	4	5	6	7	8	9	10	11	12	13	14	15	16	17	18	19	20	21	22	23	24	25	26	27	28	29	30	31	32	33	34
Venue	H	A	H	A	H	A	H	A	H	A	H	A	A	H	A	H	A	A	H	A	H	A	H	A	H	A	H	A	H	H	A	H	A	H
Competition	L	L	L	L	L	L	L	L	L	L	L	L	L	L	L	L	L	L	L	L	L	L	L	L	L	L	L	L	L	L	L	L	L	L
Result	L	W	L	W	D	D	W	D	W	W	W	W	L	W	D	W	D	L	W	W	W	W	D	L	D	L	W	W	W	W		W	W	W

Goalkeepers
Timo Hildebrand
Michael Langer

Defenders
Markus Babbel
Andreas Beck
Arthur Boka
Mathieu Delpierre
Tobias Feisthammel
Fernando Meira
Ricardo Osorio
Serdar Tasci

Midfielders
Daniel Bierofka
Antonio da Silva
Alexander Farnerud
Christian Gentner
Heiko Gerber
Roberto Hilbert
Thomas Hitzlsperger
Sami Khedira
Ludovic Magnin
Silvio Meissner
Pavel Pardo

Forwards
Jeronimo Cacau
Mario Gomez
Benjamin Lauth
Bernd Nehrig
Marco Streller
Jon Dahl Tomasson

KEY: ■ On all match ◄◄ Subbed or sent off (Counting game) ▸▸ Subbed on from bench (Counting Game) ▸◄ Subbed on and then subbed or sent off (Counting Game) ☐ Not in 16
■ On bench ◄ Subbed or sent off (playing less than 70 minutes) ▸ Subbed on (playing less than 70 minutes) ▸▸ Subbed on and then subbed or sent off (playing less than 70 minutes)

GERMANY - VfB STUTTGART

SCHALKE 04

Final Position: 2nd

NICKNAME: KONIGSBLAUE

KEY: ☐ Won ☐ Drawn ☐ Lost

Attendance

#					Result	Scorers	Attendance
1	grpr1	Eintr Frankfurt	H	D	1-1	Hal.Altintop 31	61,482
2	grpr1	Alem Aachen	A	W	1-0	Rodriguez 53	21,300
3	grpr1	W Bremen	H	W	2-0	Kuranyi 7, Hal.Altintop 72	61,000
4	ucrl1	Nancy	H	W	1-0	Larsen 86	45,878
5	grpr1	Hertha Berlin	A	L	0-2		60,000
6	grpr1	Wolfsburg	H	W	2-0	Kuranyi 56, Lincoln 88	60,000
7	ucrl2	Nancy	A	L	1-3	Bordon 77	18,029
8	grpr1	B Leverkusen	A	L	1-3	Bordon 6	22,500
9	grpr1	Hamburg	A	W	2-1	Hal.Altintop 16, Bordon 53	57,000
10	grpr1	Hannover 96	H	W	2-1	Bajramovic 17, Kobiashvili 27	61,000
11	grpr1	Stuttgart	A	L	0-3		50,000
12	grpr1	Bayern Munich	H	D	2-2	Lovenkrands 13, Kobiashvili 20	61,482
13	grpr1	B M'gladbach	A	W	2-0	Ze Antonio 11 og, Varela 31	53,000
14	grpr1	Mainz	H	W	4-0	Kuranyi 13, 32, Hal.Altintop 22, 67	61,000
15	grpr1	Cottbus	A	W	4-2	Ham.Altintop 4, Kuranyi 11, Pander 50, Kobiashvili 83	17,210
16	grpr1	Bochum	H	W	2-1	Rafinha 19, Lovenkrands 27	61,000
17	grpr1	Nurnberg	A	D	0-0		45,000
18	grpr1	B Dortmund	H	W	3-1	Pander 14, Kuranyi 25, Lovenkrands 47	61,482
19	grpr1	Arminia B	A	W	1-0	Bajramovic 81	26,601
20	grpr1	Eintr Frankfurt	A	W	3-1	Varela 16, Kuranyi 70, 90	51,500
21	grpr1	Alem Aachen	H	W	2-1	Rafinha 23 pen, Sichone 74 og	61,482
22	grpr1	W Bremen	A	W	2-0	Lovenkrands 20, 73	42,100
23	grpr1	Hertha Berlin	H	W	2-0	Kuranyi 64, Lovenkrands 75	61,482
24	grpr1	Wolfsburg	A	D	2-2	Kuranyi 10, 29	28,346
25	grpr1	B Leverkusen	H	L	0-1		61,482
26	grpr1	Hamburg	H	L	0-2		61,482
27	grpr1	Hannover 96	A	D	1-1	Hal.Altintop 2	49,000
28	grpr1	Stuttgart	H	W	1-0	Krstajic 75	61,482
29	grpr1	Bayern Munich	A	L	0-2		69,000
30	grpr1	B M'gladbach	H	W	2-0	Asamoah 57, Kuranyi 71	61,482
31	grpr1	Mainz	A	W	3-0	Kuranyi 10, Asamoah 34, Lincoln 71	20,300
32	grpr1	Cottbus	H	W	2-0	Rost 59 og, Bordon 63	61,058
33	grpr1	Bochum	A	L	1-2	Kuranyi 8	31,328
34	grpr1	Nurnberg	H	W	1-0	Kuranyi 64	61,482
35	grpr1	B Dortmund	A	L	0-2		80,708
36	grpr1	Arminia B	H	W	2-1	Lincoln 11, Hal.Altintop 16	61,482

LEAGUE APPEARANCES, BOOKINGS AND CAPS

	AGE (on 01/07/07)	IN NAMED 18	APPEARANCES	COUNTING GAMES	MINUTES ON PITCH	YELLOW CARDS	RED CARDS	CAPS THIS SEASON	NATIONAL SIDE
Goalkeepers									
Manuel Neuer	21	34	27	27	2430	1	0	-	Germany
Frank Rost	34	15	7	7	630	0	0	-	Germany
Defenders									
Mathias Abel	26	11	1	0	10	0	0	-	Germany
Sebastian Boenisch	20	26	8	1	217	1	0	-	Germany
Jose Marcelo Bordon	31	28	28	27	2483	7	0	-	Brazil
Tim Hoogland	22	25	9	2	292	0	0	-	Germany
Benedikt Howedes	19	1	0	0	0	0	0	-	Germany
Mladen Krstajic	33	27	27	25	2345	3	1	7	Serbia
Christian Pander	23	16	16	14	1310	0	0	-	Germany
Rafinha	21	33	31	29	2679	9	0	-	Brazil
Dario Rodriguez	32	33	26	22	2087	4	0	-	Uruguay
Midfielders									
Hamit Altintop	24	33	31	15	1697	4	0	6	Turkey
Zlatan Bajramovic	27	32	27	20	1944	7	0	-	Bosnia
Alex Baumjohann	20	8	1	0	26	0	0	-	Germany
Fabian Ernst	28	27	26	24	2214	8	0	-	Germany
Markus Heppke	21	6	1	0	1	0	0	-	Germany
Levan Kobiashvili	29	30	29	22	2143	6	0	6	Georgia
Timo Kunert	20	9	1	0	1	0	0	-	Germany
Lincoln	28	23	23	20	1845	4	1	-	Brazil
Mesut Ozil	18	32	19	6	882	1	0	-	Germany
Gustavo A Varela	29	21	18	9	1023	2	0	-	Uruguay
Forwards									
Halil Altintop	24	34	34	19	2154	3	0	1	Turkey
Gerald Asamoah	28	13	13	0	520	1	0	2	Germany
Christian Erwig	23	5	1	0	4	0	0	-	Germany
Kevin Kuranyi	25	34	34	32	2889	6	0	5	Germany
Soren Larsen	25	16	11	0	191	0	0	-	Denmark
Peter Lovenkrands	27	24	15	1580	1	0	3		Denmark

TEAM OF THE SEASON

D Christian Pander CG: 14 DR: 131

M Hamit Altintop CG: 15 SD: 57

D Rafinha CG: 29 DR: 99

M Levan Kobiashvili CG: 22 SD: 41

F Kevin Kuranyi CG: 32 SR: 192

G Manuel Neuer CG: 27 DR: 115

D Jose Marcelo Bordon CG: 27 DR: 91

M Fabian Ernst CG: 24 SD: 38

F Peter Lovenkrands CG: 15 SR: 263

D Mladen Krstajic CG: 25 DR: 90

M Lincoln CG: 20 SD: 33

MONTHLY POINTS TALLY

AUGUST	7	78%
SEPTEMBER	3	50%
OCTOBER	6	50%
NOVEMBER	13	87%
DECEMBER	7	78%
JANUARY	6	100%
FEBRUARY	7	58%
MARCH	4	33%
APRIL	9	75%
MAY	6	67%

LEAGUE GOALS

	PLAYER	MINS	GOALS	S RATE
1	Kuranyi	2889	15	192
2	Altintop, Hal	2154	7	307
3	Lovenkrands	1580	6	263
4	Lincoln	1845	3	615
5	Kobiashvili	2143	3	714
6	Bordon	2483	3	827
7	Asamoah	520	2	260
8	Varela	1023	2	511
9	Pander	1310	2	655
10	Bajramovic	1944	2	972
11	Rafinha	2679	2	1339
12	Altintop, Ham	1697	1	1697
13	Rodriguez	2087	1	2087
	Other		1	
	TOTAL		**50**	

TOP POINT EARNERS

	PLAYER	GAMES	AV PTS
1	Peter Lovenkrands	15	2.40
2	Levan Kobiashvili	22	2.36
3	Christian Pander	14	2.21
4	Manuel Neuer	27	2.15
5	Mladen Krstajic	26	2.12
6	Rafinha	29	2.10
7	Hamit Altintop	15	2.07
8	Lincoln	20	2.05
9	Kevin Kuranyi	32	2.03
10	Zlatan Bajramovic	20	2.00
	CLUB AVERAGE:		**2.00**

DISCIPLINARY RECORDS

	PLAYER	YELLOW	RED	AVE
1	Zlatan Bajramovic	7	0	277
2	Fabian Ernst	8	0	316
3	Rafinha	9	0	334
4	J Marcelo Bordon	7	0	354
5	Levan Kobiashvili	6	0	357
6	Lincoln	4	1	369
7	Hamit Altintop	4	0	424
8	Gustavo A Varela	2	0	511
9	Gerald Asamoah	1	0	520
10	Dario Rodriguez	4	0	521
11	Mladen Krstajic	3	1	586
12	Halil Altintop	3	0	718
13	Kevin Kuranyi	6	0	722
	Other	3	0	
	TOTAL	**67**	**2**	

KEY GOALKEEPER

Manuel Neuer

Goals Conceded in the League	21	Counting Games League games when player was on pitch for at least 70 minutes	27
Defensive Rating Ave number of mins between League goals conceded while on the pitch	115	Clean Sheets In games when player was on pitch for at least 70 minutes	13

KEY PLAYERS - DEFENDERS

Christian Pander

Goals Conceded Number of League goals conceded while the player was on the pitch	10	Clean Sheets In League games when player was on pitch for at least 70 minutes	8
Defensive Rating Ave number of mins between League goals conceded while on the pitch	131	Club Defensive Rating Average number of mins between League goals conceded by the club this season	95

	PLAYER	CON LGE	CLEAN SHEETS	DEF RATE
1	Christian Pander	10	8	131 mins
2	Rafinha	27	12	99 mins
3	Jose Marcelo Bordon	27	12	91 mins
4	Mladen Krstajic	26	9	90 mins

KEY PLAYERS - MIDFIELDERS

Hamit Altintop

Goals in the League	1	Contribution to Attacking Power Average number of minutes between League team goals while on pitch	56
Defensive Rating Average number of mins between League goals conceded while on the pitch	113	Scoring Difference Defensive Rating minus Contribution to Attacking Power	57

	PLAYER	LGE GOALS	DEF RATE	POWER	SCORE DIFF
1	Hamit Altintop	1	113	56	57 mins
2	Levan Kobiashvili	3	97	56	41 mins
3	Fabian Ernst	0	105	67	38 mins
4	Lincoln	3	92	59	33 mins

KEY PLAYERS - GOALSCORERS

Kevin Kuranyi

Goals in the League	15	Player Strike Rate Average number of minutes between League goals scored by player	192
Contribution to Attacking Power Average number of minutes between League team goals while on pitch	56	Club Strike Rate Average number of minutes between League goals scored by club	57

	PLAYER	LGE GOALS	POWER	STRIKE RATE
1	Kevin Kuranyi	15	56	192 mins
2	Peter Lovenkrands	6	49	263 mins
3	Halil Altintop	7	56	307 mins
4	Lincoln	3	59	615 mins

Kevin Kuranyi

SQUAD APPEARANCES

Match	1	2	3	4	5	6	7	8	9	10	11	12	13	14	15	16	17	18	19	20	21	22	23	24	25	26	27	28	29	30	31	32	33	34	35	36
Venue	H	A	H	H	A	H	A	A	A	H	A	H	A	H	A	H	A	H	A	A	H	A	H	A	H	H	A	H	A	H	A	H	A	H	A	H
Competition	L	L	L	L	E	L	E	L	L	L	L	L	L	L	L	L	L	L	L	L	L	L	L	L	L	L	L	L	L	L	L	L	L	L	L	L
Result	D	W	W	W	L	W	L	L	W	W	L	D	W	W	W	W	D	W	W	W	W	W	W	D	L	L	D	W	L	W	W	W	L	W	L	W

Goalkeepers
Manuel Neuer
Frank Rost

Defenders
Mathias Abel
Sebastian Boenisch
Jose Marcelo Bordon
Tim Hoogland
Benedikt Howedes
Mladen Krstajic
Christian Pander
Rafinha
Dario Rodriguez

Midfielders
Hamit Altintop
Zlatan Bajramovic
Alex Baumjohann
Fabian Ernst
Markus Heppke
Levan Kobiashvili
Timo Kunert
Lincoln
Mesut Ozil
Gustavo A Varela

Forwards
Halil Altintop
Gerald Asamoah
Christian Erwig
Kevin Kuranyi
Soren Larsen
Peter Lovenkrands

KEY: ■ On all match ◄◄ Subbed or sent off (Counting game) ▸▸ Subbed on from bench (Counting Game) ▸▸ Subbed on and then subbed or sent off (Counting Game) □ Not in 16
□ On bench ◄ Subbed or sent off (playing less than 70 minutes) ▸ Subbed on (playing less than 70 minutes) ▸▸ Subbed on and then subbed or sent off (playing less than 70 minutes)

WERDER BREMEN

Final Position: 3rd

NICKNAME: FISCHKOPPE   KEY: ☐ Won ☐ Drawn ☐ Lost   Attendance

#					Score	Scorers	Attendance
1	grpr1	Hannover 96	A	W	4-2	Diego 19, Almeida 79, Klose 85, Jensen 90	49,000
2	grpr1	B Leverkusen	H	W	2-1	Klose 26, Hugo Almeida 77	39,600
3	grpr1	Schalke	A	L	0-2		61,000
4	ecgpa	Chelsea	A	L	0-2		32,135
5	grpr1	Stuttgart	H	L	2-3	Hilbert 4 og, Zidan 31	40,000
6	grpr1	Hamburg	A	D	1-1	Borowski 58	57,000
7	ecgpa	Barcelona	H	D	1-1	Puyol 56 og	41,256
8	grpr1	B M'gladbach	H	W	3-0	Hunt 33, Schulz 35, Diego 38	38,000
9	grpr1	Bochum	A	W	6-0	Hunt 6, Schulz 61, Vranjes 76, Diego 77, Fritz 88, Naldo 90	31,328
10	ecgpa	Levski Sofia	H	W	2-0	Naldo 45, Diego 73	36,246
11	grpr1	Bayern Munich	H	W	3-1	Diego 11, Wome 34, Lucio 62	42,500
12	grpr1	Mainz	A	W	6-1	Klose 13, 21, Hunt 20, 75, Naldo 80, Diego 89	20,300
13	ecgpa	Levski Sofia	A	W	3-0	Mihaylov 33 og, Baumann 35, Frings 37	36,000
14	grpr1	Cottbus	H	D	1-1	Klasnic 76	35,000
15	grpr1	Nurnberg	A	W	2-1	Frings 32, Diego 79	35,000
16	grpr1	B Dortmund	H	L	1-3	Klose 30	42,100
17	grpr1	Alem Aachen	A	D	2-2	Mertesacker 47, Klose 81	20,800
18	ecgpa	Chelsea	H	W	1-0	Mertesacker 26	40,000
19	grpr1	Arminia B	H	W	3-0	Klose 29, 45, Hunt 75	40,000
20	grpr1	Hertha Berlin	H	W	3-1	Diego 23 pen, Klose 32, 40	39,000
21	ecgpa	Barcelona	A	L	0-2		98,787
22	grpr1	Eintr Frankfurt	A	W	6-2	Naldo 3, 31, 48, D.Jensen 11, Vranjes 86, Diego 90	51,400
23	grpr1	Wolfsburg	H	W	2-1	D.Jensen 16, Naldo 86	39,584
24	grpr1	Hannover 96	H	W	3-0	Borowski 5, Hugo Almeida 67, Mertesacker 74	40,000
25	grpr1	B Leverkusen	A	W	2-0	Klose 15, Hugo Almeida 78	22,500
26	grpr1	Schalke	H	L	0-2		42,100
27	grpr1	Stuttgart	A	L	1-4	Diego 21	58,000
28	ucrl1	Ajax	H	W	3-0	Mertesacker 48, Naldo 54, Frings 71	38,150
29	grpr1	Hamburg	H	L	0-2		42,100
30	ucrl2	Ajax	A	L	1-3	Hugo Almeida 14	35,227
31	grpr1	B M'gladbach	A	D	2-2	Wome 11, Vranjes 84	50,644
32	grpr1	Bochum	H	W	3-0	Hunt 25, 73, 77	40,156
33	ucrl1	Celta Vigo	A	W	1-0	Hugo Almeida 84	20,000
34	grpr1	Bayern Munich	A	D	1-1	Rosenberg 66	69,000
35	ucrl2	Celta Vigo	H	W	2-0	Hugo Almeida 48, Fritz 61	28,000
36	grpr1	Mainz	H	W	2-0	Vranjes 60, Diego 90	39,450
37	grpr1	Cottbus	A	D	0-0		20,344
38	ucqfl1	AZ Alkmaar	A	D	0-0		16,000
39	grpr1	Nurnberg	H	W	1-0	Rosenberg 75	42,100
40	ucqfl2	AZ Alkmaar	H	W	4-1	Borowski 16, Klose 36, 62, Diego 82	35,000
41	grpr1	B Dortmund	A	W	2-0	Klose 28, Diego 39	80,500
42	grpr1	Alem Aachen	H	W	3-1	D.Jensen 50, Rosenberg 56, Diego 90	40,300
43	ucsfl1	Espanyol	A	L	0-3		35,000
44	grpr1	Arminia B	A	L	2-3	Klose 59, Hugo Almeida 74	26,601
45	ucsfl2	Espanyol	H	L	1-2	Hugo Almeida 4	37,000
46	grpr1	Hertha Berlin	A	W	4-1	Rosenberg 19, 50, 82, Diego 60	74,220
47	grpr1	Eintr Frankfurt	H	L	1-2	Hunt 34	42,100
48	grpr1	Wolfsburg	A	W	2-0	Rosenberg 54, 87	28,000

LEAGUE APPEARANCES, BOOKINGS AND CAPS

	AGE (on 01/07/07)	IN NAMED 18	APPEARANCES	COUNTING GAMES	MINUTES ON PITCH	YELLOW CARDS	RED CARDS	CAPS THIS SEASON	NATIONAL SIDE
Goalkeepers									
Andreas Reinke	46	34	3	3	270	0	0	-	Germany
Tim Wiese	25	32	31	31	2790	2	1	-	Germany
Defenders									
Leon Andreasen	24	15	4	0	98	0	0	2	Denmark
Per Mertesacker	22	26	25	24	2165	2	0	5	Germany
Naldo	24	32	32	32	2875	7	0	2	Brazil
Peter Niemeyer	23	13	3	1	109	0	0	-	Germany
Patrick Owomoyela	27	15	9	3	429	1	0	-	Germany
Petri Pasanen	26	33	17	8	974	3	0	7	Finland
Christian Schulz	24	28	19	7	1006	1	0	-	Germany
Pierre Nlend Wome	28	30	28	24	2337	8	0	1	Cameroon
Midfielders									
Kevin Artmann	21	0	0	0	0	0	0	-	Germany
Frank Baumann	31	18	17	9	1066	5	0	-	Germany
Amaury Bischoff	20	4	0	0	0	0	0	-	France
Tim Borowski	27	17	17	11	1264	5	0	3	Germany
R da C Santos Diego	22	33	33	33	2935	10	0	6	Brazil
Torsten Frings	30	33	33	33	2970	10	0	10	Germany
Clemens Fritz	26	32	32	31	2813	12	0	7	Germany
Daniel Jensen	28	24	23	12	1490	4	0	8	Denmark
Jurica Vranjes	27	33	25	8	1263	3	0	-	Croatia
Forwards									
M Hugo Almeida	23	32	28	7	1203	6	0	1	Portugal
Aaron Hunt	20	31	28	14	1660	5	0	-	Germany
Ivan Klasnic	27	16	12	2	447	0	0	3	Croatia
Miroslav Klose	29	33	31	29	2692	1	1	7	Germany
Jerome Polenz	20	6	0	0	0	0	0	-	Germany
Markus Rosenberg	24	17	14	2	564	0	0	6	Sweden
Kevin Schindler	19	7	1	0	6	0	0	-	Germany
Mohammed Zidan	25	7	5	2	234	0	0	-	Egypt

TEAM OF THE SEASON

D Per Mertesacker CG: 24 DR: 94
M Daniel Jensen CG: 12 SD: 47
D Pierre Nlend Wome CG: 24 DR: 80
M Clemens Fritz CG: 31 SD: 42
F Aaron Hunt CG: 14 SR: 184
G Tim Wiese CG: 31 DR: 79
D Naldo CG: 32 DR: 75
M Torsten Frings CG: 33 SD: 39
F Miroslav Klose CG: 29 SR: 207
D Christian Schulz* CG: 7 DR: 83
M Santos Diego CG: 33 SD: 33

MONTHLY POINTS TALLY

AUGUST	6	67%
SEPTEMBER	4	44%
OCTOBER	9	100%
NOVEMBER	8	53%
DECEMBER	9	100%
JANUARY	6	100%
FEBRUARY	1	8%
MARCH	8	67%
APRIL	9	75%
MAY	6	67%

LEAGUE GOALS

	PLAYER	MINS	GOALS	S RATE
1	Klose	2692	13	207
2	Diego	2935	13	225
3	Hunt	1660	9	184
4	Rosenberg	564	8	70
5	Naldo	2875	6	479
6	Hugo Almeida	1203	5	240
7	Vranjes	1263	4	315
8	Jensen, D	1490	4	372
9	Schulz	1006	2	503
10	Borowski	1264	2	632
11	Mertesacker	2165	2	1082
12	Wome	2337	2	1168
13	Zidan	234	1	234
	Other		3	
	TOTAL		74	

TOP POINT EARNERS

	PLAYER	GAMES	AV PTS
1	Daniel Jensen	12	2.17
2	Per Mertesacker	24	2.08
3	Tim Wiese	31	2.03
4	Miroslav Klose	29	2.00
5	Torsten Frings	33	2.00
6	Clemens Fritz	31	2.00
7	Pierre Nlend Wome	24	1.96
8	Santos Diego	33	1.91
9	Naldo	32	1.88
10	Aaron Hunt	14	1.79
	CLUB AVERAGE:		1.94

DISCIPLINARY RECORDS

	PLAYER	YELLOW	RED	AVE
1	Miguel H Almeida	6	0	240
2	Clemens Fritz	12	0	312
3	Petri Pasanen	3	0	324
4	Santos Diego	10	0	326
5	Aaron Hunt	5	0	332
6	Torsten Frings	10	0	371
7	Pierre Nlend Wome	8	0	389
8	Tim Borowski	5	0	421
9	Daniel Jensen	4	0	496
10	Naldo	7	0	575
11	Jurica Vranjes	3	0	631
12	Frank Baumann	5	0	1066
13	Per Mertesacker	2	0	1082
	Other	4	2	
	TOTAL	84	2	

KEY GOALKEEPER

Tim Wiese

Goals Conceded in the League	35	Counting Games League games when player was on pitch for at least 70 minutes	31
Defensive Rating Ave number of mins between League goals conceded while on the pitch	79	Clean Sheets In League games when player was on pitch for at least 70 minutes	10

KEY PLAYERS - DEFENDERS

Per Mertesacker

Goals Conceded Number of League goals conceded while the player was on the pitch	23	Clean Sheets In League games when player was on pitch for at least 70 minutes	10
Defensive Rating Ave number of mins between League goals conceded while on the pitch	94	Club Defensive Rating Average number of mins between League goals conceded by the club this season	76

	PLAYER	CON LGE	CLEAN SHEETS	DEF RATE
1	Per Mertesacker	23	10	94 mins
2	Pierre Nlend Wome	29	8	80 mins
3	Naldo	38	11	75 mins
4	Petri Pasanen	15	2	64 mins

KEY PLAYERS - MIDFIELDERS

Daniel Jensen

Goals in the League	4	Contribution to Attacking Power Average number of minutes between League team goals while on pitch	35
Defensive Rating Average number of mins between League goals conceded while on the pitch	82	Scoring Difference Defensive Rating minus Contribution to Attacking Power	47

	PLAYER	LGE GOALS	DEF RATE	POWER	SCORE DIFF
1	Daniel Jensen	4	82	35	47 mins
2	Clemens Fritz	1	82	40	42 mins
3	Torsten Frings	1	78	39	39 mins
4	Ribas da Cunha Santos Diego	13	73	40	33 mins

KEY PLAYERS - GOALSCORERS

Aaron Hunt

Goals in the League	9	Player Strike Rate Average number of minutes between League goals scored by player	184
Contribution to Attacking Power Average number of minutes between League team goals while on pitch	43	Club Strike Rate Average number of minutes between League goals scored by club	40

	PLAYER	LGE GOALS	POWER	STRIKE RATE
1	Aaron Hunt	9	43	184 mins
2	Miroslav Klose	13	39	207 mins
3	Ribas da Cunha Santos Diego	13	40	225 mins
4	Daniel Jensen	4	35	372 mins

Miroslav Klose

SQUAD APPEARANCES

Match	1 2 3 4 5	6 7 8 9 10	11 12 13 14 15	16 17 18 19 20	21 22 23 24 25	26 27 28 29 30	31 32 33 34 35	36 37 38 39 40	41 42 43 44 45	46 47 48
Venue	A H A A H	A H H A H	H A A H A	H A H H H	A A H H A	H A H H A	A H A A H	H A A H H	A H A A H	A H A
Competition	L L L C L	L C L L C	L L C L L	L L C L L	C L L L L	L L E L E	L L E L E	L L E L E	L L E L E	L L L
Result	W W L L L	D D W W W	W W W D W	L D W W W	L W W W W	L L W L L	D W W D W	W D D W W	W W L L L	W L W

Goalkeepers
Andreas Reinke
Tim Wiese

Defenders
Leon Andreasen
Per Mertesacker
Naldo
Peter Niemeyer
Patrick Owomoyela
Petri Pasanen
Christian Schulz
Pierre Nlend Wome

Midfielders
Kevin Artmann
Frank Baumann
Amaury Bischoff
Tim Borowski
R da C Santos Diego
Torsten Frings
Clemens Fritz
Daniel Jensen
Jurica Vranjes

Forwards
M Hugo Almeida
Aaron Hunt
Ivan Klasnic
Miroslav Klose
Jerome Polenz
Markus Rosenberg
Kevin Schindler
Mohammed Zidan

KEY: ■ On all match   ◀◀ Subbed or sent off (Counting game)   ▶▶ Subbed on from bench (Counting Game)   ▷▷ Subbed on and then subbed or sent off (Counting Game)   ☐ Not in 16
    ■ On bench   ◀◀ Subbed or sent off (playing less than 70 minutes)   ▶▶ Subbed on (playing less than 70 minutes)   ▷▷ Subbed on and then subbed or sent off (playing less than 70 minutes)

GERMANY - WERDER BREMEN

BAYERN MUNICH

Final Position: **4th**

NICKNAME: DIE ROTEN   KEY: ☐ Won ☐ Drawn ☐ Lost   Attendance

#	Comp	Opponent		Result	Scorers	Attendance
1	grpr1	B Dortmund	H W	2-0	Makaay 24, Schweinsteiger 55	69,000
2	grpr1	Bochum	A W	2-1	Makaay 43, Lahm 65	31,328
3	grpr1	Nurnberg	H D	0-0		69,000
4	ecgpb	Spar Moscow	H W	4-0	Pizarro 48, Santa Cruz 51, Schweinsteiger 71, Salihamidzic 84	66,000
5	grpr1	Arminia B	A L	1-2	van Bommel 6	26,601
6	grpr1	Alem Aachen	H W	2-1	Pizarro 39, van Bommel 54	69,000
7	ecgpb	Inter Milan	A W	2-0	Pizarro 81, Podolski 90	79,000
8	grpr1	Wolfsburg	A L	0-1		30,000
9	grpr1	Hertha Berlin	H W	4-2	Makaay 10, Sagnol 14, Pizarro 54, Podolski 78	69,000
10	ecgpb	Sp Lisbon	A W	1-0	Schweinsteiger 19	45,000
11	grpr1	W Bremen	A L	1-3	Makaay 37	42,500
12	grpr1	Eintr Frankfurt	H W	2-0	Makaay 24, van Bommel 29	69,000
13	ecgpb	Sp Lisbon	H D	0-0		66,000
14	grpr1	Schalke	A D	2-2	Ottl 45, Makaay 52	61,482
15	grpr1	Hannover 96	H L	0-1		69,000
16	grpr1	B Leverkusen	A W	3-2	Salihamidzic 33, Demichelis 83, Pizarro 86	22,500
17	grpr1	Stuttgart	H W	2-1	Makaay 27, Pizarro 36	69,000
18	ecgpb	Spar Moscow	A D	2-2	Pizarro 22, 39	25,000
19	grpr1	Hamburg	A W	2-1	Makaay 57, Pizarro 78	57,000
20	grpr1	B M'gladbach	H D	1-1	Demichelis 23	69,000
21	ecgpb	Inter Milan	H D	1-1	Makaay 62	66,000
22	grpr1	Cottbus	H W	2-0	Schweinsteiger 42, Van Buyten 54	69,000
23	grpr1	Mainz	A W	4-0	Salihamidzic 31, Makaay 45, Pizarro 64, Schweinsteiger 65	20,300
24	grpr1	B Dortmund	A L	2-3	Van Buyten 25, Makaay 42	80,708
25	grpr1	Bochum	H D	0-0		60,000
26	grpr1	Nurnberg	A L	0-3		47,000
27	grpr1	Arminia B	H W	1-0	Makaay 8	69,000
28	grpr1	Alem Aachen	A L	0-1		20,832
29	eckl1	Real Madrid	A L	2-3	Lucio 24, van Bommel 88	80,000
30	grpr1	Wolfsburg	H W	2-1	Podolski 26 pen, van Bommel 55	69,000
31	grpr1	Hertha Berlin	A W	3-2	Salihamidzic 30, Podolski 31, Makaay 68	74,220
32	eckl2	Real Madrid	H W	2-1	Makaay 1, Lucio 66	66,000
33	grpr1	W Bremen	H D	1-1	Podolski 7	69,000
34	grpr1	Eintr Frankfurt	A L	0-1		51,500
35	grpr1	Schalke	H W	2-0	Makaay 3, Salihamidzic 78	69,000
36	ecqfl1	AC Milan	A D	2-2	Van Buyten 73, 90	60,000
37	grpr1	Hannover 96	A W	2-1	Demichelis 52, Schweinsteiger 70	49,000
38	ecqfl2	AC Milan	H L	0-2		66,000
39	grpr1	B Leverkusen	H W	2-1	van Bommel 30, Makaay 47	69,000
40	grpr1	Stuttgart	A L	0-2		57,400
41	grpr1	Hamburg	H L	1-2	Pizarro 35	69,000
42	grpr1	B M'gladbach	A D	1-1	Makaay 12	54,067
43	grpr1	Cottbus	A W	3-0	Makaay 32 pen, Van Buyten 35, Santa Cruz 61	22,450
44	grpr1	Mainz	H W	5-2	Santa Cruz 30, Scholl 33, van Bommel 38, Karimi 63, Pizarro 74	69,000

LEAGUE APPEARANCES, BOOKINGS AND CAPS

	AGE (on 01/07/07)	IN NAMED 18	APPEARANCES	COUNTING GAMES	MINUTES ON PITCH	YELLOW CARDS	RED CARDS	CAPS THIS SEASON	NATIONAL SIDE
Goalkeepers									
Bernd Dreher	42	5	1	1	90	0	0	-	Germany
Oliver Kahn	38	33	32	32	2880	4	0	-	Germany
Michael Rensing	23	30	1	1	90	0	0	-	Germany
Defenders									
Philipp Lahm	23	34	34	33	3022	3	0	9	Germany
Christian Lell	22	24	12	8	761	2	0	-	Germany
Lucio	29	28	26	25	2272	2	0	6	Brazil
Willy Sagnol	30	23	23	23	2032	9	0	8	France
Daniel Van Buyten	29	32	31	30	2727	4	0	7	Belgium
Midfielders									
Sebastian Deisler	27	4	4	0	136	0	0	-	Germany
Martin Demichelis	26	30	26	15	1740	9	0	-	Argentina
Julio Dos Santos	24	16	4	0	10	1	0	-	Paraguay
Stephan Furstner	19	7	1	0	4	0	0	-	Germany
Andreas Gorlitz	25	15	11	1	385	1	0	-	Germany
Owen Hargreaves	26	12	9	7	718	2	0	5	England
Matts Hummels	18	7	1	0	39	0	0	-	Germany
Ali Karimi	28	27	13	4	660	0	0	-	Iran
Andreas Ottl	22	31	24	18	1845	4	0	-	Germany
Hasan Salihamidzic	30	31	29	21	2123	7	0	1	Bosnia
Mehmet Scholl	36	24	14	0	306	1	0	-	Germany
B Schweinsteiger	22	27	27	25	2242	8	1	8	Germany
Mark van Bommel	30	29	29	26	2488	14	1	-	Holland
Forwards									
Stefan Maierhofer	24	4	2	0	13	0	0	-	Austria
Roy Makaay	32	34	33	27	2598	2	0	-	Holland
L C Ngwat-Mahop	19	2	1	0	3	0	0	-	Cameroon
Claudio Pizarro	28	34	33	20	2152	2	0	1	Peru
Lukas Podolski	22	23	22	9	1128	2	0	6	Germany
Roque Santa Cruz	25	32	26	11	1194	1	0	1	Paraguay

TEAM OF THE SEASON

Daniel Van Buyten **CG:** 30 **DR:** 77 (D)
Andreas Ottl **CG:** 18 **SD:** 39 (M)
Lucio **CG:** 25 **DR:** 75 (D)
Hasan Salihamidzic **CG:** 21 **SD:** 31 (M)
Roy Makaay **CG:** 27 **SR:** 162 (F)
Oliver Kahn **CG:** 32 **DR:** 77 (G)
Philipp Lahm **CG:** 33 **DR:** 75 (D)
Bastian Schweinsteiger **CG:** 25 **SD:** 21 (M)
Claudio Pizarro **CG:** 20 **SR:** 269 (F)
Willy Sagnol **CG:** 23 **DR:** 70 (D)
Mark van Bommel **CG:** 26 **SD:** 17 (M)

MONTHLY POINTS TALLY

Month		Pts	%
AUGUST		7	78%
SEPTEMBER		3	33%
OCTOBER		6	67%
NOVEMBER		10	67%
DECEMBER		7	78%
JANUARY		1	17%
FEBRUARY		6	50%
MARCH		7	58%
APRIL		6	50%
MAY		7	78%

LEAGUE GOALS

	PLAYER	MINS	GOALS	S RATE
1	Makaay	2598	16	162
2	Pizarro	2152	8	269
3	van Bommel	2488	6	414
4	Podolski	1128	4	282
5	Salihamidzic	2123	4	530
6	Schweinsteiger	2242	4	560
7	Demichelis	1740	3	580
8	Van Buyten	2727	3	909
9	Santa Cruz	1194	2	597
10	Scholl	306	1	306
11	Karimi	660	1	660
12	Ottl	1845	1	1845
13	Sagnol	2032	1	2032
	Other		1	
	TOTAL		55	

TOP POINT EARNERS

	PLAYER	GAMES	AV PTS
1	Andreas Ottl	18	2.17
2	Hasan Salihamidzic	21	1.90
3	Martin Demichelis	15	1.87
4	Mark van Bommel	26	1.77
5	Oliver Kahn	32	1.75
6	Willy Sagnol	23	1.74
7	Philipp Lahm	33	1.73
8	Roy Makaay	27	1.70
9	Daniel Van Buyten	30	1.70
10	Claudio Pizarro	20	1.65
	CLUB AVERAGE:		1.76

DISCIPLINARY RECORDS

	PLAYER	YELLOW	RED	AVE
1	Mark van Bommel	14	1	248
2	Martin Demichelis	9	0	248
3	Willy Sagnol	9	0	254
4	Bas Schweinsteiger	8	1	373
5	Christian Lell	2	0	380
6	Hasan Salihamidzic	7	0	424
7	Owen Hargreaves	2	0	718
8	Oliver Kahn	4	0	720
9	Andreas Ottl	4	0	922
10	Philipp Lahm	3	0	1007
11	Claudio Pizarro	2	0	1076
12	Lukas Podolski	2	0	1128
13	Roque Santa Cruz	1	0	1194
	Other	8	0	
	TOTAL	75	2	

KEY GOALKEEPER

Oliver Kahn

Goals Conceded in the League	37	Counting Games League games when player was on pitch for at least 70 minutes	32
Defensive Rating Ave number of mins between League goals conceded while on the pitch	77	Clean Sheets In League games when player was on pitch for at least 70 minutes	8

KEY PLAYERS - DEFENDERS

Daniel Van Buyten

Goals Conceded Number of League goals conceded while the player was on the pitch	35	Clean Sheets In League games when player was on pitch for at least 70 minutes	7
Defensive Rating Ave number of mins between League goals conceded while on the pitch	77	Club Defensive Rating Average number of mins between League goals conceded by the club this season	76

	PLAYER	CON LGE	CLEAN SHEETS	DEF RATE
1	Daniel Van Buyten	35	7	77 mins
2	Lucio	30	6	75 mins
3	Philipp Lahm	40	7	75 mins
4	Willy Sagnol	29	5	70 mins

KEY PLAYERS - MIDFIELDERS

Andreas Ottl

Goals in the League	1	Contribution to Attacking Power Average number of minutes between League team goals while on pitch	48
Defensive Rating Average number of mins between League goals conceded while on the pitch	87	Scoring Difference Defensive Rating minus Contribution to Attacking Power	39

	PLAYER	LGE GOALS	DEF RATE	POWER	SCORE DIFF
1	Andreas Ottl	1	87	48	39 mins
2	Hasan Salihamidzic	4	88	57	31 mins
3	Bastian Schweinsteiger	4	77	56	21 mins
4	Mark van Bommel	6	71	54	17 mins

KEY PLAYERS - GOALSCORERS

Roy Makaay

Goals in the League	16	Player Strike Rate Average number of minutes between League goals scored by player	162
Contribution to Attacking Power Average number of minutes between League team goals while on pitch	53	Club Strike Rate Average number of minutes between League goals scored by club	55

	PLAYER	LGE GOALS	POWER	STRIKE RATE
1	Roy Makaay	16	53	162 mins
2	Claudio Pizarro	8	53	269 mins
3	Mark van Bommel	6	54	414 mins
4	Hasan Salihamidzic	4	57	530 mins

Mark van Bommel & Roy Makaay

SQUAD APPEARANCES

Match	1	2	3	4	5		6	7	8	9	10		11	12	13	14	15		16	17	18	19	20		21	22	23	24	25		26	27	28	29	30		31	32	33	34	35		36	37	38	39	40		41	42	43	44
Venue	H	A	H	H	A		H	A	A	H	A		A	H	H	A	H		A	H	A	A	H		H	H	A	A	H		A	H	A	A	H		A	H	H	A	H		A	A	H	H	A		H	A	A	H
Competition	L	L	L	C	L		L	C	L	L	C		L	L	C	L	L		L	L	C	L	L		C	L	L	L	L		L	L	L	C	L		L	C	L	L	L		C	L	C	L	L		L	L	L	L
Result	W	W	D	W	L		W	W	L	W	W		L	W	D	D	L		W	W	D	W	D		D	W	W	L	D		L	W	L	L	W		W	W	D	L	W		D	W	L	W	L		L	D	W	W

Goalkeepers

Bernd Dreher
Oliver Kahn
Michael Rensing

Defenders

Philipp Lahm
Christian Lell
Lucio
Willy Sagnol
Daniel Van Buyten

Midfielders

Sebastian Deisler
Martin Demichelis
Julio Dos Santos
Stephan Furstner
Andreas Gorlitz
Owen Hargreaves
Matts Hummels
Ali Karimi
Andreas Ottl
Hasan Salihamidzic
Mehmet Scholl
B Schweinsteiger
Mark van Bommel

Forwards

Stefan Maierhofer
Roy Makaay
L C Ngwat-Mahop
Claudio Pizarro
Lukas Podolski
Roque Santa Cruz

KEY: ■ On all match ◄◄ Subbed or sent off (Counting game) ►► Subbed on from bench (Counting Game) ►► Subbed on and then subbed or sent off (Counting Game) □ Not in 16
■ On bench ◄◄ Subbed or sent off (playing less than 70 minutes) ►► Subbed on (playing less than 70 minutes) ►► Subbed on and then subbed or sent off (playing less than 70 minutes)

GERMANY - BAYERN MUNICH

BAYER LEVERKUSEN

Final Position: 5th

NICKNAME: BAYER-LOWEN

KEY: ☐ Won ☐ Drawn ☐ Lost

Attendance

#		Opponent			Result	Scorers	Attendance
1	grpr1	Alem Aachen	H	W	3-0	Ramelow 32, Castro 45, Rolfes 60	22,500
2	grpr1	W Bremen	A	L	1-2	Freier 15 pen	39,600
3	grpr1	Wolfsburg	H	D	1-1	Juan 49	22,500
4	ucrl1	Sion	A	D	0-0		11,000
5	grpr1	Eintr Frankfurt	A	L	1-3	Madouni 52	42,000
6	grpr1	Hannover 96	A	D	1-1	Barbarez 37	36,000
7	ucrl2	Sion	H	W	3-1	Voronin 62, Ramelow 76, Schneider 86 pen	22,500
8	grpr1	Schalke	H	W	3-1	Castro 28, 47, Ramelow 56	22,500
9	grpr1	Stuttgart	A	L	0-3		35,000
10	ucgpb	Club Brugge	A	D	1-1	Schneider 35	20,000
11	grpr1	Hamburg	H	L	1-2	Voronin 40	22,500
12	grpr1	B M'gladbach	A	W	2-0	Babic 12, Voronin 74	51,217
13	grpr1	Mainz	H	D	1-1	Barbarez 45	22,500
14	grpr1	Bochum	A	W	3-1	Barbarez 7, Voronin 32, Barnetta 71	21,000
15	grpr1	Bayern Munich	H	L	2-3	Kiessling 48, Athirson 80	22,500
16	grpr1	Nurnberg	A	L	2-3	Madouni 7, 68	37,143
17	ucgpb	Tottenham	H	L	0-1		22,500
18	grpr1	Cottbus	H	W	3-1	Barbarez 19, Rolfes 66, Voronin 79	22,500
19	ucgpb	Din Bucharest	A	L	1-2	Barbarez 22	12,000
20	grpr1	Arminia B	A	D	0-0		22,000
21	grpr1	Hertha Berlin	H	W	2-1	Freier 33, Babic 80	22,500
22	ucgpb	Besiktas	H	W	2-1	Schneider 78, Barbarez 87	22,500
23	grpr1	B Dortmund	A	W	2-1	Voronin 24, Kiessling 74	66,155
24	grpr1	Alem Aachen	A	W	3-2	Schneider 44, 57, Voronin 55	21,000
25	grpr1	W Bremen	H	L	0-2		22,500
26	grpr1	Wolfsburg	A	L	2-3	Kaluzny 29, Hofland 71 og	16,621
27	grpr1	Eintr Frankfurt	H	D	2-2	Jones 40 og, Kiessling 90	22,000
28	ucrl1	Blackburn	H	W	3-2	Callsen-Bracker 18, Ramelow 43, Schneider 56	22,500
29	grpr1	Hannover 96	H	L	0-1		22,500
30	ucrl2	Blackburn	A	D	0-0		25,124
31	grpr1	Schalke	A	W	1-0	Kiessling 85	61,482
32	grpr1	Stuttgart	H	W	3-1	Voronin 19, Freier 22, Juan 61	22,500
33	ucrl1	Lens	A	L	1-2	Haggui 51	29,200
34	grpr1	Hamburg	A	D	0-0		55,337
35	ucrl2	Lens	H	W	3-0	Voronin 36, Barbarez 55, Juan 70	22,500
36	grpr1	B M'gladbach	H	W	1-0	Voronin 90	22,500
37	grpr1	Mainz	A	W	3-1	Barbarez 42, 45, Schneider 53	20,300
38	ucqfl1	Osasuna	H	L	0-3		22,500
39	grpr1	Bochum	H	L	1-4	Kiessling 61	22,500
40	ucqfl2	Osasuna	A	L	0-1		19,800
41	grpr1	Bayern Munich	A	L	1-2	Voronin 60	69,000
42	grpr1	Nurnberg	H	W	2-0	Schneider 20, 59	22,500
43	grpr1	Cottbus	A	L	1-2	Kiessling 44	18,904
44	grpr1	Arminia B	H	L	1-2	Barbarez 30	22,500
45	grpr1	Hertha Berlin	A	W	3-2	Callsen-Bracker 13, Voronin 34, Schneider 64 pen	54,820
46	grpr1	B Dortmund	H	W	2-1	Kiessling 45, Rolfes 54	22,500

LEAGUE APPEARANCES, BOOKINGS AND CAPS

	AGE (on 01/07/07)	IN NAMED 18	APPEARANCES	COUNTING GAMES	MINUTES ON PITCH	YELLOW CARDS	RED CARDS	CAPS THIS SEASON	NATIONAL SIDE
Goalkeepers									
Rene Adler	22	13	11	11	990	0	0	-	Germany
Hans-Jorg Butt	33	32	22	21	1918	2	1	-	Germany
Erik Domaschke	21	1	0	0	0	0	0	-	Germany
Benedikt Fernandez	22	22	2	1	151	0	0	-	Germany
Defenders									
Athirson M Oliveira	30	24	12	1	456	1	0	-	Brazil
J-I Callsen-Bracker	22	25	15	10	989	4	0	-	Germany
Gonzalo Castro	20	27	26	24	2256	10	1	-	Germany
Karim Haggui	23	30	25	18	1905	12	1	-	Tunisia
Juan	28	28	28	27	2474	6	0	4	Brazil
A Reda Madouni	26	29	14	10	978	4	0	-	France
Roque Junior	30	1	1	0	22	0	0	-	Brazil
Fredrik Stenman	24	34	13	8	776	1	0	-	Sweden
Assimou Toure	19	6	1	0	45	0	0	-	Togo
Midfielders									
Marko Babic	26	29	24	19	1822	5	1	7	Croatia
Sergei Barbarez	35	33	32	29	2632	10	0	3	Bosnia
Tranquillo Barnetta	22	30	30	21	2144	6	0	3	Switzerland
Pierre De Wit	19	11	4	0	34	0	0	-	Germany
Paul Freier	27	31	31	18	1911	6	2	-	Germany
Thomas Hubener	25	2	0	0	0	0	0	-	Germany
Carsten Ramelow	33	14	13	9	1017	6	2	-	Germany
Simon Rolfes	25	34	34	32	2955	2	0	-	Germany
Bernd Schneider	33	31	31	31	2743	7	0	7	Germany
Pirmin Schwegler	20	29	21	13	1232	2	0	-	Switzerland
Forwards									
Stefan Kiessling	23	32	32	15	1829	4	1	-	Germany
Michal Papadopulos	22	19	7	0	113	0	0	-	Czech Republic
Andriy Voronin	27	32	31	20	2065	9	0	5	Ukraine

TEAM OF THE SEASON

- **D** Gonzalo Castro — CG: 24 DR: 66
- **M** Marko Babic — CG: 19 SD: 14
- **D** Juan — CG: 27 DR: 65
- **M** Bernd Schneider — CG: 31 SD: 13
- **F** Andriy Voronin — CG: 20 SR: 206
- **G** Hans-Jorg Butt — CG: 21 DR: 59
- **D** Karim Haggui — CG: 18 DR: 65
- **M** Simon Rolfes — CG: 32 SD: 8
- **F** Stefan Kiessling — CG: 15 SR: 261
- **D** Ahmed Reda Madouni* — CG: 10 DR: 61
- **M** Tranquillo Barnetta — CG: 21 SD: 7

MONTHLY POINTS TALLY

AUGUST	4	44%
SEPTEMBER	1	17%
OCTOBER	6	50%
NOVEMBER	7	47%
DECEMBER	7	78%
JANUARY	3	50%
FEBRUARY	4	33%
MARCH	10	83%
APRIL	3	25%
MAY	6	67%

LEAGUE GOALS

	PLAYER	MINS	GOALS	S RATE
1	Voronin	2065	10	206
2	Kiessling	1829	7	261
3	Barbarez	2632	7	376
4	Schneider	2743	6	457
5	Madouni	978	3	326
6	Freier	1911	3	637
7	Castro	2256	3	752
8	Rolfes	2955	3	985
9	Ramelow	1017	2	508
10	Babic	1822	2	911
11	Juan	2474	2	1237
12	Athirson	456	1	456
13	Callsen-Bracker	989	1	989
	Other		1	
	TOTAL		51	

TOP POINT EARNERS

	PLAYER	GAMES	AV PTS
1	Marko Babic	19	1.79
2	Juan	27	1.74
3	Andriy Voronin	20	1.70
4	Gonzalo Castro	24	1.67
5	Bernd Schneider	31	1.65
6	Simon Rolfes	32	1.59
7	Karim Haggui	18	1.56
8	Pirmin Schwegler	13	1.46
9	Hans-Jorg Butt	22	1.45
10	Paul Freier	19	1.42
	CLUB AVERAGE:		1.50

DISCIPLINARY RECORDS

	PLAYER	YELLOW	RED	AVE
1	Carsten Ramelow	6	2	145
2	Karim Haggui	12	1	173
3	Paul Freier	6	2	273
4	Gonzalo Castro	10	1	282
5	Andriy Voronin	9	0	295
6	A Reda Madouni	4	0	326
7	Sergei Barbarez	10	0	329
8	J-I Callsen-Bracker	4	0	329
9	Marko Babic	5	1	364
10	Stefan Kiessling	4	1	365
11	Bernd Schneider	7	0	457
12	Juan	6	0	494
13	Tranquillo Barnetta	6	0	536
	Other	8	1	
	TOTAL	97	9	

KEY GOALKEEPER

Hans-Jorg Butt

Goals Conceded in the League	32	Counting Games League games when player was on pitch for at least 70 minutes	21
Defensive Rating Ave number of mins between League goals conceded while on the pitch	59	Clean Sheets In League games when player was on pitch for at least 70 minutes	4

KEY PLAYERS - DEFENDERS

Gonzalo Castro

Goals Conceded Number of League goals conceded while the player was on the pitch	34	Clean Sheets In League games when player was on pitch for at least 70 minutes	6
Defensive Rating Ave number of mins between League goals conceded while on the pitch	66	Club Defensive Rating Average number of mins between League goals conceded by the club this season	62

	PLAYER	CON LGE	CLEAN SHEETS	DEF RATE
1	Gonzalo Castro	34	6	66 mins
2	Juan	38	7	65 mins
3	Karim Haggui	29	6	65 mins
4	Ahmed Reda Madouni	16	2	61 mins

KEY PLAYERS - MIDFIELDERS

Marko Babic

Goals in the League	2	Contribution to Attacking Power Average number of minutes between League team goals while on pitch	56
Defensive Rating Average number of minutes between League goals conceded while on the pitch	70	Scoring Difference Defensive Rating minus Contribution to Attacking Power	14

	PLAYER	LGE GOALS	DEF RATE	POWER	SCORE DIFF
1	Marko Babic	2	70	56	14 mins
2	Bernd Schneider	6	68	55	13 mins
3	Simon Rolfes	3	65	57	8 mins
4	Tranquillo Barnetta	1	61	54	7 mins

KEY PLAYERS - GOALSCORERS

Andriy Voronin

Goals in the League	10	Player Strike Rate Average number of minutes between League goals scored by player	206
Contribution to Attacking Power Average number of minutes between League team goals while on pitch	51	Club Strike Rate Average number of minutes between League goals scored by club	56

	PLAYER	LGE GOALS	POWER	STRIKE RATE
1	Andriy Voronin	10	51	206 mins
2	Stefan Kiessling	7	53	261 mins
3	Sergei Barbarez	7	59	376 mins
4	Bernd Schneider	6	55	457 mins

Andriy Voronin

SQUAD APPEARANCES

Match	1 2 3 4 5	6 7 8 9 10	11 12 13 14 15	16 17 18 19 20	21 22 23 24 25	26 27 28 29 30	31 32 33 34 35	36 37 38 39 40	41 42 43 44 45	46
Venue	H A H A A	A H H A A	H A H A H	A H H A A	H H A A H	A H H H A	A H A A H	H A H H A	A H A H A	H
Competition	L L L E L	L E L L E	L L L L L	L E L E L	L E L L L	L L E L E	L L E L E	L L E L E	L L L L L	L
Result	W L D D L	D W W L D	L W D W L	L L W L D	W W W W L	L D W L D	W W L D W	W W L L L	L W L L W	W

Goalkeepers
Rene Adler
Hans-Jorg Butt
Erik Domaschke
Benedikt Fernandez

Defenders
Athirson M Oliveira
J-I Callsen-Bracker
Gonzalo Castro
Karim Haggui
Juan
A Reda Madouni
Roque Junior
Fredrik Stenman
Assimou Toure

Midfielders
Marko Babic
Sergei Barbarez
Tranquillo Barnetta
Pierre De Wit
Paul Freier
Thomas Hubener
Carsten Ramelow
Simon Rolfes
Bernd Schneider
Pirmin Schwegler

Forwards
Stefan Kiessling
Michal Papadopulos
Andriy Voronin

KEY: ■ On all match   ◄◄ Subbed or sent off (Counting game)   ►► Subbed on from bench (Counting Game)   ►› Subbed on and then subbed or sent off (Counting Game)   □ Not in 16
  ▨ On bench   ◄ Subbed or sent off (playing less than 70 minutes)   ›› Subbed on (playing less than 70 minutes)   ›› Subbed on and then subbed or sent off (playing less than 70 minutes)

GERMANY - BAYER LEVERKUSEN

NUREMBURG

Final Position: **6th**

NICKNAME: DER CLUB7 KEY: ☐ Won ☐ Drawn ☐ Lost Attendance

#				Result	Scorers	Attendance
1	grpr1	Stuttgart	A W	3-0	Vittek 36, Schroth 45, Saenko 78	40,000
2	grpr1	B M'gladbach	H W	1-0	Schroth 5	46,780
3	grpr1	Bayern Munich	A D	0-0		69,000
4	grpr1	Bochum	H D	1-1	Polak 30	45,000
5	grpr1	Cottbus	A D	1-1	Mnari 10	16,900
6	grpr1	Mainz	H D	1-1	Polak 24	35,000
7	grpr1	Arminia B	H D	1-1	Polak 39	39,788
8	grpr1	Eintr Frankfurt	A D	2-2	Saenko 5, Pinola 48	46,000
9	grpr1	B Dortmund	H D	1-1	Mnari 59 pen	42,500
10	grpr1	Hertha Berlin	A L	1-2	Banovic 48	40,000
11	grpr1	W Bremen	H L	1-2	Banovic 90 pen	35,000
12	grpr1	Alem Aachen	A D	1-1	Galasek 29	20,800
13	grpr1	B Leverkusen	H W	3-2	Vittek 11, Schroth 47, Saenko 85	37,143
14	grpr1	Wolfsburg	A D	1-1	Reinhardt 7	20,000
15	grpr1	Schalke	H D	0-0		45,000
16	grpr1	Hamburg	A D	0-0		55,000
17	grpr1	Hannover 96	H W	3-1	Banovic 31, Schroth 55, Mnari 90	30,000
18	grpr1	Stuttgart	H W	4-1	Saenko 25, Gresko 50, Schroth 69, Magnin 76 og	35,082
19	grpr1	B M'gladbach	A D	0-0		33,116
20	grpr1	Bayern Munich	H W	3-0	Saenko 13, Schroth 71, Vittek 86	47,000
21	grpr1	Bochum	A W	2-0	Saenko 88, 90	18,110
22	grpr1	Cottbus	H W	1-0	Beauchamp 73	40,580
23	grpr1	Mainz	A L	1-2	Saenko 64	20,300
24	grpr1	Arminia B	A L	2-3	Banovic 16, Engelhardt 83	18,444
25	grpr1	Eintr Frankfurt	H D	2-2	Spycher 80 og, Vittek 87	44,055
26	grpr1	B Dortmund	A D	0-0		80,100
27	grpr1	Hertha Berlin	H W	2-1	Galasek 4, Engelhardt 60	45,649
28	grpr1	W Bremen	A L	0-1		42,100
29	grpr1	Alem Aachen	H W	1-0	Pagenburg 12	44,298
30	grpr1	B Leverkusen	A L	0-2		22,500
31	grpr1	Wolfsburg	H D	1-1	Wolf 23	44,000
32	grpr1	Schalke	A L	0-1		61,482
33	grpr1	Hamburg	H L	0-2		47,000
34	grpr1	Hannover 96	A W	3-0	Mintal 54, Engelhardt 62, Banovic 90	49,000

LEAGUE APPEARANCES, BOOKINGS AND CAPS

	AGE (on 01/07/07)	IN NAMED 18	APPEARANCES	COUNTING GAMES	MINUTES ON PITCH	YELLOW CARDS	RED CARDS	CAPS THIS SEASON	NATIONAL SIDE
Goalkeepers									
Daniel Klewer	30	34	1	0	62	1	0	-	Germany
Raphael Schafer	28	34	34	33	2998	3	0	-	Germany
Defenders									
Michael Beauchamp	26	29	18	13	1362	2	0	-	Australia
Marco Engelhardt	26	11	11	7	779	3	0	-	Germany
Leandro Glauber	23	24	20	17	1620	2	0	-	Brazil
Marek Nikl	31	24	7	3	336	1	0	-	Czech Republic
Thomas Paulus	25	19	5	0	58	0	0	-	Germany
Javier Horacio Pinola	24	32	32	29	2712	9	0	-	Argentina
Dominik Reinhardt	22	30	30	28	2583	3	0	-	Germany
Matthew Spiranovic	19	15	8	2	367	1	0	-	Australia
Andreas Wolf	25	32	32	32	2853	13	0	-	Germany
Midfielders									
Ivica Banovic	26	34	25	5	891	4	0	-	Croatia
Tomas Galasek	34	32	32	31	2726	5	1	6	Czech Republic
Vratislav Gresko	29	18	14	8	834	1	0	2	Slovakia
Jan Kristiansen	25	29	20	10	1116	1	0	2	Denmark
Marek Mintal	29	15	13	7	790	1	0	5	Slovakia
Jawhar Mnari	30	23	23	18	1813	1	1	-	Tunisia
Jan Polak	26	30	30	18	1825	4	0	9	Czech Republic
Forwards									
Leon Benko	23	15	7	0	74	0	0	-	Croatia
Chhunly Pagenburg	20	22	10	1	328	0	0	-	Germany
Ivan Saenko	24	32	32	29	2657	4	0	2	Russia
Markus Schroth	32	31	31	26	2474	3	0	-	Germany
Gerald Sibon	33	20	10	0	228	0	0	-	Holland
Robert Vittek	25	24	24	24	2116	5	0	5	Slovakia

TEAM OF THE SEASON

D Andreas Wolf CG: 32 DR: 105
M Jawhar Mnari CG: 18 SD: 56
D Javier Horacio Pinola CG: 29 DR: 100
M Tomas Galasek CG: 31 SD: 29
F Ivan Saenko CG: 29 SR: 332
G Raphael Schafer CG: 33 DR: 93
D Dominik Reinhardt CG: 28 DR: 95
M Jan Polak CG: 18 SD: -3
F Markus Schroth CG: 26 SR: 412
D Michael Beauchamp CG: 13 DR: 90
M Jan Kristiansen* CG: 10 SD: 27

MONTHLY POINTS TALLY

AUGUST		7	78%
SEPTEMBER		3	33%
OCTOBER		3	33%
NOVEMBER		5	33%
DECEMBER		5	56%
JANUARY		4	67%
FEBRUARY		9	75%
MARCH		5	42%
APRIL		4	33%
MAY		3	33%

LEAGUE GOALS

	PLAYER	MINS	GOALS	S RATE
1	Saenko	2657	8	332
2	Schroth	2474	6	412
3	Banovic	891	5	178
4	Vittek	2116	4	529
5	Engelhardt	779	3	259
6	Mnari	1813	3	604
7	Polak	1825	3	608
8	Galasek	2726	2	1363
9	Pagenburg	328	1	328
10	Mintal	790	1	790
11	Gresko	834	1	834
12	Beauchamp	1362	1	1362
13	Reinhardt	2583	1	2583
	Other		2	
	TOTAL		41	

TOP POINT EARNERS

	PLAYER	GAMES	AV PTS
1	Jawhar Mnari	19	1.63
2	Andreas Wolf	32	1.50
3	Ivan Saenko	29	1.48
4	Markus Schroth	26	1.46
5	Michael Beauchamp	13	1.46
6	Dominik Reinhardt	28	1.46
7	Tomas Galasek	31	1.42
8	Robert Vittek	24	1.38
9	Raphael Schafer	33	1.36
10	Javier Horacio Pinola	29	1.34
	CLUB AVERAGE:		1.41

DISCIPLINARY RECORDS

	PLAYER	YELLOW	RED	AVE
1	Andreas Wolf	13	0	219
2	Ivica Banovic	4	0	222
3	Marco Engelhardt	3	0	259
4	Javier H Pinola	9	0	301
5	Robert Vittek	5	0	423
6	Tomas Galasek	5	1	454
7	Jan Polak	4	0	456
8	Ivan Saenko	4	0	664
9	Michael Beauchamp	2	0	681
10	Marek Mintal	1	0	790
11	Leandro Glauber	2	0	810
12	Markus Schroth	3	0	824
13	Vratislav Gresko	1	0	834
	Other	8	1	
	TOTAL	64	2	

KEY GOALKEEPER

Raphael Schafer

Goals Conceded in the League	32	Counting Games League games when player was on pitch for at least 70 minutes	33
Defensive Rating Ave number of mins between League goals conceded while on the pitch	93	Clean Sheets In League games when player was on pitch for at least 70 minutes	12

KEY PLAYERS - DEFENDERS

Andreas Wolf

Goals Conceded Number of League goals conceded while the player was on the pitch	27	Clean Sheets In League games when player was on pitch for at least 70 minutes	12
Defensive Rating Ave number of mins between League goals conceded while on the pitch	105	Club Defensive Rating Average number of mins between League goals conceded by the club this season	95

	PLAYER	CON LGE	CLEAN SHEETS	DEF RATE
1	Andreas Wolf	27	12	105 mins
2	Javier Horacio Pinola	27	10	100 mins
3	Dominik Reinhardt	27	11	95 mins
4	Michael Beauchamp	15	6	90 mins

KEY PLAYERS - MIDFIELDERS

Jawhar Mnari

Goals in the League	3	Contribution to Attacking Power Average number of minutes between League team goals while on pitch	64
Defensive Rating Average number of mins between League goals conceded while on the pitch	120	Scoring Difference Defensive Rating minus Contribution to Attacking Power	56

	PLAYER	LGE GOALS	DEF RATE	POWER	SCORE DIFF
1	Jawhar Mnari	3	120	64	56 mins
2	Tomas Galasek	2	97	68	29 mins
3	Jan Kristiansen	0	101	74	27 mins
4	Jan Polak	3	76	79	-3 mins

KEY PLAYERS - GOALSCORERS

Ivan Saenko

Goals in the League	8	Player Strike Rate Average number of minutes between League goals scored by player	332
Contribution to Attacking Power Average number of minutes between League team goals while on pitch	71	Club Strike Rate Average number of minutes between League goals scored by club	71

	PLAYER	LGE GOALS	POWER	STRIKE RATE
1	Ivan Saenko	8	71	332 mins
2	Markus Schroth	6	79	412 mins
3	Robert Vittek	4	62	529 mins
4	Jawhar Mnari	3	64	604 mins

Markus Schroth

SQUAD APPEARANCES

Match	1	2	3	4	5	6	7	8	9	10	11	12	13	14	15	16	17	18	19	20	21	22	23	24	25	26	27	28	29	30	31	32	33	34
Venue	A	H	A	H	A	H	H	A	H	A	H	A	H	A	H	A	H	H	A	H	A	H	A	A	H	A	H	A	H	A	H	A	H	A
Competition	L	L	L	L	L	L	L	L	L	L	L	L	L	L	L	L	L	L	L	L	L	L	L	L	L	L	L	L	L	L	L	L	L	L
Result	W	W	D	D	D	D	D	D	D	L	L	D	W	D	D	D	W	W	D	W	W	W	L	L	D	D	W	L	W	L	D	L	L	W

Goalkeepers

Daniel Klewer

Raphael Schafer

Defenders

Michael Beauchamp

Marco Engelhardt

Leandro Glauber

Marek Nikl

Thomas Paulus

Javier Horacio Pinola

Dominik Reinhardt

Matthew Spiranovic

Andreas Wolf

Midfielders

Ivica Banovic

Tomas Galasek

Vratislav Gresko

Jan Kristiansen

Marek Mintal

Jawhar Mnari

Jan Polak

Forwards

Leon Benko

Chhunly Pagenburg

Ivan Saenko

Markus Schroth

Gerald Sibon

Robert Vittek

KEY: ■ On all match   ◀◀ Subbed or sent off (Counting game)   ▶▶ Subbed on from bench (Counting Game)   ▶▶ Subbed on and then subbed or sent off (Counting Game)   ☐ Not in 16
■ On bench   ◀◀ Subbed or sent off (playing less than 70 minutes)   ▶▶ Subbed on (playing less than 70 minutes)   ▶▶ Subbed on and then subbed or sent off (playing less than 70 minutes)

GERMANY - NUREMBURG

HAMBURG SV

Final Position: 7th

NICKNAME: HSV KEY: ☐ Won ☐ Drawn ☐ Lost   Attendance

#		Opponent	H/A	Result	Scorers	Attendance
1	ecql1	Osasuna	H	D	0-0		47,458
2	grpr1	Arminia B	H	D	1-1	Sanogo 67	49,713
3	grpr1	Cottbus	A	D	2-2	Sanogo 39, de Jong 72	21,000
4	ecql2	Osasuna	A	D	1-1	de Jong 74	18,766
5	grpr1	Hertha Berlin	H	D	1-1	Sanogo 18	52,000
6	ecgpg	Arsenal	H	L	1-2	Sanogo 90	51,258
7	grpr1	B Dortmund	A	L	0-1		80,000
8	grpr1	W Bremen	H	D	1-1	Reinhardt 68	57,000
9	ecgpg	CSKA Moscow	A	L	0-1		23,000
10	grpr1	Eintr Frankfurt	A	D	2-2	Ljuboja 51, Sanogo 69	45,000
11	grpr1	Schalke	H	L	1-2	Trochowski 30	57,000
12	ecgpg	Porto	A	L	1-4	Trochowski 89	31,109
13	grpr1	B Leverkusen	A	W	2-1	Guerrero 71, 86	22,500
14	grpr1	Hannover 96	H	D	0-0		57,000
15	ecgpg	Porto	H	L	1-3	Van der Vaart 62	51,000
16	grpr1	Wolfsburg	A	L	0-1		25,000
17	grpr1	Stuttgart	A	L	0-2		45,000
18	grpr1	B M'gladbach	H	D	1-1	Levels 65 og	57,000
19	grpr1	Mainz	A	D	0-0		20,300
20	ecgpg	Arsenal	A	L	1-3	Van der Vaart 4	59,962
21	grpr1	Bayern Munich	H	L	1-2	Van der Vaart 18 pen	57,000
22	grpr1	Bochum	A	L	1-2	Ljuboja 42	25,000
23	ecgpg	CSKA Moscow	H	W	3-2	Berisha 28, Van der Vaart 84, Sanogo 90	49,649
24	grpr1	Nurnberg	H	D	0-0		55,000
25	grpr1	Alem Aachen	A	D	3-3	Berisha 32, Benjamin 67, Ljuboja 76	20,500
26	grpr1	Arminia B	A	D	1-1	Ljuboja 10	26,601
27	grpr1	Cottbus	H	D	1-1	Sorin 4 pen	52,484
28	grpr1	Hertha Berlin	A	L	1-2	Laas 33	47,354
29	grpr1	B Dortmund	H	W	3-0	Van der Vaart 11 pen, Benjamin 40, Mahdavikia 89	57,000
30	grpr1	W Bremen	A	W	2-0	Van der Vaart 42 pen, 87	42,100
31	grpr1	Eintr Frankfurt	H	W	3-1	Van der Vaart 7, Trochowski 77, Olic 90	57,000
32	grpr1	Schalke	A	W	2-0	Van der Vaart 71, Olic 81	61,482
33	grpr1	B Leverkusen	H	D	0-0		55,337
34	grpr1	Hannover 96	A	D	0-0		49,000
35	grpr1	Wolfsburg	H	W	1-0	Mahdavikia 60	57,000
36	grpr1	Stuttgart	H	L	2-4	Jarolim 66, Olic 76	57,000
37	grpr1	B M'gladbach	A	W	1-0	Guerrero 90	54,067
38	grpr1	Mainz	H	D	2-2	Sorin 23 pen, Guerrero 83	57,000
39	grpr1	Bayern Munich	A	W	2-1	Van der Vaart 71, Guerrero 75	69,000
40	grpr1	Bochum	H	L	0-3		57,000
41	grpr1	Nurnberg	A	W	2-0	Van der Vaart 39, Jarolim 41	47,000
42	grpr1	Alem Aachen	H	W	4-0	Olic 15, 27, Sorin 54, 87	57,000

LEAGUE APPEARANCES, BOOKINGS AND CAPS

	AGE (on 01/07/07)	IN NAMED 18	APPEARANCES	COUNTING GAMES	MINUTES ON PITCH	YELLOW CARDS	RED CARDS	CAPS THIS SEASON	NATIONAL SIDE
Goalkeepers									
Sascha Kirschstein	27	23	9	9	810	1	1	-	Germany
Frank Rost	34	17	17	17	1518	0	0	-	Germany
Stefan Wachter	29	26	9	8	732	0	0	-	Germany
Defenders									
Mathias Abel	26	11	7	4	405	0	0	-	Germany
Timothee Atouba	25	21	21	19	1771	5	2	-	Cameroon
Rene Klingbeil	26	27	8	5	515	1	0	-	Germany
Vincent Kompany	21	6	6	6	540	1	0	2	Belgium
Joris Mathijsen	27	32	32	31	2835	4	0	11	Holland
Bastian Reinhardt	31	26	25	23	2155	2	0	-	Germany
Volker Schmidt	28	7	3	2	208	1	0	-	Germany
Juan Pablo Sorin	31	19	19	13	1433	4	0	-	Argentina
Midfielders									
Anis Ben-Hatira	18	9	5	1	160	0	1	-	Germany
Collin Benjamin	28	27	21	20	1853	4	1	-	Namibia
Nigel de Jong	22	21	18	13	1296	7	0	7	Holland
Guy Demel	26	8	8	4	567	3	1	-	Ivory Coast
Benny Feilhaber	22	16	9	6	638	0	0	6	United States
Mario Fillinger	22	11	9	3	445	2	0	-	Germany
David Jarolim	28	30	30	27	2543	15	1	6	Czech Republic
Markus Karl	21	10	2	0	12	0	0	-	Germany
Alexander Laas	23	33	21	13	1338	3	0	-	Germany
Mehdi Mahdavikia	29	30	27	19	1875	6	1	2	Iran
Piotr Trochowski	23	31	26	11	1485	3	0	4	Germany
Rafael Van der Vaart	24	26	26	25	2183	6	1	6	Holland
Raphael Wicky	30	26	14	10	906	2	0	4	Switzerland
Forwards									
Besart Berisha	21	16	12	2	351	0	0	-	Albania
Jose Paolo Guerrero	23	26	20	4	763	4	0	-	Peru
Benjamin Lauth	25	11	6	1	226	0	1	-	Germany
Danijel Ljuboja	29	16	16	10	988	1	0	2	Serbia
Ivica Olic	27	16	15	11	1109	1	0	5	Croatia
Boubacar Sanogo	24	33	31	16	1852	5	0	1	Ivory Coast

TEAM OF THE SEASON

G Frank Rost CG: 17 DR: 101

D Timothee Atouba CG: 19 DR: 118
D Bastian Reinhardt CG: 23 DR: 93
D Joris Mathijsen CG: 31 DR: 85
D Juan Pablo Sorin CG: 13 DR: 84

M Alexander Laas CG: 13 SD: 32
M Rafael Van der Vaart CG: 25 SD: 29
M David Jarolim CG: 27 SD: 17
M Collin Benjamin CG: 20 SD: 17

F Ivica Olic* CG: 11 SR: 221
F Boubacar Sanogo CG: 16 SR: 463

MONTHLY POINTS TALLY

Month		Points	%
AUGUST		3	33%
SEPTEMBER		2	22%
OCTOBER		4	44%
NOVEMBER		2	13%
DECEMBER		2	22%
JANUARY		2	33%
FEBRUARY		9	75%
MARCH		5	56%
APRIL		10	67%
MAY		6	67%

LEAGUE GOALS

	PLAYER	MINS	GOALS	S RATE
1	Van der Vaart	2183	8	272
2	Guerrero	763	5	152
3	Olic	1109	5	221
4	Ljuboja	988	4	247
5	Sorin	1433	4	358
6	Sanogo	1852	4	463
7	Trochowski	1485	2	742
8	Benjamin	1853	2	926
9	Mahdavikia	1875	2	937
10	Jarolim	2543	2	1271
11	Berisha	351	1	351
12	de Jong	1296	1	1296
13	Laas	1338	1	1338
	Other		1	
	TOTAL		**42**	

TOP POINT EARNERS

	PLAYER	GAMES	AV PTS
1	Juan Pablo Sorin	13	1.92
2	Frank Rost	17	1.88
3	Timothee Atouba	19	1.74
4	Alexander Laas	13	1.62
5	Rafael Van der Vaart	25	1.52
6	Nigel de Jong	13	1.46
7	Collin Benjamin	20	1.45
8	Bastian Reinhardt	23	1.39
9	David Jarolim	28	1.36
10	Joris Mathijsen	31	1.35
	CLUB AVERAGE:		**1.32**

DISCIPLINARY RECORDS

	PLAYER	YELLOW	RED	AVE
1	David Jarolim	15	1	169
2	Guy Demel	3	1	189
3	Jose P Guerrero	4	0	190
4	Nigel de Jong	7	0	216
5	Timothee Atouba	5	2	354
6	Mehdi Mahdavikia	6	1	375
7	Rafael V der Vaart	6	1	436
8	Alexander Laas	3	0	446
9	Raphael Wicky	2	0	453
10	Boubacar Sanogo	5	0	463
11	Collin Benjamin	4	1	463
12	Juan Pablo Sorin	4	0	477
13	Rene Klingbeil	1	0	515
	Other	13	1	
	TOTAL	**78**	**8**	

KEY GOALKEEPER

Frank Rost

Goals Conceded in the League	15	Counting Games League games when player was on pitch for at least 70 minutes	17
Defensive Rating Ave number of mins between League goals conceded while on the pitch	101	Clean Sheets In League games when player was on pitch for at least 70 minutes	9

KEY PLAYERS - DEFENDERS

Timothee Atouba

Goals Conceded Number of League goals conceded while the player was on the pitch	15	Clean Sheets In League games when player was on pitch for at least 70 minutes	10
Defensive Rating Ave number of mins between League goals conceded while on the pitch	118	Club Defensive Rating Average number of mins between League goals conceded by the club this season	82

	PLAYER	CON LGE	CLEAN SHEETS	DEF RATE
1	Timothee Atouba	15	10	118 mins
2	Bastian Reinhardt	23	10	93 mins
3	Joris Mathijsen	33	12	85 mins
4	Juan Pablo Sorin	17	6	84 mins

KEY PLAYERS - MIDFIELDERS

Alexander Laas

Goals in the League	1	Contribution to Attacking Power Average number of minutes between League team goals while on pitch	63
Defensive Rating Average number of mins between League goals conceded while on the pitch	95	Scoring Difference Defensive Rating minus Contribution to Attacking Power	32

	PLAYER	LGE GOALS	DEF RATE	POWER	SCORE DIFF
1	Alexander Laas	1	95	63	32 mins
2	Rafael Van der Vaart	8	99	70	29 mins
3	David Jarolim	2	82	65	17 mins
4	Collin Benjamin	2	80	63	17 mins

KEY PLAYERS - GOALSCORERS

Ivica Olic

Goals in the League	5	Player Strike Rate Average number of minutes between League goals scored by player	221
Contribution to Attacking Power Average number of minutes between League team goals while on pitch	58	Club Strike Rate Average number of minutes between League goals scored by club	71

	PLAYER	LGE GOALS	POWER	STRIKE RATE
1	Ivica Olic	5	58	221 mins
2	Rafael Van der Vaart	8	70	272 mins
3	Boubacar Sanogo	4	84	463 mins
4	Piotr Trochowski	2	74	742 mins

Rafael van der Vaart

SQUAD APPEARANCES

Match	1	2	3	4	5	6	7	8	9	10	11	12	13	14	15	16	17	18	19	20	21	22	23	24	25	26	27	28	29	30	31	32	33	34	35	36	37	38	39	40	41	42
Venue	H	H	A	A	H	H	A	H	A	A	H	A	A	H	H	A	A	H	A	A	H	A	H	H	A	A	H	A	H	A	H	A	H	A	H	H	A	H	A	H	A	H
Competition	C	L	L	C	L	C	L	L	C	L	L	C	L	L	C	L	L	L	L	C	L	L	C	L	L	L	L	L	L	L	L	L	L	L	L	L	L	L	L	L	L	L
Result	D	D	D	D	D	L	L	D	L	D	L	L	W	D	L	L	L	D	D	L	L	L	W	D	D	D	D	L	W	W	W	W	D	D	W	L	W	D	W	L	W	W

Goalkeepers
Sascha Kirschstein
Frank Rost
Stefan Wachter
Defenders
Mathias Abel
Timothee Atouba
Rene Klingbeil
Vincent Kompany
Joris Mathijsen
Bastian Reinhardt
Volker Schmidt
Juan Pablo Sorin
Midfielders
Anis Ben-Hatira
Collin Benjamin
Nigel de Jong
Guy Demel
Benny Feilhaber
Mario Fillinger
David Jarolim
Markus Karl
Alexander Laas
Mehdi Mahdavikia
Piotr Trochowski
Rafael Van der Vaart
Raphael Wicky
Forwards
Besart Berisha
Jose Paolo Guerrero
Benjamin Lauth
Danijel Ljuboja
Ivica Olic
Boubacar Sanogo

KEY: ■ On all match ◄◄ Subbed or sent off (Counting game) ►► Subbed on from bench (Counting Game) ►► Subbed on and then subbed or sent off (Counting Game) ☐ Not in 16
■ On bench ◄◄ Subbed or sent off (playing less than 70 minutes) ►► Subbed on (playing less than 70 minutes) ►► Subbed on and then subbed or sent off (playing less than 70 minutes)

GERMANY - HAMBURG SV

VfL BOCHUM

Final Position: 8th

NICKNAME: VFL

KEY: ☐ Won ☐ Drawn ☐ Lost

Attendance

				Result	Scorers	Attendance
1	grpr1	Mainz	A L	1-2	Zdebel 86	20,300
2	grpr1	Bayern Munich	H L	1-2	Fabio Junior 52	31,328
3	grpr1	Cottbus	H L	0-1		21,000
4	grpr1	Nurnberg	A D	1-1	Gekas 10	45,000
5	grpr1	Arminia B	H W	2-1	Fabio Junior 58, Ilicevic 73	20,318
6	grpr1	Alem Aachen	A L	1-2	Gekas 36	21,300
7	grpr1	W Bremen	H L	0-6		31,328
8	grpr1	B Dortmund	A D	1-1	Gekas 30	75,100
9	grpr1	Wolfsburg	H L	0-1		18,650
10	grpr1	Hannover 96	A W	2-0	Drsek 4, Gekas 76	28,000
11	grpr1	B Leverkusen	H L	1-3	Ilicevic 48	21,000
12	grpr1	Hertha Berlin	A D	3-3	Gekas 37, Misimovic 45, 48	28,000
13	grpr1	Eintr Frankfurt	H W	4-3	Misimovic 29 pen, Maltritz 33, Butscher 36, Gekas 46	21,260
14	grpr1	Schalke	A L	1-2	Gekas 49	61,000
15	grpr1	Hamburg	H W	2-1	Dabrowski 5, Misimovic 70	25,000
16	grpr1	Stuttgart	A L	0-1		45,000
17	grpr1	B M'gladbach	H W	2-0	Gekas 45, Kahe 85 og	30,500
18	grpr1	Mainz	H L	0-1		20,487
19	grpr1	Bayern Munich	A D	0-0		60,000
20	grpr1	Cottbus	A D	0-0		11,650
21	grpr1	Nurnberg	H L	0-2		18,110
22	grpr1	Arminia B	A W	3-1	Gekas 3, 10, Dabrowski 51	21,025
23	grpr1	Alem Aachen	H D	2-2	Gekas 25, Epalle 53	21,350
24	grpr1	W Bremen	A L	0-3		40,156
25	grpr1	B Dortmund	H W	2-0	Gekas 48, 83	31,278
26	grpr1	Wolfsburg	A L	1-3	Gekas 66	15,743
27	grpr1	Hannover 96	H W	2-0	Gekas 36, Epalle 43	24,117
28	grpr1	B Leverkusen	A W	4-1	Haggui 8 og, Yahia 16, Gekas 22, 89	22,500
29	grpr1	Hertha Berlin	H L	1-3	Gekas 1	27,181
30	grpr1	Eintr Frankfurt	A W	3-0	Gekas 32, Epalle 58, 69	47,962
31	grpr1	Schalke	H W	2-1	Misimovic 33, Gekas 41	31,328
32	grpr1	Hamburg	A W	3-0	Gekas 61, Grote 66, Misimovic 80 pen	57,000
33	grpr1	Stuttgart	H L	2-3	Schroder 4, Maltritz 42	31,328
34	grpr1	B M'gladbach	A W	2-0	Dabrowski 24, Wosz 82	50,001

LEAGUE APPEARANCES, BOOKINGS AND CAPS

	AGE (on 01/07/07)	IN NAMED 18	APPEARANCES	COUNTING GAMES	MINUTES ON PITCH	YELLOW CARDS	RED CARDS	CAPS THIS SEASON	NATIONAL SIDE
Goalkeepers									
Alexander Bade	36	16	5	5	450	0	0	-	Germany
Jaroslav Drobny	27	17	17	17	1530	2	0	-	Czech Republic
Peter Skov-Jensen	36	16	12	12	1080	0	0	-	Denmark
Defenders									
Phillip Bonig	27	33	30	26	2478	6	1	-	Germany
Heiko Butscher	26	26	30	13	1279	2	0	-	Germany
Pavel Drsek	30	33	27	14	1434	2	0	-	Czech Republic
Daniel Imhof	29	18	7	1	261	0	0	-	Canada
Benjamin Lense	28	12	8	8	720	2	0	-	Germany
Marcel Maltritz	28	31	31	30	2750	8	1	-	Germany
Martin Meichelbeck	30	22	9	2	236	0	0	-	Germany
David Pallas	26	12	8	7	652	0	1	-	Switzerland
Anthar Yahia	25	16	16	14	1344	2	0	-	Algeria
Midfielders									
Chris Dabrowski	29	33	31	26	2421	6	0	-	Germany
Joel Epalle	29	17	17	15	1400	2	0	-	Cameroon
Dennis Grote	20	22	16	7	899	3	0	-	Germany
Ivo Ilicevic	20	29	19	1	604	0	0	-	Croatia
Zvjezdan Misimovic	25	30	30	30	2600	5	0	6	Bosnia
Oliver Schroder	27	29	28	26	2428	2	0	-	Germany
Filip Trojan	24	29	26	17	1787	1	0	-	Czech Republic
Dariusz Wosz	38	5	1	0	21	0	0	-	Germany
Tomasz Zdebel	33	32	32	31	2813	13	0	-	Poland
Forwards									
Benjamin Auer	26	9	2	1	91	0	0	-	Germany
Tommy Bechmann	25	11	11	1	331	2	0	-	Denmark
Fabio Junior	29	27	16	11	1020	1	0	-	Brazil
Theofanis Gekas	27	32	32	31	2778	0	0	5	Greece
Sebastian Hille	26	1	1	0	14	0	0	-	Germany
Thomas Rathgeber	22	7	1	0	11	0	0	-	Germany
Joris Van Hout	30	28	13	0	168	0	0	-	Belgium

TEAM OF THE SEASON

G Peter Skov-Jensen CG: 12 DR: 49

D Anthar Yahia CG: 14 DR: 84
D Marcel Maltritz CG: 30 DR: 61
D Pavel Drsek CG: 14 DR: 59
D Phillip Bonig CG: 26 DR: 56

M Joel Epalle CG: 15 SD: 26
M Oliver Schroder CG: 26 SD: 15
M Zvjezdan Misimovic CG: 30 SD: 11
M Tomasz Zdebel CG: 31 SD: -1

F Theofanis Gekas CG: 31 SR: 132
F Fabio Junior* CG: 11 SR: 510

MONTHLY POINTS TALLY

AUGUST		0	0%
SEPTEMBER		4	44%
OCTOBER		1	11%
NOVEMBER		7	47%
DECEMBER		6	67%
JANUARY		1	17%
FEBRUARY		5	42%
MARCH		3	33%
APRIL		12	80%
MAY		6	67%

LEAGUE GOALS

	PLAYER	MINS	GOALS	S RATE
1	Gekas	2778	21	132
2	Misimovic	2600	6	433
3	Epalle	1400	4	350
4	Dabrowski	2421	3	807
5	Ilicevic	604	2	302
6	Fabio Junior	1020	2	510
7	Maltritz	2750	2	1375
8	Wosz	21	1	21
9	Grote	899	1	899
10	Butscher	1279	1	1279
11	Yahia	1344	1	1344
12	Drsek	1434	1	1434
13	Schroder	2428	1	2428
	Other		1	
	TOTAL		**47**	

TOP POINT EARNERS

	PLAYER	GAMES	AV PTS
1	Anthar Yahia	14	1.71
2	Joel Epalle	15	1.60
3	Jaroslav Drobny	17	1.59
4	Oliver Schroder	26	1.58
5	Theofanis Gekas	31	1.45
6	Zvjezdan Misimovic	30	1.40
7	Marcel Maltritz	31	1.35
8	Heiko Butscher	13	1.31
9	Tomasz Zdebel	31	1.26
10	Christophe Dabrowski	26	1.19
	CLUB AVERAGE:		**1.32**

DISCIPLINARY RECORDS

	PLAYER	YELLOW	RED	AVE
1	Tomasz Zdebel	13	0	216
2	Dennis Grote	3	0	299
3	Marcel Maltritz	8	1	305
4	Phillip Bonig	6	1	354
5	Benjamin Lense	2	0	360
6	C Dabrowski	6	0	403
7	Zvjezdan Misimovic	5	0	520
8	Heiko Butscher	2	0	639
9	David Pallas	0	1	652
10	Anthar Yahia	2	0	672
11	Joel Epalle	2	0	700
12	Pavel Drsek	2	0	717
13	Jaroslav Drobny	2	0	765
	Other	4	0	
	TOTAL	**57**	**3**	

407

KEY GOALKEEPER

Peter Skov-Jensen

Goals Conceded in the League	22	Counting Games League games when player was on pitch for at least 70 minutes	12
Defensive Rating Ave number of mins between League goals conceded while on the pitch	49	Clean Sheets In League games when player was on pitch for at least 70 minutes	1

KEY PLAYERS - DEFENDERS

Anthar Yahia

Goals Conceded Number of League goals conceded while the player was on the pitch	16	Clean Sheets In League games when player was on pitch for at least 70 minutes	7
Defensive Rating Ave number of mins between League goals conceded while on the pitch	84	Club Defensive Rating Average number of mins between League goals conceded by the club this season	61

	PLAYER	CON LGE	CLEAN SHEETS	DEF RATE
1	Anthar Yahia	16	7	84 mins
2	Marcel Maltritz	45	8	61 mins
3	Pavel Drsek	24	2	59 mins
4	Phillip Bonig	44	5	56 mins

KEY PLAYERS - MIDFIELDERS

Joel Epalle

Goals in the League	4	Contribution to Attacking Power Average number of minutes between League team goals while on pitch	56
Defensive Rating Average number of mins between League goals conceded while on the pitch	82	Scoring Difference Defensive Rating minus Contribution to Attacking Power	26

	PLAYER	LGE GOALS	DEF RATE	POWER	SCORE DIFF
1	Joel Epalle	4	82	56	26 mins
2	Oliver Schroder	1	71	56	15 mins
3	Zvjezdan Misimovic	6	70	59	11 mins
4	Tomasz Zdebel	1	62	63	-1 mins

KEY PLAYERS - GOALSCORERS

Theofanis Gekas

Goals in the League	21	Player Strike Rate Average number of minutes between League goals scored by player	132
Contribution to Attacking Power Average number of minutes between League team goals while on pitch	59	Club Strike Rate Average number of minutes between League goals scored by club	62

	PLAYER	LGE GOALS	POWER	STRIKE RATE
1	Theofanis Gekas	21	59	132 mins
2	Joel Epalle	4	56	350 mins
3	Zvjezdan Misimovic	6	59	433 mins
4	Fabio Junior	2	102	510 mins

Tomasz Zdebel & Theofanis Gekas

SQUAD APPEARANCES

Match	1	2	3	4	5	6	7	8	9	10	11	12	13	14	15	16	17	18	19	20	21	22	23	24	25	26	27	28	29	30	31	32	33	34
Venue	A	H	H	A	H	A	H	A	H	A	H	A	H	A	H	A	H	H	A	A	H	A	H	A	H	A	H	A	H	A	H	A	H	A
Competition	L	L	L	L	L	L	L	L	L	L	L	L	L	L	L	L	L	L	L	L	L	L	L	L	L	L	L	L	L	L	L	L	L	L
Result	L	L	L	D	W	L	L	D	L	W	L	D	W	L	W	L	W	L	D	D	L	W	D	L	W	L	W	L	W	L	W	W	L	W

Goalkeepers
Alexander Bade
Jaroslav Drobny
Peter Skov-Jensen

Defenders
Phillip Bonig
Heiko Butscher
Pavel Drsek
Daniel Imhof
Benjamin Lense
Marcel Maltritz
Martin Meichelbeck
David Pallas
Anthar Yahia

Midfielders
Chris Dabrowski
Joel Epalle
Dennis Grote
Ivo Ilicevic
Zvjezdan Misimovic
Oliver Schroder
Filip Trojan
Dariusz Wosz
Tomasz Zdebel

Forwards
Benjamin Auer
Tommy Bechmann
Fabio Junior
Theofanis Gekas
Sebastian Hille
Thomas Rathgeber
Joris Van Hout

KEY: ■ On all match ◄◄ Subbed or sent off (Counting game) ▸▸▸ Subbed on from bench (Counting Game) ▸▸ Subbed on and then subbed or sent off (Counting Game) □ Not in 16
■ On bench ◄ Subbed or sent off (playing less than 70 minutes) ▸▸ Subbed on (playing less than 70 minutes) ▸ Subbed on and then subbed or sent off (playing less than 70 minutes)

GERMANY - VfL BOCHUM

BORUSSIA DORTMUND

Final Position: **9th**

NICKNAME: DIE SCHWARZ-GELBEN   KEY: ☐ Won ☐ Drawn ☐ Lost   Attendance

1	grpr1	**Bayern Munich**	A L	0-2	69,000
2	grpr1	**Mainz**	H D	1-1 Amedick 76	70,100
3	grpr1	**Stuttgart**	A W	3-1 Magnin 20, Kringe 32, Frei 88	38,000
4	grpr1	**Hamburg**	H W	1-0 Worns 82	80,000
5	grpr1	**B M'gladbach**	A L	0-1	54,000
6	grpr1	**Hannover 96**	H D	2-2 Smolarek 5, 76	66,100
7	grpr1	**Cottbus**	A W	3-2 Brzenska 1, 57, Frei 59	19,699
8	grpr1	**Bochum**	H D	1-1 Smolarek 35	75,100
9	grpr1	**Nurnberg**	A D	1-1 Tinga 87	42,500
10	grpr1	**Arminia B**	H D	1-1 Frei 90 pen	72,000
11	grpr1	**Alem Aachen**	H D	0-0	65,000
12	grpr1	**W Bremen**	A W	3-1 Frei 7, Tinga 53, Kruska 84 pen	421,000
13	grpr1	**Hertha Berlin**	H L	1-2 Frei 21 pen	70,000
14	grpr1	**Eintr Frankfurt**	A D	1-1 Smolarek 79	51,000
15	grpr1	**Wolfsburg**	H W	1-0 Smolarek 90	62,000
16	grpr1	**Schalke**	A L	1-3 Frei 83	61,482
17	grpr1	**B Leverkusen**	H L	1-2 Amedick 85	66,155
18	grpr1	**Bayern Munich**	H W	3-2 Frei 12, 56, Tinga 59	80,708
19	grpr1	**Mainz**	A L	0-1	20,300
20	grpr1	**Stuttgart**	H L	0-1	63,600
21	grpr1	**Hamburg**	A L	0-3	57,000
22	grpr1	**B M'gladbach**	H W	1-0 Frei 19	73,600
23	grpr1	**Hannover 96**	A L	2-4 Smolarek 88, Kringe 90	43,852
24	grpr1	**Cottbus**	H L	2-3 Frei 42, 86	64,100
25	grpr1	**Bochum**	A L	0-2	31,278
26	grpr1	**Nurnberg**	H D	0-0	80,100
27	grpr1	**Arminia B**	A L	0-1	26,601
28	grpr1	**Alem Aachen**	A W	4-1 Worns 14, Frei 54, 58, Tinga 61	20,800
29	grpr1	**W Bremen**	H L	0-2	80,500
30	grpr1	**Hertha Berlin**	A W	1-0 Brzenska 49	64,382
31	grpr1	**Eintr Frankfurt**	H W	2-0 Frei 39, 60	80,708
32	grpr1	**Wolfsburg**	A W	2-0 Smolarek 12, Valdez 90	30,000
33	grpr1	**Schalke**	H W	2-0 Frei 44, Smolarek 85	80,708
34	grpr1	**B Leverkusen**	A L	1-2 Smolarek 79	22,500

LEAGUE APPEARANCES, BOOKINGS AND CAPS

	AGE (on 01/07/07)	IN NAMED 18	APPEARANCES	COUNTING GAMES	MINUTES ON PITCH	YELLOW CARDS	RED CARDS	CAPS THIS SEASON	NATIONAL SIDE
Goalkeepers									
Soren Pirson	21	31	0	0	0	0	0	-	Germany
Roman Weidenfeller	26	34	34	34	3060	2	0	-	Germany
Defenders									
Martin Amedick	24	26	18	12	1162	0	0	-	Germany
Markus Brzenska	23	33	25	20	1915	8	0	-	Germany
Philipp Degen	24	30	27	22	2116	7	0	5	Switzerland
Marc Heitmeier	22	1	0	0	0	0	0	-	Germany
Uwe Hunemeier	21	24	1	0	1	0	0	-	Germany
Sebastian Kehl	27	9	6	1	253	1	0	-	Germany
Patrick Kohlmann	24	1	0	0	0	0	0	-	Germany
Christoph Metzelder	26	19	19	16	1493	1	0	4	Germany
Christian Worns	35	26	24	24	2150	1	0	-	Germany
Midfielders									
Leonardo Dede	29	30	30	28	2600	2	1	-	Brazil
Daniel Gordon	22	6	5	0	106	0	0	-	Germany
Florian Kringe	24	34	34	31	2901	3	0	-	Germany
Marc-Andre Kruska	20	33	31	27	2507	10	0	-	Germany
Steven Pienaar	25	30	25	17	1729	2	0	1	South Africa
Lars Ricken	30	21	13	4	550	1	0	-	Germany
Nuri Sahin	18	33	24	8	1186	0	0	1	Turkey
Sahr Senesie	22	1	0	0	0	0	0	-	Sierra Leone
Sebastian Tyrala	19	21	6	0	120	0	0	-	Germany
Forwards									
Matthew Amoah	26	18	9	2	261	0	0	-	Ghana
Alexander Frei	27	32	32	28	2603	9	0	5	Switzerland
David Odonkor	23	3	2	1	115	0	0	5	Germany
Kosi Saka	21	6	6	0	82	0	0	-	Congo DR
Ebi Smolarek	26	30	30	24	2251	3	0	7	Poland
Tinga	27	31	31	29	2697	8	0	2	Brazil
Nelson Haedo Valdez	23	29	29	15	1722	6	1	-	Paraguay

TEAM OF THE SEASON

D Christian Worns CG: 24 DR: 82
M Steven Pienaar CG: 17 SD: 34
D Markus Brzenska CG: 20 DR: 73
M Marc-Andre Kruska CG: 27 SD: 15
F Alexander Frei CG: 28 SR: 162
G Roman Weidenfeller CG: 34 DR: 71
D Philipp Degen CG: 22 DR: 68
M Leonardo Dede CG: 28 SD: 0
F Ebi Smolarek CG: 24 SR: 250
D Christoph Metzelder CG: 16 DR: 64
M Florian Kringe CG: 31 SD: -9

MONTHLY POINTS TALLY

AUGUST	4	44%
SEPTEMBER	4	44%
OCTOBER	5	56%
NOVEMBER	6	40%
DECEMBER	3	33%
JANUARY	3	50%
FEBRUARY	3	25%
MARCH	1	8%
APRIL	9	75%
MAY	6	67%

LEAGUE GOALS

	PLAYER	MINS	GOALS	S RATE
1	Frei	2603	16	162
2	Smolarek	2251	9	250
3	Tinga	2697	4	674
4	Brzenska	1915	3	638
5	Amedick	1162	2	581
6	Worns	2150	2	1075
7	Kringe	2901	2	1450
8	Valdez	1722	1	1722
9	Kruska	2507	1	2507
10	Meier	0	0	
11	Metzelder, C	1493	0	
12	Odonkor	115	0	
13	Pienaar	1729	0	
	Other		0	
	TOTAL		**40**	

TOP POINT EARNERS

	PLAYER	GAMES	AV PTS
1	Steven Pienaar	17	**1.82**
2	Markus Brzenska	20	**1.65**
3	Alexander Frei	28	**1.50**
4	Marc-Andre Kruska	27	**1.48**
5	Tinga	29	**1.45**
6	Christian Worns	24	**1.42**
7	Leonardo Dede	29	**1.31**
8	Ebi Smolarek	24	**1.29**
9	Roman Weidenfeller	34	**1.29**
10	Florian Kringe	31	**1.23**
	CLUB AVERAGE:		**1.29**

DISCIPLINARY RECORDS

	PLAYER	YELLOW	RED	AVE
1	Markus Brzenska	8	0	239
2	Nelson H Valdez	6	1	246
3	Marc-Andre Kruska	10	0	250
4	Alexander Frei	9	0	289
5	Philipp Degen	7	0	302
6	Tinga	8	0	337
7	Lars Ricken	1	0	550
8	Ebi Smolarek	3	0	750
9	Steven Pienaar	2	0	864
10	Leonardo Dede	2	1	866
11	Florian Kringe	3	0	967
12	Christoph Metzelder	1	0	1493
13	Roman Weidenfeller	2	0	1530
	Other		1	
	TOTAL	**63**	**2**	

KEY GOALKEEPER

Roman Weidenfeller

Goals Conceded in the League	43	Counting Games League games when player was on pitch for at least 70 minutes	34
Defensive Rating Ave number of mins between League goals conceded while on the pitch	71	Clean Sheets In League games when player was on pitch for at least 70 minutes	9

KEY PLAYERS - DEFENDERS

Christian Worns

Goals Conceded Number of League goals conceded while the player was on the pitch	26	Clean Sheets In League games when player was on pitch for at least 70 minutes	7
Defensive Rating Ave number of mins between League goals conceded while on the pitch	82	Club Defensive Rating Average number of mins between League goals conceded by the club this season	71

	PLAYER	CON LGE	CLEAN SHEETS	DEF RATE
1	Christian Worns	26	7	82 mins
2	Markus Brzenska	26	7	73 mins
3	Philipp Degen	31	5	68 mins
4	Christoph Metzelder	23	5	64 mins

KEY PLAYERS - MIDFIELDERS

Steven Pienaar

Goals in the League	0	Contribution to Attacking Power Average number of minutes between League team goals while on pitch	57
Defensive Rating Average number of mins between League goals conceded while on the pitch	91	Scoring Difference Defensive Rating minus Contribution to Attacking Power	34

	PLAYER	LGE GOALS	DEF RATE	POWER	SCORE DIFF
1	Steven Pienaar	0	91	57	34 mins
2	Marc-Andre Kruska	1	86	71	15 mins
3	Leonardo Dede	0	74	74	0 mins
4	Florian Kringe	2	69	78	-9 mins

KEY PLAYERS - GOALSCORERS

Alexander Frei

Goals in the League	16	Player Strike Rate Average number of minutes between League goals scored by player	162
Contribution to Attacking Power Average number of minutes between League team goals while on pitch	83	Club Strike Rate Average number of minutes between League goals scored by club	74

	PLAYER	LGE GOALS	POWER	STRIKE RATE
1	Alexander Frei	16	83	162 mins
2	Ebi Smolarek	9	64	250 mins
3	Tinga	4	72	674 mins
4	Florian Kringe	2	78	1450 mins

Alexander Frei

SQUAD APPEARANCES

Match	1	2	3	4	5		6	7	8	9	10		11	12	13	14	15		16	17	18	19	20		21	22	23	24	25		26	27	28	29	30		31	32	33	34
Venue	A	H	A	H	A		H	A	H	A	H		H	A	H	A	H		A	H	H	A	H		A	H	A	H	A		H	A	A	H	A		H	A	H	A
Competition	L	L	L	L	L		L	L	L	L	L		L	L	L	L	L		L	L	L	L	L		L	L	L	L	L		L	L	L	L	L		L	L	L	L
Result	L	D	W	W	L		D	W	D	D	D		D	W	L	D	W		L	L	W	L	L		L	W	L	L	L		D	L	W	L	W		W	W	W	L

Goalkeepers
Soren Pirson
Roman Weidenfeller

Defenders
Martin Amedick
Markus Brzenska
Philipp Degen
Marc Heitmeier
Uwe Hunemeier
Sebastian Kehl
Patrick Kohlmann
Christoph Metzelder
Christian Worns

Midfielders
Leonardo Dede
Daniel Gordon
Florian Kringe
Marc-Andre Kruska
Steven Pienaar
Lars Ricken
Nuri Sahin
Sahr Senesie
Sebastian Tyrala

Forwards
Matthew Amoah
Alexander Frei
David Odonkor
Kosi Saka
Ebi Smolarek
Tinga
Nelson Haedo Valdez

KEY: ■ On all match   ◄◄ Subbed or sent off (Counting game)   ▶▶ Subbed on from bench (Counting Game)   ▶▶ Subbed on and then subbed or sent off (Counting Game)   ☐ Not in 16
     ☐ On bench   ◄◄ Subbed or sent off (playing less than 70 minutes)   ▶▶ Subbed on (playing less than 70 minutes)   ▶▶ Subbed on and then subbed or sent off (playing less than 70 minutes)

GERMANY - BORUSSIA DORTMUND

HERTHA BERLIN

Final Position: 10th

NICKNAME: FROSCHE   KEY: ☐ Won ☐ Drawn ☐ Lost   Attendance

#		Opponent			Score	Scorers	Attendance
1	grpr1	Wolfsburg	A	D	0-0		23,496
2	grpr1	Hannover 96	H	W	4-0	Pantelic 20, 63, Dardai 31, Ebert 76	37,166
3	ucql2	Ameri Tbilisi	A	D	2-2	Lakic 35, Pantelic 84	4,000
4	grpr1	Hamburg	A	D	1-1	Gimenez 64	52,000
5	ucrl1	Odense	H	D	2-2	Gimenez 38, Boateng 50	12,800
6	grpr1	Schalke	H	W	2-0	Gimenez 39, 50	60,000
7	grpr1	Mainz	A	D	1-1	Boateng 55	20,300
8	ucrl2	Odense	A	L	0-1		15,000
9	grpr1	Stuttgart	H	D	2-2	Friedrich 9, Pantelic 14	48,637
10	grpr1	Bayern Munich	A	L	2-4	Fathi 58, Pantelic 73	69,000
11	grpr1	B M'gladbach	H	W	2-1	Dardai 48, Okoronkwo 70	43,604
12	grpr1	Cottbus	A	L	0-2		17,525
13	grpr1	Nurnberg	H	W	2-1	Pantelic 30, 65	40,000
14	grpr1	Arminia B	A	D	2-2	Gilberto 45, Gimenez 58	20,000
15	grpr1	Bochum	H	D	3-3	Pantelic 10, Van Burik 59, Neuendorf 80	28,000
16	grpr1	B Dortmund	A	W	2-1	Schmidt 10, Gilberto 15	70,000
17	grpr1	Alem Aachen	H	W	2-1	Pantelic 41, Dejagah 62	35,000
18	grpr1	W Bremen	A	L	1-3	Simunic 24	39,000
19	grpr1	B Leverkusen	A	L	1-2	Pantelic 22	22,500
20	grpr1	Eintr Frankfurt	H	W	1-0	Gimenez 63	40,000
21	grpr1	Wolfsburg	H	W	2-1	Gimenez 27, Pantelic 86 pen	40,272
22	grpr1	Hannover 96	A	L	0-5		30,584
23	grpr1	Hamburg	H	W	2-1	Friedrich 78, Mineiro 90	47,354
24	grpr1	Schalke	A	L	0-2		61,482
25	grpr1	Mainz	H	L	1-2	Dardai 22	35,473
26	grpr1	Stuttgart	A	D	0-0		41,000
27	grpr1	Bayern Munich	H	L	2-3	Gimenez 59, Van Burik 82	74,220
28	grpr1	B M'gladbach	A	L	1-3	Gimenez 56	40,518
29	grpr1	Cottbus	H	L	0-1		51,831
30	grpr1	Nurnberg	A	L	1-2	Gimenez 69	45,649
31	grpr1	Arminia B	H	D	1-1	Ebert 71	41,512
32	grpr1	Bochum	A	W	3-1	Gimenez 57, Dardai 65, Ede 90	27,181
33	grpr1	B Dortmund	H	L	0-1		64,382
34	grpr1	Alem Aachen	A	W	4-0	Gilberto 6, Gimenez 48, Pantelic 77, Basturk 80	20,800
35	grpr1	W Bremen	H	L	1-4	Gilberto 63	74,220
36	grpr1	B Leverkusen	H	L	2-3	Pantelic 32, Gimenez 51	54,820
37	grpr1	Eintr Frankfurt	A	W	2-1	K.Boateng 48, Pantelic 87	50,500

LEAGUE APPEARANCES, BOOKINGS AND CAPS

	AGE (on 01/07/07)	IN NAMED 18	APPEARANCES	COUNTING GAMES	MINUTES ON PITCH	YELLOW CARDS	RED CARDS	CAPS THIS SEASON	NATIONAL SIDE
Goalkeepers									
Christian Fiedler	32	32	32	32	2880	1	0	-	Germany
Kevin Stuhr-Ellegaard	24	28	2	2	180	0	0	-	Denmark
Defenders									
Jerome Boateng	18	11	10	6	653	3	0	-	Germany
Sofian Chahed	24	22	20	16	1563	4	2	-	Germany
Malik Fathi	23	33	31	24	2355	6	0	2	Germany
Arne Friedrich	28	26	26	25	2295	5	0	6	Germany
Christopher Samba	23	13	8	0	99	1	0	-	France
Christopher Schorch	18	5	2	0	18	0	0	-	Germany
Josip Simunic	29	25	25	24	2175	7	3	7	Croatia
Dick Van Burik	33	28	28	26	2379	8	0	-	Holland
AWallschlager	21	2	1	0	2	0	0	-	Germany
Midfielders									
Yildiray Basturk	28	19	19	15	1438	2	0	3	Turkey
K-P Boateng	20	22	21	12	1454	8	0	-	Germany
Pal Dardai	31	28	28	26	2412	4	0	-	Hungary
Patrick Ebert	20	32	19	8	1057	2	0	-	Germany
Gilberto	30	30	30	29	2595	5	0	6	Brazil
Mineiro	31	14	10	7	765	1	0	5	Brazil
Christian Muller	23	15	7	0	126	0	0	-	Germany
Andreas Neuendorf	32	28	18	2	477	6	0	-	Germany
Andreas Schmidt	33	22	12	10	879	0	0	-	Germany
Forwards									
Ellery Cairo	28	20	11	3	496	1	0	-	Holland
Ashkan Dejagah	20	27	22	15	1474	5	1	-	Iran
Chinedu Ede	20	22	14	3	540	1	0	-	Germany
Christian Gimenez	32	30	28	23	2150	3	0	-	Argentina
Srdjan Lakic	23	23	11	1	322	1	0	-	Croatia
Solomon Okoronkwo	20	11	6	2	229	1	1	-	Nigeria
Marko Pantelic	28	32	32	27	2546	6	0	7	Serbia

TEAM OF THE SEASON

G Christian Fiedler CG: 32 DR: 58

D Josip Simunic CG: 24 DR: 65
D Sofian Chahed CG: 16 DR: 60
D Dick Van Burik CG: 26 DR: 55
D Arne Friedrich CG: 25 DR: 52

M Yildiray Basturk CG: 15 SD: 0
M Gilberto CG: 29 SD: -4
M Kevin-Prince Boateng CG: 12 SD: -7
M Pal Dardai CG: 26 SD: -11

F Christian Gimenez CG: 23 SR: 179
F Marko Pantelic CG: 27 SR: 195

MONTHLY POINTS TALLY

Month	Points	%
AUGUST	5	56%
SEPTEMBER	4	67%
OCTOBER	4	33%
NOVEMBER	11	73%
DECEMBER	3	33%
JANUARY	3	50%
FEBRUARY	4	33%
MARCH	0	0%
APRIL	7	58%
MAY	3	33%

LEAGUE GOALS

	PLAYER	MINS	GOALS	S RATE
1	Pantelic	2546	13	195
2	Gimenez	2150	12	179
3	Dardai	2412	4	603
4	Gilberto	2595	4	648
5	Ebert	1057	2	528
6	Boateng, K	1454	2	727
7	Friedrich	2295	2	1147
8	Van Burik	2379	2	1189
9	Okoronkwo	229	1	229
10	Neuendorf	477	1	477
11	Ede	540	1	540
12	Mineiro	765	1	765
13	Schmidt	879	1	879
	Other		4	
	TOTAL		**50**	

TOP POINT EARNERS

	PLAYER	GAMES	AV PTS
1	Yildiray Basturk	15	1.60
2	Ashkan Dejagah	15	1.53
3	Malik Fathi	24	1.50
4	Kevin-Prince Boateng	12	1.50
5	Marko Pantelic	27	1.48
6	Christian Gimenez	23	1.43
7	Arne Friedrich	25	1.40
8	Sofian Chahed	16	1.38
9	Dick Van Burik	26	1.35
10	Gilberto	29	1.34
	CLUB AVERAGE:		**1.29**

DISCIPLINARY RECORDS

	PLAYER	YELLOW	RED	AVE
1	Andreas Neuendorf	5	0	95
2	Kevin-P Boateng	8	0	207
3	Jerome Boateng	3	0	217
4	Josip Simunic	7	3	241
5	Ashkan Dejagah	5	1	245
6	Sofian Chahed	4	2	260
7	Dick Van Burik	8	0	297
8	Malik Fathi	6	0	392
9	Arne Friedrich	5	0	459
10	Ellery Cairo	1	0	496
11	Marko Pantelic	6	0	509
12	Gilberto	5	0	519
13	Patrick Ebert	2	0	528
	Other	12	0	
	TOTAL	**77**	**6**	

KEY GOALKEEPER

Christian Fiedler

Goals Conceded in the League	49	Counting Games League games when player was on pitch for at least 70 minutes	32
Defensive Rating Ave number of mins between League goals conceded while on the pitch	58	Clean Sheets In League games when player was on pitch for at least 70 minutes	6

KEY PLAYERS - DEFENDERS

Josip Simunic

Goals Conceded Number of League goals conceded while the player was on the pitch	33	Clean Sheets In League games when player was on pitch for at least 70 minutes	5
Defensive Rating Ave number of mins between League goals conceded while on the pitch	65	Club Defensive Rating Average number of mins between League goals conceded by the club this season	55

	PLAYER	CON LGE	CLEAN SHEETS	DEF RATE
1	Josip Simunic	33	5	65 mins
2	Sofian Chahed	26	2	60 mins
3	Dick Van Burik	43	4	55 mins
4	Arne Friedrich	44	5	52 mins

KEY PLAYERS - MIDFIELDERS

Yildiray Basturk

Goals in the League	1	Contribution to Attacking Power Average number of minutes between League team goals while on pitch	62
Defensive Rating Average number of mins between League goals conceded while on the pitch	62	Scoring Difference Defensive Rating minus Contribution to Attacking Power	0

	PLAYER	LGE GOALS	DEF RATE	POWER	SCORE DIFF
1	Yildiray Basturk	1	62	62	0 mins
2	Gilberto	4	56	60	-4 mins
3	Kevin-Prince Boateng	2	53	60	-7 mins
4	Pal Dardai	4	54	65	-11 mins

KEY PLAYERS - GOALSCORERS

Christian Gimenez

Goals in the League	12	Player Strike Rate Average number of minutes between League goals scored by player	179
Contribution to Attacking Power Average number of minutes between League team goals while on pitch	61	Club Strike Rate Average number of minutes between League goals scored by club	61

	PLAYER	LGE GOALS	POWER	STRIKE RATE
1	Christian Gimenez	12	61	179 mins
2	Marko Pantelic	13	60	195 mins
3	Pal Dardai	4	65	603 mins
4	Gilberto	4	60	648 mins

Marko Pantelic, Christian Gimenez & Jerome Boateng

SQUAD APPEARANCES

Match	1	2	3	4	5	6	7	8	9	10	11	12	13	14	15	16	17	18	19	20	21	22	23	24	25	26	27	28	29	30	31	32	33	34	35	36	37
Venue	A	H	A	A	H	H	A	A	H	A	H	A	H	A	H	A	H	A	A	H	H	A	H	A	H	A	H	A	H	A	H	A	H	A	H	H	A
Competition	L	L	E	L	E	L	L	E	L	L	L	L	L	L	L	L	L	L	L	L	L	L	L	L	L	L	L	L	L	L	L	L	L	L	L	L	L
Result	D	W	D	D	D	W	D	L	D	L	W	L	W	D	D	W	W	L	L	W	W	L	W	L	L	D	L	L	L	L	D	W	L	W	L	L	W

Goalkeepers
Christian Fiedler
Kevin Stuhr-Ellegaard

Defenders
Jerome Boateng
Sofian Chahed
Malik Fathi
Arne Friedrich
Christopher Samba
Christopher Schorch
Josip Simunic
Dick Van Burik
A Wallschlager

Midfielders
Yildiray Basturk
K-P Boateng
Pal Dardai
Patrick Ebert
Gilberto
Mineiro
Christian Muller
Andreas Neuendorf
Andreas Schmidt

Forwards
Ellery Cairo
Ashkan Dejagah
Chinedu Ede
Christian Gimenez
Srdjan Lakic
Solomon Okoronkwo
Marko Pantelic

KEY: ■ On all match ◀◀ Subbed or sent off (Counting game) ▶▶ Subbed on from bench (Counting Game) ▶▶ Subbed on and then subbed or sent off (Counting Game) □ Not in 16
■ On bench ◀◀ Subbed or sent off (playing less than 70 minutes) ▶▶ Subbed on (playing less than 70 minutes) ▶▶ Subbed on and then subbed or sent off (playing less than 70 minutes)

GERMANY - HERTHA BERLIN

HANNOVER 96

Final Position: 11th

NICKNAME: DIE ROTEN   **KEY:** ☐ Won ☐ Drawn ☐ Lost   Attendance

1	grpr1	W Bremen	H L	2-4	Stajner 41, Hashemian 66	49,000
2	grpr1	Hertha Berlin	A L	0-4		37,166
3	grpr1	Alem Aachen	H L	0-3		30,087
4	grpr1	Wolfsburg	A W	2-1	Brdaric 50, 62	21,000
5	grpr1	B Leverkusen	H D	1-1	Brdaric 74	36,000
6	grpr1	B Dortmund	A D	2-2	Hashemian 74, Huszti 78	66,100
7	grpr1	Eintr Frankfurt	H D	1-1	Hashemian 20	34,021
8	grpr1	Schalke	A L	1-2	Rosenthal 51	61,000
9	grpr1	Hamburg	A D	0-0		57,000
10	grpr1	Bochum	H L	0-2		28,000
11	grpr1	Bayern Munich	A W	1-0	Huszti 43	69,000
12	grpr1	Stuttgart	H L	1-2	Rosenthal 13	28,847
13	grpr1	B M'gladbach	A W	1-0	Balitsch 50	38,000
14	grpr1	Mainz	H W	1-0	Hashemian 75	27,000
15	grpr1	Cottbus	A W	1-0	Cherundolo 22	10,000
16	grpr1	Arminia B	H D	1-1	Brdaric 68	33,000
17	grpr1	Nurnberg	A L	1-3	Wolf 4	30,000
18	grpr1	W Bremen	A L	0-3		40,000
19	grpr1	Hertha Berlin	H W	5-0	Vinicius 16, 37, Fahrenhorst 45, Rosenthal 64, Lala 76	30,584
20	grpr1	Alem Aachen	A W	4-1	Yankov 5, Rosenthal 24, Huszti 31 pen, Stajner 90	20,800
21	grpr1	Wolfsburg	H D	2-2	Balitsch 22, Fahrenhorst 62	35,244
22	grpr1	B Leverkusen	A W	1-0	Rosenthal 7	22,500
23	grpr1	B Dortmund	H W	4-2	Huszti 56 pen, Stajner 69, Bruggink 76, 78	43,852
24	grpr1	Eintr Frankfurt	A L	0-2		40,038
25	grpr1	Schalke	H D	1-1	Tarnat 4	49,000
26	grpr1	Hamburg	H D	0-0		49,000
27	grpr1	Bochum	A L	0-2		24,117
28	grpr1	Bayern Munich	H L	1-2	Bruggink 43	49,000
29	grpr1	Stuttgart	A L	1-2	Cherundolo 61	53,000
30	grpr1	B M'gladbach	H W	1-0	Bruggink 31	42,784
31	grpr1	Mainz	A W	2-1	Bruggink 26, Yankov 50	20,300
32	grpr1	Cottbus	H W	2-0	Vinicius 37, Bruggink 83	43,509
33	grpr1	Arminia B	A L	1-3	Rosenthal 30	26,600
34	grpr1	Nurnberg	H L	0-3		49,000

LEAGUE APPEARANCES, BOOKINGS AND CAPS

	AGE (on 01/07/07)	IN NAMED 18	APPEARANCES	COUNTING GAMES	MINUTES ON PITCH	YELLOW CARDS	RED CARDS	CAPS THIS SEASON	NATIONAL SIDE
Goalkeepers									
Robert Enke	29	34	34	34	3060	1	0	2	Germany
Richard Golz	39	31	0	0	0	0	0	-	Germany
Defenders									
Christoffer Andersson	28	27	6	3	295	0	0	-	Sweden
Steve Cherundolo	28	33	33	31	2882	3	1	1	United States
Frank Fahrenhorst	29	30	26	18	1682	6	1	-	Germany
Soren Halfar	20	13	3	0	18	0	0	-	Germany
Moritz Marheineke	22	3	0	0	0	0	0	-	Germany
Jonas Troest	22	3	1	0	32	0	0	-	Denmark
Bergantin Vinicius	26	32	30	29	2675	2	0	-	Brazil
Tobias Willers	20	1	0	0	0	0	0	-	Germany
Dariusz Zuraw	34	31	24	22	1994	2	0	-	Poland
Midfielders									
Hanno Balitsch	26	33	33	31	2867	10	0	-	Germany
Johannes Dietwald	22	1	0	0	0	0	0	-	Germany
Szabolcs Huszti	24	31	31	27	2538	5	0	-	Hungary
Altin Lala	31	21	17	13	1245	5	0	5	Albania
Jan Rosenthal	21	32	29	20	2080	1	0	-	Germany
Silvio Schroter	28	31	21	1	661	1	0	-	Germany
Michael Tarnat	37	28	28	27	2468	8	1	-	Germany
Chavdar Yankov	22	34	28	17	2036	3	0	-	Bulgaria
Forwards									
Thomas Brdaric	32	12	11	5	670	1	0	-	Germany
Arnold Bruggink	29	33	32	17	2001	2	0	-	Holland
Vahid Hashemian	30	33	31	16	1791	2	0	-	Iran
Erik Jendrisek	20	24	9	0	163	0	0	-	Slovakia
Fabian Montabell	22	7	2	0	10	0	0	-	Germany
Sebastian Stachnik	21	4	0	0	0	0	0	-	Germany
Jiri Stajner	31	34	34	21	2221	3	0	3	Czech Republic
G H Thorvaldsson	25	9	7	1	217	0	0	2	Iceland

TEAM OF THE SEASON

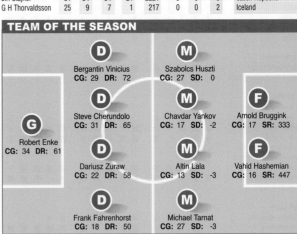

G Robert Enke — CG: 34 DR: 61

D Bergantin Vinicius — CG: 29 DR: 72
D Steve Cherundolo — CG: 31 DR: 65
D Dariusz Zuraw — CG: 22 DR: 58
D Frank Fahrenhorst — CG: 18 DR: 50

M Szabolcs Huszti — CG: 27 SD: 0
M Chavdar Yankov — CG: 17 SD: -2
M Altin Lala — CG: 13 SD: -3
M Michael Tarnat — CG: 27 SD: -3

F Arnold Bruggink — CG: 17 SR: 333
F Vahid Hashemian — CG: 16 SR: 447

MONTHLY POINTS TALLY

AUGUST	0	0%
SEPTEMBER	5	56%
OCTOBER	2	22%
NOVEMBER	9	60%
DECEMBER	4	44%
JANUARY	3	50%
FEBRUARY	10	83%
MARCH	2	22%
APRIL	6	40%
MAY	3	33%

LEAGUE GOALS

	PLAYER	MINS	GOALS	S RATE
1	Bruggink	2001	6	333
2	Rosenthal	2080	6	346
3	Brdaric	670	4	167
4	Hashemian	1791	4	447
5	Huszti	2538	4	634
6	Stajner	2221	3	740
7	Vinicius	2675	3	891
8	Fahrenhorst	1682	2	841
9	Yankov	2036	2	1018
10	Balitsch	2867	2	1433
11	Cherundolo	2882	2	1441
12	Lala	1245	1	1245
13	Tarnat	2468	1	2468
	Other		0	
	TOTAL		40	

TOP POINT EARNERS

	PLAYER	GAMES	AV PTS
1	Chavdar Yankov	17	1.76
2	Szabolcs Huszti	27	1.59
3	Arnold Bruggink	17	1.53
4	Bergantin Vinicius	29	1.52
5	Jan Rosenthal	20	1.45
6	Vahid Hashemian	16	1.44
7	Steve Cherundolo	31	1.42
8	Michael Tarnat	28	1.39
9	Altin Lala	13	1.38
10	Hanno Balitsch	31	1.32
	CLUB AVERAGE:		1.29

DISCIPLINARY RECORDS

	PLAYER	YELLOW	RED	AVE
1	Frank Fahrenhorst	6	1	240
2	Altin Lala	5	0	249
3	Michael Tarnat	8	1	274
4	Hanno Balitsch	10	0	286
5	Szabolcs Huszti	5	0	507
6	Silvio Schroter	1	0	661
7	Thomas Brdaric	1	0	670
8	Chavdar Yankov	3	0	678
9	Steve Cherundolo	3	1	720
10	Jiri Stajner	3	0	740
11	Vahid Hashemian	2	0	895
12	Dariusz Zuraw	2	0	997
13	Arnold Bruggink	2	0	1000
	Other	3	0	
	TOTAL	54	3	

KEY GOALKEEPER

Robert Enke

Goals Conceded in the League	50	Counting Games League games when player was on pitch for at least 70 minutes	34
Defensive Rating Ave number of mins between League goals conceded while on the pitch	61	Clean Sheets In League games when player was on pitch for at least 70 minutes	10

KEY PLAYERS - DEFENDERS

Bergantin Vinicius

Goals Conceded Number of League goals conceded while the player was on the pitch	37	Clean Sheets In League games when player was on pitch for at least 70 minutes	10
Defensive Rating Ave number of mins between League goals conceded while on the pitch	72	Club Defensive Rating Average number of mins between League goals conceded by the club this season	61

	PLAYER	CON LGE	CLEAN SHEETS	DEF RATE
1	Bergantin Vinicius	37	10	72 mins
2	Steve Cherundolo	44	10	65 mins
3	Dariusz Zuraw	34	7	58 mins
4	Frank Fahrenhorst	33	4	50 mins

KEY PLAYERS - MIDFIELDERS

Szabolcs Huszti

Goals in the League	4	Contribution to Attacking Power Average number of minutes between League team goals while on pitch	70
Defensive Rating Average number of mins between League goals conceded while on the pitch	70	Scoring Difference Defensive Rating minus Contribution to Attacking Power	0

	PLAYER	LGE GOALS	DEF RATE	POWER	SCORE DIFF
1	Szabolcs Huszti	4	70	70	0 mins
2	Chavdar Yankov	2	70	72	-2 mins
3	Altin Lala	1	59	62	-3 mins
4	Michael Tarnat	1	63	66	-3 mins

KEY PLAYERS - GOALSCORERS

Arnold Bruggink

Goals in the League	6	Player Strike Rate Average number of minutes between League goals scored by player	333
Contribution to Attacking Power Average number of minutes between League team goals while on pitch	76	Club Strike Rate Average number of minutes between League goals scored by club	74

	PLAYER	LGE GOALS	POWER	STRIKE RATE
1	Arnold Bruggink	6	76	333 mins
2	Jan Rosenthal	6	74	346 mins
3	Vahid Hashemian	4	59	447 mins
4	Szabolcs Huszti	4	70	634 mins

Jiri Stajner

SQUAD APPEARANCES

Match	1	2	3	4	5	6	7	8	9	10	11	12	13	14	15	16	17	18	19	20	21	22	23	24	25	26	27	28	29	30	31	32	33	34
Venue	H	A	H	A	H	A	H	A	A	H	A	H	A	H	A	H	A	A	H	A	H	A	H	A	H	H	A	H	A	H	A	H	A	H
Competition	L	L	L	L	L	L	L	L	L	L	L	L	L	L	L	L	L	L	L	L	L	L	L	L	L	L	L	L	L	L	L	L	L	L
Result	L	L	L	W	D	D	D	L	D	L	W	L	W	W	W	D	L	L	W	W	D	W	W	L	D	D	L	L	L	W	W	W	L	L

Goalkeepers
Robert Enke
Richard Golz

Defenders
Christoffer Andersson
Steve Cherundolo
Frank Fahrenhorst
Soren Halfar
Moritz Marheineke
Jonas Troest
Bergantin Vinicius
Tobias Willers
Dariusz Zuraw

Midfielders
Hanno Balitsch
Johannes Dietwald
Szabolcs Huszti
Altin Lala
Jan Rosenthal
Silvio Schroter
Michael Tarnat
Chavdar Yankov

Forwards
Thomas Brdaric
Arnold Bruggink
Vahid Hashemian
Erik Jendrisek
Fabian Montabell
Sebastian Stachnik
Jiri Stajner
G H Thorvaldsson

KEY: ■ On all match   ◄◄ Subbed or sent off (Counting game)   ▸▸ Subbed on from bench (Counting Game)   ▸▸ Subbed on and then subbed or sent off (Counting Game)   ☐ Not in 16
   ■ On bench   ◄◄ Subbed or sent off (playing less than 70 minutes)   ▸▸ Subbed on (playing less than 70 minutes)   ▸▸ Subbed on and then subbed or sent off (playing less than 70 minutes)

GERMANY - HANNOVER 96

ARMINIA BIELEFELD

Final Position: **12th**

NICKNAME: DIE ARMINEN   KEY: ☐ Won ☐ Drawn ☐ Lost   Attendance

#		Match		Result	Scorers	Attendance
1	grpr1	Hamburg	A	D 1-1	Eigler 32	49,713
2	grpr1	Stuttgart	H	L 2-3	Ahanfouf 11 pen, Bome 76	22,095
3	grpr1	B M'gladbach	A	L 0-1		42,000
4	grpr1	Bayern Munich	H	W 2-1	Wichniarek 25, Kamper 84	26,601
5	grpr1	Bochum	A	L 1-2	Gabriel 11	20,318
6	grpr1	Cottbus	H	W 3-1	Zuma 48, Wichniarek 62, Masmanidis 74	17,000
7	grpr1	Nurnberg	A	D 1-1	Bohme 26 pen	39,788
8	grpr1	Mainz	H	W 1-0	Westermann 72	19,260
9	grpr1	Alem Aachen	H	W 5-1	Kamper 10, 67, Kucera 18, Wichniarek 49, Eigler 85	23,538
10	grpr1	B Dortmund	A	D 1-1	Wichniarek 68	72,000
11	grpr1	Hertha Berlin	H	D 2-2	Zuma 28, Kucera 76	20,000
12	grpr1	Eintr Frankfurt	A	W 3-0	Wichniarek 26, Zuma 62, Ndjeng 84	32,000
13	grpr1	Wolfsburg	H	D 0-0		20,000
14	grpr1	W Bremen	A	L 0-3		40,000
15	grpr1	B Leverkusen	H	D 0-0		22,000
16	grpr1	Hannover 96	A	D 1-1	Ndjeng 66	33,000
17	grpr1	Schalke	H	L 0-1		26,601
18	grpr1	Hamburg	H	D 1-1	Borges 88	26,601
19	grpr1	Stuttgart	A	L 2-3	Eigler 26, Ahanfouf 87 pen	28,000
20	grpr1	B M'gladbach	H	L 0-2		23,114
21	grpr1	Bayern Munich	A	L 0-1		69,000
22	grpr1	Bochum	H	L 1-3	Wichniarek 26	21,025
23	grpr1	Cottbus	A	L 1-2	Gabriel 15	12,227
24	grpr1	Nurnberg	H	W 3-2	Kucera 44, Wichniarek 50 pen, Bohme 86	18,444
25	grpr1	Mainz	A	L 0-1		20,300
26	grpr1	Alem Aachen	A	L 0-2		20,800
27	grpr1	B Dortmund	H	W 1-0	Kamper 79	26,601
28	grpr1	Hertha Berlin	A	D 1-1	Kucera 20	41,512
29	grpr1	Eintr Frankfurt	H	L 2-4	Kucera 28, Eigler 81	24,349
30	grpr1	Wolfsburg	A	W 3-2	Westermann 8, Eigler 71, Wichniarek 86	20,941
31	grpr1	W Bremen	H	W 3-2	Westermann 30, Kamper 61, Eigler 79	26,601
32	grpr1	B Leverkusen	A	W 2-1	Wichniarek 19, Kamper 83	22,500
33	grpr1	Hannover 96	H	W 3-1	Wichniarek 22, Bohme 32, Vata 65	26,600
34	grpr1	Schalke	A	L 1-2	Kucera 90	61,482

LEAGUE APPEARANCES, BOOKINGS AND CAPS

	AGE (on 01/07/07)	IN NAMED 18	APPEARANCES	COUNTING GAMES	MINUTES ON PITCH	YELLOW CARDS	RED CARDS	CAPS THIS SEASON	NATIONAL SIDE
Goalkeepers									
Mathias Hain	34	31	31	30	2745	1	0	-	Germany
Marc Ziegler	31	33	4	3	315	0	0	-	Germany
Defenders									
Markus Bollmann	26	31	18	16	1433	4	0	-	Germany
Marcio Borges	34	13	6	5	505	3	1	-	Brazil
Petr Gabriel	34	28	22	17	1659	2	1	-	Czech Republic
Radim Kucera	33	29	27	21	2089	1	0	-	Czech Republic
Markus Schuler	29	33	30	27	2504	6	0	-	Germany
Heiko Westermann	23	34	33	32	2891	0	0	-	Germany
Midfielders									
Jorg Bohme	33	32	30	22	2198	2	0	-	Germany
Tim Danneberg	21	13	5	1	169	0	0	-	Germany
Nils Fischer	20	7	0	0	0	0	0	-	Germany
Jonas Kamper	24	33	29	10	1686	2	0	1	Denmark
Ruediger Kauf	32	32	32	32	2866	6	0	-	Germany
David Kobilyk	26	22	15	5	627	1	0	-	Czech Republic
Umit Kocin	19	3	0	0	0	0	0	-	Turkey
Bernd Korzynietz	27	29	26	25	2280	4	0	-	Germany
Thorben Marx	26	32	26	8	1129	4	0	-	Germany
Marcel Ndjeng	25	20	10	2	332	0	0	-	Germany
Tobias Rau	25	6	5	4	422	0	0	-	Germany
Robert Tesche	20	8	7	5	542	0	0	-	Germany
Kamil Vacek	20	1	0	0	0	0	0	-	Czech Republic
Fatmir Vata	35	11	9	2	357	0	0	-	Albania
Forwards									
Abdelaziz Ahanfouf	29	8	6	0	217	1	0	-	Morocco
Christian Eigler	23	31	27	9	1266	1	0	-	Germany
Ioannis Masmanidis	24	27	22	9	1187	4	0	-	Germany
Artur Wichniarek	30	33	32	25	2429	5	0	-	Poland
Sibusiso Zuma	32	26	24	17	1810	3	0	-	South Africa

TEAM OF THE SEASON

D Radim Kucera **CG:** 21 **DR:** 69
M Jorg Bohme **CG:** 22 **SD:** 0

D Markus Schuler **CG:** 27 **DR:** 65
M Ruediger Kauf **CG:** 32 **SD:** -1
F Artur Wichniarek **CG:** 25 **SR:** 242

G Mathias Hain **CG:** 30 **DR:** 59

D Markus Bollmann **CG:** 16 **DR:** 65
M Bernd Korzynietz **CG:** 25 **SD:** -15
F Sibusiso Zuma **CG:** 17 **SR:** 603

D Heiko Westermann **CG:** 32 **DR:** 61
M Jonas Kamper* **CG:** 10 **SD:** 0

MONTHLY POINTS TALLY

AUGUST		1	11%
SEPTEMBER		6	67%
OCTOBER		7	78%
NOVEMBER		6	40%
DECEMBER		2	22%
JANUARY		1	17%
FEBRUARY		0	0%
MARCH		6	50%
APRIL		7	58%
MAY		6	67%

LEAGUE GOALS

	PLAYER	MINS	GOALS	S RATE
1	Wichniarek	2429	10	242
2	Eigler	1266	6	211
3	Kamper	1686	6	281
4	Kucera	2089	6	348
5	Bohme	2198	4	549
6	Zuma	1810	3	603
7	Westermann	2891	3	963
8	Ahanfouf	217	2	108
9	Ndjeng	332	2	166
10	Gabriel	1659	2	829
11	Vata	357	1	357
12	Borges	505	1	505
13	Masmanidis	1187	1	1187
	Other		0	
	TOTAL		**47**	

TOP POINT EARNERS

	PLAYER	GAMES	AV PTS
1	Radim Kucera	21	1.62
2	Markus Bollmann	16	1.44
3	Jorg Bohme	22	1.36
4	Heiko Westermann	32	1.31
5	Sibusiso Zuma	17	1.29
6	Artur Wichniarek	25	1.28
7	Ruediger Kauf	32	1.28
8	Petr Gabriel	17	1.18
9	Mathias Hain	30	1.17
10	Markus Schuler	27	1.00
	CLUB AVERAGE:		**1.24**

DISCIPLINARY RECORDS

	PLAYER	YELLOW	RED	AVE
1	Marcio Borges	3	1	126
2	Thorben Marx	4	0	282
3	Ioannis Masmanidis	4	0	296
4	Markus Bollmann	4	0	358
5	Markus Schuler	6	0	417
6	Ruediger Kauf	6	0	477
7	Artur Wichniarek	5	0	485
8	Petr Gabriel	2	1	553
9	Bernd Korzynietz	4	0	570
10	Sibusiso Zuma	3	0	603
11	David Kobilyk	1	0	627
12	Jonas Kamper	2	0	843
13	Jorg Bohme	2	0	1099
	Other	3	0	
	TOTAL	**49**	**2**	

KEY GOALKEEPER

Mathias Hain

Goals Conceded in the League	46	Counting Games — League games when player was on pitch for at least 70 minutes	30
Defensive Rating — Ave number of mins between League goals conceded while on the pitch	59	Clean Sheets — In League games when player was on pitch for at least 70 minutes	4

KEY PLAYERS - DEFENDERS

Radim Kucera

Goals Conceded — Number of League goals conceded while the player was on the pitch	30	Clean Sheets — In League games when player was on pitch for at least 70 minutes	5
Defensive Rating — Ave number of mins between League goals conceded while on the pitch	69	Club Defensive Rating — Average number of mins between League goals conceded by the club this season	62

	PLAYER	CON LGE	CLEAN SHEETS	DEF RATE
1	Radim Kucera	30	5	69 mins
2	Markus Schuler	38	6	65 mins
3	Markus Bollmann	22	2	65 mins
4	Heiko Westermann	47	5	61 mins

KEY PLAYERS - MIDFIELDERS

Jonas Kamper

Goals in the League	6	Contribution to Attacking Power — Average number of minutes between League team goals while on pitch	62
Defensive Rating — Average number of mins between League goals conceded while on the pitch	62	Scoring Difference — Defensive Rating minus Contribution to Attacking Power	0

	PLAYER	LGE GOALS	DEF RATE	POWER	SCORE DIFF
1	Jonas Kamper	6	62	62	0 mins
2	Jorg Bohme	4	62	62	0 mins
3	Ruediger Kauf	0	62	63	-1 mins
4	Bernd Korzynietz	0	63	78	-15 mins

KEY PLAYERS - GOALSCORERS

Artur Wichniarek

Goals in the League	10	Player Strike Rate — Average number of minutes between League goals scored by player	242
Contribution to Attacking Power — Average number of minutes between League team goals while on pitch	67	Club Strike Rate — Average number of minutes between League goals scored by club	65

	PLAYER	LGE GOALS	POWER	STRIKE RATE
1	Artur Wichniarek	10	67	242 mins
2	Jorg Bohme	4	62	549 mins
3	Sibusiso Zuma	3	75	603 mins
4	Bernd Korzynietz	0	78	0 mins

Jonas Kamper & Artur Wichniarek

SQUAD APPEARANCES

Match	1	2	3	4	5	6	7	8	9	10	11	12	13	14	15	16	17	18	19	20	21	22	23	24	25	26	27	28	29	30	31	32	33	34
Venue	A	H	A	H	A	H	A	H	H	A	H	A	H	A	H	A	H	H	A	H	A	H	A	H	A	A	H	A	H	A	H	A	H	A
Competition	L	L	L	L	L	L	L	L	L	L	L	L	L	L	L	L	L	L	L	L	L	L	L	L	L	L	L	L	L	L	L	L	L	L
Result	D	L	L	W	L	W	D	W	W	D	D	W	D	L	D	D	L	D	L	L	L	L	L	W	L	L	W	D	L	W	W	W	W	L

Goalkeepers
Mathias Hain
Marc Ziegler

Defenders
Markus Bollmann
Marcio Borges
Petr Gabriel
Radim Kucera
Markus Schuler
Heiko Westermann

Midfielders
Jorg Bohme
Tim Danneberg
Nils Fischer
Jonas Kamper
Ruediger Kauf
David Kobilyk
Umit Kocin
Bernd Korzynietz
Thorben Marx
Marcel Ndjeng
Tobias Rau
Robert Tesche
Kamil Vacek
Fatmir Vata

Forwards
Abdelaziz Ahanfouf
Christian Eigler
Ioannis Masmanidis
Artur Wichniarek
Sibusiso Zuma

KEY: ■ On all match ■ On bench | ◄◄ Subbed or sent off (Counting game) ◄◄ Subbed or sent off (playing less than 70 minutes) | ►► Subbed on from bench (Counting Game) ►► Subbed on (playing less than 70 minutes) | ►► Subbed on and then subbed or sent off (Counting Game) ►► Subbed on and then subbed or sent off (playing less than 70 minutes) | □ Not in 16

GERMANY - ARMINIA BIELEFELD

ENERGIE COTTBUS

Final Position: **13th**

NICKNAME: ENERGIE

KEY: ☐ Won ☐ Drawn ☐ Lost

Attendance

#				Score	Scorers	Attendance
1	grpr1	B M'gladbach	A L	0-2		48,000
2	grpr1	Hamburg	H D	2-2	Munteanu 57 pen, Radu 69	21,000
3	grpr1	Bochum	A W	1-0	da Silva 85	21,000
4	grpr1	Mainz	H W	2-0	Radu 47, Munteanu 60	16,000
5	grpr1	Nurnberg	H D	1-1	Baumgart 83	16,900
6	grpr1	Arminia B	A L	1-3	Munteanu 22	17,000
7	grpr1	B Dortmund	H L	2-3	da Silva 3, Munteanu 89 pen	19,699
8	grpr1	Alem Aachen	A W	2-1	Munteanu 65, Rost 75	20,300
9	grpr1	Hertha Berlin	H W	2-0	Gunkel 65, Shao 82	17,525
10	grpr1	W Bremen	A D	1-1	Kioyo 49	35,000
11	grpr1	Eintr Frankfurt	H L	0-1		13,000
12	grpr1	Wolfsburg	A D	0-0		15,000
13	grpr1	Schalke	H L	2-4	Radu 28, 30	17,210
14	grpr1	B Leverkusen	A L	1-3	Munteanu 50	22,500
15	grpr1	Hannover 96	H L	0-1		10,000
16	grpr1	Bayern Munich	A L	1-2	Baumgart 53	69,000
17	grpr1	Stuttgart	H D	0-0		12,000
18	grpr1	B M'gladbach	H W	3-1	Radu 33, 39, Munteanu 90	13,044
19	grpr1	Hamburg	A D	1-1	Munteanu 8	52,484
20	grpr1	Bochum	H D	0-0		11,650
21	grpr1	Mainz	A L	1-4	Radu 20	20,300
22	grpr1	Nurnberg	A L	0-1		40,580
23	grpr1	Arminia B	H W	2-1	Kukielka 62, Radu 66	12,227
24	grpr1	B Dortmund	A W	3-2	Munteanu 6, 56 pen, Shao 65	64,100
25	grpr1	Alem Aachen	H L	0-2		15,200
26	grpr1	Hertha Berlin	A W	1-0	Radu 47	51,831
27	grpr1	W Bremen	H D	0-0		20,344
28	grpr1	Eintr Frankfurt	A W	3-1	Radu 58, Preuss 76 og, Munteanu 90	45,074
29	grpr1	Wolfsburg	H W	3-2	Radu 20, Munteanu 56, Kioyo 57	16,293
30	grpr1	Schalke	A L	0-2		61,058
31	grpr1	B Leverkusen	H W	2-1	Radu 7, Gunkel 85	18,904
32	grpr1	Hannover 96	A L	0-2		43,509
33	grpr1	Bayern Munich	H L	0-3		22,450
34	grpr1	Stuttgart	A L	1-2	Radu 19	56,000

LEAGUE APPEARANCES, BOOKINGS AND CAPS

	AGE (on 01/07/07)	IN NAMED 18	APPEARANCES	COUNTING GAMES	MINUTES ON PITCH	YELLOW CARDS	RED CARDS	CAPS THIS SEASON	NATIONAL SIDE
Goalkeepers									
Tomislav Piplica	38	34	34	34	3060	2	0	-	Bosnia
Gerhard Tremmel	28	32	0	0	0	0	0	-	Germany
Defenders									
Mario Cvitanovic	32	17	17	17	1530	3	0	-	Croatia
Vragel da Silva	33	25	25	18	1805	9	0	-	Brazil
Arne Feick	19	3	2	1	97	1	1	-	Germany
Mariusz Kukielka	30	32	32	32	2864	6	0	-	Poland
Kevin McKenna	26	29	29	29	2610	6	0	-	Canada
Igor Mitreski	28	28	27	26	2361	6	0	6	Macedonia
Benjamin Schuckel	26	3	1	0	45	1	0	-	Germany
Santos di B Sidney	27	16	1	1	90	1	0	-	Brazil
Daniel Ziebig	24	32	24	16	1662	8	1	-	Germany
Midfielders									
Tomasz Bandrowski	22	21	12	4	440	1	0	-	Poland
Daniel Gunkel	27	29	27	6	1061	4	0	-	Germany
Vlad Munteanu	26	33	33	29	2719	5	0	-	Romania
Timo Rost	28	32	31	28	2604	10	0	-	Germany
Sebastian Schuppan	20	1	0	0	0	0	0	-	Germany
Jiayi Shao	27	34	29	7	1218	2	0	-	China
Ervin Skela	30	10	7	1	313	1	0	4	Albania
Zoltan Szelesi	25	29	22	19	1790	5	0	1	Hungary
Forwards									
Lawrence Aidoo	25	16	1	0	53	1	1	-	Ghana
Steffen Baumgart	35	33	33	10	1367	5	0	-	Germany
Lars Jungnickel	25	3	1	0	21	0	0	-	Germany
Marco Kintzel	31	31	16	4	675	2	0	-	Germany
Francis Kioyo	27	29	29	21	2192	2	0	-	Cameroon
Sergiu Marian Radu	29	34	34	31	2927	3	0	-	Romania
Stiven Rivic	21	17	7	0	100	1	0	-	Croatia
Przemyslaw Trytko	19	3	0	0	0	0	0	-	Poland

TEAM OF THE SEASON

G Tomislav Piplica
CG: 34 DR: 62

D Kevin McKenna
CG: 29 DR: 65

D Vragel da Silva
CG: 18 DR: 64

D Mariusz Kukielka
CG: 32 DR: 63

D Daniel Ziebig
CG: 16 DR: 63

M Zoltan Szelesi
CG: 19 SD: -16

M Vlad Munteanu
CG: 29 SD: -20

M Timo Rost
CG: 28 SD: -22

M Jiayi Shao*
CG: 7 SD: -14

F Sergiu Marian Radu
CG: 31 SR: 225

F Francis Kioyo
CG: 21 SR: 1096

MONTHLY POINTS TALLY

AUGUST	4	44%
SEPTEMBER	4	44%
OCTOBER	6	67%
NOVEMBER	2	13%
DECEMBER	1	11%
JANUARY	4	67%
FEBRUARY	4	33%
MARCH	7	58%
APRIL	9	75%
MAY	0	0%

LEAGUE GOALS

	PLAYER	MINS	GOALS	S RATE
1	Radu	2927	13	225
2	Munteanu	2719	12	226
3	Gunkel	1061	2	530
4	Shao	1218	2	609
5	Baumgart	1367	2	683
6	da Silva	1805	2	902
7	Kioyo	2192	2	1096
8	Rost	2604	1	2604
9	Kukielka	2864	1	2864
10	McKenna	2610	0	
11	Mitreski	2361	0	
12	Piplica	3060	0	
13	Rivic	100	0	
	Other		0	
	TOTAL		**37**	

TOP POINT EARNERS

	PLAYER	GAMES	AV PTS
1	Mario Cvitanovic	17	1.41
2	Vlad Munteanu	29	1.38
3	Francis Kioyo	21	1.33
4	Kevin McKenna	29	1.31
5	Timo Rost	28	1.29
6	Sergiu Marian Radu	31	1.26
7	Mariusz Kukielka	32	1.25
8	Vragel da Silva	18	1.22
9	Tomislav Piplica	34	1.21
10	Daniel Ziebig	17	1.18
	CLUB AVERAGE:		**1.21**

DISCIPLINARY RECORDS

	PLAYER	YELLOW	RED	AVE
1	Daniel Ziebig	8	1	184
2	Vragel da Silva	9	0	200
3	Timo Rost	10	0	260
4	Daniel Gunkel	4	0	265
5	Steffen Baumgart	5	0	273
6	Jiayi Shao	4	0	304
7	Marco Käntzel	2	0	337
8	Zoltan Szelesi	5	0	358
9	Igor Mitreski	6	0	393
10	Kevin McKenna	6	0	435
11	Mariusz Kukielka	6	0	477
12	Mario Cvitanovic	3	0	510
13	Vlad Munteanu	5	0	543
	Other	7	0	
	TOTAL	**80**	**1**	

KEY GOALKEEPER

Tomislav Piplica

Goals Conceded in the League	49	Counting Games League games when player was on pitch for at least 70 minutes	34
Defensive Rating Ave number of mins between League goals conceded while on the pitch	62	Clean Sheets In League games when player was on pitch for at least 70 minutes	8

KEY PLAYERS - DEFENDERS

Kevin McKenna

Goals Conceded Number of League goals conceded while the player was on the pitch	40	Clean Sheets In League games when player was on pitch for at least 70 minutes	8
Defensive Rating Ave number of mins between League goals conceded while on the pitch	65	Club Defensive Rating Average number of mins between League goals conceded by the club this season	62

	PLAYER	CON LGE	CLEAN SHEETS	DEF RATE
1	Kevin McKenna	40	8	65 mins
2	Vragel da Silva	28	4	64 mins
3	Mariusz Kukielka	45	8	63 mins
4	Daniel Ziebig	26	5	63 mins

KEY PLAYERS - MIDFIELDERS

Jiayi Shao

Goals in the League	2	Contribution to Attacking Power Average number of minutes between League team goals while on pitch	81
Defensive Rating Average number of mins between League goals conceded while on the pitch	67	Scoring Difference Defensive Rating minus Contribution to Attacking Power	-14

	PLAYER	LGE GOALS	DEF RATE	POWER	SCORE DIFF
1	Jiayi Shao	2	67	81	-14 mins
2	Zoltan Szelesi	0	61	77	-16 mins
3	Vlad Munteanu	12	59	79	-20 mins
4	Timo Rost	1	62	84	-22 mins

KEY PLAYERS - GOALSCORERS

Sergiu Marian Radu

Goals in the League	13	Player Strike Rate Average number of minutes between League goals scored by player	225
Contribution to Attacking Power Average number of minutes between League team goals while on pitch	79	Club Strike Rate Average number of minutes between League goals scored by club	80

	PLAYER	LGE GOALS	POWER	STRIKE RATE
1	Sergiu Marian Radu	13	79	225 mins
2	Vlad Munteanu	12	79	226 mins
3	Francis Kioyo	2	78	1096 mins
4	Timo Rost	1	84	2604 mins

Daniel Gunkel & Mariusz Kukielka

SQUAD APPEARANCES

Match	1	2	3	4	5	6	7	8	9	10	11	12	13	14	15	16	17	18	19	20	21	22	23	24	25	26	27	28	29	30	31	32	33	34
Venue	A	H	A	H	H	A	H	A	H	A	H	A	H	A	H	A	H	H	A	H	A	A	H	A	H	A	H	A	H	A	H	A	H	A
Competition	L	L	L	L	L	L	L	L	L	L	L	L	L	L	L	L	L	L	L	L	L	L	L	L	L	L	L	L	L	L	L	L	L	L
Result	L	D	W	W	D	L	L	W	W	D	L	D	L	L	L	L	D	W	D	D	L	L	W	W	L	W	D	W	W	L	W	L	L	L

Goalkeepers
Tomislav Piplica
Gerhard Tremmel

Defenders
Mario Cvitanovic
Vragel da Silva
Arne Feick
Mariusz Kukielka
Kevin McKenna
Igor Mitreski
Benjamin Schuckel
Santos di B Sidney
Daniel Ziebig

Midfielders
Tomasz Bandrowski
Daniel Gunkel
Vlad Munteanu
Timo Rost
Sebastian Schuppan
Jiayi Shao
Ervin Skela
Zoltan Szelesi

Forwards
Lawrence Aidoo
Steffen Baumgart
Lars Jungnickel
Marco Kintzel
Francis Kioyo
Sergiu Marian Radu
Stiven Rivic
Przemyslaw Trytko

KEY: ■ On all match ◄◄ Subbed or sent off (Counting game) ►► Subbed on from bench (Counting Game) ►► Subbed on and then subbed or sent off (Counting Game) ☐ Not in 16
■ On bench ◄◄ Subbed or sent off (playing less than 70 minutes) ►► Subbed on (playing less than 70 minutes) ►► Subbed on and then subbed or sent off (playing less than 70 minutes)

EINTRACHT FRANKFURT

Final Position: **14th**

NICKNAME: DIE EINTRACHT   **KEY:** ☐Won ☐Drawn ☐Lost   Attendance

#		Opponent		Result	Scorers	Attendance
1	grpr1	Schalke	A D	1-1	Amanatidis 72	61,482
2	grpr1	Wolfsburg	H D	0-0		40,000
3	grpr1	Mainz	A D	1-1	Amanatidis 25	20,300
4	ucrl1	Brondby	H W	4-0	Thurk 49 pen, 71 pen, 78, Kohler 90	35,000
5	grpr1	B Leverkusen	H W	3-1	Takahara 54, Thurk 70, Ochs 84	42,000
6	grpr1	Stuttgart	A D	1-1	Meier 88	40,000
7	ucrl2	Brondby	A D	2-2	Vasoski 5, 52	14,067
8	grpr1	Hamburg	H D	2-2	Meier 36, Amanatidis 58	45,000
9	grpr1	Hannover 96	A D	1-1	Meier 55	34,021
10	ucgph	Palermo	H L	1-2	Streit 45	45,000
11	grpr1	Nurnberg	H D	2-2	Amanatidis 2 pen, Streit 56	46,000
12	grpr1	Bayern Munich	A L	0-2		69,000
13	ucgph	Celta Vigo	A D	1-1	Huber 17	10,000
14	grpr1	B M'gladbach	H W	1-0	Takahara 78	47,000
15	grpr1	Cottbus	A W	1-0	Takahara 22	13,000
16	grpr1	Arminia B	H L	0-3		32,000
17	grpr1	Bochum	A L	3-4	Streit 1, 5, Amanatidis 56	21,260
18	grpr1	B Dortmund	H D	1-1	Kyrgiakos 38	51,000
19	ucgph	Newcastle	H D	0-0		47,000
20	grpr1	Alem Aachen	A W	3-2	Takahara 14, 44, 62	20,000
21	grpr1	W Bremen	H L	2-6	Russ 4, Kyrgiakos 81	51,400
22	ucgph	Fenerbahce	A D	2-2	Takahara 7, 52	50,000
23	grpr1	Hertha Berlin	A L	0-1		40,000
24	grpr1	Schalke	H L	1-3	Takahara 48	51,500
25	grpr1	Wolfsburg	A D	2-2	Thurk 63, Meier 69	15,097
26	grpr1	Mainz	H D	0-0		51,300
27	grpr1	B Leverkusen	A D	2-2	Kyrgiakos 42, Meier 85	22,000
28	grpr1	Stuttgart	H L	0-4		46,000
29	grpr1	Hamburg	A L	1-3	Takahara 59	57,000
30	grpr1	Hannover 96	H W	2-0	Takahara 58, Thurk 75	40,038
31	grpr1	Nurnberg	A D	2-2	Kyrgiakos 26, Takahara 69	44,055
32	grpr1	Bayern Munich	H W	1-0	Preuss 78	51,500
33	grpr1	B M'gladbach	A D	1-1	Kyrgiakos 11	52,177
34	grpr1	Cottbus	H L	1-3	Meier 64	45,074
35	grpr1	Arminia B	A W	4-2	Amanatidis 10, 47 pen, Vasoski 33, Heller 90	24,349
36	grpr1	Bochum	H L	0-3		47,962
37	grpr1	B Dortmund	A L	0-2		80,708
38	grpr1	Alem Aachen	H W	4-0	Huggel 3, Vasoski 31, Takahara 57, Kohler 80	51,500
39	grpr1	W Bremen	A W	2-1	Amanatidis 14, Naldo 69 og	42,100
40	grpr1	Hertha Berlin	H L	1-2	Streit 61	50,500

LEAGUE APPEARANCES, BOOKINGS AND CAPS

	AGE (on 01/07/07)	IN NAMED 18	APPEARANCES	COUNTING GAMES	MINUTES ON PITCH	YELLOW CARDS	RED CARDS	CAPS THIS SEASON	NATIONAL SIDE
Goalkeepers									
Oka Nikolov	33	31	20	19	1732	1	0	-	Germany
Markus Pröll	27	15	14	14	1238	0	0	-	Germany
Jan Zimmermann	22	18	1	1	90	0	0	-	Germany
Defenders									
Mounir Chaftar	21	11	2	2	180	0	0	-	Germany
C M Hening Chris	28	18	13	4	557	3	0	-	Brazil
Daniyel Cimen	22	15	4	2	287	1	0	-	Germany
Michael Fink	25	30	23	21	1927	3	0	-	Germany
Sotirios Kyrgiakos	27	27	27	25	2315	3	2	7	Greece
Marko Rehmer	35	15	12	7	825	0	0	-	Germany
Christopher Reinhard	22	10	2	1	135	0	0	-	Germany
Marco Russ	21	34	27	18	1759	2	0	-	Germany
Aleksandar Vasoski	27	29	26	23	2199	3	3	3	Macedonia
Midfielders									
Francisco Copado	32	2	1	0	15	1	0	-	Germany
Alexander Huber	22	12	3	0	27	0	0	-	Germany
Benjamin Huggel	29	32	25	19	1802	5	0	-	Switzerland
Jermaine Jones	25	4	4	4	346	1	0	-	Germany
Patrick Ochs	23	30	30	28	2545	8	0	-	Germany
Christoph Preuss	25	20	14	6	683	0	0	-	Germany
Christoph Spycher	29	30	30	27	2515	1	2	6	Switzerland
Albert Streit	27	30	29	27	2470	9	0	-	Germany
Michael Thurk	31	26	24	12	1428	5	0	-	Germany
Faton Toski	20	7	2	1	81	0	0	-	Serbia
M Weissenberger	32	25	9	2	475	1	0	-	Austria
Forwards									
Ioannis Amanatidis	25	27	27	19	1875	2	0	3	Greece
Marcel Heller	21	16	11	2	411	0	0	-	Germany
Benjamin Kohler	26	30	22	8	1094	2	0	-	Germany
Alexander Meier	24	31	29	22	2183	5	1	-	Germany
Naohiro Takahara	28	30	30	24	2337	1	0	1	Japan

TEAM OF THE SEASON

G Markus Proll — CG: 14 DR: 53

D Michael Fink — CG: 21 DR: 64
D Aleksandar Vasoski — CG: 23 DR: 52
D Marco Russ — CG: 18 DR: 51
D Sotirios Kyrgiakos — CG: 25 DR: 49

M Christoph Spycher — CG: 27 SD: -5
M Patrick Ochs — CG: 28 SD: -9
M Albert Streit — CG: 27 SD: -14
M Benjamin Huggel — CG: 19 SD: -17

F Naohiro Takahara — CG: 24 SR: 212
F Ioannis Amanatidis — CG: 19 SR: 234

MONTHLY POINTS TALLY

Month		Points	%
AUGUST		3	33%
SEPTEMBER		5	56%
OCTOBER		2	22%
NOVEMBER		7	47%
DECEMBER		3	33%
JANUARY		1	17%
FEBRUARY		2	17%
MARCH		8	67%
APRIL		3	25%
MAY		6	67%

LEAGUE GOALS

	PLAYER	MINS	GOALS	S RATE
1	Takahara	2337	11	212
2	Amanatidis	1875	8	234
3	Meier	2183	6	363
4	Kyrgiakos	2315	5	463
5	Streit	2470	4	617
6	Thurk	1428	3	476
7	Vasoski	2199	2	1099
8	Heller	411	1	411
9	Preuss	683	1	683
10	Kohler	1094	1	1094
11	Russ	1759	1	1759
12	Huggel	1802	1	1802
13	Ochs	2545	1	2545
	Other		0	
	TOTAL		**45**	

TOP POINT EARNERS

	PLAYER	GAMES	AV PTS
1	Michael Fink	21	1.57
2	Michael Thurk	12	1.50
3	Naohiro Takahara	24	1.33
4	Marco Russ	18	1.33
5	Christoph Spycher	28	1.29
6	Oka Nikolov	19	1.26
7	Patrick Ochs	28	1.21
8	Ioannis Amanatidis	19	1.21
9	Albert Streit	27	1.15
10	Markus Proll	14	1.14
	CLUB AVERAGE:		**1.18**

DISCIPLINARY RECORDS

	PLAYER	YELLOW	RED	AVE
1	C Maicon H Chris	3	0	185
2	Albert Streit	9	0	308
3	Patrick Ochs	8	0	318
4	Christoph Preuss	2	0	341
5	Michael Thurk	5	0	476
6	Alexander Meier	5	1	545
7	Aleksandar Vasoski	3	3	549
8	Sotirios Kyrgiakos	3	2	578
9	Benjamin Huggel	5	0	600
10	Michael Fink	3	0	642
11	Christoph Spycher	1	2	838
12	Marco Russ	2	0	879
13	Oka Nikolov	1	0	1732
	Other	6	0	
	TOTAL	**56**	**8**	

KEY GOALKEEPER

Markus Proll

Goals Conceded in the League	23	Counting Games League games when player was on pitch for at least 70 minutes	14
Defensive Rating Ave number of mins between League goals conceded while on the pitch	53	Clean Sheets In League games when player was on pitch for at least 70 minutes	2

KEY PLAYERS - GOALSCORERS

Naohiro Takahara

Goals in the League	11	Player Strike Rate Average number of minutes between League goals scored by player	212
Contribution to Attacking Power Average number of minutes between League team goals while on pitch	61	Club Strike Rate Average number of minutes between League goals scored by club	66

	PLAYER	LGE GOALS	POWER	STRIKE RATE
1	Naohiro Takahara	11	61	212 mins
2	Ioannis Amanatidis	8	64	234 mins
3	Alexander Meier	6	72	363 mins
4	Michael Thurk	3	75	476 mins

KEY PLAYERS - DEFENDERS

Michael Fink

Goals Conceded Number of League goals conceded while the player was on the pitch	30	Clean Sheets In League games when player was on pitch for at least 70 minutes	5
Defensive Rating Ave number of mins between League goals conceded while on the pitch	64	Club Defensive Rating Average number of mins between League goals conceded by the club this season	52

	PLAYER	CON LGE	CLEAN SHEETS	DEF RATE
1	Michael Fink	30	5	64 mins
2	Aleksandar Vasoski	42	5	52 mins
3	Marco Russ	34	4	51 mins
4	Sotirios Kyrgiakos	47	5	49 mins

Naohiro Takahara

KEY PLAYERS - MIDFIELDERS

Christoph Spycher

Goals in the League	0	Contribution to Attacking Power Average number of mins between League team goals while on pitch	62
Defensive Rating Average number of mins between League goals conceded while on the pitch	57	Scoring Difference Defensive Rating minus Contribution to Attacking Power	-5

	PLAYER	LGE GOALS	DEF RATE	POWER	SCORE DIFF
1	Christoph Spycher	0	57	62	-5 mins
2	Patrick Ochs	1	51	60	-9 mins
3	Albert Streit	4	54	68	-14 mins
4	Benjamin Huggel	1	47	64	-17 mins

SQUAD APPEARANCES

Match	1 2 3 4 5	6 7 8 9 10	11 12 13 14 15	16 17 18 19 20	21 22 23 24 25	26 27 28 29 30	31 32 33 34 35	36 37 38 39 40
Venue	A H A H H	A A H H H	H A A H A	H A H H A	H A A H A	H A H A H	A H A H A	H A H A H
Competition	L L L E L	L E L E L	L E L L E	L L L D D	L E L L L	L L L L L	L L L L L	L L L L L
Result	D D D W W	D D D D L	D L D W W	L L L D D W	L D L L D	D D L L W	D W D L W	L L W W L

Goalkeepers
Oka Nikolov
Markus Proll
Jan Zimmermann

Defenders
Mounir Chaftar
C M Hening Chris
Daniyel Cimen
Michael Fink
Sotirios Kyrgiakos
Marko Rehmer
Christopher Reinhard
Marco Russ
Aleksandar Vasoski

Midfielders
Francisco Copado
Alexander Huber
Benjamin Huggel
Jermaine Jones
Patrick Ochs
Christoph Preuss
Christoph Spycher
Albert Streit
Michael Thurk
Faton Toski
M Weissenberger

Forwards
Ioannis Amanatidis
Marcel Heller
Benjamin Kohler
Alexander Meier
Naohiro Takahara

KEY: ■ On all match   ◄◄ Subbed or sent off (Counting game)   ►► Subbed on from bench (Counting Game)   ◄► Subbed on and then subbed or sent off (Counting Game)   □ Not in 16
  ■ On bench   ◄◄ Subbed or sent off (playing less than 70 minutes)   ►► Subbed on (playing less than 70 minutes)   ►► Subbed on and then subbed or sent off (playing less than 70 minutes)

GERMANY - EINTRACHT FRANKFURT

VfL WOLFSBURG

Final Position: 15th

NICKNAME: DIE WOLFE   KEY: ☐ Won ☐ Drawn ☐ Lost   Attendance

#		Opponent	H/A	W/D/L	Score	Scorers	Attendance
1	grpr1	Hertha Berlin	H	D	0-0		23,496
2	grpr1	Eintr Frankfurt	A	D	0-0		40,000
3	grpr1	B Leverkusen	A	D	1-1	Madouni 70 og	22,500
4	grpr1	Hannover 96	H	L	1-2	Krzynowek 52	21,000
5	grpr1	Schalke	A	L	0-2		60,000
6	grpr1	Bayern Munich	H	W	1-0	Hanke 36	30,000
7	grpr1	B M'gladbach	A	L	1-3	Madlung 16	45,096
8	grpr1	Stuttgart	H	D	1-1	Hanke 25	21,927
9	grpr1	Bochum	A	W	1-0	Krzynowek 24	18,650
10	grpr1	Hamburg	H	W	1-0	Hanke 19	25,000
11	grpr1	Mainz	A	W	2-1	Hanke 4 pen, Lamprecht 84	20,000
12	grpr1	Cottbus	H	D	0-0		15,000
13	grpr1	Arminia B	A	D	0-0		20,000
14	grpr1	Nurnberg	H	D	1-1	Menseguez 75	20,000
15	grpr1	B Dortmund	A	L	0-1		62,000
16	grpr1	Alem Aachen	H	L	1-2	Madlung 50	20,000
17	grpr1	W Bremen	A	L	1-2	Boakye 41	39,584
18	grpr1	Hertha Berlin	A	L	1-2	Madlung 18	40,272
19	grpr1	Eintr Frankfurt	H	D	2-2	Klimowicz 8, Hanke 73	15,097
20	grpr1	B Leverkusen	H	W	3-2	Hanke 16, 37, Klimowicz 72	16,621
21	grpr1	Hannover 96	A	D	2-2	Klimowicz 3, Krzynowek 25	35,244
22	grpr1	Schalke	H	D	2-2	Klimowicz 56, 89	28,346
23	grpr1	Bayern Munich	A	L	1-2	Makiadi 79	69,000
24	grpr1	B M'gladbach	H	W	1-0	Makiadi 65	21,343
25	grpr1	Stuttgart	A	D	0-0		48,000
26	grpr1	Bochum	H	W	3-1	Boakye 21, Madlung 26, Marcelinho 83	15,743
27	grpr1	Hamburg	A	L	0-1		57,000
28	grpr1	Mainz	H	W	3-2	Klimowicz 42, Marcelinho 80, 87	19,011
29	grpr1	Cottbus	A	L	2-3	Boakye 65, Makiadi 90	16,293
30	grpr1	Arminia B	H	L	2-3	Marcelinho 18, Boakye 53	20,941
31	grpr1	Nurnberg	A	D	1-1	Krzynowek 18	44,000
32	grpr1	B Dortmund	H	L	0-2		30,000
33	grpr1	Alem Aachen	A	D	2-2	Lamprecht 81, Klimowicz 85	20,800
34	grpr1	W Bremen	H	L	0-2		28,000

LEAGUE APPEARANCES, BOOKINGS AND CAPS

	AGE (on 01/07/07)	IN NAMED 18	APPEARANCES	COUNTING GAMES	MINUTES ON PITCH	YELLOW CARDS	RED CARDS	CAPS THIS SEASON	NATIONAL SIDE
Goalkeepers									
Simon Jentzsch	31	34	34	34	3060	1	0	-	Germany
Andre Lenz	33	32	0	0	0	0	0	-	Germany
Defenders									
D Martins Costa Alex	27	18	4	3	265	0	0	-	Portugal
Kevin Hofland	28	30	30	29	2669	12	0	-	Holland
Alexander Madlung	24	29	29	25	2465	5	0	2	Germany
Uwe Mohrle	27	34	22	20	1890	1	0	-	Germany
Facundo Quiroga	29	27	26	25	2256	7	1	-	Argentina
Michael Stegmayer	22	23	11	8	759	2	0	-	Germany
Peter van der Heyden	30	19	18	17	1496	2	0	3	Belgium
Midfielders									
Marian Hristov	33	5	2	0	60	1	0	-	Bulgaria
Miroslav Karhan	31	29	12	3	535	1	0	-	Slovakia
Jacek Krzynowek	31	32	32	28	2637	2	0	-	Poland
Chris Lamprecht	22	22	10	0	225	2	0	-	Germany
Cedric Makiadi	23	31	30	23	2209	1	0	-	Congo DR
Marcelinho	32	17	17	16	1456	4	0	-	Brazil
Jonathan Santana	25	23	18	11	1170	1	0	-	Argentina
Hans Sarpei	31	28	24	12	1287	3	0	5	Ghana
Pablo Thiam	33	12	6	1	215	2	0	-	Guinea
Tom van der Leegte	30	32	32	30	2809	12	0	-	Holland
Forwards									
Isaac Boakye	25	26	24	11	1289	1	0	-	Ghana
Mike Hanke	23	23	22	14	1499	1	0	3	Germany
Kamani Hill	21	15	9	0	155	0	0	1	United States
Rick Hoogendorp	32	17	8	2	366	1	0	-	Holland
Diego F Klimowicz	32	21	21	19	1795	2	0	-	Argentina
Juan C Menseguez	23	27	23	5	1030	0	0	-	Argentina

TEAM OF THE SEASON

Position	Player	Stats
D	Uwe Mohrle	CG: 20 DR: 78
D	Facundo Quiroga	CG: 25 DR: 70
D	Alexander Madlung	CG: 25 DR: 66
D	Kevin Hofland	CG: 29 DR: 63
G	Simon Jentzsch	CG: 34 DR: 68
M	Jacek Krzynowek	CG: 28 SD: -14
M	Hans Sarpei	CG: 12 SD: -14
M	Marcelinho	CG: 16 SD: -14
M	Tom van der Leegte	CG: 30 SD: -15
F	Mike Hanke	CG: 14 SR: 214
F	Diego F Klimowicz	CG: 19 SR: 256

MONTHLY POINTS TALLY

Month		%
AUGUST	3	33%
SEPTEMBER	3	33%
OCTOBER	4	44%
NOVEMBER	9	60%
DECEMBER	0	0%
JANUARY	1	17%
FEBRUARY	5	42%
MARCH	7	78%
APRIL	4	27%
MAY	1	11%

LEAGUE GOALS

	PLAYER	MINS	GOALS	S RATE
1	Hanke	1499	7	214
2	Klimowicz	1795	7	256
3	Boakye	1289	4	322
4	Marcelinho	1456	4	364
5	Madlung	2465	4	616
6	Krzynowek	2637	4	659
7	Makiadi	2209	3	736
8	Lamprecht	225	2	112
9	Menseguez	1030	1	1030
10	Mohrle	1890	0	
11	Muller	0	0	
12	Platins	0	0	
13	Quiroga	2256	0	
	Other		0	
	TOTAL		36	

TOP POINT EARNERS

	PLAYER	GAMES	AV PTS
1	Mike Hanke	14	1.43
2	Hans Sarpei	12	1.25
3	Facundo Quiroga	26	1.23
4	Jacek Krzynowek	28	1.14
5	Marcelinho	16	1.13
6	Tom van der Leegte	30	1.13
7	Peter van der Heyden	17	1.12
8	Alexander Madlung	25	1.12
9	D Fernando Klimowicz	19	1.11
10	Uwe Mohrle	20	1.10
	CLUB AVERAGE:		1.09

DISCIPLINARY RECORDS

	PLAYER	YELLOW	RED	AVE
1	Kevin Hofland	12	0	222
2	Tom v der Leegte	12	0	234
3	Facundo Quiroga	7	1	282
4	Marcelinho	4	0	364
5	Michael Stegmayer	2	0	379
6	Hans Sarpei	3	0	429
7	Alexander Madlung	5	0	493
8	Miroslav Karhan	1	0	535
9	Peter v der Heyden	2	0	748
10	Diego F Klimowicz	2	0	897
11	Jonathan Santana	1	0	1170
12	Isaac Boakye	1	0	1289
13	Jacek Krzynowek	2	0	1318
	Other	4	0	
	TOTAL	58	1	

KEY GOALKEEPER

Simon Jentzsch

Goals Conceded in the League	45	Counting Games League games when player was on pitch for at least 70 minutes	34
Defensive Rating Ave number of mins between League goals conceded while on the pitch	68	Clean Sheets In League games when player was on pitch for at least 70 minutes	9

KEY PLAYERS - DEFENDERS

Uwe Mohrle

Goals Conceded Number of League goals conceded while the player was on the pitch	24	Clean Sheets In League games when player was on pitch for at least 70 minutes	8
Defensive Rating Ave number of mins between League goals conceded while on the pitch	78	Club Defensive Rating Average number of mins between League goals conceded by the club this season	68

	PLAYER	CON LGE	CLEAN SHEETS	DEF RATE
1	Uwe Mohrle	24	8	78 mins
2	Facundo Quiroga	32	7	70 mins
3	Alexander Madlung	37	7	66 mins
4	Kevin Hofland	42	6	63 mins

KEY PLAYERS - MIDFIELDERS

Jacek Krzynowek

Goals in the League	4	Contribution to Attacking Power Average number of minutes between League team goals while on pitch	79
Defensive Rating Average number of mins between League goals conceded while on the pitch	65	Scoring Difference Defensive Rating minus Contribution to Attacking Power	-14

	PLAYER	LGE GOALS	DEF RATE	POWER	SCORE DIFF
1	Jacek Krzynowek	4	65	79	-14 mins
2	Hans Sarpei	0	85	99	-14 mins
3	Marcelinho	4	52	66	-14 mins
4	Tom van der Leegte	0	70	85	-15 mins

KEY PLAYERS - GOALSCORERS

Mike Hanke

Goals in the League	7	Player Strike Rate Average number of minutes between League goals scored by player	214
Contribution to Attacking Power Average number of minutes between League team goals while on pitch	71	Club Strike Rate Average number of minutes between League goals scored by club	82

	PLAYER	LGE GOALS	POWER	STRIKE RATE
1	Mike Hanke	7	71	214 mins
2	Diego Fernando Klimowicz	7	81	256 mins
3	Isaac Boakye	4	85	322 mins
4	Marcelinho	4	66	364 mins

Marcelinho

SQUAD APPEARANCES

Match	1	2	3	4	5	6	7	8	9	10	11	12	13	14	15	16	17	18	19	20	21	22	23	24	25	26	27	28	29	30	31	32	33	34
Venue	H	A	A	H	A	H	A	H	A	H	A	H	A	H	A	H	A	A	H	H	A	H	A	H	A	H	A	H	A	H	A	H	A	H
Competition	L	L	L	L	L	L	L	L	L	L	L	L	L	L	L	L	L	L	L	L	L	L	L	L	L	L	L	L	L	L	L	L	L	L
Result	D	D	D	L	L	W	L	D	W	W	W	D	D	D	L	L	L	L	D	W	D	D	L	W	D	W	L	W	L	L	D	L	D	L

KEY: On all match · Subbed or sent off (Counting game) · Subbed on from bench (Counting Game) · Subbed on and then subbed or sent off (Counting Game) · Not in 16 · On bench · Subbed or sent off (playing less than 70 minutes) · Subbed on (playing less than 70 minutes) · Subbed on and then subbed or sent off (playing less than 70 minutes)

GERMANY - VfL WOLSBURG

MAINZ

Final Position: 16th

NICKNAME: DIE NULLFUNFER   KEY: ☐ Won ☐ Drawn ☐ Lost   Attendance

				Result	Scorers	Attendance
1	grpr1	Bochum	H W	2-1	Damm 29, Azaouagh 72	20,300
2	grpr1	B Dortmund	A D	1-1	Edu 77	70,100
3	grpr1	Eintr Frankfurt	H D	1-1	Jovanovic 84	20,300
4	grpr1	Cottbus	A L	0-2		16,000
5	grpr1	Hertha Berlin	H D	1-1	Bakary Diakite 49	20,300
6	grpr1	Nurnberg	A D	1-1	Babatz 85	35,000
7	grpr1	Alem Aachen	H L	1-3	Rose 29	20,300
8	grpr1	Arminia B	A L	0-1		19,260
9	grpr1	W Bremen	H L	1-6	Azaouagh 74	20,300
10	grpr1	B Leverkusen	A D	1-1	Szabics 28	22,500
11	grpr1	Wolfsburg	H L	1-2	Szabics 7	20,000
12	grpr1	Schalke	A L	0-4		61,000
13	grpr1	Hamburg	H D	0-0		20,300
14	grpr1	Hannover 96	A L	0-1		27,000
15	grpr1	Stuttgart	H D	0-0		20,300
16	grpr1	B M'gladbach	A D	1-1	Jovanovic 89	44,157
17	grpr1	Bayern Munich	H L	0-4		20,300
18	grpr1	Bochum	A W	1-0	Rose 38	20,487
19	grpr1	B Dortmund	H W	1-0	Andreasen 61 pen	20,300
20	grpr1	Eintr Frankfurt	A D	0-0		51,300
21	grpr1	Cottbus	H W	4-1	Andreasen 7, Zidan 22, 39 pen, 60	20,300
22	grpr1	Hertha Berlin	A W	2-1	Zidan 55 pen, Andreasen 65	35,473
23	grpr1	Nurnberg	H W	2-1	Zidan 20, 27	20,300
24	grpr1	Alem Aachen	A L	1-2	Zidan 15	20,832
25	grpr1	Arminia B	H W	1-0	Andreasen 51 pen	20,300
26	grpr1	W Bremen	A L	0-2		39,450
27	grpr1	B Leverkusen	H L	1-3	Zidan 76	20,300
28	grpr1	Wolfsburg	A L	2-3	Zidan 22 pen, 79	19,011
29	grpr1	Schalke	H L	0-3		20,300
30	grpr1	Hamburg	A D	2-2	Zidan 12, Gerber 59	57,000
31	grpr1	Hannover 96	H L	1-2	Zidan 81	20,300
32	grpr1	Stuttgart	A L	0-2		56,000
33	grpr1	B M'gladbach	H W	3-0	Zidan 32 pen, Ruman 45, Feulner 72	20,300
34	grpr1	Bayern Munich	A L	2-5	Amri 55, Feulner 76	69,000

LEAGUE APPEARANCES, BOOKINGS AND CAPS

	AGE (on 01/07/07)	IN NAMED 18	APPEARANCES	COUNTING GAMES	MINUTES ON PITCH	YELLOW CARDS	RED CARDS	CAPS THIS SEASON	NATIONAL SIDE
Goalkeepers									
Dimo Wache	33	30	26	26	2340	1	0	-	Germany
Christian Wetklo	27	28	8	8	720	1	0	-	Germany
Defenders									
Leon Andreasen	24	15	15	15	1318	7	1	2	Denmark
Doo-Ri Cha	26	27	12	8	726	0	0	-	South Korea
Christian Demirtas	23	25	22	21	1937	1	0	-	Germany
Ralph Gunesch	23	23	9	8	721	0	0	-	Germany
Nikolce Noveski	28	31	31	31	2790	4	0	-	Macedonia
Marco Rose	30	28	28	26	2432	7	1	-	Germany
Neven Subotic	18	2	1	1	90	0	0	-	United States
Benjamin Weigelt	24	29	10	6	662	0	0	-	Germany
Midfielders									
Otto Addo	32	4	2	0	49	0	0	-	Ghana
Mimoun Azaouagh	24	28	27	18	1952	6	0	-	Germany
Christof Babatz	32	17	13	7	809	0	0	-	Germany
Markus Feulner	25	33	30	19	2221	8	0	-	Germany
Manuel Friedrich	27	32	32	32	2880	0	0	7	Germany
Petr Ruman	30	19	17	7	919	2	0	-	Czech Republic
Elkin Soto	26	9	8	6	582	1	0	-	Colombia
Mario Vrancic	18	4	2	0	68	0	0	-	Germany
Forwards									
Chadli Amri	22	21	15	7	859	1	0	-	Algeria
Conor Casey	25	3	2	0	28	0	0	-	United States
Tobias Damm	23	10	8	1	343	0	0	-	Germany
Bakary Diakite	26	10	9	5	581	2	0	-	Germany
Goncalves Edu	25	15	14	4	682	0	0	-	Brazil
Fabian Gerber	27	32	31	22	2191	4	0	-	Germany
Ranisav Jovanovic	26	27	26	4	832	2	0	-	Serbia
Marius Niculae	26	10	6	0	161	0	0	-	Romania
Milorad Pekovic	29	33	29	20	2076	8	0	-	Serbia
Imre Szabics	26	24	20	11	1166	1	0	-	Hungary
Damir Vrancic	21	13	5	2	211	1	0	-	Croatia
Mohammed Zidan	25	16	15	15	1307	0	0	-	Egypt

TEAM OF THE SEASON

Christian Demirtas — D — CG: 21 DR: 62
Markus Feulner — M — CG: 19 SD: -31
Nikolce Noveski — D — CG: 31 DR: 59
Manuel Friedrich — M — CG: 32 SD: -34
Mohammed Zidan — F — CG: 15 SR: 100
Dimo Wache — G — CG: 26 DR: 57
Leon Andreasen — D — CG: 15 DR: 57
Mimoun Azaouagh — M — CG: 18 SD: -55
Imre Szabics* — F — CG: 11 SR: 583
Marco Rose — D — CG: 26 DR: 50
Petr Ruman* — M — CG: 7 SD: 19

MONTHLY POINTS TALLY

Month		
AUGUST	5	56%
SEPTEMBER	2	22%
OCTOBER	0	0%
NOVEMBER	2	13%
DECEMBER	2	22%
JANUARY	6	100%
FEBRUARY	10	83%
MARCH	3	25%
APRIL	1	8%
MAY	3	33%

LEAGUE GOALS

	PLAYER	MINS	GOALS	S RATE
1	Zidan	1307	13	100
2	Andreasen	1318	4	329
3	Jovanovic	832	2	416
4	Szabics	1166	2	583
5	Azaouagh	1952	2	976
6	Feulner	2221	2	1110
7	Rose	2432	2	1216
8	Damm	343	1	343
9	Diakite	581	1	581
10	Edu	682	1	682
11	Babatz	809	1	809
12	Amri	859	1	859
13	Ruman	919	1	919
	Other		1	
	TOTAL		34	

TOP POINT EARNERS

	PLAYER	GAMES	AV PTS
1	Leon Andreasen	15	1.53
2	Christian Demirtas	21	1.38
3	Mimoun Azaouagh	18	1.33
4	Mohammed Zidan	15	1.33
5	Markus Feulner	19	1.11
6	Dimo Wache	26	1.08
7	Nikolce Noveski	31	1.06
8	Manuel Friedrich	32	1.03
9	Marco Rose	26	1.00
10	Fabian Gerber	22	0.91
	CLUB AVERAGE:		1.00

DISCIPLINARY RECORDS

	PLAYER	YELLOW	RED	AVE
1	Leon Andreasen	7	1	164
2	Milorad Pekovic	8	0	259
3	Markus Feulner	8	0	277
4	Bakary Diakite	2	0	290
5	Marco Rose	7	1	304
6	Mimoun Azaouagh	6	0	325
7	Ranisav Jovanovic	2	0	416
8	Petr Ruman	2	0	459
9	Fabian Gerber	4	0	547
10	Elkin Soto	1	0	582
11	Mohammed Zidan	2	0	653
12	Nikolce Noveski	4	0	697
13	Christian Wetklo	1	0	720
	Other	4	0	
	TOTAL	58	2	

KEY GOALKEEPER

Dimo Wache

Goals Conceded in the League	41	Counting Games League games when player was on pitch for at least 70 minutes	26
Defensive Rating Ave number of mins between League goals conceded while on the pitch	57	Clean Sheets In League games when player was on pitch for at least 70 minutes	5

KEY PLAYERS - DEFENDERS

Christian Demirtas

Goals Conceded Number of League goals conceded while the player was on the pitch	31	Clean Sheets In League games when player was on pitch for at least 70 minutes	7
Defensive Rating Ave number of mins between League goals conceded while on the pitch	62	Club Defensive Rating Average number of mins between League goals conceded by the club this season	53

	PLAYER	CON LGE	CLEAN SHEETS	DEF RATE
1	Christian Demirtas	31	7	62 mins
2	Nikolce Noveski	47	7	59 mins
3	Leon Andreasen	23	5	57 mins
4	Marco Rose	48	3	50 mins

KEY PLAYERS - MIDFIELDERS

Petr Ruman

Goals in the League	1	Contribution to Attacking Power Average number of minutes between League team goals while on pitch	57
Defensive Rating Average number of mins between League goals conceded while on the pitch	76	Scoring Difference Defensive Rating minus Contribution to Attacking Power	19

	PLAYER	LGE GOALS	DEF RATE	POWER	SCORE DIFF
1	Petr Ruman	1	76	57	19 mins
2	Markus Feulner	2	61	92	-31 mins
3	Manuel Friedrich	0	53	87	-34 mins
4	Mimoun Azaouagh	2	59	114	-55 mins

KEY PLAYERS - GOALSCORERS

Mohammed Zidan

Goals in the League	13	Player Strike Rate Average number of minutes between League goals scored by player	100
Contribution to Attacking Power Average number of minutes between League team goals while on pitch	65	Club Strike Rate Average number of minutes between League goals scored by club	90

	PLAYER	LGE GOALS	POWER	STRIKE RATE
1	Mohammed Zidan	13	65	100 mins
2	Imre Szabics	2	194	583 mins
3	Mimoun Azaouagh	2	114	976 mins
4	Markus Feulner	2	92	1110 mins

Mohammed Zidan

SQUAD APPEARANCES

Match	1	2	3	4	5	6	7	8	9	10	11	12	13	14	15	16	17	18	19	20	21	22	23	24	25	26	27	28	29	30	31	32	33	34
Venue	H	A	H	A	H	A	H	A	H	A	H	A	H	A	H	A	H	A	H	A	H	A	H	A	H	A	H	A	H	A	H	A	H	A
Competition	L	L	L	L	L	L	L	L	L	L	L	L	L	L	L	L	L	L	L	L	L	L	L	L	L	L	L	L	L	L	L	L	L	L
Result	W	D	D	L	D	D	L	L	L	D	L	L	D	L	D	D	L	W	W	D	W	W	W	L	W	L	L	L	L	D	L	L	W	L

Goalkeepers
Dimo Wache
Christian Wetklo

Defenders
Leon Andreasen
Doo-Ri Cha
Christian Demirtas
Ralph Gunesch
Nikolce Noveski
Marco Rose
Neven Subotic
Benjamin Weigelt

Midfielders
Otto Addo
Mimoun Azaouagh
Christof Babatz
Markus Feulner
Manuel Friedrich
Petr Ruman
Elkin Soto
Mario Vrancic

Forwards
Chadli Amri
Conor Casey
Tobias Damm
Bakary Diakite
Goncalves Edu
Fabian Gerber
Ranisav Jovanovic
Marius Niculae
Milorad Pekovic
Imre Szabics
Damir Vrancic
Mohammed Zidan

KEY: ■ On all match   ◄◄ Subbed or sent off (Counting game)   ►► Subbed on from bench (Counting Game)   ►► Subbed on and then subbed or sent off (Counting Game)   ☐ Not in 16
  ☐ On bench   ◄ Subbed or sent off (playing less than 70 minutes)   ►► Subbed on (playing less than 70 minutes)   ►► Subbed on and then subbed or sent off (playing less than 70 minutes)

ALEMANNIA AACHEN

Final Position: **17th**

NICKNAME: KARTOFFELKAFER   KEY: ☐ Won ☐ Drawn ☐ Lost   Attendance

1	grpr1	**B Leverkusen**	A	L	0-3	22,500
2	grpr1	**Schalke**	H	L	0-1	21,300
3	grpr1	**Hannover 96**	A	W	3-0 Schlaudraff 15, Dum 47, Plasshenrich 72	30,087
4	grpr1	**B M'gladbach**	H	W	4-2 Reghecampf 7 pen, Schlaudraff 31, 84,	
					Ebbers 51	21,300
5	grpr1	**Bayern Munich**	A	L	1-2 Dum 38	69,000
6	grpr1	**Bochum**	H	W	2-1 Schlaudraff 48, Rosler 49	21,300
7	grpr1	**Mainz**	A	W	3-1 Stehle 33, Rosler 38, Ebbers 78	20,300
8	grpr1	**Cottbus**	H	L	1-2 Reghecampf 17	20,300
9	grpr1	**Arminia B**	A	L	1-5 Plasshenrich 46	23,538
10	grpr1	**Stuttgart**	H	L	2-4 Rosler 28, Ibisevic 86	21,000
11	grpr1	**B Dortmund**	A	D	0-0	65,000
12	grpr1	**Nurnberg**	H	D	1-1 Plasshenrich 90	20,800
13	grpr1	**W Bremen**	H	D	2-2 Rosler 33, Schlaudraff 68	20,800
14	grpr1	**Hertha Berlin**	A	L	1-2 Lehmann 45	35,000
15	grpr1	**Eintr Frankfurt**	H	L	2-3 Schlaudraff 32, Fiel 81	20,000
16	grpr1	**Wolfsburg**	A	W	2-1 Reghecampf 72, Herzig 78	20,000
17	grpr1	**Hamburg**	H	D	3-3 Reghecampf 62, Fiel 77, Reinhardt 90	20,500
18	grpr1	**B Leverkusen**	H	L	2-3 Reghecampf 9 pen, Ibisevic 30	21,000
19	grpr1	**Schalke**	A	L	1-2 Ibisevic 17	61,482
20	grpr1	**Hannover 96**	H	L	1-4 Reghecampf 26 pen	20,800
21	grpr1	**B M'gladbach**	A	D	0-0	52,000
22	grpr1	**Bayern Munich**	H	W	1-0 Klitzpera 10	20,832
23	grpr1	**Bochum**	A	D	2-2 Ibisevic 35, Lehmann 59	21,350
24	grpr1	**Mainz**	H	W	2-1 Schlaudraff 47, Ibisevic 49	20,832
25	grpr1	**Cottbus**	A	W	2-0 Rosler 28, Pinto 90	15,200
26	grpr1	**Arminia B**	H	W	2-0 Schlaudraff 70, Reghecampf 75 pen	20,800
27	grpr1	**Stuttgart**	A	L	1-3 Sichone 59	43,000
28	grpr1	**B Dortmund**	H	L	1-4 Ibisevic 63	20,800
29	grpr1	**Nurnberg**	A	L	0-1	44,298
30	grpr1	**W Bremen**	A	L	1-3 Pinto 2	40,300
31	grpr1	**Hertha Berlin**	H	L	0-4	20,800
32	grpr1	**Eintr Frankfurt**	A	L	0-4	51,500
33	grpr1	**Wolfsburg**	H	D	2-2 Lehmann 65 pen, Nemeth 68	20,800
34	grpr1	**Hamburg**	A	L	0-4	57,000

LEAGUE APPEARANCES, BOOKINGS AND CAPS

	AGE (on 01/07/07)	IN NAMED 18	APPEARANCES	COUNTING GAMES	MINUTES ON PITCH	YELLOW CARDS	RED CARDS	CAPS THIS SEASON	NATIONAL SIDE
Goalkeepers									
Marcus Hesse	23	9	2	2	180	0	0	-	Germany
Kristian Nicht	25	29	18	17	1541	0	1	-	Germany
Stephan Straub	26	28	16	14	1337	0	0	-	Germany
Defenders									
Mirko Casper	25	27	7	2	263	1	0	-	Germany
Sascha Dum	20	24	22	10	1152	7	1	-	Germany
Matthias Heidrich	29	24	10	2	402	1	0	-	Germany
Nico Herzig	23	31	27	24	2248	7	1	-	Germany
Alexander Klitzpera	29	29	24	20	1957	5	1	-	Germany
Jeffrey Leiwakabessy	26	34	34	34	3028	4	0	-	Holland
Moises Sichone	30	31	21	11	1718	6	0	-	Zambia
Thomas Stehle	26	30	19	15	1606	5	0	-	Germany
Midfielders									
Cristian Fiel	27	30	30	13	1589	3	0	-	Germany
Matthias Lehmann	24	34	30	23	2196	4	0	-	Germany
Emil Noll	28	12	7	1	153	0	0	-	Germany
Sergio Pinto	26	31	29	18	1923	10	0	-	Portugal
Reiner Plasshenrich	30	18	18	16	1484	1	0	-	Germany
L Reghecampf	31	33	32	23	2337	5	0	-	Romania
Forwards									
Marius Ebbers	29	27	27	17	1890	2	0	-	Germany
Vedad Ibisevic	22	32	24	11	1385	4	0	-	Bosnia
Manuel Junglas	18	2	1	0	2	0	0	-	Germany
Erwin Koen	28	1	1	0	15	1	0	-	Holland
Emmanuel Krontiris	24	7	5	0	118	1	0	-	Germany
Szilard Nemeth	28	6	4	0	78	0	0	1	Slovakia
Abdulkadir Ozgen	20	6	2	0	6	0	0	-	Turkey
Marco Quotschalla	18	5	2	0	13	0	0	-	Germany
Sascha Rosler	29	30	30	27	2479	6	1	-	Germany
Jan Schlaudraff	23	28	28	25	2382	4	0	3	Germany

TEAM OF THE SEASON

D
Alexander Klitzpera
CG: 20 **DR:** 46

M
Reiner Plasshenrich
CG: 16 **SD:** -5

D
Thomas Stehle
CG: 15 **DR:** 45

M
Laurentiu Reghecampf
CG: 23 **SD:** -17

F
Vedad Ibisevic*
CG: 11 **SR:** 230

G
Stephan Straub
CG: 14 **DR:** 58

D
Nico Herzig
CG: 24 **DR:** 44

M
Sergio Pinto
CG: 18 **SD:** -18

F
Jan Schlaudraff
CG: 25 **SR:** 297

D
Jeffrey Leiwakabessy
CG: 34 **DR:** 43

M
Cristian Fiel
CG: 13 **SD:** -25

MONTHLY POINTS TALLY

AUGUST	3	33%
SEPTEMBER	6	67%
OCTOBER	3	33%
NOVEMBER	3	20%
DECEMBER	4	44%
JANUARY	0	0%
FEBRUARY	5	42%
MARCH	9	75%
APRIL	0	0%
MAY	1	11%

LEAGUE GOALS

	PLAYER	MINS	GOALS	S RATE
1	Schlaudraff	2382	8	297
2	Reghecampf	2337	7	333
3	Ibisevic	1385	6	230
4	Rosler	2479	5	495
5	Plasshenrich	1484	3	494
6	Lehmann	2196	3	732
7	Dum	1152	2	576
8	Fiel	1589	2	794
9	Ebbers	1890	2	945
10	Pinto	1923	2	961
11	Nemeth	78	1	78
12	Stehle	1606	1	1606
13	Sichone	1718	1	1718
	Other		2	
	TOTAL		**45**	

TOP POINT EARNERS

	PLAYER	GAMES	AV PTS
1	Stephan Straub	14	1.50
2	Reiner Plasshenrich	16	1.25
3	Jan Schlaudraff	25	1.24
4	Nico Herzig	24	1.21
5	Laurentiu Reghecampf	23	1.13
6	Moises Sichone	17	1.12
7	Sascha Rosler	27	1.11
8	Marius Ebbers	17	1.06
9	Jeffrey Leiwakabessy	34	1.00
10	Thomas Stehle	15	1.00
	CLUB AVERAGE:		**1.00**

DISCIPLINARY RECORDS

	PLAYER	YELLOW	RED	AVE
1	Sascha Dum	7	1	144
2	Sergio Pinto	10	0	192
3	Nico Herzig	7	1	281
4	Moises Sichone	6	0	286
5	Thomas Stehle	5	0	321
6	Alexander Klitzpera	5	1	326
7	Vedad Ibisevic	4	0	346
8	Sascha Rosler	6	1	354
9	L Reghecampf	5	0	467
10	Cristian Fiel	3	0	529
11	Matthias Lehmann	4	0	549
12	Jan Schlaudraff	4	0	595
13	J Leiwakabessy	4	0	757
	Other	3	1	
	TOTAL	**73**	**5**	

KEY GOALKEEPER

Stephan Straub

Goals Conceded in the League	23	Counting Games League games when player was on pitch for at least 70 minutes	14
Defensive Rating Ave number of mins between League goals conceded while on the pitch	58	Clean Sheets In League games when player was on pitch for at least 70 minutes	6

KEY PLAYERS - DEFENDERS

Alexander Klitzpera

Goals Conceded Number of League goals conceded while the player was on the pitch	42	Clean Sheets In League games when player was on pitch for at least 70 minutes	4
Defensive Rating Ave number of mins between League goals conceded while on the pitch	46	Club Defensive Rating Average number of mins between League goals conceded by the club this season	43

	PLAYER	CON LGE	CLEAN SHEETS	DEF RATE
1	Alexander Klitzpera	42	4	46 mins
2	Thomas Stehle	35	4	45 mins
3	Nico Herzig	50	5	44 mins
4	Jeffrey Leiwakabessy	70	6	43 mins

KEY PLAYERS - MIDFIELDERS

Reiner Plasshenrich

Goals in the League	3	Contribution to Attacking Power Average number of minutes between League team goals while on pitch	64
Defensive Rating Average number of mins between League goals conceded while on the pitch	59	Scoring Difference Defensive Rating minus Contribution to Attacking Power	-5

	PLAYER	LGE GOALS	DEF RATE	POWER	SCORE DIFF
1	Reiner Plasshenrich	3	59	64	-5 mins
2	Laurentiu Reghecampf	7	44	61	-17 mins
3	Sergio Pinto	2	40	58	-18 mins
4	Cristian Fiel	2	41	66	-25 mins

KEY PLAYERS - GOALSCORERS

Vedad Ibisevic

Goals in the League	6	Player Strike Rate Average number of minutes between League goals scored by player	230
Contribution to Attacking Power Average number of minutes between League team goals while on pitch	65	Club Strike Rate Average number of minutes between League goals scored by club	66

	PLAYER	LGE GOALS	POWER	STRIKE RATE
1	Vedad Ibisevic	6	65	230 mins
2	Jan Schlaudraff	8	58	297 mins
3	Laurentiu Reghecampf	7	61	333 mins
4	Reiner Plasshenrich	3	64	494 mins

Sergio Pinto & Vedad Ibisevic

SQUAD APPEARANCES

Match	1	2	3	4	5	6	7	8	9	10	11	12	13	14	15	16	17	18	19	20	21	22	23	24	25	26	27	28	29	30	31	32	33	34
Venue	A	H	A	H	A	H	A	H	A	H	A	H	H	A	H	A	H	H	A	H	A	H	A	H	A	H	A	H	A	A	H	A	H	A
Competition	L	L	L	L	L	L	L	L	L	L	L	L	L	L	L	L	L	L	L	L	L	L	L	L	L	L	L	L	L	L	L	L	L	L
Result	L	L	W	W	L	W	W	L	L	L	D	D	D	L	L	W	D	L	L	L	D	W	D	W	W	L	L	L	L	L	L	L	D	L

Goalkeepers

Marcus Hesse
Kristian Nicht
Stephan Straub

Defenders

Mirko Casper
Sascha Dum
Matthias Heidrich
Nico Herzig
Alexander Klitzpera
Jeffrey Leiwakabessy
Moises Sichone
Thomas Stehle

Midfielders

Cristian Fiel
Matthias Lehmann
Emil Noll
Sergio Pinto
Reiner Plasshenrich
L Reghecampf

Forwards

Marius Ebbers
Vedad Ibisevic
Manuel Junglas
Erwin Koen
Emmanuel Krontiris
Szilard Nemeth
Abdulkadir Ozgen
Marco Quotschalla
Sascha Rosler
Jan Schlaudraff

KEY: ■ On all match | ◄◄ Subbed or sent off (Counting game) | ►► Subbed on from bench (Counting Game) | ►► Subbed on and then subbed or sent off (Counting Game) | Not in 16
■ On bench | ◄◄ Subbed or sent off (playing less than 70 minutes) | ►► Subbed on (playing less than 70 minutes) | ►► Subbed on and then subbed or sent off (playing less than 70 minutes)

GERMANY - ALEMANNIA AACHEN

BORUSSIA MONCHENGLADBACH

Final Position: **18th**

NICKNAME: DIE FOLEN (THE FOALS)   KEY: ☐ Won ☐ Drawn ☐ Lost   Attendance

#					Scorers	Attendance
1	grpr1	Cottbus	H W	2-0	Svensson 51, Neuville 61 pen	48,000
2	grpr1	Nurnberg	A L	0-1		46,780
3	grpr1	Arminia B	H W	1-0	Kahe 60	42,000
4	grpr1	Alem Aachen	A L	2-4	Kahe 51, 90	21,300
5	grpr1	B Dortmund	H W	1-0	Kahe 39	54,000
6	grpr1	W Bremen	A L	0-3		38,000
7	grpr1	Wolfsburg	H W	3-1	Kluge 34, Neuville 35, Degen 84	45,096
8	grpr1	Hertha Berlin	A L	1-2	Neuville 62	43,604
9	grpr1	B Leverkusen	H L	0-2		51,217
10	grpr1	Eintr Frankfurt	A L	0-1		47,000
11	grpr1	Schalke	H L	0-2		53,000
12	grpr1	Hamburg	A D	1-1	Neuville 84	57,000
13	grpr1	Hannover 96	H L	0-1		38,000
14	grpr1	Stuttgart	A L	0-1		46,000
15	grpr1	Bayern Munich	A D	1-1	Delura 33	69,000
16	grpr1	Mainz	H D	1-1	Demirtas 16 og	44,157
17	grpr1	Bochum	A L	0-2		30,500
18	grpr1	Cottbus	A L	1-3	Degen 79	13,044
19	grpr1	Nurnberg	H D	0-0		33,116
20	grpr1	Arminia B	A W	2-0	Insua 28, Jansen 89	23,114
21	grpr1	Alem Aachen	H D	0-0		52,000
22	grpr1	B Dortmund	A L	0-1		73,600
23	grpr1	W Bremen	H D	2-2	Delura 18, Rafael 90	50,644
24	grpr1	Wolfsburg	A L	0-1		21,343
25	grpr1	Hertha Berlin	H W	3-1	Rafael 32, 69, Delura 86	40,518
26	grpr1	B Leverkusen	A L	0-1		22,500
27	grpr1	Eintr Frankfurt	H D	1-1	Insua 89	52,177
28	grpr1	Schalke	A L	0-2		61,482
29	grpr1	Hamburg	H L	0-1		54,067
30	grpr1	Hannover 96	A L	0-1		42,784
31	grpr1	Stuttgart	H L	0-1		48,014
32	grpr1	Bayern Munich	H D	1-1	Kluge 52	54,067
33	grpr1	Mainz	A L	0-3		20,300
34	grpr1	Bochum	H L	0-2		50,001

LEAGUE APPEARANCES, BOOKINGS AND CAPS

	AGE (on 01/07/07)	IN NAMED 18	APPEARANCES	COUNTING GAMES	MINUTES ON PITCH	YELLOW CARDS	RED CARDS	CAPS THIS SEASON	NATIONAL SIDE
Goalkeepers									
Christofer Heimeroth	25	34	7	6	599	0	0	-	Germany
Kasey Keller	37	28	28	27	2461	0	0	3	United States
Defenders									
Kasper Bogelund	26	23	21	19	1795	3	0	-	Denmark
Marvin Compper	22	27	23	17	1758	3	0	-	Germany
Steve Gohouri	26	15	14	14	1255	6	2	4	Ivory Coast
Thomas Helveg	36	15	8	6	577	1	1	3	Denmark
Marcell Jansen	21	23	23	23	2059	3	0	8	Germany
Tim Rubink	19	1	1	0	45	0	0	-	Germany
Bo Svensson	27	25	19	14	1449	3	0	-	Denmark
Jose Ze Antonio	30	31	30	30	2700	3	0	-	Portugal
Midfielders									
Alex Baumjohann	20	5	3	0	55	0	0	-	Germany
Hassan El Fakiri	30	31	18	12	1306	4	0	3	Norway
Robert Flessers	20	14	6	2	262	0	0	-	Germany
Federico Insua	27	34	32	23	2446	4	0	-	Argentina
Oliver Kirch	24	17	14	11	1101	1	0	-	Germany
Peer Kluge	26	29	25	23	2093	8	0	-	Germany
Tobias Levels	20	24	12	10	915	1	0	-	Holland
Marko Marin	18	4	4	2	241	0	0	-	Germany
Eugen Polanski	21	30	22	13	1501	4	0	-	Poland
Sebastian Svard	24	10	9	3	472	2	0	-	Denmark
Bernd Thijs	29	18	14	10	999	0	0	-	Belgium
Mikkel Thygesen	22	11	5	0	197	0	0	1	Denmark
J van den Bergh	20	2	1	0	45	0	0	-	Germany
Forwards									
David Degen	24	22	18	5	676	4	0	-	Switzerland
Michael Delura	22	28	28	17	1884	3	0	-	Germany
C E de Souza Kahe	24	33	26	14	1590	3	0	-	Brazil
Moses Lamidi	19	6	5	1	215	1	0	-	Nigeria
Oliver Neuville	34	16	16	9	1014	0	0	3	Germany
Nando Rafael	23	25	19	14	1323	5	0	-	Angola
Wesley Sonck	28	12	7	3	333	1	0	-	Belgium
Vaclav Sverkos	23	10	6	2	222	0	0	-	Czech Republic

TEAM OF THE SEASON

D Bo Svensson CG: 14 DR: 85
M Oliver Kirch* CG: 11 SD: -36
D Marvin Compper CG: 17 DR: 76
M Peer Kluge CG: 23 SD: -56
F C E de Souza Kahe CG: 14 SR: 397
G Kasey Keller CG: 27 DR: 72
D Kasper Bogelund CG: 19 DR: 74
M Federico Insua CG: 23 SD: -62
F Nando Rafael CG: 14 SR: 441
D Marcell Jansen CG: 23 DR: 71
M Hassan El Fakiri CG: 12 SD: -65

MONTHLY POINTS TALLY

Month		
AUGUST	6	67%
SEPTEMBER	3	33%
OCTOBER	3	33%
NOVEMBER	1	7%
DECEMBER	2	22%
JANUARY	1	17%
FEBRUARY	5	42%
MARCH	4	33%
APRIL	0	0%
MAY	1	11%

LEAGUE GOALS

	PLAYER	MINS	GOALS	S RATE
1	Neuville	1014	4	253
2	Kahe	1590	4	397
3	Rafael	1323	3	441
4	Delura	1884	3	628
5	Degen	676	2	338
6	Kluge	2093	2	1046
7	Insua	2446	2	1223
8	Svensson	1449	1	1449
9	Jansen	2059	1	2059
10	Keller	2461	0	
11	Kirch	1101	0	
12	Lohe	0	0	
13	Lamidi	215	0	
	Other		0	
	TOTAL		22	

TOP POINT EARNERS

	PLAYER	GAMES	AV PTS
1	C E de Souza Kahe	14	1.21
2	Michael Delura	17	1.00
3	Hassan El Fakiri	12	1.00
4	Eugen Polanski	13	1.00
5	Federico Insua	23	0.96
6	Bo Svensson	14	0.93
7	Kasey Keller	27	0.89
8	Marcell Jansen	23	0.87
9	Jose Ze Antonio	30	0.87
10	Kasper Bogelund	19	0.84
	CLUB AVERAGE:		0.76

DISCIPLINARY RECORDS

	PLAYER	YELLOW	RED	AVE
1	Steve Gohouri	6	2	156
2	David Degen	4	0	169
3	Sebastian Svard	2	0	236
4	Peer Kluge	8	0	261
5	Nando Rafael	5	0	264
6	Thomas Helveg	1	1	288
7	Hassan El Fakiri	4	0	326
8	Eugen Polanski	4	0	375
9	Bo Svensson	3	0	483
10	C E de Souza Kahe	3	0	530
11	Marvin Compper	3	0	586
12	Kasper Bogelund	3	0	598
13	Federico Insua	4	0	611
	Other	11	0	
	TOTAL	61	3	

KEY GOALKEEPER

Kasey Keller

Goals Conceded in the League	34	Counting Games League games when player was on pitch for at least 70 minutes	27
Defensive Rating Ave number of mins between League goals conceded while on the pitch	72	Clean Sheets In League games when player was on pitch for at least 70 minutes	7

KEY PLAYERS - DEFENDERS

Bo Svensson

Goals Conceded Number of League goals conceded while the player was on the pitch	17	Clean Sheets In League games when player was on pitch for at least 70 minutes	5
Defensive Rating Ave number of mins between League goals conceded while on the pitch	85	Club Defensive Rating Average number of mins between League goals conceded by the club this season	69

	PLAYER	CON LGE	CLEAN SHEETS	DEF RATE
1	Bo Svensson	17	5	85 mins
2	Marvin Compper	23	2	76 mins
3	Kasper Bogelund	24	5	74 mins
4	Marcell Jansen	29	6	71 mins

KEY PLAYERS - MIDFIELDERS

Oliver Kirch

Goals in the League	0	Contribution to Attacking Power Average number of minutes between League team goals while on pitch	100
Defensive Rating Average number of mins between League goals conceded while on the pitch	64	Scoring Difference Defensive Rating minus Contribution to Attacking Power	-36

	PLAYER	LGE GOALS	DEF RATE	POWER	SCORE DIFF
1	Oliver Kirch	0	64	100	-36 mins
2	Peer Kluge	2	83	139	-56 mins
3	Federico Insua	2	81	143	-62 mins
4	Hassan El Fakiri	0	65	130	-65 mins

KEY PLAYERS - GOALSCORERS

Carlos Eduardo de Souza Kahe

Goals in the League	4	Player Strike Rate Average number of minutes between League goals scored by player	397
Contribution to Attacking Power Average number of minutes between League goals while on pitch	113	Club Strike Rate Average number of minutes between League goals scored by club	133

	PLAYER	LGE GOALS	POWER	STRIKE RATE
1	Carlos Eduardo de Souza Kahe	4	113	397 mins
2	Nando Rafael	3	120	441 mins
3	Michael Delura	3	104	628 mins
4	Peer Kluge	2	139	1046 mins

Kasper Bogelund & Nando Rafael

SQUAD APPEARANCES

Match	1	2	3	4	5		6	7	8	9	10		11	12	13	14	15		16	17	18	19	20		21	22	23	24	25		26	27	28	29	30		31	32	33	34
Venue	H	A	H	A	H		A	H	A	H	A		H	A	H	A	A		H	A	A	H	A		H	A	H	A	H		A	H	A	H	A		H	H	A	H
Competition	L	L	L	L	L		L	L	L	L	L		L	L	L	L	L		L	L	L	L	L		L	L	L	L	L		L	L	L	L	L		L	L	L	L
Result	W	L	W	L	W		L	W	L	L	L		L	D	L	L	D		D	L	L	D	W		D	L	D	L	W		L	D	L	L	L		L	D	L	L

Goalkeepers
Christofer Heimeroth
Kasey Keller

Defenders
Kasper Bogelund
Marvin Compper
Steve Gohouri
Thomas Helveg
Marcell Jansen
Tim Rubink
Bo Svensson
Jose Ze Antonio

Midfielders
Alex Baumjohann
Hassan El Fakiri
Robert Flessers
Federico Insua
Oliver Kirch
Peer Kluge
Tobias Levels
Marko Marin
Eugen Polanski
Sebastian Svard
Bernd Thijs
Mikkel Thygesen
J van den Bergh

Forwards
David Degen
Michael Delura
C E de Souza Kahe
Moses Lamidi
Oliver Neuville
Nando Rafael
Wesley Sonck
Vaclav Sverkos

KEY: ■ On all match   ◄◄ Subbed or sent off (Counting game)   ►► Subbed on from bench (Counting Game)   ►◄ Subbed on and then subbed or sent off (Counting Game)   □ Not in 16
■ On bench   ◄ Subbed or sent off (playing less than 70 minutes)   ►► Subbed on (playing less than 70 minutes)   ►► Subbed on and then subbed or sent off (playing less than 70 minutes)

GERMANY - BORUSSIA MONCHENGLADBACH

FRENCH LEAGUE ROUND-UP

FINAL LEAGUE TABLE

	P	HOME W	D	L	F	A	AWAY W	D	L	F	A	TOTAL F	A	DIF	PTS
Lyon	38	12	6	1	32	14	12	3	4	32	13	64	27	37	81
Marseille	38	14	2	3	35	16	5	5	9	18	22	53	38	15	64
Toulouse	38	10	4	5	26	17	7	3	9	18	26	44	43	1	58
Rennes	38	10	6	3	24	15	4	9	6	14	15	38	30	8	57
Lens	38	9	8	2	28	16	6	4	9	19	25	47	41	6	57
Bordeaux	38	12	3	4	25	12	4	6	9	14	23	39	35	4	57
Sochaux	38	10	6	3	24	17	5	6	8	22	31	46	48	-2	57
Auxerre	38	10	7	2	20	13	3	8	8	21	28	41	41	0	54
Monaco	38	9	5	5	26	18	4	7	8	19	20	45	38	7	51
Lille	38	9	5	5	26	16	4	6	9	19	27	45	43	2	50
St Etienne	38	11	0	8	31	24	3	7	9	21	26	52	50	2	49
Le Mans	38	7	10	2	25	18	4	6	9	20	28	45	46	-1	49
AS Nancy	38	12	2	5	26	19	1	8	10	11	25	37	44	-7	49
Lorient	38	8	6	5	17	13	4	7	8	16	27	33	40	-7	49
PSG	38	7	5	7	24	23	5	7	7	18	19	42	42	0	48
Nice	38	8	8	3	27	19	1	8	10	7	21	34	40	-6	43
Valenciennes	38	7	8	4	18	16	4	2	13	18	32	36	48	-12	43
Troyes	38	8	7	4	29	23	1	5	13	10	31	39	54	-15	39
Sedan	38	4	10	5	23	22	3	4	12	23	36	46	58	-12	35
Nantes	38	4	8	7	15	23	3	5	11	14	26	29	49	-20	34

CLUB STRIKE FORCE

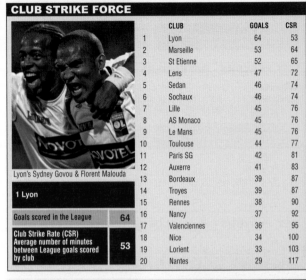

Lyon's Sydney Govou & Florent Malouda

	CLUB	GOALS	CSR
1	Lyon	64	53
2	Marseille	53	64
3	St Etienne	52	65
4	Lens	47	72
5	Sedan	46	74
6	Sochaux	46	74
7	Lille	45	76
8	AS Monaco	45	76
9	Le Mans	45	76
10	Toulouse	44	77
11	Paris SG	42	81
12	Auxerre	41	83
13	Bordeaux	39	87
14	Troyes	39	87
15	Rennes	38	90
16	Nancy	37	92
17	Valenciennes	36	95
18	Nice	34	100
19	Lorient	33	103
20	Nantes	29	117

1 Lyon

Goals scored in the League	64
Club Strike Rate (CSR) Average number of minutes between League goals scored by club	53

CLUB DISCIPLINARY RECORDS

Monaco's Leko: 15 cards

1 AS Monaco

League Yellow	82
League Red	7
League Total	89
Cards Average in League Average number of minutes between a card being shown of either colour	38

	CLUB	Y	R	TOTAL	AVE
1	AS Monaco	82	7	89	38
2	Troyes	81	6	87	39
3	Toulouse	79	4	83	41
4	Lille	77	4	81	42
5	Bordeaux	78	2	80	42
6	Nancy	74	7	81	42
7	Valenciennes	77	4	81	42
8	Nice	73	5	78	43
9	Marseille	72	3	75	45
10	Nantes	72	3	75	45
11	Lens	69	5	74	46
12	Paris SG	69	4	73	46
13	Le Mans	69	1	70	48
14	St Etienne	64	4	68	50
15	Lyon	66	1	67	51
16	Rennes	61	3	64	53
17	Sochaux	62	1	63	54
18	Sedan	58	5	63	54
19	Auxerre	58	4	62	55
20	Lorient	42	3	45	76

CLUB DEFENCES

	CLUB	LGE	CS	CDR
1	Lyon	27	15	126
2	Rennes	30	16	114
3	Bordeaux	35	17	97
4	AS Monaco	38	14	90
5	Marseille	38	11	90
6	Nice	40	13	85
7	Lorient	40	15	85
8	Lens	41	15	83
9	Auxerre	41	14	83
10	Paris SG	42	12	81
11	Lille	43	13	79
12	Toulouse	43	15	79
13	Nancy	44	13	77
14	Le Mans	46	9	74
15	Sochaux	48	12	71
16	Valenciennes	48	11	71
17	Nantes	49	10	69
18	St Etienne	50	10	68
19	Troyes	54	9	63
20	Sedan	58	6	58

Lyon's Squillaci wins an aerial battle

1 Lyon

Goals conceded in the League	27
Clean Sheets (CS) Number of league games where no goals were conceded	15
Club Defensive Rate (CDR) Average number of minutes between League goals conceded by club	126

PLAYER NATIONALITIES

Overseas country with the most player appearances in the French League - Brazil

691 league appearances by Brazilian players

	COUNTRY	PLAYERS	IN SQUAD	LGE APP	% LGE ACT	CAPS	MOST APP	APP
1	France	365	8541	6574	63.15	78	Ulrich Rame	100
2	Brazil	29	778	691	6.99	6	Vitorino Hilton	97.4
3	Senegal	25	536	407	4.05	1	Habib Beye	94.7
4	Ivory Coast	11	333	313	3.1	16	Ndri Romaric	90.4
5	Cameroon	14	340	244	2.33	0	Achille Emana	93.7
6	Mali	9	235	196	1.96	0	Adama Coulibaly	86.8
7	Nigeria	7	221	192	1.92	0	Taye Ismaila Taiwo	97
8	Morocco	12	239	196	1.8	0	Mickael Chretien	86.8
9	Algeria	9	235	193	1.8	0	Nadir Belhadj	90.1
10	Guinea	8	219	175	1.67	0	Pascal Feindouno	85.8
11	Argentina	10	222	171	1.64	0	Mauro Cetto	76.3
12	Czech Republic	7	177	152	1.32	37	David Rozehnal	97.4
13	Sweden	4	111	108	1.03	28	Johan Elmander	74.8
14	Serbia	6	115	95	0.98	22	Nenad Kovacevic	76.3
15	Portugal	3	95	88	0.91	9	Pauleta	78.3
16	Congo	3	84	79	0.8	0	H Nkolongo Ilunga	94.6
17	Holland	2	59	59	0.66	2	Mario Melchiot	77.3
18	Belgium	3	99	85	0.63	12	Luigi Pieroni	54
19	Tunisia	6	97	85	0.6	0	David Jemmali	68.3
20	Switzerland	6	90	55	0.54	14	Stephan Lichtsteiner	48.6

CLUB MAKE-UP – HOME AND OVERSEAS PLAYERS

1 Lens

46.7% of appearances by overseas players

	CLUB	OVERSEAS	HOME	% OVERSEAS	% LGE ACT	MOST APP	APP
1	Lens	14	16	46.7	64.3	Vitorino Hilton	97.4
2	AS Monaco	18	17	51.4	58.6	Flavio Roma	100
3	Nantes	22	15	59.5	57.2	Alioum Saidou	81.4
4	Lille	15	17	46.9	53.0	Tony Mario Sylva	86.3
5	Le Mans	10	19	34.5	50.3	Ndri Romaric	90.4
6	Marseille	12	17	41.4	48.5	Taye Ismaila Taiwo	97
7	Bordeaux	12	17	41.4	46.9	F Vieira Jussie	79.1
8	Paris SG	12	18	40	46.0	David Rozehnal	97.4
9	Rennes	15	19	44.1	41.7	Mario Melchiot	77.3
10	Lyon	13	18	41.9	41.6	Cris	84.2
11	Sochaux	10	19	34.5	41.3	Guirane N'Daw	92.5
12	St Etienne	12	14	46.2	39.2	H Nkolongo Ilunga	94.6
13	Auxerre	12	17	41.4	37.6	Kanga Akale	81.1
14	Nancy	10	18	35.7	37.2	Mickael Chretien	86.8
15	Toulouse	8	25	24.2	33.6	Achille Emana	93.7
16	Troyes	12	20	37.5	31.4	Ibrahima Faye	76.9
17	Sedan	9	20	31	25.9	Nadir Belhadj	90.1
18	Nice	9	17	34.6	25.0	Bakary Kone	76.7
19	Valenciennes	7	20	25.9	24.4	Eric Chelle	68.9
20	Lorient	7	23	23.3	22.1	Rafik Saifi	87.7

CHART-TOPPING MIDFIELDERS

1 Tiago - Lyon	
Goals scored in the League	4
Defensive Rating Av number of mins between League goals conceded while on the pitch	137
Contribution to Attacking Power Average number of minutes between League team goals while on pitch	52
Scoring Difference Defensive Rating minus Contribution to Attacking Power	85

	PLAYER	CLUB	GOALS	DEF RATE	POWER	S DIFF
1	Cardoso Tiago	Lyon	4	137	52	85
2	Etienne Didot	Rennes	1	150	80	70
3	P Juninho	Lyon	10	126	57	69
4	Diego Fernando Perez	AS Monaco	2	142	74	68
5	Florent Malouda	Lyon	10	117	52	65
6	Jeremy Toulalan	Lyon	0	112	56	56
7	Geraldo Wendel	Bordeaux	5	112	71	41
8	Nenad Kovacevic	Lens	0	100	69	31
9	Samir Nasri	Marseille	3	88	61	27
10	Lorik Cana	Marseille	2	84	59	25
11	Jean Makoun	Lille	1	94	70	24
12	Bruno Cheyrou	Rennes	3	113	89	24
13	Oliver Sorlin	Rennes	0	106	82	24
14	Fernando Menegazzo	Bordeaux	2	120	97	23
15	Eric Carriere	Lens	2	97	79	18

CHART-TOPPING GOALSCORERS

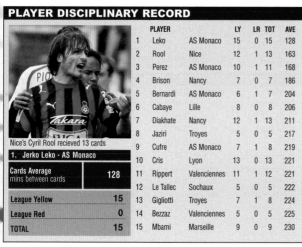

1 Pauleta - Paris SG	
Goals scored in the League	15
Contribution to Attacking Power Average number of minutes between League team goals while on the pitch	99
Club Strike Rate (CSR) Average minutes between League goals scored by club	83
Player Strike Rate Average number of minutes between League goals scored by player	178

	PLAYER	CLUB	GOALS: LGE	POWER	CSR	S RATE
1	Pauleta	Paris SG	15	99	83	178
2	John Utaka	Rennes	11	74	90	209
3	Joseph-Desire Job	Sedan	9	64	74	214
4	Ismael Bangoura	Le Mans	12	72	76	216
5	Libano Batista Grafite	Le Mans	12	75	76	225
6	Johan Elmander	Toulouse	11	77	79	231
7	Steve Savidan	Valenciennes	13	97	95	232
8	Ireneusz Jelen	Auxerre	10	75	83	250
9	P Juninho	Lyon	10	57	53	253
10	Florent Malouda	Lyon	10	52	53	258
11	Aruna Dindane	Lens	11	75	72	259
12	Jimmy Briand	Rennes	9	88	90	266
13	Pierre-Andre Gignac	Lorient	9	91	103	274
14	Gregory Pujol	Sedan	9	67	74	278
15	Mamadou Niang	Marseille	10	76	64	289

CHART-TOPPING DEFENDERS

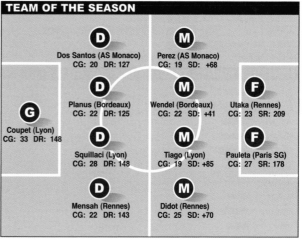

1 Squillaci- Lyon	
Goals Conceded in the League The number of League goals conceded while he was on the pitch	17
Clean Sheets In games when he played at least 70 mins	12
Club Defensive Rating Average mins between League goals conceded by the club this season	126
Defensive Rating Average number of minutes between League goals conceded while on pitch	148

	PLAYER	CLUB	CON: LGE	CS	CDR	DEF RATE
1	Sebastien Squillaci	Lyon	17	12	126	148
2	John Mensah	Rennes	14	11	114	143
3	Jacques Faty	Rennes	14	8	114	137
4	Manuel Dos Santos	AS Monaco	16	12	90	127
5	Marc Planus	Bordeaux	16	11	97	125
6	Cris	Lyon	23	13	126	125
7	Erik Edman	Rennes	20	12	114	125
8	Mario Melchiot	Rennes	21	13	114	125
9	Eric Abidal	Lyon	22	11	126	124
10	Anthony Reveillere	Lyon	21	9	126	116
11	Onyekachi Apam	Nice	16	10	85	115
12	Gregory Bourillon	Rennes	18	9	114	111
13	Franck Jurietti	Bordeaux	23	13	97	108
14	Efstathios Tavlaridis	Lille	18	8	79	103
15	Francois Modesto	AS Monaco	21	9	90	97

CHART-TOPPING GOALKEEPERS

1 Coupet - Lyon	
Counting Games Games in which he played at least 70 minutes	33
Goals Conceded in the League The number of League goals conceded while he was on the pitch	20
Clean Sheets In games when he played at least 70 mins	15
Defensive Rating Average number of minutes between League goals conceded while on pitch	148

	PLAYER	CLUB	CG	CONC	CS	DEF RATE
1	Gregory Coupet	Lyon	33	20	15	148
2	Simon Pouplin	Rennes	38	30	16	114
3	Remy Riou	Lorient	22	19	11	104
4	Olivier Sorin	Auxerre	20	18	9	100
5	Ulrich Rame	Bordeaux	38	35	17	97
6	Hugo Lloris	Nice	37	37	13	90
7	Cedric Carasso	Marseille	38	38	11	90
8	Flavio Roma	AS Monaco	38	38	14	90
9	Tony Mario Sylva	Lille	33	33	13	89
10	Charles-Hubert Itandje	Lens	38	41	15	83
11	Yohann Pele	Le Mans	27	30	8	83
12	Mickael Landreau	Paris SG	38	42	12	81
13	Nicolas Douchez	Toulouse	36	42	14	77
14	Teddy Richert	Sochaux	38	46	13	74
15	Nicolas Penneteau	Valenciennes	31	38	9	73

PLAYER DISCIPLINARY RECORD

	PLAYER		LY	LR	TOT	AVE
1	Leko	AS Monaco	15	0	15	128
2	Rool	Nice	12	1	13	163
3	Perez	AS Monaco	10	1	11	168
4	Brison	Nancy	7	0	7	186
5	Bernardi	AS Monaco	6	1	7	204
6	Cabaye	Lille	8	0	8	206
7	Diakhate	Nancy	12	1	13	211
8	Jaziri	Troyes	5	0	5	217
9	Cufre	AS Monaco	7	1	8	219
10	Cris	Lyon	13	0	13	221
11	Rippert	Valenciennes	11	1	12	221
12	Le Tallec	Sochaux	5	0	5	222
13	Gigliotti	Troyes	7	1	8	224
14	Bezzaz	Valenciennes	5	0	5	225
15	Mbami	Marseille	9	0	9	230

Nice's Cyril Rool recieved 13 cards

1. Jerko Leko - AS Monaco	
Cards Average mins between cards	128
League Yellow	15
League Red	0
TOTAL	15

TEAM OF THE SEASON

D Dos Santos (AS Monaco) CG: 20 DR: 127

M Perez (AS Monaco) CG: 19 SD: +68

D Planus (Bordeaux) CG: 22 DR: 125

M Wendel (Bordeaux) CG: 22 SD: +41

F Utaka (Rennes) CG: 23 SR: 209

G Coupet (Lyon) CG: 33 DR: 148

D Squillaci (Lyon) CG: 28 DR: 148

M Tiago (Lyon) CG: 19 SD: +85

F Pauleta (Paris SG) CG: 27 SR: 178

D Mensah (Rennes) CG: 22 DR: 143

M Didot (Rennes) CG: 25 SD: +70

LYON

Final Position: 1st

NICKNAME: LES GONES KEY: ☐ Won ☐ Drawn ☐ Lost Attendance

#	Comp	Opponent	H/A	Result	Scorers	Attendance
1	frpr1	Nantes	A	W 3-1	Benzema 3, Squillaci 64, Fred 88	36,000
2	frpr1	Toulouse	H	D 1-1	Malouda 83	39,280
3	frpr1	Bordeaux	A	W 2-1	Fred 27, Wiltord 85	32,008
4	frpr1	Nice	A	W 4-1	Malouda 48, Benzema 67, 90 pen, Tiago 73	13,814
5	frpr1	Troyes	H	W 2-0	Cris 15, Juninho 86	37,391
6	ecgpe	Real Madrid	H	W 2-0	Fred 11, Tiago 30	40,013
7	frpr1	Lorient	A	W 3-1	Tiago 6, Fred 61, Malouda 64	15,230
8	frpr1	Lille	H	W 4-1	Malouda 5, Juninho 51, Fred 63, 69	40,165
9	ecgpe	Ste Bucharest	A	W 3-0	Fred 43, Tiago 55, Benzema 89	28,000
10	frpr1	Sochaux	A	W 1-0	Wiltord 78	18,788
11	frpr1	St Etienne	H	W 2-0	Tiago 64, Juninho 88	39,218
12	ecgpe	Dinamo Kiev	A	W 3-0	Juninho 31, Kallstrom 38, Malouda 50	30,000
13	frpr1	Marseille	A	W 4-1	Juninho 20, 77, Benzema 47, Kallstrom 86	57,376
14	frpr1	Nancy	H	W 1-0	Carew 13	40,298
15	ecgpe	Dinamo Kiev	H	W 1-0	Benzema 14	35,000
16	frpr1	Rennes	A	L 0-1		28,499
17	frpr1	Valenciennes	H	W 2-1	Cris 83, Squillaci 85	39,833
18	frpr1	Sedan	A	W 1-0	Abdou 79 og	21,025
19	ecgpe	Real Madrid	A	D 2-2	Carew 11, Malouda 31	78,677
20	frpr1	Auxerre	H	W 1-0	Malouda 25	39,576
21	frpr1	Le Mans	A	W 1-0	Wiltord 56	15,106
22	ecgpe	Ste Bucharest	H	D 1-1	Diarra 12	30,000
23	frpr1	Paris SG	H	W 3-1	Wiltord 45, Cris 86, Malouda 87	36,072
24	frpr1	Lens	A	W 4-0	Juninho 22, 61, Malouda 34, Cris 50	40,038
25	frpr1	AS Monaco	H	D 0-0		38,225
26	frpr1	Toulouse	A	L 0-2		33,940
27	frpr1	Bordeaux	H	L 1-2	Fred 63	35,305
28	frpr1	Nice	H	D 1-1	Baros 39	33,971
29	frpr1	Troyes	A	L 0-1		14,009
30	frpr1	Lorient	H	W 1-0	Fred 7	37,976
31	frpr1	Lille	A	W 2-1	Fred 83, Squillaci 88	17,092
32	eckl1	Roma	A	D 0-0		55,000
33	frpr1	Sochaux	H	D 3-3	Baros 39, Wiltord 89, Juninho 90 pen	40,363
34	frpr1	St Etienne	A	W 3-1	Kallstrom 27, Tiago 36, Fred 46	35,201
35	eckl2	Roma	H	L 0-2		41,000
36	frpr1	Marseille	H	D 1-1	Baros 19	38,930
37	frpr1	Nancy	A	W 3-0	Baros 35, Kallstrom 75, Fred 80	19,919
38	frpr1	Valenciennes	A	D 0-0		15,999
39	frpr1	Sedan	H	W 1-0	Ben Arfa 44	37,539
40	frpr1	Rennes	H	D 0-0		39,848
41	frpr1	Auxerre	A	D 0-0		16,141
42	frpr1	Le Mans	H	W 2-1	Fred 38, Malouda 67	40,167
43	frpr1	Paris SG	A	D 1-1	Juninho 90	41,577
44	frpr1	Lens	H	W 3-0	Govou 20, Juninho 37, Diarra 45 pen	38,213
45	frpr1	AS Monaco	A	L 0-1		13,145
46	frpr1	Nantes	H	W 3-1	Malouda 21, 65, Benzema 83	40,149

LEAGUE APPEARANCES, BOOKINGS AND CAPS

	AGE (on 01/07/07)	IN NAMED 18	APPEARANCES	COUNTING GAMES	MINUTES ON PITCH	YELLOW CARDS	RED CARDS	CAPS THIS SEASON	NATIONAL SIDE
Goalkeepers									
Gregory Coupet	34	33	33	33	2970	0	0	9	France
Remi Vercoutre	27	33	5	5	450	1	0	-	France
Defenders									
Eric Abidal	27	35	33	30	2747	1	0	10	France
Jeremie Berthod	23	21	10	7	739	2	0	-	France
Claudio Cacapa	31	18	6	5	511	2	0	-	Brazil
Francois Clerc	24	34	21	13	1331	1	0	5	France
Cris	30	34	32	32	2880	14	0	-	Brazil
Patrick Muller	30	25	10	9	819	2	0	6	Switzerland
Anthony Reveillere	27	34	30	26	2445	5	0	-	France
Sebastien Squillaci	26	34	28	28	2520	0	0	1	France
Midfielders									
Hatem Ben Arfa	20	18	13	3	535	1	0	-	France
Mahamadou Diarra	26	2	2	2	180	0	0	-	Mali
Alou Diarra	25	19	15	8	875	3	0	3	France
Fabio Santos	26	12	8	4	424	0	0	-	Brazil
P Juninho	32	33	31	27	2537	9	1	-	Brazil
Kim Kallstrom	24	35	33	16	1821	3	0	7	Sweden
Florent Malouda	27	36	35	25	2588	9	0	11	France
Loic Remy	20	8	6	1	198	1	0	-	France
Cardoso Tiago	26	30	27	19	1928	9	0	9	Portugal
Jeremy Toulalan	23	35	32	26	2480	8	0	4	France
Forwards									
Milan Baros	25	14	12	6	717	3	0	7	Czech Republic
Karim Benzema	19	22	21	9	1153	0	0	2	France
Gregory Bettiol	21	5	4	0	84	0	0	-	France
John Alieu Carew	27	11	9	3	482	0	0	4	Norway
Fred	23	22	20	11	1144	5	0	5	Brazil
Sydney Govou	27	29	28	18	1877	4	0	5	France
Sylvain Wiltord	33	25	22	10	1172	0	0	5	France

TEAM OF THE SEASON

G Gregory Coupet CG: 33 DR: 148

D Sebastien Squillaci CG: 28 DR: 148
D Cris CG: 32 DR: 125
D Eric Abidal CG: 30 DR: 124
D Francois Clerc CG: 13 DR: 121

M Kim Kallstrom CG: 16 SD: 107
M Cardoso Tiago CG: 19 SD: 85
M Juninho CG: 27 SD: 69
M Florent Malouda CG: 25 SD: 65

F Fred* CG: 11 SR: 104
F Sydney Govou CG: 18 SR: 1877

MONTHLY POINTS TALLY

Month		Points	%
AUGUST		10	83%
SEPTEMBER		12	100%
OCTOBER		9	100%
NOVEMBER		9	75%
DECEMBER		10	83%
JANUARY		1	11%
FEBRUARY		7	58%
MARCH		7	78%
APRIL		9	60%
MAY		7	58%

LEAGUE GOALS

	PLAYER	MINS	GOALS	S RATE
1	Fred	1144	11	104
2	Juninho	2537	10	253
3	Malouda	2588	10	258
4	Benzema	1153	5	230
5	Wiltord	1172	5	234
6	Baros	717	4	179
7	Tiago	1928	4	482
8	Cris	2880	4	720
9	Kallstrom	1821	3	607
10	Squillaci	2520	3	840
11	Carew	482	1	482
12	Ben Arfa	535	1	535
13	Diarra	875	1	875
	Other		1	
	TOTAL		**63**	

TOP POINT EARNERS

	PLAYER	GAMES	AV PTS
1	Francois Clerc	13	2.46
2	Kim Kallstrom	16	2.31
3	Florent Malouda	25	2.20
4	Cris	32	2.19
5	Gregory Coupet	33	2.18
6	Sebastien Squillaci	28	2.18
7	Eric Abidal	30	2.13
8	Jeremy Toulalan	26	2.12
9	Cardoso Tiago	19	2.11
10	Pernambucano Juninho	27	2.11
	CLUB AVERAGE:		**2.13**

DISCIPLINARY RECORDS

	PLAYER	YELLOW	RED	AVE
1	Cris	14	0	221
2	Milan Baros	3	0	239
3	Cardoso Tiago	9	0	241
4	Fred	5	0	286
5	Alou Diarra	3	0	291
6	Juninho	9	1	317
7	Jeremie Berthod	2	0	369
8	Patrick Muller	2	0	409
9	Florent Malouda	9	0	431
10	Jeremy Toulalan	8	0	496
11	Claudio Cacapa	2	0	511
12	Hatem Ben Arfa	1	0	535
13	Sydney Govou	4	0	625
	Other	10	0	
	TOTAL	**81**	**1**	

KEY GOALKEEPER

Gregory Coupet

Goals Conceded in the League	20	Counting Games League games when player was on pitch for at least 70 minutes	33
Defensive Rating Ave number of mins between League goals conceded while on the pitch	148	Clean Sheets In games when player was on pitch for at least 70 minutes	15

KEY PLAYERS - DEFENDERS

Sebastien Squillaci

Goals Conceded Number of League goals conceded while the player was on the pitch	17	Clean Sheets In League games when player was on pitch for at least 70 minutes	12
Defensive Rating Ave number of mins between League goals conceded while on the pitch	148	Club Defensive Rating Average number of mins between League goals conceded by the club this season	126

	PLAYER	CON LGE	CLEAN SHEETS	DEF RATE
1	Sebastien Squillaci	17	12	148 mins
2	Cris	23	13	125 mins
3	Eric Abidal	22	11	124 mins
4	Francois Clerc	11	6	121 mins

KEY PLAYERS - MIDFIELDERS

Kim Kallstrom

Goals in the League	3	Contribution to Attacking Power Average number of minutes between League team goals while on pitch	44
Defensive Rating Average number of mins between League goals conceded while on the pitch	151	Scoring Difference Defensive Rating minus Contribution to Attacking Power	107

	PLAYER	LGE GOALS	DEF RATE	POWER	SCORE DIFF
1	Kim Kallstrom	3	151	44	107 mins
2	Cardoso Tiago	4	137	52	85 mins
3	Pernambucano Juninho	10	126	57	69 mins
4	Florent Malouda	10	117	52	65 mins

KEY PLAYERS - GOALSCORERS

Fred

Goals in the League	11	Player Strike Rate Average number of minutes between League goals scored by player	104
Contribution to Attacking Power Average number of minutes between League team goals while on pitch	44	Club Strike Rate Average number of minutes between League goals scored by club	53

	PLAYER	LGE GOALS	POWER	STRIKE RATE
1	Fred	11	44	104 mins
2	Pernambucano Juninho	10	57	253 mins
3	Florent Malouda	10	52	258 mins
4	Cardoso Tiago	4	52	482 mins

Fred

SQUAD APPEARANCES

Match	1 2 3 4 5	6 7 8 9 10	11 12 13 14 15	16 17 18 19 20	21 22 23 24 25	26 27 28 29 30	31 32 33 34 35	36 37 38 39 40	41 42 43 44 45	46
Venue	A H A A H	H A H A A	H A A H H	A H A A H	A H H A H	A H H A H	A A H A H	H A A H H	A H A H A	H
Competition	L L L L L	C L L C L	L C L L L	L L L C L	L C L L L	L L L L L	L C L L C	L L L L L	L L L L L	L
Result	W D W W W	W W W W W	W W W W W	L W W D W	W D W W D	L L D L W	W D D W L	D W D W D	D W D W L	W

Goalkeepers
Gregory Coupet
Remi Vercoutre

Defenders
Eric Abidal
Jeremie Berthod
Claudio Cacapa
Francois Clerc
Cris
Patrick Muller
Anthony Reveillere
Sebastien Squillaci

Midfielders
Hatem Ben Arfa
Mahamadou Diarra
Alou Diarra
Fabio Santos
P Juninho
Kim Kallstrom
Florent Malouda
Loic Remy
Cardoso Tiago
Jeremy Toulalan

Forwards
Milan Baros
Karim Benzema
Gregory Bettiol
John Alieu Carew
Fred
Sydney Govou
Sylvain Wiltord

KEY: ■ On all match ◄◄ Subbed or sent off (Counting game) ►► Subbed on from bench (Counting Game) ►► Subbed on and then subbed or sent off (Counting Game) □ Not in 16
■ On bench ◄◄ Subbed or sent off (playing less than 70 minutes) ►► Subbed on (playing less than 70 minutes) ►► Subbed on and then subbed or sent off (playing less than 70 minutes)

MARSEILLE

Final Position: **2nd**

NICKNAME: l'OM   KEY: ☐ Won ☐ Drawn ☐ Lost   Attendance

1	frpr1	Sedan	A D	**0-0**	22,779
2	ucql1	Young Boys	A D	**3-3** Zubar 18, Niang 43, 56	10,000
3	frpr1	Rennes	H W	**2-0** Pagis 38, Maoulida 84	55,711
4	frpr1	Auxerre	A W	**3-0** Ribery 45, Maoulida 49, Pagis 69	19,415
5	ucql2	Young Boys	H D	**0-0**	50,000
6	frpr1	Le Mans	H W	**2-0** Bamogo 69, Niang 78 pen	52,672
7	frpr1	Paris SG	A W	**3-1** Niang 7 pen, Nasri 67, Pagis 89	44,431
8	ucrl1	Mlada Boleslav	H W	**1-0** Bamogo 31	21,000
9	frpr1	Bordeaux	H W	**2-1** Pagis 48, Taiwo 55	55,000
10	frpr1	Nantes	A L	**1-2** Niang 77	35,068
11	ucrl2	Mlada Boleslav	A L	**2-4** Maoulida 13, Taiwo 55	5,000
12	frpr1	Toulouse	H W	**3-0** Taiwo 44, Bamogo 45, Cana 46	48,833
13	frpr1	Lens	A D	**1-1** Niang 63 pen	40,567
14	frpr1	Lyon	H L	**1-4** Bamogo 69	57,376
15	frpr1	Nice	A L	**1-2** Pagis 61	15,030
16	frpr1	Lorient	H L	**0-1**	45,000
17	frpr1	Lille	A L	**0-1**	17,351
18	frpr1	Valenciennes	H W	**1-0** Pagis 60	46,484
19	frpr1	Troyes	A D	**1-1** Maoulida 60	18,579
20	frpr1	Sochaux	A L	**0-1**	19,986
21	frpr1	AS Monaco	H W	**2-1** Pagis 37, Niang 76	47,708
22	frpr1	Nancy	A L	**0-2**	20,081
23	frpr1	St Etienne	H W	**2-1** Cisse 9, Pagis 63	53,614
24	frpr1	Rennes	A W	**2-0** Cisse 57, Maoulida 90	29,144
25	frpr1	Auxerre	H W	**3-1** Ribery 8, 38, Taiwo 87	30,000
26	frpr1	Le Mans	A L	**0-2**	15,976
27	frpr1	Paris SG	H D	**1-1** Cisse 68	58,000
28	frpr1	Bordeaux	A L	**0-1**	32,200
29	frpr1	Nantes	H D	**0-0**	49,507
30	frpr1	Toulouse	A L	**0-3**	35,164
31	frpr1	Lens	H L	**0-1**	51,718
32	frpr1	Lyon	A D	**1-1** Niang 86	38,930
33	frpr1	Nice	H W	**3-0** Niang 5, 40, Civelli 15	50,007
34	frpr1	Lorient	A L	**1-2** Cisse 80 pen	15,752
35	frpr1	Lille	H W	**4-1** Niang 8 pen, 90, Civelli 37, 63	53,000
36	frpr1	Valenciennes	A D	**0-0**	16,398
37	frpr1	Troyes	H W	**2-1** Cisse 54, Mbami 85	47,708
38	frpr1	Sochaux	H W	**4-2** Cana 13, Cisse 69, Nasri 73, Ribery 85	54,702
39	frpr1	AS Monaco	A W	**2-1** Ribery 44, Niang 83 pen	16,401
40	frpr1	Nancy	H W	**2-1** Niang 77 pen, Cisse 81	46,464
41	frpr1	St Etienne	A W	**2-1** Cisse 54, Valbuena 85	34,466
42	frpr1	Sedan	H W	**1-0** Nasri 61	53,604

LEAGUE APPEARANCES, BOOKINGS AND CAPS

	AGE (on 01/07/07)	IN NAMED 18	APPEARANCES	COUNTING GAMES	MINUTES ON PITCH	YELLOW CARDS	RED CARDS	CAPS THIS SEASON	NATIONAL SIDE
Goalkeepers									
Cedric Carasso	25	38	38	38	3420	2	0	-	France
Sebastien Hamel	31	35	0	0	0	0	0	-	France
Defenders									
Habib Beye	30	36	36	36	3240	7	0	3	Senegal
Alain Cantareil	23	17	3	1	130	0	0	-	France
Bostjan Cesar	24	29	7	7	630	2	0	6	Slovenia
Renato Civelli	23	32	21	19	1755	4	1	-	Argentina
Julien Rodriguez	29	16	16	14	1320	2	0	-	France
Taye Ismaila Taiwo	22	37	37	36	3281	3	2	-	Nigeria
Ronald Zubar	21	34	34	33	2986	4	1	-	France
Midfielders									
Salim Arrache	24	13	5	0	38	0	0	-	Algeria
Garry Bocaly	19	8	3	3	252	1	0	-	France
Lorik Cana	23	33	33	32	2856	10	0	-	Bosnia
Thomas Deruda	20	7	3	0	93	0	0	-	France
Sabri Lamouchi	35	6	5	3	294	2	0	-	France
Modeste Mbami	24	33	30	17	2072	9	0	-	Cameroon
Samir Nasri	20	37	37	29	2834	1	0	3	France
Salomon Olembe	26	29	14	1	403	0	0	-	Cameroon
Wilson Oruma	30	26	19	8	899	1	0	-	Nigeria
Franck Ribery	24	25	25	23	2151	6	0	8	France
Mathieu Valbuena	22	25	15	1	362	1	0	-	France
Forwards									
Habib Bamogo	25	18	15	1	525	2	0	-	France
Djibril Cisse	25	21	21	15	1515	5	0	5	France
Toifilou Maoulida	28	35	34	10	1537	5	0	-	France
Mame N'Diaye	21	2	1	1	90	0	0	-	Senegal
Mamadou Niang	27	37	36	33	2892	8	0	3	Senegal
Michael Pagis	33	35	34	14	1939	6	1	-	France

TEAM OF THE SEASON

G Cedric Carasso CG: 38 DR: 90

D Taye Ismaila Taiwo CG: 36 DR: 96
D Renato Civelli CG: 19 DR: 92
D Habib Beye CG: 36 DR: 92
D Julien Rodriguez CG: 14 DR: 88

M Samir Nasri CG: 29 SD: 27
M Lorik Cana CG: 32 SD: 25
M Franck Ribery CG: 23 SD: 14
M Modeste Mbami CG: 17 SD: 3

F Djibril Cisse CG: 15 SR: 189
F Michael Pagis CG: 14 SR: 242

MONTHLY POINTS TALLY

AUGUST		10	83%
SEPTEMBER		6	67%
OCTOBER		4	33%
NOVEMBER		4	33%
DECEMBER		6	50%
JANUARY		6	67%
FEBRUARY		2	17%
MARCH		4	33%
APRIL		10	83%
MAY		12	100%

LEAGUE GOALS

	PLAYER	MINS	GOALS	S RATE
1	Niang	2892	10	289
2	Cisse	1515	8	189
3	Pagis	1939	8	242
4	Ribery	2151	5	430
5	Maoulida	1537	4	384
6	Bamogo	525	3	175
7	Civelli	1755	3	585
8	Nasri	2834	3	944
9	Taiwo	3281	3	1093
10	Cana	2856	2	1428
11	Valbuena	362	1	362
12	Mbami	2072	1	2072
13	N'Diaye	90	0	
	Other		0	
	TOTAL		51	

TOP POINT EARNERS

	PLAYER	GAMES	AV PTS
1	Michael Pagis	14	1.93
2	Julien Rodriguez	14	1.93
3	Renato Civelli	20	1.90
4	Modeste Mbami	17	1.82
5	Samir Nasri	29	1.76
6	Franck Ribery	23	1.74
7	Taye Ismaila Taiwo	37	1.73
8	Djibril Cisse	15	1.73
9	Lorik Cana	32	1.72
10	Habib Beye	36	1.69
	CLUB AVERAGE:		1.68

DISCIPLINARY RECORDS

	PLAYER	YELLOW	RED	AVE
1	Modeste Mbami	9	0	230
2	Habib Bamogo	2	0	262
3	Michael Pagis	6	1	277
4	Djibril Cisse	5	0	303
5	Bostjan Cesar	2	0	315
6	Renato Civelli	4	1	351
7	Lorik Cana	10	0	357
8	Franck Ribery	6	0	358
9	Toifilou Maoulida	5	0	384
10	Mamadou Niang	8	0	413
11	Julien Rodriguez	2	0	660
12	Ronald Zubar	4	1	746
13	Habib Beye	7	0	810
	Other	7	2	
	TOTAL	77	5	

KEY GOALKEEPER

Cedric Carasso

Goals Conceded in the League	38	Counting Games League games when player was on pitch for at least 70 minutes	38
Defensive Rating Ave number of mins between League goals conceded while on the pitch	90	Clean Sheets In League games when player was on pitch for at least 70 minutes	11

KEY PLAYERS - DEFENDERS

Taye Ismaila Taiwo

Goals Conceded Number of League goals conceded while the player was on the pitch	34	Clean Sheets In League games when player was on pitch for at least 70 minutes	11
Defensive Rating Ave number of mins between League goals conceded while on the pitch	96	Club Defensive Rating Average number of mins between League goals conceded by the club this season	90

	PLAYER	CON LGE	CLEAN SHEETS	DEF RATE
1	Taye Ismaila Taiwo	34	11	96 mins
2	Renato Civelli	19	3	92 mins
3	Habib Beye	35	11	92 mins
4	Julien Rodriguez	15	3	88 mins

KEY PLAYERS - MIDFIELDERS

Samir Nasri

Goals in the League	3	Contribution to Attacking Power Average number of minutes between League team goals while on pitch	61
Defensive Rating Average number of mins between League goals conceded while on the pitch	88	Scoring Difference Defensive Rating minus Contribution to Attacking Power	27

	PLAYER	LGE GOALS	DEF RATE	POWER	SCORE DIFF
1	Samir Nasri	3	88	61	27 mins
2	Lorik Cana	2	84	59	25 mins
3	Franck Ribery	5	79	65	14 mins
4	Modeste Mbami	1	79	76	3 mins

KEY PLAYERS - GOALSCORERS

Djibril Cisse

Goals in the League	8	Player Strike Rate Average number of minutes between League goals scored by player	189
Contribution to Attacking Power Average number of minutes between League team goals while on pitch	58	Club Strike Rate Average number of minutes between League goals scored by club	64

	PLAYER	LGE GOALS	POWER	STRIKE RATE
1	Djibril Cisse	8	58	189 mins
2	Michael Pagis	8	66	242 mins
3	Mamadou Niang	10	76	289 mins
4	Franck Ribery	5	65	430 mins

Michael Pagis and Mamadou Niang

SQUAD APPEARANCES

Match	1 2 3 4 5	6 7 8 9 10	11 12 13 14 15	16 17 18 19 20	21 22 23 24 25	26 27 28 29 30	31 32 33 34 35	36 37 38 39 40	41 42
Venue	A A H A H	H A H H A	A H A H A	H A H A A	H A H A H	A H A H A	H A H A H	A H H A H	A H
Competition	L E L L E	L L E L L	E L L L L	L L L L L	L L L L L	L L L L L	L L L L L	L L L L L	L L
Result	D D W W D	W W W W L	L W D L L	L L W D L	W L W W W	L D L D L	L D W L W	D W W W W	W W

Goalkeepers
Cedric Carasso
Sebastien Hamel

Defenders
Habib Beye
Alain Cantareil
Bostjan Cesar
Renato Civelli
Julien Rodriguez
Taye Ismaila Taiwo
Ronald Zubar

Midfielders
Salim Arrache
Garry Bocaly
Lorik Cana
Thomas Deruda
Sabri Lamouchi
Modeste Mbami
Samir Nasri
Salomon Olembe
Wilson Oruma
Franck Ribery
Mathieu Valbuena

Forwards
Habib Bamogo
Djibril Cisse
Toifilou Maoulida
Mame N'Diaye
Mamadou Niang
Michael Pagis

KEY: ■ On all match   ◄◄ Subbed or sent off (Counting game)   ►► Subbed on from bench (Counting Game)   ►► Subbed on and then subbed or sent off (Counting Game)   ☐ Not in 16
   ▢ On bench   ◄◄ Subbed or sent off (playing less than 70 minutes)   ►► Subbed on (playing less than 70 minutes)   ►► Subbed on and then subbed or sent off (playing less than 70 minutes)

TOULOUSE

Final Position: **3rd**

NICKNAME: LE TEFECE   KEY: ☐ Won ☐ Drawn ☐ Lost   Attendance

#						Attendance
1	frpr1	Bordeaux	A	L	0-2	30,186
2	frpr1	Lyon	A	D	1-1 Fabinho 90	39,280
3	frpr1	Nice	H	W	1-0 Mathieu 44	17,837
4	frpr1	Troyes	A	W	2-1 Battles 19, Emana 56	8,976
5	frpr1	Nancy	H	D	2-2 Battles 11, Akpa-Akpro 90	14,872
6	frpr1	Lille	A	W	3-1 Fabinho 16, 38, Emana 25	12,961
7	frpr1	Lorient	H	D	0-0	13,961
8	frpr1	Marseille	A	L	0-3	48,833
9	frpr1	Valenciennes	H	W	3-0 Battles 9, Mansare 12, Ebondo 29	21,904
10	frpr1	AS Monaco	A	W	3-1 Bergougnoux 11, Elmander 85, Emana 90	7,903
11	frpr1	Sochaux	H	L	1-2 Battles 21	20,846
12	frpr1	St Etienne	A	L	0-3	30,022
13	frpr1	Sedan	H	W	3-1 Fabinho 45, Elmander 49, 71	14,461
14	frpr1	Auxerre	A	L	0-1	9,138
15	frpr1	Rennes	H	W	1-0 Bergougnoux 64 pen	15,674
16	frpr1	Lens	H	L	0-1	17,040
17	frpr1	Le Mans	A	L	0-2	9,470
18	frpr1	Nantes	H	L	0-4	16,812
19	frpr1	Lyon	H	W	2-0 Emana 57, Elmander 81	33,940
20	frpr1	Paris SG	A	D	0-0	29,538
21	frpr1	Nice	A	W	1-0 Elmander 23	8,802
22	frpr1	Troyes	H	D	1-1 Arribage 27	15,046
23	frpr1	Nancy	A	L	1-2 Bergougnoux 90	16,596
24	frpr1	Lille	H	W	1-0 Tafforeau 90 og	16,252
25	frpr1	Lorient	A	W	1-0 Paulo Cesar 54 pen	12,311
26	frpr1	Marseille	H	W	3-0 Elmander 38, 48, Emana 62	35,164
27	frpr1	Valenciennes	A	D	0-0	13,721
28	frpr1	AS Monaco	H	D	1-1 Mathieu 26	27,595
29	frpr1	Sochaux	A	L	2-4 Mansare 88, Emana 90	11,485
30	frpr1	St Etienne	H	W	1-0 Elmander 71	25,888
31	frpr1	Sedan	A	W	2-0 Paulo Cesar 77, Ebondo 84	15,424
32	frpr1	Auxerre	H	W	2-0 Emana 6, Mansare 30	22,404
33	frpr1	Rennes	A	L	2-3 Emana 29, Fabinho 76	27,477
34	frpr1	Paris SG	H	L	1-3 Mansare 7	30,594
35	frpr1	Lens	A	L	0-2	38,896
36	frpr1	Le Mans	H	L	0-1	18,042
37	frpr1	Nantes	A	D	0-0	30,000
38	frpr1	Bordeaux	H	W	3-1 Elmander 37, 49, 71	32,008

LEAGUE APPEARANCES, BOOKINGS AND CAPS

	AGE (on 01/07/07)	IN NAMED 18	APPEARANCES	COUNTING GAMES	MINUTES ON PITCH	YELLOW CARDS	RED CARDS	CAPS THIS SEASON	NATIONAL SIDE
Goalkeepers									
Benoit Benvegnu	22	34	2	2	180	0	0	-	France
Nicolas Douchez	27	37	36	36	3240	0	0	-	France
Defenders									
Dominique Arribage	36	35	35	35	3150	10	0	-	France
Lucien Aubey	23	18	16	16	1415	1	0	-	France
Alseni Camara	20	10	0	0	0	0	0	-	Guinea
Walid Cherfa	21	7	4	2	242	0	0	-	France
Daniel Congre	22	20	17	16	1477	1	0	-	France
Issou Malia Dao	23	19	9	9	810	5	0	-	France
Albin Ebondo	23	35	35	34	3092	7	1	-	France
Mohamed Fofana	22	28	7	5	537	0	0	-	France
Jeremy Mathieu	23	32	32	29	2701	10	0	-	France
Midfielders									
Laurent Battles	31	34	31	21	2051	4	1	-	France
Alexandre Bonnet	20	32	13	2	351	0	0	-	France
Kevin Constant	20	9	2	0	4	0	0	-	France
Nicolas Dieuze	28	37	37	36	3233	8	0	-	France
Achille Emana	25	36	36	36	3206	10	0	-	Cameroon
F A Felix Fabinho	27	37	30	21	2217	3	0	-	Brazil
Paulo Cesar	28	17	17	14	1317	0	0	-	Brazil
Francois Sirieix	26	32	22	10	1173	3	0	-	France
Nabil Taider	24	11	5	0	25	1	0	-	France
Forwards									
J-Louis Akpa-Akpro	22	15	10	0	316	0	0	-	France
Bryan Bergougnoux	24	33	9	1	1206	3	0	-	France
Johan Elmander	26	32	32	28	2550	1	1	6	Sweden
Pavel Fort	24	14	10	2	268	2	1	-	Czech Republic
Fode Mansare	25	34	32	27	2494	10	0	-	Guinea
Xavier Pentecote	23	11	5	0	105	0	0	-	France
Francileudo Santos	28	4	4	0	123	0	0	-	Tunisia

TEAM OF THE SEASON

D Daniel Congre CG: 16 DR: 92

M Fabio A Felix Fabinho CG: 21 SD: 15

D Dominique Arribage CG: 35 DR: 80

M Paulo Cesar CG: 14 SD: 5

F Johan Elmander CG: 28 SR: 231

G Nicolas Douchez CG: 36 DR: 77

D Jeremy Mathieu CG: 29 DR: 77

M Achille Emana CG: 36 SD: 4

F Fode Mansare CG: 27 SR: 623

D Albin Ebondo CG: 34 DR: 77

M Nicolas Dieuze CG: 36 SD: 4

MONTHLY POINTS TALLY

Month		Pts	%
AUGUST		7	58%
SEPTEMBER		5	56%
OCTOBER		6	50%
NOVEMBER		6	50%
DECEMBER		0	0%
JANUARY		8	67%
FEBRUARY		9	75%
MARCH		2	22%
APRIL		9	60%
MAY		4	33%

LEAGUE GOALS

	PLAYER	MINS	GOALS	S RATE
1	Elmander	2550	11	231
2	Emana	3206	8	400
3	Fabinho	2217	5	443
4	Battles	2051	4	512
5	Mansare	2494	4	623
6	Bergougnoux	1206	3	402
7	Paulo Cesar	1317	2	658
8	Mathieu	2701	2	1350
9	Ebondo	3092	2	1546
10	Akpa-Akpro	316	1	316
11	Arribage	3150	1	3150
12	Aubey	1415	0	
13	Benvegnu	180	0	
	Other		0	
	TOTAL		**43**	

TOP POINT EARNERS

	PLAYER	GAMES	AV PTS
1	F A Felix Fabinho	21	**1.86**
2	Johan Elmander	28	**1.71**
3	Daniel Congre	16	**1.69**
4	Fode Mansare	27	**1.59**
5	Jeremy Mathieu	29	**1.55**
6	Dominique Arribage	35	**1.51**
7	Lucien Aubey	16	**1.50**
8	Laurent Battles	22	**1.50**
9	Paulo Cesar	14	**1.50**
10	Albin Ebondo	35	**1.49**
	CLUB AVERAGE:		**1.53**

DISCIPLINARY RECORDS

	PLAYER	YELLOW	RED	AVE
1	Issou Malia Dao	5	0	162
2	Fode Mansare	10	0	249
3	Jeremy Mathieu	10	0	270
4	Dom Arribage	10	0	315
5	Achille Emana	10	0	320
6	Albin Ebondo	7	1	386
7	Francois Sirieix	3	0	391
8	B Bergougnoux	3	0	402
9	Nicolas Dieuze	8	0	404
10	Laurent Battles	4	1	410
11	F A Felix Fabinho	3	0	739
12	Johan Elmander	1	1	1275
13	Lucien Aubey	1	0	1415
	Other	1	0	
	TOTAL	**76**	**3**	

KEY GOALKEEPER

Nicolas Douchez

Goals Conceded in the League	42	Counting Games League games when player was on pitch for at least 70 minutes	36
Defensive Rating Ave number of mins between League goals conceded while on the pitch	77	Clean Sheets In League games when player was on pitch for at least 70 minutes	14

KEY PLAYERS - DEFENDERS

Daniel Congre

Goals Conceded Number of League goals conceded while the player was on the pitch	16	Clean Sheets In League games when player was on pitch for at least 70 minutes	9
Defensive Rating Ave number of mins between League goals conceded while on the pitch	92	Club Defensive Rating Average number of mins between League goals conceded by the club this season	81

	PLAYER	CON LGE	CLEAN SHEETS	DEF RATE
1	Daniel Congre	16	9	92 mins
2	Dominique Arribage	39	14	80 mins
3	Jeremy Mathieu	35	12	77 mins
4	Albin Ebondo	40	13	77 mins

KEY PLAYERS - MIDFIELDERS

Fabio Alves Felix Fabinho

Goals in the League	5	Contribution to Attacking Power Average number of minutes between League team goals while on pitch	73
Defensive Rating Average number of mins between League goals conceded while on the pitch	88	Scoring Difference Defensive Rating minus Contribution to Attacking Power	15

	PLAYER	LGE GOALS	DEF RATE	POWER	SCORE DIFF
1	Fabio Alves Felix Fabinho	5	88	73	15 mins
2	Paulo Cesar	2	87	82	5 mins
3	Achille Emana	8	78	74	4 mins
4	Nicolas Dieuze	0	80	76	4 mins

KEY PLAYERS - GOALSCORERS

Johan Elmander

Goals in the League	11	Player Strike Rate Average number of minutes between League goals scored by player	231
Contribution to Attacking Power Average number of minutes between League team goals while on pitch	77	Club Strike Rate Average number of minutes between League goals scored by club	79

	PLAYER	LGE GOALS	POWER	STRIKE RATE
1	Johan Elmander	11	77	231 mins
2	Achille Emana	8	74	400 mins
3	Fabio Alves Felix Fabinho	5	73	443 mins
4	Laurent Battles	4	82	512 mins

Achille Emana and Johan Elmander

SQUAD APPEARANCES

Match	1	2	3	4	5	6	7	8	9	10	11	12	13	14	15	16	17	18	19	20	21	22	23	24	25	26	27	28	29	30	31	32	33	34	35	36	37	38
Venue	A	A	H	A	H	A	H	A	H	A	H	A	H	A	H	H	A	H	H	A	A	H	A	H	A	H	A	H	A	H	A	H	A	H	A	H	A	H
Competition	L	L	L	L	L	L	L	L	L	L	L	L	L	L	L	L	L	L	L	L	L	L	L	L	L	L	L	L	L	L	L	L	L	L	L	L	L	L
Result	L	D	W	W	D	W	D	L	W	W	L	L	W	L	W	L	L	L	W	D	W	D	L	W	W	W	D	D	L	W	W	W	L	L	L	L	D	W

Goalkeepers
Benoit Benvegnu
Nicolas Douchez

Defenders
Dominique Arribage
Lucien Aubey
Alseni Camara
Walid Cherfa
Daniel Congre
Issou Malia Dao
Albin Ebondo
Mohamed Fofana
Jeremy Mathieu

Midfielders
Laurent Battles
Alexandre Bonnet
Kevin Constant
Nicolas Dieuze
Achille Emana
F A Felix Fabinho
Paulo Cesar
Francois Sirieix
Nabil Taider

Forwards
J-Louis Akpa-Akpro
Bryan Bergougnoux
Johan Elmander
Pavel Fort
Fode Mansare
Xavier Pentecote
Francileudo Santos

KEY: ■ On all match   ◄◄ Subbed or sent off (Counting game)   ►► Subbed on from bench (Counting Game)   ►► Subbed on and then subbed or sent off (Counting Game)   □ Not in 16
■ On bench   ◄ Subbed or sent off (playing less than 70 minutes)   ►► Subbed on (playing less than 70 minutes)   ►► Subbed on and then subbed or sent off (playing less than 70 minutes)

RENNES

Final Position: 4th

NICKNAME: LES ROUGES ET NOIRS **KEY:** ☐ Won ☐ Drawn ☐ Lost Attendance

1	frpr1	Lille	H L	**1-2** Monterrubio 55	22,497
2	frpr1	Marseille	A L	**0-2**	55,711
3	frpr1	AS Monaco	H D	**1-1** Briand 85	25,877
4	frpr1	Valenciennes	A L	**1-3** Briand 22	14,061
5	frpr1	Sochaux	H W	**2-1** Jeunechamp 52, Monterrubio 61	21,526
6	frpr1	Nancy	A D	**0-0**	16,529
7	frpr1	St Etienne	H D	**0-0**	24,842
8	frpr1	Sedan	A L	**0-1**	9,863
9	frpr1	Auxerre	H W	**3-1** Utaka 38, 79, Marveaux 45	20,610
10	frpr1	Nice	H W	**1-0** Monterrubio 57	22,978
11	frpr1	Paris SG	A L	**0-1**	37,648
12	frpr1	Lyon	H W	**1-0** M'Bia 12	28,499
13	frpr1	Lens	A D	**0-0**	32,214
14	frpr1	Le Mans	H D	**1-1** Marveaux 88	24,373
15	frpr1	Toulouse	A L	**0-1**	15,674
16	frpr1	Nantes	H W	**2-0** Melchiot 38, Cheyrou 79	29,093
17	frpr1	Bordeaux	A W	**2-1** Marveaux 9, Utaka 61	21,929
18	frpr1	Troyes	H D	**1-1** Briand 71	21,896
19	frpr1	Lorient	A D	**0-0**	15,618
20	frpr1	Marseille	H L	**0-2**	29,144
21	frpr1	AS Monaco	A W	**2-0** Briand 49, Didot 79	6,866
22	frpr1	Valenciennes	H W	**1-0** Danze 5	22,052
23	frpr1	Sochaux	A D	**0-0**	10,477
24	frpr1	Nancy	H D	**1-1** Utaka 85	22,893
25	frpr1	St Etienne	A W	**3-1** Utaka 14, 58, Marveaux 61	28,389
26	frpr1	Sedan	H L	**0-2**	22,032
27	frpr1	Auxerre	A L	**0-1**	7,863
28	frpr1	Nice	A D	**1-1** Briand 15	10,875
29	frpr1	Paris SG	H W	**1-0** Briand 75	27,085
30	frpr1	Lens	H W	**1-0** Utaka 29	27,108
31	frpr1	Le Mans	A D	**0-0**	12,683
32	frpr1	Lyon	A D	**0-0**	39,848
33	frpr1	Toulouse	H W	**3-2** Briand 62 pen, Marveaux 75, Cheyrou 86	27,477
34	frpr1	Nantes	A W	**2-0** Utaka 54, Briand 58	35,616
35	frpr1	Bordeaux	H D	**0-0**	28,368
36	frpr1	Troyes	A D	**2-2** Briand 24, Utaka 29	11,247
37	frpr1	Lorient	H W	**4-1** Melchiot 1, Cheyrou 52, Utaka 77, Jeunechamp 87	29,425
38	frpr1	Lille	A D	**1-1** Utaka 73	14,809

LEAGUE APPEARANCES, BOOKINGS AND CAPS

	AGE (on 01/07/07)	IN NAMED 18	APPEARANCES	COUNTING GAMES	MINUTES ON PITCH	YELLOW CARDS	RED CARDS	CAPS THIS SEASON	NATIONAL SIDE
Goalkeepers									
Simon Pouplin	22	38	38	38	3420	1	0	-	France
Defenders									
Guillaume Borne	18	12	8	6	596	0	0	-	France
Gregory Bourillon	23	23	23	22	2009	4	0	-	France
Erik Edman	28	30	30	25	2506	6	0	7	Sweden
Jacques Faty	23	29	24	20	1931	4	0	-	France
Cyril Jeunechamp	31	15	10	8	763	4	0	-	France
Mario Melchiot	30	30	30	29	2643	1	0	2	Holland
John Mensah	24	25	23	22	2014	4	0	-	Ghana
J-J Perrier-Doumbe	28	11	2	1	124	0	0	-	Cameroon
Midfielders									
Kevin Bru	18	4	2	0	16	0	0	-	France
Bruno Cheyrou	29	37	35	32	2962	5	1	-	France
Romain Danze	20	24	20	12	1208	1	0	-	France
Etienne Didot	23	25	25	25	2250	4	0	-	Senegal
Papacouli Diop	21	1	1	0	1	0	0	-	Senegal
Stephane M'Bia	21	35	30	18	1961	7	1	-	Cameroon
Sylvain Marveaux	21	30	28	7	1152	4	0	-	France
Arnold Mvuemba	22	4	1	0	56	0	0	-	France
Oliver Sorlin	28	32	32	28	2655	4	0	-	France
Forwards									
Jimmy Briand	22	37	35	25	2399	7	0	-	France
Jires Ekoko	19	8	3	0	26	0	0	-	Congo DR
Julian Esteban	20	3	1	0	4	0	0	-	Switzerland
Youssouf Hadji	27	16	13	8	769	1	0	2	Morocco
Olivier Monterrubio	30	16	13	11	953	0	0	-	France
Daniel Moreira	29	34	29	16	1650	2	0	-	France
Moussa Sow	21	27	14	1	328	1	0	-	France
Olivier Thomert	27	11	11	5	738	0	0	-	France
John Utaka	25	35	35	23	2308	1	0	2	Nigeria

TEAM OF THE SEASON

G Simon Pouplin — CG: 38 DR: 114

D John Mensah — CG: 22 DR: 143
D Jacques Faty — CG: 20 DR: 137
D Mario Melchiot — CG: 29 DR: 125
D Erik Edman — CG: 25 DR: 125

M Romain Danze — CG: 12 SD: 86
M Etienne Didot — CG: 25 SD: 70
M Bruno Cheyrou — CG: 32 SD: 24
M Oliver Sorlin — CG: 28 SD: 24

F John Utaka — CG: 23 SR: 209
F Jimmy Briand — CG: 25 SR: 266

MONTHLY POINTS TALLY

AUGUST	1	8%
SEPTEMBER	5	42%
OCTOBER	6	67%
NOVEMBER	5	42%
DECEMBER	8	67%
JANUARY	6	67%
FEBRUARY	5	42%
MARCH	4	44%
APRIL	11	73%
MAY	6	50%

LEAGUE GOALS

	PLAYER	MINS	GOALS	S RATE
1	Utaka	2308	11	209
2	Briand	2399	9	266
3	Marveaux	1152	5	230
4	Monterrubio	953	3	317
5	Cheyrou	2962	3	987
6	Jeunechamp	763	2	381
7	Melchiot	2643	2	1321
8	Danze	1208	1	1208
9	M'Bia	1961	1	1961
10	Didot	2250	1	2250
11	Diop	1	0	
12	Edman	2506	0	
13	Ekoko	26	0	
	Other		0	
	TOTAL		38	

TOP POINT EARNERS

	PLAYER	GAMES	AV PTS
1	John Utaka	24	1.79
2	Etienne Didot	25	1.76
3	John Mensah	22	1.73
4	Romain Danze	12	1.67
5	Mario Melchiot	29	1.66
6	Oliver Sorlin	28	1.64
7	Jacques Faty	20	1.60
8	Bruno Cheyrou	33	1.52
9	Simon Pouplin	38	1.50
10	Jimmy Briand	25	1.48
	CLUB AVERAGE:		1.50

DISCIPLINARY RECORDS

	PLAYER	YELLOW	RED	AVE
1	Cyril Jeunechamp	4	0	190
2	Stephane M'Bia	7	1	245
3	Sylvain Marveaux	4	0	288
4	Jimmy Briand	7	0	342
5	Erik Edman	6	0	417
6	Jacques Faty	4	0	482
7	Bruno Cheyrou	5	1	493
8	Gregory Bourillon	4	0	502
9	John Mensah	4	0	503
10	Etienne Didot	4	0	562
11	Oliver Sorlin	4	0	663
12	Youssouf Hadji	1	0	769
13	Daniel Moreira	2	0	825
	Other	4	1	
	TOTAL	60	3	

KEY GOALKEEPER

Simon Pouplin

Goals Conceded in the League	30	Counting Games — League games when player was on pitch for at least 70 minutes	38
Defensive Rating — Ave number of mins between League goals conceded while on the pitch	114	Clean Sheets — In League games when player was on pitch for at least 70 minutes	16

KEY PLAYERS - DEFENDERS

John Mensah

Goals Conceded — Number of League goals conceded while the player was on the pitch	14	Clean Sheets — In League games when player was on pitch for at least 70 minutes	11
Defensive Rating — Ave number of mins between League goals conceded while on the pitch	143	Club Defensive Rating — Average number of mins between League goals conceded by the club this season	114

	PLAYER	CON LGE	CLEAN SHEETS	DEF RATE
1	John Mensah	14	11	143 mins
2	Jacques Faty	14	8	137 mins
3	Mario Melchiot	21	13	125 mins
4	Erik Edman	20	12	125 mins

KEY PLAYERS - MIDFIELDERS

Romain Danze

Goals in the League	1	Contribution to Attacking Power — Average number of minutes between League team goals while on pitch	86
Defensive Rating — Average number of mins between League goals conceded while on the pitch	172	Scoring Difference — Defensive Rating minus Contribution to Attacking Power	86

	PLAYER	LGE GOALS	DEF RATE	POWER	SCORE DIFF
1	Romain Danze	1	172	86	86 mins
2	Etienne Didot	1	150	80	70 mins
3	Bruno Cheyrou	3	113	89	24 mins
4	Oliver Sorlin	0	106	82	24 mins

KEY PLAYERS - GOALSCORERS

John Utaka

Goals in the League	11	Player Strike Rate — Average number of minutes between League goals scored by player	209
Contribution to Attacking Power — Average number of minutes between League team goals while on pitch	74	Club Strike Rate — Average number of minutes between League goals scored by club	90

	PLAYER	LGE GOALS	POWER	STRIKE RATE
1	John Utaka	11	74	209 mins
2	Jimmy Briand	9	88	266 mins
3	Bruno Cheyrou	3	89	987 mins
4	Romain Danze	1	86	1208 mins

Jimmy Briand

SQUAD APPEARANCES

Match	1 2 3 4 5	6 7 8 9 10	11 12 13 14 15	16 17 18 19 20	21 22 23 24 25	26 27 28 29 30	31 32 33 34 35	36 37 38
Venue	H A H A H	A H A H H	A H A H A	H A H A H	A H A H A	H A A H H	A A H A H	A H A
Competition	L L L L L	L L L L L	L L L L L	L L L L L	L L L L L	L L L L L	L L L L L	L L L
Result	L L D L W	D D L W W	L W D D L	W W D D L	W W D D W	L L D W W	D D W W D	D W D

Goalkeepers: Simon Pouplin

Defenders: Guillaume Borne, Gregory Bourillon, Erik Edman, Jacques Faty, Cyril Jeunechamp, Mario Melchiot, John Mensah, J-J Perrier-Doumbe

Midfielders: Kevin Bru, Bruno Cheyrou, Romain Danze, Etienne Didot, Papacouli Diop, Stephane M'Bia, Sylvain Marveaux, Arnold Mvuemba, Oliver Sorlin

Forwards: Jimmy Briand, Jires Ekoko, Julian Esteban, Youssouf Hadji, Olivier Monterrubio, Daniel Moreira, Moussa Sow, Olivier Thomert, John Utaka

KEY: ■ On all match · ■ On bench · ◀◀ Subbed or sent off (Counting game) · ◀ Subbed or sent off (playing less than 70 minutes) · ▶▶ Subbed on from bench (Counting Game) · ▶ Subbed on (playing less than 70 minutes) · ▶▶ Subbed on and then subbed or sent off (Counting Game) · ▶▶ Subbed on and then subbed or sent off (playing less than 70 minutes) · ☐ Not in 16

FRANCE - RENNES

LENS

Final Position: **5th**

NICKNAME: LES SANG ET OR   KEY: ☐ Won ☐ Drawn ☐ Lost   Attendance

					Score		Attendance
1	frpr1	Troyes	H	W	1-0	Dindane 36	32,131
2	frpr1	Lille	A	L	0-4		16,619
3	frpr1	Lorient	H	D	1-1	Dindane 41	31,843
4	frpr1	St Etienne	A	L	2-3	Ilan 74 og, Jussie 78 pen	27,828
5	frpr1	Valenciennes	H	W	3-0	Dindane 8, 23, Demont 29	34,927
6	ucrl1	Eth Achnas	A	D	0-0		1,300
7	frpr1	Sochaux	A	W	3-0	Dindane 10, Keita 55, Jussie 59	12,363
8	frpr1	AS Monaco	H	W	1-0	Jussie 5 pen	31,828
9	ucrl2	Eth Achnas	H	W	3-1	Dindane 10, Jemaa 62, Cousin 64	27,171
10	frpr1	Nancy	A	L	1-2	Jussie 71 pen	18,017
11	frpr1	Marseille	H	D	1-1	Dindane 79 pen	40,567
12	frpr1	Sedan	A	D	2-2	Dindane 4, Keita 30	12,639
13	frpr1	Auxerre	H	W	1-0	Demont 61	31,808
14	ucgpd	Osasuna	H	W	3-1	Dindane 15, Cousin 69 pen, Boukari 82	26,000
15	frpr1	Paris SG	A	W	3-1	Cousin 49, 67, Thomert 80	35,894
16	frpr1	Rennes	H	D	0-0		32,214
17	frpr1	Nantes	H	W	2-0	Coulibaly 1, Keita 82	33,128
18	ucgpd	Odense	A	D	1-1	Jemaa 87	7,707
19	frpr1	Le Mans	A	D	1-1	Thomert 41	9,217
20	ucgpd	Parma	H	L	1-2	Cousin 19	32,341
21	frpr1	Bordeaux	H	W	3-0	Hilton 39, Cousin 59, Jemaa 87	30,279
22	frpr1	Toulouse	A	W	1-0	Jemaa 90	17,040
23	ucgpd	Heerenveen	A	L	0-1		17,000
24	frpr1	Lyon	H	L	0-4		40,038
25	frpr1	Nice	A	W	2-1	Jussie 73 pen, Dindane 77	10,128
26	frpr1	Lille	H	D	1-1	Jussie 83	39,460
27	frpr1	Lorient	A	L	0-1		13,117
28	frpr1	St Etienne	H	D	3-3	Seydou.Keita 66, 90, Coulibaly 88	30,989
29	frpr1	Valenciennes	A	W	3-1	Carriere 28, Seydou.Keita 45, Jemaa 90	16,513
30	frpr1	Sochaux	H	W	3-1	Hilton 28, Seydou.Keita 30, Dindane 57	31,122
31	ucrl1	Panathinaikos	H	W	3-1	Jemaa 49, 70, Dindane 90 pen	40,000
32	frpr1	AS Monaco	A	D	0-0		10,677
33	ucrl2	Panathinaikos	A	D	0-0		30,000
34	frpr1	Nancy	H	D	2-2	Dindane 18, Seydou.Keita 24 pen	32,143
35	frpr1	Marseille	A	W	1-0	Dindane 60 pen	51,718
36	ucrl1	B Leverkusen	H	W	2-1	Monterrubio 17, Cousin 70 pen	29,200
37	frpr1	Sedan	H	D	1-1	Seydou.Keita 28	29,939
38	ucrl2	B Leverkusen	A	L	0-3		22,500
39	frpr1	Auxerre	A	L	0-1		9,580
40	frpr1	Paris SG	H	L	1-2	Rozehnal 51 og	37,808
41	frpr1	Rennes	A	L	0-1		27,108
42	frpr1	Nantes	A	D	0-0		33,193
43	frpr1	Le Mans	H	W	2-0	Carriere 56, Seydou.Keita 89	35,319
44	frpr1	Bordeaux	A	L	0-1		32,253
45	frpr1	Toulouse	H	W	2-0	Seydou.Keita 82, Cousin 89 pen	38,896
46	frpr1	Lyon	A	L	0-3		38,213
47	frpr1	Nice	H	D	0-0		38,468
48	frpr1	Troyes	A	L	0-3		13,719

LEAGUE APPEARANCES, BOOKINGS AND CAPS

	AGE (on 01/07/07)	IN NAMED 18	APPEARANCES	COUNTING GAMES	MINUTES ON PITCH	YELLOW CARDS	RED CARDS	CAPS THIS SEASON	NATIONAL SIDE
Goalkeepers									
Sebastien Chabbert	28	32	0	0	0	0	0	-	France
Charles-Hubert Itandje	24	38	38	38	3420	2	0	-	France
Defenders									
Patrick Barul	29	33	12	6	699	3	0	-	France
Milan Bisevac	23	11	9	6	648	1	0	2	Serbia
Adama Coulibaly	26	36	33	33	2970	3	0	-	Mali
Yohan Demont	29	36	35	33	2984	11	0	-	France
Nicholas Gillet	30	26	8	5	536	3	0	-	France
Vitorino Hilton	29	37	37	37	3330	4	0	-	Brazil
Marco Ramos	24	29	27	23	2204	9	1	-	Portugal
Damien Tixier	27	14	6	4	425	0	0	-	France
Gregory Vignal	25	14	9	6	622	3	1	-	France
Kamil Zayatte	22	1	1	0	1	0	0	-	Guinea
Midfielders									
Abdoulrazak Boukari	20	34	29	3	1055	2	0	-	France
Eric Carriere	34	35	32	21	2137	0	0	-	France
Mounir Diane	25	7	4	0	74	0	0	-	Morocco
Seyadou Keita	27	33	30	26	2419	6	1	-	Mali
Sidi Yaya Keita	22	35	24	15	1460	7	1	-	Mali
Nenad Kovacevic	26	31	31	27	2515	7	2	8	Serbia
Jonathan Lacourt	20	5	3	1	129	1	0	-	France
Forwards									
Daniel Cousin	30	30	30	16	1851	7	0	-	Gabon
Aruna Dindane	26	35	34	31	2851	8	0	5	Ivory Coast
Issam Jemaa	23	28	27	5	938	4	0	3	Tunisia
Ferreira Vieira Jussie	23	21	21	16	1579	3	0	-	Brazil
Kevin Monnet-Paquet	18	12	5	0	44	0	0	-	France
Olivier Monterrubio	30	16	16	12	1222	1	0	-	France
Adel Taarabt	18	2	1	0	4	0	0	-	Algeria
Olivier Thomert	27	18	17	11	1187	1	0	-	France

TEAM OF THE SEASON

G Charles-Hubert Itandje CG: 38 DR: 83

D Yohan Demont CG: 33 DR: 87
D Vitorino Hilton CG: 37 DR: 83
D Adama Coulibaly CG: 33 DR: 80
D Marco Ramos CG: 23 DR: 78

M Nenad Kovacevic CG: 27 SD: 31
M Eric Carriere CG: 21 SD: 18
M Sidi Yaya Keita CG: 15 SD: 9
M Seyadou Keita CG: 26 SD: -7

F Aruna Dindane CG: 31 SR: 259
F F Vieira Jussie CG: 16 SR: 263

MONTHLY POINTS TALLY

AUGUST		4 33%
SEPTEMBER		9 100%
OCTOBER		5 42%
NOVEMBER		8 67%
DECEMBER		9 75%
JANUARY		2 22%
FEBRUARY		8 67%
MARCH		4 44%
APRIL		4 27%
MAY		4 33%

LEAGUE GOALS

	PLAYER	MINS	GOALS	S RATE
1	Dindane	2851	11	259
2	Keita, Seydou	2419	7	345
3	Jussie	1579	6	263
4	Cousin	1851	4	462
5	Jemaa	938	3	312
6	Keita, Sidi	1460	3	486
7	Thomert	1187	2	593
8	Carriere	2137	2	1068
9	Coulibaly	2970	2	1485
10	Demont	2984	2	1492
11	Hilton	3330	2	1665
12	Itandje	3420	0	
13	Gillet	536	0	
	Other		0	
	TOTAL		**44**	

TOP POINT EARNERS

	PLAYER	GAMES	AV PTS
1	Daniel Cousin	16	1.75
2	Ferreira Vieira Jussie	16	1.75
3	Nenad Kovacevic	29	1.66
4	Yohan Demont	33	1.58
5	Eric Carriere	21	1.57
6	Sidi Yaya Keita	15	1.53
7	Charles-Hubert Itandje	38	1.50
8	Adama Coulibaly	33	1.48
9	Aruna Dindane	31	1.48
10	Vitorino Hilton	37	1.46
	CLUB AVERAGE:		**1.50**

DISCIPLINARY RECORDS

	PLAYER	YELLOW	RED	AVE
1	Gregory Vignal	3	1	155
2	Issam Jemaa	4	0	234
3	Marco Ramos	9	1	244
4	Daniel Cousin	7	0	264
5	Nenad Kovacevic	7	2	279
6	Sidi Yaya Keita	7	1	365
7	Yohan Demont	11	0	373
8	Aruna Dindane	8	0	475
9	Seyadou Keita	6	1	483
10	F Vieira Jussie	3	0	526
11	Azak Boukari	2	0	527
12	Nicholas Gillet	3	0	536
13	Olivier Thomert	2	0	593
	Other	14	0	
	TOTAL	**86**	**6**	

KEY GOALKEEPER

Charles-Hubert Itandje

Goals Conceded in the League	41	Counting Games League games when player was on pitch for at least 70 minutes	38
Defensive Rating Ave number of mins between League goals conceded while on the pitch	83	Clean Sheets In League games when player was on pitch for at least 70 minutes	15

KEY PLAYERS - DEFENDERS

Yohan Demont

Goals Conceded Number of League goals conceded while the player was on the pitch	34	Clean Sheets In League games when player was on pitch for at least 70 minutes	13
Defensive Rating Ave number of mins between League goals conceded while on the pitch	87	Club Defensive Rating Average number of mins between League goals conceded by the club this season	83

	PLAYER	CON LGE	CLEAN SHEETS	DEF RATE
1	Yohan Demont	34	13	87 mins
2	Vitorino Hilton	40	15	83 mins
3	Adama Coulibaly	37	13	80 mins
4	Marco Ramos	28	10	78 mins

KEY PLAYERS - MIDFIELDERS

Nenad Kovacevic

Goals in the League	0	Contribution to Attacking Power Average number of minutes between League team goals while on pitch	69
Defensive Rating Average number of mins between League goals conceded while on the pitch	100	Scoring Difference Defensive Rating minus Contribution to Attacking Power	31

	PLAYER	LGE GOALS	DEF RATE	POWER	SCORE DIFF
1	Nenad Kovacevic	0	100	69	31 mins
2	Eric Carriere	2	97	79	18 mins
3	Sidi Yaya Keita	3	69	60	9 mins
4	Seyadou Keita	7	73	80	-7 mins

KEY PLAYERS - GOALSCORERS

Aruna Dindane

Goals in the League	11	Player Strike Rate Average number of minutes between League goals scored by player	259
Contribution to Attacking Power Average number of minutes between League team goals while on pitch	75	Club Strike Rate Average number of minutes between League goals scored by club	72

	PLAYER	LGE GOALS	POWER	STRIKE RATE
1	Aruna Dindane	11	75	259 mins
2	Ferreira Vieira Jussie	6	65	263 mins
3	Seyadou Keita	7	80	345 mins
4	Daniel Cousin	4	77	462 mins

Aruna Dindane

SQUAD APPEARANCES

Match	1 2 3 4 5	6 7 8 9 10	11 12 13 14 15	16 17 18 19 20	21 22 23 24 25	26 27 28 29 30	31 32 33 34 35	36 37 38 39 40	41 42 43 44 45	46 47 48
Venue	H A H A H	A A H H A	H A H H A	H H A A H	H A A H A	H A H A H	H A A H A	E L E L L	H H A A H	A A H A H	A H A
Competition	L L L L L	E L L E L	L L L E L	L L E L E	L L E L L	L L L L L	E L E L L	E L E L L	L L L L L	L L L
Result	W L D L W	D W W W L	D D W W W	D W D D L	W W L L W	D L D W W	W D D D W	W D L L L	L D W L W	L D L

Goalkeepers
Sebastien Chabbert
Charles-Hubert Itandje

Defenders
Patrick Barul
Milan Bisevac
Adama Coulibaly
Yohan Demont
Nicholas Gillet
Vitorino Hilton
Marco Ramos
Damien Tixier
Gregory Vignal
Kamil Zayatte

Midfielders
Abdoulrazak Boukari
Eric Carriere
Mounir Diane
Seyadou Keita
Sidi Yaya Keita
Nenad Kovacevic
Jonathan Lacourt

Forwards
Daniel Cousin
Aruna Dindane
Issam Jemaa
Ferreira Vieira Jussie
Kevin Monnet-Paquet
Olivier Monterrubio
Adel Taarabt
Olivier Thomert

KEY: ■ On all match   ◄◄ Subbed or sent off (Counting game)   ►► Subbed on from bench (Counting Game)   ►► Subbed on and then subbed or sent off (Counting Game)   □ Not in 16
   ■ On bench   ◄◄ Subbed or sent off (playing less than 70 minutes)   ►► Subbed on (playing less than 70 minutes)   ►► Subbed on and then subbed or sent off (playing less than 70 minutes)

FRANCE - LENS

BORDEAUX

Final Position: 6th

NICKNAME: GIRONDINS

KEY: ☐ Won ☐ Drawn ☐ Lost

#				Score	Scorers	Attendance
1	frpr1	Toulouse	H W	2-0	Chamakh 58, Faubert 88	30,186
2	frpr1	Lorient	A W	1-0	Micoud 44	15,180
3	frpr1	Lyon	H L	1-2	Faubert 4	32,008
4	frpr1	Lille	A L	0-3		15,003
5	frpr1	Nice	H W	3-2	Darcheville 41, 64 pen, Wendel 44	20,178
6	ecgpc	Galatasaray	A D	0-0		45,514
7	frpr1	Marseille	A L	1-2	Chamakh 63 pen	55,000
8	frpr1	Troyes	H W	2-1	Darcheville 49, Wendel 49	18,623
9	ecgpc	PSV Eindhov	H L	0-1		26,000
10	frpr1	Valenciennes	A L	0-2		15,040
11	frpr1	AS Monaco	H W	1-0	Perea 69	22,146
12	ecgpc	Liverpool	H L	0-1		29,963
13	frpr1	Sochaux	A L	1-2	Ducasse 90	13,475
14	frpr1	Sedan	H W	3-1	Wendel 45, Micoud 46, Darcheville 52 pen	20,836
15	ecgpc	Liverpool	A L	0-3		41,978
16	frpr1	Nancy	A L	1-2	Darcheville 31	18,041
17	frpr1	Auxerre	H D	0-0		22,025
18	frpr1	Paris SG	A W	2-0	Wendel 27, Laslandes 86	38,394
19	ecgpc	Galatasaray	H W	3-1	Alonso 22, Laslandes 47, Faubert 50	25,000
20	frpr1	St Etienne	H W	1-0	Alonso 69	29,702
21	frpr1	Lens	A L	0-3		30,279
22	ecgpc	PSV Eindhov	A W	3-1	Faubert 7, Dalmat 25, Darcheville 37	26,000
23	frpr1	Rennes	H L	1-2	Darcheville 68	21,929
24	frpr1	Nantes	A D	0-0		26,490
25	frpr1	Le Mans	H W	1-0	Cid 59	20,392
26	frpr1	Lorient	H D	1-1	Chamakh 86	19,809
27	frpr1	Lyon	A W	2-1	Francia 2 pen, Micoud 26	35,305
28	frpr1	Lille	H L	0-1		23,453
29	frpr1	Nice	A L	1-2	Micoud 34	10,898
30	frpr1	Marseille	H W	1-0	Faubert 74	32,200
31	ucrl1	Osasuna	H D	0-0		20,000
32	frpr1	Troyes	A L	0-1		10,401
33	ucrl2	Osasuna	A L	0-1		14,000
34	frpr1	Valenciennes	H W	2-1	Fernando Menegazzo 24 pen, Jussie 43	22,371
35	frpr1	AS Monaco	A D	0-0		11,456
36	frpr1	Sochaux	H W	2-0	Micoud 45, Cavenaghi 90	25,128
37	frpr1	Sedan	A D	1-1	Darcheville 27	16,994
38	frpr1	Auxerre	A D	0-0		14,556
39	frpr1	Paris SG	H D	0-0		31,731
40	frpr1	Nancy	H W	3-0	Chamakh 17, 43, Cavenaghi 54	21,732
41	frpr1	St Etienne	A W	2-0	Fernando Menegazzo 50, Obertan 90	27,851
42	frpr1	Lens	H W	1-0	Jussie 13	32,253
43	frpr1	Rennes	A D	0-0		28,368
44	frpr1	Nantes	H L	0-1		27,432
45	frpr1	Le Mans	A D	1-1	Perea 68	14,072
46	frpr1	Toulouse	A L	1-3	Wendel 16	32,008

LEAGUE APPEARANCES, BOOKINGS AND CAPS

	AGE (on 01/07/07)	IN NAMED 18	APPEARANCES	COUNTING GAMES	MINUTES ON PITCH	YELLOW CARDS	RED CARDS	CAPS THIS SEASON	NATIONAL SIDE
Goalkeepers									
Ulrich Rame	34	38	38	38	3420	5	0	-	France
Mathieu Valverde	24	34	0	0	0	0	0	-	France
Defenders									
Gerald Cid	24	12	10	10	900	2	0	-	France
Joseph Enakarhire	24	26	16	11	1227	3	0	-	Nigeria
Julien Faubert	23	26	26	25	2271	4	1	1	France
Carlos Henrique	24	25	15	15	1334	3	0	-	Brazil
David Jemmali	32	29	28	24	2282	8	1	-	France
Franck Jurietti	32	31	29	27	2492	6	0	-	France
Florian Marange	21	32	24	18	1828	3	0	-	France
Marc Planus	25	26	23	22	2012	4	0	-	France
Midfielders									
Alejandro Alonso	25	38	30	15	1872	6	0	-	Argentina
Stephane Dalmat	28	15	13	3	463	0	0	-	France
Pierre Ducasse	20	24	12	7	764	1	0	-	France
Fernando Menegazzo	26	32	32	27	2643	6	1	1	Brazil
Juan-Pablo Francia	22	20	9	3	443	0	0	-	Argentina
Ted Lavie	21	2	0	0	0	0	0	-	France
Rio Mavuba	23	34	32	24	2406	6	0	3	France
Johan Micoud	33	32	32	28	2615	8	0	-	France
Vladimir Smicer	34	13	3	0	54	1	0	-	Czech Republic
Geraldo Wendel	25	33	29	22	2142	7	0	-	Brazil
Forwards									
Fernando Cavenaghi	23	15	9	1	279	1	0	-	Argentina
Marouane Chamakh	23	29	29	19	1995	7	0	-	Morocco
Jean-Cl. Darcheville	31	26	23	11	1374	5	0	-	France
Ferreira Vieira Jussie	23	16	16	10	1127	2	0	-	Brazil
Lilian Laslandes	35	16	11	4	585	1	0	-	France
Gabriel Obertan	18	19	17	1	427	0	0	-	France
Edixon Perea	23	27	17	4	608	1	0	-	Colombia

TEAM OF THE SEASON

D Marc Planus — CG: 22 DR: 125
M Geraldo Wendel — CG: 22 SD: 41
D Julien Faburet — CG: 25 DR: 94
M Alejandro Alonso — CG: 15 SD: 32
F J-C Darcheville* — CG: 11 SR: 196
G Ulrich Rame — CG: 38 DR: 97
D Carlos Henrique — CG: 15 DR: 111
M Fernando Menegazzo — CG: 27 SD: 23
F M Chamakh — CG: 19 SR: 399
D Franck Jurietti — CG: 27 DR: 108
M Johan Micoud — CG: 28 SD: 13

MONTHLY POINTS TALLY

Month		Points	%
AUGUST		6	50%
SEPTEMBER		6	50%
OCTOBER		6	67%
NOVEMBER		7	58%
DECEMBER		4	33%
JANUARY		4	44%
FEBRUARY		6	50%
MARCH		5	56%
APRIL		11	73%
MAY		2	17%

LEAGUE GOALS

	PLAYER	MINS	GOALS	S RATE
1	Darcheville	1374	7	196
2	Chamakh	1995	5	399
3	Wendel	2142	5	428
4	Micoud	2615	5	523
5	Faubert	2271	3	757
6	Cavenaghi	279	2	139
7	Perea	608	2	304
8	Jussie	1127	2	563
9	F Menegazzo	2643	2	1321
10	Obertan	427	1	427
11	Francia	443	1	443
12	Laslandes	585	1	585
13	Ducasse	764	1	764
	Other		2	
	TOTAL		**39**	

TOP POINT EARNERS

	PLAYER	GAMES	AV PTS
1	Geraldo Wendel	22	1.91
2	Alejandro Alonso	15	1.80
3	Marouane Chamakh	19	1.68
4	Marc Planus	22	1.64
5	Carlos Henrique	15	1.53
6	David Jemmali	25	1.52
7	Ulrich Rame	38	1.50
8	Franck Jurietti	27	1.48
9	Johan Micoud	28	1.46
10	Fernando Menegazzo	27	1.41
	CLUB AVERAGE:		**1.50**

DISCIPLINARY RECORDS

	PLAYER	YELLOW	RED	AVE
1	David Jemmali	8	1	285
2	Alejandro Alonso	6	0	312
3	Johan Micoud	8	0	326
4	Marouane Chamakh	7	0	332
5	Jean-C Darcheville	5	0	343
6	Geraldo Wendel	7	0	357
7	F Menegazzo	6	1	440
8	Carlos Henrique	3	0	444
9	Gerald Cid	2	0	450
10	Rio Mavuba	6	0	481
11	Franck Jurietti	6	0	498
12	F Vieira Jussie	2	0	563
13	Julien Faubert	4	1	567
	Other	18	0	
	TOTAL	**88**	**3**	

KEY GOALKEEPER

Ulrich Rame

Goals Conceded in the League	35	Counting Games League games when player was on pitch for at least 70 minutes	38
Defensive Rating Ave number of mins between League goals conceded while on the pitch	97	Clean Sheets In League games when player was on pitch for at least 70 minutes	17

KEY PLAYERS - DEFENDERS

Marc Planus

Goals Conceded Number of League goals conceded while the player was on the pitch	16	Clean Sheets In League games when player was on pitch for at least 70 minutes	11
Defensive Rating Ave number of mins between League goals conceded while on the pitch	125	Club Defensive Rating Average number of mins between League goals conceded by the club this season	97

	PLAYER	CON LGE	CLEAN SHEETS	DEF RATE
1	Marc Planus	16	11	125 mins
2	Carlos Henrique	12	8	111 mins
3	Franck Jurietti	23	13	108 mins
4	Julien Faubert	24	13	94 mins

KEY PLAYERS - MIDFIELDERS

Geraldo Wendel

Goals in the League	5	Contribution to Attacking Power Average number of minutes between League team goals while on pitch	71
Defensive Rating Average number of mins between League goals conceded while on the pitch	112	Scoring Difference Defensive Rating minus Contribution to Attacking Power	41

	PLAYER	LGE GOALS	DEF RATE	POWER	SCORE DIFF
1	Geraldo Wendel	5	112	71	41 mins
2	Alejandro Alonso	1	110	78	32 mins
3	Fernando Menegazzo	2	120	97	23 mins
4	Johan Micoud	5	100	87	13 mins

KEY PLAYERS - GOALSCORERS

Jean-Claude Darcheville

Goals in the League	7	Player Strike Rate Average number of minutes between League goals scored by player	196
Contribution to Attacking Power Average number of minutes between League team goals while on pitch	76	Club Strike Rate Average number of minutes between League goals scored by club	87

	PLAYER	LGE GOALS	POWER	STRIKE RATE
1	Jean-Claude Darcheville	7	76	196 mins
2	Marouane Chamakh	5	99	399 mins
3	Geraldo Wendel	5	71	428 mins
4	Johan Micoud	5	87	523 mins

Jean-Claude Darcheville

SQUAD APPEARANCES

Match	1	2	3	4	5	6	7	8	9	10	11	12	13	14	15	16	17	18	19	20	21	22	23	24	25	26	27	28	29	30	31	32	33	34	35	36	37	38	39	40	41	42	43	44	45	46
Venue	H	A	H	A	H	A	A	H	H	A	H	H	A	H	A	A	H	H	H	A	A	H	A	H	H	H	A	H	A	H	H	A	A	H	A	H	A	A	H	H	A	H	A	H	A	A
Competition	L	L	L	L	L	C	L	L	C	L	L	C	L	L	C	L	L	L	C	L	L	C	L	L	L	L	L	L	L	L	E	L	E	L	L	L	L	L	L	L	L	L	L	L	L	L
Result	W	W	L	L	W	D	L	W	L	L	W	L	L	W	L	L	D	W	W	W	L	W	L	D	W	D	W	L	L	W	D	L	L	W	D	W	D	D	D	W	W	W	D	L	D	L

Goalkeepers

Ulrich Rame

Mathieu Valverde

Defenders

Gerald Cid

Joseph Enakarhire

Julien Faubert

Carlos Henrique

David Jemmali

Franck Jurietti

Florian Marange

Marc Planus

Midfielders

Alejandro Alonso

Stephane Dalmat

Pierre Ducasse

Fernando Menegazzo

Juan-Pablo Francia

Ted Lavie

Rio Mavuba

Johan Micoud

Vladimir Smicer

Geraldo Wendel

Forwards

Fernando Cavenaghi

Marouane Chamakh

Jean-Claude Darcheville

Ferreira Vieira Jussie

Lilian Laslandes

Gabriel Obertan

Edixon Perea

KEY: ■ On all match   ◄◄ Subbed or sent off (Counting game)   ▷▷ Subbed on from bench (Counting Game)   ▷▷ Subbed on and then subbed or sent off (Counting Game)   □ Not in 16

■ On bench   ◄◄ Subbed or sent off (playing less than 70 minutes)   ▷▷ Subbed on (playing less than 70 minutes)   ▷▷ Subbed on and then subbed or sent off (playing less than 70 minutes)

FRANCE - BORDEAUX

SOCHAUX

Final Position: 7th

NICKNAME: LES LIONCEAUX   KEY: ☐ Won ☐ Drawn ☐ Lost   Attendance

1	frpr1	St Etienne	A W	2-1	Leroy 22, Zairi 74	32,786
2	frpr1	Auxerre	H D	1-1	Birsa 52	14,759
3	frpr1	Sedan	A D	1-1	Quercia 15	11,227
4	frpr1	Paris SG	H W	3-2	Ziani 29, 81, Sene 35	16,317
5	frpr1	Rennes	A L	1-2	Alvaro Santos 55	21,526
6	frpr1	Lens	H L	0-3		12,363
7	frpr1	Le Mans	A D	2-2	Quercia 1, Sene 70	9,452
8	frpr1	Lyon	H L	0-1		18,788
9	frpr1	Nantes	A W	2-0	Afolabi 27, Santos 48	26,904
10	frpr1	Bordeaux	H W	2-1	Alvaro 3, Birsa 68	13,475
11	frpr1	Toulouse	A W	2-1	Alvaro 31 pen, Ziani 86	20,846
12	frpr1	Troyes	H W	1-0	N'Daw 67	16,740
13	frpr1	Nice	A D	0-0		10,688
14	frpr1	Lille	H D	0-0		12,397
15	frpr1	Lorient	A W	3-1	Le Tallec 22, 25, Ziani 44 pen	12,513
16	frpr1	Marseille	H W	1-0	Afolabi 76	19,986
17	frpr1	Valenciennes	A D	0-0		12,889
18	frpr1	AS Monaco	A L	0-3		11,292
19	frpr1	Nancy	H W	2-1	Ziani 61, 65 pen	17,700
20	frpr1	Auxerre	A L	0-1		7,066
21	frpr1	Sedan	H D	1-1	Alvaro Santos 62	9,903
22	frpr1	Paris SG	A D	0-0		31,119
23	frpr1	Rennes	H D	0-0		10,477
24	frpr1	Lens	A L	1-3	Tosic 84	31,122
25	frpr1	Le Mans	H W	2-0	Alvaro Santos 13 pen, Yebda 78 og	9,996
26	frpr1	Lyon	A D	3-3	Alvaro Santos 8, Ziani 28 pen, Grax 85	40,363
27	frpr1	Nantes	H L	1-2	Santos 33 pen	14,664
28	frpr1	Bordeaux	A L	0-2		25,128
29	frpr1	Toulouse	H W	4-2	Grax 21, 55, Leroy 32, Isabey 63	11,485
30	frpr1	Troyes	A W	1-0	Pitau 32	11,554
31	frpr1	Nice	H D	1-1	Dagano 70	16,759
32	frpr1	Lille	A L	0-2		15,454
33	frpr1	Lorient	H D	1-1	Grax 73	13,952
34	frpr1	Marseille	A L	2-4	Leroy 5, Rodriguez 90 og	54,702
35	frpr1	Valenciennes	H W	1-0	Le Tallec 88	15,657
36	frpr1	AS Monaco	H W	2-1	Toure 29 og, Grax 81	13,451
37	frpr1	Nancy	A L	2-5	Birsa 44, Dagano 89	19,503
38	frpr1	St Etienne	H W	1-0	Le Tallec 18	19,738

LEAGUE APPEARANCES, BOOKINGS AND CAPS

	AGE (on 01/07/07)	IN NAMED 18	APPEARANCES	COUNTING GAMES	MINUTES ON PITCH	YELLOW CARDS	RED CARDS	CAPS THIS SEASON	NATIONAL SIDE
Goalkeepers									
Jeremy Gavanon	23	31	1	0	11	0	0	-	France
Teddy Richert	32	38	38	38	3409	2	0	-	France
Defenders									
Rabiu Afolabi	27	37	34	32	2953	7	0	-	Nigeria
Jeremie Brechet	27	30	28	27	2489	3	0	-	France
Fousseni Diawara	26	11	2	1	105	1	0	-	France
Souleymane Diawara	28	3	3	3	270	1	0	-	Senegal
Hakim El Bounadi	20	15	3	3	270	1	0	-	France
Stephane Pichot	30	32	31	30	2709	7	0	-	France
Lionel Potillon	33	23	8	7	660	0	0	-	France
Dusko Tosic	22	33	26	24	2226	6	0	3	Serbia
Midfielders									
Phillipe Brunel	34	17	9	2	390	1	1	-	France
Mickael Isabey	32	35	32	8	1378	1	0	-	France
Jerome Leroy	32	34	30	26	2448	3	0	-	France
Valery Mezague	23	22	9	0	169	1	0	-	Cameroon
Guirane N'Daw	23	38	37	35	3165	4	0	-	Senegal
Romain Pitau	29	33	33	28	2650	3	0	-	France
Badara Sene	22	26	25	20	1951	5	0	-	Senegal
Jaouad Zairi	25	3	3	3	270	1	0	-	Morocco
Karim Ziani	24	33	33	28	2687	5	0	-	France
Forwards									
Alvaro Santos	27	30	28	17	1782	1	0	-	Brazil
Valter Birsa	20	33	30	11	1656	1	0	4	Slovenia
Moumouni Dagano	26	13	13	2	581	0	0	-	Burkina Faso
Mevlut Erding	20	10	4	0	71	0	0	-	France
Sebastien Grax	23	14	13	6	729	0	0	-	France
Anthony Le Tallec	22	30	25	9	1112	5	0	-	France
Robin Previtali	20	2	1	0	18	0	0	-	France
Julien Quercia	20	29	26	11	1386	3	0	-	France

TEAM OF THE SEASON

G Teddy Richert   CG: 38   DR: 74

D Rabiu Afolabi   CG: 33   DR: 77
D Jeremie Brechet   CG: 27   DR: 71
D Dusko Tosic   CG: 24   DR: 67
D Stephane Pichot   CG: 30   DR: 66

M Badara Sene   CG: 20   SD: 4
M Karim Ziani   CG: 28   SD: 2
M Guirane N'Daw   CG: 35   SD: -2
M Jerome Leroy   CG: 26   SD: -5

F Alvaro Santos   CG: 17   SR: 254
F Valter Birsa   CG: 11   SR: 552

MONTHLY POINTS TALLY

AUGUST	8	67%
SEPTEMBER	1	8%
OCTOBER	9	100%
NOVEMBER	8	67%
DECEMBER	7	58%
JANUARY	2	22%
FEBRUARY	5	42%
MARCH	3	33%
APRIL	5	33%
MAY	9	75%

LEAGUE GOALS

	PLAYER	MINS	GOALS	S RATE
1	Alvaro Santos	1782	7	254
2	Ziani	2687	7	383
3	Grax	729	5	145
4	Le Tallec	1112	4	278
5	Birsa	1656	3	552
6	Leroy	2448	3	816
7	Dagano	581	2	290
8	Quercia	1386	2	693
9	Sene	1951	2	975
10	Afolabi	3027	2	1513
11	Zairi	270	1	270
12	Isabey	1378	1	1378
13	Tosic	2226	1	2226
	Other		2	
	TOTAL		**42**	

TOP POINT EARNERS

	PLAYER	GAMES	AV PTS
1	Badara Sene	20	1.80
2	Jerome Leroy	26	1.69
3	Rabiu Afolabi	33	1.64
4	Jeremie Brechet	27	1.63
5	Guirane N'Daw	35	1.51
6	Teddy Richert	38	1.50
7	Karim Ziani	28	1.43
8	Romain Pitau	28	1.39
9	Alvaro Santos	17	1.35
10	Stephane Pichot	30	1.33
	CLUB AVERAGE:		**1.50**

DISCIPLINARY RECORDS

	PLAYER	YELLOW	RED	AVE
1	Anthony Le Tallec	5	0	222
2	Dusko Tosic	6	0	371
3	Stephane Pichot	7	0	387
4	Badara Sene	5	0	390
5	Rabiu Afolabi	7	0	432
6	Julien Quercia	3	0	462
7	Karim Ziani	5	0	537
8	Guirane N'Daw	4	0	791
9	Jerome Leroy	3	0	816
10	Jeremie Brechet	3	0	829
11	Romain Pitau	3	0	883
12	Mickael Isabey	1	0	1378
13	Valter Birsa	1	0	1656
	Other	3	0	
	TOTAL	**56**	**0**	

KEY GOALKEEPER

Teddy Richert

Goals Conceded in the League	46	Counting Games League games when player was on pitch for at least 70 minutes	38
Defensive Rating Ave number of mins between League goals conceded while on the pitch	74	Clean Sheets In League games when player was on pitch for at least 70 minutes	13

KEY PLAYERS - DEFENDERS

Rabiu Afolabi

Goals Conceded Number of League goals conceded while the player was on the pitch	39	Clean Sheets In League games when player was on pitch for at least 70 minutes	12
Defensive Rating Ave number of mins between League goals conceded while on the pitch	77	Club Defensive Rating Average number of mins between League goals conceded by the club this season	71

	PLAYER	CON LGE	CLEAN SHEETS	DEF RATE
1	Rabiu Afolabi	39	12	77 mins
2	Jeremie Brechet	35	9	71 mins
3	Dusko Tosic	33	7	67 mins
4	Stephane Pichot	41	9	66 mins

KEY PLAYERS - MIDFIELDERS

Badara Sene

Goals in the League	2	Contribution to Attacking Power Average number of minutes between League team goals while on pitch	88
Defensive Rating Average number of mins between League goals conceded while on the pitch	92	Scoring Difference Defensive Rating minus Contribution to Attacking Power	4

	PLAYER	LGE GOALS	DEF RATE	POWER	SCORE DIFF
1	Badara Sene	2	92	88	4 mins
2	Karim Ziani	7	72	70	2 mins
3	Guirane N'Daw	1	71	73	-2 mins
4	Jerome Leroy	3	69	74	-5 mins

KEY PLAYERS - GOALSCORERS

Alvaro Santos

Goals in the League	7	Player Strike Rate Average number of minutes between League goals scored by player	254
Contribution to Attacking Power Average number of minutes between League team goals while on pitch	66	Club Strike Rate Average number of minutes between League goals scored by club	74

	PLAYER	LGE GOALS	POWER	STRIKE RATE
1	Alvaro Santos	7	66	254 mins
2	Karim Ziani	7	70	383 mins
3	Valter Birsa	3	78	552 mins
4	Julien Quercia	2	77	693 mins

Jeremie Brechet

SQUAD APPEARANCES

Match	1	2	3	4	5	6	7	8	9	10	11	12	13	14	15	16	17	18	19	20	21	22	23	24	25	26	27	28	29	30	31	32	33	34	35	36	37	38
Venue	A	H	A	H	A	H	A	H	A	H	A	H	A	H	A	H	A	A	H	A	H	A	H	A	H	A	H	A	H	A	H	A	H	A	H	H	A	H
Competition	L	L	L	L	L	L	L	L	L	L	L	L	L	L	L	L	L	L	L	L	L	L	L	L	L	L	L	L	L	L	L	L	L	L	L	L	L	L
Result	W	D	D	W	L	L	D	L	W	W	W	W	D	D	W	W	D	L	W	L	D	D	D	L	W	D	L	L	W	W	D	L	D	L	W	W	L	W

Goalkeepers
Jeremy Gavanon
Teddy Richert

Defenders
Rabiu Afolabi
Jeremie Brechet
Fousseni Diawara
Souleymane Diawara
Hakim El Bounadi
Stephane Pichot
Lionel Potillon
Dusko Tosic

Midfielders
Phillipe Brunel
Mickael Isabey
Jerome Leroy
Valery Mezague
Guirane N'Daw
Romain Pitau
Badara Sene
Jaouad Zairi
Karim Ziani

Forwards
Alvaro Santos
Valter Birsa
Moumouni Dagano
Mevlut Erding
Sebastien Grax
Anthony Le Tallec
Robin Previtali
Julien Quercia

KEY: ■ On all match · ◀◀ Subbed or sent off (Counting game) · ▶▶ Subbed on from bench (Counting Game) · ▶▶ Subbed on and then subbed or sent off (Counting Game) · ☐ Not in 16
☐ On bench · ◀◀ Subbed or sent off (playing less than 70 minutes) · ▶▶ Subbed on (playing less than 70 minutes) · ▶▶ Subbed on and then subbed or sent off (playing less than 70 minutes)

FRANCE - SOCHAUX

AUXERRE

Final Position: 8th

NICKNAME: AJA   KEY: ☐ Won ☐ Drawn ☐ Lost   Attendance

#							Attendance
1	frpr1	**Valenciennes**	H	D	1-1	Mignot 50	11,076
2	frpr1	**Sochaux**	A	D	1-1	Mathis 13	14,759
3	frpr1	**Marseille**	H	L	0-3		19,415
4	ucql2	**OFK Belgrado**	H	W	5-1	Mathis 21, Jelen 45, Pieroni 82, 85, 90	11,000
5	frpr1	**Nancy**	A	L	0-1		18,215
6	frpr1	**AS Monaco**	H	W	2-1	Cheyrou 27, Jelen 58	11,860
7	ucrl1	**Dinamo Zagreb**	A	W	2-1	Jelen 43, Niculae 72	30,000
8	frpr1	**St Etienne**	A	W	3-2	Mathis 40, Akale 84, Cheyrou 90	30,188
9	frpr1	**Sedan**	H	D	2-2	Pedretti 23, Pieroni 74	7,498
10	ucrl2	**Dinamo Zagreb**	H	W	3-1	Jelen 35, 41, Mathis 69	10,000
11	frpr1	**Nantes**	H	W	1-0	Niculae 39	8,549
12	frpr1	**Rennes**	A	L	1-3	Mathis 90	20,610
13	ucgpa	**Maccabi Haifa**	A	L	1-3	Niculae 29	8,000
14	frpr1	**Paris SG**	H	D	0-0		14,146
15	frpr1	**Lens**	A	L	0-1		31,808
16	frpr1	**Le Mans**	H	L	2-3	Akale 56, Pieroni 79 pen	7,000
17	frpr1	**Bordeaux**	A	D	0-0		22,025
18	frpr1	**Toulouse**	H	W	1-0	Pieroni 47	9,138
19	ucgpa	**Rangers**	H	D	2-2	Jelen 31, Niculae 76	8,305
20	frpr1	**Lyon**	A	L	0-1		39,576
21	ucgpa	**Partizan**	A	W	4-1	Cheyrou 18, Niculae 24, Akale 36, Pieroni 82	7,000
22	frpr1	**Nice**	H	D	0-0		6,252
23	frpr1	**Troyes**	A	D	3-3	Jelen 53, 84, Akale 90	16,891
24	ucgpa	**Livorno**	H	L	0-1		8,000
25	frpr1	**Lorient**	H	W	2-1	Akale 21, Jelen 53	6,049
26	frpr1	**Lille**	A	D	1-1	Akale 55	14,665
27	frpr1	**Sochaux**	H	W	1-0	Jelen 85	7,066
28	frpr1	**Marseille**	A	L	1-3	Jelen 16	30,000
29	frpr1	**Nancy**	H	W	2-0	Akale 33, Kahlenberg 36	6,150
30	frpr1	**AS Monaco**	A	L	1-2	Akale 90	8,102
31	frpr1	**St Etienne**	H	D	1-1	Akale 18	13,158
32	frpr1	**Sedan**	A	D	2-2	Niculae 14, 89	12,610
33	frpr1	**Nantes**	A	D	1-1	Cheyrou 18	28,307
34	frpr1	**Rennes**	H	W	1-0	Jelen 66	7,863
35	frpr1	**Paris SG**	A	W	1-0	Kaboul 41	33,036
36	frpr1	**Lens**	H	W	1-0	Kahlenberg 16	9,580
37	frpr1	**Le Mans**	A	D	2-2	Akale 65, Kaboul 71	13,712
38	frpr1	**Bordeaux**	H	D	0-0		14,556
39	frpr1	**Toulouse**	A	L	0-2		22,404
40	frpr1	**Lyon**	H	D	0-0		16,141
41	frpr1	**Nice**	A	D	0-0		10,936
42	frpr1	**Troyes**	H	W	1-0	Jelen 81	10,731
43	frpr1	**Lorient**	A	L	1-2	Jelen 20	12,412
44	frpr1	**Lille**	H	W	2-1	Kahlenberg 15, Jelen 79	7,667
45	frpr1	**Valenciennes**	A	W	3-1	Niculae 17, Kahlenberg 20, Lejeune 90	15,681

LEAGUE APPEARANCES, BOOKINGS AND CAPS

	AGE (on 01/07/07)	IN NAMED 18	APPEARANCES	COUNTING GAMES	MINUTES ON PITCH	YELLOW CARDS	RED CARDS	CAPS THIS SEASON	NATIONAL SIDE
Goalkeepers									
Anthony Basso	27	14	0	0	0	0	0	-	France
Fabien Cool	34	18	18	18	1620	2	0	-	France
Denis Petric	19	9	0	0	0	0	0	-	Slovenia
Olivier Sorin	26	20	20	20	1800	1	0	-	France
Defenders									
Stephane Grichting	28	22	18	16	1522	2	1	4	Switzerland
Jean-Sebastien Jaures	29	33	27	25	2276	4	0	-	France
Younes Kaboul	21	31	31	28	2535	5	1	-	France
Omar Kalabane	26	17	12	9	905	1	0	-	Guinea
Baptiste Martin	22	24	8	3	327	1	0	-	France
Jean Pascal Mignot	26	27	27	25	2315	10	0	-	France
Johan Radet	30	16	10	6	645	3	1	-	France
Bacary Sagna	24	38	38	38	3411	4	0	-	France
Midfielders									
Kanga Akale	26	36	36	26	2734	3	1	1	Ivory Coast
Issa Ba	25	22	19	3	521	1	0	-	Senegal
Benoit Cheyrou	26	34	34	32	2940	6	1	-	France
Thomas Kahlenberg	24	30	29	20	2002	2	0	8	Denmark
Lionel Mathis	25	20	20	12	1269	5	0	-	France
Benoit Pedretti	26	31	31	29	2657	7	0	-	France
Frederic Thomas	26	36	30	25	2372	4	0	-	France
Alain Traore	18	12	4	0	107	0	0	-	Burkina Faso
Krisztian Vadocz	22	2	0	0	0	0	0	-	Hungary
Forwards									
Ludovic Genest	19	7	0	0	0	0	0	-	France
Ireneusz Jelen	26	32	32	26	2507	0	0	-	Poland
Kevin Lejeune	22	21	9	0	125	0	0	-	France
Moussa N'Diaye	28	24	15	1	432	3	0	-	Senegal
Daniel Niculae	24	33	30	10	1525	1	0	3	Romania
Luigi Pieroni	26	18	17	7	985	2	0	6	Belgium

TEAM OF THE SEASON

G Olivier Sorin — CG: 20 DR: 100

D Jean Pascal Mignot — CG: 25 DR: 85
D Younes Kaboul — CG: 28 DR: 84
D Jean-Sebastien Jaures — CG: 25 DR: 84
D Stephane Grichting — CG: 16 DR: 84

M Frederic Thomas — CG: 25 SD: 10
M Benoit Pedretti — CG: 29 SD: 8
M Kanga Akale — CG: 26 SD: 6
M Thomas Kahlenberg — CG: 20 SD: 0

F Ireneusz Jelen — CG: 26 SR: 250
F Daniel Niculae — CG: 10 SR: 381

MONTHLY POINTS TALLY

AUGUST	2	17%
SEPTEMBER	7	78%
OCTOBER	4	33%
NOVEMBER	4	33%
DECEMBER	6	50%
JANUARY	6	67%
FEBRUARY	3	25%
MARCH	9	100%
APRIL	4	27%
MAY	9	75%

LEAGUE GOALS

	PLAYER	MINS	GOALS	S RATE
1	Jelen	2507	10	250
2	Akale	2734	9	303
3	Niculae	1525	4	381
4	Kahlenberg	2002	4	500
5	Pieroni	985	3	328
6	Mathis	1269	3	423
7	Cheyrou	2940	3	980
8	Kaboul	2535	2	1267
9	Lejeune	125	1	125
10	Mignot	2315	1	2315
11	Pedretti	2657	1	2657
12	Petric	0	0	
13	N'Diaye	432	0	
	Other		0	
	TOTAL		**41**	

TOP POINT EARNERS

	PLAYER	GAMES	AV PTS
1	Kanga Akale	27	1.67
2	Jean Pascal Mignot	25	1.60
3	Olivier Sorin	20	1.60
4	Benoit Pedretti	29	1.59
5	Frederic Thomas	25	1.52
6	Younes Kaboul	28	1.50
7	Thomas Kahlenberg	20	1.50
8	Ireneusz Jelen	26	1.46
9	Bacary Sagna	38	1.42
10	Benoit Cheyrou	33	1.36
	CLUB AVERAGE:		**1.42**

DISCIPLINARY RECORDS

	PLAYER	YELLOW	RED	AVE
1	Johan Radet	3	1	215
2	Lionel Mathis	5	0	253
3	J Pascal Mignot	10	0	289
4	Benoit Cheyrou	6	1	420
5	Benoit Pedretti	7	0	442
6	Luigi Pieroni	2	0	492
7	Issa Ba	1	0	521
8	Frederic Thomas	4	0	593
9	Younes Kaboul	5	1	633
10	Kanga Akale	3	1	683
11	Jean-Seb Jaures	4	0	758
12	Stephane Grichting	2	1	761
13	Fabien Cool	2	0	810
	Other	9	0	
	TOTAL	**63**	**5**	

KEY GOALKEEPER

Olivier Sorin

Goals Conceded in the League	18	Counting Games	League games when player was on pitch for at least 70 minutes	20
Defensive Rating	Ave number of mins between League goals conceded while on the pitch	100	Clean Sheets	In League games when player was on pitch for at least 70 minutes	9

KEY PLAYERS - DEFENDERS

Jean Pascal Mignot

Goals Conceded	Number of League goals conceded while the player was on the pitch	27	Clean Sheets	In League games when player was on pitch for at least 70 minutes	11
Defensive Rating	Ave number of mins between League goals conceded while on the pitch	85	Club Defensive Rating	Average number of mins between League goals conceded by the club this season	83

	PLAYER	CON LGE	CLEAN SHEETS	DEF RATE
1	Jean Pascal Mignot	27	11	85 mins
2	Younes Kaboul	30	9	84 mins
3	Jean-Sebastien Jaures	27	10	84 mins
4	Stephane Grichting	18	6	84 mins

KEY PLAYERS - MIDFIELDERS

Frederic Thomas

Goals in the League	0	Contribution to Attacking Power	Average number of minutes between League team goals while on pitch	84
Defensive Rating	Average number of mins between League goals conceded while on the pitch	94	Scoring Difference	Defensive Rating minus Contribution to Attacking Power	10

	PLAYER	LGE GOALS	DEF RATE	POWER	SCORE DIFF
1	Frederic Thomas	0	94	84	10 mins
2	Benoit Pedretti	1	88	80	8 mins
3	Kanga Akale	9	88	82	6 mins
4	Thomas Kahlenberg	4	91	91	0 mins

KEY PLAYERS - GOALSCORERS

Ireneusz Jelen

Goals in the League	10	Player Strike Rate	Average number of minutes between League goals scored by player	250
Contribution to Attacking Power	Average number of minutes between League team goals while on pitch	75	Club Strike Rate	Average number of minutes between League goals scored by club	83

	PLAYER	LGE GOALS	POWER	STRIKE RATE
1	Ireneusz Jelen	10	75	250 mins
2	Kanga Akale	9	82	303 mins
3	Daniel Niculae	4	80	381 mins
4	Lionel Mathis	3	84	423 mins

Kanga Akale

SQUAD APPEARANCES

Match	1 2 3 4 5	6 7 8 9 10	11 12 13 14 15	16 17 18 19 20	21 22 23 24 25	26 27 28 29 30	31 32 33 34 35	36 37 38 39 40	41 42 43 44 45
Venue	H A H H A	H A A H H	H A A H A	H A H H A	A H A H H	A H A H A	H A A H A	H A H A H	A H A H A
Competition	L L L E L	L E L L E	L L E L L	L L L E L	E L L E L	L L L L L	L L L L L	L L L L L	L L L L L
Result	D D L W L	W W W D W	W L L D L	L D W D L	W D D L W	D W L W L	D D D W W	W D D L D	D W L W W

Goalkeepers
Anthony Basso
Fabien Cool
Denis Petric
Olivier Sorin

Defenders
Stephane Grichting
Jean-Sebastien Jaures
Younes Kaboul
Omar Kalabane
Baptiste Martin
Jean Pascal Mignot
Johan Radet
Bacary Sagna

Midfielders
Kanga Akale
Issa Ba
Benoit Cheyrou
Thomas Kahlenberg
Lionel Mathis
Benoit Pedretti
Frederic Thomas
Alain Traore
Krisztian Vadocz

Forwards
Ludovic Genest
Ireneusz Jelen
Kevin Lejeune
Moussa N'Diaye
Daniel Niculae
Luigi Pieroni

KEY: ■ On all match ◄◄ Subbed or sent off (Counting game) ►►| Subbed on from bench (Counting Game) ►► Subbed on and then subbed or sent off (Counting Game) □ Not in 16
■ On bench ◄◄ Subbed or sent off (playing less than 70 minutes) ►► Subbed on (playing less than 70 minutes) ►► Subbed on and then subbed or sent off (playing less than 70 minutes)

FRANCE - AUXERRE

MONACO

Final Position: **9th**

NICKNAME: LES ROUGE ET BLANC **KEY:** ☐ Won ☐ Drawn ☐ Lost

					Attendance
1	frpr1	Nancy	A L	0-1	17,515
2	frpr1	St Etienne	H L	1-2 Gerard 86 pen	17,510
3	frpr1	Rennes	A D	1-1 Koller 12	25,877
4	frpr1	Sedan	H W	2-1 Kallon 31, Modesto 43	9,603
5	frpr1	Auxerre	A L	1-2 Nimani 60	11,860
6	frpr1	Paris SG	H L	1-2 Kallon 32	12,000
7	frpr1	Lens	A L	0-1	31,828
8	frpr1	Le Mans	H W	2-1 Toure 9, Menez 81	9,895
9	frpr1	Bordeaux	A L	0-1	22,146
10	frpr1	Toulouse	H L	1-3 Di Vaio 13	7,903
11	frpr1	Nantes	A L	0-1	28,745
12	frpr1	Nice	H D	0-0	15,981
13	frpr1	Troyes	A W	4-0 Gakpe 19, Meriem 72 pen, Toure 84, Di Vaio 90	11,436
14	frpr1	Lorient	H D	2-2 Toure 6, Menez 49	9,830
15	frpr1	Lille	A D	1-1 Gakpe 36	13,193
16	frpr1	Valenciennes	H W	3-0 Toure 36, Gakpe 46, Koller 62	12,277
17	frpr1	Marseille	A L	1-2 Di Vaio 57	47,708
18	frpr1	Sochaux	H W	3-0 Leko 5, Menez 58, Toure 87	11,292
19	frpr1	Lyon	A D	0-0	38,225
20	frpr1	St Etienne	A W	1-0 Koller 65	32,518
21	frpr1	Rennes	H L	0-2	6,866
22	frpr1	Sedan	A W	1-0 Koller 1	10,851
23	frpr1	Auxerre	H W	2-1 Gakpe 35, Piquionne 63 pen	8,102
24	frpr1	Paris SG	A L	2-4 Piquionne 49, Koller 86	34,171
25	frpr1	Lens	H D	0-0	10,677
26	frpr1	Le Mans	A W	2-0 Piquionne 15, Perez 48	10,388
27	frpr1	Bordeaux	H D	0-0	11,456
28	frpr1	Toulouse	A D	1-1 Koller 76	27,595
29	frpr1	Nantes	H W	2-1 Perez 34, Givet 43	9,493
30	frpr1	Nice	A D	1-1 Plasil 79	13,524
31	frpr1	Troyes	H D	0-0	9,311
32	frpr1	Lorient	A D	0-0	14,213
33	frpr1	Lille	H W	3-1 Meriem 42, Monsoreau 67, Menez 75	10,004
34	frpr1	Valenciennes	A D	2-2 Menez 46, Koller 66	15,816
35	frpr1	Marseille	H L	1-2 Menez 11	16,401
36	frpr1	Sochaux	A L	1-2 Piquionne 44	13,451
37	frpr1	Lyon	H W	1-0 Menez 57	13,145
38	frpr1	Nancy	H W	2-0 Koller 9, Piquionne 54	7,918

LEAGUE APPEARANCES, BOOKINGS AND CAPS

	AGE (on 01/07/07)	IN NAMED 18	APPEARANCES	COUNTING GAMES	MINUTES ON PITCH	YELLOW CARDS	RED CARDS	CAPS THIS SEASON	NATIONAL SIDE
Goalkeepers									
Flavio Roma	33	38	38	38	3420	3	0	-	Italy
Stephane Ruffier	20	33	0	0	0	0	0	-	France
Defenders									
Fabian Guedes Bolivar	26	34	34	34	3060	3	0	-	Brazil
Leandro Cufre	29	25	20	19	1755	7	1	-	Argentina
Manuel Dos Santos	33	34	25	20	2040	1	0	-	France
Gael Givet	25	33	32	27	2642	3	0	1	France
Francois Modesto	28	36	25	22	2044	3	0	-	France
Sylvain Monsoreau	26	32	30	26	2432	4	0	-	France
Massamba Sambou	20	14	4	4	348	1	0	-	Senegal
Olivier Veigneau	21	1	1	0	58	0	0	-	France
Midfielders									
Djamel Bakar	18	4	2	0	30	1	0	-	-
Lucas Bernardi	29	16	16	16	1432	6	1	-	Argentina
Serge Gakpe	20	26	23	13	1425	5	0	-	France
Lopez Segurra Gerard	28	12	6	0	105	2	0	-	Spain
Jerko Leko	27	29	28	19	1920	15	0	7	Croatia
Camel Meriem	27	30	25	16	1701	0	0	-	France
Diego Fernando Perez	27	26	25	19	1853	10	1	-	Uruguay
Juan Pablo Pino	20	11	8	0	252	0	0	-	Colombia
Jaroslav Plasil	25	35	30	18	1950	4	1	10	Czech Republic
Gneri Yaya Toure	24	28	27	16	1874	2	1	-	Ivory Coast
Forwards									
Marco Di Vaio	30	16	14	4	588	0	0	-	Italy
David Gigliotti	22	1	1	1	80	1	1	-	France
Sebastien Grax	23	10	4	0	100	0	0	-	France
Mohammed Kallon	27	20	12	1	518	0	1	-	Sierra Leone
Jan Koller	34	33	32	22	2364	3	0	9	Czech Republic
Nicolas Maurice-Belay	22	2	2	0	40	0	0	-	France
Jeremy Menez	20	32	29	15	1894	6	0	-	France
Frederic Nimani	18	3	3	0	66	0	0	-	France
Frederic Piquionne	28	14	14	10	1037	1	0	-	France
Gonzalo Vargas	25	22	8	3	402	0	0	-	Uruguay

TEAM OF THE SEASON

D — Manuel Dos Santos CG: 20 DR: 127
D — Francois Modesto CG: 22 DR: 97
G — Flavio Roma CG: 38 DR: 90
D — Gael Givet CG: 27 DR: 91
D — Fabian Guedes Bolivar CG: 34 DR: 90
M — Diego Fernando Perez CG: 19 SD: 68
M — Camel Meriem CG: 16 SD: 32
M — Serge Gakpe CG: 13 SD: 18
M — Jerko Leko CG: 19 SD: 15
F — Jeremy Menez CG: 15 SR: 270
F — Jan Koller CG: 22 SR: 295

MONTHLY POINTS TALLY

AUGUST		4	33%
SEPTEMBER		3	25%
OCTOBER		0	0%
NOVEMBER		6	50%
DECEMBER		7	58%
JANUARY		6	67%
FEBRUARY		7	58%
MARCH		5	56%
APRIL		7	47%
MAY		6	50%

LEAGUE GOALS

	PLAYER	MINS	GOALS	S RATE
1	Koller	2364	8	295
2	Menez	1894	7	270
3	Piquionne	1037	5	207
4	Toure	1874	5	374
5	Gakpe	1425	4	356
6	Di Vaio	588	3	196
7	Kallon	518	2	259
8	Meriem	1701	2	850
9	Perez	1853	2	926
10	Nimani	66	1	66
11	Gerard	105	1	105
12	Leko	1920	1	1920
13	Plasil	1950	1	1950
	Other		3	
	TOTAL		45	

TOP POINT EARNERS

	PLAYER	GAMES	AV PTS
1	Jan Koller	22	1.64
2	Serge Gakpe	13	1.62
3	Manuel Dos Santos	20	1.60
4	Diego Fernando Perez	20	1.60
5	Jeremy Menez	15	1.53
6	Francois Modesto	22	1.45
7	Jerko Leko	19	1.42
8	Gael Givet	27	1.41
9	Fabian Guedes Bolivar	34	1.38
10	Sylvain Monsoreau	26	1.38
	CLUB AVERAGE:		1.34

DISCIPLINARY RECORDS

	PLAYER	YELLOW	RED	AVE
1	Jerko Leko	15	0	128
2	Diego F Perez	10	1	168
3	Lucas Bernardi	6	1	204
4	Leandro Cufre	7	1	219
5	Serge Gakpe	5	0	285
6	Jeremy Menez	6	0	315
7	Jaroslav Plasil	4	1	390
8	Mohammed Kallon	0	1	518
9	Sylvain Monsoreau	4	0	608
10	Gneri Yaya Toure	2	1	624
11	Francois Modesto	3	0	681
12	Jan Koller	3	0	788
13	Gael Givet	3	0	880
	Other	8	0	
	TOTAL	76	6	

KEY GOALKEEPER

Flavio Roma

Goals Conceded in the League	38	Counting Games League games when player was on pitch for at least 70 minutes	38
Defensive Rating Ave number of mins between League goals conceded while on the pitch	90	Clean Sheets In League games when player was on pitch for at least 70 minutes	14

KEY PLAYERS - DEFENDERS

Manuel Dos Santos

Goals Conceded Number of League goals conceded while the player was on the pitch	16	Clean Sheets In League games when player was on pitch for at least 70 minutes	12
Defensive Rating Ave number of mins between League goals conceded while on the pitch	127	Club Defensive Rating Average number of mins between League goals conceded by the club this season	90

	PLAYER	CON LGE	CLEAN SHEETS	DEF RATE
1	Manuel Dos Santos	16	12	127 mins
2	Francois Modesto	21	9	97 mins
3	Gael Givet	29	10	91 mins
4	Fabian Guedes Bolivar	34	13	90 mins

KEY PLAYERS - MIDFIELDERS

Diego Fernando Perez

Goals in the League	2	Contribution to Attacking Power Average number of minutes between League team goals while on pitch	74
Defensive Rating Average number of mins between League goals conceded while on the pitch	142	Scoring Difference Defensive Rating minus Contribution to Attacking Power	68

	PLAYER	LGE GOALS	DEF RATE	POWER	SCORE DIFF
1	Diego Fernando Perez	2	142	74	68 mins
2	Camel Meriem	2	100	68	32 mins
3	Serge Gakpe	4	89	71	18 mins
4	Jerko Leko	1	91	76	15 mins

KEY PLAYERS - GOALSCORERS

Jeremy Menez

Goals in the League	7	Player Strike Rate Average number of minutes between League goals scored by player	270
Contribution to Attacking Power Average number of minutes between League team goals while on pitch	65	Club Strike Rate Average number of minutes between League goals scored by club	76

	PLAYER	LGE GOALS	POWER	STRIKE RATE
1	Jeremy Menez	7	65	270 mins
2	Jan Koller	8	65	295 mins
3	Serge Gakpe	4	71	356 mins
4	Gneri Yaya Toure	5	78	374 mins

Jan Koller

SQUAD APPEARANCES

Match	1	2	3	4	5	6	7	8	9	10	11	12	13	14	15	16	17	18	19	20	21	22	23	24	25	26	27	28	29	30	31	32	33	34	35	36	37	38
Venue	A	H	A	H	A	H	A	H	A	H	A	H	A	H	A	H	A	H	A	A	H	A	H	A	H	A	H	A	H	A	H	A	H	A	H	A	H	H
Competition	L	L	L	L	L	L	L	L	L	L	L	L	L	L	L	L	L	L	L	L	L	L	L	L	L	L	L	L	L	L	L	L	L	L	L	L	L	L
Result	L	L	D	W	L	L	L	W	L	L	L	D	W	D	D	W	L	W	D	W	L	W	W	L	D	W	D	D	W	D	D	D	W	D	L	L	W	W

Goalkeepers
Flavio Roma
Stephane Ruffier
Defenders
Fabian Guedes Bolivar
Leandro Cufre
Manuel Dos Santos
Gael Givet
Francois Modesto
Sylvain Monsoreau
Massamba Sambou
Olivier Veigneau
Midfielders
Djamel Bakar
Lucas Bernardi
Serge Gakpe
Lopez Segurra Gerard
Jerko Leko
Camel Meriem
Diego Fernando Perez
Juan Pablo Pino
Jaroslav Plasil
Gneri Yaya Toure
Forwards
Marco Di Vaio
David Gigliotti
Sebastien Grax
Mohammed Kallon
Jan Koller
Nicolas Maurice-Belay
Jeremy Menez
Frederic Nimani
Frederic Piquionne
Gonzalo Vargas

KEY:
■ On all match
⊞ On bench
◄◄ Subbed or sent off (Counting game)
◄◄ Subbed or sent off (playing less than 70 minutes)
►► Subbed on from bench (Counting Game)
►► Subbed on (playing less than 70 minutes)
►► Subbed on and then subbed or sent off (Counting Game)
►► Subbed on and then subbed or sent off (playing less than 70 minutes)
□ Not in 16

LILLE

Final Position: 10th

NICKNAME: LES DOGUES
KEY: ☐ Won ☐ Drawn ☐ Lost
Attendance

#	Comp	Opponent		Result	Scorers	Attendance
1	frpr1	Rennes	A W	2-1	Bodmer 8, Keita 41	22,497
2	frpr1	Lens	H W	4-0	Bodmer 12, Odemwingie 32, 56, 66	16,619
3	frpr1	Paris SG	A L	0-1		35,077
4	ecql2	FK Rabotnicki	A W	1-0	Audel 18	6,000
5	frpr1	Bordeaux	H W	3-0	Cabaye 27, Bodmer 41, Odemwingie 57	15,003
6	frpr1	Nantes	A D	1-1	Odemwingie 9	24,708
7	ecgph	Anderlecht	A D	1-1	Fauverge 80	21,107
8	frpr1	Toulouse	H L	1-3	Tavlaridis 31	12,961
9	frpr1	Lyon	A L	1-4	Cris 23 og	40,165
10	ecgph	AC Milan	H D	0-0		35,000
11	frpr1	Nice	H W	1-0	Fauverge 67	13,088
12	frpr1	Troyes	A D	1-1	Keita 46	18,272
13	ecgph	AEK Athens	H W	3-1	Robail 64, Gygax 82, Makoun 90	32,000
14	frpr1	Lorient	H W	1-0	Bodmer 35	12,752
15	frpr1	Le Mans	A D	1-1	Keita 4	10,126
16	ecgph	AEK Athens	A L	0-1		32,000
17	frpr1	Valenciennes	A W	3-0	Fauverge 23, Odemwingie 60, Cabaye 90	16,530
18	frpr1	Marseille	H W	1-0	Bodmer 45	17,351
19	frpr1	Sochaux	A D	0-0		12,397
20	ecgph	Anderlecht	H D	2-2	Odemwingie 28, Fauverge 47	35,000
21	frpr1	AS Monaco	H D	1-1	Bodmer 76	13,193
22	frpr1	Nancy	A W	3-1	Bodmer 62, Debuchy 68, Youla 90	19,589
23	ecgph	AC Milan	A W	2-0	Odemwingie 7, Keita 67	27,067
24	frpr1	St Etienne	H D	2-2	Bodmer 21, Keita 52	14,134
25	frpr1	Sedan	A L	0-2		12,105
26	frpr1	Auxerre	H D	1-1	Youla 50	14,665
27	frpr1	Lens	A D	1-1	Bastos 70	39,460
28	frpr1	Paris SG	H W	1-0	Makoun 75	12,950
29	frpr1	Bordeaux	A W	1-0	Chamakh 77	23,453
30	frpr1	Nantes	H D	0-0		14,750
31	frpr1	Toulouse	A L	0-1		16,252
32	frpr1	Lyon	H L	1-2	Audel 50	17,092
33	eckl1	Man Utd	H L	0-1		41,000
34	frpr1	Nice	A L	1-2	Cabaye 62	11,369
35	frpr1	Troyes	H W	4-0	Keita 15, 33, Dumont 18, 46	13,715
36	eckl2	Man Utd	A L	0-1		75,182
37	frpr1	Lorient	A D	0-0		13,551
38	frpr1	Le Mans	H L	0-2		14,136
39	frpr1	Valenciennes	H L	0-2		14,778
40	frpr1	Marseille	A L	1-4	Bastos 11 pen	53,000
41	frpr1	Sochaux	H W	2-0	Fauverge 48, Mirallas 65	15,454
42	frpr1	AS Monaco	A L	1-3	Keita 83	10,004
43	frpr1	Nancy	H L	0-1		15,352
44	frpr1	St Etienne	A L	1-2	Mirallas 59	29,154
45	frpr1	Sedan	H W	2-1	Bastos 28 pen, Keita 43	14,027
46	frpr1	Auxerre	A L	1-2	Keita 28	7,667
47	frpr1	Rennes	H D	1-1	Fauverge 90	14,809

LEAGUE APPEARANCES, BOOKINGS AND CAPS

	AGE (on 01/07/07)	IN NAMED 18	APPEARANCES	COUNTING GAMES	MINUTES ON PITCH	YELLOW CARDS	RED CARDS	CAPS THIS SEASON	NATIONAL SIDE
Goalkeepers									
Gregory Malicki	33	35	6	5	468	0	0	-	France
Tony Mario Sylva	32	34	33	33	2952	1	0	1	Senegal
Defenders									
Michel F Bastos	23	29	25	14	1722	4	0	-	Brazil
Mathieu Chalme	26	34	30	23	2285	3	0	-	France
Conceicao Emerson	21	3	2	1	85	0	1	-	Brazil
Peter Franquart	22	13	7	7	630	0	0	-	France
Stephan Lichtsteiner	23	34	24	15	1661	4	0	-	Switzerland
Nicolas Plestan	26	28	23	22	2014	4	1	-	France
Rafael Schmitz	26	33	24	21	2037	5	1	-	Brazil
Gregory Tafforeau	30	35	34	32	2991	1	0	-	France
Efstathios Tavlaridis	27	34	21	20	1865	4	0	-	Greece
Milivoje Vitakic	30	6	3	1	150	0	0	-	Serbia & Montenegro
Midfielders									
Mathieu Bodmer	24	32	32	24	2386	4	0	-	France
Yohan Cabaye	21	26	22	17	1648	8	0	-	France
Mathieu Debuchy	21	24	22	14	1449	1	0	-	France
Stephane Dumont	24	21	18	12	1215	0	1	-	France
Henri Ewane-Elong	21	2	1	1	90	0	0	-	Cameroon
Daniel Gygax	25	5	2	0	58	0	0	4	Switzerland
Jean Makoun	24	34	33	32	2942	8	0	2	Cameroon
Ludovic Obraniak	22	17	17	5	876	2	0	-	France
Adil Rami	-	2	2	2	180	0	0	-	France
Forwards									
Johan Audel	23	7	4	2	199	0	0	-	France
Nicolas Fauverge	22	32	28	2	866	6	0	-	France
C Kamulete-Makiese	19	3	3	0	30	0	0	-	France
Abdul Kader Keita	25	37	36	26	2649	5	0	3	Ivory Coast
Kevin Mirallas	19	29	23	6	1036	4	0	-	Belgium
Peter Odemwingie	25	30	28	19	1760	4	0	-	Nigeria
Mathieu Robail	22	12	10	4	567	0	0	-	France
Souleymane Youla	25	26	16	2	640	4	0	-	Guinea

TEAM OF THE SEASON

G Tony Mario Sylva CG: 33 DR: 89

D Michel F Bastos CG: 14 DR: 107
D Efstathios Tavlaridis CG: 20 DR: 103
D Gregory Tafforeau CG: 32 DR: 90
D Mathieu Chalme CG: 23 DR: 87

M Jean Makoun CG: 32 SD: 24
M Mathieu Bodmer CG: 24 SD: 15
M Yohan Cabaye CG: 17 SD: 4
M Stephane Dumont CG: 12 SD: 0

F Peter Odemwingie CG: 19 SR: 293
F Abdul Kader Keita CG: 26 SR: 294

MONTHLY POINTS TALLY

Month		%
AUGUST	9	75%
SEPTEMBER	4	33%
OCTOBER	5	56%
NOVEMBER	8	67%
DECEMBER	5	42%
JANUARY	7	78%
FEBRUARY	1	8%
MARCH	4	44%
APRIL	3	20%
MAY	4	33%

LEAGUE GOALS

	PLAYER	MINS	GOALS	S RATE
1	Keita	2649	9	294
2	Bodmer	2386	8	298
3	Odemwingie	1760	6	293
4	Fauverge	866	4	216
5	Cabaye	1648	3	549
6	Bastos	1722	3	574
7	Youla	640	2	320
8	Mirallas	1036	2	518
9	Dumont	1215	2	607
10	Audel	199	1	199
11	Debuchy	1449	1	1449
12	Tavlaridis	1865	1	1865
13	Makoun	2942	1	2942
	Other		0	
	TOTAL		**43**	

TOP POINT EARNERS

	PLAYER	GAMES	AV PTS
1	Peter Odemwingie	19	1.58
2	M Fernandes Bastos	14	1.57
3	Efstathios Tavlaridis	20	1.55
4	Mathieu Bodmer	24	1.54
5	Abdel Kader Keita	26	1.50
6	Stephan Lichtsteiner	15	1.47
7	Jean Makoun	32	1.47
8	Tony Mario Sylva	33	1.45
9	Mathieu Chalme	23	1.39
10	Nicolas Plestan	23	1.35
	CLUB AVERAGE:		**1.32**

DISCIPLINARY RECORDS

	PLAYER	YELLOW	RED	AVE
1	Nicolas Fauverge	7	0	144
2	Souleymane Youla	5	0	160
3	Yohan Cabaye	11	0	206
4	Efs Tavlaridis	11	1	233
5	Kevin Mirallas	4	0	259
6	Rafael Schmitz	5	1	339
7	Jean Makoun	11	0	367
8	Nicolas Plestan	6	1	402
9	S Lichtsteiner	5	0	415
10	Michel F Bastos	4	0	430
11	Ludovic Obraniak	2	0	438
12	Peter Odemwingie	4	0	440
13	Abdel Kader Keita	8	0	529
	Other	16	1	
	TOTAL	**99**	**4**	

KEY GOALKEEPER

Tony Mario Sylva

Goals Conceded in the League	33	Counting Games League games when player was on pitch for at least 70 minutes	33
Defensive Rating Ave number of mins between League goals conceded while on the pitch	89	Clean Sheets In League games when player was on pitch for at least 70 minutes	13

KEY PLAYERS - GOALSCORERS

Peter Odemwingie

Goals in the League	6	Player Strike Rate Average number of minutes between League goals scored by player	293
Contribution to Attacking Power Average number of minutes between League team goals while on pitch	65	Club Strike Rate Average number of minutes between League goals scored by club	76

	PLAYER	LGE GOALS	POWER	STRIKE RATE
1	Peter Odemwingie	6	65	293 mins
2	Abdul Kader Keita	9	73	294 mins
3	Mathieu Bodmer	8	70	298 mins
4	Yohan Cabaye	3	82	549 mins

KEY PLAYERS - DEFENDERS

Michel Fernandes Bastos

Goals Conceded Number of League goals conceded while the player was on the pitch	16	Clean Sheets In League games when player was on pitch for at least 70 minutes	7
Defensive Rating Ave number of mins between League goals conceded while on the pitch	107	Club Defensive Rating Average number of mins between League goals conceded by the club this season	79

	PLAYER	CON LGE	CLEAN SHEETS	DEF RATE
1	Michel Fernandes Bastos	16	7	107 mins
2	Efstathios Tavlaridis	18	8	103 mins
3	Gregory Tafforeau	33	12	90 mins
4	Mathieu Chalme	26	9	87 mins

KEY PLAYERS - MIDFIELDERS

Jean Makoun

Goals in the League	1	Contribution to Attacking Power Average number of minutes between League team goals while on pitch	70
Defensive Rating Average number of mins between League goals conceded while on the pitch	94	Scoring Difference Defensive Rating minus Contribution to Attacking Power	24

	PLAYER	LGE GOALS	DEF RATE	POWER	SCORE DIFF
1	Jean Makoun	1	94	70	24 mins
2	Mathieu Bodmer	8	85	70	15 mins
3	Yohan Cabaye	3	86	82	4 mins
4	Stephane Dumont	2	57	57	0 mins

Peter Odemwingie and Abdel Kader Keita

SQUAD APPEARANCES

Match	1 2 3 4 5	6 7 8 9 10	11 12 13 14 15	16 17 18 19 20	21 22 23 24 25	26 27 28 29 30	31 32 33 34 35	36 37 38 39 40	41 42 43 44 45	46 47
Venue	A H A A H	A A H A H	H A H H A	A A H A H	H A A H A	H A H A H	A H H A H	A A H H A	H A H A H	A H
Competition	L L L C L	L C L L C	L L C L L	C L L L C	L L C L L	L L L L L	L L C L L	C L L L L	L L L L L	L L
Result	W W L W W	D D L L D	W D W W D	L W W D D	D W W D L	D D W W D	L L L L W	L D L L L	W L L L W	L D

Goalkeepers
Gregory Malicki
Tony Mario Sylva

Defenders
Michel F Bastos
Mathieu Chalme
Conceicao Emerson
Peter Franquart
Stephan Lichtsteiner
Nicolas Plestan
Rafael Schmitz
Gregory Tafforeau
Efstathios Tavlaridis
Milivoje Vitakic

Midfielders
Mathieu Bodmer
Yohan Cabaye
Mathieu Debuchy
Stephane Dumont
Henri Ewane-Elong
Daniel Gygax
Jean Makoun
Ludovic Obraniak
Adil Rami

Forwards
Johan Audel
Nicolas Fauverge
C Kamulete-Makiese
Abdul Kader Keita
Kevin Mirallas
Peter Odemwingie
Mathieu Robail
Souleymane Youla

KEY: ■ On all match ■ On bench ◄◄ Subbed or sent off (Counting game) ◄◄ Subbed or sent off (playing less than 70 minutes) ▸▸ Subbed on from bench (Counting Game) ▸▸ Subbed on (playing less than 70 minutes) ▸▸ Subbed on and then subbed or sent off (Counting Game) ▸▸ Subbed on and then subbed or sent off (playing less than 70 minutes) □ Not in 16

St ETIENNE

Final Position: **11th**

NICKNAME: LES VERTS   KEY: ☐ Won ☐ Drawn ☐ Lost   Attendance

#					Result	Scorers	Attendance
1	frpr1	Sochaux	H	L	1-2	Piquionne 16	32,786
2	frpr1	AS Monaco	A	W	2-1	Feindouno 11, Piquionne 71	17,510
3	frpr1	Nancy	H	W	1-0	Ilan 63	30,610
4	frpr1	Lens	H	W	3-2	Demont 17 og, Ilan 45, Feindouno 52	27,828
5	frpr1	Sedan	A	D	2-2	Piquionne 2, Feindouno 68 pen	12,542
6	frpr1	Auxerre	H	L	2-3	Ilan 8, Dernis 46	30,188
7	frpr1	Rennes	A	D	0-0		24,842
8	frpr1	Paris SG	H	W	1-0	Ilan 38	25,734
9	frpr1	Lyon	A	L	1-2	Hautcoeur 67	39,218
10	frpr1	Le Mans	H	W	2-0	Cerdan 3 og, Piquionne 68	28,461
11	frpr1	Troyes	A	L	1-3	Feindouno 39	13,071
12	frpr1	Toulouse	H	W	3-0	Hognon 10, Gomis 22, 86	30,022
13	frpr1	Nantes	A	D	2-2	Feindouno 45, Hagnon 90	32,404
14	frpr1	Nice	H	W	2-1	Piquionne 19, Feindouno 26	26,707
15	frpr1	Bordeaux	A	L	0-1		29,702
16	frpr1	Lorient	H	W	2-0	Heinz 50, Piquionne 66	24,892
17	frpr1	Lille	A	D	2-2	Ilan 7, 65	14,134
18	frpr1	Valenciennes	H	W	3-0	Ilan 35, Feindouno 79, Landrin 82	27,957
19	frpr1	Marseille	A	L	1-2	Heinz 45	53,614
20	frpr1	AS Monaco	H	L	0-1		32,518
21	frpr1	Nancy	A	W	2-0	Ilan 56, Gomis 70	17,816
22	frpr1	Lens	A	D	3-3	Gomis 15, Heinz 23, 44	30,989
23	frpr1	Sedan	H	L	1-2	Gomis 9	24,838
24	frpr1	Auxerre	A	D	1-1	Moussilou 75	13,158
25	frpr1	Rennes	H	L	1-3	Gomis 34	28,389
26	frpr1	Paris SG	A	W	2-0	Perquis 31, Ilan 44	38,857
27	frpr1	Lyon	H	L	1-3	Gomis 79	35,201
28	frpr1	Le Mans	A	L	1-2	Gomis 81	14,066
29	frpr1	Troyes	H	W	3-1	Feindouno 2, Gomis 17, Guarin Vasquez 49	27,225
30	frpr1	Toulouse	A	L	0-1		25,888
31	frpr1	Nantes	H	W	2-1	Hognon 26, Gomis 33	33,606
32	frpr1	Nice	A	L	1-2	Diatta 46	12,405
33	frpr1	Bordeaux	H	L	0-2		27,851
34	frpr1	Lorient	A	D	0-0		15,055
35	frpr1	Lille	H	W	2-1	Moussilou 30, 61	29,154
36	frpr1	Valenciennes	A	L	0-1		15,393
37	frpr1	Marseille	H	L	1-2	Feindouno 69	34,466
38	frpr1	Sochaux	A	L	0-1		19,738

LEAGUE APPEARANCES, BOOKINGS AND CAPS

	AGE (on 01/07/07)	IN NAMED 18	APPEARANCES	COUNTING GAMES	MINUTES ON PITCH	YELLOW CARDS	RED CARDS	CAPS THIS SEASON	NATIONAL SIDE
Goalkeepers									
Jeremie Janot	29	38	36	36	3240	1	0	-	France
Jessy Moulin	21	2	0	0	0	0	0	-	France
Jody Viviani	25	34	2	2	180	0	0	-	France
Defenders									
Zoumana Camara	28	36	36	36	3240	7	0	-	France
Mouhamadou Dabo	20	22	14	12	1177	3	1	-	Senegal
Lamine Diatta	31	35	25	24	2173	1	1	-	Senegal
Fousseni Diawara	26	17	3	2	214	0	0	-	France
Vincent Hognon	32	37	34	31	2886	3	0	-	France
H Nkolongo Ilunga	25	36	36	36	3235	4	0	-	Congo
Damien Perquis	23	34	20	7	833	2	0	-	France
Midfielders									
Moustapha Bayal Sall	21	15	3	1	117	0	0	-	Senegal
Daniel Ruben Bilos	26	17	14	0	371	1	0	2	Argentina
Geoffrey Dernis	26	30	28	14	1812	4	0	-	France
Pascal Feindouno	26	36	36	33	2934	5	0	-	Guinea
F A Guarin Vasquez	21	26	18	5	879	6	0	-	Colombia
Yohan Hautcoeur	25	34	23	7	893	1	0	-	France
Christophe Landrin	30	34	31	28	2557	6	0	-	France
Loic Perrin	21	10	10	10	888	1	0	-	France
Julien Sable	26	34	32	27	2599	6	0	-	France
Forwards									
Maodomalick Faye	19	2	1	0	1	0	0	-	Senegal
Bafetibis Gomis	21	35	30	16	1646	3	0	-	France
Marek Heinz	29	31	28	8	1191	3	0	1	Czech Republic
Aruajo Ilan	26	33	33	27	2631	4	0	-	Brazil
Matt Moussilou	25	15	11	2	406	0	0	-	France
Frederic Piquionne	28	18	18	14	1400	3	2	-	France
Lamine Sakho	29	5	2	0	14	0	0	-	Senegal

TEAM OF THE SEASON

Jeremie Janot (G) — CG: 36 DR: 67

Lamine Diatta (D) — CG: 24 DR: 77
Vincent Hognon (D) — CG: 31 DR: 68
Herita Nkolongo Ilunga (D) — CG: 36 DR: 67
Zoumana Camara (D) — CG: 36 DR: 67

Geoffrey Dernis (M) — CG: 14 SD: 13
Christophe Landrin (M) — CG: 28 SD: 13
Pascal Feindouno (M) — CG: 33 SD: 8
Julien Sable (M) — CG: 27 SD: 5

Bafetibis Gomis (F) — CG: 16 SR: 164
Frederic Piquionne (F) — CG: 14 SR: 233

MONTHLY POINTS TALLY

AUGUST		9	75%
SEPTEMBER		2	22%
OCTOBER		6	50%
NOVEMBER		7	58%
DECEMBER		7	58%
JANUARY		4	44%
FEBRUARY		4	33%
MARCH		3	33%
APRIL		4	27%
MAY		3	25%

LEAGUE GOALS

	PLAYER	MINS	GOALS	S RATE
1	Gomis	1646	10	164
2	Ilan	2631	9	292
3	Feindouno	2934	9	326
4	Piquionne	1400	6	233
5	Heinz	1191	4	297
6	Moussilou	406	3	135
7	Hognon	2886	3	962
8	Perquis	833	1	833
9	Guarin Vasquez	879	1	879
10	Hautcoeur	893	1	893
11	Dernis	1812	1	1812
12	Diatta	2173	1	2173
13	Landrin	2557	1	2557
	Other		0	
	TOTAL		50	

TOP POINT EARNERS

	PLAYER	GAMES	AV PTS
1	Christophe Landrin	28	1.54
2	Julien Sable	27	1.52
3	Frederic Piquionne	15	1.47
4	Lamine Diatta	24	1.38
5	Jeremie Janot	36	1.33
6	Vincent Hognon	31	1.32
7	Herita Nkolongo Ilunga	36	1.31
8	Aruajo Ilan	27	1.30
9	Geoffrey Dernis	14	1.29
10	Zoumana Camara	36	1.28
	CLUB AVERAGE:		1.29

DISCIPLINARY RECORDS

	PLAYER	YELLOW	RED	AVE
1	F A Guarin Vasquez	6	0	146
2	Frederic Piquionne	3	2	280
3	Mouhamadou Dabo	3	1	294
4	Marek Heinz	3	0	397
5	Damien Perquis	2	0	416
6	Christophe Landrin	6	0	426
7	Julien Sable	6	0	433
8	Geoffrey Dernis	4	0	453
9	Zoumana Camara	7	0	462
10	Bafetibis Gomis	3	0	548
11	Pascal Feindouno	5	0	586
12	Aruajo Ilan	4	0	657
13	H Nkolongo Ilunga	4	0	808
	Other	7	1	
	TOTAL	63	4	

KEY GOALKEEPER

Jeremie Janot

Goals Conceded in the League	48	Counting Games League games when player was on pitch for at least 70 minutes	36
Defensive Rating Ave number of mins between League goals conceded while on the pitch	67	Clean Sheets In League games when player was on pitch for at least 70 minutes	9

KEY PLAYERS - DEFENDERS

Lamine Diatta

Goals Conceded Number of League goals conceded while the player was on the pitch	28	Clean Sheets In League games when player was on pitch for at least 70 minutes	8
Defensive Rating Ave number of mins between League goals conceded while on the pitch	77	Club Defensive Rating Average number of mins between League goals conceded by the club this season	68

	PLAYER	CON LGE	CLEAN SHEETS	DEF RATE
1	Lamine Diatta	28	8	77 mins
2	Vincent Hognon	42	8	68 mins
3	Herita Nkolongo Ilunga	48	9	67 mins
4	Zoumana Camara	48	9	67 mins

KEY PLAYERS - MIDFIELDERS

Geoffrey Dernis

Goals in the League	1	Contribution to Attacking Power Average number of minutes between League team goals while on pitch	62
Defensive Rating Average number of minutes between League goals conceded while on the pitch	75	Scoring Difference Defensive Rating minus Contribution to Attacking Power	13

	PLAYER	LGE GOALS	DEF RATE	POWER	SCORE DIFF
1	Geoffrey Dernis	1	75	62	13 mins
2	Christophe Landrin	1	73	60	13 mins
3	Pascal Feindouno	9	73	65	8 mins
4	Julien Sable	0	66	61	5 mins

KEY PLAYERS - GOALSCORERS

Bafetibis Gomis

Goals in the League	10	Player Strike Rate Average number of minutes between League goals scored by player	164
Contribution to Attacking Power Average number of minutes between League team goals while on pitch	74	Club Strike Rate Average number of minutes between League goals scored by club	65

	PLAYER	LGE GOALS	POWER	STRIKE RATE
1	Bafetibis Gomis	10	74	164 mins
2	Frederic Piquionne	6	53	233 mins
3	Aruajo Ilan	9	65	292 mins
4	Pascal Feindouno	9	65	326 mins

Matt Moussilou

SQUAD APPEARANCES

Match	1	2	3	4	5	6	7	8	9	10	11	12	13	14	15	16	17	18	19	20	21	22	23	24	25	26	27	28	29	30	31	32	33	34	35	36	37	38
Venue	H	A	H	H	A	H	A	H	A	H	A	H	A	H	A	H	A	H	A	H	A	A	H	A	H	A	H	A	H	A	H	A	H	A	H	A	H	A
Competition	L	L	L	L	L	L	L	L	L	L	L	L	L	L	L	L	L	L	L	L	L	L	L	L	L	L	L	L	L	L	L	L	L	L	L	L	L	L
Result	L	W	W	W	D	L	D	W	L	W	L	W	D	W	L	W	D	W	L	L	W	D	L	D	L	W	L	L	W	L	W	L	L	D	W	L	L	L

Goalkeepers
Jeremie Janot
Jessy Moulin
Jody Viviani

Defenders
Zoumana Camara
Mouhamadou Dabo
Lamine Diatta
Fousseni Diawara
Vincent Hognon
H Nkolongo Ilunga
Damien Perquis

Midfielders
Moustapha Bayal Sall
Daniel Ruben Bilos
Geoffrey Dernis
Pascal Feindouno
F A Guarin Vasquez
Yohan Hautcoeur
Christophe Landrin
Loic Perrin
Julien Sable

Forwards
Maodomalick Faye
Bafetibis Gomis
Marek Heinz
Aruajo Ilan
Matt Moussilou
Frederic Piquionne
Lamine Sakho

KEY: On all match — Subbed or sent off (Counting game) — Subbed on from bench (Counting Game) — Subbed on and then subbed or sent off (Counting Game) — Not in 16
On bench — Subbed or sent off (playing less than 70 minutes) — Subbed on (playing less than 70 minutes) — Subbed on and then subbed or sent off (playing less than 70 minutes)

FRANCE - St ETIENNE

LE MANS

Final Position: **12th**

NICKNAME: LE MUC KEY: ☐ Won ☐ Drawn ☐ Lost   Attendance

1 frpr1	**Nice**	H W	**1-0**	Grafite 17	9,574
2 frpr1	**Troyes**	A D	**2-2**	Bangoura 4, 9	8,749
3 frpr1	**Valenciennes**	H W	**3-2**	Romaric 36, Samassa 52, Bangoura 79	9,456
4 frpr1	**Marseille**	A L	**0-2**		52,672
5 frpr1	**Lorient**	H D	**1-1**	Grafite 49	9,653
6 frpr1	**Sedan**	A W	**2-1**	Bangoura 4, Paulo Andre 26	9,774
7 frpr1	**Sochaux**	H D	**2-2**	Samassa 15, Fanchone 67	9,452
8 frpr1	**AS Monaco**	A L	**1-2**	Romaric 24 pen	9,895
9 frpr1	**Nancy**	H D	**0-0**		9,090
10 frpr1	**St Etienne**	A L	**0-2**		28,461
11 frpr1	**Lille**	H D	**1-1**	Grafite 12	10,126
12 frpr1	**Auxerre**	A W	**3-2**	Bangoura 14, 80 pen, 90	7,000
13 frpr1	**Paris SG**	H D	**1-1**	Lucau 35	12,983
14 frpr1	**Rennes**	A D	**1-1**	Sessegnon 45	24,373
15 frpr1	**Lens**	H D	**1-1**	Bangoura 22	9,217
16 frpr1	**Lyon**	H L	**0-1**		15,106
17 frpr1	**Nantes**	A D	**0-0**		24,357
18 frpr1	**Toulouse**	H W	**2-0**	Basa 30, Romaric 76	9,470
19 frpr1	**Bordeaux**	A L	**0-1**		20,392
20 frpr1	**Troyes**	H W	**2-0**	Matsui 7, 87	8,525
21 frpr1	**Valenciennes**	A D	**1-1**	De Melo 88	11,716
22 frpr1	**Marseille**	H W	**2-0**	Fanchone 36, Grafite 82 pen	15,976
23 frpr1	**Lorient**	A L	**1-2**	Grafite 45	12,303
24 frpr1	**Sedan**	H W	**3-2**	Samassa 13, Romaric 66, Grafite 72	9,143
25 frpr1	**Sochaux**	A L	**0-2**		9,996
26 frpr1	**AS Monaco**	H L	**0-2**		10,388
27 frpr1	**Nancy**	A D	**1-1**	Grafite 72	18,124
28 frpr1	**St Etienne**	H W	**2-1**	Coutadeur 42, Bangoura 51	14,066
29 frpr1	**Lille**	A W	**2-0**	Bangoura 67, Grafite 90	14,136
30 frpr1	**Auxerre**	H D	**2-2**	Bangoura 46, De Melo 51	13,712
31 frpr1	**Paris SG**	A L	**1-2**	Grafite 29	42,368
32 frpr1	**Rennes**	H D	**0-0**		12,683
33 frpr1	**Lens**	A L	**0-2**		35,319
34 frpr1	**Lyon**	A L	**1-2**	Grafite 64	40,167
35 frpr1	**Nantes**	H D	**1-1**	Matsui 26	13,303
36 frpr1	**Toulouse**	A W	**1-0**	Grafite 81	18,042
37 frpr1	**Bordeaux**	H D	**1-1**	Grafite 58	14,072
38 frpr1	**Nice**	A D	**3-3**	Romaric 35, Bangoura 60, Matsui 63	11,522

LEAGUE APPEARANCES, BOOKINGS AND CAPS

	AGE (on 01/07/07)	IN NAMED 18	APPEARANCES	COUNTING GAMES	MINUTES ON PITCH	YELLOW CARDS	RED CARDS	CAPS THIS SEASON	NATIONAL SIDE
Goalkeepers									
Yohann Pele	24	30	29	27	2499	1	0	-	France
Rodolphe Roche	28	34	11	10	921	0	0	-	France
Defenders									
Marko Basa	24	35	35	33	3042	5	0	-	Serbia
Laurent Bonnart	27	20	20	18	1698	1	0	-	France
Jean Calve	23	34	20	13	1279	3	0	-	France
S Ibrahima Camara	22	28	19	17	1604	2	0	-	Guinea
Gregory Cerdan	24	32	26	20	1945	2	0	-	France
Yannick Fischer	32	26	15	6	849	1	0	-	France
Gregory Louiron	26	2	1	0	18	0	0	-	France
Paulo Andre	23	7	5	5	433	1	0	-	Brazil
Olivier Thomas	32	35	33	29	2717	7	0	-	France
Midfielders									
Mathieu Coutadeur	21	37	31	24	2326	1	0	-	France
Guillaume Loriot	21	15	6	2	259	1	0	-	France
Cyriaque Louvion	19	22	15	12	1154	3	0	-	France
Daisuke Matsui	26	29	27	18	1808	6	0	-	Japan
Stephane Sessegnon	23	31	31	25	2376	7	1	-	Benin
Hassan Yebda	23	1	1	0	22	0	0	-	France
Forwards									
Ismael Bangoura	22	33	33	28	2603	6	0	-	Guinea
Philippe Celdran	33	1	0	0	0	0	0	-	France
Vinicius De Melo	22	18	17	6	795	2	0	-	Brazil
Abdou Dieye	19	2	0	0	0	0	0	-	France
Martin Douillard	22	28	16	4	577	1	0	-	France
James Fanchone	27	23	20	5	844	1	0	-	France
Libano Batista Grafite	20	34	34	28	2702	6	0	-	Brazil
Chigury Lucau	22	18	14	1	461	1	0	-	Congo
Ndri Romaric	24	35	35	34	3090	8	0	1	Ivory Coast
Mamadou Samassa	21	31	27	11	1597	2	0	-	France

TEAM OF THE SEASON

G Yohann Pele CG: 27 DR: 83

D Sory Ibrahima Camara CG: 17 DR: 94
D Marko Basa CG: 33 DR: 82
D Olivier Thomas CG: 29 DR: 79
D Gregory Cerdan CG: 20 DR: 67

M Stephane Sessegnon CG: 25 SD: 0
M Cyriaque Louvion CG: 12 SD: -5
M Daisuke Matsui CG: 18 SD: -9
M Mathieu Coutadeur CG: 24 SD: -9

F Ismael Bangoura CG: 28 SR: 216
F L Batista Grafite CG: 28 SR: 225

MONTHLY POINTS TALLY

AUGUST		7	58%
SEPTEMBER		5	42%
OCTOBER		2	22%
NOVEMBER		6	50%
DECEMBER		4	33%
JANUARY		7	78%
FEBRUARY		3	25%
MARCH		7	78%
APRIL		2	13%
MAY		6	50%

LEAGUE GOALS

	PLAYER	MINS	GOALS	S RATE
1	Bangoura	2603	12	216
2	Grafite	2702	12	225
3	Romaric	3090	5	618
4	Matsui	1808	4	452
5	Samassa	1597	3	532
6	De Melo	795	2	397
7	Fanchone	844	2	422
8	Paulo Andre	433	1	433
9	Lucau	461	1	461
10	Coutadeur	2326	1	2326
11	Sessegnon	2376	1	2376
12	Basa	3042	1	3042
13	Bonnart	1698	0	
	Other		0	
	TOTAL		**45**	

TOP POINT EARNERS

	PLAYER	GAMES	AV PTS
1	Sory Ibrahima Camara	17	1.53
2	Jean Calve	13	1.46
3	Yohann Pele	27	1.44
4	Ismael Bangoura	28	1.43
5	Marko Basa	33	1.33
6	Daisuke Matsui	18	1.33
7	Olivier Thomas	29	1.31
8	Mathieu Coutadeur	24	1.29
9	Ndri Romaric	34	1.26
10	Stephane Sessegnon	25	1.24
	CLUB AVERAGE:		**1.29**

DISCIPLINARY RECORDS

	PLAYER	YELLOW	RED	AVE
1	Steph Sessegnon	7	1	297
2	Daisuke Matsui	6	0	301
3	Cyriaque Louvion	3	0	384
4	Ndri Romaric	8	0	386
5	Olivier Thomas	7	0	388
6	Vinicius De Melo	2	0	397
7	Jean Calve	3	0	426
8	Ismael Bangoura	6	0	433
9	L Batista Grafite	6	0	450
10	Chigury Lucau	1	0	461
11	Martin Douillard	1	0	577
12	Marko Basa	5	0	608
13	Mamadou Samassa	2	0	798
	Other	9	0	
	TOTAL	**66**	**1**	

KEY GOALKEEPER

Yohann Pele

Goals Conceded in the League	30	Counting Games League games when player was on pitch for at least 70 minutes	27
Defensive Rating Ave number of mins between League goals conceded while on the pitch	83	Clean Sheets In League games when player was on pitch for at least 70 minutes	9

KEY PLAYERS - DEFENDERS

Sory Ibrahima Camara

Goals Conceded Number of League goals conceded while the player was on the pitch	17	Clean Sheets In League games when player was on pitch for at least 70 minutes	6
Defensive Rating Ave number of mins between League goals conceded while on the pitch	94	Club Defensive Rating Average number of mins between League goals conceded by the club this season	74

	PLAYER	CON LGE	CLEAN SHEETS	DEF RATE
1	Sory Ibrahima Camara	17	6	94 mins
2	Marko Basa	37	9	82 mins
3	Olivier Thomas	34	8	79 mins
4	Gregory Cerdan	29	4	67 mins

KEY PLAYERS - MIDFIELDERS

Stephane Sessegnon

Goals in the League	1	Contribution to Attacking Power Average number of minutes between League team goals while on pitch	84
Defensive Rating Average number of mins between League goals conceded while on the pitch	84	Scoring Difference Defensive Rating minus Contribution to Attacking Power	0

	PLAYER	LGE GOALS	DEF RATE	POWER	SCORE DIFF
1	Stephane Sessegnon	1	84	84	0 mins
2	Cyriaque Louvion	0	67	72	-5 mins
3	Daisuke Matsui	4	60	69	-9 mins
4	Mathieu Coutadeur	1	68	77	-9 mins

KEY PLAYERS - GOALSCORERS

Ismael Bangoura

Goals in the League	12	Player Strike Rate Average number of minutes between League goals scored by player	216
Contribution to Attacking Power Average number of minutes between League team goals while on pitch	72	Club Strike Rate Average number of minutes between League goals scored by club	76

	PLAYER	LGE GOALS	POWER	STRIKE RATE
1	Ismael Bangoura	12	72	216 mins
2	Libano Batista Grafite	12	75	225 mins
3	Daisuke Matsui	4	69	452 mins
4	Ndri Romaric	5	77	618 mins

Mamadou Samassa and Ismael Bangoura

SQUAD APPEARANCES

Match	1	2	3	4	5	6	7	8	9	10	11	12	13	14	15	16	17	18	19	20	21	22	23	24	25	26	27	28	29	30	31	32	33	34	35	36	37	38
Venue	H	A	H	A	H	A	H	A	H	A	H	A	H	A	H	H	A	H	A	H	A	H	A	H	A	H	A	H	A	H	A	H	A	A	H	A	H	A
Competition	L	L	L	L	L	L	L	L	L	L	L	L	L	L	L	L	L	L	L	L	L	L	L	L	L	L	L	L	L	L	L	L	L	L	L	L	L	L
Result	W	D	W	L	D	W	D	L	D	L	D	W	D	D	D	L	D	W	L	W	D	W	L	W	L	D	W	W	D	L	D	L	L	L	D	W	D	D

Goalkeepers
Yohann Pele
Rodolphe Roche

Defenders
Marko Basa
Laurent Bonnart
Jean Calve
S Ibrahima Camara
Gregory Cerdan
Yannick Fischer
Gregory Louiron
Paulo Andre
Olivier Thomas

Midfielders
Mathieu Coutadeur
Guillaume Loriot
Cyriaque Louvion
Daisuke Matsui
Stephane Sessegnon
Hassan Yebda

Forwards
Ismael Bangoura
Philippe Celdran
Vinicius De Melo
Abdou Dieye
Martin Douillard
James Fanchone
Libano Batista Grafite
Chigury Lucau
Ndri Romaric
Mamadou Samassa

KEY: ■ On all match ◄◄ Subbed or sent off (Counting game) ►◄ Subbed on from bench (Counting Game) ►► Subbed on and then subbed or sent off (Counting Game) □ Not in 16
■ On bench ◄◄ Subbed or sent off (playing less than 70 minutes) ►► Subbed on (playing less than 70 minutes) ►► Subbed on and then subbed or sent off (playing less than 70 minutes)

FRANCE - LE MANS

NANCY

Final Position: **13th**

NICKNAME: ASNL   KEY: ☐ Won ☐ Drawn ☐ Lost   Attendance

#		Opp			Result	Scorers	Attendance
1	frpr1	AS Monaco	H	W	1-0	Zerka 53	17,515
2	frpr1	Sedan	H	W	3-1	Gavanon 77, Curbelo 79, Dosunmu 88	17,310
3	frpr1	St Etienne	A	L	0-1		30,610
4	frpr1	Auxerre	H	W	1-0	Gavanon 73 pen	18,215
5	frpr1	Toulouse	A	D	2-2	Kim 52, Curbelo 62	14,872
6	ucrl1	Schalke	A	L	0-1		45,878
7	frpr1	Rennes	H	D	0-0		16,529
8	frpr1	Paris SG	A	D	0-0		34,103
9	ucrl2	Schalke	H	W	3-1	Andre Luiz 17, Curbelo 24, Dia 69	18,029
10	frpr1	Lens	H	W	2-1	Gavanon 25 pen, Sauget 58	18,017
11	frpr1	Le Mans	A	D	0-0		9,090
12	frpr1	Nantes	H	W	1-0	Chretien 53	18,225
13	frpr1	Lyon	A	L	0-1		40,298
14	ucgpe	Wisla Krakow	H	W	2-1	Berenguer 11, 58	18,000
15	frpr1	Bordeaux	H	W	2-1	Puygrenier 15, Zerka 54 pen	18,041
16	frpr1	Lorient	A	L	0-2		12,233
17	frpr1	Troyes	H	W	1-0	Puygrenier 76	17,168
18	ucgpe	Basel	A	D	2-2	Kim 31, Berenguer 34	14,497
19	frpr1	Valenciennes	A	L	0-1		13,241
20	ucgpe	Feyenoord	H	W	3-0	Puygrenier 23, Bahia 43 og, Zerka 66 pen	19,840
21	frpr1	Lille	H	L	1-3	Gavanon 51	19,589
22	frpr1	Nice	A	D	0-0		9,421
23	ucgpe	Blackburn	A	L	0-1		12,568
24	frpr1	Marseille	H	W	2-0	Gavanon 42, Kim 70	20,081
25	frpr1	Sochaux	A	L	1-2	Puygrenier 11	17,700
26	frpr1	Sedan	A	D	2-2	Chretien 45, Puygrenier 74	10,493
27	frpr1	St Etienne	H	L	0-2		17,816
28	frpr1	Auxerre	A	L	0-2		6,150
29	frpr1	Toulouse	H	W	2-1	Curbelo 14, Fortune 76	16,596
30	frpr1	Rennes	A	D	1-1	Kim 55	22,893
31	ucrl1	Shakhtar Don	A	D	1-1	Fortune 81	23,000
32	frpr1	Paris SG	H	L	0-3		19,252
33	ucrl2	Shakhtar Don	H	L	0-1		18,000
34	frpr1	Lens	A	D	2-2	Fortune 6, Hadji 89	32,143
35	frpr1	Le Mans	H	D	1-1	Macaluso 36	18,124
36	frpr1	Nantes	A	L	1-2	Brison 38	32,626
37	frpr1	Lyon	H	L	0-3		19,919
38	frpr1	Lorient	H	L	0-1		18,370
39	frpr1	Troyes	A	D	0-0		18,327
40	frpr1	Bordeaux	A	L	0-3		21,732
41	frpr1	Valenciennes	H	W	1-0	Gavanon 39 pen	19,505
42	frpr1	Lille	A	W	1-0	Dia 74	15,352
43	frpr1	Nice	H	W	3-0	Fortune 28, Gavanon 30 pen, Kim 38	18,583
44	frpr1	Marseille	A	L	1-2	Puygrenier 80	46,464
45	frpr1	Sochaux	H	W	5-2	Fortune 19, 79, Puygrenier 31, Gavanon 67, Sauget 90	19,503
46	frpr1	AS Monaco	A	L	0-2		7,918

LEAGUE APPEARANCES, BOOKINGS AND CAPS

	AGE (on 01/07/07)	IN NAMED 18	APPEARANCES	COUNTING GAMES	MINUTES ON PITCH	YELLOW CARDS	RED CARDS	CAPS THIS SEASON	NATIONAL SIDE
Goalkeepers									
Gennaro Bracigliano	27	10	10	9	855	0	0	-	France
Damien Gregorini	28	16	16	15	1410	0	0	-	France
Johan Lapeyre	21	30	2	0	75	0	0	-	France
Olivier Sorin	26	16	12	12	1080	0	0	-	France
Defenders									
A L S do Nascimento	27	35	33	22	2213	8	0	-	Brazil
Jonathan Brison	24	23	20	12	1307	7	0	-	France
Mickael Chretien	23	35	35	32	2968	1	0	-	Morocco
Pape Diakhate	23	33	33	30	2749	13	1	-	Senegal
Cedric Lecluse	35	22	14	9	787	4	1	-	France
Damian Macaluso	27	19	9	5	476	1	0	-	Uruguay
Sebastien Puygrenier	25	32	30	30	2688	9	0	-	France
David Sauget	27	35	31	24	2356	4	1	-	France
Midfielders									
Pascal Berenguer	26	35	28	13	1507	4	1	-	France
Frederic Biancalani	32	32	20	15	1497	3	0	-	France
Emmanuel Duchemin	28	25	24	12	1377	5	1	-	France
Benjamin Gavanon	26	37	36	30	2913	5	1	-	France
Rachid Hamdani	22	6	2	0	45	0	0	-	France
Landry N'Guemo	21	33	22	14	1355	2	0	-	Cameroon
Moncef Zerka	25	16	16	7	932	3	0	-	France
Forwards									
Basile Camerling	20	4	1	0	21	0	0	-	France
Gaston Curbelo	31	37	35	28	2643	8	1	-	France
Issiar Dia	20	27	27	15	1655	4	0	-	France
Tosin Dosunmu	26	17	11	0	228	0	0	-	Nigeria
Marc-Antoine Fortune	25	16	15	13	1241	0	0	-	France
Youssouf Hadji	27	17	14	9	973	3	0	2	Morocco
Carlos H Dias Kim	27	29	28	22	2152	3	1	-	Brazil

TEAM OF THE SEASON

G Olivier Sorin   CG: 12   DR: 135

D Mickael Chretien   CG: 32   DR: 87
D Sebastien Puygrenier   CG: 30   DR: 81
D Pape Diakhate   CG: 30   DR: 78
D David Sauget   CG: 24   DR: 78

M Benjamin Gavanon   CG: 30   SD: 6
M Frederic Biancalani   CG: 15   SD: -5
M Landry N'Guemo   CG: 14   SD: -17
M Pascal Berenguer   CG: 13   SD: -23

F Marc-A Fortune   CG: 13   SR: 248
F Carlos H Dias Kim   CG: 22   SR: 538

MONTHLY POINTS TALLY

Month		Pts	%
AUGUST		9	75%
SEPTEMBER		3	33%
OCTOBER		7	58%
NOVEMBER		6	50%
DECEMBER		4	33%
JANUARY		1	11%
FEBRUARY		5	42%
MARCH		1	11%
APRIL		7	47%
MAY		6	50%

LEAGUE GOALS

	PLAYER	MINS	GOALS	S RATE
1	Gavanon	2913	8	364
2	Puygrenier	2688	6	448
3	Fortune	1241	5	248
4	Kim	2152	4	538
5	Curbelo	2643	3	881
6	Zerka	932	2	466
7	Sauget	2356	2	1178
8	Chretien	2968	2	1484
9	Dosunmu	228	1	228
10	Macaluso	476	1	476
11	Hadji	973	1	973
12	Brison	1307	1	1307
13	Dia	1655	1	1655
	Other		0	
	TOTAL		**37**	

TOP POINT EARNERS

	PLAYER	GAMES	AV PTS
1	Pascal Berenguer	14	**1.64**
2	Landry N'Guemo	14	**1.64**
3	Frederic Biancalani	15	**1.53**
4	Gaston Curbelo	28	**1.50**
5	Olivier Sorin	12	**1.42**
6	Mickael Chretien	32	**1.34**
7	Pape Diakhate	30	**1.33**
8	Benjamin Gavanon	30	**1.33**
9	Carlos H Dias Kim	22	**1.32**
10	A L S do Nascimento	22	**1.32**
	CLUB AVERAGE:		**1.29**

DISCIPLINARY RECORDS

	PLAYER	YELLOW	RED	AVE
1	Cedric Lecluse	4	1	157
2	Jonathan Brison	7	0	186
3	Pape Diakhate	13	1	211
4	E Duchemin	5	1	275
5	Pascal Berenguer	4	1	301
6	A L S d Nascimento	8	0	316
7	Youssouf Hadji	3	0	324
8	Gaston Curbelo	8	1	330
9	Seb Puygrenier	9	0	384
10	Moncef Zerka	3	0	466
11	Damian Macaluso	1	0	476
12	Carlos H Dias Kim	3	1	538
13	David Sauget	4	1	589
	Other	15	1	
	TOTAL	**87**	**8**	

KEY GOALKEEPER

Olivier Sorin

Goals Conceded in the League	8	Counting Games League games when player was on pitch for at least 70 minutes	12
Defensive Rating Ave number of mins between League goals conceded while on the pitch	135	Clean Sheets In League games when player was on pitch for at least 70 minutes	7

KEY PLAYERS - DEFENDERS

Goals Conceded Number of League goals conceded while the player was on the pitch	34	Clean Sheets In League games when player was on pitch for at least 70 minutes	13
Defensive Rating Ave number of mins between League goals conceded while on the pitch	87	Club Defensive Rating Average number of mins between League goals conceded by the club this season	77

	PLAYER	CON LGE	CLEAN SHEETS	DEF RATE
1	Mickael Chretien	34	13	87 mins
2	Sebastien Puygrenier	33	12	81 mins
3	Pape Diakhate	35	12	78 mins
4	David Sauget	30	8	78 mins

KEY PLAYERS - MIDFIELDERS

Benjamin Gavanon

Goals in the League	8	Contribution to Attacking Power Average number of minutes between League team goals while on pitch	91
Defensive Rating Average number of mins between League goals conceded while on the pitch	97	Scoring Difference Defensive Rating minus Contribution to Attacking Power	6

	PLAYER	LGE GOALS	DEF RATE	POWER	SCORE DIFF
1	Benjamin Gavanon	8	97	91	6 mins
2	Frederic Biancalani	0	78	83	-5 mins
3	Landry N'Guemo	0	79	96	-17 mins
4	Pascal Berenguer	0	71	94	-23 mins

KEY PLAYERS - GOALSCORERS

Marc-Antoine Fortune

Goals in the League	5	Player Strike Rate Average number of minutes between League goals scored by player	248
Contribution to Attacking Power Average number of minutes between League team goals while on pitch	73	Club Strike Rate Average number of minutes between League goals scored by club	92

	PLAYER	LGE GOALS	POWER	STRIKE RATE
1	Marc-Antoine Fortune	5	73	248 mins
2	Benjamin Gavanon	8	91	364 mins
3	Carlos Henrique Dias Kim	4	82	538 mins
4	Gaston Curbelo	3	88	881 mins

Benjamin Gavanon

SQUAD APPEARANCES

Match	1 2 3 4 5	6 7 8 9 10	11 12 13 14 15	16 17 18 19 20	21 22 23 24 25	26 27 28 29 30	31 32 33 34 35	36 37 38 39 40	41 42 43 44 45	46
Venue	H H A H A	A H A H H	A H A H H	A H A A H	H A A H A	A H A H A	A H H A H	A H H A H	H A H A H	A
Competition	L L L L L	E L L E L	L L L E L	L L E L E	L L E L L	L L L L L	E L E L L	L L L L L	L L L L L	L
Result	W W L W D	L D D W W	D W L W W	L W D L W	L D L W L	D L L W D	D L L D D	L L L D L	W W W L W	L

Goalkeepers

Gennaro Bracigliano

Damien Gregorini

Johan Lapeyre

Olivier Sorin

Defenders

A L S do Nascimento

Jonathan Brison

Mickael Chretien

Pape Diakhate

Cedric Lecluse

Damian Macaluso

Sebastien Puygrenier

David Sauget

Midfielders

Pascal Berenguer

Frederic Biancalani

Emmanuel Duchemin

Benjamin Gavanon

Rachid Hamdani

Landry N'Guemo

Moncef Zerka

Forwards

Basile Camerling

Gaston Curbelo

Issiar Dia

Tosin Dosunmu

Marc-Antoine Fortune

Youssouf Hadji

Carlos H Dias Kim

KEY: ■ On all match ◄◄ Subbed or sent off (Counting game) ►► Subbed on from bench (Counting Game) ►◄ Subbed on and then subbed or sent off (Counting Game) □ Not in 16
■ On bench ◄◄ Subbed or sent off (playing less than 70 minutes) ►► Subbed on (playing less than 70 minutes) ►► Subbed on and then subbed or sent off (playing less than 70 minutes)

LORIENT

Final Position: **14th**

NICKNAME: LES MERLUS   KEY: ☐ Won ☐ Drawn ☐ Lost   Attendance

#		Opponent			Score	Scorers	Attendance
1	frpr1	Paris SG	A	W	3-2	Fiorese 32, 53, Saifi 73	36,215
2	frpr1	Bordeaux	H	L	0-1		15,180
3	frpr1	Lens	A	D	1-1	Jallet 71	31,843
4	frpr1	Nantes	H	W	3-1	Gignac 2, 15, 27	14,718
5	frpr1	Le Mans	A	D	1-1	Morel 60	9,653
6	frpr1	Lyon	H	L	1-3	Ciani 69	15,230
7	frpr1	Toulouse	A	D	0-0		13,961
8	frpr1	Troyes	H	D	0-0		10,839
9	frpr1	Nice	A	L	0-3		10,115
10	frpr1	Lille	A	L	0-1		12,752
11	frpr1	Valenciennes	H	W	1-0	Saifi 43	13,556
12	frpr1	Marseille	A	W	1-0	Gignac 48	45,000
13	frpr1	Nancy	H	W	2-0	Le Pen 66, Namouchi 88	12,233
14	frpr1	AS Monaco	A	D	2-2	Namouchi 22, Le Pen 48	9,830
15	frpr1	Sochaux	H	L	1-3	Marchal 1	12,513
16	frpr1	St Etienne	A	L	0-2		24,892
17	frpr1	Sedan	H	W	2-0	Gignac 22, Saifi 28	11,466
18	frpr1	Auxerre	A	L	1-2	Gignac 13	6,049
19	frpr1	Rennes	H	D	0-0		15,618
20	frpr1	Bordeaux	A	D	1-1	Saifi 36	19,809
21	frpr1	Lens	H	W	1-0	Saifi 50	13,117
22	frpr1	Nantes	A	W	2-0	Gignac 21, Abriel 53	29,860
23	frpr1	Le Mans	H	W	2-1	Fischer 51 og, Marlet 88	12,303
24	frpr1	Lyon	A	L	0-1		37,976
25	frpr1	Toulouse	H	L	0-1		12,311
26	frpr1	Troyes	A	L	0-3		9,485
27	frpr1	Nice	H	D	0-0		12,461
28	frpr1	Lille	H	D	0-0		13,551
29	frpr1	Valenciennes	A	D	0-0		15,359
30	frpr1	Marseille	H	W	2-1	Saifi 59, Le Pen 73	15,752
31	frpr1	Nancy	A	W	1-0	Saifi 68 pen	18,370
32	frpr1	AS Monaco	H	D	0-0		14,213
33	frpr1	Sochaux	A	D	1-1	Gignac 56	13,952
34	frpr1	St Etienne	H	D	0-0		15,055
35	frpr1	Sedan	A	L	1-3	Taider 41	11,522
36	frpr1	Auxerre	H	W	2-1	Gignac 11, Le Pen 85	12,412
37	frpr1	Rennes	A	L	1-4	Ewolo 22	29,425
38	frpr1	Paris SG	H	L	0-1		15,621

LEAGUE APPEARANCES, BOOKINGS AND CAPS

	AGE (on 01/07/07)	IN NAMED 18	APPEARANCES	COUNTING GAMES	MINUTES ON PITCH	YELLOW CARDS	RED CARDS	CAPS THIS SEASON	NATIONAL SIDE
Goalkeepers									
Fabien Audard	29	12	12	11	1001	0	0	-	France
Lionel Cappone	28	31	5	4	372	0	1	-	France
Remy Riou	19	27	22	22	1980	1	0	-	France
Defenders									
Fabrice Abriel	27	38	38	38	3413	4	0	-	France
Anis Ayari	25	8	2	0	56	0	0	-	Tunisia
Marc Boutruche	30	13	8	4	520	0	0	-	France
Mickael Ciani	23	33	33	32	2947	3	1	-	France
Benjamin Genton	27	32	7	3	335	1	0	-	France
Christophe Jallet	23	37	36	34	3117	4	0	-	France
Sylvain Marchal	27	35	35	31	2919	9	0	-	France
Carl Medjani	22	23	9	7	684	0	0	-	France
Midfielders									
Oscar Ewolo	28	30	29	25	2344	3	0	-	Congo
Ulrich Le Pen	33	31	31	26	2563	3	0	-	France
Yazid Mansouri	29	34	32	25	2474	0	1	-	Algeria
Jeremy Morel	23	31	29	27	2523	3	0	-	France
Guillaume Moullec	26	37	22	15	1487	2	0	-	France
Hamed Namouchi	23	25	23	6	1089	2	0	3	Tunisia
Stephane Pedron	36	6	3	0	21	0	0	-	France
Nabil Taider	24	17	11	2	416	0	0	-	France
Farid Talhaoui	25	2	1	0	18	0	0	-	Morocco
Diego Yesso	22	10	1	0	1	0	0	-	France
Forwards									
Rahmane Barry	20	20	13	2	405	0	0	-	Senegal
Kemal Bourhani	25	15	13	0	338	0	0	-	France
Fabrice Fiorese	31	9	7	1	251	1	0	-	France
Pierre-Andre Gignac	22	37	37	27	2473	2	0	-	France
A David M'Bodji	22	9	7	0	199	1	0	-	France
Steve Marlet	33	29	22	2	577	1	0	-	France
Rafik Saifi	32	38	37	30	3000	2	0	-	Algeria

TEAM OF THE SEASON

Remy Riou G — CG: 22 DR: 104

Fabrice Abriel D — CG: 38 DR: 87
Mickael Ciani D — CG: 32 DR: 92
Christophe Jallet D — CG: 34 DR: 86
Sylvain Marchal D — CG: 31 DR: 81

Jeremy Morel M — CG: 27 SD: 9
Oscar Ewolo M — CG: 25 SD: 0
Yazid Mansouri M — CG: 25 SD: -5
Ulrich Le Pen M — CG: 26 SD: -13

P-Andre Gignac F — CG: 27 SR: 274
Rafik Saifi F — CG: 30 SR: 428

MONTHLY POINTS TALLY

AUGUST	7	58%
SEPTEMBER	3	25%
OCTOBER	3	33%
NOVEMBER	7	58%
DECEMBER	4	33%
JANUARY	7	78%
FEBRUARY	3	25%
MARCH	6	50%
APRIL	6	50%
MAY	3	25%

LEAGUE GOALS

	PLAYER	MINS	GOALS	S RATE
1	Gignac	2473	9	274
2	Saifi	3000	7	428
3	Le Pen	2563	4	640
4	Fiorese	251	2	125
5	Namouchi	1089	2	544
6	Taider	416	1	416
7	Marlet	577	1	577
8	Ewolo	2344	1	2344
9	Morel	2523	1	2523
10	Marchal	2919	1	2919
11	Ciani	2947	1	2947
12	Jallet	3117	1	3117
13	Abriel	3413	1	3413
	Other		0	
	TOTAL		**32**	

TOP POINT EARNERS

	PLAYER	GAMES	AV PTS
1	Pierre-Andre Gignac	27	**1.56**
2	Yazid Mansouri	25	**1.56**
3	Jeremy Morel	27	**1.48**
4	Oscar Ewolo	25	**1.44**
5	Rafik Saifi	30	**1.40**
6	Ulrich Le Pen	26	**1.38**
7	Mickael Ciani	33	**1.33**
8	Christophe Jallet	34	**1.32**
9	Remy Riou	22	**1.32**
10	Fabrice Abriel	38	**1.29**
	CLUB AVERAGE:		**1.29**

DISCIPLINARY RECORDS

	PLAYER	YELLOW	RED	AVE
1	Sylvain Marchal	9	0	324
2	Hamed Namouchi	2	0	544
3	Steve Marlet	1	0	577
4	Mickael Ciani	3	1	736
5	Guillaume Moullec	2	0	743
6	Christophe Jallet	4	0	779
7	Oscar Ewolo	3	0	781
8	Jeremy Morel	3	0	841
9	Fabrice Abriel	4	0	853
10	Ulrich Le Pen	3	0	854
11	Pierre-Andre Gignac	2	0	1236
12	Rafik Saifi	2	0	1500
13	Remy Riou	1	0	1980
	Other	0	1	
	TOTAL	**39**	**2**	

KEY GOALKEEPER

Remy Riou

Goals Conceded in the League	19	Counting Games League games when player was on pitch for at least 70 minutes	22
Defensive Rating Ave number of mins between League goals conceded while on the pitch	104	Clean Sheets In League games when player was on pitch for at least 70 minutes	11

KEY PLAYERS - DEFENDERS

Mickael Ciani

Goals Conceded Number of League goals conceded while the player was on the pitch	32	Clean Sheets In League games when player was on pitch for at least 70 minutes	14
Defensive Rating Ave number of mins between League goals conceded while on the pitch	92	Club Defensive Rating Average number of mins between League goals conceded by the club this season	85

	PLAYER	CON LGE	CLEAN SHEETS	DEF RATE
1	Mickael Ciani	32	14	92 mins
2	Fabrice Abriel	39	15	87 mins
3	Christophe Jallet	36	14	86 mins
4	Sylvain Marchal	36	12	81 mins

KEY PLAYERS - MIDFIELDERS

Jeremy Morel

Goals in the League	1	Contribution to Attacking Power Average number of minutes between League team goals while on pitch	100
Defensive Rating Average number of mins between League goals conceded while on the pitch	109	Scoring Difference Defensive Rating minus Contribution to Attacking Power	9

	PLAYER	LGE GOALS	DEF RATE	POWER	SCORE DIFF
1	Jeremy Morel	1	109	100	9 mins
2	Oscar Ewolo	1	83	83	0 mins
3	Yazid Mansouri	0	107	112	-5 mins
4	Ulrich Le Pen	4	85	98	-13 mins

KEY PLAYERS - GOALSCORERS

Pierre-Andre Gignac

Goals in the League	9	Player Strike Rate Average number of minutes between League goals scored by player	274
Contribution to Attacking Power Average number of minutes between League team goals while on pitch	91	Club Strike Rate Average number of minutes between League goals scored by club	103

	PLAYER	LGE GOALS	POWER	STRIKE RATE
1	Pierre-Andre Gignac	9	91	274 mins
2	Rafik Saifi	7	96	428 mins
3	Ulrich Le Pen	4	98	640 mins
4	Oscar Ewolo	1	83	2344 mins

Pierre-Andre Gignac

SQUAD APPEARANCES

Match	1	2	3	4	5	6	7	8	9	10	11	12	13	14	15	16	17	18	19	20	21	22	23	24	25	26	27	28	29	30	31	32	33	34	35	36	37	38
Venue	A	H	A	H	A	H	A	H	A	A	H	A	H	A	H	A	H	A	H	A	H	A	H	A	H	A	H	H	A	H	A	H	A	H	A	H	A	H
Competition	L	L	L	L	L	L	L	L	L	L	L	L	L	L	L	L	L	L	L	L	L	L	L	L	L	L	L	L	L	L	L	L	L	L	L	L	L	L
Result	W	L	D	W	D	L	D	D	L	L	W	W	W	D	L	L	W	L	D	D	W	W	W	L	L	L	D	D	D	W	W	D	D	D	L	W	L	L

Goalkeepers

Fabien Audard
Lionel Cappone
Remy Riou

Defenders

Fabrice Abriel
Anis Ayari
Marc Boutruche
Mickael Ciani
Benjamin Genton
Christophe Jallet
Sylvain Marchal
Carl Medjani

Midfielders

Oscar Ewolo
Ulrich Le Pen
Yazid Mansouri
Jeremy Morel
Guillaume Moullec
Hamed Namouchi
Stephane Pedron
Nabil Taider
Farid Talhaoui
Diego Yesso

Forwards

Rahmane Barry
Kemal Bourhani
Fabrice Fiorese
Pierre-Andre Gignac
A David M'Bodji
Steve Marlet
Rafik Saifi

KEY: ■ On all match ◄◄ Subbed or sent off (Counting game) ▸▸ Subbed on from bench (Counting Game) ▸▸ Subbed on and then subbed or sent off (Counting Game) □ Not in 16
■ On bench ◄◄ Subbed or sent off (playing less than 70 minutes) ▸▸ Subbed on (playing less than 70 minutes) ▸▸ Subbed on and then subbed or sent off (playing less than 70 minutes)

PARIS St GERMAIN

Final Position: **15th**

NICKNAME: PSG   KEY: ☐ Won ☐ Drawn ☐ Lost   Attendance

#		Opponent			Result	Scorers	Attendance
1	frpr1	Lorient	H	L	2-3	Frau 28, Pancrate 45	36,215
2	frpr1	Valenciennes	A	D	0-0		15,545
3	frpr1	Lille	H	W	1-0	Pauleta 58	35,077
4	frpr1	Sochaux	A	L	2-3	Pauleta 69, 74	16,317
5	frpr1	Marseille	H	L	1-3	Pauleta 22 pen	44,431
6	ucrl1	Derry City	A	D	0-0		3,000
7	frpr1	AS Monaco	A	W	2-1	Rozehnal 41, Hellebuyck 53	12,000
8	frpr1	Nancy	H	D	0-0		34,103
9	ucrl2	Derry City	H	W	2-0	Cisse 6, Pauleta 41	7,000
10	frpr1	St Etienne	A	L	0-1		25,734
11	frpr1	Sedan	H	W	4-2	Frau 4, Yepes 48, Pauleta 56, 72 pen	36,329
12	ucgpg	Rap Bucharest	A	D	0-0		15,000
13	frpr1	Auxerre	A	D	0-0		14,146
14	frpr1	Rennes	H	W	1-0	Diane 43	37,648
15	frpr1	Lens	H	L	1-3	Armand 26	35,894
16	frpr1	Le Mans	A	D	1-1	Kalou 10 pen	12,983
17	frpr1	Bordeaux	H	L	0-2		38,394
18	ucgpg	Hapo Tel-Aviv	H	L	2-4	Frau 14, Pauleta 25	35,000
19	frpr1	Nantes	A	D	1-1	Kalou 1	32,104
20	ucgpg	Mlada Boleslav	A	D	0-0		5,000
21	frpr1	Lyon	A	L	1-3	Pauleta 59	36,072
22	ucgpg	Panathinaikos	H	W	4-0	Pauleta 29, 47, Kalou 52, 54	20,000
23	frpr1	Nice	H	D	0-0		28,341
24	frpr1	Troyes	A	D	1-1	Diane 47	12,046
25	frpr1	Valenciennes	H	L	1-2	Pauleta 90 pen	27,866
26	frpr1	Toulouse	H	D	0-0		29,538
27	frpr1	Lille	A	L	0-1		12,950
28	frpr1	Sochaux	H	D	0-0		31,119
29	frpr1	Marseille	A	D	1-1	Pauleta 73	58,000
30	frpr1	AS Monaco	H	W	4-2	Diane 4, Roma 34 og, Gallardo 82, C.Rodriguez 84	34,171
31	ucrl1	AEK Athens	A	W	2-0	Traore 45, Mendy 88	30,000
32	frpr1	Nancy	A	W	3-0	Pauleta 70 pen, Frau 85, Gallardo 88	19,252
33	ucrl2	AEK Athens	H	W	2-0	Frau 42, Mendy 90 pen	25,000
34	frpr1	St Etienne	H	L	0-2		38,857
35	frpr1	Sedan	A	L	0-2		15,851
36	ucrl1	Benfica	H	W	2-1	Pauleta 36, Frau 41	35,000
37	frpr1	Auxerre	H	L	0-1		33,036
38	ucrl2	Benfica	A	L	1-3	Pauleta 32	65,000
39	frpr1	Rennes	A	L	0-1		27,085
40	frpr1	Lens	A	W	2-1	Diane 2, Armand 71	37,808
41	frpr1	Le Mans	H	W	2-1	Luyindula 56, Diane 80	42,368
42	frpr1	Bordeaux	A	D	0-0		31,731
43	frpr1	Nantes	H	W	4-0	Pauleta 16, 64, Rothen 42, Luyindula 65	42,744
44	frpr1	Toulouse	A	W	3-1	Luyindula 31, Cisse 43, Rothen 90	30,594
45	frpr1	Lyon	H	D	1-1	Cisse 47	41,577
46	frpr1	Nice	A	L	0-1		12,271
47	frpr1	Troyes	H	W	2-1	Pauleta 71 pen, 77	40,816
48	frpr1	Lorient	A	W	1-0	Pauleta 53	15,621

LEAGUE APPEARANCES, BOOKINGS AND CAPS

	AGE (on 01/07/07)	IN NAMED 18	APPEARANCES	COUNTING GAMES	MINUTES ON PITCH	YELLOW CARDS	RED CARDS	CAPS THIS SEASON	NATIONAL SIDE
Goalkeepers									
Mickael Landreau	28	38	38	38	3420	0	0	2	France
Defenders									
Sylvain Armand	26	36	36	36	3234	5	0	-	France
J-H Bilayi Ateba	25	1	1	1	90	0	0	-	Cameroon
Boukary Drame	21	33	20	12	1377	4	0	-	France
Bernard Mendy	25	35	28	27	2467	6	1	-	France
David Rozehnal	26	37	37	37	3330	4	0	10	Czech Republic
Mamadou Sakho	17	2	0	0	0	1	0	-	France
Sammy Traore	25	29	22	15	1507	6	0	-	Mali
Mario Yepes	31	26	24	19	1855	3	0	-	Colombia
Midfielders									
Albert Baning	22	11	1	1	81	1	0	-	Cameroon
Clement Chantome	19	31	20	13	1254	4	0	-	France
Edouard Cisse	29	36	34	30	2828	9	0	-	France
Jeremy Clement	22	9	9	8	778	1	0	-	France
Vikash Dhorasoo	33	3	3	2	238	0	0	-	France
Marcelo Gallardo	31	15	13	6	722	3	0	-	Argentina
David Hellebuyck	28	22	11	6	655	0	0	-	France
Youssouf Mulumbu	20	28	12	9	897	4	1	-	Congo DR
Paulo Cesar	28	16	8	4	434	0	0	-	Brazil
Cristian Rodriguez	21	28	25	3	743	3	0	-	Uruguay
Jerome Rothen	29	27	27	25	2277	6	0	-	France
Forwards									
Amara Diane	24	33	33	10	1593	6	1	1	Ivory Coast
Pierre-Alain Frau	27	25	25	14	1615	2	1	-	France
Bonaventure Kalou	29	32	27	11	1858	6	0	2	Ivory Coast
Peguy Luyindula	28	14	14	11	1025	2	1	-	France
David N'Gog	18	5	4	0	65	0	0	-	France
Fabrice Pancrate	27	19	15	5	626	1	0	-	France
Pauleta	34	35	33	27	2588	5	1	-	Portugal

TEAM OF THE SEASON

Position	Player	Stats
G	Mickael Landreau	CG: 38 DR: 81
D	Boukary Drame	CG: 13 DR: 91
D	Sylvain Armand	CG: 37 DR: 85
D	David Rozehnal	CG: 37 DR: 85
D	Sammy Traore	CG: 16 DR: 84
M	Youssouf Mulumbu*	CG: 9 SD: 20
M	Jerome Rothen	CG: 25 SD: 16
M	Edouard Cisse	CG: 31 SD: 3
M	Clement Chantome	CG: 14 SD: -28
F	Pauleta	CG: 28 SR: 178
F	Peguy Luyindula	CG: 11 SR: 341

MONTHLY POINTS TALLY

Month		%
AUGUST	4	33%
SEPTEMBER	4	44%
OCTOBER	7	58%
NOVEMBER	2	17%
DECEMBER	2	22%
JANUARY	2	17%
FEBRUARY	7	58%
MARCH	0	0%
APRIL	13	87%
MAY	7	58%

LEAGUE GOALS

	PLAYER	MINS	GOALS	S RATE
1	Pauleta	2678	15	178
2	Diane	1593	4	398
3	Luyindula	1025	3	341
4	Frau	1615	3	538
5	Gallardo	722	2	361
6	Kalou	1948	2	974
7	Rothen	2277	2	1138
8	Cisse	2918	2	1459
9	Armand	3324	2	1662
10	Hellebuyck	655	1	655
11	Pancrate	716	1	716
12	Rodriguez, C	743	1	743
13	Yepes	1855	1	1855
	Other		1	
	TOTAL		**40**	

TOP POINT EARNERS

	PLAYER	GAMES	AV PTS
1	Boukary Drame	12	1.92
2	Pierre-Alain Frau	15	1.60
3	Jerome Rothen	25	1.48
4	Sammy Traore	15	1.47
5	Edouard Cisse	30	1.33
6	David Rozehnal	37	1.30
7	Mickael Landreau	38	1.26
8	Pauleta	27	1.22
9	Sylvain Armand	36	1.17
10	Mario Yepes	19	1.11
	CLUB AVERAGE:		**1.26**

DISCIPLINARY RECORDS

	PLAYER	YELLOW	RED	AVE
1	Marcelo Gallardo	3	0	240
2	Youssouf Mulumbu	4	1	299
3	Amara Diane	6	1	318
4	Sammy Traore	6	0	319
5	Edouard Cisse	9	0	324
6	Clement Chantome	4	0	336
7	Peguy Luyindula	2	1	341
8	Cristian Rodriguez	3	0	371
9	Bonaventure Kalou	6	0	389
10	Bernard Mendy	6	1	426
11	Pauleta	5	1	446
12	Pierre-Alain Frau	2	1	538
13	Jerome Rothen	6	0	569
	Other	18	0	
	TOTAL	**80**	**6**	

KEY GOALKEEPER

Mickael Landreau

Goals Conceded in the League	42	Counting Games League games when player was on pitch for at least 70 minutes	38
Defensive Rating Ave number of mins between League goals conceded while on the pitch	81	Clean Sheets In League games when player was on pitch for at least 70 minutes	12

KEY PLAYERS - DEFENDERS

Boukary Drame

Goals Conceded Number of League goals conceded while the player was on the pitch	16	Clean Sheets In League games when player was on pitch for at least 70 minutes	7
Defensive Rating Ave number of mins between League goals conceded while on the pitch	91	Club Defensive Rating Average number of mins between League goals conceded by the club this season	83

	PLAYER	CON LGE	CLEAN SHEETS	DEF RATE
1	Boukary Drame	16	7	91 mins
2	Sylvain Armand	39	13	85 mins
3	David Rozehnal	39	12	85 mins
4	Sammy Traore	19	5	84 mins

KEY PLAYERS - MIDFIELDERS

Youssouf Mulumbu

Goals in the League	0	Contribution to Attacking Power Average number of minutes between League team goals while on pitch	69
Defensive Rating Average number of mins between League goals conceded while on the pitch	89	Scoring Difference Defensive Rating minus Contribution to Attacking Power	20

	PLAYER	LGE GOALS	DEF RATE	POWER	SCORE DIFF
1	Youssouf Mulumbu	0	89	69	20 mins
2	Jerome Rothen	2	91	75	16 mins
3	Edouard Cisse	2	88	85	3 mins
4	Clement Chantome	0	84	112	-28 mins

KEY PLAYERS - GOALSCORERS

Pauleta

Goals in the League	15	Player Strike Rate Average number of minutes between League goals scored by player	178
Contribution to Attacking Power Average number of minutes between League team goals while on pitch	99	Club Strike Rate Average number of minutes between League goals scored by club	83

	PLAYER	LGE GOALS	POWER	STRIKE RATE
1	Pauleta	15	99	178 mins
2	Peguy Luyindula	3	56	341 mins
3	Amara Diane	4	66	398 mins
4	Pierre-Alain Frau	3	67	538 mins

Pauleta and Pierre-Alain Frau

SQUAD APPEARANCES

Match	1 2 3 4 5	6 7 8 9 10	11 12 13 14 15	16 17 18 19 20	21 22 23 24 25	26 27 28 29 30	31 32 33 34 35	36 37 38 39 40	41 42 43 44 45	46 47 48
Venue	H A H A H	A A H H A	H A A H H	A H H A A	A H H A H	H A H A H	A A H H A	H H A A A	H A H A H	A H A
Competition	L L L L L	E L L E L	L E L L L	L L E L E	L E L L L	L L L L L	E L E L L	E L E L L	L L L L L	L L L
Result	L D W L L	D W D W L	W D D W L	D L L L D	L W D D L	D L D D W	W W W L L	W L L L W	W D W W D	L W W

Goalkeepers
Mickael Landreau

Defenders
Sylvain Armand
J-H Bilayi Ateba
Boukary Drame
Bernard Mendy
David Rozehnal
Mamadou Sakho
Sammy Traore
Mario Yepes

Midfielders
Albert Baning
Clement Chantome
Edouard Cisse
Jeremy Clement
Vikash Dhorasoo
Marcelo Gallardo
David Hellebuyck
Youssouf Mulumbu
Paulo Cesar
Cristian Rodriguez
Jerome Rothen

Forwards
Amara Diane
Pierre-Alain Frau
Bonaventure Kalou
Peguy Luyindula
David N'Gog
Fabrice Pancrate
Pauleta

KEY: ■ On all match ◄◄ Subbed or sent off (Counting game) ►► Subbed on from bench (Counting Game) ►► Subbed on and then subbed or sent off (Counting Game) □ Not in 16
■ On bench ◄ Subbed or sent off (playing less than 70 minutes) ►► Subbed on (playing less than 70 minutes) ►► Subbed on and then subbed or sent off (playing less than 70 minutes)

FRANCE - PARIS St GERMAIN

NICE

Final Position: **16th**

NICKNAME: LES AIGLONS   KEY: ☐ Won ☐ Drawn ☐ Lost   Attendance

1 frpr1	Le Mans	A	L	0-1		9,574
2 frpr1	Nantes	H	D	1-1	Ederson 53	12,943
3 frpr1	Toulouse	A	L	0-1		17,837
4 frpr1	Lyon	H	L	1-4	Vahirua 26	13,814
5 frpr1	Bordeaux	A	L	2-3	Varrault 28, Ederson 77 pen	20,178
6 frpr1	Troyes	A	L	0-2		8,809
7 frpr1	Valenciennes	H	W	2-0	Varrault 84, Bellion 90	9,905
8 frpr1	Lille	A	L	0-1		13,088
9 frpr1	Lorient	H	W	3-0	Bellion 12, 50, Kone 76	10,115
10 frpr1	Rennes	A	L	0-1		22,978
11 frpr1	Marseille	H	W	2-1	Rool 24, Ederson 90 pen	15,030
12 frpr1	AS Monaco	A	D	0-0		15,981
13 frpr1	Sochaux	H	D	0-0		10,688
14 frpr1	St Etienne	A	L	1-2	Rool 45	26,707
15 frpr1	Sedan	H	D	2-2	Kone 56, Kante 77	9,028
16 frpr1	Auxerre	A	D	0-0		6,252
17 frpr1	Nancy	H	D	0-0		9,421
18 frpr1	Paris SG	A	D	0-0		28,341
19 frpr1	Lens	H	L	1-2	Kone 25	10,128
20 frpr1	Nantes	A	L	0-1		29,000
21 frpr1	Toulouse	H	L	0-1		8,802
22 frpr1	Lyon	A	D	1-1	Kone 34	33,971
23 frpr1	Bordeaux	H	W	2-1	Ederson 11, 25	10,898
24 frpr1	Troyes	H	W	3-0	Laslandes 45, 60, Ederson 77	11,711
25 frpr1	Valenciennes	A	W	1-0	Kone 33 pen	15,208
26 frpr1	Lille	H	W	2-1	Kone 42, 81	11,369
27 frpr1	Lorient	A	D	0-0		12,461
28 frpr1	Rennes	H	D	1-1	Vahirua 46	10,875
29 frpr1	Marseille	A	L	0-3		50,007
30 frpr1	AS Monaco	H	D	1-1	Laslandes 10	13,524
31 frpr1	Sochaux	A	D	1-1	Bellion 67	16,759
32 frpr1	St Etienne	H	W	2-1	Bellion 69, 80 pen	12,405
33 frpr1	Sedan	A	D	1-1	Kone 87 pen	18,200
34 frpr1	Auxerre	H	D	0-0		10,936
35 frpr1	Nancy	A	L	0-3		18,583
36 frpr1	Paris SG	H	W	1-0	Vahirua 1	12,271
37 frpr1	Lens	A	D	0-0		38,468
38 frpr1	Le Mans	H	D	3-3	Bellion 30 pen, 54, Vahirua 43	11,522

LEAGUE APPEARANCES, BOOKINGS AND CAPS

	AGE (on 01/07/07)	IN NAMED 18	APPEARANCES	COUNTING GAMES	MINUTES ON PITCH	YELLOW CARDS	RED CARDS	CAPS THIS SEASON	NATIONAL SIDE
Goalkeepers									
Damien Gregorini	28	19	0	0	0	0	0	-	France
Lionel Letizi	34	16	1	1	90	0	0	-	France
Hugo Lloris	20	38	37	37	3330	0	0	-	France
Defenders									
Jacques Abardonado	29	31	30	27	2491	3	0	-	France
Onyekachi Apam	20	29	22	20	1847	6	0	-	Nigeria
Rod Fanni	25	36	36	32	2982	7	1	-	France
Ismael Gace	20	9	0	0	0	0	0	-	France
Cedric Kante	27	31	30	29	2656	7	0	-	France
T Scotto Di Porfirio	28	18	6	1	118	0	0	-	France
Cedric Varrault	27	32	32	27	2622	2	2	-	France
Olivier Veigneau	21	30	18	3	677	1	0	-	France
Anthar Yahia	25	15	9	8	732	1	0	-	Algeria
Midfielders									
Florent Balmont	27	32	32	28	2679	8	1	-	France
Drissa Diakite	22	24	21	14	1468	6	0	-	Mali
Olivier Echouafni	34	37	33	28	2708	5	0	-	France
H Campos Ederson	21	31	30	16	1933	2	0	-	Brazil
Cyril Rool	32	25	25	22	2123	12	1	-	France
Mahamane Traore	18	14	4	0	114	1	0	-	Mali
Forwards									
David Bellion	24	30	30	10	1655	0	0	-	France
Souleymane Camara	24	35	14	0	260	1	0	-	Senegal
Bakary Diakite	26	7	4	3	297	2	0	-	Germany
Bakary Kone	25	33	33	26	2623	2	0	1	Ivory Coast
Kamel Larbi	22	15	4	1	117	0	0	-	Algeria
Lilian Laslandes	35	16	16	15	1389	3	0	-	France
Matt Moussilou	25	20	19	6	899	2	0	-	France
Marama Vahirua	27	36	32	6	1558	2	0	-	France

TEAM OF THE SEASON

G Hugo Lloris CG: 37 DR: 90

D Onyekachi Apam CG: 20 DR: 115
D Cedric Kante CG: 29 DR: 88
D Cedric Varrault CG: 27 DR: 81
D Rod Fanni CG: 32 DR: 80

M Drissa Diakite CG: 14 SD: 5
M H Campos Ederson CG: 16 SD: -8
M Olivier Echouafni CG: 28 SD: -13
M Florent Balmont CG: 28 SD: -13

F Bakary Kone CG: 26 SR: 327
F Lilian Laslandes CG: 15 SR: 463

MONTHLY POINTS TALLY

AUGUST		1	8%
SEPTEMBER		3	25%
OCTOBER		6	67%
NOVEMBER		3	25%
DECEMBER		3	25%
JANUARY		1	11%
FEBRUARY		12	100%
MARCH		2	22%
APRIL		7	47%
MAY		5	42%

LEAGUE GOALS

	PLAYER	MINS	GOALS	S RATE
1	Bellion	1655	8	206
2	Kone	2623	8	327
3	Ederson	1933	6	322
4	Vahirua	1558	4	389
5	Laslandes	1389	3	463
6	Rool	2123	2	1061
7	Varrault	2622	2	1311
8	Kante	2656	1	2656
9	S Di Porfirio	118	0	
10	Traore, M.	114	0	
11	Veigneau	677	0	
12	Yahia	732	0	
13	Letizi	90	0	
	Other		0	
	TOTAL		**34**	

TOP POINT EARNERS

	PLAYER	GAMES	AV PTS
1	Lilian Laslandes	15	1.60
2	Drissa Diakite	14	1.43
3	Onyekachi Apam	20	1.35
4	Florent Balmont	29	1.31
5	Bakary Kone	26	1.31
6	Olivier Echouafni	28	1.25
7	Cedric Kante	29	1.24
8	Jacques Abardonado	27	1.15
9	Hugo Lloris	37	1.14
10	Cedric Varrault	28	1.11
	CLUB AVERAGE:		**1.13**

DISCIPLINARY RECORDS

	PLAYER	YELLOW	RED	AVE
1	Cyril Rool	12	1	163
2	Drissa Diakite	6	0	244
3	Florent Balmont	8	1	297
4	Onyekachi Apam	6	0	307
5	Rod Fanni	7	1	372
6	Cedric Kante	7	0	379
7	Matt Moussilou	2	0	449
8	Lilian Laslandes	3	0	463
9	Olivier Echouafni	5	0	541
10	Cedric Varrault	2	2	655
11	Olivier Veigneau	1	0	677
12	Anthar Yahia	1	0	732
13	Marama Vahirua	2	0	779
	Other	7	0	
	TOTAL	**69**	**5**	

KEY GOALKEEPER

Hugo Lloris

Goals Conceded in the League	37	Counting Games League games when player was on pitch for at least 70 minutes	37
Defensive Rating Ave number of mins between League goals conceded while on the pitch	90	Clean Sheets In League games when player was on pitch for at least 70 minutes	13

KEY PLAYERS - DEFENDERS

Onyekachi Apam

Goals Conceded Number of League goals conceded while the player was on the pitch	16	Clean Sheets In League games when player was on pitch for at least 70 minutes	10
Defensive Rating Ave number of mins between League goals conceded while on the pitch	115	Club Defensive Rating Average number of mins between League goals conceded by the club this season	85

	PLAYER	CON LGE	CLEAN SHEETS	DEF RATE
1	Onyekachi Apam	16	10	115 mins
2	Cedric Kante	30	10	88 mins
3	Cedric Varrault	32	10	81 mins
4	Rod Fanni	37	10	80 mins

KEY PLAYERS - MIDFIELDERS

Drissa Diakite

Goals in the League	0	Contribution to Attacking Power Average number of minutes between League team goals while on pitch	86
Defensive Rating Average number of mins between League goals conceded while on the pitch	91	Scoring Difference Defensive Rating minus Contribution to Attacking Power	5

	PLAYER	LGE GOALS	DEF RATE	POWER	SCORE DIFF
1	Drissa Diakite	0	91	86	5 mins
2	Honorato Campos Ederson	6	84	92	-8 mins
3	Olivier Echouafni	0	87	100	-13 mins
4	Florent Balmont	0	76	89	-13 mins

KEY PLAYERS - GOALSCORERS

Honorato Campos Ederson

Goals in the League	6	Player Strike Rate Average number of minutes between League goals scored by player	322
Contribution to Attacking Power Average number of minutes between League team goals while on pitch	92	Club Strike Rate Average number of minutes between League goals scored by club	100

	PLAYER	LGE GOALS	POWER	STRIKE RATE
1	Honorato Campos Ederson	6	92	322 mins
2	Bakary Kone	8	104	327 mins
3	Lilian Laslandes	3	92	463 mins
4	Cyril Rool	2	117	1061 mins

Bakary Kone and David Bellion

SQUAD APPEARANCES

Match	1	2	3	4	5	6	7	8	9	10	11	12	13	14	15	16	17	18	19	20	21	22	23	24	25	26	27	28	29	30	31	32	33	34	35	36	37	38
Venue	A	H	A	H	A	A	H	A	H	A	H	A	H	A	H	A	H	A	H	A	H	A	H	H	A	H	A	H	A	H	A	H	A	H	A	H	A	H
Competition	L	L	L	L	L	L	L	L	L	L	L	L	L	L	L	L	L	L	L	L	L	L	L	L	L	L	L	L	L	L	L	L	L	L	L	L	L	L
Result	L	D	L	L	L	L	W	L	W	L	W	D	D	L	D	D	D	D	L	L	L	D	W	W	W	W	D	D	L	D	D	W	D	D	L	W	D	D

Goalkeepers
Damien Gregorini
Lionel Letizi
Hugo Lloris

Defenders
Jacques Abardonado
Onyekachi Apam
Rod Fanni
Ismael Gace
Cedric Kante
T Scotto Di Porfirio
Cedric Varrault
Olivier Veigneau
Anthar Yahia

Midfielders
Florent Balmont
Drissa Diakite
Olivier Echouafni
H Campos Ederson
Cyril Rool
Mahamane Traore

Forwards
David Bellion
Souleymane Camara
Bakary Diakite
Bakary Kone
Kamel Larbi
Lilian Laslandes
Matt Moussilou
Marama Vahirua

KEY: ■ On all match ◀◀ Subbed or sent off (Counting game) ▶▶ Subbed on from bench (Counting Game) ▶▶ Subbed on and then subbed or sent off (Counting Game) ☐ Not in 16
■ On bench ◀◀ Subbed or sent off (playing less than 70 minutes) ▶▶ Subbed on (playing less than 70 minutes) ▶▶ Subbed on and then subbed or sent off (playing less than 70 minutes)

FRANCE - NICE

VALENCIENNES

Final Position: **17th**

NICKNAME: LES ATHENIENS KEY: ☐ Won ☐ Drawn ☐ Lost Attendance

1 frpr1	Auxerre	A D	1-1	Savidan 42	11,076
2 frpr1	Paris SG	H D	0-0		15,545
3 frpr1	Le Mans	A L	2-3	Savidan 9, 26	9,456
4 frpr1	Rennes	H W	3-1	Dufresne 62 fk, 71, Bezzaz 90	14,061
5 frpr1	Lens	A L	0-3		34,927
6 frpr1	Nantes	H W	1-0	Savidan 37	14,295
7 frpr1	Nice	A L	0-2		9,905
8 frpr1	Bordeaux	H W	2-0	Chelle 70, Bourgeois 90	15,040
9 frpr1	Toulouse	A L	0-3		21,904
10 frpr1	Troyes	H W	3-1	Roudet 32, 53, Dossevi 77	13,378
11 frpr1	Lorient	A L	0-1		13,556
12 frpr1	Lille	H L	0-3		16,530
13 frpr1	Lyon	A L	1-2	Savidan 76	39,833
14 frpr1	Marseille	A L	0-1		46,484
15 frpr1	Nancy	H W	1-0	Savidan 1	13,241
16 frpr1	AS Monaco	A L	0-3		12,277
17 frpr1	Sochaux	H D	0-0		12,889
18 frpr1	St Etienne	A L	0-3		27,957
19 frpr1	Sedan	H W	2-1	Savidan 12 pen, Mater 18	13,766
20 frpr1	Paris SG	A W	2-1	Savidan 60, Roudet 87	27,866
21 frpr1	Le Mans	H D	1-1	Roudet 39	11,716
22 frpr1	Rennes	A L	0-1		22,052
23 frpr1	Lens	H L	1-3	Savidan 59 pen	16,513
24 frpr1	Nantes	A W	5-2	Savidan 18, 49, 71, 87, Dufresne 75	24,751
25 frpr1	Nice	H L	0-1		15,208
26 frpr1	Bordeaux	A L	1-2	Dossevi 82	22,371
27 frpr1	Toulouse	H D	0-0		13,721
28 frpr1	Troyes	A W	3-1	Bezzaz 37, Roudet 67, Dufresne 86	13,572
29 frpr1	Lorient	H D	0-0		15,359
30 frpr1	Lille	A W	2-0	Doumeng 77, Hassli 90	14,778
31 frpr1	Lyon	H D	0-0		15,999
32 frpr1	Marseille	H D	0-0		16,398
33 frpr1	Nancy	A L	0-1		19,505
34 frpr1	AS Monaco	H D	2-2	Haddad 84, Chelle 88	15,816
35 frpr1	Sochaux	A L	0-1		15,657
36 frpr1	St Etienne	H W	1-0	Paauwe 53	15,393
37 frpr1	Sedan	A D	1-1	Hassli 49	14,812
38 frpr1	Auxerre	H L	1-3	Bratu 79	15,681

LEAGUE APPEARANCES, BOOKINGS AND CAPS

	AGE (on 01/07/07)	IN NAMED 18	APPEARANCES	COUNTING GAMES	MINUTES ON PITCH	YELLOW CARDS	RED CARDS	CAPS THIS SEASON	NATIONAL SIDE
Goalkeepers									
Willy Grondin	32	32	7	7	630	0	0	-	France
Nicolas Penneteau	26	31	31	31	2790	1	0	-	France
Defenders									
Eric Chelle	29	28	28	25	2334	3	1	-	Mali
Maxence Flachez	34	34	34	34	3038	7	0	-	France
Ludovic Liron	29	24	13	0	336	1	0	-	France
Rudy Mater	26	37	37	31	2994	9	0	-	France
Abdeslam Ouaddou	28	10	10	9	816	0	0	-	Morocco
Guillaume Rippert	22	35	33	28	2659	11	1	-	France
Orlando Silvestri	34	5	5	4	426	0	0	-	France
Dame Traore	21	2	1	0	45	0	0	-	France
Midfielders									
Yacine Bezzaz	25	29	20	10	1127	5	0	-	Algeria
Freddy Bourgeois	30	14	9	3	448	0	0	-	France
Thomas Dossevi	28	33	20	4	604	1	0	-	Togo
Geoffrey Doumeng	26	37	32	22	2280	4	0	-	France
Rudy Haddad	22	36	29	12	1586	3	0	-	France
Khaled Kharroubi	23	17	10	3	469	0	0	-	France
Patrick Paauwe	31	29	29	23	2304	7	1	-	Holland
Sebastien Roudet	26	32	30	23	2185	5	0	-	France
Jose Saez	25	31	21	13	1349	4	1	-	France
Mody Traore	26	24	19	11	1156	2	0	-	France
Forwards									
Florin Bratu	27	26	22	9	1162	2	0	-	Romania
Laurent Dufresne	35	24	23	23	2039	2	0	-	France
Eric Hassli	26	28	21	4	862	3	0	-	France
Sebastian Heitzmann	27	2	1	1	71	0	0	-	France
Da R do N Jeovanio	29	10	9	9	777	2	0	-	Brazil
Steve Savidan	29	34	34	34	3019	5	0	-	France

TEAM OF THE SEASON

Nicolas Penneteau **CG: 31 DR: 73**
Rudy Mater **CG: 31 DR: 78**
Maxence Flachez **CG: 34 DR: 72**
Guillaume Rippert **CG: 28 DR: 71**
Eric Chelle **CG: 25 DR: 64**
Patrick Paauwe **CG: 23 SD: -4**
Geoffrey Doumeng **CG: 22 SD: -10**
Sebastien Roudet **CG: 23 SD: -21**
Rudy Haddad **CG: 12 SD: -38**
Steve Savidan **CG: 34 SR: 232**
Laurent Dufresne **CG: 23 SR: 509**

MONTHLY POINTS TALLY

AUGUST	5	42%
SEPTEMBER	6	50%
OCTOBER	3	33%
NOVEMBER	3	25%
DECEMBER	4	33%
JANUARY	4	44%
FEBRUARY	3	25%
MARCH	5	56%
APRIL	6	40%
MAY	4	33%

LEAGUE GOALS

	PLAYER	MINS	GOALS	S RATE
1	Savidan	3019	13	232
2	Roudet	2185	5	437
3	Dufresne	2039	4	509
4	Dossevi	604	2	302
5	Hassli	862	2	431
6	Bezzaz	1127	2	563
7	Chelle	2334	2	1167
8	Bourgeois	448	1	448
9	Bratu	1162	1	1162
10	Haddad	1586	1	1586
11	Doumeng	2280	1	2280
12	Paauwe	2304	1	2304
13	Mater	2994	1	2994
	Other		0	
	TOTAL		**36**	

TOP POINT EARNERS

	PLAYER	GAMES	AV PTS
1	Patrick Paauwe	24	1.33
2	Laurent Dufresne	23	1.30
3	Rudy Mater	31	1.19
4	Steve Savidan	34	1.18
5	Maxence Flachez	34	1.18
6	Geoffrey Doumeng	22	1.14
7	Nicolas Penneteau	31	1.13
8	Guillaume Rippert	28	1.04
9	Eric Chelle	26	1.04
10	Rudy Haddad	12	1.00
	CLUB AVERAGE:		**1.13**

DISCIPLINARY RECORDS

	PLAYER	YELLOW	RED	AVE
1	Guillaume Rippert	11	1	221
2	Yacine Bezzaz	5	0	225
3	Jose Saez	4	1	269
4	Eric Hassli	3	0	287
5	Patrick Paauwe	7	1	288
6	Rudy Mater	9	0	332
7	Da R do N Jeovanio	2	0	388
8	Maxence Flachez	7	0	434
9	Sebastien Roudet	5	0	437
10	Rudy Haddad	3	0	528
11	Geoffrey Doumeng	4	0	570
12	Mody Traore	2	0	578
13	Florin Bratu	2	0	581
	Other	12	1	
	TOTAL	**76**	**4**	

KEY GOALKEEPER

Nicolas Penneteau

Goals Conceded in the League	38	Counting Games League games when player was on pitch for at least 70 minutes	31
Defensive Rating Ave number of mins between League goals conceded while on the pitch	73	Clean Sheets In League games when player was on pitch for at least 70 minutes	9

KEY PLAYERS - DEFENDERS

Rudy Mater

Goals Conceded Number of League goals conceded while the player was on the pitch	38	Clean Sheets In League games when player was on pitch for at least 70 minutes	12
Defensive Rating Ave number of mins between League goals conceded while on the pitch	78	Club Defensive Rating Average number of mins between League goals conceded by the club this season	71

	PLAYER	CON LGE	CLEAN SHEETS	DEF RATE
1	Rudy Mater	38	12	78 mins
2	Maxence Flachez	42	10	72 mins
3	Guillaume Rippert	37	8	71 mins
4	Eric Chelle	36	6	64 mins

KEY PLAYERS - MIDFIELDERS

Patrick Paauwe

Goals in the League	1	Contribution to Attacking Power Average number of minutes between League team goals while on pitch	96
Defensive Rating Average number of mins between League goals conceded while on the pitch	92	Scoring Difference Defensive Rating minus Contribution to Attacking Power	-4

	PLAYER	LGE GOALS	DEF RATE	POWER	SCORE DIFF
1	Patrick Paauwe	1	92	96	-4 mins
2	Geoffrey Doumeng	1	71	81	-10 mins
3	Sebastien Roudet	5	66	87	-21 mins
4	Rudy Haddad	1	75	113	-38 mins

KEY PLAYERS - GOALSCORERS

Steve Savidan

Goals in the League	13	Player Strike Rate Average number of minutes between League goals scored by player	232
Contribution to Attacking Power Average number of minutes between League team goals while on pitch	97	Club Strike Rate Average number of minutes between League goals scored by club	95

	PLAYER	LGE GOALS	POWER	STRIKE RATE
1	Steve Savidan	13	97	232 mins
2	Sebastien Roudet	5	87	437 mins
3	Laurent Dufresne	4	75	509 mins
4	Rudy Haddad	1	113	1586 mins

Steve Savidan

SQUAD APPEARANCES

Match	1	2	3	4	5	6	7	8	9	10	11	12	13	14	15	16	17	18	19	20	21	22	23	24	25	26	27	28	29	30	31	32	33	34	35	36	37	38
Venue	A	H	A	H	A	H	A	H	A	H	A	H	A	A	H	A	H	A	H	A	H	A	H	A	H	A	H	A	H	A	H	H	A	H	A	H	A	H
Competition	L	L	L	L	L	L	L	L	L	L	L	L	L	L	L	L	L	L	L	L	L	L	L	L	L	L	L	L	L	L	L	L	L	L	L	L	L	L
Result	D	D	L	W	L	W	L	W	L	W	L	L	L	L	W	L	D	L	W	W	D	L	L	W	L	L	D	W	D	W	D	D	L	D	L	W	D	L

Goalkeepers
Willy Grondin
Nicolas Penneteau

Defenders
Eric Chelle
Maxence Flachez
Ludovic Liron
Rudy Mater
Abdeslam Ouaddou
Guillaume Rippert
Orlando Silvestri
Dame Traore

Midfielders
Yacine Bezzaz
Freddy Bourgeois
Thomas Dossevi
Geoffrey Doumeng
Rudy Haddad
Khaled Kharroubi
Patrick Paauwe
Sebastien Roudet
Jose Saez
Mody Traore

Forwards
Florin Bratu
Laurent Dufresne
Eric Hassli
Sebastian Heitzmann
Da R do N Jeovanio
Steve Savidan

KEY: ■ On all match ◄◄ Subbed or sent off (Counting game) ►► Subbed on from bench (Counting Game) ►► Subbed on and then subbed or sent off (Counting Game) ☐ Not in 16
■ On bench ◄◄ Subbed or sent off (playing less than 70 minutes) ►► Subbed on (playing less than 70 minutes) ►► Subbed on and then subbed or sent off (playing less than 70 minutes)

FRANCE - VALENCIENNES

TROYES

Final Position: 18th

NICKNAME: TROYES   KEY: ☐ Won ☐ Drawn ☐ Lost   Attendance

					Attendance
1 frpr1	**Lens**	A L	0-1		32,131
2 frpr1	**Le Mans**	H D	2-2	Sanz 49, Bangoura 80	8,749
3 frpr1	**Nantes**	A D	1-1	Guillon 63 og	27,452
4 frpr1	**Toulouse**	H L	1-2	Nivet 67	8,976
5 frpr1	**Lyon**	A L	0-2		37,391
6 frpr1	**Nice**	H W	2-0	Gigliotti 52, Nivet 75 pen	8,809
7 frpr1	**Bordeaux**	A L	1-2	Gigliotti 9	18,623
8 frpr1	**Lorient**	A D	0-0		10,839
9 frpr1	**Lille**	H D	1-1	Nivet 40	18,272
10 frpr1	**Valenciennes**	A L	1-3	Sanz 40	13,378
11 frpr1	**St Etienne**	H W	3-1	Danic 55, Amzine 74, Gigliotti 85	13,071
12 frpr1	**Sochaux**	A L	0-1		16,740
13 frpr1	**AS Monaco**	H L	0-4		11,436
14 frpr1	**Nancy**	A L	0-1		17,168
15 frpr1	**Marseille**	H D	1-1	Lachuer 17	18,579
16 frpr1	**Sedan**	A W	2-1	Ba 39, Danic 70	14,291
17 frpr1	**Auxerre**	H D	3-3	Lachuer 18, Gigliotti 44, 69	16,891
18 frpr1	**Rennes**	A D	1-1	Gigliotti 5	21,896
19 frpr1	**Paris SG**	H D	1-1	Ba 74	12,046
20 frpr1	**Le Mans**	A L	0-2		8,525
21 frpr1	**Nantes**	H W	1-0	Sanz 86	10,511
22 frpr1	**Toulouse**	A D	1-1	Barbosa 6	15,046
23 frpr1	**Lyon**	H W	1-0	Nivet 90	14,009
24 frpr1	**Nice**	A L	0-3		11,711
25 frpr1	**Bordeaux**	H W	1-0	Gigliotti 66	10,401
26 frpr1	**Lorient**	H W	3-0	Danic 1, 70, Gigliotti 38	9,485
27 frpr1	**Lille**	A L	0-4		13,715
28 frpr1	**Valenciennes**	H L	1-3	Gigliotti 90	13,572
29 frpr1	**St Etienne**	A L	1-3	Nivet 42 pen	27,225
30 frpr1	**Sochaux**	H L	0-1		11,554
31 frpr1	**AS Monaco**	A D	0-0		9,311
32 frpr1	**Nancy**	H D	0-0		18,327
33 frpr1	**Marseille**	A L	1-2	Jaziri 79	47,708
34 frpr1	**Sedan**	H W	3-2	Barbosa 31, Matuidi 73, 82	11,877
35 frpr1	**Auxerre**	A L	0-1		10,731
36 frpr1	**Rennes**	H D	2-2	Paisley 18, Bangoura 26	11,247
37 frpr1	**Paris SG**	A L	1-2	Nivet 22	40,816
38 frpr1	**Lens**	H W	3-0	Danic 8, Matuidi 54, Lachuer 56	13,719

LEAGUE APPEARANCES, BOOKINGS AND CAPS

	AGE (on 01/07/07)	IN NAMED 18	APPEARANCES	COUNTING GAMES	MINUTES ON PITCH	YELLOW CARDS	RED CARDS	CAPS THIS SEASON	NATIONAL SIDE
Goalkeepers									
Kevin Grau	27	2	2	2	180	0	0	-	France
Ronan Le Crom	32	35	35	34	3108	1	0	-	France
Quentin Westberg	21	30	2	1	132	0	0	-	United States
Defenders									
Nabil Berkak	23	20	9	7	686	0	0	-	Morocco
Ibrahima Faye	27	31	31	29	2629	8	0	-	Senegal
Demetrius Ferreira	33	25	24	23	2097	7	1	-	Brazil
Auriol Guillaume	27	16	9	4	417	0	0	-	France
Blaise Kouassi	32	26	19	15	1518	3	1	-	Ivory Coast
Jean-Louis Montero	36	3	3	3	270	1	0	-	France
Gregory Paisley	30	32	31	31	2772	7	1	-	France
Gael Sanz	30	18	15	14	1301	5	0	-	France
Midfielders									
Gharib Amzine	34	32	23	16	1699	4	1	-	Morocco
Cedric Barbosa	31	32	30	24	2314	7	0	-	France
Eloge Enza Yamissi	24	31	29	16	1896	2	1	-	France
Yann Lachuer	35	38	37	27	2747	3	0	-	France
Jonathan Lacourt	20	28	16	4	737	2	0	-	France
Blaise Matuidi	20	34	34	30	2849	6	0	-	France
Benjamin Nivet	30	31	31	27	2583	5	0	-	France
Forwards									
Georges Ba	28	13	8	1	248	1	0	-	Ivory Coast
Ibrahima Bangoura	24	35	27	9	1383	2	0	-	Guinea
Sebastien Dallet	33	20	13	4	549	0	0	-	France
Gael Danic	25	37	32	21	2244	4	0	-	France
David Gigliotti	22	30	29	14	1792	7	1	-	France
Sebastien Grax	23	1	0	0	0	0	0	-	France
Ziad Jaziri	28	24	23	7	1086	5	0	-	Tunisia
Marek Saganowski	28	6	6	0	114	1	0	-	Poland
J Santos de A Weldon	26	5	3	1	94	0	0	-	Brazil

TEAM OF THE SEASON

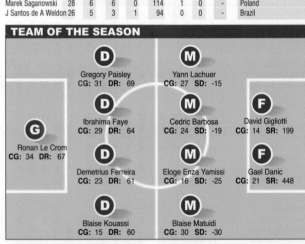

Ronan Le Crom G — CG: 34 DR: 67

Gregory Paisley D — CG: 31 DR: 69
Ibrahima Faye D — CG: 29 DR: 64
Demetrius Ferreira D — CG: 23 DR: 61
Blaise Kouassi D — CG: 15 DR: 60

Yann Lachuer M — CG: 27 SD: -15
Cedric Barbosa M — CG: 24 SD: -19
Eloge Enza Yamissi M — CG: 16 SD: -25
Blaise Matuidi M — CG: 30 SD: -30

David Gigliotti F — CG: 14 SR: 199
Gael Danic F — CG: 21 SR: 448

MONTHLY POINTS TALLY

AUGUST	2	17%
SEPTEMBER	4	33%
OCTOBER	4	44%
NOVEMBER	1	8%
DECEMBER	6	50%
JANUARY	4	44%
FEBRUARY	9	75%
MARCH	0	0%
APRIL	5	33%
MAY	4	33%

LEAGUE GOALS

	PLAYER	MINS	GOALS	S RATE
1	Gigliotti	1792	9	199
2	Nivet	2583	6	430
3	Danic	2244	5	448
4	Sanz	1301	3	433
5	Lachuer	2747	3	915
6	Matuidi	2849	3	949
7	Ba	248	2	124
8	Bangoura	1383	2	691
9	Barbosa	2314	2	1157
10	Jaziri	1086	1	1086
11	Amzine	1699	1	1699
12	Paisley	2772	1	2772
13	Perez	0	0	
	Other		0	
	TOTAL		**38**	

TOP POINT EARNERS

	PLAYER	GAMES	AV PTS
1	Gael Danic	21	1.24
2	Eloge Enza Yamissi	17	1.18
3	Gharib Amzine	17	1.18
4	Yann Lachuer	27	1.11
5	Gregory Paisley	31	1.10
6	Ibrahima Faye	29	1.07
7	Ronan Le Crom	34	1.06
8	Cedric Barbosa	24	1.04
9	Blaise Matuidi	30	0.97
10	Benjamin Nivet	27	0.96
	CLUB AVERAGE:		**1.03**

DISCIPLINARY RECORDS

	PLAYER	YELLOW	RED	AVE
1	Ziad Jaziri	5	0	217
2	David Gigliotti	7	1	224
3	Gael Sanz	5	0	260
4	Demetrius Ferreira	7	1	262
5	Ibrahima Faye	8	0	328
6	Cedric Barbosa	7	0	330
7	Gharib Amzine	4	1	339
8	Gregory Paisley	7	1	346
9	Jonathan Lacourt	2	0	368
10	Blaise Kouassi	3	1	379
11	Blaise Matuidi	6	0	474
12	Benjamin Nivet	5	0	516
13	Gael Danic	4	0	561
	Other	8	1	
	TOTAL	**78**	**6**	

KEY GOALKEEPER

Ronan Le Crom

Goals Conceded in the League	46	Counting Games League games when player was on pitch for at least 70 minutes	34
Defensive Rating Ave number of mins between League goals conceded while on the pitch	67	Clean Sheets In League games when player was on pitch for at least 70 minutes	9

KEY PLAYERS - DEFENDERS

Gregory Paisley

Goals Conceded Number of League goals conceded while the player was on the pitch	40	Clean Sheets In League games when player was on pitch for at least 70 minutes	8
Defensive Rating Ave number of mins between League goals conceded while on the pitch	69	Club Defensive Rating Average number of mins between League goals conceded by the club this season	63

	PLAYER	CON LGE	CLEAN SHEETS	DEF RATE
1	Gregory Paisley	40	8	69 mins
2	Ibrahima Faye	41	7	64 mins
3	Demetrius Ferreira	34	4	61 mins
4	Blaise Kouassi	25	4	60 mins

KEY PLAYERS - MIDFIELDERS

Yann Lachuer

Goals in the League	3	Contribution to Attacking Power Average number of minutes between League team goals while on pitch	80
Defensive Rating Average number of mins between League goals conceded while on the pitch	65	Scoring Difference Defensive Rating minus Contribution to Attacking Power	-15

	PLAYER	LGE GOALS	DEF RATE	POWER	SCORE DIFF
1	Yann Lachuer	3	65	80	-15 mins
2	Cedric Barbosa	2	60	79	-19 mins
3	Eloge Enza Yamissi	0	61	86	-25 mins
4	Blaise Matuidi	3	64	94	-30 mins

KEY PLAYERS - GOALSCORERS

David Gigliotti

Goals in the League	9	Player Strike Rate Average number of minutes between League goals scored by player	199
Contribution to Attacking Power Average number of minutes between League team goals while on pitch	89	Club Strike Rate Average number of minutes between League goals scored by club	87

	PLAYER	LGE GOALS	POWER	STRIKE RATE
1	David Gigliotti	9	89	199 mins
2	Benjamin Nivet	6	95	430 mins
3	Gael Danic	5	83	448 mins
4	Yann Lachuer	3	80	915 mins

David Gigliotti and Yann Lachuer

SQUAD APPEARANCES

Match	1	2	3	4	5	6	7	8	9	10	11	12	13	14	15	16	17	18	19	20	21	22	23	24	25	26	27	28	29	30	31	32	33	34	35	36	37	38
Venue	A	H	A	H	A	H	A	A	H	A	H	A	H	A	H	A	H	A	H	A	H	A	H	A	H	H	A	H	A	H	A	H	A	H	A	H	A	H
Competition	L	L	L	L	L	L	L	L	L	L	L	L	L	L	L	L	L	L	L	L	L	L	L	L	L	L	L	L	L	L	L	L	L	L	L	L	L	L
Result	L	D	D	L	L	W	L	D	D	L	W	L	L	L	D	W	D	D	D	L	W	D	W	L	W	W	L	L	L	L	D	D	L	W	L	D	L	W

Goalkeepers
Kevin Grau
Ronan Le Crom
Quentin Westberg

Defenders
Nabil Berkak
Ibrahima Faye
Demetrius Ferreira
Auriol Guillaume
Blaise Kouassi
Jean-Louis Montero
Gregory Paisley
Gael Sanz

Midfielders
Gharib Amzine
Cedric Barbosa
Eloge Enza Yamissi
Yann Lachuer
Jonathan Lacourt
Blaise Matuidi
Benjamin Nivet

Forwards
Georges Ba
Ibrahima Bangoura
Sebastien Dallet
Gael Danic
David Gigliotti
Sebastien Grax
Ziad Jaziri
Marek Saganowski
J Santos de A Weldon

KEY: ■ On all match　◄◄ Subbed or sent off (Counting game)　►► Subbed on from bench (Counting Game)　►► Subbed on and then subbed or sent off (Counting Game)　□ Not in 16
■ On bench　◄◄ Subbed or sent off (playing less than 70 minutes)　►► Subbed on (playing less than 70 minutes)　►► Subbed on and then subbed or sent off (playing less than 70 minutes)

FRANCE - TROYES

SEDAN

Final Position: **19th**

NICKNAME: LES SANGLIERS   KEY: ☐ Won ☐ Drawn ☐ Lost   Attendance

1	frpr1	**Marseille**	H D	0-0		22,779
2	frpr1	**Nancy**	A L	1-3	Pujol 13	17,310
3	frpr1	**Sochaux**	H D	1-1	Lachor 87	11,227
4	frpr1	**AS Monaco**	A L	1-2	Boutabout 82	9,603
5	frpr1	**St Etienne**	H D	2-2	Noro 9, 47	12,542
6	frpr1	**Le Mans**	H L	1-2	Belhadj 77	9,774
7	frpr1	**Auxerre**	A D	2-2	Pujol 43, Marin 50	7,498
8	frpr1	**Rennes**	H W	1-0	Noro 39 pen	9,863
9	frpr1	**Paris SG**	A L	2-4	Lachor 19, Boutabout 90	36,329
10	frpr1	**Lens**	H D	2-2	Lemoigne 64, Mokake 90	12,639
11	frpr1	**Bordeaux**	A L	1-3	Belhadj 17	20,836
12	frpr1	**Nantes**	H D	1-1	Pujol 61	15,469
13	frpr1	**Toulouse**	A L	1-3	Boutabout 65	14,461
14	frpr1	**Lyon**	H L	0-1		21,025
15	frpr1	**Nice**	A D	2-2	Job 16, Pujol 87	9,028
16	frpr1	**Troyes**	H L	1-2	Pujol 72	14,291
17	frpr1	**Lorient**	A L	0-2		11,466
18	frpr1	**Lille**	H W	2-0	Pujol 28, Marin 31	12,105
19	frpr1	**Valenciennes**	A L	1-2	Job 68	13,766
20	frpr1	**Nancy**	H D	2-2	Marin 20 pen, Job 30	10,493
21	frpr1	**Sochaux**	A D	1-1	Job 21	9,903
22	frpr1	**AS Monaco**	H L	0-1		10,851
23	frpr1	**St Etienne**	A W	2-1	Job 47, Diatta 70 og	24,838
24	frpr1	**Le Mans**	A L	2-3	Job 38 pen, Ouadah 90	9,143
25	frpr1	**Auxerre**	H D	2-2	Sartre 19, Job 23	12,610
26	frpr1	**Rennes**	A W	2-0	Pujol 14, Boutabout 86	22,032
27	frpr1	**Paris SG**	H W	2-0	Landreau 7 og, Boutabout 73	15,851
28	frpr1	**Lens**	A D	1-1	Pujol 1	29,939
29	frpr1	**Bordeaux**	H D	1-1	Boutabout 46	16,994
30	frpr1	**Nantes**	A W	1-0	Ducourtioux 60	35,553
31	frpr1	**Toulouse**	H L	0-2		15,424
32	frpr1	**Lyon**	A L	0-1		37,539
33	frpr1	**Nice**	H D	1-1	Echouafni 90 og	18,200
34	frpr1	**Troyes**	A L	2-3	Lachor 54, Job 67	11,877
35	frpr1	**Lorient**	H W	3-1	Marin 45, Noro 74, Ciani 88 og	11,522
36	frpr1	**Lille**	A L	1-2	Pujol 12	14,027
37	frpr1	**Valenciennes**	H D	1-1	Job 63	14,812
38	frpr1	**Marseille**	A L	0-1		53,604

LEAGUE APPEARANCES, BOOKINGS AND CAPS

	AGE (on 01/07/07)	IN NAMED 18	APPEARANCES	COUNTING GAMES	MINUTES ON PITCH	YELLOW CARDS	RED CARDS	CAPS THIS SEASON	NATIONAL SIDE
Goalkeepers									
Patrick Regnault	33	30	29	29	2610	0	0	-	France
Stephane Trevisan	33	35	9	9	810	0	0	-	France
Defenders									
Nadjim Abdou	22	26	16	11	1133	4	0	-	France
Jean-Michel Badiane	24	31	19	11	1180	2	0	-	France
Nadir Belhadj	25	37	37	33	3080	2	0	-	Algeria
David Ducourtioux	29	37	37	36	3274	3	0	-	France
David Hamed	33	12	3	1	202	0	0	-	France
Jeremy Henin	29	21	20	20	1800	4	0	-	France
Yoann Lachor	31	37	30	27	2594	6	0	-	France
Romain Sartre	24	24	24	24	2122	2	0	-	France
Steven Thicot	20	8	3	1	190	0	0	-	France
Alledine Yahia	25	14	12	12	1066	0	0	-	Tunisia
Midfielders									
Morgan Amalfitano	22	31	31	25	2468	6	1	-	France
Christophe Bastien	31	11	3	0	99	1	1	-	France
Aliou Cisse	31	19	11	4	566	4	1	-	Senegal
Fabrice Jau	28	34	22	6	961	2	0	-	France
Jerome Lemoigne	24	13	11	7	755	2	0	-	France
Nicolas Marin	26	31	28	9	1685	5	0	-	France
Marcus Mokake	25	29	8	2	397	1	0	-	Cameroon
Stephane Noro	27	17	16	9	1042	3	0	-	France
Abdelnasser Ouadah	31	17	13	8	840	2	0	-	Algeria
Forwards									
Mansour Boutabout	28	37	36	17	2100	3	1	-	Algeria
Eyemen Henaini	23	5	4	0	65	0	0	-	France
Joseph-Desire Job	29	27	25	18	1926	3	0	-	Cameroon
Nicolas Maurice-Belay	22	31	30	19	1958	3	0	-	France
Gregory Pujol	27	36	36	23	2507	0	1	-	France

TEAM OF THE SEASON

D Alledine Yahia — CG: 12 DR: 82
D Romain Sartre — CG: 24 DR: 66
G Stephane Trevisan — CG: 9 DR: 90
D Nadir Belhadj — CG: 33 DR: 64
D David Ducourtioux — CG: 36 DR: 59
M Abdelnasser Ouadah — CG: 8 SD: 17
M Stephane Noro — CG: 9 SD: -15
M Morgan Amalfitano — CG: 25 SD: -24
M Nicolas Marin — CG: 9 SD: -29
F Joseph-Desire Job — CG: 18 SR: 214
F Gregory Pujol — CG: 23 SR: 278

MONTHLY POINTS TALLY

AUGUST		2	17%
SEPTEMBER		5	42%
OCTOBER		1	11%
NOVEMBER		2	17%
DECEMBER		3	25%
JANUARY		2	22%
FEBRUARY		7	58%
MARCH		5	56%
APRIL		4	27%
MAY		4	33%

LEAGUE GOALS

	PLAYER	MINS	GOALS	S RATE
1	Job	1926	9	214
2	Pujol	2507	9	278
3	Boutabout	2100	6	350
4	Noro	1042	4	260
5	Marin	1685	4	421
6	Lachor	2594	3	864
7	Belhadj	3080	2	1540
8	Mokake	397	1	397
9	Lemoigne	755	1	755
10	Ouadah	840	1	840
11	Sartre	2122	1	2122
12	Ducourtioux	3274	1	3274
13	Hamed	202	0	
	Other		0	
	TOTAL		**42**	

TOP POINT EARNERS

	PLAYER	GAMES	AV PTS
1	Alledine Yahia	12	1.25
2	Joseph-Desire Job	18	1.17
3	Mansour Boutabout	18	1.11
4	Nicolas Maurice-Belay	19	1.00
5	Gregory Pujol	24	1.00
6	Romain Sartre	24	1.00
7	Nadir Belhadj	33	0.97
8	Morgan Amalfitano	26	0.96
9	Yoann Lachor	27	0.96
10	David Ducourtioux	36	0.94
	CLUB AVERAGE:		**0.92**

DISCIPLINARY RECORDS

	PLAYER	YELLOW	RED	AVE
1	Aliou Cisse	4	1	113
2	Nadjim Abdou	4	0	283
3	Nicolas Marin	5	0	337
4	Stephane Noro	3	0	347
5	Morgan Amalfitano	6	1	352
6	Jerome Lemoigne	2	0	377
7	Abdel Ouadah	2	0	420
8	Yoann Lachor	6	0	432
9	Jeremy Henin	4	0	450
10	Fabrice Jau	2	0	480
11	Mans Boutabout	3	1	525
12	J-Michel Badiane	2	0	590
13	Joseph-Desire Job	3	0	642
	Other	10	1	
	TOTAL	**56**	**4**	

KEY GOALKEEPER

Stephane Trevisan

Goals Conceded in the League	9	Counting Games League games when player was on pitch for at least 70 minutes	9
Defensive Rating Ave number of mins between League goals conceded while on the pitch	90	Clean Sheets In League games when player was on pitch for at least 70 minutes	4

KEY PLAYERS - DEFENDERS

Alledine Yahia

Goals Conceded Number of League goals conceded while the player was on the pitch	13	Clean Sheets In League games when player was on pitch for at least 70 minutes	3
Defensive Rating Ave number of mins between League goals conceded while on the pitch	82	Club Defensive Rating Average number of mins between League goals conceded by the club this season	58

	PLAYER	CON LGE	CLEAN SHEETS	DEF RATE
1	Alledine Yahia	13	3	82 mins
2	Romain Sartre	32	4	66 mins
3	Nadir Belhadj	48	7	64 mins
4	David Ducourtioux	55	6	59 mins

KEY PLAYERS - MIDFIELDERS

Abdelnasser Ouadah

Goals in the League	1	Contribution to Attacking Power Average number of minutes between League team goals while on pitch	76
Defensive Rating Average number of mins between League goals conceded while on the pitch	93	Scoring Difference Defensive Rating minus Contribution to Attacking Power	17

	PLAYER	LGE GOALS	DEF RATE	POWER	SCORE DIFF
1	Abdelnasser Ouadah	1	93	76	17 mins
2	Stephane Noro	4	65	80	-15 mins
3	Morgan Amalfitano	0	58	82	-24 mins
4	Nicolas Marin	4	51	80	-29 mins

KEY PLAYERS - GOALSCORERS

Joseph-Desire Job

Goals in the League	9	Player Strike Rate Average number of minutes between League goals scored by player	214
Contribution to Attacking Power Average number of minutes between League team goals while on pitch	64	Club Strike Rate Average number of minutes between League goals scored by club	74

	PLAYER	LGE GOALS	POWER	STRIKE RATE
1	Joseph-Desire Job	9	64	214 mins
2	Stephane Noro	4	80	260 mins
3	Gregory Pujol	9	67	278 mins
4	Mansour Boutabout	6	77	350 mins

David Ducourtioux and Nicolas Marin

SQUAD APPEARANCES

Match	1	2	3	4	5	6	7	8	9	10	11	12	13	14	15	16	17	18	19	20	21	22	23	24	25	26	27	28	29	30	31	32	33	34	35	36	37	38
Venue	H	A	H	A	H	H	A	H	A	H	A	H	A	H	A	H	A	H	A	H	A	H	A	A	H	A	H	A	H	A	H	A	H	A	H	A	H	A
Competition	L	L	L	L	L	L	L	L	L	L	L	L	L	L	L	L	L	L	L	L	L	L	L	L	L	L	L	L	L	L	L	L	L	L	L	L	L	L
Result	D	L	D	L	D	L	D	W	L	D	L	D	L	L	D	L	L	W	L	D	D	L	W	D	L	W	W	D	D	W	L	L	D	L	W	L	D	L

Goalkeepers

Patrick Regnault

Stephane Trevisan

Defenders

Nadjim Abdou

Jean-Michel Badiane

Nadir Belhadj

David Ducourtioux

David Hamed

Jeremy Henin

Yoann Lachor

Romain Sartre

Steven Thicot

Alledine Yahia

Midfielders

Morgan Amalfitano

Christophe Bastien

Aliou Cisse

Fabrice Jau

Jerome Lemoigne

Nicolas Marin

Marcus Mokake

Stephane Noro

Abdelnasser Ouadah

Forwards

Mansour Boutabout

Eyemen Henaini

Joseph-Desire Job

Nicolas Maurice-Belay

Gregory Pujol

KEY: ■ On all match ◄◄ Subbed or sent off (Counting game) ►► Subbed on from bench (Counting Game) ►» Subbed on and then subbed or sent off (Counting Game) ☐ Not in 16
■ On bench ◄ Subbed or sent off (playing less than 70 minutes) ► Subbed on (playing less than 70 minutes) » Subbed on and then subbed or sent off (playing less than 70 minutes)

FRANCE - SEDAN

NANTES

Final Position: **20th**

NICKNAME: LES CANARIS   KEY: ☐ Won ☐ Drawn ☐ Lost   Attendance

1 frpr1	**Lyon**	H L	**1-3**	Boukhari 2	36,000
2 frpr1	**Nice**	A D	**1-1**	Rossi 87	12,943
3 frpr1	**Troyes**	H D	**1-1**	Kouassi 4 og	27,452
4 frpr1	**Lorient**	A L	**1-3**	Da Rocha 12	14,718
5 frpr1	**Lille**	H D	**1-1**	Payet 67	24,708
6 frpr1	**Valenciennes**	A L	**0-1**		14,295
7 frpr1	**Marseille**	H W	**2-1**	Payet 37, Norbert 48	35,068
8 frpr1	**Auxerre**	A L	**0-1**		8,549
9 frpr1	**Sochaux**	H L	**0-2**		26,904
10 frpr1	**Nancy**	A L	**0-1**		18,225
11 frpr1	**AS Monaco**	H W	**1-0**	Rossi 26	28,745
12 frpr1	**Sedan**	A D	**1-1**	Payet 43	15,469
13 frpr1	**St Etienne**	H D	**2-2**	Cubilier 38, Boukhari 86	32,404
14 frpr1	**Lens**	A L	**0-2**		33,128
15 frpr1	**Paris SG**	H D	**1-1**	Da Rocha 75	32,104
16 frpr1	**Rennes**	A L	**0-2**		29,093
17 frpr1	**Le Mans**	H D	**0-0**		24,357
18 frpr1	**Bordeaux**	H D	**0-0**		26,490
19 frpr1	**Toulouse**	A W	**4-0**	Rossi 61, Cetto 67, Oliech 76, Diallo 85	16,812
20 frpr1	**Nice**	H W	**1-0**	Pieroni 90	29,000
21 frpr1	**Troyes**	A L	**0-1**		10,511
22 frpr1	**Lorient**	H L	**0-2**		29,860
23 frpr1	**Lille**	A D	**0-0**		14,750
24 frpr1	**Valenciennes**	H L	**2-5**	Keseru 78, Guillon 86	24,751
25 frpr1	**Marseille**	A D	**0-0**		49,507
26 frpr1	**Auxerre**	H D	**1-1**	Keseru 75	28,307
27 frpr1	**Sochaux**	A W	**2-1**	Payet 22, Keseru 50	14,664
28 frpr1	**Nancy**	H W	**2-1**	Diallo 34, Fae 73	32,626
29 frpr1	**AS Monaco**	A L	**1-2**	Da Rocha 13	9,493
30 frpr1	**Sedan**	H L	**0-1**		35,553
31 frpr1	**St Etienne**	A L	**1-2**	Diallo 28	33,606
32 frpr1	**Lens**	H D	**0-0**		33,193
33 frpr1	**Paris SG**	A L	**0-4**		42,744
34 frpr1	**Rennes**	H L	**0-2**		35,616
35 frpr1	**Le Mans**	A D	**1-1**	Keseru 90	13,303
36 frpr1	**Bordeaux**	A W	**1-0**	Oliech 78	27,432
37 frpr1	**Toulouse**	H D	**0-0**		30,000
38 frpr1	**Lyon**	A L	**1-3**	Diallo 51	40,149

LEAGUE APPEARANCES, BOOKINGS AND CAPS

	AGE (on 01/07/07)	IN NAMED 18	APPEARANCES	COUNTING GAMES	MINUTES ON PITCH	YELLOW CARDS	RED CARDS	CAPS THIS SEASON	NATIONAL SIDE
Goalkeepers									
Fabien Barthez	36	14	14	14	1240	0	0	-	France
Vincent Briant	21	13	8	8	720	0	0	-	France
Tony Heurtebis	32	29	7	6	560	0	0	-	France
Vladimir Stojkovic	23	12	10	10	900	0	0	9	Serbia
Defenders									
Mauro Cetto	25	30	29	28	2571	7	2	-	Argentina
Eric Cubilier	28	20	19	15	1598	3	0	-	France
Kevin Das Neves	21	15	9	6	596	3	0	-	France
Karim El Mourabet	20	17	7	4	446	1	0	-	France
Loic Guillon	25	36	26	20	1982	4	0	-	France
Soilyho Mete	19	3	1	0	23	0	0	-	France
Jean-Jacques Pierre	24	26	25	25	2238	4	0	-	Haiti
Nicolas Savinaud	31	28	20	11	1232	1	0	-	France
Franck Signorio	25	30	27	21	2212	4	0	-	France
Midfielders									
Bocundji Ca	20	21	9	6	639	2	0	-	Guinea-Bissau
Aurelien Capoue	25	13	10	5	511	1	0	-	France
Frederic Da Rocha	32	33	31	23	2270	3	0	-	France
Milos Dimitrijevic	23	22	16	6	813	1	0	-	Serbia
Emerse Fae	23	24	24	22	2077	5	0	2	Ivory Coast
Guillaume Norbert	26	24	19	11	1337	3	0	-	France
Alioum Saidou	29	34	33	30	2785	9	0	-	Cameroon
William Vainqueur	18	11	9	3	482	1	0	-	France
Christian Wilhelmsson	27	14	13	8	837	2	0	8	Sweden
Jaouad Zairi	25	10	8	4	432	0	0	-	Morocco
Forwards									
Nourdine Boukhari	27	12	9	1	355	1	0	-	Morocco
Mamadou Diallo	25	33	31	20	2127	4	0	-	Mali
Claudiu Andrei Keseru	20	26	22	8	1139	1	0	-	Romania
Dennis Oliech	22	26	23	5	965	2	0	-	Kenya
Dimitri Payet	20	30	30	23	2139	4	0	-	France
Luigi Pieroni	26	17	14	6	862	2	0	6	Belgium
Julio Hernan Rossi	30	29	24	11	1390	4	1	-	Argentina

TEAM OF THE SEASON

G — Fabien Barthez CG: 14 DR: 56

D — Jean-Jacques Pierre CG: 25 DR: 86
D — Mauro Cetto CG: 28 DR: 73
D — Eric Cubilier CG: 15 DR: 69
D — Loic Guillon CG: 20 DR: 68

M — Emerse Fae CG: 22 SD: -11
M — Alioum Saidou CG: 30 SD: -42
M — Frederic Da Rocha CG: 23 SD: -51
M — Guillaume Norbert CG: 11 SD: -85

F — Dimitri Payet CG: 23 SR: 534
F — Mamadou Diallo CG: 20 SR: 531

MONTHLY POINTS TALLY

AUGUST		2	17%
SEPTEMBER		4	44%
OCTOBER		3	25%
NOVEMBER		3	25%
DECEMBER		5	42%
JANUARY		3	33%
FEBRUARY		3	25%
MARCH		6	67%
APRIL		1	7%
MAY		5	42%

LEAGUE GOALS

	PLAYER	MINS	GOALS	S RATE
1	Keseru	1139	4	284
2	Diallo	2127	4	531
3	Payet	2139	4	534
4	Rossi	1390	3	463
5	Da Rocha	2270	3	756
6	Boukhari	355	2	177
7	Oliech	965	2	482
8	Pieroni	862	1	862
9	Norbert	1337	1	1337
10	Cubilier	1598	1	1598
11	Guillon	1982	1	1982
12	Fae	2077	1	2077
13	Cetto	2571	1	2571
	Other		0	
	TOTAL		**28**	

TOP POINT EARNERS

	PLAYER	GAMES	AV PTS
1	Emerse Fae	22	1.23
2	Dimitri Payet	23	1.17
3	Loic Guillon	20	1.15
4	Jean-Jacques Pierre	25	1.12
5	Alioum Saidou	30	1.07
6	Mauro Cetto	29	1.03
7	Mamadou Diallo	20	0.95
8	Frederic Da Rocha	23	0.91
9	Fabien Barthez	14	0.86
10	Julio Hernan Rossi	12	0.83
	CLUB AVERAGE:		**0.89**

DISCIPLINARY RECORDS

	PLAYER	YELLOW	RED	AVE
1	Kevin Das Neves	3	0	198
2	Julio Hernan Rossi	4	1	278
3	Mauro Cetto	7	2	285
4	Alioum Saidou	9	0	309
5	Bocundji Ca	2	0	319
6	Emerse Fae	5	0	415
7	C Wilhelmsson	2	0	418
8	Luigi Pieroni	2	0	431
9	Guillaume Norbert	3	0	445
10	Dennis Oliech	2	0	482
11	William Vainqueur	1	0	482
12	Loic Guillon	1	0	495
13	Aurelien Capoue	1	0	511
	Other	25	0	
	TOTAL	**70**	**3**	

KEY GOALKEEPER

Fabien Barthez

Goals Conceded in the League	22	Counting Games League games when player was on pitch for at least 70 minutes	14
Defensive Rating Ave number of mins between League goals conceded while on the pitch	56	Clean Sheets In League games when player was on pitch for at least 70 minutes	3

KEY PLAYERS - DEFENDERS

Jean-Jacques Pierre

Goals Conceded Number of League goals conceded while the player was on the pitch	26	Clean Sheets In League games when player was on pitch for at least 70 minutes	9
Defensive Rating Ave number of mins between League goals conceded while on the pitch	86	Club Defensive Rating Average number of mins between League goals conceded by the club this season	69

	PLAYER	CON LGE	CLEAN SHEETS	DEF RATE
1	Jean-Jacques Pierre	26	9	86 mins
2	Mauro Cetto	35	10	73 mins
3	Eric Cubilier	23	3	69 mins
4	Loic Guillon	29	5	68 mins

KEY PLAYERS - MIDFIELDERS

Emerse Fae

Goals in the League	1	Contribution to Attacking Power Average number of minutes between League team goals while on pitch	90
Defensive Rating Average number of mins between League goals conceded while on the pitch	79	Scoring Difference Defensive Rating minus Contribution to Attacking Power	-11

	PLAYER	LGE GOALS	DEF RATE	POWER	SCORE DIFF
1	Emerse Fae	1	79	90	-11 mins
2	Alioum Saidou	0	69	111	-42 mins
3	Frederic Da Rocha	3	68	119	-51 mins
4	Guillaume Norbert	1	63	148	-85 mins

KEY PLAYERS - GOALSCORERS

Julio Hernan Rossi

Goals in the League	3	Player Strike Rate Average number of minutes between League goals scored by player	463
Contribution to Attacking Power Average number of minutes between League team goals while on pitch	115	Club Strike Rate Average number of minutes between League goals scored by club	117

	PLAYER	LGE GOALS	POWER	STRIKE RATE
1	Julio Hernan Rossi	3	115	463 mins
2	Mamadou Diallo	4	106	531 mins
3	Dimitri Payet	4	101	534 mins
4	Frederic Da Rocha	3	119	756 mins

Fabien Barthez and Loic Guillon

SQUAD APPEARANCES

Match	1 2 3 4 5	6 7 8 9 10	11 12 13 14 15	16 17 18 19 20	21 22 23 24 25	26 27 28 29 30	31 32 33 34 35	36 37 38
Venue	H A H A H	A H A H A	H A H A H	A H H A H	A H A H A	H A H A H	A H A H A	A H A
Competition	L L L L L	L L L L L	L L L L L	L L L L L	L L L L L	L L L L L	L L L L L	L L L
Result	L D D L D	L W L L L	W D D L D	L D D W W	L L D L D	D W W L L	L D L L D	W D L

Goalkeepers
Fabien Barthez
Vincent Briant
Tony Heurtebis
Vladimir Stojkovic

Defenders
Mauro Cetto
Eric Cubilier
Kevin Das Neves
Karim El Mourabet
Loic Guillon
Soilyho Mete
Jean-Jacques Pierre
Nicolas Savinaud
Franck Signorio

Midfielders
Bocundji Ca
Aurelien Capoue
Frederic Da Rocha
Milos Dimitrijevic
Emerse Fae
Guillaume Norbert
Alioum Saidou
William Vainqueur
Christian Wilhelmsson
Jaouad Zairi

Forwards
Nourdine Boukhari
Mamadou Diallo
Claudiu Andrei Keseru
Dennis Oliech
Dimitri Payet
Luigi Pieroni
Julio Hernan Rossi

KEY: ■ On all match ◄◄ Subbed or sent off (Counting game) ►► Subbed on from bench (Counting Game) ►► Subbed on and then subbed or sent off (Counting Game) ☐ Not in 16
■ On bench ◄◄ Subbed or sent off (playing less than 70 minutes) ►► Subbed on (playing less than 70 minutes) ►► Subbed on and then subbed or sent off (playing less than 70 minutes)

FRANCE - NANTES

CHAMPIONS LEAGUE ROUND-UP

Football was not just on the back pages last season after the Serie A match fixing scandal and police action in and outside grounds at Champions League games.

Uefa found itself thwarted by the courts in its wish to exclude from the Champions League, those sides penalised for match fixing. One of the clubs involved, AC Milan, were reinstated and went on to win the entire competition; all had their sentences commuted. Eventually, Fiorentina were deducted 15 points; AC Milan were deducted 8 points; Lazio were deducted 3 points and Reggina lost 11 points.

The competition also suffered from crowd trouble, often involving British fans - but not always correctly interpreted by the Police. Man United fans suffered tear gas and truncheon-wielding police whilst playing Lille in Lens. Missiles were thrown when United visited Roma following a warning to beware of the Italian club's notorious 'Ultras'.

Spurs fans complained of over-reaction by Spanish police in Seville in the Uefa Cup. Finally Uefa's show-piece occasion was marred by ticketing complaints before the game and forgeries at the barrier. Fans with legitimate tickets missed the game; others with forgeries got in at the Greek national stadium which lacked basic turnstiles.

A Liverpool supporter argues his case with Greek police

CLUB STRIKE FORCE

	CLUB	GOALS	CSR
1	Real Madrid	18	40
2	Man Utd	23	46
3	Barcelona	14	51
4	Valencia	19	52
5	Bayern Munich	16	56
6	AC Milan	23	58
7	Lyon	12	60
8	Liverpool	22	61
9	Chelsea	17	63
10	AEK Athens	11	65
11	Benfica	11	65
12	Porto	11	65
13	Steaua Bucharest	11	65
14	Roma	13	69
15	Arsenal	13	69
16	Shakhtar Donetsk	9	70
17	Spartak Moscow	9	70
18	W Bremen	7	77
19	Anderlecht	7	77
20	Galatasaray	8	90
21	Hamburg	8	90
22	Dinamo Kiev	7	90
23	Bordeaux	6	90
24	Celtic	8	90
25	Olympiakos	6	90
26	FC Copenhagen	8	90
27	Lille	9	90
28	Inter Milan	7	102
29	CSKA Moscow	6	105
30	PSV Eindhoven	8	112
31	Levski Sofia	5	144
32	Sp Lisbon	3	180

Real Madrid's Raul and Ruud van Nistelrooy

1 Real Madrid	
Goals in the Champions League	18
Club Strike Rate (CSR) Average number of minutes between League goals scored by club	40

CLUB DEFENCE

	CLUB	CONCEDED	CS	CDR
1	Arsenal	6	4	150
2	Lyon	5	5	144
3	CSKA Moscow	5	5	126
4	AC Milan	11	8	122
5	Barcelona	6	4	120
6	Chelsea	9	4	120
7	Lille	7	3	115
8	Liverpool	12	7	112
9	W Bremen	5	3	108
10	Inter Milan	7	3	102
11	Porto	7	3	102
12	Valencia	11	4	90
13	Sp Lisbon	6	2	90
14	Man Utd	13	4	83
15	PSV Eindhoven	11	4	81
16	Bayern Munich	11	4	81
17	Benfica	9	3	80
18	Bordeaux	7	1	77
19	Roma	12	5	75
20	FC Copenhagen	10	3	72
21	Celtic	10	4	72
22	AEK Athens	10	3	72
23	Real Madrid	12	1	60
24	Spartak Moscow	12	0	52
25	Steaua Bucharest	14	0	51
26	Olympiakos	11	0	49
27	Anderlecht	11	0	49
28	Galatasaray	13	1	48
29	Shakhtar Donetsk	13	1	48
30	Hamburg	16	1	45
31	Levski Sofia	19	1	37
32	Dinamo Kiev	18	0	35

Arsenal's Kolo Toure and Philippe Senderos

1 Arsenal	
Goals conceded in the Champions League	6
Club Defensive Rate (CDR) Average number of minutes between goals conceded by club	150

CLUB DISCIPLINARY RECORD

Razvan Rat outmuscles Valencia's David Villa

	CLUB	Y	R	TOT	CA
1	Shakhtar Donetsk	21	2	23	27
2	Steaua Bucharest	23	0	23	31
3	Lille	23	1	24	33
4	Olympiakos	15	0	15	36
5	Roma	24	0	24	37
6	Hamburg	16	3	19	37
7	Bayern Munich	20	2	22	40
8	Inter Milan	15	3	18	40
9	Sp Lisbon	13	0	13	41
10	Lyon	17	0	17	42
11	Celtic	17	0	17	42
12	CSKA Moscow	15	0	15	42
13	Dinamo Kiev	14	1	15	42
14	Galatasaray	13	2	15	42
15	Valencia	23	0	23	43
16	Chelsea	24	0	24	45
17	AEK Athens	16	0	16	45
18	W Bremen	12	0	12	45
19	Anderlecht	11	1	12	45
20	Man Utd	21	1	22	49
21	Real Madrid	12	1	13	55
22	Levski Sofia	12	1	13	55
23	Liverpool	24	0	24	56
24	Arsenal	16	0	16	56
25	Spartak Moscow	11	0	11	57
26	Barcelona	12	0	12	60
27	Benfica	12	0	12	60
28	Porto	12	0	12	60
29	FC Copenhagen	11	0	11	65
30	AC Milan	19	1	20	67
31	Bordeaux	7	1	8	67
32	PSV Eindhoven	9	2	11	81

1 Shakhtar Donetsk	
Yellow	21
Red	2
Cards Average Average number of minutes between a card being shown of either colour	27

PLAYER DISCIPLINARY RECORD

	PLAYER	CLUB	Y	R	TOT	Avge
1	D Pizarro	Roma	5	0	5	100
2	D Albelda	Valencia	5	0	5	108
3	M van Bommel	B Munich	4	1	5	135
4	E Tavlaridis	Lille	3	1	4	138
5	R Ayala	Valencia	5	0	5	144
6	M Sissoko	Liverpool	4	0	4	151
7	V Love	CSKA Mosc	3	0	3	156
8	T Henry	Arsenal	3	0	3	166
9	J Toulalan	Lyon	3	0	3	169
10	S Perrotta	Roma	4	0	4	172
11	Brandao	S Donetsk	3	0	3	175
12	S Ramos	Real Madrid	3	0	3	180
13	A Tymoschuk	S Donetsk	3	0	3	180
14	Z Ibrahimovic	Inter Milan	2	1	3	184
15	M Diarra	Real Madrid	2	1	3	196
16	J Cesar	AEK Athens	3	0	3	204
17	P Scholes	Man Utd	3	1	4	206
18	A Kader Keita	Lille	3	0	3	207
19	R Rocha	Benfica	3	0	3	210
20	F Malouda	Lyon	3	0	3	210
21	S Ghionea	S Bucharest	3	0	3	210
22	A Gilardino	AC Milan	3	0	3	215
23	Schweinsteiger	B Munich	2	1	3	221
24	Berezoutski	CSKA Mosc	2	0	2	227
25	Katsouranis	Benfica	3	0	3	232
26	K Miller	Celtic	2	0	2	234

1 David Pizarro

1 David Pizarro	
Yellow	5
Red	0
Cards Average Average number of minutes between a card being shown of either colour	100

CHART-TOPPING GOALSCORERS

1 Ruud van Nistelrooy

Goals in Chapions League	6
Contribution to Attacking Power (AP) Average number of minutes between League team goals while on pitch	40
Player Strike Rate (SR) Average number of minutes between League goals scored by player	96

	PLAYER	TEAM	G	AP	SR
1	van Nistelrooy	Real Madrid	6	40	96
2	Morientes	Valencia	7	42	98
3	Crouch	Liverpool	7	45	111
4	Raul	Real Madrid	5	37	120
5	Kaka	AC Milan	10	57	132
6	Inzaghi	AC Milan	6	62	136
7	Pizarro	B Munich	4	62	155
8	Villa	Valencia	5	52	157
9	Drogba	Chelsea	6	61	175
10	Dica	St Bucharest	4	64	177

CHART-TOPPING MIDFIELDERS

1 Rodrigo Taddei

Goals scored in the Champions League	2
Defensive Rating Av number of mins between goals conceded while on the pitch	234
Contribution to Attacking Power Average number of minutes between team goals while on pitch	64
Scoring Difference Defensive Rating minus Contribution to Attacking Power	170

	PLAYER	CLUB	G	DR	AP	SD
1	Rodrigo Taddei	Roma	2	234	64	170
2	Gennaro Gattuso	AC Milan	0	208	54	154
3	Max Tonetto	Roma	0	210	63	147
4	Gilberto Silva	Arsenal	1	185	74	111
5	Simone Perrotta	Roma	1	172	62	110
6	Florent Malouda	Lyon	2	152	57	100

CHART-TOPPING DEFENDERS

Habib Kolo Toure

Goals Conceded in the Competition The number of goals conceded while he was on the pitch	5
Clean Sheets In games when he played at least 70 mins	4
Defensive Rating Average number of minutes between goals conceded while on pitch	167
Club Defensive Rating Average mins between goals conceded by the club this season	150

	PLAYER	CLUB	Conc	CS	CDR	DR
1	Habib Kolo Toure	Arsenal	5	4	150	167
2	Cris	Lyon	4	5	144	157
3	Eric Abidal	Lyon	4	5	144	148
4	Steve Finnan	Liverpool	8	6	115	138
5	Nemanja Vidic	Man Utd	5	4	83	135
6	Paolo Maldini	AC Milan	6	4	125	132

CHART-TOPPING GOALKEEPERS

1 Jens Lehmann

Goals conceded in the Champions League	5
Counting Games Competition games when he played at least 70 minutes	8
Clean Sheets In games when he played at least 70 mins	3
Defensive Rating Average number of minutes between League goals conceded while on pitch	144

	PLAYER	CLUB	CG	Conc	CS	DR
1	Jens Lehmann	Arsenal	8	5	3	144
2	Jose Reina	Liverpool	14	9	7	143
3	Nelson Dida	AC Milan	13	9	7	131
4	Gregory Coupet	Lyon	7	5	4	126
5	Igor Akinfeev	CSKA Moscow	7	5	5	126

TEAM OF THE SEASON

LEHMANN	ARSENAL	M 1080 DR 216
FINNAN	LIVERPOOL	M 1107 DR 138
VIDIC	MAN UTD	M 675 DR 135
TOURE	ARSENAL	M 837 DR 167
CRIS	LYON	M 630 DR 157
TADDEI	ROMA	M 704 SD 170
GATTUSO	AC MILAN	M 1044 SD 154
GILBERTO	ARSENAL	M 741 SD 111
MALOUDA	LYON	M 630 SD 100
KAKA	AC MILAN	M 1322 SR 132
VAN NISTELROOY	REAL MADRID	M 581 SR 96

KEY: DR = Defensive Rate, SD = Scoring Difference AP = Attacking Power SR = Strike Rate, M = Minutes played in Champions League proper.

The Champions League Team of the Season shows a 4-4-2 of the best players in the competition based upon the selection criteria used for the chart-toppers. The players selected are taken from the lists for each 'last 16' club except that to get into the Team of the Season you must have played at least 500 minutes in the competition. The other restriction is that we are only allowing one player from each club in each position. So the maximum number of players one club can have in the divisional team is four.

• **The Champions League team's goalkeeper** is the player with the highest *Defensive Rating*

• **The Champions League team's defenders** are also tested by *Defensive Rating*, i.e. the average number of minutes between league goals conceded while on the pitch.

• **The Champions League team's midfield** are selected on their *Scoring Difference*, i.e.their *Defensive Rating* minus their *Contribution to Attacking Power* (average number of minutes between league goals scored while on the pitch. It takes no account of assists.

• **The Champions League team strikeforce** is made up of the striker with the highest Strike Rate (the average number of minutes per goals scored) together with the striker with the highest total goals in the competition, in this case Kaka.

LEADING PLAYER APPEARANCES

	PLAYER	GAMES	TIME		PLAYER	GAMES	TIME
1	Ricardo Kaka	15	1322	17	Frank Lampard	11	1019
2	Jose Reina	14	1290	18	Raul Albiol	11	970
3	Andrea Pirlo	14	1207	19	Steven Gerrard	12	968
4	Jamie Carragher	13	1200	20	Cristiano Ronaldo	11	957
5	Nelson Dida	13	1187	21	Michael Essien	10	930
6	Clarence Seedorf	14	1147	22	Dirk Kuyt	11	928
7	Steve Finnan	12	1107	23	Heurelho Gomes	10	900
8	Xabi Alonso	15	1104	24	Alexander Doni	10	900
9	Daniel Agger	12	1097	25	Santitiage Canizares	10	900
10	Edwin van der Sar	12	1080	26	Daniel Van Buyten	10	900
11	John Arne Riise	12	1071	27	Ricardo Carvalho	10	900
12	Marek Jankulovski	13	1061	28	Timmy Simons	10	900
13	Wayne Rooney	12	1060	29	Cesc Fabregas	10	897
14	Didier Drogba	12	1051	30	Michael Ballack	10	884
15	Gennaro Gattuso	13	1044				
16	Michael Carrick	12	1027				

Champions League Group A

GROUP A TABLE		P	W	D	L	F	A	DIF	PTS
	Chelsea	6	4	1	1	10	4	6	13
	Barcelona	6	3	2	1	12	4	8	11
	W Bremen	6	3	1	2	7	5	2	10
	Levski Sofia	6	0	0	6	1	17	-16	0

WERDER BREMEN

	PLAYER	POS	AGE	APP	MINS ON	GOALS	CARDS(Y/R)		HOME COUNTRY
1	Clemens Fritz	MID	26	6	540	0	1	0	Germany
2	Naldo	DEF	24	6	540	1	1	0	Brazil
3	Ribas Santos Diego	MID	22	6	540	1	1	0	Brazil
4	Torsten Frings	MID	30	6	540	1	2	0	Germany
5	Miroslav Klose	ATT	29	6	529	0	0	0	Germany
6	Per Mertesacker	DEF	22	5	450	1	0	0	Germany
7	Tim Wiese	GK	25	5	450	0	0	0	Germany
8	Pierre Nlend Wome	DEF	28	5	388	0	2	0	Cameroon
9	Tim Borowski	MID	27	4	360	0	1	0	Germany
10	Aaron Hunt	ATT	20	5	275	0	0	0	Germany
11	Frank Baumann	MID	31	3	252	1	3	0	Germany
12	Miguel Hugo Almeida	ATT	23	4	190	0	0	0	Portugal
13	Christian Schulz	DEF	24	3	184	0	0	0	Germany
14	Daniel Jensen	MID	28	2	168	0	0	0	Denmark
15	Jurica Vranjes	MID	27	2	162	0	1	0	Croatia
16	Ivan Klasnic	ATT	27	6	149	0	0	0	Croatia
17	Petri Pasanen	DEF	26	2	96	0	0	0	Finland
18	Andreas Reinke	GK	46	1	90	0	0	0	Germany
19	Leon Andreasen	DEF	24	2	31	0	0	0	Denmark
20	Mohammed Zidan	ATT	25	1	5	0	0	0	Egypt
21	Patrick Owomoyela	DEF	27	1	1	0	0	0	Germany

LEVSKI SOFIA

	PLAYER	POS	AGE	APP	MINS ON	GOALS	CARDS(Y/R)		HOME COUNTRY
1	Elin Topuzakov	DEF	30	8	720	0	1	0	Bulgaria
2	Richard Eromoigbe	MID	23	8	720	0	0	0	Nigeria
3	Cedric Bardon	ATT	30	8	700	2	0	0	France
4	Igor Tomasic	DEF	30	8	686	0	2	0	Bulgaria
5	Daniel Borimirov	MID	37	8	680	0	2	0	Bulgaria
6	Hristo Yovov	ATT	29	8	648	0	0	0	Bulgaria
7	Stanislav Angelov	DEF	29	7	597	0	1	0	Bulgaria
8	Zhivko Milanov	DEF	22	7	593	0	2	0	Bulgaria
9	Georgi Petkov	GK	31	6	540	0	1	0	Bulgaria
10	Dimitar Telkiyski	MID	30	7	463	1	0	0	Bulgaria
11	Lucio Wagner	MID	31	4	359	0	1	1	Bulgaria
12	Valeri Domovchiyski	ATT	21	5	313	1	0	0	Bulgaria
13	Lucio	DEF	31	2	180	0	1	0	Bulgaria
14	Emil Angelov	ATT	26	3	140	0	0	0	Bulgaria
15	Mitrev	GK	20	2	135	0	0	0	Bulgaria
16	Georgi Ivanov	ATT	30	4	117	0	1	0	Bulgaria
17	Nikolay Dimitrov	ATT	19	3	92	0	0	0	Bulgaria
18	Miroslav Ivanov	MID	25	2	48	0	0	0	Bulgaria
19	Milan Koprivarov	MID	23	3	45	0	0	0	Bulgaria
20	Nikolay Mihaylov	GK	19	1	45	0	0	0	Bulgaria
21	Mariyan Ognyanov	ATT	18	2	38	1	0	0	Bulgaria
22	Lachezar Baltanov	ATT	18	1	32	0	0	0	Bulgaria
23	Veselin Minev	DEF	26	1	28	0	0	0	Bulgaria

QUALIFYING - second round — L1 L2

Levski — 4-0 Sioni — 2-0 2-0

QUALIFYING - third round

Levski — 4-2 Chievo — 2-0 2-2

Barcelona 5 Levski Sofia 0
Iniesta 7, Giuly 39
Puyol 49, Eto'o 58,
Ronaldinho 90
91,326

Ronaldinho gains the final goal of five as Levski Sofia are shown to be out of their class in this company. Barca share their goals around with even skipper Puyol netting after a Ronaldinho free kick is fumbled

Chelsea 2 W Bremen 0
Essien 24
Ballack 68 pen
32,135

Levski Sofia 1 Chelsea 3
Ognyanov 89
Drogba 39, 52, 68
27,950

W Bremen 1 Barcelona 1
Puyol 56 og
Messi 89
41,256

Chelsea 1 Barcelona 0
Drogba 46
45,999

W Bremen 2 Levski Sofia 0
Naldo 45, Diego 73
36,246

Barcelona 2 Chelsea 2
Deco 3,
Gudjohnsen 58
Lampard 52
Drogba 90
98,000

A thriller as Deco's early strike is answered by an impossible chip from Lampard and after former Blue Gudjohnsen slots Barca in front, Drogba levels at the last

Levski Sofia 0 W Bremen 3
Mihaylov 33 og
Baumann 35
Frings 37
36,000

Levski Sofia 0 Barcelona 2
Giuly 5, Iniesta 65
43,340

W Bremen 1 Chelsea 0
Mertesacker 26
40,000

Barcelona 2 W Bremen 0
Ronaldinho 13
Gudjohnsen 18
98,787

Chelsea 2 Levski Sofia 0
Shevchenko 27
Wright-Phillips 83
33,358

Three of the top teams in Europe contest Group A. The intense rivalry between Chelsea and Barca is renewed with Mourinho's side winning in London after a turn and shot from Didier Drogba. They snatch a last-minute draw in Spain. A goal from central defender Per Mertesacker beats Chelsea to keep Bremen in touch until the final game.

Champions League Group B

GROUP B TABLE		P	W	D	L	F	A	DIF	PTS
	Bayern Munich	6	3	3	0	10	3	7	12
	Inter Milan	6	3	1	2	5	5	0	10
	Spartak Moscow	6	1	2	3	7	11	-4	5
	Sporting Lisbon	6	1	2	3	3	6	-3	5

SPARTAK MOSCOW

	PLAYER	POS	AGE	APP	MINS ON	GOALS	CARDS(Y/R)		HOME COUNTRY
1	Roman Pavlyuchenko	ATT	25	7	602	3	0	0	Russia
2	Radoslav Kovac	DEF	27	7	601	1	0	0	Czech Republic
3	Santos Mozart	MID	27	7	574	1	2	0	Brazil
4	Martin Jiranek	DEF	28	7	570	0	1	0	Czech Republic
5	Vladimir Bystrov	MID	23	7	562	0	2	0	Russia
6	Martin Stranzl	DEF	27	6	540	0	1	0	Austria
7	Yegor Titov	MID	31	6	540	0	0	0	Russia
8	Voizech Kovalewski	GK	30	5	450	0	0	0	Poland
9	Antonio Geder	DEF	29	5	446	0	1	0	Brazil
10	Roman Shishkin	DEF	20	5	420	0	0	0	Russia
11	Clemente Rodriguez	DEF	25	4	315	0	1	0	Argentina
12	Denis Boyarintsev	MID	29	4	297	2	0	0	Russia
13	Serghei Covalciuc	MID	25	3	201	0	0	0	Moldova
14	Maksym Kalinichenko	MID	28	4	185	2	2	0	Ukraine
15	Shiskin	DEF	20	2	180	0	0	0	Russia
16	Zuev	GK	26	2	180	0	1	0	Russia
17	Fernando Cavenaghi	ATT	23	2	131	0	0	0	Argentina
18	Quincy Owusu-Abeyie	ATT	21	3	73	0	0	0	Holland
19	Nikita Bazhenov	ATT	22	2	33	0	0	0	Russia
20	Dmitri Torbinskiy	MID	23	1	14	0	0	0	Russia
21	Aleksei Rebko	MID	21	1	11	0	0	0	Russia
22	Rebko	MID	21	1	4	0	0	0	Russia
23	Artem Dzyuba	DEF	18	1	1	0	0	0	Russia

SPORTING LISBON

	PLAYER	POS	AGE	APP	MINS ON	GOALS	CARDS(Y/R)		HOME COUNTRY
1	Alexandre Ricardo	GK	31	6	540	0	0	0	Portugal
2	Joao Moutinho	MID	20	6	540	0	1	0	Portugal
3	Tonel	DEF	27	6	507	0	1	0	Portugal
4	Rodrigo Alvaro Tello	MID	27	6	461	0	1	0	Chile
5	Liedson da Silva Muniz	ATT	29	5	450	0	3	0	Brazil
6	Nani	MID	20	6	424	1	1	0	Portugal
7	Daniel Quesnel Yannick	MID	21	5	383	0	0	0	Portugal
8	Veloso	MID	21	5	376	0	2	0	Portugal
9	Marco Caneira	DEF	28	5	374	1	0	0	Portugal
10	Anderson Correa Polga	DEF	28	3	270	0	0	0	Brazil
11	Polga	MID	28	3	270	0	1	0	Brazil
12	Carlos Humberto Paredes	MID	30	5	254	0	1	0	Paraguay
13	Barbosa Alecsandro	ATT	26	6	252	0	0	0	Brazil
14	Miguel Custodio	MID	24	2	180	0	2	0	Portugal
15	Carlos Martins	MID	25	3	125	0	0	0	Portugal
16	Fernando Pereira Ferreira	DEF	28	2	102	0	0	0	Portugal
17	Carlos Bueno	ATT	27	2	101	1	0	0	Uruguay
18	Pontus Farnerud	MID	27	2	95	0	0	0	Sweden
19	Ronny Heberson	DEF	21	1	90	0	0	0	Brazil
20	Miguel Garcia	DEF	24	2	72	0	0	0	Portugal
21	Leandro Romagnoli	MID	26	1	65	0	0	0	Argentina
22	Joao Alves	MID	26	1	9	0	0	0	Portugal

QUALIFYING - second round   **L1 L2**

Sheriff   1-1 Sp Moscow   1-1   0-0
Moscow win on away goals

QUALIFYING - third round

Liberec   1-2 Spartak Moskva   0-0   1-2

Bayern Munich   **4 Spartak Moscow**   **0**
Pizarro 48
Santa Cruz 51
Schweinsteiger 71
Salihamidzic 84   66,000

Bastian Schweinsteiger is congratulated by Owen Hargreaves after scoring the third goal in Bayern's demolition of Spartak Moscow with Mark van Bommel dominant in midfield for his new side

Sp Lisbon   **1 Inter Milan**   **0**
Caneira 64   30,000

Inter Milan   **0 Bayern Munich**   **2**
     Pizarro 81, Podolski 90
      79,000

Spartak Moscow   **1 Sp Lisbon**   **1**
Boyarintsev 4   Nani 59
      75,101

Inter Milan   **2 Spartak Moscow**   **1**
Cruz 2, 9   Pavlyuchenko 54
      40,000

Julio Cruz; twice on target for Inter

Sp Lisbon   **0 Bayern Munich**   **1**
     Schweinsteiger 19
      45,000

Bayern Munich   **0 Sp Lisbon**   **0**
      66,000

Spartak Moscow   **0 Inter Milan**   **1**
     Cruz 2
      60,000

Inter Milan   **1 Sp Lisbon**   **0**
Crespo 36   40,000

Spartak Moscow   **2 Bayern Munich**   **2**
Kalinichenko 16   Pizarro 22, 39
Kovac 72   25,000

Bayern Munich   **1 Inter Milan**   **1**
Makaay 62   Vieira 90
      66,000

Sp Lisbon   **1 Spartak Moscow**   **3**
Bueno 31   Pavlyuchenko 7
     Kalinichenko 16
     Boyarintsev 89
      37,000

European giants Inter Milan and Bayern Munich dominate Group B. Bayern begin with South American duo Claudio Pizarro and Roque Santa Cruz launching a 4-0 demolition of Spartak Moscow. Inter lose to a volley by Sporting's Marco Caneira and Bayern at home but still progress easily. Spartak's 3-1 win in Lisbon snaps up the Uefa spot.

Champions League Group C

GROUP C TABLE		P	W	D	L	F	A	DIF	PTS
	Liverpool	6	4	1	1	11	5	6	13
	PSV	6	3	1	2	6	6	0	10
	Bordeaux	6	2	1	3	6	7	-1	7
	Galatasaray	6	1	1	4	7	12	-5	4

BORDEAUX

	PLAYER	POS	AGE	APP	MINS ON	GOALS	CARDS(Y/R)	HOME COUNTRY
1	Ulrich Rame	GK	34	6	540	0	1 0	France
2	Julien Faubert	DEF	23	6	478	2	1 0	France
3	David Jemmali	DEF	32	5	448	0	0 0	France
4	Geraldo Wendel	MID	25	5	427	0	1 0	Brazil
5	Jean-Claude Darcheville	ATT	31	6	416	1	1 0	France
6	Rio Mavuba	MID	23	5	377	0	0 0	France
7	Johan Micoud	MID	33	5	376	0	0 0	France
8	Franck Jurietti	DEF	32	4	343	0	1 0	France
9	Pierre Ducasse	MID	20	4	293	0	1 0	France
10	Florian Marange	DEF	21	3	270	0	0 0	France
11	Joseph Enakarhire	DEF	24	3	270	0	1 0	Nigeria
12	Lilian Laslandes	ATT	35	5	250	1	0 0	France
13	Fernando Menegazzo	MID	26	3	246	0	0 1	Brazil
14	Carlos Henrique	DEF	24	2	180	0	0 0	Brazil
15	Gerald Cid	DEF	24	2	180	0	0 0	France
16	Marc Planus	DEF	25	2	180	0	0 0	France
17	Marouane Chamakh	ATT	23	4	167	0	0 0	Morocco
18	Alejandro Alonso	MID	25	2	152	1	0 0	Argentina
19	Edixon Perea	ATT	23	4	127	0	0 0	Colombia
20	Stephane Dalmat	MID	28	3	108	1	0 0	France
21	Gabriel Obertan	ATT	18	2	88	0	0 0	France

GALATASARAY

	PLAYER	POS	AGE	APP	MINS ON	GOALS	CARDS(Y/R)	HOME COUNTRY
1	Faryd Mondragon	GK	36	7	630	0	0 0	Colombia
2	Rigobert Song	DEF	31	6	540	0	0 0	Cameroon
3	Stjepan Tomas	DEF	31	6	487	0	1 1	Croatia
4	Sasa Ilic	MID	29	7	464	2	0 0	Serbia
5	Akman Ayhan	MID	30	5	450	0	2 0	Turkey
6	Junichi Inamoto	MID	27	5	450	1	2 0	Japan
7	Turan Arda	MID	20	6	409	0	1 1	Turkey
8	Umit Karan	ATT	30	6	387	2	0 0	Turkey
9	Haspolati Cihan	MID	27	7	377	0	1 0	Turkey
10	Gokhan Hasan Sas	MID	30	5	368	1	3 0	Turkey
11	Sabri	MID	22	4	360	0	1 0	Turkey
12	Orhan Ak	DEF	27	4	345	0	1 0	Turkey
13	Sarioglu Sabri	MID	22	3	270	0	0 0	Turkey
14	Hakan Sukur	ATT	35	5	267	0	0 0	Turkey
15	Buruk Okan	MID	33	2	180	1	1 0	Turkey
16	Ates Necati	ATT	27	4	176	1	0 0	Turkey
17	Tolga Seyhan	MID	30	2	135	0	0 0	Turkey
18	Penbe Ergun	MID	35	2	112	0	0 0	Turkey
19	Oztorun Ferhat	DEF	20	1	90	0	0 0	Turkey
20	Topal	MID	21	3	89	0	0 0	Turkey
21	Ucar Ugur	DEF	20	2	82	0	0 0	Turkey
22	Marcelo Carrusca	MID	23	2	79	0	0 0	Argentina
23	Emre Asik	DEF	33	1	45	0	0 0	Turkey
24	Hasan Kabze	ATT	25	1	30	0	0 0	Turkey
25	Mehmet Guven	MID	19	1	16	0	0 0	Turkey
26	Ozcan Ozgurcan	ATT	19	1	7	0	0 0	Turkey

Galatasaray 0 **Bordeaux** 0
45,514

PSV Eindhoven 0 **Liverpool** 0
35,000

Bordeaux 0 **PSV Eindhoven** 1
Vayrynen 65
26,000

Liverpool 3 **Galatasaray** 2
Crouch 8, 52   Karan 59, 64
Luis Garcia 14   41,976

Crouch starts his impressive challenge to top the Champions League scoring charts with a brace against Galatasaray. But it needs another from Garcia and a brilliant save from Reina to keep out Hakan Sukar's late header for the Reds to claim all three points

Bordeaux 0 **Liverpool** 1
Crouch 58
29,963

Galatasaray 1 **PSV Eindhoven** 2
Ilic 19   Kromkamp 59
Kone 72
45,000

Liverpool 3 **Bordeaux** 0
Luis Garcia 23, 76
Gerrard 71   41,978

PSV Eindhoven 2 **Galatasaray** 0
Simons 59, Kone 84   35,000

PSV confirm qualification from Group C with a double over the Turks. They fight back from a goal down in Turkey with strikes from Jan Kromkamp and Arouna Kone in game three. In the return, Phillip Cocu's parried header is turned in by Timmy Simons (pictured) before Kone again adds a second

Bordeaux 3 **Galatasaray** 1
Alonso 22   Inamoto 73
Laslandes 47
Faubert 50   25,000

Liverpool 2 **PSV Eindhoven** 0
Gerrard 65, Crouch 88
41,948

Galatasaray 3 **Liverpool** 2
Necati 24, Okan 28,   Fowler 22, 90
Ilic 79   23,000

PSV Eindhoven 1 **Bordeaux** 3
Alex 87   Faubert 7, Dalmat 25
Darcheville 37
26,000

PSV and Liverpool draw their opening encounter in Eindhoven before both collecting three wins to take the top two places in Group C.
Once qualified, PSV relax and Julien Faubert begins Bordeaux's first half rout in Holland, which ends in a 1-3 win, to take the Uefa Cup spot. Galatasaray beat Liverpool to no avail.

Champions League Group D

GROUP D TABLE

	P	W	D	L	F	A	DIF	PTS
Valencia	6	4	1	1	12	6	6	13
Roma	6	3	1	2	8	4	4	10
Shakhtar Donetsk	6	1	3	2	6	11	-5	6
Olympiakos	6	0	3	3	6	11	-5	3

SHAKHTAR DONETSK

	PLAYER	POS	AGE	APP	MINS ON	GOALS	CARDS(Y/R)		HOME COUNTRY
1	Razvan Rat	DEF	26	7	629	0	1	1	Romania
2	Anatoliy Tymoschuk	MID	28	6	540	0	3	0	Ukraine
3	Brandao	ATT	27	7	526	0	3	0	Brazil
4	Fernandinho	MID	22	6	518	2	1	0	Brazil
5	Ciprian Marica	ATT	21	7	513	4	2	0	Romania
6	F Da Silva Matuzalem	MID	27	6	507	1	2	0	Brazil
7	Darijo Srna	MID	25	5	450	0	1	0	Croatia
8	Tomas Hubschman	DEF	25	5	405	1	3	0	Czech Republic
9	Bohdan Shust	GK	21	4	360	0	1	0	Ukraine
10	Dmytro Chygrynskiy	DEF	20	4	360	0	0	0	Ukraine
11	Mariusz Lewandowski	MID	28	4	360	0	2	0	Poland
12	Rodrigues Jadson	ATT	23	6	331	1	0	0	Brazil
13	Blumer Elano	MID	26	5	275	0	0	0	Brazil
14	Julius Aghahowa	ATT	25	6	206	0	0	0	Nigeria
15	Igor Duljaj	MID	27	4	197	0	0	0	Serbia
16	Dmytro Shutkov	GK	35	2	180	0	0	0	Ukraine
17	Kucher	MID	24	2	180	0	1	0	Ukraine
18	Vyacheslav Sviderskiy	DEF	28	2	165	0	1	1	Ukraine
19	Jose Leonardo	DEF	21	1	90	0	0	0	Brazil
20	Stipe Pletikosa	GK	28	1	90	0	0	0	Croatia
21	Andriy Vorobiei	ATT	28	2	23	0	0	0	Ukraine
22	Oleksiy Hai	MID	24	2	9	0	0	0	Ukraine

OLYMPIAKOS

	PLAYER	POS	AGE	APP	MINS ON	GOALS	CARDS(Y/R)		HOME COUNTRY
1	Antonios Nikopolidis	GK	36	6	540	0	1	0	Greece
2	Predrag Djordjevic	MID	34	6	514	0	1	0	Serbia
3	Ieroklis Stoltidis	MID	32	6	511	0	0	0	Greece
4	Rivaldo	ATT	35	6	448	0	0	0	Brazil
5	Nery Castillo	MID	23	5	429	3	1	0	Uruguay
6	Michal Zewlakow	DEF	31	5	405	0	1	0	Poland
7	Michalis Konstantinou	ATT	29	6	391	2	2	0	Cyprus
8	Julio Cesar Correa	DEF	28	6	478	0	0	0	Brazil
9	Milos Maric	MID	25	5	373	0	3	0	Serbia
10	Anastasios Pantos	DEF	31	4	293	0	2	0	Greece
11	Athanasios Kostoulas	DEF	31	3	270	0	1	0	Greece
12	Didier Domi	DEF	29	3	262	0	0	0	France
13	Georgios Anatolakis	DEF	33	4	223	0	0	0	Greece
14	Grigorios Georgatos	MID	34	3	188	0	1	0	Greece
15	Pantelis Kafes	MID	29	3	151	0	0	0	Greece
16	Yiannis Okkas	ATT	30	3	112	0	0	0	Cyprus
17	Haruna Babangida	MID	0	2	111	0	0	0	Nigeria
18	Abdeslam Ouaddou	DEF	28	1	90	0	1	0	Morocco
20	Patsatzoglou	MID	0	1	64	0	0	0	Greece
21	Christos Patsatzoglou	DEF	28	1	45	0	0	0	Greece
22	Felix Borja	ATT	24	4	42	0	0	0	Ecuador
23	Ioannis Taralidis	MID	26	0	0	0	0	0	Greece
24	Tomislav Butina	GK	32	0	0	0	0	0	Croatia

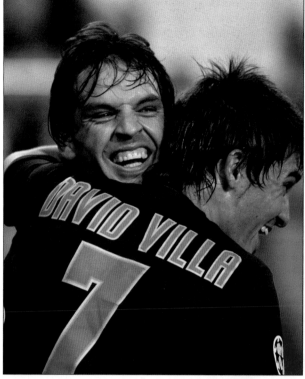

QUALIFYING - third round

			L1	L2
Shakhtar	4-2	Legia	1-0	3-2

Olympiakos 2 **Valencia** 4
Konstantinou 28 — Morientes 34, 39, 89
Castillo 66 — Albiol 86
34,500

Roma 4 **Shakhtar Donetsk** 0
Taddei 67, Totti 76
De Rossi 79, Pizarro 89 — 75,000

Shakhtar Donetsk 2 **Olympiakos** 2
Hubschman 34 — Konstantinou 24
Marica 70 — Castillo 68
20,000

Valencia 2 **Roma** 1
Angulo 13, Villa 29 — Totti 18 pen
48,000

Olympiakos 0 **Roma** 1
Perrotta 76

Valencia 2 **Shakhtar Donetsk** 0
Villa 31, 45

The in-form David Villa strikes for Valencia, dribbling around Shakhtar's keeper Stipe Pletikosa in the 35th minute of a home tie. He heads a second from new team-mate Joaquin's teasing cross before halftime. It's the Spanish side's third straight win

Roma 1 **Olympiakos** 1
Totti 66 — Cesar 18
40,000

Shakhtar Donetsk 2 **Valencia** 2
Jadson 2 — Morientes 18
Fernandinho 28 — Ayala 68
25,000

Argentinian centre back Ayala (pictured with team-mate Edu) is the surprise scorer who salvages a point for the Spanish side after twice falling behind. The second Ukrainian goal is a 30-metre swerver which leaves Canizares for dead

Shakhtar Donetsk 1 **Roma** 0
Marica 61 — 25,000

Valencia 2 **Olympiakos** 0
Angulo 45
Morientes 46 — 35,000

Olympiakos 1 **Shakhtar Donetsk** 1
Castillo 54 — Matuzalem 27
31,000

Roma 1 **Valencia** 0
Panucci 13 — 45,000

With Valencia and Roma both hitting form and four goals in their opening games, Group D looks easy to call. David Villa trumps a penalty from Roma's Francesco Totti to give Valencia the early bragging rights over their rivals. Ukrainians Shakhtar drop out with only two defeats but their 1-0 win over Roma earns their Uefa Cup place

Champions League Group E

	P	W	D	L	F	A	DIF	PTS
Lyon	6	4	2	0	12	3	9	14
Real Madrid	6	3	2	1	14	8	6	11
Steaua Buchuresti	6	1	2	3	7	11	-4	5
Dynamo Kiev	6	0	2	4	5	16	-11	2

GROUP E TABLE

STEAUA BUCHAREST

	PLAYER	POS	AGE	APP	MINS ON	GOALS	CARDS(Y/R)	HOME COUNTRY
1	Banel Nicolita	MID	22	8	720	0	1 0	Romania
2	Dorin Goian	MID	26	8	720	0	3 0	Romania
3	Nicolae Dica	MID	27	8	710	4	2 0	Romania
4	Petre Marin	DEF	33	7	630	1	1 0	Romania
5	Sorin Ghionea	DEF	28	7	630	1	3 0	Romania
6	Ion Sorin Paraschiv	MID	26	8	617	1	1 0	Romania
7	Valentin Badea	ATT	24	7	489	4	0 0	Romania
8	Alberto Carlos Fernandes	GK	27	5	450	0	2 0	Congo DR
9	Florin Lovin	MID	25	7	419	0	1 0	Romania
10	Mihai Nesu	DEF	24	4	358	0	2 0	Romania
11	Daniel Oprita	ATT	25	8	309	0	2 0	Romania
12	Vasilica Cristocea	MID	26	5	308	0	0 0	Romania
13	Cornel Cernea	GK	31	3	270	0	2 0	Romania
14	Stellian Stancu	DEF	25	3	270	0	0 0	Romania
15	Ovidiu Petre	MID	25	6	264	0	2 0	Romania
16	Cyril Thereau	ATT	24	6	242	0	0 0	France
17	Klemi Rahamin Saban	DEF	27	2	148	0	0 0	Israel
18	Gabriel Bostina	MID	30	3	146	0	0 0	Romania
19	Mirel Matei Radoi	DEF	26	2	101	0	1 0	Romania
20	Eugen Baciu	DEF	25	2	91	0	0 0	Romania
21	Gigel Coman	MID	28	2	28	0	0 0	Romania

DYNAMO KIEV

	PLAYER	POS	AGE	APP	MINS ON	GOALS	CARDS(Y/R)	HOME COUNTRY
1	Atanda Yussuf	MID	22	7	630	0	2 0	Nigeria
2	Oleg Gusev	MID	24	7	585	0	2 0	Ukraine
3	Maksim Shatskikh	ATT	28	7	520	4	2 0	Uzbekistan
4	Oleksander Shovkovski	GK	32	6	517	0	0 1	Ukraine
5	Marjan Markovic	DEF	25	5	420	0	0 0	Serbia
6	Rodrigo da Costa	DEF	26	5	404	0	2 0	Brazil
7	Artem Milevskiy	ATT	22	5	373	1	1 0	Ukraine
8	Badr El Kaddouri	MID	26	4	360	0	1 0	Morocco
9	Dantas Bispo Rodolfo	DEF	24	5	348	0	0 0	Brazil
10	Valentin Belkevich	MID	34	5	295	0	0 0	Belarus
11	Taras Mikhalik	MID	23	4	287	0	0 0	Ukraine
12	Diogo Rincon	ATT	27	4	273	0	1 0	Brazil
13	Sergei Rebrov	ATT	33	4	272	1	0 0	Ukraine
14	Goran Gavrancic	DEF	28	4	271	0	1 0	Serbia
15	Andriy Nesmachniy	DEF	28	3	270	0	0 0	Ukraine
16	Carlos Correa	MID	26	4	266	0	0 0	Brazil
17	Goran Sablic	DEF	27	2	180	0	0 0	Croatia
18	Giacomace Freitas Kleber	MID	23	3	161	0	1 0	Brazil
19	Florin Cernat	MID	27	2	153	1	0 0	Romania
20	Ruslan Rotan	MID	25	2	91	0	0 0	Ukraine
21	Lutsenko	GK	33	1	90	0	0 0	Ukraine
22	Mandzyuk	MID	21	1	57	0	0 0	Ukraine
23	Jose Moreno	ATT	26	1	30	0	0 0	Colombia
24	Oleksandr Rybka	GK	20	1	21	0	0 0	Ukraine
25	Harrison Otalvaro	MID	21	1	18	0	0 0	Colombia
26	Oleksandr Aliyev	ATT	22	1	10	0	0 0	Ukraine
27	Maris Verpakovskis	ATT	27	1	5	0	0 0	Latvia

QUALIFYING - second round		L1	L2
Metalurgs	1-8 Dynamo Kyiv	1-4	0-4
Gorica	0-5 Steaua	0-2	0-3

QUALIFYING - third round			
Dynamo Kyiv	5-3 Fenerbahce	3-1	2-2
Standard	3-4 Steaua	2-2	1-2

Dinamo Kiev   1   **Steaua Bucharest**   4
Rebrov 16   Ghionea 3, Badea 24
Dica 43, 79
30,000

Lyon   2   **Real Madrid**   0
Fred 11, Tiago 30   40,013

Real Madrid   5   **Dinamo Kiev**   1
van Nistelrooy 19, 70 pen   Milevskiy 48
Raul 27, 61, Reyes 45   70,000

It was the the Ruud and Raul show at the Bernabeu as Kiev were thumped and lost keeper Shovkovskiy to a red card for hauling down van Nistelrooy, who promptly got up to claim the fifth goal

Steaua Bucharest   0   **Lyon**   3
     Fred 43
     Tiago 55, Benzema 89
     28,000

Dinamo Kiev   0   **Lyon**   3
     Juninho 31, Kallstrom 38
     Malouda 50
     30,000

Steaua Bucharest   1   **Real Madrid**   4
Badea 64   Sergio Ramos 9
     Raul 34, Robinho 56
     van Nistelrooy 76
     20,000

Lyon   1   **Dinamo Kiev**   0
Benzema 14   35,000

Real Madrid   1   **Steaua Bucharest**   0
Nicolita 70 og   69,000

Real Madrid   2   **Lyon**   2
Diarra 39,   Carew 11
van Nistelrooy 83   Malouda 31
     78,677

Steaua Bucharest   1   **Dinamo Kiev**   1
Dica 69   Cernat 29
     20,000

Cernat (right) helps earn a rare point for Group E's bottom club, Dinamo Kiev

Dinamo Kiev   2   **Real Madrid**   2
Shatskikh 13, 27   Ronaldo 86, 88 pen
     33,000

Lyon   1   **Steaua Bucharest**   1
Diarra 12   Dica 2
     30,000

Lyon feel their dominance of French football should bring Champions League glory and kick-off with an impressive win over Madrid after goals by Fred and Tiago. Real bounce back with a 5-1 thrashing of whipping boys Dinamo Kiev and a 4-1 away win over Steaua as van Nistelrooy hits four group goals to secure their place in the last 16

Champions League Group F

GROUP F TABLE

	P	W	D	L	F	A	DIF	PTS
Man Utd	6	4	0	2	10	5	5	12
Celtic	6	3	0	3	8	9	-1	9
Benfica	6	2	1	3	7	8	-1	7
FC Copenhagen	6	2	1	3	5	8	-3	7

BENFICA

	PLAYER	POS	AGE	APP	MINS ON	GOALS	CARDS(Y/R)		HOME COUNTRY
1	Joaquim Manuel Sampaio	GK	31	8	720	0	0	0	Portugal
2	Konstantinos Katsouranis	MID	28	8	696	0	3	0	Greece
3	Nuno Gomes	ATT	30	8	693	3	0	0	Portugal
4	Anderson Luisao	DEF	26	7	630	0	0	0	Brazil
5	Ricardo Rocha Azevedo	DEF	28	7	630	0	3	0	Portugal
6	Armando Teixeira Petit	MID	30	7	606	1	1	0	Portugal
7	Leo	DEF	21	6	540	1	1	0	Brazil
8	Simao Sabrosa	MID	27	6	530	0	0	0	Portugal
9	Augusto Nelson	DEF	24	6	469	1	1	0	Portugal
10	Nuno Assis	MID	29	7	452	0	0	0	Portugal
11	Paulo Jorge	ATT	26	6	442	0	1	0	Portugal
12	Cleber Anderson	DEF	27	4	351	0	0	0	Brazil
13	Fabrizio Miccoli	ATT	28	5	314	2	1	0	Italy
14	Eduardo Alcides	DEF	22	3	270	0	1	0	Brazil
15	Manuel Rui Costa	MID	35	2	155	1	0	0	Portugal
16	Hateni Manu	MID	24	2	100	0	0	0	Portugal
17	Georgios Karagounis	MID	30	3	91	0	0	0	Greece
18	Manuel dos Santos	MID	0	1	69	0	0	0	France
20	Andrei Kariaka	MID	29	2	45	1	0	0	Russia
21	Jose Fonseca	ATT	27	2	36	0	0	0	Mexico
22	Beto	MID	30	2	24	0	0	0	Brazil
23	Pedro Mantorras	ATT	25	4	22	0	0	0	Angola
24	Marco Ferreira	MID	29	1	21	0	0	0	Brazil
25	Jose Francisco Guzman	ATT	27	2	14	0	0	0	Mexico

FC COPENHAGEN

	PLAYER	POS	AGE	APP	MINS ON	GOALS	CARDS(Y/R)		HOME COUNTRY
1	Atiba Hutchinson	MID	24	8	720	1	1	0	Canada
2	Brede Hangeland	MID	26	8	720	1	1	0	Norway
3	Jesper Christiansen	GK	29	8	720	0	0	0	Denmark
4	Michael Gravgaard	DEF	29	8	720	0	0	0	Denmark
5	Tobias Linderoth	MID	28	8	720	0	1	0	Sweden
6	Lars Jacobsen	DEF	27	8	685	0	1	0	Denmark
7	Michael Silberbauer	MID	25	8	646	1	2	0	Denmark
8	Marcus Allback	ATT	33	7	618	3	2	0	Sweden
9	Hjalte Bo Norregaard	MID	26	6	419	0	1	0	Denmark
10	Oscar Wendt	DEF	21	4	349	0	1	0	Sweden
11	Andre Bergdolmo	DEF	35	4	344	0	0	0	Norway
12	Fredrik Berglund	ATT	28	8	342	0	0	0	Sweden
13	Jesper Gronkjaer	MID	29	4	313	1	1	0	Denmark
14	William Kvist	MID	22	7	269	0	0	0	Denmark
15	Razak Pimpong	MID	24	4	128	0	0	0	Ghana
16	Martin Bergvold	MID	23	4	97	0	0	0	Denmark
17	Mads Jorgensen	MID	28	1	90	0	0	0	Denmark
18	Dan Thomassen	DEF	26	3	20	0	0	0	Denmark
19	Benny Gall	GK	36	0	0	0	0	0	Denmark

QUALIFYING - second round

	L1	L2
FC Copenhagen 4-2 MyPa	2-0	2-2

QUALIFYING - third round

	L1	L2
Austria Wien 1-4 Benfica	1-1	0-3
FC Copenhagen 3-2 Ajax	1-2	2-0

FC Copenhagen 0 **Benfica** 0
40,000

Man Utd 3 **Celtic** 2
Saha 30 pen, 40   Vennegoor 21
Solskjaer 47   Nakamura 43
74,031

Benfica 0 **Man Utd** 1
Saha 60
61,000

Celtic 1 **FC Copenhagen** 0
Miller 36 pen
57,598

Celtic 3 **Benfica** 0
Miller 56, 66
Pearson 90
58,313

Miller puts Celtic in a strong position at the halfway stage of the group with a brace of goals in a comprehensive win over Group F rivals Benfica. The two sides trade possession and attacks in an even first half before Miller pounces on a rare Nakamura mishit to score the first goal. His breakaway second goal stops Benfica's revival before Pearson strikes

Man Utd 3 **FC Copenhagen** 0
Scholes 39, O'Shea 46
Richardson 83
72,020

Benfica 3 **Celtic** 0
Caldwell 10 og
Nuno Gomes 22, Kariaka 76
49,000

FC Copenhagen 1 **Man Utd** 0
Allback 73
40,000

Allback's goal threatens United's progress from the group

Benfica 3 **FC Copenhagen** 1
Leo 14, Miccoli 16, 37   Allback 89
47,500

Celtic 1 **Man Utd** 0
Nakamura 81
60,632

FC Copenhagen 3 **Celtic** 1
Hutchinson 2,   Jarosik 75
Gronkjaer 27, Allback 57
41,500

Man Utd 3 **Benfica** 1
Vidic 45, Giggs 61,   Nelson 27
Saha 75
74,955

Scottish champions Celtic thrice concede three goals in defeats yet are still the first team qualified after a Shunsuke Nakamura-inspired 1-0 win over Manchester United in game five. United also lose in Copenhagen but qualify top after battling back from one down against Benfica in the final game. Benfica finish third on goal difference.

Champions League Group G

GROUP G TABLE

	P	W	D	L	F	A	DIF	PTS
Arsenal	6	3	2	1	7	3	4	11
FC Porto	6	3	2	1	9	4	5	11
CSKA Moscow	6	2	2	2	4	5	-1	8
Hamburg	6	1	0	5	7	15	-8	3

CSKA MOSCOW

	PLAYER	POS	AGE	APP	MINS ON	GOALS	CARDS(Y/R)	HOME COUNTRY
1	Alexei Berezoutski	DEF	25	7	630	0	0 0	Russia
2	Igor Akinfeev	GK	21	7	630	0	0 0	Russia
3	Daniel Carvalho	MID	24	7	598	2	0 0	Brazil
4	Deividas Semberas	DEF	28	7	585	0	1 0	Lithuania
5	Yuri Zhirkov	MID	28	7	585	1	2 0	Russia
6	Elvir Rahimic	MID	31	6	540	0	2 0	Bosnia
7	Yevgeny Aldonin	MID	27	7	515	0	0 0	Russia
8	Vagner Love	ATT	23	6	468	1	3 0	Brazil
9	Vassili Berezoutski	DEF	25	6	454	0	0 0	Russia
10	Sergei Ignashevitch	DEF	27	5	450	0	1 0	Russia
11	Milos Krasic	MID	22	7	415	0	0 0	Serbia
12	Dudu Cearense	MID	24	6	390	1	2 0	Brazil
13	Ivica Olic	ATT	27	7	238	1	1 0	Croatia
14	Jo	ATT	20	2	96	0	0 0	Brazil
15	Serguei Dadu	ATT	26	1	90	0	0 0	Moldova
16	Anton Grigoriev	DEF	21	1	82	0	0 0	Russia
17	Ivan Taranov	MID	21	3	80	0	0 0	Russia
18	Kochubey	MID	20	2	69	0	1 0	Russia
19	Chidi Odiah	DEF	23	1	9	0	0 0	Nigeria
20	Rolan Gusev	MID	29	2	6	0	0 0	Russia

HAMBURG

	PLAYER	POS	AGE	APP	MINS ON	GOALS	CARDS(Y/R)	HOME COUNTRY
1	Boubacar Sanogo	ATT	24	8	638	2	1 0	Ivory Coast
2	Mehdi Mahdavikia	MID	29	8	621	0	2 0	Iran
3	Piotr Trochowski	MID	23	8	557	1	1 0	Germany
4	Bastian Reinhardt	DEF	31	6	540	0	0 0	Germany
5	Joris Mathijsen	DEF	27	6	540	0	1 0	Holland
6	Rafael Van der Vaart	MID	24	5	450	3	2 0	Holland
7	David Jarolim	MID	28	5	442	0	1 0	Czech Republic
8	Nigel de Jong	MID	22	5	429	1	1 0	Holland
9	Danijel Ljuboja	ATT	29	6	404	0	1 0	Serbia
10	Sascha Kirschstein	GK	27	5	369	0	1 1	Germany
11	Vincent Kompany	DEF	21	5	350	0	0 0	Belgium
12	Stefan Wachter	GK	29	4	349	0	0 0	Germany
13	Raphael Wicky	MID	30	5	305	0	0 0	Switzerland
14	Timothee Atouba	DEF	25	4	265	0	1 1	Cameroon
15	Juan Pablo Sorin	DEF	31	3	249	0	1 0	Argentina
16	Guy Demel	MID	26	3	233	0	1 0	Ivory Coast
17	Jose Paolo Guerrero	ATT	23	7	219	0	0 0	Peru
18	Collin Benjamin	MID	28	3	215	0	1 0	Namibia
19	Benny Feilhaber	MID	22	3	158	0	0 0	United States
20	Mario Fillinger	MID	22	2	135	0	1 0	Germany
21	Besart Berisha	ATT	21	2	116	1	0 0	Albania
22	Benjamin Lauth	ATT	25	4	103	0	0 1	Germany
23	Alexander Laas	MID	23	1	90	0	0 0	Germany
24	Rene Klingbeil	DEF	26	2	57	0	0 0	Germany

QUALIFYING - third round   L1   L2

Hamburg   1-1 Osasuna   0-0 1-1
Hamburg win on away goals

CSKA Moskva   5-0 Ruzomberok   3-0 2-0

Hamburg   1 **Arsenal**   2
Sanogo 90   Gilberto Silva 12 pen
               Rosicky 53
               51,258

Porto   0 **CSKA Moscow**   0
               40,000

Arsenal   2 **Porto**   0
Henry 38, Hleb 48
               59,861

CSKA Moscow   1 **Hamburg**   0
Dudu Cearense 59
               23,000

CSKA Moscow   1 **Arsenal**   0
Carvalho 24
               36,500

Carvalho's 24th minute free kick proves to be the winner on a freezing night in Moscow. It frustrates Arsenal with Henry convinced he has scored only to be booked for handball, while Toure hits the net but is ruled offside

Porto   4 **Hamburg**   1
L.Lopez 14, 81   Trochowski 89
Lucho Gonzalez 45 pen
Postiga 69
               31,109

Arsenal   0 **CSKA Moscow**   0
               60,003

Hamburg   1 **Porto**   3
Van der Vaart 62   Lucho Gonzalez 44
               L.Lopez 61
               Bruno Moraes 88
               51,000

Arsenal   3 **Hamburg**   1
van Persie 52,   Van der Vaart 4
Eboue 83, Baptista 88
               59,962

CSKA Moscow   0 **Porto**   2
               Quaresma 2
               Lucho Gonzalez 61
               30,000

Porto's players celebrate Gonzalez' goal in Moscow

Hamburg   3 **CSKA Moscow**   2
Berisha 28   Olic 23 pen
Van der Vaart 84   Zhirkov 65
Sanogo 90
               49,649

Porto   0 **Arsenal**   0
               41,500

Hamburg are humbled in Group G, losing their first five games to finish bottom. CSKA Moscow look favourites with two wins and two draws after four games but lose their last two, throwing away a 2-1 lead in the final seven minutes in Hamburg, and have to settle for a Uefa Cup spot behind Arsenal and Porto

Champions League Group H

GROUP H TABLE		P	W	D	L	F	A	DIF	PTS
	AC Milan	6	3	1	2	8	4	4	10
	Lille	6	2	3	1	8	5	3	9
	AEK Athens	6	2	2	2	6	9	-3	8
	Anderlecht	6	0	4	2	7	11	-4	4

AEK ATHENS

	PLAYER	POS	AGE	APP	MINS ON	GOALS	CARDS(Y/R)		HOME COUNTRY
1	Bruno Cirillo	DEF	30	8	720	1	2	0	Italy
2	Nikolaos Liberopoulos	MID	31	8	668	2	2	0	Greece
3	Stefano Sorrentino	GK	28	7	630	0	0	0	Italy
4	Julio Cesar	MID	27	8	613	4	3	0	Brazil
5	Nikolaos Georgeas	DEF	30	6	540	0	1	0	Greece
6	Moises Emerson	MID	35	6	475	0	1	0	Brunei
7	Vasilios Zikos	MID	33	5	450	0	0	0	Greece
8	Daniel Tozser	MID	22	7	430	0	1	0	Hungary
9	Traianos Dellas	DEF	31	5	414	0	1	0	Greece
10	Martin Pautasso	DEF	28	4	330	0	0	0	Argentina
11	Pantelis Kapetanos	ATT	24	5	314	1	1	0	Greece
12	Evangelos Moras	DEF	25	4	283	0	1	0	Greece
13	S Papaststhopoulos	DEF	19	3	270	0	1	0	Greece
14	Vladimir Ivic	MID	30	4	237	1	0	0	Serbia
15	Vassilis Lakis	MID	30	5	210	1	0	0	Greece
16	Perparim Hetemaj	MID	20	4	194	0	0	0	Finland
17	Panagiotis Lagos	MID	21	3	188	0	0	0	Greece
18	Gustavo Manduca	MID	27	3	180	0	0	0	Brazil
19	Ifeanyi Udeze	DEF	26	2	180	0	1	0	Nigeria
20	Stavros Tziortziopoulos	DEF	28	3	178	0	1	0	Greece
21	Andrija Delibasic	ATT	26	4	164	0	0	0	Serbia
22	Elias Kiriakidis	MID	21	4	91	0	0	0	Greece
23	Dionisios Chiotis	GK	30	1	90	0	0	0	Greece
24	Dimitrris Koutroumanos	DEF	20	1	64	0	0	0	Greece
25	Leonidas Kabantais	ATT	25	1	7	0	0	0	Greece

ANDERLECHT

	PLAYER	POS	AGE	APP	MINS ON	GOALS	CARDS(Y/R)		HOME COUNTRY
1	Bart Goor	MID	34	6	540	0	2	0	Belgium
2	Mohamed Tchite	ATT	23	6	540	0	1	0	Congo DR
3	Oliver Deschacht	DEF	26	6	540	0	0	0	Belgium
4	Anthony Vanden Borre	DEF	19	6	527	1	2	0	Belgium
5	Lucas Biglia	MID	21	6	516	0	1	0	Argentina
6	Daniel Zitka	GK	32	5	450	0	0	0	Czech Republic
7	Mbark Boussoufa	ATT	22	6	383	0	1	0	Holland
8	Mark De Man	DEF	24	4	360	0	0	0	Belgium
9	Nicolas Pareja	DEF	23	4	360	1	0	0	Argentina
10	Ahmed Hassan	ATT	32	5	347	0	2	0	Egypt
11	Roland Juhasz	DEF	24	5	294	1	0	0	Hungary
12	Jelle van Damme	DEF	23	3	267	0	1	1	Belgium
13	Nicolas Frutos	ATT	26	3	258	2	0	0	Argentina
14	Yves Vanderhaeghe	MID	37	4	205	0	0	0	Belgium
15	Cristian Leiva	MID	29	1	90	0	0	0	Argentina
16	Davy Schollen	GK	31	1	90	0	0	0	Belgium
17	Mbo Mpenza	ATT	30	2	76	2	1	0	Belgium
18	Serhat Akin	ATT	26	2	59	0	0	0	Turkey
19	Jonathan Legear	ATT	20	4	35	0	0	0	Belgium

QUALIFYING - third round   **L1**   **L2**

Hearts   1-5 AEK   1-2   0-3

AC Milan   **3 AEK Athens**   **0**
Inzaghi 17
Gourcuff 41, Kaka 76 pen   45,000

Anderlecht   **1 Lille**   **1**
Pareja 42   Fauverge 80
    21,107

AEK Athens   **1 Anderlecht**   **1**
Julio Cesar 28   Frutos 25
    35,618

Lille   **0 AC Milan**   **0**
    35,000

Anderlecht   **0 AC Milan**   **1**
    Kaka 58
    20,129

Lille   **3 AEK Athens**   **1**
Robail 64, Gygax 82   Ivic 68
Makoun 90   32,000

Robail gets on the end of Keita's low cross to break the deadlock in a defence-dominated match in France. It starts a run of goals with Ivic thumping a shot past a static Sylva in the Lille goal to level, before Keita sets up Gygax and Makoun makes sure for Lille

AC Milan   **4 Anderlecht**   **1**
Kaka 6 pen, 22, 56   Juhasz 61
Gilardino 88   42,300

AEK Athens   **1 Lille**   **0**
Liberopoulos 74   32,000

AEK Athens   **1 AC Milan**   **0**
Julio Cesar 32   70,000

AEK Athens triumph over AC Milan with a 32nd minute free kick from Cesar proving the difference. It lifts them to second place and raises their qualification hopes.
Inzhagi gets on the end of three clear chances for Milan but finds Sorrentino in excellent form in the AEK goal

Lille   **2 Anderlecht**   **2**
Odemwingie 28,   Mpenza 38, 48
Fauverge 47   35,000

AC Milan   **0 Lille**   **2**
    Odemwingie 7, Keita 67
    27,067

Anderlecht   **2 AEK Athens**   **2**
Vanden Borre 37   Lakis 75, Cirillo 81
Frutos 63   18,000

Lille's unlikely win in Milan underlines their key qualities; a strong defence and a battling spirit. Milan can afford to field a weakened side in this tie after a Kaka hat-trick against AEK earns them passage by game four.
AEK would still pip Lille but can only draw their last game in Anderlecht, so drop into the Uefa Cup

Champions League Last 16

1. CELTIC v AC MILAN

Celtic give AC Milan a ferocious test over both legs of this last 16 game before succumbing in extra time.
Shunsuke Nakamura's free-kick offers Jan Vennegoor of Hesselink the best first leg chance at Celtic Park while Artur Boruc has to make a sharp save from Alberto Gilardinho.
Kaka is the difference in a tight game at the San Siro. The Brazilian hits the bar before the 90 minutes are up. It is a different result in the third minute of extra time when Kaka runs from distance, holding off Neil Lennon before slipping the ball through the legs of Boruc

| Celtic | 0 | AC Milan | 0 |
| 58,785 | | | |

| AC Milan | (0) 1 | Celtic | (0) 0 |
| Kaka 93 | | | 65,000 |

2. PSV EINDHOVEN v ARSENAL

Brazilian centre back Alex is the man of both matches as PSV spring a surprise to beat a confident Arsenal.
Henry and Rosicky go close for Arsenal, who dominate the first leg in Holland but end up losing to a low long-range drive by Ecuadorian Edison Mendez. PSV's lead looks fragile for the return trip to London and Alex is unlucky to see his header fly into his own net from a corner. Heurelho Gomes makes a vital save from Emmanuel Adebayor to keep the deficit to one and Alex scores his second of the match – in Arsenal's net this time – to put PSV through

| PSV Eindhoven | 1 | Arsenal | 0 |
| Mendez 61 | | | 35,000 |

Arsenal	(1) 1	PSV Eindhoven	(2) 1
Alex 58 og			Alex 83
			60,073

CELTIC

	PLAYER	POS	AGE	APP	MINS ON	GOALS	CARDS(Y/R)	HOME COUNTRY
1	Artur Boruc	GK	27	8	750	0	1 0	Poland
2	Lee Naylor	DEF	27	8	750	0	1 0	England
3	Stephen McManus	DEF	24	8	732	0	3 0	Scotland
4	Neil Lennon	MID	36	8	716	0	2 0	N Ireland
5	Shunsuke Nakamura	MID	29	8	662	2	1 0	Japan
6	Paul Telfer	DEF	35	6	519	0	0 0	Scotland
7	Kenny Miller	ATT	27	8	469	3	2 0	Scotland
8	Aiden McGeady	MID	21	6	458	0	1 0	Rep of Ireland
9	Evander Sno	MID	20	5	413	0	2 0	Holland
10	Thomas Gravesen	MID	31	6	407	0	1 0	Denmark
11	Jan Vennegoor	ATT	28	4	390	1	0 0	Holland
12	Gary Caldwell	DEF	26	4	360	0	0 0	Scotland
13	Maciej Zurawski	ATT	30	5	310	0	0 0	Poland
14	Jiri Jarosik	MID	29	6	285	1	1 0	Czech Republic
15	Mark Wilson	DEF	23	3	231	0	0 0	Scotland
16	Shaun Maloney	ATT	24	5	230	0	1 0	Scotland
17	Darren O'Dea	DEF	20	3	228	0	0 0	Rep of Ireland
18	Dianbobo Balde	DEF	31	2	180	0	0 0	France
19	Stephen Pearson	MID	24	4	119	1	1 0	Scotland
20	Craig Beattie	ATT	23	2	41	0	0 0	Scotland

ARSENAL

	PLAYER	POS	AGE	APP	MINS ON	GOALS	CARDS(Y/R)	HOME COUNTRY
1	Cesc Fabregas	MID	20	10	897	2	1 0	Spain
2	Habib Kolo Toure	DEF	26	10	837	0	0 0	Ivory Coast
3	Alexander Hleb	MID	26	10	805	1	3 0	Belarus
4	Gilberto Silva	MID	30	9	741	1	1 0	Brazil
5	Jens Lehmann	GK	37	8	720	0	0 0	Germany
6	Emmanuel Eboue	DEF	24	6	540	1	0 0	Ivory Coast
7	Robin van Persie	ATT	23	8	540	2	0 0	Holland
8	William Gallas	DEF	29	8	539	0	0 0	France
9	Emmanuel Adebayor	ATT	23	8	538	0	0 0	Togo
10	Tomas Rosicky	MID	26	6	520	1	1 0	Czech Republic
11	Justin Hoyte	DEF	22	6	513	0	1 0	England
12	Thierry Henry	ATT	29	7	500	1	3 0	France
13	Gael Clichy	DEF	21	6	460	0	1 0	France
14	Johan Djourou	DEF	20	5	434	0	1 0	Switzerland
15	Fredrik Ljungberg	MID	30	5	346	1	0 0	Sweden
16	Mathieu Flamini	MID	23	6	304	1	1 0	France
17	Manuel Almunia	GK	30	2	180	0	0 0	Spain
18	Philippe Senderos	DEF	22	2	180	0	2 0	Switzerland
19	Julio Baptista	MID	25	4	113	1	0 0	Brazil
20	Denilson	MID	19	1	90	0	0 0	Brazil
21	Theo Walcott	MID	18	6	69	0	1 0	England
22	Jeremie Aliadiere	ATT	24	2	18	0	0 0	France
23	Vassiriki Abou Diaby	MID	21	1	15	0	0 0	France
24	Alexandre Song	MID	19	1	1	0	0 0	Cameroon

Champions League Last 16

3. LILLE v MANCHESTER UNITED

The quick thinking of Ryan Giggs and his free kick causes a rumpus in northern France.
He punishes a Lille foul in the first leg, catching Tony Mario Sylva still organising his wall. Lille, who had earlier seen a Peter Odemwingie header disallowed for a push on Nemanja Vidic, argue that Giggs' goal should not stand and seem about to walk off in protest.
The away win makes United's second leg a tame affair and Henrik Larsson settles it in his last game on loan at Old Trafford in the 72nd minute. The winner is a trademark header from Cristiano Ronaldo's cross

Lille	0	Man Utd	1
			Giggs 83
			41,000
Man Utd	(2) 1	**Lille**	(0) 0
Larsson 71			75,182

4. REAL MADRID v BAYERN MUNICH

A late strike by former Barcelona star Mark van Bommel turns into the crucial goal that sends Real Madrid out and Bayern through.
His goal comes in the 88th minute of the first leg and pulls Real back to 3-2. Two goals by Raul and a third from Ruud van Nistelrooy, answered by one from Lucio, probably make Real favourites before van Bommel's strike. Roy Makaay scores the fastest-ever Champions League goal after just 11 seconds to get Bayern off to the perfect start at home. Bayern extend their lead when Lucio scores his second of the tie, so van Nistelrooy's penalty is not enough.

Real Madrid	3	Bayern Munich	2
Raul 10, 28,			Lucio 24
van Nistelrooy 34			van Bommel 88
			80,000
Bayern Munich	(2) 2	**Real Madrid**	(3) 1
Makaay 1, Lucio 66			van Nistelrooy 83 pen
			66,000
Bayern win on away goals			

LILLE

	PLAYER	POS	AGE	APP	MINS ON	GOALS	CARDS(Y/R)		HOME COUNTRY
1	Gregory Tafforeau	DEF	30	9	810	0	2	0	France
2	Jean Makoun	MID	24	9	767	1	3	0	Cameroon
3	Mathieu Chalme	DEF	26	9	749	0	1	0	France
4	Nicolas Plestan	DEF	26	8	720	0	2	0	France
5	Tony Mario Sylva	GK	32	7	630	0	1	0	Senegal
6	Mathieu Bodmer	MID	24	7	628	0	0	0	France
7	Abdul Kader Keita	ATT	25	7	622	1	3	0	Ivory Coast
8	Peter Odemwingie	ATT	25	8	603	2	0	0	Nigeria
9	Efstathios Tavlaridis	DEF	27	7	555	0	3	1	Greece
10	Yohan Cabaye	MID	21	7	440	0	3	0	France
11	Mathieu Debuchy	MID	21	5	296	0	1	0	France
12	Rafael Schmitz	DEF	26	4	276	0	0	0	Brazil
13	Nicolas Fauverge	ATT	22	7	251	2	1	0	France
14	Mathieu Robail	ATT	22	5	220	1	1	0	France
15	Gregory Malicki	GK	33	2	180	0	0	0	France
16	Ludovic Obraniak	MID	22	2	178	0	0	0	France
17	Souleymane Youla	ATT	25	5	176	0	1	0	Guinea
18	Stephane Dumont	MID	24	2	163	0	0	0	France
19	Kevin Mirallas	ATT	19	4	150	0	0	0	Belgium
20	Michel Fernandes Bastos	DEF	23	4	125	0	0	0	Brazil
21	Johan Audel	ATT	23	2	106	1	0	0	France
22	Stephan Lichtsteiner	DEF	23	2	93	0	1	0	Switzerland
23	Milivoje Vitakic	DEF	30	1	90	0	0	0	Serbia
24	Daniel Gygax	MID	25	1	13	1	0	0	Switzerland

REAL MADRID

	PLAYER	POS	AGE	APP	MINS ON	GOALS	CARDS(Y/R)		HOME COUNTRY
1	Roberto Carlos	DEF	34	8	688	0	2	0	Brazil
2	Iker Casillas	GK	26	7	630	0	0	0	Spain
3	Gonzalez Raul	ATT	30	7	601	5	1	0	Spain
4	Mahamadou Diarra	MID	26	7	588	1	2	1	Mali
5	Ruud van Nistelrooy	ATT	31	7	581	6	0	0	Holland
6	Fabio Cannavaro	DEF	33	6	540	0	2	0	Italy
7	Sergio Ramos	DEF	26	6	540	1	3	0	Spain
8	Emerson Ferreira da Rosa	MID	31	6	466	0	0	0	Brazil
9	Jose Maria Guti	MID	30	7	455	0	1	0	Spain
10	Ivan Helguera	DEF	32	5	450	0	0	0	Spain
11	Robinho	ATT	23	7	349	1	0	0	Brazil
12	David Beckham	MID	32	6	332	0	0	0	England
13	Miguel Torres	DEF	21	3	270	0	0	0	Spain
14	Antonio Cassano	ATT	24	4	195	0	0	0	Italy
15	Alvaro Mejia	DEF	25	2	180	0	0	0	Spain
16	Fernando Gago	MID	21	2	164	0	0	0	Argentina
17	Jose Antonio Reyes	MID	23	4	164	1	0	0	Spain
18	Ronaldo	ATT	30	4	139	2	1	0	Brazil
19	Gonzalo Higuain	ATT	19	2	97	0	0	0	Argentina
20	Cicinho	DEF	27	1	90	0	0	0	Brazil
21	Diego Lopez	GK	25	1	90	0	0	0	Spain
22	Michel Salgado	DEF	31	1	90	0	0	0	Spain
23	Miguel Nieto	ATT	21	1	73	0	0	0	Spain
24	Ruben De la Red	MID	22	1	69	0	0	0	Spain
25	Raul Bravo	DEF	26	1	32	0	0	0	Spain
26	Javi Garcia	MID	20	1	21	0	0	0	Spain
27	Borja Valero	MID	22	1	17	0	0	0	Spain

Champions League Last 16

5. ROMA v LYON

Roma's strong season continues as Francesco Totti scores the breakthrough goal in Lyon to condemn the French Champions.
Lyon are confident after outclassing Madrid in the group matches and look to have done the hard work with a goalless draw in Rome. However, Totti scores with a powerful header from Max Tonetto's run and cross in the second leg. Lyon now need two to win the tie and Juninho urges them forward from midfield, but Mancini's drive into the top corner helps Roma claim their first Champions League quarter-final slot

Roma	0	Lyon	0
			55,000

Lyon	(0) 0	Roma	(0) 2
		Totti 22, Mancini 44	
			41,000

6. BARCELONA v LIVERPOOL

The tie of the round pitches the last two winners together with holders Barcelona favourites against Liverpool.
The first leg in Spain proves decisive with Deco scoring Barca's first goal against Liverpool in four attempts – a header from Gianluca Zambrotta's cross. The Reds strike back when Craig Bellamy's header is carried over the line by Victor Valdes. They grab an unexpected winner as Bellamy sets up John Arne Riise for a fierce drive. Barca are outplayed in the return but cause Anfield flutters as Eidur Gudjohnsen dribbles past Pepe Reina to score the only goal

Barcelona	1	Liverpool	2
Deco 14		Bellamy 43, Riise 74	
			88,000

Liverpool	(2) 0	Barcelona	(1) 1
		Gudjohnsen 75	
			45,000

Liverpool win on away goals

LYON

	PLAYER	POS	AGE	APP	MINS ON	GOALS	CARDS(Y/R)		HOME COUNTRY
1	Cris	DEF	30	7	630	0	1	0	Brazil
2	Florent Malouda	MID	27	7	630	2	3	0	France
3	Gregory Coupet	GK	34	7	630	0	0	0	France
4	Cardoso Tiago	MID	26	8	606	2	1	0	Portugal
5	Eric Abidal	DEF	27	7	593	0	0	0	France
6	Pernambucano Juninho	MID	32	7	567	1	2	0	Brazil
7	Jeremy Toulalan	MID	23	7	508	0	3	0	France
8	Francois Clerc	DEF	24	6	459	0	0	0	France
9	Sebastien Squillaci	DEF	26	5	450	0	0	0	France
10	Fred	ATT	23	5	413	2	1	0	Brazil
11	Sydney Govou	ATT	27	5	382	0	1	0	France
12	Anthony Reveillere	DEF	27	6	375	0	2	0	France
13	Sylvain Wiltord	ATT	33	6	281	0	0	0	France
14	Patrick Muller	DEF	30	3	270	0	0	0	Switzerland
15	Kim Kallstrom	MID	24	6	264	1	2	0	Sweden
16	Alou Diarra	MID	25	5	218	1	0	0	France
17	John Alieu Carew	ATT	27	2	154	1	0	0	Norway
18	Karim Benzema	ATT	19	3	102	2	0	0	France
19	Claudio Cacapa	DEF	31	1	90	0	1	0	Brazil
20	Hatem Ben Arfa	MID	20	1	90	0	0	0	France
21	Jeremie Berthod	DEF	23	1	90	0	0	0	France
22	Remi Vercoutre	GK	27	1	90	0	0	0	France
23	Milan Baros	ATT	25	1	17	0	0	0	Czech Republic
24	Loic Remy	MID	20	1	11	0	0	0	France

BARCELONA

	PLAYER	POS	AGE	APP	MINS ON	GOALS	CARDS(Y/R)		HOME COUNTRY
1	Deco	MID	29	8	720	2	1	0	Portugal
2	Ronaldinho	ATT	27	8	720	2	0	0	Brazil
3	Victor Valdes	GK	25	8	720	0	0	0	Spain
4	Carlos Puyol	DEF	29	8	703	1	1	0	Spain
5	Rafael Marquez	DEF	28	6	512	0	0	0	Mexico
6	Andres Iniesta	MID	23	8	482	2	0	0	Spain
7	Gianluca Zambrotta	DEF	30	6	458	0	1	0	Italy
8	Thiago Motta	MID	24	6	440	0	2	0	Brazil
9	Eidur Gudjohnsen	ATT	28	8	397	3	1	0	Iceland
10	Xavi Hernandez	MID	27	7	396	0	1	0	Spain
11	Lionel Messi	MID	20	5	386	1	1	0	Argentina
12	Ludovic Giuly	MID	30	8	368	2	0	0	France
13	Gio Van Bronckhorst	DEF	32	4	326	0	1	0	Holland
14	Lilian Thuram	DEF	35	4	268	0	1	0	France
15	Presas Oleguer	DEF	27	5	236	0	0	0	Spain
16	Samuel Eto'o	ATT	26	3	214	1	0	0	Cameroon
17	Juliano Belletti	DEF	31	2	180	0	1	0	Brazil
18	Sylvinho	DEF	33	2	172	0	0	0	Brazil
19	Edmilson	MID	30	2	124	0	1	0	Brazil
20	Javier Saviola	ATT	25	1	82	0	0	0	Argentina
21	Santiago Ezquerro	ATT	30	2	16	0	0	0	Spain

Champions League Last 16

7. INTER MILAN v VALENCIA

Valencia knock out the runaway Serie A leaders by scoring twice in the first leg to take a vital draw back to Spain.
They twice come from behind in the San Siro; first after Esteban Cambiasso heads in a rebound to give a dominant Inter side the lead. David Villa levels with a 30 metre free kick against the run of play. When Brazilian Maicon scores for Inter after a right wing run, David Silva strikes in the 86th minute to make it 2-2. In the second leg, Dejan Stankovic gives Inter midfield control but Santiago Canizares and some valiant defending see Valencia through, sparking an ugly on-field fight.

Inter Milan	2	Valencia	2
Cambiasso 28, Maicon 76		Villa 64, Silva 89	
			65,000

Valencia	(2) 0	Inter Milan	(2) 0
			53,000

Valencia win on away goals

8. PORTO v CHELSEA

Jose Mourinho won the Champions League with Porto in 2004 and returned there with Chelsea for the last 16 game.
Porto start the stronger at home in the first leg when Raul Meireles gives them a 12th minute lead. Ukrainian Andriy Shevchenko shows his Champions League pedigree by levelling four minutes later to ensure a draw.
Ricardo Quaresma finishes calmly after racing clear in the second leg to give Porto a lead. Arjen Robben replies three minutes into the second half with a soft shot spilled by the visiting keeper before Michael Ballack settles it

Porto	1	Chelsea	1
Meireles 12		Shevchenko 15	
			49,000

Chelsea	(1) 2	Porto	(1) 1
Robben 48, Ballack 79		Quaresma 15	
			39,041

INTER MILAN

	PLAYER	POS	AGE	APP	MINS ON	GOALS	CARDS(Y/R)		HOME COUNTRY
1	Douglas Maicon	DEF	25	8	720	1	2	0	Brazil
2	Javier Zanetti	DEF	33	8	641	0	1	0	Argentina
3	Ivan Cordoba	DEF	30	7	630	0	2	0	Colombia
4	Dejan Stankovic	MID	28	7	616	0	1	0	Serbia
5	Olivier Dacourt	MID	32	7	572	0	0	0	France
6	Zlatan Ibrahimovic	ATT	25	7	552	0	2	1	Sweden
7	Julio Cesar	GK	27	6	540	0	0	0	Brazil
8	Marco Materazzi	DEF	33	6	540	0	2	0	Italy
9	Luis Figo	MID	34	7	454	0	1	0	Portugal
10	Hernan Crespo	ATT	31	6	355	1	0	0	Argentina
11	Patrick Vieira	MID	31	4	337	1	1	1	France
12	Nicolas Burdisso	DEF	26	5	304	0	1	0	Argentina
13	Fabio Grosso	DEF	29	6	288	0	0	1	Italy
14	Julio Cruz	ATT	32	4	228	3	0	0	Argentina
15	Walter Samuel	DEF	29	3	181	0	1	0	Argentina
16	Francesco Toldo	GK	35	2	180	0	1	0	Italy
17	Scherer Maxwell	MID	25	2	164	0	0	0	Brazil
18	Mariano Gonzalez	MID	26	3	139	0	0	0	Argentina
19	Leite Adriano	ATT	25	3	106	0	0	0	Brazil
20	Santiago Hernan Solari	MID	30	4	103	0	0	0	Argentina
21	Marco Andreolli	DEF	21	1	90	0	0	0	Italy
22	Alvaro Recoba	ATT	31	2	78	0	0	0	Uruguay
23	Esteban Cambiasso	MID	26	2	39	1	0	0	Argentina

PORTO

	PLAYER	POS	AGE	APP	MINS ON	GOALS	CARDS(Y/R)		HOME COUNTRY
1	Bruno Eduardo Alves	DEF	25	8	720	0	1	0	Portugal
2	da Silva Arruda Helton	GK	29	8	720	0	0	0	Brazil
3	Lucho Gonzalez	MID	26	8	720	3	0	0	Argentina
4	Pepe	DEF	24	8	720	0	2	0	Brazil
5	Ricardo Quaresma	ATT	23	8	676	2	2	0	Portugal
6	da Silva Paulo Assuncao	MID	27	7	630	0	1	0	Brazil
7	Lisandro Lopez	ATT	24	8	587	3	0	0	Argentina
8	Jose da Silva Bosingwa	MID	24	6	540	0	0	0	Portugal
9	Raul Meireles	MID	24	7	487	1	1	0	Portugal
10	Fucile	MID	22	5	450	0	2	0	Uruguay
11	Helder Postiga	ATT	24	6	419	1	0	0	Portugal
12	Marek Cech	DEF	24	5	272	0	0	0	Slovakia
13	Luis Anderson	ATT	19	3	197	0	0	0	Brazil
14	Vieira Adriano	ATT	28	4	144	0	1	0	Brazil
15	Ricardo Miguel Costa	DEF	26	2	135	0	1	0	Portugal
16	dos Santos Moraes	ATT	22	6	98	1	1	0	Brazil
17	Roosevelt Ezequias	DEF	26	1	90	0	0	0	Brazil
18	Tarik Sektioui	ATT	30	1	90	0	0	0	Morocco
19	Jorginho	ATT	30	3	78	0	0	0	Brazil
20	Jorge Fucile Perdomo	DEF	22	1	63	0	0	0	Uruguay
21	Barreto da Silva Ibson	MID	23	2	40	0	0	0	Brazil
22	Osorio Alan	MID	27	2	33	0	0	0	Brazil
23	Adelino Vieirinha	MID	21	1	11	0	0	0	Portugal

Champions League Quarter Finals

1. AC MILAN v BAYERN MUNICH

Early strikes by Champions League winner Clarence Seedorf with a second from Filippo Inzaghi help AC Milan's experience tell against Bayern Munich.

The first leg's result favours the Germans, who twice draw level thanks to late goals from Belgian centre half Daniel van Buyten. He strikes in the 78th minute to cancel out Andrea Pirlo's opener for Milan and again after Kaka's penalty has regained the lead.

However, Milan are the better side and prove it in the second leg with Seedorf, firing home before claiming an assist for Inzaghi's goal

AC Milan	2	Bayern Munich	2
Pirlo 40, Kaka 84 pen		Van Buyten 73, 90	
		60,000	

Bayern Munich	(2) 0	AC Milan	(2) 2
		Seedorf 27, Inzaghi 3	
		66,000	

2. PSV EINDHOVEN v LIVERPOOL

Without the hero of the last tie, the injured Alex, PSV look a shadow of the side that won through to the quarters.

The tie is as good as over after the first leg with Liverpool coasting to a 3-0 victory. After Heurelho Gomes brilliantly saves a header from Jamie Carragher, Steven Gerrard goes one better with a diving header into the corner to leave Gomes standing. John Arne Riise scores with his normal spectacular rocket before Peter Couch adds the third.

The second leg is an anti-climax and PSV never threaten Liverpool's progress.

PSV Eindhoven	0	Liverpool	3
36,500			
		Gerrard 27, Riise 49, Crouch 63	

Liverpool	(3) 1	PSV Eindhoven	(0) 0
Crouch 68			41,447

BAYERN MUNICH

	PLAYER	POS	AGE	APP	MINS ON	GOALS	CARDS(Y/R)		HOME COUNTRY
1	Daniel Van Buyten	DEF	29	10	900	2	2	0	Belgium
2	Oliver Kahn	GK	38	9	810	0	0	0	Germany
3	Philipp Lahm	DEF	23	9	810	0	0	0	Germany
4	Willy Sagnol	DEF	30	9	781	0	1	0	France
5	Lucio	DEF	29	8	720	2	1	0	Brazil
6	Hasan Salihamidzic	MID	30	10	696	1	2	0	Bosnia
7	Mark van Bommel	MID	30	8	675	1	4	1	Holland
8	Bastian Schweinsteiger	MID	22	8	663	2	2	1	Germany
9	Roy Makaay	ATT	32	8	646	2	0	0	Holland
10	Claudio Pizarro	ATT	28	10	622	4	0	0	Peru
11	Andreas Ottl	MID	22	7	540	0	2	0	Germany
12	Lukas Podolski	ATT	22	7	459	1	1	0	Germany
13	Owen Hargreaves	MID	26	5	450	0	1	0	England
14	Martin Demichelis	MID	26	6	293	0	2	0	Argentina
15	Roque Santa Cruz	ATT	25	7	275	1	0	0	Paraguay
16	Christian Lell	DEF	22	4	234	0	0	0	Germany
17	Michael Rensing	GK	23	1	90	0	0	0	Germany
18	Julio Dos Santos	MID	24	2	71	0	1	0	Paraguay
19	Mehmet Scholl	MID	36	4	58	0	1	0	Germany
20	Ali Karimi	MID	28	2	21	0	0	0	Iran
21	Andreas Gorlitz	MID	25	2	20	0	0	0	Germany
22	Sebastian Deisler	MID	27	1	12	0	0	0	Germany

PSV EINDHOVEN

	PLAYER	POS	AGE	APP	MINS ON	GOALS	CARDS(Y/R)		HOME COUNTRY
1	Heurelho Gomes	GK	26	10	900	0	0	0	Brazil
2	Timmy Simons	MID	30	10	900	1	0	0	Belgium
3	Carlos Salcido	DEF	27	9	810	0	3	0	Mexico
4	Edison Mendez	MID	28	9	729	1	1	0	Ecuador
5	Alex	DEF	25	8	720	2	0	0	Brazil
6	Arouna Kone	ATT	23	9	690	2	0	0	Ivory Coast
7	Jan Kromkamp	DEF	26	8	652	1	1	0	Holland
8	Jefferson Farfan	ATT	22	8	644	0	0	0	Peru
9	Phillip Cocu	MID	36	7	630	0	0	0	Holland
10	Jason Culina	MID	26	8	585	0	0	0	Australia
11	Ibrahim Afellay	MID	21	5	358	0	0	0	Holland
12	Mika Vayrynen	MID	25	8	337	1	1	0	Finland
13	Manuel da Costa	DEF	21	4	334	0	0	0	Portugal
14	Diego Tardelli	ATT	22	5	316	0	0	0	Brazil
15	Michael Reiziger	DEF	34	3	270	0	0	0	Holland
16	Csaba Feher	MID	31	4	240	0	2	0	Hungary
17	Xiang Sun	DEF	25	4	190	0	0	0	China PR
18	Eric Addo	DEF	28	4	149	0	0	0	Ghana
19	Ismael Aissati	MID	18	5	114	0	0	0	Morocco
20	Patrick Kluivert	ATT	31	3	114	0	1	0	Holland
21	Michael Lamey	DEF	27	1	85	0	0	1	Holland
22	Dirk Marcellis	DEF	19	1	63	0	0	1	Holland
23	Rens van Eijden	MID	20	1	20	0	0	0	Holland
24	Roy Beerens	ATT	19	2	18	0	0	0	Holland

Champions League Quarter Finals

3. ROMA v MANCESTER UNITED

Roma	**2**	Man Utd	**1**
Taddei 43, Vucinic 66		Rooney 60	
			77,000

Man Utd	(1) **7**	Roma	(2) **1**
Carrick 11, 60		De Rossi 69	
Smith 17, Rooney 19			
Ronaldo 44, 49, Evra 81			74,476

A record knock-out score propels Manchester United through to the semi-finals as they smash Roma 7-1 in the second leg.

United are reduced to ten men after Paul Scholes is sent off in Rome as fans clash on the terraces. They came back from one down with Wayne Rooney scoring his first goal in Europe since his debut hat-trick for the team, although Roma persevere to win 2-1.

The second leg sees United on top early through Michael Carrick's improvised strike. Alan Smith finishes off a glorious passing move and Rooney flicks home a third before the 20th minute. Cristiano Ronaldo adds two of the four scored in the second half

4. CHELSEA v VALENCIA

Chelsea	**1**	Valencia	**1**
Drogba 53		Silva 30	
			38,065

Valencia	(1) **1**	Chelsea	(1) **2**
Morientes 32		Shevchenko 52	
		Essien 90	
			53,000

The closest tie of the round comes as Chelsea snatch victory from the jaws of extra time in Valencia's Mestela Stadium.

David Silva gives the Spanish side a well-deserved lead with an unstoppable strike past Petr Cech on the half hour mark. Chelsea respond both sides of half time and draw level when Didier Drogba nods home. The second leg sees Fernando Morientes converting a cross in the 32nd minute. Andriy Shevchenko stabs home an equaliser and the game looks destined for extra time when Michael Essien's shot defeats Santiago Canizares at the near post

ROMA

	PLAYER	POS	AGE	APP	MINS ON	GOALS	CARDS(Y/R)		HOME COUNTRY
1	Alexander Doni	GK	27	10	900	0	0	0	Brazil
2	Daniele De Rossi	MID	22	10	879	2	2	0	Italy
3	Christian Panucci	DEF	34	9	810	1	1	0	Italy
4	Francesco Totti	ATT	30	9	799	4	2	0	Italy
5	Christian Chivu	DEF	26	8	720	0	0	0	Romania
6	Rodrigo Taddei	MID	27	8	704	2	1	0	Brazil
7	Simone Perrotta	MID	29	9	691	1	4	0	Italy
8	Max Tonetto	MID	32	7	630	0	2	0	Italy
9	Philippe Mexes	DEF	25	7	630	0	2	0	France
10	Alessandro Mancini	DEF	26	7	594	1	1	0	Brazil
11	Marco Cassetti	DEF	30	8	582	0	2	0	Italy
12	David Marcelo Pizarro	MID	27	7	501	1	5	0	Chile
13	Matteo Ferrari	DEF	27	6	473	0	1	0	Italy
14	Alberto Aquilani	MID	22	5	259	0	1	0	Italy
15	Mirko Vucinic	ATT	23	6	254	1	0	0	Montenegro
16	Christian Wilhelmsson	MID	27	3	163	0	0	0	Sweden
17	Ricardo Faty	DEF	20	3	84	0	0	0	France
18	Valerio Virga	ATT	21	1	82	0	0	0	Italy
19	Vincenzo Montella	ATT	33	3	69	0	0	0	Italy
20	Aleandro Rosi	MID	20	4	46	0	0	0	Italy
21	Okaka Chuka Stefano	ATT	17	3	29	0	0	0	Nigeria
22	Rodrigo Defendi	DEF	21	1	1	0	0	0	Brazil

VALENCIA

	PLAYER	POS	AGE	APP	MINS ON	GOALS	CARDS(Y/R)		HOME COUNTRY
1	Raul Albiol	MID	21	11	970	0	0	0	Spain
2	Santiago Canizares	GK	37	10	900	0	1	0	Spain
3	Luis Garcia Miguel	DEF	27	9	810	0	0	0	Portugal
4	Emiliano Moretti	DEF	26	9	796	0	1	0	Italy
5	David Villa	ATT	25	10	785	5	1	0	Spain
6	Roberto Ayala	DEF	34	8	720	1	5	0	Argentina
7	Fernando Morientes	ATT	31	9	686	7	0	0	Spain
8	David Silva	MID	21	10	682	3	1	0	Spain
9	Miguel Angel Angulo	ATT	30	9	665	0	1	0	Spain
10	David Albelda	MID	29	6	540	0	5	0	Spain
11	Sanchez Joaquin	MID	26	8	482	0	0	0	Spain
12	Edu	MID	29	5	412	0	1	0	Brazil
13	David Navarro	DEF	27	4	356	0	0	0	Spain
14	Carlos Marchena	DEF	27	3	270	0	1	0	Spain
15	Rodriguez Vicente	ATT	25	4	241	0	0	0	Spain
16	Hugo Viana	MID	24	7	190	0	0	0	Portugal
17	Asier Del Horno	DEF	26	2	180	0	1	0	Spain
18	Curro Torres	DEF	30	2	180	0	0	0	Spain
19	Miguel Pallardo	MID	20	2	179	0	1	0	Spain
20	Ruben Baraja	MID	31	2	123	0	0	0	Spain
21	Jorge Lopez	MID	28	5	114	0	0	0	Spain
22	Francesco Tavano	ATT	28	2	106	0	0	0	Italy
23	Jaime Gavilan	MID	22	3	99	0	0	0	Spain
24	Mario Regueiro	MID	28	5	97	0	0	0	Uruguay
25	David Cerra	DEF	23	1	90	0	1	0	Spain
26	Ludovic Butelle	GK	24	1	90	0	0	0	France
27	Nacho Insa	MID	21	1	64	0	0	0	Spain

Champions League Semi-Final

Manchester United v AC Milan

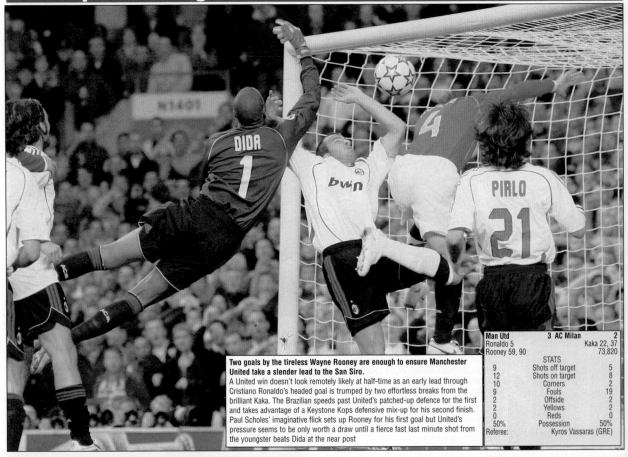

Man Utd	3	AC Milan	2
Ronaldo 5		Kaka 22, 37	
Rooney 59, 90			73,820

STATS

Man Utd		AC Milan
9	Shots off target	5
12	Shots on target	8
10	Corners	2
9	Fouls	19
2	Offside	2
2	Yellows	2
0	Reds	0
50%	Possession	50%
Referee:		Kyros Vassaras (GRE)

Two goals by the tireless Wayne Rooney are enough to ensure Manchester United take a slender lead to the San Siro.

A United win doesn't look remotely likely at half-time as an early lead through Cristiano Ronaldo's headed goal is trumped by two effortless breaks from the brilliant Kaka. The Brazilian speeds past United's patched-up defence for the first and takes advantage of a Keystone Kops defensive mix-up for his second finish. Paul Scholes' imaginative flick sets up Rooney for his first goal but United's pressure seems to be only worth a draw until a fierce fast last minute shot from the youngster beats Dida at the near post.

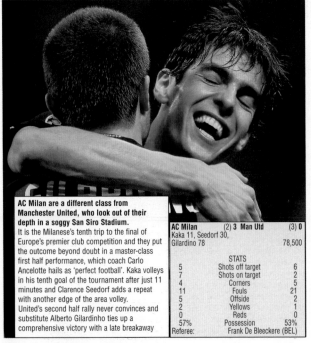

AC Milan are a different class from Manchester United, who look out of their depth in a soggy San Siro Stadium.

It is the Milanese's tenth trip to the final of Europe's premier club competition and they put the outcome beyond doubt in a master-class first half performance, which coach Carlo Ancelotte hails as 'perfect football'. Kaka volleys in his tenth goal of the tournament after just 11 minutes and Clarence Seedorf adds a repeat with another edge of the area volley. United's second half rally never convinces and substitute Alberto Gilardinho ties up a comprehensive victory with a late breakaway

AC Milan	(2) 3	Man Utd	(3) 0
Kaka 11, Seedorf 30,			
Gilardino 78			78,500

STATS

AC Milan		Man Utd
5	Shots off target	6
7	Shots on target	2
4	Corners	5
11	Fouls	21
5	Offside	2
2	Yellows	1
0	Reds	0
57%	Possession	53%
Referee:		Frank De Bleeckere (BEL)

MANCHESTER UNITED

	PLAYER	POS	AGE	APP	MINS ON	GOALS	CARDS(Y/R)		HOME COUNTRY
1	Edwin van der Sar	GK	36	12	1080	0	0	0	Holland
2	Wayne Rooney	ATT	21	12	1060	4	1	0	England
3	Michael Carrick	MID	25	12	1027	2	1	0	England
4	Cristiano Ronaldo	MID	22	11	957	2	3	0	Portugal
5	Paul Scholes	MID	32	11	825	1	3	1	England
6	Rio Ferdinand	DEF	28	9	765	0	1	0	England
7	John O'Shea	DEF	26	11	683	1	0	0	Rep of Ireland
8	Nemanja Vidic	DEF	25	8	675	1	1	0	Serbia
9	Gabriel Ivan Heinze	DEF	29	8	638	0	2	0	Argentina
10	Wes Brown	DEF	27	7	630	0	0	0	England
11	Ryan Giggs	MID	33	8	600	2	1	0	Wales
12	Darren Fletcher	MID	23	9	561	0	1	0	Scotland
13	Gary Neville	DEF	32	6	540	0	0	0	England
14	Louis Saha	ATT	28	8	466	4	0	0	France
15	Patrice Evra	DEF	26	7	391	1	3	0	France
16	Ole Gunnar Solskjaer	ATT	34	6	293	1	1	0	Norway
17	Mikael Silvestre	DEF	29	3	270	0	1	0	France
18	Henrik Larsson	ATT	35	2	163	1	0	0	Sweden
19	Alan Smith	ATT	26	4	144	1	1	0	England
20	Kirran Richardson	MID	22	4	46	1	1	0	England
21	Ji-Sung Park	MID	26	1	9	0	0	0	South Korea

Champions League Semi-Final

Chelsea	1	Liverpool	0
J.Cole 29			39,483

	STATS	
9	Shots off target	5
4	Shots on target	4
1	Corners	5
9	Fouls	19
5	Offside	2
0	Yellows	1
0	Reds	0
48%	Possession	52%
Referee:		Markus Merk (GER)

Joe Cole slides in to give Chelsea a rare advantage over Liverpool in their Champions League tussles.
On his first start in the competition Cole races in to put away a low cross from Didier Drogba, whose powerful run and turn on the right flank exposes Daniel Agger.
Pepe Reina makes two fine saves from Frank Lampard and Javier Mascherano and John Arne Riise are both guilty of giving the ball away in dangerous positions as Liverpool contribute to Chelsea's dominance on the night. Chelsea keep an important clean sheet when Petr Cech dives to save Steven Gerrard's edge of the area shot

CHELSEA

	PLAYER	POS	AGE	APP	MINS ON	GOALS	CARDS(Y/R)		HOME COUNTRY
1	Didier Drogba	ATT	29	12	1051	6	2	0	Ivory Coast
2	Frank Lampard	MID	29	11	1019	1	3	0	England
3	Michael Essien	MID	24	10	930	2	3	0	Ghana
4	Ricardo Carvalho	DEF	29	10	900	0	0	0	Portugal
5	Michael Ballack	MID	30	10	884	2	2	0	Germany
6	John Terry	DEF	26	10	852	0	3	0	England
7	Ashley Cole	DEF	26	9	817	0	2	0	England
8	Andriy Shevchenko	ATT	28	10	762	3	0	0	Ukraine
9	Petr Cech	GK	27	8	750	0	1	0	Czech Republic
10	Claude Makelele	MID	34	9	703	0	1	0	France
11	John Obi Mikel	MID	20	9	584	0	1	0	Nigeria
12	Khalid Boulahrouz	DEF	25	5	434	0	0	0	Holland
13	Paulo Ferreira	DEF	28	6	383	0	0	0	Portugal
14	Joe Cole	MID	25	7	381	1	2	0	England
15	Arjen Robben	MID	23	8	353	1	2	0	Holland
16	Lassana Diarra	MID	22	5	323	0	2	0	France
17	Salomon Kalou	ATT	21	11	279	0	0	0	Ivory Coast
18	Henrique Hilario	GK	31	3	270	0	0	0	Portugal
19	Wayne Bridge	DEF	26	3	270	0	0	0	England
20	Geremi Nitjap	DEF	28	2	93	0	0	0	Cameroon
21	Carlo Cudicini	GK	33	1	90	0	0	0	Italy
22	Shaun Wright-Phillips	MID	25	6	82	1	0	0	England

Chelsea	1	Liverpool	0
J.Cole 29			39,483
	Liverpool win 4-1 on penalties		

	STATS	
7	Shots off target	6
6	Shots on target	4
5	Corners	6
32	Fouls	21
3	Offside	5
2	Yellows	1
0	Reds	0
54%	Possession	46%
Referee:		Manuel Mejoto Gonzales (ESP)

The two English semi-finalists are all level on aggregate after a great Agger finish from a cleverly worked Liverpool free-kick.
The Reds have the best of the chances on the night with Dirk Kuyt heading against the bar and also putting an extra time rebound into the net only to be ruled narrowly offside. At the other end the screening work of Javier Mascherano and four defiant defensive performances led by man-of-the-match Jamie Carragher, keep Chelsea's attack toothless.
A tight match comes down to penalties and Pepe Reina's reputation as a superb spot-kick keeper is enhanced with saves from Arjen Robben and Geremi to put Liverpool through

CHAMPIONS LEAGUE FINAL

AC Milan v Liverpool

AC Milan	2	Liverpool	1
Inzaghi 45, 82		Kuijt 89	
		74,000	

	STATS	
1	Shots off target	6
3	Shots on target	4
4	Corners	6
15	Fouls	27
3	Offside	3
2	Yellows	2
0	Reds	0
53%	Possession	47%
Referee:	Herbert Fandel (GER)	

In a reverse of the 2005 final, Pippo Inzaghi struck twice to give AC Milan revenge for their defeat in Istanbul.

Liverpool fans descended on Athens in their thousands, which led to a ticketing rumpus as some fans with legitimate tickets missed the game, while others with forgeries found a way into the stadium.

Allied to crowd scenes in Lille and Rome earlier in the competition, it has given Uefa's organising committee some issues to address for the future.

On the pitch, Liverpool played Stevie Gerrard in a central position ahead of the midfield.

Prompted by Jermaine Pennant, the Reds were the best side in the first half, without making many chances for lone striker Dirk Kuyt.

They were punished for their caution when Andrea Pirlo's free kick deflected in off Inzaghi's back just before half time in an outrageous piece of luck.

The Champions League's star performer and top scorer Kaka had one moment of class in a more even second half, slipping Inzaghi clear to round Pepe Reina for a more traditional finish.

Rafa Benitez had already deployed Peter Crouch and Kuyt pulled one back in the last minute but it was too late.

AC MILAN

	PLAYER	POS	AGE	APP	MINS ON	GOALS	CARDS(Y/R)		HOME COUNTRY
1	Ricardo Kaka	MID	25	15	1322	10	2	0	Brazil
2	Andrea Pirlo	MID	28	14	1207	1	0	0	Italy
3	Nelson Dida	GK	33	13	1187	0	0	0	Brazil
4	Clarence Seedorf	MID	31	14	1147	3	1	0	Holland
5	Marek Jankulovski	MID	30	13	1061	0	2	0	Czech Republic
6	Gennaro Gattuso	MID	29	13	1044	0	3	0	Italy
7	Massimo Ambrosini	MID	30	12	872	0	2	0	Italy
8	Filippo Inzaghi	ATT	33	12	816	6	0	0	Italy
9	Paolo Maldini	DEF	39	9	794	0	2	0	Italy
10	Massimo Oddo	DEF	31	7	656	0	0	0	Italy
11	Alessandro Nesta	DEF	31	8	648	0	0	0	Italy
12	Alberto Gilardino	ATT	24	11	646	2	3	0	Italy
13	Dario Simic	DEF	31	7	544	0	0	0	Croatia
14	Cafu	DEF	37	8	462	0	0	0	Brazil
15	Kakha Kaladze	DEF	29	7	439	0	1	0	Georgia
16	Daniele Bonera	DEF	26	6	419	0	2	1	Italy
17	Christian Brocchi	MID	31	8	402	0	0	0	Italy
18	Yoann Gourcuff	MID	20	8	370	1	0	0	France
19	Ricardo Oliveira	ATT	27	6	293	0	1	0	Brazil
20	Alessandro Costacurta	DEF	41	3	225	0	0	0	Italy
21	Serginho	MID	36	3	201	0	0	0	Brazil
22	Zeljko Kalac	GK	34	3	193	0	0	0	Australia
23	Marco Borriello	ATT	25	3	95	0	0	0	Italy
24	Giuseppe Favalli	DEF	35	4	93	0	0	0	Italy

LIVERPOOL

	PLAYER	POS	AGE	APP	MINS ON	GOALS	CARDS(Y/R)		HOME COUNTRY
1	Jose Reina	GK	24	14	1290	0	1	0	Spain
2	Jamie Carragher	DEF	29	13	1200	0	1	0	England
3	Steve Finnan	DEF	31	12	1107	0	1	0	Rep of Ireland
4	Xabi Alonso	MID	25	15	1104	0	2	0	Spain
5	Daniel Agger	DEF	22	12	1097	1	2	0	Denmark
6	John Arne Riise	MID	26	12	1071	2	0	0	Norway
7	Steven Gerrard	MID	27	12	968	3	0	0	England
8	Dirk Kuyt	ATT	26	11	928	1	3	0	Holland
9	Jermaine Pennant	MID	24	14	833	0	2	0	England
10	Peter Crouch	ATT	26	14	780	7	0	0	England
11	Boudewijn Zenden	MID	30	11	729	0	2	0	Holland
12	Momo Sissoko	MID	22	9	605	0	4	0	France
13	Craig Bellamy	ATT	27	12	542	2	1	0	Wales
14	Javier Luis Garcia	MID	29	7	462	3	0	0	Spain
15	Sami Hyypia	DEF	33	5	450	0	1	0	Finland
16	Javier Mascherano	MID	23	4	374	0	3	0	Argentina
17	Alvaro Arbeloa	DEF	24	5	363	0	1	0	Spain
18	Fabio Aurelio	DEF	27	5	322	0	0	0	Brazil
19	Mark Gonzalez	MID	22	8	267	0	0	0	Chile
20	Robbie Fowler	ATT	32	4	181	2	0	0	England
21	Stephen Warnock	DEF	25	3	121	0	0	0	England
22	Gabriel Paletta	DEF	21	2	103	0	0	0	Argentina
23	Jerzy Dudek	GK	34	1	90	0	0	0	Poland
24	Lee Peltier	MID	20	1	90	0	0	0	England
25	Danny Guthrie	MID	20	1	65	0	0	0	England
26	Harry Kewell	MID	27	1	32	0	0	0	Australia
27	Miguel Roque	DEF	18	1	6	0	0	0	Spain

CHAMPIONS LEAGUE FINAL

I meant that one: Inzaghi slips through the centre of the stretched Liverpool defence and is unerringly found by Kaka. Reina is quickly out of his goal but the veteran striker's instincts are too sharp and he easily takes the ball past the diving keeper and slides it home before racing for the corner flag

The evergreen Milan captain Paolo Maldini lifts the Champions League trophy he first won in 1989, to the delight of Rino Gattuso who revelled in their revenge over Liverpool

THE UEFA CUP

1ST ROUND

	AGG		LEG1	LEG2
Chornomorets	1-4 H. Tel-Aviv		0-1	1-3
Braga (aet)	3-2 Chievo		2-0	1-2
Levadia	1-3 Newcastle		0-1	1-2
Molde	0-2 Rangers		0-0	0-2

After a nervy draw in Norway, Rangers put in a confident first half at Ibrox to secure their place in the group stages. Buffel converts a Smith cross before captain Barry Ferguson ties it up with a second goal just before the interval

Standard	0-4 Celta		0-1	0-3
M. Haifa	4-2 Litex		1-1	3-1
Derry	0-2 PSG		0-0	0-2
Hertha	2-3 OB		2-2	0-1
Legia	1-2 Austria		1-1	0-1
Panathinaikos	2-1 Zaporizhya		1-1	1-0
Loko. Moscow	2-3 Zulte-Waregem		2-1	0-2
Hearts	0-2 Sparta		0-2	0-0
Fenerbahce	5-1 Randers		2-1	3-0
Salzburg	2-4 Blackburn		2-2	0-2

Schalke	2-3 Nancy		1-0	1-3
Achnas	1-3 Lens		0-0	1-3
Liberec	4-1 Crvena Zvezda		2-0	2-1
AZ	4-3 Kayserispor		3-2	1-1
Rubin	0-2 Parma		0-1	0-1
Eintracht	6-2 Br‾ndby		4-0	2-2
Rapid B'rst (aet)	3-1 Nacional		1-0	2-1
Besiktas (aet)	4-2 CSKA Sofia		2-0	2-2
Set´bal	0-3 Heerenveen		0-3	0-0
Marseille	3-4 Mlad· Boleslav		1-0	2-4

Atvidaberg	0-8 Grasshoppers		0-3	0-5
Atromitos	1-6 Seville		1-2	0-4

Holders Seville romp through to a 6-1 aggregate win over Greek side Atromitos with Fabiano scoring twice in the second leg as the Spaniards turn on the style in front of their own fans

GROUP A

Livorno   **2**   **Rangers**   **3**
C.Lucarelli 33 pen, 89   Adam 27
     Boyd 29 pen, Novo 35
13,200

Maccabi Haifa   **3**   **Auxerre**   **1**
Masudi 13, Boccoli 56,   Niculae 29
Colautti 58   8,000

Partizan   **1**   **Livorno**   **2**
Mirosavljevic 70   Amelia 88
12,170

Rangers   **2**   **Maccabi Haifa**   **0**
Novo 5, Adam 89 pen   43,062

Adam scores from the spot to gain a win for Rangers against Maccabi Haifa after Boyd misses an earlier penalty

Auxerre   **2**   **Rangers**   **2**
Jelen 31, Niculae 76   Novo 61, Boyd 84
8,305

Maccabi Haifa   **1**   **Partizan**   **0**
Anderson 21   13,000

Livorno   **1**   **Maccabi Haifa**   **1**
C.Lucarelli 20   Colautti 90
7,874

Partizan   **1**   **Auxerre**   **4**
Nebojsa.Marinkovic 5   Cheyrou 18, Niculae 24
     Akale 36, Pieroni 82
7,000

Auxerre   **0**   **Livorno**   **1**
     C.Lucarelli 59
8,000

Rangers   **1**   **Partizan**   **0**
Hutton 55   45,129

On paper a competitive group but Rangers quickly emerge as favourites by beating their two main rivals in the first two games.
Livorno follow that Rangers defeat with two draws but win in Auxerre to claim third spot while Maccabi Haifa impress with a 3-1 win over Auxerre to finish runners-up

GROUP A TABLE

	P	W	D	L	DIF	PTS
Rangers	4	3	1	0	4	10
M Haifa	4	2	1	1	1	7
Livorno	4	1	2	1	0	5
Auxerre	4	1	1	2	0	4
Partizan	4	0	1	3	-5	1

GROUP B

Besiktas   **0**   **Tottenham**   **2**
     Ghaly 31, Berbatov 63
26,800

Club Brugge   **1**   **B Leverkusen**   **1**
Clement 47   Schneider 35
20,000

Dinamo Bucharest   **2**   **Besiktas**   **1**
Cristea 21   Deivson 58
Niculescu 87 pen   10,000

Tottenham   **3**   **Club Brugge**   **1**
Berbatov 17, 73   Salou 14
Keane 63   35,716

B Leverkusen   **0**   **Tottenham**   **1**
     Berbatov 36
22,500

Club Brugge   **1**   **Dinamo Bucharest**   **1**
Vermant 62 pen   Niculescu 33
18,713

Besiktas   **2**   **Club Brugge**   **1**
Akin 32   Balaban 14 pen
Ricardinho 70 pen   19,668

Dinamo Bucharest   **2**   **B Leverkusen**   **1**
Niculescu 37, 73   Barbarez 22
12,000

B Leverkusen   **2**   **Besiktas**   **2**
Schneider 78   Ricardinho 90 pen
Barbarez 87   22,500

Tottenham   **3**   **Dinamo Bucharest**   **1**
Berbatov 16,   Mendy 90
Defoe 39, 50   34,004

Defoe scores twice and hits the bar as Spurs record an easy win over Dinamo Bucharest at White Hart lane to secure top spot. The in-form Berbatov opens the scoring against the Romanians with a 20-yard sizzler

Tottenham's' long-awaited return to European football results in an impressive 100% record in Group B. Ghaly and Berbatov score to gain a difficult away win over Besiktas and they never look back. Romanian side Dinamo Bucharest win two of their remaining games to go second while Leverkusen scrape third on four points

GROUP B TABLE

	P	W	D	L	DIF	PTS
Tottenham	4	4	0	0	7	12
D Bucharest	4	2	1	1	0	7
B Leverkusen	4	1	1	2	-1	4
Besiktas	4	1	0	3	-3	3
Club Brugge	4	0	2	2	-3	2

GROUP C

AZ Alkmaar   **3**   **Braga**   **0**
Arveladze 36, Koevermans 74
Schaars 79   13,534

Slovan Liberec   **0**   **Seville**   **0**
     8,000

Braga   **4**   **Slovan Liberec**   **0**
Chavez 30, Marcel 33
Cesinha 54 pen, Gama 90   15,000

Grasshoppers   **2**   **AZ Alkmaar**   **5**
Biscotte 29,   Arveladze 49, de Zeeuw 56
Eduardo 61   Dembele 78, 90
     Martens 90
5,000

Seville   **2**   **Braga**   **0**
Fabiano 40, Chevanton 76   40,000

Slovan Liberec   **4**   **Grasshoppers**   **1**
Blazek 7, Zapotocny 31   Schwegler 9
Papousek 68, Frejlach 90   6,670

AZ Alkmaar   **2**   **Slovan Liberec**   **2**
Steinsson 69   Zapotocny 25
Jenner 89   Papousek 85
15,745

Grasshoppers   **0**   **Seville**   **4**
     Daniel Alves 12, 53
     Chevanton 62, Kepa 84
7,300

Braga   **2**   **Grasshoppers**   **0**
Pinto 61, Castanheira 90   10,500

Seville   **1**   **AZ Alkmaar**   **2**
Chevanton 52 pen   Arveladze 62, 90
20,000

Georgia international striker Shota Arveladze scores a double as AZ take the honours at cup holders Seville

The form teams AZ and Seville are both sure of the next round before their head-to-head. Grasshoppers lose all four games to leave Portugal's Braga to claim third spot ahead of Slovakia's Liberec by beating their rivals 4-0 at home with goals from Chavez and Gama, and two more made in Brazil from Marcel and Cesinha

GROUP C TABLE

	P	W	D	L	DIF	PTS
AZ Alkmaar	4	3	1	0	7	10
Seville	4	2	1	1	5	7
Braga	4	2	0	2	6	6
Liberec	4	1	2	1	-1	5
Grasshoppers	4	0	0	4	-12	0

GROUP D

Odense   **1**   **Parma**   **2**
Hansen 7   Dessena 40, Budan 50
12,559

Osasuna   **0**   **Heerenveen**   **0**
     20,000

Heerenveen   **0**   **Odense**   **2**
     Lekic 45, 59
17,500

Lens   **3**   **Osasuna**   **1**
Dindane 15,   Valdo 46
Cousin 69 pen,
Boukari 82   26,000

Odense   **1**   **Lens**   **2**
Grahn 58   Jemaa 87
7,707

Parma   **2**   **Heerenveen**   **1**
Budan 24, 73   Pranjic 21
3,632

Lens   **1**   **Parma**   **2**
Cousin 19   Dedic 77, Paponi 90
32,341

Osasuna   **3**   **Odense**   **1**
Punal 29, 67, Romeo 87   Punal 75 og
13,000

Osasuna striker Lopez scores two first-half goals to set up a crucial victory against an already-qualified Parma side

Heerenveen   **1**   **Lens**   **0**
Alves 90   17,000

Parma   **0**   **Osasuna**   **3**
     David Lopez 33, 44
     Juanfran 82
3,109

Osasuna and Parma confirm their favourites' status by qualifying first and second. However, Osasuna need to win their last game in Italy to make sure of progressing. Lens sneak through with the best record of the other three teams, all stuck on four points and can thank in-form striker Aruna Dindane for launching a 3-1 win over Osasuna

GROUP D TABLE

	P	W	D	L	DIF	PTS
Parma	4	3	0	1	0	9
Osasuna	4	2	1	1	3	7
Lens	4	1	1	2	0	4
Odense	4	1	1	2	-1	4
Heerenveen	4	1	1	2	-2	4

Trabzonspor	2-2 Osasuna (ag)	2-2	0-0
Basel	7-2 Rabotnicki	6-2	1-0
West Ham	0-4 Palermo	0-1	0-3
Loko Sofia	2-2 Feyenoord (ag)	2-2	0-0
Ru~omberok	1-2 Club Brugge	0-1	1-1
Sion	1-3 Leverkusen	0-0	1-3

Bayer Leverkusen are made to fight hard for their 3-1 aggregate against Swiss side. Schneider slots home a late penalty to secure a place in the next round for the Bundesliga club. Sion have two players sent-off late on

GROUP E

Basel 1 **Feyenoord** 1
Eduardo 60 / Huysegems 76
16,000

Wisla Krakow 1 **Blackburn** 2
Cantoro 28 / Savage 56, Bentley 89
14,000

Blackburn 3 **Basel** 0
Tugay 75, Jeffers 89 pen McCarthy 90
13,789

Nancy 2 **Wisla Krakow** 1
Berenguer 11, 58 / Brozek 32
18,000

Basel 2 **Nancy** 3
Chipperfield 32, / Kim 31, Berenguer 34
Sterjovski 56
14,497

Feyenoord 0 **Blackburn** 0
35,000

Nancy 3 **Feyenoord** 0
Puygrenier 23
Bahia 43 og, Zerka 66 pen
19,840

Wisla Krakow 3 **Basel** 1
Brozek 11, 83, Paulista 71 / Petric 8
12,000

Blackburn 1 **Nancy** 0
Neill 90
12,568

Neill's superb turn and shot from the edge of the area deep into stoppage time settles a match that seems certain to finish goalless after both keepers produce a string of vital saves. Friedel shines for Blackburn, while Lapeyre is outstanding on his debut for Nancy

Feyenoord 3 **Wisla Krakow** 1
Hofs 16, de Guzman 41, / Brozek 23
Charisteas 67
24,000

Blackburn set down an early marker with a win in Krakow and a late rush of goals at home to Basel but Feyenoord hold them to a draw. Nancy also have two wins and a draw and the French and English sides meet to decide the group. Rovers snatch a narrow 1-0 win at Ewood Park to top the table. Feyenoord finish third after winning their last game.

GROUP E TABLE

	P	W	D	L	DIF	PTS
Blackburn	4	3	1	0	5	10
Nancy	4	2	1	1	3	7
Feyenoord	4	1	2	1	-1	5
Wisla	4	1	0	3	-2	3
Basel	4	0	2	2	-5	2

Partizan	4-3 Groningen	4-2	0-1
Xanthi	4-8 Dinamo Bucuresti	3-4	1-4

The fleet-footed Niculescu scores a brace in goals in both legs as Dinamo Bucuresti hammer Greek side Xanthi 8-4 on aggregate

GROUP F

Austria Vienna 1 **Zulte-Waregem** 4
Lasnik 22 / Matthys 33, 56, 69
Vandendriessche 90
11,100

Sparta Prague 0 **Espanyol** 2
Luis Garcia 17 pen, Riera 85
11,020

Ajax 3 **Austria Vienna** 0
Huntelaar 35, 68,
Manucharyan 65
30,000

Zulte-Waregem 3 **Sparta Prague** 1
Roussel 4, Meert 17, / Lustrinelli 85
Repka 63 og
6,000

Espanyol 6 **Zulte-Waregem** 2
Corominas 9 / Matthys 17
Pandiani 14, 83 / D'Haene 62
Luis Garcia 19, 27 pen, 73
10,000

Garcia helps himself to a hat-trick as Espanyol hit Zulte-Waregem for six

Sparta Prague 0 **Ajax** 0
12,230

Ajax 0 **Espanyol** 2
Pandiani 36, Corominas 77
41,248

Austria Vienna 0 **Sparta Prague** 1
Repka 11
10,000

Espanyol 1 **Austria Vienna** 0
Pandiani 57
5,580

Zulte-Waregem 0 **Ajax** 3
Huntelaar 3, 57
Heitinga 83
12,000

Espanyol are a 100% team in Group F and goals from Pandiani and Corominas despatch closest rivals, Ajax, in Holland. Austria Vienna finish pointless, leaving Belgian club Zulte-Waregem to pip Sparta Prague to third place (by beating them 3-1) despite being off the pace in their domestic league.

GROUP F TABLE

	P	W	D	L	DIF	PTS
Espanyol	4	4	0	0	9	12
Ajax	4	2	1	1	4	7
Zulte-Waregem	4	2	0	2	-2	6
Sparta	4	1	1	2	-3	4
Austria	4	0	0	4	-8	0

Slavia	0-2 Tottenham	0-1	0-1

Jenas scores the winner in a dull first leg in Prague and then Tottenham struggle to score at home until Keane notches his first goal of the season

Artmedia	3-5 Espanyol	2-2	1-3

GROUP G

Panathinaikos 2 **Hapoel Tel-Aviv** 0
Chen 47 og, Romero 64
100

Rapid Bucharest 0 **Paris SG** 0
15,000

Hapoel Tel-Aviv 2 **Rapid Bucharest** 2
Barda 10, Badir 33 / Zicu 14, Buga 53
13,000

Mlada Boleslav 0 **Panathinaikos** 1
Salpiggidis 64
5,000

Toama's quickfire double gives Hapoel Tel-Aviv an early advantage at Paris St Germain. The French side hit back to equalise but Badir restores the visitors' lead and Barda makes it four.

Paris SG 2 **Hapoel Tel-Aviv** 4
Frau 14, Pauleta 25 / Toama 2, 6
Badir 44, Barda 57
35,000

Rapid Bucharest 1 **Mlada Boleslav** 1
M..Constantin 52 / Raijnoch 42
10,000

Mlada Boleslav 0 **Paris SG** 0
5,000

Panathinaikos 0 **Rapid Bucharest** 0
15,000

Hapoel Tel-Aviv 1 **Mlada Boleslav** 0
Barda 27 / Kysela 39
10,000

Paris SG 4 **Panathinaikos** 0
Pauleta 29, 47, Kalou 52, 54
20,000

The tightest group in the competition sees Paris St Germain and Hapoel Tel-Aviv progressing with only five points. Panathinaikos manage seven points but are comprehensively beaten in Paris with Pauleta in striking form. Rapid Bucharest draw every game and finish just ahead of Czech side Mlada Bolesla, who have three draws

GROUP G TABLE

	P	W	D	L	DIF	PTS
Panathinaikos	4	2	1	1	-1	7
Paris SG	4	1	2	1	2	5
H Tel-Aviv	4	1	2	1	0	5
R Bucharest	4	0	4	0	0	4
Mlada B	4	0	3	1	-1	3

Wisla (aet)	2-1 Iraklis	0-1	2-0
Livorno	3-0 Pasching	2-0	1-0
Dinamo Zagreb	2-5 Auxerre	1-2	1-3
Start	2-9 Ajax	2-5	0-4

aet - After extra time
(ag) - Won on away goals

Competition rules:
40 clubs go through to the Group Stage in eight groups of five teams, each playing two home and two away games. The top three clubs in each group go through to the Round of 32, joined by the eight third-placed clubs from the Champions League Group Stage.

GROUP H

Eintr Frankfurt 1 **Palermo** 2
Streit 45 / Brienza 49, Zaccardo 87
45,000

Newcastle 1 **Fenerbahce** 0
Sibierski 79
30,035

Celta Vigo 1 **Eintr Frankfurt** 0
Perera 11 / Huber 17
10,000

Palermo 0 **Newcastle** 1
Luque 37
16,904

Fenerbahce 3 **Palermo** 0
Appiah 20, Lugano 62
Sanli 83
45,000

Fenerbahce's Lugano celebrates the goal that condemns Italy's Palermo team to defeat in Istanbul. His goal, added to the earlier effort from Ghanaian captain Appiah, ensures a Group H win and proves the key result in Fenebahce's progress through in third place

Newcastle 2 **Celta Vigo** 1
Sibierski 37, Taylor 86 / Canobbio 9
25,079

Celta Vigo 1 **Fenerbahce** 0
Canobbio 77
10,000

Eintr Frankfurt 0 **Newcastle** 0
47,000

Fenerbahce 2 **Eintr Frankfurt** 2
Tuncay Sanli 64 / Takahara 7, 52
Semih Senturk 83
50,000

Palermo 1 **Celta Vigo** 1
Tedesco 70 / Baiano 83
10,222

Newcastle are the fourth British side to top a table in the group stages of the Uefa Cup after beating experienced European campaigners Fenerbahce and Celta Vigo. Sibierski scores some vital goals, while Albert Luque makes a rare appearnce to hit the winner against Palermo. Fenerbahce and Celta qualify ahead of Palermo.

GROUP H TABLE

	P	W	D	L	DIF	PTS
Newcastle	4	3	1	0	3	10
Celta Vigo	4	1	2	1	0	5
Fenerbahce	4	1	1	2	1	4
Palermo	4	1	1	2	-3	4
Eintracht	4	0	3	1	-1	3

ROUND OF 32

The eight third-placed clubs from the Champions League Groups to join the 24 Uefa Cup sides through from the Group Stage are: Werder Bremen, Spartak Moscow, Bordeaux, Shakhtar Donetsk, Steaua Bucharest, Benfica, CSKA Moscow, and AEK Athens

AEK Athens	0	Paris SG	2
		Traore 45, Mendy 88	
			30,000

Paris SG	(2) 2	AEK Athens	(0) 0
Frau 42, Mendy 90 pen			25,000

B Leverkusen	3	Blackburn	2
Callsen-Bracker 18,		Bentley 39	
Ramelow 43,		Nonda 86	
Schneider 56			22,500

Blackburn	(2) 0	B Leverkusen	(3) 0
			25,124

Benfica	1	Dinamo Bucharest	0
Miccoli 90			35,000

Benfica fall behind to Dinamo's early second leg goal scored by Munteanu but a whipped cross from man-of-the-match Simao is headed home by Anderson before Katsouranis gets on the end of another Simao cross to crush the Romanian side's hopes

Dinamo Bucharest	(0) 1	Benfica	(1) 2
Munteanu 23		Anderson 50	
		Katsouranis 64	
			15,300

Bordeaux	0	Osasuna	0
			20,000

Osasuna	(0) 1	Bordeaux	(0) 0
Nekounam 120			14,000

CSKA Moscow	0	Maccabi Haifa	0
			19,000

Maccabi Haifa	(0) 1	CSKA Moscow	(0) 0
Colautti 14			14,000

Fenerbahce	3	AZ Alkmaar	3
Metin 28, 75,		de Zeeuw 15	
Tuncay Sanli 66		Boukhari 62, Jenner 63	
			38,000

AZ Alkmaar	(3) 2	Fenerbahce	(3) 2
Martens 64, Opdam 86		Tumer 21, Alex 34	
			16,191

Hapoel Tel-Aviv	2	Rangers	1
Toama 43, Dago 76		Novo 53	
			13,000

Rangers	(1) 4	Hapoel Tel-Aviv	(2) 0
Ferguson 24, 73,			
Boyd 35, Adam 90			46,213

Captain Ferguson leads by example with two goals as Rangers trounce Israeli rivals, overcoming a 2-1 first leg deficit. Rangers keeper McGregor is red-carded and misses the next round

Livorno	1	Espanyol	2
Galante 82		Pandiani 28 pen, Moha 59	
		game played behind closed doors	

Espanyol	(2) 2	Livorno	(1) 0
Lacruz Gomez 16			
Coriminas 49			10,000

Espanyol's Moroccan Mohamed El Yaagoubi congratulates Pandiani after a successful penalty that helps earn an away leg win in Italy.
The Spanish side finish the job with LaCruz Gomez and Coriminas scoring for the Parakeets at home

Shakhtar Donetsk	1	Nancy	1
Srna 84		Fortune 81	
			23,000

Nancy	(1) 0	Shakhtar Donetsk	(1) 1
		Fernandinho 70	
			18,000

W Bremen	3	Ajax	0
Mertesacker 48,			
Naldo 54, Frings 71			38,150

Ajax	(0) 3	W Bremen	(3) 1
Leonardo 3,		Hugo Almeida 14	
Huntelaar 60, Babel 74			35,227

Braga	1	Parma	0
Silva 81			6,127

Parma	(0) 0	Braga	(1) 1
		Diego 89	
			3,861

Lens	3	Panathinaikos	1
Jemaa 49, 70,		Salpiggidis 65	
Dindane 90 pen			40,000

Panathinaikos	(1) 0	Lens	(3) 0
			30,000

Lens do the hard work in the first leg, with two Jemaa strikes. The Tunisian scores either side of Panathinaikos' reply through Salpingidis but Dindane's late penalty gives Lens the edge

Spartak Moscow	1	Celta Vigo	1
Kalinichenko 62		Nunez 41	
			30,000

Celta Vigo	(1) 2	Spartak Moscow	(1) 1
Nene 19, Jonathan 78		Titov 88	
			7,000

Steaua Bucharest	0	Seville	2
28,000		Poulsen 41, Kanoute 76 pen	

Seville	(2) 1	Steaua Bucharest	(0) 0
Kerzhakov 45			25,000

Zulte-Waregem	1	Newcastle	3
D'Haene 68		Dindeleux 47 og	
		Martins 59 pen,	
		Sibierski 76	
			8,015

Newcastle	(3) 1	Zulte-Waregem	(1) 0
Martins 68			30,083

LAST 16

Braga	2	Tottenham	3
Paulo Jorge 76,		Keane 57, 90	
Carlos 81		Malbranque 72	
			15,000

Tottenham	(3) 3	Braga	(2) 2
Berbatov 28, 42,		Huddlestone 24 og	
Malbranque 76		Amaral 61	
			33,761

Braga's spectacular quarry stadium hosts a first leg of fluctuating fortunes. Spurs' Robbie Keane and Steed Malbranque give the visitors a two-goal lead, but Keane needs a 92nd minute winner after Braga level. Dimitar Berbatov scores a brace in Spurs' home leg

Celta Vigo	0	W Bremen	1
		Hugo Almeida 84	
			20,000

W Bremen	(1) 2	Celta Vigo	(0) 0
Hugo Almeida 48			
Fritz 61			28,000

A headed goal in each leg of the tie by Portuguese striker Almeida is Bremen's passport into the quarter finals. He tucks away Wome's cross in Spain for a late away goal and adds a second half goal at home to leave Celta Vigo needing three

Lens	2	B Leverkusen	1
Monterrubio 17		Haggui 51	
Cousin 70 pen			29,200

B Leverkusen	(1) 3	Lens	(2) 0
Voronin 36, Barbarez 55			
Juan 70			22,500

Ukrainian Voronin's drive gives Leverkusen the impetus in their second leg against Lens. Barbarez snaps up a rebound to make Lens' job harder and defender Juan settles it by heading home a Voronin corner

Maccabi Haifa	0	Espanyol	0
			15,000

Espanyol	(0) 4	Maccabi Haifa	(0) 0
De La Pena 53, Tamudo 59,			
Luis Garcia 61, Pandiani 90			16,000

No goals in the first 143 minutes of this tie and then Espanyol hit four in the final 37 minutes. Ivan De la Pena scores the breakthrough goal from distance early in the second half and the floodgates open

Seville	2	Shakhtar Donetsk	2
Marti 8 pen,		Hubschman 19	
Maresca 88 pen		Matuzalem 60 pen	
			35,000

Shakhtar Donetsk	(2) 2	Seville	(2) 3
Matuzalem 49,		Maresca 53, Palop 90	
Elano 83		Chevanton 106	
			30,000

Shakhtar stun holders Seville by drawing 2-2 in Spain. Palop keeps Seville in the tie with a 94th minute second leg equaliser in the Ukraine to force extra time and Uruguayan Ernesto Chevanton then adds a winner

Paris SG	2	Benfica	1
Pauleta 36, Frau 41		Simao Sabrosa 10	
			35,000

Benfica	(1) 3	Paris SG	(2) 1
Simao 12, 89 pen,		Pauleta 32	
Petit 27			65,000

Benfica's star winger Simao holds his nerve to score an 89th minute penalty in a tight tie against PSG. The French lead 2-1 from the first leg but Portugal draw level on aggregate and it's all square until the late spot kick.

Rangers	1	Osasuna	1
Hemdani 90		Raul Garcia 17	
			50,290

Osasuna	(1) 1	Rangers	(1) 0
Webo 71			35,000

Osasuna are the better side in Glasgow, scoring through Garcia's sharp header. Hemdani's late equaliser for Rangers isn't enough as Webo's second leg goal puts Osasuna through more comfortably than the scoreline suggests

Newcastle	4	AZ Alkmaar	2
Steinsson 7 og, Dyer 22		Arveladze 31	
Martins 23, 37		Koevermans 73	
			28,452

AZ Alkmaar	(2) 2	Newcastle	(4) 0
Arveladze 14, Koevermans 56			16,401

Newcastle striker Martins rips AZ Alkmaar apart in the first leg at St James' Park, scoring twice and setting up a 4-1 halftime lead. Other missed chances cost Newcastle dear when Koevermans adds a second away goal and AZ win 2-0 at home in Holland

QUARTER-FINALS

AZ Alkmaar	0	W Bremen	0
			16,000

W Bremen	(0) 4	AZ Alkmaar	(0) 1
Borowski 16, Klose 36, 62		Dembele 32	
Diego 82			35,000

Germany's World Cup stars Borowski and Klose drive Bremen into the semis with three second leg goals. Borowski's opener is levelled by Dembele before two Klose strikes - a poke home and a header – settle it for Bremen before Diego adds a late fourth

B Leverkusen	0	Osasuna	3
		Cuellar 1, D Lopez 72	
		Webo 73	
			22,500

Osasuna	(3) 1	B Leverkusen	(0) 0
Juanlu 62			19,800

A first minute first leg Cuellar header from a corner sets Osasuna on their way and two more away goals effectively end Leverkusen's interest in this tie. Gomez scores a rebound goal in the home tie to put the Spanish side in the semi-finals

Espanyol	3	Benfica	2
Tamudo 15,		Nuno Gomes 63	
Nelson 33 og, Pandiani 58		Simao 65	
			20,000

Benfica	(2) 0	Espanyol	(3) 0
			40,000

Espanyol strike first through Tamudo and cruise into a three goal lead with a Riera shot and a header from tournament top-scorer Pandiani. Benfica respond through Nuno Gomes and Simao, but can't score in the second leg

Seville	2	Tottenham	1
Kanoute 19 pen		Keane 2	
Kerzhakov 36			40,000

Tottenham	(1) 2	Seville	(2) 2
Defoe 65		Malbranque 3 og	
Lennon 67		Kanoute 8	
			35,284

Keane gives Spurs a dream start in Seville with his ninth goal in as many games. A bad penalty call against keeper Robinson sees Kanoute (pictured) level against his former side before Kerzhakov heads a winner. A second leg draw earns Seville the tie

SEMI-FINALS

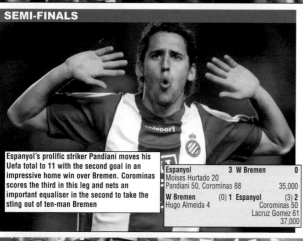

Espanyol's prolific striker Pandiani moves his Uefa total to 11 with the second goal in an impressive home win over Bremen. Corominas scores the third in this leg and nets an important equaliser in the second to take the sting out of ten-man Bremen

Espanyol	3	W Bremen	0
Moises Hurtado 20			
Pandiani 50, Corominas 88			35,000

W Bremen	(0) 1	Espanyol	(3) 2
Hugo Almeida 4		Corominas 50	
		Lacruz Gomez 61	
			37,000

Osasuna	1	Seville	0
Soldado 55			19,500

Seville	(0) 2	Osasuna	(1) 0
Fabiano 37, Renato 53			45,000

Uefa Cup holders Seville will travel to Hampden Park to defend the trophy. Osasuna hold a narrow first leg lead through Soldado in an all-Spanish affair. It never looks enough as Fabiano drives home a goal to level the tie, before Renato's volley wins it

Espanyol	2	Seville	2
Riera 28,		Adriano Correia 18	
Jonatas 115		Kanoute 105	
			50,000
Seville win 3-1 on penalties			

Seville keeper Palop saves three shoot-out penalties as the holders become only the second club to retain the Uefa Cup despite twice losing the lead to Espanyol in a thrilling all-Spanish final in Glasgow. Espanyol finish the match with ten men following Hurtado's second-half dismissal but don't give up the fight with Jonatas advancing to grab a late extra-time equaliser when his deflected shot makes it 2-2 and takes the game to penalties. Palop then performs his heroics between the posts

EUROPEAN LEAGUES ROUND-UP

FINAL PREMIERSHIP LEAGUE TABLE - TOP THREE

		HOME					AWAY					TOTAL		
	P	W	D	L	F	A	W	D	L	F	A	F	A	DIF	PTS
Man Utd	38	15	2	2	46	12	13	3	3	37	15	83	27	56	89
Chelsea	38	12	7	0	37	11	12	4	3	27	13	64	24	40	83
Liverpool	38	14	4	1	39	7	6	4	9	18	20	57	27	30	68

FINAL DUTCH LEAGUE TABLE - TOP THREE

		HOME					AWAY					TOTAL		
	P	W	D	L	F	A	W	D	L	F	A	F	A	DIF	PTS
PSV	34	15	0	2	53	14	8	6	3	22	11	75	25	50	75
Ajax	34	12	3	2	44	12	11	3	3	40	23	84	35	49	75
AZ	34	10	6	1	44	13	11	3	3	39	18	83	31	52	72

FINAL FRENCH LEAGUE TABLE - TOP THREE

		HOME					AWAY					TOTAL		
	P	W	D	L	F	A	W	D	L	F	A	F	A	DIF	PTS
Lyon	38	12	6	1	32	14	12	3	4	32	13	64	27	37	81
Marseille	38	14	2	3	35	16	5	5	9	18	22	53	38	15	64
Toulouse	38	10	4	5	26	17	7	3	9	18	26	44	43	1	58

FINAL GERMAN LEAGUE TABLE - TOP THREE

		HOME					AWAY					TOTAL		
	P	W	D	L	F	A	W	D	L	F	A	F	A	DIF	PTS
VfB Stuttgart	34	12	3	2	30	13	9	4	4	31	24	61	37	24	70
Schalke 04	34	13	2	2	30	11	8	3	6	23	21	53	32	21	68
Werder Bremen	34	11	1	5	33	18	9	5	3	43	22	76	40	36	66

FINAL ITALIAN LEAGUE TABLE - TOP THREE

		HOME					AWAY					TOTAL		
	P	W	D	L	F	A	W	D	L	F	A	F	A	DIF	PTS
Inter Milan	38	15	3	1	42	19	15	4	0	38	15	80	34	46	97
Roma	38	13	4	2	43	12	9	5	5	31	22	74	34	40	75
Lazio*	38	10	6	3	25	9	8	5	6	34	24	59	33	26	62

FINAL SPANISH LEAGUE TABLE - TOP THREE

		HOME					AWAY					TOTAL		
	P	W	D	L	F	A	W	D	L	F	A	F	A	DIF	PTS
Real Madrid	38	12	4	3	32	18	11	3	5	34	22	66	40	26	76
Barcelona	38	14	5	0	41	12	8	5	6	37	21	78	33	45	76
Seville	38	15	2	2	41	13	6	6	7	23	22	64	35	29	71

CLUB STRIKE FORCE

Ajax players celebrate after scoring a goal

1 Ajax

Club Strike Rate (CSR) Average number of minutes between League goals scored by club		36

	CLUB	LEAGUE GOALS	CSR
1	Ajax	84	36
2	AZ Alkmaar	83	36
3	PSV Eindhoven	75	40
4	W Bremen	76	40
5	Man Utd	83	41
6	Inter Milan	80	42
7	Barcelona	78	43
8	Twente	67	45
9	Roma	74	46
10	Stuttgart	61	50
11	Real Madrid	66	51
12	Heerenveen	60	51
13	Chelsea	64	53
14	Seville	64	53
15	Lyon	64	53
16	Arsenal	63	54
17	Feyenoord	56	54
18	Fiorentina	62	55
19	Bayern Munich	55	55
20	Groningen	54	56

Goals scored in the League   84

CLUB DEFENCES

1 Chelsea

Club Defensive Rate (CDR) Average number of minutes between League goals conceded by club		142

	CLUB	CONCEDED	CLEAN SH	CDR
1	Chelsea	24	22	142
2	Liverpool	27	20	126
3	Man Utd	27	16	126
4	Lyon	27	15	126
5	PSV Eindhoven	25	17	122
6	Rennes	30	16	114
7	Fiorentina	31	19	110
8	Barcelona	33	15	103
9	Getafe	33	15	103
10	Lazio	33	18	103
11	Roma	34	14	100
12	Inter Milan	34	15	100
13	AZ Alkmaar	31	16	98
14	Arsenal	35	12	97
15	Seville	35	14	97
16	Bordeaux	35	17	97
17	Everton	36	14	95
18	AC Milan	36	17	95
19	Nuremberg	32	12	95
20	Schalke	32	14	95

Chelsea's John Terry battles for the ball

Goals conceded Number of goals conceded in League games	24
Clean Sheets (CS) Number of league games where no goals were conceded	22

PLAYER NATIONALITIES

1 Country with the most player representation across major European leagues - Italy

Number of players	436	International appearances 06-07	116
Number of occasions in squad	10640	Total minutes played	602886
Actual League appearances	8297	% of European League action	14.32

	COUNTRY	NO OF PLAYERS	CAPS	IN SQUAD	LGE APP	MINS PLAYED	% LGE ACT
1	Italy	436	116	10640	8297	602886	14.32
2	France	447	146	10225	7982	578338	13.73
3	Spain	313	144	8038	6107	441047	10.47
4	Holland	384	183	7756	5943	437311	10.39
5	England	304	166	5253	4440	332443	7.9
6	Germany	289	164	5581	4008	289764	6.88
7	Brazil	138	123	3377	2904	216895	5.15
8	Argentina	77	44	1980	1588	115001	2.73
9	Belgium	62	61	1300	1019	69827	1.66
10	Portugal	45	67	1064	862	60227	1.43
11	Ivory Coast	29	46	800	741	54837	1.3
12	Senegal	34	1	787	635	47715	1.13
13	Denmark	47	106	922	698	46116	1.1
14	Czech Republic	36	102	863	662	45478	1.08
15	Serbia	32	72	754	635	44516	1.06
16	Nigeria	26	1	646	554	39526	0.94
17	Cameroon	34	0	672	527	37538	0.89
18	Sweden	26	79	605	500	36798	0.87
19	Rep of Ireland	28	79	563	485	36313	0.86
20	Australia	25	33	589	453	35826	0.85

CLUB MAKE-UP – HOME AND OVERSEAS PLAYERS

1 Club which used the most overseas players in league action - Arsenal

Overseas players in named 16s	30	Home country players in named 16s	8
Percent of overseas players	78.9	Percent of League action	99.02
Most appearances	Jens Lehmann	% of match time played	94.7

	CLUB	OVERSEAS	HOME	% OVERSEAS	% LGE ACT	MOST APP	% APP
1	Arsenal	30	8	78.9	99.02	Jens Lehmann	94.7
2	Inter Milan	27	7	79.4	95.45	Javier Zanetti	91.6
3	Blackburn	23	10	69.7	81.04	Brad Friedel	98.7
4	Bolton	23	6	79.3	78.23	Jussi Jaaskelainen	100
5	Cottbus	17	11	60.7	69.4	Tomislav Piplica	89.5
6	PSV Eindhoven	23	13	63.9	66.83	Timmy Simons	89.5
7	Fulham	24	10	70.6	73.07	Brian McBride	84.7
8	Chelsea	22	10	68.8	71.07	Michael Essien	86.8
9	Hamburg	18	17	51.4	62.72	Joris Mathijsen	88.1
10	Villarreal	23	7	76.7	69.84	Diego Forlan	88.1
11	Heerenveen	18	16	52.9	60.64	Brian Vandenbussche	90.4
12	Celta Vigo	25	11	69.4	67.03	Diego Placente	87.8
13	Wolfsburg	17	12	58.6	59.74	Tom van der Leegte	82.1
14	B M'gladbach	20	15	57.1	59.73	José Ze Antonio	78.9
15	Schalke	13	17	43.3	59.1	Rafinha	78.3
16	Roda JC Kerk	15	9	62.5	58.89	Davy De Fauw	86.3
17	Liverpool	23	14	62.2	65.74	Jose Reina	92.1
18	Reading	19	13	59.4	65.28	Ivar Ingimarsson	100
19	Atl Madrid	25	8	75.8	65.26	Leonardo Franco	82.9
20	Everton	19	11	63.3	64.31	Joseph Yobo	100

CLUB DISCIPLINARY RECORDS

Madrid's Cannavaro is shown a red card

	Yellow cards	117
	Red cards	11
	Total	128

1 Real Madrid

Cards Average in League		
Average number of minutes between a card being shown of either colour		26

	CLUB	Y	R	TOTAL	AVE
1	Real Madrid	117	11	128	26
2	Deportivo	115	11	126	27
3	Atl Madrid	114	10	124	27
4	R Santander	114	9	123	27
5	Levante	112	13	125	27
6	Osasuna	112	6	118	28
7	Real Zaragoza	110	8	118	28
8	Messina	107	13	120	28
9	Ascoli	107	8	115	29
10	Espanyol	104	9	113	30
11	Celta Vigo	101	11	112	30
12	Seville	96	11	107	31
13	Valencia	101	9	110	31
14	Reggina	104	5	109	31
15	Real Betis	95	11	106	32
16	Parma	99	6	105	32
17	Catania	95	11	106	32
18	Siena	92	12	104	32
19	Atalanta	94	7	101	33
20	Villarreal	95	5	100	34

PLAYER DISCIPLINARY RECORD

Tough tackling Garcia in a action for Celta

1 Garcia - Celta Vigo

Cards Average		
mins between cards		89
League Yellow		9
League Red		2
TOTAL		11

	PLAYER	CLUB	Y	R	TOTAL	AVE
1	Garcia	Celta Vigo	9	2	11	89
2	Beckham	Real Madrid	12	1	13	108
3	Tacchinardi	Villarreal	10	0	10	110
4	Minieri	Ascoli	8	2	10	125
5	Leko	AS Monaco	15	0	15	128
6	Codrea	Siena	10	1	11	131
7	Helguson	Fulham	10	1	11	133
8	Marti	Seville	10	1	11	143
9	Luccin	Atl Madrid	15	3	18	145
10	Diogo	Real Zaragoza	16	2	18	147
11	Doni	Atalanta	13	0	13	158
12	Murillo	Athl Bilbao	16	1	17	162
13	Rool	Nice	12	1	13	163
14	Pinilla	Gimnastic	10	0	10	164
15	Deco	Barcelona	14	1	15	165
16	Ardito	Torino	10	1	11	166
17	Tamas	Celta Vigo	11	2	13	167
18	Contra	Getafe	9	1	10	167
19	Perez	AS Monaco	10	1	11	168
20	Jarolim	Hamburg	14	1	15	169
			(mimimum of ten cards)			

TEAM OF THE SEASON

CECH		
CHELSEA		
CG	19	DR	190

ALEXIS		
GETAFE		
CG	23	DR	162

ALEX		
PSV EINDHOVEN		
CG	27	DR	167

TERRY		
CHELSEA		
CG	27	DR	172

AGGER		
LIVERPOOL		
CG	23	DR	197

TIAGO		
LYON		
CG	19	SD	+84

MAKELELE		
CHELSEA		
CG	24	SD	+134

GIGGS		
MAN UTD		
CG	22	SD	+104

RIISE		
LIVERPOOL		
CG	27	SD	+91

KOEVERMANS		
AZ ALKMAAR		
CG	20	AP	34

ALVES		
HEERENVEEN		
CG	30	SR	79

The European Team of the Season shows a 4-4-2 of the best players in the major European Leagues based upon the selection criteria used for the chart-toppers. The players selected are taken from the lists for each club except that to get into this Team of the Season you must have played at least 17 Counting Games in league matches (roughly half the league season) and not 12 as is the case in the club lists. The other restriction is that we are only allowing one player from each club in each position.
· **The Top team's goalkeeper** is the player with the highest *Defensive Rating*
· **The Top team's defenders** are also tested by *Defensive Rating*, i.e. the average number of minutes between league goals conceded while on the pitch.
· **The Top team's midfield** are selected on their *Scoring Difference*, i.e.their *Defensive Rating* minus their *Contribution to Attacking Power* (average number of minutes between league goals scored while on the pitch. It takes no account of assists.
· **The Top team strikeforce** is made up of the striker with the highest *Strike Rate* (his average number of minutes between league goals scored while on the pitch) together with the striker with the highest *Contribution to Attacking Power.*

CHART-TOPPING POINT EARNERS

	PLAYER	TEAM	GAMES	POINTS	AVE
1	Patrick Vieira	Inter Milan	19	53	2.79
2	Ryan Giggs	Man Utd	22	56	2.55
3	Koevermans	AZ Alkmaar	20	49	2.45
4	A Mancini	Roma	21	50	2.38
5	Alex	PSV Eindhoven	27	64	2.37
6	M Diarra	Real Madrid	27	64	2.37
7	M Ballack	Chelsea	22	52	2.36
8	L Kobiashvili	Schalke	22	52	2.36
9	D de Zeeuw	AZ Alkmaar	25	57	2.28
10	R Babel	Ajax	23	52	2.26
11	J Edmilson	Barcelona	19	43	2.26
12	F Liverani	Fiorentina	24	54	2.25
13	R Zomer	Twente	26	58	2.23
14	F Malouda	Lyon	25	55	2.20
15	A Ottl	Bayern Munich	18	39	2.17
16	G Pandev	Lazio	23	50	2.17
17	J Navas	Seville	24	52	2.17
18	R Osorio	Stuttgart	21	45	2.14
19	T Rosicky	Arsenal	18	38	2.11
20	A Gilardino	AC Milan	20	42	2.10
	(Selection limited to top player per club)				

1 Vieira - Inter Milan

Counting Games		
Played at least 70mins.		19
Total Points		
Taken in Counting Games		53
Average points per game		
Taken in Counting Games		2.79

MOST MISSED PLAYERS

	PLAYER	TEAM	AVERAGE	CLUB	DIFF
1	Fabio Liverani	Fiorentina	2.25	1.53	0.72
2	Patrick Mtiliga	NAC Breda	1.9	1.26	0.64
3	A Gamberini	Fiorentina	2.07	1.53	0.54
4	Goran Pandev	Lazio	2.17	1.63	0.54
5	Tomas Ujfalusi	Fiorentina	2.03	1.53	0.5
6	A Gilardino	AC Milan	2.1	1.61	0.49
7	G Zuiverloon	Heerenveen	2.1	1.62	0.48
8	Daniele Bonera	AC Milan	2.09	1.61	0.48
9	Moises Hurtado	Espanyol	1.75	1.29	0.46
10	M Jankulovski	AC Milan	2.04	1.61	0.43
11	Javi Venta	Villarreal	2.06	1.63	0.42
12	Shay Given	Newcastle	1.55	1.13	0.42
13	T Atouba	Hamburg	1.74	1.32	0.42
14	Ruben Cani	Villarreal	2.05	1.63	0.42
15	Geraldo Wendel	Bordeaux	1.91	1.5	0.41
16	Andreas Ottl	Bayern Munich	2.17	1.76	0.41
17	Manuel Pasqual	Fiorentina	1.94	1.53	0.41
18	A Mancini	Roma	2.38	1.97	0.41
19	Michael Fink	Eintr Frankfurt	1.57	1.18	0.39
20	Sebastian Frey	Fiorentina	1.92	1.53	0.39
	(No limit on the number of players per club selected)				

1 Liverani - Fiorentina

Average points		2.25
Club average		1.53
Difference		0.72

CHART-TOPPING GOALSCORERS

1 Afonso Alves - Heerenveen	
Goals scored in the League	34
Contribution to Attacking Power Average number of minutes between League team goals while on pitch	48
Player Strike Rate Average number of minutes between League goals scored by player	79
Club Strike Rate (CSR) Average minutes between League goals scored by club	51

	PLAYER	CLUB	GOALS	POWER	CSR	S RATE
1	Afonso Alves	Heerenveen	34	48	51	79
2	Danny Koevermans	AZ Alkmaar	22	34	36	100
3	Frederic Kanoute	Seville	22	48	53	117
4	Christian Rigano	Messina	19	86	97	118
5	Francesco Totti	Roma	25	44	47	120
6	Jefferson Farfan	PSV Eindhoven	21	38	40	121
7	Ruud van Nistelrooy	Real Madrid	25	52	51	127
8	Klaas-Jan Huntelaar	Ajax	21	38	36	127
9	Ronaldinho	Barcelona	21	40	43	130
10	Theofanis Gekas	Bochum	21	59	62	132
11	Cristiano Lucarelli	Livorno	20	86	85	133
12	Blaise N'Kufo	Twente	22	46	45	134
13	Diego Milito	Real Zaragoza	23	62	62	136
14	Wesley Sneijder	Ajax	18	38	36	138
15	Lionel Messi	Barcelona	14	45	43	142
16	Luca Toni	Fiorentina	16	55	56	144
17	Zlatan Ibrahimovic	Inter Milan	15	41	43	144
18	Danko Lazovic	Vitesse Arnhem	19	56	61	146
19	Didier Drogba	Chelsea	20	52	53	147
20	Mark Viduka	Middlesbrough	14	54	77	148

The Chart-topping Goalscorers measures the players by Strike Rate. They are most likely to be Forwards but Midfield players and even Defenders do come through the club tables. It is not a measure of the number of League goals scored - although that is also noted - but how often on average they have scored.

CHART-TOPPING MIDFIELDERS

1 Makelele - Chelsea	
Goals scored in the League	1
Defensive Rating Av number of mins between League goals conceded while on the pitch	189
Contribution to Attacking Power Average number of minutes between League team goals while on pitch	55
Scoring Difference Defensive Rating minus Contribution to Attacking Power	134

	PLAYER	CLUB	GOALS	DEF R	POWER	SCORE DIFF
1	Claude Makelele	Chelsea	1	189	55	134
2	Ryan Giggs	Man Utd	4	143	39	104
3	Cristiano Ronaldo	Man Utd	17	139	39	100
4	John Arne Riise	Liverpool	1	151	60	91
5	Frank Lampard	Chelsea	11	141	52	89
6	Paul Scholes	Man Utd	6	129	41	88
7	Cardoso Tiago	Lyon	4	137	52	85
8	Demy de Zeeuw	AZ Alkmaar	5	119	37	82
9	Timmy Simons	PSV Eindhoven	5	122	40	82
10	Patrick Vieira	Inter Milan	1	120	40	80
11	Michael Carrick	Man Utd	3	119	40	79
12	David Marcelo Pizarro	Roma	1	123	46	77
13	Michael Essien	Chelsea	2	129	52	77
14	Michael Ballack	Chelsea	0	126	49	77
15	Stefano Mauri	Lazio	6	128	54	74
16	Steven Gerrard	Liverpool	7	133	59	74
17	Edison Mendez	PSV Eindhoven	5	111	38	73
18	Moraes Edmilson	Barcelona	0	120	47	73
19	Phillip Cocu	PSV Eindhoven	7	112	41	71
20	Etienne Didot	Rennes	1	150	80	70

The Divisional Round-up charts combine the records of chart-topping keepers, defenders, midfield players and forwards, from every club in the division.. The one above is for **the Chart-topping Midfielders**. The players are ranked by their Scoring Difference although other attributes are shown for you to compare.

TOP LEAGUES IN EUROPE

	UEFA Cup Group Phase	Pts	Champions League Group Phase	Pts	UEFA Cup Round of 32	Pts	Champions League last 16	Pts
England	Tottenham Blackburn Newcastle	3	Liverpool Chelsea Man United Arsenal	8	Tottenham Newcastle Blackburn	3	Liverpool Chelsea Man United Arsenal	8
Spain	Espanyol Seville Osasuna Celta Vigo	4	Barcelona Valencia Real Madrid	6	Espanyol Seville Osasuna Celta Vigo	4	Valencia Barcelona Real Madrid	6
Italy	Livorno Palma Palermo	3	AC Milan Roma Inter Milan	6	Livorno Palma	2	AC Milan Roma Inter Milan	6
France	Lens Paris St G Nancy Auxerre	4	Lyon Lille Bordeaux (U)	6	Lens Paris St G Nancy Bordeaux (U)	4	Lyon Lille	4
Germany	B Levekusen Eintracht Frankfurt	2	Bayern Munich Hamburg W Bremmen (U)	6	B Levekusen W Bremmen (U)	2	Bayern Munich	2
Holland	AZ Alkmaar Ajax Feyenoord Heerenveen	4	PSV	2	AZ Alkmaar Ajax Feyenoord (Disq.)	3	PSV	2
Portugal	Braga	1	FC Porto Benfica (U) Sporting Lisbon	6	Benfica (U) Braga	2	FC Porto	2
Scotland	Rangers	1	Celtic	2	Rangers	1	Celtic	2
Greece	Panathinaikos	1	Olympiakos AEK Athens (U)	4	Panathinaikos AEK Athens(U)	2		
Romania	Dinamo Bucharest Rapid Bucharest	2	Steaua Bucharest (U)	2	Dinamo Bucharest Steaua Bucharest	2		
Ukraine			Shakhtar Donetsk (U) Dinamo Kiev	4	Shakhtar Donetsk (U)	1		
Russia			CSKA Moscow (U) Spartak Moscow(U)	4	CSKA Moscow (U) Spartak Moscow(U)	2		
Turkey	Fenebache Besiktas	2	Galatasaray	2	Fenebache	1		
Belgium	Zulte Waregem Club Brugge	2	Anderlecht	2	Zulte Waregem	1		
Israel	Maccabi Haifa Hapoel Tel Aviv	2			Maccabi Haifa Hapoel Tel Aviv	2		
Denmark	Odense Boldklub	1	FC Copenhagen	2				
Czech Republic	Sparta Prague Mlada Bloeslav	2						
Switzerland	Basel Grasshoppers	2						
Bulgaria			Levski Sofia	2				
Slovakia	Liberic	1						
Austria	Austria Vienna	1						
Serbia	Partizan Belgrade	1						
Poland	Wisla Krakow	1						

(U) shows clubs qualifying for Uefa Cup round of 32 from Champions League Group phase

CHART-TOPPING DEFENDERS

1 Agger - Liverpool	
Goals conceded in the League	11
Clean Sheets In games when he played at least 70 mins	15
Defensive Rating Average number of minutes between League goals conceded while on pitch	197
Club Defensive Rating Average mins between League goals conceded by the club this season	126

	PLAYER	CLUB	CON: LGE	CS	CDR	DEF RATE
1	Daniel Agger	Liverpool	11	15	126	197
2	John Terry	Chelsea	14	16	142	172
3	Alex	PSV Eindhoven	15	15	122	167
4	Ruano Alexis	Getafe	13	13	103	162
5	Gary Neville	Man Utd	13	11	126	152
6	Sebastien Squillaci	Lyon	17	12	126	148
7	John Mensah	Rennes	14	11	114	143
8	Nemanja Vidic	Man Utd	15	11	126	142
9	Ricardo Carvalho	Chelsea	19	16	142	138
10	Jacques Faty	Rennes	14	8	114	137
11	Stefano Lucchini	Empoli	15	11	83	136
12	Jamie Carragher	Liverpool	22	19	126	135
13	E Sanchez Cribari	Lazio	15	13	106	135
14	Matteo Ferrari	Roma	16	11	103	133
15	Steve Finnan	Liverpool	22	18	126	131
16	Lilian Thuram	Barcelona	15	12	103	130
17	Jan Kromkamp	PSV Eindhoven	18	11	122	130
18	Rio Ferdinand	Man Utd	23	14	126	127
19	Alessandro Gamberini	Fiorentina	19	14	113	127
20	Manuel Dos Santos	AS Monaco	16	12	90	127

The **Chart-topping Defenders** are resolved by their Defensive Rating, how often their team concedes a goal while they are playing. All these rightly favour players at the best performing clubs because good players win matches. However, good players in lower-table clubs will chart where they have lifted the team's performance.

CHART-TOPPING GOALKEEPERS

1 Cech - Chelsea	
Counting Games Games where he played at least 70 minutes	19
Goals Conceded in the League The number of League goals conceded while he was on the pitch	9
Clean Sheets In games when he played at least 70 mins	12
Defensive Rating Average number of minutes between League goals conceded while on pitch	190

	PLAYER	CLUB	CG	CONC	CS	DEF RATE
1	Petr Cech	Chelsea	19	9	12	190
2	Gregory Coupet	Lyon	33	20	15	148
3	Jose Reina	Liverpool	35	23	19	136
4	Heurelho Gomes	PSV Eindhoven	32	24	16	120
5	Nelson Dida	AC Milan	25	19	13	118
6	Edwin van der Sar	Man Utd	32	25	12	115
7	Alexander Doni	Roma	32	25	13	115
8	Manuel Neuer	Schalke	27	21	13	115
9	Simon Pouplin	Rennes	38	30	16	114
10	Tim Howard	Everton	36	29	14	111
11	Sebastian Frey	Fiorentina	38	31	19	110
12	Roberto Abbondanzieri	Getafe	35	30	14	107
13	Thomas Sorensen	Aston Villa	28	24	12	106
14	Remy Riou	Lorient	22	19	11	104
15	Victor Valdes	Barcelona	38	33	15	103
16	Vladan Kujovic	Roda JC Kerk	20	18	10	103
17	Leonardo Franco	Atl Madrid	31	28	11	101
18	Olivier Sorin	Auxerre	20	18	9	100
19	Sebastian Viera	Villarreal	27	25	11	99
20	Angelo Peruzzi	Lazio	26	24	11	99

The **Chart-topping Goalkeepers** are positioned by their Defensive Rating. We also show Clean Sheets where the team has not conceded and the Keeper has played all or most (at least 70 minutes) of the game. Only one keeper is selected from each club unless they have played the requisite number of counting games.

UEFA last 16	Pts	Champ's L. Q-finals	Pts	UEFA Q. finals	Pts	Champ's L.S-finals	Pts	UEFA Semi-finals	Pts	Champ's L.Final	Pts	UEFA Final Winners	TOTAL	
Tottenham Newcastle	2	L'pool Chelsea Man Utd	6	Tottenham	1	L'pool Chelsea Man Utd	6			Liverpool	2		39 England	(3)
Es'yol Seville O'suna C Vigo	4	Valencia	2	Espanyol Seville O'suna	3			Seville O'suna Espanyol	3			Seville Osasuna 3	35 Spain	(1)
		AC Milan Roma	4			AC Milan	2			AC Milan	4		27 Italy	(2)
Lens Paris St G	2												20 France	(4=)
B Levekusen W Bremmen (U)	2	Bayern Munich	2	W Bre'men (U) B L'kusen	2			W Bremmen (U)	1				19 Germany	(4=)
AZ Alkmaar	1	PSV	2	AZ Alkmaar	1								15 Holland	(6)
Benfica (U) Braga	2			Benfica (U)	1								14 Portugal	(8)
Rangers	1												7 Scotland	(15=)
													7 Greece	(13=)
													6 Romania	(7)
Shakhtar Donetsk (U)	1												6 Ukraine	(17=)
													6 Russia	(10=)
													5 Turkey	(17=)
													5 Belgium	(12)
Maccabi Haifa	1												5 Israel	(21=)
													3 Denmark	(24)
													2 Czech Rep	(15=)
													2 Switzerland	(9)
													3 Bulgaria	(10=)
													1 Slovakia	(17=)
													1 Austria	(20)
													1 Serbia	(21)
													1 Poland	(-)

Top Leagues in Europe

This chart sees how different country's leagues fared in cross-border rivalries. Picking up from the Champions League and UEFA Cup Group Phases we've noted every surviving club. 24 leagues feature initially and it's gradually whittled down to two winners.

Each league wins one point for every survivor in the UEFA Cup each round and two points in the Champions League.

EURO 2008 Qualifying

GROUPS A and B

GROUP A

Qualifying table as of August 1 2007

	P	W	D	L	GF	GA	Dif	Pts
Poland	9	6	1	2	15	7	8	19
Serbia	7	4	2	1	10	4	6	14
Portugal	7	4	2	1	15	5	10	14
Finland	8	4	2	2	9	5	4	14
Belgium	8	2	1	5	5	10	-5	7
Armenia	7	2	1	4	3	7	-4	7
Kazakhstan	8	1	3	4	5	11	-6	6
Azerbaijan	8	1	2	5	4	17	-13	5

RESULTS TO AUGUST 1 2007

Belgium	0	Kazakhstan	0

Poland	1	Finland	3

Gargula 89
Litmanen 54, 76 pen,
Vayrynen 84
15,000

Serbia	1	Azerbaijan	0

Zigic 72
40,000

Armenia	0	Belgium	1

Van Buyten 41
8,000

Azerbaijan	1	Kazakhstan	0

Ladaga 16
Byakov 36
20,000

Finland	1	Portugal	1

Johansson 22
Nuno Gomes 42
38,015

Poland	1	Serbia	1

Matusiak 30
Lazovic 71
5,000

Armenia	0	Finland	0

7,500

Kazakhstan	0	Poland	1

Smolarek 52
18,000

Portugal	3	Azerbaijan	0

Ronaldo 25, 63,
Carvalho 31
20,000

Serbia	1	Belgium	0

Zigic 54
35,000

Belgium	3	Azerbaijan	0

Simons 24 pen,
Vandenbergh 47,
Dembele 82
12,000

Kazakhstan	0	Finland	2

10,000
Litmanen 27,
Hyypia 65

Poland	2	Portugal	1

Smolarek 9, 18
Nuno Gomes 90
40,000

Serbia	3	Armenia	0

D.Stankovic 54 pen,
Lazovic 62, Zigic 90
20,000

Belgium	0	Poland	1

37,578
Matusiak 19

Finland	1	Armenia	0

Nurmela 10
9,445

Portugal	3	Kazakhstan	0

Simao Sabrosa 8, 84,
Ronaldo 30

Kazakhstan	2	Serbia	1

Ashirbekov 47,
Zhumaskaliev 61
Zigic 68
10,000

Poland	5	Azerbaijan	0

Bak 3, Dudka 6,
Lobodzinski 34,
Krzynowek 58,
Kazmierczak 84
15,000

Portugal	4	Belgium	0

Nuno Gomes 53,
Ronaldo 55, 75,
Quaresma 69
47,009

Azerbaijan	1	Finland	0

Imamaliev 83
14,000

Poland	1	Armenia	0

Zurawski 26
15,000

Serbia	1	Portugal	1

Jankovic 37
Tiago 5
51,300

Azerbaijan	1	Poland	3

SubaÃjic 6
Smolarek 63,
Krzynowek 66, 90
20,000

Belgium	1	Portugal	2

Fellaini 55
Nani 43, Postiga 64
45,000

Finland	0	Serbia	2

33,615
Jankovic 3,
M.Jovanovic 86

Kazakhstan	1	Armenia	2

Baltiyev 88 pen
Arzumanyan 31,
Ovsepyan 39 pen
10,000

Armenia	1	Poland	0

H.Mkhitaryan 66
8,000

Finland	2	Belgium	0

Johansson 27,
A.Eremenko Jr 71
30,000

Kazakhstan	1	Azerbaijan	0

Baltiyev 53
Nadirov 30
10,000

CRISTIANO RONALDO

In Ronaldo, Portugal have the star performer in this group.

The tricky winger has continued his good form with Manchester United into the Portuguese international side. He and Quaresma are more important to the side with their main scorer of recent years, Pauleta, now retired.

Ronaldo had scored an incredible five goals in six qualifying matches including two against Azerbaijan and Belgium, as well as having had more shots, 26, than anyone else in the competition at the end of the 2006/07 season.

GROUP A FIXTURES AUG – NOV

22 Aug	Finland	v	Kazakhstan
22 Aug	Armenia	v	Portugal
22 Aug	Belgium	v	Serbia
8 Sep	Azerbaijan	v	Armenia
8 Sep	Serbia	v	Finland
8 Sep	Portugal	v	Poland
12 Sep	Armenia	v	Azerbaijan
12 Sep	Finland	v	Poland
12 Sep	Kazakhstan	v	Belgium
12 Sep	Portugal	v	Serbia
13 Oct	Azerbaijan	v	Portugal
13 Oct	Belgium	v	Finland
13 Oct	Armenia	v	Serbia
13 Oct	Poland	v	Kazakhstan
17 Oct	Kazakhstan	v	Portugal
17 Oct	Azerbaijan	v	Serbia
17 Oct	Belgium	v	Armenia
17 Nov	Serbia	v	Kazakhstan
17 Nov	Finland	v	Azerbaijan
17 Nov	Portugal	v	Armenia
17 Nov	Poland	v	Belgium
21 Nov	Azerbaijan	v	Belgium
21 Nov	Serbia	v	Poland
21 Nov	Portugal	v	Finland
21 Nov	Armenia	v	Kazakhstan

GROUP B

QUALIFYING TABLE AT AUGUST 2007

	P	W	D	L	GF	GA	Dif	Pts
France	7	6	0	1	15	2	13	18
Italy	7	5	1	1	13	6	7	16
Scotland	7	5	0	2	13	6	7	15
Ukraine	6	4	0	2	8	6	2	12
Lithuania	7	2	1	4	4	7	-3	7
Georgia	8	2	0	6	13	14	-1	6
Faroe Islands	8	0	0	8	2	27	-25	0

RESULTS TO AUGUST 2007

Faroe Islands	0	Georgia	6

Kankava 16, Iashvili 18,
S.Arveladze 37, 63, 82,
Kobiashvili 51 pen

Georgia	0	France	3

70,000
Malouda 7, Saha 16,
Asatiani 46 og

Italy	1	Lithuania	1

Inzaghi 29
Danilevicius 21
70,000

Scotland	6	Faroe Islands	0

Fletcher 7, McFadden 10,
Boyd 24 pen, 38,
K.Miller 30 pen,
O'Connor 85
50,059

France	3	Italy	1

Govou 2, 56, Henry 17
Gilardino 19
78,800

Lithuania	1	Scotland	2

Miceika 85
Dailly 46, K.Miller 62
6,500

Ukraine	3	Georgia	1

Shevchenko 31,
Rotan 61, Rusol 78
S.Arveladze 38,
Demetradze 60

Faroe Islands	0	Lithuania	1

1,982
Skerla 89

Italy	2	Ukraine	0

Oddo 71 pen, Toni 79
49,149

Scotland	1	France	0

G.Caldwell 67
57,000

GARY CALDWELL

A win over France is a real scalp and the Scots defence proved greater than the sum of its parts with Caldwell scoring that crucial goal from Hartley's corner.

France	5	Faroe Islands	0

Saha 2, Henry 22,
Anelka 77,
Trezeguet 78, 84
18,800

Georgia	1	Italy	3

Shashiashvili 26
De Rossi 18,
Camoranesi 63,
Perrotta 71
50,000

Ukraine	2	Scotland	0

Kucher 60,
Shevchenko 90 pen
55,000

Faroe Islands	0	Ukraine	2

717
Yezerskiy 20,
Gusev 57

Lithuania	0	France	1

8,000
Anelka 73

Scotland	2	Georgia	1

Boyd 11,
Beattie 89
S.Arveladze 40
50,850

Georgia	3	Faroe Islands	1

Siradze 25,
Iashvili 46, 90 pen
R.Jacobsen 57
15,000

Italy	2	Scotland	0

Toni 12, 70
37,500

Ukraine	1	Lithuania	0

Gusev 47
33,600

Faroe Islands	1	Italy	2

R.Jacobsen 77
Inzaghi 12, 48
5,987

France	2	Ukraine	0

Ribery 57, Anelka 71
78,000

Lithuania	1	Georgia	0

Mikoliunas 78
6,000

Faroe Islands	0	Scotland	2

4,063
Maloney 31,
O'Connor 35

France	1	Georgia	0

Nasri 33
23,000

Lithuania	0	Italy	2

8,000
Quagliarella 31, 45

THIERRY HENRY

Former Arsenal legend Henry will enjoy linking up with fellow frenchmen Ludovic Guily and Eric Abidal at new club Barcelona in the 2007/2008 season.

After an injury disrupted season in 06/07, Henry will be hoping to recapture his form of old and win the La Liga title in his first season with Barca.

The clinical finisher's injuries have also held back his international appearances for France, only managing to make four appearances in Les Bleus campaign by the end of 2006/07.

GROUP B FIXTURES AUG – NOV

8 Sep	Georgia	v	Ukraine
8 Sep	Scotland	v	Lithuania
8 Sep	Italy	v	France
12 Sep	Ukraine	v	Italy
12 Sep	France	v	Scotland
12 Sep	Lithuania	v	Faroe Islands
13 Oct	Scotland	v	Ukraine
13 Oct	Italy	v	Georgia
13 Oct	Faroe Islands	v	France
17 Oct	Georgia	v	Scotland
17 Oct	Ukraine	v	Faroe Islands
17 Oct	France	v	Lithuania
17 Nov	Lithuania	v	Ukraine
17 Nov	Scotland	v	Italy
21 Nov	Italy	v	Faroe Islands
21 Nov	Georgia	v	Lithuania
21 Nov	Ukraine	v	France

EURO 2008 Qualifying — GROUPS C and D

GROUP C

QUALIFYING TABLE AT AUGUST 2007

	P	W	D	L	GF	GA	Dif	Pts
...eece	7	6	0	1	12	5	7	18
...osnia	7	4	1	2	14	14	0	13
...rkey	6	4	1	1	16	6	10	13
...orway	7	4	1	2	17	6	11	13
...ungary	7	2	0	5	7	14	-7	6
...alta	7	1	1	5	5	15	-10	4
...oldova	7	0	2	5	4	15	-11	2

RESULTS TO AUGUST 2007

...ungary 1 Norway 4
...era 90 — Solskjaer 15, 54, Stromstad 32, MG.Pedersen 41
...000

...alta 2 Bosnia 5
...ace 6, M.Mifsud 85 — Barbarez 4, Hrgovic 10, 45, Muslimovic 48, 50
...000

...oldova 0 Greece 1
Liberopoulos 77
...000

...osnia 1 Hungary 3
...simovic 64 — Huszti 36, Gera 47, Dardai 49
...000

...orway 2 Moldova 0
...romstad 74, ...ersen 79
23,848

...rkey 2 Malta 0
...hat 56, Metin 79

...reece 1 Norway 0
...atsouranis 33
25,000

...ungary 0 Turkey 1
Tuncay Sanli 41
...500

...oldova 2 Bosnia 3
...ogachiov 13, 32 — Misimovic 62, Grlic 68
...000

...osnia 0 Greece 4
Charisteas 8 pen, Patsatzoglou 82, Samaras 85, Katsouranis 90
...000

...alta 2 Hungary 1
...hembri 14, 53 — Torghelle 19
5,000

...rkey 5 Moldova 0
...ukur 35, 37 pen, 43, 73, ...ncay Sanli 68

AKAN SUKUR
...urkey's veteran goalscorer, now in his ...ird stint with Galatasaray, has over 100 ...aps and more than 50 goals for his ...ountry. He found the net five times in the ...06/07 campaign and is still the Turks' ...isman.

...eece 1 Turkey 4
...giakos 5 — Tuncay Sanli 27, Unal 55, Metin 70, Gokdeniz 81
...742

...dova 1 Malta 1
...ureanu 85 — Mallia 73
5,000

...rway 1 Bosnia 2
...ew 50 pen — Misimovic 18, Damjanovic 33
...987

Hungary 2 Moldova 0
Epureanu 9 og, Gera 63
5,000

Malta 0 Greece 1
15,000 — Basinas 66 pen

Turkey 2 Norway 2
Hamit.Altintop 72, 90 — Brenne 31, Andresen 40

Bosnia 3 Turkey 2
Muslimovic 27, Dzidic 45, Custovic 90 — Sukur 13, Sabri 39
35,000

Greece 2 Hungary 0
Gekas 16, Seitaridis 29
27,000

Norway 4 Malta 0
Haestad 31, Helstad 73, Iversen 79, JA.Riise 90
16,364

Bosnia 1 Malta 0
Muslimovic 6
15,000

Greece 2 Moldova 1
Charisteas 30, Liberopoulos 90 — Frunza 80
20,000

Norway 4 Hungary 0
Iversen 22, Braaten 57, Carew 60, 78
19,000

ANGELOS CHARISTEAS
Feyenoord front man Charisteas played a part in six of Greece's qualifying matches in the 2006/07 season. The striker managed to score two goals in appearances and was the season's top scorer for his club, Feyenoord, with nine league goals.

Charisteas was the hero in Euro 2004 in Portugal after scoring three including the final winner for Greece, and should be back for Austria-Switzerland

GROUP C FIXTURES AUG – NOV

8 Sep	Moldova	v	Norway
8 Sep	Hungary	v	Bosnia
8 Sep	Malta	v	Turkey
12 Sep	Norway	v	Greece
12 Sep	Turkey	v	Hungary
12 Sep	Bosnia	v	Moldova
13 Oct	Moldova	v	Turkey
13 Oct	Hungary	v	Malta
13 Oct	Greece	v	Bosnia
17 Oct	Turkey	v	Greece
17 Oct	Bosnia	v	Norway
17 Oct	Malta	v	Moldova
17 Nov	Moldova	v	Hungary
17 Nov	Norway	v	Turkey
17 Nov	Greece	v	Malta
21 Nov	Turkey	v	Bosnia
21 Nov	Malta	v	Norway
21 Nov	Hungary	v	Greece

GROUP D

QUALIFYING TABLE AT AUGUST 2007

	P	W	D	L	GF	GA	Dif	Pts
Germany	7	6	1	0	29	4	25	19
Czech Republic	7	4	2	1	15	4	11	14
Rep of Ireland	7	4	1	2	12	8	4	13
Slovakia	7	3	0	4	16	13	3	9
Wales	6	2	1	3	8	9	-1	7
Cyprus	6	1	1	4	9	16	-7	4
San Marino	6	0	0	6	1	36	-35	0

RESULTS TO AUGUST 2007

Czech Republic 2 Wales 1
Lafata 76, 89 — Jiranek 85 og
16,204

Germany 1 Rep of Ireland 0
Podolski 57
52,000

Slovakia 6 Cyprus 1
Skrtel 9, Mintal 33, 56, Sebo 43, 49, Karhan 52 — Yiasoumi 90
5,000

San Marino 0 Germany 13
Podolski 12, 42, 64, 70, Schweinsteiger 29, 48, Klose 30, 45, Ballack 35, Hitzlsperger 66, 71, Friedrich 87, Schneider 90
5,019

Slovakia 0 Czech Republic 3
27,683 — Sionko 10, 24, Koller 57

Cyprus 5 Rep of Ireland 2
M.Konstantinou 10, 16, 50 pen, C.Charalampides 60, 75 — Ireland 8, Dunne 44
12,000

Czech Republic 7 San Marino 0
Kulic 15, Polak 22, Baros 28, 68, Koller 43, 52, Jarolim 49
9,514

Wales 1 Slovakia 5
Bale 37 — Svento 14, Mintal 32, 38, Karhan 51, Vittek 59
28,493

Rep of Ireland 1 Czech Republic 1
Kilbane 62 — Koller 64
35,500

KEVIN KILBANE
Ireland's new managerial partnership of Steve Staunton and Sir Bobby Robson got off to a dreadful start but a draw with the Czechs in Dublin, courtesy of a Kilbane goal, was the start of a return to form.

Slovakia 1 Germany 4
Varga 58 — Podolski 13, 72, Ballack 25, Schweinsteiger 36
27,500

Wales 3 Cyprus 1
Koumas 33, Earnshaw 39, Bellamy 72 — Okkas 83
20,456

Cyprus 1 Germany 1
Okkas 43 — Ballack 15
15,000

Rep of Ireland 5 San Marino 0
Simoncini 7 og, Doyle 24, Robbie.Keane 31, 58 pen, 85
34,018

San Marino 1 Rep of Ireland 2
Manuel.Marani 86 — Kilbane 49, Ireland 90
3,294

Cyprus 1 Slovakia 3
Aloneftis 45 — Vittek 54, Jakubko 77
2,696

Czech Republic 1 Germany 2
Baros 77 — Kuranyi 42, 62
17,821

Rep of Ireland 1 Wales 0
Ireland 39
72,539

Czech Republic 1 Cyprus 0
Kovac 22
9,310

Rep of Ireland 1 Slovakia 0
Doyle 13
71,297

Wales 3 San Marino 0
Giggs 3, Bale 20, Koumas 62 pen
18,752

Germany 6 San Marino 0
Kuranyi 45, Jansen 52, Frings 54 pen, 63, Gomez 65, Fritz 67
43,967

Wales 0 Czech Republic 0
30,714

Germany 2 Slovakia 1
Durica 10 og, Hitzlsperger 43 — Metzelder 20 og
51,500

LUCAS PODOLSKI
Revitalised by Jurgen Klinsmann at the World Cup, Germany are Europe's form team and still playing with the same attacking verve. Unsurprising as Klinsmann's assistant, Joachim Low is now head coach and keeping to his philosophy; they had scored 29 goals in the 2006/07 season – 12 more than any other team so far in qualifying. Podolski, only hit four for Bayern last season but leads the German scoring list with seven although Kuranyi looks the form striker.

GROUP D FIXTURES AUG – NOV

22 Aug	San Marino	v	Cyprus
8 Sep	San Marino	v	Czech Rep
8 Sep	Wales	v	Germany
8 Sep	Slovakia	v	Rep of Ireland
12 Sep	Czech Rep	v	Rep of Ireland
12 Sep	Slovakia	v	Wales
12 Sep	Cyprus	v	San Marino
13 Oct	Cyprus	v	Wales
13 Oct	Rep of Ireland	v	Germany
13 Oct	Slovakia	v	San Marino
17 Oct	Germany	v	Czech Rep
17 Oct	Rep of Ireland	v	Cyprus
17 Oct	San Marino	v	Wales
17 Nov	Czech Rep	v	Slovakia
17 Nov	Germany	v	Cyprus
17 Nov	Wales	v	Rep of Ireland
21 Nov	Cyprus	v	Czech Rep
21 Nov	Germany	v	Wales
21 Nov	San Marino	v	Slovakia

EURO 2008 Qualifying

GROUPS E and F

GROUP E

QUALIFYING TABLE AT AUGUST 2007

	P	W	D	L	GF	GA	Dif	Pts
Croatia	7	5	2	0	16	4	12	17
Israel	8	5	2	1	17	7	10	17
Russia	7	4	3	0	11	1	10	15
England	7	4	2	1	12	2	10	14
FR Macedonia	7	2	1	4	6	7	-1	7
Estonia	7	0	0	7	0	14	-14	0
Andorra	7	0	0	7	1	28	-27	0

RESULTS TO AUGUST 2007

Estonia 0 **Macedonia** 1
Sedloski 73

England 5 **Andorra** 0
Crouch 5, 66,
Gerrard 13,
Defoe 38, 47
56,290

Estonia 0 **Israel** 1
5,000 Colautti 8

Israel 4 **Andorra** 1
Benayoun 9, Fernandez 84
Ben Shushan 11,
Gershon 43 pen,
Tamuz 69

Macedonia 0 **England** 1
16,500 Crouch 46

PETER CROUCH
Not as good in the air as he might be,
better on the ground than you think…
Crouch top scored for Liverpool with 18 in
the 2006/07 season and is the only striker
in form for England.

Russia 0 **Croatia** 0
27,500

Croatia 7 **Andorra** 0
Petric 12, 37, 48, 50,
Klasnic 58,
Balaban 62,
Modric 83
20,000

England 0 **Macedonia** 0
72,062

Russia 1 **Israel** 1
Arshavin 5 Ben Shushan 84
22,000

Andorra 0 **Macedonia** 3
Pandev 13,
Noveski 16,
1,000 I.Naumovski 31

Croatia 2 **England** 0
Da Silva 60,
G.Neville 69 og
38,000

Russia 2 **Estonia** 0
Pogrebnik 78,
Sychev 90
20,000

Israel 3 **Croatia** 4
Colautti 8, 89, Srna 35 pen,
Benayoun 68 Eduardo 39, 54, 72

Macedonia 0 **Russia** 2
Bystrov 18,
16,000 Arshavin 32

Croatia 2 **Macedonia** 1
Srna 58, Sedloski 38
Eduardo 88 25,000

Estonia 0 **Russia** 2
9,000 Kerzhakov 66, 78

Israel 0 **England** 0
35,000

Andorra 0 **England** 3
Gerrard 54, 76,
12,800 Nugent 90

Israel 4 **Estonia** 0
Tal 19, Colautti 29,
Sahar 77, 80 23,658

Estonia 0 **Croatia** 1
9,000 Eduardo 32

Macedonia 1 **Israel** 2
Stojkov 13 Itzhaki 11,
14,500 Colautti 44

Russia 4 **Andorra** 0
Kerzhakov 8, 16, 49,
Sychev 71 22,000

Andorra 0 **Israel** 2
1,000 Tamuz 37, Colautti 53

Croatia 0 **Russia** 0
38,000

Estonia 0 **England** 3
J.Cole 37,
11,000 Crouch 54, Owen 62

MICHAEL OWEN
A lot rests on Owen, who has lost some
pace but not his striking instinct as
McClaren needs a reliable source of
goals. The forward has been at the
forefront of England's attack for nearly a
decade, despite still being relatively
young.
The Newcastle striker had been out of
action since injuring his knee in Germany
at the 2006 World Cup, but a late return
to fitness in the 2006/07 season, meant
Owen received a call-up to the England
squad for the summer's qualifier against
Estonia. The forward repaid his England
coach by scoring on his return to the
international side courtesy of Beckham's
cross.

GROUP E FIXTURES AUG – NOV

22 Aug	Estonia	v	Andorra
8 Sep	England	v	Israel
8 Sep	Russia	v	Macedonia
8 Sep	Croatia	v	Estonia
12 Sep	Andorra	v	Croatia
12 Sep	Macedonia	v	Estonia
12 Sep	England	v	Russia
13 Oct	England	v	Estonia
17 Oct	Croatia	v	Israel
17 Oct	Macedonia	v	Andorra
17 Oct	Russia	v	England
17 Nov	Macedonia	v	Croatia
17 Nov	Israel	v	Russia
17 Nov	Andorra	v	Estonia
21 Nov	England	v	Croatia
21 Nov	Israel	v	Macedonia
21 Nov	Andorra	v	Russia

GROUP F

QUALIFYING TABLE AT AUGUST 2007

	P	W	D	L	GF	GA	Dif	Pts
Sweden	7	6	0	1	17	4	13	18
Spain	7	5	0	2	13	6	7	15
Northern Ireland	6	4	1	1	10	7	3	13
Denmark	6	3	1	2	9	5	4	10
Liechtenstein	7	1	1	5	4	18	-14	4
Iceland	7	1	1	5	5	15	-10	4
Latvia	6	1	0	5	4	7	-3	3

RESULTS TO AUGUST 2007

Latvia 0 **Sweden** 1
9,000 Kallstrom 39

N Ireland 0 **Iceland** 3
Thorvaldsson 18,
Hreidarsson 20,
14,500 E.Gudjohnsen 37

Spain 4 **Liechtenstein** 0
Torres 20, 62,
Villa 45,
Luis Garcia 66 10,000

Iceland 0 **Denmark** 2
Rommedahl 5,
10,007 Tomasson 33

N Ireland 3 **Spain** 2
D.Healy 19, 64, 79 Xavi 14,
15,000 Villa 52

Sweden 3 **Liechtenstein** 1
Allback 2, 70, M.Frick 27
Rosenberg 88 17,735

Denmark 0 **N Ireland** 0
41,482

Latvia 4 **Iceland** 1
Karlsons 14,
Verpakovskis 15, 25,
Visnakovs 52 7,500

Sweden 2 **Spain** 0
Elmander 10,
Allback 82 33,056

Iceland 1 **Sweden** 2
Vidarsson 6 Kallstrom 8,
8,725 Wilhelmsson 59

Liechtenstein 0 **Denmark** 4
D.Jensen 29,
Gravgaard 32,
3,000 Tomasson 51, 64

N Ireland 1 **Latvia** 0
D.Healy 35 14,500

Liechtenstein 1 **N Ireland** 4
Burgmeier 90 D.Healy 52, 75, 82,
4,340 McCann 90

Spain 2 **Denmark** 1
Morientes 33, Gravgaard 48
Villa 45 75,000

DAVID VILLA
There are a host of hot Strike Rates in La
Liga but none of the top six are Spanish
and the national side are struggling for a
striking partnership. In the 2006/07
campaign, Luis Aragones left out Torres in
favour of the Valencia partnership of
Morientes and Villa, and then switched to
Villa and a potent midfield. The striker has
responded with seven goals for his
country in qualifying so far.

Liechtenstein 1 **Latvia** ?
M.Frick 17 1,68?

N Ireland 2 **Sweden** ?
D.Healy 31, 58 Elmander 2?
14,50?

Spain 1 **Iceland** ?
Iniesta 81 20,00?

Iceland 1 **Liechtenstein** ?
B.Gunnarsson 27 Rohrer 6?
5,13?

Latvia 0 **Spain** ?
Villa 4?
9,000 Xavi 6?

Latvia 0 **Denmark** ?
9,000 Rommedahl 15, 1?

Liechtenstein 0 **Spain** ?
3,000 Villa 8, 1?

Sweden 5 **Iceland** ?
Allback 11, 51,
Svensson 42,
Mellberg 45,
Rosenberg 50 33,35?

DAVID HEALY
The star of the qualification competition a?
the halfway stage was Northern Ireland's
Healy. Lawrie Sanchez had constructed a?
team with a sound tactical plan behind a?
inspired striker.
At the end of the 2006/07 season, the
team were playing well and Healy was in
top quality form, after firing in nine goals
from 22 attempts on goal (16 on target).
The team now has to overcome the loss
of inspirational coach Lawrie Sanchez
after he agreed to takeover as Manager o?
Fulham in the Premiership for the 2007/0?
league campaign.
There is also a tough run second half to
the campaign.

GROUP F FIXTURES AUG – NOV

22 Aug	N Ireland	v	Liechtenstein?
8 Sep	Sweden	v	Denmark
8 Sep	Latvia	v	N Ireland
8 Sep	Iceland	v	Spain
12 Sep	Iceland	v	N Ireland
12 Sep	Spain	v	Latvia
12 Sep	Denmark	v	Liechtenstei?
13 Oct	Liechtenstein	v	Sweden
13 Oct	Iceland	v	Latvia
13 Oct	Denmark	v	Spain
17 Oct	Sweden	v	N Ireland
17 Oct	Liechtenstein	v	Iceland
17 Oct	Denmark	v	Latvia
17 Nov	Spain	v	Sweden
17 Nov	N Ireland	v	Denmark
17 Nov	Latvia	v	Liechtenste?
21 Nov	Spain	v	N Ireland
21 Nov	Sweden	v	Latvia
21 Nov	Denmark	v	Iceland

EURO 2008 Qualifying — GROUP G and ROUND UP

GROUP G

QUALIFYING TABLE AT AUGUST 2007

	P	W	D	L	GF	GA	Dif	Pts
Romania	7	5	2	0	14	4	10	17
Bulgaria	7	4	3	0	11	4	7	15
Holland	6	4	2	0	8	2	6	14
Albania	7	2	3	2	8	6	2	9
Belarus	7	2	1	4	10	15	-5	7
Slovenia	7	1	1	5	5	12	-7	4
Luxembourg	7	0	0	7	1	14	-13	0

RESULTS TO AUGUST 2007

Belarus 2 **Albania** 2
Kalachev 2, Skela 7 pen,
Mak.Romaschenko 24 Hasi 86
30,000

Luxembourg 0 **Holland** 1
8,000 Mathijsen 18

Romania 2 **Bulgaria** 2
Rosu 40, M.Petrov 82, 84
Marica 55 15,000

Albania 0 **Romania** 2
Dica 65,
10,000 Mutu 75 pen

Bulgaria 3 **Slovenia** 0
Bojinov 58,
M.Petrov 72,
Telkiyski 81 16,543

Holland 3 **Belarus** 0
van Persie 32, 79,
Kuyt 90 35,000

DIRK KUYT
Kuyt's rampant striking with Feyenoord has been blunted by Premiership defences. His 12 league goals came at a Strike Rate of one every 214 minutes and he was an unused sub in Holland's 0-0 draw with Romania.

Bulgaria 1 **Holland** 1
M.Petkov 11 van Persie 61
30,547

Romania 3 **Belarus** 1
Mutu 7, Kornilenko 20
Marica 10, Goian 76 12,000

Slovenia 2 **Luxembourg** 0
Novakovic 30,
Koren 44 3,500

Belarus 4 **Slovenia** 2
Kulchy 23, Cesar 23,
Kornilenko 52, 60, Lavric 43
Korytko 85 20,000

Holland 2 **Albania** 1
van Persie 14, Curri 67
Dede 41 og 40,000

Luxembourg 0 **Bulgaria** 1
6,000 Tunchev 26

Albania 0 **Slovenia** 0
10,000

Holland 0 **Romania** 0
49,000

Luxembourg 1 **Belarus** 2
Sagramola 68 Kalachev 25,
3,000 Kutuzov 54

Bulgaria 0 **Albania** 0
25,000

Romania 3 **Luxembourg** 0
Mutu 26,
Contra 56,
Marica 90 12,000

Slovenia 0 **Holland** 1
10,000 Van Bronckhorst 85

Albania 2 **Luxembourg** 0
Kapllani 38,
Haxhi 57 8,000

Belarus 0 **Bulgaria** 2
27,000 Berbatov 28, 46

Slovenia 1 **Romania** 2
Vrsic 90 Tamas 52,
6,000 Nicolita 69

Bulgaria 2 **Belarus** 1
M.Petrov 10, Vasiliuk 5 pen
C.Yankov 40 20,000

Luxembourg 0 **Albania** 3
Skela 25,
2,000 Kapllani 36, 72

Romania 2 **Slovenia** 0
Mutu 40,
Contra 70 22,000

ROBIN VAN PERSIE
Marco Van Basten's Dutch side struggled in the 2006/07 season and were outside the qualifying places and short on goals. The manager called back former stars such as Seedorf and Bouma in an attempt to revive his side. He also made his peace with Madrid's goalscoring hero van Nistelrooy, who should now return to Oranje.

More importantly, for their future is the form and return to fitness of van Persie. His metatarsal-breaking celebration cost the Dutch their most potent striker. He top-scored with four goals in qualifying in 2006/07 and had the best Strike Rate in the Premiership with his 11 goals coming at one every 132 minutes.

GROUP G FIXTURES AUG – NOV

8 Sep Belarus v Romania
8 Sep Netherlands v Bulgaria
8 Sep Luxembourg v Slovenia
12 Sep Slovenia v Belarus
12 Sep Bulgaria v Luxembourg
12 Sep Albania v Netherlands
13 Oct Romania v Netherlands
13 Oct Belarus v Luxembourg
13 Oct Slovenia v Albania
17 Oct Luxembourg v Romania
17 Oct Netherlands v Slovenia
17 Oct Albania v Bulgaria
17 Nov Bulgaria v Romania
17 Nov Albania v Belarus
17 Nov Netherlands v Luxembourg
21 Nov Belarus v Netherlands
21 Nov Romania v Albania
21 Nov Slovenia v Bulgaria

FIFA RANKINGS

RANK AUG 06	COUNTRY	RANK JULY 07	COUNTRY	CHANGE	
1	Brazil	1	Italy	Up	1
2	Italy	2	France	Up	2
3	Argentina	3	Brazil	Down	-2
4	France	4	Germany	Up	5
5	England	5	Argentina	Down	-2
6	Holland	6	Portugal	Up	3
7	Spain	7	Spain	Level	0
8	Portugal	8	England	Down	-3
9	Germany	9	Holland	Down	-3
10	Czech Rep	10	Czech Republic	Level	0
11	Nigeria	11	Croatia	Up	10
12	Cameroon	12	Romania	Up	14
13	Switzerland	13	Ukraine	Up	1
14	Uruguay	14	Cameroon	Down	-2
15	Ukraine	15	Greece	Up	17
16	Mexico	16	USA	Up	7
17	Denmark	17	Sweden	Up	3
18	Ivory Coast	18	Poland	Up	12
19	Paraguay	19	Ghana	Up	6
20	Sweden	20	Ivory Coast	Down	-2
21	Croatia	21	Turkey	Up	7
22	Rep of Guinea	22	Serbia	Up	12
23	USA	23	Scotland	Up	17
24	Egypt	24	Russia	Up	9
25	Ghana	25	Switzerland	Down	-12
26	Romania	26	Mexico	Down	-10
27	Ecuador	27	Denmark	Down	-10
28	Turkey	28	Bosnia	Up	14
29	Columbia	29	Northern Ireland	Up	43
30	Poland	30	Uruguay	Down	-16
31	Tunisia	31	Columbia	Down	-2
32	Greece	32	Nigeria	Down	-21
33	Russia	33	Bulgaria	Up	3
34	Serbia	34	Israel	Up	17
35	Senegal	35	Morocco	Up	4
36	Bulgaria	36	Norway	Up	13
37	Australia	37	Paraguay	Down	-18
38	Rep of Ireland	38	Rep of Ireland	Level	0
39	Morocco	39	Egypt	Down	-15
40	Scotland	40	Japan	Up	8
41	Peru	41	Slovakia	Up	2
42	Bosnia	42	Finland	Up	25
43	Slovakia	43	Senegal	Down	-8
44	Chile	44	Ecuador	Down	-17
45	Iran	45	Tunisia	Down	-14
46	Togo	46	Costa Rica	Up	1
47	Costa Rica	47	Iran	Down	-2
48	Japan	48	Australia	Down	-11
49	Norway	49	Mali	Down	11
50	Guatemala	50	Rep of Guinea	Down	-28

NORTHERN IRELAND ON THE UP
The FIFA Rankings were widely criticised before the last World Cup. Not least by the coach of the hosts, Jurgen Klinsmann, who lashed back when he was being lambasted for letting Germany drop down to the 20 mark in the pre-tournament gloom about his side's prospects.

Fifa revamped their criteria for August 2006 and this is a study of the movement of the teams over the last 11 months.

The two fastest risers, Northern Ireland and Scotland have both lost their managers. Lawrie Sanchez (pictured) to Fulham and Walter Smith to Rangers, showing the lure of club football over the international variation of the game.

INTERNATIONAL RESULTS
POLAND - SERBIA - PORTUGAL

POLAND

MANAGER: Leo Beenhakker
CAPTAIN: Maciej Zurawski
FIFA RANKING (July 2007): 18
EURO 2008: Group A
TOP SCORER: Smolarek 4
TOTAL SHOTS: 81
TOTAL CARDS: 10

1	Denmark	A	L	0-2
2	Finland	H	L	1-3
3	Serbia	H	D	1-1
4	Kazakhstan	A	W	1-0
5	Portugal	H	W	2-1
6	Belgium	A	W	1-0
7	Estonia	H	W	4-0
8	Slovakia	A	D	2-2
9	Azerbaijan	H	W	5-0
10	Armenia	H	W	1-0
11	Azerbaijan	A	W	3-1
12	Armenia	A	L	0-1

Results above, include friendlies, while player charts are purely based on Euro 2008 qualifying games.

Jacek Bak

	PLAYER	POS	AGE	APP	MINS ON	GOALS	CARDS(Y/R)		CLUB
1	Jacek Bak	DEF	34	9	784	1	0	0	Al-Rayyan
2	Maciej Zurawski	ATT	30	9	667	1	0	0	Celtic
3	Michal Zewlakow	DEF	31	7	630	0	0	0	Anderlecht
4	Mariusz Lewandowski	MID	28	7	569	0	1	0	Shakhtar Donetsk
5	Marcin Wasiliewski	DEF	27	7	559	0	0	0	Anderlecht
6	Jacek Krzynowek	MID	31	7	546	3	0	0	Wolfsburg
7	Jakub Blaszczykowski	DEF	21	8	484	0	2	0	B Dortmund
8	Ebi Smolarek	ATT	26	6	465	4	0	0	B Dortmund
9	Artur Boruc	GK	27	5	450	0	0	0	Celtic
10	Dariusz Dudka	DEF	23	5	450	1	0	0	Wisla Krakow
11	Arek Radomski	MID	30	4	360	0	0	0	Austria Wien
12	Grzegorz Bronowicki	DEF	26	4	360	0	1	0	Legia Warsaw
13	Radoslaw Sobelewski	MID	30	6	336	0	1	0	Wisla Krakow
14	Wojciech Kowalewski	GK	30	3	270	0	2	0	Spartak Moscow
15	Michal Golinski	MID	26	3	251	0	0	0	Groclin
16	Grzegorz Rasiak	ATT	28	3	242	0	0	0	Southampton
17	Lukasz Gargula	MID	26	4	227	1	0	0	GKS Belchatow
18	Radoslaw Matusiak	ATT	25	4	216	2	0	0	Palermo
19	Wojciech Lobodzinski	MID	21	3	183	1	0	0	Zaglebie Lubin
20	Przemyslaw Kazmierczak	MID	25	4	145	1	0	0	Pogon Szczecin

SERBIA

MANAGER: Javier Clemente
CAPTAIN: Dejan Stankovic
FIFA RANKING (July 2007): 22
EURO 2008: Group A
TOP SCORER: Zigic 4
TOTAL SHOTS: 73
TOTAL CARDS: 16

The best defence in the group marshalled by two top of the top club performers in Europe; Mladen Krstajic from Schalke 04 and Nemanja Vidic from Manchester United. For goals they may be overly reliant on the height of Nikola Zigic

1	Czech Republic	A	W	3-1
2	Azerbaijan	H	W	1-0
3	Poland	A	D	1-1
4	Belgium	H	W	1-0
5	Armenia	H	W	3-0
6	Norway	H	D	1-1
7	Kazakhstan	A	L	1-2
8	Portugal	H	D	1-1
9	Finland	A	W	2-0

Vladimir Stojkovic

	PLAYER	POS	AGE	APP	MINS ON	GOALS	CARDS(Y/R)		CLUB
1	Vladimir Stojkovic	GK	23	7	630	0	0	0	Vitesse
2	Mladen Krstajic	DEF	33	6	540	0	0	0	Schalke
3	Nenad Kovacevic	MID	26	6	540	0	1	0	Lens
4	Dejan Stankovic	MID	28	6	527	1	3	0	Inter Milan
5	Marko Pantelic	ATT	28	7	512	0	1	0	Hertha Berlin
6	Nikola Zigic	ATT	26	5	449	4	0	1	Crvena Zvezda
7	Marjan Markovic	DEF	25	5	373	0	1	0	Dimamo Kiev
8	Ivica Dragutinovic	DEF	31	4	360	0	1	0	Seville
9	Milan Stepanov	DEF	24	4	360	0	0	0	Trabzonspor
10	Nemanja Vidic	DEF	25	4	360	0	1	0	Man Utd
11	Igor Duljaj	MID	27	6	343	0	1	0	Shakhtar Donetsk
12	Milos Krasic	MID	22	3	264	0	1	0	Serbia & Mont
13	Ognijen Koroman	MID	28	6	261	0	1	0	Terek Groznyi
14	Danko Lazovic	ATT	24	7	235	2	0	0	PSV
15	Bosko Jankovic	MID	23	3	219	2	1	0	Palermo
16	Dusko Tosic	DEF	22	2	173	0	0	0	Sochaux
17	Aleksander Trisovic	MID	23	3	161	0	0	0	Red Star Belgrade
18	Ivan Ergic	DEF	26	5	149	0	0	0	Basel
19	Aleksandar Lukovic	MID	24	1	90	0	0	0	Udinese
20	Antonio Rukavina	DEF	23	1	90	0	0	0	FK Partizan

PORTUGAL

MANAGER: Luis Felipe Scolari
CAPTAIN: Jorge Andrade
FIFA RANKING (July 2007): 6
EURO 2008: Group A
TOP SCORER: Ronaldo 5
TOTAL SHOTS: 57
TOTAL CARDS: 17

Dropped points away in a defeat to leaders Poland and two draws with the other main contenders Serbia and Finland. However, the run in sees home fixtures against all three main rivals

1	Denmark	A	L	2-4
2	Finland	A	D	1-1
3	Azerbaijan	H	W	3-0
4	Poland	A	L	1-2
5	Kazakhstan	H	W	3-0
6	Brazil	A	W	2-0
7	Belgium	H	W	4-0
8	Serbia	A	D	1-1
9	Belgium	A	W	2-1
10	Kuwait	A	D	1-1

Ricardo Carvalho

	PLAYER	POS	AGE	APP	MINS ON	GOALS	CARDS(Y/R)		CLUB
1	Pereira Ricardo	GK	31	7	630	0	0	0	Sp Lisbon
2	Ricardo Carvalho	DEF	29	6	540	1	1	0	Chelsea
3	Nuno Gomes	ATT	30	6	515	3	0	0	Benfica
4	Luis Garcia Miguel	DEF	27	6	483	0	0	0	Valencia
5	Cristiano Ronaldo	MID	22	6	476	5	2	0	Man Utd
6	Cardoso Tiago	MID	26	7	438	1	0	0	Lyon
7	Armando Teixeira Petit	MID	30	5	412	0	1	0	Benfica
8	Anderson Deco	MID	29	5	408	0	0	0	Barcelona
9	Paulo Ferreira	DEF	28	4	360	0	1	0	Chelsea
10	Simao Sabrosa	MID	27	4	360	2	2	0	Benfica
11	Jorge Andrade	DEF	29	4	284	0	0	0	Deportivo
12	Francisco Costinha	MID	32	3	225	0	1	0	Dinamo Moscow
13	Nuno Valente	DEF	32	3	224	0	0	0	Everton
14	Ricardo Rocha	DEF	28	3	214	0	2	0	Tottenham
15	Nani	MID	20	5	203	1	1	0	Man United
16	Quaresma	ATT	23	3	201	1	1	0	Porto
17	Joao Moutinho	DEF	20	3	182	0	0	0	Sporting
18	Marco Caneira	DEF	28	3	155	0	0	0	Valencia
19	Fernando Meira	DEF	29	2	105	0	0	0	Stuttgart
20	Raul Meireles	MID	24	2	104	0	0	0	Porto

INTERNATIONAL RESULTS

FRANCE

MANAGER: Raymond Domenech
CAPTAIN: Patrick Vieira
FIFA RANKING (July 2007): 2
EURO 2008: Group B
TOP SCORER: Anelka 3
TOTAL SHOTS: 79
TOTAL CARDS: 3

A shock defeat against Scotland in Glasgow but made up for it by beating Italy in their previous game as revenge for the World Cup final defeat

1	Bosnia	A W	2-1
2	Georgia	A W	3-0
3	Italy	H W	3-1
4	Scotland	A L	0-1
5	Faroe Islands	H W	5-0
6	Greece	H W	1-0
7	Argentina	H L	0-1
8	Lithuania	A W	1-0
9	Austria	H W	1-0
10	Ukraine	H W	2-0
11	Georgia	H W	1-0

Lilian Thuram

	PLAYER	POS	AGE	APP	MINS ON	GOALS	CARDS(Y/R)		CLUB
1	Lilian Thuram	DEF	35	7	630	0	0	0	Barcelona
2	Florent Malouda	MID	27	7	599	1	0	0	Lyon
3	Eric Abidal	DEF	27	6	540	0	0	0	Lyon
4	William Gallas	DEF	29	6	540	0	1	0	Arsenal
5	Claude Makelele	MID	34	6	507	0	0	0	Chelsea
6	Franck Ribery	MID	24	6	497	1	0	0	Marseille
7	Gregory Coupet	GK	34	5	450	0	0	0	Lyon
8	Willy Sagnol	DEF	30	5	438	0	0	0	Bayern Munich
9	Jeremy Toulalan	MID	23	4	360	0	0	0	Lyon
10	Patrick Vieira	MID	31	4	360	0	0	0	Juventus
11	Thierry Henry	ATT	29	4	330	2	1	0	Arsenal
12	Nicolas Anelka	ATT	28	4	284	3	0	0	Bolton
13	Francois Clerc	MID	24	3	192	0	0	0	Lyon
14	Mickael Landreau	GK	28	2	180	0	0	0	Nantes
15	Louis Saha	ATT	28	4	177	2	0	0	Man Utd
16	Samir Nasri	MID	20	2	170	1	0	0	Marseille
17	Sydney Govou	ATT	27	4	158	2	0	0	Lyon
18	David Trezeguet	ATT	29	2	91	2	0	0	Juventus
19	Alou Diarra	MID	25	1	90	0	1	0	Lyon
20	Jean-Alain Boumsong	DEF	27	1	90	0	0	0	Juventus

ITALY

MANAGER: Roberto Donadoni
CAPTAIN: Fabio Cannavaro
FIFA RANKING (July 2007): 1
EURO 2008: Group B
TOP SCORERS: Toni, Inzaghi 3
TOTAL SHOTS: 59
TOTAL CARDS: 10

With a new coach in Roberto Donadoni, to add to their reputation as slow starters in international tournaments, Italy began with two bad results. However, they have a vast array of Serie A talent to call upon and should be favourites for Euro 2008

1	Croatia	H L	0-2
2	Lithuania	H D	1-1
3	France	A L	1-3
4	Ukraine	H W	2-0
5	Georgia	A W	3-1
6	Turkey	H D	1-1
7	Scotland	H W	2-0
8	Faroe Islands	A W	2-1
9	Lithuania	A W	2-0

Gianluigi Buffon

	PLAYER	POS	AGE	APP	MINS ON	GOALS	CARDS(Y/R)		CLUB
1	Gianluigi Buffon	GK	29	7	630	0	0	0	Juventus
2	Fabio Cannavaro	DEF	33	7	613	0	1	0	Real Madrid
3	Massimo Oddo	DEF	31	6	540	1	0	0	Lazio
4	Andrea Pirlo	MID	28	7	527	0	1	0	AC Milan
5	Gennaro Gattuso	MID	29	6	476	0	3	0	AC Milan
6	Gianluca Zambrotta	DEF	30	5	450	0	2	0	Barca
7	Simone Perrotta	MID	29	5	397	1	2	0	Roma
8	Daniele De Rossi	MID	22	6	395	1	0	0	Roma
9	Marco Materazzi	DEF	33	5	352	0	0	0	Inter Milan
10	Luca Toni	ATT	30	3	260	3	0	0	Fiorentina
11	Filippo Inzaghi	ATT	33	5	256	3	0	0	AC Milan
12	Andrea Barzagli	DEF	26	3	205	0	0	0	Palermo
13	Alessandro Del Piero	ATT	32	4	193	0	0	0	Juventus
14	Mauro Camoranesi	MID	30	3	191	1	0	0	Juventus
15	Fabio Grosso	DEF	29	2	180	0	0	0	Inter Milan
16	Antonio Cassano	ATT	24	2	162	0	0	0	Real Madrid
17	Antonio Di Natale	ATT	29	2	119	0	0	0	Udinese
18	Alberto Gilardino	ATT	24	2	108	1	1	0	AC Milan
20	Fabio Quagliarella	MID	23	3	99	2	0	0	Sampdoria

SCOTLAND

MANAGER: Alex McLeish
CAPTAIN: Barry Ferguson
FIFA RANKING (July 2007): 23
EURO 2008: Group B
TOP SCORER: Boyd 3
TOTAL SHOTS: 52
TOTAL CARDS: 15

Alex McLeish realised the difficulty of the task when he traded jobs with Walter Smith. Scotland had been revitalised by Smith before he was coaxed away to Rangers and expectations, dulled by Bertie Vogts spell in charge, were high again - even against the top two sides in the world

1	Faroe Islands	H W	6-0
2	Lithuania	A W	2-1
3	France	H W	1-0
4	Ukraine	A L	0-2
5	Georgia	H W	2-1
6	Italy	A L	0-2
7	Austria	A W	1-0
8	Faroe Islands	A W	2-0

David Weir

	PLAYER	POS	AGE	APP	MINS ON	GOALS	CARDS(Y/R)		CLUB
1	Craig Gordon	GK	24	7	630	0	0	0	Hearts
2	David Weir	DEF	37	7	630	0	0	0	Rangers
3	Paul Hartley	MID	30	7	628	0	0	0	Celtic
4	Barry Ferguson	MID	29	5	450	0	2	0	Rangers
5	Gary Naysmith	DEF	28	5	450	0	1	0	Everton
6	Graham Alexander	DEF	35	5	450	0	0	0	Preston
7	Kenny Miller	ATT	27	5	419	2	2	0	Rangers
8	Darren Fletcher	MID	23	5	382	1	2	0	Celtic
9	Steven Pressley	DEF	33	4	355	0	0	1	Celtic
10	Kris Boyd	ATT	23	6	324	3	0	0	Rangers
11	Stephen McManus	DEF	24	4	272	0	0	0	Celtic
12	Christian Dailly	DEF	33	3	270	1	2	0	West Ham
13	Gary Caldwell	DEF	26	3	270	1	1	0	Celtic
14	James McFadden	ATT	24	4	253	1	2	0	Everton
15	Lee McCulloch	MID	29	3	227	0	1	0	Wigan
16	Gary Teale	ATT	28	5	224	0	0	0	Derby
17	Garry O'Connor	ATT	24	3	139	2	0	0	Birmingham
18	Nigel Quashie	MID	28	2	125	0	0	0	West Ham
19	Scott Brown	MID	22	2	117	0	0	0	Celtic
20	Shaun Maloney	ATT	24	3	102	1	0	0	Aston Villa

INTERNATIONAL RESULTS

GREECE

MANAGER: Otto Renhagel
CAPTAIN: Angelos Basinas
FIFA RANKING (July 2007): 15
EURO 2008: Group C
TOP SCORERS: Charisteas, Liberopoulos Katsouranis 2
TOTAL SHOTS: 44
TOTAL CARDS: 10

The winners of Euro 2004 have lifted their FIFA Ranking in the past three years since and built on regular Champions League action for their top club sides.

1	England	A L	0-4
2	Moldova	A W	1-0
3	Norway	H W	1-0
4	Bosnia	A W	4-0
5	France	A L	0-1
6	South Korea	H L	0-1
7	Turkey	H L	1-4
8	Malta	A W	1-0
9	Hungary	H W	2-0
10	Moldova	H W	2-1

Giorgos Karagounis

	PLAYER	POS	AGE	APP	MINS ON	GOALS	CARDS(Y/R)		CLUB
1	Giorgos Karagounis	MID	30	6	574	0	1	0	Benfica
2	Angelos Basinas	MID	31	6	540	1	2	0	Mallorca
3	Konstantinos Katsouranis	MID	28	6	540	2	1	0	Benfica
4	Sotirios Kyrgiakos	MID	28	6	540	1	0	0	Frankfurt
5	Angelos Charisteas	ATT	27	6	510	2	0	0	Feyenoord
6	Giourkas Seitaridis	MID	26	6	506	1	1	0	Atletico Madrid
7	Antonios Nikopolidis	GK	36	5	450	0	0	0	Olympiakos
8	Ioannis Amanatidis	MID	25	6	373	0	0	0	Frankfurt
9	Panagiotis Fyssas	MID	32	4	325	0	1	0	Hearts
10	Vassillis Torossidis	MID	22	4	305	0	0	0	Olympiakos
11	Georgios Samaras	ATT	22	5	291	1	1	0	Man City
12	Theofanis Gekas	MID	27	4	269	1	0	0	Bayer Leverkusen
13	Traianos Dellas	MID	29	3	260	0	0	0	AEK Athens
14	Stylianos Giannakopoulos	MID	33	6	227	0	0	0	Bolton
15	Georgios Anatolakis	DEF	33	3	182	0	1	0	Olympiakos
16	Konstantinos Chalkias	GK	33	2	180	0	0	0	Aris
17	Christos Patsatzoglou	DEF	28	3	117	1	0	0	Greece
18	Nikolaos Liberopoulos	MID	32	2	116	2	0	0	AEK Athens

BOSNIA

MANAGER: Fuad Muzurovic
CAPTAIN: Zvjezdan Misimovic
FIFA RANKING (July 2007): 28
EURO 2008: Group C
TOP SCORERS: Muslinov 4
TOTAL SHOTS: 56
TOTAL CARDS: 17

Competing at international level since 1995 after the split-up of Yugoslavia, Bosnia & Herzegovina were close to reaching Euro 2004. They achieved a famous win over Turkey in Sarajevo 3-2 but also surprised Norway in a 2-1 away victory

1	France	H L	1-2
2	Malta	A W	5-2
3	Hungary	H L	1-3
4	Moldova	A D	2-2
5	Greece	H L	0-4
6	Norway	A W	2-1
7	Turkey	H W	3-2
8	Malta	H W	1-0

Zvjezdan Misimovic

	PLAYER	POS	AGE	APP	MINS ON	GOALS	CARDS(Y/R)		CLUB
1	Zvjezdan Misimovic	MID	25	7	630	3	1	0	Nuremberg
2	Mirko Hrgovic	MID	28	7	607	2	1	0	Hajduk Split
3	Zlatan Muslimovic	ATT	26	4	359	4	0	0	Atalanta
4	Vedin Music	DEF	34	5	347	0	0	0	Treviso
5	Zlatan Bajramovic	MID	27	4	346	0	0	0	Schalke 04
6	Dario Damjanovic	MID	26	4	315	1	1	0	Hajduk Split
7	Kenan Hasagic	GK	27	4	314	0	0	0	Gaziantepspor
8	Mladen Bartolovic	ATT	30	5	305	0	0	0	Hajduk Split
9	Sasa Papac	DEF	27	4	289	0	0	1	Rangers
10	Adnan Guso	GK	31	3	270	0	0	0	Pandurii Targu-Ju
11	Sergei Barbarez	MID	36	3	245	1	2	0	Bayer Leverkusen
12	Ivan Radeljic	ATT	26	3	224	0	0	0	Slaven Belupo
13	Ivica Grlic	ATT	31	3	195	1	0	0	Duisburg
14	Branimir Bajic	DEF	27	2	180	0	0	0	Koblenz
15	Elvir Rahimic	MID	30	2	180	0	0	0	CSKA Moscow
16	Emir Spahic	DEF	26	2	180	0	3	0	Lokomotive M.
17	Darko Maletic	MID	26	3	169	0	0	0	Partizan Belgrade
18	Dalibor Silic	DEF	28	2	158	0	1	0	Sironki Brijeg
19	Dzemal Berberovic	DEF	25	2	147	0	0	0	Litex Lovech
20	Vule Trivunovic	DEF	24	2	118	0	0	0	Khimki

TURKEY

MANAGER: Faith Terim
CAPTAIN: Hakan Suker
FIFA RANKING (July 2007): 21
EURO 2008: Group C
TOP SCORERS: Hakan Suker 5
TOTAL SHOTS: 52
TOTAL CARDS: 8

A 4-1 away win over fierce rivals Greece is the highlight of the Turkish campaign so far. This is an experienced side led by Hakan Suker and Rustu Recber drawn mainly from the big Istanbul clubs

1	Luxembourg	A W	1-0
2	Malta	H W	2-0
3	Hungary	A W	1-0
4	Moldova	H W	5-0
5	Italy	A D	1-1
6	Georgia	A L	0-4
7	Greece	A W	4-1
8	Norway	H D	2-2
9	Bosnia	A L	2-3
10	Brazil	A D	0-0

Hamit Altintop

	PLAYER	POS	AGE	APP	MINS ON	GOALS	CARDS(Y/R)		CLUB
1	Hamit Altintop	MID	25	6	540	2	1	0	Schalke 04
2	Mehmet Aurelio	MID	29	6	540	0	2	0	Fenerbahce
3	Hakan Sukur	ATT	35	6	523	5	0	0	Galatasaray
4	Gokhan Zan	DEF	25	5	450	0	1	0	Besiktas
5	Tuncay Sanli	ATT	25	5	449	3	0	0	Fenerbahce
6	Sarioglu Sabri	DEF	22	5	436	1	1	0	Galatasaray
7	Ibrahim Uzulmez	MID	32	4	360	0	0	0	Besiktas
8	Recber Rustu	GK	34	4	360	0	0	0	Fenerbahce
9	Servet Cetin	DEF	26	3	270	0	0	0	Sivasspor
10	Gokdeniz Karadeniz	MID	27	5	255	1	0	0	Trabzonspor
11	Arda Turin	MID	20	3	221	0	1	0	Galatasaray
12	Tumer Metin	MID	32	3	214	2	0	0	Fenerbahce
13	Servet Cetin	DEF	26	2	180	0	0	0	Galatasaray
14	Volkan Demirel	GK	25	2	180	0	1	0	Fenerbahce
15	Huseyin Cimsir	MID	28	4	108	0	0	0	Trabzonspor
16	Mehmet Topuz	ATT	23	2	91	0	0	0	Kayserispor
17	Can Arat	DEF	23	1	90	0	0	0	Fenerbahce
18	Emre Asik	DEF	33	1	90	0	1	0	Galatasaray
19	Emre Belozoglu	MID	26	1	90	0	0	0	Newcastle
20	Ergun Penbe	DEF	35	1	90	0	0	0	Galatasaray

INTERNATIONAL RESULTS

GERMANY

MANAGER: Joachim Low
CAPTAIN: Michael Ballack
FIFA RANKING (July 2007): 4
EURO 2008: Group D
TOP SCORERS: Podolski 7
TOTAL SHOTS: 91
TOTAL CARDS: 11

Easily the top scorers in the qualifying tournament with Joachim Low sticking largely by the stars of Germany 2008 but with Kevin Kuranyi back in the attack

1	Sweden	H W	3-0
2	Rep of Ireland	H W	1-0
3	San Marino	A W	13-0
4	Georgia	H W	2-0
5	Slovakia	A W	4-1
6	Cyprus	A D	1-1
7	Switzerland	H W	3-1
8	Czech Republic	A W	2-1
9	Denmark	H L	0-1
10	San Marino	H W	6-0
11	Slovakia	H W	2-1

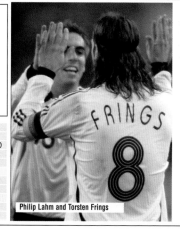

Philip Lahm and Torsten Frings

	PLAYER	POS	AGE	APP	MINS ON	GOALS	CARDS(Y/R)		CLUB
1	Philip Lahm	DEF	23	7	609	0	0	0	Bayern Munich
2	Torsten Frings	MID	30	7	601	2	0	0	Werder Bremen
3	Jens Lehmann	GK	37	6	540	0	1	0	Arsenal
4	Bernd Schneider	MID	33	6	515	1	2	0	B Leverkusen
5	Miroslav Klose	ATT	29	6	478	2	2	0	W Bremen
6	Marcell Jansen	DEF	21	5	450	1	1	0	B M'gladbach
7	Bastian Schweinsteiger	MID	22	5	436	3	1	0	Bayern Munich
8	Michael Ballack	MID	30	5	405	3	0	0	Chelsea
9	Manuel Friedrich	DEF	27	4	360	0	0	0	Mainz
10	Per Mertesacker	DEF	22	4	360	0	0	0	W Bremen
11	Lukas Podolski	ATT	22	4	337	7	0	0	Bayern Munich
12	Clemens Fritz	DEF	27	4	302	1	1	0	W Bremen
13	Thomas Hitzlsperger	MID	25	5	289	3	0	0	Stuttgart
14	Arne Friedrich	DEF	28	3	270	1	0	0	Hertha Berlin
15	Christophe Metzelder	DEF	26	3	270	0	0	0	B Dortmund
16	Kevin Kuranyi	ATT	25	3	212	3	0	0	Schalke
17	Timo Hildebrand	GK	28	1	90	0	0	0	Stuttgart
18	Oliver Neuville	ATT	34	2	76	0	0	0	B M'gladbach
19	David Odonkor	ATT	23	3	73	0	1	0	Real Betis
20	Mario Gomez	ATT	22	2	58	1	0	0	Stuttgart

CZECH REPUBLIC

MANAGER: Karel Bruckner
CAPTAIN: Tomas Rosicky
FIFA RANKING (July 2007): 10
EURO 2008: Group D
TOP SCORERS: Koller 4
TOTAL SHOTS: 94
TOTAL CARDS: 7

A second retirement from the inspirational Pavel Nedved and a disappointing World Cup hasn't stalled Karel Bruckner's ability to make the most of a limited squad. Still reliant on the tall Jan Koller up front

1	Serbia	H L	1-3
2	Wales	H W	2-1
3	Slovakia	A W	3-0
4	San Marino	H W	7-0
5	Rep of Ireland	A D	1-1
6	Denmark	H D	1-1
7	Belgium	A W	2-0
8	Germany	H L	1-2
9	Cyprus	H W	1-0
10	Wales	A D	0-0

Jan Koller

	PLAYER	POS	AGE	APP	MINS ON	GOALS	CARDS(Y/R)		CLUB
1	Jan Koller	ATT	34	7	630	4	1	0	Monaco
2	Marek Jankulovski	DEF	30	7	630	0	1	0	AC Milan
3	Petr Cech	GK	25	7	630	0	0	0	Chelsea
4	Tomas Ujfalusi	DEF	29	7	623	0	0	0	Fiorentina
5	Tomas Rosicky	MID	26	7	602	0	0	0	Arsenal
6	David Rozehnal	DEF	26	7	585	0	0	0	Paris SG
7	Jan Polak	MID	26	6	495	1	1	0	Nuremberg
8	Jaroslav Plasil	MID	25	7	441	0	0	0	Monaco
9	Martin Jiranek	DEF	28	5	424	0	0	0	Spartak Moscow
10	Milan Baros	ATT	25	5	382	3	0	0	Lyon
11	Tomas Galasek	MID	34	4	332	0	1	0	Nuremberg
12	Radoslav Kovac	DEF	27	5	218	1	1	0	Spartak Moscow
13	David Jarolim	MID	28	4	215	1	0	0	Hamburg
14	Marek Kulic	ATT	31	4	188	1	0	0	Sparta Prague
15	Libor Sionko	MID	30	3	166	2	0	0	Austria Vienna
16	Zdenek Grygera	DEF	27	3	107	0	0	0	Ajax
17	Tomas Sivok	MID	23	1	83	0	0	0	Udinese
18	David Lafata	ATT	25	2	61	2	0	0	Austria Vienna
19	Jiri Stajner	ATT	31	2	59	0	0	0	Hannover 96
20	Tomas Zapotocny	DEF	26	1	45	0	0	0	Udinese

REPUBLIC OF IRELAND

MANAGER: Steve Staunton
(with Sir Bobby Robson)
CAPTAIN: Robbie Keane
FIFA RANKING (July 2007): 38
EURO 2008: Group D
TOP SCORERS: Keane, Ireland 3
TOTAL SHOTS: 33
TOTAL CARDS: 14

A side filled with Premiership stalwarts who should be capable of giving the Czechs a battle for the second qualification spot behind Germany. They could do with Damien Duff staying fit though

1	Holland	H L	0-4
2	Germany	A L	0-1
3	Cyprus	A L	2-5
4	Czech Republic	H D	1-1
5	San Marino	H W	5-0
6	San Marino	A W	2-1
7	Wales	H W	1-0
8	Slovakia	H W	1-0
9	Ecuador	A D	1-1

Damien Duff

	PLAYER	POS	AGE	APP	MINS ON	GOALS	CARDS(Y/R)		CLUB
1	Steve Finnan	DEF	31	7	630	0	0	0	Liverpool
2	Damien Duff	MID	28	7	616	0	0	0	Newcastle
3	Kevin Kilbane	MID	30	7	598	2	1	0	Wigan
4	John O'Shea	DEF	26	7	585	0	1	0	Man United
5	Richard Dunne	DEF	27	6	527	1	2	1	Man City
6	Robbie Keane	ATT	26	6	539	3	1	0	Tottenham
7	Lee Carsley	MID	33	5	409	0	1	0	Everton
8	Paul McShane	DEF	21	5	405	0	1	0	West Brom
9	Shay Given	GK	31	4	360	0	0	0	Newcastle
10	Stephen Ireland	MID	20	4	297	3	0	0	Man City
11	Michael Doyle	MID	25	4	244	2	0	0	Reading
12	Jonathan Douglas	MID	25	4	218	0	1	0	Leeds Utd
13	Aiden McGeady	MID	21	5	209	0	0	0	Celtic
14	Wayne Henderson	GK	23	2	180	0	0	0	Preston
15	Andy O'Brien	DEF	28	3	172	0	0	0	Portsmouth
16	Andrew Reid	MID	24	2	161	0	0	0	Charlton
17	Shane Long	ATT	20	2	98	0	0	0	Reading
18	Clinton Morrison	ATT	28	1	90	0	0	0	Crystal Palace
19	Patrick Kenny	GK	28	1	90	0	0	0	Sheff Utd

INTERNATIONAL TEAMS

INTERNATIONAL RESULTS

CROATIA

MANAGER: Slaven Bilic
CAPTAIN: Nico Kovac
FIFA RANKING (July 2007): 11
EURO 2008: Group E
TOP SCORER: Eduardo Da Silva 6
TOTAL SHOTS: 63
TOTAL CARDS: 3

Ahead in a World Cup semi in 1998 and on the wrong end of an in-form Wayne Rooney in Euro 2004, Croatia look likely qualifiers. The emergence of new Arsenal signing Eduardo Da Silva and Mladen Petric gives them a cutting edge

1 Italy	A	W	2-0
2 Russia	A	D	0-0
3 Andorra	H	W	7-0
4 England	H	W	2-0
5 Israel	A	W	4-3
6 Norway	H	W	2-1
7 Macedonia	H	W	2-1
8 Estonia	A	W	1-0
9 Russia	H	D	0-0

Eduardo

	PLAYER	POS	AGE	APP	MINS ON	GOALS	CARDS(Y/R)		CLUB
1	Vedran Corluka	DEF	21	7	630	0	0	0	Dinamo Zagreb
2	Luka Modric	MID	21	7	630	1	0	0	Dinamo Zagreb
3	Nico Kovac	MID	35	7	608	0	2	0	Red Bull Salzburg
4	Niko Kranjcar	ATT	22	7	565	0	0	0	Portsmouth
5	Josip Simunic	DEF	29	6	540	0	0	0	Hertha Berlin
6	Robert Kovac	DEF	33	6	540	0	0	0	B Dortmund
7	Stipe Pletikosa	GK	28	6	540	0	0	0	Spartak Moscow
8	Eduardo	ATT	24	6	476	5	0	0	Dinamo Zagreb
9	Dario Simic	DEF	31	5	450	0	0	0	AC Milan
10	Mladen Petric	ATT	26	6	350	4	0	0	B Dortmund
11	Marko Babic	MID	26	7	241	0	0	0	B Leverkusen
12	Darijo Srna	MID	25	4	229	2	0	0	Shakhtar Donetsk
13	Ivan Klasnic	ATT	27	2	177	1	0	0	W Bremen
14	Milan Rapaic	MID	33	3	177	0	0	0	Standard Liege
15	Jerko Leko	MID	27	6	162	0	1	0	Monaco
16	Ivica Olic	ATT	27	4	137	0	0	0	Hamburg
17	Bosko Balaban	ATT	28	3	116	1	0	0	Club Brugge
18	Anthony Seric	DEF	28	1	90	0	0	0	Panathinaikos
19	Goran Sabljic	DEF	27	1	90	0	0	0	Dinamo Kiev
20	Vedran Runje	GK	31	1	90	0	0	0	Besiktas

ISRAEL

MANAGER: Dror Kashtan
CAPTAIN: Yossi Benayoun
FIFA RANKING (July 2007): 34
EURO 2008: Group E
TOP SCORERS: Colautti 6
TOTAL SHOTS: 54
TOTAL CARDS: 18

Dogged in qualifying in the most competitive group for the World Cup. They missed out by the narrowest margin despite being unbeaten in the group. They have already showed England how hard they are to beat

1 Estonia	A	W	1-0
2 Andorra	H	W	4-1
3 Russia	A	D	1-1
4 Croatia	H	L	3-4
5 Ukraine	H	D	1-1
6 England	H	D	0-0
7 Estonia	H	W	4-0
8 Macedonia	A	W	2-1
9 Andorra	A	W	2-0

Yossi Benayoun

	PLAYER	POS	AGE	APP	MINS ON	GOALS	CARDS(Y/R)		CLUB
1	Dudu Aouate	GK	29	8	720	0	0	0	Racing Santander
2	Idan Tal	MID	31	7	626	1	2	0	Bolton
3	Roberto Colautti	ATT	24	7	615	6	2	0	Maccabi Haifa
4	Yossi Benayoun	MID	27	7	592	2	2	0	West Ham
5	Walid Badir	MID	32	8	589	0	1	0	Hapoel Tel Aviv
6	Tal Ben-Haim	DEF	25	6	540	0	2	0	Bolton
7	Yoav Ziv	DEF	26	6	540	0	1	0	Beitar Jerusalem
8	Shimon Gershon	DEF	29	5	405	1	0	0	Beitar Jerusalem
9	Gal Alberman	MID	23	7	380	0	1	0	Beitar Jerusalem
10	Omri Afek	DEF	28	4	360	0	0	0	Beitar Jerusalem
11	Amit Ben Shushan	ATT	21	6	353	2	1	0	Beitar Jerusalem
12	Toto Tamuz	ATT	19	6	305	2	0	0	Beitar Jerusalem
13	Arik Benado	DEF	33	3	270	0	1	0	Beitar Jerusalem
14	Yuval Shpungin	DEF	19	3	270	0	1	0	Maccabi Tel Aviv
15	Yaniv Katan	ATT	26	5	207	0	0	0	West Ham
16	Adoram Keisi	DEF	25	2	180	0	0	0	Maccabi Haifa
17	Barat Itzhaki	ATT	22	2	165	1	1	0	Beitar Jerusalem
18	Tomer Ben-Yosef	DEF	27	2	135	0	0	0	Beitar Jerusalem
19	Pini Balili	ATT	27	2	129	0	0	0	Slvasspor
20	Ben Sahar	ATT	17	3	76	0	0	0	Chelsea

RUSSIA

MANAGER: Guus Hiddink
CAPTAIN: Andre Arshavin
FIFA RANKING (July 2007): 24
EURO 2008: Group E
TOP SCORER: Kerzhakov 4
TOTAL SHOTS: 71
TOTAL CARDS: 11

Still to play England twice at the halfway stage, the Russians hold the key to this group. The Moscow clubs have recently had some success in European cups and they make up the majority of Guus Hiddink's squad

1 Latvia	H	W	1-0
2 Croatia	H	D	0-0
3 Israel	H	D	1-1
4 Estonia	H	W	2-0
5 Macedonia	A	W	2-0
6 Holland	A	L	1-4
7 Estonia	A	W	2-0
8 Andorra	H	W	4-0
9 Croatia	A	D	0-0

Andrei Arshavin

	PLAYER	POS	AGE	APP	MINS ON	GOALS	CARDS(Y/R)		CLUB
1	Andrei Arshavin	MID	26	7	629	2	1	0	Zenit St P'burg
2	Sergei Ignashevitch	DEF	27	6	540	0	0	0	CSKA Moscow
3	Alexander Anyukov	MID	24	6	495	0	0	0	Zenit St P'burg
4	Alexei Berezutsky	DEF	25	6	495	0	1	0	CSKA Moscow
5	Igor Akinfeev	GK	21	5	450	0	0	0	CSKA Moscow
6	Vassili Berezutsky	DEF	25	5	450	0	0	0	CSKA Moscow
7	Petr Bystrov	MID	27	5	419	1	0	0	Dinamo Moscow
8	Yuri Zhirkov	MID	23	5	402	0	0	0	CSKA Moscow
9	Dinyar Bilyaletdinov	MID	22	5	388	0	0	0	Loko Moscow
10	Igor Semshov	MID	29	5	374	0	1	0	Torpedo Moscow
11	Alexander Kerzhakov	ATT	24	5	312	5	1	0	Seville
12	Yevgeny Aldonin	MID	27	3	253	0	0	0	CSKA Moscow
13	Dmitri Torbinskiy	MID	23	3	225	0	1	0	Spartak Moscow
14	Pavel Pogrebnyak	ATT	23	4	196	1	1	0	Zenit St P'burg
15	Denis Kolodin	DEF	25	2	180	0	0	0	Dinamo Moscow
16	Vyacheslav Malafeev	MID	28	2	180	0	0	0	Zenit St P'burg
17	Yegor Titov	MID	31	2	180	0	0	0	Spartak Moscow
18	Marat Izmailov	MID	24	2	124	0	0	0	Loko Moscow
19	Dmitri Sychev	ATT	23	5	114	2	1	0	Spartak Moscow
20	Alexei Smertin	MID	32	1	90	0	0	0	Fulham

INTERNATIONAL RESULTS

SWEDEN - SPAIN - NORTHERN IRELAND

SWEDEN

MANAGER: Lars Lagerback
CAPTAIN: Fredrik Ljungberg
FIFA RANKING (July 2007): 17
EURO 2008: Group F
TOP SCORER: Allback 5
TOTAL SHOTS: 57
TOTAL CARDS: 11
Apart from a shock defeat to Northern Ireland, the Swedes have a 100% record and expect to qualify

1	Germany	A	L	0-3
2	Latvia	A	W	1-0
3	Liechtenstein	H	W	3-1
4	Spain	H	W	2-0
5	Iceland	A	W	2-1
6	Ivory Coast	A	L	0-1
7	Venezuela	A	L	0-2
8	Ecuador	A	L	1-2
9	Ecuador	A	D	1-1
10	Egypt	A	L	0-2
11	N Ireland	A	L	1-2
12	Iceland	H	W	5-0

Marcus Allback and Markus Rosenberg

	PLAYER	POS	AGE	APP	MINS ON	GOALS	CARDS(Y/R)	CLUB
1	Petter Hansson	DEF	30	6	540	0	0 0	Heerenveen
2	Niclas Alexandersson	MID	35	6	510	0	0 0	IFK Gothenburg
3	Erik Edman	DEF	28	5	450	0	1 0	Rennes
4	Mikael Nilsson	MID	29	5	450	0	0 0	Panathinaikos
5	Fredrik Ljungberg	MID	30	5	415	0	0 0	Arsenal
6	Johan Elmander	ATT	26	5	413	2	1 0	Toulouse
7	Rami Shaaban	GK	32	4	360	0	0 0	Fredrikstad
8	Olof Mellberg	DEF	29	4	339	1	0 0	Aston Villa
9	Tobias Linderoth	MID	28	4	331	0	0 0	FC Copenhagen
10	Marcus Allback	ATT	33	4	330	5	0 0	FC Copenhagen
11	Kim Kallstrom	MID	24	5	276	2	0 0	Lyon
12	Christian Wilhelmsson	MID	27	5	258	1	1 0	Nantes
13	Daniel Andersson	MID	29	4	223	0	1 0	Malmo
14	Zlatan Ibrahimovic	ATT	25	3	198	0	1 0	Inter Milan
15	Andreas Isaksson	GK	25	2	180	0	0 0	Man City
16	Anders Svensson	MID	30	3	154	0	2 0	Elfsborg
17	Markus Rosenberg	ATT	24	3	111	2	0 0	Ajax
18	Karl Svensson	MID	23	2	110	1	0 0	Rangers
19	Mikael Antonsson	DEF	26	1	90	0	0 0	Panathinaikos
20	Teddy Lucic	DEF	34	1	90	0	0 0	Gothenburg

SPAIN

MANAGER: Luis Aragones
CAPTAIN: Iker Casillas
FIFA RANKING (July 2007): 7
EURO 2008: Group F
TOP SCORER: Villa 7
TOTAL SHOTS: 99
TOTAL CARDS: 17
Perpetual under-achievers, they are having a shaky time in their group, losing to Northern Ireland and struggling to narrow wins over the bottom three

1	Iceland	A	D	0-0
2	Liechtenstein	H	W	4-0
3	N Ireland	A	L	2-3
4	Sweden	A	L	0-2
5	Argentina	H	W	2-1
6	Romania	H	L	0-1
7	England	A	W	1-0
8	Denmark	H	W	2-1
9	Iceland	H	W	1-0
10	Latvia	A	W	2-0
11	Liechtenstein	A	W	2-0

Iker Casillas

	PLAYER	POS	AGE	APP	MINS ON	GOALS	CARDS(Y/R)	CLUB
1	David Villa	ATT	25	7	587	7	1 0	Valencia
2	Iker Casillas	GK	26	6	540	0	0 0	Real Madrid
3	Sergio Ramos	DEF	21	6	494	0	1 0	Real Madrid
4	Carlos Puyol	DEF	29	5	450	0	2 0	Barcelona
5	Andres Iniesta	ATT	0	6	434	1	1 0	Barcelona
6	Xavi Hernandez	MID	27	5	419	2	1 0	Barcelona
7	David Albelda	MID	29	6	418	0	1 0	Valencia
8	Carlos Marchena	DEF	27	4	360	0	1 0	Valencia
9	Xabi Alonso	MID	25	6	339	0	1 0	Liverpool
10	Joan Capdevila	DEF	29	5	327	0	1 0	Villarreal
11	Fernando Torres	ATT	23	5	317	2	0 0	Atl Madrid
12	David Silva	MID	21	3	256	0	0 0	Valencia
13	Cesc Fabregas	MID	20	4	234	0	1 0	Arsenal
14	Francisco Javi Navarro	DEF	33	2	180	0	0 0	Seville
15	Pablo Ibanez	DEF	25	2	180	0	0 0	Atletico Madrid
16	Raul	ATT	30	2	180	0	0 0	Real Madrid
17	Luis Garcia	MID	29	5	166	1	1 0	Liverpool
18	Miguel Angulo	ATT	30	4	162	0	1 0	Spain
19	Sanchez Joaquin	MID	25	2	136	0	0 0	Valencia
20	Guerrero Antonio Lopez	MID	25	2	129	0	1 0	Atletico Madrid

NORTHERN IRELAND

MANAGER: Nigel Worthington
CAPTAIN: Aaron Hughes
FIFA RANKING (July 2007): 29
EURO 2008: Group F
TOP SCORER: Healy 9
TOTAL SHOTS: 45
TOTAL CARDS: 10
Healy's golden touch must adapt to Nigel Worthington. The key to the group may be November 17 when Spain host Sweden and the province play their toughest remaining home game against Denmark. If results go their way it could set up a last fixture in Spain with both sides level

1	Finland	A	W	2-1
2	Iceland	H	L	0-3
3	Spain	H	W	3-2
4	Denmark	A	D	0-0
5	Latvia	H	W	1-0
6	Wales	H	D	0-0
7	Liechtenstein	A	W	4-1
8	Sweden	H	W	2-1

David Healy

	PLAYER	POS	AGE	APP	MINS ON	GOALS	CARDS(Y/R)	CLUB
1	Aaron Hughes	DEF	27	6	540	0	0 0	Aston Villa
2	Stephen Craigan	DEF	30	6	540	0	0 0	Motherwell
3	Steven Davis	MID	22	6	540	0	0 0	Aston Villa
4	Maik Taylor	GK	35	6	529	0	1 0	Birmingham
5	David Healy	ATT	27	6	518	9	1 0	Leeds Utd
6	Jonny Evans	DEF	0	5	450	0	1 0	Man United
7	Keith Gillespie	MID	32	5	450	0	2 0	Sheff Utd
8	Mike Duff	DEF	28	5	375	0	2 0	Burnley
9	Chris Baird	DEF	25	4	360	0	0 0	Southampton
10	Sammy Clingan	MID	0	4	325	0	0 0	Nottm Forest
11	Damien Johnson	MID	28	4	304	0	1 0	Birmingham
12	Kyle Lafferty	ATT	0	6	295	0	1 0	Burnley
13	Chris Brunt	MID	22	2	156	0	0 0	Sheff Wed
14	Warren Feeney	ATT	26	6	135	0	1 0	Luton
15	James Quinn	ATT	32	3	124	0	0 0	Northampton
16	Grant McCann	MID	27	2	114	1	0 0	Barnsley
17	Anthony Capaldi	MID	25	1	75	0	0 0	Plymouth
18	Stuart Elliott	ATT	28	1	62	0	0 0	Hull City
19	Steve Jones	ATT	30	2	34	0	0 0	Burnley
20	Roy Carroll	GK	29	1	11	0	0 0	West Ham

INTERNATIONAL TEAMS

INTERNATIONAL RESULTS

ROMANIA · BULGARIA · HOLLAND

ROMANIA

MANAGER: Victor Piturca
CAPTAIN: Cristian Chivu
FIFA RANKING (July 2007): 12
EURO 2008: Group G
TOP SCORER: Mutu 4
TOTAL SHOTS: 67
TOTAL CARDS: 18

Former Chelsea striker Adrian Mutu is in form for Fiorentina in Serie A and is hitting goals for his country. A healthy sprinkling of players from the big leagues plus a youthful set from the Bucharest clubs

1	Cyprus	H W	2-0
2	Bulgaria	H D	2-2
3	Albania	A W	2-0
4	Belarus	H W	3-1
5	Spain	A W	1-0
6	Moldova	A W	2-0
7	Holland	A D	0-0
8	Luxembourg	H W	3-0
9	Slovenia	A W	2-1
10	Slovenia	H W	2-0

Christian Chivu and Adrian Mutu

	PLAYER	POS	AGE	APP	MINS ON	GOALS	CARDS(Y/R)		CLUB
1	Adrian Mutu	ATT	28	7	605	4	1	0	Fiorentina
2	Bogdan Lonut Lobont	GK	29	6	540	0	1	0	Dinamo Buch'est
3	Cosmin Marius Contra	DEF	31	6	540	2	2	0	Getafe
4	Gabriel Tamas	DEF	23	6	535	1	3	1	Celta Vigo
5	Razvan Rat	DEF	26	6	527	0	1	0	Shakhtar Donetsk
6	Ciprian Marica	MID	21	7	508	3	0	0	Shakhtar Donetsk
7	Christian Chivu	DEF	26	5	450	0	0	0	Roma
8	Paul Codrea	MID	26	5	434	0	2	0	Siena
9	Dimitru Laurentiu Rosu	MID	31	7	397	1	1	0	Recreativo
10	Dorin Goian	MID	25	4	360	1	2	0	Steaua Buch'est
11	Florentin Petre	ATT	31	4	324	0	0	0	CSKA Sofia
12	Niculae Dica	MID	27	3	235	1	1	0	Steaua Buch'est
13	Razvan Cocsis	MID	24	4	215	0	0	0	Loko Moscow
14	Banel Nicolita	MID	22	3	196	1	1	0	Romania
15	Mirel Matei Radoi	DEF	26	2	180	0	0	0	Steaua Buch'est
16	Ianis Zicu	MID	23	3	177	0	0	0	Dinamo Buch'est
17	Daniel Niculae	ATT	24	3	108	0	0	0	Auxerre
18	Stefan Radu	MID	20	2	103	0	0	0	Dinamo Buch'est
19	Petre Marin	DEF	33	2	102	0	0	0	Steaua Buch'est
20	Danut Coman	GK	28	1	90	0	0	0	Rapid Buch'est

BULGARIA

ASST. MANAGER: Dimitar Penev
CAPTAIN: Dimitar Berbatov
FIFA RANKING (July 2007): 33
EURO 2008: Group G
TOP SCORER: Martin Petrov 4
TOTAL SHOTS: 45
TOTAL CARDS: 12

Hristo Stoichkov resigned as manager in April, following criticism of the former star's coaching style. He had fallen out with previous captain Stiliyan Petrov and now Dimitar Berbatov is skipper

1	Wales	A D	0-0
2	Romania	A D	2-2
3	Slovenia	H W	3-0
4	Holland	H D	1-1
5	Luxembourg	A W	1-0
6	Slovakia	A L	1-3
7	Latvia	H W	2-0
8	Albania	H D	0-0
9	Belarus	A W	2-0
10	Belarus	H W	2-1

Martin Petrov

	PLAYER	POS	AGE	APP	MINS ON	GOALS	CARDS(Y/R)		CLUB
1	Alexandar Tunchev	DEF	26	6	540	1	2	0	CSKA Sofia
2	Dimitar Ivankov	GK	31	6	540	0	1	0	Kayserispor
3	Stiliyan Petrov	MID	28	6	540	0	1	0	Aston Villa
4	Dimitar Berbatov	ATT	26	6	511	2	0	0	Tottenham
5	Stanislav Angelov	DEF	29	6	472	0	1	0	Levski Sofia
6	Radostin Kishishev	MID	32	7	441	0	0	0	Charlton
7	Dimitar Telkiyski	MID	33	6	389	1	0	0	Levski Sofia
8	Chavdar Yankov	MID	23	5	381	1	2	0	Hannover 96
9	Lucio Wagner	DEF	31	4	360	0	0	0	Levski Sofia
10	Martin Petrov	MID	28	4	323	4	0	0	Atletico Madrid
11	Hristo Yovov	MID	29	6	320	0	0	0	Levski Sofia
12	Igor Tomasic	DEF	30	3	270	0	0	0	Levski Sofia
13	Lucio Wagner	DEF	31	3	270	0	0	0	Levski Sofia
14	Valeri Bojinov	ATT	21	5	210	1	1	0	Juventus
15	Elin Topouzakov	DEF	30	2	180	0	0	0	Levski Sofia
16	Emil Gargarov	MID	26	2	180	0	0	0	Strasbourg
17	Zoran Jankovic	MID	33	2	113	0	0	0	Litex
18	Georgi Peev	MID	28	2	109	0	1	0	Amkar Perm
19	Blagoy Georgiev	MID	25	2	97	0	0	0	Red Star Belgrade

HOLLAND

MANAGER: Marco van Basten
CAPTAIN: Andre Arshavin
FIFA RANKING (July 2007): 24
EURO 2008: Group G
TOP SCORER: van Persie 4
TOTAL SHOTS: 101
TOTAL CARDS: 10

Marco van Basten is still ringing the changes but not finding the formula for goals. Defensively strong and unbeaten at the halfway stage of qualification

1	Rep of Ireland	A W	4-0
2	Luxembourg	A W	1-0
3	Belarus	H W	3-0
4	Bulgaria	A D	1-1
5	Albania	H W	2-1
6	England	H D	1-1
7	Russia	H W	4-1
8	Romania	H D	0-0
9	Slovenia	A W	1-0
10	South Korea	A W	2-0
11	Thailand	A W	3-1

Ryan Babel

	PLAYER	POS	AGE	APP	MINS ON	GOALS	CARDS(Y/R)		CLUBS
1	Joris Mathijsen	DEF	27	6	540	1	1	0	Hamburg
2	Edwin van der Sar	GK	36	5	450	0	0	0	Man Utd
3	Wesley Sneijder	MID	23	5	440	0	1	0	Ajax
4	Gio Van Bronckhorst	DEF	32	5	427	1	1	0	Barcelona
5	Denny Landzaat	MID	31	5	415	0	1	0	Wigan
6	Arjen Robben	MID	23	4	360	0	0	0	Chelsea
7	Ryan Babel	ATT	20	6	356	0	0	0	Ajax
8	Robin van Persie	MID	23	4	346	4	1	0	Arsenal
9	Andre Ooijer	DEF	32	4	315	0	0	0	Blackburn
10	Dirk Kuijt	ATT	26	4	284	0	0	0	Liverpool
11	Klaas Jan Huntelaar	ATT	23	3	256	0	0	0	Ajax
12	Nigel de Jong	DEF	22	3	230	0	1	0	Hamburg
13	John Heitinga	DEF	23	3	229	0	0	0	Ajax
14	Khalid Boulahrouz	DEF	25	3	204	0	0	0	Chelsea
15	Wilfred Bouma	DEF	29	2	180	0	0	0	Aston Villa
16	Urby Emanuelson	DEF	21	4	169	0	0	0	Ajax
17	Stijn Schaars	MID	23	3	108	0	0	0	AZ Alkmaar
18	Tim de Cler	DEF	28	2	101	0	0	0	AZ Alkmaar
19	Kew Jaliens	DEF	28	1	90	0	1	0	AZ Alkmaar
20	Maarten Stekelenburg	GK	24	1	90	0	0	0	Ajax

INTERNATIONAL RESULTS

ENGLAND

MANAGER: Steve McClaren
CAPTAIN: John Terry
FIFA RANKING (July 2007): 8
EURO 2008: Group E
TOP SCORER: Crouch 4
TOTAL SHOTS: 83
TOTAL CARDS: 13

McClaren's uneasy start has made second place the qualification target as he tries to blend top club stars into a side that plays well against less blessed opponents

1	Greece	H	W	4-0
2	Andorra	H	W	5-0
3	Macedonia	A	W	1-0
4	Macedonia	H	D	0-0
5	Croatia	A	L	0-2
6	Holland	A	D	1-1
7	Spain	H	L	0-1
8	Israel	A	D	0-0
9	Andorra	A	W	3-0
10	Brazil	H	D	1-1
11	Estonia	A	W	3-0

Steve McClaren

	PLAYER	POS	AGE	APP	MINS ON	GOALS	CARDS(Y/R)		CLUB
1	John Terry	DEF	26	7	630	0	0	0	Chelsea
2	Paul Robinson	GK	27	7	630	0	0	0	Tottenham
3	Steven Gerrard	MID	27	6	540	3	2	0	Liverpool
4	Frank Lampard	MID	29	6	533	0	0	0	Chelsea
5	Ashley Cole	DEF	26	5	450	0	3	0	Chelsea
6	Peter Crouch	ATT	26	5	428	4	2	0	Liverpool
7	Owen Hargreaves	MID	26	4	360	0	0	0	Bayern Munich
8	Rio Ferdinand	DEF	28	4	360	0	1	0	Man Utd
9	Stewart Downing	MID	22	6	336	0	0	0	Middlesbrough
10	Wayne Rooney	ATT	26	4	315	0	2	0	Man Utd
11	Phil Neville	DEF	30	3	226	0	0	0	Everton
12	Jermain Defoe	ATT	26	6	220	2	0	0	Tottenham
13	Aaron Lennon	MID	20	4	213	0	0	0	Tottenham
14	Michael Carrick	MID	25	3	187	0	0	0	Man Utd
15	Andrew Johnson	ATT	26	4	182	0	0	0	Everton
16	Gary Neville	DEF	32	2	180	0	0	0	Man Utd
17	Ledley King	DEF	26	2	180	0	0	0	Tottenham
18	Wes Brown	DEF	27	2	180	0	1	0	Man Utd
19	Jamie Carragher	DEF	29	2	163	0	1	0	Liverpool
20	Wayne Bridge	DEF	26	1	90	0	0	0	Chelsea

WALES

MANAGER: John Toshak
CAPTAIN: Craig Bellamy
FIFA RANKING (July 2007): 75
EURO 2008: Group D
TOP SCORER: Koumas, Bale 2
TOTAL SHOTS: 59
TOTAL CARDS: 8

The retirement of Ryan Giggs leaves a wealth of youngsters, mainly from lower league clubs, and two potent strikers in Craig Bellamy and Robert Earnshaw

1	Bulgaria	H	D	0-0
2	Czech Republic	A	L	1-2
3	Brazil	H	L	0-2
4	Slovakia	H	L	1-5
5	Cyprus	H	W	3-1
6	Liechtenstein	H	W	4-0
7	N Ireland	A	D	0-0
8	Rep of Ireland	A	L	0-1
9	San Marino	H	W	3-0
10	New Zealand	H	D	2-2
11	Czech Republic	H	D	0-0

Craig Bellamy and Ryan Giggs

	PLAYER	POS	AGE	APP	MINS ON	GOALS	CARDS(Y/R)		CLUB
1	Craig Bellamy	ATT	27	6	539	1	0	0	Blackburn
2	Simon Davies	MID	27	6	537	0	1	0	Fulham
3	Lewin Nyatanga	DEF	18	6	478	0	0	0	Derby
4	Carl Robinson	MID	30	5	449	0	1	0	Toronto
5	Daniel Gabbidon	DEF	27	4	360	0	0	0	West Ham
6	James Collins	DEF	23	4	360	0	0	0	West Ham
7	Samuel Ricketts	DEF	25	4	348	0	1	0	Hull City
8	Jason Koumas	MID	27	4	345	2	3	0	West Brom
9	Gareth Bale	DEF	17	4	343	2	0	0	Southampton
10	Ryan Giggs	MID	33	4	340	1	0	0	Man Utd
11	Joe Ledley	MID	20	5	228	0	0	0	Cardiff
12	Carl Fletcher	MID	27	3	180	0	1	0	Crystal Palace
13	Danny Coyne	GK	33	2	180	0	0	0	Burnley
14	Paul Jones	GK	40	2	180	0	0	0	QPR
15	Richard Duffy	DEF	21	2	168	0	0	0	Portsmouth
16	Steve Evans	DEF	28	2	152	0	0	0	Wrexham
17	Robert Earnshaw	ATT	26	4	149	1	0	0	Norwich
18	Craig Morgan	MID	21	1	90	0	0	0	Peterborough
19	Lewis Price	GK	22	1	90	0	0	0	Ipswich
20	Wayne Hennessey	GK	20	1	90	0	0	0	Wolves

BELGIUM

MANAGER: Rene Vandereycken
CAPTAIN: Bart Goor
FIFA RANKING (July 2007): 71
EURO 2008: Group A
TOP SCORER: 5 players 1 goal each
TOTAL SHOTS: 50
TOTAL CARDS: 22

Fifth placed in Group A and out of the qualification running, Belgium seem unable to trouble the four quality teams and were soundly beaten 4-0 by Portugal. Daniel Van Buyten is playing well for Bayern but the team is short of goals

1	Kazakhstan	H	D	0-0
2	Armenia	A	W	1-0
3	Serbia	A	L	0-1
4	Azerbaijan	H	W	3-0
5	Poland	H	L	0-1
6	Czech Republic	H	L	0-2
7	Portugal	A	L	0-4
8	Portugal	H	L	1-2
9	Finland	A	L	0-2

Daniel Van Buyten

	PLAYER	POS	AGE	APP	MINS ON	GOALS	CARDS(Y/R)		CLUB
1	Stijn Stijnen	GK	26	8	720	0	0	0	Club Brugge
2	Timmy Simons	MID	31	7	630	1	1	0	PSV Eindhoven
3	Carl Hoefkens	MID	28	7	540	0	1	0	Stoke
4	Daniel Van Buyten	DEF	29	6	540	1	1	0	Bayern Munich
5	Thomas Vermaelen	DEF	21	6	494	0	1	0	Ajax
6	Karel Geraerts	MID	25	6	465	0	1	0	Standard Liege
7	Emile Mpenza	ATT	28	5	424	0	0	0	Man City
8	Bart Goor	MID	34	5	379	0	1	0	Anderlecht
9	Steven Defour	ATT	19	4	284	0	1	0	Standard Liege
10	Philippe Clement	DEF	33	3	270	0	0	0	Club Brugge
11	Gaby Mudingayi	MID	25	4	250	0	0	0	Lazio
12	Jelle Van Damme	DEF	23	4	249	0	3	0	Anderlecht
13	Moussa Dembele	ATT	20	4	244	1	0	1	AZ Alkmaar
14	Marouane Fellaini	MID	18	3	231	1	2	1	Standard Liege
15	Mark De Man	MID	24	3	226	0	1	0	Anderlecht
16	Peter Van der Heyden	DEF	30	2	180	0	0	0	Wolfsburg
17	Luigi Pieroni	ATT	26	5	171	0	1	0	Auxerre
18	Anthony Vanden Borre	DEF	19	4	170	0	1	0	Anderlecht
19	Philippe Leonard	DEF	33	2	169	0	1	0	Feyenoord
20	Kevin Vandenbergh	ATT	24	3	153	1	0	0	Genk

INTERNATIONAL RESULTS

DENMARK

MANAGER: Morten Olsen
CAPTAIN: Jon Dahl Tomasson
FIFA RANKING (July 2007): 27
EURO 2008: Group F
TOP SCORER: Tomasson 4
TOTAL SHOTS: 55
TOTAL CARDS: 7
A good side on paper but struggling to qualify in a tough group

1	Poland	H	W	2-0
2	Portugal	H	W	4-2
3	Iceland	A	W	2-0
4	N Ireland	H	D	0-0
5	Liechtenstein	A	W	4-0
6	Czech Republic	A	D	1-1
7	United States	A	L	1-3
8	El Salvador	A	L	0-1
9	Honduras	A	D	1-1
10	Australia	A	W	3-1
11	Spain	A	L	1-2
12	Germany	A	W	1-0
13	Latvia	A	W	2-0

Jon Dahl Tomasson

	PLAYER	POS	AGE	APP	MINS ON	GOALS	CARDS(Y/R)		CLUB
1	Daniel Agger	DEF	22	5	450	0	0	0	Liverpool
2	Jon Dahl Tomasson	ATT	30	5	450	4	1	0	Stuttgart
3	Lars Jacobsen	DEF	27	5	450	0	0	0	FC Copenhagen
4	Martin Jorgensen	MID	31	5	405	0	0	0	Fiorentina
5	Thomas Sorensen	GK	31	5	382	0	0	0	Aston Villa
6	Christian Poulsen	MID	27	4	360	0	0	0	Seville
7	Michael Gravgaard	DEF	29	4	360	2	0	0	FC Copenhagen
8	Thomas Kahlenberg	MID	24	5	338	0	0	0	Auxerre
9	Daniel Jensen	MID	28	5	336	1	1	0	W. Bremen
10	Dennis Rommedahl	ATT	28	4	302	3	1	0	Charlton
11	Niclas Jensen	DEF	32	4	271	0	1	1	FC Copenhagen
12	Jesper Gronkjaer	MID	30	2	121	0	0	0	FC Copenhagen
13	Jesper Christiansen	GK	29	2	113	0	0	0	FC Copenhagen
14	Nicklas Bendtner	ATT	19	3	94	0	0	0	Birmingham
15	Jan Kristiansen	DEF	25	1	90	0	0	0	Nuremberg
16	Martin Laursen	DEF	35	1	90	0	0	0	Aston Villa
17	Claus Jensen	MID	29	3	72	0	0	0	Fulham
18	Thomas Gravesen	MID	31	1	69	0	0	0	Celtic
19	Peter Lovenkrands	ATT	27	1	54	0	0	0	FC Shalke
20	Rasmus Wurtz	MID	23	1	31	0	0	0	Aalborg BK

FINLAND

MANAGER: Roy Hodgson
CAPTAIN: Jari Litmanen
FIFA RANKING (July 2007): 42
EURO 2008: Group A
TOP SCORER: Litmanen 3
TOTAL SHOTS: 54
TOTAL CARDS: 10
Well-travelled English coach Roy Hodgson is 18 months into the task of getting Finland into their first ever major championship finals. They are holding their own in a tough group but the 2-0 home defeat to Serbia was damaging

1	N Ireland	H	L	1-2
2	Poland	A	W	3-1
3	Portugal	H	D	1-1
4	Armenia	A	D	0-0
5	Kazakhstan	A	W	2-0
6	Armenia	H	W	1-0
7	Azerbaijan	A	L	0-1
8	Serbia	H	L	0-2
9	Belgium	H	W	2-0

Jari Litmanen

	PLAYER	POS	AGE	APP	MINS ON	GOALS	CARDS(Y/R)		CLUB
1	Hannu Tihinen	DEF	8	8	720	0	0	0	Anderlecht
2	Jussi Jaaskelainen	GK	32	8	720	0	0	0	Bolton
3	Tonni Kallio	DEF	28	8	720	0	1	0	BSC Young Boys
4	Joonas Kolkka	ATT	32	8	659	0	0	0	Feyenoord
5	Mika Vayrynen	ATT	25	8	657	1	2	0	PSV Eindhoven
6	Markus Heikkinen	MID	28	7	630	0	1	0	Luton
7	Petri Pasanen	DEF	26	7	630	0	1	0	W. Bremen
8	Sami Hyypia	DEF	33	7	630	1	2	0	Liverpool
9	Jonatan Johansson	ATT	31	7	503	2	0	0	Malmo
10	Jari Litmanen	ATT	36	6	466	3	1	0	Malmo
11	Aleksei Eremenko Jr	ATT	24	5	300	1	2	0	FC Saturn
12	Jari Ilola	MID	28	3	224	0	0	0	Elfsborg IF
13	Mika Nurmela	ATT	35	5	216	1	0	0	HLK Helsinki
14	Teemu Tainio	MID	27	3	207	0	0	0	Tottenham
15	Shefki Kuqi	ATT	30	6	190	0	0	0	Crystal Palace
16	Ari Nyman	DEF	23	2	180	0	0	0	FC Thun
17	Mikael Forssell	ATT	26	6	169	0	0	0	Birmingham
18	Roman Eremenko	MID	20	1	90	0	0	0	Udinese
19	Aki Riihilahti	MID	30	2	9	0	0	0	Djurgardens
20	Magnus Bahne	GK	28	0	0	0	0	0	Halmstad BK

NORWAY

MANAGER: Aje Hareide
CAPTAIN: Martin Andresen
FIFA RANKING (July 2007): 36
EURO 2008: Group C
TOP SCORER: Iverson, Carew 3
TOTAL SHOTS: 83
TOTAL CARDS: 9
A handful of strong performers from the Premiership in John Carew, Morten Gamst Pedersen, Ole Gunnar Solskjaer and John Arne Riise and home-based players make up a squad capable of qualifying

1	Brazil	H	D	1-1
2	Hungary	A	W	4-1
3	Moldova	H	W	2-0
4	Greece	A	L	0-1
5	Serbia	A	D	1-1
6	Croatia	A	L	1-2
7	Bosnia	H	L	1-2
8	Turkey	A	D	2-2
9	Malta	H	W	4-0
10	Hungary	H	W	4-0

Ole Gunnar Solskjaer

	PLAYER	POS	AGE	APP	MINS ON	GOALS	CARDS(Y/R)		CLUB
1	Brede Hangeland	DEF	26	7	630	0	0	0	FC Copenhagen
2	Erik Hagen	DEF	32	7	630	0	2	0	Zenit St P'burg
3	Kristofer Haestad	MID	24	7	536	1	1	0	Start
4	John Alieu Carew	ATT	27	6	506	3	0	0	Aston Villa
5	John Arne Riise	MID	26	5	450	1	0	0	Liverpool
6	Martin Andresen	MID	30	5	450	1	0	0	Brann
7	Thomas Myhre	GK	33	5	450	0	0	0	Charlton
8	Morten Gamst Pedersen	ATT	25	5	412	1	0	0	Blackburn
9	Fredrik Stromstad	MID	25	5	361	2	0	0	Start
10	Jarl Andre Storbaek	DEF	28	4	348	0	0	0	Valerenga
11	Steffen Iversen	ATT	30	6	311	3	0	0	Rosenborg BK
12	Anders Rambekk	DEF	30	3	264	0	0	0	Lillestrom
13	Ole Gunnar Solskjaer	ATT	34	3	225	2	0	0	Man Utd
14	Bjorn Helge Riise	MID	24	2	180	0	0	0	Lillestrom
15	Hakon Opdal	GK	25	2	180	0	0	0	Brann
16	Trond Andersen	MID	32	2	180	0	1	0	Wimbledon
17	Marius Johnsen	DEF	25	2	154	0	1	0	Cologne
18	Simen Brenne	ATT	26	3	125	1	1	0	Lillestrom
19	Daniel Braaten	MID	25	4	113	1	0	0	Rosenborg BK
20	Frode Johnsen	ATT	33	2	90	0	0	0	Rosenborg BK

INTERNATIONAL RESULTS
BRAZIL - ARGENTINA - USA

BRAZIL

MANAGER: Dunga
CAPTAIN: Lucio
FIFA RANKING (July 2007): 3
Finished the season with a surprise defeat to Mexico in the Copa America. Dunga has spread the net to look at Brazilians playing outside the big clubs. He has now lost two of his first 12 games in charge, the first to former Brazil coach, Big Phil Scolari's Portugal.

1 Norway	A	D	1-1
2 Argentina	H	W	3-0
3 Wales	A	W	2-0
4 Ecuador	H	W	2-1
5 Switzerland	A	W	2-1
6 Portugal	H	L	0-2
7 Chile	H	W	4-0
8 Ghana	H	W	1-0
9 England	A	D	1-1
10 Turkey	H	D	0-0
11 Mexico	H	L	0-2
12 Chile	H	W	3-0

Vagner Love

	PLAYER	POS	AGE	APP	MINS ON	GOALS	CARDS(Y/R)		CLUB
1	Gilberto Silva	MID	30	11	851	0	1	0	Arsenal
2	Juan	DEF	28	10	843	0	0	0	B Leverkusen
3	Robinho	ATT	23	11	758	3	2	0	Real Madrid
4	Gilberto	DEF	31	9	703	0	1	0	Hertha Berlin
5	Kaka	MID	25	9	653	4	0	0	AC Milan
6	Elano	MID	26	11	597	2	1	0	Shakhtar Don.
7	Mineiro	MID	31	7	587	0	1	0	Hertha Berlin
8	Vagner Love	ATT	23	8	565	2	0	0	CSKA Moscow
9	Lucio	DEF	31	6	540	0	1	0	Bayern Munich
10	Alex	DEF	25	6	462	0	1	0	PSV Eindhoven
11	Ronaldinho	ATT	27	7	455	2	0	0	Barcelona
12	Doni	GK	27	4	360	0	0	0	Roma
13	Edmilson	MID	31	6	354	0	0	0	Barcelona
14	Dudu	MID	24	8	323	0	0	0	CSKA Moscow
15	Fred	ATT	23	5	315	1	0	0	Lyon
16	Helton	GK	29	3	270	0	0	0	Porto Moscow
17	Alfonso Alves	ATT	26	6	226	0	1	0	Heerenveen
18	Julio Cesar	GK	27	2	180	0	0	0	Inter Milan
19	Heurelho Gomes	GK	26	2	180	0	0	0	PSV Eindhoven
20	Daniel Alves	DEF	24	3	166	0	2	0	Seville

ARGENTINA

MANAGER: Alfio Basile
CAPTAIN: Roberto Ayala
FIFA RANKING (July 2007): 5
Alfio Basile is in his second spell as Argentinian coach, taking over from Jose Pekerman after the World Cup. It follows a successful spell in charge of home side Boca Juniors.
He has largely stayed with the team he inherited, elavating Carlos Tevez and Lionel Messi to regulars and bringing back Pablo Aimar and Juan Sebastian Veron to an experienced midfield. He called for Tevez and Javier Mascherano to leave the Premiership and switch to Italy or Spain.

1 Brazil	A	L	0-3
2 Spain	A	L	1-2
3 France	A	W	1-0
4 Chile	H	D	0-0
5 Switzerland	A	D	1-1
6 United States	H	W	4-1
7 Colombia	H	W	4-2

Pablo Aimar

	PLAYER	POS	AGE	APP	MINS ON	GOALS	CARDS(Y/R)		CLUB
1	Abbondanzieri	GK	34	6	540	0	0	0	Getafe
2	Roberto Ayala	DEF	34	6	540	0	1	0	Valencia
3	Gabriel Milito	DEF	26	6	540	0	3	0	Real Zaragoza
4	Lionel Messi	MID	20	5	403	0	0	0	Barcelona
5	Luiz Gonzalez	MID	26	5	381	0	0	0	Porto
6	Carlos Tevez	ATT	23	5	380	2	0	0	West Ham
7	Javier Zanetti	DEF	33	4	360	0	0	0	Inter Milan
8	Gabriel Heinze	DEF	29	4	360	0	1	0	Man Utd
9	Javier Mascherano	MID	23	5	338	0	0	0	Liverpool
10	Estaban Cambiasso	MID	26	4	302	0	0	0	Inter Milan
11	Juan Riquelme	MID	29	3	270	2	1	0	Boca Juniors
12	Hernan Crespo	ATT	32	4	257	3	0	0	Inter Milan
13	Fernando Gago	MID	21	3	184	0	1	0	Real Madrid
14	Juan Sebastian Veron	MID	32	2	166	0	1	0	Estudientes
15	Fabricio Coloccini	DEF	25	1	90	0	0	0	Deportivo
16	Daniel Diaz	DEF	28	1	90	0	0	0	Boca Juniors
17	Hugo Ibarra	DEF	33	1	90	0	0	0	Boca Juniors
18	Nicolas Burdisso	DEF	26	1	90	0	0	0	Inter Milan
19	Diego Milito	ATT	28	7	80	1	1	0	Real Zaragoza
20	Pablo Aimar	MID	27	3	77	1	0	0	Real Zaragoza

USA

MANAGER: Bob Bradley
CAPTAIN: Carlos Bocanegra
FIFA RANKING (July 2007): 16
Bob Bradley took over as coach from Bruce Arena in December 2006 and led them to triumph in the CONCACAF Gold Cup. His first loss came in the Copa America against a strong Argentinian side. Bradley, who previously managed Chicago Fire, Metrostars and Chivas in the MLS, has Carlos Bocanegra as his skipper

1 Denmark	H	W	3-1
2 Mexico	H	W	2-0
3 Ecuador	H	W	3-1
4 Guatemala	H	D	0-0
5 China PR	H	W	4-1
6 Guatemala	H	W	1-0
7 Trinidad & Tobago	H	W	2-0
8 El Salvador	H	W	4-0
9 Panama	A	W	2-1
10 Argentina	A	L	1-4
11 Paraguay	H	L	1-3

Carlos Bocanegra

	PLAYER	POS	AGE	APP	MINS ON	GOALS	CARDS(Y/R)		CLUB
1	Jonathan Bornstein	DEF	22	8	720	1	2	0	Chivas USA
2	Landon Donovan	ATT	25	8	629	7	0	0	Los Ang. Galaxy
3	Benny Feilhaber	MID	22	8	597	1	0	0	Hamburg
4	Jimmy Conrad	DEF	30	6	540	1	0	0	Kansas C Wizards
5	Tim Howard	GK	23	6	495	0	0	0	Everton
6	Eddie Johnson	MID	23	8	477	2	0	0	Leeds
7	Carlos Bocanegra	DEF	28	5	450	1	2	0	Fulham
8	DaMarcus Beasley	MID	25	5	436	3	0	0	Man City
9	Clint Dempsey	MID	22	6	429	2	1	0	Fulham
10	Kasey Keller	GK	37	5	405	0	0	0	B. Monchen'bach
11	Taylor Twellman	ATT	27	7	381	1	0	0	New England Rev.
12	Bobby Convey	MID	24	6	362	0	0	0	Reading
13	Oguchi Onyewu	DEF	25	4	360	1	3	1	Newcastle
14	Jay DeMerit	DEF	27	5	343	0	1	0	Watford
15	Justin Mapp	MID	22	4	341	0	0	0	Chicago Fire
16	Ben Olsen	MID	30	5	298	0	0	0	DC United
17	Jonathan Spector	DEF	21	5	271	0	0	0	West Ham
18	Ricardo Clark	MID	24	3	170	1	0	0	Houston Dynamo
19	Drew Moor	DEF	23	1	90	0	0	0	FC Dallas
20	Marvel Wynn	DEF	21	1	90	0	0	0	Toronto FC

INTERNATIONAL TEAMS

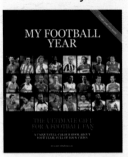